Australia

Justine Vaisutis
Lindsay Brown, Jayne D'Arcy, Katja Gaskell, Sarah Gilbert, Paul Harding,
Virginia Jealous, Rowan McKinnon, Olivia Pozzan, Charles Rawlings-Way,
Rowan Roebig, Tom Spurling, Regis St Louis, Penny Watson, Meg Worby

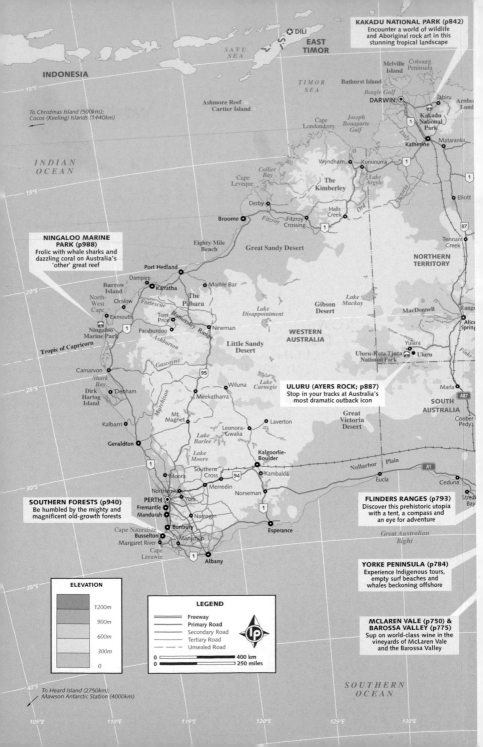

KAKADU NATIONAL PARK (p842)
Encounter a world of wildlife and Aboriginal rock art in this stunning tropical landscape

NINGALOO MARINE PARK (p988)
Frolic with whale sharks and dazzling coral on Australia's 'other' great reef

ULURU (AYERS ROCK; p887)
Stop in your tracks at Australia's most dramatic outback icon

SOUTHERN FORESTS (p940)
Be humbled by the mighty and magnificent old-growth forests

FLINDERS RANGES (p793)
Discover this prehistoric utopia with a tent, a compass and an eye for adventure

YORKE PENINSULA (p784)
Experience Indigenous tours, empty surf beaches and whales beckoning offshore

MCLAREN VALE (p750) & BAROSSA VALLEY (p775)
Sup on world-class wine in the vineyards of McLaren Vale and the Barossa Valley

To Christmas Island (500km);
Cocos (Keeling) Islands (1440km)

To Heard Island (2750km);
Mawson Antarctic Station (4000km)

ELEVATION

1200m
900m
600m
300m
0

LEGEND

Freeway
Primary Road
Secondary Road
Tertiary Road
Unsealed Road

0 ——— 400 km
0 ——— 250 miles

INDONESIA
EAST TIMOR
DILI
SAVU SEA
TIMOR SEA
INDIAN OCEAN
SOUTHERN OCEAN
NORTHERN TERRITORY
WESTERN AUSTRALIA
SOUTH AUSTRALIA
Great Australian Bight

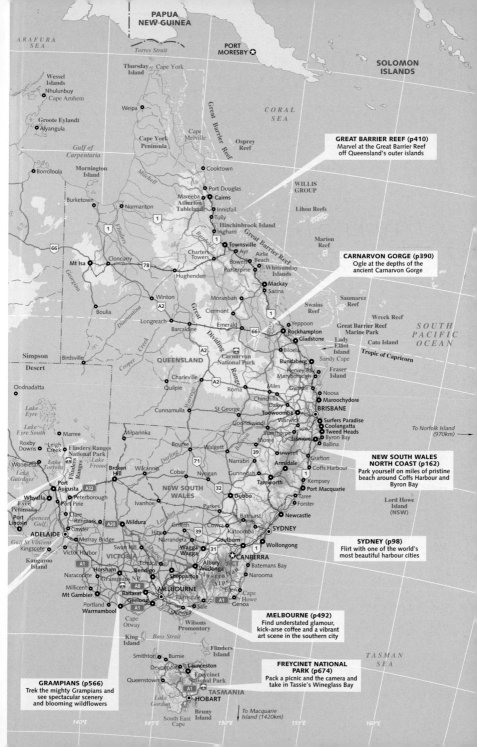

GREAT BARRIER REEF (p410)
Marvel at the Great Barrier Reef off Queensland's outer islands

CARNARVON GORGE (p390)
Ogle at the depths of the ancient Carnarvon Gorge

NEW SOUTH WALES NORTH COAST (p162)
Park yourself on miles of pristine beach around Coffs Harbour and Byron Bay

SYDNEY (p98)
Flirt with one of the world's most beautiful harbour cities

MELBOURNE (p492)
Find understated glamour, kick-arse coffee and a vibrant art scene in the southern city

FREYCINET NATIONAL PARK (p674)
Pack a picnic and the camera and take in Tassie's Wineglass Bay

GRAMPIANS (p566)
Trek the mighty Grampians and see spectacular scenery and blooming wildflowers

On the Road

JUSTINE VAISUTIS
Coordinating Author
Brunswick Street (p510) is my favourite Melbourne strip; it's colourful and diverse and, in true Melbourne style, embraces everyone from yuppies to ferals. On a Saturday night when the street throbs with fun, this iconic tiled couch on the corner of Westgarth St provides a moment of calm before the next party swings by.

LINDSAY BROWN One of the fun things to do at the Devil's Marbles (p862) is hunt out the celebrities: a small band of famous stationary stones that always end up on postcards and tourist brochures. The list includes the impossibly round, the precarious balancers, the rudely anatomical, and this pair of overexposed oddballs.

KATJA GASKELL My absolute all-time favourite Sunday morning Sydney hang-out is Nielsen Park (p118). This harbour beach has it all; calm waters for swimming, shady breakfast and newspaper spots and a shark net! It's also very 'Sydney', with distant cityscape views, sailboats and ferries criss-crossing in front of the beach, and seaplanes flying overhead.

JAYNE D'ARCY Does checking out one waterfall after another cause waterfallitis? Not if you come from drought-stricken Victoria. Here's one of the zillion watery beauties in Queensland's Atherton Tablelands (p456).

SARAH GILBERT Here I am before a portrait of Les Murray, a wonderful Australian poet and one of my favourites. Canberra is perfect for gallery and museum hopping, and on this day I was escaping from the 40°C heat outside. Les is hung in all his glory in the new National Portrait Gallery (p272).

PAUL HARDING If there's one thing the locals in the Top End love, it's fishing. Especially barramundi fishing. On a billabong near Litchfield (p839) I spent an afternoon casting a lure. We pulled in a dozen decent-sized barra (releasing all but one each). Now I know what all the fuss is about!

VIRGINIA JEALOUS It's one of those crazy weather days on Western Australia's south coast. Clouds loom, rain squalls and five minutes later the sun's out. On the Bibbulmun Track (p898) near Denmark there's the sound of surf, birdsong and small animals scrabbling in the bush – with not another person in sight. Magic!

OLIVIA POZZAN
Flying the flag at the Tip of Australia (p481) was an exhilarating experience; the climax to an epic overland journey through Cape York's wild and untamed wilderness. After days bouncing over rugged dirt roads and braving croc-infested rivers I felt as wild and feral as the land – and proud of it!

ROWAN MCKINNON Tasmania's Cradle Mountain alpine region is breathtaking, with incredibly pure cold air that numbs your ears and nose – hard to believe it was snowing in mid-summer. This is one end of the famous six-day Overland Track (p632), one of the world's great bushwalks and a rite of passage for many Australians.

CHARLES RAWLINGS-WAY
Cultured South Australia has a refreshing dearth of tacky 'big' tourist attractions (banana, pineapple, koala etc). But this one snuck in under the door: Larry the Lobster (p764) in Kingston SE. And, I suppose, as far as accurate supersizings of Australian beasts goes, Larry is fairly authentic! (My baby daughter seemed suitably impressed.)

ROWAN ROEBIG Catching a ferry on the Brisbane River is far too picturesque to be plainly termed 'public transport'. It was a gorgeous sunny November day and I had just finished a lap of the city walking tour (p312) featured in this guide. The mighty Story Bridge was my backdrop. Sure beats the bus!

TOM SPURLING My wife came up from Melbourne for a few days, so I took her to see the Big Mango (p412). You can imagine how excited she was! On the highway outside Bowen, this oversized fruit was a delicious distraction en route to nearby Rose Bay.

REGIS ST LOUIS After a long day driving over corrugated roads, we came across this remote campsite, which we had all to ourselves, right beside a billabong (hint: it's south of Old Halls Creek). The allure of the Kimberley (p995): there's so much to discover.

MEG WORBY We thought we might see brumbies under the searing outback sun of the Flinders Ranges (p793)…but all we saw were wedge-tailed eagles soaring on their 2m wingspans past the crags of 600 million-year-old Wilpena Pound, a herd of six emus running past, and a muscular red roo. I was happy with that.

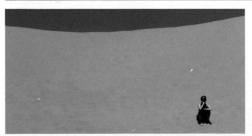

PENNY WATSON I am plonked on one of the stunning Perry Sand Hills (p256), 6km north of Wentworth on the road to Broken Hill. These glorious orange dunes date back 40,000 years. They're also searingly hot and my tootsies are burning.

For full author biographies see p1082.

Australia Highlights

Australia is one hot spot, but why is it that people are headed to the land down under in droves?

We asked some fellow Australians why they love this vast brown land we call home. They've packed their 4WDs and headed off into the outback, snorkelled, dived and surfed their way along the coast and explored ancient forests and Indigenous art centres. Here are their top picks.

Welcome, enjoy and explore, and find out why Lonely Planet calls Australia home.

JULIET COOMBE

ULURU, NORTHERN TERRITORY

If you're looking for a place that makes you feel like you're in an ancient universe, then Uluru (p887) in the Northern Territory is the place for you! This ancient, sacred Indigenous place is an awe-inspiring natural phenomenon, and its undeniable air of spirituality and sheer presence are simply incredible! Uluru will hold you in a trance because of the way the rock seems to throb and move from sunrise to sundown. It's the time, light and space of the majestic Uluru that really makes it rock.
The ancient Pitjantjatjara and Yankunytjatjara Aboriginal peoples protect Uluru and want to share their beautiful home with you.

Catherine Freeman, Former Olympian

RICHARD I ANSON

THE WHITSUNDAYS, QUEENSLAND

The Whitsundays (p408) are one of the best areas to visit in the world. Try to get away from the big island resorts and visit the little places. The best way is to get onto a boat and cruise around. There are plenty of charters going out every day. If your budget allows, there are boats you can rent and skipper yourself – absolutely magic. Anchoring for the night in a secluded bay with no one around under a million stars is about as good as it gets. And if you go at the right time of year you will see whales migrating, dolphins swimming, turtles cruising by. It is truly paradise! I think I'll head up there again myself – see you out there.

Jimmy Barnes, Musician

ANDREW BAIN

VALLEY OF THE GIANTS, WESTERN AUSTRALIA

Ancient tingle trees – the locals in Walpole (p944) say they make you 'tingle all over' and it's true. Walk among trees so tall they used to take pictures of cars sitting in their hollow trunks, see the sapphire flash of a tiny iridescent fairy wren, small and surprising like the strange native orchids that arrive in spring. Swim in the warm-at-the-top-cold-underneath expanse of the Frankland River, while tall karri trees as ghostly as cathedral candles come right to the edge. Then drink some truly great local wine, watch the forest go dark, listen to the roar of the ocean, and the next day let the tourist information people at Walpole happily top you up with many more ideas.

Moira Finucane, Writer & Performer

BOB BROWN

PETER PTSCHELINZEW

LIFFEY VALLEY, TASMANIA

The Aborigines called Drys Bluff 'Taytikitikheeker', and the Liffey River (p690), which tumbles around it, 'Tellerpanger'. The Bluff towers 1000m above my little red-roofed house and the river is home to platypuses, blackfish and native hens. There is a peregrine falcon's nest in the sandstone outcrop, halfway up, and on top in a jumble of boulders is the rock-wall remains of a trapper's hut. Up here the winter turns the farm into a skating rink, the wallabies dot the snow-flecked alpine meadows and the waratahs wait to flower. Once, beneath a full moon, I walked to the summit, getting home as the eastern sky was streaked with the red of the dawning day.

Bob Brown, Federal Politician, Greens

TIWI ISLANDS, NORTHERN TERRITORY

As a Tiwi man who is often away from the community, when I return home the first places I visit are the art centres. These are always a hive of activity and a popular place for children to play and to be educated about Tiwi art and culture. I recommend to anyone visiting the Tiwi Islands (p835) that a visit to one of the art centres is a must. You haven't seen the Territory till you've seen the Tiwi Islands.

Tristan Mungatopi, Young Indigenous Writer

GARY HUTCHINGS

WUJAL WUJAL, QUEENSLAND

Last wet season I had the pleasure and fortune to travel with the circus to Wujal Wujal (p472), north of the Daintree, to perform and teach the gorgeous kids from the various Kuku-yalanji communities. This place is full of my favourite things: beautiful people; warm damp air; deafening sounds of pelting rains and forest life singing with gusto; great puddles to dance in after the rain; smells of rich fecund earth; stunning watering holes to swim in with big boulders to lie on and massive trees to climb; the juice and flesh of young green coconuts to gorge on; mountains of mangosteens and rambutans; and a tranquil beach on which to welcome the sun of each new day.

Rockie Stone, Circus Oz Performer

WILL MINSON

CARRICKALINGA BEACH, SOUTH AUSTRALIA

Carrickalinga (p753) is an hour-and-a-half drive southeast of Adelaide along the Fleurieu Peninsula. As you drive to the world-famous McLaren Vale wineries, be sure to drive a little further to Carrickalinga. The beaches here are the most superb in the state. The beautifully clear water allows beachgoers to swim in luxury. Snorkelling and spear fishing can be done with great ease and leisure due to the superb underwater visibility. The fish are numerous and not too hard to catch either. If you have the opportunity to get in a boat I strongly recommend you do so, as the fishing in the waters off Carrickalinga and nearby Normanville and Lady Bay is some of the best in South Australia.

Will Minson, Aussie Rules Footballer

KENNY BEDFORD

ERUB, QUEENSLAND

Maiem! This is how we welcome and greet visitors at Erub (Darnley Island; p482), located in the far northeastern corner of the Torres Strait. I share my island community with about 400 other Erubians, most of them my extended family. Living on a remote island at the apex of the Great Barrier Reef can be as idyllic as it sounds but island life has its challenges too, most of them linked to the isolation factor. Some of the reasons I feel very fortunate to be living on Erub include the access I have to my cultural elders, the beautiful and resourceful environment at our doorstep, the relatively relaxed lifestyle we enjoy and the feel-good sense of belonging Erub provides me.

Kenny Bedford, Torres Strait Islands Deputy Mayor

OLIVER STREWE

THE ROAD FROM KUNUNURRA TO WYNDHAM, WESTERN AUSTRALIA

The road to Wyndham (p1013) traverses Miriwoong country into Balanggara country. Its incredible beauty is juxtaposed with its remoteness and its difficult history. Snaking your way west you are watched by the vast array of granite ridges worn bare over thousands of years, witnessed by thousands of generations of the owners of this country. Wyndham appears – a rough frontier past, an uneasy existence, a humble and subtle present. Climbing the Five Rivers Lookout, the curve of the world is revealed as five vast river systems carve their way back into the earth. It is absurdly and terrifyingly beautiful.

Steve Kinnane, Writer & Researcher

RICHARD NEBESKY

GREAT OCEAN ROAD, VICTORIA

The Great Ocean Road (p551) loops and curls along Victoria's coastline, with hypnotically beautiful glimpses of surf beaches and golden sands on one side and dense rainforests on the other. For me, it is more than a road, it's a portal to how I would like to spend my life – paddling in rock pools at sunset, eating fish and chips on the sand, drinking cold beer on the terrace of a country pub, or just sunbaking on a giant rock like an ancient lizard in the bush, listening to the cacophony of birdsong.

Jill Dupleix, Food Writer

AA WORLD TRAVEL LIBRARY / ALAMY

KANGAROO VALLEY, NEW SOUTH WALES

My favourite place out of the water is somewhere I go to relax and take a complete break from the demands of life. Kangaroo Valley (p232) slows you down, encourages you to take a deep breath and appreciate the incredible beauty of the environment. Tucked between the South Coast and the Southern Highlands, it's surrounded by escarpments of volcanic rock. Like a gateway to another world, the road in descends quickly, dry scrub becomes lush temperate rainforest and the air becomes moister and cooler. With activities such as bushwalking, kayaking, golf and tennis, the valley is a wonderful place for the whole family, or for a romantic escape.

Layne Beachley, World Champion Surfer & Author

Contents

Regional Map Contents

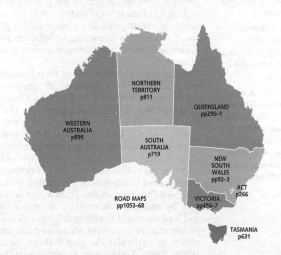

Destination Australia

Cut from the ancient Gondwana continent more than 45 million years ago, Australia's identity, both geographic and cultural, has been forged by millennia of survival and isolation. Vulnerable to violent climatic extremes, this savvy landscape learned to manipulate voracious fires, long droughts and desperate floods to carve some of the world's most dramatic terrain. These origins, harsh, resilient and beautiful, remain emblematic of the diversity of life Australia has created ever since. Leap to the present and you'll discover it in the Australian people – it hides behind the larrikin wit and amicable informality that sucks you in before your eyes can arch in surprise. It's no wonder locals, visitors and admirers from afar are driven to call Australia home.

Australia's greatest enigma is its extremes. The driest and flattest continent on earth is also home to the colossal rainforests of Cape Tribulation, laden with prehistoric and impenetrable flora. Nearby the world's largest coral reef adorns 2300km of coastline. This underwater jungle teems with life and colours unheralded above ground. The diverse coastline that buffers this immense island from the ocean bleeds into thick Australian bush with towering eucalypts and old-growth forests before petering out into the vast ochre outback of the interior. At its heart the iconic Uluru overwhelms visitors with its bulk, rising 348m from the earth and burying almost twice as much of itself beneath. Nearby the domed buttresses of the Olgas huddle close around cut gorges and valleys, and the largest, Mt Olga, soars 1066m above sea level. Decades of crafted marketing and cinematography have paraded images of Kakadu and the Top End on screens of all sizes across the world. But none can invoke the magic of Aboriginal cultures that have lived there for more than 50,000 years, or the 530 plus bird, reptile, fish and mammal species that call it home.

Australians' love for home is matched by an intense curiosity of the foreign and their cities are in a constant state of flux, absorbing fresh influences from far corners of the globe. But this country hates the generic and so its cities remain distinct: Sydney is a luscious tart, Melbourne a subtle glamour puss, Brisbane a blithe playmate, Adelaide a gracious dame and Perth a free spirit. In between are coastal villages and spreads, hinterland towns and outback communities defining their own patch of utopia.

Australians are shameless in their belief that theirs is the lucky country. But pride is served with an equal measure of reality. Just as climate was the dominant influence in Australia's beginnings, so too it remains core to the country's fears and psyche. As the world grapples with climate change, Australians feel it more tangibly than most. Vast regions are enduring a decade-long drought and the need for rain is a burning issue for much of the country. Using water sparingly is now common practice for most Australians and enforced restrictions have adapted behaviours in an effort to cope. Threatened with extinction, the vibrant life on the Great Barrier Reef is dependent on halting global warming. As temperatures rise, bushfires have shifted from a part of summer life to an unfathomable fear. By and large, Australians are eager for environmental policies that will lead the world to tackle this most global of problems. But in the competing market of current affairs and industry lobbying, more immediate needs, in particular the global financial crisis, have taken precedence. When Kevin Rudd swept to victory in the November 2007 election, a

FAST FACTS

Population: 21,824,140

GDP growth: 1.8% (2008), 0% (2009)

Inflation: 2.5%

Unemployment: 5.7%

Average gross weekly income (full-time work): $1183

Tourism generates over $8.1 billion annually (0.9% of Australia's GDP).

Australia's coastline is 25,800km long and is dusted with over 7000 beaches.

Australia currently exports around 715 million litres of wine per year, with a value of $2.6 billion.

Australia has almost 112,600 surf life savers, who collectively spend some 1.4 million hours patrolling Australian beaches, where they rescue approximately 10,000 people per year.

mood of hope and inspiration awakened in parts of the population that had become dormant and numb. He promptly delivered by ratifying the Kyoto Protocol and issuing a public and emotive apology to the Indigenous peoples of Australia. Immigration policies affecting refugees were also addressed and suddenly many Australians found in their Prime Minister a tenacity to embrace the future. But the tendency for politicians to be inhibited by, well politics, is universal, and after racing to victory on a campaign of environmental responsibility, the inevitable reality of a population laden with mortgages and financial uncertainty has taken precedence. Concerns about job security, education and health reign on the street and in the halls of parliament. Despite the polls consistently showing that Australians want strong action on climate change, the government announced a modest target to reduce emissions by five to 15 per cent by 2020. Though interest rates plummeted in the first half of 2009, providing welcome relief to home owners and the promise of a salvaged economy, the reality of economic empires crumbling around the globe has ensured many Australians remain anxious about their future.

But Australians are a hardy lot, and in tough times resilience and compassion dictate the population's behaviour. Personal fears were relegated to obscurity in the aftermath of the tragic Victorian bushfires of February 2009, which claimed more than 170 lives and wiped towns from existence. Within one week this disparate community of 21 million raised over $100 million in an act of solidarity and sympathy. By the end of week two it had passed $200 million. And this one example returns us to the beauty and inimitability of Australia. You have only to determine how to take it all in: overload your senses, witness unforgettable imagery, learn from the earliest cultures, dine on the world's most diverse cuisine, mingle with a population that already considers you a mate and ponder it all amid space and isolation you couldn't begin to imagine.

Getting Started

Australia is so vast and diverse it fulfils the full spectrum of adventure fantasies. A well-developed tourism industry and ample information provides options for travellers on all budgets and enables you to land in any city or well-touristed destination with little more than your first night's accommodation sorted. An intrepid road trip through the outback or tropical Top End requires more investigation and planning. The most important thing to remember is that Australia is big – *really* big – so time is of the essence. Think about what you want to see and how you're going to get there, and then make sure you don't underestimate how long you'll need for your visit.

WHEN TO GO

See Climate (p1024) for information.

Truth be told, any time is a good time to be *somewhere* in Australia. When it's cold down south, it's magnificent in the north and the Centre; when it's too hot and sweaty up north, the southern states are at their natural finest. There are also the numerous festivals and other public spectacles on show every month to lure you.

The seasons in Australia are the antitheses of those in Europe and North America. Summer is December to February; the weather and longer daylight hours are tailor-made for swimming and other outdoor activities across much of the country. Summer is also school-holiday period and consequently high season for most places. Unless you want to compete with hordes of grimly determined local holidaymakers at every turn, avoid Australia's prime destinations during the peaks of school holidays (January) and public holidays. See p1032 for more information. During these times, you're also likely to encounter spontaneous rises in the price of everything from accommodation to petrol.

If weather is your main determinant then the best way to decide when to go is to first decide where you're going in Australia. Check the Geography and Climate headings at the start of regional chapters in this book for more specific information. Winter, from June to August, is officially designated the tourism low season for most of the country, but not the Northern Territory, Queensland and top of Western Australia. Winter in this northern stretch offers respite from the humidity of the wet season (which runs roughly from October to March, with the heaviest rain falling from January onwards; the

---

DON'T LEAVE HOME WITHOUT...

- A willingness to use 'mate', 'no worries' and 'she'll be right' liberally
- An appetite for seafood, steak, beer (other than Fosters), barbecues and fresh fruit
- A travel insurance policy (p1032) covering skydiving, bungee jumping, diving, skiing, abseiling and white-water rafting
- Warm clothes because winter does actually occur in Australia...well, down south anyway
- Extra-strength insect repellent to fend off merciless flies and mosquitoes (p1027)
- Sunscreen, sunglasses and a hat to deflect fierce UV rays (p1078)
- A towel and bathers/togs/swimmers/swimming costume/cossie/trunks/Speedos/budgie smugglers...for the beach
- Good maps for outback meanders and binoculars for the wildlife while you're there

Dry lasts from April to September) and the temperatures are highly agreeable. It's also when roads and tracks are most accessible up north. Autumn (March to May) and spring (September to November) both enjoy a lack of climatic extremes everywhere.

COSTS & MONEY

Australia is affordable by Western European and American standards, but certainly not a budget destination compared to say Southeast Asia. Your biggest costs will be accommodation and transport.

If you're a midrange traveller hiring a car, seeing the sights, staying in hotels and motels, and enjoying the fabulous food and grog, budget for $150 per person per day but add $50 to $100 for cities and well-touristed areas. In remote areas such as Far North Queensland and the Kimberley bank on spending $250 to as much as $500 per day with 4WD hire and petrol. Escalated petrol prices make multiweek, remote road trips in a 4WD an expensive affair, but small, economical 2WDs elsewhere are still wallet-friendly.

Travellers with a demanding brood in tow will find there are many ways to keep kids inexpensively satisfied, including beach and park visits, camping grounds and motels with pools and games rooms, kids' menus and youth/family concessions for attractions. For more information on travelling with children, see p1024.

If you camp or stay in hostels, cook your own meals, restrain your urge for entertainment and move around by public transport, you could probably eke out an existence on $80 per day; for a budget that realistically enables you to have a good time, aim for $100 to $120 per day.

TRAVEL LITERATURE

Australia's enormity of social and geographical extremes – from cityscapes to isolation, yuppies to nomads, outback to the reefs – can be hard to wrap your head around. Fortunately, some inspiring, thought-provoking and just plain entertaining books have been written about this country.

Peter Carey demonstrates his art for wit and characters in *Theft: A Love Story* (2006) about the shambling existence of a famous Sydney artist, long since fallen off his perch.

Burke's Soldier (2003) by Alan Atwood is a historical account of the Burke and Wills expedition and Australia in the 1860s through the eyes of John King – the sole survivor of the mission.

Carpentaria (2006) by indigenous writer Alexis Wright is set on the Gulf of Carpentaria and aptly captures the distance – socially and environmentally – of remote Australia from its cities. It's also highly recommended as an audiobook for long road trips.

Set in Queensland's Darling Downs region, *The White Earth* (2004) by Andrew McGahan is a beautiful and brutal work of fiction about a young boy facing an immense inheritance of land, as well as the bloody history and contemporary racial struggles attached to it.

A Fraction of the Whole (2008) by Steve Toltz follows the path of three generations of one family, with criminal and undeniably Australian overtones. It's a confronting, descriptive and excellent read.

Knockabout Girl (2007) by Pip Newling is an endearing and humorous account of the author's experience moving to Halls Creek in remote Western Australia at the age of 23.

The Songlines (1986) by Bruce Chatwin combines a fictional and nonfictional account of the author's trip to Australia and his research and insights in outback and Indigenous cultures, issues and religion.

HOW MUCH?

Coffee $2.80-3.50

Stubby of bottled beer $3-5

Toasted foccacia or wrap $7

1L of petrol $1.15-1.50

Metropolitan train ticket $3.50-6.50

TOP PICKS

AUSTRALIA

MUST-SEE MOVIES

If you're in need of instant inspiration, these quintessential Australian films, which range from intelligent and insightful to uber-cheesy, will fill your head with larrikin wit, breathtaking landscapes and urban Aussie culture. See p48 for some reviews of these and other films.

- **Australia** (2008) Director: Baz Luhrmann
- **Beneath Clouds** (2002) Director: Ivan Sen
- **The Black Balloon** (2008) Director: Elissa Down
- **Gallipoli** (1981) Director: Peter Weir
- **Jindabyne** (2006) Director: Ray Lawrence

- **Rabbit-Proof Fence** (2002) Director: Phillip Noyce
- **The Sound of One Hand Clapping** (1998) Director: Richard Flanagan
- **Ten Canoes** (2006) Director: Rolf de Heer
- **The Year My Voice Broke** (1987) Director: John Duigan

TOP SOUNDTRACKS

A respectable Australian road trip deserves an authentic soundtrack. Get a head full of these iconic albums before and after you arrive to capture the memories, landscapes, events and characters on your trip. See p51 for more musical inspiration.

- **Chisel** (1991) Cold Chisel
- **Claim** (1989) Not Drowning Waving
- **Diesel & Dust** (1987) Midnight Oil
- **Hourly Daily** (1996) You Am I
- **John Butler** (2000) John Butler
- **Songs from the South: The Best of Paul Kelly** (1997) Paul Kelly

- **Wait Long by the River and the Bodies of Your Enemies Will Float By** (2005) The Drones
- **When the Flood Comes** (2008) The Audreys
- **White Moth** (2007) Xavier Rudd
- **Wide Open Road** (2008) Compilation by some of Australia's best artists

TOP FESTIVALS

Australians celebrate at the drop of a hat. Music and art feature highly on the festival calendar, but cultural celebrations get plenty of attention too. Joining the following festivities will show visitors Australia's energy and diversity at its finest.

- **Big Day Out** (p1030) In Sydney, Melbourne, Adelaide, Perth and the Gold Coast in January.
- **Sydney Gay & Lesbian Mardi Gras** (p124) In Sydney in February.
- **Ten Days on the Island** (p647) In Hobart in March.
- **East Coast International Blues & Roots Music Festival** (p198) Held over Easter in Byron Bay.

- **Melbourne International Film Festival** (p516) In July and August in Melbourne.
- **Garma Festival** (p814) In August in Arnhem Land.
- **Alice Desert Festival** (p870) In September in Alice Springs.
- **Woodford Folk Festival** (p356) In December in the Sunshine Coast hinterland.
- **WOMADelaide** (p735) In Adelaide in March.

Around Australia in 80 Days (2004) by Jonathon Green is essential reading for anyone planning to eat/sleep/live out of their vehicle while touring Australia, with 20,000km worth of wit, advice and inspiration.

For comfortably predictable reading, pick up a copy of Bill Bryson's *Down Under* (2001, also titled *In a Sunburned Country*), or Mark Dapin's *Strange Country: Travels In A Very Different Australia* (2008).

INTERNET RESOURCES

Australian Newspapers Online (www.nla.gov.au/npapers) National Library–maintained listing of Australian newspaper websites.

Australian Tourist Commission (www.australia.com) Official tourism site run by the federal government with nationwide info for visitors.

Bureau of Meteorology (www.bom.gov.au) Great for checking weather anywhere around the country.

Department of the Environment & Heritage (www.environment.gov.au/parks/index.html) Links to info on Australia's national parks and reserves.

Lonely Planet (www.lonelyplanet.com) Get quick Australian info and inspiration from the 'Destinations' tab, a rundown of guidebooks from the bookshop, accommodation reviews and bookings from 'Hotels and hostels', and travellers trading information on the Thorn Tree.

Itineraries
CLASSIC ROUTES

The Surf & Sun Run is 2864km of bare blissful beaches, dense national parks, dizzying theme parks, serious surfing, marine wonders and urban fun. You might do it in a fortnight, but what a waste – take a month or two and chill out.

THE SURF & SUN RUN
Six to Eight Weeks/Sydney to Cairns

Lured by sun and surf, both international and domestic travellers hug the east coast between Sydney and Cairns, making it the most well-trodden path in Australia.

Start with the bright lights and glitz of **Sydney** (p98) and then meander north along the Pacific Hwy through central and northern New South Wales (NSW). Hang out in the **Hunter Valley** (p168) for vino-quaffing and national-park tramping, and stop for water sports in family-friendly **Port Stephens** (p174), **Myall Lakes National Park** (p177) and **Coffs Harbour** (p186). Skip up to **Byron Bay** (p195) for New Age indulgences and great beaches, then head over the Queensland border into the honey-hued, surf-addicted **Gold Coast** (p333). Pause in **Brisbane** (p297) and then amble up through **Noosa** (p349) and the glorious **Sunshine Coast** (p344).

The Bruce Hwy wends along the stunning coast into the far north. Nature lovers should visit the whale-watching haven of **Hervey Bay** (p362) and then make their way further north, up to the blissful **Whitsunday Islands** (p408), the coral charms of the **Great Barrier Reef** (p442) and the scuba-diving nexus of **Cairns** (p436).

BEST OF THE WEST TO THE OUTBACK

Six to Eight Weeks/Perth to Alice Springs

This route gives you the best of the country's lush southwest and then takes you through the burnt, bare and beautiful outback. Start in **Perth** (p900) and exhaust all of your urban urges in the great pubs, galleries, bars and restaurants. Then snake your way south via the stunning beaches of Cape Naturaliste, before camping out in **Margaret River** (p938). Go surfing and winery-hopping before continuing south to **Augusta** (p940) and magnificent Cape Leeuwin, where whales drop by. Meander through the giant old-growth forests of the southwest and rest a while in **Albany** (p948) for its historic architecture and world-class diving. Follow the southern coast to **Esperance** (p951) where you can visit seals, penguins and seabirds in the Archipelago of the Recherche.

Bid the coast farewell for a spell and head north to the iconic outback town of **Kalgoorlie-Boulder** (p956). Play 'wild west', succumb to hedonism and buy a miner a beer. Then hit the Eyre Hwy and follow it through to South Australia (SA), past the Nullarbor Plain and into the coastal towns, surfing beaches and fishing hideouts that skirt the Great Southern Bight. Pause in ambient **Port Lincoln** (p789) for fishing expeditions and all things tuna related, and then climb north to **Port Augusta** (p787).

Hit the Stuart Hwy – a must for avid road trippers – and journey up to the opal-tinted dugout town of **Coober Pedy** (p802). You're now well and truly into an 'outback odyssey' and the obvious route is through the Simpson Desert to awe-inspiring **Uluru (Ayers Rock)** (p887) and the spectacular, vertigo-inducing **Watarrka (Kings Canyon) National Park** (p884). Finish up in the desert oasis of **Alice Springs** (p863), in the heart of the steep-sided **MacDonnell Ranges** (p876).

Pack a tent, do your homework (p74) and bid the neighbours farewell for a while – this route takes in around 4750km of the best of the southwest and the outback's big empty. Make the most out of the landscape and take a good two months.

THE GIANT LOOP
Six Months/Sydney to Sydney

After bidding *au revoir* to **Sydney** (p98) and following your suntanned nose up the east coast into Queensland (see p26), veer west from **Townsville** (p413) towards the tunnel-threaded Queensland mining town of **Mt Isa** (p392). Settle in for the long, red drive (via **Tennant Creek**; p860) in the red centre, where you can inspect **Alice Springs** (p863) and the awesome splendour of **Uluru (Ayers Rock)** (p887) before dog-legging it up to **Darwin** (p816). Cross into Western Australia (WA) for a pit stop at pretty **Kununurra** (p1014), then negotiate the Great Northern Hwy to the cosmopolitan beachside getaway of **Broome** (p998).

Take a peninsula sidetrack to the snorkel-friendly **Cape Range National Park** (p988) and the marine brilliance of **Ningaloo Reef** (p988), followed by a date with a bottlenose dolphin at **Monkey Mia** (p978). Continue south to the 'life is a beach' city of **Perth** (p900) and the latte-flavoured enclave of **Fremantle** (p920), then wine away the hours at **Margaret River** (p938) until you're ready to tackle the flat immensity of the **Nullarbor Plain** (p962).

In South Australia (SA) bushwalkers can trudge towards the challenging **Flinders Ranges** (p793), while tipplers can refuel their palates in the **Barossa Valley** (p775). Beyond **Adelaide** (p724) it's a shortish trek into Victoria (Vic) to check out surfboard-strewn **Torquay** (p552) and cultured **Melbourne** (p492), from where there's a ferry to **Devonport** (p691), your gateway to the stunning island highlights of **Tasmania** (p629).

Further along the Victorian coast, enjoy the secluded wilderness of **Wilsons Promontory National Park** (p617) and spend a couple of days somewhere along **Ninety Mile Beach** (p621), then cruise around **Narooma** (p236) on the southern NSW coast, and bask in idyllic **Jervis Bay** (p233). After you've detoured to the national capital, **Canberra** (p267), return to the bright lights of Sydney.

Experiencing the furthest reaches of the land can mean tallying up over 14,000km of highway, not counting side trips to beaches, forests, mountains, reefs, towns... Where you start and finish is up to your imagination, but allow for around six months of discovery.

ROADS LESS TRAVELLED

VINEYARDS, RIVERS, MOUNTAINS & GORGES   Eight weeks/Adelaide to Rockhampton

This trip shies from the norm but packs in much of Australia's diversity. Start in **Adelaide** (p724) for gracious architecture and uncrowded beaches. Duck down to the vineyards of **McLaren Vale** (p750) before ambling up to those in the **Barossa Valley** (p775). Then hit the Murray and make your way along the Sunraysia Hwy to **Mildura** (p573). Take a paddle boat down the Murray River and an Indigenous tour to **Mungo National Park** (p264). Head into the vast New South Wales (NSW) outback and course the Silver City Hwy to **Broken Hill** (p259), with its rich history of artists, poets and Aboriginal culture, as well as mining.

From here follow the Barrier Hwy east to Dubbo's outstanding **Western Plains Zoo** (p219). Then take the Newell Hwy north onto the Oxley Hwy for a few days of boot scootin' in **Tamworth** (p206). Chart a course for the breathtaking **Waterfall Way** (p210), pop into picturesque **Bellingen** (p211) and then hightail it to the New Age, lush, remote **Far North Coast Hinterland** (p201) and **Byron Bay** (p195).

Carve back inland through the mountainous and woody **Gold Coast Hinterland** (p342) to the Best of All Lookout (it really is?!) in **Springbrook National Park** (p343). Take the inland routes through the **Darling Downs** (p356) for wine tasting, Queensland style. Flit through **Toowoomba** (p358) and drive through the Great Dividing Range to **Roma** (p359) before hiding out in **Carnarvon National Park** (p390) to marvel at the jaw-dropping 30km-long, 200m-high Carnarvon Gorge. Then wrap things up with die-hard country music and the best steak you've ever eaten in **Rockhampton** (p385).

Escape the coast and muddle your way through South Australia's vineyards; Victoria's fertile Murray towns; and New South Wales' amber outback and rich, New Age hinterland. Add two spectacular national parks in Queensland before landing on the coast again. Eight weeks will do this 3700km route justice.

ACROSS THE CONTINENT   One to Two Months/Cairns to Perth

If you prefer solitude and travelling rough you'll love the Australian outback, which is criss-crossed with roads and tracks, some sealed and others little more than a pair of dirty ruts. There are many potential hazards in heading off the beaten track, so wherever you go, make sure you're well informed and fully prepared – see Extra Precautions for Outback Driving (p88) for more information.

Few roads are less travelled than this monster 4560km trail from the tidal rivers of the Gulf Savannah to the pounding surf at the bottom of Western Australia, with undulating desertscapes in between. Conditions can be unpredictable, so plan on taking up to two months.

The following is a long, difficult route from the tropics to the Indian Ocean. Start in **Cairns** (p436), gateway to the arduous Mulligan Hwy that (in case you're interested) snakes towards the tip of **Cape York** (p476). Head west from Cairns to **Normanton** (p434), the biggest town in the Gulf of Carpentaria region, then south down the Matilda Hwy to the mining rough house of **Mt Isa** (p392).

To the southwest is the frontier outback town of Urandangi, after which you run into the **Plenty Hwy** (p86), a monotonous – or to some, gloriously desolate – road with plenty of bone-jolting challenges (4WD recommended). Over 500km later you'll hit the Stuart Hwy and then the dead-centre city of **Alice Springs** (p863).

The Lasseter Hwy turn-off takes you to weighty **Uluru (Ayers Rock)** (p887) and the captivating **Kata Tjuta (the Olgas)** (p889) rock formations, beyond which is the beginning of the **Great Central Rd** (p85). This lonely trail, suitable for well-prepared 2WDs and lined with saltbush, spinifex and desert oaks, stretches 750km to the tiny gold-mining town of **Laverton** (p961), from where it's another 400km to the gold-mining concern of **Kalgoorlie-Boulder** (p956). Finally, the ocean beckons from behind the beaches of Scarborough and Cottesloe in **Perth** (p900).

TAILORED TRIPS

BEST WORLD HERITAGE HIKING & CAMPING

Australia's full of gems. Let's start in the west with the stunning peninsulas, rich marine park and Indigenous cultural tours of **Shark Bay** (p976) and the colossal domes of the **Bungle Bungles** in **Purnululu National Park** (p1013).

The sultry Top End is home to the world-famous **Kakadu National Park** (p842), full of rare species and ancient rock art.

Far North Queensland encompasses the enormous **Wet Tropics World Heritage Area** (p468), sheltering a huge array of flora and fauna. Offshore the wilderness is just as rich beneath the waves along the **Great Barrier Reef** (p410). Potter south and you'll discover **Fraser Island** (p367), the world's largest sand island, brimming with forests, mineral lakes and wildlife.

In the Central Eastern Rainforest Reserves in NSW there's **Nightcap** (p203), **Border Ranges** (p204) and **Mt Warning National Parks** (p204); all prime bushwalking territory. New England boasts the dramatic, rugged **Gibraltar Range** and **Washpool National Parks** (p213), **Richmond Range National Park** (p214) and the superb **Dorrigo National Park** (p211).

Then there's the glorious Tasmanian wilderness, with the mighty rivers and snow-capped summits of **Franklin-Gordon Wild Rivers National Park** (p709), pristine lakes of **Cradle Mountain-Lake St Clair National Park** (p710), glacial landscape of the **Walls of Jerusalem National Park** (p696) and virgin rainforest of **Southwest National Park** (p713).

THE CULINARY CRUSADE

If gastronomic pleasures are your caper then Australia is your Arcadia. In Western Australia (WA) you can mix superlative wines with marinated marron (see p66) in the wineries surrounding **Margaret River** (p938). If nothing appeals to you more than following your bouquet-detecting schnozz, head to the stalwart of the country's internationally praised viticulture scene – South Australia's (SA) **Barossa Valley** (p775), where the 60-plus wineries release more bottled varieties than you can pop a cork at. The roll-call of SA's worthy vine-covered bits continues to the north in the Riesling-proficient **Clare Valley** (p780).

Another prominent wine-making region is the **Hunter Valley** (p168) in NSW, producing outstanding Shiraz and Semillon varieties. The rustic Victorian district **Rutherglen** (p582) specialises in fortified wines like Muscat, Tokay and port that owe a debt to its hot climate. In **Melbourne** (p522), locals rate their need to dine out on an even keel with oxygen, and global flavours and exquisite Mod Oz are up for grabs for every budget. **Sydney** (p131) rivals, of course, but with a voguish cutting edge. Queensland's **Noosa** (p353) is a breeding ground for culinary inventiveness; and for salt-of-the-earth organic cuisine done with pure class, head to **Byron Bay** (p195).

The region around **Pipers River** (p680) in Tasmania releases many superb vintages that are characterised by their full, fruity flavours.

CAPERS FOR THE KIDS

Australia's smorgasbord of natural and artificial sights makes it one giant playground for kids. Get them giddy on the feisty rides and theme parks of Queensland's **Gold Coast** (p333) and then temper the experience with the bounty of wildlife opportunities: go whale watching in **Albany** (p948) or **Hervey Bay** (p363) and then get them up close and personal with furred, feathered and finned critters from around the globe at Queensland's world-famous **Australia Zoo** (p346), New South Wales' **Western Plains Zoo** (p219) and Victoria's **Werribee Open Range Zoo** (p538).

A refreshing ocean dip must be near the top of everyone's outdoor-activities list, with beaches such as those at **Merimbula** (p237) and **Coffs Harbour** (p187) in NSW, **Cottesloe Beach** (p914) in Western Australia, **Barwon Heads** (p542) in Victoria, and numerous seaside spots on Queensland's **Sunshine Coast** (p344).

In Tasmania, the **West Coast Wilderness Railway** (p707) is an unforgettable ride across some of the west coast's most exhilarating terrain, which lies stretched out between Queenstown and Strahan. There's also stage-managed fun at period places like Swan Hill's **Pioneer Settlement** (p578), with seats up for grabs on a paddle steamer, vintage cars and horse-drawn wagons; or Ballarat's **Sovereign Hill** (p586), with period-dressed gold-digging fun.

Don't forget the urban fun – there is plenty of hands-on exploration to be found at the **Melbourne Museum** (p509) and at the **Art Gallery of NSW** (p114).

THE FESTIVAL FRENZY

Australians will seize on just about any excuse for a celebration, and while you're visiting this country it only makes sense to follow the light-hearted, self-indulgent lead of its inhabitants. The year gets off to a champagne-swilling start when fireworks explode high above Sydney Harbour on **New Year's Eve** (p124). The new year is also vigorously celebrated further south during the **Hobart Summer Festival** (p646), when Taswegians stuff themselves with food, wine and song.

In late January the streets of Tamworth in NSW are littered with broken guitar strings and broken hearts during its famous **Country Music Festival** (p206), while Sydney vamps itself up in February for the **Gay & Lesbian Mardi Gras** (p136).

The exuberant **Adelaide Festival of Arts** (p734) and its eccentric sibling, **Adelaide Fringe** (p734), fill the South Australian capital with culture and idiosyncratic performances in February and March. And in April in Victoria, Melbourne repeatedly smacks its own funny bone with the outstanding **International Comedy Festival** (p515).

In September, the **Brisbane Riverfestival** (p315) captivates the city with 10 days of performance, art and celebrations, and the city gets a musical work out during October's **Livid** (p315) festival.

In the Northern Territory, the **Garma Festival** (p814), held in August, celebrates Indigenous culture in Arnhem Land.

History Dr Michael Cathcart

INTRUDERS ARRIVE

By sunrise the storm had passed. Zachary Hicks was keeping sleepy watch on the British ship *Endeavour* when suddenly he was wide awake. He summoned his captain, James Cook, who climbed into the brisk morning air to a miraculous sight. Ahead of them lay an uncharted country of wooded hills and gentle valleys. It was 19 April 1770. In the coming days Cook began to draw the first European map of Australia's eastern coast. He was mapping the end of Aboriginal supremacy.

Two weeks later Cook led a party of men onto a narrow beach. As they waded ashore, two Aboriginal men stepped onto the sand, and challenged the intruders with spears. Cook drove the men off with musket fire. For the rest of that week, the Aborigines and the intruders watched each other warily.

Cook's ship *Endeavour* was a floating annexe of London's leading scientific organisation, the Royal Society. The ship's gentlemen passengers included technical artists, scientists, an astronomer and a wealthy botanist named Joseph Banks. As Banks and his colleagues strode about the Aborigines' territory, they were delighted by the mass of new plants they collected. (The showy banksia flowers, which look like red, white or golden bottlebrushes, are named after Banks.)

The local Aborigines called the place Kurnell, but Cook gave it a foreign name: he called it 'Botany Bay'. The fertile eastern coastline of Australia is now festooned with Cook's place names – including Point Hicks, Hervey Bay (after an English admiral), Endeavour River and Point Solander (after one of the *Endeavour*'s scientists).

When the *Endeavour* reached the northern tip of Cape York, blue ocean opened up to the west. Cook and his men could smell the sea-route home. And on a small, hilly island ('Possession Island'), Cook raised the Union Jack. Amid volleys of gunfire, he claimed the eastern half of the continent for King George III.

Cook's intention was not to steal land from the Aborigines. In fact he rather idealised them. 'They are far more happier than we Europeans', he wrote. 'They think themselves provided with all the necessaries of Life and that they have no superfluities.' At most, his patriotic ceremony was intended to contain the territorial ambitions of the French, and of the Dutch, who had visited and mapped much of the western and southern coast over the previous two centuries. Indeed, Cook knew the western half of Australia as 'New Holland'.

Dr Michael Cathcart wrote the History chapter. Michael teaches history at the Australian Centre, the University of Melbourne. He is well known as a broadcaster on ABC Radio National and presented history programs on ABC TV. For more information about Michael, see p1086.

The brilliant classic biography of Cook is JC Beaglehole's *The Life of Captain James Cook* (1974). Beaglehole also edited Cook's journals. There are several biographies online, including the excellent http://en.wikipedia. org/wiki/James_Cook.

TIMELINE

50,000 years ago	1616	1770
The first Aborigines arrive by sea in northern Australia. The country is home to giant marsupials including a wombat the size of a rhinoceros. Today's central deserts are places of lush forests and teeming lakes.	The Dutch trading route across the Indian Ocean to Indonesia utilises winds called 'the Roaring Forties'. These winds bring Captain Dirk Hartog to the Western Australian coast.	Captain James Cook is the first European to map the eastern coast, which he names 'New South Wales'. He returns to England with news that he has found an ideal place for settlement at 'Botany Bay'.

CONVICT BEGINNINGS

Eighteen years after Cook's arrival, in 1788, the English were back to stay. They arrived in a fleet of 11 ships, packed with supplies including weapons, tools, building materials and livestock. The ships also contained 751 convicts and around 250 soldiers, officials and their wives. This motley 'First Fleet' was under the command of a humane and diligent naval captain, Arthur Phillip. As his orders dictated, Phillip dropped anchor at Botany Bay. But the paradise that had so delighted Joseph Banks filled Phillip with dismay. The country was marshy, there was little healthy water, and the anchorage was exposed to wind and storm. So Phillip left his floating prison and embarked in a small boat to search for a better location. Just a short way up the coast his heart leapt as he sailed into the finest harbour in the world. There, in a small cove, in the idyllic lands of the Eora people, he established a British penal settlement. He renamed the place after the British Home Secretary, Lord Sydney.

The intruders set about clearing the trees and building shelters and were soon trying to grow crops. Phillip's official instructions urged him to colonise the land without doing violence to the local inhabitants. Among the Aborigines he used as intermediaries was an Eora man named Bennelong, who adopted many of the white man's customs and manners. For many years Bennelong lived in a hut on the finger of land now known as Bennelong Point, the site of the Sydney Opera House. But his people were shattered by the loss of their lands. Hundreds died of smallpox, and many of the survivors, including Bennelong himself, succumbed to alcoholism and despair.

So what kind of society were the British trying to create? Robert Hughes' bestseller *The Fatal Shore* (1987) depicts convict Australia as a terrifying 'Gulag' where the British authorities tormented rebels, vagrants and criminals. But other historians point out that powerful men in London saw transportation as a scheme for giving prisoners a new and useful life. Indeed, under Governor Phillip's authority, many convicts soon earned their 'ticket of leave', a kind of parole which allowed them to live where they wished and to seek work on their own behalf.

But the convict system could also be savage. Women (who were outnumbered five to one) lived under constant threat of sexual exploitation. Female convicts who offended their gaolers languished in the depressing 'female factories'. Male re-offenders were cruelly flogged and could even be hanged for such crimes as stealing.

In 1803 English officers established a second convict settlement in Van Diemen's Land (later called Tasmania). Soon, re-offenders filled the grim prison at Port Arthur (p667) on the beautiful and wild coast near Hobart. In time, others would endure the senseless agonies of Norfolk Island prison (p226) in the remote Pacific.

So miserable were these convict beginnings, that Australians long regarded them as a period of shame. But things have changed: today most white

A likable observer of the settlement was Watkin Tench. His vivid journal is available as *1788* (edited by Tim Flannery).

The website www .portarthur.org.au is a vital guide for the visitor to this powerful historical site, where a tragic massacre occurred in 1996.

1788	1789	1804
The First Fleet brings British convicts and officials to the lands of the Eora people, where Governor Arthur Phillip establishes a penal settlement. He calls it 'Sydney'.	An epidemic of smallpox devastates the Aboriginal groups around Sydney. British officers report that Aborigines' bodies are rotting in every bay of the harbour.	In Van Diemen's Land (now called Tasmania), David Collins moves the fledgling convict colony from Risdon Cove to the site of modern Hobart.

Australians are inclined to brag a little if they find a convict in their family tree. Indeed, Australians annually celebrate the arrival of the First Fleet at Sydney Cove on 26 January 1788, as 'Australia Day'.

FROM SHACKLES TO FREEDOM

At first, Sydney and the smaller colonies depended on supplies brought in by ship. Anxious to develop productive farms, the government granted land to soldiers, officers and settlers. After 30 years of trial and error, the farms began to flourish. The most irascible and ruthless of these new landholders was John Macarthur. Along with his spirited wife Elizabeth, Macarthur pioneered the breeding of merino sheep on his verdant property near Sydney.

Macarthur was also a leading member of the 'Rum Corps', a clique of powerful officers who bullied successive governors (including William Bligh of *Bounty* fame) and grew rich by controlling much of Sydney's trade, notably rum. But the Corps' racketeering was ended in 1810 by a tough new governor named Lachlan Macquarie. Macquarie laid out the major roads of modern-day Sydney, built some fine public buildings (many of which were designed by talented convict-architect Francis Greenway) and helped to lay the foundations for a more civil society.

Macquarie also championed the rights of freed convicts, granting them land and appointing several to public office. But Macquarie's tolerance was not shared by the 'Exclusives'. These landholders, middle-class snobs and senior British officials observed a rigid expatriate class system. They shunned ex-prisoners, and scoffed at the distinctive accent and easy-going manners of these new Australians.

By now, word was reaching England that Australia offered cheap land and plenty of work, and adventurous migrants took to the oceans in search of their fortunes. At the same time the British government continued to transport prisoners.

In 1825 a party of soldiers and convicts established a penal settlement in the territory of the Yuggera people, close to modern-day Brisbane. Before long this warm, fertile region was attracting free settlers, who were soon busy farming, grazing, logging and mining.

TWO NEW SETTLEMENTS: MELBOURNE & ADELAIDE

In the cooler grasslands of Tasmania, the sheep farmers were also thriving. In the 1820s, they waged a bloody war against the island's Aborigines, driving them to the brink of extinction. Now these settlers were hungry for more land. In 1835 an ambitious young men named John Batman sailed to Port Phillip Bay on the mainland. On the banks of the Yarra River, he chose the location for Melbourne, famously announcing 'This is the place for a village'. Batman persuaded local Aborigines to 'sell' him their traditional lands (a whopping 250,000 hectares) for a crate of blankets, knives and knick-knacks. Back in

Tasmania's Aborigines were separated from the mainland when sea levels rose after the last Ice Age.

1820s	1829	1835
In Van Diemen's Land, Aborigines and settlers clash in the Black Wars. The bloody conflict devastates the Aboriginal population. Only a few remnants survive.	Captain James Stirling heads a private company that founds the settlement of Perth on Australia's west coast in Noongar country. The surrounding land is arid, retarding development of the colony.	The young John Batman sails from Van Diemen's Land to Port Phillip, where he negotiates a land deal with elders of the Kulin nation. The settlement of Melbourne follows that same year.

Sydney, Governor Bourke declared the contract void, not because it was unfair, but because the land officially belonged to the British Crown. Bourke proved his point by granting Batman some prime acreage near Geelong.

At the same time, a private British company settled Adelaide in South Australia (SA). Proud to have no links with convicts, these God-fearing folks instituted a scheme under which their company sold land to well-heeled settlers, and used the revenue to assist poor British labourers to emigrate. When these worthies earned enough to buy land from the company, that revenue would in turn pay the fare of another shipload of labourers. This charming theory collapsed in a welter of land speculation and bankruptcy, and in 1842 the South Australian Company yielded to government administration. By then miners had found rich deposits of silver, lead and copper at Burra, Kapunda and the Mount Lofty Ranges, and the settlement began to pay its way.

The level of frontier violence is disputed in the acrimonious and highly political 'history wars', as detailed in Stuart Macintyre's The History Wars *(2003).*

THE SEARCH FOR LAND CONTINUES

Each year, settlers pushed deeper into Aboriginal territories in search of pasture and water for their stock. These men became known as squatters (because they 'squatted' on Aboriginal lands) and many held this territory with a gun. To bring order and regulation to the frontier, from the 1830s, the governments permitted the squatters to stay on these 'Crown lands' for payment of a nominal rent. Aboriginal stories tell of white men slaughtering groups of Aborigines in reprisal for the killing of sheep or settlers. Later, across the country, people also tell stories of black resistance leaders, including Yagan of Swan River, Pemulwuy of Sydney and Jandamarra, the outlaw-hero of the Kimberley.

In time, many of the squatters reached a compromise with local tribes. Aborigines took low-paid jobs on sheep and cattle stations as drovers and domestics. In return they remained on their traditional lands, adapting their cultures to their changing circumstances. This arrangement continued in outback pastoral regions until after WWII.

The newcomers had fantasised about the wonders waiting to be discovered from the moment they arrived. Before explorers crossed the Blue Mountains west of Sydney in 1813, some credulous souls imagined that China lay on the other side. Then explorers, surveyors and scientists began trading theories about inland Australia. Most spoke of an Australian Mississippi. Others predicted desert. An obsessive explorer named Charles Sturt (there's a fine statue of him looking lost in Adelaide's Victoria Sq) believed in an almost mystical inland sea.

Exploration inspired Patrick White's Voss *(1957), revered by some as the great Australian novel.*

The explorers' expeditions inland were mostly journeys into disappointment. But Australians made heroes of explorers who died in the wilderness (Ludwig Leichhardt, and the duo of Burke and Wills are the most striking examples). It was as though the Victorian era believed that a nation could not be born until its men had shed their blood in battle – even if that battle was with the land itself.

1836	1851	1854
Colonel William Light chooses the site for Adelaide on the banks of the River Torrens in the lands of the Kaurna people. Unlike Sydney, all the settlers are free and willing immigrants, many of them Christian.	Prospectors find gold in central Victoria, triggering a great gold rush, which brings youthful settlers from across the world. At the same time, the eastern colonies exchange rule by the governor for democracy.	Angered by the hefty cost of gold-mining licences, miners stage a protest at the Eureka Stockade near Ballarat. Several rebels are killed and others are charged with treason. Public opinion supports the rebels.

GOLD & REBELLION

Transportation of convicts to eastern Australia ceased in the 1840s. This was just as well: in 1851 prospectors discovered gold in New South Wales (NSW) and central Victoria. The news hit the colonies with the force of a cyclone. Young men and some adventurous women from every social class headed for the diggings. Soon they were caught up in a great rush of prospectors, entertainers, publicans, sly-groggers (illicit liquor-sellers), prostitutes and quacks from overseas. In Victoria, the British governor was alarmed – both by the way the Victorian class system had been thrown into disarray, and by the need to finance law and order on the goldfields. His solution was to compel all miners to buy an expensive monthly licence, partly in the hope that the lower orders would return to their duties in town.

But the lure of gold was too great. In the reckless excitement of the gold-fields, the miners initially endured the thuggish troopers who enforced the government licence. After three years, however, the easy gold at Ballarat was gone, and miners were toiling in deep, water-sodden shafts. They were now infuriated by a corrupt and brutal system of law which held them in contempt. Under the leadership of a charismatic Irishman named Peter Lalor, they raised their own flag, the Southern Cross, and swore to defend their rights and liberties. They armed themselves and gathered inside a rough stockade at Eureka, where they waited for the government to make its move.

In the predawn of Sunday 3 December 1854, a force of troopers attacked the stockade. It was all over in 15 terrifying minutes. The brutal and one-sided battle claimed the lives of 30 miners and five soldiers. But democracy was in the air and public opinion sided with the miners. When 13 of the rebels were tried for their lives, Melbourne juries set them free. Many Australians have found a kind of splendour in these events: the story of the Eureka Stockade is often told as a battle for nationhood and democracy – again illustrating the notion that any 'true' nation must be born out of blood. But these killings were tragically unnecessary. The eastern colonies were already in the process of establishing democratic parliaments, with the full support of the British authorities. In the 1880s Peter Lalor himself became Speaker of the Victorian parliament.

The gold rush had also attracted boatloads of prospectors from China. These Asians sometimes endured serious hostility from whites, and were the victims of ugly race riots on the goldfields at Lambing Flat (now called Young) in NSW in 1860–61. Chinese precincts soon developed in the back-streets of Sydney and Melbourne, and popular literature indulged in tales of Chinese opium dens, dingy gambling parlours and brothels. But many Chinese went on to establish themselves in business and, particularly, in market gardening. Today the busy Chinatowns of the capital cities and the presence of Chinese restaurants in towns across the country are reminders of the vigorous role of the Chinese in Australia since the 1850s.

The Goldfields of Victoria website, www.goldfields.org.au, is a fabulous tourist guide. The key attraction is Sovereign Hill at Ballarat.

There's a good Chinese museum in Melbourne; see www.chinesemuseum.com.au.

1861	1872	1880
The explorers Burke and Wills become the first Europeans to cross the continent from south to north. Their expedition is an expensive debacle that costs several lives, including their own.	Engineer Charles Todd builds a telegraph line from Adelaide to Darwin. From there it joins an undersea cable to Java linking Australia to a European network. The age of electronic information is born.	Police capture the notorious bushranger Ned Kelly at the Victorian town of Glenrowan. Kelly is hanged as a criminal – and remembered ever afterwards as a folk hero.

Gold and wool brought immense investment and gusto to Melbourne and Sydney. By the 1880s they were stylish modern cities, with gaslights in the streets, railways, electricity and that great new invention, the telegraph. In fact, the southern capital became known as 'Marvellous Melbourne', so opulent were its theatres, hotels, galleries and fashions. But the economy was overheating. Many politicians and speculators were engaged in corrupt land deals, while investors poured money into wild and fanciful ventures. It could not last.

MEANWHILE, IN THE WEST...

Western Australia (WA) lagged behind the eastern colonies by about 50 years. Though Perth was settled by genteel colonists back in 1829, their material progress was handicapped by isolation, Aboriginal resistance and the arid climate. It was not until the 1880s that the discovery of remote goldfields promised to gild the fortunes of the isolated colony. At the time, the west was just entering its own period of self-government, and its first premier was a forceful, weather-beaten explorer named John Forrest. He saw that the mining industry would fail if the government did not provide a first-class harbour, efficient railways and reliable water supplies. Ignoring the threats of private contractors, he appointed the brilliant engineer CY O'Connor to design and build each of these as government projects. O'Connor's final scheme was a 560km pipeline and a series of mighty pumping stations that would drive water uphill from the coast to the dry goldfields round Kalgoorlie. As the work neared completion, O'Connor was subjected to merciless slander in the capitalist press. In 1902 the tormented man rode into the surf at South Fremantle and shot himself. A lonely statue in the waves marks the spot. His great pipeline continues to pump water into the thirsty gold cities of central WA.

GROWING NATIONALISM

By the end of the 19th century, Australian nationalists tended to idealise 'the bush' and its people. The great forum for this 'bush nationalism' was the massively popular *Bulletin* magazine. Its politics were egalitarian, democratic and republican, and its pages were filled with humour and sentiment about daily life, written by a swag of writers, most notably Henry Lawson and AB 'Banjo' Paterson.

Central to the *Bulletin's* ethos was the idea of 'mateship'. At its most attractive, mateship was a sense of brotherhood reinforced by a profound egalitarianism. But there was also a deeply chauvinistic side to mateship. This was represented in the pages of the *Bulletin*, where cartoons and stories often portrayed women as sexy maidens or nagging wives. It parodied Aborigines as amiable simpletons and it represented the Chinese as goofballs or schemers. A more bruised and knowing account of women and the bush appeared in the short stories of Barbara Baynton.

Acclimatisation societies of the 19th century tried to replace the 'inferior' Australian plants and animals with 'superior' European ones. Such cute 'blessings' as rabbits and foxes date from this time.

For more on the painters and writers of the colonial bush legend, see www.cultureandrecreation.gov.au/articles/bush.

1895	1901	1915
Publication of AB 'Banjo' Paterson's ballad 'The Man from Snowy River'. Paterson and his rival Henry Lawson lead the literary movement that creates the legend of the Australian bush.	The Australian colonies form a federation of states. The federal parliament sits in Melbourne, where it passes the Immigration Restriction Act – the 'White Australia Policy'.	On 25 April, in the second year of the Great War, the Australian and New Zealand Army Corps (Anzac) joins an ambitious British attempt to invade Turkey. This military disaster spawns a nationalist legend.

The 1890s were also a time of great trauma. As the speculative boom came crashing down, unemployment and hunger dealt cruelly with working-class families in the eastern states. However, Australian workers had developed a fierce sense that they were entitled to share in the country's prosperity. As the depression deepened, trade unions became more militant in their defence of workers' rights. At the same time, activists intent on winning legal reform established the Australian Labor Party (ALP).

Some people feared that the nation was about to descend into revolution. But there was a broad liberal consensus in Australia that took democracy and fairness for granted. So the new century was ushered in, not with bombs, but with fireworks.

NATIONHOOD

On 1 January 1901 Australia became a federation. When the bewhiskered members of the new national parliament met in Melbourne, their first aim was to protect the identity and values of a European Australia from an influx of Asians and Pacific Islanders. Their solution was a law which became known as the White Australia Policy. It became a racial tenet of faith in Australia for the next 70 years.

For whites who lived inside the charmed circle of citizenship, this was to be a model society, nestled in the skirts of the British Empire. Just one year later, white women won the right to vote in federal elections. In a series of radical innovations, the government introduced a broad social welfare scheme and it protected Australian wage levels with import tariffs. Its radical mixture of capitalist dynamism and socialist compassion became known as the 'Australian settlement'.

Meanwhile, most Australians lived on the coastal 'edge' of the continent. So forbidding was the arid, desolate inland, that they called the great dry Lake Eyre 'the Dead Heart' of the country. It was a grim image – as if the heart muscle, which should pump the water of life through inland Australia, was dead. But one prime minister in particular, the dapper Alfred Deakin, dismissed such talk. He led the 'boosters' who were determined to triumph over this tyranny of the climate. Even before Federation, in the 1880s, Deakin championed irrigated farming on the Murray River at Mildura. Soon the district was green with grapevines and orchards. Today, this massively productive region is facing an ecological crisis as the Murray River struggles to meet the great demands made upon its waters; see Murray in Meltdown (p771).

The most accessible version of the Anzac legend is Peter Weir's Australian epic film *Gallipoli* (1981), with a cast that includes a young Mel Gibson.

ENTERING THE WORLD STAGE

Living on the edge of a dry and forbidding land, and isolated from the rest of the world, most Australians took comfort in the knowledge that they were a dominion of the British Empire. When war broke out in

1919	**1929**	**1932**
Australian aviators Ross and Keith Smith become national heroes after they fly from England to Australia.	America's Great Depression spreads to Australia, where many working-class families are thrown into poverty. The violence and suffering of this period imprint themselves on the public memory.	NSW firebrand premier Jack Lang is upstaged when a right-wing activist named Francis de Groot, wearing military uniform and riding a horse, cuts the ribbon to open the Sydney Harbour Bridge.

Europe in 1914, thousands of Australian men rallied to the Empire's call. They had their first taste of death on 25 April 1915, when the Australian and New Zealand Army Corps (the Anzacs) joined thousands of other British and French troops in an assault on the Gallipoli Peninsula in Turkey. It was eight months before the British commanders acknowledged that the tactic had failed. By then 8141 young Australians were dead. Before long the Australian Imperial Force was fighting in the killing fields of Europe. By the time the war ended, 60,000 Australian men had died. Ever since, on 25 April, Australians have gathered at war memorials around the country for the sad and solemn services of Anzac Day.

In the 1920s Australia embarked on a decade of chaotic change. Cars began to rival horses on the highway. In the new cinemas, young Australians enjoyed American movies. In an atmosphere of sexual freedom not equalled until the 1960s, young people partied and danced to American jazz. At the same time, popular enthusiasm for the British Empire grew more intense – as if imperial fervour were an antidote to grief. As radicals and reactionaries clashed, Australia careered wildly through the 1920s until it collapsed into the abyss of the Great Depression in 1929. World prices for wheat and wool plunged. Unemployment brought its shame and misery to one in three households. Once again working people experienced the cruelty of a system which treated them as expendable. For those who were wealthy – or who had jobs – the Depression was hardly noticed. In fact, the extreme deflation of the economy actually meant that the purchasing power of their wages was enhanced.

Don't miss Phar Lap himself. This stuffed horse is a seriously odd spectacle. The legend is explored at www.museum.vic.gov .au/pharlap.

In the midst of the Depression-era hardship, sport brought escape to a nation in love with games and gambling. A powerful chestnut horse called Phar Lap won race after race, culminating in an effortless and graceful victory in the 1930 Melbourne Cup. (This annual event is still known as 'the race that stops a nation'.) In 1932 the great horse travelled to the racetracks of America, where he mysteriously died. In Australia, the gossips insisted that the horse had been poisoned by envious Americans. And the legend grew of a sporting hero cut down in his prime. Phar Lap was stuffed and is a revered exhibit at the Melbourne Museum.

The year 1932 saw accusations of treachery on the cricket field. The English team, under their captain Douglas Jardine, employed a violent new bowling tactic known as 'bodyline'. The aim was to unnerve Australia's star batsman, the devastatingly efficient Donald Bradman. The bitterness of the tour provoked a diplomatic crisis with Britain, and became part of Australian legend. And Bradman batted on. When he retired in 1948 he had an unsurpassed career average of 99.94 runs.

1939	1941	1945
Prime Minister Robert Menzies announces that Britain has gone to war with Hitler's Germany and that 'as a result, Australia is also at war'.	The Japanese attack Pearl Harbor and sweep through Southeast Asia. Australia discovers that it has been abandoned by Britain, its traditional ally. Instead, it welcomes US forces, which are based in Australia.	The war ends. Australia adopts a new slogan 'Populate or Perish!' Over the next 30 years more than two million immigrants arrive. One-third are British.

WAR WITH JAPAN

After 1933, the economy began to recover. The whirl of daily life was hardly dampened when Hitler hurled Europe into a new war in 1939. Though Australians had long feared Japan, they took it for granted that the British navy would keep them safe. In December 1941, Japan bombed the US Fleet at Pearl Harbor. Weeks later, the 'impregnable' British naval base in Singapore crumbled, and before long thousands of Australians and other Allied troops were enduring the savagery of Japanese prisoner-of-war camps.

As the Japanese swept through Southeast Asia and into Papua New Guinea, the British announced that they could not spare any resources to defend Australia. But the legendary US commander General Douglas MacArthur saw that Australia was the perfect base for American operations in the Pacific. In a series of fierce battles on sea and land, Allied forces gradually turned back the Japanese advance. Importantly, it was the USA, not the British Empire, which saved Australia. The days of the alliance with Britiain alone were numbered.

A wonderful novel set in wartime Brisbane is *Johnno* (1975) by David Malouf, one of Australia's best writers.

VISIONARY PEACE

When WWII ended, a new slogan rang through the land: 'Populate or Perish!' The Australian government embarked on an ambitious scheme to attract thousands of immigrants. With government assistance, people flocked from Britain and from non-English speaking countries. They included Greeks, Italians, Slavs, Serbs, Croatians, Dutch and Poles, followed by Turks, Lebanese and many others. These 'new Australians' were expected to assimilate into a suburban stereotype known as the 'Australian way of life'.

This was the great era of the 'nuclear family', in which Australians basked in the prosperity of a 'Long Boom'. Many migrants found jobs in the growing manufacturing sector, in which companies such as General Motors and Ford operated with generous tariff support. In addition, the government embarked on audacious public works schemes, notably the mighty Snowy Mountains Hydro-Electric Scheme in the mountains near Canberra. Today, environmentalists point out the devastation caused by this huge network of tunnels, dams and power stations. But the Snowy scheme was an expression of a new-found optimism and testifies to the cooperation among the men of many nations who laboured on the project. At the same time, there was growing world demand for Australia's primary products: metals, wool, meat and wheat. In time Australia would even become a major exporter of rice to Japan.

This era of growth and prosperity was dominated by Robert Menzies, the founder of the modern Liberal Party and Australia's longest-serving prime minister. Menzies was steeped in British history and tradition, and liked to play the part of a sentimental monarchist. He was also a vigilant opponent of communism. As Asia succumbed to the chill of the Cold War, Australia and New Zealand entered a formal military alliance with the USA – the 1951

1956	1965	1967
The Olympic Games are held in Melbourne where the Olympic flame is lit by young running champion Ron Clarke.	Prime Minister Menzies commits Australian troops to the American war in Vietnam, and divides the nation.	In a national referendum, white Australians vote overwhelmingly to give citizenship to Aborigines.

Anzus security pact. When the USA hurled its righteous fury into a civil war in Vietnam, Menzies committed Australian forces to the battle, introducing conscription for military service overseas. The following year Menzies retired, leaving his successors a bitter legacy. The antiwar movement split Australia.

There was a feeling too among many artists, intellectuals and the young that Menzies' Australia had become a rather dull, complacent country, more in love with American and British culture than with its own talents and stories. In an atmosphere of youthful rebellion and new-found nationalism, the Labor Party was elected to power in 1972 under the leadership of a brilliant, idealistic lawyer named Gough Whitlam. In just four short years his government transformed the country. He ended conscription and abolished all university fees. He introduced a free universal health scheme, no-fault divorce, the principle of Aboriginal land rights and equal pay for women. The White Australia Policy had been gradually falling into disuse; under Whitlam it was finally abandoned altogether. By now, around one million migrants had arrived from non-English speaking countries, and they had filled Australia with new languages, cultures, foods and ideas. Under Whitlam this achievement was embraced as 'multiculturalism'.

By 1975 the Whitlam government was rocked by a tempest of inflation and scandal. At the end of 1975 his government was controversially dismissed from office by the governor general. But the general thrust of Whitlam's social reforms was continued by his successors. The principle of Aboriginal land rights was expanded. From the 1970s, Asian immigration increased, and multiculturalism became a new Australian orthodoxy. China and Japan far outstripped Europe as major trading partners – Australia's economic future lay in Asia.

Two very different, intelligent introductions to Australian history are Stuart Macintyre's A Concise History of Australia *and Geoffrey Blainey's* A Shorter History of Australia.

CHALLENGES

Today Australia faces new challenges. In the 1970s the country began dismantling its protectionist scaffolding. New efficiency brought new prosperity. At the same time, wages and working conditions, which were once protected by an independent tribunal, became more vulnerable as egalitarianism gave way to competition. And after two centuries of development, the strains on the environment were starting to show – on water supplies, forests, soils, air quality and the oceans (see Environmental Challenges, p60).

Under the conservative John Howard, Australia's second-longest serving prime minister (1996–2007), the country grew closer than ever to the USA, joining the Americans in their war in Iraq. The government's harsh treatment of asylum seekers, its refusal to acknowledge the reality of climate change, its anti-union reforms and the prime minister's lack of empathy with Aborigines dismayed more liberal-minded Australians. But Howard presided over a period of economic growth that emphasised the values of self-reliance, and won him continuing support in middle Australia.

1975	1979	1983
Against a background of radical reform and uncontrolled inflation, Governor-General Sir John Kerr sacks Labor's Whitlam government and orders a federal election, which the conservatives win.	Despite heated protests, the federal government grants authorisation for the Ranger consortium to mine uranium in the Northern Territory.	Tasmanian government plans for a hydroelectric dam on the wild Franklin River dominate a federal election campaign. Supporting a 'No Dams' policy, Labor's Bob Hawke becomes prime minister.

By 2007, Howard was losing touch with a changing society. In December that year he was defeated in a bid to win a fifth term in office, suffering the indignity of losing his own seat. The victorious Labor Government, led by the youthful Kevin Rudd, immediately set a tone of reform and reconciliation when the new prime minister issued a formal apology to the Aborigines for the injustices they had suffered over the past two centuries. Though it promised sweeping reforms in environment and education, the Rudd government found itself faced with a crisis when the world economy crashed in 2008. It soon became clear that the spectacular growth since the 1980s had been funded by a bottomless hole of debt. Australia, like the rest of the world, now faced three related challenges – climate change, a diminishing oil supply and a shrinking economy. To some commentators, the world economy would soon be 'back to normal'. But other observers argued that the era of unregulated markets was over. What comes next, for Australia and for the world, remains to be seen.

In remote parts of Australia, many Aborigines still speak their traditional languages rather than English.

1992	2000	2007
The High Court of Australia recognises the principle of native title in the Mabo decision.	The Sydney Olympic Games are a triumph of spectacle and good will. Aboriginal running champ Cathy Freeman lights the flame.	Kevin Rudd is elected Australian prime minister. Marking a change of direction from his conservative predecessor, Rudd says 'Sorry' to Aborigines and ratifies the Kyoto Protocol on climate change.

The Culture

LIFESTYLE

Australians have been sold to the world as outdoorsy, sporty, big-drinking, thigh-slapping country folk, but, despite the stereotypes, most Australians live in cities, watch a lot more sport than they play and wouldn't be seen dead in an Akubra hat. The feature that unites Australians is diversity – it's near impossible to define a typical Australian. Extrapolating from statistics, if you looked into an Australian lounge room you might be surprised by what you found.

The Great Australian Dream of owning an oversized house and carport on a quarter-acre block has meant that sprawling suburbia is endemic in Australian towns and cities. Inside the average middle-class suburban home, you'll probably find a married heterosexual couple, though it is becoming increasingly likely that they will be de facto or in their second marriage. Australian law doesn't recognise gay marriages, but in November 2008, the Australian parliament passed laws that recognised same-sex couples in federal law, offering them the same rights as unmarried heterosexual couples in areas such as taxation, social security and health care.

Our 'Mum and Dad' will have an average of two children (1.93 to be exact, and probably called Lilly, Mia, Lachlan or Jack), although the number of childless couples rose by 30% in the last decade. The average full-time worker increasingly spends more time at work, averaging 41 hours and earning $1,145 gross per week. And while 60 used to be the average age for retirement, 20% of Australians over 65 continue to work.

Some great Australian inventions include the half-car-half-truck ute (utility vehicle), the bionic ear, the black box flight recorder, the note-pad and the wine cask.

The typical family owns two TV sets and a computer. They'll have a barbecue in the backyard and a pet Labrador. What rubbish the dog doesn't eat is recycled – 99% of Australians recycle their rubbish. Like most Australians, our family probably loves the sun. Australians have the highest rate of skin cancer in the world, with one in two people affected. Our family heads to the beach every holiday, and at weekends they probably watch sport, go to the movies or head to the shops. However, don't get the idea that they're particularly active: Australia's obesity rate has soared in the last 20 years, with statistics showing that more than seven million Australians over the age of 18 are overweight or obese. This figure amounts to approximately 40% of the adult population and represents an increase of 2.8 million over the previous 15 years.

Our family not only travels domestically, they also love to travel overseas. With over four million overseas trips made annually, figures suggest there's a need to leave Australia in order to understand what Australia is. That said, about half of these trips are to Fiji, New Zealand, the UK, USA and parts of Indonesia – where Australians don't face language difficulties and can mingle with hordes of other Australians. It's also probably fair to say that Australia has produced some of the most successful travel businesses in the world: Flight Centre, Intrepid and Lonely Planet, to name a few.

A middle-Australia couple likes a few quiet ones down the pub, which may equate to a few louds ones depending on where you're from. Australia has consistently ranked fourth in beer consumption for many years, drinking an average of 107 litres per person per year, compared to the Czechs who take top honours with an average of 160 litres per person per year.

POPULATION

According to the Australian Bureau of Statistics, the population in early 2009 was around 21.7 million and is growing faster than that of any other wealthy country, swelling by 250,000 each year. Population density is among the lowest in the world, with an average of 2.5 people per square kilometre – no one's within cooee in the outback. Most people live along the eastern seaboard, between Melbourne and Brisbane, with a smaller concentration on the coastal region in and around Perth. Despite the extraordinarily low population density, population policy is fiercely debated in Australia. Some opponents of increased immigration argue that the dry Australian landscape and overcrowded cities can't sustain more people; others say that population growth is an economic imperative.

MULTICULTURALISM

Australia enjoys a diverse multicultural make-up, encompassing a wealth of ideas, cuisines and lifestyle opportunities. It's a harmonious country, but rare bouts of racial tensions mar the good intentions and accepting nature of most Australians. The source of such angst is generally a cocktail of ignorance and socioeconomic frustrations rather than inherent prejudice. Similarly, racism can be overt in remote areas where the extent of multiculturalism is low if not entirely absent. In 2007 the federal government implemented an Australian values test for aspiring citizens, sparking massive debate about how to quantify and test for such a nebulous notion.

The last census (2006) revealed that 24% of the population is foreign-born and another fifth of the population had at least one parent born overseas. Every two minutes and 36 seconds Australia gains another international migrant. Many foreign-born Australians came from Italy and Greece after WWII, but recent immigrants have mostly come from New Zealand and the UK, as well as China, Vietnam, Africa and India, among many other places. You'll enjoy this diversity most in urban areas and cities; in regional settings the population is far more of an Anglo-monoculture. Some 2.2% of the population identifies itself as of Aboriginal origin. Australia's other Indigenous people, Torres Strait Islanders, are primarily a Melanesian people, living in north Queensland and on the islands of the Torres Strait between Cape York and Papua New Guinea.

RELIGION

Historians and sociologists generally portray Australians as an irreligious bunch. The truth may be more that religion's institutional forms are struggling, but spirituality – usually grounded in place and land – is important to many Australians' being. Australians are relatively shy about their spirituality; they're less inclined to trumpet spiritual encounters, such as with American televangelists, preferring to keep their faith to themselves. The largest religious affiliations in the country are Catholic (27%), Anglican (21%) and other Christian denominations (21%), with non-Christian religions including Buddhism (2%) and Islam (1.5%) making up another 5% of Australians. Some 16% of Australians described themselves as having no religion in the most recent census. Proponents of New Age spirituality pervade many religious classifications, so you might meet a vegetarian Catholic who meditates, who has more than a few self-help titles on the bookshelf.

Portraits from a Land Without People (John Ogden, 2008) is one of the most significant and powerful anthologies of photographs of Aboriginal and Torres Strait Islander cultures that has been published.

Aboriginal Dreaming

Traditional Aboriginal religious beliefs centre on the continuing existence of spirit beings that lived on earth during the creation time (or Dreamtime), which occurred before the arrival of humans. These beings created all the features of the natural world and were the ancestors of all living things. They took different forms but behaved as people do, and as they travelled about they left signs to show where they had passed.

Despite being supernatural, the ancestors were subject to ageing and eventually returned to the sleep from which they'd awakened at the dawn of time. Here their spirits remain as eternal forces that breathe life into the newborn and influence natural events. Each ancestor's spiritual energy flows along the path it travelled during the Dreamtime and is strongest at the points where it left physical evidence of its activities, such as a tree, hill or claypan. These features are called sacred sites. These days the importance of sacred sites is more widely recognised among the non-Aboriginal community, and most state governments have legislated to give these sites a measure of protection.

Every person, animal and plant is believed to have two souls – one mortal and one immortal. The latter is part of a particular ancestral spirit and returns to the sacred sites of that ancestor after death, while the mortal soul simply fades into oblivion. Each person is spiritually bound to the sacred sites that mark the land associated with his or her spirit ancestor. It is the individual's obligation to help care for these sites by performing the necessary rituals and singing the songs that tell of the ancestor's deeds. By doing this, the order created by that ancestor is maintained.

Each person has their own totem, or Dreaming. These totems are the links between the people and their spirit ancestors, and they take many forms, such as trees, snakes, fish and birds. Songs explain how the landscape contains these powerful creator ancestors, who can exert either a benign or a malevolent influence. They also have a practical meaning, telling of the best places and times to hunt, and where to find water in drought years. They can also specify kinship relations and identify correct marriage partners.

SPORT

Although Australia is a relatively new nation, its inhabitants constantly vie for kudos by challenging formidable and well-established sporting opponents around the globe in just about any event they can attempt. Often this approach pays off, and the country holds its own against bigwigs such as the USA, Russia and China. This kind of success is not often accompanied by modesty; for example, although the Olympic Games are theoretically about 'participation', many Australians will be quick to point out that coming fifth on the Beijing medal tally is a pretty impressive effort for a country of 21.5 million. This will be closely followed by a vitriolic rant of frustration that Great Britain came fourth.

Big international events aside, Australia's everyday heroes are found in the number-one-watched sport: Australian Rules football. Originally exclusive to Victoria, the Australian Football League (AFL; www.afl.com.au) is overrepresented in Melbourne (with nine of the 16 teams) and there are no teams from Tasmania, the Northern Territory (NT) or the Australian Capital Territory (ACT). However, some teams – notably Essendon, Richmond and Port Adelaide – run Indigenous programs designed to promote the sport in communities, and all teams recruit Indigenous players, praising their unique vision (kicking into a space for a team-mate to run into) and skills. The most spectacular aspects of the game are the long kicking, the high marking and the brutal collisions. Crowd participation is high, with 'Carn the [insert team nickname]' and 'Baaalll... You're joking umpire' voiced times 50,000 merging into a roar that upsets dogs in suburban backyards for kilometres around.

Approximately 66% of the Australian population aged 15 and over participates in sport or recreation – mostly walking or aerobics.

While Melburnians refuse to acknowledge it (or do so with a scowl akin to that directed at an unfaithful spouse), there are other footballs. The National Rugby League (NRL; www.nrl.com.au) is the most popular sporting competition north of the Murray River. Undoubtedly the highlight of the season is the annual State of Origin series. To see one of these games is to acquire a grim appreciation of Newton's laws of motion: a force travelling in one direction can only be stopped with the application of an equal and opposite force. It's terrifying stuff. If Newton had been hit by a Queensland second-rower rather than an apple, science would have been very much the poorer.

Australians who play rugby union argue that theirs is the dominant code. The national team, the Wallabies, has won the William Webb Ellis trophy (or Rugby World Cup trophy) with sufficient frequency for Australians to refer to it as 'Bill'. The glory days are beginning to look like a distant memory however; the Wallabies were runners-up to England in 2003 (more vitriolic rants of frustration) and failed to make the top four in 2007. In between times, the Bledisloe Cup (www.rugby.com.au) games against New Zealand are the most anticipated fixtures and form part of a Tri Nations tournament that also includes South Africa. The same countries also share a club competition, the ever-popular Super 14, which includes four Australian teams: the Waratahs (Sydney), the Reds (Brisbane), the Brumbies (ACT) and the Western Force (Perth).

The Socceroos finally qualified for the World Cup in 2006 after a 32-year history of almost-but-not-quite getting there. For years local soccer floundered as young players chose the better competition and contracts on offer in Europe, but the national A-League (www.a-league.com.au) has enjoyed increased support and attention in recent years and seems to be an effective vehicle to develop home-grown talent for home-grown competition.

Girt by sea and pocked with public pools, Australia has fostered a population that can swim (see www.swimming.org.au). But broad shoulders and tiny waists are only the half of it. Add superskintight bodysuits modelled using three-D body scans and water-resistant fabric technology for a truer picture. Australia's greatest ever swimmer is Dawn Fraser, who is known nationally simply as 'Our Dawn'. Australia's greatest male swimmer is Our Ian (Thorpe; known as Thorpie or the Thorpedo), who retired in 2006 at the age of 24.

The Australian cricket team dominated both test and one-day cricket for much of the naughties, holding the number-one world ranking for the best part of a decade. The lack of competition had many Aussies barracking for Australia's opponents – until early 2007. Now Australian cricket is reeling from its quadruple loss. Joining the hat trick of players exiting the game in 2007 – once-in-a-lifetime legend Shane Warne, Glenn McGrath and Damien Martyn – was the Mexican wave. Cricket Australia, which instituted the ban, acknowledged that it could be construed as 'the fun police gone wrong' but explained that it was the only way to stop people throwing things. A dismal performance in early 2009 saw the Australian team lose convincingly at home against a formidable South Africa and flounder against New Zealand – once considered good only for batting practice. Consequently the new threat may be spectators throwing things at the Australian team.

Come January, tennis shoes melt to the outer courts and games get cancelled for the heat. The Australian Open (www.ausopen.com.au) is one of four tennis tournaments that comprise the Grand Slam, and it attracts more people to Australia than any other sporting event. In the men's competition, last won by an Australian back in 1976, Lleyton Hewitt has been Australia's great hope in recent years. In the women's game, Sam Stosur has been climbing the ranks but the celebrated comeback kid is Jelena Dokic. Vilified for her erratic departure from Australia in 2001 under the influence of her father, Jelena was once ranked number four in the world but spiralled out of competition. In 2009 she recaptured Australians' hearts after ditching dad and fighting her way back into top competition in true Little Aussie Battler style.

On the first Tuesday in November the nation stops for a horse race, the Melbourne Cup (www.racingvictoria.net.au). In Melbourne it's cause to have a day off. Australia's most famous Cup winner was Phar Lap, who won in 1930 before dying of a mystery illness in America. Phar Lap is now a prize

The first organised group of Australian cricketers to play overseas was a side composed entirely of Australian Aborigines, which toured England in 1868.

exhibit in the Melbourne Museum (p509). Makybe Diva is the event's most recent star, for winning three in a row before retiring in 2005, but also for being a shining example of that great Australian tradition for 1) stupid racehorse names and 2) taking or jumbling up letters from the owners' names to make a new name ('Makybe Diva' comes from the first two letters of five of the owners' employees: Maureen, Kylie, Belinda, Diane and Vanessa).

Australian netball's biggest rivalry is with New Zealand's Silver Ferns. There are 1.2 million netballers in the country, which makes it Australia's most popular participation sport (see www.netball.com.au). Women's basketball (www.wnbl.com.au) is also popular; the Australian Opals won silver at the 2000, 2004 and 2008 Olympic Games and won the 2006 World Cup. Lauren Jackson is considered the best Australian female player of all time and one of the best players in the world. In the men's basketball (www.nbl.com.au), Andrew Bogut is the big name and a bigger man. The men's hockey team (www.hockey.org.au) finally won gold at the Athens Olympics. The annual Rip Curl Pro Surf & Music Festival (formerly known as the Bells Beach Surf Classic) has been held at Victoria's Bells Beach since 1961. The Sydney to Hobart Yacht Race (www.rolexsydneyhobart.com) is on each Boxing Day, and the Formula One Grand Prix (www.grandprix.com.au) takes place in Melbourne every March.

Sport is the most watched TV programming after news and current affairs (which is 15 minutes of general news and 15 minutes of sports news). The field is well propped with financial support too; the federal government kicks in over $200 million annually. But there's always room to improve, which means Aussies still pass as underdogs – thus giving legitimacy to continued devotion to the proliferation of sport.

ARTS

At least 3.5 million Australians (roughly 16% of the population) work in the arts and culture sector.

Australians are conspicuous in their support for sport (it's hard to ignore a green-and-gold mob yelling 'oi oi oi'), but statistics also reveal them to have a quiet love affair with the arts. Statistics show that in an average year, approximately 23% of Australians visit art galleries, museums and/or live music performances, 35% visit a zoo or aquarium and 65% head to the cinema. Australian households also spend around $14.7 billion on culture…but this last figure encompasses CDs, televisions and pay TV subscriptions, and almost 45% of the population attends at least one sporting event each year, so perhaps the country has some ground to cover before reaching cultural pacesetter status.

Cinema

Although it was one of the first established in the world, the Australian film industry really kicked off when social upheaval and cultural re-examination in the '60s and '70s led to the establishment of the Australian Film Commission, a cinematic forum for Australians to thrash out issues of identity. *Walkabout,* in the early '70s, was one of the first films to explore Indigenous Australia. Other films focused on revisiting colonisation, war and the country's relationship with England; examples are *Gallipoli* and *Breaker Morant,* which mythologised the gung-ho Aussie male as pawn of the British Empire. *Mad Max* and *Mad Max II* were genre-busters that referenced Australia's car culture, and they were box-office hits that did well overseas – to everyone's surprise.

Government tax incentives in the early '80s introduced investor clout, spurring on a handful of hopefuls desperate to secure the international success of the Mad Max movies. Examples include the appalling *Mad Max III,* and *Crocodile Dundee* (still Australia's highest-grossing film) – movies that did nothing to hose down stereotypes of stubbled Aussie blokes.

In the late '80s and '90s the spotlight was turned home to the suburban quarter-acre block, where the larrikin Aussie battler fought for a 'fair go' in side-splitting satirical celebrations of Australian myths and stereotypes. The best of these were *Muriel's Wedding* and *The Castle*. At the same time, powerful films such as *Ghosts of the Civil Dead* and Jane Campion's *Sweetie* showed that Australians could do more than take the piss out of themselves.

The presence of Fox Studios Australia (Sydney, New South Wales), Warner Roadshow Studios on the Gold Coast (Queensland) and Central City Studios (Melbourne, Victoria) has attracted big-budget US productions such as *Where the Wild Things Are* and *Ghost Rider* to the country. While the economic benefits are many, the local industry can only dream of the 80% box-office share that US releases claim in Australia.

In recent years most films made for an Australian audience have abandoned the worn-out ocker stereotypes and started to explore the country's diversity. Indigenous stories have found a mainstream voice on the big screen, with films such as *The Tracker*, *Beneath Clouds*, *Rabbit-Proof Fence* and *Samson & Delilah* illustrating a nation starting to come to terms with its racist elements. Cultural and gender stereotypes continue to erode in a genre of intimate dramas exploring the human condition, such as *Lantana* and *Suburban Mayhem*, *The Black Balloon* and *Unfinished Sky*. Australian film has also made its mark in the genre of animation with the uber-popular box-office hit *Happy Feet* and Adam Elliot's more subtle, yet similarly Oscar-winning *Harvey Crumpet*. Elliot's *Mary & Max* also opened the 2009 Sundance Film Festival.

Literature

Stories and ballads in early postcolonial literature mythologised the hardships of pioneers and unjust governments. Nationalism was a driving force, especially in the late 1800s with the celebration of the country's centenary (1888), and at Federation (1901). AB 'Banjo' Paterson was the bush poet of the time, famous for his poems 'The Man from Snowy River' and 'Clancy of the Overflow', and the lyrics to 'Waltzing Matilda'. Henry Lawson, a contemporary of Paterson's, wrote short stories evoking the era; one of his best, *The Drover's Wife,* is a moving tale of the woman's lot in the settler life. Barbara Baynton wrote first-hand of a woman's perpetual struggle against Australian conditions; her writings are also collected in a book of short stories, *Bush Studies* (1902). All these stories helped establish the motifs of traditional Australian literature: the desert as 'heart' of a nation, the hardworking Aussie 'battler' as soldier against adversity.

By the 1940s a modernist movement known as the Angry Penguins charged onto the scene, headed by Max Harris and his magazine, *Angry Penguins*. It set out to deflower the conservative European-style expression that dominated Australian art and literature, determining a 'mythic sense of geographical and cultural identity'. The inevitable backlash took shape in the famous Ern Malley affair. Two traditionalist poets gleaned lines from disparate sources and submitted them as poems purporting to be the works of a recently deceased poet by the name of Ern Malley. The poems were published in *Angry Penguins* in 1944 and enthusiastically received. The pranksters believed their hoax discredited the modernist movement; however, the publishers stayed firm in their belief the poems had literary merit. Analysis of the hoax continues today, most recently in Peter Carey's novel *My Life as a Fake* (2003), which beautifully frames the relationship between art and artist, truth and fiction.

In the postwar era Australian writers began to re-evaluate their colonial past. Patrick White, the country's only winner of the Nobel Prize for Literature (not counting South African–born JM Coetzee, who recently emigrated to Adelaide), helped turn the tables on earlier writers' romanticism with *Voss*

The Quarterly Essay (www.quarterlyessay .com) is one of Australia's most respected political journals, featuring essays from the cream of the legal, arts, politics and other industries.

AUSTRALIANA ON THE BIG SCREEN *Jeanie Menzies*

Once upon a time Australia used to parody itself on film and, apparently, we still do! *Australia* (2008), Baz Luhrmann's newest Spectacular Spectacular was canned by critics, however, the ringmaster has had the last laugh. The only film to gross more in Australian film history is *Crocodile Dundee*, an equally cringeworthy delight. The following are other Australian films that may not have caught Oprah's attention, but give an insight into different aspects of the Australian psyche.

- **Beautiful** (2009, director Dean O'Flaherty) A wonderful cast brings to life this plot full of secrets, lies and intrigues. Set in middle-class suburbia, families and neighbourhoods are brought undone when teenage girls start disappearing off the streets.

- **The Square** (2008, director Nash Edgerton) Set on the Central Coast of New South Wales, this Nash and Joel Edgerton story follows the life of a family man whose life is torn asunder when his desperate lover takes her husband's illegal gains in a bid for a new life.

- **The Black Balloon** (2008, director Elissa Down) A beautiful story about a teenage boy dealing with not only his coming of age but also the responsibility of sharing the care of his mentally challenged brother and the implications and the pressure that this places on his, and his family's life.

- **Unfinished Sky** (2007, director Peter Duncan) The story of a farmer (played by William McInnes) who unwillingly takes in an illegal immigrant who has been kept as a prostitute in a brothel. A cross between a thriller and a love story.

- **Little Fish** (2005, director Rowan Woods) Cate Blanchett may be a red-carpet glamour girl but her roles like Tracy in Little Fish have confirmed her as a formidable talent…and a bloody great Australian. Tracy is a former addict trying to stay straight in the midst of the Cabramatta (Sydney) drug scene. If you don't shed a tear in the school hall scene, you don't have a heart.

- **Chopper** (2000, director Andrew Dominik) The story of Mark 'Chopper' Read (you may call him 'uncle chop chop') is an oldie, by film standards, but a goodie. More Australian Psycho than psyche, Eric Bana's portrayal has become legendary and as with many rotten scoundrels, Chopper will go down in history with the Ned Kellys and Jesse Jameses of the world. While you're in Australia, check out his art. Just don't get too close.

- **Two Hands** (1999, director Gregor Jordan) Heath Ledger at his vulnerable best with Rose Byrne. This film shows what the fuss was about. Ledger finds himself spiralling into a world far more foreboding than his innocence could possibly imagine.

(1957) and his deeply despair-inducing *The Tree of Man* (1955). Later novelists such as Booker Prize–winner Thomas Keneally keenly felt the devastation and angst of Indigenous Australians, as depicted in his excellent novel *The Chant of Jimmie Blacksmith* (1972; it was also made into an important film).

Australia's literary scene, long dominated by writers of British and Irish descent, has evolved to reflect the country's multicultural make-up. Many Indigenous writers focus on coming to terms with identity in often intensely personal autobiographies. Sally Morgan's *My Place* (1987) is one of the most popular books ever written by an Indigenous Australian, along with Ruby Langford's *Don't Take Your Love to Town*, a moving autobiography of courage in adversity. *When the Pelican Laughed* (1988), by Alice Nannup, Lauren Marsh and Steve Kinnane, is a captivating account of Alice Nannup's life in WA. *The Town Grew up Dancing – The Life & Art of Wenten Rubuntja* (2002), by W Rubuntja with Jenny Green, is a travelogue through time of one Arrernte man's life and his town, Alice Springs. Rubuntja was an artist, activist, elder statesman and ambassador for his people. Kim Scott's excellent *Benang* (1999) is a challenging but rewarding read about Indigenous identity. Part fiction and part fact it touches on the author's own mixed heritage and the complex legacies and issues most Indigenous people face today. Malaysian-born Australian Hsu-Ming Teo's *Love and Vertigo* took out the *Australian/Vogel* literary award in 1999, while Hong Kong-born Brian Castro shared the award in 1982 for *Birds of Passage*. Castro's novels, including *Shanghai Dancing* (2003), often explore issues of diversity and identity.

Other contemporary authors, such as Peter Carey and David Malouf, frequently focus on fictitious reinterpretations of Australian history to examine perceptions of the individual and society. Carey, Australia's best-known novelist and two-time winner of the prestigious Booker Prize, writes knockout books; among his finest are *Oscar & Lucinda* (1988) and *True History of the Kelly Gang* (2000). The works of Thea Astley and Tim Winton – winners of Australia's most prestigious literary award, the Miles Franklin – and other talented and accomplished authors such as Robert Drewe and Kate Grenville usually focus on human relations but have a strong sense of the Australian landscape.

For a country founded on crime and convicts it's only fitting that crime is a healthy component of Australian literature. Look for anything by Shane Maloney, Kerry Greenwood, Peter Temple and Garry Disher.

Australian children's literature is popular worldwide. Classics such as Norman Lindsay's *The Magic Pudding* (1918) and May Gibbs' *Complete Adventures of Snugglepot and Cuddlepie* (1942) captivated imaginations by bringing the Australian bush to life. In *Bib & Bub: Their Adventures* (1925) Gibbs pits gumnut babies Snugglepot and Cuddlepie against the Australian bogeyman, the bunyip. *Possum Magic* (1983) by Mem Fox reignited an interest in Australian bush creatures after a long hiatus; her picture book *Hattie & the Fox* (1986) has also become a modern classic. Jeannie Baker's sublime picture books convey environmental messages through collages; look for *Hidden Forest* (2000) and *Belonging* (2004). Pamela Allen's books are frequently shortlisted for Children's Book of the Year awards for early readers, as are Emily Rodda's. Libby Gleeson writes delightful picture books, as well as stories for older readers. For young adults, John Marsden's sci-fi *Tomorrow* series has gained a loyal following. Morris Gleitzman is deservedly popular: *Toad Surprise* is his 28th bluntly humorous book. Paul Jennings is an award-winning author for kids whose gross-out books are worthy of your bookshelf. Parents of teen boys have Matthew Reilly to thank for encouraging them to read via his adventure-packed books. Sonya Hartnett's work for teen readers is also consistently good, look for the acclaimed *Thursday's Child* (2000) and *Forest* (2001).

Great for long flights, Australia's bestselling author, Bryce Courtenay, pumps out brick-sized blockbusters, such as *Matthew Flinders' Cat* (2002) and *The Persimmon Tree* (2007).

> Join the six million plus Australians volunteering around the country annually: from hunkering beneath a dragon's body during Chinese New Year celebrations or assisting disabled kids to ride horses, to bush regeneration and wildlife surveying. Look for opportunities at www .govolunteer.com.au.

Music

Australian rock was born on the sticky carpet of Australia's pubs in the conservative climate of the flare-wearing '70s. This thriving live-music scene was thrashed out in local watering holes and popularised by the hugely successful *Countdown* (1974–87), a music-TV show that had the nation's attention every Sunday evening with a parade of one-hit wonders and local music. Eff-off rock legends AC/DC started out in the early '70s; their 1980 album *Back in Black* blitzed, with some 10 million sales in the US alone. Cold Chisel also started out around that time, and their gravely Aussie blokedom and earnest rock was an instant success; *Cold Chisel* and *East* are their best albums. Paul Kelly's first forays into the music scene were in the '70s, too, though his solo album *Post* (1985) put his passionate folk-ballad blend on the map. Midnight Oil's politico-pop peaked at the time of *Diesel and Dust* (1987), while the Go Betweens – one of Australia's most artistically successful bands – endured

AUSTRALIANA ON THE PAGE Katie Horner

■ **Breath** (Tim Winton; 2008) Described as a coming-of-age tale set in a small town on the coast; a surfie, recounts his life. Filled with Winton's typically evocative descriptions and imagery, this time with the wild sea at centre stage.

■ **Ghostlines** (Nick Gadd; 2008) Based in inner-suburban Melbourne, a boy dies after being hit by a train. Local journalist Phillip Trudeau uncovers more than meets the eye when he investigates the death. A suspenseful page-turner.

■ **The Household Guide to Dying** (Debra Adelaide; 2008) Don't let the title put you off. Yes Delia is dying, but she is also a mother, wife and advice columnist for a paper. Black comedy in all its glory, with a pithy, jigsaw-type plot.

■ **The Rip** (Robert Drewe; 2008) A collection of powerful short stories based on and around the Australian coast. Like the sea, easy to dip in and out of. Makes for great beach reading.

■ **Vertigo** (Amanda Lohrey; 2008) A couple decide on a sea change and move to the country. Their expectations of a quiet life are stretched when they encounter fire, drought and their own emotional quandaries.

the whole decade before splitting in 1989. Nick Cave & the Bad Seeds are among a number of indie performers who came to prominence in the late '80s and left in a diaspora of Aussie talent in the '80s.

By the late '80s – notably, around the time that *Countdown* wound down – Australian popular music began to be dominated by the lucrative ditty-pop market. Enter Kylie Minogue; one-time fluffy-haired nymphet from *Neighbours*, she first hit the music stage with 'Locomotion' in 1987, and, as they say, the rest is history. John Farnham released *Whispering Jack* in 1986 and it became the biggest-selling album in Australian history.

Throughout the '90s it seemed that everybody had a box of vinyl and moonlighted as a DJ. This scene was dominated by loungey remixes and electronic beats that followed and reinterpreted overseas trends. The beginning of the millennium saw a backlash of sorts, with a rock revival. Melbourne band Jet led the charge, with other bands such as Augie March, Wolfmother, The Drones, Powderfinger, The Vines, You Am I and Eskimo Joe working the scene. Adelaide trio the Hilltop Hoods have become hip-hop's most commercially successful band; for an overview of the hip-hop scene, see www.ozhiphop.com.

In recent years Australian acts have again begun to thrive, and in so doing represent the country's diverse culture. After the harder edges of the '80s and '90s, the sounds that are now evolving pay homage to the down-to-earth ideals of those rock roots while forging new ground, both at home and on the world stage. The Presets, Architecture In Helsinki and Sneaky Sound System keep club floors jumping; for something even more progressive, check out Empire of the Sun.

Roots-based music has also progressed with artists such as the John Butler Trio, Xavier Rudd, Pete Murray and the Waifs offering sounds that reflect an earthier side of Aussie life. Landing in a number of genres and not entirely in one, The Cat Empire's musical blend, harmonies and instrumentation represent Australia's increasingly celebrated cultural melting pot.

Less affected by trends, Australian country and jazz are ever-popular genres that have developed distinctive qualities. Country ranges from the traditional twang of artists such as Keith Urban (now Mr Nicole Kidman), Lee Kernaghan and Kasey Chambers, to alt-country wonders including

the Warumpi Band (Too Much Harmony), Tex, Don & Charlie and Tim
Rogers (kind of alt-country-pop). The term 'jazz' is barely elastic enough to
encompass the diverse improvisatory scene. Traditional jazz artists include
Don Burrows, James Morrison, Vince Jones and Paul Grabowsky, while the
Necks stretch the jazz moniker with their ambient noodling.

Contemporary indigenous music is thriving, and the annual Deadly
awards (http://deadlys.vibe.com.au) are a good place to find out who's setting the pace. Jimmy Little, a country-folk stalwart, began his career in the
'50s; the Lifetime Achievement award is named in his honour. Indigenous
music finally hit the mainstream in the '90s, thanks largely to the immense
popularity of Yothu Yindi and the single 'Treaty', lifted from their excellent
album Tribal Voice (1991). Archie Roach is best known for albums such
as Journey (2007), his latest, and Charcoal Lane (1992), arguably his best.
With fellow singer-songwriter and partner Ruby Hunter, Archie has toured
globally and collaborated on various performance projects; check out Ruby
(2006), a collaboration between the two and jazz great Paul Grabowsky and
his Australian Art Orchestra. Compelling singer-storyteller Kev Carmody
and the multitalented Christine Anu are worth looking out for; so too are
the Pigram Brothers and their album Under the Mango Tree (2006), and any
recordings from the (now defunct) alt-rock band Broken English. Marshall
Whyler and Ash Dargan, Indigenous musicians from central Australia, both
create beautiful sounds by combining didgeridoo, trance and electronica.
In 2008 Geoffrey Gurrumul Yunupingu stopped the music world in its
tracks with his album Gurrumul, sung entirely in Aboriginal languages
including Galpu, Djambarrpuynu and Gumatj. Blind from birth and heart-
wrenchingly shy, Yunupingu has become a household name in Australia
and toured the world.

> 'The term
> 'jazz' is
> barely elastic
> enough to
> encompass
> the diverse
> improvisa-
> tory scene.'

If you're in Alice Springs pop into the Central Australian Aboriginal Media
Association (p874) for a concentrated collection of Indigenous music.

Local radio stations have a content quota to play at least 15% Australian
music, but for a 100% dose, tune into the national youth radio station Triple
J (www.triplej.net.au/homeandhosed) for 'Home and Hosed', 9pm to 11pm
Monday to Thursday. Also check out the TV program Message Stick (www
.abc.net.au/message) for 100% Indigenous arts and music information. See
Festivals & Events in individual state and territory chapters for information
about Australia's many fabulous live-music festivals.

Theatre & Dance

Like most art forms in Australia, the country's performing arts were built
on European traditions. Over time, both theatre and dance have developed
into unique practices that have defined themselves through talented local
playwrights, actors, designers, dancers, directors, composers, choreographers
and musicians. Australia has a broad range of companies – both fully funded
and independent – and an abundance of venues to play out any drama.

Australian theatre has a long association with vaudeville, which flourished in the late 19th century. The bawdy combination of comic skits and
music entertained the influx of miners who'd arrived during the gold rush.
The theatre scene turned the corner in 1967 when Betty Burstall founded
La Mama theatre (p532) in Melbourne, which spawned the Australian
Performers Group – later known as the Pram Factory. The Pram Factory
was dedicated to producing works written by Australians such as David
Williamson and Stephen Sewell, set in Australia and using the Australian
vernacular. At around the same time Sydney established the Belvoir Street
Theatre Company (p140), which also continues to perform outstanding
Australian works. And just when things might have been getting too serious,

AUSTRALIANA ON THE SPEAKERS *Jeanie Menzies*

It's a hot summer's evening. You're trying to pretend you can keep cool by lying very still. The scene from your window is that of a Mambo shirt; power lines, Holdens and veneered houses. The hum of a lawnmower overpowers ABC radio's cricket coverage. Take time to reflect on the Oz artists who have been bold enough to expose and embrace both the beauty and the grit of this suburban lifestyle without a hint of cultural cringe, just a lot of heart.

- **Australian Crawl** *Sons of Beaches* (1982); key track 'Daughters of the Northern Coast'
- **Cold Chisel** *Circus Animals* (1982); key track 'You Got Nothing I Want'
- **The Go Betweens** *16 Lovers Lane* (1988); key track 'Spring Rain'
- **Hunters & Collectors** *Human Frailty* (1986); key track 'Say Goodbye'
- **Midnight Oil** *10-1* (1982); key track 'Power and the Passion'
- **Paul Kelly** *Gossip* (1986); key track 'Before Too Long'
- **Skyhooks** *Living in the 70's* (1974); key track 'You Just Like Me Cause I'm Good In Bed'
- **The Whitlams** *Undeniably* (1994); key track 'I Make Hamburgers'

Barry Humphries (aka Dame Edna) stormed Australian stages with his (her) inimitable satire of the Australian housewife, among other characters. The respected Bell Shakespeare Company formed in 1990 and continues to perform Shakespearean and other classically themed works.

These days, artistic merit increasingly holds hands with celebrity. Major theatre companies are using actors with overseas credibility, and not necessarily in acting roles; the Sydney Theatre Company's artistic directors are Cate Blanchett and husband (and playwright) Andrew Upton.

The 1990s hosted a revival in musical theatre, with wildly successful productions such as *Bran Nue Day* (a work about Australian Aboriginality, now also a film) and the Peter Allen story *The Boy from Oz,* which also hit Broadway.

Australia's exuberant dance scene is well versed in both classical and contemporary styles: check out Australia Dancing (www.australiadancing.org) for up-to-date information on companies and performances. Classically, the Australian Ballet (www.australianballet.com.au), established in 1964, is considered to be among the world's finest companies. Dance has long been influenced by Aboriginal traditions too; this is most accessible through the stellar Sydney-based Bangarra Dance Theatre (www.bangarra.com.au), which performs stories and characters of the Dreaming. Melbourne's contemporary company Chunky Move (www.chunkymove.com) is enjoying great success. It's been pushing the boundaries since 1998, redefining contemporary dance and popularising the medium with vital choreography, clever concepts firmly anchored in popular culture and extraordinary dancers. The nexus between dance and theatre, physical theatre, is best represented by Melbourne company Kage (www.kagephysicaltheatre.com).

The Australia Council funds a number of major state theatre and dance companies. If you add to that the huge number of independent companies and venues that produce works that, collectively, fill the gaps left by the mainstream, you have the vibrant, multilayered landscape of Australia's performing arts.

Visual Arts

Paintings in the early days of colonial Australia depicted the landscape through European eyes. It wasn't until the 1880s, in tune with the growing nationalist movement, that Australian-born artists began to capture the unique qualities of the Australian light and landscape. Members of the group known as the Heidelberg School, artists such as Tom Roberts and Arthur Streeton created a heroic national iconography from sheep-shearing scenes and visions of a wide brown land that offered opportunity to all. By the 1940s a cultural re-evaluation had taken place with the modernist movement known as the Angry Penguins at the helm. This movement threw romantic Impressionist convention out and introduced a period of modernism; Arthur Boyd, Sir Sidney Nolan (who painted the well-known Ned Kelly series), Albert Tucker and Joy Hester were the main players.

Contemporary Australian artists are strongly concerned with an Australian sense of place and are actively engaged in the more universal concerns of our contemporary, globalised world. Artists such as Jeffrey Smart and photographer Bill Henson are well known for their explorations of the urban environment. Other artists comment on the practice of making art and the relationship between the real and the represented. The impact of technology is a common theme of such artists as Patricia Piccinini and Ron Mueck, Martine Corompt and Sam Jinks, who are empowered by the digital world as well as thoughtfully engaged with the ethical dilemmas it generates. Cross-cultural investigations are regularly represented, with artists drawing on a range of personal cultural perspectives to find their own expressive language. To the 2009 Venice Biennale, Australia sent Shaun Gladwell to exhibit his work *MADDESTMAXIMVS*, a compilation of videos, sound, photographic and sculptural works based on the Australian landscape. Also there was a group exhibition from artists Vernon Ah Kee, Ken Yonetani, Claire Healy and Sean Cordeiro, with works and installations focused on displacement, Indigenous and environmental issues.

Aboriginal Art

Indigenous culture has brought huge benefits to Australia's art. Visual imagery is a fundamental part of Indigenous life; it's a connection between past and present, the supernatural and the earthly, and the people and the land. The early forms of Indigenous artistic expression were rock carvings (petroglyphs), body painting and ground designs.

Arnhem Land, in Australia's tropical Top End, is an area of rich artistic heritage. Some of the rock-art galleries in the huge sandstone Arnhem Land plateau are at least 18,000 years old, and range from hand prints to paintings of animals, people, mythological beings and European ships. Two of the finest sites, Ubirr and Nourlangie in Kakadu National Park, are accessible to visitors. The art of the Kimberley is perhaps best known for its images of the Wandjina, a group of ancestral beings who came from the sky and sea and were associated with fertility. The superb galleries at Laura on the Cape York Peninsula, in north Queensland, are also among the finest in the country. Among the many creatures depicted on the walls are the Quinkan spirits.

Painting in central Australia has flourished to such a degree that it is now an important source of income for Indigenous communities. It has also been an important educational tool for children, through which they can learn different aspects of religious and ceremonial knowledge. Western Desert painting, also known as 'dot' painting, has partly evolved from 'ground paintings', which formed the centrepiece of dances and songs. These 'paintings' were made from pulped plant material and the designs were made on the ground using dots of this mush. Dot paintings depict Dreaming stories.

Bark painting is an integral part of the cultural heritage of Arnhem Land Indigenous people, and one of its main features is the use of *rarrk* (cross-hatching) designs. These identify particular clans and are based on body paintings handed down through generations.

Dollar Dreaming – Inside the Aboriginal Art World (Benjamin Genocchio 2008) is an exposé of the booming Aboriginal Art industry, from its humble beginnings to its controversial and complex present.

Environment Dr Tim Flannery

Dr Tim Flannery wrote the Environment chapter. He is a naturalist, explorer and writer, and was named Australian of the Year in 2007. For more information about Tim, see p1086.

Australia's plants and animals are just about the closest things to alien life you are likely to encounter on Earth. That's because Australia has been isolated from the other continents for a very long time – at least 45 million years. The other habitable continents have been able to exchange various species at different times because they've been linked by land bridges. Just 15,000 years ago it was possible to walk from the southern tip of Africa right through Asia and the Americas to Tierra del Fuego. Not Australia, however. Its birds, mammals, reptiles and plants have taken their own separate and very different evolutionary journey, and the result today is the world's most distinct – and one of its most diverse – natural realms.

The first naturalists to investigate Australia were astonished by what they found. Here the swans were black – to Europeans this was a metaphor for the impossible – while mammals such as the platypus and echidna were discovered to lay eggs. It really was an upside-down world, where many of the larger animals hopped, where each year the trees shed their bark rather than their leaves, and where the 'pears' were made of wood.

If you are visiting Australia for a short time, you might need to go out of your way to experience some of the richness of the environment. That's because Australia is a subtle place, and some of the natural environment – especially around the cities – has been damaged or replaced by trees and creatures from Europe. Places like Sydney, however, have preserved extraordinary fragments of their original environment that are relatively easy to access. Before you enjoy them though, it's worthwhile understanding the basics about how nature operates in Australia. This is important because there's nowhere like Australia, and once you have an insight into its origins and natural rhythms, you will appreciate the place so much more.

A UNIQUE ENVIRONMENT

There are two really big factors that go a long way towards explaining nature in Australia: its soils and its climate. Both are unique. Australian soils are the more subtle and difficult to notice of the two, but they have been fundamental in shaping life here. On the other continents, in recent geological times processes such as volcanism, mountain building and glacial activity have been busy creating new soil. Just think of the glacier-derived soils of North America, north Asia and Europe. They feed the world today, and were made by glaciers grinding up rock of differing chemical composition over the last two million years. The rich soils of India and parts of South America were made by rivers eroding mountains, while Java in Indonesia owes its extraordinary richness to volcanoes.

Uluru (Ayers Rock) is often thought to be the world's largest monolith. In fact, it only wins second place. The biggest is Mt Augustus (Burringurrah) in Western Australia, which is 2½ times the size.

All of these soil-forming processes have been almost absent from Australia in more recent times. Only volcanoes have made a contribution, and they cover less than 2% of the continent's land area. In fact, for the last 90 million years, beginning deep in the age of dinosaurs, Australia has been geologically comatose. It was too flat, warm and dry to attract glaciers, its crust too ancient and thick to be punctured by volcanoes or folded into mountains. Look at Uluru (Ayers Rock; p887) and Kata Tjuta (the Olgas; p889). They are the stumps of mountains that 350 million years ago were the height of the Andes. Yet for hundreds of millions of years they've been nothing but nubs.

Under such conditions no new soil is created and the old soil is leached of all its goodness by the rain, and is blown and washed away. Even if just 30cm of rain falls each year, that adds up to a column of water 30 million km high passing through the soil over 100 million years, and that can do a great deal of leaching! Almost all of Australia's mountain ranges are more than 90 million years old, so you will see a lot of sand here, and a lot of country where the rocky 'bones' of the land are sticking up through the soil. It is an old, infertile landscape, and life in Australia has been adapting to these conditions for aeons.

Australia's misfortune in respect to soils is echoed in its climate. In most parts of the world outside the wet tropics, life responds to the rhythm of the seasons – summer to winter, or wet to dry. Most of Australia experiences seasons – sometimes very severe ones – yet life does not respond solely to them. This can clearly be seen by the fact that although there's plenty of snow and cold country in Australia, there are almost no trees that shed their leaves in winter, nor do any Australian animals hibernate. Instead there is a far more potent climatic force that Australian life must obey: El Niño.

The cycle of flood and drought that El Niño brings to Australia is profound. Our rivers – even the mighty Murray River, the nation's largest river, which runs through the southeast – can be miles wide one year, yet you can literally step over its flow the next. This is the power of El Niño, and its effect, when combined with Australia's poor soils, manifests itself compellingly. As you might expect from this, relatively few of Australia's birds are seasonal breeders, and few migrate. Instead, they breed when the rain comes, and a large percentage are nomads, following the rain across the breadth of the continent.

So challenging are conditions in Australia that its birds have developed some extraordinary habits. The kookaburras, magpies and blue wrens you are likely to see – to name just a few – have developed a breeding system called 'helpers at the nest'. The helpers are the young adult birds of previous breedings, which stay with their parents to help bring up the new chicks. Just why they should do this was a mystery, until it was realised that conditions in Australia can be so harsh that more than two adult birds are needed to feed the nestlings. This pattern of breeding is very rare in places like Asia, Europe and North America, but it is common in many Australian birds.

Australia is, of course, famous as the home of the kangaroo (roo) and other marsupials. Unless you visit a wildlife park, such creatures are not easy to see as most are nocturnal. Their lifestyles, however, are exquisitely attuned to Australia's harsh conditions. Have you ever wondered why kangaroos, alone among the world's larger mammals, hop? It turns out that hopping is the most efficient way of getting about at medium speeds. This is because the energy of the bounce is stored in the tendons of the legs – much like in a pogo stick – while the intestines bounce up and down like a piston, emptying and filling the lungs without needing to activate the chest muscles. When you travel long distances to find meagre feed, such efficiency is a must.

Marsupials are so energy-efficient that they need to eat one-fifth less food than equivalent-sized placental mammals (everything from bats to rats, whales and ourselves). But some marsupials have taken energy efficiency much further. If you visit a wildlife park or zoo you might notice that faraway look in a koala's eyes. It seems as if nobody is home – and this in fact is near the truth. Several years ago biologists announced that koalas are the only living creatures that have brains that don't fit their skulls. Instead they have a shrivelled walnut of a brain that rattles around in a fluid-filled cranium. Other researchers have contested this finding, however, pointing out that the brains of the koalas examined for the study may have shrunk because these organs are so soft. Whether soft-brained or empty-headed, there is no doubt that the koala is not the Einstein of the animal world, and we now believe that it has sacrificed its brain to energy efficiency. Brains cost a lot to

In *The Weather Makers*, Tim Flannery argues passionately for the urgent need to address – NOW –the implications of a global climate change that is damaging all life on Earth and endangering our very survival. It's an accessible read.

The website of the Australian Museum (www.australianmuseum.net.au) holds a wealth of info on Australia's animal life from the Cretaceous period till now. Kids will love the online games, fact files and movies.

R Strahan's *The Mammals of Australia* is a complete survey of Australia's somewhat cryptic mammals. Every species is illustrated, and almost everything known about them is covered in the individual species accounts, which have been written by the nation's experts.

run – our brains typically weigh 2% of our body weight, but use 20% of the energy we consume. Koalas eat gum leaves, which are so toxic that koalas use 20% of their energy just detoxifying this food. This leaves little energy for the brain, and living in the tree tops where there are so few predators means that they can get by with few wits at all.

The peculiar constraints of the Australian environment have not made everything dumb. The koala's nearest relative, the wombat (of which there are three species), has a large brain for a marsupial. These creatures live in complex burrows and can weigh up to 35kg, making them the largest herbivorous burrowers on Earth. Because their burrows are effectively air-conditioned, they have the neat trick of turning down their metabolic activity when they are in residence. One physiologist, who studied their thyroid hormones, found that biological activity ceased to such an extent in sleeping wombats that, from a hormonal point of view, they appeared to be dead! Wombats can remain underground for a week at a time, and can get by on just a third of the food needed by a sheep of equivalent size. One day, perhaps, efficiency-minded farmers will keep wombats instead of sheep. At the moment, however, that isn't possible; the largest of the wombat species, the northern hairy-nose, is one of the world's rarest creatures, with only around 100 surviving in a remote nature reserve in central Queensland.

Among the more common marsupials you might catch a glimpse of in the national parks around Australia's major cities are the species of antechinus. These nocturnal, rat-sized creatures lead an extraordinary life. The males live for just 11 months, the first 10 of which consist of a concentrated burst of eating and growing. Like teenage males, the day comes when their minds turn to sex, and in the antechinus this becomes an obsession. As they embark on their quest for females they forget to eat and sleep. Instead they gather in logs and woo passing females by serenading them with squeaks. By the end of August – just two weeks after they reach 'puberty' – every male is dead, exhausted by sex and by carrying around swollen testes. This extraordinary life history may also have evolved in response to Australia's trying environmental conditions. It seems likely that if the males survived mating, they would compete with the females as they tried to find enough food to feed their growing young. Basically, antechinus dads are disposable. They do better for antechinus posterity if they go down in a testosterone-fuelled blaze of glory.

One thing you will see lots of in Australia are reptiles (see p1077). Snakes are abundant, and they include some of the most venomous species known. Where the opportunities to feed are few and far between, it's best not to give your prey a second chance, hence the potent venom. Around Sydney and other parts of Australia, however, you are far more likely to encounter a harmless python than a dangerously venomous species. Snakes will usually leave you alone if you don't fool with them. Observe, back quietly away and don't panic, and most of the time you'll be OK.

Some visitors mistake lizards for snakes, and indeed some Australian lizards look bizarre. One of the more abundant is the sleepy lizard. These creatures, which are found throughout the southern arid region, look like animated pine cones. They are the Australian equivalent of tortoises, and are harmless. Other lizards are much larger. Unless you visit the Indonesian island of Komodo you will not see a larger lizard than the desert-dwelling perentie. These beautiful creatures, with their leopard-like blotches, can grow to more than 2m long, and are efficient predators of introduced rabbits, feral cats and the like.

Australia's plants can be irresistibly fascinating. If you happen to be in the Perth area in spring it's well worth taking a wildflower tour. The best flowers grow on the arid and monotonous sand plains, and the blaze of colour

H Cogger's *Reptiles and Amphibians of Australia* is a bible to those interested in Australia's reptiles, and useful protection for those who are definitely not. This large volume will allow you to identify the species, and you can wield it as a defensive weapon if necessary.

The saltwater crocodile is the world's largest living reptile – males can reach a staggering 6m long.

produced by the kangaroo paws, banksias and similar native plants can be dizzying. The sheer variety of flowers is amazing, with 4000 species crowded into the southwestern corner of the continent. This diversity of prolific flowering plants has long puzzled botanists. Again, Australia's poor soils seem to be the cause. The sand plain is about the poorest soil in Australia – it's almost pure quartz. This prevents any single fast-growing species from dominating. Instead, thousands of specialist plant species have learned to find a narrow niche, and so coexist. Some live at the foot of the metre-high sand dunes, some on top, some on an east-facing slope, some on the west and so on. Their flowers need to be striking in order to attract pollinators, for nutrients are so lacking in this sandy world that even insects such as bees are rare.

> The Australian Conservation Foundation (ACF; www.acfonline.org.au) is Australia's largest non-government organisation involved in protecting the environment.

If you do get to walk the wildflower regions of the southwest, keep your eyes open for the sundews. Australia is the centre of diversity for these beautiful, carnivorous plants. They've given up on the soil supplying their nutritional needs and have turned instead to trapping insects with the sweet globs of moisture on their leaves, and digesting them to obtain nitrogen and phosphorus.

If you are very lucky, you might see a honey possum. This tiny marsupial is an enigma. Somehow it gets all of its dietary requirements from nectar and pollen, and in the southwest there are always enough flowers around for it to survive. But no-one knows why the males need sperm larger even than those of the blue whale, or why their testes are so massive. Were humans as well endowed, men would be walking around with the equivalent of a 4kg bag of potatoes between their legs!

CURRENT ENVIRONMENTAL ISSUES

Headlining the environmental issues facing Australia's fragile landscape at present are climate change, water scarcity, nuclear energy and uranium mining. All are interconnected. For Australia, the warmer temperatures resulting from climate change spell disaster to an already fragile landscape. At the time of research, Australia was suffering its worst drought on record. Dams throughout the country are at record lows and mandatory water restrictions have been imposed. A 2°C climb in average temperatures on the globe's driest continent will result in an even drier southern half of the country and greater water scarcity. Scientists also agree that hotter and drier conditions will exacerbate bushfire conditions and increase cyclone intensity, two natural phenomena that have cost lives and a great deal of money to the Australian public; see When Larry Showed Up (p431) and Bushfires & Blizzards (p1028).

> The Climate Project trains ordinary citizens (in the US, Australia and the UK, so far) to become Climate Change Messengers who present the information delivered by Al Gore in the documentary, *An Inconvenient Truth*. For more, go to www .theclimateproject.org.

MALAISE OF THE MURRAY-DARLING

The Murray-Darling is Australia's largest river system. Ranked 15th in the world, it flows through South Australia (SA), New South Wales (NSW), the Australian Capital Territory (ACT), Victoria and Queensland, covering an area of 1.05 million sq km – roughly 14% of Australia. Aside from quenching around a third of the country's agricultural and urban thirsts, it also irrigates precious rainforests, wetlands, subtropical areas and scorched arid lands. But the Murray-Darling is sick and parched. Leading scientists estimate that unless 1500 gigalitres of water (think Sydney Harbour and then multiply it by three) are returned to the Murray River alone, it won't be able to recover and its water will simply become too salty for use (see Murray in Meltdown, p771). Wetland areas around the Darling River that used to flood every five years are now likely to do so every 25 years, and prolific species are threatened with extinction. In 2008, state, territory and federal governments agreed to develop the Basin Plan, a strategy for sustainable management of water resources in the Murray-Darling Basin; it is due to commence in 2011.

ENVIRONMENTAL CHALLENGES

The European colonisation of Australia, commencing in 1788, heralded a period of catastrophic environmental upheaval, with the result that Australians today are struggling with some of the most severe environmental problems to be found anywhere. It may seem strange that a population of just twenty million, living in a continent the size of the USA minus Alaska, could inflict such damage on its environment, but Australia's long isolation, its fragile soils and difficult climate have made it particularly vulnerable to human-induced change.

Damage to Australia's environment has been inflicted in several ways, the most important being the introduction of pest species, destruction of forests, overstocking rangelands, inappropriate agriculture and interference with water flows.

Beginning with the escape of domestic cats into the Australian bush shortly after 1788, a plethora of vermin – from foxes to wild camels and cane toads – have run wild in Australia, causing extinctions in the native fauna. One out of every 10 native mammals living in Australia prior to European colonisation is now extinct, and many more are highly endangered. Extinctions have also affected native plants, birds and amphibians.

The destruction of forests has also had a profound effect on the environment. Most of Australia's rainforests have suffered clearing, while conservationists fight with loggers over the fate of the last unprotected stands of 'old growth'.

Many Australian rangelands have been chronically overstocked for more than a century, the result being the extreme vulnerability of both soils and rural economies to Australia's drought and flood cycle, as well as the extinction of many native species. The development of agriculture has involved land clearance and the provision of irrigation, and here again the effect has been profound. Clearing of the diverse and spectacular plant communities of the Western Australian wheat belt began just a century ago, yet today up to one-third of that country is degraded by salination of the soils. Between 70kg and 120kg of salt lies below every square metre of the region,

The 2007 discovery of the rare Moggridgea tingle spider (which dates back 140 million years) in the Walpole Wilderness Area may alter the entire management of southern Western Australia's karri and tingle forests.

Australia is a heavy greenhouse gas emitter because it relies on coal and other fossil fuels for its energy supplies. The most prominent and also contentious alternative energy source is nuclear power, which creates less greenhouse gases and relies on uranium, in which Australia is rich. But the radioactive waste created by nuclear power stations can take thousands of years to become harmless. Moreover, uranium is a finite energy source (as opposed to yet-cleaner and renewable energy sources such as solar and wind power), and even if Australia were to establish sufficient nuclear power stations now to make a real reduction in coal-dependency, it would be years before the environmental and economic benefits were realised.

Uranium mining itself also produces polarised opinions. Because countries around the world are also looking to nuclear energy, Australia finds itself in a position to increase exports of one of its top-dollar resources. But uranium mining in Australia has been met with fierce opposition for decades, not only because the product is a core ingredient of nuclear weapons, but also because much of Australia's uranium supplies sit beneath sacred Indigenous land. Supporters of increased uranium mining and export suggest that the best way to police the use of uranium is to manage its entire life cycle; that is to sell the raw product to international buyers, and then charge a fee to accept the waste and dispose of it. Both major political parties consider an expansion of Australia's uranium export industry to be inevitable for economic reasons.

NATIONAL & STATE PARKS

Australia has more than 500 national parks – nonurban protected wilderness areas of environmental or natural importance. Each state defines and runs its own national parks, but the principle is the same throughout Australia.

and clearing of native vegetation has allowed water to penetrate deep into the soil, dissolving the salt crystals and carrying brine towards the surface.

In terms of financial value, just 1.5% of Australia's land surface provides over 95% of its agricultural yield, and much of this land lies in the irrigated regions of the Murray-Darling Basin. This is Australia's agricultural heartland, yet it too is under severe threat from salting of soils and rivers. Irrigation water penetrates into the sediments laid down in an ancient sea, carrying salt into the catchments and fields; see Malaise of the Murray-Darling (p59). The Snowy River in NSW and Victoria also faces a huge battle for survival.

Despite the enormity of the biological crisis engulfing Australia, governments and the community have been slow to respond. It was in the 1980s that coordinated action began to take place, but not until the '90s that major steps were taken. The establishment of **Landcare** (www.landcareaustralia .com.au), an organisation enabling people to effectively address local environmental issues, and the expenditure of over $2 billion through the federal government initiative **Caring for our Country** (www.nrm.gov.au) have been important national initiatives. Yet so difficult are some of the issues the nation faces that, as yet, little has been achieved in terms of halting the destructive processes.

Individuals are also banding together to help. Groups such as **Bush Heritage Australia** (www.bushherit age.org.au) and **Australian Wildlife Conservancy** (AWC; www.australianwildlife.org) allow people to donate funds and time to conserving native species. Some such groups have been spectacularly successful; AWC, for example, already manages many endangered species over its 25,000 sq km holdings.

So severe are Australia's problems that it will take a revolution before they can be overcome, for sustainable practices need to be implemented in every arena of life – from farms to suburbs and city centres. Renewable energy, sustainable agriculture and water use lie at the heart of these changes, and Australians are only now developing the road map to sustainability that they so desperately need if they are to have a long-term future on the continent.

National parks include rainforests, vast tracts of empty outback, strips of coastal dune land and rugged mountain ranges.

Public access is encouraged as long as safety and conservation regulations are observed. In all parks you're asked to do nothing to damage or alter the natural environment. Camping grounds (often with toilets and showers), walking tracks and information centres are often provided for visitors. In most national parks there are restrictions on bringing in pets.

State parks and state forests are other forms of nature reserves; owned by state governments, they have fewer regulations than national parks. Although state forests can be logged, they are often recreational areas with camping grounds, walking trails and signposted forest drives. Some permit horses and dogs.

For the addresses of national and state park authorities, see the National Parks section in each destination chapter.

Ecotourism Australia (www.ecotourism.org.au) has an accreditation system for environmentally friendly and sustainable tourism in Australia.

WATCHING WILDLIFE

Some regions of Australia offer unique opportunities to see wildlife, and one of the most fruitful is Tasmania. The island is jam-packed with wallabies, wombats and possums, principally because foxes, which have decimated marsupial populations on the mainland, were slow to reach the island state (the first fox was found in Tasmania only as recently as 2001!). It is also home to the Tasmanian devil – the Australian hyena, but less than one-third the size of its African ecological counterpart. They're common on the island, and in some national parks you can watch them tear apart road-killed wombats. Their squabbling is fearsome, the shrieks ear splitting. It's the nearest thing Australia can offer to experiencing a lion

---

RESPONSIBLE BUSHWALKING

You can help preserve the ecology and beauty of Australia by keeping in mind the following when you're out hiking:

■ Don't pee or poo within 100m of any water sources. Doing so can lead to the transmission of serious diseases, and it also pollutes precious water supplies.

■ Wash at least 50m from any water sources, and use a biodegradable detergent.

■ It's best not to cut wood for fires in popular bushwalking areas as this can cause rapid deforestation. Instead, use a stove that runs on kerosene, methylated spirits or some other liquid fuel. Avoid stoves powered by disposable butane gas canisters.

■ It's important to stick to existing tracks when you're walking, as hillsides and mountain slopes are prone to erosion.

---

kill on the Masai Mara. Unfortunately, Tassie devil populations are being decimated by the devil facial tumour disease; see Tigers & Devils (p698).

For those intrigued by the diversity of tropical rainforests, Queensland's World Heritage sites are well worth visiting. Birds of paradise, cassowaries and a variety of other birds can be seen by day, while at night you can search for tree-kangaroos (yes, some kinds of kangaroo do live in the tree tops). In your nocturnal wanderings you are highly likely to see curious possums, some of which look like skunks, and other marsupials that today are restricted to a small area of northeast Queensland. Fossils from as far afield as western Queensland and southern Victoria indicate that such creatures were once widespread.

Australia's deserts are a real hit-and-miss affair as far as wildlife is concerned. If you're visiting in a drought year, all you might see are dusty plains, the odd mob of kangaroos and emus, and a few struggling trees. Return after big rains, however, and you'll encounter something close to a Garden of Eden. Fields of white and gold daisies stretch endlessly into the distance, perfuming the air. The salt lakes fill with fresh water, and millions of water birds – pelicans, stilts, shags and gulls – can be seen feeding on the superabundant fish and insect life of the waters. It all seems like a mirage, and like a mirage it will vanish as the land dries out, only to spring to life again in a few years or a decade's time. For a more reliable bird-watching spectacular, Kakadu (p842) is well worth a look, especially towards the end of the dry season around November.

The largest creatures found in the Australian region are marine mammals such as whales and seals, and there is no better place to see them than South Australia. During springtime southern right whales crowd into the head of the Great Australian Bight. You can readily observe them near the remote Aboriginal community of Yatala as they mate, frolic and suckle their young. Kangaroo Island (p756), south of Adelaide, is a fantastic place to see seals and sea lions. There are well-developed visitor centres to facilitate the viewing of wildlife, and nightly penguin parades occur at some places where the adult blue penguins make their nest burrows. Kangaroo Island's beaches are magical places, where you're able to stroll among fabulous shells, whale bones and even jewel-like leafy sea dragons amid the sea wrack.

The fantastic diversity of Queensland's Great Barrier Reef is legendary, and a boat trip out to the reef from Cairns or Port Douglas is unforgettable. Just as extraordinary but less well known is the diversity of Australia's southern waters; the Great Australian Bight is home to more kinds of marine creatures than anywhere else on Earth. A stroll along any beach, from Cape Leeuwin

Some of Australia's most beautiful national parks are included on the World Heritage Register, a UN register of natural and cultural places of world significance. See http://whc.unesco.org for more information about these sites.

The Wilderness Society focuses on protection of wilderness and forests; visit www.wilderness .org.au.

at the tip of Western Australia to Tasmania, is likely to reveal glimpses of that diversity in the shape of creatures washed up from the depths. The exquisite shells of the paper nautilus are occasionally found on the more remote beaches, where you can walk the white sand for kilometres without seeing another person.

TEN GOOD REASONS TO VISIT A NATIONAL PARK

Park Name	Best Time to Visit	Features	Activities	Page Reference
Coorong National Park (SA)	Nov-Mar	Wetlands of international importance, evocative dunes, lagoons, freshwater soaks, ephemeral lakes, water birds and pelicans	Canoeing, fishing, swimming, walking, 4WDing	p764
Freycinet National Park (Tasmania)	Year-round	Gorgeous beaches, rocky peaks, stunning Wineglass Bay	Bushwalking, swimming, canoeing, kayaking, fishing, camping, wildlife watching	p674
Girringun National Park (Queensland)	May -Sep	The knockout Wallaman Falls (at their fullest Nov-Feb), dense rainforest, endangered cassowaries, open ridges, deep gullies and laden creeks	Camping, bushwalking, overnight hikes, wildlife watching	p425
Grampians National Park (Victoria)	Year-round	Wide open vistas, dense forests, abundant native flora and fauna, waterfalls	Bushwalking, sightseeing, rock climbing, abseiling, camping	p566
Innes National Park (SA)	Oct to Mar	Spectacular coastal scenery, indigo waters, sheer cliffs, intimate sandy coves, prolific wildlife	Bushwalking, surfing, fishing, reef diving	p786
Kakadu National Park (NT)	Apr-Sep	Australia's largest national park, World Heritage–listed landscapes, bird watching, rock-art sites, diverse habitats	Aboriginal tours, stunning bushwalks, bird watching, 4WDing, camping	p842
Karijini National Park (WA)	Aug-Sep	Stunning gorges, spectacular waterfalls, sublime natural swimming pools carved from rocks, impressive views of four gorges from Oxers Lookout	Rigorous but breathtaking walks, splendid swimming opportunities	p989
Kosciuszko National Park (NSW)	Year-round	Australia's highest mountain, snowfields in winter, wildflowers in January	Skiing, snowboarding, bushwalking, mountain biking, canoeing, white-water rafting, abseiling	p242
Mungo National Park (NSW)	May-Aug	Remote pristine outback territory, dry Lake Mungo, massive sand dunes concealing ancient remains, Aboriginal heritage	Award-winning eco-tours, 4WDing	p264
Moreton Island National Park (Queensland)	Year-round	Freshwater lagoons, towering sand dunes, wildflowers, ruins of forts, miles of sandy beaches, the Tangalooma Wrecks off Flinders Reef	Superb coastal walks, snorkelling, scuba diving	p331

The whole eastern half of the Northern Territory is designated as the Arnhem Land Aboriginal Reserve. Apart from a few areas, it's not open to independent travellers.

If your visit extends only as far as Sydney, however, don't give up on seeing Australian nature. The Sydney sandstone – which extends approximately 150km around the city – is one of the most diverse and spectacular regions in Australia. In springtime, spectacular red waratahs abound in the region's parks, while the woody pear (a relative of the waratah) that so confounded the early colonists can also be seen, alongside more than 1500 other species of flowering plants. Even in a Sydney backyard you're likely to see more reptile species (mostly skinks) than can be found in all of Great Britain – so keep an eye out!

Food & Drink

Once upon a time in a decade not so far away Australians proudly survived and thrived on a diet of 'meat and three veg'. Fine fare was a Sunday roast that *wasn't* cooked to carcinogenic stages and lasagne was considered exotic. Fortunately the country's culinary sophistication has evolved and, mirroring the population's cheeky and disobedient disposition, contemporary Australian cuisine now thrives on breaking rules and conventions. The Australian propensity to absorb global influences and infuse them into a local equivalent is spurred by an inquisitive dining public willing to give anything new, and better, a go. The result is dynamic and constantly surprising cuisine and what's hot this morning may be dated by tomorrow – or, more likely, reinvented and improved.

To a large degree immigration has been the key to Australia's culinary bloom. A significant influx of migrants from Europe, Asia, the Middle East and, increasingly, Africa in the last 60 years has introduced new ingredients and new ways to use existing staples. But urban Australians have become culinary snobs along the way, and in order to wow the socks off fussy and demanding diners, restaurants must succeed in fusing contrasting ingredients and traditions into ever more innovative fare. The phrase Modern Australian (Mod Oz) has been coined to describe the cuisine. Laksas, curries and marinara pastas are now old-school 'pub grub'. If it's a melange of East and West, it's Mod Oz. If it's not authentically French or Italian, it's Mod Oz – the term is an attempt to classify the unclassifiable. As Australians' appetite for diversity and invention grows, so do the avenues of discovery. Cookbooks and foodie magazines are bestsellers, and Australian celebrity chefs – sought overseas – reflect Australia's multiculturalism in their background and dishes.

If all this sounds overwhelming, fear not. You'll find that dishes are characterised by bold and interesting flavours and fresh ingredients rather than fussy or cluttered creations. Spicing ranges from gentle to extreme, coffee is great (though it still reaches its greatest heights in the cities), wine is world renowned, seafood is plentiful and meats are tender, full flavoured and usually bargain priced. The range of food in Australia is its greatest culinary asset – all palates, be they timid or brave, shy or inquisitive, are well catered for.

> Tipping is not expected in Australia, but it is common practice when service is acceptable or better. Around 5% to 10% is appreciated, perhaps more if your kids (or fellow adults) have gone crazy and trashed the dining room.

STAPLES & SPECIALITIES

Seafood is iconic in Australian cuisine, and little compares to what's hauled from some of the purest waters you'll find anywhere. Despite its abundance it's usually cooked with passion and care.

Connoisseurs prize Sydney rock oysters, a species that actually lives right along the New South Wales (NSW) coast and even in Western Australia (WA). Giving them a run for their money are the oysters grown in seven

> Australians consume more than 206,000 tonnes of seafood per year. Along the coast, head to a seafood co-op, where you can gorge on a five-star meal for a one-star budget.

TALKING STRINE

The opening dish in a three-course meal is called the entrée, the second course (the North American entrée) is called the main course and the sweet bit at the end is called dessert, sweets, afters or pud. In lesser restaurants, of course, it's called desert.

When an Australian invites you over for a baked dinner it might mean a roast lunch. Use the time as a guide – dinner (the evening meal) is normally served after 6pm. By 'tea' they could be talking dinner or they could be talking tea. A coffee definitely means coffee, unless it's after a hot date when you're invited up to a prospect's flat.

Australian Gourmet Pages
(www.australiangour
metpages.com.au) is
a website devoted to
wine, food, restaurants
and more run by a *Vogue
Entertaining + Travel*
contributor. Subscription
is free.

different regions in South Australia (SA), and Tasmania's Pacific oysters.
Tassie is also known for trout, salmon and abalone. There are sea scallops from Queensland and estuary scallops from Tasmania and SA. Rock
lobsters are fantastic and fantastically expensive, and mud crabs, despite
the name, are a sweet delicacy. The crayfish and prawns of Mandurah in
WA are so good that they're shipped to Japan. Another odd-sounding
delicacy is 'bugs' – like shovel-nosed lobsters without a lobster's price
tag; try the Balmain and Moreton Bay varieties. Marron are prehistoric-
looking freshwater crayfish from WA, while their smaller cousins, yabbies,
can be found throughout the southeast. Prawns are incredible, particularly
sweet school prawns or the eastern king (Yamba) prawns found along the
northern NSW coast. Add to that countless wild fish species including prized
barramundi from the Northern Territory (NT). Even fish considered run-
of-the-mill such as snapper, trevally or whiting taste fabulous just slapped
on a barbecue.

Before buying fresh seafood to prepare yourself, take a minute to read the
Sustainable Seafood Guide (www.acfonline.org.au/uploads/res/res_ocean-
wisebrochure.pdf), a publication put together by the Australian Conservation
Foundation and the Australian Marine Conservation Society to inform
consumers of the most sustainable seafood to purchase and eat.

Almost everything eaten from the land was introduced. Even superexpen-
sive truffles are harvested in Tasmania and WA. Australia is huge (similar
in size to the continental USA) and it varies so much in climate, from the
tropical north to the temperate south, that at any time of the year there's an
enormous variety of produce on offer. Fruit is a fine example. In summer,
fruit bowls overflow with nectarines, peaches and cherries, and mangoes are
so plentiful that Queenslanders actually get sick of them. The Murray River
gives rise to vast orchards of citrus fruits, grapes, stone fruits and melons.
Tasmania's cold climate means its strawberries and stone fruits are sublime.
Lamb from Victoria's lush Gippsland is highly prized, the veal of White
Rocks in WA is legendary, and the tomatoes of SA are the nation's best. On
the topic of vine produce from SA, the state's wine industry is something
of a giant and SA reds in particular have made their way to bottle shops the
world over.

There's a brilliant and growing farmhouse cheese movement, and the
produce is great. Keep an eye out for goats-milk cheese from Gympie
(Queensland), Kytren (WA) and Kervella (WA), cheddar from Pyengana
(Tasmania) and the Hunter Valley (NSW), sheeps-milk cheese from Highland
Farm, washed rind from Milawa (Victoria), and anything from Woodside
Cheesewrights (SA) or Bruny Island (Tasmania), among others. The King
Island Dairy (Tasmania) has been wowing Australian taste buds for years
with its blue-veined and triple-cream brie (it also comes in the single-cream
variety). Tasmania alone now produces 50 cheese varieties.

Before you arrive, famil-
iarise yourself with good
Australian fare by poring
through the recipes in
Every Day by acclaimed
Sydney chef Bill Granger,
the master of laid-back
cuisine.

Anything another country does, Australia does too. Vietnamese, Japanese,
Fijian, Italian – no matter where it's from, there's an expat community and
interested locals desperate to cook and eat it. Dig deep enough, and you'll
find Jamaicans using scotch-bonnet peppers and Tunisians making tajine.
And you'll usually find that their houses are the favourite haunts of their
locally raised friends.

In cities and urban centres you'll be able to get your hands on any variety
of meat, fruit, veg and dairy by popping down to the local supermarket or
fresh-food market. Owing to their populations, Sydney and Melbourne boast
the widest variety of markets and produce, but the metropolitan sprawl along
coastal areas provides ample vendors. Seafood is always freshest close to the
source, and as Australia's an island, it's plentiful.

BUSH TUCKER: AUSTRALIAN NATIVE FOODS *Janelle White*

Did you know, there are around 350 food plants that are native to the Australian bush? Perhaps the best known is the macadamia nut, which was first commercially planted in the 1880s and decades later developed into a multi-million-dollar industry in Hawaii. Bush foods (also known as bush tucker) include an impressive variety of plant and animal products and most are still harvested from the wild by Indigenous Australians. Many early explorers and settlers failed to realise the full potential of these foods. Seeing the world through Eurocentric eyes, they favoured known species, dismissing the native vegetation as being of no economic or nutritional worth. Yet today an interest in the unique flavours and health benefits of bush foods is generating a broader market.

Bush foods provide a real taste of Australia's landscapes: piquant dried fruits and lean meats of the desert; shellfish and fish of the saltwater country; delicate alpine berries and mountain peppers of the high country; and varied citrus flavours, fruits and herbs of the rainforests. This cuisine is based on Indigenous Australians' expert understanding of the natural environment, founded on cultural knowledge handed down over generations. Years of trial and error has ensured a rich appreciation of these foods and mastery of their preparation. Ancestral connections are still strong and the collecting and eating of foods from one's traditional country makes people healthy and feel good.

Harvesting of bush foods for commercial return has been occurring for about 30 years. In central Australia it is mainly carried out by middle-aged and senior Aboriginal women. Here and in other regions, bush meats such as kangaroo, emu and crocodile, fish such as barramundi and bush fruits including desert raisins, quandongs, riberries, and Kakadu plums are seasonally hunted and gathered for personal enjoyment, as well as to supply local, national and international markets. Bush-food plants are also increasingly being cultivated in gardens for a developing native-foods industry.

Native Australian–cuisine restaurants are few, but typically offer a rich array of intense flavours and dishes with intriguing names. In Canberra, enjoy a predinner desert-lime spritzer while dipping wattleseed damper in bush-tomato dukkah at Ironbark (p282). Try cured crocodile with strawberry eucalypt and a lilly pilly macadamia nut salad at Brisbane's Tukka (p320), or kangaroo fillets with quandong chilli glaze at Ochre Restaurant (p446) in Cairns. Desserts are often a highlight, with temptations such as the gumleaf-scented creme caramels and wild-rosella cheesecake with wattleseed ice cream and passionberry sauce on offer at Red Ochre Grill (p873) in Alice Springs... Yum!

For a better understanding of the value of these foods to Aboriginal people, take a bush-tucker tour with Beanies, Baskets & Bushtucker (p870) in Alice Springs or Bookabee Tours (p734) in Adelaide.

Janelle is an applied anthropologist, currently completing a PhD on Aboriginal peoples' involvement in a variety of desert-based bush produce industries, including bush foods, bush medicines and bush jewellery. She lives and works between Adelaide and territory 200km northwest of Alice Springs.

At home, Australians' taste for the unusual usually kicks in at dinner only, although often for a weekend lunch as well. Most people still eat cereal, toast and fruit for breakfast, or perhaps eggs and bacon at weekends. They devour sandwiches (including panini, focaccias, toasted Turkish bread, and pita wraps), salads and sushi for lunch, and then eat anything and everything in the evening. Yum cha (the classic southern-Chinese feast incorporating a diversity of small dishes) is hugely popular as a breakfast or lunch option with urban locals, particularly at weekends. The barbecue is iconic and virtually mandatory for any home with a garden. In summer it's used frequently at dinner time to grill burgers or rissoles (the Aussie version is similar to a burger), sausages, steaks, lamb chops, chicken, seafood, and veggie, meat or seafood skewers. Year-round, weather permitting, it's pulled out at weekends for casual Sunday lunches with friends and family.

Chalk and Cheese by Will Studd contains everything you ever wanted to know about boutique cheese and cheesemakers in Australia's blossoming industry.

DRINKS

No matter what your poison, you're in the right country if you're after a drink. Long recognised as some of the finest in the world, wine is now one of Australia's top exports. In fact, if you're in the country's southern climes, you're probably not far from a wine region right now. As the public develops a more demanding palate, local beers are rising to the occasion, with a growing wealth of flavours and varieties available.

Most beers have an alcohol content between 3.5% and 5.5%. That's less than many European beers but more than most in North America. Light beers contain under 3% alcohol and are finding favour with people observing the stringent drink-driving laws.

The terms for ordering beer varies with the state. In NSW you ask for a 'schooner' (425mL) if you're thirsty and a 'middy' (285mL) if you're not quite so dry. In Victoria and Tasmania it's a 'pot' (285mL), and in most of the country you can just ask for a beer and wait to see what turns up. Pints (425mL or 568mL, depending on where you are) aren't as common, though Irish pubs and European-style ale houses tend to offer pints for homesick Poms.

Coffee has become an Australian addiction; there are Italian-style espresso machines in virtually every cafe, boutique roasters are all the rage and, in urban areas, the qualified barista (coffee maker) is virtually the norm. Sydney and Melbourne have borne a whole generation of coffee snobs, but Melbourne easily takes top billing as Australia's coffee capital. The cafe scene there rivals the most vibrant in the world – the best way to immerse yourself is by wandering the city centre's cafe-lined lanes. You'll also find decent stuff in most other cities, and there's a 20% chance of good coffee in many rural areas.

An essential website for beer lovers is www .microbrewing.com.au; devoted to the Australian industry, it lists microbreweries, books on the subject and beer-award festivals.

Figures from the Australian Bureau of Statistics show that approximately 1.3 million cups of coffee are sold in Australia every day.

CELEBRATIONS

Food and festivities in Australia are strongly linked, with celebrations often including equal amounts of food and alcohol. A birthday could be a barbecue (barbie, BBQ) of steak or prawns, washed down with a beverage or two. Traditionally, weddings have always been a slap-up dinner affair, although increasingly common are variations on the norm, such as cocktail receptions – less formal affairs that dish up hors d'oeuvres, tapas and finger food. Cultural backgrounds are also an influence, and if you've never

---

ORGANIC HOTSPOTS

Australia is increasingly a producer of organic food – that is, food that has grown or produced without the use of pesticides or chemicals. Organic retailers are prevalent in Sydney and Melbourne and becoming more common in cities and towns elsewhere. The NSW north coast is something of an organic-produce hub, and Byron Bay (p195) is the HQ.

Keep an eye out for the following on your travels:

- **Afghan Traders** (p873) in Alice Springs
- **Bangalow Farmers Market** (p202) in Bangalow
- **Billy Kwong** (p133) in Sydney
- **Ceres Community Environment Park** (p513) in Melbourne
- **Good Life** (p740) in Adelaide
- **Green Garage** (p200) in Byron Bay
- **Lentil as Anything** (p525) in Melbourne
- **Lismore Farmers Market & Organic Market** (p203) in Lismore
- **Mondo Organics** (p320) in Brisbane
- **Noosa Organika** (p353) in Noosa
- **Organic Market & Café** (p747) in the Adelaide Hills
- **West End Green Flea Markets** (p325) in Brisbane

NEW BREWS

In urban pubs you'll find anything from one to eight boutique beers complementing the standard tap draughts, and microbrewers are popping up as fast as hops after rain. While you're out and about, keep an eye out for the following breweries or their delectable product:

- **Blue Sky Brewery** (p447)
- **Bright Brewery** (p610)
- **Matso's Broome Brewery** (p1004)
- **Mudgee Brewery** (p221)
- **Potters Brewery** (p170)
- **Steam Exchange Brewery** (p755)
- **Tanglehead Brewery** (p950)
- **Wicked Ale Brewery** (p938)
- **Wig & Pen** (p283)

---

been to a Greek or Italian wedding you need to start making some new mates. Christenings or naming ceremonies are more sober; they're usually casual affairs with finger food, cake, coffee and tea after the ceremony.

Food tourism and food festivals are hugely popular. Melbourne, for instance, has its own month-long food-and-wine festival in March (p515). There are harvest festivals in wine regions, and various communities, such as the Clare Valley (p781), hold annual events. For more, see Top Food Festivals, p72.

For many an event, especially in the warmer months, Australians fill the car with an Esky (an ice chest, to keep everything cool), tables, chairs and a cricket set or footy, and head off for a barbie by the lake/river/beach. If there's a total fire ban (which occurs increasingly each summer), the food is precooked and the barbie becomes more of a picnic, but the essence remains the same.

Christmas in Australia is in midsummer and, in keeping with the warm weather, is less likely to involve a traditional European baked dinner than a barbecue, full of seafood and quality steak. Prawn prices skyrocket, chicken may be eaten with champagne at breakfast, and the main meal is usually in the afternoon, after a swim and before a really good, long siesta. If there's an exception to this rule it's Melbourne, which frequently produces winter weather on Christmas Day (regardless if there's a heatwave either side) and consequently facilitates a traditional baked dinner.

Various ethnic groups have their own celebrations. The Indian community brings out all the colour of the old country and the stickiest of sweets during Diwali, Greeks embrace any chance to hold a spit barbecue and the Chinese go off during their annual Spring Festival (Chinese New Year) every January or February (it changes with the lunar calendar).

WHERE TO EAT & DRINK

Typically, a restaurant meal in Australia is a relaxed affair. You'll probably order within 15 minutes, and see the first course 20 minutes later. The main will arrive about half an hour after that.

A competitively priced place to eat is a club (RSL or Surf Life Saving clubs are good bets), where you order at the kitchen – usually a staple such as a fisherman's basket, steak, or chicken parmigiana – take a number and wait until it's called out over the counter or intercom. You pick up the meal

Quaff by Peter Forrestal is the quintessential guide to the best wines available in Australia for $10, $15 and over $15 a bottle, including over 400 local and imported labels.

Useful websites for organic cuisine in Australia include www .organicfoodmarkets.com .au, www.farmersmar kets.org.au/finder/nsw .jsp and www.organ icwine.com.au yourself, saving the restaurant on staffing costs and you on your total bill. These clubs are popular local haunts in regional areas so you'll also be adding to your cultural education.

Pub meals (often referred to as counter meals, even if you sit at a table) are also good value, and standards such as gourmet sausages and mash, pizza,

---

WINE REGIONS

Most Australian states now nurture wine industries. Some are almost 200 years old and some are blossoming babes. Most wineries have small cellar doors where you can taste for free or a minimal fee. If you like the wine, you're generally expected to buy.

Although plenty of good wine comes from big producers with economies of scale on their side, the most interesting wines are usually made by small vignerons, where you pay a premium; the gamble means the pay-off in terms of flavour is often greater. Almost half the cost of wine is due to a high-taxing program courtesy of the Australian government.

Chapters on each state go into greater detail, but the following rundown should give you a head start.

Australian Capital Territory

Canberra is surrounded by a burgeoning number of small but excellent wineries making their mark. See Wineries of the ACT (p287) for pointers.

New South Wales

In NSW the Hunter Valley is the oldest wine region in Australia – it first had vines in the 1820s. The lower region is best known for Shiraz and unwooded Semillon, and the Upper Hunter wineries specialise in Cabernet Sauvignon and Shiraz, with forays into Verdelho and Chardonnay; see p170 and p173.

Further inland are award-winning wineries at Griffith (p253), Mudgee (p221) and Orange (p216).

Queensland

The Darling Downs is the heartland of Queensland's boutique wine industry and Stanthorpe is the centre of it; see Granite Belt Wineries (p357).

South Australia

Purists will rave about Shiraz and Cabernet Sauvignon from Coonawarra (p769), Riesling from the Clare Valley (p782), and Shiraz from the Barossa Valley (p775). SA is Australia's vinous heartland (visit the National Wine Centre in Adelaide, p730), but there are many more regions that produce fine wine.

Tasmania

In Tassie there are highly regarded wineries in Pipers River (p680) and the Tamar Valley (p687) and a burgeoning wine industry in the Coal River Valley around Richmond (p655).

Victoria

Just out of Melbourne, the Yarra Valley (p543) is one of Victoria's most important wine-growing regions, producing excellent Chardonnay and Pinot Noir. The same varieties are grown in lesser quantities on the Mornington Peninsula (p545). Wineries in Rutherglen (p582) produce superb fortified wines as well as Shiraz and Durif.

Victoria has over 500 wineries; see Yarra Valley Wineries (p543) and Rutherglen Reds (p582) for more information.

Western Australia

Margaret River is synonymous with incredible wine. The competition is stiff and the region has attracted international awards in recent years. The Cabernets and Chardonnays produced here are among the world's best; see Wining & Dining (p939) for more information.

Tucked into old-growth forest territory, Pemberton (p942) is peppered with wineries specialising in Cabernet Sauvignon, Merlot, Pinot Noir, Sauvignon Blanc and Shiraz.

Mt Barker (p947) on the South Coast is another budding wine region.

pasta and salads go for $15 to $20. In cities you'll also find pubs that pride themselves on their food – much like a British gastropub. Prices are higher, but the food is top-notch restaurant quality.

If a restaurant says it's BYO, you're allowed to bring your own alcohol. If the place also sells alcohol, the BYO bit is usually limited to bottled wine only (no beer, no casks) and a corkage charge is added to your bill. The cost is either per person or per bottle and ranges from nothing to $15 per bottle in fancy places.

Most restaurants open around noon for lunch and from 6pm for dinner. Australians usually eat lunch shortly after noon, and dinner bookings are usually made between 6.30pm and 8pm, though in major cities some restaurants stay open past 10pm. Australians also love to eat breakfast out and cafes serve morning fare from approximately 8am on weekends, earlier on week days. Cafes tend to be all-day affairs that either close around 5pm or continue into the night. Pubs usually serve food from noon to 2pm and 6pm to 8pm. Pubs and bars often open for drinking at lunchtime and continue well into the evening, particularly from Thursday to Saturday. For this book, eating venues are open for breakfast, lunch and dinner unless otherwise stated.

The James Halliday Australian Wine companion is a best-selling tome on the country's local plonk, with information about wineries thrown in.

Quick Eats

There's not a huge culture of street vending in Australia, though you may find a pie or coffee cart in some places. In cities the variety of quick eats is great; gourmet sandwich bars and delis, globally inspired takeaways, bakeries and sushi or salad bars. Elsewhere the options are more limited and traditional, such as a milk bar, which serves old-fashioned hamburgers (with bacon, egg, pineapple and beetroot if you want) and other takeaway foods. Fish and chips is still hugely popular, the fish most often a form of shark (often called flake; don't worry, it can be delicious) either grilled or dipped in batter and fried, and ideal for eating at the beach on a Friday night.

If you're at a rugby league or Aussie Rules football match, a beer, meat pie and bag of hot chips are as compulsory as wearing your team's colours to the game.

Pizza is one Australia's most popular fast foods. Most pizzas that are home delivered are of the American style (thick and with lots of toppings) rather than Italian style; that said, wood-fired, thin, Neapolitan-style pizza can easily be found, even in country towns.

delicious is a monthly magazine published by the Australian Broadcasting Corporation (ABC) listing recipes, restaurant reviews, food and wine trends, and foodie-related travel articles.

VEGETARIANS & VEGANS

You're in luck: most cities have a substantial number of local vegetarians, which means you're well catered for. Cafes always seem to have vegetarian options, and even the best restaurants may have a separate veg menu. Take care with risotto and soups, though, as meat stock is often used.

Vegans will find the going much tougher, but local Hare Krishna restaurants or Buddhist temples often provide relief, and there are usually dishes that are vegan-adaptable at restaurants.

Both vegetarians and vegans are likely to have difficulty finding a decent meal in remote areas. The rule of thumb is that the greater the resident population the greater your chances of finding good vegetarian or vegan fare.

Happy Cow (www.happy cow.net/australia/) lists vegetarian and vegetarian-friendly restaurants, with reader reviews and recommendations, by destination throughout Australia.

EATING WITH KIDS

Dining with children in Australia is relatively easy. At all but the flashiest places children are commonly seen. Kids are usually more than welcome at cafes, while bistros and clubs often see families dining early. Many fine-dining restaurants discourage small children (assuming that they're all ill behaved).

TOP FOOD FESTIVALS

Australia has a multitude of festivals to keep gastronomes gambolling year-round.

- **Sardine Festival** (WA; p924) A gourmet seafood fiesta held in January.
- **Festivale** (Tasmania; p684) Takes place over three days in February.
- **Melbourne Food & Wine Festival** (Victoria; p515) Melbourne's main gastronomical celebration (and that's a big call) features events throughout the city and is internationally renowned; takes place in March.
- **Barossa Vintage Festival** (SA; p777) Beginning Easter Monday every second year, this festival lasts a whole week.
- **Clare Valley Gourmet Weekend** (SA; p781) Held on a long weekend in May.
- **Taste of Byron** (NSW; p198) A celebration of the Byron region's organic and home-grown produce at the end of September.
- **Jazz in the Vines** (NSW; p171) A food, wine and jazz combo held in NSW's vino heartland in October.
- **Taste Festival** (Tasmania; p647) A week-long event seeing in the New Year.

Most places that do welcome children don't have kids' menus, and those that do usually offer everything straight from the deep fryer – crumbed chicken and chips etc. You might be best finding something on the normal menu (say a pasta or salad) and asking the kitchen to adapt it to your child's needs.

The best news for travelling families is that there are plenty of free or coin-operated barbecues in parks. Note that these will be in high demand at weekends and on public holidays.

Vegemite is a good source of vitamin B, which the body requires after heavy alcohol consumption. Australians consume more than 22 million jars of the stuff every year.

HABITS & CUSTOMS

As a nation, Australians aren't really a fussy lot. And that extends to the way they approach dining; it's usually a casual affair, and even at the finest of restaurants a jacket is virtually never required (but certainly isn't frowned upon). Table manners however are the norm; talking with your mouth full is considered uncouth and fingers should be used only for food that can't be tackled another way. That said, in pubs, cafes and other casual eateries it's perfectly acceptable to eat your chips or burger with your hands.

If you're invited to someone's house for dinner, always take a gift. Even if the host downright refuses when asked in advance, take a bottle of wine, some flowers or a box of chocolates.

'Shouting' is a revered custom where people rotate paying for a round of drinks. Just don't leave before it's your turn to buy! At a toast, everyone should touch glasses and look each other in the eye as they clink – failure to do so is reported to end in seven years' bad sex. On the other hand, a firm look may guarantee seven years of mind-blowing sex. Many drinks/cheers and looks may even ensure mind-blowing sex with someone at your table.

Australians like to linger a bit over coffee, and linger longer while drinking beer. And they tend to take quite a bit of time if they're out to dinner.

Smoking is banned in all eateries, bars, clubs and pubs, so sit outside if you love to puff.

The Cook's Companion by Stephanie Alexander is Australia's single-volume answer to Delia Smith's oeuvre. If it's in here, most Australians have probably seen it or eaten it.

COOKING COURSES

Many good cooking classes are run by food stores such as **Simon Johnson** (☎ 02-8244 8240; 181 Harris St, Pyrmont) in Sydney, and the **Essential Ingredient** (☎ 03-9827 9047; www.theessentialingredient.com.au; Prahran Market, Elizabeth St, Prahran) in Melbourne.

Others are run by markets, such as the Sydney Seafood School (p115) or the Queen Victoria Market Cooking School (p506) in Melbourne.

For a more comprehensive list of cooking schools in Australia, click onto www.classic.com.au/wizard/schools.htm.

More courses for culinary inspiration:

Bangalow Cooking School (p202)

Daniel Alps at Strathlyn (p688) Set in a vineyard, this highly regarded restaurant runs good cooking courses.

Le Cordon Bleu (☎ 08-8346 3700; www.lecordonbleu.com.au; Sydney & Adelaide) The original must-do French course is available thanks to a joint venture down under. Courses from 10 weeks to five years (part-time).

Mondo Organics (p320) This much-loved organic restaurant in Brisbane holds cooking courses that attract pupils from all over the city.

EAT YOUR WORDS

For a bit more insight into Australian cuisine, stick your nose into one or more of these books.

Australian Regional Food Guide (www.australianregionalfoodguide.com) By Sally and Gordon Hammond. A great guide to where to buy good food at the source as you travel around.

Cheap Eats The *Age* publishes an annual guide to great meals for under $30 in and around Melbourne.

Good Food Guide The *Age* and the *Sydney Morning Herald* both put out annual restaurant guides that rate over 400 restaurants in Victoria and NSW respectively.

Penguin's Good Australian Wine Guide An annual publication with lots of useful information on many readily available wines.

> Curtis Stone is one of Australia's most successful culinary exports, having been voted by the US magazine *People* as one of the sexiest men alive. His cooking isn't bad either, check out www.curtisstone.com.

Food Glossary

Australians love to shorten everything, including people's names, so expect many other words to be abbreviated. Some words you might hear:

barbie – a barbecue (BBQ), where (traditionally) smoke and overcooked meat are matched with lashings of coleslaw, potato salad and beer

Chiko roll – a fascinating large, spring-roll-like pastry for sale in takeaway shops; best used as an item of self-defence rather than eaten

moo-juice – milk

middy – a medium-sized glass of beer (NSW)

nummies – delicious, can be an adjective or a noun

pav – pavlova, the meringue dessert topped with cream, passionfruit and kiwi fruit or other fresh fruit

pie floater – a meat pie served floating in thick pea soup (SA)

pot – a medium-sized glass of beer (Victoria, Tasmania)

sanger/sando/sambo – a sandwich

sausage roll – an Australian treasure consisting of seasoned minced meat encased in a roll of pastry; found in most country bakeries

schooner – a big glass of beer (NSW), but not as big as a pint

snag – (aka surprise bag); sausage

snot block – a vanilla slice

spag bol – spaghetti bolognese

Tim Tam – a commercially produced chocolate biscuit that lies close to the heart of most Australians; best consumed as a Tim Tam shooter (also known as a Tim Tam bomb or exploding Tim Tam), where the two diagonally opposite corners of the rectangular biscuit are nibbled off, and a hot drink (tea is the true aficionado's favourite) is sucked through the fast-melting biscuit like a straw – ugly but good

Driving in Australia

With its vast distances, long stretches of road and off-the-beaten-track sights, Australia explored by road guarantees an experience unlike any other. Diverting from the well-serviced east coast will reveal vast tracts of country without comprehensive or convenient public transport and many travellers find that the best way to see the place is to purchase or hire a car. It's certainly the only way to get to those interesting out-of-the-way places without taking a tour.

DRIVING LICENCE

You must hold a current driving licence that has been issued in English from your home country in order to drive in Australia. If the licence from your home country is not issued in English, you will also need to carry an International Driving Permit, issued in your home country, at all times.

CHOOSING A VEHICLE

The type of vehicle you choose will depend on the kind of travel you have planned.

4WD

Four-wheel drives are a good choice for outback travel as they can access almost any track you're likely to come across. Their larger size means there is ample room for luggage and perhaps even space to sleep in the back. However, they're not as good for city driving and parking, they have poorer fuel economy and can be noisy, and may cost more to hire or buy than you are prepared to pay.

2WD

Depending on where you want to travel, a 2WD vehicle may suffice. Two-wheel drives are cheaper to hire, buy and run than 4WDs and are more readily available. Most are quite fuel efficient. Common 2WD models are well known by mechanics and spare parts are cheaper. They are also be easier to sell, as the market for standard 2WDs is broad. While 2WDs can be driven down most dirt roads, they can't access as many places as a 4WD. The storage space in a 2WD is also much less than a campervan or 4WD, with no room to sleep.

Campervan

All the creature comforts are at your fingertips in a campervan; they usually have a sink, fridge, cupboard space, beds, kitchen and general equipment, and provide a space to relax when breaking your journey. This can be a hindrance as anywhere you drive, even short day trips or down to the pub for dinner, you'll be lugging everything including the kitchen sink with you. Campervans are also slower than other means of travel and use more fuel. They generally can't be taken on dirt roads and are not great for city driving. Hi-tops can be difficult to drive in high winds and even tricky on the open road (pop-top vans are easier to drive). Campervans also feel extremes in temperature: in hot weather they can feel like an oven, and in the cold they can be freezing.

Motorcycle

Motorcycles can be a unique, dare we say romantic way to travel in Australia. The climate is good for bikes for much of the year, and the many small trails from the road into the bush lead to perfect spots to spend the night. Bikes are also a great way to avoid congested city traffic. However, Australia is not as bike-friendly as Europe, for example in terms of driver awareness, so riders need to be alert and aware at all times. The amount of luggage and supplies you can carry is limited and you are also more exposed to the elements. It is advised that travellers don't use this form of transport in central and northern Australia during the summer months, due to the extreme heat. See p82 for more information on driving hazards for motorcyclists.

Bringing your own motorcycle into Australia will entail an expensive shipping exercise, valid registration in the country of origin and a Carnet de Passages en Douane (CPD) – an internationally recognised customs document that allows the holder to import their vehicle without paying customs duty or taxes. To get one, apply to a motoring organisation or association in your home country. You'll also need a riders licence and a helmet. A fuel range of 350km will cover fuel stops up the centre and on Hwy 1 around the continent. The long, open roads are tailor-made for large-capacity machines above 750cc.

BUYING A VEHICLE

Buying your own vehicle to travel around in gives you the freedom to go where and when the mood takes you. Owning the vehicle you're driving also means you don't have to worry about having to pay excess for any minor damage to the car, as you would with a rental car. And buying a vehicle may work out to be cheaper in the long run.

Always read the fine print when buying a car. See Where & When to Buy (p76) for organisations that can check to ensure the car you're buying is fully paid for and owned by the seller.

The downsides of buying a vehicle include having to deal with confusing and expensive registration, roadworthy certificates and insurance. You'll have to keep the vehicle maintained yourself, and selling the vehicle may be more difficult than expected. Some dealers will sell you a car with an undertaking to buy it back at an agreed price, but don't accept verbal guarantees – get it in writing.

What to Look for

If a car has been regularly serviced it should be in reasonable mechanical condition – a good start is with the car's service record. Other things to check include:

- tyre tread
- number of kilometres
- rust damage
- accident damage
- oil should be translucent and honey-coloured
- coolant should be clean and not rusty in colour
- engine condition; check for fumes from engine, smoke from exhaust while engine is running and engines that rattle or cough
- exhaust system should not be excessively noisy or rattle when engine is running
- windscreen should be clear with no cracks or chip marks

When test-driving the car, listen for body noises and changes in engine noise. Check for oil and petrol smells, leaks and overheating. Check that the instruments and controls in the car work, including the heating, air-con and windscreen wipers. Check all the seatbelts work. The brakes should pull the car up straight, without pulling, vibrating or making any noise. Gears should change smoothly and quietly. Steering should also be smooth and quiet. If the

LRP RIP

In 2002 Australia discontinued the use of leaded fuel and introduced lead replacement petrol (LRP) to cater to older-model cars unable to run on unleaded petrol (ULP) – the cars in question are those pre-1986 vehicles that need lead or lead substitute in their fuel to prevent erosion of the engine valve seats. However, LRP has now been entirely phased out. In lieu of an expensive engine overhaul, drivers of older cars that relied on LRP will have to fill up with unleaded or premium unleaded petrol (generally, the higher the octane rating the better) and then manually top up their tanks with a valve-protecting additive. This additive comes in a small plastic dispenser and is sold at most service stations.

If you're planning to buy a car in Australia that was manufactured before 1986, look up the model on the website of the **Australian Institute of Petroleum** (www.aip.com.au/health/lead_guide) to see whether it accepts ULP or not. If it doesn't, and you're planning a long road trip through remote areas, stock up on the additive before heading off, as we encountered several roadhouses in central Australia that had sold out of the product.

car bounces and is extremely rough, it may be worth getting the suspension checked. Check that all the brake lights, headlights and indicators work.

It is always best to have the car checked by an independent expert. Auto clubs (p80) offer vehicle checks, and road transport authorities (p78) have lists of licensed garages.

Check the prices of the make, model and year of any vehicle you are considering with online dealers, online papers such as the **Trading Post** (www .tradingpost.com.au), or in local newspapers to get an idea of the average price for this type of vehicle. Or look at **Red Book** (www.redbook.com.au) and the auto club websites.

Where & When to Buy

There are a number of options for buying a secondhand vehicle. Keep in mind that it will cost more than the negotiated price as you'll have to factor in extra costs such as stamp duty, registration, transfer fee, insurance and maintenance. Main cities are obviously the best places to look. Cairns is a hotspot; many travellers end a south to north journey and want to sell vehicles along with equipment. And, during northern Australia's wet season, there are fewer tourists around and car yards are often full of secondhand vehicles.

PRIVATE ADS

Buying privately can be time consuming as you will usually have to travel around to look at your options. Given the extra risks and hassles involved when you buy privately, you should expect a lower price than that charged by a licensed dealer.

The seller should provide you with a roadworthy certificate, but you won't get a cooling-off period or a statutory warranty. It'll also be your responsibility to make sure that the car is not stolen and that there's no money owing on it. Contact one of the following organisations to check this officially:

REVS (☎ 133 230; www.revs.nsw.gov.au) ACT, NSW and NT.
REVS (☎ 131 304; www.fairtrading.qld.gov.au) Queensland; through the Office of Fair Trading.
REVS (☎ 1300 304 024; https://bizline.commerce.wa.gov.au/revs/) WA; through the Department of Commerce.
Registration Status Service (☎ 1300 851 225; www.transport.tas.gov.au) Tasmania.
Vehicles Securities Register (☎ 131 084; www.ecom.transport.sa.gov.au) SA.
Vehicles Securities Register (☎ 131 171; www.vicroads.vic.gov.au) Victoria; through VicRoads.

BACKPACKERS

Accommodation notice boards, especially those in hostels, and online notice boards such as **Travellers Contact Point** (www.taw.com.au) and the Thorn Tree travel forum at www.lonelyplanet.com are good places to find vehicles for sale. Tour desks also often have notice boards.

Ride sharing is also a good way to split costs and environmental impact with other travellers. Notice boards are good places to find ads, as well as online classifieds.

Aussie Carpool (www.aussiecarpool.com)
Catch A Lift (www.catchalift.com)
MySpareSeat (www.myspareseat.com)
Need A Ride (www.needaride.com.au)

DEALERS

Buying from a licensed dealer does give you more protection. They are obliged to guarantee that no money is owing on the car and you're usually allowed a cooling-off period (usually three days). Depending on the age of the car and the kilometres travelled, you may also receive a statutory warranty. You will need to sign an agreement for sale; make sure you understand what is says before you sign.

Some companies offer buyback deals, where they guarantee to buy the vehicle back from you within a set time frame for a fraction of the price you pay. This may be useful if you have trouble selling the car, or getting a roadworthy certificate once you've finished with it. While the dealers are obliged to buy the vehicle back, any damage or out of the ordinary maintenance costs will have to be met by you.

Don't buy any extras such as extended warranties without doing your research first. Look at what's covered and how that compares to the price of the additional warranty, and then at what could go wrong with the car and how much it will cost to repair it anyway.

TRAVELLERS' MARKETS

Cairns, Sydney, Darwin and Perth (cities where travellers commonly begin or finish their travels) are the best places to buy or sell a vehicle, with Cairns highly regarded as a buyer's market.

Australia's largest backpacker car market is the **Kings Cross Car Market** (☎ 1800 800 188; www.carmarket.com.au; 110 Bourke Street Woolloomooloo) in Sydney. It's likely these cars have been around Australia several times so it can be a risky option.

Paperwork
REGISTRATION

When you buy a vehicle in Australia, you need to transfer the vehicle registration into your own name within 14 days. Each state has slightly different requirements and different organisations to do this. Similarly, when selling a vehicle you need to advise the state or territory road transport authority (p78) of the change of name. In Queensland before advertising a car for sale you need to obtain and display a safety certificate. In NSW, NT, SA, Tasmania and WA you do not need to provide a roadworthy certificate. In Victoria you are required to provide a roadworthy certificate, or you can remove the plates, cancel the registration, and sell the car without a certificate.

You'll have to make sure you consider the following things when registering your new car:

Transfer of registration form In NSW, NT, Queensland, Tasmania, Victoria and WA, you and the seller need to complete and sign this form. In the ACT and SA there is no transfer form, but you and the seller need to fill in and sign the reverse of the current registration certificate.

Roadworthy certificate In the ACT, if the vehicle is more than six years old it will need a roadworthy certificate. In NSW, NT, SA, Tasmania and WA you do not need to provide a roadworthy certificate. In Queensland a safety certificate has replaced the roadworthy certificate and needs to be provided. In Victoria a roadworthy certificate is required.
Gas certificate In Queensland if a vehicle runs on gas, a gas certificate (dated less than three months before date of transfer) must be provided by the seller and shown to transfer the registration.
Immobiliser fitting In WA it is compulsory to have an approved immobiliser fitted to most vehicles before transfer of registration will be allowed; this is the responsibility of the buyer. (Note that motorcycles are exempt.)

Registering a vehicle in a different state to the one it was previously registered in can be extremely difficult, time consuming and expensive. A roadworthy certificate or equivalent is required.

Registration is usually renewed annually Australia-wide. This generally requires no more than payment of the registration fee. However, some states have extra requirements:

NSW Vehicle roadworthy inspections are required annually once the vehicle is five years old.
NT Vehicle roadworthy inspections are required once the vehicle is three years old. Vehicles older than three years, but less than 10 years old, require a roadworthy inspection every two years until they reach their 10th year. Vehicles over 10 years old require a roadworthy inspection every year.
SA You can pay for three, six, nine or 12 months registration.
Tasmania You can pay for six or 12 months registration.

ROAD TRANSPORT AUTHORITIES
For more information about processes and costs, visit the websites or contact the road transport authority in each state/territory:
Rego ACT (☎ 13 22 81; www.rego.act.gov.au) ACT.
Roads & Traffic Authority NSW (☎ 13 22 13; www.rta.nsw.gov.au) NSW.
Northern Territory Department of Planning & Infrastructure (☎ 1300 654 628; www.dpi.nt.gov.au) NT
Queensland Transport (☎ 132 3 80; www.transport.qld.gov.au) Queensland.
Department for Transport, Energy & Infrastructure (☎ 13 10 84, 1300 360 067; www.transport.sa.gov.au) SA.
Department of Infrastructure, Energy & Resources (☎ 1300 135 513; www.transport.tas.gov.au) Tasmania
VicRoads (☎ 13 11 71; www.vicroads.vic.gov.au) Victoria.
Department for Planning & Infrastructure (☎ 13 11 56; www.dpi.wa.gov.au) WA.

ROADWORTHY CERTIFICATES
If the vehicle you are considering does not have a current roadworthy certificate, it is worth having a roadworthy check done or requesting that the seller have one done before you buy. This will cost between $60 and $100 (not including repairs) but can save you money on hidden costs. Road transport authorities have lists of licensed vehicle testers.

RENTING A VEHICLE
Hire
The biggest advantage of hiring is that you avoid the messy problems that come with buying a vehicle such as obtaining roadworthy certificates, registering and selling it. Larger car-rental companies have drop offs in major cities and towns so you don't need to waste time backtracking.

For cheaper alternatives to the car-hire prices charged by big-name international firms, try one of the many local outfits. Remember, though, that if you want to travel a significant distance you will want unlimited kilometres, and that cheap car hire often comes with serious restrictions.

Most companies require the driver to be over the age of 21, though in some cases it may be 18, and in others 25.

While hiring can seem like an easier alternative, it does come with its own set of issues, including overly complex contracts, gaps in insurance cover, hidden fees and fine print. Some suggestions to assist in the process of hiring a car include the following:

- Get a copy of the contract and read it carefully.
- Check what the bond entails. Some companies may require a signed credit-card slip, others may actually charge your credit card; if this is the case, find out when you'll get a refund.
- Ask if unlimited kilometres are included and if not, what the extra charge per kilometre is.
- Find out what excess you will pay and if this can be lowered by an extra charge per day. Check if your personal travel insurance covers you for motor vehicle accidents and rental insurance excess.
- Check for any exclusions. Some companies won't cover single vehicle accidents (eg if you hit a kangaroo), accidents occurring while the car is being reversed or damage occurring on unsealed roads. Check whether you are covered on unavoidable unsealed roads, such as gaining access to campgrounds. Some companies also exclude parts of the car from cover, such as the underbelly, tyres and windscreen or any damage from immersion in water.
- At pick-up inspect the vehicle for any damage. Make a note of anything on the contract before you sign.
- Ask about procedures in the event of a breakdown or accident.
- If you can, return the vehicle during business hours and insist on an inspection in your presence.
- If you have a complaint, contact the office of consumer affairs of the state or territory you are in.

There are a huge number of rental companies. Useful sites offering last-minute discounts:

Carhire.com (www.carhire.com.au)
Drive Now (www.drivenow.com.au)
Webjet (www.webjet.com.au)

4WD & CAMPERVAN HIRE

A small 4WD such as a Suzuki Vitara or Toyota Rav4 cost between $85 and $100 a day. A Toyota Landcruiser is at least $150, which should include insurance and some free kilometres (100km to 200km a day, or sometimes unlimited).

Check the insurance conditions carefully, especially the excess, as it can be onerous – in the NT $5000 is typical, but this can often be reduced to around $1000 (or even to nil) by paying an extra daily charge (around $50). Even for a 4WD, insurance offered by most companies may not cover damage caused travelling 'off-road', meaning anywhere that isn't a maintained bitumen or dirt road.

Hertz, Budget and Avis have 4WD rentals, with one-way rentals possible between the eastern states and the NT. **Britz** (☎ 00 800 200 80 801, 1800 331 454; www .britz.com.au) hires out fully equipped 2WD and 4WD campervans. Rates start from around $50 (two-berth) or $70 (four-berth) per day for a minimum hire of five days (with unlimited kilometres), but the price escalates dramatically in peak season. It costs extra per day to reduce the insurance excess from $5000 to a few hundred dollars. One-way rentals are also possible.

Many other places rent campervans, especially in Tasmania and the Top End. Check out **Backpacker Campervans** (☎ 1800 670 232; www.backpackercampervans .com). Some campervan rental companies targeted specifically at backpackers don't maintain their vehicles as well as the bigger companies. Always ask when the last service and roadworthy certificate were completed before handing over your money and heading onto the wide open road.

Relocations

Relocations are a great way to get cheap deals, although they don't allow for much flexibility when it comes to time. Most of the large hire companies offer relocation deals. **Standbycars** (www.standbycars.com.au) and **Drive Now** (www .drivenow.com.au) are recommended companies, advertising a range of deals. It's also worth contacting individual companies, such as **Apollo** (www.apollocamper .com) and **Britz** (www.britz.com.au), directly. Shop around to find the best deal and one that suits your travel plans.

INSURANCE

With the exception of NSW, third-party personal injury insurance is included in the vehicle registration cost, ensuring that every registered vehicle carries at least minimum insurance. (If registering in NSW you will need to arrange this privately.) We recommend extending that minimum to at least third-party property insurance – minor collisions can be amazingly expensive.

When it comes to hire cars, understand your liability in the event of an accident. Rather than risk paying out thousands of dollars, you can take out your own comprehensive car insurance or (the usual option) pay an additional daily amount to the rental company for an 'insurance excess reduction' policy. This reduces the excess you must pay in the event of an accident from between $2000 and $5000 to a few hundred dollars.

Be aware that if travelling on dirt roads you will not be covered by insurance unless you have a 4WD. Also, most companies' insurance won't cover the cost of damage to glass (including the windscreen) or tyres.

AUTO CLUBS

The various automobile clubs in each state are a great resource for travellers when it comes to insurance and state regulations, driving maps and roadside assistance. A membership to one of these clubs at around $100 to $150 can save a lot of trouble if things go wrong mechanically. If you are a member of an auto club in your country of residence check to see if reciprocal rights are offered in Australia.

The Australian auto clubs listed below generally offer reciprocal rights in other states and territories so you are covered Australia-wide if you join one. You should confirm this at the time of joining.

AAA (Australian Automobile Association; ☎ 02-6247 7311; www.aaa.asn.au)

AANT (Automobile Association of the Northern Territory; ☎ 08-89813 837; www.aant.com.au)

NRMA (☎ 13 11 22; www.mynrma.com.au) Operates in NSW and the ACT.

RAC (Royal Automobile Club of WA; ☎ 13 1703; www.rac.com.au)

RACQ (Royal Automobile Club of Queensland; ☎ 13 19 05; www.racq.com.au)

RACT (Royal Automobile Club of Tasmania; ☎ 13 27 22; www.ract.com.au)

RACV (Royal Automobile Club of Victoria; ☎ 13 72 28; www.racv.com.au)

ROAD RULES

Australians drive on the left-hand side of the road and all cars are right-hand drive. An important road rule is 'give way to the right' – if an intersection is unmarked (unusual), you must give way to vehicles entering the intersection from your right.

The general speed limit in built-up and residential areas is 50km/h, although in many cases it's 40km/h, so keep an eye out for signs. Near schools, the limit is 40km/h in the morning and afternoon. On the open highway it's usually 100km/h or 110km/h. In the NT speed limits on the open road are either 110km/h or 130km/h. Pay close attention to signage while driving; the police have speed radar guns and cameras and are fond of using them in strategically concealed locations.

Oncoming drivers who flash their lights at you may be giving you a friendly warning of a speed camera ahead, or they may be telling you that your headlights are not on. It's polite to wave back if someone does this. Try not to get caught doing it yourself, since it's illegal.

All new cars in Australia have seat belts back and front and it's the law to wear them; you're likely to get a fine if you don't. Small children must be belted into an approved safety seat.

Drink-driving is a real problem, especially in country areas. Serious attempts to reduce the resulting road toll are ongoing and random breath-tests are not uncommon in built-up areas. If you're caught with a blood-alcohol level of more than 0.05% expect a hefty fine and the loss of your licence. Note also that talking on a mobile phone while driving is illegal in Australia.

Australian police operate mobile and roadside speed cameras. If you are caught speeding you will be heavily fined. The police also operate breathalyser and drug check-points on Australian roads and penalties for being under the influence of alcohol or drugs while driving are severe. Police can randomly pull any driver over for a breathalyser or drug test.

For more information, see the rules and regulations sections of the road transport authorities' websites (p78).

Parking

One of the major problems with driving around cities such as Sydney and Melbourne (or popular tourist towns such as Byron Bay) is finding somewhere to park. Even if you do find a spot there's likely to be a time restriction, meter (or ticket machine) or both. It's one of the great rorts in Australia that for overstaying your welcome (even by five minutes) in a space that may cost only a few dollars to park in, local councils are prepared to fine you anywhere from $50 to $120. Also note that if you park in a 'clearway' your car will be towed away or clamped – look for signs. In the cities there are large multi-storey car parks where you can park all day for between $10 and $25.

Many towns in NSW have a peculiar form of reverse-angle parking, a recipe for disaster if ever there was one. If in doubt, park your car in the same direction and at the same angle as other cars.

ROAD CONDITIONS

Australia has few multilane highways, although there are stretches of divided road (four or six lanes) in some particularly busy areas, including the Princes Hwy from Murray Bridge to Adelaide, most of the Pacific Hwy from Sydney to Brisbane, and the Hume Hwy and Princes and Calder Fwys in Victoria. Elsewhere the major roads are all sealed two-laners.

You don't have to get far off the beaten track to find dirt roads. In fact, anybody who sets out to see the country in reasonable detail should expect some dirt-road travelling. And if you seriously want to explore the more remote Australia, you'd better plan on having a 4WD and a winch. Look out for potholes and rough surfaces, roads changing surfaces without notice, soft and broken edges and single-lane bridges.

In the outback, if you plan on driving through pastoral stations and Aboriginal communities you must get permission first. This is actually for

---

OUTBACK ROAD SHOW

On many outback highways you'll see thundering road trains – huge trucks (a prime mover plus two or three trailers) up to 50m long. These things don't move over for anyone and it's like something out of a *Mad Max* movie to have one bearing down on you at 120km/h. When you see a road train approaching on a narrow bitumen road, slow down and pull over – if it has to put its wheels off the road to pass you, the resulting shower of stones will almost certainly smash your windscreen. When trying to overtake one, allow plenty of room (about a kilometre) to complete the manoeuvre. Road trains throw up a lot of dust on dirt roads, so if you see one coming it's best to pull over and stop until it's gone past.

And while you're on outback roads, don't forget to give the standard bush wave to oncoming drivers – it's simply a matter of lifting the index finger off the steering wheel to acknowledge your fellow motorist.

---

your safety; many international travellers have tackled this rugged landscape on their own and required complicated rescues after getting lost or breaking down.

Australian drivers are generally a courteous bunch, but risks can be posed by rural petrolheads, inner-city speedsters and, particularly, drunk drivers. Driving on dirt roads can also be tricky if you're not used to them.

Preparations & Practicalities

If you stick to main highways on the southern and eastern coasts of Australia you'll be in for a fairly comfortable ride with regular opportunities to stop, refuel, snack and stretch. Obviously the further off the beaten track you get the more prepared you'll need to be. Regardless of where you're headed always carry plenty of water, a first aid kit, a good set of maps, a torch and spare batteries. Also carry essential tools, a spare tyre (two if possible), a tyre pressure gauge and an air pump. It's a good idea to take basic parts specific to your car, such as a spare fan belt and radiator hose especially on roads where traffic is light and garages are few and far between. If you're travelling long distances in remote areas take extra fuel if possible.

In addition, when travelling in the outback, take a compass, a shovel for if you get bogged, an off-road jack, and a snatchem strap for quick, easy extraction when you're stuck (only useful as long as there's another vehicle to pull you out).

HAZARDS & PRECAUTIONS

Be wary of driver fatigue; driving long distances (particularly in hot weather) can be so tiring that you might fall asleep at the wheel. It's not uncommon and the consequences can be unthinkable. So on a long haul, stop and rest every two hours or so – it's a good idea to do some exercise, change drivers or have a coffee. Carry a mobile phone if possible, but be aware that there isn't always coverage in country areas. Be careful overtaking road trains; you'll need distance and plenty of speed. On single-lane roads you'll need to get right off the road when one approaches to avoid collision.

Motorcyclists should be particularly aware of dehydration in the dry, hot air – carry at least 5L of water on remote roads in central Australia and drink plenty of it, even if you don't feel thirsty. If riding in Tasmania (a top motorcycling destination) or southern or eastern Victoria, you should be prepared for rotten weather in winter and rain at any time of the year. It's worth carrying some spares and tools even if you don't know how to use them, because someone else often does. Carry a workshop manual for your bike and spare elastic (octopus) straps for securing your gear.

The roadkill that you see a lot of in the outback and alongside roads in many other parts of the country is mostly the result of cars and trucks hitting animals at night. It's a huge problem in Australia, particularly in the NT, Queensland, NSW, SA and Tasmania. Many Australians avoid travelling altogether once the sun drops because of the risks posed by animals on the roads.

Kangaroos are common hazards on country roads, as are cows and sheep in the unfenced outback – hitting an animal of this size can make a real mess of your car. Kangaroos are most active around dawn and dusk. They often travel in groups, so if you see one hopping across the road in front of you, slow right down, as its friends may be just behind it.

If you're travelling at night and a large animal appears in front of you, hit the brakes, dip your lights (so you don't continue to dazzle and confuse it) and only swerve if it's safe to do so – numerous travellers have been killed in accidents caused by swerving to miss animals.

If you hit an animal while driving pull it off the road. This prevents further injury to it from another car and also prevents the next car from having a potential accident. If the animal is only injured and is small, perhaps an orphaned joey (baby kangaroo), wrap it in a towel or blanket and call the relevant wildlife rescue line:

Fauna Rescue South Australia (☎ 08-8289 0896; www.faunarescue.org.au)

New South Wales Wildlife Information and Rescue Service (☎ 1300 094 737; www .wires.org.au)

Northern Territory Wildlife Rescue Hotline Darwin (☎ 0409 090 840); Katherine (☎ 0412 955 336); Alice Springs (☎ 0419 221 128)

Queensland Parks & Wildlife Service (☎ 1300 130 372; www.epa.qld.gov.au)

Tasmania Parks & Wildlife Service (☎ 1300 135 513, 03-6233 6556; www.parks.tas.gov.au)

Western Australia Department of Environment and Conservation (☎ 08-9474 9055, marine emergencies 08-9483 6462; www.dec.wa.gov.au)

Wildlife Victoria (☎ 13 000 94535; www.wildlifevictoria.org.au)

ENVIRONMENTAL CONCERNS

A few simple actions can help minimise the impact your journey has on the environment.

- Ensure your vehicle is properly serviced and tuned.
- Travel as light as you can.
- Drive slowly; many vehicles use 25% more fuel at 110km/h than at 90km/h.
- Avoid hard acceleration and heavy braking.
- Use air-conditioning only when absolutely necessary.
- Stay on designated roads and vehicle off-road tracks. Do not drive on walking tracks, and where possible, avoid driving on vegetation.
- Drive in the middle of tracks to minimise track widening and damage.
- Avoid shining high beams or spotlights on wildlife.
- Cross creeks at designated areas.
- Consider ride sharing where possible (see p77).

For more information, see www.greenvehicleguide.gov.au.

OUTBACK TRAVEL

You can drive all the way around Australia on Hwy 1 and through the centre from Adelaide to Darwin without leaving sealed roads. However, if you really want to see outback Australia, there are plenty of routes that breathe new life into the phrase 'off the beaten track'.

SYDNEY TO MELBOURNE VIA THE PRINCES HWY

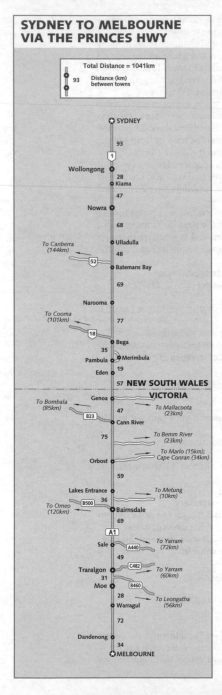

Total Distance = 1041km

93 Distance (km) between towns

⊙ SYDNEY

93

1

Wollongong ⊙
28
⊙ Kiama

47

Nowra ⊙

68

To Canberra (144km) → ⊙ Ulladulla
48
52
⊙ Batemans Bay

69

Narooma ⊙

To Cooma (101km) → 77

18
⊙ Bega
35
Pambula ⊙ ⊙ Merimbula
19
Eden ⊙

57 **NEW SOUTH WALES**

VICTORIA

To Bombala (85km) → Genoa ⊙
B23
47 → To Mallacoota (23km)
⊙ Cann River

75 → To Bemm River (23km)

→ To Marlo (15km); Cape Conran (34km)
Orbost ⊙

59

Lakes Entrance ⊙ → To Metung (10km)
B500
36
To Omeo (120km) → ⊙ Bairnsdale

69

A1

Sale ⊙ → To Yarram (72km)
A440
49
Traralgon ⊙ → To Yarram (60km)
C482
31
Moe ⊙
B460
28 → To Leongatha (56km)
⊙ Warragul

72

Dandenong ⊙
34
⊙ MELBOURNE

While you may not need a 4WD or fancy equipment to tackle most of these roads, you do need to be carefully prepared for the isolation and lack of facilities. Vehicles should be in good condition and have reasonable ground clearance. Always carry a tow rope so that some passing good Samaritan can pull your broken-down car to the next garage. If you're travelling extensively in the outback, on sealed roads, a campervan with a fridge is a must. If you're planning to veer onto unsealed roads extensively then a 4WD with a fridge will be necessary, and (yes again) always carry plenty of water.

When travelling to very remote areas, such as the central deserts, it's advisable to carry a high-frequency (HF) radio transceiver equipped to pick up the Royal Flying Doctor Service bases. A satellite phone and Global Positioning System (GPS) finder or Emergency Position-Indicating Radio Beacon (EPIRB) can also be handy. Of course, all this equipment comes at a cost, but travellers have perished in the Australian desert after breaking down.

Do not attempt the tougher routes during the hottest part of the year (October to April inclusive) – apart from the risk of heat exhaustion, simple mishaps can lead to tragedy at this time. Conversely, there's no point going anywhere on outback dirt roads if there has been recent flooding. Get local advice before heading off into the middle of nowhere.

If you do run into trouble in the back of beyond, don't wander off – stay with your car. It's easier to spot a car than a human from the air, and you wouldn't be able to carry a heavy load of water very far anyway. SA police suggest you carry two spare tyres (for added safety) and, if stranded, try to set fire to one of them (let the air out first) – the pall of smoke will be seen for miles.

Outback Tracks
Birdsville Track
Running 517km from Marree in SA to Birdsville just across the border of Queensland, this old droving trail (p398) is one of Australia's best-known outback routes. It's generally feasible to travel it in any well-prepared, conventional vehicle.

Canning Stock Route
This old 1700km-long cattle-droving trail runs southwest from Halls Creek to Wiluna in WA. The route crosses the Great Sandy Desert and

Gibson Desert and, since the track is entirely unmaintained, it's a route to be taken very seriously. Like the Simpson Desert crossing, you should travel only in a well-equipped 4WD party. Nobody does this trip in summer.

Gibb River Road

This 'short cut' between Derby and Kununurra runs through the heart of the spectacular Kimberley in northern WA – it's approximately 660km, compared with about 920km via Hwy 1 (see p1008). The going is much slower but the surroundings are so beautiful you'll probably find yourself lingering anyway. Although badly corrugated in places, it can usually be negotiated without too much difficulty by conventional vehicles in the dry season (May to November); it's impassable in the Wet.

Great Central Road (Outback Way)

This route runs west from Uluru to Laverton in WA, from where you can drive down to Kalgoorlie and on to Perth. The road is well maintained and is normally OK for conventional vehicles, but it's pretty remote. It passes through Aboriginal land for which travel permits must be obtained in advance – see Permits, p813 (NT) and p897 (WA) for details. It's almost 1500km from Yulara (the town nearest Uluru) to Kalgoorlie. For 300km, from near the Giles Meteorological Station, this road and the Gunbarrel Hwy run on the same route. Taking the old Gunbarrel (to the north of Warburton) to Wiluna in WA is a much rougher trip requiring a 4WD.

See p962 for more information.

Mulligan Highway

This road goes all the way up to the tip of Cape York (p476) and has a number of river crossings, such as the Jardine, that can only be made in the dry season. Only those in 4WD vehicles should consider the journey to Cape York, via any route. The shortest route from Cairns is 1000km, but a worthwhile alternative is Cooktown to Musgrave via Lakefield National Park, which then meets up with the main route.

Oodnadatta Track

Running mainly parallel to the old Ghan railway line through outback SA, this track (p802) is comprehensively bypassed by the

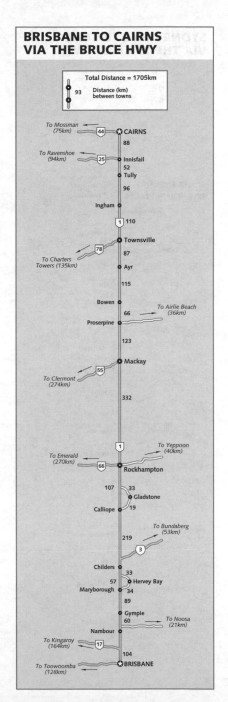

BRISBANE TO CAIRNS VIA THE BRUCE HWY

Total Distance = 1705km

93 Distance (km) between towns

To Mossman (75km) — 44 — ✪ CAIRNS

88

To Ravenshoe (94km) — 25 — ● Innisfail

52

● Tully

96

Ingham ●

1 110

● Townsville

78

87

To Charters Towers (135km)

● Ayr

115

Bowen ●

66 — To Airlie Beach (36km)

Proserpine ●

123

● Mackay

55

To Clermont (274km)

332

1

To Yeppoon (40km)

To Emerald (270km) — 66 — Rockhampton

107   33

● Gladstone

Calliope ● 19

To Bundaberg (53km)

219

3

Childers ●

33

57   ● Hervey Bay

Maryborough ● 34

89

● Gympie

60 — To Noosa (21km)

Nambour ●

To Kingaroy (164km) — 17

104

To Toowoomba (128km) — ✪ BRISBANE

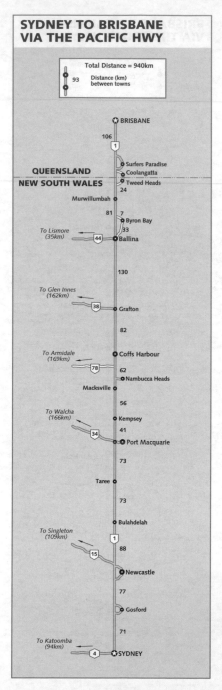

SYDNEY TO BRISBANE VIA THE PACIFIC HWY

Total Distance = 940km

93 Distance (km) between towns

BRISBANE

106

1

QUEENSLAND

Surfers Paradise
Coolangatta
NEW SOUTH WALES   Tweed Heads
24

Murwillumbah

81 7
Byron Bay
33
To Lismore
(35km)   44 Ballina

130

To Glen Innes
(162km)
38 Grafton

82

To Armidale
(169km)   Coffs Harbour
78 62
Nambucca Heads
Macksville

56
To Walcha
(166km)   Kempsey
41
34 Port Macquarie

73

Taree

73

Bulahdelah
To Singleton
(109km)   1
15 88

Newcastle

77

Gosford

71
To Katoomba
(94km)   4 SYDNEY

sealed Stuart Hwy to the west. It's 429km from Marree to Oodnadatta, then another 216km to the Stuart Hwy at Marla. So long as there is no rain, any well-prepared conventional vehicle should be able to manage this fascinating route.

Plenty & Sandover Highways

These remote routes run east from the Stuart Hwy north of Alice Springs to Boulia or Mt Isa in Queensland. They're normally suitable for conventional vehicles, but are often rough.

Simpson Desert

The route crossing the Simpson Desert from the Stuart Hwy to Birdsville (p399) is a real test of both driver and vehicle. A 4WD is definitely required and you should be in a party of at least three vehicles equipped with HF radio or EPIRB.

Strzelecki Track

This track (p807) covers much the same territory through SA as the Birdsville Track, starting south of Marree at Lyndhurst and going to Innamincka, 460km northeast and close to the Queensland border. It was at Innamincka that the hapless explorers Burke and Wills died. This route has been much improved due to work on the Moomba gas fields.

Tanami Track

Turning off the Stuart Hwy just north of Alice Springs, this route goes northwest across the Tanami Desert to Halls Creek in WA. The road has received extensive work and conventional vehicles are normally OK, although there are sandy stretches on the WA side and it's very corrugated if it hasn't been graded for a while. Be warned that the Rabbit Flat roadhouse in the middle of the desert is open only from Friday to Monday, so if you don't have long-range fuel tanks, plan your trip accordingly. Get advice on road conditions in Alice Springs.

MAINTENANCE & RUNNING COSTS

Maintenance and running costs will depend on the age and condition of the car. It's a good idea to check the oil and water regularly (in older cars every day). Also check the tyre pressure regularly (including the spare tyre). The manufacturer should specify what the ideal pressure is (often detailed on the inside of the driver's door). Vehicles should be serviced every six months or 10,000km; a basic service

ROAD DISTANCES (KM)

MAINLAND AUSTRALIA

	Adelaide	Albany	Alice Springs	Birdsville	Brisbane	Broome	Cairns	Canberra	Cape York	Darwin	Kalgoorlie	Melbourne	Perth	Sydney	Townsville
Albany	2649														
Alice Springs	1512	3573													
Birdsville	1183	3244	1176												
Brisbane	1942	4178	1849	1573											
Broome	4043	2865	2571	3564	5065										
Cairns	3079	5601	2396	1919	1705	4111									
Canberra	1372	4021	2725	2038	1287	5296	2923								
Cape York	4444	6566	3361	2884	2601	5076	965	3888							
Darwin	3006	5067	1494	2273	3774	1844	2820	3948	3785						
Kalgoorlie	2168	885	3092	2763	3697	3052	5234	3540	6199	4896					
Melbourne	728	3377	2240	1911	1860	4811	3496	637	4461	3734	2896				
Perth	2624	411	3548	3219	4153	2454	6565	3996	7530	4298	598	3352			
Sydney	1597	4246	3109	2007	940	5208	2634	289	3599	3917	3765	862	3869		
Townsville	3237	5374	2055	1578	1295	3770	341	2582	1306	2479	4893	3155	5349	2293	
Uluru	1559	3620	441	1617	2290	3012	2837	2931	3802	1935	3139	2287	3595	2804	2496

TASMANIA

	Bicheno	Cradle Mountain	Devonport	Hobart	Launceston
Cradle Mountain	383				
Devonport	283	100			
Hobart	186	296	334		
Launceston	178	205	105	209	
Queenstown	443	69	168	257	273

These are the shortest distances by road; other routes may be considerably longer.
For distances by coach, check the companies' leaflets.

will cost $100 to $150. Keep water and/or coolant on hand. Note that you should *never* try to open the radiator cap while the engine is hot as the boiling water may burst up, burning you badly. (Newer cars usually have a coolant reservoir avoiding the need to check the water level via the radiator.)

Fuel & Spare Parts

Fuel (predominantly unleaded and diesel) is available from service stations sporting well-known international brand names. LPG (liquefied petroleum gas) is not always stocked at more remote roadhouses; if you're on gas it's safer to have dual-fuel capacity.

Prices vary from place to place but basically fuel is heavily taxed and continues to hike up, much to the disgust of local motorists. Unleaded petrol is now hovering between $1.25 and $1.55. Once out into the country, prices soar – in outback Northern Territory (NT) and Queensland they can go as high as $2.20 a litre. Distances between fill-ups can be long in the outback but there are only a handful of tracks where you'll require a long-range fuel tank. On main roads there'll be a small town or roadhouse roughly every 150km to 200km. Note, though that while many roadhouses on main highways are open 24 hours, this does not apply to every fuel stop and you can't always rely on a service station being open in the dead of night.

The further you get from the cities, the better it is to be in a Holden or a Ford. If you're in an older vehicle that's likely to require a replacement part, life is much simpler if it's a make for which spare parts are more readily available. VW Kombi vans were once the quintessential backpackers' wheels, but they're notoriously bad for breaking down and difficult to find parts for, and so are a poor choice for remote Australia.

EXTRA PRECAUTIONS FOR OUTBACK DRIVING

You need to be particularly organised and vigilant when travelling in the outback, due to the scorching temperatures, long distances between fuel stops and remoteness. The previous hints apply as well as the following suggestions:

- Always carry plenty of water. In warm weather allow 5L per person per day and an extra amount for the radiator, carried in several containers.
- Carry food and water in case of a breakdown.
- Have your vehicle serviced and checked before you leave. It is a good idea to inflate your tyres to the recommended levels for the terrain you're travelling on.
- Report your route and schedule to the police or a friend or relative.
- Load your vehicle evenly, with heavy items inside and light items on the roof rack.
- Check road conditions before travelling. Roads that are passable in the dry season (March to November) can disappear beneath water during the Wet.
- Check the weather conditions ahead – heavy rain will make many of the roads impassable when wet.
- Check locations and opening times of service stations and carry spare fuel and provisions – fill-ups can be infrequent.
- Mobile phones are often out of range and useless in the outback. An extra safety net is to hire a satellite phone, high frequency (HF) radio or Emergency Position-Indicating Radio Beacon (EPIRB).
- Reduce speed on unsealed roads as traction is decreased and braking distances increase. Dirt roads are often corrugated. The best way to deal with this is to keep an even speed.
- Dust on outback roads can obscure your vision. Stop and wait for it to settle.
- Take note of the water level markers at creek crossings to gauge the water's depth before you proceed. Do not attempt to cross flooded bridges or causeways unless you are sure of the depth and any road damage.
- If your vehicle is struggling through deep sand, deflating your tyres a bit will help. If you do get stuck, don't attempt to get out by revving the engine as this will cause the wheels to dig in deeper.
- In an emergency, stay with your vehicle – it's easier to spot than you are. But don't sit inside it as it will become an oven in hot weather.

Resources

Australian Bureau of Meteorology (www.bom.gov.au) Up-to-date weather reports.
Motorcycle Riders Association of Australia Inc (MRAA; http://mraa.org.au) Nonprofit organisation's website has useful information on motorcycle travel in Australia.
NT Road Conditions Hotline (☎ 1800 246 199; www.roadreport.nt.gov.au)
South Australia Road Conditions Hotline (☎ 1300 361 033)
Queensland Road Condition Reporting Service (www.racq.com.au) Information is under Trip Planning/Road Conditions.
WA Road Conditions Hotline (☎ 13 81 38; www.mainroads.wa.gov.au)

Carbon offsets

Various organisations use 'carbon calculators' that allow travellers to offset the level of greenhouse gases they are responsible for with financial contributions. Some Australian-based organisations:
CarbonNeutral (www.carbonneutral.com.au)
Carbon Planet (www.carbonplanet.com)
Elementree (www.elementree.com.au)
Greenfleet (www.greenfleet.com.au)

GLOSSARY

bogged – stuck in mud, gravel, sand, or clay

cooling-off period – the amount of time a buyer is legally allowed to withdraw from a contract of sale

extended warranty – a policy protecting the car owner against mechanical failure and breakdowns

hi-top – a variety of campervan with more facilities than a normal van but fewer than a full caravan

pop-top – a caravan with a roof that can be raised for headroom and ventilation

registration – the annual fee payable to register a vehicle with the official government body; required to keep a vehicle on the road

relocation – a deal offered by some hire companies whereby the driver can pick up a vehicle at one point and drop off at another

road trains – trucks with trailers; can be up to 50m long

roadworthy certificate – a document issued by licensed operators specifying that a vehicle meets certain requirements

safety certificate – equivalent of a roadworthy certificate in Queensland

snatchem strap – a recovery tool for quick, easy extraction when you're stuck, made of thick seatbelt-webbing type material, usually 10m to 15m long, with a reinforced loop at each end

stamp duty – government tax, which is added on to the sale of motor vehicles

statutory warranty – legal obligation requiring licensed dealers to fix certain problems occurring in a vehicle for up to three months after the sale of the vehicle

transfer fee – the charge for changing the ownership details of a vehicle

New South Wales

Sometimes reserved, more often outrageously outgoing, but always welcoming, New South Wales (NSW) is endlessly fascinating. The country's most populous state and the birthplace of the modern nation, it's a state rich in history (both Aboriginal and European), geography and contrasts. And of course it's home to stunning Sydney, the nation's capital in all but name.

Diversity reigns supreme here. South of the enchanting harbour, languid coastal towns hug the rugged coastline and deliver increasingly deserted and beautiful beaches. Still further south the Snowy Mountains lure ski bunnies in winter and ramblers in summer. Towns founded by gold miners and graziers pepper the heart of the state, and to the far west the arid lunar landscape of the outback beckons and beguiles. In the north, the classic Aussie surf culture dominates and alternative hinterland lifestyles rub shoulders with million-dollar beach houses. And in almost every corner you'll find incredible national parks to explore: some World Heritage listed and some that look like they should be.

NSW has something to offer every traveller. Gastronomes love Sydney's world-class restaurants and the Hunter Valley's award-winning wines; adrenalin junkies get their kicks canyoning, skiing, surfing, bushwalking, cycling, diving and whale watching. Backpackers live it up in campervans barrelling along the east coast, and culture buffs devour the many museums, galleries and ancient Indigenous sites that are woven into the magnificent landscape.

But wherever you choose to travel you can be certain of two things: the road is always easy and the welcome is always warm.

HIGHLIGHTS

- Fall in love with **Sydney** (p98) and her heartbreaking harbour
- Be inspired by the dramatic scenery and empty spaces of **Broken Hill** (p259)
- Hire a houseboat and wind your way along the twisting, tapering, magical **Hawkesbury River** (p151)
- Dip your toes in the pure white sand and sapphire waters of **Jervis Bay** (p233)
- Discover boutique wineries among the jacaranda-lined lanes of **Wollombi** (p172) and the vineyards of the **Lower Hunter Valley** (p168)
- Make a beeline for the beautiful beaches, terrific surf and laid-back organic lifestyle of **Byron Bay** (p195)
- Meet the enchanting Three Sisters in the spectacular **Blue Mountains** (p153)
- Ski, snowboard, bushwalk and camp the lofty heights of **Kosciuszko National Park** (p242)

| ■ TELEPHONE CODE: 02 | ■ POPULATION: 6.9 MILLION | ■ AREA: 900,628 SQ KM |

HISTORY

On 19 April 1770 Lieutenant (later Captain) James Cook of the British Navy climbed onto the deck of his ship *Endeavour* and spied land. Ten days later he dropped anchor at Botany Bay and declared the area New South Wales. His arrival caused much alarm to the Aboriginal people living in the area, for as Cook noted in his journal: 'All they seemed to want was for us to be gone.'

But in 1788 the British were back to stay. Under the command of naval Captain Arthur Phillip, the 'First Fleet' numbered 751 convicts and children and around 250 soldiers, officials and their wives. Upon arriving at Botany Bay, Phillip was rather disappointed by what he saw and ordered the ships to sail north, where he found 'the finest harbour in the world'. The date of the landing was 26 January, an occasion that is remembered each year (although not without some protest) with a public holiday known as Australia Day.

Early days of settlement were difficult and famine threatened the population in 1790, but by the early 1800s Sydney was a bustling port. A space in the bush had been cleared for vegetable gardens, new houses, warehouses and streets – and windmills seemed to occupy the top of every hill. In 1793 Phillip returned to London, having done what had been asked of him, but his plans to create a vigorous new society in Australia had begun to unravel owing to the self-serving military officers who had gained control of Government House. London was having none of it and in 1809 dispatched Governor Lachlan Macquarie to restore the rule of law, and under his guidance Sydney flourished.

By the 1830s the general layout of NSW was understood, and the Blue Mountains had been penetrated. In addition the Lachlan, Macquarie, Murrumbidgee and Darling river systems had been explored.

Over the next 60 or so years, the rapid expansion of the NSW economy resulted in good wages, social mobility and increasingly strong unions, all of which fed the belief that Australia might become 'the working man's paradise'. But employers were anxious to keep wage costs low, and the appeal of cheap Asian or Islander labour was irresistible. Immigration was encouraged, and against this background the popular Sydney magazine the *Bulletin* was founded in 1880 and ran until January 2008. Originally intended to be a journal of political and business commentary, the magazine quickly developed a strong nationalist, anti-imperialist and racist voice that championed a version of Australian nationalism that was working class, male, white and republican.

On 1 January 1901, NSW and the other colonies federated to form the nation of Australia, which remained part of the British Empire. In 1914, as citizens of the Empire, thousands of Australian men volunteered to fight in the Australian Imperial Force when WWI broke out. They did the same again during WWII, after which the Australian government embarked on a massive immigration program, attracting migrants from Britain and mainland Europe. These 'new Australians' had a huge impact on NSW, especially in the irrigation farms of the Riverina, in the building of the great Snowy Mountains Hydro-Electric Scheme, in the large industrial centres and in Sydney itself. By the 1970s Australia had abolished its old policies of racial discrimination and declared itself to be a multicultural country.

Sydney is now a confident world city. In 2000 it welcomed the new millennium by hosting a spectacularly successful Olympic Games. But ugly race riots on Sydney's Cronulla Beach in 2005 laid bare the tensions between some old and new Australians. Overwhelmingly, however, the people of NSW are unerringly warm and open to travellers, and they maintain a profound and enduring culture of goodwill and good sense.

GEOGRAPHY & CLIMATE

NSW divides roughly into four regions: the coastal strip; the Great Dividing Range about 100km inland from the coast; the Blue Mountains west of Sydney; and the Snowy Mountains in the south.

West of the Great Dividing Range is farming country: dry western plains that cover two-thirds of the state. The plains fade into the barren outback in the far west, where summer temperatures can soar to over 40°C. The major rivers are the Murray and the Darling (which wanders westward across the plains). As a general rule, it gets hotter the further north you go and drier the further west. In winter the Snowy Mountains live up to their name.

Sydney has a temperate climate, rarely dropping below 10°C at night. Summer temperatures can hit 40°C, but the average summer maximum is 25°C. Winters often see substantial rain; bring an umbrella.

NEW SOUTH WALES

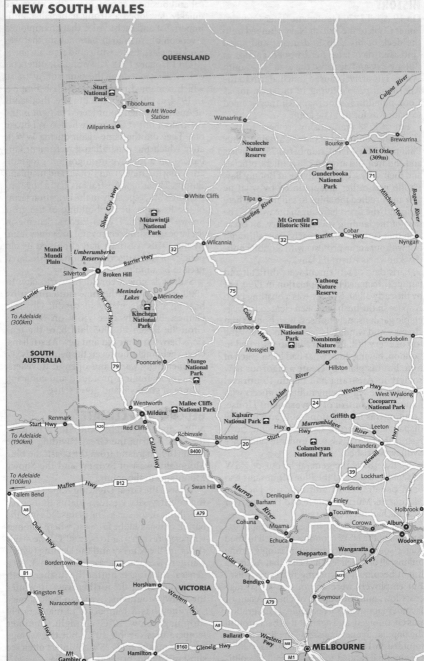

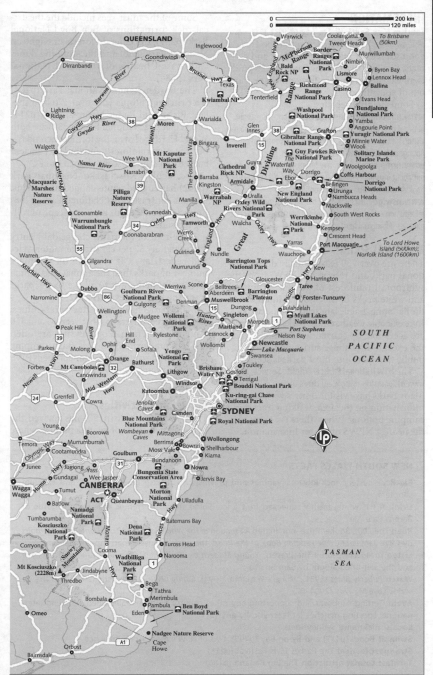

NEW SOUTH WALES

INFORMATION

Tourism New South Wales (☎ 02-9931 1111; www .visitnsw.com.au), the state's tourism body, is a good source for information, ideas and contacts. Lonely Planet's *New South Wales* guide is an excellent resource for getting the most out of your time.

Some helpful websites:

www.nationalparks.nsw.gov.au Information about national park access (including access for mobility-impaired visitors), camping permits, walking tracks, conservation, Aboriginal heritage and children's activities.

www.nrma.com.au If you're hiring or buying a car, find out about insurance, road maps and guides. You can also book accommodation and tours online.

www.nsw.gov.au Bypass the boring parliamentary information and check out the leads to festivals, markets, galleries, Aboriginal heritage and more.

NATIONAL PARKS

There are over 780 exceptionally diverse national parks and reserves in NSW, from the subtropical rainforest of the Border Ranges and white peaks of the Snowy Mountains to the haunting, fragile landscapes of the outback. In reasonable weather most parks and reserves are accessible by conventional vehicle. With the exception of those surrounding Sydney, public transport into most parks is scarce.

The **NSW National Parks & Wildlife Service** (NPWS; www.nationalparks.nsw.gov.au) does an excellent job. Many parks have visitor centres with detailed information on the area, walking tracks and camping options. Where there isn't one, visit the nearest NPWS office for information.

Some of the must-sees include the theatrical rock formations of Ben Boyd National Park (p239), the emerald forests of Nightcap National Park (p203) and the stunning dunes and coastal heaths of Hat Head National Park (p184).

The Border Ranges National Park (p204) is a twitcher's utopia with over 170 bird species. Richmond Range National Park (p214) and Willandra National Park (p254) are both World Heritage listed, the former encompassing forgotten rainforests and the latter ancient lakes fringed by crescent-shaped dunes.

Spectacular Kosciuszko National Park (p242) has rugged white-capped mountains. In stark contrast, Sturt National Park (p258) protects an enormous arid landscape of rolling red sand dunes.

Forty-four of the parks charge daily entry fees, generally $7 per car (less for motorcycles and pedestrians). If you plan on visiting a number of parks then the annual pass, which gives unlimited entry to all the state's parks is worthwhile; prices start at $22.

Many parks have campsites with facilities; some are free, others cost between $5 and $10 a night per person. Popular sites are often booked out during holidays. Bush camping is allowed in some parks; contact the NPWS office for regulations.

ACTIVITIES
Australiana Activities

The town of Wooli (p190) has revived the oddly named sport of goanna pulling, where

---

NEW SOUTH WALES FACTS

Eat Rock oysters, rock lobsters, yabbies and prawns; also Turkish bread 'sangers' and Tim Tam shooters

Drink A flat white, freshly squeezed fruit juice, Shiraz from the Hunter Valley and a bottle of Barons Pale Ale

Read The 2008 Booker Prize–nominated *A Fraction of the Whole* by Steve Toltz, *Unreliable Memoirs* by Clive James and *The Penguin Book of the Road,* the perfect Aussie road-trip companion

Listen to *Apocalypso* by The Presets, *Young Modern* by Silverchair, *Chimney's Afire* by Josh Pyke and the self-titled album by Sam Sparro

Watch *Puberty Blues* (1981), *Muriel's Wedding* (1994), *Candy* (2006), *Newcastle* (2008) and the TV series *Love My Way* (2004–07)

Avoid Getting sunburnt and supporting any other country than Australia when watching international sporting matches (at least vocally anyway)

Locals' nickname Sydneysiders

Swim at Bondi (p117) and Byron Bay (p195), two of NSW's most iconic beaches

Strangest festival The Parkes Elvis Festival (p218)

Tackiest tourist attraction The Big Banana (p186)

ABORIGINAL NEW SOUTH WALES

On the beaches and rocky outcrops of Sydney Harbour, the Eora people and their neighbours hunted and fished for thousands of years. A person travelling around the harbour in Aboriginal times would have encountered several different peoples. Each group maintained their own distinct beliefs or 'Dreaming'. And each spoke their own language – including Dharug, Tharawal, Gundungurra and Kuring-gai. This linguistic diversity was found across the entire continent.

The Aborigines' world changed forever on 19 April 1770, when Lieutenant James Cook of the British Navy sailed into Botany Bay. The story goes that Cook, his head filled with notions of 'noble savages', was respectful towards the Indigenous population and later reported back on their peaceable nature.

However, when Captain Phillip's penal settlement came to town, kidnappings and punishment became the norm, with the explicit aim of terrifying Aborigines into submission. Smallpox, introduced by the invaders, also decimated the local population, which had no resistance to such a disease. But there was resistance in other forms: Aboriginal freedom-fighting groups began to spring up, led by storied indigenous figures including Bennelong, Pemulwuy and Mosquito, a warrior from a Broken Bay people. The freedom fighters were eventually crushed as the settlers resorted to ever more barbaric methods to achieve total domination.

There were somewhere between 500,000 and one million Aboriginal peoples in Australia before the British arrived, and more than 250 regional languages. Sydney Cove had an Indigenous population of around 3000, using three main languages encompassing several dialects and subgroups. Kuring-gai (derived from the nomenclature 'Koori') was generally spoken on the northern shore, Tharawal along the coast south of Botany Bay, and Dharug and its dialects near the Blue Mountains.

Quite a few words from NSW Aboriginal language are still in common usage in Australian English, including galah, kookaburra, dingo, koala, wallaby and billabong.

Today there are an estimated 148,200 Aboriginal people in NSW, and the Sydney region is estimated to have over 40,000 Indigenous inhabitants, mostly descended from migratory inland peoples.

NSW is littered with opportunities to gain a deeper understanding of Indigenous culture and heritage. Aboriginal rock art and engravings can be seen in Bondi (p117), Ku-ring-gai Chase National Park (p150), the Blue Mountains (p154) and in Brisbane Water National Park (p162), near Gosford.

The NSW outback has many sites of Aboriginal heritage, including Mt Gunderbooka (p257) and the wonderful Mt Grenfell Historic Site (p259).

There are many acclaimed galleries focusing on Aboriginal art in Sydney (p142) and Broken Hill (p261).

But the best way to experience indigenous culture is at a cultural centre. Trips to the Muru Mittigar Aboriginal Cultural Centre (p156) in Penrith, the Aboriginal Cultural Centre & Keeping Place (p209) in Armidale, and the Umbarra Cultural Centre (p237) near Bermagui will provide a deeper appreciation of the way the traditional custodians of those areas used the land, and of their life and heritage.

There are also highly recommended Aboriginal tours throughout the state listed under individual towns and parks in this chapter.

For more information, go to www.visitnsw.com.au and follow the links to Aboriginal Culture under Activities and Attractions, or www.indigenoustourism.australia.com for links to Indigenous-owned and -operated tour and accommodation operators, as well as artists and art organisations.

---

grown men and women wearing leather harnesses try to pull each other's heads off.

Blokes and sheilas compete for titles such as 'Chick's Ute' and 'Feral Ute' at Deniliquin's Ute Muster (p255), and at Lightning Ridge's annual Great Goat Race (p223) locals and tourists don crash helmets and, erm, race goats.

Bushwalking

Almost every national park has marked trails or wilderness walking opportunities, ranging from short stomps to longer, more challenging treks.

In Sydney, it's worth picking up a copy of *Sydney's Best Harbour & Coastal Walks* published by the *Sydney Morning Herald*. It includes the must-do 6km Bondi to Coogee Coastal Walk (p117) and the beautiful 10km Manly Scenic Walkway (p121) in addition to wilder walks.

Near Sydney, the wilderness areas of Royal National Park (p147) hide dramatic cliff-top walks including a 28km coastal walking trail. There are smaller bushwalks around the inlets of Broken Bay in Ku-ring-gai Chase National Park (p150). If you're up for a lengthy trek, tackle the Great North Walk (p163) between Sydney and Newcastle.

West of Sydney, the sandstone bluffs, eucalyptus forests and wildflowers of the Blue Mountains (p155) make for a breathtaking experience, as does the walk to the summit of Australia's highest peak, Mt Kosciuszko (2228m), in Kosciuszko National Park (p242).

In the state's northwest, Warrumbungle National Park (p222), with its volcanic peaks, has over 30km of trails to keep you hale and strong. Keen trampers should try the 15km Syndicate Ridge Walking Trail near Bellingen (p212), the 42km Six Foot Track (p161) to the Jenolan Caves, or the spectacular 50km Nadgee Howe Wilderness Walk trail in Ben Boyd National Park (p239).

Outdoor stockists are good sources of bushwalking information. Also try the **NPWS** (www.nationalparks.nsw.gov.au) and the **Confederation of Bushwalking Clubs NSW** (www.bushwalking.org.au).

Lonely Planet's *Walking in Australia* provides maps and descriptions of 17 major trails throughout NSW.

Canyoning

Canyoning combines rock climbing, abseiling, swimming and bushwalking, with lots of rock scrambling and jumping in water. If negotiating narrow crevices while getting soaking wet sounds fun (it is!), then consider the Blue Mountains (p156), where there are trips to suit most levels.

There's also great abseiling to be found in the Snowy Mountains, particularly around Jindabyne (p241).

Cycling

Cycling in Sydney's kamikaze traffic is no fun, so head off-road on a mountain bike instead. The national parks around Sydney, the Blue Mountains (p153) and the Great North Road around the Hawkesbury River (p152) offer stunning challenges. In the southeast,

mountain biking is a warm-weather favourite in Thredbo (p244).

Bicycle NSW (Map pp102-3; ☎ 02-9218 5400; www.bicyclensw.org.au; Level 5, 822 George St, Sydney) provides information and guides for cycling routes throughout the state, as well as the bimonthly magazine *Australian Cyclist*.

The **Bicycles Network Australia** (www.bicycles.net.au) website is useful, as is Lonely Planet's *Cycling Australia*.

Diving & Snorkelling

There are over 30 diving destinations in Sydney alone. See Sydney's Best Beaches p118 for a list of the best shore and boat dives.

North of Sydney try Broughton Island near Port Stephens (p174), while Fish Rock Cave off South West Rocks (p184) is renowned for its excellent diving, with shells, schools of clownfish and humpback whales. Swim with grey nurse sharks at The Pinnacles near Forster (p177) and leopard sharks at Julian Rocks Marine Reserve off Byron Bay (p197). Good dive schools can be found at Coffs Harbour (p187) and Byron Bay (p197).

On the South Coast popular diving spots include Jervis Bay (p233), pretty Montague Island (p236) and Merimbula (p237).

Diving outfits typically offer four-day **PADI courses** (Professional Association of Diving Instructors; www.padi.com).

Skiing & Snowboarding

Snowfields criss-cross the NSW–Victoria border. The season is relatively short (mid-June to early September) and snowfalls can be unpredictable. Cross-country skiing is popular and most resorts offer lessons and equipment.

The Snowy Mountains (p239) boasts popular resorts including Charlotte Pass, Perisher Blue, Selwyn and Thredbo.

Skiing Australia (www.skiingaustralia.org.au) details the major resorts and race clubs.

Surfing & Swimming

For the low-down on Sydney's top surfing and swimming spots, see p120 and p121.

You can also fine-tune your surfing skills (or indeed learn some) at Newcastle (p165), Port Macquarie (p181) and Coffs Harbour (p187). Crescent Head (p183) is the long-boarding capital of Australia, and the gnarly swells at Angourie Point (p192) are for seasoned surfers and/or nutcases only. Further north, you can hang ten at Lennox Head (p194) and Byron Bay (p198).

The South Coast is literally awash with great surf beaches, particularly around Wollongong (p228), Ulladulla (p234) and Merimbula (p237).

Useful websites include www.realsurf.com and www.coastalwatch.com.

NSW has some 2137km of coastline and 721 ocean beaches, so it goes without saying that practically any coastal town can satisfy the need of swimmers. There are innumerable lakes and rivers and most towns have an Olympic-sized outdoor swimming pool.

Whale & Dolphin Watching

Every year between late May and late November, southern right and humpback whales migrate along Australia's southern coast between the Antarctic and warmer waters. Get up close to these magnificent creatures on a whale-watching cruise; good spots are Eden (p238) in southern NSW and along the mid-north coast of NSW at Coffs Harbour (p186) and Port Stephens (p174).

Dolphins can be seen year-round at many places along the NSW coast, such as Jervis Bay (p233), Port Stephens (p174) and Byron Bay (p195), and they've even been seen at Bondi Beach (p117).

White-Water Rafting, Kayaking & Canoeing

For rafting, try the upper Murray near Jindabyne (p240), and Coffs Harbour (p186).

There is stunning sea kayaking at Byron Bay (p197), Lord Howe Island (p224), Yamba (p192) and Batemans Bay (p235). You can also kayak around Sydney Harbour (p119).

For canoeing, head to Barrington Tops National Park (p176), Myall Lakes National Park (p177), Bellingen (p211) and Kangaroo Valley (p232). Contact the **New South Wales Canoeing Association** (☎ 02-8116 9727; www.nswcanoe .org.au) for info on courses and hire in Sydney, or buy *The Canoeing Guide to NSW*.

TOURS

NSW offers tours to suit all tastes and budgets: wineries, outback, whale watching, skiing, bushwalking, eco-certified, Aboriginal heritage, surfing and more.

In Sydney, take your pick from bus, walking or harbour tours (p122). Various companies operate tours to popular destinations such as the Blue Mountains (p156) and the Hunter Valley (p171).

From Port Stephens (p175), Port Macquarie (p181) and Coffs Harbour (p187) there are dolphin- and whale-watching tours aplenty.

Ecotours and mountain-bike tours of the far north hinterland are the speciality from Byron Bay (p198), while the Snowy Mountains offer Indigenous snowshoeing tours (p245).

Award-winning tours from Broken Hill (p262) are the best way for time-strapped travellers to experience the haunting and dramatic NSW outback.

GETTING THERE & AROUND

Sydney's **Kingsford Smith Airport** (☎ 02-9667 9111; www.sydneyairport.com.au) is the main port of call for most international visitors to Australia. By car and motorcycle, you'll probably reach NSW via the Hume Hwy if you're coming from the south, or via the Pacific Hwy if you're coming from the north. The Princes Hwy heads south from Sydney along the state's southern coast.

Air

Virgin Blue (☎ 13 67 89; www.virginblue.com.au), **Jetstar** (☎ 13 15 38; www.jetstar.com.au) and **Qantas** (☎ 13 13 13; www.qantas.com.au) fly all over Australia; fares are cheaper if booked online.

Regional Express (Rex; ☎ 13 17 13; www.regional express.com.au) flies to rural destinations throughout NSW.

Bus

More towns in NSW are serviced by bus than any other public transport. If you want to make multistop trips, look for cheap stopover deals rather than buying separate tickets. In remote areas school buses may be the only option; the drivers will usually pick you up, but they're not obliged to.

The main companies servicing the NSW coast are **Greyhound** (☎ 1300 473 946; www.greyhound .com.au) and **Premier Motor Service** (☎ 13 34 10; www .premierms.com.au). Fares and stops for both companies are interchangeable, but Greyhound is often ever so slightly more expensive. Fares purchased online are usually marginally cheaper than over-the-counter tickets.

Smaller regional operators running key routes or covering a lot of ground:

Busways (☎ 02-4368 2277; www.busways.com.au) Connects the central coast.

Murrays Coaches (☎ 13 22 59; www.murrays.com.au) Runs between Sydney and Canberra.

Port Stephens Coaches (☎ 02-4982 2940; www .pscoaches.com.au) Runs between Sydney, Port Stephens and Newcastle.

Transborder (☎ 02-6241 0033; www.transborder.com .au) From Canberra to Thredbo.

Train

CountryLink (☎ 13 22 32; www.countrylink.info), the state rail service, will take you to many sizeable towns in NSW, in conjunction with connecting buses. You need to book in advance by phone, online or in person at one of Sydney's CountryLink Travel Centres – Central Station (Map pp102–3) or Town Hall Station (Map pp102–3). CountryLink offers 1st- and economy-class tickets, as well as a quota of discount and multistop tickets: the Backtracker Pass offers unlimited travel on the CountryLink network, including the Gold Coast and Byron Bay, from $275 for one month.

CityRail (☎ 13 15 00; www.cityrail.info), the Sydney metropolitan service, runs frequent commuter-style trains south through Wollongong to Bomaderry; west through the Blue Mountains to Katoomba and Lithgow; north to Newcastle; and southwest through the Southern Highlands to Goulburn. CityRail has an **information booth** (Map pp102-3; ☎ 13 15 00; www.131500.com.au; Wharf 5; ☻ 9.05am-4.50pm) at Circular Quay.

SYDNEY

pop 4.35 million

Sydney is the capital that all other cities love to hate; with stunning surf and buttery beaches, glorious weather and glamorous people, world-class restaurants and outrageously fashionable bars, she seemingly has it all. And, damn it, doesn't she know it.

Built around one of the most beautiful natural harbours in the world, Sydney's shimmering soul reveals an iconic landscape that to many signifies 'Australia'. The Harbour Bridge, the Opera House, myriad sandstone headlands, lazy bays and scalloped shorelines are breathtakingly beautiful. But while her neighbours might snipe that Sydney is all about fleeting physical fun, Sydneysiders know that there's more to this city than her good looks (even if Bondi Beach on a Saturday afternoon argues otherwise). She's Australia's oldest, largest and most diverse city with captivating monuments, urban galleries, magnificent museums, a vivacious performing arts scene and an edgy multiculturalism that injects colour to her outer suburbs. Give it a couple of days and you'll quickly realise that there's so much more to Sydney than soy lattes and sunbathing. Give it any longer and you'll probably never want to leave.

HISTORY

The Sydney region is the ancestral home of the Eora people (the Kuring-gai, Birrabirragal and Cadi peoples) who possessed an intimate understanding of environmental sustainability, spoke three distinct languages, and maintained sophisticated sacred and artistic cultures. In 1788 Captain Arthur Phillip established Australia's first European settlement here, and the Eora were soon stripped of legal rights to their land, systematically incarcerated, and killed or driven away by force.

Early Sydney bumbled through near-starvation and rum-fuelled political turmoil; things didn't boom until the 1850s gold rush, when Sydney's population doubled ina decade.

In the 20th century, post-WWII immigrants from the UK, Ireland and the Mediterranean brought spirit and prosperity to Sydney. Hosting the 2000 Olympic Games thrust Sydney into the global limelight for celebratory reasons, and the simmering racial tensions that exploded into mob violence on the southern beaches in late 2005 did the same for horrific ones.

ORIENTATION

Central Sydney is relatively small and easy to navigate, but the city does sprawl; Greater Sydney covers more than 1200 sq km from Botany Bay to the south, the Blue Mountains to the west and Pittwater to the north.

At the heart of the city is Sydney Harbour (Port Jackson); the city centre runs from The Rocks and Circular Quay to Central Station in the south. The harbour divides Sydney into north and south, with the Sydney Harbour Bridge and the Harbour Tunnel connecting the two shores. Immediately west is Darling Harbour, while to the east lies Darlinghurst, Kings Cross and Paddington.

Head further southeast along the coast and you'll find the archetypal beach suburbs of Bondi and Coogee. Sydney's Kingsford Smith Airport is 10km south of the city centre. West of the centre are the gentrified suburbs of Pyrmont, Glebe and Balmain. The inner west includes Newtown and Leichardt. The suburbs north of the bridge are known collectively as the North Shore, with the sandy stretch of Northern Beaches running north from the suburb of Manly.

Maps

Lonely Planet's *Sydney City Map* has detailed coverage of central Sydney and the Blue Mountains. If you're driving, a *Sydney UBD* street directory (around $35) is invaluable.

Department of Lands (Map pp102-3; ☎ 02-9228 6666; www.lands.nsw.gov.au; 1 Prince Albert Rd, Sydney; ☿ 8.30am-4.30pm Mon-Fri) Topographic map heaven.

Map World (Map pp102-3; ☎ 02-9261 3601; www.mapworld.com.au; 280 Pitt St, Sydney; ☿ 9am-5.30pm Mon-Fri, 10am-3.45pm Sat) All you need to ensure you don't get lost.

INFORMATION
Bookshops

Ariel (Map pp102-3; ☎ 02-9332 4581; www.arielbooks.com.au; 42 Oxford St, Paddington; ☿ 9am-midnight) Hip bookshop good for art, film, fashion, design and travel guides.

Berkelouw Books (Map pp102-3; ☎ 02-9360 3200; www.berkelouw.com.au; 19 Oxford St, Paddington; ☿ 9am-11pm Sun-Thu, to midnight Fri & Sat) Rare, out-of-print, secondhand and new books, and a cafe.

Dymocks (Map pp102-3; ☎ 02-9235 0155; www.dymocks.com.au; 424-28 George St, Sydney; ☿ 8.30am-6.30pm Mon-Wed & Fri, to 9pm Thu, 9am-6pm Sat, 10am-5.30pm Sun) Mainstream titles, stationery and a cafe.

Gleebooks (Map p108; ☎ 02-9660 2333; www.gleebooks.com.au; 49 Glebe Point Rd, Glebe; ☿ 9am-9pm) Fabulous independent bookshop that stocks just about everything.

Kinokuniya (Map pp102-3; ☎ 02-9262 7996; www.kinokuniya.com; Level 2, TGV, 500 George St, Sydney; ☿ 10am-7pm Mon-Wed, Fri & Sat, to 9pm Thu, to 6pm Sun) Sydney's biggest bookshop.

Emergency

Lifeline (☎ 13 11 14; www.lifeline.com.au) Telephone counselling services round the clock, including suicide prevention.

National Roads & Motorists Association (NRMA; Map pp102-3; ☎ 13 11 22; www.nrma.com.au; 74-6 King St, Sydney; ☿ 9am-5pm Mon-Fri) Car insurance and roadside service.

Police (☎ 000; www.police.nsw.gov.au) Day St (Map pp102-3; 192 Day St, Sydney); Kings Cross (Map p106; 1-15 Elizabeth Bay Rd); The Rocks (Map pp102-3; 132 George St)

Rape Crisis Centre (☎ 02-9819 7357, 1800 424 017; www.nswrapecrisis.com.au)

Internet Access

Internet cafes are common in Sydney, especially in Kings Cross, Chinatown and Bondi. Rates are $2 to $3 an hour. Plenty of hostels and hotels offer internet access to their guests.

Global Gossip (☎ 1300 738 353; per hr $3; ☿ 9am-midnight) Bondi (Map p107; 37 Hall St); George St (Map pp102-3; 760 George St, Sydney); Kings Cross (Map p106; 63 Darlinghurst Rd) Traveller-friendly chain.

Internet World (Map pp102-3; ☎ 02-9262 9700; 369 Pitt St, Sydney; per hr $2; ☿ 24hr) Fast servers under fluoro light.

Internet Resources

For more information on Sydney, check out the following websites:

www.cityofsydney.nsw.gov.au City news and views.
www.sydney.citysearch.com.au Events and listings.
www.timeoutsydney.com.au Excellent weekly guide to what's on in the city.
www.twothousand.com.au Snapshot of Sydney's subculture.
www.visitnsw.com.au Info on Sydney and NSW, including events.

Medical Services

Kings Cross Travellers' Clinic (Map p106; ☎ 02-9358 3066; www.travellersclinic.com.au; 13 Springfield Ave, Kings Cross; ☿ 9am-1pm & 2-6pm Mon-Fri, 10am-noon Sat) Vaccinations, medications, dive medicals and morning-after pill scripts; bookings advised.

St Vincent's Hospital (Map p106; ☎ 02-8382 1111; www.stvincents.com.au; 390 Victoria St, Darlinghurst; ☿ 24hr emergency)

Sydney Children's Hospital (Map pp100-1; ☎ 02-9382 1111; www.sch.edu.au; High St, Randwick; ☿ 24hr kids' emergency)

Sydney Hospital & Sydney Eye Hospital (Map pp102-3; ☎ 02-9382 7111; www.sesahs.nsw.gov.au/sydhosp; 8 Macquarie St, Sydney; ☿ 24hr emergency)

Travel Doctor (Map pp102-3; ☎ 02-9221 7133; www.traveldoctor.com.au; Level 7, 428 George St, Sydney; ☿ 9am-5.30pm Mon-Wed & Fri, to 8pm Thu, to 1pm Sat) Travel shots and medical advice.

Money

There are plenty of ATMs throughout Sydney; both **American Express** (Map pp102-3; ☎ 1300 139 060; 50 Pitt St, Sydney; ☿ 9.30am-4pm Mon-Thu, to 5pm Fri) and

(Continued on page 109)

SYDNEY

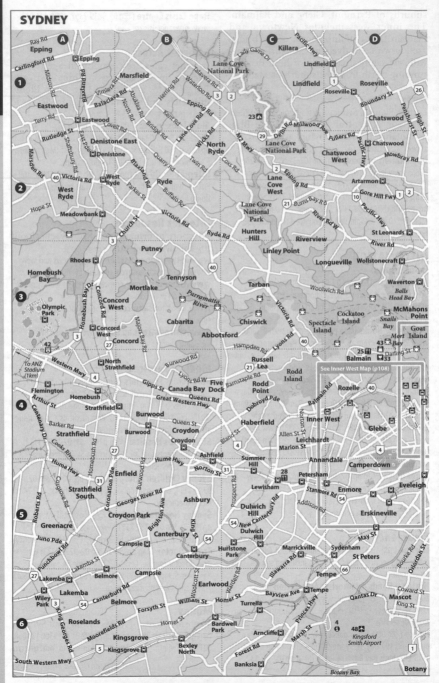

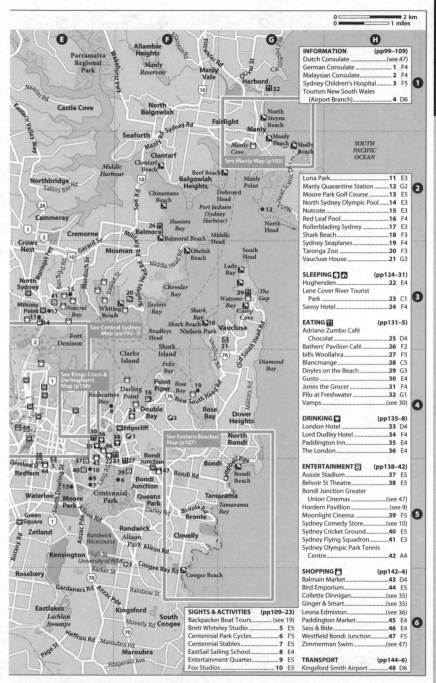

CENTRAL SYDNEY

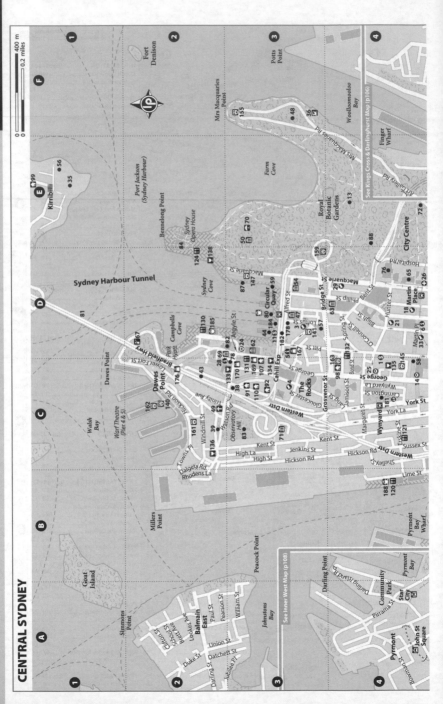

See Kings Cross & Darlinghurst Map (p106)

See Inner West Map (p108)

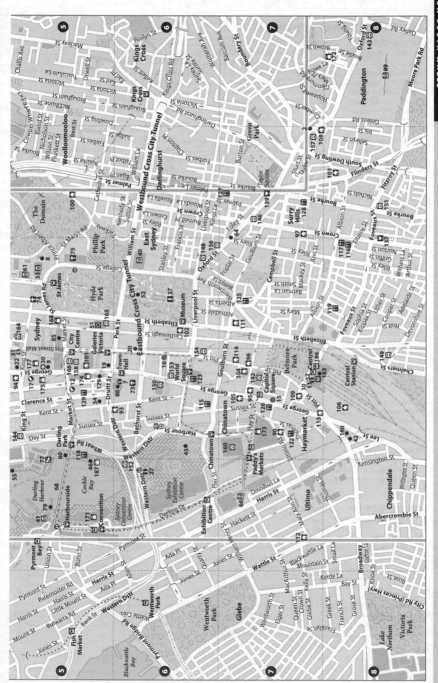

NEW SOUTH WALES

CENTRAL SYDNEY (pp102–3)

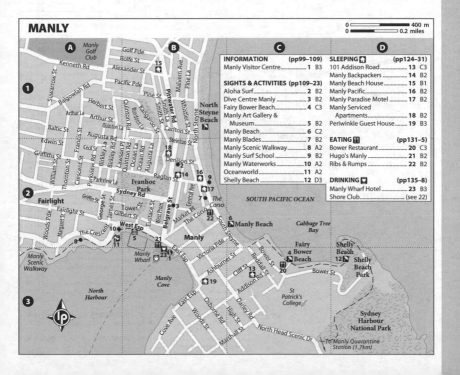

NEW SOUTH WALES

KINGS CROSS & DARLINGHURST

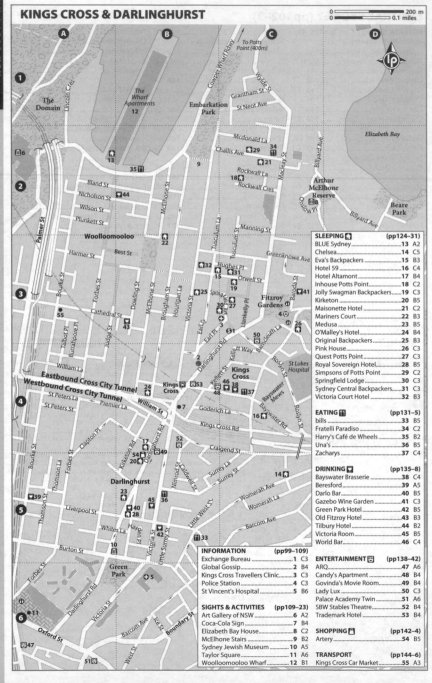

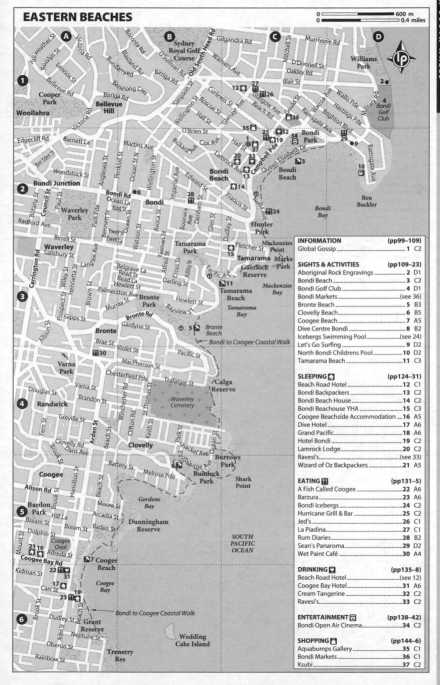

EASTERN BEACHES

INFORMATION	(pp99–109)
Global Gossip	1 C2

SIGHTS & ACTIVITIES	(pp109–23)
Aboriginal Rock Engravings	2 D1
Bondi Beach	3 C2
Bondi Golf Club	4 D1
Bondi Markets	(see 36)
Bronte Beach	5 B3
Clovelly Beach	6 B5
Coogee Beach	7 A5
Dive Centre Bondi	8 B2
Icebergs Swimming Pool	(see 24)
Let's Go Surfing	9 D2
North Bondi Childrens Pool	10 D2
Tamarama Beach	11 C3

SLEEPING	(pp124–31)
Beach Road Hotel	12 C1
Bondi Backpackers	13 C2
Bondi Beach House	14 C2
Bondi Beachouse YHA	15 C3
Coogee Beachside Accommodation	16 A5
Dive Hotel	17 A6
Grand Pacific	18 A6
Hotel Bondi	19 C2
Lamrock Lodge	20 C2
Ravesi's	(see 33)
Wizard of Oz Backpackers	21 A5

EATING	(pp131–5)
A Fish Called Coogee	22 A6
Barzura	23 A6
Bondi Icebergs	24 C2
Hurricane Grill & Bar	25 C2
Jed's	26 C1
La Piadina	27 C1
Rum Diaries	28 B2
Sean's Panorama	29 D2
Wet Paint Café	30 A4

DRINKING	(pp135–8)
Beach Road Hotel	(see 12)
Coogee Bay Hotel	31 A6
Cream Tangerine	32 C2
Ravesi's	33 C2

ENTERTAINMENT	(pp138–42)
Bondi Open Air Cinema	34 C2

SHOPPING	(pp144–6)
Aquabumps Gallery	35 C1
Bondi Markets	36 C1
Ksubi	37 C2

NEW SOUTH WALES

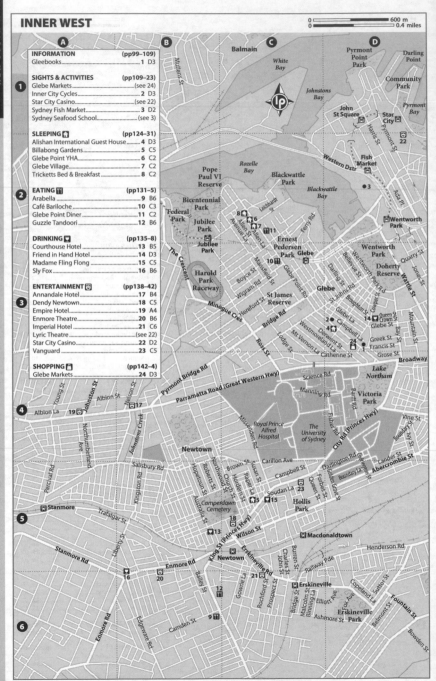

INNER WEST

0   600 m
0   0.4 miles

(Continued from page 99)

Travelex (Map pp102-3; ☎ 02-9264 1267; Shop W64, Queen Victoria Building, George St, Sydney; ☼ 8am-6pm Mon-Wed & Fri, to 7.30pm Thu, 11am-4pm Sat, noon-5pm Sun) have city branches. Seven-day exchange bureaus:
Central Station (Map pp102-3; Coach Terminal; ☼ 9am-4pm)
Circular Quay (Map pp102-3; Wharf 6; ☼ 8am-9.30pm)
Kings Cross (Map p106; cnr Springfield Ave & Darlinghurst Rd; ☼ 8am-midnight)

Post
Stamps are sold at post offices, Australia Post retail outlets in most suburbs and most newsagencies.
General Post Office (GPO; Map pp102-3; ☎ 13 13 18; www.auspost.com.au; 1 Martin Pl, Sydney; ☼ 8.15am-5.30pm Mon-Fri, 10am-2pm Sat)
Poste Restante Service (Map pp102-3; ☎ 13 13 18; www.auspost.com.au; 310 George St, Sydney; ☼ 8.15am-5.30pm Mon-Fri, 10am-2pm Sat) Bring identification to collect mail.

Tourist Information
City Host Information Kiosks (☼ 9am-5pm) Circular Quay (Map pp102-3; cnr Pitt & Alfred Sts, Sydney); Martin Place (Map pp102-3; btwn Elizabeth & Castlereagh Sts, Sydney); Town Hall (Map pp102-3; cnr Druitt & George Sts, Sydney)
Sydney Visitor Centres (www.sydneyvisitorcentre.com;); Darling Harbour (Map pp102-3; ☎ 02-9240 8788; Palm Grove; ☼ 9.30am-5.30pm) Information on *everything*; also acts as an accommodation agency; The Rocks (Map pp102-3; ☎ 02-9240 8788; www.sydneyvisitorcentre .com; cnr Argyle & Playfair Sts, The Rocks; ☼ 9.30am-5.30pm Mon-Fri).
Tourism New South Wales (☎ 02-9931 1111; www .visitnsw.com.au; ☼ 9am-5pm Mon-Fri); airport (Map pp100-1; ☎ 02-9667 6050; International Arrivals, Terminal 1; ☼ 5am-11pm) State-wide accommodation and travel advice.
Tourist Information Service (☎ 02-9669 5111; ☼ 7am-10pm) Information and accommodation telephone service.
Travellers' Information Service (Map pp102-3; ☎ 02-9281 9366; Sydney Coach Terminal, Eddy Ave, Haymarket; ☼ 6am-8pm Mon-Fri, to 6pm Sat & Sun) Accommodation bookings, coach tickets, public transport information and maps.

Travel Agencies
Travellers Contact Point (Map pp102-3; ☎ 1300 855 569; www.travellers.com.au; Level 7, 428 George St, Sydney; ☼ 9am-6pm Mon-Fri, 10am-4pm Sat) Backpacker agency that holds mail and has a good bulletin board.

YHA Membership & Travel Centre (Map pp102-3; ☎ 02-9261 1111; www.yha.com.au; 422 Kent St, Sydney; ☼ 9am-5pm Mon-Wed & Fri, to 6pm Thu, 10am-2pm Sat) Offers travel packages and YHA bookings worldwide; also try the travel agent in the Sydney Central YHA (see p125).

SIGHTS
Sydney's jam-packed with things to see and do, much of which doesn't cost a cent. But if you're planning to see an exceptional number of museums, attractions and tours, check out the **Smartvisit card** (☎ 1300 661 711; www.seesydneycard.com).

The vast majority of sights and museums in Sydney have good disabled access.

Sydney Harbour
Sydney's stunning harbour (officially Port Jackson) is the city's heart and soul. Stretching 20km inland to the mouth of the Parramatta River, it's peppered with islands, coves, beaches and bays, some insanely busy and others virtually deserted.

North Head (Map pp100-1) and **South Head** (Map pp100-1) form the gateway to the harbour. Close to South Head at the harbour entrance, **Camp Cove** (Map pp100-1) is a particularly photogenic swimming beach and where Arthur Phillip first landed. The fortunately shark-netted **Shark Beach** (Map pp100-1) at Nielsen Park is similarly sublime. For the most part the harbour beaches tend to be far calmer than their frenzied ocean cousins. On the North Shore try **Manly Cove**, **Reef Beach**, **Clontarf Beach**, **Chinamans Beach** and **Balmoral Beach** (all Map pp100-1).

SYDNEY HARBOUR NATIONAL PARK
This **park** (Map pp100-1) protects scattered pockets of harbourside bushland with magical walking tracks, lookouts, Aboriginal engravings and historic sites. Its southern side incorporates South Head and **Nielsen Park**; on the North Shore it includes **North Head**, **Dobroyd Head**, **Middle Head** and **Bradleys Head**.

Five harbour islands also form part of the park: **Clark Island** off Darling Point, **Shark Island** off Rose Bay, **Rodd Island** in Iron Cove, **Goat Island** and the small fortified **Fort Denison** (Map pp100-1) off Mrs Macquaries Point. Run by the Sydney Harbour Federation Trust, **Cockatoo Island** (Map pp100-1; ☎ 02-8969 2100; www.cockatooisland.gov.au; adult/child/family $18/14/60; ☼ tours 11.15am & 1.15pm Sun), a former convict prison, shipyard and industrial school for girls, is a fascinating industrial relic. Take a guided tour (p123) or camp overnight ($75 per night).

Except for Goat Island, which is currently off-limits, the harbour islands are open to visitors. The NPWS runs a number of tours, including hour-long Fort Denison **heritage tours** (adult/child $27/17; 12.15pm & 2.30pm daily, 10.45am Wed-Sun) – book at the **Sydney Harbour National Park Information Centre** (Map pp102-3; ☎ 02-9247 5033; www.environment.nsw.gov.au/national parks; 110 George St, The Rocks; 9.30am-4.30pm Mon-Fri, 10am-4.30pm Sat & Sun).

Matilda Cruises (Map pp102-3; ☎ 02-9264 7377; www.matilda.com.au; adult/child $17/15; every 45min from 9.45am departing Circular Quay & Pier 26, Darling Harbour) runs ferries to Shark Island. You can catch a water taxi from Circular Quay to Rodd and Clark islands (see p145); they incur a $7 landing fee per person, also payable at Cadman's Cottage. Cockatoo Island can be reached by ferry from Circular Quay.

SYDNEY OPERA HOUSE

Millions over budget, years overdue and a scandalous political affair that forced architect Jørn Utzon to resign before the building's completion: it's fair to say that Sydney's **opera house** (Map pp102-3; ☎ 02-9250 7111; www.sydneyop erahouse.com; Bennelong Pt, Circular Quay E, Sydney) had a troubled youth. Today, however, this visionary building is Australia's most recognisable icon and since its official opening in 1973 millions have admired its soaring shell-like exterior.

The building is said to have drawn inspiration from orange segments, snails, palm fronds, sails and Mayan temples. Less poetically it's been likened to a 'nun's scrum' and

Clive James called it an 'Olivetti Lettera 22 typewriter full of oyster shells left after an office party'. He quickly changed his mind, however, when he saw it 'for what it is: an epic poem'.

However you view the building, there's no denying that it's impressive: the 67m-high roof features 27,230 tonnes of Swedish tiles – 1,056,000 of them in total. Sadly, Jørn Utzon died in 2008 having never seen the finished design in person.

There are four main auditoriums for dance, concerts, opera and theatre events, plus the left-of-centre Studio for emerging artists; get your tickets at the **box office** (☎ 02-9250 7777; 9am-8.30pm Mon-Sat, 2hr pre-show Sun).

One hour opera house **tours** (☎ 02-9250 7250; adult/concession $23/16; 9am-5.30pm) take you from 'front of house' to backstage, excluding theatres in rehearsal use. Let them know in advance if you require wheelchair access. Public transport to Circular Quay is the best way to get here, but if you're driving there's a **car park** (☎ 02-9247 7599; nightly rate $32; 6.30am-1am) under the building (enter via Macquarie St).

SYDNEY HARBOUR BRIDGE

Sydneysiders simply adore their **bridge** (Map pp102-3). Dubbed the 'coat hanger' this colossal steel-arch bridge, held together by almost six million hand-driven rivets, links the CBD with the North Sydney business district. It took eight years to build and was finally completed in 1932 – at a cost of $20 million. The city took 60 years to pay it off.

There are many ways to experience this favourite Sydney icon – you can drive over it, climb up it, travel by train across it or sail underneath it – but the best way to fully

---

STAYING IN SYDNEY

Let's face it: Sydney is a bloody long way from anywhere, so once you've arrived you might as well stick around for a while. If you are planning on putting down roots then you'll most likely need a job; the free monthly **Jobmap** (www.jobmap.com) magazine is invaluable both for finding employment and helping to navigate boring but important issues such as Tax File Numbers, insurance and visa extensions. *TNT Magazine* also has job listings.

Cityhobo (www.cityhobo.com) is a comprehensive website for sussing out what neighbourhood you would like – and can afford – to live in. Check www.domain.com.au and the Saturday edition of the *Sydney Morning Herald* for rental properties, as well as **Gumtree** (www.gumtree.com.au), which is also good for finding cheap furniture to kit out your apartment (most units come unfurnished). Be warned that Sydney's rental market can be brutal and there's a lot of competition; once you find a place you like, you'll need to pay six to eight weeks' rent in advance and most landlords will require some kind of reference letter to ensure you won't run off with the curtains.

SYDNEY IN...

Three Days

Start your time in Sydney the way that all Sydneysiders begin their day with a flat white and breakfast. Fortified, head to the harbour and get blown away by the stunning views on a **Bridge Climb** (p123). Ramble around **The Rocks** (below) and wind your way over to the **Sydney Opera House** (opposite), stopping in at the **Museum of Contemporary Art** (p112) on your way. Kick back in the **Royal Botanic Gardens** (p114), but keep an eye out for the flying foxes.

On day two goofy-foot it over to **Bondi** (p117) for a surf lesson followed by the **Coastal Walk** (p117) to Coogee. Fill up on fish for lunch at the **Sydney Fish Market** (p115) and then wander the arty streets of **Glebe** (p117) or **Balmain** (p117), both of which offer ample opportunities for an early evening drink or two.

Start day three with some window shopping along **Oxford Street** (p116) followed by a bike ride and picnic in **Centennial Park** (p116). In the evening head to **Surry Hills** (p116) for dinner, drinks and a play at the **Belvoir St Theatre** (p140).

One Week

It's easy to fill another four days in Sydney – lunch, beaches, swimming and views in **Manly** (p119) alone will take up one. Don't miss **Taronga Zoo** (p118), the **Sydney Aquarium** (p114) or the history-rich **Australian Museum** (p114).

Catch a ferry and camp out at **Cockatoo Island (p109)**, take high tea in the **Queen Victoria Building** (p144) and max out your credit card in the **Strand Arcade** (p144).

Get out of town to meet the Three Sisters in the **Blue Mountains** (p153) or spend a lazy day or two cruising up the **Hawkesbury River** (p151).

---

appreciate the bridge is on foot. Staircases climb up from both shores leading to a footpath running the length of the eastern side. A cycle way wheels along the western side. You can climb the southeastern pylon to the **Pylon Lookout** (Map pp102-3; ☎ 02-9240 1100; www .pylonlookout.com.au; adult/child $10/4; ☻ 10am-5pm), or ascend the great arc on a bridge climb (see p123).

On New Year's Eve the bridge takes centre stage with an impressive kaleidoscopic fireworks display.

The Rocks

The site of Sydney's first European settlement has evolved unrecognisably from its squalid origins. Early residents lived cheek by jowl in filthy alleyways festering with disease, prostitution and crime. Sailors, whalers and street gangs roamed the streets, boozing and brawling in the grimy harbourside pubs.

The Rocks remained a commercial and maritime hub until shipping services sailed away from Circular Quay in the late 1800s. A bubonic plague outbreak in 1900 furthered the decline and when construction began on the Harbour Bridge in the 1920s, entire streets were demolished.

It wasn't until the 1970s that The Rocks' cultural and architectural heritage was recognised and efforts were made to preserve and redevelop the area. Some argue that the result is a sanitised, 'olde worlde' tourist trap, but there's no denying that the area holds a certain charm, especially once you leave the main drag for the narrow backstreets.

Built in 1816, **Cadman's Cottage** (Map pp102-3; ☎ 02-9247 5033; www.environment.nsw.gov .au; 110 George St, The Rocks; ☻ 9.30am-4.30pm Mon-Fri, 10am-4.30pm Sat & Sun) is Sydney's oldest house. Its namesake, John Cadman, was the government coxswain. Water police detained criminals here in the late 1840s and it was later converted into a home for retired sea captains. Today it is home to the Sydney Harbour National Park Information Centre (p110). Further along George St is the tourist-oriented weekend Rocks Market (see p143).

In a restored 1850s sandstone warehouse, the **Rocks Discovery Museum** (Map pp102-3; ☎ 1800 067 676; www.rocksdiscoverymuseum.com; Kendall Lane, The Rocks; admission free; ☻ 10am-5pm) delves into the area's history and provides a sensitive insight into the lives of the Cadigal people, The Rocks' original inhabitants.

Beyond the **Argyle Cut** (Map pp102–3), an impressive tunnel excavated by convicts, is **Millers Point**, a relaxed district of early colonial homes. **Argyle Place** (Map pp102–3) is an English-style village green overlooked by the 1840 **Garrison Church** (Map pp102–3), the colony's first military church.

The 1850s, copper-domed, Italianate **Sydney Observatory** (Map pp102–3; ☎ 02-9921 3485; www.sydneyobservatory.com.au; Watson Rd, Millers Point; admission free; ☼ 10am-5pm) stands atop Observatory Park. Inside there's a 3-D **Space Theatre** (adult/child/family $7/5/20; ☼ 2.30pm & 3.30pm daily, plus 11am & noon Sat & Sun) and an interactive Australian astronomy exhibition. Squint at galaxies far, far away during night viewings (adult/child/family tickets cost $15/10/45); bookings are required.

In the old military hospital building nearby, the **SH Ervin Gallery** (Map pp102–3; ☎ 02-9258 0173; www.nsw.nationaltrust.org.au/ervin.html; Watson Rd, Millers Point; adult/child $6/4; ☼ 11am-5pm Tue-Sun) exhibits Australian art, including the fun and oft-controversial annual Salon des Refusés, an alternative collection from the hundreds of entries to the annual Archibald and Wynne art prizes.

The wharves around Dawes Point have emerged from prolonged decay into a cultural hub. Walsh Bay's Pier 4 houses the renowned Sydney Theatre Company (p140), the excellent **Bangarra Dance Theatre**, the **Australian Theatre for Young People (ATYP)** and the **Sydney Dance Company**. The impressive Sydney Theatre (p140) is across the road.

CIRCULAR QUAY

Built around Sydney Cove, Circular Quay is one of the city's main focal points, as well as a major public transport hub, with ferry quays, bus stops, a train station and the **Overseas Passenger Terminal** (Map pp102–3). European settlement grew around the Tank Stream, which now trickles underground into the harbour near Wharf 6. For many years Circular Quay was also Sydney's port, but these days it's more of a recreational space, with harbour walkways, grassy verges, outstanding restaurants and buskers of unpredictable merit.

The cavernous 1885 **Customs House** (Map pp102–3; ☎ 02-9242 8595; www.cityofsydney.nsw.gov.au/customshouse; 31 Alfred St, Sydney; admission free; ☼ 8am-midnight Mon-Fri, 10am-midnight Sat, 11am-5pm Sun, library 10am-7pm Mon-Fri, 11am-4pm Sat & Sun) houses the Customs House Library. Under the glass floor

of the foyer is a geeky (but undeniably impressive) 1:500 model of Sydney.

MUSEUM OF CONTEMPORARY ART

In 2008 Sydney's Chamber of Commerce recognised the **MCA** (Map pp102–3; ☎ 02-9245 2400; www.mca.com.au; 140 George St, The Rocks; admission free; ☼ 10am-5pm) as the city's most popular museum. Innovative and challenging, the ever-changing exhibitions from Australia and overseas are hip, thought provoking and often controversial. There are also excellent permanent exhibitions of Aboriginal art.

Central Sydney

Central Sydney stretches from Circular Quay in the north to Central Station in the south. The business district has traditionally sat at the northern end, but is gradually creeping southwards. For a lofty city view, take a trip up **Sydney Tower** (Map pp102–3; Centrepoint, 100 Market St, Sydney; adult/child/student $25/15/20; ☼ 9am-10.30pm).

Sydney lacks a true civic centre, but **Martin Place** (Map pp102–3) comes close. This grand pedestrian mall extends from Macquarie St to George St and is lined with monumental financial buildings and the Victorian colonnaded General Post Office. In the centre is a cenotaph commemorating Australia's war dead.

Sydney's elaborate 1874 **Town Hall** (Map pp102–3) is a few blocks south of here on the corner of George and Druitt Sts. Currently undergoing major renovations, the building is due to reopen in late 2009. Next door, the Anglican **St Andrew's Cathedral** (Map pp102–3), was consecrated in 1868, making it Australia's oldest cathedral. Across the road from the Town Hall, and taking up an entire city block, is the Queen Victoria Building (QVB; p144), Sydney's most sumptuous shopping complex. Running a close second is the ornate Strand Arcade (p144) between Pitt St Mall and George St.

The grand **State Theatre** (Map pp102–3; ☎ 02-9373 6862; www.statetheatre.com.au; 49 Market St, Sydney; adult/child $12/8; ☼ 11.30am-3pm Mon-Fri) was built in 1929. There are 45-minute group and self-guided tours, but even a quick peek at the glittering foyer is worthwhile.

Breathing life into the city's lacklustre southwestern zone are Sydney's blink-and-you'll-miss-it **Spanish Quarter** (Map pp102–3) along Liverpool and Kent Sts, and thriving **Chinatown** (Map pp102–3), a tight bundle of restaurants, shops and barbecue-duck-scented alleyways around Dixon St. Chinatown goes berserk during Chinese New Year (late January/early February), when dancing lions roam the lantern-covered streets and dragon-boat races take over Darling Harbour.

On the eastern edge of the city centre is the formal **Hyde Park** (Map pp102–3), which has a grand avenue of trees, delightful fountains and a giant public chessboard. Wander into the dignified **Anzac Memorial** (Map pp102-3; ☎ 02-9267 7668; www.anzacmemorial.nsw.gov.au; admission free; ☻ 9am-5pm), with an interior dome studded with one star for each of the 120,000 NSW citizens who served in WWI. The pines near the entrance grew from seeds gathered at Gallipoli. **St Mary's Cathedral** (Map pp102–3) overlooks the park from the east, while the 1878 **Great Synagogue** (Map pp102-3; ☎ 02-9267 2477; www.greatsynagogue.org.au; 187a Elizabeth St, Sydney; adult/child $5/3; ☻ tours noon Tue & Thu) stands to the west.

Macquarie Place & Around

Narrow lanes lead south from Circular Quay towards the city centre. At the corner of Loftus and Bridge Sts is **Macquarie Place** (Map pp102–3), a leafy public square proudly displaying a cannon and an anchor from the First Fleet flagship, HMS *Sirius*, and an 1818 obelisk (cleverly positioned to disguise a sewer vent) etched with road distances to various points in the nascent colony.

Inside the old Water Police Station (1858) nearby, the **Justice & Police Museum** (Map pp102-3; ☎ 02-9252 1144; www.hht.net.au; cnr Albert & Phillip Sts, Sydney; adult/child/family $8/4/17; ☻ 10am-5pm Sat & Sun, daily Jan) shines the spotlight on disreputable activities, with exhibits of confiscated weapons, 'most wanted' mug shots and gruesome forensic evidence form Sydney's most bloody crimes. Wheelchair access is to the ground floor only, but Braille and audio guides are available.

MUSEUM OF SYDNEY
Built on the site of Sydney's first (and infamously pungent) Government House (1788), this thoroughly engaging **museum** (Map pp102-3; ☎ 02-9251 5988; www.hht.net.au; cnr Bridge & Phillip Sts, Sydney; adult/child/family $10/5/20; ☻ 9.30am-5pm) brings the city's early history to life through whispers, arguments, gossip, artefacts and state-of-the-art installations. The sculpture in the forecourt symbolises the meeting of cultures that occurred when Cook and co first dropped anchor.

MACQUARIE STREET
A crop of early public buildings graces Macquarie St, defining the city's edge from Hyde Park to the Opera House. Many of these buildings were commissioned by Lachlan Macquarie, the first NSW governor to have a vision of Sydney beyond its convict origins. He enlisted convict architect Francis Greenway to help realise his plans.

Two Greenway gems front onto Queens Square at Hyde Park's northern end: built in 1819 **St James' Church** (Map pp102–3) is Sydney's oldest church; the **Hyde Park Barracks Museum** (Map pp102-3; ☎ 02-8239 2311; www.hht.net .au; adult/child/family $10/5/20; ☻ 9.30am-5pm), was also built in 1819. The barracks functioned as convict quarters for Anglo-Irish sinners (1819–48), an immigrant depot (1848–86) and government courts (1887–1979) before its current incarnation: a window into everyday convict life.

Nearby are the deep verandahs and formal colonnades of the twin 1816 buildings of the **Mint** (Map pp102-3; ☎ 02-8239 2288; www .hht.net.au; admission free; ☻ 9am-5pm Mon-Fri) and **Parliament House** (Map pp102-3; ☎ 02-9230 2111; www.parliament.nsw.gov.au; admission free; ☻ 9.30am-4.30pm Mon-Fri). They were originally wings of the infamous Rum Hospital, which was built by two Sydney merchants in 1816 in return for a monopoly on the rum trade. You can watch the elected representatives outdo each other when parliament sits, or take a guided tour of the two chambers (call for bookings and times). Wheelchair access is available by prior arrangement.

Next to Parliament House, the **State Library of NSW** (Map pp102-3; ☎ 02-9273 1414; www.sl.nsw .gov.au; ☻ 9am-8pm Mon-Thu, to 5pm Fri, 10am-5pm Sat & Sun) holds over five million tomes, the smallest being a tablet-sized Lord's Prayer, and hosts innovative exhibitions in its **galleries** (☻ 9am-5pm Mon-Fri, 11am-5pm Sat & Sun). Disabled access is excellent.

At the top of Bridge St, the **Sydney Conservatorium of Music** (see p141 for musical recital details) was the Greenway-designed stables and servants' quarters for Macquarie's planned Government House. Macquarie was usurped as governor before the house could be finished, partly because of the project's extravagance.

Built between 1837 and 1845, the regal **Government House** (Map pp102–3; ☎ 02-9931 5222; www.hht.net.au; admission free; ☒ 10am-3pm Fri-Sun, grounds to 4pm daily, 45min tours from 10.30am) was designed by British architect Edward Blore, who was also involved in the design for Buckingham Palace. Unless there's an official event happening, you can tour the fussy furnishings.

The **Domain** (Map pp102–3) is a pleasant grassy area east of Macquarie St that was set aside by Governor Phillip for public recreation. In front of the Art Gallery, the unfailingly eccentric **Speakers' Corner** (☒ noon-4pm Sun) doesn't draw crowds like it used to, but there is always someone eager to have their voice heard.

AUSTRALIAN MUSEUM
Come face to face with some of Australia's deadliest creatures, including funnel webs (spiders) and salties (estuarine crocodiles), at this natural history **museum** (Map pp102–3; ☎ 02-9320 6000; www.amonline.net.au; 6 College St, Sydney; adult/child/family $12/6/30, extra for special exhibits; ☒ 9.30am-5pm); fortunately they're all behind glass. There are also excellent Aboriginal exhibitions, self-guided tours and Indigenous performances on Sunday (noon and 2pm), plus good wheelchair access.

ART GALLERY OF NSW
This **gallery** (Map p106; ☎ 02-9225 1744; www.artgallery.nsw.gov.au; Art Gallery Rd, The Domain; admission free, varied costs for touring exhibitions; ☒ 10am-5pm Thu-Tue, to 9pm Wed, free guided tours 11am, 1pm & 2pm) plays a prominent and gregarious role in Sydney society. Highlights include outstanding permanent displays of 19th- and 20th-century Australian art, Aboriginal and Torres Strait Islander art, 15th- to 19th-century European and Asian art, and blockbuster international touring exhibitions. The headline-grabbing Archibald Prize exhibits here annually, with portraits of the famous and not-so-famous bringing out the art critic in everyone.

On Wednesday evenings Sydneysiders skip the pub for **art.afterhours** (☒ 5-9pm): talks, documentary screenings, concerts and, of course, art. Kids love **GalleryKids** (☒ 2-3pm Sun) programs where workshops, performances and guided tours with costumed actors feed their imaginations. There are also programs for the deaf and visually impaired. Wheelchair access is good.

ROYAL BOTANIC GARDENS
The **gardens** (RBG; Map pp102–3; ☎ 02-9231 8111; www.rbgsyd.nsw.gov.au; Mrs Macquaries Rd; admission free; ☒ 7am-sunset) were established in 1816 as the colony's vegetable patch and are now Sydney's favourite communal backyard. Signs encourage visitors to 'smell the roses, hug the trees, talk to the birds and picnic on the lawns'. Take a free **guided walk** (☒ 10.30am daily & 1pm Mon-Fri), departing from the **Gardens Shop**. A trackless train does a circuit if you're feeling weary.

Highlights include the rose garden, the ancient Wollemi Pine, the succulent garden, the glass pyramid at the **Tropical Centre** (adult/child $5.50/3.30; ☒ 10am-4pm) and a spooky, swooping bat colony. Management periodically tries to oust the bats (they destroy the vegetation), but they just keep hanging around. Actually, calling them bats is a misnomer – they're grey-headed flying foxes (*Pteropus policephalus*) – and they take to the skies in their hundreds come dusk when they fly southeast to feast on Centennial Park's fruit trees.

Most RBG paths are wheelchair accessible.

Darling Harbour
What was once industrial docklands is today a rambling, purpose-built waterfront tourist park on the city's western edge. Although slick – think fountains, sculptures and sailcloth – the rejuvenation has scrubbed away much of the area's charm and character (and greenery). That said, the snazzy cafes and bars of the **Cockle Bay Wharf** (Map pp102–3) and **King St Wharf** (Map pp102–3) precincts have injected some much-needed 'oomph' into the area.

A stroll across **Pyrmont Bridge** (Map pp102–3), the world's first electric swing bridge, leads you into Pyrmont, home of the overrated Harbourside Shopping Centre and the Sydney Fish Market (opposite). Nearby bigger fish play at the **Star City Casino** (Map p108; ☎ 02-9777 9000; www.starcity.com.au; 80 Pyrmont St, Pyrmont; ☒ 24hr).

Darling Harbour and Pyrmont are serviced by ferry, monorail, Metro Light Rail (MLR) and the Sydney Explorer bus. A dinky people-mover **train** (adult/child $5/4; ☒ 10am-6pm) connects the sights; the Sydney Visitor Centre (p109) is underneath the highway, next to the Imax cinema.

SYDNEY AQUARIUM
Kids and adults wander goggle-eyed through underwater glass tunnels at this ever-popular **aquarium** (Map pp102–3; ☎ 02-8251 7800;

DISCOUNT SYDNEY SIGHTSEEING

The Historic Houses Trust's **Ticket Through Time** (☎ 02-8239 2288; www.hht.net.au/visiting; adult/child/family $30/15/60) gets you into all 11 of the HHT's houses and museums in the Sydney area – including the Museum of Sydney, the Mint, the Justice & Police Museum and the Hyde Park Barracks Museum – and is valid for three months from the first visit.

The **See Sydney & Beyond Card** (☎ 1300 661 711; www.seesydneycard.com) offers admission to over 40 attractions, including sightseeing tours, harbour cruises, museums, historic buildings and wildlife parks. Prices for one-/two-/three-/seven-day cards are $75/135/165/225 for adults and $55/79/95/160 for children. The two-/three-/seven-day cards are also available with public transport included for $175/225/299 for adults and $99/125/199 for children. Cards are available online or at the Sydney Visitor Centres (p109).

www.sydneyaquarium.com.au; Aquarium Pier, Darling Harbour; adult/child/family $30/14/63; ☒ 9am-10pm, last admission 9pm), celebrating the rich and colourful diversity of Australian marine life. Don't miss the kaleidoscopic colours of the Great Barrier Reef exhibit, the platypuses and crocodiles at the Southern and Northern Rivers display, and Pig and Wuru, two orphaned – and very cute – dugongs that now call the aquarium home.

AUSTRALIAN NATIONAL MARITIME MUSEUM

Play out your naval battle fantasies at this thematic **museum** (Map pp102-3; ☎ 02-9298 3777; www.anmm.gov.au; 2 Murray St, Pyrmont; admission free, special exhibits adult/child/family from $10/6/20; ☒ 9.30am-5pm) that explores Australia's inextricable relationship with the sea – from Aboriginal canoes to surf culture and the Navy. There's good disabled access to the museum, but not to the boats moored out the front. Regular guided tours are available.

POWERHOUSE MUSEUM

This excellent and progressive **museum** (Map pp102-3; ☎ 02-9217 0111; www.powerhousemuseum.com; 500 Harris St, Ultimo; adult/child/family $10/5/25, extra for special exhibits; ☒ 10am-5pm) whirs away inside the former power station for Sydney's defunct tram network, and celebrates science, design, history, fashion, space, innovation and sustainability. The eclectic exhibitions cover everything from Japanese fashion to Australia in the '80s.

CHINESE GARDEN OF FRIENDSHIP

Built according to the balanced principles of yin and yang, these **gardens** (Map pp102-3; ☎ 02-9281 6863; www.darlingharbour.com; adult/child/family $6/3/15; ☒ 9.30am-5pm) are an oasis of tranquillity in the otherwise built-up Darling Harbour. Designed by architects from Guangzhou (Sydney's sister city) for Australia's 1988 bicentenary, the garden interweaves pavilions, waterfalls, lakes and paths.

SYDNEY FISH MARKET

This cavernous **market** (Map p108; ☎ 02-9004 1100; www.sydneyfishmarket.com.au; cnr Pyrmont Bridge Rd & Bank St, Pyrmont; ☒ 7am-4pm) is where Sydneysiders head to buy their Christmas lunch: in 2008 120,000 dozen oysters, 200 tonnes of snapper and 170 tonnes of prawns were purchased over the festive period. But this market is always busy – over 15 million kilograms of seafood are shipped through here annually. There are plenty of fishy restaurants, a deli, a wine centre, a sushi bar and an oyster bar. Arrive early to catch the noisy wholesale fish auctions or take a behind-the-scenes **auction tour** (adult/child $20/10; ☒ 6.50-8.30am Mon-Fri) – it's best to book in advance and you must wear closed-toe shoes. You can also sign yourself up for seafood cooking classes at the **Sydney Seafood School** (☎ 02-9004 1111; classes from $80). It's west of Darling Harbour on Blackwattle Bay; the MLR stops outside.

Kings Cross

Stylish and sleazy, decadent and depraved, colourful Kings Cross rides high above the CBD under the neon glare of the oversized **Coca-Cola sign** (Map p106), which is as much a Sydney icon as LA's Hollywood sign. It's an intense, densely populated domain that prompted notorious artist and writer Donald Friend to comment: 'In the Cross, everyone is wicked.'

Once home to grand estates and stylish apartments, the neighbourhood took a left turn in the 1930s when wine-soaked intellectuals, artists, musicians, pleasure-seekers and ne'er-do-wells claimed the streets for their own. The neighbourhood's reputation for vice was sealed during the Vietnam War, when American sailors flooded the Cross with a tide of bawdy debauchery.

Today the streets retain an air of seedy hedonism, but along with the strip joints and shabby drinking dens there are classy restaurants, cool bars and boutique hotels. Sometimes the razzle-dazzle has a sideshow appeal; sometimes walking up Darlinghurst Rd promotes pity. Either way, it's never boring.

The gracious tree-lined streets of neighbouring **Potts Point** (off Map p106) and **Elizabeth Bay** (Map p106) feature well-preserved Victorian, Edwardian and art deco houses and flats. Built between 1835 and 1839, the grand neoclassical **Elizabeth Bay House** (Map p106; ☎ 02-9356 3022; www .hht.net.au; 7 Onslow Ave, Elizabeth Bay; adult/child/family $8/4/17; ⏰ 9.30am-4pm Fri-Sun) was once the finest house in the colony and later the scene of wild bohemian parties.

Possibly the only word in the world containing eight 'O's, **Woolloomooloo** (Map p106), down **McElhone Stairs** (Map p106) from the Cross, was once a slum full of drunks, sailors and drunk sailors. Things are begrudgingly less pugilistic these days – the pubs are relaxed and **Woolloomooloo Wharf** (Map p106) contains some excellent restaurants. Nearby, the infamously lowbrow and exceedingly popular Harry's Café de Wheels (p132) dishes up pie floaters and more.

It's a 15-minute walk to the Cross from the city, or you could jump on a train. Buses 327, 324, 325-6 and 311 from the city also pass through here.

Inner East

The spirited backbone of the Inner East is **Oxford Street** (Map pp102–3), a long string of shops, cafes, bars and clubs that exudes a flamboyance largely attributable to Sydney's gay community. The Sydney Gay & Lesbian Mardi Gras (p124) gyrates through in late February or early March each year.

Oxford St runs all the way from Hyde Park to Centennial Park, continuing to Bondi Junction. Confusingly, street numbers recommence east of South Dowling St, the Darlinghurst–Paddington border. Bus 378 from Railway Sq and buses 333, 380 and 389 from Circular Quay run the length of Oxford St.

Wedged between Oxford and William Sts, the **Sydney Jewish Museum** (Map p106; ☎ 02-9360 7999; www.sydneyjewishmuseum.com.au; 148 Darlinghurst Rd, Darlinghurst; adult/child/family $10/6/22; ⏰ 10am-4pm Sun-Thu, to 2pm Fri, closed Jewish holidays) displays evocative, powerful exhibits on Australian Jewish history and the Holocaust.

South of Darlinghurst is **Surry Hills** (Map pp102–3), home to a raffish mishmash of style-conscious urbanites and a swag of great restaurants and bars. It was once the undisputed centre of Sydney's rag trade and print media, and many of its warehouses have been converted to slick apartments. Preserved as a temple to rock-and-roll artistry, the **Brett Whiteley Studio** (Map pp100-1; ☎ 02-9225 1881; www.brettwhiteley.org; 2 Raper St, Surry Hills; admission free; ⏰ 10am-4pm Sat & Sun) exhibits some of Whiteley's most raucous paintings. Get in early for weekend discussions, performances, readings and workshops. Surry Hills is a short walk east of Central Station or south from Oxford St. Catch buses 301, 302 or 303 from Circular Quay.

Next door to Surry Hills, gentrified **Paddington** (Map pp102–3), aka 'Paddo', is an elegant suburb of restored terrace houses on steep leafy streets. Paddington was built for aspiring Victorian artisans, but the lemming-like rush to the outer suburbs after WWII turned it into Australia's worst slum. Renewed passion for Victorian architecture (and the realisation that the outer suburbs were deathly dull) fuelled Paddington's 1960s resurgence. By the '90s, real estate was out of reach for all but the lucky and the loaded.

The best time to explore Paddington is on Saturday when the Paddington Market (p143) is pumping.

Victoria Barracks (Map pp102-3; ☎ 02-9339 3330; www.awm.gov.au; cnr Oxford St & Greens Rd, Paddington; museum adult/child $2/1; ⏰ 10am-1pm Thu, to 4pm Sun, Mar-Nov) is a tightly managed malarial vision from the peak of the British Empire. Thursday's tours (10am) of the Georgian buildings take in a flag-raising ceremony, a marching band (subject to availability) and the paraphernalia-packed war museum.

Just southeast of Paddington is Sydney's biggest park, the leafy 220-hectare **Centennial Park** (Map pp100–1), which has running, cycling, skating and horse-riding tracks, duck ponds, barbecue sites and sports pitches.

Near Moore Park, much of the former Sydney Showgrounds has been converted into the private **Fox Studios** (Map pp100–1) and the **Entertainment Quarter** (Map pp100–1; ☎ 02-8117 6700; www.entertainmentquarter.com.au; ☼ 10am–late), which is not nearly as entertaining as it promises. That said, there are cinemas, a bowling alley, bars and restaurants here, as well as Aussie Stadium and the Sydney Cricket Ground (SCG). **Tours** (☎ 1300 724 737; www.sydneycricket ground.com.au; adult/child/family $25/17/65; ☼ 10am, noon & 2pm Mon-Fri, 10am Sat) take you behind the scenes.

Eastern Suburbs

Handsome **Rushcutters Bay** (Map pp100–1) is a five-minute walk east of Kings Cross; its harbourside park is a great place to stretch your legs and a family-friendly spot for the New Year's Eve fireworks. The eastern suburbs extend east from here – a shimmering, conservative conglomeration of SUVs, mortgage madness and skinny soy decaf lattes. The harbour-hugging New South Head Rd passes through **Double Bay** (Map pp100–1) – otherwise known as 'Double Pay' – and pretty **Rose Bay** (Map pp100–1) before climbing east into the chichi suburb of **Vaucluse** (Map pp100–1).

Built in fits and starts between 1805 and the early 1860s, the semi-Gothic Australiana **Vaucluse House** (Map pp100–1; ☎ 02-9388 7922; www .hht.net.au; Wentworth Rd, Vaucluse; adult/child/family $8/4/17; ☼ 9.30am-4.30pm Fri-Sun) is Sydney's last remaining 19th-century harbourside estate. The mishmash of styles, incomplete reception rooms and corridors that lead nowhere reflect the social decline of the explorer and once revered statesman William Charles Wentworth, who lived here from 1827 to 1862 with his equally amoral wife. The Bondi Explorer bus (p122) stops outside.

At the entrance to the harbour is **Watsons Bay** (Map pp100–1), a snug community with restored fisherman's cottages, a palm-lined park and a couple of nautical churches. Nearby **Camp Cove** (Map pp100–1) is one of Sydney's best harbour beaches. **South Head** (Map pp100–1) has great views across the harbour entrance to North Head and Middle Head. **The Gap** (Map pp100–1) is an epic cliff-top lookout where sunrises, sunsets and suicide leaps occur with similar frequency.

Buses 324 and 325 from Circular Quay service the eastern suburbs via Kings Cross. Grab a seat on the left heading east to snare the best views.

Eastern & Southern Beaches

Bondi (Map p107) lords it over every other beach in the city, despite not being the best one for a swim, a surf or a place to park. Still, there are many reasons why this is Sydney's most popular beach, and the crashing waves, flashy cafes and beautiful people are just some of them.

The suburb itself has a unique atmosphere due to its mix of old Jewish and other European communities, dyed-in-the-wool Aussies, New Zealanders who never went home, working travellers and way too many wannabe models and actors.

The stunning 6km **Bondi to Coogee Coastal Walk** leads south from Bondi Beach along the cliff tops to Coogee via Tamarama, Bronte and Clovelly Beaches, interweaving panoramic views, swimming spots and foodie delights.

Most of Bondi's pubs, bars and restaurants are set back from the beach, located along Campbell Pde and Hall St. Nearby are Bondi's Sunday Markets (p143), plus some very faint Eora **Aboriginal rock engravings** (Map p107) north of the beach near the cliffs at the Bondi Golf Club – the name 'Bondi' derives from an Aboriginal word for the sound of the surf.

Catch bus 333, 380 or L94 from the city or bus 381 from Bondi Junction to get to the beach.

Inner West

West of the centre is the higgledy-piggledy peninsula suburb of **Balmain** (Map pp100–1). It was once a notoriously rough neighbourhood of dockyard workers, but has been transformed into an artsy, middle-class area of restored Victoriana flush with pubs, cafes and trendy shops. Don't miss the Saturday market (p143). Catch a ferry from Circular Quay or buses 432 from Railway Sq or 441/2 from the QVB.

Bohemian **Glebe** (Map p108) lies just southwest of the centre, boasting a large student population, a cafe-lined main street, a tranquil Buddhist temple and some excellent bookshops. Saturday's Glebe markets (p143) overrun Glebe Public School. Glebe is a smoggy 10-minute walk from Central Station along Broadway. Bus 433 from Millers Point runs via George St along Glebe Point Rd. The MLR also services Glebe.

NEW SOUTH WALES

SYDNEY'S BEST BEACHES

Sydneysiders swim before, after or instead of going to work. Most beaches are clean, easily accessible and patrolled by surf lifesavers. Many beaches are topless, a couple are nude – do as locals do!

- **Best for fish and chips:** Split in two by an unfeasibly picturesque rocky outcrop, Balmoral (Map pp100–1) is a popular North Sydney haunt for swimming, kayaking and windsurfing. There are also some fabulous fish and chip shops. Catch bus 246 from Wynyard, then bus 257 from Spit Junction.

- **Best for people watching:** Hit Bondi (Map p107) on a summer's day and it feels like the whole of Sydney has gathered to sunbathe, surf and scope out the talent. Catch bus 333 or 380 from the city, or bus 381 from Bondi Junction.

- **Best for families:** Norfolk Island pines and sandstone headlands hug the bowl-shaped park behind Bronte (Map p107), a small family-oriented beach that has a playground, rock pool and sandy cafes. Catch bus 378 from Railway Sq.

- **Best for snorkelling:** More like a giant ocean pool, the crystal clear waters of Clovelly (Map p107) is heaven for snorkellers. Keep an eye out for Bluey, the resident blue groper. Catch bus 339 from Central Station.

- **Best for star spotting:** Palm Beach (Map p148), aka 'Palmy', is a 2.3km strip of golden sand that's home to some of Sydney's most expensive reál estate, glamorous residents and the stickiest sand. Catch bus L90 from Wynyard Station.

- **Best for harbour swims:** In Nielsen Park, stunning Shark Beach (Map pp100–1) has shady grounds, picnic facilities and calm waters that are protected by a shark net during the summer months. Catch bus 325 from Circular Quay.

South of Sydney Uni is **Newtown** (Map p108), a melting pot of social and sexual subcultures, students and media types with a penchant for DIY. King St, its relentlessly urban main drag, is full of funky clothes stores, bookshops, ethnic eateries and cool cafes. Although fast becoming gentrified, Newtown retains an irrepressible dose of grunge. Take the train, or bus 422/3, 426 or 428 from Circular Quay to King St.

West of Glebe is predominantly Italian **Leichhardt** (Map pp100–1), which is increasingly popular with students and young families. Norton St is the place for pizza, pasta and slick Mediterranean style. Bus 413 from Wynyard and buses 436, L38 and 440 from Circular Quay service Leichhardt.

North Shore

On the northern side of the Harbour Bridge is **North Sydney** (Map pp102–3), a high-rise office centre with little to tempt the traveller. **McMahons Point** is a low-key, forgotten suburb below the western side of the bridge. There's a row of cheery alfresco cafes on Blues Point Rd, running down to Blues Point Reserve on Lavender Bay.

At the end of Kirribilli Point, just east of the bridge, are **Admiralty House** (Map pp102–3) and **Kirribilli House** (Map pp102–3), the Sydney residences of the Governor General and Prime Minister respectively.

On the eastern shore of Lavender Bay, the maniacal grin of the **Luna Park** (Map pp100–1; ☎ 02-9922 6644; www.lunaparksydney.com; 1 Olympic Pl, Milsons Point; admission free, multiride passes from $20; ☯ 10am-9pm Sun-Thu, to 11pm Fri & Sat Dec-Feb, 11am-4pm Mon, to 10pm Fri & Sat, 10am-6pm Sun Mar-Nov) clown is the gateway to all manner of nausea-inducing fairground rides.

East of here are the upmarket suburbs of **Neutral Bay**, **Cremorne** and **Mosman** (all Map pp100–1), with picturesque coves and harbourside parks. Ferries from Circular Quay service these suburbs. On the northern side of Mosman is impossibly pretty **Balmoral**, which faces Manly across Middle Harbour.

In a superb setting, **Taronga Zoo** (Map pp100–1; ☎ 02-9969 2777; www.zoo.nsw.gov.au; Bradleys Head Rd, Mosman; adult/child/family $39/19/99; ☯ 9am-5pm) has some 4000 critters (from seals, tigers and monkeys to koalas, echidnas and platypuses), all well cared for and in decent habitats, although none can compete with the harbour views from the giraffe enclosure. Twilight concerts take place in the zoo during February and March.

Zoo ferries depart Circular Quay's Wharf 2 half-hourly from 7.15am on weekdays and from 8.45am on Saturday and Sunday. The zoo is on a fairly steep slope, so if you arrive by ferry, take the **Sky Safari cable car** (included in admission) or bus 238 to the top entrance and work your way downhill. A **Zoo Pass** (adult/child/family $44/22/117), sold at Circular Quay and elsewhere, includes return ferry rides and zoo admission. The nightly **Roar & Snore** (☎ 02-9978 4791; adult/child from $216/167) is an overnight family experience with a night-time safari, buffet dinner and tents under the stars. Breakfast and behind-the-scenes tours arrive with the dawn.

Manly

Laid-back Manly may only be a 30-minute ferry ride from Sydney's CBD, but it feels like another world. This narrow peninsula near North Head boasts ocean and harbour beaches, excellent surfing and a distinct personality all of its own.

On the harbour side, the **Manly visitor centre** (Map p105; ☎ 02-9976 1430; www.manlyaustralia.com.au; Manly Wharf, Manly; ⏱ 9am-5pm Mon-Fri, 10am-4pm Sat & Sun), just outside the ferry wharf, has free pamphlets along with information on the Manly Scenic Walkway. There is also a range of cafes, pubs and restaurants here. West of the wharf is **Oceanworld** (Map p105; ☎ 02-8251 7877; www.oceanworld.com.au; W Esplanade, Manly; adult/child/family $19/10/46; ⏱ 10am-5.30pm), where you can get up close and alarmingly personal with giant stingrays, turtles, shoals of fish and Maia the shark in the underwater tunnels. Next door, the beachy **Manly Art Gallery & Museum** (Map p105; ☎ 02-9976 1420; www.manlyaustralia.com/manlyartgallery; W Esplanade, Manly; admission free; ⏱ 10am-5pm Tue-Sun) holds over 2000 historic photographs, including prints of the eyebrow-raising first daylight swim at Manly Beach in 1902.

Behind the gallery is the not-to-be-missed 10km Manly Scenic Walkway (see Walking Tour, p121), which has a 2km-long wheelchair-accessible path. Bring water and snacks as there are no shops along the way.

Manly's harbour is separated from the ocean by the **Corso**, a pedestrianised strip of surf shops, burger joints, juice bars and cafes that have not been entirely kind to the strip's heritage character. At the southern

end of the beach, a footpath follows the ocean shoreline around a small headland to tiny **Fairy Bower Beach** and lovely **Shelly Beach**, which is great for snorkelling.

North Head Scenic Dr provides stunning ocean, harbour and city views. Along this route you'll find the **Manly Quarantine Station** (Map pp100-1; ☎ 02-9977 5145; www.qstation.com.au), where disease-riddled migrants were isolated between 1832 and 1984. The once decaying station has been revamped and visitors can wander around part of the compound or jump on the bus that leaves the visitor car park every half hour from 8.30am to 10pm. There are also **day tours** (adult $35; ⏱ 2.30pm Sun) and spooky adults-only **ghost tours** (adult $44; ⏱ 8pm Wed & Thu, 9pm Sat).

To get to Manly, catch the ferry, bus E69 from Wynyard, or buses 169 or 151 from the QVB.

Northern Beaches

Extending north from Manly, Sydney's northern **beaches** form a continuous 30km stretch of sleepy 'burbs, craggy headlands and over 20 beaches, including **Freshwater, Curl Curl, Dee Why, Collaroy, Narrabeen** and **Warriewood** beaches (all Map p148). At the end of the line is well-heeled **Palm Beach**: *Home and Away* fans will definitely recognise the area. Of the more spectacular beaches, **Whale, Avalon** and **Bilgola** rank highly. Buses 169 and 136 run from Manly Wharf to Dee Why and Curl Curl respectively. Bus L90 runs from Wynyard station to Palm Beach.

ACTIVITIES
Canoeing & Kayaking

Contact the **New South Wales Canoeing Association** (☎ 02-8116 9727; www.nswcanoe.org.au) for information on canoeing.

Natural Wanders (☎ 02-9899 1001; www.kayaksydney.com; per person from $90; ⏱ 6.30-10am) has exhilarating morning harbour kayaking tours. Or you can hire a kayak – single or tandem – from **OzPaddle Rose Bay** (☎ 0416 239 543; www.ozpaddle.com.au; per hour from $20).

Cycling

The best spot to get some spoke action in this bike-unfriendly city is Centennial Park. **Bicycle NSW** (Map pp102-3; ☎ 02-9281 5400; www.bicyclensw.org.au; fl 5, 822 George St, Sydney) publishes *Cycling Around Sydney*, which details 30 classic city rides.

NEW SOUTH WALES

Many cycle-hire shops require a hefty deposit on a credit card.

Centennial Park Cycles (Map pp100-1; ☎ 02-9398 5027; www.cyclehire.com.au; Centennial Park; per hr/day from $15/50; ☺ 9am-5pm, last hire 4pm) Located 100m past intersection of Grand and Hamilton Drs.

Inner City Cycles (Map p108; ☎ 02-9660 6605; www .innercitycycles.com.au; 151 Glebe Point Rd, Glebe; per day/week $33/88; ☺ 9.30am-6pm Mon-Wed & Fri, to 7pm Thu, to 4pm Sat, 11am-3pm Sun)

Diving

Sydney's best shore dives are to be found at Gordons Bay north of Coogee (Map p107), Shark Point in Clovelly (Map p107) and Ship Rock in Cronulla (Map p148). Popular boat-dive sites include Wedding Cake Island off Coogee (Map p107), The Heads (Map pp100–1) and off Royal National Park (Map pp92–3).

Dive Centre Bondi (Map p107; ☎ 02-9369 3855; www.divebondi.com.au; 198 Bondi Rd, Bondi; ☺ 8.30am-6pm Mon-Fri, from 7.30am Sat & Sun) Four-day PADI course from $425; shore and boat dives.

Dive Centre Manly (Map p105; ☎ 02-9977 4355; www.divesydney.com.au; 10 Belgrave St, Manly; ☺ 8.30am-6pm Mon-Fri, from 7.30am Sat & Sun) Similar rates and offerings as its sister office in Bondi.

Golf

There are more than 80 golf courses in the metropolitan area, though many are members only. Book to play on public courses (especially at weekends).

Bondi Golf Club (Map p107; ☎ 02-9130 1981; www .bondigolf.com.au; 5 Military Rd, North Bondi; 18 holes $20; ☺ 7am-sunset Mon, Tue, Thu & Fri, from 10.30am Wed, 12.30pm-sunset Sat & Sun)

Moore Park Golf Course (Map pp100-1; ☎ 02-9663 1064; www.mooreparkgolf.com.au; cnr Anzac Pde & Cleveland St, Moore Park; 18 holes Mon-Fri $45, Sat & Sun $55; ☺ 6am-10pm)

Horse Riding

Centennial Stables (Map pp100-1; ☎ 02-9360 5650; www.centennialstables.com.au; Pavilion B, cnr Cook & Lang Rds, Centennial Park; per hr incl equipment $95; ☺ 9am-5pm) Conducts one-hour horse rides around leafy Centennial Park. Other stables at the centre also conduct rides; equine familiarity is not required.

Eastside Riding Academy (☎ 02-9360 7521; www .eastsideriding.com.au)

Moore Park Stables (☎ 02-9360 8747; www.moore parkstables.com.au)

In-Line Skating

Scoot and skate along the beach promenades at Bondi and Manly, and the paths around Centennial Park.

Manly Blades (Map p105; ☎ 02-9976 3833; www .manlyblades.com.au; 2/49 North Steyne, Manly; hire per hr from $20; ☺ 9am-6pm) Excellent blades and gear; it also has a shop in the Entertainment Quarter, Moore Park.

Rollerblading Sydney (Map pp100-1; ☎ 0411 872 022; www.rollerbladingsydney.com.au; Milsons Point Station; per 1hr/2hr $55/99; ☺ 7am-9pm Mon-Fri, 8am-6pm Sat & Sun) Lessons, quality skates and protective gear.

Sailing

Sydney has dozens of yacht clubs and sailing schools. Even if you have wobbly sea legs, an introductory lesson is a super way to see the harbour.

Eastsail Sailing School (Map pp100-1; ☎ 02-9327 1166; www.eastsail.com.au; D'Albora Marina, New Beach Rd, Rushcutters Bay; 3hr cruise per person from $109; ☺ 9am-6pm) A sociable outfit offering cruises and introductory courses from $500.

Sydney by Sail (Map pp102-3; ☎ 02-9280 1110; www .sydneybysail.com.au; Festival Pontoon, National Maritime Museum, Darling Harbour; 3hr tour $150, course $425; ☺ 9am-5pm) Daily harbour sailing tours and introductory sailing courses.

Scenic Flights

See Sydney's sights from up high with **Sydney Seaplanes** (Map pp100-1; ☎ 02-9388 1978, 1300 732 752; www.seaplanes.com.au; Lyne Park, Rose Bay; 15min scenic flights per person from $160; ☺ times vary according to flights & weather conditions). Flights to the Hunter Valley and Newcastle are also available, as are Fly & Dine packages to ritzy waterfront restaurants.

Surfing

On the eastern beaches hang ten at Bondi, Tamarama and Coogee, or Maroubra and Cronulla in the south. The North Shore is home to a dozen gnarly breaks between Manly and Palm Beach, including Curl Curl, Dee Why, Narrabeen, Mona Vale and Newport.

Aloha Surf (Map p105; ☎ 02-9977 3777; www.aloha .com.au; 44 Pittwater Rd, Manly; board hire half/full day $20/40; ☺ 9am-6pm) Longboards, shortboards, bodyboards.

Let's Go Surfing (Map p107; ☎ 02-9365 1800; www .letsgosurfing.com.au; 128 Ramsgate Ave, Bondi; 2hr lesson incl board & wetsuit adult/child from $79/40; ☺ 9am-6pm) Excellent small-group lessons. Board and wetsuit hire is $25 for two hours.

Manly Surf School (Map p105; ☎ 02-9977 6977; www.manlysurfschool.com; North Steyne Surf Club, Manly; lessons per hr incl board & wetsuit adult/child $55/45; ☽ 9am-6pm) Small-group surf lessons.

Swimming

There are over 100 public swimming pools in Sydney and many beaches have protected ocean swimming pools. The harbour beaches offer sheltered and shark-netted swimming, but nothing beats (or cures a hangover faster) than being pounded by Pacific Ocean waves. Always swim within the flagged lifeguard-patrolled areas and be wary of rips: they can be lethal.

Outdoor city pools:

Andrew 'Boy' Charlton Pool (Map pp102-3; ☎ 02-9358 6686; www.abcpool.org; 1c Mrs Macquaries Rd, The Domain; adult/child $6/4; ☽ 6am-8pm Sep-Apr) A 50m outdoor heated saltwater pool, one of Sydney's best.

Icebergs (Map p107; ☎ 02-9130 4804; 1 Notts Ave, Bondi Beach; adult/child $5/3; ☽ 6am-6.30pm Mon-Wed & Fri, from 6.30am Sat & Sun) Watch the sunrise over Bondi while swimming laps in this 50m ocean pool.

North Sydney Olympic Pool (Map pp100-1; ☎ 02-9955 2309; www.northsydney.nsw.gov.au; Alfred St South, Milsons Point; adult/child $6/3; ☽ 5.30am-9pm Mon-Fri, 7am-7pm Sat & Sun) Next to Luna Park, right on the harbour.

WALKING TOUR

One of Sydney's many beautiful trails, the Manly Scenic Walkway tracks west from Manly around North and Middle Harbour, past waterside mansions and harbour viewpoints and through rugged Sydney Harbour National Park (wear sturdy shoes) finishing at Spit Bridge. Take water and grab a snack or picnic before you leave; there are no shops en route.

To get there, catch the Manly ferry, bus 151 from the QVB, or bus 169 or E69 from Wynyard.

Check the surf at **Manly Beach** (**1**; p119), then cruise down the Corso to **Oceanworld** (**2**; p119) on West Esplanade. Scan the view through the

> **WALK FACTS**
>
> **Start** Manly Beach
> **Finish** Spit Bridge
> **Distance** 10km
> **Duration** three to four hours

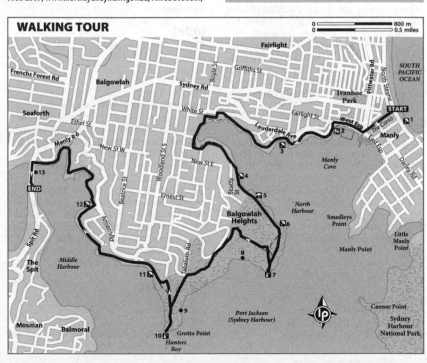

Heads from **Fairlight Beach (3)** and the yachts tugging on their moorings near **Forty Baskets Beach (4)**. Cackling kookaburras mock you as you enter the **Sydney Harbour National Park (5**; p109) and approach **Reef Beach (6)**, also known as Pirates Camp. The track becomes steep, sandy and rocky further into the park – look for wildflowers, fat goannas sunning themselves and spiders in bottlebrush trees. The views from **Dobroyd Head (7)** are frameworthy. Check out the deserted **1930s sea shanties (8)** at the base of Crater Cove cliff, and the **Aboriginal rock carvings (9)** on an unsigned ledge left of the track before the **Grotto Point Lighthouse (10)** turnoff. Quiet, calm **Castle Rock Beach (11)** is at the western end of the national park. Munch your picnic at **Clontarf Beach (12)**. From the southern end of the **Spit Bridge (13)**, head back to the city on bus 151, 169 or E69.

SYDNEY FOR CHILDREN

Sydney is heaven for ankle-biters. There are plenty of activities on offer, particularly during the school holidays (December/January, April, July and September). Check www.sydney forkids.com.au and the kids' section of *Time Out* magazine. The free *Sydney's Child* and *Kid Friendly* magazines also have listings.

Beach-wise there are plenty of options, but some of the best include Balmoral Beach, Shelly Beach and Dee Why on the north shore and Clovelly Beach, Bronte Beach and the North Bondi Children's Pool on the eastern beaches.

Otherwise, Sydney Aquarium (p114), Taronga Zoo (p118), Oceanworld (p119) and Luna Park (p118) are sure-fire crowd pleasers, as are the twisting, turning water slides at **Manly Waterworks** (Map p105; ☎ 02-9949 1088; www .manlywaterworks.com; cnr West Esplanade & Commonwealth Pde, Manly; per hr/day $15/20; ☉ 10am-5pm Sat & Sun).

The Sunday afternoon GalleryKids program at the Art Gallery of NSW (p114) includes dance, stories, magic, cartoons, Aboriginal performance, costumed tour guides and exhibition-specific events. The Sydney Opera House (p110) runs the Kids at the House program, featuring everything from lullabies, tutus and African rhythms to puppeteers, drama and dance. There's also the Babies' Proms Orchestra (orchestral nursery rhyme and picture-book accompaniment) and introductory ballet with Australian Ballet dancers.

There are several wildlife parks on Sydney's fringes that give kids the chance to get close to Australia's iconic wildlife, including the **Koala Park Sanctuary** (Map p148; ☎ 02-9484 3141; www.koalaparksanctuary.com.au; 84 Castle Hill Rd, West Pennant Hills; adult/child $19/9; ☉ 9am-5pm) and **Featherdale Wildlife Park** (Map p148; ☎ 02-9622 1644; www.featherdale.com.au; 217-229 Kildare Rd, Doonside; adult/child/family $20/10/58), where kids can pet the wallabies, feed the kangaroos and get within range of the reptiles.

Fans of the dinky-di Aussie classic *Snugglepot & Cuddlepie* can visit **Nutcote** (Map pp100-1; ☎ 02-9953 4453; www.maygibbs.com; 5 Wallaringa Ave, Neutral Bay; adult/child/family $8/3/17; ☉ 11am-3pm Wed-Sun), the former home of celebrated children's author May Gibbs set in a peaceful garden oasis perfect for picnics.

Jellibeanz Babysitting (☎ 1300 799 860; www .jellibeankidz.com) supplies babysitters and nannies across Sydney. Babysitters are $20 per hour; a $30 agency fee applies. It can also organise nannies. **Care For Kids** (www.care forkids.com.au) is an online database that will identify nannies and babysitters working in your area, all of whom are represented by agencies.

TOURS

There are countless tours available in Sydney. You can book most of them at the visitor centres (p109).

City Bus Tours

Bondi Explorer (☎ 13 15 00; www.sydneybuses.info; adult/child/family $39/19/97; ☉ 8.45am-4.15pm) Hop-on, hop-off 19-stop loop (two hours) from Circular Quay to Kings Cross, Double Bay, Rose Bay, Vaucluse, Watsons Bay, the Gap, Bondi Beach and Coogee, returning to the city along Oxford St. Buses depart every 30 minutes; buy your ticket on board or at STA offices.

Sydney Explorer (☎ 13 15 00; www.sydneybuses .info; adult/child/family $39/19/97; ☉ 8.40am-5.20pm) The red hop-on, hop-off explorer bus visits 27 of Sydney's best attractions starting from Circular Quay through Kings Cross, Chinatown, Darling Harbour, The Rocks and across the Harbour Bridge. Tickets include discounted entry to attractions. Buses depart every 20 minutes.

Cycling Tours

Bonza Bike Tours (Map pp102-3; ☎ 02-9247 8800; www.bonzabiketours.com; 30 Harrington St, The Rocks; adult/child from $89/69; ☉ 10.30am & 2.15pm) Various options for exploring Sydney on two wheels, including the three-to-four-hour 'Sydney Classic'.

ALL ABOARD

Get your sea legs ready and hop aboard one of the following:

- **Cockatoo Island** (Map pp100–1) Recently opened to the public, intriguing Cockatoo Island is the largest island in Sydney Harbour and was once an imperial prison, industrial school, reformatory and shipyard. Ferries depart from Circular Quay Wharf 5.

- **Palm Beach** (Map p148) Hop on the ferry at Palm Beach Jetty and wind your way along this ridiculously pretty route past The Basin, Mackerel Beach and the majestic shores of Ku-ring-gai Chase National Park.

- **Parramatta** (Map pp100–1) This relaxed one-hour journey from Circular Quay explores Sydney's backwaters via a sleek catamaran. Those with a sporting interest can hop off early and explore the Sydney Olympic Park (ferry tickets include a bus through the Olympic village).

- **Manly Ferry** (Map p105) The ferry to Manly is a compulsory Sydney activity – it's also the best way to soak up million-dollar views on a shoestring budget. If it's choppy the trip past the heads makes for a hair-raising (and stomach-churning) ride.

Sydney Bike Tours (Map pp102–3; ☎ 02-9252 5505; www.sydneybiketours.net.au; Shop 120, Clocktower Bldg, 25 Argyle St, The Rocks; 3-4hr tours per person from $49; ☽ 9am & 2pm daily, also 6pm Tue, Thu & Sun) Travellers rave about these guided bike tours; choose from three different tour options.

Harbour Cruises

Backpacker Boat Tours (Map pp100–1; ☎ 0404 026 678; www.backpackerboattours.com; Rose Bay Wharf; per person $100; ☽ 10am) Six-hour cruises stopping off for lunch at the Fish Market, dips in the ocean and a beer in Watson's Bay. Price includes lunch and pick up from most hostels.

Captain Cook Cruises (Map pp102–3; ☎ 02-9206 1111; www.captaincook.com.au; Jetty 6, Circular Quay; adult/child/family from $28/15/59; ☽ 8.30am-6pm) Range of harbour cruise options; also at Aquarium Wharf, Darling Harbour.

Matilda Cruises (Map pp102–3; ☎ 02-9264 7377; www.matilda.com.au; Pier 26, Aquarium Wharf, Darling Harbour; adult/child from $35/30; ☽ 9.30am-5.30pm) Hop-on, hop-off harbour explorer trips plus catamaran, yacht and ferry cruises. Cocktail dinner cruises also available.

Sydney Ferries (Map pp102–3; ☎ 02-9246 8363; www.sydneyferries.info/cruises.htm; Wharf 4, Circular Quay; adult/child $30/15; ☽ 1.30pm Mon-Sat) Ninety-minute harbour cruises that come with live commentary and a souvenir badge.

Tribal Warrior (Map pp102–3; ☎ 02-9699 3491; www.tribalwarrior.org; Eastern Pontoon, Circular Quay; adult/child $55/45; ☽ 12.45pm Tue-Sat) See Sydney through Aboriginal eyes; includes authentic cultural performances.

Walking Tours

Aboriginal Heritage Tour (Map pp102–3; ☎ 02-9231 8134; www.rbgsyd.nsw.gov.au; adult/child $25/13; ☽ 1hr tours 2pm Fri) Discover the Botanic Garden's rich Indigenous heritage and get to sample Australian bush foods on tours led by the garden's Aboriginal Education Officer.

Aboriginal Heritage – Walk The Rocks (Map pp102–3; ☎ 0403 686 433; adult/child $23/12) Walkabouts exploring Sydney's Aboriginal history. One hour tours depart from The Rocks Visitor Centre; check there for times.

Bounce Walking Tours (Map pp102–3; ☎ 1300 665 365; www.bouncewalkingtours.com.au; adult/concession from $25/20; ☽ 2-3hr tours daily, times vary according to tour) Fun guided walks departing from the Opera House. The Crimes & Passions Tour (Kings Cross) is especially popular.

BridgeClimb (Map pp102–3; ☎ 02-8274 7777; www.bridgeclimb.com; 5 Cumberland St, The Rocks; adult $179-295, child $109-195; ☽ 3½hr tours 7am-7pm) Choose between the original climb (up and over the top) and the Discovery Climb that walks you through the inner workings of the bridge.

Sydney Architecture Walks (Map pp102–3; ☎ 02-8239 2211; www.sydneyarchitecture.org; adult/concession $25/20; ☽ 2hr walks) Four themed walks guided by young archi-buffs. Tours depart from the Museum of Sydney.

Other Tours

Maureen Fry (☎ 02-9660 7157; www.ozemail.com.au/~mpfry; 2hr tours for 10 people $200) The omniscient Maureen runs introductory tours to Sydney, from The Rocks to Macquarie St to Paddington. Mainly for groups; individuals by arrangement.

Urban Walkabout Tours (☎ 1300 660 624; www.urbanwalkabouttours.com; 2-3hr tours per person from $75) Uncover Sydney's sartorial secrets with these three fashion-forward tours.

NEW SOUTH WALES

FESTIVALS & EVENTS

Sydney's social calendar is packed with festivals and special goings-on year-round. Visitor information centres will be able to advise you about what's on or check the listings in *Time Out* magazine.

January

Australia Day (www.australiaday.gov.au) Australia celebrates the green and gold on 26 January with regattas, barbecues and fireworks.

Flickerfest (www.flickerfest.com.au) Open-air international short-film festival at Bondi Pavilion.

Sydney Festival (www.sydneyfestival.org.au) This calendar highlight floods the city streets and parks with art, including free outdoor concerts in the Domain.

February

Chinese New Year (www.cityofsydney.nsw.gov.au/cny) Chinatowns hosts colourful parades and performances in late January or early February.

Sydney Gay & Lesbian Mardi Gras (www.mardigras.org.au) Late February or early March. The highlight of this world-famous festival is the flamboyant Oxford St parade.

Tropfest (www.tropfest.com) The world's largest short-film festival judged by international superstars such as Geoffrey Rush and Baz Luhrmann.

March & April

Australian Fashion Week (www.rafw.org.au) Sydney struts her stuff at Circular Quay in late April.

Royal Easter Show (www.eastershow.com.au) Twelve-day agricultural show and funfair at Homebush Bay.

May

Sydney Writers' Festival (www.swf.org.au) Celebrates the literary in Sydney with guest authors, talks and forums.

June

Sydney Biennale (www.biennaleofsydney.com.au) Epic international art festival held in even-numbered years at venues and locations across the city.

Sydney Film Festival (www.sydneyfilmfestival.org) A 14-day orgy of cinema held at the State Theatre and other cinemas across town.

July

Yulefest (www.katoomba-nsw.com/yulefest.html) The Blue Mountains celebrates Christmas in July.

August

City to Surf Run (http://city2surf.sunherald.com.au) This 14km-long fun run takes place on the second Sunday in August and attracts a mighty 40,000 nutcases who run from Hyde Park to Bondi Beach.

September

Rugby League Grand Final (www.nrl.com) The two best teams left standing in the National Rugby League (NRL) meet to decide who's best.

October

Good Food Month (http://gfm.smh.com.au) Yummy month-long celebration of food and wine with street festivals, cooking classes and farmers markets.

Manly Jazz Festival (www.manly.nsw.gov.au/manly jazz) Labour Day long weekend. The jazz is mostly free.

November

Sculpture by the Sea (www.sculpturebythesea.com) In mid-November the Bondi to Coogee coastal walk is transformed into an outdoor sculpture gallery.

December

Boxing Day On 26 December boats crowd Sydney Harbour to farewell the yachts competing in the gruelling Sydney to Hobart Yacht Race (http://rolexsydneyhobart.com).

New Year's Eve The Rocks, Kings Cross and Bondi Beach heave with alcohol-fuelled celebrations on 31 December. The Harbour Bridge goes off with a bang.

SLEEPING

Sydney has beds to suit everyone, from backpacker hotels and boutique B&Bs to unassuming motels, Aussie pubs and high-end harbour-view hotels. The city gets busy between November and February when you can expect prices to jump by as much as 40% from the normal rates quoted here. Conversely, bargains can be found during the slower winter months when the southerlies roll into town. Booking through an accommodation agency such as Tourism New South Wales (p109) can sometimes land you a discount.

Sydney's neighbourhoods are very distinct so it's worth reading up on areas before you unpack your bag. Party people should head for Kings Cross, Darlinghurst, Paddington, Bondi or the hostels around Central Station. Shoppers and sightseers should book in at The Rocks or the CBD, while those looking for something quieter would do well to try Glebe, Potts Point, Surry Hills or Manly.

In this section, a budget room is classified as up to $60/110 per night for a single/double. Midrange doubles cost between $111 and $200; top-end doubles start at $201 a night. Serviced apartments usually sleep more than two people – good value for groups and families.

Budget

CENTRAL SYDNEY & CHINATOWN

Westend Backpackers (Map pp102-3; ☎ 02-9211 4588, 1800 013 186; www.legendhasitwestend.com.au; 412 Pitt St, Sydney; dm/d with bathroom from $24/82; 🖳) This colossal hostel sleeps 350 backpackers over 13 floors in two-, four-, and eight-bed dorms. There's also the insanely popular 28-bed 'Church' – fortunately it's well ventilated.

Harbour City Backpackers (Map pp102-3; ☎ 02-9380 2922; www.harbourcitybackpackers.com.au; 50 Sir John Young Cres, Woolloomooloo; dm $24-28, d & tw from $75; 🖳) Travellers either love this cavernous Woolloomooloo hostel or say it's too big, but whatever your size preference there's no denying the warm welcome and squeaky-clean facilities.

Base Backpackers (Map pp102-3; ☎ 02-9267 7718; www.stayatbase.com; 477 Kent St, Sydney; dm $26-34, s & d $90-120; 🖂 🖳) The flashy Base chain maintains its high standards in this slick city hostel. The girls-only 'sanctuary' (complete with complimentary Aveda kits) is a winner, but even if you pick the mixed dorms you won't be slumming it.

Wake Up! (Map pp102-3; ☎ 02-9288 7888; www.wakeup.com.au; 509 Pitt St, Sydney; dm from $28, d & tw from $98; 🖂 🖳) A perennial favourite with backpackers is this mammoth hostel housed within a converted 1900s department store. Convivial, colourful and with the best backpacker bar in town, visitors inevitably find themselves staying far longer than they had originally planned.

Railway Square YHA (Map pp102-3; ☎ 02-9281 9666; www.yha.com.au; 8-10 Lee St, Haymarket; dm $31-42, d $88-111; 🖂 🖳 🐾) A historic 1904 train shed has been converted into this friendly hostel. Rooms are simple and bright, but the best are those hidden within old 'red rattler' train carriages on the former Platform Zero.

Chamberlain Hotel (Map pp102-3; ☎ 02-9288 0888; www.chamberlainhotel.com.au; 428 Pitt St, Haymarket; dm/d $35/100) The once dingy 'Dingo' is now a snazzy drinking den with accommodation to match. Opt for the doubles, which bizarrely can sleep three and come with fridge and TV.

Sydney Central YHA (Map pp102-3; ☎ 02-9218 9000; www.yha.com.au; 11 Rawson Pl, Haymarket; dm from $36, d & tw from $102; 🅿 🖂 🖳 🐾) Sydney's biggest hostel is also one of the city's most popular. But it's not the bright rooms and excellent kitchen that draw the crowds (although these certainly help) – it's the fabulous rooftop pool that's perfect for making faces at the office workers in the tower across the street.

Sydney Harbour YHA (Map pp102-3; ☎ 02-9261 1111; www.sydneyharbouryha.com.au; 110 Cumberland St, The Rocks; dm/d with bathroom from $42/139; 🖂 🖳) Due to open in November 2009, this hostel in the heart of The Rocks promises to be one of Sydney's best. Built to 'float' above the 'Dig Site', where much of the early colony's history has been discovered, the eco-oriented hostel boasts excellent rooms with Opera House and harbour views and what looks like being the best roof terrace in town.

KINGS CROSS

Pink House (Map p106; ☎ 02-9358 1689, 1800 806 385; www.pinkhouse.com.au; 6-8 Barncleuth Sq, Kings Cross; dm/d incl breakfast from $24/75; 🖳) Travellers love the Pink House (yep, it's a pink house) with its laid-back hippy vibe more akin to student digs than a Kings Cross hostel. It has welcoming communal areas, generous dorm rooms and three leafy patios perfect for dealing with the effects of the night before.

Sydney Central Backpackers (Map p106; ☎ 02-9358 6600; www.sydneybackpackers.com.au; 16 Orwell St, Kings Cross; dm/d $27/70) The ramshackle, boardinghouse feel only adds to the holiday vibe of the Sydney Central. Brightly painted walls accompany the retro communal areas and while the dorm rooms are tight (think twice before packing that extra pair of shoes), they're perfectly fine for a short stay.

Original Backpackers (Map p106; ☎ 02-9356 3232, 1800 807 130; www.originalbackpackers.com.au; 160-162 Victoria St, Kings Cross; dm/s/d $30/70/80; 🖳) This rambling old-school hostel has been housing travellers for over 25 years and remains a firm backpacker favourite. There are 176 beds spread across two character-laden Victorian houses, and some rooms even have private balconies.

Jolly Swagman Backpackers (Map p106; ☎ 02-9358 6400, 1800 805 870; www.jollyswagman.com.au; 27 Orwell St, Kings Cross; dm/d incl breakfast $30/80; 🖳) The guests at this multicoloured hostel tend to be as lively as the psychedelic murals (wallflowers look elsewhere). There's an endless array of fun and games on the menu, including the infamous Beer and Pizza Tuesday.

Eva's Backpackers (Map p106; ☎ 02-9358 2185, 1800 802 517; www.evasbackpackers.com.au; 6-8 Orwell St, Kings Cross; dm/d incl breakfast $30/84; 🖳) Super-slick Eva caters to the flashpacker crowd. There are no 24-hour parties here, just immaculate bedrooms, tip-top bathrooms and a cosy common room with fireplace. There's also a fabulous rooftop terrace with photo-worthy city views.

O'Malley's Hotel (Map p106; ☎ 02-9357 2211; www
.omalleyshotel.com.au; 228 William St, Kings Cross; s/d/tr incl
breakfast $79/79/99) This jovial Irish pub has tra-
ditionally decorated, well-furnished rooms
upstairs that are surprisingly quiet, given the
William St location and nightly twiddle-dee-
dee live music downstairs. The harbour view
suite (room 319) is a winner.

Royal Sovereign Hotel (Map p106; ☎ 02-9331 3672;
306 Liverpool St, Darlinghurst; d $99) Positioned directly
above one of Sydney's favourite pubs (BYO
earplugs), the nine rooms won't win any design awards, but the once-hip contemporary
colour palate is pleasant enough. The communal bathrooms are immaculate.

BONDI

Bondi Backpackers (Map p107; ☎ 02-9130 4660;
www.bondibackpackers.com.au; 110 Campbell Pde, Bondi;
dm/d/tr incl breakfast $25/55/81; 🖳) If you can nab
a room at the front of the building then
you're in for a treat, as this is the only
hostel positioned smack bang opposite the
beach. Otherwise the rooms are a little down
at heel, but ideally located for maximising
sunbaking time.

Lamrock Lodge (Map p107; ☎ 02-9130 5063, 1800
625 063; www.lamrocklodge.com; 19 Lamrock Ave, Bondi; dm/
d from $26/66; 🖳) On a quiet residential street,
the mazelike Lamrock offers well-equipped
rooms not far from the beach. There aren't
as many bathrooms as you might expect (or
need), but they are squeaky clean.

Bondi Beachouse YHA (Map p107; ☎ 02-9365 2088;
www.bondibeachouse.com.au; 63 Fletcher St, Bondi; dm/d
from $28/70; Ⓟ 🖳) The ever-excellent YHA
outdoes itself with a fabulous rooftop terrace
that comes complete with spa. The staff are
great, there's free snorkelling and surfboards,
and you're only a hop, skip and splash from
the surf.

Hotel Bondi (Map p107; ☎ 02-9130 3271; www
.hotelbondi.com.au; 178 Campbell Pde, Bondi; s/d/tr from
$50/105/115; Ⓟ 🞐) Rooms in the 'Pink Palace'
might be stuck in a 1980s time warp (think
pink wallpaper and artwork in bold, primary
colours), but if you wangle a room with a
beach view then you'll be laughing. The pub
downstairs is one of the loudest in Bondi,
which may or may not be a good thing.

Beach Road Hotel (Map p107; ☎ 02-9130 7247; www.
beachrdhotel.com.au; 71 Beach Rd, Bondi; s/d with bathroom
$70/85; 🞐) Ideally placed for two of Bondi's
favourite activities – beach and beer –
this cheerful hotel forms part of a huge,

lively pub. Rooms are clean and bright with
the odd splash of maritime-inspired decor.

COOGEE

Wizard of Oz Backpackers (Map p107; ☎ 02-9315 7876;
www.wizardofoz.com.au; 172 Coogee Bay Rd, Coogee; dm
$25-45; 🖳) There's no place like home but
you'd be hard pressed to find a better budget
option while in Coogee. Clean, secure and
just moments from the sand, this place is
quiet by day (everyone's at the beach), but
the large communal areas liven up at night.

Grand Pacific (Map p107; ☎ 02-9665 6301; fax 02-
9665 6203; 136a Beach S, Coogee; s/d/tr from $45/65/85)
Peeling paint, mismatched curtains, retro
carpet and creaking stairs make this the
perfect place for shooting a horror movie.
Grand it most certainly ain't, but it's definitely quirky – and wait until you meet the
long-stay residents.

Coogee Beachside Accommodation (Map p107;
☎ 02-9315 8511; www.sydneybeachside.com.au; 178
Coogee Bay Rd, Coogee; d & tw $50-120) Run by the
same folk that look after the Wizard of Oz,
this two-storey beach house has been converted into homely budget accommodation.
Rooms are well proportioned, the bathrooms
sparkle and the shaded garden is ideal for a
post-surf and -sun beer.

GLEBE & NEWTOWN

Glebe Village (Map p108; ☎ 02-9660 8133, 1800 801 983;
www.glebevillage.com; 256 Glebe Point Rd, Glebe; dm/s/d
incl breakfast from $24/65/80; 🖳) Kick back at this
laid-back hostel spread across four character-
rich Victorian terraced houses. The recently
renovated rooms are all polished floorboards,
exposed brickwork and quirky furnishings,
and the tree-covered courtyard was made for
whiling away sunny afternoons.

Alishan International Guest House (Map p108;
☎ 02-9566 4048; www.alishan.com.au; 100 Glebe Point
Rd, Glebe; dm $25, s/d/f from $60/80/154; Ⓟ 🖳) The
recently refurbished rooms and central Glebe
location make this friendly international guest
house a good deal. There's a huge kitchen,
barbecue area and decent lounge.

Glebe Point YHA (Map p108; ☎ 02-9692 8418; www
.yha.com.au; 262-264 Glebe Point Rd, Glebe; dm $26-34, d $72-
80; 🖳) It's unlikely to win any design awards,
but this boxy hostel does at least guarantee
clean rooms and shared bathrooms, YHA-
style. The staff are friendly, there's a rooftop
terrace and the atmosphere's perfect for those
looking for a more chilled hostel option.

Billabong Gardens (Map p108; ☎ 02-9550 3236, 1800 806 419; www.billabonggardens.com.au; 5-11 Egan St, Newtown; dm/s/d/tr/f from $27/50/70/90/110; **P ⬜ ☀**) This three-part hostel (one-third motel, two-thirds Victorian terrace) is a bit of a mish-mash, but the huge variety of spotless rooms makes this a popular choice for musos, media types and wandering urbanites. Party people should head elsewhere.

MANLY
Manly Backpackers (Map p105; ☎ 02-9977 3411, 1800 662 500; www.manlybackpackers.com.au; 24-28 Raglan St, Manly; dm/d from $20/55; **P ⬜**) It's fun with a capital 'F' at Manly's most reliable budget option, which is housed within a converted ambulance station. The best rooms open onto balconies where the party contin-ues long after the boozy evening activities have officially finished. Take advantage of the good weekly rates; you *will* stay longer than planned.

Manly Beach House (Map p105; ☎ 02-9977 7050; www.manlybeachhouse.com.au; 179 Pittwater Rd, Manly; s/d/tr $50/60/85; **P ⬜**) A hit with travellers, this homely guest house is just minutes from the beach. Some of the nine bedrooms look weary, but your hosts are some of the friendliest in town. Good long-stay deals in winter.

Manly Serviced Apartments (Map p105; ☎ 02-9977 3411; www.manlyservicedapartments.com.au; 29-33 Pittwater Rd, Manly; apt from $99; **P**) Run by the folks at Manly Backpackers, these self-contained studio apartments are the perfect option for those looking for peace and quiet: they're sim-ple, clean and secure.

NORTH SHORE
Collaroy Beachouse YHA (Map p148; ☎ 02-9981 1177; www.sydneybeachouse.com.au; 4 Collaroy St, Collaroy; dm/d from $26/70; **P ⬜ ☀**) If you're bombing around the northern beaches, this breezy hos-tel will make you feel at home. There are free surfboards, bikes and snorkelling gear if the Pacific is calling your name, or you can hang out by the rooftop pool.

Glenferrie Lodge (Map pp102-3; ☎ 02-9955 1685, 1800 121 011; www.glenferrielodge.com; 12a Carabella St, Kirribilli; dm/s/d/f incl breakfast from $45/69/129/229; **⬜**) Ignore the ridiculous sculpture that stands outside this 1880s house and focus instead on the generous rooms, spotless shared bathrooms and excellent location – close to Milsons Point Station and Kirribilli ferry pier.

Midrange
CITY CENTRE, THE ROCKS & CIRCULAR QUAY
Lord Nelson Brewery Hotel (Map pp102-3; ☎ 02-9251 4044; www.lordnelson.com.au; 19 Kent St, The Rocks; d with/without bathroom $190/130; **☒**) Built in 1841, this boutique sandstone hotel claims to be the oldest in Sydney. It's been beautifully reno-vated and each bedroom showcases a slice of history, with either the original stone wall or dormer window on display.

Australian Hotel (Map pp102-3; ☎ 02-9247 2229; www.australianheritagehotel.com; 100 Cumberland St, The Rocks; d incl breakfast $135) Say goodbye to contemporary blah design and hello to Aussie charm at this hotel in the heart of The Rocks. The nine cosy rooms (shared bathrooms) feature antique fur-niture and there's a breezy living room, too.

B&B Sydney Harbour (Map pp102-3; ☎ 02-9247 1130; www.bedandbreakfastsydney.com; 140-142 Cumberland St, The Rocks; s/d incl breakfast from $140/155; **P ☒**) Occupying a lovely corner in The Rocks is this gorgeous guest house that dates back to the late 1800s. The nine bedrooms are named after famous Australians and are charming without being twee. Breakfasts are served in the leafy courtyard garden.

Russell (Map pp102-3; ☎ 02-9241 3543; www.therussell.com.au; 143a George St, The Rocks; d incl breakfast from $150, with bathroom $235; **☒**) We love a hotel with a story and the Russell has one of the best in town – room 8 is reportedly haunted by a 19th-century sea captain! The other rooms might not receive paranormal visitors, but don't let that deter you: this is an excellent hotel in a brilliant location.

Vibe Hotel (Map pp102-3; ☎ 02-8272 3300; www.vibehotels.com.au; 111 Goulburn St, Sydney; d from $165; **P ☒ ⬜ ☀**) In a city where hushed tones and minimalist decor are the norm, Vibe stands out (literally) thanks to its neon-pink sofas, lime-green armchairs and bold, stripy bed linen. The 'Vibe Out' space (complete with lava lamp) is positively Austin Powers. Good weekend rates.

CHINATOWN & DARLING HARBOUR AREA
Pensione Hotel (Map pp102-3; ☎ 02-9265 8888; www.pensione.com.au; 631-635 George St, Haymarket; s/d/t/f $99/115/140/170; **⬜**) Run by the group that owns ubertrendy Kirketon (p129), this is budget boutique chic. Housed within an elegantly re-worked post office, the rooms are small (some are *very* small) but comfortable. Aim for a rear room – George St traffic grumbles at night.

Capitol Square Hotel (Map pp102-3; ☎ 02-9211 8633; www.rydges.com/capitolsquare; cnr George & Campbell Sts, Haymarket; d from $105; P ⊠ 🖵) The colour scheme may be unnervingly similar to a certain Swedish super store, but don't let that put you off. Rooms are tidy and bright and the deluxe rooms come with balconies. Wheelchair access is available; frequent internet deals.

Aaron's Hotel (Map pp102-3; ☎ 02-9281 5555; www.aaronshotel.com.au; 37 Ultimo Rd, Haymarket; s/d from $115/135; ⊠ 🖵) Deceptively large is this renovated 19th-century building that features spacious, clean and light-filled rooms. It's a hit with backpackers, families and groups, particularly the courtyard rooms that look and feel positively penthouse-esque.

Metro Hotel Sydney Central (Map pp102-3; ☎ 02-9281 6999; www.metrohospitalitygroup.com; 431-439 Pitt St, Haymarket; d from $135; P ⊠ 🖵 🛋) Centrally located, the courteous Metro has newly refurbished, modern deluxe rooms and Brett Whiteley prints along the corridors. The open-air rooftop pool should clinch the deal.

Vulcan Hotel (Map pp102-3; ☎ 02-9211 3283; www.vulcanhotel.com.au; 500 Wattle St, Ultimo; d from $139; P ⊠) If you like your design contemporary then the Vulcan is sure to please. An old pub and a row of terraced houses have been woven together to form a grey-and-white boutique bolt-hole that channels a cool vibe minus any pretensions.

KINGS CROSS & AROUND
Maisonette Hotel (Map p106; ☎ 02-9357 3878; www.maisonettehotel.com; 31 Challis Ave, Potts Point; s/d/tr/f incl breakfast from $65/120/150/165) You get bang for your buck at the Maisonette, a cheery hotel in the heart of Potts Point. Sure, it could do with a lick of paint and the carpet's a little frayed, but the spacious rooms are welcoming and the location rocks.

Hotel 59 (Map p106; ☎ 02-9360 5900; www.hotel59.com.au; 59 Bayswater Rd, Kings Cross; s/d/f incl breakfast $88/110/132; ⊠) Without doubt one of the friendliest places in town is this lovely family-run hotel. The nine rooms may hark back to a time when Wham! and crimped hair were in vogue, but they are spotless and oddly charming. The central location only adds to the appeal.

Victoria Court Hotel (Map p106; ☎ 02-9357 3200; www.victoriacourt.com.au; 122 Victoria St, Potts Point; d incl breakfast $99-330; P ⊠) Decorated to within an inch of its life, this welcoming guest house fills a pair of three-storey 1881 brick terrace houses. The 25 rooms have private bathrooms, TV and

plenty of flowery soft furnishings. The deluxe rooms come with a leafy private terrace.

Springfield Lodge (Map p106; ☎ 02-8307 4000; www.springfieldlodge.com.au; 9 Springfield Av, Potts Point; s/d/f $105/120/170) This double-fronted 1930s house hides a great midrange surprise; extensively renovated in 2007, the compact but tidy rooms still look brand new. The rooms towards the rear of the building are larger and quieter.

Quest Potts Point (Map p106; ☎ 02-8988 6999; www.questpottspoint.com.au; 15 Springfield Ave, Potts Point; d from $135; P ⊠ 🖵 🛋) Housed with an attractive art deco building are 68 individually designed serviced apartments styled in earthy hues, bold patterns and dramatic prints. The executive suites have stunning harbour-view terraces, but there's also a cheaper rooftop option.

Mariners Court (Map p106; ☎ 02-9358 3888; www.marinerscourt.com.au; 44-50 McElhone St, Woolloomooloo; d/tr/f incl breakfast $154/174/198; P 🖵) Shipshape rooms and a stellar location around the corner from celeb hangout Woolloomooloo Wharf make this hidden gem a winner. There are lots of other added bonuses, too: the espresso machine at breakfast and the harbour glimpses from the 3rd-floor terrace.

Simpsons of Potts Point (Map p106; ☎ 02-9356 2199; www.simpsonshotel.com; 8 Challis Ave, Potts Point; d incl breakfast $175-330; P ⊠ 🖵) This handsome building had been carved up into apartments until it was painstakingly restored in the late 1980s. Today the heritage-listed building offers 14 luxurious rooms with fireplaces, balconies and antique prints. Enjoy complimentary port in the elegant lounge and delicious breakfasts in the sunny conservatory.

DARLINGHURST & SURRY HILLS
Chelsea (Map p106; ☎ 02-9380 5994; www.chelsea.citysearch.com.au; 49 Womerah Ave, Darlinghurst; s/d from $94/143; 🖵) The charming Chelsea guest house occupies adjoining Victorian terrace houses down a quiet, leafy street in Darlinghurst. There are 13 rooms styled in either French provincial or contemporary design; our favourite is room 13 for its private courtyard. Breakfast is served on the sun-drenched terrace.

City Crown Motel (Map pp102-3; ☎ 02-9331 2433; www.citycrownmotel.com.au; 289 Crown St, Surry Hills; d from $115; P ⊠ 🖵) This friendly family-run motel is regularly booked solid, which is hardly surprising given its fabulous Surry Hills location. Rooms are simple but welcoming and the bathrooms have recently been replaced. Prices double during Mardi Gras.

Hotel Altamont (Map p106; ☎ 02-9360 6000; www
.altamont.com.au; 207 Darlinghurst Rd, Darlinghurst; d from
$129; P 🅇 💻) Party like a rock star at the
Altamont, once the venue of choice for the
likes of the Rolling Stones and Madonna –
albeit before it was a hotel. The popular Loft
Suite was once the VIP Room for the Cauldron
Nightclub, accessible only via a hidden stairway.
Doubles are swish and expensive-looking.

Kirketon (Map p106; ☎ 02-9332 2011; www.kirke
ton.com.au; 229 Darlinghurst Rd, Darlinghurst; d from $155;
P 🅇 💻) This modernist boutique hotel ticks
all the right design boxes: minimalist interiors,
cool local artwork and high-end furnishings.
The standard rooms are small but the location
in the heart of Darlinghurst means you won't
spend much time indoors.

PADDINGTON & WOOLLAHRA

Hughenden (Map pp100-1; ☎ 02-9363 4863; www.hugh
endenhotel.com.au; 14 Queen St, Woollahra; s/d incl breakfast
from $148/188; P 🅇 💻) This quirky Italianate
guest house features individually designed
rooms with antique bric-a-brac flourishes;
some have balconies. Paddington is just a
stone's throw away, but there's Sunday high
tea, poetry readings and Sir Victor the nocturnal pianist to keep you amused at home.

Sullivans Hotel (Map pp102-3; ☎ 02-9361 0211;
www.sullivans.com.au; 21 Oxford St, Paddington; d/tr/f from
$165/180/180; P 🅇 💻 🅢) This well-managed
hotel in 'Paddinghurst' checks in more nationalities than the UN. There are 64 tidy rooms,
an army of friendly staff and a pretty central
courtyard complete with solar-heated swimming pool (perfect for cooling off after a day's
shopping on Oxford St).

EASTERN SUBURBS

Savoy Hotel (Map pp100-1; ☎ 02-9326 1411; www
.savoyhotel.com.au; 41-45 Knox St, Double Bay; d $125-155,
f $195-260; P 🅇) Sitting pretty among the ge-
nerically good-looking in Double Bay's coffee strip, the Savoy's rooms offer unexpected
amounts of individual character. Atrium-view
rooms are the cheapest; strive for an executive balcony room or a suite looking towards
the harbour.

BONDI

Bondi Beach House (Map p107; ☎ 0417 336 444; www
.bondibeachhouse.com.au; 28 Sir Thomas Mitchell Rd, Bondi;
s/d from $95/140) Without doubt one of the
best-kept secrets in Bondi is this little gem
located just 100m from the beach. There

are 10 beautifully presented rooms (some
with private bathroom), two well-equipped
kitchens, an inviting lounge area and a huge
sun-drenched deck.

COOGEE

Dive Hotel (Map p107; ☎ 02-9665 5538; www.dive
hotel.com.au; 234 Arden St, Coogee; d & tw incl breakfast
$165-280; 🅇 💻) Behind the modern exte-
rior lies a refurbished Victorian home with
polished wooden floorboards, plush carpets
and a light-filled communal dining area.
Rooms are modern with designer bathrooms; if you're feeling flush splash out on
an ocean-view room.

MANLY

Periwinkle Guest House (Map p105; ☎ 02-9977 4668;
www.periwinkle.citysearch.com.au; 18-19 East Esplanade,
Manly; s/d incl breakfast from $115/139; P) In a
quiet corner of Manly, two Federation-style
houses have been combined to create this
relaxed guest house with 17 pretty bedrooms. Plump for a room on the top floor
facing Manly Cove or our favourite, room
7, which is perfectly positioned for catching
the winter sun.

101 Addison Road (Map p105; ☎ 02-9977 6216;
www.bb-manly.com; 101 Addison Rd, Manly; d $150-170)
Behind a huge frangipani tree, this pretty
four-star B&B has just two romantic rooms
and snug communal areas. If it's not beach
weather, plunk on the grand-piano ivories,
perfect your chess moves or catch the sea
breeze on the verandah. Book well ahead.

Manly Paradise Motel (Map p105; ☎ 02-9977 5799;
www.manlyparadise.com.au; 54 North Steyne, Manly; d/f from
$160/210; P 🅇 🅢) This angular building on
the beachfront holds well-appointed rooms
of varying shapes and sizes (tip: the rooms
towards the back of the building are bigger).
None comes with an ocean view, but the
rooftop pool most definitely does.

Top End

CITY CENTRE

Hyde Park Inn (Map pp102-3; ☎ 02-9264 6001; www
.hydeparkinn.com.au; 271 Elizabeth St, Sydney; s/d/f incl
breakfast from $176/193/209; P 🅇 💻) The Hyde
Park Inn has had a makeover and what a
transformation: the 1980s colour palette has
been replaced with neutral tones, contemporary furnishings and all manner of high-tech
gadgets. The deluxe rooms have balconies
overlooking Hyde Park.

NEW SOUTH WALES

Blacket (Map pp102-3; ☎ 02-9279 3030; www
.theblacket.com; 70 King St, Sydney; d from $230; ✂ ☐)
This very cool urban retreat hides stylish
suites, slick, minimalist design and its very
own underground nightclub – hide the backpack before checking in here. Check online
for late bargains.

Hilton (Map pp102-3; ☎ 02-9266 2000; www
.sydney.hilton.com; 488 George St, Sydney; d from $270;
P ✂ ☐ ☒) This Hilton is a whole lot
classier than the one who regularly graces
the pages of celebrity magazines. The rooms
are contemporary, chic and surprisingly spacious, while the fabulous Zeta Bar (p135) is
reason alone to check in.

Establishment Hotel (Map pp102-3; ☎ 02-9240
3100; www.establishmenthotel.com; 5 Bridge Lane, Sydney;
d from $365; ✂ ☐) Still one of the hippest
hotels in town, Establishment continues to
lure the superstars, supermodels and those
who just wish they were. The guest rooms
are all beautifully decorated but the New
York–style penthouse suites are simply
sublime.

KINGS CROSS AREA & WOOLLOOMOOLOO

Inhouse Potts Point (Map p106; ☎ 0406 316 609; www
.inhouse.net.au; 2/8 Rockwall Cres, Potts Point; d from $225;
✂ ☐) For those tired of big hotels (or ho-
tels full stop), look no further than this one-
bedroom apartment housed within an 1891
heritage-listed Victorian townhouse. With
12ft-high ceilings, Tasmanian oak parquetry
floors and oodles of good design, this is luxury
travel at its very best.

BLUE Sydney (Map p106; ☎ 02-9331 9000; www.tajho
tels.com/sydney; 6 Cowper Wharf Rd, Woolloomooloo; d from
$360; P ✂ ☐ ☒) Stay here for the night and
boast that you slept next to Russell Crowe (he
owns one of the apartments at the end of the
wharf). But even if he's not your cup of tea,
you're sure to enjoy the boutique sensibilities
of this Taj-owned hotel.

DARLINGHURST

Medusa (Map p106; ☎ 02-9331 1000; www.medusa
.com.au; 267 Darlinghurst Rd, Darlinghurst; d from $310;
✂ ☐) Behind the raspberry pink exterior
of a Victorian townhouse lies Sydney's
most style-conscious hotel. Each of the 17
rooms at Medusa has been individually designed using bold colours and custom-made
furnishings, including chaise longues and
'capsule' kitchenettes. Dogs are welcome;
children less so.

PADDINGTON

Manor House (Map pp102-3; ☎ 02-9380 6633; www
.manorhouse.com.au; 86 Flinders St, Paddington; d $250-400;
✂ ☐ ☒) For old-world charm look no fur-
ther than this elegant 19-room mansion just
off Oxford St. The chandeliers, antiques and
grand mahogany beds are in keeping with
the period of the property that was originally
built for one of Sydney's first lord mayors. The
indoor plunge pool is pure decadence.

EASTERN SUBURBS

Ravesi's (Map p107; ☎ 02-9365 4422; www.ravesis.com
.au; cnr Campbell Pde & Hall St, Bondi; d from $240; ✂ ☐)
The rooms above Bondi's favourite drinking
den are a world apart from the boozy Saturday
night shenanigans downstairs. Modern and
spacious, the bedrooms boast Juliet balconies, individual art works and ocean views
to die for.

GLEBE

our pick **Tricketts Bed & Breakfast** (Map p108; ☎ 02-
9552 1141; www.tricketts.com.au; 270 Glebe Point Rd, Glebe;
s/d incl breakfast from $176/198; P ☐) Rich in his-
tory, this gorgeous 1880s merchant's mansion was earmarked for demolition before Liz
Trickett came to its rescue and returned the
building to its former glory. Today the seven
large rooms are beautifully decorated with
antiques and Persian rugs. Be sure to visit the
living room (the former ballroom): the ceiling
is spectacular.

MANLY

Manly Pacific (Map p105; ☎ 02-9977 7666; www.novo
telmanlypacific.com.au; 55 North Steyne, Manly; d from $220;
P ✂ ☐ ☒) Manly's biggest hotel is so close
to the beach you almost feel like you're sleeping in the surf, especially if you opt for one of
the newly refurbished ocean-view rooms.

Camping

Sydney's camping and caravan parks are a fair
way out of town; the following are up to 17km
from the city centre. Note that peak seasons
(such as Christmas) see rate hikes.

Lane Cove River Tourist Park (Map pp100-1; ☎ 02-
9888 9133, 1300 729 133; www.lcrtp.com.au; Plassey Rd,
North Ryde; unpowered/powered sites from $34/36, cabins
from $121; P ✂ ☐ ☒) Just 10km north of
Sydney among bushland and eucalypt forests is this cheery, eco-certified site with good
facilities, including over 150 caravan sites,
plus cabins.

Grand Pines Tourist Park (Map p148; ☎ 02-9529 7329; www.thegrandpines.com.au; 289 The Grand Pde, Sans Souci; powered sites $40, cabins from $69; (P) (□)) This friendly caravan park is 17km south of Sydney (you can actually see the CBD from the park) on beautiful Botany Bay, but it has no tent sites.

Sydney Lakeside Holiday Park (Map p148; ☎ 02-9913 7845; www.sydneylakeside.com.au; Lake Park Rd, North Narrabeen; unpowered/powered sites $45/50, cabins from $210; (P) (✕) (□)) You're surrounded by 21 beaches at this well-managed place 17km north of Sydney's CBD. If roughing it doesn't appeal, there are good cabins and lakeside 'villas'.

EATING

If there's one thing Sydney does well it's food. Brunches, lunches, morning tea, high tea, pre-dinner appetisers, get-me-through-the-afternoon snacks or just plain old dinner, this city knows how to eat and you will rarely (and we mean hardly ever) have a bad meal.

You're also spoilt for choice: an abundance of fresh produce, innovative and highly competitive chefs and a multicultural melange has resulted in a dining arena where just about everything is on the menu.

City Centre, The Rocks & Circular Quay

You'll find everything in the city centre from frenzied lunchtime sandwich shops to some of Sydney's best culinary experiences. The numerous building food courts cater for the budget-conscious, while the harbour hides upmarket Mod Oz restaurants.

Central Baking Depot (Map pp102-3; ☎ 02-9290 2229; 37-39 Erskine St, Sydney; light meals $6-10; (✕) breakfast & lunch Mon-Fri) Once upon a time the best bakeries were confined to outside Sydney's business district, but fortunately all that has changed. The savoury offerings here are good (pies, pizzas, sandwiches), but the sweet treats are totally moreish.

Plan B (Map pp102-3; ☎ 02-9283 3450; 204 Clarence St, Sydney; light meals $6-10; (✕) breakfast & lunch Mon-Fri) Owned by the folks who run Becasse, one of Sydney's finest dining establishments, is this shoebox cafe that serves incredible Wagyu beef burgers. It also offers gourmet panini, sausage rolls, pastries, cakes and muffins.

Via Abercrombie (Map pp102-3; ☎ 02-9251 0000; 1 Abercrombie Lane, Sydney; sandwiches $6-13; (✕) breakfast & lunch Mon-Fri) The best sandwiches in town are the ones made in this hole-in-the-wall cafe located down a narrow alley. The bread is homemade and the chilli chicken (its speciality) is delicious. Expect queues at lunchtime.

Cafe Sydney (Map pp102-3; ☎ 02-9251 8683; 5th fl, Customs House, 31 Alfred St, Sydney; mains $32-39; (✕) lunch Mon-Fri & Sun, dinner Mon-Sat) The amazing rooftop location above Customs House is spectacular, but if views of the harbour don't sell Cafe Sydney the food definitely will. The seasonal menu reflects a strong seafood theme, with freshly shucked oysters, seared scallops and tandoori-roasted blue-eye cod all making regular appearances.

Guillaume at Bennelong (Map pp102-3; ☎ 02-9241 1999; Sydney Opera House, Bennelong Point, Sydney; mains $35-42; (✕) lunch Thu & Fri, dinner Mon-Sat) Indulge in master chef Guillaume Brahimi's delectable creations under the sails of the city's most famous landmark. Snuggle into a banquette or sit yourself next to the window, and don't leave without trying the basil-infused tuna with mustard seed and soy vinaigrette.

Rockpool (Map pp102-3; ☎ 02-9252 1888; 107 George St, The Rocks; mains $52-59; (✕) dinner Tue-Sat) Chef Neil Perry's innovative take on cooking results in modern seafood creations that consistently wow the critics. Even those on a budget can enjoy his work: grab a seat at the bar and order the Moroccan fish burger ($15) or half a dozen oysters.

Quay (Map pp102-3; ☎ 02-9251 5600; Level 3, Overseas Passenger Terminal, The Rocks; 4-course menu $145; (✕) lunch Tue-Fri, dinner daily) Peter Gilmore's cooking is imaginative, delicate and beautifully executed. Add to this the iconic Sydney views and outstanding wine list and you've got a dining experience to remember. The two-course set lunch ($75 per person) is an excellent deal.

Chinatown & Darling Harbour

Head to Chinatown for cheap and cheerful yum cha, noodles and barbecue duck, and to Darling Harbour for views and good (but pricier) food.

Chinese Noodle Restaurant (Map pp102-3; ☎ 02-9281 9051; Shop 7, Prince Centre, 8 Quay St, Chinatown; mains $4-12; (✕) lunch & dinner) It's cramped and crowded, but this lively restaurant also serves up some of the best (northern-style) steamed dumplings this side of Beijing. The handmade thick, wheat noodles and the braised eggplant and potato are similarly tasty. The entrance is on Thomas St.

Marigold (Map pp102-3; ☎ 02-9281 3388; Levels 4 & 5, 683-689 George St, Sydney; mains $4-15; ☢ lunch & dinner) Yum cha trolleys clatter endlessly around this noisy Chinese restaurant that spills over two floors. Choose from over 100 different yum cha; get there early as this place fills up quickly.

Din Tai Fung (Map pp102-3; ☎ 02-9264 6010; World Square Shopping Centre, 644 George St, Sydney; mains $4-16; ☢ lunch & dinner) The immensely popular Taipei-based global chain has set up shop in Sydney and not surprisingly there are queues day and night. But the wait is worth it especially if you choose the expertly crafted *xiaolongbao* ('little dragon buns'). Ridiculously delicious.

BBQ King (Map pp102-3; ☎ 02-9267 2586; 18-20 Goulburn St, Chinatown; mains $8-20; ☢ lunch & dinner) Chinatown's favourite late-night spot to chow down is low on frills but big on flavour, with royal portions of roast duck, suckling pig and other Cantonese staples. Open until 2am, it's popular with late-night revellers and chefs who come for a bottle of Tsingtao once their own kitchens have closed.

Blackbird (Map pp102-3; ☎ 02-9283 7385; Cockle Bay Wharf, Darling Harbour; mains $16-33) This place is fun, funky and a little quirky with hearty bowls of pasta, New York–style pizzas and big burgers on the menu. Popular with students for the daily $12 specials, it's a great place to fill up before a night out.

Bungalow 8 (Map pp102-3; ☎ 02-9299 4660; King St Wharf, 3 Lime St, Darling Harbour; mains $17-24; ☢ lunch & dinner) The bamboo and rattan decor are evocative of an snazzy island resort, but the views are pure Sydney. The menu has something for everyone but focuses primarily on seafood. Tuesday is all-you-can-eat mussel night ($22 per person).

Kings Cross, Potts Point & Woolloomooloo

Cool cafes, even cooler restaurants and late-night fast-food joints populate the Cross.

Harry's Café de Wheels (Map p106; ☎ 02-9357 3074; Cowper Wharf Roadway, Woolloomooloo; mains $5-10) You've not been to Australia until you've had a pie, and Harry's serves up some of the best. For over 50 years, cabbies, sailors and Saturday night party people have slurred orders over Harry's famous counter.

Zacharys (Map p106; ☎ 02-9380 4500; 28-30 Bayswater Rd, Kings Cross; mains $15-24; ☢ dinner Tue-Sun) It's not surprising that this diner-cum-bar in central Kings Cross is so popular – Thursday is all-you-can-eat pizza night ($22 per person). But

this is no fast-food joint: the low-slung sofas and rich timber finishes lend an air of sophistication while the masses tuck in.

Fratelli Paradiso (Map p106; ☎ 02-9357 1744; 12 Challis Ave, Potts Point; mains $17-29; ☢ breakfast & lunch daily, dinner Mon-Fri) This stylish banquette-lined trattoria is so Italian it should be in Rome. The menu is in Italian, the staff are Italian and the food is so damn tasty it can only be Italian. Try the melt-in-your-mouth calamari or the ravioli with veal, but be prepared to queue: locals love this spot.

Darlinghurst, Surry Hills & East Sydney

Head to Victoria St in Darlinghurst or explore the side streets of Surry Hills – many of the best eateries sit within converted warehouses stretching down to Central Station.

our pick Bodega (Map pp102-3; ☎ 02-9212 7766; 216 Commonwealth St, Surry Hills; mains $8-16; ☢ lunch Thu & Fri, dinner Mon-Sat) For Argentine tapas with a rock 'n' roll attitude, head to this hip Surry Hills joint. The best seats in the house are at the bar where you can watch the chefs (and co-owners) dish up empanadas, *morcilla* (Spain's black pudding) and smoked chorizo. No bookings so arrive early.

Pizza Mario (Map pp102-3; ☎ 02-9332 3633; Shop 9, 417-421 Bourke St, Surry Hills; mains $11-25; ☢ dinner) This is the only pizzeria in Sydney to be given the seal of approval from the *Associazione Vera Pizza Napoletana* – the governing Naples body established to ensure *pizzaioli* (pizza makers) aren't corrupting the trade. Not surprisingly, the pizzas are kickin' (as is the tiramisu).

Una's (Map p106; ☎ 02-9360 6885; 340 Victoria St, Darlinghurst; mains $12-22) It's not often you'll see someone sporting lederhosen in Sydney, but you will at Una's. This is the place to fill up on hearty, home-style European dishes such as *spätzle*, Hungarian goulash and the world's biggest schnitzels.

Phamish Asian Cuisine (Map pp102-3; ☎ 02-9357 2688; 109/50 Burton St, Darlinghurst; mains $13-20; ☢ dinner) Packed most nights, locals claim this busy Vietnamese restaurant to be the best in Sydney. Menu favourites include duck pancakes, salt-and-pepper squid and Bodhi ricepaper rolls.

bills (Map p106; ☎ 02-9360 9631; 433 Liverpool St, Darlinghurst; mains $14-27; ☢ breakfast & lunch) Bill Granger dishes up popular scramble-for-a-table breakfasts. Sweetcorn fritters with roast tomato, spinach and bacon is a Sunday morning Sydney staple. Also in Surry Hills (Map pp102–3) at 359 Crown St, and Woollahra (Map pp100–1) at 118 Queen St.

Billy Kwong (Map pp102–3; ☎ 02-9332 3300; 3/355 Crown St, Surry Hills; mains $19-50; ☽ dinner) Owned by celebrity chef Kylie Kwong, this stylish carbon-neutral eatery is modelled on a traditional Chinese teahouse. The menu features only local and organic produce, and includes dishes such as steamed scallop wontons with Sichuan chilli oil and Kylie's signature dish: crispy-skin duck with plum sauce.

Longrain (Map pp102–3; ☎ 02-9280 2888; 85 Commonwealth St, Surry Hills; mains $20-50; ☽ lunch Mon-Fri, dinner daily) Inside a century-old, wedge-shaped warehouse is one of Sydney's coolest Asian fusion restaurants. Urbanites flock to the communal wooden tables for the fabulous Thai-inspired dishes – the soft-shell crab is divine. No reservations so hang out and look beautiful at the cocktail bar.

Paddington, Woollahra & Eastern Suburbs

Gusto (Map pp100–1; ☎ 02-9361 5640; 2a Heely St, Five Ways, Paddington; mains $6-14) While the neighbouring cafes have empty tables aplenty, Gusto is standing room only. At weekends half of Paddington piles in for egg, ham and tomato breakfast rolls, slices of quiche with salad or a strong short black. The deli is stocked with cheeses, hams, olives and more.

Jones the Grocer (Map pp100–1; ☎ 02-9362 1222; 68 Moncur St, Woollahra; mains $10-15; ☽ breakfast & lunch) JTG offers high-end groceries, cookbooks and gourmet goodies galore. Munch into a caramel slice with a serious coffee at the cafe, then double wrap some double brie for a Centennial Park picnic.

Vamps (Map pp100–1; ☎ 02-9331 1032; 227 Glenmore Rd, Paddington; mains $30-34; ☽ breakfast & lunch Sat & Sun, dinner Tue-Sat) Don't let the name put you off: this is a lovely French bistro. The menu is old school so if you're hankering after *duck a l'orange* or *coquilles St Jacques* (scallops served on the shell with a mornay sauce) then look no further. The three-course prix-fixe menu is a steal ($40 per person).

Doyles on the Beach (Map pp100–1; ☎ 02-9337 2007; 11 Marine Pde, Watsons Bay; mains $30-60; ☽ lunch & dinner) There may well be better places for seafood, but few can compete with Doyles' location or its history – this restaurant first opened in 1885. Catching the harbour ferry to Watsons Bay for a seafood lunch is a quintessential Sydney experience.

Bondi

The restaurants lining Campbell Pde are for the most part best avoided. Head instead down the many side streets where you'll find an abundance of options, from celeb favourites to a bag of takeaway fish and chips on the beach.

Rum Diaries (Map p107; ☎ 02-9300 0440; 288 Bondi Rd, Bondi; mains $5-20; ☽ dinner) It's cool, it's intimate and it has 91 different rums from all over the world on its menu. It also has an innovative tapas menu. Try 'the Diaries' – a three-step appetiser comprising grilled chorizo, a shot of dark rum and a chaser of caramelised pear.

Jed's (Map p107; ☎ 02-9365 0022; 60 Warners Ave, Bondi; mains $8-20; ☽ breakfast & lunch) A local favourite, this ultra-laid-back cafe in North Bondi features all the usual breakfast suspects with some tasty alternatives such as Jamaican porridge. The Brekky Bowl – half granola, half bircher topped with lashings of yoghurt, berries and rhubarb – is delicious.

La Piadina (Map p107; ☎ 02-9300 0160; 106 Glenayr Ave, Bondi; mains $9-12) A piadina is a filled flat bread common in northern Italy, and the Zizioli brothers are the only ones serving them in Sydney. Fillings include prosciutto, rocket, mozzarella and *ndjua*, a kind of spicy sausage. Have them for breakfast, lunch or dinner, but whatever you do have them – they're delicious!

Hurricane's Grill & Bar (Map p107; ☎ 02-9130 7101; 126 Roscoe St, Bondi; mains $18-54) Good luck getting a seat at this hugely popular steakhouse that specialises in juicy Australian beef steaks and racks of ribs marinated and grilled in a secret basting sauce. If you can't stand the queue, there's a takeaway window (Hurricanes Express) next door with a pared-down menu.

Sean's Panaroma (Map p107; ☎ 02-9365 4924; 270 Campbell Pde, Bondi; mains $25-36; ☽ lunch Fri-Sun, dinner Wed-Sat) Sean Moran's ever-changing menu hangs on swinging squares of chalked blackboard in this modest but romantic diner. Come for the ocean views, hearty seasonal dishes and friendly service.

Bondi Icebergs (Map p107; ☎ 02-9365 9000; 1 Notts Ave, Bondi; mains $38-97; ☽ lunch & dinner Tue-Sun) When Hollywood A-listers come to town they head immediately to Icebergs. Something of a Sydney institution, this snazzy restaurant has phenomenal views across Bondi Beach, an excellent menu specialising in seafood and Wagyu steaks, and a superb wine list.

Coogee & Bronte

A Fish Called Coogee (Map p107; ☎ 02-9664 7700; 229 Coogee Bay Rd, Coogee; pay per weight of fish; ☽ lunch & dinner) This upmarket fish and chipper offers much more than your standard deep-fried cod. There's everything from barbecued shrimp and peppered marlin to swordfish and garlic prawns. Eat in or grab a bag and find a patch of sand.

Barzura (Map p107; ☎ 02-9665 5546; 64 Carr St, Coogee; mains $15-29) Sandy beachside cafe by day, stylish waterfront diner by night, this Coogee favourite has all bases covered. The daytime menu is varied, and the evening speciality is grilled kangaroo fillet with roast pumpkin, caramelised onion and red wine poached pears.

Wet Paint Café (Map p107; ☎ 02-9369 4634; 50 MacPherson St, Bronte; mains $18-26; ☽ dinner Tue-Sat) Away from the beachside strip is this cosy restaurant that's hugely popular with locals. The menu is modern Australian but with a Creole twist; try the signature Louisiana stuffed chicken.

Glebe, Newtown, Balmain & Petersham

The inner west is a fabulous melting pot of cultures and cuisine, with much to tempt both novice foodies and dedicated gourmets. Try Glebe for laid-back cafes, Newtown for eclectic ethnic eateries, Leichhardt for Italian fare, Petersham for Portuguese and Balmain for the best cakes in town.

Café Bariloche & Patisserie (Map p108; ☎ 02-9660 3524; 333 Glebe Point Rd, Glebe; mains $4-6; ☽ breakfast & lunch) Everything about this blink-and-you'll-miss-it cafe is authentic small-town Argentina, from the no-frills decor and the modest window display to the delicious beef-mince empanadas. Stuffed with paprika, cumin, egg and green olives, they are the best in town.

Guzzle Tandoori (Map p108; ☎ 02-9557 3537; 453 King St, Newtown; mains $7-15; ☽ dinner) The restaurant's not pretty, but you're not here for the decor: you're here for the cheap and very cheerful (halal) Pakistani/Indian food. Squeeze in next to the cabbies (it's a taxi driver fave) and order a beef vindaloo or butter chicken accompanied by freshly made naan bread.

Arabella (Map p108; ☎ 02-9550 1119; 12/489-491 King St, Newtown; mains $7-24; ☽ lunch Fri-Sun, dinner daily) Bringing a touch of Beirut to Sydney is this lively modern Lebanese restaurant that serves up falafel and fried kibbe with fervour. It's BYO and there's no corkage fee, so you've no excuses not to shake it when the belly dancing starts.

Adriano Zumbo Café Chocolat (Map pp100-1; ☎ 02-9810 7318; 296 Darling St, Balmain; mains $9-16; ☽ breakfast & lunch) Adriano Zumbo's cakes and pastries have the critics raving, so head to this newly opened cafe and see what all the fuss is about. Indulge in a *dulce de leche* éclair or one of the witty desserts such as 'The Younger Years', served in a kidney dish complete with syringe.

Blancmange (Map pp100-1; ☎ 02-9568 4644; 1 Station St, Petersham; mains $18-25; ☽ dinner Tue-Sat) This good-looking bistro prides itself on simple honest food using great produce. The modern European menu is not extensive (there are just four entrées and mains), but it changes regularly. Check out the cool artwork by the likes of Ben Quilty and Bill Henson while waiting for your order.

Glebe Point Diner (Map p108; ☎ 02-9660 2646; 407 Glebe Point Rd, Glebe; mains $18-30; ☽ lunch Thu-Sun, dinner Wed-Sat) The ceilings are high, the walls striped and the lampshades oversized, but this quirky design belies a diner where everything from the hand-churned butter to the pasta is made from scratch. The food is simple and soulful, while the signature dish of roast chook with bread sauce is sensational.

North Shore & Manly

Bower Restaurant (Map p105; ☎ 02-9977 5451; 7 Marine Pde, Manly; mains $12-30; ☽ breakfast & lunch daily, dinner Thu) Folks queue along the wall outside the Bower on weekends hoping to a nab a spot inside or outside for a slap-up meal or the Big Bower Breakfast. Positioned just metres from the gorgeous Shelly Beach, you can take a dip until your table number is called.

Ribs & Rumps (Map p105; ☎ 02-9977 3476; 35 South Steyne, Manly; mains $15-28; ☽ lunch & dinner) A great one for the guys (and girls with man-size appetites) is this lively top-floor diner overlooking the beach. Expect sizzling steaks, finger-licking ribs and precariously stacked burgers with all the trimmings.

Hugo's Manly (Map p105; ☎ 02-8116 8555; Manly Wharf, East Esplanade, Manly; mains $16-30; ☽ lunch & dinner) Hugo's might not flip the best pizzas in town (although they're pretty bloody good), but it does so with an attitude that leaves you thinking 'So what?' That's what happens when you have stellar views, first-rate cocktails and staff that look like they've just stepped off the catwalk.

Bathers' Pavilion Café (Map pp100-1; ☎ 02-9969 5050; 4 The Esplanade, Balmoral; mains $16-34; ☉ lunch & dinner) Gazing out over Balmoral Beach from within the confines of this iconic Spanish Mission–style restaurant is a true Sydney experience. The well-heeled North Shore crowd favours the restaurant next door, but the cafe section serves equally tasty food with a more affordable price tag.

Pilu at Freshwater (Map pp100-1; ☎ 02-9938 3331; Moore Rd, Freshwater; mains $37-44; ☉ lunch Wed-Sun, dinner Tue-Sat) Housed within a heritage-listed beach house overlooking the ocean is this multi-award winning Sardinian restaurant. Specialities include the oven-roasted suckling pig, but your best bet is to plump for the tasting menu ($100) and thereby eliminate any possible order envy.

DRINKING

Ever since the days of the 'six o'clock swill', the hour-long after-work speed-drinking session before the bars shut at 6pm, pubs have played an important part in Sydney's social scene. Today the bars are open much later and new licensing laws promise to bring more choice to a scene that's still largely dominated by sports and pokie-machine venues. That said, more and more small, independent bars are springing up creating a bar stool for everyone in Sydney. Unless otherwise specified, admission to bars and pubs listed here is free.

City Centre & The Rocks

The Rocks is littered with rambling old pubs, all claiming to be Sydney's oldest. It gets busy here on weekends and St Patrick's Day (17 March).

Australian Hotel (Map pp102-3; ☎ 02-9247 2229; 100 Cumberland St, The Rocks; ☉ 11.30am-midnight Mon-Sat, to 10pm Sun) Beer geeks rejoice! Not only is this pub one of the oldest in Sydney (check out the 1930s bathrooms), but it also boasts more than 90 Aussie boutique beers. Keeping with the antipodean theme, the Australian also fires up pizzas topped with kangaroo, emu and saltwater crocodile.

Opera Bar (Map pp102-3; ☎ 02-9250 7777; Sydney Opera House, Bennelong Pt, Sydney; ☉ 11.30am-midnight Mon-Thu & Sun, to 1am Fri & Sat) The Opera Bar puts all other beer gardens to shame. Spilling into the harbour with the Opera House on one side and the Harbour Bridge on the other, this outdoor drinking den has it all. Live music in the evenings will keep you there till closing.

Ivy Bar (Map pp102-3; ☎ 02-9240 3000; 330 George St, Sydney; ☉ 5pm-late) The newly opened Ivy has celebs scrambling for their high heels. This multilevel playground holds countless bars and restaurants, a ballroom and an LA-inspired rooftop pool where girls strut their stuff in teeny bikinis.

Lord Nelson Brewery Hotel (Map p102-3; ☎ 02-9251 4044; 19 Kent St, The Rocks; ☉ 11am-11pm Mon-Sat, noon-10pm Sun) Sydney's oldest boutique brewery (the 'Nello' first started brewing back in 1986) is the only place you'll find 'Nelson's Blood'. If that doesn't appeal, there are five other award-winning ales to choose from and beds upstairs (p127) if you can't face the journey home.

Fortune of War Hotel (Map pp102-3; ☎ 02-9247 2714; 137 George St, The Rocks; ☉ 9am-11pm Mon-Thu, to midnight Fri, to 1am Sat & Sun) The title of 'Sydney's oldest pub' is a highly contested one, but this 1828 drinking den might just take the prize. This hamper-style bar was the first and last port of call for soldiers. It retains much of its original charm and, by the looks of things, some of the original punters, too.

Zeta Bar (Map pp102-3; ☎ 02-9265 6070; 4th fl, Hilton Hotel, 488 George St, Sydney; ☉ 5pm-late Mon-Sat) The Zeta is all about cocktails, but not the kind that come with umbrellas. This place introduced molecular mixology to Australia, the art of flambéing fruit before adding it to drinks. Not convinced? Order a scorched pink grapefruit and lavender martini and see how quickly you change your mind.

Argyle Hotel (Map pp102-3; ☎ 02-9247 5500; 18 Argyle St, The Rocks; ☉ 11am-midnight Sun-Tue, to 3am Wed-Sat) For a guaranteed great night out in The Rocks, head to this lively pub tucked away down a cobblestone path. The courtyard heaves on weekends and sometimes the patrons do too.

Establishment Hotel (Map pp102-3; ☎ 02-9240 3000; 252 George St, Sydney; ☉ 11am-late Mon-Fri, 6pm-late Sat) This is where Sydney's cashed-up crowd comes to swill cocktails, seal deals and scout talent. There's a 42m-long marble bar, a swish courtyard and a leather lounge, as well as the popular nightclub Tank.

Kings Cross, Darlinghurst & Surry Hills

All-night party people flock to the Cross where drinking and stripping dens stand in equal numbers along Darlinghurst Rd, the trashy main drag. But you'll also find cool bars around here, particularly in Surry Hills.

GAY & LESBIAN SYDNEY

Gay is the new (and old, actually) straight in Sydney; gay and lesbian culture forms a vocal, vital part of the city's social fabric. Traditionally Oxford St (Map pp102–3) has been the centre of the gay community, but an influx of 'straight' venues has diluted the scene and sadly the mix isn't always a harmonious one.

Gay venues are scattered around the city, although you'll still find many along the city end of Oxford St. Newtown is home to Sydney's lesbian scene.

Gay beach life focuses on **Tamarama** (Map p107), **Lady Bay** (Map pp100–1) and the little-known **Obelisk Beach** (Map pp100–1) in Mosman (the last two are nude beaches). Also check out **Red Leaf Pool** (Map pp100–1) and **Andrew 'Boy' Charlton Pool** (p121).

Sydney's famous **Gay & Lesbian Mardi Gras** (☎ 02-9568 8600; www.mardigras.org.au) started in 1978 as a political march commemorating New York's Stonewall riots. It has evolved into a month-long arts festival that culminates in a flamboyant themed street parade on the first Saturday in March. The rampant 200-float parade begins on Elizabeth St around 7.30pm and cavorts the length of Oxford St. Around 700,000 spectators line the streets.

For counselling and referral, call the **Gay & Lesbian Counselling Service of NSW** (☎ 02-8594 9596; www.glcsnsw.org.au). **Gay & Lesbian Tourism Australia** (www.galta.com.au) has a wealth of information about gay and lesbian travel in Australia.

The following represent old favourites and newer haunts; check out the free gay media including *SX*, the *Sydney Star Observer*, *Lesbians on the Loose* and *Cherrie* for more comprehensive listings and information on rotating club nights.

ARQ (Map p106; ☎ 02-9380 8700; www.arqsydney.com.au; 16 Flinders St, Darlinghurst; admission Thu/Fri/Sat/Sun free/$10/25/5; ❂ 9pm-6am Thu & Fri, 10pm-9am Sat, 9pm-9am Sun) This flash megaclub is where folks come to dance till dawn, usually aided by something a touch stronger than a beer. There's a recovery room, two dance floors, drag shows and foam parties.

Colombian Hotel (Map pp102-3; ☎ 02-9360 2151; 117 Oxford St, Darlinghurst; admission free-$20; ❂ 9am-6am) Open until the wee small hours, this vibrant gay venue is where folk of all persuasions

Gazebo Wine Garden (Map p106; ☎ 02-9357 5333; 2 Elizabeth Bay Rd, Elizabeth Bay; ❂ 3pm-midnight Mon-Thu, from noon Fri-Sun) You've got to love a place that divides its wine list into sections including 'Unpronounceable' and 'Slurpable'. With moss-covered walls and taxidermy hanging from the ceilings, a night out at this Kings Cross oasis is only ever going to be fantastic.

Bayswater Brasserie (Map p106; ☎ 02-9357 2177; 32 Bayswater Rd, Kings Cross; ❂ 5pm-late Mon-Sun) Order the most obscure cocktail you know, but it's unlikely you'll flummox the bartenders at the award-winning Bays – these guys know how to fix drinks. The cool art deco space buzzes with trendy types on weekends; mid-week it's perfect for a relaxed martini or two.

The Victoria Room (Map p106; ☎ 02-9357 4488; Level 1, 235 Victoria St, Darlinghurst; ❂ 6pm-midnight Tue-Thu, to 2am Fri & Sat, 2pm-midnight Sun) Plush Chesterfields, art nouveau wallpaper, dark-wood panelling and bamboo screens – this place is 1920s Bombay gin palace meets Hong Kong opium den. Don your white linen suit and Panama hat and order a Raspberry Debonair.

The Beresford (Map p106; ☎ 02-9357 1111; 354 Bourke St, Darlinghurst; ❂ noon-late) After a $35 million rebuild the once dingy Beresford is back and sparkling. The gleaming island bar stocks every drink imaginable, while the beer garden promises to be one of the best in town once the creepers grow. There's also a critic-pleasing trattoria.

The World Bar (Map p106; ☎ 02-8324 0100; 24 Bayswater Rd, Kings Cross; ❂ 12.30pm-late) Offering four floors of alcohol-fuelled mayhem and madness is this down-to-earth backpacker favourite in the heart of the Cross. With entertainment alternating between live music, indie, dance and hip hop, the World rocks out every night of the week.

Mille Vini (Map pp102-3; ☎ 02-9357 3366; 397 Crown St, Surry Hills; ❂ 6pm-11pm Tue-Thu, to midnight Fri, from 2pm Sat & Sun) Mille Vini – or Milli Vanilli as it's known locally – might not have the 1000 wines it promises, but the list is nevertheless impressive. The two-storey wine bar is cool and sophisticated, tempting gourmands with the promise of fine *vini* and *spuntini* (Italian snacks).

stumble into when they're not quite ready to go home. Sweaty bodies dance to the latest chart tunes; others sit slurring at the bar.

Exchange Hotel (Map pp102-3; ☎ 02-9331 2956; www.exchangehotel.biz; 34 Oxford St, Darlinghurst; admission Exchange free, Q Bar free-$20, Phoenix $5-10) Q Bar (open 10pm until late) upstairs pumps hot house nightly; the Phoenix club (also open 10pm until late) downstairs is the sticky, sexy home to an alternative gay crowd (that means no Cher or Kylie). Sandwiched in between, the Exchange (open until 4am Monday to Friday, and 6am Saturday and Sunday) is a regulation beery pub.

Green Park Hotel (Map p106; ☎ 02-9380 5311; 360 Victoria St, Darlinghurst; admission free; ⏰ 10pm-1am Mon-Sat, noon-midnight Sun) Something of a Sydney institution is this Darlo pub where a 30-something gay clientele mingles with musos, suits, students and locals with ease. Grab a pew around the blue-tiled bar or head into the newly renovated beer garden.

Imperial Hotel (Map p108; ☎ 02-9519 9899; 35 Erskineville Rd, Erskineville; admission free; ⏰ 3pm-midnight Sun-Wed, to 2.30am Thu, to 6am Fri & Sat) The art deco Imperial's drag shows inspired *Priscilla, Queen of the Desert* (the opening scene was filmed here). At the time we visited, the Imperial was undergoing massive refurbishment (including the installation of some much-needed air-conditioning), but will be open by the time you read this.

Oxford Hotel (Map pp102-3; ☎ 02-9331 3467; 134 Oxford St, Taylor Sq, Darlinghurst; admission free-$10) The ever-lovin' Oxford is a Taylor Sq beacon. Recently refurbished, downstairs is beer-swilling and mannish, and open 24 hours. The 1st-floor Supper Club (open 7pm until late Wednesday to Sunday) offers sophisticated live entertainment, the 2nd-floor Polo Lounge (open 6pm until late Tuesday to Sunday) resembles an old-school gentlemen's club, while in the basement Gilligans (open 10pm until late Thursday to Saturday) is all about drinking and dancing.

The Sly Fox (Map p108; ☎ 02-9557 1016; 199 Enmore Rd, Newtown; admission free; ⏰ 10am-4am Mon-Thu, to 6am Fri, to midnight Sun) Sydney's main lesbian hang-out with pool tables and drag performances; Wednesday night is laydees night.

Darlo Bar (Map p106; ☎ 02-9331 3672; cnr Darlinghurst Rd & Liverpool St, Darlinghurst; ⏰ 10am-midnight Mon-Sat, noon-midnight Sun) Occupying its own tiny block, the Darlo's triangular retro room is a magnet for thirsty urban bohemians with something to read or a hankering for pinball or pool. The green and pink outdoor patio is a must-see, and if you're lucky you'll score a table.

Paddington & Woollahra

Paddington Inn (Map pp100-1; ☎ 02-9380 5913; 338 Oxford St, Paddington; ⏰ noon-midnight Sun-Thu, to 1am Fri & Sat) This 1850s pub hasn't changed much outside, but the interiors have been revamped and re-styled with curvy banquettes, cherry red walls and vaguely dangerous-looking light fixtures. Popular with locals, it's a place where girls wear hair product and the guys even more.

Lord Dudley Hotel (Map pp100-1; ☎ 02-9327 5399; 236 Jersey Rd, Woollahra; ⏰ 11am-11pm Mon-Wed, to midnight Thu-Sat, noon-10pm Sun) As close to a British pub as you're going to find in Sydney, the Lord Dudley is the place to head for real English ale in dimpled pint glasses. Best enjoyed on a winter's day when the open fire is roaring.

London (Map pp100-1; ☎ 02-9331 3200; 85 Underwood St, Paddington; ⏰ noon-midnight Mon-Sat, to 10pm Sun) Among the designer boutique shops of William St, the London draws a fashionable crowd that heads upstairs to kick back in the intimate lounge area. Downstairs punters vie for a stool at one of the circular tables and watch – or try to ignore – sport on the big screen.

Woolloomooloo

Old Fitzroy Hotel (Map p106; ☎ 02-9356 3848; 129 Dowling St, Woolloomooloo; ⏰ 11am-midnight Mon-Fri, from noon Sat, 3-10pm Sun) Is it a pub? A theatre? A bistro? Actually it's all three. Grab a bowl of laksa, assess the acting talent of tomorrow and wash it all down with a beer. The outdoor deck is unbeatable on a steamy summer night; in winter there's a fire going and a supply of marshmallows for you to roast.

Tilbury Hotel (Map p106; ☎ 02-9368 1955; 12-18 Nicholson St, Woolloomooloo; ⏰ 8am-midnight Mon-Fri, from 9am Sat, 10am-10pm Sun) Once the dank domain of burly sailors and salty ne'er-do-wells, the Tilbury now sparkles with one of the best

NEW SOUTH WALES

beer gardens in town. It attracts a well-heeled crowd that camps out back under the frangipani and olive trees or on the deck for one of the regular barbecues.

Bondi & Coogee

Cream Tangerine (Map p107; ☎ 02-9300 8471; Swiss Grand Hotel, cnr Curlewis St & Campbell Pde, Bondi; ☼ noon-late Wed-Sun) Bringing a touch of glamour to summertime drinking in Bondi is this place set on the terrace of the Swiss Grand Hotel. There's an extensive drinks menu (a martini for every meal of the day), DJs and sunken sofas for watching the sunset.

Ravesi's (Map p107; ☎ 02-9365 4422; cnr Campbell Pde & Hall St, Bondi; ☼ 10am-1am Mon-Sat, to midnight Sun) It's never too early for a drink at Ravesi's and at weekends the crowd throbs. Upstairs is the newly opened Drift Bar that is a touch more sophisticated than the downstairs pub, but not quite as exclusive as it would like to be.

Beach Road Hotel (Map p107; ☎ 02-9130 7247; 71 Beach Rd, Bondi; ☼ 10am-2.30am Mon-Fri, 9am-12.30am Sat, 10am-10pm Sun) Weekends at this big, yellow, boxy pub are a boisterous multilevel alcoholiday, with Bondi types (bronzed, buff and brooding) and woozy out-of-towners playing pool, drinking beer and digging live bands and DJs.

Coogee Bay Hotel (Map p107; ☎ 02-9665 0000; cnr Coogee Bay Rd & Arden St, Coogee; ☼ 9am-3am) The rambling, rowdy Coogee Bay Hotel caters to all types with a beach bar, sports bar, beer garden, garden bar, lounge and nightclub. Come here for the beers and the view over the beach; steer clear of the ice cream.

Balmain, Newtown & Glebe

For a low-key drink head to the inner west: Newtown's King St has plenty of good boozers as do Glebe Point Rd and Balmain's Darling St.

London Hotel (Map pp100-1; ☎ 02-9555 1377; 234 Darling St, Balmain; ☼ 11am-midnight Mon-Sat, noon-10pm Sun) Once the drinking den of choice for The Sydney Push, a group of left-wing intellectuals and writers including Germaine Greer and Clive James, the London Hotel is now a locals' favourite for the great range of Oz beers on tap and the much-coveted balcony seats with views of the Bridge.

Courthouse Hotel (Map p108; ☎ 02-9519 8273; 202 Australia St, Newtown; ☼ 10am-midnight Mon-Sat, to 10pm Sun) A true local where folks from all walks of life congregate at the bar and bond over a beer.

Inside the carpets are stained, sport plays on TV and the pokies are blaring, so head to the beer garden instead.

Friend in Hand Hotel (Map p108; ☎ 02-9660 2326; 58 Cowper St, Glebe; ☼ 8am-late Mon-Sat, from 10am Sun) This is not the place to come for a quiet drink (or a first date). Eating competitions, comedy nights, hula-hoop spin-offs and poetry slams are sure to cut into your drinking time. Make sure you don't miss the legendary crab racing held every Wednesday (7.30pm).

Madame Fling Flong (Map p108; ☎ 02-9565 2471; 169 King St, Newtown; ☼ 5pm-late) Newtown's best (and only) cocktail bar has got that scruffy Inner West thing going on with its retro lounge and shabby-chic decor. On Tuesday nights the Flong screens art-house movies from 8.30pm, but book ahead as seating is limited.

North Shore & Manly

Manly Wharf Hotel (Map p105; ☎ 02-9977 1266; E Esplanade, Manly; ☼ 11.30am-midnight Mon-Sat, 11am-10pm Sun) The fabulously well-designed Manly Wharf Hotel is the kind of place that makes you want to pack up your bags and move to Sydney permanently. On the harbour side of Manly, it's perfect for watching the ferries roll in while tucking into sunny afternoon beers.

Shore Club (Map p105; ☎ 02-9977 6322; 36-38 South Steyne, Manly; ☼ 11am-late Mon-Wed, to 2am Thu-Sat, to midnight Sun) The island bar of this Miami Beach–style boozer is staffed by a bevy of bleached blondes in short shorts who serve tongue-in-cheek cocktails such as the Pool Boy. Show off your dance moves in the Sound Bar.

Newport Arms Hotel (Map p148; ☎ 02-9977 4900; cnr Beaconsfield & Kalinya Sts, Newport; ☼ 10am-midnight Mon-Thu, to 1am Fri & Sat, to 10pm Sun) The mammoth beer garden buzzes with bronzed Aussies discussing surf boat competitions and comparing ocean swim times. Ignore them and enjoy the beautiful views over Pittwater instead. The Garden Bistro serves up good pub grub.

ENTERTAINMENT

Sydney has an energetic and often underrated arts, entertainment and music scene. It's vibrant, eclectic and constantly changing, with innovative and eclectic theatre, a healthy live music scene (rock, jazz, classical and everything in between) and numerous showcases for the city's visual and performing arts. Outdoor cinemas and sports stadiums cater to families.

For comprehensive entertainment information pick up a copy of *Time Out* magazine. Cinema listings can be found in Sydney's daily newspapers, and the Metro section in Friday's *Sydney Morning Herald* details entertainment listings. Free weekly street magazines such as *Drum Media, 3D World* and *Brag* specialise in gig and club information. Tickets for most shows can be purchased directly from venues or the following distributors:

Moshtix (Map pp102-3; ☎ 02-9209 4614; www .moshtix.com.au; Red Eye Records, 370 Pitt St; ☩ 9am-6pm Mon-Wed & Fri, to 9pm Thu, to 5pm Sat, 11am-5pm Sun) Servicing alternative music venues.

Ticketek (Map pp102-3; ☎ 13 28 49; www.ticketek .com.au; 195 Elizabeth St; ☩ 9am-5pm Mon-Wed, to 7pm Thu & Fri, to 4pm Sat)

Ticketmaster (Map pp102-3; ☎ 13 61 00; www .ticketmaster.com.au; State Theatre, 49 Market St; ☩ 9am-5pm Mon-Fri)

Nightclubs

Trademark Hotel (Map p106; ☎ 02-9326 0633; 1 Bayswater Rd, Kings Cross; admission $10-20; ☩ 5pm-late Thu-Sun) There are two parts to Sydney's latest favourite late-night wonderland: the Piano Room and the Lounge. The former is where Stevie Wonder played an impromptu gig when he came to town and the Lounge is where 20- and 30-somethings shimmy to dance and electro funk.

Oxford Art Factory (Map pp102-3; ☎ 02-9332 3711; 38-46 Oxford St, Darlinghurst; admission free-$28; ☩ 9pm-late Wed-Sat, 7pm-late Sun) Bringing some serious New York style to Darlinghurst is this multifunctional space offering everything from live indie gigs and burlesque nights to international DJs spinning Baltimore beats. Expect cool kids in low-slung skinnies and Wayfarers.

Chinese Laundry (Map pp102-3; ☎ 02-8295 9950; 111 Sussex St, Sydney; admission $10-20; ☩ 9pm-5am Fri & Sat) One of the longest-running clubs in Sydney, this underground warren has plenty of nooks and crannies to get lost in. Local and international DJs spin floor-filling house, electro, techno, hip hop and break beats over three dance floors.

Lady Lux (Map p106; ☎ 02-9361 5000; 2 Roslyn St, Potts Point; admission free-$20; ☩ 10pm-6am Fri-Sun) This glam venue attracts a stylish crowd with its boudoir-inspired decor and supersexy house beats. Sip expertly made cocktails amid the plush surroundings and nurse those stiletto-wearing feet – the girls who come here wouldn't be seen wearing anything else.

Candy's Apartment (Map p106; ☎ 02-9380 5600; 22 Bayswater Rd, Kings Cross; admission free-$15; ☩ 8pm-3am Thu, to 6am Fri & Sat) It's dark and very sweaty in this subterranean venue with two bars, a dance floor and a space for bands to play (Aussie acts Wolfmother and the Presets have both graced Candy's stage). At weekends they pack 'em in and you'll find plenty of guys and gals scanning the crowd hoping they won't go home alone.

Cinemas

Unless otherwise stated, tickets generally cost $15 to $17 for an adult and $10 to $13 for a child. Most cinemas have a cheap night when tickets are discounted by around a third.

Bondi Junction Greater Union Cinemas (Map pp100-1; ☎ 02-9209 4614; www.greaterunion.com; Level 6, 500 Oxford St, Bondi Junction) Within the colossal Westfield Bondi Junction (p144) 11 cinemas screen all the latest Hollywood blockbusters.

Dendy Opera Quays (Map pp102-3; ☎ 02-9247 3800; www.dendy.com.au; Shop 9, 2 Circular Quay E) Right on the harbour is this classy cinema where you can enjoy a glass of wine with your arthouse flick. There's also a Dendy cinema in Newtown (Map p108; ☎ 02-9550 5699; 261-263 King St).

George Street Cinemas (Map pp102-3; ☎ 02-9273 7333; www.greaterunion.com.au; 505-525 George St) Three huge complexes screening nonstop Hollywood fare.

Chauvel Cinema (Map pp102-3; ☎ 02-9361 5398; www.chauvelcinema.net.au; cnr Oxford St & Oatley Rd, Paddington) Inside the Paddington Town Hall ballroom, the Chauvel focuses on indie films, but also screens mainstream movies.

Govinda's Movie Room (Map p106; ☎ 02-9380 5155; www.govindas.com.au; 112 Darlinghurst Rd, Darlinghurst; dinner & movie $29; ☩ 6-11pm) The Hare Krishna Govinda's is an all-you-can-gobble vegetarian smorgasbord, including admission to the mainstream movie room upstairs.

IMAX (Map pp102-3; ☎ 02-9281 3300; www.imax .com.au; 31 Wheat Rd, Darling Harbour; adult/child $20/15) Watch supersized films on an eight-storey screen with both kid-friendly docs (sharks, space, haunted castles etc) and grown-up films (U2, Batman). Many are in 3-D.

Palace Academy Twin (Map p106; ☎ 02-9361 4453; www.palacecinemas.com.au; 3a Oxford St, Paddington) The cinema of choice for art-house and foreign film enthusiasts, the Palace is also home to the annual Mardi Gras, French, Spanish and Italian film festivals (in February, March, May and September respectively).

Palace Verona (Map p102-3; ☎ 02-9360 6099; www.palacecinemas.com.au; 17 Oxford St, Paddington) Just down the road from the affiliated Academy Twin (p139), the Verona screens international, art-house, documentary and independent films. There's also a cafe and bar, so you can sit, sip and scrutinise the films.

Moonlight Cinema (Map pp100-1; ☎ 1300 551 908; www.moonlight.com.au; Centennial Park, Oxford St; adult/concession $15/13; ☽ dusk late Nov-early Mar) Nothing says summer's arrived quite like the open-air cinema season. Bring a rug, picnic and friends and watch everything from *Breakfast at Tiffany's* to *Zoolander* on the huge outdoor screen. Buy tickets online, by phone or at the gate from 7pm (subject to availability). Enter the park at Woollahra Gate.

Open Air Cinema (Map pp102-3; ☎ 1300 366 649; www.stgeorge.com.au/openair; Mrs Macquaries Point, Royal Botanic Gardens; adult/concession $24/22; ☽ box office 6.30pm, screenings 8.30pm Jan & Feb) This three-storey screen rises from the harbour with the Bridge as its backdrop. Book tickets early: the season sells out within days.

Bondi Open Air Cinema (Map p107; ☎ 02-9209 4614; www.bondiopenair.com.au; Bondi Pavilion, Bondi; ☽ dusk late Jan-mid Mar) Enjoy open-air screenings at the ocean's edge. Bookings essential.

Theatre

Many theatres have cheap midweek pay-what-you-can (minimum price $10 per ticket) and under-30 deals.

Belvoir St Theatre (Map pp100-1; ☎ 02-9699 3444; www.belvoir.com.au; 25 Belvoir St, Surry Hills; adult $29-54, concession $23-33; ☽ box office 9.30am-6pm Mon & Tue, to 7.30pm Wed-Sat, 2.30-7.30pm Sun) Upstairs the Belvoir stages tried-and-tested plays favoured by left-leaning intellectuals, while the Downstairs Theatre is renowned for experimenting with new works by up-and-coming writers, all under the watchful eye of Director Neil Armfield.

SBW Stables Theatre (Map p106; ☎ 02-8002 4772; www.griffintheatre.com.au; 10 Nimrod St, Kings Cross; concession $44/33; ☽ box office 10am-2pm Mon, 11am-6pm Tue-Fri, 10am-4pm Sat & 1hr before performances) Home to the Griffin Theatre Company, this quirky, intimate theatre (it seats just 120) is *the* home for new writing. It's also where many actors started out – Cate Blanchett and David Wenham both trod the boards here before conquering Hollywood.

Sydney Comedy Store (Map pp100-1; ☎ 02-9357 1419; www.comedystore.com.au; Entertainment Quarter, 122 Lang Rd, Moore Park; tickets $15-30; ☽ box office 10am-6pm Mon, to midnight Tue-Sat) This purpose-built comedy hall lures big-time Australian and overseas comics, including Edinburgh Festival stand-ups, and nurtures new talent with open-mic and 'New Comics' nights.

Sydney Theatre (Map pp102-3; ☎ 02-9250 1999; www.sydneytheatre.org.au; 22 Hickson Rd, Walsh Bay; tickets $35-130; ☽ box office 9am-8.30pm Mon-Sat, 3-5.30pm Sun) The resplendent Sydney Theatre at the base of Observatory Hill puts 896 bums on seats for specialist drama and dance. Wharf 1 stages reliably good theatre; Wharf 2 is more experimental.

Sydney Theatre Company (Map pp102-3; ☎ 02-9250 1777; www.sydneytheatre.com.au; Pier 4, Hickson Rd, Walsh Bay; tickets from $30; ☽ box office 9am-7pm Mon, to 8.30pm Tue-Fri, from 11am Sat, 2hr pre-show Sun) Working in tandem with the Sydney Theatre across the road, Artistic Directors Cate Blanchett and Andrew Upton lead the way for Sydney's premier theatre company.

Studio (Map p102-3; ☎ 02-9250 7777; www.sydneyoperahouse.com; Sydney Opera House, Bennelong Point, Circular Quay E; tickets $24-85; ☽ box office 9am-8.30pm Mon-Sat) The smallest venue in the Opera House is the most experimental with an eclectic mix of quirky performances: bawdy cabaret, small theatrical productions, new music performances and shows for kids.

Major theatres hosting West End and Broadway musicals, opera and concerts (tickets from $50 to $150):

Capitol Theatre (Map pp102-3; ☎ 02-9320 5000; www.capitoltheatre.com.au; 13 Campbell St, Haymarket; ☽ box office 9am-5pm Mon-Fri)

Lyric Theatre (Map p108; ☎ 02-9657 8500; www.lyrictheatre.com.au; Star City Casino, 80 Pyrmont St, Pyrmont) Bookings through Ticketmaster (p139).

State Theatre (Map pp102-3; ☎ 02-9373 6655; www.statetheatre.com.au; 49 Market St; ☽ box office 9am-5pm Mon-Fri, to 8pm performance nights)

Theatre Royal (Map pp102-3; ☎ 02-9224 8444; www.theatreroyal.net.au; MLC Centre, 108 King St) Bookings through Ticketek (p139).

Live Music
CLASSICAL

City Recital Hall (Map pp102-3; ☎ 02-8256 2222; www.cityrecitalhall.com; Angel Pl, Sydney; tickets free-$80; ☽ box office 9am-5pm Mon-Fri, 3½hr pre-show Sat & Sun) Classically configured, this custom-built 1200-seat venue boasts near-perfect acoustics. Top-billing companies here include the Sydney Conservatorium of Music and

Sydney Symphony, plus touring international ensembles, soloists and opera singers. The Little Lunch Music is a good deal ($10 per person).

Sydney Conservatorium of Music (Map pp102-3; ☎ 02-9351 1438; www.music.usyd.edu.au; cnr Bridge & Macquarie Sts; tickets free-$45; ⚇ box office 9am-5pm Mon-Fri) 'The Con's' annual student/teacher performance program includes choral, jazz, opera and chamber recitals, and free lunchtime and 'Cocktail Hour' concerts.

Sydney Opera House (Map pp102-3; ☎ 02-9250 7777; www.sydneyoperahouse.com; Bennelong Point, Circular Quay E; ticket prices vary with shows; ⚇ box office 9am-8.30pm Mon-Sat) As well as theatre and dance, the Opera House (p110) regularly hosts the following classy classicists: **Australian Chamber Orchestra** (☎ 02-8274 3800; www.aco.com.au); **Musica Viva** (☎ 02-8394 6666; www.mva.org.au); **Opera Australia** (☎ 02-9699 1099; www.opera-australia.org.au); **Sydney Philharmonic Choirs** (☎ 02-9251 2024; www.sydneyphilharmonia.com.au); and **Sydney Symphony** (☎ 02-8215 4600; www.sydneysymphony.com)

JAZZ & BLUES

Basement (Map pp102-3; ☎ 02-9251 2797; www.thebasement.com.au; 29 Reiby Pl, Circular Quay; tickets from $39; ⚇ noon-1.30am Mon-Thu, to 2.30am Fri, 7.30pm-3am Sat, 7pm-1am Sun) Sydney's premier jazz venue has played host to all the greats from Dizzy Gillespie to Herbie Hancock, but it's not all scat – funk, blues, rock and reggae also feature on the musical menu with big international and local names. Book a table by the stage.

Empire Hotel (Map p108; ☎ 02-9557 1701; www.empirelive.com.au; cnr Parramatta Rd & Johnston St, Annandale; tickets free-$20; ⚇ 9am-3pm Mon-Sat, 10am-midnight Sun) The Empire's 300-capacity bar gets down 'n' dirty with Sydney's best blues and roots. Local bands with loyal followings play free gigs; listen out for international artists and regular metal, ska, rockabilly, country-and-western and swing dancing nights!

ROCK

Enmore Theatre (Map p108; ☎ 02-9550 3666; www.enmoretheatre.com.au; 118-132 Enmore Rd, Newtown; tickets $20-80; ⚇ box office 9am-5pm Mon-Fri, 10am-2pm Sat) Originally a vaudeville playhouse, the elegantly wasted Enmore now hosts alt-cum-mainstream rockers such as Franz Ferdinand, Belle and Sebastian, the John Butler Trio and Martha Wainwright. The 1600-capacity theatre feels like an old-time movie hall, complete with lounge areas and balconies.

Vanguard (Map p108; ☎ 02-9557 7992; www.thevanguard.com.au; 42 King St, Newtown; dinner & show per person from $36, general admission $10-40; ⚇ dinner from 7pm, music from 8pm) A 1920s jazz club feel sets the perfect stage for singer songwriters such as Anthony and the Johnsons and Elvis Costello. Most seats are reserved for dinner-and-show punters, but standing tickets are available.

Annandale Hotel (Map p108; ☎ 02-9550 1078; www.annandalehotel.com; 17 Parramatta Rd, Annandale; tickets free-$20; ⚇ 11am-midnight Tue-Sat, to 10pm Sun, to 11pm Mon) The reigning home of Sydney rock'n'roll, the 'Dale hosts fledgling local acts as well as high-profile Aussie and international bands. Dedicated musos, students and laid-back locals swig VB in between sets by Jet, Thirsty Merc and the Vines.

Metro (Map pp102-3; ☎ 02-9550 3666; www.metrotheatre.com.au; 624 George St, Sydney; tickets $20-60; ⚇ box office 10am-7pm Mon-Fri, noon-7pm Sat) Hip international acts such as the Ting Tings and Razorlight grace the Metro's stage, but if moshing is not your thing then fear not: you can watch the action while propping up the bar. Theatre-style tiers, air-con and super sound and visibility.

Gaelic Club (Map pp102-3; ☎ 02-9211 1687; www.thegaelic.com; 64 Devonshire St, Surry Hills; tickets $10-30; ⚇ varies with shows) Surry Hills' live music stalwart, the no-nonsense Gaelic is all about the music. The split-level, multipurpose venue is where you can catch the next big thing or those who've already made it.

Hopetoun Hotel (Map pp102-3; ☎ 02-9361 5257; www.myspace.com/hopetounhotel; 416 Bourke St, Surry Hills; tickets free-$15; ⚇ 3pm-midnight Mon-Sat, to 10pm Sun) Once the uncontested crucible for new Sydney rock bands, the booze-and-bands 'Hoey' still delivers the local goods to an intimate crowd.

Hordern Pavilion (Map pp100-1; ☎ 02-9383 4000; www.playbillvenues.com; 1 Driver Ave, Moore Park; tickets $68-125; ⚇ varies with shows) Snow Patrol, Lily Allen, the Presets and other big, respectably commercial names play to big audiences in this big space.

Sydney Entertainment Centre (Map pp102-3; ☎ 02-9320 4200; www.sydentcent.com.au; 35 Harbour St, Darling Harbour; ticket prices vary with shows; ⚇ box office 9am-5pm Mon-Fri) Sydney's largest indoor venue holds 12,000 howling rock fans and hosts massive international acts when they're in town. Like most monster venues, the sound quality leaves a little to be desired.

Spectator Sports

Like most Australians, Sydneysiders are passionate about sport. But nothing gets the red-blooded Aussie male going (or grabs newspaper headlines) quite like the **National Rugby League** (NRL; www.nrl.com.au; Ticketek tickets $10-55). The season unfolds at suburban stadiums and **Aussie Stadium** (Map pp100-1; ☎ 02-9360 6601; www.aussiestadium.com; Driver Ave, Moore Park), with September finals. The fever-inducing NSW versus Queensland State of Origin series is played annually.

From March to September, the 2005 premiers Sydney Swans play in the **Australian Football League** (AFL; www.afl.com.au; Ticketmaster tickets $20-40) at the **Sydney Cricket Ground** (Map pp100-1; ☎ 02-9360 6601; www.sydneycricketground.com.au; Driver Ave, Moore Park) and **ANZ Stadium** (off Map pp100-1; ☎ 02-8765 2000; www.anzstadium.com.au; Olympic Blvd, Homebush Bay).

The **National Basketball League** (NBL; www.nbl.com.au; Ticketmaster tickets $10-60) has struggled recently owing to financial woes, but the season dribbles on from April to November.

The **cricket** (www.cricket.com.au) season runs from October to March. The Sydney Cricket Ground (above) plays host to Sheffield Shield (interstate competition) matches and sell-out international Test, one-day and Twenty20 matches.

Tennis NSW (☎ 1800 153 040; www.tennisnsw.com.au) has info on local tournaments and international events at the **Sydney Olympic Park Tennis Centre** (Map pp100-1; ☎ 02-9764 1999; www.sydneyolympicpark.com.au; Rod Laver Dr, Olympic Park, Homebush).

Out on the harbour, the 18ft-skiff racing season runs from September to March. The **Sydney Flying Squadron** (Map pp100-1; ☎ 02-9955 8350; www.sydneyflyingsquadron.com.au; 76 McDougall St, Milsons Point; adult/child $20/6; ☻ 2-4.30pm Sat Sep-Mar) conducts viewings.

SHOPPING

Shopping in Sydney is a mixed bag: fast and furious among the department, chain and high-end shops of the city centre, while neighbourhoods such as Paddington and Newtown offer a distinctly more leisurely (and enjoyable) retail experience.

Head to Oxford St (Paddington) for upmarket boutiques and high-street shops, Queen St (Woollahra) for art and antiques, Transvaal Ave (Double Bay) for high-end labels, King St (Newtown) for independent designers and arty bookshops, and the streets of Surry Hills for off-beat designer furniture and fashion.

In town, the corner of Kent and Bathurst Sts is home to a number of outdoor shops, but also check out Sydney's markets. Around The Rocks is where you'll find all manner of 'Australiana' ranging from Aboriginal artwork to Akubras, but it can be expensive.

Serious shoppers should pick up a free **Urban Walkabout** (www.urbanwalkabout.com) map, divided according to neighbourhood, which delivers the inside scoop on Sydney's shopping secrets.

Late-night shopping is on Thursday, when most shops stay open until 9pm.

Art

Aquabumps Gallery (Map p107; ☎ 02-9130 7788; 151 Curlewis St, Bondi) Photographer/surfer Eugene Tan has been snapping photos of Sydney's sunrises, surf and sand for 10 years and his colourful prints hang in this cool space, a splash from Bondi Beach.

Artery (Map p106; ☎ 02-9380 8234; Shop 2, 221 Darlinghurst Rd, Darlinghurst) This low-key gallery works with established and up-and-coming contemporary central Australian artists. The tiny space has over 300 colourful artworks at any one time; many are refreshingly affordable.

Gannon House (Map pp102-3; ☎ 02-9251 4474; 45 Argyle St, The Rocks) Purchasing works directly from Aboriginal communities, Gannon House represents prominent artists such as Gloria Petyarre and other lesser-known names. You'll also find Aboriginal artefacts as well as contemporary white Australian art.

Gavala (Map pp102-3; ☎ 02-9212 7232; Shop 131, Harbourside Centre, Darling Harbour) Aboriginal-owned store sells only authentic Indigenous products that are licensed, authorised or purchased directly from artists and communities. It stocks

---

BUYING INDIGENOUS ART

Most of Sydney's incredible Indigenous art comes from elsewhere in Australia. To ensure you're not perpetuating non-Indigenous cash-ins on Aboriginal art's popularity, make sure you're buying from an authentic dealer selling original art. If the gallery doesn't pay their artists up front, ask exactly how much of your money will make it back to the artist or community. Another good test is to request some biographical info on the artists – if the vendor can't produce it, keep walking.

paintings, weavings, didgeridoos, boomerangs, masks, jewellery and more.

Hogarth Galleries (Map pp102-3; ☎ 02-9360 6839; 7 Walker Lane, Paddington) This privately run gallery has been supporting and promoting Aboriginal art for over 30 years, in addition to exhibiting works by Australian artists including Sidney Nolan.

Australiana

Australian Wine Centre (Map pp102-3; ☎ 02-9247 2755; Shop 3, Goldfields House, 1 Alfred St, Circular Quay) This basement shop is packed with quality Australian and New Zealand wine, as well as a healthy dose of beer and spirits. There's something for every budget, including a large selection of the highly coveted Robert Parker 95+ wines.

Flame Opals (Map pp102-3; ☎ 02-9247 3446; 119 George St, The Rocks) Shimmering opals are sold in all shapes and sizes at this outlet, and prices range from about $20 to 'If you have to ask, you can't afford it'. There's a tax-free concession for overseas customers.

RM Williams (Map pp102-3; ☎ 02-9262 2228; 389 George St, Sydney) The unofficial uniform for urban cowboys and country folk, this hardwearing outback gear is so quintessentially Australian it even has its own starring role in Baz Luhrmann's epic *Australia*. Favourites include oilskin jackets, leather work boots and Nicole Kidman–inspired blouses and jackets.

Clothing

Bird Emporium (Map pp100-1; ☎ 02-8399 0230; 380 Cleveland St, Surry Hills) Fabulous eco emporium of fashion, fabrics and homewares created by Byron Bay–based designer Rachel Bending, whose company is entirely carbon neutral.

Ksubi (Map p107; ☎ 02-9300 8233; 82 Gould St, Bondi) Pronounced 'soobie', this denim and streetwear label was founded by a couple of Sydney surfer boys in 2000 and is now de rigueur among eastern suburbs hipsters.

Leona Edmiston (Map pp100-1; ☎ 02-9331 7033; 88 William St, Paddington) Leona Edmiston's flirty, feminine frocks are elegant and highly wearable; a favourite among celebs and 'normal' gals alike.

More Aussie talent:

Collette Dinnigan (Map pp100-1; ☎ 02-9360 6691; 33 William St, Paddington) Frills and sequins as worn on the red carpet.

Ginger & Smart (Map pp100-1; ☎ 02-9380 9966; 27 William St, Paddington) Sexy, chic, modern designs for women.

Sass & Bide (Map pp100-1; ☎ 02-9360 3900; 132 Oxford St, Paddington) Highly coveted denim label.

Zimmerman Swim (Map pp100-1; ☎ 02-9387 5111; Shop 3048, Westfield Bondi Junction, 500 Oxford St, Bondi Junction) Itsy bitsy bikinis as modelled by the Bondi beautiful.

Markets

Balmain Market (Map pp100-1; ☎ 0418 765 736; 223 Darling St, Balmain; 🕑 8am-4pm Sat) Set in the shady grounds of St Andrews Congregational, stalls sell arts, crafts, books, clothing, plants, and fruit and veg.

Bondi Markets (Map p107; ☎ 02-9315 8988; Bondi Beach Public School, cnr Campbell Pde & Warners Ave, Bondi; 🕑 10am-4pm Sun) When school's out the yard fills up with stalls selling everything from vintage clothing and bric-a-brac to wooden frames and jewellery. It's great for grabbing a bargain from up-and-coming fashion designers.

Glebe Markets (Map p108; ☎ 0419 291 449; Glebe Public School, cnr Glebe Point Rd & Derby Pl, Glebe; 🕑 10am-4pm Sat) Inner-city hippies flock here for vintage duds, new designers, arts and crafts, a chai latte and restorative massage. Live bands add to the festival vibe.

Paddington Market (Map pp100-1; ☎ 02-9331 2923; St John's Church, 395 Oxford St, Paddington; 🕑 10am-4pm Sat) Born in 1973 Sydney's most attended weekend market has been the launching pad for some of Australia's high-profile fashion labels. Some 250 stalls flog jewellery, homewares, beauty products, art, palmistry and more. Parking is miserable – take public transport.

Paddy's Markets (Map pp102-3; ☎ 1300 361 589; cnr Hay & Thomas Sts, Haymarket; 🕑 9am-5pm Thu-Sun) Among the dozens of stalls selling flashing toys, cheap backpacks and mobile phone covers, you'll find Ugg boots and other Aussie sheepskin memorabilia for a fraction of the price sold in shops.

Rocks Market (Map pp102-3; ☎ 02-9240 8717; George St, The Rocks; 🕑 10am-5pm Sat & Sun) Under a canopy of white sails, 150 stalls vie for tourists' attention with homemade jams, frames, photography, Indigenous artwares and other presents for folks back home.

Shopping Centres & Department Stores

David Jones (Map pp102-3; ☎ 02-9266 5544; 65-77 Market St, Sydney) In two enormous city buildings, DJs is Sydney's premier department store. The Market St store has menswear, electrical and a highbrow food court; Castlereagh St has women's and children's wear.

NEW SOUTH WALES

Queen Victoria Building (QVB; Map pp102-3; ☎ 02-9264 9209; 455 George St, Sydney) Completed in 1898 this Victorian masterpiece occupies an entire city block. Die-hard shoppers will no doubt find something to buy, but we say forget the shops and focus instead on the intricate tiled floors, stained-glass windows and magnificent central dome.

Strand Arcade (Map pp102-3; ☎ 02-9232 4199; 412-414 George St, Sydney) The last remaining arcade of the five originally built in Sydney, the Strand matches the QVB in terms of splendour but wins in the style stakes; the shopping options here are much better.

Westfield Bondi Junction (Map pp100-1; ☎ 02-9947 8000; 500 Oxford St, Bondi Junction) The super-shiny Westfield sucks you in and spins you round its 300 shops over six sprawling levels. The trick is finding your way out again.

GETTING THERE & AWAY
Air
Sydney's Kingsford Smith Airport (Map pp100-1; ☎ 02-9667 9111; www.sydneyairport.com.au) is Australia's busiest. It's only 10km south of the city centre, making access easy, but this also means that flights cease between 11pm and 5am due to noise regulations. The T1 (international) terminal is a 4km bus ($6) or train ($14, or $6 if you are transferring between flights) ride from the T2 (domestic) and T3 (Qantas domestic) terminals.

You can fly into Sydney from all the usual international points and from within Australia. **Qantas** (☎ 13 13 13; www.qantas.com.au), **Jetstar** (☎ 13 15 38; www.jetstar.com.au) and **Virgin Blue** (☎ 13 67 89; www.virginblue.com.au) have frequent flights to other capital cities. Smaller Qantas-affiliated airlines fly to smaller Oz destinations.

For further details on air travel within Australia, see p97. For air travel to/from Australia, see p1046.

Bus
All private interstate and regional bus travellers arrive at **Sydney Coach Terminal** (Map pp102-3; ☎ 02-9281 9366; Central Station, Eddy Ave; ⏰ 6am-10.30pm). Sample destinations include Brisbane ($140, 17 hours), Byron Bay ($130, 13½ hours), Canberra ($36, four hours) and Melbourne ($85, 13 hours).

The government's CountryLink rail network is also complemented by coaches. Most buses stop in the suburbs on the way in and out of Sydney. If you hold a VIP or YHA discount card, shop around the major bus companies with offices here:
Firefly (☎ 1300 730 740; www.fireflyexpress.com.au)
Greyhound (☎ 13 14 99; www.greyhound.com.au)
Murrays (☎ 13 22 51; www.murrays.com.au)
Premier (☎ 13 34 10; www.premierms.com.au)

Train
Sydney's main rail terminus for CountryLink interstate and regional services is **Central Station** (Map pp102-3; ☎ 13 22 32; www.countrylink.info; Eddy Ave; ⏰ staffed ticket booths 6am-10pm, ticket machines 24hr). Call for information, reservations and arrival/departure times. CountryLink discounts often nudge 40% on economy fares – sometimes cheaper than buses!

Sample train fares (without discount) include Brisbane ($100, 14 hours), Canberra ($40, 4½ hours) and Melbourne ($95, 11 hours).

GETTING AROUND
For information on buses, ferries and trains call the **Transport Infoline** (☎ 13 15 00; www.131500 .com.au).

To/From the Airport
One of the easiest ways to get to and from the airport is with a shuttle company such as **Kingsford Smith Transport** (KST; ☎ 02-9666 9988; www.kst.com.au; one-way/return $13/22; ⏰ 5am-11pm), which services hotels in the city, Kings Cross and Darling Harbour. Bookings are essential.

The **Airport Link** (☎ 02-8337 8417; www.airportlink .com.au; one way/return from Central Station to domestic terminal $15/22, to international terminal $15/23; ⏰ 5am-midnight) train runs to and from the airport terminals every 10 to 15 minutes.

Taxi fares from the airport are approximately $25 to $35 to Circular Quay, $40 to $50 to North Sydney and Bondi, and $60 to Manly.

Boat
FERRY
Sydney's most civilised and popular transport option, harbour ferries and RiverCats (to Parramatta) depart from Circular Quay. Most ferries operate between 6am and midnight; those servicing tourist attractions operate shorter hours. The **Ferry Information Office** (Map pp102-3; ☎ 13 15 00; www.sydneyferries.info; ⏰ 7am-5.45pm Mon-Sat, 8am-5.45pm Sun) at Circular Quay has details. Many ferries have connecting bus services.

A one-way inner-harbour ride on a regular ferry costs $5/3 adult/concession. A one-way RiverCat ride to Parramatta (50 minutes, every 50 minutes) costs $8/4 adult/concession.

WATER TAXI

Water taxis ply dedicated shuttle routes; rides to/from other harbour venues can be booked.

Watertours (Map pp102-3; ☎ 02-9211 7730; www .watertours.com.au; 9.30am-late) Opera House to Darling Harbour $15/10 adult/child; one-hour harbour tours $35/20 adult/child; Nightlights tours $20/15.

Yellow Water Taxis (Map pp102-3; ☎ 02-9555 9778, 1300 138 840; www.yellowwatertaxis.com.au; 9am-late) Circular Quay to Darling Harbour $15/10 adult/child; 45-minute harbour tours $30/20.

Bus

Sydney buses run almost everywhere; Bondi Beach, Coogee and parts of the North Shore are serviced only by bus. Nightrider buses operate skeletally after regular services cease around midnight.

The main city bus stops are Circular Quay, Wynyard Park (York St) and Railway Sq. Buy tickets from newsagents, 7-Elevens, Bus TransitShops and on some buses. Pay the driver as you enter, or dunk prepaid tickets in ticket machines by the doors. Fares start at $2. There's a **Bus TransitShop** (Map pp102-3; www.syd neybuses.info; cnr Alfred & Loftus Sts; 7am-7pm Mon-Fri, 8.30am-5pm Sat & Sun) at Circular Quay, and there are others at the Queen Victoria Building (Map pp102–3), Railway Sq (Map pp102–3) and Wynyard Station (Map pp102–3).

Bus routes starting with an X indicate express routes; those with an L have limited stops. Some buses are PrePay, meaning that you must purchase a ticket before boarding the bus. Most buses depart the city on George or Castlereagh Sts, ploughing down George or Elizabeth Sts on the way back in.

Car & Motorcycle

Cars are good for day trips out of town, but drive in the city and you'll spend more time looking for somewhere to park (and pay through the nose for it) than you will anything else.

BUYING OR SELLING A CAR

If you can successfully navigate the secondhand car industry then you can land yourself a good deal. Parramatta Rd is lined with used-car lots, but also check the **Trading Post** (www.tradingpost.com .au), a weekly rag available at newsagents, and www.carsales.com.au for secondhand vehicles. For more information on buying or selling a vehicle, see Driving in Australia, p74.

The **Kings Cross Car Market** (Map p106; ☎ 1800 808 188; www.carmarket.com.au; 110 Bourke St, Woolloomooloo; 9am-5pm) can be a good spot to buy and sell a car; see p77.

RENTAL

The hire car business is a competitive one and some deals will see you driving away in a zippy small car for as little as $30 per day. Rates sometimes include insurance and unlimited kilometres; some companies require you to be over 25 years old. At the time of writing, petrol cost around $1.30 per litre but prices fluctuate regularly (a favourite Sydney talking point). William St, near Kings Cross, has numerous car (and campervan) rental dealerships targeting backpackers.

Standbycars (☎ 1300 789 059; www.standbycars .com) has cheap last-minute deals on cars and campervans, and specialises in car relocations, whereby you return a rental vehicle to its original location after a one-way rental; see p78 for more information.

No Birds (☎ 02-9360 3622; www.nobirds.com.au) has a flock of Toyota Corollas available at some of the best prices in town.

Major rental agencies with offices in Sydney:

Avis (☎ 13 63 33; www.avis.com.au)
Budget (☎ 1300 362 848; www.budget.com.au)
Europcar (☎ 1300 131 390; www.europcar.com.au)
Hertz (☎ 13 30 39; www.hertz.com.au)
Thrifty (☎ 1300 367 227; www.thrifty.com.au)

ROAD TOLLS

Driving around Sydney can be expensive owing to the plethora of toll roads. There's a $4 southbound toll on the Sydney Harbour Bridge and Tunnel. If you're heading from the North Shore to the eastern suburbs, it's easier to take the tunnel. There's a $5 northbound toll on the Eastern Distributor and the Cross City Tunnel costs $4 one way. Sydney's main motorways (M2, M4, M5 and M7) are also tolled ($3 to $6), as are the Lane Cove Tunnel and Flacon St Gateway.

You can pay cash on the Eastern Distributor, M4, M5 and M2, but all other roads are electronically operated. Some car hire companies offer an e-Tag allowing you to zoom through and pay the accumulated toll fees when you return your car. Otherwise look into getting an **e-Pass** (www .roamexpress.com.au), a temporary toll pass. Check www.rta.nsw.gov.au for the latest info.

Fare Deals

The **SydneyPass** (www.sydneypass.info) offers three, five or seven days' unlimited travel over eight days on STA buses, ferries and within the rail network's Red TravelPass zone (inner suburbs). Passes include the Airport Express, Sydney and Bondi Explorer buses, RiverCats and three STA-operated harbour cruises. They cost $110/55/275 per adult/child/family (three days), $145/70/365 (five days) and $165/80/410 (seven days). Buy passes from STA offices, train stations, Bus TransitShops, the Sydney Ferry ticket offices at Circular Quay and Manly Wharf, and from Airport Express and Explorer bus drivers.

There is a range of TravelPasses for unlimited rail, bus and ferry rides at cheap weekly rates, with various colour-coded grades offering combinations of distance and service. A weekly Red TravelPass (inner suburbs), available at train stations, STA offices, Bus TransitShops and newsagents, costs $38/19 adult/concession.

If you're just catching buses, a TravelTen ticket from newsagents and Bus TransitShops offers 10 discounted bus trips and allows you to use the PrePay only buses. There are various colour codes for different distances: a Red TravelTen ticket (inner suburbs) costs $34/17 adult/concession. FerryTen tickets from the Circular Quay ticket office are also good value – 10 inner-harbour rides for $34/17 adult/concession. DayTripper tickets letting you ride most inner-suburban trains, buses and ferries cost $17/9 adult/concession.

Several transport-plus-entry tickets available from the Circular Quay Ferry Information Office (p144) work out cheaper than catching a return ferry and paying entry separately. These include the **ZooPass** (adult/child/family $44/22/117) and the **Wild Australia Pass** (adult/child/family $55/28/128), which includes entry to Sydney Wildlife World and the Aquarium.

Monorail & Metro Light Rail (MLR)

The privately operated **Metro Monorail** (☎ 02-8584 5288; www.metrotransport.com.au; circuit $5, day pass adult/family $10/23; ☽ every 3-5min 7am-10pm Mon-Thu, to midnight Fri & Sat, 8am-10pm Sun) is an elevated electronic worm circling around Darling Harbour and the city. The full loop takes about 14 minutes.

Run by the same company, the futuristic **Metro Light Rail** (MLR; Zone 1 adult/concession $3/2, Zone 1 & 2 adult/concession $4/3, day pass adult/concession $9/7; ☽ 24hr, every 10-15min 6am-midnight, every 30min midnight-6am) glides between Central Station and Pyrmont via Chinatown and Darling Harbour. The Zone 2 service beyond Pyrmont to Lilyfield stops at 11pm Sunday to Thursday, midnight Friday and Saturday. Purchase tickets on board.

Note that the SydneyPass isn't valid on the monorail or the MLR.

Taxi

Taxis and cab ranks proliferate in Sydney. Flag fall is $3.10, then it's $1.85 per kilometre (plus 20% from 10pm to 6am). The waiting charge is 80c per minute. Passengers must also pay bridge, tunnel and road tolls (even if you don't incur them 'outbound', the returning driver will incur them 'inbound').

The four major taxi companies offering phone bookings ($2 fee):

Legion (☎ 13 14 51)
Premier Cabs (☎ 13 10 17)
Silver Service (☎ 13 31 00)
Taxis Combined (☎ 13 33 00)

Train

Sydney's vast suburban rail network bumbles along, providing good service for some areas and absolutely none whatsoever for the northern and southern beaches, Balmain or Glebe. All suburban trains stop at Central Station, and usually one or more of the other seven City Circle stations, too.

Trains run from around 5am to midnight. At weekends and after 9am on weekdays you can buy an off-peak return ticket, valid until 4am the next day, for little more than a standard one-way fare.

You'll find 24-hour ticket machines in most stations, but human ticket tellers are usually available, too. If you have to change trains, buy a ticket to your ultimate destination, but don't exit the transfer station en route or your ticket will be invalid.

For train information, visit the **CityRail Information Booth** (Map pp102-3; ☎ 13 15 00; www.131500.com.au; Wharf 5, Circular Quay; ☽ 9.05am-4.50pm).

AROUND SYDNEY

Sydney's extensive urban sprawl eventually dissolves into superb national parks and historic small towns. North of Sydney, where the Hawkesbury River meets the sea, lies Ku-ring-gai Chase National Park, a dense cluster of forests, creeks and sheltered coves with a rich Aboriginal heritage. To the south, Royal National Park – the second-oldest national park in the world – hides lost-to-the-world beaches, rainforest pockets and precipitous cliffscapes. The wooded foothills of the Great Dividing Range sit to the west of Sydney and climb to the magnificent Blue Mountains. Inland the rolling hills and fertile soils of Macarthur Country support old Macquarie towns established in the early days of settlement.

BOTANY BAY

In May 1787 the First Fleet left Britain for Australia, bound for Botany Bay. Upon arriving, however, it was discovered that the sandy infertile soil was unsuitable for settlement and the decision was made to move to the natural harbour of Port Jackson to the north.

Today Botany Bay, on the city's southern fringe, is a smoke-stacked industrial heartland that bears little resemblance to the landscape that first confronted Cook when he stepped ashore. Despite the refineries, however, Botany Bay still has scenic stretches and continues to hold a special place in Australian history. Joseph Banks, Cook's expedition's naturalist, named the bay for the many botanical specimens he found here.

Botany Bay National Park (cars $7, pedestrians & cyclists free; 🕑 7am-7.30pm Sep-May, to 5.30pm Jun-Aug) occupies both headlands of the bay – 458 hectares of bushland and coastal walking tracks, picnic areas, sheltered coves and beaches. A sandstone obelisk marks Cook's landing place in Kurnell, on the southern side of the park. The **Discovery Centre** (☎ 02-9668 2000; www.environment.nsw.gov.au/nationalparks; Cape Solander Dr, Kurnell; admission free; 🕑 11am-3pm Mon-Fri, 9am-4pm Sat & Sun) focuses on the first contact between Aboriginal people and the crew of the *Endeavour*. There's also information on the geography of the region. The entry fee for cars applies only on the southern headland – pedestrian access is free. Most of the walking tracks begin close to the park entrance, so you might as well park outside. To get here via public transport, catch the train to Cronulla, then **Crowthers Buslink** (☎ 02-9523 4047; www.buslink.net.au) bus 987 from Cronulla train station 10km away (one way adult/child $4/2, 20 minutes, roughly every hour 6.20am to 6.20pm).

La Perouse, on the northern headland, is named after the French explorer who arrived in 1788, just six days after the arrival of the First Fleet. La Perouse and his men camped at Botany Bay for a few weeks before sailing off into the Pacific, never to be seen again. The **La Perouse Museum & Visitors Centre** (☎ 02-9311 3379; www.environment.nsw.gov.au; Cable Station, Anzac Pde, La Perouse; adult/child/family $6/3/13; 🕑 10am-4pm Wed-Sun), housed inside the old cable station (1882), charts the course of La Perouse's fateful expedition, and also hosts changing exhibitions on local history and environment. It is well worth a visit.

About 50m offshore at La Perouse sits the strange **Bare Island** (☎ 02-9247 5033; www.nationalparks.nsw.gov.au; tours adult/concession/family $10/8/25; 🕑 tours 1.30, 2.30 & 3.30pm Sun), famous for appearing in *Mission: Impossible II*. Originally built in 1885 to discourage a sea attack (which never materialised), today the decaying concrete fort is a museum. A 45-minute guided tour is the only way to access the island.

Bus 394 runs from Circular Quay to La Perouse (one way adult/child $5/3, 45 minutes, every 20 minutes).

ROYAL NATIONAL PARK

The 15,080-hectare **Royal National Park** (cars $11, pedestrians & cyclists free; 🕑 gates to park areas locked at 8.30pm daily) was established in 1879, making it the oldest national park in the world after Yellowstone in the USA. Here you'll find pockets of subtropical rainforest, windblown coastal scrub, sandstone gullies dominated by gum trees, fresh- and saltwater wetlands, and isolated beaches. Traditionally the home of the Dharawal people, there are also numerous Aboriginal sites and artefacts.

The national park begins at Port Hacking, 30km south of Sydney, and stretches 20km further south. Its main road detours to Bundeena, a small town on Port Hacking, the starting point for kayaking tours of the park and the 17km-long **Bundeena-Maianbar Heritage Walk**.

The sandstone plateau at the northern end of the park is an ocean of low scrub, the fuel for three voracious bushfires in recent years. The most serious one (1994) destroyed 95% of the park.

AROUND SYDNEY

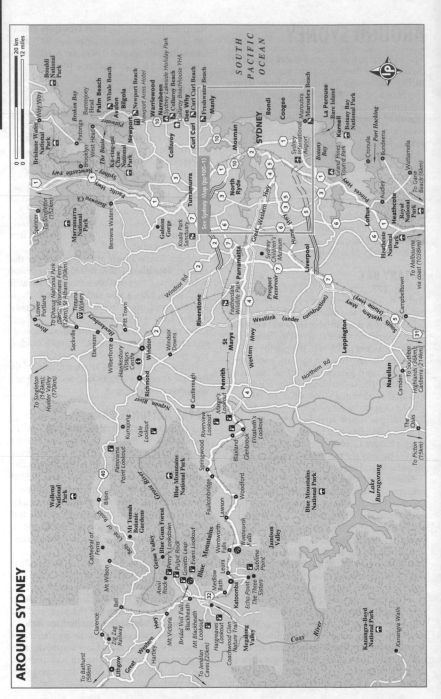

Within the park there's sheltered swimming at Wattamolla and Bonnie Vale, and good surf at Garie Beach, Era and Burning Palms. At the historic **Audley Boat Shed** (☎ 02-9545 4967; Farnell Rd, Audley; ⏰ 9am-5pm Mon-Sat, to 5.30pm Sun) you can hire rowboats, canoes and kayaks ($20/40 per hour/day), aqua bikes ($15 per 30 minutes) and bicycles ($16/34 per hour/day) and paddle up Kangaroo Creek or the Hacking River.

A walking and cycling trail follows the Hacking River south from Audley; others pass tranquil freshwater swimming holes. The spectacular two-day, 28km **coast track** hugs the park's eastern boundary and is highly recommended.

The **visitor centre** (☎ 02-9542 0648; www.environ ment.nsw.gov.au/nationalparks; Farnell Ave, Audley; ⏰ 9am-4pm) can assist with camping permits, maps and bushwalking details.

Sleeping & Eating

Garie Beach YHA (☎ 02-9261 1111; Garie Beach, Royal National Park; dm $14) This 12-bunk hostel is low on frills (there's no phone, electricity or showers), but if you're looking to get away from it all then you couldn't pick a better spot. It's utterly secluded and close to one of the best surf beaches in NSW. Bring all your food with you. Book via the YHA Membership & Travel Centre (p109) or the Cronulla Beach YHA. It's a 1.5km walk from Garie Beach car park, a 10km coastal walk from Otford train station, or a 15km coastal walk from Bundeena.

Cronulla Beach YHA (☎ 02-9527 7772; www.cronulla beachyha.com; 40-42 Kingsway, Cronulla; dm/d/f $30/95/145; 🖳) Run by two gregarious brothers, this is a top spot for cheerful vibes, honing your surfing skills or hooking up with fellow coastal trail walkers. The rooms are well kitted out with wardrobes and safes.

Beachhaven Bed & Breakfast (☎ 02-9544 1333; www.beachhavenbnb.com.au; 13 Bundeena Dr, Bundeena; d incl breakfast $275-300; 🐾 🖳) The faux-Tudor mansion won't be everyone's cup of tea, but the location on heavenly Hordens Beach is stunning. There are two royally appointed suites, a barbecue and a lovely sea-view deck for evening drinks.

There's a drive-in **camp site** (☎ 02-9542 0683; adult/child $14/7, vehicle fee $11) at Bonnie Vale near Bundeena, but you must book in advance. If you're walking, you can camp along the coastal trail and at Uloola on the western side

of the park; grab a permit ($5 per person per night) from the visitor centre.

Passionfruit Café (☎ 02-9527 6555; 46-48 Brighton St, Bundeena; mains $5-20; ⏰ breakfast & lunch daily, dinner Tue-Fri) The busiest joint in town is this cheerful cafe that dishes up old-school fuel: burgers, pies, lasagne and yummy cakes.

Getting There & Away

From Sydney, take the Princes Hwy south and turn off at Farnell Ave, south of Loftus, to the park's northern end – it's about a 45-minute drive from the city. If you're driving north from Wollongong, don't miss the famous 665m-long curving Sea Cliff Bridge section of Lawrence Hargrave Dr between Clifton and Coalcliff.

The most scenic route into the park is to take the CityRail train (one way adult/child $5/3, one hour, every 20 minutes) to Cronulla and then jump aboard a **Cronulla National Park Ferry** (☎ 02-9523 2990; www.cronullaferries.com.au; Cronulla Wharf) to Bundeena (one way adult/child $6/3, 30 minutes, hourly). Cronulla Wharf is off Tonkin St just below the train station. This outfit also runs three-hour **Port Hacking Scenic Cruises** (adult/child/family $18/13/50; ⏰ 10.30am daily Sep-May, 10.30am & 1.30pm Sun-Wed & Fri Jun-Aug). Alternatively, Loftus, Engadine, Heathcote, Waterfall and Otford train stations are on the park boundary and have trails leading into the park. Loftus is closest to the visitor centre (6km).

PARRAMATTA

pop 148,323

These days it's all about harbour views, but early colonists much preferred the fertile pastures of Parramatta, 24km west of the city centre, to the rowdy, narrow streets around Port Jackson. By 1792 the area was home to 1970 people, compared with just 1170 on the coast.

More recently, however, folk living in Parramatta and other western Sydney suburbs have been labelled (usually by poncey central Sydneysiders) as flannel-shirt-wearing AC/DC fans. While this may have been true in the 1980s when local rugby league team, the mullet-proud Parramatta Eels, topped the league tables, those stereotypes no longer hold any merit. Today Parramatta has successfully established itself as Sydney's second CBD and is fast developing its own art, theatre and festival scene to boot.

NEW SOUTH WALES

The name Parramatta is a Dharug Aboriginal name meaning 'the place where eels lie down'.

Although modernity reigns, a clutch of colonial buildings remains; the **Parramatta Heritage Centre** (☎ 02-8839 3311; www.parracity.nsw .gov.au; 346a Church St; ☺ 9am-5pm) can steer you towards the city's attractions.

Established in 1799 **Old Government House** (☎ 02-9635 8149; www.nsw.nationaltrust.org.au; Parramatta Park; adult/concession/family $8/5/18; ☺ 1hr tours 10am-4.30pm Tue-Fri, 10.30am-4.30pm Sat & Sun) is Australia's oldest public building. For seven decades it was the country retreat of early colony governors looking to escape the bawdy, crime-ridden streets of Sydney. It is now a carefully maintained museum. Nearby on O'Connell St, **St John's Cemetery** dates back to 1790 and is the resting ground for many of Australia's earliest settlers: you'll find graves of governors' wives, notable citizens and First Fleet convicts.

Elizabeth Farm (☎ 02-9635 9488; www.hht.net .au; 70 Alice St, Rosehill; adult/concession/family $8/4/17; ☺ 9.30am-4pm Fri-Sun) is the oldest surviving homestead (1793) in Australia. Built by renegade pastoralist/rum trader/wool merchant John Macarthur, it is now a hands-on museum chock-full of history. Recline on the furniture and thumb voyeuristically through Elizabeth Macarthur's letters.

Nearby **Hambledon Cottage** (☎ 02-9635 6924; 63 Hassall St; adult/child $4/2; ☺ 11am-4pm Wed, Thu, Sat & Sun) was built in 1824 for the Macarthurs' daughter's governess, and was later used as weekend lodgings.

In 1789 ex-convict James Ruse was chosen by Governor Phillip to run a trial in self-sufficiency, and was given **Experiment Farm Cottage** (☎ 02-9635 5655; www.nsw.nationaltrust.org .au; 9 Ruse St; adult/concession/family $6/4/14; ☺ 10.30am-3.30pm Tue-Fri, 11am-3.30pm Sat & Sun). By 1791 Ruse had successfully farmed the 30-acre site and subsequently became Australia's first private farmer.

Getting There & Around

The most pleasant route to Parramatta is by RiverCat from Circular Quay (one way adult/child $8/4, 55 minutes). Otherwise catch a train from Central Station (one way adult/child $4/2, 30 minutes). By car, exit the city via Parramatta Rd and detour onto the Western Motorway tollway ($3) at Strathfield.

CAMDEN AREA

About 50km southwest of Sydney, Camden is a peaceful agrarian town that played a pivotal role in the birth of the Australian wool, wine and wheat industries. Several heritage-listed buildings remain.

Built in the 1890s as a workman's cottage, **John Oxley Cottage** (☎ 02-4658 1370; Camden Valley Way, Elderslie; ☺ 9.30am-4pm) today houses the visitor centre. It's on the town's northern outskirts.

The 400-hectare **Mount Annan Botanic Garden** (☎ 02-4648 2477; www.rbgsyd.nsw.gov.au/mount_annan; Mt Annan Dr, Mt Annan; admission car/pedestrian $9/3; ☺ 10am-5pm) is the native-plant branch of Sydney's Royal Botanic Gardens and claims to be the largest botanic garden in the southern hemisphere. With 4000 species on 1000 acres, the claim seems entirely plausible.

North of Camden, pretty **Cobbitty Village** was first settled in 1812 and many of the original homes still stand. A morning craft and local produce **market** is held on the first Saturday of every month (except January and February).

South of Camden is **Picton**, reportedly one of the most haunted towns in Australia. A handful of significant buildings remain, including the old post office where you'll find the **Wollondilly visitor centre** (☎ 02-4677 8313; www.visitwollondilly.com.au; cnr Argyle & Menangle Sts; ☺ 9am-5pm). Pick up the *Historic Picton Walking Tour* pamphlet and when dusk falls join historian Liz Vincent on one of her spine-chilling **Ghost Tours** (☎ 02-4677 2044; www .lizvincenttours.com.au; ☺ 8pm Fri & Sat). The historic **George IV Inn** (☎ 02-4677 1415; www.georgeiv.com.au; 180 Argyle St; d without bathroom from $55) has simple pub-style accommodation.

CityRail trains run from Sydney's Central Station to Picton (one way adult/child $10/5, roughly hourly). They also run to Campbelltown (one way adult/child $7/3, half-hourly). **Busways'** (☎ 02-4625 8922; www.bus ways.com.au) bus 890 and 895 run to Camden (one way adult/child $5/3, 25 minutes, half-hourly). Bus 31 runs from Camden to Cobbitty Village (adult/child $2/1).

KU-RING-GAI CHASE NATIONAL PARK

Just 24km north of the city centre, this 15,000-hectare **national park** (per car $11; ☺ sunrise-sunset) offers Sydneysiders endless opportunities to commune with nature. The park borders Broken Bay's southern edge and Pittwater's western shore, and is a mixture of drowned river valley estuaries, steep sandstone cliffs and plateaus. There are some excellent walking trails here, including the **Aboriginal Heritage Track**, an easy 1km path that leads past a fantastic Aboriginal engraving site. There are also cycling and horse-riding trails, picnic areas and spectacular views of Broken Bay, particularly from West Head at the park's northeastern tip.

The **Kalkari discovery centre** (☎ 02-9472 9300; www.nationalparks.nsw.gov.au; Ku-ring-gai Chase Rd; ⏰ 9am-5pm) runs guided tours. It's about 2.5km into the park from the Mt Colah entrance. The road descends from Kalkari to **Bobbin Head picnic area** and **Bobbin Head Information Centre** (☎ 02-9472 8949; www.nationalparks.nsw.gov.au; Bobbin Head Rd; ⏰ 10am-4pm) at the old Bobbin Head Inn on Cowan Creek, then climbs to the Turramurra entrance. Contact **Empire Marinas** (☎ 02-9457 9011; www.empiremarinas.com.au; ⏰ 8am-4pm) at Bobbin Head for information on boat hire. Sharks in Broken Bay make for a risky swim, but there's a netted area at the Basin if you simply must cool off.

Sleeping

Pittwater YHA Hostel (☎ 02-9999 5748; www.yha.com.au; Ku-ring-gai Chase National Park; dm $25-28, d & tw $65-72) Undoubtedly one of the most picturesque hostel locations can be found here at this basic but comfy hostel. The outstanding Pittwater views, isolated bush setting and friendly wildlife make it a must for nature lovers. Bookings are essential. To get here, take the ferry from Church Point to Halls Wharf, then trek 15 minutes up the hill.

Basin campsites (☎ 02-9974 1011; www.basincampground.com.au; Ku-ring-gai Chase National Park; per night adult/child $14/7) Camping is permitted at the Basin (bookings essential) on the western side of Pittwater. Getting there requires a 2.5km walk from West Head Rd, or a ferry or water-taxi ride from Palm Beach.

Getting There & Away

There are four road entrances to the park: Mt Colah on the Pacific Hwy; Turramurra in the southwest; and Terrey Hills and Church Point in the southeast.

The **Palm Beach Ferry Service** (☎ 02-9974 2411; www.palmbeachferry.com.au) leaves Palm Beach Wharf in Pittwater for the Basin every hour on the hour (adult/child $14/7). **Peninsula Water Taxis** (☎ 0415 408 831) operates services on demand between Church Point Ferry Wharf, Palm Beach and over the whole of Pittwater.

To get to Palm Beach, take bus 190 or L90 from Wynyard Station (one way adult/child $6/3, 1½ hours, half-hourly). From Turramurra Station, **Shorelink Buses** (☎ 02-9457 8888; www.shorelink.com.au) runs bus 577 every hour to the park entrance (one way adult/child $4/2, 20 minutes, hourly). From here it's about 3km to Bobbin Head.

HAWKESBURY RIVER

Less than an hour from Sydney the slow-roaming Hawkesbury River is a favourite weekend destination for stressed-out city folk. The river – one of the longest in eastern Australia – flows past honeycomb-coloured cliffs, historic townships and riverside hamlets into bays and inlets and between a series of national parks.

The fertile farming country around the Hawkesbury sustains vineyards, vegetable farms, flower acreages and alpaca studs. Contact **Hawkesbury Harvest** (☎ 0406 237 877; www.hawkesburyharvest.com.au) for information on wine and farm trails.

HAWKESBURY HOUSEBOATS

The best way to experience the Hawkesbury is on a houseboat. Expect rates to skyrocket during summer and school holidays, but most outfits offer affordable low-season, midweek and long-term rental specials. As a rough guide, a two-/four-/six-berth boat for three nights costs from $650/780/1190 between May and September, with prices doubling during summer.

Most companies base themselves at Brooklyn. The following are some of the main players:

- **Able Hawkesbury River Houseboats** (☎ 02-4566 4306, 1800 024 979; www.hawkesburyhouseboats.com.au; 3008 River Rd, Wisemans Ferry)

- **Brooklyn Marina** (☎ 02-9985 7722; www.brooklynmarina.com.au; 45 Brooklyn Rd, Brooklyn)

- **Holidays Afloat** (☎ 02-9985 7368; www.holidaysafloat.com.au; 65 Brooklyn Rd, Brooklyn)

- **Ripples Houseboats** (☎ 02-9985 5555; www.ripples.com.au; 87 Brooklyn Rd, Brooklyn)

SOLOMON WISEMAN

Born in 1777 in Essex, England, Solomon Wiseman was a true wheeler-dealer. As captain of a small sloop that cruised the English Channel, he was employed by the British government to carry spies to the French coast. Never one to pass up a moneymaking opportunity, Wiseman also did a neat trade in rum and brandy. His booze cruise came to an end, however, in 1806 when he was caught by revenue officers who found both contraband spirits and a handful of passengers who turned out to be French spies. Solomon was thus sent to the colony for life, arriving in 1806.

Whether or not there is much truth in the above story is debatable, but it's the one that larger-than-life Wiseman liked to tell over a drink or two. What is true, however, is that he received his ticket-of-leave in June 1810, his absolute pardon in 1812 and was later granted 200 acres on the Hawkesbury. Wiseman built his house (now Wisemans Inn; see below) in 1826 and soon after established the ferry service, which still runs today.

The **Riverboat Postman** (☎ 02-9985 7566; www .hawkesburyriverferries.com.au; Riverboat Postman Wharf, Brooklyn; adult/child/family $50/30/130; ⌚ 9.30am Mon-Fri), Australia's last operating mail boat, chugs 40km up the Hawkesbury as far as Marlow, near Spencer. There are additional 'coffee cruises' during summer.

Near Brooklyn is the brilliant **Peats Bite** (☎ 02-9985 9040; www.peatsbite.com.au; Sunny Corner; set menu per person $120; ⌚ lunch Thu-Sat). This restaurant has been operated by the same family since 1981. Guests are encouraged to linger over a long lunch, take a dip in the pool between courses and shimmy on the dance floor when Tammy gets up to sing. Access is by boat only.

Further upstream a narrow forested waterway diverts from the Hawkesbury and peters down to the chilled-out river town of **Berowra Waters**, where a handful of businesses, boat sheds and residences cluster around the free, 24-hour ferry across Berowra Creek. If you feel like exploring, rev the river in an outboard dinghy from the **Berowra Waters Marina** (☎ 02-9456 7000; www.barbecueboat.info; 199 Bay Rd, Berowra Waters; per half day $75; ⌚ 8am-5pm). Nearby, elegant **Berowra Waters Inn** (☎ 02-9456 1027; www .berowrawatersinn.com; 4/5/6 courses $125/135/150; ⌚ lunch Fri-Sun, dinner Thu-Sat) is one of the region's best restaurants. The restaurant is only accessed by boat.

CityRail trains run from Sydney's Central Station to Berowra (one way adult/child $6/3, 45 minutes, roughly hourly) and on to Brooklyn's Hawkesbury River Station (one way adult/child $7/4, one hour). Berowra Station is a solid 6km trudge from Berowra Waters. **Hawkesbury Cruises** (☎ 02-9985 9900; www.hawkesburycruises.com.au) runs water taxis on demand to anywhere along the river.

The lively riverside hamlet of **Wisemans Ferry** spills over a bow of the Hawkesbury River where it slides east towards Brooklyn. The surrounding area is the scene of the convict-built **Great North Road**, originally constructed to link Sydney with the Hunter Valley. Today it is a pretty back route to the north. Some 15km of the original road has been preserved and offers an excellent mountain-bike trail.

The town's social hub is the historic sandstone **Wisemans Inn** (☎ 02-4566 4301; www.wise mansinnhotel.com.au; Old Northern Rd, Wisemans Ferry; d with/without bathroom $90/75), which has decent pub rooms and a bistro (mains $16 to $28; open for lunch and dinner) oozing country singers and dozens of bikies at weekends. The prettiest access is from the east, via Old Wisemans Ferry Rd, wedged between Dharug National Park and the river. Two free 24-hour ferries connect the Wisemans Ferry river banks.

Largely unsealed but photogenic roads on both sides of the Macdonald River run north from Wisemans Ferry to tiny **St Albans** in Darkinung tribal country. The colourful flags on the hill mark the **St Albans Gallery** (☎ 02-4568 2286; ⌚ 11am-5pm Fri-Sun), which has quirky exhibitions of local jewellery, glass, painting, sculpture and Indigenous art.

WINDSOR & RICHMOND
On the banks of the Hawkesbury River, the once grand **Windsor** (population 1670) is the third-oldest place of British settlement. The town still boasts a handful of original buildings, but there's no denying that much of the town's charm has been swallowed up by the ever-creeping urban sprawl.

Designed by convict architect Francis Greenway, **Windsor Courthouse** (☎ 02-4577 3023; cnr North Pitt & Court Sts) was built in 1822 for a cost of £1800. Nearby the convict-built **St Matthew's Anglican Church** (☎ 02-4577 3193; Moses St; ⏰ 10am-3pm, services 8am, 10am & 5.30pm Sun) held its first service in September 1821. It remains the oldest Anglican church in Australia.

The reputedly haunted **Macquarie Arms Hotel** (☎ 02-4577 2206; 99 George St; ⏰ 10am-midnight) has been calling last orders since 1815. The interiors retain much of their country-town charm; unfortunately the beer garden and bistro (mains $13 to $29; open lunch and dinner) don't.

The **Hawkesbury Regional Museum** (☎ 02-4560 4655; www.hawkesburyhistory.org.au/museum; 7 Thompson Sq; admission free; ⏰ 10am-4pm Wed-Sun) offers a slice of early pioneer life. The **Hawkesbury Regional Gallery** (☎ 02-4560 4441; www.hawkesbury.com.au; Level 1, Deerubbin Centre, 300 George St; admission free; ⏰ 10am-4pm Mon & Wed-Fri, to 3pm Sat & Sun) is Windsor's cultural centre with art exhibitions, literary launches, film screenings and kids' events.

Five kilometres west of Windsor is **Richmond** (population 5560), first settled in 1794. Like its neighbour the town has suffered from its now suburban location, but has managed to cling onto some noteworthy buildings, including the 1878 **courthouse** and **police station** (☎ 02-4578 0731; cnr Market & Windsor Sts).

Built in 1845 by local George Bowman for his daughter's wedding to a penniless reverend, **St Andrew's Church** (☎ 02-4578 3820; www.richmonduniting.org.au; Market St; ⏰ services 8.30am, 9.45am & 6pm Sun) retains some of its original features. One of the more remarkable buildings is a heritage-listed 1817 weatherboard cottage that today houses Richmond's **NPWS Office** (☎ 02-4588 5247; www.npws.nsw.gov.au; Bowmans Cottage, 370 George St; ⏰ 9am-4.30pm Mon-Fri).

Halfway between Richmond and Windsor, the **Hawkesbury visitor centre** (☎ 02-4578 0233; www.hawkesburytourism.com.au; Ham Common Park, Hawkesbury Valley Way, Clarendon; ⏰ 9am-5pm Mon-Fri, to 4pm Sat & Sun) handles accommodation bookings.

CityRail trains run from Sydney's Central Station to Windsor (one way adult/child $7/3, 70 minutes, roughly hourly) and Richmond (one way adult/child $7/4, 80 minutes, roughly hourly).

BLUE MOUNTAINS

Within striking distance of Sydney is the spectacular wilderness area of the Blue Mountains. For more than a century these mountains – in reality a series of hills shaped by dramatic gorges – have been luring Sydneysiders up from the sweltering plains with promises of cool-climate relief, stunning scenery and fabulous bushwalking opportunities. The slate-coloured haze that gives the mountains their name comes from a fine mist of oil exuded by eucalyptus trees.

The mountains, part of the Great Dividing Range, begin 65km inland rising to a 1100m-high sandstone plateau riddled with valleys eroded into the stone over millennia. For years these mountains formed an impenetrable barrier to colonial expansion from Sydney as numerous attempts to find a route through failed. Many settlers also had the rather bizarre notion that China – and freedom – lay on the other side. It wasn't until 1813 that European explorers Blaxland, Lawson and Wentworth successfully traversed the mountains. Today the Great Western Hwy follows their route through the hilltop towns of – surprise, surprise – Blaxland, Lawson and Wentworth Falls.

There are three beautiful national parks in the area, the most accessible of which is the Blue Mountains National Park, which protects large tracts of gullies and gums north and south of the Great Western Hwy. Absorb the park's jaw-dropping scenery at the numerous drive-up lookouts, or get among the greenery on established bushwalking trails. Southwest of here is Kanangra Boyd National Park, accessible from Oberon or Jenolan Caves. Launch into a bushwalk, descend into limestone caverns or check out the amazing Kanangra Walls plateau, encircled by sheer cliffs. At nearly 500,000 hectares, Wollemi National Park, north of Bells Line of Road, is the state's largest forested wilderness area with rugged bushwalking and native critters aplenty.

Entry to these national parks is free unless you enter the Blue Mountains National Park at Bruce Rd, Glenbrook ($7 per car, walkers free). For more information (including camping) contact the **NPWS Visitor Centre** (☎ 02-4787 8877; www.nationalparks.nsw.gov.au; Govetts Leap Rd, Blackheath; ⏰ 9am-4.30pm), about 2.5km off the Great Western Hwy and 10km north of Katoomba.

Climate

Be prepared for a climatic shift as you ascend to the Blue Mountains – swelter in Coogee, shiver in Katoomba. The mountains are promoted as a cool-climate attraction, but visit at any time: summer days are hazy perfection, while autumn fogs make

Katoomba an eerily atmospheric place. Winter days can be sunny and sometimes bring snow.

Getting There & Away

If travelling by car follow the signs from the city to Parramatta. At Strathfield turn onto the Western Motorway tollway (M4; $3), which becomes the Great Western Hwy west of Penrith.

To reach Bells Line of Road (see p162), head out on Parramatta Rd, and from Parramatta drive northwest on the Windsor Rd to Windsor. The Richmond Rd from Windsor becomes the Bells Line of Road west of Richmond.

CityRail trains regularly service Leura, Katoomba, Blackheath, Mt Victoria and Lithgow.

Getting Around

The **Blue Mountains Bus Company** (☎ 02-4751 1077; www.bmbc.com.au) has services from Valley Heights (near Springwood) to Mt Victoria, stopping pretty much everywhere in between. Check the website for details and schedules.

There are train stations in Blue Mountains towns along the Great Western Hwy. Trains run roughly every hour between stations east of Katoomba, and roughly every two hours between stations to the west.

RediCar (☎ 02-4751 8920; 42 Great Western Hwy, Valley Heights; ☒ 9am-5pm Mon-Fri, to noon Sat) hires out cars from $66 per day.

GLENBROOK TO WENTWORTH FALLS

From **Marge's Lookout** and **Elizabeth's Lookout** near Glenbrook there are super views back to Sydney. The section of the Blue Mountains National Park south of Glenbrook contains **Red Hands Cave**, an old Aboriginal shelter with hand stencils on the walls. It's an easy 7km return walk southwest of the **Glenbrook NPWS centre** (☎ 02-4739 2950; ☒ Sat & Sun) on the Great Western Hwy.

Celebrated artist, author and bon vivant Norman Lindsay, famed for his racy artworks and children's tale *The Magic Pudding*, lived in Faulconbridge from 1912 until his death in 1969. His home and studio is now the **Norman Lindsay Gallery & Museum** (☎ 02-4751 1067; www.normanlindsay.com.au; 14 Norman Lindsay Cres, Faulconbridge; adult/child/family $9/6/24; ☒ 10am-4pm), with a significant collection of his paintings, watercolours, drawings and sculptures. There is a very good

cafe (☎ 02-4751 9611; mains $12-25; ☒ breakfast & lunch) on site and you can overnight in the grounds in a cosy **cottage** (d $120-150).

The quiet and ecofriendly **Hawkesbury Heights YHA** (☎ 02-4754 5621; www.yha.com.au; 836 Hawkesbury Rd, Hawkesbury Heights; dm/d from $24/48) sits tucked away in the bush 11km northeast of Springwood. It has solar power, comfortable rooms and sensational valley views. You need wheels to get here; the reception is in the red-brick house on the main road.

As you head into Wentworth Falls, you'll get your first real taste of Blue Mountains scenery: views to the south open out across the majestic Jamison Valley. Wentworth Falls itself launches a plume of fraying droplets over a 300m drop – check it out from Falls Rd. This is also the starting point for a network of walking tracks that delves into the sublime Valley of the Waters, with waterfalls, gorges, woodlands and rainforests.

Campsites are accessible by road at Euroka Clearing (vehicle/adult/child $7/10/5) near Glenbrook, and Murphys Glen near Woodford. Check track/road condition updates and collect permits for Euroka Clearing at the Richmond NPWS Office (p153).

LEURA

pop 4385

Leura, with its pretty tree-lined streets, art deco houses and grand Victorian verandahs, is one of the most charming and attractive villages in the Blue Mountains. Without the Great Western Hwy running through its centre it's managed to maintain a sense of exclusivity, which is reflected in the upmarket boutiques and restaurants that line the **Mall**. The **Leura Visitors Gateway** (☎ 02-4784 3443; www.bluemountainsway.com.au; 121 The Mall; ☒ 9am-5pm) books accommodation and tours, organises car hire and has a local art gallery next door.

The **Leuralla Toy & Railway Museum** (☎ 02-4784 1169; www.toyandrailwaymuseum.com.au; 36 Olympian Pde; adult/child $12/6; ☒ 10am-5pm) is set amid 12 acres of handsome gardens in a heritage-listed home. The museum houses a huge collection of toys, including antique dolls and teddy bears, old tin toys, model trains and railway memorabilia.

Designed in the 1930s by famous Danish landscaper Paul Sorensen, **Everglades Gardens** (☎ 02-4784 1938; www.everglades.org.au; 37 Everglades Ave; adult/child $7/3; ☒ 10am-5pm Oct-Mar, to 4pm Apr-Sep) is a National Trust property and Leura's

---

FOOTING IT IN THE BLUE MOUNTAINS

The roads across the mountains offer tantalising glimpses of the majesty of the area, but the only way to really experience the Blue Mountains is on foot. There are walks lasting from a few minutes to several days. The two most popular areas are Jamison Valley, south of Katoomba, and Grose Valley, east of Blackheath. The area south of Glenbrook is also good.

Blackheath's Blue Mountains Heritage Centre (p160) is a good source of information for long hikes; for shorter walks, ask at Katoomba's Echo Point Visitor Centre (p156). It's rugged country, and it's not unheard for walkers to lose their way, so it's imperative to get reliable information, not to go alone and to tell someone where you're going. People have perished by skipping one of these three necessities. Many Blue Mountains watercourses are polluted, so you must sterilise water or take your own. Most importantly, be prepared for rapid weather changes.

Guided bushwalking can be arranged through companies in Katoomba (see p156).

Good walking books on the area include *Exploring the Blue Mountains* (Key Guide; $30) and *Walks in the Blue Mountains National Park* (Neil Paton; $11).

---

horticultural heartland. **Sublime Point** is a dramatic clifftop lookout south of Leura offering alternative (albeit distant) views of the Three Sisters. Further north is **Gordon Falls Reserve**, an idyllic picnic spot. From here you can trek the steep Prince Henry Cliff Walk, or take the Cliff Drive 4km west past Leura Cascades to Katoomba's Echo Point.

Sleeping & Eating

Greens of Leura B&B (☎ 02-4784 3241; www .thegreensleura.com.au; 24-26 Grose St; d incl breakfast with/ without bathroom $175/145; ☐) Inside this pretty pink weatherboard cottage are five luxury bedrooms each named after a British author (Austen, Bronte etc). Some have four-poster beds, others French doors leading onto the garden. There's also a living room and billiards room with full-sized snooker table.

Leura House (☎ 02-4784 2035; www.leurahouse .com.au; 7 Britain St; s/d from $135/168) Built in the 1880s this dramatic Italianate house was a country residence, a boarding house and a nunnery before being transformed into a hotel. The hotel's decor is as quirky as its history, but the rooms are attractive and the gardens captivating.

Cafe Bon Ton (☎ 02-4782 4377; 192 The Mall, cnr Megalong St; mains $10-37) Indulge in banana pancakes for breakfast, a smoked-salmon panini for lunch and slow-braised pork cheeks for dinner at this convivial cafe on the edge of the roundabout. The leafy courtyard is ideal for alfresco dining.

Le Gobelet (☎ 02-4787 1919; 131 The Mall; mains $24-32; ☽ dinner Thu-Mon) For a unique dining experience head to this French restaurant (it's the one painted bright purple) at the top of the Mall. Run by a husband-and-wife team, the service can be haphazard and the language colourful but the food is absolutely beautiful. Bring a sense of humour.

Most of Leura's eateries charge an extra 10% on Sunday and an extra 15% on holidays.

Getting There & Around

The direct route to the Blue Mountains from Sydney is via Parramatta Rd, detouring onto the tolled Western Motorway (M4; $3) at Strathfield.

CityRail trains run from Sydney's Central Station to Leura (adult/child $12/6, two hours, hourly). The Blue Mountains Bus Company (opposite) connects Leura to other Blue Mountains towns.

KATOOMBA
pop 7623

Grand old Katoomba has long been a popular holiday destination. During the 1920s and '30s the steep streets were lined with handsome residences, splendid art deco buildings and wealthy Sydneysiders seeking fun and frivolity. Today the mountain town retains much of its charm, character and architecture, but there's no denying that some of the shine has rubbed away, leaving a town that is distinctly more bohemian than bourgeois. That said the setting is still spellbinding, no more so than when the streets are bathed in swirling mists. Right in town there are astonishing valley views alongside a quirky miscellany of good restaurants, hippy cafes, bawdy pubs, classy hotels, galleries, shops, buskers, homeless people, artists and a seemingly never-ending throng of tourists.

NEW SOUTH WALES

MURU MITTIGAR ABORIGINAL CULTURAL CENTRE

On your way out to the Blue Mountains take a few hours out in Penrith to visit the **Muru Mittigar Aboriginal Cultural Centre** (☎ 02-4729 3277; www.murumittigar.com.au; 89-151 Old Castlereigh Rd, Castlereagh; ☺ 9am-4pm Mon-Fri, 10am-2pm Sat, by appointment Sun), which was opened as an Aboriginal Meeting Place in 1998 to acknowledge the Dharug people as the traditional custodians of the region. The Cultural Museum here showcases the art and stories of the Dharug people as well as the rich diversity of Indigenous peoples throughout Australia. An outdoor amphitheatre plays host to traditional dance performances, where local guides also play the didgeridoo and explain the story of its creation and significance. Cultural tours are offered, and a cafe on site serves bush tucker, so you can scoff that side of roo or wallaby you've always wanted.

The centre is an hour's drive west of Sydney and an hour's drive east of Katoomba.

Katoomba's crowning glory is **Echo Point**, where a series of sensational viewing platforms transport your gaze out over the Jamison Valley. The impressive Three Sisters rock formation towers over the scene. Legend has it that a sorcerer turned the Three Sisters to stone in order to protect them from the unwanted advances of three young men. Unfortunately for the sisters, however, the sorcerer died before he could reverse the spell.

Echo Point draws busloads of tourists, which can really spoil the serenity – arrive early before they do.

To the west of town is the very good **Scenic World** (☎ 02-4780 0200; www.scenicworld.com.au; cnr Cliff Dr & Violet St; cable-car return adult/child $19/10; ☺ 9am-5pm), with an 1880s railway descending the 52-degree incline to the valley floor and an elevated boardwalk through the rainforest. The eco-certified venue also has a glass-floored **Scenic Skyway** cable car floating out across the valley.

Information

There are numerous banks and ATMs on Katoomba St.

Blue Mountains Accommodation Booking Service (☎ 02-4782 2652; www.bluemountainsbudget.com; 157 Lurline St; ☺ 10.30am-5.30pm) Free accommodation-booking service.

Blue Mountains District Anzac Memorial Hospital (☎ 02-4784 6500; fax 02-4784 6980; cnr Woodlands Rd & Great Western Hwy; ☺ 24hr emergency)

Echo Point Visitor Centre (☎ 1300 653 408, 02-4739 6787; www.visitbluemountains.com.au; Echo Point; ☺ 9am-5pm)

Katoomba Book Exchange (☎ 02-4782 9997; 34 Katoomba St; per 15min $3; ☺ 10am-6pm) Internet access with a free cup of tea.

Activities

BUSHWALKING

Unless the weather is dire, a mountain bushwalk is mandatory. Head for Jamison Valley, south of Katoomba, or Grose Valley, northeast of Katoomba and east of Blackheath. The area south of Glenbrook is also worthwhile.

The Echo Point Visitor Centre (left) has information on short and day walks; the Blue Mountains Heritage Centre in Blackheath (p160) supplies longer walk details.

Guided bushwalking or bushcraft tours can be arranged (see below); rates range from $55 to $175 per day.

ABSEILING, CANYONING & ROCK CLIMBING

The following offer climbing, hiking and cycling; prices indicate easy or beginner grades (more advanced = more dollars). The following all offer YHA member discounts.

Australian School of Mountaineering (☎ 02-4782 2014; www.asmguides.com; 166 Katoomba St; ☺ 8.30am-5.30pm) Full-day abseiling ($145) or canyoning ($165), plus two-day bush-survival courses ($425).

Blue Mountains Adventure Company (☎ 02-4782 1271; www.bmac.com.au; 84a Bathurst Rd; ☺ 9am-5pm) Abseiling (from $145), canyoning (from $165) and rock climbing (from $175).

High 'n' Wild Mountain Adventures (☎ 02-4782 6224; www.high-n-wild.com.au; 3/5 Katoomba St; ☺ 9am-5pm) Half-/full-day abseiling (from $99/145) and climbing ($159/179), and full-day canyoning ($179).

Tours

Australian Eco Adventures (☎ 02-9971 2402; www.ozeco.com.au; adult/child $170/130; ☺ 7am) Eco-certified luxury day tours of the Blue Mountains departing from Sydney (maximum 16 people). Includes breakfast, buffet lunch and champagne.

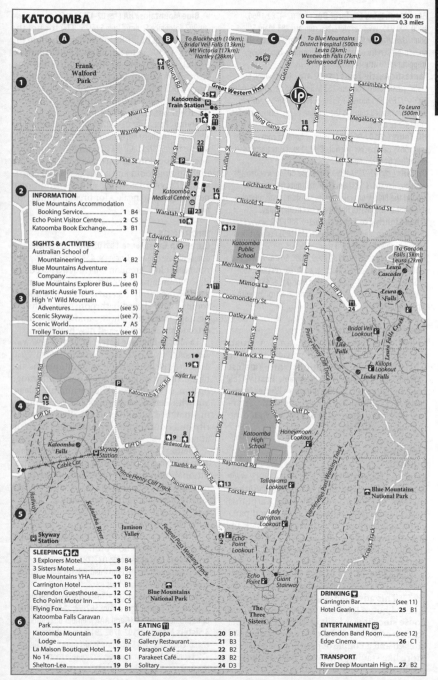

KATOOMBA

INFORMATION
Blue Mountains Accommodation
    Booking Service.............................**1** B4
Echo Point Visitor Centre.............**2** C5
Katoomba Book Exchange............**3** B1

SIGHTS & ACTIVITIES
Australian School of
    Mountaineering.........................**4** B2
Blue Mountains Adventure
    Company.....................................**5** B1
Blue Mountains Explorer Bus .....(see 6)
Fantastic Aussie Tours....................**6** B1
High 'n' Wild Mountain
    Adventures................................(see 5)
Scenic Skyway................................(see 7)
Scenic World....................................**7** A5
Trolley Tours..................................(see 6)

SLEEPING
3 Explorers Motel.............................**8** B4
3 Sisters Motel..................................**9** B4
Blue Mountains YHA......................**10** B2
Carrington Hotel..............................**11** B1
Clarendon Guesthouse..................**12** C2
Echo Point Motor Inn.....................**13** C5
Flying Fox..**14** B1
Katoomba Falls Caravan
    Park..**15** A4
Katoomba Mountain
    Lodge..**16** B2
La Maison Boutique Hotel.............**17** B4
No 14..**18** C1
Shelton-Lea......................................**19** B4

EATING
Café Zuppa......................................**20** B1
Gallery Restaurant.........................**21** B3
Paragon Café...................................**22** B2
Parakeet Café..................................**23** B2
Solitary...**24** D3

DRINKING
Carrington Bar...............................(see 11)
Hotel Gearin....................................**25** B1

ENTERTAINMENT
Clarendon Band Room ....(see 12)
Edge Cinema...................................**26** C1

TRANSPORT
River Deep Mountain High **27** B2

Blue Mountains Explorer Bus (☎ 02-4782 1866, 1300 300 915; www.explorerbus.com.au; 283 Main St; adult/child/family $34/17/85; ☺ 9.45am-5.15pm) Hop-on hop-off service on an hourly Katoomba–Leura loop, stopping at 30 attractions.

Fantastic Aussie Tours (☎ 02-4782 1866; www.fantastic-aussie-tours.com.au; 283 Main St; adult/child/family $70/49/189; ☺ tours 11.15am-5.15pm Mon-Sat, office 9am-5pm) Coach tours to the Jenolan Caves; price includes entrance to caves.

HQ Tours (☎ 02-9666 8433; www.hqtours.com.au; day tours $89) Backpacker-friendly Blue Mountains tours, also departing from Sydney.

Oztrails (☎ 02-9387 8390, 0411 288 805; www.oztrails.com.au; day tours $83) Small-group tours from Sydney around the Blue Mountains sights, finishing with a ferry ride on the Parramatta River back to Circular Quay.

Tread Lightly Eco Tours (☎ 02-4788 1229; www.treadlightly.com.au; 2hr/day tours $35/185) Eco-certified guided bushwalks and 4WD tours.

Trolley Tours (☎ 02-4782 7999, 1800 801 577; www.trolleytours.com.au; 258 Main St; adult/concession $20/15; ☺ hourly 9.15am-4.15pm Mon-Fri, 9.45am-3.45pm Sat & Sun) A bus masquerading as a trolley, with piped commentary.

Festivals & Events

Every year between June and August, the Blue Mountains enjoy out-of-kilter Christmas-style celebrations with **Yulefest** (☎ 1300 653 408; www.bluemts.com.au). Festivities reach a pagan peak at **Katoomba's Winter Magic Festival** (21 June), with a street parade, market stalls and general frivolity to welcome the winter solstice.

Sleeping

BUDGET

Katoomba Mountain Lodge (☎ 02-4782 3933; www.katoombamountainlodge.com.au; 31 Lurline St; dm/s/d from $20/48/68; ☐) Stuck in a 1970s time warp, this hostel boasts naff wallpaper, faux-wood panelling and the kind of artwork you'd pick up at a car boot sale – but we love it! Friendly, roomy and with lovely views, this is a great (and quirky) budget option.

ourpick No 14 (☎ 02-4782 7104; www.bluemts.com.au/no14; 14 Lovel St; dm $22, d with/without bathroom $69/59) This adorable yellow-painted weatherboard house has been operating as a guest house since it was built in 1913. The dorms are cute and cosy, and there's a well-equipped kitchen and a couple of inviting living areas. More like staying with your best mate than in a hostel.

Blue Mountains YHA (☎ 02-4782 1416; www.yha.com.au; 207 Katoomba St; dm/d from $27/75; ☐) It's not the most inviting building in town, but behind the austere 1930s exterior hides a much-lauded hostel that boasts spotless bedrooms and enormous common areas filled with beanbags, pool tables and even a pinball machine. The open fire (and central heating) make it the ideal winter destination.

Flying Fox (☎ 02-4782 4226; www.theflyingfox.com.au; 190 Bathurst Rd; dm/d/tr $28/71/87, camping with/without tent $18/25; ☐) This small, welcoming hostel has colourful dorms, a roaring log fire in the living room and a sun-drenched courtyard. It's very laid-back and the additional perks such as pancakes for breakfast only add to its appeal.

MIDRANGE

Clarendon Guesthouse (☎ 02-4782 1322; www.clarendonguesthouse.com.au; 68 Lurline St; d $90-176; ☐ ☻) The rambling old Clarendon is as much a part of the Blue Mountains as the Three Sisters…almost. This wonderfully eccentric hotel has budget rooms (with shared bathroom) chock-full of heritage in the main house and spotless modern rooms in the annexed new building.

La Maison Boutique Hotel (☎ 02-4782 4996; www.lamaison.com.au; 175-177 Lurline St; s incl breakfast $90-230, d incl breakfast $98-300) Not as 'boutique' as the name might suggest, it's a good midrange option nevertheless. The rooms are pleasant with decent bathrooms and occasionally mismatched furniture. The hallways are eerily quiet during the day but things liven up at night.

Shelton-Lea (☎ 02-4782 9883; www.sheltonlea.com; 159 Lurline St; r incl breakfast $120-340) This traditional mountain cottage has been tweaked to create three bedrooms, each with its own sitting area and small kitchenette. There's a hint of art deco in the decor and lots of frilly furnishings.

There are three comfortable and affordable motels close to Echo Point.

Echo Point Motor Inn (☎ 02-4782 2088; www.echopointmotel.com; 18 Echo Point Rd; s/d from $80/90) Rooms with and without views.

3 Explorers Motel (☎ 02-4782 1733; www.3explorers.com.au; 197 Lurline St; s/d from $82/98; ☒ ☐) Floral print proliferation; NRMA and AAA member discounts.

3 Sisters Motel (☎ 02-4782 2911; www.threesistersmotel.com.au; 348 Katoomba St; d/f from $110/140; ☒) Funky retro neon sign; the serviceable rooms have less funk.

TOP END

Carrington Hotel (☎ 02-4782 1111; www.thecarrington .com.au; 15-47 Katoomba St; d incl breakfast $125-490) The Grand Old Lady of the mountains has a long and colourful history, having provided accommodation to road-weary travellers since 1880. Beautifully refurbished in the 1990s she now offers a wide range of indulgent heritage-infused rooms. The ballroom and dining room are equally splendid.

CAMPING

Katoomba Falls Caravan Park (☎ 02-4782 1835; www.bmcc.nsw.gov.au; Katoomba Falls Rd; unpowered/powered sites from $27/29, cabins from $77) A rather soulless park, but it's Katoomba's only camping option.

Eating

Most of Katoomba's eateries charge an extra 10% on Sunday and many shut for Christmas and during January.

Paragon Café (☎ 02-4782 2928; 65 Katoomba St; mains $10-20; ⏲ breakfast & lunch Tue-Sun) Established in 1916, Paragon has been serving drinks and selling homemade chocolates to the blue rinse brigade for almost a century. The original booths, wood panelling and framed photos of movie stars make this charming cafe a compulsory Blue Mountains experience.

Parakeet Café (☎ 02-4782 1815; 195b Katoomba St; mains $11-19; ⏲ breakfast & lunch Wed-Mon) This colourful cafe dishes up hearty staples along with the odd surprise such as the tempura hoki with chips. There are a couple of couches, a courtyard out back and wireless internet access.

Cafe Zuppa (☎ 02-4782 9247; 36 Katoomba St; mains $13-18) This friendly mountain cafe brews excellent coffees and hot chocolates. The belly-warming burgers and sandwiches are foolproof, but the more experimental dishes are sometimes hit-and-miss.

Gallery Restaurant (☎ 02-4782 1220; 98 Lurline St; 2/3 courses $51/66; ⏲ dinner Thu-Sat) This French-focused restaurant forms part of the Fine Art Gallery housed within a grand old Katoomba residence. Wander through the gallery between courses and admire (or buy, depending on how much wine you've consumed) the paintings, sculptures and glassware on display.

Solitary (☎ 02-4782 1164; 90 Cliff Dr; 2/3 courses $55/66; ⏲ lunch Sat & Sun, dinner Wed-Sun) The weatherboard cottage now called Solitary has been serving refreshments to Blue Mountain visitors since 1913. Today this oh-so-pretty restaurant offers the same amazing views but with a Mod Oz menu. The adjoining kiosk offers all-day brunches and lunches that are easier on the wallet.

Drinking & Entertainment

Hotel Gearin (☎ 02-4782 4395; 273 Great Western Hwy; admission free; ⏲ 7am-2am Mon-Thu, to 3am Fri & Sat, 10am-10pm Sun) This art deco watering hole is one of the liveliest in town, with trivia nights, live music, pool comps and Sunday afternoon jazz. It's owned by actor Jack Thompson – reason enough for a beer and a $5 steak.

Carrington Bar (☎ 02-4782 1111; 15-47 Katoomba St; admission free; ⏲ 9.30am-1.30am Mon-Thu, to 4.30am Fri & Sat, to 11pm Sun) The lowbrow wing of the upper-crust hotel, this is the place for shooters, schooners and rugby on the three large plasma TVs. There's a nightclub upstairs on Saturday night (admission $5). The less sport-oriented City Bank Bar at the bottom of the main hotel driveway has live entertainment at weekends.

Clarendon Band Room (☎ 02-4782 1322; 68 Lurline St; admission $15-50; ⏲ live music Wed-Sat night) Everything from Australian folk and pop to jazz and rock is performed on the Clarendon stage. Dinner-and-dance shows are usually double the ticket price.

Edge Cinema (☎ 02-4782 8900; www.edgecinema.com .au; 225 Great Western Hwy; adult/child $14/10; ⏲ 10am-late) A giant screen shows mainstream flicks plus a 40-minute Blue Mountains documentary (adult/child $15/10). Budget Tuesdays features flicks for $9 per person.

Getting There & Around

CityRail runs to Katoomba from Sydney's Central Station (one way adult/child $12/6, two hours, hourly).

The Blue Mountains Bus Company (p154) services Katoomba en route from Mt Victoria to the north (one way adult/child $7/4, 40 minutes, three daily Monday to Friday) and Springwood to the east (one way adult/child $9/5, 50 minutes, nine daily Monday to Saturday). The Blue Mountains Explorer Bus and Trolley Tours (both opposite) track the highlights through Katoomba and Leura.

River Deep Mountain High (☎ 02-4782 6109; www.rdmh.com.au; 2/187 Katoomba St; half/full day $28/50; ⏲ 9am-5pm) rents out all-terrain mountain bikes and runs mountain-biking tours (half/full day from $110/180).

Katoomba-Leura-Wentworth Falls Taxis (☎ 02-4782 1311) services its monikers.

BLACKHEATH AREA

Leura may be more affluent and Katoomba definitely sees more crowds, but neat and petite Blackheath is simply lovely. Although no longer the secret it once was, visitors still only trickle into town rather than arrive by the noisy, gas-guzzling coach load. Come for the excellent dining and accommodation options, the art galleries and cafes, and the stunning scenery. It's also a good base for visiting the Grose and Megalong Valleys.

East of town are lookouts at **Govetts Leap** (comparable to the Three Sisters in terms of 'wow' factor), **Bridal Veil Falls** (the highest in the Blue Mountains) and **Evans Lookout**. To the northeast, via Hat Hill Rd, are **Pulpit Rock**, **Perry's Lookdown** and **Anvil Rock**. There are steep walks into the Grose Valley from Govetts Leap; Perry's Lookdown is the start of the shortest route (five hours one way) to the magical **Blue Gum Forest**. From Evans Lookout there are tracks to Govetts Leap (1½ hours one way) and to **Junction Rock**, continuing to the Blue Gum Forest (six hours one way).

To the west and southwest lie the **Kanimbla** and **Megalong Valleys**, with spectacular views from **Hargreaves Lookout**. Register your walk and get trail-condition updates from the **Blue Mountains Heritage Centre** (☎ 02-4787 8877; www.nationalparks.nsw.gov.au; Govetts Leap Rd; ☺ 9am-4.30pm) near the entrance to Govetts Leap.

Sleeping & Eating

Glenella Guesthouse (☎ 02-4787 8352; www.glenellabluemountainshotel.com.au; 56-60 Govetts Leap Rd; d incl breakfast $100-160) Gorgeous Glenella has long played an important – and lively – part in Blackheath's history. Today it's run by a friendly Welsh couple who have refreshed and restored this celebrated home to create seven comfortable bedrooms. There's also a large living area and a restaurant (dinner Thursday to Sunday, lunch Saturday and Sunday).

Gardners Inn (☎ 02-4787 6400; www.gardnersinn.com.au; 255 Great Western Hwy; s/d incl breakfast with bathroom $160/250, without bathroom $130/180) Across from Blackheath Station, this is the oldest licensed hotel (1831) in the Blue Mountains. It's just benefited from a $6 million refurbishment, which means that the rooms are modern and bright, although a smidgen of heritage charm remains. Good online deals.

Jemby-Rinjah Eco Lodge (☎ 02-4787 7622; www.jembyrinjahlodge.com.au; 336 Evans Lookout Rd; standard/deluxe cabins from $170/219) These eco-cabins are lodged so deeply in the bottlebrush you'll have to bump into one to find it. One- and two-bedroom weatherboard cabins are jauntily designed; the deluxe models have Japanese plunge-style spas.

There are free campsites at Perry's Lookdown and Acacia Flat, near the Blue Gum Forest in the Grose Valley.

Victory Café (☎ 02-4787 6777; 17 Govetts Leap Rd; mains $10; ☺ breakfast & lunch, dinner Fri & Sat) At the entrance to the cavernous antiques emporium, the Victory is where folk come for coffee and to catch up on local news. The Mod Oz menu is straightforward and wholesome.

Ashcroft's (☎ 02-4787 8297; 18 Govetts Leap Rd; 2/3 courses $68/80; ☺ dinner Wed-Sun, lunch Sun) This multi-award-winning restaurant experiments with European, Middle Eastern, Asian and Australian cuisine in a gallery-like setting. There's an excellent wine list, and the paintings and photography on display are all for sale.

Also available:

Blackheath Caravan Park (☎ 02-4787 8101; Prince Edward St; unpowered/powered sites $25/31, cabins from $46) Small, clean and good value.

Piedmont Inn Pizza Restaurant (☎ 02-4787 7769; 248 Great Western Hwy; mains $12) Great pizzas.

Getting There & Away

CityRail trains run to Blackheath from Sydney's Central Station (one way adult/child $14/7, 2¼ hours, hourly).

The Blue Mountains Bus Company (p154) services Blackheath, Govetts Leap Rd, Evans Lookout Rd and Hat Hill Rd en route from Mt Victoria to the north (one way adult/child $6/3, 15 minutes, three daily Monday to Friday) and Katoomba to the south (one way adult/child $7/4, 25 minutes, 11 daily Monday to Friday, four Saturday, two Sunday).

MEGALONG VALLEY

Unless you walk in or take Katoomba's Scenic Railway, the only way you'll see a Blue Mountains gorge from the inside is in the Megalong Valley. This is straw-coloured rural Australia, a real departure from the quasi-suburbs strung along the ridgeline. The 600m **Coachwood Glen Nature Trail**, 2km before Werribee, features dripping fern dells, stands of mountain ash and sun-stained sandstone cliffs.

The **Megalong Australian Heritage Centre** (☎ 02-4787 8188; www.megalong.cc; Megalong Rd; adult/child/family $8/5/20; ☺ 9am-5pm) is a display farm heaven for little tackers – visitors can feed and pat sheep, ducks, ponies and alpacas. There's guided horse riding ($45/85 per person for one/two hours), plus farm shows and activities during school holidays.

The **farm accommodation** (unpowered sites per 2 people $24, dm $20, d incl breakfast $85) comprises campsites, basic dorm beds and B&B guest house rooms.

Werribee Trail Rides (☎ 02-4787 9171; www.aus tralianbluehorserides.com.au; Megalong Rd; 30min/2hr rides $30/90; ☺ 10am-5pm) offers horse-riding packages to suit everyone. See the area pioneer-style by adding your weight to a two-day/one-night 'Pub Crawl' ride.

MT VICTORIA, HARTLEY & LITHGOW

With a charming alpine air, **Mt Victoria** (population 828) sits at 1043m and is the highest town in the mountains. Historic buildings dominate and include **St Peter's Church** (1874) and the **Toll Keepers Cottage** (1849).

Nothing is far from the train station, where the **Mt Victoria Museum** (☎ 02-4787 1210; Mt Victoria Railway Station; adult/child $3/50c; ☺ 2-5pm Sat & Sun) is chock-full of quirky Australiana including old farm equipment, taxidermy and Ned Kelly's sister's bed. Inside an old public hall, the 130-seat **Mount Vic Flicks** (☎ 02-4787 1577; www.bluemts .com.au/mountvic; Harley Ave; adult/child $10/8; ☺ noon-8.30pm Fri-Sun, from 10.30am Thu) is a wonderful step back in time. With ushers, a piano player and door prizes you'll soon forget what you came to see.

The best pub in the area by a mountain mile, the 1878 **Imperial Hotel** (☎ 02-4787 1878; www.hotelimperial.com.au; 1 Station St, Mt Victoria; d with/ without bathroom incl breakfast from $99/60) has budget and basic downstairs rooms and grand ones above. The bar has live music and log fires, and the kitchen (mains $17 to $24) cooks solid pub grub.

About 12km past Mt Victoria, on the western slopes of the range, is the tiny, sandstone 'ghost' town of **Hartley**, which flourished from the 1830s but declined when bypassed by the railway in 1887. It's been well preserved and a number of historic buildings remain, including several private homes and inns.

The **NPWS Information Centre** (☎ 02-6355 2117; www.nationalparks.nsw.gov.au; ☺ 10am-1pm & 2-4.20pm) is in the old Farmer's Inn (1845). You can explore Hartley for free or take a 20-minute guided tour of the 1837 **Greek Revival Courthouse** (tours $6; ☺ hourly 10am-3pm).

A further 14km on from Hartley in the western foothills of the Blue Mountains is **Lithgow** (population 11,298), a sombre coal-mining town popular with trainspotters for its **Zig Zag Railway** (☎ 02-6355 2955; www.zigzagrailway.com.au; Clarence Station, Bells Line of Road; adult/child/family $25/13/63; ☺ 11am, 1pm, 3pm & 4.45pm), which sits just 10km east of town. Built in the 1860s to transport the Great Western Railway tracks down from the mountains into Lithgow, today it zigzags tourists gently down the precipice (1½-hour return trip).

CityRail trains run to Mt Victoria from Sydney's Central Station (one way adult/child $14/7, 2½ hours, hourly). The Blue Mountains Bus Company (p154) runs to Mt Victoria from Katoomba (one way adult/child $6/3, 15 minutes, four daily Monday to Friday). CityRail trains run to Lithgow from Sydney's Central Station (one way adult/child $18/9, three hours, hourly).

JENOLAN CAVES

The story behind the discovery of **Jenolan Caves** (☎ 02-6359 3911; www.jenolancaves.org.au; Jenolan Caves Rd; admission with tour adult/child/family from $25/18/59; ☺ 9.30am-5.30pm) is the stuff of legends: local pastoralist James Whalan stumbled across the prehistoric caves while tracking the escaped convict and cattle rustler James McKeown, who is thought to have used the caves as a hideout.

Originally named Binoomea or 'Dark Places' by the Gundungurra people, these spellbinding caves took shape more than 400 million years ago and are one of the most extensive and complex limestone cave systems in the world.

There are over 350 caves in the region, although only a handful is open to the public. You must take a tour to see them; the most comprehensive tours include the two-hour **Legends, Mysteries & Ghosts Tour** (per person $38; ☺ 8pm Sat). A number of the caves are also open for spelunking adventures (from $60), where you don a boiler suit and squeeze yourself through narrow tunnels with only a headlamp to guide you.

The **Six Foot Track** from Katoomba to the Jenolan Caves is a fairly challenging 45km three-day hike. Consult the Echo Point Visitor Centre (p156) before you attempt anything.

DETOUR: BELLS LINE OF ROAD

This back road (Map p148) between Richmond and Lithgow is the most scenic route across the Blue Mountains. It's highly recommended if you have your own transport. There are fine views towards the coast from Kurrajong Heights on the eastern slopes of the range, there are orchards around Bilpin, and there's sandstone cliff and bush scenery all the way to Lithgow.

Midway between Bilpin and Bell, the delightful **Mt Tomah Botanic Gardens** (☎ 02-4567 2154; www.mounttomahbotanicgarden.com.au; Bells Line of Road; adult/child/family $6/3/11; ☽ 10am-4pm Apr-Sep, to 5pm Oct-Mar) is a cool-climate annexe of Sydney's Royal Botanic Gardens. As well as native plants there are displays of exotic cold-climate species, including some magnificent rhododendrons. Parts of the park are wheelchair accessible.

North of Bells Line of Road, and a 10-minute drive north of Mt Tomah, at the little town of **Mt Wilson** are formal gardens and the nearby **Cathedral of Ferns** – a wet rainforest remnant with tree ferns and native doves exploding from the foliage. It's an almost unbearably serene 10-minute stroll.

The grand, but somewhat eerie, **Jenolan Caves House** (☎ 02-6359 3322; www.jenolancaves.house .com.au; Jenolan Caves Rd; d $90-285) offers nostalgic accommodation to suit most budgets.

Jenolan Caves Cottages (☎ 02-6359 3911; www .jenolancaves.org.au; Jenolan Caves Rd; cottages sleeping 6-8 people $100-135, Bellbird Cottage $168-198), about 8km north of the caves, offers eight comfortable, self-contained cottages and the beautifully renovated 1930s Bellbird Cottage.

The caves are 30km from the Great Western Hwy. The narrow Jenolan Caves Rd becomes a one-way system between 11.45am and 1.15pm daily, running clockwise from the caves out through Oberon.

NORTH COAST

It's no wonder that the NSW north coast is one of the most celebrated road trips in Oz. This idyllic stretch of coastline from Sydney to Tweed Heads is a magical blend of sea and sand, sparkling lakes, enchanting national parks, rootsy towns and alternative lifestyles.

Leaving Sydney the coast rolls gently north. Craggy headlands and golden beaches dominate a landscape that's broken only by seaside towns and surf settlements, which become increasingly languorous the further north you travel. To the west green fields roll inland, melting into the ancient forests and charming hill towns of the beautiful hinterland. Many travellers head straight to New Age Byron Bay tempted by its organic, ecofriendly lifestyle, but take your time on the road and you'll discover that this corner of NSW has so much more to offer: from the vineyards of the Hunter Valley and deep blue basins of the Myall Lakes to spectacular World Heritage rainforests and sun-blessed coastal parks peppered with idyllic coves and great surf.

At times you'll feel like the only person on the road, for despite the well-trodden path the trail only ever gets busy when passing through the inevitable network of urban centres (keep moving!). But whatever your final destination remember to occasionally put away the map, close your guidebook and see where the road takes you; it's unlikely you'll be disappointed.

SYDNEY TO NEWCASTLE

Between Broken Bay and Newcastle the central coast springs to life with a combination of splendid lakes, golden surf beaches and lush national parks, which are marred only by the predictable swathes of housing.

The largest town in the area is hilly **Gosford**, where the **Gosford visitor centre** (☎ 02-4343 4444, 1300 130 708; www.cctourism.com.au; 200 Mann St; ☽ 9.30am-4pm Mon-Fri, to 1.30pm Sat) covers all of the central coast.

Southwest of Gosford rambling trails run through rugged sandstone in **Brisbane Water National Park** (www.nationalparks.nsw.gov.au). The **Bulgandry Aboriginal Engraving Site** is 3km south of the Pacific Hwy on Woy Woy Rd. CityRail trains stop at Wondabyne train station inside the park upon request. Southeast of Gosford, **Bouddi National Park** extends north along the coast from the mouth of Brisbane Water and has excellent coastal bushwalking and camping. The Gosford **NPWS Office** (☎ 02-4320 4200; www.nationalparks.nsw.gov.au; Suite 36-38, 207 Albany St North; ☽ 8.30am-4.30pm Mon-Fri) provides permits for both parks.

A favourite retreat for actors, writers and other luvvies is the National Trust–listed village of **Pearl Beach**, on the eastern edge of Brisbane Water National Park.

CityRail trains run from Sydney to Gosford (adult/child $8.60/4.30, 1½ hours).

NEWCASTLE
pop 493,466

Sydney may possess the glitz and the glamour, but Newcastle has the down-to-earth larrikin charm. This is the kind of place where you can grocery shop barefoot, go surfing in your lunch hour and quickly become best buddies with the person sitting next to you in the bar.

This easygoing, 'no worries' attitude has been shaped by Newcastle's rough-and-tumble past; it was originally the destination for the worst-behaved convicts. Today it continues to be the largest coal export harbour in the world, but the city is undergoing something of a renaissance. Wharf rejuvenation projects are breathing new life into the harbour and an eclectic and innovative arts scene is injecting colour and culture into the streets.

Swim or surf at the popular beaches and soak in ocean baths, explore the outstanding heritage architecture in the CBD and window shop along funky Darby St. Dine on fish and chips, watch the tankers chug along the horizon and catch some live music. Whatever you do, however, don't just pass through – Newcastle is easily worth a couple of days or more.

Orientation

The city centre is bordered by the Hunter River to the north and the ocean to the east. The train station, bus terminal, post office and banks are located at the CBD's northeastern corner.

Hunter St runs down the length of the peninsula and is the city's major shopping street. On the banks of the Hunter River, the wharf area of Honeysuckle Dr is undergoing major development with new restaurants and bars constantly springing up. Running south, colourful Darby St is lined with cafes, restaurants, galleries and boutique shops.

Information

There are ATMs all around town and Hunter St Mall meets most needs. Most locals head to Charlestown Sq (in Charlestown to the southeast) for luxury items.

John Hunter Hospital (☎ 02-4921 3000; Lookout Rd, New Lambton) Has emergency care.

Juicy Beans Café (☎ 02-4929 4988; 365 Hunter St; per 30min $2; 🕑 6.30am-4.30pm Mon-Fri, 7.30am-2pm Sat) Internet access and wi-fi.

Newcastle Region Library (☎ 02-4974 5300; Laman St; per 30min $3; 🕑 9.30am-8pm Mon-Fri, to 2pm Sat) Internet access for emails.

Visitor Information Centre (☎ 02-4974 2999; 361 Hunter St; 🕑 9am-5pm Mon-Fri, 10am-3pm Sat & Sun)

Sights

Get your bearings (and your heart racing) with a climb up 180 steps to the top of the 40.3m-high **Queens Wharf Tower** (Queens Wharf; admission free; 🕑 8am-dusk) for a 360-degree view of the city.

From here, hot foot it along the **Bathers Way**, a 5km coastal walk that stretches from the lighthouse at Nobbys Head to Glenrock Reserve and includes Fort Scratchley (p165). The **Newcastle East Heritage Walk** is a 3km self-guided tour exploring Newcastle's architecture and history. Maps for both walks are available from the visitor centre.

BEACHES

At the northeastern tip, the gentle curve of **Nobby's Beach** makes this one of the city's prettiest stretches of coast. Surfers should head to the northern end to tackle the fast left-hander known as the Wedge. Around the corner a wonderful multicoloured art deco facade hides the ocean baths, perfect for those paranoid about sharks.

Newcastle Beach satisfies swimmers and surfers, the chugging cargo ships on the horizon provoking some interesting holiday snaps.

GREAT NORTH WALK

Looking to stretch the legs? The Great North Walk should do the trick. This 250km trail begins in central Sydney and, after a short ferry ride, follows natural bushland the entire way to Newcastle. While not strictly a wilderness walk, there's adequate greenery along the way and it can be walked in any season.

The best track reference, *The Great North Walk* by walk originators Garry McDougall and Leigh Shearer-Heriot, is out of print, but libraries stock copies. The Department of Lands (see p99) produces maps of the route in 'Discovery Kit' form ($11), available by calling **Sydney Map Sales** (☎ 02-9236 7720).

NEW SOUTH WALES

NEWCASTLE

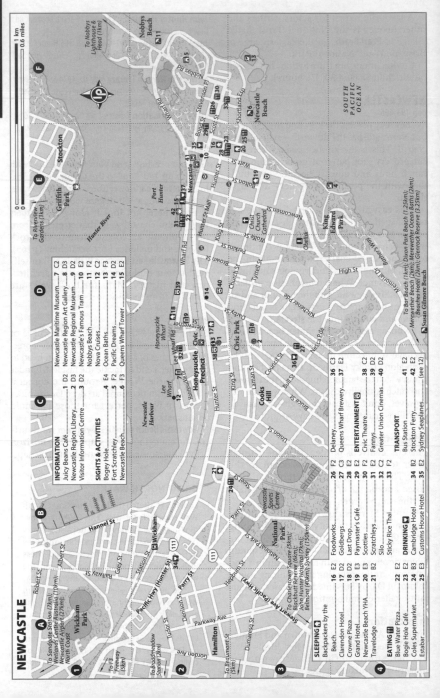

INFORMATION

Juicy Beans Café	1 D2
Newcastle Region Library	2 D3
Visitor Information Centre	3 E2

SIGHTS & ACTIVITIES

Bogey Hole	4 E4
Fort Scratchley	5 F2
Newcastle Beach	6 F3

Newcastle Maritime Museum	7 C2
Newcastle Region Art Gallery	8 D3
Newcastle Regional Museum	9 D2
Newcastle's Famous Tram	10 E2
Nobbys Beach	11 F2
Nova Cruises	12 C2
Ocean Baths	13 F3
Pacific Dreams	14 D2
Queens Wharf Tower	15 E2

SLEEPING 🛏

Backpackers by the Beach	16 E2
Clarendon Hotel	17 D2
Crowne Plaza	18 D2
Grand Hotel	19 E3
Newcastle Beach YHA	20 F2
Travelodge	21 E3

EATING 🍴

Blue Water Pizza	22 E2
Bogie Hole Café	23 E2
Coles Supermarket	24 B3
Estabar	25 E3

Foodworks	26 F2
Goldbergs	27 D2
Last Drop	28 E2
Paymaster's Café	29 E3
Scotties	30 F2
Scratchleys	31 E2
Silo	32 C2
Sticky Rice Thai	33 F2

DRINKING 🍷

Cambridge Hotel	34 B2
Customs House Hotel	35 E2

Delaney	36 C3
Queens Wharf Brewery	37 E2

ENTERTAINMENT 🎭

Civic Theatre	38 C2
Fannys	39 D2
Greater Union Cinemas	40 D2

TRANSPORT

Bus Station	41 E2
Stockton Ferry	42 E2
Sydney Seaplanes	(see 12)

South of here, below King Edward Park, the convict-carved **Bogey Hole** is Australia's oldest ocean bath. Scramble around the rocks and under the headland to **Susan Gilmore Beach**, where swimwear is optional (and not encouraged).

Merewether Beach is Newcastle's most consistent surfing beach and home to four-time world champion Mark Richards. Also popular are the surfing breaks at **Bar Beach** and **Dixon Park Beach**. The absurdly large **ocean baths** (100m x 50m) is where the Merewether Mackerels Winter Swimming Club splashes about; they mark the opening of the winter swimming season by dumping big blocks of ice into the water.

Frequent local buses from the CBD run as far south as Bar Beach, but only the 207 continues to Merewether.

FORT SCRATCHLEY

Occupying one of Newcastle's best vantage points, the recently reopened **Fort Scratchley** (☎ 02-4974 5000; www.fortscratchley.com.au; Nobbys Rd; admission free; ☒ 10am-4pm Wed-Mon) played a vital role in defending the city when a Japanese submarine attacked Newcastle on 8 June 1942. A free map will guide you around the barracks and defence structures, but if you want to delve into the underground maze of tunnels then you must join a tour (adult/child $8/4, one hour).

NOBBYS HEAD

Nobbys was an island until it was joined to the mainland in 1846 to create a singularly pretty (and long) **sand spit**. It was twice its current height before being reduced to 28m above sea level in 1855 in an effort to keep the wind in the sails of the ships as they turned into the harbour. The walk along the spit towards the lighthouse is exhilarating as waves crash about your ears and joggers jostle your elbows.

MUSEUMS

Admire works by Australian artists including Brett Whiteley, Sidney Nolan and Russell Drysdale in the **Newcastle Region Art Gallery** (☎ 02-4974 5100; www.newcastle.nsw.gov.au/discover_newcastle/region_art_gallery; Laman St; admission free; ☒ 10am-5pm Tue-Sun), which also hosts travelling exhibitions throughout the year.

The **Newcastle Regional Museum** (☎ 02-4974 1400; www.nrmuseum.com.au; Honeysuckle Precinct) was closed at the time of writing, but is due to reopen in a new space in 2010.

Explore maritime memorabilia at the **Newcastle Maritime Museum** (☎ 02-4929 2588; www.maritimecentrenewcastle.org.au; 3 Honeysuckle Dr; adult/child $10/5; ☒ 10am-4pm Tue-Sat), including old captains' logs, photographs, uniforms, and the flotsam and jetsam washed up with shipwrecks.

WILDLIFE

The **Wetlands Centre Australia** (☎ 02-4951 6466; www.wetlands.org.au; Sandgate Rd, Sandgate; adult/child $9/4; ☒ 10am-5pm Mon-Fri, from 9am Sat & Sun) was born out of a desperate bid to stop the highway storming through the guts of this former rubbish tip. Now it's 45 hectares of swampy wonderland, home to over 250 wildlife species. Mosquitoes are plentiful, so you'd best keep on walking, cycling or **canoeing** (2-person per 2hr $15; ☒ 10am-2pm). The centre is a short walk from Sandgate train station.

Set in a bushland reserve, **Blackbutt Reserve** (☎ 02-4904 3344; www.newcastle.nsw.gov.au/environment/blackbutt_reserve; Carnley Ave, Kotara; admission free; ☒ 9am-5pm) is a fabulous place for the nippers, with nature trails, wildlife exhibits, playgrounds and all manner of animals: koalas, wombats, emus, kangaroos and more.

Activities

SURFING

Newcastle is all about surfing. Avoid dropping-in on the locals with some lessons:

Newcastle Surf School (☎ 0405 500 469; lessons $40) Beginners to advanced lessons.

Pacific Dreams (☎ 02-4926 3355; 7 Darby St; day hire $50) Rents secondhand fibreglass boards and far less painful soft boards.

Redhead Mobile Surf School (☎ 02-4944 9585; www.redheadsurfschool.com.au; lessons $45, 2hr wetsuit & board hire $25) Maximum of five people per group.

Surfest Surf School (☎ 0410 840 155; www.surfestsurfschool.com; lessons $30) Held at Nobbys Beach; buy four lessons and get one free.

HANG-GLIDING

Air Sports (☎ 0412 607 815; www.air-sports.com.au; flights from $165) Offers tandem hang-gliding flights.

Tours

Heliservices (☎ 02-4962 5188; scenic flights from $69) Aerial tours of Newcastle, the Hunter Valley and Port Stephens.

THE CAMPERVAN CRUISE

The east-coast run from Sydney to Cairns is one of the most popular campervan routes in Australia. The Pacific and Bruce Hwys barrel up the coast, providing a continuous corridor of bitumen accessible to vehicles of all shapes and sizes. The opportunities for bush camping in national parks and more comfortable camping in private camping grounds is abundant, and you'll be hard-pressed not to find either on a nightly basis. There are also wonderful, tarred diversions such as the glorious Waterfall Way (p210). Off tributaries like this are dirt tracks into the hinterland and its national parks. These vary in condition, and the camping options become more rudimentary and less prolific. But that's no reason not to explore them; just seek local advice about the road conditions before heading right off the beaten track. Enjoy!

Newcastle's Famous Tram (☎ 02-4977 2270; Newcastle Station, Brewery Wharf Rd, Crowne Plaza Wharf Rd; adult/child $15/6; ⏱ 11am & 1pm) Hour-long tours of Newcastle's surf and sights accompanied by an entertaining commentary.

Nova Cruises (☎ 0400 381 787; Lee Wharf; from $50) Harbour cruises, Hunter River tours and whale-watching expeditions (May to October).

Festivals & Events

Surfest (☎ 02-4929 5833) Australia's largest surfing event for men and women held at Merewether Beach in March.

Shoot Out Film Festival (☎ 02-4940 8152) Filmmakers have 24 hours to shoot a short film in mid-July.

Newcastle Jazz Festival (www.newcastlejazz.com.au) A weekend of doo-wop and bebop in late August.

Mattara – Festival of Newcastle (www.mattarafestival.org.au) Newcastle's largest festival; early October.

This Is Not Art Festival (☎ 02-4927 0675; www.thisisnotart.org) In early October, an independent arts and new media festival for emerging and established writers, artists and music makers.

Rainbow Festival (www.rainbowvisions.org.au) An October festival celebrating Hunter gays and lesbians.

Sleeping

Terraces for Tourists (☎ 02-4929 4575; www.terracesfortourists.com.au) does what it says and rents terraced houses for tourists.

BUDGET

Newcastle Beach YHA (☎ 02-4925 3544; www.yha.com.au; 30 Pacific St; dm/s/d from $28/47/67; 🖥) In a heritage-listed old gentlemen's club is this excellent hostel with large light-filled rooms, a grand, old wood-panelled living room and more organised activities than there are days in the year. Almost.

Backpackers by the Beach (☎ 02-4926 3472, 1800 008 972; www.backpackersbythebeach.com.au; 34 Hunter St; dm/d without bathroom $28/66; 🖥) With just 40 beds this homely hostel is terrific: close to the beach, friendly and perfectly placed for nights on the town. Rooms are on the small side but are bright and clean, and some have ocean glimpses.

The Grand Hotel (☎ 02-4929 3489; www.thegrandhotelnewcastle.com.au; 32 Church St; d $70-80) Rooms above this Federation-style pub are a hodgepodge of shapes and sizes stuffed with mismatched furniture. They're nothing flash but they are well equipped.

MIDRANGE

Travelodge (☎ 02-4926 3777, 1300 886 886; www.travelodge.com.au; 15 Steel St; r from $135; 🖵 🖥 🖳 🏊) You know what you're getting with this chain, but the newly refurbished rooms are a cut above others of a similar ilk. While the architecture may lack inspiration, the outdoor pool is a big plus.

Riverview Gardens (☎ 02-4928 3048; www.riverviewgardens.com.au; 98 Fullerton St, Stockton; d incl breakfast $130-150) This pretty B&B in Newcastle's only northern suburb has just two bedrooms. Expect homemade scones upon arrival and a cooked breakfast that will see you through until dinnertime.

Clarendon Hotel (☎ 02-4927 0966; www.clarendonhotel.com.au; 347 Hunter St; d $150-180; 🖵 🖥) The Clarendon does boutique chic in this old art deco building. Rooms feature contemporary hues with bold artwork and modern furnishings; some even have balconies. The bar downstairs is less stylish but equally convivial.

TOP END

Crowne Plaza (☎ 02-4907 5000; www.crowneplaza.com.au; Wharf Rd; d incl breakfast from $270; 🖵 🖥 🏊) This is your best top-end bet in a city sadly lacking in high-end options. Located on the foreshore, many rooms have lovely views but the best one is from the outdoor swimming pool that overlooks the harbour.

Eating

Head to Darby St for funky cafes, Honeysuckle Dr for swanky bars with water views, Hunter St for its backpacker-friendly cafes and Beaumont St for cheap eats (Thai, Indian etc). Check out www.eatlocal.com.au for restaurant listings. Get groceries at **Foodworks** (60-62 Scott St) and **Coles** (King St).

ourpick Scotties (☎ 02-4926 3780; 36 Scott St; mains $7-15) Locals love this laid-back place for its fish and chips, burgers and old-fashioned milkshakes. Takeaway or eat in at one of the rickety tables and watch the people pass by.

Last Drop (☎ 02-4926 3470; 37 Hunter St; dishes $9-12; ☺ breakfast & lunch Mon-Sat) A fabulous funky cafe that's big on service, good food and great coffee. The Turkish sandwiches are best enjoyed on the comfy couch out back.

Estabar (☎ 02-4927 1222; cnr Ocean St & Shortland Esplanade; meals from $10) Head here for gooey chocolate cakes, homemade gelati and Spanish-style hot chocolates. If you're a savoury kind of guy or girl, then opt for the chorizo and chickpea hot pot – it rocks.

Goldbergs (☎ 02-4929 3122; 137 Darby St; mains $11-18) This Darby St favourite is always busy and we're not surprised. A large and varied menu, huge portions, a leafy courtyard and battered leather sofas keep folk coming back again and again.

Sticky Rice Thai (☎ 02-4927 0200; 19 Scott St; mains $12-19; ☺ lunch & dinner) Beach-style Thai served up with typical Novocastrian zest and five beers on tap.

Paymaster's Café (☎ 02-4925 2600; 18 Bond St; mains $14-40; ☺ breakfast & lunch Wed-Sun, dinner Wed-Sat) White linen tablecloths, wicker chairs and heritage surrounds make dining here an absolute delight – and that's before you've even sampled the excellent Asian-inspired menu.

Bogie Hole Café (☎ 02-4929 1790; cnr Hunter & Pacific Sts; mains $15-24) Within splashing distance of Newcastle Beach, this summery corner cafe offers bikini-friendly lunches and heavier hide-behind-your-towel dishes such as crumbed calamari and lasagne.

Blue Water Pizza (☎ 02-4929 5686; Queens Wharf; mains $16-25; ☺ lunch & dinner) Bright and brassy, this lively waterfront eatery is the place to come for wood-fired pizza, particularly on a Monday when all pies are a bargain $14.

Scratchleys (☎ 02-4929 1111; 200 Wharf Rd; mains $25-40; ☺ lunch & dinner) This glass-fronted block stretches out over the water and is popular for business lunches, romantic dinners and family celebrations (think golden oldies toasting their 40th wedding anniversary). The extensive menu is sure to please seafood lovers.

Silo (☎ 02-4926 2828; 1 Honeysuckle Dr; mains $30-39; ☺ breakfast Sat & Sun, lunch & dinner daily) Laughter refracts from the red-and-silver wallpaper and ricochets off the glass chandeliers. Silo specialises in local produce and sports a tremendous selection of beers, cocktails, liqueurs and spirits in general. A DJ spins up a storm Friday and Saturday night (from 9.30pm) and on lazy Sunday afternoons.

Drinking & Entertainment

The bars around Hunter St are popular with students and heave during term time (Wednesday night is student night). If your university days are a distant memory, head to Honeysuckle Dr. For a rundown of upcoming events, pick up a copy of *Drum Media*.

Beaches Hotel (☎ 02-4963 1574; www.thebeachhotel.com.au; cnr Frederick & Ridge Sts, Merewether) There is only one place to be seen on a Sunday afternoon and that is at this quintessential Newcastle pub overlooking the beach.

Queens Wharf Brewery (☎ 02-4929 6333; www.qwb.com.au; 150 Wharf Rd) If the beaches are empty then check the Brewery, one of Newcastle's most popular pubs with over 40 craft beers. Sunday afternoons drift into evening with live music on the wharf.

Delaney (☎ 02-4929 1627; 134 Darby St) Something of a Newcastle institution, the 'Del' is grotty and grimy but it does guarantee a cracking night out. Friendly staff, friendly punters and excellent live music make this pub a hard act to follow.

Cambridge Hotel (☎ 02-4962 2459; 789 Hunter St) Block out the spewy scent saturating the carpet – by midnight you won't even notice. It's renowned for secret gigs where big acts will rock up to do an unadvertised show.

Customs House Hotel (☎ 02-4925 2585; www.customshouse.net.au; 1 Bond St) The shaded courtyard is a great spot for an afternoon bevvy; inside the bar is all polished floorboards, low-lying banquettes and dressed-up Novocastrians strutting their stuff.

Fannys (☎ 02-4929 2025; 311 Wharf Rd; ☺ 8pm-3am Wed, to 3.30am Fri & Sat) See boys and gals out on the razzle-dazzle wearing their shortest skirts and strongest aftershave. A strict dress code applies (yes, really!).

Civic Theatre (☎ 02-4974 2166; www.civictheatrenew
castle.com.au; 375 Hunter St) The Civic hosts theatre, musicals, concerts and dance in a typically evocative Newcastle heritage building.

Greater Union Cinemas (☎ 02-4926 2233; www
.greaterunion.com.au; 183-185 King St) For a more subdued evening, head to the movies.

Getting There & Away
AIR
Newcastle's main **airport** (☎ 02-4928 9800; www
.newcastleairport.com.au) is at Williamtown, about
15km north of the city.

Virgin Blue (☎ 13 67 89; www.virginblue.com.au)
and **Jetstar** (☎ 13 15 38; www.jetstar.com.au) fly to
Brisbane and Melbourne, and **Qantas** (☎ 13
13 13; www.qantas.com.au) flies to Sydney as well.
Aeropelican (☎ 02-4928 9600; www.aeropelican.com.au)
and **Brindabella Airlines** (☎ 1300 668 824; www.brind
abellaairlines.com.au) also fly here from Canberra,
Port Macquarie, Coffs Harbour and Brisbane.
Sydney Seaplanes (☎ 02-9388 1978, 1300 732 752)
flies from Rose Bay in Sydney to Newcastle
Harbour (from $150, 30 minutes).

BUS
All local and long-distance buses leave
from Newcastle Station. **Greyhound** (☎ 13 14
99) goes to Byron Bay (adult/child $106/92)
and Sydney (adult/child $49/41).

Premier Motor Service (☎ 13 34 10) travels through to Brisbane daily for slightly
less than Greyhound. **Port Stephens Coaches**
(☎ 02-4982 2940) has daily services to Fingal
Bay (adult/child $12/6), and **Busways** (☎ 02-
4983 1560) runs to Forster (adult/child $36/18)
and Sydney daily.

CAR
Major companies with airport offices:
Avis (☎ 13 63 33)
Budget (☎ 1300 362 868)
Europcar (☎ 13 13 90)
Hertz (☎ 13 30 39)
Thrifty (☎ 1300 367 227)

TRAIN
All CountryLink trains stop at Broadmeadow,
just west of town, and run up and down
the coast to Coffs Harbour (adult/child
$55/36). Change at either Casino or Grafton
for Byron Bay (adult/child $75/54). Trains
also head inland to Tamworth (adult/child
$37/27) and leave directly from Newcastle
Station for Sydney (adult/child $18/9).

Plenty of CityRail trains head daily to
Sydney and northwest to Maitland, Dungog
and Scone.

Getting Around
Port Stephens Coaches (☎ 02-4982 2940) runs to
and from the airport almost hourly, with reduced trips at the weekend (per person $5, 35
minutes). Otherwise, call a **cab** (☎ 13 33 00).

All travel on the blue and white buses
around the city centre is free.

Newcastle Buses & Ferries (☎ 13 15 00) offers
a late-night bus service (adult/child $8/4)
around Newcastle and across to Stockton.
The Stockton Ferry departs Queens Wharf
every half hour from 5.15am (one way
adult/child $2/1).

LOWER HUNTER VALLEY
Wine first arrived in Australia in 1788 when
Captain Arthur Phillip planted the first vines
in Sydney (no doubt he thought that establishing the first European settlement at Port
Jackson might be an easier task with a glass of
red in hand). Unfortunately he had little luck
and it wasn't until James Busby – the father
of the Australian wine industry – put pen to
paper and told the masses how to grow grapes
that the country's viticulture truly began.

In the Hunter Valley it was a free settler
by the name of George Wyndham who first
got things going; in 1828 he cleared some
land, planted some vines and Wyndham
Estate was born. By the 1860s there were
20 sq km of vineyards under cultivation in
the area, although many of these wineries
gradually declined. It wasn't until nearly a
century later that winemaking again became
an important industry.

Today there are over 140 wineries in the
area and the best-known varietals are the
Hunter Semillon and Shiraz. The rigid few
will grab a copy of the *Hunter Valley Wine
Country Visitor Guide*. The rest will get to
know the biggies, and then go looking for
the boutiques.

Orientation & Information
Most of the Lower Hunter's attractions
lie in an area bordered to the north by the
New England Hwy and to the south by the
Wollombi–Maitland Rd.

The **Hunter Valley Wine Country Visitor Centre**
(☎ 02-4990 0900; www.winecountry.com.au; 455 Wine
Country Dr; ◯ 9am-5.30pm Mon-Fri, to 5pm Sat, to 4pm Sun)

LOWER HUNTER VALLEY

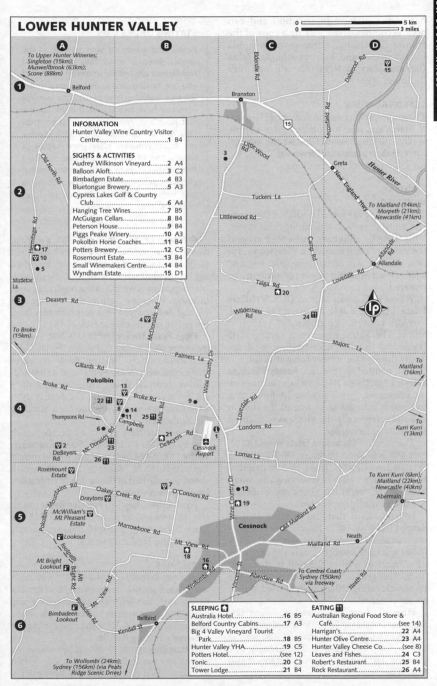

0 — 5 km
0 — 3 miles

INFORMATION
Hunter Valley Wine Country Visitor
    Centre....................................**1** B4

SIGHTS & ACTIVITIES
Audrey Wilkinson Vineyard........**2** A4
Balloon Aloft.............................**3** C2
Bimbadgen Estate......................**4** B3
Bluetongue Brewery...................**5** A3
Cypress Lakes Golf & Country
    Club....................................**6** A4
Hanging Tree Wines...................**7** B5
McGuigan Cellars.......................**8** B4
Peterson House..........................**9** B4
Piggs Peak Winery....................**10** A3
Pokolbin Horse Coaches...........**11** B4
Potters Brewery.......................**12** C5
Rosemount Estate.....................**13** B4
Small Winemakers Centre.........**14** B4
Wyndham Estate......................**15** D1

SLEEPING
Australia Hotel.........................**16** B5
Belford Country Cabins.............**17** A3
Big 4 Valley Vineyard Tourist
    Park..................................**18** B5
Hunter Valley YHA...................**19** C5
Potters Hotel.......................(see 12)
Tonic.......................................**20** C3
Tower Lodge...........................**21** B4

EATING
Australian Regional Food Store &
    Café...............................(see 14)
Harrigan's...............................**22** A4
Hunter Olive Centre.................**23** A4
Hunter Valley Cheese Co.........(see 8)
Leaves and Fishes....................**24** C3
Robert's Restaurant.................**25** B4
Rock Restaurant......................**26** A4

has oodles of local information and can book accommodation. Pick up a copy of the *Hunter Blackboard*, a free monthly guide to new wines and local events. **Red Zebra Childcare Agency** (☎ 0419 411 636) will look after the under agers.

SEASONAL WORK
The grape-picking season runs from January to March and June to August. March to June is olive-picking season. Contact the **National Harvest Labour Information Service** (☎ 1800 062 332) for seasonal work information.

Sights
WINERIES
The following are just a handful of the many Hunter wineries with welcoming cellar doors. Visit these by all means, but a tour around the vineyards will uncover a wine for everyone, whether you favour boutique, organic, aged, award-winning or simply white more than red.

Where it all began back in 1828, **Wyndham Estate** (☎ 02-4938 3444; 700 Dalwood Rd, Dalwood; ◷ 9.30am-4.30pm) is the birthplace of Australian Shiraz. The 'Shiraz Experience' tasting plate is essential to fully understanding the drop. Tours through the winery leave at 11am.

First planted in 1866, the **Audrey Wilkinson Vineyard** (☎ 02-4998 7411; www.audreywilkinson.com.au; DeBeyers Rd; ◷ 9am-5pm Mon-Fri, from 9.30am Sat & Sun) is believed to be one of the first in Pokolbin; ironically the vines were planted by a lifelong teetotaller.

The name of **Bimbadgen Estate Wines** (☎ 02-4998 4650; www.bimbadgen.com.au; 790 McDonalds Rd; ◷ 10am-5pm) derives from the Aboriginal term meaning 'a place of good view', although 'spectacular' might have been more apt. Its wines are equally impressive.

Legend has it that the hanging tree of **Hanging Tree Wines** (☎ 02-4998 6601; www.hangingtreewines.com.au; 294 O'Connors Rd, Pokolbin; ◷ 11am-5pm Fri-Sun) was once used to dangle the carcasses of animals as well as the odd bushranger. Today this gem of a winery offers one of the most welcoming cellar doors housed within an old cowshed.

One of Australia's leading wineries, **Rosemount Estate** (☎ 02-4998 6670; www.rosemountestate.com.au; McDonalds Rd, Pokolbin; ◷ 10am-5pm) is wonderfully attitude-free. The friendly cellar door staff will indulge both seasoned and novice oenophiles.

McGuigan Cellars (☎ 02-4998 7400; www.mcguiganwines.com.au; cnr Broke & McDonalds Rds, Pokolbin; tours $3; ◷ 9.30am-5pm, tours noon Mon-Fri, 11am & noon Sat & Sun) is the culmination of the McGuigan family's 55-year involvement in the Australian wine industry. The wine is affordable, very quaffable and best enjoyed with some nibbles from the neighbouring cheese factory (p172).

Piggs Peake Winery (☎ 02-6574 7000; www.piggspeake.com; 697 Hermitage Rd, Pokolbin; ◷ 10am-5pm) is one to watch. Priding itself on non-traditional winemaking practices, its limited-edition, unwooded wines are causing quite a stir in the viniculture world. The dessert styles have fabulous names: anyone for a Suckling Pig Zinfandel?

Pressed for time and can't decide which winery to visit? Head to the **Small Winemakers Centre** (☎ 02-4998 7668; www.smallwinemakerscentre.com.au; McDonalds Rd, Pokolbin; ◷ 10am-5pm), which showcases the best of the bunch from smaller, lesser-known wineries.

For bubbles, head to **Peterson House** (☎ 02-4998 7881; www.petersonhouse.com.au; cnr Broke Rd & Wine Country Dr, Pokolbin; ◷ breakfast & lunch) and sample its sparkling (and still) wines.

BREWERIES
Bluetongue Brewery (☎ 02-4998 7777; www.hunterresort.com.au/bluetongue/index.htm; Hunter Resort, Hermitage Rd, Pokolbin; ◷ 10am-late) brews up award-winning beers and a supremely refreshing alcoholic ginger beer to boot. Taste the range using the brewery's Tasting Paddle.

Potters Brewery (☎ 02-4991 7922; www.hunterbeer.com.au; Wine Country Dr, Nulkaba; tours $10; ◷ tours noon, 2pm & 4pm) is the Hunter's first microbrewery. Join a tour to see how it all works and get three free tastings, or just work your way through all six in the Old Brickworks Brasserie next door.

Activities

Balloon Aloft (☎ 02-4991 1995, 1800 028 568; www.balloonaloft.com; 1443 Wine Country Dr, North Rothbury; flights from $295) Sunrise flights over the vineyards.

Cypress Lakes Golf & Country Club (☎ 02-4993 1555; www.cypresslakes.com.au; cnr McDonalds & Thompsons Rds, Pokolbin; 18 holes $90-110). Soft spikes and collar required.

Hunter Valley Cycling (☎ 0428 281 480; www .huntervalleycycling.com.au; adult/child from $30/20) Mountain and tandem bikes delivered to your doorstep.

Tours

There are tours galore in the Hunter; get a full list from the Hunter Valley Wine Country visitor centre (p168).

Aussie Wine Tours (☎ 0412 735 809; www.aussiewine tours.com.au) Family-run day tours from $50.

Boutique Wine Tours (☎ 02-9499 5444; www .boutiquewinetours.com.au; from $99) Small group tours and customised itineraries.

Hunter Vineyard Tours (☎ 02-4991 1659; www. huntervineyardtours.com.au) Day tours $60, with lunch $90.

Pokolbin Horse Coaches (☎ 0408 161 133; www .pokolbinhorsecoaches.com.au; 426 McDonalds Rd; from $45) Half- and full-day tours in a horse-drawn carriage.

Festivals & Events

See www.winecountry.com.au/events for a full listing.

A Day on the Green (www.adayonthegreen.com.au) A series of summer vineyard concerts that have featured everyone from Leonard Cohen to Lionel Richie.

Opera in the Vineyards (www.wyndhamestate.com) Opera under the stars and plenty of award-winning wine.

Lovedale Long Lunch (www.lovedalelonglunch.com .au) A progressive lunch held over one weekend in May.

Jazz in the Vines (www.jazzinthevines.com.au) A day of food, wine, jazz and sunshine among the vines; held late October.

Sleeping

Beds get booked up well in advance during holidays and on weekends, so make sure you plan ahead. Many hotels raise prices on weekends; base yourself at Cessnock for budget and midrange accommodation.

Hunter Valley YHA (☎ 02-4991 3278; www.yha.com .au; 100 Wine Country Dr, Nulkaba; dm/s/d from $29/65/77; 🖳) This homely log cabin with pretty valley views is your best budget option. The 13 simple rooms are spotlessly clean, and a handful of doubles even have shoebox-sized private baths. There are organised wine tours and packages that include return transfers from Sydney (from $149). One room has disabled access.

Australia Hotel (☎ 02-4990 1256; 136 Wollombi Rd, Cessnock; d/tr without bathroom incl breakfast $60/100) The rooms above this local watering hole look a bit weary, but are perfectly adequate for resting your woozy wine head. The sparkling new bathrooms will make you feel much better in the morning. The reception is in the motel behind the pub.

Potters Hotel (☎ 02-4991 7922; www.pottersbrew ery.com.au; Wine Country Dr, Nulkaba; dm $99, d $120-240; 🖳 🖳) Simple, motel-style accommodation can be found within this collection of low-lying brick buildings. The rooms are fuss-free but tidy and perfectly placed for when the beer tasting (opposite) gets out of hand. The dorm room 'package' includes one main meal and a free drink.

Belford Country Cabins (☎ 02-6574 7100; www .belfordcabins.com.au; 659 Hermitage Rd, Pokolbin; d from $100; 🖳 🖳) Your only neighbours here are the possums, kangaroos and other bush-dwelling critters (snakes!). Choose one of five roomy self-contained cabins that sleep up to six. Each cabin comes with a private barbecue plus all manner of kiddie paraphernalia (cots etc).

Tonic (☎ 02-4930 9999; 251 Talga Rd, Lovedale; d incl breakfast $425; 🖳 🖳) The six rooms in this very cool boutique hotel come with everything (and we mean *everything*), most of which is available to buy. The artwork, slippers, candles and even the ironing board are yours for a price – just leave the king-sized bed behind.

Tower Lodge (☎ 02-4998 7022; www.towerlodge.com .au; Halls Rd, Pokolbin; d incl breakfast from $595; 🖳 🖳) There are 10 luxurious rooms to choose from, each furnished with antiques, artworks and the biggest bathrooms in the world (or at least the Hunter). The Chairman's Suite, a freestanding complex with its own small tower and vineyard-viewing platform, is bound to impress.

Big 4 Valley Vineyard Tourist Park (☎ 02-4990 2573; www.valleyvineyard.com.au; 137 Mt View Rd, Cessnock; powered sites $30, deluxe cabins $65; 🖳 🖳) A spacious, orderly park with a pool and on-site Thai restaurant. It's ideally placed for the wineries.

Eating

You can't have fine wine without fine dining, and many of the bigger wineries have excellent restaurants attached. Pokolbin Village offers cheaper fare, or grab a picnic and find a shady spot.

Hunter Valley Cheese Co (☎ 02-4998 7744; McGuigan Complex, McDonalds Rd; ◷ 9am-5.30pm) Fantastic European-style cheeses including the fabulously rich and creamy Hunter Gold Washed Rind. There's also gourmet produce such as whisky marmalade and ready-made picnic hampers.

Hunter Olive Centre (☎ 02-4998 7524; Pokolbin Estate Vineyard, 298 McDonalds Rd; ◷ 10am-5pm) Local jams, preserves, conserves, mustards, vinegars, chutneys and dozens and dozens of olives.

Australian Regional Food Store & Café (☎ 02-4998 6800; McDonalds Rd; mains $11-23; ◷ breakfast & lunch) Next to the Small Winemakers Centre, this is the place to stock up on Aussie fare to accompany the wines you've just bought. Alternatively have cake in the cafe overlooking the bushland.

Rock Restaurant (☎ 02-4998 6968; 576 DeBeyers Rd; mains $14-69; ◷ lunch & dinner) By day Rock operates as the Firestick Café with light lunches and wood-fired pizzas. The evening menu is contemporary Australian with a French twist. The restaurant is attached to the Poole's Rock Winery estate.

Robert's Restaurant (☎ 02-4998 7330; Halls Rd; mains $38-56; ◷ lunch & dinner) Set on the Tower Estate within a delightful National Trust slab cottage (c 1876), Robert's is one of the Hunter's finest restaurants. The menu is traditional European and award-winningly delicious.

Also available:

Harrigan's (☎ 02-4998 4000; Broke Rd; mains $17-28) Bangers and mash, fish and chips and other pub fare.

Leaves & Fishes (☎ 02-4930 7400; 737 Lovedale Rd, Lovedale) Fish farmed from the restaurant's own lake. Two-course minimum ($58).

Getting There & Around

Rover Coaches (☎ 02-4990 1699) runs a coach from Sydney daily (adult/child $40/20) with drop-offs in Cessnock and throughout the Lower Hunter Valley vineyards, as well as full-day wine-tasting tours ($40 to $120). It also has multiple daily services to Maitland (adult/child $6/3) and Newcastle (adult/child $6/3). Buses leave from the Hunter Valley Wine Country Visitor Centre (p168). CityRail runs trains from Newcastle to/from Maitland ($5, 30 minutes).

WOLLOMBI

pop 264

Established in 1830 the oh-so-pretty town of Wollombi is well worth a visit, particularly in spring when the jacaranda trees are in full bloom. Historic sandstone buildings, independent wineries and a handful of excellent eateries make this a lovely day trip. One option is to travel north from Sydney through Wollombi along the convict-built Great North Rd (p152) on your way to the Hunter Valley.

For a lesson in local history, head to the **Wollombi Courthouse** (cnr Wollombi & Broke Rds; adult/child $2/1; ◷ Fri-Mon 11am-3pm, to 4pm Sat & Sun), where old photos, cooking equipment, dental tools (including yellow-stained teeth) and old grocery store ledgers fill the rooms. The original prisoners exercise yard is attached. Stop in at **Undercliff Winery & Gallery** (☎ 02-4998 3322; www .undercliff.com.au; ◷ 10am-5pm) and sample its very good Shiraz. Undercliff also offers boutique accommodation for up to six people in the **Settlers Cottage** (r from $160), built in 1847.

On the main drag, **Gray's Inn** (☎ 02-4998 3312; www.graysinnwollombi.com.au; Wollombi Rd; d $80-120) offers three lovely sunny rooms furnished with antiques. Diagonally opposite, **Café Wollombi** (☎ 02-4998 3220; Wollombi Rd; mains $13-30; ◷ breakfast & lunch daily, dinner Fri & Sat) serves light lunches (salads, sandwiches etc) and hearty dinners on a wisteria-covered verandah.

Wollombi lies at the southern entrance to the Hunter Valley on the Great North Rd, 130km from Sydney and 28km south of Cessnock.

UPPER HUNTER VALLEY

Dark craggy hills cradle the Upper Hunter providing a striking backdrop to the region's vineyards. But it's not all about wine here; in stark contrast to the 100-plus vineyards of its lower neighbour, the Upper Hunter is home to only a handful of wineries spread across the valley. This is horse country and the area surrounding Scone is one of the largest horse-breeding regions in the world. There are also some excellent national parks here and only a handful of visitors.

A particularly scenic route into the Upper Hunter from Sydney follows the winding Putty Rd from Windsor to Singleton, passing through some of the most breathtaking sections of Wollemi and Yengo National Parks.

Sights
WINERIES
They specialise in Cabernet Sauvignon and Shiraz, so forget Merlot, but do dabble in the Verdelho and Chardonnay.

Arrowfield Estate (☎ 02-6576 4041; www.arrowfield estate.com.au; 3483 Golden Hwy, Jerry's Plain; ☼ 10am-5pm) produces prize-worthy wines (the estate has won over 1300 awards) in a stunning location; it's the only winery in the Hunter Valley actually located on the Hunter River.

The Chardonnays are the flagship at **Catherine Vale** (☎ 02-6579 1334; www.catherinevale .com.au; 656 Milbrodale Rd, Bulga; ☼ 10am-5pm), but this small family-run vineyard also produces Verdelho, the Italian red varieties Dolcetto and Barbera plus late-harvest Semillon.

Cruikshank Wines & Callatoota Estate (☎ 02-6547 8149; 2656 Wybong Rd, Wybong; ☼ 9am-5pm) is unique in that absolutely everything takes place on the property, from grape pressing through to marketing. Visitors can not only taste the wine but also help bottle it.

Bordered by the Wollemi National Park and with sweeping panoramas of the Goulburn River, **James Estate** (☎ 02-6547 5168; www.james tatewines.com.au; 951 Bylong Valley Way, Baerami; ☼ 10am-4.30pm) offers views as formidable as its wines.

OLIVE GROVES
The Hunter Valley's olive industry continues to grow; you'll find the largest groves at Merriwa and Denman. **Pukara Estate** (☎ 02-6547 1055; www.pukaraestate.com.au; 1440 Denman Rd, Muswellbrook; ☼ 9.30am-4.30pm) produces a range of extra-virgin olive oils, flavoured oils, olives, tapenades, relishes and more, all produced on site.

GOULBURN RIVER NATIONAL PARK
The river is the star attraction of this park and is of great significance to the Aboriginal people who once used the valley as a trading route – look out for rock-art paintings mostly in the form of hand stencils, lines, arrows and circles. Wombats, wallabies and wallaroos like to graze on the grassy riverbanks; water dragons and platypuses make the occasional appearance. **Mt Dangar** offers views over the Hunter Valley.

There are a number of short bush walks to various lookouts and several basic **campsites** (☎ 02-6372 7199); Spring Gully and Big River Camp are right on the river and are good spots for swimming and rafting.

The park is 35km southwest of Merriwa. Access is from the road south to Wollar and Bylong. All roads in the park are unsealed; check conditions after heavy rains. Mudgee **NPWS** (☎ 02-6372 7199) and **Mudgee visitor centre** (☎ 02-6372 1020; www.visitmudgeeregion.com.au; 84 Market St, Mudgee; ☼ 9am-5pm) can provide information.

BURNING MOUNTAIN
Off the New England Hwy, 20km north of Scone is an underground **coal seam** that's been smoking 30m below the surface for some 5500 years. The fire smoulders at a rate of about 1m per year, and so far it has shifted 150m since it was first identified in 1829. A steep 3.5km-return walking track leads up through the nature reserve to puffing vents.

Festivals & Events
Held in the first two weeks of May, the **Scone & Upper Hunter Horse Festival** (www.sconehorsefesti val.com) celebrates all things equine. The highlight for lonely lads and ladies is the B&S (Bachelor and Spinster) Ball.

Sleeping
Middlebrook Station (☎ 02-6545 0389; www.mid dlebrookstation.com; Middlebrook Rd, Scone; d from $88; ⛾) Ideal for city slickers looking for a rural retreat is this working farm just 10km from Scone. The 70-year-old woolshed now houses 12 comfortable rooms and there's a well-equipped shared kitchen plus two living rooms with fabulous views.

Airlie House Motor Inn (☎ 02-6545 1488; www .airliehouse.com.au; 229 New England Hwy; s/d/tw/f $92/105/115/150; ⛾ ⛳) Once home to the town doctor, this 1895 building is not your average motel. Stay in one of the guest suites or pick a modern motel unit.

Willowgate Hall (☎ 02-6545 9378; www.willowgate hall.com.au; 91 Kingdon St, Scone; d incl breakfast $135-145) Built in 1873 this elegant stucco-fronted building was once the cultural centre of Scone. The current owners have expertly renovated the hall to provide five comfortable bedrooms decked out in all manner of country florals. Dinner can be arranged by prior appointment.

Sandy Hollow Tourist Park (☎ 02-6547 4575; www .sandyhollow.com.au; Golden Hwy; sites $19-25, d cottages $90-150, cabins $80-90; ⛾ ⛳) A wide range of accommodation options in a beautiful setting makes this the ideal jumping-off point for touring the area.

Getting There & Around

Greyhound (☎ 1300 473 946) has daily bus services between Scone and Sydney (adult/child $86/75) and Newcastle (adult/child $62/53).

CountryLink (☎ 13 22 32) runs a daily train service between Scone and Sydney (adult/child $48/28).

NEWCASTLE TO PORT MACQUARIE

Port Stephens & Around

pop 63,408

Port Stephens is an area, not a town, which often confuses people. The stunning sheltered bay incorporates a string of coastal towns populated by welcoming locals with a passion for their local environment. An hour's drive north of Newcastle, the bay occupies a submerged valley that stretches more than 20km inland.

On the southern shore lies the unofficial capital, Nelson Bay, along with beach and bayside towns including Shoal Bay and Anna Bay. On the northern shore (officially Myall Lakes, terrain confusingly overseen by a separate visitor centre) is Tea Gardens and Hawks Nest. Though the towns on either side of the port practically look each other in the eye, they are only accessible by car via a 45-minute round trip or – for passengers only – via an hour-long (albeit very scenic) ferry ride.

Both sides are popular boating, fishing and family holiday spots and the port itself is home to some 160 bottlenose dolphins and – during the migrating season (from late May to July heading north and from September to November heading south) – thousands of passing whales. The area offers all kinds of adventure activities and several near-deserted beaches fringed by bungalows.

INFORMATION

CTC@Tea Gardens (☎ 02-4997 0749; shop 4, Myall Plaza, Tea Gardens; per hr $10) Internet access.

Internet Café (☎ 02-4984 2088; shop 13, Cascade Walk, off Stockton St; per hr $6; ☉ 9am-5pm Mon-Fri, 11am-4pm Sat, noon-4pm Sun)

Port Stephens Visitor Information Centre (☎ 1800 808 900; www.portstephens.org.au; Victoria Pde, Nelson Bay) Near d'Albora Marina.

Tea Gardens Visitor Information Centre (☎ 02-4997 0111; Myall Rd, Tea Gardens)

SIGHTS & ACTIVITIES

On the main road heading into **Nelson Bay**, **Port Stephens Winery** (☎ 02-4982 6411; www.port stephenswinery.com; Bob's Farm, 3443 Nelson Bay Rd) is a good place to stop for lunch – or if you have a designated driver – a drink. The winery has a huge cellar door and is the new home of Murray's Craft Brewing Co. Be warned: Murray's Grand Cru, a hybrid of Belgian Trippel and Golden Strong Ale styles, has won awards. Declining a second can be difficult.

Closer to Nelson Bay, on the southern side of the Tomaree Peninsula, **One Mile Beach** is a gorgeous semicircle of velvety sand and crystalline water, favoured by surfers, beachcombers and idle romantics…some of whom are nude by the time you reach **Samurai Beach**.

Further south, you can hang loose at the surfside village of **Anna Bay**, with both surf and bay beaches. It's backed by the incredible **Stockton Bight**, the longest moving sand dunes in the southern hemisphere, stretching 35km to Newcastle. The tourist board refers to the dunes as *Mad Max*–style, but think *Lawrence of Arabia* – more Sahara than outback. At the far west end of the beach, the wreck of the *Sygna* languishes in the water.

About half an hour by boat from Nelson Bay, **Broughton Island** is uninhabited except for muttonbirds, a scarcity of penguins and an enormous diversity of fish species. The diving is great and the beaches are incredibly secluded.

The restored 1872 **Inner Lighthouse** at Nelson Head has a small **museum**, with displays on the area's history, and tearooms with inspiring views of Port Stephens.

At the mouth of the Myall River, on the northern side of Port Stephens, are the small, pretty towns of **Tea Gardens**, on the river, and **Hawks Nest**, on the beach. **Jimmy's Beach** at Hawks Nest fronts a glasslike stretch of water, while **Bennett's Beach** has great views of Broughton Island and Cabbage Tree Island, the only forested island off the NSW coast.

Activities available through the visitor information centre include fishing and helicopter rides, and tours of Barrington Tops National Park, Hunter Valley wineries and Maitland architecture.

Or try the following:

Port Stephens Parasailing (☎ 02-4982 2808; www .portstephensparasailing.com.au) Solo ($84) or tandem ($139) flights 150m above the water.

Pro Dive Nelson Bay (☎ 02-4981 4331; www.prodive nelsonbay.com; D'Albora Marina, Nelson Bay; ☉ 9am-5pm Mon-Fri, 6.30am-5pm Sat & Sun) PADI course $450.

Sahara Trails (☎ 02-4981 9077; www.saharatrails.com; 9 Port Stephens Dr, Nelson Bay) A one-hour horse ride is $50.

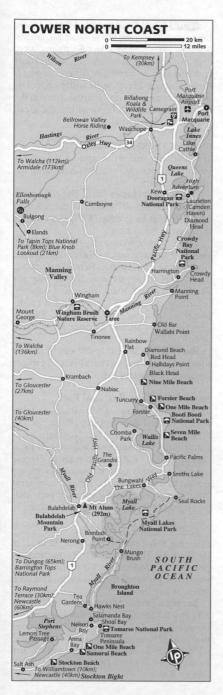

LOWER NORTH COAST

0 ——— 20 km
0 ——— 12 miles

TOURS

4WD Tours R Us & Quad Bike King (☎ 02-4919 0088; www.quadbikeking.com.au; 1½hr tours $110) Has 4WDs, bushmobiles and quad bikes.

Blue Water Sea Kayaking (☎ 0405 033 518; www.kayakingportstephens.com.au) Dolphin tours are adult/child $45/25 and champagne sunset tours $35/20.

Moonshadow Cruises (☎ 02-4984 9388; www.moonshadow.com.au; 3hr whale tour adult/child $60/25, dolphin tour $26/14) Ecocertified cruises on big catamarans.

Thundacraft (☎ 0400 382 028; www.thundaraft.com.au) Wave-jumping rides ($65) and whale-watching tours ($75).

SLEEPING

In Nelson Bay, Gowrie Ave and Government St – between Stockton and Church Sts – are lined with motels and hotels. Shoal Bay, virtually a suburb of Nelson Bay, has accommodation, shops and restaurants. Anna Bay is the closest hamlet to One Mile Beach. **Winning Holidays** (☎ 02-4984 0100; www.winningholidays.com.au; 19 Stockton St, Nelson Bay) has prolific holiday-rental listings.

Melaleuca Surfside Backpackers (☎ 02-4981 9422; www.melaleucabackpackers.com.au; 2 Koala Pl, One Mile Beach; camping per person $18, dm/d $32/100) It's all mates and smiles at this excellent backpacker retreat, spread across a large green property. Camping is 'free range' on a grassy oval and cabins are made of glorious rust-red timber. It's wheelchair-friendly and the koalas dig it, too.

O'Carrollyns At One Mile Beach (☎ 02-4982 2801; www.ocarrollyns.com.au; 5 Koala Pl, One Mile Beach; dm/d from $45/140; 🖰 🖵) O'Carrollyns' eight cabins are laid out in a distinctly bush setting – complete with grunting koalas and frogs – and it's 600m from the beach down a little track. Digs have mezzanine bedrooms and five-star energy ratings and are wheelchair friendly. The owners are a wealth of local info.

Seabreeze Hotel (☎ 02-4916 4606; Government Rd, Nelson Bay; standard/deluxe d $75/85) A tidy pub within walking distance to Nelson Bay's shops and marina. The standard rooms might be small and basic but they have private bathrooms. Pub grub and pool are a staple in Red Bellies bistro (open for lunch and dinner).

Santa Catalina (☎ 02-4981 1519; 9 Shoal Bay Rd, Shoal Bay; apt $90-150; 🖰 🖵) This cute block of weatherboard apartments is blessed with a dose of 1970s retro character. The self-contained apartments sleep two to five, have a decent-sized kitchen and open-plan lounge. Ask for one overlooking the beach (30m away) or the pool. The shops are close, too.

NEW SOUTH WALES

Tea Gardens Club Inn (☎ 02-4997 0911; ww.teagardensclubinn.com.au; Yalinbah St, Tea Gardens; r from $99; ⊠) Behind the bowls club, this sturdy motel has good-sized rooms with creature comforts and spas. Some rooms have sliding doors right onto the bowling green – you can watch the greenkeepers battle with the birds in the morning.

Shoal Bay Resort & Spa (☎ 1800 181 810, 02-4981 1555; www.shoalbayresort.com; Beachfront, Shoal Bay; apt from $209; ⊠ ☒) Praise be to the gods of pampering: they surely had a hand in this classy number. A range of rooms treats fussy tushes and if you really want to impress, opt for a 'heritage suite' with ocean views.

Also recommended:

Halifax Holiday Park (☎ 1800 600 201; Beach Rd, Little Beach, Nelson Bay; powered sites from $30, cabins $59-165; ⊠) Excellent cabins right on the beach.

Jimmy's Beach Caravan Park (☎ 02-4997 0466; www.jimmysbeachcaravanpark.com.au; Coorilla St, Hawks Nest; campsites/cabins $27/135) A eucalypt-studded setting close to the beach.

Samurai Beach YHA (☎ 02-4982 1921; www.yha .com.au; Frost Rd, Anna Bay; dm $27, d with/without bathroom$80/60; ⌨ ☒) Bungalow dorms in a lovely rainforest setting.

EATING

Red Neds Gourmet Pies (☎ 02-4984 1355; shop 3, 17-19 Stockton St, Nelson Bay; pies $4-5; ☽ 6am-5pm) The lobster, prawn and barramundi pies are second only to the Japanese Wagyu, cheese and onion pies. And the ostrich, coconut cream and parmesan pies. And the… With more than 50 varieties on the menu it's hard to choose.

Café Sea (☎ 02-4997 2744; 43 Booner St, Hawks Nest) This simple sky-blue cafe has market umbrellas and a patio for alfresco dining. Southeast Asian cuisine is the house speciality.

Mod Thai Food & Noodle Bar (☎ 02-4984 4222; shop 12, Nelson Bay Cinema Complex, Stockton St, Nelson Bay; ☽ lunch & dinner Mon-Sun) Keeping things simple yet delicious, this little restaurant packs in a hungry crowd of locals and tourists on most evenings. The fried fish red curry ($17) is a speciality. One main feeds two people.

Elena's on the Bay (☎ 02-4984 1203; d'Albora Marina, Nelson Bay; ☽ lunch & dinner) This sunny waterfront restaurant, where boating types gravitate at the end of the day, has a short and sweet menu with seafood favourites including garlic prawns ($18), seafood platters ($30) and fish and chips ($15). The salty breeze goes nicely with a crisp Chardonnay.

ourpick Ritual Organics (☎ 02-4981 5514; shop 1 & 2, Austral St Shopping Village, Nelson Bay; degustation menu $85; ☽ dinner) Port Stephens' very own molecular gastronomist fuses flavours and textures to challenge diners' expectations: chicken breast with white chocolate jus, for example. With 16 small courses, the biggest surprise will be finishing the meal! Reservations essential.

GETTING THERE & AROUND

When driving, follow the signs for Nelson Bay on the southern shore or Tea Gardens on the northern shore.

Port Stephens Coaches (☎ 02-4982 2940; www.ps coaches.com.au) runs daily from all the towns of Port Stephens to Sydney ($37), and services the coast to Newcastle.

To drive from Nelson Bay to Tea Gardens, you have to backtrack to Raymond Terrace. Alternatively, **Port Stephens Ferry Service** (☎ 0412 682 117, 0419 417 689) departs Nelson Bay for Tea Gardens at 8.30am, noon and 3.30pm, returning at 10am, 2.30pm and 5pm (additional services during summer and Easter). The trip takes around an hour (return fare adult/child/family $20/10/50).

Shoal Bay Bike Hire (☎ 02-4981 4121; cnr Shoal Bay & Government Rds, Shoal Bay) rents bikes to explore the good network of paths.

Barrington Tops National Park

This World Heritage–listed wilderness lying on the rugged Barrington Plateau rises to a height of almost 1600m. Northern rainforest butts into southern sclerophyll here, creating one of Australia's most diverse ecosystems, with giant strangler figs, mossy Antarctic beech forests, limpid rainforest swimming holes and pocket-sized pademelons (note: it is illegal to put pademelons in your pocket).

Bushwalks, mountain biking, horse riding, canoeing, fishing and 4WDing are the order of the day here. The **Barrington Trail** is particularly popular for 4WDing, but it's closed during winter. Be prepared for cold snaps, and even snow, at any time.

Barrington Outdoor Adventure Centre (☎ 02-6558 2093; www.boac.com.au, www.canoebarrington.com.au; 126 Thunderbolts Way; 1-/2-day tours $130/335) specialises in downhill mountain-biking adventures and white water kayaking. Or hire canoes and kayaks (one-day hire canoe/kayak $50/$80) and go it alone.

There's also a self-contained cabin in the park for rent from $80 per night. It's BYO everything and sleeps five. Camping is possible throughout the park (adult/child per night $10/5). The most popular grounds are at Devils Hole and Gloucester River. There's also camping at Little Murray and Junction Pools, although you need to walk in or have a 4WD to get there.

Alternatively, the **Barringtons Country Retreat** (☎ 02-4995 9269; www.thebarringtons.com.au; 194 Chichester Dam Rd, Bandon Grove via Dungog; d for 2 nights $120-310) has 25 lodges and six cabins hidden in the foothills of the park; some have spas and log fires. Dinner and B&B packages are an option.

Day tours to **Barrington Tops** (☎ 1300 130 647; www.barringtontops.com.au) can be organised through the Port Stephens (p174), Dungog and Gloucester visitor centres. Also pick up a *Farm Trail* map for the low-down on producers of alpaca wool, goats cheese and wine.

The park can be accessed from Scone, Dungog and Gloucester. For more information contact **Gloucester NPWS** (☎ 02-6538 5300).

Myall Lakes National Park & Around

These stunning **lakes** (entry per car $7) form the largest natural freshwater system in NSW. Pooling in deep blue basins, they weave around clumps of forest and small settlements.

In the south, the road from Hawks Nest to Mungo Brush reveals scenery ideal for bushwalks through coastal rainforest and beach dunes, and wildflower spotting. There are numerous waterside campsites, some only accessible by boat. **Mungo Brush campsite** (adult/child $10/5) on the main road is a beautiful option, right on the lake. Further along, the NPWS operates a **punt** (car/passenger $5/2; 🕐 8am-6pm) crossing to Bombah Point, a short but pretty ride.

Canoes, sailboards, bikes and runabouts are available at **Bombah Point**. Here you'll also find **Bombah Point Eco Cottages** (☎ 02-4997 4401; www.bombah.com.au; 969 Bombah Point Rd; d $210-260), an environmentally friendly and romantic getaway.

Alternatively, **Eco Point Myall Shores Resort** (☎ 1300 769 566; www.ecopoint.com.au; Myall Lakes National Park, Bombah Point; powered campsites $35, cabins/ villas $40-460; 🖳) on the edge of the lake has a huge range of cabins and villas.

The best way from Bombah Point to Seal Rocks is to continue on the partially sealed road to Bulahdelah, follow the Pacific Hwy

2km north then turn off onto the **Lakes Way**, which ribbons its way through magnificent scenery past the tallest tree in NSW, the 400-year-old **Grandis**, and the Seal Rocks turn-off (for which you will need a 4WD) towards Forster-Tuncurry.

The best beaches are in the north around secluded **Seal Rocks**, an idyllic cove embodying the Australian ideal of utopia – few people, gorgeous views, great surf, magical flora and fauna and little to do but swim and sit. The historic **lighthouse** here is well worth the walk to witness the rocks that have claimed many ships over the last 150 years. Even better, spend a weekend in one of the three old lighthouse keeper's cottages at **Sugarloaf Point lighthouse accommodation** (☎ 02-4997 6590; www .sealrockslighthouseaccommodation.com.au, www.srla.com.au; 6-person cottage for 2 nights from $250). If the crashing waves and wildlife aren't distracting enough, each cottage has queen beds, plasma televisions, DVD players and barbecues. The **Seal Rocks Camping Reserve** (☎ 1800 112 234, 02-4997 6164; www. sealrockscampingreserve.com.au; Kinka Rd; powered campsites/ cabins from $28/70) has tidy cabins, a manicured-to-bowling-green-perfection lawn and a blissful location right on the beach.

A touch further north, the **NPWS** (☎ 02-6591 0300; www.nationalparks.nsw.gov.au; Ruins Camping Ground, Booti Booti National Park, The Lakes Way, Pacific Palms) has information on the many local national parks, including **Booti Booti National Park** (adult/child per night $14/7, vehicle per day $7).

Sundowner Tiona Tourist Park (☎ 02-6554 0291; The Lakes Way, Pacific Palms; powered sites/dm/cabin from $22/23/70) sits between tranquil Wallis Lake and the energetic ocean of Seven Mile Beach on the last stretch of road before Forster. Stop by the **Green Cathedral**, an open-air sanctuary paying more homage to nature than any god.

The view from **Cape Hawke**, just south of Forster, is a 360-degree panorama of the confluence of lakes, ocean, forest and teeny towns.

Forster-Tuncurry
pop 18,372

Separated by the sea entrance to Wallis Lake, these twin towns have 'waterfront potential' stamped all over them: they're just waiting for a cash injection and the right town planner. In the meantime it's a great hub for exploring not only the lakes, but also a string of spectacular beaches along an unhurried and unpretentious coastline.

Forster (*fos*-ter), on the southern side of the entrance, is the big brother of the pair. The helpful **visitor centre** (☎ 02-6554 8799; Little St, Forster) is on the pretty street that runs beside the lake. There's internet access at **Boxfish Café** (☎ 02-6557 2577; shop 4, 2-6 Wharf St, Forster).

Tobwabba Art (☎ 02-6554 5755; www.tobwabba .com.au; 10 Breckenridge St, Forster; admission free; ☽ 10am-4.30pm Mon-Fri) is owned by the Worimi people of the Great Lakes region. The centre exhibits their paintings and artefacts. It is run by volunteers so the opening hours can be erratic.

Beaches are of the highest quality in this area, with **Nine Mile Beach** the pick of the surf spots, **Forster Beach** a good family option with its swimming pools, and **One Mile Beach** also popular. The **Surf School** (☎ 02-6554 7811; 33 Wharf St, Forster; 1-5 lessons $50-180) meets at the surf club on One Mile Beach.

Various cruise operators and boat hire facilities can be found along Little St. **Dive Forster** (☎ 02-6554 7478; www.diveforster.com.au; Fisherman's Wharf, Forster; swimmers/nonswimmers $70/40) runs swim-with-the-dolphins tours. It also offers scuba dives and has limited accommodation.

Catering to backpackers, **Lakes & Ocean Hotel** (☎ 02-6554 6005; 10 Little St, Forster; r $40) has basic pub rooms with shared bathrooms. Opt for a room on the verandah with a lake view, pelicans and all. Another option is **Barkley Inn** (☎ 02-6555 2552; www.barkleyinn.com.au; 38 Head St, Forster; r from $75; ☒ ☒), with neat and petite rooms and plenty of sunlight.

Dorsal Boutique Hotel (☎ 02-6554 8766; www.dor salhotel.com.au; 1 West St, Forster; r from $180; ☒ ☐) is a newish establishment in an enviable position right on Forster Beach. The alfresco terrace cafe is a serene place to start the day. Breakfast is included.

Coffee Grind Café (☎ 02-6557 5155; 59 Wharf St, Forster; ☽ breakfast & lunch) is a hidey-hole on the main street serving excellent coffee and a great Aussie snack – ham, cheese and pineapple toasties ($7).

Reef Bar & Grill (☎ 02-6555 7092; Wharf St, Forster; mains $15) is a popular local haunt with great steaks, seafood and watery views that will keep punters ordering 'just one more' drink.

Over the bridge in Tuncurry, the **Bell Vue Hotel-Motel** (☎ 02-6554 6577; www.bellevuehotel tuncurry.com; Manning St, Tuncurry) has pub meals, rooms and live music. Thursday nights are, erm, big!

CountryLink (☎ 13 22 32; www.countrylink.info) runs north to Taree ($5, 40 minutes) and south to Sydney ($40, six hours). **Busways** (☎ 1800 043 263; www.busways.com.au) runs to Taree ($15), Hawks Nest ($26) and Sydney ($55).

Manning Valley

From Forster-Tuncurry the Pacific Hwy swings inland to **Taree** (population 16,621), a large town serving the farms of the fertile Manning Valley. Its sprawling green riverbanks are reminiscent of English countryside. The **Taree visitor centre** (☎ 1800 182 733, 02-6592 5444; 21 Manning River Dr) is at the northern end of town.

Further west up the valley, **Wingham Brush Nature Reserve**, a patch of idyllic rainforest near the timber town of Wingham, is home to giant, otherworldly Moreton Bay figs and flocks of flying foxes. Just past it, **Mick Tuck Reserve** on the Manning River is a picnic paradise.

Near Wingham, **Tinonee** is a tiny heritage town. It features the usual Sunday drive crafts-and-souvenir shop, a museum and the highlight – the 22-seat **Terrace Cinema** (☎ 02-6553 1428; 1 Mill St, Tinonee). This little gem is the world's second-smallest cinema, set in a charming 1860s weatherboard house. Unfortunately it's only available for group bookings.

The Coastal Way

This meandering route has sweet sleepy towns and good surf, particularly at **Old Bar**, on the coast near Taree. Just south there's a lagoon for swimming at **Wallabi Point**.

Across the river – but a hefty drive because there is no bridge shortcut – is **Harrington**. As much to support the retailers as for the view, keep driving through the developing estates and past the faux Irish pub into the original village, which has an eye-popping inlet and beach. The **Harrington Hotel** (☎ 02-6656 1205; 30 Beach St; mains $15; ☽ lunch & dinner) is a beauty. The expansive bistro has glorious water views and upstairs there are wonderfully creaky old pub rooms (singles/doubles $45/55).

Crowdy Head is the prettiest of the nearby settlements, with sweeping views from the 1878 **lighthouse** out to sea and overlooking Crowdy Head National Park.

You can avoid the Pacific Hwy by taking the unsealed, but well maintained, Crowdy Head Rd to **Diamond Head** and **Laurieton** through the national park and rainforest. Pitch a tent at one of the isolated bush or beach campsites.

Kylie's Beach campsite (adult/child per night $10/5, car per day $7) is a hang-out for seemingly tame kangaroos. Be sure to bring your own water.

Wedged between Dooragan National Park and the ocean is **Camden Haven**, where quaint towns cluster around the wide sea entrance of **Queens Lake**. You can get a jaw-dropping eyeful of the scenery from Laurieton Lookout, inside **Dooragan National Park**, 5km up a winding wooded road.

Your final march up the coastline will take you past the biggest town, **Lake Cathie** (*cat*-eye), where a gleaming salt marsh estuary backing onto the beach is warm and shallow, ideal for a relaxing swim.

PORT MACQUARIE

pop 39,508

If Port, as it's affectionately known, had a 'big banana' or a 'big pineapple' like other Australian cities, it would probably have a bigger tourist profile. Mercifully, on both counts, the city has never had to manufacture its appeal, reclining as it does over a spectacular headland at the entrance to the subtropical coast. The palm trees, rolling parklands, hefty koala population and beach coves here do a good job of camouflaging swank restaurants and fine accommodation, and this balance of greenery and infrastructure, combined with a placid ambience that belies its size, makes it an ideal holiday destination.

Port was founded in 1821 as a penal colony for slack convicts who found life in Sydney Cove too easy. The heavy-duty past is still visible in the frontier architecture (Port was the third town to be established on the Australian mainland), but these days idle Aussies choose to serve time here.

Information

Network Video & Internet Café (☎ 02-6583 4667; 17 Short St; per hr $4; ☼ 10am-7.30pm Mon-Fri, to 8.30pm Sat & Sun)
NPWS office (☎ 02-6586 8300; 152 Horton St)
Visitor centre (☎ 1300 303 155; www.portmac quarieinfo.com.au; cnr Gordon & Gore Sts)

Sights

MUSEUMS & HISTORIC BUILDINGS

In the town centre you'll find a host of colonial buildings including convict-built **St Thomas' Anglican Church** (Hay St), the 1835 **Garrison shopping precinct** (cnr Clarence & Hay Sts), the 1869 **old courthouse** (☎ 02-6584 1818; Clarence St; adult/child $2/50c; ☼ 10am-4pm Mon-Sat) and the 1836 **Port Macquarie Historical Society Museum** (☎ 02-6583 1108; 22 Clarence St; adult/child $5/4; ☼ 9.30am-4.30pm Mon-Sat).

Up on the point, the old pilot's cottage (1882) houses the **Maritime Museum** (☎ 02-6583 1866; 6 William St; adult/child $4/2; ☼ 10am-4pm Mon-Sat). At the **Town Wharf**, there's a second maritime museum, **Pilot's Boatshed Museum** (☎ 02-6584 2987; entry by donation; ☼ 10am-2pm Sun-Fri), or step back in time cruising on the **MV Wentworth** (☎ 02-6584 2987; ☼ Tue & Thu), a restored 1948 vessel.

The **Alma Doepel** (☎ 02-6581 8000; Lady Nelson Wharf; adult/child $3/1; ☼ 9am-3pm) is a resplendent three-masted trading vessel built in 1903, now spending its retirement as Port Macquarie's centrepiece.

WILDLIFE & NATURE RESERVES

Two car ferries cross the Hastings River to **Limeburners Creek Nature Reserve** where you can spend the day swimming, bushwalking and wildlife watching.

Port Macquarie shares its beautiful gum trees with one of Australia's icons, the koala. Unfortunately, many end up at the **Koala Hospital** (☎ 02-6584 1522; www.koalahospital.org.au; Roto House, Lord St; admission by donation; ☼ feeding 8am & 3pm), which you can visit. **Billabong Koala & Wildlife Park** (☎ 02-6585 1060; www.billabongkoala.com .au; 61 Billabong Dr; adult/child $18/11; ☼ 8am-4.30pm, feeding 3pm) is a wonderful family experience.

Sea Acres Rainforest Centre (☎ 02-6582 3355; Pacific Dr; adult/child $8/4; ☼ 9am-4.30pm) protects 72 hectares of coastal rainforest alive with birds, goannas, brush turkeys and, unfortunately, mosquitoes. There's a wheelchair-accessible boardwalk, leafy rainforest cafe and excellent guided tours.

ARTS & CULTURE

The **Glasshouse** (☎ 02-6581 8066; www.glasshouse .org.au; cnr Clarence & Hay Sts; ☼ 9am-5.30pm Mon-Fri, to 4pm Sat & Sun) opened in July 2009 in the heart of Port, and is the new talk of the town. The funky building, modelled on environmental sustainability, houses the regional art gallery, museum and two theatres.

OTHER SIGHTS

For those looking for answers beyond the horizon, sneak a peek through the telescope at the **astronomical observatory** (☎ 02-6583 1933; www.pmobs .org.au; Rotary Park, William St; adult/child $8/5; ☼ 7.30pm Wed & Sun Apr-Sep, 8.15pm Wed Oct-Mar) on one of its its public viewing and presentation nights.

NEW SOUTH WALES

PORT MACQUARIE

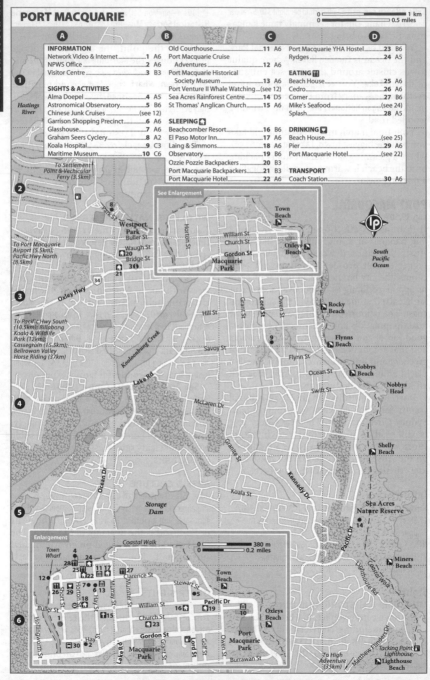

INFORMATION
Network Video & Internet..............**1** A6
NPWS Office....................................**2** A6
Visitor Centre.................................**3** B3

SIGHTS & ACTIVITIES
Alma Doepel...................................**4** A5
Astronomical Observatory.............**5** B6
Chinese Junk Cruises................(see 12)
Garrison Shopping Precinct...........**6** A6
Glasshouse.....................................**7** A6
Graham Seers Cyclery.....................**8** A2
Koala Hospital................................**9** C3
Maritime Museum........................**10** C6

Old Courthouse............................**11** A6
Port Macquarie Cruise
    Adventures..............................**12** A6
Port Macquarie Historical
    Society Museum.......................**13** A6
Port Venture II Whale Watching...(see 12)
Sea Acres Rainforest Centre.........**14** D5
St Thomas' Anglican Church.........**15** A6

SLEEPING
Beachcomber Resort.....................**16** B6
El Paso Motor Inn.........................**17** A6
Laing & Simmons..........................**18** A6
Observatory..................................**19** B6
Ozzie Pozzie Backpackers.............**20** B3
Port Macquarie Backpackers.........**21** B3
Port Macquarie Hotel...................**22** A6

Port Macquarie YHA Hostel.........**23** B6
Rydges...**24** A5

EATING
Beach House.................................**25** A6
Cedro..**26** A6
Corner...**27** B6
Mike's Seafood........................(see 24)
Splash..**28** A5

DRINKING
Beach House............................(see 25)
Pier...**29** A6
Port Macquarie Hotel...............(see 22)

TRANSPORT
Coach Station..............................**30** A6

Several wineries are scattered around. A reputation as the region's pioneering vineyard has made **Cassegrain** (☎ 02-6582 8377; www.casse grainwines.com.au; 764 Fernbank Creek Rd; ☒ 9am-5pm), 15km out of town, a favourite. The **Ça Marche Restaurant** (☎ 02-6582 8320; mains $30; ☒ lunch daily, dinner Fri) here has won awards.

Activities

The **Coastal Walk**, hugging 9km of shoreline from Westport Park in town to Tacking Point Lighthouse, is Port's latest ode to nature. It wends in and around bays and beaches, passing historic sites, picnic spots and excellent places to swim.

High Adventure (☎ 0429 844 961; www.highad venture.com.au; tandem flights from $160) delivers adrenalin and dramatic landscapes courtesy of hang-gliding.

Readers rave about **Bellrowan Valley Horse Riding** (☎ 02-6587 5227; www.bellrowanvalley.com.au; 334 Crows Rd, Bellrowan Valley; 1hr per person $55) in the hinterland, 30 minutes' drive from Port Macquarie.

Edge Experience (☎ 0427 324 009; www.edgeexperi ence.com.au; full-day tours from $100) offers adventure-combo tours that mix mountain biking and abseiling. There's also a twilight eco-tour.

More active pursuits:
Graham Seers Cyclery (☎ 02-6583 2333; Port Marina; 1hr $15, half-/full-day $25/40) Bike hire.
Port Macquarie Surf School (☎ 02-6585 5453; www .portmacquariesurfschool.com.au; 2hr lessons from $40)

Tours

The following tours depart from the Town Wharf (Clarence St):
Chinese Junk Cruises (☎ 0409 744 270; www .junkcruises.com.au; adult/child $25/15; ☒ Fri & Sun) Two-hour lunch cruises, including fish and chips.
Port Macquarie Cruise Adventures (☎ 02-6583 8483, 1300 555 890; www.cruiseadventures.com.au; 90min per person from $12) Dolphin- and whale-watching tours, nature, sunset and oyster-farm tours.
Port Venture II Whale Watching (☎ 1300 795 577; adult/child $49/39) Dolphin- and whale-watching tours.

Sleeping

For holiday apartment rentals, get in touch with **Laing & Simmons** (☎ 02-6583 7733; www.port realestate.net; cnr William & Horton Sts).

BUDGET

Ozzie Pozzie Backpackers (☎ 1800 620 020, 02-6583 8133; www.ozziepozzie.com; 36 Waugh St; dm $29, d with/ without bathroom $85/75; ☒) Not far from the visi

tor centre, this small, charming and colourful hostel with spotless bathrooms and a cosy TV room has dorms arranged around a wee courtyard. Breakfast is free, bike hire is $5.

Port Macquarie YHA Hostel (☎ 1800 880 008, 02-6583 5512; www.yha.com.au; 40 Church St; dm/tw/d $30/70/89, d with bathroom $95; ☒) The sunflower-yellow weatherboard is starting to look a tiny bit tired but the orderly four- to six-bed dorms, lounge and open kitchen make this a friendly little place for quality downtime.

Port Macquarie Backpackers (☎ 02-6583 1791; www.portmacquariebackpackers.com.au; 2 Hastings River Dr; s/d $31/45; ☒ ☒) On a busy intersection, this cheerful place has small clean dorms, a great host and free breakfast.

Port Macquarie Hotel (☎ 02-6580 7888; www.mac quariehotel.com; cnr Horton & Clarence Sts; d with/without bathroom $80/55) Much of Port Macquarie's live music and nightlife happens in the bar downstairs making this a great option if you plan to stumble home to bed after a Bundy Rum or two. Expect a bit of noise and larrikinism on the weekends.

MIDRANGE

El Paso Motor Inn (☎ 02-6584 1021; www.elpasomo torinn.com.au; 29 Clarence St; r from $125; ☒ ☒) This kitsch Mexicana motel holds its own as a cheap and cheerful one-stop shop in the centre of town, complete with palm trees, terracotta decor and a swimming pool. It has beach access and does a penny-pincher dinner and B&B packages.

our pick **Observatory** (☎ 1300 888 305, 02-6586 8000; www.observatory.net.au; 40 William St; apt from $129; ☒ ☒ ☒) Soft tones, suede couches and glass doors that open onto beach-view balconies make these apartments and hotel rooms extremely comfortable. The same-sameness of them is a tad clinical, but they're great value if you pay the low walk-in rate.

Beachcomber Resort (☎ 02-6584 1881; www .beachcomberresort.com.au; 54 William St; apt from $130; ☒ ☒ ☒) This low-rise condo-block has spiffy apartments with kitchenettes and bright, open living spaces. There's a barbecue courtyard, and Town Beach is across the way.

TOP END

Rydges (☎ 02-6589 2888; www.rydges.com; 1 Hay St; r from $155; ☒ ☒ ☒) With a day spa and coffee bar to hand, this hotel is a home-away-from-home for folk used to the good things in life.

It's right on the water in the middle of town and the room rates increase with the better views. The rooftop swimming pool enables many laps of luxury.

Eating

Mike's Seafood (☎ 02-6583 7721; shop 4, 13 Hay St; mains $11; ☼ lunch & dinner) We love the slogan – 'It's all good!' And it is. This great little takeaway specialises in paper parcels of fishy goodness. After 4.30pm on Tuesday it's 'buy one, get another for a buck' night.

ourpick **Beach House** (☎ 02-6584 5692; Horton St; mains $14-29; ☼ lunch & dinner) Take in the water views from the sea of seats outside and launch into a lavish prawn and mango platter, satay skewers or a wrap. Stick around for beer and a burger, oysters and wine or a gourmet pizza for dinner.

Cedro (☎ 02-6583 5529; 70 Clarence St; mains $16) If the goats-cheese scrambled eggs doesn't tempt you at breakfast time, turn up at lunch for delectable Moroccan lamb. Still not convinced? Pop in on Friday evening for tapas and live music.

Corner (☎ 02-6583 3300; cnr Clarence & Munster Sts; mains $18) This trendy eatery a block or two away from the town centre is bright, airy and open with plenty of pavement for sitting outside. Specialities include hearty gourmet salads, big enough to eat as mains.

Splash (☎ 02-6584 4027; 3/2 Horton St; meals $25-30; ☼ lunch & dinner) The verandah view across Town Green to the water provides the perfect setting for a treat-yourself dinner. Seafood is the chef's special talent, from the simple (grilled dory and chips) to the exceptional (king prawns and goats-cheese gnocchi). Lunch set menus ($20) are a cheaper option.

Drinking & Entertainment

Things can get rowdy at weekends, especially during 'schoolies' week in summer.

Pier (☎ 02-6584 2800; 72 Clarence St; ☼ 11am-late) It's amazing what a facelift will do for a dowdy old pub. This place is now the haunt of 30-somethings still kicking up their heels (and a few years away from needing facelifts themselves).

ourpick **Beach House** (☎ 02-6584 5692; Horton St; ☼ 11am-late) The enviable position right on the grassy water's edge makes this beautiful pub perfect for lazy afternoon drinks. As the wee hours draw near, folk fasten their beer goggles and mingle on black-leather couches inside.

Port Macquarie Hotel (☎ 02-6583 1011; cnr Horton & Clarence Sts; ☼ 10am-late) The old man of Port's pubs, this place simmers with afternoon drinkers and picks up for live bands at weekends and trivia on Sunday.

Getting There & Away

AIR
Qantas (☎ 13 13 13; www.qantas.com.au) and **Virgin Blue** (☎ 13 67 89; www.virginblue.com.au) fly to Sydney in an hour for around $120 and $98 respectively. **Brindabella Airlines** (☎ 1300 668 824; www.brindabellaairlines.com.au) flies to Coffs Harbour ($115, 30 minutes).

BUS
Greyhound (☎ 1300 GREYHOUND/1300 473 946; www.greyhound.com.au) buses run to Sydney ($72, 7½ hours) and Coffs Harbour ($53, three hours). **Premier Motor Service** (☎ 13 34 10; www.premierms.com.au) buses run to Sydney ($68, 6½ hours) and Coffs Harbour ($42, two hours). **Keans** (☎ 02-6543 1322; www.keans.com.au) buses run to Tamworth. Most coaches stop at the **coach station** (28 Hayward St).

FERRY & BICYCLE
Settlement Point ferry (cars $3, passengers free) operates 24 hours. A 10-minute trip on a flat punt gives you access to the north beach and Pilots Beach. If you have a 4WD you can drive to Point Plomer and on over unsealed roads north to Crescent Head (opposite).

Prefer to cycle? Head to Graham Seers Cyclery (p181).

PORT MACQUARIE TO COFFS HARBOUR

Kempsey
pop 27,387

About 45km north of Port Macquarie, Kempsey is a large rural town serving the farms of the Macleay Valley. It is home to the fabled **Akubra** (www.akubra.com.au) hat, the headwear of choice for a swag of Aussie icons – from Paul 'Crocodile Dundee' Hogan and singer John 'Whispering Jack' Farnham to former prime minister John Howard (when he wanted to bond with little Aussie battlers). The factory is not open to the public, but the local department store will happily fit out those wanting an iconic Aussie souvenir.

Country-music legend the late Slim Dusty (who also favoured an Akubra), was born here. The wheels are in (very slow) motion for the opening of a **Slim Dusty Heritage Centre**

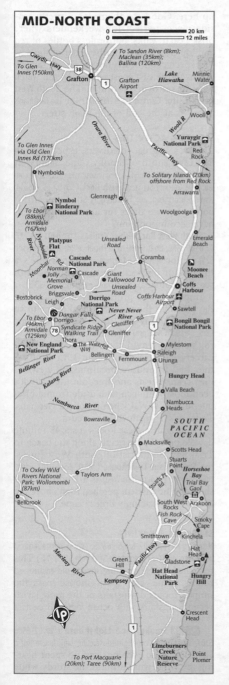

MID-NORTH COAST

0 ——— 20 km
0 ——— 12 miles

To Sandon River (8km);
Maclean (35km);
Ballina (120km)

Gwydir Hwy

To Glen
Innes (150km)

To Glen
Innes via Old Glen
Innes Rd (170km)

38

Grafton

Grafton
Airport

Lake
Hiawatha

Minnie
Water

Wooli R

Wooli

Yuraygir
National Park

Orara River

Nymboida

Red
Rock

Pacific Hwy

To Solitary Islands (20km)
offshore from Red Rock

Arrawarra

Glenreagh

Nymbol
Binderay
National Park

To Ebor
(88km);
Armidale
(167km)

Woolgoolga

Emerald
Beach

Platypus
Flat

Unsealed
Road

Cascade
National Park

Coramba

Moonee
Beach

Norman
Jolly
Memorial
Grove

Cascade

Giant
Tallowood Tree

Coffs
Harbour

Briggsvale

Unsealed
Road

Coffs Harbour
Airport

Bostobrick

Leigh

Dorrigo
National Park

Sawtell

To Ebor
(46km);
Armidale
(125km)

Dangar Falls

Dorrigo

Never Never
River

Gleniffer

78

Syndicate Ridge
Walking Trail

Gleniffer

Bongil Bongil
National Park

New England
National Park

Thora

The Waterfall
Way

Bellingen

Mylestom

Raleigh

Fernmount

Urunga

Bellinger River

Kalang River

Hungry Head

Valla

Valla Beach

Nambucca River

Nambucca
Heads

Bowraville

SOUTH
PACIFIC
OCEAN

Macksville

Scotts Head

Stuarts
Point

To Oxley Wild
Rivers National
Park; Wollombi
(87km)

Taylors Arm

Horseshoe
Bay

Stuarts
Pt
Rd

Trial Bay
Gaol

Bellbrook

South West
Rocks

Arakoon

Fish Rock
Cave

Smoky
Cape

Smithtown

Kinchela

Macleay River

Green
Hill

Gladstone

Hat
Head

Pacific Hwy

Hat Head
National
Park

Hungry
Hill

Kempsey

Crescent
Head

To Port Macquarie
(20km); Taree (90km)

Limeburners
Creek
Nature
Reserve

Point
Plomer

(☎ 02-6562 6533; www.slimdustycentre.com.au; Old Kempsey Showgrounds).

The **Kempsey visitor centre** (☎ 1800 642 480, 02-6563 1555; Pacific Hwy) is at a rest stop on the south side of town, sharing space with a **sheep shearer's museum** (adult/child $4/2; ☻ 10am-4pm).

Sample bush tucker – or learn to throw a boomerang – at **Wigay Aboriginal Culture Park** (☎ 02-6560 2946; http://wigay.nciwiki.com.au; 58 Sea St).

The turn-off to Crescent Head is near the visitor centre in Kempsey. Alternatively, from the north take the very scenic Belmore Rd, which leaves the Pacific Hwy at Seven Oaks and follows the Macleay River.

Cavanaghs (☎ 02-6562 7800; www.cavanaghs.com.au) run buses to South West Rocks from Kempsey train station.

Crescent Head & Around
pop 1966

This little hideaway, 18km southeast of Kempsey, is the kind of sleepy place you'd come to write a book. Failing that, how about learning to ride a longboard? The town is the surf longboarding capital, and it's here that the Malibu surfboard gained prominence in Australia during the '60s. Today many come just to watch the longboard riders surf the epic waves of **Little Nobby's Junction**. There's also good shortboard riding off Plomer Rd.

For holiday rentals, try **Point Break Realty** (☎ 1800 352 272, 02-6566 0306; www.pointbreakrealty.com.au; Rankine St). For shorter stays, **Mediterranean Motel** (☎ 02-6566 0303; www.crescentheadaccommodation.com.au; 35 Pacific St; d $85; ❄ 🖵 🛱) offers comfy and spotless rooms. The cleaners are a wealth of local knowledge.

ourpick **Bush 'n' Beach Motel** (☎ 1800 007 873; www.surfaris.com; 353 Loftus Rd; dm/d $25/60; 🛱 🖵), better known as Surfari Central, is the perfect place for keen surfers to stay. These guys started the original Sydney-Byron surf tours and have now based themselves in Crescent Head because 'the surf is guaranteed every day'. The rooms are clean and comfortable with bathrooms and some wicked wall murals. Surf-and-stay packages are a speciality.

The **Crescent Tavern** (☎ 02-6566 0166; 2 Main St; ☻ lunch & dinner) has cold beer and a sun-soaked deck. Below, a wood-fired pizza shop makes a mean capricciosa.

ourpick **Mongrel** (7 Main St) is worth a visit to see who will sell you a dozen of the freshest Sydney Rock oysters you can eat for $6.50 – the perfect beach snack.

Right on the beach, **Crescent Head Holiday Park** (☎ 02-6566 0261; Pacific St; campsites/cabins from $17/79; 💻) is a lovely spot to pitch a tent. The reception doubles as a cafe with espresso coffee, wraps and sandwiches as well as a heart-starting breakfast egg-and-bacon roll for $4.50.

For a bit of adventure take the partly un-sealed but well-kept Loftus Rd from Crescent Head to South West Rocks alongside the pretty-as-a-picture Belmore and Macleay rivers.

The road detours through gorgeous riverside **Gladstone**, which is worth a stop for a meal.

our pick **Heritage Hotel** (☎ 02-6567 4444; www.heritagehotel.net.au; 21 Kinchela St; 🕑 lunch & dinner), an excellent eatery on the water's edge, conjures up beer-battered fish and chips ($16), rocket and Cajun chicken salad ($19) or salmon fillet on polenta ($28) in an idyllic beer garden.

Nearby, the **Old Lodge Gallery & Riverbank Café** (☎ 02-6567 4366; 8 Kinchela St; 🕑 breakfast & lunch) does sumptuous scones.

Busways (☎ 1800 043 263; www.busways.com.au) buses run from Crescent Head to Kempsey.

Hat Head National Park

This coastal **park** (per car per day $7) of 6500 hectares runs north from near Hat Head to **Smoky Cape** (south of Arakoon), protecting scrubland, swamps and some excellent beaches backed by one of the largest dune systems in NSW. Rising up from the generally flat landscape is **Hungry Hill**, near Hat Head, and sloping Hat Head itself, where there's a walking track.

The wonderfully isolated village of **Hat Head**, surrounded by the national park, is much smaller and quieter than Crescent Head with its own natural beauty. At the end of town, a picturesque wooden footbridge crosses the aqua-green salt marsh ocean inlet. The water is so clear you can see fish darting around. **Hat Head Coastal Café** (☎ 02-6567 7555; 40 Straight St) is the go-to spot for holiday-house rentals and information. **Hat Head Holiday Park** (☎ 02-6567 7501; campsites/cabins $21/80) is close to the sheltered bay and footbridge. You can camp (adult/child $5/3) at **Hungry Head**, 5km south of Hat Head.

Hat Head and the national park are accessible from the hamlet of Kinchela, on the road between Kempsey and South West Rocks.

South West Rocks & Around

pop 4612

South West Rocks is at the end of a headland, ensuring only those willing to divert off the highway, then backtrack to it, end up here. Good for them. It's a pretty seaside place, perfect for weekenders where brisk beach walks, bottomless bottles of red and top-notch food are the order of the day. The spectacular beach here is one of the few places on the east coast where you can watch the sun set over the water. The **South West Rocks Visitor Centre** (☎ 1800 642 480; The Boatman's Cottage) is at the end of the main street.

SIGHTS & ACTIVITIES

The area is great for divers, especially **Fish Rock Cave**, south of Smoky Cape. **South West Rocks** (☎ 02-6566 6474; www.southwestrocksdive.com.au; 5/98 Gregory St) and **Fish Rock** (☎ 02-6566 6614; www.fishrock.com.au; 134 Gregory St) dive centres both offer two dives for around $120. Both have accommodation.

South West Rocks River Cruises (☎ 0401 163 237, 02-6566 6386; Boat Shed, New Entrance Rd; 2hr per person $25) explores the Macleay River. There's a three-hour barbecue cruise complete with scotch fillet steak and jacket potato ($35).

Imposing and profoundly historic, Trial Bay occupies the west headland of the town and the **Trial Bay Gaol** (☎ 02-6566 6168; adult/child $8/5; 🕑 9am-4.30pm) dominates the area. Pity (or perhaps envy) the wretched souls incarcerated here during the 19th century; they had to endure breathtaking views of the ocean, forests and freedom. Actually it's been mostly unoccupied, aside from a brief interlude in WWII when it housed Germans. Today it's a worthwhile museum.

From South West Rocks it's a 45-minute dawdle past the surf club along the beach to Trial Bay. Southeast of South West Rocks, the **Smoky Cape Lighthouse** (☎ 02-6566 6301; adult/child $15/7; 🕑 tours 1pm Wed) is a landmark that shouldn't be missed, perched high above the ocean on a bracingly breezy cape.

SLEEPING & EATING

Heritage (☎ 02-6566 6625; www.heritageguesthouse.com.au; 21-23 Livingstone St; d from $115; 🖨) This renovated 1880s house has lovely, old-fashioned rooms, some with spas. Choose from the simpler rooms downstairs or the more lavish versions upstairs with ocean views. Breakfast is included.

our pick **Smoky Cape Lighthouse** (☎ 02-6556 6301; www.smokycapelighthouse.com; Lighthouse Rd; d $187) Romantic evenings can be spent hearing the wind whip around the sturdy white lighthouse-keeper's building just a few metres from the lighthouse itself. The views are also fuel for passion.

Arakoon State Conservation Area (adult camping $18-24, child $9), behind the gaol, is a magnificent campsite sits on the peninsula affording generous beach views.

Horseshoe Bay Beach Park (☎ 02-6566 6370; www.horseshoebaypark.com.au; Livingstone St; powered sites/vans/cabins $32/50/80) Planted a hop and a skip from the main street and right on sheltered Town Beach, the 82 sites and 12 cabins at this fine caravan park are in understandably high demand during the summer holidays.

Surf Club (☼ 4-9pm Fri-Sun Dec-Feb) This club on Horseshoe Bay is the best place in town for a beer with an ocean view. Unpretentious meals including roast ($13) and shepherds pie ($8) are a Sunday must.

Seabreeze Hotel (☎ 02-6566 6909; www.seabreeze beachhotel.com.au; Livingstone St; mains $8-18; ☼ lunch & dinner; ☒ ▣) This place serves scrubbed-up pub nosh on pleasant decks. The clean rooms with private balconies – some with ocean views – are a good cheap sleep option (single/double from $65/80).

South West Woks (☎ 02-6566 6655; Gregory St; mains $10-23; ☼ dinner) This is a good option for a cheap night out. Take a bottle of wine (it's BYO) and choose from a varied Asian menu sporting the likes of Vietnamese favourite *pho bo* (beef and noodle soup) and Thai staple pad Thai noodle. Tables are alfresco.

Geppys (☎ 02-6566 6169; cnr Livingstone & Memorial Sts; mains $20; ☼ dinner) This cosmopolitan restaurant is signed up to the slow-food movement; tuck into a whole baked snapper, mussel and chilli spaghetti, cheesy gnocchi or calf's liver and polenta.

GETTING THERE & AWAY
Cavanaghs (☎ 02-6562 7800; www.cavanaghs.com.au) runs to Kempsey, leaving from the town bus stop at Horseshoe Bay.

Nambucca Heads
pop 17,896

Map reading around Nambucca's labyrinth of streets might be nauseating but that's a minor pay-off in a town idyllically strewn over a dramatically curling headland interlaced with the estuaries of the Nambucca River. It is spacious, sleepy and unspoilt with one of the coast's prettiest foreshores.

Nambucca Heads visitor centre (☎ 02-6568 6954; cnr Riverside Dr & Pacific Hwy) doubles as the main bus terminal and has a nice spot on the estuary. **Computing Innovations** (☎ 02-6568 5411; shop 4, Nambucca Plaza; per hr $8; ☼ 9am-5pm Mon-Fri, to noon Sat) has internet.

SIGHTS & ACTIVITIES
From the visitor centre, the newly extended **Gulmani Boardwalk** stretches 3km along the foreshore, through parks and bushland, and over pristine sand and waterways. It's the perfect introduction to the town.

Of the numerous lookouts, **Captain Cook Lookout**, with its 180-degree vista, best exploits the staggering views.

The only patrolled beach in town is **Main Beach**. Beilby's and **Shelly Beaches** are just to the south, closer to the river mouth – where the best surf is – and can be reached by going past the Captain Cook Lookout.

Located near the foreshore, the **V-Wall** is a clever snapshot of life. Here you can read graffitied memoirs from newlyweds, newly borns and travellers who have left their colourful mark. Pick up a paintbrush and make your mark. Worth a visit is **Headland Historical Museum** (☎ 02-6569 5698; Main Beach; adult/child $2/50c; ☼ 2-4pm Wed, Sat & Sun), with local-history exhibits, including a collection of more than 1000 photos.

SLEEPING
Nambucca Riverview Lodge (☎ 02-6568 6386; www .here.com.au/riverview; 4 Wellington Dr; d $90; ☒) Built in 1887, this old pub was, for many years, one of only a few buildings on the rise of a hill overlooking the foreshore. Today the double-decker hotel has eight unique rooms, all with balcony views. Each is stuffed with charming furniture, plus TV, DVD and lounge.

Marcel Towers (☎ 02-6568 7041; www.marceltowers .com.au; Wellington Dr; d from $95; ☒ ▣) The decor at these holiday apartments might be somewhat passé, but the balcony views over a restaurant-studded foreshore soon make up for it. Apartments are clean and available for overnight stays.

Headland Holiday Village (☎ 02-6568 6547; www .headlandtouristpark.com.au; Liston St; unpowered/powered sites from $18/20, vans/cabins from $40/70) On the peak of the headland, this grassy knoll has a bird's-eye view of passing whales. It has clean and orderly facilities and decent cabins.

EATING

Terry Catherine's (☎ 02-6569 4422; 5 Mann St; mains $14-28; ☯ lunch & dinner) This BYO establishment has gorgeous views from the back verandah and cosy couches when the weather turns. The raison toast stack with bananas, maple syrup and walnuts ($10) is a fine way to start the day.

Bluewater Brasserie (☎ 02-6568 6394; V-Wall Tavern; Wellington Dr; mains $18; ☯ lunch & dinner) A legion of outdoor tables on the wide balcony at this tavern makes for long, easy, boozy lunches and balmy dinners. Salads, steaks and seafood adorn the menu, and it's family friendly.

Ocean Chill Restaurant (☎ 02-6568 8877; Ridge St; lunch mains $19-21, dinner $29; ☯ lunch Wed & Fri, dinner Tue-Sat) Set in the bushy urban streets, this contemporary restaurant has all the telltale signs of people who know food and service. For lunch indulge in swimmer crab omelette with coriander, baby spinach and lemongrass. For dinner, it's a toss-up between lamb rack, pork belly and roast chicken.

Matilda's (☎ 02-6568 6024; Wellington Dr; mains $25-39; ☯ lunch Tue-Wed, dinner Mon-Sat) Saved up for a seafood feast? Go no further. This cute little shack juggles good old-fashioned beachfront character with food and service know-how. A front porch allows diners to catch a few rays as they indulge in their favourite fish.

GETTING THERE & AWAY

Nearly all southbound buses stop outside the **visitor centre** (cnr Riverside Dr & Pacific Hwy), northbound ones at the shopping centre nearby. **Keans** (☎ 02-6543 1322; www.keans.com.au) runs four times a week to Tamworth. **Premier Motor Service** (☎ 13 34 10; www.premierms.com.au) runs to Sydney ($61, eight hours) and Byron Bay ($56, five hours). **Greyhound** (☎ 1300 GREYHOUND/1300 473 946; www.greyhound.com.au) also runs to Sydney ($85, eight hours) and Byron Bay ($82, 5½ hours).

The train station is about 3km out of town. **CountryLink** (☎ 13 22 23; www.countrylink.info) has trains to Coffs Harbour ($5, 40 minutes) and Sydney ($68, 8½ hours).

Between Nambucca Heads and Coffs Harbour, detour off the highway onto the Waterfall Way (p210) to explore beautiful Bellingen (p211) and Dorrigo (p210). A partly sealed road continues north from Dorrigo and swings east into Coffs Harbour via beautiful winding rainforest roads and a huge tallow wood tree, 56m high and more than 3m in diameter.

COFFS HARBOUR

pop 64,910

Coffs Harbour has always had to work hard to tart up its image. Where other coastal towns have the ready-made aesthetic of a main street slap-bang on the waterfront, Coffs has an inland city centre, a town 'jetty' (albeit with some great restaurants) that isn't actually on the water, and a semi-enclosed marina. On the flipside, the city has a string of fabulous beaches and a preponderance of water-based activities, action sports and wildlife encounters, making it hugely popular with families and the 'middle-Australian' market.

Orientation

The town is split into three areas, making it infamously tedious to navigate between the jetty, the town centre and beaches. Harbour Dr is the spine of main activity. It runs from the town centre to the jetty and marina. The Pacific Hwy turns into Grafton St and then Woolgoolga Rd on its run north through town.

Information

Jetty Village Internet Shop (☎ 02-6651 9155; Jetty Village, Harbour Dr; per hr $7; ☯ 9am-7pm Mon-Fri, to 4pm Sat &Sun)

Main post office (Park Beach Plaza shopping centre)

Visitor centre (☎ 1300 369 070, 02-6652 1522; www .coffscoast.com.au; Pacific Hwy)

Sights

Coffs Harbour boasts a ferrous-concrete **Big Banana** (☎ 02-6652 4355; www.bigbanana.com; Pacific Hwy; ☯ 9am-4.30pm) that's hailed by many as a national icon. This joint, built in 1964, actually started the craze for 'Big Things' in Australia (just so you know who to blame or praise).

Clumps of indigenous scrub and rainforest mingle with foreign foliage at the beautiful **North Coast Botanic Gardens** (☎ 02-6648 4188; Hardacre St; admission by donation; ☯ 9am-5pm), which is bordered on three sides by Coffs Creek. Paths criss-cross beneath the lush canopy, kookaburras laugh from up high, and there is a vast grassy lawn just begging for frisbee action. Passing by the entrance is the 6km **Coffs Creek Habitat Walk**. It starts opposite the **council chambers** (Coff St) and finishes near the sea.

At the **Pet Porpoise Pool** (☎ 02-6652 2164; www .petporpoisepool.com; Orlando St; adult/child $27/14; ☯ 9am-4pm, last entry 2.30pm) dolphins and seals interact with the public during acrobatic shows at 10am and 1pm.

The harbour's northern breakwater runs out onto **Muttonbird Island**, named for more than 12,000 pairs of birds who migrate here from late August to early April, with cute offspring visible in December and January. It marks the southern boundary of the **Solitary Islands Marine Park**, where warm tropical currents meet temperate southern currents, attracting unusual varieties of fish and great scuba diving.

At **Legends Surf Museum** (☎ 02-6653 6536; 18 Gaudrons Rd; adult/child $5/2; ☺ 10am-4pm), over 160 boards are on display as well as hundreds of surfing photos. It's 100m off the Pacific Hwy 10km north of Coffs; look for signs.

BEACHES

Sweeping **Park Beach** attracts plenty of swell along with punters and lifeguards from October to April. **Jetty Beach** is just south and a safer option. **Diggers Beach** – to the north – is partly nudist and sensational (for the surf), and **Macauleys Headland** also offers good surf. **Moonee Beach** lies 14km further north and **Emerald Beach** is a further 6km.

GALLERIES

Although housed in an administrative-looking council office block, **Coffs Harbour Regional Gallery** (☎ 02-6648 4861; cnr Coff & Duke Sts; ☺ 10am-4pm Tue-Sat, noon-4pm Sun) is first-rate, embracing regional and international artists.

Activities

Promenade Canoes (☎ 02-6651 1032; The Promenade, 321 Harbour D; single/double/triple canoes per hr $15/20/25, 3rd hr freer; ☺ 9.30am-5pm Fri-Mon, daily during holidays) hires canoes for 5km, self-guided trips along scenic Coffs Creek in the heart of town.

Valery Horse Trails (☎ 02-6653 4301; www.valery trails.com.au; 758 Valery Rd, Valery; 2hr rides $30) has 60 'well disciplined horses' and plenty of acreage to explore.

Liquid Assets Adventure Tours & Beach Shop (☎ 02-6658 0850; www.surfrafting.com; 38 Harbour Dr) keeps thrill junkies giddy with sea kayaking, surf rafting, surf lessons and kayaking in Bongil Bongil National Park (all $50 for a full day). it also offers , white-water rafting on the Nymboida River (half day $80) and skydives (from $239).

Coffs City Skydivers (☎ 02-6651 1167; www .coffsskydivers.com.au; Coffs Harbour airport; tandem jumps $325) satisfies all urges to fling yourself from a plane.

More active options:
East Coast Surf School (☎ 02-6651 5515; www .eastcoastsurfschool.com.au; Diggers Beach; 2½hr lessons per person from $55) Adults' and kids' surf camps.
Jetty Dive Centre (☎ 02-6651 1611; www.jettydive .com.au; 398 Harbour Dr) PADI backpacker dive courses from $215; Solitary Island diving $295.

Tours

Bark Hut Mountain Bike Rides (☎ 02-6653 4822, 0411 569 649; with/without bike hire $99/69) Guided rides. Picnic lunch included.
Pacific Explorer Whale Watching (☎ 02-6652 8988; 2-3hr from $20) A 10m sailing catamaran limited to 23 passengers.
Spirit of Coffs Harbour Cruises (☎ 02-6650 0155; shop 5, Coffs Harbour Marina) Dolphin swims ($33) and cruises.

Festivals & Events

Pittwater to Coffs Yacht Race (www.pittwatertocoffs .com.au) New Year. Starts in Sydney, finishes here.
Sawtell Chilli Festival (www.sawtellchillifestival.com .au) Early July.
Coffs Harbour International Buskers' Festival (www.coffsharbourbuskers.com) Late September and not to be missed.
Coffs Coast Food & Wine Festival Early November.
Gold Cup (☎ 02-6652 1488) Early August. Coffs' premier horse race.

Sleeping

Pacific Property & Management (☎ 1800 658 569, 02-6652 1466; www.coffsholidayrentals.com.au; 101 Park Beach Rd) has holiday-rental listings and internet access.

BUDGET

Aussitel Backpackers Hostel (☎ 1800 330 335, 02-6651 1871; www.aussitel.com; 312 Harbour Dr; dm/d $28/70; ☐ ☒) Don't be put off by the exterior. This capacious brick house, with homely dorms and a shady courtyard, is a hub for backpackers of all shapes and sizes, codes and creeds. Diving specialists are on site (PADI courses from $295) with accommodation specials for divers.

our pick **Coffs Harbour YHA** (☎ 02-6652 6462; www .yha.com.au; 51 Collingwood St; dm/d with bathroom from $29/85; ☐ ☒) With service and amenities like these, it's a wonder hotels don't go out of business. The dorms and doubles with bathrooms are spacious and modern, and the TV lounge and kitchen are immaculate. You can hire surfboards and bikes.

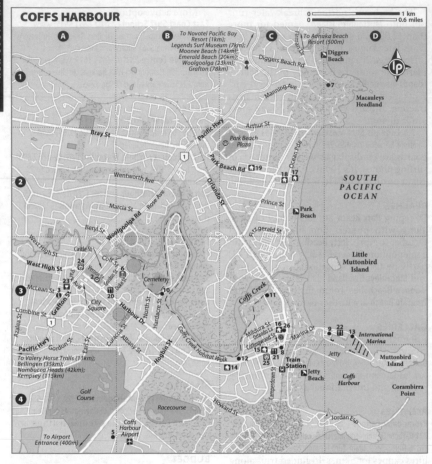

COFFS HARBOUR

To Novotel Pacific Bay Resort (1km);
Legends Surf Museum (7km);
Moonee Beach (14km);
Emerald Beach (20km);
Woolgoolga (23km);
Grafton (78km)

To Aanuka Beach Resort (500m)

To Valery Horse Trails (13km);
Bellingen (35km);
Nambucca Heads (42km);
Kempsey (115km)

To Airport Entrance (400m)

Hoey Moey Pub (☎ 02-6651 7966; Ocean Pde; s/d $50/60) You can hear the waves roll in from these motel-style backpacker rooms nicely located between the pub and the main beach. You can also hear your mates in the beer garden.

MIDRANGE & TOP END

Ocean Paradise Motel (☎ 02-6652 5133; www.ocean paradisecoffs.com; cnr Ocean Pde & Park Beach Rd; r from $70; 🖥 🛋) Towering palms and a lush garden give this cheerful motel a leg-up. It has quiet rooms with kitchenettes. The central lawn and pool are family friendly.

Caribbean Motel (☎ 02-6652 1500; www.stayincoffs .com.au; 353 Harbour Dr; r from $85; 🍴 🛋) Within strolling distance to the jetty, this motel complex has modern rooms, some with balconies or spas, plus great-value one-bedroom suites with kitchenettes.

Aanuka Beach Resort (☎ 02-6652 7555; www .aanuka.com.au; 11 Firman Dr; r from $123; 🍴 🖥 🛋) It might be out of town, but this luxurious resort, set amid luscious foliage, has excellent studios and apartments, all with spas and dishy interiors. It sits on a quiet neck of Diggers Beach and has tennis courts and an award-winning restaurant.

Novotel Pacific Bay Resort (☎ 1300 363 360, 02-6659 7000; cnr Pacific Hwy & Bay Dr; r from $149; 🍴 🖥 🛋) The colossal Novotel is lavishly sprawled around a nine-hole golf course. The penthouse suites each have a rooftop eating area and outdoor spa tub.

Eating

The Jetty and the Promenade boast the best dining options. Most of the CBD closes down around 6pm. Kitchens start closing around 8.30pm, so come early or make a reservation.

JETTY

Crying Tiger (☎ 02-6650 0195; 382 Harbour Dr; mains $15-27; ⏰ dinner) Swimming in ambience and fragrant smells, the Crying Tiger keeps inquisitive diners happy with red-duck curry and king prawns in lime leaf and coconut. You can turn the chilli gauge as high or low as you like.

Foreshore Café (☎ 02-6652 3127; 394 Harbour Dr; ⏰ breakfast & lunch) Crowds flock to this spacious cafe with big wooden tables, both inside and out, and a menu to suit all tastes. The Thai green curry is a winner ($16).

Piccolo (☎ 02-6651 9599; 390 Harbour Dr; mains $23-33; ⏰ dinner Tue-Sat) Cushioned window seats add to the allure of this cute and contemporary Italian eatery. Entrées include a leek, goats cheese and mushroom tartlet or for main, veal scaloppine in lemon and white wine sauce.

MARINA

Fisherman's Co-op (☎ 02-6652 2811; 69 Marina Dr; meals $10; ⏰ lunch & dinner) Once *the* place to head for grilled or battered catch of the day in a cardboard box, this place is nowadays a bit of a tourist trap.

Wild Harvest (☎ 02-6651 6888; Marina Dr; cafe mains $10-17, restaurant $12-27) An upscale fish-and-chips and seafood place. There's an upper and lower deck but the difference between the two is minimal, save for the extra dollars you pay for the view.

PROMENADE

Mangrove Jacks (☎ 02-6652 5517; The Promenade Centre, Harbour Dr; mains $25; ⏰ breakfast & lunch daily, dinner Tue-Sat) Overlooking a quiet bend of Coffs Creek, this restaurant serves sultry gourmet dinners. Brekkie and lunch are more casual.

CITY

Cocoa (☎ 02-6650 9417; Harbour Dr; mains $8-13; ⏰ breakfast & lunch) The bright and gleaming modern decor and excellent coffee make this place a hot spot for Coffs' business set and pram brigade. Or maybe it's the breakfast on offer; the fruit salad and fresh yoghurt is good.

Drinking & Entertainment

See Thursday's edition of the *Coffs Harbour Advocate* for live-music listings.

Coast Hotel (☎ 02-6652 3007; 2 Moonee St; ⏰ 11am-late) Formerly the Old Fitzroy Hotel, this place has been purpose-renovated to supply lovers of a lazy afternoon in a beer garden with a venue. It has landscaped decking and cool breakaway areas so you can kick back on a couch if the mood takes you. The food is great, too.

Hoey Moey Pub (☎ 02-6651 7966; Ocean Pde; ⏰ 10am-late) The massive inner beer 'garden' gives a good indication of how much this place kicks off in the summer. Pool comps, live music (Wednesday to Sunday) and terrifying karaoke sessions are the norm.

More pub sessions and live music:

Coffs Hotel (☎ 02-6652 3817; cnr Pacific Hwy & West Harbour Dr; ⏰ 11am-1am) Irish pub with bands, several bars, DJs and mad Friday nights.

Pier Hotel (☎ 02-6652 2110; cnr Hood St & Harbour Dr; ⏰ 10am-1am) Unrenovated; grizzly regulars and cover bands. Pure Australiana.

NEW SOUTH WALES

Getting There & Away

AIR

Virgin Blue (☎ 13 67 89; www.virginblue.com.au) flies to Sydney ($85, one hour) and **Qantas** (☎ 13 13 13; www.qantas.com.au) also makes the trip ($105, one hour). **Brindabella Airlines** (☎ 1300 668 824; www .brindabellaairlines.com.au) flies to Port Macquarie ($120, 30 minutes).

BUS

Buses leave from the visitor centre.

Greyhound (☎ 1300 GREYHOUND/1300 473 946; www .greyhound.com.au) runs to Port Macquarie ($55, 2¾ hours) and Byron Bay ($65, four hours). **Premier Motor Service** (☎ 13 34 10; www.premierms .com.au) runs to Port Macquarie ($45, 2½ hours) and Byron Bay ($48, five hours).

Keans (☎ 02-6543 1322; www.keans.com.au) has two services a week to Bellingen, Dorrigo and Armidale. **Busways** (☎ 02-6652 2744; www.busways .com.au) has four buses daily to Bellingen ($10, one hour). **Ryans Buses** (☎ 02-6652 3201; www.ryans busservice.com.au) runs to Grafton ($23) via various small towns and beaches. **Sawtell Coaches** (☎ 02-6653 3344; www.sawtellcoaches.com.au) runs to Sawtell ($7).

TRAIN

CountryLink (☎ 13 22 32; www.countrylink.info) trains head to Grafton ($12, 90 minutes), Sydney ($67, nine hours) and Casino ($25, three hours).

Getting Around

Hostel shuttles meet all long-distance buses and trains.

Coffs Bike Hire (☎ 02-6652 5102; cnr Orlando & Collingwood Sts; per day $25) rents mountain bikes.

The major car-rental companies have offices in town and/or at the airport. **Coffs District Taxi Network** (☎ 13 10 08) operates a 24-hour cab service.

COFFS HARBOUR TO BYRON BAY

If you want to avoid big city centres such as Coffs, **Woolgoolga** (also known as Woopi; population 4715), a coastal town just north of Coffs, is a good option. It's known for its surf-and-Sikh community.

As you drive by on the highway you're sure to notice the impressive **Guru Nanak Temple**, a Sikh *gurdwara* (place of worship). Don't confuse it with the **Raj Mahal**, a defunct emporium with two decrepit elephant statues out the front.

Drive straight through town for a magnificent view of the group of five islands in the **Solitary Islands Marine Park**.

The **Woolgoolga Beach Caravan Park** (☎ 02-6654 1373; Beach St; unpowered sites/cabins from $26/58) right on the beach can't be beaten on position.

Neither can **Bluebottles Brasserie** (☎ 02-6654 1962; cnr Wharf & Beach Sts; mains $24-28; ☷ breakfast & lunch Mon-Sat, dinner Fri & Sat), a happening place that serves fine seafood and hosts live jazz sessions. **Possum Café** (☎ 02-6654 2807; Beach St; mains $4-14; ☷ breakfast & lunch Tue-Sun) is a more casual affair serving Turkish bread toasties, salads, burgers and fresh sandwiches.

Red Rock (population 274) is a sleepy village with an inlet and surrounds so gorgeous it's worth trekking 3km off the highway. It is a site sacred to the Gunawarri people. Soak up the sun or catch a fish while camping at **Red Rock Caravan Park** (☎ 02-6649 2730; 1 Lawson St, Red Rock; campsites/cabins from $16/50, cottages $80).

The 20,000-hectare **Yuraygir National Park** (per car per day $7) covers the 60km stretch of coast north from Red Rock. The isolated beaches are outstanding and there are some bushwalking paths where you can view endangered coastal emus. Walkers can bush camp in basic campsites (adult/child $10/5 per night) at Station Creek in the southern section; at the Boorkoom and Illaroo rest areas in the central section; on the north bank of the Sandon River; and at Red Cliff at the Brooms Head end of the northern section. These are accessible by car; there is also a free walk-in campsite at Shelly Beach.

Nearby **Wooli** (population 600) hosts the **Australian Goanna Pulling Championships** (☎ 02-6649 7540) in June. Rather than ripping the eponymous animal to shreds, participants, squatting on all fours, attach leather harnesses to their heads and engage in a cranial tug-of-war.

The **Solitary Islands Marine Park Resort** (☎ 1800 003 031, 02-6649 7519; North St; sites/cabins from $23/75) here has a mouthful of a name and lovely cabins in a scrubby bush setting.

Grafton

pop 22,812

Grafton is not so much a blast from the past as a serene gust or a puff. Nestled into a quiet bend of the Clarence River, the town's charming grid of wide streets, grand pubs and splendid old houses capture an era that is hard to garner in beachside towns. It's also the 1963 founding home of hang-gliding, though you'll have to go elsewhere to partake in the sport.

FAR NORTH COAST

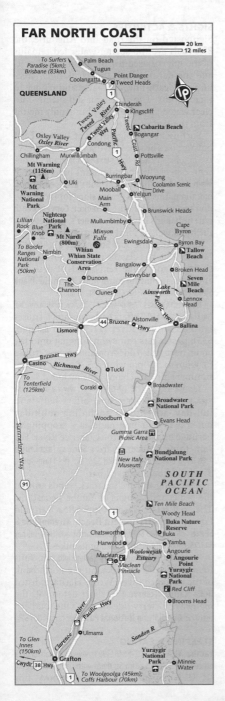

The helpful, award-winning **Clarence River visitor centre** (☎ 02-6642 4677; www.clarencetourism.com; cnr Spring St & Pacific Hwy) is south of town. There's also a **NPWS office** (☎ 02-6641 1500; Level 3, 49 Victoria St).

The local arts scene manifests itself in **Grafton Artsfest** (www.artsfestgrafton.com), held twice yearly with workshops and exhibitions.

Victoria St is the town's historical focal point, providing fascinating glimpses of 19th-century architecture, including the **courthouse** (1862), **Roches Family Hotel** (1870) and the **Anglican Cathedral** (1884).

The **Grafton Regional Gallery** (☎ 02-6642 3177; 158 Fitzroy St; admission by donation; ☽ 10am-4pm Tue-Sun) hosts quality works from galleries around NSW. **Georgies at the Gallery** (☎ 02-6642 6996; ☽ lunch & dinner Tue-Sat, lunch Sun) is touted as one of the best cafes in the state as voted by patrons.

Susan Island, in the middle of the river, is home to the biggest fruit-bat colony in the southern hemisphere. Their evening departure is a spectacular summer sight. Access to the river is by boat or canoe; you can hire a tinny from **Seelands Boat Hire** (☎ 02-6644 9381; 67 Old Punt Rd; per day $60), 6km north of Grafton.

Atmospheric accommodation includes the fantastic, historic **Roches Family Hotel** (☎ 02-6644 2866; www.roches.com.au; 85 Victoria St; s/d incl breakfast $26/40), with spruced-up pub rooms, a cafe and a beer garden. It's worth calling in just for a peek at the croc in the public bar. **Arcola B&B** (☎ 02-6643 2331; www.arcola.com.au; 150 Victoria St; s/d $100/150), at the end of the street on the water's edge, is a romantic old home with a delightful garden.

Regional Express (Rex; ☎ 13 17 13; www.regionalexpress.com.au) flies to Sydney ($150, two hours). **Busways** (☎ 02-6642 2954; www.busways.com.au) runs to Yamba and Maclean. **Ryans Buses** (☎ 02-6652 3201; www.ryansbusservice.com.au) has four buses daily to Coffs Harbour ($23) via various small towns and beaches. **Greyhound** (☎ 1300 GREYHOUND/1300 473 946; www.greyhound.com.au) has buses to Byron Bay ($55, 3¼ hours) and Coffs Harbour ($40, 1¼ hours). **Premier Motor Service** (☎ 13 34 10; www.premierms.com.au) has buses to Byron Bay ($45, 3½ hours) and Coffs Harbour ($32, two hours). **Northern Rivers Buslines** (☎ 02-6626 1499; www.nrbuslines.com.au) has buses to Ballina, Lennox Head, Byron Bay and Murwillumbah. Buses stop at the train station.

CountryLink (☎ 13 22 32; www.countrylink.info) has trains to Sydney ($72, 10½ hours) and Casino ($13, 1½ hours) and buses to Coffs Harbour ($12, 1½ hours).

NEW SOUTH WALES

Around Grafton

There's an interesting route from Grafton to Armidale (p208) via Nymboida and Ebor, passing turn-offs to Dorrigo (p210) and the New England and Cathedral Rock National Parks (p210). Heading west to Glen Innes (p212), the Gwydir Hwy passes through the superb Washpool and Gibraltar Range National Parks (p213).

Heading north on the Pacific Hwy it's worth taking a small detour to **Ulmarra** (population 1586), a heritage-listed town with a river port. There's a quaint old corner **pub** (☎ 02-6644 5305; 2 Coldstream St; ☽ lunch & dinner Fri & Sat) with a wrought-iron verandah, pub rooms (singles/doubles $35/60) and a greener-than-green beer garden that stretches down to the Clarence River. The river can be crossed by car ferry 1km north of town.

Maclean (population 3250) is a picturesque little town that takes its Scottish heritage seriously. It sweeps alongside a lazy sprawl of the delta in vaguely Celtic fashion and, true enough, with your Glenmorangie goggles (firmly) fastened, you might mistake the Clarence River for a highland loch. The **Clarence Coast visitor centre** (☎ 02-6645 4121; Ferry Park, Pacific Hwy, Maclean), at the edge of town, can help with accommodation.

Yamba & Angourie

Once a sleepy little fishing town, **Yamba** (population 6464) is slowly distancing itself from this reputation by attracting a fan base that has cottoned-on to the merits of beaches on three fronts, a relaxed pace and excellent food without encroaching development.

Its southern neighbour **Angourie** (population 169) is home to NSW's first National Surfing Reserve and has always been a hot spot for experienced surfers (the type who were born on a board, wear helmets and leap off rocks). It complements Yamba's can-do attitude by remaining a small chilled-out place. Apart from the surf, the only sign of development is the Pacific St home (mansion) of Gordon Merchant, founder of the surf brand Billabong, who grew up here (and who, by all accounts, still gets around in boardshorts).

There is no visitor centre (yet), but **Yamba YHA** (☎ 02-6646 3991; www.yambabackpack ers.com.au; 26 Coldstream St) has the low-down on everything.

SIGHTS & ACTIVITIES

Signposted on the road into Angourie, the **Blue Pools** are the spring-water-fed remains of the quarry used for the breakwall. Locals and the daring climb the 'chalk-line', 'tree-line' or 'death-line' cliff-faces and plunge to their depths. The saner can slip silently into clear water, surrounded by bush, only metres from the surf.

Surfing for the big boys is at **Angourie Point** but Yamba's beaches have something for everyone else. When the surf is flat **Pippi's** is decent, especially when dolphins hang around. **Main Beach** is the busiest with an ocean pool, banana palms and a grassy slope for those who don't want sand up their clacker. **Convent Beach** is a sunbaker's haven and **Turner's**, protected by the breakwall, is ideal for surf lessons.

Yamba-Angourie Surf School (☎ 02-6646 1496; 2hr lessons $50) has classes run by a former pro surfer. To go it alone, rent boards of all shapes and sizes, including mini-mals, from the **Plank Shop** (☎ 02-6645 8362; Clarence St, Yamba).

Rockfish Cruises (☎ 0447 458 153; www.rockfish.com.au; The Marina, Yamba Rd) offers barbecue-lunch cruises on the Clarence River (11.30am to 2.30pm, $35); passengers can swim clinging onto the boom nets. It also does romantic sunset cruises (3.30pm to 5.30pm winter, 5.30pm to 7.30pm summer) for $55, champagne included.

Yamba Kayak (☎ 02-6646 1137; www.yambakayak .com.au; Whiting Beach car park) offers half- and full-day adventures including multiday pubcrawls – or pub paddles – stopping at heritage hotels along the Clarence River. For something cruisier board a **Sunday Jazz Cruise** (☎ 0408 664 556; adult/child $25/13; ☽ 11am-3pm). The boat has a licensed bar.

A walking and cycling track wends around the peaks and troughs of Yamba's coastline. The prettiest bit is from Pippi's Beach around Lovers Point to Convent Beach. **Xtreme Cycle & Skate** (☎ 02-6645 8879; 34 Coldstream St; adult half/full day $15/25, child half/full day $10/15) rents bikes.

A passenger-only **ferry** (adult/child $8/3) runs four times daily to Iluka, on the north bank of the Clarence River. World Heritage–listed **Iluka Nature Reserve** is a short detour off the highway or a ferry ride away; it's the southern end of **Bundjalung National Park** (per car per day $7).

SLEEPING & EATING

Yamba YHA (☎ 02-6646 3991; www.yambabackpack ers.com.au; 26 Coldstream St; dm/d with bathroom $28/78; ☒ ☐ ☖) Spankingly new and groovy, this is a purpose-built hostel with a downstairs bar and restaurant. Upstairs there's a rooftop deck, pool and barbecue area. It's family run and extremely welcoming. After sampling one of Shane's welcome tours, you're guaranteed to extend your stay.

Pacific Hotel (☎ 02-6646 2466; 18 Pilot St, Yamba; dm $35, r with/without bathroom $120/60) This is a fabulous pub overlooking the ocean, with bright bunk rooms and handsome hotel rooms. It would be remiss to come to Yamba without sampling a beer with this kind of view but the food is also exceptional – a lofty step above the usual pub nosh.

Angourie Rainforest Resort (☎ 02-6646 8600; www .angourieresort.com.au; 166 Angourie Rd, Angourie; r with/ without breakfast from $160/140; ⛽ 🖳 🖭) A little piece of paradise sidled up to 600 hectares of fauna. Luxuries include a pool, tennis court, restaurant and day spa. Extras include a pristine rainforest aroma and resident birds and lizards.

Sounds Lounge Café (☎ 02-6646 3909; 16 Yamba Rd, Yamba; mains $5-18; ⛽ breakfast & lunch; 🖳) In a corner position with a couple of shady trees, this cafe serves up tasty focaccias, wraps, panini and eggs of all description, plus fresh OJ.

El Pirata (☎ 02-6646 3276; 6 Clarence St, Yamba; ⛽ dinner Tue-Sun) For sublime dining, this is a fabulous tapas bar serving authentic hot and cold Spanish dishes including *jamon* (ham), chorizo, oily garlic prawns and cheesy stuffed peppers ($8 to $17). The staff is as enthusiastic as the diners are after sinking a sangria or two.

Frangipan (☎ 02-6646 2553; www.frangipan.com.au; 11-13 The Crescent, Angourie; mains $28; ⛽ lunch Sat & Sun, dinner Tue-Sat) Spend big at this award-winning restaurant. Alternatively, sample the excellent share plates with prosciutto, fetta, semidried tomatoes, olives and dips.

GETTING THERE & AWAY
Busways (☎ 02-6645 8941; www.busways.com.au) runs to Grafton and Maclean. **Northern Rivers Buslines** (☎ 02-6626 1499; www.nrbuslines.com.au) runs to Ballina and Lismore.

CountryLink (☎ 13 22 32; www.countrylink.info) runs buses to Grafton ($10, 50 minutes), Lennox Head ($13, 2¼ hours) and Byron Bay ($14, three hours). **Greyhound** (☎ 1300 GREYHOUND/1300 473 946; www.greyhound.com.au) stops at the YHA on its way to Byron Bay ($50, three hours), Coffs Harbour ($50, two hours) and Sydney ($113, 10½ hours).

Ballina
pop 36,784
At the mouth of the Richmond River, Ballina is spoilt for white sandy beaches and crystal-clear waters. If it were not so close to Byron it would be a tourist haven in its own right. Instead, it is somewhere between a commercial centre and a wannabe tourist lure, maintaining a coastal ambience without tarting itself up for the holiday bucks.

The **Ballina visitor centre** (☎ 02-6686 3484; www .discoverballina.com; cnr Las Balsas Plaza & River St) is at the eastern end of town. **Happy Buddha Coffee & Internet Café** (☎ 02-6686 5783; 178 River St; per hr $6) has internet.

SIGHTS & ACTIVITIES
Behind the visitor centre, the **Naval & Maritime Museum** (☎ 02-6681 1002; Regatta Ave; adult/child $2/1; ⛽ 9am-4pm) has a remarkable collection of model ships. There are also the remains of a balsawood raft that drifted across the Pacific from Ecuador as part of the Las Balsas expedition in 1973.

White and sandy, **Shelly Beach** is patrolled, and glassy **Shaws Bay Lagoon** is popular with families.

The **Big Prawn** (Pacific Hwy) is beached unceremoniously next to a transit centre at the town's southern entry. It's only worth stopping at if you need seafood from the co-op below.

Ballina is renowned for its great walking and bike tracks. Hire bikes from **Jack Ransom Cycles** (☎ 02-6686 3485; 16 Cherry St; per day $18).

Richmond River Cruises (☎ 02-6687 5688; Regatta Ave; 2hr tours adult/child $25/13) is the most established cruise service and is wheelchair friendly. It has lunch and dinner cruises, as well as morning and afternoon tea cruises.

SLEEPING & EATING
Ballina Travellers Lodge YHA (☎ 02-6686 6737; www .yha.com.au, www.ballinatravellerslodge.com.au; 36-38 Tamar St; dm $28, d $115-130; ⛽ 🖭) In a quiet residential street, this lodge combines motel and hostel guests. It is clean and comfortable and the owners are a good source of info.

Ballina Heritage Inn (☎ 02-6686 0505; www .ballinaheritageinn.com.au; 229 River St; d with/without spa $129/109; ⛽) In the centre of town, this tidy inn has neat, bright and comfortable rooms that are a significant leap in quality from the nearby motels.

NEW SOUTH WALES

Ballina Manor (☎ 02-6681 5888; www.ballinamanor .com.au; 25 Norton St; r from $165; 🗶) This grand old dame of hospitality was once a school but has since been converted into a luxurious guest house filled to the hilt with restored 1920s furnishings, carpets and curtains. Though antique in design, all rooms are indulgent: the best room has a four-poster bed and spa.

Evolution Espresso Bar (☎ 02-6681 4095; Martin St; 🕑 7.30am-4pm Mon-Wed, to late Thu & Fri, 9am-late Sat; 🖳) Sniff hard enough and the fresh coffee aroma emanating from this cool little cafe might lead you off the highway. It has light meals, cakes, couches and a bar looking towards Richmond River.

La Cucina di Vino (☎ 02-6618 1195; cnr Martin & Fawcett Sts; mains $14-25; 🕑 lunch & dinner) Water views and an open corner locale make this Italian restaurant an excellent venue for a long lunch. Short on time? There's pizza too.

Also available:

Brundah (☎ 02-6686 8166; www.babs.com.au/brun dah; 37 Norton St; s/d $145/189; 🗶) Heritage-listed B&B with tranquil gardens. Breakfast included.

Wicked (☎ 02-6686 2564; 37 Cherry St; mains $19-30; 🕑 lunch Tue-Fri, dinner Tue-Sat) Huge menu to suit all tastes.

GETTING THERE & AWAY

Virgin Blue (☎ 13 67 89; www.virginblue.com.au) and **Jetstar** (☎ 13 15 38; www.jetstar.com.au) fly to Sydney ($70, 1½ hours). The **Rex** (☎ 13 17 13; www.regionalexpress.com.au) service is slower ($130, two hours). **Qantas** (☎ 13 13 13; www.qantas.com.au) flies to Melbourne ($173, two hours).

Greyhound (☎ 1300 GREYHOUND/1300 473 946; www.greyhound.com.au) stops at the Big Prawn on its way to Brisbane ($50, four hours), Coffs Harbour ($55, three hours) and Sydney ($120, 12 hours). **Premier Motor Service** (☎ 13 34 10; www .premierms.com.au) stops at the Ampol Pied Pier on its way to Brisbane ($37, 4½ hours), Coffs Harbour ($45, 4¾ hours) and Sydney ($90, 11 hours).

Northern Rivers Buslines (☎ 02-6626 1499; www .nrbuslines.com.au) has buses to Lismore, Lennox Head and Evans Head. **Blanch's Bus Service** (☎ 02-6686 2144; www.blanchs.com.au) operates a service to Lennox Head ($7), Mullumbimby ($10), Byron Bay ($10) and Bangalow ($8). All stop on Tamar St. **CountryLink** (☎ 13 22 32; www .countrylink.info) buses head to Evans Head ($5, 35 minutes), Lennox Head ($5, 15 minutes) and Lismore ($5, 50 minutes).

If you're driving to Byron Bay, take the coast road through Lennox Head. It's shorter and much prettier than the highway.

Lennox Head
pop 6618

Recently classified as a protected National Surfing Reserve – à la the surfing mecca of Angourie – Lennox Head is home to picturesque coastline with some of the best surf on the coast, including long right-hander breaks. Its blossoming food scene combined with a laid-back atmosphere makes it an alternative to its boisterous well-touristed neighbour Byron, 17km north.

Stunning **Seven Mile Beach** runs along parallel to the main street. The best places for a dip are at the north end near the surf club or at the southern end in The Channel. **Port Morton lookout** is a whale-and-dolphin-spotting high point.

Lake Ainsworth, a lagoon just back from the surf club, is made brown by tannins from the tea trees along its banks, which also make swimming here beneficial to the skin. If the wind's up, **Wind & Water Action Sports** (☎ 0419 686 188; www.windnwater.net; 1hr kite-boarding lesson $79, 1hr windsurfing lesson plus 4hr hire $80, 2hr private surf lesson $80) has good equipment.

For holiday rentals contact the **Professionals** (☎ 02-6687 7579; www.lennoxheadrealestate.com.au; 66 Ballina St).

Lennox Lodge (☎ 02-6687 7210; www.lennoxlodge .com.au; 20 Byron St; s/d $25/80; 🖳 🐾) is a motel-style backpackers daubed in mustard paint and dotted with palm trees and frangipanis. The atmosphere is relaxed and with a maximum of four people to each room, with bathroom, it's comfortable.

The YHA-affiliated **Lennox Head Beach House** (☎ 02-6687 7636; www.yha.com.au; 3 Ross St; dm/d $30/72) has immaculate rooms and a great vibe. For $5 you can use the boards, sailboards and bikes.

Lake Ainsworth Caravan Park (☎ 02-6687 7249; www.bscp.com.au/lakeainsworth.htm; Pacific Pde; unpowered/powered sites $24/27, cabins from $60) sits on flat, green grass just opposite the beach.

Lime, Lime, Lime (☎ 02-6687 7132; 70 Ballina St; 🕑 breakfast & lunch) serves good cafe fare including bacon, pesto and avocado toasties ($10) and smoothies.

Ruby's by the Sea (☎ 02-6687 5769; 17-19 Pacific Pde; entrées $13, mains $20; 🕑 lunch & dinner), within the Lennox Point Hotel, cooks up gastro-bistro fare – Monday night is pasta night, Tuesday is curry.

Premier Motor Service (☎ 13 34 10; www.premierms.com.au) stops here on request; pick up is from the CountryLink Coach Stop. **Blanch's Bus Service** (☎ 02-6686 2144; www.blanchs.com.au) operates a service to Ballina ($7), Mullumbimby ($10) and Byron Bay ($8).

BYRON BAY
pop 18,890

Byron Bay's reputation precedes it like no other place in Australia: it's a gorgeous town where the trademark laid-back, New Age populace lives an escapist, organic lifestyle against a backdrop of evergreen hinterland and never-ending surfable coastline.

With such a heady high rap in mind, the pitfall lies in arriving in this utopia along with every other backpacker on the coast, and wondering what all the fuss is about. Never fear, the sensation doesn't last long. Byron's unique vibe has a way of converting even the most cynical with its long days, balmy weather, endless beaches, delightful accommodation, delectable food, delirious nightlife, ambling milieu and the charisma and hospitality of the local community.

It's an addiction that's hard to kick; many simply don't. A weekend turns into a week, a week into a month… Before you know it, dreadlocks are a serious consideration.

Information

Backpackers World (☎ 02-6685 8858; www.backpackersworld.com.au; shop 6, 75 Jonson St) Info and tours for budget travellers.

Byron Bus & Backpacker Centre (☎ 02-6685 5517; 84 Jonson St) Low-down on transport, accommodation and activities.

Global Gossip (☎ 02-6680 9140; www.globalgossip.com; 84 Jonson St; per hr $3; ☽ 8.30am-11pm) Internet.

Visitor centre (☎ 02-6680 9271; 80 Jonson St) A wealth of information.

Sights
CAPE BYRON

The grandfather of the 'mad, bad and dangerous to know' poet Lord Byron was a renowned navigator in the 1760s, and Captain Cook named this spot, Australia's most easterly, after him. (A star-struck clerk in Sydney thought the grandson was the one being honoured, and named the streets – and the town – after poets: Keats, Jonson, Shelley.)

The views from the summit are spectacular, particularly if you've just burnt breakfast off on the climbing track from Clarkes Beach. Ribboning around the headland, it dips and (mostly) soars its way to the lighthouse. The surrounding ocean also jumps to the tune of dolphins and migrating humpback whales in June and July. Towering over all is the 1901 **lighthouse** (☎ 02-6685 6585; Lighthouse Rd; ☽ 8am-sunset), Australia's most easterly and powerful. The Cape Byron Walking Track continues around the northeastern side of the cape, delving into **Cape Byron State Conservation Park**, where you'll stumble across bush turkeys and wallabies. En route, photo-hungry walkers can work the lens at **Captain Cook Lookout**. You can also drive right up to the lighthouse and pay $7 for the privilege of parking (or nothing at all if you park 300m below).

BEACHES

Main Beach, immediately in front of town, is terrific for people watching and swimming. At the western edge of town, **Belongil Beach** is clothing optional. **Clarkes Beach**, at the eastern end of Main Beach, is good for surfing, but the best surf is at the next few beaches: the **Pass**, **Wategos** and **Little Wategos**.

Tallow Beach is an amazing stretch that extends 7km south of Cape Byron to a rockier patch around **Broken Head**, where a succession of small beaches dots the coast before opening onto **Seven Mile Beach**, which goes all the way to Lennox Head (opposite).

The suburb of **Suffolk Park** (with more good surf, particularly in winter) starts 3km south of town. **Kings Beach**, a popular gay beach, is just off Seven Mile Beach Rd near the Broken Head Holiday Park.

Activities

Most activity operators offer free pick-up from local accommodation. It's cheapest to book through hostels.

Want to run away and join **Circus Arts** (☎ 02-6685 6566; www.circusarts.com.au; 17 Centennial Circuit), 2km west of town? Choose between flying trapeze ($45) and circus skills ($20) classes.

ALTERNATIVE THERAPIES

Byron is the alternative-therapy heartland. The *Body & Soul* guide, available from the visitor centre, is a handy guide to therapies on offer.

NEW SOUTH WALES

BYRON BAY

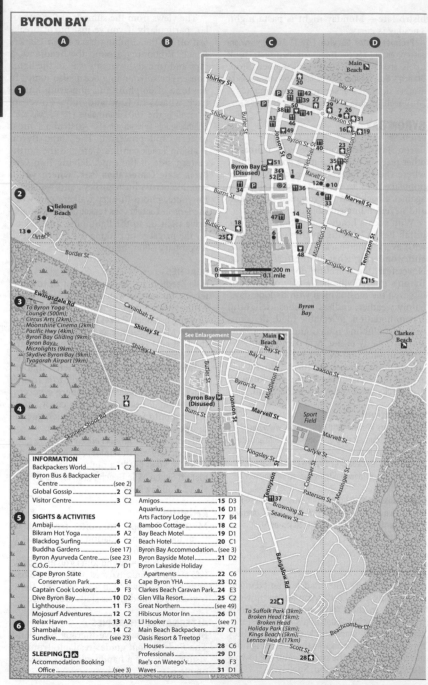

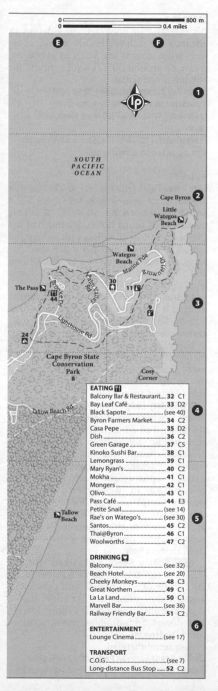

Ambaji (☎ 02-6685 6620; www.ambajihouseofwellbe
ing.com; 1st floor, 1 Marvell St; treatments from $65;
🕙 10am-4pm Mon-Sat, 11am-3pm Sun) Craniosacral
balancing, aqua balance healing and more.
Bikram Hot Yoga (☎ 02-6685 6334; www.bikramyo
gabyronbay.com.au; 35 Childe St; 90min class $18)
Buddha Gardens (☎ 02-6680 7844; www.buddhagar
densdayspa.com.au; Arts Factory Village, 15 Gordon St; treatments from $80; 🕙 10am-6pm) Balinese-style day spa.
Byron Ayurveda Centre (☎ 02-6680 8788; www
.ayurvedahouse.com.au; shop 6, Middleton St; treatments
from $45; 🕙 9am-6pm Mon-Sat) Indian medicinal
therapies and organic products.
Byron Yoga Lounge (☎ 0402 770 441; www.byroniy
engaryoga.com; 1 Banksia Dr; classes from $8) Daily classes.
Relax Haven (☎ 02-6685 8304; Belongil Beachouse,
Childe St; 🕙 10am-8pm) Flotation tanks (one hour $35)
and massage (one hour $55). Female therapists.
Shambala (☎ 02-6680 7791; www.shambala.net.au; 4
Carlyle St; treatments from $45; 🕙 9am-7pm) Massage,
reflexology and acupuncture.

DIVING & SNORKELLING

About 3km offshore, Julian Rocks Marine
Reserve blends cold southerly and warm
northerly currents, attracting a profusion of
marine species and divers alike.

Reputable diving companies:
Dive Byron Bay (☎ 1800 243 483, 02-6685 8333;
www.byronbaydivecentre.com.au; 9 Marvell St) PADI
courses from $395, dives from $90.
Sundive (☎ 1800 008 755; www.sundive.com.au; Middleton St) PADI courses from $395, snorkelling $50.

FLYING

Byron Bay Gliding (☎ 02-6684 7572; www.byron
baygliding.com; Tyagarah Airport) Flights over coast and
hinterland; 30 minutes from $150.
Byron Bay Microlights (☎ 0407 281 687; Tyagarah
Airport) Whale watching from $170.
Skydive Byron Bay (☎ 02-6684 1323; www.sky
divebyronbay.com; Tyagarah Airport;14,000ft jump $299)
Australia's highest dive.

KAYAKING

Exhibitionist dolphins enhance scenic, half-
day kayaking tours in and around Cape
Byron Marine Park. Tours generally go for
$50 to $60 per adult, less for children.
Cape Byron Kayaks (☎ 02-6680 9555; www.capeby
ronkayaks.com)
Dolphin Kayaking (☎ 02-6685 8044; www.dolphin
kayaking.com.au)
Gosea Kayaks (☎ 0416 222 344; www.goseakayakby
ronbay.com.au; 🕙 9.30am & 2pm)

Mother Earth Kayak Tours (☎ 0431 945 338; www
.motherearthkayaktours.com.au) Inlet and hinterland tours.

SURFING
Byron Bay waves are often quite mellow. Most
hostels provide free boards to guests.
Blackdog Surfing (☎ 02-6680 9828; www.blackdog
surfing.com; shop 8, The Plaza, Jonson St) Three-hour
lesson $60, three days $135.
C.O.G (☎ 02-6680 7066; 31 Lawson St) Rents boards for
$25 per day.
Kool Katz (☎ 02-6685 5169; www.koolkatzsurf.com)
Half-day lessons $49, three days $115.
Mojosurf Adventures (☎ 1800 113 044; www
.mojosurf.com; Marvell St) Half-day lessons $65; two-to-
five day, all-inclusive surf trips $195 to $635.
Samudra (☎ 02-6685 5600; www.samudra.com.au)
Surf-and-yoga retreats.

Tours
The following offer small-group tours into the
north coast hinterland:
Byron Bay Eco Tours (☎ 02-6685 4030; www
.byron-bay.com/ecotours; tours $85; ☷ 10am) Excellent
commentary.
Byron Bay Wildlife Tours (☎ 0429 770 686; www
.byronbaywildlifetours.com; adult/child $50/25) Platypus
and wildlife spottings guaranteed.
Jim's Alternative Tours (☎ 02-6685 7720; www
.jimsalternativetours.com; tours $35) Entertaining tours
(with soundtrack!) to Nimbin.
Mountain Bike Tours (☎ 1800 122 504, 0429 122
504; www.mountainbiketours.com.au; tours $99) Environ-
mentally friendly bike tours.
Night Vision Walks (☎ 02-6687 4237; www
.visionwalks.com; adult/child from $60/44) See nocturnal
animals in their natural habitat.

Festivals & Events
**East Coast International Blues & Roots Music
Festival** (☎ 02-6685 8310; www.bluesfest.com.au) Held
over Easter, this international jam attracts high-calibre
international performers and local heavyweights. Book
early.
Splendour in the Grass (www.splendourinthegrass
.com) Held in July, this popular indie music festival
treats punters to funk, electronica, folk, rock, hip hop
etc. Book early.
Byron Bay Writers Festival (☎ 02-6685 5115; www
.byronbaywritersfestival.com.au) In late July/early August,
top-shelf writers and literary followers gather from across
Australia.
Taste of Byron (www.atasteofbyron.com) This celebration of produce from the Northern Rivers region rumbles
the tummy in September.

Sleeping
It's essential to book accommodation in
advance for school holidays and summer, when rooms are full and tariffs increase by around 30%. Useful contacts for
holiday-house rental:
Byron Bay Accommodation (☎ 02-6680 8666; www
.byronbayaccom.net) Run by the visitor centre.
LJ Hooker (☎ 02-6685 7300; www.ljhooker.com; 4/31
Lawson St)
Professionals (☎ 02-6685 6552; www.byronbaypro
.com.au; cnr Lawson & Fletcher Sts)

BUDGET
Cape Byron YHA (☎ 1800 652 627, 02-6685 8788; www
.yha.com.au; cnr Byron & Middleton Sts; dm $25, d
with/without bathroom from $90/80; ⌨ ⧉) This
purpose-built hostel is one tidy ship and has
five-bed, uncramped dorms with lockers and
fans. The doubles and twins are also spacious, and one has a bathroom. The kitchen
and TV room are tight, but there's a sunny
courtyard to compensate.
Aquarius (☎ 02-6685 7663; www.aquarius-backpack
ers.com.au; 14-16 Lawson St; dm/d from $30/80, motel d from
$120; ✄ ⌨ ⧉) This motel-style backpack-
ers overflows with the comings and goings
of hyperactive, excitable travellers. There's
plenty of communal space – including a
bar – ensuring those going it solo can find
mates. Self-contained apartments also available (doubles from $140).
Arts Factory Lodge (☎ 02-6685 7709; www.artsfac
tory.com.au; Skinners Shoot Rd; dm/d from $31/95, campsites
$16; ⌨ ⧉) For an archetypal Byron experi-
ence, pull up stumps here. The complex has
didgeridoo lessons and yoga and meditation
workshops delivered in a serene hippie-esque
setting on a picturesque swamp. Choose from
colourful six- to 10-bed dorms, teepees or
wagons. Couples can opt for 'cube' rooms
(aptly titled), island retreat canvas huts or the
pricier love shack with bathroom. Be warned;
some folk have complained of encountering
small rodents here.
ourpick Main Beach Backpackers (☎ 1800
150 233, 02-6685 8695; cnr Lawson & Fletcher Sts; dm
$33, d $70-80; ⌨) This small and personable
hostel makes guests feel like more than a
number with friendly staff, a sunny lounge,
and dorms and doubles reminiscent of
comfy bedrooms.
Also recommended:
Clarkes Beach Caravan Park (☎ 02-6685 6496;
www.northcoastparks.com.au/clarkes; off Lighthouse Rd;

unpowered sites/cabins from $30/110) Tightly packed cabins and sites in a bush setting.

Great Northern (☎ 02-6685 6454; Jonson St; s/d $60/70) Spartan rooms above this classic pub.

MIDRANGE

Amigos (☎ 02-6680 8622; www.amigosbb.com; 32 Kingsley St; s/d from $88/108) Soaked in south-of-the-border flavours, this cute TV-free B&B has three bedrooms with crisp white linen and South American spreads. There are hammocks out the back.

our pick **Bamboo Cottage** (☎ 02-6685 5509; www .byron-bay.com/bamboocottage; 76 Butler St; r from $99) Featuring global charm and wall hangings, Bamboo Cottage treats guests to individually styled rooms with Asian overtones in a home-away-from-home atmosphere. It's on the quiet side of the tracks.

Glen Villa Resort (☎ 02-6685 7382; www.byron bayresorts.com/glenvilla; Butler St; d cabin from $110; 🞬 🖳 🖭) Though slightly militant with its 'two people only' rule, this well-maintained cabin park is clean, comfortable and secure. It's off the main traffic route so it is last to fill up, and blissfully peaceful.

Byron Bayside Motel (☎ 02-6685 6004; www.byron baysidemotel.com.au; 14 Middleton St; s/d $110/115) These spotless rooms have small kitchenettes and full laundries; ideal for campers looking for downtime. It's central, comparatively cheap and takes security seriously.

Oasis Resort & Treetop Houses (☎ 1800 336 129, 02-6685 7390; www.byronbayoasisresort.com.au; 24 Scott St; apt from $135; treetop apt from $205; 🞬 🖭) This compact resort is engulfed by palms and has sizeable one- and two-bedroom apartments with big balconies. Even better are the apartments sitting atop the tree canopies with outdoor spas and ocean views. All units are immaculate and kitted out in cheery decor.

Bay Beach Motel (☎ 02-6685 6090; www.baybeach motel.com.au; 32 Lawson St; r $155-180, 2-bed apt from $235; 🞬 🖭) Unpretentious but smart, this white-brick hotel with contemporary furnishings is close to town, but not so close that party-goers keep guests awake.

More midrangers:

Byron Lakeside Holiday Apartments (☎ 02-6680 9244; www.byronlakeside.com; 5 Old Bangalow Rd; 4-night apt from $540; 🞬 🖳 🖭) Stylish holiday village with superb apartments.

Hibiscus Motor Inn (☎ 02-6685 6195; 33 Lawson St; d $155; 🞬 🖭) A basic but central motel with friendly owners.

TOP END

Beach Hotel (☎ 02-6685 6402; www.beachhotel .au; Bay St; r incl breakfast from $260; 🞬 🖭) This classy beachfront joint has garden-view rooms doused in forest greens and polished wood, with marble bathrooms and Thai silk cushions. Top of the food chain are the ocean-view loft rooms and the 'east coast suite'.

More top-enders:

Rae's on Watego's (☎ 02-6685 5366; www.raes.com .au; 8 Marine Pde, Wategos Beach; price on application; 🞬 🖭) One of Australia's best.

Waves (☎ 1800 040 151; www.wavesresorts.com .au; Lawson St; d apt from $250; 🞬) Cushy, boutique penthouse and studio apartments in the heart of Byron.

Eating

RESTAURANTS

Most restaurant kitchens close by 9pm.

Lemongrass (☎ 02-6680 8443; Lawson Arcade, 3/17 Lawson St; mains $13-20; 🕑 lunch Mon-Fri, dinner daily) All your favourite Vietnamese dishes, from ricepaper rolls and beef *pho* to green pawpaw salad and prawn fried rice.

Kinoko Sushi Bar (☎ 02-6680 9044; 7/23 Jonson St; 🕑 lunch & dinner) Choo choo choose something from the sushi train or let the Japanese chef slice up a plate of fresh sashimi. This is a lively place where the Asahi also goes down well.

Casa Pepe (☎ 02-6685 7121; cnr Byron & Middleton Sts; mains $18-26; 🕑 dinner Tue-Sat) It's strictly vegetarian, but this cosy restaurant is worthy of all dietary persuasions. Happy patrons sit in the sheltered courtyard and tuck into pizzas, pies, soups and tofu burgers for lunch and smart pastas for dinner.

our pick **Balcony Bar & Restaurant** (☎ 02-6680 9666; cnr Lawson & Johnson Sts; mains $20-30) Amid voyeuristic seating or cosy, obese cushions, the Balcony dishes up Ottoman overtones and fabulous fare for breakfast and lunch, and midnight tapas to soak up the cocktails.

Olivo (☎ 02-6685 7950; 34 Jonson St; mains $27-31; 🕑 dinner) Chic and snug with global flavours such as baked eggplant stuffed with tomato, raisins and cinnamon, and duck confit with wild rice, grape and pistachio pilaf.

Dish (☎ 02-6685 7320; cnr Jonson & Marvell Sts; mains $27-38; 🕑 dinner) Ivy-clad walls and floor-to-ceiling glass create an atrium atmosphere at this dishy restaurant. The equally sophisticated cuisine includes pan-roasted eye fillet with potato, onion and bacon croquette.

ourpick **Petit Snail** (☎ 02-6685 8526; 5 Carlyle St; entrées $15, mains $35; ☒ dinner) An intimate restaurant is off the main beat serving up traditional French cuisine such as wild rabbit terrine and duck confit in orange sauce.

Rae's on Watego's (☎ 02-6685 5366; Marine Pde, Wategos Beach; entrées $32, mains $45; ☒ lunch & dinner) Save this exquisite restaurant with a terrace overlooking the ocean for a very special occasion. With the sound of surf providing ambience and the seafood platter providing the impetus, this is one to remember.

More fine dining:

Black Sapote (☎ 02-6680 8016; 21 Fletcher St; tapas $8-13; ☒ lunch & breakfast daily, dinner Wed-Sat) A groovy bar atmosphere with an inspired menu.

Mokha (☎ 02-6685 7726; shop 2, Lawson St; mains $16-23) Eclectic Euro–Middle Eastern menu and a wine list as long as your arm.

CAFES

Like most of Byron's cafes the following are open for breakfast and lunch only.

Pass Café (☎ 02-6685 6074; 1 Brooke Dr; mains $8-15) One of the best cafes in Byron with a super outdoor deck surrounded by trees and birdlife. The fare includes avocado on toast and fresh squeezed juices.

Mary Ryan's (☎ 02-6685 8183; shop 5, 21-25 Fletcher St; mains $8-16) Snuggled up to the ABC bookshop, this literary cafe provides coffee drinkers with a caffeine high. Speaking of high, the ceilings are, leaving plenty of wall space for artworks.

ourpick **Bay Leaf Café** (☎ 02-6685 8900; Marvell St; mains $10-18) Locals flock to this teeny, bohemian cafe that packs a punch for its small size. Best meal of the day is breakfast: the fresh stewed rhubarb, yoghurt and pistachios shouldn't be missed.

QUICK EATS

Local takeaways litter Jonson St.

Mongers (☎ 02-6680 8080; Bay Lane; mains $10-18; ☒ lunch & dinner) This little eatery turns out boxed-up gourmet fish and chips in a casual environment.

Thai@Byron (☎ 02-6680 6737; shop 10, Feros Arcade; mains $17-22; ☒ lunch Mon-Fri, dinner daily) Authentic Thai food.

SELF-CATERING

Byron Farmers Market (☎ 02-6685 9792; Butler St; ☒ 8-11am Thu & Sat) Great for picking up delicious local produce.

Green Garage (☎ 02-6680 8577; www.greengarage .com.au; 68 Tennyson St; ☒ 7am-7pm) Organic goodies.

Santos (☎ 02-6685 7071; 105 Jonson St; ☒ 8.30am-6pm Mon-Fri, 9am-5pm Sat, 9am-4pm Sun) Organic grocer.

Woolworths (☎ 02-6685 7292; The Plaza, Jonson St; ☒ 8am-9pm)

Drinking & Entertainment

Byron's nightlife is the best on the north coast. For info on live music at the assortment of pubs, check the gig guide in Thursday's *Byron Shire News* and Bay 99.9FM for various events.

Railway Friendly Bar (☎ 02-6685 7662; Jonson St; ☒ 11am-late) This indoor-outdoor pub draws everyone from grey pensioners and lobster-red British tourists to acid-soaked hippies and high-on-life earth mothers. Its cosy interior is the old railway station. The front beer garden, conducive to boozy afternoons, has live music most nights.

Balcony (☎ 02-6680 9666; cnr Lawson & Jonson Sts; ☒ 8am-11pm) With its verandah poking out amid the palm trees, this fine bar-cum-restaurant is the place to park yourself. Choose from stools, chairs or sofas while working through the long wine list.

Great Northern (☎ 02-6685 6454; Byron St; ☒ noon-late) You won't need your fancy duds at this brash and boisterous pub. It's loud and beery most nights and even louder when hosting headline acts. Live music almost nightly.

ourpick **Beach Hotel** (☎ 02-6685 6402; cnr Jonson & Bay Sts; ☒ 11am-late) The mother ship of all pubs is close to the main beach and is shot through with a fabulously infectious atmosphere that makes everyone your best mate. There's live music and DJs some nights.

More drinking:

Cheeky Monkeys (☎ 02-6685 5886; 115 Jonson St; ☒ 7pm-3am) A backpackers bonanza – and dare we say it, wet T-shirt comps.

La La Land (☎ 02-6680 7070; 6 Lawson St; ☒ 5pm-late) Soft couches, sinful lighting, slinky young things.

Marvell Bar (☎ 02-6685 7320; cnr Jonson & Marvell Sts; ☒ 6pm-midnight) Cocktails, sushi and plenty of style.

CINEMAS

In summer **Moonshine Cinema** (☎ 02-6685 8000; www.myspace.com/moonshinecinema; Byron Bay Beach Resort, Bayshore Dr; adult/child $10/8) screens latest release, art-house and classic films in tropical surrounds.

The Arts Factory's **Lounge Cinema** (☎ 02-6680 9055; Skinners Shoot Rd; admission $10) screens Hollywood fodder as well as art-house flicks and classic reruns.

Getting There & Away

AIR

The closest commercial airport is at Ballina (p193), but most people use the larger Coolangatta airport on the Gold Coast (p333).

BUS

Long-distance buses stop along Jonson St. **Greyhound** (☎ 1300 GREYHOUND/1300 473 946; www .greyhound.com.au) has daily services to Brisbane ($45, 3¼ hours), Coffs Harbour ($65, 4¼ hours) and Sydney ($130, 13½ hours). **Premier Motor Service** (☎ 13 34 10; www.premierms .com.au) has buses to Brisbane ($29, 3½ hours), Coffs Harbour ($48, five hours) and Sydney ($90, 12 hours). **Northern Rivers Buslines** (☎ 02-6626 1499; www.nrbuslines.com.au) has buses to Lismore, Murwillumbah and Brunswick Heads. **Blanch's Bus Service** (☎ 02-6686 2144; www .blanchs.com.au) operates a service to Ballina ($10), Mullumbimby ($7), Lennox Head ($8) and Bangalow ($7). The **Nimbin Tours & Shuttle Bus** (☎ 02-6680 9189; www.nimbintours.com) runs to Uki ($25) and Byron Bay ($14) with optional stops at Mt Warning. The bus leaves from the Byron visitor centre.

Shuttle services:

Byron easyBus (☎ 02-6685 7447; www.byroneasybus .com.au) Brisbane ($50), Gold Coast ($35) and Ballina airport ($16).

Xcede Byron Bay (☎ 02-6620 9200; www.xcede.com .au) Ballina airport (from $18), Gold Coast and Coolangatta ($40).

Getting Around

Byron Bay Taxis (☎ 02-6685 5008) On call 24 hours.
C.O.G (☎ 02-6680 7066; 31 Lawson St) Rents bikes for adult/child $20/18 per day and can advise about trails.

BYRON BAY TO TWEED HEADS

The Pacific Hwy continues north to the Queensland border at Tweed Heads. For a detour through the town of **Mullumbimby** ('Mullum'; population 3655) take Gulga Rd and rejoin the highway via the pretty Coolamon Scenic Dr. This serene town is a coast-hinterland hybrid with a cosmopolitan spread of cafes, bistros and pubs.

On the Old Pacific Hwy, only slightly north, beautiful Brunswick Heads reaps a bounty of fresh oysters and mud crabs from its peaceful Brunswick River inlets and beaches. The 1940s **Hotel Brunswick** (☎ 02-6685 1236; www.hotelbrunswick.com.au; Mullumbimby St; s/d

$55/85) is a sight to behold and a destination unto itself. It has decent pub rooms and the restaurant (mains $20; open for lunch and dinner) serves great nosh. There's live music Thursday to Sunday.

Take the Chinderah Bypass halfway between Brunswick Heads and Murwillumbah to the town of **Mooball** and its legendary **Moo Moo Café** (☎ 02-6677 1230; Tweed Valley Way; mains $8-13; ☺ breakfast & lunch). It is famous for its bovine obsession, with cow and farm kitsch aplenty.

Tweed Heads (population 51,788) marks the southern end of the Gold Coast strip. At Point Danger, the towering **Captain Cook Memorial** straddles the state border. Tweed Heads accommodation options spill over into Coolangatta (p341) and up into the Gold Coast, where there's more choice.

FAR NORTH COAST HINTERLAND

Beach bums and surfers might not credit it, but there are people who not so secretly regard the hinterland – as opposed to Byron Bay – as the jewel in the Far North Coast crown.

Just minutes from Byron, the greener-than-green undulating landscape is a crocheted rug of lush rainforest, pastoral lands, striped orchards and stands of eucalypt, all navigable via pretty winding roads, the kind best driven in an antique convertible with a gingham-covered picnic basket on the back seat.

Characteristic towns hide in among the foliage offering an eclectic take on small-town life. The hippie haven of Nimbin is the most popular, but towns such as Bangalow, with its esteemed bookshop and gourmand restaurants, exemplify the trend for combining the laid-back lifestyle of the country with the cultural idiosyncrasies and creature comforts of the big smoke.

The hinterland also boasts The Border Ranges, Mt Warning and Nightcap National Parks, which form part of the World Heritage–listed rainforests of the Central Eastern Rainforest Reserves. With a combined total of 42, 264 hectares, the parks are a haven for walking and camping, and a bounty of Aboriginal history and culture.

BANGALOW

pop 1753

Boutiques, fine eateries, bookshops and an excellent pub – a mere 14km from Byron Bay. Beautiful Bangalow, with its character-laden main street, is the kind of place that turns Sydneysiders into tree-changers.

There's a good weekly **farmers market** (Byron St; 8-11am Sat) and a praised **cooking school** (02-6687 2799; www.bangalowcookingschool.com).

Stately old **Riverview Guesthouse** (02-6687 1317; www.riverviewguesthouse.com.au; 99 Byron St; r with/without bathroom $195/180) sits on the river's edge ensuring guests see platypuses and oversized lizards as they take on breakfast. It's the stuff of B&B dreams.

Ate (02-6687 1010; 33 Byron St; mains $23-36; breakfast & lunch) is great for sipping coffee on the verandah or dining in for inventive dishes along the lines of marinated grilled quail with chickpeas and pancetta. Upstairs, **Satiate** (degustation from $55; dinner Tue-Sat) does a designer set menu and chic cocktails.

Gluten-free, organic and sublimely tasty wraps, salads, rolls and produce are up for grabs at **Bangalow Basics** (02-6687 1428; 29 Byron St; breakfast & lunch) and **Urban Café** (02-6687 2678; 33 Byron St; mains $12-16; breakfast & lunch), which changes its stripes at night to become **Bang Thai** (02-6687 2000; mains $18; dinner Thu-Sat), with all the faves including Mussuman curry.

our pick **Fresca** (02-6687 1711; www.fresca.net.au; Byron St; mains $20-33; lunch & dinner) at Bangalow Hotel is a classy place with just the right amount of cool. Reserve a table on the deck for a leisurely antipasto ($20).

Blanch's Bus Service (02-6686 2144; www.blanchs .com.au) operates a service to Ballina ($8) and Byron Bay ($7).

LISMORE

pop 37,894

Lismore, the hinterland's commercial centre, appears to have been dropped into its green surroundings without ruffling the feathers of the pristine hinterland. The town itself sits on the Wilson River, though it has yet to take advantage of this, and is otherwise beautified by a liberal supply of heritage and art deco buildings, and a thriving artistic community. Students from Southern Cross University add to the town's eclecticism.

The **Lismore visitor centre** (1300 369 795; www .visitlismore.com.au; cnr Molesworth & Ballina Sts) has inter-net ($6 per hour) and a rainforest display ($1). Kids groove on the **Heritage Park** playground and skate park, next to the centre. The diminutive **Lismore Regional Art Gallery** (02-6622 2209; 131 Molesworth St; admission by donation; 10am-4pm Tue-Fri, 10.30am-4pm Sat) has just enough space for two visiting exhibitions, but the curators do it justice by showing excellent works.

The **Koala Care & Research Centre** (02-6622 1233; Rifle Range Rd; admission $3; tours 10am & 2pm Mon-Fri, 10am Sat) is home to recovering koalas and well worth a visit. To get a glimpse of platypuses, head to the northern end of Kadina St and walk up to **Tucki Tucki Creek** at dawn or sunset. You can also spot fuzzy grey bums-in-the-gums at **Tucki Tucki Nature Reserve** (02-6627 0200; Wyrallah Rd), about 16km south of town.

A pleasant walking track skirts the river. Along the way you'll pass a **bush-tucker garden**, nurturing the once daily diet of the Widjabal people, the traditional owners of the land.

Sleeping

Melville House (02-6621 5778; 267 Ballina St; s/d without bathroom $60/80, s with bathroom $90-110, d with bathroom $120-140;) Chequered tiles in the kitchen, antique clocks in the hall, marble bathrooms and cut glass on the windows: this excellent B&B is a slice of vintage Australiana. No-frills rooms also available (singles/doubles $45/50).

Winsome Hotel (02-6622 1112; Bridge St; d $75) In a beautiful old heritage building, the double and twin rooms here are clean and cheerful with shared bathrooms. Bands and DJs turn up the volume on the weekends.

Karinga Motel (02-6621 2787; www.karingamotel .com; 258 Molesworth St; s/d $79/115;) This central motel has not only had a facelift; the rooms have been fully refurbished and a funky pool and spa installed.

Lismore Palms Caravan Park (02-6621 7067; www.lismorepalms.com.au; 42-48 Brunswick St; unpowered sites/cabins from $15/60;) Grassy plots on the pretty Wilson River make this the nicest of Lismore's caravan parks.

Eating

our pick **Blue Tongue** (02-6622 0750; 43 Bridge St; mains $8-15; breakfast & lunch Wed-Sun) One of a couple of worthy cafes on the quieter side of the river, this one is in a wonderfully worn building. Great BLATs, toasted Turkish sandwiches and fine coffee can be enjoyed in a sunny courtyard out the back.

Sweet Pea Café (☎ 02-6622 1146; 13 Woodlark St; mains $10-15; ☻ 7.30am-6pm Mon-Wed, to 9pm Sat, 10am-6pm Sun; ▣) This upbeat vegetarian restaurant has a counter full of healthy comfort food including gourmet pies and soups. The gelato is made on the premises and the coffee is locally grown.

Left Bank Café (☎ 02-6622 2338; 133 Molesworth St; mains $12-22; ☻ breakfast & lunch Mon-Sat, dinner Fri & Sat) Attached to the gallery, this bright, open cafe serves artistic works of its own, such as zucchini, mint and feta frittata. You can dine in the shaded courtyard or glassy interior.

Lismore stages its **farmers market** (☎ 02-6621 5916; ☻ 8am-noon Sat) and **Organic Market** (☎ 02-6628 2391; ☻ 8-11am Tue) at the showground, off the Nimbin Rd.

Also recommended is **Lismore Pie Cart** (☎ 02-6622 2946; 11 Magellan St; ☻ 6am-5pm Mon-Fri), which serves homemade pies, mashed potato, mushy peas and gravy.

Getting There & Around
Rex (☎ 13 17 13; www.regionalexpress.com.au) flies to Sydney ($130, 1¾ hours).

Greyhound (☎ 1300 GREYHOUND/1300 473 946; www.greyhound.com.au) has daily buses to Byron Bay ($50, two hours). Locally based **Northern Rivers Buslines** (☎ 02-6626 1499; www.nrbuslines.com.au) runs to Ballina, Lennox Head, Byron Bay, Murwillumbah, Brunswick Heads, Grafton ($28), Casino ($11), Maclean ($20) and Tenterfield ($33). **CountryLink** (☎ 13 22 32; www.countrylink.info) buses head to Byron Bay ($7, 45 minutes) and Murwillumbah ($13, 1¼ hours). All leave from the transit centre.

There are also 24-hour **taxis** (☎ 13 10 08).

AROUND LISMORE
The **Channon** is an intimate village between Nimbin and Lismore. Time your visit for the second Sunday of each month for the 'mother of all markets' (say the locals).

NIGHTCAP NATIONAL PARK
This 8080-hectare park, south of Murwillumbah and north of Lismore, borders Nimbin and the Channon. It was World Heritage–listed in 1989 and is home to diverse subtropical rainforests and many species of wildlife. With NSW's highest annual rainfall, the park has spectacular waterfalls, gorgeous green gullies and sheer cliffs. The exposed rock pinnacles of the **Sphinx** can be seen from Lismore.

Mt Nardi offers a challenging climb (800m), and the NPWS office in the visitor centre in Murwillumbah (p204) has information on walks and picnics.

The historic **Nightcap Track** (16km) passes through both the state conservation area and Nightcap National Park and was originally used by postal workers in the late 19th and early 20th century. **Rummery Park** is not far of the road down from the falls and is a well-provided picnic spot with barbecues and cold showers. **Peate's Mountain Lookout**, just on from Rummery Park, gives you a great panoramic view from Jerusalem Mountain in the north, to Byron Bay in the east. There's a platypus-viewing platform at Rocky Creek Damn picnic area.

Southeast of the forest, **Mud Manor Forest Retreat** (☎ 02-6688 2205; www.mudmanor.com; r $120; ▣ ▣) has a permaculture garden and rooms with hand-crafted luxuries, spas and large decks. Breakfast is included.

NIMBIN
pop 1318
A trip in Nimbin, or rather, a trip *to* Nimbin – is, erm, *high*-ly recommended for anyone visiting the Far North Coast. Wordplays aside, this strange little place, a hangover from an experimental 'Aquarius Festival' in the '70s, still feels like a social experiment where anything goes. Reefers included. But it's not all dreadlocks and tie-dye. A day or two here will reveal a growing artist community, a New Age culture and welcoming locals. The **visitor centre** (☎ 02-6689 1388; 80 Cullen St) has great local info.

Sights & Activities
The wacky and wonderful **Nimbin Museum** (☎ 02-6689 1123; 62 Cullen St; admission free; ☻ 9am-5pm) pays homage to crashed kombis in psychedelic garb and the pursuit of 'loving the child within yourself'. Across the street, the **Hemp Embassy** (☎ 02-6689 1842; Cullen St; ☻ 9am-5pm) features none-too-subtle displays about hemp and marijuana, and might be banned under (more) despotic regimes. Smokers are welcome at the coffee shop next door.

Nimbin Artists Gallery (☎ 02-6689 1444; 49 Cullen St; ☻ 10am-4pm) packs an eclectic collection of local art into a modest space. **Djanbung Gardens** (☎ 02-6689 1755; www.permaculture.com.au; 74 Cecil St; admission free; ☻ 10.30am-3pm Tue-Sat, tours 11am Wed & Sat) is a permaculture education centre, cafe and bookshop.

The **Candle Factory** (☎ 02-6689 1010; www
.nimbincandles.com.au; Old Butter Factory; admission free;
🕑 9am-5pm Mon-Fri, 11am-4pm Sat & Sun) drips with
colourful characters – and the wax that forms
candles sold across the country. The colourful
Nimbin Market is on the third and fifth Sunday
of the month.

Nimbin Mardi Grass, held over the first weekend in May, showcases some of the country's
finest endurance talent in the **hemp olympix**.

Avid **Wwoofers** (Willing Workers on Organic Farms;
www.wwoof.com.au) can lend a hand at one of
Nimbin's numerous organic farms.

Sleeping, Eating & Drinking

Nimbin Hotel (☎ 02-6689 1246; Cullen St; per person
$25; 💻) Nimbin's local boozer has basic pub
rooms with shared bathrooms. Downstairs
there's hearty pub nosh for lunch and dinner
and cold schooners on a fantastic rear deck.

YHA Nimbin Rox Hostel (☎ 02-6689 0022; www
.yha.com.au; 74 Thorburn St; dm/d from $25/59; 💻 🖭)
Tumbling down a landscaped native garden,
this excellent hostel has clean and contemporary accommodation and spectacular
national-park views. One dorm is suitable
for wheelchairs. There are also safari tents
($55) and campsites (from $15).

Rainbow Café (☎ 02-6689 1997; 70 Cullen St; mains
$6-13; 🕑 breakfast & lunch) Murals cover the walls
of this thumping Nimbim institution serving
generous burgers, wraps, nachos and salads.
The leafy courtyard has a familiar whiff.

Nimbin Trattoria & Pizzeria (☎ 02-6689 1427;
70 Cullen St; mains $10-20; 🕑 lunch Fri-Sun, dinner
daily) Outstanding pizzas ($3 a slice or $8
for three) and delicious pastas. Live music
every Thursday.

More options:

Grey Gum Lodge (☎ 02-6689 1713; 2 High St; d $65;
🐾) A worn and creaky house with comfy beds.

Rainbow Retreat Backpackers (☎ 02-6689 1262;
www.rainbowretreat.net; 75 Thorburn St; campsites/dm/d
$13/20/25, cabins $40; 💻) A serene retreat for hippies
at heart.

Getting There & Away

The **Nimbin Tours & Shuttle Bus** (☎ 02-6680
9189; www.nimbintours.com) runs to Uki ($25)
and Byron Bay ($14) with optional stops
at Mt Warning. The bus leaves from the
visitor centre. **Wallers Bus Company** (☎ 02-
6687 8550; www.nimbingoodtimes.com) has buses to
Lismore, Uki, Murwillumbah and the Mt
Warning turn-off.

Jim's Alternative Tours (p198) is a long-
running Byron outfit with a party bent.

BORDER RANGES NATIONAL PARK

This 31,729-hectare **World Heritage area** (per
car per day $7) covers the NSW side of the
McPherson Range, with the park's wetter
areas protecting large tracts of superb rainforest; more than 170 Australian bird species
have been identified here.

The eastern section is the most accessible
via the gravel **Tweed Range Scenic Drive**, which
begins at Barkers Vale, 40km southwest of
Murwillumbah. The drive loops through the
park from Lillian Rock to Wiangaree, through
mountain forest most of the way, with steep
hills and breathtaking lookouts over the
Tweed Valley to Mt Warning and the coast.

There are basic **NPWS campsites** (adult/child
$5/3) on the Scenic Dr at Sheepstation Creek,
15km north of the turn-off at Wiangaree,
and Forest Tops, 6km further on. There's
free camping at Byrill Creek, on the eastern
side of Mebbin State Forest.

MT WARNING NATIONAL PARK

Although only 2455 hectares, this is the most
dramatic feature of the hinterland, with Mt
Warning (1156m) towering over the valley. The peak is the first part of mainland
Australia to be touched by sunlight each day.
More than 60,000 people a year make the
4.4km, five-hour round-trip trek to the top
from Breakfast Creek.

You should be aware that, under the law
of the local Bundjalung people, only specifically chosen people are allowed to climb the
mountain and consequently they ask you not
to go, out of respect.

The **Mt Warning Holiday Park** (☎ 02-6679 5120;
www.mtwarningholidaypark.com; 153 Mt Warning Rd; unpowered sites/cabins from $18/65), on the Mt Warning
approach road, has good kitchen facilities and
a well-stocked kiosk.

Wallers Bus Company (☎ 02-6687 8550; www
.nimbingoodtimes.com) buses run from Lismore and
Nimbin to Dum Dum, the tiny town at the turn-
off for Mt Warning, and Murwillumbah.

MURWILLUMBAH

pop 6868

Murwillumbah is gleefully free of precocious-
ness. Sitting calmly, as it does, on the banks of
the Tweed River, it's a great base for exploring the river country, Mt Warning National

Park and the surrounding NSW–Queensland Border Ranges. The town, an agricultural focal point for the region, is old-school with a charming main street and hills flanked with heritage facades. Views of Mt Warning peek around every corner. **Murwillumbah visitor centre** (☎ 02-6672 1340; www.tweedcoolangatta.com.au; cnr Alma St & Tweed Valley Way) has national park info.

Sights

The exceptional **Tweed River Regional Art Gallery** (☎ 02-6670 2790; www.tweed.nsw.gov.au/artgallery; cnr Mistral Rd & Tweed Valley Way; admission free; ☿ 10am-5pm Wed-Sun) is an architectural delight and home to some of Australia's finest in a variety of media.

The small **Murwillumbah Museum** (☎ 02-6672 1865; 2 Queensland Rd; adult/child $2/1; ☿ 11am-3pm Wed-Fri & 4th Sun of month) is housed in a beautiful old building and features a solid account of local history and an interesting radio room.

Just north of town, **Tropical Fruit World** (☎ 02-6677 7222; www.tropicalfruitworld.com.au; Duranbah Rd; adult/child $33/16; ☿ 10am-4.30pm) allegedly has the world's largest collection of tropical fruit, along with plantation safaris, tastings and a jungle cruise. Plan for at least half a day to make the most of the pricey entry.

Sleeping & Eating

Mount Warning-Murwillumbah YHA (☎ 02-6672 3763; www.yha.com.au; 1 Tumbulgum Rd; dm/d from $32/67) This former river captain's home now houses a colourful waterfront hostel with eight-bed dorms. There's free ice cream at night plus canoe and bike hire.

Imperial Hotel (☎ 02-6672 2777; 115 Main St; s/d with shared bathroom $35/50, d $65) It's hard to miss this pink pub on the main street. The grand old pub rooms are shabby chic without even trying. Downstairs is a decent bistro.

Murwillumbah Motor Inn (☎ 02-6672 2022; www.murwillumbahmotorinn.com.au; 17 Byangum Rd; d $104-113; ✄ 🖳 🖭) These clean and comfortable rooms are a great option away from the town centre. The deluxe rooms have flat-screen televisions. There's a pleasant courtyard out the back.

New Leaf Café (☎ 02-6672 2667; shop 10, Murwillumbah Plaza; meals $5-15; ☿ breakfast & lunch) The food here is creative and vegetarian, with plenty of Middle Eastern flavours and salads on offer. Dine inside, alfresco, or takeaway.

Sugar Beat (☎ 02-6672 2330; shop 2, 6-8 Commercial Rd; mains $10; ☿ breakfast & lunch Mon-Sat) Whether it be for cake and coffee, or a longish lunch,

this is a fine place to park yourself by the sunny window or on a bench in the corner. The menu boasts vegetarian fare but the burgers are mighty fine too.

Flamingos Café (☎ 02-6672 5492; 91 Main St; mains $10-29; ☿ lunch Mon-Fri, dinner daily) The somewhat extroverted decor in this happening little eatery makes for a lively dining experience. The pizza toppings are generous and the vegetarian choices exemplary.

Getting There & Away

Northern Rivers Buslines (☎ 02-6626 1499; www.nrbuslines.com.au) runs to Lismore, Byron Bay and Brunswick Heads. **Wallers Bus Company** (☎ 02-6687 8550; www.nimbingoodtimes.com) has buses to Lismore, Nimbin, Uki and Dum Dum, the tiny town at the turn-off for Mt Warning.

Greyhound (☎ 1300 GREYHOUND/1300 473 946; www.greyhound.com.au) runs to Coolangatta ($30, 30 minutes) and Byron Bay ($20, one hour).

Premier Motor Service (☎ 13 34 10; www.premierms.com.au) has buses to Tweed Heads ($7, 30 minutes) and Byron Bay ($18, one hour).

CountryLink (☎ 13 22 32; www.countrylink.info) buses run to Byron Bay ($7, one hour), Tweed Heads ($5, 30 minutes) and Brisbane ($16, 1¾ hours).

NEW ENGLAND

New England misses out on the kind of exposure Australia's desert landscapes and vast coastlines attract, but the area's rolling green hills and farmland, autumnal foliage and vast tracts of bushland are at least as worthy of exploration.

The verdant scenery prompted the original settlers to name the area New England in 1839. In the northern 'highlands' especially, images of Britain still raise their head. Mist settles in the cool-climate hilltops and valleys, little churches sit in oak-studded paddocks and winding roads navigate impossibly green landscapes.

Curiously some of the small country towns along the New England Hwy, the region's main thoroughfare, show signs that this nostalgia might verge on obsession. Place names and traditions have been transplanted straight out of Scotland and England, and the architecture – including Tudor pubs and a castle – slots in surreally next to typically Australian eucalypt trees and corrugated iron sheds.

The bigger towns of Tamworth and Armidale, though resplendent with heritage architecture, are less enamoured with their past, more focused on a future that can draw tourists.

The region has a string of national parks including Bald Rock and Washpool National Parks in the north. On the Waterfall Way linking Armidale and Coffs Harbour, Guy Fawkes River, Cathedral Rock, New England and Oxley Wild Rivers National Parks feature granite outcrops, unforgettably deep gorges and waterfalls.

On the Fossickers Way, north of Tamworth, you'll need to get out the shovel and dig a little deeper, as each town carries its own signature gem.

TAMWORTH
pop 42,499

Country music kicks this town along like a line of boot-scooters but don't expect Nashville-style roadhouses and Route 66 scenery. This pretty place is wonderfully green with a marvellously tree-filled main street that makes you wonder where Jackie Cole, Keith Urban and Slim Dusty found their inspiration – most likely from the agricultural scene. The country-music capital of Oz has a vibrant nightlife and an emerging wine scene, as well as the rather large golden guitar. They may not wear chaps but you'll sure see some boots.

Information

To get into the string of things, drop into the guitar-shaped visitor centre (☎ 02-6767 5300; www .visittamworth.com.au; cnr Peel & Murray Sts) and check out the Walk a Country Mile Museum (adult/child $5/4.50). Café Latte (☎ 02-6766 1373; 345 Peel St) in the Atrium Shopping Centre has internet.

Sights

If the names Tex Morton, Buddy Williams and Smoky Dawson mean anything to you, then the Australian Country Music Foundation (☎ 02-6766 9696; www.acmf.org.au; 93 Brisbane St; adult/child $6/4; ⏰ 10am-4pm Mon-Fri, to 1pm Sat) will too. This is a country music great Hall of Fame (in the making) with photographs, historic video and film footage, music and souvenirs.

The Big Golden Guitar Tourist Centre (☎ 02-6765 2688; www.biggoldenguitar.com.au; New England Hwy; ⏰ 9am-5pm) has a cafe and a shop where you can stock up on all-important golden-guitar

snow cones. When you've finished, check out the Wax Museum (adult/child $8/4).

Tamworth Regional Gallery (☎ 02-6767 5459; www .tamworthregionalgallery.com.au; 466 Peel St; ⏰ 10am-5pm Tue-Fri, to 4pm Sat), in new purpose-built premises next to the library, has some interesting local bequeaths.

Oxley Marsupial Park (Endeavour Dr; ⏰ 8am-5pm) has over-friendly cockatoos and other native animals as well as barbecues and picnic shelters. The park joins the Kamilaroi walking track.

Grab a bottle of wine and follow jacaranda-lined White St to the very top, where you'll reach Oxley Scenic Lookout (Scenic Rd). This is the best seat in the house as the sun goes down over Tamworth and the surrounding Liverpool Ranges.

Festivals & Events

Held at the end of January, New England's biggest annual party, the Country Music Festival, lasts 10 days. There are over 800 acts, of which 75% are free. If you missed it, get along to Hats Off to Country Music in July.

Sleeping

Unless you book years in advance, you'll be lucky to find a bed or campsite during the festival when prices skyrocket. However, the council makes large areas of river land available to campers, where it's rough and rowdy but fun.

Tudor Hotel (☎ 02-6766 9564; 327 Peel St; s/d $50/60) Brash and ballsy but lots of fun, this hotel on the main street is the pick of the pubs in terms of accommodation, a feeling enhanced significantly after alcoholic beverages are consumed.

Good Companions Hotel (☎ 02-6766 2850; 9 Brisbane St; r from $90) Just around the corner from Peel St, the 'Goodies' is a cleverly renovated bright and funky hotel unrecognisable from its former self. The bar downstairs mixes cocktails. Bless.

Quality Hotel Powerhouse (☎ 02-6766 7000; www .qualityhotelpowerhouse.com.au; New England Hwy; r $150-190; ❄ ⚐) This large and comfortable hotel extends along the northern entry to town. It has all the mod cons including wi-fi and a flash restaurant called Monty's.

More options:

Austin Tourist Park (☎ 1800 826 967, 02-6766 2380; www.austintouristpark.com.au; 581 Armidale Rd; unpowered/powered sites $25/29, cabins $62-105; ❄ ⚐)

Tamworth YHA (☎ 02-6761 2600; www.yha.com.au; 169 Marius St; dm/d $26/58; ❄ ⚐) On a busy street but neat as a pin. Contacts for Jackaroo & Jillaroo School (opposite).

Eating

Filling Groovy (☎ 02-6766 5600; 412 Peel St; ⓨ breakfast & lunch) With an emphasis on healthy and filling, this bright little cafe runs the gamut of salad-stuffed baguettes, wraps and sandwiches that go down a treat with smoothies and fresh juices.

Tudor Hotel (☎ 02-6766 2930; 327 Peel St; mains $9-24; ⓨ lunch & dinner) Choose from the bistro menu downstairs where tables spill out onto the street or head upstairs (via the elevator) to the rooftop bar where the barbecue beckons.

Immrama (☎ 02-6761 3504; 306 Peel St; ⓨ breakfast & lunch) If the couches and coffee tables in this cafe don't help you kick back and relax then the long list of 'well-being' and 'relaxation' teas might. It also serves organic coffee, cake and a seasonal lunch menu.

SSS BBQ Barns (☎ 02-6762 2238; cnr Craigends Lane & New England Hwy; mains $22; ⓨ dinner) Decked out in all kinds of miscellany and memorabilia, this lively restaurant-bar is the perfect place to ingest a big bit of beef.

Entertainment

For live country music, check Thursday's *Northern Daily Leader*. Dress codes are stricter in Tamworth than elsewhere in the region – after all, cowboys never go out smelling like cow poop.

Imperial Hotel (☎ 02-6766 2613; www.imperialhotel.com.au; cnr Brisbane & Marius Sts; ⓨ 11am-late) This is where the young folk tend to hang out. You can catch local live acts on weekends in Studio 181.

Central Hotel (☎ 02-6766 2160; cnr Brisbane & Peel Sts; ⓨ 11am-1am) More of a laid-back affair, the Central Hotel, with its old-school, art deco exterior, pulls an older crowd and bands or a DJ on weekends. You'll make friends here whether you like it or not.

Getting There & Around

Qantas (☎ 13 13 13; www.qantas.com.au) flies to Sydney ($120, one hour).

Greyhound (☎ 1300 GREYHOUND/1300 473 946; www.greyhound.com.au) has daily services along the New England Hwy to Armidale ($50, 2½ hours) and through to Sydney ($110, 7¼ hours). **Keans** (☎ 02-6545 1945; www.keans.com.au) runs to Coffs Harbour, Port Macquarie and south to Scone once a week.

Tamworth Buslines (☎ 02-6762 3999; www.tamworthbuslines.com.au) operates extensively throughout town; stops are obvious.

AROUND TAMWORTH

Keen on a bit of mustering, milking, shearing, shoeing and even lamb slaughtering? **Leconfield Jackaroo & Jillaroo School** (☎ 02-6769 4328; 'Bimboola', Kootingal; 5-day course $625) will have you sorting the cowboys from the girls' blouses in no time.

THE FOSSICKERS WAY

You're now heading into gemstone territory. The **Fossickers Way** scenic route begins about 60km southeast of Tamworth at Nundle and continues through Manilla, 191km north to Warialda, then 124km east through Inverell (p213) to Glen Innes (p212). **Nundle** is a charming town coveted for its tranquil locale between the Great Dividing Range and Peel River. There are a couple of decent museums and some cute little old wares shops. The **visitor centre** (☎ 02-6769 3158; 96 Jenkins St) is part of Café Nundle.

ourpick **Peel Inn** (☎ 02-6769 3377; www.peelinn.com.au; s $35-60, d $65-80) is an excellent place for hunkering down in retro pub rooms after a slab of steak. Breakfast is included and dearer rooms score a bathroom. Meals are $12 to $28, and the inn is open for lunch and dinner. For a touch of romance **Jenkins St Guest House** (☎ 0439 693 111; www.jenkinsstguesthouse.com.au; 85 Jenkins St; r from $150) has wood floors and colonial homewares.

Out of town climb **Hanging Rock** for views to swoon over or get fishy at Arc-En-Ciel **Trout Farm** (☎ 02-6769 3665; www.rainbowtrout.com.au; Morrisons Gap Rd; ⓨ 10am-4pm Sun, Mon & Wed-Fri).

Australia's **national paragliding championships** are held in February and March at **Manilla**, 44km north of Tamworth. **Manilla Paragliding** (☎ 02-6785 6545; www.flymanilla.com) offers tandem flights from $160. The town itself is a glimmer of its former glory, but the three remaining pubs stand defiantly on the main street, and the area is also a fishing utopia. Grab your bait and licence, and a greasy takeaway from **North Manilla Store** (☎ 02-6785 1900), just north of the bridge, before heading to **Lake Keepit** (☎ 02-6769 7605) or north to **Warrabah National Park** (☎ 02-6773 7000; campsites per adult/child $5/3) for the big bites.

Settled in the 1830s, **Barraba**, with its old wide streets and elegant awnings, was put on the map during the gold-fever days of the late 1800s. Its location, on the Peel Fault line made for excellent fossicking. If the fever takes hold travel 3km north, turn right onto Woodsreef Rd, go 14km more and you will

NEW SOUTH WALES

come to **Ironbark Goldfield and Woodsreef Reserve**, where you can get cracking with the shovel, pick and pan. **Millie's Park Vineyard**, also north of town, has wines, a barbecue area and a nature walk. The **visitor centre** (☎ 02-6782 1255; www.barraba.org; 116 Queen St) has a leaflet detailing a Heritage Walk.

Andy's Backpackers (☎ 02-6782 1916; www .andysbackpackers.com.au; 98 Queen St; dm $25; 🖳) is the 'living room' of Barraba where drop-ins are welcome whether for a bed, meal, game of chess (Friday nights) or just a chat. Drop a few dollars on the counter and help yourself to a cold stubby! Andy can organise bushwalking, horse riding and fossicking tours.

Bingara, a small town straddling the Gwydir River, is a nice place to stop over. The **visitor centre** (☎ 02-6724 0066; www.bingara.nsw.gov.au; 74 Maitland St) is situated in the Roxy Theatre, a Greek-influenced, refurnished, art deco cinema. It is still used today for films, concerts and theatrical pursuits.

There are 3000 acres for horse riding in the area, but most people want to swim with the horses at **Gwydir River Trail Rides** (☎ 02-6724 1562; www.gwydirrivertrailrides.com.au; 17 Keera St; 2½hr trail ride $55, half-day canoe hire $30). For fair-dinkum Aussieness, complete the five-day Jackeroo/ Jillaroo Adventure ($580). You will come back able to ride a horse, crack a whip and brand cattle among other things.

The **Fossickers Way Motel** (☎ 02-6724 1373; www .bingaramotel.com.au; Finch St; s/d $60/80; 🌣) is one of the few hotels on the main road between Tamworth and Warialda. It's neat and comfortable, and sits just across the road from the Gwydir River. Take time out for a star gaze.

URALLA
pop 3847

This historic town, halfway between Brisbane and Sydney, is Captain Thunderbolt territory. The famed bushranger's six-year career included several episodes of holding up Uralla publicans and then spending the proceeds on beer. He was killed here in 1870 and is buried in the John St cemetery (see p210).

The **visitor centre** (☎ 02-6778 4496; www.uralla .com; 104 Bridge St) can point you in the right direction for fossicking. It has a cafe and internet access.

McCrossin's Mill Museum (☎ 02-6778 3022; cnr Bridge & Salisbury Sts; admission $4; 🌣 noon-5pm Mon-Fri, from 10am Sat & Sun) is where you can view Captain Thunderbolt's muzzle loader and

revolver and learn about the evolution of the cricket bat.

Uralla has a couple of antique and old-ware shops and the antiquarian **Burnet's Books** (☎ 02-6778 4682; www.burnetsbooks.com.au; 46 Bridge St; 🌣 9am-6pm).

An interesting loop goes southeast from Uralla to **Gostwyck**, an Australian sheep station that looks like an English country squire's hamlet, complete with a photogenic vine-covered chapel. From there, go via **Dangar Falls** up to Armidale.

Sleeping & Eating

Bushranger Motor Inn (☎ 02-6778 3777; www .bushrangermotorinn.com.au; 37 Bridge St; s/d $90/100; 🌣) This is a clean and comfortable motel with queen-sized beds. Ask for a room away from the main road through town and for a little extra cash, a spa.

Surfing Cow Café (Bridge St; 🌣 breakfast & lunch Wed-Sun) Established in 2008 'and still going strong' this cruisy cafe serves high-tin cakes, frittatas, gourmet pies ($5) and souvlaki lamb wraps ($9). The chai latte is quality, too.

Top Pub (☎ 02-6778 4110; www.toppuburalla.com .au; 23-27 Bridge St; mains $17-30; 🌣 lunch & dinner) At the top of the main street, this popular drinking hole has a great beer garden and the fabulous Funk Lush Room restaurant. Stay the night in a cheaper pub room or in the minimotel out the back with enormous, bold bathrooms and funky paintwork (singles $35 to $55, doubles $70).

Getting There & Away

Keans (☎ 02-6545 1945; www.keans.com.au) travels to Coffs Harbour, Port Macquarie and Tamworth twice a week. **Greyhound** (☎ 1300 GREYHOUND/1300 473 946; www.greyhound.com.au) travels to Tenterfield ($75, 3½ hours), Tamworth ($50, 1¼ hours) and Sydney ($125, 8½ hours). **Edwards** (☎ 02-6772 3116; www.edwardscoaches.com.au) does a school run to Armidale.

ARMIDALE
pop 21,451

Armidale's heritage buildings, gardens and moss-covered churches look like the stage-set for a period drama. This olde-worlde scenery coupled with spectacular autumn foliage plays a big part in attracting people to this regional centre blessed with some of Australia's best grazing country. It also boasts private schools and the New England University, recession-proof institutions that attract professionals and ensure arts and culture prosper. Excellent delis and coffee shops point to a food scene worthy of exploring, too.

The **visitor centre** (☎ 1800 627 736, 02-6772 4655; www.armidaletourism.com.au; 83 Marsh St) is at the bus station. The **library** (Faulkner St; ☺ 10am-6pm Mon-Fri, to 1pm Sat) has free internet access.

Sights & Activities

There are some elegant old buildings around the town centre. Pick up the heritage walking-tour pamphlet from the visitor centre.

At the southern edge of town the **New England Regional Art Museum** (Neram; ☎ 02-6772 5255; www.neram.com.au; Kentucky St; admission free; ☺ 10am-5pm Tue-Fri, 9am-4pm Sat & Sun) has a sizeable permanent collection and good contemporary exhibitions in pleasant grounds. It also houses the **Museum of Printing** (☺ 10.30am-3.30pm), a cafe and souvenir shop.

Next door, the **Aboriginal Cultural Centre & Keeping Place** (☎ 02-6771 3606; 128 Kentucky St; www.acckp.com.au; art exhibits $2-5; ☺ 9am-4pm Mon-Fri, 10am-2pm Sat & Sun) will broaden your perception of Indigenous art, and enable the kids to make their own with the help of a resident artist.

Grass-roots Eco-store (☎ 02-6771 4406; www.grassrootsecostore.com.au; 160 Rusden St ☺ 9am-5pm Tue-Fri, to 1pm Sat, to 3pm Mon) is full to the brim with produce to bring out the inner greenie: fair-trade toys, organic beauty products, sustainable clothing and other guilt-free goods.

Free **heritage bus tours** (☎ 1800 627 736; ☺ 10am) of Armidale depart from the visitor centre; bookings essential. The visitor centre also has details of heritage walks around town. Better still, get on a bike from the Armidale Bicycle Centre (p210).

Sleeping

There are motels around the visitor centre and on Barney St. Head out of town on the Glen Innes Rd to find doubles under $70.

Cameron Lodge Motor Inn (☎ 02-6772 2351; cnr Dangar & Barney Sts; s/d $70/80; ☒) It's hard to go past this faux Georgian hotel conveniently located just one block from the main strip, across the road from the park. The rooms are clean and well priced.

ourpick **Lindsay House** (☎ 02-6771 4554; www.lindsayhouse.com.au; 128 Faulkner St; d from $120; ☐) Immerse yourself in a past when beds were four-poster, ceilings were ornate, furniture was beautifully crafted and port was served

in the evening. This lovely old home is as restful and recuperative as it is grand. Breakfast is included.

Armidale Pines Motel (☎ 02-6772 0625; www.armidalepinesmotel.com; 141 Marsh St; r from $130; ☒ ☒) Slap bang in the middle of town, guests at this spick-and-span motel will reap the benefits of a fresh decor, new furnishings and a contemporary colour scheme. Long-haulers will appreciate the kitchenettes and shared guest laundry.

Also available:

Pembroke Tourist & Leisure Park & YHA (☎ 02-6772 6470; www.pembroke.com.au, www.yha.com.au; 39 Waterfall Way; unpowered/powered sites $20/25; dm $30, cabins from $62; ☐ ☒) Friendly and leafy with a hostel wing.

Smith House (☎ 02-6772 0652; www.smithhouse.com.au; 100 Barney St; s/d incl breakfast $45/65; ☐) Purpose-built as a university residence, this place has great facilities.

Eating & Drinking

Goldfish Bowl (☎ 02-6771 3271; Dangar St; mains $6-9; ☺ breakfast & lunch) So-called because caffeine-fiends queue up along Dangar St staring in at the baristas who make this well-executed little drinkery tick. (That's our take on it.)

ourpick **Bottega Café & Delicatezza** (☎ 02-6772 6262; 2/14 Moore St; ☺ breakfast & lunch Mon-Sat) A haunt not just for foodies, but for hungries too. This cafe has tables and shelves stocked with gourmet produce and a deli full of charcuterie and cheese. On the menu, breakfast doesn't get better than homemade baked beans with bacon and toast ($6).

White Bull (☎ 02-6772 3833; www.whitebullhotel.com; 117 Marsh St; ☺ lunch & dinner) Armidale's telltale blue-grey bricks are still in place but the White Bull hasn't been shy giving the interior a makeover. This is a pub worthy of a bit of lippy, with couches for chilling, a bar with boutique beers and a bistro menu that rises above the usual pub grub.

Getting There & Around

The airport is 5km southeast of town. **Qantas** (☎ 13 13 13; www.qantas.com.au) flies to Sydney ($120, 1¼ hours).

Greyhound (☎ 1300 GREYHOUND/1300 473 946; www.greyhound.com.au) runs to Glen Innes ($56, 1¼ hours), Tamworth ($50, 1½ hours) and Sydney ($125, 9½ hours). **Keans** (☎ 02-6545 1945; www.keans.com.au) runs to Coffs Harbour twice a week.

THUNDERBOLT

Born to an Irish convict in 1835, dead by 36. A typical timeline for your average Aussie bushranger. Supported by the poorer locals, their legends still ignite a sense of 'them-and-us' only possible in a population grown from a convict state. Frederick Ward, aka Thunderbolt, inspired the public imagination even further by escaping the inescapable Cockatoo Island Gaol in Sydney Harbour, not once but twice. Swimming to shore in Balmain, he survived the next six years by intercepting and robbing the wealthy aristocrats as they travelled past his bush hideouts throughout the Hunter Valley and New England. Stop at his many lookouts, inspect his hideout north of Tenterfield (the scene of his shooting), and mourn his passing over a beer at **Thunderbolt's Pub** (☎ 02-6778 4048; cnr Bridge & Hill Sts, Uralla) before checking out his grave on the edge of Uralla Cemetery on John St.

CountryLink (☎ 13 22 32; www.countrylink.info) runs daily to Tamworth ($14, two hours), Broadmeadow-Newcastle ($56, 5¾ hours) and Sydney ($67, 8¼ hours).

Edwards (☎ 02-6772 3116; www.edwardscoaches.com.au) runs a local bus service about town. For taxi services, call **Armidale Radio Taxis** (☎ 02-6771 1455). You can rent a bike from **Armidale Bicycle Centre** (☎ 02-6772 3718; 244 Beardy St; per hr/day $5.50/22).

THE WATERFALL WAY

If you're into touring, point the car in this direction. The **Waterfall Way** (www.visitwaterfallway.com.au) is an awe-inspiring scenic drive from inland Armidale to coasty Coffs Harbour – and what a ride. Not only does the journey traverse the gamut of spectacular World Heritage–listed national parks full of magnificent gorges, waterfalls and rare and endangered plants and animals, it passes through characteristic old towns including sleepy hillside Dorrigo and charm-your-socks-off Bellingen. You can easily drive the 168km to the coast in a day but, as this is one of the loveliest parts of NSW, why not take a few?

From Armidale, the road heads east 40km to **Wollomombi Falls**, one of Australia's highest. Tame paths lead to nearby lookouts and more strenuous multiday tracks head down into the wilderness gorges of **Oxley Wild Rivers National Park**. On the southwest edge of the park is **Apsley Falls**.

New England National Park, 12km off the Waterfall Way and on a good gravel road, is home to platypuses and glider possums and is one of the few core refuges in the world for the very rare, 80-million-year-old Antarctic Beech tree. Over 20km of bushwalking trails mostly begin from wheelchair-accessible **Point Lookout**. There are nearby cabins and sites at **Thungutti camping area** (☎ 02-6657 2309; campsite per adult/child $5/3, cabins $35-90).

Cathedral Rock National Park (☎ 02-6657 2309; campsite per adult/child $5/3) has precariously balanced huge boulders and wetland swamps perfect for bird-watching; camping is also available. Near Ebor township, **Ebor Falls** is a spectacular part of **Guy Fawkes River National Park**, deep in gorge country that's popular for canoeing and bushwalking. Access is from **Hernani**, 15km northeast of Ebor, then it's another 30km to **Chaelundi rest area** (☎ 02-6657 2309; campsite per adult/child $5/3) for camping and trailheads. There are great views from **Misty Creek Lookout**, or stop to have a look at the little old **graveyard** nearby.

Dorrigo
pop 2400

Set on the T-junction of two wider-than-wide streets, Dorrigo is a pretty little place, home to laid-back and affable locals. One gets the sense that this might be the next Bellingen in terms of food and wine, but it hasn't quite happened yet. The winding roads that lead here from Armidale, Bellingen and Coffs Harbour, however, reveal rainforests, mountain passes and waterfalls – some of the most dramatic scenery in NSW.

The **visitor centre** (☎ 02-6657 2486; 36 Hickory St) is run by helpful volunteers. The town's main attraction is the Dorrigo Rainforest Centre (see opposite) and **Dangar Falls**, which cascade over a series of rocky shelves before plummeting into a pristine gorge. A lookout provides Kodak moments, and you can swim beneath the falls if you have a yen for glacial bathing.

SLEEPING & EATING

Gracemere Grange (☎ 02-6657 2630; www.gracemeregrange.com.au; 325 Dome Rd; s/tw/d from $40/70/80) Out of town, this hospitable B&B has cosy upstairs bedrooms with slanted, attic-style roofs, and a double with bathroom and a skylight for views of the twinkling canopy. Breakfast is included.

Heritage Hotel Motel (☎ 02-6657 2016; cnr Cudgery & Hickory Sts; dm from $45, r with bathroom from $75) The charm of this almighty pub's exterior might not be echoed in the public bar or the rear dining room. Upstairs, however, the bedrooms, some with bathrooms, have been tastefully renovated to provide wholesome country hospitality. Double doors open onto the wide-girthed verandah for a sweeping main-street vista.

Dots on Cudgery (☎ 02-6657 2304; 15/12 Cudgery St; ✆ breakfast & lunch) Emu burgers, salt-and-pepper crocodile and kangaroo-loin fillet grace a menu devoted to gourmet bush food at this simple cafe on Dorrigo's main street. Aboriginal art, leather goods and knick-knacks also on sale.

GETTING THERE & AWAY
Twice a week **Keans** (☎ 02-6543 1322; www.keans .com.au) buses run to Bellingen, Coffs Harbour and Armidale.

Dorrigo National Park
The most accessible of Australia's World Heritage–listed rainforests, this national park is simply stunning, encompassing around 120 bird species and numerous walking tracks. The turn-off to the park is just south of Dorrigo. The **Rainforest Centre** (☎ 02-6657 2309; Dome Rd; ✆ 9am-4.30pm), at the park entrance, has information about the park's various ecosystems and can advise you on which walk to conquer given the weather and time of year. The **Lyrebird Link Track** is an easy 400m stroll but the highlight is the **Skywalk**, a walkway jutting over the rainforest canopy with jaw-dropping views of the ranges beyond. Those interested in dawn and dusk photography should note that the skywalk is accessible after hours.

Bellingen
pop 12,985

Buried in foliage on a hillside by the banks of the Bellinger River, this gorgeous town dances to the beat of its own bongo drum, attracting a populace of artists, academics and those drawn to a more organic lifestyle. Thick with gourmet cuisine and accommodation, Bellingen has just a hint of unpretentious chic, distinguishing it from the 'hippie haven' it was a decade or two ago.

INFORMATION
There's an excellent community website at www.bellingen.com.
Bellingen Book Nook (☎ 02-6655 9372; 25 Hyde St) Bookworm heaven.
Technicality (☎ 02-6655 1121; 7d Church St; per hr $6) Internet access.

SIGHTS & ACTIVITIES
First up, head to the magnificent **Hammond & Wheatley Emporium** (Hyde St), formerly an old department store. It has been beautifully restored and now houses a shop selling stylish duds, as well as an art gallery and cafe.

The historic **Old Butter Factory** (☎ 02-6655 2260; 1 Doepel St; ✆ 9.30am-5pm) houses craft shops, a gallery, opal dealers, a masseur and a great cafe.

From December to March a huge colony of flying foxes descends on **Bellingen Island**.

Bellingen Canoe Adventures (☎ 02-6655 9955; 4 Tyson St, Fernmount; day tours per adult/child $77/39) operates wonderful guided canoe tours on the Bellinger River, including full-moon tours (adult/child $22/17).

Heartland Didgeridoos (☎ 02-6655 9881; 2/25 Hyde St) sent the first didg into space. The Indigenous owners have a growing international reputation.

On the second and fourth Saturday of the month, the **Natural Produce Market** holds court at the Bellingen Showground. On the third Saturday of the month, the lively **Community Market** does the same at Bellingen Park.

FESTIVALS & EVENTS
Bellingen Jazz & Blues Festival (www.bellingenjazz festival.com.au) Features a strong line-up of jazz names in mid-August.
Global Carnival (www.globalcarnival.com) A three-day musical festival in early October.

SLEEPING
Bellingen YHA (☎ 02-6655 1116; www.yha.com.au; 2 Short St; dm/d $28/72, s/d campsites $15/25; 💻) This renovated two-storey weatherboard overlooking the pristine river valley attracts backpackers via the grapevine and then keeps them here with its tranquil, engaging atmosphere.

Federal Hotel (☎ 02-6655 1003; www.federalhotel.com .au; 77 Hyde St; dm/s/d $40/65/80; 📶) This beautiful old pub has refurbished weatherboard rooms that open onto a balcony with a sweeping view of the main street. Downstairs there is a lively pub scene, and Relish Bar & Grill (☎ 02-6655 1003; meals $14; open for lunch & dinner).

Maddefords Cottages (☎ 02-6655 9866; www.mad defordscottages.com.au; 224 North Bank Rd; d $145; 🗷) These polished mountain cabins have cosy interiors with country furnishings and big, sunny windows. Timber balconies overlook a private valley tumbling below, and your first night includes a sizeable brekkie hamper.

EATING & DRINKING

There are plenty of excellent options to choose from in this hedonistic town.

Tuckshop Bellingen (☎ 02-6655 0655; 63 Hyde St; 🕑 8am-5pm Mon-Fri, to 2pm Sat) If only all tuckshops were like this. This incy wincy cafe serves great coffee and a delicious line-up of breakfast and lunch options. Try the bacon, egg and roast tomato on Turkish ($10) or polenta with chargrilled vegetable, pesto, prosciutto and bocconcini ($4.50).

our pick Lodge 241 (☎ 02-6655 2470; Hyde St; 🕑 from 8.30am Wed-Sun) A pew at this excellent cafe is golden. Chess players gather here on a Sunday to soak up the atmosphere while locals line up along a communal table and imbibe great coffee. The menu ranges from soup of the day with sourdough ($9) to rocket, basil, pesto and ricotta gnocchi ($16).

No 2 Oak St (☎ 02-6655 9000; 2 Oak St; mains $30-35; 🕑 dinner Wed-Sat) Housed in a timber cottage, this award-winning restaurant specialises in Australian cuisine with a French twist – slow-cooked Burrawong rabbit with sweet potato, mushroom, apple and braising jus for example.

More options:

Bellingen Gelato Bar (☎ 02-6655 1870; 101 Hyde St; 🕑 10am-6pm) A 1950s-America-styled cafe with sensational homemade ice cream and outdoor tables.

Little Red Kitchen (☎ 02-6655 1551; 111 Hyde St; 🕑 5-9pm Wed-Mon) A pizza and pasta shop with gourmet toppings.

GETTING THERE & AWAY

Keans (☎ 02-6543 1322; www.keans.com.au) has twice-weekly services to Coffs Harbour, Dorrigo and Armidale.

Around Bellingen

There are some beautiful spots waiting to be discovered in the surrounding valleys. The most accessible is the hamlet of **Gleniffer**, 10km

to the north and clearly signposted from North Bellingen. There's a good swimming hole in the **Never Never River** behind the small Gleniffer School of Arts at the crossroads. Then you can drive around Loop Rd, which takes you to the foot of the New England tableland – a great drive for which words don't do justice.

If you want to sweat, tackle the **Syndicate Ridge Walking Trail**, a strenuous 15km-long, seven- to eight-hour walk from Gleniffer to the Dorrigo plateau following the route of a tramline once used by timber cutters. There's a very steep 1km climb on the way up. To get to the start, take the Gordonville Rd, turning into Adams Lane soon after crossing the Never Never River. The walking track commences at the first gate.

NORTH OF ARMIDALE

Businesses with names such as Glen This and Wee That hint at the Scottish heritage of **Glen Innes** (population 5944) – and a Caledonian-culture-consumed populace. It's not surprising though, as even the architecture on the main street has an earthy northern ambience. The Tudor-style **visitor centre** (☎ 02-6730 2400; www.gle ninnestourism.com) is on the New England Hwy.

Frustrated by the lack of pagan activity back in the Stone and Bronze Ages, the town went about erecting its own impressive **Standing Stones**, off the eastern end of the Gwydir Hwy. Devonshire Tea is served in the little Crofters Cottage.

The town centre is full of heritage buildings. The **Land of the Beardies History House** (☎ 02-6732 1035; cnr West Ave & Ferguson St; adult/child $6/1; 🕑 10am-noon & 1-4pm) fills an old hospital to bursting with eclectic artefacts of old Glen Innes. If you fancy saddling up, take a **pub crawl on horseback** (☎ 02-6732 1599; www.pubcrawl sonhorseback.com.au; Bullock Mountain Homestead; 2-/4-day ride $395/1480) or bag a bed at **Bullock Mountain Homestead** (www.bullockmountainhomestead.com; s/d $45/80), where they offer rides ($30 per hour) and fossicking tours ($10).

The **Australian Celtic Festival** (www.australiancelt icfestival.com), held April-May each year, features many grown men in medieval dress poking each other with big sticks (in the jousting competition). But the **Beardies Festival** (www .beardiesfestival.com) at the end of October is where you will see the beard-growing competition – open to both men and women.

There are several motels along the highway. The **Lodge** (☎ 02-6732 2922; 160 Church St; r with/without air-con $104/94; (⊠) has a Tudor facade with newly renovated rooms. Alternatively, **Kings Plains Castle** (☎ 02-6733 6808; Kings Plain Rd; ☯ Thu-Sun) has taken the Scottish theme to great heights. Phone ahead for accommodation prices.

In an old butcher shop fit-out, the **Tasting Room** (☎ 02-6732 6500; 296 Grey St; ☯ 8.30am-5pm Mon-Fri, to 2pm Sat) does breakfast and gourmet sandwiches.

Dramatic, forested and wild, **Gibraltar Range National Park** (per car per day $7) and **Washpool National Park** (per car per day $7) lie south and north of the Gwydir Hwy, about 80km east of Glen Innes on the road to Grafton. There are two camping area; **Mulligans** (adult/child $10/5) is near Little Dandahra Creek, which is ideal for swimming. Of the many walks, the 100km **World Heritage Walk** is a standout.

Inverell, on the Gwydir Hwy, might not be that aesthetically fabulous but the sapphires for which the area is famed certainly are. You can pick up a map of the area's fossicking sites at the **visitor centre** (☎ 02-6728 8161; www.inverell -online.com.au; Campbell Station). All fossicked out? Sample the olive oil at **Gwydir Grove** (☎ 02-6721 2727; 35 Brissett St; ☯ 8.30am-5pm Mon-Fri).

Built on an extinct volcano, **Blair Athol Estate** (☎ 02-6722 4288; www.babs.com.au/blairathol; Warialda Rd; d from $130) has stunning grounds peppered with a rich mix of flora from Himalayan cedars to boabs. Breakfast is included.

Further northwest, **Kwiambal National Park** (admission free), pronounced kigh-*am*-bal, sits at the junction of the Macintyre and Severn Rivers. Largely undiscovered, it is an important conservation area for the tumbledown gum and Caley's ironbark.

TENTERFIELD
pop 3172

At the junction of the New England and Bruxner Hwys, Tenterfield is the hub of a region boasting a smattering of characteristic villages and 10 national parks. In the town itself you can have fun wandering around historic buildings and getting into the gourmet cuisine.

The **visitor centre** (☎ 02-6736 1082; www.tenterfield .com; 157 Rouse St) has bushwalking guides and can book tours to nearby national parks.

There is plenty of work fruit picking on farms near town from October through to May. To pick stone fruit, cherries, tomatoes and grapes, contact Barbara at **Tenterfield Lodge & Caravan Park** (☎ 02-6736 1477).

The **Tenterfield Saddler** (☎ 02-3252 9549; 123 High St; ☯ 10am-4pm), celebrated by Peter Allen (who was born here) in his eponymous song, is still open for business. About 12km out on the road north to Liston lies **Thunderbolt's Hideout**, where bushranger Captain Thunderbolt did just that. On your way check out the **Tenterfield Weather Rock** near the baths.

The king of 4WD and motorbike parks is **Rover Park** (☎ 02-6737 6862; www.roverpark.com.au; Rover Park Rd; campsites $30, on-site vans $60, bunkhouse $70), 35km east of Tenterfield on Casino Rd. It has more than 300km of 4WD tracks to traverse.

Bald Rock National Park (per car per day $7) is 29km northeast of Tenterfield. You can hike to the top of Australia's largest exposed granite monolith (which looks like a stripy little Uluru) and **camp** (adult/child $10/5) near the base.

Motels line Rouse St leading south out of town or try **Deloraine B&B** (☎ 02-6736 2777; 14 Clarence St; r from $140), a characteristic old heritage roadhouse with some lovely antique-filled rooms. The owners provide dinner for latecomers ($15) and breakfast is included. **Tenterfield Lodge & Caravan Park** (☎ 02-6736 1477; www.tenterfieldbiz.com/tenterfieldlodge; 2 Manners St; unpowered/powered sites $14/19, dm from $23, vans $35, cabins $50-65; (🖳)) is a friendly place with a range of accommodation.

Kurrajong Downs Winery (☎ 02-9736 4590; www .kurrajongdownswines.com; Kurrajong Downs Rd; ☯ 9am-4pm Thu-Mon) sits on a lovely elevated plot. Its wide verandahs and wine-striped outlook make a good spot for coffee and cake or lunch.

Buses leave town from the **Community Centre** (Manners St). **Greyhound** (☎ 1300 GREYHOUND/1300 473 946; www.greyhound.com.au) runs to Tamworth ($81, 4¾ hours) and Sydney ($130, 12 hours). **Northern Rivers Buslines** (☎ 02-6626 1499; www.nrbuslines.com.au) has buses to Casino and Lismore ($33).

CountryLink (☎ 13 22 32; www.countrylink.info) buses run south to Glen Innes ($12, 1¼ hours), and to Armidale ($31, 2¾ hours) where you can change for Sydney ($67, 8¼ hours).

TENTERFIELD TO CASINO

The winding road to Casino leads through the quietly beautiful Upper Clarence cattle country. The rolling hills are easy on the eyes, even if dinner time is hard on the grazing inhabitants.

Clarence River Wilderness Lodge (☎ 02-6665 1337; www.clarenceriver.com; Paddy's Flat Rd; campsites from $5, bushman huts $75, cabins $180) is up a rough but scenic road 30km from Tabulam. It has a beautiful river gorge with great swimming, plus bushwalking, platypus-spotting, canoe and kayak expeditions, and gold fossicking. Lights are solar-powered, hot water is wood-fired, and guests need to bring bedding, food and drinks.

Richmond Range National Park contains some of the best-preserved old-growth rainforest in NSW. The 15,712-hectare park is part of a World Heritage–listed preserve showing-off what this part of Australia looked like before settlement. There is a good two-hour circular walk through the foliage from the Cambridge Plateau picnic area (some sections are steep) and basic campsites at **Peacock Creek** (campsites adult/child $5/3). The park is 45km west of Casino via the Bruxner Hwy (which goes to Tenterfield); turn north onto Cambridge Plateau Dr.

Casino (population 11,186) celebrates its **beef festival** (www.casinobeefweek.com.au) in late May and early June, but otherwise it's really just a useful transport hub.

CENTRAL WEST

The Central West's relative proximity to Sydney and its population of eager tree-changers, weekend-awayers and holiday-homers has no doubt given many of the agricultural cities and towns just beyond the Blue Mountains a leg-up.

The university city of Bathurst is also a rev-head's haven, Orange has an inordinate number of lauded chefs and restaurants, Mudgee is a small town with a big nose for wine, and Dubbo has joined the milieu with a brand new cultural centre.

The stately buildings, grandiose wide streets, parks, and vivid and well-tended English gardens align these cities with a past built on gold-mining and bushranger folk-lore, but this history is best explored in the smaller hill towns where wide verandahs and old pubs are often coupled with a decent cafe or restaurant and local B&B.

Further west, Forbes and Parkes were united by the radio telescope made famous by the movie *The Dish* until Elvis fever gave the latter town something of its own to focus on. Drive further west and the rolling agri-cultural heartland transforms into vast plains and finally the harsher outback soil of the far west.

BATHURST
pop 37,508

There are two sides to Bathurst. Primarily, it is Australia's oldest inland settlement, boasting European trees, a cool climate and a beautiful, manicured central square where formidable Victorian buildings can snap you back to the past. But it's also the bastion of Australian motor sport, hosting numerous events.

The **visitor centre** (☎ 02-6332 1444; www.visit bathurst.com.au; Kendall Ave) is helpful. Internet access is free at the **Bathurst Library** (☎ 02-6332 2130; 70-78 Keppel St).

Sights & Activities

See *Tyrannosaurus rex*, Australia's only com-plete skeleton, at the **Australian Fossil & Mineral Museum** (☎ 02-6331 5511; www.somervillecollection .au; 224 Howick St; adult/child/family $8/4/20; 10am-4pm Mon-Sat, 11am-2pm Sun). You'll also see the inter-nationally renowned Somerville Collection and over 6000 fossils from every period of the earth's history. It's fantastic.

The **Bathurst Regional Art Gallery** (☎ 02-6333 6555; 70-78 Keppel St; admission free; 10am-5pm Tue-Sat, 11am-2pm Sun) has a dynamic collection of work, featuring local artists as well as exciting touring exhibitions.

The **courthouse** (Russell St), from 1880, is the most impressive of Bathurst's historical build-ings and houses the small **Historical Museum** (☎ 02-6330 8455; adult/child/family $3/2/8; 10am-4pm Tue, Wed & Sat, 11am-2pm Sun).

Ben Chifley, prime minister from 1945 to 1949, lived in Bathurst, and the mod-est **Chifley Home** (☎ 02-6332 1444; 10 Busby St; adult/child/family $7/4.50/18; 10am-2pm Sat-Mon) is on display.

Rev-heads will enjoy the **National Motor Racing Museum** (☎ 02-6332 1872; Pit Straight; adult/ child/family $8/3/17; 9am-4.30pm). The 6.2km **Mt Panorama Motor Racing Circuit** is the venue for the **Bathurst Motorsport Spectacular** in October. You can drive around the circuit, but only up to an unthrilling 60km/h.

Perhaps a little more hair-raising, **Panorama Trike Tours** (☎ 02-6331 9629, 0422 182 020; reggiet rickes@bigpond.com; 3 passengers from $10) takes punt-ers on an open-air Chopper 4 ride around the circuit. Helmets and leather provided.

Sleeping

Commercial Hotel (☎ 02-6331 2712; http:// commercialhotel.6te.net; 135 George St; dm/s/d $25/35/55) This quaint old pub in the heart of town has a cosy bar downstairs and small but inviting rooms upstairs, opening onto a verandah.

Russells (☎ 02-6332 4686; www.therussells.com.au; 286 William St; s/d/tr $75/100/140; 🏊) This quaint cottage accommodation comes with a cooked breakfast and warm hospitality. It is set in a lovely garden close to the centre.

Accommodation Warehouse (☎ 02-6332 2801; www.accomwarehouse.com.au; 121a Keppel St; s/d $80/116) A soaring, historic brick building with arched windows and Juliet balconies, this place has a selection of lovely self-contained apartments, or stylish rooms with shared kitchen.

Big 4 Bathurst Holiday Park (☎ 02-6331 8286; www.bathurstholidaypark.com.au; Sydney Rd; 2-person powered sites/cabins from $29/65; 🏊) A well-equipped park with a cute, red-topped, corrugated-iron colonial cabin is the main caravan and camping option. Prices increase when the races are on.

Eating

Yummy Noodle (☎ 02-6331 3018; 96 William St; meals $9-11; 🕐 lunch & dinner) A variety of laksas, rice and noodles packaged ideally for eating in the park across the road.

our pick **Church Bar** (☎ 02-6334 2300; 1 Ribbon Gang Lane; mains $14-20; 🕐 lunch & dinner Tue-Sat, lunch Sun) This restored 1850s church now attracts punters praying to a different deity: the god of wood-fired pizza. The soaring ceilings and verdant courtyard off William St make it one of the region's best eating and socialising venues.

Ellie's Café (☎ 02-6332 1707; 108 William St; mains $15; 🕐 breakfast & lunch daily, dinner Thu-Sat) Ellie's patrons spill out onto the main street below the Royal Hotel. The lunch menu is popular with Bathurst's suited set seeking sunshine and coffee.

Getting There & Away

Selwood's (☎ 02-6362 7963; www.selwoods.com.au) buses leave daily for Sydney (1¼ hours) from **Acropole Café** (cnr William & Howick Sts). **CountryLink** (☎ 13 22 32; www.countrylink.info) trains go to Sydney ($38, five hours) and Dubbo ($19, two hours). CountryLink's XPT also stops here on the daily Sydney ($32, 3½ hours) and Dubbo ($29, three hours) service.

Rex (☎ 13 17 13; www.regionalexpress.com.au) flies to Sydney ($100, 45 minutes).

AROUND BATHURST

The region north of Bathurst is good driving territory with beautiful scenery, parks and reserves and a handful of quaint little towns – such as **O'Connell**, **Sofala** and **Hill End** – that owe their existence to the gold-mining days. While the populations have long since dwindled, the remaining old timbered houses, pubs and for that matter, locals, make for hospitable pit stops. For longer stays there are two **NPWS camping grounds** (☎ 02-6337 8206; unpowered sites adult/child $7/4, powered sites $10/5) and the **Royal Hotel** (☎ 02-6337 8261; Beyers Ave; r from $40) in Hill End. The **Old Sofala Gaol & Cottage** (☎ 02-6337 7064; www.oldsofala gaol.com.au; Barkly St; s/d $65/70) is a fun option.

The famous **Abercrombie Caves** (☎ 02-6368 8603; self-guided/guided tours $13/16; 🕐 9am-5pm) is south of Bathurst. The complex has one of the world's largest natural tunnels, the Grand Arch. The Jenolan Caves (p161) are also in the region. **Jenolan Adventure** (☎ 1300 763 311; www.jenolancaves.org.au) hosts caving and abseiling tours throughout the 40km of multilevelled caves and passages. There's **accommodation** (☎ 02-6368 8603; campsites per person/family $10/24, standard/deluxe cabins $50/90) near the cave, with good facilities nearby.

ORANGE

pop 33,182

There might be pears, apples and stone fruit aplenty in the surrounding orchards, but it just so happens the town was named after Prince William of Orange. It's now a dedicated food-and-wine hub with four distinct seasons – and a food festival for each. The city's parks and gardens are a kaleidoscope of colours throughout the year, with cold winters bringing occasional snowfalls. Bush poet AB 'Banjo' Paterson was born here.

Information

DNA Coffee (☎ 02-6363 1400; Orange City Centre, 190 Anson St; per hr $5) Internet access.

Orange visitor centre (☎ 02-6393 8226, 1800 069 466; www.orange.nsw.gov.au; Byng St) Local produce, history and information.

SEASONAL WORK

The autumn apple-, cherry- and grape-picking season lasts for about six weeks. The **National Harvest Labour Information Service** (☎ 1800 062 332; www.jobsearch.gov.au/harvesttrail) can help you find work or ask at the visitor centre for orchards with accommodation.

Sights & Activities

Next to the visitor centre, **Orange Regional Gallery** (☎ 02-6393 8136; Civic Sq; admission free; ☽ 10am-5pm Tue-Sat, 1-4pm Sun) has an ambitious, varied program of exhibitions and some Australian masters.

The **Botanic Gardens** (☎ 02-6361 5186; Kearneys Dr; admission free; ☽ 7.30am-dusk) was established in 1982 to preserve the native woodlands of the area. It's on Clover Hill (with good views between the trees), 2km north of the city.

Orange has a reputation for distinctive cool-climate wines, with many award-winning vineyards. Get a map and summary for each vineyard from the visitor centre. **Word of Mouth Wines** (☎ 02-6365 3509; www.wordofmouthwines .com.au; Pinnacle Rd; ☽ 9am-5pm Fri-Sun) is highly recommended; after visiting pop across the road to **Brangayne of Orange** (☎ 02-6365 3229; 837 Pinnacle Rd; www.brangayne.com; ☽ 9am-5pm).

Australia's first real gold rush took place at **Ophir**, 27km north of Orange along mostly unsealed roads. It's still popular with fossickers today. Southwest of Orange, **Mt Canobolas** forms part of an extensive volcanic chain stretching 3000km along Australia's eastern seaboard. The flora and fauna, waterfalls, picnic areas, spectacular views, walking trails and bike paths make this great exploratory territory. Kayaks are available for hire on **Lake Canobolas** (☎ 0428 645 301, 02-6364 5301; Lake Canobolas Rd; per hr from $10; ☽ dawn-dusk).

Festivals & Events

Testament to its 'foodie' reputation, Orange now has four seasonal **festivals** (www.tasteorange .com.au) where the region's producers make star appearances: **Slow Summer**, in early February, **F.O.O.D Week** (www.orangefoodweek.com.au) in mid-April, **Frost Fest** in early August and **Wine Week** in late October.

Local produce can be foraged at the popular **farmer's market** (☎ 0425 259 350; Orange Regional Gallery North Ct, ☽ 8.30am-noon) held on the second Saturday of the month – if it's wet the market's in the Orange Showground.

Sleeping & Eating

Duntryleague Guesthouse (☎ 02-6362 3822; www.dun tryleague.com.au; Woodward St; s/d hotel $100/120, B&B from $120/140; ☒) Found at the end of a rambling tree-lined drive, this grand mansion (1876) has capacious rooms with four-poster beds as well as simpler hotel versions. It's right on the golf course.

Town Square Motel (☎ 02-6369 1444; 246 Anson St; s/d $105/118; ☒) Just off the main street this clean and comfortable hotel, painted white and green, has fluffy pillows, doonas and a chock-full mini bar. The adjoining **Balcony Restaurant** (mains $15-28) does a great eggplant parmigiana and is one of the few venues open on Sunday night.

Black Sheep Inn (☎ 02-6369 0662; www.blacksheep inn.com.au; 91 Heifer Station Ln; s/d $150/195) Off Forbes Rd, the owners of this quirky B&B have turned the corrugated-iron sheep shed into smart sleeping quarters. Breakfast is three courses. Prices go up on weekends.

our pick Union Bank (☎ 02-6361 4441; cnr Sale & Byng Sts; mains $18-27; ☽ lunch & dinner Mon-Sat, lunch Sun) This upmarket and rather groovy cellar door and wine bar has more than 500 wine labels, any of which can be enjoyed with a cheese platter or antipasto plate featuring trout tartare with pickled cucumber and tuna-stuffed baby peppers.

Hotel Canobolas (☎ 02-6362 2444; cnr Summer St & Lords Pl; ☽ 10am-late) A good pub for a relaxed beer, with park views and windows opening onto the footpath. The bar snacks are good value.

The Orange region is known for its many 'chef's hat' award-winning restaurants:

Lolli Redini (☎ 02-6361 7748; 48 Sale St; mains $30; ☽ dinner Tue-Sat) Italian.

Selkirks (☎ 02-6361 1179; 179 Anson St; 2/3 courses $66/77; ☽ lunch Fri, dinner Tue-Sat) In a lovely old sandstone house, boasting local and seasonal produce.

Tonic (☎ 02-6366 3811; cnr Pym & Victoria Sts, Millthorpe; ☽ breakfast & lunch Sat & Sun, dinner Thu-Sat) Modern Australian in a cute out-of-the-way location.

Getting There & Away

Rex (☎ 13 17 13; www.regionalexpress.com.au) flies to Sydney ($135, one hour). The airport is 13km southeast of Orange. Locally based **Selwood's** (☎ 02-6362 7963; www.selwoods.com.au) buses leave daily for Sydney (four hours) from the train station and twice midweekly to Bathurst (45 minutes) from **Hotel Canobolas** (248 Summer St). **CountryLink** (☎ 13 22 32; www.countrylink.info) trains go to Sydney ($38, five hours) and Dubbo ($19, two hours).

CANOWINDRA

pop 1511

The teeny town of Canowindra, 32km north of Cowra, is the perfect laid-back weekender. It has a heritage-listed main street where a surprising number of art galleries make for a leisurely meander.

The **Old Vic Inn** (☎ 02-6344 1009; www.oldvicinn.com
.au; 56 Gaskill St; r with/without bathroom $129/90) serves
as the town's information hub, with a restaurant and B&B accommodation. For a little
more space and romance, **Everview Retreat**
(☎ 02-6344 3116; www.everview.com.au; 72 Cultowa
Lane; d from $210; 🌀) has luxury stone cottages
equipped with spas, DVDs, the works.

The town is the self-proclaimed ballooning
capital of Australia. **Aussie Balloontrek** (☎ 02-6361
2552; www.aussieballoontrek.com.au; Nanami Lane; flights from
$160) can get you high with a barbecue-and-
champagne breakfast. **Tom's Waterhole Winery**
(☎ 02-6344 1819; www.tomswaterhole.com.au; Longs
Corner Rd; 🕑 10am-4pm) has a cellar door and a
cafe serving ploughman's lunches. **Balloon Joy
Flights** (www.balloonjoyflights.com.au) operates from
the same establishment.

Taste Canowindra (☎ 02-6344 2332; www.taste
canowindra.com.au; 42 Ferguson St; 🕑 10am-4pm) hosts
regional wine tastings, art-and-craft exhibitions, and the occasional live band. Coffee
and cake is served all day.

COWRA
pop 10,457

History buffs will be prone to various states
of excitability in Cowra, a town with a unique
story. Ever since August 1944, when 1000
Japanese prisoners broke out of a prisoner-of-
war camp here (231 of them died, along with
four Australians), Cowra has aligned itself
with Japan and the cause of world peace.

The **visitor centre** (☎ 02-6342 4333; www.cowratour
ism.com.au; Olympic Park, Mid Western Hwy; 🕑 9am-4pm)
shows an excellent nine-minute holographic
film about the break-out scene. **Ideal Tours**
(☎ 02-6341 3350; 1 Kendal St) runs tours of wineries and other local attractions.

The **Cowra Cork & Fork** (www.cowrashow
.com) wine and food festival, held in early
November, brings all the region's produce
to the one place on the one day.

Sights & Activities

Built as a token of Cowra's connection with
Japanese POWs (but with no overt mention
of the war or the break-out), the **Japanese
Garden** (☎ 02-6341 2233; Binni Creek Rd; adult/child $9/5;
🕑 8.30am-5pm) and the attached cultural cen-
tre, with its collection of *ukiyo-e* paintings
depicting everyday events in pre-industrial
Japan, are well worth visiting. A **sakura matsuri** (cherry-blossom festival) is held around
September/October.

The Australian and Japanese **war cemeteries** are 5km south of town; many of those
who died were very young. A nearby **memorial** marks the site of the break-out, and you
can still see the camp foundations.

One of the darkest places for stargazing
in all of Australia is **Darby Falls Observatory**
(☎ 02-6345 1900; Mt McDonald Rd; adult/child $10/7;
🕑 7-10pm, 8.30-11pm summer). From town, follow
Wyangala Dam Rd for 22km and turn onto
Mt McDonald Rd, then follow the signs.

The **Cowra Regional Art Gallery** (☎ 02-6340 2190;
www.cowraartgallery.com.au; 77 Darling St; admission free;
🕑 10am-4pm Tue-Sat, 2-4pm Sun). Displays a permanent collection and exhibitions.

In the heart of town, the **Mill** (☎ 02-6341
4141; www.windowrie.com.au; 6 Vaux St; 🕑 11am-5pm) is
Cowra's oldest building, where the millstone
first turned in 1861. The region's Chardonnay
has tickled many a palate; enjoy it here with
a cheese platter. On the edge of town 4km
along Boorowa Rd, the **Quarry** (☎ 02-6342 3650;
🕑 lunch Tue-Sun, dinner Fri & Sat) cellar-door restaurant is set amid the vineyards, and the cuisine
is well regarded.

Sleeping & Eating

Breakout Motel (☎ 02-6342 6111; www.breakoutmotel
.com.au; 181 Kendal St; s/d from $95/98; 🌀 🖳) This is
a modern and quite delightful place, right in
the centre, with atmospheric slate, blue and
beige decor.

Vineyard Motel (☎ 02-6342 3641; www.vineyard
motel.com.au; Chardonnay Rd; s/d from $105/115, d with spa
$140; 🌀 🖳) The Lachlan Valley vineyard views
from this boutique hotel, 4km from town, are
so mesmerising that the plastic flowers and
lace doilies can be forgiven.

La-Vita (☎ 02-6341 1511; 127 Kendal St; 🕑 breakfast &
lunch) This place is on the main street with market umbrellas and table settings in the front
courtyard. The menu includes hearty soups,
quiche, focaccias and good espresso coffee.

Apsara (☎ 02-6342 2212; 69 Kendal St; mains $9-17;
🕑 lunch & dinner Mon-Sat) It might look like one
of the many takeaway shops on the main
street, but Apsara serves up a mean selection
of Thai dishes in a casual setting. The Thai
green curry with basil is a goer.

our pick Neila (☎ 02-6341 2188; 5 Kendal St; mains
$29; 🕑 dinner Thu-Sat) On Cowra's main drag, this
small gem, with a contemporary Australian
menu, is a tribute to the quality of food in
the region. Opening times can be erratic so
book ahead.

Getting There & Away

CountryLink (☎ 13 22 32; www.countrylink.info) has daily services to Sydney ($43, 5¾ hours).

YOUNG
pop 12,035

Come to Young in spring and you'll be welcomed by the dazzling pink, red and green hues of the region's cherry orchards. On the edge of the western slopes of the Great Dividing Range, this is Australia's 'cherry capital'. Prunes are also an important local industry, but 'prune capital' doesn't have quite the same ring.

The **visitor centre** (☎ 02-6382 3394; Lovell St) is housed in the old railway station and has a list of orchards where you can pick your own fruit. The cherry harvest is in November and December. In January other stone fruits are harvested and in February the prune harvest begins. The **Ready Workforce office** (☎ 02-6382 4728; 145 Boorowa St) can help you find fruit-picking work.

There are about 15 small vineyards in the area producing award-winning cool-climate wines, including the excellent **Lindsay's Woodonga Hill** (☎ 02-6382 2972; 1101 Cowra Rd; ❨ 9am-5pm), northeast of Young, and **Grove Estate Wines** (☎ 02-6382 6999; www.groveestate.com.au; Murringo Rd; ❨ 10am-4pm).

The **Lambing Flat Folk Museum** (☎ 02-6382 2248; Campbell St; adult/child $4/1; ❨ 10am-4pm) displays artefacts from the goldfields, including the remarkable 'Roll Up' banner carried by European miners in protest against the Chinese in 1861. The Sydney Chinese community raised money to build the **Chinese Tribute Garden** (Pitstone Rd; admission free), a tranquil spot featuring a pagoda and dam, to remember the contribution the Chinese miners made.

Young hosts the **Cherry Festival** on the first weekend in December. For fruit-inspired produce, head to **JD's Jam Factory** (☎ 02-6382 4060; Lot 1, Grenfell Rd).

Young Affordable Accommodation (☎ 02-6382 2444; Campbell St & Olympic Hwy; s/d/f $33/48/65) is a decent option for penny pinchers. It has discount rates for longer term 'cherry pickers'.

Colonial Motel (☎ 02-6382 2822; Olympic Hwy; s/d/tw from $79/89/97) has decent-sized, clean and comfortable rooms, some of them with spa baths. The owners are exceptionally welcoming.

Young Tourist Park (☎ 02-6382 2190; Zouch St; camp-sites per adult $25, cabins $65; ☒) is a comfortable camping option that has drive-through sites with bathrooms for caravans.

On the main street **Provedore Café** (☎ 02-6382 7255; 126 Boorowa St; ❨ breakfast & lunch Mon-Sat) serves eggs Benedict, toasted sandwiches and a mean cappuccino in a pleasant atmosphere. Or try **Café de Jour** (☎ 02-6382 1413; cnr Lovell & Zouch Sts; mains $21-29; ❨ lunch & dinner Tue-Sat), a lovely restaurant run by an amiable couple.

our pick **Zouch** (☎ 02-6382 2775; www.zouch.com.au; 26 Zouch St; ❨ lunch & dinner Mon & Thu-Sat) is great for somethingmore gourmet. It's in the old hall across the road from Café de Jour and features exceptional decor and a lauded menu.

FORBES
pop 9361

You might recognise Forbes from the popular Australian film *The Dish*, where much of the filming took place? Maybe not. Perched on the banks of the Lachlan River and Forbes Lake, Forbes is spectacularly pretty, retaining much of its 19th-century flavour thanks to its beautifully restored buildings.

The **visitor centre** (☎ 02-6852 4155; cnr Newell Hwy & Union St) is inside the old train station and has local art exhibits and a DVD about local legend Ben Hall, a landowner who became Australia's first official bushranger. He was betrayed and shot near Forbes and is buried in the town's cemetery; people still miss him, if the notes on his grave are anything to go by. The **Forbes Museum** (☎ 02-6851 6600; adult/child $2/1; ❨ 2-4pm) houses Ben Hall relics and other memorabilia.

The **Bushrangers Hall of Fame** (☎ 02-6851 1881; 135 Lachlan St; adult/child $5/3; ❨ 10am-6pm), in the Albion Hotel, has guided tours of old underground tunnels that were used to transfer gold from banks into waiting coaches. Balcony rooms with shared bathrooms are available upstairs (doubles $25).

our pick **Mezzanine Style** (☎ 02-6851 4056; 23 Rankin St; ❨ breakfast & lunch) has an unimpressive exterior but the spacious interior with a mezzanine level is relaxed with great food such as a Portuguese chicken burger or teriyaki steak sandwich.

PARKES
pop 14,846

Parkes was content being known as the home of the radio telescope made famous by the film *The Dish*, until hundreds of Elvis impersonators started coming to town. Now the King's birthday is the focal weekend for this sleepy town. The **visitor centre** (☎ 02-6863 8860;

www.visitparkes.com.au; cnr Newell Hwy & Thomas St) is in Kelly Reserve.

Along the Newell Hwy on the Dubbo side of town, the **Sir Henry Parkes Museum** (☎ 02-6862 3509; admission $5; 🕙 10am-3.30pm Mon-Sat) is more like someone's house than a traditional exhibition space. Walk through the 'moat cottage', a replica of Sir Henry Parkes' birthplace.

The **Radio Telescope**, built by the Commonwealth Scientific & Industrial Research Organisation (CSIRO) in 1961, is 6km east of the Newell Hwy, about 20km north of Parkes. As one of the world's most powerful telescopes it has helped Australian radio astronomers become leaders in their field, and brought pictures of the *Apollo 11* moon landing to an audience of 600 million people.

Although the telescope is off-limits, you can get close enough for a good look, and the **Dish CSIRO visitor centre** (☎ 02-6861 1777; www .csiro.au/parkesdish; admission free; 🕙 8.30am-4.15pm) has hands-on displays and visual effects; 3-D films (adult/child $6.50/5) screen throughout the day.

The **Parkes Elvis Festival** (www.parkeselvisfestival .com.au), on the second weekend in January, is growing into one of the weirdest and wackiest festivals in the country. An influx of King lookalikes invades the town to celebrate his birthday with street parades, concerts, talent quests and busking. Don't forget your blue suedes!

Just off the main street, the **Coachman Hotel Motel** (☎ 02-6862 2622; www.coachman.com.au; 48-54 Welcome St; s/d $85/90; 🞭 🖳 🗩) is a well-kept establishment with a swimming pool, restaurant, digital TV and internet access. It's a good option for Gen Y and Xers who prefer a bit of nightlife.

Just a few metres north of the visitor centre is the small, quiet and pretty **Currajong Tourist Park** (☎ 02-6862 3400; Newell Hwy; campsites per adult $20, cabins/cottages $45/75; 🞭 🗩), with a spacious aviary to keep you entranced.

The **Dish Café** (☎ 02-6862 1566; Parkes Radio Telescope, Telescope Rd; meals $6-13) has close-up views of the dish and a healthy selection of breakfast and lunch dishes. Eat indoors or out.

DUBBO
pop 39,499

Dubbo has long been known as the home of the grand Western Plains Zoo. Now the rural centre and transport crossroads on the northern fringe of the Central West region has another string to its bow – the Western Plains Cultural Centre. For locals it has inspired a new era of arts and culture and hard-to-come-by statewide attention.

The **visitor centre** (☎ 1800 674 443, 02-6801 4450; www.dubbotourism.com.au; cnr Macquarie St & Newell Hwy) is in a park at the northern end of town. *Photo News* is a free paper with good local info.

Sights

With over 1500 animals, **Western Plains Zoo** (☎ 02-6882 5888; www.zootopia.com.au; Obley Rd; 2-day adult/child/family pass $39/19/84; 🕙 9am-5pm, last entry 4pm) is Dubbo's star attraction. You can walk the 6km trail, hire a bike ($15) or join the crawling line of cars. Guided walks (adult/child $10/5) start at 6.45am every weekend. Book ahead (☎ 02-6881 1488) for special animal encounters: Wild Africa (adult/child $29/19, 10.45am), Big Cats ($59 per person, Thursday to Tuesday) and Giraffes ($5 per person).

The exciting new **Western Plains Cultural Centre** (☎ 02-6801 4444; www.wpccdubbo.org.au; 76 Wingewarra St; admission free; 🕙 10am-4pm Wed-Mon), incorporating Dubbo Regional Museum and Gallery, is housed in a swanky architectural space cleverly incorporating the main hall of Dubbo's former high school. The combination befits the centre's exhibitions, both contemporary and historic. There's an innovative dedicated children's gallery, so mums and dads can wander the gallery sans sleeve-tugging.

The **Old Dubbo Gaol** (☎ 02-6801 4460; 90 Macquarie St; adult/child $15/5; 🕙 9am-4.30pm) is now a museum. 'Animatronic' characters tell their stories – you hear from a condemned man due for a meeting with the gallows. Creepy but authentic.

The **NPWS** (☎ 02-6841 0921) runs **Starry Starry Night Walks** (adult/child/family $10/5/20; 🕙 8pm summer) along the Macquarie River, which are perfect for spotting resident marsupials. Meet at the visitor centre. **Dubbo Observatory** (☎ 02-6885 3022; 17 Camp Rd; adult/child/family $20/10/50) also partakes in a bit of stargazing in two sessions each evening, minus the animals.

About 2km beyond the Western Plains Zoo, **Dundullimal** (☎ 02-6884 9984; Obley Rd; adult/child $8/4; 🕙 10am-4pm Tue-Thu) is a National Trust timber-slab homestead built in the 1840s showcasing some of the earliest forms of permanent European housing in NSW.

NEW SOUTH WALES

Red Earth Estate Vineyard (☎ 02-6885 6676; www.redearthestate.com.au; 18 Camp Rd; ⊙ 10am-5pm Thu-Tue), just past the zoo, is one of numerous vineyards with lunchtime platters and free tastings.

Sleeping

De Russie Boutique Hotel (☎ 02-6882 7888; www.derussiehotels.com.au; 95 Cobra St; r from $105; ⊠ 🖳 🖻) This place has a hotel-standard facade but inside the rooms are equipped with top-notch furniture, linen and appliances. It's one of the nicer options in town.

Westbury Guesthouse (☎ 02-6884 9445; westbury dubbo@bigpond.com; cnr Brisbane & Wingewarra Sts; s/d $110/140; ⊠) This lovely old heritage home (1910) has spacious rooms, all with bathrooms, and a shared lounge and kitchen. Longer-term stays attract discounts.

Dubbo City Caravan Park (☎ 02-6882 4820; www.dubbocaravanpark.com.au; Whylandra St; powered sites/cabins from $24/55; ⊠ 🖻) On the riverbank and an easy walk across the bridge into town, this busy spot has a barbecue area, kids playground, and cabins nestled between trees.

Eating

our pick **Two Doors Tapas & Wine Bar** (☎ 02-6885 2333; www.twodoors.com.au; 215b Macquarie St; tapas $9-19; ⊙ lunch & dinner Mon-Sat) Kick back with a drink in a leafy courtyard below street level, while munching on, say, the chargrilled sirloin with Roquefort cream sauce.

Grape Vine Café (☎ 02-6884 7354; 144 Brisbane St; mains $11-15; ⊙ breakfast & lunch) In a cute two-storey terrace, this place serves fresh soup, pasta and cakes in a coffee-house atmosphere or the lovely courtyard.

Outlook Café (☎ 02-6884 7977; 76 Wingewarra St; mains $12-16; ⊙ breakfast & lunch) Set in the light and airy foyer of the Western Plains Cultural Centre, there's no better place than this to indulge in salt-and-pepper squid salad or chilli-and-garlic-prawn linguini. In summer, the floor-to-ceiling windows allow a good view of the cricket ground.

Getting There & Around

Rex (☎ 13 17 13; www.regionalexpress.com.au) flies to Sydney ($115, 1¼ hours) and Dubbo ($220, 1¼ hours). **Qantas** (☎ 13 13 13; www.qantas.com.au) flies to Sydney ($115, one hour). **Air Link** (☎ 02-6884 2435; www.airlinkairlines.com.au) has charter flights to Cobar, Bourke and Lightning Ridge via Walgett and Coonamble.

The **CountryLink** (☎ 13 22 32; www.countrylink.info) XPT trains run to Sydney ($55, 6¾ hours).

Darrell Wheeler Cycles (☎ 02-6882 9899; 25 Bultje St; ⊙ Mon-Sat) rents out mountain bikes for $15 per day.

WELLINGTON
pop 8406

At the junction of the Macquarie and Bell Rivers, and surrounded by verdant hills and scenery, Wellington is a pleasant spot with a dazzling set of attractions. The helpful **visitor centre** (☎ 02-6845 1733; www.visitwellington.com.au) is in beautiful Cameron Park.

The **Wellington Caves & Phosphate Mine** (☎ 02-6845 1418; Gaden Cave adult/child $14/9, Cathedral Cave or mine $16/10; ⊙ tours daily; ⊠) was discovered in 1830 by a colonist, George Ranken, when he accidentally fell into one of the caves. These exquisite and unusual formations, subterranean waters, marsupial fossils and 'living fossils' are an absolute highlight. Cathedral Cave is famous for its majestic 32m-wide and 15m-high stalagmite!

Twenty minutes from town, **Burrendong Botanic Garden & Arboretum** (☎ 02-6846 7454; www.burrendongarboretum.org; per car $4; ⊙ 7.30am-sunset) is an area overlooking Lake Burrendong that has been transformed into a wonderland of native vegetation with 50,000 plants. There are self-guided walks and a picnic area, plus wallabies, kangaroos, echidnas and emus.

Also check out **Lake Burrendong**, which holds 3½ times the volume of water in Sydney Harbour.

One of the few good eating options, **Cactus Café & Gallery** (☎ 02-6845 4647; Warne St; ⊙ from 10am Wed-Sun) is in a Spanish Mission–style building where you can eat indoors among gifts and knick-knacks or outside under a lovely arbour.

Wellington Caves Holiday Complex (☎ 02-6845 2970; www.wellington.nsw.gov.au; Caves Rd; powered/unpowered sites $23/18, cabins/units $55/60; 🖻) has all the mod cons, with campsites and cabins hidden between the trees around a golf course.

MUDGEE
pop 8726

Mudgee is an Aboriginal word for 'nest in the hills', a fitting name for this quaint little grid of a town with vineyards on its edge and rolling hills wherever you turn. The wineries come hand in hand with excellent cuisine making it a popular weekend getaway where gastronomic exploration is central to the experience.

The **visitor centre** (☎ 1800 816 304, 02-6372 1020; www.visitmudgeeregion.com.au; 84 Market St), near the post office, can help with wine-tasting jaunts. The **NPWS** (☎ 02-6372 7199) is in Church St.

Sights
WINERIES

Mudgee's 40-plus vineyards are clustered in two groups north and southeast of town. This makes them ideal for cycling between as long as you don't get the wobbles. The vintage is later than the Hunter Valley because of Mudgee's higher altitude. The region is well known for its Shiraz, Cabernet Sauvignon and a blend of the two.

Logan (☎ 02-6373 1333; Castlereagh Hwy) is a new kid on the block with an impressive cellar door. Its floor-to-ceiling windows and extravagant deck make the most of the beautiful hillside scenery. It serves cheese platters and coffee, too.

Get some old-fashioned winery atmosphere at **Pieter Van Gent** (☎ 02-6373 3807; 141 Black Springs Rd; ☽ 9am-5pm Mon-Sat, 10.30am-4pm Sun), where tastings can be taken in old choir stalls, and the muscat is the nectar of the gods. It also offers bicycle wine tours with a picnic lunch, a wine collection service and special tastings in the barrel room at 11.30am Saturday.

Petersons Glenesk Estate (☎ 02-6373 3184; www.petersonswines.com.au; Black Springs Rd; ☽ 10am-5pm) is one of the smaller establishments, conducive to smaller groups and personalised tastings. To recuperate, there's a lovely deck overlooking the vineyards.

There's a **wine festival** (www.mudgeewine.com.au) throughout September.

Sleeping & Eating

Mudgee Vineyard Motor Inn (☎ 02-6372 1022; 252 Henry Lawson Dr; r from $85; ☽ ☐ ☞) Located only a couple of minutes' drive from town, this is an attractive place in the heart of the vineyards with pretty rooms and great views.

Cobb & Co Boutique Hotel (☎ 02-6372 7245; www.cobbandcocourt.com.au; 97 Market St; r $145-215) In the centre of town, this place has the mod cons elegantly suited to its heritage style.

Mudgee Riverside Caravan & Tourist Park (☎ 02-6372 2531; www.mudgeeriverside.com.au; 22 Short St; powered/unpowered sites $23/20, cabins/villas $65/80; ☒) Central and leafy, this pleasant park has an aviary, self-contained cabins and a camp kitchen with an open fire.

our pick Butcher Shop Café (☎ 02-6372 7373; 49 Church St; mains $7-15; ☽ breakfast & lunch daily, dinner Fri & Sat) A hip eatery in an old butchery with stained glass and interesting artwork. The delicious fare is understated and nicely presented.

Wineglass Bar & Grill (entrées $17, mains $32, light lunches $10) Downstairs in the Cobb & Co building, this place the serves meals in a lovely courtyard next to the atmospheric bar.

High Valley Wine & Cheese Co (☎ 02-6372 1011; 137 Cassilis Rd; mains $24-29; ☽ 10am-5pm Mon-Fri, from 8.30am Sat & Sun in summer) In a beautiful stone-and-corrugated-iron building, this foodie stop has a produce shop and a vine-laden verandah under which you can indulge in coffee and cake, rare-roast-beef open sandwiches or cheese and antipasto plates for two.

our pick Deebs Kitchen (☎ 02-6373 3133; Cassilis Rd; ☽ lunch Sat & Sun, dinner Sat, to mid-Feb–mid Jan) A lovely couple run this gorgeous, hidden-away restaurant where Mediterranean cuisine (with a Lebanese skew) and plenty of wine is served in the garden.

Also worthy:

Mudgee Brewery (☎ 02-6372 1222; 4 Church St; ☽ 10am-4pm Sat) For those who prefer beer to Beaujolais.

Roth's Wine Bar (☎ 02-6372 1222; 30 Market St; ☽ 5pm-late Thu-Sat) Oldest wine bar in NSW, with an atmosphere to show for it.

Getting There & Away

CountryLink (☎ 13 22 32; www.countrylink.info) buses to Lithgow connect with Sydney trains ($38, five hours). **Air Link** (☎ 02-6884 2435; www.airlinkairlines.com.au) has charter flights to Sydney.

GULGONG
pop 1907

This gorgeous time-warped town once featured alongside author Henry Lawson on the $10 note. Today the narrow, rambling streets, classified by the National Trust, are not so done-up that they have lost their charm. The **visitor centre** (☎ 02-6374 1202; 109 Herbert St) has guides to some terrific walks.

The huge **Gulgong Pioneer Museum** (☎ 02-6374 1513; 73 Herbert St; adult/child $10/3.50; ☽ 9am-5pm) has one of the most eclectic and chaotic collections of artefacts in the state.

Author Henry Lawson spent part of his childhood here, and the **Henry Lawson Centre** (☎ 02-6374 2049; 147 Mayne St; adult/child $4/2.50; ☽ 10am-3.30pm Tue-Sat, to 1pm Sun & Mon) looks at his early memories of the town. Originally built from bark, the **opera house** (☎ 02-6374 1162;

99-101 Mayne St) is one of the oldest surviving theatres in Australia and still holds several performances a year. **Cudgegong Gallery** (☎ 02-6374 1630; 102 Herbert St; ☺ 10am-5.30pm) has the most beautiful ceramics collection you're likely to see.

Ten Dollar Town (☎ 02-6374 1204; www.tendollar townmotel.com.au; cnr Mayne & Medley Sts; s/d $101/111) has a heritage facade and a rear garden and sitting area to make you feel at home.

The **Butcher Shop Café** (☎ 02-6374 2322; 113 Mayne St; mains $8-21; ☺ lunch & dinner) is a delightful little, erm, former butcher shop, cleverly transformed. It serves a hearty array of food all chalked up on the blackboard. The melts and toasties are especially good.

CountryLink (☎ 13 22 32; www.countrylink.info) runs daily buses to Mudgee ($5, 20 minutes).

NORTHWEST

People tend to put pedal to the metal driving through this flat archetypal Australian landscape, possibly because they have Queensland beaches on their minds.

The Newell Hwy, the through-route from Victoria, passes through star-gazing Coonabarabran, the cotton-picking centre of Narrabri, and the burgeoning Aboriginal art hub of Moree, before hitting the border at Goondiwindi. The roads in between are flanked by crops of cotton, canola and, increasingly, olive groves, offering a glimpse of an arid landscape worked for its agricultural rewards.

If Queensland isn't on the itinerary, chances are Lightning Ridge is. Like other Australian mining communities, the town throws up as many characters as it does gems.

West of Coonabarabran, Warrumbungle National Park is one of the most popular in NSW with camping, walking, stargazing and a wealth of Aboriginal culture and history. Similarly, Moree has some intriguing Aboriginal sites, largely undiscovered by tourists. You'll have to be adventurous or curious to track them down.

NEWELL HIGHWAY

The Newell Hwy is the quickest route between Melbourne and Brisbane, briefly joining the Oxley Hwy from Tamworth at **Coonabarabran** (population 2609), the gateway

to the Warrumbungles. The helpful **visitor centre** (☎ 02-6842 1441; www.coonabarabran.com; Newell Hwy) is south of the clock tower.

Wattagan Estate Winery (☎ 02-6842 2456; Oxley Hwy; ☺ 10am-5pm Fri-Mon) has delicious port, crisp Chardonnay and ample emu-oil products.

The area's roadsides are home to the **World's Largest Virtual Solar System Drive** (www .solarsystemdrive.com), with interpretative boards and 'planets' spread out 38 million times smaller than in outer space.

Head to **Siding Spring Observatory** (☎ 02-6842 6211; www.sidingspringexploratory.com.au; National Park Rd; tours adult/child $5.50/3.50; ☺ 9.30am-4pm Mon-Fri, 10am-2pm Sat & Sun), 27km west of town in the Warrumbungle Range, for some of the world's major, and Australia's largest, telescopes. Alternatively, phone local stargazer Peter Starr (seriously) who conducts night-time **telescopic viewings** (☎ 0488 425 112).

The **Crystal Kingdom** (☎ 02-6842 1927; www .crystalkingdom.com.au; Newell Hwy) displays the 'Mineral of the Warrumbungles' including the world's most colourful zeolite crystals and fossil specimens.

The **Imperial Hotel** (☎ 02-6842 1023; 70 John St; s/d $30/35, d with bathroom $55) has good pub rooms that open onto the balcony, and a full breakfast for $8. Alternatively, the **Country Garden Motel** (☎ 02-6842 1711; cnr John & Edward Sts; s/d from $73/85; ☒ ☐ ☒) has a central swimming pool, and large clean rooms and bathrooms.

Snap, crackle, pop went the Warrumbungle Volcano as it erupted more than 13 million years ago, forming the spectacular granite domes of the **Warrumbungle National Park** (per car $7). Sitting 33km west of Coonabarabran, this 23,311-hectare park has 43km of bushwalking trails and explosive wildflower displays during spring. Park fees are payable at the **NPWS visitor centre** (☎ 02-6825 4364) in the park; some sights also have camp fees (adult/child from $5/$3). Ask the centre about the **Warrumbungle Tara Cave Walk & Sundancin' Tour**, which is guided by local Kamilaroi people, including Aboriginal elders. The tour encompasses a walk through **Tara Cave**, a significant Aboriginal site that was occupied for over 4000 years, and insight into the traditional use of the land. For the Sundancin' section of the tour, you'll need your own wheels to follow a ranger to the Sandstone Caves in the **Pilliga Nature Reserve**. Be warned that it can get cold here, even in summer.

Park yourself at **Mountain View Hotel/Motel** (☎ 02-6848 1017; s/d $45/60) in wee Tooraweenah, at the foot of the Warrumbungles. Digs can also be found at **Timor Country Cabins** (☎ 02-6842 1055; www.coonabarabran.com/timor; National Park Rd; 2-night d from $100), two romantic cottages dwarfed by the Timor Rock.

Narrabri (population 6102), the cotton-growing centre, is home to the **Australian Cotton Centre** (☎ 02-6792 6443; www.australiancottoncentre.com .au; Newell Hwy; adult/child $8/5.50; ☒ 8.30am-4.30pm), dedicated to the region's big cash crop. FYI: one standard 225kg bale of cotton can be made into 3085 nappies. Some 20km west, the **Australia Telescope** (☎ 02-6790 4070; Yarrie Lake Rd; admission free; ☒ sunrise-sunset) comprises an array of radio telescopes used to map the universe. The **visitor centre** (☎ 02-6799 6760; www .narrabri.nsw.gov.au; Newell Hwy) has displays and a shop and sits on the riverfront where there's a swimming beach and picnic tables. **Joblink** (☎ 02-6792 5188; 5/100 Maitland St) can help with cotton jobs; also check out the government's **National Harvest Labour Information Service** (☎ 1800 062 332; www.jobsearch.gov .au/harvesttrail).

Sawn Rocks, a pipe-organ formation about 40km northeast of Narrabri (20km unsealed), is the most accessible and popular part of **Mt Kaputar National Park**. The southern part of the park has dramatic lookouts, climbing, bushwalking and camping.

Moree (population 13,976), a large town on the Gwydir River, has the **Hot Artesian Pool Complex** (☎ 02-6757 3450; www.mpsc.nsw.gov.au; cnr Anne & Gosport Sts; adult/child $6/4; ☒ 6am-8.30pm Mon-Fri, 7am-7pm Sat & Sun), where locals frolic in the hotter of the artesian pools (42°C).

In one of the town's attractive historic buildings, **Moree Plains Gallery** (☎ 02-6757 3320; cnr Frome & Herber Sts; ☒ 9am-5pm Mon-Fri, 10am-2pm Sat) has an inspiring collection of Aboriginal art by some of the country's best artists. For a more local take, check out **Yaama Maliyaa Arts** (☎ 02-6752 1813; 29 Herber St); the friendly owner is also a good source of info on local Aboriginal sites.

our pick **Café 2500** (☎ 02-6752 6700; 123 Balo St; ☒ breakfast & lunch Mon-Fri, breakfast Sat) would be at home in Sydney's groovier suburbs with excellent coffee, cakes, sandwiches and light meals.

Cotton-related work is available from March to May for skilled workers. Anyone can partake in cotton chipping from November to January or olive- and pecan-picking from April to August. Contact **Joblink** (☎ 02-6752 8488) for further info on Project Harvest, or check the **National Harvest Labour Information Service** (www.jobsearch.gov.au/harvesttrail).

CASTLEREAGH HIGHWAY

The Castlereagh Hwy forks off the Newell at pretty **Gilgandra** (population 4526), and runs north into rugged opal country towards the Queensland border. Just north of Gilgandra, pull off the highway at the spot where, in 1818, John Oxley spat the dummy. Expecting to find a giant inland sea, he instead discovered that the Macquarie River petered out into a boggy marsh. The town was also the starting point for the Coo-ee March, a WWI recruiting drive to Sydney, led by a butcher and his brother.

West of here, the prolific bird life of 220,000-hectare **Macquarie Marshes Nature Reserve** is best seen during breeding season (usually spring, but it varies with water levels).

Lightning Ridge
pop 2746

Know what a 'ratter', a 'rough' and a 'blower' are? Opal lingo, that's what. Near the Queensland border, this strikingly imaginative mining community (one of the world's few sources of black opals) has real frontier spirit, home to eccentric artisans, true-blue bushies and a general unconventional collective.

The town was named after an unfortunate event in 1963 when a flock of sheep, their drover and his faithful dog were struck down by lightning. Their singed woolly carcasses were still wafting with smoke when the town took its name from the event.

The fossicking season kicks off over the Easter long weekend, when you can prove your worth at the **Great Goat Race**. Catch a feral beast, give it some racing lessons, let it go with 50 other goats, and bet money on it.

Several **underground mines** and **opal show-rooms** are open to the public, and there's a **gem festival** every July. In an example of the community's spirit, locals have mapped out four **Car Door Explorer** touring routes around town, using car doors as markers. Get details from the **Lightning Ridge visitor centre** (☎ 02-6829 1670; www.lightningridge.net.au; Morilla St).

Visit the **Walk-In Mine** (☎ 02-6829 0473; Bald Hill; adult/child $8/3; ☒ 9am-4.30pm) to get a feel for the type of environment encountered by the average opal miner.

NEW SOUTH WALES

The **Black Queen** (☎ 02-6829 0980; www.black queen.com.au; Red Car Door E; admission $7) is a quirky antique lamp museum with more than 200 magnificent kerosene lamps from the last 300 years.

There are **Hot Artesian Bore Baths** (Pandora St; admission free; ☽ 24hr). We have four words: warm artesian water, free.

Do a bit of fossicking with **Black Opal Tours** (☎ 02-6829 0368; www.blackopaltours.com; adult/child $25/10; ☽ tours 8.30am, 9.30am & 1.30pm).

Glengarry Hilton (☎ 02-6829 3983; per person $16) is somewhere to write home about. It's a tin shed of a pub in the Glengarry Opal Fields, frequented by lots of local characters. There are four bunk rooms and a double room, and breakfast is included. If you hadn't guessed, the name is tongue-in-cheek.

Lorne Station (☎ 02-6829 1869; off Opal St; unpowered/powered sites $12/18, bunkhouse r $35, self-contained cottages $50-130; ⊠ ⊡) is a 10,000-hectare property with an intriguing variety of accommodation. The lovely owner conducts free opal field walking tours.

Chats On Opal (☎ 02-6829 4228; 4 Opal St; mains $8-16; ☽ breakfast & lunch) is a colourful place serving gourmet sandwiches, cakes and decent coffee. It's a good place to watch the world go by.

CountryLink (☎ 13 22 32; www.countrylink.info) buses run to Dubbo ($27, 4¼ hours). **Air Link** (☎ 02-6884 2435; www.airlinkairlines.com.au) has charter flights to Walgett, Coonamble and Sydney via Dubbo.

LORD HOWE ISLAND

pop 350

Shhh! Lord Howe Island is one of Australia's best-kept coastal secrets – Lord how we love it! About 500km east of Port Macquarie and 770km northeast of Sydney, this gorgeous, subtropical island remains remarkably pristine. Listed on the World Heritage Register for its rare bird and plant life, the island is a haven for ecotourists and those seeking a *real* holiday. Many visitors (numbers are limited to 400 at any one time) are repeat customers, returning for a dose of the island's barefoot, first-name hospitality, empty beaches and balmy vibes.

The island is far from a budget destination, although prices fall considerably in winter. Unless you have a boat you'll have to fly here, and both food and accommodation are limited and pricey. But there's plenty of family-friendly stuff to do here if you're feeling lively.

Orientation & Information

Crescent-shaped Lord Howe wraps itself around a lagoon, fringed by coral reefs. The island is lorded over by three peaks: **Mt Lidgbird** (777m) and **Mt Gower** (875m) in the south, and the astonishing spike of **Ball's Pyramid** (551m) jagging up from the sea 23km to the southeast. The island is about 11km long by 3km wide; most accommodation and services are located in the flat area north of the airport. Island time is GMT plus 10½ hours – 30 minutes ahead of Sydney (the same as Sydney in summer).

The island **visitor centre** (☎ 1800 240 937, 02-6563 2114; www.lordhoweisland.info; cnr Lagoon & Middle Beach Rds; ☽ 9.30am-2.30pm Mon-Fri, to 2pm Sun; ⊡) is inside the Lord Howe Island Museum, and has internet access.

Near the corner of Ned's Beach and Lagoon Rds there's a post office, general store and two banks (no ATMs). Some businesses have Eftpos facilities.

Sights & Activities

Between September and April, Lord Howe becomes a rabbling gaggle of nesting seabirds – a bird-nerd's wonderland! Check out the birdlife on **bushwalks** along the coast and through the hills and rainforest. The summit climb up Mt Gower (eight to 10 hours return) is a candidate for Australia's best one-day walk. The steep hike will either cure or initiate vertigo; you must be accompanied by a licensed guide (see Tours, opposite).

Fish feeding causes a splash in the Ned's Beach shallows, and you can **snorkel** among vivid tropical fish and coral just offshore. Hire a mask, snorkel, fins and wetsuit at the beach using an honesty box system. There's good **surf** at Blinky Beach, and off the island's western shore is the world's southernmost **coral reef**, sheltered by a wide lagoon popular for **sea kayaking**. You can also inspect the sea life from above via a **glass-bottom boat** (see Tours, opposite). If you really want to get among it, **Howea Divers** (☎ 02-6563 2290; www.howeadivers.com .au) runs 'Discover Scuba' dives ($130) and boat dives around the island (from $75).

The **Lord Howe Island Museum** (☎ 02-6563 2114; www.lordhoweisland.info; cnr Lagoon & Middle Beach Rds;

admission free; 9.30am-2.30pm Mon-Fri, to 2pm Sun) is behind the visitor centre, and will give you a good rundown on island geography and natural history.

Tours

Thompson's General Store (02-6563 2155; Neds Beach Rd; 9am-5pm) takes bookings for tours and activities from fishing charters to nature walks. Alternatively, try the following:

LHI Environmental Tours (02-6563 2214; www .lordhoweislandtours.com) Treks up Mt Gower ($50 per person), plus glass-bottom boat trips with snorkelling ($35). Kayaking trips also available.

Sea to Summit Expeditions (02-6563 2218; http://seatosummit.googlepages.com) Locally run guided climbs up Mt Gower ($40 per person), plus fishing trips (four/six hours per person $90/110).

Sleeping & Eating

Camping is prohibited on the island, and all accommodation must be booked in advance. There are 18 lodge and self-contained apartment businesses here, some of which close in winter or lower their rates. Eating out is expensive; bookings are essential. Keep an eye out for 'Fish Fries' ($50) held on various nights at various resort restaurants, plus the bowls club and golf course – they offer all-you-can-eat seafood fresh off the boat (the local kingfish is brilliant). Most places on the island aren't air-conditioned – it rarely gets too hot, cold or humid here.

Ocean View Apartments (02-6563 2041; www .lordhoweisland.info/oceanview; Ocean View Dr; d $160, f apt from $300;) In truth, these self-contained apartments don't have ocean views, and the interiors are underwhelming, but they do have tennis courts and a swimming pool.

Capella Lodge (02-9918 4355; www.lordhowe .com; Salmon Beach; s/d incl breakfast & dinner from $590/1180;) Big money has been splashed around here to create a luxury haven for the cash-rich and time-poor. The views here are worth the outlay, and meals at the restaurant are outstanding.

Arajilla Retreat (1800 063 928, 02-6563 2002; www.arajilla.com.au; Old Settlement Beach; s/d incl meals from $825/1040) This plush, upmarket resort is set amid kentia-palm forest and pampers guests with opulent suites and family-friendly apartments. Rates include all meals, mountain bikes, snorkelling gear and other active necessities. It also has a good (but pricey) restaurant.

Pinetrees (02-6563 2177; www.pinetrees.com.au; Lagoon Beach; 5 nights per person from $1015) Affordable by Lord Howe standards, Pinetrees lodge occupies an old homestead and has decent units or cottages. Rates include all meals.

Eating options other than at resorts:

Humpty Micks Cafe (02-6563 2287; Ned's Beach Rd; mains $8-18) Opposite the post office; fab smoothies, wraps and burgers.

Coral Café (02-6563 2488; cnr Lagoon & Middle Beach Rds; mains $12-22; breakfast & lunch daily, dinner Thu & Sun) Part of the visitor centre and museum complex; low-key ambience with good-quality cafe food.

Pandanus (02-6563 2400; Anderson Rd; mains $25-35; lunch Thu-Sat, dinner daily Jan & Feb, Mon-Sat Mar-Dec) Impressive wine list and zingy à la carte Italian.

Getting There & Away

QantasLink (13 13 13; www.qantas.com.au) has daily flights from Sydney (from $880 return), and weekend flights from Brisbane (from $960 return). There are also seasonal weekly flights from Port Macquarie from February to June, and September to December. Flight time from the mainland is around two hours.

Flight and accommodation packages are the best option. Winter prices start at $1100 for seven nights. Package providers:

Fastbook Pacific Holidays (1300 361 153, 02-9080 1600; www.fastbook.com.au)

Orient Pacific (1800 808 055; 03-8662 7350; www .orientpacific.com.au)

Oxley Travel (1800 671 546, 02-6583 1955; www .oxleytravel.com.au)

Getting Around

You can hire bicycles (per day/week $8/50) and cars (per day $50) on the island, but a bicycle is all you really need and most accommodation places will happily drive you anywhere. There's a 25km/h speed limit on the island. There aren't many streetlights – bring a torch!

NORFOLK ISLAND

6723 / pop 2120

Norfolk Island is a pine-studded speck adrift in the South Pacific Ocean, 1600km northeast of Sydney and 1000km northwest of Auckland. It's the largest of a cluster of three islands emerging from the underwater Norfolk Ridge, which stretches from New Zealand to New Caledonia, the closest landfall, almost 700km north.

NEW SOUTH WALES

Norfolk Island is administered as an Australian external territory. It elects its own nine-member legislative assembly to govern its affairs and is not subject to Australian tax laws – there's a strip of duty-free outlets in Burnt Pine, and a sprinkling of millionaires living here. Tourism accounts for more than 90% of the local economy, but it's not a cheap destination. Airfares are expensive, and there's no budget accommodation available.

History

Norfolk Island, which appears never to have been settled by Polynesians, was first eye-balled by Captain James Cook on 10 October 1774. Fifteen convicts were among the first settlers who arrived on 6 March 1788, only weeks after the First Fleet reached Port Jackson to settle Sydney. But food shortages, shipwrecks and native timber that proved too brittle for building caused the settlers to give up and move to New Norfolk in Van Diemen's Land (Tasmania).

After 11 years of abandonment, the colonial authorities tried again in 1825. Governor Darling planned this second penal settlement as 'a place of the extremest punishment short of death'. Under such notorious sadists as Commandant John Giles Price, Norfolk became known as 'hell in the Pacific'.

The second penal colony lasted until 1855, when the prisoners were shipped off to Van Diemen's Land and Queen Victoria handed the island over to the descendants of the mutineers from the HMS *Bounty*, who had outgrown their adopted Pitcairn Island. About a third of the present population is descended from the 194 Pitcairners and their Tahitian wives who arrived on 8 June 1856.

Orientation & Information

The island measures only 8km by 5km, with vertical cliffs defining much of the coastline. Kingston, the principal settlement in convict days and now largely an open-air museum, is on the charmingly named Slaughter Bay on the island's south coast. The service town of Burnt Pine is in the centre of the island, near the airport, while Norfolk Island National Park encompasses the hillier northern part of the island. Island time is GMT plus 11½ hours – 1½ hours ahead of Sydney (30 minutes ahead in summer).

The **visitor centre** (☎ 6723-22 147; www.norfolkisland.com.au; Taylors Rd, Burnt Pine; ☾ 8.30am-5pm Mon-Fri, to 3pm Sat & Sun) is next to the post office. **Westpac Bank** (☎ 6723-22 120) and the **Commonwealth Bank** (☎ 6723-22 144) have branches nearby, the latter with an ATM. Most shops have Eftpos. Norfolk Telecom's **Communications Centre** (☎ 6723-22 244; New Cascade Rd; ☾ 9am-5pm Mon-Fri; ☐) has internet access.

Other online resources include www.norfolkbedbank.com and www.gonorfolkisland.com.

VISAS

All Norfolk Island visitors must have a valid passport and a return airline ticket. Australian and New Zealand passport holders don't require visas, but all other nationalities must obtain an Australian entry visa before flying. Australian citizens who don't have a passport can obtain a 'Document of Identity' through Australia Post.

Sights & Activities

Kingston, knocked-up by convicts of the second penal colony, is Norfolk's star attraction. Many historic buildings have been restored – the best of these, along Quality Row, still house the island's administrators, as well as four small-but-engaging **museums** (☎ 6723-23 788; www.museums.gov.nf; single/combined ticket $10/25; ☾ 11am-3pm).

By the shore are the ruins of an early pentagonal prison, a lime pit (into which convict murder victims were sometimes thrown) and the **convict cemetery**. Among the subterranean here are 105-year-old Thomas Wright, a convict who at 101 was sentenced to 14 years!

Spend an hour poking around the **Bounty Folk Museum** (☎ 6723-22 592; www.lareau.org/bfm.html; Middlegate Rd; admission $10; ☾ 10am-4pm), crammed with motley convict-era and *Bounty* souvenirs.

Fletcher's Mutiny Cyclorama (☎ 6723-23 871; www.norfolkcyclorama.nlk.nf; Queen Elizabeth Ave; per person from $11; ☾ 9am-5pm Mon-Sat, 10am-3pm Sun) is a 360-degree panoramic painting depicting the *Bounty* mutiny and Norfolk Island history. The admission price depends on the size of your group.

West of Burnt Pine, the amazing **St Barnabas Chapel** (Douglas Dr; admission free) was built by the (Anglican) Melanesian Mission, which was based on the island from 1866 to 1920.

It's never really closed; just shut the door behind you.

Covering 650 hectares of the island's north, **Norfolk Island National Park** (www.environ ment.gov.au/parks/norfolk) offers various bushwalking tracks, with awesome views from Mt Pitt (316m) and Mt Bates (318m). There's a sheltered beach at **Emily Bay** in the south, from where glass-bottom boats depart to ogle the coral below.

Snorkelling around the Kingston breakwall is worthwhile; hire gear in Burnt Pine. Alternatively, several companies arrange snorkelling, diving and fishing trips, including **Bounty Divers** (☎ 6723-24 375; www.bountydivers.com).

Tours

Norfolk Touring Co (☎ 6723-22 232; www.nor folktouring.com) Wide-ranging tours with either a local, cultural, historic, relaxing or adventurous bent. Prices start at $32.

Pinetree Tours (☎ 6723-22 424; www.pinetreetours .com) Day/night cultural tours from $34/40; 4WD tours also available.

Sleeping

There is plenty of accommodation on Norfolk; check out www.norfolkisland.com.au for listings. All accommodation must be booked in advance. Most visitors come on package deals, starting from around $1000 for seven nights in winter and around $1460 in summer, sometimes including car hire and breakfast. **Norfolk & Pacific Holidays** (☎ 1800 111 653; www.norfolkpacific .com.au) is a good starting point.

Hillcrest (☎ 6723-22 255; www.hillcrest.nf; Taylors Rd; r $85-175) Catering to most budgets, this place has motel-style units, spa suites, self-contained apartments and cottages. Most of the rates include breakfast.

Anson Bay Lodge (☎ 6723-22 897; www.ansonbay lodge.com; Anson Bay; r incl car hire from $110) Reasonable and reliable, Anson Bay Lodge has two self-contained units with decent facilities and a lovely one-bedroom cottage.

Christians of Bucks Point (☎ 6723-23 833; www .christians.nf; r from $365) This restored three-bedroom house (sleeping up to six) is good value if you're travelling with some buddies. Car hire and the first morning's breakfast are often included. Beware: frills and floral prints.

More accommodation options:

By the Bay (☎ 6723-22 730; www.bythebay.nf; r incl car hire $360) Jaunty timber cottages on five private acres.

Hibiscus Island Resort (☎ 6723-22 325; www .hibiscus.nf; s/d incl car hire from $94/134) Moderate motel-style accommodation.

Eating

History-themed 'progressive' dinners ($50) at islanders' homes and the local 'Fish Fry' ($50) at Puppy's Point can be booked through the visitor centre.

Brewery Bar & Bistro (☎ 6723-23 515; Douglas Dr; meals $10-20; ☽ lunch & dinner) Opposite the airport, this brewery plates up affordable counter meals and bubbles its own beer.

Homestead Restaurant (☎ 6723-22 068; Hundred Acres; mains from $24; ☽ lunch Wed-Mon) Out of town near the gates to the Rocky Point Reserve, the Homestead serves a bang-up lunch.

Hilli Lounge & Wine Bar (☎ 6723-24 270; Queen Elizabeth Ave; mains $30; ☽ dinner) Good food and cosy surroundings.

Mariah's Bar & Grill (☎ 6723-222 55; Hillcrest, Taylors Rd; mains $25-35; ☽ lunch & dinner) One of Norfolk's best foodie options, Mariah's serves excellent Mod Oz cuisine with camera-worthy views over Phillip Island.

Taylors Rd has cafes for coffee and lunch ($10 to $15), including **Golden Orb Bookshop Cafe** (☎ 6723-24 295) and **Cafe Tempo** (☎ 6723-23 773).

Getting There & Away

The island is a 2½-hour flight from east-coast Australia, 1¾ hours from Auckland. Flights can be booked as part of flight-accommodation package deals. There's a departure tax of $30, payable at the airport or in advance at the visitor centre; some packages incorporate this into the cost.

Air New Zealand (☎ in New Zealand 0800 737 000; www.airnewzealand.co.nz) Flies from Auckland on Wednesday and Sunday. Return fares start at around NZ$730.

Norfolk Air (☎ 1800 612 960; www.norfolkair.com) Flies from Sydney and Brisbane on Wednesday, Friday, Saturday and Sunday; from Melbourne on Friday; and from Newcastle on Monday. Return fares start at around $830 ex-Sydney, $730 ex-Brisbane.

Getting Around

Car hire can be organised at the airport or through **Advance Hire Cars** (☎ 6723-23 119; advance@ ninet.nf; Taylors Rd, Burnt Pine) for as little as $20 a day. The speed limit for most of the island is 50km/h. Cows have right of way on island roads – you'll be $300 poorer if you hit one!

Bicycle hire can be arranged through the visitor centre.

SOUTH COAST

If a road trip takes your fancy you've come to the right place. The South Coast, breathtaking in the extreme, stretches 400km by road to the Victorian border through rolling dairy country, blast-from-the-past heritage towns, stunning national parks and rugged coastline. Though the main thoroughfare, the Princes Hwy, projects a lot of this scenery onto your windscreen, the South Coast is undoubtedly best experienced by dipping on and off the road well travelled. It's on the backroads and byways that isolated beaches, pristine campsites and remote lighthouses reveal themselves.

The South Coast's pit stops hold their own, too. The holiday-hectic, coastal hubs of Wollongong, Kiama, Batemans Bay, Narooma and Merimbula cater to holiday-makers of all budgets with restaurants and bars to match. Alternatively put the brakes on the pace in the beautiful little beachside nooks of Gerroa, Jervis Bay, Bermagui and Eden, where the comforts of the city cater to a quieter crowd just as partial to a day's fishing as an espresso coffee.

The inland towns of Berry, Kangaroo Valley and Braidwood, to name a few, manage to compete with their coastal counterparts with top-notch restaurants, heritage buildings and vineyards.

With time on your hands, the region is inundated with activities, be it kayaking and scuba diving, hiking and camping, bike-riding and boating. If you pack one thing, make it your binoculars – whales are quite fond of the South Coast, too.

WOLLONGONG

pop 277,972

The 'Gong', 80km south of Sydney, is the envy of many cities. Sure, it has restaurants, bars, arts, culture and entertainment, that's easy enough. But it also enjoys a laid-back, beachside lifestyle impossible to match anywhere inland. Just to rub it in, Sydney is easily accessible by local rail.

There are 17 patrolled beaches – all unique – and a spectacular sandstone escarpment that runs from the Royal National Park south past Wollongong and Port Kembla. The Grand Pacific Dr makes the most of the landscape and the whole combination makes for a host of outdoor activities: excellent surf, safe

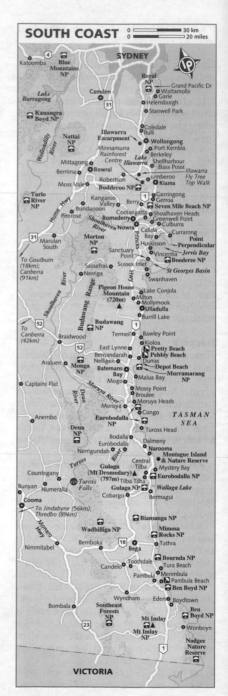

beaches, bushwalks and sky-high adventures to name a few.

Orientation & Information

Crown St is the main street in town. Between Kembla and Keira Sts is a two-block pedestrian mall, badly in need of an update. Keira St is part of the Princes Hwy. Through-traffic bypasses the city on the Southern Fwy.

Network Café (☎ 02-4228 8686; upstairs, 157 Crown St; per hr $3.50; ☽ 9.45am-6pm Mon-Wed & Fri, to 8.30pm Thu, to 4pm Sat) Internet access.

NPWS office (☎ 02-4223 3000; 84 Crown St)

Wollongong visitor centre (☎ 02-4227 5545, 1800 240 737; www.tourismwollongong.com; 93 Crown St) Books accommodation.

Sights

Wollongong's fishing fleet is based at the southern end of the harbour, **Belmore Basin**. There's a fishing cooperative here (with a fish market and a couple of cafes) and an 1872 **lighthouse** on the point. Nearby, on the headland, is the newer **Breakwater Lighthouse**.

North Beach and **Wollongong City Beach** have breaks suitable for all visitors and are walking distance from the city centre. Look for the Acids Reef break on North Beach for more of a challenge. Up the coast, the options are varied and less crowded, with fun beach breaks at **Coledale** and **Bulli** beaches, and reef breaks at **Sharkies** (also at Coledale) and **Headlands**. The risk of meeting a finned friend at Sharkies is minimal, but surfers have occasionally encountered humpback whales surfacing close to shore.

Check out www.wannasurf.com for a full rundown on local waves and a five-day forecast.

Along the highway, **Nan Tien Buddhist Temple** (☎ 02-4272 0600; www.nantien.org.au; Berkeley Rd, Berkeley; ☽ 9am-5pm Tue-Sun) has weekend retreats, vegetarian cooking classes, meditation and t'ai chi.

Southwest of Wollongong, the **Illawarra Escarpment** is a state recreation area. There's no vehicle access, but the spot is good for bushwalking. The Wollongong NPWS office (above) can provide information on bush camping.

Just south of Wollongong, **Lake Illawarra** is very popular for water sports, including windsurfing. Further south is **Shellharbour**, a popular holiday resort, now overrun with tacky housing estates.

Activities

Taupu Surf School (☎ 02-4268 0088; www.taupusurf school.com; 1/3 lessons $59/$159; ☽ Mon-Sat) runs courses at Thirroul and North Wollongong.

A bird's-eye view of the coastline is perhaps the best. **Sydney Hang Gliding Centre** (☎ 02-4294 4294; www.hanggliding.com.au; ☽ 8am-8pm) has tandem flights ($195) from breathtaking Bald Hill at Stanwell Park. If the adrenalin still hasn't kicked in, you can skydive from 14,000ft and land in the sand with **Skydive the Beach** (☎ 1300 663 634; www.skydivethebeach.com; Stuart Park; tandem jumps from $275; ☽ 8am-6pm Mon-Fri, to 2pm Sat & Sun).

Sleeping

The visitor centre can make accommodation reservations.

Wollongong YHA & Kieraview Accommodation (☎ 02-4229 9700; www.yha.com.au; 75-79 Keira St; dm/d $30/110; ▣) This complex contains the well-equipped and friendly YHA hostel, which caters to students and backpackers in tidy four-bed dorms. It's also home to Kieraview, which have double and family rooms with verandahs and kitchenettes. They are clean but soulless and a tad overpriced.

Novotel Northbeach (☎ 02-4226 3555; www.novotel.com.au; 2-14 Cliff Rd; r from $199; ✖ ▣ ▣) Wollongong's flashiest joint is all class. The spacious and comfortable rooms have balconies with ocean or escarpment views. Breakfast is included.

Coledale Beach Camping Reserve (☎ 02-4267 4302; Beach Rd, Coledale; unpowered/powered sites from $20/25) Small and right on the beach, this is one of the best urban camping spots on the coast.

Eating

Keira St has the greatest concentration of restaurants, especially north of the mall.

Old Siam Style (☎ 02-4226 6388; 157 Keira St; entrées $8, mains $14; ☽ lunch & dinner) One of the newer restaurants on the Keira St strip, this spacious place with all the trimmings serves up exquisite authentic Thai dishes, orchids and all.

Diggies (☎ 02-4226 2688; www.diggies.com.au; 1 Cliff Rd, North Beach; entrées $9-19, mains $15-21) With a view to the rolling waves, this is the perfect spot for feasting any time of day. Friday and Saturday evening is tapas time. On Sunday arvo during summer, cocktails and tunes are let loose on the deck.

NEW SOUTH WALES

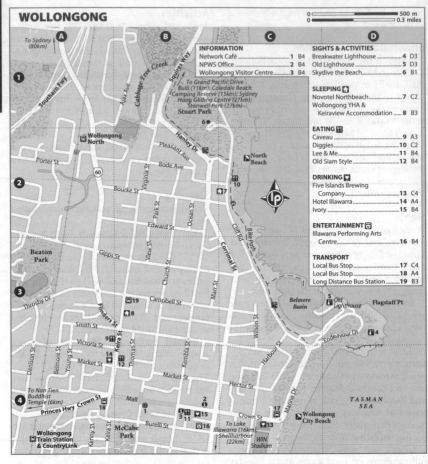

WOLLONGONG

our pick **Lee & Me** (☎ 02-4244 0695; www.leeandme .com.au; 87 Crown St; ☼ breakfast & lunch) A cafe and art and clothing store in a two-storey heritage building. There's nothing quite like dining on a mushroom and goats-cheese omelette on the sunny verandah, then shopping in the upstairs boutique on a full stomach.

Caveau (☎ 02-4226 4855; www.caveau.com.au; 122-124 Keira St; 2-/3-/7-course degustation $57/70/90; ☼ dinner) Sitting unpretentiously on Keira St, this lauded restaurant washed in a soft amber glow serves gourmet treats such as mushroom ravioli with asparagus and shaved truffle.

Drinking & Entertainment

Five Islands Brewing Company (☎ 02-4220 2854; WIN Entertainment Centre, cnr Crown & Harbour Sts; ☼ 11am-1am) This slick bar has nine fine draught beers including a Pig Dog Pilsner, named after the owner (an ex–St George rugby player).

Hotel Illawarra (☎ 02-4229 5411; www.hotelil lawarra.com.au; cnr Market & Keira Sts; ☼ 11am-late) Best suited to the cocktail-sipping funky set, this complex has the red-hued Amber bar and Cucina Illawarra, which dishes up Mediterranean fare, tapas-style.

Ivory (☎ 02-4226 4305; 90 Crown St; ☼ 8am-late Wed-Sat) This glitzy nightclub starts its week as a uni hang-out – with free pizzas after 11pm – and ends it as a party spot with two floors, two atmospheres and a lot of skirt.

Illawarra Performing Arts Centre (IPAC; ☎ 02-4226 3366; www.ipac.org.au; 32 Burelli St) This cultural injection presents excellent theatre, dance and music, including topical productions.

Getting There & Away

All long-distance buses leave from the **long distance bus station** (☎ 02-4226 1022; cnr Keira & Campbell Sts). **Greyhound** (☎ 1300 GREYHOUND/1300 473 946; www .greyhound.com.au) has buses to Gerroa ($15, 45 minutes) and Sydney ($17, two hours). **Premier Motor Service** (☎ 13 34 10; www.premierms.com.au) has buses to Sydney ($16, two hours) and Eden ($67, seven hours). **Murrays** (☎ 13 22 51; www.mur rays.com.au) travels to Moss Vale ($20, 1¼ hours) and Canberra ($33, 3¼ hours). **CountryLink** (☎ 13 22 32; www.countrylink.info) runs buses to Moss Vale ($9, 1¼ hours) from outside the train station, and links with **CityRail** (☎ 13 15 00; www.cityrail.info) to Sydney's Central Station ($10, 1½ hours). CityRail also runs south to Kiama, Gerringong and Bomaderry/Nowra.

Getting Around

Two local bus companies, **Premier Illawarra** (☎ 02-4271 1322; www.premierillawarra.com.au) and **Dions** (☎ 02-4254 4888; www.dions.com.au), service the local area. The main stops are on Marine Dr, and the corner of Crown and Keira Sts.

Bringing a bike on the train from Sydney is a great way to get around; a cycle path runs from the city centre north to Bulli and south to Port Kembla.

WOLLONGONG TO NOWRA

This region has some great beaches, state forests, and, in the ranges to the west, the big **Morton National Park**. It's a popular family-holiday area, but it isn't yet as crowded as parts of the north coast and much of the tourism is confined to weekenders from Sydney. **Lake Illawarra** is popular for water sports.

Further south is **Shellharbour**, a popular holiday resort and one of the oldest towns along the coast (its name comes from the number of shell middens, remnants of Aboriginal feasts, that the early Europeans found here). There are beaches on the Windang Peninsula north of the town and scuba diving off **Bass Point** to the south.

Kiama & Around

Right on the water's edge with good beaches and surf, **Kiama** (population 12,286) hasn't had to work hard for its share of glory. What it has done is admirable and tasteful, making this one of the best stops on the South Coast. The **visitor centre** (☎ 02-4232 3322, 1300 654 262; www.kiama .com.au) is on Blowhole Point, so called because of a **blowhole** that can spurt water 60m.

There's a good **lookout** from the top of Saddleback Mountain, and waves at **Surf** and **Bombo Beaches**.

Amid the flora and fauna of the Southern Highlands, about 14km inland from Kiama, the brand-new **Illawarra Fly Tree Top Walk** (☎ 1300 362 881; www.illawarrafly.com; 182 Knights Hill Rd, Knights Hill; adult/child/family $19/9/49; ☺ 9am-7pm) takes visitors on a 500m elevated walk to the edge of the forest with spectacular Illawarra and ocean views. Nearby **Minnamurra Rainforest Centre** (☺ 9am-5pm) has two stunning nature walks and a **NPWS visitor centre** (☎ 02-4236 0469) in beautiful **Budderoo National Park** (☎ 02-4236 0469; per car $11). On the way you'll pass through the old village of **Jamberoo**, which has a nice pub.

South along the coast, **Gerringong** and **Gerroa** have their fair share of picture-postcard scenery. There's good surf at **Werri Beach**, 10km south in Gerringong, and **Surf Camp Australia** (☎ 1800 888 732; www.surfcamp.com.au; 2 lessons $90) gives surf lessons on beautiful Seven Mile Beach in Gerroa. There are camping parks on both sides of Crooked River here.

Kiama Backpackers (☎ 02-4233 1881; 31 Bong Bong St, Kiama; dm/s/d $25/30/60; ☐) is a decidedly drab building but has clean male and female dorms. The **Grand Hotel** (☎ 02-4232 1037; 49 Manning St, Kiama; s/d $40/70) also caters to backpackers with basic rooms. Bands crank up the volume on Saturday night.

Bellevue Accommodation (☎ 02-4232 4000; 21 Minnamurra St, Kiama; r from $170) hosts guests in luxury serviced apartments in a two-storey 1890s heritage manor. It has ocean views and is a short walk to the main street.

The modern **Kiama Harbour Cabins** (☎ 1800 823 824; Blowhole Point, Kiama; 1-bedroom cabins from $185) are in the best position in town and have barbecues on the front verandahs, which overlook the beach and the ocean pool.

our pick **Seahaven Café** (☎ 02-4234 3796; 19 Riverleigh Ave, Gerroa; lunch $14-29, dinner $18-32) is one of the South Coast's best cafe-cum-restaurants, with gourmet food, tasteful decor and a seaside setting. From the lunch menu, try the fresh ricepaper rolls of smoked salmon, avocado, rocket and mango chutney.

Greyhound (☎ 1300 GREYHOUND/1300 473 946; www.greyhound.com.au) buses run from Gerroa to Wollongong ($15, 45 minutes) and Sydney ($19, three hours), and from Kiama to

Wollongong ($15, 30 minutes) and Sydney ($19, 2½ hours). **Premier Motor Service** (☎ 13 34 10; www.premierms.com.au) buses run to Eden ($67, seven hours) and Sydney ($23, 2½ hours). **Kiama Coachlines** (☎ 02-4232 3466; www.kiamacoach lines.com.au) runs to Gerroa, Gerringong and Minnamurra (via Jamberoo).

Frequent **CityRail** (☎ 13 15 00; www.cityrail .info) trains run to Wollongong, Sydney and Bomaderry/Nowra.

If you're driving, take the beach detour via Gerringong and Gerroa and rejoin the high-way either in Berry or just north of Nowra.

Berry
pop 1485

Berry has metamorphosed from a small retiree kind of town into a must-do South Coast stop. Inland and about 20km north of Nowra, it has a plethora of great eating venues, two pubs fit for shouting a round or two, and a smattering of National Trust–classified buildings.

Pottering Around (☎ 02-4464 2177; 97-99 Queen St), opposite the Great Southern Hotel, has some tourist information, or try www.berry.net.au.

Mild to Wild (☎ 02-4464 2211; 84 Queen St) organ-ises adventure tours such as a pedal, picnic and plunge ($110).

The **Treat Factory** (☎ 02-4464 1112; www.treatfac tory.com.au; Old Creamery Lane; 9.30am-4.30pm Mon-Fri, 10am-4pm Sat & Sun) is chock-full of nostalgic lol-lies such as rocky road and liquorice.

There are several nearby wineries. **Hotel Berry** (☎ 02-4464 1011; 120 Queen St; 11am Sat) runs a short and sweet wine tour ($25), but you need to book ahead.

Accommodation is abundant in Berry, but prices rise at weekends. Holiday apartments can be booked through **Elders Real Estate** (☎ 02-4464 1600; 121 Queen St).

Hotel Berry (☎ 02-4464 1011; 120 Queen St; s/d $70/110) is a popular local watering hole with standard but large pub bedrooms with shared bathroom facilities. Its rear dining room serves grilled steaks and other pub grub.

A step up are the stylish rooms (some with a spa) at the **Village Boutique Motel** (☎ 02-4464 3570; www.berrymotel.com.au; 72-76 Queen St; d from $155;).

our pick Hungry Duck (☎ 02-4464 2323; 85 Queen St; mains $9-28; dinner Wed-Sat, lunch Sun) is one of the newer additions to Berry's foodie scene, with a contemporary Asian menu served tapas-style. Try the *sung choi bao* of braised oxtail, fresh ginger and wild mushroom.

There are scenic roads from Berry to pretty Kangaroo Valley. **Premier Motor Service** (☎ 13 34 10; www.premierms.com.au) has buses to Kiama ($16, 30 minutes), Nowra ($16, 25 minutes) and Sydney ($23, three hours).

Kangaroo Valley
pop 320

Unbelievably picturesque Kangaroo Valley is pegged in by a fortress of rainforest-covered cliffs and the valley floor is carpeted by cow-dotted pasturelands, river gums and gurgling creeks. The slow country town of Kangaroo Valley itself has an excellent pub, bakery and general store, plus the odd feel-good shop and gallery to satiate wealthy Sydneysiders who populate the town at the weekend.

The formal entry to the valley is the cas-tellated sandstone-and-iron **Hamden Bridge** (1898), a few kilometres north of the town. The beach just below the bridge is a good spot for a swim. Next to the bridge is the walkabout **Pioneer Museum Park** (☎ 02-4465 1306; Hampden Bridge, Moss Vale Rd; adult/child/family $4/2.50/10; 10am-4pm Fri-Mon Oct-Easter, 11am-3pm Fri-Mon Easter-Sep), which provides a visual encounter with rural life in the late 19th century.

If you want to get a little more personal with the landscape, go canoeing, mountain biking and bushwalking in and around the Shoalhaven and Kangaroo Rivers. **Kangaroo Valley Escapes** (☎ 0400 651 170; Moss Vale Rd; half-day tours $50-80, overnight $65-180) offers environmen-tally conscious guided tours that you design yourself, combining various rigorous activi-ties. **Kangaroo Valley Safaris** (☎ 02-4465 1502; www .kangaroovalleycanoes.com.au; 2210 Moss Vale Rd; full-day safaris $35-70) rents canoes and bikes (half/full day $35/50) and runs overnight canoe camp-ing trips (2-/3-day trips $85/125).

Hamden Cottage B&B (☎ 02-4465 1502; 2210 Moss Vale Rd; d $180) is a pretty little house near the Hamden Bridge with a rear garden that attracts wallabies. Breakfast is included.

There's a carpet of flat, lush grass to pitch a tent at **Glenmack Park** (☎ 02-4465 1372; www.glen mack.com.au; 215 Moss Vale Rd; unpowered/powered sites $16/24, cabins with/without bathroom $70/50), or you can take the more comfortable option of a cabin. Trees and ducks dominate here, and you can light a campfire (such a rarity!), but there's an undercover barbecue if things get too rough.

The **Friendly Inn Hotel** (☎ 02-4465 1355; 159 Moss Vale Rd; mains $15-25; lunch & dinner) is Kangaroo Valley's heartbeat, a classic country boozer, ever-so-subtly renovated to retain its local character. The rear grassy beer garden has gorgeous views or sit on the sunny pub verandah to people watch.

Kennedy's Bus Service (☎ 1300 133 477; www.kennedystours.com.au) has daily buses to Moss Vale via Fitzroy Falls, and Nowra via Cambewarra.

NOWRA
pop 27,478

Nowra sits about 17km from the coast and is the largest town in the Shoalhaven area. Although it's not top of the pops in terms of beach holidays, it is a handy base for excursions to beaches and villages around the region.

The **Shoalhaven visitor centre** (☎ 1300 662 808; www.shoalhavenholidays.com.au; Princes Hwy; 🖳) is just south of the bridge. There's also a **NPWS office** (☎ 02-4423 2170; 55 Graham St).

The 6.5-hectare **Nowra Wildlife Park** (☎ 02-4421 3949; www.nowrawildlifepark.com.au; Rock Hill Rd, North Nowra; adult/child $16/8; 🕑 9am-5pm), on the north bank of the Shoalhaven River, is a hang-out for mammals, birds and reptiles. It has a fully catered campsite (adult/child $8/6).

Love jumping out of planes? **Nowra Skydive** (☎ 0419 446 904; www.shoal.net.au/~skydivenowra/; Braidwood Rd) has tandem ($330) and static-line ($450) jumps from 10,000ft.

The relaxing **Ben's Walk** starts at the bridge near Scenic Dr and follows the south bank of the Shoalhaven River (6km return). North of the river, the circular 5.5km **Bomaderry Creek Walking Track** runs through sandstone gorges from a trailhead at the end of Narang Rd.

Shoalhaven River Cruises (☎ 0429 981 007; www.shoalhavenrivercruise.com; 2hr cruise $22) has great river tours that leave from the wharf, near the visitor centre.

There are decent motel rooms at **Riverhaven Motel** (☎ 02-4421 2044; www.riverhaven.com.au; 1 Scenic Dr; s/d $65/75), while **Whitehouse** (☎ 02-4421 2084; www.whitehouseguesthouse.com; 30 Junction St; s/d/tr from $90/110/130) is a homely and family-friendly guest house. Ship-shape **Shoalhaven Caravan Village** (☎ 02-4423 0770; 17 Terara Rd; unpowered/powered sites $19/22, cabins $60) backs onto the river.

In an old fire brigade building, **Red Raven** (☎ 02-4423 3433; 55 Junction St; mains $20-28; 🕑 lunch Wed-Fri, dinner Tue-Sat) dishes up distinctly Aussie flavours such as roasted kangaroo fillets with polenta chips. Alternatively, the old renovated **Boatshed Restaurant** (☎ 02-4421 2419; 10

Wharf Rd; entrées $15, mains $30; 🕑 breakfast Sat & Sun, lunch & dinner Thu-Mon) serves excellent food with a river view.

Premier Motor Service (☎ 13 34 10; www.premierms.com.au) runs buses to Sydney ($23, three hours) and Eden ($53, six hours). **Kennedy's Bus Service** (☎ 1300 133 477; www.kennedystours.com.au) has daily buses to Kangaroo Valley, Moss Vale, Greenwell Point and Culburra.

The **train station** (☎ 02-4423 0141) is at Bomaderry. Frequent **CityRail** (☎ 13 15 00; www.cityrail.info) services run to Kiama, Wollongong and Sydney.

An interesting and mainly unsealed road runs from Nowra to Braidwood, through Morton National Park and the hamlets of Sassafras and Nerriga.

AROUND NOWRA

East of Nowra, the Shoalhaven River meanders through dairy country in a system of estuaries and wetlands, finally reaching the sea at Crookhaven Heads.

Greenwell Point, on the estuary about 15km east of Nowra, is a quiet, pretty fishing village specialising in fresh oysters. The little kiosk near the pier has fresh fish and chips for $8.

Further around the inlet there's great **surfing** at **Crookhaven Heads** (Crooky) or **Culburra Beach**, where you can rent a hot-pink, Gidget-esque **surf shack** (☎ 0400 606 990; www.gidgetgoestoculburra.com.au; 78 Park Row; per night $230). Also try **Warrain Beach**, which is protected from wind by the headland. There are camping grounds and, for landlubbers, walking tracks to the lighthouse.

On the north side of the estuary, just before Shoalhaven Heads, is **Historic Coolangatta Estate Winery** (☎ 02-4448 7131; www.coolangattaestate.com.au; 1335 Bolong Rd, Shoalhaven Heads; 🕑 10am-5pm), a slick winery with a golf course, a good restaurant open for lunch and accommodation (singles/doubles from $110/130) in convict-built buildings.

At **Shoalhaven Heads**, sandbars form a bridge between the river and the sea. There's a motel, a caravan park and an excellent **surf beach** here, but for a picnic or a swim keep on trucking north to the **Seven Mile Beach National Park** (admission free), one of the largest stretches of natural coastal-dune vegetation in the state.

JERVIS BAY

South of Nowra, Jervis Bay is a scenically opulent and unmissable stretch of coastline with white sandy beaches, bushland, forest and a protected marine park. **Huskisson** (population 1593), one of the oldest towns on the bay, has a handful of excellent eating venues, plenty of adventure-based activity and delightful surrounds that make it a great place to spend a night or two.

The **Lady Denman Heritage Complex** (☎ 02-4441 5675; www.ladydenman.asn.au; Dent St; adult/child $10/5; ☯ 10am-4pm) has interesting history on Jervis Bay and a maritime museum. On the first Saturday of each month it hosts a **growers market**.

June to November is prime whale time in Jervis Bay, and **Dolphin Watch Cruises** (☎ 1800 246 010t; www.dolphinwatch.com.au; 50 Owen S) has the best reputation for dolphin (adult/child $25/15, two hours) and whale-watching (adult/child $65/35, three hours, May to November) tours. Jervis Bay is also popular with divers. For dives see **Dive Jervis Bay** (☎ 02-4441 5255; www.divejervisbay.com; 64 Owen St; 1/2 dives for $100/170).

Remarkable **Booderee National Park** (2-day car entry $10) occupies Jervis Bay's southeastern spit, a stunning area combining heathland, small rainforest pockets, sparkling water, white sandy beaches and a botanic garden. In 1995 the Wreck Bay Aboriginal community won a land claim and now jointly administers the vast park. There are walks aplenty, basic campsites and, off Jervis Bay Rd, **Scottish Rocks** and **Murrays Beach** are exceptionally beautiful secluded spots. Get maps and info from **Booderee visitor centre** (☎ 02-4443 0977; www.booderee.gov.au; Jervis Bay Rd) at the park entrance. South of Huskisson, **Hyams Beach** is spectacularly white and secluded.

There's substantial accommodation in Huskisson and Vincentia; book ahead for weekends and holidays, when prices soar.

Husky Pub (☎ 02-4441 5001; Owen St; s/d $50/70) is a good-time joint with decent rooms, live music and tip-top bay views. **Huskisson B&B** (☎ 02-4441 7551; www.huskissonbnb.com.au; 12 Tomerong St; r from $185; ✕) is a quaint weatherboard place with bright and airy eclectic rooms containing comfy beds and fluffy towels.

our pick **Paperbark Camp** (☎ 1300 668 167; www.paperbarkcamp.com.au; 571 Woollamia Rd; d from $320; ☯ Sep-Jun) is ecotourism at its luxury best: five-star accommodation in 12 safari-style tents with outdoor showers. The camp's **Gunyah Restaurant** (☎ 02-4441 7299; entrées $25, mains $35; ☯ dinner) sits among the treetops, attracting romantics, and the odd possum.

Supply (☎ 02-4441 5815; shop 1, 54 Owen St; ☯ breakfast & lunch) has fresh and healthy fodder and juices echoed in the floor-to-ceiling shelves of produce and a bay of fresh fruit and vegetables.

AROUND JERVIS BAY

Ulladulla (population 10,298) itself doesn't have much to offer. There is, however, good swimming and surfing nearby at **Mollymook beach**, just north of town. Or head to **Pigeon House Mountain**, which has a fantastic walk (below).

If you do spend a night, try **Traveller's Rest Accommodation** (☎ 02-4454 0500; www.southcoastbackpackers.com; 63 Pacific Hwy, Ulladulla; dm/d $25/55). At the other end of the budget scale, welcoming **Ulladulla Guest House** (☎ 02-4455 1796; www.guesthouse.com.au; 39 Burrill St, Ulladulla; r from $218; ✕ ☎)

PIGEON HOUSE MOUNTAIN

'Everyone must do it,' said the amiable owner of Ulladulla Guest House in his hard-to-pick accent, 'but unfortunately, some people, they drive right past'. It was a small lament, maybe even a throwaway line, but it worked a treat. Climbing Pigeon House Mountain (720m) in the far south of Morton National Park might be the kind of upper-thigh workout that isn't called for on holiday, but the rewards make any huffing and puffing worthwhile.

The main access road leaves the highway about 8km south of Ulladulla, then it's a rough and rocky 26km drive to the picnic area at the start of the track. The return walk takes three to four hours but plan for longer; the summit is barbaric-yawp territory where the rest of the world rolls out from under your feet in all directions.

On a clear day, Gulaga (Mt Dromedary) sticks its head towards the south and to the northwest is Point Perpendicular. In between, a canopy of stunning national park vegetation spreads out like a blanket, occasionally making creases in the steep gorges carved by the Clyde River and flattening out over the elongated plateaus of Byangee Walls and the Castle.

People with a fear of heights should avoid the final section; and be sure to take water as there is none available.

has local and international art lining the walls and a fantastic French restaurant (open for dinner Thursday to Sunday).

our pick **Cupitt's Winery & Restaurant** (☎ 02-4455 7888; www.cupittwines.com.au; 60 Washburton Rd, Ulladulla; ☺ lunch Wed-Sun, dinner Fri & Sat) For a little piece of Provence. make a pit stop at this glorious spot and enjoy some of the most respected cuisine this side of Sydney and wine tasting in the restored 1851 creamery.

Premier Motor Service (☎ 13 34 10; www.premierms .com.au) has buses to Eden ($44, 4¾ hours) and Sydney ($33, five hours). **Priors Scenic Express** (☎ 1800 816 234) heads to local towns, including Milton and Burrill Lake.

Further south, beautiful, coastal **Murramarang National Park** (per car per day $7) is home to wild kangaroos and lorikeets and the protected **Murramarang Aboriginal Area**, which contains ancient middens and other Indigenous cultural treasures. Inside the park, stunning **Pretty** (☎ 02-4457 2019; unpowered sites adult/child $10/5, powered sites $14/7), **Pebbly** (☎ 02-4478 6023; adult/child $10/5) and **Depot Beach** (☎ 02-4478 6582; unpowered sites adult/child $10/5, powered sites $14/7) camping grounds are idyllic locations close to the surf (Pebbly is the most popular for surfing). Pretty Beach is the most accessible. No caravans are allowed at Pebbly Beach.

BATEMANS BAY
pop 10,845

The good beaches and a luscious estuary in this fishing port have given it a leg-up to become one of the South Coast's largest holiday centres. But the town and waterfront are lacklustre, and the food scene is yet to take off.

The **visitor centre** (☎ 1800 802 528; Princes Hwy) has local art for sale. **Live Fire** (☎ 02-4472 2006; shop 1, 6 Orient St; per 20min $2) has internet access.

Corrigans Beach is the closest patch of sand to the town centre. South of here is a series of small beaches nibbled into the rocky shore. Surfers flock to **Surf Beach**, **Malua Bay** and **Broulee**, which has a small wave when everywhere else is flat. For the experienced, the best surfing in the area is at **Pink Rocks** (near Broulee). For amateurs **Soulrider Surf School** (☎ 02-4478 6297; www.soulrider.com.au; 1hr adult/child $40/35) conducts lessons on Surf Beach.

On the north side of the Clyde River estuary, just across the bridge, there are a couple of **boat hire** places. Several boats offer cruises up the estuary from the ferry wharf just east of the bridge, including **Merinda Cruises** (☎ 02-4472

4052; 3hr cruise adult/child $27/14; ☺ 11.30am). **Region X** (☎ 0400 184 034; www.regionxrivers.com; tours $145-440; ▓) hosts morning ($77) and evening ($99) sea kayaking tours with an eco bent.

Holiday apartments are profuse; letting agents include **Nola Debney Real Estate** (☎ 02-4472 1218; www.beachfrontholidays.com.au).

The central **Clyde River Motor Inn** (☎ 02-4472 6444; www.clydemotel.com.au; 3 Clyde St; s/d from $85/89) is excellent value, with good river rooms and townhouses. If you're cashed up, try the **Esplanade Motor Inn** (☎ 02-4472 0200; www.esplanade.com.au; 23 Beach Rd; d from $125) for river views that kick butt.

Alternatively, gather your mates and hire a houseboat. **Bay River Houseboats** (☎ 02-4472 5649; www.bayriverhouseboats.com.au; Wray St) and **Clyde River Houseboats** (☎ 02-4472 6369; www.clyderiverhouseboats .com.au) lease six-/eight-berth boats from $560 for four nights (Monday to Friday).

North St Café & Bar (☎ 02-4472 5710; North St, Batemans Bay; ☺ breakfast & lunch Mon-Sat, dinner Fri & Sat) is a refreshingly funky little den with great coffee and a tasty selection of salads and light lunches. It's a neat place for a wine, too. Also check out **Monet's Café Restaurant** (☎ 02-4472 5717; 3/1 Orient St; mains $18; ☺ breakfast & lunch Mon-Sat, dinner Thu-Sat).

Premier Motor Service (☎ 13 34 10; www.pre mierms.com.au) runs to Eden ($37, 3½ hours) and Sydney ($43, 5¾ hours). **Murrays** (☎ 13 22 51; www.murrays.com.au) runs to Narooma ($24, 1½ hours) and Canberra ($22, 2½ hours).

AROUND BATEMANS BAY

About 60km inland from Batemans Bay, on the scenic road to Canberra, is **Braidwood**, home to many old buildings and a burgeoning food scene.

our pick **Albion Café** (☎ 02-4842 1422; 119 Wallace St; ☺ breakfast & lunch) is a fine example: a corner pub conversion complete with floorboards, open fire, excellent coffee and a breakfast menu that includes corn fritters with bacon, poached egg, spinach and spicy tomato chutney.

From November to February there's peach-picking work in the peaceful little town of **Araluen**, 26km south of Braidwood on the road to Moruya. **Araluen Valley Hotel** (☎ 02-4846 4023; Main Rd; s/d $45/70) has all the info and back-to-basics pub rooms.

There's unspoilt coast down the side roads south of **Moruya**, including **Eurobodalla National Park**, an area of many lakes, bays and inlets backed by spotted-gum forests that stretch down past Narooma. Don't miss the incredible

NEW SOUTH WALES

rock formations at **Bingie Bingie Point** or the 7.5km **Bingie Dream Track**. Contact the Narooma NPWS (below) for more information.

Inland from Moruya, **Deua National Park** is a mountainous wilderness area (122,033 hectares) with gentle and swift-running rivers (good for canoeing or floating on a lilo), some challenging walks and a network of limestone caves. **Deua River** (campsites adult/child $5/3) and **Berlang camping grounds** (campsites adult/child $5/3) make good bases for activities.

NAROOMA
pop 3100

Narooma is a sleepy little seaside town with a large number of retiree residents adding to its snail-paced leisurely atmosphere. It's also one of the prettier coastal towns boasting the attractive Wagonga River inlet, a picturesque bridge and relatively little development.

The **visitor centre** (☎ 1800 240 003, 02-4476 2881; www.naturecoast-tourism.com.au; Princes Hwy), incorporating the **Lighthouse Museum**, is just south of the bridge.

Narooma is an access point for Deua, Gulaga and Wadbilliga National Parks, and there's a **NPWS office** (☎ 02-4476 0800; www.nationalparks.nsw.gov.au; cnr Graham & Burrawang Sts).

Cruise inland up the Wagonga River on the **Wagonga Princess** (☎ 02-4476 2665; 3hr cruise adult/child $33/22; ☺ 1pm). **Boat hire** and **fishing charters** are available along Riverside Dr.

Heading north over the bridge, take the first two right turns to **Mills Bay Boardwalk**, a 5km wheelchair- and pram-friendly walking track where you can spot large schools of fish and stingrays.

For **surfing**, Mystery Bay, between Cape Dromedary and Corunna Point, is rocky but good, as is Handkerchief Beach. More relaxing **swims** can be had at the south end of Bar Beach. From there it's a short stroll up to **Bar Rock Lookout** for a view of Montague Island (right). The clear waters around the island are good for **diving**, especially from February to June when you can snorkel with the fur seals.

Island Charters Narooma (☎ 02-4476 1047; www.islandchartersnarooma.com) offers diving ($85), snorkelling ($75), kayaking (adult/child $45/40) and·whale watching ($80/55). Attractions in the area include grey nurse sharks, fur seals and the wreck of the SS *Lady Darling*. For the cheapest deal, book tours at the visitor centre.

Narooma Real Estate (☎ 02-4476 2169), opposite the visitor centre, rents holiday accommodation.

Narooma YHA (☎ 02-4476 3287; www.yha.com.au; 243 Princes Hwy; dm/d $32/75; ⌨) has comfortable, clean motel-style rooms and fun hosts. **Lynch's Hotel** (☎ 02-4476 2001; 135 Wagonga St; s/d $50/80) is an old-school place in the heart of town, with lovely rooms, and shared kitchen and bathroom facilities. Downstairs is a cute restaurant open for dinner.

Whale Motor Inn (☎ 02-4476 2411; www.whalemotorinn.com; 104 Wagonga St; d $120; ⌨ ⌨) offers the best all-round views of Narooma. It has large, clean renovated rooms with balconies, and a nice restaurant.

ourpick **Pelican's** (☎ 02-4476 2403; Riverside Dr; mains $13-32; ☺ breakfast & lunch Tue-Sun, dinner Fri, Sat & holidays), jutting idly into the lovely river frontage on the Marina, is the pick of local fare. The bouillabaisse with crusty bread is a rare treat.

Quarterdeck Marina (☎ 02-4476 2723; 13 Riverside Dr; mains $22; ☺ breakfast & lunch Wed-Mon), with its colourful maritime decor, serves ah-me-hearties breakfasts and fresh seafood lunches on a great deck overhanging the river.

Premier Motor Service (☎ 13 34 10; www.premierms.com.au) has buses to Eden ($25, 12½ hours), Sydney ($56, 7½ hours) and Melbourne ($65, 10 hours). Buses stop outside Lynch's Hotel. **Murrays** (☎ 13 22 51; www.murrays.com.au) runs to Batemans Bay ($24, 1½ hours) and Canberra ($33, 4½ hours).

AROUND NAROOMA

About 10km offshore from Narooma, **Montague Island** was once an important source of food for local Aborigines (who called it Barunguba) and is now a nature reserve. **Little penguins** nest here; the best time to see them is spring. Many other seabirds and hundreds of fur seals also call the island home, and there's a historic **lighthouse**.

Narooma Charters (☎ 0407 909 111; adult/child/family $130/99/430) operates a daily four-hour boat trip to Montague Island including a NPWS tour. Take the afternoon trip if you want to see the little penguins.

Off the highway, 15km south of Narooma, **Central Tilba** is perched on the side of **Gulaga** (Mt Dromedary; 797m). It's a delightful 19th-century gold-mining boomtown. There's information and a town guide at **Bates Emporium** (☎ 02-4473 7290; Bates St), at the start of the main street. Further along are several craft, antique and gift shops, galleries, and food venues including the **ABC Cheese Factory** (☎ 02-4473 7387; ☺ 8am-5pm), where you can chow down on cheddar.

Nearby **Gulaga National Park** includes Gulaga Flora Reserve, a large portion of Gulaga and the former **Wallaga Lake** national park. Trees now block the views from the summit of Gulaga, but there are many sites of Aboriginal significance worth experiencing. For an expert tour visit **Umbarra Cultural Centre** (☎ 02-4473 7232; www.umbarra.com.au; ☺ 9am-5pm Mon-Fri, to 4pm Sat & Sun), run by the Yuin people from the Wallaga Lake Koori community. It is 3km from the highway towards Wallaga Lake, a worthy scenic drive in its own right.

On the Princes Hwy is **Cobargo**, another unspoilt old town. Near here is the main 2WD access point to rugged **Wadbilliga National Park**, a subalpine wilderness area of 98,530 hectares.

Bermagui
pop 1298

South of the beautiful bird-filled Wallaga Lake and off the Princes Hwy, Bermagui is a pretty fishing port with a main street that hums to the sound of small-town contentment. The new purpose-built **information centre** (☎ 02-6493 3054; www.bermagui.net; Bunga St) with its museum and discovery centre is a sign that tourists are finally appreciating it too.

There are several **walks** around Bermagui (including an 8km coast walk to Wallaga Lake), good **surfing** at Camel Rock and Cuttagee beaches, and a spectacular **beach rock pool**.

Julie Rutherford Real Estate (☎ 02-6493 3444; www.julierutherford.com.au) can assist with lettings. One option is **Seaview Flats** (per week $385), a row of blue-and-white two-bedroom beach huts on the main road into town.

our pick **Bermagui Beach Hotel** (☎ 02-6493 4206; 10 Lamont St; dm $20-40; d $60-175; ✿) is a gorgeous old place with the best views in town. Stay here to tap into the local scene. The suites have spas, and, like the motel rooms, include bathrooms and TV. The dorms have shared bathrooms.

Zane Grey Park (☎ 02-6493 4382; www.zanegreytouristpark.com.au; Lamont St; powered/unpowered sites $23/19, cabins $45-85) has a prime position on Dickson's Point overlooking Horseshoe Bay.

Snazzy **Morrisons on Lamont** (☎ 02-6493 3165; Lamont St; entrées $15, mains $22; ☺ dinner) cooks seafood delights such as Eden mussels with tomato, dill and baby caper sauce.

SOUTH TO THE VICTORIAN BORDER

Running along 20km of beautiful coastline, **Mimosa Rocks National Park** (per car $7) is 5802 hectares of earthly paradise with dense and varied bush, caves, headlands and beaches with crystal-clear water. There are basic **campsites** (adult/child $10/5) at **Aragunnu Beach**, **Picnic Point**, and **Middle** and **Gillards Beaches**. The Narooma **NPWS office** (☎ 02-4476 0800; www.nationalparks.nsw.gov.au) has more info.

Taking in most of the coast from Merimbula north to Tathra (on beautiful Sapphire Coast Dr), **Bournda National Park** (per car $7) is a 2378-hectare park with good beaches, freshwater lagoons and several walking trails. **Camping** (adult/child $10/5) is permitted at Hobart Beach, on the southern shore of the big **Wallagoot Lagoon**. Contact the **Merimbula NPWS office** (☎ 02-6495 5000) for more information.

Merimbula
pop 3851

The surplus of nondescript hotels and holiday apartments lining the sloping main street of Merimbula still manage to play second fiddle to the town's impressive inlet (or lake). The rocking boat masts and sky-blue water – catering to fisherfolk throwing in a line wherever they please – make this popular holiday place very easy on the eye.

The **visitor centre** (☎ 02-6495 1129; www.sapphirecoast.com.au; cnr Market & Beach Sts; per 15min $2) has internet access. The **NPWS office** (☎ 02-6495 5000; cnr Merimbula & Sapphire Coast Drs) provides information on bushwalking.

SIGHTS & ACTIVITIES

At the wharf on the eastern point is the small **Merimbula Aquarium** (☎ 02-6495 4446; Lake St; adult/child $12/7; ☺ 10am-5pm). There are good views across the lake from near here and the jetty is a popular fishing spot.

Merimbula Divers Lodge (☎ 1800 651 861; www.merimbuladiverslodge.com.au; 15 Park St) has PADI-certificate courses ($460), shore dives, three wreck dives and a cave dive.

Merimbula Marina (☎ 02-6495 1686; Merimbula jetty) runs three-hour reef cruises (adult/child $40/30), two-hour dolphin cruises ($25/20) and whale-watching cruises (from $40/25) from September to November. There's **boat hire** at the Merimbula Marina jetty ($25 per 30 minutes).

West of the bridge, just off the causeway, a magnificent 1.75km **boardwalk** takes nature lovers and morning people hopping and skipping around mangroves, oyster farms and melaleucas.

Nearby **Pambula Beach** is quiet, in a suburban kind of way, with a pretty main street.

SLEEPING & EATING

Letting agents for the area include **Merimbula Lake Accommodation Centre** (☎ 02-6495 1522; Market St).

Wandarrah YHA Lodge (☎ 02-6495 3503; www .yha.com.au; 8 Marine Pde; dm/d from $24/60) This clean place, with a good kitchen and hanging-out areas, is near the surf beach and the bus stop. Pick-ups by arrangement or let the staff know if you're arriving late.

Merimbula Gardens Motel (☎ 02-6495 5900; 36 Merimbula Dr; s/d $65/70; ⚗ ▣ ▣) Though there are no gardens to speak of, this old-school motel is one of the cheaper options in the heart of town. Rooms are basic but clean and comfortable.

Merimbula Lakeview Hotel (☎ 02-6495 1202; Market St; r from $89) This waterfront establishment has stylish rooms with all the motel trimmings; a handful have good views. Come summertime, they're close to the beer garden…which may be good or bad. The Lakeview bistro (mains $12 to $30) has upmarket pub food and an open fire in winter.

our pick Cantina Tapas & Wine Bar (☎ 02-6495 1085; 58 Market St; tapas from $7; ☽ lunch & dinner) This atmospheric little hidey-hole in the centre of town dishes up tasty plates of salt-and-pepper calamari, fried chorizo and lamb souvlaki. Not hungry? The bar has a good vibe also.

Zanzibar Café (☎ 02-6495 3636; cnr Main & Market Sts; entrées $16-25, mains $25-33; ☽ dinner Tue-Sat) Serving up a seafood hot pot for two ($75) filled with king prawns, Eden black mussels and Balmain bugs, this contemporary restaurant is the ideal romantic night out.

GETTING THERE & AWAY

Rex (☎ 13 17 13; www.regionalexpress.com.au) flies to Melbourne ($140, 1½ hours) and Sydney ($140, 1¾ hours). The airport is 1km out of town on the road to Pambula.

Premier Motor Service (☎ 13 34 10; www.premierms .com.au) has buses to Eden ($7, 25 minutes), Melbourne ($56, 8½ hours) and Sydney ($67, 8½ hours). They stop near the lakeside BP.

CountryLink (☎ 13 22 32; www.countrylink.info) runs

to Canberra ($34, four hours), and **Deane's** (☎ 02-6495 6452; www.deanestransitgroup.com.au) runs to Pambula, Bega and Eden.

Eden

pop 3006

Eden lives up to its namesake. Once a haven for fisherfolk and woodchippers, this charming seaside town is now squarely on the itinerary for those looking to laze a day away on the town's 1.5km beach or explore the surrounding national parks and wilderness areas. Whale watching is big on the agenda and you're likely to hear a bit about former resident Benjamin Boyd, a 19th-century entrepreneur, landowner and magnate whose failed whaling boom enterprise – Boydtown – can still be visited.

The helpful **visitor centre** (☎ 02-6496 1953; Mitchell St) is in the same building as the library, which has internet access.

The **Killer Whale Museum** (☎ 02-6496 2094; 94 Imlay St; adult/child $8/2; ☽ 9.15am-4.45pm Mon-Sat, 11am-5pm Sun) is often derided as a little old hat. You decide. The skeleton of Old Tom, a killer whale and local legend is housed there.

In October and November, **Cat Balou Cruises** (☎ 0427 962 027; www.catbalou.com.au; Main Wharf; adult/child $65/55) has whale-spotting cruises. At other times, dolphins, fur seals and seabirds can usually be seen during the shorter bay cruise ($30/17).

Ocean Wilderness (☎ 02-6495 3669; www.oceanwil derness.com.au) has kayaking trips through Ben Boyd National Park and Twofold Bay ($80), two-hour whale-watching tours during whale season ($40) and a day trip to Davidson Whaling Station ($125).

Boydtown, off the highway 10km south of Eden, has relics of Ben Boyd's stillborn empire.

See the sea through a rocky reef aquarium at the new **Sapphire Coast Marine Discovery Centre** (☎ 02-6496 1699; www.edenmarinediscovery.org.au; Main Wharf; ☽ 1-4pm Wed-Sun) and sign up for a rocky shore ramble (adult/child $5/1) or group snorkelling trip ($25).

Eden comes alive at the start of November with the annual **Whale Festival** (www.edenwhale festival.com).

The **Great Southern Hotel** (☎ 02-6496 1515; www .greatsoutherninn.com.au; 121 Imlay St; dm/s/d/f $20/30/60/80) has good-value shared pub rooms and newly renovated backpacker accommodation. The pub grub downstairs is hearty and the rear deck is a winner.

At Boydtown, the **Seahorse Inn** (☎ 02-6496 1361; d from $175), overlooking Twofold Bay, is a lavish boutique hotel with all the trimmings. It's worth popping into the bar for a stickybeak.

Eden Tourist Park (☎ 02-6496 1139; Aslings Beach Rd; www.edentouristpark.com.au; unpowered/powered sites from $20/23, cabins from $57) is neat, trim and in a prime position on a spit separating stunning Aslings Beach from Lake Curalo.

our pick **Taste of Eden** (☎ 02-6496 1304; Main Wharf; mains $18) is an atmospheric, tiny cafe with a seafaring decor serving a good selection of seafood, including fresh local mussels with white wine, chilli and lemon.

The corner locale of the **Wharfside Café** (☎ 02-6496 1855; Main Wharf; mains $10-18) makes it ideal for lazy coffee in the sun or dishes such as macadamia-and-parmesan-crusted fish or Sichuan fish and prawn salad.

Premier Motor Service (☎ 13 34 10; www.premierms .com.au) has buses to Melbourne ($56, eight hours) and Sydney ($69, 10 hours). **Deane's** (☎ 02-6495 6452; www.deanestransitgroup.com.au) runs to Merimbula, Pambula and Bega. They stop opposite the Caltex service station. Bus bookings can be made at the visitor centre.

Ben Boyd National Park & Around

Protecting some relics of Ben Boyd's operations, this national park (10,485 hectares), stretching north and south along the coast on either side of Eden, has dramatic coastline, bush and walking territory. The southern access road is the sealed Edrom Rd, off the Princes Hwy 19km south of Eden.

Wonboyn Rd is 4km south of Edrom Rd, and gives access to Nadgee Nature Reserve and to **Wonboyn**, a small settlement on Wonboyn Lake at the northern end of the reserve. Many roads in the parks have unsealed sections that can be slippery after rain.

Nadgee Nature Reserve, stretching from the southern tip of Ben Boyd National Park to the Victorian border, is one of Australia's spectacularly wild and remote wilderness areas. Such is the importance of this pristine environment that general access is only allowed as far as the ranger station near the Merrica River, 7km from Newton's Beach. To really get a feel for the breathtaking scenery, a limited number of visitors can apply for a permit. Most do so to experience the **Nadgee Howe Wilderness Walk**, 50km of remote heathlands, windswept beaches and coastal lagoons.

Walk-in campsites are also available. Contact the Merimbula **NPWS** (☎ 02-6495 5000; www.environ ment.nsw.gov.au/nationalparks) for info or download a permit application.

SNOWY MOUNTAINS

The Snowies, as they are known, form part of the Great Diving Range where it straddles the NSW–Victorian border and also the Australian Alps stretching north to the ACT border and south to the Victorian Alps. This larger region boasts five of the highest peaks on the mainland, and the Snowies themselves lays claim to *numero uno*, Mt Kosciuszko (koz-zy-*os*-ko), at 2228m. In its entirety, the region is mainland Australia's only true Alpine area, and as such, can expect snow falls from early June to late August.

Kosciuszko National Park, NSW's largest at 673,492 hectares, dominates the Snowies in all seasons. The Snowy Mountains Hwy and Alpine Way worm their way through the park providing spectacular scenery and access to the tiny towns of the famed Snowy Mountain Scheme. In winter, the bigger towns of Jindabyne and Cooma become hives of activity when day-trippers and holidaymakers pass through on their way to live it up in the snow towns of Thredbo and Perisher Blue.

Getting There & Away

Cooma is the eastern gateway to the Snowy Mountains. The most spectacular mountain views can be enjoyed from the Alpine Way (sometimes closed in winter), running between Khancoban, on the western side of the national park, and Jindabyne. You'll need a car to use this road. There are restrictions on car use in the national park during the ski season; check with the NPWS or visitor centres at Cooma or Jindabyne before entering.

If you are just going to one place to ski, then public transport is an option. Otherwise, you'll need a car, which does let you fully appreciate the region.

COOMA
pop 6587

You could 'coo-ee' down the main street of Cooma in summer and not raise an eyebrow. But proximity to the snowfields keeps

NEW SOUTH WALES

this little town punching above its weight during winter. It imbues the best of 'country town' and 'mountain momma', with good places to hang out, an attractive centre and a laid-back vibe.

The **visitor centre** (☎ 1800 636 525; www.visitcooma .com.au; 119 Sharp St; per hr $6) makes accommodation bookings and has internet access.

Sights & Activities

On the Monaro Hwy, 2km north of the town centre, the **Snowy Mountains Scheme Information Centre** (☎ 1800 623 776; www.snowyhydro.com.au; admission free) has the best info on this feat of engineering; the dams and hydroelectric plant took 25 years and more than 100,000 people to build.

The **Cooma Monaro Railway** (☎ 02-6452 7791; 11am, 1pm & 2pm Sat & Sun summer, 1pm & 2pm Sun winter) runs train rides to Snowy Junction (adult/child $6/4), Bunyan ($12/8) and Chakola ($18/12) aboard restored 1923 CPH rail motors. Ring ahead (☎ 0417 061 699) for midweek rides.

Next to functioning Cooma Gaol is the new **NSW Department of Corrective Services Museum** (☎ 02-6452 5974; 1 Vale St; admission free; 12.30-3.30pm Tue-Fri, from 9.30am Sat) exhibiting artefacts from convict time through to the present prison system. Inmates conduct tours and sell their art and craft.

Sleeping & Eating

Bunkhouse Motel (☎ 02-6452 2983; www.bunkhouse motel.com.au; 28 Soho St; winter dm/s/d $30/45/65) This is good value for money in Cooma – a neat, friendly place with a slightly cramped and rustic feel. All rooms have cooking facilities.

Royal Hotel (☎ 02-6452 2132; www.royalhotelcooma .com; 59 Sharp St; s/d $35/55) The oldest licensed hotel in Cooma is a beautiful old sandstone place with decent pub rooms, open fires, shared bathrooms and a great verandah. Lambies Grill is a fine place for a pub meal and a beer.

Snowtels Caravan Park (☎ 02-6452 1828; www.snowtels.com.au; 286 Sharp St; unpowered/powered sites $19/23, cabins from $42) On the highway, 1.5km west of town, this is a big, well-equipped place.

Kuma Pies & Pastries (☎ 02-6452 6337; 180 Sharp St; breakfast & lunch) This cosy slip of a cafe has bar stools where patrons can sit and munch on a 'bushman' pie (cheese, bacon and beef) or a 'drover' (beef, mushy peas and bacon) for under $5. It also does decent coffee.

Pastry Box Patisserie (☎ 02-6452 5159; 100 Sharp St; breakfast & lunch) Opens at about 6am (knock and the pastry chef will let you in) with a selection of French pastries, chicken-and-tarragon pies, wraps, flans and sandwiches.

Lott (☎ 02-6452 1414; 177 Sharp St; breakfast & lunch daily, dinner Fri) In a kitted-out corner shop, Cooma's foodie hub has excellent coffee, hearty snacks, light lunches and pastries and is a provedore of all kinds of gourmet goodies perfect for picnics.

Getting There & Away

The airport is about 10km southwest of Cooma on the Snowy Mountains Hwy but at the time of writing, operators had stopped flying here.

Murrays (☎ 13 22 51; www.murrays.com.au) buses run from Canberra via Cooma ($41), Jindabyne ($41) and Bullocks Flat ($41) to Thredbo ($53). It also has day returns to Thredbo ($72) and Perisher Blue ($59), with lift passes and equipment packages available. **Transborder** (☎ 02-6241 0033; www.transborder.com.au) and **Greyhound Ski Express** (☎ 1300 GREYHOUND/1300 473 946; www.greyhound.com.au) have similar itineraries and package deals.

Snowliner Coaches (☎ 02-6452 1584; www.snowliner .com.au) do a public-accessible school run to Jindabyne ($15) and back.

CountryLink (☎ 132 232; www.countrylink.info) runs year-round to Canberra ($14, two hours) and Sydney Central ($21, 7½ hours). Snowboards and skis are not permitted on board.

Victoria's **V/Line** (☎ 13 61 96; www.vline.com .au) has a twice-weekly run from Melbourne to Canberra via Cooma (9¼ hours). The trip from Melbourne takes you by train to Bairnsdale, then by bus.

Heading to Batemans Bay, you can travel via Numeralla to Braidwood on a partly sealed road skirting Deua National Park. If you're heading to Bega, be warned that there's no petrol until Bemboka.

JINDABYNE
pop 1903

Jindabyne has a split personality. As the closest town to Kosciuszko National Park's major ski resorts, it sleeps more than 20,000 visitors in winter. But in summer the crowds go elsewhere and the town reverts to its relatively peaceful small-town self, where fishing is the mainstay activity.

Information

Koscom (☎ 02-6456 2766; shop 17, Nugget's Crossing, per hr $10) Has internet access. The post office is located behind the centre.

Nugget's Crossing (Kosciuszko Rd) The town's main shopping centre is near the visitor centre with three banks, cafes and shops.

Snowy Region visitor centre (☎ 02-6450 5600; www.nationalparks.nsw.gov.au; Kosciuszko Rd) This impressive centre is operated by the NPWS. There are display areas, a cinema and a good cafe.

Summer Activities

Jindabyne Adventure Booking (☎ 1300 736 581; 2 Thredbo Tce) has various tours and packages, including wake boarding, mountain biking, white-water rafting, abseiling and guided walks to the top of Mt Kosciuszko. It also rents bikes (adult/child per hour $15/10, per day $40/30).

Steve Williamsons Fishing Adventures (☎ 02-6456 1551; shop 1, Snowline Centre, Kosciuszko Rd) conducts tours including a *Jindabyne – the movie* – boat tour through the old and new lake townships and to Curiosity Rocks and Church Rocks.

Paddy Pallin (☎ 1800 623 459; www.paddypallin.com.au; cnr Kosciuszko & Thredbo Rds; ☼ 9am-5pm summer, 8am-6pm Mon-Thu, 7.30am-midnight Fri, to 7pm Sat & Sun winter) is a kitted-out adventure centre 2.5km from Jindabyne, just past the Thredbo Rd turn-off.

Among the dozens of local adventure companies:

Snowy River Horseback Adventure (☎ 02-6457 8393; www.snowyriverhorsebackadventure.com.au; half-day rides $95) Experienced riders. Also two- to five-day treks.

Upper Murray Rafting (☎ 1800 677 179; www.raftingsnowymountains.com.au; half-day trips $65) White-water rafting.

Sleeping

The influx of snow bunnies in winter sends prices through the roof, so book ahead. Agents for holiday rental include **Jindabyne & Snowy Mountains Accommodation Centre** (☎ 1800 527 622; www.snowaccommodation.com.au) and **Visit Snowy Mountains** (☎ 02-6457 7132; www.visitsnowymountains.com.au). Many lodges have ski gear and accommodation packages.

Carinya Alpine Village (☎ 02-6456 2252; www.carinya-village.com.au; Carinya Lane; winter bunkrooms per person $25-44, apt per person from $160) Off the Snowy River Way, this budget abode with four- to 10-bed apartments has no pretensions. It's

homely and basic – ideal for those who prefer boarding to critiquing furniture.

Snowy Mountains Backpackers (☎ 1800 333 468; www.snowybackpackers.com.au; 7-8 Gippsland St; summer dm/d $25/60, winter dm $30-42, d $90-130, family dm $160-220; ☐) Perhaps the best winter value in Jindabyne, this well-oiled machine has clean rooms, internet ($3 per 20 minutes), rooms with bathrooms and service with a smile. The way a backpackers should be.

Banjo Paterson Inn (☎ 1800 046 275; www.banjopatersoninn.com.au; 1 Kosciuszko Rd; summer r from $79, winter $130-230) The best rooms at this lakefront place have balconies and bathrooms. Other facilities include a rowdy bar (see below) and Clancy's restaurant. It might look a little washed out in summer but it's a lively establishment come snowtime.

Lake Jindabyne Hotel/Motel (☎ 1800 646 818; Kosciuszko Rd; s/d $80/90; ☒) A big place by the lake in the centre of town, this has a heated pool, a spa, sauna and bar (see below).

Eating & Drinking

Café Susu (☎ 02-6456 1503; 8 Gippsland St; ☼ 8am-8.30pm) Near the backpackers, this place has cheap and tasty breakfast dishes ($8 to $10), salads, burgers and other light meals.

Café Darya (☎ 02-6457 1867; Snowy Mountains Plaza; mains $13-28) Tucked away on the upper level this Persian restaurant is a treat for those who find it. Fill up on slow-cooked lamb shank in Persian spices and rose petals or, for something lighter, a trio of award-winning dips.

Angie's Italian Kitchen (☎ 02-6456 2523; Snowy Mountains Plaza; mains $20; ☼ lunch & dinner) Ignore the nearby Italian competitors: this cosy eatery with an outdoor deck and water views dishes up authentic Italian dishes such as black mussels with tomato and garlic, homemade ravioli and wood-fired pizzas.

Banjo Paterson Inn (☎ 1800 046 275; www.banjopatersoninn.com.au; 1 Kosciuszko Rd; mains $20; ☼ lunch & dinner) This is a popular establishment where locals flock for a piss-up in the main bar (don't mind the big screens and poker machines). For a quieter tipple, slip next door for a glass of wine at Clancy's.

Lake Jindabyne Hotel/Motel (☎ 1800 646 818; Kosciuszko Rd; ☼ lunch & dinner) With its massive bar and eating area, this place is purpose-built for packing people in. It's party-central in winter. In summer the big beer deck has the best lake views in town.

NEW SOUTH WALES

KOSCIUSZKO NATIONAL PARK

It would be short-sighted to visit the jewel in NSW's national-park crown – home to Australia's highest mountain, **Mt Kosciuszko** (2228m) – and to focus purely on the snow. Sure the mountain welcomes throngs of ski bunnies in winter, but this natural park, covering 673,492 hectares and stretching 150km from north to south, has so many varied attractions that it takes visits in all seasons to really gauge its full potential.

Scenic drives reveal a wonderland of alpine and subalpine flora and fauna. This is the only place on the planet, for example, where you'll find the rare mountain pygmy possum. Come spring and summer, pristine walking trails and campsites can be appreciated when spectacular alpine flowers are in full bloom. Mystical caves, limestone gorges, historic huts and homesteads are also ripe for discovery.

In some parts, the ghostly dead-white trunks of eucalypts bare witness to a treacherous bushfire in 2003, from which a huge swathe of land is still recovering.

Despite this, the park has recently been National Heritage listed. It has also lured pundits of another sport – cyclists addicted to the calf-burning sensation of those winding uphill climbs.

Orientation & Information

Mt Kosciuszko and the main ski resorts are in the south-central area of the park. From Jindabyne, Kosciuszko Rd leads to the resorts of Smiggin Holes (30km), Perisher Valley (33km) and Charlotte Pass (40km), with a turn-off before Perisher Valley to Guthega and Mt Blue Cow. From Jindabyne, the Alpine Way leads to Thredbo (33km) and on to Khancoban (103km).

The main NPWS visitor centre for the park is at Jindabyne (p241). There's an **education centre** (☎ 02-6451 3700) at Sawpit Creek (15km from Jindabyne), which runs programs during school holidays, and visitor centres at Khancoban in the west of the park, and Yarrangobilly Caves and Tumut (p246) in the north.

For a great park map and information, pick up a free copy of *Kosciuszko Today* at the visitor centres.

Entry to the national park costs $27 a day per car in winter and $16 at other times. If you intend to stay a while, buy the $190 annual parks permit, which gives you unlimited access to every national park in NSW.

SEASONAL WORK

Thredbo employs about 200 year-round full-time staff and close to 750 in winter. For job vacancies and info, **Snowy Staff** (☎ 02-6457 1950; www.snowystaff.com.au; Nuggets Crossing, Jindabyne) is a one-stop shop. Also check out www.thredbo.com.au/about-thredbo/snow-jobs. The noticeboard at Thredbo supermarket in the village centre also posts jobs and accommodation.

For seasonal job vacancies and information in Perisher Blue, check out www.perisherjobs.com.au. Foreign applicants need a working visa; however, Perisher Blue can apply for sponsored work visas.

Fruit-picking work is also available in Batlow; see p246.

Skiing

With a short season (early June to late August) and unpredictable snowfalls, this is not the Swiss Alps. But don't be put off. Thredbo has forked out a fortune to automate its snowmaking machines (ensuring 25% of rideable terrain is covered), and Perisher Blue has upgraded its facilities to enable more reliable connections between major chairlifts. If the outcome is not exactly 100%-guaranteed snow, it's a pretty good start.

Off the slopes there's lively nightlife, excellent restaurants, and a plethora of facilities and activities catering for families. Both Thredbo and Perisher Blue have a designated kids skiing program, crèches and day care.

On the downside, the resorts tend to be particularly crowded at weekends and the short season means operators have to get their returns quickly, so costs are high. (There's a running joke among Australians that it is cheaper to fly to New Zealand to ski.)

For snow and road reports, contact the visitor centres at **Thredbo** (☎ 1900 934 320) and **Perisher Blue** (☎ 1900 926 664) or try www.ski.com.au. Also tune into 97.7 Snow FM locally.

Sleeping

There's no longer a problem finding accommodation in summer, especially at the year-round resort of Thredbo (p244). The Alpine Way between Jindabyne and Thredbo is similarly punctuated with cosy B&Bs and resorts. In all cases the off-season prices will

KOSCIUSZKO NATIONAL PARK

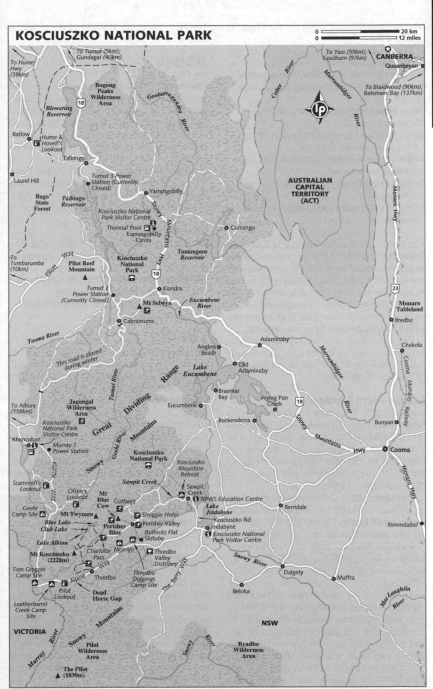

be considerably lower, some less than half the peak-season prices.

Travel agents in most regions book accommodation and ski packages. Useful contacts:

Jindabyne & Snowy Mountains Accommodation Centre (☎ 1800 527 622; www.snowaccommodation .com.au)

Snowy Mountains Holiday Centre (☎ 1800 641 064; www.smhc.com.au)

Snowy Mountains Reservation Centre (☎ 1800 020 622; www.snowholidays.com.au)

Thredbo Accommodation (☎ 1800 801 982; www .accommodationthredbo.com.au)

Thredbo Resort Centre (☎ 1300 020 589; www .thredbo.com.au)

Visit Snowy Mountains (☎ 02-6457 7132; www .visitsnowymountains.com.au)

The only formal camping area is **Kosciuszko Mountain Retreat** (☎ 02-6456 2224; www.kositreat.com .au; unpowered/powered sites from $25/35, cabins from $115), but in such a pristine environment it would be a shame not to sample at least one of the 48 free campsites spread throughout the park, most of them accessible by 2WD and equipped with toilet, picnic and barbecue facilities.

For a real high-country experience, bunker down in one of the historic homesteads run by the NPWS. The Tumut visitor centre (p246) has all the info.

Getting There & Around
Murrays (☎ 13 22 51; www.murrays.com.au) runs from Canberra to Cooma ($41), Jindabyne ($41), Bullocks Flat (for Skitube; $41) and Thredbo ($53). It also has day returns from Canberra to Thredbo ($72) and Perisher Blue ($59), with lift passes and equipment hire packages available.

Transborder (☎ 02-6241 0033; www.transborder.com .au), **SkiBus** (☎ 02-6456 2957; www.skibus.net.au) and **Greyhound Ski Express** (☎ 1300 GREYHOUND/1300 473 946; www.greyhound.com.au) have similar deals.

Snowliner Coaches (☎ 02-6452 1584; www.snow liner.com.au) does a public-accessible school run to Jindabyne ($15).

Several coach companies operate shuttle services from the **Snowy Region visitors centre** (☎ 1800 004 439) in Jindabyne to the skifields.

In winter you can normally drive as far as Perisher Valley, but snow chains must be carried in 2WD vehicles – even when there's no snow – and fitted where directed. The penalty if you're caught without them is more than $300. The simplest, safest way to get to Perisher Valley and Smiggin Holes in winter is to take the Skitube train (opposite).

THREDBO
pop 477

Thredbo (☎ 1300 020 589; www.thredbo.com.au) is oft lauded as Australia's number-one ski resort. At 1370m it not only has the longest runs and some of the best skiing, the village itself is eye candy compared with other Australian ski villages, the blue, green and grey tones ensuring chalets and lodges blend with the surrounding snow gums and alpine flora. And, of course, Thredbo is an all-season resort, so if you can't afford it in winter, summer has a lot to offer, too.

Information
Hot Shots (☎ 02-6457 6422; 1st fl, Upper Concourse, Alpine Hotel; per 5min $1.50) Unfathomably expensive internet access.
Thredbo Leisure Centre (☎ 02-6459 4100, 02-6459 4151; Friday Dr) The low-down on everything.
Thredbo visitor centre (☎ 02-6459 4294; Friday Dr) Good for accommodation.

Activities
Thredbo's skiing terrain is roughly 16% beginner, 67% intermediate and 17% advanced; no matter what category you fit into you should try to have a crack at a long run. The **Supertrail** (3.7km) begins at Australia's highest lifted point, then drops 670m through some pretty awesome scenery. From up here you can also take the 5km easy **Village Trail** to Friday Flats, or black-run junkies can crank it up a notch on the 5.9km hair-raiser from **Karels T-Bar** right down to Friday Flats. These back-valley slopes are best in the morning; head to the front valley in the afternoon for more freestyle action. For lift ticket prices see opposite.

The slopes are also popular in summer when the **scenic chairlift** (adult/child return $28/14) and **Bobsled** (1/6/10 rides $6/30/44) are in action.

Thredbo Leisure Centre (☎ 02-6459 4100, 02-6459 4151; Friday Dr) organises all sorts of activities, summer and winter, including hiking, mountain biking, canoeing, white-water rafting, abseiling and horse riding. **Thredbo Snow Sports Outdoor Adventures** (☎ 02-6459 4044; www.thredbo.com.au) has a diverse range of high-energy activities including snowshoeing, snow climbing, telemark and back-country alpine touring.

SKI COSTS

During peak season at Thredbo, an adult one-/five-day lift ticket costs $97/412. Children's tickets cost $53/236. Group lessons (including lift tickets) cost from $135/86 for adults/children.

During peak season at Perisher Blue an adult one-/five-day lift ticket costs $98/431, or $102/528 including return Skitube tickets (see below). Children's tickets cost $43/250 or $55/299. Group lessons (including lift passes) for adults/children start at $139/94 per person, less for beginners.

Boots, skis and stocks can be hired for $68/46 per day for adults/children, and snowboards and boots for $78/60.

In warmer climes conquer Mt Kosciuszko on a **guided walk** (☎ 1300 020 589; adult/child $36/24; ☯ 10am-3pm Sat, Sun, Tue & Thu Nov-Apr) or a once-in-a-lifetime **Sunrise tour** (tour incl champagne breakfast $146; ☯ Sun Jan-Apr).

There are beautiful mountain-fed **rock pools** at Woodridge near the end of Mountain Dr. Take the track on your right after the gate, cross the bridge and the pool is on your left. Otherwise **Snowmakers Pond** is on the left when you enter the village. It's warmer and has a pontoon.

Sleeping

The following places are open in both summer and winter.

Thredbo YHA Lodge (☎ 02-6457 6376; www.yha.com .au; 8 Jack Adams Path; winter dm/d, $145/163, r with bathroom $179, summer dm/d $30/69, r with bathroom $80; ☐) The best value on the mountain, this YHA is well appointed, with great common areas, a good kitchen and a balcony. Peak-season adults must be full YHA members.

Aneeki Lodge (☎ 0417 479 581; www.aneeki.com .au; 9 Bobuck Lane, winter 2-night d per person $170-340, summer d $190) One of the cheapest lodges on the mountain.

Thredbo Alpine Hotel (☎ 1800 026 333; Friday Dr; winter s/d from $190/270, summer r from $105; ☯ ☐ ☎) The only hotel on the mountain has suitably flash rooms. Breakfast is included.

Candlelight Lodge (☎ 1800 020 900; www.candle lightlodge.com.au; 32 Diggings Tce; winter s/d from $200/240, summer from $95/125) Founded by Hungarian immigrants this Tyrolean lodge has great rooms, all with views. The restaurant's fondue is fabulous.

Eating & Drinking

Gourmet 42 (☎ 02-6457 7500; 100 Mowamba Pl, Village Sq; mains $10-15; ☯ breakfast & lunch) Hungover boarders and sleepy bar staff rock up to this small cafe for excellent coffee, soup and pasta.

Aprés Bar (☎ 02-6457 6222; The Denman, Diggings Tce; ☯ 6pm-late) Cosy couches and crimson leather poufs are crammed together in this cosy over-25s atmosphere. The tunes are spot-on and vino by the glass is affordable.

Berntis Bar (☎ 02-6457 6332; 4 Mowomba Pl; ☯ 6pm-late) The winter steakhouse and year-round tapas bar are the starting points for a good night out at this locals-recommend-it hang-out.

Also try:

Altitude 1380 (☎ 02-6457 6190; Village Sq; ☯ breakfast & lunch) Reliable lively eatery.

Credo (☎ 02-6457 6844; www.credo.com.au; Diggings Tce; mains $20; ☯ dinner) Seductive – whether by cocktails or double-roasted duck.

PERISHER BLUE

elev 1680m

Perisher Valley, Smiggin Holes, Mt Blue Cow and Guthega make up the massive resort of **Perisher Blue** (☎ 02-6459 4495, 1300 655 811; www .perisherblue.com.au). Guthega (1640m) and Mt Blue Cow (1640m) are mainly day resorts, so they're smaller and less crowded. Mt Blue Cow is accessible via the **Skitube** (☎ 1300 655 822; same-day return adult/child/family $42/23/99, open return $55/37/141), Perisher Blue's most underrated drawcard. Simply park the car at **Bullocks Flat** (Alpine Way), buy a ticket, board the train and within 15 minutes you're on the slopes. Blue Cow doesn't have the village ambience of Thredbo, but there are alpine and cross-country runs, valley and bowl skiing and snowboarding areas (dude!). For lift ticket prices see above.

For something entirely different, local Aboriginal Dreamtime expert Rod Mason conducts **Indigenous Snowshoeing Tours** (☎ 1300 655 822; tours $30; ☯ every full moon).

Most accommodation is in Perisher Valley and Smiggin Holes. The following rates include either breakfast and lunch or breakfast and dinner. Winter only.

NEW SOUTH WALES

THREDBO TRAGEDY

On a winter's night in July 1997, when most of Thredbo's residents were sleeping soundly, the Kosciuszko Alpine Way embankment, running across the upper edge of the village, collapsed, taking with it two snow lodges and 2000 cu metres of liquefied soil. Courtesy of a media throng that engulfed the ski village, Australians sat around the breakfast table the next morning and watched as rescue teams, working around the clock, removed victims from the debris. The only survivor, Stuart Diver, lay trapped under the rubble next to his dead wife for hours before being miraculously rescued. His courageous story became the subject of endless tabloid coverage and somewhat inevitably, a TV movie. He remains the name and face of the first disaster of its kind in Australia.

For Thredbo folk, memories of that terrible night and the people who lost their lives remain in the tapestry of the landscape. The **Thredbo Landslide Memorial** can be seen along Bobuck Lane where the two lodges, Carinya and Bimbadeen, once stood. The 18 posts used in the construction of the platform signify the 18 lives lost.

Sundeck Hotel (☎ 02-6457 5222; www.sundeck hotel.com.au; Kosciuszko Rd; 2-night d/tw per person from $375-645) Australia's highest hotel, and one of Perisher's oldest lodges, has a comfy bar and great views over the Quad 8 Express.

Other recommendations:

Aurora Ski Club (☎ 0412 363 206; www.ski.com.au; Perisher Valley; 2-night d per person $230-320) Budget – book early.

Heidi's Chalet (☎ 1800 252 668; www.heidis.com .au; Munyang Rd, Smiggin Holes; 2-night apt $1200-1800) Four-person apartments a short snowplough to the ski lifts.

CHARLOTTE PASS
elev 1780m

At the base of Mt Kosciuszko, **Charlotte Pass** (www .charlottepass.com.au) is one of the highest, oldest and most isolated ski resorts in Australia, and in winter you have to 'snowcat' (use oversnow transport) the last 8km from Perisher Valley ($50 each way; book ahead). Five lifts service rather short but uncrowded runs, and this is good ski-touring country. It's also marketing itself as a good base for summer activities.

Accommodation includes the grand **Kosciuszko Chalet** (☎ 1800 026 369; www.charlottepass .com.au; Fri & Sat r per person incl 2 meals & transfer $520-720) and the cheaper **Alitji Alpine Lodge** (☎ 02-6457 5024; www.ski.com.au; r $120-200).

THE ALPINE WAY

From **Khancoban**, this spectacular route runs through dense forest, around the southern end of Kosciuszko National Park to Thredbo and on to Jindabyne. All vehicles have to carry chains in winter, which can be hired at **Khancoban Lakeside Caravan Resort** (☎ 02-6076 9488; www.klcr.com

.au; 1362 Alpine Way) and dropped off at **Margaritta Hire** (☎ 02-6456 1959; 8 Kosciuszko Rd, Jindabyne) or vice versa. Motorbikes are not permitted along the Alpine Way from June to October.

Two of the best mountain views are from **Scammell's Lookout**, just off the Alpine Way at a good picnic spot and **Olsen's Lookout**, 10km off the Alpine Way on the Geehi Dam dirt road.

Geehi campsite, right on Swampy Plain River, is one of the loveliest in the park with resident kangaroos.

In winter, check conditions at Khancoban or Jindabyne. There's no fuel available between Khancoban and Thredbo (71km). If you're driving between Khancoban and Jindabyne you can get a free transit pass, but if you stop en route you must have a day pass (winter/nonwinter $27/16).

TUMUT & AROUND

In **Tumut** (population 5925), the **visitor centre & NPWS office** (☎ 02-6947 7025; www.tumut.nsw.gov.au; 5 Adelong Rd) are in the refurbished Old Butter Factory north of the town centre.

Batlow, on one side of a bowl-shaped valley, is an apple-orchard town, where picking and pruning work is usually available year-round. Contact **Riverina Community College** (☎ 02-6947 3886; Wynyard Centre, Wynyard St, Tumut; ☽ Mon-Fri) or check out the **National Harvest Labour Information Service** (☎ 1800 062 332; www.jobsearch.gov.au/harvesttrail).

Nearby is **Hume & Hovell's Lookout**, where the two explorers did just that in 1824.

In Tumbarumba, the **Pioneer Women's Hut** (☎ 02-6948 2635; Wagga Rd; ☽ 10am-5pm Sat & Sun, to 4pm Wed) is praised as one of Australia's most interesting small museums.

SOUTHWEST & THE MURRAY

This wide, endless country is rarely the first destination on a visitor's itinerary, but nor should it be the last. Between Sydney and Albury, a string of atmospheric old inland towns straddles the Hume Hwy, each of them with a claim to some kind of fame, be it bushrangers, drought, rich grazing land or old money.

Northwest of the highway, the land flattens out, becoming incrementally redder and drier. The Murray and Murrumbidgee rivers that make up the Riverina district not only offer respite in a harsh landscape, but an income through farming and agricultural practices centred on irrigation. Success stories can be seen in the lush vineyards and orchards around the immigrant foodie hubs of Griffith and Mildura on the Victorian side.

In the eclectic collection of smaller towns, rural folk are having a tougher time with farming practices changing, and drought and salinity threatening the country. Even so, curious travellers will find these places have a story to tell.

Getting There & Around

Several roads run through the southwest, the Hume Hwy being the major one. There are quieter routes such as Olympic Way, which runs through Cowra, Wagga Wagga and Albury. Routes to Adelaide include the Sturt Hwy through Hay and Wentworth. You'll also pass through the southwest if travelling between Brisbane and Melbourne on the Newell Hwy.

Major bus routes cross the region, running from Sydney and Brisbane to both Melbourne and Adelaide. Melbourne to Sydney bus services run on the Hume Hwy and trains run close to it.

HUME HIGHWAY

Like all big swaths of four-lane bitumen, the Hume Hwy, running nearly 900km from Sydney to Melbourne, is somewhat lacking in aesthetic appeal. Sure, visitors will spot some of Australia's most beloved animals – kangaroos, wombats and koalas – but they're likely to be roadkill. Despite this, the highway is easily navigable and an effortless way to traverse the country by car. It also provides

an opportunity, via myriad signposted scenic routes, to visit small towns.

Much of the highway is speed limited to 110km/h, which is rigorously enforced by speed cameras and roadside police cars. Take heed for safety reasons but also for the back pocket. Speeding fines are hefty.

The highway was named after Hamilton Hume, the first Australian explorer who, along with William Hovell, 'discovered' much of the land straddling the highway.

SYDNEY TO GOULBURN

The large towns of **Mittagong** and **Bowral** adjoin each other just off the Hume Hwy.

The **Southern Highlands Visitors Information Centre** (☎ 02-4871 2888, 1300 657 559; www.southern -highlands.com.au; 62-70 Main St, Mittagong) has comprehensive information.

For two weeks over September and October, Bowral bursts into vivid hues during the **Bowral Tulip Time Festival** (☎ 1300 657 559; www.tuliptime.net.au).

Bowral is also where the late great cricketer Sir Donald Bradman, undoubtedly Australia's greatest sporting hero and legendary to the point of sainthood, spent his boyhood. There's a cricket ground here and fans pay homage at the **Bradman Museum of Cricket** (☎ 02-4862 1247; www.bradman.com.au; St Jude St, Bowral; adult/child/family $12/5/35; ☻ 10am-5pm), which has an engrossing collection of Ashes and Don-centric memorabilia that even cricket-loathers admit is worthwhile.

This pocket of the Hume is popular with Sydney day-trippers and overnighters, and has a good dining and B&B scene. **Fountaindale Grand Manor** (☎ 02-4885 1111; www.fountaindale .au; Illawarra Hwy, Robertson; r $110-120) is a commanding English manor (1924) with lavish rooms. Breakfast is included.

Striping the paddocks in the hilly countryside are about 15 vineyards with cellar-door sales and tasting. Top spots for lunch include **Centennial Vineyards** (☎ 02-4861 8700; www.centennial .net.au; Centennial Rd; ☻ 10am-7pm), which has a flash restaurant open 11am to 5pm (closed Tuesday) or **Southern Highland Wines** (☎ 02-4686 2300; www.shw.com.au; Oldbury Rd; ☻ 10am-5pm Sat & Sun) with its tasty cafe. **McVitty Grove Estate** (☎ 02-4878 5044; www.mcvittygrove.com.au; Oldbury Rd; ☻ 10am-5pm Fri-Sun) scores points for its stunning views.

The convoluted but spectacular, limestone **Wombeyan Caves** (☎ 02-4843 5976; www.npws.nsw.gov .au; Wombeyan Caves Rd; adult/child/family $13/8/30, with tour $16/10/39; 9am-5pm Mon-Fri, to 4pm Sat & Sun) are at the end of an unsealed mountain road 65km northwest of Mittagong. Nearby are walking trails and plenty of wildlife.

A little further south along the Hume is tiny but heritage-classified **Berrima**, founded in 1829. It's full of art galleries, tourist-trapping antique shops, historic buildings and fine food and wine. The gorgeous old sandstone **White Horse Inn** (02-4877 1204; www.whitehorseinn.com.au; Market Pl; s $70-135, d $80-150) has four tasteful motel rooms and a fabulous restaurant open for breakfast, lunch and dinner (mains $17 to $32), and Devonshire tea.

Three kilometres north of Berrima, **Berkelouw's Book Barn & Café** (02-4877 1370; www.berkelouw.com.au; Old Hume Hwy; 9.30am-4.30pm Mon-Fri, to 5pm Sat & Sun) stocks secondhand and antiquated tomes.

South of Berrima is the small, appealing town of **Bundanoon**, one of the gateways to the vast and unruly **Morton National Park**, which has the deep gorges and high sandstone plateaus of the **Budawang Range**. The **NPWS visitor centre** (02-4887 7270; www.nationalparks.nsw.gov.au; Nowra Rd, Fitzroy Falls) is at the park entrance and has information on walking and hiking.

Bundanoon YHA (02-4883 6010; www.yha.com.au; 115 Railway Ave; unpowered sites $31, dm/d $28/67) occupies a fastidiously restored Edwardian guest house, complete with shady verandah and gallons of gingham. It's close to the village where **Ye Olde Bike Shoppe & Café** (02-4883 6043; 9 Church St; 9.30am-4.30pm Mon-Fri, 9am-5pm Sat & Sun) has bikes for hire ($19 per hour, half/full day $28/$45).

CountryLink (132 232; www.countrylink.info) runs from Bundanoon to Wollongong ($10, two hours) and Sydney Central ($21, two hours).

GOULBURN & AROUND

Goulburn (population 20,127) makes the headlines as the worst of the country's drought-stricken cities but it also lays claim to being Australia's first inland city. The old town centre, studded with historic buildings, is worth a stroll, and alfresco dining and lattes are becoming mainstays of the city's food scene. Curiously, wood-fired pizzas in particular are in stiff competition!

The **Goulburn visitor centre** (02-4823 4492, 1800 353 646; www.igoulburn.com; 201 Sloane St) has regional information and free internet access.

First stop should be **Old Goulburn Brewery** (02-4821 6071; http://goulburnbrewery.servebeer.com;

23 Bungonia Rd; s/d/tw $66/110/110; 11am-4pm), where you can see the workings of a brewery and, more importantly, sip on a beer. It also has cheap and cheerful 1830s brewer's cottage accommodation.

The three-storey-high **Big Merino** (02-4821 6071; www.thebigmerino.com.au; cnr Hume & Sowerby Sts; admission free; 8.30am-5.30pm) has been spruced up after moving to greener pastures 500m from its old paddock near Goulburn's southern exit.

The **Goulburn Club** (02-4821 2043; 19 Market St; 5pm-late Thu-Sat) is a groovy hub that prides itself on live music and boutique brewed beer rather than big screens and poker machines. Art and photography exhibitions line the walls.

About 40km southeast of Goulburn and abutting Morton National Park, **Bungonia State Conservation Area** (02-4844 4277; www.nationalparks.nsw.gov.au; 838 Lookdown Rd) has a dramatic forested gorge, deep caves and a cool camping area with hot showers, toilets, a communal kitchen and gas barbecues. Walking is the mainstay activity.

YASS & AROUND

Yass (population 5333) is pretty and quiet (thanks to the highway bypass). But it's also atmospheric, laced with heritage buildings, and shops and pubs of the wide-verandah variety.

Yass Valley visitor centre (02-6226 2557; www.yassvalley.nsw.gov.au; 259 Comur St) is in Coronation Park. Next door, the **Yass & District Museum** (02-6226 2577; adult/child $3/1; 10am-4pm Sat & Sun summer) has a model reconstruction of the town in the 1890s – check at the visitors centre for off-season opening hours. Hume's house, the 1835 **Cooma Cottage** (02-6226 1470; adult/child $4/2; 10am-4pm Thu-Sun), is on the Yass Valley Way on the Sydney side of town.

The **Hume & Hovell Walking Track**, which follows the route chosen by Hume and his sometime partner in exploration, William Hovell, has some half-day and longer walks that begin at Cooma Cottage.

At the start of November the **Wine, Roses & All That Jazz Festival** features live music, gourmet food and wine tasting at 25 cellar doors.

About 57km southeast of Yass, along some partly dirt roads, the limestone **Careys Cave** (02-6227 9622; www.weejaspercaves.com; adult/child $11/7) is at **Wee Jasper**.

our pick **Long Track Pantry** (02-6945 4144; www.longtrackpantry.com.au; Riverside Dr, Jugiong; breakfast & lunch, Wed-Mon) provides a rarefied country experience. This renovated old general store turned coffee stop and cafe is between Yass and Gundagai; take the Jugiong exit off the Hume Hwy.

GUNDAGAI
pop 1998

Gundagai, on the Murrumbidgee River, is relaxed and one of the more interesting small towns along (or bypassed by) the Hume with fascinating bushranger and Aboriginal history.

The **visitor centre** (☎ 02-6944 0250; www.gundagai .nsw.gov.au; 249 Sheridan St) is on the grand main street. Housed within is **Rusconi's Marble Masterpiece**, a cathedral model that relentlessly plays 'Along the Road to Gundagai', so that you'll likely hum it mindlessly for days.

The **Prince Alfred Bridge** (closed to traffic so you can walk it) is the star of Gundagai's sights. It crosses the flood plain of the Murrumbidgee River. Running alongside it is a stretch of the longest wooden railway track in NSW.

Green Dog Gallery (☎ 02-6944 1479; Sheridan St; ⌚ 10.30am-5.30pm Thu-Sat) and **Lannigan Abbey & Bandamora Art Gallery** (☎ 02-6944 2852; www.laniganabbey.com.au; 72 First Ave; ⌚ 9am-5pm) are worth a bo peep. The former has B&B accommodation.

Gold rushes and bushrangers were part of the town's colourful early history. The notorious bushranger Captain Moonlight was tried in Gundagai's 1859 **courthouse** and is now buried in the town. While you're in the cemetery, check out the **monument to Yarri**, an Aborigine who saved dozens of locals when the area flooded in the early 1800s.

The **Mt Parnassus lookout** has picnic facilities and good 360-degree views over the town and surrounds; take the steep walk (or drive) up Hanley St.

About 8km east of town, the **Dog on the Tuckerbox** is Gundagai's most famous monument. A sculpture of a dog from a 19th-century bush ballad, it is well-known along the Hume Hwy. It is mostly a petrol-and-sausage-roll pit stop, but Coffee Guru serves decent espresso coffee.

Just 6km out of town, **Gundagai Wines** (☎ 0419 220 711; Nangus Rd; ⌚ 10.30am-4.30pm Fri-Sun) has a gorgeous corrugated-iron-shed cellar door set among a rose garden. On the last Sunday of each month, pop in for lunchtime wood-fired pizza.

The **Snake Gully Cup**, in mid-November, is a highly prized local racing carnival (see Picnic Races, p250) that straddles two days. On a Celtic note, the **Turning Wave festival** (www.turn ingwave.org.au) is a folksy folk favourite.

Touches such as a swimming pool, spa and bar make **Poet's Recall** (☎ 02-6944 1777; cnr West & Punch Sts; s/d $75/95; ☒) the best motel in town. The restaurant dishes up roasts and other homestyle meals.

In South Gundagai, the **Old Bridge Inn** (☎ 02-6944 4250; 1 Tumut St; s/d $80/130) is a lovely 1850s building with relaxed B&B accommodation, an excellent restaurant open for lunch and dinner (mains $15 to $30) and amiable owners.

Gundagai Tourist Park (☎ 02-6944 4440; Nangus Rd; unpowered/powered sites $24/28, cabins $75) has well-presented vans and cabins and is situated near the river and the local swimming pool.

ALBURY
pop 46,282

This major regional centre on the Murray River, just below the big Hume Weir, sits on the state border opposite its Victorian twin, Wodonga (p583). Given its history, heritage buildings and river orientation, Albury is the more interesting and aesthetically pleasing part of the conurbation. It's a good base for trips to the snowfields and high country of both Victoria and NSW; the vineyards around Rutherglen (Victoria); and for exploring the upper Murray River. It's also a good spot to break the journey between Sydney and Melbourne.

Information

Gateway visitor centre (☎ 1300 796 222; www .destinationalburywodonga.com.au; Lincoln Causeway) Part of a large 'island' between Albury and Wodonga.
Library Museum (☎ 02-6023 8333; cnr Kiewa & Swift Sts; admission free) Free internet access.

Sights & Activities

Albury's fabulous new state-of-the-art **Library Museum** (☎ 02-6023 8333; cnr Kiewa & Swift Sts; admission free; ⌚ 10.30am-5pm Mon-Fri, to 4pm Sat & Sun), dubbed the 'living room', blends book borrowing, magazine browsing and net surfing with exhibitions and local history including Aboriginal culture and 20th-century migration into the area.

The newly renovated **Albury Regional Art Gallery** (☎ 02-6051 3480; 546 Dean St; admission free;

PICNIC RACES

Care for a bet on the nags? Here's a tip: get along to a picnic race day. Held annually in a large number of country towns, these community race meets are the lifeblood of the rural social calendar and a bloody good bash for everyone else. They are traditionally held on a Friday and are the only day of the year when farmers and graziers feel at liberty to swap their work attire for a pair of polished RM Williams boots and a chambray shirt. Today, town and city folk are cottoning on to the fun and some picnic race days are held on a Saturday.

Expect to see a fraternity of frocked-up women gathered around gourmet picnic hampers, Akubra-donned men downing cold beer at the outdoor bar and a bustling betting ring. Some tracks are better than others (Yass' Marchmont track has a back straight hidden from public view, prompting endless rumours of jockey-swapping), but all of them kick up enough dust to raise a whoop or whimper from the barracking-mad punters in the (often) not-so-grand stands. Pluck that little dress out of the backpack and try your luck with Fashions on the Field.

Race days that coincide with Melbourne's November Spring Racing Carnival are particularly good fun. See the racing diary at www.racingnsw.com.au or contact visitors centres.

10am-5pm Mon-Thu, to 7pm Fri, to 4pm Sat, noon-4pm Sun) has a small permanent collection featuring works by Russell Drysdale and Fred Williams, contemporary Australian photography, a reading room and a cafe.

For a cleansing river swim, turn right into **Noreuil Park** in Albury, just before the Lincoln Causeway, where there's a **river swimming pool**, or try the **loop**, a magical 20-minute float (on your back) around a big bend that ends close to where you began. Though the low water level means it no longer plies the river, the paddle steamer **PS Cumberoona** (☎ 02-6021 1113) is moored here. Also here is the tree marked by explorer William Hovell on his 1824 expedition with Hume from Sydney to Port Phillip.

The **Botanic Gardens** (4 hectares), at the northern end of Wodonga Pl, are old, formal and beautiful – a heritage walk is available from the visitor centre. During summer the gardens and nearby Hovell Tree Park host **Cinema under the Stars** (☎ 02-6023 8111; admission free; sunset).

In November the annual **Ngangirra Festival**, which features Aboriginal art, music, dance and language, is held at Mungabareena Reserve.

There are numerous **bike and walking tracks** in and around Albury. The **Canoe Guy** (☎ 02-6041 1822; thecanoeguy@hotmail.com; 301 Macauley St; half/full day $25/35) organises canoe trips on the Murray, including a two-day camping trip to nearby Howlong ($70).

See over 120 bird species in their native habitat at the **Wonga Wetlands** (☎ 02-6051 3800; www.wongawetlands.nsw.gov.au; Riverina Hwy, Splitters Creek), an innovative project to restore local wetlands using treated waste water. Call for tour information.

Oz E Wildlife (☎ 02-6040 3677; Ettamogah; adult/child $10/5; 9am-5pm), 11km north on the Hume Hwy, is a sanctuary for sick and injured local wildlife. The roos will enjoy your company.

About 8km north, the lopsided **Ettamogah Pub** (☎ 02-6026 2366; www.ettamogah.com; Burma Rd, Tabletop) is a real-life re-creation of a famous Aussie cartoon pub by Albury-born Ken Maynard.

Sleeping

Some motels are on busy streets such as Hume and Young and suffer from noise, especially from flatulent trucks.

Sodens Hotel Motel (☎ 02-6021 2400; cnr David & Wilson Sts; s/d $45/50, with bathroom and breakfast $50/60) Two blocks from the main street, this is an old-style pub with a grandiose verandah. It has 50 rooms – within stumbling distance of the beer garden – that cater to backpackers.

Country Comfort (☎ 02-6021 5366; www.countrycomfort.com.au; cnr Dean & Elizabeth Sts; r from $130;) Albury's tallest building is also its most popular hotel. It has all the expected mod cons plus a restaurant and cocktail bar. It's on the main street.

Albury Motor Village YHA (☎ 02-6040 2999; www.yha.com.au; 372 Wagga Rd; powered sites $20, dm/d/cabins $32/65/65;) About 4.5km north of the centre, this is a tidy park with a range of cabins, vans and backpacker beds in clean dorms.

Eating & Drinking

Dean St is a long strip of takeaways, cafes, restaurants and nightlife.

Simply Fed (☎ 02-6021 0144; shop 9, AMP Lane; ☺ breakfast & lunch Mon-Sat) Off Dean St, this cute cafe with a hint of Melbourne laneway culture about it has a counter full of tasty, filling lunches such as lasagne, as well as sandwiches and salads.

our pick **Baan Sabai Jai** (☎ 02-6021 2250; 459 Smollett St; mains $9; ☺ lunch & dinner Mon-Sat) This excellent restaurant with a traditional food cart on the front pavement has stolen the hearts and appetites of locals with its authentic Thai dishes. Fly by or eat in.

Electra Café (☎ 02-6021 7200; 3/441 Dean St; mains $17; ☺ Wed-Sun) This place has excellent coffee, a sunny footpath eating area, and poached eggs and grilled-mushroom breakfasts worth pulling off the highway for.

Star Hotel (☎ 02-6021 2745; 502 Guinea St) This local favourite has a huge beer garden out the back and a front bar with pool tables where the gregarious owners will keep you entertained. It's a little off the main drag but worth the walk down Olive St.

Getting There & Away

The **airport** (Borella Rd) is 10 minutes out of town. **Rex** (☎ 13 17 13; www.regionalexpress.com .au) flies to Sydney ($115, 1¼ hours) and Melbourne ($106, one hour). **Brindabella Airlines** (☎ 1300 668 824; www.brindabellaairlines .com.au) flies to Canberra ($120, 45 minutes). **Virgin Blue** (☎ 13 67 89; www.virginblue.com.au) flies to Sydney ($110, one hour).

Greyhound (☎ 1300 GREYHOUND/1300 473 946; www .greyhound.com.au) has coaches to Melbourne ($42, 3¾ hours), Wagga Wagga ($35, 1½ hours) and Sydney ($65, 8½ hours).

The **CountryLink** (☎ 13 22 32; www.countrylink .info) XPT train runs north to Wagga ($19, 1¼ hours) and Sydney ($72, eight hours), and south to Melbourne ($47, 3½ hours). CountryLink buses run to Echuca ($32, 4¼ hours) three times a week (from the train station bus stop). **V/Line** (☎ 13 61 96; www.vline .com.au) trains run to Melbourne ($30).

WAGGA WAGGA
pop 46,735

The Murrumbidgee River squiggles around the northern end of 'Wagga' like a snake in an Aboriginal painting. Its wide-girthed eucalypts and sandy banks add an understated beauty to a place already prettied by wide tree-lined streets and lovely gardens. Meaning 'place of many crows' in the language of the local Wiradjuri people, 'Wagga' is the state's largest inland city.

Orientation & Information

The long main street, Baylis St, which runs north from the train station, becomes Fitzmaurice St at the northern end. The **visitor centre** (☎ 1300 100 122; www.visitwaggawagga.com .au; Tarcutta St) is close to the river.

There's internet access at **Wagga Systems** (☎ 02-6925 8861; 114 Fitzmaurice St; per hr $6; ☺ 10am-5pm).

Sights & Activities

The Civic Centre houses the excellent **Wagga Wagga Art Gallery** (☎ 02-6926 9660; www.waggaart gallery.org; admission free; ☺ 10am-5pm Tue-Sat, noon-4pm Sun), home to the wonderful **National Art Glass Gallery**.

The **Botanic Gardens** (Macleay St; ☺ sunrise-sunset) has a small **zoo**, geese and peacocks roam free, and there's a free-flight aviary. The entrance is just before the archway telling you you're entering Lord Baden Powell Dr, which itself leads to a good lookout and the scenic **Captain Cook Drive**.

Wagga Beach at the end of Tarcutta St is a good swimming option by the river.

Wagga is a major centre for **livestock sales** (Boman industrial area); you can watch farmers sell cattle on Monday in an amphitheatre-style ring, and sheep by the thousands on Thursday.

The **Museum of the Riverina** (☎ 02-6925 2934; Baden Powell Dr; admission free; ☺ 10am-5pm Tue-Sat, noon-4pm Sun) operates from both the Civic Centre and the Botanic Gardens; the latter site focuses on Wagga's people, places and events and includes a **Sporting Hall of Fame**.

The **Wiradjuri Walking Track** is a 30km circuit beginning from the visitor centre (get your map there) that includes some good lookouts and places of Aboriginal significance.

Out of town, the **Wagga Wagga Winery** (☎ 02-6922 1221; www.waggawaggawinery.com.au; Gundagai Rd; ☺ 11am-10pm) has delicious barbecue meals (from $17). Closer to home Charles Sturt University also has an award-winning **winery** (☎ 02-6933 2435; www.csu.edu.au/winery; McKeown Dr; ☺ 11am-5pm Mon-Fri, to 4pm Sat & Sun) and excellent cheese tastings and tours at 1pm.

Sleeping

There are many motels in town, especially along Tarcutta St.

Romano's Hotel (☎ 02-6921 2013; www.romanoshotel.com.au; cnr Fitzmaurice & Sturt Sts; s/d/tw without bathroom $38/50/50, d with bathroom$78) This is an airy old pub with high ceilings, quaint rooms, grand beds and old bathrooms – ask for a room on the quieter 2nd floor.

Dunns B&B (☎ 02-6925 7771; www.dunnsbedandbreakfast.com.au; 63 Mitchelmore St; s/d $110/112) A pristinely decorated federation home with three rooms with bathrooms and the use of a private balcony and sitting room. Breakfast is included.

Prince of Wales Motel (☎ 02-6921 7016; www.princeofwalesmotel.com.au; 143 Fitzmaurice St; r from $117; 🖳) This place is in the heart of town. The quaint pub facade is matched by cosy rooms, some equipped with spas and minibars.

Wagga Wagga Beach Caravan Park (☎ 02-6931 0603; www.wwbcp.com.au; 2 Johnston St; sites per adult $19, standard/deluxe cabins $65/75; 🌊) This park has a swimming beach fashioned from the river bank and plenty of cabins.

Eating

Cache Store of Food (☎ 02-6921 2916; 236 Baylis St; dishes $7-15; 🕐 breakfast & lunch) Located opposite Myer on the main street, this cafe has the creative sandwich, mini pizza and pastry market covered. The coffee is good and there are tables aplenty inside and out.

Café Lulaba (☎ 02-6931 8903; 10 Best St; mains $11-16; 🕐 breakfast & lunch Tue-Sat, dinner Fri) It's known for its dhal curry, but how could you go past the quiche? It's a cheery spot with a large zebra watching over you.

Magpies Nest (☎ 02-6933 1523; 20 Pine Gully Rd; mains $22-33; 🕐 lunch Wed-Sun, dinner Wed-Sat) A delightful restaurant set in a restored 1860s stone stable overlooking the Murrumbidgee River and surrounded by olive groves and vineyards. The fare is regional with a hint of Tuscany, and my, it's good.

Three Chefs (☎ 02-6921 5897; 70 Morgan St; mains $28-37; 🕐 breakfast daily, lunch Wed-Fri, dinner Mon-Sat) A white-tablecloth, fine-dining place, Three Chefs has kept a warm and comfortable atmosphere. The restaurant has a penchant for delicious 'desert spring rolls' with fillings that change weekly. The lounge bar is open from noon Thursday and Friday, from 5pm Saturday.

Getting There & Away

Qantas (☎ 13 13 13; www.qantas.com.au) flies to Sydney ($115, 1¼ hours), and **Rex** (☎ 13 17 13; www.regionalexpress.com.au) flies to Melbourne ($133, 1¼ hours) and Sydney ($114, 1¼ hours).

CountryLink (☎ 13 22 32; www.countrylink.info) buses leave from **Wagga train station** (☎ 13 22 32, 02-6939 5488), where you can make bookings. The XPT runs to Albury ($19, 1¼ hours), Melbourne ($63, five hours) and Sydney Central ($63, 6¾ hours). **Greyhound** (☎ 1300 GREYHOUND/1300 473 946; www.greyhound.com.au) runs to Sydney ($35, 7½ hours) and Melbourne ($45, six hours).

Firefly Express (☎ 1300 730 740; www.fireflyexpress.com.au) coaches run to Sydney ($50, 6¼ hours) and Melbourne ($45, 5½ hours).

JUNEE
pop 3744

Once known as the 'Rail Centre of the South', Junee is a small, friendly country town with an extraordinary number of impressive buildings. Get tourist information and a map from the board on Seignior St and from **Broadway Museum** (☎ 02-6924 1832; Broadway St; admission free; 🕐 10am-4pm Wed-Sun) and coffee shop, where there's a collection of historical artefacts and some tasteful antiques.

Built in 1884, the mansion of **Monte Cristo** (☎ 02-6924 1637; www.montecristo.com.au; Monte Cristo Rd; adult/child $10/5; 🕐 10am-4pm) is open for self tours and Devonshire tea. It was the home of a shrewd landowner named Christopher Crawley who haunts the place apparently.

Built in 1947, the **Railway Roundhouse** (☎ 02-6924 2909; www.rhta-junee.org; Harold St; adult/child/family $6/4/16; 🕐 noon-4.30pm Tue-Thu, from 9.30am Sat & Sun), a giant turntable with 42 train-repair bays, is the only surviving, working one of its kind in Australia. Railway enthusiasts should visit the Roundhouse Museum in the same complex.

Junee Liquorice & Chocolate Factory (☎ 02-6924 3574; www.greengroveorganics.com; 45-61 Lord St; adult/child $4/2; 🕐 10am-4pm) makes a show out of creating liquorice and chocolate in the old Junee Flour Mill (1935). An excellent cafe and gift shop are all part of the fun.

Junee boasts some magnificent old pubs with massive verandahs dripping with iron lace. The 1915 **Commercial Hotel** (cnr Lorne & Waratah Sts) still has a busy bar crowded with after-work drinkers. The **Loftus** (☎ 02-6924 1511; 6 Humphreys St) was the town's grandest hotel, with a frontage running for an entire block. The film *The Crossing*, starring Russell Crowe, was filmed there.

Across the tracks, the **Junee Hotel** (☎ 02-6924 1124; Seignior St; s/d/tr $30/40/60) was built in 1876. The pub hasn't had a lot done to it over the years, but that means the original fittings are still intact. Cheap pub rooms are available.

Loftus B&B (☎ 02-6924 1511; 6 Humphreys St; s/tw $80/150, d with bathroom $95) is a 112-year-old pub located in the centre of town, complete with sweeping staircases and an endless balcony. Breakfast is included.

our pick Loftus on Humphreys (☎ 02-6924 2555; mains $15-29; ⏲ 10am-late Tue-Sat, 11am-3pm Sun, 10am-3pm Mon), a surprisingly upmarket restaurant, bar and cafe, is downstairs from the B&B and run by the same hard-working people. The dinner menu includes roo wrapped in bacon!

LEETON
pop 6828

The first of the Walter Burley Griffin–designed towns, Leeton remains close to the architect's original vision: beautiful wide streets, a grand roundabout and avenues of huge palm trees. Its future as headquarters of the Murrumbidgee Irrigation Area (MIA) is precipitous given the drought in this rice-growing region.

The **visitor centre** (☎ 02-6953 6481; www.leeton tourism.com.au; 10 Yanco Ave), in a beautiful heritage homestead, has maps for forest drives and heritage walks.

With the recent drought, the Riverina's crops have seen better times, none more so than the rice industry. Even so, see how the industry operates at the **SunRice Centre** (☎ 02-6953 0596; www.sunrice.com.au; Calrose St; admission free; ⏲ 9am-5pm Mon-Fri), which has presentations at 9.30am and 2.45pm.

Lillypilly Estate (☎ 02-6953 4069; www.lillypilly .com; 279 Lillypilly Rd; ⏲ 10am-5pm Mon-Sat) and **Toorak Wines** (☎ 02-6953 2333; www.toorakwines.com.au; Toorak Rd; ⏲ 9am-5.30pm Mon-Sat) are two local wineries open for tastings and sales.

GRIFFITH
pop 16,182

You're just as likely to see Indians as Italians on Griffith's wide leafy main street, a tribute to the cultural eclecticism in this small but sophisticated town. Add to the mix an influx of South Korean tourists seeking fruit-picking work and it really brings home the point. Griffith is the wine-and-food capital of the Riverina, with vineyards, cafes and restaurants offering renowned variety and quality.

Information

Grapes and other crops provide year-round harvest jobs, but some periods are slower than others. Check first. Lack of transport around Griffith's farms and orchards can make job seeking difficult. Having your own vehicle is a distinct advantage. **Summit Personnel** (☎ 02-6964 2718; griffith@summitpersonnel.com.au; 86 Yambil St) and **Skilled** (☎ 02-6964 2547; tphilpott@skilled.com.au; 102 Yambil St) can sort you out.

Griffith visitor centre (☎ 02-6962 4145; www .griffith.com.au; cnr Banna & Jondaryan Aves) Fronted by a life-size, WWII Fairey Firefly plane.

Library (☎ 02-6962 2515; 449 Banna Ave; per hr $1) Internet access.

Riverina NPWS office (☎ 02-6966 8100; www.npws .nsw.gov.au; 200 Yambil St) Information on nearby national parks.

Sights & Activities

High on a hill north of the town centre, **Pioneer Park Museum** (☎ 02-6962 4196; cnr Remembrance & Scenic Drs; adult/child $9/5; ⏲ 9.30am-4pm) is a re-creation of an early Riverina village, with an old hospital, a music room and other fascinating displays in original old buildings.

Further along Scenic Dr the **Sir Dudley de Chair Lookout** has a panoramic view and is near the **Hermit's Cave**.

Riverina Grove (☎ 02-6962 7988; www.riverinagrove .com.au; 4 Whybrow St) is a produce mecca with everything from marinated feta to homemade jams and chutney.

Though small, the art deco **Griffith Regional Art Gallery** (☎ 02-6962 5991; 167-185 Banna Ave; admission by gold coin donation; ⏲ 10am-5pm Wed-Fri, to 3pm Sat & Sun) has a lovely sense of space and excellent changing exhibitions.

Nearby at Darlington Point **Altina Wildlife Park** (☎ 0412 060 342; www.altinawildlife.com; Waddi Roadhouse, 7 Sturt Hwy; ⏲ daily by appointment) is 207 hectares of natural bush on the banks of the Murrumbidgee where the exotic residents, including giraffes, bison and camels, live in natural enclosures.

The Griffith area also has a large number of award-winning wineries:

Australian Old Vine Wine (☎ 02-6963 5239; Farm 271 Rosetto Rd, Beelbangera; ⏲ 10am-4pm) Boutique – these guys still hand-pick their grapes (and sometimes help help).

McWilliam's Hanwood Estate (☎ 02-6963 3400; Jack McWilliam Rd, Hanwood; ⏲ tastings 10am-4pm Mon-Fri, to 5pm Sat) The oldest (1913).

Westend Estate (☎ 02-6969 0800; Brayne Rd; ⏲ 8am-5pm Mon-Fri, 9am-5pm Sat, 10am-4pm Sun)

In early June, **UnWINEd** (www.unwined-riverina.com) is a festival of food and wine with tutored tastings, languid lunches and live music at various venues.

Sleeping

our pick **Myalbangera Outstation** (☎ 0428 130 093; hhtp://myalbangera.com; Farm 1646, Rankin Springs Rd, Yenda; dm $19-25, d $40-45; ☒) An excellent backpacker option, located about 12km out of town in an iconic Australiana setting. The owners know the lay of the land and can assist with work and transfers from town.

Hotel Victoria (☎ 02-6962 1299; www.hotelvictoria.com.au; 384 Banna Ave; s/d $85/100; ☒ ☐) The Victoria features bright corridors, cheerful rooms, good bathrooms and friendly staff. Breakfast is included. Downstairs there is a bistro with a chargrill.

Griffith Motor Inn (☎ 02-6962 1800; 96 Banna Ave; s/d $86/93; ☒ ☐ ☒) This central, small place with a smattering of palm trees is clean, comfortable and reasonably priced. Its Kolours restaurant is approved by locals.

Tourist Caravan Park (☎ 02-6964 2144; 919 Willandra Ave; s/d caravans $20/25, sites with bathroom $27/30, s cabins $40-60, d $50-77; ☒) This convenient caravan park is small and organised, and has grassy sitting areas.

There are a number of other backpacker options in Griffith:

Alberta Lodge (☎ 02-6964 6288; 87 Canal St; dm/d $30/35) Closest to the city centre. Weekly rates available.

Shearer's Quarters at Pioneer Park Museum (☎ 02-6962 4196; Remembrance Dr; s $15) Cheapest nightly option. Weekly rates available.

Eating

Banna Ave is dotted with 'true-blue' Italian pizza and pasta shops.

Miei Amici Café (☎ 02-6962 5999; 350 Banna St; dishes $6-12; ☾ breakfast & lunch Mon-Sat) This tiny place has simple but delicious breakfasts; or pull up a seat on the footpath for coffee and one of the best carrot cakes around.

La Tavola (☎ 02-6962 7777; 188 Banna Ave; ☾ lunch & dinner) A cheery restaurant dishing up chicken *al funghi* ($20), pepper steak ($22), saltimbocca ($20), a darn good La Tavola Special pizza ($12 to $25) and the like.

Marcos Restaurant (☎ 02-6964 3438; 10/454 Banna Ave; mains $15-30; ☾ dinner Mon-Sat) This contemporary Australian restaurant is one of the snazzier options in town with a menu that includes crab-and-rocket fettuccini, wasabi oysters, and bacon-wrapped eye fillet steak. It's hidden up a little staircase a few metres from the Grand Hotel.

our pick **La Scala** (☎ 02-6962 4322; 455b Banna Ave; dishes $26; ☾ dinner Tue-Sat) Hidden down steps and behind an old pink door, this cellar has a great reputation and an extensive local wine list.

For something lighter:

Bertoldo's Bakery (☎ 02-6964 2514; 324 & 150 Banna Ave; ☾ breakfast & lunch) Italian patisserie and panetteria.

La Piccola Italian Deli (☎ 02-6964 7266; Banna Ave; ☾ breakfast & lunch) Takeaway focaccias $9.

Getting There & Away

Rex (☎ 13 17 13; www.regionalexpress.com.au) flies to Sydney ($135, 1¼ hours).

All buses, except CountryLink (which stops at the train station), stop at the **Griffith Travel & Transit Centre** (☎ 02-6962 7199; Banna Ave) in the same building as the visitor centre. Services run daily to Adelaide ($140, 12 hours), Melbourne ($35, nine hours), Sydney ($90, 10 hours) and Mildura ($75, six hours).

There's **Griffith Taxis** (☎ 13 10 08) and an **airport express bus service** (☎ 0418 696 280).

WILLANDRA NATIONAL PARK

This World Heritage–listed national park, on the plains 174km northwest of Griffith, has been carved from a huge sheep station on a system of lakes. Though often dry, the lakes, especially **Hall's Lake**, sometimes become temporary wetlands and bird life is abundant. During spring there are magnificent displays of wildflowers, and emus and kangaroos can be found on the open plains throughout the year.

The historical interest of Willandra centres on the wool industry and station life, although there were certainly Aboriginal societies in the area. In 1869 some enterprising Melbourne grocers formed the sheep station Big Willandra – the national park (19,385 hectares), formed in 1972, is less than 10% of Big Willandra.

There is a **campsite** (adult/child $3/2) on Willandra Creek, with pit toilets and fireplaces. Bring your own drinking water. **Griffith NPWS office** (☎ 02-6966 8100; 200 Yambil St) has more info.

HAY

pop 2636

Hay's friendly main street attracts its fair share of people, it being the heart and soul of a huge rural area that stretches flat to the horizon in every direction.

The **visitor centre** (☎ 02-6993 4045; www.hay.nsw.gov.au; 407 Moppett St) is helpful. **Hay NPWS office** (☎ 02-6990 8200; www.environment.nsw.gov.au; Murray

St) has quality information on guided walks through the region's Cocoparra, Mungo, Kalvarr and Colambeyan national parks.

Sights & Activities

Shearers enjoy legendary status in this part of Australia; the innovative **Shear Outback** (☎ 02-6993 4000; cnr Sturt & Cobb Hwys; adult/child $15/8; ☼ 9am-5pm) is devoted to these colourful characters.

Hay housed three internment camps during WWII, and the **Hay POW & Internment Camp Interpretive Centre** (☎ 02-6993 4045; Murray St; admission $2; ☼ 9am-5pm), at the 1882 railway station, tells the stories of the 'Dunera boys', and Japanese and Italian internees.

Impressive old buildings in town include **Bishop's Lodge** (☎ 02-6993 1727; Roset St; admission $5; ☼ 2-4.30pm Mon-Sat), a mansion built entirely of corrugated iron as a residence for the Anglican bishop in 1888. The **Old Hay Gaol** (Church St; adult/child $4/1; ☼ 9am-5pm) has had many uses but is now a museum.

The **Booligal Sheep Races** in October attract big crowds.

Sleeping & Eating

Bank B&B (☎ 02-6993 1730; www.users.tpg.com.au/users/tssk; 86 Lachlan St; s/d $80/120; ✄) On the main street, this charming B&B, in an 1891 mansion, has a gorgeous lounge and balcony area, oodles of character and modern facilities.

Saltbush Motor Inn (☎ 02-6993 4555; www.saltbush motorinn.com.au; 193 Lachlan St; s/d $92/98; ☀) New on the scene, this ship-shape establishment has all the mod cons including a saltwater swimming pool and barbecue.

Felicity's Guesthouse (☎ 02-6993 4028; Wooloondool; r $100) About 10km out on the road to Maude, this tranquil and private guest house has river views, birdlife and extensive gardens. Guests can cook their own breakfast and make use of the barbecue.

Long Paddock Café (☎ 02-6993 1128; 131 Lachlan St; ☼ breakfast & lunch) This is the best food option in Hay, with plenty of tables and a selection of tasty gourmet burgers, focaccias and sandwiches. Plans for a new grill and evening opening hours are afoot.

Getting There & Away

CountryLink (☎ 13 22 32; www.countrylink.info) XPT trains run to both Sydney ($81, 13 hours) and Melbourne ($88, 12 hours) via Cootamundra (which explains the lengthy journey time).

DENILIQUIN & AROUND
☎ 03

Deniliquin (population 7431), or 'Deni', as it's known, is an attractive old town, set on a grid beside a wide bend of the Edward River. It's the shopping, eating and drinking hub for the larger agricultural region and home to the famed and ever-growing local ute muster.

Sights & Activities

The **visitor centre** (☎ 1800 650 712; www.deniliquin. nsw.gov.au) is part of the attractive **Peppin Heritage Centre** (☎ 1800 650 712, 03-5898 3120; George St; admission by gold coin donation), which is devoted to the wool industry with in good historical displays.

The **Island Sanctuary**, on the river bank in town, has a pleasant walking track among the river red gums, which joins the historic town and heritage walk (maps available at the visitor centre). It's home to plenty of wildlife including kangaroos, possums and birds.

For swimming, head to **McLean Beach**, one of Australia's finest river beaches, with golden sand, picnic facilities and a walking track.

Some 92km east of Deniliquin and on the Newell Hwy, Jerilderie is immortalised by the bushranger Ned Kelly, who held up the whole town for three days in 1879. Kelly relics can be seen in **Willows Museum & Ned Kelly Post Office** (☎ 03-5886 1511; Powell St; admission by donation; ☼ 9.30am-4pm). The town is 109km south of Narrandera.

Fstivals & Events

Deniliquin holds an annual **Ute Muster** (www.deniutemuster.com.au), which attracts people from across the country for an action-packed weekend in their utes – 7242 of them at last record-breaking count! The event is part of the **Play on the Plains Festival** (☎ 03-5881 3388), held on the Labour Day long weekend in October, which celebrates Aussie culture with live music, celebrity guests, carnivals and bull-rides.

Sleeping & Eating

Coach House (☎ 03-5881 1011; 99 End St; s/d $65/67) Considering its clean and spacious rooms, this place is very reasonably priced. Adjoining the motel is Taylors restaurant and bar, popular for its decent pub meals and lively atmosphere.

Riverview Motel (☎ 03-5881 2311; www.riverview motel.com.au; 1 Butler St; s/d $69/79; ☀ ▢) These spacious rooms have private porches overlooking speckled gum trees and the Edward River. It's a serene option away from the main street.

NEW SOUTH WALES

Riverside Caravan Park (☎ 03-5881 1284; www .deniliquinriversidecaravanpark.com.au; 20 Davidson St; cabins $65-130, unpowered/powered sites per person $10/22; 🖳 🌉) This campsite on the river bank has classy cabins and mod cons including a swimming pool. It's a short walk from the main street.

our pick Crossing Café (☎ 03-5881 7827; Peppin Heritage Centre; mains $25-30; 🕙 lunch Tue-Sun, dinner Fri & Sat) This place has an outdoor deck overlooking an idyllic riverside setting. The menu focuses on quality rather than quantity. Think gourmet: the eggs Benedict with homemade hollandaise is particularly worthwhile.

Getting There & Away

Long-distance buses stop on Whitelock St, opposite Gorman Park. **CountryLink** (☎ 13 22 32; www.countrylink.info) buses run to Wagga ($46, 3½ hours), linking with the XPT train to Sydney Central ($63, 6¾ hours), and to Albury ($26, 3½ hours), linking with the XPT to Melbourne ($47, 3½ hours). **V/Line** (☎ 13 61 96; www.vline.com.au) coaches run to Melbourne ($23, four hours).

ALONG THE MURRAY

Most of the major river towns are on the Victorian side (see p573), but it's easy to hop back and forth across the river. You can cross the border at the twin towns of Moama (NSW) and Echuca (Victoria).

The **visitor centre** (☎ 1800 804 446, 03-5480 7555; www.echucamoama.com; 2 Heygarth St, Echuca) serves both towns and is located in Echuca beside the bridge that crosses into NSW. Ask about trips on the paddle steamers that ply these waters (reminders of when the Murray and Darling Rivers were the main highways of communication and trade).

Downstream from Albury (p249) is **Corowa**, a wine-producing centre, whose Lindemans winery dates from 1860. **Tocumwal**, on the Newell Hwy, is a quiet riverside town with sandy beaches and a big fibreglass Murray cod in the town square. The cod- and carp-stuffed Murray River has some good beaches.

WENTWORTH

☎ 03 / pop 1303

Complete with a proud old wharf, the colonial river port of Wentworth lies at the impressive confluence of the Murray and Darling Rivers, 30km northwest of Mildura (p573) on the fringe of the desert. Enormous river red gums shade the banks, and there are numerous lookouts and walking tracks. The town's streets are dotted with restored colonial buildings.

The **visitor centre** (☎ 03-5027 3624; www .wentworth.nsw.gov.au; 66 Darling St) is next to the old courthouse.

You can see some local history in the **Old Wentworth Gaol** (☎ 03-5027 3327; Beverley St; adult/child $6/free; 🕙 10am-5pm) and across the road in the interesting **Folk Museum & Pioneer World** (☎ 03-5027 3160; adult/child $5/2; 🕙 10am-4pm). The latter has eclectic exhibitions including a megafauna replica display and a collection of photos of the paddle steamers that once made this a major port.

Take a cardboard box for some desert tobogganing action at **Perry Sand Hills**, amazing orange sand dunes dating back 40,000 years. They're 6km north of town, off the road to Broken Hill.

Harry Nanya Tours (☎ 03-5027 2076; www.harry nanyatours.com.au; adult/child from $155/100) runs day (April to October) and sunset (November to March) tours with Aboriginal guides into Mungo National Park (p264). Pick-ups are available or tag along with your own car (adult/child $80/40).

Wentworth Central Motor Inn (☎ 03-5027 3777; www.fringeofthedesert.com.au; 43 Adams St; s/d $60/70; ❌ 🌉) has a restaurant, leafy courtyard complete with a cafe, and pleasant enough hotel rooms.

A more historical option is a room at **Avoca-On-Darling** (☎ 03-5027 3020; www.users.bigpond .com/lawsavoca; off Low Darling Rd; per person $110) guest house, an 1800s heritage homestead 26km from Wentworth on the gum-laden banks of the river junction. A self-contained cook's cottage ($150), jackeroo's quarters ($25 per person) and campsites (powered/unpowered $25/15) are also available. Alternatively, visit for a Devonshire tea and tour ($15).

Plenty of houseboats are available for long meanders down both rivers. **Sunraysia Houseboats** (☎ 03-5027 3621; www.sunraysiahouse boats.com) has the biggest fleet or ask at the visitor centre.

OUTBACK

Clumps of grey saltbush hole-punch the red landscape out here and if you concentrate hard enough you can imagine yourself superimposed onto the world's biggest

Aboriginal dot painting, a canvas reaching as far as the eye can see.

If you've made it this far, you ought to be congratulated. NSW is rarely credited for its far west outback corner but it should be. The harsh dry landscape either sucks you in or spits you out depending on its mood. Whatever it has in store, it is guaranteed to be an adventure.

The mining town of Broken Hill is its unique heart-centre, close to the much-photographed town of Silverton; handy for forays into national parks; and a good base for road trips to Tibooburra, the hottest town in the state, and beyond to Cameron Corner at the intersection of NSW, Queensland and South Australia (SA), a milestone of sorts marked by nothing but the feat of arriving there.

Further afield are the unique towns of White Cliffs and Lightning Ridge (p223), where there is more to do underground than above. Like everywhere in the outback, the people here are larger than life, hardened as much by the intense summer heat as they are softened by the eccentricities of actually living here.

Seek local advice if you want to venture onto unsealed roads, even in a 4WD. Although the country is flat to the horizon there are plenty of birds, mobs of emus, cattle, feral goats and kangaroos along the roadside to watch – and to watch out for! Not to mention drifts of fine sand that can be as difficult to navigate as floodplains.

BOURKE
pop 2145

Immortalised for Australians in the expression 'back of Bourke' – that is, anything in the middle of nowhere – this town sits on the edge of the outback. Beyond Bourke, green pastoral lands stop abruptly, settlements are few, and the country is flat, brown and alluring. Sprawled along the beautiful Darling River, Bourke is historic and quaint, but come 6pm, its metal-shuttered shop windows point to an element of social unrest.

The **visitor centre** (☎ 02-6872 1222; www.visit bourke.com; Anson St; ☯ closed Sun summer) has an excellent leaflet called *Bourke Mud Map Tours*, detailing walks and drives of interest.

Theres seasonal fruit- and cotton-picking work available November to January, and May to October; contact **Bourke Joblink** (☎ 02-6870 1041; www.joblinkplus.com.au; 26 Oxley St) for information.

The very worthwhile **Back O' Bourke Exhibition Centre** (☎ 02-6872 1321; www.backobourke.com.au; Kidman Way; adult/child/family $20/10/70) follows the legends of the back country – both Indigenous and settler – through interactive installations and innovative visuals.

The historical and agricultural **Mateship Country Tours** (☎ 02-6872 2280; www.visitbourke.com; adult/child $22/11; ☯ 2pm Mon-Fri, 9.30am Sat) last 3½ hours.

The impressive **three-tiered wharf** at the northern end of Sturt St is a faithful reconstruction of the original (built in 1897), and, on the river, the **PV Jandra** (☎ 02-6872 1321; Kidman's Camp Tourist Park; adult/child $14/12; ☯ 9am & 3pm) offers one-hour cruises on a replica of an 1895 paddle wheeler.

Contact the **NPWS office** (☎ 02-6872 2744; 51 Oxley St) for visits to the Aboriginal art sites at **Gunderbooka**, the newest outback national park. There's camping at Dry Tank (adult/child $5/3) or try the shearer's quarters (doubles $80).

Bourke's Historic Cemetery (Kidman Way) is peppered with epitaphs saying 'perished in the bush', and tells a thousand stories about the many cultures and creeds buried here. Professor Fred Hollows, the eye surgeon who was determined to help restore the sight of people going needlessly blind, is buried here, after his decades of work in the region.

Sleeping & Eating

Gidgee Guesthouse (☎ 02-6870 1017; www.gidgeeguest house.com.au; 17 Oxley St; dm/s/d $28/40/70; ☐) The tired old London Bank building is actually a guest house with homely rooms around a peaceful native garden. It has canoes for hire.

Port O'Bourke Hotel (☎ 02-6872 2544; 32 Mitchell St; s/d $50/80; ☼) This cheerful place has a large grassy beer garden – with a pet rabbit – and OK pub meals that are included in the tariff.

Bourke Riverside Motel (☎ 02-6872 2539; www .bourkeriversidemotel.com; 3 Mitchell St; s/d $105/110; ☼ ☐ ☻) An oasis in the desert, this rambling historic motel with an enchanting riverside garden has eclectic rooms with antique furniture and an array of good and bad artwork.

Morrall's Bakery (☎ 02-6872 2086; 37 Mitchell St; ☯ 6am-4pm Mon-Fri, to 2pm Sat) Tuck into a Back o' Bourke lamb pie here.

Getting There & Away

Air Link (☎ 02-6884 2435; www.airlinkairlines.com .au) has charter flights to Cobar and Dubbo. **CountryLink** (☎ 13 22 32; www.countrylink.info) buses

NEW SOUTH WALES

run to Dubbo ($57, 4½ hours). **Bourke Courier Service** (☎ 02-6872 2092; cnr Oxley & Richard Sts) sells bus and plane tickets.

A **road condition report** (☎ 02-6872 2055, 0419 722 055) is posted at service stations. All unsealed roads are closed when wet.

BACK O' BOURKE – CORNER COUNTRY

Ever read the classic Australian novel *Wake in Fright*? Perhaps you should. Or not, depending on your perspective. Out here, it's a different world; both harsh and peaceful, stretching forever to the endless sky. This far-western corner of NSW is a semidesert of red plains, heat, dust and flies. But it's also cattle and sheep country, where the properties are huge.

West of Bourke, the 395km to Tibooburra via tiny Wanaaring is a challenging, unsealed road; north on the Silver City Hwy it's mostly sealed but monstrous after rain. Along the Queensland border is the 5400km dingo-proof fence, patrolled daily by boundary riders.

Tiny **Tibooburra**, the hottest town in the state, boasts two rough-around-the-edges sandstone pubs, a small drive-in cinema and a landscape of large red rock formations known as 'granites'. The large **NPWS office** (☎ 08-8091 3308; Briscoe St) with its adjoining Courthouse Museum is a good source of information on many things local including **Sturt National Park**, on the northern edge of town. The **Keeping Place** (☎ 08-8091 3435) features Indigenous artefacts and art from the Wadigali, Wangkumara and Malyangaba peoples.

Granites Motel & Caravan Park (☎ 08-8091 3477; Brown St; unpowered/powered sites $6/18, cabins $55-88, motel s/d from $72/88; ✖ ♨) has cheery rooms, pleasant cabins and a three-bedroom cottage ($130).

The **Family Hotel** (☎ 08-8091 3314; cabins $70, r $30), with its bar adorned in paintings by one-time resident artist Clifton Pugh, has basic rooms out the back and practical cabins over the road.

Out of town in Sturt National Park, glorious Mt Wood Historic Homestead provides the impetus for a real outback stay (see below).

Dead Horse Gully (adult/child $5/3, car $7) is a basic NPWS camping ground 1km north of town; you'll need to bring drinking water (as you should everywhere).

You can normally reach Tibooburra (driving slowly and carefully) from Bourke or Broken Hill in a conventional vehicle, except after rain (which is pretty rare). The road from Broken Hill is partly sealed.

South of Tibooburra, **Milparinka**, once a gold town, now consists of little more than a solitary hotel and an old sandstone building. A better stop between Tibooburra and Broken Hill is the **Packsaddle Roadhouse**, providing petrol, food, beer and camping facilities ($12) to weary (or thirsty) travellers.

Sturt National Park

Taking in vast stony plains, the towering red-sand hills of the great Strzelecki Desert and the unusual flat-topped mesas around Olive Downs, this **park** (admission $7) covers 325,329 hectares of classic outback terrain. Thanks to the protection of the dingo-proof fence, there are large populations of western grey and red kangaroos.

The national park has 300km of drivable tracks, camping areas and walks. The NPWS at Tibooburra (left) has brochures for each. A favourite destination for visitors is

---

CORNER ACCOMMODATION

If you have managed to get this far after four hours on the red raw road from Broken Hill or Bourke, you'll be primed for adventure. What few people know when they come to a halt in the dusty streets of Tibooburra (above), is that just a few kilometres out of town a true icon of the outback awaits. **Mt Wood Historic Homestead** sits on the edge of Sturt National Park surrounded by broad horizons by day and a galaxy of stars by night. The former sheep station is now run by the NPWS and the homestead, with its wide verandahs and high ceilings, is primed for accommodation. Resident park ranger Ingrid has set up a sanctuary for injured and orphaned kangaroos and the surrounding creeks and scrubland of the national park provide plenty of room for exploring. Ring ahead for opportunities to live and work on the homestead in exchange for bed and board. Shorter stays are $60 per room (with two or three beds) per night with a minimum two nights. Plans are afoot for Nearby Olive Hill Downs to open for guests also. Contact Tibooburra NPWS (above) for information and bookings.

Cameron Corner. A post marks the spot where Queensland, SA and NSW meet. The Corner is reached by a well-signposted dirt road (allow two hours). In the Queensland corner, vine-covered **Cameron Corner Store** (☎ 08-8091 3872) has fuel, meals, accommodation and good advice on road conditions.

BARRIER HIGHWAY & AROUND

The Barrier Hwy is the main sealed route in the state's west, heading from Nyngan 594km through to Broken Hill. It's an alternative route to Adelaide and the most direct route between Sydney and Western Australia. For road conditions phone ☎ 08-8082 6660 or 08-8082 6699.

Cobar is a bustling mining town with a productive copper mine. It's littered with interesting buildings, including the splendid **Great Western Hotel** (1898), with its enormous iron-lace verandah, and the old **courthouse and cop station** (Barton St). The **visitor centre** (☎ 02-6836 2448; Barrier Way) is in the Great Cobar Heritage Centre, where **Cobar Museum** (adult/child/family $8/6/18; ☯ 8.30am-5pm) has sophisticated displays on the environment, local Aboriginal life and the early Europeans.

The **Town & Country Motor Inn** (☎ 02-6836 1244; 52 Marshall St; s/d from $95/115; ✕ ▢ ▣) has smart and crisply clean rooms behind a treed garden, and you can walk across the courtyard to **Giovanni's** (mains $26; ☯ dinner).

On the road south to Hillston get a glimpse into the raw **New Cobar Open Cut Gold Mine** from Fort Bourke Lookout, which has a 150m viewing platform.

About 32km northwest of the Barrier Hwy (signposted), **Mt Grenfell Historic Site** protects well-preserved and brilliantly coloured Aboriginal rock art in several caves along a watered gully, an important place for its Aboriginal owners, the Ngiyampaa Wangaaypuwan people. Contact the **NPWS** (☎ 02-6836 2692; Barton St) or the **Cobar Aboriginal Lands Council** (☎ 02-6836 1144) for more information.

There are few stranger places in Australia than the tiny opal-mining town of **White Cliffs**, located about 91km northwest of Wilcannia. Surrounded by some of the harshest country the outback has to offer, many residents in this pot-holed landscape have moved underground to escape temperatures that soar to 50°C. You can inspect some of their homes with **Parkers'**

Dug-Out Home Tours (☎ 08-8091 6635; adult/child $5/free). You can also try fossicking for the world-renowned local opals around the old diggings, but watch the kids around those deep, unfenced holes.

White Cliffs Underground Motel (☎ 08-8091 6677; www.undergroundmotel.com.au; s/d $79/99; ▢ ▣) was custom built with a tunnelling machine. It has wide corridors, a lively dining room and delightfully comfortable silent rooms. Claustrophobics can stay in the two above-ground rooms.

Simmering in the sun, **White Cliffs Opal Pioneer Reserve** (☎ 08-8091 6649; powered sites $12) has sites on flat dusty earth.

Mutawintji National Park

This exceptional 69,000-hectare park lies in the Byngnano Range – the eroded and sculptured remains of a 400-million-year-old seabed. Its stunning gorges and rock pools teem with wildlife, and the mulga plains here stretch to the horizon.

The Malyangapa and Bandjigali peoples have lived in the area for more than 8000 years, and there are important rock engravings, stencils, paintings and scattered remains of their day-to-day life.

You can camp at **Homestead Creek** (adult/child $5/3), but you will need to bring your own food. Check road-closure info on ☎ 08-8082 6660, 13 27 01 or 08-8091 5155.

BROKEN HILL
☎ 08 / pop 18,854

The massive silver skimp dump forming the background of Broken Hill's town centre accentuates the unique character of this desert location known as Silver City, and remains a stark reminder of the area's vibrant – if colossal – mining history. Though set in the barren and dry environment, at least a day's driving from the nearest capital city, Broken Hill is a fascinating destination for its comfortable, oasis-like existence.

Some of the state's best national parks are in the area, plus interesting near-ghost towns. Elements of 'traditional' Australian culture that are disappearing in other cities can still be found in Broken Hill, showing the sensibilities that come with access to a huge, unpopulated landscape. This has also inspired a major arts centre, with poets, writers, artists and sculptors offering a surprisingly different and delightful view of the great outback.

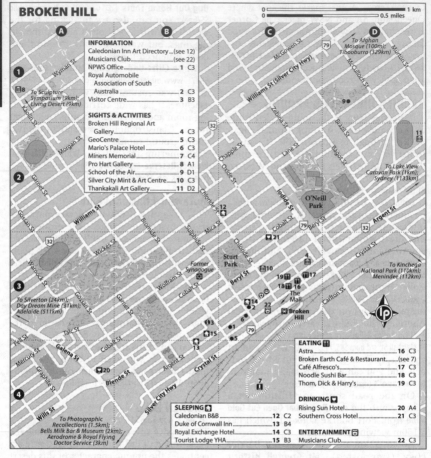

BROKEN HILL

INFORMATION
Caledonian Inn Art Directory	...(see 12)	
Musicians Club	(see 22)	
NPWS Office	1	C3
Royal Automobile Association of South Australia	2	C3
Visitor Centre	3	B3

SIGHTS & ACTIVITIES
Broken Hill Regional Art Gallery	4	C3
GeoCentre	5	C3
Mario's Palace Hotel	6	C3
Miners Memorial	7	C4
Pro Hart Gallery	8	A1
School of the Air	9	D1
Silver City Mint & Art Centre	10	C3
Thankakali Art Gallery	11	D2

EATING
Astra	16	C3
Broken Earth Café & Restaurant	(see 7)	
Café Alfresco's	17	C3
Noodle Sushi Bar	18	C3
Thom, Dick & Harry's	19	C3

SLEEPING
Caledonian B&B	12	C2
Duke of Cornwall Inn	13	B4
Royal Exchange Hotel	14	C3
Tourist Lodge YHA	15	B3

DRINKING
Rising Sun Hotel	20	A4
Southern Cross Hotel	21	C3

ENTERTAINMENT
Musicians Club	22	C3

History

A boundary rider, Charles Rasp, laid the foundations in Broken Hill that took Australia from an agricultural country to an industrial nation. In 1885 he discovered a silver lode and formed the Broken Hill Proprietary Company (which now goes by the name of BHP Billiton). It ultimately became Australia's largest company and an international giant.

Early conditions in the mine were appalling. Hundreds of miners died and many more suffered from lead poisoning and lung disease. This gave rise to the other great force in Broken Hill, the unions. Many miners were immigrants, but all were united in their efforts to improve conditions. The Big Strike of 1919–20 lasted for over 18 months, but the miners achieved a 35-hour week and the end of dry drilling.

Today the world's richest deposits of silver, lead and zinc are still being worked here. However, all of the mining operations are slowly being wound down and the gold of tourism is replacing the silver of the ground.

Orientation & Information

The city is laid out in a grid, with the streets named after metals and their compounds. Argent St is the main street.

Caledonian Inn Art Directory (☎ 08-8087 1945; www .caledonianbnb.com.au; 140 Chloride St; ⏰ 10am-6pm) Local art hangings with mud maps to relevant galleries.

Musicians Club (☎ 08-8088 1777; 267 Crystal St; per hr $10) Internet access.

NPWS office (☎ 08-8080 3200; 183 Argent St) Local national-park inquiries and bookings.

Royal Automobile Association of South Australia (Raasa; ☎ 08-8088 4999; 320 Argent St) Reciprocal service to other auto-club members.

Visitor centre (☎ 08-8088 3560; www.visitbroken hill.com.au; cnr Blende & Bromide Sts) Call in here to pick up a copy of the excellent free booklet *Broken Hill, the Accessible Outback*, which is full of helpful regional information. The adjoining cafe is one of the few places open on Sunday.

Sights

Many sights are closed sporadically during summer.

MINING

The first mines were walk-in, pick-and-shovel horrors. For an amazing experience, tour the historic **Day Dream Mine** (☎ 08-8088 5682; underground tours adult/child $20/19, surface $7/3.50; ☼ tours 10am-3.30pm, 10am & 11.30am summer), where you squeeze down the steps with your helmet-light quivering on your head. Sturdy footwear is essential. It's a scenic 20-minute drive off the Silverton road.

Teetering atop the huge silver skimp dump is the moving **Line of Lode Miners Memorial** (☎ 08-8087 1318; Federation Hill; admission $2.50; ☼ 9am-5pm, later summer). It houses the impressively stark Cor-Ten steel memorial to the 900 miners who have died since Broken Hill first became a mining town. Inside the monument, a sobering series of plaques for each year itemise an appalling litany of gruesome deaths. The neighbouring Line of Lode Visitor Centre makes an excellent sunrise or sunset vantage point over Broken Hill, and the Broken Earth Café & Restaurant (p262) is next door.

GALLERIES

With its dramatic scenery and empty spaces, Broken Hill is an inspiring place, and, unsurprisingly, is home to an abundance of galleries, including the **Pro Hart Gallery** (☎ 08-8088 2992; 108 Wyman St; admission $4; ☼ 9am-5pm Mon-Sat & school holidays, 1.30-5pm Sun). Pro Hart, who died early in 2006, was a former miner and is Broken Hill's best-known artist. Aside from housing his excellent work, the gallery holds a superb collection of Australian art (such as

Brett Whiteley's *Nude*, Norman Lindsay's *Selena* and Albert Tucker's *Australian Girl in Paris*) and several works by international artists such as Pablo Picasso and Salvador Dalí.

The must-see **Broken Hill Regional Art Gallery** (☎ 08-8088 6897; 404-408 Argent St; admission by donation; ☼ 10am-5pm) is now housed in the beautifully restored Sully's Emporium. It is the oldest regional gallery in NSW and holds 1500 works in its permanent collection.

Thankakali Art Gallery (☎ 08-8087 6111; cnr Buck & Beryl Sts; ☼ 8am-2.30pm Mon-Thu) is the Aboriginal cultural centre, located in an old brewery. It has an extensive gallery and a range of hand-painted arts, crafts and didgeridoos by local artists.

On Argent St ring the buzzer on the door for a peek at the murals in Mario's Palace Hotel (p262).

OTHER SIGHTS

The **Royal Flying Doctor Service** (☎ 08-8080 1714; www.flyingdoctors.org; aerodrome; adult/child $5.50/2.20; ☼ 9am-5pm Mon-Fri, 11am-4pm Sat & Sun) exhibition includes the fascinating Mantle of Safety Museum, with lots of quirky stories and things to see. Tours run during the week, or visit the museum at any time.

For a back-to-school experience, sit in on **School of the Air** (Lane St; admission $4.40; ☼ broadcasts 8.30am school days), which broadcasts to kids in isolated homesteads.

The wonderful **Photographic Recollections** (☎ 08-8087 9322; Old Central Power Station, Eyre St; adult/child $5/2; ☼ 10am-4.30pm Mon-Fri, 1-4.30pm Sat & Sun) exhibition is a pictorial history of Broken Hill.

GeoCentre (☎ 08-8087 6538; cnr Bromide & Crystal Sts; adult/child $3.50/2.50; ☼ 10am-4.45pm Mon-Fri, 1-4.45pm Sat & Sun) is an interactive geology museum, with beautiful and rare minerals and crystals on display and lots of touch-and-feel exhibits. It's also home to a 42kg silver nugget.

On the other side of the hill, the old commercial hub of Patton St is a slice of 1950s nostalgia. Sip on a 'soda spider' in a high-topped glass at **Bells Milk Bar & Museum** (☎ 08-8087 5380; www.bellsmilkbar.com.au; 60 Patton St).

Silver City Mint & Art Centre (☎ 08-8088 6166; 66 Chloride St; ☼ 10am-4pm Mon-Sat, 1-4pm Sun) is home to a chocolate factory and the Big Picture (admission $5), the largest continuous canvas in Australia, an amazing 100m-by-12m diorama of the Broken Hill outback.

The **Afghan Mosque** (cnr Williams & Buck Sts; admission $2.50; 2-4pm Sun) is a simple corrugated-iron building erected around 1891. Afghani cameleers helped open up the outback; the mosque was built on the site of a camel camp.

Star of the hit Australian movie *The Adventures of Priscilla, Queen of the Desert*, **Mario's Palace Hotel** (08-8088 1699; cnr Argent & Sulphide Sts) is an impressive old pub (1888) with an elaborate cast-iron verandah – the longest in the state and now heritage listed by the National Trust. With the passing of the legendary Mario, the hotel has fallen into troubled times (and disrepair) but the extravagant murals can still be viewed. Anyone wanting an experience as opposed to comfort and service can try for a room ($37), although accommodation is usually reserved for workers.

The **St Pats Day Races** (www.stpatricks.org.au; Broken Hill Racecourse) in March is an iconic annual event.

Tours

Two-hour guided walks (for a donation) of Broken Hill commence from the tourist centre at 10am Monday, Wednesday and Friday (not in summer).

Broken Hill's Outback Tours (1800 670 120) Deluxe 4WD tours of the area for up to nine days.

Bush Mail Run (0411 102 339; adult $120; 7am-4pm Wed & Sat) The 4WD outback mail-delivery service covers 550km, stopping at isolated homesteads for the occasional cuppa.

Mine tours (08-8087 2484) Day Dream Mine ($65) and Silverton ($106) tours depart daily at 9.30am. Call ahead for reservation and pick-up.

Tri State Safaris (08-8088 2389; www.tristate.com.au) Half- to 18-day tours to places such as Corner Country, Birdsville and the Simpson Desert.

Sleeping

Tourist Lodge YHA (08-8088 2086; www.yha.com.au; 100 Argent St; dm/s/d $25/40/60;) This popular and central YHA has a laid-back atmosphere and is set around a charming courtyard with a small pool. Tours and bike rental can be arranged.

Caledonian B&B (08-8087 1945; www.caledonianbnb.com.au; 140 Chloride St; s/d $65/75;) This B&B is in a refurbished pub (1898) known as 'the Cally'. The decor and garden are a little cluttered and the owner a tad chatty but the rooms are super clean and comfortable.

Duke of Cornwall Inn (08-8087 8495; 76 Argent St; d from $70;) On the main street with terrific views across to the silver dump from the

balcony, this two-storey, heritage hotel is the perfect immersion into Broken Hill's history. The halls are lined with interesting artefacts, heirlooms and clippings and the rooms, with basic bathrooms, are dotted with antiques. The pragmatic owners do train station pick-ups.

our pick Royal Exchange Hotel (08-8087 2308; www.royalexchangehotel.com; 320 Argent St; d $205, with balcony $260;) This beautifully restored 1930s hotel with an art deco bent is an accommodation oasis in the heart of town.

Lake View Caravan Park (08-8088 2250; 1 Mann St; sites/cabins $22/62, r from $97;) Looking down on Imperial Lake, you're high enough for cooling breezes, and the park is dotted with grass patches and trees.

Eating

Thom, Dick & Harry's (08-8088 7000; 354 Argent St; breakfast & lunch Mon-Sat) A narrow shop cluttered with stylish kitchenware and gourmet produce. Sit in amongst it for a decent coffee and delicious baguette, sanger, wrap or Turkish (around $8).

Noodle Sushi Bar (08-8087 6734; 351 Argent St; meals $10; lunch & dinner) Every country town should have one of these. This clean and friendly eat-in or takeaway restaurant dishes up a vast array of noodles – Hokkien, Mongolian and Singapore to name a few – plus nasi goreng, curry laksa and stir-fried veg.

Café Alfresco's (08-8087 5599; cnr Argent & Oxide Sts; mains $12-27; lunch & dinner) The service ticks along at an outback pace but this place still pulls an unfussy crowd pining for plates of pancakes, roasts, salads, pasta dishes and gourmet pizzas.

our pick Broken Earth Café & Restaurant (08-8087 1318; Line of Lode visitor centre; entrées $20, mains $38; closed Sun in summer) With its stunning views over Broken Hill, airy modern design and eclectic gourmand menu, this gets a big thumbs up. There's all-day coffee and cakes, too.

Astra (08-8087 5428; 393 Argent St; entrées $21, mains $34; lunch & dinner) This restaurant and wine bar with tables and chairs outside has a diverse menu including eye fillet steak, duck confit stack and chicken schnitzel. Service is a notch above.

Drinking & Entertainment

Broken Hill stays up late and people feel safe here, so you'll find pubs doing a roaring trade on Thursday, Friday and Saturday. The nightlife slows down considerably in summer.

OUTBACK DUSK & DAWN

One of the most brilliant experiences at Broken Hill is a sunset or sunrise at the **Sculpture Symposium** on the highest hilltop 9km from town. The sculptures are the work of 12 international artists who carved the huge sandstone blocks on site. The colours of the stone change constantly with the light, a vision matched by 360-degree views. The symposium is part of the 2400-hectare **Living Desert**, featuring a 2km cultural trail through protected native flora, a Sturt desert pea display, an Aboriginal story pole and picnic and barbecue area. The visitor centre has gate keys and directions to drive to the top (per car $10), where there's wheelchair access to the sculptures. Or take the second exit (also $10) through the Living Desert for a 20-minute climb to the sculpture site from the lower car park.

Rising Sun Hotel (☎ 08-8087 4856; 2 Beryl St; ☯ 10am-late) Has free games of pool and gets very lively on Friday night.

Southern Cross Hotel (☎ 08-8088 4122; 357 Cobalt St; ☯ 10am-midnight) Here you'll find a mellow atmosphere with '70s- and '80s-style music, a pool table and a decent pub menu.

Musicians Club (☎ 08-8088 1777; 267 Crystal St; ☯ 10am-midnight Mon-Thu, to 1am Fri & Sat, to 11pm Sun; ▣) A jolly place with a heaving mix of young and old. Country, blues and rock 'n' roll music bands play at weekends while the drinks flow. Two-up (gambling on the fall of two coins) is played on Friday and Saturday night from 10pm to 2am.

Getting There & Around

Rex (☎ 13 17 13; www.regionalexpress.com.au) flies to Adelaide ($145, 1¼ hours), Sydney ($231, 2¾ hours) and Dubbo ($212, two hours).

Buses arrive at the visitor centre. **CountryLink** (☎ 13 22 32) runs the *Broken Hill Outback Explorer* to Sydney ($118, 13½ hours). A coach departing from the visitor centre connects with the Dubbo XPT to Sydney ($118, 16½ hours). The **CountryLink booking office** (☎ 08-8087 1400; ☯ 8am-5pm Mon-Fri) is at the train station.

The **Indian Pacific** (☎ 13 21 47; www.trainways.com .au) goes east to Sydney ($129, 16 hours), south to Adelaide ($60, 6¾ hours) and west to Perth ($246, 47 hours).

A free bus services some of the clubs from 6pm to midnight. **Murton's Citybus** (☎ 08-8087 3311; www.murtons.com.au) operates four routes around Broken Hill, or you can call a **taxi** (☎ 08-8087 2222).

AROUND BROKEN HILL
Silverton

☎ 08 / pop about 50 people & 1 donkey

It's absolutely obligatory to visit Silverton, an old silver-mining town where you walk inside a Drysdale painting and discover the charm of the outback. Silverton's fortunes peaked in 1885, when it had a population of 3000, but in 1889 the mines closed and the people (and some houses) moved to the new boom town at Broken Hill.

Today it's a ghost town with a new lease of life due to the spirits at the pub (beer too) and a small community of artists, a couple of whom have studios here. The basic **visitor centre** (☎ 08-8088 7566) is in the Beyond 39 Dips shop, a reference to the roller-coaster road from Broken Hill. It has walking-tour maps.

Silverton is the setting of films such as *Mad Max II* and *A Town Like Alice*. The popular **Silverton Hotel** (☎ 08-8088 5313; Layard St; ☯ 9am-9pm) displays film memorabilia and a litany of miscellany typifying Australia's peculiar brand of larrikin humour. The pub has accommodation in the 'grave yard', a collection of beer-garden cabins (singles/doubles $33/44).

It's hard to believe the **Old Silverton Gaol** (adult/child $3/50c; ☯ 9.30am-4.30pm) housed 14 cells. Today the tiny building is home to a museum with photos and memorabilia of the early prison days. The new **School Museum** (adult/child $4/50c) is another history pit stop.

Barrier Range Camel Safaris (☎ 08-8088 5316; tours from $15, 2hr sunset treks $65), on the road to Silverton, runs a variety of camel tours from Silverton on friendly and quiet camels.

Silverton Tea Rooms (☎ 08-8088 6601; ☯ breakfast & lunch Tue-Sun), with 'cafe' sprawled across the corrugated iron roof, has a menu with staples such as Gun Shearers Pie ($13) and Bushman's Burger ($10). It also has collections of old wares dug up in the area.

The road beyond Silverton becomes isolated and vast almost immediately, but it's worth driving 5km to **Mundi Mundi Lookout**

NEW SOUTH WALES

PHONES, TIMES & FOOTBALL

When the NSW government refused to give Broken Hill the services it needed, saying the town was just a pinprick on the map, the Barrier Industrial Council replied that Sydney was also a pinprick from where it was, and Broken Hill would henceforth be part of SA. Since the town was responsible for much of NSW's wealth there was an outcry, the federal government stepped in, and Broken Hill was told it was to remain part of NSW. In protest, the town adopted SA time, phone area code, and football, playing Australian Rules from then on.

Tourists beware: time in Broken Hill is Central Standard Time (CST), 30 minutes later than the surrounding area on Eastern Standard Time (EST); you're in the 08 phone code region; and don't talk about rugby in the pub.

---

where the view over the **Mundi Mundi Plain** is so extensive it reveals the curvature of the Earth. About 8km further, **Umberumberka Reservoir** is a popular picnic spot.

Menindee Lakes

Menindee Lakes are a series of nine natural, ephemeral lakes adjacent to the Darling River that have been dammed to ensure year-round water. There's a helpful **visitor centre** (☎ 08-8091 4274; www.outbacknow.com; Menindee St). **River Lady Tours** (☎ 0427 195 336) has daytime, sunset cruises and camp-oven dinner cruises, departing from Lake Wetherell weir.

Copi Hollow Caravan Park (☎ 08-8091 4880; Menindee-Broken Hill Rd; campsites/cabins $20/40) is set around a lovely tree-lined swimming hole at the far end of the lakes and has great fishing, waterskiing and bushwalking.

Kinchega National Park (admission per car $7) is close to Menindee, and the lakes here are a haven for bird life. There are three well-marked driving trails through the park, and accommodation is available at the **shearers' quarters** (adult/child $17/9), which can be booked at Broken Hill NPWS office (see p261). There are also three **campsites** (adult/child $5/3). If you're driving, call **roads info** (☎ 08-8087 0660, 08-8091 5155).

MUNGO NATIONAL PARK

This remote, beautiful and important place covers 27,850 hectares of the Willandra Lakes World Heritage area. The echoes of over 400 centuries of continuous human habitation are almost tangible in **Lake Mungo**, a dry lake that is the site of the oldest archaeological finds in Australia as well as being the longest continual record of Aboriginal life (the world's oldest recorded cremation has been found here). A 25km semicircle ('lunette') of huge sand dunes has been created by the unceasing westerly wind, which continually exposes fabulously

ancient remains. These shimmering white dunes are known as the **Walls of China**.

Mungo is 110km from Mildura and 150km from Balranald on good, unsealed roads that become instantly impassable after rain. These towns are the closest places selling fuel.

Harry Nanya Tours (☎ 03-5027 2076; www.harrynanya tours.com.au) runs daily tours to Mungo National Park from Mildura (p573) and Wentworth (p256), and employs Aboriginal guides who give cultural information. Indigenous-owned **My Country Enterprise Tours** (☎ 0401 919 275; www.my countryenterprises.com) runs a five-day walking tour that includes a nocturnal tour of the Mungo lunette. Ring ahead for price and dates.

The **NPWS office** (☎ 03-5021 8900), on the corner of the Sturt Hwy at Buronga, near Mildura, has park information. There's a visitor centre (not always staffed) in the park, by the old Mungo woolshed; pay your day-use fee here.

From here a road leads across the dry lake bed to the Walls of China, and you can drive a complete 70km signposted loop of the dunes when it's dry. There's a self-guided drive brochure at the visitor centre. Alternatively take the 2.5km Grassland Nature Trail direct from Main Camp or the 2.5km Foreshore Walk from the visitor centre.

In school holidays accommodation fills up. **Mungo Lodge** (☎ 03-5029 7297; www.mungolodge .com.au; cabins with bathroom $240, self-contained $340), on the Mildura road, about 4km from the visitor centre has cute cabins with all the mod cons and a flash restaurant (book ahead).

In the park, **Main Camp** (adult/child $5/3, car $7) is 2km from the visitor centre, and **Belah Camp** (adult/child $5/3, car $7) is on the eastern side of the dunes. Bookings not required. Accommodation is also available at the **shearers' quarters** (adult/child $20/5.50), which has five rooms, a communal kitchen and bathroom, and barbecue area. It's BYO bed linen.

Australian Capital Territory

The Australian Capital Territory (ACT) was born of a dispute between Sydney and Melbourne, each competing to become the capital of the newly independent and federated Australia. Neither could bear for the other to triumph, so when a compromise was reached, a small chunk was carved out of New South Wales' Limestone Plains 280km southwest of Sydney and 150km inland from the coast. This became the site for Canberra, and the country's smallest self-governing territory.

The city of Canberra is a monument to the young country's aspirations, its urban landscape expertly designed to show off the nation's democratic and cultural institutions. The city is an excellent destination for museum addicts, with wonderful fine art and historical collections. Canberra is the nation's political heart – its restaurants buzz with power-lunchers hammering out strategy, while at the city's bars political reporters hang about hoping for a bit of gossip or a wine-fuelled indiscretion. The population is both richer and better educated than the national average. The ACT is known for its liberal politics, becoming the first jurisdiction to vote a woman its head of government and enacting progressive legislation on everything from gay unions and women's rights to porn and marijuana.

The almost too-tidy town is cradled by mountain ranges and hills covered in bushland, beyond which are several charming villages and a growing number of cold-climate wineries. Half of the territory is protected as national park or reserve, with plenty to attract hikers, campers and nature-lovers of all kinds.

HIGHLIGHTS

- Stroll the corridors of creativity in the **National Gallery of Australia** (p272)
- Lose yourself for days or silently stand for the last post at the **Australian War Memorial** (p273)
- Spot kangaroos and Aboriginal rock art in **Namadgi National Park** (p288)
- Marvel at Australia's moving-picture and sound recording history at the **National Film & Sound Archive** (p275)
- Negotiate the network of Australiana in the **National Museum of Australia** (p272)
- Paddle, cycle, skate, walk or run around **Lake Burley Griffin** (p272)
- Ogle at the architectural splendour of **Parliament House** (p273)

National Film & Sound Archive;
National Museum of Australia ★ ★ Australian War Memorial
Lake Burley Griffin ★ ★ ★ National Gallery of Australia
Parliament House
★ Namadgi National Park

| ■ TELEPHONE CODE: 02 | ■ POPULATION: 347,800 | ■ AREA: 2366 SQ KM |

AUSTRALIAN CAPITAL TERRITORY

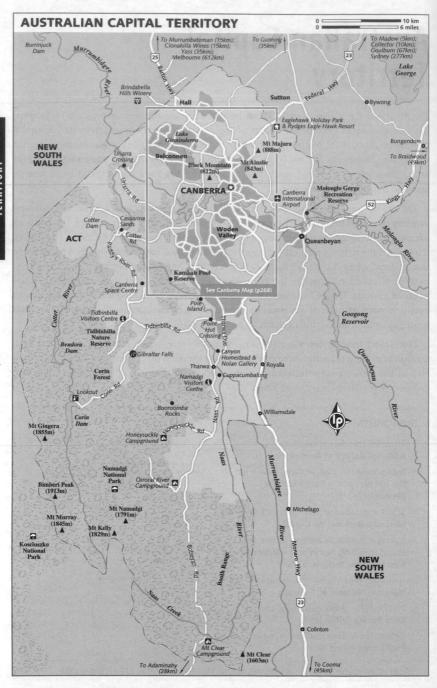

AUSTRALIAN CAPITAL TERRITORY

| 0 | 10 km |
| 0 | 6 miles |

Burrinjuck Dam

Murrumbidgee River

To Murrumbateman (15km);
Clonakilla Wines (15km);
Yass (35km);
Melbourne (612km)

To Gunning (35km)

To Madew (5km);
Collector (10km);
Goulburn (67km);
Sydney (277km)

Lake George

25

23

Brindabella Hills Winery

Hall

Sutton

Federal Hwy

Bywong

Eaglehawk Holiday Park
& Rydges Eagle Hawk Resort

NEW SOUTH WALES

Lake Ginninderra

Belconnen

Mt Majura (888m)

Bungendore

To Braidwood (49km)

Uriarra Crossing

Black Mountain (812m)

Mt Ainslie (843m)

CANBERRA

Uriarra Rd

Canberra International Airport

Molonglo Gorge Recreation Reserve

52

Kings Hwy

Cotter Dam

Casuarina Sands

ACT

Cotter Rd

Woden Valley

Canberra Space Centre

Paddy's River Rd

Molonglo River

Queanbeyan

Cotter River

Kambah Pool Reserve

See Canberra Map (p268)

Googong Reservoir

Bendora Dam

Tidbinbilla Visitors Centre

Tidbinbilla Nature Reserve

Pine Island

Tidbinbilla Rd

Point Hut Crossing

Tharwa Dve

Queanbeyan River

Gibraltar Falls

Tharwa

Lanyon Homestead & Nolan Gallery

Royalla

Corin Forest

Corin Rd

Namadgi Visitors Centre

Cuppacumbong

Lookout

Corin Dam

Booroomba Rocks

Williamsdale

Mt Gingera (1855m)

Honeysuckle Campground

Honeysuckle Rd

Namadgi National Park

Naas Rd

Bimberi Peak (1913m)

Orroral River Campground

Mt Murray (1845m)

Mt Namadgi (1791m)

Michelago

Mt Kelly (1829m)

Murrumbidgee River

Kosciuszko National Park

Booth Range

Monaro Hwy

Naas River

Bobayan Rd

NEW SOUTH WALES

23

Naas Creek

Colinton

Mt Clear Campground

Mt Clear (1603m)

To Adaminaby (28km)

To Cooma (45km)

CANBERRA

pop 339,500

A tranquil artificial lake, an enormous flag flying above and huge avenues fanning out from its centre: Canberra, like other purpose-built capitals, can seem big on architectural symbolism and low on spontaneity. But behind its slightly sterile exterior the city has plenty going on. Apart from its world-class museums and galleries – which alone justify a visit – the city boasts a lively bar scene (if only from Thursday to Saturday), and a vibrant live music culture fuelled by the city's university students. Canberra's museums host gaggles of school kids, bussed in from all over the country to pay homage to the nation's icons and celebrate its history, while the fine permanent collection and frequent international blockbuster exhibitions at the National Gallery draw visitors from around Australia. During parliamentary-sitting weeks the town hums with the business of national politics, but it can feel a bit dead during university holidays, especially around Christmas and New Year.

HISTORY

For over 20,000 years the Ngunnawal Aboriginal people made this country their home. The people were nomadic by necessity, but the seasonal abundance of foods, such as the yam daisies of the plains and the Bogong moths of the high country, occasioned large gatherings. 'Canberra' or 'Kanberra' is believed to be an Aboriginal term for 'meeting place'.

European settlement began in the 1820s and many Ngunnawal people ended up working on expansive sheep stations. They withstood the trials of white settlement – persecution, introduced diseases, official neglect and massive environmental change – and have increased their profile in recent years.

When Australia's separate colonies were federated in 1901 and became states, the decision to build a national capital was written into the constitution. In 1908 the site was selected, and in 1911 the Commonwealth government created the Federal Capital Territory (changed to the Australian Capital Territory in 1938).

Canberra took over from Melbourne as the seat of national government in 1927, but the city's expansion really got under way after WWII – in the next decade the population trebled to 39,000.

The western and southern outskirts of the city were struck by devastating bushfires in January 2003. The fires claimed four lives, 530 homes, 30 farms and the historic Mt Stromlo Observatory, and decimated large swaths of Namadgi National Park. Almost all of the 5500 hectares of Tidbinbilla Nature Reserve, including most wildlife, were destroyed. The regeneration of the fire-scorched landscape, however, began quickly and the area is well worth exploring.

CLIMATE

Summer days across the ACT range from comfortably warm to uncomfortably hot, though the temperature doesn't often top 40°C. Winter days here are invariably cool and sometimes gloriously sunny, with little wind, and often kick off with early morning frost and fog – winter nights hover around 0°C during July.

ORIENTATION

Think crop circles in suburbia and you have an aerial picture of this city, conceived on an architect's drawing board with the aid of ruler, compass and protractor. Two great road axes, Kings and Commonwealth Aves, converge at the apex of Capital Hill, which, with Constitution Ave, create Walter Burley Griffin's parliamentary triangle. Kings and Commonwealth Aves span Canberra's central water feature – Lake Burley Griffin – complete with spout, and all roads end with roundabouts.

The main axis starts north of the city where the Federal and Barton Hwys converge into Northbourne Ave which then runs south through the suburbs of Downer, Dickson and Braddon before entering Civic, the city centre. After circling City Hill this axis road becomes Commonwealth Ave and heads across Lake Burley Griffin to Capital Hill.

Capital Hill is encircled by State Circle and Capital Circle, Parkes Way skirts the northern shore of the lake and the rest of the city is made up of suburban satellites, each with their own town centres.

Maps

The **National Roads & Motorists' Association** (NRMA; Map p270; ☎ 02-6240 4630; 6 City Walk, Canberra Centre, Civic; ☽ 9am-5pm Mon-Fri) has the *Canberra &*

AUSTRALIAN CAPITAL TERRITORY

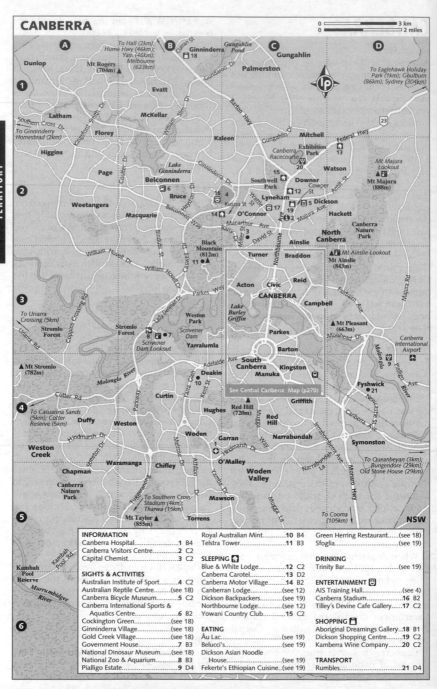

CANBERRA

0   3 km
0   2 miles

AUSTRALIAN CAPITAL TERRITORY FACTS

Eat Italian, Malaysian, Turkish, Chinese, vegetarian, seafood…
Drink 'Middy' (285mL) or 'schooner' (425mL) of Wig and Pen Velvet Cream Stout
Read *How to be a Megalomaniac* by Mungo MacCallum, *The Point* by Marion Halligan, poems by Judith Wright
Listen to Udo (pop, jazz, funk), The Gadflys (pop, rock, punk)
Watch Anything at the National Film & Sound Archive (p275)
Avoid Swimming in algal blooms, hailstorms
Locals' nickname Pubes (public servants)
Swim at Cotter River (p287), overflowing with cool clean water and lined by serene picnic spots
Strangest festival SCOTT Australian 24 Hour Mountain Bike Championships (p278), in October, in which thousands of entrants tackle Stromlo Forest on two wheels for 24 hours of hardship; smarter folk do it in teams
Tackiest tourist attraction Gold Creek Village (p288) souvenir shops

Southeast map ($7; free if you belong to an affiliated motoring organisation), good for tours of the city and surrounding area. The Canberra Visitors Centre (p271) stocks good city maps and maps for bushwalking in Namadgi National Park ($4.50). **Map World** (Map p270; ☎ 02-6230 4097; Jolimont Centre, 65 Northbourne Ave, Civic) and the Namadgi Visitor Centre (p288) stock regional topographic maps.

INFORMATION
Bookshops
Dymocks (Map p270; ☎ 02-6257 5057; 177 City Walk, Civic) Large, central bookshop with latest releases.
Electric Shadows Bookshop (Map p270; ☎ 02-6248 8352; 40 Mort St, Braddon; ⏰ 9am-7pm Mon-Thu, 9am-8pm Fri & Sat, 11am-6pm Sun) This bookshop specialises in books on theatre and film, plus gay and lesbian books and rentable art-house DVDs.
National Library Bookshop (Map p270; ☎ 02-6262 1424; Parkes Pl, Parkes) Stocks exclusively Australian books, including a superb range of fiction.
Smiths Alternative Bookshop (Map p270; ☎ 02-6247 4459; 76 Alinga St, Civic) Sells everything from New Age 'science' to gay and lesbian literature.

Emergency
Dial ☎ 000 for ambulance, fire or police.
Canberra Rape Crisis Centre (☎ 02-6247 2525) Help 24 hours.
Lifeline (☎ 13 11 14) Crisis counselling available 24 hours.

Internet Access
Public libraries, the Canberra Centre (p285), the interstate bus terminal at the Jolimont Centre (p286) and some hostels have public internet access.
Bytes Internet Cafe (Map p270; ☎ 02-6248 9155; 7 Akuna St, Civic; per hr $5; ⏰ 7am-11pm) Underneath the YHA Hostel – coffee and food available.

Internet Resources
Canberra Arts Marketing (www.canberraarts.com.au) Comprehensive events listings.
Canberra Bed & Breakfast Network (www.canberra bandb.com) B&B options in and around Canberra.
National Capital Authority (www.nationalcapital.gov .au) Good for capital history and facts.
Visit Canberra (www.visitcanberra.com.au) What to eat, see, drink and do in Canberra.

Medical Services
Canberra Hospital (Map p268; ☎ 02-6244 2222, emergency dept ☎ 02-6244 2611; Yamba Dr, Garran)
Capital Chemist O'Connor (Map p268; ☎ 02-6248 7050; Sargood St; ⏰ 9am-11pm); Kingston (Map p270; ☎ 02-6295 9146; 58 Giles St; ⏰ 8.30am-7pm Mon-Fri, 10am-4pm Sat & Sun)
Travellers' Medical & Vaccination Centre (Map p270; ☎ 02-6257 7156; 5th fl, 8-10 Hobart Pl, Civic; ⏰ 8.30am-4.30pm Mon-Fri, to 7pm Thu) Appointments essential.

Money
Major banks and ATMs are abundant. Foreign exchange bureaus include the following:
American Express (Amex; Map p270; ☎ 1300 139 060; Petrie Plaza, Civic; ⏰ 9.30am-4pm Mon-Thu, 9.30am-5pm Fri) Located inside a branch of the Westpac bank.
Travelex (Map p270; ☎ 1800 637 642; Canberra Centre, Bunda St, Civic; ⏰ 9am-5pm Mon-Fri, 9.30am-12.30pm Sat) Inside the Harvey World Travel office.

AUSTRALIAN CAPITAL TERRITORY

CENTRAL CANBERRA

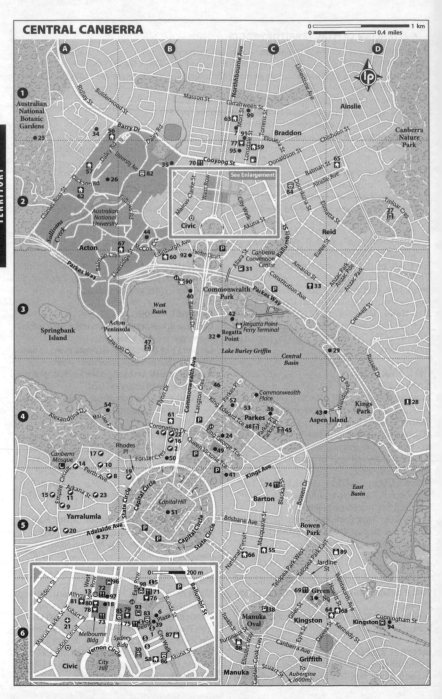

AUSTRALIAN CAPITAL TERRITORY

Post

Main post office (☎ 13 13 18; 53-73 Alinga St, Civic)
Pick up your poste restante here. Mail can be addressed:
poste restante Canberra GPO, Canberra, ACT 2601.

Tourist Information

Canberra Visitors Centre (Map p268; ☎ 1300 554
114, 02-6205 0044; www.visitcanberra.com.au; 330 Northbourne Ave, Dickson; ◷ 9am-5.30pm Mon-Fri, to 4pm Sat

& Sun) For a wealth of information on the region, head to
this centre, operated by the ACT's peak tourist information
body, the Canberra Tourism & Events Corporation.

Citizens Advice Bureau ACT (Map p270; ☎ 02-6248
7988; www.citizensadvice.org.au; New Griffin Centre,
Genge St, Civic; ◷ 10am-4pm Mon, Tue, Thu & Fri, to
1pm Wed) The helpful people here can provide you with
plenty of information on the community services and
facilities available in the ACT.

SIGHTS

Canberra's significant edifices, museums and galleries are dotted around Lake Burley Griffin. Wheelchair-bound visitors will find that most sights are fully accessible.

Those keen on visiting Questacon (p274), the Australian Institute of Sport (AIS; p275) and Cockington Green (p288) should pick up a **3-in-1 Ticket** (adult/child/concession/family $47.50/27/33/128.50), which gives access to all three attractions; buy it at any of the sites or the visitors centre.

Bus 34 is handy for many of the following sights.

Lake Burley Griffin

Named after Canberra's architect, **Lake Burley Griffin** (Map p270) was filled by damming the Molonglo River in 1963 with the 33m-high Scrivener Dam. Around its 35km-long shore are many places of interest.

Built in 1970 to mark the bicentenary of Cook's landfall, the **Captain Cook Memorial Water Jet** (Map p270; ☻ 10am-noon & 2-4pm, also 7-9pm daylight-saving months) flings a 6-tonne column of water up to 147m into the air, and sometimes gives free showers, despite its automatic switch-off in strong winds. There is a skeleton globe at nearby **Regatta Point** on which Cook's three great voyages are traced; also close is the **National Capital Exhibition** (Map p270; ☎ 02-6257 1068; Barrine Dr; admission free; ☻ 9am-5pm), displaying the city's history. Further east is the stone-and-slab **Blundells' Cottage** (Map p270; ☎ 02-6257 1068; Wendouree Dr; adult/child/family $4/2/10; ☻ 11am-4pm), built in 1860 to house workers on the surrounding estate and now a reminder of the area's early farming history.

On Aspen Island is the 50m-high **National Carillon** (Map p270; ☎ 02-6257 1068), a gift from Britain on Canberra's 50th anniversary in 1963. The tower has 55 bronze bells, weighing from 7kg to 6 tonnes each, making it one of the world's largest musical instruments. Daily recitals are held – call ahead or check www.nationalcapital.gov .au then hit 'visiting' to download the latest schedule.

On the northern shore fronting Old Parliament House is **Reconciliation Place** (Map p270), where artwork represents the nation's commitment to the cause of reconciliation between Indigenous and non-Indigenous Australians.

National Museum of Australia

This **museum** (☎ 1800 026 132, 02-6208 5000; www .nma.gov.au; Lawson Cres, Acton Peninsula; admission free; ☻ 9am-5pm) is one big abstract Australian storybook. Using creativity, controversy, humour and self-contradiction, the National Museum dismantles national identity and in the process provokes visitors to come up with ideas of their own. There are lots of attendants on hand to help you navigate exhibitions on environmental change, Indigenous culture, national icons and more, and you can take one-hour **guided tours** (adult/child/family $7.50/5/20). Don't miss the introductory film, shown in a small rotating theatre at the start of the exhibition rooms, which is an enjoyable audiovisual taste of the range of artefacts on show and how they form part of Australia's national identity.

Bus 34 runs here. There's also a free bus on weekends and public holidays, departing regularly from 10.30am from platform 7 in the **Civic bus interchange** (Map p270).

National Gallery of Australia

The **national gallery** (Map p270; ☎ 02-6240 6502; www.nga.gov.au; Parkes Pl, Parkes; permanent collection admission free; ☻ 10am-5pm) has a stunning collection of over 100,000 works of art representing four major areas: Aboriginal & Torres Strait Islander, Australian (from colonial to contemporary), Asian and international. Treasures range from traditional Aboriginal art to the controversial *Blue Poles* by Jackson Pollock. The spectacular Art of the Indian Subcontinent gallery showcases one of the largest subcontinent collections outside of India.

There's also a striking Sculpture Garden, drawings, photographs, furniture, ceramics, fashion, textiles and silverware. Visiting exhibitions usually attract an admission fee. In addition to regular all-inclusive **guided tours** (☻ 11am & 2pm), there's also a **tour** (☻ 11am Thu & Sun) focusing on Aboriginal and Torres Strait Islander art. Visually impaired visitors should ask about the *Braille Guide*.

National Portrait Gallery

This **gallery** (Map p270; ☎ 02-6102 7000; www.portrait .gov.au; Parkes Pl, Parkes; admission free; ☻ 10am-5pm) tells the story of Australia through its faces – from colonial portraits of the nation's founding families to Bill Henson's photographs of Australian conductor Simone Young and shots of celebrities such as Cate Blanchett and AC/DC's Angus Young. The several hundred works on show also tell the story of the evolution of portraiture, from wax cameos of Aboriginal tribespeople to a day-glo Nick Cave. The collection used to be housed at Old Parliament House, and this beautiful new purpose-built gallery is a treat in itself – it's made from wood and stone from every state and territory and its gardens are planted with varieties from all over the country.

Australian War Memorial

In a stately position, overlooking Anzac Pde and Lake Burley Griffin, the magnificent **war memorial** (Map p270; ☎ 02-6243 4211; www.awm.gov .au; Treloar Cres, Campbell; admission free; ☼ 10am-5pm) is one of the finest museums in the country. This genuinely moving memorial provides a fascinating insight into how battle forged Australia's national identity, with an enormous collection of pictures, dioramas, relics and exhibitions that detail and humanise wartime events. For military-history fans, there's also plenty of weaponry and uniforms – most of the heavy machinery is arrayed in Anzac Hall, which features an impressive **sound-and-light show** (☼ hourly from 10am). Entombed among the mosaics of the Hall of Memory is the Unknown Australian Soldier, whose remains were returned from a WWI battlefield in 1993 and who symbolises all Australian war casualties. Even if you're not a history buff, the engaging and affecting contents of this massive edifice are sufficient for two full days of exploration.

There are free 90-minute guided tours; alternatively, purchase the *Self-Guided Tour* leaflet ($3).

Along Anzac Pde, which is Canberra's broad commemorative way, there are 11 poignant memorials to various campaigns and campaigners.

Australian National Botanic Gardens

Spread over 90 invigorating hectares on Black Mountain's lower slopes are these beautiful **gardens** (Map p270; ☎ 02-6250 9450; www.anbg.gov.au/anbg; Clunies Ross St, Acton; admission free; ☼ 8.30am-5pm Feb-Dec, to 6pm Mon-Fri & 8pm Sat & Sun Jan), devoted to the growth, study and promotion of Australian floral diversity. While enjoying the gardens' tranquillity, take the **Aboriginal Plant Use Walk** (1km, 45 minutes), which passes through the cool

Rainforest Gully. The Eucalypt Lawn is peppered with 600 species of this quintessential Aussie tree.

The **visitors centre and bookshop** (☼ 9.30am-4.30pm) is the departure point for free **guided walks** (☼ 11am & 2pm, also 10am summer). Nearby is **Hudsons in the Gardens** (☎ 02-6248 9680; mains $10-15; ☼ breakfast & lunch), a pleasant cafe with a verdant aspect.

Parliament House

The symbolic and extravagant **Parliament House** (Map p270; ☎ 02-6277 5399; www.aph.gov.au; admission free; ☼ 9am-5pm) opened in 1988 after a $1.1 billion construction project. The building is dug into Capital Hill, its roof covered in grass and topped by an 81m-high flagpole with a flag the size of a double-decker bus. The rooftop lawns are easily accessible, encompass 23 hectares of landscaped gardens, and provide superb 360-degree views of the city. See Design for a Nation (p274) for specifics about the magnificent interior.

Free 45-minute **guided tours** (☼ every 30min 9am-4pm) are available on non-sitting days and 20-minute tours on sitting days, but you're welcome to self-navigate and watch parliamentary proceedings from the public galleries. Tickets for question time (2pm on sitting days) in the House of Representatives are free but must be booked through the **Sergeant at Arms** (✆02-6277 4889); tickets aren't required for the Senate chamber.

Old Parliament House

The venerable **Old Parliament House** (Map p270; ☎ 02-6270 8222; www.oph.gov.au; King George Tce, Parkes; adult/concession/family $2/1/5; ☼ 9am-5pm) was the seat of government from 1927 to 1988 and is a great place to get a whiff of bygone parliamentary activity. In 2009, Old Parliament House was transformed into the **Museum of Australian Democracy** (www.moadoph.gov.au). The exhibits place Australia's tradition in the context of the broader history of democracy, spanning the globe over two millennia. Notable items in the collection include a 1653 coin minted by Oliver Cromwell and the headdress worn by an Aboriginal elder as she performed the Welcome to Country for parliament's opening in 2008, on the day the prime minister, Kevin Rudd, made his historic apology to Australia's indigenous peoples for past wrongs committed against them.

DESIGN FOR A NATION

Opened in 1988, Parliament House was designed by Romaldo Giurgola of Mitchell, Giurgola & Thorp architects, winners of a design competition that attracted 329 entries from 28 countries. Its splendid interior incorporates different combinations of Australian timbers in each main section and more than 3000 original artworks.

The structure was built into the hillside and covered by grass to preserve the site's original landscape. Great swathes of neatly clipped lawn gently rise over the roof where a shiny metallic flagpole soars 81m to hoist a flag the size of a double-decker bus; a monumental, if unintentional, tribute to the Aussie backyard, the galvanised Hill's hoist and a beach towel.

The main axis of Parliament House runs northeast–southwest in a direct line with Old Parliament House, the Australian War Memorial and Mt Ainslie, Burley Griffin's original 'land axis'. Two high, granite-faced walls curve out from the axis to the corners of the building; the House of Representatives (east of the walls) and the Senate (to the west) are linked to the centre by covered walkways.

Enter the building across the 90,000-piece **forecourt mosaic** by Michael Nelson Tjakamarra – the theme of which is 'a meeting place', representing possum and wallaby Dreaming – and through the white marble Great Verandah at the northeastern end of the main axis. In the foyer, the grey-green marble columns symbolise a forest, and marquetry wall panels are inlaid with designs of Australian flora.

The first floor overlooks the Great Hall and its 20m-long tapestry was inspired by the original Arthur Boyd painting of eucalypt forest hanging outside the hall. Beyond it is the Members' Hall. In the public gallery above the Great Hall is the 16m-long embroidery, created by more than 500 members of the Embroiders Guild of Australia. Both works make subtle references to European settlement.

The Great Hall is the centre of the building, with the flagpole above it and passages to chambers on each side. One of only four known copies of the 1297 issue of the Magna Carta is on display here – so close you could almost touch it, if it wasn't for the gas-filled, glass casing. South of the Members' Hall are the committee rooms and ministers' offices; visitors are welcome to view committee rooms and attend some of the proceedings.

Parked on the lawn in front of Old Parliament House is the **Aboriginal Tent Embassy** – an important site in the struggle for equality and representation for Indigenous Australians.

National Zoo & Aquarium

Nestled behind Scrivener Dam is this wonderful **zoo and aquarium** (Map p268; ☎ 02-6287 8400; www.nationalzoo.com.au; Lady Denman Dr, Yarralumla; adult/child/concession/family $29/17/24/84; ☼ 10am-5pm), to which you should definitely devote a few hours. It has a roll call of fascinating animals, ranging from capuchins to sharks, and includes Australia's largest collection of big cats, including tigons (the unnatural result of breeding tiger-lion crosses in captivity, a practice thankfully discontinued). Heavily promoted are the additional tours where you can cuddle a cheetah ($150) or take a **tour** (adult/child from $125/65) behind the scenes to handfeed a tiger, and much more.

Questacon – National Science & Technology Centre

The hands-on **National Science & Technology Centre** (Questacon; Map p270; ☎ 1800 020 603, 02-6270 2800; www.questacon.edu.au; King Edward Tce, Parkes; adult/child/concession/family $18/12/13/49; ☼ 9am-5pm) is a child magnet, with its lively, educational and just-plain-fun interactive science and technology exhibits. Kids can explore the physics of sport, athletics and fun parks, cause tsunamis and take shelter from cyclones and earthquakes. Exciting science shows, presentations and puppet shows are included in the admission price.

Canberra Museum & Gallery

This stylish **museum and gallery** (Map p270; ☎ 02-6207 3968; www.museumsandgalleries.act.gov.au/museum/index.asp; Civic Sq, London Circuit, Civic; admission free; ☼ 10am-5pm Tue-Fri, noon-5pm Sat & Sun) is ostensibly devoted to Canberra's social history and visual arts. The highlight is the Nolan Collection, a changing collection of the painter Sidney Nolan's work, including his wonderful paintings of Ned Kelly, Australia's most famous and beloved outlaw.

National Film & Sound Archive

This excellent **archive** (Map p270; ☎ 02-6248 2000; www.nfsa.afc.gov.au; McCoy Circuit, Acton; admission free; ☺ 9am-5pm Mon-Fri, 10am-5pm Sat & Sun) preserves Australian moving-picture and sound recordings for posterity. Highlights include the absorbing permanent exhibition *Sights + Sounds of a Nation,* and 100 years of audio and visual recordings, from Norman Gunston's idiosyncratic interviews to the 1943 Oscar-awarded propaganda flick *Kokoda Front Line.* There are also temporary exhibitions, talks and film screenings.

Lookouts

Black Mountain (812m), northwest of the city, is topped by the 195m-high **Telstra Tower** (Map p268; ☎ 02-6219 6111; Black Mountain Dr; adult/child & concession $7.50/3; ☺ 9am-10pm), which has a great vista from 66m up its shaft. In the northeast, **Mt Ainslie** (843m) has fine views day and night; walking tracks start behind the War Memorial, climb Mt Ainslie and end at **Mt Majura** (888m).

High Court of Australia

The grandiose **high court** (Map p270; ☎ 02-6270 6811; www.hcourt.gov.au; Parkes Pl, Parkes; admission free; ☺ 9.45am-4.30pm Mon-Fri, closed public holidays) was dubbed 'Gar's Mahal' when it opened in 1980, a reference to Sir Garfield Barwick, chief justice during the building's construction.

The rarefied heights of the foyer (that's a 24m-high ceiling!) and main courtroom are in keeping with the building's name and position as the highest court in the Australian judicial system. Have a chat to a knowledgeable attendant about judicial life and check out the murals and paintings adorning the walls.

National Library of Australia

The **National Library** (Map p270; ☎ 02-6262 1111; www.nla.gov.au; Parkes Pl, Parkes; admission free; ☺ main reading room 9am-9pm Mon-Thu, to 5pm Fri & Sat, 1.30-5pm Sun) was established in 1901 and has since accumulated over six million items, most of which can be accessed in one of eight reading rooms. Be sure to check out the **Exhibition Gallery** (admission free; ☺ 9am-5pm) highlighting the library's diverse visual treats. Bookings are required for the

free, customised **guided tours** (☎ 02-6262 1271) or you can simply join the **Behind-the-Scenes Tour** (☺ 12.30pm Thu).

National Archives of Australia

Canberra's original post office now houses the **National Archives** (Map p270; ☎ 02-6212 3600; www.naa .gov.au; Queen Victoria Tce, Parkes; admission free; ☺ 9am-5pm), a repository for Commonwealth government records in the form of personal papers, photographs, films, maps and paintings. There are short-term special exhibits, but the centrepiece exhibit is the Federation Gallery and its original charters, including Australia's 1900 Constitution Act and the 1967 amendment ending constitutional discrimination against Aboriginal people. Records of military service and emigration can be accessed for those keen on exploring their ancestry.

Australian National University

The attractive grounds of the **ANU** (Map p270; ☎ 02-6125 5111; Acton; www.anu.edu.au), founded in 1946, lie between Civic and Black Mountain and make for a pleasant wander. Drop into the **Drill Hall Gallery** (☎ 02-6125 5832; Kingsley St; admission free; ☺ noon-5pm Wed-Sun) to see special exhibitions and paintings from the university's art collection; a permanent fixture is the near-phosphorescent hue of Sidney Nolan's *Riverbend.* Collect the ANU *Sculpture Walk* brochure for a fine-arts appreciation of the university grounds.

Australian Institute of Sport

The country's elite and aspiring-elite athletes hone their sporting prowess at the **AIS** (Map p268; ☎ 02-6214 1444; www.ausport.gov.au/tours; Leverrier Cres, Bruce). The 90-minute **tours** (adult/child/concession/family $16/9/11/44; ☺ 10am, 11.30am, 1pm & 2.30pm) are led by resident athletes, with information on training routines and diets, displays on Australian champions and the Sydney Olympics, and interactive exhibits where you can publicly humble yourself at basketball, rowing and skiing.

Other Attractions

While they are not open to the public, you can sneak a peek through the gates of the prime minister's official residence, the **Lodge** (Map p270; Adelaide Ave, Deakin), and the governor-general's official residence, **Government House** (Map p268; Dunrossil Dr, Yarralumla). **Scrivener Dam lookout** (Map p268) gives a good view of both.

The **Royal Australian Mint** (Map p268; ☎ 02-6202 6800; www.ramint.gov.au; Denison St, Deakin; admission free; ⏱ 9am-4pm Mon-Fri, 10am-4pm Sat & Sun) is Australia's biggest money-making operation. Its gallery showcases the history of Australian coinage; here you can learn about the 1813 'holey dollar' and its enigmatic offspring, the 'dump'.

Several of Canberra's 80-odd diplomatic missions are architecturally interesting and periodically open to the public. The **Thai embassy** (Map p270; Empire Circuit, Yarralumla), with its pointy orange-tiled roof, is reminiscent of Bangkok temples. The **Papua New Guinea high commission** (Map p270; ☎ 02-6273 3322; Forster Cres, Yarralumla) resembles a *haus tamberan* (spirit house) from the Sepik region and has a **cultural display** (⏱ 9am-1pm & 2-4pm Mon-Fri).

The 79m-tall **Australian-American Memorial** (Map p270; Kings Ave, Russell), a pillar topped by an eagle, recognises US support for Australia during WWII.

The **Church of St John the Baptist** (Map p270; Constitution Ave, Reid) was finished in 1845, its stained-glass windows donated by pioneer families. The adjoining **St John's Schoolhouse Museum** (Map p270; ☎ 02-6249 6839; Constitution Ave, Reid; admission by donation; ⏱ 10am-noon Wed, 2-4pm Sat & Sun) houses memorabilia from Canberra's first school.

The **Canberra Bicycle Museum** (Map p268; ☎ 02-6247 1363; 3 Rosevear Pl; admission by donation; ⏱ 10am-4pm Wed, 11am-3pm Sat) has an astonishing collection of old clankers including a penny farthing and the aptly named Boneshaker. If bicycles aren't your thing, you can take a look at some slightly more updated technology and learn about Australian innovative scientific research – such as gene technology and climate research – at **CSIRO Discovery** (Map p270; ☎ 02-6246 4646; www.discovery.csiro.au; Clunies Ross St, Acton; adult/child/family $8/5/20; ⏱ 9am-5pm Mon-Fri, 11am-3pm Sun).

ACTIVITIES

Canberra's lakes, mountains and climate offer abundant bushwalking, swimming, cycling and other activities.

Boating

Lake Burley Griffin Boat Hire (Map p270; ☎ 02-6249 6861; www.actboathire.com; Acton Jetty, Civic; ⏱ 9am-5pm Mon-Fri, 8am-dusk Sat & Sun, closed May-Aug) has canoe, kayak and paddleboat hire ($28 per hour).

Bushwalking

Tidbinbilla Nature Reserve (p288), southwest of the city, has marked walking tracks. Another great area for bushwalking is **Namadgi National Park** (p288), one end of the challenging 655km-long Australian Alps Walking Track.

Local bushwalking maps are available at Map World (p267) and **Mountain Designs** (Map p270; ☎ 02-6247 7488; 6 Lonsdale St, Braddon). The *Namadgi National Park* map ($4.40), available from the Canberra and Namadgi Visitor Centres, details 22 walks.

Cycling

Canberra has one of the most extensive cycle-path networks of any Australian city, with dedicated routes making it almost possible to tour the entire city without touching a road. The visitors centre sells the *Canberra Cycleways* map ($6) and *Canberra & Queanbeyan Cycling & Walking Map* ($8), the latter published by **Pedal Power ACT** (www.pedalpower.org.au).

Mr Spokes Bike Hire (Map p270; ☎ 02-6257 1188; www.mrspokes.com.au; Barrine Dr, Civic; ⏱ 9am-5pm Wed-Sun, daily during school holidays) is near the Acton Park ferry terminal; bike hire per hour/half day/full day costs $15/25/35. Canberra YHA Hostel (p279), and Victor Lodge (p280) also rent out bikes. **Row'n'Ride** (☎ 0410 547 838) delivers bicycles (hire per day/week $39/95) to your door and **Brindabella Bike Tours** (☎ 02-6242 6276, 0407 426 276; www.brindabellabiketours.com) runs cycling tours.

Swimming

There are 25m and 50m heated indoor swimming pools at the **Canberra International Sports & Aquatics Centre** (Map p268; ☎ 02-6251 7888; www.csiac.com.au; 100 Eastern Valley Way, Bruce; adult/child $5/4; ⏱ 6am-9pm Mon-Fri, 7am-7pm Sat & Sun).

You can also have a splash at the **Canberra Olympic Pool** (Map p270; ☎ 02-6248 6799; Allara St, Civic; adult/child $5.10/3.40; ⏱ 6am-8.30pm Mon-Thu, to 7.50pm Fri, 7am-6pm Sat, 8am-6pm Sun) and the National Trust-listed 75-year-old **Manuka Swimming Pool** (Map p270; ☎ 02-6295 1349; Manuka Oval, Manuka; adult/child $4/3; ⏱ 6.30am-7pm Mon-Fri, 8am-7pm Sat & Sun Nov-Mar, usually closed Apr-Oct).

See Murrumbidgee River Corridor (p287) for more on inviting waterholes around the city.

WALKING TOUR

Canberra is widely spread, but many of its major attractions are in or near the parliamentary triangle defined by Lake Burley Griffin, Commonwealth Ave and Kings Ave.

The focus of the triangle is **Parliament House** (**1**; p273) on Capital Hill. Heading north from here along Commonwealth Ave towards the lake, you'll pass the New Zealand, Canadian and UK high commissions on your left. Turn right (east) at Coronation Dr to King George Tce to learn about Australia's democracy at **Old Parliament House** (**2**; p273) and the **Aboriginal Tent Embassy** (**3**; **p274**).

Head southeast along King George Tce and turn left at Parkes Pl, across King Edward Tce, to the **National Portrait Gallery** (**4**; p272), where you'll find plenty of famous faces. Just beyond it, towards the Lake, you'll see the grand **High Court of Australia** (**5**; p275), with its ornamental watercourse bubbling alongside the path to the entrance. Next door is the wonderful **National Gallery of Australia** (**6**; p272), where you can imbibe caffeine as well as culture.

Follow Parkes Pl down to the shores of **Lake Burley Griffin** (**7**; p272) where you'll see and perhaps hear the **National Carillon** (**8**; p272) on Aspen Island. Turn left towards Commonwealth Place where you can explore indigenous issues through art at **Reconciliation Place** (**9**; p272).

Cross diagonally (northwest) over the lawns to **Questacon** (**10**; p274), Canberra's interactive science museum. From here you should cross Parkes Pl (northwest) to arrive at the **National Library of Australia** (**11**; p275). Head back up Parkes Pl to Coronation Dr, crossing the busy Commonwealth Ave and heading north to the art nouveau classic **Hyatt Hotel Canberra** (**12**; p281) for a well-earned refreshment.

CANBERRA FOR CHILDREN

The hyperactive demands of children are easily met in Canberra. There's lots of free stuff and

---

WALK FACTS

Start/Finish Capital Hill
Distance 6km
Duration 2 to 3 hours

AUSTRALIAN CAPITAL TERRITORY

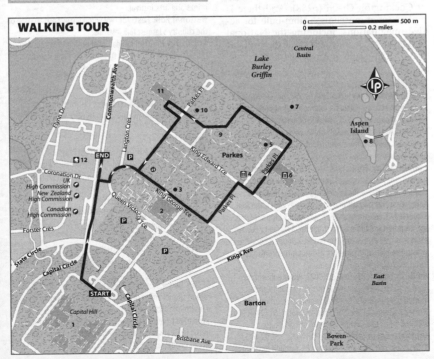

outdoor activities; but beware, some of the big-ticket attractions have big-ticket prices and strategically placed souvenir shops. Also watch out for the family-ticket small print where more than two kids is considered a rort.

The visitors centre has the brochure **Kidfriendly** (www.kidfriendly.com.au), a *Parks & Playgrounds* leaflet and a map of skate parks.

For fresh air and exercise, stroll through the lovely Australian National Botanic Gardens (p273). Take budding Attenboroughs to the tooth and claw distractions of the National Zoo & Aquarium (p274). Or drape them in a python at the Australian Reptile Centre (p288). The littlest littlies will appreciate a spin on Civic's landmark **merry-go-round** (Map p270; cnr Petrie Plaza & City Walk; per child $3; 10am-4pm Mon-Thu, 10am-7pm Fri, 9.30am-4pm Sat, 11am-3pm Sun).

Energy levels can also be accommodated by swimming at a pool or waterhole (p276), or by hiring bikes (p276).

For hands-on scientific fun, visit Questacon (p274), the interactive science museum. Another place with a child-friendly scientific bent is CSIRO Discovery (p276).

Miniature steam-train rides can be taken at Cockington Green (p288). And there is a plethora of museums custom-built for active imaginations, including the National Dinosaur Museum (p288) and the brilliant National Museum of Australia (p272).

TOURS

Aquila Helicopters (02-0412 066 766; www.aquila helicopters.com.au; Canberra International Airport; flights $440 for groups of up to 3 people) For aerial views.

Balloon Aloft (02-6285 1540; www.canberrabal loons.com.au; rides from adult/child $270/200) For quieter aerial views.

Canberra Day Tours (02-0418 455 099; www .canberradaytours.com.au) Shuttles you around various capital sites all day for adult/child $35/15, including entry fees. This hop-on hop-off service is called the Red Explorer bus and there are five services kicking off from the Melbourne Building, Northbourne Ave, Civic. The first service leaves at 9.30am, the last at 2.30pm. Check the website or pick up a brochure at the visitors centre for a timetable.

Go Bush Tours (02-6231 3023; www.gobushtours .com.au) Reputable tailored excursions around Canberra, including a circuit of city lookouts, and explorations of Namadgi National Park ($100 half-day tours, $130 full day with lunch). It has a wheelchair-accessible vehicle.

Southern Cross Yacht Club (Map p270; 02-6273 1784; www.cscc.com.au; 1 Mariner Pl, Yarralumla; adult/ child $15/9) Provides a sightseeing cruise aboard the MV *Southern Cross* departing 3pm daily.

SS Maid Marion (02-0418 828 357; adult/child $12/5) Operates one-hour pirate-themed cruises that pick-up/drop-off at lakeside locales such as Regatta Point ferry terminal, the National Library and the National Museum.

FESTIVALS & EVENTS
January
Summernats Car Festival (www.summernats.com.au) Revs up over three days in January at Exhibition Park.

Australia Day Live (www.australiadaylive.gov.au) The annual 25 January live concert on the lawns of Federal Parliament featuring the hottest names in Australian music.

February
National Multicultural Festival (www.multicultural festival.com.au) Celebrated over 10 days in February.

Royal Canberra Show (www.rncas.org.au/showweb site/main.html) The country meets the city at the end of February.

March & April
Celebrate Canberra (www.celebratecanberra.com.au) The city's extended birthday party, with a day-long food, drinks and arts festival.

National Folk Festival (www.folkfestival.asn.au) One of the country's largest folk festivals.

Anzac Day National holiday held on April 25, commemorating the armed services. Dawn services and marches held at the Australian War Memorial.

June
National Capital DanceSport Championships Competition ballroom dancing at its glitziest best.

July
Vivid National Photography Festival Exhibitions, conferences and events throughout the city, include giant images projected onto the city's landmark buildings.

September–November
Canberra International Film Festival (www.canber rafilmfestival.com.au) A 10-day international film festival held in October/November.

Floriade (www.floriadeaustralia.com) Held in September/ October and dedicated to Canberra's spectacular spring flowers.

SCOTT (www.scott24hr.com.au) Largest mountain bike race in the southern hemisphere, held over two days in early to mid-October.

Stonefest (www.stonefest.com.au) Big-time two-day music festival staged at the end of October at the University of Canberra.

AUSTRALIAN CAPITAL TERRITORY

HUMORISTS OF THE HOUSE

To look at them, Australia's politicians seem a respectable enough bunch, but a close examination of the parliamentary debating record tells a different tale. There it says the senate is made up of 'unrepresentative swine', the opposition are a pack of 'dullards, mugs and scumbags', while the government is a 'conga line of suck-holes'.

Debate in Canberra's parliament can be heated indeed. Australia inherited its system of government from England, and along with it the daily spectacle known as Question Time. The idea is that the members ask questions of one another, illuminating for both the press gallery and the public the policies of the day. But a good day is when the political jousting switches to vaudeville and insults fly, roars of indignation rise up from the opposite benches, and the house – often known as the 'bear pit' – is on fire.

When William McMahon (prime minister 1971–72) bemoaned, 'Sometimes I am my own worst enemy', his opposite number, conservative James Killen, shot back, 'Not while I'm here you're not'.

Conservative Peter Costello (treasurer 1996–2007) addressed his colleagues thus: 'Let me remind the very voluble Leader of the Opposition, "The Skipper", and his crew on Gilligan's Island over there...'

Not even the press gallery is immune from attack. 'In my experience,' declared James Killen of one hack, 'that journalist could not be relied upon to report accurately a minute's silence.'

The Labor Party's Paul Keating (prime minister 1991–96) was perhaps the undisputed master of the one-liner. 'Howard will wear his leadership like a crown of thorns, and in the parliament I'll do everything to crucify him', he warned the then-member of the Opposition, John Howard (prime minister 1996–2007). Keating meant what he said, greeting Howard with 'Come in, sucker', and accusing him of 'slithering out of the Cabinet room like a mangy maggot'.

Howard's predecessors did even worse, with Keating calling one 'a gutless spiv', while declaring that debating another was 'like being flogged with a warm lettuce'.

While those on the other side of politics may prefer to find him entirely unfunny, Keating's lines were so legendary that they became the basis for a successful stage show, *Keating! The Musical*.

These days, things are a little less colourful. His colleagues have labelled the current PM, Kevin Rudd, a 'toxic bore in the parliament', but his deputy, Julia Gillard, is quite spicy, referring to the Opposition as 'a hopeless rabble and a joke' and describing one member as a 'mincing poodle'.

SLEEPING

Northbourne Ave is strung with nondescript but serviceable hotels, while the neighbourhoods around Capital Hill, particularly in the politician-favoured domains of Kingston and Barton, are within easy distance of the city's museums and other sights. Canberra's accommodation is busiest during parliamentary sitting days, which means booking ahead on weekdays and some great discounts on weekends. Many hotels offer special deals on internet bookings.

Most places can supply cots and a room or two suitable for a family-sized stay. Travellers with limited mobility will find that few places outside top-end accommodation have true barrier-free rooms.

Budget

Civic Pub (Map p270; ☎ 02-6248 6488; 8 Lonsdale St, Braddon; dm $25, tw $70) These basic rooms with bunks and shared bathrooms make an acceptable option if the city's hostels are full. There's no kitchen but the pub downstairs sells $5 steaks.

Canberra YHA Hostel (Map p270; ☎ 02-6248 9155; www.yha.com.au; 7 Akuna St, Civic; dm $27-36, d/f $93/142; ⊠ ⌨ ⌕) This bright, well-run hostel has an impressive list of services including an indoor pool and Jacuzzi, 24-hour reception, laundry, bar, self-catering kitchen and cable TV. It remains fond of backpackers, but has all the facilities (except parking) to attract families seeking central, reasonably priced rooms.

Dickson Backpackers (Map p268; ☎ 02-6262 9922; www.dicksonbackpackers.com.au; 4/14 Woolley St, Dickson; dm $35, d & tw $88; ⊠ ⌨) This new backpackers, in the heart of Canberra's Chinatown, boasts comfortable bunks (spring mattresses and warm coverings), a large kitchen and games room, and pleasing oriental decor. Go for a room with windows – the ones without are a little dingy.

Victor Lodge (Map p270; ☎ 02-6295 7777; www
.victorlodge.com.au; 29 Dawes St, Kingston; dm $36, s/d
$75/92; P 🖳) This place offers mainly private
rooms, but has a few dorm beds. It makes a
good option if you need to park a vehicle
and it is very handy to the Kingston cafes
and shops. The rooms are compact and the
bathrooms shared. There's linen provided,
use of a commercial kitchen, a barbecue area,
continental breakfasts and bicycle hire, plus a
helping hand if you need info on local attractions. They'll pick you up from the Jolimont
Centre or the train station if need be; otherwise catch bus 38, 39 or 80 from Civic.

HALLS OF RESIDENCE
Some of the ANU's halls of residence, nestled
in the campus' leafy grounds, rent out rooms
from late November to late February during
uni holidays. Most offer similar facilities; room
prices start around $50 ($15 more for B&B).

Bruce Hall (Map p270; ☎ 02-6267 4000) and **Burton
& Garran Hall** (Map p270; ☎ 02-6267 4333) are at the
northern end of Daley Rd. The affiliated **Ursula
College** (Map p270; ☎ 02-6279 4303) and **John XXIII
College** (Map p270; ☎ 02-6279 4905) are opposite
Sullivans Creek. Civic is a brisk 15-minute
walk across campus.

CAMPING
Canberra Motor Village (Map p268; ☎ 02-6247 5466;
www.canberravillage.com; Kunzea St, O'Connor; unpowered/
powered site $23/30, d $98-135; P 🐾) Attractively
positioned in a peaceful, bush hillside setting 6km northwest of Civic, this place has
an abundance of amenities, motel rooms and
self-contained cabins ($97 to $170) in various
sizes. Note no pets allowed.

Canberra Carotel (Map p268; ☎ 02-6241 1377; www
.carotel.com.au; Federal Hwy, Watson; unpowered/powered site
$25/29, d $79-244; P 🐾 🖳) This is a large caravan park and motel complex on the northern
outskirts of town. The complex looks a little
ordinary on its 22 acres with not enough trees,
but the reception-shop is friendly and the
cabins are good value, especially for larger
families and groups.

Eaglehawk Holiday Park (off-Map p268; ☎ 02-6241
6411; www.eaglehawk.contact.com.au; Federal Hwy, Sutton;
camp/caravan site $28/30, cabins $88-150; P 🖳) This
friendly highwayside complex is only 12km
north of the centre, just over the NSW border. It
has plenty of sheltered midrange accommodation and recreation facilities and is pet friendly.
Meals are available at the pub next door.

Midrange
The Canberra Visitors Centre (p271) can
often provide a midrange or top-end room
cheaper than standby rates and the rack
rates mentioned here. Prices vary, depending on the season and whether parliament
is sitting.

Blue & White Lodge (Map p268; ☎ 02-6248 0498; blue
andwhitelodge@bigpond.com; 524 Northbourne Ave, Downer;
s/d/f $95/110/130; P 🐾) The Hellenic columns
and Mediterranean colour scheme at this
impeccable B&B pay tribute to the friendly
owners' Greek roots. The comfortable rooms,
some with shared bathrooms, are neat as a pin
and come with a delicious cooked breakfast
for $10. The owners also manage the neigh-
bouring Canberran Lodge.

Canberran Lodge (Map p268; 528 Northbourne Ave,
Downer; s/d/f $95/110/130; P 🐾) Managed by the
owners of neighbouring Blue & White Lodge,
this a similarly styled place, where the family-
sized rooms are en suite. Make inquiries at the
Blue & White Lodge, where you will also find
your breakfast dining room.

Northbourne Lodge (Map p268; ☎ 02-6257 2599;
522 Northbourne Ave, Downer; s/d $80/100; P 🐾) This
terracotta-coloured B&B provides good-value
accommodation with private bathrooms, and
a $15 optional breakfast. The owners have a
wealth of ideas for what to do in Canberra,
and speak several languages, including French
and Chinese.

our pick **University House** (☎ 02-6125 5211; www
.anu.edu.au/unihouse; 1 Balmain Cres, Acton; s $81-136,
d $125-177; P 🐾) This 1950s-era building,
with furniture to match, resides in the bushy
grounds of ANU and is favoured by some
politicians during sitting weeks. The spacious
rooms and two-bedroom apartments can be
hired with or without breakfast and come with
a small balcony from where you can watch
donnish professors come and go. There's
also a pleasant courtyard in which to let your
thoughts wander, a fine restaurant, cafe and
a good selection of wine in the cellar.

Yowani Country Club (Map p268; ☎ 02- 6241 3377;
www.yowani.com.au; 455 Northbourne Ave, Lyneham; d
$112-134, extra person $15; P 🐾 ♿) This club,
complete with golf course and bowling
green, offers accommodation in spacious
and comfortable, if somewhat characterless,
apartments (one of which is wheelchair-
accessible). The club has a restaurant and
is also an easy walk from the Asian eateries
of Dickson.

Motel Monaro (Map p270; ☎ 02-6295 2111; www
.bestwestern.com.au/motelmonaro; 27 Dawes St, Kingston;
s/d from $105/116; P ✗ 🖳) This newly redeco-
rated motel is on a quiet street a short stroll
from the coffee-scented Kingston shopping
centre. It is run by the same convivial folk
who manage Victor Lodge (opposite) next
door. It has a couple of large rooms that are
ideal for groups. Book ahead when parliament is sitting.

Olims Hotel Canberra (Map p270; ☎ 1800 475 337,
02-6243 0000; www.olimshotel.com; cnr Ainslie & Limestone
Aves, Braddon; d $115-170; P ✗ 🖳) This 1927
National Trust–listed building and its later
refurbishments look a little worse for wear
on the outside, but the well-appointed rooms
surround a nice, terraced courtyard garden.
There are standard rooms, superior rooms
and 1st-floor, self-contained 'loft' rooms with
balconies overlooking the inner garden.

Brassey (Map p270; ☎ 02-6273 3766; www.brassey
.net.au; Belmore Gardens & Macquarie St, Barton; s $150-168,
d $165-188; P ✗) This charming and historic
hotel is an easy walk from Parliament House,
the National Gallery and other museums. The
rooms are spacious and decorated in a stately,
mock-1920s style. Room rates include a buffet
breakfast and free use of nearby tennis courts,
while Manuka Pool is a short walk away.

Marque (Map p270; ☎ 02-6249 1411; 102 Northbourne
Ave; s/d $159-189; P ✗ 🖳) This comfort-
able if non-descript hotel at the Civic end
of Northbourne Ave offers large rooms with
queen-size beds – go for one of the rooms with
a small balcony overlooking the big outdoor
swimming pool. A buffet breakfast is on offer
for $15.

Ginninderry Homestead (off-Map p268; ☎ 02-
6254 6464, 0438 547 764; www.ginninderry.com.au; 468
Parkwood Rd via MacGregor; s/d $175-280; P ✗ 🖳)
This award-winning and green-rated heritage B&B is a 20-minute drive out of town.
Its gardens are quite magnificent and the
airy rooms are all decorated with antique
furniture. There are also tennis courts and
some friendly dogs.

Top End

Diamant (Map p270; ☎ 02-6175 2222; www.diamant.com
.au; 15 Edinburgh Ave, Civic; d $185-280; P ✗ 🖳 🖳)
This hip new boutique hotel is tucked away
in a quiet corner of Civic, not far from the
National Museum. Its 80 rooms have all been
decorated with an eye for detail: printed wallpaper on the ceilings, mini fish-scale tiles in

the bathrooms and flat-screen TVs. The restaurant offers fine contemporary Australian
cuisine and the Parlour Room wine bar (p284)
is its own buzzing little scene.

Realm (Map p270; ☎ 02-6163 1800; www.hotel
realm.com.au; 18 National Circuit, Barton; d $225-275;
P ✗ 🖳 🖳) This brand new, high-rise ultramodern five-star joint aims to impress,
from the soaring atrium lobby to the spacious double rooms overlooking Capital
Hill. Mostly servicing business guests, it's
an easy distance from the museums on King
Edward Tce.

Hyatt Hotel Canberra (Map p270; ☎ 02-6270
1234; www.canberra.park.hyatt.com; Commonwealth Ave,
Yarralumla; r from $350; P ✗ 🖳) This beautifully
restored, luxurious, art deco hotel boasts an
impressive spa, gym and pool, a cigar bar,
restaurant and round-the-clock room service. High tea in the hotel's elegant lounge is
a Canberra institution. Try for a room with
a view of the lake, and ask about the various
B&B packages.

EATING

Canberrans fork in food and fork out cash at
several hundred diverse eateries. Dining hubs
include Civic, Kingston, Manuka and Griffith.
There's also a fantastic Asian strip on Woolley
St in Dickson and a growing trend of excellent
options throughout the suburbs.

On Monday and Sunday nights tumble-
weeds roll through town and it can be hard
to find a restaurant that's open.

Civic

Within and around Civic you'll find everything from burger joints to no-fuss Italian
restaurants and trendy Asian eateries.

our pick **Sammy's Kitchen** (Map p270; ☎ 02-6247
1464; Canberra Centre, Bunda St; mains $9-23; 🕑 lunch &
dinner) This place, now in new digs, has been
serving up delicious, cheap and plentiful
Chinese and Malay dishes for years. Don't
miss out on the prawn sambal ($18) or the
Mongolian lamb ($15).

la pasa (Map p270; ☎ 02-6248 6288; Shop 1 Alinga St;
mains $11-17; 🕑 lunch & dinner) This Singaporean
beauty woks up superb Malaysian meals including a variety of fiery laksas, chilli prawns,
and beef *rendang* (spicy coconut-milk curry).
There are several vegetarian options and
good-value boxed lunches for $7.

Lemon Grass (Map p270; ☎ 02-6247 2779; 65 London
Circuit; mains $14-18; 🕑 lunch Mon-Fri, dinner Mon-Sat)

This dependable Thai institution offers a long list of vegetarian, stir-fry, curry and seafood dishes. You can bring your own wine and beer, and if you're a fan of king prawns order the *goong gratiam* (garlic prawns) with pepper and steamed vegetables.

Gus' Café (Map p270; ☎ 02-6248 8118; cnr Garema Pl & Bunda St, mains $17-29) Founded by Gus, a homesick Viennese, this cafe was one of the city's first and is about as close to European bohemia as Canberra gets. The exhaustive menu offers all-day breakfast, sandwiches and an array of hot dinners, along with good vegetarian and gluten-free options. There are plenty of outdoor tables, and the kitchen never closes before 10pm.

Tosolini's (Map p270; ☎ 02-6247 4317; cnr London Circuit & East Row; mains $23-33) This cafe has a loungey feel inside and plenty of al fresco tables, with a varied menu of pastas and rich, meaty dishes. Lighter meals include sandwiches and salads, and there are a few vegetarian dishes available. The cakes are scrumptious.

Courgette (Map p270; ☎ 02-6247 4042; 54 Marcus Clarke St, Civic; mains $23-32; ⊗ lunch Mon-Fri, dinner Mon-Sat) This fine French-influenced establishment may be named after a vegetable, but meat gets top billing here, from pan-seared calf liver to wonderful prawn ravioli. Frequented by an older clientele, this restaurant is earnest but low key and offers a splendid assortment of mature wines by the glass or bottle.

Fast food is on the menu at the Canberra Centre's **food hall** (Map p270; Bunda St; meals $6-12), including sushi, kebabs, burgers, laksa, gourmet rolls and smoothies.

Manuka

Southeast of Capital Hill is the multicuisine culture of Manuka shopping centre, an upmarket hub for diplomats and other suits. Try French, Spanish, Turkish, Italian, Lebanese, Vietnamese, Indonesian, and more, in the local eateries.

Kushi (Map p270; ☎ 02-6295 7122; Style Arcade, Franklin St; mains $8-17; ⊗ lunch Tue-Fri & Sun, dinner Tue-Sat) Kushi specialises in South Indian cuisine and has a comprehensive menu of vegetarian and meat dishes from Goan vindaloo and Keralan fish curries to lamb Madras. Bring a group of friends and take an inexpensive epicurean excursion of this other Deep South. There's a popular lunch buffet on Sunday ($17).

Ironbark (Map p270; ☎ 02-6239 7143; 17 Franklin St; mains $12-32; ⊗ lunch Tue-Sun, dinner Wed-Sun) If you

ever wondered what the Australian coat of arms tastes like, Ironbark's kangaroo fillet wrapped in emu prosciutto should satisfy your curiosity. This place takes its bush food seriously, with native Australian ingredients featuring in every dish – even the wattle-seed ice cream.

Verve Café (Map p270; ☎ 02-6239 4666; Cnr Franklin St & Flinders Way; mains $13-34) This small licensed cafe serves up a global menu, from gourmet burgers and fish and chips to Thai noodles and Asian duck rolls. The brunch is impressive, offering bircher muesli, pancakes, and eggs served with chorizo and roast mushrooms.

Alanya (Map p270; ☎ 02-6295 9678; Style Arcade, Franklin St; mains $23-30; ⊗ lunch Tue-Fri, dinner Tue-Sat) This long-standing, award-winning Turkish restaurant has been feeding its fans authentic delights for over 20 years. The brief but tasty menu includes vegetarian options, plates to share and stand-alone mains such as the excellent *hünkar beğendi* (diced lamb on a bed of eggplant).

Legends (Map p270; ☎ 02-6295 3966; Franklin St; mains $25-30; ⊗ lunch Mon-Fri, dinner Mon-Sat) This lively Spanish restaurant is upstairs in the Capital Cinema Centre. House specialities include paella (a vegetarian version is available) and *bacalao* (dried salted cod), and there are lots of delicious tapas (from $12) to nibble. There's also the odd bit of live flamenco guitar most nights.

Kingston

Kingston's cafes, bars and restaurants surround the leafy Green Sq and continue right around the perimeter of the shopping centre.

Portia's Place (Map p270; ☎ 02-6239 7970; 11 Kennedy St; mains $12.50-26; ⊗ lunch Sun-Fri, dinner daily) During sitting weeks, you'll often find parliamentary powerbrokers fine-tuning their strategy over steaming noodles or Peking duck at this popular local Chinese restaurant.

La Capanna (Map p270; ☎ 02-6239 6712; 32 Giles St; mains $14-27; ⊗ lunch & dinner) This traditional trattoria serves classic pastas and stonefired pizzas, along with a few meat and fish dishes. Try the pasta with king prawns and mussels.

Silo (Map p270; ☎ 02-6260 6060; 36 Giles St; mains $15-24; ⊗ breakfast & lunch Tue-Sat) This accomplished bakery-cafe can be standing room only during the breakfast and lunch rushes, when locals line up to buy the exquisite homemade tarts and breads. The egg dishes feature original twists such as chilli jam. If the place is full, try Idelic, just down the road, where the coffee and brunch are also good.

Artespresso (Map p270; ☎ 02-6295 8055; 31 Giles St; mains $26-30; ☺ lunch Mon-Fri, dinner Mon-Sat) This sun-filled bistro-style eatery has contemporary art on the walls, but the paintings get scant attention from diners absorbed in delights such as the superb seafood pie filled with tender scallops, prawns and cod.

Dickson

Dickson's eclectic shopping precinct is dominated by an Asian smorgasbord where Chinese, Thai, Laotian, Vietnamese, Korean, Japanese, Indian, Turkish and Malaysian restaurants compete with such odd bedfellows as McDonald's and an Irish pub.

Sfoglia (Map p268; ☎ 02-6262 5538; 57 Woolley St; mains $8-14; ☺ breakfast & lunch) A relaxed cafe where you'll find a hearty cooked breakfast and strong coffee to kick-start your day or a focaccia to give you a lunchtime boost.

Âu Lac (Map p268; ☎ 02-6262 8922; 39 Woolley St; mains $10-14; ☺ lunch Tue-Sun, dinner daily) This simple Vietnamese vegetarian restaurant employs soya bean as a culinary chameleon, making it pretend to be a beef curry, fried fish or honey-roast chicken. The meals are tasty and the service is quick. A value lunch-box special is $7.

Dickson Asian Noodle House (Map p268; ☎ 02-6262 5903; 29 Woolley St; mains $12-15; ☺ lunch & dinner) This perennially popular Laotian and Thai cafe is usually booked up towards the end of the week, though thankfully there's always takeaway. Within minutes of ordering, eat your fill of wok-fried, Hokkien-style or soup-laden noodles. Pick of the menu is the addictive combination laksa.

Belluci's (Map p268; ☎ 02-6257 7788; cnr Cape & Woolley Sts; mains $12-35; ☺ lunch & dinner) This slick modern pub offers casual dining (tapas, burgers and fish and chips) at the bar and outside tables, as well as a slightly more sophisticated restaurant setting with menu to match (pasta, seafood and steaks). On Fridays and Saturdays there's live music and dancing.

Fekerte's Ethiopian Cuisine (Map p268; ☎ 02-6262 5799; 2 Cape St; mains $25; ☺ lunch Tue-Fri, dinner Tue-Sat) This African gem weaves culinary magic with authentic Ethiopian cuisine along the lines of thick stews, spicy curries and moreish *injera* (Ethiopian flat bread). It's like comfort food, only far more interesting and from another continent.

Around Canberra

Café in the House (Map p270; ☎ 02-6270 8156; Old Parliament House, King George Tce, Parkes; mains $10-25; ☺ lunch Sun-Mon & dinner Fri) Enjoy white linen service in the delightful surrounds of Old Parliament House.

Green Herring Restaurant (Map p268; ☎ 02-6230 2657; Ginninderra Village, O'Hanlon Pl, Nicholls; mains $28-31; ☺ lunch Fri-Sun, dinner Tue-Sat) This place offers rustic cosiness in a 120-year-old slab hut. Don't be put off by the name – it serves Mod Oz with creative flourishes, exceptional desserts, and has a separate vegetarian menu.

Ottoman (Map p268; ☎ 02-6273 6111; Cnr Broughton & Blackall Sts, Barton; mains $29-45; ☺ lunch Tue-Fri, dinner Tue-Sat) One of Canberra's finest restaurants, serving sophisticated Turkish cuisine to the city's hungriest power-lunchers.

Aubergine (off-Map p270; ☎ 02-6260 8666; 18 Barker St, Griffith; mains $32; ☺ lunch Wed-Sun, dinner Mon-Sun) Another fine-dining favourite, with inventive dishes such as pumpkin and roast-lobster risotto flavoured with ginger. It's worth saving room for the delectably rich desserts – try the rhubarb and pistachio pie.

DRINKING

Pubs and bars are mostly concentrated in Civic, but there are also some in the northern suburbs of Dickson and O'Connor and across the lake in Kingston that merit a visit. During the summer, when the university students are out of town, the bar scene goes a bit limp, while between Christmas and New Year many places shut down for several days.

Wig & Pen (Map p270; ☎ 02-6248 0171; cnr Alinga St & West Row, Civic) This little brewery and pub has its two-room interior packed out on Friday nights by thirsty office workers who also enjoy the hearty pub meals ($10 to $12). It produces several styles of beer, including real English ale.

Phoenix (Map p270; ☎ 02-6247 1606; 21 East Row, Civic) Regulars don't think twice about coming back to this pub after rising from the ashes of the night before, and we love it too. It's a staunch supporter of new local musos, and has a mellow atmosphere, rustic decorations and armchairs that incline you towards pondering life for the night.

Knightsbridge Penthouse (Map p270; ☎ 02-6262 6221; 34 Mort St, Braddon) It's about as chic as Canberra gets – which is surprisingly chic. This opulent den of a bar is cleverly illuminated by optic fibres and serves dishy cocktails to dishy folk. It's New Orleans Gothic meets Bret Easton Ellis.

Belgian Beer Cafe (Map p270; ☎ 02-6260 6511; 29 Jardine St, Kingston) With 33 bottled Belgian beers and five on tap, this is the place to quench a thirst and educate a palate.

Parlour Wine Bar (Map p270; ☎ 02-6162 3656; www.parlour.net.au; 16 Kendall Lane, Civic; ☺ noon-late Tue-Thu, to 3am Fri & Sat, to midnight Sun) Modern banquettes share the polished wood floor with well-stuffed chesterfield lounges in this contemporary take on the Victorian smoking lounge, located in the same building as the Diamant Hotel. Views over the lake complement the list of local, Australian and international wines, not to mention the killer cocktails.

Trinity Bar (Map p268; ☎ 02-6262 5010; www.lovetrinitybar.com; 28 Challis St, Dickson; ☺ 3pm-late Tue-Sun) Sleek, DJ-equipped Trinity has fine vodkas, martinis and cocktails to sample, plus beer pulled from ceiling-hung taps. Look for the deep-red lighting and the tri-stripe symbol on the wall – they're the only signs directing strangers to this out-of-the-way haunt.

Muddle Bar (Map p268; ☎ 02-6262 7898; www.muddlebar.com; Shop 8, West Row, Civic; ☺ 4pm-late Mon-Sat) This bar in the Melbourne Building fills with lively after-office drinkers who get stuck into the happy-hour cocktails and the sophisticated bar snacks with alacrity.

Hippo Bar (Map p270; ☎ 02-6257 9090; www.hippobar.com.au; 17 Garema Pl, Civic; ☺ 5pm-late Wed-Sat) Chilled-out Hippo is indeed hip and appropriately cosy for a lounge-bar. The red poufs are accosted by a young crowd of cocktail slurpers who file in for Wednesday-night jazz.

For a Guinness and Irish-themed schmaltz head to **PJ O'Reilly's** (Map p270; ☎ 02-6230 4752; www.pjoreillys.com.au; Melbourne Bldg, cnr Alinga St & West Row, Civic; ☺ 10am-late), endearingly referred to by the locals as Plastic McPaddy's; the **Durham Castle Arms** (Map p270; ☎ 02-6295 1769; www.thedurham.com.au; Green Sq, Kingston; ☺ noon-late), a cosy village-pub wannabe in the middle of cafe-filled Kingston; or **King O'Malley's** (Map p270; ☎ 02-6257 0111; www.kingomalleys.com.au; 131 City Walk, Civic; ☺ 11am-midnight), where there's cheap, hearty meals and free live music nearly every night.

ENTERTAINMENT

Canberra has always been curiously good at nurturing its music talent, and they pop up around town. You'll find entertainment listings in Thursday's *Canberra Times* and in the free monthly street mag *bma*. **Ticketek** (Map p270; ☎ 02-6219 6666; www.ticketek.com.au; Akuna St, Civic) sells tickets to all major events.

Nightclubs

icbm & Meche (Map p270; ☎ 02-6248 0102; 50 Northbourne Ave, Civic; Meche Sat $10-12; ☺ icbm 7pm-late, Meche midnight-3am Wed-Sat) Young drinking crowds attend this clubbing complex, with the music-blasted bar icbm downstairs and the dancehall Meche upstairs. Hosting the odd international DJ the complex diversifies with Wednesday comedy nights.

Cube (Map p270; ☎ 02-6257 1110; www.cubenightclub.com.au; 33 Petrie Plaza, Civic; ☺ 8pm-late Thu-Sun) Revellers throw themselves onto the bed-sized lounges to take a break from the dance floor at this hetero-friendly gay club, which goes from relaxed games of pool in the early evening to riotous partying well into the wee hours.

Cinemas

Dendy Canberra Centre (Map p270; ☎ 02-6221 8900; www.dendy.com.au; 2nd fl, Canberra Centre, 148 Bunda St, Civic; adult/concession $15/12.50) Canberra's newest cinema is also the last bastion for independent and art-house cinema in the city. Tuesday is discount day.

Greater Union (Map p270; ☎ 02-6295 9042; www.greaterunion.com.au; cnr Canberra Ave & Furneaux St, Manuka; adult/child $17/13) This venue screens mainstream releases. Other multiplex cinemas can be found within Canberra's various suburban shopping malls.

Theatre

Canberra Theatre Centre (Map p270; ☎ box office 1800 802 025, 02-6275 2700; www.canberratheatre.org.au; Civic Sq, London Circuit, Civic; ☺ box office 9am-5.30pm Mon-Sat) This centre is the hub of live theatre in Canberra and the dramatic goings-on range from Shakespeare to Circus Oz and Indigenous dance troupes. Information and tickets are supplied by Canberra Ticketing in the adjacent North Building.

Gorman House Arts Centre (Map p270; ☎ 02-6249 7377; www.gormanhouse.com.au; Ainslie Ave, Braddon) This arts centre hosts various theatre and dance companies that regularly stage their own self-hatched productions, including the innovative moves of the Australian Choreographic Centre (☎ 02-6247 3103).

Live Music

Many pubs have free live music.

Tilley's Devine Cafe Gallery (Map p268; ☎ 02-6249 1543; www.tilleys.com.au; cnr Wattle & Brigalow Sts, Lyneham; admission $20-40; 🕑 shows from 9pm) People of all ages breeze in and out of Tilley's cool, clean-air interior, with its scuffed furniture, dark booths and eclectic menu of local and international musicians and comedians. It also does poetry nights, writers sessions and great cooked breakfasts.

ANU Union Bar (Map p270; ☎ 02-6125 2446; www.anu union.com.au; Union Court, Acton; admission $5-20; 🕑 gigs from 8pm) A mainstay of Canberra's music scene, the Uni Bar has energetic live music bouncing off its walls and into the ears of sozzled students up to three times a week during the semester. Significant student discounts usually apply to gigs. It's also a good place for a game of pool and a drink.

Transit Bar (Map p270; ☎ 02-6162 0899; 7 Akuna St, Civic; 🕑 12pm-late Mon-Sat, 2pm-late Sun) Tucked under the youth hostel, this bar stocks an excellent range of international bottled beers and live music from hip-hop to punk by local bands and overseas acts.

Hippo Bar (Map p270; ☎ 02-6257 9090; 17 Garema Pl, Civic) This is another good place for emerging live music, where you can hear jazz and turntable sounds.

Sport

The Canberra Raiders are the home-town rugby league side and during the season (from March to September) they play regularly at **Canberra Stadium** (Map p268; ☎ 02-6256 6700; www .canberrastadium.com; Battye St, Bruce; 🅿). Also laying tackles at Canberra Stadium are the ACT Brumbies rugby union team, who play in the international Super 14 competition (February to May). From October to February, catch the super-successful women's basketball team, the Canberra Capitals, at **Southern Cross Stadium** (off-Map p268; ☎ tickets 02-6253 3066; cnr Cowlishaw St & Athllon Dr, Greenway; 🅿); their compatriots, the AIS, play at the **AIS Training Hall** (Map p268; ☎ 02-6214 1201; Leverrier Cres, Bruce; 🅿).

SHOPPING

Clothing shops for all budgets are concentrated in the city centre, but if you want to splash some cash in chic boutiques head to Manuka Shopping Centre (Map p270) and Kingston, or try on some of the local designers who have shops along Lonsdale St in Braddon. For multicultural groceries and Asian goods head to Dickson Shopping Centre (Map p268). Canberra is a crafty city and a good place for picking up creative gifts and souvenirs from galleries, museum shops and markets. For Aboriginal art see Gold Creek Village (p288).

Canberra Centre (Map p270; ☎ 02-6247 5611; Bunda St, Civic) The city's biggest shopping centre boasts numerous speciality stores, including fashion boutiques, food emporia, jewellery shops and several chain stores. The ground-floor information desk can help with wheelchair and stroller hire.

Craft ACT (Map p270; ☎ 02-6262 9993; www.craftact .org.au; 1st fl, North Bldg, London Circuit, Civic) It's well worth visiting this venue for the wonderful exhibitions of contemporary work, including cutting-edge designs in the form of bags, bowls, pendants and prints.

Old Bus Depot Markets (Map p270; ☎ 02-6292 8391; www.obdm.com.au; Wentworth Ave, Kingston; 🕑 10am-4pm Sun) This popular, decade-old indoor market specialises in handcrafted goods and regional edibles, including the output of the Canberra district's 20-plus wineries.

Gorman House Arts Centre Markets (Map p270; ☎ 02-6249 7377; Gorman House Arts Centre, Ainslie Ave, Braddon; 🕑 10am-4pm Sat) Art, craft, tarot, massages, vintage goods and the odd burst of entertainment liven up the courtyards of this heritage precinct.

Kamberra Wine Company (Map p268; ☎ 02-6262 2333; www.kamberra.com.au; cnr Northbourne Ave & Flemington Rd, Lyneham; 🕑 10am-5pm) A winery and part-time gallery, this complex showcases the district's fine cool-climate wines.

GETTING THERE & AWAY
Air

Canberra International Airport (Map p268; ☎ 02-6275 2236) is serviced by **Qantas** (Map p270; ☎ 13 13 13, TTY 1800 652 660; www.qantas.com.au; Jolimont Centre, Northbourne Ave, Civic) and **Virgin Blue** (☎ 13 67 89; www.virginblue.com.au), with direct flights to Adelaide, Brisbane, Melbourne and Sydney.

Brindabella Airlines (☎ 1300 668 824; www .brindabella-airlines.com.au) flies between Canberra, Albury-Wodonga, Brisbane, Port Macquarie, Coffs Harbour and Newcastle.

Bus

The **interstate bus terminal** (Map p270; Northbourne Ave, Civic) is at the Jolimont Centre, and has showers, left-luggage lockers, public internet access and free phone lines to the visitor information centre and some budget accommodation. Inside is **Guidepost Travel** (Map p270; ☎ 02-6249 6006; 65 Northbourne Ave, Civic), which handles **CountryLink** (www.countrylink.info) train/coach tickets and books seats on most bus services.

Greyhound Australia (Map p270; ☎ 1300 473 946; ☷ Jolimont Centre branch 6am-9.30pm) has frequent services to Sydney ($36, four hours) and also runs to/from Adelaide ($180, 18 hours) and Melbourne ($85, nine hours). In winter there are services to Cooma, Jindabyne and Thredbo.

Murrays (Map p270; ☎ 13 22 51; www.murrays.com.au; ☷ Jolimont Centre branch 7am-7pm) has daily express services running to Sydney (adult $36, 3¼ hours) and also runs to Batemans Bay ($22, 2½ hours), Narooma ($33, 4½ hours) and Wollongong ($33, 3½ hours).

Transborder (☎ 02-6241 0033; www.transborder .com.au) runs daily to Yass ($14, 50 minutes). Its Alpinexpress service runs to Thredbo ($65, three hours) via Jindabyne ($45, 2½ hours) daily.

Car & Motorcycle

The Hume Hwy connects Sydney and Melbourne, passing 50km north of Canberra. The Federal Hwy runs north to connect with the Hume near Goulburn and the Barton Hwy meets the Hume near Yass. To the south, the Monaro Hwy connects Canberra with Cooma.

Rental car prices start at around $50 a day. Major companies with city-centre offices and desks at the airport include the following:

Avis (Map p270; ☎ 13 63 33, 02-6249 6088; 17 Lonsdale St, Braddon)

Budget (Map p270; ☎ 1300 362 848, 02-6257 2200; Rydges Lakeside Hotel, 1 London Circuit, Civic)

Hertz (Map p270; ☎ 13 30 39, 02-6257 4877; 32 Mort St, Braddon)

Thrifty (Map p270; ☎ 13 61 39, 02-6247 7422; 29 Lonsdale St, Braddon)

Another option is locally-owned **Rumbles** (Map p268; ☎ 02-6280 7444; 11 Paragon Mall, Gladstone St, Fyshwick). Its office is usually open only on weekdays (weekends by appointment).

Train

Kingston train station (Wentworth Ave), is the city's rail terminus. You can book trains and connecting buses inside the station at the **CountryLink travel centre** (☎ 13 22 32, 02-6295 1198; ☷ 6am-5pm Mon-Sat, 10.30am-5.30pm Sun), and Guidepost Travel (left).

CountryLink trains run to/from Sydney (adult/child $40/27, four hours, two or three daily). There's no direct train to Melbourne, but a CountryLink coach to Cootamundra links with the train to Melbourne (adult/child $102/51, nine hours, one daily); the service leaves the Jolimont Centre at 10am. A daily **V/Line** (☎ 02-13 61 96; www.vline.com.au) Canberra Link service involves a train between Melbourne and Albury-Wodonga, then a connecting bus to Canberra ($45, 8½ hours).

GETTING AROUND
To/From the Airport

Canberra International Airport is in Pialligo, 8km southeast of the city. Taxi fares to the city centre average $28. **Airliner** (☎ 02-6299 3722; www.airliner.com.au) runs a regular bus service ($9, 20 minutes, 11 per day Monday to Friday) from bay 6 of the Civic bus interchange.

Car & Motorcycle

Canberra's road system is as circuitous as a politician's answer to a straight question. That said, the wide and relatively uncluttered main roads make driving easy, even at so-called 'peak-hour' times. A map is essential.

Public Transport
BUS

Canberra's public transport provider is the **ACT Internal Omnibus Network** (Action; ☎ 13 17 10; www.action.act.gov.au). The main bus interchange is along Alinga St, East Row and Mort St. Visit the **information kiosk** (Map p270; East Row, Civic; ☷ 7.15am-5pm) for free route maps and timetables.

You can buy single-trip tickets (adult/concession $3/1.50), but a better bet for most visitors is to buy a daily ticket (adult/concession $6.60/3.30). Prepurchase tickets are available from Action agents (including the visitors centre and some newsagents). You can also buy them on board from the driver.

WINERIES OF THE ACT

It's been a slow and steady process but Canberra's wine region is finally attracting worldwide recognition for the cool-climate vinos produced here. In particular the area knocks out wonderful Riesling, Shiraz and Chardonnay.

There are over 30 cellar doors to go knocking on; click onto www.canberrawines.com.au or ask at the visitor centre (p271) for detailed information. Otherwise, these are a good start:

- **Brindabella Hills Winery** (Map p266; ☎ 02--6230 2583; www.brindabellahills.com.au; Woodgrove Cl, Hall; ◷ cellar door 10am-5pm Sat & Sun) This sizeable vineyard has been operating for more than 20 years. Set on a beautiful ridge, it has won awards for its Shiraz, Cabernet Sauvignon and Riesling.

- **Clonakilla Wines** (Map p266; ☎ 02--6277 5877; www.clonakilla.com.au; Crisps Lane, Murrumbateman; cellar door 11am-5pm) Boutique winery producing a handful of highly sought varieties.

- **Lake George Winery** (☎ 02--9948 4676; Federal Hwy, Lake George; www.lakegeorgewinery.com.au; ◷ cellar door 9am-5pm) Overlooking the now drought-parched bed of Lake George, this winery produces fine Pinot Noir, Chardonnay, Pinot Grigio and Shiraz. It also has a restaurant, **grape-foodwine** (◷ 9am-5pm Fri-Sun)

- **Pialligo Estate** (Map p268; ☎ 02--6247 6060; www.pialligoestate.com.au; 18 Kallaroo Rd, Pialligo; ◷ cellar door 10am-5pm) Within stumbling distance to Canberra, this winery unfurls over a pleasant estate, with a green-certified **cafe** (◷ 11am-5pm Wed-Sun) serving fabulous mains ($30) to soak up the vino.

AUSTRALIAN CAPITAL TERRITORY

Action also offers several tourist routes (buses 33, 34, 40 and 80) that service most of Canberra's tourist attractions.

Taxi

Taxis Combined (☎ 13 22 27) has vehicles with access for wheelchairs. There's a convenient **taxi rank** (Bunda St) outside the Greater Union cinema.

AROUND CANBERRA

For information and maps on attractions around Canberra, including the unspoiled bushland just outside the outer urban limits, head to the visitors centre (p271).

SOUTH & WEST OF THE CITY – THE WILD SIDE

Murrumbidgee River Corridor

About 66km of the **Murrumbidgee River** flows through the ACT, and along with major tributaries of the **Molonglo** and **Cotter Rivers**, it provides great riverside picnic locations and swimming spots. Pick up a map and brochure at the Canberra Visitors Centre (p271) and explore the waters of: **Uriarra Crossing**, 24km northwest of the city, on the Murrumbidgee near its meeting with the Molonglo River; **Casuarina Sands**, 19km west of the city at the meeting of the Cotter and Murrumbidgee Rivers; **Kambah Pool Reserve**, another 14km upstream on the Murrumbidgee; **Cotter Dam**, 23km west of the city on the Cotter River and with a camping ground; **Pine Island** and **Point Hut Crossing**, upstream of Kambah Pool Reserve on the Murrumbidgee; and **Gibraltar Falls**, roughly 45km southwest of the city.

On the banks of the Murrumbidgee, 20km south of Canberra, is the beautiful **Lanyon Homestead** (Map p266; ☎ 02-6237 5136; Tharwa Dr; adult/concession/family $7/5/15; ◷ 10am-4pm Tue-Sun).

Near Tharwa is **Cuppacumbalong** (Map p266; ☎ 02-6237 5116; Naas Rd; ◷ 11am-5pm Wed-Sun & public holidays), a 1922 homestead and heritage garden reincarnated as a quality Australian craftware studio and gallery.

Space Observatories

The **Canberra Space Centre** (Map p266; ☎ 02-6201 7880; www.cdscc.nasa.gov; off Paddy's River Rd; admission free; ◷ 9am-5pm) resides in the grounds of the Canberra Deep Space Communication Complex, 40km southwest of the city. Pride of place goes to Deep Space Station 43, a 70m-diameter dish that has communicated with the likes of Voyager 1 and 2, Galileo and various Mars probes. There are displays of spacecraft and deep-space tracking technology, plus a piece of lunar basalt scooped up by Apollo XI in 1969. A theatre continuously screens short films on space exploration.

Tidbinbilla & Namadgi

Tidbinbilla Nature Reserve (Map p266; ☎ 02-6205 1233; www.environment.act.gov.au; off Paddy's River Rd) is just 45km southwest of the city and is threaded with bushwalking tracks. There are kangaroos and emus and it's a great spot to view platypuses and lyrebirds at dusk. Call for information on ranger-guided activities on weekends and school holidays.

Corin Forest (Map p266; ☎ 02-6235 7333; www .corin.com.au; Corin Rd), roughly 50km southwest of the city, is a mountain recreation facility surrounded by Tidbinbilla Reserve. There's a 1.2km bobsled track and a flying fox, both open year-round; a water slide in summer; and a 'snowplay' area in winter. See the website for prices and special packages.

Namadgi National Park (Map p266; www.environ ment.act.gov.au) includes eight peaks higher than 1700m and offers excellent opportunities for bushwalking, mountain biking, fishing, horseback riding and viewing Aboriginal rock art. For more information, visit the **Namadgi Visitor Centre** (☎ 02-6207 2900; Naas Rd, Tharwa; ☾ 9am-4pm Mon-Fri, 9am-4.30pm Sat & Sun), 2km south of the Tharwa township. **Camping** (unpowered sites per person $3-5) is available at Honeysuckle Creek, Mt Clear and Orroral River; book through the visitor centre.

NORTH & EAST OF THE CITY
Gold Creek Village

The attractions at **Gold Creek Village** (Map p268; ☎ 02-6253 9780; www.goldcreekvillage.com.au; Gold Creek Rd, Barton Hwy, Nicholls; admission free; ☾ 10am-5pm) are a combination of colonial kitsch and genuinely interesting exhibits that will keep the kids occupied.

Little tackers will also ogle at the big bones at the **National Dinosaur Museum** (Map p268; ☎ 02-6230 2655; www.nationaldinosaurmuseum.com.au; adult/child/family $10.50/7.50/34; ☾ 10am-5pm).

The **Australian Reptile Centre** (Map p268; ☎ 02-6253 8533; adult/child/concession/family $7.50/6/7/29; ☾ 10am-5pm) is a fascinating showcase of reptilian life. Behind glass you can see tree skinks and scrub pythons, plus the world's four deadliest land snakes.

Cockington Green (Map p268; ☎ 02-6230 2273; www.cockingtongreen.com.au; adult/child/family $15/8/42; ☾ 9.30am-5pm) is an immaculately groomed, too-quaint-for-its-own-good English village in miniature, coupled with miniature steam-train rides.

Nearby is the **Aboriginal Dreamings Gallery** (Map p268; ☎ 02-6230 2922; 19 O'Hanlon Pl, Nicholls) with an excellent selection of Aboriginal artwork that includes didgeridoos and bark paintings.

SURROUNDING TOWNS & VILLAGES

A number of NSW towns lie just over the border and are intrinsically linked to the national capital, many of them offering charming country-style accommodation as well as fine food and wine.

Collector, on the Federal Highway not long after the turn-off from the Hume, is where you'll find the famed **Lynwood Café** (☎ 02-4848 0200; 1 Murray St; mains $14-$25; ☾ 10am-5pm Thu-Sun & public holidays), serving gourmet country meals and selling delicious homemade jams and chutneys, as well as the charmingly eccentric **Bushranger Hotel**, (☎ 02-4848 0071; 24 Church St; s/d $45/$75), which in 1865 was held up by feared highwaymen Ben Hall and John Gilbert.

At **Murrumbateman** (20 minutes' drive from Canberra along the Barton Hwy), there are wineries as well as chic B&Bs such as the **Schönegg Guesthouse** (☎ 02-6227 0344; www.schon egg.com.au; 381 Hillview Dr, Murrumbateman; r from $180; ⚒) and ecofriendy **Redbrow Garden** (☎ 02-6226 8166; www.redbrowgarden.com.au; 1143 Nanima Rd, Murrumbateman; r from $195).

Queanbeyan is a thriving country town with inexpensive motel accommodation; try the **Mid City Motor Inn** (☎ 02-6297 7366; 215 Crawford St, Queanbeyan; s/d $90/100; ⚒) if you run out of options in Canberra.

Bungendore is a very attractive village, 35km east of Canberra, which bustles on weekends but sleeps during the week. There are galleries and antique stores aplenty to keep the cardigan crowd amused and bemused, but the highlight would have to be the **Bungendore Wood Works Gallery** (☎ 02-6238 1682; www.bwoodworks.com.au; cnr Malbon & Ellendon Sts, Bungendore). As well as showcasing superb works crafted from Australian timber there are changing exhibits of contemporary Australian artists.

The best place to stay in the region is the **Old Stone House** (☎ 02-6238 1888; www.theoldstonehouse .com.au; 41 Molonglo St, Bungendore; r $200; ⓟ ⚒), a charismatic 1867 granite-block house offering B&B in four antique-furnished rooms.

Queensland

Occupying Australia's northeastern corner, this vast state is awash with dazzling landscapes, vibrant cities and 300 days of sunshine a year. It's also home to some of the country's most notable highlights, from the golden beaches of the Sunshine Coast and the luminous green of the Daintree rainforest to the clear blue waters of the Great Barrier Reef.

It hides some of the country's lesser-known treasures, delivering wow-factor with gusto. You only have to peel back the postcard to find corners seemingly untouched by other visitors – spectacular national parks with tumbling waterfalls, white sandy beaches fringed by kaleidoscopic coral, vibrant and unique Aboriginal festivals and jaw-dropping sunsets.

Brisbane will delight city slickers with its lively, cosmopolitan atmosphere and, in the north, Cairns is a travellers' mecca. Between the two are strings of towns and islands, each with its own flavour but all brimming with Queenslander hospitality.

For the active traveller there are oodles of opportunities for white-water rafting, scuba diving, snorkelling, bushwalking, horse riding, surfing, bungee jumping, abseiling... The state is also home to more tours accredited under the national Eco Certification Program than any other, so you can safely explore, rather than exploit, this beautiful state.

QUEENSLAND

HIGHLIGHTS

- Scale Brisbane's **Story Bridge** (p310), one of three licensed bridge climbs in the world
- Set up tent in the jaw-dropping environs of **Boodjamulla (Lawn Hill) National Park** (p435) in the Gulf Savannah
- Chill with a kangaroo or cuddle a koala at the hands-on, ecofriendly **Australia Zoo** (p346), home of the late Steve Irwin
- Walk along the **North Gorge Headlands** (p329) on North Stradbroke Island and spot dolphins, manta rays, turtles and whales
- Swim under moonlight at **Lake Eacham** (p459) near Yungaburra
- Pitch a tent in the rainforests of **Lamington National Park** (p343) and walk the 21km Border Track between Queensland and New South Wales
- Sail the azure seas around the **Whitsunday Islands** (p408) and snorkel off the Great Barrier Reef
- Listen to Nugal-warra elder Willie Gordon from **Guurrbi Tours** (p474) tell stories at his ancestral rock-art sites near Hopevale, just outside of Cooktown

| ■ TELEPHONE CODE: 07 | ■ POPULATION: 4.3 MILLION | ■ AREA: 1,740,000 SQ KM |

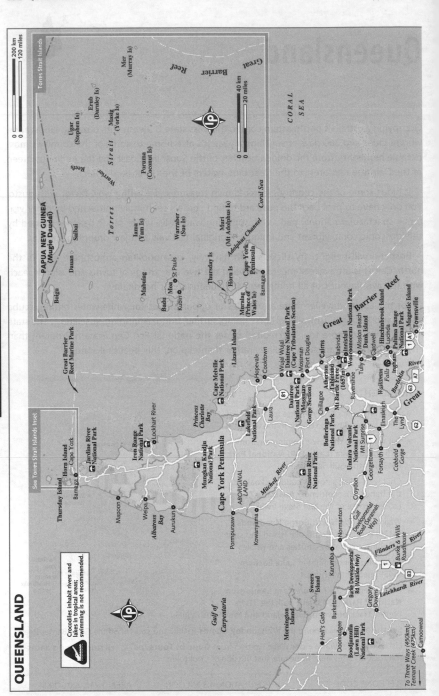

QUEENSLAND

Crocodiles inhabit rivers and lakes in tropical areas; swimming is not recommended.

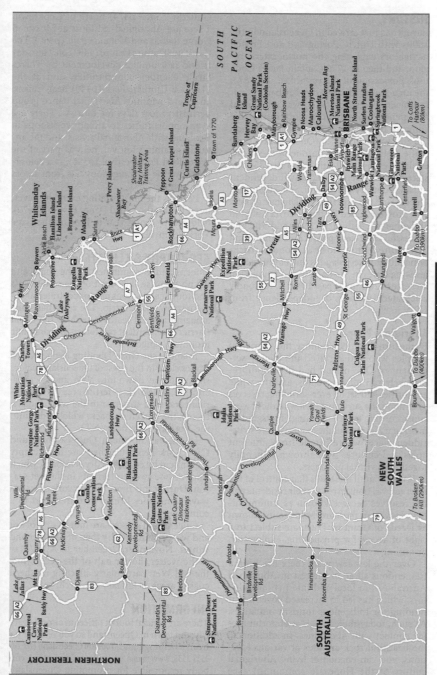

HISTORY

Europeans first arrived in Queensland in the 1600s with Dutch, Portuguese and French navigators exploring the northeastern region, and then in 1770 Captain James Cook took possession of the east coast. By 1825, the area that is modern-day Brisbane's central business district (CBD) was established as a penal colony for the more intractable convicts. Despite fierce Aboriginal resistance, the area was later settled (Queensland's early white settlers indulged in one of the greatest land grabs of all time) and in 1859 the state became a separate colony independent of New South Wales (NSW). Since that time, Queensland has experienced dynamic growth and progress, aided by the discovery of gold and other minerals in the 1860s and '70s, and successful sugar-cane production. Mining and agriculture continue to be an economic backbone today. Queensland is one of the fastest-growing states in Australia with a population increase of 20% in the past 10 years. It proudly celebrated 150 years of independence from NSW in 2009.

Aboriginal People

By the turn of the 19th century, the Aboriginal peoples who had survived the bloody settlement of Queensland had been comprehensively run off their lands, and the white authorities had set up ever-shrinking reserves to contain the survivors. A few of these were run according to well meaning, if misguided, missionary ideals, but the majority were strife-ridden places where people from different areas and cultures were thrown unhappily together as virtual prisoners.

It wasn't until the 1980s that control of the reserves was transferred to their residents and the reserves became known as 'communities'. However, these freehold grants, known as Deeds of Grant in Trust, are subject to a right of access for prospecting, exploration or mining.

Over the last few years there has been a tremendous surge in interest in Aboriginal Australia from local and international visitors, which has led to increased government funding for Indigenous tourism initiatives. As such, today there are great opportunities for contact with Aborigines. In addition to the beautiful rock-art sites at various locations, you can encounter living Aboriginal culture at the Hopevale community (see Guurrbi Tours, p474) north of Cooktown. There are Aboriginal-led tours at Mossman Gorge (p466) and Malanda Falls (p460). The Gab Titui Culture Centre (p482) on Thursday Island is a unique development by Torres Strait Islander communities, and at the Tjapukai Cultural Park (p440) near Cairns, an award-winning Aboriginal dance group performs most days for tourists. There are even opportunities to attend workshops in Brisbane with Aboriginal artists, and the annual Dreaming festival, held as part of the Woodford Folk Festival (p356), is a colourful showcase of Indigenous arts from across the country.

Perhaps the most exciting event, however, is the Laura Aboriginal Dance Festival (p479), held every second year in June on the Cape York Peninsula.

GEOGRAPHY & CLIMATE

Queensland is dominated by the coast, and it's no surprise that most of the settlements and tourist attractions are concentrated along the narrow coastal strip. The coast has some amazing natural features such as the Great Barrier Reef, verdant rainforests and dramatic mountain ranges.

Inland is the Great Dividing Range, which comes close to the coast of Queensland before slicing its way down into NSW and Victoria, and the tablelands – fertile areas of flat agricultural land that run to the west. Finally, there's the barren outback, which fades into the Northern Territory (NT).

In the far northern Gulf Country and Cape York Peninsula there are huge empty regions cut by countless dry riverbeds, which can become swollen torrents in the wet season. During this time, the network of waterways sometimes brings road transport to a complete halt.

Queensland seasons are more a case of hot and wet or cool and dry than of summer and winter. November/December to April/May is the wetter, hotter half of the year, while the real Wet, particularly affecting northern coastal areas, is January to March.

INFORMATION

There are official tourist offices in almost every city and town in Queensland so you're never far from a helping hand. **Tourism Queensland** (☎ 07-3535 3535; www.tq.com.au) is the government-run body responsible for promoting Queensland interstate and overseas. **Sunlover Holidays** (☎ 13 88 33; www.sunloverholidays.com) offices are located in state capitals for booking accommodation and tours. **Queensland Holidays** (www.queensland holidays.com.au) is aimed solely at tourists and is a great resource for planning your trip. The travel information section of its website (www .accessiblequeensland.com) is a decent source for visitors with disabilities.

Families with young children can check out the **Bub Hub** (www.bubhub.com.au) website, which lists everything from clinic contacts and locations to prenatal care to activities for newborns and toddlers, or call the **Child Care Information Service** (Map pp302-3; ☎ 1800 637 711, 07-3224 4557; www.communities.qld.gov.au/childcare; 4th fl, 111 George St, Brisbane).

For travelling safe in Queensland check out www.police.qld.gov.au/toursafe. For those travellers heading up to Far North Queensland, www.safetraveltnq.com.au is helpful if you're planning on exploring the area by 4WD.

For comprehensive information about the state, it's worth picking up a copy of Lonely Planet's *Queensland & the Great Barrier Reef* guidebook.

Some other useful contacts are the **Environmental Protection Agency** (☎ 13 13 04; www.epa.qld.gov.au) and **Royal Automobile Club of Queensland** (RACQ; ☎ 13 19 05; www.racq.com.au).

NATIONAL PARKS

There are some 220 national parks and state forests dotted around Queensland, and while some comprise only a single hill or lake, others are major wilderness areas. Many islands, expanses of water and stretches of coast are national parks.

Three of the most spectacular national parks inland are: Lamington (p343), on the forested rim of an ancient volcano on the NSW border; Carnarvon (p390), with its 30km gorge southwest of Rockhampton; and, near Mackay, rainforested Eungella (p404) swarms with wildlife.

On the coast, the Great Sandy National Park (Cooloola, p356) is a mesmerising tangle of mangroves, rivers and forest and, of course, there's the jewel in Queensland's crown – the Great Barrier Reef Marine Park (see p410).

The **Queensland Parks & Wildlife Service** (QPWS; ☎ 13 13 04; www.epa.qld.gov.au) website has details of activities, safety and history of the parks and you can search by region. If you're keen to do more than just have a holiday, the QPWS also runs volunteer programs in many of the national parks.

ACTIVITIES
Bushwalking

The bigger national parks have kilometres of marked walking tracks and there are excellent bushwalking opportunities in many parts of the state and national parks, and state forests year-round. Among the favourites are: Gold Coast Hinterland's 54km Great Walk (p343); Carnarvon (p390); Hinchinbrook Island's Thorsborne Trail (p427); Wooroonooran (p432), which contains Queensland's highest peak, Mt Bartle Frere (1657m); and the traditional walking trails of the Jirrbal and Mamu Aboriginal people.

QUEENSLAND FACTS

Eat Moreton Bay bugs, prawns, mud crabs and barramundi (especially at Lake Tinaroo), Rockhampton steak, Bowen mangoes, bananas and macadamia nuts

Drink Pots of XXXX beer, Bundaberg Rum, Granite Belt wines and mango wine

Read John Birmingham's *He Died with a Felafel in His Hand*, Andrew Stafford's *Pig City*, Chloe Hooper's *The Tall Man* and Thea Astley's *Drylands*

Listen to The Grates' *Teeth Lost, Hearts Won* (2008), the Gin Club's *Junk* (2008), the Boat People's *Chandeliers* (2008) and Kate Miller-Heidke's *Curiouser* (2008)

Watch *Australia* (2008), *Radiance* (1998), *Cane Toads* (1988), *Dead Calm* (1989) and *Finding Nemo* (2003)

Avoid Surfers Paradise during Schoolies Week, cane toads, sunburn, stingers and crocs

Locals' nickname Cane toads, banana benders

Swim at Fraser Island's Lakes McKenzie and Wabby (p368), Sunshine Coast's Peregian (p348) and Noosa (p349) beaches, Great Keppel Island (p388) and along the Great Barrier Reef

Best festivals Biennial Laura Aboriginal Dance Festival (p479) in June, Woodford Folk Festival (p356) in late December, and Brisbane's Riverfestival and National Festival of Beers (p315) in September

Tackiest tourist attraction Big Gumboot (p427).

SOUTH SEA ISLANDER AUSTRALIANS

A group of people that played an important, if tragic, part in shaping Queensland's history are the South Sea Islander Australians who were brought over between 1863 and 1904 to provide cheap labour on the sugar-cane plantations. Many of them were kidnapped, or 'blackbirded', from their islands and were forced to work in virtual slavelike conditions once they arrived.

'In many ways our grandfathers were the foundation of the sugar-cane industry', says John Pene-Fonmosa whose grandfather was blackbirded after leaving his island home of Rotuma for Fiji. 'They cleared the fields, cut the cane and crushed it. They were the pillars of the industry.'

These people were termed 'Kanakas', the Polynesian word for man, which took on derogatory connotations when hijacked by Europeans. In total, an estimated 60,000 islanders were shipped to Australia, but as unions began to call for white-only labour, many were sent home.

'Of course, some got a taste for the Western lifestyle and didn't want to leave so they ran away', says John, who is from the Bundjalung tribal area, south of Brisbane, where most of the community are a mix of the Bundjalung Aboriginal Nation and the South Sea Islands. 'And for some, if the captain of the ship hadn't properly logged where each individual was from, they couldn't even get home.'

Many who remained experienced unemployment, racism and government neglect, and it wasn't until 1994 that the federal government recognised Australian South Sea Islanders as a distinct cultural group. It took another five years for the Queensland government to do the same.

The Queensland government has also developed the Great Walks of Queensland: six tracks designed to allow walkers to experience rainforests and bushlands without disturbing the ecosystem. They include the Whitsundays, Sunshine Coast Hinterland, Mackay Highlands, Fraser Island, Gold Coast Hinterland and the Wet Tropics (tropical North Queensland). Contact **QPWS** (☎ 13 13 04; www.epa.qld.gov.au) for more information. **Queensland Walks** (www.queenslandwalks.com.au) is a helpful website set up by Tourism Queensland.

Camping

There are some stunning spots to pitch a tent in Queensland and many of the state and national parks have camping grounds with toilets, showers and sometimes even an electric barbecue.

Among those recommended are the QPWS camping ground on Snapper Island (p468), the shaded beach sites on Noah Beach (p470) and Binna Burra campsite (p344), which has permanent safari-style tents within a rainforest setting.

There are often privately run camping grounds, motels and lodges on the park fringes.

In order to camp anywhere in a national park you will need a permit. You can self-register at a handful of sites, but for the vast majority you will need to purchase a permit in advance, either by calling QPWS or booking online. Camping in national parks and state forests costs $4.85/19.40 per person/family per night. Popular parks fill up at holiday times, so it pays to book well in advance.

Diving & Snorkelling

The Queensland coast is an Aladdin's cave of spectacular dive sites and there are dozens of operators vying to teach you or provide you with the ultimate dive safari. Learning here is fairly inexpensive – PADI (Professional Association of Diving Instructors) courses range from two to five days and cost anything between $300 and $700 – and you usually do a good part of your learning in the warm waters of the Great Barrier Reef itself.

Almost every major town along the coast has one or more dive schools (the three most popular places are Airlie Beach, Cairns and Townsville), but standards vary from place to place and course to course. Good instructors move around from company to company, so ask around to see which company is currently well regarded.

When choosing a course, look at how much of your open-water experience will be out on the reef. Many budget courses only offer shore dives, which are frequently less interesting, whereas the more expensive options can include two days aboard a boat and reef dives. Normally you have to show you can tread water for 10 minutes and swim 200m before you can start a course. Most schools require a medical, which usually costs extra (from $70 to $130).

While school standards are generally high, each year a number of newly certified divers are stricken with 'the bends' and end up in the decompression chamber in Townsville. This potentially fatal condition is caused by bubbles of nitrogen that form in the blood when divers ascend too quickly to the surface – always ascend slowly and, on dives over 9m in depth, take a rest stop en route to the surface.

For divers, trips and equipment hire are available just about everywhere. You'll need evidence of your qualifications, and some places may also ask to see your diving log book. You can snorkel just about everywhere, too. There are coral reefs off some mainland beaches and around several of the islands, and many day trips out to the Great Barrier Reef provide snorkelling gear free.

Extreme Sports

Queensland has its fair share of activities to satisfy thrill-seekers. Bungee jumping and similar adrenalin-charged rides can be found at major tourist stops, such as Surfers Paradise, Airlie Beach and Cairns. If you need something a tad more heart-stopping, then there are opportunities for parachuting, skydiving and even canopy surfing. Two of the best spots to jump out of a plane are Caloundra (p346) and Mission Beach (p428).

Sailing & Fishing

Sailing enthusiasts will find plenty of places with boats and/or sailboards for hire, both along the coast and inland. Manly (near Brisbane), Airlie Beach and the Whitsunday Islands are probably the biggest centres and you can indulge in almost any type of boating or sailing. The Whitsundays, with their plentiful bays and relatively calm waters, are particularly popular for sailing; day trips start at $100 and overnight trips from $250. Bareboat charters (sailing yourself) are also possible from $500 per day.

Fishing is one of Queensland's most popular sports and you can hire fishing gear and/or boats in many places. Fraser Island, Karumba, Cooktown and North Stradbroke Island are some good spots. The Great Barrier Reef has traditionally been a popular fishing ground, but a recent overhaul of the zoning laws has tightened the area that can be fished. For comprehensive information on where and when you can fish, contact the **Great Barrier Reef Marine Park Authority** (☎ 07-4750 0700; www.gbrmpa.gov.au), based at Reef HQ (p415) in Townsville.

Surfing

There are some fantastic breaks along Queensland's southeastern coast, most notably at Coolangatta (p341), Burleigh Heads (p340), Surfers Paradise (p336), North Stradbroke Island (p329), Noosa (p349) and Town of 1770 (p383). Surf shops in these areas generally offer board hire, or you can buy cheap secondhands. If you've never hit the surf before, it's a good idea to have a lesson or two.

Swimming

North of Fraser Island the beaches are sheltered by the Great Barrier Reef, so they're great for swimming, and the clear waters are justly deserving of their reputation. There is also a

QUEENSLAND

DIVING IN QUEENSLAND – FIVE OF THE BEST

- **Osprey Reef** (p440) Take a live-aboard trip out to this action- (and shark-) packed, vertical-wall dive site around 350km from Cairns.

- **Heron Island** (p383) This exclusive and tranquil coral cay sits amid a huge spread of reef. You can step straight off the beach and join a crowd of colourful fish here.

- **Lady Elliot Island** (p381) The most southerly of the Great Barrier Reef islands and also a coral cay. It's home to 19 highly regarded dive sites, so it's hard to know where to begin.

- **Lizard Island** (p475) Remote and rugged, Lizard Island boasts what are arguably Australia's best-known dive sites – Cod Hole, famous for its resident giant and docile potato cod, and Pixie Bommie.

- **HMAS Brisbane** (p347) This sunk, old Australian warship is the hottest dive spot in Queensland. Easily accessible off the Sunshine Coast, it has a flourishing artificial reef teeming with marine life.

LOADS OF TOADS

Queenslanders have several nicknames, but perhaps the most curious one is 'cane toad', after the amphibious critters that were introduced to Australia in 1935 in an attempt to control the native cane beetle. These creatures are not a pretty sight: dry and warty skin, heavy-ridged eyes and poisonous glands across their backs would make any girl looking for her prince run a mile. But fairy tales aside, the cane toads have proved to be absolutely useless; they ignored the pesky cane grub and instead focused on reproducing. From an original batch of just 101 toads, there are now over 200 million of these long-legged creatures hopping around Australia – an invasion that has seen the populations of native snakes and goanna lizards decline. Indeed, the problem got so bad that a millionaire pub owner introduced a beer-for-a-bag-of-toads bounty that even got the support of the Royal Society for the Prevention of Cruelty to Animals (RSPCA). There's also a Stop the Toad Foundation in Western Australia, raising funds for barrier fencing to keep the state cane-toad free. But it seems that not everyone hates them: Queensland's representative rugby league team has chosen the cane toad as its unofficial mascot and they have even been listed by the National Trust of Queensland as a state icon. Warts and all.

---

fantastic abundance of good freshwater swimming spots around the state. Box jellyfish are a serious problem from Rockhampton north between October and April; see Stingers, p386, for more information. Be careful of estuarine crocs swimming in the coastal waters north of Rockhampton and their freshwater cousins living in the rivers and swamps of Cape Tribulation.

White-Water Rafting & Canoeing

The Tully and North Johnstone Rivers between Townsville and Cairns are the big ones for white-water rafting. You can do day trips from around $150.

Sea-kayaking is also a popular option, with various trips running from Cairns, Mission Beach, Cape Tribulation, Noosa and Maroochydore.

Coastal Queensland is full of waterways and lakes you can explore, so there's never a shortage of canoeing territory. You can rent canoes or join canoe tours in several places including Noosa, Surfers Paradise, Townsville and Cairns.

TOURS

Queensland has more tours and activities accredited by the national **Eco Certification Program** (www.ecotourism.org.au) than any other state and many are listed throughout this chapter and in the GreenDex (p1112). However, many nonaccredited tour operators have jumped on the eco bandwagon of late, and they're not always what they seem. It's worth asking what their ecopolicies are before signing up.

Although choosing a tour operator can often be a hit-and-miss affair, you'll find some of the best the state has to offer mentioned throughout the chapter. Good online resources for tours include www.queenslandholidays.com.au and www.sunloverholidays.com.

GETTING THERE & AROUND

Most travellers will arrive in Queensland from NSW, and while your car or bus can legally be inspected crossing the border, it hardly ever happens. You probably won't even notice that you've passed from one state to the other. Brisbane (p325) is the main port of call for flights into Queensland and is the main international airport for the state, but Cairns and Gold Coast airports also receive international flights. For more information, see the Transport chapter (p1046).

Air

National carriers, **Qantas Airways** (☎ 13 13 13; www.qantas.com.au), **Jetstar** (☎ 13 15 38; www.jetstar.com.au) and **Virgin Blue** (☎ 13 67 89; www.virginblue.com.au), fly to Queensland's major cities. **Tiger Airways** (☎ 03-9335 3033; www.tigerairways.com) is the new kid on the block with flights to the Gold Coast, Rockhampton, Sunshine Coast and Mackay from Melbourne or Adelaide.

There are also smaller airlines, including charter flights, operating up and down the coast, across the Cape York Peninsula and into the outback. **Alliance Airlines** (☎ 07-4750 1300; www.allianceairlines.com.au) offers charter flights between Brisbane, Mt Isa, Townsville and Cairns.

Boat

In the past travellers have managed to travel along the coast or even over to Papua New Guinea or Darwin by crewing on the numerous yachts and cruisers that sail Queensland waters. It's still possible to do, but it's not easy. Ask at harbours, marinas or sailing clubs. Manly (near Brisbane), Airlie Beach, Townsville and Cairns are good places to try. You'll normally have to contribute some money for your passage.

Bus

Greyhound Australia (☎ 1300 GREYHOUND/1300 473 946; www.greyhound.com.au), the largest bus company in Australia, offers comprehensive coverage of Queensland and all the major tourist destinations, as well as excellent interstate connections.

The busiest route is up the coast on the Bruce Hwy from Brisbane to Cairns – there are various passes that cover this route, allowing multiple stops along all or part of the coast. Useful passes for Queensland include Greyhound's 'Mini Traveller Pass', which gives you 45 days hop-on, hop-off travel from Sydney to Cairns for $357. Check the Greyhound Australia website for more details. See the Transport chapter (p1070) for more information on interstate bus passes.

Premier Motor Service (☎ 13 34 10; www.premierms.com.au) also covers the route between Melbourne, Sydney, Brisbane and Cairns with fewer services than Greyhound, but often considerably cheaper fares.

Car

The roads in Queensland are in good condition, particularly along the coastal highways and main thoroughfares in the hinterland and outback. However, they can often turn into badly maintained sealed roads or dirt tracks in the more remote areas of the state. For car hire information see individual destinations.

Train

Queensland Rail (☎ 13 22 32, 1300 131 722; www.traveltrain.com.au) operates numerous services throughout Queensland. The main railway line is the Brisbane to Cairns run, which is serviced by the *Tilt Train,* a high-speed connection that operates three times weekly, and the *Sunlander,* a more leisurely option with three services weekly. There are also inland services from Brisbane to Charleville, Brisbane to Longreach and Charleville, and from Townsville to Mt Isa, plus a more regular *Tilt Train* service between Brisbane and Rockhampton. More detail is listed under the relevant destinations.

BRISBANE

pop 1.86 million

Blessed with an abundance of sunshine and spectacular waterways, Brisbane is surging forward as a modern metropolis with a new air of confidence and style. Rapid inner-city development, a swelling population and a cosmopolitan upswing have given it greater stature in recent times, yet it retains the friendliness and relaxed attitude it has always been praised for.

Locally known as Brissie (or Brisvegas), it's the nation's third-largest destination and deserves all acclaim for being a dazzling river city. Sleek catamaran ferries glide up and down the Brisbane River, which snakes its way around shiny CBD buildings and sprawling subtropical parklands, under the mighty Story Bridge, past colossal rock faces at Kangaroo Point, and out to magical Moreton Bay.

For a city with less than two million inhabitants, it punches well above its weight for cosmopolitan offerings: world-class art galleries, rocking live-music venues and a thriving restaurant scene with year-round outdoor dining. It is consistently a front runner in the 'Australia's fastest growing city' stakes with up to 900 people moving there every week. The temperate climate and clear blue skies are irresistible for some, along with its distinct lack of pretentiousness. During its so-called 'winter', when you're basking in sunshine on the verandah of an old Queenslander home while 'southerners' shiver, it's easy to see why the Brisbane lifestyle has become so desirable.

HISTORY

Aboriginal inhabitants knew the area later known as Brisbane as Mian-jin, meaning 'place shaped like a spike'. The first white settlement here was established at Redcliffe on Moreton Bay in 1824 – a penal colony for difficult convicts from the Botany Bay colony in NSW. After struggling with inadequate water supplies and hostile Aboriginal groups, the colony was relocated to safer territory on the banks of the Brisbane River, before the whole colony idea was abandoned in 1839.

QUEENSLAND

Moreton Bay was opened to free settlers in 1842. This marked the beginning of Brisbane's rise to prominence and the beginning of the end for the region's Aboriginal peoples.

Brisbane prospered during the 20th century, and in more recent times, hosted the 1982 Commonwealth Games, 1988 World Expo and 2001 Goodwill Games.

ORIENTATION

Brisbane's city centre or CBD is bounded by a U-shaped loop of the Brisbane River. Your best starting point is pedestrianised Queen St Mall, the city's main retail strip, which runs from Edward St up to the former Treasury Building (casino) and Victoria Bridge to South Bank.

Across Victoria Bridge are South Brisbane and the South Bank Parklands. Further southwest is West End. Ann St runs northeast of the CBD into the bar/nightclub precinct of Fortitude Valley, and the Story Bridge connects 'the Valley' with Kangaroo Point.

The Roma Street Transit Centre, where you'll arrive if you're coming by bus, train or airport shuttle, is on Roma St, about 500m northwest of the CBD.

Brisbane airport is about 15km northeast of the city. There are shuttles to and from the city (see p327).

Maps

You can pick up free maps with detail of the CBD from one of the visitors centres, but for more comprehensive city coverage get a copy of *Brisbane Compact Map* ($6.95) or *Brisbane and Region Handy Map* ($6.95), both by Hema Maps. Other good options include *Brisbane Suburban Map* by UBD ($7.95) and Gregory's *Brisbane Street Directory* ($24.95).

The definitive guide to Brisbane's streets is UBD's *Brisbane Street Directory* (known locally as 'Refidex'; $34.95), which includes maps of the Gold and Sunshine Coasts.

INFORMATION
Bookshops

Archives Fine Books (Map pp302-3; ☎ 07-3221 0491; www.archives.com.au; 40 Charlotte St, Brisbane) Independent bookstore with a reputed one million secondhand titles.

Bent Books (Map pp300-1; ☎ 07-3846 5004; www.bentbooks.com.au; 205a Boundary St, West End) Cute shop for rare and secondhand.

Folio Books (Map pp302-3; ☎ 07-3221 1368; www.foliobooks.com.au; 80 Albert St, Brisbane) Art and design specialists.

World Wide Maps & Guides (Map pp302-3; ☎ 07-3221 4330; www.worldwidemaps.com.au; shop 30, Anzac Square Arcade, 267 Edward St, Brisbane) Small but well stocked with travel guides and maps.

Emergency
Ambulance (☎ 000)
Fire (☎ 000)
Lifeline (☎ 13 11 14)
Police (☎ 000) city centre (Map pp302-3; ☎ 07-3258 2582; 46 Charlotte St); Fortitude Valley (Map pp300-1; ☎ 07-3131 1055; cnr Brookes & Wickham Sts); headquarters (Map pp302-3; ☎ 07-3364 6464; 200 Roma St)
RACQ (☎ 13 19 05) city centre (Map pp302-3; ☎ 07-3872 8465; GPO Bldg, 261 Queen St); Fortitude Valley (Map pp302-3; ☎ 07-3872 8429; 300 St Pauls Tce) Roadside service.

Internet Access

Most backpacker hostels and hotels offer internet access and many have wireless; a few are free of charge. Internet cafes are scattered around the city centre; rates are $4 to $6 per hour.

Global Gossip city centre (Map pp302-3; ☎ 07-3229 4033; 290 Edward St; ☉ 9am-11pm Mon-Sat, 10am-10pm Sun); Fortitude Valley (Map pp302-3; ☎ 07-3666 0800; 312 Brunswick St; ☉ 9am-11pm) Plenty of terminals; cheap-call phone booths (Valley only).

Internet City (Map pp302-3; ☎ 07-3003 1221; 4th fl, 132 Albert St; ☉ 24hr) More than 60 terminals.

Internet Resources
www.brisbane247.com Complete entertainment guide.
www.brisbane-australia.com General visitor info.
www.brisbane.citysearch.com.au Latest information on dining, drinking and dancing venues.
www.ourbrisbane.com Extensive online city guide.

Media
Brisbane Times (www.brisbanetimes.com.au) Up-to-the-minute online news.
Courier Mail (www.news.com.au/couriermail) Brisbane's daily tabloid newspaper.
Rave (www.ravemag.com.au) Weekly street press with music news and gig guide.
Time Off (www.timeoff.com.au) Free weekly mag listing Brisbane's gigs.

Medical Services
Brisbane Sexual Health Clinic (Map pp302-3; ☎ 07-3837 5611; 1st fl, 270 Roma St, Brisbane; ☉ 8.30am-4.30pm Mon, Tue & Fri, to noon Wed, 10am-4.30pm Thu) Free check-ups for travellers.

(Continued on page 305)

BRISBANE

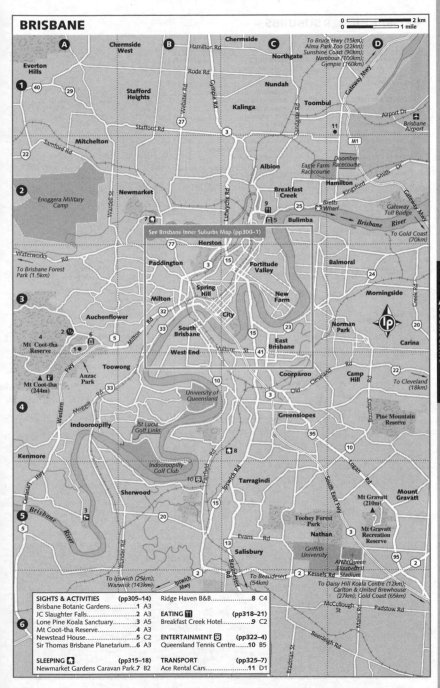

See Brisbane Inner Suburbs Map (pp300–1)

QUEENSLAND

SIGHTS & ACTIVITIES	(pp305–14)
Brisbane Botanic Gardens	1 A3
JC Slaughter Falls	2 A3
Lone Pine Koala Sanctuary	3 A5
Mt Coot-tha Reserve	4 A3
Newstead House	5 C2
Sir Thomas Brisbane Planetarium	6 A3
SLEEPING 🏠	(pp315–18)
Newmarket Gardens Caravan Park	7 B2

Ridge Haven B&B	8 C4
EATING 🍴	(pp318–21)
Breakfast Creek Hotel	9 C2
ENTERTAINMENT 🎭	(pp322–4)
Queensland Tennis Centre	10 B5
TRANSPORT	(pp325–7)
Ace Rental Cars	11 D1

BRISBANE INNER SUBURBS

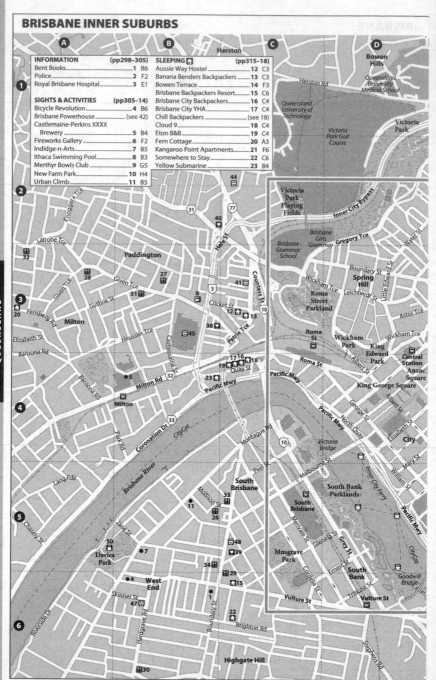

INFORMATION	(pp298–305)
Bent Books	1 B6
Police	2 F2
Royal Brisbane Hospital	3 E1

SIGHTS & ACTIVITIES	(pp305–14)
Bicycle Revolution	4 B6
Brisbane Powerhouse	(see 42)
Castlemaine-Perkins XXXX Brewery	5 B4
Fireworks Gallery	6 F2
Indidge-n-Arts	7 B5
Ithaca Swimming Pool	8 B3
Merthyr Bowls Club	9 G5
New Farm Park	10 H4
Urban Climb	11 B5

SLEEPING	(pp315–18)
Aussie Way Hostel	12 C3
Banana Benders Backpackers	13 C3
Bowen Terrace	14 F3
Brisbane Backpackers Resort	15 C6
Brisbane City Backpackers	16 C4
Brisbane City YHA	17 C4
Chill Backpackers	(see 18)
Cloud 9	18 C4
Eton B&B	19 C4
Fern Cottage	20 A3
Kangaroo Point Apartments	21 F6
Somewhere to Stay	22 C6
Yellow Submarine	23 B4

QUEENSLAND

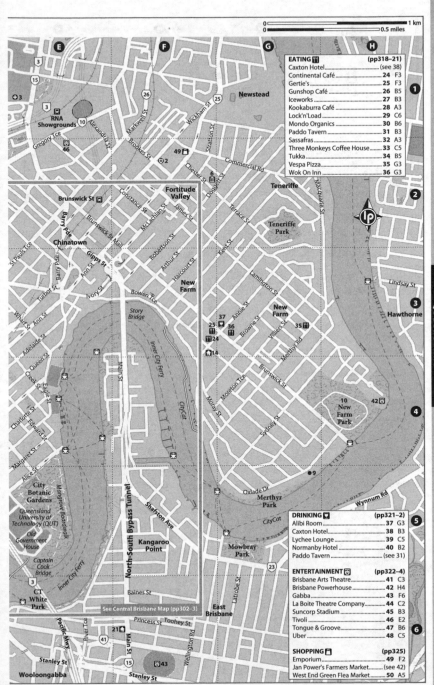

QUEENSLAND

EATING 🍴	(pp318–21)
Caxton Hotel	(see 38)
Continental Café	24 F3
Gertie's	25 F3
Gunshop Café	26 B5
Iceworks	27 B3
Kookaburra Café	28 A3
Lock'n'Load	29 C6
Mondo Organics	30 B6
Paddo Tavern	31 B3
Sassafras	32 A3
Three Monkeys Coffee House	33 C5
Tukka	34 B5
Vespa Pizza	35 G3
Wok On Inn	36 G3

DRINKING 🍷	(pp321–2)
Alibi Room	37 G3
Caxton Hotel	38 B3
Lychee Lounge	39 C5
Normanby Hotel	40 B2
Paddo Tavern	(see 31)

ENTERTAINMENT 🎭	(pp322–4)
Brisbane Arts Theatre	41 C3
Brisbane Powerhouse	42 H4
Gabba	43 F6
La Boite Theatre Company	44 C2
Suncorp Stadium	45 B3
Tivoli	46 E2
Tongue & Groove	47 B6
Uber	48 C5

SHOPPING 🛍	(pp325)
Emporium	49 F2
Jan Power's Farmers Market	(see 42)
West End Green Flea Market	50 A5

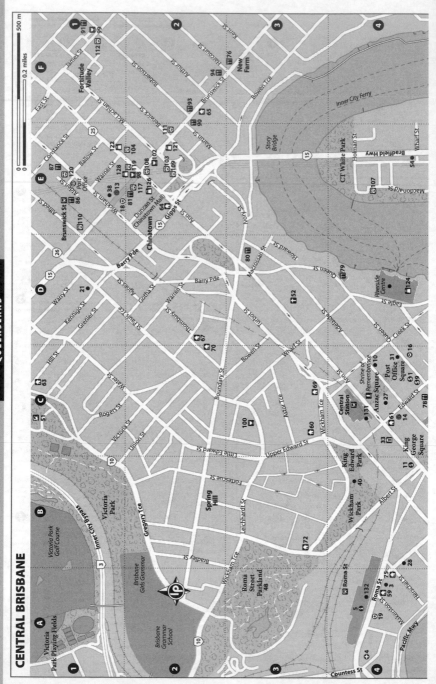

CENTRAL BRISBANE

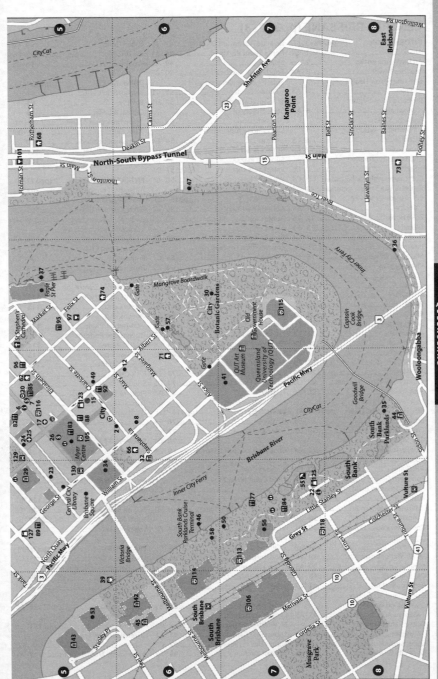

CENTRAL BRISBANE (pp302–3)

QUEENSLAND

(Continued from page 298)

Dr Deb's the Travel Doctor (Map pp302-3; ☎ 07-3221 9066; 5th fl, 247 Adelaide St, Brisbane; ✆ 8am-5pm Mon & Fri, to 7pm Tue & Wed, to 4pm Thu, 8.30am-2pm Sat) Vaccinations and medical advice.

Pharmacy On the Mall (Map pp302-3; ☎ 07-3221 4585; Queen St Mall, 141 Queen St, Brisbane; ✆ 7am-9pm Mon-Thu, to 9.30pm Fri, 8am-9pm Sat, 8.30am-6pm Sun)

Queensland Statewide Sexual Assault Helpline (☎ 1800 010 120; ✆ 7.30am-midnight)

Royal Brisbane Hospital (Map pp300-1; ☎ 07-3636 8111; cnr Butterfield St & Bowen Bridge Rd, Herston; ✆ 24hr switchboard & casualty ward)

Travel Clinic (Map pp302-3; ☎ 07-3211 3611, after hours 07-3831 9999; 1st fl, 245 Albert St, Brisbane; ✆ 7.30am-7pm Mon-Thu, to 6pm Fri, 8.30am-5pm Sat, 9.30am-5pm Sun) General medical services and vaccinations.

Money

There are foreign-exchange bureaus in the domestic and international terminals at Brisbane airport, as well as ATMs that take most international credit cards. Most banks have exchange bureaus and ATMs.

Amex (Map pp302-3; ☎ 1300 139 060, 07-3229 3926; 260 Queen St, Brisbane) Located within the Westpac bank.

Change Group (Map pp302-3; ☎ 07-3221 3562; shop 255, Wintergarden Centre, Queen St Mall, Brisbane)

Commonwealth Bank (Map pp302-3; ☎ 13 22 21, 07-3237 3499; 240 Queen St, Brisbane)

Travelex (Map pp302-3; ☎ 07-3210 6325; Shop 149f, Myer Centre, Queen St Mall, Brisbane)

Post

Main post office (GPO; Map pp302-3; ☎ 13 13 18; 261 Queen St, Brisbane; ✆ 7am-6pm Mon-Fri)

Post office (Post Shop; Map pp302-3; ☎ 13 13 18; 2nd fl, Wintergarden Centre, Queen St Mall, Brisbane; ✆ 9am-5pm Mon-Fri, to 12.30pm Sat)

Tourist Information

Brisbane Transit Visitor Information (Map pp302-3; ☎ 07-3236 2020; 3rd fl, Roma Street Transit Centre, Roma St, Brisbane; ✆ 7am-6.30pm Mon-Fri, 7.30am-6pm Sat & Sun) Information counter specialising in backpacker travel, tours and accommodation in much of Queensland.

Brisbane Visitor Information & Booking Centre (Map pp302-3; ☎ 07-3006 6290; www.visitbrisbane .com.au; Queen St Mall, Brisbane; ✆ 9am-5.30pm Mon-Thu, to 7pm Fri, to 5pm Sat, 9.30am-4.30pm Sun) Great one-stop information centre in the middle of the mall near Wintergarden has all you'll need to know about Brisbane.

EPA Customer Service Centre (Map pp302-3; ☎ 07-3227 8185; www.epa.qld.gov.au; 160 Ann St, Brisbane; ✆ 8.30am-5pm Mon-Fri) The Environment Protection Agency's information centre provides maps, brochures and camping permits for Queensland's national parks and state forests.

South Bank visitor information centre (Map pp302-3; ☎ 07-3867 2051; Stanley Street Plaza, South Bank Parklands; ✆ 9am-5pm) Information on South Bank activities and the place to buy tickets for entertainment events.

Travel Agencies

Beaches Travel (Map pp302-3; ☎ 07-3008 7100; 154b Roma St, Brisbane) Specialising in jobs for backpackers.

STA Travel (Map pp302-3; ☎ 07-3229 2499; www .statravel.com.au; shop G11, Queen Adelaide Bldg, 59 Adelaide St, Brisbane)

Trailfinders (Map pp302-3; ☎ 1300 651 900, 07-3229 0887; www.trailfinders.com.au; 101 Adelaide St, Brisbane)

YHA Travel (Map pp302-3; ☎ 07-3236 1680; 450 George St, Brisbane) Tours, YHA membership and YHA hostel bookings.

SIGHTS

Most of Brisbane's historical and colonial sights are in the city centre (also called the CBD). The surrounding inner-city suburbs offer loads of attractions and activities: South Bank's galleries and arts centres; Fortitude Valley/New Farm's gritty cafes, bars and live-music venues; and West End's bohemian vibe. The freebie brochure **Brisbane's Living Heritage Network Experience Guide** (www.brisbanelivingheritage .com), available from the visitor information centres, highlights many of the sights Brisbane has to offer.

City Centre
CITY HALL & AROUND

The majestic old **Brisbane City Hall** (Map pp302-3; ☎ 07-3403 8888; www.brisbane.qld.gov.au/cityhall; btwn Ann & Adelaide Sts, Brisbane; admission free; ✆ lift & viewing tower 10am-3pm), opened in 1930, is slowly sinking and suffering concrete cancer. At the time we passed through, Brisbane City Council announced it was closing City Hall for up to three years from December 2009. Savour what you can from the outside; the four clock faces on each side of the tower are the largest in Australia and, until the Sydney Opera House was completed in 1971, Brisbane's City Hall was the most expensive building in the country. It was the tallest building in the city until 1973.

Next to City Hall is the recently re-developed **King George Square**, a popular CBD meeting place with an underground bus station.

QUEENSLAND

Housed within the old School of Arts, a short walk east of King George Sq, is the **Footsteps Gallery** (Map pp302-3; ☎ 07-3229 0395; 166 Ann St, Brisbane; admission free; ☺ 8am-5pm Mon-Fri), established to support emerging artists from the Aboriginal and Torres Strait Islander communities. It hosts monthly exhibitions of Indigenous art and is one of the better spots for purchasing handmade Aboriginal souvenirs.

TREASURY BUILDING & AROUND

The most grand and impressive of the city's historical architecture is the state government's **Former Treasury Building** (Map pp302-3), now Conrad Treasury casino. An imposing Italian Renaissance–style building, it was once regarded as a symbol of self-government (the proclamation of the federation of the Australian Commonwealth was read from a balcony here in 1901), but now offers a very different form of freedom: 24-hour gambling.

In the block southeast of the casino is the equally magnificent former **Land Administration Building** (Map pp302-3), which has been transformed into a luxury five-star hotel under the Conrad Treasury banner (p318).

To the south of the casino is the **Commissariat Stores Building** (Map pp302-3; ☎ 07-3221 4198; 115 William St, Brisbane; adult/child $5/2.50; ☺ 10am-4pm Tue-Fri), of which the first two floors were constructed entirely by convict labour in 1829. A Queensland government storehouse until 1951 and now a museum, the guided tours offer a thorough insight into Brisbane's gruesome penal history.

PARLIAMENT HOUSE & BOTANIC GARDENS

With its unique roof made from Mt Isa copper, **Parliament House** (Map pp302-3; ☎ 07-3406 7111; www.parliament.qld.gov.au; cnr Alice & George Sts, Brisbane; admission free; ☺ 9am-5pm Mon-Fri) is where you can watch state politicians trade legislation and insults from the public balcony on sitting days. The French Renaissance–style building dates from 1868 and is one of Brisbane's treasured historical landmarks. Free tours leave on demand from 9am to 4.15pm Monday to Friday and 10am to 2pm weekends, unless parliament is sitting.

The spacious **City Botanic Gardens** (Map pp302-3; ☎ 07-3403 0666; Albert St, Brisbane; admission free; ☺ 24hr, free guided tours 11am & 1pm Mon-Sat) is a regular chill-out spot for CBD workers

and students craving fresh air and beautiful views of the Kangaroo Point cliffs. Set alongside a curve in the Brisbane River, the gardens form Brisbane's oldest park and are filled with walking trails, green lawns, bamboo gardens, bunya pines, macadamia trees and Moreton Bay figs. The pretty **Mangrove Boardwalk**, a wooden walkway skirting the riverbank on the eastern rim, is lit up until midnight, affording good opportunities to spot possums.

ROMA STREET PARKLAND

Located on 16 hectares, **Roma Street Parkland** (Map pp302-3; ☎ 07-3006 4546; romastreetparkland.com; 1 Parkland Blvd; admission free; ☺ 24hr, free guided tours 10am & 2pm) is allegedly the world's largest subtropical garden in a city centre. Formerly the site of a market and later a railway yard, the parkland features 40 varieties of Australian native trees, a lake, three waterfalls, a playground and public barbecues.

Southeast of Roma St Parkland in Wickham Park stands the **Old Windmill** (Map pp302-3; Wickham Tce), which was first constructed by convicts as a mill for grinding grains. Built in 1828 it's just a fraction older than the Commissariat Stores, making it the oldest surviving building in Brisbane. It is closed to the public.

East of Roma St Parkland heading towards Fortitude Valley is **St John's Cathedral** (Map pp302-3; ☎ 07-3835 2231; 373 Ann St, Brisbane; admission free; ☺ 9.30am-4.30pm), a fine example of 19th-century Gothic Revival architecture. The building was recently completed according to its original design, 102 years after construction commenced.

South Bank

QUEENSLAND CULTURAL CENTRE

The vast Queensland Cultural Centre forms the city's cultural backbone and comprises two art galleries, a performing arts centre, museum and the state library. The precinct's stunning architecture, landscaping and riverside location are must-sees – even from the outside.

The most recent addition to this group of buildings is the world-class **Queensland Gallery of Modern Art** (GoMA; Map pp302-3; ☎ 07-3840 7303; www.qag.qld.gov.au; Stanley Pl, South Brisbane; admission free; ☺ 10am-5pm Mon-Fri, 9am-5pm Sat & Sun). It opened in 2006 and is the nation's largest modern art gallery, focusing on art, including cinematic and multimedia, from the last 30 years. Pablo

Picasso and Andy Warhol temporary exhibitions have been major attractions for the gallery since its opening, creating renewed excitement about Brisbane's arts scene. Eye-opening permanent displays include a life-size statue of a seal balancing a piano on its nose.

Standing beside GoMA is the impressive **State Library of Queensland** (Map pp302–3) and the **Queensland Art Gallery** (Map pp302–3; ☎ 07-3840 7303; Stanley Pl, South Brisbane; admission free; ☟ 10am-5pm Mon-Fri, 9am-5pm Sat & Sun). There are some particularly enjoyable permanent collections that include prominent Aboriginal artists and paintings by Queenslander Ian Fairweather.

An entrée to Queensland's history and cultural identity, the **Queensland Museum** (Map pp302–3; ☎ 07-3840 7555; www.southbank.qm.qld.gov .au; cnr Grey & Melbourne Sts, South Brisbane; admission free; ☟ 9.30am-5pm) houses a diverse range of displays including the Discover Queensland exhibition and the Museum Zoo, which houses over 700 prehistoric and modern animals from dung beetles to dinosaurs. Upstairs, there's a sobering display on Australia's endangered species and on the 4th floor is the museum's Dandiiri Maiwar Aboriginal and Torres Straits Islander Cultures Centre. Often packed with school kids is the very fun **Sciencentre** (www.southbank.qm.qld.gov.au/sciencentre; adult/child/family $11/8/33), a hands-on science exhibit with interactive displays and optical illusions. Blast out of the blocks and check your speed in the 10m interactive dash or make your own whirlpool at the water world exhibits – it's an educational funhouse.

SOUTH BANK PARKLANDS

Swarming with locals and day-trippers is **South Bank Parklands** (Map pp302–3; ☎ 07-3867 2051; www .visitsouthbank.com.au; admission free; ☟ sunrise-sunset) on the banks of the Brisbane River, an enormously popular family area with blooming arbours, cafes and restaurants, picnic spots, tropical gardens and walkways. Built on a former World Expo site, the scenic Clem Jones Promenade is the real winner here with spectacular views across the river to the CBD. In-line skaters, cyclists and skateboarders are permitted.

The latest attraction in the parklands is the **Wheel of Brisbane** (Map pp302–3; ☎ 07-3844 3464; www.worldtouristattractions.com.au; South Bank Parklands; adult/child/private $15/10/95; ☟ 10am-10pm Mon-Thu, 9am-midnight Fri & Sat, 9am-10pm Sun) with its London Eye–style prime riverfront views. The fully enclosed, air-conditioned capsules rise to nearly 60m but the experience is all over in 13 minutes. Book online for a 10% discount.

At the heart of the gardens is **Streets Beach** (Map pp302–3), an artificial subtropical swimming hole that ambles its way through the park before opening up into a vast lagoon. It even has its own lifeguards! Behind the beach, running parallel to the parklands, is **Little Stanley Street**, a lively strip of gourmet eateries, boutique shops and pubs.

The **Suncorp Piazza** (Map pp302–3) screens international sporting events, free movies during the school holidays and short films during festival periods. It also acts as a concert venue and a place for impromptu performances by street artists.

Naval enthusiasts will enjoy the **Queensland Maritime Museum** (Map pp302–3; ☎ 07-3844 5361; Sidon St, South Brisbane; adult/child/family $7/3.50/16; ☟ 9.30am-4.30pm, last entry 3.30pm). The highlight is the gigantic HMAS *Diamantina*, a restored WWII frigate that you can clamber aboard and explore.

To get to South Bank jump on a CityCat or Inner City Ferry (there are three jetties along the riverbank; see p327) or walk across the **Goodwill Bridge** that links South Bank to the City Botanic Gardens. Buses and trains also run here from Roma St or Central Stations.

Inner North
FORTITUDE VALLEY

Fortitude Valley is loud, proud and the place to party all night in Brisbane. The heart of the Valley is the **Brunswick Street Mall** (Map pp302–3), a pedestrianised strip where coffee shops thrive by day and bars buzz at night with live music and DJ beats. On weekends, bleary-eyed shoppers congregate for the **Valley Markets** (Brunswick St Mall & Chinatown Mall, Fortitude Valley; ☟ 8am-4pm Sat, to 5pm Sun).

At the Wickham St end of the mall is **McWhirter's Marketplace** (Map pp302–3), a Brisbane landmark with an impressive art-deco corner facade.

Running parallel to the Brunswick St Mall is **Chinatown** (Map pp302–3; Duncan St, Fortitude Valley), a compact but lively strip of affordable restaurants, Asian supermarkets and clothes boutiques.

The **Institute of Modern Art** (Map pp302–3; ☎ 07-3252 5750; www.ima.org.au; 420 Brunswick St, Fortitude Valley; admission free; ☟ 11am-5pm Tue, Wed, Fri & Sat, to 8pm Thu) is a not-for-profit gallery where all exhibitions are free of charge.

> **SAVING THE MUSIC**
>
> Musicians, live-music fans and club owners in Fortitude Valley united for the 'Save the Music' campaign in 1999 after residents of the flashy Sun apartments on Brunswick St complained about noise coming from the neighbouring Empire Hotel and Press Club. Archaic state-government restrictions on amplified noise favoured the complainants and nearly forced the closure of the venues. The entertainment industry rallied and a petition of more than 20,000 signatures was handed to the state government and Brisbane City Council – the start of a long campaign to protect the rights of artists.
>
> Eventually, seven years later in 2006, council introduced 'special entertainment precinct' zoning regulations for the region, the first of its kind in Australia. Valley venues are now exempt from noise restrictions covering the rest of the city, have their own 'music venues local law' regulated by council, and any new residential buildings require extensive noise insulation.

NEW FARM

Fashionable New Farm, just east of the Valley along Brunswick St, is bursting with coffee shops, wine bars and restaurants to cater for its new cashed-up residents. Further southeast heading towards the Brisbane River is **New Farm Park** (Map pp300–1), a spacious parkland with playgrounds, picnic areas and scenic river frontage.

On the eastern fringes of New Farm Park stands the **Brisbane Powerhouse** (Map pp300-1; ☎ 07-3358 8600; 119 Lamington St, New Farm; ☯ farmers market 6am-noon 2nd & 4th Sat every month), a former power station that's been superbly transformed into a contemporary arts centre. The Powerhouse hosts a range of visual arts and music and comedy performances, and has two restaurants. If you haven't got tickets for a show, it's still worth seeing the building for its rustic architecture, preserved graffiti walls and river views.

NEWSTEAD

Occupying a beautiful hilltop spot near the Brisbane River is the city's oldest domestic dwelling, picturesque **Newstead House** (Map p299; ☎ 07-3216 1846; www.newsteadhouse.com.au; Breakfast Creek Rd, Newstead; adult/child/family $4/2/10; ☯ 10am-4pm Mon-Fri, 2-5pm Sun). Built in 1846, the house is now a museum and the rooms are decorated with Victorian furnishings, antiques and period displays. The surrounding lawns offer lovely river views.

The excellent **Fireworks Gallery** (Map pp300-1; ☎ 07-3216 1250; 52a Doggett St, Newstead; ☯ 10am-6pm Mon-Fri, to 4pm Sat) is a commercial space dedicated to contemporary Australian and Aboriginal art. Life-size sculptures of emus made from barbed wire were on display when we passed through.

Mt Coot-tha Reserve

About 7km west of the city centre is Mt Coot-tha Reserve (Map p299), an expansive bush and parkland area peppered with picnic spots and more than 50km of trails for walkers, horse riders and cyclists.

A must-see is the lookout at the top of the mountain that brings spectacular views of Brisbane – on a clear day you can see all the way to Moreton Bay in the east and the Glass House Mountains to the west. The lookout is reached via Sir Samuel Griffith Dr and has wheelchair access.

Just north of the road to the lookout is the turn-off to **JC Slaughter Falls** (3.4km), reached by a short walking track. Also here is the **Aboriginal Art Trail** (1km circuit). If you have a car, or are an ambitious cyclist, then it's worth trying the road around the reserve for some very pretty vistas.

At the foot of the mountain are the lush **Brisbane Botanic Gardens** (☎ 07-3403 2535; admission free; ☯ 8.30am-5.30pm Sep-Mar, 8am-5pm Apr-Aug, free guided walks 11am & 1pm Mon-Sat),which extend for 52 hectares and include over 20,000 species of plants. It's a wonderful spot for a picnic (there are shaded areas and toilets) or ideal for simply wandering through the many gardens. Highlights include the fragrant plant and herb garden, tropical dome and bonsai house.

At the entrance to the gardens is the **Sir Thomas Brisbane Planetarium** (☎ 07-3403 2578; www .brisbane.qld.gov.au/planetarium; ☯ 10am-4.15pm Tue-Fri, 11am-8.15pm Sat, to 4.15pm Sun), the only standalone planetarium in Australia and a wonderland for budding Neil Armstrongs. The observatory has a variety of telescopes and one of the resident astronomers can help pinpoint stars and intergalactic beings. There are also regular shows inside the **Cosmic Skydome**

QUEENSLAND

(adult/child/family $12.70/7.40/34.20),which journey into outer space and are narrated by the likes of Harrison Ford and Ewan McGregor.

Bus 471 ($2.90, 25 minutes, hourly) runs from Adelaide St, opposite King George Sq and stops at the Botanic Gardens before continuing on to the lookout at Mt Coot-tha. The last bus returning to the city leaves at 4.10pm on weekdays and 5.05pm on weekends.

D'Aguilar Range

The mountain tops and forest flats of the D'Aguilar Range National Park (Map p328) provide a magnificent 50,000 hectare home for wildlife just 12km from the city centre. The range is a succession of protected areas comprising Brisbane Forest Park, Bunyaville and Mt Mee. Hidden within the natural bushland are remote gorges, expanses of subtropical rainforest and eucalypt woodland. The wildlife is rich with owls, bowerbirds, cockatoos and an estimated 90 species of reptiles and amphibians. There are numerous walking trails varying in length and degree of difficulty.

The **Brisbane Forest Park information centre** (☎ 1300 130 372; 60 Mt Nebo Rd; ☒ 9am-4.15pm Mon-Fri, to 4.30pm Sat & Sun) sits at the park entrance and has information about **bush camping** (per person/family $5/19) and maps of walking trails, but it does not sell camping permits. If you plan to camp then you must get your permit through the **EPA** (☎ 13 13 04; www.epa.qld.gov.au) before arrival and you'll need a vehicle – camping areas cannot be accessed by foot.

To get here catch bus 385 ($3.80, 30 minutes) from King George Sq bus station. The bus stops near the visitors centre and the last departure back to the city is at 4.48pm weekdays and at 3.53pm on weekends. The actual walking trails are a fair distance from the visitors centre, so if you're planning on attacking them it's best to have your own transport.

Wildlife Sanctuaries
LONE PINE KOALA SANCTUARY
Cuddling a koala at **Lone Pine** (Map p299; ☎ 07-3378 1366; www.koala.net; Jesmond Rd, Fig Tree Pocket; adult/child/family $20/15/52, photo with koala $15; ☒ 8.30am-5pm) and getting your photo taken with one of the cute, fuzzy creatures has long been a must-do when in southeast Queensland. Situated 11km southwest of the city centre, Lone Pine

was established in 1927 as the world's first koala sanctuary with just two koalas; these days there are 130 and it's still the world's largest sanctuary of its kind. You can hand-feed kangaroos and emus or get an up-close look at wombats, Tasmanian devils and other native animals. If you pack your lunch there are numerous picnic and barbecue areas on the beautiful 20-hectare riverside setting.

The most enjoyable way to get here is with **Mirimar Cruises** (Map pp302-3; ☎ 1300 729 742; adult/child/family incl park entry $50/30/145),which departs daily at 10am from the Queensland Cultural Centre pontoon on the boardwalk outside the State Library, next to Victoria Bridge, returning at 2.45pm.

Alternatively, express bus 430 ($3.40, 35 minutes) leaves hourly from platform B4 at Queen St Mall bus station between 8.45am and 3.40pm daily.

ALMA PARK ZOO
Lone Pine is not the only place where you can hang out with koalas in Brisbane. This friendly **zoo** (Map p328; ☎ 07-3204 6566; www.almaparkzoo.com.au; Alma Rd, Dakabin; adult/child/family $28/19/75; ☒ 9am-5pm, last entry 4pm) lies 28km north of the city centre off the Bruce Hwy (exit Boundary Rd) and is home to a large number of exotic and Australian animals. You can enter the koala enclosure at 2.30pm daily and take as many photos as you like for free, and if you're brave, hold a snake or baby crocodile at the reptile presentation (11.30am and 3pm). Baboons, a Malaysian sun bear and the latest addition of ring-tailed lemurs all hail from foreign shores. You can touch and feed many of the animals between 11am and 3pm – animal feed bags cost $3.

The zoo train (on the Caboolture line) runs from Central Station departing daily at 9.07am ($4.80, 45 minutes) and connects with the free zoo bus at Dakabin station. The bus departs the zoo at 1.30pm daily to connect with the 1.47pm service from Dakabin back to the city.

DAISY HILL KOALA CENTRE
The bushland of Daisy Hill is a vital koala habitat – these cute creatures have become a threatened species in the southeast Queensland bioregion. This conservation **centre** (Map p328; ☎ 1300 130 372; www.epa.qld.gov.au; Daisy Hill Rd, Daisy Hill Forest Reserve; admission free; ☒ 10am-4pm) is roughly 25km southeast of Brisbane. The surrounding area provides plenty of opportunity to spot koalas in the wild.

Getting here via public transport is not easy. Catch the Logan City bus 555 and change at the Hyperdome for buses 572 or 574; it's a 1.5km walk from where the bus drops you off to the entrance. You can also visit the centre with Araucaria Ecotours (p314).

ACTIVITIES

With average maximum temperatures in summer around 29°C and dropping to just 21°C in winter, Brisbane residents are largely outdoor types. The city centre, South Bank and surrounding areas are popular training grounds for joggers, cyclists, walkers and in-line skaters. Adventure sports lovers will feel right at home with renowned outdoor rock climbing sites and oodles of river-based activities.

Story Bridge Adventure Climb

Fast becoming a Brisbane must-do, the **bridge climb** (Map pp302-3; ☎ 1300 254 627; www .sbac.net.au; 170 Main St, Kangaroo Point; adult $89-130, child $75-110) offers breathtaking views of the city. Established in 2005, it is only the third licensed bridge climb experience in the world (the other two being in Sydney and Auckland) and you can climb at dawn, during the day, or at the recommended twilight time slot. The 900m climb takes place on the southern half of the bridge and reaches heights of 80m above the Brisbane River. Tours last 2½ hours and bookings are essential. Prices differ according to time of day, with twilight tours being the most expensive.

CityCat

Ditching the tourist bus and catching one of the sleek CityCat ferries down the Brisbane River has become the sightseeing journey of choice for visitors to the city. Passengers can stand on the open-air front deck of the blue, white and yellow catamarans and glide under the Story Bridge to South Bank and the city centre. They run every 15 to 30 minutes, between 5.40am and 11.45pm, from the University of Queensland in the southwest to Apollo Rd, Bulimba, and back (a little over one hour each way). There are 15 terminals in total including New Farm Park, North Quay (for the Queen St Mall), Riverside (for the CBD) and West End. The CityCats are wheelchair accessible at the University of Queensland, Guyatt Park, North Quay, South Bank 1 and 2, Hawthorne and Apollo Rd.

Cycling

Getting on your bike is a popular pursuit in Brisbane with more than 550km of bikeways – any of them on the riverside. Check out the city council's **Our Brisbane** (www.ourbrisbane.com/transport/bicycles) cycling website for the best bike routes, maps and general information.

Bicycles are allowed on Citytrains, except on weekdays during peak hours (7am to 9.30am going into the CBD and 3pm to 6.30pm heading out of the CBD). You can take bikes on CityCats and ferries for free.

Brisbane bike rentals:

Bicycle Revolution (Map pp300-1; ☎ 07-3342 7829; www.bicyclerevolution.org.au/wp; 294 Montague Rd, West End; per day $25) Friendly community shop with a great range of recycled bikes assembled by staff with reconditioned parts.

Riverlife Adventure Centre (Map pp302-3; ☎ 07-3891 5766; www.riverlife.com.au; Naval Stores, River Tce, Kangaroo Point; per 1½hr $15, per day $40) Range includes mountain, tandem and kick bikes (a bicycle-scooter hybrid).

Valet Cycle Hire (Map pp302-3; ☎ 0408 003 198; www.cyclebrisbane.com; Alice St entrance, City Botanic Gardens; 1st hr $18, extra hr $6, per day $42) All kinds of bikes including tandems and children's can be delivered to your door for a minimal charge.

Rock Climbing & Abseiling

A spectacular sight at night with its floodlit vertical rock face, the **Kangaroo Point Cliffs** (Map pp302-3) on the southern banks of the Brisbane River offer excellent outdoor climbing and abseiling during the day. The 20m cliffs are the result of extensive quarrying for about 150 years (1826–1976) and its distinctive stone was used in some of Brisbane's earliest buildings, such as the Commissariat Stores Building.

The **Riverlife Adventure Centre** (Map pp302-3; ☎ 07-3891 5766; www.riverlife.com.au; Naval Stores, River Tce, Kangaroo Point; per lesson $34; ⌚ rock climbing 5-6.30pm Fri-Sun, abseiling 3-4.30pm daily) is ideally located to provide lessons. **Adventures Around Brisbane** (☎ 07-3870 3223; www.adventuresaroundbrisbane.com.au; climbing $25; ⌚ 6-9pm Wed) holds rock-climbing introductory courses and meets at the base of the cliffs. It also has an introduction to abseiling course every Saturday from 8.30am to 11.30am.

Other operators:

Adventure Seekers (☎ 1300 855 859; www.adventureseekers.com.au) Runs abseiling and rock climbing at Kangaroo Point seven days a week at 8.30am, 1pm and 5.30pm. Book 24 hours in advance.

Urban Climb (Map pp300-1; ☎ 07-3844 2544; www
.urbanclimb.com; Unit 2, 220 Montague Rd, West End;
adult/child/family $18/16/88; ⊙ noon-10pm Mon-Fri,
10am-6pm Sat & Sun) Large indoor climbing wall.

Riverlife Adventure Centre

Opened in 2005, this diverse **centre** (Map pp302-3;
☎ 07-3891 5766; www.riverlife.com.au; Naval Stores, River
Tce, Kangaroo Point; ⊙ 9am-5pm Mon-Thu, to 10pm Fri
& Sat, to 7pm Sun) offers a wealth of river- and
land-based activities. Group kayaking lessons along the Brisbane River are held daily
at 1pm ($34), Tuesdays and Thursdays at
7pm ($45), or you can hire your own ($25 for
1½ hours). The paddle and prawns ($69; 1½
hours kayaking followed by beer and prawns
on the riverfront deck) on Friday nights
from 7pm gets rave reviews. On Thursdays
at noon you can participate in traditional
Aboriginal song and dance performances
(adult/child $45/25) with members of the
Nunukul, Yuggera, Yugimbir and Nugi
tribes. Performances ($65 per person) are
also held on Saturday at 7pm; bookings are
essential.

To get here catch the ferry to the Thornton
St ferry terminal and follow the signs south
along the river for 380m.

Swimming

A good central place for a quick (and free)
dip is the artificial Streets Beach (p307) on
the banks of the Brisbane River at South Bank.
Lifeguards are on duty from 7am to 7pm in
the warmer months, and until midnight in
December and January.

Other recommended swimming centres:
Ithaca Swimming Pool (Map pp300-1; ☎ 07-3369
2624; entrance on Caroline St, Paddington; adult/child
$4.10/3.90; ⊙ 5.30am-7pm Mon-Fri, 8am-6pm Sat
& Sun) Backpacker-friendly 25m outdoor pool opposite
Suncorp Stadium.
Splash Leisure Centenary Fitness Centre (Map
pp302-3; ☎ 07-3831 7665; 400 Gregory Tce, Spring Hill;
adult/child $5/4; ⊙ 5.30am-7.30pm Mon-Fri, 6.30am-
6pm Sat, 7am-6pm Sun) An Olympic-sized lap pool, kids'
pool and diving pool with high tower.

In-line Skating

Skaters reclaim the streets on Wednesday
nights with **Planet Inline** (☎ 07-3217 3571; www
.planetinline.com) skate tours starting at 7.15pm
from the top of the Goodwill Bridge ($15).
It also runs a Saturday morning breakfast
club tour ($15), and Sunday afternoon tours

that differ each week and last about three
hours ($15).

You can hire skates and equipment from
Skatebiz (Map pp302-3; ☎ 07-3220 0157; www.skate
biz.com.au; 101 Albert St, Brisbane; per 2/24hr $13/20;
⊙ 9am-5.30pm Mon-Thu, to 9pm Fri, to 4pm Sat,
10am-4pm Sun).
Riverlife Adventure Centre (Map pp302-3; ☎ 07-
3891 5766; www.riverlife.com.au; Naval Stores, River Tce,
Kangaroo Point) has in-line skate hire for $20 for
1½ hours or $40 for four hours.

Aboriginal Workshops

Learn how to make and paint your own didgeridoo or boomerang at **Indidge-n-Arts** (Map
pp300-1; ☎ 1800 893 896, 07-3846 0455; 270 Montague
Rd, West End; lessons $20-89; ⊙ 9am-5pm). You can
also learn traditional weaving and jewellery-
making techniques and the venue has an
art gallery with proceeds of sales returning directly to the artists. It also holds
Aboriginal cultural tours to Mt Coot-tha
(p308) where you can have a go at throwing
a boomerang.

Bowls

Lawn bowls has shed its traditional image
of cucumber sandwiches and ancient men
in white suits to become a popular weekend
activity for Brisbane's young and old. Leading
the charge is the **Merthyr Bowls Club** (Map pp300-1;
☎ 07-3358 1291; Oxlade Dr, New Farm; per person from $20),
on the banks of the Brisbane River. It's packed
at weekends with punters trying to bowl in a
straight line after a snag and a stubby, courtesy of the cheap Sunday arvo barbecue.

Other Activities

Relax and enjoy tranquillity as you exercise
with free **tai chi classes** in the Botanic Gardens
(p306) on Tuesdays and Thursdays from
12.30pm to 1.30pm. There are also classes
at 8am on Saturdays in New Farm Park ($5
per person).

Thrill seekers can take to the skies
over Brisbane with any of the following
companies:
Antique Airways (☎ 07-3204 1933; www.users
.bigpond.com/antiqueairways) Enjoy the rush of flying in
the open cockpit of a 1940s Tiger Moth plane from $125.
Fly Me to the Moon (☎ 07-3423 0400; www
.flymetothemoon.com.au) Balloon flights over Brisbane
from $298.
Ripcord Sky Divers (☎ 07-3399 3552; www.ripcord
-skydivers.com.au) Tandem and solo skydiving from $330.

QUEENSLAND

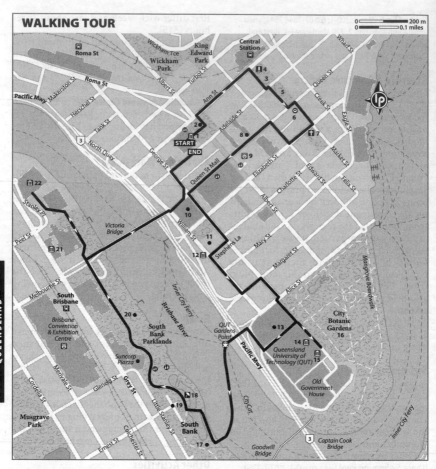

WALKING TOUR

The city centre and South Bank are relatively flat and walker-friendly. Taking a hike around the major retail strips, historic buildings and riverside landscapes is a great way to get your bearings. The city council produces the free *Brisbane's Living Heritage Network Experience Guide* (with a map of inner-city sights) and the *Gonewalking* brochure that lists more than 60 free walks conducted by volunteers and walk organisers. The following 5km to 6km walk takes anything from a couple of hours to a full day.

Start your expedition at the imposing classical-style **Brisbane City Hall (1**; p305), where you can buff up on the city's history and soak in the spectacular views from the top of the

bell tower. Walk through the recently redeveloped **King George Square (2)**, head up Ann St and cross Edward St into **Anzac Square (3)**, where city workers chill out on the grassy patches. At the northwestern end of the park, the **Shrine of Remembrance (4)** is a Greek Revivalist cenotaph where an eternal flame burns in remembrance of Australian soldiers who died in WWI.

Head over the pedestrian bridge at the eastern corner of the square, which connects Anzac Sq to **Post Office Square (5)**. Continue heading southeast, across Queen St, to Brisbane's magnificent, historic **General Post Office (6)**, which is still in use. Walk down the small alley that skirts the eastern side of the post office through to Elizabeth St. Cross the road and explore the beautiful **St Stephen's**

WALK FACTS

Start/finish Brisbane City Hall
Distance 5km to 6km
Duration two to five hours

Cathedral (7) and the adjoining St Stephen's Chapel. Built in 1850, the chapel is Brisbane's oldest church and was designed by English architect Augustus Pugin, who designed London's Houses of Parliament. The cathedral was built in 1874.

From the cathedral, head southwest down Elizabeth St, then turn right onto Edward St and left into the **Queen Street Mall (8)**. This busy pedestrian mall is the commercial centre of Brisbane, and is lined with fine facades dating back to Australia's federation, including the glorious frontage of the old **Regent Theatre (9)**.

Walk the length of Queen St Mall until you reach George St. Diagonally opposite you'll see the unmistakable Italian-Renaissance **Treasury Building (10**; p306), housing a casino. Turn left onto George St and you'll pass another building from the same era, the **Land Administration Building (11**; p306), now the Conrad Treasury hotel. Take the small alley just south of the hotel (Stephens Lane) onto William St and head right, passing the historic **Commissariat Stores Building (12**; p306).

Continue down William St, turn left up Margaret St and right onto George St. Cross Alice St to take in the splendour of Queensland's regal copper-topped **Parliament House (13**; p306). Further south is the impressive **QUT Art Museum (14)** and the **Old Government House (15)**, built in 1860. From here you can stroll through the **City Botanic Gardens (16**; p306) and take the weight off your feet for a while under a magnificent Moreton Bay fig.

Once rested, head back through the QUT campus towards the river and catch a ferry from QUT Gardens Point ferry stop to South Bank 2. This will land you at the southern end of the **South Bank Parklands (17**; p307). Meander north along the modernist walkway, past **Streets Beach (18**; p307) and **Stanley Street Plaza (19)**. Just beyond here, tucked away among the trees, is an ornate wooden **Nepalese Pagoda (20)**, built during the Brisbane 1988 Expo. Past the Queensland Cultural Centre, be sure to pop into the **Queensland Museum (21**; p307) and the **Queensland Gallery of Modern Art (22**; p306).

Once you've exhausted these, cross the Victoria Bridge back into the CBD, back past the former Treasury Building, turning left onto George St. Turn right onto Adelaide St and one block will land you back at your starting point at the Brisbane City Hall.

BRISBANE FOR CHILDREN

From toddlers to teenagers, there's no shortage of places to keep youngsters busy (and parents happy) in Brisbane.

The spacious inner-city parks are your best place to start. South Bank Parklands (p307) have a smattering of playgrounds and the Wheel of Brisbane (p307) would be the highlight of any kids' day out. Streets Beach (p307) is also located here with a shallow paddling pool for really small tots. In the **Roma Street Parkland** (Map pp302–3) there are free *Out and About with Bub* guided walks for parents and under fives every Wednesday and Friday at 10am, leaving from the Melange Café. **New Farm Park** (Map pp300–1) is another good option with its excellent playground, easily accessible via CityCat.

You can't go wrong taking the kids to South Bank. Always a big hit with the little ones is the Sciencentre (p307) in the Queensland Museum with its mind-boggling fun displays. The museum also runs entertaining educational activities during the school holidays for kids aged three to 14. The Queensland Gallery of Modern Art (p306) Children's Art Centre is a good educational option. It offers hands-on activities and workshops, and there are artist-run programs that introduce children to exhibitions on selected Sundays. **Hands on Art** (Map pp302–3; ☎ 07-3844 4589; www.handsonart.org.au; Boardwalk Riverkids Arts Centre, South Bank Parklands; admission free; ☯ 10am-5pm Mon-Fri school holidays, 10am-5pm Wed-Fri school days), at the southern end of the South Bank Parklands, is a nonprofit centre for innovative art activities where kids can get mucky with paint and clay. The centre caters for children aged four to 14 and bookings are essential.

Departing from outside the State Library at South Bank, a river cruise to the Lone Pine Koala Sanctuary (p309) is guaranteed to win parents brownie points.

If heading out Mt Coot-tha way, the Sir Thomas Brisbane Planetarium (p308) has a special children's show, *Secret of the Dragon*, a magical tale of two children taken on a dragon ride to explore the universe. It is showing on Saturdays and Sundays at 11.30am.

The **Brisbane City Council** (www.brisbane.qld.gov .au) runs Chill Out, a program of activities for 10 to 17 year olds during the school holidays including everything from adventure mountain biking to African drum making. During school term, check out www.ourbrisbane .com/lifestyle/topics/kids for the latest listings of activities.

For child-care listings see www.ourbrisbane .com/businesses/browse/all/6308 or contact the Child Care Information Service (p293).

TOURS
Brewery Tours
'Make it a XXXX mate.' Utter this famous phrase to any Brisbane bartender and you'll receive a pot of Queensland's finest golden nectar. If you reckon it's a good drop, get along to the **Castlemaine-Perkins XXXX Brewery** (Map pp300-1; ☎ 07-3361 7597; www.xxxx.com.au; cnr Black & Paten Sts, Milton; adult/child $20/12; ☺ tours 75min, every hr 10am-4pm Mon-Fri, plus 6pm Wed, 10.30am, 11am & noon Sat). The popularity of the XXXX tours among backpackers might have something to do with the four free pots of beer at the end of the tour (over 18s only) and you can stay in the Ale House bar for a few extra pots at regular prices. The brewery is a 20-minute walk west from the Roma Street Transit Centre or you can take the Citytrain to Milton station.

Brewers of VB, the **Carlton & United Brewhouse** (off Map p299; ☎ 07-3826 5858; www.carltonbrewhouse .com.au; cnr Darlington Dr & Cuthbert St, Yatala; adult/child $20/12; ☺ tours 10am, noon & 2pm Mon-Fri, noon & 2pm Sat) is 40km south of the city centre on the way to the Gold Coast. It is the largest brewery in Queensland producing 570 million litres of beer per year.

City Tours
Brisbane Lights Tours (☎ 07-3822 6028; adult/child from $60/25) Tour departs at 6.30pm nightly (pick-up from your hotel included in price) and covers a dozen city landmarks, dinner or refreshments at Mt Coot-tha Lookout and a CityCat cruise.

Brisbane Photo Walks (☎ 0433 745 533; www .brisbanephotowalks.com.au; 2hr tour & photo CD $150; ☺ 9am & 1pm Mon-Fri) Guided city tour with your own personal paparazzo to capture the moments. A CD of the photos is delivered to your hotel within 48 hours.

City Sights bus tour (Map pp302-3; ☎ 13 12 30; adult/child day ticket $25/20; ☺ every 45min 9am-3.45pm) Hop-on, hop-off bus departs from outside Post Office Sq (Queen St) and shuttles around 19 of the city's

major landmarks. Day tickets can be bought on the bus. The same ticket covers you for unlimited use of CityCat services.

Ghost Tours (☎ 07-3344 7265; www.ghost-tours.com .au; walking tours from $25, coach tours adult/child from $65/60) Visit alleged haunted sites and hear ghost stories on these spooky tours of Brisbane's city centre, cemeteries and the old Boggo Rd jail.

River Cruises
If a cruise on a CityCat leaves you wanting more, several companies run longer trips on the Brisbane River.

Kookaburra River Queens (Map pp302-3; ☎ 07-3221 1300; www.kookaburrariverqueens.com; lunch/ dinner cruise per person $55/75) Enjoy a seafood buffet lunch (two hours) or an evening meal (2½ hours) on a paddle wheeler as it coasts lazily up and down the river. Cruises depart from Eagle St Pier, on the eastern side of the city. Boarding is at 11.45am daily for the lunch cruise and at 7pm Sunday to Thursday (and public holidays) for the dinner cruise. On Friday and Saturday nights the evening cruise departs at 6.45pm ($10 extra).

Mirimar Cruises (Map pp302-3; ☎ 1300 729 742; www.mirimar.com; 90min cruise per adult/child/family $25/12/70, wildlife cruise $50/30/145) The *Mirimar* cruises 19km upstream to the Lone Pine Koala Sanctuary (p309) departing from the Queensland Cultural Centre pontoon outside the State Library at South Bank daily at 10am. You can take the one-way 90-minute cruise, or the return trip including entry to the sanctuary.

River City Cruises (Map pp302-3; ☎ 0428 278 473; www.rivercitycruises.com.au; South Bank Parklands Cruise Terminal Jetty A; adult/child/family $25/15/60; ☺ 10.30am & 12.30pm) Relax and enjoy the captain's commentary on these 90-minute cruises.

Hinterland Tours
Araucaria Ecotours (☎ 07-5544 1283; www.learna boutwildlife.com; adult/child from $88/58) Ecotours include birdwatching ($132), a three-day tour to World Heritage rainforests (from $418) and a weekend budget wildlife camp ($176).

Aries Tours (☎ 07-5594 9933; www.ariestours.com; adult/child from $80/40) The pick of the offerings from this ecocertified company is the glow-worm tour to Natural Bridge in Springbrook National Park.

Bushwacker Ecotours (☎ 1300 559 355, 07-3871 0057; www.bushwacker-ecotours.com.au; adult/child from $115/95) Day tours and overnight trips to southeast Queensland national parks.

FESTIVALS & EVENTS
Brisbane's most popular events and festivals are listed on the **city council's website** (www.our

brisbane.com/whats-on). The staff at the Brisbane Visitor Information & Booking Centre (p305) can help you with any enquiries.

January

Brisbane International (www.brisbaneinternational .com.au) Professional tennis tournament attracting the world's best, held prior to the Australian Open, at the new Queensland Tennis Centre.

Cockroach Races (www.cockroachraces.com.au) A hilarious Australia Day (26 January) tradition at the Story Bridge Hotel (see p321). Entrants are encouraged to bring their own roach, or you can choose from the house stable. Proceeds go to charity.

February

Chinese New Year Held in Fortitude Valley's Chinatown Mall; expect loads of firecrackers and dancing dragons.

Tropfest (www.tropfest.com) Nationwide short-film festival telecast live at the Suncorp Piazza at South Bank in late February.

March

Brisbane Comedy Festival Four-week festival featuring local and international comedians at the Brisbane Powerhouse.

April

Queensland Winter Racing Carnival (www.queens landracing.com.au) The state's major horse racing carnival held from early April to mid-July. The biggest day is the Stradbroke Handicap in early June.

May

Urban Country Festival (www.urbancountry.com.au) Four-day country music festival with up to 500 artists held 45 minutes north of Brisbane in Caboolture.

June

Brisbane Pride Festival (www.pridebrisbane.org.au) Brisbane's annual gay and lesbian celebration held over four weeks. Fair Day in mid-June features a parade through the city streets.

Out of the Box (www.outoftheboxfestival.com.au) Biennial festival of performing and visual art for kids aged three to eight. Held on even-numbered years.

July

Brisbane International Film Festival (www.biff.com .au) Ten days of quality films starting in late July.

Queensland Music Festival (www.queenslandmu sicfestival.com.au) Statewide festival with styles ranging from classical to contemporary, held over two weeks on odd-numbered years.

August

'Ekka' Royal National Agricultural Show (www .ekka.com.au) Country and city come together for Queensland's largest annual event, the Ekka. Plenty of animal pavilions, fun park rides and fashion shows.

September

Brisbane Riverfestival (www.riverfestival.com.au) Brisbane's major festival of the arts held over 10 days. Don't miss the spectacular Riverfire sky show on the Brisbane River.

Brisbane Writers Festival (www.brisbanewriters festival.com.au) Queensland's premier literary event.

National Festival of Beers (www.nfb.com.au) An annual event since 1990, this three-day booze-up is at the Story Bridge Hotel (see p321) in mid-September.

Valley Fiesta (www.valleyfiesta.com.au) Rock bands and dance acts take over Fortitude Valley's Brunswick St and Chinatown malls for Brisbane's biggest free festival of music.

October

Brisbane Cabaret Festival (www.brisbanecabaretfesti val.com) Dazzling 10-day event of sexy and slick performances in the city's best venues.

December

Christmas Festival (www.visitsouthbank.com.au) Three days of festive cheer held during the week before Christmas at South Bank.

SLEEPING

Comfortable and affordable accommodation options in Brisbane, particularly for budget travellers, have improved out of sight in recent years. New and renovated inner-city hostels, designed for the increasingly fussy flashpacker, have everything a traveller needs – they're central, modern, fun and secure. For those with slightly deeper pockets, the city centre has an excellent range of middle to top-end hotels close to the city sights and public transport connections.

If you're in Brisbane to party, head for Fortitude Valley or the strip of hostels on Upper Roma St, Petrie Terrace. New Farm is perfect if you want to be close to the Valley's pubs and clubs, but far enough away to ensure quiet surrounds. The midrange hotels around Spring Hill and Wickham Tce are walking distance to the city, but also reasonably quiet at night. Kangaroo Point is the place to stay if you're in town to see international cricket or Australian Rules football at the Gabba.

QUEENSLAND

The Brisbane Visitor Information & Booking Centre (p305) has brochures and information on accommodation in Brisbane and up and down the coast.

For the following listings, expect to pay more in December and January.

Budget

CITY CENTRE

Base Central (Map pp302-3; ☎ 1800 242 273, 07-3211 2433; www.stayatbase.com; 308 Edward St, Brisbane; dm $26-33, s $45, d & tw $70; ❄ 💻) Formerly Palace Backpackers, this massive 97-year-old building with a rickety old lift is overdue for an interior refurb and won't win awards for cleanliness, but can't be beaten for location. The basement level Down Under Bar & Grill (p321) is party central – dancing on tables is a nightly ritual.

Base Embassy (Map pp302-3; ☎ 1800 242 273, 07-3002 5777; www.stayatbase.com; 214 Elizabeth St, Brisbane; dm $28-33, d & tw $80-95; ❄ 💻) The sister hotel of Base Central, just five minutes' walk away.

Tinbilly (Map pp302-3; ☎ 1800 446 646, 07-3238 5888; www.tinbilly.com; 466 George St, Brisbane; dm $30-34, d & tw $115; ❄ 💻) Right across from the Roma Street Transit Centre, this brightly coloured party hostel has modern interiors and soundproof windows in rooms to block out traffic noise. In-room safes and internet terminals on three levels are a bonus. All the action is in the ground floor bar where food is served from 10am to 8.30pm.

FORTITUDE VALLEY & NEW FARM

Bunk Backpackers (Map pp302-3; ☎ 1800 682 865; www.bunkbrisbane.com.au; cnr Ann & Gipps Sts, Fortitude Valley; dm $27-31, s $76, d & tw $96, tr $110, loft apt $150; P ❄ 💻 🛗) Located within stumbling distance from the Valley's pubs and clubs, Bunk ticks all the boxes. Set in a mammoth building, rooms have a refreshing earthy feel with terracotta-coloured walls, impressive wooden floors and green bed linen. On the ground level there's a heated pool and spa, an awesome beer garden, and you can party all night at the adjoining Birdie Num Num nightclub.

Bowen Terrace (Map pp300-1; ☎ 07-3254 0458; www.bowentceaccommodation.com; 365 Bowen Tce, New Farm; s $38-40, d $60-70, deluxe $80-90; P 💻 🛗) A beautifully restored old home, this hotel is tucked away in a quiet area of New Farm. The friendly owners have installed TVs and bar fridges in every room and there's a lovely back deck overlooking the pool. Excellent value for money.

PETRIE TERRACE & UPPER ROMA STREET

Aussie Way Hostel (Map pp300-1; ☎ 07-3369 0711; http://users.bigpond.net.au/aussieway; 34 Cricket St, Petrie Terrace; dm/s/d $26/46/66; ❄ 💻) An old colonial home (built in 1872) converted into a hostel, Aussie Way is a reliable option with clinically clean, air-conditioned rooms. Guests love the swimming pool out the back and it's a short stroll to all the beer-fuelled shenanigans on Caxton St.

Banana Benders Backpackers (Map pp300-1; ☎ 07-3367 1157; www.bananabenders.com; 118 Petrie Tce, Petrie Terrace; dm $26-28, tw & d $64-70, 1-bedroom apt per week from $350; 💻) Anything but a party hostel, this chilled-out backpackers is super-friendly and features a back balcony with stunning views of the hilly surrounding suburbs. Dorms are spacious but some of the double rooms are on the small side. There's a job club here and it's also a WWOOF (Willing Workers on Organic Farms) agent.

Yellow Submarine (Map pp300-1; ☎ 07-3211 3424; www.yellowsubmarinebackpackers.com; 66 Quay St, Petrie Terrace; dm $27-29, tw/d $66/69; ❄ 💻 🛗) Never mind the graffitied walls and creaky staircases, Yellow Submarine is as homely as they come. The courtyard, barbecue area and swimming pool are fantastic in summer, and there's a log fireplace for cool winter nights. Some rooms have air-conditioning.

our pick **Chill Backpackers** (Map pp300-1; ☎ 1800 851 875, 07-3236 0088; www.chillbackpackers.com; 328 Upper Roma St, Brisbane; dm $28-35, d & tw $89, tr $105; P ❄ 💻) This garish aqua building on the CBD fringe delivers city and river views from its sun-lounge deck like no other Brisbane hostel. All rooms are super clean, modern and have shared bathrooms, and the kitchen is fully equipped. There's a movie room too, but you're better off kicking back with a cocktail on the fabulous deck.

More budget options:

Brisbane City Backpackers (Map pp300-1; ☎ 1800 062 572; www.citybackpackers.com; 380 Upper Roma St, Brisbane; dm $21-31, s $99, tw & d $79-99; ❄ 💻) Dirt-cheap dorms and free internet.

Brisbane City YHA (Map pp300-1; ☎ 07-3236 1004; www.yha.com.au; 392 Upper Roma St, Brisbane; dm $33, tw & d $78; P ❄ 💻) Recently renovated with 500 more beds.

Cloud 9 (Map pp300-1; ☎ 1800 256 839, 07-3236 2333; www.cloud9backpackers.com.au; 350 Upper Roma

St, Brisbane; dm $17-28; (💻) No single or double rooms here, only dorm rooms – some without windows.

SPRING HILL

Kookaburra Inn (Map pp302-3; ☎ 1800 733 533, 07-3832 1303; www.kookaburra-inn.com.au; 41 Phillips St, Spring Hill; s/d $55/72) The Kookaburra's rooms are a little tight on space but excellent value if you're looking for a quiet place close to the CBD. The 19 rooms all come with a fridge and ceiling fans, or you can pay a little extra for the air-conditioned double.

Annie's Inn (Map pp302-3; ☎ 07-3831 8684; 405 Upper Edward St, Spring Hill; s $65, d & tw $75-85) This pale pink and baby blue B&B is a gloriously kooky place somewhat reminiscent of staying with a mad great aunt. Old family portraits in the main hallway give a homely feel and the rooms, although a bit tired looking, are very cosy.

WEST END

Somewhere to Stay (Map pp300-1; ☎ 1800 812 398, 07-3846 2858; www.somewheretostay.com.au; 47 Brighton Rd, West End; dm $19-27, s $44-49, tw & d $54-84; 💻 🛏) Big and breezy, there are more than 50 rooms in this enormous white Queenslander home with a very laid-back vibe. Rooms are stock standard; the incredible hilltop views make you want to stay a little longer.

Brisbane Backpackers Resort (Map pp300-1; ☎ 1800 626 452, 07-3844 9956; www.brisbanebackpackers .com.au; 110 Vulture St, West End; dm $26-30, tw & d $84; P 🞩 💻 🛏) There's a cheery buzz around the reception and mess area/beer garden of this colourful hostel swarming with backpackers. Rooms have bathrooms, balconies and TVs; guests take full advantage of the large swimming pool and tennis court. The cafes and pubs of South Bank are very close by.

Midrange

FORTITUDE VALLEY

Central Brunswick Apartments (Map pp302-3; ☎ 07-3852 1411; www.centralbrunswickhotel.com.au; 455 Brunswick St, Fortitude Valley; r $120-150; P 🞩) These modern serviced apartments, a favourite with business travellers, have fully-equipped kitchens with microwaves and handy extras such as ironing boards and hairdryers. Meeting and function rooms are available; after the deals go down, guests head for the gym, sauna and spa.

UPPER ROMA STREET

Eton B&B (Map pp300-1; ☎ 07-3236 0115; www.eton.com .au; 436 Upper Roma St, Petrie Terrace; s $115, d & tw $125-145;

1-bedroom apt per week $595-700; P 🞩) If Upper Roma St's party hostels are not your cup of tea, head further along to this colonial-style home. There are five bedrooms (with en suites) and an attic apartment all decorated in heritage style. Travellers with laptops can use the wireless internet ($5 per day); the back courtyard garden is a relaxing spot to log on.

SPRING HILL

Soho Motel (Map pp302-3; ☎ 07-3831 7722; www.so hobrisbane.com.au; 333 Wickham Tce, Spring Hill; s from $99, tw & d from $112; P 🞩 💻) Rooms at Soho are bordering on the shoebox variety, but it's a good central option for shorter stays. Free wireless internet in every room and in-house movies (also free) are unusually generous benefits compared to most city hotels.

Best Western Gregory Terrace (Map pp302-3; ☎ 07-3832 1769; www.bestwestern.com.au/gregoryterrace; 397 Gregory Tce, Spring Hill; r $130-180; P 🞩 🛏) This rooms at this reliable chain option are a good option for families.

Dahrl Court Apartments (Map pp302-3; ☎ 07-3830 3400; www.dahrlcourt.com.au; 45 Phillips St, Spring Hill; apt $135, 1-/2-bedroom townhouse $150/165; P 🞩) These elegant self-contained apartments tucked away in a leafy corner of Spring Hill are some of the best in town. Tastefully decorated with modern kitchen appliances and designer bathrooms, they offer incredible value for money. For a private balcony or courtyard, upgrade to one of the town houses.

Inchcolm Hotel (Map pp302-3; ☎ 07-3226 8888; www .inchcolmhotel.com.au; 73 Wickham Tce, Spring Hill; r from $160; 🞩 🛏) This renovated block of medical offices has been restored into a very classy boutique hotel. The building is heritage listed – even the doors for the rooms are originals from the 1920s. All rooms have TVs, minibars and ultramodern bathrooms, and wireless internet is available on request. You've got to love a hotel with a rooftop swimming pool.

KANGAROO POINT

Southern Cross Motel & Apartments (Map pp302-3; ☎ 07-3391 2881; www.motelsoutherncross.com .au; 715-747 Main St, Kangaroo Point; s/d/tr $89/98/129; P 🞩) Location close to the Gabba is convenient for sports fans; Family-sized and studio apartments also available.

Kangaroo Point Apartments (Map pp300-1; ☎ 1800 676 855, 07-3391 6855; www.kangaroopoint .com; 819 Main St, Kangaroo Point; apt per night/week from $99/595; P 🞩 🛏) Super-slick and spotlessly clean, these four-star premium apartments have been given a thorough refurb. White tiles and shiny steel kitchen fittings give a sterile vibe; inviting sofas cosy things up. Spacious and downright luxurious.

Il Mondo (Map pp302-3; ☎ 07-3392 0111; www.il mondo.com.au; 23-35 Rotherham St, Kangaroo Point; r $129-169, apt from $189; P ⌘ 🖳 🖳) Corporate clientele shack up at Il Mondo, where self-contained units have been tastefully decorated with contemporary furniture and bold lashings of colour. Oddly enough, there's complimentary bicycle hire, but you won't need it to get to one of Brisbane's best pubs – the Story Bridge Hotel is just across the street.

PADDINGTON
Fern Cottage (Map pp300-1; ☎ 07-3511 6685; www .ferncottage.net; 89 Fernberg Rd, Paddington; s/d from $120/150; ⌘) Those preferring green suburban surrounds will adore this very homely B&B within a charming Queenslander house. There's a range of pretty bedrooms with individual outdoor patios. Your hosts, Geoff and Mary, also offer free wireless internet access.

ANNERLEY
Ridge Haven B&B (Map p299; ☎ 07-3391 7702; 374 Annerley Rd, Annerley; s $130-190, d $140-200; P ⌘) Located 10 minutes' drive south of the city, Ridge Haven B&B is set in a gorgeous Victorian home filled with old-world character. The owner, Morna, will make you feel welcome and loves to cook gourmet breakfasts. Free wireless internet access is a bonus.

Top End
Quay West Suites Brisbane (Map pp302-3; ☎ 1800 672 726, 07-3853 6000; reservations@qwsb.mirvac.com.au; 132 Alice St, Brisbane; apt from $189; P ⌘ 🖳 🖳) Half of the five-star apartments here are privately owned and have been finished to a standard worthy of the price tag. Every luxury imaginable is at your fingertips and the unobstructed views of the City Botanic Gardens are a special touch.

Conrad Treasury (Map pp302-3; ☎ 1800 506 889, 07-3306 8888; www.conradtreasury.com.au; 130 William St, Brisbane; r from $295; P ⌘) One for the high rollers, Conrad Treasury is as posh as they make them. This beautiful building, next to the casino, once housed the Land Administration Offices and has been carefully restored to its former opulent grandeur. Now darling, would you prefer the park or city view?

Also recommended:
Abbey Apartments (Map pp302-3; ☎ 07-3236 0600; www.abbeyhotel.com.au; 160 Roma St, Brisbane; 1-bedroom apt per night/week $200/980; P ⌘ 🖳 🖳) Plush CBD apartments; call for last-minute deals.
Stamford Plaza Brisbane (Map pp302-3; ☎ 07-3221 1999; www.stamford.com.au/spb; cnr Edward & Margaret Sts, Brisbane; r from $250; P ⌘ 🖳) Five-star luxury rooms plus a gymnasium, business centre and three restaurants.

Camping
Newmarket Gardens Caravan Park (Map p299; ☎ 07-3356 1458; www.newmarketgardens.com.au; 199 Ashgrove Ave, Ashgrove; unpowered/powered sites $28/30, caravans $47, cabins $81-101; P 🖳) Here at the closest caravan park to the city centre (4km north) there's room for 100 caravans, motorhomes and tents. You're all sorted for facilities: there's a laundromat, kiosk, internet terminals and wireless hot spot, even TV hire. Cabins have air-conditioning and are wheelchair accessible. Buses to the city centre stop right outside.

EATING
No need to drag the tables and chairs inside for winter: Brisbane's climate allows year-round outdoor dining. The city's restaurant scene has raised its sophistication level of late and many of the following eateries have spacious courtyards, gardens and open-air settings. Pricey, more conservative establishments can be found in the CBD; Fortitude Valley, New Farm and West End are where it's at for more adventurous, contemporary culinary spots.

City Centre
Govindas (Map pp302-3; ☎ 07-3210 0255; 1st fl, 99 Elizabeth St; Sun feasts $5; ✆ lunch Mon-Sat, dinner Fri, Sun feast from 5pm) Cheap and healthy Hare Krishna eats; expect to queue at lunchtime for the popular $10 all-you-can-eat vegetarian buffet. Smiley staff also serve snacks, salads and desserts.

Java Coast Café (Map pp302-3; ☎ 07-3211 3040; 340 George St; dishes $6-13; ✆ breakfast & lunch Mon-Fri) Huge Texas muffins at Java Coast are a scrummy bargain if you're on the go, or walk down the alley to the surprisingly spacious outdoor garden if you have time to chill. The gourmet burgers and salads are winners.

Spoon Deli Espresso (Map pp302-3; ☎ 07-3012 7322; cnr Albert & Charlotte Sts; dishes $7-15; ☽ breakfast & lunch) Breezy and unpretentious, this small health-food cafe serves up chunky fruit salads and vegie breakfasts for city workers. Watching what you eat? There are fresh juices and low-fat foods aplenty; tarts and slices too for a sugar hit.

Verve Café (Map pp302-3; ☎ 07-3221 5691; 109 Edward St; mains $15-21; ☽ lunch Mon-Fri, dinner Mon-Sat) This cavernous bar-cafe-restaurant where the cool kids hang has work by local artists for sale on the exposed brick walls. Food is modern Italian – blue-cheese risotto, and goats-cheese gnocchi are the big sellers. There's acoustic music on Thursday nights and DJs on Friday nights.

Customs House Brasserie (Map pp302-3; ☎ 07-3365 8921; 399 Queen St; mains $29-34; ☽ breakfast Sun, lunch daily, dinner Tue-Sat) Few restaurants in Brisbane have open-air settings quite like the majestic Customs House, overlooking the Brisbane River and Story Bridge. The Queensland prawn and crab tian with roasted tomato and avocado, and the seared scallops are divine options. Go on, splash out.

E'cco (Map pp302-3; ☎ 07-3831 8344; 100 Boundary St; mains $39-43; ☽ lunch Tue-Fri, dinner Tue-Sat) A slick bistro set within a converted tea warehouse near the Story Bridge, E'cco has won dozens of awards for its innovative, gourmet cuisine. Field mushrooms with olive toast, rocket, parmesan, truffle oil and lemon is the staff's recommendation from the menu.

There are several **food courts** (Map pp302-3; dishes $5-15; ☽ 9am-5pm; Broadway Centre lower fl; Myer Centre level E; Queens Plaza lower fl; Wintergarden Centre ground fl) serving up sushi, kebabs and dozens of international dishes. More take-away options are in Brisbane Sq, facing the Treasury casino.

Fortitude Valley & New Farm

Fatboy's Café (Map pp302-3; ☎ 07-3252 3789; 323 Brunswick St, Fortitude Valley; dishes $4-20; ☽ daily, 24hrs Fri-Sun) The $4 breakfast at Fatboy's is legendary: eggs, bacon, sausage, tomato and toast served any time (add just $1 after 5pm). It's easily the best value hangover cure in town and it's located smack bang in the action in the Brunswick St Mall.

Gertie's (Map pp300-1; ☎ 07-3358 5088; www.gerties .com.au; 699 Brunswick St, New Farm; dishes $6-16; ☽ dinner Tue-Thu, lunch & dinner Fri-Sun) A super-cool tapas bar and lounge, the massive bi-fold windows here offer a fabulous breezy feel. Best bets on the menu include the beef and oregano meatballs, and Peking duck rolls.

BurgerUrge (Map pp302-3; ☎ 07-3254 1655; 542 Brunswick St, New Farm; dishes $8-13; ☽ lunch & dinner Tue-Sun) A pint-sized gourmet burger bar with monster-size varieties; a popular choice is the lamb burger with grilled haloumi, caramelised onion, pesto and relish. Vegetarians devour the roasted aubergine burgers, with goats cheese and sun-dried tomatoes.

Lucky's Trattoria (Map pp302-3; ☎ 07-3252 2353; shop 14, Central Brunswick, 455 Brunswick St, Fortitude Valley; dishes $10-29; ☽ dinner 6pm-late) This gritty diner has been serving up authentic pasta and pizza in the Valley since 1974 and the original Italian owners still run the business. It's BYO and there's a bottle shop right next door.

Tibetan Kitchen (Map pp302-3; ☎ 07-3358 5906; 454 Brunswick St, Fortitude Valley; mains $12-15, banquets $24; ☽ dinner) Launch into a variety of zingy curries at this colourful restaurant serving Tibetan, Sherpa, Indian and Nepalese food. For larger groups, the banquet is the way to go. Afterwards, the Brunswick St Mall night-life is a short stroll downhill.

Continental Café (Map pp300-1; ☎ 07-3254 0377; 21 Barker St, New Farm; dishes $15-26; ☽ breakfast Sun, lunch & dinner daily) The 'Continental classics' menu is the popular pick at this busy European-themed cafe, including a delicious soy-lime chicken breast with coconut risotto and steamed bok choy. Tasty veg options include spinach lasagne with grilled spring vegetables.

Vespa Pizza (Map pp300-1; ☎ 07-3358 4100; 148 Merthyr Rd, New Farm; mains $18-20; ☽ lunch Fri, dinner daily) No chance of a boring selection like the big pizza chains here: Vespa's wood-fired varieties are certainly unique. Big sellers include the streaky bacon and red currant with camembert, and the cinnamon roast butternut pumpkin with dried chilli and feta.

our pick Garuva Hidden Tranquillity Restaurant & Bar (Map pp302-3; ☎ 07-3216 0124; www.garuva .com.au; 324 Wickham St, Fortitude Valley; mains $20; ☽ dinner) This genuine gem of the Valley restaurant scene has the ultimate chilled-out vibe: dimly lit private booths with cushioned seating are partitioned with white silk curtains. All dishes are the same price including the delicious lamb curry and warm Thai beef salad. The cocktail bar out the back is a good option if you missed out on a booking (essential).

Also recommended:

Spoon Deli Café (Map pp302-3; ☎ 07-3257 1750; 22 James St, Fortitude Valley; breakfast $10-19, mains $14-21; ☽ 5.30am-7pm Mon-Fri, to 6pm Sat & Sun) Upmarket deli with delicious salads and monster breakfasts.

Urban Grind (Map pp302-3; www.urbangrind.com. au; 530 Brunswick St, New Farm; ☽ breakfast & lunch Mon-Fri, breakfast Sat & Sun) Cute coffee house with a serve-yourself fruit toast counter and sun deck.

Wok On Inn (Map pp300-1; ☎ 07-3254 2546; 728 Brunswick St, New Farm; dishes $9-11; ☽ lunch & dinner Mon-Fri, dinner Sat & Sun) Simple, budget noodle bar with dishes cooked to order.

South Bank

Café San Marco (Map pp302-3; ☎ 07-3846 4334; South Bank Parklands; mains $17-25; ☽ lunch & dinner) Food and service matter little with a riverside location this good. If the food still matters, go for the rare peppered salmon with polenta crisp or the lemon peppered calamari. Smashing city views, too.

There's a small outdoor **food court** (Map pp302-3; South Bank Parklands), where you can pick up a cheapie lunch ($15 and under).

West End

Three Monkeys Coffee House (Map pp300-1; ☎ 07-3844 6045; 58 Mollison St; dishes $6-15) A family business for 14 years, Three Monkeys serves it up supersized – piping hot coffee and spicy chai come in soup bowls. Hide away in the cosy den, or wolf down your chocolate cake on the bench outside.

Gunshop Café (Map pp300-1; ☎ 07-3844 2241; 53 Mollison St; dishes $8-32; ☽ breakfast & lunch daily, dinner Tue-Sat) West End's gourmet breakfast specialists churn out potato-feta hash browns by the hundreds, particularly on weekends when this upmarket retro place is crammed. How about vodka cured ocean trout with poached eggs? There's great coffee, and a range of tasty beers and wines to wash it all down.

Lock'n'Load (Map pp300-1; ☎ 07-3844 0142; www .locknloadbistro.com.au; 142 Boundary St; mains $12-29; ☽ breakfast, lunch & dinner Tue-Sun) Pub-style grub goes down a treat at this bistro which also stocks a huge selection of international and Australian handcrafted beer brands. Live reggae, funk or soul music on Sundays.

Mondo Organics (Map pp300-1; ☎ 07-3844 1132; www.mondo-organics.com.au; 166 Hardgrave Rd; dishes $16-34; ☽ lunch & dinner Tue-Fri, dinner Sat) Doubling as an organic cooking school, you

know they're serious about quality produce at Mondo. It's an elegant, fine-dining setup (think crisp white linens) where you'll be served sustainable beef and lamb, or wild line-caught fish. Organic wines are served in Riedel crystalware: it's posh with a conscience.

Tukka (Map pp300-1; ☎ 07-3846 6333; www.tukkar estaurant.com.au; 145b Boundary St; mains $30; ☽ dinner) If you don't mind eating animals that are on Australia's coat of arms, this upmarket restaurant serves them up with flair. Emu and kangaroo fillet are mains, or for something lighter, chow down on the Tasmanian possum entrée. Tried crocodile? Here's your chance.

Paddington

Sassafras (Map pp300-1; ☎ 07-3369 0600; 88 Latrobe Tce; dishes $8-17; ☽ breakfast & lunch) This delightful little cafe, great for vegetarian options, has good-value meals for those on a tight budget. Scrambled tofu on Turkish bread goes down well, or the goats-cheese omelette with roast capsicum and spinach will fill the gaps.

Kookaburra Café (Map pp300-1; ☎ 07-3369 2400; 280 Given Tce; meals $12-30; ☽ lunch & dinner) A gigantic 50-piece pizza, supposedly Australia's biggest, is slightly oversized unless you're in a group of 10 (or attempting a Guinness world record), so lucky there's regular-sized pizza, pasta and salads here too. The outdoor courtyard makes dining in worthwhile.

Iceworks (Map pp300-1; ☎ 07-3367 9800; www.iceworks .com.au; cnr Given Tce & Dowse St; mains $16-28; ☽ lunch & dinner) You guessed it: this place was formerly an ice factory (1926–96) and reopened as a swanky bar-lounge-restaurant in 2008 with cool light-blue-and-white modern decor. Coffin Bay shucked oysters or Szechuan spiced calamari are popular shared-food options, or sit back with your sparkling white and gaze out through the enormous bi-fold windows towards Suncorp Stadium.

The bar menus at the **Caxton Hotel** (Map pp300-1; ☎ 07-3369 5544; 38 Caxton St; mains $20-35; ☽ lunch & dinner) and the **Paddo Tavern** (Map pp300-1; ☎ 07-3369 0044; 186 Given Tce; mains $12-20; ☽ lunch & dinner) offer good pub grub. The Paddo's $5.45 roast lunch (served seven days) is brilliant value.

Breakfast Creek

Breakfast Creek Hotel (Map p299; ☎ 07-3262 5988; 2 Kingsford Smith Dr; dishes $13-25, steaks $28-37; ☽ lunch

& dinner) A stunning French Renaissance–style building constructed in 1889, the Brekky Creek is probably Brisbane's most famous pub. It also cooks the best steaks in town (ask any local!); modern extensions to the old building offer excellent outdoor dining, perfect for demolishing a juicy grain-fed Wagyu rump.

Self-Catering

There's a **Coles Express** (Map pp302-3; Queen St) and a **Woolworths** (Map pp302-3; Edward St) in the city centre. In Fortitude Valley, there's a **Foodworks** (Map pp302-3; Brunswick St Station Mall) as you exit the train station, and a great produce market inside **McWhirter's Markets** (Map pp302-3; cnr Brunswick & Wickham Sts).

DRINKING

Many of Brisbane's best-known watering holes have been given major makeovers in recent times to introduce more outdoor seating, bigger beer gardens and slicker designs. Be aware there is an indoor smoking ban in place, and a 3am lockout at some bars. The best areas for pubs and bars are Fortitude Valley, New Farm, West End and Paddington. CBD bars cater mainly to the after-work crowd.

Bowery (Map pp302-3; ☎ 07-3252 0202; 676 Ann St, Fortitude Valley; ⏰ 5pm-3am Tue-Sun) Smartly dressed bartenders shake up deceptively potent cocktails at this multi-award-winning bar. The Bowery is long, thin and tight on space; cool inner-city types wedge themselves into booths as live jazz bands bust out tunes on a tiny stage near the entrance. Spruce up; door security can be snooty.

Press Club (Map pp302-3; ☎ 07-3852 1216; 339 Brunswick St, Fortitude Valley; ⏰ 7pm-late Mon & Tue, from 6pm Wed, Thu & Sun, from 5pm Fri & Sat) A huge leap forward in Brisbane bar design and decor when it first opened 10 years ago, Press Club still scrubs up OK against its sexy Valley rivals. Rich, maroon-coloured walls and leather seating banks provide a dark, sophisticated atmosphere, and the open-air courtyard is a welcome new addition. DJs most nights; occasional live funk and jazz bands.

Cru Bar & Cellar (Map pp302-3; ☎ 07-3252 2400; 22 James St, Fortitude Valley; ⏰ 11am-late Mon-Fri, 8.30am-1am Sat & Sun) A mind-boggling menu of 400 wines is on offer at this classy bar, which also features a very impressive on-site cellar for connoisseurs. Sommeliers can help you with

gourmet food and wine matching. It could be a little heavy on the wallet, but irresistible.

Lychee Lounge (Map pp300-1; ☎ 07-3846 0544; 2/94 Boundary St, West End; ⏰ 3pm-midnight Mon-Thu, to 1am Fri-Sun) This stylish little cocktail bar in West End's main drag pumps out jazzy lounge music all night long. Wacky designers were let loose on this place – barramundi-skin walls and Barbie-doll-head chandeliers are as quirky as it gets. Brilliant!

Belgian Beer Café (Map pp302-3; ☎ 07-3221 0199; cnr Edward & Mary Sts, Brisbane; ⏰ 11.30am-late) A brassy city-centre pub, there are 30 Belgian nectars to sample here with Hoegaarden, Leffe Blonde and others on tap. Bartenders recommend trying one of Belgium's premium golden pale ales, Duvel.

Alibi Room (Map pp300-1; ☎ 07-3358 6133; 720 Brunswick St, New Farm; ⏰ 8am-midnight Sun-Thu, to 1am Fri & Sat) Kitschy trinkets are scattered around this fun retro bar, which is a popular hangout for New Farm locals. The downstairs tiki bar houses Alibi's ultimate tacky attraction – a mini in-house waterfall.

Story Bridge Hotel (Map pp302-3; ☎ 07-3391 2266; 200 Main St, Kangaroo Point; ⏰ 10am-midnight Mon-Thu, to 1.30am Fri & Sat, 8am-midnight Sun) Situated under the Story Bridge, this giant hotel has three lively bars, a restaurant (great steaks!) and plenty of open breezy spaces. The swingin' Up The River jazz band have been the resident Sunday act for well over a decade – catch them from 3pm in the Outback Bar.

Caxton Hotel (Map pp300-1; ☎ 07-3369 5544; 38 Caxton St, Petrie Terrace; ⏰ 11.30am-late) Jersey-wearing sports lovers unite at the Caxton to watch rugby and cricket on big screens and have a sly punt on the ponies while they're there. It's a massive hotel, also serving pub grub. Security guys at the entrance might look you up and down and make you wait – just 'cause they can.

Sportsman's Hotel (Map pp302-3; ☎ 07-3831 2892; 130 Leichhardt St, Spring Hill; ⏰ 10am-late) A popular gay venue, this lively no-frills pub is famous for 'camp karaoke' and fabulous drag shows. There are also pool tables and hearty pub fare. On Leichhardt St, look out for the birdcagelike front smoking area.

Other places to wet your whistle:
Down Under Bar & Grill (Map pp302-3; ☎ 07-3002 5740; cnr Ann & Edward Sts, Brisbane; ⏰ 4pm-late Mon & Tue, from noon Wed-Fri, from 5pm Sat & Sun) So many backpackers dance on tables here, they've installed safety bars. Located under Base Central (p316).

QUEENSLAND

Normanby Hotel (Map pp300-1; ☎ 07-3831 3353; 1 Musgrave Rd, Red Hill; ⏲ 11am-midnight Mon & Tue, to 1am Wed & Thu, to 3am Fri-Sun) Classic old pub with an enormous beer garden.

Paddo Tavern (Map pp300-1; ☎ 07-3369 0044; 186 Given Tce, Paddington; ⏲ 10am-late) Saddle up for a beer and a steak at this massive pub where bar staff wear cowboy hats.

ENTERTAINMENT

Most touring international bands have Brisbane on their radar and the city's nightclubs regularly attract top-class DJs. Theatres, cinemas and other performing-arts venues are among Australia's biggest and best.

Pick up one of the free entertainment papers: **Time Off** (www.timeoff.com.au), **Rave** (www.ravemagazine.com.au) or **Scene** (www.scenemagazine.com.au). The fortnightly **Q news** (www.qnews.com.au) covers events on the gay and lesbian scene and **Queensland Pride** (www.qlp.e-p.net.au) takes in the whole of the state.

The **Courier-Mail** (www.news.com.au/courier mail) has daily arts and entertainment listings or otherwise check the **Brisbane Times** (www.brisbane times.com.au).

Ticketek (☎ 13 19 31; www.ticketek.com.au) is a centralised phone-booking agency that handles bookings for many of the major events, sports and performances. You can pick up tickets from the **Ticketek booth** (Map pp302-3; Elizabeth St), at the back of the Myer Centre, or at the South Bank visitor information centre (p305).

Nightclubs

Spruce up and head straight to Fortitude Valley for Brisbane's multilevel superclubs. Most are open Wednesday to Sunday nights – some are free to enter but others charge up to $20. If a big-name DJ is playing, tickets skyrocket. Photo ID is an absolute must and remember that some places are sticklers for dress codes. The 3am lockout is in force at most clubs.

Family (Map pp302-3; ☎ 07-3852 5000; www.the family.com.au; 8 McLachlan St, Fortitude Valley; ⏲ 9pm-5am Fri-Sun) Glam up baby: this four-level giant is Brisbane's biggest party nightclub. The main room pumps out trance, house and electro; international DJs are on the bill most Saturday nights. You might even see the occasional acrobat or percussion player accompanying the DJs. Sunday is 'fluffy' gay night.

Alhambra Lounge (Map pp302-3; ☎ 07-3216 0226; www.alhambralounge.com; 12 McLachlan St, Fortitude Valley; ⏲ 9pm-5am Thu-Sun) Next door to Family, this place caters to clubbers who have outgrown their glow sticks. Themed around a Spanish castle, the dark red interiors are filled with sofas and private booths. Tunes are typically break-beat, house and new-school funk.

Empire (Map pp302-3; ☎ 07-3852 1216; www.empire hotel.com.au; 339 Brunswick St, Fortitude Valley; ⏲ 5pm-3am Mon-Fri, noon-5am Sat & Sun) The Empire's street-level corner bar is a popular spot for kick-starting a night out. People who like their beats hard go upstairs to the moon bar for drum and bass.

Uber (Map pp300-1; ☎ 07-3846 6680; www.uber.net.au; 100 Boundary St, West End; ⏲ 7pm-late Wed-Sat) This superstylish club has free entry every night, which means you might catch an international touring DJ for nothing. The design is pure glamour with copper, stainless steel and dark wood fittings. The front bar is for lounging; hit the dance floor in the back room.

Beat Mega Club (Map pp302-3; ☎ 07-3852 2661; www.thebeatmegaclub.com.au; 677 Ann St, Fortitude Valley; ⏲ 8pm-5am) Every single night of the year, the Beat is open and firing on all cylinders. Popular with the gay and lesbian crowd, there are regular drag performances, five dance floors, six bars and some extremely hardcore techno. Free before 10.30pm.

More clubs:

Wickham Hotel (Map pp302-3; ☎ 07-3852 1301; 308 Wickham St, Fortitude Valley; ⏲ 10am-midnight Sun & Mon, to 2am Tue-Thu, to 5am Fri & Sat) Brisbane's most popular gay and lesbian venue; there are drag shows Tuesday to Friday nights.

Zuri (Map pp302-3; ☎ 07-3257 4999; www.zuri.com.au; 1/367 Brunswick St, Fortitude Valley; ⏲ 5.30pm-1am Wed & Thu, 4.30pm-4am Fri, 6.30pm-4am Sat, 4.30pm-midnight Sun) Lavishly decorated wine and cocktail bar.

Birdie Num Num (Map pp302-3; ☎ 07-3257 3644; www.birdeenumnum.com.au; 608 Ann St, Fortitude Valley; ⏲ 2pm-1am Sun-Thu, to 5am Fri & Sat) Part of the Bunk Backpackers complex, it's filled with backpackers and students nightly.

Cinemas

The **Palace Centro** (Map pp302-3; ☎ 07-3852 4488; 39 James St, Fortitude Valley) plays good art-house films and the cheapest cinema for mainstream flicks is **South Bank Cinema** (Map pp302-3; ☎ 07-3846 5188; cnr Grey & Ernest Sts, South Bank).

Catch an outdoor flick at the **Brisbane Powerhouse** (Map pp300-1; www.brisbanepowerhouse .org; 119 Lamington St, New Farm) during the summer months courtesy of the **Moonlight Cinema** (☎ 1300 551 908; www.moonlight.com.au).

Mainstream cinemas on Queen St Mall:

Birch, Carroll & Coyle (Map pp302-3; ☎ 07-3027 9999; 3rd fl, Myer Centre, Queen St Mall, Brisbane) Mainstream blockbusters.

Regent Cinema (Map pp302-3; ☎ 07-3027 9999; 167 Queen St, Brisbane) A classic gothic cinema worth visiting for the building alone.

Theatre

South Bank's venues stage most of the mainstream productions, but there are some excellent more intimate theatres around the inner city. The **Queensland Cultural Centre** (☎ 13 62 46) has a 24-hour phone line that handles bookings for events at South Bank theatres and other venues and events nationally.

Queensland Performing Arts Centre (Map pp302-3; ☎ 07-3840 7444; www.qpac.com.au; cnr Grey & Melbourne Sts, South Bank; Ⓟ) Blockbuster musicals, orchestral performances, dance and other theatre is staged at this colossal centre. There are four world-class concert venues for everything from French ballet to *Chicago*.

Brisbane Powerhouse (Map pp300-1; ☎ 07-3358 8622; box office 07-3358 8600; www.brisbanepowerhouse .org; 119 Lamington St, New Farm; Ⓟ ☒) Emerging theatre and visual arts are performed within the graffitied walls of the robust Powerhouse building. Photography displays, cabaret feasts, live comedy and experimental music are regular features here.

Queensland Conservatorium (Map pp302-3; ☎ 07-3735 6241; 16 Russell St, South Bank) The delicate notes of violins and dramatic crescendos of orchestral drums ring out from the Conservatorium, also the state's leading classical music school. Located at South Bank, it presents around 200 performances a year including jazz and opera.

La Boite Theatre Company (Map pp300-1; ☎ 07-3007 8600; www.laboite.com.au; Roundhouse Theatre, 6-8 Musk Ave, Kelvin Grove) This intimate venue was purpose-built for theatre-in-the-round. The company produces plays by Australian and international playwrights; ask about discounts for under-30s.

Judith Wright Centre of Contemporary Arts (Map pp302-3; ☎ 07-3872 9000; www.judithwrightcentre.com; 420 Brunswick St, Fortitude Valley) A medium-sized (300 seats maximum) creative space for

cutting-edge performances: contemporary dance and world music, Indigenous theatre, circus and visual arts.

Also recommended:

Brisbane Arts Theatre (Map pp300-1; ☎ 07-3369 2344; 210 Petrie Tce, Petrie Terrace) Small community theatre; catch improvisation troupes, children's theatre or classic plays.

QUT Gardens Theatre (Map pp302-3; ☎ 07-3138 4455; Queensland University of Technology, 2 George St, Brisbane; Ⓟ) Set within a university campus, productions are anything but amateur. Expect to see Australia's best professional stage actors.

Live Music

Local acts the Grates, Shane Nicholson and Katie Noonan have been flying the flag for Brisbane on the national music scene in recent years. Fortitude Valley has the majority of Brisbane's rock and dance venues, though there are a few others in West End, New Farm and Kangaroo Point. Smaller venues have free entry, but expect to pay anything from $6 to $30 for live gigs and significantly more for international touring bands.

Zoo (Map pp302-3; ☎ 07-3854 1381; 711 Ann St, Fortitude Valley) A long-standing supporter of independent music: most touring Australian bands have earned their stripes playing the Zoo at some stage in their career. A midsized venue with a well-raised stage, acts range from hip hop, rock and dub to acoustic, folk and reggae.

Ric's Café (Map pp302-3; ☎ 07-3854 1772; 321 Brunswick St, Fortitude Valley) Squeeze in if you can: this tiny but very cool venue in the Brunswick St Mall has indie, rock and acoustic acts playing every night of the week. There's outside seating and a balcony upstairs for some breathing space.

Troubadour (Map pp302-3; ☎ 07-3252 2626; 2nd fl, 322 Brunswick St, Fortitude Valley; ☒ Wed-Sun) Fitted out with grimy old lounges and plenty of kitsch art, this intimate venue is a great place to catch solo and acoustic artists.

Tongue & Groove (Map pp300-1; ☎ 07-3846 0334; 63 Hardgrave Rd, West End) A cool but unpretentious bar boasting an eclectic line-up of music playing its basement-level stage. You'll hear blues, jazz, funk and maybe a few killer dance beats.

Tivoli (Map pp300-1; ☎ 07-3852 1711; 52 Costin St, Fortitude Valley) International artists such as Nick Cave and Noel Gallagher have graced

QUEENSLAND

BRIS-BAND'S WALK OF FAME

It won't ever match Hollywood Blvd for glamour but Brisbane's Brunswick St Mall has its very own **Valley Walk of Fame** honouring the city's seminal and most successful musical acts. Located at the top of the mall, near the Royal George pub, are 10 plaques for bands that called Brisbane home, at least for the formative years of their careers. Long before the tight pants and disco beats of *Saturday Night Fever*, the **Bee Gees** lived just north of Brisbane in Redcliffe where they honed their harmonies from 1958 until cracking the UK charts in the mid-'60s. Punk legends the **Saints** formed here in 1974, a band Bob Geldof is quoted as saying 'changed rock music in the '70s' along with the Sex Pistols and the Ramones. The **Go-Betweens** were an internationally influential rock band during the 1980s and were the first band chosen for the Walk of Fame following the untimely death of Brisbane-based singer Grant McLennan in 2006. Another singer not known for his Brisbane roots, **Keith Urban** grew up just north of the city in Caboolture. He started winning talent quests there at age eight and more recently, won a Grammy Award in 2008 for Best Male Country Vocal Performance. Popsters **Savage Garden** formed in 1993 after guitarist Daniel Jones placed an ad in a Brisbane street press magazine. Singer Darren Hayes responded and together they went on to sell 25 million albums worldwide. Other bands on the Walk of Fame include 15-time ARIA-award-winning rock band **Powderfinger**, electro-rockers **Regurgitator**, '90s indie band **Custard**, '70s group **Railroad Gin** and local act **Blowhard**.

---

the stage at this elegant, old art deco venue built in the early 20th century. Hosting a range of touring acts, you're likely to see quality comedy here, too.

Brisbane Jazz Club (Map pp302-3; ☎ 07-3391 2006; 1 Annie St, Kangaroo Point; cover $10-15) Perched on the riverside, this little old wooden boatshed comes alive at night as Brisbane's best port for traditional, swing and contemporary jazz. Known for its friendly atmosphere and lively gigs, the club hosts all the big names in jazz. Views from the river deck are magnificent.

Brisbane Convention & Exhibition Centre (Map pp302-3; ☎ 07-3308 3000; cnr Merivale & Glenelg Sts, South Bank; P) Brisbane's largest multifunctional entertainment complex.

More live-music venues:

Brisbane Powerhouse (Map pp300-1; ☎ 07-3358 8600; 119 Lamington St, New Farm) Has live music on Sunday afternoons.

Globe (Map pp302-3; ☎ 1300 762 545; 220 Brunswick St, Fortitude Valley) An old cinema converted into a live-music venue; gigs on weekends.

Sport

Brisbanites are fanatical about sport, particularly the variety that involves 'wielding the willow' and 'bowling a bouncer'. At the start of every summer, the first international test cricket match of the season is always played at the famous **Gabba** (Map pp300-1; ☎ 07-3008 6166; www.thegabba.org.au; Vulture St, Woolloongabba) ground. The drama unfolds over five days, or there are shorter versions of the game to

check out. One-day internationals and the slog-fest Twenty20 matches (lasting about three hours) are usually played between January and March.

The Gabba is also a home ground for the Brisbane Lions, an Australian Football League (AFL) team. Watch them in action, often at night under lights, between March and September.

One of the fiercest rivalries in Australian sport is the State of Origin rugby league match held at least once a year at the 'cauldron', **Suncorp Stadium** (Map pp300-1; ☎ 07-3331 5000; www.suncorpstadium.com.au; Castlemaine St, Milton), between the mighty maroons (Queensland) and the blues (NSW). The local rugby league team, the Brisbane Broncos, play home games at Suncorp Stadium and it also hosts international tests.

The Queensland Reds, the state's rugby union team, contests the Super 14 competition at Suncorp against provincial sides from Australia, New Zealand and South Africa between March and May.

Also calling Suncorp home is the Queensland Roar soccer (football) team, attracting massive crowds in recent years. The domestic soccer season lasts from August to February.

The new **Queensland Tennis Centre** (Map p299; ☎ 07-3120 7999; www.queenslandtenniscentre.com.au; 190 King Arthur Tce, Tennyson), featuring the 5500-seat Pat Rafter Arena, hosts the Brisbane International in January.

QUEENSLAND

SHOPPING

Lovers of fashion can splash out at a range of high-end boutiques and designer stores in Brisbane. The Queen St Mall and Myer Centre in the CBD have large chain stores, upmarket outlets and the obligatory tourist tat. Smaller independent and specialist shops are in Fortitude Valley.

Tribal Galleries (Map pp302-3; ☎ 07-3236 1700; 376 George St, Brisbane) There are Indigenous artefacts aplenty here, including didgeridoos that the staff claim have been hollowed the proper way – by termites. Works come with a certificate of authenticity and the money goes straight back to the artist.

TCB on Brunswick (Map pp302-3; ☎ 07-3231 1367; 315 Brunswick St, Fortitude Valley) An arcade of chic boutiques between the Brunswick St and Chinatown malls, TCB is the place to find too-cool-for-school streetwear, shoes and sunglasses. Occasionally you'll find displays of emerging fashion designed by university students.

(M)art & Gallery Artisan (Map pp302-3; ☎ 07-3215 0808; 381 Brunswick St, Fortitude Valley) A creative wonderland of one-off and obscure pieces made by Queensland and other Australian designers. Choose from designer jewellery, accessories and ceramics.

Emporium (Map pp300-1; 1000 Ann St, Fortitude Valley) This retail centre has more than 35 boutique shops and eateries. Check out Coaldrake's, a well-stocked family-owned bookshop with an espresso bar, or grab a Turkish pizza at Mecca Bah.

Blonde Venus (Map pp302-3; ☎ 07-3216 1735; 707 Ann St, Fortitude Valley) This boutique outlet for women stocks up-and-coming Australian designers such as Dhini, Carl Kapp and Arnsdorf. Great for unique, cutting-edge styles.

Globe Trekker (Map pp302-3; ☎ 07-3221 4476; 142 Albert St, Brisbane) Excellent selection of outdoor gear including tents, sleeping bags, backpacks and camping equipment.

Markets

Valley Markets (Map pp302-3; Brunswick St Mall & Chinatown Mall, Fortitude Valley; ☑ 8am-4pm Sat, 9am-4pm Sun) Hang with the hungover locals at these very cool, and often packed, markets. Perfect for secondhand clothes, books, CDs and jewellery.

South Bank Lifestyles Markets (Map pp302-3; South Bank Parklands; ☑ 5-10pm Fri, 11am-5pm Sat, 9am-5pm Sun) This tourist market is full of boomer-angs, stuffed kangaroos, tarot readers and opal traders.

West End Green Flea Markets (Map pp300-1; Davies Park, cnr Montague Rd & Jane St, West End; ☑ 6am-2pm Sat) A delightfully hippy market where organic foods, gourmet stalls, herbs and flowers jostle for space with bric-a-brac and buskers.

Jan Power's Farmers Market (Map pp300-1; Brisbane Powerhouse, 119 Lamington St, New Farm; ☑ 6am-noon 2nd & 4th Sat of month) Fancy some purple carrots or blue bananas? This market, with more than 100 stalls, has some of the most unusual produce available. Also great for regular coloured flowers, cheeses, coffees and fish.

Riverside Centre Market (Map pp302-3; Riverside Centre, 123 Eagle St, Brisbane; ☑ 7am-4pm Sun) Good craft stalls, including glassware, metalwork and photography.

GETTING THERE & AWAY

Air

Brisbane's main airport (Map p299) is about 16km northeast of the city centre at Eagle Farm and has separate international and domestic terminals about 2km apart, linked by the **Airtrain** (☎ 07-3215 5000; www.airtrain.com.au; per person $4; ☑ every 30min 6am-8pm). From the international terminal there are frequent flights to Asia, Europe, the Pacific Islands, North America, New Zealand and Papua New Guinea. See p1046 for details of international airlines that service Brisbane.

Domestic airlines servicing Brisbane include **Qantas** (Map pp302-3; ☎ 13 13 13; www.qantas.com.au; 247 Adelaide St, Brisbane; ☑ 8.30am-5pm Mon-Fri, 9am-1pm Sat), **Virgin Blue** (☎ 13 67 89; www.virginblue.com.au), **Jetstar** (☎ 13 15 38; www.jetstar.com.au) and **Tiger Airways** (☎ 03-9335 3033; www.tigerairways.com).

Bus

Brisbane's main terminus and booking office for all long-distance buses and trains is the **Roma Street Transit Centre** (Map pp302-3; Roma St, Brisbane), about 500m west of the city centre. The centre has an accommodation booking service, shops and food outlets.

You'll find booking desks for the bus companies on the third level of the centre. **Greyhound Australia** (☎ 1300 GREYHOUND/1300 473 946, 07-3236 3035; www.greyhound.com.au) is the main company on the Sydney–Brisbane run ($140, 17 hours), but **Premier Motor Service** (☎ 13 34 10; www.premierms.com.au) often has considerably cheaper deals on this route. You can

QUEENSLAND

also travel between Brisbane and Melbourne ($220, 28 to 33 hours) or Adelaide ($290, 39 to 43 hours), although competitive airfares may enable you to fly for the same price or less.

Destination	Price ($)	Duration (hr)
Airlie Beach	200	18
Bundaberg	85	7
Cairns	280	30
Hervey Bay	65	6
Longreach	150	17
Mackay	180	17
Noosa Heads	55	2½
Rockhampton	100	12
Surfers Paradise	30	1½
Townsville	250	23

Car & Motorcycle

There are several major routes into and out of the Brisbane metropolitan area. The major north–south route, the M1, connects the Pacific Motorway in the south with the Bruce Hwy in the north.

Coming from the Gold Coast, the Pacific Motorway splits into two at Eight Mile Plains. From here, the South East Freeway (M3) runs right into the centre, skirting along the riverfront on the western side of the CBD, before emerging on the far side as the Gympie Arterial Rd.

If you're just passing through, take the Gateway Motorway (M1) at Eight Mile Plains, which bypasses the city centre to the east and crosses the Brisbane River at the Gateway Bridge ($2.90 toll). From either direction, the Eagle Farm exit on the northern side of the bridge provides a quick route to Fortitude Valley and the city centre. Just north is the turn-off to Brisbane airport. The Gateway Motorway and Gympie Arterial Rd meet in Bald Hills, just south of the Pine River, and merge to form the Bruce Hwy.

HIRE

All of the major companies – **Hertz** (☎ 13 30 39), **Avis** (☎ 13 63 33), **Budget** (☎ 1300 362 848), **Europcar** (☎ 1300 131 390) and **Thrifty** (☎ 1300 367 227) – have offices at the Brisbane airport terminals and throughout the city.

There are also some smaller companies in Brisbane, which advertise cheaper deals:
Abel Rent A Car (Map pp302–3; ☎ 1800 131 429, 07-3236 1225; www.abel.com.au; ground fl, Roma Street Transit Centre, Brisbane)

Ace Rental Cars (Map p299; ☎ 1800 620 408, 07-3862 2158; www.acerentals.com.au; 330 Nudgee Rd, Hendra)

Train

The **Roma Street Transit Centre** (Map pp302–3; Roma St, Brisbane) is Brisbane's main station for long-distance trains. For any information and reservations, call into the **Queensland Rail Travel Centre** (☎ 13 16 17; www.qr.com.au; Central Station Map pp302–3; ☎ 07-3235 1323; ground fl, Central Station, 305 Edward St, Brisbane; ☺ 8am-5pm Mon-Fri; Roma Street Transit Centre Map pp302–3; ☎ 07-3235 1331; Roma St, Brisbane; ☺ 6.30am-5pm Mon-Fri, 6.30am-1pm Sat, 6.30-11am Sun). It is also possible to make reservations online or over the phone.

CountryLink (☎ 13 22 32; www.countrylink.info.au) has a daily XPT (express passenger train) service between Sydney and Brisbane (economy/1st class/sleeper $135/155/235). The northbound service runs overnight, and the southbound service runs during the day. Each one takes 14 hours.

Concessions are available for children under 16 years, students with a valid ISIC card and senior citizens.

Services within Queensland:
Spirit of the Outback Brisbane to Longreach via Rockhampton twice weekly (economy seat/economy sleeper/1st-class sleeper $185/240/375, 24 hours).

Sunlander Brisbane to Cairns via Townsville (economy seat/economy sleeper/1st-class sleeper/Queenslander class $210/270/415/760, 30 hours). The exclusive Queenslander class includes restaurant meals and historical commentary.

Tilt Train Brisbane to Cairns (business seat only $310, 24 hours) and Brisbane to Rockhampton (economy seat/business seat $100/155, eight hours).

Westlander Brisbane to Charleville via Roma (economy seat/economy sleeper/1st-class sleeper $100/160/245, 17 hours).

GETTING AROUND

Brisbane boasts an efficient public transport network. Information on bus, train and ferry routes and connections can be obtained by calling **TransLink** (☎ 13 12 30; www.translink.com.au; ☺ 24hr).

Bus and ferry information is available at the Brisbane Visitor Information & Booking Centre (p305), the information centre at the Queen St Mall bus station (Map pp302–3), King George Sq bus station (Map pp302–3) and the Queensland Rail Travel Centre (above).

Fares on buses, trains and ferries operate on a zone system. There are 23 zones in total, but the city centre and most of the inner-city suburbs fall within Zone 1, which translates into a single fare of $2.40/1.20 per adult/child.

If you're going to be using public transport more than once on any single day, it's worth getting a **daily ticket** (zone 1 adult/child $4.80/2.40, zone 2 $5.80/2.90, zone 3 $6.80/3.40), which allows you unlimited transport on all buses, trains and ferries.

You can also purchase **off-peak daily tickets** (zone 1 adult/child $3.60/1.80, zone 2 $4.40/2.20, zone 3 $5.10/2.60), which allow unlimited transport but only between 9am and 3.30pm and after 7pm from Monday to Friday, and all weekend.

A pre-paid **Go Card** (adult/child $10/5) can be purchased and topped up at the information centres and convenience stores.

To/From the Airport

The easiest way to get to and from the airport is the **Airtrain** (☎ 1800 119 091; www.airtrain .com.au; ticket $14; ☻ every 30min 5.20am-8pm Mon-Fri, 6am-8pm Sat & Sun), which runs between the airport and the Roma Street Transit Centre (p325) and Central Station. There are also half-hourly services to the airport from Gold Coast Citytrain stops. **Coachtrans** (☎ 07-3358 9700; www.coachtrans.com.au) runs the half-hourly **Skytrans** (per adult/child to city $12/8, to Gold Coast accommodation $39/18; ☻ 5.45am-midnight) shuttle bus between the airport, Brisbane and the Gold Coast. A taxi into the centre from the airport will cost around $35.

Boat

In addition to the CityCats (p310), the Inner City Ferries zigzag back and forth across the river between North Quay, near the Victoria Bridge, and Mowbray Park. Services start at 6am and run till about 11pm. There are also several cross-river ferries; most useful is the Eagle St Pier to Thornton St (Kangaroo Point) service.

Like all public transport, fares are based on zones (zone 1 adult/child $2.40/1.80, daily ticket $4.80/2.40).

Bus

The Loop, a free bus service that circles the city area – stopping at QUT, Queen St Mall, City Botanic Gardens, Central Station and Riverside – runs every 10 minutes on weekdays between 7am and 6pm.

The main stop for local buses is in the underground Queen St Mall bus station (Map pp302–3), where there's an information

centre, and King George Sq bus station (Map pp302–3). You can also pick up many buses from the colour-coded stops along Adelaide St, between George and Edward Sts.

Buses generally run every 10 to 30 minutes Monday to Friday, from 5am till about 11pm, and with the same frequency on Saturday morning (starting at 6am). Services are less frequent at other times, and cease at 9pm Sunday and midnight on other days.

Car & Motorcycle

There is ticketed two-hour parking on many streets in the CBD and in the inner suburbs, but the major thoroughfares become clearways (ie parking is prohibited) during the morning and afternoon peak hours. If you do park in the street, pay close attention to the times on the parking signs, as Brisbane's parking inspectors take no prisoners. Parking is cheaper around South Bank than the city centre but is free in the CBD during the evening.

Taxi

It's easy to find a cab around the city centre during the day. There are taxi ranks at the transit centre and at the top end of Edward St, by the junction with Adelaide St. You might have a tough time hailing one late at night in Fortitude Valley. There's a rank near the corner of Brunswick and Ann Sts, but expect queues to get longer the later it gets.

The two major taxi companies here are **Black & White Cabs** (☎ 13 32 22) and **Yellow Cab Co** (☎ 13 19 24).

Train

The fast Citytrain network has seven lines, which run as far as Gympie North in the north (for the Sunshine Coast) and Robina in the south (for the Gold Coast). All trains go through Roma St, Central and Brunswick St Stations.

MORETON BAY

The Brisbane River winds its way east of the city centre for about 20km and enters Moreton Bay, which stretches from Caloundra in the north to the Gold Coast in the south. Few marine parks have an island

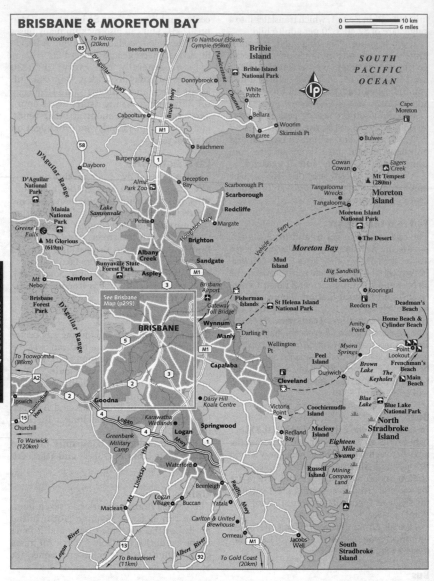

BRISBANE & MORETON BAY

for every day of the year but with some 365, this one has the perfect number.

Moreton Bay is separated from the Pacific Ocean by four sand islands: Moreton Island and Bribie Island to the north, and North and South Stradbroke Islands towards the south. The most popular of these is North Stradbroke Island with its great surfing

beaches, visible marine life and a new wave of sophisticated dining and accommodation options. On Moreton Island, wild dolphin feeding is the major attraction.

Tours

Humpback whales are a regular sight in the bay between June and November when they migrate to and from their southern feeding grounds. Moreton Bay also has the largest resident population of bottlenose dolphins in the world (more than 300).

Dolphin Wild (☎ 07-3880 4444; www.dolphinwild .com.au; adult/child/family incl lunch $110/60/290) Departing from Redcliffe, these full-day ecotours include a cruise to Moreton Island with commentary from a marine naturalist and guided snorkel tours (adult/child $20/10) around the Tangalooma wrecks.

Manly Eco Cruises (☎ 07-3396 9400; www.manlye cocruises.net; adult/child $99/44) Ride on the catamaran boom nets, enjoy free canoe rides or sit back on the MV *Getaway* and spot marine life. The two-hour Sunday barbecue breakfast tour is especially popular (adult/child $29/14).

NORTH STRADBROKE ISLAND
pop 2016

Saturated with natural beauty, North Stradbroke is a subtropical sand island close to Brisbane that feels a world away from the mainland.

Affectionately referred to as 'Straddie' by the friendly locals, the island is mostly undeveloped but has a few small settlements popular with southeast Queenslanders seeking a chilled-out weekend getaway.

A bridge (via Russell Island) was almost approved in the early 1980s, but thankfully the idea was canned – easier access would diminish its quiet charm. A 30-minute water taxi or 45-minute car barge from Cleveland, 30km southeast of Brisbane, remains the preferred passage.

Surfers come for the awesome breaks around Point Lookout, which is also a regular spot for sighting dolphins, turtles and manta rays. Between June and November, hundreds of humpback whales can also be seen here.

Those seeking a freshwater dip venture to the lakes in the middle of the island, and the southeastern coast is a playground for 4WD drivers.

Orientation & Information

There are three main settlements on the island that are all grouped towards the northern end. Point Lookout on the surf side is the major tourist destination, while Dunwich, on the western coast, is where the ferries dock. Amity Point is a small village on the northwestern tip. The southern part of the island is closed to visitors because of sand mining.

Although quiet most of the year, the population can swell significantly at Christmas,

Easter and during school holidays, so book accommodation well in advance.

If planning to camp, get information and permits on the way to the ferries at Cleveland's **Redlands on Moreton Bay Visitor Centre** (☎ 1300 667 386; www.more2redlands.com.au; shop 2/152 Shore St West, Cleveland; ☻ 9am-5pm Mon-Fri, to 3pm Sat & Sun) or on the island at **Straddie Holiday Parks** (☎ 1300 551 253; www.straddieholiday parks.com.au; Junner St, Dunwich; ☻ 7.30am-4pm Mon-Fri, 7.to 2pm Sat), which is 200m from the ferry terminal in Dunwich. Those with a 4WD will need to obtain a permit ($45) from one of the centres.

Sights & Activities

At **Point Lookout**, the breathtaking **North Gorge Headlands Walk** is an absolute must for any visitor to Straddie. Turtles, dolphins and manta rays can be spotted any time of year from the wooden boardwalk that skirts the rocky outcrops and the view from the headland down Main Beach is utterly jaw-dropping.

There are several gorgeous **beaches** huddled around Point Lookout. A patrolled swimming area, Cylinder Beach is popular with families and is flanked by Home Beach and Deadman's Beach. Further around the point, Frenchman's Beach is another peaceful secluded spot if you don't mind the occasional nudist passing by. On the eastern side, surfers and bodyboarders descend on **Main Beach** in search of the ultimate wave, while fishing fanatics take their 4WD vehicles down the strip of beach that extends towards **Eighteen Mile Swamp**.

No trip to Straddie is complete without a refreshing swim in a freshwater lake. East of Dunwich, the aptly named **Brown Lake** is the colour of stewed tea owing to the native tea trees that line the waters. There are picnic tables, barbecues and a toilet at the lake.

It can be thirsty work, but grabbing your water bottle and following the 2.6km (40-minute) bush track to the sparkling **Blue Lake** is a rewarding experience. Wildlife such as forest birds and reptiles can be spotted on the way. The path for vehicles is closed. Further north, the **Keyholes** is a freshwater system of lakes and lagoons where you can listen to the surf just metres away.

Used mainly for ferry access to the mainland, **Dunwich** is also a handy spot for picking up supplies at the convenience store and bakery. The small but impressive **North**

QUEENSLAND

Stradbroke Island Historical Museum (☎ 07-3409 9699; 15-17 Welsby St; adult/child $3.30/1.10; ☑ 10am-2pm Wed, Fri & Sat) has curious displays such as items retrieved from shipwrecks and a giant skull of a sperm whale that washed up on Main Beach in 2004.

For a greater sense of seclusion, **Amity Point** is a lovely, quiet place for fishing and snorkelling in calmer waters.

Anglers can hire fishing gear from **Straddie Super Sports** (☎ 07-3409 9252; 18 Bingle Rd, Dunwich) from $10 per day (plus a $30 deposit) and sea kayaks cost $50 per day. Surfboards, snorkelling equipment and bicycles can be hired at **Straddie Adventures** (☎ 07-3409 8414; www .straddieadventures.com.au; 112 East Coast Rd, Point Lookout), which also offers sea-kayaking trips around Straddie for $60 and sandboarding for $30. Based at Manta Lodge YHA (below), Manta Scuba Centre offers snorkelling for $55/80 per single/double, inclusive of a two-hour boat trip and all the gear. Open-water three-day dive courses cost $450, or a trip with two dives for certified divers is $160.

Tours

Stradbroke Island 4WD Tours (☎ 07-3409 8051; straddie4wd@bigpond.com; half-day tours adult/child $35/20, full-day tours adult/child $85/55) Tours to beaches and lakes with an option to go beach fishing.

Straddie Guides (☎ 07-3415 3106; www.straddie guides.com; half-day tours $49, full-day whale-watching tours $69) Half-day 4WD tours include exploring the beaches and a trip to a freshwater lake. Whale-watching tours are May to November only.

Sleeping

HOTELS

Manta Lodge (☎ 07-3409 8888; www.mantalodge.com .au; 1 East Coast Rd, Point Lookout; dm $28, tw & d $70) Set behind Home Beach, rooms at Straddie's only backpacker hostel are very basic and a little grimy but you're well compensated by the convenient on-site dive school which runs daily scuba and snorkelling trips. There are four-, six- and eight-bed dorms and guests can lounge around the comfy common area or take advantage of the free pool tables. Snorkelling hire packs for $20 per day include a mask, snorkel and fins.

Domain Stradbroke Resort (☎ 07-3415 0000; www .stradbrokedomain.com; 43-47 East Coast Rd, Point Lookout; cabins from $144; ☒ ☒) These self-contained modern shacks and villas in bushy surrounds near Home Beach are the most stylish on the island. The cute shacks are ideal for singles or couples with open-plan living and beds in the loft, or for larger groups the villas sleep up to 12 people. Both options have all mod cons and outdoor decks. Cheaper rates for longer stays.

our pick Stradbroke Island Beach Hotel & Spa Resort (☎ 07-3409 8188; www.stradbrokehotel.com.au; East Coast Rd, Point Lookout; r from $165) The daggy, old brown-brick Straddie Pub at Point Lookout was knocked down in 2006 and replaced with this dazzling modern complex comprising a bar, restaurant, hotel and spa. Spotlessly clean rooms have blond-wood tones, top-grade kitchen and bathroom fittings and flat-screen TVs. The extra $40 for sea views is money well spent but the best view of all is free downstairs at the open-air bar. Be there for sunset!

Anchorage on Straddie (☎ 07-3409 8266; www .anchorage.stradbrokeresorts.com.au; East Coast Rd, Point Lookout; 1-/2-bedroom units $170/280, studios $160; ☒) The friendly managers of these self-contained apartments keep the place shipshape and there's a boardwalk from the hotel grounds straight to the beach. For sea views, ask for a room on the third level.

Whale Watch Resort (☎ 1800 450 004, 07-3409 8555; www.whalewatchresort.com.au; Samarinda Dr, Point Lookout; 2/5 nights from $380/950; ☒ ☒ ☒) Features spacious interiors and ocean views from private patios.

For longer stays, enquire about holiday homes at **Dolphin Holiday Accommodation** (☎ 07-3409 8455; www.straddie.info; 1 Endeavour St, Point Lookout).

CAMPING

Beachfront camping sites are packed in peak season and bookings should be made well in advance. The five serviced camping grounds (near the beach) and two foreshore sites (on the beach) are run by **Straddie Holiday Parks** (☎ 1300 551 253; www.straddieholidayparks.com .au; unpowered/powered/foreshore sites from $24/28/14). Cylinder Beach at Point Lookout is the most popular serviced site with amenity blocks and laundry facilities, but expect to pay up to $42 per night for a powered site in peak season. Adder Rock and Thankful Rest are the other serviced sites at Point Lookout, or there are quieter grounds at Amity Point and Dunwich (Bradbury's Beach). Foreshore campsites at Main Beach and Flinders Beach are accessible by 4WD only.

Eating
Oceanic Gelati Bar (☎ 07-3415 3222; 19 Mooloomba Rd, Point Lookout; ☽ 9.30am-5pm) A sprightly ice-cream-parlour-cum-coffee-shop where gelati is made on the premises. Folks take their ice creams to the grassy hillside opposite for views over Frenchman's Beach.

Look Café Bar (☎ 07-3415 3390; www.lookcafe bar.com; 29 Mooloomba Rd, Point Lookout; dishes $10-25; ☽ breakfast & lunch daily, dinner Thu-Sat) If you can manage to take your eyes off the dreamy ocean view and take a look at the menu, this cafe serves up tasty breakfasts and summery Mod Oz mains to a soundtrack of smooth jazzy tunes. The prawn and avocado salad with roast capsicum and orange segments is the chef's tip.

La Focaccia (☎ 07-3409 8778; Anchorage on Straddie, East Coast Rd, Point Lookout; mains $19-30; ☽ dinner) For a sophisticated dining experience, La Focaccia is one of the island's finest. Service is snappy, the wine list is superb and seafood rules here – try the Straddie chilli prawns tossed with glass noddles and coriander, or a gourmet marinara pizza like no other.

There is a **Foodworks** (☎ 07-5493 6387; 2 Endeavour St, Point Lookout; ☽ 7am-9pm) convenience store, but it's worth bringing grocery supplies from the mainland.

Other options:

Amis (☎ 07-3409 8600; www.amisrestaurant.com.au; 21 Cumming Pde, Point Lookout; dishes $17-31; ☽ dinner Wed-Sat) High-class restaurant with ocean views.

Domain Café (☎ 07-3415 0090; 43-47 East Coast Rd, Point Lookout; mains $12-25; ☽ breakfast & lunch) Casual alfresco dining at Domain Stradbroke Resort (opposite).

Getting There & Away
The gateway to North Stradbroke Island is the seaside town of Cleveland. Regular city train services run from Central or Roma St stations in Brisbane to Cleveland station ($4.80, one hour), from where you can get a bus (free if you show your train ticket) to the ferry terminal. Buses to the terminal are infrequent so a taxi is a good option (five minutes).

Stradbroke Ferries (☎ 07-3286 2666; www.strad brokeferries.com.au) runs a water taxi to Dunwich almost every hour from about 6am to 6.30pm (adult/child return $17/10, 25 minutes). It also has a slightly less frequent vehicle ferry (return per vehicle including passengers $135; return walk-on passengers $11, 50 minutes) from around 5.30am to 5.30pm.

The **Stradbroke Flyer** (☎ 07-3821 3821; www .flyer.com.au) runs an almost hourly catamaran service from Cleveland to One Mile Jetty (Dunwich) from around 5am to 7.30pm (adult/child return $19/11, 20 minutes). A courtesy bus is available from Cleveland train station to the ferry terminal.

Sea Stradbroke (☎ 07-3488 9777; www.bigredcat .com.au) has a Big Red Cat vehicle and passenger ferry departing Cleveland daily from 5.30am to 7pm (return per vehicle $135, including passengers; return walk-on passengers $11, 50 minutes).

Getting Around
North Stradbroke Island Bus Services (☎ 07-3415 2417; www.stradbrokebuses.com) meets the water taxis (not the vehicle ferries) at Dunwich and One Mile Jetty between 7.25am and 6.55pm and run across to Point Lookout and Amity Point ($8.60 return). Remember to tell the driver where you want to get off. The last bus to Dunwich leaves Point Lookout around 6.15pm. There's also the **Stradbroke Cab Service** (☎ 0408 193 685), which charges $55 to $60 from Dunwich to Point Lookout.

MORETON ISLAND
pop 250

City life rapidly fades from memory when you're cruising on the ferry from Brisbane out to this sand island north of Stradbroke. Day-trippers, campers and folks staying at the island's resort love to explore its extremes, diving deep into crystal clear waters to view marine life or rising to the summits of enormous sand dunes for tobogganing. It's comforting to know Moreton Island's miles of sandy beaches, prolific birdlife, sparkling lagoons and precious bushland are well protected – more than 90% is designated national park. The island has a colourful history, from evidence of early Aboriginal settlements to being the site of Queensland's first and only whaling station, which operated between 1952 and 1962.

Orientation & Information
There are no paved roads on Moreton Island, but 4WDs can travel along the beaches and a few cross-island tracks. Vehicle permits for the island cost $38 and are available from the barge operator or from the EPA Customer Service Centre in Brisbane (p305). If you don't have a 4WD, there are lots of good

walking trails and decommissioned 4WD roads. Maps for walkers and 4WDs are available from the Marine Education & Conservation Centre (below).

Tangalooma is the island's tourist resort and there are three other small settlements on the west coast. **Bulwer** sits near the north-western tip, **Cowan Cowan** between Bulwer and Tangalooma, and **Kooringal** is near the southern tip. There is a convenience store and two cafes at the resort, but best to bring food supplies from the mainland.

Sights & Activities

The main attraction is the **wild dolphin feeding**, which takes place every evening around sunset at the Tangalooma resort. Between five and nine dolphins swim in from the ocean to take fish from the hands of volunteer feeders, but you need to be a guest at the resort with a 'dolphin feeding package' to be involved. Day visitors to Tangalooma are welcome to watch from the jetty. The resort also organises **whale-watching cruises** between June and October for $58.

Just north of the resort off the coast are the **Tangalooma Wrecks**, which provide excellent snorkelling and diving. You can hire gear from **Dive In Sports** (☎ 07-3410 6924; Tangalooma Wild Dolphin Resort; ☒ 8am-5pm) on the resort grounds. **Tangatours** (☎ 07-3410 6927; www.tanga tours.com.au; Tangalooma) offers jet-ski tours ($120, 40 minutes) and sunset kayaking (from $45) and has a kids' club ($10 per hour). Next to the resort near the ferry terminal is the **Marine Education & Conservation Centre** (☒ 10am-noon & 1-5pm), which has interesting displays of marine and bird life.

You don't need to be an expert climber to conquer the highest coastal sand hill in the world, **Mt Tempest** (280m), located north of the resort in the centre of the island. Built in 1857, **Cape Moreton Lighthouse** at the northern tip is the oldest operating lighthouse in Queensland, and is the place to come for great views if the whales are passing by. Near the lighthouse is the tiny **Moreton Island National Park information centre** (☎ 07-3408 2710), which has some cultural and historical displays.

Tours

Moreton Bay Escapes (☎ 1300 559 355; www .moretonbayescapes.com.au; adult/child/family from Brisbane incl lunch $149/129/379) A certified ecotour,

the one-day Moreton Island 4WD tour includes sandboarding, tobogganing, marine wildlife watching and a picnic lunch.

Sunrover Expeditions (☎ 1800 353 717, 07-3880 0719; www.sunrover.com.au; 1-/2-/3-day tour per person from $120/195/295, plus $20 per day national park entrance fee) Ecotours run as day trips or camping safaris departing from Brisbane's Roma Street Transit Centre.

Sleeping

Tangalooma Wild Dolphin Resort (☎ 1300 652 250, 07-3268 6333; www.tangalooma.com; r from $290; ☒ ☒) Situated at the old whaling station on the waterfront, there's a huge range of ritzy rooms here including some particularly posh new serviced apartments. Some rooms are noticeably older, but all have modern facilities and contemporary decor. Around the bar, guests sip on cocktails at picnic tables and laze around on grassy patches leading onto the beach.

There are nine **camping grounds** (☎ 13 13 04; www.epa.qld.gov.au; per person/family $4.85/20), including four right on the beach. Those sites not on the beach have water, toilets and cold showers. Camping permits must be obtained prior to arriving on the island as there is no self-registration on site or on the ferries. These can be obtained from the EPA Customer Service Centre (p305) in Brisbane.

Getting There & Around

The **Tangalooma Flyer** (☎ 1300 652 250, 07-3268 6333; www.tangalooma.com; adult/child return day-trip from $40/25; ☒ 7.30am, 10am & 5pm daily, plus 12.30pm Mon, Sat & Sun) is the resort's fast catamaran. It departs from Holt St, off Kingsford Smith Dr in Eagle Farm, Brisbane. A bus ($14) departs Brisbane's Roma Street Transit Centre at 9am to catch the 10am boat. Bookings are essential.

The vehicle ferry **Micat** (☎ 07-3909 3333; www .micat.com.au; return adult/child $45/30, vehicle with 2 passengers $190-220; ☒ 8.30am) leaves from 14 Howard Smith Dr, Lyton, at the Port of Brisbane, and arrives on the beach at Tangalooma Wrecks. Return times from the island are irregular – call ahead.

There is no 4WD hire on the island unless you are a guest at the Tangalooma Resort. There is one 4WD taxi driver operating **Moreton Island Tourist Services** (☎ 07-3408 2661; www.moretonisland.net.au).

BRIBIE ISLAND
pop 16,460

Queensland's only offshore island linked to the mainland by bridge, Bribie is 70km north of Brisbane at the top end of Moreton Bay. Like Stradbroke and Moreton, it is a sand island with protected bushland areas but is far more developed due to its easy accessibility. Popular with grey nomads and those seeking the laid-back island lifestyle, there are some beautifully remote **QPWS camping areas** (☎ 13 13 04; www.epa.qld.gov.au; per person/family $4.85/20) on the western and northern coasts. Acess is by 4WD only and you must book ahead before arriving.

There is no 4WD hire on the island and 4WD permits ($36 per week) should be purchased from the **Bongaree Caravan Park** (☎ 07-3408 1054; Welsby Pde, Bongaree) as soon as you arrive. There's a **ranger station** (☎ 07-3408 8451) at White Patch on the southeastern fringes of the park, and you can pick up 4WD maps ($8) and other information at the friendly **Bribie Island information centre** (☎ 07-3408 9026; www.bribie.com.au; Benabrow Ave, Bellara; ❍ 9am-4pm Mon-Fri, to 3pm Sat, 9.30am-1pm Sun).

If you're not camping, the **Inn Bongaree** (☎ 07-3410 1718; www.innbongaree.com.au; 25 Second Ave, Bongaree; s/d/tr $40/50/60) is a no-frills hotel two minutes' walk from the beach.

There are plenty of takeaway outlets around Bellara and Bongaree, and the **Surf Club** (☎ 07-3408 2141; First Ave, Woorim; mains $17-25; ❍ 10am-midnight Mon-Sat, from 7.30am Sun) has a bar and bistro with lovely views of Moreton Island.

There are frequent Citytrain services between Brisbane and Caboolture. A Trainlink bus runs between Caboolture station and Bribie Island.

GOLD COAST

Be prepared to show plenty of skin and wear your finest 'bling': the Gold Coast is southeast Queensland's glitzy beach-holiday hot spot. The 70km stretch of coastline from South Stradbroke Island to Rainbow Bay on the NSW border attracts a staggering four million sun-seeking visitors every year.

The coastline is studded with high-rise apartment blocks, has a Las Vegas–style flashy feel and is famous for million-dollar theme parks where tourists get their thrills on roller coasters and waterslides.

This city also has a reputation for enormous shopping malls and tacky tourist traps, but the Gold Coast's original attraction is by far the best of them all – the beach. Up to 15,000 people per year are moving to this city just to be close to it; throw in around 290 days of sunshine annually and you've got one very enticing tropical destination.

Outside of gaudy Surfers Paradise are laid-back neighbourhoods such as Burleigh Heads and Coolangatta, which offer breezy oceanfront cafes, lively pubs and, of course, great surfing breaks.

Dangers & Annoyances

Car theft is a problem around Southport and Surfers Paradise – park in well-lit areas and don't leave valuables in your vehicle.

Between mid-November and mid-December tens of thousands of school leavers descend on the Gold Coast for Schoolies Week, a month-long party that's great fun for those celebrating but can be hell for everyone else.

Getting There & Around

Based at Coolangatta, the Gold Coast airport is serviced by **Qantas** (☎ 13 13 13; www.qantas.com .au), **Virgin Blue** (☎ 13 67 89; www.virginblue.com.au), **Jetstar** (☎ 13 15 38; www.jetstar.com.au) and **Tiger Airways** (☎ 03-9335 3033; www.tigerairways.com).

The **Gold Coast Tourist Shuttle** (☎ 1300 655 655, 07-5574 5111; www.gcshuttle.com.au; one way per adult/child/family $18/9/45) will meet your flight and drop you at most Gold Coast accommodation.

Citytrain services link Brisbane to Helensvale station ($9, one hour), Nerang station ($10, 70 minutes) and Robina station ($12, 75 minutes) roughly every half hour. **Surfside Buslines** (☎ 13 12 30, 07-5571 6555; www.surfside.com.au) runs buses from the train stations down to Surfers ($3 to $4) and beyond, and to the theme parks. You can buy individual fares or get an Ezy Pass ($26) for three days' unlimited travel, or a weekly pass ($45).

Coachtrans (☎ 1300 664 700, 07-3358 9700; www.coachtrans.com.au) runs transfers between Brisbane airport and most Gold Coast accommodation (one way adult/child $39/18). It also offers the Gold Coast Super Pass, which includes return airport transfers, unlimited coach transfers between Gold Coast

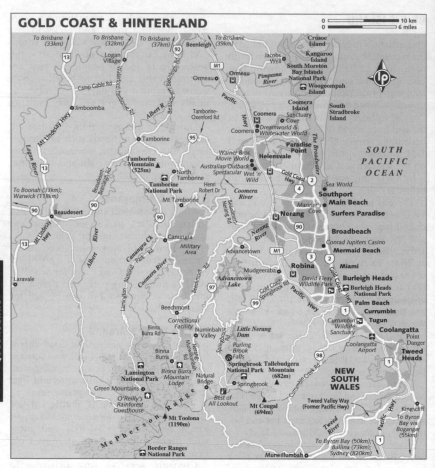

GOLD COAST & HINTERLAND

accommodation and theme parks, and unlimited use of the Surfside bus network (three-day adult/child $114/57).

SOUTHPORT & MAIN BEACH

The northern gateway to the Gold Coast, Southport (population 24,100) is a residential and business district known for its shopping centres and family-friendly vibe. It is sheltered from the ocean by a long sand bar known as the Spit, home to one of the big theme parks, Sea World. Directly southeast is Main Beach, where apartment blocks are many and golden sand stretches for miles.

There are ATMs dotted along Scarborough St and the **Gold Coast Hospital** (☎ 07-5519 8211; 108 Nerang St, Southport) is here.

Sights & Activities

The ocean side of the spit is a popular fishing spot and from here you can see across the channel to South Stradbroke Island. Opposite the entrance to Sea World (opposite), in the car park of Phillip Park, is the start of the **Federation Walk**, a pretty 3.7km trail that winds its way through patches of littoral rainforest and down to the Gold Coast Oceanway.

Near the start of the walk is the upmarket shopping and dining complex **Marina Mirage**; a **farmers market** is held at the nearby Mariner's Cove on the first and third Saturday of each month. **Tallship Cruises** (☎ 07-5532 2444; www.tallship.com.au; adult/child $99/69; ☯ 9am) runs day trips from Mariner's Cove to McLarens Landing

Resort on South Stradbroke Island. Lunch is included.

At the **Mariner's Cove Booking Office** (☎ 07-5571 1711; ⏲ 8.30am-4.30pm) you can arrange most of the following activities:

Gold Coast Helitours (☎ 07-5591 8457; www.gold coasthelitours.com.au; adult/child 30min ride $135/105) Departs from Mirage Heliport.

Jet Ski Safaris (☎ 07-5526 3111; www.jetskisafaris .com.au; 1hr $200) Take a 20km ride up to South Stradbroke Island.

Wahoo Fishing Adventures (☎ 1300 492 466; www .wahoocharters.com.au; half/full day per person $140/190; ⏲ 6am) Fishing trips for singles and groups and night charters on request.

Sleeping & Eating

our pick **Trekkers** (☎ 1800 100 004, 07-5591 5616; www .trekkersbackpackers.com.au; 22 White St, Southport; dm $27, d & tw $70; 🖳 🛋) The friendly owner, Cliff, welcomes guests at this homely hostel set in an old Queenslander house. He recently gave the rooms a lick of paint; the place looks spiffy and polished wooden floors throughout give it extra points for cleanliness. Guests are offered a free breakfast of coffee and cereal to be enjoyed by the pool or pianola. Thumbs up!

Aquarius (☎ 1800 229 955, 07-5527 1300; www .aquariusbackpackers.com.au; 44 Queen St, Southport; dm $27, d & tw $70; 🖳 🛋) Party hostels that are clean with modern facilities can be hard to come by on the Coast, but Aquarius is a cut above. Rooms are small but tidy and sliding doors link the spacious TV room with an outdoor area for shooting pool. Fire up the barbecue and let the pool party begin.

Main Beach Tourist Park (☎ 1800 444 474, 07-5581 7722; www.gctp.com.au/main; 3600 Main Beach Pde; unpowered/powered sites from $31/34, cabins from $136; 🖳 🛋) Pack your surfboard: this excellent site is the closest tourist park to Surfers Paradise (3km)

GOLD COAST THEME PARKS

The roller coasters and waterslides at these American-style theme parks offer so much dizzying action, keeping your lunch down can be a constant battle. Discount tickets are sold in most tourist offices. The Fun Pass (adult/child $147/93) allows one single-day entry into Movie World, Sea World and Wet 'n' Wild over a five-day period.

Australian Outback Spectacular (☎ 13 33 86, 07-5519 6200; www.myfun.com.au; Entertainment Rd, Oxenford; adult/child incl dinner $99/65; ⏲ 6.15pm Tue-Sun) Between Movie World and Wet 'n' Wild, this is not actually a theme park but rather a 1½-hour dinner and show in a 1000-seat arena. The venue captures the spirit of the Australian outback with displays of brilliant horsemanship, stampeding cattle and even a little boot scootin' to music written by Australian country singer Lee Kernaghan. You're given a stockman's hat to keep; dinner is three courses of outback tucker.

Dreamworld (☎ 07-5588 1111; www.dreamworld.com.au; Pacific Hwy, Coomera; adult/child $67/43; ⏲ 10am-5pm) Home to the Big 6 Thrill Rides, including the Giant Drop and Tower of Terror. Get your photo taken with a Bengal tiger at Tiger Island.

Sea World (☎ 07-5588 2222, show times 07-5588 2205; www.myfun.com.au; Sea World Dr, The Spit, Main Beach; adult/child $67/43; ⏲ 10am-5pm) See polar bears, sharks and performing dolphins at this aquatic park, or ride one of the original Gold Coast roller coasters, the Corkscrew. Catch up with Bert and Ernie at the new Sesame Street Beach.

Warner Bros Movie World (☎ 07-5573 8485; www.myfun.com.au; Pacific Hwy, Oxenford; adult/child $67/43; ⏲ 10am-5pm) Movie-themed shows, rides and attractions including the Batwing Spaceshot and Lethal Weapon roller coaster.

Wet 'n' Wild (☎ 07-5573 2255; www.myfun.com.au; Pacific Hwy, Oxenford; adult/child $47/30; ⏲ 10am-5pm Feb-Apr & Sep-Dec, to 4pm May-Aug, to 9pm 27 Dec-25 Jan) The ultimate waterslide here is the Kamikaze where you plunge down an 11m drop in a two-person tube at 50km/h. This vast water fun park also has slippery slides, white-water rapids and tube rides, and latest-release films are shown at Dive 'n' Movies.

WhiteWater World (☎ 1800 073 300, 07-5588 1111; www.whitewaterworld.com.au; Dreamworld Parkway, Coomera; adult/child $43/28; ⏲ 10.30am-4.30pm) Connected to Dreamworld, this park features the Cave of Waves, Pipeline Plunge and more than 140 water activities and slides. A World Pass (adult/child $77/55 for one day, $99/$66 for two days) ensures entry to Dreamworld and WhiteWater World.

and is right opposite Main Beach. There's plenty of shade for pitching a tent, cabins have good decks, and all guests can use the free wireless internet.

C Espresso Bar (☎ 07-5591 6377; 56 Scarborough St, Southport; mains $9-15; ✆ breakfast & lunch Mon-Sat) If passing through the Southport town centre, stop off at this petite cafe for a fresh fruit juice or tasty pasta. Local workers gobble up fresh salads and rib-eye steak sandwiches.

Seaway Kiosk (☎ 07-5591 6970; Seaworld Dr, The Spit, Main Beach; meals from $10; ✆ breakfast & lunch) Famous for fresh crab-meat sandwiches and prawn rolls, this cafe at the tip of the Spit is always full to the gills.

Also recommended:

Harbour Side Resort (☎ 07-5591 6666; www .harboursideresort.com.au; 132 Marine Pde, Southport; apt from $99; P ✆ ✆) Basic apartments, good for families.

Peter's Fish Market (☎ 07-5591 7747; 120 Sea World Dr, Main Beach; meals $10, fish & chips $7.50; ✆ 9am-7.30pm) Competitive prices for prawns, crabs and fish fillets.

SURFERS PARADISE & BROADBEACH

Some say the 'Surfers' prefer other beaches and the 'Paradise' is tragically lost, but there's no denying this wild and trashy party zone attracts phenomenal visitor numbers all year round. Spend-happy tourists flock here for the dizzying mix of nightclubs, bars, shopping malls, fun rides and maybe a bit of beach time when the hangover kicks in.

For backpackers, Surfers Paradise (population 18,500) is *the* place to party on the coast – most hostels organise pub-crawls to ensure guests are soaked in revelry, and probably beer, every night. At year's end, school-leavers from across Australia descend on Surfers for a few weeks of frantic fun. Schoolies Week is a riotous time, and there's always 'toolies' (over-aged gate crashers) adding fuel to the fire.

Directly south is Broadbeach (population 3800) where the decibel level is considerably lower, but it offers some chic restaurants and a gorgeous stretch of golden beach.

Orientation & Information

The centre of the action is Cavill Ave, a pedestrianised strip leading to the beach. One block in from the Esplanade is Orchid Ave, the nightclub and bar strip. The following are all based in Surfers Paradise.

Email Centre (☎ 07-5538 7500; shop 51/3-15 Orchid Ave, Surfers Paradise; per hr $5; ✆ 8.30am-10pm Mon-Sat, 9am-10pm Sun) Internet access.

Gold Coast Accommodation Service (☎ 07-5592 0067; www.goldcoastaccommodationservice.com; shop 1, 1 Beach Rd, Surfers Paradise) Accommodation booking service.

Gold Coast Tourism Bureau (☎ 07-5538 4419; www.goldcoasttourism.com.au; Cavill Ave Mall, Surfers Paradise; ✆ 8.30am-5pm Mon-Fri, to 5pm Sat, 9am-4pm Sun) Helpful information booth with super-friendly staff.

Surfers Paradise Day & Night Medical Centre (☎ 07-5592 2299; 3221 Surfers Paradise Blvd, Surfers Paradise; ✆ 7am-11pm) Medical centre and pharmacy.

Travellers Central (☎ 1800 359 830, 07-5592 2911; Surfers Paradise Transit Centre, Beach Rd, Surfers Paradise) Accommodation and tour bookings service for backpackers.

UAE X Change (☎ 07-5538 2995; shop 22, Centre Arcade, 3131 Gold Coast Hwy, Surfers Paradise; ✆ 9am-9pm) Foreign currency exchange.

Sights

Surfers is all about going out until stupid o'clock, recovering, and doing it all again. That said, there are a couple of sober attractions well worth a look.

The 360-degree views of the Gold Coast from the observation level of **QDeck** (☎ 1300 473 325, 07-5582 2777; Surfers Paradise Blvd, Surfers Paradise; adult/child/family $19/10/47; ✆ 9am-9pm Sun-Thu, to midnight Fri & Sat) are brilliant for gaining perspective and orientation. The deck is 230m high on the 77th level of Q1 Tower, and is accessed by one of the world's fastest elevators. The Qbar has DJs on Friday and Saturday nights.

Further inland, the **Gold Coast Art Gallery** (☎ 07-5581 6567; 135 Bundall Rd, Surfers Paradise; ✆ 10am-5pm Mon-Fri, 11am-5pm Sat & Sun) features two main galleries displaying works by established Australian and international artists.

Activities
SURFING

Most surf schools aim to have you standing up and catching waves in your first lesson. They charge between $45 and $55 for a two-hour group lesson. Surfboard and wetsuit hire is also available.

Cheyne Horan School of Surf (☎ 1800 227 873, 0403 080 484; www.cheynehoran.com.au; ✆ lessons 10am & 2pm) Lessons for beginners held daily. Coaches are trained by Cheyne, a former world-champion surfer.

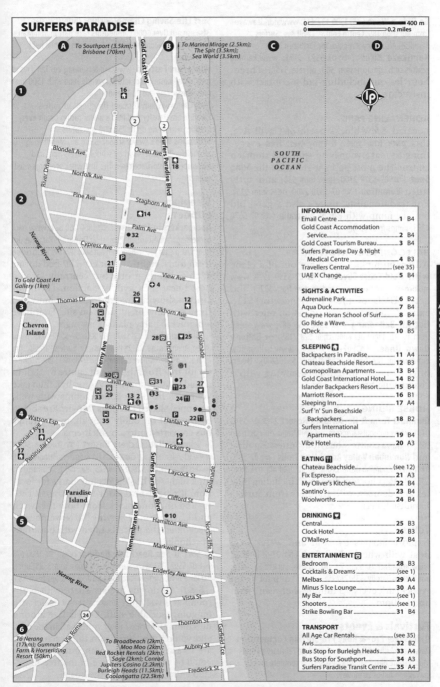

SURFERS PARADISE

INFORMATION

Email Centre	**1**	B4
Gold Coast Accommodation Service	**2**	B4
Gold Coast Tourism Bureau	**3**	B4
Surfers Paradise Day & Night Medical Centre	**4**	B3
Travellers Central	(see 35)	
UAE X Change	**5**	B4

SIGHTS & ACTIVITIES

Adrenaline Park	**6**	B2
Aqua Duck	**7**	B4
Cheyne Horan School of Surf	**8**	B4
Go Ride a Wave	**9**	B4
QDeck	**10**	B5

SLEEPING

Backpackers in Paradise	**11**	A4
Chateau Beachside Resort	**12**	B3
Cosmopolitan Apartments	**13**	B4
Gold Coast International Hotel	**14**	B2
Islander Backpackers Resort	**15**	B4
Marriott Resort	**16**	B1
Sleeping Inn	**17**	A4
Surf 'n' Sun Beachside Backpackers	**18**	B2
Surfers International Apartments	**19**	B4
Vibe Hotel	**20**	A3

EATING

Chateau Beachside	(see 12)	
Fix Espresso	**21**	A3
My Oliver's Kitchen	**22**	B4
Santino's	**23**	B4
Woolworths	**24**	B4

DRINKING

Central	**25**	B3
Clock Hotel	**26**	B3
O'Malleys	**27**	B4

ENTERTAINMENT

Bedroom	**28**	B3
Cocktails & Dreams	(see 1)	
Melbas	**29**	A4
Minus 5 Ice Lounge	**30**	A4
My Bar	(see 1)	
Shooters	(see 1)	
Strike Bowling Bar	**31**	B4

TRANSPORT

All Age Car Rentals	(see 35)	
Avis	**32**	B2
Bus Stop for Burleigh Heads	**33**	A4
Bus Stop for Southport	**34**	A3
Surfers Paradise Transit Centre	**35**	A4

Go Ride a Wave (☎ 1300 132 441; www.gorideawave .com.au; shop 189, Centro Centre, Cavill Ave, Surfers Paradise) Also a popular place for surfboard hire.

Kamikaze Kites (☎ 07-5592 5171; www.kamika zekites.com; group lesson $80, private $150) Three-hour lessons including radio contact with instructor.

ADRENALINE PARK

Located a few blocks north of Cavill Ave, this **park** (cnr Cypress & Ferny Aves) has everything to make your head spin and stomach churn. The most popular rides are the **Sling Shot** (☎ 07-5570 2700; rides from $30) and aptly titled **Vomatron** (☎ 07-5570 2700, rides from $15). For traditionalists, there's also a good old bungee jump with **Bungy Australia** (☎ 07-5570 4833; jumps from $99).

BALLOONING & SKYDIVING

Adrenalin junkies can jump out of a plane with **Gold Coast Skydive** (☎ 07-5599 1920; www .goldcoastskydive.com.au; tandem dive from $325) and get a DVD of the experience for $115 extra. A more leisurely ride is on offer with **Hot Air Ballooning** (☎ 1300 766 887; www.hotair .com.au; 1hr flight per adult/child $285/185) or **Balloon Down Under** (☎ 07-5593 8400; www.balloondow nunder.com; 1hr flight per adult/child $310/200). Both offer early morning flights, ending with a champagne breakfast.

HORSE RIDING

Gumnuts Farm & Horseriding Resort (☎ 07-5543 0191; www.gumnutsfarm.com.au; adult/child 2hr ride from $65/45) has a courtesy bus from Surfers Paradise and **Numinbah Valley Adventure Trails** (☎ 07-5533 4137; www.numinbahtrails.com; adult/child 4hr trek from $75/65) offers horse-riding tours including billy tea and damper, with transfers from Surfers Paradise hotels.

Tours

Explore Surfers by land and water in a boat with wheels. **Aqua Duck** (☎ 07-5539 0222; www.aquaduck.com.au; 7a, Orchid Ave, Surfers Paradise; adult/child/family $35/26/95) tours depart from Appel Park every 75 minutes between 10am and 5.30pm.

Festivals & Events

Quicksilver Pro- & Roxy Pro-Surfing Competition (www.quicksilverpro.com.au) From late February to mid-March some of the world's best surfers compete for big waves and big prize money.

Surf Life-Saving Championships (http://aussies .slsa.asn.au) Over 6000 competitors take part in Iron Man, boat crew, ski paddler and beach running events; held mid-March.

Wintersun Festival (www.wintersun.org.au) Ten days of rock 'n' roll nostalgia in late May/early June with 1500 hot rods, classic cars and 100 bands.

IndyCar (www.indy.com.au) The streets of Surfers Paradise are transformed into a motor racing circuit every October, attracting up to 250,000 spectators.

Schoolies Week (www.schoolies.org.au) Month-long alcohol-fuelled party held by school-leavers from mid-November to mid-December. The first week sees organised events.

Sleeping
BUDGET

Backpackers in Paradise (☎ 1800 268 621; www.back packersinparadise.com; 40 Peninsular Dr, Surfers Paradise; dm from $20, d & tw $70, 1-bedroom apt $80; 🖥 🖹) Choose from four-, eight-, 12- or even 20-bed dorms at this slightly grotty but centrally located hostel near the Cavill Ave action. The mini-cinema showing free movies is a bonus and there's a convenient store on site. Staff have a nightclub party plan, every night.

Sleeping Inn (☎ 1800 817 832, 07-5592 4455; www .sleepinginn.com.au; 26-28 Peninsular Dr, Surfers Paradise; dm from $27, d with/without bathroom $88/78; 🖹) Be picked up for free from the transit centre by staff in an old white limousine (yes, really), then take your pick from the comfy rooms with well-equipped shared kitchens. Movies are shown by the pool or, oddly enough, in an orange bus converted into a minicinema.

Islander Backpackers Resort (☎ 07-5538 8000; www.islander.com.au; cnr Beach Rd & Surfers Paradise Blvd, Surfers Paradise; dm $28, d & tw $85; 🖥 🖹) This faded pink high-rise hostel gets full marks for location: it's right next door to the transit centre and only one block from both the beach and Cavill Ave. If staying in November or December, the place is filled with hundreds of schoolies.

Surf 'n' Sun Beachside Backpackers (☎ 1800 678 194, 07-5592 2363; www.surfnsun-goldcoast.com; 3323 Surfers Paradise Blvd, Surfers Paradise; dm $32, d & apt from $85; 🖥 🖹) All dorms are six-share with bathrooms at this slightly shabby party hostel with outgoing, sociable staff. Guests laze around the common area or play volleyball in the pool and you're only 30m from the beach. There are TVs in every dorm room, but chances are you'll be taking advantage of the free nightclub entry organised by the hostel.

MIDRANGE

Cosmopolitan Apartments (☎ 1300 553 800, 07-5570 2311; 3142 Gold Coast Hwy, Surfers Paradise; apt from $105 ⊠ ⊠) The apartments here are all privately owned so some have a fresh modern feel, while others are still stuck in the '80s. The location is primo (close to Cavill Ave) and you can fry yourself on the rooftop sun deck.

Surfers International Apartments (☎ 1800 891 299, 07-5579 1299; www.surfers-international.com.au; 7-9 Trickett St, Surfers Paradise; 1-/2-bedroom apt from $115/160; P ⊠) Only metres from the beach, these self-contained apartments have exceptional ocean views, even by Surfers Paradise standards. Rooms are privately owned so decor and facilities vary. The two-bedroom apartments are spacious; great for families.

our pick **Vibe Hotel** (☎ 07-5539 0444; www.vibe hotels.com.au; 42 Ferny Ave, Surfers Paradise; d/tr/ste from $125/169/385; ⊠ ⊡ ⊠) A high-rise on the Nerang River, Vibe's lime-and-chocolate-brown exterior and bright seaside-themed lobby decor make surrounding hotels seem bland. The luxurious rooms are tastefully decorated and have all mod cons, and the poolside bar rocks. Reception staff? Outstanding.

Other recommendations:

Chateau Beachside Resort (☎ 1800 807 336, 07-5538 1022; www.chateaubeachside.com.au; cnr Elkhorn Ave & The Esplanade, Surfers Paradise; d from $120, 1-bedroom apt from $150; P ⊠ ⊠) Directly opposite the beach; studio apartments have air-con.

Gold Coast International Hotel (☎ 1800 074 020, 07-5584 1200; www.gci.com.au; 7 Staghorn Ave, Surfers Paradise; d from $159; P ⊠ ⊠) High-standard rooms with three restaurants on site.

TOP END

Marriott Resort (☎ 07-5592 9800; www.marriott.com/oolsp; 158 Ferny Ave, Surfers Paradise; d/ste from $275/460; P ⊠ ⊠) Five-star accommodation with immaculate rooms and decadent extras such as the resort's private beach with saltwater lagoon and artificial coral reef for snorkelling (among 400 fish!). Restaurants on site include a Japanese steakhouse.

Eating

Quantity over quality is often the case at Surfers' many eateries, but there are a few exceptions.

My Oliver's Kitchen (☎ 07-5553 1904; cnr Hanlan St & The Esplanade, Surfers Paradise; mains $11-21) Located at the Surfers Paradise Surf Life Saving Club, My Oliver's Kitchen serves breakfast fry-ups all day and the equally greasy lunch menu (11am to 4pm) has nothing over $10. Stick around for a beer at the 'Champions' bar.

Sage (☎ 07-5538 9938; cnr Surf Pde & Queensland Ave, Broadbeach; mains $14-29; ☽ 7am-late) Vodka oyster shots are the entrée of choice at this award-winning alfresco restaurant with bubbly staff. For mains, there are thick and tender steak cuts and plenty of seafood dishes. Discounts between 5pm and 6pm nightly.

Moo Moo (☎ 07-5539 9952; Broadbeach on the Park, 2685 Gold Coast Hwy, Broadbeach; mains $30-60; ☽ lunch & dinner) Nightmarish for vegetarians, heavenly for carnivores, Moo Moo is *the* steak restaurant on the coast. Staff recommend the spice-rubbed 1kg Wagyu rump roast for two to four people. Before dinner, pull up a cow-skin-covered bar stool for cocktails or zesty wines.

For cheap and cheerful try **Santino's** (☎ 07-5527 5273; 3 Orchid Ave, Surfers Paradise; meals $10-13) pizza and pasta or **Chateau Beachside** (☎ 07-5526 9994; cnr Elkhorn Ave & The Esplanade, Surfers Paradise; meals from $8) for its famous $13 all-you-can-eat breakfast. **Fix Espresso** (☎ 07-5504 5332; shop G4, 64 Ferny Ave, Surfers Paradise; dishes $4-8; ☽ 7.30am-3.30pm) is a great grab-and-go option. There's a **Woolworths** (Centro Surfers Paradise, Cavill Mall, Surfers Paradise) supermarket for self caterers.

Drinking

O'Malleys (☎ 07-5570 4075; level 1, 1 Cavill Ave, Surfers Paradise; ☽ 10.30am-late) Always rowdy and popular with the student crowd, there's live entertainment five nights a week in this Irish-themed pub. The deck overlooks the boozy mayhem on Cavill Ave and the Esplanade.

Minus 5 Ice Lounge (☎ 07-5527 5571; Circle on Cavill, Cavill Ave, Surfers Paradise; 30min adult/child $30/15; ☽ 11am-late) Gimmicky but kinda fun if you don't mind the cover charge, *everything* is made of ice at this bar: your glass, the seats and the vodka-stocked bar. There are even ice sculptures imported from Canada.

Central (☎ 07-5592 3228; 27 Orchid Ave, Surfers Paradise) DJs bust out smooth beats at Central way before the nightclubs open their doors. This lounge and cocktail bar with outdoor seating also offers a cheap lunch menu, though most prefer three courses of mojitos.

Clock Hotel (☎ 07-5539 0344; 3282 Surfers Paradise Blvd, Surfers Paradise) Easily recognisable with its gaudy clock tower exterior, this three-level pub is a good central meeting place for a beer and cheap steak. There's outdoor seating and DJs on Friday and Saturday nights.

QUEENSLAND

Entertainment

The majority of Surfers' nightlife is centred on or around Orchid Ave. If you're up for partying with other backpackers, Wednesday, Friday and Saturday nights see the **Wicked Club Crawl** (☎ 07-5580 8422; www.wickedclubcrawl .com.au; ☺ 5pm-late), which goes to five clubs for $35. Otherwise, cover charges start at $10, and remember that photo ID is a must.

Melbas (☎ 07-5538 7411; 46 Cavill Ave, Surfers Paradise; ☺ 8pm-5am) Have a flutter on the poker machines then fritter away your cash on cocktails at this glamorous nightclub, the Gold Coast's longest standing (since 1981). The downstairs bar has live bands on Sunday nights.

Strike Bowling Bar (☎ 1300 787 453; Circle on Cavill, 35 Cavill Ave, Surfers Paradise; game & shoe hire from $12; ☺ 10am-late) A bowling alley and nightclub merged into one, Strike has music-video screens, club-style lighting and a well-stocked bar. A fun night out.

Shooters (☎ 07-5592 1144; Mark Complex, Orchid Ave, Surfers Paradise; ☺ 8pm-5am) Within this Wild West saloon bar you'll find a cigar lounge, sports bar, pool tables and dance floors playing the latest top 40 tunes.

Cocktails & Dreams (☎ 07-5592 1955; level 1, Mark Complex, Orchid Ave, Surfers Paradise; ☺ 9pm-late Wed & Thu, to 5am Fri & Sat) This two-level megaclub draws a huge crowd of folks for shmoozing in the downstairs lounge bar and grooving in the upstairs main room. Fashion police at the door insist guys wear collared shirts.

Bedroom (☎ 07-5582 6188; 26 Orchid Ave, Surfers Paradise) Recline on one of the queen-sized beds or pull shapes on the dance floor at this oh-so-sexy superclub. Recently renovated and housing a thumping sound system; catch international DJs on weekends.

More entertainment:

Conrad Jupiters Casino (☎ 07-5592 8100; www .conrad.com.au; Broadbeach Island, Gold Coast Hwy, Broadbeach; admission free; ☺ 24hr) Live music and dinner shows.

My Bar (☎ 07-5592 1144; Mark Complex, Orchid Ave, Surfers Paradise; ☺ 9pm-5am Thu-Sun) Lounge bar favoured by the over-25 crowd.

Getting There & Around

Long-distance buses stop at the **Surfers Paradise Transit Centre** (Beach Rd, Surfers Paradise). **Greyhound Australia** (☎ 1300 GREYHOUND/1300 473 946, 07-5531 6677) and **Premier Motor Service** (☎ 13 34 10; www .premierms.com.au) have frequent services to/from

Brisbane ($20, 90 minutes). The bus stops for Burleigh Heads and Southport are on Ferny Ave.

Local car-rental outfits that consistently offer good deals include **All Age Car Rentals** (☎ 07-5570 1200, 07-5527 6044; Surfers Paradise Transit Centre, Beach Rd, Surfers Paradise; per day from $19), **Avis** (☎ 07-5539 9388; cnr Cypress & Ferny Aves, Surfers Paradise; per day from $38) and **Red Rocket Rentals** (☎ 07-5538 9074; 2735 Gold Coast Hwy, Broadbeach; per day from $29). Insurance costs extra.

The major taxi companies servicing the area are **Regent Taxis** (☎ 13 62 94), **Gold Coast Taxis** (☎ 13 10 08) and **Silver Service Taxis** (☎ 13 31 00).

See the Gold Coast Getting There & Around section (p333) for more transport information.

BURLEIGH HEADS
pop 8459

Directly in between Surfers Paradise and Coolangatta lies gorgeous Burleigh Heads, a rocky headland linked to a strip of coastline popular with holidaying families and hard-core surfers. The headland provides a legendary right-hand point break for fast barrel rides, and the beach is also one of the nicest for bathing on the Gold Coast.

The town itself has some of the Gold Coast's best dining options with sunny cafes and open-air beachfront restaurants. You can get national park information about the headland from the **QPWS Information Centre** (☎ 07-5535 3032; 1711 Gold Coast Hwy; ☺ 9am-4pm).

Sights & Activities

A walk around the headland through **Burleigh Heads National Park** is a must for any visitor – it's a 27-hectare eucalypt forest reserve with plenty of birdlife and several walking trails. The natural rock slides and water cascades at the **Currumbin Rock Pools** are wonderful in the summer months.

There are two excellent wildlife sanctuaries in the vicinity. The **Currumbin Wildlife Sanctuary** (☎ 1300 886 511, 07-5534 0803; www.cws.org.au; Gold Coast Hwy, Currumbin; adult/child $39/21; ☺ 8am-5pm) has Australia's biggest rainforest aviary where you can hand feed rainbow lorikeets. There's also kangaroo feeding, photo opportunities with koalas, Aboriginal dance displays and a Snakes Alive show. The Wildnight Adventure (adult/child $52/27) at 7pm is an excellent 2½-hour guided tour to see nocturnal animals by torchlight. To get here catch a Surfside bus

---

THE GOLD COAST GODFATHER

Former pro-surfer Michael 'Munga' Barry is a local legend in the surfing community of Burleigh. A winner of world surfing championship tour events in Japan and South Africa in the 1990s, he was affectionately dubbed a 'godfather' by his peers on the world surfing circuit for initiating charity work on the tour. He established giveaways and celebrity auctions, often donating his own surfboards to help disadvantaged people in Bali, Fiji, Tahiti and Hawaii. Since retiring from the circuit in 2000, Munga has operated the **Godfathers of the Ocean Surf School** (☎ 07-5593 5661, 0410 504 979; www.godfathersoftheocean.com; adult/child $45/40; ☺ 2hr group lessons 10am, noon, 2pm & 4pm) on Burleigh Beach, personally taking first-time surfers out to catch their first wave.

---

700 from Surfers Paradise or 765 from Robina train station.

Opened by the doctor who first succeeded in breeding platypuses, the **David Fleay Wildlife Park** (☎ 07-5576 2411; West Burleigh Rd; adult/child/family $17/8/43; ☺ 9am-5pm) is an important education and conservation centre for the duck-billed creatures. It's also home to many other native Australian animals including the endangered inland desert bilby.

The **Hot Stuff Surf Shop** (☎ 07-5535 6899; 1969 Gold Coast Hwy) rents out surfboards (mostly long boards) per half/full day for $30/40.

Sleeping & Eating

Burleigh Palms (☎ 07-5576 3955; www.burleighpalms .com; 1849 Gold Coast Hwy; 1-bedroom apt per night/week from $120/490, 2-bedroom apt from $150/600; P ☐ ☒) These self-contained family units are ideally located near the local shops and there's a private walkway through to Burleigh Beach. Rooms have open-plan living/kitchen/dining and large TVs; ask the owner Kae about wireless internet for a small charge.

Hillhaven Holiday Apartments (☎ 07-5535 1055; www.hillhaven.com.au; 2 Goodwin Tce; r per week from $750; P ☐) This upmarket 10-storey building near the headland has two- and three-bedroom self-contained apartments that are individually furnished, with various balcony sizes. It's set back 150m from the beach, but the ocean view is 10 out of 10.

Bluff (☎ 07-5576 6333; 1/66 Goodwin Tce, Burleigh Heads; dishes $8-33) Always buzzing, the Bluff has you covered for heart-starter morning coffees and scrumptious breakfasts in a breezy spot across from the beach. You won't find another Moreton Bay bug and prawn gourmet pizza quite like they have here – deelish!

ourpick **Mermaids Dining Room & Bar** (☎ 07-5520 1177; 31 Goodwin Tce, Burleigh Heads; dishes $14-36) So close to the waves you could almost reach out and pluck a surfer from their board, this restaurant with a stunning sea-view terrace is located on the rocks at the southern end of Burleigh Beach. Breakfasts include a 'Queensland fruit plate' or classic eggs Benedict; feast on fresh king prawns, reef fish or scallops for mains.

Also recommended:

Burleigh Beach Tourist Park (☎ 07-5581 7755; www. gctp.com.au/burly; Goodwin Tce; unpowered/powered sites $27/32, cabins $132, villas $180; ☒ ☐) Council-owned park for caravans and camping; perfectly placed for the beach. Free wireless internet.

Surf Club Burleigh Heads (☎ 07-5520 2972; cnr Goodwin Tce & Gold Coast Hwy; meals $6-26) Grab a cheap burger from the takeaway counter downstairs or enjoy tasty pub grub upstairs with unobstructed ocean views.

COOLANGATTA
pop 5439

The most southerly seaside town before crossing into NSW, Coolangatta has a laid-back charm and friendly community vibe. This border town was the site for Queensland's very first surf life saving club in 1909, and its north-facing beaches remain some of the best for surfing on the coast. Southeast Queensland residents love taking holidays here, spending a relaxing week or two in one of the many high-rise apartments far from the wild nightlife at the northern end of the Gold Coast.

On the main shopping drag is the **Gold Coast Information & Booking Centre** (☎ 1300 309 440; www.verygoldcoast.com.au; shop 22, Showcase on the Beach, Griffith St, Coolangatta; ☺ 8.30am-5pm Mon-Fri, 9am-3pm Sat), which can provide local info. You can get online at the **Coolangatta Internet Café** (☎ 07-5599 2001; cnr Griffith & Warner Sts; per hr $7; ☺ 8.30am-6pm Mon-Fri, to 5pm Sat & Sun).

There are some fantastic views down the coast from **Point Danger**, the headlands at the end of the state line. Snapper Rocks, Rainbow Bay, Kirra and Greenmount are renowned for their excellent **surf**. Around the corner, south of Snapper Rocks and Point Danger, lies the popular beach break of Duranbah locally known as D-bah. The Gold Coast city council's sand-dredging operation at the mouth of the Tweed River in 2001 led to the formation of the **Superbank**, an unintentional gift to the surfing community. Sand was pumped north of the river mouth, creating a 2km sandbank and killer waves all the way from Snapper Rocks to Kirra if there's a decent easterly swell. Surfboards are available to rent from $30 per day from **Retro Groove** (☎ 07-5599 3952; 4/33 McLean St) or **Walkin' on Water Surf School** (☎ 07-5534 1886, 0418 780 311; www.walkinonwater.com), which also offers lessons to surfers of all levels.

Sleeping & Eating

Coolangatta YHA (☎ 07-5536 7644; www.coolangattayha.com; 230 Coolangatta Rd, Bilinga; dm $24-29, d $56-63; P ☐ ☒) Noise from the airport and highway might be a problem here and it's quite a hike from the beach, but this YHA has always been popular with surfers. Rooms are very basic and the free breakfast of toast, yoghurt and fruit juice is a bonus. Super friendly staff organise shuttle buses to Snapper Rocks and hire boards for $25 per day.

Kirra Beach Tourist Park (☎ 07-5581 7744; www.gctp.com.au/kirra; Charlotte St, Kirra; unpowered/powered sites $27/30, cabins from $59, villas $125; ☒) A sprawling park with grassy sites and loads of shady trees; there's good wheelchair access here, too. Book well ahead if planning to stay in December/January.

ourpick Café d'bar (☎ 1300 766 301; www.cafedbar.com.au; 275 Boundary St, Coolangatta; meals $6-15; ☙ breakfast & lunch) A cafe and art gallery in one, you can have a gourmet meal here with ocean views over Point Danger, then browse through the beach-themed photos and paintings all produced by local artists. Budding artists can enrol in art workshops held on site.

Crave (☎ 07-5589 6888; www.thecoolyhotel.com.au; Coolangatta Hotel, cnr Marine Pde & Warner St; mains from $12; ☙ lunch & dinner daily, breakfast Sat & Sun) The Cooly Hotel's restaurant, directly across from the beach, has been revamped with a stylish new interior and plenty of outdoor tables. The lunch menu offers the best bargains with chicken parmigianas or seafood baskets for $15.

Also recommended:

Bella Mare (☎ 07-5599 2755; www.bellamare.com.au; cnr Hill & Boundary Sts; r per 3 nights/week from $387/763, villas from $492/1008; P ☒ ☒) Modern self-contained family apartments in a Mediterranean-style building, just 50m from the beach.

Markwell Café & Bar (☎ 07-5536 4544; 64 Griffith St; mains $10-35) All seafood here is wild caught; mains include deep-fried coconut prawns dipped in beer batter, served with curry mayonnaise.

GOLD COAST HINTERLAND

Those who dare to venture inland from the beach and high-rise apartments are richly rewarded in the densely forested hinterland, an unspoilt environment often overlooked by visitors darting up and down the Gold Coast Hwy. The mountain air and enchanting bushwalking trails seem a world away from the hubbub on the coastline, but it's only a short drive via Mudgeeraba or Nerang to reach tranquillity. The seven national parks and 16 conservation parks cover 30,000 hectares of subtropical rainforests, mountain streams, waterfalls, spectacular lookouts and some wonderful pockets for wildlife.

Tours

Winding your way around the mountain and valley roads is great fun in a hire car, or take a tour if you'd prefer an experienced navigator. See p314 for hinterland tours departing from Brisbane.

Bushwacker Ecotours (☎ 1300 559 355; www.bushwacker-ecotours.com.au; adult/child from $115/95) A range of ecotours including day-long bushwalks and overnight rainforest jungle camps.

Scenic Hinterland Day Tours (☎ 07-5531 5536, 07-5538 2899; www.hinterlandtours.com.au; adult/child from $65/39) Ecotours exploring Lamington, Springbrook and Tamborine Mountain.

Southern Cross 4WD Tours (☎ 07-5574 5041; www.sc4wd.com.au; half-day tours adult/child $85/45, full-day tours $132/75) Guided 4WD tours to Tamborine Mountain and Lamington National Park including meals and wine tasting.

TAMBORINE MOUNTAIN

Just 36km northwest from Southport stands Tamborine Mountain (525m), a small plateau community known for its quaint shops

QUEENSLAND

selling homemade sweets and Australiana-themed craft souvenirs. Grey nomads love this place for its kitschy offerings and heritage feel, and there are some beautiful natural settings in **Tamborine National Park** (1500 hectares). Spectacular cascades at **Witches Falls**, **Cameron Falls** and **Curtis Falls** are accessed via walking trails, and the **Cedar Creek Falls** track (900m return) is one of the most popular in the area, leading you past gently tumbling falls and rock pools (some wheelchair access).

The **visitor information centre** (☎ 07-5545 3200; Doughty Park, Main Western Rd, North Tamborine; ☺ 10am-3.30pm Mon-Fri, 9.30am-3.30pm Sat & Sun) has plenty of information about the national park, which happens to be Queensland's oldest.

Take a swig of award-winning lemon liqueur at **Tamborine Mountain Distillery** (☎ 07-5545 3452; 87-91 Beacon Rd, North Tamborine; ☺ 10am-3pm Wed-Sun), a quirky boutique distiller that manufactures its own schnapps and other spirits from organically grown fruits.

Tamborine Mountain Caravan & Camping (☎ 07-5545 0034; Thunderbird Park, Tamborine Mountain Rd, Mt Tamborine; unpowered/powered sites $18/22) is a lovely wooded camping ground with a freshwater swimming creek.

SPRINGBROOK NATIONAL PARK

The breathtaking landscape of Springbrook is a remnant of the huge shield volcano that centred on nearby Mt Warning in NSW more than 20 million years ago. The national park is directly west of Coolangatta, just 29km from Mudgeeraba or 42km from Nerang. It's a natural wonderland for hikers with excellent walking trails through cool-temperate and eucalypt forests offering a mosaic of gorges, cliffs and waterfalls.

The park is divided into four reserves. The **Springbrook Plateau** is a 900m-high section with numerous waterfalls and spectacular lookouts. The village of Springbrook is balanced right on the edge of the plateau and there are several places where you can get the giddy thrill of leaning right out over the edge, including **Purling Brook Falls**, **Canyon Lookout** and **Best of All Lookout**. The pathway to Best of All Lookout is home to several ancient Antarctic beech trees.

The friendly folks at the **ranger's office and works depot** (☎ 07-5533 5147; 87 Carrick's Rd, Springbrook; ☺ variable hours) have copies of walking track leaflets and there's an un-staffed **information centre** (Old School Rd) near Hardy's Lookout.

You can pitch a tent at the grassy **Settlement Campground** (sites per person/family $4.85/20), off Carricks Rd, which has 11 sites including four for caravans. There is little shade and no showers, but there is a barbecue area and toilet block. You need to book in advance through **QPWS** (☎ 13 13 04; www.qld.gov.au/camping).

[our pick] **Mouses House** (☎ 07-5533 5192; www.mouseshouse.com.au; 2807 Springbrook Rd, Springbrook; r from $235, 2 nights from $390) will adored by those seeking a romantic retreat in the mountains. Linked by rainforest boardwalks, there are 11 luxury chalets here with double spas and wood fires. The A-frame wooden chalets look like they should be covered in snow on the Swiss Alps, but somehow Springbrook's lush greenery is perfectly fitting.

The beautiful **Natural Bridge** section, off the Nerang–Murwillumbah road, has a 1km walking circuit leading to a rock arch spanning a water-formed cave, which is home to a huge colony of glow-worms. Swimming in the creek is no longer allowed and rangers do enforce fines.

The **Mt Cougal** section, accessed via Currumbin Creek Rd, has several waterfalls and swimming holes. The **Numinbah** forest reserve was recently added as the fourth section of the national park.

LAMINGTON NATIONAL PARK

This precious ecological giant west of Springbrook is part of a Unesco World Heritage site and is Queensland's best known protected area. The 200 sq km park covers much of the McPherson Range and adjoins the Border Ranges National Park in NSW. Most of the park is lying on a 900m plateau characterised by beautiful gorges, waterfalls, thick subtropical rainforests and stunning bushwalking trails.

The two most popular and accessible sections of the park are **Binna Burra** and **Green Mountains**, both reached via narrow winding roads from Canungra. The drive to Green Mountains is a little challenging at times due to blind curves around the mountains, but extremely rewarding. Binna Burra can also be reached from Nerang.

There are numerous walking tracks within the park and the latest attraction for experienced hikers is the **Great Walk** (opened in 2008), a three-day 54km path that leads to the Springbrook Plateau. Other favourites include the excellent **tree-top canopy walk** along a

QUEENSLAND

series of rope-and-plank suspension bridges at Green Mountains, and the 21km **Border Track** that follows the dividing range between NSW and Queensland and links Binna Burra to the O'Reilly's Rainforest Guesthouse.

Walking trail guides are available from the **ranger stations** (Binna Burra ☎ 07-5533 3584; ⏰ 7.30am-4pm Mon-Fri, 9am-3pm Sat & Sun; Green Mountains ☎ 07-5544 0634; ⏰ 8am-3.30pm Mon-Fri, 9am-3pm Sat & Sun). Opening times vary at weekends.

Sleeping & Eating

O'Reilly's Rainforest Guesthouse (☎ 1800 688 722, 07-5544 0644; www.oreillys.com.au; Lamington National Park Rd; s/d/ste incl breakfast from $145/250/450; 🖳) This classic guest house at Green Mountains has been attracting visitors for over 90 years. The Retreat Restaurant has an old-world atmosphere and the rooms are looking a little tired, but views from the nearby pool and observation deck are simply stunning. The resort's Rainforest Room bar is open from 4pm daily and there are a multitude of activities and tours to enjoy.

Binna Burra Mountain Lodge (☎ 1300 246 622, 07-5533 3622; www.binnaburralodge.com.au; Binna Burra Rd, Binna Burra; d with/without bathroom incl breakfast from $240/180) This venerable mountain resort sits on a magical spot with commanding views from its Clifftop Dining Room and surrounding cabins. Built in 1933 by two pioneering conservationists, the original cabins remain today (number five was the first one built). There are also luxurious modern cabins with bathrooms and balconies. The dining room buffet dinner is $38.

Just 500m down the road from Binna Burra Mountain Lodge is a **campsite** (☎ 1800 074 260, 07-5533 3622; www.binnaburralodge.com.au; Binna Burra Rd, Binna Burra; unpowered/powered sites $24/30, 2-/4-/6-person safari tents $55/75/90) operated by the lodge. There are permanent safari-style tents or you can pitch your own.

There is also a **QPWS camping ground** (☎ 13 13 04; www.qld.gov.au/camping; sites per person/family $4.85/20) as you head down the hill from O'Reilly's. There are plenty of spots for tents and caravans (and a toilet/shower block) but permits must be obtained in advance from the ranger at Green Mountains (above) or by booking online.

Getting There & Away

Australian Day Tours (☎ 07-3003 0700, 1300 363 436; adult/child $84/52) runs daily tours from Brisbane

to O'Reilly's, leaving Brisbane's Roma Street Transit Centre at 8.30am and arriving back around 6pm.

Mountain Coach Company (☎ 07-5524 4249; return day trip per adult/child/family $58/35/155) has a daily service from the Gold Coast to O'Reilly's via Tamborine Mountain (three hours). If you want to use this service to stay overnight at O'Reilly's, the cost is $40 each way.

SUNSHINE COAST

A seemingly endless summer and waxed-down surfer chic make life a breeze on the Sunshine Coast. A short drive north of Brisbane, this fast-growing region is a permanent home for lucky locals and retirees, and a thriving holiday spot for Aussie families from further south.

The classic beach suburbs of Caloundra, Maroochydore and Mooloolaba – just north of Brisbane – are icons dipped in working-class bronze and zinc. If you prefer a little more froth in your cappuccino, then head further north for the boutique delights of Noosa, a blue-chip beach town at the tip of the Great Sandy National Park, surrounded by rainforest and circled by property sharks.

From here it's a short drive inland and upwards to the Glass House Mountains and the lush Sunshine Coast hinterland. Explore pretty little semirural villages and tackle a section of the spectacular, 86km-long Great Walk. And if you're within dancing distance around New Year, don't miss the mind-blowing Woodford Folk Festival.

To pay tribute to an iconic modern-day Australian, every year thousands of foreign visitors spend a memorable day at the Australia Zoo, a wonderful all-in-one animal-Irwin experience.

Getting There & Around

AIR

Jetstar (☎ 13 15 38; www.jetstar.com.au) and **Virgin Blue** (☎ 13 67 89; www.virginblue.com.au) have multiple daily connections between the **Sunshine Coast Airport** (☎ 07-5453 1500; www.sunshinecoastairport .com; Friendship Ave, Marcoola), near Maroochydore, and Sydney and Melbourne. Both airlines also offer a twice-weekly service to Adelaide. **Tiger Airways** (☎ 03-9335 3033; www.tigerairways.com) runs a daily flight to Melbourne and Sydney.

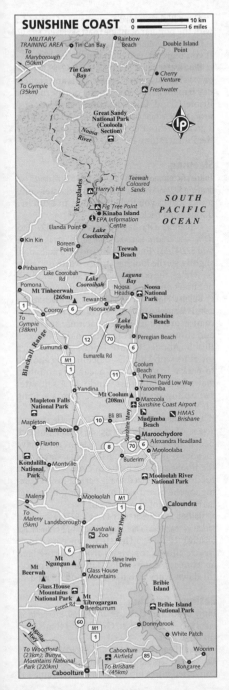

SUNSHINE COAST

BUS
Greyhound Australia (☎ 13 14 99; www.greyhound.com
.au) and **Premier Motor Service** (☎ 13 34 10; www.pre
mierms.com.au) have daily services from Brisbane
to Maroochydore ($21, 1½ hours). Premier
also offers a hop-on, hop-off backpacker bus
that covers the entire length of coastline between Brisbane and Cairns. At the time of
writing, a three-stop pass cost $198, while a
six-month unlimited-stop pass (in one direction) cost $251.

   Sunbus (☎ 07-5450 7888; www.translink.com.au)
buzzes frequently between Caloundra and
Noosa ($6, 1½ hours), and also runs regu-
lar buses from Noosa to the train station
at Nambour on the Bruce Hwy ($5.20, one
hour), via Eumundi and Yandina.

   Henry's (☎ 07-5474 0199), **Noosa Transfers &
Charters** (☎ 07-5449 9782; noosatransfers@powerup.com
.au) and **Col's Airport Shuttle** (☎ 07-5450 5933; www
.airshuttle.com.au) offer transfers from Sunshine
Coast Airport and Brisbane to Sunshine Coast
locations. The cost per adult/child is around
$45/25. Sunshine Coast Airport to Noosa
costs around $22.

TRAIN
Citytrain has services from Nambour to
Brisbane ($11.60, two hours). Trains also
go to Beerwah ($7.60, 1½ hours), near
Australia Zoo.

GLASS HOUSE MOUNTAINS
pop 660
Rising high above the green subtropical hinterland are the 16 volcanic crags known as the
Glass House Mountains. Mt Beerwah (556m),
the highest of these ethereal cornices, is the
mother according to Dreamtime mythology.
These stunning natural formations lend an
eerie otherworldliness to a region brimming
with life.

   Reach the Glass House Mountains National
Park via a series of sealed and unsealed roads
off Steve Irwin Dr. Coming from the Bruce
Hwy, take the Landsborough exit.

   Hikers are spoilt for choice here; grab a
map from the **EPA** (☎ 07-5494 3983; 61 Bunya St,
Maleny; ☻ 7am-3.30pm) in Maleny. If you're in
a hurry, the **Glass House Mountains lookout** provides a fine view of the peaks and the distant
beaches. The **lookout circuit** (800m) is a short
and steep walking track that leads through
open scribbly gum forest and down a wet gully
before circling back.

QUEENSLAND

For something more intense, check out the 1.4km (return) hike to the summit of **Mt Ngungun** (253m). It has impressive views of the four major peaks and a bit of challenging hiking – keep the kids close as the steep trail passes close to the cliff line and can be slippery.

For some mountainside *parkour*, otherwise known as 'bouldering', leg it up **Tibrogargan** (3km return) and **Beerwah** (2.6km return); you'll need good shoes and leg muscles to spring up the patches of loose rock.

Just north of Beerwah is the justifiably famous **Australia Zoo** (☎ 07-5494 1134; www.australia zoo.com.au; Steve Irwin Way, Beerwah; adult/child/family $49/29/146; ⏰ 9am-4.30pm), a homage to wildlife superenthusiast Steve Irwin and home to a remarkable assortment of critters. This is not the usual passive zoo experience, but rather an exotic animal extravaganza featuring the 'Crocoseum', Tiger Temple, armfuls of Australian natives and enough slimy-faced, beady-eyed beauties to keep the kids busy all day long. Courtesy buses are available from throughout the Sunshine Coast.

The fine country swill hall at **Glasshouse Mountains Tavern** (☎ 07-5493 0933; 10 Reed St, Glass House Mountains; mains $12-23; ⏰ lunch & dinner) serves good pub grub and icy cold glasses of beer. Visiting in winter? Take your red wine and beef sausages by the fireplace.

CALOUNDRA
pop 45,444

The Sunshine Coast's southernmost suburb is a sprawling beach community of seven surf beaches linked up by a fine promenade running north to Currimundi. With loads of beachfront cafes – and a grand backdrop of the Glass House Mountains – Caloundra makes an ideal base for beach-loving families and those wanting to keep life pretty simple.

Bulcock Beach near the main street is the most popular for sunbathing, surfing and windsurfing. The biggest crowds are found at **King's Beach**, while **Dicky**, **Moffat**, **Currimundi**, **Wurtulla** and **Buddina Beaches** at the northern end of Caloundra's coastline are also worth visiting. **Q Surf School** (☎ 0404 869 622; www.qsurf school.com) arranges day trips from Brisbane for $150 including two lessons, lunch and transfers. **Beach Beat** (☎ 07-5491 4711; 112 Burcock St; surf/body boards per day $40/30; ⏰ 9am-5pm) is just one of a few places to rent boards.

Get a flightless bird's-eye view of Caloundra with the popular **Sunshine Coast Skydivers** (☎ 07-5437 0211; Caloundra Aerodrome; tandem jumps from $200). If you regret it, you didn't make it.

Blue Water Kayak Tours (☎ 07-5494 7789; half-/full-day tours $65/130, minimum 2 people) runs an excellent day trip for active souls to the northern tip of Bribie Island. **Caloundra Cruise** (☎ 07-5492 8280; www.caloundracruise.com; adult/child/family $16/8/40) has a great 2½-hour eco-explorer cruise through the Pumicestone Passage.

Sleeping
Tourist Accommodation (☎ 07-5499 7655; 84 Omrah Ave; dm/tw/d $22/46/55; 🖳) This simple hostel-cum-motel makes you feel like you're an extra in a budget surf flick.

Caloundra City Backpackers (☎ 07-5499 7655; www.caloundracitybackpackers.com.au; 84 Omrah Rd; dm/tw/d $22/45/55) Functional and ultraclean, if slightly sterile looking (think white on white on white); the doubles have en suites and TVs, but book ahead as there are only four.

Belaire Place (☎ 07-5491 8688; www.belaireplace .com; 34 Minchinton St; r from $120; 🅿 🖳) Feel fresher than a prince in these spacious, sparkling and sunny apartments overlooking Bulcock Beach. Abodes feature bright and modern interiors with kitchens, balconies big enough to park a truck on, and ocean or mountain views from plate-glass windows. A saltwater swimming pool and on-site gym are icing on the cake.

La Promenade (☎ 07-5499 7133; www.lapromenade .com.au; 4 Tay Ave; r from $130; 🅿 🖳) Near Bulcock Beach, these upmarket waterfront units have mosquito nets covering the beds, terracotta tile floors and spa baths in every room. The rooftop family-sized spa is perfect for stargazing, or the boardwalk overlooking the water is fine for a coffee and stroll.

Rolling Surf Resort (☎ 07-5491 9777; www.rolling surfresort.com; Levuka Ave, King's Beach; 1-/2-bedroom apt $180/200; 🅿 🖳 🖳) This slick choice on King's Beach affords top views from sharp-edged apartments. It suits stylish families and party-till-dawn types who like their pool heated.

Eating & Drinking
Dicky Beach Surf Club (☎ 07-5491 6078; Coochin St; mains $12; ⏰ lunch & dinner) Good food that's easy on the wallet.

Tanja's Beach Pavilion (☎ 07-5499 6600; 8 Levuka Ave, King's Beach; mains $12-32) A classic beach pavilion converted into a hip modern eatery, Tanja's is ideal for perving on King's Beach bodies while feasting on fine, freshly grilled seafood.

Above Board (☎ 07-5491 6388; shop 8, The Esplanade; mains $14-30) A sophisticated menu and relaxed vibe greet you at this trendy eatery. You can rock up in jeans and dine on mahi mahi fillets with macadamia pesto dressing. Brekky and lunch are simpler, but equally delicious.

CBX (☎ 07-5439 4555; 12 Bulcock St) Queensland's only beer 'exchange' sees prices fluctuate as quickly as the crowd in a sudden 6ft South Pacific swell.

Getting There & Away

The **bus terminal** (Comma Tce) is one block back from Bulcock Beach. **Sunbus** (☎ 13 12 30) runs shuttles to Noosa ($5.80, 1½ hours) that stop in Maroochydore ($3.20, 50 minutes).

MAROOCHY
pop 46,611

The Sunshine Coast suburbs of Maroochydore, Alexandra Headland and Mooloolaba, collectively known as Maroochy, were once bastions of the Australian surfing scene, but these days their coastal charm is giving way to a steady suburban sprawl. The beaches themselves are still spot on though, and the buzz in the shops and cafes fronting the azure sea makes the district of Maroochy a reliable summer getaway. Try Cotton Tree Beach for a more chilled-out beach break, or wander inland to the ginger 'hood of Buderim for a taste of the 1950s.

Maroochydore takes its name from the local Aboriginal word *murukutchi-da*, meaning 'home of the black swan', but nowadays you're more likely to spot just a few stray 'birds' on the beach.

Information
Maroochy Tourism Information Booths (www .discovermaroochy.com.au, www.tourismsunshinecoast .com.au) Mooloolaba (☎ 07-5478 2233; cnr Brisbane Rd & First Ave, Mooloolaba; ☒ 9am-5pm); Maroochydore airport (☎ 07-5448 9088; Friendship Dr, Marcoola; ☒ 9.30am-3pm)
Maroochy Visitors Centre (☎ 1800 882 032, 07-5479 1566; www.maroochytourism.com; cnr Sixth Ave & Melrose St, Maroochydore; ☒ 9am-5pm Mon-Fri, to 4pm Sat & Sun) Free accommodation booking service.

Sights & Activities
Mooloolaba is perhaps the hippest of the bunch, owing to the longest beaches, most

consistent surf and its plethora of cafes, shops and colourful rental houses. The Wharf is ideal for kids.

Swim with sloppy-kissing seals, dive with sharks and psyche out psychedelic fish at **Underwater World** (☎ 07-5444 8488; The Wharf, Mooloolaba; adult/child/family $27/16/73; ☒ 9am-6pm), Queensland's largest oceanarium. The adjoining **Scuba World** (☎ 07-5444 8598; www.scubaworld .com.au; The Wharf, Mooloolaba; dives from $90; ☒ 10am-5pm) arranges coral dives off the coast and a popular wreck dive of the sunken ex-HMAS *Brisbane* ($150 for a half-day trip including two dives).

The **Aussie Sea Kayak Company** (☎ 07-5477 5355; www.ausseakayak.com.au; The Wharf, Mooloolaba; 4hr tour $65, 2hr sunset paddle $45) is a highly reputable company that can also arrange multiday missions to North Stradbroke, Fraser and Moreton Islands.

Steve Irwin's Whale One (☎ 1300 274 539; www .whaleone.com.au; adult/child/family $125/75/320) runs whale-watching cruises in September and October for those who can't make it north to Hervey Bay.

Pin Cushion, near the mouth of the Maroochy River, is probably the top **surf break** in this excellent stretch for surfing, but most visitors head to the more easily accessed Maroochy and Memorial Ave. For the inexperienced, **Robbie Sherwell's XL Surfing Academy** (☎ 07-5478 1337; 63 Oloway Cres, Alexandra Headland; 1hr lesson private/group $70/30) runs popular introductory lessons. You can rent boards from **Beach Beat** (☎ 07-5443 2777; 164 Alexandra Pde, Alexandra Headland; surfboards/body boards per day $35/25; ☒ 9am-5pm).

Sleeping
Cotton Tree Beachouse Backpackers (☎ 07-5443 1755; www.cottontreebackpackers.com; 15 The Esplanade, Cotton Tree; dm/s/d $22/44/50) Maroochy's backpacker pulse is found at peaceful Cotton Tree. Here, young travellers enjoy a tree-lined beach frontage, plus free use of kayaks, bikes and boogie boards. Rooms are bright and breezy, and the adjacent park and river lend Cotton Tree all the charm of a watercolour painting.

Mooloolaba Beach Backpackers (☎ 07-5444 3399; www.mooloolababackpackers.com; 75 Brisbane Rd, Mooloolaba; dm/d $29/70; ☐ ☒) The serviceable backpacker digs here are clean and the location is handy – set back just a few blocks from the beach.

QUEENSLAND

Heritage Motor Inn (☎ 07-5443 7355; heritagemotorinn@hotmail.com; 69 Sixth Ave, Mooloolaba; r from $145; ❌ ❑) Well located, well proportioned, and well and truly kitsch, the Heritage is a genuine and friendly beach motel, close to the action and spotlessly clean.

Coral Sea Apartments (☎ 07-5479 2999; www.coralsea-apartments.com; 35-37 Sixth Ave, Maroochydore; apt per week from $1380; ❌ ❑) These spacious apartments, close to the Maroochy Surf Life Saving Club, are a great option for small families or self-caterers.

Landmark Resort (☎ 1800 888 835; www.landmarkresort.com.au; cnr The Esplanade & Burnett St, Mooloolaba; 1-/2-bedroom apt from $210/280; ❌ ❑) The Landmark boasts the best ocean views in town, and it is a mere stumble down the stairs to the trendy dining set. The rooftop has the makings of a debauched lagoon-shaped pool party, with barbecue, spa and heaps of sun.

Cotton Tree Caravan Park (☎ 1800 461 253; www.maroochypark.qld.gov.au; Cotton Tree Pde, Cotton Tree; unpowered/powered sites from $25/28, cabins $125-160) Best avoided in summer, this large caravan park at the mouth of the Maroochy River is a grassy, beachside gem.

Eating

Sister Organic (☎ 07-5479 4911; shop 1, 13 The Esplanade, Cotton Tree; meals $8-18; ☯ breakfast & lunch) This excellent new cafe is like a cute younger sibling to the bland high-rise eateries further south – plus it's totally organic. The imaginative breakfast menu includes delicious homemade baked beans on sourdough, and scrambled polenta and chorizo. There's also quality coffee and juices.

Cracked Pepper (☎ 07-5452 6700; shop 1, Mooloolaba International, cnr Venning St & The Esplanade, Mooloolaba; mains $10-20) Sophisticated cafe fare is served at this popular restaurant with copious outdoor seating facing Mooloolaba's main promenade.

Boat Shed (☎ 07-5443 3808; The Esplanade, Cotton Tree; mains $22-34; ☯ lunch daily, dinner Mon-Sat) This classic Maroochy seafood joint sits proudly on the banks of the river beneath a sprawling cotton tree. The coconut-battered prawns are delectable, while anything fresh from the rod is sure to please. Noneaters rejoice: the outdoor lounges will have you throwing back the cocktails in stargazing comfort.

Bella Venezia (☎ 07-5444 5844; 95 The Esplanade, Mooloolaba; mains $25-38; ☯ lunch & dinner)

Mooloolaba's fanciest restaurant is an Italian love affair starring *ravioli alla sambuca* and *risotto nera* (squid-ink risotto). The recently added wine bar has fortnightly tastings and live music on Wednesday nights.

Also recommended:

Raw Energy (☎ 07-5444 2111; Shop 3, The Esplanade, Mooloolaba; dishes $6-15; ☯ breakfast & lunch) A buzzing cafe chain with a reputation for standout vegetarian fare, fresh juices and smoothies.

Sunshine Plaza (Horton Pde, Maroochydore; meals $5-8) Takeaway and supermarket.

Drinking

Mooloolaba SLSC (☎ 07-5444 1300; The Esplanade, Mooloolaba; ☯ 10am-10pm Sun-Thu, to midnight Fri & Sat) So you want to drink, eat and party like a local? Get to your nearest surf club! Right on the beach, Mooloolaba's has floor-to-ceiling windows affording stunning views during the day and suntanned dance floor antics by night.

Getting There & Away

Long-distance buses stop at the **Suncoast Pacific bus terminal** (☎ 07-5443 1011; First Ave, Maroochydore), just off Aerodrome Rd.

AROUND MAROOCHY

Coolum and **Peregian Beaches** are both favourites with local surfers when there's good swell. **Point Perry** is a wonderful vantage point for that seminal Aussie summer snap, while intrepid photographers (and anyone else for that matter) can climb **Mt Coolum** (208m) for bird's-eye vistas. Get details at the **visitor information office** (David Low Way; ☯ 9am-1pm Mon-Sat) – look for it off the main drag from Maroochy towards Coolum and Peregian.

Coolum Beach Caravan Park (☎ 1800 461 474; David Low Way, Coolum; unpowered/powered sites $24/27) is beachfront and basic, with plenty of grass to shake the sand from your undies.

On Peregian Beach, the best sleeping bet is the crisp, clean and spacious **Pacific Blue Apartments** (☎ 07-5448 3611; www.pacificblueapartments.com.au; 236 David Low Way, Peregian Beach; apt $120-180; ❑). For dinner, come to **My Place** (☎ 07-5446 4433; David Low Way; mains $15-20; ☯ 7am-11pm) for the ocean views, cocktails and Mediterranean cuisine.

Sol Bar (☎ 07-5446 2333; cnr Beach Rd & David Low Way) is a godsend for city-starved indie rockers. A constantly surprising line-up performs, while punters enjoy an array of international beers.

NOOSA

pop 34,539

If Noosa isn't the hippest beachside destination in Australia, then we give up! The brightest light on the Sunshine Coast has bloody close to the lot: superb north-facing surf beaches, a pristine waterway in Noosa Sound, haute couture on Hastings St, beds for all budgets, fab local markets – and all this encircled by a resplendent national park.

And despite gobsmacking property and cocktail prices, Noosa remains the domain of the outdoor enthusiast. Bypass the year-round be-seen scene of Noosa Heads for the epic and empty North Shore, where you can hike, sail, paddle, and, of course, surf your pants off in a fauna-filled biosphere. For those with big wheels to burn, the area across the Noosa River is preserved as the Cooloola Section of the Great Sandy National Park – you can ride this wilderness all the way to Fraser Island.

Just remember you're in Noosa, ladies and gentlemen, so whatever you do, please do it in style.

Orientation

It's easy to get disoriented when driving in Noosa – over 100 roundabouts mean more than 300 choices to make! In short, get a map.

A number of communities surround Noosa River yet Noosa, to many, still means Hastings St. Further west is Noosa Spit, reached via a footpath from the far west end of Hastings St. Tucked around the headland to the east in Noosa National Park are superb walking tracks and quiet stretches of sand ending at funky little Sunshine Beach, which is ideal for longer stays.

Most of the accommodation options are a few minutes' drive from Noosa Heads along the mouth of the Noosa River in Noosaville or Tewantin. You'll also find restaurants clustered around Gympie Tce and Thomas St in Noosaville.

Uphill from Noosa Heads is Noosa Junction, home to the post office, supermarkets, shops and a cinema.

Information

You will find banks and ATMs in Noosa Junction and Hastings St.

Adventure Travel Bugs (☎ 1800 666 720, 07-5474 8530; 9 Sunshine Beach Rd, Noosa Junction; per hr $2; ⊗ 8am-8pm Mon-Fri, 9am-7pm Sat & Sun) Internet access and super-friendly budget tours and ticket-booking service.

EPA centre (☎ 07-5447 3243; ⊗ 9am-3pm) Located at the main entrance to Noosa National Park, 2km southwest of town.
Noosa Visitor Information Centre (☎ 1800 448 833, 07-5447 4988; www.tourismnoosa.com.au; Hastings St; ⊗ 9am-5pm) A helpful service.
Post office (☎ 07-5473 8591; 91 Noosa Dr)

Sights

You don't so much see as be seen in Noosa. Stroll the pretty streets, beaches and waterways, and shop for a polka-dotted parasol, organic cotton dress or custom-made longboard.

Boutique shopping is found on **Hastings St** in Noosa Heads. Here you'll also find **Noosa Main Beach** and the main entrance to **Noosa National Park** (☎ 07-5447 3243; ⊗ 9am-3pm). The 2km-long park has fine walks, great coastal scenery and a string of popular bays for surfing on the northern side – when there's good swell, don't miss an iconic Australian afternoon at Tea Tree Bay or Little Cove. **Sunshine Beach** is a popular destination for a morning stroll – the monstrous shore-break and bluebottles will keep the kids giddily on their toes. Charming **Alexandria Bay**, on the eastern side of the national park, is for both naturists and nature enthusiasts.

Art lovers can pick up information on the excellent **Sunshine Coast Gallery Trail** from the visitors centre.

Activities

Noosa River is excellent for canoeing and kayaking. It's possible to follow it up past beautiful homes through to Lakes Cooroibah and Cootharaba, and the Cooloola Section of the Great Sandy National Park to just south of Rainbow Beach Rd. **Ocean & River Kayak Tours** (☎ 0418 787 577; www.learntosurf.com) offers two-hour sea-kayaking tours ($66) around Noosa National Park and Noosa River – if you're lucky, you'll see turtles and dolphins. Tours meet at Noosa Woods.

For the hard-core paddler, **Peterpan Adventure Travel** (☎ 1800 777 115; www.peterpans .com; shop 3, 75 Noosa Dr, Noosa Junction; per person $160) offers three-day canoe tours into the national park, including tents and equipment.

For a more sedate experience, hop aboard **Noosa Ferry Cruises** (☎ 07-5449 8442; all day pass adult/ child/family $20/5.50/45; ⊗ departs 10 times daily), which chugs (or, rather, motors) the 40 minutes between the Sheraton Hotel and Tewantin.

QUEENSLAND

QUEENSLAND

NOOSA

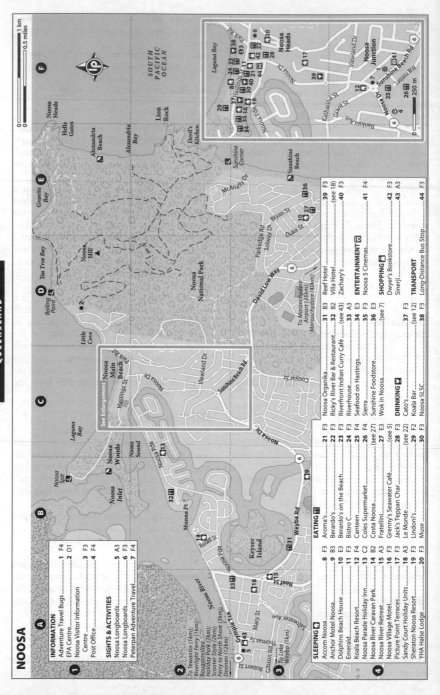

INFORMATION

Adventure Travel Bugs	**1** F4
EPA Centre	**2** D1
Noosa Visitor Information Centre	**3** F3
Post Office	**4** F4

SIGHTS & ACTIVITIES

Noosa Longboards	**5** A3
Noosa Longboards	**6** F3
Peterpan Adventure Travel	**7** F4

SLEEPING 🛏

Accom Noosa	**8** F3
Anchor Motel Noosa	**9** B3
Dolphins Beach House	**10** E3
Emerald	**11** F3
Koala Beach Resort	**12** F4
Noosa Parade Holiday Inn	**13** C2
Noosa River Caravan Park	**14** B2
Noosa River Retreat	**15** A3
Noosa Village Motel	**16** F3
Picture Point Terraces	**17** F3
Sandy Court Holiday Units	**18** A3
Sheraton Noosa Resort	**19** F3
YHA Halse Lodge	**20** F3

EATING 🍴

Aroma's	**21** F3
Berardo's	**22** F3
Berardo's on the Beach	**23** F3
Bistro C	**24** F3
Canteen	**25** F4
Coles Supermarket	**26** F4
Costa Noosa	(see 27)
Fratellini	**27** E3
Grenny's Seawater Café	(see 5)
Jack's Teppan Char	**28** F3
Le Monde	**29** F2
Lindoni's	**30** F3
Muse	**31** B3
Noosa Organika	**31** B3
Ricky's River Bar & Restaurant	**32** B2
Riverfront Indian Curry Café	(see 43)
Riverhouse	**33** A3
Seafood on Hastings	**34** E3
Sierra	**35** F3
Sunshine Foodstore	**36** E7
Wok in Noosa	(see 7)

DRINKING 🍷

Cato's	**37** F3
Koala Bar	(see 12)
Noosa SLSC	**38** F3

ENTERTAINMENT 🎭

Reef Hotel	**39** F3
Villa Hotel	(see 18)
Zachary's	**40** F3
Noosa 5 Cinemas	**41** F4

SHOPPING 🛍

Dwyer's Bookstore	**42** F3
Sinerji	**43** A3

TRANSPORT

Long-Distance Bus Stop	**44** F3

To Tewantin (1km);
Riverlight Ferry (1km);
Bougainvillea
Holiday Park (2km);
Scooter Style (2km);
Ferry to North Shore (3km);
Doonan (12km)

To Lake
Weyba (1km)

SOUTH PACIFIC OCEAN

Noosa Heads
Hells Gates
Alexandria Beach
Alexandria Bay
Devil's Kitchen
Lion Rock
Boiling Point
Tea Tree Bay
Granite Bay
Little Cove
Noosa Hill
Noosa National Park
Sunshine Corner
Sunshine Beach

To Maroochydore
Airport (35km);
Maroochydore (40km)

Noosa Spit
Noosa Inlet
Noosa Sound
Noosa Woods
Laguna Bay
Munna Pt
Keyser Island
Noosa River
Noosa Main Beach
Laguna Bay
Noosa Heads
Noosa Junction

See Enlargement

GOOFY OR NATURAL? SURFING'S NOT FOR KOOKS

Marching down to Noosa's Little Cove, the conditions are officially 'cranking' – the best in six months. We paddle out the back (I can do that bit easily enough), and join 30-odd locals. One seven-year-old punk does a 360-degree turn that nearly rips my head off then a silver bearded senior citizen walks the plank of his bright-yellow longboard and gives me a wave from deep inside a curling tube. Everyone's throwing long-distance high-fives and patting themselves on the back just for being here, out in the ocean, on this cloudless January day.

My deltoids are burning, my lower back aching, but this is a day to savour. For the record, I catch four waves, stand up twice, nosedive thrice and love every single minute. Give me a week, and I'll be hangin' (something) loose.

Unspoilt Noosa National Park offers peaceful, peeling right-hand waves for all levels, though it can be fickle in winter. On the northern coast of the headland, good surfers look to Boiling Point and Tea Tree. Little Cove and Granite Bay are the pick of the point breaks for grommets. Sunshine Beach, and in particular Sunshine Corner, is a heavy wave best left to the experts, while Noosa Spit, on the far end of Hastings St, is protected from the rips and makes an ideal place to 'un-kook' yourself (ie learn to surf).

The luxury surfing travel company, **Tropic Surf** (www.tropicsurf.net) is based in Noosa, and its offshoot **Wave Sense** (☎ 07-5474 9076, 1800 249 076; www.wavesense.com.au) runs private lessons for $150 for two hours – a great option for families or those looking to really improve their surfing. Mostly based around Noosa Spit, other options include **Go Ride a Wave** (☎ 1300 132 441; www .gorideawave.com.au), **Noosa Surf Lessons** (☎ 0412 330 850; www.noosasurflessons.com.au) and **Merrick's Learn to Surf** (☎ 0418 787 577; www.learntosurf.com.au). Two-hour group lessons on longboards cost around $55. They all meet at Noosa Woods, just off Hastings St.

For something extra soulful, have a go at self-explanatory **Standup Paddle Surfing** (☎ 0412 175 233; www.standuppaddlesurfing.com.au) – or look for the dude surfing Main Beach with his pet dog beside him!

If you want to hire equipment, **Noosa Longboards** (www.noosalongboards.com; Noosa Heads ☎ 07-5447 2828; 64 Hastings St; Noosaville ☎ 07-5474 2722; 187 Gympie Tce) has boards for $35/50 per half/full day. You can also grab a boogie board here ($15/20).

Guides are friendly and knowledgeable. The sunset cruise ($20) is a thirst-quenching BYO affair.

Noosa Kite Surfing (☎ 0438 747 801; www.noosakite surfing.com.au; 2hr lesson $140) runs lessons around Lake Weyba at the mouth of the river.

Tours

A number of tour operators offer trips from Noosa to Fraser Island via the Cooloola Coast. All include the major Fraser Island highlights.

Beyond Noosa (☎ 1800 657 666; www.beyondnoosa .com.au; afternoon tours adult/child from $69/45; 🖳 🐾) Relaxed ecotours of the Noosa everglades.

Fraser Island Adventure Tours (☎ 07-5444 6957; www.fraserislandadventuretours.com.au; adult/child $159/115) An industry award-winner that includes a delicious barbecue lunch.

Fraser Island Excursions (☎ 07-5449 0393; www .fraserislandexcursions.com.au; tours $189) Small day tours take place in comfortable 4WD minibuses, and include a gourmet lunch and a glass of tipple.

Festivals & Events

In the first week of January, the **Great Noosa Campout** (www.thegreatnoosacampout.com; Eumundi-Noosa Rd, Doonan) is a new music festival that takes place in nearby Doonan. Otherwise, the **Noosa Long Weekend** (www.noosalongweekend .com) is actually 10 days of fine food, fashion and frivolity in June/July, while the **Noosa Jazz Festival** (www.usmevents.com.au/noosajazz) continues its international surge for four days in late August.

Sleeping

Most accommodation in Noosa is in self-contained units, although there are several backpacker hostels and caravan parks. Accommodation prices soar around school holidays and Christmas; book ahead at these times.

BUDGET

Noosa is not all about the bling. In fact, budget travellers have some fine options.

ourpick Dolphins Beach House (☎ 07-5447 2100; www.dolphinsbeachhouse.com; 14 Duke St, Sunshine Beach; dm/d/apt $27/65/70; 💻 💷) Up there with the better backpacker joints on the east coast, Dolphins is a peaceful retreat set in lush tropical gardens. The self-contained dorms are neat and spacious, with their own share of a large Queenslander balcony, while the doubles are decked for travelling lovers. A very short walk to the beach or the Sunshine cafe strip, the real difference here is the absence of a bar. The travel-savvy owners know it all in a good way.

Koala Beach Resort (☎ 1800 357 457, 07-5447 3355; www.koala-backpackers.com; 44 Noosa Dr, Noosa Junction; dm $27, tw & d $70; 💻 💷) It's a touch impersonal and scruffy, but if we didn't include this Koala branch we'd likely get chastised by raucous guests three months into an East Coast bender. It's well situated in Noosa Junction, close to shops and Sunshine. The dorms are massive, the parties carry on.

YHA Halse Lodge (☎ 1800 242 567, 07-5447 3377; www.halselodge.com.au; 2 Halse Lane, Noosa Heads; dm/d $32/82; 💻) In a word, busy. Climb the steep driveway to find a fine white Queenslander and one of the coast's most famous traveller rest stops. The big balcony and bar teem with cool-seeking backpackers. The dorms are nothing special, but this doesn't seem to repel the masses from booking online well in advance. Best of all, it's right downtown. Guests can use surfboards free of charge. The kitchen serves tasty, cheap meals ($9 to $12).

Sandy Court Holiday Units (☎ 07-5449 7225; fax 07-5473 0397; 30 James St, Noosaville; units $80-120; 💷) As far as cheap, self-contained beds in Noosaville go, Sandy Court gets our vote. Down a quiet residential street, these minihouses with full kitchen, living room and one or two bedrooms are great value, though fairly hot and old fashioned.

MIDRANGE & TOP END

Accommodation on Hastings St can be ridiculously expensive, but the tariffs drop markedly along Gympie Tce, the riverside main road through Noosaville. For private units to rent, call **Accom Noosa** (☎ 1800 072 078; www.accomnoosa.com.au; shop 5, Fairshore Apartments, Hastings St, Noosa Heads). There's often a three-night minimum stay for these.

Anchor Motel Noosa (☎ 07-5449 8055; www.anchormotelnoosa.com.au; cnr Anchor St & Weyba Rd, Noosaville; r from $100; 💷 💷) Motel ahoy! The Anchor pushes the nautical theme hard and starboard, with porthole windows, blue sailor-striped doonas and various underwater motifs. Rooms are neat and still new enough, plus there's a small pool with a real Jacuzzi! It's centrally located between Hastings St and Noosa Junction.

Noosa River Retreat (☎ 07-5474 2811; www.noosariverretreat.net; cnr Weyba Rd & Reef St, Noosaville; 1-bedroom units $130; 💷 💻 💷) Your buck goes a long way at this orderly complex, which houses spacious, spick-and-span units. On site are a central barbecue and laundry and the corner units are almost entirely protected by small native gardens.

Noosa Village Motel (☎ 07-5447 5800; www.noosavillage.com; 10 Hastings St; r from $130; 💷) Save your pennies for a few Noosa iced teas by staying at this good-value joint right on Hastings St. Set inside a bright-blue-and-yellow, boxlike motel, rooms are large, if a little plain, and feature wall-length windows.

Noosa Parade Holiday Inn (☎ 07-5447 4177; www.noosaparadeholidayinn.com; 51 Noosa Pde, Noosa Heads; r $190; 💷 💷) Close to Hastings St, this is a surprisingly bright and spacious motel, with cool, tiled rooms offering some of the better value in this part of town.

Sheraton Noosa Resort (☎ 07-5449 4888; www.starwoodhotels.com/sheraton; 14-16 Hastings St, Noosa Heads; r $290-540; 💷 💻 💷) No surprises in this superb downtown five-star hotel that has stylish suede suites (no seriously, they're stylish), with extra-special beds. There are four bars, three restaurants (start your day at Cato's), and state-of-the-nation gym facilities. Book online or get fleeced.

Emerald (☎ 1800 803 899, 07-5449 6100; www.emeraldnoosa.com.au; 42 Hastings St, Noosa Heads; r from $370; 💷 💻 💷) The ethereal white, angular rooms at Emerald are smoother than a Noosa iced tea. The self-contained rooms are magazine-cover cool, and suit newlyweds and long-time lovers. Dine downstairs on seafood at Rococo (mains $25 to $38), just because you can.

Picture Point Terraces (☎ 07-5449 2433; www.picturepointterraces.com.au; 47 Picture Point Cres, Noosa Heads; 2-/3-bedroom apt from $475/575; 💷 💻 💷) Peer over the rainforest and down to Laguna Bay from these modern apartments up high behind the Reef Hotel. It's perfect for families or a group of young party pirates who should make full use of the private spa bath on the balcony.

CAMPING

Noosa River Caravan Park (☎ 07-5449 7050; Russell St, Noosaville; unpowered/powered sites $21/23; 🖳)) On Munna Point, this gets the prize for location. Book well ahead.

Bougainvillea Holiday Park (☎ 1800 041 444, 07-5447 1712; jsjs@optusnet.com.au; 141 Cooroy-Noosa Rd, Tewantin; unpowered/powered sites $30/34, cabins $65-135; 🔲 🖳) Enjoy manicured lawns and spotless facilities at the sharpest campsite in town.

Eating

Maybe it's the weather, maybe it's the sea, maybe it's the happy hour just gone, but Noosa is a fabulous place to eat out.

NOOSA HEADS & HASTINGS STREET

Hastings St and the Noosa Head area is where to head for sophisticated dining.

Aroma's (☎ 07-5474 9788; 32 Hastings St; mains $10-20) Eating comes shortly after meeting and greeting at Noosa's premier street-side cafe. Once business has been attended to, cute strangers perved upon and the children settled, try the fab shared meze platter, an endless assortment of coffee drinks, great open sandwiches or a stiff cocktail at sunset.

Sierra (☎ 07-5447 4800; 10 Hastings St; mains $15-25) Sierra is a rocking little cafe-bar serving strong fruit daquiris to shoeless chess players and tanned newspaper browsers. The food is also spot-on, including such glorious tropical concoctions as grilled prawns with Cajun banana and black sticky rice.

Bistro C (☎ 07-5447 2855; On the Beach, Hastings St; mains $16-32) Even the patrons look edible at the famed little Bistro C right on Noosa Main Beach. The whole baby barramundi fried in lime and palm sugar is suitably sumptuous. Vegies can slurp on the linguini with baby bocconcini, pine nuts, rocket and basil oil. It's that place with the famous people sculptures.

Jack's Teppan Char (☎ 07-5474 9555; 50 Hastings St; mains $18-28; 🕑 lunch & dinner Tue-Sun) Noosa's very own brewery – Laguna Bay – now has its very own teppan-yaki restaurant serving char-grilled goodness in a hip cocktail-induced atmosphere. The vegetarian udon is deliciously crunchy and the noodles perfectly sweet and sticky, while the chicken teriyaki is outstanding. Serves are not huge, so dig into the extensive entrée menu. Best of all, the adjoining bottle shop keeps the price of the booze down.

Le Monde (☎ 07-5449 2366; Hastings St; mains $18-32) A recent facelift has merely fixed a permanent smile on Noosa's beloved Le Monde, still the cafe of choice for those who know about those kinds of things! An extraordinarily long menu – juicy burgers, fine pasta, all manner of seafood and curries – hides the secret agenda of this open-air glam spot, which is to simply sip the day away. Regular live music means you can often sip the night away too.

Muse (☎ 07-5447 2433; 8 Hastings St, Noosa Heads; meals $25-35; 🕑 dinner) Upon entry through the waterfall windows, you know you're in Noosa's new king of stylish dining. If the pleasures of the sea are not your thing, then how about roasted venison with sweet potato and pecan pie? Or triple-orange glazed duck? You get the idea: it's fancy.

Berardo's (☎ 07-5447 5666; Hastings St, Noosa Heads; mains $26-33; 🕑 dinner) Find subtropical sex appeal dished up in slithers of truffle polenta and quail crépinette. The seafood hotpot is fragrant, the beach just across the road. There's a grand piano in the centre of the rooftop garden and enough style to sink some petits fours from the elegant dessert menu.

Also recommended:

Berardo's on the Beach (☎ 07-5477 5666; On the Beach, Hastings St; mains $15-30) The more relaxed Berardo's.

Lindoni's (☎ 07-5447 5111; Hastings St, Noosa Heads; mains $25-35; 🕑 dinner) Australian-style Italian.

Seafood on Hastings (☎ 07-5474 5210; 2 Hastings St, Noosa Heads; mains $10-18; 🕑 lunch & dinner) Brand new takeaway fish and chip joint, with fresh and local written all over it.

NOOSAVILLE

Check out the strip along Thomas St or Gibson St. Many places here are BYO, so stock up on wine and beer beforehand.

Grenny's Seawater Café (☎ 07-5449 7215; 197 Gympie Tce, Noosaville; meals $8-20) Grenny's is full of young families, very young couples and relaxed locals eating simple, sizeable seafood meals, including humungous fish sandwiches.

our pick **Riverhouse** (☎ 07-5449 7441; 301 Weyba Rd, Noosaville; mains $26-36; 🕑 dinner daily, lunch Sun) Understated, underrated Riverhouse has a stylish Queensland sensibility, with a bright, open aspect on a street away from the Noosaville drag. Staff are warm and non-intrusive, while the seasonal menu includes buttery Wagyu steak, organic chicken and ham hock terrine with fig chutney and angel shell pasta with croutons, tomato, rocket, fresh basil and dollops of sweet olive oil.

Ricky's River Bar & Restaurant (☎ 07-5447 2455; Noosa Wharf, 2 Quamby Pl; mains $27-36; ✆ noon-midnight) This culinary surprise down by the Noosa River serves up fine local produce in a simply elegant setting. It's hard to outdo a bowl of Noosa spanner crab spaghettini with a chilled glass of Chardonnay. Try to at least arrive by boat.

Also recommended:

Noosa Organika (☎ 07-5442 4973; Weyba Rd, Noosaville) Grocer and cafe of the future!

Riverfront Indian Curry Café (☎ 07-5449 7708; shop 10, 203 Gympie Tce, Noosaville; mains $10-20) Cheap, cheerful Indian cafe. Ten buck thalis? You heard.

NOOSA JUNCTION & SUNSHINE BEACH

Eating options in Noosa Junction tend to be casual affairs, popular with locals, long-stay visitors and self-caterers. Sunshine Beach has just one small strip of restaurants on Duke St, right above the beach.

Costa Noosa (☎ 07-5474 9222; 26 Duke St, Sunshine Beach; ✆ breakfast & lunch) Coffee lovers unite! Busy young staff prepare killer coffee in every blend, in every way, in this cool open-plan cafe.

Canteen (☎ 07-5447 5400; 4-6 Sunshine Beach Rd, Noosa Junction; dishes $8-15; ✆ breakfast & lunch; ▯) Oddly located beside the TAB is this very popular breakfast joint that throws up new ideas such as bacon minitartlets with eggs. Loads of healthy options, plus 30 minutes free internet.

Sunshine Foodstore (☎ 07-5474 5611; 46 Duke St, Sunshine Beach; dishes $8-16; ✆ breakfast & lunch) Multipurpose food stores like these are just so happy summer holidays! While awaiting plates of pesto-laden scrambled eggs or mouth-wrenching ciabatta, bright-eyed news fiends scour headlines from behind enormous juice cups and designer sunnies.

Wok in Noosa (☎ 07-5448 0372; 77 Noosa Dr, Noosa Junction; mains $12-22; ✆ lunch & dinner) Opposite Koala Beach Resort is this authentic and snappy Thai and Malaysian joint. Highly recommended are Fu's Seafood Sambal and the vegie pad thai.

Fratellini (☎ 07-5474 8080; 36 Duke St, Sunshine Beach; mains $12-26) This mostly Italian restaurant is the pick of the Sunshine Beach cafe stretch, partly for the food, partly for the party mood. The

friendly kitchen pumps out delicious homemade pasta and crispy-thin pizza.

Self-caterers should head to the **Coles Supermarket** (Noosa Fair Shopping Centre, Lanyana Way, Noosa Junction).

Drinking & Entertainment

Both Sierra (p353) and Le Monde (p353) have live music some nights.

Noosa SLSC (☎ 07-5474 5688; Noosa Main Beach, Hastings St; ✆ 11am-midnight) Feel like a single-minded surfing mogul millionaire after a few jars in the $6 million, almost-famous Noosa Surf Life Saving Club. The views are unbelievable, as is the fact that pokies are played so close to paradise!

Zachary's (☎ 07-5447 3211; 30 Hastings St, Noosa Heads; ✆ noon-midnight) Noosa Heads' Zachary's offers an alternative for electronic kids who still love eating great pizza, chugging cocktails and checking people out. The walls are dark red, the day beds made of velvet, and the overall preparty bravado is very hard to resist.

Koala Bar (☎ 07-5447 3355; 44 Noosa Dr, Noosa Junction; ✆ noon-2am) Meet a partner with a use-by date at the free-spirited, lemon-and-salted backpacker bar par excellence. Sweaty bands bang out all-too-familiar tunes, but you've gotta love the dedication of the beer-swilling temporary expats.

Villa Hotel (☎ 07-5430 5555; Mary St, Noosaville; ✆ 11am-midnight) A recent overhaul has granted Noosaville a reliable, all-purpose boozer – and a decent alternative for your beer and pool money. There are new double rooms starting at $90.

Reef Hotel (☎ 07-5447 4477; 9 Noosa Dr, Noosaville; ✆ 11am-midnight Sun-Thu, to 3am Fri & Sat) Classic country meets coast at the grandstanding Reef Hotel, a multifloored long-time favourite. The downstairs club cranks until 3am on Friday and Saturday nights. During the day, patrons watch or gamble on sport, munch hearty pub meals and spread sand all over the place.

Cato's (☎ 07-5449 4888; 12-14 Hastings St, Noosa Heads; ✆ noon-midnight) This firmly established wine bar gets packed on warm summer nights by masters of the smart casual. Whirling fans keep the breeze running down the polo tops of the 30-plus crowd, as you peruse the 30-strong wine list and spill your own life story. The regular live music gets loud!

Noosa 5 Cinemas (☎ 1300 366 339; 29 Sunshine Beach Rd, Noosa Junction) This plush, comfortable cinema screens the latest blockbusters.

Shopping

Sinerji (☎ 07-5449 9808; shop 5, Gympie Tce, Noosaville) A generation from Hastings St, this shop sells locally designed fabrics and jewellery made from natural, organic materials. It's fair trade and fairly priced.

Dwyer's Bookstore (☎ 07-5474 9989; Shop 5, Laguna, Hastings St, Noosa Heads) Stocks a good range of new fiction.

Getting There & Around

Long-distance buses stop at the bus stop near the corner of Noosa Dr and Noosa Pde; see p345 for fares. Most hostels have courtesy pick-ups, except YHA Halse Lodge, which is 100m away.

Sunbus has frequent services to Maroochydore ($5, one hour), and links up with the major parts of Noosa. From Christmas until early January, and over Easter, free shuttle buses run every 10 to 15 minutes between Noosa Junction, Noosa Heads and Tewantin.

Noosa Bike Hire (☎ 07-5474 3322; www.noosabike hire.com; per 4hr/day $39/49) is available at YHA Halse Lodge (p352) and various other outlets. It even delivers bikes to your door. Noosa is ideal for scootering around, and the bad-arse bikes available from **Scooter Style** (☎ 0404 861 322; www.scooterstyle.com.au; 175 Eumundi Rd, Noosaville; per day from $55) are in excellent nick.

Riverlight Ferry (☎ 07-5449 8442; one way per adult/child/family $12/4/27, day pass $18/5/40) operates ferries between Noosa Heads and Tewantin, with services running six to 10 times a day. The **Other Car Rental Company** (☎ 07-5447 2831; per day from $50) delivers cars and 4WDs to your door.

COOLOOLA COAST

Running from its southern tip at Noosa to Rainbow Beach in the north is 50km of gloriously undeveloped Cooloola Coast. Wildlife abounds, but a fair amount of 4WD through traffic means your starry nights are not always spent in silence.

Nevertheless, travelling north in this direction is a real buzz, as you forego the bitumen for low tidal highways, passing the Teewah Coloured Sands and the wreck of the *Cherry Venture*, swept ashore in 1973.

Lake Cooroibah

Where Noosa River widens into the wondrous Lake Cooroibah, you'll find surprisingly thick bushland – a popular base for engaging with the natural environment.

Lake Cooroibah is about 2km north of Tewantin. From the end of Moorindil St in Tewantin, you can catch the **Noosa North Shore Ferry** (☎ 07-5447 1321; one way per pedestrian/car $1/5; ☯ 5.30am-10.20pm Sun-Thu, 5am-12.20am Fri & Sat) up to the lake in a conventional vehicle and camp along sections of the beach.

The refreshingly feral **Gagaju Backpackers** (☎ 1300 302 271, 07-5474 3522; www.travoholic.com/gagaju; 118 Johns Dr, Tewantin; unpowered sites $10, dm $15) is a riverside ecowilderness camp with basic dorms constructed out of recycled timber. There's a somewhat hands-off managerial approach, unless a good party is involved! Don't forget to bring food and mozzie repellent. A courtesy shuttle runs to and from Noosa twice a day.

A touch more luxury is found at the **Noosa North Shore Retreat** (☎ 07-5447 1706; www.noosa northshore.com.au; Beach Rd; unpowered/powered sites from $16/22, r from $110, cabins from $120; ☢ ☲). Choose from a tent or a shiny motel room then break up your day with stints paddling around the lake, bushwalking or tracking marsupials solely for patting purposes. There's also a **pub** (mains $10-20; ☯ lunch & dinner).

Lake Cootharaba

A little further northwest of Tewantin is Lake Cootharaba. This pretty water reserve is some 10km long and 5km across. Here you enter the Noosa Everglades and chilled inland communities such as the one at **Boreen Point**.

From Boreen Point, an unsealed road leads another 5km up to **Elanda Point**, where there's a **ranger's station** (☎ 07-5485 3245; Elanda Point; ☯ 7am-4pm), and the headquarters of the **Elanda Point Canoe Company** (☎ 1800 226 637, 07-5485 3165; www.elanda.com.au/noosa; Elanda Point; canoes per day $50). Unguided safaris are available on request.

The **Apollonian Hotel** (☎ 07-5485 3100; Laguna St, Boreen Point; mains $12-24; ☯ lunch & dinner) is the pride of Boreen Point. Set inside a quintessential Queenslander, this sturdy timber pub serves tasty food to casual diners intoxicated by country charm. The rooms (dorm/double without bathroom $30/50) are neat and quiet.

QUEENSLAND

Great Sandy National Park (Cooloola)

This 54,000-hectare national park stretching east and north of the lakes sports a varied wilderness of mangroves, forest and heathland that is traversed by the Noosa River. It's great fun to explore the region with a jeep (available in Noosa, p355) and you can drive through the park all the way to Rainbow Beach (p360) to the north. Other activity options include kayaking and some fantastic walking trails starting from Elanda Point on the shore of Lake Cootharaba, including the 46km Cooloola Wilderness Trail to Rainbow Beach and a 7km trail to the **EPA information centre** (☎ 07-5449 7364; ❉ 8am-4pm) at Kinaba Island.

The park contains about 15 **EPA camping grounds** (sites per person/family $4.50/18), including Fig Tree Point at Lake Cootharaba's northern edge; Harry's Hut, 4km further up the river; and Freshwater, about 6km south of Double Island Point on the beach. You must purchase permits for all camping grounds along the river at Elanda Point's **ranger's station** (☎ 07-5485 3245; Elanda Point; ❉ 7am-4pm). You can purchase permits for Harry's Hut, Fig Tree Point, Freshwater and all beach camping at the **EPA Great Sandy Information Centre** (☎ 07-5449 7792; 240 Moorindil St, Tewantin; ❉ 7am-4pm), which can also provide information on park access, tide times and fire bans within the park. Apart from Harry's Hut and Freshwater, all sites are accessible by hiking or river only.

SUNSHINE COAST HINTERLAND

When the rain hits Noosa, or the tourists get restless, many make the short trip inland to **Eumundi**, a charming artsy town 18km to the west. Try to time your visit for the world-famous **market** (❉ 8am-2pm Wed, 6am-2pm Sat), where you'll find everything from homemade cheese graters to aromatic sneeze abaters, plus clothing, food and music in the 200-plus stalls. Sunbus 631 and 630 ($4, one hour, roughly hourly) will take you here from Noosa Heads. There's also a night market on Friday and Saturdays during December and January.

If you find you don't want to leave, **Hidden Valley B&B** (☎ 07-5442 8685; www.eumundibed.com; 39 Caplick Way; r $175-195, railway carriages from $105; ☒) is a peaceful solution (go for the Hinterland Retreat!) with cooking courses available for guests ($95).

Inland from **Nambour**, the Blackall Range creates a scenic hinterland with rather chintzy rustic villages. The scenic Mapleton–Maleny road runs along the ridge of the range, past rainforests at **Mapleton Falls National Park**, 4km northwest of Mapleton. You can now walk all the way to the bottom of the falls – well worth it for a spectacularly refreshing swim.

Kondalilla National Park is 3km northwest of Montville. Both Mapleton and Kondalilla waterfalls plunge more than 80m, and their lookouts offer wonderful forest views.

The largest town in the region is **Maleny**, a green and scenic mountain town famous for its 'co-op' spirit. To get a good sample of Maleny's characters, try the **Up Front Club** (☎ 07-5494 2592; 31 Main St; dishes $9-18) for organic tofu burgers and hand-clapping folk gigs. Gourmet travellers should try the **Terrace** (☎ 07-5494 3700; cnr Mountain View Rd & Landsborough Hwy; mains $26-36) for award-winning seafood and Glass House views.

Midway between Mapleton and Maleny is **Montville**, a dinky trinket town popular with short-term visitors escaping the steamy cool. There's an antique clock emporium, candy-making display centre, cafes, pubs and a contender for 'best view from a car park'. The area is brimming with B&Bs – ask the **information centre** (☎ 07-5478 5544; 168 Main St; ❉ 10am-4pm) for up-to-date listings and vacancies. We liked **Secrets on the Lake** (☎ 07-5478 5888; www.secretsonthe lake.com.au; 207 Narrows Rd; midweek/weekend $320/370; ☒), a handcrafted, tree-house kingdom.

A little further west through the Blackall Ranges is **Kenilworth**, a friendly 'outdoorsy' village in the Mary River Valley.

If you're within shouting distance of the Sunshine Coast around New Year, do yourself a favour and unplug at the **Woodford Folk Festival** (www.woodfordfolkfestival.com), a soul-soaring cavalcade of good vibes and world-class musical performance, just southwest of Maleny. For the duration of the 10-day, kid-friendly party, Woodford becomes the second-biggest city in Queensland.

DARLING DOWNS

Queensland's breadbasket is a rich pastoral tapestry of rolling greens and grainy hues that make a relaxing detour by car, bus or lazy outstretched thumb. Its mineral-laden Granite Belt supports an up-and-coming wine region

---

GRANITE BELT WINERIES

The cluster of vineyards scattered around the elevated plateau of the Great Dividing Range constitutes Queensland's best-known wine district. Moseying from one winery to the next amid some spectacular scenery is a must for visitors to the area.

Grapes were first grown in the district in the 19th century, but the wine industry really took off after WWII when Italian immigrants were brought into the countryside to work on the farms. These forced émigrés flourished, and there are now some 40 wineries dotted around the New England Hwy between Cottonvale and Wallangara.

Heading south from Stanthorpe, some of the best include the following:

Lucas Estate (☎ 07-4683 6365; Donges Rd, Severnlea; ☺ 10am-5pm)
Mountview (☎ 07-4683 4316; Mt Stirling Rd, Glen Aplin; ☺ 9.30am-4.30pm Fri-Sun)
Ballandean Estate (☎ 07-4684 1226; Sundown Rd, Ballandean; ☺ 9am-5pm)
Symphony Hill Wines (☎ 07-4684 1388; 2017 Eukey Rd, Ballandean; ☺ 10am-5pm)
Pyramids Rd Wines (☎ 07-4684 5151; Pyramids Rd, Wyberba; ☺ 10am-4.30pm Sat & Sun)
Bald Mountain Winery (☎ 07-4684 3186; Hickling Lane, Wallangara; ☺ 10am-5pm)

If you would rather not drive yourself, **Grape Escape** (☎ 1300 361 150; www.grapeescape.com.au; per person $75) operates tours to five wineries, including lunch, from Stanthorpe.

---

and a thriving fruit industry (ably supported by young itinerant workers). The dramatic boulder and bush landscapes of Girraween and Sundown National Parks attract walkers and wildflower hunters alike, while the stately city of Toowoomba is famed for its gardens and plantation houses.

Closer to the coast, the Bunya Mountains National Park is filled with high-altitude pines and prehistoric grasses that skirt the Great Dividing Range. Inland, huge sheep and cotton farms run west into the outback where you can leave your ride in the highest gear and roll out into the great unknown.

Getting There & Away

Greyhound Australia (☎ 1300 GREYHOUND/1300 473 946; www.greyhound.com.au) has connections from Brisbane to Toowoomba ($15, two hours), Miles ($52, 5½ hours), Roma ($73, eight hours) and Stanthorpe ($69, 4½ hours).

Crisps' Coaches (☎ 07-4661 8333; www.crisps.com .au) is the biggest local operator, offering services from Brisbane to Goondiwindi ($70, 5¼ hours) and Stanthorpe ($60, 3½ hours).

The **Queensland Rail** (☎ 13 22 32, 1300 131 722; www.traveltrain.com.au) *Westlander* runs twice weekly from Brisbane to Charleville (economy seat/sleeper $102/160, 17 hours) on Tuesday and Thursday, returning on Wednesday and Friday, stopping in Toowoomba (economy seat/sleeper $32/90, four hours) and Roma (economy seat/sleeper $73/132, 11 hours).

STANTHORPE
pop 4271

Most travellers bypass Warwick, the state's second-oldest city, in favour of Stanthorpe, a pretty highland town in southwest Queensland that gets seriously chilly in winter. Stanthorpe is also the centre of the boutique wine-growing region set in the elevated plateau of the Great Dividing Range known as the Granite Belt.

The annual **Brass Monkey Festival** is celebrated here every July where more unusual grape varieties are quaffed in merry abundance.

This is a great place to find steady work from October to mid-June in the surrounding orchards and vineyards; see Granite Belt Wineries, p371. **OzJobs** (☎ 07-4681 3746; cnr Railway & Rogers Sts) can help with placements on farms and vineyards, or otherwise keep an eye out at Backpackers of Queensland (below).

If you yawn at the whiff of a Chardonnay or Shiraz, perhaps the **Strange Bird Alternative Wine Trail** will sing a more palatable tune. Sample Tempranillo, Barbera, Viognier and other grapes more suited to the intense Granite Belt climate. Maps are available at the visitors centre, or check out www.granitebeltwinecountry.com.au.

Sleeping

Backpackers of Queensland (☎ 0429 810 998; www .backpackersofqueensland.com.au; 80 High St; per week $170) Something of a halfway house for young workers, this clean, efficient place insists on a minimum one-week stay (May to September) in five-bed dorms with en suite bathrooms. While the digs, the $5 meals and en suite dorms are all enticing, many travellers are put off by the cantankerous management.

Happy Valley (☎ 07-4681 3250; www.happyvalleyretreat.com; Glenlyon Dr; r $88-170) This delightful resort boasts 20 luxury timber cabins on 30 acres of dense bush held in check by granite outcrops. Every cabin has a private bathroom and open fireplace (prices jump on Saturday nights). The on-site Homestead restaurant serves country breakfasts daily, and a gourmet lunch menu for day visitors on weekends. Prices increase during public holidays.

Escape on Tully (☎ 07-4683 7000; www.escapeontully.com; 934 Mt Tully Rd; d $180) A real surprise 12km from town is this secluded B&B with a north-facing deck and haunting bush views. Silence abounds, especially from the bottom of your claw-foot bath tub.

Girraween Environmental Lodge (☎ 07-4684 5138; www.girraweenlodge.com.au; Pyramids Rd, Ballandean; cabins $190) This is an ecofriendly bushland retreat set on 400 acres adjacent to the national park. The self-contained timber cabins have private decks with barbecues. There's an outdoor spa and plunge pool.

Camping options:

Blue Topaz Caravan Park (☎ 07-4683 5279; New England Hwy, Severnlea; powered sites $15, cabins $50) Good for families; pets are welcome.

Top of the Town Caravan Village (☎ 07-4681 4888; fax 07-4681 4222; 10 High St; powered sites $24, cabins from $100; 🖥 🐾) An excellent alternative for seasonal workers. A cute six-person cottage costs $180 per night.

Eating

Anna's Restaurant (☎ 07-4681 1265; cnr Wallangarra Rd & O'Mara Tce; dishes $9-17; 🕑 dinner Mon-Sat) Anna's has long served honest Italian inside a cosy Queenslander. The weekend buffets (adult/child $28/14) are a hit with locals who gorge on antipasto platters, hearty pasta and a vast array of veal, poultry and seafood dishes. Blessed by BYO.

Barrel Room Café (☎ 07-4684 1226; Ballandean Estate, Sundown Rd, Ballandean; mains $10-20; 🕑 9am-5pm) Lining the walls in this rustic cafe are 130-year-old, floor-to-ceiling wooden barrel lids, creating the perfect atmosphere for an antipasto platter ($30) and a bottle (or two) of the winery's excellent vino.

Cooks, Gluttons & Gourmets (☎ 07-4681 2377; 137a High St; mains $12-24; 🕑 lunch & dinner) A celebrity chef is all that's missing from this warm, casual Mod Oz eatery. The food is classy; a towering plate of Atlantic salmon and prawns comes served on handmade pappardelle, and the tea-smoked kangaroo fillet is tender and delicious. A mid-afternoon quiche ($10) hits the spot.

TOOWOOMBA

pop 95,265

It might sound like it belongs in the middle of nowhere, but Toowoomba (meaning 'reeds in the swamp') is a provincial town just 128km west of Brisbane. Queensland's largest inland city dangles on the edge of a plateau of the Great Dividing Range, some 700m above breathtaking Lockyer Valley. The cooler climate produces an array of dazzling gardens. Toowoomba's most famous export is the humble lamington. The city is in full bloom in September for the fabulous **Carnival of Flowers** (www.tcof.com.au).

Information

Coffee On Line (☎ 07-4639 4686; 12 Russell St; per hr $6; 🕑 8.30am-8pm Mon-Fri, to 7pm Sat, 10am-7pm Sun) Internet access.

EPA (☎ 07-4639 4599; 158 Hume St; 🕑 8.30am-5pm Mon-Fri)

Toowoomba Visitor Information Centre (☎ 07-4639 3797; www.toowoomba.qld.gov.au; 86 James St; 🕑 9am-5pm)

Sights

The ever-expanding **Cobb & Co Museum** (☎ 07-4639 1971; 27 Lindsay St; adult/child $8/4; 🕑 10am-4pm) is more than a collection of carriages and traps from the horse-drawn age; it's also a showcase for Toowoomba's Indigenous and multicultural communities, and includes a children's play area. **Queen's Park** (cnr Lindsay & Campbell Sts) houses the botanic gardens, although some might prefer the beautiful **Ju Raku En Japanese Garden** (☎ 07-4631 2627; West St; 🕑 7am-dusk), with its 3km of walking trails, waterfalls and streams.

Sleeping & Eating

Be sure to book ahead during September's Carnival of Flowers festival.

A Raceview Motor Inn (☎ 07-4634 6777; 52 Hursley Rd; r from $65; 🐾 🖥 🐾) This motel across the street from the Clifford Park Racetrack offers solid rooms – some with track views so good you can see the horses. Families and groups will appreciate the self-contained units with bunks sleeping up to six, and the saltwater swimming pool. One of your better budget bets.

Vacy Hall (☎ 07-4639 2055; www.vacyhall.com.au; 135 Russell St; r $100-200) Just uphill from the town centre, this magnificent 1880s mansion offers 12 heritage-style rooms of the highest standard. The priciest digs come with working fireplaces and huge verandahs, making for a romantic evening. The extensive grounds are worth a stroll.

Central Plaza Hotel (☎ 07-4688 5333; 523 Ruthven St; 1-/2-/3-bedroom apt $160/275/350; 🅿 🖳) This award-winning new hotel complex sets the benchmark for four-star accommodation in the Toowoomba region. The colourful apartments are well designed, with spacious bathrooms and firm, chiropractic beds.

Spotted Cow (☎ 07-4632 4393; cnr Ruthven & Campbell Sts; mains $12-20; 🕑 breakfast Sat & Sun, lunch & dinner daily) If you like your pubs restored and your steaks juicy (700g of Kimberley red T-bone anyone?) then it's worth a night out at this Toowoomba institution. There's a fantastic wine list of Aussie labels and plenty of beers on tap.

ourpick Oxygen Café (☎ 07-4613 1131; 517 Ruthven St; mains $15-25; 🕑 breakfast & lunch Mon-Sat) Run by a smooth operator who inverted the organic vibe from the big cities to Toowoomba, Oxygen Café is an impressive cafe by any stretch of the map. The rotating menu includes a sweet chickpea curry, healthy salads and pies, eggs all ways and killer juices made from fresh, local produce. There's a stack of magazines to spread out across the cool, stone benches while you digest the green power.

GPO Café & Bar (☎ 07-4659 9240; 1/140 Margaret St; mains $15-25; 🕑 breakfast & lunch daily, dinner Tue-Sat) Slick and modern with a stainless-steel bar and airy dining room, GPO's surrounds reflect the kind of food served: big on flavour and very inner city. Corn, crab and chilli chowder comes with a polenta muffin, or try a gourmet burger. Grab a coffee in the morning or a brew come dark.

Swish Cafe (☎ 07-4763 1200; Central Plaza Hotel, 523 Ruthven St; meals $15-30) Downstairs at the Central Plaza Hotel is this modern restaurant and tapas bar that boasts a huge open-plan wine cellar and a lengthy Mod Oz menu. Great for a drink, a formal meal or a quick coffee. The breakfast menu is very good.

TOOWOOMBA TO ROMA

About 45km west of Toowoomba is the **Jondaryan Woolshed Complex** (☎ 07-4692 2229; www.jondaryanwoolshed.com; Evanslea Rd; adult/child self-guided tours $9/5, guided tours $13/8; 🕑 9am-5pm, tours 1pm Wed-Fri, 10.30am & 1pm Sat, Sun & school holidays), which displays antique tractors and obscure farm machinery. There are daily blacksmithing and shearing demonstrations – check the website for times. To really get into the pioneering spirit, try spending a night in the shearers' quarters (adult/child $15/8) or one of the cabins (up to four people $40). Or you can pseudo-camp in pre-erected safari tents ($20 per person), which come complete with mattress.

A further 167km west on the main street in Miles is **Dogwood Crossing** (☎ 07-4627 2455; 🕑 8.30am-5pm Mon-Fri, 9am-4pm Sat & Sun), a $1.6 million community project that combines visual arts, social history and literature into a museum, gallery, library and multimedia resource centre. You can bed down for the night in a refurbished, underground bunker at **Possum Park** (☎ 07-4627 1651; Leichhardt Hwy; d $77). Munitions were stored in these bunkers during WWII as part of Australia's prepared last line of defence against the advancing Japanese.

ROMA
pop 5436

An early Queensland settlement, and now the centre of a sheep- and cattle-raising district, Roma also has some curious small industries. There's enough oil in the area to support a small refinery, but the gas deposits are even larger and Roma contributes to Brisbane's supply through a 450km pipeline.

The major landmark in Roma is the **Big Rig Complex** (☎ 07-4622 4355; www.thebigrig.com .au; Warrego Hwy; adult/child $10/7, combined entry & night show $16/11; 🕑 9am-5pm, night show 7pm daily Apr-Nov, Wed & Sun Dec-Mar), a museum of oil and gas exploration centred on the old, steam-operated oil rig at the eastern edge of town. There's also a nightly sound-and-light show. The **visitor information centre** (☎ 1800 222 399; Warrego Hwy; 🕑 9am-5pm) can help with accommodation, especially handy if you're stopping here en route to the Carnarvon Gorge (p390).

Easter In the Country is Roma's annual week-long celebration of country music and life in western Queensland.

QUEENSLAND

FRASER COAST

A visit to Australia's famous Fraser is a highlight of any Kombi-crushing itinerary along the eastern seaboard. Grotty budgeteers cram side by side in dusty 4WDs with jolly grey nomads and amateur dingo-spotters feasting on a million stars. On a breathtaking bush walk or on sparkling blue Lake McKenzie, you'll meet honeymooners on hiatus from luxury rainforest retreats and families navigating the golden Sandy Cape Straits.

You can enter Fraser Island via tripped-out Rainbow Beach, a bona fide surf town with colourful sands and luminous locals, or through the caravan community of Hervey Bay, a sleeping tourism giant with thumping backpacker bars and a seemingly endless esplanade. From July to October you can also spot migrating whales here – it's serious heart-in-the-mouth stuff.

Further north is the fertile Bundaberg region, where sugar cane grows taller than trees and little-visited sections of the Great Barrier Reef beckon from beneath bright coral cays. Backpackers can easily pick up hard work here, then blow their earnings on buckets of thick, sickly sweet Bundaberg rum. Fear not the fermenting hangover though – you're on Queensland time now.

GYMPIE
pop 11,100

Roughly 80km northwest of Noosa, Gympie was a vital gold mining town at the turn of the 19th century that substantially boosted Queensland's coffers. For that reason, there's some stately charm in this low-lying valley town, but not much else for travellers.

The principal reminder of Gympie's illustrious past is the **Gympie Gold Mining & Historical Museum** (☎ 07-5482 3995; 215 Brisbane Rd; adult/child/family $8.80/4.40/24; ☼ 9am-4.30pm), which holds a diverse collection of mining equipment and steam engines. There's also a weeklong **Gold Rush Festival** (www.goldrush.org .au) every October.

For sleeping, the **Gympie Muster Inn** (☎ 07-5482 8666; 21 Wickham St; d $120; ⚡), which has big rooms with light decor and plump settees, along with cable TV, makes a good overnight resting spot. Gympie has a handful of other motels and caravan parks on and just off the main drag (the Bruce Hwy). These cost between $80 and $150.

Greyhound Australia (☎ 1300 GREYHOUND/1300 473 946; www.greyhound.com.au) serves Gympie from Noosa ($17, two hours, three daily) and Hervey Bay ($22, 1½ hours, frequent). All long-distance coaches stop at the Gympie Transit Centre. You'll also find buses to Rainbow Beach ($16, 1¾ hours, three daily weekdays) depart from here.

RAINBOW BEACH
pop 1100

Seventy-two shades of sand form the spectacular 'rainbow' cliffs, but the beauty of this still tiny coastal hamlet is the more substantial pot of gold. This beauty spot on the cheek of the Inskip Peninsula is a great place to try your foot at surfing, access Fraser Island or to just recharge your travel-logged batteries.

Despite its close proximity to tourist central, Rainbow Beach is still pretty much a sand-sprinkled main street and a long beach – 4WDs can traverse it all the way to Double Island Point, the premier surf break 13km to the south and, with a little luck, Noosa.

Other highlights include dipping your toes in pretty Seary's Creek, tumbling down the great windswept Carlo Sandblow and breakfasting with dolphins at Tin Can Bay.

Activities

Without a 4WD, beach options are limited to the patrolled surf beach at the end of town. For those not wishing to hire a 4WD (see opposite), **Surf & Sand Safaris** (☎ 07-5486 3131; www .surfandsandsafaris.com.au; adult/child $80/40) runs half-day 4WD tours south down the beach, taking in the lighthouse at Double Island Point and the *Cherry Venture*, a freighter that ran aground here in 1973.

Rainbow Beach Dolphin View Sea Kayaking (☎ 0408 738 192; 4hr tours per person $65) offers paddle-eye views of visiting dolphin pods. Alternatively, try surfing at the **Rainbow Beach Surf School** (per lesson $25). The best surfing is at Double Island Point, 13km to the south. You'll need a 4WD to reach it, but that should prove no hindrance to the gnarly brigade.

Birdmen and women will relish the sight of Carlo Sandblow, a 120m-high dune where the national paragliding championships are held every January. **Rainbow Paragliding** (☎ 07-5486 3048; www.paraglidingrainbow.com; glides $155) is the best operator. For a more intense vertical assault, talk to **Skydive Rainbow Beach** (☎ 0418 218 358; 8000/14,000ft dives incl DVD $305/400).

Nearby Wolf Rock is one of Queensland's finest scuba-diving sites. **Wolf Rock Dive Centre** (☎ 07-5486 8004; www.wolfrockdive.com.au) offers courses and dives at the four volcanic pinnacles off Double Island Point. Four-day PADI courses cost around $600.

Sleeping & Eating

Beds are found on Spectrum St and up the hill towards Carlo Sandblow. The three main hostels arrange self-guided tours to Fraser Island.

Pippies Beach House (☎ 1800 425 356, 07-5486 8503; www.pippiesbeachhouse.com.au; 22 Spectrum Ave; dm/d $22/60; 🕸 🔲 🐾) Pippies is the most relaxed of the side-by-side backpacker joints on Spectrum St. It has beds enough for 25 in a breezy, well-fashioned hostel that sees ramblers, surfers and underwater walkers play didgeridoo and roll it right out. There are free barbecues on Wednesday nights when on-site campers ($12) descend from a spacious garden.

Dingo's Backpacker's Resort (☎ 1800 111 126, 07-5486 8200; www.dingosresort.com; 3 Spectrum Ave; dm $23; 🕸 🔲 🐾) This trendsetting hostel is warm and welcoming to up to 150 fun-loving youngsters at a time. It may be dorms only, but they're nonetheless roomy, spotless and equipped with sinks and bathrooms. You can escape the heat in the ingenious thatched lounge fitted with strong, cotton hammocks and cool cement floors. The festive bar serves decent five-buck meals such as creamy chicken pasta bake and beefy burritos. There's a Peter Pan branch on site.

Frasers on Rainbow YHA (☎ 1800 100 170, 07-5486 8885; bookings@frasersonrainbow.com; 18 Spectrum St; dm/d from $23/60; 🕸 🔲) An impressive conversion from drab motel to fab hostel, this YHA winner features tidy dorms and fabulously comfy beds. The sprawling outdoor bar lets in anyone with an accent.

our pick **Debbie's Place** (☎ 07-5486 3506; 30 Kurana St; d/ste from $79/89; 🕸) A perfect option for those seeking an authentic coastal Queensland experience, Debbie's is a home away from mobile home. This beautiful, timber Queenslander offers private entrances and verandahs to your charming, fully self-contained room. There's a barbecue in the tropical garden with leaves at every turn. It's just around the corner from the hostels on Spectrum St; or behind the IGA. If it's full, affable Debbie can find you a home equally good nearby.

Rainbow Shores Resort (☎ 07-5486 3999; www.rainbowshores.com.au; 12 Rainbow Shores Dr; r from $120; 🕸 🐾) If you like a little luxury with your beach, you'll hit the jackpot at this sprawling resort. Accommodation options include standard holiday units, funky three-bedroom beachhouses and polished split-level villas. On site is a nine-hole golf course, barbecues and children's playground on the edge of the bush.

Plantation Resort (☎ 07-5486 8706; www.theplantationatrainbow.com.au; 1 Rainbow Beach Rd; r from $270; 🕸 🔲 🐾) Some locals fear that Plantation Resort will spell the end for the relative anonymity for Rainbow Beach, but it's hard to resist the three-bedroom penthouses ($550) here with the best sea view in town. Oh, and the swimming pool is deluxe!

Waterview Bistro (☎ 07-5486 8344; 103 Cooloola Dr; mains $15-32; 🕑 lunch & dinner Wed-Sun) Up the hill towards Carlo Sandblow is Rainbow Beach's award-winning Waterview Bistro. It's tucked beside the Rainbow Ocean Palms Resort and prepares delicious seafood, meat and pasta dishes in an informal, southern Queensland setting. From every table you can enjoy sublime views over the water to Fraser Island. Linger for dessert if you know what's good for you.

Rainbow Beach Hotel (☎ 07-5486 9090; www.rainbowhotel.com.au; 1 Rainbow Beach Rd; mains $20-35) This is a classy new enterprise that adds a touch of the city to the main drag of Rainbow Beach. The country-style Queensland facade hides an eastern Sydney interior – a rectangular, metallic bar, sun-filled cane lounge and neatly landscaped beer garden. It's worth retiring to the upstairs balcony and drawing room. The restaurant had some teething problems when we visited (both the pumpkin risotto and barramundi were cold and bland), but expect the fare to soon meet the feel.

Getting There & Around

Greyhound Australia (☎ 1300 GREYHOUND/1300 473 946; www.greyhound.com.au) and **Premier Motor Service** (☎ 13 34 10; www.premierms.com.au) have daily services from Brisbane ($38, 5½ hours).

With a 4WD it's possible to drive south along the beach to Noosa or head for Fraser Island. **Aussie Adventure 4WD Hire** (☎ 07-5486 3599; 4/54 Rainbow Beach Rd) offers 4WD vehicle hire from $125 to $200 per day. For ferry details, see p370.

QUEENSLAND

MARYBOROUGH
pop 20,521

In a region ripe for redevelopment, Maryborough is still a timeless slice of heritage country Queensland. Rows of exquisitely maintained timber Queenslanders in the town's wide leafy streets are an unmarked tourism highlight, but there's also the scenic and significant Mary River from where the state's first settlers wound their way to shore. To add to the palpable sense of yesteryear, the author of *Mary Poppins*, PL Travers, was born here in 1899.

Inside the 100-year-old City Hall is the **Maryborough visitor information centre** (☎ 1800 214 789, 07-4190 5742; City Hall, Kent St; ☿ 9am-5pm Mon-Fri, to 3pm Sat & Sun), where you can pick up comprehensive self-guided walking tours.

On the National Trust tip, **Brennan & Geraghty's Store** (☎ 07-4121 2250; 64 Lennox St; adult/child/family $5/3.50/12; ☿ 10am-3pm), which traded for 100 years before becoming a museum, is like a vintage packaging graveyard of tins, bottles and packets, all crammed onto the ceiling-high shelves. Just look how far the happy little Vegemite has come.

The **Portside Centre & Heritage Museum** (☎ 07-4190 5730; 101 Wharf St; ☿ 10am-4pm) in the historic port area has interactive displays on Maryborough's history. The **Bond Store Museum** records the colourful history of illegal booze.

Maryborough Riverboat Cruises (☎ 07-4123 1523; www.maryboroughrivercruise.com; 1hr adult/child $15/8, 2hr lunch cruise $30/15; ☿ 10am, noon & 2pm Tue-Sun) provides informed commentaries along the Mary River.

On the last weekend of the month, Maryborough goes into activities mode. On Friday night **Portside Moonlight Movies** (admission free; ☿ 5pm) screens films in a park on the shore of the Mary River near the port. On Saturday the **Ghostly Tour & Tales of the Port of Maryborough** (☎ 07-4121 4111; tour & dinner $65) departs from the visitor information centre in City Hall at dusk. The lore is pretty meaty and includes tales from beyond the grave. Then there's **Sunday in the Park** (☿ 9am-1pm Sun), which includes a concert and river cruises on the *Mary Ann*, a full-sized replica of Queensland's first steam locomotive built in Maryborough in 1873. The train also runs every Thursday. There's plenty to do for kids.

The **Royal Centrepoint Motel** (☎ 07-4121 2241; 326 Kent St; r $65; ☒) is a dusty, clapped-out, utterly charming 1920s hotel version of Maryborough high life. The spotless rooms are feeling their age, but perks such as video players and friendly hosts take up the slack. Otherwise, **Wallace Caravan Park & Units Motel** (☎ 07-4121 3970; 22 Ferry St; www.wallacecaravanpark.com; unpowered/powered sites $17/22, 2-person cabins $45-80; ☒ ☒) is leafy, pleasant and very convenient.

For a feed, try the **Port Residence** (☎ 07-4123 5001; Customs House, Wharf St; mains $12-25; ☿ lunch Wed-Mon, dinner Fri & Sat) overlooking the Mary River Parklands. The best place for a drink is the **Post Office Hotel** (☎ 07-4121 3289; cnr Bazaar & Wharf Sts), a lovely building designed by an Italian architect, Caradini, in 1889.

Getting There & Away

Maryborough's train station, Maryborough West, is 7km west of town on Lennox St. Here you'll find trains to Brisbane ($60, five hours, at least four weekly). The main bus station for long-haul trips north or south is next to the train station, but a shuttle connects both stations with town.

If you just need to get to Hervey Bay ($7, 1½ hours), catch one of the frequently departing **Wide Bay Transit** (☎ 07-4121 3719) buses from outside **City Hall** (Kent St).

HERVEY BAY
pop 52,000

Once the caravanning capital of Queensland, Hervey Bay has matured from a welfare-by-the-sea escape into a top-tourist-dollar destination thanks to its lovely sandy bay (and soothing sea breezes), energetic resort development and huge pods of humpback whales.

As the main gateway to Fraser Island (p367), the often sleepy, startlingly long Esplanade has an air of youthful anticipation as the bars and clubs crank come nightfall. Over copious icy cold pots, punters trade safari scars and dingo tales, while ex-strangers returned from moonlit rainforest rambles lather sunscreen and insect repellent across each other's slow-roasted bodies.

From July to October, fishing boats are kitted out like assault vehicles to make way for the life-affirming migration of humpback whales. This is reputedly the best viewing region in the world.

The gentle, shallow bay itself is very safe for swimming and snorkelling (especially off the end of Zephyr St in Scarness), which means many mums, dads and kids also pay Hervey Bay a seasonal visit.

Information

The main tourist office is a way out of town, but ask any downtown agency for good advice.

Great Adventures (☎ 07-4125 3601; 408 The Esplanade, Torquay; per hr $4; ☼ 8.30am-10pm) Very comprehensive booking agency with internet access; located at Koala Beach Resort.

Hervey Bay Tourism & Development Bureau (☎ 1800 811 728; www.herveybaytourism.com.au; cnr Urraween & Maryborough Rds; ☼ 8.30am-5pm Mon-Fri, 10am-4pm Sat & Sun)

Post office (☎ 07-4125 1101; 414 The Esplanade, Torquay)

Sights

Run by the Korrawinga Aboriginal Community, the **Scrub Hill Community Farm** (☎ 07-4124 6908; Scrub Hill Rd; tours per adult/child/family $17/5.50/33; ☼ by appointment) produces organic vegetables, tea-tree oil and excellent artworks, including didgeridoos.

Activities

FRASER ISLAND

Hervey Bay is great for self-drive and guided backpacker trips to Fraser Island. Prices include a 4WD vehicle (to be shared by 10 passengers) for two nights, an introductory lecture, plus camping equipment and park permits. Prices vary according to quality of vehicle and camping equipment. Here are a few good operators:

A1 Fraser Roving (☎ 1800 989 811, 07-4125 6386; www.fraserroving.com.au; trips per person $210, maximum 9 people)

Colonial Log Cabins (☎ 1800 818 280, 07-4125 1844; www.yhafraserisland.com; trips per person $379) Includes guide, plus hostel accommodation on Fraser.

Hummer Tours (☎ 1800 833 433; www.fraserexperience.com; 102 Boat Harbour Dr, Pialba; trips per person $220; ☼ 8.30am) Popular new luxury day trips, with champagne lunch, small groups and a roaring Hummer to maim, er, spot dingoes from.

Koala Adventures (☎ 1800 354 535, 07-4125 3601; www.koalaadventures.com; 408 The Esplanade, Torquay; trips per person $115, maximum 11 people)

Next Backpackers (☎ 07-4125 6600, 07-5486 8503; www.nextbackpackers.com; trips per person $255, maximum 11 people)

For more Fraser Island options, see p369.

WHALE WATCHING

After fleeing the Antarctic winter, humpback whales migrate to warmer waters off northeastern Australia, and Hervey Bay is as good a place as any in the world to witness their startling grace. Between mid-July and late October, whale-watching tours operate out of Hervey Bay daily – weather permitting. Sightings are guaranteed from 1 August to 1 November, when you get a free subsequent trip if the whales don't show.

The boats cruise from the Urangan Marina out to Platypus Bay and then zip around from pod to pod to find the most active whales. In a very competitive market, vessels offer half-day (four-hour) tours that include lunch and cost from $100 for adults and $60 for children. The larger boats run six-hour day trips and the amenities are better, but they take around two hours to reach Platypus Bay. Among the many available tours are the following:

Blue Dolphin Marine Tours (☎ 07-4124 9600; www.bluedolphintours.com.au; ☼ 7.30am) Maximum 20 passengers on a 10m catamaran.

MV Tasman Venture (☎ 1800 620 322; www.tasmanventure.com.au; ☼ 8.30am & 1.30pm) Maximum of 80 passengers, with underwater microphones and viewing windows.

SAILING

Hervey Bay is an untapped sailing paradise, with only a few operators awake to its true potential.

Fraser Island Rent-a-Yacht (☎ 1800 672 618; www.rentayacht.com.au; half/full day $130/230) Run the cool, calm waters of the Great Sandy Straits in this great-value aqua adventure.

Mango (☎ 07-4124 2832; Mango Hostel, 110 Torquay Rd; 3-night trip per person $450) The hostel plans to launch trips up the remote west coast of Fraser – did I hear the new Whitehaven Beach?

Shayla (☎ 07-4125 3727; www.shaylacruises.com.au) Excellent trips to Moon Point for around $100 per person.

CRUISES

Blue Horizon Cruises (☎ 1800 247 992; 4hr tour adult/child $80/50) offers informative cruises through the shipwrecks and coral reefs of the Great Sandy Straits. Tours leave Urangan Harbour at 10am daily.

OTHER ACTIVITIES

The fishing in and around Hervey Bay is excellent and numerous vessels operate fishing safaris. **MV Fighting Whiting** (☎ 07-4124 6599; adult/child/family $60/35/160) and **Lapu Charters** (☎ 07-4194 2440; www.lapucharters.com.au) both offer fishing

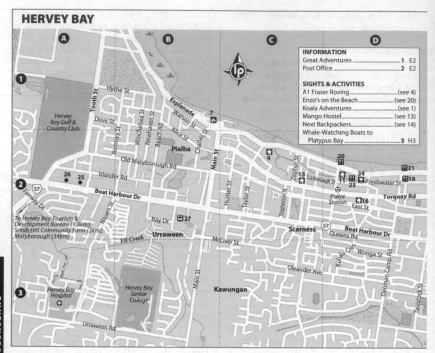

HERVEY BAY

expeditions that include lunch; Lapu Charters also arranges diving trips.

There's excellent introductory kitesurfing in the ripples off **Enzo's on the Beach** (☎ 07-4124 6375; 351a The Esplanade, Scarness; 2hr lesson $90), a cool outdoor cafe. Another cafe, **Aquavue** (☎ 07-4125 5528; www.aquavue.com.au; The Esplanade, Torquay) offers a new water activity called sea-karting ($50 per hour), where crazy cats recline in small catamarans that can hit 15 knots in good conditions.

Sleeping

Try anywhere along the Esplanade if the following places are full.

BUDGET

Most Hervey Bay hostels do pick-ups from the main bus stop, and organise trips to Fraser Island.

ourpick Woolshed Backpackers (☎ 07-4124 0677; www.woolshedbackpackers.com; 181 Torquay Rd, Scarness; dm $20-22, cabins $44-75; ⊠) Clean, simple and private, Woolshed is an escape from the hostel party circuit. The rustic farm-style cabins have tiled floors and the wooden

dorms are full of character and kitted out with outback touches such as old lanterns, Aboriginal photographs and miscellaneous horse and leather goods. The 12 cabins are on a woodsy property.

A1 Fraser Roving (☎ 1800 989 811, 07-4125 6386; www.fraserroving.com.au; 412 The Esplanade, Torquay; dm/d $20/58; ⊠ ⊠) Fraser Roving has earned a place on the backpacker grapevine. It features spartan dorms, an atmospheric bar and a location right in the heart of town. The place has a party vibe, but if you're after a quiet night there's plenty of space to buffer the noise. There are good wheelchair facilities.

Next Backpackers (☎ 07-4125 6600; www.nextback packers.com.au; 10 Bideford St, Torquay; dm $22-25, d $65; ⊠ ⊠) This award-winning budget lodging has polished floorboards, stainless-steel kitchens, a cafe and a bar that opens until midnight. The spacious dorms round off a premier backpacker experience.

Mango Hostel (☎ 07-4124 2832; www.mangohostel .com; 110 Torquay Rd; dm/d $23/55; ⊠) A quaint little Queenslander home that's popular with German guests, happy little Mango has been

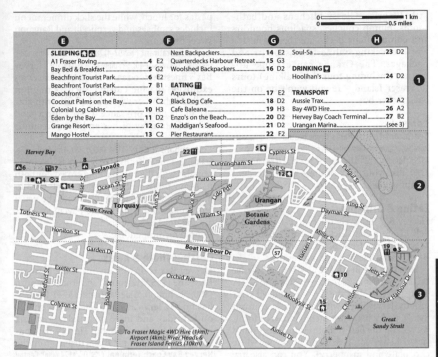

SLEEPING
A1 Fraser Roving..................................4 E2
Bay Bed & Breakfast..........................5 G2
Beachfront Tourist Park......................6 E2
Beachfront Tourist Park......................7 B1
Beachfront Tourist Park......................8 E2
Coconut Palms on the Bay...................9 C2
Colonial Log Cabins..........................10 H3
Eden by the Bay................................11 D2
Grange Resort..................................12 G2
Mango Hostel...................................13 C2
Next Backpackers..............................14 E2
Quarterdecks Harbour Retreat............15 G3
Woolshed Backpackers.......................16 D2

EATING
Aquavue...17 E2
Black Dog Cafe.................................18 D2
Cafe Baleana....................................19 H3
Enzo's on the Beach..........................20 D2
Maddigan's Seafood..........................21 D2
Pier Restaurant.................................22 F2
Soul-Sa...23 D2

DRINKING
Hoolihan's..24 D2

TRANSPORT
Aussie Trax......................................25 A2
Bay 4WD Hire...................................26 A2
Hervey Bay Coach Terminal................27 B2
Urangan Marina.........................(see 3)

QUEENSLAND

operating for nearly 20 years. The four-bed dorm is colourful, clean and comfy, while the two double rooms open onto a beautiful, leafy front verandah. The laid-back owner, Phil, is a long-time local who arranges fabulous sailing trips around Fraser.

Colonial Log Cabins (☎ 1800 818 280, 07-4125 1844; www.coloniallogcabins.com; 820 Boat Harbour Dr, Urangan; dm $25, d & tw from $48, cabins from $80; 🞭 🖳) One of our favourite budget places in Hervey Bay is YHA and fabulous, with spotless four-bed dorms, spacious cabins and villas scattered around a rare patch of bush in the 'burbs. The bar is less raucous than others of its ilk, due mostly to its laid-back crowd. Mind the possums on your way back to bed!

MIDRANGE & TOP END

Bay Bed & Breakfast (☎ 07-4125 6919; www.hervey.com .au/baybedandbreakfast; 180 Cypress St, Urangan; s $70, d $110-125; 🖳) Guests at this modern, comfortable B&B occupy cool rooms in a secluded annexe out the back (most share bathrooms). There's also a stylish share lounge, comfy couches, a guests' fridge and a lagoon-style saltwater pool outside. Children under 16 are not welcome.

Coconut Palms on the Bay (☎ 07-4124 0200; www .coconutpalmsonthebay.com.au; 335 The Esplanade, Scarness; 1-/2-bedroom apt $100/125; 🞭 🖳) A lovely couple oversees this award-winning premises down the quiet end of Scarness. The self-contained apartments are pseudo-tropical, with beautiful teak furniture and king-size beds. A dip in the saltwater pool shakes off an afternoon snooze.

Quarterdecks Harbour Retreat (☎ 07-4197 0888; www.quarterdecksretreat.com.au; 80 Moolyyir St, Urangan; 1-/2-/3-bedroom villas $160/210/240; 🞭 🖳) Our favourite fully self-contained villas back onto a nature reserve, but are still just a cooee from the beach. Private courtyards, mod cons and expansive bedrooms represent excellent value. Pets are welcome.

Eden by the Bay (☎ 07-4197 6000; 350 The Esplanade, Scarness; d $165, 1-/2-bedroom apt $185/275; 🖳) One of the better apartment hotels; across the road from the beach.

Grange Resort (☎ 07-4125 2002; www.thegrange -herveybay.com.au; cnr Elizabeth & Shell Sts, Urangan; r $170-250; 🞭 🖳) Reminiscent of a stylish desert resort, this large complex is home to fancy split-level condos filled with life's little luxuries. Glossy kitchens and bathrooms, plump couches, spacious boudoirs and commodious decks are the norm. It's worth checking online for discounts and packages. The Grange can arrange upmarket (including four-day walking) tours to Fraser Island – ie you won't be on the backpacker bus.

CAMPING
Beachfront Tourist Parks (www.beachfronttouristparks .com.au; unpowered/powered sites $20/26) Scarness (☎ 07-412); Torquay (☎ 07-4125 1578); Pialba (☎ 07-4128 1399) Take your pick of these three excellent camping sites.

Eating & Drinking
Hervey Bay has lively places to eat and drink. Self-caterers can stock up at the supermarkets inside the Centro, Urangan Central and Bay Central Plaza shopping centres.

Enzo's on the Beach (☎ 07-4124 6375; 351a The Esplanade, Scarness; mains $7-15; ☼ 6.30am-5pm; ☐) A great place to start the day – or indeed your visit to Hervey Bay – with its prime beachfront locale, perky breakfast menu and, wait for it, we reckon the *best* smoothies in Queensland (icy cold apricot, peach and honey, or white chocolate and raspberry). You can also try kayaks and kitesurfing.

Maddigan's Seafood (☎ 07-4128 4202; 401 The Esplanade, Torquay; fish & chips $8-12) Go where the locals go for their fish and seafood bits.

our pick **Black Dog Cafe** (☎ 07-4124 3177; 381 The Esplanade, Torquay; mains $10-20; ☼ lunch & dinner) Healthy Japanese-influenced cuisine, including well-priced sushi (eight pieces $6), is the emphasis at one of Hervey Bay's funkiest eateries. The menu also does a good variety of East-meets-West dishes such as fresh burgers, curries, club sambos and seafood salads. The 'young pups' menu is a plus for families.

Cafe Balaena (☎ 07-4125 4799; shop 7, Terminal Bldg, Buccaneer Ave, Urangan; mains $10-25) This efficient and friendly cafe in the heart of the Hervey Bay Marina serves gourmet croissants and outstanding fruit juices. At lunch and dinner the menu is equally trendy, boasting mountainous hot sandwiches and salads, with a good dose of fresh seafood.

Soul-Sa (☎ 07-4128 1793; 352 The Esplanade, Scarness; mains $12-28; ☼ lunch & dinner) A stylish little Asian fusion restaurant serving sizey burgers and

pastas for lunch, while the slick dinner menu includes sambal squid vermicelli and Rangoon sweet beef curry.

Pier Restaurant (☎ 07-4128 9695; 573 The Esplanade, Urangan; mains $20-40; ☼ dinner) Arguably Hervey Bay's finest seafood restaurant, the Pier serves exquisite 'marine cuisine' such as mignon scallop kebabs, or whole baked fish with ginger and peppercorn sauce. There's also a good dose of nonfishy dishes and the surrounds are classy.

Hoolihans (☎ 07-4194 0099; 382 The Esplanade, Scarness) This kitschy Irish pub is insanely popular with the backpacking crowd, for both its heavy fluids and meaty pub meals ($15 to $25). Inside the place is filled with the usual Irish maps and trinkets; the pavement seats are the ones to score come dark.

Also recommended:

Getting There & Away
Hervey Bay is on a main bus route between Brisbane ($65, 5½ hours) and Rockhampton ($80, 5½ hours). **Wide Bay Transit** (☎ 07-4121 3719) has hourly services every weekday, with five on Saturday and three on Sunday, running between Maryborough and Hervey Bay marina ($7.60, 1½ hours). Buses depart from the **Hervey Bay Coach Terminal** (☎ 07-4124 4000; Central Ave, Pialba) on Hervey Bay's west side. Hostels run shuttles to the bus terminal.

The **Queensland Rail** (☎ 13 22 32, 1300 131 722; www.traveltrain.com.au) *Sunlander* ($56, five hours) and *Tilt Train* ($55, 3½ hours) connect Brisbane with Maryborough West, where a Trainlink bus ($7.60) transfers you to Hervey Bay.

Getting Around
Most places to stay will pick you up from the bus station if you call ahead.

Bay Bicycle Hire (☎ 0417 644 814; per half/full day $15/20) rents out bicycles from various outlets along the Esplanade, or can deliver bikes to your door.

Hervey Bay has plenty of places to hire a 4WD. Loads of packages are available, but just the vehicle itself starts at around $185 per day. The following have good reputations:

Aussie Trax (☎ 1800 062 275, 07-4124 4433; 56 Boat Harbour Dr, Pialba)

Bay 4WD Hire (☎ 1800 687 178, 07-4128 2981; www .bay4wd.com.au; 52-54 Boat Harbour Dr, Pialba)

Fraser Magic 4WD Hire (☎ 07-4125 6612; www.fra ser-magic-4wdhire.com.au; Lot 11, Kruger Court, Urangan)

FRASER ISLAND
pop 360

Created by over 800,000 years of drifting sands, Fraser Island is an ecological wonderland like nowhere else on Earth. Known as K'Gari, or paradise, by the local Aboriginal people, this World Heritage–listed sand island attracts anglers, wranglers and all lovers of the natural world. It's hard to grasp the concept that this 120km-long patch of lush rainforest, staggeringly beautiful beach and mineral-rich pools of freshwater sits atop a mere pile of sand. The variety and richness of Fraser's plant and animal life, its fierce, shark-infested ocean swell, and its sandblows (dunes) that soar above 200m make this a highlight for both foreign and domestic travellers.

Before you wish upon a million stars each night, be warned that the ocean here is treacherous (if the undertow doesn't get you, the sharks certainly will!). And despite their cuddly exterior, dingoes are wild animals so your barbecue leftovers are strictly for human consumption only.

The 4WD rules the sandy tracks, and it's essential that all visitors have some understanding of how to drive one. Before crossing via ferry from either Rainbow Beach (p360) or Hervey Bay (p362), ensure also that your vehicle has suitably high clearance, and that campers have adequate food, water and fuel. Driving on Fraser all looks pretty relaxed in the brochure, but a sudden tide change or an unseen pothole can set your wheels spinning perilously. See p369 for more details.

History

Fraser Island takes its European name from James and Eliza Fraser. The captain of the *Stirling Castle* and his wife were shipwrecked on the northwest coast in 1836. He died here, and she survived with help from the local Aboriginal people.

As European settlers awoke to the value of Fraser's timber, that same tribe of Aborigines was displaced (although not without a fight) and tracts of rainforest were cleared in the search for turpentine (satiny), a waterproof wood prized by shipbuilders. The island's mineral sands were also mined for many years.

In the late 20th century the focus shifted from exploitation to protection. Sand mining ceased in 1975. Logging stopped in 1991 after the island was brought under the auspices of the EPA, as part of the Great Sandy National

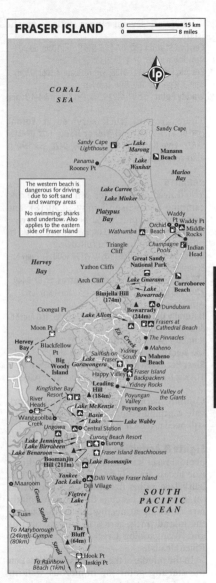

Park. In 1993 native title was recognised and the island was listed as a World Heritage area.

Information

General supplies and expensive fuel are available from stores at Cathedral Beach, Eurong, Kingfisher Bay, Happy Valley and Orchid Beach.

There are several ranger stations on the island:

Central Station (☎ 07-4127 9191; ⊙ 10am-noon)

Dundubara (☎ 07-4127 9138; ⊙ 8-9am)

Eurong (☎ 07-4127 9128; ⊙ 10.30am-3.30pm Mon, 8am-3.30pm Tue-Thu, 8am-1pm Fri)

Waddy Point (☎ 07-4127 9190; ⊙ 7-8am & 4-4.30pm)

There are tow-truck services at **Eurong** (☎ 07-4127 9188) and **Yidney Rocks** (☎ 07-4127 9167). **Five Rats** (☎ 07-4127 9499, 0428 353 164) is also recommended.

PERMITS

You'll need a permit for vehicles ($34) and camping (per person/family $4.50/18), and these must be purchased before you arrive; contact the **EPA** (☎ 13 13 04; www.epa.qld.gov.au) or purchase them from the following:

Bundaberg EPA Office (☎ 07-4131 1600; 46 Quay St, Bundaberg)

EPA Great Sandy Information Centre (☎ 07-5449 7792; 240 Moorindil St, Tewantin; ⊙ 7am-4pm) Just inland from Noosa Heads.

Naturally Queensland (☎ 07-3227 8185; 160 Ann St, Brisbane; ⊙ 8.30am-5pm Mon-Fri)

Rainbow Beach EPA Office (☎ 07-5486 3160; Rainbow Beach Rd, Rainbow Beach; ⊙ 7am-4pm)

River Heads EPA kiosk (☎ 07-4125 8485; ⊙ 6.15-11.15am & 2-3.30pm) One of the ferry departure points.

Camping permits aren't required for the private camping grounds and resorts, but you still need a vehicle permit.

Sights & Activities

From Fraser's southern tip, use the high-tide access track between Hook Point and **Dilli Village**, rather than the beach. From here on, the eastern beach is the main thoroughfare. Stock up at nearby **Eurong**, the start of the inland track, across to Central Station and Wanggoolba Creek (for the ferry to River Heads).

In the middle of the island is **Central Station**, the starting point for numerous walking trails. Signposted tracks head to the beautiful **Lakes McKenzie**, **Jennings**, **Birrabeen** (less tourists) and **Boomanjin**, in effect, giant rainwater puddles 'perched' atop a thin impermeable layer of decaying twigs and leaves. Lore has it that rich mineral sand lends the lakes anti-ageing properties.

About 4km north of Eurong along the beach is a signposted walking trail to **Lake Wabby**. An easier route is from the lookout on the inland track. Wabby is surrounded on three sides by eucalypt forest, while the fourth side is a massive sandblow, which is encroaching on the lake at a rate of about 3m a year. The lake is deceptively shallow and diving is extremely dangerous. You can often find turtles and huge catfish under the trees in the eastern corner of the lake.

Driving north along the beach you'll pass **Happy Valley**, with many places to stay, and **Eli Creek**. After rainfall this becomes a fast-moving, crystal-clear waterway that will carry you effortlessly downstream. Pretty much everyone wanders knee-deep along its pretty path. About 2km from Eli Creek is the wreck of the *Maheno*, a passenger liner that was blown ashore by a cyclone in 1935 while being towed to a Japanese scrap yard.

Roughly 5km north of the *Maheno* you'll find the **Pinnacles** (a section of coloured sand cliffs) and, about 10km beyond, **Dundubara**. Then there's a 20km stretch of beach before you come to the rocky outcrop of **Indian Head**, the best vantage point on the island. Sharks, manta rays, dolphins and (during the migration season) whales can often be spotted from the top of the headland.

From Indian Head the trail branches inland, passing the **Champagne Pools**, the only safe spot on the island for saltwater swimming. This inland road leads back to **Waddy Point** and **Orchid Beach**, the last settlement on the island. Many tracks north of this are closed for environmental protection. The 30km of beach up to **Sandy Cape**, the northern tip, with its lighthouse, is off-limits to hire vehicles. The beach from Sandy Cape to Rooney Point is closed to all vehicles, as is the road from Orchid Beach to **Platypus Bay** on the western coast.

Sleeping & Eating

Camping is by far the best way to experience the island, but come prepared or pay through the roof for supplies.

HOTELS & HOSTELS

Fraser Island Backpackers (☎ 07-4127 9144; www.fraserislandco.com.au; Happy Valley; dm $40-60; 🖳 🖭) This is a fabulous in-between option for those budget travellers keen to see and feel the island, rather than just 'do' it. Once a wilderness retreat, dorms are fitted out in nine cosy timber lodges. All meals are available (mains $10 to $20).

Eurong Beach Resort (☎ 1800 111 808, 07-4127 9122; www.fraser-is.com; Eurong; r $150; 2-bedroom apt $270; ✖ 🖳 🖳) Cheerful Eurong is the main resort on the east coast. The cheapest digs are in simple motel rooms and units, climbing in price to comfortable apartments and A-frame chalets. There's also a restaurant (mains $15 to $30), lagoon-style pool and the popular Beach Bar.

Sailfish on Fraser (☎ 07-4127 9494; www.sailfishon fraser.com.au; Happy Valley; d/f from $220/240; 🖳) This popular rainforest retreat has two-bedroom

---

NOTES FROM A SMALL ISLAND: EXPLORING FRASER

Taking care of such a precious natural landscape goes without saying, but deciding how you visit the island can make a real difference to its preservation (and your experience!). Regardless of what you choose, this is strictly 4WD territory.

Organised Tours

Package tours leave from Hervey Bay (p362), Rainbow Beach (p360) and Noosa (p349) and typically cover rainforests, Eli Creek, Lakes McKenzie and Wabby, the coloured Pinnacles and the *Maheno* shipwreck.

Advantages: Minimum fuss, plus you can return to Rainbow Beach or Noosa. Expert commentary.

Disadvantages: During peak season you could share the experience with 40 others.

We've listed a few companies below (for options based in Hervey Bay, see p363):

■ **Footprints on Fraser** (☎ 1300 765 636; www.footprintsonfraser.com.au; 4-/5-day walk $1250/1670) Get up close and personal with Fraser's unique environment when you walk the island with Footprints. The company runs four- and five-day guided walking tours that take in lake, dune and rainforest hikes.

■ **Fraser Experience** (☎ 1800 689 819, 07-4124 4244; www.safari4wdhire.com.au; 2-day tour $245) Small groups and more freedom regarding the itinerary.

■ **Kingfisher Bay Tours** (☎ 1800 072 555, 07-4120 3353; www.kingfisherbay.com; Fraser Island; adult/child day tour $165/105, 2-/3-day adventure tour from $275/355) Ranger-guided day tours in 4WDs, plus multiday adventure tours targeted at 18 to 35 year olds.

Self-Drive Backpacker Tours

Hostels organise guests into groups of about 10 per vehicle to drive their own convoy to the island and camp out, usually for two nights. Some instruction about driving 4WD vehicles is given and drivers are nominated. Booking through a local hostel reduces the risk of dodgy damage claims. Be sure to thoroughly check your vehicle beforehand.

Advantages: Cheap! You get to choose when and how you see everything and if your group is good, even getting rained on is fun.

Disadvantages: If your group doesn't get along it's a loooong three days. Inexperienced drivers mixed with booze and sand can cause headaches, or worse.

Rates hover around $185 and exclude food and fuel (usually $50 to $70). See p363 for operators.

4WD Vehicle Hire

Hire companies lease out 4WD vehicles in Hervey Bay, Rainbow Beach and on the island itself. When planning your trip, reckon on covering 20km an hour on the inland tracks and 40km an hour on the eastern beach. Most companies will help arrange ferries and permits, and hire camping gear.

Advantages: Complete freedom to roam the island, and escape the crowds.

Disadvantages: Having to drive in conditions that even experienced drivers find difficult, and being responsible for any vehicle damage.

Rates for multiday rentals start at around $185 per day depending on the vehicle. If you want to hire on the island, **Kingfisher Bay 4WD Hire** (☎ 07-4120 3366) has a medium-sized fleet, from Suzuki Sierras to Land Cruisers, all at $205 per day. Also see Getting Around in the Hervey Bay (p366) and Rainbow Beach (p361) sections for rental companies.

apartments decked out with wall-to-wall glass doors, spas and enough mod cons to keep nature at bay.

Fraser Island Beachhouses (☎ 1800 626 230, 07-4127 9205; www.fraserislandbeachhouses.com.au; Eurong Second Valley; d per 2 nights $250-350, f per 2 nights from $420; ☒) This complex contains sunny, self-contained units kitted out with polished wood, cable TVs and ocean views. Rates start with studios and climb to $600 (per two nights) for six-bed beachfront houses. Low season attracts a two-night minimum stay and high season five nights.

Kingfisher Bay Resort (☎ 1800 072 555, 07-4120 3333; www.kingfisherbay.com; Kingfisher Bay; r from $300; ☒ ☒) This elegant ecoresort has smart hotel rooms, sophisticated two- and three-bedroom timber villas (three-night minimum from $820), restaurants, bars and shops.

CAMPING

EPA camping grounds (sites per person/family $5/20) The best of these campsites, with coin-operated hot showers, toilets and barbecues, are at Waddy Point, Dundubara and Central Station. Campers with vehicles can also use the more basic grounds at Lake Boomanjin, Lake Allom and, on the western coast, Ungowa and Wathumba. There's also a hikers-only camping ground at Lake McKenzie. Camping is permitted on designated stretches of the eastern beach (you also need a permit for these). Fires are prohibited except in communal fire rings at Waddy Point and Dundubara; you need to bring your own untreated, milled timber. See p368 for information on camping permits.

Dilli Village Fraser Island (☎ 07-4127 9130; Dilli Village; unpowered sites $20, cabins $60-100) This is a tidy site perched on a gentle slope. It's run by the University of the Sunshine Coast.

Frasers at Cathedral Beach (☎ 07-4127 9177; www.fraserislandco.com.au; Cathedral Beach; unpowered/powered sites $18/28, cabins from $110) A spacious private park with abundant grassy sites and excellent facilities.

Getting There & Away

Air Fraser Island (☎ 07-4125 3600) flies out of Hervey Bay airport and lands on the island's eastern beach. Returns flights cost $70.

Vehicle ferries connect Fraser Island with River Heads, about 10km south of Hervey Bay, or further south at Inskip Point, near Rainbow Beach.

Fraser Island Barges (☎ 1800 227 437; pedestrian/vehicle with 4 passengers return $30/150) makes the 30-minute crossing from River Heads to Wanggoolba Creek on the western coast of Fraser Island. It departs daily from River Heads at 9am, 10.15am and 3.30pm, returning at 9.30am, 2.30pm and 4pm. On Saturday there's an additional 7am service, which returns at 7.30am. This company also operates the **Fraser Dawn Vehicular Ferry** (pedestrian/vehicle with 4 passengers return $22/130) from the Urangan Marina in Hervey Bay to Moon Point on Fraser Island.

Day-trippers and hikers can use the **Kingfisher Fast Cat** (☎ 1800 072 555, 07-4120 3333; adult/child return $55/28) to make the 35-minute crossing from Urangan Marina in Hervey Bay to Kingfisher Bay at 6.45am, 8.45am, noon, 4pm, 7pm and 10pm daily, returning at 7.40am, 10.30am, 2pm, 5pm, 8pm and 11.30pm daily. Those with a vehicle can use **Kingfisher Vehicular Ferry** (☎ 1800 072 555, 07-4120 3333; pedestrian/vehicle with 4 passengers return $25/145) for the 45-minute crossing from River Heads to Kingfisher Bay, departing at 7.15am, 11am and 2.30pm, and returning at 8.30am, 1.30pm and 4pm.

Coming from Rainbow Beach, **Rainbow Venture** (☎ 07-5486 3227) and **Manta Ray** (☎ 0418 872 599) both make the 15-minute crossing from Inskip Point to Hook Point on Fraser Island continuously from about 7am to 5.30pm. Both cost $85 return for a vehicle and four passengers.

CHILDERS
pop 1500

One of the sweeter stops on the heavily plied Bruce Hwy is pretty little Childers. This sugarcane town, scattered with liquorice-coloured houses and fruit-picking youth, is used by most travellers to stretch the legs or take a cafe break in the country.

Sadly, Childers is widely known for a devastating fire at the Palace Backpackers Hostel in June 2000, in which 15 backpackers died. There is now a beautiful memorial, with moving dedications to those who perished, at the **Childers Palace Memorial Art Gallery & Information Centre** (☎ 07-4126 3886; ☽ 9am-5pm Mon-Fri, to 3pm Sat & Sun), where you'll also find a good gallery.

Sleeping & Eating

If you're looking for work, stay at the **Sugarbowl Caravan Park** (☎ 07-4126 1521; 4660 Bruce Hwy; unpowered/powered sites $20/22, cabins $66; ☐ ☒), a leafy

FRUIT PICKING DOWN IN QUEENSLAND

There is seasonal fruit- and vegetable-picking work aplenty in Stanthorpe (p357), Childers (opposite) and Bundaberg (below), and during harvests these towns attract backpackers by the bucket-load. Many are hoping to pick tomatoes in exchange for a bit of cash and, even better, a second holidaymaker visa.

Here's the scoop. If you have a valid Australian work visa and do three months of harvest work, you are entitled to another year-long working visa. It sounds great, and if you can stomach the work, it is great. But before you just show up at a farm, here are a few things you should know.

Farm work can be brutal. You'll be expected to work seven days a week, and get up insanely early when it's still cold and dark – 4am anyone? It takes about three days to get used to the physical aspects of harvest work. Be prepared for a few grumpy, achy first days.

Some popular destinations, such as Stanthorpe, are basically one-traffic-light villages with little to do as far as nightlife goes. If you're only coming to work, this is fine, but if you're also looking for a bit of atmosphere, it's probably best to head to Bundy.

Most backpackers are usually hooked up with farm work directly through the hostel, which also provides transport to and from the harvest site each day. This is a major plus, as there is no public transport to the farms. Being connected to a hostel can also be helpful if you end up having a problem with your farm boss. Be warned: racism is not extinct on farms, and the occasional farmer won't hire Asians or blacks.

We hate to have to even bring the subject up, but to avoid a potentially hostile situation it's best to talk to the hostel management before signing up for work if you have any concerns whatsoever. Managers may be strict when it comes to partying, but we found many, especially the crew at the Cellblock Backpackers in Bundy (see p372), to be very sensitive to backpackers' feelings and needs.

site a little out of town. Free transfers to work are available. Rates are for two people.

The **Palace Motel** (☎ 07-4126 2244; 72 Churchill St; s/d $85/95; ❷) was rebuilt on the site of the ill-fated backpackers. It's now a serviceable motel in the centre of town.

Mango Hill B&B (☎ 07-4126 1311; www.mangohill cottages.com; 8 Mango Hill Dr; s/d/tr $90/120/140; ❷) is a collection of cane-cutter cottages 4km south of town. Rooms are decorated with handmade wooden furniture and ladles of country charm. There's an on-site organic winery.

Kape' Centro (☎ 07-4126 1916; 65 Churchill St; mains $9-15; ❷ breakfast & lunch), in the old post office building, serves a rotating menu of salads, sandwiches and a few Filipino specialities. Otherwise, turn left off the highway towards Woodgate for famed macadamia-nut ice cream at **Mammino** (☎ 07-4126 2880; 115 Lucketts Rd; ❷ 9am-6pm).

Greyhound Australia (☎ 1300 GREYHOUND/1300 473 946; www.greyhound.com.au) and **Premier Motor Service** (☎ 13 34 10; www.premierms.com.au) both stop at the Shell service station just north of town and have daily services to/from Brisbane ($75, 6½ hours), Hervey Bay ($18, one hour) and Bundaberg ($18, 1¾ hours).

BUNDABERG
pop 55,464

Iconic 'Bundy' is a proud mid-sized coastal city with a small-town country complex. Famed for its dirty, dark rum and the jovial white polar bear that flogs it, Bundaberg is passed over by many travellers despite its rare turtle population, coral-fringed coastline and distinct architectural charm.

A stint picking, packing and shellacking fruit on the farms around Bundaberg has become a rite of passage for many cash-strapped young backpackers from all corners of the working-holiday-visa world. It can be rough and ready stuff (both the work *and* the lifestyle!), but locals are for the most part endeared to a foreign accent (especially when the sweet stuff kicks in!), and most visitors have a memorable experience in this genuine, working-class Queensland town.

Information

Bundaberg Email Centre (☎ 07-4153 5007; 197 Bourbong St; per hr $4; ❷ 10am-10pm)
Bundaberg visitors centre (☎ 1300 722 099; www .bundabergregion.info; 271 Bourbong St; ❷ 9am-5pm Mon-Fri, to noon Sat & Sun)

TALKING TURTLE

You almost expect to hear the hushed commentary of David Attenborough during the egg-laying and hatching at Mon Repos, Australia's most accessible turtle rookery. But on this beach, 15km northeast of Bundaberg, it's no disappointment to be accompanied instead by the knowledgeable staff from the **EPA visitors centre** (☎ 07-4159 1652; ☼ 7.30am-4pm Mon-Fri). From November to late March, when loggerhead and other marine turtles drag themselves up the beach to lay their eggs, and the young emerge, the office organises **ranger-guided tours** (adult/child/family $10/5/22; ☼ 7pm-midnight). Bookings are mandatory through the Bundaberg visitors centre (p371). Alternatively, go with **Footprints Adventures** (☎ 07-4152 3659; www.footprintsadventures.com.au; adult/child incl transfers $46/30). Make sure you bring warm clothing, rain protection and insect repellent.

EPA (☎ 07-4131 1600; 46 Quay St)

Post Office (☎ 07-4151 6708; cnr Bourbong & Barolin Sts)

Sights & Activities

Wake up and smell the molasses! In the annals of alcohol production tours (think Guinness and Heineken in Dublin and Amsterdam respectively), it's hard to surpass the **Bundaberg Rum Distillery** (☎ 07-4131 2999; www.bundabergrum .com.au; Ave St; self-guided tour adult/child $14/7, guided tour adult/child $20/10; ☼ tours hourly 10am-3pm Mon-Fri, to 2pm Sat & Sun). Tours follow the rum's production from start to finish and, if you're over 18, you get to sample the final product. The one-hour, wheelchair-accessible tours run every hour on the hour. Note, you must wear closed-toe shoes.

On the first Friday of each month between September and April, a lovely **night market** is held at the **Riverside Parklands** along a 1km boardwalk on the banks of the Burnett River. Some 3km further from the city centre is **Baldwin Swamp** (Steindl St), an 87-hectare wetland reserve of lagoons and forest filled with birds, trees, loads of bandicoots and other furry night-time friends.

About 16km east of Bundaberg the small beach hamlet of **Bargara** entices divers and snorkellers with a dazzling bank of coral near the Barolin Rocks and in the Woongarra Marine Park. There are some good **surf breaks** here too, especially to the south of Bargara.

Bundaberg Ferry Company (☎ 07-4152 9188; 3 Quay St; 2½hr tour per adult/child/family $25/13/70; ☼ 9.30am & 1.30pm Tue, Wed, Fri & Sun, 1.30pm Sat) runs slow-paced tours to the mouth of the Burnett River.

Sleeping, Eating & Drinking

A number of illegal backpacker hostels were closed down in late 2008 (leaving unlucky travellers to sleep on the street!), so be sure to choose a legitimate operator. If you don't plan to live and work in the area, a number of good-value motels line Bourbong St, the main road into town.

Feeding Grounds Backpackers (☎ 07-4152 3659; www.footprintsadventures.com.au; 4 Hinkler Ave; dm $25) Turtles rule in this delightful, eco-minded hostel that goes against the trend in Bundaberg by offering only 18 beds in a converted family Queenslander. The country kitchen, lounge and bathroom facilities are luxurious compared to the norm. There's also a tidy guest laundry. Turtle tours leave most nights.

City Centre Backpackers (☎ 07-4151 3501; city centrebackpackers@hotmail.com; 216 Bourbong St; dm per night/week $25/135) This atmospheric, dry hostel is ironically set in an old pub in the centre of town where large rooms have high ceilings and a more subdued kind of guest. There's a hint of the Wild West looking down from the huge verandah as cool summer breezes blow in through gracious French doors.

Cellblock Backpackers (☎ 1800 837 773; www.cell block.com.au; cnr Quay & Mayborough Sts; dm per night/week $25/145; ✕ ☐ ☎) You can throw out the rule book at this heritage-listed ex-prison that piles in punters from across the world into cramped, mixed dorms on a high rotation. Sounds awful for a 10-year stretch, but for a month or so it's a serious social outing, akin to an episode of *Big Brother* 'Backpacker Special'. There's a huge open bar set beside a swimming pool – no prizes for guessing where the party ends up.

Oscar Motel (☎ 07-4152 3666; reception@oscarmotel .com.au; 252 Bourbong St; s/d $83/94; ✕ ☐ ☎) This reliable motel has a good range of rooms, from small and functional to utterly cavernous. All have cable TV and the proud and professional owners keep the whole place spotless. It has broadband internet access in rooms.

(Continued on page 381)

GREAT AUSSIE TRIPS

The magical Land of Oz, flush with natural splendour, acres of grapevines,
sublime beaches and epic distances. You've heard the sales pitch – now get
out there among it! Tour nature's highlights on an epic 'Lap of the Map',
wheel through the country's best wine regions, carve up the waves, hurl
yourself into outdoor activities or enjoy some classic Aussie experiences: the
reality leaves the marketing spin for dead!

The Ultimate Road Trip

Forget your briefcase, your Blackberry, your business suit…it's time to unwind on an epic tour of Australia's highlights and highways. On this mammoth continent, 'the road' is ingrained in the nation's collective consciousness – driving from Sydney Harbour to the Kimberley and back will really get you into the Aussie mindset.

❶ Sydney Harbour, New South Wales

When convicted murderer Francis Morgan stood on the gallows in 1797, he gazed wistfully across Sydney Harbour (p109) and uttered, 'Well, you have here indeed a most beautiful harbour.' This magical body of water is Sydney's shimmering soul.

❷ Cradle Mountain, Tasmania

Float across Bass Strait and shift down into Tassie Time. Australia's divine island state preserves some of the country's oldest forests and World Heritage–listed mountain ranges: Cradle Mountain (p710) is easily accessible and absolutely beautiful.

❸ Great Ocean Road, Victoria

A wiggly, 250km-long oceanside snake between Torquay and Warrnambool, the Great Ocean Road (p551) is one of the world's great drives. Along the way you can hit the surf, munch fresh seafood and spy migrating whales cavorting offshore.

❹ Flinders Ranges, South Australia

Three hours' drive northwest of Adelaide, the Flinders Ranges (p793) jag up from the semi-desert like a rust-coloured mirage. Rich in Indigenous culture and geologic drama, the Flinders will etch itself into your memory.

❺ Great Australian Bight, South Australia & Western Australia

The bite-shaped Great Australian Bight (p792) is a massive span of water – massive in a truly Australian way (we mean BIG!). Tackle the gun-barrel-straight highway across the Nullarbor Plain from Ceduna to Norseman and you'll see what we're talking about.

❻ The Kimberley, Western Australia

In northern WA, the Kimberley (p995) is a curious mix of seasonal extremes, rough outback towns and jaw-dropping scenery – the kind of place you think you'll trundle through in a day or two but end up exploring for weeks.

❼ Kakadu National Park, Northern Territory

Home to the Aboriginal peoples for at least 50,000 years, the World Heritage–listed Kakadu National Park (p842) tells a story of the ages, and is top of the list of essential Australian destinations.

❽ Uluru-Kata Tjuta National Park, Northern Territory

Down the Stuart Hwy from Darwin is Australia's ochre-coloured heart and the iconic Uluru-Kata Tjuta National Park (p885). You've seen the photos and the TV shows, but there's nothing quite like seeing an Uluru sunset firsthand.

❾ Great Barrier Reef, Queensland

Stretching 2300km and visible from outer space, the Great Barrier Reef (p410) is an absolute must-see. From the Torres Strait to Bundaberg, there are plenty of opportunities to experience the reef: scuba diving, snorkelling, sailing or peering through glass-bottom boats.

2

Best Wine Regions

Gone are the days of the beer-bloated Aussie and casks of rot-gut plonk. Australia now produces (and drinks) the world's best wines, and wobbling between wine-region cellar doors has become a regular local indulgence. Just make sure someone abstemious can drive you back to the hotel.

① Hunter Valley, New South Wales

Dating back to the 1820s, the Hunter Valley (p168) is the oldest wine region in Australia, bottling Australia's gift to the world – super Semillon. The local Shiraz is also worth the two-hour drive north from Sydney.

② Yarra Valley, Victoria

Chase Melbourne's Yarra River an hour north-east and you'll bump into the very boutiquey, cool-climate Yarra Valley (p543). With over 1400 hectacres under vine, this is the place for syrupy Chardonnay, complex Cabernet Sauvignon and crisp Sauvignon Blanc.

③ McLaren Vale, South Australia

The young upstart of South Australia's mu-nificent wine industry, McLaren Vale (p750) is heaps hipper than the old-school Barossa or Clare Valleys: straw-coloured hills, turquoise ocean and Shiraz worth shouting about.

④ Tamar Valley, Tasmania

A gourmet Tasmanian groove running north from Launceston towards Bass Strait, the Tamar Valley (p687) has evolved into one of Australia's premier cool-climate wine grow-ing regions, delivering superb Pinot Noir, Sauvignon Blanc and sparkling white.

East Coast Surf Safari

Strap your mini-mal to the roof rack, fire up the Kombi and cruise out into your very own *Endless Summer*. Australia's east coast has the country's most consistent and challenging surf: sand-slapping shore breaks, river-mouth sandbars and majestic point breaks. Surf's up!

❶ Bells Beach, Victoria

Little more than an hour's drive south of Melbourne is a place many consider the spitirual home of Australian surfing. Bells Beach (p553) has the country's most famous wave: a long, lavishly curling point break.

❷ Maroubra Beach, New South Wales

Just 6km south of the more famous Bondi, Maroubra Beach (p120) is where Sydney's hard-core surfers cut loose: barrelling beach breaks, edgy suburbia and the notorious 'Bra Boys'. Don't drop in on any locals.

❸ The Pass, New South Wales

Arcing into the beach from Australia's most easterly tip, the Pass (p195) point break at Byron Bay is a ripper. The crowds arrive on big days, but hopefully there'll be more dolphins than surfers here when you visit.

❹ Snapper Rocks, Queensland

Sand pumped out of the Gold Coast's Tweed River to improve navigability accidentally created the Superbank – a huge, hollow sandbar break that can allegedly be ridden for 2km. Snapper Rocks (p341) is the launch pad.

Iconic Outdoors

With all this sunshine and wide, open space, there's not much point cooping yourself up inside. Sure, the museums, galleries, bookshops and bars are fantastic, but outside is really where it's at Down Under. Hit the sand, the snow, the islands and the deserts for some definitive Australian experiences.

❶ Bondi Beach, New South Wales

Backpackers, beach breaks and bikinis – Bondi (p117) is the quintessential Australian beach, and the mandatory Sydney experience. It's also Sydney's biggest beach, so there's plenty of room to strut your stuff. Unmissable.

❷ High Country, Victoria

In winter the Victorian High Country (p602) is thick with snow and Melburnian powder-hounds. The region isn't that 'high' by world standards (1986m at the most), but the skiing at Falls Creek, Mt Buller and Mt Hotham is awesome.

❸ Wineglass Bay & Freycinet National Park, Tasmania

Hike up to the saddle and snap the perfect picture of Wineglass Bay (p674), or continue down the other side onto this gorgeous goblet of sand – surely one of the world's most photogenic beaches.

❹ Kangaroo Island, South Australia

Across Backstairs Passage, 18km from mainland South Australia, Kangaroo Island (p756) is an unspoiled, unhurried wildlife haven, with plenty of opportunities to rub shoulders with the local fauna. Straight from the Southern Ocean (or, perhaps, heaven), 'KI' seafood is superb.

❺ Margaret River, Western Australia

Whether you're after a day in the surf or a glass of fine local wine, Margaret River (p938) delivers. A three-hour hop south of Perth, the town fills to the gills over the Easter and Christmas breaks – time your visit wisely.

❻ Kings Canyon & Watarrka National Park, Northern Territory

About 200km west of Alice Springs on the (usually) dry Kings Creek, Watarrka National Park (p884) rewards intrepid travellers with eye-popping walks into and around the rim of this gaping desert chasm.

❼ Whitsunday Islands, Queensland

There are few prospects in life as tantalising as yacht hopping around the Whitsunday Islands (p408), snorkelling over coral reefs and stopping in for a meal or a massage at snazzy island resorts. Got a few spare dollars?

Australian Classics

If you find yourself with some free time between big-ticket sights, Mod Oz meals, surf sessions and long, lonesome highways, you might want to try a few things we could categorise as 'classically' Australian: the heart-pumping, the serene, the multicultural and the decadent.

① Sydney Harbour Bridge 'BridgeClimb', New South Wales

Once only painters and insane daredevils scaled the arch of Sydney's humongous Harbour Bridge, but these days anyone can tackle the 'BridgeClimb' (p123). Don a natty jumpsuit and a safety harness and up you go – Sydney never looked so good!

② Murray River Houseboating, South Australia

Old Man Murray (p770) may be getting a little short of breath, but you can still hire a houseboat and chug up and down the river for a few days. Swim, fish, relax and crack a cold beer – the Australian dream?

③ Mindil Beach Sunset Market, Northern Territory

Darwin is a surprisingly multicultural town, as a visit to the fabulous Mindil Beach Sunset Market (p833) will confirm. Grab some Thai stir-fry, Indonesian beef *rendang*, a Malaysian laksa or a Greek souvlaki and head for the beach.

④ Fremantle Sunday Sessions, Western Australia

In the most isolated city on the planet, Perth locals are delightfully self-indulgent. Sink some 'Sunday Session' beers at a Fremantle pub (p925) as the sun dips down into the Indian Ocean. Who cares about the rest of the world?

(Continued from page 372)

Inglebrae (☎ 07-4154 4003; www.inglebrae.com; 17 Branyan St; r incl breakfast $100-130; ✷) For old-world English charm in a glorious Queenslander, this delightful B&B is just the ticket. Polished timber and stained glass seep from the entrance into the rooms, which come with high beds and small antiques. Breakfasts are big and hot, and are served on the lovely verandah.

Eating & Drinking

Spicy Tonight (☎ 07-4154 3320; 1 Targo St; dishes $10-19; ✷ dinner) This unlikely Indian and Thai cross-dining experience in a crumbling old building is very popular with locals. The curries and tandoori dishes are fiery and exquisite, plus there's plenty for vegetarians.

Metro Bar (☎ 07-4151 3154; 166 Bourbong St; mains $15-20; ✷ lunch & dinner) The front bar at Metro is perfect for a breezy post-work beer on stainless steel tables and comfy black bar stools. If you get peckish, head out the back for some reasonable Australian pub food.

The Restaurant (☎ 07-4154 4589; cnr Quay & Toonburra St; mains $25-35; ✷ dinner Mon-Sat) An evening drink on the timber deck of this former rowing shed is a fabulous Bundaberg moment. Live music plays on weekends.

Central Hotel (☎ 07-4151 3159; 18 Targo St; ✷ noon-midnight Sun-Wed, to 3am Thu-Sat) Stick your elbows out and reach for the lasers at Bundy's loosest night spot where pretty young things and backpackers crowd in every weekend.

Queenslander (☎ 07-4152 4691; 61 Targo St; ✷ noon-midnight Sun-Thu, to 1am Fri & Sat) Enjoy live gigs and DJs at this pub, which rocks on every Friday and Saturday night. When the weather is fine, the gigs move into the tropical beer garden.

Moncrieff Theatre (☎ 07-4153 1985; 177 Bourbong St) Bundaberg's lovely old cinema has plays, shows and mainstream movies.

Self-caterers should head to the **IGA Supermarket** (Woongarra St).

Getting There & Away

Qantaslink (☎ 13 13 13; www.qantas.com.au) flies between Brisbane and Bundaberg for around $150.

The main bus stop in Bundaberg is **Stewart's Coach Terminal** (☎ 07-4153 2646; 66 Targo St). **Greyhound Australia** (☎ 1300 GREYHOUND/1300 473 946; www.greyhound.com.au) and **Premier Motor Service** (☎ 13 34 10; www.premierms.com.au) have daily services between Bundaberg and Brisbane

($81, seven hours), Hervey Bay ($18, 1½ hours), Rockhampton ($62, four hours) and Gladstone ($45, 2½ hours).

The **Queensland Rail** (☎ 13 22 32, 1300 131 722; www.traveltrain.com.au) *Sunlander* ($65, seven hours) and *Tilt Train* ($65, five hours) both make the journey from Brisbane to Bundaberg on their respective routes to Cairns and Rockhampton.

CAPRICORN COAST

Welcome to Capricornia. This tropic-straddling playground is an unusual post-colonial melting pot of pulsating coral shelves, world-class tropical islands and crusading cowboy yarns. There are fewer tourists than elsewhere on the coast and more options to explore, making travel here a very personal Queensland experience. From the beefy turf around Rockhampton to the peachy coastal breaks in 1770 and inland to magnificent Carnarvon Gorge, this is one of Queensland's most wonderfully varied regions – and its worst-kept secret to boot.

SOUTHERN REEF ISLANDS

Some of the Capricorn Coast's finest moments lie 80km to the northeast of Bundaberg, on these lush green-and-gold islands atop a glassy azure sea. More and more savvy travellers are doing their Great Barrier Reef thing here – and for good reason. These sparkling coral cays are as good as it gets in Australia, without nearly the same crowds, storms or miles to travel. There's the diving wilderness of Lady Elliot and Lady Musgrave, while at secluded Heron Island, you can literally wade into an underwater paradise.

The Town of 1770 is the most common stepping-off point (see p384), otherwise Hervey Bay (p362) or Bundaberg (p371). Tours to the islands ($250) stop at a number of beaches and snorkelling spots and include lunch. Alternatively, you can camp at Lady Musgrave, or style it up overnight on Lady Elliot.

Lady Elliot Island

If humans were born to scuba, we would have mutated into permanent inhabitants of this 40-hectare paradise. If you're certified (in PADI, that is), then get your East Coast travel arse here immediately. Shipwrecks, coral gardens, bommies (submerged rock)

QUEENSLAND

CAPRICORN COAST

QUEENSLAND

and blowholes: choose from 19 sites to take your remaining breath away. To add to its Crusoe chic, Lady Elliot is reached only by light plane, and you're not allowed to camp!

The recently renovated **Lady Elliot Island Resort** (☎ 1800 072 200; www.ladyelliot.com.au; per person reef unit $219, garden unit $200, eco cabin $145) has a monopoly on the island's accommodation, but is still great value for a bed on the edge of heaven. Try to make your booking online as the resort often has tailored specials inclusive of airfare, meals and diving. Basic 'eco huts' are a touch drab for the price, but the colourful reef units (two-bedroom self-contained suites) are a good deal, with the sand within stretching distance. Rates include breakfast and dinner.

Sea Air (book through the resort) flies guests in from pretty much every airport between the Gold Coast and Gladstone. Return prices are around $219/119 (adult/child).

Lady Musgrave Island

If Lady Musgrave were a literary figure, she'd be pursued the world over by an olive-skinned suitor with a tropical itch to scratch. Nobody lives here permanently though, aside from the terns, shearwaters and white-capped noddies taking time out from October to April (green turtles nest from November to February). But you should at least live here for a moment, perhaps deep inside the aqua lagoon surrounded by a dense canopy of pisonia forest: it'll make the real world feel so close. This 15-hectare national park is increasingly popular with day-trippers and campers, youngsters or oldies.

Before the 'barefoot luxury' movement, there was barefoot camping at an **EPA camping ground** (per person/family $4.50/18), which lies on the island's west side, with bush toilets and little else. Campers need a permit and must be totally self-sufficient, even bringing their own water. Fires are not allowed. Numbers are limited to 40 at any one time, so apply well ahead for a permit at the Gladstone **Environmental Protection Agency** (☎ 13 13 04; www.epa.qld.gov.au; 136 Goondoon St, Gladstone). If you made it this far (in your travels), you'll appreciate the surging peace of a night on Lady Musgrave.

The 1770 Great Barrier Reef Cruises operates great day trips from the Town of 1770; see p384.

Heron & Wilson Islands

Heron Island is quite rare on the Australian east coast – a true coral cay that lives and breathes within walking distance of the shore. Twenty-four square kilometres of reef runs out from dense vegetation (mostly pisonia trees), affording some gentle diving and snorkelling expeditions in luscious locations. There's a resort and research station on the northeastern third of the island; the remainder is national park.

Heron Island Resort (☎ 07-4972 9055, 1800 737 678; www.heronisland.com; s/d from $399/420) covers the northeastern third of the island. Its comfortable accommodation is suited to families and couples – the point suites have the best views. Prices include all meals, but guests will pay $200/100 per adult/child for launch transfer, or $440/270 for helicopter transfer. Both are from Gladstone.

Wilson Island (www.wilsonisland.com; 2-nights including transfers and all meals s/d $1600/2100), also part of a national park, is an expensive wilderness retreat with permanent tents. There are excellent beaches and superb snorkelling. The Multi-Resort package is a popular five-night stay between Heron and Wilson Islands (singles/doubles $3220/4460).

AGNES WATER & TOWN OF 1770

When a fleet of British sailors first stepped ashore this headland in, you guessed it, 1770, the local Meerooni tribe must have cursed their rotten luck. Centuries later, however, and these delightful twin towns are yet to be overwhelmed by her majesty's masses. Perhaps only a cherished absence of direct flights keeps Agnes Water (population 1619) safely off the beaten track. With just a few shops clustered behind the splendid beach, coupled with stylish rental homes, swish backpacker barns and campsites, and a few Balinese B&Bs, Agnes has a *Home & Away* kind of coastal innocence.

The Town of 1770 (population 56), 5km north of Agnes Water, is even more laid-back, consisting of just a marina and gorgeous Bustard Head. Some of Australia's finest diving is done offshore, while ecowanderers will find plenty to keep them gasping in Deepwater and Eurimbula National Parks.

For info on the area, your best bet is **Agnes Water Visitor Information Centre** (☎ 07-4974 7002; Rural Transaction Centre, Round Hill Rd).

Activities

Patrolled in summer, Agnes Water is an ideal wave for initiating yourself into the cultural and sporting phenomenon of **surfing**. Agnes Point is the pick of the breaks, particularly when there's good swell, but learners can pull in almost anywhere along the 5km beach.

Just show up in front of the **Reef 2 Beach Surf School** (☎ 07-4974 9072; www.reef2beachsurf.com; 1/10 Round Hill Rd, Agnes Water) shop to join in, or on the beach look for the group with matching yellow sun shirts. Lessons cost $22 per person for four or more students, or $55 for a private lesson. The shop also rents boards and sells mega surf gear.

Can you keep a secret, surfers? There are world-class waves out on the Great Barrier Reef, and the very experienced guys at **MV James Cook** (☎ 07-4974 9422; www.1770jamescook .com.au) will help you find them. It's $220 per person for an all-day mission. If the waves aren't pumping offshore, you can fish, dive and snorkel instead.

With it's wide open headlands, generous winds and reasonable swell, 1770 is regarded as one of the country's premier locations for one of the ocean's crazier new crazes, and you can give it a try with **Kite Surfing** (☎ 07-4974 7874; www.kitesurf1770.com.au; 3hr lesson $150).

Or ride an automatic chopper down coastal tracks, past roos, wallabies and gorgeous sea-backed scrub. The laid-back South African guide at **Scooteroo** (☎ 07-4974 7696; www.scooter rootours.com; 3hr chopper ride $65; ☼ 3pm summer, 2.30pm winter by appointment) makes the trip ultracool.

QUEENSLAND

Tours

1770 Great Barrier Reef Cruises (☎ 07-4974 9077; www.spiritof1770.com.au; Captain Cook Dr, Town of 1770; adult/child incl lunch $145/70, plus environment tax per person $5) Excellent day trips to Lady Musgrave Island including snorkelling and fishing gear. Cruises depart the Town of 1770 marina. Island camping transfers are also available for $240 per person ($260 in school holidays).

1770 Sea Quest (☎ 1800 177 011; www.1770seaquest .com.au; adult/child incl lunch $170/80) Runs top-shelf diving, snorkelling and marine education tours to the sublime Fitzroy Lagoon in the Great Barrier Reef. The advanced snorkel ($30) is a tremendous open-water excursion.

Larc Tours (☎ 07-4974 9422; www.1770larctours .com.au) It might feel a touch A-Team, but these amphibious vehicle tours to Bustard Heard and Eurimbula National Park are ecocertified and heaps of fun.

Sleeping & Eating

Sandcastles 1770 Motel & Resort (☎ 07-4974 9428; www.sandcastles1770.com.au; 1 Grahame Colyer Dr, Agnes Water; dm $25, apt from $130; 🕮 🖳 🏊) Sandcastles is a smart first port of call. It's got the Balinese boutique stamp, yet retains a minimum of fuss. The mini-apartments are Hollywood cool, with sloping ceilings, heaps of space (most sleep four to six) and splashes of pastel. Otherwise, if you're alone, broke or plain idealistic, there's a good backpacker dorm. The on-site restaurant, Kahuna's, is a hub of social activity, serving delicious pizza ($10 to $15), seafood and jugs of beer.

ourpick **1770 Southern Cross Tourist Resort** (☎ 07-4974 7225; www.1770southerncross.com; 2694 Round Hill Rd, Agnes Water; dm/d $26/65; 🖳 🏊) On the highway 2km before town is this dreamy backpacker hang-out that has an adventurous crew hanging round happily for days. Nation-themed dorm rooms surround a good-sized swimming pool and spa, and a fabulous open-air communal area with table-tennis table, pool table, a big comfy lounge area, farmhouse benches, meditation *sala*, computer terminals, spotless kitchen (with free breakfast!) and helpful reception. A free shuttle bus runs regularly to town and back, but you might find a good book by the on-site creek is all you ever needed.

1770 Backpackers (☎ 1800 121 770; www.the 1770backpackers.com.au; 22 Graham Colyer Dr, Agnes Water; dm $27) A brilliant backpacker joint in a brand new location couldn't stay out of our reach for long. The large, breezy dorms have comfy mattresses (for a dorm!) and sparkling en suite bathrooms. The communal area is con-

stantly cruisey, whether you're slung low in a hammock or sipping your BYO stubbie in the cool, cushioned area with a frayed map in hand. Reception can arrange pretty much *any*thing.

Freckles Up North (☎ 07-4974 7200; www.1770 beachsidebackpacker.com.au; 12 Captain Cook Dr, Agnes Water; dm $27) Happily accept the invitation to 'get speckled at Freckles', a brand new restaurant and pub, with a classy bistro menu and quality bar meals. The adjoining backpackers was being completed at the time of writing, but the signs are very promising indeed: spacious communal area, brand-new dorms and a yoga-centric relaxation centre.

Cool Bananas (☎ 07-4974 7600; www.coolbananas .net.au; 2 Springs Rd, Agnes Water; dm $27; 🖳) A funky exponent of Balinese open-plan living, Cool Bananas has roomy dorms, a chirping tropical garden and loads of old-school travel cred.

Mango Tree Motel (☎ 07-4974 9132; 7 Agnes St, Agnes Water; s/d $85/95; 🕮) Families and groups of holidaying friends dig this good-value motel, just 100m from the beach. Its large self-contained rooms (sleeping up to six per room) book out quickly. There's also a licensed restaurant and the option of continental breakfast with the room rate.

Beach Shacks (☎ 07-4974 9463; www.1770beachshacks .com; 578 Captain Cook Dr, Town of 1770; d from $150) These delightful Balinese-inspired units are hardly shacks: they're gorgeous, very private affairs decorated in timber, cane and bamboo. They offer grand views and are just minutes' walk from the water. An on-site bar and restaurant and a fully stocked guest kitchen give you eating options.

1770 Camping Grounds (☎ 07-4974 9286; camp ground1770@bigpond.com; Captain Cook Dr, Town of 1770; 2-person unpowered/powered sites $24/27) A large but peaceful park with sites right by the beach and plenty of shade.

Saltwater Cafe 1770 & Tree Bar (☎ 07-4974 9599; Captain Cook Dr, Town of 1770; mains $10-26; 🕙 dinner) A ramshackle, Caribbean vibe lulls diners into multiple after-dinner chasers at this classic 1770 venue. The pizzas make good beer food, but get serious and get messy in a mud crab or seared scallops.

Getting There & Away

Greyhound Australia (☎ 13 14 99; www.greyhound.com .au) has one daily bus from Bundaberg ($24, 1½ hours). Other buses are met at Fingerboard Rd in Miriam Vale by a local **shuttle service** ('Macca';

☎ 07-4974 7540; tickets $24) that makes a 30-minute drive to Agnes Water and Town of 1770.

ROCKHAMPTON
pop 66,567

Rocky is a bit rough around the edges, but mostly it's as tender as a pig dog's pot-belly. Cut-out cows circle the Capricornian administrative centre like remnants of a once great circus, but still there's something endearing about Rockhampton's crumbling deco and Queenslander buildings, cowboy-collared pub life and stiff tropical whiff along the mighty Fitzroy River. The region around Rocky is also popular for experiencing life on a true blue (green and brown) cattle station.

Rockhampton Visitor Information Centre (☎ / fax 07-4922 5339; 208 Quay St; ☩ 8.30am-4.30pm Mon-Fri, 9am-4pm Sat & Sun) is in the beautiful former Customs House.

Sights

An eclectic and satisfying snippet of Australian artwork is on display at **Rockhampton City Art Gallery** (☎ 07-4936 8248; 62 Victoria Pde; admission free; ☩ 10am-4pm Tue-Fri, 11am-4pm Sat & Sun). Sir Russell Drysdale, Sir Sidney Nolan and Albert Namatjira are part of the fine permanent collection, as are some impressive contemporary Indigenous painters. Check with the gallery for the latest temporary exhibition, for which there is usually a charge.

The **Dreamtime Cultural Centre** (☎ 07-4936 1655; Bruce Hwy; adult/child $14/6.50; ☩ 10am-3.30pm Mon-Fri, tours 10.30am & 1pm) is an easily accessible insight into Aboriginal and Torres Strait Islander heritage and history. The excellent 90-minute tours are hands on (boomerangs!) and appeal to all ages. It's about 7km north of the centre.

Rockhampton's wonderful **Botanic Gardens** (☎ 07-4922 1654; Spencer St; admission free; ☩ 6am-6pm, zoo feeding 2.30-3.30pm) is an oasis of Japanese gardens, lagoons and immaculate lawns. There is good access for those with disabilities, a kiosk, an attractive picnic area and a small zoo with koalas and a walk-through aviary.

Sleeping & Eating

As a key regional city, Rockhampton has plenty of business motels lining the highway, most with attached restaurants. Following are a few alternatives.

Heritage Hotel (☎ 07-4927 0344; 228 Quay St; dm/s/d from $20/45/60) Recently overhauled by a Melbourne duo, this huge period pub lights up its section of the Fitzroy River. The dorm rooms are large and the doubles are quiet and airy with shared bathrooms. There's a new lounge bar upstairs (poker on Thursdays), while the wooded ground-floor saloon has big-screen TVs and free video games. The elegant dining room has a terrace overlooking the river – perfect for an evening drink.

Rockhampton YHA (☎ 1800 617 194; www.yha .com.au; 60 MacFarlane St; dm $22, d $50-59; ☒ ☐ ☒) The Rocky YHA is well looked after, with a spacious lounge and dining area and a well-equipped kitchen. It has six- and nine-bed dorms as well as doubles and cabins with bathrooms, and there's a large patch of lawn

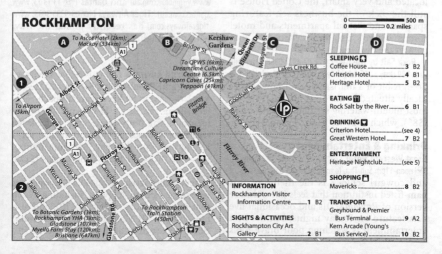

ROCKHAMPTON		0 _____ 500 m / 0 _____ 0.2 miles
SLEEPING		
Coffee House	3	B2
Criterion Hotel	4	B1
Heritage Hotel	5	B2
EATING		
Rock Salt by the River	6	B1
DRINKING		
Criterion Hotel	(see 4)	
Great Western Hotel	7	B2
ENTERTAINMENT		
Heritage Nightclub	(see 5)	
SHOPPING		
Mavericks	8	B2
INFORMATION		
Rockhampton Visitor Information Centre	1	B2
SIGHTS & ACTIVITIES		
Rockhampton City Art Gallery	2	B1
TRANSPORT		
Greyhound & Premier Bus Terminal		
Kern Arcade (Young's Bus Service)	9	A2
	10	B2

QUEENSLAND

STINGERS

It mightn't look or feel pretty, but unless you stay out of the water a 'stinger suit' is your only real protection against Queensland's lethal jellyfish (and harmful UV rays). There are two to be aware of: the rare and tiny (1cm to 2cm across) irukandji and the box jellyfish, also known as the sea wasp or stinger. They're found in coastal waters north of Rockhampton (occasionally further south) from around October to April, although the danger periods can vary.

If someone has been stung, call an ambulance or get a lifeguard (artificial respiration may be required), douse the stings with vinegar (available on many beaches or from nearby houses) and seek medical aid.

Check with lifeguards whether the stingers are out. If so, stick to the hotel pool.

---

to toss a ball around. The hostel arranges tours, has courtesy pick-ups from the bus station, and is an agent for Premier and Greyhound buses.

Ascot Hotel (☎ 07-4922 4719; www.ascothotel.com .au; 177 Musgrave St; dm/d $23/50; ✖ 🖳) Highly recommended by homesick travellers, this heartfelt backpackers set in an old pub is lovingly run by Robbie, your 'Mum' away from, well, Mum. The restaurant has a fabulous stone grill for sizzling steak and seafood. Dorms have from three to seven beds, plus there's an all-girl option. It's 2km north of the centre.

Criterion Hotel (☎ 07-4922 1225; www.thecriterion .com.au; 150 Quay St; s/d $45/65, motel r $108; ✖) Similar deal to the Heritage, with dozens of period rooms on the top two storeys and toilets down the hall. The bar is immensely popular. The excellent Bush Inn Bar & Grill ($10 to $20) serves the best pub food in town.

Coffee House (☎ 07-4927 5722; www.coffeehouse .com.au; 51 William St; r from $160; ✖ 🖳) Centrally located and very smart, the Coffee House is still the pick of the business set, featuring spacious and tasteful apartments and motel rooms. There's also an excellent cafe that stirs in the evening.

Rock Salt by the River (☎ 07-4927 0888; Riverbank Park, 189 Quay St, Riverbank Park; mains $20-35; ✖ lunch & dinner) A bit of a tourist trap, but nonetheless ideally situated by the river and starring the most mouth-watering seafood platter for two ($85), which is better suited to four!

Drinking & Entertainment

Great Western Hotel (☎ 07-4922 3888; 39 Stanley St; ✖ noon-11pm Sun-Thu, to midnight Fri & Sat) Cowboy and cowgirl schlock is the theme of this ham-fisted institution that feels like a theatre version of *Rawhide*. DJs and occasional live acts feature on Friday nights, but the best entertainment is watching poor brave fools

try to ride bucking bulls and broncos in the bullring every Wednesday.

Criterion Hotel (☎ 07-4922 1225; 150 Quay St; ✖ noon-11pm Sun-Tue, to midnight Wed-Sat) Arguably Rockhampton's favourite pub, the Criterion resonates with a good-time feel. There's live music Wednesday to Saturday nights.

Heritage Nightclub (☎ 07-4927 6996; Heritage Hotel, 228 Quay St; ✖ 9pm-4am Thu-Sat) When the pubs are shut, try this revamped club down by the river. It's got raised leather booths, a heaving dance floor and a number of enticing bars.

Shopping

Mavericks (☎ 07-4921 0622; 33 Stanley St) Pick up quality belt buckles, Akubra hats, stockman whips and other countrified regalia.

Getting There & Away
AIR

Rockhampton is serviced by **Jetstar** (☎ 13 15 38; www.jetstar.com.au), **Virgin Blue** (☎ 13 67 89; www.virginblue.com.au) and **Qantas** (☎ 13 13 13; www .qantas.com.au). **Tiger Airways** (☎ 03-9335 3033; www .tigerairways.com) has recently joined the fray, with daily flights to Melbourne.

BUS

Greyhound Australia (☎ 13 14 99; www.greyhound .com.au) and **Premier Motor Service** (☎ 13 34 10; www.premierms.com.au) have regular coach services along the Bruce Hwy, and the Rocky terminus for both carriers is at the **Mobil roadhouse** (91 George St). There are regular services to and from Mackay ($60, four hours), Brisbane ($114, 11 hours) and Cairns ($178, 18 hours).

Young's Bus Service (☎ 07-4922 3813) operates several services to Yeppoon, including a loop that includes Rosslyn Bay ($8.10), and also has buses to Mt Morgan, Monday to Friday. Buses depart from the **Kern Arcade** (Bolsover St).

TRAIN

The **Queensland Rail** (☎ 1300 131 722, 07-4932 0453; www.traveltrain.com.au) *Tilt Train* and *Sunlander* connect Rockhampton with Brisbane (from $102) and Cairns ($167). The journey takes seven to 11 hours, depending on which service you take. The *Spirit of the Outback* also connects Rockhampton with Brisbane (economy seat/sleeper $102/160, 10 hours) and Longreach (economy seat/sleeper $111/169, 10 to 11 hours) twice weekly. The train station is 450m southwest of the city centre.

AROUND ROCKHAMPTON

About 23km north in the Berserker Range are the impressive **Capricorn Caves** (☎ 07-4934 2883; www.capricorncaves.com.au; Caves Rd; adult/child $20/10; ⏱ 9am-4pm). These deeply illuminated limestone passages are particularly spectacular during the summer solstice period (1 December to 14 January), when the sun beams vertical light through the roof of the Belfry Cave. The informative one-hour Cathedral Tour is an easy guided walk that leaves on the hour.

Myella Farm Stay (☎ 07-4998 1290; www.myella.com; Baralaba Rd; 3/7 days $275/580, day trips $85; 🗙 🖵 🕾) offers a chance to stay at an authentic cattle station without having to travel all the way to 'whoop whoop'. This 1040-hectare beef property 120km southwest of Rockhampton is a fully renovated homestead, fitted with hardwood floors and pine-scented mod cons. There's plenty to do – including exploring the bush on horseback, motorcycle or 4WD and caring for orphaned joeys at the on-site kangaroo rehab centre – but some prefer just unwinding in the almost outback. Prices include free transfers from Rockhampton.

Another fine farm stay is at **Kroombit Lochenbar Station** (☎ 07-4992 2186; www.kroombit.com.au; d with/without bathroom $86/64, 2-night package from $170), 35km east of Biloela.

YEPPOON

pop 11,280

The gateway to Great Keppel Island, Yeppoon is an attractive seaside village with pleasant beaches giving way to untapped rainforest around Byfield. Travelling south, you pass Rosslyn Bay, the departure point for Great Keppel, and a lovely little emu park, before winding your way along similarly scenic coastline.

For info on the area, head to **Capricorn Coast Information Centre** (☎ 1800 675 785, 07-4939 4888; www.capricorncoast.com.au; Scenic Hwy; ⏱ 9am-5pm).

Sleeping & Eating

Emu's Beach Resort & Backpackers (☎ 1800 333 349; www.emusbeachresort.com; 92 Pattison St, Emu Park; dm/d/tr/q $25/75/90/100; 🗙 🖵 🕾) The new backpacker on the beach block is a low-key, welcoming place across the road from Emu Beach, 19km south of Yeppoon. The central pool and barbecue are built for relaxing, partying or just hanging out with the kids. Dorms are self-contained and spacious (if a touch stuffy), and the modern communal kitchen and lounge area is first rate. The apartment-sized family rooms are great value. The owners are up to date with the travel scene, and they also offer neat packages such as the Great Keppel ($109), which includes two nights' accommodation and a full-day trip to the island.

Yeppoon Surfside Motel (☎ 07-4939 1272; 1 Anzac Pde; d $90; 🗙 🕾) It is hard to miss this lime-green and galvanised steel motel at the beginning of Yeppoon's main beach road. It's a smart, modern affair with nicer-than-expected, boutique-style rooms – you get tile floors, rugs and the ubiquitous floral motel bedspread. TVs come with Austar and you can order breakfast in your room for an extra charge. The beach is just across the street.

Rydges Capricorn Resort (☎ 1800 075 902, 07-4925 2525; www.capricornresort.com; Farnborough Rd; r from $130; 🗙 🕾) This large and lavish golf resort about 8km north of Yeppoon has rooms ranging from standard hotel digs to plush self-contained apartments. There's also a gym, several bars and restaurants, and immaculate golf courses. It can have absurdly low rates if you check online.

Thai Paleao (☎ 07-4938 8550; shop 5, 24/26 Hill St, Emu Park; mains $16-25) It must be the climate that makes Thai restaurants flourish along the Queensland coast. Whatever it is, the food at friendly Thai Paleao in Emu Park is up there with the best. The tofu green curry ($27) rocks.

our pick **Megalomania** (☎ 07-4939 2333; Arthur St; mains $20-35; ⏱ 11am-late) Travel is full of pleasant surprises, like finding a restaurant as accomplished as Megalomania in a town as humble as Yeppoon. A city-meets-sea vibe is played out here beautifully behind slatted wooden blinds, across a cool stone floor. Deft, professional staff shuffle around a chic bar that wins for a cheeky glass of whatever. The menu is constantly changing, though the jewfish with mango salsa – climactic perfection – should still be there.

Getting There & Away

Young's Bus Service (☎ 07-4922 3813) operates a loop service from Rockhampton to Yeppoon, Rosslyn Bay, Emu Park and back (one way $8, daily).

AROUND YEPPOON

The rainforest scrub and rocky headlands of **Byfield National Park** provide superb Sunday arvo driving terrain, with plenty of hiking paths. There are five **camping grounds** (☎ 07-4939 3738; Farnborough Rd; unpowered/powered sites $20/23) to choose from, two of which (Nine Mile Beach and Five Rocks) require a 4WD to be accessed. When conditions are right, there's also decent surf at Nine Mile. **Byfield General Store** (☎ 07-4935 1190; Byfield Rd; ◷ 8am-6pm Wed-Mon, to 2pm Tue; ▯ ▣) doubles as an information centre.

The area is also known for the highly controversial US military training facility at **Shoalwater Bay**, which borders the forest and park, and is strictly off limits. Vocal protests over the nature of the weapons-testing program continue to agitate both the Australian and American governments.

It's worth a detour to **Nob Creek Pottery** (☎ 07-4935 1161; 216 Arnolds Rd; admission free; ◷ 9am-5pm), a working pottery and gallery nestled in leafy rainforest. The gallery showcases hand-blown glass, woodwork and jewellery, and the handmade ceramics are outstanding. The friendly owners are opening a mountain retreat – check ahead to see if it's operating yet.

Bypass the history tour and unfurl your senses in the rainforest on a silent, electric boat tour with **Waterpark Eco Tours** (☎ 07-4935 1171; www.waterparkecotours.com; 201 Waterpark Creek Rd; 2-3hr tours $25). The 97-hectare farm has a beautiful self-contained, air-conditioned timber cabin ($100) should the trees lull you to sleep.

Also recommended:

Rainforest Ranch (☎ 07-4935 1555; 76 Yaxleys Rd; d $120-180) New boutique retreat.

Ferns Hideaway (☎ 07-4935 1235; www.fernshideaway.com.au; 67 Cahills Rd; mains $13-25; ◷ lunch daily, dinner Sat, breakfast Sun) Bush oasis just north of Byfield with the region's best restaurant and unpowered sites ($24) and doubles ($100).

GREAT KEPPEL ISLAND

pop 20

Once the hedonistic getaway of the head-in-the-sand '80s, Great Keppel is back on the cool travel hot list. And not surprisingly given the 18km of fine white beaches that rival the Whitsunday isles, and sit just 13km from the mainland. Around 90% of its 14 sq km is natural bushland. Visitors can choose between pure seclusion and vibrant social activity. Backpackers looking for a cheap, semideveloped and beautiful escape are very happy here.

Sights & Activities

Snorkelling is the pastime de rigueur. Visitors usually start out investigating **Shelving Beach**, becoming progressively more adventurous as they flap and flop to **Monkey Beach** and **Clam Bay**. For really good marine life (and a sunken Taiwanese ship!), keep kicking out to Middle and Halfway Islands (see opposite).

There are several bushwalking tracks from **Fisherman's Beach**, the main beach. The longest, perhaps the most difficult, leads to the 2.5m 'lighthouse' near **Bald Rock Point** on the far side of the island (about three hours return).

With 18km of white-sand beaches, you don't need to go far for a swim. **Fisherman's Beach**, where the ferries come in, rarely gets crowded, and it's even quieter just round the corner at **Putney Beach**.

The **Watersports Hut** (☎ 07-4925 0624; Putney Beach) is just one of a few places hiring sailboards, catamarans, motorboats and snorkelling gear. It can also take you waterskiing, parasailing or camel-riding.

Keppel Reef Scuba Adventures (☎ 07-4939 5022; www.keppeldive.com; Putney Beach) on Putney Beach offers introductory dives for $120, and snorkelling trips for $40 per person.

Tours

Freedom Fast Cats (☎ 1800 336 244; Rosslyn Bay marina; adult/child $63/42) operates a coral cruise to the best location of the day (depending on tides and weather), which includes viewing through a glass-bottom boat and fish feeding. There are also afternoon and full-day cruises (adult/child $130/85, including barbecue lunch).

Sleeping

Great Keppel Island Holiday Village (☎ 07-4939 8655; www.gkiholidayvillage.com.au; dm $27, s/d tents $40/60, cabins $100) This YHA-affiliated resort caters to everyone with various types of accommo-

dation (including four- and six-bed dorms
and cabins that sleep four). It's friendly and
relaxed and has good communal facilities.

Keppel Lodge (☎ 07-4939 4251; www.keppellodge
.com.au; s/d $100/130) Four rooms to choose from
in this open-plan house – we say grab some
mates and have it all to yourselves! There's a
good-sized communal kitchen and lounge.

Svendsen's Beach (☎ 07-4938 3717; www.svend
sensbeach.com; cabins per night $285) Searching for
authenticity in your travels? This place,
named after its beachcombing host, is your
new best-kept secret. There's a minimum
three-night stay.

Eating & Drinking
The kiosk at Great Keppel Island Holiday
Village has a few essentials, but if you want
to cook bring your own supplies.

Island Pizza (☎ 07-4939 4699; The Esplanade; dishes
$6-30; ☽ dinner Tue-Sun, lunch Sat & Sun) This friendly
place prides itself on a unique healthy pizza
recipe with plenty of toppings. The pizzas are
rather pricey but still tempting.

Getting There & Away
Ferries for Great Keppel leave from Rosslyn
Bay Harbour, about 7km south of Yeppoon.
If you have booked accommodation, check
that someone will meet you on the beach to
help with your luggage.

Freedom Fast Cats (☎ 1800 336 244, 07-4933 6244;
adult/child/family return $45/25/115) departs Rosslyn
Bay at 9.15am Wednesday to Sunday, returning at 4.15pm. On Tuesday it departs
Rosslyn Bay at 10.30am and returns at 2pm.
Once on the island, **Geoff's Water Taxi** (☎ 0438
247 595) can shuffle up to four people around
for $40 total.

OTHER KEPPEL BAY ISLANDS
Although you can make day trips to the fringing coral reefs of **Middle Island** or **Halfway Island**
from Great Keppel Island (ask your accommodation or at Great Keppel Island Holiday
Village), you can also **camp** (per person/family $8/20)
on several national park islands, including
Middle, **North Keppel** and **Miall Islands**. You'll
need all your own supplies, including water.
The **EPA** (☎ in Rockhampton 07-4936 0511, in Rosslyn Bay
07-4933 6608; www.epa.qld.gov.au) has information
and permits.

Tiny, privately owned **Pumpkin Island** (☎ 07-
4939 2431; campsites $20, cabins $240-424), just south
of North Keppel, has five simple, cosy cabins

with water, solar power, kitchen and bathroom; bring food and linen.

Funtastic Cruises (☎ 0438 909 502) can organise camping drop-offs from Rosslyn Bay to
the islands.

CAPRICORN HINTERLAND
Ancient rock art, blazing green-and-orange
panoramas and gemstones loose under foot –
Central Queensland's heart lies west in the
Capricorn Hinterland. Blackdown Tableland
National Park is a brooding, powerful place,
but don't miss the opportunity to see spectacular Carnarvon National Park. While
270km inland at Emerald, you'll find yourself
in one of the world's largest gem fields. Try
to stick to the cooler months between April
and November.

Blackdown Tableland National Park
Spooky, spectacular Blackdown Tableland is
a 600m sandstone plateau that rises suddenly
out of the flat plains of central Queensland. It's
a bushwalker's heaven here, with unique wildlife and plant species and a strong Indigenous
artistic and spiritual presence. The turn-off
to the Blackdown Tableland is 11km west
of Dingo and 35km east of the coal-mining
centre of Blackwater. The 23km gravel road,
which begins at the base of the tableland, isn't
suitable for caravans and can be unsafe in
wet weather – the first 8km stretch is steep,
winding and often slippery. At the top you'll
come to the breathtaking **Horseshoe Lookout**,
with picnic tables, barbecues and toilets.
There's a walking trail to **Two Mile Falls** (2km)
starting here.

Munall Camping Ground (☎ 13 13 04; per person/
family $4.50/18) is about 8km on from Horseshoe
Lookout. It has pit toilets and fireplaces –
you'll need water, firewood and/or a fuel
stove. Bookings are advised.

Gem Fields
Queenslanders love to punt, whether it be a
horse race, a couple of flies up a wall, or a lazy
fossick for precious gems. In the fields west
of **Emerald** (named after Emerald Downs Hill
just north of town), tales of instant fortune
have a sprinkling of truth. Sapphires, rubies
and zircons to cry for have all fallen into lucky
folks' hands. In fact, the gem fields around
Anakie, Sapphire, Rubyvale and Willows are
the world's largest of their kind and renowned
for large, rare sapphires.

To go fossicking you need a **licence** (adult/family $5.80/8.20) from the Emerald Courthouse or one of the gem fields' general stores or post offices. If you just wish to dabble, you can buy a bucket of 'wash' (mine dirt in water) from one of the fossicking parks and hand-sieve and wash it. If you're serious, however, wait for a heavy rain and then keep your eye glued to the sparkling surface.

In **Anakie**, 42km west of Emerald, the **Big Sapphire Gemfields Information Centre** (☎ 07-4985 4525; 1 Anakie Rd, Anakie; ☺ 8am-6pm) has maps of the fields and fossicking licences, plus it hires out fossicking equipment. If you need a helping hand, **Jake's Fossicking Tour** (☎ 07-4985 4142; Anakie Gemfields Caravan Park, Capricorn Hwy; tours $40) leaves daily from the Anakie Gemfields Caravan Park.

Another 18km on is **Rubyvale**, the main town on the fields, and 2km further is the excellent **Miners Heritage Walk-in Mine** (☎ 07-4985 4444; Heritage Rd, Rubyvale; adult/child $10/3; ☺ 9am-5pm), which has informative 20-minute underground tours throughout the day that have you descending into a maze of tunnels 18m beneath the surface.

Rubyvale Holiday Units (☎ 07-4985 4518; www .rubyvaleholiday.com.au; 35 Heritage Rd, Rubyvale; d $85, 1-/2-bedroom apt $105/150; 🅿 🖴) has spacious motel and self-contained units, about 1km north of Rubyvale.

There are caravan-camping parks at Anakie, Rubyvale and Willows Gemfields.

Carnarvon National Park

One of the highlights of all Queensland, **Carnarvon Gorge** is a dramatic rendition of Australian natural beauty. The 30km-long, 200m-high gorge was carved out over millions of years by Carnarvon Creek and its tributaries twisting through soft sedimentary rock. What was left behind is a lush, otherwordly oasis, where life flourished, shielded from the stark terrain.

You'll find giant cycads, king ferns, river oaks, flooded gums, cabbage palms, deep pools and platypuses in the creek. It's hardly surprising that humanity has revered this place for so long – the Aboriginal rock paintings and carvings here are detailed and easily accessible – or escaped convicts and escape artists taken refuge in its nooks and crannies. The area was made a national park in 1932 after defeated farmers forfeited their pastoral leases.

For most people, Carnarvon Gorge *is* the Carnarvon National Park, because the other sections – including Mt Moffatt (where Indigenous groups lived some 19,000 years ago), Ka Ka Mundi and Salvator Rosa – have long been difficult to access. Much of that is changing now, so expect a small rise in tourism to the area.

Coming from Rolleston the road is bitumen for 70km and unsealed for 25km. From Roma via Injune and Wyseby homestead, the road is good bitumen for about 215km then unsealed and fairly rough for the last 30km. After heavy rain, both these roads can become impassable.

The entrance road leads to an **information centre** (☎ 07-4984 4505; ☺ 8-10am & 3-5pm) and scenic picnic ground. The main walking track also starts here, following Carnarvon Creek through the gorge, with detours to various points of interest. These include the **Moss Garden** (3.6km from the picnic area), **Ward's Canyon** (4.8km), the **Art Gallery** (5.6km) and **Cathedral Cave** (9.3km). Allow *at least* a whole day for a visit. Basic groceries and ice are available at Takarakka Bush Resort (see below). Petrol is not available anywhere in the gorge – fill up at Rolleston or Injune.

You cannot drive from Carnarvon Gorge to other sections of the park, although you can reach beautiful Mt Moffatt via an unsealed road from Injune (4WD necessary).

A four-night camping expedition of the entire 50km rim of the gorge is set to open in 2009; contact the information centre for details.

SLEEPING

It's best to book ahead, especially from April to October.

Takarakka Bush Resort (☎ 07-4984 4535; www .takarakka.com.au; Wyseby Rd; unpowered/powered sites $24/30, cabins $80) This picturesque campsite is perfect for families, couples and intrepid explorers. The elevated canvas cabins are airy and durable (fresh linen is $10). The private verandahs are great for kangaroo spotting. The shared cooking and bathing facilities are excellent, while the reception sells drinks, groceries, maps and ice. Takarakka is about 5km from the picnic ground.

Carnarvon Gorge Wilderness Lodge (☎ 1800 644 150; www.carnarvon-gorge.com; Wyseby Rd; cabins $210-250; ☺ Mar-Nov; 🖴) Outback chic by the billabong-full is on offer at this attractive wilderness lodge set deep in the scrub. Excellent guided tours are available, plus a full-board package for around $300.

Bookings are required for both these camping options:

Carnarvon Gorge Visitor Area & Big Bend Camping Ground (☎ 13 13 04, 07-4984 4505; www.epa.qld .gov.au; sites per person/family $4.50/18) Isolated camping ground a 10km walk up the gorge.

Mt Moffatt Camping Ground (☎ 07-4626 3581; www.epa.qld.gov.au; sites per person/family $4.50/18) Campers need to be self-sufficient and have a 4WD.

GETTING THERE & AWAY

There are no bus services to Carnarvon, so your best bet is to hire a car or to take an overnight tour from the coast.

OUTBACK

You're not a true Aussie, so says the white fella, until you've visited western Queensland. A proper noun of staggering proportions, the Outback is an awesome frontier where settler folk struck open the deep red earth and bored out a nation through myth and verse. If coastal Queenslanders try to tell you there's 'nothing out there', don't listen. This mineral-rich region is vast and wealthy; the livestock fit and full, and the Indigenous song lines run deep. Plus this ancient landscape was once the playground of marauding dinosaurs!

It's out here, past the Great Dividing Range, that the sky opens wide and the sun beats down on tough country, both relentless and beautiful, where an honest day meets a silent, starry night, and more than the occasional character. Travellers come here for the exotic and intimate Australian experience, their restlessness tamed by the sheer size of the place, the rare colours it exudes and the dusty bare earth underfoot.

Although sparsely settled, the outback is well serviced by major roads, namely the Overlander's Way (Flinders and Barkly Hwys) and the Matilda Hwy (Landsborough Hwy and Burke Developmental Rd). Once you turn off these major arteries, however, road conditions deteriorate rapidly, services are remote and you need to be fully self-sufficient, carrying spare parts, fuel and water. Also do some planning as some sights and accommodation

options (in particular the outback stations) close from November to March, the outback's hottest period.

Getting There & Away
AIR

Qantas and **QantasLink** (☎ 13 13 13; www.qantas.com.au) fly from Brisbane to Barcaldine, Blackall, Charleville, Longreach and Mt Isa. The Cairns-based **Skytrans** (☎ 1300 759 872; www.skytrans.com.au) also flies between Brisbane and various outback destinations, although less regularly, including Birdsville via Charleville, Quilpie and Windorah. It also connects Mt Isa to Cairns.

BUS

Greyhound Australia (☎ 13 14 99; www.greyhound.com.au) connects Mt Isa to Townsville ($143, 12 hours) and Brisbane ($192, 26 hours). From Mt Isa, buses continue to Three Ways in the NT.

Emerald Coaches (☎ 1800 428 737; www.emeraldcoaches.com.au) operates services from Rockhampton to Longreach at least twice each week.

TRAIN

The grandest way to travel the outback is with **Queensland Rail** (☎ 1300 131 722; www.traveltrain.com.au), which runs three services, all leaving twice weekly. The ever-popular *Spirit of the Outback* runs from Brisbane to Longreach (economy seat/sleeper $185/240, 26 hours) via Rockhampton, with connecting bus services to Winton. The *Westlander* has services from Brisbane to Charleville (economy seat/sleeper $100/160, 17 hours), with connecting bus services to Cunnamulla and Quilpie; and the *Inlander* runs from Townsville on to Mt Isa (economy seat/ sleeper $125/188, 21 hours).

CHARTERS TOWERS TO CLONCURRY

The Flinders Hwy runs a gruelling 775km stretch of mostly flat road from Charters Towers west to little Cloncurry. The highway was originally a Cobb & Co coach run, and along its length are small towns established as coach stopovers. At **Prairie**, 200km west of Charters Towers, the friendly, supposedly haunted **Prairie Hotel** (☎ 07-4741 5121; Flinders Hwy; r from $50; 🗷) is filled with memorabilia and atmosphere.

QUEENSLAND

The **Porcupine Gorge National Park** (☎ 07-4741 1113; camping per person/family $5/20) is an oasis in the dry country north of Hughenden. The best spot to go to is **Pyramid Lookout**, about 70km north of Hughenden. You can camp here and it's an easy 30-minute walk into the gorge, with some fine rock formations and a permanently running creek. The venerable **Grand Hotel** (☎ 07-4741 1588; 25 Gray St, Hughenden; r from $40; ❷) has well worn, suitably priced pub rooms and good counter meals.

Julia Creek, 144km further on, is a nowhere outback town with a smattering of motels and a caravan park. From Julia Creek, the sealed Wills Developmental Rd heads north to Normanton (432km), Karumba (494km) and Burketown (467km). See the Gulf Savannah section (p432) for more information on these towns.

CLONCURRY
pop 5200

Cloncurry is an unlikely town with a fabled flying past. At 121km east of Mt Isa, the Curry was the birthplace of the Royal Flying Doctors Service (RFDS), plus Qantas Airlines was conceived here (check out the original aircraft hanger standing at Cloncurry Shire Airport).

In the 19th century, Cloncurry was the largest producer of copper in the British empire. This historic pastoral centre is on the verge of another mining boom. Real estate prices are rocketing, and big business is hovering in the shadows.

Global warming is old news in the outback – Australia's highest recorded temperature in the shade, 53.1°C, was measured here in 1889.

John Flynn Place (☎ 07-4742 4125; Daintree St; adult/child $10/5; ❷ 8am-4.30pm Mon-Fri, 9am-3pm Sat & Sun Apr-Oct) commemorates Flynn's work in setting up the invaluable Royal Flying Doctor Service. The building incorporates an art gallery, cultural centre and theatre.

The best place to sleep is the **Wagon Wheel Motel** (☎ 07-4742 1866; 54 Ramsay St; s/d from $65/75; ❷ ❷), which is clean, comfortable and sports a friendly bar. Across the road, the **Red Rock Motel** (☎ 07-4742 2728; 56-58 Scarr St; r from $70; ❷) has excellent motel facilities. There's also the upmarket **Gidgee Inn** (☎ 07-4742 1599; www.gidgeeinn.com.au; d/tw $125/138; ❷ ❷), packed together with rammed red earth, and the **Cloncurry Caravan Park Oasis** (☎ 07-4742 1313; unpowered/powered sites $16/20, cabins from $75).

MT ISA
pop 22,600

Boisterous, prosperous Mt Isa is a long way from everywhere, and unlike anywhere else. Around the clock this wealthy mining town lights up the starry sky, as tireless miners and their machines dig deep into the night. The locals are a mix of well-to-do, how-do-*you*-do cowboys and girls and itinerant easygoing wage earners. But everyone shares the dusty heat and geographic isolation – often over multiple beers – and the sense of community is palpable.

The most pleasant surprise for first-time visitors to Isa is the stark red beauty of the place. Strange rocky formations – padded with olive-green spinifex – line the perimeter of town as deep-blue sunsets eclipse all unnatural light.

There's a surprisingly diverse ethnic mix (more than 50 nationalities have settled here for work), but don't expect an absence of racist rhetoric. Likewise Mayor John Maloney made national headlines in August 2008 when he issued a call for 'beauty disadvantaged' women to consider moving to Mt Isa to make use of the majority male population. A world away from the big cities on the coast, the Isa is nothing if not honest.

Orientation & Information
The sandy Leichhardt River separates 'townside' from 'mineside', and home from work. The Barkly Hwy, which becomes Marian St, is the main entry road. The city centre is in the area between Grace and Isa Sts, and West and Simpson Sts. **Mt Isa Airport** (☎ 07-4743 4598; Barkly Hwy) is roughly 5km from the town centre; a taxi to town costs around $20. Head to Outback at Isa (below) for tourist information.

Sights & Activities
Don't miss Mt Isa's extra-sensory sunset at the **City Lookout**, off Hilary St. It's free and hard to forget.

The Australian Tourism Award–winning **Outback at Isa** (☎ 1300 659 660, 07-4749 1555; www .outbackatisa.com.au; 19 Marian St; ❷ 8.30am-5pm) is featured on most itineraries, and for good reason, too. The hands-on museum provides a colourful, articulate and air-conditioned overview of mining, pioneering and local history. It comprises a number of galleries and experiences. The **Hard Times Mine** (adult/child $45/26) takes you 10m beneath the surface (the real mines descend up to 10 times that distance)

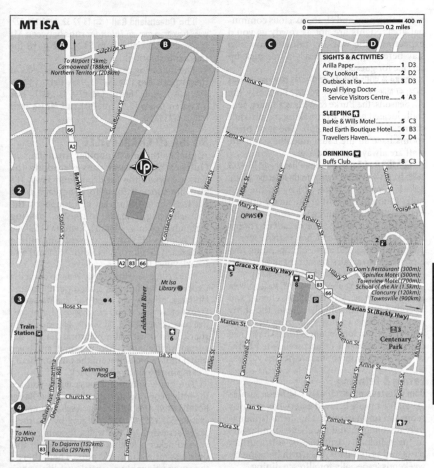

MT ISA

SIGHTS & ACTIVITIES		
Arilla Paper	**1**	D3
City Lookout	**2**	D2
Outback at Isa	**3**	D3
Royal Flying Doctor		
Service Visitors Centre	**4**	A3

SLEEPING		
Burke & Wills Motel	**5**	C3
Red Earth Boutique Hotel	**6**	B3
Travellers Haven	**7**	D4

DRINKING		
Buffs Club	**8**	C3

QUEENSLAND

to a purpose-built mine complete with fuming, roaring and rattling machinery. The fascinating **Riversleigh Fossil Centre** (adult/child $10/6.50) is also here. If you think Australia has strange animals now, then check out what *used* to roam the land. The re-creation of Australia's prehistoric fauna is the stuff of science fiction, plus you can examine actual fossils. The centre also houses the **Isa Experience Gallery** and **Outback Park** (adult/child $10/6.50), showcasing natural, Indigenous and mining heritage of Mt Isa. There's a good-value, two-day **Discovery Tour Pass** (adult/child $55/33), which combines all the attractions.

Arilla Paper (☎ 07-4743 0084; cnr Shackleton & Marian Sts) is an Indigenous women's cooperative that sells beautiful handcrafted paper made from native plants and grasses. It's great for gifts!

Also worth a peek are the **Royal Flying Doctor Service Visitors Centre** (☎ 07-4743 2800; Barkly Hwy; admission by donation $2.50; ☽ 9.30am-4.30pm Mon-Fri) and the **School of the Air** (☎ 07-4744 9100; Kalkadoon High School, Abel Smith Pde; admission by donation $2; ☽ tours 9am & 10am Mon-Fri during school term). Both put Isa's isolation into perspective.

If in town during the second week in August, saddle up for Australia's largest **rodeo** (www.isarodeo.com.au).

Sleeping

Travellers Haven (☎ 07-4743 0313; fax 07-4743 4007; 75 Spence St; dm/s/d $20/35/50; ☒ ☒) A tad worn in places, the Haven is still the only genuine budget haunt in town. Aside from the peeling floors and creaky bunks, there's a good-sized swimming pool and clean, spacious communal area. Nights are not as rowdy as you'd expect as some working miners choose to stay here long-term. There's a free pick-up service for guests.

Burke & Wills Motel (☎ 07-4743 8000; fax 07-4743 8424; 47 Miles St; r $100-150; ✖ ☒) Formerly the All Seasons, the Burke & Wills is a smart, centrally located motel, within slumping distance of the roaring Buff's Club. The neat brick rooms have all the usual amenities, and the staff are always up and about.

our pick **Red Earth Boutique Hotel** (☎ 07-4749 8888; fax 07- 4749 8899; www.redearth-hotel.com.au; cnr Rodeo Dr & West St; r $110-160; ✖) By far the best hotel in town, the staff at the newly opened Red Earth are still coming to terms with their boutique surrounds. The decadent rooms feature plush leather couches, massive street-facing balconies and an air of impending revelry. The downstairs restaurant is first class (kangaroo steak with red wine jus $28).

Spinifex Motel (☎ 07-4749 2944; 79-83 Marian St; www.spinifexmotel.com.au; r $110-180; ✖ ☒) Owned and operated by a personable couple, the shiny new Spinifex is a short walk from the town centre. The spacious, spotless rooms have tiled floors, flat-screen TVs and well-fitted bathrooms. The family rooms are honest value.

Eating & Drinking

Dom's Restaurant (☎ 07-4743 4444; Marian St; mains $15-30) Isa's most beloved eatery has recently reopened on Marian St. The menu is thankfully unchanged, and the clientele still pours in for delicious crispy pizzas, soft, buttery pasta and tasty salads. It's worth booking on weekends, especially for alfresco dining.

Buff's Club (☎ 07-4743 2365; cnr Grace & Simpon Sts; beers $5) A multipurpose, big-screen venue – and unofficial country community centre on weekends – the Carpentaria Buffalo Club sees young and old gossip, drink and gamble in air-conditioned comfort. A Friday afternoon on the deck at Buff's is a real Mt Isa moment.

Getting There & Around

Skytrans (☎ 1300 759 872; www.skytrans.com.au) operates services onnecting Mt Isa with Birdsville, Charleville and Normanton. See p391 for flight information.

Greyhound Australia (☎ 13 14 99; www.greyhound.com.au) has regular services to Townsville ($143, 11½ hours), Longreach ($104, 8½ hours) and Brisbane ($192, 26 hours).

The **Queensland Rail** (☎ 13 22 32, 1300 131 722; www.traveltrain.com.au) *Inlander* runs between Mt Isa and Townsville from $124; see p418 for more information.

The following car-hire firms have desks at the airport: **Avis** (☎ 07-4743 3733), **Hertz** (☎ 07-4743 4142) and **Thrifty** (☎ 07-4743 2911). For a taxi to town ($20 to $30) call **Mt Isa Taxis** (☎ 07-4743 2333).

MT ISA TO CHARLEVILLE

Arguably the most popular road trip in Outback Queensland runs east along the Barkly Hwy to the Landsborough Hwy. It's also the shortest route to Longreach from Mt Isa. Some 14km east of Cloncurry, the Landsborough heads southeast, passing through McKinlay (91km), Kynuna (168km) and Winton (339km), and eventually hitting Longreach (516km), Barcaldine (621km) and Charleville (1020km).

The cringe-worthy classic Aussie comedy, *Crocodile Dundee*, was filmed partly in tiny **McKinlay**, otherwise famed for the **Walkabout Creek Hotel** (☎ 07-746 8424; Landsborough Hwy; unpowered/powered sites $29/35, s/d $65/70; ✖), a hot tin shack loaded with film memorabilia and assorted Australiana. There are small and basic motel units a block west of the pub, or there's a camping ground out the back.

You know you're in **Kynuna** when you see the little neon dog atop the historic **Blue Heeler Hotel** (☎ 07-4746 8650; Landsborough Hwy, Kynuna; campsites $15, r $55-80; ✖). Judging by the messages scrawled on the walls, it seems every second ocker celeb has sipped a beer in this quintessential outback pub. Then there's the unquestionably essential surf life-saving club, where each April a surf life-saving carnival is held – you're doing well to drown. Accommodation ranges from pub rooms to spotless motel units, and campsites.

The signposted turn-off to the waterholes of **Combo Conservation Park**, which Banjo Paterson is said to have visited in 1895 before he wrote 'Waltzing Matilda', is off the highway about 12km east of Kynuna.

Winton

pop 1321

It's pioneer days at 40 paces on main street Winton, a cattle and sheep centre that dishes up tasty tourist cheese by the swag-full. Still, the population has swelled in recent years, and while the period charms may be forced, they're also mighty infectious. A short visit will have you happy snapping at the heritage buildings and brushing up on your bush poetry. When you've run out of things to do in town, plan your run with the dinosaurs.

Winton's biggest attraction is the **Waltzing Matilda Centre** (☎ 07-4657 1466; www.matildacentre .com.au; 50 Elderslie St; adult/child/family $19/8/42; ⏱ 9am-5pm), which doubles as the visitor information booth. There is a surprising number of exhibits here for a museum devoted to a song, including an indoor billabong complete with a squatter, troopers and a jolly swagman; a hologram display oozing cringe-inducing nationalism; and the **Jolly Swagman statue**, a tribute to the unknown swagmen who lie in unmarked graves in the area. The centre also houses the **Qantilda Pioneer Place**, which has a huge range of artefacts and displays on the founding of Qantas.

Find the world's biggest deck chair in the open-air **Royal Theatre** (☎ 07-4657 1296; 73 Elderslie St; adult/child $6.50/4; ⏱ screenings 8pm Wed Apr-Sep) at the rear of the Wookatook Gift & Gem. There's an old-movie-world charm in the canvas-slung chairs, corrugated tin walls and star-studded ceiling. It has a small **museum** (admission $3) in the projection room and screens old classics.

Arno's Wall (Vindex St), behind the North Gregory Hotel, is Winton's quirkiest attraction – a 70m-long work-in-progress by artist Arno Grotjahn, featuring a huge range of industrial and household items, from televisions to motorcycles, ensnared in the mortar.

About 110km southwest of Winton is the startling **Lark Quarry Dinosaur Trackways** (☎ 07-4657 1188; www.dinosaurtrackways.com.au; guided tour adult/child $10/6; ⏱ 10am, noon & 2pm), where you'll see dinosaur footprints in a prehistoric streambed beneath a manmade sheltered walkway. It requires imagination, a guided tour (and a packed lunch!), but is nonetheless a humbling travel experience. Contact the Waltzing Matilda Centre at Winton to book tours.

The annual **Bush Poetry Festival**, in July, attracts entrants from all over Australia, but Winton's major festival is the five-day **Outback Festival**, held every odd year during the September school holidays.

To nod off for the night, try heading to the **North Gregory Hotel** (☎ 1800 801 611, 07-4657 1375; 67 Elderslie St; s/d $44/55, motel units $77; ⏱), a big, friendly country pub where 'Waltzing

Matilda' was allegedly first performed on 6 April 1895, although the original building burnt down in 1900. It has dozens of comfortable, old-fashioned rooms upstairs, with clean shared facilities. There's also an excellent bistro (mains $10 to $20).

The best place for a feed is **Twilight Cafe** (☎ 07-4657 1301; 68 Elderslie St; mains $5-20; ⏱ 8am-2pm & 3-8pm). The menu is straightforward (burgers, pasta, big breakfast), but it's BYO and a photo gallery is attached.

If you didn't come this far to sleep in a mere town, try the welcoming **Carisbrooke Station** (☎ 07-4657 3885; unpowered sites per person $10; tw with/ without bathroom $70/60; ⏱), a sheep and cattle property that has camping and accommodation in self-contained units. To get there from Winton, head 35km down the Boulia road, turn left at Cork Mail Rd (unsealed) and continue another 50km.

Greyhound Australia (☎ 13 14 99; www.grey hound.com.au) connects Winton with Brisbane ($159, 19½ hours), Mt Isa ($87, six hours) and Longreach ($31, three hours).

Longreach
pop 3700

This prosperous outback town was the home of Qantas early last century, but these days it's equally famous for the Australian Stockman's Hall of Fame & Outback Heritage Centre, one of outback Queensland's biggest attractions. The Tropic of Capricorn passes through Longreach, and so do more than a million sheep and cattle.

The **Visitors Information Centre** (☎ 07-4658 3555; 99 Eagle St; ⏱ 8.30am-5pm Mon-Fri, 9am-noon Sat & Sun, closed Sat & Sun Oct-Mar) is on Eagle St.

SIGHTS

The **Australian Stockman's Hall of Fame & Outback Heritage Centre** (☎ 07-4658 2166; www.outbackheritage .com.au; Landsborough Hwy; adult/child/family $23/12/50; ⏱ 9am-5pm) is a tribute to the early stockmen and explorers (check out the nifty maps), and has a range of galleries covering Aboriginal culture and European invasion. It's 2km east of town towards Barcaldine. Admission is valid for two days.

The **Qantas Founders Outback Museum** (☎ 07-4658 3737; www.qfom.com.au; Landsborough Hwy; adult/child/family $18/9/40; ⏱ 9am-5pm) houses a life-size replica of an Avro 504K, the first aircraft owned by the fledgling airline. Interactive multimedia and working displays tell the history of Qantas. Next door, the original 1921 Qantas hangar houses a mint-condition DH-61. Towering over everything is a bright and shiny **747-200B Jumbo** (adult/child/family with museum tour $32/16/69; ✆ 9.30am, 11am, 1pm & 3pm).

TOURS

Longreach Outback Travel Centre (☎ 07-4658 1776; www.lotc.com.au; 115a Eagle St) The epicentre for travel in and around Longreach offers some excellent tours, including the Longreach Lookabout (adult/child $187/154), which takes in the town's sights and ends with a dinner cruise on the Thomson River. Alternatively, cut straight to the best bit with the evening Billabong Boat Cruise (adult/child $50/36).

Outback Aussie Tours (☎ 07-4658 3000; Landsborough Hwy) Offers extended tours within a 300km radius of Longreach, including the highly recommended five-night Legendary Longreach and Winton Tour (1/2 person from $1879/$3170, departs Wednesday). It's located at the train station.

SLEEPING & EATING

Eagle St has a number of pubs with good, cheap meals.

Longreach Outback Adventures (☎ 07-4651 1242; 18 Stork Rd; s/d $28/45; ✖ ⬛) This complex of dongas (small transportable buildings) with a common room, kitchen and laundry is a fun and friendly refuge from a lonely life on the road.

Old Time Cottage (☎ 07-4658 1550; fax 07-4658 3733; 158 Crane St; d $90; ✖) A great choice for groups and families, this quaint little corrugated-iron cottage is set in an attractive garden. Fully furnished, the self-contained cottage sleeps up to five people.

Albert Park Motor Inn (☎ 1800 812 811, 07-4658 2411; Sir Hudson Fysh Memorial Dr; s/d $99/116; ✖ ⬛) On the highway east of the centre, this good motel has spacious, four-star, well-appointed rooms, as well as pools and a spa. The motel's Oasis Restaurant (mains $15 to $30) has an elegant dining room and varied menu.

Gunnadoo Caravan Park & Cabins (☎ 07-4658 1781; 12 Thrush Rd; unpowered/powered sites $25/27, cabins $80-150; ✖ ⬛) This exceptionally neat, modern park is hard to beat for its three artesian in-ground spa pools in a cave-grotto setting.

Longreach Club (☎ 07-4658 1016; 31 Duck St; mains $17-25; ✆ lunch & dinner) Every country town worth its weight in poker machines has a club like the Longreach Club. There's a pleasant garden and formal dining room, serving staple roasts, steaks and pasta.

GETTING THERE & AWAY

Greyhound Australia (☎ 13 14 99; www.greyhound.com .au) connects Longreach with Winton ($36, three hours), Brisbane ($107, 17 hours) and Mt Isa ($101, 8½ hours). Buses stop behind the **Longreach Outback Travel Centre** (☎ 07-4658 1776; 115a Eagle St).

Emerald Coaches (☎ 07-4982 4444; www.emerald coaches.com.au) makes the twice-weekly run travelling to and from Rockhampton ($97, 9½ hours). Buses stop at Outback Aussie Tours (left).

Barcaldine
pop 1500

Barcaldine is a colourful little pub town with a long, colourful past. Popping up at the junction of the Landsborough and Capricorn Hwys 108km east of Longreach, Bar-*call*-din's wide, tree-lined streets are dotted with brightly painted colonial pubs, frequented on weekends by strong-armed farmers and pretty homestead sheilas.

The town gained a place in Australian history in 1891 when it became the headquarters of a major shearers' strike. The confrontation led to the formation of the Australian Workers' Party, now the Australian Labor Party. The organisers' meeting place was the **Tree of Knowledge**, a ghost gum planted near the train station that long stood as a monument to workers and their rights. It was tragically poisoned in 2006. Some suspect Liberal Party insiders; others blame jealous Longreach folk.

The original inhabitants of Barcaldine were the Inningai who 'disappeared' soon after explorer Thomas Mitchell arrived in 1824.

The **Visitor Information Centre** (☎ 07-4651 1724; Oak St) is next to the train station. The **Australian Workers Heritage Centre** (☎ 07-4651 2422; www.australianworkersheritagecentre.com.au; Ash St; adult/child/family $12/7.50/28; ✆ 9am-5pm Mon-Sat, 10am-5pm Sun) provides a rundown on Australian social, political and industrial movements. Set in landscaped gardens, Barcaldine's main attraction features the Australian Bicentennial Theatre, with displays tracing the history of the shearers' strike, as well as a schoolhouse, hospital and powerhouse.

Central Queensland's first artesian bore was built 26km east of Barcaldine at **Back Creek** in 1886.

A bit south of town, the **Ironbark Inn** (☎ 07-4651 2311; 115 Oak St; s/d from $69/79; ✖ ⬛) has clean, comfortable rooms set in native gardens. Liars, larrikins and legends will revel in the **3Ls Bar & Bistro** (mains $15-25), a rustic, open-shed restaurant with wooden bench tables and stockmen's ropes and branding irons on the walls. Shut up and eat your steak, mate. Other iconic iron-roofed, wooden-verandah pubs line Oak St and are well worth a crawl.

CHARLEVILLE

pop 3500

Located 760km west of Brisbane, Charleville is the grand old dame of Central Queensland and the largest town in Mulga Country. Due largely to its prime locale on the Warrego River, the town was an important centre for early explorers – Cobb & Co had their largest coach-making factory here – but the town has maintained its prosperity as a major Australian wool centre.

Through initiatives such as the Bidjara Community Development Employment Project, Charleville was long heralded as an example of 'practical reconciliation'. Yet the disbanding of Australian & Torres Strait Islander Commission (Atsic) has led to a sharp rise in unemployment and a subsequent decline in population.

The **Visitor Information Centre** (☎ 07-4654 3057; Sturt St), on the southeast side of town, offers two handy heritage trail maps to follow by either car or foot.

The finest sights in Charleville are a million miles away. The **Cosmos Centre** (☎ 07-4654 7771; www.cosmoscentre.com; adult/child/family $10/5/25, observatory session $20/13/43; ☼ 10am-6pm, night observatory variable hours), offers a spectacular view of the night sky via a high-powered telescope and an expert guide. The 90-minute sessions start soon after sunset. The centre lies 2km south of town, off Airport Dr.

The **EPA** (☎ 07-4654 1255; 1 Park St; ☼ 8.30am-4.30pm Mon-Fri) runs a captive breeding program for endangered native species. You can see yellow-footed rock wallabies and all manner of cuddly creatures at the **Bilby Show** (Racecourse Complex, Partridge St; admission $5; ☼ 6-7pm Sun, Mon, Wed & Fri Apr-Sep), which also provides a fascinating insight into its rare nocturnal namesake.

The most majestic hotel in Central Queensland, **Hotel Corones** (☎ 07-4654 1022; 33 Wills St; r $50-90; ☼) is a stunningly restored country pub. Bypass the motel rooms in favour of its resurrected upstairs interior where

rooms feature fireplaces, leadlight windows and elegant Australian antiques. You can eat in the grandiose, yet affordable dining room (mains $15 to $20) or the bare-bones public bar (mains $10 to $12).

THE CHANNEL COUNTRY

You wanted outback, did ya? Well, here it is, mate – miles and bloody square miles of it! The Channel Country is an unforgiving, eerily empty region where red sand hills, the odd wildflower and strange luminous phenomena run across prime beef-grazing land. The channels are formed by water rushing south from the summer monsoons to fill the Georgina, Hamilton and Diamantina Rivers and Cooper Creek. Despite a record-breaking deluge in 2007, rain itself rarely falls in southwest Queensland, which borders the NT, South Australia (SA) and NSW. Avoid the summer months (October to April), unless you go for searing heat and dust.

GETTING THERE & AROUND

There are no train or bus services in the Channel Country, and the closest car rental is in Mt Isa. Fools perish out here; roads are poorly marked and getting lost is easy. In fact, it's required that you write your name, destination and expected date of arrival on a blackboard at the station where you start, so search-and-rescue services can come looking if you don't show up within a few days. Some roads from the east and north to the fringes of the Channel Country are sealed, but between October and May even these can be cut off when dirt roads become quagmires. Visiting this area requires a sturdy vehicle (a 4WD if you want to get off the beaten track) with decent clearance. Always carry plenty of drinking water and petrol.

The main road through this area is the Diamantina Developmental Rd. It runs south from Mt Isa through Boulia to Bedourie, then east through Windorah and Quilpie to Charleville. It's a long and lonely 1340km, about two-thirds of which is sealed. Take extra caution when driving at dusk when the warm road attracts wild camels and kangaroos.

Mt Isa to Birdsville

It's around 300km of sealed road from Mt Isa south to Boulia, and the only facilities along the route are at **Dajarra**, which has a pub and a roadhouse.

Boulia
pop 300

The unofficial 'capital' of the Channel Country is a neat little outpost on the cusp of the great Simpson Desert. It's from here that the world's longest mail run comes to an end, some 3000km from Port Augusta in South Australia. In mid-July, Boulia hosts Australia's premier **camel racing** event.

The most famous residents of Boulia are the mysterious Min Min Lights, a supposedly natural phenomenon that occurs when the temperature plummets after dark and erratic lights appear on the unusually flat horizon.

Believe it or not, but the **Min Min Encounter** (☎ 07-4746 3386; Herbert St; adult/child $12/8; ☼ 8.30am-5pm Mon-Fri, 9am-noon Sat & Sun) feels like a Spielberg movie set, featuring sophisticated gadgetry and eerie lighting in its hourly show. Doubling as the information centre, it's classic travel kitsch and could well help you spot your own Min Min.

Hang a little prehistory around your neck with one of Boulia's more earthly **moonstones**. These beautiful stones have pyrite crystal centres sourced from the bed of an inland sea that dried up in the area about 100 million years ago.

With modern and spacious units, the **Desert Sands Motel** (☎ 07-4746 3000; fax 07-4746 3040; Herbert St; s/d $80/90; ☒) is the best place to sleep. For a drink, keep your head down at the **Australian Hotel** (☎ 07-4746 3144; Herbert St).

The sealed Kennedy Developmental Rd runs east from Boulia, 369km to Winton. The **Middleton Hotel** (☎ /fax 07-4657 3980; Kennedy Developmental Rd; s/d $55/65), 168km before Winton, is the only fuel stop en route. It serves meals daily and you can rent out simple dongas without bathrooms.

Bedourie
pop 120

From Boulia it's 200km of mainly unsealed road south to Bedourie, the administrative centre for the huge Diamantina Shire Council.

One of the finest outback pubs is Bedourie's own **Royal Hotel** (☎ 07-4746 1201; fax 07-4746 1101; Herbert St; s/d $65/75; ☒), a charming adobe brick building built in 1880. There are two motel units out the back.

Alternatively, there's a caravan park and comfortable motel units at the **Simpson Desert**

Oasis (☎ 07-4746 1291; fax 07-4746 1208; Herbert St; unpowered/powered sites $12/18, d $100; ☒), which incorporates a fuel stop, supermarket and restaurant.

Birdsville
pop 120

Off-the-beaten track travellers can't claim the title until they visit Birdsville, an iconic Australian settlement on the fringe of the Simpson Desert, and Queensland's most remote 'town'. During the first weekend in September, the annual **Birdsville Cup** (www.birds villeraces.com) horse races draw up to 7000 fans from all over the country to drink, dance and gamble for three dusty days. Parking is free for all light aircraft. In the wake of large-scale flooding in early 2009, bird enthusiasts and other curious folk flocked to Birdsville to see, among thousands of other species, coastal pelicans enjoying the Diamantina River and Eyre Creek running at capacity.

The desert throws up another surprise at the wonderful **Blue Poles Gallery** (☎ 07-4656 3099; www.birdsvillestudio.com.au; Graham St; ☼ 9am-6pm Sun-Thu, to 10pm Fri, Sat & school holidays Apr-Nov), where you can inspect and buy outback art by, among others, local artist Wolfgang John.

The **Birdsville Working Museum** (☎ 07-4656 3259; Macdonald St; adult/child $7/5; ☼ 8am-5pm Apr-Oct, tours 9am, 11am & 3pm) is an impressive private collection of droving gear, saddles, shearing equipment, wool presses, road signs, toys and trinkets. John Menzies will happily show you around his big tin shed.

Standing strong in sandstone since 1884 is the much-loved **Birdsville Hotel** (☎ 07-4656 3244; www.theoutback.com.au; Adelaide St; r $90-130; ☒). It's a humbling experience to sip a stubbie on the verandah with loose-lipped locals and big-hearted adventurers and watch the sun set deep into the desert. When you've had a gutful, the motel-style units are tasteful and spacious, while the restaurant (mains $15 to $20) is surprisingly slick. Try to arrive on a Friday when happy hour runs late and loud.

Birdsville Track

Tackling the 517km Birdsville Track was once reserved for the foolhardy and fearless, but these days it's one of Australia's favourite outback driving routes. You can even travel via 2WD, as the track is now largely baked-flat dirt. But don't get too cocky; this is still perilous country. Making the trip all the way to Maree requires a reliable vehicle and plenty of extra water, fuel and spare parts.

The easterly Outside Track is your only option, as it hugs the Stuart Stony Desert at a safe distance. The trip can be done in two days from Birdsville with an overnight stop in Mungeranie station in South Australia, where you'll find fuel, food and a hotel to rest your throbbing head. The station is a lonely 313km from Birdsville.

Before leaving Birdsville, don't forget to check in at the **Wirrarri Centre** (☎ 07-4656 3300; www.diamantina.qld.gov.au; Billabong Blvd, Birdsville; ⏲ 8.30am-6pm Mar-Oct, 8.to 4.30pm Mon-Fri Nov-Feb; 🖳); learn the lay of the road, stock up on fuel and snacks, and email someone you wish was here.

Simpson Desert National Park

So you've made it this far without too many troubles? Good, but this 200,000 sq km slab of spinifex, cane grass and enormous red sand dunes is not the place to start finding them. Out here, ranches the size of small nations muster up a living on land that refuses to yield much more than aching bones and Georgina gidgee wattle.

A 4WD is compulsory in the spectacular, waterless Simpson Desert, which occupies a sizeable piece of central Australia, and stretches across the Queensland, NT and SA borders. The Queensland section, in the state's far southwestern corner, is protected as the 10,000 sq km Simpson Desert National Park,

Only attempt to cross in parties of at least two 4WD vehicles, equipped with suitable communications. Alternatively, you can hire a satellite phone from **Birdsville police** (☎ 07-4656 3220; McDonald St) for $23 per day, which can be returned to **Maree police** (☎ 08-8675 8346) in SA. Permits are required to traverse the park, and are available from the Birdsville **EPA office** (☎ 07-4652 7333; cnr Billabong Blvd & Jardine St, Birdsville) or from the town's petrol stations. You will need to write your anticipated route and arrival time at your destination on the police blackboard, so help can be sent if you get lost – this is very, very rough country and should not be attempted by anyone without lots of outback driving experience.

For the park's SA sections, you need a separate permit, available through the **South Australian National Parks & Wildlife Service** (☎ 1800 816 078).

Birdsville to Charleville

The Birdsville Developmental Rd heads east from Birdsville, meeting the Diamantina Developmental Rd after 277km of rough gravel and sand. **Betoota** is the sole 'town' between Birdsville and Windorah, but there are no facilities here any more so motorists have to carry enough fuel to cover the 395km distance.

Windorah is often either very dry or very wet. The town's general store sells fuel and groceries. Originally built in 1878, the charming blue **Western Star Hotel** (☎ 07-4656 3166; 15 Albert St; s/d pub r $40/55, motel units $90/100; 🏊) has good pub rooms and four neat motel units. The pub swells on the Wednesday before the Birdsville Cup when it hosts **yabbie races**.

Quilpie is an opal-mining town and the railhead from which cattle are transported to the coast. It has a good range of facilities, including two pubs, a motel, a caravan park, several petrol stations and the **Quilpie Museum & Visitors Centre** (☎ 07-4656 2166; 51 Brolga St; ⏲ 8am-5pm Mon-Fri year-round, 10am-4.30pm Sat & Sun Apr-Nov). From here it's another 210km to Charleville (p397).

South of Quilpie and west of Cunnamulla are the remote **Yowah Opal Fields** and the town of **Eulo**, which cohosts the **World Lizard Racing Championships** with Cunnamulla in late August. **Thargomindah**, 130km west of Eulo, has a couple of motels and a guest house. **Noccundra**, another 145km further west, was once a busy little community. It now has just one hotel supplying basic accommodation, meals and fuel. If you have a 4WD you can continue west to Innamincka, in SA, on the rough and stony Strzelecki Track, via the site of the famous **Dig Tree**, where William Brahe buried provisions during the ill-fated Burke and Wills expedition in 1860–61.

WHITSUNDAY COAST

When Lieutenant James Cook sailed along this coast 50 days after Easter (on White Sunday) in 1770, he must have gargled with resplendent joy. The Whitsunday Islands are a travellers' wonderland where a great southern experience of sun, sand and sailing is an outstretched arm away. It was no surprise that the 'Best Job in the World' – as promoted by Tourism Queensland – was stationed here, and received a whopping 34,000 applications.

QUEENSLAND

WHITSUNDAY COAST

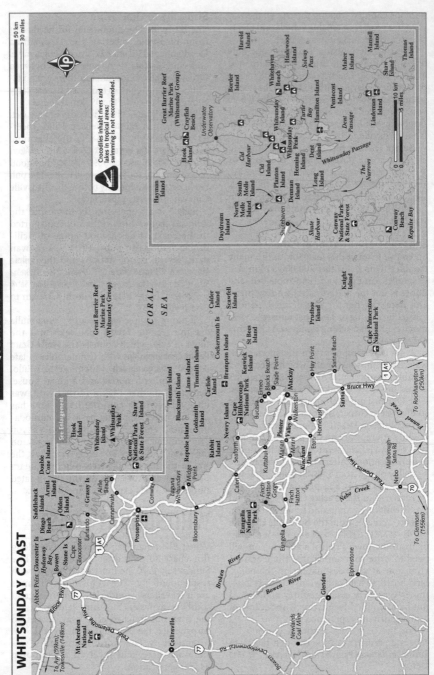

Crocodiles inhabit rivers and lakes in tropical areas; swimming is not recommended.

The Great Barrier Reef Marine Park lies just beneath its shimmering surface, while the sky shoots starry nights almost year-round. Aside from the odd untimely storm, this is a permanent holiday paradise, equally suited to the rich, the famous and the not-so-rich-or-famous!

As though it weren't enough to claim the finest tropical islands on the planet, there are also some excellent national parks in the area offering first-class bushwalking and camping.

The gateway to the islands, Airlie Beach, is also a gateway to heady good times. Those in search of solace here, be warned – a galley of restaurants, bars and backpackers ensure the wannabe stars stay out all night.

MACKAY
pop 80,000

Mackay is a tropical town with few pretensions, a slice of suburbia with a slice of pineapple. The Pioneer River runs alongside the compact, palm-lined business district that becomes a boisterous bar scene after dark. At the redeveloped marina, restaurants, themed pubs and residential apartments overlook a giant stone spit and long stretches of open beach that run all the way to glorious Cape Hillsborough National Park.

Despite its fabulous location, a night or two here en route to elsewhere is all you need. One such detour is a short trip west through the cane fields to Eungella National Park, with its famous platypuses, and the lush, hidden highlights of Finch Hatton Gorge.

Orientation & Information

The wide, easy-flowing Pioneer River wends its way through Mackay with the town settled on its southern side. Victoria St is the main strip. The marina is 3km away to the north.

EPA office (☎ 07-4944 7800; fax 07-4944 7811; cnr Wood & River Sts)

Mackay Visitor Information Centre (☎ 07-4952 2677; www.mackayregion.com; 320 Nebo Rd; ☽ 8.30am-5pm Mon-Fri, 9am-4pm Sat & Sun) About 3km south of the centre.

Paper Chain (☎ 07-4953 1331; 8a Sydney St; ☽ 8.45am-5pm Mon-Fri, 9am-12.30pm Sat & Sun) Good-quality secondhand bookshop.

Sights

Artspace Mackay (☎ 07-4957 1775; www.artspacemackay .com.au; admission free; Gordon St; ☽ 10am-5pm Tue-Sun)

upholds the strong reputation of regional Queensland art galleries, showcasing local and visiting works on the edge of the civic precinct. You can dabble in a workshop or graze at Foodspace, the in-house licensed cafe open 10am to 4pm Tuesday to Friday, from 9am on weekends. Information on the Mackay Self-Drive Art Gallery, Pottery & Craft Tour is available.

Art deco enthusiasts will love Mackay's CBD. Most of the facades are at their finest on the second storey. Noteworthy examples include the **Mackay Townhouse Motel** (Victoria St), the **Australian Hotel** (Victoria St) and the **Ambassador Hotel** (Sydney St).

Mackay Regional Botanical Gardens (☎ 07-4952 7300; Lagoon St; admission free), 3km south of the city centre, includes a lovely **Tropical Shade Garden** (☽ 8.45am-4.45pm).

Some fine beaches are within a short walk of the marina, but Mackay's best beaches, **Blacks Beach**, **Eimeo** and **Bucasia**, are about 16km north of town.

Tours

Beyond Mackay's sugar-cane sea are a superb rainforest and national park.

Jungle Johno Tours (☎ 07-4951 3728; larrikin@ mackay.net.au; adult/child/YHA member $90/50/80) Runs excellent day trips to Eungella National Park, including pick-up, morning tea and lunch.

Reeforest Adventure Tours (☎ 1800 500 353; www .reeforest.com) Offers a wide range of tours, including an Indigenous cultural tour to Cape Hillsborough National Park.

Sleeping

Hotels in Mackay fill up quick smart due to a steady influx of mine workers, so book well ahead in the high season.

BUDGET

Larrikin Lodge (☎ 07-4951 3728; fax 07-4957 2978; 32 Peel St; dm/tw $24/55) This airy, high-ceilinged timber house is a delightful place to unpack your pack. It's also home to Jungle Johno Tours (above). Call to arrange a pick-up.

Gecko's Rest (☎ 07-4944 1230; www.geckosrest.com .au; 34 Sydney St; dm/s/d $24/40/55; ☒ ▯) There's a healthy backpacker scene in this hip, downtown, art deco building. Gecko's is bright and bold, with a sensational rooftop deck and busy communal kitchen. The communal bathrooms are excellent – plenty of room to swing a cat (or a towel). There's a TV

QUEENSLAND

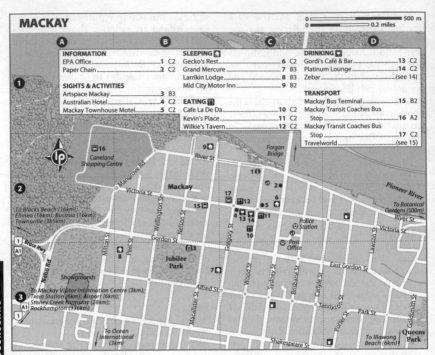

MACKAY

INFORMATION	
EPA Office	1 C2
Paper Chain	2 C2

SIGHTS & ACTIVITIES	
Artspace Mackay	3 B3
Australian Hotel	4 C2
Mackay Townhouse Motel	5 C2

SLEEPING	
Gecko's Rest	6 C2
Grand Mercure	7 B3
Larrikin Lodge	8 B3
Mid City Motor Inn	9 B2

EATING	
Cafe La De Da	10 C2
Kevin's Place	11 C2
Wilkie's Tavern	12 C2

DRINKING	
Gordi's Café & Bar	13 C2
Platinum Lounge	14 C2
Zebar	(see 14)

TRANSPORT	
Mackay Bus Terminal	15 B2
Mackay Transit Coaches Bus	
Stop	16 A2
Mackay Transit Coaches Bus	
Stop	17 C2
Travelworld	(see 15)

lounge to hook up with your next travel partner, plus central air-con. All dorms are spacious, but ask for one with a king-sized single bed.

MIDRANGE & TOP END

Mid City Motor Inn (☎ 07-4951 1666; 2 Macalister St; r $105-155; ☒ ☒) Great value standard rooms beside the river promenade make this a good bet for couples in transit.

Ocean International (☎ 1800 635 104, 07-4957 2044; www.ocean-international.com.au; 1 Bridge Rd, Illawong Beach; d $170-270; ☒ ☒ ☒) This stalwart business hotel is 3km south of the centre, close to the airport. All rooms, with tiled floors and bright aspects, face straight out to the Coral Sea. There's an excellent restaurant and cocktail bar, plus a spa and sauna.

Grand Mercure (☎ 07-4969 1000; www.mackaygrand mercure.com.au; 9 Gregory St; r $170, ste $235; ☒ ☒) This grand new complex dominates the city centre as both a social hub and luxury hotel of choice. The spa suite ($280 to $350), with panoramic plasma views, is reason enough to travel top end.

Clarion Hotel Mackay Marina (☎ 1800 386 386; www.mackaymarinahotel.com; Mulherin Dr, Mackay Harbour; d $185-350; ☒ ☒ ☒) If you prefer staying at the harbour, this is your premier choice.

Stoney Creek Farmstay (☎ 07-4954 1177; Peak Downs Hwy; campsites/dm/cottages $20/20/120) A hospitable farm offering a rare bush experience. Accommodation is in crafted cedar cottages. After a day mustering cattle, shower in the open air or stroll to your private swimming hole. The pick-up point is 28km southwest of Mackay.

Eating

Mackay has a burgeoning dining scene, thanks largely to its weather and waterfront. Keep in mind that you'll need a car to get to the marina.

Angelo's on the Marina (☎ 07-4955 5600; Mackay Marina, Mulherin Dr; mains $10-30) This big, bright and breezy Mediterranean establishment gets the nod for its hearty brekkies, and extensive range of pasta and risotto dishes. It's fully licensed, very lively after dark and there's a free courtesy bus for parties of six or more people, so join a group and enjoy.

QUEENSLAND

Cafe La De Da (☎ 07-4942 0601; 70 Wood St; meals $14-26) This sure-fire breakfast joint is colourful and, as you'd expect in this part of the world, very easygoing. The lunch menu includes curries, steaks and seafood.

Wilkie's Tavern (☎ 07-4957 2241; cnr Victoria & Gregory Sts; mains $15-25; ☒ lunch & dinner) Dark red walls and a breezy balcony – Wilkie's is a little classier than most in Mackay, although it can sound like an aviary up here with all the parrots chirping from nearby trees. A small but solid menu offers fresh fish, oysters and meats as well as a large selection of starters.

Pacino's on the Waterfront (☎ 07-4957 8131; Mackay Harbour, Mulherin Dr; mains $15-35; ☒ lunch & dinner Mon-Sat) This relaxed riverside restaurant is tucked between a string of warehouses, giving it an 'in-the-know' kind of feel. Seafood is the main fare, served in abundant and tasty quantities, sometimes tossed around in heaps of pasta or plonked on crispy pizzas.

Kevin's Place (☎ 07-4953 5835; cnr Victoria & Wood Sts; mains $18-25; ☒ lunch & dinner Mon-Fri, dinner Sat) Spicy Singaporean dishes in a colonial corner building, hyperactive waiters and warm tropical breezes take you back to a Southeast Asia of old. Kevin's Place rocks.

Lighthouse (☎ 07-4955 5022; Mulherin Dr; takeaway $7-16, mains $22-29, ☒ 6am-late) An excellent takeaway seafood spot (try the epic fish burger) with a popular, rather fancy seafood restaurant next door.

Drinking & Entertainment

Mackay is in the midst of a crackdown on public drinking. Don't fear though – there are tons of places to get boozy in private.

Gordi's Café & Bar (☎ 07-4951 2611; 85 Victoria St; ☒ 11am-midnight Sun-Thu, to 1am Fri & Sat) It may be a cafe by day, but the open windows facing Mackay's main drag provide the perfect vantage point to enjoy a cold beer. Things get busier once evening kicks in with live music and DJs upstairs (entry $10).

Satchmo's at the Reef (☎ 07-4955 6055; Mulherin Dr, Mackay Harbour; ☒ 11am-9pm) Classy Satchmo's dishes up wine, tapas and style, but lends itself to a relaxed crowd. Boaties join other locals and tourists here and live music is a regular feature on Sunday afternoon.

Platinum Lounge (☎ 07-4957 2220; 83 Victoria St; ☒ 8pm-late Sun-Tue, 6pm-late Wed-Sat) On the 1st floor above the corner of Victoria and Wood Sts, the Platinum Lounge is a good place

to unwind and to converse without shouting. Wednesday and Thursday nights are karaoke nights.

Zebar (☎ 07-4951 2611; 85 Victoria St; ☒ 3pm-late) This hyped-up cocktail bar boasts one of the coast's best beer menus.

Getting There & Away

Qantas (☎ 13 13 13; www.qantas.com.au), **Jetstar** (☎ 13 15 38; www.jetstar.com.au) and **Virgin Blue** (☎ 13 67 89; www.virginblue.com.au) all service Mackay. Flights include Brisbane, Rockhampton, Townsville and Sydney. The airport is 5km south of the city centre. **Tiger Airways** (☎ 03-9335 3033; www .tigerairways.com) has arrived in Mackay, with absurdly cheap deals from Melbourne (it doesn't fly from Sydney).

Travelworld (☎ 07-4944 2144; roseh@mkytworld .com.au; ☒ 7am-6pm Mon-Fri, to 4pm Sat) handles all transport arrangements and is located at the **Mackay Bus Terminal** (cnr Victoria & Macalister Sts), where a 24-hour cafe also sells bus tickets. **Greyhound Australia** (☎ 13 14 99; www.greyhound.com .au) and **Premier Motor Service** (☎ 13 34 10; www .premierms.com.au) connect Mackay with Cairns ($151, 12 hours), Townsville ($87, six hours), Airlie Beach ($26, two hours) and Brisbane ($180, 16 hours).

The **Queensland Rail** (☎ 1300 131 722; www .traveltrain.com.au) *Tilt Train* connects Mackay with Brisbane ($227, 12½ hours), Townsville ($101, 5½ hours) and Cairns ($178, 12 hours). The slower *Sunlander* does the same: Brisbane (economy seat/sleeper $154/212, 17 hours), Townsville (economy seat/sleeper $70/129, 6½ hours) and Cairns ($123/182, 12½ hours). The train station is at Paget, 5km south of the city centre.

Getting Around

Avis (☎ 07-4951 1266), **Budget** (☎ 07-4951 1400) and **Hertz** (☎ 07-4951 3334) have counters at the airport.

Mackay Transit Coaches (☎ 07-4957 3330) operates local buses from two bus stops in town: at the back of Canelands Shopping Centre, and from the corner of Victoria and Gregory Sts. The visitor centres have timetables.

Mackay Taxis (☎ 13 10 08) gets you to the airport, marina or train station for about $25.

AROUND MACKAY

West of Mackay is classic country Queensland. If you have time, explore these parts for a day or two.

QUEENSLAND

Pioneer Valley

Finch Hatton Gorge is a beautiful, secluded riverine located 32km northwest of Mackay. The turn-off is 1.5km before the township of Finch Hatton. It's 9km into the gorge and the last 3km are on good, unsealed roads, but heavy rain can make access difficult or impossible. A highly underrated extreme activity is **Forest Flying** (☎ 07-4958 3359; www.forestflying.com; rides $45). It's like virtual monkey play as you skim the rainforest canopy in a harness attached to a 340m-long cable. Beware the fruit-bat colony (August to May). Book ahead.

You can take a relaxed 1.6km rainforest walk to a stunning swimming hole beneath **Araluen Falls**, or a 2.6km walking trail to the **Wheel of Fire Falls**. For a peaceful sleep, stay at **Finch Hatton Gorge Cabins** (☎ 07-4958 3281; d $95; 🛇), set in enchanting subtropical surrounds, with a creek nearby.

Twenty kilometres further along is **Eungella National Park** (*young*-gulla), the kind of place to spark a mass 'mountain change'. The 'land of clouds' is situated in the Clark Ranges, and reaches 1280m at its zenith. This oldest and longest stretch of subtropical rainforest in Australia has been cut off from other rainforest areas for roughly 30,000 years, meaning there's a whole host of freaky creatures that exist nowhere else, such as the orange-sided skink and the Eungella gastric brooding frog, which incubates its eggs in its stomach and gives birth by spitting out the tadpoles!

On the trails between Eungella and **Broken River**, the real star is the world's cutest, most reclusive monotreme (egg-laying mammal). You can be fairly sure of seeing platypuses from the viewing platform near the bridge. The best times are immediately after dawn and at dusk, but you must be patient, still and half-mad. Rangers lead night walks; ask at the EPA office.

Resident goannas and brush-tailed possums enjoy the lovely **Broken River Mountain Retreat** (☎ 07-4958 4528; www.brokenrivermr.com.au; d $110-170; 🛇 🐾), which has cosy cedar cabins, a wood-finished lounge and the friendly **Platypus Lodge Restaurant & Bar** (mains $20-25). There's also the **EPA Fern Flat Camping Ground** (per person/family $4.50/18), which is reserved for walk-in campers only, near the **EPA office** (☎ 07-4958 4552; 🕙 8am-4pm) and kiosk.

Buses don't cover Finch Hatton or Eungella, so you'll need a car or an organised tour from Mackay.

AIRLIE BEACH

pop 5000

Tacky and tremendous, exploited and exploitative, Airlie Beach is not so much a stepping off point for the Whitsunday Islands, as a high-voltage launching pad! Airlie is the kind of town where humanity celebrates its close proximity to natural beauty by partying very hard, fast and frequently. The bustling backpacker set turns momentarily monolingual in the late afternoon sun – after the obligatory Whitsunday cruise – before splashing and slumping in a glorious artificial lagoon.

Airlie is a relatively tiny town that can at times feel as busy as Brisbane. Aside from the stream of budget travellers, the sailing fraternity converges here for the mainland conveniences, families flock to the fine restaurants and boutique hotels, while shrewd developers scour the coast for the next best Airlie Beach.

Orientation & Information

Shute Harbour is 12km east of the main drag, while the smaller Abel Point Marina is 1km west along a pretty promenade. A new marina is being built at the Shute Harbour end of town. Private operators dish out tourist advice along Shute Harbour Rd – use your discretion and shop around.

Destination Whitsundays (☎ 07-4946 7172; 297 Shute Harbour Rd)

EPA (☎ 07-4946 7022; fax 07-4946 7023; cnr Shute Harbour & Mandalay Rds; 🕙 9am-5pm Mon-Fri) A must-visit for info on island camping and various hikes.

Internet Centre (346 Shute Harbour Rd; per hr $4) Internet access.

Post office (☎ 13 13 18; 372 Shute Harbour Rd; 🕙 9am-5pm Mon-Fri, to 12.30pm Sat)

Activities

Sailing is the leisure activity of choice here, in all its nautical variations. Do-it-yourselfers will appreciate how easy it is to set sail unsupervised.

The Great Barrier Reef is roughly 70km offshore from Airlie Beach – most sailing trips are to a mere fringe. If you came here to see the reef (and aren't going north to Cairns), then check out the ecocertified **Fantasea Adventure Cruising** (☎ 07-4967 5455; www.fantasea.com.au; trips $209), which runs trips out to a floating pontoon at Hardy Reef. The full-day tours include a buffet lunch and four hours of snorkelling (two dives cost $100 extra). Nonswimmers will

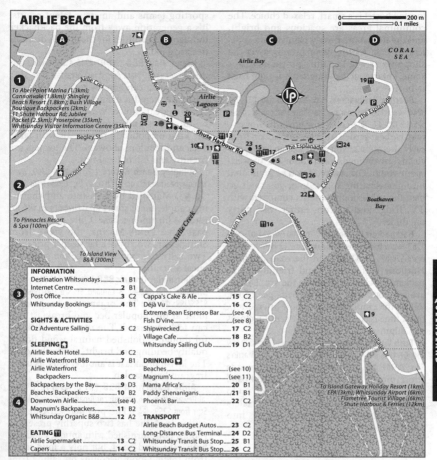

AIRLIE BEACH

INFORMATION	
Destination Whitsundays	**1** B1
Internet Centre	**2** B1
Post Office	**3** C2
Whitsunday Bookings	**4** B1

SIGHTS & ACTIVITIES	
Oz Adventure Sailing	**5** C2

SLEEPING	
Airlie Beach Hotel	**6** C2
Airlie Waterfront B&B	**7** B1
Airlie Waterfront	
Backpackers	**8** C2
Backpackers by the Bay	**9** D3
Beaches Backpackers	**10** B2
Downtown Airlie	(see 4)
Magnum's Backpackers	**11** B2
Whitsunday Organic B&B	**12** A2

EATING	
Airlie Supermarket	**13** C2
Capers	**14** C2

Cappa's Cake & Ale	**15** C2
Déjà Vu	**16** C2
Extreme Bean Espresso Bar	(see 4)
Fish D'vine	(see 8)
Shipwrecked	**17** C2
Village Cafe	**18** B2
Whitsunday Sailing Club	**19** D1

DRINKING	
Beaches	(see 10)
Magnum's	(see 11)
Mama Africa's	**20** B1
Paddy Shenanigans	**21** B1
Phoenix Bar	**22** C2

TRANSPORT	
Airlie Beach Budget Autos	**23** C2
Long-Distance Bus Terminal	**24** D2
Whitsunday Transit Bus Stop	**25** B1
Whitsunday Transit Bus Stop	**26** C2

QUEENSLAND

enjoy a Vernelike, semisubmersible vessel or seated underwater viewing chamber. Do yourself a favour though, and spend the night (dorm/king rooms $409/570).

Salty Dog Sea Kayaking (☎ 07-4946 1388; www .saltydog.com.au; day trips $125) offers guided full-day tours and kayak rental, plus longer kayak/camping missions (the six-day challenge costs $1490). It's a charming and healthy way to see the islands. Some folk go for parasailing with **Whitsunday Parasail** (☎ 07-4948 0000; per person $85), but the real hardcore kids can plummet headfirst into the Whitsundays with **Skydive Airlie Beach** (☎ 07-4946 9115; per person from $350).

For information on sailing and reef trips, see Sailing the Whitsundays, p412.

Sleeping

BUDGET

Magnum's Backpackers (☎ 1800 624 634; www.mag nums.com.au; 366 Shute Harbour Rd; dm $18, d & tw $54; 🛇 🖵) Think backpacking has evolved from its hedonistic past? Drink again! Maniacal Magnum's is a downright hotbed of Euro-teen revelry. You won't get personalised customer service, but you will get cheap, clean dorms within retching distance of the party. The better rooms are located in a slightly more subdued tropical garden out the back. Lack of security can be a concern.

Airlie Waterfront Backpackers (☎ 1800 089 000, 07-4948 1300; www.airliewaterfront.com; 6 The Esplanade; dm $25-30, d & tw with/without bathroom $110/60; 🛇 🖵) Completely overhauled in 2008, this centrally located hostel is a smart, relaxed choice. The communal areas are spacious and bright, and the dorms are freshly painted and spotlessly clean. Exiting your premises via the shopping arcade is a little postmodern for some, but overall the Waterfront is right back in business.

Beaches Backpackers (☎ 1800 636 630, 07-4946 6244; www.beaches.com.au; 356 Shute Harbour Rd; dm/d $25/80; 🟤 💻 💲) You know how this works – massive beer garden launches into action from early afternoon as you come and go from your clean, streamlined dorm room full of well-spent youth. Otherwise, if you've graduated into globetrotting coupledom, you can't go past the value double rooms equipped with TV, fridge and air-con. Either way, party on, dude.

Backpackers by the Bay (☎ 1800 646 994, 07-4946 7267; www.backpackersbythebay.com; 12 Hermitage Dr; dm/d $26/62; 🟤 💻 💲) On the road to Shute Harbour is this warm and friendly backpackers perched high above the sea. Dorms are spacious with just four beds per room. While the emphasis is on guest interaction, quiet time is equally valued. Reception closes at 7.30pm.

Bush Village Boutique Backpackers (☎ 1800 809 256, 07-4946 6177; www.bushvillage.com.au; 2 St Martin's Rd; r $78-109; 🟤 💻) A five-minute drive towards Proserpine is this neat, self-contained hostel with 'modern Aussie' cabins that sleep up to four people. It's especially good for travellers over the party scene, or young couples into each other.

MIDRANGE & TOP END

Downtown Airlie (☎ 07-4948 0599; www.downtownairlie.com; 346 Shute Harbour Rd; apt $110-220; 🟤 💻) In a prime location for perving on the creatures of the blue lagoon, this well-priced midrange hotel is ideal for couples and post-budgeteers. The mini-apartments are chic enough for Birkenstocks, but still retro enough for thongs. The bedrooms are a touch dull, but the living areas feature bright blue tiled floors, oversized suede chairs and flat-screen TVs.

Airlie Beach Hotel (☎ 1800 466 233, 07-4964 1999; www.airliebeachhotel.com.au; cnr The Esplanade & Coconut Grove; r $129-259; 🟤 💲) The ABH is an icon: a sharply presented, no-nonsense establishment, with spacious sea-facing suites, a world-class restaurant and a robust poolside social scene. Popular with professional sporting teams and amateur talent scouts, it's a generation away from the backpacker indulgence. Facilities for those with disabilities are good.

Island View B&B (☎ 07-4946 4505; www.islandviewbb.com.au; 19 Nara Ave; d incl breakfast from $140; 🟤 💲) If you can happily resist the lures of the town, then this delightful bed and breakfast is a great choice. Wake up to gorgeous hilltop views and tropical breakfasts from the king or poolside rooms, all with large beds and fabulous showers. The owners are friendly and full of local tips.

Shingley Beach Resort (☎ 07-4948 8300; www.shingleybeachresort.com; 1 Shingley Dr; studios from $150; 🟤 💲) Managed by an astute and charming couple, these smart apartments make an ideal Whitsundays base. On a grassy patch past Abel Point Marina, the views from Shingley are worthy of a far steeper price tag. Two saltwater pools enhance the generous guest amenities.

Whitsunday Organic B&B (☎ 07-4946 7151; www.whitsundaybb.com.au; 8 Lamond St; s/d incl breakfast $155/199; 🟤 💻) The 'organic' tag hangs fairly loose at this popular bed and breakfast that can feel congested. The rooms are delightful though – polished natural wood floors, quality bedding and bright, airy bathrooms. The lavish breakfast is another plus, as is the fragrant herb garden.

Airlie Waterfront B&B (☎ 07-4946 7631; www.airliewaterfrontbnb.com.au; cnr Broadwater Ave & Mazlin St; r from $259; 🟤) The premier self-catering option in Airlie has two superbly presented rooms, both furnished with antiques and spa baths. It's dead quiet, but only a loud shout from town. Good discounts on sailing trips are available to guests.

Pinnacles Resort & Spa (☎ 07-4948 4800; www.pinnaclesresort.com; 8 Lamond St; s/d/apt incl breakfast $215/285/350; 🟤 💲) One of the best in town.

CAMPING

Island Gateway Holiday Resort (☎ 07-4946 6228; www.islandgateway.com.au; Shute Harbour Rd, Jubilee Pocket; unpowered/powered sites $32/39, cabins $85-185; 🟤 💲) has shady sites and cabins just 1.5km from town.

Further down the coast, **Flametree Tourist Village** (☎ 07-4946 9388; www.flametreevillage.com.au; Shute Harbour Rd; unpowered/powered sites $19/29, cabins from $85; 🟤 💲) is in a lovely, bird-filled ecological sanctuary bordering a national park.

Eating

Airlie is developing a reputation for fine seafood restaurants, and there are plenty of good cheap eats too.

Extreme Bean Espresso Bar (☎ 07-4948 2283; 346 Shute Harbour Rd; coffees $4-5, mains $8-15; ❤ breakfast & lunch) An excellent cafe specialising in frappés, eggs Benedict and cheesecakes. Check the blackboard for scrawled specials.

Fish D'vine (☎ 07-4948 0088; Beach Plaza; mains $8-18; ❤ lunch & dinner) The darling of Airlie cheap eats is this incongruously imagined 'fish cafe and rum bar'. In the heart of the Beach Plaza, thong-clad patrons munch fresh fish handpicked from the counter and wash it down with evangelical mojitos like they were Hemingway in a shopping mall.

Village Cafe (☎ 07-4964 1121; 351 Shute Harbour Rd; mains $10-18; ❤ 8am-5.30pm) With grand plans to rule the luxury cafe world, the Village is a heaving hangover breakfast joint that rewards those who hang around for the freshly prepared lunch menu. Definitely try the lemon pepper calamari with chilli jam. The takeaway picnic boxes are a speciality.

Déjà Vu (☎ 07-4948 4309; Waters Edge Resort, 4 Golden Orchid Dr; lunch mains $12-20, dinner mains $25-40; ❤ lunch & dinner Tue-Sat) In an airy Polynesian-style thatched building overlooking a pool, the Déjà Vu sets the standard in Airlie. The menu is modern, but unpretentious, and takes its flavours from Asian and Mediterranean cuisines. The scallop pad thai is genius and the tiki torches are always firing. The slow-burning Sunday lunch (just $36 for eight courses) starts at noon; be sure to book ahead for ocean views.

Whitsunday Sailing Club (☎ 07-4946 7894; Airlie Point; mains $14-32) Canny travellers make their way to the sailing club terrace for a sunset drink and a yarn with the locals. The bistro menu is the usual Queensland coastal fare – hearty steaks and schnitzels, huge plates of fish and chips – but it's fresh, friendly and inexpensive.

our pick **Shipwrecked** (☎ 07-4946 6713; cnr Shute Harbour Rd & The Esplanade; lunch mains $20-25, dinner mains $30-45) An exceptional wine list accompanies the best seafood menu in town. The barramundi and coral trout are always safe bets, but you're on holidays, for crying out loud, so try the sweet and sultry Penang seafood curry or the Shipwrecked Platter ($135

at last count),which will easily please three fussy pescatarians.

Capers (☎ 07-4964 1777; Airlie Beachfront Hotel, The Esplanade; mains $22-40) This casual, though classy restaurant gets a huge rap from locals and tourists alike. Lots of fresh seafood along with steaks, fine cheeses and a mouth-watering array of desserts complement a good wine list and a prime people-watching locale. Grab a plump couch and get stuck right in (just like Matthew McConaughey and Kate Hudson famously did back in 2007).

Also recommended:

Airlie Supermarket (277 Shute Harbour Rd) For self-caterers.

Cappa's Cake & Ale (☎ 07-4946 5033; Pavilion Arcade; mains $6-20) Tucked in an alley behind Shute Harbour Rd in central Airlie, it has heaps of breakfast options, real bagels and great sandwiches and cocktails.

Drinking

Airlie has enough drinking holes (and enough heavy drinkers!) to keep you buried for days on end.

Mama Africa's (☎ 07-4948 0438; 263 Shute Harbour Rd; ❤ 10pm-5am) Mama's is the late-night mash-up venue of choice in Airlie Beach. Zebra crossings at every turn, wall-hung tribal things and savannah-style lounge chairs will have you settling in for longer than a drunk missionary.

Paddy Shenanigans (☎ 07-4946 5055; 366 Shute Harbour Rd; ❤ noon-1am) Irish name? Check. Irish beer? Check. Irish crowd? And Czech, German, English, Canadian, Mackay… Hundreds of loose individuals dancing like mice on a wheel and loving it? Check it out; it's right near Magnum's.

Beaches (☎ 1800 636 630, 07-4946 6244; 356 Shute Harbour Rd; ❤ 11am-midnight) Late afternoons here are heaven by some definitions. More of a sit-and-whistle than dance-ya-pants-off kind of crowd; there's also a great pool if you get too hot to handle.

Phoenix Bar (Shute Harbour Rd) Locals and curious tourists quaff drinks in more intimate surrounds at this brand-new bar, yapping about how much they're 'over' the all-night parties, before midnight kicks in, Phoenix closes and they stumble down the street to Magnum's.

Magnum's (☎ 07-4946 6266; Shute Harbour Rd; ❤ 11am-midnight) Imagine a giant bottle of champagne. Now imagine five hundred sunburned 21-somethings jumping around in a

QUEENSLAND

vast outdoor venue with cheap champagne and cheap beds. Magnum's is a classic backpacker party; we say whack it on an ironic 'do-before-you-die' list.

Getting There & Around

The closest major airports are at Proserpine and on Hamilton Island. The small **Whitsunday airport** (☎ 07-4946 9933) is about 6km southeast of town; see below for flight details.

Greyhound Australia (☎ 13 14 99; www.greyhound .com.au) and **Premier Motor Service** (☎ 13 34 10; www.premierms.com.au) have bus connections to Brisbane ($206, 19 hours), Mackay ($35, two hours), Townsville ($62, five hours) and Cairns ($126, 11 hours). The long-distance bus terminal is just off the Esplanade.

Locally, **Whitsunday Transit** (☎ 07-4946 1800) connects Proserpine (Proserpine Airport), Cannonvale, Abel Point, Airlie Beach and Shute Harbour. Buses operate daily from 6am to 10.30pm and stop along Shute Harbour Rd.

There are car-rental companies all along Shute Harbour Rd. Try **Airlie Beach Budget Autos** (☎ 07-4948 0300; 285 Shute Harbour Rd).

WHITSUNDAY ISLANDS

These 90-plus islands, most of which are uninhabited, have long sat atop Australian travellers' must-do lists. But the Whitsundays' serene blue waters now attract yachties, hotties and schoolies from all corners of the watery world.

More than 60 companies jostle to grant travellers access to these continental isles, only four of which have not been accorded national park status. Akin to the tips of coral mountains, the Whitsundays fall within the Great Barrier Reef World Heritage Area that stretches from Cape York in the north to Bundaberg in the south. Some basic greensmarts are essential: don't feed the fish, don't pet the coral; do *not* throw your empty stubby in the sea.

Warm nights, white sands and infrequent rain make these islands ideal for camping, but most visitors come to stay at the resorts scattered throughout the archipelago, where good-value package holidays can be booked in advance.

GETTING THERE & AWAY

Both **Virgin Blue** (☎ 13 67 89; www.virginblue.com.au) and **Jetstar** (☎ 13 15 38; www.jetstar.com.au) connect

Hamilton Island with Brisbane, Sydney and Melbourne. **QantasLink** (☎ 13 13 13; www.qantas .com.au) flies there from Cairns.

Island Air Taxis (☎ 07-4946 9933; Shute Harbour Rd; ☼ 7.45am-5.30pm) offers flights to Hamilton and Lindeman Islands ($75 one way per adult from Airlie Beach). **Air Whitsunday Seaplanes** (☎ 07-4946 9111; www.airwhitsunday.com.au) offers a range of excellent tours, including the fabulous Panorama Tour ($390), which flies from Airlie Beach to Heart Reef where you snorkel or scuba before returning to land four hours later. Hamilton Island is also one of the airport options available with the Aussie Airpass from Qantas, which makes getting to the Whitsundays superconvenient if you're on a tight schedule.

Fantasea Ferries (☎ 07-4967 5455; www.fantasea .com.au) has return fares to Hamilton Island or Daydream Island (adult/child $72/44) via high-speed catamaran. Ferries depart from the pier at 11 Shute Harbour Rd, Airlie Beach. Tickets can be purchased at the airport on Hamilton Island, resorts or directly from the pier at Airlie Beach. A return ticket to Airlie Beach from Hamilton Island airport costs $120.

Long Island

Some of the best walking in the Whitsundays is found on this little gem. With the majority of the island deemed national park, days here are spent wandering around the 13km of marked tracks and peering across the narrow strait from one of many fine lookouts.

Sadly, camping is no longer available, but there are still three resorts, the best of which is by far **Peppers Palm Bay** (☎ 1800 095 025, 07-4946 9233; www.peppers.com.au/palm-bay; d from $460; ✖ ⚊). The Whitsundays version of the well-regarded Peppers boutique resort group is no exception – indulgent, Thai-style cabins snuggled around blissful Palm Bay, topped off with exceptional cuisine and service. Check for standby rates.

South Molle Island

Lovers of birds and long, sandy beaches will enjoy the largest of the Molle archipelago. Nearly 15km of splendid walking tracks traverse this mountainous 4 sq km island; the highest point is Mt Jeffreys (198m), but the climb up Spion Kop is also worthwhile. There's an **EPA camping ground** (per person/family $4.50/18) in the north, where the boats come in.

The reasonable **South Molle Island Resort** (☎ 1800 075 080, 07-4946 9433; www.southmolleisland .com.au; d from $274; ❌ ▣) has a spectacular outlook across its private jetty, but the resort is overdue for a spruce-up.

Daydream Island

Daydream Island is more manufactured than dreamy, but at just 1km long and a 15-minute ferry ride from Shute Harbour, it's a good compromise for busy families. A usual day sees hordes of kids getting touchy-feely with marine life in a small lagoon, while parents and cheap singles swivel cocktail umbrellas at the bar. Loads of water-sports gear is available for hire.

Daydream Island Resort & Spa (☎ 1800 075 040, 07-4948 8488; www.daydreamisland.com; 3-night package d $910; ❌ ▣) is the tackier side of the Whitsundays, with five grades of accommodation. Still, it's efficiently operated and set in beautifully landscaped tropical gardens. There are three swimming pools, tennis courts, catamarans and faux beaches. There's also a heaven-sent kids' club.

Hook Island

Just quietly, Hook Island is a magical place. Rugged enough to keep the crowds away, but easy to get around, Hook is perhaps the finest island in the Whitsundays.

At 53 sq km, Hook Island is mainly national park and blessed with great beaches and camping grounds. The underwater traffic is stunning and light on humans. Those you do meet are usually cruising through the weekdays with chilled-out smiles. **Crayfish Beach** (campsites per person $4.50) is a gorgeous camping spot with just 12 secluded campsites. Bookings are essential and can be made through the EPA. **Camping Whitsundays** (www.campingwhitsundays.com) offers a spot on a two-night shared camping deal ($329) that includes boat transfers from Shute Harbour, food and camping equipment. Extra nights are likely.

For those who prefer a more solid ceiling, you can stay at **Hook Island Wilderness Resort** (☎ 07-4946 9380; www.hookislandresort.com; sites per person $25, dm $35, d with/without bathroom $150/100; ❌ ▣). It's clean though basic, with tiny bathrooms and a licensed restaurant (mains $15 to $25) that serves seafood, steak and pasta. It's popular with everyone from school groups to singles.

Whitsunday Island

Whitsunday Island is the largest and most celebrated of the islands, and home to **Whitehaven Beach**, arguably Australia's finest tropical beach. Boats of young and old tourists day trip here daily, but the smart ones stick around until morning. The island comprises 109 sq km and rises to 438m at **Whitsunday Peak**. There's excellent **snorkelling** off the southern end and a fine view from Hill Inlet on Tongue Point down towards pristine Whitehaven.

There are **EPA camping grounds** (per person/family $4.50/18) at Dugong, Sawmill, Nari's and Joe's Beaches in the west; at Turtle Bay and Chance Bay in the south; at the southern end of Whitehaven Beach; and at Peter Bay in the north.

Hamilton Island

Hamilton Island Resort (☎ 1800 075 110, 07-4946 9999; www.hamiltonisland.com.au; d $305-595) manages this superbusy island, which feels more like a friendly film-set town than an established resort. Development seems to go on permanently (though there's a strong whiff of the '70s in the architecture), but there is an element of the unexplored, especially on the fine hike over Passage Peak. There's also an airport, and a deluxe marina full of smiling yuppie sea cats and ageless retirees. There are excellent restaurants, bars, shops and a huge range of accommodation, from the five-star Beach Club down to the relaxed Palm Bungalows. **Lagoon 101** (18 Resort Dr; r from $580) is a swish self-catering option.

Hamilton is a ready-made day trip from Shute Harbour, and you can use some of the resort's facilities – see opposite for transport details.

A stay at potentially the most luxurious hotel in Australia, **Qualia** (☎ 1300 780 959, 07-4948 9222; www.qualia.com.au; d from $1510; ❌ ▣), requires little imagination and plenty of coin. The Leeward rooms ($1450) are like divinely presented tree houses, while the ubersexy and secluded Beach House ($3100) will satisfy and sleep four damn lucky fools.

Lindeman Island

Lovely Lindeman is mostly national park, with empty bays and 20km of impressive walking trails. Nature photographers descend for the varied island tree life and the sublime view from Mt Oldfield (210m).

QUEENSLAND

QUEENSLAND

THE GREAT BARRIER REEF

Larger than the Great Wall of China and the only living thing visible from space, the Great Barrier Reef is one of the seven wonders of the natural world. The spectacular kaleidoscope of colour stretches along the Queensland seaboard from south of the Tropic of Capricorn to the Torres Strait, south of New Guinea. It's the planet's biggest reef system, where 2900 separate reefs form an outer ribbon parallel to the coast.

At a Glance

Length: 2300km from north of Bundaberg to the Torres Strait
Width: 80km at its broadest
Distance from shore: 300km in the south, 30km in the north
Age: Estimated between 600,000 and 18 million years old (contentious)

From Little Polyps, Mighty Reefs Grow

An industrious family of tiny animals, the coral polyp is responsible for creating the Great Barrier Reef and other reefs. All corals are primitive hollow sacs with tentacles on the top, but it is the hard corals that are the architects and builders. These corals excrete a small amount of limestone as an outer skeleton that protects and supports their soft bodies. As polyps die and new ones grow on top, their billions of skeletons cement together into an ever-growing natural bulwark.

Different polyps form varying structures, from staghorn and brain patterns to flat plate or table corals. However, they all need sunlight, so few grow deeper than 30m below the surface. The coral's skeletons are white, while the reef's kaleidoscopic colours come from the living polyps.

One of the most spectacular sights on the Great Barrier Reef occurs for a few nights after a full moon in late spring or early summer, when vast numbers of corals spawn. With tiny bundles of sperm and eggs visible to the naked eye, the event resembles a gigantic underwater snowstorm.

Did You Know?

Marine environments, including coral reefs, demonstrate the greatest biodiversity of any ecosystems on earth – much more so than rainforests. The Great Barrier Reef is home to marine mammals such as whales, dolphins and dugongs (sea cows). With new varieties still being found, its flora and fauna also includes:

- 1500 species of fish
- 400 types of coral
- 4000 breeds of clams and other molluscs
- 800 echinoderms, including sea cucumbers
- 500 varieties of seaweed
- 200 bird species
- 1500 different sponges
- six types of turtle.

Sorting the Reef from the Cays

Reefs fall into three categories: barrier (or ribbon) reefs, platform reefs and fringing reefs.

The barrier reef proper lies on the outer, seaward edge of the reef system, lining the edge of the continental shelf in an often-unbroken formation.

Platform reefs grow on the land side of these barrier reefs and often support coral cay islands. These occur when the reef grows above sea level; dead coral is ground down by water action to form sand, and sometimes vegetation takes root. Many famous islands – eg Green Island near Cairns, Heron Island off Gladstone and Lady Musgrave Island north of Bundaberg – are coral cays.

Closer to shore you'll find fringing reefs surrounding the hillier, continental islands. Great Keppel, most of the Whitsundays, Hinchinbrook and Dunk, for example, were once the peaks of mainland coastal ranges, but rising sea levels submerged most of these mountains, leaving only the tips exposed.

Taking the Temperature of the Barrier Reef

Coral polyps need a water temperature of between 17.5°C and 28°C to grow and can't tolerate too much sediment. There are three main threats to the reef: land-based pollutants, over-fishing and global warming. Global warming causes parts of the world's oceans to overheat, and the rise in temperature bleaches the reef. As the brightly coloured living polyps die, only the white skeletons remain. Pollution has also poisoned some coral, plus some questions persist about the long-term effects of crown-of-thorns starfish.

Some environmentalists and scientists predict that under current conditions, coral cover within the reef may be reduced to less than 5% by 2050. Because all the living organisms in the reef are symbiotic, the diverse ecosystem we see today may be gone forever.

Fortunately it's not all doom and gloom. In 2004, the Australian government introduced new laws that increased 'no-take' zones, where it is forbidden to remove animal or plant life (eg no fishing), to 33.33% of the reef (it was previously only 4.5%). The Queensland government also unveiled the Great Barrier Reef Coast Marine Park, a state park encompassing the actual coastline from just north of Bundaberg to the tip of Cape York – a total of 3600km. And collectively the federal and Queensland governments have launched a Reef Water Quality Protection Plan in an effort to deal with land-based pollutants. On a micro level, the **Great Barrier Reef Marine Park Authority** (☎ 07-4750 0700; Reef HQ bldg, 2-68 Flinders St East, Townsville) looks after the welfare of most of the reef. It monitors bleaching and other problems and works to enforce the reef's 'no-take' zones.

This increased awareness means it's even more important to take all litter with you, even biodegradable material such as apple cores. Admire, but don't touch or harass, marine animals and be aware that if you touch or walk on coral you'll damage it.

Snorkelling and diving will get you up close and personal with the reef. However, you can also view fish and coral from a glass-bottomed or semisubmersible boat. You can visit the Reef HQ aquarium in Townsville (p415) to see a living coral reef without leaving dry land. Apart from all the psychedelically patterned tropical fish, there's the chance to swim with manta rays, squid, turtles and other marine life. There's nothing to be too alarmed about, but make sure you avoid scorpion fish, stonefish and jellyfish (see Stingers, p386). No reef shark has ever attacked a diver, and sea snakes have fangs in the back of their throats so they're no threat to humans.

You could dive here every day of your life and still not see the entire Great Barrier Reef. The best time to visit varies depending on the individual area, the weather or any recent damage, but places to start include the following:

Cairns (p440) The most common choice, so rather over-trafficked.

Cape Tribulation (p470) A couple of small operators, such as Rumrunner (p468), have started capitalising on the close proximity to the reef; a good launching pad for those wanting to experience snorkelling trips without the hordes.

Fitzroy Island (p451) Snorkel over the coral reefs amid turtles; tourist numbers are still limited.

Heron Island (p383) Popular diving resort where it's wise to book ahead.

Lady Elliot Island (p381) Shipwrecks and gorgeous coral.

Lizard Island (p475) Superb diving at the Cod Hole.

Port Douglas (p463) Gateway to the Low Isles and the Agincourt Reefs.

Yongala shipwreck (p416) One of Australia's best, off Townsville.

For more information about visiting this remarkable environment, see Lonely Planet's *Great Barrier Reef: Diving & Snorkelling*.

QUEENSLAND

SAILING THE WHITSUNDAYS

Walk down Airlie's main drag and you'll be assaulted by signed specials: 'Two-night sailing trips just $179, includes free dive!' Don't book the first thing you see, however. Cheaper companies generally have crowded boats, bland food and cramped quarters. Unfortunately no matter what price bracket you go with, bed bugs can be a reality.

The usual package is three days/two nights – really just two days as trips depart in the afternoon of the first day and return early on the third.

Most companies offer a considerably lower standby rate for last-minute bookings, so it's actually best not to book ahead unless you have your heart set on a particular boat and date. And be sure to check the weather before you commit.

Most vessels follow the fringing reef and Whitsunday Island–hopping route. Snorkelling along the fringing reef is as good, if not better (the fish are confined to a smaller space), than the real thing. Divers not able to visit the main reef elsewhere may want to book one of the trips visiting Bait Reef. Reaching Bait Reef requires 1½ hours of sailing across open water – consider seasickness tablets. Boats won't make the trip if it's too windy.

Once you've figured out what boat you'd like to sail on, you'll need to book through a travel agency such as **Whitsunday Bookings** (☎ 07-4948 2201; www.whitsundaybookings.com.au; shop 1, 346 Shute Harbour Rd, Airlie Beach) or a management company such as **Oz Adventure Sailing** (☎ 1800 359 554; www.aussiesailing.com.au; 293 Shute Harbour Rd, Airlie Beach). Both can sell berths on most vessels and will offer the same standby rates.

Expect to pay about $50 more than the prices quoted below on reef taxes and stinger suit rentals.

Avatar (2-night trips $380-459) This 18m beauty carries 26 passengers and has huge amounts of deck space for sunbathing. The *Avatar* has a reputation as an upmarket singles boat that's lots of fun. Choose from a fairly cramped, shared berth or camping ashore on one of the Whitsunday Islands – tents provided.

Iceberg (2-night trips from $350) Fast 52-footer steered by a highly accomplished crew.

Pride of Airlie (2-night trips $300) The original party boat, the *Pride of Airlie* is still exactly that: a raucous booze cruise popular with young backpackers. It carries 70 people and is good if you want to party but suffer from seasickness – both nights are spent on land (you sleep in dorms at a hostel on South Molle Island).

Ragamuffin (www.maxiaction.com.au; day trips from $156) Sail and dive from this famous Maxi yacht.

Silent Night (2-night trips $300) Small groups to suit a discerning, younger crowd.

Tall Ship Defender (www.australiantallships.com; overnight trips up to $300) Trips are for one night, but they depart at 9.30am and don't return until 4.30pm the following day. With prices often hovering around $279, the *Tall Ship* is good value. Built in 1896, the 35m-long vessel carries just 27 passengers and has lots of space.

Club Med Resort (☎ 1800 258 2633, 07-4946 9333; www.clubmed.com; packages per person per night $492; ❌ 💻 ♿) is a fun all-inclusive option. It has its own launch that connects with flights from the airport at Hamilton Island.

There is also an **EPA camping ground** (sites per person/family $4.50/18).

BOWEN

pop 11,505

Bowen is a delightful reminder of how Australian beach towns used to be – innocent, low rise and beautiful. Famed for its **Big Mango** and as a set for Baz Luhrmann's epic curiosity *Australia*, Bowen is full of 1970s coastal charm. With big weekenders, lush mangroves, and spectacular beaches – most notably Horseshoe Bay and Rose Bay – plus a dirty

great pub, Bowen is set to break box-office travel records.

Mango picking season is in November and December, but you can also pick tomatoes from September to December.

Sleeping & Eating

Bowen Backpackers (☎ 07-4786 3433; bowenback packers@bigpond.com; Herbert St; dm from $26; ❌ ♿) Located at the beach end of Herbert St (past the Grandview Hotel), this is the place to stay if you're working in the surrounding fruit farms. Rooms are neat and reasonably spacious.

Rose Bay Resort (☎ 07-4786 2402; www.rose bayresort.com.au; 2 Pandanus St, Rose Bay; apt $130-185; ❌ ♿) This place offers well-appointed (they are nicer inside than out) studio, one- and two-bedroom beachfront apartments with good swimming, snorkelling and fishing in the gorgeous Coral Sea right at your doorstep.

For dining, in Bowen try **Three Sixty on the Hill** (☎ 07-4786 6360; Margaret Reynolds Dr; mains $8-25; ✆ lunch & dinner) high atop Flagstaff Hill. It serves delicious fresh food and features stunning 360-degree views. The **Grandview Hotel** (☎ 07-4786 6360; Margaret Reynolds Dr; mains $8-25; ✆ lunch & dinner) is a charming 100-year-old pub with a slick new beer garden with a giant TV screen and sound system. There's an excellent $10 roast available on Sunday nights.

Getting There & Away

Long-distance buses stop outside **Bowen Travel** (☎ 07-4786 4022; 5 Herbert St). **Greyhound Australia** (☎ 13 14 99; www.greyhound.com.au) has services to/from Rockhampton ($96, eight hours), Airlie Beach ($26, 1½ hours) and Townsville ($43, 3½ hours).

The **Queensland Rail** (☎ 13 22 32, 1300 131 722; www.traveltrain.com.au) *Sunlander* and *Tilt Train* stop at Bootooloo Siding, 3km south of the centre. For an economy sleeper/seat on the *Sunlander,* the fare from Brisbane is $240/170.

NORTH COAST

The North Coast boasts mountain ranges, authentic outback towns and islands worth hopping to, all within reach of the vibrant city of Townsville. Townsville's waterfront stretches for miles and is hugged by hotels and pubs, trendier-every-day bars, and cafes filled with the city's easygoing people. Magnetic Island lies just offshore, and, with its 22 bays, makes an awesome place for isolated-beach-to-isolated-beach walking. Named for interfering with Captain Cook's compass, Magnetic Island is sacred to the Wulgurukaba Aboriginal people. Only a few kilometres out of Townsville, the red outback earth gets under your nails, and the outback towns of Charters Towers and Ravenswood make great diversions. Northwest of Townsville, the misty rainforest of the Paluma Range National Park stakes its claim as the southernmost part of the fantastic Wet Tropics World Heritage Area.

TOWNSVILLE
pop 164,955

There's a vibrant nightlife in Townsville, and it's no wonder: there's lots to celebrate in this smart Coral Sea–meets-outback-meets-rainforest city. Public swimming pools and grassy, tree-lined parks dot the water's edge and, perhaps surprisingly, you can expect gourmet treats, Zen-inspired waterfront dining and local breweries, all frequented by a youthful population that's a mix of students, defence force personnel (the Australian Defence Force has a large base here) and sophisticated locals. The *Yongala* shipwreck is located just 90km from Townsville, and local dive operations lead regular diving expeditions out to thi internationally regarded site.

Orientation

Townsville's Coral Sea curves are easy to admire from the red-rock Castle Hill (290m) lookout, which watches over the city and Magnetic Island. The 2.2km-long Strand runs from Ross Creek to 'kissing point', near the rock pool.

The Flinders St Mall shopping strip is on the western side of Ross Creek, as are the marina and casino, and Victoria Foot Bridge and Dean St Bridge lead to the booming Palmer St and its high-end accommodation and classy eateries zone. Car ferries to Magnetic Island leave from Ross St, an extension of Palmer St, while passenger ferries and coaches depart from the western side of Ross Creek, opposite the marina.

South of the coach terminal is the Flinders St East's nightclub and cheap-eats zone.

The train station has been relocated 2km south of the town centre.

Information
BOOKSHOPS

Jim's Book Exchange (☎ 07-4771 6020; 10/390 Flinders St Mall; ✆ 10am-4pm Mon-Fri, to noon Sun).

Mary Who? Bookshop (☎ 07-4771 3824; 414 Flinders St Mall; ✆ 9am-5.30pm Mon-Fri, to 1pm Sat & Sun) Large travel section and Australian Broadcasting Corporation (ABC) books.

INTERNET ACCESS

Internet Den (☎ 07-4721 4500; 265 Flinders St Mall; per hr $4; ✆ 9am-9pm)

Internet on the Mall (☎ 07-4721 3444; Cowboy Leagues Club, Shop 1, 335 Flinders St Mall; per hr $6; ✆ 5am-5pm)

TOWNSVILLE

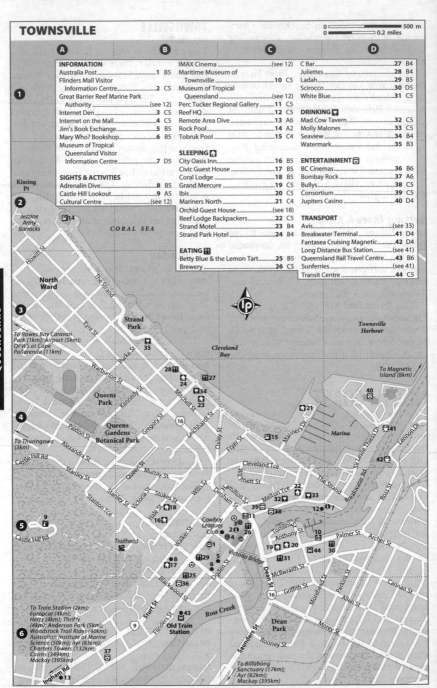

QUEENSLAND

POST
Australia Post (Post Office Plaza, shop 1, Sturt St)

TOURIST INFORMATION
Flinders Mall visitor information centre (☎ 07-4721 3660; www.townsvilleonline.com.au; Flinders St Mall; ☼ 9am-5pm Mon-Fri, to 1pm Sat & Sun) Information on diving and tours.

Great Barrier Reef Marine Park Authority (☎ 07-4750 0700; www.gbrmpa.gov.au; Reef HQ, 2-68 Flinders St East; ☼ 9am-5pm) National education centre for the Great Barrier Reef.

Museum of Tropical Queensland Visitor Information Centre (☎ 1800 801 902, 07-4721 1116; www.townsvilleonline.com.au; 70-102 Flinders St East; ☼ 9am-5pm) Good location next to museum with helpful folk with good accommodation and activities info.

QPWS (☎ 07-4722 5224; www.epa.qld.gov.au; old Quarantine Station Cape Pallarenda; ☼ 10am-4pm Mon-Fri)

Sights
REEF HQ
An enthralling way to spend a few hours, this **aquarium** (☎ 07-4750 0800; www.reefhq.com.au; 2-68 Flinders St East; adult/child/concession $25/13/19, family $37-63; ☼ 9.30am-5pm) has the best of the reef in a series of recreated reefs. Check out the turtles, sharks, rays and sawfish (a pleasant change to seeing their snout pinned to Queensland's pubs' walls). Different tours leave every half hour until 4pm. The **IMAX cinema** (☎ 07-4721 1481; Flinders St East; adult/child/concession $14/9/12; ☼ 1st show 10.45am, last show 2.45pm) is next door.

OTHER SIGHTS
The **Strand** stretches its palm-tree-lined self along the coast and is a great place to chill out with locals, including Aboriginal elders, under the fat fig trees.

The **Museum of Tropical Queensland** (☎ 07-4726 0600; www.mtq.qm.qld.gov.au; Flinders St East; adult/child/concession $12/7/8; ☼ 9.30am-5pm) is a sprawling museum filled with coral and rainforest exhibits and a homage in replica form of HMS *Pandora*, shipwrecked in 1791 after it was sent to capture the *Bounty* mutineers and find the *Bounty*. In the tropical north Queensland section you'll find answers to questions such as 'Why are the wet tropics so wet?' and see what makes the Queenslander tick.

The **Maritime Museum of Townsville** (☎ 07-4721 5251; www.townsvillemaritimemuseum.org.au; 42-68 Palmer St; adult/concession/family $6/5/15; ☼ 10am-3pm) is a smaller affair, with lighthouse memorabilia and a *Yongala* shipwreck model and display.

The **Cultural Centre** (☎ 07-4772 7679; www.cc townsville.com.au; 2-68 Flinders St East; admission $6; ☼ 9.30am-4.30pm) features an Indigenous museum-like gallery representing the Wulgurukaba people and the Bindal people, as well as Torres Strait Islander culture. This is the place to get your own very original Aboriginal art–covered cricket bat.

The **Perc Tucker Regional Gallery** (☎ 07-4727 9011; ptrg@townsville.qld.gov.au; cnr Denham St & Flinders St Mall; admission free; ☼ 10am-5pm Mon-Fri, to 2pm Sat & Sun) is an art gallery in a heritage building featuring art depicting the region. There's a good kids' bit, too.

If the temperature's right (ie the asphalt's not melting), it's worth scrambling to the top of **Castle Hill** for the view. The 2km path begins at the corner of Wills and Victoria Sts, and there's a 'goat track' from Stanley St. There's also a road, if you're driving.

The **Billabong Sanctuary** (☎ 07-4778 8344; www.billabongsanctuary.com.au; Bruce Hwy; adult/child/backpackers/family $28/17/25/88; ☼ 8am-5pm) is a 'hold-em-'n'-snap-em' ecocertified wildlife park situated 17km south of Townsville. It's filled with Aussie creatures, some of which you can hold for an extra $15. There are feeding or holding shows every 20 minutes.

At the base of Castle Hill, the four-hectare **Queens Gardens Botanical Park** (cnr Gregory & Paxton Sts) has a rainforest and black bean walk. **Anderson Park** (Gulliver St, Mundingburra) is more focused on tropical northern Queensland trees.

The headquarters for the **Australian Institute of Marine Science** (AIMS; ☎ 07-4753 4409; www.aims.gov.au) is 50km southeast of Townsville at Cape Ferguson. It runs public tours on Friday mornings from March to November.

Activities
The Strand-side **Tobruk Pool** (☎ 07-4772 6550; The Strand; adult/child $2.50/1.50; ☼ 5.30am-8pm Mon-Thu, to 6.30pm Fri, 7am-5pm Sat, 8am-5pm Sun Oct-Mar, reduced hours Apr-Sep) is a bright and lively swimming complex, buoyed by its history as the training spot for the 1952 and 1964 Australian Olympic swim teams. The B&W photo exhibition and other human fish memorabilia are worth a look.

Who needs the beach when you've got the **rock pool** (admission free; ☼ 24hr), a swimming spot surrounded by palms, play equipment and picnic tables, though the layer of sand on the pool's floor doesn't fool.

QUEENSLAND

Fancy yourself as a drover, à la Hugh Jackman in *Australia*? **Woodstock Trail Rides** (☎ 07-4778 8888; www.woodstocktrailrides.com.au; Flinders Hwy; per person incl transfers $150) offers cattle mustering on its 9000-acre property, or just head off on a trail ride (billy tea and damper included).

Those curious to know Townsville from top to bottom can try **Coral Sea Skydivers** (☎ 07-4772 4889; www.coralseaskydivers.com.au; tandem from $330). You'll be landing smack bang (and hopefully softly) in the middle of the sandy Strand.

DIVING

Aside from Coral Sea exploration, most dive companies do *Yongala* day trips, which require you to have an open-water certificate. From June to September you might be lucky enough to spot whales. The local diving industry is in a state of flux, so check with other travellers to get the low-down.

Ecocertified **Adrenalin Dive** (☎ 1300 664 600, 07-4724 0600; www.adrenalinedive.com.au; 252 Walker St; incl levies from $210) has day trips to the reef.

Remote Area Dive (☎ 07-4721 4425; www.remotear eadive.com; 25 Ingham Rd; incl levies from $239) also operates overnighters involving Aussie swags and authentic campfire meals.

Sleeping

BUDGET

our pick **Reef Lodge Backpackers** (☎ 07-4721 1112; www.reeflodge.com.au; 4 Wickham St; dm $21-25, d with/ without bathroom $78/57; 🏊 🖳) It's hard to get a bed in this bright, cheery and friendly hostel so book ahead to enjoy hammocks, concretejungle palm trees, a games room and barbecue. It's located near the action of Flinders St East.

Civic Guest House (☎ 1800 646 619, 07-4771 5381; www.civicguesthouse.com; 262 Walker St; dm $22, d/tw $70/75; 🏊 🖳 🛒) This hostel has a mixture of both classic Queenslander and motel-style rooms. Expect cleanish bathrooms, Friday night barbecues and relaxed folk running the show.

Orchid Guest House (☎ 07-4771 6683; 34 Hale St; s/d $60/80; 🏊) Clean and very blue, this neighbours Coral Lodge and, while not as frilly, is a great Queenslander to get some rest in.

Coral Lodge (☎ 1800 614 613, 07-4771 5512; www .corallodge.com.au; 32 Hale St; s/d $75/85; 🏊) As pretty as a picture, Coral Lodge looks high over Townsville and is splendid in mauve.

Strand Motel (☎ 07-4772 1977; www.strandmotel .com.au; 51 The Strand; s/d $75/85; 🏊) As the neighbouring hotels are getting bigger, this motel

stays the same, providing basic rooms (some with balconies) in a waterfront location.

MIDRANGE

Ibis (☎ 07-4753 2000; www.ibishotels.com.au; 12-14 Palmer St; d $100-220; 🏊 🖳) Welcoming staff, subdued colours and warming Aboriginal prints are features, though this 'toddler' has a few learning-to-walk scuffs on the walls. The popular Suga Train lounge bar is downstairs. Maximum of two people per room, and some ecocredentials: cross ventilation in the hall rather than air-con.

Grand Mercure (☎ 07-4753 2800; www.grandmercure .com.au; 8-10 Palmer St; studio/apt $119/139; 🏊 🖳) A newbie on the Palmer St scene, it impresses with its balconies, wood-panelled walls, tree-inspired artwork and huge bathrooms. Studios are cosy but big enough to swing a cat in. Oh, and the pool and spa are pretty special, too.

Strand Park Hotel (☎ 07-4750 7888; www.strandpark hotel.com.au; 59-60 The Strand; r $120-185; 🏊 🖳) Clean and completely self-contained rooms are good value, though on a hot day you'll probably want to head straight for the pool's coves.

City Oasis Inn (☎ 07-4771 6048; www.cityoasis .com.au; 143 Wills St; r $120-195; 🏊 🖳) The rooms in this spotless and friendly inn are hardly showing their age even though some of the original hotel was built motel-style in 1959. There are loft and self-contained (kitchenette) options. The luscious gardens hide a grassy knoll, swing seat and pool (complete with bridge).

TOP END

Mariners North (☎ 07-4722 0777; www.marinersnorth .com.au; 7 Mariners Dr; apt $225-275; 🏊 🖳) Large high-storey complex featuring bright rooms with sea views (yep, all of them), luscious in-room couches, massive kitchens and access to the 20 herbs growing down by the waterside barbecue. Topped off with tennis courts and a spa.

CAMPING

Rowes Bay Caravan Park (☎ 07-4771 3576; www.rowes baycp.com.au; Heatley Pde, Rowes Bay; unpowered/powered sites $23/29, cabins $62-77; 🖳) Leafy beachside camping ground 3km from Townsville's CBD.

Eating

Juliettes (☎ 07-4721 5577; 7/58 The Strand; ⏰ 7am-9pm Sun-Fri, 7am-10pm Sat) This is the perfect place to fill up on a cheap breakfast ($3.50 to $9) while indulging in great water views. There's also coffee, ice cream (fig or black forest anyone?) and exotic salsa yoghurt on offer.

ourpick Ladah (☎ 07-4724 0402; cnr Sturt & Stanley Sts; meals $8-17; ☺ breakfast & lunch) The menu's written on butchers' paper on the wall, but this ain't no primary-school cooking class – it's special. The cinnamon scones with jam and cream are indulgent and delicious, or try the flourless choc hazelnut mud cake. Breakfast is served all day and the coffee's great.

Betty Blue & the Lemon Tart (☎ 07-4724 2554; 254 Sturt St; meals $10-16; ☺ breakfast & lunch) Orders printed onto canvas hang artily on the walls in this 1930s shopfront cafe. Sit yourself on a large cube under a lollipop spatula and go for pricey treats such as passionfruit curd.

Brewery (☎ 07-4724 2999; www.townsvillebrewery .com.au; 252 Flinders St; meals $9-25; ☺ lunch & dinner) Make your steak a surf'n'turf with a prawn and red-claw upgrade at this former post office, now a brewery-restaurant-nightclub. The food's delicious, great value, and there's good people-spotting from the front deck.

C Bar (☎ 07-4724 0333; Gregory St Headland; mains $20-30) With watery views and savoury corn cakes or blackberry pancakes (a mere $10) for breakfast, you know things can only get better for lunch and dinner. The inspired 'grazing and sharing menu' ($24) runs from 4pm until late.

Scirocco (☎ 07-4724 4508; 61 Palmer St; mains $20-36; ☺ lunch Tue-Fri, dinner Tue-Sat) Thai and Vietnamese influences confuse themselves with the Tuscan-inspired decor, but no worries; there's mud crab and 'typhoon' barramundi on the menu.

White Blue (☎ 07-4724 4498; 13 Palmer St; mains $30-45; ☺ dinner Mon-Sat) A good Greek menu including meze and soups, a sophisticated blue-and-white atmosphere and a decent cocktail list make this a place worth diving into on busy Palmer St.

Drinking

Watermark (☎ 07-4724 4281; 72-74 The Strand; ☺ noon-midnight) Packed during weekends, this seafront bar does glam perfectly.

Seaview (☎ 07-4771 5005; cnr The Strand & Gregory St; meals $20-30) The sea views, fig tree locale and occasionally loud live music win over pub-loving locals in this sprawling drinking hub.

Mad Cow Tavern (☎ 07-4771 5727; 129 Flinders St East; ☺ 5pm-2am Thu-Sun), with its drooping fans, ceiling roses and checkered floor, is gaudy

fun, as is the Irish-themed **Molly Malones** (☎ 07-4771 3428; 87 Flinders St East; ☺ 11.30am-late Mon-Fri, 5pm-5am Sat), which also serves $10 meals.

Entertainment

Consortium (☎ 07-4724 5122; 159-165 Flinders St East; ☺ 8pm-late) This classy, dazzling establishment is run by the same folk as Watermark. It's all about chandeliers, booths done up with white lace, black vinyl and antiques, and tables that light up.

Bombay Rock (☎ 07-4724 2800; www.bombayrock .com.au; 719 Flinders St West; ☺ from 8pm Fri & Sat) Get zapped by laser lighting as you relax on comfy couches, or check out touring bands. There's a garden bar here, too.

Bullys (☎ 07-4771 5647; 108 Flinders St East; ☺ 8pm-5am Tue-Sun) Bullys is a place to party and has the interesting claim to fame of being located under Townsville's only strip club.

Other recommendations:

BC Cinemas (☎ 07-4771 4101; cnr Sturt & Blackwood Sts) Mainstream films.

Jupiters Casino (☎ 07-4722 2333; Sir Leslie Thiess Dr) One of the places Townsville is famous for.

Getting There & Away

AIR

Virgin Blue (☎ 13 67 89; www.virginblue.com.au), **Alliance Airlines** (☎ 07-4750 1300; www.allianceair lines.com.au), **Jetstar** (☎ 13 15 38; www.jetstar.com.au) and **Qantas** (☎ 13 13 13; www.qantas.com.au) – and its subsidiaries – all service Townsville.

BUS

The **long-distance bus station** (Sir Leslie Thiess Dr; lockers per day $4-6) is at Breakwater Terminal. **Greyhound Australia** (☎ 1300 GREYHOUND/1300 473 946, 07-4772 5100; www.greyhound.com.au; ☺ 6am-6pm Mon-Fri, 6am-4pm Sat & Sun) departs from here.

Destination	Price ($)	Duration (hr)
Airlie Beach	63	5
Brisbane	240	23
Cairns	73	6
Charters Towers	35	1½
Mackay	88	6
Mission Beach	56	4
Rockhampton	133	12

At the ageing **transit centre** (Plume St) you'll find an agent for **Premier Motor Service** (☎ 13 34 10, 07-4772 3905; www.premierms.com.au), which has a daily service to Cairns (adult $53, six hours), and **Douglas Coaches** (☎ 07-4787 1830), which

QUEENSLAND

connects Townsville with Charters Towers (adult/student $24/18, 1¾ hours) on weekdays at 4pm.

TRAIN

The **Queensland Rail Travel Centre** (☎ 07-4772 8358; 502 Flinders St; ☺ 8.30am-5pm Mon-Fri) is where the old train station was, about 500m south of the centre. The new railway station is halfway between Ingham Rd and the old station, on Flinders St.

The *Sunlander* connects Townsville with Brisbane (economy seat/sleeper $184/242, 24 hours), Rockhampton (economy seat $124, 11 hours) and Cairns (economy seat $64, 7½ hours). The more luxurious Queenslander class, which includes a sleeper and meals, is available on two services per week. The business-class *Tilt Train* also connects Townsville with Brisbane (economy seat $260, 18 hours) and Cairns (economy seat $95, six hours) three times a week.

The *Inlander* heads from Townsville to Mt Isa on Thursday and Sunday at 12.30pm (economy seat/sleeper $124/182).

Getting Around

Townsville's airport is 5km northwest of the city in Garbutt. A taxi costs $20, or **Abacus Charters & Tours** (☎ 1300 554 378) does airport-to-Townsville runs for $10 for one person, $15 for two.

Sunbus (☎ 07-4725 8482; www.sunbus.com.au) scoots around town; pick up info from Breakwater Terminal.

Car-rental agencies include **Avis** (☎ 13 63 33, 07-4721 2688; www.avis.com.au; 81 Flinders St), **Europcar** (☎ 1300 131 390, 07-4762 7050, 07-4760 1380; www.europcar.com.au; 305 Ingham Rd, Garbutt), **Hertz** (☎ 13 30 30, 07-4775 5950; www.hertz.com; Stinson Ave, Garbutt) and **Thrifty** (☎ 07-4725 4600; www.thrifty.com.au; 289 Ingham Rd, Garbutt).

Taxis (☎ 13 10 08, 07-4778 9500) congregate outside the Cowboy Leagues Club and the Breakwater Terminal.

MAGNETIC ISLAND

pop 2107

Magnetic Island, or 'Maggie' as she's affectionately known, is packed full of koalas, bush stone-curlews, rocky outcrops, dry forests, beautiful bays and, come school holidays, 'schoolies' and families. Day tripping to Maggie is popular for hikers, and there are some great eateries for refuelling once the hik-

ing's done. Accommodation options include a guaranteed flashpacking experience, a 'sleep near the wildlife' experience and some above-average beachfront abodes. It's the site of solar suburb (locals are installing solar panels en masse) and there are some folk here keen to inject a little more sustainable travel into the mix, so you might well find yourself swapping the Moke for an electric bike.

Orientation & Information

Magnetic Island is a triangular-shaped island just 8km off Townsville. There's one main road across the island, which goes from Picnic Bay, past Nelly and Geoffrey Bays, to Horseshoe Bay. Local buses ply the route regularly. Other roads head down to Radical Bay and there's an unsealed road from Picnic Bay to West Point. Ferries dock at Nelly Bay's flash Harbourside Plaza.

Information and maps are in the local free publications *Magnetic Island Guide* and *Magnetic Island Informer*.

Nelly Bay's Harbourside Plaza houses **Australia Post** (☎ 07-4778 5118; shop 2, 98-100 Sooning St), which does foreign-currency exchange, credit-card cash advances and poste restante.

Sights

PICNIC BAY

It isn't too exciting down this way since they moved the ferry up to Nelly Bay, but if bright lights in the distance, rather than in your face, suit you better, then head here.

Businesses in the mall aren't coping too well with the reduced clientele, but that curious elegant bird, the curlew, has made it its own. Activities in the area include swimming in the beach's stinger enclosure (November to May) or hitting balls around the nine-hole golf course at the **Magnetic Island Country Club** (☎ 07-4778 5188; Hurst St, Picnic Bay; ☺ from 8am). West is **Cockle Bay**, site of the HMS *City of Adelaide* wreck, followed by **West Point** with its sunsets and secluded beach.

NELLY BAY

This flashy harbour is where the Maggie experience begins and ends if you come by passenger or car ferry. There's also a public boat ramp, and it's chock-a-block with real estate agents, a supermarket, Moke rental outlets, resorts and cafes. Full-moon time equals party time on Nelly Bay beach.

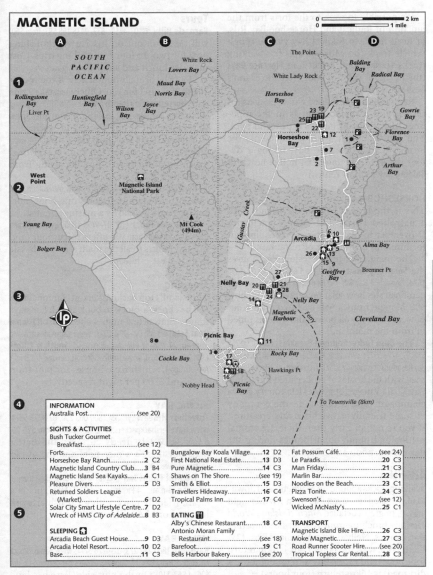

MAGNETIC ISLAND

ARCADIA

Arcadia's Friday night market is great for mingling with the locals and dining on Indonesian food. It's held at the **Returned Services League** (RSL); silence descends at 6pm as Australia's war dead are remembered. Beachwise, enjoy the great swimming and grassy, shady playground at **Alma Bay**. Nearby **Geoffrey Bay** has rock wallabies and fringes a reef, though QPWS discourages reef walking.

RADICAL BAY & THE FORTS

In 1942 Townsville took up a role as a major military base and a **forts** complex was built on Magnetic Island to spot aircraft with its two 3,000,000-candlepower searchlights.

It's possible to walk to the forts from the junction of Radical and Horseshoe Bay Rds, or head north to Radical Bay via the rough vehicle track (no Mokes). This has walking tracks to secluded **Arthur** and **Florence Bays** (the northern sides of both offer the island's best snorkelling).

Radical Bay once housed a now-demolished resort, and a replacement is in the pipe-line. In the meantime it's a peaceful spot. You can walk from Radical Bay across the headland to Horseshoe Bay, taking a de-tour down to the unofficial nudist beach of **Balding Bay** (3.4km return).

HORSESHOE BAY

This is the largest bay on the island, with a patrolled beach and stinger enclosure (November to May), water-sports equipment for hire and a gathering of restaurants.

The main road to Horseshoe Bay houses the **Solar City Smart Lifestyle Centre** (☎ 07-4758 1674; Horseshoe Bay Rd; ☒ 8am-4pm Mon-Fri), which demonstrates how solar power works and how 500 Maggie homes will be fitted with solar power (currently all power and water is piped in from the mainland).

The **Bush Tucker Gourmet Breakfast** (☎ 1800 285 577, 07-4778 5577; www.bungalowbay.com.au; 40 Horseshoe Bay Rd; adult/child/family $25/13/70; ☒ 8.30-10am Wed, Fri & Sat) with the koalas at ecocertified Bungalow Bay Koala Village (opposite) lets you try guava champagne and breakfast in the company of some friendly native birds and creatures. If you're not an early riser, there are animal petting and photo opportunities during the day (10am, noon and 2.30pm).

Activities

Walking tracks abound on Magnetic, and down-loadable maps are available from www.epa.qld .gov.au or grab a detailed *Magnetic Island World Heritage* brochure from Townsville's informa-tion centres. Nelly Bay to Arcadia is 5km (2½ hours) one way; the Forts Walk is 4km return (one hour) and Picnic Bay to West Point (on a dirt road) is 16km return (four hours).

Pleasure Divers (☎ 1800 797 797, 07-4778 5788; www .pleasuredivers.com.au; 10 Marine Pde, Arcadia; open-water course per person $329) teaches all PADI courses and offers reef, wreck and island dives.

For something different hire an electric bike from **Magnetic Island Bike Hire** (☎ 07-4758 1333; www.goelectric.com.au; Shop 5, Bright Ave, Arcadia; 0427 443 322; per day $25; ☒ Mon-Sat).

Tours

Barnacle Bill (☎ 07-4758 1837, 0438 165 581; from $60) will take you out on his 7m sports-fishing boat for two- to four-hour fishing trips. Cost includes lunch and snorkelling gear.

Got to be brutally honest here: if you're over 100kg, this ain't for you. Otherwise, take a ride with **Horseshoe Bay Ranch** (☎ 07-4778 5109; 38 Gifford St, Horseshoe Bay; rides $90), leaving at 9am and 3pm. Rides take you through bush and beach.

Magnetic Island Sea Kayaks (☎ 07-4778 5424; www .seakayak.com.au; tours from $69) runs ecocertified morning and sunset tours departing from Horseshoe Bay.

Reef Ecotours (☎ 0419 712 579; www.reefecotours.com; from $75) offers family-friendly one-hour snor-kelling tours guided by a marine scientist.

Tropicana Tours (☎ 07-4758 1800; www.tropicana tours.com.au; tours from $66) offers three-hour (and full-day) tours to all the main areas on the isle in a s-t-r-e-t-c-h jeep.

Sleeping

The island's top backpackers' accommodation can be chock-a-block so book ahead. For stays longer than a few nights check **First National Real Estate** (☎ 07-4778 5077; www.visitmagneticisland .com.au; 21 Marine Pde, Arcadia) and **Smith & Elliott** (☎ 07-4778 5570; www.smithandelliott.com.au; 4/5 Bright Ave, Arcadia), which have houses for rent from $120 and $100 per night respectively.

PICNIC BAY

Travellers Hideaway (☎ 1800 000 290, 07-4778 5314; www.travellersbackpackers.com; 32 Picnic St; dm $20-25, d $60; ☐ ☒) It needs curtains and better beds but there's a nice pool and the owner is mellow.

Tropical Palms Inn (☎ 07-4778 5076; info@tropical palmsinn.com.au; 34 Picnic St; s/d $105/115) This is a clean, friendly place with great fish artwork hanging on the walls.

NELLY BAY

Base (☎ 1800 242 273, 07-4778 5777; www.basebackpack ers.com; 1 Nelly Bay Rd; unpowered sites per person $12, dm $26, d $62-110) On the plus side, Base has loud music, cool attitudes, unique A-frame huts, beach views from the beachfront deck and loads of activity options (full-moon parties, swimming, kayaking, diving etc). However, the eight-bed dorms are crowded and the kitchens and bathrooms don't gleam with clean. 'Steal deals' include ferry transfers from Townsville and are good value.

Pure Magnetic (☎ 07-4778 5955; www.puremag netic.com; 9 The Esplanade; villas from $375; 🐾 🕹) Here you'll find scrumptious timber villas with spas, plasma TVs, decking designed for entertaining and, of course, essentials such as coffee plungers, wi-fi and access to the statue-clad pool.

ARCADIA

Arcadia Hotel Resort (☎ 1800 663 666, 07-4778 5177; www.magnums.com.au; 7 Marine Pde; dm $22-26, d $89; 🐾 💻 🕹) Attached to a pub whose weekly highlight is cane-toad races (8.15pm every Wednesday), you can't expect too much from this backpackers. However, there are two pools, a basic restaurant and the motel-style doubles at the side are good value, particularly given their proximity to Geoffrey Bay.

our pick **Arcadia Beach Guest House** (☎ 07-4778 5668; www.arcadiabeachguesthouse.com.au; 27 Marine Pde; dm $30, d $140-150; 🐾) Friendly owners have created a clean and stunningly different place to stay; from the minute the Rolls Royce picks you up from the ferry you can expect excellent hospitality and unique experiences such as turtle spotting from the balcony and eating breakfast in the large boat that sits in the front yard. There's luxury camping out the back ($60 with breakfast).

HORSESHOE BAY

Bungalow Bay Koala Village (☎ 1800 285 577, 07-4778 5577; www.bungalowbay.com.au; 40 Horseshoe Bay Rd; unpowered/powered sites $20/25, dm $24, d & tw with/without bathroom $80/58; 🐾 💻 🕹) Wake up to the sounds of Australian animals in this ecocertified YHA hostel set in a wildlife reserve. A-frames are scattered around the large property and have new flyscreens, futons and extras including reading lights. Sunday's live-music sessions liven up the bistro, which serves $10 pizzas, and even born-and-bred Aussies will enjoy time with the neighbouring koalas.

Shaws on the Shore (☎ 07-4758 1900; www.shaw sontheshore.com.au; 7 Pacific Dr; d from $185; 🕹) OK, so the T-shirts match the couches (monogrammed), and it's a little too cane and Ken Done, but the self-contained rooms are bright and very clean, and all have sea views.

Eating

Horseshoe Bay certainly leads the pack in terms of food diversity on Maggie.

PICNIC BAY

Alby's Chinese Restaurant (☎ 07-4778 5706; 6 Picnic Bay Arcade; dishes $4-16; 🕑 lunch & dinner) Alby dishes up homemade dim sims and wontons and more elaborate spreads including king prawns with chilli sauce at the BYO eatery.

Antonio Moran Family Restaurant (☎ 07-4778 5018; 10 The Esplanade; meals $15) Dine outside with the curlews at this pizza-and-pasta joint run by 'Tony Moran the Pizza Man'.

NELLY BAY

Fat Possum Café (☎ 07-4778 5409; 55 Sooning St; dishes $6-10; 🕑 breakfast & lunch; 💻) The Irish owner makes this a friendly and relaxed place to chow down on homemade cakes and slices and great coffees. Of course, there are healthier options too, such as the homemade beef -and-Guinness pie.

Man Friday (☎ 07-4778 5658; 37 Warboys St; meals $15-30; 🕑 dinner Mon-Sat) This converted beach shack in the bush serves up nachos, caters to little amigos and doesn't mind if you BYO.

Le Paradis (☎ 07-4778 5044; cnr Mandalay Av & Sooning St; mains $20-35; 🕑 lunch Fri-Sun, dinner Tue-Sat) This à la carte, BYO restaurant offers a range of French-inspired eats, and there's an attached 'kiosk' selling fresh baguettes and more.

More options:

Bells Harbour Bakery (☎ 07-4758 1870; shop 4, 98-100 Sooning St, Harbourside Plaza) Has gold-medal-winning pies.

Pizza Tonite (☎ 07-4758 1400; 53 Sooning St; pizzas $10-25; 🕑 dinner Tue-Sun) Fancy some home delivery? Pizza Tonite (and burgers and lasagne) does hostel delivery.

ARCADIA

Butler's Pantry (Bright Ave; meals $7-15; 🕑 7am-2pm) A day-long breakfast menu includes delish options such as Red Hill muesli and the Five Beach Bay breakfast.

Banister's Seafood (☎ 07-4778 5700; 22 McCabe Cres; mains $18-20; 🕑 lunch & dinner Tue-Sun) Delish fish and chips taste even better if you go for the outdoor dining option. Add some honey-ginger prawns to your order and you can't go wrong. Banister's cooks up a great mix of Asian-inspired seafood dishes, served with rice instead of chips.

HORSESHOE BAY

Noodies on the Beach (☎ 07-4778 5786; www.nood ies.com.au; 2/6 Pacific Dr; mains $10; 🕑 10am-10pm Mon-Wed & Fri, 8am-10pm Sat, 8am-3pm Sun) The island's nudist beach may be a few kilometres away, but Noodies has arguably the best coffee on the island, magazines to peruse while you're drinking it, and a book exchange.

Barefoot (☎ 07-4758 1170; 5 Pacific Dr; meals $10-30; ☺ lunch & dinner Thu-Mon) With more paintings than you can poke a stick at, it's surprising there's even room for food, but there is (and wine, too). Water watchers will love the front porch option, but the back deck is inviting, too.

Marlin Bar (☎ 07-4758 1588; 3 Pacific Dr; mains $17-22; ☺ lunch daily, dinner Tue-Sat) This lively waterfront pub has the usual variety of crumbed food and grills as well as an all-day breakfast.

Also recommended:

Swenson's (☎ 07-4778 5577; 40 Horseshoe Bay Rd; meals $16-23) At Bungalow Bay Koala Village, this place offers deck dining and $10 made-for-one pizzas, and does a roaring trade in chickpea curry.

Wicked McNasty's (☎ 07-4778 5861; 3/6 Pacific Dr; meals $7-13) A popular no-frills breakfast hang-out.

Getting There & Away

Sunferries (☎ 07-4771 3855; www.sunferries.com.au; return per person $29; ☺ 6.20am-6.40pm Mon-Fri, 7am-5.30pm Sat & Sun) operates a frequent passenger ferry from the **Breakwater Terminal** (Sir Leslie Thiess Dr, Townsville). No forward booking is required; be there 20 minutes ahead of departure. There is car parking here ($5 per day).

Fantasea Cruising Magnetic (☎ 07-4772 5422; Ross St, South Townsville; ☺ from Magnetic Island 6.15am-6.55pm Mon-Fri, 8.05am-6.55pm Sat & Sun) does the crossing eight times each weekday and seven times on weekends from the south side of Ross Creek. There's free internet for waiting passengers. It costs $156 (return) for a car (including passengers) and $22 (return) for a passenger only. The ferry docks at Magnetic Harbour in Nelly Bay.

Getting Around

Magnetic Island is ideal for cycling. Most places to stay rent bikes for around $15 a day. Otherwise **Magnetic Island Bike Hire** (☎ 07-4758 1333; www.electricbike.com.au; Arcadia Shopping Centre) charges the same, with free delivery, and it also has a range of electric bikes ($25 per day), so you can go further on less of your own steam.

The **Magnetic Island Bus Service** (☎ 07-4778 5130; fares $2-4, day pass $11) ploughs between Picnic Bay and Horseshoe Bay at least 18 times a day, meeting all ferries and stopping at, or near, all accommodation.

Mokes and scooters are also popular options, though you are not allowed to access some beaches with them. Expect to pay around $80 per day, plus extras such as petrol and a per-kilometre fee, for a Moke (mini open-air vehicle) from either **Moke Magnetic** (☎ 07-4778 5377; www.mokemagnetic.com; 112 Sooning St, Nelly Bay) or **Tropical Topless Car Rentals** (☎ 07-4758 1111; 138 Sooning St, Nelly Bay; per day from $78). Scooters are taken care of by **Road Runner Scooter Hire** (☎ 07-4778 5222; 3/64 Kelly St, Nelly Bay; per day from $30).

If you need a cab, call **Magnetic Island Taxi** (☎ 13 10 08).

NORTH COAST HINTERLAND

Just a couple of days' drive and you can swelter in Australia's famed outback. The Flinders Hwy heads 800km due west from Townsville to Cloncurry.

Ravenswood

pop 120

Ravenswood is a 44km 'detour' from the Flinders Hwy, but it's well worth the extra journey to check out this tiny chimney-pocked town. An expansive blue sky and the red, hot dirt dotted with ruins of better times make this an intriguing stop, especially if your trip coincides with April's **Cocktails in the Outback** (a big cocktail party).

If the **mining & historical museum** (☎ 07-4770 2047; adult/child $2/1; ☺ 11am-1pm) is open, call in to see how they've reconstructed the courthouse and police station. There's also a family-tracing service here too, which might come in handy if you think you've got Ravenswood blood.

For antiques and nonkitsch souvenirs visit the **pottery shop** (Thorps Bldg; ☎ 07-4770 2504; ☺ 10am-3pm), then pick up a *Heritage Trail* map ($1) and choose from the three colour-coded walking trails, ranging from half-hour strolls to three-hour walks.

Part of the scenery is the **Railway Hotel** (☎ 07-4770 2144; 1 Barton St; s/tw/d $39/77/88), where you can drool over a Wagyu beef burger and chips (mains from $10), while chatting to the amiable locals. The basic rooms upstairs have tin ceilings. You can also stay in good, old-style rooms at the **Imperial Hotel** (☎ 07-4770 2131; Macrossan St; s/d $35/60). A short drive past the council's bone-dry **camping ground** (unpowered sites $12) and you're at the shaded local **gold mine lookout**.

Charters Towers
pop 8469

You'd be forgiven for wondering what keeps Charters Towers alive, but alive it is, and it's thanks to some Australian staples: cattle and gold. Apart from truckloads of cattle bumbling through town, the town features splendid architecture, friendly locals, choice food options and a vibrant tourism industry. Ghosts apparently abound in the town's buildings; everyone has a ghost story to tell.

An Aboriginal boy, Jupiter Mosman, first found gold in town in 1871 and it didn't take long for the population to explode (to around 30,000) and for the town to become known as 'the World'. Not that that self-important name has disappeared: at night the words 'the World' shine brightly over the town from the sides of Towers Hill's massive water tanks.

INFORMATION

Charters Towers Computers (☎ 07-4787 2988; 32 Gill St; per hr $6; ☺ 9am-5pm Mon-Fri, to noon Sat) Has internet access.

Charters Towers visitor information centre (☎ 07-4761 5533; www.charterstowers.qld.gov.au; 74 Mosman St; ☺ 9am-5pm; ☐) Maps and info.

Library (☎ 07-4761 5580; 130 Gill St; per hr $5; ☺ 10am-5pm Mon-Fri, 9.30am-1pm Sat) Internet access.

SIGHTS

Wonderful buildings abound in this town; Gill and Mosman Sts have some of the best, including the **Stock Exchange Arcade**, now the scene of the **Calling of the Card** audio presentation that runs hourly from 9.40am (enter via the information centre).

The **Charters Towers Folk Museum** (☎ 07-4787 4661; 36 Mosman St; adult/child $5/3) holds a dusty collection of the town's antiques, as does the wonderful, privately owned **Miners Cottage** (☎ 0414 967 369; 26 Deane St; adult/child $4/2; ☺ 11am-2pm Mon-Fri, 9am-2pm Sat & Sun May-Oct, 9am-2pm Sat & Sun Nov-Apr), which caught a resident ghost on film. Staff here will play a few tunes on the accordion and teach you some gold-panning skills.

The **World Theatre** (82 Mosman St) was originally the Australian Bank of Commerce building (built in 1891). These days it houses a theatre, cinema and gift shop.

QUEENSLAND

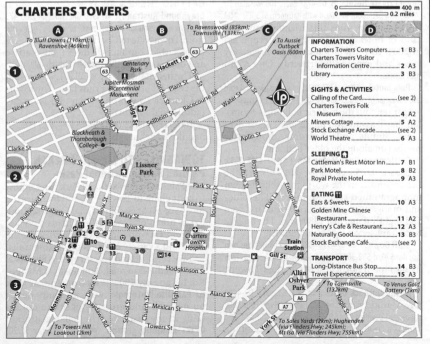

CHARTERS TOWERS

0 — 400 m
0 — 0.2 miles

INFORMATION
Charters Towers Computers........**1** B3
Charters Towers Visitor
  Information Centre..................**2** A3
Library...**3** B3

SIGHTS & ACTIVITIES
Calling of the Card...................(see 2)
Charters Towers Folk
  Museum......................................**4** A2
Miners Cottage............................**5** A2
Stock Exchange Arcade..........(see 2)
World Theatre.............................**6** A3

SLEEPING 🏠
Cattleman's Rest Motor Inn.....**7** B1
Park Motel.....................................**8** B2
Royal Private Hotel....................**9** A3

EATING 🍴
Eats & Sweets............................**10** A3
Golden Mine Chinese
  Restaurant................................**11** A2
Henry's Cafe & Restaurant......**12** A3
Naturally Good...........................**13** B3
Stock Exchange Café................(see 2)

TRANSPORT
Long-Distance Bus Stop..........**14** B3
Travel Experience.com.............**15** A3

The **Venus Gold Battery** (☎ 07-4787 4773; Millchester Rd; adult/child $12/6; ☺ hourly tours 10am-3pm Oct-Apr, 9am & 10am May-Sep) stopped crushing gold in 1973, and it's the oldest preserved battery in Australia. Imagination rules during the tour thanks to holograms on a water screen.

Towers Hill Lookout, where gold was first discovered, has wonderful views over the town towards Townsville and picnic tables and information panels. Book at the visitors centre to see a screening of the movie *Ghosts of Gold*. For something different, watch the organised chaos of the **Wednesday Cattle Sales** (Sale Yards; ☺ 9am).

FESTIVALS & EVENTS

Ten Days in the Towers (☎ 1800 449 977; www.char terstowerscountrymusic.com) is held in early May and features talent quests, a prince and princesses competition, cowgirls, tribute shows and more. **Goldfield Ashes** (www.goldfieldashes .com.au) is an amateur cricket carnival that sees at least 200 cricket teams descend on Charters Towers each Australia Day weekend (late January).

SLEEPING

Royal Private Hotel (☎ 07-4787 8688; 100 Mosman St; s/d without bathroom $30/60, d with bathroom $75-85; ☒) Julie Loughrey runs this friendly hang-out kind of hotel, built in 1888 and reopened in 2004. Its attributes include great balcony views and exposed floorboards. One room has a spa.

Park Motel (☎ 07-4787 1022; admin@parkmotel .au; 1 Mosman St; s/d $85/95; ☒ ☒) Owners may no longer rent out the historic building's rooms, but they'll assure you the resident ghost lives there. Simple and ghost-free, motel-style rooms run along the older building.

Cattleman's Rest Motor Inn (☎ 07-4787 3555; cnr Bridge & Plant Sts; s/d $93/104; ☒) This may be the only hotel in the world that sells its own monogrammed steak-knife sets. The blue-and-orange-themed rooms are clean and cool and slightly dated in a 1980s way. The on-site restaurant serves up chunky steaks.

Bluff Downs (☎ 07-4770 4084; www.bluffdowns .au; dm $20, d $90-300, campsite $20) Cattle-station living 110km northwest of Charters Towers. Call ahead.

Aussie Outback Oasis (☎ 1800 812 417, 07-4787 8722; ausaback@bigpond.net.au; Flinders Hwy, Columbia; unpowered/powered sites $20/30, cabins $100-110; ☒ ☒) This is a good-looking oasislike Big 4 camping

ground with a pillow trampoline, playground, landscaped pool/gazebo area and clean cabins that can sleep eight.

EATING

Eats & Sweets (☎ 07-4787 2667; 14 Gill St; meals $5-9) Offers yummy cakes (can do takeaway) and coffees.

Naturally Good (☎ 07-4787 4211; 58 Gills St; lunches $6; ☺ 8am-4pm Mon-Sat) Sandwiches, made-on-premises sausage rolls and pasties, and delicious sweet desserts.

Stock Exchange Café (☎ 07-4787 7954; 76 Mosman St; mains $7-11; ☺ breakfast & lunch Mon-Sat) Great for a nonfancy all-day breakfast in an airy arcade. It has a pleasant black-and-white lino and lace-curtains kind of atmosphere.

Golden Mine Chinese Restaurant (☎ 07-4787 7609; 64-66 Mosman St; meals $10-17; ☺ lunch & dinner) All-you-can-eat smorgasbord (lunch/dinner $11/14) with no fewer than 34 dishes.

Henry's Café (☎ 07-4787 4333; 82 Mosman St; mains $18-29; ☺ lunch & dinner Tue-Sun) A big, classy eatery with great-tasting mains such as its version of vegetarian lasagne. Also has mouth-watering desserts including lemon meringue.

GETTING THERE & AWAY

Greyhound Australia (☎ 1300 GREYHOUND/1300 473 946; www.greyhound.com.au) has a daily service from Townsville to Charters Towers ($35, 1½ hours), which continues to the NT. Buses arrive and depart outside the **Catholic Church** (Gill St).

The **train station** (Enterprise Rd) is 1.5km east of the centre. The *Inlander* runs from Townsville to Charters Towers on Sunday and Thursday (adult/child $27/14).

Travel Experience.com (☎ 07-4787 2622; 13 Gill St) handles travel tickets.

TOWNSVILLE TO MISSION BEACH
Paluma Range National Park

The Paluma Range National Park runs almost from Ingham to Townsville, and includes the must-see Mt Spec–Big Crystal Creek section, 62km north of Townsville. This is a pocket of rainforest with some awesome views of the coast and a variety of different walking trails.

Take the northern access route to **Big Crystal Creek**, via the 4km road, 2km north of Mt Spec Rd. It's an easy 100m walk from the car park to **Paradise Waterhole**, with its sandy beach on one side and great views of the mountains in the distance. The self-registration **QPWS camping ground** (per person/family $5/20)

CAMPERVANS

Who *isn't* driving a campervan on Queensland's North Coast and Far North Queensland roads?

Self-contained freedom on four wheels is certainly the transport mode of choice for those travelling as couples or in groups. It is a hefty initial outlay, but many find it more economical in the long run – although you will have to pay extra to stay at camping grounds in these parts. There are some unsealed roads, such as those that access Wallaman Falls (below), which are inaccessible to caravans. There are also some seriously winding roads – in the Atherton Tableland there's around 280 bends in the Gilles Hwy between Yungaburra (p458) and Gordonvale. However, getting around is mostly a cinch and allows flexibility to pull into those roadside stalls brimming with tropical fruit plus call into a multitude of waterfalls and state parks.

Taking campervans for extended periods can limit your island-hopping (eg it's $156 return on the car ferry between Townsville and Magnetic Island), but there's something innately carefree about travelling the roads with the windows down.

The **Queensland 2009 Caravan Parks & Touring Accommodation Directory** (www.caravanqld .com.au) is a handy and free dashboard companion guide; it's available at most visitor information centres in the region. For more information, see p74.

has gas barbecues, toilets and water (treat before drinking).

Leave the caravans behind to take on the windy, narrow road up to the cool mountain town of Paluma. Along the way there are a bunch of creek and swimming-hole stops, including **Little Crystal Creek**, 7km along Mt Spec Rd, which is a series of swimming holes surrounded by rainforest and looked over by a stone bridge (built in 1932).

To get to **Jourama Falls** travel 6km on a good, sealed road from the highway, though the creek at the entrance can be impassable. It's a steep walk up to the lookout; watch for Ulysses butterflies, nocturnal brown bandicoots and threatened mahogany gliders. The rock pools are good for a dip, and there are plenty of turtles to check out. The **QPWS camping ground** (per person/family $5/20) has toilets and barbecues.

Up in the tiny village of Paluma is the cool **Rainforest Inn** (☎ 07-4770 8688; www.rain forestinnpaluma.com; d $125; ✦), with brand-new, well-designed rooms and a nearby restaurant-bar. The other option is **Forest Mist Cottage B&B** (☎ 07-4770 8578; d incl breakfast $100) and its rainfor-est-view room. On the Bruce Hwy, the **Crystal Creek Caravan Park** (☎ 07-4770 8198; 8 Barrilgie Rd, Mutarnee; unpowered/powered sites $20/25, cabins $70) is in flat country and also has a petrol station and shop.

A break at **Frosty Mango** (☎ 07-4770 8184; www .frostymango.com.au; Bruce Hwy, Mutarnee; light meals $5-10; ✦ 9am-5pm) is perfect for indulging in its range of ice creams (mango included) or buying some tacky but cute souvenirs featuring the legendary 'frosty mango'.

Ingham & Around

Laid-back Ingham (population 4605) is the proud guardian of an ever-expanding wet-land, **Tyto wetlands** (Tyto Wetlands Information Centre; ☎ 07-4776 5211; www.hinchinbrooknq.com.au; cnr Cooper St & Bruce Hwy; ✦ 8.45am-5pm Mon-Fri, 9am-4pm Sat & Sun), which has been protected since 1996 and holds around 230 species of birds including far-flung guests from Siberia and Japan. Twitchers love the 120-hectare site, and, like the birds, come from around the world to visit.

Also bringing in the visitors – 20,000 of them – is Ingham's annual **Car Show** (www .inghamcarshow.com.au). Each May, car-loving hoards descend to check out the cars and participate in or watch the wet T-shirt and tattoo competitions.

In May the **Australian-Italian Festival** (www .australianitalianfestival.com.au) celebrates the fact that 60% of Ingham residents are of Italian descent. The motto is 'eat, drink and celebrate'.

The other reason to make this town a stopo-ver is to get directions to **Wallaman Falls**, which has the longest single drop of any waterfall in Australia, at 305m. Located in **Girringun National Park**, 50km west of the town (on a not-for-caravans road), the falls look their best in the Wet, though are spectacular at any time. Also there is the 2km Jinda walk. The nearby self-registration **QPWS camping ground** (per person/family $5/20) has shower facilities. Don't miss the swimming hole, which is also frequented by the occasional platypus.

It's not hard to find a decent coffee in this town of Italian descendents; try the popular **Café Fiorellis** (☎ 07-4776 2172; 5-7 Lannercost St),

QUEENSLAND

which also does great gelati. If you're staying over, art deco fans will love **Noorla Heritage Resort** (☎ 07-4776 1100; www.hotelnoorla.com.au; 5-9 Warren St; unpowered/powered sites $15/22, s $55-129, d $59-149; ☒ ☒). Once the domain for single Italian cane cutters, it now offers guests wonderfully restored high-ceilinged rooms as well as cheaper container-style rooms behind the main building. The history is on the walls in photo format. High teas are popular on Saturday and Sunday ($30 per person); book ahead to enjoy the classy surrounds.

Between Ingham and Cardwell, the Bruce Hwy climbs high above the coast with wonderful views out over the mangrove-lined waterways known as the Everglades, which separate Hinchinbrook Island from the coast.

Lucinda is a sweet-as-pie port town with one massive attribute – a 6km-long jetty used for shipping sugar. It's worth driving here just to see it.

Cardwell
pop 10,084

Spread along kilometres of crocodile-infested waters (even the public pool has a crocodile on its sign), Cardwell is the gateway to the sublime Hinchinbrook Island National Park, but has its own unique seaside, prawn-burger lovin' attitude that doesn't take long to get used to. Port Hinchinbrook Marina, 2km from the town, has a glamorous pace and doubles as the departure point for the Hinchinbrook Island ferry. Behind Cardwell is the 26km **Cardwell Forest Drive**, and you can dip into the springs and spas along the way.

The **Rainforest & Reef Information Centre** (☎ 07-4066 8601; www.greatgreenwaytourism.com; 142 Victoria St; ☽ 8.30am-5pm Mon-Fri, 9am-3pm Sat & Sun) has loads of information on the area (including Hinchinbrook Island) as well as a kiosk for national-park campsite bookings and enquiries.

SEASONAL WORK
With mod cons in the kitchen and friendly owners who think nothing of piling the troops into the bus and showing them the sights, **Cardwell Backpackers Hostel** (☎ 07-4066 8014; card wellbackpackers@bigpond.com; 178 Bowen St; dm $19-20; ☒ ☒) is the place to stay if you're in the mood for some farm work (which the owners will find for you) and fun. The warehouse-living style may not appeal to everyone – 10 in a dorm – but the atmosphere is warm and

there's a dedicated room for dirty shoes. Banana and pineapple farms provide work throughout the year.

SLEEPING & EATING
our pick **Kookaburra Holiday Park** (Hinchinbrook Hostel; ☎ 07-4066 8648; www.kookaburraholidaypark.com.au; 175 Bruce Hwy; unpowered/powered sites $22/26, dm $20, d $40-95, cabins from $60; ☒ ☒) Great grounds with roomy cabins and motel rooms in the front, and a clean dorm block and good dongas in the rear; perfect for workers who crave space and a tropical garden atmosphere.

Cardwell Central Backpackers (☎ 07-4066 8404; www.cardwellbackpackers.com.au; 6 Brasenose St; dm $20; ☒) These former squash courts tightly pack in beds and backpackers, and though the 'rain catcher' umbrellas hanging from the ceiling and the murals are bright, the dirty kitchen and flimsy curtains for privacy are disappointing.

Mudbrick Manor (☎ 07-4066 2299; www.mud brickmanor.com.au; Lot 13, Stony Creek Rd; s/d incl breakfast $90/120; ☒) The Manor's six rooms have the subtle smell of timber and smoke and the atmosphere urges you to chill out and enjoy the pool and garden courtyard. If you stay here you get to indulge in the oft-recommended in-house meals ($25).

Cardwell's eateries compete in the prawn burger stakes, but since the quality of the more expensive restaurants can be dubious, ask a local where the good chefs work these days. Try **Holy Dooly Boutique Café** (cnr Victoria & Brasenose Sts; ☽ 9am-5pm Tue-Sat) for brekky and lunch snacks, and the quiet beachfront dining option of **Cardwell Village Beachcomber Motel & Tourist Park** (☎ 07-4066 8550; 43 Marine Pde; mains $22-29; ☽ 6-8pm) for reef-and-beef grills. **Annie's Kitchen** (☎ 07-4066 8818; 107 Victoria St; mains $9-17) also gets a good rap.

GETTING THERE & AWAY
All buses between Townsville and Cairns stop in Cardwell, including **Greyhound** (☎ 1300 GREYHOUND, 1300 473 946), with services from Townsville or Cairns for $50, and **Premier Motor Service** (☎ 13 34 10; www.premierms.com.au) with services from Townsville/Cairns for $25/30. The *Sunlander* train from Townsville (two hours) or Cairns (three hours), both $40, or the business-class *Tilt Train* (from Townsville or Cairns $60) also stop in Cardwell. Contact **Queensland Rail** (☎ 1800 872 467) for bookings.

Hinchinbrook Island National Park

Hinchinbrook Island's awesome granite mountains, mangrove-lined waterways and long, picturesque beaches featured recently as the isolated island in the movie *Nim's Island*, and isolated and unspoilt it is.

All 399 sq km of the island is national park, and rugged Mt Bowen (1121m) is its highest peak. Dugongs, lizards, wallabies and the iridescent-blue Ulysses butterfly frequent the area, and if you're fortunate enough to have the time to trek the **Thorsborne Trail**, a 32km, four-day, three-night trek from Ramsay Bay to Zoe Bay and on to George Point, you might well spot them all (as well as estuarine crocodiles and ration-eating bush rats). Insect repellent is a must, as are all your food requirements, and something to purify water as you go. Following the colourful ribbons and pebbles lining the track, you'll come across plenty of places to swim, and the spectacular **Zoe Falls**. There are six **QPWS camping grounds** (adult/family $5/20) on the trail, plus two at Macushla Bay and the Haven in the north. Only 40 people are allowed on the track at any one time, so book ahead, or, if you're late but lucky you might get to replace a cancellation. Pick up leaflets from the Rainforest & Reef Information Centre (opposite) in Cardwell, or visit www.queenslandwalks.com.au for more information. **QPWS** (☎ 13 13 04; www.epa.qld.gov.au) sells permits and arranges campsite bookings.

The ferry company will check permits before you catch the ferry, and will issue you with an emergency beacon before dropping you off at one end of the island. You then make the journey back to the well-hidden **Hinchinbrook Island Wilderness Lodge** (☎ 1800 220 077, 07-4066 2000; www.hinchinbrooklodge.com.au; d $245-545; 🏊). There are two types of accommodation on offer here: beachfront cabins similar to Australian holiday houses circa 1960, or classy treetop houses, perched into granite walls. Relax by the pool under swishing fans in the circular bar-restaurant or head to stunning Orchid Beach.

GETTING THERE & AWAY

Hinchinbrook Island Ferries (07-4066 8270; www.hinchinbrookferries.com.au) has a daily service from May to October, then operates on Sunday, Wednesday and Friday from November until March; check ahead to ensure that services are running in January and February. The journey costs adult/child $125/85 return, which includes a cruise through the mangrove everglade system, time to beachcomb on Ramsay Beach and the option to grab a picnic and walk the 5.3km back to the resort, or, alternatively, be ferried back to lunch at the restaurant. It also does Thorsborne Trail one-way transfers for $85.

Tully

pop 3000

This is not only the wettest town in Australia, but also the UFO capital as well. Throw in the banana capital of Australia and you wouldn't be far wrong, and steam still billows from the Tully Sugar Mill's smoke stacks during the harvesting season. The rainfall (averaging 4000mm annually) is celebrated by the town's **Big Gumboot**, which has a green tree frog holding on tightly to its side. Climb the 7.9m boot (Tully received 7.9m of water in 1950) for town and mill views.

There's plenty of banana-related work here year-round, and workers spend their spare time **white-water rafting** or cooling off at **Tully Gorge** or **Alligators Nest** swimming hole (croc-free, thankfully, unlike the region's coastal rivers). Rafting day trips on the Tully River with **Raging Thunder Adventures** (☎ 07-4030 7990; www.ragingthunder.com.au) or **R'n'R White Water Rafting** (☎ 1800 079 039, 07-4041 9444; www.raft.com.au) cost $170 and include transfers from Cairns, Northern Beaches and Mission Beach.

Tully State Forest, 40km from Tully on Cardstone Rd, has some good rainforest walks as well as picnic facilities and river access for swimming at Tully Gorge's pebble and sand beach. There's a beautifully situated **QPWS camping ground** (adult/family $5/20) with outdoor showers, and toilets and change rooms. As warning signs declare, when the hydro-electricity company opens its floodgates the gentle burble of Tully River becomes loved-by-kayakers rapids. There are several spots to watch the rafters pass by on Cardstone Rd.

The **Tully Visitor Information Centre** (☎ 07-4068 2288; Bruce Hwy; sugar-mill tours adult/child $12/8; ⏰ 8.30am-4.45pm Mon-Fri, 9.30am-4.30pm Sat & Sun) takes bookings for 90-minute tours of the Tully Sugar Mill, which run at 10am and 11am weekdays and at 11am weekends from May to December. No kids under seven or open shoes allowed.

QUEENSLAND

QUEENSLAND

THE CASSOWARY'S PRECIOUS POO

The flightless cassowary is as tall as a grown man, has three toes, a blue-and-purple head, red wattles (fleshy lobes hanging from its neck), a helmetlike horn and unusual black feathers, which look more like ratty hair. It could certainly be confused with an ageing rocker. Traditional gender roles are reversed with the male bird incubating the egg and rearing the chicks alone. The Australian cassowary is also known as the southern cassowary, though it's only found in the north of Queensland. It begins to make sense when you realise that other species are found in Papua New Guinea – to the north of Australia.

The cassowary is a vital link in the rainforest ecosystem. It is the only animal capable of dispersing the seeds of more than 70 species of trees whose fruits are too large for other rainforest animals to digest and pass. Cassowaries swallow fruit whole and excrete the fruit's seed intact in large piles of dung, which acts as fertiliser encouraging growth of the seed. Without this process, the rainforest as we know it would look very different.

The cassowary is an endangered species; there are less than 1000 left. Its biggest threat is loss of habitat, and eggs and chicks are vulnerable to dogs and wild pigs. A number of birds are also hit by cars: heed road signs warning drivers to be cassowary-aware. You're most likely to see cassowaries around Mission Beach and the Cape Tribulation section of the Daintree National Park. They can be aggressive, particularly if they have chicks. If you feel threatened, do not run; instead give the bird right-of-way and try to keep something solid between you and it – preferably a tree.

Sleeping options include the central **Banana Barracks** (☎ 07-4068 0455; www.bananabarracks.com; 50 Butler St; dm $24-30, d $80; ☒), which, with its party atmosphere, on-site bar-restaurant (Rafters Bar), outdoor cinema and white-water rafting booking office, doesn't guarantee sleep. Over the railway tracks from town is **Greenway Caravan Park** (☎ 07-4068 2055; Murray St; unpowered/powered sites $26/28, cabins with bathroom $75; ☼ reception 8-10am & 4-6pm; ☐), which has strict opening hours and perhaps goes a little overboard with its video surveillance, but the campsites are attractive.

Greyhound Australia (☎ 1300 GREYHOUND, 1300 473 946; www.greyhound.com.au) calls into Tully from Brisbane six times daily, before reaching Mission Beach 25 minutes later. **Premier Motor Service** (☎ 13 34 10; www.premierms.com.au) has one service daily to Tully on the same route.

MISSION BEACH
pop 4000

Mission Beach covers around 14km of prime beachfront land and remnant rainforest, and incorporates the tiny towns of Wongaling and South Mission Beach in the south, larger Mission Beach in the middle, and Bingil Bay and Garners Beach in the north. This former haven for rainforest-dwelling people and wildlife (including the endangered keystone species the cassowary, see above) is rapidly developing, although in recent cases the federal government has stepped in to halt the more controversial housing developments.

Skydiving and nearby Dunk Island, with its awesome camping and walking tracks, draw travellers to the town, and some of the accommodation options make it an ideal place to hang up the backpack and take advantage of some mid-Cairns/Townsville R&R.

To avoid an unexpected meeting with a croc or stinger, don't swim in any of Mission Beach's beach creeks – stick to the swimming enclosures provided.

Information
Mission Beach Information Station (☎ 07-4068 8699; www.missionbeachinfo.com; shop 4, Wongaling Shopping Centre; per hr $5; ☼ 9am-7pm) An internet cafe with a zillion brochures and helpful staff who'll make bookings for you.

Mission Beach Visitor Information Centre (☎ 07-4068 7099; www.missionbeachtourism.com; Porter Promenade; ☼ 9am-4.45pm) Run by volunteers providing a great, free, street and business directory.

Wet Tropics Environment Centre (☎ 07-4068 7197; Porters Promenade) Displays and movies about the local environment, including, of course, the cassowary.

Activities
Mission Beach is great for the adrenalin junkie; the local hostels are experienced in encouraging guests to jump out of planes.

Paul's Extreme Skydiving (☎ 1800 005 006, 07-4051 8855; www.xtremeskydiving.com.au; 14,000ft tandem jump from $295, plus levies) also offers Tully River rafting, as does **Jump the Beach** (☎ 1800 444 568; www.jumpthebeach.com.au; 14,000ft tandem jump from $295, plus levies).

Coral Sea Kayaking (☎ 07-4068 9154, 0419 782 453; www.coralseakayaking.com; half-/full-day tours $70/118) can get you over to Dunk Island under your own steam, and **Tropical Island Mission Beach Boat Charters** (☎ 07-4068 7009; www.missionbeachcharters .com.au; 1349c Cassowary Dr; island drop-off per person from $100) can dump you on an island with a picnic hamper and camping equipment, as well as arrange QPWS camping permits.

Quick Cat (☎ 07-4068 7289; www.quickcatcruises.com .au; reef trip adult/child $160/80) runs four trips daily to Dunk Island (adult/child return $43/22) as well as day trips to the outer reef, with a 50-minute stopover on Dunk Island.

Experienced divers can dive with **Calypso Dive** (☎ 07-4068 8432; www.calypsodive.com.au; per person from $225), which operates dives to the *Lady Bowen* wreck.

Biking it around the place is possible; **Le Tour Bikes** (☎ 07-4068 9553, 0419 782 453; shop 4, Wongaling Shopping Centre) hires out bikes for $25 per day.

Sleeping
BUDGET
Absolute Backpackers (☎ 1800 688 316, 07-4068 8317; 28 Wongaling Beach Rd; dm $22-24, d $50; 🖳 🖳) The new owners are proud of the recent makeover, and it's certainly put this backpackers at the top of the list, though the rooms are slightly small. It's a clean and relaxing place to stay.

Treehouse (☎ 07-4068 7137; www.yha.com.au; Frizelle Rd, Bingil Bay; unpowered sites $14, dm/d $25/55) Those seeking a peaceful oasis may be disappointed to find themselves at sometimes-noisy Treehouse, but the timber rooms are more about letting the sounds of nature in, rather than keeping the Bali-style communal area's noise out. Great views over the rainforest and a special tree-house ambience might make up for it. There's a shuttle bus to town.

Scotty's Mission Beach House (☎ 1800 665 567, 07-4068 8676; www.scottysbeachhouse.com.au; 167 Reid Rd, Wongaling Beach; dm $22, d $52-63; 🖳 🖳 🖳) Likeminded souls take time out on hammocks over the grassy grounds and splash in the pool. Double rooms have excellent facilities including kettles, fridges and bathrooms.

MIDRANGE
our pick **Sanctuary Retreat** (☎ 07-4088 6064, 1800 777 012; www.sanctuaryretreat.com.au; Holt Rd, Bingil Bay; s/d huts $33/65, cabins $149; 🖳 🖳) This ecocertified retreat is worth crossing the continent for. From the minute you decide to walk the 1km to reception through the rainforest (or choose a 4WD pick-up), you know you're somewhere very, very special. Mozzies are out, but forest noises are in if you sleep in one of the bare-bones, flyscreen-walled platforms, or you can upgrade to one of the canopy cabins. There's yoga on offer ($12 per class; held in a specially designed yoga studio), as well as mouth-watering meals for in-house guests ($20 to $26) in the 'shoes off' restaurant.

Hibiscus Lodge B&B (☎ 07-4068 9096; www.hibis cuslodge.com.au; 5 Kurrajong Close, Wongaling Beach; s/d $105/130; 🖳 🖳) The three themed rooms are located inside a modern home and have TVs and DVD players (and a selection of DVDs) and native timber floorboards. The gazebo in the garden's rainforest is a popular place for tucking into the cooked breakfast, and the mallets are always lined up and ready for a game of croquet on the lush lawn.

Bali Hai (☎ 07-4068 9291; cnr Banfield & Wongaling Beach Rds, Wongaling Beach; cabins $125, unpowered/ powered sites $10/23) Bright, self-contained cabins that sleep up to eight, right opposite Dunk Island.

Mission Beach Ecovillage (☎ 07-4068 7534; www .ecovillage.com.au; Clump Point Rd, Mission Beach; units $165-178; 🖳 🖳) Hours and hours of work go into maintaining the wonderful gardens at this hamlet of large, self-contained units. Some have ponds, and when it gets hot the host sometimes find guests plonked in them, though it's only a short walk down a private path to the beach or to the free-form pool. If you opt for a tropical breakfast (with home-grown bananas) it can be delivered to your door.

Cassawong Cottages (☎ 07-4068 7444; www.cas sawongcottages.com.au; 47 Reid Rd, Wongaling; d $185-220; 🖳 🖳) Families are welcome at these cottages hidden in a rainforest garden by the beach. Two self-contained spa suites are designed for couples, with balconies looking out over rainforest and access to their own secluded pool, while the other four cottages have two bedrooms, toys and teddies for loan, as well as kids' DVDs and access to a walk-in pool.

QUEENSLAND

TOP END

Coco Loco (☎ 07-4068 7637; www.cocolocomissionbeach .com; 73 Holt Rd; d $180; ✸) Bold colours and rendered walls with showers built in are only part of the immense appeal of this self-contained down-to-earth residence. There's a three-night minimum stay, enough time for watergazing from the terrace and plenty of strolls down the private path to Brooks Beach.

CAMPING

Mission Beach Caravan Park (Porter Promenade; unpowered/powered sites $15/19) Council-run, character-filled caravan park right next to the beach. Doesn't take advance bookings.

Beachcomber Coconut Caravan Village (☎ 1800 008 129, 07-4068 8129; big4bccv@bigpond.com.au; Kennedy Esplanade, South Mission Beach; unpowered/powered sites $30/34, d cabins $60-170; ✸ ✿) This tree-frog-laden caravan park (there's even a giant one perched on the golf buggy) has clean and bright (blue) beachfront cabins with awesome views of Dunk Island.

Eating

Flame Café & Takeaway (☎ 07-4068 7300; shop 1, Village Green, Mission Beach; meals $10; ☯ 9am-8pm Thu-Mon, to 3pm Tue) Funky Flame serves fish burgers with grated organic beetroot and carrot, lettuce and balsamic dressing, and the chips are deliciously beer-battered. If you're hungry and it's open, you've found a winner.

Mint (☎ 07-4068 8401; Le Tour Village, Wongaling Beach; breakfasts $6-15; ☯ breakfast & lunch Mon & Wed-Fri, breakfast Sat & Sun) There's mint on the tables, the chairs are bright green and this licensed, busy brekky place serves great food in a musically enhanced environment. Yum.

Scotty's Bar & Grill (☎ 07-4068 8676; 167 Reid Rd, Wongaling Beach; meals $10-15; ☯ lunch & dinner Tue-Sun) There are no surprises at this bar-grill; it's linked to Scotty's backpackers and offers up cheap backpacker meals of the lasagne and pasta type, as well as free wine (ask when!). There's a bit of a disco in the wee hours.

Blarneys (☎ 07-4068 8472; 10 Wongaling Beach Rd, Wongaling; mains $30-34; ☯ lunch Sun, dinner Tue-Sat) The place to go if you're craving steak 'n' prawns with herb butter.

Friends (☎ 07-4068 7803; Porter Promenade, Mission Beach; mains $30-36; ☯ dinner Tue-Sat) A popular place with meals that are chock-a-block with Asian influence.

Self-caterers can find supermarkets at Mission Beach and Wongaling bus station.

Getting There & Around

Greyhound Australia (☎ 1300 GREYHOUND, 1300 473 946; www.greyhound.com.au) charges $33 to Cairns (two hours), while **Premier Motor Service** (☎ 13 34 10; www.premierms.com.au) charges $17 for the same journey. Both buses stop at Wongaling Shopping Village in Wongaling Beach. It's $54 to Townsville with Greyhound Australia or $44 with Premier.

Trans North (☎ 07-4068 7400, 0419 745 875; www .transnorth.com; fares from $3; ☯ to 5.30pm Mon-Sat) runs local buses almost every hour (except from 12.30pm to 3.30pm) between Bingil Bay and South Mission Beach; the visitor centre has timetables. For a cab, call **Mission Beach Taxis** (☎ 0429 689 366).

DUNK ISLAND
pop 55

The bird- and insect-filled island paradise of Dunk Island is only 4.5km from Mission Beach, and while the island's resort is most mentioned, the camping option gives the island experience at a fraction of the cost. The island's **rainforest walks** are invigorating, and while some run the full island circuit (9.2km), taking the sometimes-difficult track slowly lets you check out secluded beaches. See the fanning Hinchinbrook Channel from Mt Kootaloo (271m, 5.6km).

Day-trippers can enjoy the island's beaches and access the Jetty Café, or the activity-hungry can purchase a **Resort Experience Pass** (adult/child $40/20), which gives access to the resort's standard-ish butterfly pool, paddle ski use and lunch at the resort cafe or Jetty Café (where a steak sandwich normally costs $17). There are also barbecues near the camping site.

Voyages Dunk Island (☎ 07-4068 8199, 1300 134 044; www.voyages.com.au; d $332-654; ✸ ▣ ✿) offers the choice of some underwhelming garden rooms or much better white-is-light split-level options that look directly onto palm-fringed Brammo Bay. Guests can access the superb cascade pool, while the butterfly pool is looked over by a fantastic long and loungy bar.

̄ The **QPWS camping ground** (☎ 07-4068 8199; www .epa.qld.gov.au; per person/family $5/20) has nine shady bush sites beside the jetty.

Getting There & Away

From Mission Beach try **Dunk Island Ferry** (☎ 07-4068 7289; Clump Point; same-day return adult/child $52/22) or get your feet wet with **Dunk Island Express**

WHEN LARRY SHOWED UP

It was a typical Sunday in Innisfail on 19 March 2006. Families frolicked at waterfalls, communities gathered at festivals and farmers irrigated their crops. But by the following Monday morning, Cyclone Larry, a Category 4 storm, had ripped the facades and roofs off buildings, battered neighbourhoods, stripped rainforests and flattened fields at its ferocious 290km/h pace.

Unbelievably, no one died due to the speedy cyclone preparedness alerts, and sheer good fortune. But the clean up was massive: estimates suggest 15 years' worth of green vegetation growth and 350,000 cubic metres of mangled steel, household glass and remnant infrastructure were disposed of. In Innisfail shire alone, 300 homes were uninhabitable after Cyclone Larry came knocking.

Cyclone Larry also devastated the wider area between Cardwell and Cairns. Wildlife habitat corridors were affected as the cyclone left some areas of rainforest extensively damaged and the canopy destroyed. Increased light on the forest floor allowed invasive flora to intrude, thus changing the biological make-up in key habitats. The Mamu Rainforest Canopy Walkway traces Larry's path through the rainforest 30km inland from Innisfail (see below).

The reality hit home with Australians elsewhere when bananas became scarce and prohibitively expensive: indeed 80% of Australia's banana crop was lost in what was the most damaging storm to hit the nation's shores in 30 years.

With climate change and the threat of more frequent cyclones in years to come, Far North Queensland's residents and leaders are under no illusions that living in paradise can come with a price. Today, there are few physical scars left, though travellers may still come across deserted buildings, and some trees still look like they've been stripped of leaves. The population since Larry has changed too; some of the builders who came to help with repairs liked it so much that they stayed.

Water Taxi (☎ 07-4068 8310; Banfield Pde, Wongaling; same-day return adult/child $30/19).

Hinterland Aviation Air Transfer (☎ 1300 134 044) has flights from Cairns to Dunk Island for $110 one way and **Mission Beach Dunk Island Connections** (☎ 07-4095 2709; www.missionbeachdunkconnections.com.au) gets you there by bus and ferry from Cairns (one way adult/child $70/35).

DunkJet Sports (☎ 07-4068 8432) runs jet-ski tours to and around Dunk from Mission Beach, and you can also get there with Coral Sea Kayaking (p429).

MISSION BEACH TO CAIRNS

Mountains, cane fields, cane-train tracks and forest run alongside the road from Mission Beach to Cairns. For variety, take the alternative 'Canecutter Way' route to Innisfail via the cute towns of Silkwood and Mena Creek – 42km of true sugar cane country.

Mena Creek's main claim to fame is the unusual **Paronella Park** (☎ 07-4065 3225; www.paronellapark.com.au; Japoonvale Rd; adult/child/student $30/15/28; ⏱ 9am-7.30pm), which features the ruins of a Spanish castle hand-built in the 1930s. Floods, fire and moist tropics have rendered these mossy remains almost medieval.

Entry includes free camping in the adjacent caravan park and a night tour at 6.20pm and/or 8.30pm.

Off the Rails Café (☎ 07-4064 2596; meals $15; ⏱ 9am-5pm Wed-Sun), opposite South Johnstone Mill, has Mexican-inspired decor, loads of art installations and $18 'pot luck platters'. For info on sugar processing, steam trains and the slave-labour heritage of the industry, try the **Australian Sugar Industry Museum** (☎ 07-4063 2656; Bruce Hwy; adult/child/family $10/5/25; ⏱ 9am-4pm Mon-Fri, to 1pm Sat, to 11am Sun) at Mourilyan, 6km south of Innisfail.

Innisfail
pop 8989

A wonderful main street meanders through this busy farming town to the wide Johnstone River. Art deco buildings abound, as cyclones damaged many buildings in the 1920s and 1930s, and the replacements were constructed in the style of that time, turning Innisfail into the art deco capital of Australia. You can get a self-guided art deco tour map from the **Visitor Information Centre** (☎ 07-4063 2655; Bruce Hwy, Mourilyan; ⏱ 9am-5pm Mon-Fri, 9.30am-12.30pm Sat & Sun).

QUEENSLAND

Johnstone River Crocodile Park (☎ 07-4061 6202; www.crocpark.com.au; Flying Fish Point Rd; adult/child $23/12; ⏰ 8.30am-4.30pm, feeding 11am & 3pm) is a commercial croc farm, and it's also the place where many 'rogue' crocs end up. The owner is passionate about crocs; she got into the industry because they 'won' her heart.

There are plenty of hostels, and recent crackdowns by health authorities should mean some have cleaned up their act.

You can't go past **Moondarra Motel** (☎ 07-4061 7077; 21 Ernest St; s/d $70/75; ✂ 🖳) for a friendly, bright and clean place to stay. **Codge Lodge** (☎ 07-4061 8055; 63 Rankin St; dm $25, s/tw $40/60; ✂ 🖳 🕹) is made up of three Queenslanders looking out over the river. Washing and internet are free, and, wait for it, there's a dance floor.

Oh gee, a Zen hideaway with a private courtyard, packed library, great hosts and water views from almost every angle. Add to this day beds and direct access to the beach and you know you're in heaven at **Flying Fish Point Beachfront B&B** (☎ 07-4061 8934; www.beachfrontbnb .com.au; 3 Alice St, Flying Fish Point; s/d $110/150; ✂ 🕹). Nearby, **Flying Fish Point Van Park** (☎ 07-4061 3131; www.ffpvanpark.com.au; 39 Elizabeth St; unpowered/powered sites $24/28, cabins from $85) is a fisherperson's dream, with shady sites and a photo board so you can see what fish have been biting.

Flying Fish Point Café (☎ 07-4061 2180; 9 Elizabeth St, Flying Fish Point; meals $10-30; ⏰ 7am-9pm) is a post office and source of fine foods including lemon-and-pepper croc with paw-paw salad. **Jagad's Epicurean Emporium** (☎ 07-4061 1480; 49 Edith St; meals $6-11; ⏰ 7am-5pm Mon-Fri, Sat to 1pm) is dedicated to local produce, and the menu in this cute cafe includes delicious organic prawn bagels and local crocodile ravioli.

Famishes Café (☎ 07-4061 3987; 64 Edith St) does bargain breakfasts, and you can't go past the local **Returned Services League** (☎ 07-4061 1601; 18-28 Fitzgerald Esplanade) for its filling $15 meals.

Greyhound Australia (☎ 1300 GREYHOUND, 1300 473 946; www.greyhound.com.au) calls into Innisfail on the Brisbane–Cairns route with six services daily stopping at King George St. **Premier Motor Service** (☎ 13 34 10; www.premierms .com.au) has one daily service to Innisfail on the same route.

Around Innisfail

From Innisfail the Palmerston Hwy winds west up to the magical Atherton Tablelands, passing through the rainfor-est of **Wooroonooran National Park**, which has creeks, waterfalls, scenic walking tracks and a self-registration **camping ground** (per person/family $5/20) at Henrietta Creek, just off the road.

Mamu Rainforest Canopy Walkway (☎ 07-4064 5294; www.epa.qld.gov.au/mamu; Palmerston Hwy; adult/child/family $20/10/50; ⏰ 9.30am-5.30pm, last entry 4.30pm) is a 2.5km treetop walk that was built following the path Cyclone Larry (see When Larry Showed Up, p431) took through Wooroonooran National Park. It takes around 45 minutes to walk around, and includes a 100-step tower 37m above ground.

Australia's ancient landscape may not boast Himalayan highs, but Queensland's highest peak, **Mt Bartle Frere** (1657m), is definitely a challenging climb. Sitting inside Wooroonooran National Park, it falls within the dramatic Bellenden Ker range, which skirts the Bruce Hwy between Innisfail and Cairns. Experienced walkers can embark on the **Mt Bartle Frere Summit Track** (15km, two days return), which leads from the **Josephine Falls** car park to the summit. There's also an alternative 10km (eight-hour) return walk to Broken Nose. It's best that you don't walk alone and always let someone know before you go. Pick up a trail guide from the nearest visitors centre or contact **QPWS** (☎ 13 13 04; www.epa.qld.gov.au, www.queenslandwalks .com.au). Self-registration **camping** (per person/family $5/20) is permitted along the trail.

GULF SAVANNAH

The world has a different tint out here in the Gulf Savannah; the green cloud-tipped mountains and sugar-cane fields surrounding Cairns give way to one-lane roads cutting through a bushy outback populated with kangaroos and skinny cattle. You know you're there when every one of your pores is filled with red dust.

The land is populated with resource-rich towns that have been through the cycles of boom and bust over and over again. Stop by at the rusting roadhouses and you'll meet folk with stories to tell, and not too many people to tell them to (mobile phone service is nonexistent in some places). The fishing is as good as it gets in the Gulf of Carpentaria, and the hundreds of rivers and gorges will impress croc-watchers.

QUEENSLAND

The area is defined by two seasons: the Wet (December to April) and the Dry (May to November), and sensible locals stock up their cupboards in October in preparation for the roads turning into rivers and lakes. Driving is the way to see this land, but only in the Dry. For more information visit www.savannahway.com.au or www.gulf-savannah.com.au.

Getting There & Around

AIR
Savannah Aviation (☎ 07-4729 9453, 1800 455 445; www.savannah-aviation.com) runs day trips around the area.

BUS
Transnorth (☎ 1300 GREYHOUND, 1300 473 946; www .transnorthbus.com) departs 46 Spence St in Cairns for Karumba at 6.30am, stopping all towns in between on Monday, Wednesday and Friday and arriving in Karumba at 6.15pm. It returns on Tuesday, Thursday and Saturday.

CAR & MOTORCYCLE
The main sealed access to the region is from Cairns, along the Savannah Way via Georgetown and Croydon and on to Normanton, a good 450km from Cairns. Alternatively, the Burke Developmental Rd (Matilda Hwy) reaches Normanton and Cloncurry via Chillagoe (see p435) via the Burke & Wills roadhouse, but only 378km is sealed and it's mostly single-lane traffic requiring good concentration.

Cattle frequently cross the road (much of this area is made up of unfenced cattle stations) and you need to drive carefully (avoiding dawn and sunset) to avoid adding to the road kill problem. Road trains can be up to 10 cars long and out here you'll need to pull over to the side of the road to let them pass. For road conditions call ☎ 1300 130 595 or go to the **RACQ** (www.racq .com.au) website and click 'trip planning' then 'road conditions'.

TRAIN
The *Gulflander* (☎ 1300 131 722, 07-4745 1319; www.gulflander.com.au) runs from Normanton to Croydon every Wednesday from February to December at 8.30am (adult/child $60/30), and often runs special charters from Normanton to the middle-of-nowhere Critters Camp on other days.

The *Savannahlander* (☎ 1800 793 848, 07-4053 6848; www.savannahlander.com.au) runs from Cairns to Forsayth between March and December, taking four days (departing Cairns on Monday at 6.30am) to do the return trip. There are overnight trips to Mt Surprise, Undara Volcanic National Park or Cobbold Gorge by arrangement. There's a 'pub crawl' option, too.

THE SAVANNAH WAY
Undara Volcanic National Park
There's something quite amazing about these giant lava tubes, all 160km or so of them, that run underground and were formed around 190,000 years ago following a three-month eruption of a single shield volcano. The massive lava flows drained towards the sea, following the routes of ancient river beds, and while the surface of the lava cooled and hardened, hot lava continued to race through the centre of the flows, eventually leaving enormous basalt tubes. These days, they're a rare cool spot in the region, and you can be guided through them with ecocertified **Undara Experience** (☎ 1800 990 992; www.undara.com.au; half day adult/child $80/40, full day $125/63) or **Bedrock Village Caravan Park & Tours** (☎ 07-4062 3193; www.bedrockvillage.com.au; Garnet St, Mt Surprise; half day adult/child $68/34, full day $115/57).

You can sleep at **Undara Experience** (☎ 1800 990 992, 07-4097 0136; www.undara.com.au; unpowered/powered sites $22/26, budget d $60, railway carriages s/d $110/170; ❄ ▣) and enjoy its resortlike atmosphere, by-the-campfire stories, roaming wildlife, huge range of accommodation styles and railway carriage dining, though you'll save money by bringing your own food and using the barbecues. There is a small shop on site. You can also stay at nearby family-run Bedrock Village Caravan Park & Tours (above) in Mt Surprise.

Undara to Croydon
The road from Undara to the 'jewel of a town' of **Mt Surprise** is sealed in the centre, and the town welcomes you with a sculpture of a black cockatoo and a scrap-metal miner. It's a small town, with a couple of pubs and a community that loves collecting. Yes, here you can find gem collections, snake collections and even a collection of miniature horses. The snake collection/museum/camping ground, aka **Planet Earth Adventures** (☎ 07-4062 3127; 1 Cox Lane; unpowered sites $7), has a

QUEENSLAND

bunch of working backpackers and a good cafe. If it's minihorses and rare finches you like, **Mt Surprise Tourist Van Park & Motel** (☎ 1800 447 982, 07-4062 3153; d $55-82, unpowered/powered sites $16/22; ✖ ➱) has them, along with a lovely palm-fringed, shady pool. There's also the family-run **Bedrock Village Caravan Park & Tours** (☎ 07-4062 3193; www.bedrockvillage.com.au; Garnet St, Mt Surprise; cabins from $70).

The **Explorers' Loop** takes you on a 150km loop through the old gold-mining towns of **Einasleigh** and **Forsayth**. Accommodation in Forsayth, the last stop of the *Savannahlander*, is mainly at the languid **Tourist Park** (☎ 07-4062 5324; unpowered/powered sites $13/15, s/d $55/65).

Travel 40km south of Forsayth (20km on a sealed road, and 20km on dirt) and you've hit the wonderful **Cobbold Village** (☎ 1800 669 922, 07-4062 5470; www.cobboldgorge.com.au; unpowered/powered sites $14/25, s/d cabins $70/98; ▯ ➱). There's a breezy restaurant with a coffee machine on site, and basic accommodation. Nearby is Cobbold Gorge, and the only way to see it is to take a **tour** (tour adult/child $65/33), which involves getting on a 4WD bus (fondly named 'ugly') that'll take on dry rivers, then hopping on an electric boat that takes on the narrow croc-filled (of the freshwater kind), spring-fed gorge.

Georgetown is the end point of the loop, and all of a sudden you're back on the Savannah Way. There's not much here, bar a resident monitor lizard, three petrol stations, a few caravan parks and a swimming pool with free entry. The flash **Terrestrial Centre** (☎ 07-4062 1485; www.etheridge.qld.gov .au; Low St; adult/child/concession $10/8/8; ⏱ 8.30am-4.30pm Mon-Fri Oct-Mar, 8am-5pm daily Apr-Sep) houses the fossil- and gem-full **Ted Elliot Mineral Collection**. There's also internet access ($6 per hour).

Croydon
pop 255

Croydon is a tiny town near the big, refreshing **Lake Belmore**, 4km out of town. There are also some outstanding historical buildings and great local characters. It has the oldest shop in Australia (which doubles as a museum featuring goodies such as 'rat baffles'), a **swimming pool** (admission free; ⏱ 8am-6pm Mon-Fri, 9am-5pm Sat & Sun), some Chinese ruins (from the 1880s gold rush) and a new **information centre** (☎ 07-4745 6125; Samwell St; ⏱ 8am-5pm Mon-Fri Nov-Mar) with internet access.

Sleeping on the verandah is no problem at the cheery **Club Hotel** (☎ 07-4745 6184; cnr Brown & Sircom Sts; dm/s/d/units $17/40/50/100; ✖ ➱), though it's more for the drunks. There's a choice of the corrugated-iron walled rooms upstairs (one apparently inhabited by a ghost), self-contained units or motel rooms. Meals ($15) are available.

Normanton
pop 1100

Once the port for the Croydon goldfields, Normanton is now home to a humungous replica crocodile, **Krys the Savannah King**, a salty that measured 8.63m when caught in the Norman River in 1957. This largely Indigenous-populated town also has a historic **train station** with a resident (well, for half the year) brolga pair. The highlight of the town's year is the **Normanton Rodeo and Gymkhana**, held in June, which 'drags them in from all over', according to one local resident. The town's **Information Centre** (☎ 07-4745 1065; cnr Caroline & Landsborough Sts; ⏱ 9am-1pm Mon, Wed, Fri & Sat, 10am-5pm Tue, noon-4pm Thu) is also the library. If it's closed, you can get information at the **Normanton Train Station** (☎ 07-4745 1391).

For a room to snooze in and an artesian spa to soak in, try the friendly **Normanton Tourist Park** (☎ 07-4745 1121; 14 Brown St; unpowered/powered sites $20/24, s/d $55/60; ✖ ➱). According to the signs inside, the **Purple Cow Pub** (☎ 07-4745 1324; cnr Landsborough & Brown Sts) is great if you're not into 'humbugging'. Deciphering the signs on the toilets ('mangoes', 'no mangoes') can take a few minutes.

The **Albion Hotel** (☎ 07-4745 1218; Haig St; s/d $75/80) has clean, cool rooms with fridges, and the **Gulfland Motel & Caravan Park** (☎ 07-4745 1290; 11 Landsborough St; unpowered/powered sites $16/20, r $80; ✖ ➱) is easy to spot on the outskirts of town with its Big Barra. For snacks, head to the **Normanton Bakery & Café** (☎ 07-4745 1031; 26 Brodie St).

Karumba
pop 518

Karumba is famous for its fishing. There's absolutely no stopping the thousands of fisher folk who motor here in their 4WDs to slurp up the sunsets during the fishing season. The Gulf's prawn and barramundi industry is centred here, and it's the only spot of beach on the Gulf that can be accessed by sealed road (79km of it from Normanton), however, the tidal plains fill up from December to February making access impossible: check conditions first. Grey nomads fill up the caravan parks and a nearby zinc mine has added to the accommodation crunch, so if you're here during school holidays book ahead. There are two sections to Karumba: half is on the Norman River and half, and where most people stay, is Karumba Point, 6km away on the beach.

The place to watch the sun sink into the Gulf is **Sunset Tavern** (☎ 07-4745 9183; The Esplanade, Karumba Point; mains $11-25; ☽ 10am-midnight) with, you guessed it, great seafood dishes. Take a seat at an outdoor table for the sweetest sunset experience.

Accommodation options include **Ash's Holiday Units** (☎ 07-4745 9132; cnr Ward & Palmer Sts, Karumba Point; s/d $80/85; ☒ ▦), where there's also an ATM, and **Karumba Point Sunset Caravan Park** (☎ 07-4745 9277; Palmer St, Karumba Point; unpowered/powered sites $25/29, cabins $81; ☒), which has a cafe-shop out the front that serves up barra and chips and has an ATM.

NORMANTON TO CLONCURRY

The 378km of road between Normanton and Cloncurry is sealed but mostly single file, and floodway signs give you an idea of what it's like during the Wet: wet. This flat dry-grass country slowly changes into small rises and forests of termite hills. Everyone stops at the **Burke & Wills Roadhouse** (☎ 07-4742 5909; unpowered/powered sites $14/18, s/d/tr $45/55/75; ☽ 5am-10pm Mon-Fri, 5.30am-midnight Sat & Sun; ☒) to down a cool drink among noisy apostle birds. The **Quamby Hotel** (☎ 07-4742 5952; r $25; ☒) is 135km from the Burke & Wills Roadhouse and it will serve up meals ($15) if you're famished and beg for them. See p392 for information about sleeping and eating options in Cloncurry.

NORMANTON TO NORTHERN TERRITORY

While driving the unsealed, isolated and dusty stretch from Normanton to the NT, keep in mind that mad, ill-equipped explorers such as the doomed Burke and Wills walked twice these distances in summer. You can visit eerie **Camp 119**, the northernmost camp of their wretched 1861 expedition. It's signposted 37km west of Normanton.

From August to November, **Burketown** becomes the home of intrepid cloud-surfers. In the wee hours of these months the roll-ing **'morning glory' clouds** come in, and light planes zoom up into the air as the sun rises in the hope of catching one, or at least getting some good shots of their attempts. Apart from cloud-happy adventurers, Burketown attracts travellers who have read Nevil Shute's *A Town Like Alice*, part of which is set here. Don't be surprised to see wallabies meandering down its fat streets, while at night it's cane toads and bats who rule the roost.

The 130-year-old **Burketown Pub** (☎ 07-4745 5104; Beames St; dm/s/d $10/50/60, units $80-140; ☒) does a roaring dinner trade in the palm-fringed beer garden out the back. Across the park, a caravan outside **Burketown Caravan Park** (☎ 07-4745 5118) serves $8 barra burgers.

The **Doomadgee Aboriginal Community** (☎ 07-4745 8188; ☽ 8am-5pm Mon-Fri, to noon Sat), 93km west of Burketown, has a retail area and the last petrol pump for 400km. Village access is at the discretion of the community council, though there's talk of accommodation opening up. Further along is **Hell's Gate**, though its famed roadhouse closed shop in 2007. It was the last outpost of police protection for settlers heading north to Katherine in pioneer times and the scene of many ambushes as Indigenous Australians tried to stop their lands being overrun.

BURKETOWN TO CAMOOWEAL

Gregory Downs is made up of little more than **Gregory Downs Hotel** (☎ 07-4748 5566; gregory downshotel@bigpond.com; unpowered sites $15, s $40-75, d $95; ☽ 10am-10pm; ☒), by the Gregory River. There's little to do here but watch the road trains zoom past, lifting red dust again and again and staining the grass red. May Day sees life in the river during the 43km Gregory River canoe race.

Boodjamulla (Lawn Hill) National Park

This is one of those out-of-the-way places where oasis dreams can come true. After hauling the 4WD over 100km of bull dust, it's a miracle to find **Adels Grove**. Traditionally the land of the Waanyi people, you can see why they made it their home for 30,000 years. It became cattle-grazing country in the early 1800s and Albert de Lestang set up an experimental botanical gardens here at Adels Grove, though little remains of it after the site was razed by fire in the '50s. Cattle still reign in the surrounding areas, and in 1984 it was gazetted as a national park.

There are two **rock-art sites** that you can visit near the camping ground; a 20-minute walk will get you to a 3000-year-old painting of a yellow rainbow, a 5000-year-old midden and 10,000-year-old circle engravings. Amazing stuff.

In the southern part of the park, around 50km from Lawn Hill Gorge, is the World Heritage–listed **Riversleigh Fossil Field**. Some of the fossils are up to 25 million years old and include everything from giant snakes to carnivorous kangaroos.

The croc-free gorge is a short drive from **Adels Grove** (☎ 07-4748 5502; www.adelsgrove .com.au; unpowered sites $24, f $30, tents $55-200, r with air-con $100; ⏰ 8am-6.30pm; ✗), which also has a laundry, petrol pump, battery-charging service ($3) and limited internet access for laptops. The tents have beds with linen and offer great outback living; those by the river are slightly more comfortable, but with both options you'll fall asleep under a sky full of stars and wake to birdsong. There are communal bathrooms, but swimming holes are nearby. Meals are also available (mains $10).

The **QPWS campsite** (☎ 13 13 04, 07-4748 5572; per person/family $5/20) is a hop-step-and-jump from the gorge, though book ahead. Canoes (per hour $20; mornings May to October and shoulder season) can be hired by the riverbank and the 6km, two-hour return trip from the lower to the upper gorge is wonderfully relaxing. Otherwise just chill out in the nearby blissful **cascades** dipping hole, or check out the rock art.

Kingfisher Camp (☎ 07-4745 8212; www.kingfisher resort.com.au; unpowered sites per person/family $8/22) is 142km north of Boodjamulla and has 30 grassed campsites looking over a five-mile-long waterhole and boats for hire (half day $50).

GETTING THERE & AWAY

The national park is 100km west of Gregory Downs and 2WD vehicles will find this route better than the one from Mt Isa, which involves five hours and 230km of unsealed road.

Savannah Guides (www.savannah-guides.com.au) can organise half-day tours of the Riversleigh Fossil Field, and **Outback Discovery** (☎ 1300 799 443) and **Wilderness Challenge** (☎ 07-4035 4488) offer long tours that include a stop at Boodjamulla National Park.

FAR NORTH QUEENSLAND

Far North Queensland is an intoxicating mix of rainforest, strings of islands, outback, farmland and, of course, the amazing but, thanks to global warming, slowly vanishing, 345,000 sq km Great Barrier Reef Marine Park. It's certainly tourist heaven; thousands trek up and down the coast and take up both sky and scuba diving opportunities, and Cairns holds its place securely as a tropical party haven, where a 10-buck backpacker meal is just the start of your night. Day-trippers love the easy access to islands and mountain villages, while further out, Cooktown doesn't pretend to be anything other than frontier.

CAIRNS
pop 122,700

Mangrove boardwalks and croc-infested rivers by the airport, busy retail areas bursting with Ken Done clothes and stuffed koalas, and a unique tropical air make Cairns a spread-out city of surprises. The beautifully designed and perfectly located lagoon on the Esplanade is an attempt to make up for the fact that waterfront Cairns doesn't actually have a beach, and when the sun comes out so do locals and backpackers, creating a bikini-clad mirage in the city centre. Cairns can be a boom or bust town, depending on who's flying whom in; Japanese and Korean tourists are well catered for, and everyone's offered a good ol' Aussie time in the nightclubs and hostels. It's a city where the casino doubles as a rainforest, and you can walk straight from the nightclub to the pier and catch one of the many morning boats that make the daily island or reef, diving or snorkelling pilgrimage.

Orientation

Cairns' CBD sits between the waterfront Esplanade and McLeod St, and Wharf and Aplin Sts. Reef Fleet terminal is the main departure point for reef trips and Cairns' train station is hidden inside the Cairns Central Shopping Centre on McLeod St. Local buses (Sunbus) leave from the Lake St Transit Centre, while Greyhound and other regional buses leave from the Reef Fleet terminal.

Information
BOOKSHOPS
Absells Chart & Map Centre (☎ 07-4041 2699; Main St Arcade, 85 Lake St) Local and international maps, books and travel guides.

Books on Shields (☎ 07-4051 1668; www.bookson shields.com; 62 Shields St; ⊙ 10am-6pm Mon, Tue & Sat, to 8pm Wed, Thu & Fri) Huge range of foreign books and travel guides.

Bookshelf (☎ 07-4051 8569; 95 Grafton St; ⊙ 9am-5pm Mon-Thu, 9.30am-5pm Fri, 9am-2pm Sat) Second-hand books. Proceeds go to a women's shelter.

Cairns Museum (☎ 07-4051 5582; cnr Lake & Shields Sts) Books on the region's history, as well as works by local authors.

Exchange Bookshop (☎ 07-4051 1443; www .exchangebookshop.com; 78 Grafton St) New and second-hand books.

EMERGENCY
Ambulance, Fire & Police (☎ 000; ⊙ 24hr)

Police Station (☎ 000, 07-4030 7000; Sheridan St)

INTERNET ACCESS
Internet access costs $2 to $5 per hour and is available at most hostels and hotels.

Call Station (☎ 07-4052 1572; 123 Abbott St; per hr $3; ⊙ 8.30am-11.30pm)

Global Gossip (☎ 07-4031 6411; www.globalgossip .com; 125 Abbott St; ⊙ 8.30am-11pm)

Inbox C@fe (☎ 07-4041 4677; 119 Abbott St)

MEDICAL SERVICES
Cairns Base Hospital (☎ 07-4050 6333; The Esplanade) Has a 24-hour emergency service.

Cairns City 24 Hour Medical Centre (☎ 07-4052 1119; cnr Florence & Grafton Sts)

Cairns Travel Clinic (☎ 07-4041 1699; ctlmed@ ctlmedical.com.au; 15 Lake St; ⊙ 8am-6pm Mon-Fri, 9am-noon Sat)

MONEY
Most of the major banks have branches with ATMs and foreign exchange.

Currency Services Australia (☎ 07-4041 0070; 14 Spence St)

Travelex (☎ 1800 637 642; 79 Abbott St)

POST
Australia Post (☎ 13 13 18; www.auspost.com; 13 Grafton St)

TOURIST INFORMATION
Plenty of places stick up 'i' signs and call themselves 'information centres', but they're basically tour-booking agencies. The following offer unbiased information:

QPWS (☎ 07-4046 6600; www.epa.qld.gov.au; 5b Sheridan St; ⊙ 8.30am-5pm Mon-Fri) National park information and permits.

Royal Automobile Club of Queensland (RACQ; ☎ 07-4033 6433; www.racq.com.au; Stockland Shopping Centre, 537 Mulgrave Rd, Earlville) Maps and information on road conditions up to Cape York. Also has a 24-hour road-report service (☎ 1300 130 595).

Tourism Tropical North Queensland (☎ 07-4051 3588; www.tropicalaustralia.com.au; 51 The Esplanade; ⊙ 8.30am-6.30pm) Accredited and displays the authentic yellow 'i'.

TRAVEL AGENCIES
Peterpan Adventure Travel (☎ 1800 632 632; www .peterpans.com; 1st fl, 90-92 Lake St) A lively upstairs agency with internet access (per hour $1).

Trailfinders (☎ 1300 651 900, 07-4041 1199; www .trailfinders.com.au; Hides Corner, Lake St)

Travstar.com (☎ 1300 554 636, 07-4041 3409; www .travstar.com) Online travel agency specialising in the region.

Sights
You can't beat the **Cairns Foreshore Promenade** for some chilled-out Cairns fun: its main feature is a 4800 sq m saltwater swimming lagoon, and boy, is it popular when the sun comes out. Equally at home under the sun or in the tropical downpours are those gym-bunnies who run, cycle or just walk the length of the Esplanade, southeast of which is the departure point for ferries (the

---

PERFECT ONE DAY, GONE THE NEXT?

There's no pussyfooting around when it comes to Greenpeace's assessment of the future of the Great Barrier Reef. As Greenpeace climate campaigner John Hepburn says: 'The next generation may never experience the majesty and beauty of the Great Barrier Reef, which is under threat from warmer seas and ocean acidification as a result of climate change. We are rapidly running out of time to act.'

With the Great Barrier Reef attracting two million visitors per year, and contributing $2 billion in tourism dollars, global warming is going to have a serious economic effect on the region. Unless action is taken, the 'see it while it's here' comments may ring true.

QUEENSLAND

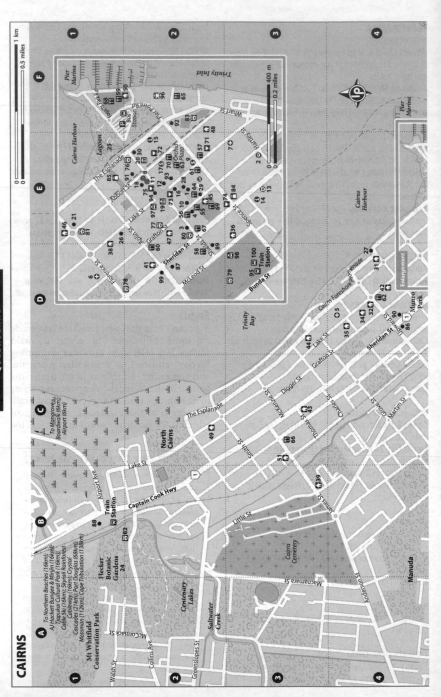

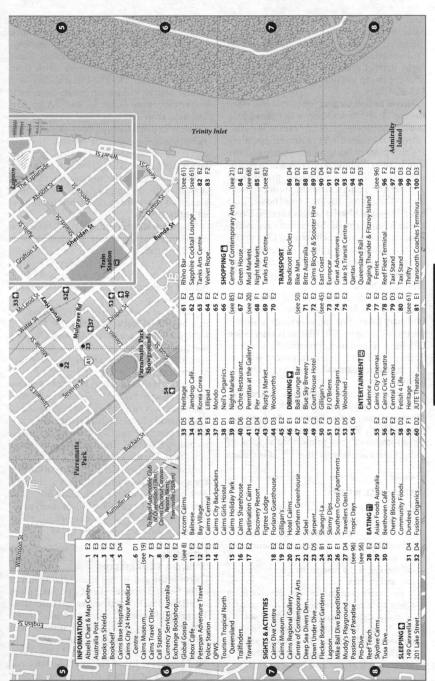

QUEENSLAND

INFORMATION
Absells Chart & Map Centre......**1**	E2
Australia Post.....................**2**	E3
Books on Shields....................**3**	E2
Bookshelf............................**4**	E2
Cairns Base Hospital................**5**	D4
Cairns City 24 Hour Medical	
Centre............................**6**	D1
Cairns Museum..................(see 19)	
Cairns Travel Clinic................**7**	E3
Call Station........................**8**	E2
Currency Services Australia..........**9**	E2
Exchange Bookshop..................**10**	E2
Global Gossip.....................(see 8)	
Inbox Café.........................**11**	E2
Peterpan Adventure Travel...........**12**	E2
Police Station.......................**13**	E3
QPWS.............................**14**	E2
Tourism Tropical North	
Queensland.......................**15**	E2
Trailfinders........................**16**	E2
Travelex..........................**17**	E2

SIGHTS & ACTIVITIES
Cairns Dive Centre..................**18**	E2
Cairns Museum.....................**19**	E2
Cairns Regional Gallery..............**20**	E2
Centre of Contemporary Arts.........**21**	E1
Deep Sea Divers Den................**22**	C5
Down Under Dive...................**23**	D5
Flecker Botanic Gardens.............**24**	B1
Lagoon...........................**25**	E1
Mike Ball Dive Expeditions...........**26**	E1
Muddy's Playground..............(see 96)	
Passions of Paradise.................**27**	D4
Pro-Dive........................(see 56)	
Reef Teach........................**28**	E2
Skydive Cairns.....................**29**	E2
Tusa Dive.........................**30**	E2

SLEEPING
149 Caravella's.....................**31**	F1
201 Lake Street....................**32**	D4
Accom Cairns......................**33**	D5
Balinese...........................**34**	D4
Bay Village........................**35**	D4
Cairns Central.....................**36**	E3
Cairns City Backpackers.............**37**	D5
Cairns Girls Hostel..................**38**	D1
Cairns Holiday Park.................**39**	B3
Cairns Sharehouse..................**40**	D6
Destination Cairns..................**41**	D2
Discovery Resort...................**42**	D4
Figtree Lodge......................**43**	C4
Floriana Guesthouse................**44**	D3
Gilligan's..........................**45**	E2
Hotel Cairns.......................**46**	E1
Northern Greenhouse...............**47**	E2
Sebel.............................**48**	F2
Serpent...........................**49**	C2
Shangri-La........................**50**	F2
Skinny Dips.......................**51**	C3
Southern Cross Apartments..........**52**	D5
Travellers Oasis....................**53**	D5
Tropic Days.......................**54**	C6

EATING
Asian Foods Australia...............**55**	E2
Beethoven Café....................**56**	E2
Cherry Blossom....................**57**	E2
Community Foods..................**58**	D2
Dundees.........................**59**	F1
Fusion Organics...................**60**	D2
Heritage..........................**61**	E2
Jamdrop Café......................**62**	D4
Korea Korea.......................**63**	D4
Lilipad............................**64**	E2
Mondo...........................**65**	F2
Neil's Organics.....................**66**	C3
Night Markets..................(see 85)	
Ochre Restaurant..................**67**	E3
Perrottas at the Gallery..........(see 20)	
Pier..............................**68**	F1
Rusty's Market.....................**69**	E2
Woolworths.......................**70**	E2
Rhino Bar.........................**61**	E2
Sapphire Cocktail Lounge........(see 61)	
Tanks Arts Centre................(see 61)	
Velvet Rope.......................**82**	B2
	83 F2

SHOPPING
Centre of Contemporary Arts.....(see 21)	
Green House.......................**84**	E3
Mud Markets.................(see 68)	
Night Markets.....................**85**	E1
Tanks Arts Centre...............(see 82)	

DRINKING
Ba8 Lounge Bar..................(see 50)	
Blue Sky Brewery..................**71**	E2
Court House Hotel.................**72**	D2
Gilligan's......................(see 45)	
PJ O'Briens.......................**73**	E2
Shenanigans......................**74**	E3
Woolshed.........................**75**	D5

ENTERTAINMENT
Cadence..........................**76**	E2
Cairns City Cinemas................**77**	E2
Cairns Civic Theatre................**78**	D2
Central Cinemas...................**79**	D3
Fetish 4 Life.......................**80**	D2
Heritage.......................(see 61)	
JUTE Theatre......................**81**	E1

TRANSPORT
Bandicoot Bicycles.................**86**	D4
Bike Man..........................**87**	D2
Britz Australia.....................**88**	B1
Cairns Bicycle & Scooter Hire........**89**	D2
East Coast.........................**90**	D4
Europcar..........................**91**	E2
Great Adventures..................**92**	F2
Lake St Transit Centre..............**93**	E2
Qantas...........................**94**	E2
Queensland Rail...................**95**	D3
Raging Thunder & Fitzroy Island	
Ferries.........................(see 96)	
Reef Fleet Terminal................**96**	F2
Taxi Stand........................**97**	D3
Taxi Stand........................**98**	D3
Thrifty............................**99**	D2
Transnorth Coaches Terminus.......**100**	D3

Trinity Inlet

Admiralty Island

Train Station

Parramatta Park Showgrounds

Parramatta Park

To Royal Automobile Club
of Queensland (3km);
Cairns Coconut Caravan
Resort (6km);
Townsville (350km)

Reef Fleet Terminal). The northern area is a particularly peaceful spot, with bird action (pelicans) and mangroves to watch over from the boardwalk. When evening descends, the night market takes over the central zone, offering cheap souvenirs, magic honey and $15 massages.

Flecker Botanic Gardens (☎ 07-4044 3398; Collins Ave, Edge Hill; ☑ 7.30am-5.30pm Mon-Fri, 8.30am-5.30pm Sat & Sun), northwest of the city centre, is dominated by the magnificent rainforest, but there are also plots of bush-tucker plants and the Gondwanan Evolutionary Trail, which begins with 415-million-year-old blue-green algae (Quaternary) and reaches its standing ovation in the Age of Angiosperms (now). Two hour-long **guided walks** (admission free; ☑ 10am & 1pm Tue & Thu) through the gardens are available, or pick up a brochure and take yourself on a self-guided walk. The licensed cafe serves not-to-be-outdone mango smoothies while the info centre has a stinging tree in captivity. Ouch.

Opposite the gardens the **Rainforest Boardwalk** leads to **Saltwater Creek** and **Centenary Lakes**. For more serious walkers, the trails throughout **Mt Whitfield Conservation Park** have several lookouts offering views of Cairns and Trinity Inlet, and there is a terrific **mangrove boardwalk** (Airport Ave) 200m before the airport.

Owned and run by Indigenous Australians, the terrific **Tjapukai Cultural Park** (☎ 07-4042 9999; www.tjapukai.com.au; Kamerunga Rd, Carevonica; adult/child/family $31/16/78, incl transfers $50/25/126; ☑ 9am-5pm) combines interesting aspects of Indigenous culture with showbiz. It includes

the creation theatre, which tells the story of creation using giant holograms and actors; there's also a dance theatre, and boomerang-and spear-throwing demonstrations (have a go!). The shop has authentic work from across the country. Shuttle-bus transfers leave Cairns hourly, picking up guests from their accommodation. Sunbus 1 and 1A go past Tjapukai as well.

Cairns Regional Gallery (☎ 07-4046 4800; www .cairnsregionalgallery.com.au; cnr Abbott & Shields Sts; adult $5; ☑ 10am-5pm Mon-Sat, 1-5pm Sun), in a gorgeous heritage building, is worth a wander. Exhibitions reflect the consciousness of the region, with an emphasis on Indigenous art. Head loft-wards to see work from local emerging artists.

The **Cairns Museum** (☎ 07-4051 5582; www.cairns museum.org.au; cnr Lake & Shields Sts; adult/child/family $5/2/12; ☑ 10am-4pm Mon-Sat) is an old-school museum housed in the former School of Arts building. If you have an interest in the history of dentistry and a love of aviation, you'll love this.

Take your knowledge of the reef to greater depths at **Reef Teach** (☎ 07-4031 7794; 85 Lake St; adult/child $15/8; ☑ 10am-9pm Mon-Sat, shows 6.30-8.30pm Mon-Sat). The lecturer explains how to identify specific types of coral and fish, and, more importantly, how to respect the reef.

The **Centre of Contemporary Arts** (☎ 07-4050 9494; www.kickarts.org.au; 96 Abbott St; admission free; ☑ 10am-5pm Tue-Sat) has two gallery levels showcasing Queensland's hottest visual artists and a gallery shop selling mostly locally made pieces, including bags made from fishing nets (ghost nets) found in the Torres Strait.

About 20km from Cairns, the **Crystal Cascades** are a series of beautiful waterfalls and pools. Avoid jumping off the rock cliffs here. The area is accessed by a 1.2km (30-minute) pathway that's suitable for wheelchairs.

For markets, see Shopping (p448).

Activities
DIVING & SNORKELLING

Cairns is the undisputed scuba-diving mecca of the Great Barrier Reef and a popular place to attain PADI open-water certification. There's a plethora of courses on offer, from budget four-day courses that combine pool training and reef dives (around $500), to four-day open-water courses ($595). Five-day courses ($540 to $715) include two days' pool theory and three days' living aboard

---

SEASONAL WORK

Cairns is one of the most popular places on the East Coast to pick up casual work in the tourism and hospitality sectors. Those bilingual in Japanese, Korean and German can pick up tour/translating work. And, of course, Cairns is a magnet for dive instructors and the like.

For those planning to stick around in Cairns for a month or more to work, dive or study, **Cairns Sharehouse** (☎ 07-4041 1875; 17 Scott St; www.cairns-sharehouse.com; s per week $100-150, tw & d per person per week $90-130; ❄ ♣) is a good option. Three weeks' rent is required up front.

CAIRNS REGION IN...

Two Days
Head way out to the iconic **Great Barrier Reef** (p442) for the day. Check out the wonderful marine life by snorkelling or diving, or stay dry in a glass-bottom boat.

Let Cairns get to know the partly exposed you at the **Cairns Foreshore Promenade's swimming lagoon** (p437). Grab a latte and read and overhear the latest gossip at **Perrottas** (p446) before pottering through the adjoining **Cairns Regional Gallery** (opposite). Drink up a view and a summery aperitif at hip bar **Ba8** (p447), before waltzing over to **Ochre Restaurant** (p446) to wrap your taste buds around some native flavours.

Four Days
On day three, head out early for a morning at the **Flecker Botanic Gardens** (opposite), where you can explore the Gondwanan Evolutionary Trail. Save the afternoon for a cultural experience at the **Tjapukai Cultural Park** (opposite). Learn about the local Indigenous people and witness some traditional dancing. Then, head back to your accommodation, freshen up and hit the **night markets** (p448) for some shopping and a massage. Brave the assortment of locals and travellers at the capacious outdoor bar at **Gilligan's** (p447). Grab a bar snack there, or go for something more substantial of the spicy Korean kind at **Korea Corea** (p446).

On day four leave the CBD and catch the **Scenic Railway** (p455) to Kuranda, walk into a flurry of winged beauties at the **Australian Butterfly Sanctuary** (p455) and get a bird's-eye rainforest view on the way back by returning on the **Skyrail** (p456). Alternatively, take an **eco-accredited tour** (p442) to the Atherton Tablelands or Cape Tribulation and the magical Daintree rainforest.

a boat, and are generally more rewarding. Before making a booking, find out whether prices include a medical check (around $55), daily reef tax ($5), passport photos (around $8), plus environmental management charges (around $10).

A selection of reputable schools:

Cairns Dive Centre (☎ 07-4051 0294; www.cairnsdive .com.au; 121 Abbott St; ⏰ 7am-5pm)

Deep Sea Divers Den (☎ 07-4046 7333; 319 Draper St; ⏰ 7am-6pm) Has seven-day/seven-night dives from $2300 where you can have 24 back-to-back dives.

Down Under Dive (☎ 1800 079 099, 07-4052 8300; www.downunderdive.com.au; 287 Draper St; ⏰ 7am-7pm) English and Japanese-speaking instructors.

Ocean Free (☎ 07-4050 0550; www.oceanfree.com.au) Certified dives from $55.

Pro-Dive (☎ 07-4031 5255; www.prodive-cairns.com .au; cnr Shields & Grafton St; ⏰ 8.30am-9pm) Japanese, German and English-speaking instructors.

Tusa Dive (☎ 07-4031 1028; www.tusadive.com; cnr Shields St & The Esplanade; ⏰ 7.30am-9pm)

More comprehensive reef trips last one to 11 days and cost roughly $200 to $3700. Live-aboard trips explore the outer and northern reefs, including Cod Hole, Homes Reef and Osprey Reef in the Coral Sea.

Operators specialising in trips for certified divers:

Mike Ball Dive Expeditions (☎ 07-4053 0500; www.mikeball.com; 143 Lake St; ⏰ 8am-5pm) Three-, four- and seven-night fly-dive trips and open-water dive courses ($385).

Passions of Paradise (☎ 1800 111 346, 07-4011 1600; www.passions.com.au; Reef Fleet Terminal; ⏰ 7am-5pm) Aimed at a fun crowd.

Reef Encounter (☎ 1800 815 811, 07-4051 5777; www.reeftrip.com) Live-aboard operator, plus open-water learn-to-dive courses (from $737) and trips from $220. Also regularly looking for 'hosties' in exchange for accommodation and diving.

ReefQuest (☎ 1800 612 223, 07-4046 7333; www.di versden.com.au) Live-aboard dive trips ($330 to $570) depart daily; learn-to-dive courses from $435; snorkelling trips $120 to $480. Japanese and German tuition available.

Rum Runner (☎ 07-4031 2920; www.rumrunner.com .au; ⏰ 9am-5pm) Two-day/one-night 'sleep on the reef' adventures.

Taka (☎ 07-4051 8722; www.takadive.com.au) Live-aboard trips to the Cod Hole, Osprey and coral and clam gardens ($900 to $1500). Underwater photography courses $200, and dive-hards can opt for a 24-dive package.

WHITE-WATER RAFTING
There's thrilling white-water rafting down the Barron, Tully, Russell and North Johnstone Rivers. For tours leaving Cairns, expect to pay about $180 for a full day to Tully, $123

QUEENSLAND

for a half day to the Barron River, $1400 for a four-day trip to North Johnstone and $155 for a full day trip to Russell. Check whether wetsuit hire (around $10) and national-park fees ($6) are included.

The major rafting companies in Cairns:

Foaming Fury (☎ 07-4031 3460; www.foamingfury .com.au)

Raging Thunder (☎ 07-4030 7990; www.ragingth under.com.au)

R'n'R (☎ 07-4051 4055; www.raft.com.au)

OTHER ACTIVITIES

AJ Hackett Bungee & Minjin (☎ 07-4057 7188; www.ajhackett.com.au; McGregor Rd, Smithfield; bungee $130, minjin swing per person $74; ☺ 10am-5pm) Give one of the 16 different jump styles a go, or swing from the trees on the minjin (a harness swing).

Cable Ski (☎ 07-4038 1304; www.cableski.com.au; Captain Cook Hwy; per hr $29; ☺ 10am-6pm Sun-Tue, Thu & Sat, to 9pm Wed & Fri) Cables pull you along to let you wakeboard, kneeboard or waterski.

Fishing Cairns (☎ 07-4041 1169; www.fishingcairns .com.au) Focuses on custom-made charters, and offers full-day estuary fishing for $155 and full-day river fishing for $170. Reef fishing (for fish including coral trout and red emperor) is from $200.

Hot Air Ballooning (☎ 1800 800 829, 07-4039 9900; www.hotair.com.au; 30min flight adult/child $190/99)

Skydive Cairns (☎ 1800 444 568, 07-4031 5499; www .skydivecairns.com.au; 82 Grafton St) Tandem jumps from 2700m $245.

Tandem Cairns (☎ 1800 805 432, 07-4015 2466; www .tandemcairns.com.au) Jumps start at 10,000ft for $244.

Cairns for Children

Muddy's playground (The Esplanade) is a great place to get saturated and it's suitable for all ages, with climbing nets, playgrounds and plenty of water-play areas. It's between Minnie and Upward Sts. Also on the Esplanade, the **Lagoon** (☺ 6am-10pm Oct-Mar, 7am-9pm Apr-Sep) is popular with kids and is patrolled all day. There are 'Tiny Tacker Tuesdays' every third Tuesday of the month at the Cairns Regional Gallery (p440) as well as theme-based workshops for children during the school holidays.

Tours

The qualified guides at **Cairns Discovery Tours** (☎ 07-4053 5259; www.cairnsdiscoverytours.com; adult/child $59/29; ☺ 12.45-6.30pm) take folk through some of the area's attractions including the Botanic Gardens, the Royal Flying Doctors Base and Palm Cove.

Down Under Tours (☎ 07-4035 5566, 1300 858 099; www.downundertours.com; day trips from $125) is one of the many tour companies that heads Kuranda-way from Cairns. Day trips feature the Kuranda Scenic Railway and Skyrail; add-ons include local attractions such as the Tjapukai Cultural Park and Cairns Tropical Zoo.

For an inland adventure, **Undara Experience** (☎ 1800 990 992, 07-4097 1900; www.undara.com.au; 2-day tour adult/child $475/238; ☺ daily Jun-Aug, Mon, Wed & Fri Sep-Mar) has coach trips to the awesome outback Undara Volcanic National Park (p433).

GREAT BARRIER REEF & ISLANDS

Reef tours usually include lunch, snorkelling gear (with dives an optional extra) and transfers. The cheapest tours start at around $80, but it's well worth spending more money for fewer passengers and a more secluded spot on the reef. An additional reef tax of $5 per person applies.

Different sections of the reef tend to be better suited for certain activities, whether it's snorkelling, or certified or introductory diving, so it pays to first determine just what it is you're after. Rates quoted here are mostly for snorkelling. See also The Great Barrier Reef, p410.

Falla (☎ 07-4041 2001; adult/child/family $89/59/240; dives from $50) The cheapest trip out. Sail to the sand spit of Upolo Cay in a classic 1950s Broome-built pearl lugger.

Ocean Spirit (☎ 1800 644 227, 07-4031 2920; adult/child incl tax and pick-up $189/95) A fast catamaran whips you out for a full day at Michaelmas Cay.

Passions of Paradise (☎ 1800 111 346, 07-4050 0676; www.passions.com.au; adult/child/family $139/89/379) Award-winning, backpacker-oriented trips to Breaking Patches and Michaelmas Cay. Takes a maximum of 80.

Reef Magic (☎ 1300 666 700, 07-4031 1588; www .reefmagiccruises.com; adult/child/family $175/90/440) Goes to Moore Reef, one of the best outer-reef sites with an observatory, fish feeding and stable platform suitable for those prone to seasickness. Look out for 'Wally', a huge fish. A snorkelling safari along a wall face is an extra $40. New boat. Recommended.

Reef Quest (☎ 1800 612 223, 07-4046 7333; www .diversden.com.au; adult/child/family from $120/85/355) One of the longstayers in the industry; has daily trips.

Seastar (☎ 07-4041 6218, 4033 0333; www.seast arcruises.com.au; adult/child $165/110, intro dives from $240) Heads to Michaelmas Cay and Hastings Reef.

A DIFFERENT KIND OF SOUVENIR

If you're looking to do more than simply soak up the sun on your travels then there are a number of ways you can leave your mark on the environment – in a good way. The **Tolga Bat Hospital** (www.tolgabathospital.org), located just outside Atherton near Cairns, is always looking for volunteers to help look after the hundreds of bats that it rescues, rehabilitates and releases every year. The winged critters are surprisingly cute and work might include feeding the 'bubs' or looking after orphaned flying foxes.

If bats aren't your thing, consider planting a tree as part of an ambitious conservation project by the **Australian Rainforest Foundation** (www.arf.net.au). Sixty bucks sees your very own tree planted along a 250km 'green corridor' between Cairns and Cardwell. This strip will become a protected wildlife area and will hopefully ensure that all rainforest wildlife, but in particular the endangered cassowary, will have a safe area in which to flourish.

Silverswift (☎ 07-4044 9944; www.quicksilver-cruises .com; adult/child $163/123, certified scuba dive incl gear from $210, 2 dives $235) A quick and new boat visits two sites close to the edge of the continental shelf where there's plenty of coloured coral. Recommended.

You can see the reef from a different view with **Down Under Helicopters** (☎ 07-4034 9000; www.dow nunderheli.com; from $282) on fly-cruise packages.

DAINTREE RIVER & CAPE TRIBULATION

Cape Tribulation is one of the most popular day-trip destinations from Cairns. Tour operators push the 'safari' angle, but the road is sealed (ie suitable for a conventional vehicle) until just before the Cape Tribulation Beach House.

Back Country Bliss Adventures (☎ 0420 101 757; www.backcountryblissadventures.com.au; Bloomfield Falls trip $199) Funky outfit with various 4WD tours plus mountain biking, bushwalking, sea-kayaking and river-drift snorkelling trips.

Billy Tea Bush Safaris (☎ 07-4032 0077; www.bil lytea.com.au; day trip adult/child $150/100; ☯ 7.10am-6.30pm) Heads into the Daintree for walks, a tropical barbecue lunch, creek-swimming and time in Cape Trib.

Cape Trib Connections (☎ 1800 838 757, 07-4041 7447; www.capetribconnections.com; day trip $119; ☯ 7.30am-6.30pm) Mossman Gorge, Cape Tribulation, Daintree and Port Douglas.

Down Under Tours (☎ 1300 858 099, 07-4035 5566; www.downundertours.com; day trips adult/child $161/81) Ecocertified tours taking in highlights of the Atherton Tablelands, Mossman Gorge, Clohesy River, Daintree River and Cape Tribulation.

ATHERTON TABLELANDS

Bandicoot Bicycle Tours (☎ 0418 967 201; www .bandicootbicycles.com; full day $109; ☯ 8am-5.30pm Mon-Fri) Bike tours to waterfalls and swimming holes.

Food Trail Tours (☎ 07-4041 1522; www.food trailtours.com.au; adult/child/family incl lunch $154/77/442; ☯ 8am-6pm Mon-Sat) Graze on macadamias, tropical-fruit wine, ice cream and coffee from around the region.

Northern Experience Eco Tours (☎ 07-4058 0268; www.northernexperience.com.au; adult/child from $99/82) Paronella Park plus Yungaburra's famous fig tree, Lake Barrine and the Babina Boulders. Lunch not included.

On the Wallaby (☎ 1800 123 311, 07-4095 2031; www.onthewallaby.com; day/overnight tours $95/165) Activity-based tours. Recommended.

Uncle Brian's Tours (☎ 07-4050 0615; www.uncle brian.com.au; adult/child $109/69; ☯ 8am-8pm Mon-Wed, Fri & Sat) Expect a singalong on your way home from this Atherton Tablelands/waterfalls tour.

Wooroonooran Safaris (☎ 1300 661 113, 07-4051 5512; www.wooroonooran-safaris.com.au; Mamu Rainforest Canopy Walkway & Wooroonooran Safari adult/child $169/85) Ecocertified tour to World Heritage–listed Wooroonooran National Park. Tours possible in seven languages. Maximum of 12 people.

COOKTOWN & CAPE YORK

Adventure North (☎ 07-4040 7500; www.adven turenorthaustralia.com; tours $209-469) One- to three-day tours to Cooktown incorporating the best Indigenous tours along the way. A range of accommodation available. One day drive-fly option.

Oz Tours (☎ 1800 079 006, 07-4055 9535; www .oztours.com.au) Purpose-built 4WDs travel to Cape York and the Gulf Savannah. Seven-day drive-fly trips from $1949, or you can return with the more expensive cargo ship option. Has advanced ecocertification.

Wilderness Challenge (☎ 07-4035 4488; www .wilderness-challenge.com.au; 3-day tours adult/child from $895/795; ☯ May-Nov) Another advanced eco-certification option with three-day rock-art, rainforest and Cooktown tours.

QUEENSLAND

GULF SAVANNAH

Oz Tours (☎ 1800 079 006, 07-4055 9535; www
.oztours.com.au; per person from $2250) Seven- to nine-
day tours taking in Undara, Georgetown, Burketown and
Boodjamulla (Lawn Hill) National Park.

Wilderness Challenge (☎ 07-4035 4488; www
.wilderness-challenge.com.au; 9-day tours adult/child from
$2895/2795; ☯ May-Oct)

Sleeping

Accommodation agencies have up-to-date
listings and can assist in locating suitable accommodation. **Destination Cairns** (☎ 1800 807 730,
07-4051 4055; www.accomcentre.com.au; cnr Sheridan & Aplin
Sts) has wheelchair access and information.
Accom Cairns (☎ 1800 079 031; www.accomcairns.com
.au; 127 Sheridan St) gives advice on midrange, top-
end and three- to six-month rental options.

Tariffs at many of the hostels include a free
dinner (in town or at the hostel's restaurant)
but keep your expectations low. The area
behind the Cairns Central Shopping Centre
between Terminus and Scott Sts is becoming
a burgeoning backpacker hub with a couple
of hostels and budget cafes. Sheridan St is
lined with $65 motels, which are often cheaper
than hostels.

BUDGET

Serpent (☎ 1800 737 736, 07-4040 7777; www.serpenthos
tel.com; 341 Lake St; dm $14-23, d & tw from $50; ☐ ☒)
Part of the Nomads chain, Serpent has a huge
pool, beach volleyball court, bar with meals
and a gathering of comfy day beds in the
breezy TV area. Rooms are brightly painted,
clean and have good mattresses. It's a fair way
out of town, at the end of the Esplanade, but
there's a frequent shuttle bus. The busy tour
desk has daily specials.

Cairns City Backpackers (☎ 1800 045 161, 07-4051
6160; www.cairnscitybackpackers.com; 274 Draper St; dm $17-
19, d $42-48; ☒) This is an earthy backpackers
where you just might find some peace and
quiet (10.30pm quiet time is strictly enforced).
Slate-floored rooms are clean, and the cheap
verandah rooms are cosy. Two kitchens and
a barbecue area make life easier.

Cairns Girls Hostel (☎ 1800 011 950, 07-4051 2016;
www.cairnsgirlshostel.com.au; 147 Lake St; dm/tw $20/48;
☒ ☐) If you don't mind being called a girl
for a few days by ever-present Dawn, you'll
fit in to this female-only hostel, though the
high ceilings don't alleviate the feeling that
it's a bit too crowded. It's tucked behind a
shopping strip.

149 Caravella's (☎ 07-4051 2431; www.caravella
.com.au; 149 The Esplanade; dm $22, d with/without bathroom
$75/60; ☐ ☒) Caravella's has clean rooms and
bathrooms and a massive kitchen to cook culinary delights. There are sprawling girls-only
dorms (no air-con) and some rooms peer onto
the Cairns foreshore, just metres away. The
booking desk does a roaring trade.

Gilligan's (☎ 07-4041 6566; www.gilligansback
packers.com.au; 57-89 Grafton St; dm $22-28, d & tw $120;
☒ ☐ ☒) This slick resort-style complex
has 500 beds, its own beauty salon, artificial
beach, tour desk and branded water. On the
down side, the 1000-capacity beer hall means
sleep might not be an option.

Tropic Days (☎ 1800 421 521, 07-4041 1521; www
.tropicdays.com.au; 28 Bunting St; unpowered sites $22,
dm $25, d $59-69; ☒ ☐ ☒) The soul sister to
Travellers Oasis, this is 10 minutes up the road
(thus further from the city centre), but similar
in vibe. Great tropical garden and the higher
priced rooms come with queen-sized beds
and TVs. There are 11 bus runs to town daily.
Monday night is $12 Aussie animal barbecue
night (croc, emu, roo and fish, though there's
a vegetarian option).

Cairns Central (☎ 07-4051 0772; cairns_central@
yhaqld.org; 20-26 McLeod St; dm $23-26, d & tw with/with-
out bathroom $72/58; ☒ ☒) This YHA has mod-
ern facilities, though some, such as the piped
music speaker system and slightly sterile
rooms lose points. Pool tables and the loggia
are good spots to hang out near the pool.

our pick **Travellers Oasis** (☎ 1800 621 353, 07-4052
1377; www.travoasis.com.au; 8 Scott St; dm/s/d $25/42/59;
☒ ☐ ☒) Expect fantastic staff, fresh-smelling
homely doubles (complete with bedside tables,
fridges and fans), and a small central pool area
surrounded by hammocks. The double rooms
are great value, the dorms have single beds
and it'll make you feel like you're in your own
timber Queenslander.

Northern Greenhouse (☎ 07-4047 7200; www.friend
lygroup.com.au; 117 Grafton St; dm $25-28, tw/f $95/120;
☒ ☐ ☒) Bright studio-style, self-contained
apartments are great value. Dorms have king
singles with great mattresses and there's a
commercial-style communal kitchen. The bar
opens at 6pm, and there's free breakfast and
airport pick-up. It's a good, lively spot for
backpackers, couples and families.

Floriana Guesthouse (☎ 07-4051 7886; maggie@
florianaguesthouse.com; 183 The Esplanade; s $69, d & tw $79-
120; ☒ ☐ ☒) Oozing charm, the charismatic
Floriana Guesthouse is caught in a 1960s time

warp but that's why we love it. The matriarch is piano-playing Maggie and she's a wealth of information about Cairns, as well as a native wildlife carer (her charges are often on site). The sweeping staircase is fit for a debutante, and lined with images of a glam Maggie and her family. It leads guests to bright, personalised rooms and self-contained flats; some have balconies with views out to sea. The communal kitchen area is within cooee of the pool.

MIDRANGE

Southern Cross Atrium Apartments (☎ 07-4031 4000; www.southerncrossapartments.com; 3-11 Water St; d $99-290; ✳ ✉) If you find yourself in one of these cool, modern self-contained apartments you'll thank yourself. Enjoy the designer kitchen in the studios, and direct access to the lap pool (one of three) from ground-floor apartments. Deluxe apartments have outdoor dining rooms, living areas and a swinging TV. It's very close to Cairns Central Shopping Centre. There's a three-night minimum stay.

Balinese (☎ 1800 023 331, 07-4051 9922; www.balinese.com.au; 215 Lake St; s, tw & d $100; ✳ ▢ ✉) It doesn't look Balinese from the outside, but some timber wall hangings do give it a slight Bali air. The basic rooms are clean, and there's a communal kitchen, laundry, minipool and internet access. Room rates include a basic breakfast and return airport transfers (7am to 7pm).

Discovery Resort (☎ 1800 672 753, 07-4044 9777; www.discoveryresort.com.au; 183-185 Lake St; d/tr $105/124; ✳ ▢ ✉) The folks here have done an excellent job refurbishing this hotel, and some rooms have extras such as wine glasses and tasteful pictures on the wall. Superior rooms look out onto saltwater pool number two. Its licensed restaurant, Rimini, serves breakfast and dinner.

Skinny Dips (☎ 07-4051 4644; www.skinnydips.com.au; 18-24 James St; s $140, d & tw $175; ✳ ▢ ✉) Gay-owned hotel catering specifically to gay travellers. The rooms have a luxury feel and come with toiletries, DVD players and sexy men on the walls (in photo form). The large pool takes centre stage, surrounded by rooms in the two-level complex. There's a smart pink bar and lounge for socialising. Rates include breakfast.

Bay Village (☎ 07-4051 4622; www.bayvillage.com.au; cnr Lake & Gatton Sts; r/apt $145/165; ✳ ▢ ✉) Owned by the same folks who own Balinese, this has more character and much more

space – the central atrium is particularly good-looking. Rooms are simple but with Balinese touches, and look out over the pool. Downstairs, the romantic Balinese-inspired Bay Leaf restaurant gets good reviews and serves breakfast, lunch and dinner. Superduper staff will organise free airport pickups and tours.

Figtree Lodge (☎ 07-4041 0000; www.figtreelodge.com.au; 253 Sheridan St; r $150, apt $125-210; ✳ ▢ ✉) Shaded walkways take you to smallwindowed, yet workable rooms, though inside has a slightly hospital-like atmosphere. The Irish restaurant downstairs and the pool area are worth a few hours.

Hotel Cairns (☎ 07-4051 6188; www.thehotelcairns.com; cnr Florence & Abbot Sts; r $165; ✉) The swish of the fan above your bed and the whispering palms outside your door will lull you to sleep, while fat showerheads will wake you up in the morning. Timber slat blinds over floor-to-ceiling windows add to the colonial look of this unique four-star hotel.

TOP END

201 Lake Street (☎ 1800 628 929, 07-4053 0100; www.201lakestreet.com.au; 201 Lake St; r/apt from $140/360; ✳ ✉) Lifted from the pages of a trendy magazine, this new apartment complex has a stellar pool and a whiff of exclusivity. Grecian white predominates and guests can choose from a smooth hotel room or contemporary apartments with an entertainment area, a plasma-screen TV and a balcony.

Sebel (☎ 07-4031 1300; www.mirvachotels.com.au; 17 Abbott St; r $230-330; ✳ ✉) This classic 1980s hotel still shines, with fab bathrooms, an on-site day spa and rooms with harbour or city views.

Shangri-La (☎ 07-4031 1411; www.shangri-la.com; Pierpoint Rd; d $235-362; ✳ ▢ ✉) Ever-so-slightly a bit too conference-oriented, this hotel nonetheless has outstanding rooms filled to the brim with luxury – from the carpet to the full-wall doors and high ceilings, it's quite extraordinary, especially if you're a lucky bunny and get an exclusive 'horizon lounge' room.

CAMPING

Cairns Holiday Park (☎ 1800 259 977, 07-4051 1467; www.cairnscamping.com.au; 12-30 Little St; unpowered sites $22-26, powered sites $28-34, cabins $50-85; ✳ ▢ ✉) More central than most, the cabins offer good value and, with a bunch of campervanners

QUEENSLAND

and camping folk offer good fun. Choose from shady sites or brand-new cabins with balconies, TVs and air-con that sleep three. There's a camp kitchen, free wireless internet and a TV room.

Cairns Coconut Caravan Resort (☎ 07-4054 6644; www.coconut.com.au; cnr Bruce Hwy & Anderson Rd; unpowered/powered sites $32/34, cabins from $60; 🖳 🖳) This is a serious spot 11km southwest of town.

Eating

Cairns is a hot-rock kind of eating town; it's extremely adaptable and willing to please international visitors' taste buds. However, in a most un-European fashion, dinner is usually served early, and most places have before-7pm specials.

RESTAURANTS

Locals have their favourites, which are actually in unexpected places such as food courts. Be brave.

Heritage (☎ 07-4031 8070; cnr Spence & Lake Sts; meals $10-15; 🕑 lunch & dinner) Ten-dollar meals that taste good? Yep, possible. The Heritage is part nightclub, part restaurant, but after your steak, wraps or Bud-battered barramundi and chips (that's Budweiser) on the fancy verandah, you might just be up for a boogie.

Perrottas at the Gallery (☎ 07-4046 4800; cnr Abbott & Shields Sts; mains $15-32) Situated in front of one of the cultural buildings of town (the Cairns Regional Gallery, p440) is fan-cooled Perrottas, where Nutella, buttermilk and trifle are not dirty words, they're breakfast. Locals check out the *Cairns Post* while sipping perfectly constructed coffee, and dinner's served until 10pm.

Pier (☎ 07-4031 4677; Pier Complex, Pier Point Rd; mains $18; 🕑 lunch & dinner) The Pier's fires burn brightly on the wooden deck that surrounds this waterfront bar-restaurant. The ice machine mesmerises as it moves ice along a perspex pipe above the bar, but if you can focus your eyes on the menu you'll find a smattering of snacks, finger foods, pizza and fish. There's a band every Sunday night from 8pm.

Mondo (☎ 07-4052 6781; Hilton Hotel, 34 The Esplanade; meals $20) The place to go if you're allergy prone, or fancy some casual waterfront dining under fairy lights. The menu is varied, from Mexican fajitas to *wagyu* burgers and Indo classics, and reasonably priced. Great for filling up when you've returned from a reef trip.

Dundees (☎ 07-4051 0399; Marlin Pde; mains $25-40) An unpretentious waterfront restaurant serving seafood chowder, smoked crocodile salad and steak cooked 'blue' (sealed both sides, room temperature in the middle). There's a delish seafood 'hot rock' option, which goes down well as you sizzle and enjoy the boat views.

Ochre Restaurant (☎ 07-4051 0100; 43 Shields St; mains $26-30; 🕑 lunch Mon-Fri, dinner daily) Red Ochre's certainly creative with its dishes: expect goodies such as emu and vermicelli spring rolls, Australian antipasto, crocodile wanton and salt-and-native-pepper crocodile and prawns. It sounds good and it is good. The Australian game platter is $48 per person, while a slice of amazing wattleseed pavlova or quandong pie with macadamia crumble costs $14. Not sure if it's Australian, but chocolate slut is also on the menu.

Cherry Blossom (☎ 07-4052 1050; cnr Spence & Lake Sts; mains $27-45; 🕑 lunch Wed-Fri, dinner Mon-Sat) Teppan-yaki reigns supreme at this upstairs Japanese restaurant reminiscent of an *Iron Chef* cook-off, with two chefs working at opposite ends of the restaurant floor. Among the authentic dishes you'll find 'Aussie animals', and they taste good.

CAFES & QUICK EATS

Jamdrop Café (☎ 07-4041 2900; 193 Lake St; breakfasts from $3; 🕑 7am-3pm Mon-Fri) An unassuming, busy joint serving bargain breakfasts and good coffee near Cairns Hospital.

Beethoven Café (☎ 07-4051 0292; 105 Grafton St; dishes $5-8; 🕑 breakfast daily, lunch Mon-Fri) Mango cheesecake anyone? Delish small cafe serving fantastic sweets, as well as healthier sandwiches such as savoury combos including *Buendnerfleisch* (air-dried beef, Swiss cheese and gherkin).

Fusion Organics (☎ 07-4051 1388; cnr Grafton & Aplin Sts; dishes $8-15; 🕑 breakfast & lunch Mon-Sat) You can't go wrong with Fusion's wholesome food and 'brain-boosting' juices, and while you're waiting, check out the travel photography that covers the walls. Bundles of allergy-free options for sensitive types.

Korea Corea (☎ 07-4031 6655; shop 32, Orchid Plaza, 79 Abbott St; mains $10; 🕑 11am-4pm & 6-9pm) Cheap, quick and tasty Korean food including spicy octopus in a stone pot, served with a smile. Locals get a discount.

Lillipad (☎ 07-4051 9565; 72 Grafton St; dishes $10-14; 🕑 7am-3pm) With massive plates carrying big feasts (pancakes, fry-ups and a huge selection of vegetarian options), there's good value to be had here, and don't miss an apple-and-mint juice ($5) to get you through the day.

The **night markets** (The Esplanade) are busy come dinner time, and self-service is all the rage.

SELF-CATERING

There's a **Woolworths** (Abbott St; ⏰ 8am-9pm Mon-Fri, 8am-5.30pm Sat, 9am-6pm Sun), plus two supermarkets in Cairns Central Shopping Centre. At **Rusty's Market** (Grafton St, btwn Shields & Spence Sts; ⏰ 5am-6pm Fri, 6am-3pm Sat, 6am-2pm Sun) multiethnic stall holders have tropical fruits piled high plus herbs, honey and pick-me-up samosas.

Niche self-catering options:

Asian Foods Australia (☎ 07-4052 1510; 101-105 Grafton St) Asian goods.

Community Foods (☎ 07-4041 5335; 74 Shields St; ⏰ 10am-6pm Mon-Fri, 9am-1pm Sat, 10am-2pm Sun) Lets you fill up your own containers with organic cereal and nut staples.

Neil's Organics (☎ 07-4051 5688; cnr James & McLeod Sts; ⏰ 9am-6pm Mon-Fri, to 3pm Sat & Sun) Organic fruit, veg and other produce.

Drinking

Drinking and getting yer kit off seem to be the rage at many of Cairns' pubs; dancing-on-the-bar comps are especially popular. The **Cairns Post** (www.cairns.com.au/entertainment) publishes *Time Out* with mainstream listings and reviews, while *Cairns Backpacker Express* will lead you in the cheap food/pole dancing comp direction.

our pick **Blue Sky Brewery** (☎ 07-4051 7290; 34-42 Lake St; meals $20; ⏰ 10am-midnight Sun-Thu, to 2am Fri & Sat) Here's a sparkling new drinking hall and brewery that caters for foodies *and* beer-lovers. A 'snow rail' keeps the average barflys' beer cool, and you can try all seven premises-made brews on a taster-tray for $16. Foodwise, the malt from the brewery goes to the tablelands cattle, which end up in the kitchen. True-blue beery beef.

Ba8 Lounge Bar (☎ 07-4052 7670; Shangri La Hotel, Pierpoint Rd; ⏰ 11am-midnight) It's all off-white couches, Indian head statues and a sparkling clean clientele here.

Gilligan's (☎ 07-4041 6566; 57-89 Grafton St; ⏰ noon-late) Here you'll find dancing podiums, hundreds of backpackers from the adjoining hostel (p444), massive TV screens and floors they'll never get the smell of beer off.

Woolshed (☎ 07-4031 6304; 24 Shields St; ⏰ to late) Once the $10 spag bol and free drink has gone down, the booths and balcony get very, very rowdy, especially on 'wet jock' comp night.

Shenannigans (☎ 07-4051 2490; 48 Spence St; ⏰ 10am-late) With a massive cool beer garden, Shags Bar is no doubt the starting point for much shenanigans. Loads of screens showing sports.

PJ O'Briens (☎ 07-4031 5333; 87 Lake St; ⏰ to late) Take a quiet snug or get rowdy on coyote-ugly night. Get your votes in for this Irish pub's weekly pole idol contest, too.

Court House Hotel (☎ 07-4031 4166; 38 Abbott St; ⏰ 10am-late) The scales of justice fly high in this heritage building (over the bright central bar, in fact), and there's an outdoor cinema. Don't miss Wednesday night's cane toad racing, and live bands on Sundays.

Entertainment

Cairns has plenty of clubs to keep you entertained into the wee hours, though because there is a high turnaround, best to ask locals what's good. Leave your flip-flops in your room. Most open around 10pm and close between 5am and 6am. Cover charges are from $5 to $10. **Fetish 4 Life** (☎ 07-4041 4161; 54 Shields St; ⏰ 9.30am-6pm daily Jan-Oct, closed Sun Nov & Dec), a funky clothes shop, sells tickets to raves plus party paraphernalia including fire sticks.

Sapphire Cocktail Lounge (☎ 07-4052 1494; cnr Lake & Aplin Sts; ⏰ 9am-late Mon-Sat, from 5pm Sun) Popular and gay-friendly; serves tapas, but gets into the cocktails as the night goes on.

Rhino Bar (☎ 07-4031 5305; cnr Lake & Spencer Sts; ⏰ 10pm-late) This is a cut-loose kinda place next to the Heritage, with less rowdy and more cheer.

Cadence (☎ 07-4051 2666; cnr The Esplanade & Shields St; ⏰ 10pm-late) Up a zillion steps the vibe is cool crossed with comfy leather lounges.

Heritage (☎ 07-4031 8070; cnr Spence & Lake St; ⏰ noon-late) Old-school fun, with indy music nights and pool on the verandah, blinds so you don't fall over, and a friendly crew.

Velvet Rope (☎ 07-4031 3383; downstairs, Cairns Casino, 28 Spence St; ⏰ 10pm-late) Velvet Rope has music as well as magician shows, so choose your night well.

You can catch a mainstream flick at **Cairns City Cinemas** (☎ 07-4031 1077; 108 Grafton St) or **Central Cinemas** (☎ 07-4052 1166; Cairns Central Shopping Centre). **End Credits Film Club** (www.endcredits.org.au) caters for art-house film buffs and shows films at the

QUEENSLAND

Botanic Gardens (p440) and **Cairns Civic Theatre** (☎ 07-4031 9933; cnr Sheridan & Florence Sts). Catch a play by a local playwright at **JUTE Theatre** (☎ 07-4050 9444; www.jute.com.au; 96 Abbott St) at the Centre of Contemporary Arts.

Tanks Arts Centre (☎ 07-4032 6600; www.tanksartscen tre.com; 46 Collins Ave, Edge Hill) hosts some of the country's finest musicians at these decommissioned tanks that also have performances and shows. Check out the program for the latest events.

Shopping

Two-dollar souvenir shops rule the Cairns roost, and there's also a sure supply of opals, Coogi, Ken Done and made-in-Korea didgeridoos and boomerangs. For an authentic termite-made didgeridoo and other Aboriginal items, your best bet is Tjapukai Cultural Park (p440).

Green House (☎ 07-4031 8787; 55 Spence St; ☼ 10am-6pm Mon-Fri, 9am-1pm Sat) An environmental shop selling candles, resin jewellery and change-your-life books, and providing information about Cairns Frog Hospital.

Centre of Contemporary Arts (☎ 07-4050 9496; 96 Abbott St; ☼ 10am-5pm Tue-Sat) It's all style at this shop, which is a great place to pick up the latest locally made designer stuff.

Tanks Arts Centre (☎ 07-4032 6600; 46 Collins Ave, Edge Hill; ☼ Apr-Nov) Hosts markets on the last Sunday of the month where you'll find everything from Samoan baskets to woodworkers, protest petitions and crystal key rings.

Head to the **night markets** (The Esplanade; ☼ 4.30-11pm) and **mud markets** (Pier Marketplace; ☼ Sat morning) for the mandatory 'Cairns Australia' T-shirt, or if you need a $15 massage or your name on a grain of rice.

Getting There & Away

AIR

Qantas (☎ 13 13 13, 07-4050 4000; www.qantas.com.au; cnr Lake & Shields Sts), **Virgin Blue** (☎ 13 67 89; www .virginblue.com.au) and **Jetstar** (☎ 13 15 38; www.jetstar .com.au) all service Cairns, with flights to/from Brisbane, Sydney, Melbourne, Darwin (including via Alice Springs) and Townsville.

Hinterland Aviation flies to Lizard Island and Dunk Island; book via **Voyages Hotels & Resorts** (☎ 1300 134 044, 02-8296 8010).

BUS

John's Kuranda Bus (☎ 0418 772 953; tickets $4) runs between Cairns and Kuranda at least twice per day, and up to five times Wednesday

to Friday. Buses depart from Cairns' Lake St Transit Centre. **Kuranda Shuttle** (☎ 07-4061 7944; tickets $4) departs Lake St Transit Centre roughly every two hours from 10am to 3pm, and Kuranda (Therwine St) at 10am, 12.15pm, 2pm and 3.45pm (the latter service does not operate on Saturday). **Transnorth** (☎ 07-4061 7944; www.transnorthbus.com; tickets $4) departs Spence St, Cairns for Kuranda at 6.45am, 8.30am, 11.30am, 1.30pm and 3pm daily. Transnorth also has departures from Cairns to the Atherton Tablelands including Mareeba, Atherton, Herberton and Ravenshoe (and Chillagoe with a separate connection). Check its website for weekday and weekend services and prices.

Long-distance buses arrive and depart at Reef Fleet Terminal.

Greyhound Australia (☎ 1300 GREYHOUND, 1300 473 946; www.greyhound.com.au; Reef Fleet Terminal) connects Cairns with Brisbane ($253, 30 hours), Rockhampton ($175, 18 hours), Airlie Beach ($113, 11 hours) and Townsville ($66, five hours).

Premier Motor Service (☎ 13 34 10; www.premierms .com.au) has buses to/from Innisfail ($17, 1½ hours), Mission Beach ($17, two hours), Tully ($24, 2½ hours), Ingham ($32, four hours) and Townsville ($53, 5½ hours).

Sun Palm Express (☎ 07-4087 2900; www.sunpalm transport.com) connects Cairns with Port Douglas ($35, 1½ hours, six daily services), Mossman ($45, 1¾ hours) and Cape Tribulation ($75, 3¼ hours, departs Cairns 7am and 1.15pm daily).

Coral Reef Coaches (☎ 07-4098 2800; www.coralreef coaches.com.au) has four services daily to Palm Cove ($20), Port Douglas ($32) and Mossman ($35, two hours).

Foaming Fury (☎ 1800 801 540, 07-4031 3460; www .foamingfury.com.au; one way $20) operates one Port Douglas shuttle daily.

Country Road Coach Lines (☎ 07-4045 2794; www .countryroadcoachlines.com.au; adult/child $72/36) runs a Cairns-to-Cooktown inland service on Wednesday, Friday and Sunday (departing at 7am, arriving at 12.15pm). A coastal service operates on Monday, Wednesday and Friday (departing at 7am, arriving at 2pm). Courtesy pick-ups are available.

CAR & MOTORCYCLE

Hiring a car or motorcycle is the best way to travel around Far North Queensland. Most companies restrict the driving of conventional vehicles to sealed roads; if you want to travel to Cooktown via the Bloomfield Track (the coastal route), hire a 4WD and check conditions.

There's a mind-numbing number of rental companies in Cairns:

Britz Australia (☎ 07-4032 2611; www.britz.com.au; 411 Sheridan St) Hires out campervans.

East Coast (☎ 1800 028 881, 07-4031 6055; www .eastcoastcarrentals.com.au; 146 Sheridan St)

Europcar (☎ 07-4051 4600; www.europcar.com.au; 9/40 Abbott St) Also has an airport desk.

Thrifty (☎ 1300 367 277; www.thrifty.com.au; cnr Sheridan & Aplin Sts)

TRAIN

The **Queensland Rail** (☎ 1800 872 467, 07-4036 9250; www.traveltrain.com.au; Cairns Central Shopping Centre, Bunda St; ☺ 9am-4.30pm Mon, 8am-4.30pm Tue-Fri, 10am Sat & Sun) *Tilt Train* runs between Cairns and Brisbane ($311, 24 hours), as does the *Sunlander* (economy seat/sleeper $212/271, 31 hours).

See p455 for information on travelling to Kuranda by train.

Getting Around
TO/FROM THE AIRPORT

The airport is about 7km from central Cairns. **Sun Palm** (☎ 07-4087 2900; www.sunpalmtransport.com; adult/child $10/5) has airport services from Cairns city to the airport from 4am to 7pm. Airport transfers can also be booked to Cairns' northern beaches ($18), Palm Cove ($18), Port Douglas ($35), Mossman ($45) and Cape Tribulation ($75, two services daily). A taxi will set you back about $15.

BICYCLE

You can hire bicycles from the following:

Bandicoot Bicycles (☎ 07-4041 0155; www.bandi cootbicycles.com; 153 Sheridan St; per day $18)

Bike Man (☎ 07-4041 5566; www.bikeman.com.au; 99 Sheridan St; per month $60)

Cairns Bicycle & Scooter Hire (☎ 07-4031 3444, 0437 115 964; 47 Shields St; per day/week $15/60) Bikes and scooters.

BUS

Sunbus (☎ 07-4057 7411; www.sunbus.com.au) runs regular services in and around Cairns, which leave from the Lake St Transit Centre, where schedules for most routes are posted. Buses run from early morning to late evening. Useful destinations include: Edge Hill (buses 6, 6a and

7), Flecker Botanic Gardens (bus 7), Machans Beach (bus 7), Holloways Beach (buses 1c, 1d and 1h), Yorkeys Knob (buses 1c, 1d and 1h), Trinity Beach (buses 2 and 2a), Clifton Beach (buses 1 and 2a) and Palm Cove (buses 1 and 2a). All are served by the (almost) 24-hour night service (N) on Friday and Saturday.

TAXI

Black & White Taxis (☎ 07-4048 8333, 13 10 08) has ranks throughout the city, including at Abbott St and Cairns Central Shopping Centre.

ISLANDS OFF CAIRNS

Cairns day trippers can easily head out to Green Island, as well as Fitzroy Island and Frankland Islands National Park for a bit of sunning, snorkelling and indulging.

Green Island

Once the site for a significant sea cucumber smoking industry, Green Island has a longer history of significance to the Gurabana Gunggandji Aboriginal people as a sacred site.

The island itself is a small, flat coral cay with boardwalks through rainforest, a luxury resort with facilities for day visitors (you can jump into its tired-looking pool, relax on its sunbeds and buy food and souvenirs from its shops) and some easily accessible coral to snorkel around. It's not all relaxing: parasailing, helicopter tours and underwater scootering (see coral without getting your hair wet) are all the rage. The local birds are keen on human food, so dining in the bird-proof cage (a bit like a reverse zoo) is recommended.

Marineland Melanesia (☎ 07-4051 4032; www .marinelandgreenisland.com; adult/child $15/7) is a tropical-themed aquarium with fish, turtles, stingrays and a skull collection (crocs and humpback whales). Crocodiles are hungry at 10.30am and 1.45pm daily. There's also a collection of Melanesian artefacts. Your ticket entitles you to re-entry throughout the day.

The luxurious **Green Island Resort** (☎ 07-4031 3300; www.greenislandresort.com.au; r $495-595; ☒ ☒) is a polished-floorboards kind of place with recently refurbished split-level rooms complete with king beds. The choice is reef suite or island suite and both are timber-infused and quite private.

Great Adventures (☎ 07-4051 0455; www.great adventures.com.au; 1 Spence St, Cairns) has regular catamaran services to Green Island ($69), departing Cairns at 8.30am, 10.30am and 1pm

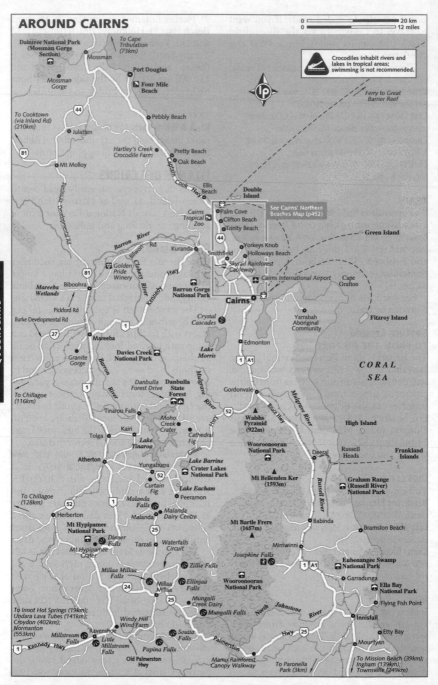

AROUND CAIRNS

0————————20 km
0————————12 miles

Crocodiles inhabit rivers and lakes in tropical areas; swimming is not recommended.

QUEENSLAND

and returning at noon, 2.30pm and 4.30pm. **Big Cat** (☎ 07-4051 0444; www.bigcat-cruises.com.au; adult/child $69/39) runs half- and full-day tours, which depart Cairns at 9am, 11am and 1pm. Prices include the use of either snorkelling gear or a spin in a glass-bottom boat. **Ocean Free** (☎ 07-4050 0550; www.oceanfree.com.au; adult/child/family schooner trips $129/85/379) sends a boutique 16.5m schooner off to Green Island and Pinnacle Reef.

Fitzroy Island National Park

Here rainforest paths meander past sleeping lizards and skinks, and beachside granite boulders older than the dinosaurs sink into the water at Nudey Beach. You'll be lucky to find a scrap of coral-free sand on the two main beaches, but the fringing coral around the island is worth donning the snorkel to see, and you don't have to do much to attract the attention of turtles. In winter (June to August) whales are spotted from the lighthouse. There's a new **resort** (☎ 07-4051 9588; www.fitzroyisland.com.au) opening on the island, but check availability before making plans. The most popular snorkelling spot is around the rocks at the nude **Nudey Beach** (1.2km from these facilities), which also has shady spots.

Walks vary in difficulty from the leisurely 20-minute **Secret Garden Walk**, with major skinks basking on rocks, to the steep two-hour climb along the **Lighthouse & Summit Trail** to the other side of the island from the resort.

At the time of research, **Raging Thunder & Fitzroy Island Ferries** (☎ 07-4030 7907; www.ragingthunder.com.au; Reef Fleet terminal, Cairns; adult/child/family return ferry $68/37/163, full-day trip adult/child $93/52) was running day trips leaving Cairns daily departing 8.30am and returning at 5.15pm, with BYO food and drinks. It is expected that when the resort opens there will be more services. Half-day trips operate on the *Thunderbolt*, which, at 80km per hour, has height and health restrictions for passengers. Transfers from Cairns and the Northern Beaches can be arranged for an additional fee, as can a half-day snorkelling tour.

Frankland Islands National Park

For a resort-free island experience try this group of five islands surrounded by little but coral and vibrant marine life. There's a camping option on **Russell Island**, but you'll need to be fully self-sufficient and have organised permits through **QPWS** (☎ 13 13 04; www.epa.qld.gov.au; per person/family $5/20) before arriving. **Frankland Island** has some good snorkelling close to a wide, sun-baked beach.

Frankland Islands Cruise & Dive (☎ 07-4031 6300; www.franklandislands.com.au; adult/child cruise & lunch only $135/95, full-day tour $165/105) runs excellent day tours, and throws in a seafood buffet, stinger/sun suits, snorkelling equipment and sun shades for families. The trip begins with a bus trip to Deeral, where you transfer to your boat on the Mulgrave River. The boat can also drop permit-holding campers off at Russell Island (adult/child $225/125).

CAIRNS' NORTHERN BEACHES
pop 12,086

Since Cairns doesn't have a beach, locals and tourists head either offshore to the islands or travel slightly north in search of golden sands. Most turn-offs from the Captain Cook Hwy lead to small communities taking advantage of an easy, relaxed seaside lifestyle. There's development along these shores, too, especially in Palm Cove, and they all have stinger nets up and running in stinger season (November to May/June). The following are listed in order from Cairns, and Sunbus (p449) travels to them all throughout the week.

Holloways Beach

The two-storey height limit on the houses fronting the beach means homeowners mightn't get the best view of the kitesurfers, but grab a bite to eat and take up your place on the narrow strip of grass between the road and the sand to watch some full-on adventure-sport action.

Strait on the Beach (☎ 07-4055 9616; 100 Oleandar St; meals $6-20; ⏲ 7.30am-6pm) is a takeaway shop and cafe on the cusp of the beach serving dhal dishes and slightly more traditional beachside meals. Eat driftwood style outside while you write 'wish you were here' on one of its 50c postcards.

Yorkeys Knob

Yorkeys is another seaside town drawing kitesurfers to its 3km stretch of beach, and yachts to its marina at Halfmoon Bay. Yacht-watch and island-gaze from the comfort of Yorkeys Knob Boating Club then tuck into masses of salt-and-pepper squid at **Driftways Restaurant** (☎ 07-4055 7711; 25-29 Buckley St; meals $15-30; ⏲ lunch & dinner). If you're driving, take a spin to the top of the knob, where the views are spectacular.

QUEENSLAND

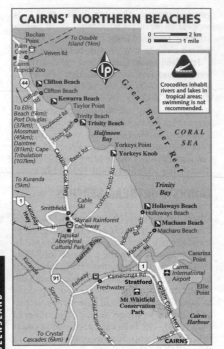

CAIRNS' NORTHERN BEACHES

The vintage villas at **Villa Marine** (☎ 07-4055 7158; www.villamarine.com.au; 8 Rutherford St; r from $89; ✿ ✧) are themed (Aboriginal, rainforest) but it's vintage kitsch at its best. You're likely to see roos and birds hanging around the grassy area around the pool, but the best bit is the owner, Peter, who organises tours at a discount and really knows his stuff. There are regular bus services (adult $3.30) into Cairns.

York Beachfront Holiday Apartments (☎ 07-4055 8733; www.yorkapartments.com.au; 61-63 Sims Esplanade; r $120; ✿ ✧) is a midsized complex with good self-contained apartments. Sliding doors open on to private balconies with sea views.

Trinity Beach

Palm trees hanging over a pleasant stretch of beach make Trinity Beach one of the faves in this coastal stretch. It's lower-key than Palm Cove but still has a growing sense of glitz and glamour about it.

Set on a bushy block, **Trinity Hideaway B&B** (☎ 07-4057 8972; www.trinityhideawaybnb.com.au; 56 Jamieson St; r with/without breakfast $100/80) is a modern, slightly suburban set-up. The owner will take you wallaby-watching if you ask.

Trinity Beach Club (☎ 07-4055 6776; www.trinity beachclub.com.au; 19-23 Trinity Beach Rd; r $130; ✿ ✧) has friendly owners and clean, self-contained rooms with balconies or courtyards and pool views. The outdoor hot tub fits 10.

It may resemble a shopping centre facade, but **Roydon** (☎ 07-4057 6512; www.roydon.com.au; 83-87 Vasey Esplanade; r $145-345; ✿ ✧) has huge two-bedroom, two-bathroom apartments, each with a serious balcony and living area, right on the beach. The neighbouring **Beachfront Apartments** (☎ 07-4057 6048; www.trinitybeachfront .com.au) have the same owners and bargain $99 standby doubles.

Menu items such as 'Bingo Bango Bonza Blue Moon Breakfast Beauty Bucko' may confuse, but rest assured, **Blue Moon Grill** (☎ 07-4057 8957; shop 6, 22-24 Trinity Beach Rd; mains $13-30) is a locals' favourite and, come afternoon, offers up a huge selection of beers.

The new **Trinity Beach Tavern** (☎ 07-4057 2900; Vasey Esplanade; mains $20-30), perched high over the road and with terrific views, serves up platters ($25) and favourites such as crumbed oysters ($8) from its all-day menu.

Clifton Beach

It's a town that's a-growing, but close to the beach it's retained its seaside appeal.

Nudging a tropical green environment park is the self-contained-unit-style accommodation at **Clifton Palms** (☎ 07-4055 3839; www .cliftonpalms.com.au; 35 Upolu Esplanade; cabins/r/units from $69/90/168; ✿ ✧). They range from one to three bedrooms, and the decor is straight out of the 1980s.

ourpick Clifton Beach Retreat (☎ 07-4059 0452, 0407 168 116; www.cliftonbeachretreat .com.au; 35 Batt St; s/d $90/95; ✧) is a fantastic purpose-built B&B with two rooms (blue- and green-themed) and private balconies facing the inviting saltwater pool. Hear the frogs calling from the neighbouring melaleuca swamp. Minimum two-night stay.

The **Argosy** (☎ 07-4055 3333; www.argosycairns.com; apt from $165; ✿ ✧) has friendly roos visiting in the morning, red-stemmed lipstick palms in the garden and the spacious water-view rooms are decked out with cane furniture.

Clifton Capers Bar & Grill (☎ 07-4059 2311; 14 Clifton Rd; mains $25; ☽ lunch Mon-Fri, dinner Mon-Sat) serves up $20 pizzas and dabbles in an international menu including Wiener schnitzel. Self-caterers can frequent the supermarket at **Clifton Village Shopping Centre** (Captain Cook Hwy).

Palm Cove

Palm Cove is a beachfront town lined with a precious pod of chunky old melaleuca trees and looks out on the tiny Double and Haycock (aka scout's hat) islands. Some of the north's top resorts make their home in Palm Cove, and there are weddings galore under the palms next to the idyllic beach. Buses from Cairns frequently negotiate the tiled 'main road' (Williams Esplanade).

At the **Village Shopping Centre** (113 Williams Esplanade) there's a post office, newsagent, moneychanger and internet access. The **Information Station** (☎ 07-4059 8700; holiday@coralhorizons.com.au; 137 Williams Esplanade) helps out with accommodation and car bookings.

Apart from beach strolls, swimming and **jet-ski trips** (☎ 07-4059 0462) to the islands, there's always a visit to **Cairns Tropical Zoo** (☎ 07-4055 3669; www.cairnstropicalzoo.com; Captain Cook Hwy; day adult/child $31/16, night adult/child $91/46; ⏱ 8.30am-10pm). It has crocodile shows (11.30am and 3pm), koala, wombat and crocodile photo sessions, and the night sessions (from 7pm to 10pm) include an all-you-can-eat dinner.

SLEEPING

Five-star resorts rule the roost here, though there are still a few bargains.

Palm Cove Accommodation (☎ 07-4055 3797, 0416 768 786; 19 Veivers Rd; d $70) If you're lucky you can claim one of these three chilled-out rooms for yourself, though being such a bargain they're often full.

Silvester Palms (☎ 07-4055 3831; www.silvesterpalms.com; 32 Veivers Rd; d $80-170; ✴ ◨) Old-school units in a double-storey block overlook the central pool. The whole shebang is covered with colourful Aussie-animal murals.

Ferntree B&B (☎ 07-4059 1603; 61-63 Cedar Rd; r $85; ⏱ Jul-Nov) Run by amiable New Zealanders who come to Palm Cove annually. You get the spotless tiled rooms, kitchen and lounge to yourself and all the ingredients to whip up breakfast.

Mango Lagoon (☎ 07-4055 3400; 81-85 Cedar Rd; d $100-150; ✴ ◨) Smart rooms with modern appliances in a Zen-inspired complex. Water flows calmly in rivers that end in lovely swimming pools. There's an on-site wellness centre and plenty of tucked-away places for relaxation.

Melaleuca Resort (☎ 07-4055 3222; www.melaleucaresort.com.au; 85-93 Williams Esplanade; r $161; ✴ ◨)

With resident green tree frogs and friendly owners, this place suits families (buckets and spades supplied!). Each of the 24 self-contained waterfront apartments has its own kitchen, balcony and laundry facilities. The pool resembles Mossman Gorge.

Peppers Beach Club & Spa (☎ 1800 134 444, 07-4059 9200; www.peppers.com.au; 123 Williams Esplanade; r $301-1373; ◨) With three pools, 200 rooms and a mother-of-pearl reception area, this is the 'mother' of main street resorts.

Angsana Resort & Spa (☎ 07-4055 3000; www.angsana.com; 1 Veivers Rd; r from $425; ✴ ◨ ◨) Its beachfront location makes it popular with wedding parties and its rooms (especially the split-level ones) are pure luxury. There are no less than 10 cushions piled up on the corner couches and a few rooms have private pools. The spa's signature treatment is the two-hour $180 body massage.

Sea Temple (☎ 1800 010 241; www.seatemple.com.au; Triton St; studios $460, apt from $580; ◨) UFO-style lights light up the sparse reception area and the studios and apartments have granite benchtops and extra-large showers. Outside it's a veritable fun park, with three different styles of pool suited to lap-lovers, lilo-floaters and playful kids.

Palm Cove Camping Ground (☎ 07-4055 3824; 149 Williams Esplanade; unpowered/powered sites $15/20) This council-owned beachfront camping ground is open but needs to work on its facilities.

EATING

CSLC (☎ 07-4059 1244; Cedar Rd; meals $16-22; ⏱ 6pm-8.30pm daily Jul-Nov, closed Mon & Tue Dec-Jun) This locals' haunt has had a massive upgrade so now there are views with the fish and prawn platters. The treed garden bar is great.

Vivo (☎ 07-4059 0944; 49 Williams Esplanade; mains $16-35) Serves up fare such as DIY garlic bread (complete with roast garlic, you sprinkle on the shaved parmesan) in a breezy Queenslander building. It's a family-friendly place to visit, with magazines and newspapers to read if you tire of the palm-tree-and-beach view.

Nu Nu (☎ 07-4059 1880; 123 Williams Esplanade; mains $20-45) There's good coffee (and mains, if you want to splash out) to be had at this luxe restaurant.

Far Horizons (☎ 07-4055 3000; www.angsana.com; cnr Veivers Rd & The Esplanade; meals $26-75) Try an 'afternoon delight' cocktail by the beach.

Self-caterers should head to the tiny **Palm Cove Supermarket** (Paradise Village; ⏱ 7.30am-7pm).

Ellis Beach

Ellis Beach is an original: uncrowded, un-populated and unbelievably perfect. It's a few minutes' drive around the headland past Palm Cove, yet feels like another world. Campervans gather at **Ellis Beach Oceanfront Bungalows** (☎ 1800 637 036, 07-4055 3538; www.ellisbeach.com; Captain Cook Hwy; unpowered sites $26, powered sites $30-38, cabins $85, bungalows $155-185; ☒), which also has perfectly acceptable cheap roadside cabins, or more upmarket beachside versions. You can't help but feel sorry for the people driving past; they don't know what they're missing.

Across the road is **Ellis Beach Bar & Grill** (☎ 07-4055 3534; Captain Cook Hwy; meals $5-22), which pumps out tasty burgers, roast chicken, fish and chips, old-fashioned milkshakes and beer. About 20 minutes' drive from Ellis Beach is **Hartley's Creek Crocodile Farm** (☎ 07-4055 3576; www.crocodileadventures.com; adult/child $31/16; ☒ 8.30am-5pm). It's a working croc farm with a wildlife section. A ticket lasts for three days and includes entry to the 11am croc feeding, the afternoon snake show, and a boat trip around the lagoon where you'll see salties being pole-fed.

KURANDA
pop 1610

Kuranda is a hop, skip and jump from Cairns, or make that a historic train journey, sky rail adventure or winding bus trip, from Cairns. The village itself is basically sprawling sets of markets nestled in a spectacular tropical rainforest setting and selling everything from made-in-China Aboriginal art to emu oil. The locals are a friendly bunch, well prepared for the hordes of tourists that arrive in the morning and depart with full bellies, bags and memory cards at almost precisely 3.30pm. There's little reason to stay overnight as this is really a day-tripper's domain.

The **Kuranda visitor information centre** (☎ 07-4093 9311; www.kuranda.org; ☒ 10am-4pm) is in Centenary Park.

Sights & Activities

Kuranda's markets are throbbing by midday, and the **Original Kuranda Rainforest Markets** (7 Therwine St; ☒ 10am-3pm) has incense sticks burning in the ground and a more authentic vibe than either the **Heritage Markets** (Rob Veivers Dr; ☒ 9.30am-3.30pm) or the **New Kuranda**

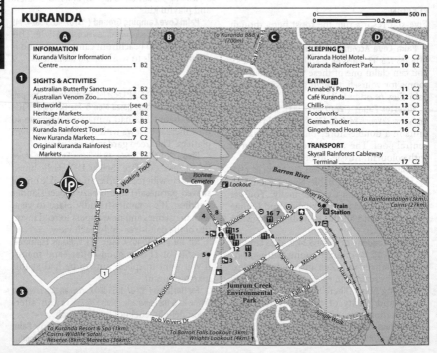

KURANDA

INFORMATION	
Kuranda Visitor Information Centre	1 B2

SIGHTS & ACTIVITIES	
Australian Butterfly Sanctuary	2 B2
Australian Venom Zoo	3 C3
Birdworld	(see 4)
Heritage Markets	4 B2
Kuranda Arts Co-op	5 B3
Kuranda Rainforest Tours	6 C2
New Kuranda Markets	7 C2
Original Kuranda Rainforest Markets	8 B2

SLEEPING	
Kuranda Hotel Motel	9 C2
Kuranda Rainforest Park	10 B2

EATING	
Annabel's Pantry	11 C2
Café Kuranda	12 C3
Chillis	13 C3
Foodworks	14 C2
German Tucker	15 C2
Gingerbread House	16 C2

TRANSPORT	
Skyrail Rainforest Cableway Terminal	17 C2

Markets (23 Coondoo St). The creative heart of Kuranda exists at the **Kuranda Arts Co-op** (☎ 07-4093 9026; www.artskuranda.asn.au; shop 6/12 Rob Veivers Dr; ☻ 10am-4pm).

Behind the train station, **Kuranda Rainforest Tours** (☎ 07-4093 7476; adult/child $14/7; ☻ hourly 10.30am-2.30pm) runs 45-minute calm-water cruises along the Barron River and you might spot a freshwater croc. Check opening times from October to March, as it doesn't operate after heavy rain.

There are several signed walks in the markets, and a short walking track through **Jumrum Creek Environmental Park**, which is off Barron Falls Rd, leads you to a big population of fruit bats.

Further down, Barron Falls Rd divides: the left fork takes you to a wheelchair accessible **lookout** over the Barron Falls, while further along the right fork brings you to **Wrights Lookout**, which looks down at Barron Gorge National Park.

There's loads of 'wildlife' in Kuranda – albeit in zoos. **Rainforestation** (☎ 07-4085 5008; www.rainforest.com.au; Kennedy Hwy; adult/child $39/20; ☻ 9am-4pm) is an enormous tourist park with a wildlife section, river cruises and an Aboriginal show. For lions, hippos and more, visit **Cairns Wildlife Safari Reserve** (☎ 07-4093 7777; www.cairnswildlifesafarireserve.com.au; Kennedy Hwy; adult/child $28/14; ☻ 9am-4.30pm).

The **Australian Butterfly Sanctuary** (☎ 07-4093 7575; www.australianbutterflies.com; 8 Rob Veivers Dr; adult/child $16/8; ☻ 10am-4pm) offers half-hour tours through its butterfly enclosure; or head next door to **Birdworld** (☎ 07-4093 9188; www.birdworldkuranda.com; Heritage Markets; adult/child $15/8; ☻ 9am-4pm), which displays 75 species of bird. The **Australian Venom Zoo** (☎ 07-4093 8905; 8 Coondoo St; adult/child $16/10; ☻ 9am-5pm) won't take up much of your time, and is a no-go zone for an arachnophobe.

Sleeping

Kuranda Rainforest Park (☎ 07-4093 7316; www.kurandarainforestpark.com.au; 88 Kuranda Heights Rd; unpowered/powered sites $24/28, s/d without bathroom $25/50, units from $90; ☒ ☒) Very basic rooms for very basic prices, and a lovely rainforest setting. The park is a 10-minute walk from town.

Kuranda Hotel Motel (☎ 07-4093 7206; cnr Arara & Coondoo Sts; s $50, d $75-85) Flash linen, tiled bathrooms and TVs with DVD players. There's a great dinner menu in the adjoining Irish-themed pub.

Kuranda B&B (☎ 07-4093 7151; kurandabed@tpgi.com.au; 28 Black Mountain Rd; s/d $110/160; ☒) This B&B has two massive rooms with big showers and rainforest-edge views from private balconies. Breakfast is included, dinner is available on request, and the walk to town will take around 20 minutes.

Kuranda Resort & Spa (☎ 07-4093 7556; www.kurandaresortandspa.com; 3 Green Hills Rd; r $139-249; ☒ ☒) There's little remaining of this complex to allow it the 'resort' tag, and though the pool area's good, the rest is a little like a withering school camp.

Eating

Gingerbread House (☎ 07-4093 9377; shop 17, 23 Coondoo St; ☻ breakfast & lunch Tue-Sun) Bakes European bread, strudels, and, as its name suggests, gingerbread.

Annabel's Pantry (☎ 07-4093 7605; Therwine St; pies $4-5; ☻ breakfast & lunch) Offering more varieties of pie than there are letters in the alphabet (29 at last count), Annabel's has come up with some creative fillings, such as the roo-filled Matilda.

Café Kuranda (☎ 07-4093 8552; 17-19 Therwine St; mains $12; ☻ breakfast & lunch) Does good coffee and good all-day breakfasts (including the delish Barbados brekky of bacon and fried bananas) in a great people-watching location.

There's a **Foodworks** (Coondoo St) supermarket. Also recommended:

Chillis (☎ 07-4093 8483; shop 5, 24 Coondoo St; meals $5-10; ☻ dinner Tue-Sun) Has curry-of-the-day specials as well as $16 hippy-chick pizzas. From the balcony you can watch brush turkeys clearing out the undergrowth.

German Tucker (☎ 07-4057 9688; Therwine St; dishes $5-14; ☻ lunch) Fat kransky sausages and lunch and beer specials for $14.

Getting There & Away

Buses are by far the cheapest way to get to Kuranda, costing $4 and departing Cairns hourly from 10.20am to 4.15pm (see p448), though the other options are more spectacular.

Kuranda Scenic Railway (☎ 1800 620 324, 07-4036 9288; www.traveltrain.com.au; adult/child/student $40/20/33) winds 34km from Cairns to Kuranda through picturesque mountains and no fewer than 15 tunnels. The trip takes 1¾ hours and trains depart from Cairns at 8.30am and 9.30am daily, returning from pretty Kuranda station at 2pm and 3.30pm.

At 7.5km long, **Skyrail Rainforest Cableway** (☎ 07-4038 1555; www.skyrail.com.au; one way adult/child/family $40/20/100, return adult/child $58/29; ◷ 8.15am-3.45pm) is one of the world's longest gondola cableways and provides a bird's-eye view over the tropical rainforest. It runs from the corner of Cairns Western Arterial Rd and the Cook Hwy in Smithfield, a northern suburb of Cairns, to Kuranda (Arara St). The journey takes about 90 minutes. It includes two stops along the way and features boardwalks that have interpretive panels and passes Barron Falls (which is reduced to a small stream in the Dry). The last departure from Cairns and Kuranda is at 3.45pm; transfers to and from the terminal (15 minutes' drive north of Cairns) and combination deals (Scenic Railway and Skyrail) are available. As space is limited, only day packs are allowed on board.

ATHERTON TABLELANDS

Waterfalls, lush green pastures complete with well-fed dairy cows and patches of remnant rainforest make up the tablelands, though the bordering areas are dramatically different; expect dry, harsh outback and much thinner cattle. The Tablelands are the site of the continent's most recent volcanic activity, some 10,000 years ago, and in some areas the altitude reaches more than 1000m. Plenty of people self-drive around the area, though since most towns are close together, bike tours are popular. Either way, allow plenty of time to visit the plethora of waterfalls and local produce outlets.

GETTING THERE & AROUND

Hire car is the ideal way to get around as there are so many stops over short distances, but **Trans North** (☎ 07-4061 7944; www.transnorthbus.com) has services departing Cairns at 8.30am, 3.15pm and 5.30pm to Mareeba ($17, one hour) and Atherton ($22, 1¾ hours). There are two services on Saturday (9.30am and 1pm) and one on Sundays and public holidays (1pm). On weekdays the 8.30am and 3.15pm buses have onward connections from Atherton to Herberton ($8, 20 minutes) and Ravenshoe ($14, 2½ hours) through **Kerry's Bus Service** (☎ 0427 841 483).

If you're travelling by car, be careful driving from Mareeba to Cairns as there are no fences and the Brahmin cattle certainly don't expect to move out of your way.

Mareeba

pop 10,800

With big cattle, wide streets and employment for seasonal workers (thanks partly to the Mareeba Mango – mango season is January to March; avocado work is available Febraury to March), Mareeba is more desert than Tablelands, but has some wonderful attractions nearby. If you're around in mid-July, don the RM Williams boots and be sure to see the **Mareeba Rodeo** (www.mareebarodeo.com.au) at Kerribee Park.

First stop is the **Mareeba Heritage Museum & Tourist Information Centre** (☎ 07-4092 5674; www.mareebaheritagecentre.com.au; Centenary Park, 345 Byrnes St; entry by donation; ◷ 8am-4pm), which has a huge room filled with displays on the area's past and present commercial industries, as well as its natural surrounds.

Jabiru Safari Lodge Mareeba Wetlands (☎ 1800 788 755, 07-4093 2514; www.jabirusafarilodge.com.au; admission free; ◷ 9am-4.30pm Apr-Dec) is a 5000-acre bird-lover's extravaganza with on-site accommodation (unpowered sites $10 per person, accommodation from $79 per person) in fantastic luxury tents (expect corrugated iron bathrooms, privacy and access to an outdoor spa), or solar-powered ecotents. Apart from birds, you might spot kangaroos and shy freshwater crocs. Boat tours cost $13 for an hour-long trip, and the cafe serves up quick meals for around $9. To reach the wetlands, turn left at the Biboohra service station on Pickford Rd, 7km north of Mareeba.

Granite Gorge (☎ 07-4093 2259; www.granitegorge.com.au; admission $5; ◷ 8.30am-5.30pm) is a privately owned nature park where you're guaranteed to see (and feed) a whole crew of rock wallabies. There are maps detailing three 1km walks, and springy folk can give rock-hopping (on the large granite boulders) a go. The camping ground (unpowered/powered sites $24/28) has a kitchen, laundry and bathroom. It's 12km west of Mareeba: follow Chewko Rd out of Mareeba for 7km, then take the turn-off to your right from there.

Ice-cold chocolate, 21 favours of coffee and a large collection of coffee faucets feature at **Coffee Works** (☎ 07-4092 4101; www.coffeeworks.com.au; 136 Mason St; tours $19; ◷ 9am-4pm). Or walk through a mango-packing factory to sample sweet mango wines at **Golden Pride Winery** (☎ 07-4093 2750; www.goldendrop.com.au; Bilwon Rd, Bilwon; mango wine per bottle $16; ◷ 8am-6.30pm). Head north on the road to Mt Molloy for 7km and turn right at Bilwon Rd – then it's another 2km to the winery.

SLEEPING & EATING

Jackaroo Motel (☎ 07-4092 2677; www.jackaroomotel.com; 340 Byrnes St; s/d $95/105; ✷ ✿) The owner's passion for continually updating the hotel means you can expect clean, modern rooms that are perhaps a bit too tidy for a real jackaroo.

Nastasi's (☎ 07-4092 2321; 210 Byrnes St; meals $4-9; ▣) Has a freezer filled with soon-to-be fried dim sims, fish and chips, eggs and bacon and burgers.

More sleeping options:

Mareeba Motor Inn (☎ 07-4092 2451; Kennedy Hwy; s/d $100/110; ✷ ▣ ✿) The biggest motel sign in town offers functional rooms and an à la carte licensed restaurant.

Riverside Caravan Park (☎ 07-4092 2309; 13 Egan St; unpowered/powered sites $18/22) Stunning poinciana trees surround this ground on the Barron River.

Chillagoe
pop 227

Caves, caves and more caves. Welcome to Chillagoe, cave capital of Far North Queensland. The town itself contains a few petrol stations, two pubs, an information office and a couple of accommodation options. Step outside the CBD to find impressive 400-million-year-old coral reefs and limestone caves, rock pinnacles and a balancing rock, Aboriginal rock art, deserted early-20th-century smelters, a Ford motor-car collection, and, to wash the dust off, a beautiful swimming hole. It's 140km west of Mareeba (15km of unsealed road) and close enough to make a day trip from Cairns during the dry season, but an overnight stay is preferable.

The **Hub** (☎ 07-4094 7111; Queen St; ✷ 8am-5pm Mon-Fri, to 3.30pm Sat & Sun) is the visitors centre, and it's here that you can book QPWS **cave tours** (tours $17) of the stunning Donna (9am), Trezkinn (11am) and Royal Arch (1.30pm) limestone caves. It's worth doing them all, if you can, and you'll also get a 20% discount if you book all three together.

The **Chillagoe Tourist Village** (☎ 07-4094 7177; Queen St; s $25, cabins from $60) has accommodation, petrol and delicious burgers and toasties near a bright bougainvillea tree. The **Chillagoe Observatory & Eco-Lodge** (☎ 07-4094 7155; info@coel .com.au; Hospital Ave; unpowered & powered sites per person $10, s/tw $30/45, d with bathroom $85-100; ✷) has more of an observatory than eco theme (stargazing costs $15/8 per adult/child) and its restaurant is open most nights.

our pick **Chillagoe Cabins** (☎ 07-4094 7206; www.chil lagoe.com; Queen St; s/d $108/140; ✷ ✿) are terrific –

modelled on rustic miners' huts, they come complete with water filters, antiques, flowers, chocolates and DVD players. The on-site restaurant serves old-fashioned outback tucker and, since the owners are wildlife carers, there's usually a collection of wildlife on the premises. The **Post Office Hotel** (☎ 07-4094 7119; Queen St; meals $10-16; ✷ lunch & dinner) has plenty of floor-to-ceiling graffiti to read while you're eating sangas, burgers, and fish and chips.

Chillagoe can be reached from Mareeba with the **Chillagoe Bus Service** (☎ 07-4094 7155; adult/child $36/18), which departs from Chillagoe post office at 7.30am Monday, Wednesday and Friday and departs Mareeba train station at 1pm on the same days.

Atherton
pop 8964

Atherton, the 'capital' of the tablelands, is a farming town with little to offer travellers but a rest in the journey, or a chance to get their hands and shoes dirty picking fruit and vegetables year-round. The **Atherton Tablelands Information Centre** (☎ 07-4091 4222; www.athertonta blelands.com.au; cnr Main & Silo Rds; ✷ 9am-5pm) has useful information including self-drive itineraries, Australia-wide booking facilities and seasonal work updates. **FNQ Computers** (☎ 07-4091 4600; cnr Mabel & Vernan Sts; per hr $5; ✷ 9am-5pm Mon-Fri, to 12.30pm Sat) has internet access.

As you approach Atherton from Herberton in the southwest, the fabulous **Hou Wang Temple** (☎ 07-4091 6945; 86 Herberton Rd; adult/child/concession/ family $10/8/8/25; ✷ 10am-4pm) is testament to the Chinese migrants who flocked to the area to search for gold in the late 1800s, and is the only Chinese temple in Australia built of corrugated iron. At the same location, **Atherton Birds of Prey** (☎ 07-4091 6945; www.birdsofprey.com.au; 86 Herberton Rd; adult/child/student/family $13/7/10/34; ✷ shows 11am & 2pm Wed-Sun Apr-Oct, Dec & Jan) presents shows with trained falcons, wedge-tailed eagles and owls. Don't miss nearby **Platypus Park** (Herberton Rd) for your chance to see a platypus family at play.

The **Crystal Caves** (☎ 07-4091 2365; www.crystal caves.com.au; 69 Main St; adult/child $20/10; ✷ 8.30am-5pm Mon-Fri, 8.30am-4pm Sat, 10am-4pm Sun) is a mineralogical museum in an artificial grotto that winds for a block under Atherton's streets, and houses rose-quartz boulders, dazzling blue topaz and assorted fossils. You must wear a torch-carrying hard hat, and the last 'miners' need to be there one hour before closing. Crack your own geode for $20 to $100.

QUEENSLAND

Travellers who stay in town for picking work usually stay at **Atherton Travellers Lodge** (☎ 07-4091 3552; 37 Alice St; dm/f $25/65, d & tw $45; 💻), a busy but relaxed workers' hostel that won't suit those with a passion for cleanliness.

Woodlands Tourist Park (☎ 1800 041 441; www .woodlandscp.com.au; 141 Herberton Rd; unpowered/powered sites $22/31, cabins/villas from $65/120; ❄ ❄) is a favourite with families thanks to its waterfall pool, playground and great kids' rooms. It also has unique refurbished miners' quarters rooms with polished floorboards.

Aromatic coffee and delectable bacon-and-cheese puffs lure the hungry to **Gallery 5** (☎ 07-4091 5576; Main St; meals $10; ☀ breakfast & lunch Mon-Sat). Self-caterers can go to the **IGA supermarket** (Main St; ☀ 7am-8pm).

Lake Tinaroo

Lake Tinaroo is mecca for the Aussie who loves nothing but setting up the tent, opening up the esky and planning for a day's fishing. The enormous artificial lake and dam were originally created for the Barron River hydroelectric power scheme, and drowned trees still poke their bones out of the water. **Tinaroo Falls**, at the northwestern corner of the lake, is the main settlement. **Tinaroo Barra Sportfishing** (☎ 07-4095 8888) will help you catch a big barra.

Near the Lake Tinaroo turn-off, **Tolga Woodworks Gallery & Café** (☎ 07-4095 4488; Kennedy Hwy, Tolga; meals $6-14; ☀ 9am-5pm) has lots of tasteful objects of desire made from Queensland timbers, and delicious gourmet meals: linger over a savoury muffin or white-chocolate cheesecake.

Tolga Lodge Backpackers (☎ 07-4095 5166; 36-38 Kennedy Hwy; dm/tw $25/60) is a new backpackers with country-style doubles, excellent dorm rooms (king singles, bedside lamps and private lockable wardrobes) and an industrial-style kitchen. It's an alternative to the Atherton Travellers Lodge and has the same owners. Luxe out in the polished timber/corrugated-iron dining room.

Optimising lake views, **Lake Tinaroo Terraces** (☎ 07-4095 8555; www.laketinarooterraces.com.au; Church St; r $79-155; ❄) presents clean and modern rooms and self-contained, two-storey terraces with two bedrooms.

Hedged by native hoop pines, **Lake Tinaroo Holiday Park** (☎ 07-4095 8232; www.discovery holidayparks.com.au; Dam Rd; unpowered/powered sites $24/30, cabins $85, units $100-200) is a family park right opposite the lake with great family rooms surrounded by trees teeming with parrots. Canoe and boat hire is available. BYO linen.

From the dam, the unsealed Danbulla Forest Dr winds 28km through the **Danbulla State Forest** beside the lake, finally emerging on the Gillies Hwy 4km northeast of Lake Barrine. The road passes five spectacular lakeside **QPWS camping grounds** (☎ 13 13 04; www.epa.qld.gov.au; per person/family $5/20) and 'day use' areas.

There's a small volcanic crater and 600m circuit walk over a basalt-pocked river at **Mobo Creek**, and 6km from the Gillies Hwy, a 100m walk takes you down to the **Cathedral Fig**, a gigantic strangler fig tree you can walk into.

Yungaburra

pop 932

Only 12km from Atherton is this friendly town, packed with cute cafes, excellent restaurants, day spas and some of the best accommodation in the region. The locals and architecture give this town its quaint village atmosphere, and it's the ideal place to hang your backpack and use as a base for the surrounding area. **Yungaburra Information Centre** (☎ 07-4095 2416; 16 Cedar St; per hr $5; ☀ 9am-5pm) has internet access.

The **Yungaburra Folk Festival** (www.yungabur rafolkfestival.org) is a fabulous community event held each October. It features music, workshops, poetry readings and kids' activities. The **Yungaburra Markets** (☎ 07-4095 2111; Gillies Hwy; ☀ 7am-noon) are held in town on the fourth Saturday of every month; at this time the town is besieged by avid craft and food shoppers. The magnificent 500-year-old **Curtain Fig** is a must-see. Looking like a *Lord of the Rings* prop, it has aerial roots that hang down to create a feathery curtain. A wheelchair-accessible viewing platform encircles the tree.

Bookish types will love **Spencer & Murphy Booksellers** (☎ 07-4095 2123; www.spencerandmur phybooksellers.com; 9 Cedar St; ☀ 10am-6pm Wed-Sun), a house transformed into a shop and packed with new and secondhand books. The owner is a hunter and collector of rare and antiquarian books, including the works of Australian writer Ion L Idriess, as well as local writers. While you're at it, grab a local Bella coffee.

SLEEPING

On the Wallaby (☎ 07-4095 2031; www
.onthewallaby.com; 34 Eacham Rd; unpowered sites $20, dm/
d $22/55, tours from $30) Comfortable and friendly,
even the green tree frogs love it here (one
lives in the didgeridoo). Doubles are cute
and comfy and there's an undeniable earthy
feel to this excellent hostel. The nightly
barbecues ($10 per person) and breakfast
($5) ensure there's a gang of folk around
the timber table (at least twice a day) and
nature-based tours run daily and include
night canoeing ($30). There are free pick-ups
from Atherton and one-way transfers from
Cairns ($25 per person).

Lake Eacham Hotel (☎ 07-4095 3515; 6 Kehoe Pl; s/d
$55/85; ⊠) This hotel creates a '50s feel in all
its tough-love, unrenovated glory. The rooms
above the pub have high ceilings and bathrooms. Meals are around $18.

Kookaburra Lodge (☎ 07-4095 3222; www.kooka
burra-lodge.com; 3 Eacham Rd; s/d $75/80; ⊠ 🖳) Amid
a large tropical garden, Kookaburra has 12
stylish rooms with shady patios fanning out
around the pale-blue pool and masses of
greenery. Breakfast is delivered to your door,
motel style, and there are big soft couches to
sink into in the communal lounge room.

Gables B&B (☎ 07-4095 2373; 5 Eacham Rd; s
$65, d with/without breakfast $95/85) This historic
Queenslander with shutter windows and
friendly hosts has two very different rooms,
including one with a spa and the other with
a '60s kitchenette and bathroom. Breakfast
consists of fresh-fruit platters, and there's a
well-stocked library for downtime.

Eden House Retreat & Mountain Spa (☎ 07-4089
7000; www.edenhouse.com.au; 20 Gillies Hwy; villas from
$140) Twelve sleek villas are divided into those
for families or couples. The king-size beds,
private courtyards, sleek sound systems and
double spas go down a treat, and for even
more luxury the on-site day spa has his-and-
hers treatments ($65 to $385). The restaurant
offers locally sourced food in a wonderfully
exclusive atmosphere.

Williams Lodge (☎ 07-4095 3449; www.williamslodge
.com; Cedar St; r $170-265; ⊠ 🖳) An immaculate
restoration of a home with a firm foot in
the town's history. Rooms here have spas,
CD players and coffee plungers. A fireplace
to get cosy by, and knockout views across
the hills from a classic verandah make this
a fine option. Rates are cheapest Sunday
to Thursday.

EATING

Whistlestop Café (☎ 07-4095 3913; 36 Cedar St; meals
$6-15; ⊙ breakfast & lunch) Gluten-free rice slice
is one of the homemade goodies on the menu
at this cute-as-pie cafe. Outside dining in the
tropical garden is recommended.

Nick's Restaurant (☎ 07-4095 3330; 33 Gillies Hwy;
mains $22; ⊙ lunch Wed-Sun, dinner Tue-Sun) Pick up
a souvenir cowbell and check out the cowbell collection at this Swiss-Italian-German
restaurant, but please resist picking on the
staff uniforms.

Flynn's (☎ 07-4095 2235; 17 Eacham Rd;
mains $27-30; ⊙ dinner Tue-Sat, lunch Sat & Sun) Between
ducking outside to pick his own vegies and running the whole place almost single-handedly,
Kiwi culinary maestro Liam has managed
to put Yungaburra on the foodies map. The
menu changes daily but expect dishes such as
duck confit and fish of the day (which could be
pan-fried sashimi-grade yellowfin tuna) with
an Italian and French accent. Reservations
are recommended.

Crater Lakes National Park & Around

The two crater lakes of Lake Barrine and
Lake Eacham make up Crater Lakes National
Park, which is part of the Wet Tropics World
Heritage Area. Both lie off the main Gillies
Hwy and are circled by walking tracks. It's
the ideal place to bring a picnic loaded with
local produce and go for a swim.

LAKE EACHAM

The morning mist lifts over Lake Eacham to
expose a large expanse of crystal-clear water
full of easy-to-spot turtles and fish. There's a
swimming pontoon and some energy is needed
to take the 3km walk around the crater lake,
while even more is needed if you decide to
walk from Yungaburra, 4km away.

Lake Eacham Tourist Park (☎ 07-4095 3730; www
.lakeeachamtouristpark.com; Lakes Dr; unpowered/powered
sites $19/22, cabins $75-85), less than 2km down
the Malanda road from Lake Eacham, is a
rambling park with an excellent camp kitchen
and entertainment provided by king parrots
and other wildlife.

Bird-lovers flock to **Chambers Wildlife
Rainforest Lodge** (☎ 07-4095 3754; www.rainforest-aus
tralia.com; Eacham Close; r $130; ⊠ 🖳 🖳), which is
embedded in the national park. Night cameras
lend a *Big Brother* atmosphere to the complex,
but don't worry, they're there to film the nocturnal animals, not the humans, and you can

QUEENSLAND

watch it live on the TV in your room. The self-contained cabins are a bit dated but have electric fireplaces. There are walking tracks on the property and landing platforms for visiting birds – all of which enjoy celebrity status (some 45 wildlife documentaries have been made here).

At **Crater Lakes Rainforest Cottages** (☎ 07-4095 2322; www.craterlakes.com.au; Eacham Close, off Lakes Dr; d incl breakfast $230; 🗷) you can sit back and relax on your balcony and let the musky rat kangaroos and pademelons come to you. The rooms are special, with wood-burner heating, spa baths, fully-fitted kitchens and a breakfast hamper for your first morning. It's no wonder that this rainforest hideaway is a popular spot for marriage proposals.

LAKE BARRINE
While no longer surrounded by tall, tall kauri pines, this popular volcanic crater lake has a 6km walking track through rainforest around it. It's 18km east of Atherton via the Gillies Hwy.

Eat up award-winning scones at **Lake Barrine Rainforest Cruise & Tea House** (☎ 07-4095 3847; Gillies Hwy; meals $6-14; ☯ breakfast & lunch) and check out the captured stinging tree, growing safely in a perspex box, or spot water dragons and tortoises on the 40-minute **cruise** (adult/child $15/8; ☯ cruises at 9.30am, 11.30am, 1.30pm & 3.15pm).

Malanda
pop 1530
Forming the eastern part of the Atherton-Yungaburra-Malanda triangle is this little town 15km south of Lake Eacham. Its claim to fame is that it has the nation's longest continually running picture theatre, the **Majestic** (established 1927), but locals are still mightily proud that Australian cricketer Don Bradman played cricket here. The **Malanda Falls Visitors Centre** (☎ 07-4096 6957; Atherton Rd; ☯ 9.30am-4.30pm) has thoughtful displays on the area's human and geological history, and runs guided **rainforest walks** (adult/child/student $15/5/10) led by members of the Ngadjonji community on Saturday and Sunday at 9.30am and 11am.

Along the Atherton road, on the outskirts of town, are **Malanda Falls**, home to saw-shelled turtles and red-legged pademelons. On the Millaa Millaa Rd, 10km from Malanda, is the tiny village of **Tarzali**, which offers some accommodation options.

Malanda Lodge Motel (☎ 07-4096 5555; www.malandalodgemotel.com.au; Millaa Millaa Rd; s/d $85/97; 🗷 🗷) is out of town and a bit dated, but has clean rooms and facilities and an à la carte restaurant. If it feels as though the solid brown-brick walls of your room are closing in, escape to the grassy gardens or the lovely refuge of the pool.

Boutique eco-accommodation doesn't get much better than the **Canopy** (☎ 07-4096 5364; www.canopytreehouses.com.au; Hogan Rd, Tarzali via Malanda; units/treehouses/family houses from $227/349/479; 🗷). This is a tree-house feast, and all the wildlife in the area is invited. The setting – 100 acres of rainforest – carries loads of native wildlife, and the view from your 'home in the trees' means sitting back on your hand-painted hemp bedspreads, or in the jacuzzi, and listening and watching. There's a minimum two-night stay. Children – recipients of wildlife-spotting certificates – are welcome.

Tree Kangaroo Café (☎ 07-4096 6658; Atherton Rd; meals $4-10; ☯ breakfast & lunch; 🖳) is next door to the environmental centre and serves stopgap food. **Malanda Dairy Centre** (☎ 07-4095 1234; 8 James St; ☯ 7.20am-3pm) has mango and macadamia nut cheesecake as well as ice cream galore. Its tours (adult/child $11/6) run Monday to Friday at 10am and 11am.

Millaa Millaa & the Waterfall Circuit
Give up any thoughts of 'seen one waterfall seen them all' and take on this 16km 'waterfall circuit' near Millaa Millaa, 24km south of Malanda. Enter the circuit by taking Theresa Creek Rd, 1km east of Millaa Millaa on Palmerston Hwy. **Millaa Millaa Falls**, the largest of the falls, has a swimming hole, change rooms and a grassy picnic spot. Continuing round the circuit, you reach **Zillie Falls**, where you can watch Teresa Creek falling into the abyss. Step down past fern fronds to the rocky **Ellinjaa Falls** before returning to the Palmerston Hwy just 2.5km out of Millaa Millaa. A further 5.5km down the Palmerston Hwy there's a turn-off to **Mungalli Falls**, 5km off the highway.

At the country-style **Mungalli Creek Dairy** (☎ 07-4097 2232; www.mungallicreekdairy.com.au; 251 Brooks Rd; meals $6-25; ☯ 10am-4pm), 3km off Palmerston Hwy, you can sample cheeses and its nine types of creamy yoghurts Sourcing organic products is a priority of the dairy and the signature dish is the cheese platter for two ($25).

A little further along the Palmerston Hwy is the Mamu Rainforest Canopy Walkway, tracing Cyclone Larry's destructive trail through the forest; see When Larry Showed Up (p431).

For a hands-on farmstay experience, try **Acton Ridge Farmstay** (☎ 07-4097 2293; www.actonridgefarmstay.com; 122 Nash Rd; adult/child over 5 $125/55), a 400-acre working farm welcoming guests. You'll make your way past the cockatoos, chooks and piglets and take part in egg collecting and milking and see a farm in action. The bedrooms are inside the homestead-style house and share a bathroom. Rates include meals.

Dairy folk and waterfall seekers gather at the **Falls Teahouse** (☎ 07-4097 2237; www.fallsteahouse.com.au; Palmerston Hwy; mains $8-20; 🕑 10am-5pm). You might try homemade pasta or sandwiches made from home-baked grain and oat bread. B&B rooms (singles/doubles/twins $95/120/120) are individually furnished with period fixtures and fittings; you can negotiate rates. It's on the turn-off to Millaa Millaa Falls.

Herberton

pop 974

Herberton is a lovely town dotted with jacaranda trees and perched on a hilly area abutting the outback. Wonderful heritage buildings line the main street, which leads to the riverside site of a former tin mine. The **visitors centre** (☎ 07-4096 2244; Great Northern Mining Centre, Jack's Rd) is located on the site of an old mine.

Lovely old pub rooms (singles/doubles $30/60) with original fittings are available at the friendly **Royal Hotel** (☎ 07-4096 2231; 42 Grace St; mains $12-16; 🕑 lunch & dinner Wed-Sun), while **Wild River Caravan Park** (☎ 07-4096 2121; 23 Holdcroft Dr; unpowered/powered sites $12/18, cabins s/d $40/60) has beautifully done-up, semi-self-contained rooms in a bush setting. Its BYO restaurant serves up pork chops and garlic prawns on Thursday and Friday nights.

Mount Hypipamee National Park

Between Atherton and Ravenshoe, the Kennedy Hwy passes the eerie, and hard to pronounce, **Mount Hypipamee crater**, which could be a scene from a sci-fi film and certainly adds some vertigo to the itinerary. It's a scenic 700m (return) walk from the picnic area, past **Dinner Falls**, to this narrow, 138m-deep crater with its moody-looking lake far below.

Ravenshoe

pop 910

Ravenshoe (pronounced hoe, not shoe) is home to 'Queensland's Highest Pub': **Hotel Tully Falls** stands proudly at the tip of this town at the grand altitude of 916m. **Ravenshoe Visitor Centre** (☎ 07-4097 7700; www.ravenshoevisitorcentre.com.au; 24 Moore St; 🕑 9am-4pm) has helpful staff and is home to the **Nganyaji Interpretive Centre**, which explains the Jirrbal people's traditional lifestyle.

Nearby, **Windy Hill Wind Farm** has 20 wind turbines producing a clean, green energy supply. You can view and hear the swishing turbines 24 hours a day from the viewing platform. Windy Hill can be reached from either the Kennedy Hwy, from Ravenshoe, or from Millaa Millaa, along the scenic Old Palmerston Hwy.

Little Millstream Falls are 2km south of Ravenshoe on the Tully Gorge Rd (which doesn't go to Tully), and **Tully Falls** are 24km south, through rainforest (watch out for cattle on the road). About 4km past Ravenshoe and 1km off the road are the 340m-high **Millstream Falls** (no swimming), created three million years ago and, during the Wet, reputedly the widest, single drop falls in Australia.

Kennedy Hwy

With water hotter than the hottest outback day (over 70°C), **Innot Hot Springs**, 32km west of Ravenshoe, is definitely worth a stop. A river spews hot water next to the **Innot Hot Springs Village** (☎/fax 07-4097 0136; unpowered/powered sites $18/22, s/d $40/55, s/d cabins $75/90; 🏊) and paying guests have free use of the park's seven **thermal pools** (nonguests adult/child $6/5; 🕑 10am-6pm), or alternatively, dig your own spa pool out of the river's sand.

The **Innot Hot Springs Hotel** (☎ 07-4097 0203; mains $20; 🕑 dinner, lunch by appointment) has a 'bar at the spa' and will have you dining under a row of bras. The hotel's '50s motel-style rooms (singles/doubles $45/55) are good value.

PORT DOUGLAS

pop 948

This is the town that Australia's southerners flock to when the temperature in their zone cools down. It cocoons visitors in tropical warmth and its balmy, breezy evenings encourage white-pants-and-gold-jewellery alfresco dining. It's an ideal set-off point for trips to the low isles and has a hospitality industry requiring staff from July to November, so some travellers stay longer than planned.

QUEENSLAND

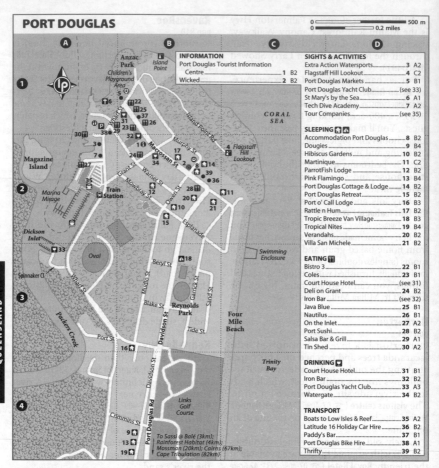

PORT DOUGLAS

0 ——————— 500 m
0 ——————— 0.2 miles

INFORMATION
Port Douglas Tourist Information
Centre 1 B2
Wicked 2 B2

SIGHTS & ACTIVITIES
Extra Action Watersports 3 A2
Flagstaff Hill Lookout 4 C2
Port Douglas Markets 5 B1
Port Douglas Yacht Club .... (see 33)
St Mary's by the Sea 6 A1
Tech Dive Academy 7 A2
Tour Companies .... (see 35)

SLEEPING
Accommodation Port Douglas 8 B2
Dougies 9 B4
Hibiscus Gardens 10 B2
Martinique 11 C2
ParrotFish Lodge 12 B2
Pink Flamingo 13 B4
Port Douglas Cottage & Lodge 14 B2
Port Douglas Retreat 15 B2
Port o' Call Lodge 16 B3
Rattle n Hum 17 B2
Tropic Breeze Van Village 18 B3
Tropical Nites 19 B4
Verandahs 20 B2
Villa San Michele 21 B2

EATING
Bistro 3 .... 22 B1
Coles 23 B1
Court House Hotel .... (see 31)
Deli on Grant 24 B2
Iron Bar .... (see 32)
Java Blue 25 B1
Nautilus 26 B1
On the Inlet 27 A2
Port Sushi 28 B2
Salsa Bar & Grill 29 A1
Tin Shed 30 A2

DRINKING
Court House Hotel 31 B1
Iron Bar 32 B2
Port Douglas Yacht Club 33 A3
Watergate 34 B2

TRANSPORT
Boats to Low Isles & Reef 35 A2
Latitude 16 Holiday Car Hire 36 B2
Paddy's Bar 37 B1
Port Douglas Bike Hire 38 A1
Thrifty 39 B2

Anzac Park
Children's Playground Area
Island Point
Wharf St
Murphy St
Island Point Rd
CORAL SEA
Magazine Island
Macrossan St
Grant St
Warner St
Flagstaff Hill Lookout
Mowbray St
Owen St
Marina Mirage
Train Station
Esplanade
Dickson Inlet
Swimming Enclosure
Oval
Beryl St
Spinnaker Cl
Mudlo St
Garrick St
Sand St
Four Mile Beach
Wharf St
Blake St
Reynolds Park
Packers Creek
Davidson St
Tide St
Trinity Bay
Port St
Links Golf Course
Crimmins St
Port Douglas Rd
To Sassi @ Balé (3km); Rainforest Habitat (4km); Mossman (20km); Cairns (67km); Cape Tribulation (82km)

Orientation & Information

Accommodation options are spread all over the region, and the larger resorts spread themselves along the 6km-long Port Douglas Rd that links Captain Cook Hwy with the town centre. Busy, centre-of-town Macrossan St links the jetty and pier with Four Mile Beach on Trinity Bay. Few hotels actually front Four Mile Beach in town, as it's been shielded from development by a golf course and parks.

There's a bunch of information centres. The **Port Douglas Tourist Information Centre** (☎ 07-4099 5599; www.tourismportdouglas.com.au; 23 Macrossan St; ⏱ 8am-6.30pm) has maps and takes tour bookings. **Wicked** (☎ 07-4099 6900; 48 Macrossan St; per hr $5; ⏱ 9am-10pm) has internet access, ice cream and secondhand books and DVDs.

Sights & Activities

On a sunny, calm day, Four Mile Beach will take your breath away; it is sand and palm trees for as far as you can see (head up to **Flagstaff Hill Lookout** for a great view). Get noisy with jet skis from **Extra Action Watersports** (☎ 07-4099 3175; www.reefsprinter.com.au; Port Douglas Slipway jetty; per 30min $85) or get on its two-hour *Reef Sprinter* reef-snorkelling trip (adult/child $100/80).

For wildlife up close, head to **Rainforest Habitat** (☎ 07-4099 3235; www.rainforesthabitat.com.au; Port Douglas Rd; adult/child/student $29/15/27; ⏱ 8am-5pm, last entry 4pm) at the Cooktown Hwy turn-off. Free guided tours leave half-hourly and take you past cassowaries, black-necked storks, crocs and tree kangaroos and give you the chance to handfeed the kangaroos. Try an interactive

QUEENSLAND

eating opportunity at **Breakfast with the Birds** (adult/child breakfast incl admission $42/21; ⏱ 8-10.30am) or **Lunch with the Lorikeets** (⏱ noon-2pm).

Dictate how much flavouring you want in your ice cup at the groovy **Port Douglas Markets** (Anzac Park; ⏱ 8.30am-1.30pm Sun), at the bottom of Macrossan St. There's a bunch of handmade items and local produce for sale as well as 20-minute massages.

Just by the market is **St Mary's by the Sea** (Anzac Park), a tiny nondenominational white-timber chapel that was built in 1911 and a nominee for prettiest church in the Land of Oz (there's a bit of a waiting list for weddings, so if you want to get hitched there, book ahead at info@portdouglasweddings.com.au).

Ever dreamed of sailing on a yacht? Well, the benevolent folk at the **Port Douglas Yacht Club** (☎ 07-4099 4386; www.portdouglasyachtclub.com.au; Wharf St) run sunset sessions each Wednesday, and it's a fun and free way to get a taste of boating life. Register at the Yacht Club at 4pm; boats leave at 5pm (BYO drinks).

Several companies offer PADI open-water certification as well as advanced dive certificates. **Tech Dive Academy** (☎ 07-4099 6880; www.tech -dive-academy.com; 3/46 Wharf St; 4-day course $760) offers a range of diving experiences, from snorkelling to night and adventure diving.

Tours

LOW ISLES TRIPS

There are several cruises to Low Isles, a small coral cay surrounded by a lagoon and topped by a lighthouse. The cay offers good snorkelling and the chance to see turtle-nesting grounds. Trips have an additional $5 marine park fee per person and leave from Marina Mirage.

Sailaway (☎ 07-4099 4772; www.sailawayportdouglas .com; adult/child/family $175/110/513) Great for families. A maximum of 33 passengers.

Shaolin (☎ 07-4099 4772; www.shaolinportdouglas .com; adult/child/family $165/100/468) A refitted Chinese junk, the *Shaolin* has snorkelling cruises (maximum 23). Sails from noon to 6.30pm.

SV Malaita (☎ 0407 130 648; www.malaita.com.au; adult/child $155/100) These trips get positive feedback. Monday to Thursday trips go island snorkelling.

Wavedancer (☎ 07-4087 2100; www.quicksilver -cruises.com; adult/child from $143/74) Recommended.

FISHING & SAILING

Reef, river and land-based fishing charters operate regularly out of Port Douglas. Prices range from $90 for a half-day group tour on the Daintree River to anywhere between $3500 and $14,000 per day on the mother ship. **Fishing Port Douglas** (☎ 0409 610 869; www.fishingportdouglas .com.au) has details. **Out 'n' About** (☎ 07-4098 5204; www.outnaboutfishing.com.au; tours from $90) specialises in estuary and reef-fishing trips.

REEF TRIPS

The unrelenting surge of visitors to the reef off Port Douglas has impacted on its general condition, and although you'll still see colourful corals and marine life, it has become patchy in parts. Reef trips generally include reef tax, snorkelling and transfers from your accommodation, plus lunch and refreshments. Add around $200/180 for an introductory/certified dive. Think about what you want out of your reef outing and then consider these recommended operators:

Aristocat (☎ 07-4099 4727; www.aristocat.com .au; adult/child $165/120) James Bond would approve. Upgraded to a new boat with a maximum of 90 passengers.

Haba (☎ 07-4098 5000; www.habadive.com.au; adult/ child $175/99) Offers a family-friendly snorkelling trip with a glass-bottom boat and visits two sites. Maximum 100 passengers.

Poseidon (☎ 1800 085 674; www.poseidon-cruises .com.au; adult/child $180/125) Fast day suiting divers.

Quicksilver (☎ 07-4087 2100; www.quicksilver-cruises .com; adult/child $202/104) The giant *Wavepiercer*, which takes over 400, visits the outer reef. Helmet diving available. Family and wheelchair friendly.

Silver Series (☎ 07-4087 2100; www.silverseries.com .au; adult/child $157/120) Heads out to Agincourt Reef System.

Synergy 2 (☎ 07-4050 0675; www.synergyreef.com.au; adult/child $260/190) Outer reef catamaran tours and limo transfers; upmarket jaunt with maximum of 12 passengers.

Tallarook (☎ 07-4099 4990; www.tallarooksail.com; adult/child $150/90) Hands-on sailing to Tongue Reef in just under two hours (maximum 25). Family-run business.

Wavelength (☎ 07-4099 5031; www.wavelength.com .au; adult/child $190/140) Snorkelling cruise only (maximum 30) to three gorgeous outer reef sites. YHA discount.

OTHER TOURS

There are numerous operators offering day trips to Cape Tribulation, some via Mossman Gorge. Many of the tours out of Cairns (p442) also do pick-ups from Port Douglas.

BTS Tours (☎ 07-4099 5665; www.btstours.com.au; adult/child/family return $54/27/150) Tours to Mossman Gorge and the Daintree River.

QUEENSLAND

Reef & Rainforest Connections (☎ 07-4099 5333; www.reefandrainforest.com.au; adult/child from $105/55) A range of day-long ecotours including Cape Trib and Bloomfield Falls, Kuranda and Mossman Gorge.

Wind Swell (☎ 0427 498 042, 07-4098 2167; www .windswell.com.au; from $100) Kitesurfing for beginners to high flyers.

Sleeping

Low-season rates (November to May) are quoted here; stand-by rates are often available. Also try www.wotif.com.au and www .lastminute.com.au.

Accommodation Port Douglas (☎ 07-4099 5355; www.accomportdouglas.com.au; 1/48 Macrossan St; ☺ 9am-5pm Mon-Sat) is an agent for many holiday rentals.

BUDGET

Dougies (☎ 1800 996 200, 07-4099 6200; www.dougies .com.au; 111 Davidson St; dm $25, d & tw $65, 'stylie' tents per person $23, unpowered sites $22; ☒ ☐ ☒) Dougies draws them in with cool pine bunk beds, free transfers to and from Cairns on Monday, Wednesday and Friday, and air-con, but there's no room for food storage, the pool's tiny and it could do with a freshen up.

ParrotFish Lodge (☎ 1800 995 011, 07-4099 5011; www.parrotfishlodge.com; 37-39 Warner St; dm $25-30, d & tw with/without bathroom $96/86; ☒ ☐ ☒) This spilt-level, purpose-built hostel is modern and beachy with vibrant blue swirling floors, mural-sized contemporary art, and a chatty bar and bistro with occasional live music. The saltwater pool is made for morning laps or an afternoon submerge.

Rattle n Hum (☎ 07-4099 5641; www.rattlenhumbar .com.au; 38 Macrossan St; dm/d with bathroom $27/80) One of the few central hostels, this simple newbie is done up with plasmas and a large open kitchen with views.

Port o' Call Lodge (☎ 1800 892 800, 07-4099 5422; www.portocall.com.au; cnr Port St & Craven Cl; dm $30-33, d $79-119; ☒ ☐ ☒) This large solar- and wind-powered, YHA ecohostel has had an environmental overhaul so expect positive things. The rooms are clean and the bistro is popular with the locals thanks to its $19 mains. Free courtesy coach to/from Cairns (Monday to Saturday) with stays of two or more nights.

MIDRANGE

Martinique (☎ 07-4099 6222; www.martinique.com.au; 66 Macrossan St; r from $129; ☒ ☒) This terracotta-coloured block contains lovely one-bedroom apartments, each with a small kitchen, cable TV (with rotating screen for whole-room viewing) and private balcony. With great hosts and a main street location close to the beach, it's a good choice. The pool has six coves and is supervised by a lavish elephant and dolphin shrine.

our pick Pink Flamingo (☎ 07-4099 6622; www .pinkflamingo.com.au; 115 Davidson St; studio r from $135, villas from $195; ☒ ☒) It's all about love at this gay-friendly miniresort, and hearts abound in the heart-shaped candelabra and statues. Adults get to enjoy the intimate tropical garden atmosphere, and the villas, with their outdoor baths, are incredibly private. The cheaper motel-style rooms have had their carports transformed into garden patios. There's also a BYO poolside bar and a tour desk. A 'shagged' sign on your door might be the fitting end to an arduous day of holidaying.

Port Douglas Retreat (☎ 07-4099 5053; www .portdouglasretreat.com.au; 31-33 Mowbray St; r from $135; ☒) Great prints above the king-sized beds, newly refurbished self-contained rooms with wicker bedheads, contemporary sleekness and courtyard dining make this a low-key, pleasant retreat. The 20m pool is lit by gas lights at night and guests are welcome to use the big barbecue.

Tropical Nites (☎ 07-4099 5666; www.tropicalnites .com.au; 119 Davidson St; townhouses from $135; ☒ ☒) These 12 townhouses feature solid timber furniture and air-con, and achieve a contemporary look with granite benchtops and stainless-steel appliances in the kitchen. They are particularly good for couples/groups wanting a long-term stay.

Villa San Michele (☎ 07-4099 4088; www.villa sanmichele.com.au; 39-41 Macrossan St; r $155-260; ☒) Four-star accommodation in well-laid-out, self-contained, tile-floored rooms. Choose from one- and two-bedroom rooms in this Tuscan-inspired, centrally located complex. There are two swimming pools and a shared courtyard area.

Hibiscus Gardens (☎ 07-4099 5315; www.hibiscus portdouglas.com.au; cnr Mowbray & Owen Sts; r from $180; ☒ ☐ ☒) This good-looking resort does tasteful rooms with Balinese furniture and bright cushions. Studio rooms face the rear garden while one-bedroom rooms overlook the pool lined with turtle sculptures and the occasional Buddha. The on-site spa specialises in Indigenous healing techniques and products.

TOP END
Verandahs (☎ 07-4099 6650; www.verandahsportdouglas
.com.au; 7 Davidson St; r $165-325; ❄ ☎) Rinse out
the coffee plunger while watching over the
lovely heated pool from these well-equipped
self-contained apartments. The glass-topped
dining table inspires convivial dining, and
the hosts are excellent sources of information
about the area.

Port Douglas Cottage & Lodge (☎ 07-4098
5432; www.portdouglascottage.com; 4 Owen St; cottage/
lodge $375/475; ❄ ☐ ☎) Beach hut meets
Queenslander in this centre-of-town cottage
and lodge. The unique timber-floored cottage
has a private plunge pool, views from the marble bath and a hidden kitchen. Expect the best
appliances and fittings and loads of privacy.

CAMPING
Tropic Breeze Van Village (☎ /fax 07-4099 5299; 24
Davidson St; unpowered sites $29, powered sites $31-34, on-site
cabins from $80; ☎) Central and close to the beach,
with shady tent sites, spotless shared bathrooms,
a camp kitchen and lots of wiry fig trees.

Eating
`our pick` **Tin Shed** (☎ 07-4099 5553; 7 Ashford Ave; mains
$15-20; ❄ 11.30am-2pm & 5.30-8.30pm) Port Douglas'
Combined Services Club is a locals' secret.
This is a rare find: bargain dining on the waterfront, and even the drinks are cheap. Sign
in, line up and order before grabbing a table
on the river- or shore-fronting deck. The
menu includes staples such as chicken Oscar
(a local favourite), steaks, salt-and-pepper
calamari, and vegetarian stir-fry, all for
under $20.

Salsa Bar & Grill (☎ 07-4099 4922; 26 Wharf St; meals
$14-33; ❄ lunch & dinner Mon-Sat) This white weath-
erboard Queenslander offers dining with the
soothing sounds of water features. There's an
Asian-Australian tinge to dishes such as croc
sausages with fragrant rice.

On the Inlet (☎ 07-4099 5255; 3 Inlet St; mains $25;
❄ lunch & dinner) Just wait till you set your eyes
on this restaurant's local 'resident', George
the Groper. He appears almost daily at 5pm;
get in early to claim your piece of deck for
viewing. Apart from George, the other hero
of this restaurant is its predinner deal (3.30pm
to 5.30pm), which gets you an icy bucket of
prawns and a drink for $18. There are two
types of dining here, fine or bar style, so take
your pick and enjoy dishes such as bang bang
prawns and chilli black-lipped mussels.

Bistro 3 (☎ 07-4099 6100; cnr Macrossan & Wharf Sts;
mains $36) Serves delicious meals (think water
chestnut and pea risotto and oven-roasted
duck) in an exclusive starched-white-napkin
atmosphere. Try the lunch menu's poached
red claw yabbies.

Nautilus (☎ 07-4099 5330; 17 Murphy St; mains $35-40;
❄ dinner) This place has an ambience to die
for. Be seated under palm trees and enjoy the
experience of being in the flame-lit rainforest
surrounds. The six-course tasting menu ($155)
features duck, bugs, prawns and more, all
matched with wines or go à la carte. Children
under eight are not accommodated.

Sassi @ Balé (☎ 07-4084 3085; 1 Balé Dr; mains $34-
60) Named after its chef, Toni Sassi, this is
a high-quality Italian restaurant where the
pasta is made on the premises and the spinach
is cooked to order. To top this, your food is
served in an exceptional dining environment
(by the pool under palm trees highlighted
by lights).

With its distinctive facade, **Iron Bar** (☎ 07-4099
4776; 5 Macrossan St; meals $10-30; ❄ lunch & dinner) serves
up $14 deals for early eaters, and, with staff
decked out in sailor outfits, the **Court House Hotel**
(☎ 07-4099 5181; cnr Macrossan & Wharf Sts; meals $15-25;
❄ lunch & dinner) has good-value meals. Self-caterers can head to **Coles** (Port Village, Macrossan St; ❄ 8am-
9pm Mon-Fri, 8am-5.30pm Sat, 9am-6pm Sun), or IGA and
Foodworks. For quick eats there's a range of
kebabs and pizza options on Grant St.

Also recommended:
Java Blue (☎ 07-4099 5814; shop 3, 2 Macrossan St;
❄ breakfast & lunch) With a long coffee menu, free-
range eggs, a main street location and good service, this
one is popular with the locals.
Deli on Grant (☎ 07-4099 5852; 11 Grant St; meals
$8-12; ❄ breakfast & lunch) Unleash the gourmand in
you with a range of boutique produce, baguettes and precooked homemade meals to take away. If you give the deli
three hours' notice it'll do you a picnic hamper.
Port Sushi (☎ 07-4099 4336; cnr Macrossan & Davidson
Sts; ❄ lunch) Japanese on the go.

Drinking
Port Douglas Yacht Club (☎ 07-4099 4386; Wharf St; www
.portdouglasyachtclub.com.au; ❄ 4pm-close Mon-Fri, noon-
close Sat & Sun) With some of the cheapest drinks
in town, drinking up the views of Dixon's
Inlet at this chilled place is easy. It's a popular hang-out for backpackers on Wednesday
nights. There's live music every Sunday from
5pm to 9pm and Australian bistro fare (cheap
fish dishes) at Spinnakers Restaurant.

QUEENSLAND

Watergate (☎ 07-4099 6665; cnr Grant & Macrossan Sts; ❀ 4pm-close) Watergate does tapas and drinks in true bronze-and-shimmer style. Port's trendsetters loll around on the chocolate couches and flitter to the long bar for cocktail ensembles.

Court House Hotel (☎ 07-4099 5181; cnr Macrossan & Wharf Sts; ❀ 10am-late) Listen to live cover-band muzak here on weekends while you take up residence on the park-bench-style tables and chairs on the street corner. Meals are good.

Iron Bar (☎ 07-4099 4776; 5 Macrossan St) The cane-toad races (every Tuesday, Thursday, Friday and Sunday) are a hoot, and if you can't get close enough in person, you can see the action from the video-cam set-up. The place itself is dark and woolshed-ish, a welcome change to the usually glam Port Douglas.

Getting There & Away

For information on getting to/from Cairns, see p448. There's a bus stop of sorts outside Paddy's Bar and some buses do Marina pick-ups.

Coral Reef Coaches (☎ 07-4098 2800; www.coral reefcoaches.com.au) connects Port Douglas with Mossman ($12, 20 minutes), Silky Oaks ($20, 30 minutes) and Cairns ($35, 1¼ hours).

Sun Palm (☎ 07-4084 2626; www.sunpalmtransport .com) runs daily services from Port Douglas to Cairns ($35, 1½ hours). Services to Mossman ($10, 20 minutes) and Cape Tribulation ($45, three hours) depart from Port Douglas at 8.30am and 3.30pm but you must book ahead.

Port Douglas BTS Bus (☎ 07-4099 5665; www .portdouglasbus.com) has three return services a day to Mossman Gorge (adult/child $17/9) and two return services a day to the Daintree River, including a one-hour cruise (adult/child $54/27).

Getting Around

Airport Connections (☎ 07-4099 5950; www.tnqshut tle.com; ❀ 3.30am-4.30pm) runs an hourly shuttle-bus service to/from Cairns airport (one way $32), and **Sun Palm** (☎ 07-4084 2626; ❀ 2.30am-8pm) runs a less frequent service (one way $35).

Coral Reef Coaches (☎ 07-4098 2800; ❀ 6.20am-3.50pm) has eight services to the airport daily (one way $32).

Sun Palm (☎ 07-4084 2626; www.sunpalmtransport .com) and **Coral Reef Coaches** (☎ 07-4098 2800) run local shuttle buses connecting Port Douglas' hotels and resorts with the beach and main

street (adult/child $4/2) half hourly from 8am to 11pm.

Pedalling around compact 'Dougie' is a sensible transport method. **Port Douglas Bike Hire Centre** (☎ 07-4099 5799; www.portdouglasbikehire .com; cnr Warner & Wharf Sts; per day from $19; ❀ 9am-5pm) has high-performance bikes for hire and offers shuttles to the 'bump track', which takes a couples of hours to cycle around. Also offers free delivery and pick-up.

For a cab contact **Port Douglas Taxis** (☎ 07-4084 2600, 13 10 08).

Port Douglas is one of the last places you can hire a 4WD before Cooktown:

Latitude 16 Holiday Car Hire (☎ 07-4099 4999; 54 Macrossan St; ❀ 8am-5pm Mon-Sat, to noon Sun)

Thrifty (☎ 07-4099 5555; www.thrifty.com; 50 Macros-san St; ❀ 7.30am-5.30pm)

MOSSMAN
pop 1740

Mossman is an unassuming town criss-crossed with cane-train tracks and featuring the wonderful **Mossman Gorge**, which draws in tourists by the 'where can I park my van'-load. There's a great 2.4km walk there, and swimming is possible, but beware of the danger of swimming after heavy rain. It's Mt Demi that you see in the town's background, and the almost century-old rain trees, behind the rail tracks, are worth tracking down.

The traditional owners of the Mossman Gorge, the Kuku-yalanji, operate **Kuku-Yalanji Dreamtime Walks** (☎ 07-4098 2595; www.yalanji.com .au; adult/child $32/19; ❀ 9am, 11am, 1pm & 3pm Mon-Sat) on the road to the gorge. The art gallery at the end of the long snake has free entry. Transfers from Port Douglas are adult/child $23/18; they leave at 8.30am and get you back to town at 11.30am.

Next to the cane-train track, **Mossman QPWS** (☎ 07-4098 2188; www.epa.qld.gov.au; ❀ 8am-4pm Mon-Fri) has maps and info.

The rooms at **Mossman Gorge B&B** (☎ 07-4098 2497; www.bnbnq.com.au/mossgorge; lot 15, Gorge View Cres; s/d $90/105) have dark timber floors, feature walls and antiques. The guest spaces are wonderful, and the views and birdlife are mesmerising. Breakfast, consisting of muffins, croissants and fruit, is included.

Get nude at **White Cockatoo** (☎ 07-4098 2222; www.thewhitecockatoo.com; 9 Alchera Dr; cabins $80-120), which celebrates its nudist season from 1 October to 1 March and runs nude tours to the Daintree and Reef. Half the premises is for clothed folk, too, and never the twain shall meet (unless they're in the same state of dress/undress). The cabins are huge.

The pies and wraps are all good and healthy at **Goodies Café** (☎ 07-4098 1118; 10 Front St; dishes $7-9; ☺ breakfast & lunch Mon-Sat), while **Raintrees Café** (☎ 07-4098 2139; 1 Front St; dishes $10; ☺ 8am-7pm Mon-Sat, to 5pm Sun) cooks up chicken, chips and burgers daily.

Getting There & Around

Coral Reef Coaches (☎ 07-4098 2800; www.coralreef coaches.com.au) stops in Mossman from Cairns ($35, two hours) and from Port Douglas ($12, 20 minutes).

Sun Palm (☎ 07-4084 2626; www.sunpalmtrans port.com) runs regular bus services between Mossman and Cairns ($45, two hours), and Port Douglas ($10, 20 minutes).

DAINTREE VILLAGE
pop 100

Surprisingly, given its tropical rainforest surrounds, **Daintree Village** (www.daintreevillage.asn.au) is not tree-covered, and you might be surprised to see cattle farms operating in large clearings next to the Daintree River. Most folk come here to see crocodiles, and there are several small operators that will take you on croc-spotting boat tours. Otherwise, there's little more on offer than birdwatching, snacking at the cafes or buying furry souvenirs.

Bruce Belcher's Daintree River Cruises (☎ 07-4098 7717; www.daintreerivercruise.com; adult/child $22/10; ☺ 8.15am-4pm) Seven tours daily; 3km north of the Cape Tribulation ferry turn-off.

Chris Dahlberg's Specialised River Tours (☎ 07-4098 7997; www.daintreerivertours.com.au; Daintree Village; 2hr tours adult/child $55/35; ☺ tours 6.30am Apr-Oct, 6am Nov-Jan) Specialises in birdwatching.

Daintree River Experience (☎ 07-4098 7480; www .daintreecruises.com.au; adult/child $50/35) Has sunrise and sunset tours on a swivel-seated birdwatching boat.

Dan Irby's Mangrove Adventures (☎ 07-4090 7017; www.mangroveadventures.com.au; tours from $50) Pick a sunrise, day or sunset tour. Open-air shallow boat with swivel seats for optimum birdwatching.

Wild Wings & Swampy Things (☎ 07-4098 6155; www.wildwings.com.au; tours $30) Recommended.

Sleeping & Eating

Red Mill House B&B (☎ 07-4098 6233; www.redmill house.com.au; Stewart St; s/d $150/180; ☒ ▣ ☒) Birds are taken very seriously at this internationally renowned birdwatching B&B, but, for some

balance, there's also a white-lipped green tree frog in the pantry. The eclectic rooms are well appointed (with bathrooms), and there's a comfortable communal lounge where you can chat to the bright, interesting hosts and other twitchers. The breakfasts are big, and while one guest – a doctor – called it a 'cholesterol pack', lighter versions are available. Families are welcome, and it's best to book ahead.

our pick Daintree Eco Lodge & Spa (☎ 07-4098 6100; www.daintree-ecolodge.com.au; 20 Daintree Rd; s/d from $510/550; ☒ ▣ ☒) Where else does your breakfast come with a free fruit platter and local yoghurt? Thanks to its position, imbedded in the rainforest, this eco lodge is always buzzing. There's Aboriginal art being created in the dining room and incense burns as you try to stop the brush turkeys from eating your breakfast before you do. The rooms have microscreens so you can hear the sounds without being eaten alive by mosquitoes, and you can expect resort essentials such as king-sized beds, flowers, and, if you're lucky, an outdoor spa. You really don't need to leave the property: there are cultural walks, the on-site spa offers treatments from $65, and the restaurant, Julaymba, offers 'spa cuisine' and specialities such as pan-fried North Queensland wild boar ($30).

Daintree Riverview Caravan Park (☎ 07-4098 6119; www.daintreeriverview.com; cnr Dagmar & Stewart Sts; unpowered/powered sites $20/25, cabins $99) Caters for budget travellers and has boat hire (half/full day $55/99).

Lunch is easy to find here: try the **Village Restaurant** (☎ 07-4098 6146; Stewart St; light meals $5-10, mains $14-30) or go for scones with jam and cream at the out-of-town, old-fashioned **Daintree Tea House Restaurant** (☎ /fax 07-4098 6161; Daintree Rd; meals from $8; ☺ lunch).

Getting a meal once the tourists have gone home can be tricky, but try **Papaya** (☎ 07-4098 6173; Stewart St; mains $18-24; ☺ lunch daily, dinner Wed-Sun), where crocodile bites and fresh sugarcane prawns are on the menu.

AROUND CAPE TRIBULATION

Rainforest, beaches, bats and some fairly hardcore driving are features of this intriguing area where tropical rainforest meets the sea. It's only accessible via cable ferry (or 4WD from Cooktown), and, adding to its mystery, it's where rainforest retreat-style accommodation regularly gets taken over by the surrounding

WORLD HERITAGE LISTING – WHAT DOES IT GUARANTEE?

Far North Queensland's Wet Tropics area has amazing pockets of biodiversity. The Wet Tropics World Heritage Area stretches from Townsville to Cooktown and covers 894,420 hectares of coastal zones and hinterland, diverse swamp and mangrove-forest habitats, eucalypt woodlands and tropical rainforest. It covers only 0.01% of Australia's surface area, but has:

- 36% of all the mammal species
- 50% of the bird species
- around 60% of the butterfly species
- 65% of the fern species.

Yep – wow!

Daintree National Park: Then & Now

The greater Daintree rainforest is protected as part of the Daintree National Park. The Daintree area has a controversial history. In 1983 the Bloomfield Track was bulldozed through sensitive lowland rainforest from Cape Tribulation to the Bloomfield River, attracting international attention to the fight to save the lowland rainforests. The conservationists lost that battle, but the publicity generated by the blockade indirectly led to the federal government's moves in 1987 to nominate Queensland's wet tropical rainforests for World Heritage listing. Despite strenuous resistance by the Queensland timber industry and state government, the area was inscribed on the World Heritage List in 1988 and commercial logging was banned.

In the mid 1980s, 1136 freehold properties were created between the Daintree River and Cape Tribulation. Since the '90s, efforts have been made by the Queensland state government and conservation agencies to buy back and rehabilitate these properties; 240 were bought back in 2004,

greenery, and the sun is rarely seen through thick foliage. Swimming holes, forest walks and wildlife spotting make this an area you're unlikely to ever forget.

About 11km before Daintree Village and 24km from Mossman is the turn-off to the **Daintree River cable ferry** (car/motorcycle $19/9, bicycle & pedestrian $2; ☯ 6am-midnight), which runs every 15 minutes and takes two minutes to cross the river into the Cape Tribulation area. After crossing the river it's another 34km by sealed road to Cape Tribulation. The Indigenous Kuku-yalanji people called the area Kulki, but the name Cape Tribulation was given by Captain Cook after his ship ran aground on Endeavour Reef.

Part of the Wet Tropics World Heritage Area, the region from Daintree River north to Cape Tribulation is famed for its ancient rainforest and the rugged mountains of **Thornton Peak** (1375m) and **Mount Sorrow** (770m).

Electricity is powered by generators and solar power in this area and few places have air-con. Cape Trib is one of the most popular day trips from Port Douglas and Cairns, and accommodation is booked solid in peak periods.

You can get fuel and supplies at **Rainforest Village** (☎ 07-4098 9015; Cape Tribulation Rd; ☯ 7am-7pm), 16km from the ferry on Cape Tribulation Rd, but self-caterers are better off coming prepared. Coral Reef Coaches and Sun Palm Express run daily bus services from Cairns to Cape Tribulation (see p448). For information on organised trips to the area, see Tours in the Cairns (p443) and Port Douglas (p463) sections.

A couple of operators offer trips out to the Great Barrier Reef from Cape Tribulation. **Rumrunner** (☎ 1800 644 227; www.rumrunner.com.au; tours adult/child $140/100) has an excellent day trip to the Mackay and Undine reefs.

The following sections chart a route from the Daintree River to Cape Tribulation.

Cape Kimberley

Take the rough Cape Kimberley Rd, 8km beyond the Daintree River crossing, to get to **Cape Kimberley Beach**, a beautiful, shimmering beach where you see Mt Alexander falling into the sea, while **Snapper Island** sits in front of you, just offshore. The small island is a national park, with a fringing reef. Access to the adding to the 81 properties purchased in the initial buy-back. The Queensland state government and Rainforest Rescue are still trying to protect a further 200 properties in the Daintree from development. The increased human population also brings dogs and traffic (neither of which mixes well with the resident cassowaries), and invasive species, including Guinea grass, Asian bramble and Singapore daisy, which have already invaded the near-pristine forests, into the area.

Check out www.rainforestrescue.org.au for more information.

What can I do?

When visiting this impossibly beautiful part of the world, *leave only footprints behind*. That's as easy as taking your rubbish with you, sticking to the designated trails and driving slowly to avoid hitting wildlife. When travelling, consider the following questions to try to minimise your 'environmental footprint':

- Does the tour I'm going on have eco-certification (www.ecotourism.org.au)?
- Are tour participants encouraged to take their rubbish with them when visiting World Heritage sites?
- Am I using natural, chemical-free toiletries while travelling?
- Are there any volunteer opportunities for me to assist with cleaning up beaches or wildlife monitoring etc?
- Is there a not-for-profit environment group to which I can donate, eg Austrop (www.austrop .org.au), the Wilderness Society (www.wilderness.org.au) or the Australian Conservation Foundation (www.acfonline.org.au)?
- Is my accommodation choice encouraging guests to recycle rubbish and reduce water consumption?

island is by private boat; Crocodylus Village (right) runs overnight sea-kayaking tours there on Monday, Wednesday and Friday. If you're organising it yourself, you'll need a permit for the **QPWS camping ground** (☎ 07-4098 2188; www.epa.qld.gov.au; per person/family $5/20) on the southwest side of Snapper Island. The campsite has a toilet and picnic tables. Be sure to take a fuel stove with you, as fires are not permitted here.

On the beach is **Koala Beach Resort** (☎ 1800 466 444, 07-4090 7500; www.koala-backpackers.com; Cape Kimberley; unpowered/powered sites $13/16, dm $25, d $50-125; 🗙 🖭), a sprawling camping ground with campsites and safari tents shaded by large trees and banana palms. Meals at the bar and restaurant are around $20, or you can buy a breakfast/dinner pack ($15).

Cow Bay

There's a footpath from the main road to beautiful Cow Bay, where you'll find rainforest logs wedged into the coral-filled sand. It's a popular fishing spot, too.

Before the turn-off to the Jindalba Boardwalk is the **Walu Wugirriga (Alexandra Range)** **lookout**, which offers marvellous views over the Alexandra Range and Snapper Island.

Get walking at the **Daintree Discovery Centre** (☎ 07-4098 9171; www.daintree-rec.com.au; adult/child/concession/family $33/14/30/78; ⏰ 8.30am-5pm), which has several rainforest walks lined with interpretive panels. If you need more information, the multilingual audio guide comes in handy (included in the entry fee unless you say no), as does the booklet, which is a useful resource for the entire trip. There's an aerial walkway that traverses the forest floor to a 23m viewing tower. The small theatre runs films such as *Australia's Deadliest Animals*. **Jindalba Boardwalk** is less than 1km down the road, and has picnic tables, a 700m walk and a longer 2.7km version.

SLEEPING & EATING

Crocodylus Village (☎ 07-4098 9166; www.crocodylus capetrib.com; Buchanan Creek Rd; dm/d $23/75; 🖳 🖭) The atmosphere's friendly at this centre-of-the-rainforest YHA hostel, especially at happy hour at the bar. Line up for $15 dinners before heading back to your safari tent to listen to the drops of rain shimmying down the surrounding trees and onto the canvas roof. Staff can arrange two-day sea-kayaking tours to Snapper Island ($199), departing Monday, Wednesday and Friday.

our pick Epiphyte B&B (☎ 07-4098 9039; www .rainforestbb.com; 22 Silkwood Rd; s $70, d $85-95) Light is the key at this wonderful, solar-powered B&B, with charming slate-floored rooms with private balconies. If the going's been tough, lie on one of the hammocks and sky gaze under the wind chimes. The cabin with a sunken bathroom is popular with honeymooners and breakfast is tropical-fruit-with-coffee style.

Prema Shanti (☎ 07-4098 9006; www.premashanti .com; 183 Turpentine Rd; per person tw/cabin $80/140) With two choices of room (boutique and off-site de-luxe), both with corrugated-iron feature walls, this yoga and meditation retreat is suitable for hard-core meditators/yoga devotees as well as travellers passing through (though you must book ahead). Some rooms are directly under the temple, making it an easy stroll to the daily 7am meditation session.

Coral Sea Views (☎ 07-4098 9058; 11 Mahogany Rd, Cow Bay; d $175) Consists of two cabins with out-standing views and a luxury camping atmos-phere. As it's powered by generator and solar, you're provided with torches and eskies (to keep the wine cold). Laze away in a hammock on the fat verandah and listen to the stereo.

Daintree Wilderness Lodge (☎ 07-4098 9105; www .daintreewildernesslodge.com.au; 83 Cape Tribulation Rd; r incl breakfast $270; 🅢) No internet, no mobile phone signal, no under-5s and plenty of nature means it's quiet here. The seven ecocabins are joined by rustic boardwalks and feature skylights for perfect fan-palm views. Add to the 'recently spotted animals' list at reception when you get back from one of the lodge's rainforest walks. Meals are available ($30 to $35).

Linc Haven Rainforest Retreat (☎ 07-4098 9155; Cape Tribulation Rd; unpowered/powered sites $19/24, cabins $100-140) This is a friendly place with a resi-dent croc (in an enclosure), roos and carpet pythons, and large, clean motel-style rooms on 20 acres. Good meals (meals $5 to $19) are served in the restaurant throughout the day.

Daintree Ice Cream Company (☎ 07-4098 9114; Cape Tribulation Rd; ice creams $5; 🕙 11am-5pm) Set in the middle of productive fruit trees, this is the ultimate in fine alfresco ice-cream eating. The ice cream of the day might be apricot, sour-sop or the chocolate-pudding-tasting black sapota. This is one place where you pray the generator keeps humming.

Fan Palm Boardwalk Café (☎ 07-4098 9243; Cape Tribulation Rd; mains $8-16) Open-air licensed cafe serving great coffee next to a boardwalk. Also organises tours.

Jambu Bar & Kitchen (☎ 07-4098 9333; lot 335, Cape Tribulation Rd; mains $15-28; 🕙 dinner) This is a light in the dark rainforest, with crisp Coral Sea–prawn pizza and kaffir-lime-tinged, reef-fish choo-chee curry. Everything is made on site.

Floravilla (☎ 07-4098 9100; Cape Tribulation Rd; mains $15-28; 🕙 lunch) To continue the theme of 'homemade ice cream capital of Australia', Betty makes 26 types of the sweet stuff, in-cluding vanilla from organic vanilla beans from down the road. On offer for lunch is quick-fried calamari, sandwiches and burgers; while you wait check out the tiny Floravilla gallery.

Cooper Creek

Cooper Creek Wilderness Cruises (☎ 07-4098 9126; www.ccwild.com; adult/child $40/30) has two-hour rainforest walks departing at 9am, 2pm and 8pm.

In a relaxed rainforest setting, **Daintree Deep Forest Lodge** (☎ 07-4098 9162; www.daintreedeepforest lodge.com.au; Cape Tribulation Rd; r $130-150) has kitch-ens set up for the gourmet traveller and fits five in the cream brick units.

Thornton Beach

Thornton Beach Bungalows (☎ 07-4098 9179; www .thorntonbeach.com; Cape Tribulation Rd; cabins/house $85/250) has two petite cabins with veran-dahs near the main road and beach, and the house, which sleeps four, is also available for a two-night minimum.

Noah Beach

Marrdja Botanical Walk is a 20-minute spin from rainforest to the mangrove-rimmed Noah Creek. A further 1.5km along is **Noah Beach Camping Area** (☎ 07-4098 0052; www.epa.qld.gov.au; per person/family $5/20), a forest-meets-sea delight. Register prior to arrival or risk having to pay $75 for one of 17 shady sites.

CAPE TRIBULATION

Volunteers from Austrop, a local conserva-tion organisation, run the **Bat House** (☎ 07-4098 0083; www.austrop.org.au; Cape Tribulation Rd; admission $4; 🕙 10.30am-3.30pm Tue-Sun), a nursery for fruit bats. The surrounding forest is slowly regenerating and there's a walk to show you the changes.

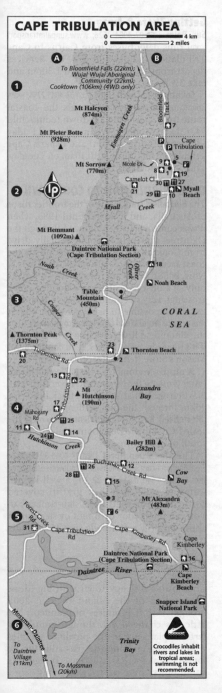

CAPE TRIBULATION AREA

Jungle Adventures (☎ 07-4098 0090; www.jungleadventurescapetrib.com.au; tours $35) runs excellent and informative night and day walks.

Cape Tribulation Horse Rides (☎ 1800 111 124, 07-4098 0030; tours $99; ☉ 8am & 1.30pm) offers horseback strolls through rainforest and paddock trails from Cape Trib Beach House. Or trade a saddle for a flying-fox harness with **Jungle Surfing Canopy Tours** (☎ 07-4098 0090; www.junglesurfingcanopytours.com; adult $85), which picks up from all accommodation; the meeting point for self-drivers is the Cape Trib pharmacy.

Sleeping & Eating

PK's Jungle Village (☎ 1800 232 333, 07-4098 0040; www.pksjunglevillage.com; Cape Tribulation Rd; unpowered sites per person $10, dm/s $23/44, d $66-115; ☒ ▣ ☒) You're not here for the boring and slightly musty rooms at PK's – you're here because that's where the bus dropped you, and you're here to party. There's music all day and nearly all night and a dance floor, airy restaurant and plenty of resortlike space.

Cape Trib Beach House (☎ 1800 111 124, 07-4098 0030; www.capetribbeach.com.au; Cape Tribulation Rd; dm $25, r $89-189, apt $249; ✗ ⬜ ⬛) The winding driveway heads straight from the main road to near the beach, past earthy dorms with slat windows and pleasant A-frames. The complex includes a small communal kitchen, and Sounds of the Water (mains $26) restaurant-bar with winged canvas roofing. Ideal for travellers who want to restore their Zen.

Cape Trib Farmstay (☎ 07-4098 0042; www.capetrib farmstay.com; Cape Tribulation Rd; d incl breakfast $130; ✗) Sleep near banana trees in one of five timber cabins (one has disabled access) with verandahs and smart bed linen. Cheaper accommodation in the farmhouse means visits from the cuddly blue heeler, Buttons. Enjoy an exotic fruit breakfast. Seasonal fruit-pickers (with work permits; call ahead for opportunities) are welcome January to May.

Rainforest Hideaway (☎ 07-4098 0108; www.rain foresthideaway.com; 19 Camelot Cl; r incl breakfast $95-135) This is a hand-built combination of timber rooms, bright colours and Easter Island sculptures designed to surprise and rejuvenate. Owner Rob is not always there, so establish contact before arriving.

Cape Trib Exotic Fruit Farm (☎ 07-4098 0057; www.capetrib.com.au; Lot 5 Nicole Dr; d $160) This place has three well-designed, ecocertified cabins on the forest's edge that run on solar power. The fruit farm runs daily tastings at 2pm (adult/child $20/10) of the home-grown fruits, though if you stay, you'll get to sample yours at breakfast. Rates go down the longer you stay.

Cape Tribulation Camping (☎ 07-4098 0077; www.capetribcamping.com.au; Cape Tribulation Rd; unpowered/powered sites $30/36, s/d $45/65) A wall of rainforest separates the campers from the beach in this well maintained park. Two-hour sea-kayaking tours are available from $45; sea-kayak hire is from $20 per hour.

Whet (☎ 07-4098 0009; Cape Tribulation Rd; mains $15-30; ✆ lunch & dinner; ⬜) This is a flash restaurant with dishes including pan-fried local tiger pawns matched with wine suggestions. There is also tapas if you happen to hit this place in the afternoon, and movies screen in the upstairs cinema.

Self-caterers can stock up at **IGA Express** (✆ 8am-7pm), which has an ATM plus a pharmacy next door (the pick-up point for Jungle Surfing Canopy Tours), and **Mason's Store** (☎ 07-4098 0070; Cape Tribulation Rd; ✆ 8.30am-8pm) is a one-stop supply shop that also runs tours.

Getting There & Away

Sun Palm (☎ 07-4084 2626; www.sunpalmtransport .com) runs daily buses from Cairns to Cape Tribulation (adult/child $75/32). Services depart from Cairns at 7am and 1.30pm and take 3½ hours.

Country Road Coach Lines (☎ 07-4045 2794; www .countryroadcoachlines.com.au) travels the coastal route from Cairns to Cooktown (adult/child $42/21) on Monday, Wednesday and Friday (departing Cairns at 7am) and departs Cape Tribulation for Cairns at 10.10am on Tuesday, Thursday and Saturday.

CAPE TRIBULATION TO COOKTOWN

The **Bloomfield Track** is one of the frontier roads of Australia, and it wasn't until 1983, when it was controversially bulldozed through the Daintree, that people could actually drive from Cooktown to Cape Tribulation via the coast (see Daintree National Park: Then & Now, p468). There are reasons why it's 4WD only: it's unsealed, there are flooded creek crossings, very steep and slippery hills and it's usually impossible to use during the Wet. It passes the **Wujal Wujal Aboriginal community** near the Bloomfield River crossing (which is tidal; if it's too deep, wait). Check road conditions at Mason's Store (left) before heading off.

A must-see along the way is **Bloomfield Falls** (after crossing the Bloomfield River turn left). North from Wujal Wujal the track heads for 46km through the tiny settlements of **Ayton (Bloomfield)**, **Rossville** and **Helensvale** to meet the sealed Cooktown Developmental Rd, 28km south of Cooktown.

The **Lion's Den Hotel** (☎ 07-4060 3911; www .lionsdenhotel.com.au; Helensvale; unpowered/powered sites $20/26, s $40, d $50-70; ⬛) is a well-known watering hole that has graffiti-covered corrugated-iron walls and a slab-timber bar. You can pitch your own tent or sleep in an above-ground safari-style tent ($70). Fuel is available.

COOKTOWN

pop 2000

Cooktown's a sleepy town with big ideas. The sealing of the inland road in 2006 brought with it promises of grandeur, but little has changed yet, though grand waterfront plans are in the pipeline. Yachties who've been cruising the seas still stop by for a chat at the RSL, the local Indigenous community, buoyed by a thriving silica

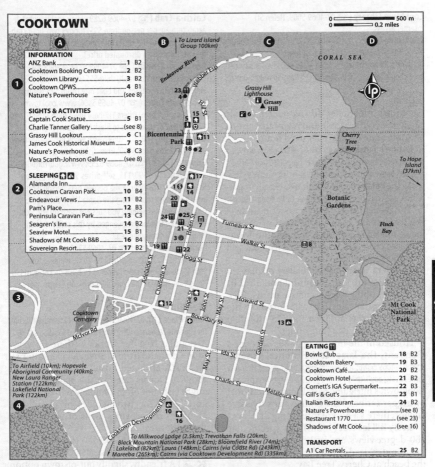

COOKTOWN

INFORMATION
ANZ Bank	**1**	B2
Cooktown Booking Centre	**2**	B2
Cooktown Library	**3**	B2
Cooktown QPWS	**4**	B1
Nature's Powerhouse	(see 8)	

SIGHTS & ACTIVITIES
Captain Cook Statue	**5**	B1
Charlie Tanner Gallery	(see 8)	
Grassy Hill Lookout	**6**	C1
James Cook Historical Museum	**7**	B2
Nature's Powerhouse	**8**	C3
Vera Scarth-Johnson Gallery	(see 8)	

SLEEPING
Alamanda Inn	**9**	B3
Cooktown Caravan Park	**10**	B4
Endeavour Views	**11**	B2
Pam's Place	**12**	B3
Peninsula Caravan Park	**13**	C3
Seagren's Inn	**14**	B2
Seaview Motel	**15**	B1
Shadows of Mt Cook B&B	**16**	B4
Sovereign Resort	**17**	B2

EATING
Bowls Club	**18**	B2
Cooktown Bakery	**19**	B3
Cooktown Café	**20**	B2
Cooktown Hotel	**21**	B2
Cornett's IGA Supermarket	**22**	B3
Gill's & Gut's	**23**	B1
Italian Restaurant	**24**	B2
Nature's Powerhouse	(see 8)	
Restaurant 1770	(see 23)	
Shadows of Mt Cook	(see 16)	

TRANSPORT
A1 Car Rentals	**25**	B2

mine, have a pride and respect in the wider community, and everyone gets around in a dusty 4WD ute. Crocodiles make their presence felt in the Endeavour River, fisher folk search the seas for the famed black marlin, and twitchers head to the wetlands for birdwatching.

Recent-history-wise, from June to August 1770, Captain Cook beached his barque *Endeavour* here, during which time the expedition's chief naturalist, Joseph Banks, collected 186 species of Australian plants from the banks of the Endeavour River and wrote the first European description of a kangaroo.

Race relations in the area turned sour a century later when Cooktown was founded

as the unruly port for the Palmer River gold rush (1873–83), where fortunes were made – and drunk – swiftly. Battle Camp, about 60km inland from Cooktown, was the site of a major battle between Europeans and Aborigines. These days it's much more relaxed. Whatever you do, try to get to Cooktown on time, as siesta is from October to June. Work is often available on banana plantations.

Information

ANZ Bank (☎ 07-4069 6522; 115 Charlotte St)
Cooktown Booking Centre (☎ 07-4069 5381; www .cooktownbookings.com.au; 132 Charlotte St; ☉ 9am-5pm Mon-Fri, to noon Sat) Tour, accommodation and transport bookings, including coaches to Cairns.

Cooktown Library (☎ 07-4069 5009; Helen St) Internet access.

Cooktown QPWS (☎ 07-4069 5777; Webber Esplanade; ☿ 8.30am-3pm Mon-Fri) Closes for lunch.

Nature's Powerhouse (☎ 07-4069 6004; www.natures powerhouse.com.au; off Walker St; ☿ 9am-5pm) Info centre.

Sights

Cooktown hibernates during winter (locals call it 'the dead season'), and many attractions and tours close or have reduced hours.

Nature's Powerhouse (☎ 07-4069 6004; www.na turespowerhouse.com.au; off Walker St; adult/child $4/free; ☿ 9am-5pm) is an environment interpretive centre in the **Botanic Gardens**, with two excellent galleries, a great bookshop and a cafe (opposite).

The **Charles Tanner Gallery** shows off Charlie the local snake man's collection of mostly local amethyst pythons, though the long-deceased cross-eyed bare-backed fruit bat will give you nightmares.

The **Vera Scarth-Johnson Gallery** displays a collection of intricate, beautiful botanical illustrations of the region's native plants. Pick up a **walking trail** map that will take you to the Coral Sea **beaches** at Finch Bay (25 minutes) and Cherry Tree Bay (one hour).

Housed in the imposing 1880s St Mary's Convent, the **James Cook Historical Museum** (☎ 07-4069 5386; jcmuseum@ecn.net.au; cnr Helen & Furneaux Sts; adult/child $10/3; ☿ 9.30am-4pm) explores Cooktown's intriguing past. From a traditional outrigger canoe to the *Endeavour*'s massive anchor, there's a host of interesting displays.

Grassy Hill lookout (162m) has spectacular 360-degree views, and its 1.5km walking trail (45 minutes) leads from the summit down to the beach at Cherry Tree Bay.

Charlotte St and Bicentennial Park have a number of interesting monuments, including the much-photographed bronze **Captain Cook statue**.

Tours

Limited tours operate from November until at least April.

Ahoy Plane Sailing Seaplanes (☎ 07-4069 5232, 0434 848 232; www.ahoyplane-sailingseaplanes.com.au; ☿ Jun-Dec) Chris flies a four-seater amphibious plane on reef and Lizard Island adventures (from $150).

Bart's Bush Adventures (☎ 07-4069 6229; www .bartsbushadventures.com.au; tours adult/child $165/85; camping safaris per day from $350) Luxury hunting and air-conditioned 4WD tours around the area. Accredited Savannah guides.

Catch-a-Crab (☎ 07-4069 6289; www.cooktowncatch acrab.com.au; per person from $95) Nicko's two-hour crab-catching tours of the Endeavour and Annan Rivers are great for kids (who get a discounted price).

Cooktown Cruises (☎ 07-4069 5712; www.cook towncruises.com.au; adult/child $55/30) Two-hour scenic Endeavour River cruises and boat hire (from $25 per hour).

Cooktown Tours (☎ 07-4069 5406; www.cooktown tours.com; ☿ 9am) Offers 1½-hour town tours (adult/child $28/17) and 2½ hour trips to Black Mountain ($55/33).

Gone Fishing (☎ 07-4069 5980; www.fishingcooktown .com; 4hr tours from $100) River fishing tours.

Guurrbi Tours (☎ 07-4069 6259; www.guurrbitours .com; 2/4hr tours $90/115, self-drives $60/80; ☿ Mon-Sat) Nugal-warra elder Willie Gordon gets personal on his award-winning tours along the Bama Way, visiting Nugal rock-art sites and helping you suss out bush tucker. Expect to have your thinking challenged by this softly spoken man. Highly recommended.

Maaramaka Tours (☎ 07-4069 5381; www.maara maka.com; 2hr tours adult/child $40/30, walking tours $80/45) Rainforest walks followed by bush tucker feasts in Hope Vale. Book at the Cooktown Booking Centre, p473.

Sleeping

Pam's Place (☎ 07-4069 5166; www.cooktownhostel.com; cnr Charlotte & Boundary Sts; dm/s $27/55, d $55-95; ☼ ☷) A popular base for workers (there's a year-round demand from the banana plantations), this YHA-affiliated hostel has a banana air about it. Dorms cater for the pickers, so you might be better off in a homely self-contained unit ($100 for two people) or elsewhere. Management provides loads of information about the area.

Alamanda Inn (☎ 07-4069 5203; phscott@tpg.com.au; cnr Hope & Howard Sts; guest house s/d $40/50, unit s/d $65/75; ☼ ☷) A friendly, slightly out-of-town option suitable for families and banana pickers who require a bit of space. The classic motel-style units have bathrooms.

Endeavour Views (☎ 07-4069 5676; cnr Charlotte & Hill Sts; cabins $88-108) Five comfortable corrugated cabins line the spot where Captain Cook drank his water back in 1770. Each has a fridge and a balcony. The self-contained unit ($150 to $170) is practically a house and has the best balcony view in town.

Seaview Motel (☎ 07-4069 5377; seaviewmotel@ bigpond.com; 178 Charlotte St; s/d from $95/115; ☼ ☷) Low-rise motel popular with families and fisher folk who plot their next day's fishing while taking dress-circle seats for one of Far North Queensland's best sunsets. A top-of-the-hill town house is available for $220.

Shadows of Mt Cook B&B (☎ 07-4069 5584; cnr Hope & Burkitt Sts; r incl breakfast $120; ☒) Nonchalant hosts, fresh rooms with Aboriginal prints and top-notch bathrooms; rooms are close to the adjoining restaurant (below) so noise may carry.

Milkwood Lodge (☎ 07-4069 5007; www.milkwood lodge.com; Annan Rd; units $130; ☒ ☒) About 2.5km south of the centre of town, these six breezy, self-contained, timber-pole cabins have bush-land spilling between them, and tranquil views. Cabins are spacious and split-level and the hosts have plenty of adventure stories to tell.

Sovereign Resort (☎ 07-4043 0500; www.sovereign -resort.com.au; cnr Charlotte & Green Sts; d $170-185; ☒ ☒) A great hotel with quality linen, air-conditioned comfort and louvred, sliding doors that look out onto the pool and palm trees. Also has a 4WD for rent.

Also recommended:

Cooktown Caravan Park (☎ 07-4069 5536; www .cooktowncaravanpark.com; 14-16 Hope St; unpowered/ powered sites $22/27) A small and friendly park set on a gorgeous bush block with wood-burning barbecues.

Peninsula Caravan Park (☎ 07-4069 5107; 64 Howard St; unpowered/powered sites $24/30, cabins $80-100) A beautiful, treed spot.

Eating

Gill's & Gut's (☎ 07-4069 5863; Fisherman's Wharf, Webber Esplanade; meals $8-17; ☙ lunch, dinner to 7.30pm) This mighty takeaway dishes up fish and chips in old-school paper parcels. The fare is spectacular – barramundi or Spanish mackerel, prawns or coral trout – but peak hour can have killer queues.

Cooktown Hotel (☎ 07-4069 5308; Charlotte St; mains $9-20; ☙ lunch & dinner) With walls lined with pictures of beer-lovin' women, and '80s Aussie music in the background, this friendly local is pretty darn authentic. Seafood-rich menu.

Cooktown Café (☎ 07-4069 6848; Charlotte St; mains $11) This is the place to go for a big fried brekky, and the coffee's decent.

Nature's Powerhouse (☎ 07-4069 6004; Walker St; meals $12-16; ☙ lunch) Head here for huge salads, gado gado, good kids' meals, homemade bread and award-winning scones. The ginger soda is refreshing.

Italian Restaurant (☎ 07-4069 6338; Charlotte St; mains $13-20; ☙ dinner Mon-Sat) For satisfying pizzas and pastas, head to this new kid on the block. Does fairly fast takeaway, too.

Bowls Club (☎ 07-4069 6173; Charlotte St; mains $17-21; ☙ lunch & dinner) Sign yourself in at the door, and join the club for the night. Apart from the enormous surf'n'turf tucker, you're able to visit the salad bar as often as you like and natter with the Cooktown regulars. Outdoor diners get a spectacular view of bowling in action.

ourpick **Shadows of Mt Cook** (☎ 07-4069 5584; cnr Hope & Burkitt Sts; mains $22-25; ☙ dinner Tue-Sat) A fantastic restaurant that will impress and surprise gourmet food lovers. There's a tinge of Bali as well as dishes such as sirloin steak with blue brie and Japanese calamari with seaweed. BYO only; book ahead.

Restaurant 1770 (☎ 07-4069 5440; 7 Webber Esplanade; mains $22-32; ☙ lunch & dinner year-round, breakfast Jun-Dec) The views at this seafood restaurant are spectacular, so get an outside table if possible and don't expect great service.

Grab supplies from **Cornett's IGA supermarket** (☎ 07-4069 5633; cnr Helen & Hogg Sts; ☙ 8am-6pm Mon-Wed, Fri & Sat, 8am-7pm Thu, 9am-5pm Sun) and **Cooktown Bakery** (☎ 07-4069 5612; cnr Hogg & Charlotte Sts; ☙ 6am-9pm Mon-Fri, to 4pm Sat & Sun).

Getting There & Around

Cooktown's airfield is 10km west of town along McIvor Rd. **Skytrans** (☎ 1800 818 405, 07-4069 5446; www.skytrans.com.au) flies up to four times a day (Monday, Tuesday, Thursday and Friday) between Cooktown and Cairns (adult/child $123/75, 35 minutes). **Cooktown Travel** (☎ 07-4069 5446) has airport transfers for $13/10 per adult/child.

Country Road Coach Lines (☎ 07-4045 2794; www .countryroadcoachlines.com.au) runs a Cooktown-to-Cairns inland service (adult/child $72/36) on Wednesday, Friday and Sunday (departing at 2.30pm and arriving in Cairns at 7pm). A coastal service operates on Tuesday, Thursday and Saturday (departing Cooktown at 7am, arriving at 1.30pm). Courtesy pick-ups are available and drop-offs to Cairns airport can be arranged.

A1 Car Rentals (☎ 1300 301 175, 07-4069 6308; 112 Charlotte St) has small, medium and large cars for hire plus 4WDs, which are ideal for a spin down to Cape Tribulation. Bookings can be made seven days a week, 24 hours a day.

There are also **taxis** (☎ 07-4069 5387) in town.

LIZARD ISLAND
pop 280

Lizard Island certainly wins points on the isolation front: it's 100km from Cooktown and the most northern Great Barrier Reef island. Divers have discovered its charm, and head 20km away to one of Australia's top dive sites, the outer reef and the **Cod Hole**, usually via live-aboard trips. Yachties are drawn here and dinghies shuttle to and from yachts moored in sparkling casuarina-lined Watson's Bay (one of 23 beaches).

There are great walks through country that switches from mangrove to rainforest to dry and rocky in mere minutes, including a hike up to **Cook's Look** (368m).

Jigurru (Lizard Island) has long been a sacred place for the Dingaal Aboriginal people. Diving tours here can be arranged through **Diving Cairns** (☎ 07-4041 7536; www.divingcairns.com.au; 4-day tours per person from $1180) and Lizard Island Resort (below).

If you don't have a yacht, your accommodation options are camping or a five-star luxury resort. The **camping ground** (per person/family $5/20) is a 10-minute walk from the resort, at the northern end of Watson's Bay. You'll need a permit from QPWS (☎ 13 13 04, 07-4069 5777; www.epa.qld.gov.au) first, and it's worth checking that the water pump, toilets and gas barbecues are working. Campers must be self-sufficient, though the resort's Marlin Bar is accessible if you're after a drink (the rest of the resort is off-limits).

Wash the sand off your feet in giant clam shells filled with water before entering your smooth-as luxury room at **Lizard Island Resort** (☎ 1800 737 678, 07-4060 3999; www.lizardisland.com.au; Anchor Bay; d from $1650; ⚄ ⚄). Rates include all meals and most activities.

Hinterland flies to Lizard Island from Cairns (one way from $245, one hour) twice a day. Ahoy Plane Sailing Seaplanes (p474) has day trips (from $465) from Cooktown and **Daintree Air Services** (☎ 07-4034 9300) has day tours from Cairns ($590).

CAIRNS TO COOKTOWN – THE INLAND ROAD

It's 332km (about four hours' drive) from Cairns to Cooktown via this cattle, cockie 'n' croc route. You can either access the Mulligan Hwy from Mareeba, or via the turn-off just before Mossman. The road travels past rugged ironbarks and cattle-trodden land before joining the Cooktown Developmental Rd at Lakeland. From here it's another 80km to Cooktown.

The tiny town of **Mount Molloy** marks the start of the Mulligan Hwy. The **National Hotel** (☎ 07-4094 1133; Main St; s/d $35/70, mains $12; ⏱ lunch & dinner) has accommodation; **Lobo Loco** (☎ 07-4094 1187; meals $10) serves up Mexican meals.

The Palmer River gold rush (1873–83) occurred about 70km to the west, throwing up the boom towns of Palmerville and Maytown; little of either remains today. You can buy horrendously expensive fuel and snacks at the **Palmer River roadhouse** (☎ 07-4060 2020; ⏱ 7.30am-9pm), which also has accommodation.

South of Cooktown the road travels through the thoroughly sinister-looking rock piles of **Black Mountain National Park** – a range of hills formed 260 million years ago and made up of thousands of granite boulders. Local Aboriginal people call it Kalcajagga, or 'place of the spears', and it's home to unique species of frog, skink and gecko.

CAPE YORK PENINSULA

Rugged and remote Cape York Peninsula has one of the wildest tropical environments on the planet. The Great Dividing Range forms the spine of the Cape, with tropical rainforests and palm-fringed beaches on its eastern flanks and sweeping savannah woodlands, dry eucalypt forests and coastal mangroves on its west. This untamed landscape undergoes an amazing transformation each year when the torrential rains and flooded rivers of the monsoonal 'wet season' form vast wetlands that isolate the region.

The overland pilgrimage to the tip of Australia is simply one of the greatest 4WD routes on the continent, an exhilarating trek into Australia's last great frontier. The challenge of rough corrugated roads, difficult creek crossings, and croc-infested rivers is part of the adventure, the cape's rich birdlife and untouched wilderness its reward. Take time to savour the experience – many of the highlights of the journey are in the unexpected and unplanned detours, and in the miles and miles of isolation.

Information & Permits

There are no official tourist information centres along the route to the cape but **Tourism Tropical North Queensland** (☎ 07-4051 3588; www.tropicalaustralia.com.au; 51 The Esplanade, Cairns; ⏱ 8.30am-6.30pm) in Cairns has comprehensive information for travel in the area. Also visit the **Queensland Parks & Wildlife Service** (QPWS; www.epa.qld.gov.au) in Cairns (p437) and Cooktown (p474) when planning your trip.

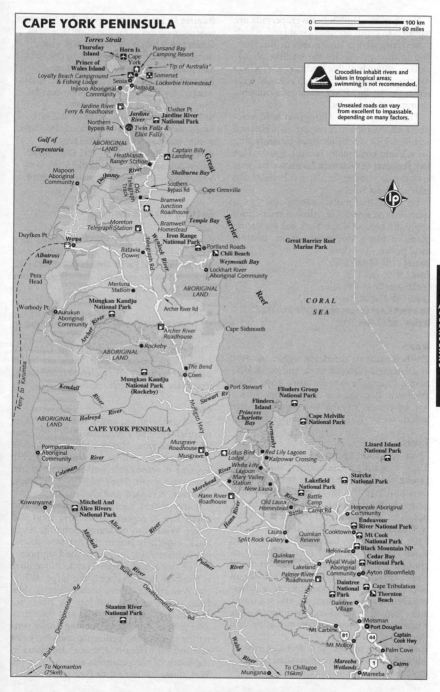

CAPE YORK PENINSULA

Crocodiles inhabit rivers and lakes in tropical areas; swimming is not recommended.

Unsealed roads can vary from excellent to impassable, depending on many factors.

North of the Dulhunty River, permits are required to camp on Aboriginal land, which is basically all the land north of the river. The Injinoo people are the traditional custodians of much of this land and the Injinoo Aboriginal Community, which runs the ferry across the Jardine River, includes a camping permit in the ferry fee.

Travelling across Aboriginal land elsewhere on the cape may require an additional permit, which can be obtained by contacting the relevant community council. See the **Cape York Peninsula Development Association Inc** (www .cypda.com.au) website for details. Permits can take up to six weeks.

Be aware that mobile-phone coverage is sporadic and unreliable. Alcohol restrictions apply throughout Cape York but vary from place to place. For information, contact local police:

Bamaga (☎ 07-4069 3156)
Coen (☎ 07-4060 1150)
Cooktown (☎ 07-4069 5320)
Laura (☎ 07-4060 3244)
Lockhart River Community (☎ 07-4060 7120)
Weipa (☎ 07-4069 9119)

MAPS

The best maps are the Hema maps *Cape York* and *Lakefield National Park*, and the RACQ maps *Cairns/Townsville* and *Cape York Peninsula*. Ron and Viv Moon's *Cape York – An Adventurer's Guide* is a comprehensive guidebook for 4WD and camping enthusiasts.

Tours

Countless tour operators run trips to the Cape – mainly from Cairns, some from Cooktown. Most tours range from six to 14 days and take five to 12 passengers. Tours generally run between April and November but dates may be affected by an early or late wet season. Places visited include Laura, Split Rock Gallery, Lakefield National Park, Coen, Weipa, the Eliot River System (including Twin Falls), Bamaga, Somerset and Cape York; Thursday Island is usually an optional extra. Many operators offer different combinations of land, air, and sea travel, and camping or motel-style accommodation. Prices include meals, accommodation and fares from Cairns.

Bart's Bush Adventures (☎ 07-4069 6229; www .bartsbushadventures.com.au; camping safaris per day from $350) A range of tours from Cooktown.

Daintree Air Services (☎ 1800 246 206, 07-4034 9300; www.daintreeair.com.au; day tours $1809) Fly to the tip.
Guides to Adventure (☎ 07-4091 1978; www .guidestoadventure.com.au; 12-/16-/22-day Cape York tours $1362/1816/2497) 4WD tag-along safaris.
Heritage Tours (☎ 07-4038 2628; www.heritagetours .com.au; 7-day budget safari $990, 7-14 day cruise/fly/ drive from $21,600) Numerous tour options.
Oz Tours Safaris (☎ 1800 079 006, 07-4055 9535; www.oztours.com.au; 7-day fly/drive from $1849, 16-day overland tours from $2725) Ecocertified tours.
Wilderness Challenge (☎ 07-4035 4488; www.wil derness-challenge.com.au; 7-day fly/drive $1895, 13-day overland safaris $2795) Excellent ecotourism accredited tours and informative guides.

Getting There & Away

AIR

QantasLink (☎ 13 13 13; www.qantas.com.au) flies daily from Cairns to Horn Island and Weipa. **Regional Pacific Airlines** (☎ 07-4040 1400; www.regionalpacific.com.au) has daily flights from Cairns to Bamaga.

BOAT

MV Trinity Bay (☎ 07-4035 1234; www.seaswift.com.au; per person tw incl meals 2-day one-way $645, 5-day return $1140) runs a weekly cargo ferry to Thursday Island and Seisia, which takes up to 38 passengers. It departs Cairns every Friday. Prices are for the high season.

CAR

Sound preparation, and a reliable 4WD, is mandatory. The Peninsula Developmental Rd is sealed from Mareeba to Lakeland while the unsealed section to Weipa (roughly 600km) is reasonably well-maintained but often corrugated. The Old Telegraph Track, however, is rugged and challenging.

Carry spares, tools and equipment, and check RACQ reports. Also carry food and water. Water can be scarce along the main track, especially late in the dry season, and roadhouses stock only basic food supplies.

The dry season from May to November is the best time to access the Cape. When the Wet arrives, rivers become impassable. Even as late as June and July the rivers are fast flowing, have steep banks and frequently alter course. The Great Dividing Range runs up the spine of the peninsula, and rivers run east and west from it. Although the rivers in the south of the peninsula flow only in the Wet, those further north flow year-round.

DETOUR: LAKEFIELD NATIONAL PARK

Lakefield National Park, Queensland's second-largest national park, is renowned for its vast river systems, spectacular wetlands and prolific birdlife. Covering more than 537,000 hectares, the park encompasses a rich and diverse landscape across the flood plains of the Normanby, Kennedy, Bizant, Morehead and Hann Rivers. This extensive river system drains into Princess Charlotte Bay on the park's northern perimeter.

Old Laura Homestead, near the junction with the Battle Camp Rd from Cooktown, was built soon after the 1873 Palmer River gold rush. The **QPWS ranger station** (☎ 07-4060 3260) is located at New Laura, about 25km north of the junction.

The best camping facilities (with toilets and showers) are at **Kalpowar Crossing** (per person/family $4.50/18) beside the Laura River. Obtain permits from the self-registration stand near the **Lakefield QPWS ranger station** (☎ 07-4060 3271; www.epa.qld.gov.au), 3km south of the camping ground.

The picturesque **Red Lily** and **White Lily Lagoons**, about 8km north of the Lakefield ranger base, attract masses of birdlife including jabirus, brolgas and magpie geese. The red lotus lilies at Red Lily Lagoon are best appreciated in the morning when the lotus blossoms are in full bloom.

Soon after **Hann Crossing** the flat, treeless landscape of **Nifold Plain** stretches from horizon to horizon, its spectacular monotony broken only by sweeping grasslands and giant termite mounds.

About 26km before Musgrave, **Lotus Bird Lodge** (☎ 07-4060 3400; www.lotusbird.com.au; Marina Plains Rd; s/d incl meals $320/516; ▨), a favourite with birdwatchers, has comfortable timber cabins overlooking a lagoon. The lodge is open from May to December.

For details on 4WD rental, see the Cairns (p448) and Cooktown (p475) sections.

LAKELAND & LAURA

At Lakeland, the Peninsula Developmental Rd (known as the PDR) heads northwest up the Cape as a wide, well-maintained dirt road. Lakeland has a general store, a small caravan park and a hotel-motel.

Leaving Lakeland you enter Quinkan country, so named for the Aboriginal spirits depicted at the rock-art sites scattered throughout this area. Unesco lists Quinkan country in the top 10 rock art regions in the world. About 50km north of Lakeland is the turn-off to **Split Rock Gallery**, the only site open to the public. The sandstone escarpments here are covered with paintings dating back 14,000 years. The **Quinkan & Regional Cultural Centre** (☎ 07-4060 3457; www.quinkancc.com .au) in Laura has more information.

Laura
pop 225

This sleepy settlement comes alive in June of odd-numbered years with the three-day **Laura Aboriginal Dance Festival** (www.quinkancc.com .au), the largest traditional Indigenous gathering in Australia.

You can fuel up at the **roadhouse** (☎ 07-4060 3419) or the **Laura Store & Post Office** (☎ 07-4060 3238). Both sell gas, ice and basic groceries.

The historic, corrugated-iron **Quinkan Hotel** (☎ /fax 07-4060 3393; Terminus St; unpowered/powered sites $20/26, r $69) burnt down in 2002 and although the rebuilt and refurbished pub is clean and functional, it lacks the rustic character of the original. The park opposite the pub has a 'lock-up' dating from the 1880s.

LAURA TO MUSGRAVE

North from Laura some of the creek crossings, such as the Little Laura and Kennedy Rivers, are great places to camp. For a scenic, alternative route to Musgrave, take the turn-off for **Lakefield National Park** (see above), about 28km north of Laura.

Staying on the Peninsula Developmental Rd brings you to a food-and-fuel (and beer) pit stop, the **Hann River Roadhouse** (☎ 07-4060 3242; Peninsula Developmental Rd; powered sites $14, r $25), 76km north of Laura.

The **Musgrave Roadhouse** (☎ /fax 07-4060 3229; musgrave.roadhouse@bigpond.com.au; unpowered sites per person $9, s/d $66/77), 80km from Hann River, was built in 1887. Originally a telegraph station, it's now a licensed cafe and roadhouse selling fuel, basic groceries and, of course, beer. Rooms are simple while the camping area is green and grassed.

MUSGRAVE TO ARCHER RIVER

Coen, the 'capital' of the Cape, is a tiny township 108km north of Musgrave.

Wunthulpu Visitor Centre (☎ 07-4060 1192), on the way into town, has historical and cultural displays, and crafts for sale. A repeater station relocated from the Overland Telegraph Line, **Coen Heritage House** has been restored as a museum.

Wash down the bull dust with a beer at the legendary **"S"Exchange Hotel** (☎ 07-4060 1133; fax 07-4060 1180; s/d from $77/99, motel $99/129; ☒). After a boozy prank the 'S' on top of the pub has become a permanent fixture.

A picturesque riverside spot for campers is at the **Bend**, about 5km north of Coen. Twenty-five kilometres north is the turn-off to the remote **Mungkan Kandju National Park**. Camping permits are located at the self-registration stand.

The **Archer River Roadhouse** (☎ 07-4060 3266; archerriverroadhouse@bigpond.com; unpowered sites per adult/child $10/5, s/d/tr $60/100/120; ☽ 7.30am-10pm), 66km north of Coen, is the last fuel stop before Bramwell Junction (170km north on Telegraph Rd) or Weipa (197km west on the PDR). Here you can tuck into the famous Archer Burger. Look for the memorial dedicated to Toots, a tough-talking woman truck driver, and a Cape York legend.

There are plenty of shady and pleasant camping locations along the river, but if you're wanting to observe life on a working cattle station, **Merluna Station** (☎ 07-4060 3209; www.merlunastation.com; unpowered sites per adult/child $10/3, safari tents per person $25, cabins $110, s/d without bathroom $66/88; ☒ ☒), about 80km northwest of the Archer River Roadhouse, has accommodation in converted workers' quarters. Guests gather in the 'wreck shed' to play pool, throw darts or sizzle a few snags on the barbie.

WEIPA
pop 2830

Weipa, the largest town in the Cape, is the site of the world's largest bauxite mine (the ore from which aluminium is processed). The traffic lights where the haul truck road crosses the Peninsula Developmental Rd are the first since Cairns, 820km south. But the strange fact that sets this coconut-palm-fringed town apart is that a person can neither be born nor buried here. Expectant mothers are flown out six weeks before giving birth, while a high water table beneath the allocated cemetery grounds disallows a normal burial.

Weipa Camping Ground & Fishing Lodge (☎ 07-4069 7871; www.campweipa.com; unpowered/powered sites $24/28, cabins $75-155; ☒), a shady spot on the beachfront, operates as the town's informal tourist office and organises mine tours ($27).

Near the shopping centre, the four-star **Heritage Resort** (☎ 07-4069 8000; www.heritageresort.com.au; Nanum; s/d $150/160; ☒ ☒) has modern comfortable rooms and a restaurant (mains $33 to $36).

ARCHER RIVER TO BRAMWELL JUNCTION

Roughly 36km north of the Archer River Roadhouse, a turn-off leads 135km through the **Iron Range National Park** to the tiny coastal settlement of Portland Roads. This park has Australia's largest area of lowland rainforest, with some animals that are found no further south in Australia. A popular campsite is **Chili Beach**, south of Portland Roads. Permits are by self-registration; for other bush camps register with the **ranger** (☎ 07-4060 7170). Otherwise, to savour a little luxury in the wilderness, stay in **Portland House** (☎ 07-4060 7193; www.portlandhouse.com.au), a self-contained beachside cottage in Portland Roads.

From Archer River, the Peninsula Developmental Rd continues towards Weipa but after 48km the **Telegraph Road** branches off north for a rough and bumpy 22km stretch to the **Wenlock River** crossing. Note the sign in the tree at the crossing that marks floodwaters of 14.3m.

On the northern bank of the Wenlock, **Moreton Telegraph Station** (☎ 07-4060 3360; more tonstation@bigpond.com.au; unpowered sites per person $10, safari tents per person $75), formerly a station on the Overland Telegraph Line, has a safari camp set-up. You can buy fuel, meals and beer, and perform basic workshop repairs. Read the witty tombstone epitaph near the station entrance.

Bramwell Junction roadhouse (☎ 07-4060 3230; unpowered sites per person $9) marks the junction of the new Southern Bypass Rd and the historic Old Telegraph Track. This is the last fuel stop before Bamaga. Fifteen kilometres before the roadhouse is the turn-off to Australia's most northern cattle station, **Bramwell Homestead** (☎ 07-4060 3300; bramwellstn@bigpond.com), which offers accommodation, camping and meals.

BRAMWELL JUNCTION TO JARDINE RIVER

After Bramwell Junction there are two possible routes to the Jardine River ferry. The longer route on the graded and reasonably well-maintained Southern and Northern Bypass Rds is quicker and avoids most of the creeks and rivers between the Wenlock and Jardine Rivers.

The more direct but far more challenging route down the **Old Telegraph Track** (commonly called the OTT or 'the Track') is where the real Cape York adventure begins.

The OTT follows the remnants of the Overland Telegraph Line, which was constructed during the 1880s to allow communications from Cairns to the Cape via a series of repeater stations and an underwater cable link to Thursday Island. The OTT is a serious 4WD experience with deep corrugations, powdery sand and difficult creek crossings (especially the **Dulhunty River** crossing).

A road leaves the OTT 2km north of the Dulhunty and heads for **Heathlands Ranger Station** (☎ 07-4060 3241), looping past the difficult Gunshot Creek crossing. Back on the OTT, the road becomes sandy for a stretch before joining the Southern Bypass Rd.

After 9km, the Northern Bypass Rd heads west to the Jardine River ferry crossing, but if you continue another 7km on the OTT you reach the turn-off to **Twin Falls & Eliot Falls**. The falls and the deep emerald-green swimming holes here are spectacular, and worth a long visit. The **camping ground** (per person/family $4.50/20) is the most popular site on the trip north. Permits are at the self-registration stand.

The old vehicular crossing of the Jardine River on the OTT is hazardous and not recommended. Access to the Jardine River Ferry is on the Northern Bypass Rd.

JARDINE RIVER

The Jardine River is Queensland's largest perennial river, spilling more fresh water into the sea than any other river in Australia. The **Jardine River Ferry & Roadhouse** (☎ 07-4069 1369; unpowered sites $10; ☼ 8am-5pm), run by the Injinoo Community Council, sells fuel and operates a ferry during the dry season ($88 return, plus $11 for trailers). The fee includes a permit for bush camping between the Dulhunty and Jardine Rivers, and in designated areas north of the Jardine.

Stretching east to the coast from the main track is the impenetrable country of **Jardine River National Park**. It includes the headwaters of the Jardine and Escape Rivers, where explorer Edmund Kennedy was killed by Aborigines in 1848.

NORTHERN PENINSULA AREA

Everything north of the Jardine River is known as the Northern Peninsula Area (NPA to the locals).

Bamaga & Seisia

The first settlement north of the Jardine River is Bamaga (population 784), home to Cape York Peninsula's largest Torres Strait Islander community. There's a small shopping centre, a hospital and an airstrip.

Five kilometres northwest of Bamaga, Seisia (population 165) overlooks the Torres Strait and is a great base from which to explore the Tip.

Cape York Adventures (☎ 07-4069 3302; www.cap eyorkadventures.com.au) has half-day and full-day fishing trips and sunset cruises.

Resort Bamaga (☎ 07-4069 3050; http://resort bamaga.com.au; r $209-229; ✗ ⌨), overlooking Mosby Creek, is the only four-star accommodation in the NPA and has a good **restaurant** (mains $20-30; ☼ breakfast & dinner daily, lunch Fri).

Seisia Holiday Park (☎ 07-4069 3243; www.sei siaholidaypark.com; unpowered/powered sites $18/24, guest house s/d $66/106, self-contained villas $150-185), next to Seisia's wharf, is a popular camping ground with good facilities and a restaurant. The park is also a booking agent for scenic flights, 4WD tours and the ferry to Thursday Island. **Loyalty Beach Campground & Fishing Lodge** (☎ 07-4069 3372; www.loyaltybeach.com; unpowered/powered sites $20/22, lodge s/d $95/120), on the beachfront 3km from the wharf, is a quieter spot.

Peddells Ferry Service (☎ 07-4069 1551; www .peddellsferry.com.au) runs regular ferries between Seisia and Thursday Island – see p483.

The Tip

From Bamaga the road north passes **Lockerbie Homestead**. The **Croc Tent** (☎ 07-4069 3210; www .croctent.com.au; ☼ 7.30am-6pm), across the road, sells souvenirs and provides an unofficial tourist information service. The road then passes through the northernmost rainforest in Australia, **Lockerbie Scrub**, before reaching a Y-junction.

QUEENSLAND

QUEENSLAND

THE JARDINES OF SOMERSET

In 1864, Captain John Jardine was selected to supervise Somerset, a government residency and remote outpost at the tip of Cape York. Big plans were afoot for Somerset – the refuge for shipwrecked sailors was earmarked to become a port for the increasing shipping trade, and the foundation for a 'Singapore' of the north. Jardine set his sons, Frank and Aleck, the task of droving a mob of cattle from Rockhampton to stock the outpost. It took 10 months to drive the cattle 2000km through searing heat, a long Wet and numerous Aboriginal attacks.

Frank Jardine's epic expedition set the tone for one of Cape York's most influential pioneers. A tough hard-headed man, Frank Jardine developed a notorious reputation as a mass-murderer of Aborigines and Islanders. He was also cited for bravery (rescuing many shipwrecked sailors), married a Samoan princess, and in 1868 took over his father's role as government resident at Somerset. He left after five years to pursue pearling interests but returned in 1877 when the government administration moved to Thursday Island (due to Somerset's poor anchorage and Thursday Island's booming pearling industry). The port never eventuated and all that's now left at Somerset are the lonely graves of Frank Jardine and his wife, Sana.

The track right leads to the pretty foreshore of **Somerset** (see The Jardines of Somerset, above). The left track leads 10km down the road to the now defunct Pajinka Wilderness Lodge. A 1km walk through the forest and along the beach (over the headland if the tide's in) takes you to **Cape York**, the northernmost 'Tip of Australia'.

On the western side of the tip, the scenic **Punsand Bay Camping Resort** (☎ 07-4069 1722; www .punsand.com.au; unpowered/powered sites per person $10/12, tents per person incl meals $130-160, air-con cabins per person incl meals $170; ⊠) is a remote haven in the wilderness. A dip in the pool, or a cold beer in the breezy restaurant, tops off the Tip experience. **Dato's Venture** (☎ /fax 07-4090 2005) operates a ferry (May to November) to Thursday and Horn Islands from here.

THURSDAY ISLAND & TORRES STRAIT ISLANDS

Australia's most northern frontier consists of over 100 islands stretching like stepping stones for 150km from the top of Cape York Peninsula to Papua New Guinea. The islands vary from the rocky, northern extensions of the Great Dividing Range, to small coral cays and rainforested volcanic mountains.

Torres Strait Islanders came from Melanesia and Polynesia about 2000 years ago, establishing a unique culture different from that found in Papua New Guinea and the Australian Aborigines.

Although **Prince of Wales Island** is the largest of the group, the administrative capital is tiny **Thursday Island** (it's only 3 sq km), 30km off the cape. Although lacking its own freshwater supply, Thursday Island (population 2550) was selected for its deep harbour, sheltered port and proximity to major shipping channels. One of 17 inhabited islands in the strait, TI (as it's locally known) was once a major pearling centre, and the legacy of that industry has resulted in a friendly, easygoing cultural mix of Asians, Europeans and Islanders.

Erub (Darnley Island as it is also known) is in the eastern group, and is of volcanic origin. It's another important island in the region as it has come into the spotlight as a campaigner for equal recognition of Torres Strait Islanders' rights.

Regular ferry services connect Seisia with Thursday and Horn Islands. To visit other inhabited Torres Strait Islands requires permission from the islands' council; contact the **Torres Strait Regional Authority** (☎ 07-4069 1247; www.tsra.gov.au; Torres Strait Haus, Victoria Pde, Thursday Island).

Sights & Activities

On Thursday Island, the **Gab Titui Cultural Centre** (☎ 07-4090 2130; www.tsra.gov.au; cnr Victoria Pde & Blackall St; ☼ 9am-5pm Mon-Sat, 2-5pm Sun) houses a modern gallery displaying the cultural history of the Torres Strait, hosts cultural events and exhibitions by local artists, and has a popular outdoor cafe.

TI's pearling heyday resulted in a number of fatalities from decompression sickness. The **Japanese Pearl Divers Memorial** at the cemetery presides over the many Japanese divers buried here. TI's war history, instead, can be experienced with a visit to **Green Hill Fort**, which was built in 1893 in response to fears of a Russian invasion. The **Torres Strait Museum**, housed in the fort, displays war paraphernalia and local artefacts.

The **Quetta Memorial Church** was built in 1893 in memory of the 134 lives lost when the *Quetta* struck an uncharted reef – and sank within three minutes. Inside the church there are memorabilia from a number of shipwrecks, including a coral-encrusted porthole recovered from the *Quetta* in 1906.

The **Heritage Museum & Art Gallery** (☎ 07-4069 2222; www.torresstrait.com.au; adult/child $6.50/3.50) at the Gateway Torres Strait Resort on Horn Island has a mine of information on the region's WWII history.

Tours

Peddells Ferry Island Tourist Bureau (☎ 07-4069 1551; www.peddellsferry.com.au; Engineers Wharf, Thursday Island; adult/child $29/15; ☼ 8.30am-5pm) offers bus tours of TI, taking in all the major tourist sites. Day trippers from Seisia have enough time to wander around town and grab lunch at one of the local pubs before catching the return ferry. Note that if you book the two-island tour, which includes a tour of Horn Island, you won't have time to stroll the streets of TI.

Tony's Island Adventures (☎ 07-4069 1965; titasey@bigpond.com) offers fishing trips and tours of various Torres Strait Islands including Friday, Hammond and Goodes Islands.

The **Gateway Torres Strait Resort** (☎ 07-4069 2222; www.torresstrait.com.au; 2hr tours adult/child $30/15) on Horn Island runs excellent tours that give a fascinating and comprehensive overview of the island's status as an advanced operational airbase during WWII.

Sleeping & Eating

Jardine Motel & Lodge (☎ 07-4069 1555; jardine motel@bigpond.com; cnr Normanby St & Victoria Pde, Thursday Island; s/d $125/222; ✖ ▯ ▣) Offers both budget accommodation and comfortable motel rooms and has a cocktail bar, bistro and restaurant.

Gateway Torres Strait Resort (☎ 07-4069 2222; www .torresstrait.com.au; Horn Island; s/d $139/159; ✖ ▣) This place has comfortable rooms and self-contained units. The resort houses the museum and organises tours.

Grand Hotel (☎ 07-4069 1557; www.grandhotelti.com .au; 6 Victoria Pde, Thursday Island; s/d from $150/170; ✖) The Grand has impressive ocean views from its bar verandah and restaurant balcony.

Federal Hotel (☎ 07-4069 1569; www.federalho telti.com.au; Victoria Pde, Thursday Island; s/d incl breakfast $160/180; ✖) Motel-style rooms, a beer garden and a mural depicting island life.

Getting There & Around

QantasLink (☎ 13 13 13; www.qantas.com.au) flies daily from Cairns to Horn Island.

Peddells Ferry Service (☎ 07-4069 1551; www .peddellsferry.com.au; Engineers Wharf, Thursday Island; adult/child $48/25) runs regular services between Seisia and Thursday Island. **McDonald Charter Boats** (☎ 1300 664 875; www.tiferry.com.au) runs ferries between TI and Horn Island, roughly hourly between 6am and 6pm ($18 one way, 20 minutes). **Rebel Marine** (☎ 07-4069 1586; rebel_marine@bigpond.com) operates a water taxi between TI and the Horn Island Airport connecting with all QantasLink flights ($18 one way). **Dato's Venture** (☎ /fax 07-4090 2005) operates ferry transfers to Thursday Island (adult/child return $100/50) and Horn Island from Punsand Bay Camping Resort (p482) from May to November.

QUEENSLAND

Victoria

It looks oh so small and unassuming on the map: a tiny state dwarfed by its western counterpart and cornered from the south and north. But don't be fooled, this slight frame simmers with enough geographic and cultural diversity to keep you engaged for weeks. Victoria shows its heftier neighbours that good things do indeed come in small(er) packages.

Melbourne, Australia's second-largest city, is the state's urban hub and the nation's artistic centre. This city is a global melting pot that has retained community spirit, where culture junkies and culinary perfectionists feast on art, music, theatre, cinema and cuisine for every budget. Australia's best baristas compete for your morning trade here, but the Melburnian pace is set to an affable amble.

Scalloping its way around coves, beaches and cliffs, the Great Ocean Road is great indeed. Wild surf pounds the shoreline and enigmatic coastal towns mingle with lush national parks.

In the High Country, brilliant autumn colours segue into snowfields and back again to sleepy summer towns, haunted by pale ghost gums. Skis get a work-out in winter, and cycling, horseback riding and cheeky weekends are the mainstays of the summer bliss.

If wild landscapes are your weakness head to the Grampians National Park, sprawled amid the dry plains of the Western District. Australia's southernmost mainland tip is the spiritually reviving Wilsons Promontory National Park. More of a cosmopolitan tourist? Duck just outside of Melbourne and sample some of Australia's finest wines in the Yarra Valley and Mornington Peninsula.

HIGHLIGHTS

- Get exquisitely lost in the wilderness of **Croajingolong National Park** (p628) and **Cape Conran Coastal Park** (p626)

- Curl your way around the magical twists of the **Great Ocean Road** (p551)

- Slip, slide and revel down the ski slopes of the **High Country** (p602)

- Make merry at music festivals at **Apollo Bay** (p556), **Lorne** (p554) and **Port Fairy** (p562)

- Experience breathtaking hikes and Aboriginal culture in the **Grampians** (p566)

- Meander the Murray on a paddle steamer in **Mildura** (p573)

- Get New Age in **Fitzroy** (p509), sun-kissed in **St Kilda** (p510) and styled up in **South Yarra** (p510)

- Achieve cultural enlightenment in Melbourne's world-renowned **Arts Precinct** (p507)

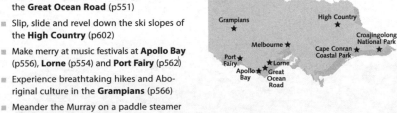

| ■ TELEPHONE CODE: 03 | ■ POPULATION: 5.4 MILLION | ■ AREA: 237,629 SQ KM |

VICTORIA FACTS

Eat Vietnamese, Thai, African, Lebanese, Greek, Italian…for a tenner
Drink Holgate White Ale (see p543)
Read *The Spare Room* by Helen Garner, *Making Modern Melbourne* by Jenny Lee or *True History of the Kelly Gang* by Peter Carey
Listen to The Cat Empire, Jet, Nick Cave, Hunters & Collectors
Watch *Three Dollars, The Hard Word, Noise*
Avoid Hook turns, tram inspectors, jay-walking tickets
Locals' nickname Mexicans
Swim at Sorrento (p546) or Queenscliff (p541) to frolic with dolphins and beautiful people
Strangest festival St Jerome's Laneway Festival (p515)
Tackiest tourist attraction Crown Casino (p507)

HISTORY

In 1803 a party of convicts, soldiers and settlers arrived at Sorrento (on the southern edge of Port Phillip Bay), but the settlement was soon abandoned. The first permanent European settlement in Victoria was established in 1834 at Portland (in the Western District) by the Henty family from Van Diemen's Land (Tasmania), some 46 years after Sydney was colonised. In 1851 Victoria won separation from New South Wales (NSW), and in that same year the rich Victorian goldfields were discovered, attracting immigrants from around the world. Towns such as Beechworth and Ballarat boomed during the gold rush, and are veritable museum pieces today. Melbourne was founded in 1835 by enterprising Tasmanians and it retains much Victorian-era charm and gold-boom 1880s architecture to this day.

The latter-half of the 20th century saw a huge influx of immigrants into Victoria, particularly Melbourne, and the city is now widely regarded as Australia's most multicultural city. It has one of the largest Greek populations per capita in the world and is heavily influenced by Italian, Eastern European and Southeast Asian cultures.

The 1990s and 21st century has seen a period of ferocious development begin – a process that continues today, and the face of the CBD (central business district) has changed and spread markedly with the boom of the Docklands, and the construction of architectural landmarks such as Federation Square.

GEOGRAPHY & CLIMATE

Victoria has a temperate four-season climate, although the distinctions between the seasons are often blurred by the unpredictability of the weather. There are three climatic regions: the southern and coastal areas, the alpine areas and the areas north and west of the Great Dividing Range. Winter is from June to August; summer December to February.

Daily summer temperatures in coastal areas average 25°C, in alpine areas 20°C and in the northwest 35°C. Daily winter temperatures average 14°C along the coast, a chillier 10°C in alpine areas and 17°C in the northwest.

Rainfall is spread fairly evenly throughout the year, although mid-January to mid-March tends to be the driest period. Victoria's wettest areas are the Otway Ranges and the High Country. Because of exposure to frequent cold fronts and southerly winds, the coastal areas are subject to the most changeable weather patterns.

The weather is generally more stable north of the Great Dividing Range. The Wimmera and Mallee regions have the lowest rainfall and the highest temperatures.

It snows during the alpine high country winter; the closest snow to Melbourne is on Mt Donna Buang (see Ski Resorts, p605).

INFORMATION

Tourism Victoria (☎ 13 28 42; www.visitvictoria.com), the state tourism body is a good source for information, ideas and contacts. Lonely Planet's *Melbourne & Victoria* guide is an excellent resource for getting the most out of your time. Some helpful websites:

Parks Victoria (☎ 13 19 63; www.parkweb.vic.gov.au) Manages Victoria's national parks.

Royal Automobile Club of Victoria (RACV; Map pp496-7; ☎ 13 72 28; www.racv.com.au; 438 Little Collins St, Melbourne) Produces the excellent *Experience Victoria* guide, full of accommodation and touring information.

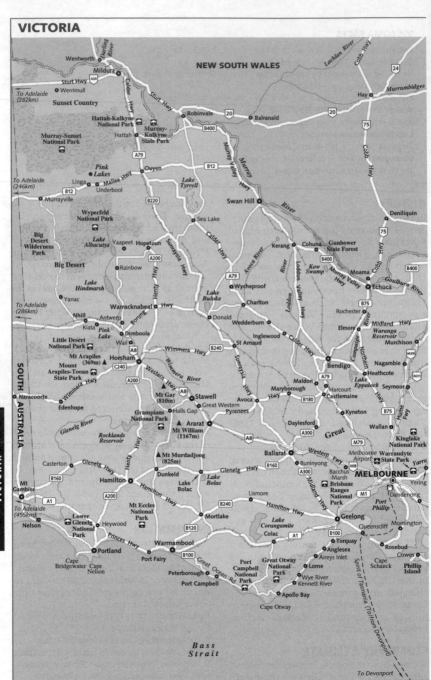

VICTORIA

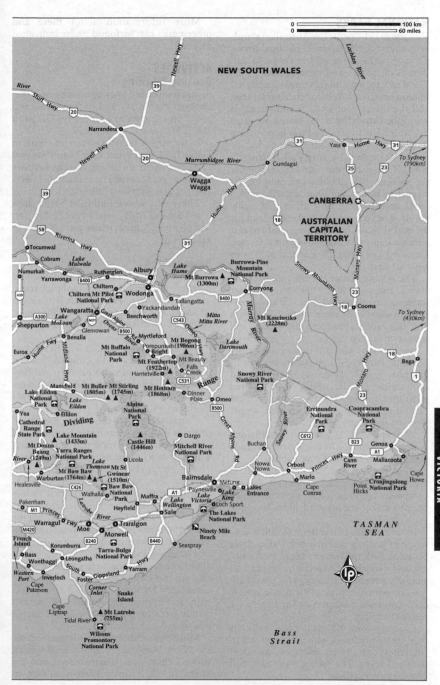

NATIONAL PARKS

Victoria may be petite (by Australian standards anyway), but it has 39 national parks, 30 state parks, three wilderness parks and dozens of marine and metropolitan parks. The whole lot amounts to approximately 4.1 million hectares, 17% of the state's total area, and the diversity of weather and terrain is vast. **Parks Victoria** (☎ 13 19 63; www.parkweb.vic.gov .au), which has a useful 24-hour information line, manages Victoria's national parks.

The Grampians National Park (Gariwerd; p566) is accessible year-round and is popular for walking, rock climbing and camping. Its staggering beauty and abundant wildlife also lends itself to long, slow drives and sightseeing. The Grampians are also excellent for an insight into Koorie heritage and culture, with the impressive Brambuk Cultural Centre, Gariwerd Dreaming Theatre and numerous rock-art sites.

The Alpine National Park (p602) is the state's largest at 646,000 hectares. In winter its frostbitten peaks lure downhill and cross-country skiers, and in summer the wildflowers and heavy forests produce great walking and mountain biking.

Another top-biller is Wilsons Promontory National Park (p617) on Australia's southernmost point. Dominated by rugged mountains, prolific wildlife and isolated coastlines, it offers superb walking, remote camping, swimming, surfing and ample wombat spotting.

Mt Arapiles (p571), in the Western District, is world famous for its huge variety of rock climbing, boasting over 2000 climbs.

Head to the Lakes National Park (p621) for boating, fishing and walking. It also encompasses breeding colonies for many bird species and there are bird hides to enjoy the view.

If you're looking for extreme isolation head to the exquisitely undeveloped Snowy River National Park (p625) for rugged bushwalking and canoeing. In the same region and similarly remote is Errinundra National Park (p625), which contains Victoria's largest cool-temperate rainforest and is known for remote camping.

Croajingolong National Park (p628) is one Australia's finest, with a huge stretch of wilderness coast, rivers, inlets and abundant flora and fauna. The fishing, swimming and canoeing are excellent.

More information about these and other parks can be found under individual sections.

ACTIVITIES
Boating & Sailing

Scenic cruises and boating options are a speciality of the Murray, and you can get out and about on the river at Mildura (p573), Swan Hill (p578) and Echuca (p580).

In the High Country you can rent boats in Eildon (p603) to explore Lake Eildon National Park, and there are fishing trips and cruises at Lakes Entrance (p622); Mallacoota Inlet is also popular with boat folk (p627).

There is a whole flotilla of yacht clubs based around Melbourne's Port Phillip Bay, and plenty of schools where you can learn to sail (p512).

Bushwalking

For national park news and updates, and detailed descriptions of national park trails, see the website of **Parks Victoria** (www.parkweb .vic.gov.au). For details of bushwalking clubs, contact **Bushwalking Victoria** (☎ 03-8846 4131; www.vicwalk.org.au).

The High Country (p602), with its spectacular alpine scenery and spring wildflowers, has a wide range of walks catering to different fitness and skill levels. Serious trekkers should head to Harrietville (p612) and Mt Hotham (p613).

If coastal treks are more your pace, head south to Wilsons Promontory National Park (p619), with marked trails that can take anywhere from a few hours to a couple of days. The landscape encompasses swamps, forests, squeaky white-sand beaches, pristine bushland teeming with wildlife, ferned valleys and coastal vistas. Some of the finest walks include the 45km Great Prom Walk and the 7km Mt Oberon Summit (see Top Five Prom Walks, p619, for more information on these and other walks).

Other popular areas to flex your calf muscles are the Otway Ranges (p554) and the Grampians National Park (Gariwerd; p566), with more than 150km of well-marked walking tracks past waterfalls and sacred Aboriginal rock-art sites.

Middle-distance walks in Victoria include the 22km Mahogany Walking Trail (p561), which begins near Warrnambool, and the 18km Mitchell River Walking Track in

ABORIGINAL VICTORIA

Aboriginal people have lived in Victoria for an estimated 40,000 years. They lived in some 38 different dialect groups that spoke 10 separate languages. These groups were further divided into clans and subclans, each with its own customs and laws, and each claiming ownership of a distinct area of land. Before British colonisation, the Yarra Valley region was occupied by members of the Woiworung clan of the Kulin Nation, known as the Wurundjeri.

As many as 100,000 Aboriginal people lived in Victoria before Europeans arrived; by 1860 there were as few as 2000 left alive. Today around 27,000 Koories (Aborigines from southeastern Australia) live in Victoria, and more than half live in Melbourne.

Many cultures have been lost, but there has been a strong movement to revive Aboriginal culture in Victoria and there are cultural centres around the state, including the excellent Brambuk Cultural Centre and Gariwerd Dreaming Theatre, both in Halls Gap (p569) in the Grampians National Park. Run by local Koorie communities, these centres provide insights into Koorie history, culture, art, music and dance, and provide tours to local rock-art sites.

In Bairnsdale the Krowathunkoolong Keeping Place (p622) is a Koorie cultural centre that explores Kurnai daily life before and after white settlement.

Based in Mildura, Harry Nanya (p574) provides acclaimed tours into Lake Mungo National Park, with excellent commentary about the traditional occupants of the land.

In Melbourne, the Ian Potter Centre: National Gallery of Victoria Australia (p504) has a renowned collection of Aboriginal and Torres Strait Islander art, while the Aboriginal Heritage Walk (p515) takes you through the story of the Boonwurrung and Woiworung peoples, on whose ancestral grounds the Royal Botanic Gardens now sit.

Melbourne itself is divided into the Kulin Nation (Wurundjeri) and the Boonwurrung peoples, and both groups are represented by female elders – Aunty Joy Murphy and Aunty Carolyn Briggs.

For more information about the history of the Victorian Indigenous people, visit the Koorie Heritage Trust Cultural Centre (p506) or the interesting and comprehensive Bunjilaka Indigenous centre at Melbourne Museum (p509).

A 'Welcome to Country' ceremony – which can vary from a speech to a traditional dance or a smoking ceremony – by an Aboriginal community is now common protocol across the state and performed at a diverse range of functions. An 'Acknowledgement Ceremony' is common at forums, whereby the first speaker pays recognition and respect to the traditional owners of the land. Similarly, a gum-leaf ceremony is common at dinners and events.

The website of **Visit Victoria** (www.visitvictoria.com) has an excellent link to Aboriginal culture, heritage, history and sites in Victoria. Another good resource is the **Aboriginal Tourism Marketing Association** (www.seeaboriginaltourism.com).

Aboriginal Melbourne – The Lost Land of the Kulin People by Gary Presland (re-released 2001) and *Aboriginal Victorians, A History Since 1800* by Richard Broome (2005) also give valuable insight into the culture and life of the region's original inhabitants.

Mitchell River National Park (p621). If you really want to work the pins, set out on the Great South West Walk (see p564), a 250km loop that starts near Portland; or the Australian Alps Walking Track, a 655km walk that traverses the Alpine National Park and starts near Walhalla (p620).

Cycling

Victoria is a great state for on- and off-road cycling and mountain biking. There is a whole network of routes that follow disused railway lines, including the Murray to Mountains Rail Trail (p601) connect-

ing Wangaratta with Beechworth and Bright, and the 30km East Gippsland Rail Trail (p622). **Railtrails Australia** (☎ 03-9306 4846; www.railtrails.org.au) describes these and other routes.

For more information on bicycle hire in Melbourne, see p511.

A few more sources of information for pedal-pushers:

Bicycle Victoria (☎ 03-8636 8888; www.bv.com.au)
Bike Paths Safe Escapes (www.bikepaths.com.au) An excellent online resource for cycling in Victoria.
Melbourne Bicycle Touring Club (☎ 03-9517 4306; www.mbtc.org.au)

Skiing & Snowboarding

Skiing in Victoria has come a long way from its modest beginnings in the 1860s when Norwegian gold miners started sliding around Harrietville in their spare time. Today it's a multimillion-dollar industry with three major and six minor ski resorts. The season officially commences the first weekend of June; skiable snow usually arrives later in the month, and often stays until the end of September. For more information see www.visitvictoria.com/ski, and consult the **Victorian Ski Report** (www.vicsnowreport.com.au).

WHERE TO SURF IN AUSTRALIA *Andrew Tudor*

Bells Beach, Cactus, Margaret River, the Superbank – mention any of them in the right company and stories of surfing legend will undoubtedly emerge. The Superbank hosts the first event on the Association of Surfing Professionals (ASP) World Tour calendar each year, and Bells Beach the second, with Bells having recently become the longest-serving host of an ASP event. Cactus dangles the lure of remote mystique, while Margaret River is a haunt for surfers chasing the bigger waves.

While the aforementioned might be jewels, they're dot points in the sea of stars that Australia has to offer. Little wonder – the coastline is vast, touching the Indian, Southern and South Pacific Oceans. With that much potential swell, an intricate coastal architecture and the right conditions, you'll find anything from innocent breaks to gnarly reefs not far from all six Australian state capitals.

For daily surf reports, cams and forecasts, look up **Coastalwatch** (www.coastalwatch.com) or for surf travel tips, the **Surfers Travel Guide** (www.thesurferstravelguide.com.au). For more information, news, events and surf schools, look up **Surfing Australia** (www.surfingaustralia.com). **RealSurf** (www.realsurf.com) is useful for surf reports.

New South Wales

It's hard to know where to begin; name practically any coastal town in NSW and there will be good surf nearby.

Popular spots:

- Manly through Avalon, otherwise known as Sydney's northern beaches (p120).
- Byron Bay (p198), Lennox Head (p194) and Angourie Point (p192) on the far north coast.
- Nambucca Heads (p185) and Crescent Head (p183) on the mid-north coast.
- The areas around Jervis Bay and Ulladulla (p234) on the south coast.

Queensland

By now every surfer in the world has heard of the Superbank (p342). Just in case you haven't, it was formed when the Tweed River entrance was dredged and a fixed sand bypass was put in place: a happy accident. The resulting sandbar is 2km long, give or take, and it's said that on the right swell you can ride a wave the entire length. The Superbank stretches from Snapper Rocks to Kirra Point, near Coolangatta, and effectively replaces the breaks of Rainbow Bay, Greenmount Point, Coolangatta Beach and the Kirra groins.

Other areas:

- Along with Superbank, Burleigh Heads (p340; surf cam and report: www.burleighcam.com.au) through to Surfers Paradise (p336) on the Gold Coast.
- North Stradbroke Island (p329) in Moreton Bay.
- Caloundra (p346), Alexandra Heads near Maroochy (p347) and Noosa (p349) on the Sunshine Coast.

Victoria

Bells Beach is arguably the spiritual home of Australian surfing; hell, there's even a museum dedicated to Australian surfing history in nearby Torquay (p552). When the wave is on, few would argue, but the break is notoriously inconsistent.

There are many other excellent breaks throughout the state. Phillip Island, the Mornington Peninsula and the Great Ocean Road are all within a two-hour drive from Melbourne.

Snowfields are scattered around the High Country northeast and east of Melbourne. The two largest ski resorts are Mt Buller (p605) and Falls Creek (p611). Mt Hotham (p613) is smaller, but has equally good skiing, while Mt Baw Baw (p615) and Mt Buffalo (p608) are smaller resorts, popular with families and less-experienced skiers. For more information see Ski Resorts, p605.

Surfing

Exposed to the chilly Southern Ocean swell, Victoria's coastline provides quality surf. Local and international surfers gravitate to

Popular spots:

- Smiths Beach on Phillip Island (p550).

- Point Leo, Flinders, Gunnamatta (p547), Rye and Portsea (p547) on the Mornington Peninsula.

- On the southwest coast, Barwon Heads (p542), Point Lonsdale (p542), Torquay (p552), Bells Beach (p553) and numerous spots along the Great Ocean Road.

Tasmania

Tasmania has some fine surfing and for years enjoyed relative anonymity among the global surf community. However, the arrival of Shipstern Bluff (p634) on the world surfing stage has blown Tassie's cover. This wave is remote and dangerous, and not recommended for the faint-hearted; indeed, it's not recommended at all unless you can magic some expert guidance.

That said, there are plenty of breaks to choose from, but be sure to pack a full-length wetsuit. Other areas:

- Marrawah (p703) on the exposed northwest coast can offer huge waves.

- St Helens (p678) and Bicheno (p676) on the east coast (surf report: www.eastsurf.com.au).

- Eaglehawk Neck (p665) on the Tasman Peninsula.

- Closer to Hobart, Cremorne Point and Clifton Beach (surf cam and news: www.coastview.com .au/site/surfing).

South Australia

The odd shark attack has made Cactus Beach (p792), west of Ceduna on remote Point Sinclair, something of a bogey for surfers (if there is such a thing). Still, it's without doubt SA's best-known surf spot and remains internationally recognised for its quality and consistency. If you're game, it'll be worth it.

Other areas to check:

- Streaky Bay (p791) and Greenly Beach (p791) on the western side of the Eyre Peninsula.

- Pennington Bay, which has the most consistent surf on Kangaroo Island (p756).

- Pondalowie Bay and Stenhouse Bay on the Yorke Peninsula tip in Innes National Park (p786).

- Victor Harbor (p753), Port Elliot (p754) and Middleton Beach at Port Elliot on the southern side of the Fleurieu Peninsula (surf cam and reports: www.surfsouthoz.com).

Western Australia

The surf on offer in WA is simply awesome. North of Perth there are reefs that produce world-class lefts, while south of Perth the coastal stretch between Capes Naturaliste and Leeuwin offers some of the world's best waves. Margaret River, Gracetown and Yallingup (see Surfing the Southwest, p937) are particular meccas. For details on the great surf WA has to offer, surf cams and reports, check out www.srosurf.com.

Other areas:

- Trigg Point and Scarborough Beach (p909), just north of Perth.

- Further north at Geraldton (p969) and Kalbarri (p974).

- Down south at Denmark (p945) on the Southern Ocean.

Torquay (p552), while nearby Bells Beach plays host to the Rip Curl Pro Tour festival every Easter.

The Shipwreck Coast (p559), stretching west from Cape Otway as far as Peterborough, offers possibly the most powerful waves in Victoria. It faces southwest and is open to the sweeping swells of the Southern Ocean. The swell is consistently up to 1m higher than elsewhere; it's the place to go if you're after big waves.

There's also good surfing at Wilsons Promontory National Park (p619). For the less experienced, popular places with surf schools include Anglesea (p554), Lorne (p554) and Phillip Island (p550).

Useful resources:

Peninsula Surf (www.peninsulasurf.com.au)

Surfing Australia (www.surfingaustralia.com)

Telephone surf reports (☎ 1900 931 996, Mornington Peninsula 1900 983 268) Updated daily.

TOURS
Eco-Certified Tours

The following companies are all eco-certified (www.ecotourism.org.au) and offer recommended tours.

Bunyip Tours (Map pp496-7; ☎ 03-9650 9680; www.bunyiptours.com; 570 Flinders St, Melbourne) One- to three-day tours of the Great Ocean Road, Grampians, Wilson's Promontory and Phillip Island.

Echidna Walkabout (☎ 03-9646 8249; www.echidnawalkabout.com.au) Small-group tours specialising in national parks and wildlife-spotting.

Eco Adventure Tours (☎ 03-5962 5115; www.ecoadventuretours.com.au) Offers guided night walks in the Yarra Valley and the Dandenong Ranges with advanced ecotourism accreditation. Ideal for animal lovers.

Go West (☎ 03-8508 9008, 1300 736 551; www.gowest.com.au) Great Ocean Road and Phillip Island Penguin Parade tours.

Other Tours

More recommended tours offering day trips to popular destinations, including the Grampians, the Great Ocean Road and the Phillip Island Penguin Parade (from around $90 per person):

Autopia Tours (☎ 03-9419 8878; www.autopiatours.com.au) Day tours to popular destinations around Melbourne.

Ecotrek: Bogong Jack Adventures (☎ 1300 948 911; www.ecotrek.com.au) Wide range of cycling, canoeing and walking tours through the Grampians, and the Murray River and High Country regions.

Wild-Life Tours (☎ 1300 661 730; www.wildlifetours.com.au) Day tours to the Great Ocean Road, Grampians and Phillip Island Penguin Parade.

GETTING THERE & AROUND

Unless you're driving, Melbourne is usually the main entry and exit point for Victoria. Bus and train services within country Victoria are operated by **V/Line** (☎ 13 61 96; www.vline.com.au); fares and routes are quoted throughout this chapter. Major bus companies operating throughout Victoria include **Greyhound** (☎ 1300 473 946; www.greyhound.com.au) and **Firefly** (☎ 1300 730 740; www.fireflyexpress.com.au). **V/Line** (☎ 13 61 96; www.vline.com.au) operates regional buses to towns throughout Victoria.

Note that there are border restrictions preventing fruit being carried into or out of Victoria in an effort to stop the spread of fruit fly; see Interstate Quarantine p1050.

See the Transport chapter (p1046), and Melbourne's Getting There & Away (p535) and Getting Around (p535) sections for more comprehensive details about boats, buses, trains and flights in and out of the state.

MELBOURNE

pop 3.9 million

Never satisfied to sit on its laurels, Melbourne is a shifting chameleon, changing its colours, style, favourites and flavours with every worthy influence in sniffing distance. Driven by the ravenous cultural appetite of a dynamic population, the city shuns fads and instead embraces the best of its evolving multiculturalism, slaps its own spin on things and then nurtures the result till it becomes a classic. One suburb may be sophisticated and slick, the next edgy and rough; one quiet and demure and its neighbour a nucleus of revelry. Ornate Victorian-era architecture and leafy boulevards reflect the city's history, and cutting-edge developments such as Federation Square, the Docklands and the Eureka Tower exemplify its enigmatic contemporary style. But, Melburnians still keep their urban frenzy to a deliciously sedate pace. Trams lumber back and forth on routes radiating out like spokes from central Melbourne, and bike lanes throughout reflect the city's love affair with cycling.

Character-filled neighbourhoods hum with life and the city produces some of the best art, music, cuisine, fashion, performance, design and ideas in the world. Melburnians are also devoted to their sport and they go ballistic around their big-ticket events such as the Australian Football League (AFL, or 'footy' to the locals) finals (p516), Spring Racing Carnival (p516), Australian Open tennis (p515) and more. They love to shop, eat and attend the myriad festivals that the city offers. You'll even find them defending the city's temperamental weather, and if you've ever experienced Melbourne's inclination to plummet from searing heat to drizzling rain in the space of an hour, you'll understand that this must be the true definition of unconditional love.

HISTORY

In May 1835 John Batman 'bought' around 240,000 hectares of land from the Aborigines of the Kulin Nation, the traditional owners. The concept of buying or selling land was foreign to the Aboriginal culture and in an extremely one-sided exchange they received some tools, flour and clothing as 'payment'.

By 1840 there were more than 10,000 Europeans living in the area around present-day Melbourne. The wealth from the goldfields built this city, known as 'Marvellous Melbourne', and this period of prosperity lasted until the depression at the end of the 1880s.

Post-WWII, Melbourne's social fabric was greatly enriched by an influx of people and cultures from around the world. Several building booms have altered the city physically and it's now a striking blend of ornate 19th-century buildings sitting alongside towering skyscrapers, and what seems like a million modern apartment complexes.

Today the city constantly rejuvenates itself through urban redevelopment. Inner-city suburbs, once the haunt of a seedy underworld, are now fashionable, hip and pricey to live in (and still a haunt of the seedy underworld).

ORIENTATION

Melbourne Airport (p535), 22km from the city centre, is Melbourne's main entry point, but Jetstar airlines also utilises Avalon Airport (p540) near Geelong. See p535 for information on travelling to/from the city's airports. If arriving by bus, you'll be dropped at the Southern Cross Railway Station's bus terminal (p535). Flinders St Station (Map pp496–7) is the main station for suburban trains.

Melbourne hugs the shores of Port Phillip Bay, with the city centre on the north bank of the Yarra River, about 5km inland. The main streets running east–west in the city's block-shaped grid are Collins and Bourke Sts, crossed by Swanston and Elizabeth Sts running north–south. The heart of the city is the Bourke St Mall, a pedestrianised shopping strip, and Chinatown along Little Bourke St.

Most places of interest to travellers are in the CBD or inner suburbs and are easily accessed by public transport.

Maps

The *Melbourne Visitors Map* is available at the Melbourne Visitor Information Centre and the Melbourne Visitor Information Booth (see Tourist Information, p503). For more comprehensive coverage, Lonely Planet also publishes the *Melbourne & Victoria City Guide* with a pull-out city map.

Street directories published by Melway (Melbourne's favourite), Gregory's and UBD are detailed and handy if you're driving. They can be purchased from newsagents and bookshops.

INFORMATION

Bookshops

Brunswick St Bookstore (Map p502; ☎ 03-9416 1030; 305 Brunswick St, Fitzroy; ⏲ 10am-11pm) A Fitzroy fixture with contemporary titles, art, literature and design tomes, plus cosy seating.

Foreign Language Bookshop (Map pp496-7; ☎ 03-9654 2883; 259 Collins St, Melbourne) Foreign-language books, dictionaries, magazines and even board games.

Readings (Map p499; ☎ 03-9347 6633; 309 Lygon St, Carlton; ⏲ 9am-11pm Mon-Sat, 10am-11pm Sun) Australian literature and music, plus art-house books and contemporary sellers.

Travellers Bookstore (Map p502; ☎ 03-9417 4179; 294 Smith St, Collingwood) Specialises in travel literature.

Emergency

Dial ☎ 000 for ambulance, fire or police.

Lifeline Counselling (☎ 13 11 14; ⏲ 24hr)

Police station (Map pp496-7; ☎ 03-9637 1100; 226 Flinders Lane; ⏲ 24hr)

Royal Women's Hospital Centre Against Sexual Assault Unit (Map pp496-7; ☎ 03-9635 3610; Level 3, Queen Victoria Centre, 210 Lonsdale St)

(Continued on page 503)

VICTORIA

MELBOURNE

VICTORIA

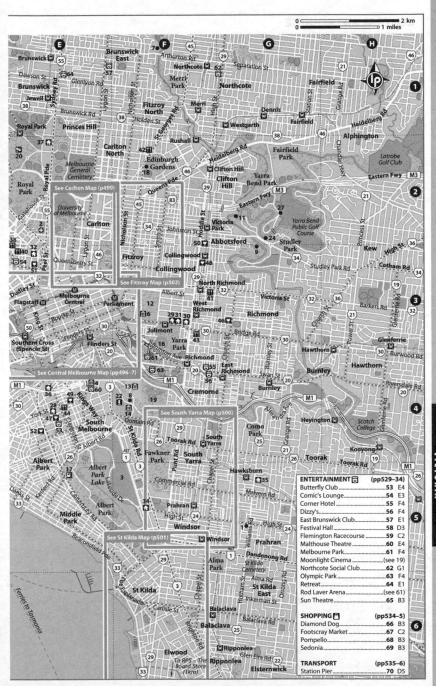

0 — 2 km
0 — 1 miles

VICTORIA

ENTERTAINMENT (pp529–34)
Butterfly Club................53 E4
Comic's Lounge...............54 E3
Corner Hotel..................55 F4
Dizzy's........................56 F4
East Brunswick Club...........57 E1
Festival Hall.................58 D3
Flemington Racecourse.........59 C2
Malthouse Theatre.............60 E4
Melbourne Park................61 F4
Moonlight Cinema...........(see 19)
Northcote Social Club.........62 G1
Olympic Park..................63 F4
Retreat.......................64 E1
Rod Laver Arena............(see 61)
Sun Theatre...................65 B3

SHOPPING (pp534–5)
Diamond Dog...................66 B3
Footscray Market..............67 C2
Pompello......................68 B3
Sedonia.......................69 B3

TRANSPORT (pp535–6)
Station Pier..................70 D5

CENTRAL MELBOURNE

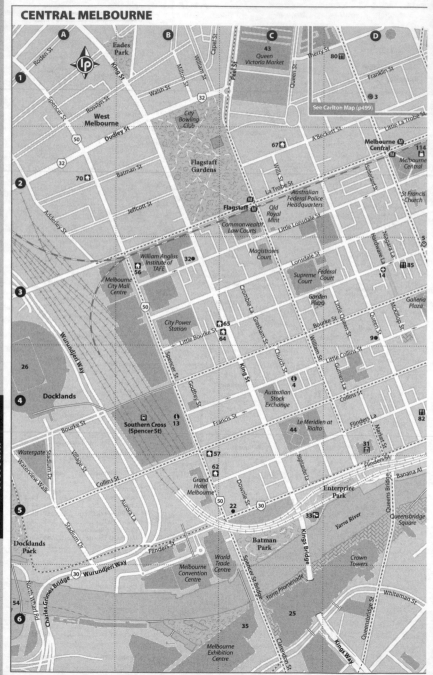

VICTORIA

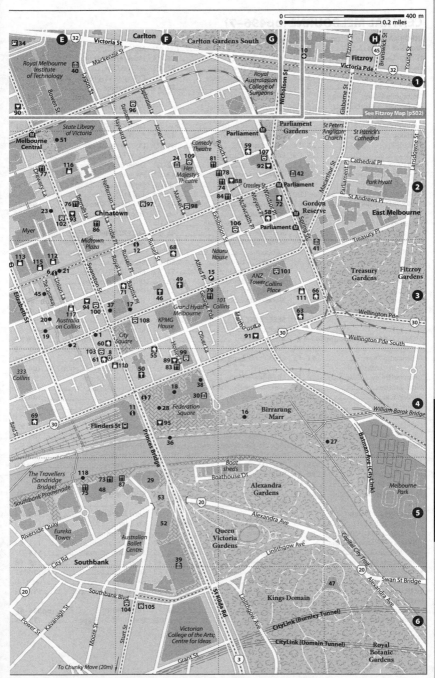

CENTRAL MELBOURNE (pp496–7)

VICTORIA

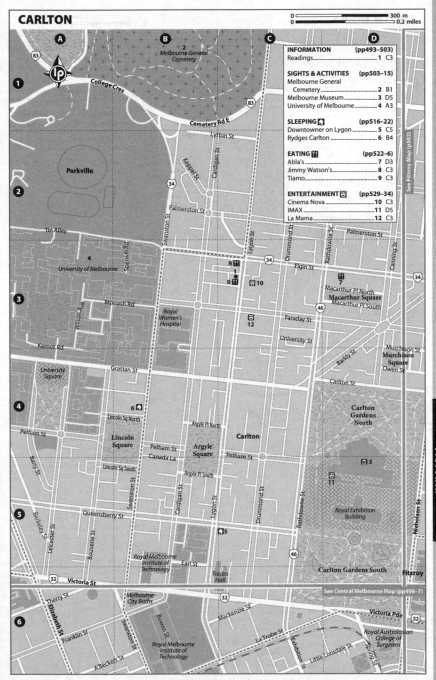

CARLTON

0 — 300 m
0 — 0.2 miles

INFORMATION	(pp493–503)
Readings	**1** C3

SIGHTS & ACTIVITIES	(pp503–15)
Melbourne General Cemetery	**2** B1
Melbourne Museum	**3** D5
University of Melbourne	**4** A3

SLEEPING	(pp516–22)
Downtowner on Lygon	**5** C5
Rydges Carlton	**6** B4

EATING	(pp522–6)
Abla's	**7** D3
Jimmy Watson's	**8** C3
Tiamo	**9** C3

ENTERTAINMENT	(pp529–34)
Cinema Nova	**10** C3
IMAX	**11** D5
La Mama	**12** C3

VICTORIA

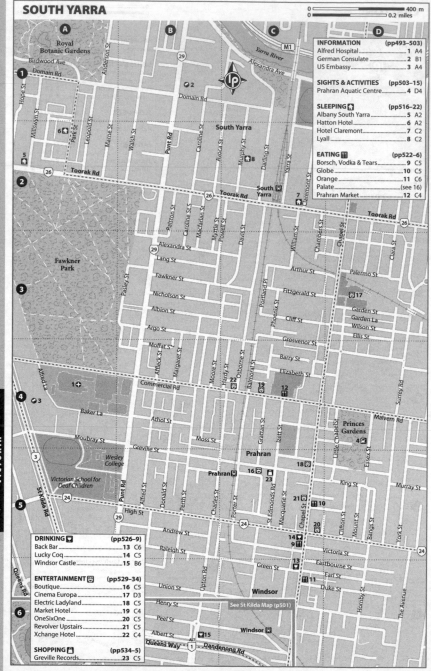

SOUTH YARRA

INFORMATION	(pp493–503)
Alfred Hospital	**1** A4
German Consulate	**2** B1
US Embassy	**3** A4

SIGHTS & ACTIVITIES	(pp503–15)
Prahran Aquatic Centre	**4** D4

SLEEPING	(pp516–22)
Albany South Yarra	**5** A2
Hatton Hotel	**6** A2
Hotel Claremont	**7** C2
Lyall	**8** C2

EATING	(pp522–6)
Borsch, Vodka & Tears	**9** C5
Globe	**10** C5
Orange	**11** C6
Palate	(see 16)
Prahran Market	**12** C4

DRINKING	(pp526–9)
Back Bar	**13** C6
Lucky Coq	**14** C5
Windsor Castle	**15** B6

ENTERTAINMENT	(pp529–34)
Boutique	**16** C5
Cinema Europa	**17** D3
Electric Ladyland	**18** C5
Market Hotel	**19** C4
OneSixOne	**20** C5
Revolver Upstairs	**21** C5
Xchange Hotel	**22** C4

SHOPPING	(pp534–5)
Greville Records	**23** C5

VICTORIA

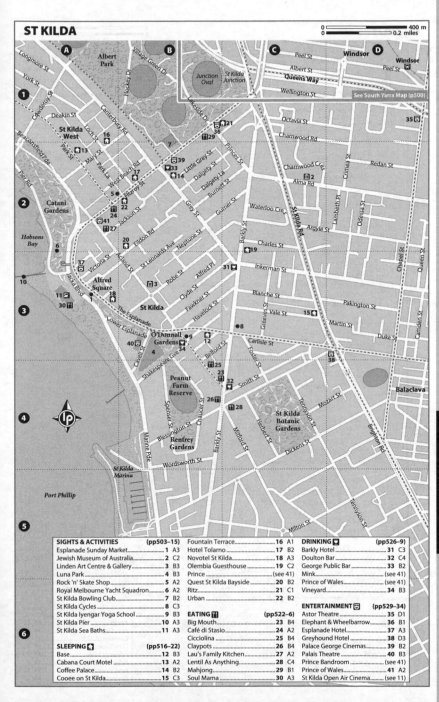

ST KILDA

0 ———— 400 m
0 ———— 0.2 miles

See South Yarra Map (p500)

VICTORIA

FITZROY

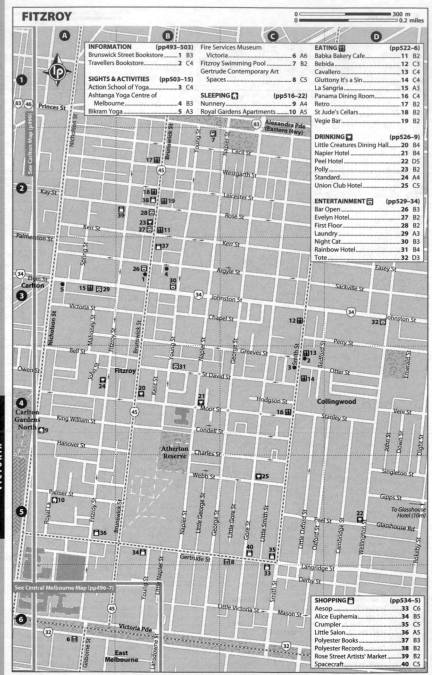

INFORMATION (pp493–503)
Brunswick Street Bookstore **1** B3
Travellers Bookstore **2** C4

SIGHTS & ACTIVITIES (pp503–15)
Action School of Yoga................**3** C4
Ashtanga Yoga Centre of
  Melbourne...............................**4** B3
Bikram Yoga **5** A3

Fire Services Museum
  Victoria..................................**6** A6
Fitzroy Swimming Pool **7** B2
Gertrude Contemporary Art
  Spaces....................................**8** C5

SLEEPING (pp516–22)
Nunnery......................................**9** A4
Royal Gardens Apartments **10** A5

EATING (pp522–6)
Babka Bakery Cafe....................**11** B2
Bebida **12** C3
Cavallero...................................**13** C4
Gluttony It's a Sin.....................**14** C4
La Sangria.................................**15** A3
Panama Dining Room................**16** C4
Retro **17** B2
St Jude's Cellars.......................**18** B2
Vegie Bar **19** B2

DRINKING (pp526–9)
Little Creatures Dining Hall......**20** B4
Napier Hotel **21** B4
Peel Hotel **22** D5
Polly..**23** B2
Standard....................................**24** A4
Union Club Hotel.......................**25** C5

ENTERTAINMENT (pp529–34)
Bar Open **26** B3
Evelyn Hotel **27** B2
First Floor..................................**28** B2
Laundry **29** A3
Night Cat **30** B3
Rainbow Hotel **31** B4
Tote **32** D3

SHOPPING (pp534–5)
Aesop..**33** C6
Alice Euphemia.........................**34** B5
Crumpler **35** C5
Little Salon...............................**36** A5
Polyester Books **37** B3
Polyester Records **38** B2
Rose Street Artists' Market **39** B2
Spacecraft.................................**40** C5

(Continued from page 493)

Travellers' Aid Society of Victoria (☎ 03-9654 2600; www.travellersaid.org.au) City Village (Map pp496-7; Level 3, 225 Bourke St); Flinders St Station (Map pp496-7); Southern Cross Station (Map pp496-7) Free assistance for stranded travellers, information, advice, showers and wheelchair-accessible toilets.

Internet Access

There are internet cafes dotted about the CBD and inner-city suburbs, and most hostels and guest houses have a few portals. Almost every hotel will have a phone jack in the room and many now have broadband or wireless access, although the latter may cost up to $10 per hour.

There are over 100 wi-fi hotspots around town; see **Azure Wireless** (www.azure.com.au) or **Wi-Fi HotSpotList** (www.wi-fihotspotlist.com/browse/au) for a full list.

A central internet cafe is **Global Gossip** (Map pp496-7; ☎ 03-9663 0511; 440 Elizabeth St, Melbourne; per hr from $2).

Media

In Melbourne, the **Age** (www.theage.com.au) is the daily broadsheet newspaper and the **Herald Sun** (www.heraldsun.com.au) is the major tabloid.

Street press thrives in Melbourne – pick up a free copy of *Beat* and *Inpress* from cafes, pubs, bookshops and record stores. They're the main music rags with listings of gigs playing around town, music news and events.

Medical Services

Alfred Hospital (Map p500; ☎ 03-9076 2000; Commercial Rd, Prahran) Twenty-four-hour emergency.
Mulqueeny Midnight Pharmacy (Map pp494-5; ☎ 03-9510 3977; cnr Williams Rd & High St, Prahran; ☾ 9am-midnight)
Royal Melbourne Hospital (Map pp494-5; ☎ 03-9342 7000; Grattan St, Parkville) Twenty-four-hour emergency.
St Vincent's Hospital (Map pp496-7; ☎ 03-9288 2211; 41 Victoria Pde, Fitzroy) Twenty-four-hour emergency.
Travellers' Medical & Vaccination Centre (TMVC; Map pp496-7; ☎ 03-9935 8100; Level 2, 393 Little Bourke St, Melbourne) Travel-related medical advice and immunisations.

Money

Foreign-exchange booths at Melbourne Airport's international terminal are open to meet all arriving flights. In the city:

American Express (Map pp496-7; ☎ 1300 139 060; Level 1, 233 Collins St, Melbourne)
Travelex (Map pp496-7; ☎ 1800 637 642; 233 Collins St, Melbourne)

Post

All suburbs have an Australia Post branch.
Melbourne GPO (General Post Office; Map pp496-7; ☎ 13 13 18; 250 Elizabeth St, Melbourne; ☾ 8.30am-5.30pm Mon-Fri, 9am-4pm Sat, 10am-4pm Sun) Poste restante available.

Tourist Information

Information Victoria (Map pp496-7; ☎ 1300 366 356; www.information.vic.gov.au; 505 Little Collins St, Melbourne) A government-run bookshop stocking a wide variety of publications about Melbourne and Victoria.
Melbourne Visitor Information Booth (Map pp496-7; Bourke St Mall, Melbourne)
Melbourne Visitor Information Centre (Map pp496-7; ☎ 03-9658 9658; www.visitmelbourne.com; Federation Sq, Melbourne; ☾ 9am-6pm) Comprehensive tourist information including excellent resources for mobility-impaired travellers.
MetShop (Map pp496-7; ☎ 13 16 38; www .metlinkmelbourne.com.au; cnr Elizabeth & Swanston Sts, Melbourne; ☾ 9am-5.30pm Mon-Fri, 9am-1pm Sat) Public transport information.

SIGHTS

Most of Melbourne's best-known sights are clustered around the city centre, but the surrounding suburbs are thick with their own character. In the alternative north you'll find Fitzroy with its fashionable Brunswick St, and Collingwood the edgier sibling. Seaside St Kilda lures weekend day-trippers for lattes and people watching. Carlton is the Italian district where Alpha Romeos growl along Lygon St, and Williamstown is a village-style port.

City Centre
FEDERATION SQUARE

A riotous explosion of steel, glass and abstract geometry, **Federation Square** (Map pp496-7; ☎ 03-9655 1900; www.federationsquare.com.au; cnr Flinders & Swanston Sts) is Melbourne's meeting hub, where thousands of locals and visitors gather in the undulating forecourt each year for regular cultural events, sporting telecasts, t'ai chi classes, twilight jazz, Afrobeats and much more. When they're not here to celebrate, protest, party or watch sport on the big telly, people fill the bars, restaurants, galleries and public lecture halls.

VICTORIA

MELBOURNE IN...

Three Days

Day one: if the weather's fine make a beeline for the sea. Jump on a tram to **St Kilda** (p510) and soak up the atmosphere of Acland and Fitzroy Sts. Indulge in wicked cakes, trek St Kilda Pier, test your carnival mettle at Luna Park and tuck into yum cha at **Mahjong** (p525) followed by a languid drink at the **George Public Bar** (p528).

Day two: start in the thick of things and do a cultural round of the central business district (CBD). Head to **Federation Square** (p503) and worship visual media at the **Australian Centre for the Moving Image** (below), then dose up on more culture at the **Ian Potter Centre: National Gallery of Victoria Australia** (below). Amble over to the **Immigration Museum** (p506) and then take a breather and a picnic in the **Royal Botanic Gardens** (p508). Spend the afternoon exploring the city's laneways and wrap things up with a fabulous dinner at **Maha** (p523).

Day three needs a dose of the north. Start at the **Melbourne Museum** (p509) or the **Royal Melbourne Zoo** (p509) and then wander over to **Brunswick Street** (p510) for the city's finest cafe and bohemian culture. If you have time, continue the foray into **Smith Street** (p510) for edgier appeal, and then scoot back to the city for **Chinatown** (p506) chow, a bout of theatre or a bar hop.

One Week

Stretch your Melbourne escapade into a week and dabble out west (see The Best of the West, p514). On day four explore **Williamstown** (p511) and take the kids to Scienceworks.

Spend day five at the **Queen Victoria Market** (p506). Sample the multicultural deli goods, stock up on organic fruit and then traipse the aisles for bargain clothing, music, shoes and souvenirs. Head to the **Melbourne Cricket Ground** (MCG; p509) and take a tour to see why this city is so nuts about sport. Finish the day with a visit to the **Australian Centre for Contemporary Art** (p507).

Day six and seven are for the leftover must-dos. Take a day's excursion to the **Great Ocean Road** (p551) or the **Yarra Valley** (p543). Hit **South Yarra** (p510) for shopping, eats and drinks on Toorak Rd, Chapel St and Greville St. Tuck into fabulous Vietnamese or Thai in **Richmond** (p525).

The **Australian Centre for the Moving Image** (ACMI; Map pp496-7; ☎ 03-8663 2200; www.acmi.net .au; ☺ 10am-6pm) is an innovative centre dedicated to the interpretation and analysis of the moving image. Housing two cinemas and a screen gallery, it hosts changing exhibitions, regular script readings and excellent minifestivals of international cinema, plus the **Melbourne Cinémathèque** (www.melbournecin ematheque.org) screenings, kids flicks, Friday-night cult films, seniors sessions and much more. ACMI's programs for young people, both film screenings and workshops, are also excellent.

The **Ian Potter Centre: National Gallery of Victoria Australia** (NGVA; Map pp496-7; ☎ 03-8620 2222; www.ngv.vic.gov.au/ngvaustralia; Federation Sq; admission free; ☺ 10am-5pm Tue-Sun) is devoted to Australian art, featuring works from the colonial to contemporary periods by celebrated artists including Sidney Nolan, Arthur Boyd, Joy Hester, Clifford Possum Tjapaltjarri, Albert Tucker, Jenny Watson, Bill Henson, Howard Arkley, Tony Clark, John Brack and Gordon Bennett.

Birrarung Marr (Map pp496-7; ☎ 03-9658 9955; Batman Ave), which means 'River of Mists' in Wurundjeri, is a park on the banks of the Yarra, providing a scenic route to the MCG via William Bark Bridge and a promenade amble to the Melbourne and Olympic Parks sporting precincts. In its centre, the **Federation Bells** (☺ 8-9am, 12.30-1.30pm, 5-6pm) ring out daily with specially commissioned contemporary compositions. An old railway building in the park, **ArtPlay** (Map pp496-7; ☎ 03-9664 7900; www.artplay.com.au) hosts creative weekend and holiday workshops for children aged between five and 12 years – bookings are essential.

The **National Design Centre** (NDC; Map pp496-7; ☎ 03-9654 6335; www.nationaldesigncentre.com; ☺ 10am-5pm Mon-Fri, noon-5pm Sat & Sun) sells, displays and interprets international and local design wares and hosts the annual Melbourne Design Festival in July.

VICTORIA

SWANSTON STREET

The 1874 **Melbourne Town Hall** (Map pp496-7; ☎ tour bookings 9658 9658; cnr Swanston & Collins Sts) was once the main concert venue in town, and has enjoyed tea with the Queen in 1954 and thousands of psychotic Beatles fans courtesy of the lads themselves appearing on the balcony in 1964. Take a free one-hour **tour** (☼ 11am & 1pm Mon-Fri) to learn more about the 'largest grand romantic organ' in the southern hemisphere.

Built in stages from 1854, the **State Library of Victoria** (Map pp496-7; ☎ 03-8664 7000; www.slv.vic.gov.au; 328 Swanston St; admission free; ☼ 10am-9pm Mon-Thu, 10am-6pm Fri-Sun) boasts a classical revival facade; millions of maps, pictures, books and other publications; and the striking, octagonal, domed **La Trobe Reading Room** to savour them in. Attached is Mr Tulk Cafe (p523).

Further along, the Edwardian baroque **Melbourne City Baths** (p512) originally served as the public baths in a bid to stop locals from washing themselves in the grotty Yarra. That was 1860; today they're a lovely spot to swim, sweat, play squash and avoid bathing in the Yarra.

Opposite Federation Square is the ornate and imposing Anglican **St Paul's Cathedral** (1880).

COLLINS STREET

Collins St is one of Melbourne's most elegant streetscapes. Its fashionable 'Paris end' is lined with plane trees (lit up beautifully with fairy lights at night), grand buildings and upmarket European boutiques (Chanel, Bally, Hermés etc). From Elizabeth to Spencer Sts, it's the haunt of bankers and stockbrokers.

Facing each other on the corners of Russell and Collins Sts are the 1873 decorative Gothic **Scots Church** (Map pp496-7; 140 Collins St) and the 1866 **St Michael's Uniting Church** (Map pp496-7; 120 Collins St), built in the Lombardic Romanesque style. The renovated **Athenaeum Theatre** (Map pp496-7; 188 Collins St) dates back to 1886 and is topped by a statue of Athena, the Greek goddess of wisdom. Across the road is the opulent **Regent Theatre** (Map pp496-7; 191 Collins St).

Block Arcade (Map pp496-7), which runs between Collins and Elizabeth Sts, was built in 1891 and is a beautifully intact 19th-century shopping arcade. It features etched-glass ceilings and mosaic floors, and magnificently detailed plasterwork. Connecting Block Arcade with Little Collins St, **Block Place** (Map pp496-7) keeps hip city cats topped up with lattes and cafe fare.

In the block between William and King Sts, the **Le Meridien at Rialto** (Map pp496-7; 495 Collins St) is an imaginative five-star hotel behind the facades of two marvellous, old Venetian Gothic buildings. These older buildings are dwarfed by the soaring **Rialto Towers** (Map pp496-7; 525 Collins St), with the justifiably popular **Melbourne Observation Deck** (Map pp496-7; ☎ 03-9629 8222; www.melbournedeck.com.au; adult/child/family $14.50/8/39.50; ☼ 10am-10pm) offering spectacular 360-degree views from the 55th floor.

BOURKE STREET

Between Swanston and Elizabeth Sts, the pedestrianised **Bourke Street Mall** (Map pp496-7) is thick with the scent of department store money laundering, and the sounds of Peruvian, New Age and unidentifiable buskers. On the corner of Bourke and Elizabeth Sts is the **GPO** (Map pp496-7; www.melbournesgpo.com), which suffered a fire in September 2001 and has risen from the ashes in its new incarnation as an agglomeration of high-end boutiques (see p534). On the other side of the mall, the **Royal Arcade** (Map pp496-7; www.royalarcade.com.au), completed in 1870, is Melbourne's oldest arcade.

Behind Little Bourke St is **Caledonian Lane** (Map pp496-7), an unofficial canvas for local street artists.

VICTORIA

CARS & TRAMS

Melbourne's notoriously confusing road rule is the 'hook turn' (which prevents turning vehicles from delaying trams). To turn right at most city intersections, pull into the left lane, at the corner of the intersection, wait until the light of the street you're turning into changes from red to green, then complete the turn. A black-and-white sign that reads 'Right Turn from Left Only' hangs from the overhead cables, identifying these intersections.

You can only overtake a tram on the left and *always* stop behind a tram when it halts to drop off or collect passengers.

SPRING STREET

The **Old Treasury** (Map pp496-7; ☎ 03-9651 2233; www .citymuseummelbourne.org; Spring St; adult/concession/family $8.50/5/18; ◷ 9am-5pm Mon-Fri, 10am-4pm Sat & Sun) is an elegant edifice built in 1862 with basement vaults to store much of the £200 million worth of gold mined from the Victorian goldfields. The **City Museum**, housed within, has three permanent exhibitions.

The 1856 **Parliament House of Victoria** (Map pp496-7; ☎ 03-9651 8911; www.parliament.vic.gov.au; Spring St) is a striking monolith of a structure preceded by a grand flourish of steps. Free half-hour **tours** (◷ 10am, 11am, 2pm, 3pm, 3.45pm weekdays when parliament is in recess; bookings required) take you through both houses and the library. Fascinating design features and the symbolism underlying much of the ornamentation are illuminated by the knowledgeable guides.

CHINATOWN

Between Exhibition and Swanston Sts on Little Bourke St, ruby-hued archways usher city-goers into a bustling strip of clattering woks, glowing neon, exotic shopfronts laced with juicy, florid ducks, and floor-to-ceiling chambers of medicinal herbs and tinctures. Melbourne's Chinatown has thrived since the 1850s, and although the opium dens, brothels and boarding houses have long made way for more salubrious enterprises, the area still maintains its entrepreneurial air.

The interesting **Chinese Museum** (Map pp496-7; ☎ 03-9662 2888; www.chinesemuseum.com.au; 22 Cohen Pl; adult/concession $7.50/5.50; ◷ 10am-5pm) documents the long history of Chinese people in Australia over five levels. The entrance of the museum is guarded by the 218kg Millennium Dragon, which snakes its way through the city streets during Chinese New Year (see p515).

QUEEN VICTORIA MARKET

Chaotic, friendly, multicultural – the **Queen Victoria Market** (Map pp496-7; ☎ 03-9320 5822; www .qvm.com.au; 513 Elizabeth St; ◷ 6am-2pm Tue & Thu, 6am-6pm Fri, 6am-3pm Sat, 9am-4pm Sun) is one of the largest open-air markets in the southern hemisphere and the grand dame of all Melbourne markets. Over 600 traders hock their wares here and it's been pushing trade for more than 125 years. You'll find everything from perfectly ripe brie to perfectly rank moccasins. An organic corridor in the fruit and vegetable section is stocked with fresh produce grown without a hint of chemicals or pesticides. The

bustling **night market** (◷ 5.30-10pm Wed) runs between late November and mid-February. The **Queen Victoria Market Cooking School** (☎ 03-9320 5835) also holds excellent and diverse cooking classes that change with the seasons.

OLD MELBOURNE GAOL

Behind its bluestone facade, this penal **museum** (Map pp496-7; ☎ 03-8663 7228; Russell St; adult/child/family $18/10/44; ◷ 9.30am-5pm) is a study in the small leaps humanity has made towards enlightenment. The dark, dank and tiny cells display plaster casts of some of the 135 prisoners who were hanged here. Ned Kelly's iconic armour and the very gallows from which he was hanged are also here. Night tours include **Ghostseekers** (www.ghostseekers.com.au; adult/child $30/22.50; ◷ monthly), which include paranormal investigations of the building. It's not recommended for children under 12; book through **Ticketek** (☎ 13 28 49; http://premier.ticketek.com.au).

IMMIGRATION MUSEUM

The inspiring **Immigration Museum** (Map pp496-7; ☎ 03-9927 2700; 400 Flinders St; adult/concession & child $6/free; ◷ 10am-5pm), in the Old Customs House (1858–70), provides a heart-rending account of Victoria's immigration history. The tears, joy, separations, reunions and difficult journeys that typify human movement are powerfully represented, and the clever multimedia displays provide insight into Melbourne's continuing multicultural mix. Contents aside, the building's Renaissance revival architecture is reason enough for a visit.

KOORIE HERITAGE TRUST CULTURAL CENTRE

Devoted to southeastern Aboriginal culture, this **centre** (Map pp496-7; ☎ 03-8622 2600; 295 King St; entry by donation; ◷ 10am-4pm Tue-Sun) preserves and popularises Koorie artefacts and art. Three galleries house significant items such as possumfur cloaks, and contemporary Aboriginal art is displayed in temporary exhibits.

DOCKLANDS

Near the rear of Southern Cross Station, **Docklands** (Map pp496-7; ☎ 1300 663 008; www.dock lands.vic.gov.au) was once a wetland and lagoon area used by Koories as a hunting ground. Until the mid-1960s it was the city's main industrial and docking area. In recent years the area has been hijacked by entrepreneurial developers and it's now a confluence of residential high rises, skirted by restaurants, businesses and bars. On paper it sounds great but the reality is sterile. One interesting landmark to note on your visit here is the utterly photogenic **Webb Bridge** (Map pp496–7), a sinuous structure designed by Robert Owen and inspired by a Koorie eel trap.

Another treat for camera junkies is the **Southern Star** (Map pp494–5; ☎ 03-8688 9688; www .thesouthernstar.com.au; adult/child $29/17; ☯ 10am-10pm), Melbourne's equivalent of the London Eye. Actually, at the time of writing it was *purely* for camera junkies given that it halted abruptly during a heat wave and refused to begin rotating again without a $20 million boost. Watch this space…

The 52,000-seat **Etihad Stadium** (Map pp496–7; ☎ 03-8625 7700) is the city's alternative footy arena, with a state-of-the-art sliding roof. Other sporting and entertainment events take place here on a regular basis. **Tours** (☎ 03-8625 7277; adult/child/family $14/7/37; ☯ 11am, 1pm & 3pm) of the stadium are conducted on weekdays, but night and weekend tours can also be arranged.

FITZROY GARDENS

The leafy **Fitzroy Gardens** (Map pp494–5; www.fitzroy gardens.com; btwn Wellington Pde & Clarendon, Lansdowne & Albert Sts) provide a luscious divide between the city centre and East Melbourne. Stately avenues lined with English elms are flanked by expansive lawns, flowerbeds and urban fugitives suffering office fatigue.

In the northwestern corner of the gardens is the **People's Path**, a circular path paved with 10,000 individually engraved bricks.

Captain Cook's Cottage (Map pp494–5; ☎ 03-9419 4677; www.cookscottage.com.au; adult/child/family $4.50/2.20/12; ☯ 9am-5pm) is the former Yorkshire home of the distinguished English navigator's parents (although the jury is still out on whether or not he ever slept there). It was dismantled, shipped to Melbourne and reconstructed stone by stone in 1934.

Southbank

Across the Yarra River from the city centre you'll find the arts precinct; the **Southgate** (www .southgate-melbourne.com.au) complex has three levels of restaurants cafes and bars, all with city skyline and river views. Further west is the 24-hour, nonstop cavalcade of illuminated excess that is the **Crown Casino & Entertainment Complex** (Map pp496–7; ☎ 03-9292 8888; www.crowncasino.com.au;

Southbank; ☯ 24hr). It's one of the largest casinos in the southern hemisphere – you'll be either spellbound or nauseated.

Across the road, the **Melbourne Exhibition Centre** (Map pp496–7; ☎ 03-9235 8000; www.mecc.com .au; 2 Clarendon St, Southbank) hosts everything from Sexpo to Santa's Kingdom.

ARTS PRECINCT

This small area on St Kilda Rd is the high-culture heart of Melbourne.

Behind an iconic waterwall, the **National Gallery of Victoria International** (NGVI; Map pp496–7; ☎ 03-8620 2222; www.ngv.vic.gov.au; 180 St Kilda Rd; general admission free, call for exhibition prices; ☯ 10am-5pm Wed-Mon) boasts an international collection that is world renowned and arguably Australia's finest. Permanent members include Rembrandt, Tiepolo, Bonnard, Monet and Modigliani. Temporary exhibitions are provocative and dynamic, and tours, talks and workshops are regular features.

The **Victorian Arts Centre** (VAC; Map pp496–7; ☎ 03-9281 8000; www.theartscentre.net.au; 100 St Kilda Rd) is made up of two separate buildings: Hamer Hall and the Theatres Building. The interiors of both buildings are stunning. **Hamer Hall** (Map pp496–7) is a major performance venue and base for the Melbourne Symphony Orchestra (MSO). The **Theatres Building** (Map pp496–7) is topped by a distinctive Eiffel-inspired spire (illuminated at night), underneath which are housed the State Theatre, the Playhouse and the George Fairfax Studio. Here you'll also find the **George Adams Gallery** and the **St Kilda Road Foyer Gallery**; both are free and have changing exhibitions. One-hour **tours** (adult/concession/family $11/8/28) of the centre are offered at noon and 2.30pm from Monday to Saturday, and a special backstage tour for over-12s only ($14) is offered at 12.15pm on Sunday. Call for bookings. There's also an arts and crafts **market** (☯ 10am-5pm Sun) in the Arts Centre undercroft, with a variety of goods on offer, many with an Australian bent.

The **Australian Centre for Contemporary Art** (Map pp494–5; ☎ 03-9697 9999; www.accaonline.org .au; 111 Sturt St; admission free; ☯ 10am-5pm Tue-Fri, 11am-6pm Sat & Sun) is one of Australia's most exciting contemporary galleries. The rust-coloured and cathedral-esque structure houses works especially commissioned for the space, plus an impressive range of works by local and international artists.

VICTORIA

THE ART OF HEIDE

Heide Museum of Modern Art (Map p537; ☎ 03-9850 1500; www.heide.com.au; 7 Templestowe Rd, Bulleen; adult/concession/child $12/8/free, extra for exhibitions; ☾ 10am-5pm Tue-Fri, noon-5pm Sat & Sun) is on the site of the former home of John and Sunday Reed, under whose patronage the likes of Sidney Nolan, John Perceval and Albert Tucker created a new movement in the Australian art world. Set in a sprawling, riverside park, Heide has an impressive collection and exceptional temporary exhibits. The museum is signposted off the Eastern Fwy. Otherwise, take an Eltham train to Heidelberg station, and catch National Bus 291 to the corner of Manningham and Templestowe Rds, and walk from there.

MELBOURNE AQUARIUM

A mesmerising marine menagerie slinks within the crystal ball of this waterside **aquarium** (Map pp496-7; ☎ 03-9620 0999; www.melbourneaquarium.com.au; King St; adult/child/concession/family $31.50/18/19.50/79; ☾ 9.30am-6pm Feb-Dec, 9.30am-9pm Jan). Get an eyeful of moray eels, giant cuttlefish, delicate sea dragons, sharks, starfish and much more. Vivid tropical fish flirt with onlookers and majestic rays soar above the domed perspex tunnel. The Antarctic section is home to King and gorgeous little Gentoo penguins and a breeding program promises tiny versions of both. It's hard to beat a dive with the sharks ($150 to $350, depending on your experience and equipment needs).

Kings Domain

Beside St Kilda Rd, which runs past the huge **Kings Domain**, stands the massive **Shrine of Remembrance** (Map pp494-5; ☾ 10am-5pm), which was built as a memorial to Victorians killed in WWI. Its design was partly based on the Temple of Halicarnassus, one of the seven ancient wonders of the world.

Near the shrine is **Governor La Trobe's Cottage** (Map pp494-5; Dallas Brooks Dr), the original Victorian government house sent out from the mother country in prefabricated form in 1840. It's positively quaint in comparison to the stretched Italianate **Government House** (Map pp494-5; ☎ National Trust 03-8663 7260; www.nattrust.com.au; Government House Dr; adult/child $15/10; ☾ guided tours Mon & Wed Feb-Nov by appointment only), where Victoria's current governor resides; it's a copy of Queen Victoria's palace on England's Isle of Wight. National Trust tours include both properties; bookings are essential.

ROYAL BOTANIC GARDENS

The finest botanic gardens in Australia, and among the best in the world, the beautifully designed **Royal Botanic Gardens** (Map pp494-5; www.rbg.vic.gov.au; admission free; ☾ 7.30am-8.30pm Nov-Mar, to 6pm Apr, Sep & Oct, to 5.30pm May-Aug) sprawl beside the Yarra River. Plants from Australia and around the world feature in mini-ecosystems, such as the cacti and succulents area, a herb garden and Australian rainforest. Take a book, a picnic or frisbee; most importantly, take your time.

Along with the abundance of plant species there's a surprising amount of wildlife, including ducks, swans and eels in and around the ornamental lake, and cockatoos, possums and flying foxes throughout the park.

The gardens are encircled by the **Tan**, a 4km running track and one of Melbourne's favourite venues for joggers and walkers (and talkers). During the summer months, the Moonlight Cinema (see Flicks Under the Stars, p532) flickers in the dark and theatre performances are staged.

A range of tours departs from the **visitors centre** (☎ 03-9252 2429; Birdwood Ave; ☾ 9am-5pm Mon-Fri, 9.30am-5pm Sat & Sun).

Along the Yarra River

Melbourne's prime natural feature, the 'mighty' Yarra River, is the butt of countless jokes but it's actually a scenic river. Parks, promenades, cycling paths, bridges and major attractions line its banks, and boat cruises depart from the banks of Federation Square (p515).

YARRA BEND PARK

Northeast of the city centre, the Yarra River is bordered by **Yarra Bend Park** (Map pp494-5; www.parkweb.vic.gov.au), much loved by runners, rowers, cyclists, picnickers, dog-walkers, families and strollers.

The **Studley Park Boathouse** (Map pp494-5; ☎ 03-9853 8707; Boathouse Rd, Studley Park; ☾ lunch Mon-Fri, 9am-11am Sat & Sun) dates back to the 1860s, and

VICTORIA

houses a restaurant, kiosk and cafe. There are also boats, canoes and kayaks available for hire (☎ 03-9852 1972; 2-person canoe per hr $28). Kane's suspension bridge takes you across to the other side of the river, and it's about a 20-minute walk from here to **Dights Falls** (Map pp494–5).

Yarra Park & Melbourne Park

Yarra Park contains the Melbourne Cricket Ground (MCG) and the Punt Road Oval (HQ for the Richmond AFL club). The adjoining Melbourne & Olympic Parks precinct contains the Melbourne Park National Tennis Centre, Olympic Park Stadium, Rod Laver Arena, Hisense Arena and several other ovals.

MELBOURNE CRICKET GROUND

The **MCG** (Map pp494–5; ☎ 03-9657 8888; www.mcg.org.au; Brunton Ave), affectionately known as 'the G', is the temple in which sports-mad Melburnians worship their heroes. The devoted come regularly, filled with hope, to watch their contemporary gladiators triumph or fall. It's one of the world's great sporting venues, and is imbued with an indefinable combination of tradition and atmosphere. You scoff? The stadium seats almost 100,000 and at a full-house AFL match or the Boxing Day Test cricket match the atmosphere is electric and the crowd deafening.

The first Australian Rules football game was played here in 1858, and in 1877 it hosted the first Test cricket match between Australia and England. Half-hour **tours** (☎ 03-9657 8879; adult/concession/family $15/11/12; ☒ 10am-3pm) are conducted on nonmatch days. Also housed within 'the G' is the **National Sports Museum** (☎ 03-9657 8879; www.nsm.org.au; adult/child/family $15/8/45; ☒ 10am-5pm), which contains Australia's largest collection of sporting artefacts and memorabilia in themed exhibitions. If sporting history tugs at your heartstrings, you'll love it. Call ahead for amended opening hours during sporting events.

Parkville & Carlton

Up the north end of town you'll find a cosmopolitan area that blends the intellectual with the recreational, and the multicultural with the mainstream.

Carlton is home to the bustling cafe strips of Drummond and Rathdowne Sts, and most importantly, Lygon St. This is the backbone of Melbourne's Italian quarter, where thousands

of Italian immigrants settled when they came to Melbourne after WWII. The strip remains one of Melbourne's liveliest, often teeming with shoppers, diners, macchiato sippers, students, film buffs and any other stereotype (or non) you can conjure.

Also in Carlton are the **Melbourne General Cemetery** (Map p499) and the gothic-style stone buildings of the **University of Melbourne** (Map p499).

ROYAL MELBOURNE ZOO

The **Royal Melbourne Zoo** (Map pp494–5; ☎ 03-9285 9300; www.zoo.org.au; Elliot Ave, Parkville; adult/child/concession/family $24/12/18/54; ☒ 9am-5pm) has been operating for more than 140 years, making it the oldest zoo in Australia, and one of the oldest in the world. Set in spacious and attractively landscaped gardens, the enclosures are simulations of the animals' natural habitats and the zoo is home to more than 320 species. Walkways pass through towering bird aviaries, a wide-open lion park, a tropical hothouse full of colourful butterflies and a gorillas' rainforest. There's also a large collection of native animals in a bush setting, a platypus aquarium, fur seals, tigers, plenty of reptiles and lots more.

In the summer months, the zoo hosts twilight concerts and there are various opportunities to sleep over inside the zoo.

MELBOURNE MUSEUM

In the middle of Carlton Gardens, **Melbourne Museum** (Map p499; ☎ 13 11 02; www.melbourne.museum.vic.gov.au; 11 Nicholson St, Carlton; adult/concession & child $8/free; ☒ 10am-5pm) provides a grand sweep of Victoria's natural and cultural histories. The emphasis is on education and interaction, and the main attractions include Bunjilaka, the Aboriginal Centre; a living forest gallery; and the Australia gallery, with an exhibit dedicated to that great Aussie icon Phar Lap, and another dedicated to the TV show *Neighbours* (filmed in Melbourne). The Children's Gallery is a great way to keep the kids entertained awhile.

Fitzroy & Collingwood

Fitzroy is where Melbourne's bohemian subculture moved when the lights got too bright in Carlton. The cafe set has also since moved in, but thankfully it still needs to share this inner-north plot with the anti-establishment, lip-studded and crimson-haired.

VICTORIA

Brunswick Street is one of Melbourne's liveliest streets, and where you'll find some of the best food, weirdest shops, most interesting people and unique clothes. In particular, the blocks on either side of the Johnston St intersection have a fascinating collection of young designer and retro clothes shops, bookshops, galleries, nurseries, pubs (the most per capita in Victoria) and, of course, more eateries than you can poke a fork at (see p524).

Smith Street forms the border between Fitzroy and Collingwood. It has an edgier milieu than Brunswick St. **Gertrude Street** connects the two at the southern end and has an increasingly well-deserved reputation for unique bars, restaurants, and local designer clothing.

Gertrude Contemporary Art Spaces (Map p502; ☎ 03-9419 3406; www.gertrude.org.au; 200 Gertrude St, Fitzroy; ☽ 11am-5.30pm Tue-Fri, 1-5.30pm Sat), is one of Melbourne's most exciting galleries. Sixteen studios promote emerging contemporary artists and the temporary exhibitions regularly provoke critical debate.

In **North Fitzroy** there are more interesting, quirky shops to explore, more historic buildings, the **Edinburgh Gardens** (Map pp494–5) and a host of gorgeous local pubs.

Richmond

As Carlton is to Italy, so Richmond is to Vietnam. There are still also many Greek Australians living here – hangers-on from the previous wave of immigrants to adopt the suburb.

The **Bridge Rd** and **Swan St** areas are something of a discount fashion centre, with shops where Australian fashion designers sell their seconds and rejects alongside the outlets of some of Melbourne's popular young designers. **Victoria St** is home to a host of cheap Vietnamese eateries; see p525.

South of the River

Welcome to the 'right' side of the river – the high-society side of town. Toorak is the ritziest suburb in Melbourne, and neighbouring suburbs Prahran and South Yarra follow closely behind. **Toorak Road** and **Chapel Street** (both Map p500) are the main strips; both are crammed with cafes, bars, restaurants, boutiques and shops, and ample ventures designed to keep the beautiful folk beautiful.

The excellent Prahran Market (p525), established in 1881, still packs in the city's gourmets

today and **Commercial Rd** is a focal point for Melbourne's gay and lesbian communities.

Running west off Chapel St, **Greville St** has a quirky collection of off-beat retro/grunge and boutique clothing shops, record shops and bookshops, and some good bars and cafes.

St Kilda

Melbourne's most famous seaside suburb maintains a perpetual state of fascinating flux. Home to Russian and Polish émigrés in the 1940s, it shifted from a prestigious address for colonial entrepreneurs to the haunt of the raffish, unkempt and experimental in the 1960s and '70s. By the '90s the suburban-macchiato crowd had begun to muscle in and a dingy flat suddenly became Melbourne's hottest property. Hotels, dance halls, sea baths, theatres, galleries and fun parks have all found their place here over the decades, and this seedy and glam, alternative and mainstream pocket remains a place of extremes. Sniff hard and you'll catch the scent of cakes, pasta, beer, roadies, sex, yoga, hair product…and the sea.

Fitzroy Street and **Acland Street** (both Map p501) are the main strips, and are packed with cafes, bars, sprawling old-school pubs and pavement tables. Acland St is particularly famed for its continental cake shops. Following **Carlisle St**, across St Kilda Rd and into Balaclava, you'll find some great Jewish bakeries and some natty boutiques and cafes.

The **Linden Art Centre & Gallery** (Map p501; ☎ 03-9209 6794; www.lindenarts.org; 26 Acland St; admission free; ☽ 1-6pm Tue-Sun) has contemporary art and a sculpture garden for children; and the excellent **Jewish Museum of Australia** (Map p501; ☎ 03-9534 0083; www.jewishmuseum.com.au; 26 Alma Rd; adult/child $10/5; ☽ 10am-4pm Tue-Thu, 11am-5pm Sun) has interactive displays relating to Jewish history and culture, plus a respected program of contemporary exhibits.

St Kilda pier (Map p501) is a favourite spot for strollers, who reward themselves with a coffee or a snack at **St Kilda Pier Pavilion**, a replica of the original 19th-century tearoom at the junction of the pier, which burnt down in 2003.

The breakwater near the pier was built in the '50s as a safe harbour for boats competing in the Olympic Games. It's now home to a colony of little penguins that have, incredibly, chosen the city's most crowded suburb in which to reside. During summer, the **Port Phillip Eco Centre** (www.ecocentre.com; adult/child $10/5) runs family tours of the St Kilda coastal environment that end up at the penguin colony. They can't guarantee a sighting, but will do their best, and all tour proceeds go towards keeping the local penguin outpost flourishing.

South of the pier the Moorish-style **St Kilda Sea Baths** (☎ 03-9593 8228, 9525 4888; www.stkildasea baths.com.au; 10-18 Jacka Blvd) contains shops, cafes and restaurants, a gym and a pricey 25m **saltwater pool** (adult/child $12/6).

Luna Park (Map p501; ☎ 03-9525 5033; www.lunapark .com.au; Lower Esplanade; unlimited ride ticket adult/child/ family $38/28/116; 🕙 11am-6pm Sat & Sun winter, 7-11pm Fri, 11am-11pm Sat, 11am-6pm Sun summer, 11am-6pm public & school holidays), a St Kilda symbol since 1912, is an old-fashioned amusement park that maintains a whiff of carny atmosphere. The old wooden roller coaster and beautifully crafted carousel are highlights, but the famous facade of a laughing Mr Moon has been the object of many a nightmare.

The **Esplanade Sunday Market** (Map p501; Upper Esplanade; 🕙 10am-5pm Sun) lines the street, featuring a range of open-air stalls selling arts and crafts, often with a New Age or Australiana slant.

Williamstown

'Willy' (Map pp494–5) is a gracious seafaring town with scenic promenades heaving with day-trippers on the weekend. Back in 1837 it was designated the main seaport on Port Phillip Bay, but became a secondary port by the 1880s.

Nelson Pl, lined with historic buildings, follows the foreshore, winding around the docklands and shipyards – the yacht clubs and marinas along the waterfront add to the maritime flavour. Between Nelson Pl and the waterfront is **Commonwealth Reserve**.

Williamstown Railway Museum (Map pp494-5; ☎ 03-9397 7412; Champion Rd; adult/child $5/2; 🕙 noon-5pm Sat & Sun, noon-4pm Mon-Fri during school holidays) has a fine collection of old steam locomotives and mini-steam-train rides for kids.

Scienceworks & Melbourne Planetarium (Map pp494-5; ☎ 03-9392 4800; http://museumvictoria.com .au/Scienceworks; 2 Booker St, Spotswood; Scienceworks adult/concession/child $8/free/free, planetarium $5/4/3.50; 🕙 10am-4.30pm) incorporates three historic buildings and keeps inquisitive grey matter occupied with interactive displays. Figure out the mysteries of the universe (or your own anatomy) by poking buttons, pulling levers, lifting flaps and learning all sorts of weird facts. The planetarium splashes the universe onto a 16m-domed ceiling.

Williamstown Ferries (Map pp494-5; ☎ 03-9517 9444, 03-9682 9555; www.williamstownferries.com.au) runs ferries between Gem Pier and Southgate, stopping at sites along the way.

ACTIVITIES
Cycling

The **Main Yarra Trail** is one of Melbourne's many inner-city bike paths along the riverside green belts. At least 20 other long urban cycle paths exist, all marked in the Melway *Greater Melbourne Street Directory*. In addition, **VicRoads** (www.vicroads.vic.gov.au) has printable maps.

Bike hire:

Rentabike (Map pp496-7 ☎ 03-9654 2762; www .rentabike.net.au; Riverbank, Federation Square; per day $35)

St Kilda Cycles (Map p501; ☎ 03-9534 3074; www.st kildacycles.com.au; 150 Barkly St, St Kilda; per day from $25)

Golf

Melbourne's sandbelt courses, such as Royal Melbourne (ranked in the world's top 10), Huntingdale and Kingston Heath are world famous. It is tough to get a round at these members' courses, but there are also plenty of public courses where anyone can play. You'll need to book on weekends. Green fees are around $25 for 18 holes, and most courses have clubs and buggies for hire. These are some good public courses close to town:

Albert Park Public Golf Course (Map pp494-5; ☎ 03-9510 5588; www.golfvictoria.com.au; Queens Rd, Albert Park; 🕙 dawn-dusk) Championship course alongside the Australian Formula One Grand Prix circuit.

Yarra Bend Public Golf Course (Map pp494-5; ☎ 03-9481 3729; Yarra Bend Rd, Fairfield; 🕙 dawn-dusk) Pick of the bunch; bookings essential.

In-line Skating

The best in-line skating tracks are found around St Kilda. **Rock 'n' Skate Shop** (Map p501; ☎ 03-9525 3434; 22 Fitzroy St, St Kilda; per hr/day $10/25; 🕙 10am-7pm Mon-Fri, 9am-7pm Sat & Sun) hires equipment that's in pretty good condition.

Lawn Bowls

Board shorts and Mambo tees sometimes outnumber pensioners in starched white in this increasingly popular Melburnian pastime. Barefoot, with a beer in one hand and a bowl in the other, they congregate on Sunday afternoons for an alternative to the pub session. And the kids aren't much better. A game costs $5 to $12 and in summer it's one of the finest ways to spend an afternoon.

Inner-city clubs:

North Fitzroy Bowls Club (Map pp494-5; ☎ 03-9481 3137; www.fvbowls.com.au; 578 Brunswick St, North Fitzroy) Bowls, barbecues and a beer garden. Bewdiful. Call for opening hours.

St Kilda Bowling Club (Map p501; ☎ 03-9537 0370; 66 Fitzroy St, St Kilda; ☾ noon-sunset Tue-Wed, Fri & Sun, till 5pm Thu Sep-Apr) A no-shoes dress code and you can also try your hand at boules.

Sailing

There are plenty of yacht clubs around the bay and races are held most weeks. Some clubs welcome visitors as crew on racing boats. Two of the biggest clubs:

Hobsons Bay Yacht Club (Map pp494-5; ☎ 03-9397 6393; www.hbyc.asn.au; 268 Nelson Pl, Williamstown) Volunteers get a go on Wednesday nights August to March.

Royal Melbourne Yacht Squadron (Map p501; ☎ 03-9534 0227; Pier Rd, St Kilda) Postcard-perfect location and crewing opportunities on Wednesdays ($15).

Swimming

The bay beaches are popular during summer. St Kilda beach is busy at the first ray of sunlight, but they all get packed bum-to-bum on scorchers.

Pools near the city:

Fitzroy Swimming Pool (Map p502; ☎ 03-9205 5180; Alexandra Pde, Fitzroy; adult/child/family $4.30/1.90/10.80; ☾ 6am-8pm Mon-Thu, 6am-7pm Fri, 8am-6pm Sat & Sun) A local fave with a toddlers' pool.

Prahran Aquatic Centre (Map p500; ☎ 03-8290 7140; www.stonnington.vic.gov.au/swim; Essex St, Prahran; adult/child/family $4.70/2.60/12.50; ☾ 6am-7.30pm Mon-Fri, 8am-6pm Sat & Sun Oct-Apr; 6-9.30am & 4.30-7.30pm Mon-Fri, 8am-10.30am Sat & Sun May-Sep)

Melbourne City Baths (Map pp496-7; ☎ 03-9663 5888; www.melbournecitybaths.com.au; 420 Swanston St; adult/child $5.10/2.40; ☾ 6am-10pm Mon-Thu, 6am-8.30pm Fri, 8am-6pm Sat & Sun) This stately swimming hall has a 30m indoor pool plus a gym, spas, saunas and squash courts.

Melbourne Sports & Aquatic Centre (MSAC; Map pp494-5; ☎ 03-9926 1555; www.msac.com.au; Albert Rd, Albert Park; adult/child $5.90/4.40; ☾ 5.30am-10pm, 7am-8pm Sat & Sun) Has a fantastic indoor 50m pool, wave pool, water slides, spa-sauna-steam room and spacious common areas. Childcare is available.

Windsurfing & Kitesurfing

South of St Kilda, Elwood is a very popular kitesurfing and windsurfing area. **RPS – the Board Store** (off Map pp494-5; ☎ 03-9525 6475; www.rpstheboardstore.com; 87 Ormond Rd, Elwood) can teach you the basics of either sport; a 90-minute windsurfing lesson will set you back $75 and a two-hour one-to-one kitesurfing lesson is $130. All gear is included in the price.

Yoga

The following places all offer drop-in classes to unkink your body. Check websites for costs and class timetables.

Action School of Yoga (Map p502; ☎ 03-9415 9798; www.actionyoga.com; Level 1, 275 Smith St, Collingwood) Teaches Iyengar yoga and has a solid reputation.

Ashtanga Yoga Centre of Melbourne (Map p502; ☎ 03-9419 1598; www.ashtangamelbourne.com.au; Level 1, 110 Argyle St, Fitzroy) Rigorous Mysore-style classes, and courses for kids and teens.

Bikram Yoga (Map p502; ☎ 03-9416 4422; www.bikramyogafitzroy.com.au; 24 Johnston St, Fitzroy) Adherents of the Bikram method will be able to sweat it out in style here.

St Kilda Iyengar Yoga School (Map p501; ☎ 03-9537 1015; www.skys.com.au; 11/82 Acland St)

WALKING TOUR

Melbourne's CBD is a warren of beautiful alleys and laneways, some cobblestoned, some bluestoned and all laden with character.

Start your foray into them at an obvious point – **Federation Square** (**1**; p503). Head east along Flinders St and then turn left onto Hosier Lane, keeping the **Forum Theatre** (**2**; p529) on your right. Depending on the hunger pangs you could pop into **MoVida** (**3**; p522) for a scrummy round of tapas, or keep moving. Turn right at Flinders Lane, left onto Russell St and then right onto Collins St. Stop a moment to admire **Scots Church** (**4**; p505) and **St Michael's Uniting Church** (**5**; p505) and make your way east along the 'Paris' end of Collins St.

Find respite from the main strip and take a left onto Alfred Pl, which leads to Little Collins St. Turn right and continue along Little Collins St, turning left onto Meyers Pl. Turn right onto Bourke St and you'll hit the eastern border of the CBD, where **Parliament House** (**6**; p506) strikes a pose.

Turn left on Spring St and left again onto Little Bourke St, past **Princess Theatre** (**7**; p532).

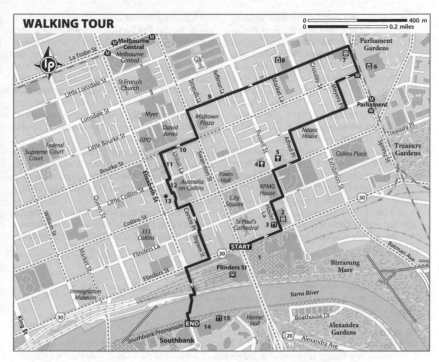

WALKING TOUR

Start Federation Square
Finish Southgate
Distance 3.5km
Duration 2½ hours

Head down Little Bourke St and stop in at the **Chinese Museum** (**8**; p506) before heading into the heart of **Chinatown** (**9**; p506).

Turn left at Swanston St and then right on Bourke St to amble through **Bourke St Mall** (**10**; p505). Ogle at the shops and people and then potter through the glorious old **Royal Arcade** (**11**; p505). Dogleg from Little Collins to **Block Place** (**12**; p505) and into **Block Arcade** (**13**; p505). Cross Collins St and head down Centre Pl and Degraves St for shoulder-to-shoulder boutiques, cafes and bars.

Turn right onto Flinders St and then cross it via the pedestrian tunnel beneath the railway tracks to reach the Yarra River. Cruise across the pedestrian bridge to **Southgate** (**14**; p507) and finish the day up with a bite to eat and a well-earned vino at **Bearbrass** (**15**; p523).

MELBOURNE FOR CHILDREN

Melbourne lays on a good spread of activities geared solely towards youngsters, from low-flying raptors and kooky science exhibits to seven-gilled sharks. During school holidays many places have tailor-made early-childhood programs, and you can always head to one of the many parks for a grassy romp.

Sights that give 'What I did on my holiday' stories backbone include the Royal Melbourne Zoo (p509), where meerkats cause great hilarity; the Werribee Open Range Zoo (p538); with its spot-the-zebra/rhino/giraffe/etc open vehicle safari; and Healesville Sanctuary (p544), the best option for getting up close to Australian native animals. Overnight camps at the zoos, such as Melbourne's 'Roar 'n' Snore' and the Open Range's 'Slumber Safari', are also lots of spooky fun.

Other educational options include Scienceworks (p511), with lots of hands-on activities, and the Melbourne Aquarium (p508), where sharks hovering overhead in the 360-degree aquarium may add weight to parental threats.

VICTORIA

Less threatening encounters with wildlife include penguin spotting with the Port Philip Eco Centre (p511) or at Phillip Island (p548). Then there's the **Collingwood Children's Farm** (Map pp494-5; ☎ 03-9417 5806; St Heliers St, Abbotsford; adult/concession/family $8/4/16; ⓥ 9am-5pm), a bucolic spot right by the Yarra River, with grazing goats, cows, lambs and ponies, all of which tolerate tiny petting hands. The farm also runs a **Farmers' Market** (admission $2; ⓥ 8am-1pm 2nd Sat of month), where you can stock up on local organic produce. In a similar vein, **Ceres Community Environment Park** (Map pp494-5; ☎ 03-9387 2609; cnr Roberts & Stewart St, Brunswick East) has plenty of room for youngsters to chase chooks while parents can chow down on delicious organic breakfasts and lunchtime baguettes.

The Ian Potter Centre (p503) and ArtPlay (p503) both have workshops and art classes for budding Rembrandts. Alternatively, take them to the **Fire Services Museum Victoria** (Map p502; ☎ 03-9662 2907; 39 Gisborne St, East Melbourne; adult/child $5/2; ⓥ 9am-3pm Thu-Fri, 10am-4pm Sun), where they can clamber on a fire truck and indulge their fire-fighter fantasies. The Children's Gallery at the Melbourne Museum (p509) has hands-on exhibits, while budding Bradmans will also love the cricket and other sporting exhibitions at the National Sports Museum (p509).

For something more riotous, Luna Park (p511) rides summon nerves of steel, and, in the depths of the Dandenongs, a day trip on steam train Puffing Billy (p544) is always a huge hit.

Get them out and about – take a frisbee, a football and a picnic and head to the **Children's Garden** (Map pp494-5; Observatory Precinct, Birdwood Ave;

THE BEST OF THE WEST Katie Horner

Melbourne's inner west has long been a favoured retreat for savvy locals with nous for the underrated, and you'd be cheating yourself if you didn't see what the fuss is about. Get started with the following bests:

To Watch

Sun Theatre (Map pp494-5; ☎ 03-9362 0999; 8 Ballarat St, Yarraville) 'Boutique' art deco gloriousness with the individual theatres named after old cinemas from around the western suburbs: Trocadero, Lyric, La Scala. Best choc-top ice-cream range in town, with lolly bags and alcohol (allowed in the cinemas) to boot. Great for a first date.

To Eat

Footscray Market (Map pp494-5; ☎ 03-9687 1205; cnr Hopkins & Leeds Sts, Footscray) Across from the station, this place is loud, pungent, and chock-a-block with food. Sample Ethiopian, Greek, Italian, Vietnamese and Chinese fare. Fish is a favourite here and so is wandering around taking it all in.

    Stefan's Pizza (Map pp494-5; ☎ 03-9315 0258; 47 Civic Pde, Altona) This place does vegan, vegetarian, gluten-free pizzas, as well as meat versions. You can choose your base: cape seed, wholemeal, low GI, sourdough or standard, and the toppings are both unique and tasty – with pine nuts, pumpkin, chilli, soy cheese and spinach. Service is fabulous and worth the trip.

To Drink

The Commercial Hotel (Map pp494-5; ☎ 03-9689 9354; 238 Whitehall St, Yarraville; ⓥ 4pm-midnight Mon, to 11pm Tue, Wed & Sun, to 3am Thu-Sat) On the outskirts of Yarraville lies a pub with good food, a range of beers on tap and drag-queen bingo if that's your fancy. A large beer garden, pool table and an array of characters from the west side make this a great watering hole.

To Browse

The unassuming suburb of Seddon is littered with west-infused, individual shops; perfect for an afternoon of browsing. For shopaholics there's the delightful **Sedonia** (Map pp494-5; ☎ 03-9689 9368; 41 Gamon St, Seddon), with many a quirky item on display from cute earrings to large poufs, and **Diamond Dog** (Map pp494-5; cnr Gamon & Charles Sts, Seddon) for funky vintage clothing. If you get hungry there's a great chippie: **Charles St Fish & Chips** (☎ 03-9689 2402; 67 Charles St, Seddon). Further up Victoria St and heading into Footscray, there's the organic grocer **Pompello** (Map pp494-5; ☎ 03-9687 2627; 164 Victoria St, Seddon).

(☯ 10am-4pm Wed-Sun; daily during Victorian school holidays) at the Royal Botanic Gardens, or any of the multitude of parks in every neighbourhood. Alternatively, head to the beach for a day of slip, slop, slap, sea and sun, or to the wave pool and waterslides of the Melbourne Sports & Aquatic Centre (p512).

For more information about local attractions and events, look for the free monthly publication **Melbourne's Child** (www.melbourneschild.com.au), which can be found in cafes and kid-oriented businesses all over town. The Melbourne Visitor Information Centre (p503) stocks *KidFriendly* and *letsgokids*, two seasonal brochures listing activities, sights and information in Victoria.

TOURS

Aboriginal Heritage Walk (☎ 03-9252 2429; www .rbg.vic.gov.au; Royal Botanic Gardens; adult/child/concession $18/9/14; ☯ tours 11am Thu & Fri Dec & Feb) This 90-minute tour takes you through the story of the Boonwurrung and Woiworung peoples, the ancestral owners of the Royal Botanic Gardens.

Blackbird Cruises (☎ 03-9689 6431; www.blackbirdcruises.com.au; adult/child from $8/4; ☯ Tue, Thu, Sat & Sun) Offers one- and two-hour cruises along the Maribyrnong River (past the Lonely Planet office!).

Chinatown Heritage Walk (☎ 03-9662 2888; www .chinesemuseum.com.au/whatson.html; 22 Cohen Pl; adult/concession from $18/15) Tours of historic Chinatown, with its atmospheric alleys and bustling vibe.

City Circle trams (www.metlinkmelbourne.com.au; admission free; ☯ 10am-6pm Sun-Wed, to 9pm Thu-Sat) Free trams with informative commentary running every 10 minutes around the city centre.

Hidden Secrets Tours (☎ 03-9329 9665; www .hiddensecretstours.com; tours $60-135) Insider tours of the city's bars, boutiques, laneways, cafes and architectural highlights.

Melbourne City Tourist Shuttle (www.thatsmelbourne .com.au/shuttle; ☯ 9.30am-4.30pm) Free and informative 90-minute tour that loops around 13 inner-city sights, including the Southern Star Observation Wheel, Melbourne Museum, the Royal Botanic Gardens and Chinatown.

Melbourne River Cruises (Map pp496-7; ☎ 03-8610 2600; www.melbcruises.com.au; Federation Wharf; adult/child/family $22/11/50) Yarra cruises.

FESTIVALS & EVENTS

There's always a festival of some sort happening in Melbourne. Many are thematic, with film, comedy, theatre, sport, food and wine enticing locals and visitors to revel in Melbourne life. Check out the free, weekly

What's on in Melbourne guide available at visitor information centres, and click onto www.melbourne.vic.gov.au/events.

January

Australian Open (www.australianopen.com) One of the four Grand Slam tennis events, held at the Melbourne Park Tennis Centre.

Big Day Out (www.bigdayout.com) Nearly 40,000 revellers cut sick to over 40 alternative international and Australian rock bands at this January event.

Midsumma Festival (www.midsumma.org.au) Held Mid-January to early February. Melbourne's annual gay and lesbian arts festival has over 100 events across the city.

February

St Jerome's Laneway Festival (www.lanewayfestival .com.au) Iconic indie festival crammed into a laneway featuring local and international music artists.

Chinese New Year (www.chinesenewyear.com.au) The smell of firecrackers mingles with aromas from food stalls as the red dragon dances past. One not to be missed.

St Kilda Festival (www.stkildafestival.com.au) This week-long celebration of local arts and culture is best when the sun's out – bring a hat and your drinking legs.

March

Australian Formula One Grand Prix (www.grandprix.com.au) Albert Park gets invaded by the thoroughbreds of the automotive world and their party-loving hangers-on.

St Patrick's Day The mother of all piss-ups is celebrated at pubs (on the 17th) throughout the city.

Melbourne Fashion Festival (www.mff.com.au) Australia's most beautiful rags adorn catwalks and runways for a week in early March.

Melbourne Food & Wine Festival (www.melbournefoodandwine.com.au) The main gastronomical event of the year takes place in February or March and is highly regarded in Australia and overseas.

Moomba (www.melbournemoombafestival.com.au) Ten days of carnivals, fireworks and an outdoor art show, as well as waterskiing, a dragon-boat festival and a street parade.

Melbourne Queer Film Festival (www.melbournequeerfilm.com.au) Australia's largest gay film festival showcases everything from full-length features and animations to experimental works.

April

Anzac Day Held on the 25 April, the day begins with a dawn service at the Shrine of Remembrance, followed by a march for returned servicemen through the city and two-up with diggers late into the night.

VICTORIA

International Comedy Festival (www.comedyfestival
.com.au) Locals are joined by a wealth of international acts
performing at venues all over the city.

May

Next Wave Festival (www.nextwave.org.au) Celebrates
challenging and engaging art forms from Melbourne's next
generation of artists. Run biannually and almost entirely by
16- to 30-year-olds.
St Kilda Film Festival (www.stkildafilmfestival.com.au)
Showcases contemporary Australian short films and videos.

July

Melbourne International Film Festival (www
.melbournefilmfestival.com.au) Two weeks of the newest
and the best in local and international film.

August

Melbourne Writers' Festival (www.mwf.com.au)
This 10-day festival covers a wide range of literary genres
and issues, with local and international authors speaking,
reading, quaffing and writing.

September

AFL Grand Final (www.afl.com.au) The AFL final is
played on the last Saturday in September and packs pubs,
bars and outdoor TV screens with festive locals.
Melbourne Fringe Festival (www.melbournefringe
.com.au) In late September to mid-October, the Fringe
starts with a parade and street party on Brunswick St.
There's events to suit a range of tastes and interests.
Royal Melbourne Show (www.royalshow.com.au) The
country comes to town for this large-scale agricultural fair
at the Royal Melbourne Showgrounds in Flemington.

October

Lygon St Festa (www.lygonstreetfesta.com.au) Celebrates Italian culture with food stalls, bands and dancers.
Melbourne International Arts Festival (www
.melbournefestival.com.au) The city's major arts event has
a program that covers theatre, opera, dance and music,
and revolves around an annual theme.

November

Spring Racing Carnival (www.springracingcarnival
.com.au) Held October to November. There are two feature
races, the Caulfield Cup (Caulfield Racecourse) and the
Melbourne Cup (Flemington Racecourse).

December

Carols by Candlelight Christmas carols under the stars
at the Sidney Myer Music Bowl.
Boxing Day Test (www.mcg.org.au) Held at the MCG,
the first day of this annual international Test match is
Boxing Day, when the G is packed.

SLEEPING

Melbourne's sleeping options are broad and
of a high standard. During major festivals
and events accommodation is scarce, so
book in advance. Similar to Sydney and other
well-touristed areas, midrange listings in
Melbourne cost between $100 and $200 for a
double room with bathroom. Anything higher
than $200 is regarded as top end; anything
less than $100 is classified as budget. Prices
listed in this chapter are for non-peak seasons.
Expect to pay a little more in summer.

Budget

There are backpacker hostels in the city centre
and most of the inner suburbs. Several of the
larger hostels have courtesy buses that will pick
you up from the bus and train terminals.

If you're planning to work or study in
Melbourne it's worth looking at **TravelandLive**
(www.travelandlive.com.au), which specialises in
short- and medium-term apartment accommodation for travellers and young international professionals working and living
in Australia.

CITY CENTRE

Nomad's Industry (Map pp496-7; ☎ 03-9328 4383, 1800
447 762; 198 A'Beckett St, Melbourne; bookings@nomadsindus
try.com; dm/d from $20/90; 🖳) The latest flashpack-
ers to open in Melbourne caters well to savvy
travellers looking for a cut above your average hostel and a cut below hotel prices. This
refurbished building has polished surfaces
throughout and a range of modern six- to
14-bed dorms, en suite dorms and en suite
doubles. If you're in a group opt for an en
suite dorm with a TV – bliss! Flash as it is (and
it is!) it's a hostel, so you won't be guaranteed
the quiet of a hotel. Nevertheless, for the location and price it gets a big thumbs up.

Melbourne Connection Travellers Hostel (Map
pp496-7; ☎ 03-9642 4464; www.melbourneconnection
.com; 205 King St, Melbourne; dm $23-27, d from $70)
This friendly hostel sticks to the smaller-
is-better mandate, and comes up trumps.
Simple, clean and uncluttered dorms, twins
and doubles all come with linen and shared
bathrooms; the basement lounge provides a
comfy night.

King Street Backpackers (Map pp496-7; ☎ 03-
9670 1111, 1800 671 115; www.kingstreetbackpackers.com
.au; 197-199 King St, Melbourne; dm $25-30, d $80; 🖳) This
friendly, efficient, clean and super-safe hostel
piles on the freebies, including pancakes on

Sunday, internet access and a decent feed of pasta on Wednesday nights. Rooms are a tad dim and sombre, but the idea is to spend time outside of the four- to eight-bed dorms (or doubles). There's also a choice between mixed and single-sex dorms.

Greenhouse Backpacker (Map pp496-7; ☎ 03-9639 6400, 1800 249 207; www.greenhousebackpacker.com.au; Level 6, 228 Flinders Lane, Melbourne; dm/s/d incl breakfast $30/65/80; 🖳) This low-key, relaxed hostel tucked above a historic laneway has tidy facilities, great common areas and a chatty and friendly vibe. The expansive rooftop garden is devoid of greenery, but on beery Fridays you won't notice.

Urban Central Backpackers (Map pp494-5; ☎ 03-9639 3700, 1800 631 288; www.urbancentral.com.au; 334 City Rd, Southbank; dm/d/f from $31/90/120; 🖳) Housed in a functional grey block monolith, this hostel is surprisingly warm, colourful, bright and trendy on the inside. The alabaster dorms are neat and tidy, there's a great bar downstairs (with dangerously cheap happy hours) and the staff are quite fabulous. You'll need to contend with several floors of fellow guests, but that might be just what you're after.

City Centre Budget Hotel (Map pp496-7; ☎ 03-9654 5401; 22 Little Collins St, Melbourne; s/d/f without bathroom $70/90/130, d with bathroom $110; 🖳) Catering to all types of holidaymakers, this independent and inconspicuous hotel is great value. The 38 rooms are fresh and sun-kissed with white linen and breezy windows – yes, real air. All share bathrooms and a rooftop boasting swing seats and umbrellas.

NORTH & WEST MELBOURNE

Melbourne Metro YHA (Map pp494-5; ☎ 03-9329 8599; www.yha.com.au; 78 Howard St, North Melbourne; dm $26-35, tw & d with/without bathroom $90/80, apt $125; 🅿 🖳) A YHA showpiece, this huge hostel is an award-winner and everyone – *everyone* – raves about it. The generous rooms and common areas provide ample space, the rooftop area is breathtaking and facilities include barbecues, a pool table and super-friendly staff.

Melbourne Oasis (Map pp494-5; ☎ 03-9328 3595; www.yha.com.au; 76 Chapman St, North Melbourne; dm $32-35, tw & d $70-76; 🅿 🖳) This YHA is smaller and older than the Melbourne Metro, but more intimate and personal in its scope. Rooms are clean and facilities include a barbecue and lovely outdoor area, bike hire, pancake brekkies and movie nights. It's also eco-certified.

FITZROY

Nunnery (Map p502; ☎ 03-9419 8637, 1800 032 635; www.nunnery.com.au; 116 Nicholson St, Fitzroy; dm $26-30, s $65-75, d & tw $75-110) Easily one of Melbourne's most atmospheric accommodation options, the Nunnery offers a range of non-en suite rooms in three different buildings. All are Victorian era, and sweeping staircases and ornate stained-glass windows are the norm. Dorms are immaculate and the guest houses and townhouses are great for those wanting more space and style.

SOUTH YARRA

Hotel Claremont (Map pp494-5; ☎ 03-9826 8000, 1300 301 630; www.hotelclaremont.com; 189 Toorak Rd, South Yarra; dm/s/d incl breakfast $42/79/89, apt $185; 🖳) This charming 1868 heritage building with high ceilings and comfortable rooms is the perfect antidote to chain motels. It's clean, welcoming and simply decorated, and the sublime lattes of South Yarra are right outside. There are also flashy, self-contained apartments with air-con and off-street parking in a separate property nearby.

ST KILDA

Ritz (Map p501; ☎ 03-9525 3501, 1800 670 364; www.ritzbackpackers.com; 169 Fitzroy St, St Kilda; dm $20-25, d from $50; 🖳) A backpacker institution, this hostel is five minutes' walk from St Kilda's heart. All rooms have wi-fi and private rooms have complimentary towels. There are freebies galore and the whole lot sits on top of a 'traditional' British pub (well, the ales are in any case).

Coffee Palace (Map p501; ☎ 03-9534 5283; www.coffeepalacebackpackers.com.au; 24 Grey St, St Kilda; dm/d from $20/60; 🖳) This rambling old-school backpackers has plenty of rooms, activities and years behind it. It has a travel desk, communal kitchen, bar, pool tables, lounge and TV room, plus a rooftop terrace with bay views. Dorms sleep from four to 10, with some for women only. There are also private rooms with shared bathrooms.

Cooee on St Kilda (Map p501; ☎ 03-9537 3777, 1800 202 500; 333 St Kilda Rd, St Kilda; dm $24-30, d/f from $105/135; 🅿 🖳) This smart hostel has outstanding facilities. Dorms are snug but thick comfy mattresses compensate, and families do well in sunny en suites containing three single beds and a double. The bright, timber-clad lounge has plenty of places to park yourself and there's even a sunny beer garden.

JUST FOR NEIGHBOURS FANS *Alan Fletcher*

For many travellers to Australia, particularly those of British origin, Melbourne is a 'must' destination because it is the home of internationally renowned TV program *Neighbours*. A visit to Melbourne would not be complete without a trip to the legendary Ramsay St. Pin Oak Ct in Vermont South is the suburban street that has been home of the show for 20 years.

The best way to see Ramsay St and have a proper *Neighbours* experience is by doing the **Official Neighbours Tour** (☎ 03-9629 5866; www.neighbourstour.com.au), which is run by Backpacker King and approved by the show's producers and the residents of Pin Oak Ct. If you're lucky you might see us filming and grab a photo and autograph. Two tours are available: the $50 tour runs twice daily Monday to Friday and visits Ramsay St and Erinsborough High School, plus the bus is met by a *Neighbours* actor. The second, more comprehensive tour, costs $65 and visits the street, the school and the outside studio sets of the Lassiters' complex, Lou's Mechanics and Grease Monkeys. This tour is also met by a *Neighbours* actor and runs on weekends and over the Christmas holidays. Official merchandise is also available on the tours and from the **Neighbours Centre** (Map pp496–7; 570 Flinders St Melbourne).

You'll also find some backpacker hostels that occasionally run in-house trips to Ramsay Street – but always check to see if it's above board and that they're a licensed operator.

If you want to make the pilgrimage yourself, Pin Oak Ct is in Vermont South (Melways map 62: E8). If you don't have wheels, take the train to Glen Waverley station and bus 888 or 889 north; get off at Vision Dr near Burwood Hwy. Tram 75 from Flinders St will take you all the way to the corner of Burwood Hwy and Springvale Rd; a short walk south takes you to Weeden Dr; Pin Oak Ct is third on the left.

When visiting Pin Oak Ct please remember to respect the privacy of the residents. Don't do anything in their street or on their properties you wouldn't be happy with in your own street or home!

Backpacker King also runs a popular **Official Neighbours Trivia Night** (☎ bookings 03-9629 5866; www.neighboursnight.com.au; $40) every Monday night, where you can meet and have photos taken with your favourite *Neighbours* actors. It's held at the **Elephant & Wheelbarrow** (Map p501; 169 Fitzroy St, St Kilda) and includes a one-hour concert by my band, Waiting Room.

Alan Fletcher has worked in every branch of the performing arts for 31 years. For the past 14 years he has played the role of Dr Karl Kennedy on Neighbours.

Base (Map p501; ☎ 03-9536 6109; www.basebackpackers.com; 17 Carlisle St, St Kilda; dm $28-34, d from $100; ✷ ▣) Boutique-meets-budget: this flashy hostel is a well-run joint with a seamless interior. The facilities are excellent, there's a whole floor devoted to female travellers, and the party vibe is warm. It's also *right* in the thick of things.

Olembia Guesthouse (Map p501; ☎ 03-9537 1412; www.olembia.com.au; 96 Barkly St, St Kilda; dm/s/d $30/80/100; Ⓟ) An elegant option for the quieter traveller, Olembia offers cosy and impeccable rooms at budget tariffs. It's charmingly dated, small and comfortable so bookings are strongly advised.

Cabana Court Motel (Map p501; ☎ 03-9534 0771; 46 Park St, St Kilda; apt from $120; Ⓟ) Low-rise and low fuss, this motel has functional apartments that sleep a squishy six or a comfy four. It's in a residential street close to Fitzroy St and great value for groups or families.

SOUTH MELBOURNE

Bev & Micks Market Hotel (Map pp494–5; ☎ 03-9690 2220; 115 Cecil St, South Melbourne; dm/d $15/40) In a converted pub, still with a working bar, this hostel is right near the bustling produce market. It's a personable place, thanks to its modest size, though it still boasts a small kitchen and communal area.

Midrange

Most of the hotels and motels in this section are rated three or four stars, and they vary in quality. Singles usually cost the same as doubles.

There are some excellent B&Bs in Melbourne, many of which are at least as comfortable as a four-star hotel but generally charge considerably less. Melbourne also has a generous range of apartment-style hotels and serviced apartments, with self-contained facilities.

Useful contacts for apartment deals:
Punt Hill (☎ 1300 731 299; www.punthill-apartments
.com.au)
Quest (☎ 1800 334 033; www.questapartments.com.au)

CITY CENTRE
Hotel Enterprize (Map pp496-7; ☎ 03-9629 6991; www
.hotelenterprize.com.au; 44 Spencer St, Melbourne; r $90-180;
P ✿) The Enterprize is a small and reason-
ably priced hotel. Don't expect fireworks – the
budget rooms are plain and well maintained
and the 'business' rooms have faux-antique
furnishings, baths and more space. Aim for a
room on the 4th floor.

Victoria Hotel (Map pp496-7; ☎ 03-9699 0000, 1800
331 147; www.victoriahotel.com.au; 215 Little Collins St,
Melbourne; s/d from $110/180; ✿ ▯ ▣) The iconic
'Vic' opened its doors in 1880, but numerous
makeovers have replaced any heritage on the
inside with a massive warren of reasonable
and clean rooms. The cheapest are as snug as
closets, but the Bellerive rooms are spacious
and bright with newish bathrooms.

City Limits (Map pp496-7; ☎ 03-9662 2544, 1800 808
651; www.citylimits.com.au; 20 Little Bourke St, Melbourne;
d & tw $120-160, tr $170-200; ✿ P) Low on fuss
but high on value, these orderly studios with
simple kitchenettes are perfect for budget-
conscious travellers looking to escape the
hostel treadmill. The double-glazed windows
do a fine job keeping the city's roar to a low
hum and parking at $15 per 24 hours is a
CBD steal.

Atlantis Hotel (Map pp496-7; ☎ 03-9600 2900; www
.atlantishotel.com.au; 300 Spencer St, Melbourne; r from $150;
P ✿ ▯) The rooms at this conveniently
situated hotel are an ocean of vanilla-sponge
beige with subtle lighting and soothing decor.
Spend a wise $20 to upgrade from a standard
room and aim high for gobsmacking views of
Telstra Dome and the Docklands.

Batman's Hill (Map pp496-7; ☎ 03-9614 6344; www
.batmanshill.com.au; 623 Collins St, Melbourne; r $155-285;
P ✿ ▯) The slick makeover that swept
through this property a few years ago is
waning a tad, but Batman's is still ideal for
travellers looking for central, comfortable
and reasonably priced digs. Opt for a Club
room for space to strew the luggage and
upgraded bathrooms.

Quest Hero (Map pp496-7; ☎ 03-8664 8500; www.questa
partments.com.au; 140 Little Collins St, Melbourne; apt from
$190; ✿ ▯) These apartments are so well
equipped that the dishwashers, beautifully
kitted kitchens, stereos and videos will daz-

zle you into ignoring the utterly nondescript
decor. Fabulous value for families.

Robinsons in the City (Map pp496-7; ☎ 03-9329 2552;
www.robinsonsinthecity.com.au; 405 Spencer St, Melbourne;
r from $200; P ✿) Sweet, neat and petite,
Robinsons sits quietly on the city fringe and
dishes up six bedrooms with modern, stylish
furnishings. The classic brickwork exterior
belies the classy innards.

Rendezvous Hotel (Map pp496-7; ☎ 03-9250 1888;
www.rendezvoushotels.com; 328 Flinders St, Melbourne; r
$240-330; ✿) Built in 1913, this regal property
occupies a plum position on Flinders St and
has the exclusive and personal ambience of a
boutique hotel but the convenience of more
than 300 contemporary rooms. Heritage-
listed charm and excellent internet package
deals get the thumbs up.

Also available:
City Square Motel (Map pp496-7; ☎ 03-9654 7011;
www.citysquaremotel.com.au; 67 Swanston St, Melbourne;
r $105-185) Central, no-frills motel.
Mercure Hotel Melbourne (Map pp496-7; ☎ 03-
9205 9999; www.accorhotels.com.au; 13 Spring St,
Melbourne; r from $145; P ✿) Clinical, functional and
comfortable hotel in the 'Paris' end of town.

CARLTON
Downtowner on Lygon (Map p499; ☎ 03-9663 5555;
www.downtowner.com.au; 66 Lygon St, Carlton; r from $140;
P ✿ ▯) This popular, amicable and per-
petually busy hotel is perched at the edge of
Melbourne's Little Italy. It's pleasantly innocuous and has a variety of rooms; the adjoining
versions are good for families.

Rydges Carlton (Map p499; ☎ 03-9347 7811;
www.rydges.com; 701 Swanston St, Carlton; r from $150;
P ✿ ▯ ▣) Polished, no-nonsense and
four-star, Rydges prides itself on good
amenities and justly so. Rooms are semi-
renovated and sleep up to three. The pricier
Parkview versions have views and more
space, and there's a heated rooftop pool and
spa-sauna room.

Vibe Hotel Carlton (Map pp494-5; ☎ 03-9380 9222;
www.vibehotels.com.au; 441 Royal Pde, Carlton North; r from
$150; P ✿ ▣) This early 1960s motel was
once glamour and high-Californian style. It
doesn't quite get there in the 21st century,
but some period charm does shine through.
Rooms have floor-to-ceiling windows and
clean lines and there's a signature '60s central pool. The location is pretty and but a
short tram ride away from Brunswick and
the city.

VICTORIA

FITZROY

Royal Gardens Apartments (Map p502; ☎ 03-9419 9888; www.questroyalgardens.com.au; 8 Royal Lane, Fitzroy; apt from $170) This rather dauntingly monumental complex of apartments is softened by hidden gardens. The comfy and contained apartments are excellent value and the larger versions are split level with bedrooms and bathrooms upstairs. Situated in a quiet nook of this happening suburb, it's so relaxed you'll feel like a local.

EAST MELBOURNE

George Powlett Apartments (Map pp494-5; ☎ 03-9419 9488; www.georgepowlett.com.au; cnr George & Powlett Sts, East Melbourne; apt $95-105; P ⊠) These studio apartments are a tad frumpy and weary, but at these rates who cares. All come with kitchenettes and some have balconies. Access to the CBD is by foot through the glorious Fitzroy Gardens and you're close enough to hear the crowds roar at the MCG. Perfect if you're not planning on spending much time in your room.

Georgian Court (Map pp494-5; ☎ 03-9419 6353; www.georgiancourt.com.au; 21 George St, East Melbourne; s $100, d $120-170; P ⊠ ⌨) Like nanna's china, some things maintain their charm despite a few chips around the edges. This gently crumbling mansion has small rooms and wonderful communal areas, reminiscent of a British period comedy. It's popular with families, rates include breakfast, and the pricier rooms come with en suite.

Knightsbridge Apartments (Map pp494-5; ☎ 03-9419 1333; www.knightsbridgeapartments.com.au; 101 George St, East Melbourne; apt $115-200; P ⊠) This spot provides well-equipped and well-furnished studio apartments, replete with thick carpets, four-poster beds and modern facilities. If you're not quick enough to score a room with a teensy courtyard, try for Room 7, 8 or 9 for the flourish of sunlight.

TOORAK & SOUTH YARRA

our pick **Albany South Yarra** (Map p500; ☎ 03-9866 4485; www.thealbany.com.au; cnr Toorak Rd & Millswyn St, South Yarra; r $100-160; P ⊠ ⌨) A glorious departure from chintz and generic comfort, the Albany has serious rock-chic cred behind its glamorous 1890s mansion facade. Myriad sleeping configurations range from old-world charm to fresh and restyled motel rooms. If the uber-cool two-bedroom penthouse is beyond your means, opt for an airy and minimal Executive room. Staff are trendy and friendly, the facilities and location are excellent and there's a rooftop pool and garden on the way.

Toorak Manor (Map pp494-5; ☎ 03-9827 2689; www.toorakmanor.net; 220 Williams Rd, Toorak; r $155-225; P ⊠) This graceful boutique hotel is set in a historic mansion and decked to the hilt in chintz and chiffon. Rooms are period-style and comfortable, and there are lovely gardens and cosy lounges.

ST KILDA

Fountain Terrace (Map p501; ☎ 03-9593 8123; www.fountainterrace.com.au; 28 Mary St, St Kilda; r incl breakfast from $140) This glorious old Victorian terrace on a residential street has seven boutique rooms lavished in brocades, silks and frills. All have been spectacularly appointed in honour of famous Aussies (top billing goes to the Melba Suite, after diva Dame Nellie) with three rooms accessing the front verandah. Book ahead.

Hotel Tolarno (Map p501; ☎ 03-9537 0200; www.hoteltolarno.com.au; 42 Fitzroy St, St Kilda; r $145-385; ⊠ ⌨) Embodying the Tardis, Hotel Tolarno houses a warren of standard rooms and suites, all dressed in bold colours (think Uluru rust and rich azure) with slick mod cons, gleaming bathrooms and a remarkable collection of art. The Fitzroy St balcony suites are for people-watchers; the executive suites at the back for sleep.

More options:

Novotel St Kilda (Map p501; ☎ 03-9525 5522; www.novotel.com; 14-16 The Esplanade, St Kilda; r from $200; P ⊠ ⌨) Generic and dependable chain hotel in a superb location.

Quest St Kilda Bayside (Map p501; ☎ 03-9593 9500; www.questapartments.com.au; 1 Eildon Rd, St Kilda; apt from $140; P ⊠ ⌨) Dependable, self-contained apartments on a charming, leafy street.

Urban (Map p501; ☎ 03-8530 8888; www.urbanstkilda.com.au; 35-37 Fitzroy St, St Kilda; r from $199; P ⊠ ⌨) A sea of blond wood, cream fabric and white tiles; comfortably corporate without breaking new style ground.

SOUTH MELBOURNE & ALBERT PARK

Sebel Albert Park & Citigate Albert Park (Map pp494-5; ☎ 03-9529 4300, 1800 633 888; www.mirvachotels.com; 65 Queens Rd, Albert Park; Citigate/Sebel r from $145/160; P ⊠ ⌨ ⌨) These two properties occupy one site on Albert Park Lake and both deliver good service, comfort and fabulous

GAY & LESBIAN MELBOURNE

Melbourne's GLBTI (gay-lesbian-bisexual-transgender-intersex) scene is like Melbourne itself – understated, slightly hard to find, but most definitely out! The free street press is a good source of information; look for *Melbourne Star* and *MCV* in various bars, clubs, bookshops and cafes, and log onto **Evolution Online** (http://eevolution.com.au).

The **ALSO Foundation** (www.also.org.au) is a very helpful community-based organisation whose website boasts a great services directory. If it's gay sounds you're after, tune in to **Joy FM** (www.joy.org.au), Melbourne's gay radio station – you'll find it at 94.9FM.

Most of the newer generation of bars and clubs in Melbourne are gay- and lesbian-friendly. St Kilda, South Yarra and Prahran are the city's main 'gay precincts', with Prahran's Commercial Rd being the traditional centre of Melbourne's gay culture. Melbourne certainly doesn't rival Sydney when it comes to gay nightlife, but it's much more relaxed than its northern sister. Other gay-friendly neighbourhoods include Collingwood and Abbotsford, with Northcote being a popular spot for lesbians.

DT's Hotel (Map pp494–5; ☎ 03-9428 5724; 164 Church St, Richmond) This small and intimate gay pub hosts some of Melbourne's best drag shows, retro nights and happy hours.

Peel Hotel (Map p502; ☎ 03-9419 4762; cnr Peel & Wellington Sts, Collingwood; admission free) The Peel is one of the best-known and most popular gay venues in Melbourne, but it also attracts a lesbian crowd. It's the last stop of a big night.

Opium Den (Map pp494–5; ☎ 03-9417 2696; www.opiumden.com.au; 176 Hoddle St, Abbotsford) Home of Melbourne's gay and lesbian Asian community, Opium Den features drag shows and live entertainment.

Glasshouse Hotel (off Map p502; ☎ 03-9419 4748; www.glass-house.com.au; 51-55 Gipps St, Collingwood) Caters for a mostly lesbian crowd with entertainment including live bands, drag kings and DJs.

Laird Hotel (Map pp494–5; ☎ 03-9417 2832; 149 Gipps St, Abbotsford; admission free) Men only. Lots of leather, moustaches, beer and brawn. Who's yer daddy?

Xchange Hotel (Map p500; ☎ 03-9867 5144; 119 Commercial Rd, Prahran; admission free-$10) A long-standing fixture on the Prahran scene, the Xchange plays host to a variety of customers and covers all the gay bases. A good, fail-safe meeting spot.

Market Hotel (Map p500; ☎ 03-9826 0933; 143 Commercial Rd, South Yarra; admission $10-20) A perennially popular nightclub with good house music keeping things going till the sun comes up, and then some.

views. Recent renovations at the Citigate elevate its neat rooms to four-star standard; the Sebel's 4½-star rooms are bigger and more vibrant.

Top End

Melbourne's top-end accommodation is varied and plentiful. There are dozens of five-star chain hotels that will find you before you find them. Generally, you'll find a range of packages and deals on offer via the internet. Parking is often of the valet variety and generally incurs a charge of between $15 and $25 per day.

CITY CENTRE

Windsor Hotel (Map pp496–7; ☎ 03-9633 6000; www.thewindsor.com.au; 103 Spring St, Melbourne; r $200-550; P ⊠ 🖳) The queen of the scene is the stately Windsor, Melbourne's 'Grand Lady', graced by old-fashioned, haute-luxe embellishments. Built in 1883 she has hosted the who's who of royalty – from Buckingham Palace to the West End to heavy metal. Her five-star rooms are simply fabulous, and no request is too great.

Hotel Lindrum (Map pp496–7; ☎ 03-9668 1111; www.hotellindrum.com.au; 26 Flinders St, Melbourne; r $425-515; P ⊠ 🖳) This opulent establishment is bathed in rich tones, suede furnishings and deliciously low lighting. Once the pool hall of legendary player Walter Lindrum, it now boasts a range of indulgent rooms, some of which have wheelchair access. Exclusive to the hilt, it's devoid of attitude or pretension.

Adelphi (Map pp496–7; ☎ 03-8080 8888; www.adelphi.com.au; 187 Flinders Lane, Melbourne; r $560-1250; P ⊠ 🖳 🛋) The landmark Adelphi is a study in minimalism and the open-plan rooms contain furnishings and fittings by internationally acclaimed architects. The effect is cutting-edge, verging on clinical. On the top floor a cantilevered lap pool allows you to swim right past the edge of the building and suspend yourself over Collins St.

SOUTH YARRA

The Hatton Hotel (Map p500; ☎ 03-9869 4800; 65 Park Street, South Yarra, r $215-350; P 🐱) This gracious, labyrinthine hotel is littered with Buddhas, intricate artworks and antiques from all corners of the globe in tasteful quantities. The effect is subtle and other-worldly. The rooms have real attention to detail, too – the Eastern Balcony Suite, featuring Asian stylings, is a highlight. Superior rooms are bathed in golden sunlight, and the simpler standard rooms are tranquil and practical.

The Lyall (Map p500; ☎ 03-9868 8222; www.thelyall.com; 14 Murphy St, South Yarra; r from $525; P 🐱 ⌨) This slick and elegant boutique property sits in a quiet, leafy street in one of Melbourne's priciest pockets. The earthy colour scheme is offset by dramatic art and the commodious rooms are appointed with fine mod cons and five-star luxuries. Discounts by as much as 50% are available on last-minute accommodation booking sites, so shop around.

ST KILDA

The Prince (Map p501; ☎ 03-9536 1111; www.theprince.com.au; 2 Acland St, St KIlda; r $270-850; P 🐱 ⌨) This fashionable study in minimalist luxury is the boutique hotel of choice for Melbourne's most chic visitors. Pared-back rooms with marble-clad bathrooms and ebony-coloured furnishings line chocolate-coloured hallways and the eating and entertainment options on site mean you need never leave its environs.

Camping

Ashley Gardens Big4 Holiday Village (off Map pp494-5; ☎ 03-9318 6866; www.aspenparks.com.au; 129 Ashley St, Braybrook; powered sites/cabins from $40/60; P 🐱 ⌨ 🐱 🐱) Only 9km from the city centre, this is a well-run, spacious park with excellent facilities. The priciest digs are state-of-the-art cabins. You can get here from the city centre via bus 220, which departs from Flinders St Station.

EATING

In this country of fabulous dining, Melbourne is unsurpassed – not only for the diversity of cuisines, restaurants, cafes, delicatessens, markets, bistros, brasseries and takeaways, but the sheer value for your buck. For $10 to $20 you can fuel up on bum-burning curry, a pub roast, gourmet pizza, fragrant Vietnamese, hearty Burmese, tangy Middle Eastern, Spanish tapas, spicy African…flavours from every corner of the globe. The variety comes in authentic packages or moulded and fused into the city's very own version of Mod Oz. Fine contemporary dining is also abundant for gastronomes with hard-to-please palates and carefree wallets.

City Centre & Docklands

Melbourne's Chinatown runs along Little Bourke St from Exhibition St to Swanston St. Chinese restaurants predominate, but you can also find Greek, Indian, Japanese and Mod Oz cuisines.

Flinders Lane, Centre Pl, Degraves St, Hardware Lane and their adjoining alleyways are packed with cafes, hole-in-the-wall favourites, restaurants and wonderful little bars. Federation Square and the Docklands also have a host of glam eateries.

MoVida (Map pp496-7; ☎ 03-9663 3038; 1 Hosier Lane, Melbourne; tapas $4-8, raciones $10-18; 🕑 lunch & dinner) Pull together a small group, book a table and share a round of the innovative tapas this subtly slick restaurant is known for; artichokes with almond sauce and manchego cheese, and Galician-cooked octopus *(pulpo)* with kipfler potatoes and paprika. MoVida is a consistent award-winner and reservations are a must. Fortunately MoVida Next Door (open for dinner Tuesday to Saturday) caters to the unorganised, with similarly divine fare and a no-bookings rule.

Portello Rosso (Map pp496-7; ☎ 03-9602 2273; 15 Warburton Lane, Melbourne; tapas $6-15, mains $14-25; 🕑 breakfast & lunch Tue-Fri, dinner Tue-Sat) A newer addition to Melbourne's tapas fascination, this smart, split-level restaurant humbly advertises itself as a pizzeria and jamon bar, but dishes including melt-in-the-mouth the zucchini flowers and artichoke stuffed with goats cheese promise so much more. The chef's five-dish surprise selection is fail-proof.

Camy Shanghai Dumpling Restaurant (Map pp496-7; ☎ 03-9663 8555; 23-25 Tattersalls Lane, Melbourne; mains $6.50-10; 🕑 lunch & dinner) If you like your dumplings hot and plentiful, your service simple, your surrounds no-nonsense and your bill bottom dollar, the Shanghai is your Shangri-

VICTORIA

La. Fifteen dumplings for six bucks is hard to beat – it's as Chinatown as it gets.

Mr Tulk Cafe (Map pp496-7; ☎ 03-8660 5700; State Library of Victoria, cnr La Trobe St & Swanston St, Melbourne; mains $10-20; ☟ breakfast & lunch Mon-Sat) Within the State Library, Mr Tulk is a warm and welcoming cafe serving good coffee and breakfasts, wine, meals and treats. It's open till 7pm on Friday for bookworms doing overtime.

Jasper Kitchen (Map pp496-7; ☎ 03-8327 2777; 489 Elizabeth St, Melbourne; lunch mains $10-15, dinner mains $25-30; ☟ breakfast daily, lunch Mon-Sat, dinner Tue-Sat) A sidestep from the Queen Victoria Market in the CBD's north, Jasper plants relaxed diners at white tables or a long communal bench and dishes up commendable mains such as salmon and chive crumbed fish burgers or chermoula marinated lamb loin. Service is exceptional.

Pellegrini's Espresso Bar (Map pp496-7; ☎ 03-9662 1885; 66 Bourke St, Melbourne; mains $12-16) This family-run 1950s-style espresso bar hasn't changed in years. A gleaming coffee machine (allegedly the first in Melbourne) churns out the good stuff and mama brews good honest pasta and sauces from scratch out the back.

Lounge (Map pp496-7; ☎ 03-9663 2916; 243 Swanston St, Melbourne; mains $12-25; ☟ lunch & dinner) Upstairs is a student stamping ground where the next generation perfect their pool and social skills. No-fuss bar service and a scrummy pub-style menu keeps them seated. Monday nights you 'pay the time', so if you order at 6.30pm your dinner will cost $6.30. Downstairs the menu is more refined and atmosphere more subdued.

Spicy Fish Restaurant (Map pp496-7; ☎ 03-9639 1885; 209 Little Bourke St, Melbourne; mains $15-25; ☟ lunch & dinner) In true Chinatown tradition the ambience at this busy Szechuan and Shanghai restaurant simmers somewhere between snappy and hectic. But the food has them lining up at the door, and justifiably so. Tables are peppered with large and steaming portions of dumplings, hot, dry and spicy chicken and squid dishes, and stir-fried vegetables. Great value and authentic flavours.

Maha (Map pp496-7; ☎ 03-9629 5900; 21 Bond St, Melbourne, mains $28-38; ☟ lunch Mon-Fri, dinner Mon-Sat) This sophisticated bar and grill occupies a subterranean pocket on unassuming Bond St and fuses tangy Middle Eastern flavours with Mediterranean overtones and local produce. The result is delicious. Make a booking for lunch or dinner and dine on 12-hour lamb

rump, onion, chick pea, mint and fazoulia *salatet* (salad) or park yourself at the bar for inexpensive meze – the slow-cooked tuna with capers and olives is spectacular.

Gingerboy (Map pp496-7; ☎ 03-9662 4200; 27-29 Crossley St, Melbourne; mains $30-35; ☟ lunch Mon-Fri, dinner Mon-Sat) Seriously trendy and touched by the disco god, Gingerboy indulges demanding city punters with aromatic cocktails and superb and contemporary Asian hawker dishes. Mains include peppered swordfish tataki or sweet and sour pork belly.

The city is treated to some great Japanese eateries, from hole-in-the-wall sushi joints to student hangouts with heartier fare. Among the best are **Kuni's** (Map pp496-7; ☎ 03-9663 7243; 56 Little Bourke St, Melbourne; mains $13-27; ☟ lunch Mon-Fri, dinner Mon-Sat) for delicate noodle dishes, and **Don Don** (Map pp496-7; ☎ 03-9670 3377; 321 Swanston St, Melbourne; mains $6-8; ☟ lunch Mon-Fri) for great *bentō* (boxed lunches).

More good central eats:

Becco (Map pp496-7; ☎ 03-9663 3000; 11-25 Crossley St, Melbourne; mains $25-30; ☟ lunch & dinner Mon-Sat) Sexy little Italian bar-restaurant package.

Il Solito Posto (Map pp496-7; ☎ 03-9654 4466; 113 Collins St, Melbourne; mains $24-35) A basement favourite serving sensational Italian staples.

Southbank

Southgate's river and city skyline views make it a prime eating destination for visitors to Melbourne. It's also close to galleries, theatres and gardens.

Blue Train Cafe (Map pp496-7; ☎ 03-9696 0440; Mid Level, Southgate; mains $9-18) Semi-alfresco with great river and city views, this loud, gay-friendly and hugely popular place dishes up earnest salads, curries, stir-fries, wood-fired pizzas and seafood at good prices. It's ideal for families and groups.

Bearbrass (Map pp496-7; ☎ 03-9682 3799; Ground fl, Southgate; mains $15) This casual riverside snug has the full complement for beautifully boozy afternoons: long bench seating for groups, outdoor tables with river and promenade views, global bar bites and inventive mains, laid-back staff and a delicious selection of local and imported beers.

Walter's Wine Bar (Map pp496-7; ☎ 03-9690 9211; Upper Level, Southgate; mains $25-35) Wine is Walter's passion and there's over 20 pages of it on the menu. You can complement that glass of Grange Hermitage with moreish Italian fare and a delicious bar menu.

VICTORIA

North Melbourne

Auction Rooms (Map pp494-5; ☎ 03-9326 7749; 103-107 Errol St, North Melbourne; mains $9-12; ✹ breakfast & lunch Tue-Sat) A little bit Soho and a whole lotta Melbourne defines this beautifully converted industrial space, where the poached eggs come with ricotta and dukkah and the toasted cheese sarni comprises taleggio with a side of sweet potato chips. The coffee is so good that fanatics won't care what's on the menu.

Courthouse Hotel (Map pp494-5; ☎ 03-9329 5394; 86 Errol St, North Melbourne; mains $22-27; ✹ lunch & dinner Mon-Sat) Fans of nouveau gastropub fare will be in heaven here – the international menu features succulent food and fine wine, and service is helpful.

Carlton

Tagged 'Little Italy' many moons ago, Lygon St now infuses a host of multicultural flavours alongside the pasta bars and Italian restaurants. You won't have difficulty getting a meal or a table here and a stroll usually involves ample invites from restaurateurs plying for business.

Tiamo (Map p499; ☎ 03-9347 5759; 303 Lygon St, Carlton; mains $11-16) This historic Lygon St institution dishes up generous portions of tasty pasta and traditional Italian cuisine. The older Italian gentlemen fastened to their espressos at the front window aren't part of the decor but they certainly add to it.

Abla's (Map p499; ☎ 03-9347 0006; 109 Elgin St, Carlton; mains $25; ✹ lunch Thu & Fri, dinner Mon-Sat) Melbourne's best-loved Lebanese restaurant is often booked solid, and the culinary genius of chef and proprietor Abla Amad's is so good it's inspired an entire cookbook. On Friday and Saturday nights there's a compulsory 13-course banquet; BYO vino and don the elasticised pants.

Jimmy Watson's (Map p499; ☎ 03-9347 3985; 333 Lygon St, Carlton; mains $25-30; ✹ lunch Mon-Sat, dinner Tue-Sat) Wine and talk are the order of the day at this long-running wine bar-restaurant. The fare is European, Middle Eastern and a dash of Mod Oz, with a nod to ingredients such as kangaroo.

Fitzroy & North Fitzroy

Brunswick St is a key box to tick on your 'eating tour of Melbourne' checklist. The prevailing mood is alternative, fashionable, multicultural and arty all at the same time, and all palates are catered for.

Bebida (Map p502; ☎ 03-9419 5260; 325 Smith St, Fitzroy; dishes $7-12; ✹ breakfast & lunch Wed-Mon, dinner Wed-Sun) This cosy bar opens its wide bay windows to let happy chatter, live music and the scent of freshly baked chorizo spill out onto the street. The food is first-rate and inexpensive, the beer selection is good and a still-warm Bebida brownie mid-morning is the stuff of chocoholic dreams.

Babka Bakery Café (Map p502; ☎ 03-9416 0091; 358 Brunswick St, Fitzroy; dishes $7-15; ✹ breakfast & lunch Tue-Sun) Famous for its breads, pastries and eternally wholesome-looking waitresses, Babka is also famous for its sensational breakfasts, massive sandwiches, blinis and borscht.

Gluttony It's a Sin (Map p502; ☎ 03-9416 0336; 278 Smith St, Collingwood; mains $10-16) It's all about the breakfasts and cakes, and boy does Gluttony live up to its name. Corn, sourdough and cheese breads spiff up seared mushrooms and eggs, but the main event is the sweet stuff; if there's a Mod Oz cake it comes in all varieties here.

our pick St Jude's Cellars (Map p502; ☎ 03-9419 7411; 389-391 Brunswick St, Fitzroy; mains $14-26; ✹ breakfast Sat & Sun, lunch & dinner Tue-Sun) An interior of industrial gloss sets the scene for fine fare and wine at stylish St Jude's. The menu allows for tapas grazing (braised artichokes, olives and parsley salad) or sturdier mains such as pork cutlet, confit of belly and sherry peppers. The service is spectacularly helpful and gracious, and a perch at the long, alabaster-tiled bar is authentically Spanish.

Cavallero (Map p502; ☎ 03-9417 1377; 300 Smith St, Fitzroy; mains $15-30; ✹ breakfast & lunch Tue-Sun, dinner Tue-Sat) The alabaster white interior of this smart Smith St option is beautifully interrupted by elegant flower arrangements and deep booth seating. The food and service are similarly appealing – with a heavy Middle Eastern bent such as ewe's fetta and eggplant with dukkah and baked eggs with flat bread.

Moroccan Soup Bar (Map pp494-5; ☎ 03-9482 4240; 183 St Georges Rd, North Fitzroy; banquet $16; ✹ dinner Tue-Sun) This squishy, brightly coloured soup bar is a vegetarian's haven. There's no menu, just the renowned owner who rattles off a list of soups, starters and heavenly North African tagine.

Panama Dining Room (Map p502; ☎ 03-9417 7663; 3rd fl, 231 Smith St, Fitzroy; mains $18-30; ✹ dinner Wed-Sun) The Euro-Fitzroy cuisine on offer in this cool, calm and collected dining room is impressive and inventive. The super-fresh and fine ingredients will knock your date's socks off and the wine list, ersatz Manhattan views and charming ambience will do the rest.

Also recommended:

La Sangria (Map p502; ☎ 03-9419 8503; 46 Johnston St, Fitzroy; tapas $6-10; ❤ dinner) Genuine Spanish tapas bar – chorizo and sangria without any fuss.

Retro (Map p502; ☎ 03-9419 9103; 413 Brunswick St, Fitzroy; mains $12-18) Relaxed, diner-style cafe with window and outdoor seating, and tasty, inexpensive nosh.

Vegie Bar (Map p502; ☎ 03-9417 6935; 380 Brunswick St, Fitzroy; mains $10-15; ❤ breakfast Sat & Sun, lunch & dinner daily) Delectable vegetarian creations and Aussie beer by the stubby.

Richmond

Victoria St is Melbourne's 'Little Saigon' and the turf between Hoddle and Church Sts is packed with Asian grocers, discount shops, fishmongers and myriad places to clack your chopsticks. Bridge Rd and Swan St offer an abundance of cafes and restaurants with plenty of global flavours.

Minh Minh (Map pp494-5; ☎ 03-9427 7891; 94 Victoria St, Richmond; mains $12-17; ❤ lunch & dinner) Minh Minh's service varies from warm and cheeky to outright rude. If it's the latter, dish it right back and concentrate on the spicy and fragrant food. The menu here is long and authentic and includes the best *laab nuea* (Lao beef salad) in Melbourne.

Richmond Hill Café & Larder (Map pp494-5; ☎ 03-9421 2808; 48 Bridge Rd, Richmond; mains $13-27; ❤ breakfast & lunch daily, dinner first Friday of the month) Carefully prepared bistro fare is served at this popular bar-restaurant and *fromagerie* (cheese shop). It's an open, unfussy space and the food is stylish Mediterranean.

South Yarra, Toorak, Prahran & Windsor

Commercial Rd features the Prahran Market and plenty of gay-friendly eateries – its sister strip is the high-profile, style-policed Greville St. South Yarra's and Toorak's affluent eateries are dotted along Toorak Rd and Chapel St. The grungier Windsor end of Chapel St is home to cafes as comfy as your cardigan.

Prahran Market (Map p500; www.prahranmarket.com.au; 163-185 Commercial Rd, Prahran; ❤ dawn-5pm Tue & Sat, dawn-6pm Thu & Fri, 10am-4pm Sun) A top-quality produce market, with several organic-produce stores (including an organic butcher), a fresh pasta shop, bountiful delis and a food court for grazing on the move.

Globe (Map p500; ☎ 03-9510 8693; 218 Chapel St, Prahran; mains $8-17; ☎ 7am-late) Get in early to secure a breakfast seat and pack an appetite for Spanish chorizo, tomato and egg bake, a Vietnamese omelette or pesto-drenched poached eggs. The burgers are stacked and by night it turns into a sultry little drinking den.

Palate (Map p500; ☎ 03-9521 5540; 132 Greville St, Prahran; mains $8-20; ❤ breakfast & lunch) Bring the Prada sunnies, the papers and an appetite if you're heading here for breakfast. For lunch bring a friend and natter over delicious risottos and pastas, and more inventive fare including chicken *bisteeya* – Middle Eastern–spiced minced chicken and almonds in puff pastry served with spicy eggplant pickle and yoghurt.

Borsch, Vodka & Tears (Map p500; ☎ 03-9530 2694; 173 Chapel St, Prahran; mains $15-25; ❤ breakfast & lunch Thu-Sun, dinner daily) A fabulous Polish place serving around 100 strains of vodka and modern Polish food. The ambience is shabby-chic with low-lighting and lots of sincere conversation.

Orange (Map p500; ☎ 03-9529 1644; 126 Chapel St, Windsor; mains $20-30; ❤ breakfast & lunch daily, dinner Wed-Sun) Orange's Bloody Mary breakfasts are a fine way to start the day (or continue the night before) and the more subtle lunch and dinner fare is inventive and delicious. By the time you've finished dinner and that bottle of plonk, the whole place gives way to its alter-ego as a bar.

St Kilda

Fitzroy and Acland Sts are where you'll find the majority of cafes and restaurants. There are some mainstays by the sea, too.

Lentil as Anything (Map p501; ☎ 03-9534 5833; 41 Blessington St, St Kilda; prices at customer's discretion; ❤ lunch & dinner) What's the clincher? Is it the organic and vegetarian ingredients? Or the Moroccan, Japanese, Indian, Vietnamese or Sri Lankan flavours? That it's a nonprofit enterprise? Or perhaps it's the fact that you decide how much your meal is worth, and that it's worth a mint.

Mahjong (Map p501; ☎ 03-9534 8833; 165 Fitzroy St, St Kilda; meals $6.50-10; ❤ lunch & dinner) If budget is an issue then plant yourself in the front of this snappy dumpling house and tuck into the well-priced bamboo baskets containing bite-size treats. Think yum-cha meets à la carte, such as *san choi bao*, shredded beef in mandarin sauce or dumplings done just about

VICTORIA

any way you like. The 'back' menu (mains $28 to $38) is superior with dishes such as lobster tail baked with spicy salt and chilli.

Claypots (Map p501; ☎ 03-9534 1282; 213 Barkly St, St Kilda; mains $10-25; ☯ lunch & dinner) This excellent restaurant can't be bothered with decor; all the effort goes into unbearably good spicy seafood claypots with African and Asian flavours. Get busy with your hands – those prawns won't shell themselves – and arrive early to beat the crowds.

Lau's Family Kitchen (Map p501; ☎ 03-8598 9880; 4 Acland St, St Kilda; mains $16-32; ☯ lunch Sun-Fri, dinner daily) Tucked into a leafy location, Lau's serves a mainly Cantonese menu. Dishes are beautifully done if not particularly exciting, with a few surprises thrown in for more adventurous diners. Super-attentive staff and the moody dark interior make for a great night out.

Cicciolina (Map p501; ☎ 03-9525 3333; 130 Acland St, St Kilda; mains $20-36; ☯ lunch & dinner) This dark and intimate, bustling institution doesn't take reservations, and it's always packed. The mod-Med menu offers prosciutto-wrapped baked figs with blue-vein cheese and earthier pastas. A snug bolt-hole of a bar out the back sorts out the queue.

Café di Stasio (Map p501; ☎ 03-9525 3999; 31 Fitzroy St, St Kilda; mains $32-38; ☯ lunch & dinner) Café di Stasio thoroughly deserves its reputation as the best Italian restaurant in Melbourne. The sublime cuisine pushes good meat dishes and the two-course lunch (including a glass of wine) is excellent value.

Also recommended:

Big Mouth (Map p501; ☎ 03-9534 4611; cnr Acland & Barkly Sts, St Kilda; mains $18) Hearty breakfasts, reliable mains and a spacious upstairs lounge-bar in an art deco package.

Soul Mama (Map p501; ☎ 03-9525 3338; Shop 10, St Kilda Sea Baths, 10 Jacka Blvd, St Kilda; meals $9-18; ☯ lunch & dinner) All-vegetarian, guilt-free, soul-warming food with unrivalled sea views.

South Melbourne

St Ali (Map pp494-5; ☎ 03-9689 2990; 12-18 Yarra Pl, South Melbourne; mains $10-15; ☯ breakfast & lunch) Locals teem into this converted warehouse cafe and educate their tastebuds with delicious Middle Eastern flavours courtesy of Lebanese pizzas, rare beef yoghurt and walnut salads, and eggs with haloumi, tomatoes, fresh mint and dukkah. They're serious about their coffee here and it's seriously good.

Self-Catering

Supermarkets, often open 24 hours or until midnight, are found in most suburbs – Coles, Safeway and IGA are the names to look out for.

Victoria St in Richmond is the place to go for cheap produce and Asian ingredients, and major markets, bursting with fresh produce and gourmet deli items, include Queen Victoria Market (p506) and Prahran Market (p525).

DRINKING

Melbourne has a famously lively drinking scene. You'll find bars hidden down tiny alleys, at the top of darkened staircases and perched atop most luxury hotels.

City Centre

Cookie (Map pp496-7; ☎ 03-9663 7660; 1st fl, 252 Swanston St, Melbourne; ☯ 11am-late) Stylish and cheeky, this bar tiles its high walls with kitschy books and vinyl, and pours fine European, Asian and Oz beers. The wine list is commendable, the Thai-inspired tapas is classy, and jeans and a T-shirt are just as welcome as designer duds.

The Toff in Town (Map pp496-7; ☎ 03-9639 8770; 2nd fl, 252 Swanston St, Melbourne; ☯ 5pm-late Sat-Thu, 3pm-late Fri) Upstairs from Cookie, this atmospheric venue is well suited to the cabaret shows it hosts, but it also works for intimate gigs by rock gods, avant-folksters or dancehall queens. The private dining carriages are intimate fun but you'll need to book in advance.

Siglo (Map pp496-7; ☎ 03-9654 6300; Level 2, 161 Spring St, Melbourne; ☯ 5pm-3am) Bless the flourish of rooftop bars in Melbourne's CBD – they bring fabulous sunsets and sky-high al-fresco cocktails to the city's drinking scene. Suits fill Siglo on a Friday night, which may lure or horrify you. Regardless, pick a time to mull over a Semillion, snack on upper-crust morsels and admire the vistas over the gracious parliament building.

Phoenix (Map pp496-7; ☎ 03-9650 4976; 82 Flinders St, Melbourne; ☯ 4pm-late Tue & Wed, noon-late Thu & Fri, 5pm-late Sat) Three levels of jungle-printed, suede-couched, polished-timbered and plush-carpeted style ensure plenty of atmosphere at this CBD fave. It's unpretentious, and everyone from high-powered suits to empty-pocketed students is able to fit right in.

VICTORIAN MICROBREWS

Victoria is blessed with a healthy scattering of boutique breweries and far healthier number of connoisseurs of the golden nectar. If you don't have the opportunity to visit the 30-plus breweries to create your short list, start with the following for a local sampler.

Bridge Road Brewers Robust Porter (see p608) A smoky molasses stew with hints of banana and cloves, and a taste vaguely like cough mixture.

Red Hill Golden Ale A dry ale, strong on hops with a restrained fruity crispness and full body.

Grand Ridge Brewery Gippsland Gold (see Grand Ridge Road, p617) A classic bitter ale with a complex nutty and burnt-honey hue.

Holgate Mt Macedon Ale (see p543) An excellent pale ale with a champagnelike fizz and light citrus finish – more sorbet than pudding.

Mountain Goat India Pale Ale Australia's first 100% certified organic beer, which may or may not enhance the full-bodied flavour, but will make you feel better about drinking it.

3 Ravens White A Belgian-style Witbier self-described as having coriander spicing.

Bellarine Brewing Co Queenscliffe Ale A delectable and refreshing pale ale with citrus and fruity flavours.

Otway Estate Prickly Moses Red Ale Gets extra thumbs up for outstanding nomenclature, but you'd drink this slightly sweet Irish-style ale even if its name was Bob.

The Beer Lovers' Guide to Victoria's Microbreweries booklet has good information and is available from Information Victoria by phoning ☎ 1300 366 356.

Order of Melbourne (Map pp496-7; ☎ 03-9663 6707; Level 2, 401 Swanston St, Melbourne; ☺ noon-11pm Mon-Wed, to 1am Thu, to 3am Fri & Sat, 3-11pm Sun) Hidden cagily above the 'Druids Club', this cavernous bar suspends industrial art from the ceiling and slips a happy, mixed crowd into cushioned corner booths. High-arched windows climb to the lofty ceiling and the bar mixes fine cocktails. A teeny bar-garden up top is open till 10pm.

Misty Place (Map pp496-7; ☎ 03-9663 9202; 3-5 Hosier Lane, Melbourne; ☺ 5pm-1am Tue-Thu, to 3am Fri, 6pm-3am Sat) Dimly lit and brightly staffed, Misty is something between a local and a sultry city bar. Equally perfect for catching up with a friend and drinking with a group, the two-roomed interior has a seating arrangement and cocktail for everyone.

Prudence (Map pp494-5; ☎ 03-9329 9267; 368 Victoria St, West Melbourne; ☺ 3pm-1am) More local watering hole than inner-city chic, gorgeous Prudence lays out a snug and delicious spread of tables, bar stools, upstairs drinking rooms and a downstairs courtyard. Groups ham it up by the open fireplace and bohemian locals concentrate on chess by the window.

Transport (Map pp496-7; ☎ 03-9658 8808; Federation Sq, Melbourne; ☺ 11am-late) This ultramodern, glass-walled pub occupies an enviable position for people-and river-watching. It's big, brassy and busy. On Friday nights it's shoulder to backbone with yuppies on the prowl.

One floor up is fine-dining at Taxi and the 3rd floor is devoted to the decadent Transit Lounge, with gorgeous leather couches, intimate corners and a spectacular wine and spirits menu.

More city drinking:

Double Happiness (Map pp496-7; ☎ 03-9650 4488; 21 Liverpool St, Melbourne; ☺ 5pm-1am Mon-Wed, 5pm-3am Thu, 4.30pm-3am Fri, 6pm-3am Sat, 6pm-1am Sun)…lies in a cocktail at this tiny, socialist-inspired space.

Tony Starr's Kitten Club (Map pp496-7; 9650 2448; Level 1, 267 Little Collins St, Melbourne; ☺ 4pm-1am Mon-Thu, to 3am Fri & Sat, 4pm-12am Sun) An unpretentious crowd, hedonistic cocktails and a cute bar with a saucy past.

Fitzroy

Fitzroy is hands-down the best pub suburb in Melbourne, but there are ample bars as well. In and around Brunswick and Smith Sts is the most obvious hunting ground.

Union Club Hotel (Map p502; ☎ 03-9417 2926; 164 Gore St, Fitzroy; ☺ 3pm-late Mon-Thu, noon-1am Fri-Sat, noon-11pm Sun) A die-hard local swimming in earthy good vibes, and happy chatter from the relaxed indie crowd. The large curved bar is one of Melbourne's best spots to park it, the food is good honest pub nosh and the beer garden is lazy Sunday begging on a hot day.

The Standard (Map p502; ☎ 03-9419 4793; 293 Fitzroy St, Fitzroy; ☺ 3-11pm Mon & Tue, noon-11pm Wed-Sat, noon-9pm Sun) Boasting one of the best beer gardens in Melbourne, the Standard is anything but its moniker. Down-to-earth bar staff and a truly eclectic crowd enhance an atmosphere defined by live music, footy on the small screen, and loud and enthusiastic chatter.

Napier Hotel (Map p502; ☎ 03-9419 4240; 210 Napier St, Fitzroy; ☟ 3-11pm Mon-Thu, 1pm-1am Fri & Sat, 1-11pm Sun) A short stroll from Brunswick St, the Napier is the archetypal 'local'. It's dark and laid-back, there's a small beer garden, the pub-grub portions are massive, and sharks wage battle around the pool tables.

Polly (Map p502; ☎ 03-9417 0880; 401 Brunswick St, Fitzroy; ☟ 5pm-1am Sun-Wed, 5pm-late Thu, 5pm-3am Fri-Sat) Polly melds a luxe sensibility and slick service with lots of ornate carved wood and plush velvet. Ease yourself into a lounge and peruse the extensive drinks list – you're not going anywhere in a hurry.

Little Creatures Dining Hall (Map p502; ☎ 03-9417 5500; 222 Brunswick St, Fitzroy; ☟ 10am-late) Fremantle's finest microbrewery has converted a huge warehouse on Brunswick Street into a relaxed, happy beer hall with long wooden tables, booth seating and warm and efficient service. Little Creatures' five brews are aptly accompanied by chermoula spiced lamb cutlets, gourmet burgers and pizzas (mains $17) and there's a small wine list for nonhop fans. It's a good spot for groups and families.

Windsor

Windsor is the southern end of Chapel St and the patch of turf to head in this part of town if you're looking for a drink without the club beats and south-of-the-river glitz.

Back Bar (Map p500; ☎ 03-9529 7899; 67 Green St, Windsor; ☟ 5pm-1am Tue-Sun) A refreshing retreat from the Chapel St glam, Back Bar is a cosy evening parlour with lavish decor. The music, lighting and attitude are mellifluous and warm.

Lucky Coq (Map p500; ☎ 03-9525 1288; 197 Chapel St, Windsor; ☟ noon-3am) Injecting just the right amount of indie-retro into this sceney pocket of Melbourne, this pub is welcome relief for those looking to enjoy a drink, a pizza and a yak with mates without having to think too carefully about their outfit.

Windsor Castle (Map p500; ☎ 03-9525 0239; 89 Albert St, Windsor; ☟ 11am-midnight Sun-Thu, to 2am Fri & Sat) Cosy nooks, sunken pits, fireplaces and flocked wallpaper make the Windsor Castle extremely attractive – if on a winter's night this way you stumble. The Castle

gets chaotic on sunny Sundays when the grass umbrellas, board shorts and bleached hair come out in force. You'll either love it or loathe it.

St Kilda

On a warm summer evening St Kilda is packed with crowded revellers – many of them English and Irish backpackers (and plenty of locals too).

Vineyard (Map p501; ☎ 03-9525 4527; 71a Acland St, St Kilda; ☟ 10am-3am) It hugs the best spot on Acland St and absolutely teems with locals, backpackers and trendy things from outside St Kilda's confines. Settle in early if you want a seat in the courtyard or even the lounge. Sunday afternoons pump.

George Public Bar (Map p501; ☎ 03-9534 8822; 127 Fitzroy St, St Kilda; ☟ 4pm-1am Mon-Wed, noon-2am Thu, noon-3am Fri & Sat, noon-1am Sun) The narrow basement bar of the George (the 'snake pit') is an unpretentious, grungy bar swarming with backpackers and the odd local. There's a pool table and bowls of fat hot chips.

Doulton Bar (Map p501; ☎ 03-9534 2200; Village Belle Hotel, 202 Barkly St, St Kilda; ☟ 9am-1am Mon-Wed, to 3am Thu & Fri, to midnight Sun) Part suburban-style bistro, part dimly lit lounge bar, the Doulton Bar caters to those craving chicken parmas, icy pints and an eyeful of St Kilda's comings and goings. Nab a spot at the curved front window with full-length Acland St views for maximum effect.

Mink (Map p501; ☎ 03-9536 1199; 2 Acland St, St Kilda; ☟ 6pm-late Thu, 6pm-3am Fri-Sun) Tucked beneath the Prince of Wales, Mink is a plush lounge-cum-bunker with plenty of dark bordello-esque corners for an intimate rendezvous (and lots of vodka).

Barkly Hotel (Map p501; ☎ 03-9525 3354; www .hotelbarkly.com; 109 Barkly St, St Kilda; ☟ 9am-3am Mon-Fri, 10am-3am Sat, 10am-1am Sun) The street-level public bar is the utopia of backpackers looking to sink a few pints, scream to the tunes on the jukebox and snog a stranger before last drinks are called. The rooftop bar feigns a bit of class, but things get messy up there, too. Nevertheless, it's worth braving for the abso-bloody-lutely spectacular sunset views.

The Esplanade Hotel (p531), **Prince of Wales** (Map p501; ☎ 03-9536 1177; 2 Acland St, St Kilda; ☟ noon-2am Mon-Thu, noon-3am Fri-Sat) and Greyhound Hotel (p531) are also St Kilda drinking institutions.

SOUTH MELBOURNE

Railway Hotel (Map pp494-5:; ☎ 03-9690 5092; 280 Ferrars St, South Melbourne; ⏰ 4pm-1am Mon-Thu, noon-1am Fri-Sat, 1-11pm Sun) Perch at the timber front bar of South Melbourne's earthiest pub for a pint of James Squire or meddle out the back in the back bar, dining room or courtyard. Retro video games complement the pool table, but socialising is the main form of entertainment here.

Maori Chief (Map pp494-5:; ☎ 03-9696 5363; 117 Moray St, South Melbourne; ⏰ 11am-11pm Mon-Thu, to 1am Fri & Sat) Eclectic and quirky are rare finds in this refined suburb, but the Maori Chief puts pure kitsch South Pacific beauties in frames on the walls, retro formica in the dining room and Monteiths ale on tap. It's one honest local with honest nosh at genuine pub prices.

George Hotel South Melbourne (Map pp494-5; ☎ 03-9686 5655; 139 Cecil St, South Melbourne; ⏰ 11.30am-1am Mon-Fri, 9.30am-1am Sat, 9.30am-11.30pm Sun) Directly opposite the South Melbourne Markets, this recent addition to South Melbourne's pub scene is ideal for sunny pub lunches with a side of people-watching. At night the mixed crowd spans families, young bloods and groups of friends catching up.

ENTERTAINMENT

Melbourne has a thriving nightlife and a lively cultural scene. The best source of 'what's on' is the *Entertainment Guide (EG)* in Friday's *Age*. *Beat* and *Inpress* are free music and entertainment publications that can be found in cafes, bars and other venues throughout the city. Also check online at www .melbourne.vic.gov.au/events and **Citysearch** (http://melbourne.citysearch.com.au).

Half-Tix (Map pp496-7; ☎ 03-9650 9420; Melbourne Town Hall, cnr Little Collins & Swanston Sts, Melbourne; ⏰ 10am-2pm Mon & Sat, 11am-6pm Tue-Thu, 11am-6.30pm Fri) Sells half-price tickets to shows and concerts on day of performance. Cash only.

Ticketek (Map pp496-7; ☎ 13 28 49; http://premier .ticketek.com.au; 225 Exhibition St, Melbourne; ⏰ 9am-5pm Mon-Fri, 9am-1pm Sat) Visit the outlet, or make phone or internet bookings for large sporting events and mainstream entertainment. There are Ticketek desks at Rod Laver Arena (p533) and the Princess Theatre (p532).

Ticketmaster (☎ 1300 136 166; www.ticketmaster .com.au) Victorian Arts Centre (Map pp496-7; Theatres Bldg, 100 St Kilda Rd, Melbourne; ⏰ 9am-9pm Mon-Sat); Athenaeum Theatre (Map pp496-7; 188 Collins St; ⏰ 9am-5pm Mon-Fri, 10am-4pm Sat) Main booking agency for theatre,

concerts, sports and other events. Book over the phone or internet, or visit an outlet. There is also a desk at Etihad Stadium (p506).

Live Music

Melbourne has long enjoyed a thriving pub-rock scene where bands such as AC/DC, Nick Cave & the Bad Seeds, Crowded House, Hunters & Collectors and Jet strummed their way into rock's rich tapestry. Legends in the domestic industry such as Paul Kelly, Lisa Miller and Tex Perkins are Melbourne-based and play regularly, as do Indigenous musicians Archie Roach and Ruby Hunter. City jazz and blues venues are also listed here. Expect to pay between zilch and $50 for live performances, but much more for international acts.

Apart from the newspapers, tune into independent radio stations **3RRR** (FM102.7; www.rrr.org .au) and **3PBS** (FM106.7) or the national **JJJ** (FM107.5; www.abc.net.au/triplej) for current gig guides.

Big venues for big names:

Festival Hall (Map pp494-5; ☎ 03-9329 9699; www .festivalhall.com.au; 300 Dudley St, West Melbourne)

Forum Theatre (Map pp496-7; www.marrinertheatres .com.au/venue_forum.jsp; cnr Russell & Flinders Sts, Melbourne) The southern-sky rendered, domed ceiling and lavishly constructed interior is as much a reason to see big name acts here as the music itself.

Palais Theatre (Map p501; ☎ 03-9525 3240; www .palaistheatre.net.au; Lower Esplanade, St Kilda) Beautiful, graceful old building.

Rod Laver Arena (p533) Headline acts in a stadium setting.

JAZZ & ACOUSTIC

Jazz cats and blues hounds will be pleased to hear that Melbourne's jazz scene is jumpin'. *EG* has listings.

Bennetts Lane (Map pp496-7; ☎ 03-9663 2856; www .bennettslane.com; 25 Bennetts Lane, Melbourne; ⏰ 8.30pm-late) Hidden down a narrow city lane, this dimly lit jazz joint is the preferred choice for the cream of local and international talent, from old-school horns and drum brushes to contemporary electronica.

Dizzy's (Map pp494-5; ☎ 03-9428 1233; www.dizzys .com.au; 381 Burnley St, Richmond; ⏰ 5.30pm-late Tue-Sun) Dizzy's offers jazz Wednesday to Sunday nights and attracts some pretty big names.

The Toff in Town Map pp496-7; ☎ 03-9639 8770; www.thetoffintown.com; 2nd fl, 252 Swanston St, Melbourne; ⏰ 5pm-late Sat-Thu, 3pm-late Fri) This sophisticated drinking and dining venue hosts live music at least four nights per week. The cabaret and jazz shows are good but sporadic – if these are your preference steer clear on Friday and Saturday nights when DJs spin until the wee hours.

Night Cat (Map p502; ☎ 03-9417 0090; www.thenight cat.com.au; 141 Johnston St, Fitzroy; ✆ 9pm-late Thu-Sun) The Cat is a large, comfortable space with a great atmosphere and skew-whiff 1950s decor (a Melbourne trademark). Bands here are big and play anything from jazz to salsa.

Manchester Lane (Map pp496-7; ☎ 03-9663 0630; www.manchesterlane.com.au; 234 Flinders Lane, Melbourne; ✆ 6pm-late Mon-Sat) Doubling as a semiformal restaurant, Manchester Lane is perfect if you're looking for dinner and a classy show. Jazz is the mainstay but other acoustic genres also get a go.

During January, February and March, the Royal Melbourne Zoo (p509) hosts the extremely popular 'Twilights' season of open-air sessions, with jazz or big bands performing on Friday, Saturday and Sunday evenings.

ROCK
City Centre
Ding Dong Lounge (Map pp496-7; ☎ 03-9662 1020; www.dingdonglounge.com.au; 18 Market Lane, Melbourne; ✆ 8pm-late Wed-Thu, to 4am Fri-Sat) This smoky, raucous, grotty bar is one of the finest spots in Melbourne to dance with pure abandon. It's so rock-and-roll it has a sister venue in New York.

Hi-Fi Bar (Map pp496-7; ☎ 03-9654 7617; www.the hifi.com.au; 125 Swanston St, Melbourne) Another fine spot to dress down for indie and alternative rock. The Hi-Fi goes for underground international and local acts with a bit of cheek – think Bon Scott tributes and Bronx rap. It's also attracted some big guns looking for an intimate venue.

Billboard the Venue (Map pp496-7; ☎ 03-9639 4000; www.billboardthevenue.com.au; 170 Russell St, Melbourne; ✆ 6pm-late) This place has been in the business for more than 40 years and has hosted everyone from Tina Turner to Carl Cox. DJs spin sets in the nightclub Thursday to Saturday.

Pony (Map pp496-7; ☎ 03-9662 1026; http://www .pony.net.au; 68 Little Collins St, Melbourne; ✆ 4pm-7am Tue-Fri, 6pm-7am Sat) If too much rock and roll is barely enough, you can party hearty at Pony. It's the kind of place where the dis-

tinction between 'riff' and ear-deafening noise is vague, but the crowds are always good fun.

Northern Suburbs
Northcote Social Club (Map pp494-5; ☎ 03-9489 3917; www.northcotesocialclub.com; 301 High St, Northcote; ✆ 4pm-midnight Mon, noon-midnight Tue-Wed & Sun, noon-3am Thu-Sat) This earthy venue is half pub, half intimate band room featuring live music most nights. A great supporter of local talent, the Northcote Social Club is also favoured by international artists.

Tote (Map p502; ☎ 03-9419 5320; www.thetotehotel .com; 71 Johnston St, Collingwood; ✆ 4pm-late Tue-Sun) A mosh pit with carpet as sticky as the tar lining the lungs of the punters. Live music – –metal, punk etc – plays every night except Monday at this stalwart.

Evelyn Hotel (Map p502; ☎ 03-9419 5500; cnr Brunswick & Kerr Sts, Fitzroy; ✆ noon-1.30am) The Evelyn attracts a mixed bag of local and international acts, and the feel is always warm and welcoming.

Retreat (Map pp494-5; ☎ 03-9380 4090; 280 Sydney Rd, Brunswick; ✆ noon-1am Mon-Thu, to 3am Fri & Sat) This big ol' rambling hotel scores on food, drink and music. Blues, roots and acoustic dominate the first half of the week and the DJs move in on the weekends. Regardless of the genre, dancing is almost mandatory and entry is around $10.

Rainbow Hotel (Map p502; ☎ 03-9419 4193; www .therainbow.com.au; 27 David St, Fitzroy; ✆ noon-midnight Mon-Tue, to 1am Wed-Sat, to 11pm Sun) This Fitzroy icon has been hosting local talent for over a decade and is a fine option for good blues, folk and jazz of the raucous energetic type. It's a small space and fills easily so start your Sunday session early.

More northern venues:

Bar Open (Map p502; ☎ 03-9415 9601; www.baropen .com.au; 317 Brunswick St, Fitzroy; ✆ 1pm-3am Mon-Sat, to 2am Sun)

East Brunswick Club (Map pp494-5; ☎ 03-9388 9794; http://eastbrunswickclub.com; 280 Lygon St, East Brunswick; ✆ 3pm-1am Mon-Fri, 1pm-1am Sat & Sun) Local acts and dirt-cheap entry.

Richmond
Corner Hotel (Map pp494-5; ☎ 03-9427 9198; www .cornerhotel.com; 57 Swan St, Richmond; ✆ 4pm-late Tue-Thu, 2pm-3am Fri-Sat, 3pm-1am Sun) A scungy pub and classic band venue that's a major player in the Melbourne music scene, host-

ing international and local acts. New indie talent is well nurtured here; ditch your attitude and fire up for a raw, loud and live good time.

St Kilda

Esplanade Hotel (Map p501; ☎ 03-9534 0211; www.espy .com.au; 11 The Esplanade, St Kilda; ☽ noon-1am Mon-Wed, noon-3am Thu-Fri, 8am-3am Sat, noon-1am Sun) A diehard rock-pig institution, the Espy is a must for lovers of cheap pots, loud live music and fabulously grungy crowds. It hosts just about every music genre (OK, so not classical) on its four stages nightly.

Prince Bandroom (Map p501; ☎ 03-9536 1168; www .princebandroom.com.au; 29 Fitzroy St, St Kilda; ☽ for shows) Check out the massive blackboard out front to see who's taking stage; you'll find the calibre is high. Above the Prince of Wales (p528), the Prince Bandroom has hosted diverse local and international acts for over 20 years.

Greyhound Hotel (Map p501; ☎ 03-9534 4189; www .greyhoundhotel.com.au; 1 Brighton Rd, St Kilda; ☽ 5pm-midnight) On Saturday nights this grotty local boozer with tonnes of rough-round-the-edges charm has drag shows. Other nights you can expect live music and cheap unpretentious drinks.

Nightclubs

Melbourne's club scene is a mixed bag, and what's here today might be gone tomorrow. Cover charges range from free to between $5 and $20. South Yarra, Fitzroy and the CBD hold the greatest concentration.

Lounge (Map pp496-7; ☎ 03-9663 2916; www.lounge .com.au; 243 Swanston St, Melbourne; ☽ Wed-Sat) Cafe by day, club by night. The crowd is an up-for-it mix of young students and the gainfully employed, and the music crosses the genres from electro to hip hop.

Revolver Upstairs (Map p500; ☎ 03-9521 5985; www.revolverupstairs.com.au; 229 Chapel St, Prahran; ☽ nightly) Cavernous Revolver is a weekend-night must for the city's party-hard crowd. A little sleazy, a little seedy and always packed, it keeps the crowd happily in the dark from Friday to Sunday. During the week it's arty and sedate.

Laundry (Map p502; ☎ 03-9419 7111; www.thelaun drybar.com.au; 50 Johnston St, Fitzroy) Comfortably shambolic and just a tad sceney, the Laundry attracts all types and does a good job of keeping the entertainment high – DJs, hip hop, 'extreme karaoke', pool tables and live music.

OneSixOne (Map p500; ☎ 03-9533 8433; www.onesix one.com.au; 161 High St, Prahran; ☽ Wed-Sat) The haunt of trendy southerners (of the river that is), this sceney club is a beautiful people's meat market. It doesn't stay refined all night though, and after the cocktails, mixed drinks and other enhancements have kicked in, the bedlam of good dance music and happy young things takes over.

Boutique (Map p500; ☎ 03-9525 2322; www.boutique .net; 132a Greville St, Prahran; ☽ Thu-Sat) This opulent little spot on a funky little strip fills its plush booths with lovely, lithe young things who are heavy on the hair product and light on the attire.

Electric Ladyland (Map p500; ☎ 03-9521 5757; www .electricladyland.com.au; Level 1, 265 Chapel St, Prahran; ☽ 5pm-3am) Practise your best pick-up lines and take a heavy wallet: Electric Ladyland is packed to the rafters with eager young things looking to hook up and be seen on Saturday nights. If the sceney-scene is your thing you'll love it. It's open nightly though and the ambience is far more subtle during the week.

First Floor (Map p502; ☎ 03-9419 6380; www.first floor393.com.au; Level 1, 393 Brunswick St, Fitzroy; ☽ Tue-Sun) A cavernous space in which to dance, drink and devote yourself to having a good time. It's a smart-looking spot, but not precious about it.

Cinemas

Melbourne has plenty of cinemas playing the latest releases; head to Village at Crown Casino, Hoyts at Melbourne Central or Greater Union on Russell St for mainstream flicks. Tickets cost around $15.50. Check the *EG* in Friday's *Age*, other newspapers or http://melbourne.citysearch.com.au/movies for screenings and times.

The following cinemas are Melbourne icons, either for their facades or for the content of their films.

Australian Centre for the Moving Image (ACMI; Map pp496-7; ☎ 03-8663 2583; www.acmi.net.au; Federation Sq, Melbourne) The fabulously high-tech cinemas here are where to go to see a mind-blowing range of films, documentaries and animated features.

Astor Theatre (Map p501; ☎ 03-9510 1414; www .astor-theatre.com; cnr Chapel St & Dandenong Rd, St Kilda) This place holds not-to-be-missed art deco nostalgia, with double features every night, of old and recent classics.

FLICKS UNDER THE STARS

Ditch the indoors on a balmy summer night for movies under the stars.

From December to March the **Moonlight Cinema** (Map pp494-5; www.moonlight.com.au; Royal Botanic Gardens; adult/child $15/10; ☾ Tue-Sun) screens newish and classic films in the Royal Botanic Gardens (enter via Gate D on Birdwood Ave, South Yarra). Bring along a rug, pillow and moonlight supper, or buy food and drinks there, and set up an outdoor living room in the middle of the gardens. **St Kilda OpenAir** (Map p501; www.stkildaopenair.com.au; St Kilda Sea Baths; adult/concession $20/14; ☾ nightly) does the same on the rooftop of the St Kilda Sea Baths from mid-January to mid-February; and **Rooftop Cinema** (Map pp494-5; www.rooftopcinema.com.au; adult/concession $18/15; ☾ Tue-Sun) screens films on top of Curtain House from November to March.

Cinema Europa (Map p500; ☎ 1300 555 400; Level 1, Jam Factory, 500 Chapel St, South Yarra) Good cafe and bar on the premises, comfy seats and art-house films.

Cinema Nova (Map p499; ☎ 03-9347 5331; www.cinemanova.com.au; 380 Lygon St, Carlton) Nova has great current film releases. Tickets are a measly $5.50 before 4pm on Monday.

Palace George Cinemas (Map p501; ☎ 03-9534 6922; 135 Fitzroy St, St Kilda) Small cinema space but a St Kilda local.

Imax (Map p499; ☎ 03-9663 5454; www.imaxmelbourne.com.au; Carlton Gardens, Carlton) Within the same complex as the Melbourne Museum, this theatre screens films in super-wide 70mm format.

Kino Cinema (Map pp496-7; ☎ 03-9650 2100; Collins Pl, 45 Collins St, Melbourne) This licensed cinema specialises in quality art-house releases, and is close to great bars, too, for after-flick drinks.

Theatre & Dance

Melbourne has a number of well-regarded theatre companies, and has one the healthiest scenes in the country, with excellent performers, a responsive public and a supportive atmosphere.

Classical music buffs must listen to the **Melbourne Chorale** (www.melbournechorale.com.au), a combination of two choirs that perform a variety of classical and modern works for voice. The **Melbourne Symphony Orchestra** (www.mso.com.au) performs regularly throughout the year; it has both a strong reputation and a keen fan base.

Musica Viva (www.mva.org.au) is one of the country's premier outfits for staging international and local ensemble music. Performances take place about once a month at the Elisabeth Murdoch Hall in the new **Melbourne Recital Centre** (Map pp496-7; cnr Southbank Blvd & Sturt St, Southbank). **Opera Australia** (www.opera-australia.org.au) also performs regularly.

The **Australian Ballet** (www.australianballet.com.au) has a good repertoire and some sterling performers, and is based in Melbourne. **Chunky Move** (Map pp496-7; ☎ 03-9645 5188; www.chunkymove.com; 111 Sturt St, Southbank) is Victoria's contemporary dance company, and dishes up a renowned repertoire of work.

The Victorian Arts Centre (p507) is Melbourne's major venue for performing arts and where the **Melbourne Theatre Company** (MTC; ☎ 03-9684 4500; www.mtc.com.au) stages around 15 productions, from contemporary to Shakespearean, each year.

The following are noteworthy venues around town for live theatre.

La Mama (Map p499; ☎ 03-9347 6142; 205 Faraday St, Carlton) This tiny, intimate forum produces new Australian works and experimental theatre, and has a reputation for developing emerging playwrights.

Malthouse Theatre (Map pp494-5; ☎ 03-9685 5111; www.malthousetheatre.com.au; 113 Sturt St, South Melbourne) An outstanding company that stages predominantly Australian works by established and new playwrights.

Princess Theatre (Map pp496-7; ☎ 03-9299 9800; 163 Spring St, Melbourne) This beautifully renovated landmark theatre is the venue for super-slick musicals.

Regent Theatre (Map pp496-7; ☎ 03-9299 9500; 191 Collins St, Melbourne) A grand old venue for musicals.

Comedy & Cabaret

Melbourne has an extremely healthy stand-up circuit and is host to April's **International Comedy Festival** (www.comedyfestival.com.au).

The following venues showcase quality comedy and some of Melbourne's most eccentric cabaret.

Butterfly Club (Map pp494-5; ☎ 03-9690 2000; 204 Bank St, South Melbourne) This adorable terrace house holds a small theatre that hosts regular cabaret performances. Show over, head out the back or upstairs to a uniquely decorated bar, where surfaces are bedecked with the kitsch, the cool and the cute.

Comic's Lounge (Map pp494-5; ☎ 03-9348 9488; www.thecomicslounge.com.au; 26 Errol St, North Melbourne) The only place in town which features daily comedy performances; acts range across the comedy spectrum and tickets cost around $25.

Last Laugh Comedy Club (Map pp496-7; ☎ 03-9650 6668; www.thecomedyclub.com.au; Athenaeum Theatre, 188 Collins St, Melbourne) Professional stand-up on Friday and Saturday nights, with dinner-and-show packages available.

Sport
FOOTBALL
Australian Rules
The **Australian Football League** (AFL; www.afl.com.au), known as 'the footy', is undoubtably the city's sporting obsession, with games at the Melbourne Cricket Ground (MCG; p509) regularly pulling crowds of between 50,000 and 90,000. If you're here between April and September try to see a match – as much for the crowd as the game. The sheer energy of the barracking at a big game is exhilarating.

Being the shrine of Aussie rules, the MCG is still widely regarded as the best place to see a game, although the smaller and more modern **Etihad Stadium** (Map pp496-7; ☎ 03-8625 7700; www.telstradome.com.au; Docklands) also hosts weekly games.

Tickets can be bought at the ground for most games, and the cheapest seats start at about $20. Booking seats in advance might be necessary at big games.

Rugby
Rugby union has been slow to catch on in AFL-obsessed Melbourne, but the MCG and Telstra Dome attract enormous crowds to international matches.

Rugby league is a NSW and Queensland game, but it is attracting a growing following in Melbourne, owing in part to the success of **Melbourne Storm** (www.melbournestorm.com.au), the only Melbourne side in the National Rugby League competition.

April to September is the season for both codes. Melbourne Storm's home matches are played at **Olympic Park** (Map pp494-5; ☎ 03-9286 1600; www.mopt.com.au; Batman Ave, Jolimont).

Soccer
Soccer (football) has always had a strong fan base in Melbourne, but Australia's international form in recent years has reinvigorated national attention for the 'real football' (we're locals, so we're allowed to say it). **Melbourne Victory** (www.melbournevictory.com.au) is the home-town hero in the national **A-League** (www.a-league.com.au) and play at Etihad Stadium. The season runs from October to May.

CRICKET
For any cricket fan a visit to the MCG (p509) is something of a pilgrimage. During summer, international Test matches and one-day internationals are played here. The cricket season in Australia is from October to March. General admission to international matches is approximately adult/child/concession/family $40/10/33/60, but finals cost more and generally require booking. The cricket event *par excellence* is the traditional Boxing Day Test.

HORSE RACING
Horse racing takes place in Melbourne throughout the year at the racecourses at Flemington, Caulfield, Moonee Valley and Sandown.

The **Melbourne Cup** (www.vrc.net.au) brings the entire nation to a standstill. It's so big it gets its own holiday in Melbourne (but not Victoria) and it's watched by millions around the world. It's always run at **Flemington Racecourse** (Map pp494–5) and always on the first Tuesday in November. The Thursday after the Cup, Oaks Day, once a 'ladies'' event, is now almost as popular – with both sexes – as the Cup.

MOTOR SPORTS
The **Australian Formula One Grand Prix** (☎ 03-9258 7100; www.grandprix.com.au) is held in Albert Park in March and the World 500cc **Motorcycle Grand Prix** (http://bikes.grandprix.com.au) races at Phillip Island in October. Tickets for the Formula One Grand Prix start at $39 for one-day general-admission and $175 for a four-day ticket.

TENNIS
For two weeks each January **Melbourne Park** (Map pp494-5; ☎ 03-9286 1600; www.mopt.com.au; Batman Ave, Jolimont) hosts the **Australian Open** (www.ausopen.org). The top tennis players from around the world come to compete in the year's first of the four Grand Slam tournaments. Tickets range from about $30 for early rounds to well over $200 for finals.

Within Melbourne Park, the **Rod Laver Arena** is an enormous arena that hosts both the Australian Open tennis and big international musos. It features a retractable roof, so weather is not an issue.

SHOPPING

This city loooooves to shop. Stores are most dense in the city centre, but South Yarra, Toorak and Fitzroy are also good for unique purchases.

Bourke St Mall is home to the city's two main department stores: **David Jones** (Map pp496-7; ☎ 03-9643 2222; 310 Bourke St, Melbourne) and **Myer** (Map pp496-7; ☎ 03-9661 1111; 314 Bourke St, Melbourne). **Melbourne Central** (Map pp496-7; ☎ 03-9922 1100; cnr Elizabeth & La Trobe Sts, Melbourne) is a shopping centre with lots of mainstream shops, especially clothing outlets. In an imposing modern complex, **QV** (Map pp496-7; ☎ 03-9658 0100; cnr Swanston & Lonsdale Sts, Melbourne) is Melbourne's freshest contender and features populist commercial options and a supermarket. **GPO** (Map pp496-7; ☎ 03-9663 0066; cnr Elizabeth & Bourke St Mall, Melbourne) houses fabulous boutiques including Akira and Veronika Maine, plus the ABC shop.

Australian

Counter (Map pp496-7; ☎ 03-9650 7775; 31 Flinders Lane, Melbourne; ⊙ noon-5pm Mon, 10am-5pm Tue-Sat) An excellent outlet for unique souvenirs, Counter sells locally crafted jewellery, ceramics, textiles, wood and glass. Each piece really is a work of art and your purchase will support the local industry.

Crumpler (Map p502; ☎ 03-9417 5338; cnr Gertrude & Smith Sts, Fitzroy) Crumpler is a local company that makes tough-as-nails bags for bicycle couriers, laptops and photography equipment. They're functional fashion accessories and 'everyone's' got a Crumpler. It's a great local souvenir you won't be ashamed to drag around the world.

RM Williams (Map pp496-7; ☎ 03-9663 7126; Melbourne Central, Lonsdale St, Melbourne) An Aussie icon, even for city slickers, this brand will kit you up with stylish essentials for working the land, including a pair of those famous boots.

Clothing & Accessories

The city is your best bet for a major wardrobe upgrade. If you've come all the way to Melbourne to buy Hermes, Prada, Chanel etc you'll find them on Collins Street between

Swanston and Spring Streets. Greville St and Chapel St between High St and Dandenong Rd in Prahran are good strips for second-hand vintage and retro gear, as well as fresh, Australian designer boutiques. Brunswick St and Gertrude Sts in Fitzroy sport designer boutiques, retro threads, street wear and rave wear. The South Yarra end of Chapel St (between High St and Toorak Rd) has long had a reputation as Melbourne's premier style strip. Hit Bridge Rd and Swan St in Richmond and Smith St in Collingwood for factory outlets.

Alice Euphemia City Centre (Map pp496-7; ☎ 03-9650 4300; Shop 6, 37 Swanston St, Melbourne); Fitzroy (Map p502; ☎ 03-9417 4300; 114 Gertrude St, Fitzroy; ⊙ noon-5pm Tue-Fri, 11am-6pm Sat) The more experimental end of Melbourne fashion gets a showing here, with inventive fabrics, cuts and finishes that aim to make you look more interesting than you might actually be. Great jewellery, too.

Little Salon (Map p502; ☎ 03-9419 7123; 71 Gertrude St, Fitzroy) Part art gallery and part retail outlet, this little shop is hipster heaven. It's wearable art: bags woven from seat belts, knitted corsages and button bracelets. Everything is locally made and extremely well priced.

Scanlon & Theodore (Map pp496-7; ☎ 03-9650 6195; 285 Little Collins St) S&T helped define the Melbourne look back in the 1980s and are still going strong with super-feminine, beautifully tailored everyday and special-occasion wear. Although now considered mainstream, this label always manage to make a statement.

Music & Books

See Bookshops (p493) for stores selling guide books, maps and other useful tourist tomes.

Greville Records (Map p500; ☎ 03-9510 3012; 152 Greville St, Prahran) One of the last bastions of the 'old' Greville St, this fabulous music shop has such a loyal following that the great Neil Young invited the owners on stage during a Melbourne concert.

Polyester Books (Map p502; ☎ 03-9419 5223; 330 Brunswick St, Fitzroy) Take kinky and rude and then go several steps beyond. This unapologetic shop specialises in literature, magazines and audiovisual materials on topics from satanic cult sex to underground comics, and everything in between.

Across the road **Polyester Records** (Map p502; ☎ 03-9419 5137; 387 Brunswick St, Fitzroy) sells independent music from around the world, plus live-music tickets.

Other

Spacecraft (Map p502; ☎ 03-9486 0010; www.space craftaustralia.com; 255 Gertrude St, Fitzroy) This is an excellent place to find a made-in-Melbourne souvenir that won't end up at the back of the cupboard. Textile artist Stewart Russell's botanical and architectural designs adorn everything from stools to socks to single-bed doonas.

Rose Street Artists Market (Map p502; ☎ 03-9419 5529; 60 Rose St, Fitzroy; ☻ 11am-5pm Sat) One of Melbourne's best and most popular art and craft markets is just a short stroll from Brunswick St. Here you'll find up to 70 stalls selling assorted wares, including jewellery, clothing, furniture, paintings, screen prints and ugly-cute toys.

Aesop City Centre (Map pp496-7; ☎ 03-9639 2436; 35 Albert Coates Lane, Melbourne); Fitzroy (Map p502; ☎ 03-9419 8356; 242 Gertrude St, Fitzroy) This home-grown skincare company specialises in products made from simple ingredients in simple packaging. The range is wide and based on botanical extracts.

GETTING THERE & AWAY

For details of international flights to/from Melbourne, see p1046.

Air

Most of the major airlines have direct international flights to **Melbourne Airport** (☎ 03-9297 1600; www.melbourneairport.com.au) in Tullamarine, 22km northwest of the city centre.

Melbourne is well connected to all other capital cities in the country and many regional centres as well. Carriers include **Qantas** (☎ 13 13 13; www.qantas.com.au), **Jetstar** (☎ 13 15 38; www.jetstar.com.au), **Virgin Blue** (☎ 13 67 89; www.virginblue.com.au), **QantasLink** (☎ 13 13 13; www.qantas.com.au), **Regional Express** (Rex; ☎ 13 17 13; www.regionalexpress.com.au) and **Tiger Airways** (☎ 03-9335 3033; www.tigerairways.com). Jetstar also has flights that operate to and from **Avalon Airport** (www.avalonairport.com.au), which is 22km north of Geelong and 56km southwest of Melbourne.

Boat

The **Spirit of Tasmania** (☎ 1800 634 906; www.spiri toftasmania.com.au) sails between Melbourne and Tasmania at 8pm nightly year-round, departing from Port Melbourne's Station Pier and the Esplanade in Devonport – both arrive at around 7am.

Bus

The long-distance bus terminal in the city centre is at the **Southern Cross Station** (Map pp496-7; Spencer St, Melbourne). **Skybus** (☎ 03-9335 2811; www .skybus.com.au) airport buses also operate from here. **Greyhound** (☎ 1300 473 946; www.greyhound.com .au) and **Premier** (☎ 13 34 10; www.premierms.com.au) both have daily services to/from Sydney ($85, 13 hours), stopping at towns along the way. **Firefly** (☎ 1300 730 740; www.fireflyexpress.com.au) also services Melbourne.

Train

Long-distance trains also operate to/from Southern Cross Station. Victoria's **V/Line** (☎ 13 61 96; www.vline.com.au) runs train services between Melbourne and regional Victoria.

CountryLink (☎ 13 22 32; www.countrylink.info) runs daily XPT trains between Melbourne and Sydney ($95, 11 hours).

GETTING AROUND
To/From the Airport

If you're driving to/from Melbourne Airport, take the tolled Tullamarine Fwy; a 24-hour Tulla Pass costs $4.30 – contact **CityLink** (☎ 13 26 29; www.citylink.com.au) for more details. From Avalon Airport take the M1 to Melbourne.

The wheelchair-accessible **Skybus** (☎ 03-9335 2811; www.skybus.com.au) operates a 24-hour shuttle bus to/from the airport and Southern Cross Station (one way $16, every 20 minutes). Buy your ticket online or from ticket booths at the airport and the station. Between 6am and 9pm you can buy it from the driver. You can take your bicycle, but the front wheel must be removed.

Avalon Airport Shuttle (☎ 03-9689 7999; www.sita coaches.com.au) meets all flights at Avalon Airport and goes to/from the city centre (one way $20, one hour).

A toll-inclusive taxi fare from Melbourne airport to the city centre costs around $60; from Avalon Airport it's around $110.

Bicycle

Melbourne's a great city for cycling, as it's reasonably flat and there are great bike paths and dedicated bike lanes on roads throughout the metropolitan area. Bicycles can be taken on suburban trains for no cost. Slippery tram tracks are a major hazard for Melbourne cyclists, though. Cross them on a sufficient angle to prevent your tyre falling into the track.

VICTORIA

For more details on cycling in Melbourne, see p511.

Car & Motorcycle

Road parking in the city costs from $2 per hour, and there's plenty of more expensive commercial car parks. Read parking signs for restrictions and times, and if your car is parked in a 'clearway' zone, which operates during peak hours, *move it* – otherwise it will be towed. The visitor information centre (p503) has information about city parking spots.

HIRE

Avis (☎ 13 63 33; www.avis.com.au), **Europcar** (☎ 1300 131 390; www.europcar.com.au), **Hertz** (☎ 13 30 39; www.hertz.com) and **Thrifty** (☎ 1300 367 227; www.thrifty.com.au) have desks at the airport and city-centre locations.

For cheap, secondhand rentals in varying conditions, try **Rent-a-Bomb** (☎ 13 15 53; www.rentabomb.com.au), which requires no bond and doesn't have a driver age limit. Rates start as low as $35 per day, but make sure you read the fine print.

TOLL ROADS

CityLink (☎ 13 26 29; www.citylink.com.au) has two main sections: the western link that runs from the Calder Hwy intersection of the Tullamarine Fwy to join the Westgate Fwy; and the southern link that runs from Kings Way, on the southern edge of the CBD, to the Monash Fwy. Both sections are toll ways.

Tolls are 'collected' electronically by overhead readers from a transponder card (an e-Tag). If you don't have an e-Tag, you can purchase a day pass ($12), which is valid for 24 hours from your first trip on any CityLink section, or a weekend pass ($12), which is valid from noon Friday to midnight Sunday. If you only intend to use the western link to travel to/from Melbourne airport, you can purchase a Tulla Pass ($4.30). Day and weekend passes can be purchased at any post office, CityLink customer service centre, over the internet or over the phone. Travel without payment and you'll cop a $100 fine.

Motorcycles can use CityLink for free.

Public Transport

Melbourne's public transport system of buses, trains and trams is privatised. For timetables, maps and fares call the **Met Information Centre** (☎ 13 16 38; www.metlinkmelbourne.com.au). The MetShop (p503) has transport information and sells tickets.

On Friday and Saturday nights after the trams, buses and trains stop running (roughly around midnight), NightRider buses depart half-hourly from City Square from 1.30am to 4.30am on Saturday mornings and till 5.30am on Sunday mornings for many suburban destinations. You need a valid metcard to travel.

TICKETS

Metcards allow you to travel on any and all Melbourne bus, train and tram services, even if you transfer from one to another. Tickets are available from Metcard vending machines and counters at train stations, on trams (tram vending machines only take coins and only dispense City Saver, two-hour and daily tickets), from retailers displaying the Met flag (usually newsagents and milk bars) and the MetShop. You can purchase tickets directly from the driver on bus services.

The metropolitan area is divided into two zones. Zone 1 covers the city and inner-suburban area (including St Kilda) and most visitors won't venture beyond that unless they're going right out of town. Adult Zone 1 two-hour/daily/weekly tickets cost $3.70/6.80/29.40.

City Saver tickets ($2.80) are fairly useless, allowing you to travel only two sections (check the maps on each tram giving this information) in the CBD without breaking your journey.

See Tours p515 for information on the free City Circle Tram and Melbourne City Tourist Shuttle.

AROUND MELBOURNE

Greater Melbourne sprawls across the top of Port Phillip Bay, only really breaking free of the urban shackles when you pass through Geelong to the Bellarine Peninsula (west) and Frankston to the Mornington Peninsula (east). The bay itself has only a tiny opening to Bass Strait between Points Nepean and Lonsdale and the two peninsulas are joined by a regular ferry service (Queenscliff–Sorrento), making it possible to do a complete circuit of the bay in a day.

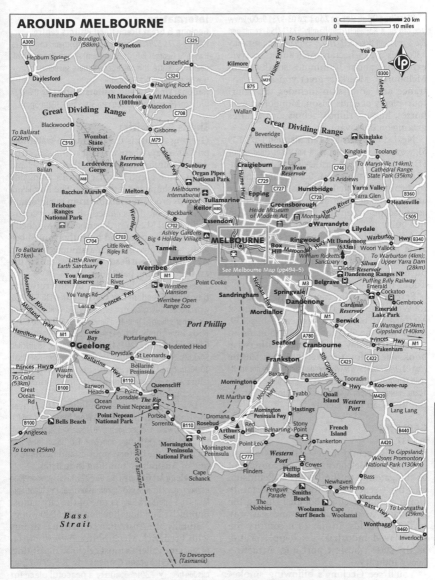

AROUND MELBOURNE

When it comes to weekends or day trips, most Melburnians stay within this curve, heading to wineries in the Yarra Valley, to historic Queenscliff or to the surf beaches of Portsea and Sorrento. Phillip Island attracts international visitors keen on the fluffy penguins, while others head for the Dandenongs or take a picnic to Hanging Rock.

MELBOURNE TO GEELONG

The one-hour drive down the Princes Fwy (M1) from Melbourne to Geelong takes you over the soaring West Gate Bridge, which provides super views over the city and Port Phillip Bay. Further along the way you pass Avalon Airport and a few interesting sights around Werribee.

VICTORIA

Werribee Open Range Zoo (☎ 03-9731 9600; www
.zoo.org.au; K Rd; adult/child/family $24/12/54, combined
zoo & mansion ticket $33/17/77; ☺ 9am-5pm, last entry
3.30pm) is a 225-hectare African-safari-style
experience about 30 minutes southwest of
Melbourne. Meerkats greet you at the entrance and admission includes the safari
tour: plenty of emus, bison, Mongolian wild
horses, hippos, rhinos, zebras and giraffes
grazing on the savannah.

Next door, **Werribee Park Mansion** (☎ 13 19
63; www.werribeepark.com.au; K Rd; adult/child/family
$13.50/7.50/32; ☺ 10am-5pm Nov-Apr, 10am-4pm Mon-
Fri & 10am-5pm Sat & Sun May-Oct) is surrounded
by beautiful formal gardens, with picnic
areas. Audio headphones re-create the 1870s
soundscape, when the Italianate mansion
was built.

Adjacent to the mansion, the **Victoria
State Rose Garden** (☎ 03-9742 4291; admission
free; ☺ 9am-5.30pm) has more than 5500 rose
bushes arranged in the shape of a giant
Tudor rose.

Several Met trains run daily from the city
to Werribee station (daily Zone 1 and 2
Metcard $10.60). From here catch bus 439,
which runs the 5km to the zoo and mansion
turn-off Monday to Saturday. Otherwise
book ahead for the **Werribee Park Shuttle**
(☎ 03-9748 5094; www.werribeeparkshuttle.com.au; adult/
child return zoo & mansion $25/15; ☺ departs 8.30am &
10am, returns 1.30pm & 4pm), which departs from
the Victorian Arts Centre.

GEELONG
pop 137,220

Victoria's second-largest city has always
been seen as Melbourne's poorer cousin, but
as the gateway to the Bellarine Peninsula
and the Great Ocean Road, it's certainly
worth a stop. Geelong boomed during the
gold rush as a major port and gateway
to the goldfields. In the 20th century the
city played industrial catch-up, serving
as the state's busiest port and attracting
heavy industry.

You'll see Geelong's billowing smoke-
stacks before you reach the city, but the sparkling waterfront redevelopment on Corio
Bay and some historic downtown buildings
should restore your faith. Geelong locals are
a parochial lot – especially when it comes to
the beloved Cats, their AFL team – and the
city centre has a pretty good nightlife and
cafe scene.

Information
Geelong & Great Ocean Road visitors centre
(☎ 03-5275 5797; www.greatoceanrd.org.au; cnr Princes
Hwy & St Georges Rd; ☺ 9am-5pm) About 7km north of
Geelong's centre, this office serves those speeding their
way to the Great Ocean Road.
National Wool Museum visitors centre (☎ 03-5227
0701; cnr Moorabool & Brougham Sts; ☺ 9.30am-5pm)

Sights & Activities
Geelong's focus is the downtown **waterfront**
on Corio Bay, where you can swim, sail, stroll
down Cunningham Pier, ride the carousel and
admire the grand historic homes alongside
modern shops and restaurants. The *Bay Walk
Bollards* brochure available from the information kiosk or, if it's closed, the visitor centre
at the Wool Museum, describes Jan Mitchell's
104 famous carved and brightly painted **bollards**, which give this area a unique character.
At nearby **Eastern Beach** you can swim by the
art deco bathing pavilion.

For a better view of the town, cruise the
bay with **Freedom Bay Cruises** (☎ 0418 522 328;
www.freedombaycruises.com.au; adult/child/family $15/7/40;
☺ departs hourly 11am-4pm holidays, Sat & Sun Sep-May).
Kids love the hand-carved **Geelong Waterfront
Carousel** (☎ 03-5224 1547; Steampacket Pl; adult/child
$4/3.50; ☺ 10.30am-5pm Mon-Fri, 10.30am-8pm Sat,
10.30am-6pm Sun), a refurbished steam-driven
merry-go-round enclosed in a modern
glass building.

In a historic bluestone building (1872) near
the waterfront, the **National Wool Museum** (☎ 03-
5227 0701; www.nwm.vic.gov.au; 26 Moorabool St; adult/child/
family $8/4/20; ☺ 9.30am-5pm Mon-Fri, 1-5pm Sat & Sun)
focuses on the history, politics and heritage of
one of Australia's founding industries.

Geelong Art Gallery (☎ 03-5229 3645; www.geelong
gallery.org.au; Little Malop St; admission free; ☺ 10am-5pm
Mon-Fri, 1-5pm Sat & Sun) is one of the city's most
impressive buildings housing over 5000 works.
Naturally, the Australian collection is strong,
with Frederick McCubbin's *A Bush Burial*
(1890) the gallery's most celebrated painting.

The 1851 **Botanic Gardens** (☎ 03-5227 0387; admission free; ☺ 7.30am-5pm) are a peaceful place for
a stroll or picnic. The '21st century' garden at
the entrance features indigenous plants from
across Australia.

Ford Discovery Centre (☎ 03-5227 8700; www
.forddiscovery.com.au; cnr Gheringhap & Brougham Sts;
adult/child/family $7/3/18; ☺ 10am-5pm Wed-Mon)
looks at the Ford motor industry then and
now, using interactive displays and exhibits.

VICTORIA

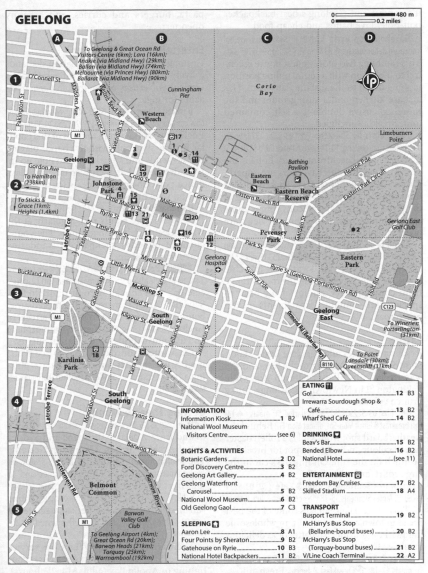

GEELONG

0 480 m
0 0.2 miles

VICTORIA

Rev-heads love the 'cars of the future' display, Bathurst-winning Falcons, a Model T Ford and crash-test dummies.

Old Geelong Gaol (☎ 03-5221 8292; cnr Myers & Swanston St; 11am-3pm Thu-& Fri, 1-4pm Sat & Sun) closed its doors to prisoners in 1991, but the old bluestone building remains and is open for tours. You can see the grim cells,

watchtowers and a gallows re-creation of the execution of James Murphy, hanged in 1863 for murdering a policeman.

Sleeping

National Hotel Backpackers (☎ 03-5229 1211; www .nationalhotel.com.au; 191 Moorabool St; dm/d $30/60) The Nash is pretty much a party pub, but it's central and Geelong's best backpacker bolt-hole. Live bands and cheap food.

Gatehouse on Ryrie (☎ 0417 545 196; www.bol .com.au/gatehouse/g.html; 83 Yarra St; s $80, d $95-120; ☐) This rambling two-storey guest house is central to the action with a commanding position looking down to the distant waterfront. Has a share kitchen and a sitting room and the more expensive double is a self-contained unit. Breakfast included.

Four Points by Sheraton (☎ 03-5223 1377; www .fourpoints.com/geelong; 10-14 Eastern Beach Rd; d $170-425; ☒) Geelong's beachfront luxury hotel is the best in town and the bay views are superb. Rooms are contemporary and packed with all mod cons, including flat-screen TVs as big as the views. Beach-facing balcony rooms come at a premium, but rooms without views are often available as packages.

Aaron Lee (☎ 03-5222 7733; www.aaronlee.com.au; cnr Western Beach Rd & Ginn Sts; studio from $155, apt $270-325; ☒) The waterfront location at this chic boutique hotel is perfect and the rooms range from contemporary studios at the back to spacious self-contained apartments on the beach road.

Eating

Restaurants, cafes and bars line Little Malop St, Moorabool St leading to the bay, and the waterfront along Eastern Beach Rd, while Pakington St in Newtown is Geelong's funky brunch epicentre.

Go! (☎ 03-5229 4752; 37 Bellarine St; meals $4-14; ☽ breakfast & lunch Mon-Sat, dinner Mon-Fri) Behind the weatherboard shopfront, Go! is a rollercoaster ride of colour and an artsy spot for breakfast or lunch on the run. On fine days eat in the large courtyard at the back.

Irrewarra Sourdough Shop & Café (☎ 03-5221 3909; 10 James St; meals $5-18; ☽ breakfast & lunch Mon-Fri) This rustic bakery makes some of the best bread in town and serves it up in wholesome sandwiches, gourmet baguettes or as delicious breakfast toast.

Sticks & Grace (☎ 03-5224 2900; 4/337 Pakington St; meals $7-18; ☽ breakfast & lunch) Fresh juices, great coffee, unbeatable bacon and eggs, and piles of pancakes make this a breakfast and brunch bonanza.

Wharf Shed Café (☎ 03-5221 6645; 15 Eastern St; mains $15-28) You can't beat the waterfront location at this casual cafe near the Eastern Beach marina. Fish and chips is a crowd favourite, but there's a good range of pizza,

pasta, burgers and curries, and a sunny open terrace.

Entertainment & Drinking

Geelong's large student population demands a lively bar and club scene. Check Friday's *Geelong Advertiser* or the freebie *Forte* magazine for gigs.

Bended Elbow (☎ 03-5229 4477; www.thebendedel bow.com.au; 69 Yarra St; meals $12-26; ☽ 10.30am-late) English brews flow from the taps of this popular British-style pub, with live bands playing on weekends and snug booths to hole up in. Upstairs Level 1 is a club space that plays dance pop. Cheap meal deals (parma night etc) on weeknights.

National Hotel (☎ 03-5229 1211; 191 Moorabool St; ☽ 11am-late) Live bands play regularly at the Nash, Geelong's rockingest pub. The young clientele includes backpackers wandering down from upstairs.

our pick **Beav's Bar** (☎ 03-5222 3366; www.beavsbar .com.au; 77 Little Malop St; ☽ 4pm-late Wed-Sat) Loungy cafe-bar with enough retro furniture to fill a Salvation Army showroom. It's tucked away behind a little red door in the back streets of Geelong's arts precinct. Very cool atmosphere and live music Friday and Saturday nights.

On winter Saturdays check to see if the mighty **Geelong Cats** (www.gfc.com.au) are playing a home game at **Skilled Stadium** (Kardinia Park; Moorabool St).

Getting There & Around

Jetstar (☎ 13 15 38; www.jetstar.com.au) has flights to and from Adelaide, Brisbane and Sydney out of Avalon Airport, 22km from Geelong. The **Avalon Airport Shuttle** (☎ 03-5278 8788; www .avalonairportshuttle.com.au) offers connections to the Great Ocean Road as far as Lorne.

V/Line (☎ 13 61 96; www.vline.com.au) trains run frequently from the **Geelong train station** (☎ 03-5226 6525; Gordon Ave) to Melbourne ($9.20, one hour).

There is a regular daily V/Line bus service to Lorne ($9, 1½ hours), with some buses continuing to Apollo Bay (adult $14, 2½ hours).

McHarry's Bus Lines (☎ 03-5223 2111; www.mchar rys.com.au) operates the Bellarine Transit service with frequent buses to Torquay and the Bellarine Peninsula. Torquay buses depart from the bus stop on Ryrie St; Bellarine-bound buses leave from Little Malop St.

Interstate buses leave from the **Busport Terminal** (cnr Brougham and Geringhap Sts).

BELLARINE PENINSULA

On the other side of Geelong, the beautiful Bellarine is a bulbous peninsula curling around to form the 'northern' entrance to Port Phillip Bay. It's a popular holiday destination with mellow seaside towns, surf beaches and some excellent wineries that make a satisfying detour on the way to the Great Ocean Road. The peninsula also has accessible diving and snorkelling sites.

Families head down here en masse during school holidays from Christmas to the end of January and over Easter, when accommodation prices soar and many caravan parks have a minimum-stay requirement.

GETTING THERE & AWAY

McHarry's Bus Lines (☎ 03-5223 2111) travels between Geelong and most peninsula towns, including Barwon Heads, Ocean Grove, Queenscliff and Point Lonsdale. A day ticket costs $6.40.

Queenscliff-Sorrento Car & Passenger Ferries (☎ 03-5258 3244; www.searoad.com.au; one way adult/child $10/8, car from $55; ☻ 7am-6pm) runs hourly services between Queenscliff and Sorrento on the Mornington Peninsula.

Queenscliff

pop 3890

This is a favourite weekender for Melbourne's chic set as the charming 19th-century Queenscliff makes the most of its historic streetscape, surf beaches and swanky cafe strip. The classic hotels, guest houses and other buildings trimmed with wrought iron along the wide main street are testament to the town's resort boom in the 1880s.

Originally Queenscliff was a base for pilot boats that steered ships through treacherous Port Phillip Heads, one of the world's most dangerous seaways, known as 'the Rip'. The coast is littered with over 200 shipwrecks.

Queenscliff visitor information centre (☎ 03-5258 4843; www.queenscliff.org; 55 Hesse St; ☻ 9am-5pm; 🖳) is in the library building in the middle of town.

SIGHTS & ACTIVITIES

Queenscliff's grandest historic buildings line beachfront Gellibrand St: the ageing **Ozone Hotel**, being refurbished at the time of research, **Lathamstowe**, **Queenscliff Hotel** and a row of old **pilots' cottages** (66-68 Gellibrand St) dating back to 1853. Pick up a heritage walk brochure from the visitor centre.

Fort Queenscliff (☎ 03-5258 1488; www.fortqueen scliff.com.au; cnr Gellibrand & King Sts; tours adult/child $10/5; ☻ tours 1pm & 3pm Sat, Sun & school holidays) was built during the 19th century to protect shipping routes between Melbourne and Geelong from a feared Russian invasion. Eighty-minute guided tours (the only way to see the fort) are of the military museum, magazine, cells and Black Lighthouse.

At the pier, the **Maritime Museum** (☎ 03-5258 3440; Wharf St; adult/child $5/3; ☎ 10.30am-4.30pm Mon-Fri, 1.30-4.30pm Sat & Sun) has a modest collection of nautical memorabilia and displays on the area's shipwrecks.

Run by rail enthusiasts, **Bellarine Peninsula Railway** (☎ 03-5258 2069; www.bpr.org.au; adult/child/family return $20/12/50; ☻ trips 11.15am & 2.45pm Sun year-round, Tue & Thu school holidays, daily 26 Dec-9 Jan, Tue-Thu, Sat & Sun 10 Jan-26 Jan) has an immaculate collection of steam trains that ply the 1¾-hour return journey to Drysdale. The *Seaside Explorer* railmotor runs the same line on Tuesday and Thursday the rest of the year.

Sea-All Dolphin Swims (☎ 03-5258 3889; www.dol phinswims.com.au; Larkin Pde; adult/child sightseeing $65/55, 3½hr swim & snorkel $120/105; ☻ morning & afternoon Sep-May) offers swims with seals and dolphins in Port Phillip Bay, and less energetic sightseeing tours from a caravan on the pier.

Queenscliff Dive Centre (☎ 03-5258 1188; www .divequeenscliff.com.au; 37 Learmonth St; per dive with/without gear $123/55, 2 dives $191/110) can get you out exploring the wrecks of the area.

FESTIVALS & EVENTS

Queenscliff Music Festival (☎ 03-5258 4816; www.qmf .net.au) is on the last weekend in November and attracts Australian and international artists of a folksy, bluesy bent.

At other times of the year, the **Blues Train** (www.thebluestrain.com.au; dinner & show $76) will get your foot tapping with irregular steam train trips that feature on-board blues and roots music and meals; check the website for dates and artists.

SLEEPING

Queenscliff Inn (☎ 03-5258 4600; www.queenscliffinn .com; 59 Hesse St; B&B d/f $130/188, YHA dm $30, s/d/f $65/80/120) This two-storey Edwardian inn is a budget travellers dream – part YHA hostel, part heritage hotel, with a choice of period-style rooms and one eight-bed dorm. Whatever your budget you can while away

VICTORIA

evenings in the beautiful lounge and drawing room, or eat in the Couta Boat Café (mains $20 to $30). Still, you should expect nothing less from Queenscliff.

Rubys B&B (☎ 03-5258 4838; 2 St Andrews St; d $100-150) This cosy B&B cottage has three well-appointed suites, two with spas and two fully self-contained. It's in a quiet street a block from the main strip.

Athelstane House (☎ 03-5258 1024; www.athelstane .com.au; 4 Hobson St; B&B d $170-230, apt $230; 🔀) Dating back to 1860, this historic building has served as a guest house for over a century. Each room has its own distinctive style, including spa, though pricier rooms have sea-view balconies. Breakfast downstairs tops off a brilliant stay as Athelstane is also one of Queenscliff's finest restaurants.

Queenscliff Tourist Parks (☎ 03-5258 1765; www .queensclifftouristparks.com.au; 134 Hesse St; unpowered/powered sites $21/26, peak season all sites $40, cabins $80-120) This big place by the water is always busy; you won't get a site in January without booking well ahead.

EATING
Hesse St has some fine cafes and restaurants, and there are more choices in the historic hotels on Gellibrand St.

Queenscliff Fish & Chips (☎ 03-5258 1312; 77 Hesse St; fish & chips $6-10; 🕙 10am-9pm) If you're after something simple, this place does a brisk trade in fried seafood.

Café Gusto (☎ 03-5258 3604; 25 Hesse St; meals $8-20; 🕙 breakfast & lunch) The luxuriant herb garden out back is a fragrant place for a lingering breakfast or lunch. Fresh local produce is prepared with inventive flair.

Vue Grand Queenscliff (☎ 03-5258 1544; www .vuegrand.com.au; 46 Hesse St; cafe mains $10-30, restaurant mains $35-45) This historic hotel's dining room drips with sophistication from its elaborate chandeliers to a menu of pan-roasted barramundi or twice-baked soufflé. Life is more casual at the hotel's streetside Café Lure, which does more simple pastas, seafood, salads and burgers.

Apostle (☎ 03-5258 3097; 79 Hesse St; www.apos tlequeenscliff.com.au; mains $15-32) In a superbly renovated 19th-century church, complete with stained-glassed rose windows and high timber ceiling, Apostle is blessed with an innovative menu of fresh seafood and Mediterranean dishes. The side terrace is a lovely place for a lunch of mixed tasting plates.

Point Lonsdale
pop 2477

Marked by a **lighthouse**, little Lonnie sits on a golden scrape of sand that looks across to Queenscliff. The **Rip View lookout** is a good spot to ponder the township after a challenging walk. The ocean beach is legendary among skilled surfers. Hidden below the lighthouse is **Buckley's Cave**, where escaped convict William Buckley lived with the Wathaurong Aboriginal people for 32 years, creating a local legend that is remembered in the phrase 'Buckley's chance' (ie very little chance).

Point Lonsdale Guest House (☎ 03-5258 1142; www .pointlonsdaleguesthouse.com.au; 31 Point Lonsdale Rd; guest house $110-150, motel $130-240; 🔀), just below the lighthouse, is a two-storey 19th-century guest house with rooms ranging from basic motel to lavish B&B.

Barwon Heads
pop 3000

Where the Barwon River meets Bass Strait, Barwon Heads is a beautiful spot with sheltered river beaches; surfers flock 2km west to **Thirteenth Beach**, and golfers flock to the sublime Thirteenth Beach links course. The town was made famous by *Seachange*, a popular TV series about a city lawyer who moves to a small beach town to escape the rat race. There are short walks around the **Bluff** (with sea-view panoramas), and scuba-diving spots under the rocky ledges below. An old wooden bridge connects Barwon Heads with the larger community of Ocean Grove.

On the town's outskirts (follow the signs 2km from the town centre) is **Jirrahlinga Koala & Wildlife Sanctuary** (☎ 03-5254 2484; www .jirrahlinga.com.au; Taits Rd; adult/child/family $15/10/50; 🕙 9am-5pm), a sweet little animal park that includes pelicans, koalas, wombats and a few other Australian natives. It's also an animal hospital involved in wildlife rescue and shelter – check the website for volunteering opportunities.

Seahaven Village (☎ 03-5254 1066; www.sea havenvillage.com.au; 3 Geelong Rd; low season r midweek $135-235, weekends $195-315; 🔀) is a cluster of colourful self-contained studios and cottages decked out in individual nautical themes.

Sprawling along the foreshore, **Barwon Heads Caravan Park** (☎ 03-5254 1115; www.barwon coast.com.au; Ewing Blyth Dr; unpowered/powered sites $22/28, peak season $38/47, cabins $75-175) featured prominently in *Seachange;* it's hard to get into in the holiday season.

The best cafes and restaurants in town are easy to find along a short stretch of Hitchcock Ave. Try the chilled **Barwon Orange** (☎ 03-5254 1090; www.barwonorange.com.au; 60 Hitchcock Ave; mains $11-25; ☺ Wed-Sun) or **Annie's Provedore** (☎ 03-5254 3233; 2/50 Hitchcock Ave; meals $8-17; ☺ 8am-5pm), a cafe-deli that specialises in local gourmet goodies.

CALDER HIGHWAY

Running northwest from Melbourne to Bendigo there's a handful of sites off the Calder Hwy.

Organ Pipes National Park (☺ 8.30am-4.30pm Mon-Fri, 8.30am-6pm Sat & Sun) has some impressive vertical basalt columns that form a natural outdoor amphitheatre.

Just north of Gisborne, exit the highway for **Mt Macedon**, a 1010m-high extinct volcano that has several walking tracks. The scenic route up Mt Macedon Rd takes you past mansions with beautiful gardens and there's a cafe and picnic grounds near the summit.

Beyond the summit turn-off, the road heads to quaint **Woodend**, or take the signed road on the right to **Hanging Rock**, a sacred site of the Wurundjeri people. The rock was a refuge for bushrangers but attained fame with Joan Lindsay's novel *Picnic at Hanging Rock* (and the subsequent film directed by Peter Weir) about the mysterious disappearance of a group of schoolgirls. In Woodend, the excellent **Holgate Brewhouse** (☎ 03-5427 3522; www.holgatebrewhouse .com; 79 High St; d $125-175), at Keatings Hotel, is a good spot to sample a locally brewed beer or even stay the night in the refitted pub. Prices include breakfast and there are packages for brewery tours and tastings.

Daily trains run to Woodend from Melbourne. From there, **Woodend Taxi** (☎ 03-5427 2641) can take you to Hanging Rock for about $18.

THE YARRA VALLEY

An hour from Melbourne, the Yarra Valley is one of Victoria's premier wine regions and a superb area for walking and cycling. This was the worst-affected area in the 2009 Black Saturday bushfires – Marysville and Kinglake were virtually destroyed by fire, but residents have vowed to rebuild.

Healesville is the main town and best base to explore the Yarra Valley as it's central to many of the wineries and is the 'capital' of the Lower Yarra Valley; **Warburton** marks the centre of the Upper Yarra Valley.

There's some good walking in national parks in the area, including **Warrandyte State Park**, **Yarra Ranges National Park** and **Kinglake National Park**. Check at the visitors centres for brochures.

INFORMATION
Warburton Water Wheel Information Centre (☎ 03-5966 9600; www.warburtononline.com; 3400 Warburton Hwy, Warburton; ☺ 11am-3pm Mon-Fri, 11am-5pm Sat & Sun)

YARRA VALLEY WINERIES

The **Yarra Valley** (www.wineyarravalley.com) has more than 80 wineries scattered around its rolling hills, and it is recognised as Victoria's oldest wine region – the first vines were planted at Yering Station in 1838. The region produces cool-climate, food-friendly drops such as Chardonnay, Pinot Noir and Pinot Gris. A small percentage of vines were damaged in the February 2009 bushfires.

Of the many food and wine festivals in the region, our favourite is **Grape Grazing** (www.grape grazing.com.au) in February, celebrating the beginning of the grape harvest.

Most wineries offer cellar door sales and tastings from 10am to 5pm daily. Worth a visit:

TarraWarra Estate (☎ 03-5957 3510; www.tarrawarra.com.au; Healesville Rd, Yarra Glen) This striking building combines an art gallery and rowdy bistro for lunch.

Coldstream Hills (☎ 03-5964 9410; www.coldstreamhills.com.au; 31 Maddens Lane, Coldstream) Chardonnay, effusive Pinot Noir and velvety Merlot are the star picks.

Rochford (☎ 03-5962 2119; www.rochfordwines.com.au; cnr Maroondah Hwy & Hill Rd, Coldstream) Large winery with restaurant and gallery, plus fine Cabernet Sauvignon and Pinot Noir.

Yering Station (☎ 03-9730 0100; www.yering.com; 38 Melba Hwy, Yering) A massive, modern complex with a fine-dining restaurant, produce store and bar; it's home to the heady Shiraz-Viognier blend and a sparkling white wine, as well as Pinot Noir, Rosé and Chardonnay. The Yarra Valley Farmers' Market is held here every third Sunday.

Yarra Valley visitor information centre (☎ 03-5962 2600; www.visityarravalley.com.au; Harker St, Healesville; ♥ 9am-5pm)

TOURS
Eco Adventure Tours (☎ 03-5962 5115; www.ecoadventuretours.com.au; adult/child $25/18) Nocturnal spotlighting walks in the Healesville and Yarra Valley area.
Yarra Valley Winery Tours (☎ 03-5962 3870; www.yarravalleywinerytours.com.au; tours $90-100) Tastings at five wineries and lunch.

GETTING THERE & AWAY
Suburban trains go as far as Lilydale (use a Zone 1 and 2 Metcard). From Lilydale station, **McKenzie's Bus Lines** (☎ 03-5962 5088; www.mckenzies.com.au) runs bus 685 to Healesville and Yarra Glen (some services continue to Healesville Sanctuary). **Martyrs** (☎ 03-5966 2035; www.martyrs.com.au) buses run to Yarra Junction and Warburton.

Healesville
pop 7355
Beloved of day-trippers and weekenders from the city, Healesville is the gateway to the Yarra Valley wineries, Yarra Ranges forest drive and north to the High Country.

One of the best places to see Australian native fauna is the **Healesville Sanctuary** (☎ 03-5957 2800; www.zoo.org.au; Badger Creek Rd, Healesville; adult/child/family $24/12/54; ♥ 9am-5pm), a wildlife park set in native bushland. The Platypus House is a top spot to see these shy creatures underwater, and you'll see koalas, kangaroos and Tasmanian devils, but the real star is the exciting **Birds of Prey** (♥ show noon & 2pm) display where predatory birds swoop, dive and attack. A number of injured or homeless animals from the 2009 bushfires were brought here for shelter.

SLEEPING, EATING & DRINKING
Healesville is the main accommodation centre for the region, though there are B&Bs scattered around the valley and many of the wineries have accommodation.
Strathvea (☎ 03-5962 4109; www.strathvea.com.au; Myers Creek Rd, Healesville; B&B $140-180) The 10 rooms at this popular heritage B&B book out well in advance for their gourmet breakfasts and tranquil gardens.
Giant Steps (☎ 1800 661 624; 336 Maroondah Hwy; mains $18-25; ♥ 10am-10pm Mon-Fri, 8am-10pm Sat & Sun) In town, the enormous boxlike Giant Steps

and Innocent Bystander winery is a great place for lunch, pizza, a lazy afternoon drink or spot of wine tasting.
Healesville Hotel (☎ 03-5962 4002; www.healesvillehotel.com.au; 256 Maroondah Hwy, Healesville; d Mon-Thu $100, Fri & Sun $130, Sat $315 with dinner; ♥ lunch & dinner) This popular foody pub does fine dining (cafe mains $8 to $16, dinner mains $24 to $30) and has an expansive beer garden to while away the afternoon. The accommodation upstairs can be noisy on busy weekends.

THE DANDENONGS
On a clear day, the Dandenong Ranges and their highest peak, Mt Dandenong (633m), can be seen from Melbourne. The landscape is a patchwork of exotics and natives with a lush understorey of tree ferns – it's the most accessible bushwalking in Melbourne's backyard.

Dandenong Ranges & Knox visitor information centre (☎ 03-9758 7522; www.dandenongrangestourism.com.au; 1211 Burwood Hwy, Upper Ferntree Gully; ♥ 9am-5pm) is outside Upper Ferntree Gully train station.

Puffing Billy (☎ 03-9754 6800; www.puffingbilly.com.au; Old Monbulk Rd, Belgrave; adult/child/family return $51/26/103) is an immensely popular steam train that snakes through lush fern gullies and bush while kids dangle arms and legs out the window. There are up to six departures between Belgrave and Gembrook during holidays, and three or four on other days; you can also ride shorter sections of line or travel one way.

Dandenong Ranges National Park, a combination of five parks, offers short walks and four-hour trails. **Sherbrooke Forest** has a towering cover of mountain ash trees. Reach the start of its eastern loop walk (10km, three hours), just 1km or so from Belgrave station, by walking to the end of Old Monbulk Rd past Puffing Billy's station. Combining this walk with a ride on *Puffing Billy* makes a great day out. Opposite the Alfred Nicholas Memorial Gardens is a **picnic ground** where crimson rosellas will peck birdseed from your hand. Walks at **Ferntree Gully National Park**, home to large numbers of lyrebirds, are 10 minutes' walk from Upper Ferntree Gully station.

William Ricketts Sanctuary (☎ 13 19 63; www.parkweb.vic.gov.au; Mt Dandenong Tourist Rd, Mt Dandenong; adult/child/family $7/5/17; ♥ 10am-4.30pm, closed on total fire ban days) features sculptures blended beautifully with damp fern gardens. Ricketts'

BLACK SATURDAY

Victoria is no stranger to bushfires. In 1939 71 people died in the Black Friday fires; in 1983 Ash Wednesday claimed 75 lives in Victoria and South Australia. But no one was prepared for the utter devastation of the 2009 bushfires that became known as Black Saturday.

On 7 February, following unprecedented heatwave temperatures in January and early February, Victoria recorded its hottest temperature on record with Melbourne exceeding 46°C and some parts of the state topping 48°C. Strong winds and tinder-dry undergrowth from years of drought meant extreme fire danger. The first recorded fires began near Kilmore and strong winds from a southerly change fanned flames towards the Yarra Ranges. Within a few devastating hours a ferocious firestorm engulfed the tiny bush towns of Marysville, Kinglake, Strathewen, Flowerdale and Narbethong, while separate fires started at Horsham, Bendigo and an area southeast of Beechworth. The fires virtually razed the towns of Marysville and Kinglake and hit so fast that many residents had no chance of escape. Many fire victims died in their homes or trapped in their cars while trying to escape, some blocked by trees fallen across the road.

Fires raged across the state for more than a month, with high temperatures, winds and practically no rainfall making it impossible for fire crews to contain the worst blazes. New fires began at Wilson's Promontory National Park (burning more than 50% of the park area), the Dandenong Ranges and the Daylesford area.

The statistics tell a tragic tale: 173 people dead (revised down from an early figure of over 200); more than 2000 homes destroyed, and an estimated 7500 people left homeless; and more than 4500 sq km burned out. What followed from the shell-shocked state and nation was a huge outpouring of grief, humanitarian aid and charity. Strangers donated tonnes of clothing, toys, food, caravans and even houses to bushfire survivors, while an appeal set up by the Australian Red Cross raised more than $300 million. Old rockers came out of retirement for a concert that filled the Melbourne Cricket Ground, celebrities appeared on televised charity appeals and major sporting events directed proceeds towards the appeal.

Firefighters from the Country Fire Authority (CFA) and Department of Sustainability & Environment (DSE) were hailed as heroes after weeks of tirelessly battling blazes and pictures of CFA volunteer David Tree giving water to a distressed koala were flashed around the globe. Hundreds of native animals, injured or left homeless, were given care and food at wildlife centres around the state. Not all of the human players were heroes. Suspected looting of fire-ravaged towns and news that some of the fires had been deliberately lit compounded the grief and anger.

A Royal Commission was established by the state government to investigate bushfire strategy and ensure lessons are learned from Black Saturday. Many residents of worst-hit towns such as Marysville and Kinglake have vowed to rebuild and be better prepared. Nature takes care of its own regeneration, but the memories of Black Saturday will never be forgotten.

work was inspired by nature and the years he spent living with Aboriginal people. Bus 688 runs here from Croydon train station.

Getting There & Away

The Met's suburban trains run on the Belgrave line to the foothills of the Dandenongs (Zone 1 and 2 Metcard). From Upper Ferntree Gully train station it's a 10-minute walk to the start of the Ferntree Gully section of the national park.

MORNINGTON PENINSULA

Ever since paddle steamers plied their way here in the 1870s, Melburnians have been heading south for this bustling summer sea-side destination. Once you leave Melbourne's urban sprawl behind at Frankston, the highway passes bayside towns such as Mt Martha, Dromana and Rosebud, but the most beautiful part is the very tip around Sorrento and Portsea and along the hilly southern surf coast around Cape Schanck and Flinders.

GETTING THERE & AROUND

Met trains run frequently from Flinders St station to Frankston train station, where the **Portsea Passenger Service** (☎ 03-5986 5666; www .grenda.com.au) runs bus 788 to/from Portsea ($5, 90 minutes). **Peninsula Bus Lines** (☎ 03-9786 7088) runs buses 782 and 783 to Flinders from Frankston train station.

VICTORIA

Car & Passenger Ferries (☎ 03-5258 3244; www
.searoad.com.au; one way adult/child $10/8, car from
$55; ☉ hourly 7am-6pm) runs daily between
Sorrento and Queenscliff. **Inter Island Ferries**
(☎ 03-9585 5730; www.interislandferries.com.au; return adult/child/bike $21/10/8) runs the triangle
between Stony Point, Cowes (on Phillip
Island) and Tankerton on French Island
for foot passengers and bicycles only. There
are at least two trips daily year-round. You
can reach Stony Point by Metlink train
from Frankston.

Sorrento
pop 1530

Victoria's first official European settlement
in 1803, Sorrento's main street is lined with
historic sandstone buildings – including
three iconic pubs – that take on a glorious warm glow in the late afternoon sun.
This is a hugely popular summer resort and
playground for Melbourne's wealthy elite.
During low tide, the **rock pool** at the back
beach is a safe spot for adults and children to
swim and snorkel, and throughout the year
you can take tours swimming with dolphins
and seals here.

Sorrento Visitor Information Centre (☎ 03-5984
1478; cnr George St & Ocean Beach Rd) is in the small
hut on the main street.

TOURS

From the visitor centre there are two-hour
walking tours (☎ 03-5984 4484; per person $30)
through historic Sorrento and along the
clifftop 'Millionaires' Walk'.

A couple of outfits offer excellent tours
swimming and snorkelling with seals and dolphins in the bay, departing from Sorrento
Pier. If you don't want to swim you can pay
less and stay aboard the boat.

Moonraker Charters (☎ 03-5984 4211; www
.moonrakercharters.com.au; adult/child sightseeing $49/39,
swimming $105/95; ☉ tours 9am & 1pm Oct-Apr)

Polperro Dolphin Swims (☎ 03-5988 8437; www
.polperro.com.au; adult/child sightseeing $55/30, swim-
ming $115; ☉ tours 8.30am & 1.30pm Oct-Apr)

SLEEPING

Prices rise with the temperature from mid-
December to the end of January, and during
Easter and school holidays when places rou-
tinely book out.

Sorrento Beach House YHA (☎ 03-5984 4323; www
.yha.com.au; 3 Miranda St; dm $30, d with/without en suite

$90/80; ☐) Buried in a bushy setting but an
easy walk to town and the beach, this hostel has the cosy feel of a family home even
though it's purpose built, and has a great
communal barbecue.

Sorrento Beach Motel (☎ 03-5984 1356; www.sorren
tobeachmotel.com.au; 780 Melbourne Rd; d $100-160, with spa
$175-215; ☐) The brightly coloured beach-box
units at this motel are a cut above most. There
are standard rooms, spacious spa rooms and
wi-fi throughout.

Whitehall Guesthouse & Oceanic Apartments
(☎ 03-5984 4166; www.oceanicgroup.com.au; 231 Ocean
Beach Rd; d $120-230, apt $210-230) The limestone,
two-storey guest house near the back beach
has dreamy views from its timber veranda,
though most rooms are small and old-style
with share bathrooms down the hall – the en
suite rooms are much roomier. Across the
road, Oceanic Apartments ditch the period
charm with spruce self-contained studios and
spa units.

Sorrento Foreshore Reserve (☎ 03-5986 8286;
Nepean Hwy; unpowered/powered sites $20/26, high sea-
son $28/35) This shire campground is wedged
between the beach and the main road into
Sorrento with hilly, bushclad sites.

EATING & DRINKING

Stringer's (☎ 03-5984 2010; 2 Ocean Beach Rd; sandwiches & snacks $4-9; ☉ breakfast & lunch) Stringer's
is a Sorrento institution with its little corner cafe serving house-made meals and
Mornington wines for sale in the attached
grocery shop.

our pick Just Fine Food (☎ 03-5984 4666; 23 Ocean
Beach Rd; mains $7-23; ☉ 9am-5pm Mon-Fri, 9am-6pm Sat)
Famous for its sublime fluffy vanilla slices
(recipe: top secret), this cafe and deli is a
top place for all-day breakfast and lunch of
open sandwiches, focaccia, antipasto and
gourmet pies.

Baths (☎ 03-5984 1500; 3278 Point Nepean Rd; mains
$20-30) The waterfront deck of the former sea
baths is the perfect spot for breakfast, lunch
or a romantic sunset dinner overlooking the
jetty and the Queenscliff ferry. The menu
has some good seafood choices and there's a
takeaway fish and chipper at the front.

Three Palms (☎ 03-5984 1057; www.threepalms
.com.au; 154-164 Ocean Beach Rd; mains $23-32; ☉ dinner
Wed-Sun, lunch Sat & Sun, daily in summer) Framed by
the namesake palms, this relaxed main street
bar and restaurant has a rocking side terrace
with a 'sarongs and thongs' ambience. The

menu is Asian fusion – ocean trout sashimi or King Island beef fillet with lemon grass panacotta to follow.

Portsea
pop 654

Wee Portsea is where Melbourne's wealthiest have gotten away from it all by building beachside mansions. Head over to the **back beach** for ocean surf – if swimming here stick between the flags. You can walk the Farnsworth Track (1.5km, 30 minutes) out to scenic **London Bridge**, a natural rock formation, and spot middens of the Boonwurrung people who once called this area home. **Front beaches** offer sheltered swimming.

Dive Victoria (☎ 03-5984 3155; www.divevictoria.com.au; 3752 Point Nepean Rd; snorkelling $60, s/d dive with gear $120/185) runs diving and snorkelling trips.

Bay Play (☎ 03-5984 0888; www.bayplay.com.au; 3755 Pt Nepean Rd) does diving and snorkelling trips and dolphin swims, as well as sea-kayaking tours (adult/child $88/55). Also rents out kayaks.

Portsea's pulse is the sprawling, half-timber **Portsea Hotel** (☎ 03-5984 2213; www.portseahotel.com.au; Point Nepean Rd; s/d from $65/110, with en suite from $125/160), an enormous pub with a great lawn and terrace area looking out over the bay. There's an excellent Mod Oz bistro (mains $18 to $34) and old-style accommodation (most rooms have shared bathroom) that increases in price based on sea views (weekend rates are higher).

Point Nepean National Park

The peninsula's tip is marked by the stunning **Point Nepean National Park** (☎ 13 19 63; www.parkweb.vic.gov.au; Point Nepean Rd, Portsea; ◷ 9am-5pm, 9am-dusk Jan), originally a quarantine station and army base. A large section of the park is a former range area and still out of bounds due to unexploded ordnance, but there's plenty to see here and long stretches of traffic-free road that make for excellent cycling. There are also plenty of **walking trails** throughout the park and at the tip is **Fort Nepean**, which was important in Australian defence from the 1880s to 1945.

Point Nepean visitor information centre (☎ 03-5984 4276; Point Nepean; adult/child/family walk or bicycle admission $8/4/20, one-way transport incl admission $11/6/26, return transport incl admission $17/10/43, bike hire per 3hr $15; ◷ 9am-6pm Jan, 9am-5pm Feb-Apr & Oct-Dec, 10am-

5pm May-Sep) will give you the low-down on the park. You can walk or cycle to the point (12km return), or take the Point Explorer, a hop-on, hop-off bus service.

Mornington Peninsula National Park

Stretching from Portsea on the sliver of coastline to Cape Schanck and inland to the Greens Bush area, this national park boasts beautiful rugged **ocean beaches**. It's possible to walk all the way from Portsea to Cape Schanck (26km, eight hours). However, swimming is dangerous at these beaches so it's advisable to keep to the lifeguard-patrolled areas at Gunnamatta and Portsea during summer.

Cape Schanck Lightstation (☎ 0500-527 891; www.austpacinns.com.au; adult/child/family lighthouse tours $14/11/38; ◷ 10am-4pm), built in 1859, is a photogenic working limestone lighthouse, with a kiosk, museum, information centre and regular guided tours. You can stay in the old lightkeeper's cottages for $150 a night.

FRENCH ISLAND
pop 89

Exposed and windswept, French Island is two-thirds national park and it retains a wonderful sense of tranquillity – you can only get here by passenger ferry so it's virtually traffic-free. The main attractions are **bushwalks**, which take in wetlands in one of Australia's largest **koala colonies**, as well as a huge variety of birds and over a hundred varieties of orchids.

Notable walks include the **Coast Wetlands Walk** (5½ hours, 14km) and **South Coast Walk** (4½ hours return, 10km), which both start and finish at Tankerton Jetty. If you bring a bike try the **Wetlands Coastal Bike Ride**, a 23km circuit that needs a good mountain bike.

The ferry docks at Tankerton, from where it's around 1km to the licensed **French Island General Store** (☎ 03-5980 1209; Lot 1, Tankerton Rd, Tankerton; bike hire half-day $30), which also serves as post office, tourist information and bike-hire centre.

TOURS

French Island Eco Tours (☎ 1300 307 054; www.frenchislandecotours.com.au; half-/full-day tour incl ferry & lunch $40/80; ◷ Thu & Sun) is one of the best ways to see the island without your own transport. Tours around the island explore McLeod Eco Farm, a former prison. Tours depart from Stony Point and Cowes.

SLEEPING & EATING
Tortoise Head Lodge (☎ 03-5980 1234; www.tortoise head.net; 10 Tankerton Rd, Tankerton; budget s/d $55/85, s/d cabins incl breakfast $80/120) A stroll from the ferry, this spot has knockout water views and is brilliant value. The cafe is open from 9.30am to 5pm daily, and does Devonshire teas and sandwiches if you're after a snack ($4 to $8).

McLeod Eco Farm (☎ 03-5980 1224; www.mcleodeco farm.com; McLeod Rd; bunk room d/q $65/110, guest house d $98) Formerly the island's prison, this organic farm offers basic bunkrooms in atmospheric old cells with kitchen facilities and lounge, but if you're after something more upmarket the guest house rooms (former officers' quarters) are cosy and include breakfast. All have shared bathrooms.

Fairhaven camping ground (☎ 03-5980 1294; www .parkweb.vic.gov.au; unpowered sites free) On the western shore where the wetlands meet the ocean, this camping ground offers a real getaway experience with little more than a compost toilet at the site. Fires aren't allowed and you must carry everything in and out. Bookings are essential.

GETTING THERE & AROUND
Inter Island Ferries (☎ 03-9585 5730; www.interisland ferries.com.au; adult/child/bike return $20/10/8) runs a service between Tankerton and Stony Point (10 minutes, at least two daily). You can reach Stony Point directly from Frankston on a Metlink train.

Unsealed roads on the island make riding tough going, but you can hire bikes ($30 per day) from the kiosk at the jetty in summer and from the general store.

PHILLIP ISLAND
pop 6700
Penguins and petrol heads have made Phillip Island what it is today. This small island was originally settled by the Boonwurrung people, who are probably the only people in history not to have attended the island's penguin parade. Instead they came for the diet of seafood and short-tailed shearwaters, both of which can still be seen from the island.

Of course, most tourists come to see those cute little penguins waddle up the beach to their burrows in the dunes every night, but the island is ruggedly handsome and has plenty to offer, including seal colonies and wild surf beaches.

The island also revs up for the Motorcycle Grand Prix; it's also a popular summer getaway, when the population more than quadruples. The main town is Cowes on the north coast, and there are small communities at Rhyll, Woolamai and Newhaven.

Information
Cowes Visitor Centre (☎ 03-5956 7447; 9197 Thompson Ave; ☼ 9am-5pm)
Phillip Island visitor information centre (☎ 1300 366 422; www.visitphillipisland.com; Phillip Island Rd, Newhaven; ☼ 9am-5pm, 9am-6pm Jan; ▯) Offers information, sells tickets to most individual attractions and has internet access.

Sights & Activities
PHILLIP ISLAND NATURE PARKS
The nature parks are three of the island's biggest attractions: the **Penguin Parade** (☎ 03-5951 2800; www.penguins.org.au; Summerland Beach; adult/child/family $20/10/50; ☼ 10am-dusk); the **Koala Conservation Centre** (☎ 03-5952 1307; adult/child/family $10/5/25; ☼ 10am-5pm, extended hr in summer), off Phillip Island Rd, with elevated boardwalks; and trips to **Churchill Island** (☎ 03-5956 7214; adult/child/family $10/5/25; ☼ 10am-4.30pm, extended hr in summer), a working farm also off Phillip Island Rd, where Victoria's first crops were planted that today features historic displays, including butter churning and blacksmithing (call ahead for times).

If you're keen on all three attractions buy the **Three Parks Pass** (adult/child/family $34/17/85), which is valid for six months (you can only visit the Penguin Parade once though) and is available at the visitors centre.

Most people come for the **Little Penguins**, the world's smallest and probably cutest of their kind. The penguin complex includes concrete amphitheatres that hold up to 3800 spectators who visit to see the little fellas just after sunset as they waddle from the sea to their land-based nests. Penguin numbers swell in summer, after breeding, but they parade year-round. You usually get a closer view from the boardwalks as they search for their burrows and mates. Bring warm clothing. There are a variety of specialised **tours** (adult $35-70) so you can be accompanied by rangers or see them from the vantage of a Skybox (an elevated platform). Be sure to book well in advance in summer.

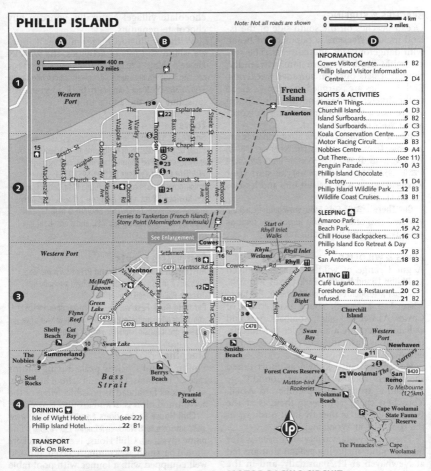

SEAL ROCKS & THE NOBBIES

The extreme southwestern tip of Phillip Island leads to the Nobbies and beyond them is **Seal Rocks**, inhabited by Australia's largest colony of fur seals. The **Nobbies Centre** (☎ 03-5951 2816; admission free; tours adult/child \$10/5; ☽ 10am-8pm summer, 10am-5pm autumn, 10am-4pm winter; 10am-6pm spring) is a sort of gigantic cafe and souvenir shop with an interpretive centre tacked on, but there are some great interactive panels and games, and the huge windows afford great views of the 6000 Australian fur seals who loll here during the October–December breeding season. You can view the seals from boardwalks or use the centre's underwater cameras to zoom in on them (\$5).

MOTOR RACING CIRCUIT

Even when the motorbikes aren't racing, petrolheads love the **Motor Racing Circuit** (☎ 03-5952 9400; www.phillipislandcircuit.com.au; Back Beach Rd; ☽ 8.30am-5.30pm Mon-Fri), which was souped up for the Australian Motorcycle Grand Prix in 1989, although the island hosted its first Grand Prix way back in 1928. The **visitor centre** (☎ 03-5952 9400; ☽ 9am-6pm) runs 45-minute **guided circuit tours** (adult/child/family \$19/10/44; ☽ tours 11am & 2pm), which include a visit to the History of Motorsport Museum, as well the chance to cut laps of the track in hotted-up V8s (one/two/three people \$210/315/365, booking essential). There's also a **go kart track** (per 10/20/30min \$28/50/65).

VICTORIA

BEACHES & SURFING

Ocean beaches on the south side of the island include **Woolamai**, a popular surf beach with dangerous rips and currents. The surf at **Smiths Beach** is more family-friendly, though it gets busy on summer weekends. Both beaches are patrolled in summer. Head to the quieter, sheltered northern beaches if you're not a strong swimmer or you worry about your kids in the surf.

Island Surfboards (www.islandsurfboards.com.au; surfing lessons $55, surfboard hire per hr/day $13/40) Smiths Beach (☎ 03-5952 3443; 65 Smiths Beach Rd); Cowes (☎ 03-5952 2578; 147 Thompson Ave) can start your waxhead career with wetsuit hire and lessons for all standards.

Out There (☎ 03-5956 6450; www.outthere.net.au; Newhaven) also offers surfing lessons as well as sea-kayaking and mountain-biking.

BIRDS & WILDLIFE

A good range of wildlife can be spotted at **Phillip Island Wildlife Park** (☎ 03-5952 2038; Thompson Ave; adult/child/family $15/8/40; ☽ 10am-5.30pm, later in summer), about 1km south of Cowes. As well as koalas, wombats, roos and wallabies there are a few harder to find critters such as Tasmanian devils, cassowaries and quolls.

Mutton birds, also known as short-tailed shearwaters, colonise the dunes around Cape Woolamai from late September to April. Your best chance of seeing them is at the Penguin Parade as they fly in at dusk, or at the rookeries at Woolamai Beach.

There's a wide variety of other water birds around, including **pelicans** that are fed at Newhaven at 11.30am daily, and in the swampland at **Rhyll Inlet** and **Rhyll Wetland**. There's a boardwalk and lookout here, and the **Oswin Roberts Walking Track** (two hours) takes you through the most important bird-watching areas.

OTHER ATTRACTIONS

Like Willy Wonka's famous factory, the **Phillip Island Chocolate Factory** (☎ 03-5956 6600; www.phillipislandchocolatefactory.com.au; 930 Phillip Island Rd, Newhaven; tours adult/child/family $12/8/36; ☽ 9am-5pm) has a few surprises. As well as free samples of handmade Belgian chocolate, there's a walk-through tour of the chocolate-making process, including a remarkable gallery of chocolate sculptures, from Michelangelo's *David* to an entire model

chocolate village! Naturally, you can buy chocolate penguins.

With an illusion maze, mini-golf, puzzle island and lots of activities, the whacky **Amaze'n Things** (☎ 03-5952 2283; www.amazenthings.com.au; 1805 Phillip Island Rd, Cowes; adult/child/family $29/20/88; ☽ 10am-6pm) fun park is great for kids, but gets the adults in, too.

Tours

Go West (☎ 1300 736 551; www.gowest.com.au; tour $109) One-day tour from Melbourne that includes lunch, entry fees and iPod commentary in several languages.

Wildlife Coast Cruises (☎ 03-5952 3501; www.wildlifecoastcruises.com.au; Rotunda Bldg, Jetty, Cowes; ☽ Nov-May) Runs a two-hour cruise from Cowes jetty around Seal Rocks (adult/child $60/40), a half-day cruise and tour of French Island ($65/45) and a one-hour bay cruise ($25/16).

Festivals & Events

Australian Motorcycle Grand Prix (www.motogp.com.au) A massive three-day event held annually in October. Phillip Island goes off!

Pyramid Rock Festival (www.thepyramidrockfestival.com) This huge music festival held over New Year's Eve attracts great Aussie bands to a scenic venue.

Sleeping

Phillip Island's prices peak during motor races, Christmas, Easter and school holidays, so book as far ahead as possible. Most of the accommodation is in and around Cowes.

Chill House Backpackers (☎ 0431 413 275; www.chillhouse.com.au; 8 Watchorn Rd; dm/d $30/70; ☐) The name says it all. Chill House is as backpackers should be: small, welcoming, relaxed, fun and well equipped with a lounge with pool table and two kitchens. It's down a side street off Settlement Rd.

San Antone (☎ 03-5952 1961; 181 Thompson Ave; dm $30, d $100-160) Quirky doesn't begin to describe these Wild West–inspired cottages, recycled sculpture garden, junk yard and the owner who built it all. The two colourful self-contained units are wonderfully decorated and super value, and there's a bunk room in a converted shed.

Phillip Island Eco Retreat & Day Spa (☎ 03-5952 6466; 181-189 Justice Rd, Cowes; d from $145; ☒) Sleep guilt-free in these two cosy spa cottages made from recycled materials and using solar water and sustainable principles. They're part of an excellent day spa with exotic treatments from $70 to $140.

There are plenty of caravan parks, mostly around Cowes, but they fill up fast in summer. Sites range from $25 to $38. **Beach Park** (☎ 03-5952 2113; www.beachpark.com.au; 2 McKenzie Rd, Cowes; powered sites $32, cabins $85-120; ☒) is a small beachfront park close to the town centre.

Also recommended:

Amaroo Park (☎ 03-5952 2548; www.amaroopark .com; 97 Church St; powered sites $35, dm $30-35, cabins $135-225; ☒) A few backpacker beds as well as deluxe cabins.

Eating & Drinking

Most dining options are in Cowes, but Rhyll has a great little waterfront dining strip and there are cafes at most of the island's tourist attractions. Cowes has two pubs – the Isle of Wight and the refurbished Phillip Island Hotel – that look out across the water and serve the usual pub fare.

Café Lugano (☎ 03-5952 5636; 71 Thompson Ave, Cowes; mains $8-17; ☣ breakfast & lunch) This cool hole-in-the-wall joint is the place to come for good coffee, or healthy lunch of focaccia, rice burger or felafel salad.

our pick **Infused** (☎ 03-5952 2665; 115 Thompson Ave; mains $17-30; ☣ lunch & dinner Wed-Mon) Locals rate the food at this slick lime-green restaurant-bar as the best on the island, and we agree. With an innovative menu – gourmet sausages, massaman curry, poached duck leg – together with a killer wine list and energetic staff, it's well worth the short walk back from the Esplanade.

Foreshore Bar & Restaurant (☎ 03-5956 9520; 11 Beach Rd, Rhyll; mains $18-34; ☣ lunch & dinner) The water views from the timber deck of this classy village pub and restaurant complement your lunchtime fish and chips or bowl of mussels. The evening has a relaxed fine-dining feel – try the juicy Phillip Island rib eye.

Getting There & Around

The best service from Melbourne to Cowes is the direct **V/Line** (☎ 13 61 96) bus departing at 3.50pm from Southern Cross Station, Monday to Friday ($11, 3½ hours).

Inter Island Ferries (☎ 03-9585 5730; www.in terislandferries.com.au; adult/child/bike return $21/10/8) runs daily between the triangle of Cowes, Stony Point (on the Mornington Peninsula) and French Island. There are at least two trips daily year-round. Foot passengers and bicycles only.

There's no public transport around Phillip Island. You can hire bicycles from **Ride On Bikes** (☎ 03-5952 2533; www.rideonbikes.com.au; 85-87 Thompson Ave, Cowes; per hr/half/full day $15/25/35).

GREAT OCEAN ROAD

Australia's most famous stretch of road winds its way almost 250km from Torquay to Warrnambool, and for once it lives up to the hype. The famous rock stacks known as the Twelve Apostles are only part of the story as you pass dramatic views of the wild coastline, classic surf beaches and seaside towns, much of it backed by lush temperate rainforest. Wind down the windows and you'll cop a unique perfume of bush and beach, gums and saltwater.

Beyond Apollo Bay, the thrashing Shipwreck Coast (from Princetown to Port Fairy) inspires spooky stories of ghosts from the bones of wrecked vessels that haunt the area. The lush Otway Ranges, stretching from Aireys Inlet to Cape Otway, offer revitalising landscapes for bushwalking and camping – most of the coastal section is now incorporated into the Great Otway National Park.

Some travellers try to do the Great Ocean Road in a day or two, but it's much better to slow the pace down and plan a few overnight stops – going for a bushwalk, a swim or koala spotting is more rewarding than the drive itself.

Getting There & Away

Interstate visitors coming from Adelaide, Brisbane or Sydney can fly into Avalon Airport, 22km from Geelong, with **Jetstar** (☎ 13 15 38; www.jetstar.com.au) and take the door-to-door **Avalon Airport Shuttle** (☎ 03-5278 8788; www.avalonairportshuttle.com.au) along the Great Ocean Road as far as Lorne.

V/Line (☎ 13 61 96; www.vline.com.au) trains from Melbourne's Southern Cross Station travel to Geelong and then connect with V/Line buses that cruise along the Great Ocean Road as far as Apollo Bay ($21), via Torquay ($9), Anglesea ($12) and Lorne ($17), four times daily Monday to Friday, and twice daily Saturday and Sunday. On Friday (and Monday during Christmas holidays), a V/Line bus continues around the coast from Apollo Bay to Port Campbell and Warrnambool.

GREAT OCEAN ROAD & SOUTHWEST COAST

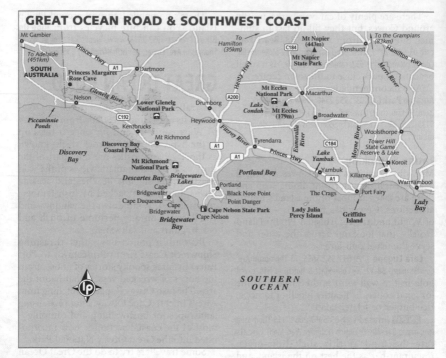

McHarry's Bus Lines (☎ 03-5223 2111; www.mcharrys .com.au) has frequent services from Geelong to Torquay ($4), Lorne ($9) and Anglesea ($5).

Tours

Several tour companies will take you out on the Great Ocean Road, many leaving from Melbourne.

Go West Tours (☎ 1300 736 551; www.gowest.com .au) Takes trips along the Great Ocean Road and to Phillip Island. Full-day Great Ocean Road tour is $105.

Groovy Grape (☎ 1800 66 11 77; www.groovygrape .com.au) Three-day Great Ocean Road and Grampians trips between Melbourne and Adelaide ($345).

Ride Tours (☎ 1800 605 120; www.ridetours.com.au; ☾ Mon, Thu & Sat) Two-day bus tours in summer for $165.

Wayward Bus (☎ 1300 653 510; www.waywardbus .com.au) Follows the southwest coast to South Australia (SA) as part of its Melbourne to Adelaide trip; you can do stopovers, too. Three-day Melbourne–Adelaide is $395.

TORQUAY
pop 9850

Victoria's undisputed surf capital heaves under the weight of surf shops and surf gear factory outlets – this is the spiritual home of

Rip Curl, but all the major names are represented here in a sort of mall for wave-lovers. Many surfers make this a first pit stop – it's a good place to stock up on gear before taking on the waves further along the road. Naturally, Torquay has some lovely beaches and surf breaks close to the busy little town centre.

Torquay visitor information centre (☎ 1300 614 219; www.greatoceanroad.org/surfcoast; Surf World, Beach Rd; ☾ 9am-5pm; ☐) is tucked in behind the main plaza and has internet access for $7 an hour.

Sights & Activities

Next to the visitor centre, **Surfworld Australia Surfing Museum** (☎ 03-5261 4606; adult/child/family $9/6/20; ☾ 9am-5pm) is a must for would-be waxheads with boards through the ages, a board-shaping workshop and plenty of footage of mountainous waves.

Torquay revolves around gorgeous local beaches: **Fisherman's Beach**, protected from ocean swells, and **Front Beach**, ringed by shady pines and sloping lawns, are ideal for families. Surf lifesavers patrol the frothing **Back**

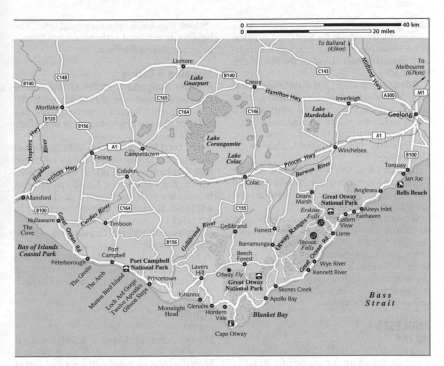

Beach during summer. **Bells Beach**, 7km southwest of Torquay, is legendary among surfers the world over for its powerful break and hosts a world-championship surfing contest every Easter.

Tiger Moth World Adventure Park (☎ 03-5261 5100; www.tigermothworld.com; 325 Blackgate Rd; adult/child under 4 $10/free; ⏰ 10am-5pm), 5km northeast of Torquay, is a giant play park with paddle boats, minigolf and daily air shows. You can also take a joy flight in a vintage aircraft (from $130).

There are plenty of opportunities in Torquay to learn to surf, hire gear and get involved in other adventure activities such as snorkelling and kayaking.

Go Ride a Wave (☎ 1300 132 441; www.gorideawave .com.au; Bell St; 2hr lessons incl hire $70, 2hr hire from $25) Hires surfing gear, sells secondhand equipment and offers lessons (cheaper with advance booking).

Southern Exposure (☎ 03-5261 9170; www.south ernexposure.com.au; 38 Bell St; lessons $55) Surfing, mountain biking and kayaking.

Torquay Surfing Academy (☎ 03-5261 2022; www .torquaysurf.com.au; 2/32 Bell St; group/private lessons $55/110) Serious surf school.

Westcoast Surf School (☎ 03-5261 2241; http://west coast.customer.netspace.net.au; lessons $55) Also offers surfing lessons, snorkelling, kayaking and rock-climbing.

Sleeping

Summer and Easter are peak times for Torquay so book well ahead, even for campsites. **Torquay Holiday Rentals** (☎ 03-5261 5579; www.torquayholidays.com.au) can help find accommodation.

Bells Beach Lodge (☎ 03-5261 7070; www .bellsbeachlodge.com.au; 51-53 Surfcoast Hwy; dm $35, d with/without en suite $95/85; 🖵) This super-chilled two-storey house faces the highway, but it's a great spot to stow your gear and catch the curl or meet like-minded souls in the backyard barbecue area. You can hire surf gear ($25) and bikes ($20) here.

Mossop's Beach Shack (☎ 0422 989 837; 21 Zeally Bay Rd; d low/high season from $80/140) Colourful self-contained beach houses close to town.

Torquay Foreshore Caravan Park (☎ 03-5261 2496; 35 Bell St; powered sites 1/2 people $15/30, cabins $75-130) Just behind Back Beach, this sprawling caravan park is the best place to pitch a tent or park a camper.

VICTORIA

Eating

There are a few cafes in the Surf City Complex, but a better place to look is across the highway around Gilbert St and on the beachfront Esplanade.

Café Moby (☎ 03-5261 2339, 41 the Esplanade; meals $5-15; ☽ breakfast & lunch) Hidden behind a sunny garden terrace, this colourful weatherboard house welcomes you with homecooked food with an international flavour – Indonesian, Vietnamese, lamb souvlaki and pasta. Great vibe.

Sandbah (☎ 03-5261 6414; 21 Gilbert St; mains $8-17; ☽ lunch & dinner) Popular hole-in-the-wall cafe serving great caffeine fixes, breakfast and toasted sandwiches.

Growlers (☎ 03-5264 8455; www.growlers.com.au; 23 the Esplanade; mains $15-32) The beach aspect and shaded verandah pulls in the punters and the innovative menu – strong on seafood – keeps them coming back. Try the seafood bisque or the tempura soft-shell crabs. A courtesy bus will pick you up and take you home, so you can give the bar a nudge.

ANGLESEA
pop 2290

This sweet little seaside village has long been a family favourite for its terrific beaches and low-key holiday feel. The town winds around the gum-green Anglesea River, and accommodation makes the most of tranquil bush settings. The town is oddly well known for the kangaroos that graze on the local golf course.

There's tourist information available from a booth across from the main shopping centre, although a more permanent visitor centre was planned at the time of writing.

Activities

You can hire surf or beach-play equipment from the **Anglesea Surf Centre** (☎ 03-5263 1530; cnr Great Ocean Rd & McMillan St) or **Go Ride a Wave** (☎ 1300 132 441; 143b Great Ocean Rd; 2hr lessons incl hire $70, 2hr hire from $25), which also gives surfing lessons.

Eco Logic Education & Environment Services (☎ 03-5263 1133; www.ecologic.net.au; walks from $10) guides kid-pleasing 'marine rock-pool rambles', night-time 'possum prowls', canoe safaris and snorkelling.

About 10km down the road at Aireys Inlet, the **Split Point Lighthouse** (☎ 1800 174 045; www.splitpointlighthouse.com.au; tours adult/child/family $12/7/35;

☽ hourly 10am-4pm) is open for guided tours. The lighthouse was used in the whacky children's program *Round the Twist*.

Sleeping & Eating

Anglesea Backpackers (☎ 03-5263 2664; anglesea backpacker@iprimus.com.au; 40 Noble St; dm/d $30/85) This brightly coloured converted house is a friendly place to crash after a day of surfing. There's one en suite double.

Surf Coast Spa Resort (☎ 03-5263 3363; www.surf coastspa.com.au; 105 Great Ocean Rd; d $160, d with spa from $200) Get pampered at this upmarket resort, which offers all sorts of health-spa add-ons to enhance your stay, from a mud wrap to full facial. Rooms range from motel-style to spa units.

Anglesea Beachfront Caravan Park (☎ 03-5263 1583; www.angleseabeachfront.com.au; 35 Cameron St; powered sites $32, cabins from $80; ☒ ☐ ☎) Lovely beachfront park with bush camping sites (all powered) and a range of cabins. Wireless internet.

LORNE
pop 967

During summer, Lorne is holiday central along this stretch of coast, but it basks in a beautiful location between the curving surf of Loutit Bay and the dense bush of the Otway Ranges. With lots of good cafes, nightlife, pier fishing, bushwalks and plenty of holiday accommodation, it's a good place to start exploring the Great Ocean Road. Over the peak Christmas/New Year season, parking space, footpath space and accommodation are scarce, but out of season it's a laid-back beach town that quietly hums along with the locals and retirees who love the good life out here.

Lorne visitor information centre (☎ 1300 891 152; www.visitsurfcoast.com; 15 Mountjoy Parade; ☽ 9am-5pm; ☐) has lots of information on walks, activities and displays on Great Ocean Road attractions.

Sights & Activities

Lorne is a good base for more than 50km of walking tracks in the eastern extremity of Great Otway National Park. **Teddy's Lookout**, just above town, has good views of the coast. **Erskine Falls**, about 10km northwest of town, is the most impressive waterfall in the area and it's an easy walk to the viewing platform or 250 steps down to the base.

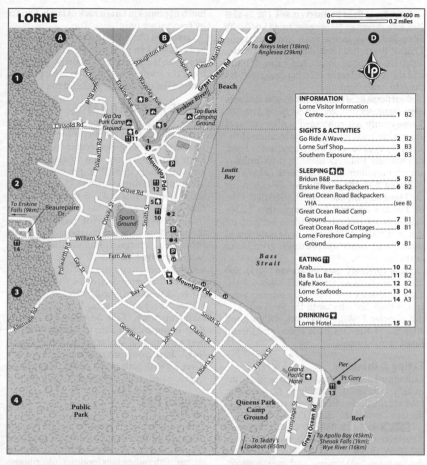

LORNE

INFORMATION
Lorne Visitor Information
Centre **1** B2

SIGHTS & ACTIVITIES
Go Ride A Wave..........................**2** B2
Lorne Surf Shop..........................**3** B3
Southern Exposure......................**4** B3

SLEEPING
Bridun B&B..................................**5** B2
Erskine River Backpackers **6** B2
Great Ocean Road Backpackers
YHA.....................................(see 8)
Great Ocean Road Camp
Ground....................................**7** B1
Great Ocean Road Cottages..........**8** B1
Lorne Foreshore Camping
Ground....................................**9** B1

EATING
Arab..**10** B2
Ba Ba Lu Bar...............................**11** B2
Kafe Kaos...................................**12** B2
Lorne Seafoods............................**13** D4
Qdos..**14** A3

DRINKING
Lorne Hotel.................................**15** B3

VICTORIA

Lorne Surf Shop (☎ 03-5289 1673; 130 Mountjoy Pde; ☼ 9am-5.30pm) hires boogie boards and wetsuits, while outfits like **Go Ride a Wave** (☎ 1300 132 441; www.gorideawave.com.au; 2hr lessons incl hire $70, 2hr hire from $25) or **Southern Exposure** (☎ 03-5261 2170; www.southernexposure.com.au; 2hr lessons $55) offer surfing lessons or hire.

Festivals & Events
Falls Festival (www.fallsfestival.com; tickets 2-/3-days incl camping $234/289) A rocking two-day music festival over New Year's is on a farm not too far from town. Assembles a top line-up of rock groups and thousands of teenagers.
Pier to Pub Swim (www.lornesurfclub.com.au) This popular event in January inspires up to 4500 swimmers to splash their way 1.2km across Loutit Bay to the Lorne Hotel.

Sleeping
Lorne locals seem to have thrown a B&B sign up on every backyard loo to create 'boutique' accommodation for the tourist throngs, but some represent poor value.

Most places are booked solid during summer holidays, but it's worth enquiring at the Lorne visitor information centre (opposite), which offers frank advice on places around town. Prices vary considerably in low and high seasons.

Erskine River Backpackers (☎ 03-5289 1496; 6 Mountjoy Pde; dm/d $25/60) Beautiful verandahs line this classic old building just steps from town and on the river. Owner Robbo runs a laid-back joint with four-bunk dorms and plenty of chill-out space.

Great Ocean Road Backpackers YHA (☎ 03-5289 1809; www.yha.com.au; 10 Erskine Ave; dm/d/f $25/75/100) Snuggled away in the bush just across the Erskine River, this relaxed two-storey timber lodge has spacious dorms, top-value doubles and the secluded scrub offering cockatoo and the odd koala sightings.

Great Ocean Road Cottages (☎ 03-5289 1070; www .greatoceanroadcottages.com; Erskine Ave; d $150-170) These comfy self-contained timber cottages enjoy a bush setting at the same location as the YHA. They're roomy, with a mezzanine level, full kitchen and verandah. In peak holiday season minimum rental is a week ($1575).

Bridun B&B (☎ 03-5289 1666; www.briden.com .au; 1 Grove Rd; d low/high season from $135/160) One of Lorne's original buildings, this 1920s classic is a weatherboard place set just off the main street. Heritage-style raw wood floors and other furnishings give it an authentic touch.

Lorne Foreshore camping ground (☎ 03-5289 1382; 2 Great Ocean Rd; sites from $25, cabins $60-120) This comprises five separate camping areas (more than 400 sites) with the head office at the popular Erskine River site. Other good sites are at Kia Ora Park and Great Ocean Road camp ground.

Eating & Drinking

Mountjoy Parade is lined with cafes and some quality restaurants catering to the summer tourist crowds. For fresh seafood off the boat, head to Lorne Seafoods at the pier.

our pick **Ba Ba Lu BAR** (☎ 03-5289 1808; www .babakubar.com.au; 6a Mountjoy Pde; tapas $5-13, mains $27-33) With an air of the Mediterranean, the inspired tapas menu and great people-watching terrace make this a Lorne favourite. Dinner mains include local seafood and Spanish cuisine.

Kafe Kaos (☎ 03-5289 2639; 52 Mountjoy Pde; lunch $9-18; ☾ breakfast & lunch) Colourful and quirky, Kaos is always buzzing with its retro style and solid menu of pancakes, wraps, burgers and smoothies.

Arab (☎ 03-5289 1435; 94 Mountjoy Pde; mains $18-26; ▣) This espresso bar has been a coffee institution for years and is well regarded for classics such as its famous apple crumble.

Qdos (☎ 03-5289 1989; www.qdosarts.com; 35 Allenvale Rd; mains $18-32; ☾ breakfast & lunch Thu-Mon, dinner Thu-Sat) A stunning architect-designed art gallery, sculpture park and cafe-bar, Qdos is well worth the short drive north of town for a lunch of pumpkin tart or rack of lamb. Dinner by reservation only.

Lorne Hotel (☎ 03-5289 1409; www.lornehotel.com.au; cnr Mountjoy Pde & Bay St; ☾ 11am-late) The huge main street pub is a good spot for a drink, especially from the rooftop beer garden. The popular bottom bar usually has weekend live music.

LORNE TO APOLLO BAY

Driving west out of Lorne, the Great Ocean Road really starts to get interesting with twists and turns revealing spectacular coastal views from lookout points and koalas hanging out of roadside trees. If you're busy rubbernecking or driving a slow vehicle, respect the traffic behind you and use the slow vehicle turn-outs!

About 3km from Lorne (signposted) is the easy 20-minute walk to the base of pretty **Sheoak Falls**. A further 13km on, the cute little hamlet of **Wye River** is well worth a stop for a swim, and more importantly a beer and lunch on the timber deck of the **Wye Beach Hotel** (☎ 03-5289 0240; Great Ocean Rd; mains $16-30; ☾ lunch & dinner). There's also a sprawling caravan park taking up much of the beachfront area here. Keep going another 5km to **Kennett River**, the best place to spot koalas on the Great Ocean Road. Park your car and wander up Grey River Rd with your neck craned. There's also a glow-worm walk after dusk – ask locally.

APOLLO BAY
pop 1370

Once a fishing town, beautiful Apollo Bay was never going to remain a secret for long, but despite creeping development it has kept its charm, with rolling hills looming over ribbons of surf beach. It's more low key than Lorne, but has a good range of accommodation and restaurants and is a jumping-off point for exploring the surrounding Great Otway National Park.

The **Great Ocean Road visitor information centre** (☎ 03-5237 6529; 100 Great Ocean Rd; ☾ 9am-5pm; ▣) is on the left as you arrive from Lorne and has displays on Aboriginal history, rainforests, shipwrecks and the building of the Great Ocean Road.

Sights & Activities

It's 1.5km from town to **Marriners Lookout** (signposted) for spectacular views of the town and coast – from the car park it's about 10 minutes' walk up to the lookout.

There's a long-running **community market** in the centre of town every Saturday morning from 8.30am.

Apollo Bay Surf & Kayak (☎ 0405 495 909; www .apollobaysurfkayak.com.au; Great Ocean Rd), opposite the visitor centre, has surfing lessons ($45), excellent seal kayak tours to the Marengo Reef Seal Colony ($55) and guided bushwalks, and also hires out boards, wetsuits, fishing rods and camping gear.

Otway Expeditions (☎ 03-5237 6341; www.otwayex peditions.tripod.com; 3hr mountain-bike tours min 6 people $65, Argo buggies $45) runs mountain-bike tours through the Otways, as well as gentle bush-bashing adventures in cross-terrain-and-water Argo buggies.

A marked multiday hike, the **Great Ocean Walk** (www.greatoceanwalk.com.au), starts at Apollo Bay and runs about 100km all the way to the Twelve Apostles. You can hop on and off the trail to do shorter walks or take on the whole trek in six days; see the website for suggestions about different legs.

Festivals & Events

Apollo Bay Music Festival (☎ 03-5237 6761; www.apol lobaymusicfestival.com; weekend passes $146), in March/ April, spans the genres from classical to rock, folk to blues and back again.

Sleeping

Apollo Bay is blessed with some excellent budget accommodation, including four back-packers and plenty of motels and B&Bs.

Surfside Backpackers (☎ 03-5237 7263; cnr Great Ocean Rd & Gambier St; dm $25, d $55-80; 🖳) This rambling, homey weatherboard has a great location with tumbling-surf views from the lounge, an eclectic vinyl collection and a front garden with barbecues and hammocks. Ask the owner about nearby self-contained flats.

YHA Eco Beach (☎ 03-5237 7899; 5 Pascoe St; dm/s/d $38/80/95; 🖳 🐾) The lounge and communal areas of this architect-designed hostel are like something out of a *Home Beautiful* magazine. It's definitely one for the flashpacker – not only luxurious but eco-designed to fit into the natural surroundings.

Haley Reef Views B&B (☎ 03-5237 7885; www.ha leyreefviews.com.au; 31 Noel St; d low/high season $110/140; 🐾) The immaculate English garden gives you an idea of the care taken with guests at this sweet little spot. It's just a short stroll to the beach, but there's an indulgent spa to relax in.

Sandpiper Motel (☎ 03-5237 6732 www.sandpiper .net.au; 3 Murray St; d low/high season from $130/165) Simple beach-style rooms in sea blues and sandy tones make for a relaxing stay at this stylish modern motel. Go for a view of the ocean or a garden deck room. Some are self-contained and there's a deluxe spa unit.

Marengo Holiday Park (☎ 03-5237 6162; www .marengopark.com.au; off Great Ocean Rd, Marengo; un-powered/powered sites $24/28, d cabins $110-135) In the 'suburb' of Marengo, 2km west of town, this meticulously run beachside park has spa-cious deluxe cabins (some with log fires and spa) and campers are well taken care of with good facilities.

Eating

Chill@The Bay (☎ 03-5237 1006; 14 Pascoe St; meals $3.50-15) This cool tapas and wine bar is a block back from the main street, so it's a quieter option. It's worth seeking out for breakfast specials – it opens ultra-early on weekends.

La Bimba (☎ 03-5237 7411; 125 Great Ocean Rd; lunch $10-21, dinner $29-34) Head upstairs to the balcony terrace to escape the main street at this artsy spot and enjoy brunch or an innovative yet unpretentious lunch. Dinner is fancier with kangaroo fillet or paella on the list.

Café Nautigals (☎ 0402 825 590; 57 Great Ocean Rd; mains $14-16; 🕑 breakfast & lunch; 🖳) With wi-fi internet ($3 for 15 minutes), this laid-back cafe is always popular with travellers for its organic coffee and cheap noodles and burgers. In the evening, the attached Thirsty Mermaid wine bar is a good place for a drink.

CAPE OTWAY

The 14km drive down to the lighthouse at Cape Otway passes through beautiful tall-timbered forest – keep an eye out for koalas hanging out of trees close to the roadside. Cape Otway's rugged coastline smashed sev-eral ships wide open in its history, but today it's a magnificent area where bushland meets the coast and forms part of the Great Otway National Park.

About 8km along Lighthouse Rd, a signpost points down an unsealed road to **Parker Hill**, **Point Franklin** and **Crayfish Beach**, all gorgeous, secluded spots for beach ambling, swimming and snorkelling. Further along, **Blanket Bay** is a National Parks campground.

VICTORIA

At the end of Lighthouse Rd is the **Cape Otway Lighthouse** (☎ 03-5237 9240; www.lightstation .com.au; Lighthouse Rd; adult/child/family $15/8/38; ⊙ 9am-5pm), Australia's oldest, dating back to 1848. The historic complex includes the old telegraph station, lightkeeper's house and a cafe with shipwreck gallery, and you can climb the decommissioned lighthouse for fine views along the coast.

The Great Ocean Road Walk passes by the lighthouse; **Rainbow Falls** is a two-hour walk from here.

Deep in the rainforest north of the Great Ocean Road (take the turn-off towards Lavers Hill), the **Otway Fly** (☎ 1800 300 477; www.otwayfly .com.au; adult/child/family $20/9/50; ⊙ 9am-5.30pm, last admission 4.30pm) is a 25m-high elevated treetop walk. The views of the forest canopy are wonderful and you can go even higher by ascending the spiral staircase to the 47m-high lookout tower. There's a visitor centre and cafe.

Sleeping

Lighthouse Keeper's Residence (☎ 03-5237 9240; www .lightstation.com; B&B d $195-300) You can spend a night in the original lighthouse keeper's residence or the more modern 'manager's residence' and, when the day-trippers depart, get a feel for the lonely life. Both are neatly furnished with a blend or heritage and mod cons and have been divided up so that you can book part of the residence or the whole place.

ourpick **Bimbi Park** (☎ 03-5237 9246; www.bim bipark.com.au; Manna Gum Dr; unpowered sites low/high season $17/25, powered sites $20/30, d cabins $50-110) Ensconced in the bush down a dirt road just 3km before the lighthouse, this serene park and horse-riding ranch is a wonderful place to stay. It has secluded bush sites, cute caravans, bunk rooms, sparkling new cabins, all with an eco-feel. There's plenty of wildlife around and bushwalks lead to remote beaches. One-hour horse rides cost $45.

There are numerous gorgeous **bush camping grounds** (sites $13) throughout the park. One of the most popular near the beach is Blanket Bay – so popular there's a ballot for sites during peak periods; book through **Parks Victoria** (☎ 13 19 63; www.parkweb.vic.gov.au).

PORT CAMPBELL NATIONAL PARK

The most photographed stretch of the Great Ocean Road offers sheer limestone cliffs towering over fierce seas. For thousands of years,

waves and tides have relentlessly sculpted the soft rock into a fascinating series of rock stacks, gorges, arches and blowholes.

The **Gibson Steps**, hand-carved into the cliffs in the 19th century (and later replaced with concrete steps), lead down to foaming Gibson Beach. This beach, and others along this stretch of coast, are unpatrolled and not recommended for swimming – you can walk along the beach, but be wary of high-tide strandings.

The **Twelve Apostles** are the best-known rock formations in Victoria. These lonely rocky stacks have been abandoned to the ocean by the eroding headland. Today their number has been whittled down to six apostles, visible from the snaking viewing platforms. There's a rather pointless walk-through visitor centre leading to boardwalks that ring the cliff tops, providing viewing platforms and seats – don't stop at the first place you come to. Sunrise is a good time for photography and to beat the crowds.

At **Loch Ard Gorge** (see The Shipwreck Coast, opposite), haunting tales of woe await. It's one of the Shipwreck Coast's most notorious sections. You can find out more at the **Port Campbell visitor information centre** (☎ 1300 137 255; www.visit 12apostles.com; 26 Morris St, Port Campbell; ⊙ 9am-5pm).

West of Port Campbell, the next piece of ocean sculpture is the **Arch**, a rocky archway offshore from Point Hesse. Nearby is **London Bridge**, albeit fallen down. It was once a double-arched rock platform linked to the mainland, but in 1990 one of the arches collapsed into the sea. Further west, beyond Peterborough, is the scenic **Bay of Islands Coastal Park**.

Tours

You can tour the coastline from the air or sea. The cheapest chopper flights last around 10 minutes.

12 Apostles Helicopters (☎ 03-5598 6161; www.12ah.com; 9400 Great Ocean Rd, Port Campbell; flights per person $100-215) Flights over the Twelve Apostles, London Bridge and Bay of Islands, recorded on a 'Skycam' video as a souvenir.

The Edge Helicopters (☎ 03-5598 8283; www .theedgehelicopters.com.au; flights per person $90-195) Based at the Twelve Apostles centre.

Port Campbell Boat Charters (☎ 0428 986 366; 155 Rounds Rd, Port Campbell; tours $50) Scenic boat tours to Twelve Apostles (four daily), plus diving, snorkelling and fishing trips.

THE SHIPWRECK COAST

The Victorian coastline between Cape Otway and Port Fairy was a notoriously dangerous stretch of water in the days of sailing ships. Navigation was exceptionally difficult due to numerous barely hidden reefs and frequent heavy fog. More than 80 vessels came to grief on this 120km stretch in just 40 years.

The most famous wreck was that of the iron-hulled clipper *Loch Ard*, which foundered off Mutton Bird Island on the final night of its voyage from England in 1878. Of the 55 people on board, only two survived. Eva Carmichael clung to wreckage and was washed into the gorge, where apprentice officer Tom Pearce rescued her. Eva and Tom were both 18 years old. The press tried to create a romantic story, but nothing actually happened. Eva soon returned to Ireland and they never saw each other again.

Divers have investigated these wrecks; relics are on display in the Flagstaff Hill Maritime Village (below) in Warrnambool.

Sleeping & Eating

Port Campbell, a pleasant little town with a safe swimming beach, is the main centre along this part of the coast and is only 12km down the road from the Twelve Apostles.

Port Campbell Hostel (☎ 03-5598 6305; www.port campbellhostel.com.au; 18 Tregea St; dm from $25, s/d $35/70) A brand-new purpose-built hostel was nearing completion when we visited and it promises to be a beauty, with thoughtful design, plenty of common areas including a barbecue deck, and a range of rooms.

Daysy Hill Country Cottages (☎ 03-5598 6226; www.daysyhillcottages.com.au; 2585 Cobden-Port Campbell Rd; d $120-195; 🐕) These hillside cedar and sandstone cottages, just a few minutes from town, are decked out in modern colonial-style country comfort. The deluxe cabins are more modern and have spas.

Port Campbell Holiday Park (☎ 1800 781 871; www .pchp.com.au; Morris St; unpowered/powered sites $26/30, cabins low/high season from $80/160) Neat, small and a two-minute walk to the beach and bottom end of town, this excellent friendly park has free wireless internet and comfy cabins.

Port Campbell has a few good eateries along Lord St, including the suave **Waves Restaurant** (☎ 03-5598 6111; 29 Lord St; mains $15-30; 🕐 lunch & dinner) and **Nico's** (☎ 03-5598 6131; 25 Lord St; pizza & pasta $14-22; 🕐 dinner), a local legend for its unusual pizza concoctions and chocolate pizza.

SOUTHWEST

The Great Ocean Road ends 12km east of Warrnambool. Here it meets the Princes Hwy, which continues west into SA. Although the dramatic coastal drive is over, it's a pretty stretch of road that passes through the traditional lands of the Gunditjmara people.

WARRNAMBOOL

pop 28,150

Once a whaling and sealing station, Warrnambool is now the major regional commercial centre of the southwest. The town sports a pleasant coastal outlook, good surf beaches and migrating whales cruising past. Its historic buildings, waterways and tree-lined streets are attractive and there's a large student population attending the Warrnambool campus of Deakin University.

Information

Warrnambool Library (☎ 03-5562 2258; 25 Liebig St; 🕐 9.30am-5pm Mon-Tue, 9.30am-6pm Wed-Fri, 10am-noon Sat; 🖳) Free internet access.

Warrnambool visitor information centre (☎ 03-5559 4620, 1800 637 725; www.visitwarrnambool.com.au; Merri St; 🕐 9am-5pm; 🖳) At Flagstaff Hill, it produces the handy *Warrnambool Visitors Guide*, has internet access and hires bikes ($20/30 per half/full day).

Sights & Activities

Warrnambool's main tourist attraction is the impressive **Flagstaff Hill Maritime Village** (☎ 1800 556 111; www.flagstaffhill.com; Merri St; adult/child/family $16/7/40; 🕐 9am-5pm), a recreated colonial village modelled on an early Australian coastal port. See the cannon and fortifications built in 1887 to withstand the perceived threat of Russian invasion. In the evening **Shipwrecked** (adult/child/family $26/14/65) is a vaguely hi-tech sound-and-laser show of the *Loch Ard*'s plunge.

VICTORIA

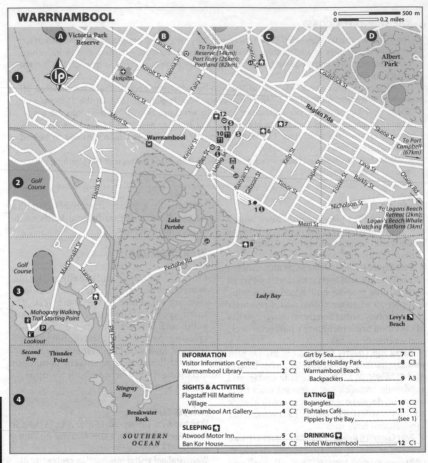

WARRNAMBOOL

INFORMATION	
Visitor Information Centre	1 C2
Warrnambool Library	2 C2
SIGHTS & ACTIVITIES	
Flagstaff Hill Maritime	
Village	3 C2
Warrnambool Art Gallery	4 C2
SLEEPING	
Atwood Motor Inn	5 C1
Ban Kor House	6 C2

Girt by Sea	7 C1
Surfside Holiday Park	8 C3
Warrnambool Beach	
Backpackers	9 A3
EATING	
Bojangles	10 C2
Fishtales Café	11 C2
Pippies by the Bay	(see 1)
DRINKING	
Hotel Warrnambool	12 C1

Warrnambool has some excellent beaches such as sheltered **Lady Bay**, the main swimming beach, which has fortifications at the breakwater at its western end. **Logan's Beach** has the best surf, and there are breaks at **Levy's Beach** and **Second Bay**. **Easyrider** (☎ 03-5521 7646; www.easyridersurfschool.com .au) offers surfing lessons (from $40) and seakayaking ($45).

Warrnambool has made a name for itself as a winter centre for **whale watching**. Southern right whales come to mate and nurse their calves in the waters off Logan's Beach from July to September. Their breaching and fluking is visible from Logan's Beach Whale Watching Platform. It's a major tourist drawcard, but you'll need 20/20 eyesight or a pair

of binoculars. **Dive Inn Charters** (☎ 0419 349 058; www.diveinncharters.com.au) runs whale-watching tours in season (one/two hours $40/70) and trips to a seal colony on Lady Julia Percy Island ($85).

Walking trails in and around Warrnambool include the 3km **Heritage Trail**. The short **Thunder Point** stroll shows off the best coastal scenery in the area; it's also the starting point for the 22km coastal **Mahogany Walking Trail**.

The **Warrnambool Art Gallery** (☎ 03-5564 7832; 165 Timor St; admission free; 10am-5pm Mon-Fri, noon-5pm Sat & Sun) is well worth a visit. The permanent Australian collection includes notables such as Tom Roberts, James Gleeson and Arthur Boyd.

Sleeping

Warrnambool Beach Backpackers (☎ 03-5562 4874; www.beachbackpackers.com.au; 17 Stanley St; dm/d $23/70; ▣) Close to the sea, this former museum (love the clocktower facade) has a huge living area with a bar, internet access (and wi-fi), kitchen and free pick-up. It's a buzzing place offering good self-contained family rooms as well as free use of mountain bikes and canoes.

Atwood Motor Inn (☎ 03-5562 7144; www.atwood motorinn.com.au; 8 Spence St; d $85-145; ▨) In a quiet side street just north of the centre, Atwood's small but attractive doubles are certainly well priced. Spa suites are also available.

Girt by Sea (☎ 0418 261 969; www.banyanplace .com.au; 52 Banyan St; d from $140) This restored 1856 sandstone home has been tastefully refurbished. Large bathrooms boast antique vanities and red Baltic pine floors. There are various suites with huge brass beds, private garden decks, plasma TVs and massage chairs. There's a large, bright guest lounge and great breakfasts.

Logans Beach Retreat (☎ 03-5561 3750; www.lo gansbeach.com.au; 7 Logans Beach Rd; 1-/2-bed apt $150/170; ▨) The two self-contained apartments at this luxury spa retreat are romantically appointed with spa baths and are superb value, with free use of the gym and discounts on spa treatments.

Surfside Holiday Park (☎ 03-5559 4700; www.surf sidepark.com.au; Pertobe Rd; sites from $28, cabins $84-113) Surfside is one of several caravan parks in town, but the location is hard to beat: between the centre and the beach and close to Lake Pertobe.

Eating & Drinking

Leibig St is the dining and entertainment heart of Warrnambool.

Fishtales Café (☎ 03-5561 2957; 63 Liebig St; mains $7-16) A cheery cafe serving burgers, fish and chips and vegetarian specials, with a sunny courtyard out the back.

Bojangles (☎ 03-5562 8751; 61 Liebig St; mains $11-18; ☖ lunch & dinner) This spiffy licensed pizza restaurant does great pastas and wood-fired pizzas, as well as steaks and grills.

Pippies by the Bay (☎ 03-5559 4600; Flagstaff Hill, Merri St; lunch $14-20, dinner $28-34) Atop Flagstaff Hill, Pippies wins the prize for best views and is a good place for lingering over breakfast or lunch while contemplating the ocean panorama. By night the restaurant serves a menu of exceptional modern Italian and seafood cuisine.

Hotel Warrnambool (☎ 03-5562 2377; cnr Koroit & Kepler Sts) This hotel, dating to 1894, is the most welcoming pub in town – an earthy, cavernous place with exposed mud bricks and railway sleepers, slouchy lounges, a billiard table, a cool corner beer garden and live music on Thursday nights and Sunday. There are 11 beers available on tap and the pub grub is good.

Getting There & Away

The **V/Line** (☎ 13 61 96) train station is on Merri St. There are daily services to Melbourne ($26, 3½ hours). Connecting V/Line buses continue form Warrnambool to Port Fairy ($3.50), Portland ($10) and Mt Gambier ($21). Weekday buses go to Ballarat ($23) and Hamilton ($8). A bus heads east along the Great Ocean Road to Apollo Bay ($16) on Monday, Wednesday and Friday, with connections to Geelong.

Christians (☎ 03-5352 1501) runs a service from Warrnambool to the Great Ocean Road to Halls Gap and Ararat on Tuesday, Friday and Sunday.

THE MAHOGANY SHIP

The Mahogany Ship is said to be a Portuguese vessel that ran aground off Warrnambool in the 1500s, and there are alleged sightings of the wreck sitting high in the dunes dating back to 1846. Portuguese naval charts from the 16th century known as the *Dieppe Maps* are said to depict parts of Australia's southern coastline, including Armstrong Bay 6km west of Warrnambool, and this has further fuelled the Mahogany Ship legend. Alternative theories claim that the Mahogany Ship was an even earlier Chinese junk. For 150 years people have been trying to find the remains of the Mahogany Ship – some say it's buried deep in the dunes or was swallowed by the sea. However, there's no direct evidence that the ship ever existed.

In any case, you can walk the Mahogany Walking Trail between Warrnambool and Port Fairy, a 22km coastal walk that passes areas of alleged sightings.

VICTORIA

TOWER HILL RESERVE

Tower Hill, 15km west of Warrnambool, is a vast caldera born in a volcanic eruption 30,000 years ago. Aboriginal artefacts unearthed in the volcanic ash show that Indigenous people lived in the area at the time. It's jointly administered by the Worn Gundidj Aboriginal Cooperative, which operates the **visitor centre** (☎ 03-5561 5315; www .worngundidj.org.au), and Parks Victoria. There are excellent day walks, including the steep 30-minute Peak Climb with spectacular 360-degree views. There's a fascinating painting in the Warrnambool Art Gallery by Eugene von Guérard of Tower Hill painted in 1855. After a century of deforestation and environmental degradation, this incredibly detailed painting was used to identify species used in a replanting program begun in 1961 when Tower Hill became a state game reserve. Since then over 300,000 trees have been replanted.

PORT FAIRY
pop 2600

Historic Port Fairy is a loveable little town, with its old bluestone and sandstone buildings, whitewashed cottages, Norfolk pine–lined streets and relaxed (often windy) seaside air. The township was settled in 1835 by whalers and sealers, and it still has a large fishing fleet. The compact town centre is along and around Sackville St.

Port Fairy Folk Festival (www.portfairyfolkfestival .com), one of Australia's biggest and best music festivals, is held on the Labour Day long weekend in early March. Accommodation for the festival is routinely booked a year in advance, and tickets usually sell out several months in advance.

Port Fairy visitor information centre (☎ 03-5568 2682; www.visitportfairy.com.au; Bank St) has plenty of info, transport bookings and clued-up staff.

Sights

Port Fairy has a rich and sometimes gloomy heritage that enraptures local history buffs. Brochures and maps from the visitor centre show the popular **Shipwreck Walk** and **History Walk** signposted around town. The **Port Fairy History Centre** (Gipps St; adult/child $3/50c; ⏱ 2-5pm Wed, Sat & Sun, daily during school holidays), housed in the old bluestone courthouse, has shipping relics, old photos and costumes, and a prisoner's cell. On **Battery Hill** there's a

lookout point, and cannons and fortifications positioned here in the 1860s. There's a lovely walk around **Griffiths Island** where the Moyne River empties into the sea. The island is connected by a footbridge and is home to a protected **mutton bird colony** and a modest **lighthouse**. The mutton birds (short-tailed shearwaters) migrate to and from their nesting grounds here like clockwork, arriving around September 22 for mating, and remaining until mid-April.

Mulloka Cruises (☎ 0408 514 382; adult/child $10/free) runs half-hour cruises of the port, bay and Griffiths Island.

You can hire surf gear and bicycles and arrange surfing lesions at **Port Fairy Surf Shop** (☎ 03-5568 2800; 33 Bank St).

Sleeping

Port Fairy Youth Hostel (☎ 03-5568 2468; www.port fairyhostel.com.au; 8 Cox St; tw/d $21/62/70, f $100-150; ▣) In the rambling 1844 home of merchant William Rutledge, this friendly and well-run hostel has a large kitchen, pool table, free cable TV and peaceful gardens. Some of the dorms are in the old stables and coachhouse – a nice touch of Port Fairy character.

Eastern Beach Holiday Units (☎ 03-5568 1117; www.port-fairy.com/easternbeach; 121 Griffiths St; d from $80) What these modern units lack in old-world style they more than make up for in price and amenities – large self-contained units with separate bedroom, lounge and kitchen. Wi-fi available.

Merrijig Inn (☎ 03-5568 2324; www.merrijiginn.com; cnr Campbell & Gipps Sts; d $130-220) Victoria's oldest inn is a classic 19th-century guest house with four spacious ground-floor en suite rooms and four tiny attic doubles – very quaint, very small! The restaurant (mains $34 to $36) is one of Port Fairy's best.

Daisies by the Sea B&B (☎ 03-5568 2355; www.port -fairy.com/daisiesbythesea; 222 Griffiths St; d $140) These modern beachfront suites, 1.5km from town on the road to the golf course, make a change from Port Fairy's heritage pads. Fresh as the sea breeze with waves crashing just 50m from your door, Daisies is a snug, appealing getaway for couples.

Gardens Caravan Park (☎ 03-5568 1060; www.port fairycaravanparks.com; 111 Griffiths St; unpowered/powered sites $26/29, cabins $90-100) The pick of several caravan parks around town, this lush site is next to the botanic gardens, 200m from the beach and a short walk to the town centre.

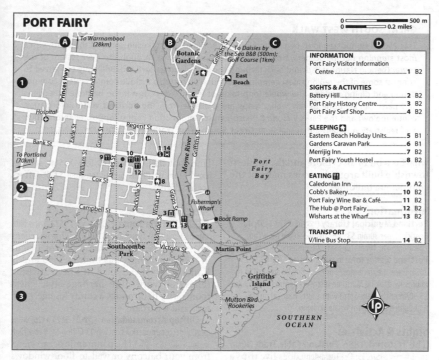

PORT FAIRY

Eating & Drinking

Port Fairy has a good range of cafes and restaurants, mostly clustered along Bank St.

Cobb's Bakery (☎ 03-5568 1713; 25 Bank St; ☾ breakfast & lunch) Locals come here for fresh-cut sandwiches, pies, pasties, burgers and, naturally, fresh bread.

The Hub @ Port Fairy (☎ 03-5568 2326; cnr Bank & Sackville Sts; mains $15-26) This popular corner cafe moonlights as an upbeat Mod Oz restaurant with a good wine list, pasta dishes and cakes.

Caledonian Inn (☎ 03-5568 1044; 41 Bank St; mains $16-22; ☾ lunch & dinner) Known to locals as the 'Stump' and claimed to be Victoria's oldest continuously licensed pub (1844), the Caledonian is a good place for a beer (Guinness on tap) and has an impressive menu of pub food, including local seafood.

Wisharts at the Wharf (☎ 03-5568 1884; 29 Gipps St; mains $17-36; ☾ lunch & dinner) Wharfside dining doesn't come prettier than this. There's a popular takeaway fish and chip and fresh seafood shop at the side, while the restaurant serves the real thing – gourmet fish and chips, whole baby snapper and tiger prawns in filo.

Getting There & Away

Several buses a day run between Port Fairy and Warrnambool ($3.50, 35 minutes), connecting with Melbourne trains. **V/Line** (☎ 13 61 96) has daily buses to Portland ($7, one hour) and Mt Gambier ($16, two hours).

PORTLAND
pop 9820

Portland has bags of history to recommend it, but driving in on the tail-end of the Great Ocean Road – passing an enormous windfarm on the way – it's hard to see the sparkle in this industrial town. One of Victoria's earliest European settlements, it was a whaling and sealing base from the early 1800s. The first permanent settlers were the Henty family, arriving from Van Diemen's Land in 1834. Mary MacKillop, Australia's first saint, came here from Melbourne in 1862 and founded Australia's first religious order. Today Portland is the only deep-water port between Melbourne and Adelaide, and home to the massive Portland Aluminium Smelter (5km from town), exporting 340,000 tonnes per year. The huge industrial

VICTORIA

GREAT SOUTH WEST WALK

This 250km signposted loop begins and ends at Portland, and takes in some of the southwest's most stunning natural scenery, from the remote, blustery coast through the river system of the Lower Glenelg National Park and back through the hinterland to Portland. Brilliantly conceived to connect some of the region's best camping grounds, you can also include comfortable accommodation and dining options. The whole loop takes at least 10 days, but it can be done in sections and parts can be done as day walks. Maps are available from the Portland visitor information centre (below) and the Parks Victoria & Nelson visitor information centre (opposite). Information and registration details are available at **Great South West Walk** (www.greatsouthwestwalk.com).

---

wharf is a bit of an eyesore and the modern township built around it hides many of the colonial-era buildings.

Information

Portland Municipal Library (☎ 03-5523 1497; 40 Bentick St; per 30min $3; ☺ 10am-5.30pm Mon-Thu, 10am-6pm Fri, 10am-1pm Sat; ☐) Internet access.

Portland visitor information centre (☎ 03-5523 2671; www.greatoceanroad.org; Lee Breakwater Rd) In the impressive-looking Maritime Discovery Centre (adult/child $5.50/free; ☺ 9am-5pm) with a nifty nautical display highlighted by a sperm whale skeleton.

Sights & Activities

The restored 1886 **Portland Cable Tram** (adult/child/family $15/6/35; ☺ 10am-4pm) does five trips a day plying an 8km circular route linking the vintage-car museum, botanic gardens, Maritime Discovery Centre and WWII memorial water tower. Passengers hop on and off as they please; it's a great way to get acquainted with the town.

The **Powerhouse Motor & Car Museum** (☎ 03-5523 5795; cnr Glenelg & Percy Sts; adult/child/family $5/1/10; ☺ 10am-4pm) has 30 vintage Australian and American vehicles and motorbikes dating from 1920.

There are some very good surfing spots around this coast, especially at sublime **Bridgewater Bay**.

It's worth the 13km drive out to 1884 **Cape Nelson Lighthouse**, as much for the sea views, rock formations and massive wind turbines as for the lighthouse itself. The Great Ocean Road Walk also passes by the lighthouse.

Like Warrnambool, Portland is a good place for **whale-watching** – southern right whales come close to the harbour on their annual migration – but here it's also possible to see blue whales feeding on the abundance of krill between November and April. They're usually too far out to see from

land, but **Heli-explore** (☎ 03-5526 5444; www.heliexplore.com.au; flights per person from $210) offers scenic flights.

Sleeping

our pick **Victoria House** (☎ 03-5521 7577; www.babs.com.au/vichouse; 5 Tyers St; s/d $130/160) This excellent two-storey Georgian bluestone hotel right in the town centre was built in 1853 and is National Trust classified. It's been stylishly renovated with nine heritage-style guest rooms with bathrooms, a comfy lounge, open fires and a garden.

Clifftop Accommodation (☎ 03-5523 1126; www.portlandaccommodation.com.au; 13 Clifton Ct; d low/high season $140/185; ☒) The panoramic ocean views from your balcony or wall-to-floor windows are superb, and the two self-contained apartments are spacious, with big brass beds, telescopes (for whale-spotting) and a modern maritime feel.

Portland Claremont Holiday Village (☎ 03-5521 7567; www.holidayvillage.com.au; 37 Percy St; unpowered/powered sites $20/25, cabins $70-125) Smack in the town centre behind a replica bluestone building.

Eating & Drinking

Although Percy St is the main shopping strip through town, with a few cafes and restaurants, the waterfront Bentick St is the best place for dining. The town's pubs – including the Gordon Hotel and Mac's – do decent bistro meals.

Kokopelli's Kafe & Ice Bar (☎ 03-5521 1200; 79 Bentick St; tapas $3-6, mains $13-25) This loungy cafe cum '70s cocktail bar does meals all day, but shines as a restaurant and bar in the evening with tapas plates, pasta and steak dishes, an open fire and cute little courtyard out the back.

Sandilands (☎ 03-5523 3319; Percy St; mains $16-35; ☺ dinner Mon-Sat) This elegant manor's imposing facade suggests stiff sophistication, but it's a relaxed fine-dining choice. Steak and seafood is the speciality, but vegetarians are well catered for here with stir-fry, pasta and risotto dishes.

Watch House Lounge Bar (☎ 03-5523 5842; 5a Cliff St; ☺ 5pm-late Wed-Sat) In a classic old bluestone building across from the harbour, this stylish wine bar is in the original 1850 watchhouse.

Getting There & Away

There are daily **V/Line** (☎ 13 61 96) buses between Portland and Port Fairy ($7, one hour), Warrnambool ($10, 1½ hours) and Mt Gambier ($9, one hour). Buses depart from Henty St.

PORTLAND TO SOUTH AUSTRALIA

From Portland, you can either go north to Heywood and rejoin the Princes Hwy to SA, or head northwest along the beautiful coastal route known as the Portland–Nelson Rd. This road runs inland from the coast, but along the way there are turn-offs leading to beaches and national parks.

Cape Bridgewater
pop 100

An essential 21km detour off the Portland–Nelson Rd is tiny Cape Bridgewater. The stunning 4km arc of **Bridgewater Bay** is one of Victoria's finest stretches of white-sand surf beach, backed by pristine dunes. The road continues on to **Cape Duquesne** where walking tracks lead to a **blowhole** and the **Petrified Forest** on the clifftop. A longer two-hour return walk takes you to a permanent **seal colony** where you can see hundreds of fur seals sunning themselves on the rocks.

The best way to visit the seal colony is by boat with **Seals by Sea Tours** (☎ 03-5526 7247; www .sealsbyseatours.com; adult/child $30/20). Departure times for the 45-minute tours vary so book ahead.

There's nowhere to camp at Cape Bridgewater, but there are some stand-out accommodation choices.

Sea View Lodge B&B (☎ 03-5526 7276; Bridgewater Rd; s/d $50/140, self-contained cottage $185) is a lovely house on the site of the original historic Sea View Hotel. As well as five cosy en suite doubles with use of the lounge, kitchen and dining areas, there's a cottage in the garden sleeping four and a two-bedroom house. Friendly owners, too.

If you have a group, book out the luxurious three-level, four-bedroom **Abalone Beach House** (☎ 0408 808 346; www.abalonehouse.com.au; Bridgewater Rd; 4-bedroom house from $200), with sensational views, log-fires and pure relaxation. It sleeps eight.

Bridgewater Bay Beach Café (☎ 03-5526 7155; 1611 Bridgewater Rd; ☺ 9am-6pm, dinner Fri & Sat) serves meals all day and hires out bikes and surfboards.

Nelson
☎ 08 / pop 226

Nelson is the last vestige of civilisation before the SA border – a riverside village with a general store, pub and a handful of accommodation places. It's a popular holiday and fishing spot at the mouth of the **Glenelg River**, which originates in the Grampians and travels more than 400km to the coast. A good chunk of the river flows through **Lower Glenelg National Park**, which is best explored by canoe.

The **Parks Victoria & Nelson visitor information centre** (☎ 03-8738 4051; 🖳) is just before the Glenelg River bridge.

Nelson Boat & Canoe Hire (☎ 03-8738 4048; www .nelsonboatandcanoehire.com.au) can rig you up for serious camping expeditions, staying at bush camps along the Glenelg River. Canoe hire costs from $40 a day.

Book a leisurely 3½-hour cruise up the Glenelg River with **Glenelg River Cruises** (☎ 03-8738 4191; adult/child $30/10). The cruise stops at the **Princess Margaret Rose Cave** (www.princessmargaret rosecave.com; adult/child/family $12/7/28), but tickets for the cave tour are separate. Cruises depart daily in summer at 1pm and on Tuesday, Wednesday, Saturday and Sunday the rest of the year. If you travel to the cave on your own, it's about 17km by road from Nelson, towards the border. If you've never had a speleological experience, take a 45-minute tour, leaving roughly hourly between 10am and 4.30pm.

The 1855 **Nelson Hotel** (☎ 03-8738 4011; www .nelsonhotel.com.au; Kellett St; d/apt from $60/135) has a stuffed pelican above the bar next to a giant crab-on-a-slab (of wood) – the rooms are more traditional but comfortable with standard pubs rooms (shared bathrooms), a cottage and self-contained apartment. The bistro serves reasonably priced pub food (mains $15 to $18, open for lunch and dinner).

VICTORIA

The **Kywong Caravan Park** (☎ 03-8738 4174; www.kywongcp.com; North Nelson Rd; unpowered/powered sites $15/20, cabins $49-70) is on 25 hectares of bushland, next to the national park and Glenelg River.

There are nine **campsites** (permits $15) in the Lower Glenelg National Park between Nelson and Dartmoor along the Glenelg River that are popular with canoeists but accessible by road, with rain-fed water tanks, toilets and fireplaces, but you need firewood. Camping permits are issued by the Parks Victoria & Nelson visitor information centre, where you can also get maps. Forest Camp South is among the nicest of these, right on the river, rich in bird life and easily accessible from Portland–Nelson Rd.

THE WIMMERA

The Wimmera is an endless expanse of wheat fields, grain silos and sheep properties bisected by the Western Hwy (A8), the main route between Melbourne and Adelaide.

The major attractions in the region are the Grampians National Park, Mt Arapiles State Park – Australia's most famous rock-climbing venue (known as Djurite to Koories) – and the Little Desert National Park. The Wimmera was the training ground for Australia's first international cricket team – an all-Aboriginal team that toured England in 1868.

Getting There & Away

The *Overland*, the Melbourne–Adelaide train, runs through the Wimmera, stopping at Ararat, Horsham and Dimboola (for confirmed bookings only), four times a week. **V/Line** (☎ 13 61 96) has train/bus services between Melbourne and major towns.

From Horsham you can take a bus north to Mildura, west to Naracoorte or south to Hamilton.

STAWELL
pop 5900

A gateway town to Grampians National Park, Stawell is nationally famous for the **Stawell Gift** (www.stawellgift.com), a 120m foot race that's Australia's richest and has been run here every Easter Monday since 1878, attracting up to 20,000 visitors. The **Stawell Gift Hall of**

Fame (☎ 03-5358 1326; Main St), alongside the oval where the race is run, was being redeveloped at the time of writing; it should be reopened by the time you read this and houses race memorabilia.

Bunjil's Shelter, along a bone-rattling bumpy road 11km south of Stawell and signposted off the road to Pomonal, is one of the most significant Aboriginal rock-art sites in the state. Bunjil is the creator spirit of the Aboriginal people of this region.

The town has a number of colonial-era heritage buildings and sites. The **Stawell visitor information centre** (☎ 1800 330 080; 50-52 Western Hwy) provides interpretive maps for town walking tours. It will also book accommodation.

There's a daily V/Line bus between Stawell and Halls Gap ($6, 35 minutes).

Sleeping & Eating

With Halls Gap, and its plethora of accommodation, only 25km away, it's hard to think of a good reason to spend the night is Stawell.

Magdala Motor Lodge (☎ 03-5358 3877; www.magdalamotorlodge.com.au; Western Hwy; s/d/f from $99/105/160; ❄ 🖳 🐾) Just outside town, Magdala has a lovely bush setting with comfortable rooms that look over a small private lake. There's a heated indoor pool and spa, tennis court and six-hole golf course, an 800m lakeside walking track, free canoe use, and a restaurant.

Stawell Park Caravan Park (☎ 03-5358 2709; fax 5358 2199; Western Hwy; unpowered/powered sites $18/20, d cabins $54-99; 🐾) This park, on 48 hectares of attractive bushland, has a pool and recreation room.

Town Hall Hotel (☎ 03-5358 1059; 62 Main St; mains $16-26; 🍴 lunch & dinner) This grand old pub opposite the town hall is a good place for pub food and relatively healthy bar meals such as focaccias and gourmet sandwiches.

GRAMPIANS NATIONAL PARK

The Grampians (known as Gariwerd to local Koories) is a bushwalkers' paradise and one of Victoria's most outstanding natural features. The rich diversity of flora and fauna, unique rock formations, Aboriginal rock art, accessible walking trails and rock-climbing sites offer something for everyone, regardless of your energy levels. The mountains are at their best in spring, when the wildflowers (including 20 species that don't exist anywhere else in the world) are at their peak. The Grampians

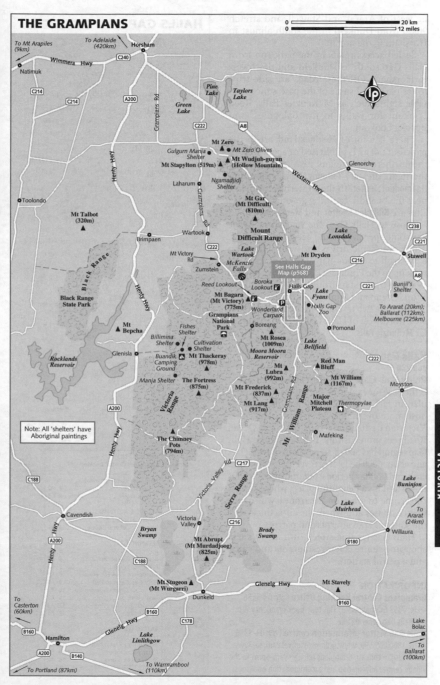

THE GRAMPIANS

0 |————————————————| 20 km
0 |————————————————| 12 miles

To Mt Arapiles (9km)
To Adelaide (420km)
Horsham
Wimmera Hwy
C240
Natimuk
C214
C214
A200

Pine Lake
Taylors Lake
Green Lake
C222
A8

Grampians Rd

Mt Zero
Gulgurn Manja Shelter
Mt Zero Olives
Mt Wudjub-guyun (Hollow Mountain)
Mt Stapylton (519m)
Glenorchy

Laharum
Ngamadjidj Shelter
Mt Gar (Mt Difficult) (810m)
Western Hwy

Toolondo
Mt Talbot (320m)
Wartook
Mount Difficult Range
Lake Lonsdale
C238

Brimpaen
C222
Mt Victory Rd
Lake Wartook
McKenzie Falls
Mt Dryden
Stawell
C221
A8

Black Range
Zumstein
Reed Lookout
Boroka Lookout
See Halls Gap Map (p568)
Halls Gap
C216
C221
Bunjil's Shelter

Black Range State Park
Mt Bagara (Mt Victory) (775m)
Lake Fyans
Halls Gap Zoo
To Ararat (20km); Ballarat (112km); Melbourne (225km)

Henty Hwy
Mt Bepcha
Grampians National Park
Wonderland Carpark
Boreang
Lake Bellfield
Pomonal
C222

Fishes Shelter
Billimina Shelter
Cultivation Shelter
Mt Rosea (1009m)
Moora Moora Reservoir

Rocklands Reservoir
Glenisla
Buandik Camping Ground
Mt Thackeray (978m)
Mt Lubra (992m)
Red Man Bluff
Mt William (1167m)
Moyston

Manja Shelter
The Fortress (875m)
Mt Frederick (837m)
Major Mitchell Plateau
Thermopylae

A200
Victoria Range
Mt Lang (917m)

Note: All 'shelters' have Aboriginal paintings

C188
The Chimney Pots (794m)
Victoria Valley Rd
C217
Serra Range
Mafeking

Lake Buninjong

Cavendish
Victoria Valley
C216
Brady Swamp
Lake Muirhead
To Ararat (24km)

Henty Hwy
Bryan Swamp
Mt Abrupt (Mt Murdadjoog) (825m)
B180
Willaura

A200
C188

Mt Stugeon (Mt Wurgarri)
Glenelg Hwy
Mt Stavely
B160

To Casterton (60km)
B160
Dunkeld
B160

Hamilton
Glenelg Hwy
Lake Linlithgow
C178
Lake Bolac

A200
B140
To Ballarat (100km)

To Portland (87km)
To Warrnambool (110km)

VICTORIA

lie west of Ararat and Stawell, and stretch 90km from Dunkeld in the south almost to Horsham in the north.

Sealed access roads in the park run from Halls Gap south to Dunkeld and northwest to Horsham. Off these roads are side trips to car parks and some of the park's most notable sights such as McKenzies Falls, Reed Lookout for walks to the Balconies, and Boroka Lookout.

There is a lot of **Aboriginal rock art** in the park, but not all is publicised or accessible. In the northern Grampians, near Mt Stapylton, the main sites are **Gulgurn Manja Shelter** and **Ngamadjidj Shelter**. In the western Grampians, near the Buandik camping ground, the main sites are **Billimina Shelter** and **Manja Shelter**.

Close to Halls Gap, the **Wonderland Range** has some spectacular and accessible scenery. There are scenic drives and walks, from an easy stroll to Venus Bath (30 minutes) to a walk up to the Pinnacles Lookout (five hours). Walking tracks start from Halls Gap, and the Wonderland and Sundial car parks.

There are two tracks from the **Zumstein picnic area**, northwest of Halls Gap, to the spectacular **McKenzie Falls**.

Halls Gap
pop 280
Pretty Halls Gap, in the heart of the Grampians, is the base for exploring the region. It's so popular, in fact, that Halls Gap and its environs host more overnight visitors than any other Victorian destination – only the Great Ocean Road sees more visitors. Figure this: the Halls Gap region has 300 or so permanent residents, and about 6000 beds! It gets very busy on weekends and holiday periods, but midweek it calms down and it's a delightful place, where kangaroos come to graze on the front lawns of the town's houses and where the air is thick with the songs of kookaburras and parrots.

Halls Gap is a one-street town with a small shopping centre, a few restaurants and cafes, and a petrol station.

INFORMATION
Grampians Central Booking Office (☎ 03-5356 4654; 7353 Grampians Rd) This tour-booking agency is in the Halls Gap general store.

Halls Gap visitor information centre (☎ 03-5356 4616, 1800 065 599; www.grampianstravel.com.au, www .visithallsgap.com.au; Grampians Rd; ☷ 9am-5pm) In the village centre; information and accommodation bookings.

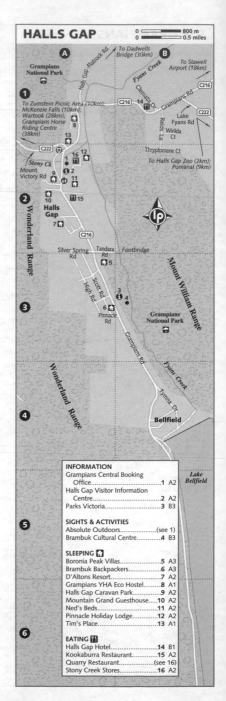

HALLS GAP

INFORMATION	
Grampians Central Booking Office................................**1** A2	
Halls Gap Visitor Information Centre......................**2** A2	
Parks Victoria.............................**3** B3	

SIGHTS & ACTIVITIES	
Absolute Outdoors....................(see 1)	
Brambuk Cultural Centre............**4** B3	

SLEEPING	
Boronia Peak Villas....................**5** A3	
Brambuk Backpackers.................**6** A3	
D'Altons Resort..........................**7** A2	
Grampians YHA Eco Hostel.........**8** A1	
Halls Gap Caravan Park..............**9** A2	
Mountain Grand Guesthouse.....**10** A2	
Ned's Beds...............................**11** A2	
Pinnacle Holiday Lodge.............**12** A2	
Tim's Place..............................**13** A1	

EATING	
Halls Gap Hotel.......................**14** B1	
Kookaburra Restaurant.............**15** A2	
Quarry Restaurant...................(see 16)	
Stony Creek Stores..................**16** A2	

Parks Victoria (☎ 03-5356 4381, 13 19 63; www
.parkweb.vic.gov.au) At the Brambuk Cultural Centre on
the southern edge of town, with maps and brochures,
camping permits and fishing licences.

SIGHTS

Don't miss a visit to the wonderful **Brambuk Cultural Centre** (☎ 03-5356 4452; www.brambuk.com.au; Grampians Rd, admission free; ☼ 9am-5pm), representing the open wings of the cockatoo (brambuk). It's a striking building that combines timeless Aboriginal motifs with contemporary design and building materials. Five Koorie communities, together with Parks Victoria, run the centre, offering insights into local culture and history through Koorie stories, art, music, dance, weapons and tools. The adjacent **Gariwerd Dreaming Theatre** (adult/child $5/3) presents both Dreamtime stories and modern informative films about the region. There are demonstrations of Koorie music and dance, organised tours of the rock-art sites, and education and holiday programs. Outside are native plants used by Aboriginal people for food and medicine.

The small **Halls Gap Zoo** (☎ 03-5356 4668; www
.hallsgapwildlife.com; Pomonal Rd; adult/child/family $16/8/40; ☼ 10am-5pm Wed-Mon), 3km southeast of Halls Gap, has lots of native and exotic animals in spacious enclosures.

TOURS

Absolute Outdoors (☎ 03-5356 4556; www.absolute outdoors.com.au; Shop 4, Stony Creek Stores) Rock-climbing, abseiling, canoeing and mountain-biking adventures.
Brambuk Cultural Centre (☎ 03-5356 4452; Grampians Rd; ☼ 9am-5pm) Offers a two-hour cultural and rock art tour (adult/child $35/22). Bookings essential.
Eco Platypus Tours (☎ 1800 819 091; www.ecoplaty pustours.com) Offers day trips to the Grampians from Melbourne for $99 per person.
Grampians Horse Riding Centre (☎ 03-5383 9255; www.grampianshorseriding.com.au; Brimpaen, Wartook Valley; 2hr rides $65; ☼ rides 10am & 2pm) Provides opportunities to explore forests and valleys on horseback, 38km northwest of Halls Gap.
Grampians Mountain Adventure Company (☎ 03-5383 9218, www.grampiansadventure.com.au; half-/full-day instruction $75/125) Rock-climbing and abseiling adventures tailored to suit those who fancy the vertical world, assisted by accredited instructors.
Grampians Personalised Tours & Adventures (☎ 0429 954 686, 03-5356 4654; www.grampianstours .com; half-/full-day tours $79/149) Offers a range of 4WD tours and guided bushwalks, as well as multiday walks.

Wildlife Tours (☎ 03-9741 6333; www.wildlifetours .com.au) Two-/three-day tours combining the Great Ocean Road and the Grampians for $160/199 per person.

SLEEPING
Budget
Brambuk Backpackers (☎ 03-5356 4250; www .brambuk.com.au; Grampians Rd; dm $22-25, d $65; ☒) Opposite the Brambuk Cultural Centre and Aboriginal-owned and run, this place is light and airy with a mellow friendly feel and mountain views.

Ned's Beds (☎ 03-5356 4516; www.grampiansback packers.com.au; 2 Heath St; dm/d $23/60) Budget accommodation in several houses around Halls Gap.

Tim's Place (☎ 03-5356 4288; www.timsplace.com .au; Grampians Rd; dm/s/d $25/50/65; ☒) Tim's Place is terrific little backpackers, with great facilities and lots of local knowledge from the friendly owner.

our pick Grampians YHA Eco-Hostel (☎ 03-5356 4544; www.yha.com.au; cnr Grampians Rd & Buckler St; dm/d/f $30/79/103; ☒) This architecturally designed and ecofriendly YHA is bright, modern and beautifully equipped. There are two- or four-bed dorms, spacious lounge and kitchen areas, and the hosts often provide freshly baked bread, freshly laid eggs and fresh herbs.

Midrange
our pick D'Altons Resort (☎ 03-5356 4666; www.dal tonsresort.com.au; 48 Glen St; standard/deluxe cottages from $100/120; ☒) These delightful timber cottages spread up the hill, away from the main road, between the gums and kangaroos. They have cosy fires, big lounge chairs and little verandahs. There's a tennis court and laundry.

Pinnacle Holiday Lodge (☎ 03-5356 4249, 1800 819 283; www.pinnacleholiday.com.au; 21-45 Heath St; 1-/2-bed unit $107/155, motel d $149-167; ☒ ☒) Right behind the Stony Creek cafe strip but shielded from the main street, this spacious property has comfy self-contained units and swanky motel spa suites with flat-screen TVs and gas log fires. The indoor pool, and tennis courts and barbecue areas add to the bush-resort feel.

Boronia Peak Villas (☎ 03-5356 4500; www.boronia peakvillas.com.au; cnr Grampians & Tandara Rds; 2-/3-bed villas from $130/220; ☒ ☒) With a lovely bush setting, these cottages offer excellent self-contained accommodation from standard and family units to super-deluxe spa units.

VICTORIA

Mountain Grand Guesthouse (☎ 03-5356 4232; www.mountaingrand.com; Grampians Rd; s/d incl breakfast & dinner $160/206) This gracious timber guest house prides itself on being an old-fashioned lodge, where breakfast and dinner is included, encouraging guests to mingle and relax. The bedrooms are fresh and colourful with their own spacious bathrooms.

Camping

Parks Victoria (☎ 03-5356 4381, 13 19 63; www .parkweb.vic.gov.au) Located at the Brambuk Cultural Centre, Parks Victoria manages 11 campsites with toilets and fireplaces, but you need to bring your own drinking water. Permits ($13) cover one car and up to six people. Bush camping is permitted except in the Wonderland Range area, around Lake Wartook, and in marked parts of the Serra, Mt William and Victoria Ranges. Check with the rangers before heading off.

Halls Gap Caravan Park (☎ 03-5356 4251; www .hallsgapcaravanpark.com.au; Dunkeld Rd; unpowered/ powered sites from $20/25, cabins $60-110) Occupying a large part of the town centre, this park has good camping, a range of cabins, a tennis court and a gymnasium.

EATING

The little group of shops known as Stony Creek Stores has a bakery and a couple of good cafes.

Halls Gap Hotel (☎ 03-5356 4566; 2262 Grampians Rd; mains $14-23; ⏱ lunch & dinner) Although a couple of kilometres north of the main strip, the local pub serves generous portions of bistro food and is a social place for a beer after bushwalking.

Quarry Restaurant (☎ 03-5356 4858; Stony Creek Stores; mains $18-38; ⏱ lunch & dinner Wed-Mon) Well known for quality Mod Oz cuisine – kangaroo fillets and lemon pepper barramundi – Quarry is near Sony Creek Stores.

Kookaburra Restaurant (☎ 03-5356 4222; 127 Grampians Rd; mains $19-31; ⏱ dinner Tue-Sun, lunch Sat & Sun) After 30 years, this place is still a Halls Gap institution for its crispy-skinned duckling and juicy steaks. Book ahead for dinner.

GETTING THERE & AWAY

V/Line (☎ 13 61 96) has a daily train/coach service from Melbourne to Halls Gap ($27, 4½ hours), but it's painfully slow, with changes required at Ballarat and Stawell.

Three daily buses run between Halls Gap and Stawell ($6, 35 minutes).

Christians Bus Company (☎ 03-5352 1501) runs a service between Ararat and Warrnambool, stopping at Halls Gap, Hamilton and Port Fairy.

Mt Zero

Planted in 1953, the olive grove at **Mt Zero Olives** (☎ 03-5383 8280; www.mountzeroolives.com; Mt Zero Rd; ⏱ 10am-5pm) produces olives, olive oils (including infused varieties), tapenades and other gourmet products in a picturesque setting. There are tastings and farm-gate sales daily, and an excellent cafe that opens on weekends and holidays. It's on the northern fringe of Grampians National Park.

HORSHAM

pop 14,125

Mark Twain came here in 1896 and commented that 'Horsham sits in a plain which is as level as a floor'. Twain clearly hadn't been to Australia's outback. First settled in 1841, Horsham is the main commercial centre of the Wimmera and a busy service town that makes a good base for visiting Mt Arapiles State Park and Little Desert National Park. It also boasts one of the finest public golf courses in regional Victoria, though the clubhouse burned down in the 2009 bushfires.

The **Horsham visitor information centre** (☎ 03-5382 1832, 1800 633 218; www.visithorsham.com .au; 20 O'Callaghan's Pde; ⏱ 9am-5pm) books accommodation and has internet access ($3 for 30 minutes).

The **Horsham Art Gallery** (☎ 03-5382 5575; www .horsham.net.au/gallery; 80 Wilson St; adult/child $2/free; ⏱ 10am-5pm Tue-Fri, 1-4.30pm Sat & Sun) houses an impressive collection of works by significant Australian artists, as well as changing contemporary exhibitions.

Sleeping & Eating

Royal Hotel (☎ 03-5382 1255; 132 Firebrace St; d $55) This historic hotel has a beer garden and simple rooms upstairs – though it can get rowdy till late on Friday and Saturday nights. The popular bistro (mains $12 to $27) serves traditional steaks and pasta dishes for lunch and dinner.

Horsham Motel (☎ 03-5382 5555; 5 Dimboola Rd; s/d $68/78; ▨) Opposite May Park, this is an affordable set of ground-floor motel units.

VICTORIA

Horsham House (☎ 03-5382 5053; www.horsham house.com.au; 27 Roberts Ave; r incl breakfast $140-160; ⊠) There's a mix of antiques and modern amenities in this grand balconied house (1905) in the centre of town. There are two guest rooms in the house and a self-contained cottage with spa overlooking a rose garden – popular with honeymooners.

Horsham Riverside Caravan Park (☎ 03-5382 3476; www.horshamcaravanpark.ymca.org.au; 188-190 Firebrace St; unpowered/powered sites $21/25, d cabins $68) This is a great little spot between the botanic gardens and the river, with shady sites, good facilities and bike hire.

Oasis of Wellbeing (☎ 03-5382 0068; 48 Wilson St; mains $8.50-16.50; ⊗ 9.30am-6pm Mon-Fri) Funky, New Age cafe serving filo wraps, focaccias, quiche and curries. The setting is like someone's home with a gallery out the back, and massage and head spas are available.

Getting There & Away
V/Line (☎ 13 61 96) operates three or four services daily from Melbourne: there's one only direct train (the *Overland* en route to Adelaide), while others change to buses at Ballarat or Ararat ($31, four to 6½ hours).

Firefly Express (www.fireflyexpress.com.au) and **Greyhound Australia** (www.greyhound.com.au) pass through Horsham daily on their Melbourne–Adelaide run. The bus terminal is outside Horsham's old **police station** (24 Roberts Ave).

To get to the Grampians, take the V/Line bus to Stawell and another bus from there to Halls Gap.

MT ARAPILES STATE PARK
Mt Arapiles, 37km west of Horsham and 12km west of Natimuk, is Australia's premier rock climbing venue, with more than 2000 climbs from basic to advanced. The park is also popular for walks. There are two short and steep walking tracks from Centenary Park to the top of Arapiles – or you can drive up.

Tiny **Natimuk** (www.natimuk.com) is the main base for climbers, with accommodation, a pub with motel units and adventure outfits.

The **Natimuk Climbing Company** (☎ 03-5387 1558; www.climbco.com.au; 117 Main St, Natimuk) and **Arapiles Climbing Guides** (☎ 03-5384 0376; http:// users.netconnect.com.au/~climbacg) offer climbing and abseiling instruction.

Arapiles Mountain Shop (☎ 03-5387 1529; 67 Main St, Natimuk) sells and hires climbing equipment.

Sleeping & Eating
Duffholme Cabins (☎ 03-5387 4246; Natimuk-Goroke Rd; d $41, extra adult $12) This self-contained cottage, surrounded by wildlife with views of Mt Arapiles, sleeps seven. Ring to make arrangements (it's not staffed).

Camping ground (Centenary Park; campsites per 2 people $2) Known locally as 'the Pines', this is a popular spot at the base of the mountain.

Natimuk Lake Caravan Park (☎ 0407 800 753, jmellis37@bigpond.com; Lake Rd; unpowered/powered sites $14/20) Beside Lake Natimuk, about 4km north of Natimuk, this camping area has barbecues and laundry but no cabins.

Getting There & Away
The weekday **bus service** (☎ 0428 861 160) between Horsham and Naracoorte will drop you at Mt Arapiles on request ($10).

DIMBOOLA
pop 1495

This tiny town was made famous by Jack Hibberd's play *Dimboola*, and the subsequent 1979 John Duigan film of the same name about a country wedding. The huge, historic Dimboola Hotel (where the film was shot), with its spectacular balcony and turret, was gutted by fire in 2003 and has since lain dormant.

There's tourist information and internet access at the **Dim-e-Shop** (☎ 03-5389 1588; 109 Lloyd St), which keeps erratic hours.

Today the town suffers from the drought – the Wimmera River is virtually bone dry here – and is best known as a gateway to the Little Desert National Park, which starts 4km south of town. **Pink Lake** is a colourful salt lake beside the Western Hwy about 9km northwest of Dimboola.

Ebenezer Aboriginal Mission Station was established in Antwerp, 18km north of Dimboola, in 1859. The remains of the station are signposted off the Dimboola–Jeparit road.

Sleeping & Eating
Dimboola Riverside Caravan Park (☎ 03-5389 1416; dimboolacaravanpark@bigpond.com; 2 Wimmera St; unpowered/powered sites $18/23, cabins $70) The grounds of this park beside the Wimmera River are shaded by eucalypt and pine trees. The owners also run the secluded Pondoroo Bush Retreat, where self-contained units cost $90 a double, and lead two-hour

VICTORIA

walking tours into the national park ($10 per person).

Riverside Host Farm (☎ 03-5389 1550; Riverside Rd; sites/cabins $20/77; ⊠) This lovely property sits between lavender fields and the banks of the Wimmera River – if there's water in it you can hire canoes. The covered camp kitchen and barbecue area is very social.

Victoria Hotel (☎ 03-5389 1630; 32 Wimmera St; s/d $35/60) A well-preserved 1924 pub with a fantastic lace-trimmed, vine-covered verandah and basic but clean rooms upstairs. The bar or bistro ($4 to $20) is the best place in town for lunch or dinner.

LITTLE DESERT NATIONAL PARK

This national park may not, initially, appear very desertlike, as there's a rich diversity of plants and wildflowers. Two sealed roads between the Western and Wimmera Hwys pass through the park, or you can take the good gravel road from Dimboola. The best-known of the residents here is the mallee fowl.

There are short walks in the eastern block. Longer walks leave from the camping ground south of Kiata, including a 12km trek south to the Salt Lake; always carry water and notify **Parks Victoria** (☎ 13 19 63) before you set out.

Little Desert Lodge (☎ 03-5391 5232; www .littledesertlodge.com.au; unpowered/powered sites $15.50/18.50, dm $20, s/d incl breakfast from $90/115; ⊠) is set in natural bushland on the edge of the national park, 16km south of Nhill, and has a range of accommodation, a bar and restaurant, barbecue area and campfire. There's a mallee fowl aviary (adult/child $10/5) on the property and 4WD tours into the park (half/three-quarter day $50/55), and evening spotlight walks.

Parks Victoria (☎ 13 19 63; Nursery Rd, Wail) has camping grounds at Horseshoe Bend and Ackle Bend, both on the Wimmera River south of Dimboola, and another about 10km south of Kiata. Sites have drinking water, toilets and fireplaces.

THE MALLEE

The Mallee takes its name from the mallee scrub that once covered the region. Mallee gums are canny desert survivors – 1000-year-old root systems are not uncommon – and

for the Aborigines the region yielded plentiful food. The sky seems vast as you drive through the area, surrounded by horizon, dead-flat semi-arid land and twisted mallee scrub. The Mallee includes the one genuinely empty part of the state (wilderness known as Sunset Country) and the sense of isolation and expanse is exhilarating – you don't have to visit central Australia to get a taste of the outback.

The farmers of this district have been doing it hard after years of drought, and consequently many towns are also failing. In just 150 years many small towns in this region have been founded, prospered, peaked and now lie all but abandoned, decaying in the mallee scrub.

BIG DESERT WILDERNESS PARK

This 113,500-hectare park is a desert wilderness with no roads, tracks, facilities or water. Walking and camping are permitted but only for the experienced and totally self-sufficient. In summer, temperatures are usually way too high for bushwalking. Notify the **Yaapeet ranger's office** (☎ 03-5395 7221) before heading off.

The area is mostly sand dunes, red sandstone ridges and mallee, but there's an abundance of flora and fauna, and some unusual wildlife, such as Mitchell's hopping mouse.

A dry-weather road from Murrayville on the Mallee Hwy (B12) to Nhill separates this park from the **Wyperfeld National Park**. Parts of the road are very rough and may be impassable after rain.

There are basic free campsites at Big Billy Bore, the Springs, Moonlight Tank and Broken Bucket Reserve, all on the eastern side of the park.

MURRAY-SUNSET NATIONAL PARK

The 663,000-hectare park is arid and mainly inaccessible. An unsealed road leads from Linga on the Mallee Hwy up to the **Pink Lakes** at the southern edge of the park, where there's a basic camping ground. Beyond this you must have a 4WD. The **Shearer's Quarters** (☎ 03-5028 1218; groups $57) has basic accommodation on the park's western side, sleeping up to 14 people.

For more information contact the rangers in **Underbool** (☎ 03-5094 6267; Fasham St) on the Mallee Hwy, or in **Werrimull** (☎ 03-5028 1218) on the northern side of the park.

VICTORIA

THE MURRAY RIVER

State border, irrigation lifeline and recreational hub for waterskiers, canoeists and campers, the Murray River is Australia's most important inland waterway. Separating Victoria and NSW, the Murray flows from its source high in the Great Dividing Range in northeastern Victoria to Encounter Bay in SA, a journey of more than 2700kms, making it the third-longest navigable river in the world.

Some of Australia's earliest explorers travelled along the river, and long before roads and railways crossed the land, the Murray's paddle steamers carried supplies to and from remote sheep stations. Today you can ride on paddle steamers at Mildura, Swan Hill and, more notably, Echuca. The Murray River region is one of the country's most productive agricultural districts, thanks to the endless sunshine and the wonders of irrigation. Approaching from the south, through the drought-stricken Wimmera/Mallee district, the contrast couldn't be starker – vineyards, avocadoes, citrus and almond groves cover countless thousands of hectares, all vividly green and surreal in this semi-arid emptiness.

Before poker machines were introduced into Victoria in 1990, many of the 'twin' river towns on the NSW side made a fortune from punters travelling across by the busload to gamble on their 'pokies'. Now they're on both sides and gambling has spread like a plague through Victoria.

MILDURA
pop 30,000

Mildura is a real oasis town. It's as isolated as anywhere you'll find in Victoria and after driving for hours past desolate, drought-plagued farmlands, the lush green orchards and huge vineyards loom up in the windscreen like an apparition.

The town developed in the late 1880s when William Chaffey pioneered the irrigation system. As well as being one of the richest agricultural areas in Australia and manna for travellers looking for fruit-picking work, it's also a thriving tourist town with lush golf courses, art deco buildings, river cruises and as much sunshine as anywhere in the state. Once a citrus-growing region, Mildura (meaning 'red soil') and neigh-

bouring Gol Gol and Wentworth in NSW are now largely given over to viticulture. It's good news for casual workers – Mildura is one of the most productive fruit-picking regions in Australia.

Information

Café de la Rue (☎ 03-5023 5800; www.cafedelarue .com.au; 51 Deakin Ave; per 30 min $1; ☽ 9am-8pm Mon-Fri, 10am-6pm Sat & Sun; 🖳) Coffee, books and internet access at $1 per half hour and you can plug your own laptop in or use wi-fi.

Mildura visitor information centre (☎ 03-5018 8380; www.visitmildura.com.au; cnr Deakin Ave & Twelfth St) In the Alfred Deakin Centre – which includes the municipal library (internet access $1 per 15 minutes), Mildura Waves Aquatic Centre and Canoe Tree Café – it has an accommodation booking service and a display on local history, ecology and Aboriginal culture.

Sights & Activities

The excellent **Mildura Arts Centre & Rio Vista** (☎ 03-5018 8322; 199 Cureton Ave; adult/child $3.50/free; ☽ 10am-5pm) complex combines an art gallery, theatre and historical museum at Rio Vista, a former home of pioneer William B Chaffey. This grand homestead has been beautifully preserved. The interior is set up as a series of displays depicting 19th-century life, with period furnishings, costumes, photos and an interesting collection of memorabilia. The adjacent modern gallery features changing exhibitions.

Available from the information centre, *The Chaffey Trail* brochure guides you around some of Mildura's more interesting sights, including the **Mildura Wharf**, the **weir** and **lock**, **Mildara Winery** and the **Old Psyche Bend Pump Station**.

PADDLE-STEAMER CRUISES

Cruises depart from the Mildura Wharf.
PS Melbourne (☎ 03-5023 2200; Mildura Wharf; 2hr cruise adult/child $25/10; ☽ cruises 10.50am & 1.50pm Sun-Thu) The famous PS *Melbourne* is the only paddle steamer in Victoria still driven by steam power – watch the operator stoke the original boiler with wood. On Friday and Saturday the same two-hour cruises are on PV *Rothbury*.
PV Rothbury (☎ 03-5023 2200; Mildura Wharf) Offers five-hour winery cruises (adult/child $60/28) at 10.30am on Thursday, three-hour dinner cruises ($58/26) at 7pm on Thursday, and a 3½-hour lunch cruise ($26/10) at 11.30am on Tuesday – you buy your own lunch at the Gol Gol Hotel. Dinner cruises also depart on PV *Mundoo*.

THE MURRAY RIVER

VICTORIA

Tours

Several Aboriginal operators run tours. The best-known of these is **Harry Nanya** (☎ 03-5027 2076; www.harrynanyatours.com.au), whose tours include an excellent day trip to Mungo National Park (adult/child $155/100) in NSW. Tag-along tours (bring your own vehicle) cost $80/40.

Discover Mildura (☎ 03-5024 7448; www.discov ermildura.com.au; day trips per person $110; ☼ Tue, Wed, Thu, Sun) Varieties of day tours taking in wineries, restaurants and paddle steamers.

Mildura Ballooning (☎ 03-5024 6848; www.mildura ballooning.com.au; adult/child $285/165) Dawn hot-air balloon flights over the Murray with champagne breakfast.

MurrayTrek Tours (☎ 1800 797 530; sunset tour $130) Evening 4WD tour to Mungo National Park with dinner.

Wild Side Outdoors (☎ 03-5024 3721; www.wild sideoutdoors.com.au; sunset canoe tour $25) Based in Red Cliffs, just south of town, this outfit offers Murray canoe trips, walking and cycling tours.

Sleeping

BUDGET

Mildura has a half-dozen hostels and budget guest houses, all geared towards backpackers looking for seasonal work. All offer cheap weekly rates and can help find fruit-picking and labouring work.

Mildura International Backpackers (☎ /fax 5021 0133; 5 Cedar Ave; dm per night/week $25/129; ☐) Basic but friendly house where the rooms have two beds (not bunks). The owners will help you find work for a $7 finders/transport fee.

Oasis Backpackers (☎ 03-5022 8255; oasis@bigpond .net.au; 230-232 Deakin Ave; dm/d per week $140/300; ☐ ☒) Mildura's best-equipped backpacker hostel has a great pool and patio bar area, ultra-modern kitchen, free internet and the owners can provide plenty of seasonal work – as a result the minimum stay here is a week.

MIDRANGE & TOP END

Kar-Rama Motor Inn (☎ 03-5023 4221; karrama@ncable .com.au; 153 Deakin Ave; s/d $62/70; ☒ ☒) Highly affordable and central motel just south of the main strip with plain but tidy rooms and a pool.

Acacia Holiday Apartments (☎ 03-5023 3855; www .acaciaapartments.com.au; 762 Calder Hwy; cabins $78-102, 1/2-bed apt $95/104; ☒ ☒) Southwest of the centre on the Calder Hwy, these large self-contained one-, two- and three-bedroom units offer out-

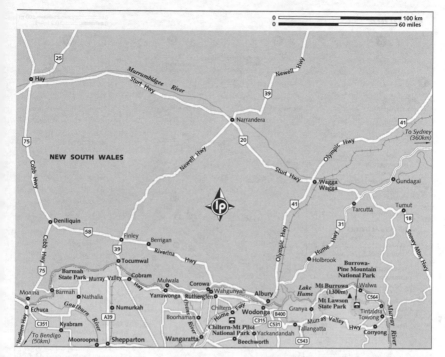

standing value for money if you're in a group or family, or staying more than a couple of days. Apartments have kitchens and lounges with free cable TV, and are arrayed around a swimming pool.

Grand Hotel (☎ 03-5023 0511; www.mildura grandhotel.com.au; Seventh St; d $100-200, ste $230-400; ❄ 🖥 ⚲) The Grand dominates Mildura's main strip, occupying a whole city block overlooking the Murray. It's Mildura's top address, as much for its historic legacy as its modern amenities. Since 1891 it has played host to prime ministers, governors-general and VIPs, and today the renovated rooms have an understated elegance. There's a gym, spa and sauna.

Penny's Cottage (☎ 03-5021 4043; www.pennyscot tage.com.au; 173a Eighth St; d $130, incl breakfast $165) In a delightful original baby-blue timber house, Penny's Cottage is fully self-contained with a backyard, colonial-era decor and two queen bedrooms.

our pick Cameron's Mildura Apartments (☎ 03-5021 2876; www.cameronsmildura.com.au; 16 Olive Ave; d incl breakfast $165-180; ❄ 🖥) These two apartments are spectacular in their design and decoration – an unlikely mix of corrugated iron, stone and recycled timber, with a lilac, mauve and canary-yellow colour scheme in the 'Shed' and a redder-than-red tartan theme in the 'Highlander'. They feature king beds, plasma TVs, modern kitchens, double spas and showers.

Acacia Houseboats (☎ 03-5022 1510; www.acacia boats.com.au; 3 nights for 2 people from $600) Acacia has a number of lovely houseboats accommodating up to 10 people, with everything supplied except food and drink. A group can rent a 10-berth houseboat for a weekend (three nights) for $1400.

CAMPING

Apex RiverBeach Holiday Park (☎ 03-5023 6879; www.apexriverbeach.com.au; Cureton Ave; unpowered/powered sites $19/22, d cabins/villas from $63/78; ❄ 🖥) Thanks to a fantastic location on sandy Apex Beach just outside town, this bush park is always popular – prices are 25% higher during school holidays. There are campfires, a bush kitchen, barbecue area, boat ramp, good swimming, a cafe and wireless internet access.

VICTORIA

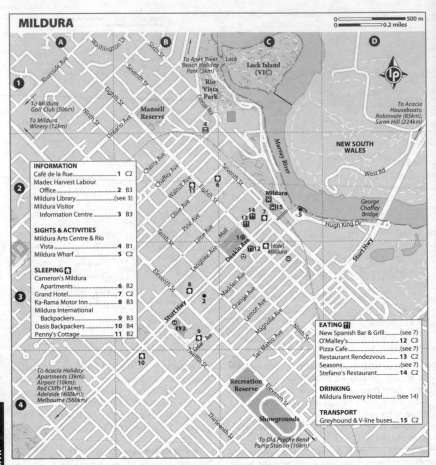

MILDURA

0 — 500 m
0 — 0.2 miles

Eating

Mildura is famous for Italian raconteur Stefano de Pieri, who has single-handedly stamped the town on the foodie map. The Grand Hotel on Deakin Avenue is culinary ground zero with Pizza Café, Seasons and Pieri's own Stefano's all sharing the address.

Aside from the gourmet dining strip on Langtree St, there are dinner cruises aboard the paddle steamer PV *Rothbury* on Thursdays (see p573).

Restaurant Rendezvous (☎ 03-5023 1571; 34 Langtree Ave; mains $19-35; ☷ lunch Mon-Fri, dinner Mon-Sat) Almost swallowed up by the Grand, the warm, casual atmosphere of this long-running place complements the perfectly prepared seafood, grills, pastas, crepes and unusual specials.

O'Malley's (☎ 03-5021 4236; 56 Deakin Ave; mains $20-26; ☷ lunch & dinner Mon-Sat) This Irish pub does hearty counter meals (beef and Guinness pie, lamb shanks etc) and packs them in for $9 lunches and half-price dinners on Wednesday (before 7pm).

New Spanish Bar & Grill (☎ 03-5023 0511; Grand Hotel, cnr Deakin Ave & Seventh St; mains $27-38; ☷ dinner Tue-Sun) Part of the Grand, this place keeps it simple with quality steaks and barbecue food, including kangaroo and Mallee rump. A carnivore's haven.

ourpick Stefano's Restaurant (☎ 03-5023 0511; Grand Hotel, cnr Deakin Ave & Seventh St; set menu $95; ☷ dinner Mon-Sat) Descend into the former un-

VICTORIA

derground wine cellar to see Stefano work his magic with his five-course northern Italian dinners. This intimate dining experience is the star attraction at the Grand Hotel – book well in advance.

Drinking

Mildura Brewery Hotel (☎ 03-5022 2988; www.mildurabrewery.com.au; 20 Langtree Ave; ◷ Tue-Sun) Set in the former Astor cinema in the same block as the Grand Hotel, this is Mildura's trendiest nightspot. Shiny stainless-steel vats, pipes and brewing equipment make a great backdrop to the stylish lounge, and the beers brewed here – honey wheat beer and Mallee Bull among them – are superb.

Getting There & Away

AIR

Mildura airport – Victoria's busiest regional airport – is about 10km west of the town centre, off the Sturt Hwy (A20). **Regional Express** (REX; ☎ 13 17 13; www.rex.com.au) operates daily services between Mildura and Melbourne, as well as many regional centres. **Qantas** (☎ 13 13 13; www.qantas.com.au) and **Virgin Blue** (☎ 13 67 89; www.virginblue.com.au) also fly between Mildura and Melbourne.

TRAIN & BUS

Long-distance buses operate from a depot at the train station on Seventh St, but there are currently no passenger train services from here.

Murraylink is a **V/Line** (☎ 13 61 96) bus service that runs four times a week, connecting all the towns along the Murray River, with connections at Bendigo, Swan Hill and Echuca. V/Line also has a train/bus service to/from Melbourne ($37, 7½ hours) to Mildura, via Swan Hill and Bendigo.

Greyhound Australia (☎ 1300 473 946; www.greyhound.com.au) has daily services between Mildura and Adelaide ($67, 5½ hours) or Sydney ($149, 16 hours).

MILDURA TO SWAN HILL

The most direct trip to Swan Hill takes you over the Murray River into NSW and along the Sturt Hwy to **Robinvale**, a small river town and wine region, before getting back on the Murray Valley Hwy on the Victoria side.

Hattah-Kulkyne National Park

South of Mildura off the Calder Hwy, the Hattah-Kulkyne National Park has dry, sandy mallee-scrub country and fertile riverside areas, lined with red gum, black box, wattles and bottlebrush. The **Hattah Lakes** system fills when the Murray floods, and is great for bird-watching.

The access road is at **Hattah**, 70km south of Mildura on the Calder Hwy. The visitor information centre is 5km into the park. There are two **nature drives**, the Hattah and the Kulkyne, and a network of old camel tracks. Contact **Parks Victoria** (☎ 13 19 63; www.parkweb.vic.gov.au) or the **Hattah ranger's office** (☎ 03-5029 3253).

There are camping facilities at Lake Hattah and Lake Mournpoul, but limited water. Camping is also possible anywhere along the Murray River frontage.

SWAN HILL
pop 9700

Swan Hill is a languid riverside community without the tourist hype of Mildura or Echuca, but still boasting a few sights such as Australia's oldest re-created pioneer museum. It was named by intrepid explorer Major Thomas Mitchell in 1836, after he was kept awake by swans in the nearby lagoon. Today it's an important regional centre surrounded by irrigated farmlands. Fruit-pickers can find work on farms about 25km west of Swan Hill around Nyah.

The **Swan Hill Region information centre** (☎ 03-5032 3033, 1800 625 373; www.swanhillonline.com; cnr McCrae & Curlewis Sts; ▣) has maps and loads of tourist brochures.

VICTORIA

SEASONAL WORK

Mildura is king of the casual fruit-picking industry in northwest Victoria. Harvest season runs from January through March, but casual work on farms and orchards is available year-round. Some farmers allow camping but often you'll need to stay in town, so transport may be necessary. Backpacker hostels in Mildura can help line up work and arrange transport (usually for a fee).

Madec Harvest Labour Office (☎ 03-5021 3472; www.madec.edu.au; 126-130 Deakin Ave) has comprehensive listings of fruit-picking work.

Sights & Activities

Swan Hill's major attraction, the **Pioneer Settlement** (☎ 03-5036 2410; www.pioneersettle ment.com.au; Horseshoe Bend; adult/child $22.60/12; 9.30am-4pm) is an enjoyable re-creation of a paddle-steamer riverside port town. The dusty old-time streets feature shops, an old school and church, vintage car rides, Aboriginal keeping place and the fascinating Kaiser Stereoscope. PS *Gem*, one of the largest river boats to have served on the Murray, was being renovated at the time of research.

The paddle steamer PS *Pyap* makes one-hour **cruises** (adult/child $16.80/10; cruises 2.30pm, also 10.30am Sat, Sun & school holidays) along the Murray. Every night at dusk a 45-minute **sound-and-light show** (adult/child $16.80/10) brings the historic old town to life. There are cheaper combination packages if you want to do the cruise and sound-and-light show with your entry ticket.

Murray Downs Resort (☎ 1800 807 574; www .murraydownsresort.com.au; Murray Downs Dr; 9/18 holes $20/35, club hire $22) is 5km east of the town in NSW, but is regarded as a Swan Hill club and boasts one of the finest public resort golf courses in Victoria.

Sleeping & Eating

Most backpackers looking for fruit-picking work head out to the small communities of Nyah and Nyah West, which have several backpacker hostels, all of which can help you find work.

Pioneer Settlement Lodge (☎ 03-5032 1093; Horseshoe Bend; dm/d $28/65) Although geared to school and community groups, this rambling riverside lodge attached to the Pioneer Settlement is worth trying, especially during school holidays. It's pretty basic (BYO linen), but there are comfortable lounge and kitchen areas and a barbecue pit, and the location is great.

Pioneer Station Motor Inn (☎ 03-5032 2017; 421 Campbell St; s/d $88/99;) Swan Hill's best-value motel is close to the town centre and the riverside. The adjacent Carriage Restaurant is a training ground for chefs from the Swan Hill International College.

Riverside Caravan Park (☎ 03-5032 1494; www .swanhillriverside.com.au; 1 Monash Dr; unpowered/powered site from $26/29, cabins $85-125;) On the river across from town and close to the Pioneer Settlement, Riverside is in a great spot.

Jilarty Gelato Bar (☎ 03-5033 0042; 233 Campbell St; daily from 8.30am) Fabulous Italian-style gelati with local fruit flavours. Everything is made on site and there's also great coffee and Spanish churros.

Spoons Riverside (☎ 03-5032 2601; Horseshoe Bend, 121 Monash Dr; meals $15-27; lunch daily, dinner Thu-Sun) The location alone is enough to lure you to this licensed cafe-restaurant with its timber deck overlooking the river and Pioneer Settlement. As well as light lunches and innovative dinners, there's a deli selling fresh produce.

Java Spice (☎ 03-5033 0511; www.javaspice.com.au; 17 Beveridge St; mains $20-27; lunch Thu, Fri & Sun, dinner Tue-Sun) Dining under open-sided, thatched and teak wood huts in the tropical garden, you'll think you've been transported to Southeast Asia. Along with Thai favourites such as green curry and tom yum are Indonesian, Balinese and Japanese dishes. Authentic flavours and takeaway is available.

Getting There & Away

V/Line (☎ 13 61 96) trains run several times daily between Melbourne and Swan Hill ($30, 4½ hours) via Bendigo. There are daily Murraylink buses between Swan Hill and Mildura ($22, three hours), Echuca ($14, 2½ hours) and Albury-Wodonga ($33, six hours).

ECHUCA
pop 12,360

Echuca is Australia's paddle-steamer capital and it's still quite a sight to see the old boats moored around the historic wharf – and even better if you happen to be gliding downriver on a houseboat of your own. The name means 'the meeting of the waters', as this is where the Goulburn and Campaspe Rivers join the Murray River. While undeniably touristy, Echuca has an authentic charm, several serious restaurants and gourmet delis for the travelling gastronome, and it's a good place to stock up on supplies if you're going camping or canoeing on the Murray.

The town was founded in 1853 by ex-convict Harry Hopwood. At the peak of the riverboat era there were more than 100 paddle steamers plying the water between Echuca and outback sheep stations. The Melbourne–Echuca railway line opened in 1864 and within a decade the boom years of the riverboat trade had ended.

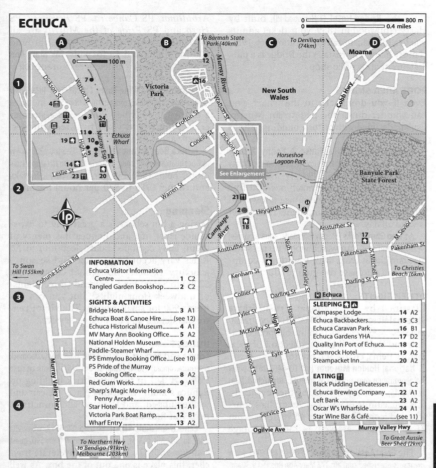

ECHUCA

Information

Echuca visitor information centre (☎ 03-5480 7555, 1800 804 446; www.echucamoama.com; 2 Heygarth St) Has an accommodation booking service.

Tangled Garden Bookshop (☎ 03-5480 1333; 495-497 High St; �9am-5.30pm Mon-Sat, 11am-4pm Sun; 🖳) Books, art supplies and internet access ($2 per 15 minutes).

Sights

HISTORIC PORT OF ECHUCA

Echuca's star attraction is the **old port area** (☎ 03-5482 4248; www.portofechuca.org.au; 52 Murray Esplanade; adult/child/family $12/8/35, with paddle-boat cruise $28/14/74; �9am-5pm), where paddle steamers dock and you really can feel transported back to the heyday of the river. It's not a theme park – everything here is original.

You can wander along Murray Esplanade and visit the shops, blacksmith and old hotels for free, or the wharf walk 'passport' gives admission to the wharf area, the Star Hotel and the Bridge Hotel.

There's a booking office is at the entrance to the **Echuca Wharf**, or buy tickets in the gift shop on Murray Esplanade. In the wharf's cargo shed, dioramas depict life on the river boats and restored historic **paddle steamers** are moored alongside the wharf. At the **steam display**, you can see all sorts of pumps and steam engines – they're usually fired up on weekends. Across the road at the **Star Hotel** (1867) you can escape through the underground tunnel that helped drinkers avoid the police when the pub was a 'sly grog shop'.

VICTORIA

At the **Bridge Hotel** (1 Hopwood Pl), built by Harry Hopwood in 1859, your ticket admits you to a historic upstairs re-creation of a 19th-century home. Downstairs the Bridge is a pub, restaurant and coffee shop.

PORT AREA SIGHTS
Even if you don't take in the wharf, you can wander down the pedestrian Murray Esplanade, lined with historic buildings, shops and restaurants.

Sharp's Magic Movie House & Penny Arcade (☎ 03-5482 2361; www.sharpsmoviehouse.com.au; Murray Esplanade; adult/child/family $15/10/45; ☺ 9am-5pm) has authentic penny-arcade machines and free fudge tasting. The movie house shows old movies using original equipment. Your ticket is valid all day.

At **Red Gum Works** (Murray Esplanade; admission free; ☺ 9am-4pm) you can watch wood turners and blacksmiths at work with traditional equipment, and purchase red-gum products.

OTHER SIGHTS
Classified by the National Trust, **Echuca Historical Museum** (☎ 03-5480 1325; 1 Dickson St; adult/child $3.50/1; ☺ 11am-3pm) is in the old police station and lock-up. It has a collection of local history items, charts and photos.

National Holden Museum (☎ 03-5480 2033; www .holdenmuseum.com.au; 7-11 Warren St; adult/child/family $7/3/15; ☺ 9am-5pm) One for the rev-heads, this museum is devoted to Australia's four-wheeled icon. There's over 40 vehicles, from FJ to Monaro, as well as racing footage and photos.

The **Great Aussie Beer Shed** (☎ 03-5480 6904; www .greataussiebeershed.com.au; 377 Mary Ann Rd; ☺ 9.30am-5pm Sat & Sun, public & school holidays) is a wall-to-wall shrine to beer cans – mostly Australian – in a huge shed; it's the result of 30 years of collecting and one dates back to Federation.

Activities
A paddle-steamer cruise along the Murray is pretty much obligatory here, and at least five steamers offer daily cruises; head down to the river and check out the sailing times. **PS Emmylou** (☎ 03-5480 2237; 1hr cruise adult/child $23/10) is a fully restored paddle steamer driven by an original engine. Overnight cruises are also available.

Hour-long cruises are offered by several paddle steamers whose booking offices are on Murray Esplanade. PS *Alexander*

Arbuthnot, PS *Canberra*, PS *Pevensey*, PS *Hero* and PS *Pride of the Murray* are all in regular service and cruises cost around $20 for adults and $9 for kids. **MV Mary Ann** (☎ 03-5480 2200) is a cruising restaurant offering lunch and dinner cruises.

Echuca Moama Wine Tours (☎ 03-5480 1839; www .echucamoamawinetours.com.au; tours from $85) includes a tour of the Echuca Port, paddle-steamer cruise, lunch and visits to three wineries. Great value.

Echuca Boat & Canoe Hire (☎ 03-5480 6208; www .echucaboatcanoehire.com; Victoria Park boat ramp) has motor boats ($40/150 per hour/day), kayaks and canoes ($16 to $30 per hour) for hire.

Sleeping
Hiring a houseboat is a great way to experience river life, and Echuca has plenty of them! Fully equipped boats sleep four to 12. Rates vary according to size and season – a luxury 12-berth houseboat coasts from $2200 to $3600 for a weekend (three nights) or midweek (four nights), but you can pay from $900 for smaller boats. The visitor centre has details and a booking service.

BUDGET
Echuca Backpackers (☎ 03-5480 7866; www.backpack ersechuca.com.au; 410-424 High St; dm $25, s/d with en suite $55/60; ☒ ☐) In the huge brick building on Echuca's main street, this place is clean and well equipped, and the staff can sometimes help you find work.

Echuca Gardens YHA (☎ 03-5480 6522; www.yha .com.au; 103 Mitchell St; dm $30, d wagon from $90, guest house from $120; ☐) Run by an inveterate traveller, this place is one out of the box. As well as dorms in the little 135-year-old worker's cottage, there are private 'gypsy wagons' in the garden and a two-bedroom guest house upstairs. The exotic garden boasts ponds, statues, a vegie patch, chooks and fruit trees.

Shamrock Hotel (☎ 03-5482 2247; 583 High St; s/d from $30/60) This friendly pub has clean rooms with shared bathrooms and a parma and pot thrown in. Live music on weekends.

MIDRANGE
Campaspe Lodge (☎ 03-5482 1087; www.echucahotel .com; 567-571 High St; d weekdays/weekends $95/125, 2-bedroom apt $220; ☒) Behind the Echuca Hotel, this group of motel units is great value, with private verandahs, huge windows to take in

VICTORIA

the view of the Campaspe River, and all mod cons. The two-bedroom units are fully self-contained and sleep up to six.

Steampacket Inn (☎ 03-5482 3411; www.steam packetinn.com.au; 37 Murray Esplanade; B&B d $139-169; 🔀) Staying in the old port area is all part of the Echuca experience and this 19th-century, National Trust–classified B&B has all the old-world charm, linen and lace, and brass bedsteads you could ask for. Request the large corner rooms with views of the wharf. The lounge room is cosy and downstairs in the tearoom meals are served on fine china.

Quality Inn Port of Echuca (☎ 03-5482 5666; porte chu@fc-hotels.com.au; 465 High St; d $165-190; 🔀 🖵 🐾) This huge luxury motel has swish rooms, a large heated pool and gym, and barbecue areas. In-room comforts include queen beds and wireless internet.

CAMPING
Five kilometres east of town is the camping area **Christies Beach** (free), on the banks of the Murray. It's a lovely spot with signposted access from Simmies Rd. There are pit toilets, but bring water and firewood.

Echuca Caravan Park (☎ 03-5482 2157; www.echu cacaravanpark.com.au; 51 Crofton St; unpowered/powered sites $29/30, d cabins $90-125; 🔀 🐾) Beside the river just a short walk from town, the facilities here are first class, with modern timber camp kitchens, resort pool, large grassy areas and magnificent shady river red gums.

Eating & Drinking
our pick **Oscar W's Wharfside** (☎ 03-5482 5133; www .oscarws.com.au; 101 Murray Esplanade; tapas $5-9, dinner mains $29-43; 🕙 lunch & dinner) If you're visiting the port area it's hard to miss Oscar's, and even harder not to be drawn in to the terrace or a table by the window overlooking the river. There's a real sense of style here and tapas plates offer a chance to sample the local ingredients prepared with a Mediterranean flavour. For dinner try crispy-skinned Murray cod with smoked yabbie and squid-ink pasta.

Black Pudding Delicatessen (☎ 03-5482 2244; 525a High St; meals $6-15; 🕙 breakfast & lunch) This High St deli is a great place for a lazy breakfast, light lunch and fresh produce such as cheeses and preserves. Grab a hamper for a picnic.

Star Wine Bar & Café (☎ 03-5480 1181; 45 Murray Esplanade; mains $20-32; 🕙 breakfast & lunch daily, dinner Fri & Sat) Part of the Star Hotel, it offers snacks

and light meals, and dinner at weekends. The lunchtime gourmet burgers are tempting. The moody bar has some interesting art works, with a patio at the back, and there's a cafe at the front (High St) serving sandwiches and gourmet pies.

Echuca Brewing Company (☎ 03-5482 4282; www .echucabrewingco.co.au; 609 High St; mains $20-27; 🕙 from 10am daily) Although the boutique beer was brewed off-site when we visited, a brewery is being built here, and the bistro serves up perfect beer accompaniments – steaming mussels, steaks and pasta.

Left Bank (☎ 03-5480 3772; 551 High St; mains $24-38; 🕙 dinner Tue-Sat) Start with a Bloody Mary oyster shooter before tucking into the crispy-skin duck with Asian greens and Madeira wine fumet, or the degustation menu. Outstanding food and service, and worth the splurge.

Getting There & Away
V/Line (☎ 13 61 96) has daily train services to/ from Melbourne ($21, 3½ hours). V/Line's Murraylink buses run daily from the train station, connecting Echuca with Wodonga ($24, three hours), Swan Hill ($14, 2½ hours) and Mildura ($31, 6½ hours). A daily service is available to destinations in southern NSW.

BARMAH STATE PARK
About 40km northeast of Echuca via the Cobb Hwy in NSW, Barmah is a significant wetland area of Murray River flood plains. It's the largest remaining red gum forest in Australia, and the swampy understorey usually floods in winter, creating a breeding area for many fish and birds.

The park entry is down a sealed road about 5km north of the tiny township of Barmah (turn at the pub and shop). From the day-use area, the cruise boat **Kingfisher** (☎ 03-5869 3399; www.kingfishercruises.com.au; adult/ child/family $23/18/82; 🕙 cruises 11am Mon, Wed, Thu, Sat & Sun) runs informative two-hour cruises.

The park is popular for bird-watching, fishing, walking and bush camping. **Gondwana Canoe Hire** (☎ 03-5869 3347), 4km past Barmah, hires canoes (per hour/day $35/60).

You can camp for free anywhere in the park or at the Barmah Lakes' camping area, which has tables, barbecue areas and pit toilets.

RUTHERGLEN REDS

Rutherglen's wineries produce superb fortifieds (port, muscat and tokay) and some potent Durifs and Shirazs – among the biggest, baddest and strongest reds. Some of the best:

All Saints (☎ 02-6035 2222; www.allsaintswine.com.au; All Saints Rd, Wahgunyah; ☯ 9am-5.30pm Mon-Sat, 10am-5.30pm Sun) Fairy-tale castle, restaurant and cheese tasting.

Buller Wines (☎ 1300 794 183; www.buller.com.au; Three Chain Rd; ☯ 9am-5pm Mon-Sat, 10am-5pm Sun) Fine Shiraz, plus a bird park.

Morris (☎ 02-6026 7303; www.morriswines.com; Mia Mia Rd; ☯ 9am-5pm Mon-Sat, 10am-5pm Sun)

Pfeiffer (☎ 02-6033 2805; www.pfeifferwines.com.au; Distillery Rd, Wahgunyah; ☯ 9am-5pm Mon-Fri, 10am-5pm Sun)

Rutherglen Estates (☎ 02-6032 8516; www.rutherglenestates.com.au; Tuileries Complex, Drummond St; ☯ 10am-6pm) Closest winery to town.

Stanton & Killeen Wines (☎ 02-6032 9457; www.stantonandkilleenwines.com.au; Jacks Rd; ☯ 9am-5pm Mon-Sat, 10am-5pm Sun)

Vintara (☎ 0447 327 517; www.vintara.com.au; Fraser Rd; ☯ 10am-5pm) Includes Bintara Brewery.

Warrabilla Wines (☎ 02-6035 7242; www.warrabillawines.com.au; Murray Valley Hwy; ☯ 10am-5pm) Small winery producing quality reds.

RUTHERGLEN
☎ 02 / pop 1990

Rutherglen has some gold-rush era buildings gracing the town, but the big draw is its position at the centre of one of northern Victoria's finest wine-growing districts. Some 26 wineries dot the surrounding area, four of which are within walking distance of town.

Rutherglen Wine Experience (☎ 02-6033 6300, 1800 622 871; www.rutherglenvic.com; 57 Main St; ☯ 9am-5pm; 🖳) combines the visitor information centre with a cafe and wine-tasting room, with free tastings of local fortifieds. You can hire bikes for winery touring ($30 per day) or pick up the heritage walks brochure. It can also provide information about Rutherglen's busy calendar of wine and food events, including **Tastes of Rutherglen** in March and **Winery Walkabout** in June.

Grapevine Getaways (☎ 02-6032 8577; www.grapevinegetaways.com.au; 72 Murray St; half-/full-day tours $35/45) runs knowledgeable personalised tours visiting up to eight wineries.

Sleeping

Victoria Hotel (☎ 02-6032 8610; www.victoriahotelrutherglen.com.au; 90 Main St; s/d $35/70, d with bathroom $90; ⊠) Front rooms at this beautiful old National Trust–classified place have bathrooms and views over Main St from its broad verandah. The town's original morgue is out the back! The bistro serves hearty meals ($12 to $26).

Motel Woongarra (☎ 02-6032 9588; www.motelwoongarra.com.au; cnr Main & Drummond Sts; s/d/f from

$75/85/104; ⊠ 🖳 ⊠) Close to the centre of town, and opposite Buller Estate, friendly Woongarra has spacious, tidy rooms, wi-fi and a pool.

Tuileries (☎ 02-6032 9033; www.tuileriesrutherglen.com.au; 13 Drummond St; B&B d $175, with dinner $265; ⊠ ⊠) All rooms are individually decorated in bright contemporary tones at this luxurious place attached to the Jolimont Cellars. There's a guest lounge, tennis court and an excellent restaurant and cafe.

Rutherglen Caravan & Tourist Park (☎ 02-6032 8577; www.rutherglentouristpark.com; 72 Murray St; unpowered/powered sites $18/24, d cabins $51-94) This friendly park with good facilities sits on the banks of Lake King (dry at the time of research), close to the golf course and swimming pool. The owners also run winery tours.

Eating

There's a great cafe scene along Main St, plus takeaway places and spots to fill a picnic hamper. Many of the wineries have restaurants overlooking vineyards, lakes and rivers serving lunch and/or dinner, although the atmosphere can suddenly change when a wine-tour bus pulls up. A good one close to town is Tuileries (see above).

Parkers Pies (☎ 02-6032 9605; 86-88 Main St; pies $4-6; ☯ 8am-4.30pm Mon-Sat, 9am-4pm Sun) If you think a pie is a pie, this award-winning local institution might change your mind.

Forks & Corks (☎ 02-6032 7662; 82 Main St; mains $10-30; ☯ lunch daily, dinner Fri & Sat) This is a bright, airy place that has artworks on the

VICTORIA

walls and serves simple, well-prepared favourites such as fish and chips, curries and pastas. The service is relaxed and cheerful, and the wine list offers some interesting local selections.

Beaumont's Café (☎ 02-6032 7428; www.beaumontscafe.com.au; 84 Main St; mains $16-34; ☾ lunch Fri & Sat, dinner Tue-Sat) Beaumont's offers fine Mod Oz dining in a contemporary dining room and courtyard. Mediterranean and Asian influences produce an interesting menu that features chicken tagine and homemade gnocchi.

Getting There & Away

V/Line (☎ 13 61 96) has one daily bus to Wangaratta ($4, 30 minutes) connecting with the train to Melbourne on Wednesday, Friday and Saturday.

The daily Murraylink bus connecting Wodonga with Mildura stops at Rutherglen. The bus stop is at the western end of Main St.

CHILTERN
pop 1060

Like an old-time movie set, tiny Chiltern is one of Victoria's most historic and charming colonial townships. Its two main streets are lined with 19th-century buildings, antique shops and a couple of pubs – authentic enough that the town is often used as a film set for period pieces.

Chiltern visitor information centre (☎ 03-5726 1611; 30 Main St; ☾ 10am-4pm) has information about the region and bird-watching opportunities in the nearby **Chiltern Mt Pilot National Park**.

Atheneum Museum (☎ 03-5726 1467; Conness St; adult/child $2/free; ☾ 10am-4pm Sat & Sun) is housed in the former town hall (1866).

Star Hotel/Theatre (☎ 03-5726 1395; cnr Main & Conness Sts; adult/child $5/2; ☾ by appointment) was once the centrepiece of Chiltern's social and cultural life. The grapevine in the courtyard is in the *Guinness World Records* as the largest in the southern hemisphere – you can sneak a peek down the laneway at the side.

Mulberry Tree (☎ 03-5726 1277; 28-30 Conness St; d $160-180) is a charming B&B in an old bank building with two cute rooms; one is self-contained with lounge and open fire. Even if you don't stay, the garden cafe is a great place for coffee, sandwiches or Devonshire tea.

WODONGA
☎ 02 / pop 29,700

The border town of Wodonga is separated from its twin, Albury, by the Murray River. Although a busy little town with a lake formed off Wodonga Creek, most of the attractions and the best of the accommodation are on the NSW side in Albury (p249).

Across the causeway, the **Gateway visitor information centre** (☎ 1300 796 222; www.alburywodongaaustralia.com.au; ☾ 9am-5pm) has info about Victoria and NSW.

For 24 years from the end of WWII, **Bonegilla**, 10km east of Wodonga, was Australia's first migrant reception centre, providing accommodation and training for some 320,000 migrants. At the **Bonegilla Migrant Experience** (☎ 02-6023 2327; Bonegilla Rd; admission free) you can visit some of the preserved buildings and see photos and historical references.

WODONGA TO CORRYONG

The Murray Valley Hwy continues east of Wodonga through tiny **Tallangatta**. In the 1950s the rising waters of the Mitta Mitta River, a tributary of Lake Hume, flooded following construction of the Hume Weir at Tallangatta. Most of the township had already been relocated to New Tallangatta. There's a lookout point 7km east of the town, from which you can see the streetscape of Old Tallangatta, especially if the waters are low.

There's a turn-off 15km west of Tallangatta to the town of **Granya**. The road to the north rejoins the Murray River and follows it to **Towong** and **Corryong**, a popular flyfishing area where the fast-flowing Murray comes down from the mountains. **Tintaldra** is worth a detour if you have a day or two to spare. Rupert Bunny (1864–1947), the famous Australian artist, spent time here in the 1920s, and painted *The Murray at Tintaldra*.

GOLDFIELDS

The Central Victoria region was literally built on gold. From those heady gold rush days of the 1850s came major regional towns such as Bendigo, Ballarat and Castlemaine, which still boast impressive Victorian-era buildings. Smaller towns such as Maldon and Maryborough make the most of their historic past, while Daylesford and Hepburn

THE EUREKA REBELLION

Life on the goldfields was a great leveller, erasing social distinctions as doctors, merchants, ex-convicts and labourers toiled side by side in the mud. But as the easily won gold began to run out, the diggers recognised the inequalities between themselves, the privileged few who held land and the government.

The limited size of claims and the inconvenience of licence hunts (see Gold Fever, p588), coupled with police brutality and taxation without political representation, fired the unrest that led to the Eureka Rebellion.

In September 1854 Governor Hotham ordered the hated licence hunts to be carried out twice weekly. In the following October a miner was murdered near a Ballarat hotel after an argument with the owner, James Bentley. Bentley was found not guilty by a magistrate (and business associate), and a group of miners rioted and burned his hotel. Bentley was retried and found guilty, but the rioting miners were also jailed, which fuelled their distrust of authority.

Creating the Ballarat Reform League, the diggers called for the abolition of licence fees, a miner's right to vote and increased opportunities to purchase land.

On 29 November 1854 about 800 miners, led by Irishman Peter Lalor, burnt their licences at a mass meeting and built a stockade at Eureka, where they prepared to fight for their rights.

On 3 December the government ordered troopers to attack the stockade. There were only 150 diggers within the barricades at the time and the fight lasted only 20 minutes, leaving 30 miners and five troopers dead.

The short-lived rebellion was ultimately successful. The miners won the sympathy of Victorians and the government chose to acquit the leaders of the charge of high treason.

The licence fee was abolished. A miner's right, costing one pound a year, gave the right to search for gold and to fence in, cultivate and build a dwelling on a moderate-sized piece of land – and to vote. The rebel leader Peter Lalor became a member of parliament some years later.

Springs are popular for their liquid gold – abundant mineral springs and the spa centres that have grown around them.

Linking these towns is rolling farmland, productive wine country and dramatic landscapes, ranging from the green forests of the Wombat Ranges to red earth, bush scrub and granite country up around Inglewood.

The region is easily accessible from Melbourne by road on the Calder Hwy or by V/Line train direct to Castlemaine and Bendigo. The **Goldfields Tourist Route** takes in all the major gold-rush centres, and is great for bike touring and horse riding.

The old diggers found most of the gold, but there's still gold around, and metal detectors and prospecting gear can be bought or hired in many towns.

BALLARAT
pop 78,220

Ballarat vies with Bendigo as Victoria's largest inland city (Ballarat just wins out) and is famous as the site of the Eureka Stockade, a battle between miners and authorities that was the birth of the labour movement in Australia

(see above). The city was built on gold and today makes the most of the legacy with the Sovereign Hill gold-mining village and the Eureka Centre.

The area around Ballarat was known to the local Koories as 'Ballaarat', meaning 'resting place'. Around 25 pre-European clans identify themselves collectively as the Wathaurong people. European pastoralists arrived in 1837 and the discovery of gold at nearby Buninyong in 1851 saw thousands of diggers flock to the area. After alluvial goldfields were played out, deep shaft mines were sunk, striking incredibly rich quartz reefs that were worked until the end of WWI.

Ballarat's former prosperity is reflected in the wealth of impressive Victorian-era buildings. Ballarat's 100-year-old **Begonia Festival**, in early March, attracts thousands of visitors.

Information

Ballarat visitor information centre (☎ 03-5320 5741, 1800 446 633; www.visitballarat.com.au; cnr Eureka & Rodier Sts; 🖳) Out of the town centre at the Eureka Centre, but there's a small information booth at the Art Gallery of Ballarat (p586). Internet access ($2 per 15 minutes).

BALLARAT

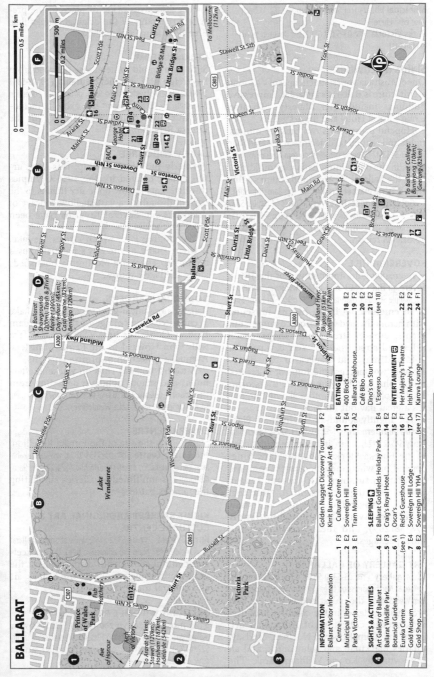

INFORMATION
Ballarat Visitor Information	
Centre....................................	1 F3
Municipal Library...................	2 E2
Parks Victoria........................	3 E1

SIGHTS & ACTIVITIES
Art Gallery of Ballarat............	4 F3
Ballarat Wildlife Park.............	5 F3
Botanical Gardens...................	6 A1
Eureka Centre.................	(see 1)
Gold Museum..........................	7 E4
Gold Shop..............................	8 E2

Golden Nugget Discovery Tours..	9 F2
Kirrit Barreet Aboriginal Art &	
Cultural Centre.......................	10 E4
Sovereign Hill.........................	11 E4
Tram Musuem.........................	12 A2

SLEEPING
Ballarat Goldfields Holiday Park..	13 E4
Craig's Royal Hotel.................	14 E2
Oscar's..................................	15 E2
Reid's Guesthouse..................	16 F1
Sovereign Hill Lodge...............	17 D4
Sovereign Hill YHA..........	(see 17)

EATING
400 Block..............................	18 E2
Ballarat Steakhouse................	19 F2
Café Bibo..............................	20 E2
Dino's on Sturt.......................	21 E2
L'Espresso.....................	(see 18)

ENTERTAINMENT
Her Majesty's Theatre.............	22 E2
Irish Murphy's........................	23 F2
Karova Lounge.......................	24 F1

VICTORIA

Municipal library (cnr Sturt & Camp Sts; 🖳) Check your email here.

Parks Victoria (☎ 03-5333 6782; cnr Doveton North & Mair Sts)

Sights & Activities

One of Australia's finest streetscapes of Victorian architecture is Ballarat's **Lydiard St**. Impressive buildings include Her Majesty's Theatre, Craig's Royal Hotel and the art gallery.

Hopeful prospectors can pick up miners' rights and rent metal detectors at the **Gold Shop** (☎ 03-5333 4242; www.thegoldshop.com.au; 8a Lydiard St North), in the old Mining Exchange building.

At the Ballarat Showgrounds there's a fine **Trash & Trivia market** (Creswick Rd; ⏰ 8am-1pm Sun).

Golden Nugget Discovery Tours (☎ 03-5332 9199; 404 Peel St; day tours $115-149) runs historical tours of Ballarat and the surrounding goldfields region.

SOVEREIGN HILL

A re-created gold-mining town of the 1860s, **Sovereign Hill** (☎ 03-5331 1944; www.sovereignhill.com .au; Magpie St; adult/child/family $38/17/96; ⏰ 10am-5pm) is an entertaining living history museum, with actors dressed in period costumes, authentic pioneer streetscapes, shops, coach rides and street theatre. You can pan for gold and may find a speck or two. There are also two underground tours of re-created mines plus a gold pour, which transforms $50,000 of liquid gold into a 3kg bullion bar. It's a great day out for kids.

The nightly sound-and-light show **Blood on the Southern Cross** (☎ 03-5333 5777; adult/child/family $45/25/122) is an impressive simulation of the Eureka Stockade battle. Show times depend on when the sun sets: 9.15pm and 10.30pm in summer; 6.45pm and 8pm in winter. Bookings are essential. Note that combined Sovereign Hill entry and show tickets are available (adult/child/family $78/38/209), and there are dinner and show packages.

ART GALLERY OF BALLARAT

This **gallery** (☎ 03-5320 5858; www.balgal.com; 40 Lydiard St North; admission free; ⏰ 9am-5pm, guided tours 2pm Wed-Sun) is the oldest and one of the best provincial galleries in the country. It houses a wonderful collection of Australian art, including Tom Roberts, Norman Lindsay, Charles Blackman and John Brack, and an 1895 work by Koorie William Barak. The gallery also gives pride of place to the preserved remnants of the original Eureka flag. Free iPod tours are available.

GOLD MUSEUM

Sitting on an old mine across the road from Sovereign Hill, the **Gold Museum** (☎ 03-5331 1944; Bradshaw St; adult/child $9/5, or free with Sovereign Hill ticket; ⏰ 9.30am-5.20pm) has exhibits including nuggets, coins and a display on the Eureka Rebellion.

LAKE WENDOUREE

Formerly the Black Swamp, this large artificial lake created for the 1956 Olympics rowing events is now bone-dry thanks to the current drought – a vast shallow concave of dried-out silt. Several firearms have been found in the dry lake bed.

Wendouree Pde, which circles the lake, is where many of the city's palatial houses are found. There are old timber boat sheds along the lake's shores.

BOTANICAL GARDENS

Ballarat's botanical gardens are beside Lake Wendouree. The cottage of the poet Adam Lindsay Gordon is here. Come face to face with John Howard in the Prime Ministers' Avenue, a collection of bronze portraits.

A tourist **tramway** runs on weekend afternoons and school holidays, departing from the **tram museum** (☎ 03-5334 1580; www.btm.org.au; South Gardens Reserve, Lake Wendouree).

EUREKA CENTRE

Standing on the site of the Eureka Rebellion, the **Eureka Centre** (☎ 03-5333 1854; www.eurekaballarat.com; Eureka St; adult/child/family $8/4/22; ⏰ 9am-4.30pm) has multimedia galleries simulating the famous battle.

KIRRIT BARREET ABORIGINAL ART & CULTURAL CENTRE

Kirrit Barreet (☎ 03-5332 2755; www.aboriginalballarat .com.au; 403-407 Main Rd; admission free) is an excellent cultural centre with displays about the local Wathaurong people, Koorie history, art and cultural tours.

BALLARAT WILDLIFE PARK

This most attractive **zoo** (☎ 03-5333 5933; www .wildlifepark.com.au; cnr York & Fussell Sts; adult/child/family $22/14/65) has native animals, reptiles and a few exotics.

VICTORIA

Sleeping

BUDGET

Sovereign Hill YHA (☎ 03-5333 3409; www.sovereignhill .com.au; Magpie St; dm/s/d $25/38/58; ☒) This cute but very compact YHA cottage has just four rooms around a central kitchen/dining area. It's part of the Sovereign Hill Lodge complex.

Reid's Guesthouse (☎ 03-5332 3461; 128 Lydiard St North; dm/s/d $26/36/75) Near the railway station, this 1886 guest house retains many of its original features – the foyer has splendid Art Nouveau ceiling murals and leadlight windows. The en suite doubles are good value.

MIDRANGE & TOP END

Sovereign Hill Lodge (☎ 03-5333 3409; www.sovereign hill.com.au; Magpie St; B&B lodge s/d/f from $115/135/190, heritage rooms $165-195; ☒) Overlooking Sovereign Hill, accommodation here ranges from standard motel rooms to the plusher heritage rooms with Victorian-era furnishings and some with spa bath.

Oscar's (☎ 03-5331 1451; www.oscarshotel.com.au; 18 Doveton St; d $150-200, spa room $225; ☐ ☒) The 13 rooms of this attractive art deco hotel have been tastefully refurbished to include double showers and spas (watch a flat-screen TV from your spa), and broadband internet connections.

Craig's Royal Hotel (☎ 03-5331 1377; www .craigsroyal.com; 10 Lydiard St South; d $230-450; ☒) The best of the grand old pubs was so named after it hosted visits by the Prince of Wales and Duke of Edinburgh. It's a wonderful Victorian building with old-fashioned opulence and some creaky floorboards, but the rooms have been beautifully refurbished with king beds, heritage furnishings and marble bathrooms.

CAMPING

Ballarat Goldfields Holiday Park (☎ 03-5332 7888, 1800 632 237; www.ballaratgoldfields.com.au; 108 Clayton St; powered sites $32, cabins $70-160; ☒) Close to Sovereign Hill, with a good holiday atmosphere. The cabins are like miners' cottages, and some have three bedrooms.

Eating

The main cafe scene is the '400 Block' on Sturt St, where tables spill out along with the coffee aroma.

L'Espresso (☎ 03-5333 1789; 417 Sturt St; mains $10-22; ☼ breakfast & lunch) This Ballarat mainstay is a trendy, friendly and atmospheric Italian-style cafe and record shop – you can choose from the whopping selection of jazz and blues CDs while you wait for your espresso or pasta.

Café Bibo (☎ 03-5331 1255; 205 Sturt St; mains $11-20; ☼ breakfast & lunch) This retro cafe is lined with copies of 1960s *Women's Weekly* magazines and shelves of decorated coffee cups belonging to the regulars. The breakfast is so good you'll be back for lunch.

Dino's on Sturt (☎ 03-5332 9711; www.ballarat .com/dinos; 212 Sturt St; mains $13-24; ☼ 10.30am-late) Welcoming, child-friendly and relaxed licensed Mediterranean restaurant with a menu of gourmet pies, lamb shanks, pizza, pasta and risotto.

Ballarat Steakhouse (☎ 03-5332 6777; 10 Grenville St; mains $20-35; ☼ dinner) The best steaks in town can be found on the grill at this upmarket meat-lovers' paradise. As well as prime cuts, lamb chops and spare ribs, sauces include creamy garlic and Danish blue cheese.

Drinking & Entertainment

With its large student population, Ballarat has a lively nightlife.

Irish Murphy's (☎ 03-5331 4091; 36 Sturt St; ☼ to 3am Wed-Sun) Snug and cosy downstairs and with live music from Thursday to Sunday, this friendly Irish pub is the best place in town for a night out.

Karova Lounge (☎ 03-5332 9122; cnr Fielding & Camp Sts; ☼ 9am-late Wed-Sat) Ballarat's best alternative and original live music venue showcases local and top touring bands in grungy, industrial style.

Her Majesty's Theatre (☎ 03-5333 5800; www.her maj.com; 17 Lydiard St South) This is Ballarat's main venue for the performing arts. The website has events listings.

Getting There & Around

There are at least 10 daily **V/Line** (☎ 13 61 96) trains from Melbourne to Ballarat ($11, 1½ hours). Trains and buses continue on to Ararat ($9, one hour) and Stawell ($12, 1½ hours). V/Line also has daily bus services to Geelong ($8, 1½ hours), Bendigo ($13, two hours), Daylesford ($7, 45 minutes), Castlemaine ($9, 1½ hours) and Mildura ($33, seven hours).

Greyhound Australia (☎ 13 14 99) buses stop at the train station on the Melbourne–Adelaide run.

VICTORIA

GOLD FEVER

In May 1851 EH Hargraves discovered gold near Bathurst in New South Wales (NSW), and sensational accounts of the find caused thousands of people to drop everything to try their luck. Sydney was virtually denuded of workers, and when news of the discovery reached Melbourne the same exodus threatened there.

A reward was offered to anyone who could find gold within 300km of Melbourne. Within a week, gold was discovered in the Yarra River, but the find was soon eclipsed by a more significant discovery at Clunes. Prospectors headed to central Victoria as fresh gold finds became an almost weekly occurrence.

In September 1851 Ballarat produced the biggest discovery, followed by other significant finds at Bendigo, Mt Alexander, Beechworth, Walhalla, Omeo and in the hills and creeks of the Great Dividing Range. By the end of 1851 about 250,000 ounces of gold had been claimed. Farms and businesses lost their workforces and were often abandoned. Hopeful miners came from England, Ireland, Europe, China and the failing goldfields of California; during 1852 about 1800 people arrived in Melbourne each week.

The government imposed a licence fee of 30 shillings a month for all prospectors. This entitled the miners to an 8-sq-foot claim in which to dig for gold and it provided the means to enforce improvised law. Any miner without a licence could be fined or imprisoned. Although this later caused serious unrest, it was successful in averting the lawlessness that had characterised the California rush.

Gold fever meant backbreaking work, unwholesome food, hard drinking and primitive dwellings, and while amazing wealth came to some, it remained the elusive dream for others – for every success story, there were hundreds more of hardship, despair and death.

The gold rush had its share of rogues, including the notorious bushrangers, but it also had its heroes: the martyrs of the Eureka Stockade, a miners' rebellion that eventually forced political change in the colony (see The Eureka Rebellion, p584).

The gold rush ushered in a fantastic era of growth and material prosperity for Victoria, opening up vast areas of country previously unexplored by colonists.

In the first 12 years of the rush, Victoria's population rose from 77,000 to 540,000. To cope with the moving population and the tonnes of gold and supplies, the development of roads and railways was accelerated.

The mining companies that followed the independent diggers invested heavily in the region over the next couple of decades. The huge shantytowns of tents, bark huts, raucous bars and police camps were eventually replaced by timber and stone buildings, which became the foundation of many of Victoria's provincial cities.

The gold towns reached the height of splendour in the 1880s. Gold gradually lost its importance, but by then the gold towns had stable populations plus agriculture and other activities to maintain economic prosperity.

The local bus line covers most of the town; timetables are available at the visitor information centre.

The **Airport Shuttlebus** (☎ 03-5333 4181; www.airportshuttlebus.com.au) goes direct to Melbourne airport from Ballarat train station (adult/child $28/15, seven daily).

For a cab, call **Ballarat Taxis** (☎ 13 10 08).

DAYLESFORD & HEPBURN SPRINGS
pop 3670

Set among the idyllic hills, lakes and forests of the central highlands, delightful Daylesford and Hepburn Springs form the 'spa centre of Victoria', and have developed into quite the bohemian weekend getaway, though the area's mineral springs have been attracting fashionable Melburnians since the 1870s. Daylesford is an intriguing mix of alternative-lifestylers, tree-changers and old-timers, and has a thriving gay and lesbian scene. The **ChillOut Festival** (www.chilloutfestival.com.au) in March is a glam gay and lesbian event with music, stalls and a street parade attracting up to 25,000 people.

Daylesford is set around pretty Lake Daylesford. Its two main streets, Raglan and Vincent, are major cafe strips. Vincent St turns into Hepburn Rd at the roundabout and takes you straight through Hepburn Springs and down to the original spa resort.

Information

Bookbarn (☎ 03-5348 3048; 1 Leggatt St, Daylesford; ☺ 10am-5pm) Excellent secondhand bookshop by Lake Daylesford.

Daylesford Library (☎ 03-5348 2800; cnr Bridport & Albert Sts, Daylesford; ☺ 10am-6pm Mon-Fri, 10am-1pm Sat; ▣) Free internet.

Daylesford visitor information centre (☎ 03-5321 6123; www.visitdaylesford.com; 98 Vincent St, Daylesford; ▣) Staff are knowledgeable and helpful. Internet access costs $6 an hour.

Sights & Activities

The historic **Hepburn Bathhouse & Spa** (☎ 03-5348 8888; www.hepburnspa.com.au; Mineral Springs Reserve, Hepburn Springs) specialises in hydrotherapy treatments using the pure mineral water, pumped from ancient underground cavities. A 20-minute mineral spa starts at $75, and there are flotation tanks, vanilla milk baths and massage therapy. Around the spa are picnic areas and several **mineral springs** where you can fill your own bottles – most are slightly effervescent with a vaguely metallic aftertaste. There are some good **walking trails**; pick up maps and guides from the visitors centre.

The **Convent Gallery** (☎ 03-5348 3211; www.theconvent.com.au; 7 Daly St, Daylesford; admission $5; ☺ 10am-4pm) is a magnificent 19th-century convent that's been lovingly converted into an art gallery with changing exhibitions, a cafe and the Altar Bar.

Boats and canoes can be hired at **Lake Daylesford**, which is also ringed by a walking trail. Or head out to the even prettier **Jubilee Lake**, a popular local swimming hole about 3km southeast of town.

The **Daylesford Museum** (☎ 03-5348 1453; 100 Vincent St, Daylesford; adult/child $3/1; ☺ 1.30-4.30pm Sat & Sun), next to the visitor centre, houses local historical society memorabilia.

Daylesford Spa Country Railway (☎ 03-5348 1759; www.dscr.com.au; Daylesford train station; adult/child/family $8/6/20; ☺ 10am-2.45pm Sun) operates one-hour rides five times every Sunday on old railway trolleys and restored trains. The **Daylesford Sunday Market** (☺ 8am-2pm Sun) is held at the train station.

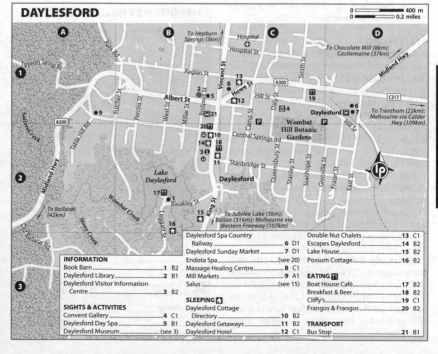

DAYLESFORD

The beautiful **Wombat Hill Botanic Gardens** (Central Springs Rd) is worth a stroll for its many oak, pine and cypress trees.

Chocolate Mill (☎ 03-5476 4208; www.chocmill.com .au; 5451 Midland Hwy, Mt Franklin; ☽ 10am-4.45pm Tue-Sun, Mar-Jan) is worth the 10-minute drive from Daylesford. You can watch the Belgian chocolates being made by hand (tour at 11.30am).

You could just about fit a Boeing 747 in the enormous **Mill Markets** (☎ 03-5348 4332; www.millmarkets.com.au; 105 Central Springs Rd, Daylesford; ☽ 10am-6pm), housing a mind-boggling collection of furniture, collectables, antiques, books and retro fashions. There's a cafe to break up the browsing.

Sleeping

Bookings for the region's charming guest houses, cottages and B&Bs (many charging 30% more on weekends and stipulating a minimum two-night stay) can be made through agencies in Daylesford.

Daylesford Cottage Directory (☎ 03-5348 1255; www .cottagedirectory.com.au; 16 Hepburn Rd, Daylesford)

Daylesford Getaways (☎ 03-5348 4422; www .dayget.com.au; 123 Vincent St)

Escapes Daylesford (☎ 03-5348 1448; www.escapes daylesford.com.au; 94 Vincent St)

DAYLESFORD

Double Nut Chalets (☎ 0418 938 954; www.doublenut .com; 5 Howe St; d incl breakfast $140, weekend $380) The four chalets are spacious and the tasteful suites have gable ceilings and kitchenette, in a lovely garden right in town.

Possum Cottage (☎ 03-5348 3173; www.lake daylesfordcottage.com.au; 33 Leggatt St, d from $215) In a fabulous lakeside location, this self-contained cottage has a comfortable lounge with wood heater and great balcony.

Lake House (☎ 03-5348 3329; www.lakehouse.com .au; King St; d incl breakfast & dinner from $260; ☒) Set in rambling gardens with bridges, waterfalls and cockatoos, these welcoming units around the lake are made for relaxation. There's a guest lounge, tennis court and the ultimate pampering of Salus healing spring waters.

Jubilee Lake Holiday Park (☎ 03-5348 2186; www .jubileelake.com.au; 151 Kale Rd; unpowered/powered sites $30/36, cabins $95-150; ☒ ▣) Set in bushland on the edge of pretty Jubilee Lake, this is the best park in the region. Canoe hire is available and lower rates apply out of summer high season.

HEPBURN SPRINGS

Daylesford Wildwood YHA (☎ 03-5348 4435; Daylesford@ yahvic.org.au; 42 Main Rd; dm/s/d $22/35/54, d with bathroom $70; ☒) This charming weatherboard cottage has a homey lounge and comfy beds. Some of the private rooms have iron-frame beds and garden views.

Continental House (☎ 03-5348 2005; www.con tinentalhouse.com.au; 9 Lone Pine Ave; s/d $45/80) This 'vegan life sanctuary' is a rambling, timber guest house with a laid-back alternative vibe, a cafe serving excellent buffets, a lovely open-verandah sitting room, yoga classes and shiatsu massage courses. BYO linen and yoga pants.

Mooltan Guesthouse (☎ 03-5348 3555; www .mooltan.com.au; 129 Main Rd; midweek s/d from $65/95, weekend from $95/120) This inviting Edwardian country home has large lounge rooms, a billiard table and tennis court. Bedrooms open onto a broad verandah overlooking the Mineral Springs Reserve. There are special weekend packages and spa rooms; the cheapest rooms have share facilities.

Shizuka Ryokan (☎ 03-5348 2030; www.shizuka.com .au; Lakeside Dr; s/d from $130/260) Inspired by traditional places of renewal and rejuvenation in

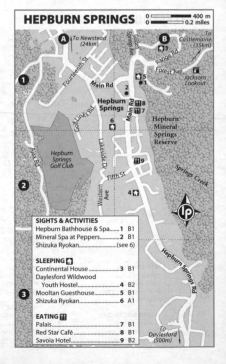

HEPBURN SPRINGS

0 — 400 m
0 — 0.2 miles

SIGHTS & ACTIVITIES
Hepburn Bathhouse & Spa......1 B1
Mineral Spa at Peppers..........2 B1
Shizuka Ryokan...................(see 6)

SLEEPING ⌂
Continental House.................3 B1
Daylesford Wildwood
  Youth Hostel.....................4 B2
Mooltan Guesthouse..............5 B1
Shizuka Ryokan....................6 A1

EATING ⊞
Palais.............................7 B1
Red Star Café......................8 B1
Savoia Hotel.......................9 B2

VICTORIA

PAMPERING SOAKS

The Daylesford and Hepburn Springs region is well known for its rejuvenating mineral spa treatments. Along with a soak or facial, you can fork out plenty of money for herbal treatments, massage and mudpacks.

Daylesford Day Spa (☎ 03-5348 2331; www.daylesforddayspa.com.au; 25 Albert St, Daylesford) Start with a vitamin-rich mud body mask and steam in a body-care cocoon, before a scalp massage and Vichy shower.

Endota Spa (☎ 03-5348 1169; www.endota.com.au; cnr Vincent St & Central Springs Rd, Daylesford) Hot stones and Hawaiian *lomi lomi* massage

Hepburn Bathhouse & Spa (☎ 03-5348 8888; www.hepburnspa.com.au; Hepburn Mineral Springs Reserve, Hepburn Springs) Where it all began in 1896, this renovated resort specialises in hydrotherapy and vanilla milk baths.

Massage Healing Centre (☎ 03-5348 1099; www.massagehealingcentre.com.au; 5/11 Howe St, Daylesford) For a modest, down-to-earth alternative to the glitz-and-glam spa resorts listed here, try this place.

Mineral Spa at Peppers (☎ 03-5348 6200; www.thesprings.com.au; Springs Retreat, 124 Main Rd, Hepburn Springs) Have an algae gel wrap, based on an ancient Chinese treatment, then move into the lavender steam room, or take a soft pack float.

Salus (☎ 03-5348 3329; www.lakehouse.com.au; Lake House, King St, Daylesford) The pampering starts as you walk through a small rainforest to your exotic jasmine-flower bath in a cedar-lined tree house overlooking the lake.

Shizuka Ryokan (☎ 03-5348 2030; www.shizuka.com.au; 7 Lakeside Dr, Hepburn Springs) Shiatsu massage, geisha facials and spa treatments with natural sea salts and seaweed extracts, ginseng and green tea at this Japanese-style country spa retreat.

Japan, this minimalist getaway has six rooms with private Japanese gardens, tatami matting and plenty of green tea. Packages can include a superb Japanese dinner and breakfast with various massage treatments.

Eating & Drinking
DAYLESFORD
Vincent St and its side streets have some great cafes.

Breakfast & Beer (☎ 03-5348 1778; 117 Vincent St; mains $7-26; ✆ Wed-Sun) Straight out of a Belgian backstreet, this inspired European-style cafe stocks fine local and imported beers, and a boutique menu strong on local produce.

Cliffy's (☎ 03-5348 3279; 28 Raglan St; mains $9-20; ✆ breakfast & lunch daily, dinner Sat) Behind the vine-covered verandah of this local legend is an old-world shop crammed with organic vegies, cheeses, preserves and the spicy aromas of fruit chutney and fresh coffee. To one side, the cafe (menus on old grocery bags) serves great breakfasts, pies and baguettes.

Boat House Café (☎ 03-5348 1387; mains $15-22; ✆ breakfast & lunch Mon-Sun, dinner Sat & Sun) This perennial favourite is in an old boat shed. The setting is lovely – you can nibble nachos out on the deck and watch the swans on the lake.

Frangos & Frangos (☎ 03-5348 2363; 82 Vincent St; mains $16-32; ✆ breakfast Fri & Sat, lunch Fri-Sun) Ensconced in a corner building on the main drag, Frangos has a popular licensed cafe serving coffee and light meals, a main dining room serving fine European-inspired cuisine and a gelati bar.

Lake House (☎ 03-5348 3329; www.lakehouse.com.au; King St; mains $32-38) Daylesford's much-lauded Lake House restaurant is among the best in Victoria. The beautiful dining room overlooks Lake Daylesford or you can take luncheon on the outdoor deck. The seasonal menu uses the freshest produce in Mod Oz preparations such as kangaroo with mango chutney. Reservations are essential.

HEPBURN SPRINGS
our pick **Red Star Café** (☎ 03-5348 2297; www.redstar.com.au; 115 Main Rd; mains $10-20; ✆ 8am-4pm daily, dinner Fri & Sat) This old weatherboard shopfront feels like someone's home, with loungy couches, great music, a garden out the back and a funky local vibe. It's *the* place for all-day breakfasts, lunch of smoked salmon and asparagus tart, antipasto or laksa.

Savoia Hotel (☎ 03-5348 2314; 69 Main Rd; mains $14-25; ✆ lunch & dinner) Hepburn's local pub serves filling bistro meals.

Palais (☎ 03-5348 4849; www.thepalais.com.au; 111 Main Rd; mains $19-25; ✆ dinner Thu-Sun) This dazzlingly atmospheric 1920s theatre building is a restaurant, cafe and cocktail bar. Enjoy the lamb rendang or asparagus, pumpkin and goat's cheese lasagne, then relax in

VICTORIA

lush lounge chairs, play pool or even dance. The Palais is a country staple on the live music circuit and hosts some of Australia's best acts.

Getting There & Around

Daily **V/Line** (☎ 13 61 96) train/coach services connect Melbourne to Daylesford ($10, two hours) by train to Woodend or Ballarat and then bus to Daylesford. Weekday V/Line buses run from Daylesford to Ballarat ($7), Castlemaine ($4) and Bendigo ($7). The buses run from Bridport St opposite the fire station.

It's a pleasant 45-minute walk between Daylesford and Hepburn Springs. A shuttle bus runs between the Daylesford visitor information centre and Hepburn Springs spa complex four times each weekday.

CASTLEMAINE

pop 7250

Castlemaine is a relaxed country town that's home to artists, long-time locals, hippies and tree-changers. It also has some splendid colonial architecture and gardens. The discovery of gold at Specimen Gully in 1851 radically altered the pastoral landscape of the Castlemaine region, as 30,000 diggers worked goldfields known collectively as the Mt Alexander Diggings. The town grew up around the government camp and soon became the marketplace for all the goldfields of central Victoria. While not as commercialised as Daylesford or Maldon, Castlemaine (the 'Hot Rod Capital of Australia') still gets its share of day-trippers but retains its authentic country-town feel.

Castlemaine hosts the **State Festival** (www.castlemainefestival.com.au) in March/April in odd-numbered years, one of Victoria's leading arts events.

Information

Book Heaven (☎ 03-5472 4555; 47 Main Rd, Campbells Creek) Awesome secondhand bookshop crammed with 90,0000 titles!

Castlemaine visitor information centre (☎ 03-5470 6200, 1800 171 888; www.maldoncastlemaine.com; Mostyn St) In the superb Castlemaine market building.

GCom Internet (☎ 03-5470 6690; 155 Barker St; ⏰ 9.30am-5.30pm Mon-Fri, 9.30am-noon Sat; 🖳) High-speed internet at $5 per hour.

Sights & Activities

Dating from 1861, **Buda** (☎ 03-5472 1032; www.budacastlemaine.org; cnr Hunter & Urquhart Sts; adult/child/family $9/4/20; ⏰ noon-5pm Wed-Sat, 10am-5pm Sun) was home to a Hungarian silversmith and his descendants for 120 years. The family's art and craft collections and personal belongings are on display.

The impressive **Castlemaine Art Gallery & Historical Museum** (☎ 03-5472 2292; www.castlemainegallery.com; 14 Lyttleton St; adult/student/family $4/2/8; ⏰ 10am-5pm Mon-Fri, noon-5pm Sat & Sun), in a superb art deco building, has a collection of colonial and contemporary Australian art including works by Frederick McCubbin and Tom Roberts; downstairs is a local history museum.

The last prisoners moved out of the imposing **Old Castlemaine Gaol** (☎ 03-5472 5311; www.oldcastlemainegaol.com.au; cnr Bowden & Charles Sts; adult/child/family $7/5/15; ⏰ guided tours 11.15am & 2.15pm Mon-Fri) in 1990. Today you can take a guided tour of the old cells, gallows and watchtowers, and there's a small cafe.

The **Castlemaine Botanic Gardens** are among the best in regional Victoria.

The famous **Restorers Barn** (☎ 03-5470 5667; www.restorersbarn.com.au; 129-133 Mostyn St; ⏰ 10am-5.30pm Mon-Fri, 10am-4pm Sat & Sun) is literally dripping interesting bric-a-brac, collectables and tools.

In the evening, catch a live band or film at the historic **Theatre Royal** (☎ 03-5472 1196; www.theatreroyal.info; 28 Hargraves St).

The **Victorian Goldfields Railway** (☎ 03-5475 2966; www.vgr.com.au; adult/child/family $27/13/60; ⏰ Wed & Sun, Sat during school holidays) does return steam-train rides between Castlemaine and Maldon, passing through the Muckleford Forest. On operating days there are usually three trains a day, which make a one hour stopover at each end for sightseeing. For an extra charge you can ride in the first-class carriage ($40/23/93). Steam-train tragics from all over the world come to ride this baby.

About 10km northwest of Castlemaine, the **Harcourt** region is known as Victoria's 'apple centre', but in recent years it has also developed as an excellent mini wine region – the tourist office can provide a map and a list of cellar doors. Check out **Bress** (☎ 03-5474 2262; www.bress.com.au; 3894 Calder Hwy; ⏰ 11am-5pm Sat & Sun), a combined winery and cidery.

Sleeping

The free **Mount Alexander accommodation booking service** (☎ 03-5470 5866, 1800 171 888; www.maldoncastlemaine.com) covers Castlemaine, Maldon and surrounds.

Midland Private Hotel (☎ 03-5472 1085; www.themidland.com.au; 2 Templeton St; s $90, d $140-180, apt d $250) This lace-decked hotel, which has been sheltering travellers since 1879, features a magnificent art deco entrance foyer and dining room, and a lounge with open fireplaces.

Castle Motel (☎ 03-5472 2433; www.castlemotel.com.au; Duke St; s/d/f $100/110/130; ✖ ☻) This is a central, classic 1960s-era roadside motel with spacious self-contained rooms with fridges, satellite TV and a pool and spa. Weekday rates are slightly lower.

ourpick **Theatre Royal Back Stage** (☎ 03-5472 1196; www.theatreroyal.info; 28 Hargraves St; d incl breakfast $220-240). It's a unique experience staying in the backstage area of the 1854 theatre building. The two suites are compact, but beautifully decorated with period furniture and cinema memorabilia, and are literally right behind the velvet curtain – you can clearly hear any performances – though the rate includes admission to all movies screened during your stay. The suites can be rented together for $240 (sleeping four) plus you get the 'Harry Potter' single (under the stairs) free.

Castlemaine Gardens Caravan Park (☎ 03-5472 1125; www.castlemainegardenscaravanpark.com; Doran Ave; unpowered/powered sites $23/28, cabins $80-90) Beautifully situated next to the Botanic Gardens and public swimming pool, this leafy park has a camp kitchen, barbecues and recreation hut.

Eating

Mostyn St is Castlemaine's eat street, with a nice knot of eateries east of Hargraves St.

Capones (☎ 03-5470 5705; 50 Hargraves St; mains $12-19; ☽ dinner) Reliable wood-fired pizzas and pastas done gangster-style.

Tog's Café (☎ 03-5470 5090; 58 Lyttleton St; mains $14-26; ☽ breakfast & lunch daily, dinner Fri & Sat) Fashionable Tog's is a local favourite, with a warm welcome, open fireplaces and artworks on the walls. Great for a light lunch, coffee and cake.

Saff's Café (☎ 03-5470 6722; 64 Mostyn St; mains $17-23; ☽ breakfast & lunch) Another local institution, Saff's serves the best coffee and breakfast fare

in town, excellent homemade bread, cakes and savouries.

Getting There & Away

Daily **V/Line** (☎ 13 61 96) trains run hourly between Melbourne and Castlemaine ($12, 1½ hours) and continue on to Bendigo ($4) and Swan Hill ($21). There's one bus a day to Daylesford ($4) and Ballarat ($9), and at least three daily to Maldon.

MALDON

pop 1220

Like a pop-up folk museum, charming Maldon is a well-preserved relic of the goldmining era, with a 19th-century streetscape, but it's very much a living town that reverts to a haven of peace when the weekend tourists depart. The population is a fraction of the 20,000 who once worked here in the heady gold-rush days. These days antique stores, cafes and cute shops make for a quaint afternoon stroll, and you can travel between Maldon and Castlemaine on a restored steam train.

The helpful **Maldon visitor information centre** (☎ 03-5475 2569; www.maldoncastlemaine.com; High St; 🖳) has a small interpretive display and internet access ($3 for 30 minutes). Behind the visitor centre, the **historical museum** (☎ 03-5474 1633; adult/child $3/1; ☽ 1.30-4pm Mon-Fri, 1.30-5pm Sat & Sun), in the 19th-century market building, displays local artefacts and mining memorabilia.

You can take a candle-lit tour of 1880s-era **Carmen's Tunnel Goldmine** (☎ 03-5475 2656; adult/child $5/2; ☽ tours 1.30, 2.30 & 3.30pm Sat & Sun), off Parkin's Reef Rd about 3km south of town. Railway buffs will enjoy the **Victorian Goldfields Railway** (☎ 03-5475 2966; www.vgr.com.au; Hornsby St), which has classic steam trains running to Castlemaine (see opposite). Historic **Porcupine Township** (☎ 03-5475 1000; www.porcupinetownship.com.au; Bendigo Rd; adult/child/family $10/6/30; ☽ 10am-5pm) is a quaint re-creation of a gold-mining village.

South of town, the excellent **Penny School Gallery & Café** (☎ 03-5475 1911; www.pennyschoolgallery.com.au; 11 Church St; lunch $9.50-18.50; ☽ 11am-5pm Mon-Thu, 11am-10pm Fri-Sun) features changing exhibitions by well-known Australian artists, and a good cafe.

Folk-music fans will enjoy the annual **Maldon Folk Festival** (www.maldonfolkfestival.com) held in early November.

VICTORIA

Sleeping

Heritage Cottages of Maldon (☎ 03-5475 1094; www.heritagecottages.com.au) manages many of the area's self-contained cottages and historic B&Bs.

Mrs Gilmore's (☎ 03-5475 2216; Main St; d/tr $88/110; ⊠) This excellent budget option is in the unlikely setting of a former garage (the pumps are still out the front). The MG room is the funkiest.

Maldon's Eaglehawk (☎ 03-5475 2750; www .maldoneaglehawk.com; 35 Reef St; s/d from $95/105; ⊠ ⊠) Beautiful heritage units here are set in delightful grounds with little alcoves overlooking the pool, barbecue nooks and vine-trimmed verandahs.

Calder House (☎ 0407 506 395; www.calderhouse .com.au; 44 High St; d $130-160) Step back in time at this formal and grand 1860s B&B. Some rooms are a bit twee with their antique furnishings, but are very 'Maldon' and feature four-poster beds, claw-foot baths and views to a lovely garden.

Maldon Caravan Park (☎ /fax 5475 2344; Hospital St; unpowered/powered sites from $22/25, d cabins $75; ⊠) In town but backing up to the bush, this friendly park has a camp kitchen, barbecues and swimming pool next door.

Parks Victoria (☎ 13 19 63, Bendigo 5430 444; www .parkweb.vic.gov.au) manages the Butts Reserve campsite in the Maldon Historic Reserve with toilets and picnic tables (free; no permits required). From Maldon, head west along Franklin St and follow the signs to Mt Tarrengower.

Eating

Main St is peppered with cafes between the antique shops, and the local pubs do honest counter meals.

Berryman's Café & Tearooms (☎ 03-5475 2904; 30 Main St; meals $5-10; ⊠ breakfast & lunch) Disappear into this classic old-style tearoom for a slice of lemon tart or enjoy a light lunch on the footpath.

Bean There Café (☎ 0419 102 723; 44-46 Main St; meals $5-12; ⊠ breakfast & lunch Wed-Sun) The yabbie and scallop pies are hard to resist, but there's also good coffee, focaccias and desserts at this relaxed cafe and wine bar.

Two Fat Men (☎ 03-5475 2504; 24 High St; mains $18-29; ⊠ Wed 6-9pm, Thu-Sun 10am-9pm) Maldon's best bet for an evening meal, Two Fat Men lovingly prepares Asian-influenced dishes such as tempura prawns and Mod Oz such

as peppered kangaroo steak, washed down with local wines.

Getting There & Away

Castlemaine Bus Lines (☎ 03-5472 1455; www.cas tlemainebuslines.com.au) runs at least three buses daily between Castlemaine and Maldon ($3.20), connecting with trains to and from Melbourne.

MARYBOROUGH

pop 7700

In 1854 gold was discovered around here at White Hills and Four Mile Flat. A police camp at the diggings was named Maryborough, and at the height of the gold rush the population was over 40,000. Today the town is a small commercial centre in the 'Golden Triangle' – a popular gold prospecting region bordered by Avoca, Castlemaine and Wedderburn – and still boasts some fine 19th-century buildings.

The **Maryborough visitor information centre** (☎ 03-5460 4511, 1800 356 511; www.visitmaryborough .com.au; cnr Alma & Nolan Sts; ⊠ 9am-5pm; ⌨) has a gallery and a replica of the famous Welcome Stranger gold nugget, discovered near here in 1869. There's internet access and a library in the same complex.

Maryborough's main attraction is the magnificent 1892 **Maryborough Railway Station** (☎ 03-5461 4683; Burns St; ⊠ 10am-5pm Mon, Wed & Sun, 10am-10pm Thu-Sat), which Mark Twain once described as 'a train station with a town attached'. Passenger trains don't stop any more, but the building houses an excellent antiques and fine-art emporium, gallery, wine centre and cafe.

Worsley Cottage (☎ 03-5461 2800; 3 Palmerston St; adult/child $3/1; ⊠ 10am-noon Tue & Thu, 2-4pm Sun), dating from 1894, is the historical society museum.

If you'd like to learn the tricks to unearthing a gold nugget, **Coiltek Gold Centre** (☎ 03-5460 4700; www.coiltek.com.au; 6 Drive-in Crt; ⊠ 9am-5pm) runs full-day prospecting tours (one/two people $120/200), which include hire of a metal detector and showing you what to look for. They also sell and hire out prospecting gear.

Sleeping & Eating

Maryborough has a handful of standard motels near the centre. High St is the place for cafes, bakeries and pubs serving counter meals.

Bull & Mouth Hotel (☎ 03-5461 3636; www.bulland mouth.com.au; cnr High & Nolan Sts) Maryborough's grandest hotel was closed for renovations at the time of research while the owners upgrade the old pub rooms to boutique-style en suite rooms. Those, and the downstairs bistro, should be open by the time you read this.

Fiorini's Guest House & Gardens (☎ 03-5461 1054; www.fiorini.com.au; 35 Tuaggra St; d incl breakfast $150; 🗷) This quirky art deco place is right in the centre, but you can hide away in the rambling garden and kick back in the retro self-contained guest rooms.

Maryborough Caravan Park (☎ 03-5460 4848; www.maryboroughcaravanpark.com.au; 7 Holyrood St; unpowered/powered sites $20/24, cabins $60-95; 🗷) Right in town and beside Lake Victoria, this pleasant family park offers Maryborough's cheapest accommodation with budget cabins.

Station Café (☎ 03-5461 4683; mains $9-25; 🕑 Sun & Mon 10am-5.30pm, Thu-Sat 10am-10pm) At the historic train station, this licensed cafe has a tapas bar six days a week and a carvery restaurant from 6pm three nights a week.

Getting There & Away

Maryborough is connected by bus to Castlemaine and Ballarat. From Melbourne, take the train to Castlemaine, and then a bus to Maryborough ($17, 2¾ hours).

BENDIGO
pop 76,000

When gold was discovered at Ravenswood in 1851, thousands converged on the fantastically rich Bendigo Diggings. The arrival of Chinese miners in 1854 had a lasting effect on Bendigo, which maintains a rich Chinese heritage.

During the boom years between the 1860s and 1880s, mining companies poured money into the town, resulting in the Victorian architecture that graces Bendigo's streets today. By the 1860s diggers were no longer tripping over surface nuggets and deep mining began. Local legend has it that you can walk underground from one side of the town to the other. These days the town is a prosperous provincial centre with fine public gardens, statues and buildings, a bohemian cafe and restaurant scene, and one of Victoria's best regional art galleries. Among Central Victoria's most likeable cities, Bendigo has lots of historical attractions, arcades and alleyways, and plenty for you to explore for a few days.

Information

Bendigo visitor information centre (☎ 03-5434 6060, 1800 813 153; www.bendigotourism.com; 51-67 Pall Mall; 🕑 9am-5pm) In the historic former post office, the visitor centre features a hands-on interpretive centre and the excellent free 'Making a Nation' exhibition. Here you can buy the Bendigo Experience Pass (adult/child/family $45/24.50/110), which gives admission to four of Bendigo's main attractions: Bendigo Pottery Museum, Central Deborah Gold Mine, Golden Dragon Museum and Talking Tram tours.

Renaissance Computers (☎ 03-5442 5856; 70 Pall Mall; per hr $6; 🕑 9.30am-5.30pm Mon-Fri) Internet access.

Sights

It's hard to miss the soaring steeple of the magnificent **Sacred Heart Cathedral** (www.sand .catholic.org.au/cathedral; cnr Wattle & High Sts). It's a superb piece of architecture and a walk down its central aisle below the high-vaulted ceiling and superb stained-glass windows is a religious experience.

The magnificent **Shamrock Hotel** (cnr Pall Mall & Williamson St), built in 1897, is a fine example of elaborate Italianate late-Victorian architecture and one of many impressive colonial buildings in the city centre. The story goes that floors were regularly washed down to collect gold dust brought in on miners' boots.

The 500m-deep **Central Deborah Goldmine** (☎ 03-5443 8322; www.central-deborah.com; 76 Violet St; adult/child/family $24/12/60; 🕑 9.30am-5pm), worked on 17 levels, became operational in the 1940s and was connected with two Deborah shafts that date back to the 1860s. About one tonne of gold was removed before it closed in 1954. The mine is one of Bendigo's major tourist attractions, with exhibits and photographs from the mid-1800s onwards. After donning hard hats and lights, you're taken 61m down the shaft to inspect the ongoing operations, complete with drilling demonstrations. There's a combined ticket (adult/child $34/18.50) for the mine tour plus a ride on the Talking Tram.

Bendigo's tram system was closed down in 1972, but Bendigo residents took direct action and resuscitated the trams, which now run as a tourist feature. The **Bendigo Talking Tram** (☎ 03-5443 2821; www.bendigotram ways.com; 1 Tramways Ave; adult/child/family $14/8.50/40;

VICTORIA

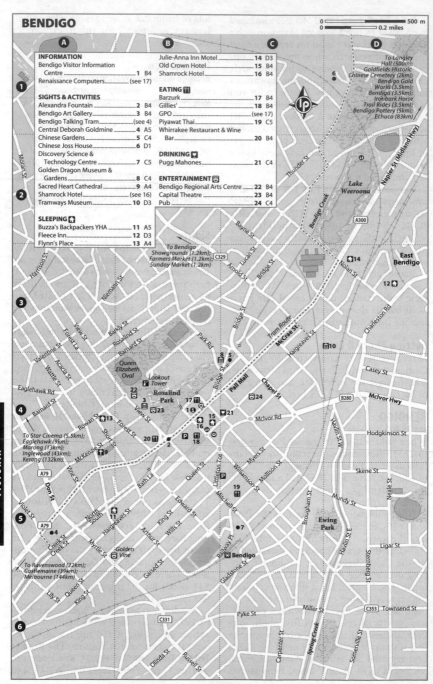

BENDIGO

INFORMATION
Bendigo Visitor Information
  Centre **1** B4
Renaissance Computers .... (see 17)

SIGHTS & ACTIVITIES
Alexandra Fountain **2** B4
Bendigo Art Gallery **3** B4
Bendigo Talking Tram .... (see 4)
Central Deborah Goldmine **4** A5
Chinese Gardens **5** C4
Chinese Joss House **6** D1
Discovery Science &
  Technology Centre **7** C5
Golden Dragon Museum &
  Gardens **8** C4
Sacred Heart Cathedral **9** A4
Shamrock Hotel .... (see 16)
Tramways Museum **10** D3

SLEEPING
Buzza's Backpackers YHA **11** A5
Fleece Inn **12** D3
Flynn's Place **13** A4

Julie-Anna Inn Motel **14** D3
Old Crown Hotel **15** B4
Shamrock Hotel **16** B4

EATING
Barzurk **17** B4
Gillies' **18** B4
GPO .... (see 17)
Piyawat Thai **19** C5
Whirrakee Restaurant & Wine
  Bar **20** B4

DRINKING
Pugg Mahones **21** C4

ENTERTAINMENT
Bendigo Regional Arts Centre **22** B4
Capital Theatre **23** B4
Pub **24** C4

9.30am-4pm) runs with a commentary from the Central Deborah Goldmine, through the centre of the city, out to the **Tramways Museum** (admission free) and on to the Chinese Joss House. It leaves the mine every half hour, or five minutes later from **Alexandra fountain** in Charing Cross.

One of Victoria's largest regional galleries, the **Bendigo Art Gallery** (☎ 03-5443 4991; www .bendigoartgallery.com.au; 42 View St; admission by donation) has an outstanding collection of 19th-century European, colonial and contemporary Australian art, and regular touring exhibitions from overseas. Guided tours run at 2pm daily. Enter the permanent collection via the cafe at the rear.

Bendigo's proud Chinese heritage can be explored at the wonderful **Golden Dragon Museum & Chinese Gardens** (☎ 03-5441 5044; www .goldendragonmuseum.org; 5-13 Bridge St; adult/child/ family $8/4/20; 9.30am-5pm). Two enormous processional dragons, Old Loong (the world's oldest) and Sun Loong (the world's longest), reside here. Old Loong arrived in 1892 for the annual Bendigo Easter Festival, and Sun Loong took over in 1970 when Old Loong retired. The museum traces the involvement of the Chinese community in the development of Bendigo. Across the road are the pretty ornamental **Chinese gardens** and there's a tearoom serving light meals and yum cha.

The **Chinese Joss House** (☎ 03-5442 1685; Finn St; adult/child $5/3; 11am-4pm Wed, Sat & Sun), at the end of the tramline, is one of the few practising joss houses (Chinese temples) in Victoria.

The **Goldfields Historic Chinese Cemetery** (White Hills Cemetery, Holdsworth Rd) is the oldest and most significant of its kind in Australia, with a prayer oven where paper money for the spirits of the dead was burnt.

The oldest working pottery in Australia (1858), **Bendigo Pottery** (☎ 03-5448 4404; www .bendigopottery.com.au; 146 Midland Hwy, Epsom; 9am-5pm) is 6km north of the town centre. There's an interpretive museum (adult/child $7/4), but it's also worth just wandering through the display galleries and historic kilns and watching the potters at work. There's a cafe and you can buy pieces at factory prices.

The huge **Discovery Science & Technology Centre** (☎ 03-5444 4400; www.discovery.asn.au; 7 Railway Pl; adult/child/family $9.50/7/30; 10am-4pm) has a wide range of interesting and educational exhibits, including a planetarium.

Bendigo Showgrounds is the venue for the **Sunday Market** (8.30am-3pm) and, on the second Saturday each month, the **Farmers Market** (8am-1pm).

Activities

Ironbark Horse Trail Rides (☎ 0407 349 928; www.bwc .com.au/ironbark; Lot 2 Watson St, White Hills; rides per hr/day $38/115) organises various horse rides including the Great Australian Pub Ride to Allies Hotel in Myers Flat (with lunch $85).

Also located in the Ironbark complex is **Bendigo Gold World** (☎ 03-5448 4140; www.bendigo gold.com.au; Watson St), which operates fossicking and detecting tours (per half-day $150) into the bush, and hires out prospecting equipment.

Balloon Flights of Bendigo (☎ 03-544 1127; www.balloonflightsvic.com.au; sunrise flight, breakfast & champagne $280) offers bird's-eye views of the Bendigo environs.

Central Wine Tours (☎ 03-5447 4814; www.central winetours.com.au; half-day tours $55-95, full-day $120) runs tours to the Bendigo region wineries; some tours include lunch.

Festivals

Bendigo's busy schedule of festivals includes the **Bendigo Agricultural Show** (www .bendigoshow.org.au) held in October, and the **Bendigo Cup** (www.racingvictoria.net.au/vcrc/bend igo), part of the Spring Racing Carnival held in November. The biggest, however, is the **Bendigo Easter Festival** (www.bendi goeasterfestival.or.au), attracting thousands of visitors with its carnival atmosphere and procession of Chinese dragons, including Sun Loong, the longest imperial dragon in the world.

Sleeping

There's an **accommodation booking service** (☎ 03-5444 4445, 1800 813 153) at the visitor information centre (p595).

BUDGET

Buzza's Backpackers YHA (☎ 03-5443 7680; bendigo@ yhavic.org.au; 33 Creek St S; dm/s/d/f $27/46/64/76;) This small, homey hostel is in a weatherboard cottage in a great central location. It's been opened up inside to make bright cheery rooms with all the usual amenities, including bike hire.

Fleece Inn (☎ 03-5443 3086; 139 Charleston Rd; dm/s/ d/f $33/50/74/104; 🐱) This 140-year-old former pub has dorm rooms with partitioned-off beds, cosy private rooms (share facilities), communal kitchen and a huge back courtyard with lounge area, TV and barbecues. Smart rooms are up the grand original timber staircase.

Old Crown Hotel (☎ 03-5441 6888; 238 Hargreaves St; r per person $45) This ultra-central pub has clean old-style rooms with share facilities. There are two-bed and four-bed rooms.

MIDRANGE & TOP END

Shamrock Hotel (☎ 03-5443 0333; www.hotelshamrock .com.au; cnr Pall Mall & Williamson St; d $120-175, ste $225) One of Bendigo's historic icons, the Shamrock is a stunning Victorian building with stained glass, original paintings, fancy columns and a *Gone with the Wind*–style staircase. The refurbished upstairs rooms range from small standard rooms to more spacious deluxe and spa suites.

Julie-Anna Inn Motel (☎ 03-5442 5855; www .julieanna.com.au; 268 Napier St; d $144-161, ste $209; 🐱 🖳 🐾) One of Bendigo's better motels enjoys a good location across from Lake Weeroona. The spacious units open onto an attractive central courtyard, with a grand dining room at the end, and there luxurious spa units and suites.

Flynn's Place (☎ 03-5444 001; www.flynnsplace .au; 104 Short St; d $165-195; 🐱 🖳) The two modern self-contained apartments at Flynn's are sleekly fitted out and furnished in a historic building, with queen beds, widescreen TVs, DVDs, sound systems and free broadband internet. It's conveniently central, around the corner from the art gallery.

Langley Hall (☎ 03-5443 3693; www.innhouse.com .au/langleyhall.html; 484 Napier St; d from $175; 🐱) Built in 1904 this Edwardian mansion offers unfussy opulence and heritage furnishings, but with modern comforts. Sweep up the grand staircase to magnificent suites, opening onto expansive verandahs. Downstairs, enjoy the elegant and comfortable parlour, drawing room and billiards room.

Eating

Bendigo has an excellent range of cafes, pubs and restaurants, most in the convenient block bounded by Pall Mall, Bull St, Hargreaves St and Mitchell St. Tiny Bath Lane also has a couple of good daytime cafes.

Gillies' (Hargreaves St Mall) The pie window on the corner of the mall here is a Bendigo institution, and the pies are as good as you'll find.

Barzurk (☎ 03-5442 4032; 66 Pall Mall; lunch $7-19, dinner $16-28; 🕑 lunch daily, dinner Wed-Sun) A trendy but casual streetside cafe-bar with pressed-tin ceilings and courtyard out the back. Even light meals are filling and the menu includes Thai, pasta, risotto and gourmet pizza.

GPO (☎ 03-5443 4343; www.gpobendigo.com.au; Pall Mall; mains $10-39; 🕑 lunch & dinner) Next door to Barzurk but made for a more classy night out, the food and atmosphere here is superb and rated highly by locals. Moroccan spiced chicken and pistachio dukkah-crusted lamb grace the Mediterranean menu, or go for the innovative pizzas and pasta or tapas. The bar is a chilled place for a drink.

Piyawat Thai (☎ 03-5444 4450; 136 Mollison St; mains $14-20; 🕑 dinner Tue-Sun) Tucked away in a cosy house a couple of blocks south of the centre, this authentic Thai restaurant serves fabulously fragrant curries, noodles and Thai stir-fries at affordable prices. Takeaway is available.

Whirrakee Restaurant & Wine Bar (☎ 03-5441 5557; www.whirrakeerestaurant.com.au; 17 View St; mains $22-38; 🕑 lunch & dinner Tue-Sat) In another of Bendigo's historic buildings with a view to Alexandra fountain, the French-influenced menu features Wagyu beef and tortellini of blue swimmer crab. Downstairs there's a small wine bar with cosy sofas.

Drinking & Entertainment

With lots of university students, Bendigo has a lively nightlife – uni nights are Tuesday and Thursday.

Pugg Mahones (☎ 03-5443 4916; www.puggs.com.au; 224 Hargreaves St) Holding court on the corner of Bendigo's very short club strip, the Guinness flows freely at Puggs. Great atmosphere, beer garden and live music Thursday to Saturday.

Pub (☎ 03-5443 4079; 173 Hargreaves St; 🕑 Tue-Sat) Bendigo's premier live-rock venue is a grungy club showcasing touring acts from all over Australia.

Capital Theatre (☎ 03-5434 6100; www.capital.com .au; 50 View St) Alongside the art gallery, the impressive Capital, with its facade of Corinthian pillars, is Bendigo's main venue for the performing arts. Check the website for a calendar of theatre, music and dance.

VICTORIA

Star Cinema (☎ 0408 337 277; www.starcinema.org
.au; Eaglehawk Town Hall, Peg Leg Rd, Eaglehawk; adult/child
$13/7) Classic and art-house flicks.

Getting There & Away

V/Line (☎ 13 61 96; www.vline.com.au) runs at least
15 trains daily from Melbourne ($16, two
hours) via Castlemaine ($4) and Kyneton
($6). Two services continue on to Swan Hill
($18). Train/bus services go to Mildura ($32,
five hours) via Swan Hill. Weekday bus services run to Ballarat ($13) and Geelong ($23),
and there's daily services to Echuca ($5).

Bendigo Airport Service (☎ 03-5444 3939; www.
bendigoairportservice.com.au; adult/child one way $38/15)
runs a shuttle direct to Melbourne airport
and back four times on weekdays and
three times on weekends, via Castlemaine
and Kyneton.

GOULBURN VALLEY & HUME HIGHWAY REGION

The Hume Hwy (M31) is the multilane link
between Melbourne and Sydney via Albury-
Wodonga. You can put your foot down for
most of the way as it isn't particularly scenic and the speed limit is usually 110km,
but there are a few attractions just off the
freeway. To the east are the foothills of
Victoria's High Country: get off at Seymour
for Mansfield and Mt Buller, or Wangaratta
for Mt Hotham and Falls Creek.

West of the Hume is the Goulburn Valley,
Victoria's fruit bowl and a popular area for
seasonal work. The valley's other main crop
is wine, and several wineries are worth a
visit, notably the impressive Tahbilk and
Mitchelton wineries near Nagambie.

River Country Adventours (☎ 03-5852 2736;
www.adventours.com.au) runs canoe and camping safaris on the Goulburn and Murray
rivers from Seymour, Shepparton, Wyuna
and other sites. Guided or self-guided safaris
start from $80 a day to $275 for a three-day
trip at private riverside camps.

SHEPPARTON
pop 27,700

Relaxed 'Shep' is the regional centre of the
Goulburn Valley, where the Goulburn and
Broken Rivers meet. This is the heart of a

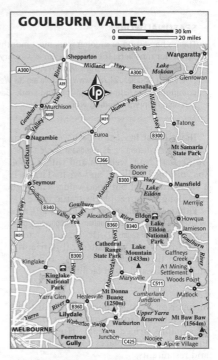

rich fruit growing region – the giant SPC
Ardmona cannery is here – so for travellers
fruit-picking work is the main attraction.

The **Bangerang Cultural Centre** (☎ 03-5831
1020; Parkside Dr; admission free; ⏱ 9am-4pm Mon-Fri),
west of the highway about 4km north of
town, has displays on the area's original
Koorie owners.

Information

Cyber Bunker (☎ 03-5832 4880; 135 Maud St; per hr
$6; 🖳) Internet cafe popular with gamers.
Greater Shepparton visitor information centre
(☎ 1800 808 839, 5831 4400; www.greatershepparton
.com.au; 534 Wyndham St; ⏱ 9am-5pm) At the southern
end of the Victoria Park Lake, the visitor centre has a free
accommodation booking service.

Sleeping

Shepparton Backpackers (☎ 03-5831 6556; www.shep
partonbackpackers.com.au; 139 Numurkah Rd; dm/d $25/80;
🖳) This well-equipped and busy backpacker
hostel caters to working travellers. Weekly
rates are cheaper. It's on the highway about
3km north of town, tucked away behind a
car wash.

VICTORIA

SEASONAL WORK

There's harvesting or pruning work most months of the year in the Shepparton area and it's well set up for travellers. The main season is January to May (apples, peaches and pears) and there's pruning work available from May to August.

CVGT (☎ 1300 724 788; www.cvgt.com.au; cnr Welsford & Sobraon St) runs a harvest hotline and has comprehensive listings of fruit-picking work. Backpacker hostels in Shepparton and Mooroopna can also help with finding work.

Tirana Motor Inn (☎ 03-5831 1766; www.tiranamotorinn.websyte.com.au; 33 Wyndham St; s/d $85/95; ❌ 🖳 🖳) Clean, well run and with a pool, spa, disabled facilities and wi-fi, Tirana is a standard motel but good value. The high wall along the street blocks traffic noise.

Victoria Lake Holiday Park (☎ 03-5821 5431; www.viclakeholidaypark.com.au; Wyndham St; unpowered/powered sites $23/25, d cabins $75-110) Beside Victoria Lake (dry when we visited), this friendly place on the highway has grass and trees, bicycle paths and good facilities.

Eating

Shepparton's central pubs, Hotel Australia and Victoria Hotel among them, offer reasonably priced meals. High St and Fryers St are the places to look for cafes and restaurants.

Moo Joose Café (☎ 03-5831 2275; Fryers St; meals $5-10; ❤ 10am-4pm Tue-Sun) Shep's funkiest cafe is themed around dairy cows – thousands of bottles (from a failed attempt to market alcoholic flavoured milk) line the black and white walls and stuffed cows guard the espresso machine. Great coffee, milkshakes (25 flavours) and light meals.

Letizia's Café Bar Restaurant (☎ 03-5831 8822; 67 Fryers St; mains $10-30; ❤ lunch & dinner Tue-Sun) With yum cha, mezes, pasta and Asian-influenced dishes (including Japanese bento boxes), Letizia's has an international selection in a casual, relaxed atmosphere. Great for lunch on the run.

Cellar 47 (☎ 03-5831 1882; 170 High St; mains $20-30; ❤ lunch daily, dinner Mon-Sat) This smart restaurant with its sleek black-and-glass bar is one of Shepparton's finest and a long-standing favourite. The menu features Italian and Australian dishes, including steaks, pasta and gourmet pizzas.

Getting There & Away

Shepparton train station is east of the town centre. There are daily **V/Line** (☎ 13 61 96)

trains and buses to/from Melbourne ($18, 2½ hours).

V/Line buses also connect with Wodonga ($17) and Benalla ($6) daily, and Bendigo ($8) twice a week.

NAGAMBIE
pop 1380

Nagambie is on the shores of **Lake Nagambie**, created by the construction of the Goulburn Weir in 1887. This area's main attractions are its wineries and water sports.

The **Nagambie visitor information centre** (☎ 03-5794 2647, 1800 444 647; www.nagambielaketourism.com.au; 145 High St; ❤ 9am-5.30pm) has a great range of information, along with free tastings and a small shop selling souvenirs and maps.

Two of the best-known wineries in Victoria, **Tahbilk Winery** (☎ 03-5794 2555; www.tahbilk.com.au; ❤ 9am-5pm Mon-Fri, 10am-5pm Sat & Sun), off Goulburn Valley Hwy, and **Mitchelton Wines** (☎ 03-5736 2221; www.mitchelton.com.au; Mitchellstown Rd; ❤ 10am-5pm), are just south of town. Tahbilk also opens onto the **Wetlands Wildlife Reserve** (adult/child $5/free, wetland cruise $10; ❤ 11am-4pm Mon-Fri, 10.30am-4.30pm Sat & Sun), entered via the Wetlands Café.

GLENROWAN
pop 320

Ned Kelly's legendary bushranging exploits came to their bloody end here in 1880. The story of Ned and his gang has become an industry in this one-street town – a short detour off the highway – and you can't drive through Glenrowan without being confronted by the legend or his souvenirs.

At the Glenrowan Tourist Centre, **Ned Kelly's Last Stand** (☎ 03-5766 2367; www.glenrowantouristcentre.com.au; 41 Gladstone St; adult/child/family $22/17/55; ❤ every half hr 9.30am-4.30pm) is an over-the-top animated theatre where Ned's story is told in a series of rooms by a cast of surprisingly lifelike computerised characters and culminating in a smoky shootout and the hanging (it may be too scary for young children). You can browse the shop and small exhibition of memorabilia and paintings for free. You can also pick up a map here detailing the important sites leading up to the shootout.

The 400-million-year-old **Warby Range State Park** extends about 25km north of Glenrowan and provided Ned Kelly and his gang with many vantage points. There's a free **camping area** in the park at Wenhams.

Sleeping & Eating

There are a couple of cafes and old-style tearooms along the main street, as well as a handful of motels and B&Bs.

Glenrowan Kelly Country Motel (☎ 03-5766 2202; www.kellycountrymotel.com; 44 Gladstone St; s/d/f from $50/70/90; ⊠ ⊠) Spacious rooms overlook a small garden and barbecue area. The owners will pick you up from Wangaratta if you book ahead.

Glenrowan Tourist Park (☎ 03-5766 2288; www.glenrowanpark.com.au; Old Hume Hwy; unpowered/powered sites $15/25, cabins $70-110; ⊠ ⊠) In a peaceful bushland setting at the foot of the Warby Ranges 2km north of town, this welcoming park has had a complete refit in recent years.

Glenrowan Hotel (☎ 03-5766 2255; 46 Gladstone St; mains $10-22; ⊗ lunch & dinner) There's mercifully no Kelly paraphernalia on the walls at this typical country pub (the building dates from well after Kelly's time). You can get a decent meal here and there's a beer garden.

WANGARATTA
pop 16,850

The Ovens and King Rivers meet at Wangaratta (known locally as 'Wang'). Its name comes from two local Aboriginal words meaning 'resting place of cormorants'. Although a base for surrounding attractions and gateway to the Great Alpine Rd and High Country snowfields, Wangaratta is a typical modern town. The main claim to fame here is the almost-world-famous **Wangaratta Jazz Festival** (☎ 1800 803 944; www.wangaratta-jazz.org.au), which attracts jazz players and buffs from around Australia and the world in early November.

The **Wangaratta visitor information centre** (☎ 03-5721 5711, 1800 801 065; www.visitwangaratta .com.au; Murphy St; ⊠) has a display on the jazz fest and internet access ($4 per hour).

Sights & Activities

At the **Wangaratta Cemetery** you'll find the grave of notorious bushranger Dan 'Mad Dog' Morgan. It contains most of Morgan's remains: his head was taken to Melbourne for a study of the criminal mind, and the scrotum was supposedly fashioned into a tobacco pouch.

A bicycle and walking trail, the **Murray to Mountains Rail Trail** (www.railtrail.com.au) connects Wangaratta with Beechworth and Bright using disused railway lines. Maps are available at the information centre. You can hire bikes from **Dean Woods** (☎ 1800 353 123; www .deanwoods.com.au; 6-8 Handley St; per day/week $29/160; ⊗ 8.30am-5.30pm Mon-Fri, 9am-1pm Sat).

THE KELLY GANG

Bushranger and outlaw though he was, Ned Kelly is Australia's greatest folk hero, and his life and death are embraced as part of the national culture. He's inspired a range of artists, including author Peter Carey, who wrote *True History of the Kelly Gang,* and painter Sidney Nolan, who produced a series of iconic works.

Before he became a cult hero, Edward 'Ned' Kelly was a common horse thief. Born in 1855 Ned was first arrested when he was 14 and spent the next 10 years in and out of jail. In a shoot-out at Stringybark Creek, Ned and his gang killed three police officers, and a reward was posted for their capture. The gang robbed banks at Euroa and Jerilderie, making a mockery of the police by locking them in their own cells and wearing their uniforms during the hold-up.

On 27 June 1880 the gang held 60 people captive in a hotel at Glenrowan. Surrounded by police, the gang was under siege for hours while wearing heavy armour made from ploughshares. Ned, wearing his now-famous helmet and chest armour, was shot in the legs and captured, and his gang, along with several hostages, was killed.

Ned Kelly was brought to Melbourne, tried and hanged on 11 November 1880. His last words were said to be 'Such is life'. His death mask, armour and the gallows on which he died are on display in the Old Melbourne Gaol (p506).

Sleeping & Eating

Millers Cottage (☎ 03-5721 5755; www.millerscottage
.com.au; 26 Parfitt Rd; s/d from $55/65; ✗ ✦) On the
northern side of town, this well-priced motel
has small but comfortable rooms and a large
garden, pool, playground and barbecue.

Painters Island Caravan Park (☎ 03-5721 3380;
www.paintersislandcaravanpark.com.au; Pinkerton Cres;
unpowered & powered sites from $26, cabins $60-145;
✗ ✦ ✦) Set on 10 hectares on the banks
of the Ovens River, just two minutes from
town, this impressive park has a playground,
barbecue, camp kitchen, wi-fi and a good
range of cabins.

Tread (☎ 03-5721 4635; www.treadrestaurant.com.au;
56-58 Faithfull St; tapas $5-10, mains $23-27; ✦ 10am-late
Wed-Fri, 8.30am-late Sat, 8.30am-5pm Sun; ✦) With its
broad timber deck hanging over the Ovens
River and a combination of tapas plates,
contemporary Australian cuisine and fine
wines, Tread is Wangaratta's newest and
best dining experience. It's equally good for
coffee, weekend breakfasts or light lunch.

Vine Hotel (☎ 03-5721 2605; www.thevinehotel.com
.au; 27 Detour Rd; mains $14-28; ✦ lunch & dinner) This
charming old pub hasn't changed much since
Ned Kelly drank here. Check out the small
history museum in the cavernous cellar.

Getting There & Away

Wangaratta train station is just west of the
town centre in Norton St. There's one direct
V/Line (☎ 13 61 96) train daily from Melbourne
($22, 2½ hours) continuing on to Albury;
all other services require changing to a
bus at Seymour. There's one V/Line bus
daily from Wangaratta to Rutherglen ($4,
30 minutes).

THE HIGH COUNTRY

The Great Dividing Range – Australia's eastern spine – curls around Victoria from the
Snowy Mountains to the Grampians, peak-
ing in the spectacular High Country. This
is Victoria's mountain playground, attracting skiers and snowboarders in winter and
bushwalkers and mountain-bikers in summer. Although not particularly high – the
highest point, Mt Bogong, only reaches
1986m – the mountain air is clear and invigorating and the scenery spectacular.

Although there are plenty of activities
on offer, it's the ski resorts that really pull
the crowds. Skiers and snowboarders flock
from Melbourne and the outlying areas
to Mt Buller, Mt Hotham and Falls Creek
in particular, all of which have good on-
mountain infrastructure. The ski season
officially launches, with or without snow,
on the Queen's Birthday long weekend in
June and runs until mid-September. The
best deals are to be found in June and
September (low season), with late July to
August (high season) the busiest and most
expensive time.

Away from the mountain-tops, the High
Country offers plenty of summer activities
such as horse riding, canoeing, abseiling
and mountain-bike riding, or more restful pastimes such as touring wineries and
gourmet regions such as Milawa, King Valley
and Beechworth.

Eildon and the gateway towns (Mansfield,
Myrtleford, Harrietville and Bright) are in
the northwestern foothills. Omeo is the High
Country's southeastern gateway town.

Declared a national park in December
1989, the 646,000-hectare **Alpine National
Park** joins the high country areas of Victoria,
NSW and the Australian Capital Territory
(ACT). Recreation and ecotourism opportunities in the area are outstanding, particularly snow sports in the winter. Dispersed
bush camping is available in areas running
off 4WD and walking tracks, while on principal roads the use of designated camping
areas is encouraged. The area's many walking tracks include the **Australian Alps Walking
Track**, which extends 655km through the park
from Walhalla to the outskirts of Canberra.
In spring and summer the slopes are carpeted with beautiful wildflowers. More
than 1100 plant species have been recorded
in the park, including 12 that are unique
to Australia.

Many of the walks in this area are described in detail in Lonely Planet's *Walking
in Australia* guide.

Getting There & Away

V/Line (☎ 13 61 96) operates services to major
alpine towns, and there are also connecting services from Benalla and Wangaratta.
Services vary seasonally.

During winter the roads can become impassable. Check road condi-
tions with the **Official Victorian Snow Report**
(www.vicsnowreport.com.au/report.html) before head-

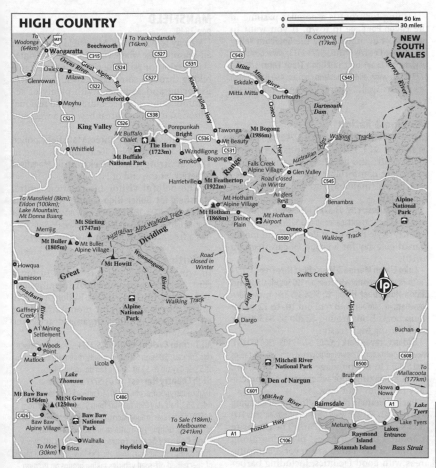

HIGH COUNTRY

ing out. Snow chains, widely available for hire, must be carried during winter even if there's no snow – heavy penalties apply if you don't.

EILDON
pop 740

The little one-pub town of Eildon was built in the 1950s to house Eildon Dam project workers. Sitting on the edge of the 'pondage', it's a popular recreation, fishing and holiday base for Lake Eildon, one of Victoria's favourite water-sports playgrounds, with a shoreline of over 500km and a water level that's somehow resisting the drought. The surrounding **Lake Eildon National Park** protects 27,750 hectares of bushland adjoining the lake.

The small **Eildon visitor information centre** (☎ 03-5774 2909; www.lakeeildon.com; Main St; ☿ 10am-2pm) has local information and houseboat hire.

Activities

Kids love the touch-and-feel tanks at the **Freshwater Discovery Centre** (☎ 03-5774 2950; Goulburn Valley Hwy; adult/child $7/4.50; ☿ 11am-4pm Fri-Mon, 11am-4pm daily during school holidays) at Snobb's Creek about 5km west of town .

A range of horse trail rides catering for all levels is offered by **Rubicon Valley Horse-riding** (☎ 03-5773 2292; www.rubiconhorseriding.com. au; Rubicon Rd, Thornton; per 2hr/half/full day $65/90/165). Introductory rides for beginners start at $45.

Fishing for trout is a popular pastime in the **Eildon Pondage** in town. If you want to practise your angling, try the **Goulburn Valley Fly Fishing Centre** (☎ 03-5773 2513; www.goulburnv lyflyfishing.com.au) or the **Eildon Trout Farm** (☎ 03-5773 2377; www.eildontroutfarm.com.au; 460 Back Eildon Rd; ☺ 9am-5pm), where you're guaranteed a catch.

Sleeping & Eating
Golden Trout Hotel-Motel (☎ 03-5774 2508; 1 Riverside Dr; d $75-85; ⊠) The local pub is the town's social centre and the attached wing of motel rooms are comfortable. The pub has a decent bistro (mains $10 to $30) with a nice sun deck.

Robyn's Nest (☎ 03-5779 1064; www.robyns-nest .com.au; 13 High St; cottage for up to 5 $225) This plush country-style B&B up at Peppin Point makes a great getaway for a group (it can sleep up to 10).

Lake Eildon Marina & Houseboat Hire (☎ 03-5774 2107; www.houseboatholidays.com.au; 190 Sugarloaf Rd) and **Eildon Houseboat Hire** (☎ 0438 345 366; www.eildon houseboathire.com.au) both rent out 10- to 12-berth houseboats from around $2200 to $4500 per week during high season.

Eildon Caravan Park (☎ 03-5774 2105, 1800 651 691; www.eildoncp.com; unpowered/powered sites $30/40, cabins from $110) On the pondage near Eildon Dam, this is a relaxing spot where you can practically fish from your tent.

Parks Victoria manages the **Fraser Camping Area** (☎ 0437 351 909; www.parkweb.vic.gov.au; sites $17) in Lake Eildon National Park. The campsite is about 14km northwest of Eildon along Skyline Drive. There are several camping areas with good facilities, including barbecues and picnic shelters, and lake access. A small shop open in peak season has basic provisions and information, but camping permits must be booked and paid for in advance.

There are several cafes and takeaways in the town's tiny shopping centre.

Vicki & Albert's (☎ 03-5774 2865; Hillside Ave; mains $18-29; ☺ dinner Thu-Mon) This rustic family restaurant does takeaway pizzas, local trout dishes, steaks and stir-fries.

Getting There & Away
McKenzie's (☎ 03-5962 5088; www.mckenzies.com .au) has a daily bus service from Melbourne to Eildon (one way $23, three hours) via Marysville and Alexandra.

MANSFIELD
pop 2840

Gateway to Mt Buller, Mansfield is a vibrant all-seasons base where you can organise winter skiing trips, or go horse riding or mountain-biking through some fabulous high country in spring and summer. With plenty of accommodation, good restaurants and regional wineries, it makes a great base for a weekend or a longer stay.

The graves of the three Mansfield police officers killed by Ned Kelly and his gang in 1878 at Stringybark Creek rest in **Mansfield cemetery**, at the end of Highett St.

The helpful visitor information centre, **Mansfield-Mt Buller High Country Reservations** (☎ 03-5775 7000, 1800 039 049; www.mansfield-mtbuller .com.au; Old Railway Station, Maroondah Hwy; ☺ 9am-5pm), has a free accommodation booking service.

Activities
In winter, several ski hire shops in town rent out ski and snowboard equipment and chains for trips to Mt Buller. At other times, horse riding and mountain-biking are the most popular organised activities from Mansfield.

All Terrain Cycles (☎ 03-5775 2724; www.allterraincy cles.com.au; 58 High St) Hires quality mountain bikes from $45 per day up to $110 for the top downhill bikes.

High Country Horses (☎ 03-5777 5590; www .highcountryhorses.com.au; 10 McCormacks Rd, Merrijig; 2hr rides $65, half-day $90, full-day from $160, overnight from $450) Offers rides around Merrijig and overnight trips across Mt Stirling, camping in a cattleman's hut at Razorback.

High Country Scenic Tours (☎ 03-5777 5101; www .highcountryscenictours.com.au; ☺ Nov-May) Has a range of specialised off-road vehicles taking groups on exciting day and overnight tours of Victoria's high country, priced from $200 per person.

McCormacks Mountain Valley Trail Rides (☎ 03-5775 2886; www.mountainvalleytrailrides.com; 2hr rides $65, half/full day $90/160, 2-day rides from $410) Has a range of High Country trail rides.

Watson's Mountain Country Trail Rides (☎ 03-5777 3552; www.watsonstrailrides.com.au; 3 Chains Rd, Boorolite; 1/2hr ride $35/60).

Sleeping
Mansfield Backpackers' Inn & Travellers Lodge (☎ 03-5775 1800; www.mansfieldtravellodge.com; 112 High St; dm summer/winter $25/30, d $95/105, f $160/180; ⊠) This restored heritage building has a spotless backpacker section with a well-equipped kitchen, lounge, laundry and drying room.

SKI RESORTS

Victoria's ski resorts offer some excellent downhill and cross-country skiing. The resorts have webcams showing conditions or you can contact the **Victorian Ski Report** (☎ 1902 240 523; www .vicsnowreport.com.au) for 24-hour road, snow and weather reports.

Mt Baw Baw (see p615) and Mt Buffalo (p608) are strictly for beginners. Mt Buller (below) and Falls Creek (p611) are glamorous resorts where fashion-conscious snow-bunnies ski during the day and party hard at night. Mt Hotham (p613) has a slightly more rustic and earthy feel, but offers some of the best downhill trails and lifts. Next door, pretty Dinner Plain (p614) is popular with cross-country skiers and as an accommodation base for Mt Hotham skiers.

The following snowfields offer cross-country skiing, but accommodation is nearby off the mountain.

Lake Mountain (☎ 03-5963 3288) Ski region, 120km northeast of Melbourne via Marysville, with 37km of beginner to advanced cross-country trails.

Mt Bogong Tough back-country skiing on Mt Bogong, Victoria's highest mountain. Accessed via Mt Beauty, 350km northeast of Melbourne, and requires a long hike.

Mt Donna Buang The closest snowfield to Melbourne, 95km east via Warburton, for sightseeing and tobogganing.

All the ski resorts are working hard to attract summer visitors, when the wildflowers are in bloom and the walking and mountain-biking opportunities are many. Mt Buller and Dinner Plain especially are becoming renowned for mountain-biking. During January a few ski lifts run for walkers and mountain-bikers.

Adjacent motel rooms are modern and neat (prices drop midweek).

Wappan Station (☎ 03-5778 7786; www.wappansta tion.com.au; Royal Town Rd, Maindample; shearer's quarters adult/child $35/20, cottage d from $100; 🐾) Experience life on a 40.5-sq-km sheep and cattle farm at Wappan Station, on the banks of Lake Eildon. The renovated self-contained cottages have a two-night minimum stay.

Tavistock House (☎ 03-5775 1024; www.tavistock house.com.au; cnr High & Highett Sts; d midweek $120, d week end $135-150) In the centre of town, this lovely conversion of the historic former Westpac building has three spacious boutique rooms decked out in Victorian-era style (no TV, phone or radio here).

Highton Manor (☎ 03-5775 2700; www.hightonmanor .com.au; 140 Highton Lane; stable/manor d $120/225; 🐾) Built in 1896, this stately two-storey manor has motel-style rooms in the former stables and lavish period rooms in the main house. The impressive gardens are great for a stroll.

Eating

Mansfield Regional Produce Store (☎ 03-5889 1404; 68 High St; mains $7-15; ☻ breakfast & lunch Tue-Sun) This barnlike rustic shop, with its array of delicious homemade produce and artisan breads, is a great place to pick up gourmet supplies but also a popular local cafe hangout with fine coffee and baguettes.

Mansfield Hotel (☎ 03-5775 2101; 86 High St; mains $15-26; ☻ lunch & dinner) The flashiest of Mansfield's pubs has a huge dining room and extensive, innovative bistro menu to go with it. Pull up a couch by the fireplace in winter or eat out in the sunny beer terrace in summer.

Deck on High (☎ 03-5775 1144; 13-15 Main St; mains $12-30; ☻ Wed-Mon) This loungy open-fronted restaurant-cafe specialises in all things Asian, from Thai curries to noodle boxes and Oriental tapas. Good food, great atmosphere.

Getting There & Away

V/Line (☎ 13 61 96) buses run twice daily (once Sunday) from Melbourne ($21, three hours). **Mansfield-Mt Buller Bus Lines** (☎ 03-5775 2606; www .mmbl.com.au) runs buses for skiers seven times per day from Mansfield to Mt Buller (adult/ child return $50/34).

MT BULLER
elev 1805m

Three hours' drive from Melbourne, Mt Buller is Victoria's largest ski resort and most popular year-round mountain destination. There's an extensive lift network, including a chairlift that takes you from the day car park directly to the slopes. Cross-country trails link Mt Buller and Mt Stirling.

VICTORIA

The downhill skiing area is 180 hectares (snow making covers 44 hectares), and runs are divided into 25% beginner, 45% intermediate and 30% advanced, with a vertical drop of 400m. There are several cool terrain parks for snowboarders. The Horse Hill chairlift operates daily in summer from 26 December until 1 February, and then weekends until Easter for mountain-bikers and walkers.

In summer there's a **bike shuttle** (☎ 03-5777 5529; per ride $12; ☒ 3 daily) from the Mirimbah Store at the base of the mountain.

Information

Mt Buller Resort Management Board (☎ 03-5777 6077; www.mtbuller.com.au; ☒ 8.30am-5pm Mon-Fri in ski season, 10am-4pm Sat & Sun in summer) Shares premises with the village post office on Summit Rd. In winter the information office is at the Clock Tower. There's internet access in the Abom complex. Gate admission fees during the ski season are $34 per car for the day car park; more for longer stays. Lift tickets for a full day cost adult/child $96/52. Discounts apply for university students. Sightseeing tickets cost $21/13.

Sleeping

There are over 7000 beds on the mountain. **High Country Reservations** (☎ 1800 039 049) and **Mt Buller Alpine Reservations** (☎ 03-5777 6633; www.mtbuller reservations.com.au) book lodge accommodation.

Mt Buller YHA Lodge (☎ 03-5777 6181; mtbuller@ yhavic.org.au; The Ave; dm midweek/weekend $77/85) Open only during the ski season, this is a bargain for solo travellers. Although the dorms are small, there's quality bedding, good facilities and friendly staff.

Duck Inn (☎ 03-5777 6236; www.duckinnmtbuller .com; 18 Goal Post Rd; dm/d from $80/100) An intimate and very affordable guest house with a range of accommodation from dorm rooms to doubles. There's a good restaurant here and a ski-hire shop.

Andre's at Buller (☎ 03-5777 6966; www.andresat buller.com; Cobbler Lane; d incl breakfast in summer from $180, ski season $270-480) The luxurious architecturally designed Andre's is open year-round and boasts an excellent ski-in, ski-out position during winter and glorious summer sunsets.

Eating

There's a licensed supermarket in the Moloney's building in the village centre (closed in summer), and various fast-food eateries on the slopes and in the village, including **Cattleman's Café** (☎ 03-5777 7800; Bourke St; mains $6-22).

Loft Lounge & Signature Restaurant (☎ 03-5777 6377; 8 Breathtaker Rd; mains $17-33; ☒ dinner daily winter, Wed-Sun summer) At the Breathtaker All Suite Hotel, the Loft Lounge & Bar is open in summer and the fine-dining restaurant, Signature, is open in winter. Magnificent views, great atmosphere and a delicious fusion of Asian, European and Mod Oz cuisine.

Pension Grimus (☎ 03-5777 6396; Breathtaker Rd; mains $18-40; ☒ dinner daily, lunch Sat & Sun winter) Traditional Austrian fare includes Wiener schnitzel and Salzburger *nockerl* (hazelnut and choc-chip soufflé). Pension Grimus also has very comfortable boutique apartments.

Getting There & Around

Mansfield-Mt Buller Buslines (☎ 03-5775 2606, winter 5775 6070; www.mmbl.com.au) runs a winter Melbourne–Mt Buller service (adult/child return $110/70) and year-round daily buses from Mansfield to Mt Buller (adult/child return $50/34).

Ski-season car parking is below the village; a 4WD taxi service transports people to their village accommodation.

Day-trippers park in the Horse Hill day car park and take the quad chairlift into the skiing area, or there's a free day-tripper shuttle-bus service between the day car park and the village. Ski hire and lift tickets are available at the base of the chairlift.

KING VALLEY

On the back road between Mansfield and Wangaratta, the King Valley is a prosperous wine region noted for its Italian varietals and cool-climate wines such as Sangiovese, Barbera, sparkling Prosecco and Pinot Grigio. Most of the region's 20 or so wineries are around Whitfield on the King River just north of the Alpine National Park and about 60km northeast of Mansfield.

Among the best are **Dal Zotto Estate** (☎ 03-5729 8321; www.dalzotto.com.au; Main Rd, Whitfield; ☒ 10am-5pm), which also has the excellent Rinaldo's Restaurant, serving North Italian cuisine; **Pizzini** (☎ 03-5729 8278; www.pizzini.com .au; 175 King Valley Rd, Whitfield; ☒ 10am-5pm); and **Chrismont** (☎ 5729 8220; 51 Upper King River Rd, Cheshunt; ☒ 11am-5pm), which also has a modern guest house among the vines.

Milawa/Oxley Gourmet Region

At the north end of the King Valley, tiny **Milawa** has had a renaissance as a regional gourmet centre, boasting notable wineries, fine restaurants and several local food producers – a perfect stop on the way to the snowfields.

Brown Brothers (☎ 03-5720 5547; www.brownbroth ers.com.au; Bobinawarrah Rd, Milawa; ☒ 9am-5pm) produced its first vintage in 1889 and is still run by the same family. The swanky complex features a tasting room, an excellent restaurant, and picnic and barbecue facilities.

Milawa Mustard (☎ 03-5727 3202; www.milawamus tard.com.au; Old Emu Inn, The Cross Roads, Milawa; ☒ 10am-5pm) offers tastings of 18 seeded mustards. The **Olive Shop** (☎ 03-5727 3887; www.theoliveshop.com.au; Snow Rd, Milawa; ☒ 10am-4pm Mon-Wed, to 5pm Thu-Sun) has locally produced olive oil for sale as well as delicious tapenades and exotic spices.

The excellent **Milawa Cheese Company** (☎ 03-5727 3588; www.milawacheese.com.au; Factory Rd, Milawa; ☒ 9am-5pm), 2km north of Milawa, offers cheese tastings and a bakery and cafe. It excels at soft and washed-rind cheeses. The **restaurant** (☎ 03-5727 3589; mains $20-25; ☒ lunch daily) here is fabulous – a must-stop on the 'Gourmet Road'. For good measure, in the same building is **Milawa Chocolates** (☎ 03-5727 3500; ☒ 10am-5pm Fri-Wed), offering handmade chocolates.

In **Oxley**, it's worth a stop for a coffee or light meal en route to the snow (or all those other gourmet delights) at the **King River Café** (☎ 03-5727 3461; Snow Rd, Oxley; mains $11-26; ☒ lunch Mon, lunch & dinner Wed-Sun), an unassuming but inviting place in an old general store, serving scrumptious lunches bringing together much of the region's famous produce. Ask about the attached self-contained accommodation.

BEECHWORTH
pop 2650

Beechworth is a living legacy of the 1860s gold-rush era and one of Victoria's most pleasing historic townscapes. Many of the distinctive honey-coloured public buildings remain, including the courthouse and jail where Ned Kelly was charged and remanded for the murder of three Mansfield policemen.

Information

Beechworth visitor information centre (☎ 03-5728 8065, 1300 366 321; www.beechworthonline.com.au; 103 Ford St) In the Old Shire Hall, it books accommodation and activities, and has information on scenic walks and wineries in the area.

Neighbourhood Centre (☎ 03-5728 2386; 30 Ford St; per 30min $4; ☒ 9am-5pm Mon-Fri, 10am-4pm Sat & Sun) Internet access in a 100-year-old Methodist church.

Sights & Activities

Beechworth's **historic and cultural precinct** (☎ 1300 366 321; precinct ticket adult/child/family $14/9/28) consists of many interesting old buildings, including the excellent **Burke Museum** (☎ 03-5728 8067; Loch St; adult/child/family $6/4/11; ☒ 9am-5pm). Named after Robert O'Hara Burke, the explorer of Burke and Wills fame who was the police superintendent at Beechworth from 1854 to 1858, it shows gold-rush relics and an arcade of shopfronts preserved as they were over 140 years ago.

The **Beechworth Courthouse** (Ford St; adult/child/ family $6/4/11; ☒ 9am-5pm) is notable for Ned Kelly's first court appearance. See the cell where Ned was held in the basement behind the **Shire Hall**.

The new **Chinese Cultural Centre** (☎ 03-5728 2866; adult/child/family $2/1/5; ☒ 10am-4pm Wed-Mon) displays the history of the 6000 Chinese who came to the area in the 1850s to seek their fortune.

The **Powder Magazine** (Gorge St; adult/child/family $3/2/6) was an 1859 storage area for gunpowder. View the *Echoes of History* video at the **1858 Town Hall** (Ford St) roughly half-hourly.

The visitor centre runs two-hour interpretive **walking tours** (adult/child/family $8/5/15; ☒ 10.30am & 1pm) covering the gold rush and Ned Kelly's connections to town.

Some of Beechworth's spooky past comes to life in the recommended walking tours offered by **Beechworth Ghost Tours** (☎ 0447 432 816; www .beechworthghosttours.com; adult/child/family $20/12/60) at La Trobe, a former lunatic asylum. The 1½-hour tours start at dusk. Book ahead.

Sleeping

There's a host of B&Bs and self-contained cottages in the area. The visitor centre will book for you.

Old Priory (☎ 03-5728 1024; www.oldpriory.com .au; 8 Priory Lane; dm/s/d $40/50/80, cottages $115) This historic convent is a big spooky old place that's often used by school groups, but it's the cheapest in Beechworth and has lovely gardens and a range of rooms.

La Trobe at Beechworth (☎ 03-5720 8050; www.latrobe.edu.au/beechworthhotel; Albert Rd; d $115-225) What was once the 1867 Beechworth Lunatic Asylum is now part of La Trobe University and accommodates up to 200 people. It includes a spa resort, cottages and lodge rooms.

Lake Sambell Caravan Park (☎ 03-5728 1421; www.caravanparkbeechworth.com.au; Peach Dr; unpowered/powered sites $21/25, cabins $70-90; 🖳) This shady park next to beautiful Lake Sambell has great facilities including camp kitchen and wi-fi. The sunsets reflected in the lake are spectacular.

Eating & Drinking

The intersection of Ford and Camp Sts is the town centre and you'll find lots of cafes, restaurants and pubs a short walk away in any direction.

Beechworth Provender (☎ 03-5728 2650; 18 Camp St) Gourmet deli specialising in local produce such as Milawa cheeses, wines, chutneys and antipasto.

Beechworth Bakery (☎ 03-5728 1132; 27 Camp St; light meals $2-8; 🕙 6am-7pm) Popular with locals and tourists, this famous bakery is great for pies and pastries, cakes and sandwiches.

Green Gecko Cafe (☎ 03-57 28 2470; 78 Ford Street; meals $5-15; 🕙 breakfast & lunch Tue-Sun) Funky little lunch spot with good coffee, burgers and salads.

Green Shed Bistro (☎ 03-5728 2360; 37 Camp St; mains $18-25; 🕙 lunch Fri-Sun, dinner Fri-Sun) This former printing house is now a rustic little restaurant (think exposed brickwork and concrete floor) serving French-style cuisine from the busy open kitchen.

Bridge Road Brewers (☎ 03-5728 2103; www .bridgeroadbrewers.com.au; Ford St; 🕙 11am-5pm Mon-Sat, Sun noon-11pm) Behind the imposing Tanswells Commercial Hotel, Beechworth's microbrewery produces some excellent beers, with tastings and cellar-door sales.

Getting There & Away

V/Line (☎ 13 61 96) has daily train/bus services from Melbourne via Wangaratta or Seymour ($26, 3½ hours). **Wangaratta Coachlines** (☎ 03-5722 1843) runs to major centres nearby.

YACKANDANDAH

☎ 02 / pop 660

An old gold-mining town nestled amid beautiful hills and valleys east of Beechworth, Yackandandah has been classified by the National Trust. The **Yackandandah visitor information centre** (☎ 02-6027 1988; www.uniqueyackandan dah.com.au; High St) issues the free *A Walk in High Street* and *Yackandandah Touring Guide*.

Karr's Reef Gold Mine (☎ 0408 975 991; tours adult/child $18.50/16.50; 🕙 tours 10am, noon, 2pm & 4pm Sat-Tue

& Fri) is an old gold mine dating from 1867. On the two-hour tour you don a hard hat and descend into the tunnels and learn a bit about the mine's history.

The studio-gallery **Kirby's Flat Pottery** (☎ 02-6027 1416; 🕙 10.15am-5.30pm Sat & Sun), 4km south of Yackandandah, is worth a visit.

Beside pretty Yackandandah Creek but close to the town, the well-equipped **Yackandandah Holiday Park** (☎ 02-6027 1380; www.yhp.com.au; Taymac Dr; unpowered/powered sites $24/28, cabins $85-120) is a little oasis of greenery and autumn colours.

The 1863 **Star Hotel** (☎ 02-6027 1493; 30 High St), known locally as the 'top pub', is an old country pub with good meals.

MYRTLEFORD

pop 2730

Near the foot of Mt Buffalo, Myrtleford is yet another 'gateway to the alps'. The helpful **Alpine Visitor Centre** (☎ 1800 991 044; www.vis itmyrtleford.com.au; Great Alpine Rd; 🕙 9am-5pm) has information and a booking service for the area and a great cafe.

Feed the horses and fluffy alpacas at **Myrtle Creek Farmstay Cottages** (☎ 03-5753 4447; www .myrtlecreekcottages.com; 5 Myrtleford-Stanley Rd, Mudgegonga; d $130), a hands-on farmstay on a working sheep and cattle farm. The self-contained log cabins, each with a spa and well-equipped kitchen, sleep up to eight and are great for families.

MT BUFFALO

elev 1500m

Beautiful Mt Buffalo, Victoria's smallest ski resort, is four hours' drive from Melbourne and managed by Parks Victoria. The **resort** (www.mtbuffaloresort.com.au) seems beset with bad luck: the Cresta Valley ski lodge was destroyed by fire in December 2006, and after trading at a loss for many years, the magnificent 1910 Mt Buffalo Chalet has now closed indefinitely. A private operator still manages the ski lifts. There are a few downhill runs, a tobogganing area and some cross-country trails that are popular with beginners, but these days Buffalo is as much a summer resort for hiking and biking.

There are two skiing areas: Cresta Valley and Dingo Dell. **Cresta Valley** is the main area, has five lifts and is the starting point for many of the cross-country trails. **Dingo Dell** is ideal for beginners and has a day-visitor shelter with a kiosk and ski school. It's usually open only on weekends.

The admission fee to Mt Buffalo National Park is $10 per car ($13 in winter, but only if ski lifts are operating), payable at the Mt Buffalo Entrance Station. Lift tickets cost adult/child $49/29.

Activities

Adventure Guides Australia (☎ 03-5728 1804; www .adventureguidesaustralia.com.au) offers abseiling, caving and rock-climbing alpine-style from $77/165 for a half/full day, as well as beginner lessons from $45 for two hours. It also runs a cross-country ski school and offers ski touring.

Eagle School of Microlighting (☎ 03-5750 1174; www.eagleschool.com.au) has exhilarating 20-minute tandem flights over Mt Buffalo Gorge for $130, and flying lessons for $150 per hour.

High Country Cycle Tours (☎ 03-5722 1994; www .highcountrycycletours.com.au) offers a mountain-biking descent of Mt Buffalo (with transport up from Bright or nearby towns) for $95/65 per half/full day.

Sleeping

Remote camping is possible at Rocky Creek, which has pit toilets only. **Parks Victoria** (☎ 03-5756 2328; www.parkweb.vic.gov.au) issues permits at the Mt Buffalo Entrance Station. **Lake Catani** (sites $16) has an all-season camping ground, with toilets and showers.

Getting There & Around

There is no public transport to the plateau, though from Melbourne a daily **V/Line** (☎ 13 61 96) train to Wangaratta and bus to Bright can drop you at Porepunkah, near the base of the mountain.

BRIGHT

pop 2110

Famous for its glorious autumn colours, Bright is a popular year-round destination in the foothills of the alps and a gateway to Mt Hotham and Falls Creek. Skiers make a beeline through Bright in winter, but it's a lovely base for exploring the Alpine National Park, paragliding, fishing and kayaking on local rivers, bushwalking and exploring the region's wineries. Plentiful accommodation and sophisticated restaurants complete the picture.

Information

Alpine visitor information centre (☎ 1800 111 885; www.visitalpinevictoria.com.au; 119 Gavan St; 🖳) Has a busy accommodation booking service, Parks Victoria information and the attached Riverdeck Café. Internet access costs $6 per hour.

Bright Internet Café (☎ 03-5750 1244; 4 Ireland St; per hr $6 🕙 10am-9pm; 🖳) Upstairs at the backpackers.

Sights & Activities

There are walking trails around Bright, including the 3km loop **Canyon Walk**, which starts from Star Rd Bridge and follows the Ovens River. The 4km **Cherry Walk** heads from Centenary Park in the other direction along the Ovens, and a 6km track to **Wandiligong** follows Morses Creek.

You could spend an hour or two getting lost among the antiques, retro stuff, junk and collectables at the **Old Tobacco Sheds** (☎ 03-5755 2344; Great Alpine Rd; 🕙 10am-5pm). There's a small gold and tobacco museum here.

The **Murray to Mountains Rail Trail** (www.railtrail .com.au) travels 30km from the old train station to Myrtleford via Porepunkah. You can hire mountain bikes, tandems and kids' bikes from **Cyclepath** (☎ 03-5750 1442; www.cyclepath.com.au; 74 Gavan St; hire per hr from $16, per half/full day from $20/28).

Bright is a popular base for paragliding, with enthusiasts catching the thermals from nearby Mystic Mountain. **Alpine Paragliding** (☎ 03-5755 1753; www.alpineparagliding.com; 100 Gavan St; 🕙 Oct-Jun) offers tandem flights from $130 and paragliding courses. **Eagle Microlights** (☎ 03-5750 1174; www.eagleschool.com.au) has tandem microlight flights from $70, and **5 Star Adventure Tours** (☎ 03-5759 2555; www.5staradventure.com.au) can organise a range of activities, including half-day kayak trips with gourmet lunch.

Sleeping

Bright has plenty of accommodation, but book ahead.

Bright Hikers Backpackers Hostel (☎ 03-5750 1244; www.brighthikers.com.au; 4 Ireland St; dm/s/d/tr $25/40/60/90; 🖳) Right in the centre of town, this, clean, well-set-up hostel has a cosy lounge, a great old-style verandah and bike hire ($20 per day).

Elm Lodge Motel (☎ 03-5755 1144; www.elmlodge .com.au; 2 Wood St; d $73-120, 8-bed cottage $240; 🐾) This slightly quirky set of burgundy units in a restored 1950s pine mill has rooms for all budgets, from a shoebox cheapie to spacious two-bedroom, self-contained apartments with polished floorboards, and spa rooms. The resourceful owners run limousine winery tours (from $75).

Odd Frog (☎ 03-5755 2123; www.theoddfrog.com; 3 McFadyens Lane; d $150-195, q $250) Designed and built by the young architect-interior designer owners, these contemporary, ecofriendly studios feature light, breezy spaces and fabulous outdoor decks. The design is fabulous with clever use of the hilly site featuring sculptural steel-frame foundations and flying balconies.

Mine Manager's House (☎ 03-5755 1702; www .brightbedandbreakfast.com.au; 30 Coronation Ave; cottage from $165, d from $180) Dating from 1892 and now sumptuously restored to the smallest detail, this traditional B&B offers couples a complete experience. Enjoy warm hospitality, beautiful rooms and a delightful English garden. The claw-foot bath in the self-contained cottage offers an extra treat.

Bright Backpackers Outdoor Inn (☎ 03-5755 1154; www.brightbackpackers.com.au; 106 Coronation Dr; unpowered/powered sites $26/30, s/d cabins $27/44; 🖳) This basic but laid-back and well-equipped park at the foot of Mystic Mountain is popular with paragliders. Free wi-fi.

Bright Caravan Park (☎ 03-5755 1141; www.bright caravanpark.com.au; Cherry Ave; unpowered/powered sites from $30/35, cabins $70-155; 🖳) Straddling pretty Morses Creek, this lovely park is five minutes' walk to the shops.

Eating & Drinking

Ireland St, south of the roundabout, has a string of cafes and takeaways. The Riverdeck Café, beside the visitor centre, is worth a coffee for the riverside location alone.

Wine & Cheese Bar (☎ 03-5759 2555; Shop 3, 104 Gavan Street; snacks & platters $5-25; 🕑 10am-3pm, dinner Fri & Sat) Regional produce from Milawa and local wineries is on offer here during the day. Innovative evening meals include Scandinavian-style rainbow trout.

Sasha's of Bright (☎ 03-5750 1711; 2d Anderson St; mains $25-36; 🕑 dinner) Hearty old-style European cooking with Wiener schnitzel, Hungarian goulash, dumplings and apple strudel.

our pick **Simone's Restaurant** (☎ 03-5755 2266; 98 Gavan St; mains $28-35; 🕑 dinner Tue-Sun) For 20 years owner-chef Patrizia Simone has been serving outstanding Italian food, with a focus on local ingredients and seasonal produce, in the rustic dining room of this heritage-listed house. This is one of regional Victoria's great restaurants and well worth the splurge. Bookings are essential.

Bright Brewery (☎ 03-5755 1301; www.bright -brewery.com.au; 121 Great Alpine Rd; 🕑 from noon) Next to the visitor centre, this boutique brewery produces wonderful Belgian-style beers, amber ale and a robust porter. If you can't decide, try a tasting tray at the bar. There are guided tours of the brewing process on Friday at 3pm ($8) and live music on Sunday afternoons.

Getting There & Away

V/Line (☎ 13 61 96) runs two daily train/coach services from Melbourne with a change at Seymour ($27, 4½ hours). Alternatively, take the train to Wangaratta and the bus ($8) from there. During the ski season a regular bus operates from Bright to Mt Hotham (adult/child return $40/50, 1½ hours).

MT BEAUTY
pop 1700

Mt Beauty and its twin town of Tawonga South are the gateways to the Falls Creek ski resort and the Bogong High Plains.

The **Mt Beauty Visitor Information Centre** (☎ 1800 111 885; www.visitmtbeauty.com.au; 31 Bogong High Plains Rd; 🕑 9am-5pm; 🖳) has an accommodation booking service. The information centre also houses displays that highlight the region's history and has internet access ($4 per half hour).

The **Mt Beauty Music Festival** (www.muscimuster .org.au) brings together folk, blues and country musicians in April.

Activities

The 2km **Tree Fern Walk** and the longer **Peppermint Walk** both start from Mountain Creek Picnic and Camping Ground, on Mountain Creek Rd, off the Kiewa Valley Hwy. About 1km south of Bogong Village (towards Falls Creek), the 1.5km return **Fainter Falls Walk** takes you to a pretty cascade. For information on longer walks in the area, visit the Alpine Discovery Centre.

Rocky Valley Bikes (☎ 03-5754 1118; www.rockyval ley.com.au; Kiewa Valley Hwy) offers mountain-biking for all levels, with bike hire from $30 per day up to $45 for cross-country bikes. Also has internet access.

Bogong Horseback Adventures (☎ 03-5754 4849; www.bogonghorse.com.au; Mountain Creek Rd; 2hr/3hr/full-day trips $80/95/190) runs excellent trail rides over the Bogong High Plains, including packhorse rides lasting three to seven days (from $1050).

The Kiewa Valley is world-renowned for trout fishing from spring to autumn. For fly-fishing trips, try **Angling Expeditions** (☎ 03-5754 1466; www.anglingvic.com.au).

Sleeping

Baensch's Lodge (☎ 03-5754 4041; 16 St Bernard Dr, Tawonga South; summer s/d from $50/70, winter $75/96) At this price you mightn't expect much, but this simple 18-bed lodge is a terrific place for self-caterers, with a kitchen, lounge and laundry. There's no one on site so book ahead.

Snowgum Motel (☎ 03-5754 4508; www.snowgum motel.com.au; 245-247 Kiewa Valley Hwy; summer s/d/f $85/95/130, ski season $105/125/195; 🅰) Snowgum is a standard roadside motel, but it's well kept with good facilities, including plasma TVs, a pool, and bocce and croquet sets.

Dreamers (☎ 03-5754 1222; www.dreamers1.com; Kiewa Valley Hwy; d $200-590) Each of Dreamer's stunning self-contained eco apartments offer something special and architecturally unique. Sunken lounges, open fireplaces, loft bedrooms and balcony spas are just some of the highlights. Great views and a pretty lagoon complete a dreamily romantic experience.

Mount Beauty Holiday Centre (☎ 03-5754 4396; www.holidaycentre.com.au; Kiewa Valley Hwy; unpowered/powered sites $26/28, cabins $90-130) This family caravan park is close to the town centre and has river frontage and an interesting range of cabins.

Eating & Drinking

Mt Beauty Bakery & Café (☎ 03-5754 4870; cnr Hollands & Kiewa Sts; meals $4-12; ☺ 7am-6.30pm) Right in town, this sunny cafe is a great place for breakfast or lunch, with a range of cakes, focaccias and antipasto.

Bogong Hotel (☎ 03-5754 4482; 169 Kiewa Valley Hwy; mains $18-27; ☺ dinner daily, lunch in season) The obvious spot for a beer, this country pub is in Tawonga and has a relaxed bistro and views of the snow-capped mountains from the verandah. The cheaper bar meals and Bogong burgers are a steal.

Roi's Diner Restaurant (☎ 03-5754 4495; 177 Kiewa Valley Hwy, Tawonga; mains $26-30; ☺ dinner Thu-Sun) An unassuming timber shack on the highway, Roi's is an award-winning restaurant offering exceptional modern Italian cuisine that belies its location.

Getting There & Away

V/Line (☎ 13 61 96) operates a train/bus service from Melbourne via Wangaratta ($31, twice weekly). **Falls Creek Coach Service** (☎ 03-5754 4024; www.fallscreekcoachservice.com.au) operates daily buses to Albury (one way/return $18/27) and to Falls Creek daily in winter ($33/52).

FALLS CREEK
elev 1780m

Falls Creek is the most fashion-conscious and upmarket ski resort in Australia, combining a picturesque alpine setting among the snow gums with impressive skiing and infamous après-ski entertainment. Hordes of city folk make the 4½-hour journey from Melbourne at weekends during the ski season.

The skiing is spread over two main areas, the **Village Bowl** and **Sun Valley**. There are 19 lifts: 17% beginner, 60% intermediate and 23% advanced runs. The downhill area covers 451 hectares with a vertical drop of 267m. Night skiing in the Village Bowl operates several times a week.

You'll also find some of Australia's best **cross-country skiing** here. A trail leads around Rocky Valley Pondage to old cattlemen's huts, and the more adventurous can tour to the white summits of Nelse, Cope and Spion Kopje. These also provide walking routes in summer. The summit chairlift operates from 27 December to mid-January for walkers and mountain-bike riders.

Information

Falls Creek visitor information centre (☎ 03-5758 3224; www.fallscreek.com.au) On the right-hand side at the bottom of the Falls Express chairlift, it has plenty of information on the whole alpine region. The daily admission fee is $31 per car, $10/5 per adult/child bus passenger during the ski season only. There are full-day lift tickets (adult/child/youth $97/49/82), and combined lift-and-lesson packages ($146/99/124). One-day cross-country trail fees are adult/child/family $12/6/30.

Frying Pan Inn (☎ 03-5758 3390; Falls Creek Rd; 🅰) 'Friars', in the Bowl, has broadband internet for $2 for 15 minutes.

Sleeping

Accommodation can be booked through **Falls Creek Central Reservations** (☎ 03-5758 3733, 1800 033 079; www.fallscreek.com.au; Bogong High Plains Rd) and **Mountain Multiservice** (☎ 03-5758 3499, 1800 465 666; www.mountainmultiservice.com.au; Schuss St).

Alpha Lodge (☎ 03-5758 3488; www.alphaskilodge
.com.au; 5 Parallel St; summer bunkroom/d $58/78, ski season
$218/260) This spacious lodge, open year-round,
has a sauna, a large lounge with panoramic
views and a sizeable communal kitchen.
Bunkrooms sleep four, while doubles have
en suite.

Viking Alpine Lodge (☎ 03-5758 3247; www.viking
lodge.com.au; 13 Parallel St; s/d summer $60/78, ski season per
person $60-120) Viking offers good-value accom-
modation all year with excellent communal
facilities including lounge, kitchen and great
views. Ski in, ski out.

Cedarwood (☎ 03-5758 3393; www.cedarwood
fallscreek.com; 5 Schuss St; d summer $190-230, ski season
$255-840) Cedarwood, open all year, has 27
apartments ranging from small studios with
bathroom and kitchenette to palatial self-
contained suites with three bedrooms, two
bathrooms, full kitchen and laundry.

Eating & Drinking

Milch Café Wine Bar (☎ 0408 465 939; 4 Schuss St; mains
$12-24) The hip place to see and be seen, this
bar-restaurant offers flavoursome Middle
Eastern meze and a good wine list. In winter,
the bar is packed with skiers conducting post-
mortems of their runs.

Huski Produce Store (☎ 03-5758 3863; www
.huski.com.au; 3 Sitzmark St; mains $16-32) At Huski
Lodge & Day Spa, the produce store in
Falls Creek's newest and trendiest designer
apartment building offers some of the best
casual eating and fine dining on the mountain. Gourmet deli goods and takeaway are
also available.

Mo's Restaurant at Feathertop (☎ 03-5758 3232; 14
Parallel St; mains $16-32; ☾ dinner) This inviting res-
taurant at the Feathertop Lodge features red-
gum furniture, leather Chesterfield couches,
private alcoves and mood lighting.

Man Hotel (☎ 03-5758 3326; 20 Slalom St; mains
$17-29; ☾ lunch Sat & Sun, dinner daily) A favourite
venue for pizzas and pub-style meals, as well
as copious drinking and live music in the
Red Room.

Getting There & Around

Falls Creek is 375km and a 4½-hour drive
from Melbourne. During the winter, **Falls
Creek Coach Service** (☎ 03-5754 4024; www.fallscreek
coachservice.com.au) operates daily buses between
Falls Creek and Melbourne (one way/return
$95/154) and also runs services to and from
Albury ($54/86) and Mt Beauty ($33/52).

The **Over-Snow Taxi service** (return $32) operates
between the car parks and the lodges from
8am to midnight (until 2am on Friday night).
Car parking for day visitors is at the base of
the village, next to the ski lifts. A free shuttle
operates around the resort itself.

If you want to ski Mt Hotham for the day,
jump on the Helicopter Lift Link for $125
return if you have a valid lift ticket.

HARRIETVILLE
pop 280

Harrietville is a pretty little **town** (www.harriet
ville.com) nestled on the Ovens River below
Mt Feathertop. It the last stop before
the start of the winding road up to Mt
Hotham. During ski season a bus shuttles between the town and Mt Hotham,
making it a good spot for slightly cheaper
off-mountain accommodation.

Ski and wheel-chain hire is available from
Hoy's (☎ 03-5779 2658).

Harrietville is the starting and finishing point for various **alpine walking tracks**,
including the popular Mt Feathertop
walk, Razorback Ridge and Dargo High
Plains walks. The town is also developing as a mountain-biking centre – you can
hire bikes ($30/40 per half/full day) from
Snowline Hotel.

In late November the annual **Blue Grass
Festival** (http://bluegrass.org.au/Festivals/harrietville/index.
cfm) takes over the town.

Sleeping & Eating

Snowline Hotel (☎ 03-5759 2524; www.snowlinehotel
.com.au; Great Alpine Rd; s/d from $70/90) The Snowline
has been operating for over 100 years, and
offers inexpensive off-mountain accommodation in comfortable motel rooms. The pub
bistro (mains $15 to $30) is gaining a loyal
following, especially for its chicken parma
and Tasmanian Angus steak.

Shady Brook Cottages (☎ 03-5759 2741; www
.shadybrook.com.au; Mountain View Walk; 1-/2-bed cottage from $105/140; ☐ ✖) A magnificent gar-
den envelopes this lovely, peaceful group of
self-contained country-style cottages. Two
come with spa and all have balconies and
mod cons.

Pick & Shovel Cottage (☎ 03-5759 2627; www.pick
andshovel.com.au; 1 Pick & Shovel Rise; d midweek/weekend
incl breakfast from $135/145; ☒) This lovely old-
world cottage offers privacy and comfort.
Sleeps up to six people.

GREAT ALPINE ROAD

The Great Alpine Rd is one of the great car and motorcycle-touring routes of Victoria. Though not as famous as the Great Ocean Road, it is no less spectacular, travelling 308km from Wangaratta in the state's northeast to Bairnsdale in Gippsland, and can be traversed in either direction. From Wangaratta, the route can take in scenic detours through the Oxley/Milawa Gourmet Food Region, historic Beechworth and wineries in the Gapsted area. The road travels southeasterly through picturesque Bright at the base of Mt Buffalo to Harrietville on the edge of the Alpine National Park. The climb up to Mt Hotham, around hairpin turns and over razorback ridges, with mountain tops tumbling away in every direction, is awe-inspiring. After Hotham and Dinner Plain villages, the road descends into pretty Omeo, past historic goldfields, then follows the Tambo River to Bruthen and Bairnsdale.

The route is also popular with cyclists who can connect with the 94km **Murray to Mountains Rail Trail** (www.railtrail.com.au) in Wangaratta or Bright.

Big Shed Café (☎ 03-5759 2672; Great Alpine Rd, Smoko; meals $6-18; ☺ breakfast & lunch Wed-Mon) You can't miss this giant roadside restaurant in the beautifully named hamlet of Smoko, 7km north of Harrietville. The former tobacco shed is having another reincarnation as a popular gourmet cafe.

Bella's (☎ 03-5759 2750; 231 Great Alpine Rd; meals $7-14 ☺ breakfast & lunch Thu-Tue) For an all-day breakfast or lunch of antipasto, damper rolls and pizza with a glass of local wine, this welcoming cafe is Harrietville's best.

MT HOTHAM
elev 1868m
Serious hikers, skiers and snowboarders head to Mt Hotham, the starting point for some stunning alpine walks between November and May, and home to 320 hectares of downhill runs, with a vertical drop of 428m. About 80% of the ski trails are intermediate or advanced. The Big D is open for **night skiing** every Wednesday and Saturday.

Off-piste skiing in steep and narrow valleys is good. **Cross-country skiing** is also good, with 35km of trails winding through tree-lined glades.

The most popular walk is to Mt Feathertop, but there are many others to choose from.

Information
Mt Hotham Alpine Resort Management (☎ 03-5759 3550; www.mthotham.com.au; ☺ 8am-5pm daily ski season, Mon-Fri other times) At the village administration centre. The ski-season admission fee is $34 per car and $11.50/6.25 per adult/child bus passenger. Lift tickets per adult/child/youth cost $97/49/82. Lift-and-lesson packages start from $146 for adults. Rates are slightly cheaper in June and September.

Sleeping
Only a handful of lodges are open year-round. There are three booking agencies: **Mt Hotham Reservation Centre** (☎ 1800 354 555; www.hotham.com.au; Hotham Central) operates year-round; **Mt Hotham Accommodation Service** (☎ 03-5759 3636, 1800 032 061; www.mthothamaccommodation.com.au; Lawlers Apartments) operates during ski season only; and **Mt Hotham Central Reservations** (☎ 03-5759 3522, 1800 657 547; www.mthotham-centralres.com.au) can book local and off-mountain accommodation throughout the year.

Leeton Lodge (☎ 03-5759 3683; www.leetonlodge.com; Dargo Ct; summer per adult/child $35/20) Classic family ski club lodge with 30 beds, cooking facilities and good views. Open year-round.

Asgaard Alpine Club (☎ 1300 767 434; www.asgaard.com.au; Great Alpine Rd; dm per person low/high ski season $63/95, 4-share with bathroom $230/360) In a central location with terrific facilities, this is another great-value option. BYO linen.

Gravbrot Ski Club (☎ 1300 735 358; www.gravbrot.com; Great Alpine Rd; midweek/weekend per person $105/125) The price at this homey place includes all meals and pre-dinner nibbles, making it startlingly good value for the ski fields. Wireless internet available. BYO linen.

Tanderra Ski Lodge (☎ 1800 819 410; www.tanderahotham.com.au; Great Alpine Rd; 4-bed room weekend low/high ski season $285/725) Tanderra has excellent facilities and offers good value.

Eating & Drinking
General (☎ 03-5759 3523; Great Alpine Rd; mains $11-16; ☺ lunch & dinner; ▯) Usually the only place to stay open all summer, the 'Gen' does tasty pizzas and counter meals, and is a popular watering hole during ski season. Free wireless internet.

VICTORIA

Summit Bar (☎ 03-5759 3503; Snowbird Inn, Great Alpine Rd) Can get rather raucous, being the bar of choice for the young snowboarding pack, especially during its daily Jug Frenzy sessions.

Some of the better eateries in the winter months are **Swindlers** (☎ 03-5759 4421; Hotham Central), which is also the place for an après-ski *Glühwein*; the Austrian-inspired **Zirky's** (☎ 03-5759 3542; Great Alpine Rd), sometimes open on summer weekends; and **Chiones** (☎ 03-5759 3626; Hotham Central), which features an impressive Mod Oz menu and a lovely deck overlooking the slopes.

Getting There & Around

Mt Hotham is 373km northeast of Melbourne and reached via the Hume Fwy (M31) and Harrietville (4½ hours), or via the Princes Hwy (A1) and Omeo (5½ hours). Contact **Mount Hotham Alpine Resort Management Board** (☎ 03-5759 3550; www.mthotham.com.au) to check winter road conditions before deciding which route to take (chains must be carried).

In winter, **Snowball Express** (☎ 03-9370 9055, 1800 659 009; www.snowballexpress.com.au) has daily buses from Melbourne to Mt Hotham ($160 return, 6½ hours), via Wangaratta, Myrtleford, Bright and Harrietville.

A free shuttle runs frequently around the resort from 7am to 3am; a separate shuttle service also operates to Dinner Plain. The free 'zoo cart' takes skiers from their lodges to the lifts between 8am and 6pm.

Mt Hotham Airport (☎ 03-5159 6777) services Mt Hotham and Dinner Plain, but it's currently only served by charter flight company **Australasian Jet** (www.ausjet.com.au).

The **Helicopter Lift Link** (☎ 03-5759 4444; return $125, with a lift ticket) takes six minutes to fly to Falls Creek (on clear days).

DINNER PLAIN

elev 1520m

Dinner Plain is a stylish alpine **resort** (www.visitdinnerplain.com) that's lovely in both winter and summer, though it's much more a summer activities destination than Hotham village, 11km away. The entire village, inspired by early cattle farmers' huts, was built in the mid-1980s from corrugated iron and local timber and stone, and exudes a relaxed, intimate feel.

There are excellent **cross-country trails** around the village, including the Hotham–Dinner Plain Ski Trail (10km one way). There is a beginners' poma lift; one-day tickets cost $52/31 per adult/child.

Get information from the **visitor centre** (☎ 1300 734 365; www.visitdinnerplain.com) in the village centre.

Pinnacle DP (☎ 03-5159 6450; 🕑 8am-6pm) has full hire options, and Dinner Plain Ski School has ski and snowboard packages available. It's a short 20-minute drive to Mount Hotham or visitors can use the convenient shuttle-bus service.

The soothing Japanese bathing experience is available at **Onsen Retreat & Spa** (☎ 03-5150 8880; www.onsen.com.au; Big Muster Dr; 🕑 11am-7pm summer, 7am-9pm winter), along with a pampering array of spa treatments from hot stone therapy to body wraps and massage. The onsen bath is $40, or free if you've booked a treatment (from $70).

In summer the village is an ideal base for hiking on the plateau – Parks Victoria notes are available from information centres in Bright and Omeo.

Specialising in mountain-bike hire and tours, **Adventures with Altitude** (☎ 03-5159 6608; www.adventureswithaltitude.com.au; bike hire per hr $15, half/full day $40/60) provides all the gear and trail maps. Guided mountain-bike tours start at $80/120 per half/full day (up to multiday trips) and they also organise guided bushwalks and horse riding.

To get started on two wheels, a new **mountain-bike park** (per day $40; 🕑 weekends) has 5km of downhill and cross-country trails and jumps.

Sleeping & Eating

There are 200 chalets and lodges to choose from – for bookings contact either **Dinner Plain Central Reservations** (☎ 03-5159 6451, 1800 670 019; www.dinnerplain.com; Big Muster Dr) or **Dinner Plain Accommodation** (☎ 03-5159 6696; www.accommdinnerplain.com.au; Big Muster Dr).

our pick **Currawong Lodge** (☎ 03-5159 6452, 1800 635 589; www.currawonglodge.com.au; Big Muster Dr; summer s/d $75/120, ski season 2-night minimum d $195) Currawong Lodge welcomes you with a huge communal lounge-and-kitchen area with a monster open fireplace, TV, DVD and stereo. There's a laundry and spa for those aching post-ski muscles. All rooms have bathrooms, and towels and linen are provided. At this price you can ski with a conscience.

Rundell's Alpine Lodge (☎ 03-5159 6422; www.rundells.com.au; Big Muster Dr; summer s/d $139/195, ski season 2-night minimum $369/539; 🚭) Originally an

VICTORIA

Australian Army retreat, this sprawling complex is a well-run hotel with all the comforts – spa, sauna and restaurant-bar – but a definite lack of pretension. The restaurant and cafe (mains $15 to $36) here is open year-round.

Dinner Plain Hotel (☎ 03-5159 6462; mains $9-18) The barn-sized local pub is the social hub of Dinner Plain and a friendly place to hang out, with roaring open fires and a bistro serving good pub grub.

OMEO
pop 230

Nestled among hills thick with bushland, historic Omeo comes as a bit of a surprise after the winding drive from the coast or High Country. This is the southern access route to Mt Hotham and the main town on the eastern section of the Great Alpine Road. The road is sometimes snowbound in winter; always check conditions before heading this way. In the gold-rush days of the 1850s, Omeo had the toughest and most remote goldfields in the state. The **Omeo visitor information centre** (☎ 03-5159 1679; www.omeoregion.com.au; 152 Day Ave; ⊗ 10am-3pm) is next to the bank on the main street.

The **German Cuckoo Clock Shop** (☎ 03-5159 1552; Great Alpine Rd; ⊗ 9.30am-5.30pm) is worth a look. The Historical Park has a mud map to the **Oriental Claims Walk**.

Snug as a Bug Motel (☎ 03-5159 1311; www.mo telomeo.com.au; 188 Great Alpine Rd; d/f from $80/160) has a range of accommodation in lovely country-style historic buildings. There are family motel rooms, the main guest house, a cute self-contained cottage and the two-room Omeo Backpackers (doubles $65).

Golden Age Hotel (☎ 03-5159 1344; Day Ave; s/d $95/109, d with spa $147) is a beautiful art deco pub with stylish B&B rooms upstairs. Its bar features old photos and the restaurant (mains $15 to $25) serves reliable fare of steaks, salads and gourmet pizzas.

The scenic Victoria Falls Camping Area, off the Great Alpine Rd, 18km west of Omeo, has pit toilets and a picnic area. **Omeo Caravan Park** (☎ 03-5159 1351; Old Omeo Hwy; unpowered/powered sites $22/25, d cabins $80-90) is about 2km from town in a pretty area alongside the Livingstone River. Bike hire available.

Twinkles Café (☎ 03-5159 1484; 174 Day Ave; meals $5-12; ⊗ breakfast & lunch) is the place for a coffee or toasted sandwich, but Omeo's fine dining can be found at **Mesley's Restaurant** (☎ 03-5159 1400; 166 Day St; mains $26-30; ⊗ dinner Tue-Sun) in a historic timber-and-shingle shopfront.

Getting There & Away
Omeo Bus Lines (☎ 0427 017 732) has one bus on weekdays only between Omeo and Bairnsdale ($17, two hours). **O'Connell's Bus Lines** (☎ 0428 591 377; www.omeobus.com.au) operates a summer Alps Link service between Omeo and Bright ($9) via Mt Hotham and Dinner Plain on Monday and Friday. A winter service to Dinner Plain and Mt Hotham operates from Friday to Sunday.

ANGLERS REST

Beside the Cobungra River, about 30km north of Omeo, you'll find the legendary **Blue Duck Inn Hotel** (☎ 03-5159 7220; www.blueduckinn.com.au; Omeo Hwy; d $120, per extra person $40), popular with fly-fishers, canoeists and bushwalkers. Comfy self-contained cabins sleep up to eight. The hotel serves superb country meals and there's a good riverside barbecue area.

MT BAW BAW
elev 1564m

This small ski resort, in the centre of the Baw Baw National Park, is a relaxed option for beginners and families. There are good beginner-to-intermediate runs, plus a couple of harder runs, and it's a good spot for hiking and mountain-biking in the summer months. The downhill skiing area is 25 hectares with a vertical drop of 140m. It also has plenty of **cross-country skiing** trails, including one that connects to the Mt St Gwinear trails.

Mt Baw Baw Alpine Resort Management Board (☎ 03-5165 1136; www.mountbawbaw.com.au), in the centre of the village, provides tourist information and accommodation bookings. Several ski-hire places operate during the season, including **Mt Baw Baw Ski Hire** (☎ 03-5165 1120; www.bawbawskihire.com.au), which also books accommodation. Ski season admission fees are $25/35 weekdays/weekends per car for the day car park. During summer admission is $5. The ski lifts operate only if there is snow; day tickets cost $59/39 per adult/child.

There's an **accommodation booking service** (☎ 1300 651 136; accommodation@mountbawbaw.com.au). In the ski season, ski-club accommodation is available from about $50/25 per adult/child (minimum two nights).

VICTORIA

Kelly's Lodge (☎ 03-5165 1129; www.kellyslodge .com.au; Frosti Lane; 4-person r summer $100, ski season $330-500) is a super-friendly self-contained chalet with four rooms, each with four beds. It's one of the few lodges open year-round and there's a cafe.

GIPPSLAND

With the Great Ocean Road on the other side of Melbourne, Gippsland doesn't get the rave reviews it richly deserves. Sprawling across the southeastern corner of Australia, this diverse region is packed full of national parks, lakes, deserted coastline and some of the most absorb-

ing wilderness, scenery and wildlife on the continent. The western part is divided into the Latrobe Valley, a relatively dull coal-mining and electricity-generating centre, and South Gippsland, which includes the beautiful Wilsons Promontory National Park. East Gippsland, backed by the wild forests of the Great Dividing Range, in-cludes the stunning Lakes District and the Wilderness Coast.

Getting There & Away

The two major routes are the Princes Hwy/ M1 and the South Gippsland Hwy. Most minor roads are unsealed and some roads in state parks are closed during the wetter winter months. Check road conditions and

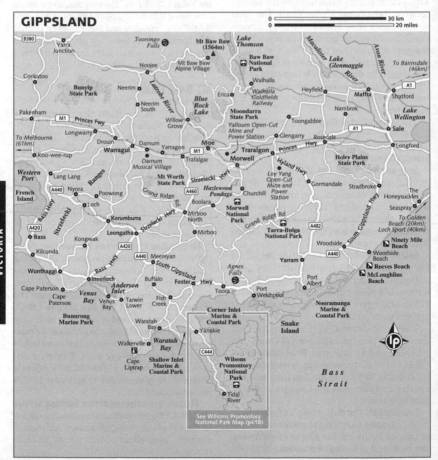

GRAND RIDGE ROAD

The spectacular Grand Ridge Rd winds along the top of the Strzelecki Ranges, running from midway between Warragul and Korumburra to midway between Traralgon and Yarram, providing a fabulous excursion through fertile farmland that was once covered with forests of giant mountain ash trees. Pick it up north of Korumburra or south of either Trafalgar or Moe. The only place of any size along the route is the pretty township of **Mirboo North**, home to Gippsland's only brewery, the unassuming **Grand Ridge Brewery** (☎ 03-5668 1647; www.grand-ridge.com.au) in the historic Butter Factory building.

One of the last remnants of original southern Gippsland forest is tucked in a rainforest gully 30km south of Traralgon in the **Tarra-Bulga National Park**. Camping isn't allowed in the park, but you can stroll to the **Cyathea Falls** and the 2km **Fern Gully Nature Walk**.

---

seasonal closures with **Parks Victoria** (☎ 13 19 63; www.parkweb.vic.gov.au) and keep an eye out for logging trucks.

BUSES

V/Line (☎ 13 61 96) has daily bus services along the Princes Hwy (A1) from Bairnsdale to Narooma in NSW and also Lakes Entrance via Lake Tyers. Another service, which runs twice a week, follows the Princes Hwy as far as Cann River, then goes north to Canberra. **Premier** (☎ 13 34 10; www.premierms.com.au) has a daily service from Melbourne via the Princes Hwy to Sydney ($83, 19½), stopping at Gippsland towns along the way.

There are also regular V/Line buses from Traralgon to Sale via Maffra; Melbourne to Yarram, which stop along the South Gippsland Hwy; and Melbourne to Inverloch, which stop along the Bass Hwy.

Omeo Bus Lines (☎ 03-5159 4231) runs services between Bairnsdale and Omeo ($31) on weekdays.

TRAINS

Bairnsdale is the end of the V/Line train link from Melbourne. Daily services from Melbourne to Bairnsdale ($26, 3¾ hours) stop at all major towns along the Princes Hwy.

SOUTH GIPPSLAND

From Melbourne, the South Gippsland Hwy passes through the beautiful 'blue' rounded hills of the Strzelecki Ranges and is the quickest route to Wilsons Promontory. An alternative coastal route is even more scenic, with some stunning ocean views and beautiful seaside towns from Cape Paterson to Venus Bay and Waratah Bay.

Korumburra

pop 3150

The first sizeable town along the South Gippsland Hwy is Korumburra, situated on the edge of the Strzelecki Ranges. **Prom Country Information Centre** (☎ 03-5655 2233, 1800 630 704; www.promcountrytourism.com.au; South Gippsland Hwy) is on the way out of town next to Coal Creek.

Coal Creek Village (☎ 03-5655 1811; www.coal creekvillage.com.au; admission free; 🕙 10am-4.30pm Thu-Mon) is a re-creation of a 19th-century mining town. V/Line coaches from Melbourne's Southern Cross Station stop outside en route to Leongatha and Yarram.

Volunteers operate the **South Gippsland Railway** (☎ 03-5658 1111, 1800 442 211; www.sgr.org.au; adult/child/family return $13/8/42), which runs heritage diesel trains along scenic tracks from Korumburra to Leongatha and Nyora on Sunday and public holidays (four services).

Wilsons Promontory National Park

With some of Victoria's best bushwalking country, wonderful beaches and abundant wildlife, 'the Prom' is one of the most popular national parks in all of Australia. Much of it is true wilderness, with only one sealed road on the park's western side. The wildlife around Tidal River is very tame: kookaburras and rosellas lurk expectantly (resist the urge to feed them), and wombats waddle out of the undergrowth seemingly oblivious to the campers and day-trippers.

Wilsons Promontory was an important area for the Kurnai and Boonwurrung Aborigines, and middens have been found in many places, including Cotters and Darby Beaches, and Oberon Bay. The southern-most part of mainland Australia, the Prom once formed a land bridge that allowed people to walk to Tasmania.

VICTORIA

WILSONS PROMONTORY NATIONAL PARK

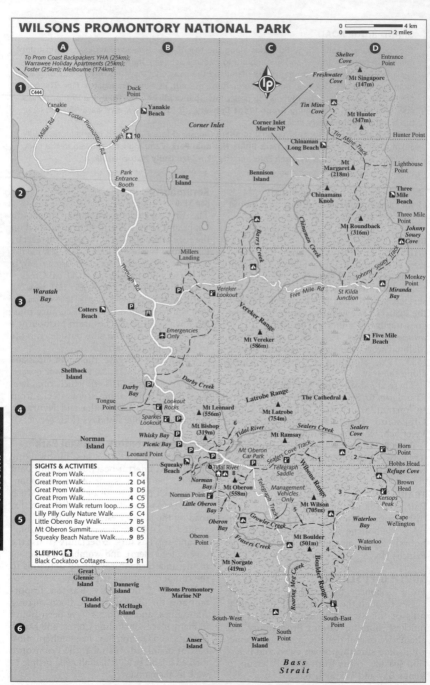

0 ————— 4 km
0 ————— 2 miles

To Prom Coast Backpackers YHA (25km);
Warrawee Holiday Apartments (25km);
Foster (25km); Melbourne (174km);

A **B** **C** **D**

Shelter Cove
Entrance Point

Freshwater Cove
Mt Singapore (147m)

Tin Mine Cove

Duck Point
Yanakie Beach

Yanakie
Foster Promontory Rd
Millar Rd
Foley Rd
10

Corner Inlet

Corner Inlet Marine NP

Mt Hunter (347m)
Hunter Point

Tin Mine Track

Chinaman Long Beach

Lighthouse Point

Mt Margaret (218m)

Park Entrance Booth

Long Island

Bennison Island

Chinamans Knob

Three Mile Beach

Three Mile Point

Johnny Souey Cove

Chinaman Creek

Mt Roundback (316m)

Millers Landing

Vereker Lookout

Barry Creek

Five Mile Rd
St Kilda Junction

Johnny Souey Track

Monkey Point

Miranda Bay

Waratah Bay

Cotters Beach

Through Rd

Vereker Range

Mt Vereker (586m)

Five Mile Beach

Emergencies Only

Shellback Island

Darby Creek

Latrobe Range

The Cathedral

Darby Bay
Tongue Point

Lookout Rocks

Sparkes Lookout

Whisky Bay
Picnic Bay

Norman Island

Leonard Point

Mt Leonard (556m)

Mt Bishop (319m)

Mt Latrobe (754m)

Tidal River

Mt Ramsay

Sealers Creek

Sealers Cove

Sealers Cove Track

Horn Point

Hobbs Head
Refuge Cove

6

Squeaky Beach

Tidal River

Mt Oberon Car Park

Telegraph Saddle

Wilsons Range

Brown Head

Kersops Peak

9

8

Norman Bay

Mt Oberon (558m)

Management Vehicles Only

Mt Wilson (705m)

Norman Point

Little Oberon Bay

7

Telegraph Track

Growler Creek

Waterloo Bay

Cape Wellington

Oberon Bay

5

Oberon Point

Mt Boulder (501m)

Waterloo Point

Frasers Creek

Mt Norgate (419m)

Roaring Meg Creek

Boulder Range

South-East Point

Great Glennie Island

Dannevig Island

Wilsons Promontory Marine NP

Citadel Island

McHugh Island

South-West Point

South Point

Anser Island

Wattle Island

Bass Strait

SIGHTS & ACTIVITIES	
Great Prom Walk	1 C4
Great Prom Walk	2 D4
Great Prom Walk	3 D5
Great Prom Walk	4 C5
Great Prom Walk return loop	5 C5
Lilly Pilly Gully Nature Walk	6 C4
Little Oberon Bay Walk	7 B5
Mt Oberon Summit	8 C5
Squeaky Beach Nature Walk	9 B5

SLEEPING	
Black Cockatoo Cottages	10 B1

VICTORIA

TOP FIVE PROM WALKS

From November to Easter a free shuttle bus operates between the Tidal River visitors' car park and the Mt Oberon car park (a nice way to start the Prom Circuit Walk).

Great Prom Walk This is the most popular long-distance hike, a moderate 45km circuit across to Sealers Cove from Tidal River, down to Refuge Cove, Waterloo Bay, the lighthouse and back to Tidal River via Oberon Bay. Allow two to three days, and coordinate your walks with tide times, as creek crossings can be hazardous. It's possible to visit or stay at the lighthouse by prior arrangement with the park office.

Lilly Pilly Gully Nature Walk An easy 5km (two-hour) walk through heathland and eucalypt forests, with lots of wildlife.

Mt Oberon Summit Starting from the Mt Oberon car park, this moderate-to-hard 7km (2½-hour) walk is an ideal introduction to the Prom with panoramic views from the summit. The free Mt Oberon shuttle bus can take you to the car park and back.

Little Oberon Bay An easy-to-moderate 8km (three-hour) walk over sand dunes covered in coastal tea trees with beautiful views over Little Oberon Bay.

Squeaky Beach Nature Walk Another easy 5km return stroll through coastal tea trees and banksias to a sensational white-sand beach.

The Prom was ravaged by fire in 2009, with some 25,000 hectares burnt out around the eastern and northern sides of the park. Fortunately the fire was halted before it reached the main accommodation base at Tidal River, and the park reopened a month later.

The only access road leads to **Tidal River** on the western coast, which has the Parks Victoria office and education centre, a petrol station, general store (with internet access), open-air cinema (summer only), campsites, cabins, lodges and facilities.

INFORMATION

Parks Victoria (☎ 03-5680 9555, 1800 350 552; www .parkweb.vic.gov.au; Tidal River; ⏰ 8am-4.30pm) Takes accommodation reservations and issues camping permits for outside the Tidal River area. Day entry to the park is $10, which is included in camping fees.

ACTIVITIES

Bushwalking

The Prom's diverse walking tracks will take you through swamps, forests, marshes, valleys of tree ferns and long beaches lined with sand dunes. The park office has details of walks, from 15-minute strolls to overnight and longer hikes. For some serious exploration, buy a copy of *Discovering the Prom* ($15).

The northern area of the park is much less visited. Most walks in this 'wilderness zone' are overnight or longer, and mainly for experienced bushwalkers. Wood fires are not permitted anywhere in the park.

Surfing

There's excellent surfing at Tidal River. Experienced surfers can get waves at Squeaky Beach, Darby Bay and elsewhere, but these are unpatrolled areas with strong currents, and are potentially very dangerous. **Offshore Surf School** (☎ 03-5680 8580; www.surfingaustralia.com.au), based in Inverloch, can arrange surfing lessons at Wilson's Prom.

SLEEPING

Hostels

Prom Coast Backpackers YHA (☎ 03-5682 2171; http:// gippsland.com/web/warraweeholidayapartments; 40 Station Rd, Foster; dm/d/f $30/70/89) There are no hostels in the park, but nearby Foster has this cosy renovated cottage with kitchen and lounge that sleeps 10. Ask the friendly owners about a lift to the Prom ($20 per person each way).

Warrawee Holiday Apartments (☎ 03-5682 2171; d/f from $100/130) Self-contained apartments next to Prom Coast Backpackers and under the same management.

Huts, Cabins & Units

Apart from bush camping, the only accommodation in the park is at Tidal River and it must be booked well in advance in summer through **Parks Victoria** (☎ 03-5680 9555, 13 19 63). There are basic huts (four to six beds from $62 to $95) in the park, units ($118), self-contained, two-bedroom cabins ($163) and safari tents ($250).

Nearby Yanakie offers several comfortable accommodation options for those day-tripping into the Prom.

VICTORIA

Black Cockatoo Cottages (☎ 03-5687 1306; www .blackcockatoo.com; 60 Foley Rd, Yanakie; d $140) Black Cockatoo Cottages offers glorious views of the Prom without leaving your very comfortable bed. These self-contained cottages are private and stylish.

Camping
Bookings are essential for Tidal River's 450 campsites during holiday periods. Sites for up to three adults (or two adults and two children) and one car cost $23, plus $5 per extra adult. There are 20 powered sites that cost $50 for up to eight people and one vehicle. Another 11 bush-camping areas around the Prom all have pit or compost toilets and most have water. Overnight hikers need camping permits (adult/child $7/4), which should be booked ahead through the park office.

GETTING THERE & AWAY
There's no direct public transport between Melbourne and the Prom, but the **Wilson's Promontory Bus Service** (☎ 13 16 38) operates from Foster to Tidal River (via Fish Creek) on Friday at 7pm, returning on Sunday at 2.35pm. This service connects with the V/Line bus from Melbourne at Fish Creek.

WEST GIPPSLAND & THE LATROBE VALLEY
From Melbourne, the Princes Hwy follows the power lines past dairy country to their source in the Latrobe Valley. The working-class region between Moe and Traralgon contains one of the world's largest deposits of brown coal, which is consumed by massive power stations at Yallourn, Morwell and Loy Yang, which produce up to 85% of Victoria's electricity.

Walhalla
pop 18

Tiny Walhalla, 46km north of Moe and reached via a gorgeous 13km winding road from Rawson, was one of Victoria's great gold-mining towns in the 19th century, producing one of the world richest gold-bearing reefs. Today fewer than 20 people live in this picturesque **town** (www.walhalla.org.au) – less than 0.5% of the 5000 residents of the area in its gold-era heyday. Despite the inevitable heritage decor (the sepia-photo salesman has evidently been in town), it remains one

of the most scenic and isolated of Victoria's historic towns. Remarkably, mains electricity only reached here 10 years ago. Today it's a year-round destination, especially with the opening of the South Face Rd connecting nearby Rawson with Mt Baw Baw.

Bushfires in 2006 came perilously close to Walhalla, burning out much of the surrounding bushland, but the area was mercifully untouched by the devastating 2009 fires.

SIGHTS & ACTIVITIES
Crossing Stringer's Creek near the band rotunda, you can follow the **Tramline Walkway**, passing a number of sights, including the Long Tunnel Mine. Heading south, the tramway leads to the 680km **Australian Alps Walking Track** (www.australianalps.deh.gov.au/parks/walktrack), which goes all the way to Canberra. The first 40km of the trail takes you to Baw Baw and can be done in two days.

There are small **museums** in the old post office and fire station. Walhalla's historic **cemetery** is worth a look. The slope is so steep that some of the dead were buried sideways.

Long Tunnel Extended Gold Mine (☎ 03-5165 6259; adult/child/family $15/12/36), off the Walhalla–Beardmore Rd, produced 13.7 tonnes of gold (more than $50 million in today's value). Guided tours run at 1.30pm weekdays and noon, 2pm and 3pm on Saturday, Sunday and during school holidays.

You can take a one-hour diesel train ride on the historic **Walhalla Goldfields Railway** (☎ 03-5126 4201, recorded info 9513 3969; www.walhallarail.com; adult/child/family return $18/13/40). Trains depart at 11am, 1pm and 3pm from the Walhalla station at the entry to town on Wednesday, Saturday, Sunday and public holidays (daily during school holidays).

TOURS
Copper Mine Adventure (☎ 03-5134 6875; www.moun taintopexperience.com; tour $20) operates rugged 1½-hour 4WD trips along old coach roads to a disused mine, on Wednesday and most weekends. The same company also does half-day tours of mining ghost towns in the area ($200 per vehicle, up to four passengers).

Walhalla Ghost Tours (☎ 03-5165 6250; www.wal hallaghosttour.info; adult/child $20/15) is a two-hour night walk with spooky stories of Walhalla's supernatural past. It's held on the first three Saturdays of each month – bookings are essential.

SLEEPING & EATING
Windsor House B&B (☎ 03-9882 5985, 03-5165 6237; www
.windsorhouse.com.au; B&B d from $160) Spectacular
Windsor House dates from Walhalla's heyday
in 1878, and is listed by the National Trust.
The guest house has been lovingly restored,
with four-poster beds, open fires and a library
of old books.

Walhalla Star Hotel (☎ 03-5165 6262; www.starho
tel.com.au; Main Rd; B&B d $199, with dinner $299) The
rebuilt historic Star offers stylish boutique
accommodation with king-size beds and
sophisticated designer decor making good
use of local materials such as corrugated iron
water tanks. Nonguests should reserve a table
for dinner at the classic Parker's restaurant
(mains $29 to $31) within the hotel, or you
can get good coffee, cakes and gourmet pies
at the attached Greyhorse Café (open 11am
to 2pm; meals $4 to $8).

Walhalla Lodge Family Hotel (☎ 03-5165 6226;
mains $12-20; ☽ lunch & dinner Wed-Mon) Prints of old
Walhalla decorate the cosy one-room 'Wally
Pub', serving reasonable pub fare.

There's free camping at **North Gardens**, on
Stringer's Creek just north of town, with
toilets barbecues and fireplaces. The nearest
caravan parks are in Rawson.

THE LAKES DISTRICT
The Gippsland Lakes comprise the largest
inland waterway system in Australia. There
are three main lakes that interconnect: Lake
King, Lake Victoria and Lake Wellington.
The 'lakes' are lagoons, separated from
the ocean by a narrow strip of sand dunes
known as Ninety Mile Beach. The dunes
were artificially breached at Lakes Entrance
in 1889 to allow ocean-going fishing boats
to shelter in the placid waters. Despite
nearby Bairnsdale and the Princes Hwy,
the 600-sq-km Lakes area is remote, with
just a half-dozen access points including
Metung, Paynesville, Loch Sport and Lakes
Entrance. Only those with a boat can truly
appreciate this wonderful lakes system. The
Lakes National Park protects 2400 hectares
of native habitat.

Sale
pop 13,336
Sale is the centre of the **Gippsland Wetlands** of
lakes, waterways and billabongs. Although
this once-busy port town, active during the
paddle-steamer era, has a few 19th-century
buildings, there's little to excite the traveller
today. Two kilometres south of Sale, on the
South Gippsland Hwy, is the Sale Common
Wildlife Refuge with a wetlands boardwalk.

The **Wentworth visitor information centre**
(☎ 1800 677 520; www.tourismwellington.com.au; 8
Foster St; 🖳) is on the Princes Hwy at the entrance to town. Near the visitor centre, the
Port of Sale is a redeveloped marina area with
boardwalks, cafes, galleries and a canal leading out to the Gippsland Lakes.

Ninety Mile Beach
Ninety miles (144km) of pristine and seamless sandy beach is backed by dunes, swamp-
lands and lagoons, stretching from Seaspray
to Lakes Entrance. The beach is great for
surf fishing and walking, but can be dangerous for swimming – except at Seaspray,
where it's patrolled.

Free **camping** is permitted at designated sites along the coastal strip between
Seaspray, Golden Beach and Loch Sport, and
there are free showers at the camping area at
Paradise Beach. Seaspray has a general store,
the **Seaspray Caravan Park** (☎ 03-5146 4364; sites
$20, d cabins from $60) and the quirky **Ronnie's Tea
Rooms** (☎ 03-5146 4420; 13 Trood St; ☽ morning &
afternoon tea).

Kangaroos graze on front lawns at **Loch
Sport**, surrounded by lake, ocean and bush,
with some good swimming areas. **Loch Sport
Holiday Park** (☎ 03-5146 0264; www.lochsportpark
.com.au; Charles St; unpowered/powered sites $30/35, cabins
$70-80), on Lake Victoria, is a well-equipped
park. **Marina Hotel** (☎ 03-5146 0666; mains $16-28;
☽ lunch & dinner) has great sunset views and
good fresh seafood.

A spit of land surrounded by lakes and
ocean, **Lakes National Park** covers 2390 hectares
of coastal bushland and is reached by road
from Loch Sport, or by boat from Paynesville
(5km). The **Parks Victoria office** (☎ 03-5146 0278)
is at the park entrance near Loch Sport. The
only camping is at Emu Bight.

Mitchell River National Park
About 42km northwest of Bairnsdale, this
park has some beautiful green valleys, camping areas and lovely hiking, including the
two-day, 18km **Mitchell River Walking Track**.
Its best-known feature is the **Den of Nargun**,
a small cave that, according to Aboriginal
stories, is haunted by a strange, half-stone
creature, the Nargun.

VICTORIA

Bairnsdale
pop 10,900

Bustling Bairnsdale is the major town of this district and the southern end of the Great Alpine Rd. The **Bairnsdale visitor information centre** (☎ 03-5152 3444, 1800 637 060; www.lakesand wilderness.com.au; 240 Main St; ☺ 9am-5pm) can book accommodation. With the coast less than 20 minutes away, there's no real reason to stay overnight.

The **Krowathunkoolong Keeping Place** (☎ 03-5152 1891; 37-53 Dalmahoy St; adult/child $4/3; ☺ 9am-5pm Mon-Fri), behind the train station, is a Koorie cultural centre that explores Kurnai daily life before and after white settlement.

On the edge of town, the **MacLeod Morass Boardwalk** is a wetland reserve with walking tracks and bird hides.

Howitt Park is the starting point for the **East Gippsland Rail Trail** (www.eastgippslandrailtrail.com), a popular bike and walking track that leads 30km northeast to Bruthen and on through state forest to Lakes Entrance.

Mitchell Gardens Holiday Park (☎ 03-5152 4654; www.mitchellgardens.com.au; unpowered/powered sites $22/26, d cabins $65-106; ☒), east of town on the Mitchell River, is a shady park with pool and jetty.

Metung
pop 730

Curling around Bancroft Bay, Metung is one of the prettiest spots on the Gippsland Lakes – the unhurried charm of this picturesque village is contagious, its shoreline dotted with jetties and small wooden craft.

Metung Visitor Centre (☎ 03-5156 2969; www .metungtourism.com.au; 50 Metung Rd; ☺ 9am-5pm) can book cruises and help with accommodation.

Boats (from $90 per day), yachts ($500 per day) and sailing lessons ($150/200 for four/eight hours) are available from **Riviera Nautic** (☎ 03-5156 2243; www.rivieranautic.com.au; 185 Metung Rd).

Lakes Director (☎ 03-5156 2628; adult/child $42/free; ☺ 3pm Tue, Thu, Sat) has a 2½-hour 'happy hour' cruise to Lakes Entrance and back.

For a dip, head to the safe **swimming beach** next to Lake King Jetty.

At high noon pelicans fly in from all around like bomber planes for the fish issued outside the Metung Hotel. Pelicans can tell the time, or at least know where to get a good feed.

SLEEPING & EATING

Accommodation is available through **Metung Accommodation** (Slipway Villas; ☎ 03-5156 2861; www .metungaccommodation.com.au). There's no camping in Metung itself.

Arendell Holiday Units (☎ 03-5156 2507; www .arendellmetung.com.au; 30 Mairburn Rd; 1-/2-bedroom units from $90/100; ☒) These comfortable timber cottages are very 1970s, but they're comfortable enough and good value outside the peak seasons.

Metung Galley (☎ 03-5156 2330; 3/59 Metung Rd; lunch $10-18, dinner $20-32) Locals rate this as Metung's best dining and it's hard to argue. Fresh local seafood and Gippsland lamb feature on the Mediterranean-influenced menu, but the all-day fare makes it perfect for breakfast or a light lunch, too.

Metung Hotel (☎ 03-5156 2206; Kurnai Ave; meals $18-30; ☺ lunch & dinner) The local pub revels in its prime position with a large wooden deck literally hanging over the water. It serves agreeable bistro food, from a bowl of steamed mussels to marinated lamb.

Lakes Entrance
pop 5550

With the shallow Cunninghame Arm waterway separating town from the crashing ocean beaches, Lakes Entrance basks in an undeniably pretty location, but in holiday season it's a packed-out tourist town with a graceless strip of motels, caravan parks, minigolf courses and souvenir shops lining the Esplanade. Still, the bobbing fishing boats, fresh seafood and cruises out to Metung and Wyanga Park Winery should win you over, and out of season there's an unhurried pace and accommodation bargains.

INFORMATION

Hai Q (☎ 03-5155 4247; cnr Myer St & the Esplanade; internet per 30 min $5)

Lakes Entrance visitor information centre (☎ 03-5155 1966, 1800 637 060; www.lakes-entrance.com; cnr Princes Hwy & Marine Pde) Has plenty of information and books accommodation.

ACTIVITIES

A wooden footbridge crosses the Cunninghame Arm inlet from the east of town to the ocean and squintingly big **Ninety Mile Beach**. From December to Easter paddle boats, canoes and sailboats can be hired by the footbridge.

There's bike hire available at **Bicycle Passion** (☎ 03-5155 3033; 229 Esplanade; per hr/day $10/24; ⏰ 10am-6pm Mon-Fri, 9am-noon Sat) opposite Ferryman's.

Lakes Entrance is the perfect place to embark on an organised cruise. There are ticket booths at Post Office Jetty:

Corque (☎ 03-5155 1508; www.wyangapark.com.au) Fabulous 4½-hour lunch cruise to Wyanga Park Winery (adult/child $50/25) at 11am and dinner cruise ($75) on Friday and Saturday nights. On Thursday the lunch cruise starts at 9.30am and stops in at Metung ($55).

Lonsdale Cruises (☎ 0413 666 638; Post Office Jetty; 3hr cruise adult/child $45/25; ⏰ 1pm) Scenic cruises out to Metung and Lake King on a former Queenscliff–Sorrento passenger ferry.

Mulloway Fishing Charters (☎ 03-5155 3304, 0427 943 154) Three-hour fishing cruises ($50) on the lake from the jetty opposite 66 Marine Pde.

Peels Tourist & Ferry Services (☎ 03-5155 1246; Post Office Jetty) Daily two-hour cruises at 10am and 2pm (adult/child $40/20) and daily four-hour lunch cruise to Metung (adult/child $44/13) at 11am.

SLEEPING

Nondescript motels and small van parks line the Esplanade. Most offer decent discounts outside the peak school holiday periods.

Riviera Backpackers (☎ 03-5155 2444; www.yha .com.au; the Esplanade; dm/s/d from $22/35/50; 🖥 🏊) The YHA is a good, clean hostel with a large kitchen and pool table. V/Line and other buses stop nearby on the Esplanade.

Kalimna Woods (☎ 03-5155 1957; www.kalimna woods.com.au; Kalimna Jetty Rd; d $115, with spa $155; 🐾) These charming one- and two-bedroom log cottages are in a beautiful bush setting of rainforest, gardens, possums and birds, but only 2km from the town centre. The spa rooms add that little extra romance to the log fires and country-style furniture.

Goat & Goose (☎ 03-5155 3079; www.goatandgoose .com; 16 Gay St; d incl breakfast $140-210) Spectacular ocean views of Bass Strait are maximised at this wonderfully unusual, multistorey, timber pole-framed house. The owners are friendly, all the rooms have spas, and a cooked breakfast on the balcony is part of the service.

Eastern Beach Caravan Park (☎ 1800 761 762; www .easternbeach.com.au; unpowered/powered sites $25/30; 🖥) This small park has a fine location away from the hubbub of town in a bush setting back from Eastern Beach. A walking track takes you into town (30 minutes). There's free wireless internet, barbecues and a kids' playground.

EATING

With one of Australia's largest commercial fishing fleets, Lakes Entrance is a great place for fresh fish and chips. Grab a bundle, sit lakeside and fend off the seagulls. You can buy fresh shellfish (prawns and bugs) direct from boats (look for signs) or from Ferryman's (below). The Fisherman's Co-op has moved its seafood sales from the wharf to shop 5 in the Safeway complex.

Six Sisters & a Pigeon (☎ 03-5155 1144; 567 Esplanade; meals $6-16; ⏰ lunch & dinner) The name alone should guide you to this quirky licensed cafe on the Esplanade opposite the footbridge. It has good coffee, breakfasts and lunches of focaccias, baguettes and light mains with an Asian-Italian influence.

our pick **Waterwheel Beach Tavern** (☎ 03-5156 5855; 577 Beach Rd, Lake Tyers; mains $17-28; ⏰ lunch & dinner) It's worth the trip out to Lake Tyers, 10 minutes' drive from Lakes Entrance, for lunch or dinner on the deck at the Waterwheel. The setting is superb (lakeside overlooking the ocean) and the food is classy but unpretentious.

Ferryman's Seafood Café (☎ 03-5155 3000; www .ferrymans.com.au; Esplanade; mains $17-32) It's hard to beat the ambience of dining on the deck of this floating cafe-restaurant, which will fill you to the gills with the freshest fish and seafood preparations, including good ol' fish and chips. Downstairs you can buy fresh seafood, including prawns and crayfish (from 8.30am to 5pm).

Miriam's Restaurant (☎ 03-5155 3999; cnr Esplanade & Bulmer St; mains $22-35; ⏰ dinner) The upstairs dining room at Miriam's overlooks the Esplanade, and the Gippsland steaks and local seafood dishes are excellent.

EAST GIPPSLAND & THE WILDERNESS COAST

Beyond Lakes Entrance stretches a wilderness area of spectacular coastal national parks and old-growth forest. Much of this region wasn't cleared for agriculture and contains some of the most remote and pristine national parks in the state, making logging in these ancient forests a hot issue.

Orbost is the main town and gateway to the Snowy River and Errinundra National Parks, but it's beyond here that things start to get interesting. The magnificent coastal areas of Cape Conran, Mallacoota and Croajingolong are all uncrowded, unspoiled

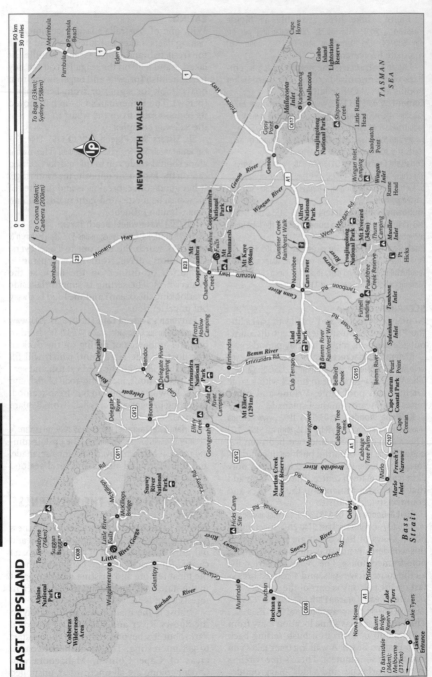

and undeveloped, and even on the highway the winding forest drive to the state's most easterly point is magnificent.

Buchan
pop 230
Leaving the coast, Buchan is a beautiful town in the foothills of the Snowy Mountains about 56km north of Lakes Entrance, famous for its intricate limestone cave system that has been open to visitors since 1913.

Guided tours, alternating between **Royal Cave** and **Fairy Cave**, are run by **Parks Victoria** (☎ 03-5162 1900; 45min tours adult/child/family $14/8/38; ☒ 10am, 11.15am, 1pm, 2.15pm & 3.30pm Oct-Easter, 11am, 1pm & 3pm Easter-Sep). Combined cave tours are slightly cheaper. The rangers also offer hard-hat guided tours to **Federal Cave** during the high season.

SLEEPING
Buchan Lodge Backpackers (☎ 03-5155 9421; www .buchanlodge.com; Saleyard Rd; dm $20) This log cabin-style place has a spacious but cosy living area, including a well-equipped kitchen, large dining room and barbecue. Dorm beds only.

Buchan Caves Caravan Park (☎ 03-5162 1900; Buchan Caves Reserve; unpowered/powered sites $18/24, cabins/safari tents $72/140; ☒) Why not stay right next to the caves at this serene Parks Victoria camping ground? The self-contained cabins sleep up to five, and the new 'wilderness retreats' – elevated tents – sleep two.

Snowy River National Park
Dominated by gorges carved by the Snowy River, this is one of Victoria's most isolated and spectacular parks.

The main access roads are Buchan–Jindabyne Rd (Gelantipy Rd) from Buchan and Bonang Rd (C612) from Orbost, and they are joined by McKillops Rd in the north, crossing the Snowy River at **McKillops Bridge**.

About 25km before the bridge, on the Gelantipy Rd, are **Little River Falls** and **Little River Gorge** lookouts. The latter, a 500m-deep gorge, is the deepest in Victoria.

Bushwalking and canoeing are popular, but be prepared as conditions can change suddenly. The classic canoe or raft trip down the Snowy River, from McKillops Bridge to a finish point near Buchan, takes at least four days.

There are campsites, toilets, fireplaces and river beaches along McKillops Bridge.

For information contact the park offices at **Buchan** (☎ 03-5162 1900), **Orbost** (☎ 03-5161 1222) or **Bairnsdale** (☎ 03-5152 0600).

Karoonda Park (☎ 03-5155 0220; www.karoon dapark.com; Gelantipy Rd, Gelantipy; dm/s/d/cabins incl breakfast $24/40/58/95 ☒ ☐ ☒) is a working sheep-and-cattle property 40km north of Buchan. Fully catered packages are available (three-course meals $14) and the owners may have work going. Snowy River Expeditions runs activities such as white-water rafting, abseiling, horse riding and caving from here.

Errinundra National Park
The Errinundra Plateau contains Victoria's largest cool-temperate rainforest. The national park covers just 25,100 hectares and sadly many adjoining areas are being logged.

The Bonang Rd passes the western side of the park, while the Errinundra Rd, from Club Terrace, runs through the centre. Both roads are unsealed, steep, winding and often closed in winter – check with Parks Victoria at **Bendoc** (☎ 02-6458 1456), **Cann River** (☎ 03-5158 6351) or **Orbost** (☎ 03-5161 1222; cnr Nicholson & Salisbury Sts).

Camping areas are at Delegate River on the Gap Rd connecting Bonang Rd with Bendoc; Frosty Hollow on the Hensleigh Creek Rd; Ada River on the Errinundra Rd; and at Goongerah. There's a petrol station and general store at **Bonang**, a pub at Bendoc and another at **Delegate River**.

Orbost
pop 2100
Orbost services the surrounding farming and forest areas. Most travellers fly through as the Princes Hwy passes just south of the town, while the Bonang Rd heads north towards the Snowy River and Errinundra National Parks, and Marlo Rd follows the Snowy River south to Marlo and continues along the coast to Cape Conran.

Orbost visitor information centre (☎ 03-5154 2424; cnr Nicholson & Clarke Sts; ☒ 9am-5pm) is in the historic 1872 Slab Hut.

The impressive **Orbost Exhibition Centre** (☎ 03-5154 2634; www.orbostexhibitioncentre.org; Clarke St; adult/ child $4/free; ☒ 10am-4pm Mon-Sat, 1-4pm Sun), next to the visitor centre, showcases stunning works by local timber artists.

VICTORIA

The town has a caravan park and a couple of motels. **Club Hotel** (☎ 03-5154 1003; 63 Nicholson St; s/d $25/40) has the cheapest rooms around – typical cheery pub rooms with shared bathrooms, as well as bistro meals and Chinese takeaway.

Marlo
pop 350

Rather than barrel down the highway from Orbost to Mallacoota, turn off to Marlo, a sleepy holiday town at the mouth of the Snowy River just 15km south of Orbost. It's a lovely spot, popular with anglers, and the road continues on to Cape Conran before rejoining the highway.

The main attraction here is the **PS Curlip** (☎ 03-5154 1699; www.paddlesteamercurlip.com.au; adult/child/family $28/14/66; ⏰ 11.30am & 2.30pm Wed-Sun), a recreation of an 1890 paddle steamer that once chugged up the Snowy River to Orbost. The vessel was rebuilt as a community project.

Marlo has a couple of caravan parks and motels. **Tabbara Lodge** (☎ 03-5154 8231; 1 Marlo Rd; d $80; ☒) is a friendly place with spacious self-contained rooms around shady gardens containing barbecues and a playground.

You can't beat an afternoon beer from the expansive wooden verandah of the **Marlo Hotel** (☎ 03-5154 8201; www.marlohotel.com.au; 17 Argyle Pde; d from $110, with spa $130) with a sublime view of the Snowy River emptying into the sea. The boutique rooms here are above average for a pub – some with spa – and the restaurant serves local seafood such as gummy shark and king prawns (mains $12 to $29).

Cape Conran Coastal Park

Cape Conran is one of the most beautiful spots in the state. The 19km coastal route from Marlo to Cape Conran is especially pretty and there are some great beaches. Be sure to stop at **French's Narrows**, a pretty system of lakes that's home to countless water birds.

A rough track 4km east leads from the cape to the mouth of the Yeerung River, which is another good spot for swimming, canoeing and fishing. There are no shops at Cape Conran – bring provisions and drinking water. There's good surfing at West Cape beach. **Cabbage Tree Palms** is a short, partly unsealed, detour off the road between Cape Conran and the Princes Hwy to Victoria's only stand of native palms – a tiny rainforest oasis.

SLEEPING

Parks Victoria (☎ 03-5154 8438; www.conran.net.au; Yeerung Rd) manages the excellent accommodation at Cape Conran.

Cape Conran Cabins (4-person cabins low/high season $90/138, safari tents $140) These large rustic cabins are fantastic, resembling oversized cubby houses with lofty mezzanine sleeping areas that can sleep up to eight. They have a remote, airy, beachcomber feel and are just a short walk to the beach. They come with kitchen, verandah and cute outdoor (but private) dunny and shower. Nearby are spacious elevated safari tents – no en suite or kitchen but very cool.

Banksia Bluff Camping Area (sites for up to 4 people low/high season $17/23) Right on the foreshore, the camping ground has toilets, cold showers and fireplaces; bring drinking water if you don't like the taste of bore water. There's a ballot system during peak periods.

Cann River
pop 250

Cann River is at the junction of the Princes and Monaro Hwys heading north into NSW. There are petrol stations, motels, a supermarket, pub and caravan park here, as well as several places to grab a quick bite, so it's a good place to break the journey and stretch your legs.

Coopracambra National Park

Remote Coopracambra (38,300 hectares) retains its original ecosystem virtually intact and supports many rare and endangered species. The landscape is rugged and spectacular, with deep gorges where the earliest fossil evidence of four-footed creatures was discovered. The only access is a 4WD track, which runs from the Monaro Hwy to Genoa. **Beehive Falls** are 2km from the Monaro Hwy, 28km north of Cann River.

Mallacoota
pop 1100

One of Gippsland's true gems, little Mallacoota is Victoria's most easterly town, snuggled on the vast Mallacoota Inlet and surrounded by the tumbling hills and beachside dunes of beautiful Croajingolong National Park. Those prepared to come this far are treated to long empty ocean surf beaches, tidal river mouths and swimming, fishing and boating on the inlet.

VICTORIA

On the road in from Genoa you pass turn-offs to **Gypsy Point** and **Karbeethong**, beautiful little communities on the inlet with accommodation. Mallacoota itself has a good range of accommodation, cafes and a pub. At Christmas and Easter it's a crowded family holiday spot – it's certainly no secret – but most of the year it's pretty quiet and very relaxed.

INFORMATION
Mallacoota Information Shed (☎ 03-5158 0800; www.visitmallacoota.com.au; Main Wharf; ☼ 10am-4pm) Brightly painted shed on the wharf with helpful volunteer staff, maps and advice.
Parks Victoria (☎ 03-5161 9500; cnr Buckland & Allan Drs) Opposite the wharf.

ACTIVITIES
The sublime 300km shoreline of Mallacoota Inlet is backed by national park. There are plenty of great short **walks** (from 30 minutes to four hours) around town, the inlet and in the bush – maps are available from the Information Shed.

There's sometimes **surf** at Bastion Point and always excellent **swimming** at Betka Beach where the Betka river mouth runs with the tide. Ask directions to **Tip Beach** (also called Secret Beach), an unofficial nudist beach off Nelson Dr.

One of the great pastimes here is to hire a boat (no licence required) and travel up the inlet. Cut the engine, drop anchor and listen for a moment to the quiet sounds of the birds and the breeze through the trees of the national park. Then dive in for the most delicious nudie swim. There are many public jetties where you can tie your boat up and come ashore for picnic tables and toilets. Hire boats from **Mallacoota Hire Boats** (☎ 0438 447 558; Main Wharf) for $55 for two hours and $15 per extra hour. They also rent fishing rods for $10.

Hit the water under your own steam with **Blue Ocean Kayaks** (☎ 0429 028 017; half/full day $70/100).

A number of operators offer boat cruises; most require advance booking:
MV Loch-Ard (☎ 03-5158 0764; Main Wharf; adult/child 2hr cruise $25/10, 3hr cruise $38/12) Runs several inlet cruises with wildlife spotting.
Porkie Bess (☎ 03-5158 0109, 0408 408 094; 2hr cruise $25, fishing trip $50) A 1940s wooden boat offering fishing trips and cruises around the lakes, and ferry services for hikers ($20 per person, minimum four).

Rumbottle's Wilderness River Cruises (☎ 03-5158 8291; Gipsy Point Wharf; 2½hr cruise adult/child $15/18; ☼ 1.30pm Sun, Tue, Fri) Eco-cruises spotting sea eagles on the Genoa River and Maramingo Creek.
Wilderness Coast Ocean Charters (☎ 03-5158 0701, 0418 553 809; wildcoast@dragnet.com.au) Runs trips to Gabo Island ($60, minimum seven) and may run trips down the coast to view the seal colony off Wingan Inlet if there's enough demand.

SLEEPING
Prices vary significantly with the seasons; book ahead for Christmas or Easter. There are no backpacker hostels, but some of the half-dozen caravan parks offer budget cabins or bunkrooms. **Mallacoota Houseboats** (☎ 03-5158 0775; 3-night minimum $850) are a great way to explore the magic waterways. They sleep up to six.

Mallacoota Hotel Motel (☎ 03-5158 0455; www.mallacootahotel.com.au; 51-55 Maurice Ave; s/d from $70/90; 🅿 🐾) The most central of Mallacoota's numerous motels, and attached to the local pub, the rooms here are comfortable, well equipped and reasonably priced. The bistro is good with mains around $16 to $35 and a big outdoor terrace.

our pick **Adobe Mudbrick Flats** (☎ 03-5158 0329; www.adobeholidayflats.com.au; 17 Karbeethong Ave; 2-/4-bed apt $80/100) A labour of love by Margaret and Peter Kurz, these unique mud-brick flats are something special. With an emphasis on recycling and eco-friendliness, there's solar hot water and guests are encouraged to compost their kitchen scraps. Birds, lizards and possums can be hand-fed outside your door. The array of whimsical apartments are comfortable, well equipped and incredibly cheap. A real find.

Karbeethong Lodge (☎ 03-5158 0411; www.karbeethonglodge.com.au; 16 Schnapper Point Dr; d with/without bathroom from $95/75) This delightful early-1900s timber guest house has uninterrupted views over Mallacoota Inlet from the broad verandahs. Karbeethong is perfect for self-caterers, with a large communal kitchen and the guest lounge and dining room have open fires and period furnishings.

Mallacoota Foreshore Caravan Park (☎ 03-5158 0300; www.mallacootaholidaypark.com.au; unpowered/powered sites $17/21; 🐾) Curling around the inlet, the grassy sites here morph into one of Victoria's most sociable and scenic caravan parks with sublime views of the inlet and its resident population of black swans and pelicans. No cabins, but the best of Mallacoota's many parks for campers.

EATING

Croajingolong Café (☎ 03-5158 0098; Allan Dr; mains $5-15; ☺ breakfast & lunch Tue-Sun) This friendly cafe is a perfect place to linger over a latte and watch the world move slowly by. Wi-fi hotspot.

Lucy's (☎ 03-5158 0666; 64 Maurice Ave; mains $9-19; ☺ 8am-8pm; ▣)) Lucy is gaining a heady reputation for her homemade rice noodles, dumplings and abalone. A tasty bowl of noodles is great value at $9 and it's a good spot for breakfast on the terrace. Internet access is $2 for 15 minutes.

Tide Restaurant & Bar (☎ 03-5158 0100; cnr Maurice Ave & Allan Dr; mains $19-26; ☺ dinner from 6pm) Tide serves quality seafood from its prime lakeside position. Dine on the deck and arrive early for happy hour drinks from 5pm.

GETTING THERE & AWAY

Mallacoota is 23km off the Princes Hwy from Genoa. From Melbourne you can catch a daily **V/Line** (☎ 13 61 96) train to Bairnsdale and bus to Genoa ($48 one way, 7½ hours), then get the **Mallacoota-Genoa Bus Service** (☎ 0408 315 615), which meets the V/Line coach on Monday, Thursday and Friday, plus Sunday during school holidays ($3.40 one way, bookings essential).

Croajingolong National Park

The coastal wilderness park of Croajingolong (87,500 hectares) is one of Australia's finest national parks. It stretches for about 100km from Bemm River to the NSW border and includes unspoiled beaches, inlets and forests. The 200m sand dunes at Thurra are the highest on the mainland. Mallacoota Inlet is the largest and most accessible area. There's plentiful wildlife in the park, including huge goannas.

Walkers must be suitably equipped for long-distance walking, with sufficient maps and information on conditions. Contact **Parks Victoria** (☎ Cann River 03-5158 6351, Mallacoota 03-5158 0219) for information, camping permits and track notes. All access roads from the Princes Hwy, except Mallacoota Rd, are unsealed and can be very rough; check conditions with Parks Victoria.

The main camping areas are at Wingan Inlet, Shipwreck Creek, Thurra River and Mueller Inlet. You may need to bring water so check with Parks Victoria. During peak season there's a ballot system for campsites, but space is usually reserved at Wingan Inlet for walk-ins; camping fees cost up to $21 a site.

Point Hicks was the first part of Australia to be spotted by Captain Cook in 1770. Experience the windy and isolated ruggedness at **Point Hicks Lighthouse** (☎ 03-5158 4268; www.pointhicks.com.au; up to 6 people $230-300), with ocean views and wood fires. There's a two-night minimum stay and prices are higher on weekends; bring all your own food. There's also a bungalow ($80 for two) and camping. There's a rugged access road leading 45km from Cann River.

Tasmania

Dazzlin' Tassie is brilliant, beautiful and accessible. It's compact enough to 'do' in a few weeks and layered enough to keep bringing you back. The island state has exquisite beaches, jagged mountain ranges, rarefied alpine plateaus, plentiful wildlife and vast tracts of virgin wilderness, much of it within a World Heritage area. Tasmania produces some of the world's great gourmet food and wine, and has a flourishing arts scene and a burgeoning urban cool.

For too long Australian mainlanders derided their compatriots across Bass Strait, partly because Tasmania took a long time to emerge from the ignominy of its grim past. The first 100 years of European settlement were mired in violence and deprivations imposed upon the island's Indigenous peoples and convicts, and there remains a pervading sense of melancholy and loss. But this is only part of Tasmania's confounding enigma. It's where the courses of mighty rivers were changed to generate hydro-electricity, where railways were built across impossible terrain and where miners and pioneers eked out meagre means in the most hostile and isolated environments. It's a land of contradictions – of wilderness and logging trucks, wildlife and road kill, where the relics of a cruel history are all the more affecting because they're so heartbreakingly beautiful.

Tassie's bushwalking, cycling, rafting and kayaking opportunities rank among the best on the planet. See voluptuous Wineglass Bay, brilliant Bay of Fires and the ragged craggy glory of Cradle Mountain. Come and camp out, or doss down in some superb boutique hotel accommodation. Tasmania is still Australia, but beguilingly, bewitchingly, a little different.

HIGHLIGHTS

- Surf the crowd around the stalls at Hobart's Saturday morning **Salamanca Market** (p644)
- Walk the **Overland Track** (p713), the essential Tasmanian bushwalk and Aussie rite of passage
- Ponder what was at **Port Arthur** (p667), the infamous penal settlement
- Pack a picnic and hike into photogenic **Wineglass Bay** (p674)
- Idle a while atop the oddball geologic formations at Wynyard's **Table Cape** (p701) and **The Nut** (p702) at Stanley
- Ride the chairlift high over Launceston's gorgeous **Cataract Gorge** (p681)
- Taste and graze through the wonderful wineries and restaurants of **Tamar Valley** (p687)
- Retrace the old inland coach route past historic sandstone buildings in the **Midlands** (p668)

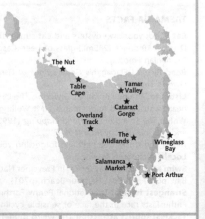

■ TELEPHONE CODE: 03   ■ POPULATION: 500,300   ■ AREA: 68,322 SQ KM

HISTORY

There were perhaps 10,000 Aborigines living on Tasmania when Dutchman Abel Janszoon Tasman became the first European to sight the island. His ships first came upon the island's northwest coast on 24 November 1642 and then skirted around the southern and southeastern coastlines. He named the island Van Diemen's Land after the Dutch East Indies' governor. Since Tasman's voyages yielded nothing of value for the Dutch East India Company, European contact with the island ceased for more than another century until the British arrived at Sydney Cove in 1788 – Van Diemen's Land would become a convenient pit stop en route to New South Wales (NSW). In 1798 Matthew Flinders circumnavigated Van Diemen's Land, proving it was an island.

In 1803 Risdon Cove, on the Derwent River, became the site of Australia's second British colony. The settlement moved a year later to the present site of Hobart, where fresh water ran plentifully off Mt Wellington.

Convicts accompanied the first settlers as labourers, but the grim penal settlements weren't built until later: on Sarah Island in Macquarie Harbour in 1822, on Maria Island in 1825 and at Port Arthur in 1830. In subsequent decades, Van Diemen's Land became infamous for the most apocalyptic punishments and deprivations exacted on convicts anywhere in the British colonies – the most fearsome, terrible of destinations. By the 1850s every second islander was a convict and Van Diemen's Land had whole industries exploiting the misery of convict labour. Hobart Town and Launceston festered with disease, prostitution and drunken lawlessness.

In 1856 the 'social experiment' of convict transportation to Van Diemen's Land was abolished. In an effort to escape the stigma of its horrendous penal reputation, Van Diemen's Land renamed itself Tasmania, after the Dutchman. By this time, however, the island's Aborigines had been practically annihilated by a mixture of concerted ethnic cleansing, disease, forced labour and ultimately doomed resettlement and assimilation schemes; see The Sorry Story of Tasmania's Aborigines, p660.

The 1870s and '80s saw prospectors arrive after gold was discovered, and the state's rugged and remote west was opened up by miners and timber workers seeking Huon pine, myrtle and sassafras. So began the exploitation of Tasmania's natural resources. In the 1960s and '70s conservationists fought unsuccessfully to stop the hydroelectric flooding of Lake Pedder. In the 1980s the issue flared again, this time the fledgling Green movement successfully campaigned against flooding the Franklin River for similar purposes. The tug-of-war between conservation groups and industry (especially logging and mining) remains *the* most divisive issue on Tasmanian political, economic and social agendas; see Deforestation in Tasmania, p664.

GEOGRAPHY & CLIMATE

Tasmania's northern and southeastern coastal areas have fertile, undulating countryside and

---

TASMANIA FACTS

Eat Shuck your own oysters and eat sunset fish 'n' chips anywhere by the water

Drink A 10-ounce (285mL) glass of beer (Cascade in the south, Boag's in the north) or a cheeky Tasmanian Pinot

Read Richard Flanagan's *Gould's Book of Fish,* Henry Reynolds' *Fate of a Free People* and David Owen's *Thylacine*

Listen to Monique Brumby's *Thylacine,* The Drones' *Gala Mill* (recorded in an old mill at Cranbrook near Swansea) and Augie March's 'Mt Wellington Reverie' from *Moo You Bloody Choir*

Watch *The Sound of One Hand Clapping* (1998), *For the Term of His Natural Life* (TV series, 1983) and *The Tale of Ruby Rose* (1988)

Avoid Log trucks, road kill and forgetting your wetsuit

Locals' nickname Taswegians

Swim at Wineglass Bay (p674) in Freycinet National Park (as if you could *not* come here!), Binalong Bay (p678) and Boat Harbour Beach (p701)

Strangest festival The National Penny Farthing Championships at Evandale (p691) – dozens of enthusiasts race in the face of sensible cycling

Tackiest tourist attraction The weird model village of Lower Crackpot at Tasmazia (p697)

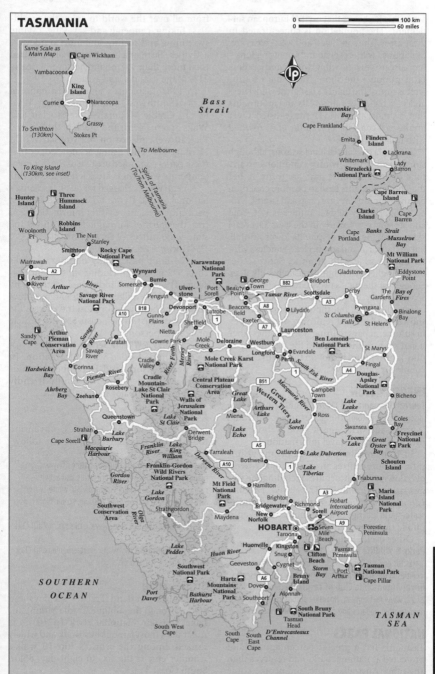

TASMANIA

0 — 100 km
0 — 60 miles

Bass Strait

Same Scale as Main Map

Cape Wickham
Yambacoona
King Island
Currie · Naracoopa
Grassy
Stokes Pt

To Smithton (130km)

To Melbourne

To King Island (130km, see inset)

Spirit of Tasmania (To/from Melbourne)

Killiecrankie Bay
Cape Frankland
Emita · Flinders Island · Lackrana
Whitemark · Lady Barron
Strzelecki National Park

Cape Barren Island
Clarke Island
Cape Barren

Cape Portland
Banks Strait
Musselroe Bay
Mt William National Park

Hunter Island
Three Hummock Island
Woolnorth Pt
Robbins Island
The Nut · Stanley
Smithton
Rocky Cape National Park
Wynyard
Somerset · Burnie
Marrawah
Arthur River
Arthur River
Penguin
Ulverstone
Savage River National Park
B18
A10
Devonport
Gunns Plains
Nietta
Sheffield
Gladstone
Bridport
B82
George Town
Beauty Point
Port Sorell
Beaconsfield
Exeter
Lulworth
A8
Tamar River
Scottsdale
Derby
The Gardens
Bay of Fires
Pyengana
Binalong Bay
St Columba Falls
St Helens
Narawntapu National Park

Sandy Cape
Arthur Pieman Conservation Area
Corinna
Savage River
Waratah
Gowrie Park
Cradle Valley
Pieman River
Rosebery
Zeehan
Queenstown
Strahan
Cape Sorell
Macquarie Harbour
Ahrberg Bay
Hardwicke Bay

Mole Creek
Deloraine
Westbury
Longford
Perth
Evandale
Mole Creek Karst National Park
Cradle Mountain-Lake St Clair National Park
Central Plateau Conservation Area
Walls of Jerusalem National Park
Great Lake
Miena
Arthurs Lake
Lake Echo
B51
Western Tiers
Launceston
South Esk River
Ben Lomond National Park
St Marys
Fingal
Douglas-Apsley National Park
A4
Campbell Town
Bicheno
Ross
Lake Sorell
Swansea
Coles Bay
Freycinet National Park
Great Oyster Bay
Schouten Island

Macquarie River
Lake Leake
Tooms Lake
Great Oyster Bay

Lake St Clair
Derwent Bridge
Franklin River
Lake King William
Franklin-Gordon Wild Rivers National Park
Tarraleah
A5
Oatlands · Lake Dulverton
Bothwell
A10
Lake Tiberias
A3
Triabunna
Maria Island National Park

Southwest Conservation Area
Gordon River
Strathgordon
Lake Gordon
Mt Field National Park
Hamilton
Brighton
Bridgewater
New Norfolk
Richmond
Sorell
Hobart International Airport
A9
Forestier Peninsula
Derwent River
Maydena
Olga River

Lake Pedder
Huon River
Huonville
Kingston
Snug
Cygnet
Clifton Beach
Storm Bay
Tasman Peninsula
Port Arthur
Tasman National Park
Cape Pillar
Seven Mile Beach
Taroona
HOBART

Southwest National Park
Geeveston
Hartz Mountains National Park
A6
Dover
Southport
Bruny Island
Alonnah
South Bruny National Park
Tasman Head
D'Entrecasteaux Channel

SOUTHERN OCEAN

Port Davey
Bathurst Harbour
South West Cape
South Cape
South East Cape

TASMAN SEA

TASMANIA

632 TASMANIA •• Information

accessible harbours that invited European settlement. The population is concentrated in these areas. The southwest and west coasts are, by contrast, wild, desolate and remote regions – monstrous seas, howling winds and endless rains pummel the shore. Tasmania's southwest is one of the planet's last great wilderness areas – a region of rainforests and mountains that is almost all World Heritage–listed. Over on the east coast it's dry, sunny and crowded with holidaymakers.

Tasmania has four distinct seasons, although storms can deliver wintry conditions at any time of year. Summer days are warm rather than hot and nights tend to be more cool than balmy. Autumn days are crisp and sunny, with occasional frosty nights. Winter is wet, cold and stormy, particularly in the west. Overcast skies cloak the east, despite its lower rainfall, but in the north and south, clear, windless winter days sparkle with promise. Snow settles on the higher peaks but it's usually only deep enough for the state's two ski resorts to operate spasmodically. Spring is windy and storms still sweep the island, but the sun shines between showers and hints at returning summer. Even in summer it pays to bring warm clothes since it can snow in the west and the mountains in mid-January (and be hot on the north coast, a couple of hours' drive away).

INFORMATION

Tourism Tasmania (☎ 1300 827 743, 03-6230 8235; www .discovertasmania.com), the government-operated tourism authority, has a good website and provides loads of travel information.

In Tasmania itself, there are helpful visitor information centres in most major towns, overflowing with brochures including the free newspapers *Tasmanian Travelways*, *Treasure Island* and *Explore Tasmania*, all containing state-wide listings of accommodation, events, public transport and vehicle hire.

Other useful information sources:

Parks & Wildlife Service (☎ 1300 315 513; www .parks.tas.gov.au) Details walks, campsites, activities and facilities in the state's magical national parks and reserves.
Royal Automobile Club of Tasmania (RACT; ☎ 13 27 22; www.ract.com.au) Roadside automotive assistance, road weather updates and general travel information.

NATIONAL PARKS

Tasmania has a greater percentage of land protected as national parks and reserves than any other Australian state, and people come from all over the world to enjoy the world-class hiking, canoeing and kayaking, caving, swimming and surfing, and other outdoorsy activities. Tasmania has 19 national parks that total more than 1.4 million hectares – nearly 21% of the island's land area.

In 1982 Tasmania's four largest national parks (Southwest, Franklin-Gordon Wild Rivers, Cradle Mountain-Lake St Clair and Walls of Jerusalem) and much of the Central Plateau were placed on the Unesco World Heritage list. This listing acknowledges that these parks combined are one of the last great temperate wilderness areas left in the world.

An entry fee is charged for all of Tasmania's national parks. Passes are available at most park entrances, many visitor information centres, the *Spirit of Tasmania* ferries and at the state-wide offices of **Service Tasmania** (☎ 1300 135 513; www.service.tas.gov.au).

A 24-hour pass to any number of parks costs $22 per car (including up to eight passengers) or $11 per individual (arriving by bus, or for bushwalkers, cyclists and motorcyclists). The best value for most travellers is the eight-week pass, which costs $56 per vehicle or $28 per person.

The **Parks & Wildlife Service** (www.parks.tas.gov .au) website is loaded with information. In the peak season (mid-December to mid-February) rangers run free family-friendly activities at the major national parks.

ACTIVITIES

For information on activities, adventure tourism and tour operators, see the following websites:

Networking Tasmanian Adventures (www.tasma nianadventures.com.au) Lists operators and activities, categorised as either 'wild' (scuba diving, white-water rafting, abseiling etc) or 'mild' (fishing, scenic flights, river cruises etc).
Parks & Wildlife Service (www.parks.tas.gov.au) Click on 'Recreation'.
Tourism Tasmania (www.discovertasmania.com) Click on 'Activities & Attractions'.

Bushwalking

Tasmania's Overland Track – six days and 65km through the sublime Cradle Mountain-Lake St Clair National Park (p710) – is Australia's most famous bushwalk and widely ranked among the world's top 10 walks. Another epic is the six- to eight-day, 85km South Coast Track.

Lonely Planet's *Walking in Australia* has info on some of Tasmania's best (longer) walks. Some of Tassie's wilderness areas can be experienced on much shorter walks: Parks & Wildlife Service's *60 Great Short Walks* brochure (free from visitor information centres) lists the state's best short walks from 10-minute strolls to day-long hikes. Check the **Parks & Wildlife Service** (www.parks.tas.gov.au) website for more information.

On long walks remember that in any Tasmanian season a beautiful day can quickly turn ugly, so warm clothing, waterproof gear, a tent, map and compass are essential. **Tasmap** (www.tasmap.tas.gov.au) produces excellent maps available online or from visitor information centres. In Hobart you'll also find them at **Service Tasmania** (Map p640; ☎ 1300 135 513; www.service.tas.gov.au; 134 Macquarie St; ⏰ 8.15am-5pm Mon-Fri) and the **Tasmanian Map Centre** (Map p640; ☎ 03-6231 9043; www.map-centre.com.au; 100 Elizabeth St; ⏰ 9.30am-5.30pm Mon-Fri, 10am-4pm Sat), as well as state-wide outdoor stores.

Shops that sell outdoor gear are common in Hobart and Launceston and they have shelves full of books on walking in Tasmania. Some youth hostels also hire out equipment and/or run guided bushwalking tours.

Fishing

For all things fishy in Tasmania, go to www.fishing.tas.gov.au.

Tasmania's Lake Country on the Central Plateau features glacial lakes, crystal-clear streams and world-class trout fishing. There are dozens of operators that can help you organise guides, lessons or fishing trips – **Trout Guides & Lodges Tasmania** (www.troutguidestasmania.com.au) is a great starting point.

Meanwhile on the east coast charter fishing is big business. See www.fishnet.com.au for a directory of operators.

Rafting & Sea-Kayaking

The Franklin River is famous for full-bore white-water rafting (p710) and the Parks & Wildlife website has good information. Other rivers offering rapid thrills include the Derwent (upstream from Hobart) the Picton (southwest of Hobart) and the Mersey in the north.

Sea-kayaking centres include Kettering southeast of Hobart (p658), from where you can explore the D'Entrecasteaux Channel, Bruny Island and the southwest coast; and Coles Bay, the launching place for Freycinet Peninsula

explorations (p674). You can also have a paddle around the Hobart docks (p644).

Sailing

The D'Entrecasteaux Channel and Huon River south of Hobart are wide, deep and tantalising places to set sail, with more inlets and harbours than you could swing a boom at. For casual berths in Hobart (overnight or weekly), contact the **Royal Yacht Club of Tasmania** (☎ 03-6223 4599; www.ryct.org.au) in Sandy Bay, or **Tasports** (☎ 1300 366 742; www.tasports.com.au), which manages berths in Hobart city and ports around Tasmania.

If you're an experienced sailor, hire a yacht from **Yachting Holidays** (☎ 03-6224 3195; www.yachtingholidays.com.au), based in Hobart. Charter of a six-berth vessel is $700 per day, with reduced rates for long rentals or in the off-peak (April to November) period. Skippered charter is also available.

Scuba Diving

Despite the chilly water there are some excellent diving opportunities, particularly on the east coast. A new artificial site was created by the scuttling of the *Troy D* in 2007 off the west coast of Maria Island – see www.troyd.com.au for information on diving and permits. Rocky Cape on the north coast offers marine life aplenty, while shipwrecks abound around King and Flinders Islands.

Tasmanian diving courses are considerably cheaper than on the mainland. Contact operators at the Bay of Fires (p679), Eaglehawk Neck (p666), Bicheno (p676) and King Island (p715). Equipment can be hired from licensed divers from dive shops around the state – **Tassie Divers** (www.tassiedivers.com) lists accredited operators, shops and clubs.

Surfing

Tasmania has dozens of brilliant surfing spots with point and reef breaks as well as river mouths. Don't think of going in with anything less than a full-length steamer because the water is friggin' cold! Close to Hobart, the most reliable spots are Clifton Beach and Goats Beach (unsigned) en route to South Arm. The southern beaches on Bruny Island (p659), particularly Whalebone Point in Cloudy Bay, offer consistent swell. The east coast from Bicheno north to St Helens has solid beach breaks when conditions are working. At Marrawah (p703) on the west coast the waves are often towering – hard-core lines all the way to South America! Shipstern Bluff is a two-hour walk into the Tasman National Park on the Tasman Peninsula south of Port Arthur around Raoul Bay, and is allegedly Australia's heaviest wave – wicked! Kids riding esky lids would be better suited to the east coast's numerous beach breaks.

Websites with surf reports and conditions updates include www.tassiesurf.com and www.coastview.com.au. See also Where to Surf in Australia, p490.

Swimming

The north and east coasts offer countless sheltered, white-sand beaches with excellent swimming, but you'll find the water rather cold. Some of the most beautiful swimming beaches include Wineglass Bay (p674), Bay of Fires (watch for rips; p679), Binalong Bay outside St Helens (p678), and lovely Boat Harbour Beach (p701) and Penguin Beach (p698).

For safe sea swimming around Hobart, skip the urban beaches and head south to the beaches at Kingston Beach or Blackmans Bay (p657), or east to Seven Mile Beach (p657). The surf on the open west-coast beaches can be very dangerous and the beaches aren't patrolled – play it safe.

TOURS

Travel agents can arrange package deals from the mainland including transport to Tasmania (by air or sea), car rental and accommodation. Contact Tourism Tasmania (p632).

There are many in-bound Tasmanian operators vying hard in a competitive business for your tourist dollars, so shop around and compare products. Tour operators can shunt you around to the highlights or provide you with authentic wilderness or activ-

---

SYDNEY TO HOBART YACHT RACE

The **Sydney to Hobart Yacht Race** (www
.rolexsydneyhobart.com), the world's greatest
and most treacherous open-ocean yacht
race, winds up at Hobart's Constitution Dock
around New Year's Eve after a full-tilt sprint
down Australia's southeast coast. As the
storm-battered maxis limp across the finish
line, champagne corks pop and sailors turn
the town upside down. It's a great few days
to spend in Hobart when you can watch the
New Year's Eve fireworks across the water,
chow down on first-class food and wine at
the Taste Festival (p646) and count spinnakers on the river as the yachts make their up
the Derwent to Constitution Dock.

---

ity-based experiences. Most trips depart from Hobart, but some operators use Devonport or Launceston as a base. Businesses are listed in the relevant sections of this chapter. Some other suggestions:

Bottom Bits Bus (☎ 1800 777 103, 03-6224 2316; www.bottombitsbus.com.au) One- to 10-day small-group trips out of Hobart, most of which take in the far south. Affiliated with Smash & Grab (below).

Craclair Tours (☎ 03-6424 7833; www.craclair.com.au) Guided four- to 16-day walking tours and treks around the Cradle Mountain and Walls of Jerusalem areas and longer treks along the South Coast Track.

Escape Tours Tasmania (☎ 1800 133 555, www.es capetourstasmania.com.au) One-, four- and five-day tours of essential Tassie highlights (Cradle Mountain, Freycinet National Park, Port Arthur etc).

Island Cycle Tours (☎ 1300 880 334, 03-6234 4951; www.islandcycletours.com) Hobart-based guided cycling trips – Mt Wellington descents, day trips, combined walking/cycling and cycling/sea-kayaking tours, and gourmet bike rides. Affiliated with Under Down Under (opposite).

Jump Tours (☎ 03-6273 6918, 0422 120 630; www .jumptours.com) Cheeky new start-up getting rave reviews that focuses on youth- and backpacker-oriented three- and five-day Tassie tours.

Smash & Grab (☎ 1800 777 103; www.tourstasmania .com.au) Hobart-based one-, two-, three- and five-day tours to the hot spots (Port Arthur, Cradle Mountain, Wineglass Bay etc) with multilingual guides.

Tarkine Trails (☎ 03-6223 5320; www.tarkinetrails .com.au) Green-focused group offering guided walks in the Tarkine wilderness, the Walls of Jerusalem and the Overland Track.

TASafari (☎ 1300 882 415, 03-6395 1577; www .tasafari.com.au) Ecoaccredited three-day eastern tours

---

TASTING TASSIE

Tasmania has very successfully reinvented itself in the last decade or so as premier foodie destination, and sampling the tasty local fare is a real highlight – fresh seafood, berries, stone fruit, dairy products and cool-climate wines are abundant and simply outstanding. To bone up on the best of the state's wine and foodie fare read Graeme Phillip's **Eat Drink Tasmania** (www.eatdrinktasmania .com.au), updated annually and available for $20 from visitor information centres, newsagents and bookshops. There's also Tourism Tasmania's *Farm Gate Guide* brochure that you can pickup at visitor information centres or download from www.discovertasmania.com/brochures. The **Taste Festival** (www.tastefestival.com.au) on the Hobart waterfront between 28 December and 3 January showcases the best of Tasmania's food and wine. Try the paella with mussels and chorizo with a local Sauvignon Blanc. Tasty…

(from Hobart), five-day western tours (from Launceston) or nine-day combined tours from either city.

Tasmanian Expeditions (☎ 1300 666 856, 03-6339 3999; www.tas-ex.com) Excellent range of state-wide activity-based tours, from half-day to 16 days: bushwalking, river-rafting, rock climbing, cycling and kayaking, or a combo of these.

Under Down Under (☎ 1800 064 726, 03-6362 2237; www.underdownunder.com.au) Nature-based, backpacker-friendly trips, including two- to nine-day tours of the east coast, west coast and the Tarkine wilderness. Tour fees refunded for photographed thylacine sightings!

GETTING THERE & AWAY

Tasmania's quarantine service rigorously protects the state's disease-free agriculture – all visitors (including those from mainland Australia) must dispose of all plants, fruits and vegetables prior to or upon arrival.

If you're travelling in a group or family and want to take a vehicle to Tasmania, the cheapest option is to combine cheap airline tickets with Virgin Blue or Jetstar for the bulk of the group, and car and driver-only passage on the ferry from Melbourne (right).

Air

There are no direct international flights to/from Tasmania. Airlines flying between Tasmania and mainland Australia:

Jetstar (☎ 13 15 38; www.jetstar.com.au) Direct flights from Melbourne, Sydney and Brisbane to Hobart and Launceston.

Qantas (☎ 13 13 13; www.qantas.com.au) Direct flights from Sydney and Melbourne to Hobart, and from Melbourne to Launceston. QantasLink (the regional subsidiary) flies between Melbourne and Devonport.

Regional Express (REX; ☎ 13 17 13; www.regional express.com.au) Flies from Melbourne to Burnie and King Island.

Virgin Blue (☎ 13 67 89; www.virginblue.com.au) Direct flights from Melbourne, Sydney, Brisbane and Adelaide to Hobart, and from Melbourne and Sydney to Launceston.

Boat

The **Spirit of Tasmania** (☎ 1800 634 906; www.spirit oftasmania.com.au) operates two ferries that cruise nightly between Melbourne and Devonport in both directions, usually departing at 9pm and taking about 10 hours shore to shore. Additional daytime sailings are scheduled during peak and shoulder seasons. Fares vary for travel in peak (mid-December to late January), shoulder (late January to April, and September to mid-December) and off-peak (May to August) seasons. There's a range of cabin and seat options, and child, student, pensioner and senior discounts apply. Some cabins are wheelchair-accessible. And you can bring your car!

The Devonport terminal is on The Esplanade in East Devonport (Map p692); the Melbourne terminal is at Station Pier in Port Melbourne (Map pp494–5). Standard one-way adult fares are as follows; limited 'Ship Saver' fares are cheaper.

Fare type	Peak ($)	Shoulder ($)	Off-peak ($)
Ocean-view recliner seat	202	170	148
4-berth cabin	258	236	226
Twin cabin	308	263	252
Daytime sailings (unallocated seating only)	179	128	122
Standard vehicles & campervans (up to 5m)	65	65	65
Motorbikes	45	45	45
Bicycles	6	6	6

TASMANIA

GETTING AROUND

Air

Air travel within Tasmania is uncommon, but bushwalkers sometimes use light air services to/from the southwest. **Par Avion** (☎ 1800 144 460, 03-6248 5390; www.paravion.com.au) and **Tasair** (☎ 1800 062 900, 03-6248 5088; www.tasair.com.au) fly between Hobart and remote Melaleuca (for the South Coast Track) one way/return for $195/370 and $214/395 respectively.

There are also air links from mainland Tasmania to King Island (p716) and Flinders Island (p717).

Bicycle

Tassie is a good size for exploring by bicycle and is a perennial favourite with visiting touring cyclists. Though beware – some areas are pretty hilly and the weather can be unpredictable but the routes are scenic and the towns aren't too far apart. You can hire touring bikes in Hobart (p644) and Launceston (p687). Cycling between Hobart and Launceston via either coast (the east coast is a cycling favourite) usually takes 10 to 14 days. For a full 'Lap of the Map', allow 18 to 28 days.

If you're planning a trip on the island, **Bicycle Tasmania** (www.biketas.org.au) is a solid source of information, including state-wide bike shop listings.

Bus

The main bus lines are **Redline Coaches** (☎ 1300 360 000, 03-6336 1446; www.tasredline.com .au) and **TassieLink** (☎ 1300 300 520, 03-6230 8900; www.tassielink.com.au) and between them they cover most of the state, running along most major highways year-round (though their weekend services are less frequent). Redline services the Midland Hwy between Hobart and Launceston, the north coast between Launceston and Smithton, north from Launceston to George Town, and to the east coast. TassieLink runs from both Hobart and Launceston to the west and to the east coast, from Hobart to Port Arthur, and south from Hobart down the Huon Valley. Redline's Main Road Express connects Bass Strait ferry arrivals/departures in Devonport to Launceston, Hobart and Burnie.

Over summer, TassieLink buses also run to popular bushwalking destinations. Special fares that enable you to be dropped off at the start of a walk and picked up at the end

are offered. Check the TassieLink website and click on 'Walking Track Links' for more information.

Additionally, **Metro Tasmania** (☎ 13 22 01; www.metrotas.com.au) runs regular services south from the Hobart as far as Woodbridge and Cygnet, and north to Richmond and New Norfolk. Smaller operators service important tourist routes – see relevant chapter sections for details.

Bus fares in Tasmania are quite reasonable: a one-way trip between Devonport and Launceston is around $20 and takes 1½ hours, Hobart to Launceston is $31 (2½ hours) and Hobart to Devonport is $52 (four hours).

BUS PASSES

TassieLink has an Explorer Pass for seven/10/14/21 days that must be used within 10/15/20/30 days and costs $208/248/286/329. Available from travel agents or directly from TassieLink, the pass is valid on all scheduled services for unlimited kilometres. Ask for timetables in advance or check TassieLink's website to plan your itinerary.

Similarly, Redline offers the Tassie Pass for unlimited travel for seven/10/14/21 days at a cost of $135/160/185/219. The Redline network isn't as comprehensive as TassieLink's, so compare timetables and assess your options.

Car, Campervan & Motorcycle

Tassie is ideal for travelling by road, whether by car, campervan or motorcycle. The distances are relatively short, fuel is readily available and the driving conditions are generally pretty good. You can bring vehicles across on the ferry from the mainland, but renting may be cheaper, particularly for shorter trips, and rates are usually more affordable here than on the mainland. If you're renting, always ask your hirer's policy on driving on unsealed roads because quite a few of Tasmania's natural attractions are reached by dirt road. Generally the deal is that you'll void your insurance if you get off the bitumen, but life's all about weighing up calculated risks, huh?

There are few road hazards but watch out for wildlife and avoid driving between dusk and dawn when critters are active (road kill is ubiquitous). One-lane bridges on country roads and log trucks speeding around sharp corners also demand caution. In cold weather, be wary of 'black ice' on shady mountain passes.

Big international players like Avis, Budget, Europcar and Thrifty have booking desks at airports and in major towns, with standard rates for small-car hire from $50 to $80 per day in high season. By booking well in advance, for a week's hire or more, car-hire rates can fall dramatically, especially outside high season. Web engines like **Vroom Vroom Vroom** (www.vroomvroomvroom.com.au) compare rental deals and can turn up some bargains.

Small local firms rent older cars for as little as $35 a day, depending on the season and rental length. They'll often ask for a bond of $300 or more. Some companies let you collect your car from the airport or ferry terminal. Some operators:

Lo-Cost Auto Rent (www.locostautorent.com) Hobart (Map p640; ☎ 03-6231 0550; 105 Murray St); Launceston (Map p682; ☎ 03-6334 3437; 80 Tamar St); Devonport (Map p692; ☎ 03-6427 0796; 5 Murray St)

Rent-a-Bug (www.rentabug.com.au) Hobart (Map p640; ☎ 03-6231 0300; 105 Murray St); Launceston (Map p682; ☎ 03-6334 3437; 80 Tamar St); Devonport (Map p692; ☎ 03-6427 9034; 5 Murray St)

Selective Car Rentals (Map p640; ☎ 1800 300 102, 03-6234 3311; www.selectivecarrentals.com.au; 47 Bathurst St, Hobart)

Well-surfaced scenic roads and relatively light traffic make motorcycling in Tasmania fantastic. Contact **Tasmanian Motorcycle Hire** (☎ 03-6391 9139; www.tasmotorcyclehire.com.au) if you want to make like Wyatt and Billy from *Easy Rider*.

Campervanning is hugely popular in Tasmania, with hundreds of white vans tootling along the roads. With loads of camping grounds, free-camping areas and a generally laissez-faire attitude to bunking down by the roadside, Tassie is *the* place for a campervanning holiday. And with a bed and a bus rolled into one, they're economical, too (from around $80 per day). Generally you get what you pay for with a rental camper, and for any more than a cosy couple you probably want to upgrade from the basic entry-level vehicle. The big players are **Britz** (☎ 1800 468 082; www.britz .com.au) and **Maui** (☎ 1300 363 800; www.maui.com.au), and there are specialist campervan-rental web engines like **Fetch** (www.fetchcampervanhire.com.au), **Cheap Motorhome Hire** (www.cheaptasmaniamotorhome hire.com.au) and **Getabout Oz** (www.getaboutoz.com). Reliable local hirers:

Campervan Hire Tasmania (☎ 03-6391 9357; www .campervanhiretasmania.com)

Tasmanian Campervan Hire (☎ 03-6248 9623; www.tascamper.com)

Tasmanian Campervan Rentals (☎ 03-6248 5638; www.tasmaniacampervanrentals.com.au)

HOBART

pop 200,525

Hobart rocks! It's Australia's second-oldest city and southernmost capital, lying at the foothills of Mt Wellington on the banks of the Derwent River. The waterfront areas around Sullivans Cove – Macquarie Wharf, Constitution Dock, Salamanca Place and Battery Point – are simply gorgeous with their neat Georgian buildings and the towering bulk of Mt Wellington behind. The town's rich colonial heritage and natural charms are accented by a spirited, rootsy atmosphere: festivals, superb restaurants and hip urban bars abound. Hobartians are super-relaxed, very friendly and have none of the haughtiness of the Melbourne and Sydney gentry. They hang out in cafes and pubs, joking and idly watching the daily rush, dressed ready for their next wilderness expedition. On summer afternoons the sea breeze blows and yachts tack across the river. On winter mornings the pea-soup 'Bridgewater Jerry' fog lifts to reveal the snow-capped summit of the mountain.

HISTORY

The seminomadic Mouheneer people were the original inhabitants of the area. Risdon Cove on the Derwent's eastern shore was the first European settlement in 1803, but just a year later the settlers decamped to the site of present-day Hobart.

Britain's jails were overflowing with criminals in the 1820s, and so tens of thousands of convicts were chained together into rotting hulks and transported to Hobart Town to serve their sentences in vile conditions. By the 1850s Hobart was rife with sailors, soldiers, whalers, ratbags and prostitutes shamelessly boozing, brawling and bonking in and around countless harbour-side taverns.

The city has only ever partially sobered up – anytime is beer-o'clock at legendary Knopwood's – and today's criminals are more likely to be white-collared. Skeletons rattle in closets, but Hobart's shimmering beauty and relaxed vibe make it easy to forget they're there.

TASMANIA

HOBART

0 ————— 500 m
0 ————— 0.2 miles

The Gobles (1km);
Adelph Court YHA
(1km); Graham Court
Apartments (1km)

To Elwick Cabin &
Tourist Park (7km);
Moorilla Estate (11km);
Cadbury Chocolate
Factory (14km);
Launceston (197km)

To Royal Tasmanian
Botanical Gardens
(200m)

To Tasman Bridge (400m);
Barilla Holiday Park (12km);
Airport (15km); Seven
Mile Beach (15km);
Clifton Beach (20km);
Richmond (26km);
Port Arthur (99km);
East Coast

See Central Hobart Map (p640)

To Cascade Brewery (1.5km);
Female Factory (1.5km);
Mt Wellington (20km)

To Mt Nelson (7km); Kingston (10km); Huonville
(29km); Kettering (31km); The Southeast

To Taroona (5km);
Kingston (8km)

INFORMATION
RACT Travelworld 1 B2
STA Travel 2 C6

SIGHTS & ACTIVITIES
St George's Anglican Church 3 C4

SLEEPING ⌂
Battery Point Manor 4 D4
Corinda's Cottages 5 C2
Edinburgh Gallery 6 B4
Grosvenor Court 7 B5
Hobart Hostel 8 B3
Lodge on Elizabeth 9 B2
Mayfair Plaza Hotel 10 C5
Narrara Backpackers 11 B3
Pickled Frog 12 B3
Woolmers Inn 13 B4

EATING 🍴
Annapurna 14 A1
Fresco Market 15 A2
Kaos Café 16 B2
Onba ....(see 14)
Raincheck Lounge 17 A1
Restaurant 373 .... 18 A1
South Hobart Food Store 19 A5

DRINKING 🍷
Lizbon 20 B2
Shipwrights Arms Hotel 21 D4
Soak@Kaos ....(see 16)

ENTERTAINMENT 🎭
Republic Bar & Café 22 A2
State Cinema 23 A1

TRANSPORT
Airporter Shuttle Bus ....(see 24)
Redline Coaches ....(see 24)
Transit Centre 24 B4

TASMANIA

ORIENTATION

The compact and navigable city centre has a grid of one-way streets encircling the Elizabeth St Mall. The visitor information centre, banks and the main post office are on Elizabeth St, while the main shopping area extends west from the Mall.

Salamanca Place, an impressive row of sandstone Georgian warehouses, lines the southern fringe of Sullivans Cove, the city's harbour and social epicentre. Just south of Salamanca Place is Battery Point, Hobart's increasingly gentrified early colonial district. South of Battery Point is cashed-up Sandy Bay, home to the University of Tasmania and the landmark/eyesore Wrest Point Casino.

The northern side of the city is bounded by the Queen's Domain (usually just called 'The Domain'), a bushy hillock that harbours the excellent Botanical Gardens. From here the Tasman Bridge arcs across the river to the eastern shore and the airport 16km away.

Maps

The visitor information centre issues simple city maps. For more comprehensive coverage try the *Hobart & Surrounds Street Directory* ($22) or the UBD *Tasmania Country Road Atlas* ($31), available at larger newsagents and bookshops. Travellers with physical disabilities should check out the useful *Hobart CBD Mobility Map* from the visitor information centre.

Maps sources in Hobart:

Hobart visitor information centre (Map p640; ☎ 03-6230 8233; www.hobarttravelcentre.com.au; cnr Davey & Elizabeth Sts; ☒ 8.30am-5.30pm Mon-Fri, 9am-5pm Sat, Sun & public holidays; ▣) Brochures, maps and information.

Service Tasmania (Map p640; ☎ 1300 135 513; www.service.tas.gov.au; 134 Macquarie St; ☒ 8.15am-5pm Mon-Fri)

Tasmanian Map Centre (Map p640; ☎ 03-6231 9043; www.map-centre.com.au; 100 Elizabeth St; ☒ 9.30am-5.30pm Mon-Fri, 10am-4pm Sat) Bushwalking maps and Lonely Planet guides.

INFORMATION

Bookshops

Fullers Bookshop (Map p640; ☎ 03-6224 2488; www.fullersbookshop.com.au; 140 Collins St; ☒ 9am-6pm Mon-Fri, to 5pm Sat, 10am-4pm Sun) Great range of literature and travel guides, plus a cafe upstairs.

Hobart Book Shop (Map p640; ☎ 03-6223 1803; www.hobartbookshop.com.au; 22 Salamanca Sq; ☒ 9am-6pm Mon-Fri, to 5pm Sat, 10am-5pm Sun) Tasmania-centric titles, Tassie writers and secondhand selections.

Wilderness Society Shop (Map p640; ☎ 03-6234 9370; www.wilderness.org.au; Shop 8, The Galleria, 33 Salamanca Pl; ☒ 9am-6pm Mon-Fri, to 5pm Sat & Sun) Environmental publications, wildlife posters, DVDs, maps and calendars.

Emergency

Hobart Police Station (Map p640; ☎ 03-6230 2111; www.police.tas.gov.au; 43 Liverpool St; ☒ 24hr)

Police, fire & ambulance (☎ 000)

HOBART IN...

Two Days

Stroll around the pretty colonial cottages and laneways of **Battery Point** (p642) and grab lunch or coffee 'n' cake at **Jackman & McRoss** (p651). Wander down to beautiful **Salamanca Place** (p642) and see **Salamanca Arts Centre** (p642). Look through the **Maritime Museum of Tasmania** (p643) and the **Tasmanian Museum & Art Gallery** (p643) before a saunter along the Sullivans Cove waterfront and fish 'n' chips for dinner at **Fish Frenzy** (p650) on Elizabeth Pier. Head to **Knopwood's Retreat** (p652), the quintessential Hobart pub, for a few after-dinner beers.

On day two, recover with coffee and eggs Benedict at **Retro Café** (p651) then join the freewheelin' **Mt Wellington Descent** (p644) for a coast down to the coast. Back at sea level dig into dinner, drinks and some live music at **Republic Bar & Café** (p653) in North Hobart.

Four Days

With bit more time on your hands, head out to **Moorilla Estate** (p643) for a long boozy lunch, or cruise south down the D'Entrecasteaux Channel to **Peppermint Bay** (p646). Snooze the afternoon away on the sunny lawns of the **Botanical Gardens** (p644) before a classy dinner at **Marque IV** (p651).

On day four visit the nearby historic town of **Richmond** (p655) for fabulous photo opportunities or the waterfalls and peaks of glorious **Mt Field National Park** (p656).

TASMANIA

lonelyplanet.com

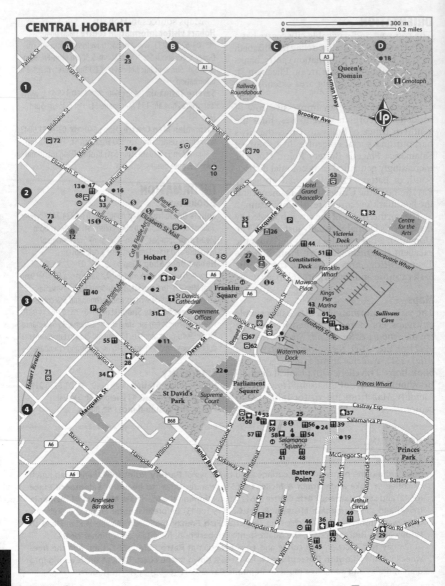

CENTRAL HOBART

TASMANIA

Internet Access

Internet cafes charge $5 to $6 per hour.

Drifters Internet Café (Map p640; ☎ 03-6224 6286; www.errolflynn.com.au; Shop 9, 33 Salamanca Pl; ☺ 9am-6.30pm)

Mouse on Mars (Map p640; ☎ 03-6231 5421; www .mouseonmars.com.au; 1st fl, 112 Liverpool St; ☺ 10am-10pm) State-wide wi-fi hot spots.

Service Tasmania (Map p640; ☎ 1300 135 513; www .service.tas.gov.au; 134 Macquarie St; ☺ 8.15am-5pm Mon-Fri) Free 30-minute access.

State Library (Map p640; ☎ 03-6233 7529; www .statelibrary.tas.gov.au; 91 Murray St; ☺ 9.30am-6pm Mon-Thu, to 9pm Fri, to 12.30pm Sat) Offers 30 minutes of free internet access for Australians; $5.50 for international visitors.

Internet Resources

Hobart City (www.hobartcity.com.au)
Tasmania's South (www.tasmaniasouth.com)

Media

Pick up free tourist publications highlighting Hobart's attractions from the visitor information centre. Hobart's long-running newspaper, the **Mercury** (www.themercury.com.au) is thin on quality global reportage but handy for what's on where – Thursday's edition lists entertainment options. The free monthly entertainment rag **Sauce** (www.sauce.net.au) provides detailed arts listings.

Medical Services

Chemist on Collins (Map p640; ☎ 03-6235 0257; www.chemistoncollins.com.au; 93 Collins St; ☼ 9am-5.30pm Mon-Thu, to 6pm Fri, 9.30am-4pm Sat)
City Doctors & Travel Clinic (Map p640; ☎ 03-6231 3003; www.citydoctors.com.au; 93 Collins St; ☼ 9am-5pm Mon-Fri) Standard consultation $60.

Royal Hobart Hospital (Map p640; ☎ 03-6222 8423; www.dhhs.tas.gov.au; 48 Liverpool St; ☼ 24hr) Argyle St emergency entry.

Money

The major banks have branches on or near the Elizabeth St Mall, plus suburban branches. There are ATMs in all major shopping precincts.

Post

General Post Office (GPO; Map p640; ☎ 13 13 18; www.austpost.com.au; cnr Elizabeth & Macquarie Sts; ☼ 8.30am-5.30pm Mon-Fri)

Tourist Information

Hobart visitor information centre (Map p640; ☎ 03-6230 8233; www.hobarttravelcentre.com.au; cnr Davey & Elizabeth Sts; ☼ 8.30am-5.30pm Mon-Fri, 9am-5pm Sat, Sun & public holidays; ☐) Brochures, maps, information and state-wide tour and accommodation bookings.
YHA (Map p640; ☎ 03-6234 9617; www.yha.com.au; 1st fl, 28 Criterion St; ☼ 9am-5pm Mon-Fri) YHA's Tasmanian HQ.

TASMANIA

Travel Agencies

Qantas Travel Centre (Map p640; ☎ 03-6237 4900; www.qantas.com.au; 130 Collins St; ☯ 9am-5pm Mon-Fri)

RACT Travelworld (Map p638; ☎ 13 27 22, 03-6232 6300; www.ract.com.au; cnr Murray & Patrick Sts; ☯ 8.45am-5pm Mon-Fri)

STA Travel (Map p638; ☎ 1300 360 960; www.statravel.com.au; Student Union Bldg, University of Tasmania, Sandy Bay; ☯ 9am-5pm Mon-Fri)

SIGHTS

The city centre and waterfront areas of Hobart are very picturesque, and all the places of interest are in easy walking distance of each other. You'll need wheels to explore the city outskirts and visit the historic houses and wineries of the Hobart environs. Make the effort to get up to the Mt Wellington summit from where, if you squint, you can almost see China.

Salamanca Place

This picturesque row of four-storey sandstone warehouses on Sullivans Cove (Map p640) is a wonderful example of Australian colonial architecture and the best-preserved and most cohesive historic urban precinct in all of the country. Salamanca Place was the hub of old Hobart Town's trade and commerce, but by the mid-20th century many of these 1830s whaling-era buildings had become decrepit ruins. The 1970s saw the dawning of Tasmania's sense of 'heritage', from which flowed a push to revive the warehouses as home to restaurants, cafes, bars and shops – an evolution that continues today. The development of the quarry behind the warehouses into **Salamanca Square** has bolstered the atmosphere.

Operating behind the scenes here is a vibrant and creative arts community. The non-profit **Salamanca Arts Centre** (Map p640; ☎ 03-6234 8414; www.salarts.org.au; 77 Salamanca Pl; ☯ shops & galleries 9am-6pm) occupies seven Salamanca warehouses and is home to 75-plus arts organisations and individuals, including shops, galleries, studios, performing arts venues and public spaces.

To reach Salamanca Place from Battery Point, descend the well-weathered **Kellys Steps**, wedged between warehouses halfway along the main block of buildings.

Battery Point

An empty rum bottle's throw from the once notorious Sullivans Cove waterfront is a nest of tiny 19th-century cottages and laneways, packed together like herring fillets in a can. This is the old maritime village of **Battery Point** (Map p640; www.batterypoint.net) and its name derives from the 1818 gun battery that stood on the promontory, protecting Hobart Town from nautical threats both real and imagined.

You can follow our walking tour (p645) or spend a few hours exploring on your own. Battery Point's liquored-up ale houses on **Hampden Rd** have been refitted as groovy cafes and classy restaurants, and cater to a rather more gracious and dignified clientele. Stumble up Kellys Steps from Salamanca Place and dogleg into **South St** where red lights once burned night and day and many a lonesome sailor sought the refuge of a buxom maiden. Spin around the picturesque **Arthur Circus**, check out **St George's Anglican Church** (Map p638) on Cromwell St or shamble down **Napoleon St** (Map p638) to the waterfront where the rigging of tethered yachts' sings and clatters with the wind. For a fortifying stout, duck into the salty 1846 **Shipwrights Arms Hotel** (p652) on Trumpeter St.

Narryna Heritage Museum (Map p640; ☎ 03-6234 2791; www.nationaltrust.org.au; 103 Hampden Rd; adult/concession/child/family $6/3/5/12; ☯ 10.30am-5pm Tue-Fri, 2-5pm Sat & Sun, closed Jul) is a stately Georgian sandstone-fronted mansion (pronounced 'Narrina') built in 1836, set in beautiful grounds with a wonderful collection of artefacts.

Historic Buildings

Hobart has more than 90 buildings classified by the National Trust – 60 of these are on Macquarie and Davey Sts. This stock of amazingly well-preserved old buildings makes Hobart exceptional among Australian cities. The intersection of Macquarie and Murray Sts features a gorgeous sandstone edifice on each corner. For detailed information contact the **National Trust** (Map p640; ☎ 03-6223 5200; www.nationaltrust.org.au; cnr Brisbane & Campbell Sts; ☯ 9am-1pm Mon-Fri) or pick up the *Hobart's Historic Places* brochure from the visitor information centre.

See the court rooms, and grim cells and gallows of the **Penitentiary Chapel Historic Site** (Map p640; ☎ 03-6231 0911; www.penitentiarychapel.com; cnr Brisbane & Campbell Sts; tours adult/concession/child/family $8/6/6/16; ☯ tours 10am, 11.30am, 1pm & 2.30pm). Writer TG Ford mused: 'As the Devil was going through Hobart Gaol, he saw a solitary cell; and the Devil was pleased for it gave him a hint, for improving the prisons in hell'. For extra frisson take the excellent one-hour National Trust–run **Ghost Tour** (☎ 0417 361 392; www.hobartghosts.com; adult/concession/family $10/8/25; ☾ 8.30pm) held most nights (bookings essential).

One in four convicts transported to Van Diemen's land were women, and the **Female Factory** (off Map p638; ☎ 03-6223 1559; www.femalefactory.com.au; 16 Degraves St, South Hobart; tours adult/concession/child/family $10/8/5/25; ☾ 9am-4pm, 1hr tour 9.30am, extra 2pm tour Dec-Apr), 2.5km southwest of the city centre, was where Hobart's female convicts were incarcerated. Tour bookings are essential.

Take a backstage tour of Hobart's prestigious **Theatre Royal** (Map p640; www.theatreroyal.com.au; 29 Campbell St; 1hr tours adult/concession/child $8/6/6; ☾ tours 10.30am & 2pm Mon, Wed & Fri), built in 1837 and Australia's oldest continually operating theatre.

Presiding over an oak-studded park adjacent to Salamanca Place is the low-lying, sandstone **Parliament House** (Map p640; ☎ 03-6233 2200; www.parliament.tas.gov.au; Salamanca Pl; 45min tours free; ☾ tours 10am & 2pm Mon-Fri), completed in 1840 and originally used as a customs house. Tours don't run when parliament is in session.

There are free 20-minute tours of Hobart's grand **Town Hall** (Map p640; ☎ 03-6238 2711; www.hobartcity.com.au; 50 Macquarie St; ☾ tours 2.45pm Tue, 10.45am Thu). It was built in 1864 and styled on the Rome's stunning Palazzo Farnese. Tours depart from the Macquarie St foyer.

Museums

The excellent **Tasmanian Museum & Art Gallery** (Map p640; ☎ 03-6211 4177; www.tmag.tas.gov.au; 40 Macquarie St; admission free; ☾ 10am-5pm) is installed in Hobart's oldest building, the Commissariat Store (1808). The museum features Aboriginal displays, colonial relics and shifting exhibitions, while the gallery curates a collection of Tasmanian colonial art. There are free guided tours at 2.30pm from Wednesday to Sunday.

Hobart is still the staging post for many voyages into the Southern Ocean and Antarctic, and its unbreakable bond with the sea is celebrated at the fascinating **Maritime Museum of Tasmania** (Map p640; ☎ 03-6234 1427; www.maritimetas.org; 16 Argyle St; adult/concession/child/under 12/family $7/5/4/free/16; ☾ 9am-5pm). There are wonderful collections of old photos, paintings, models and relics – just try resisting ringing the huge brass bell from the *Rhexenor*. Upstairs you'll find the **Carnegie Gallery** (admission free; ☾ 9am-5pm) with its exhibitions of contemporary Tasmanian art, craft, design and photography.

Tastes of Hobart
CADBURY CHOCOLATE FACTORY

For years kids have been pestering their parents to do the famous tour of the **Cadbury Chocolate Factory** (off Map p638; ☎ 1800 627 367, 03-6249 0333; www.cadbury.com.au; 100 Cadbury Rd, Claremont; adult/child under 13 $7.50/free; ☾ 8am-4pm Mon-Fri except public holidays, 9am-3pm Jun-Aug), 15km north of the city centre. However, recent health-department regulations have put paid to the factory tours, so chocoholics and wannabe Willy Wonkas must now content themselves with 'a comprehensive talk and short film' in the Cadbury Visitor Centre…oooh! You can still stuff your pockets with cheap choc products, and there's a cafe and souvenir shop. Bookings are essential. Some tour companies offer excursions that incorporate the Cadbury Chocolate Factory (see p646), or book directly with Cadbury and make your own way there.

CASCADE BREWERY

The **Cascade Brewery** (off Map p638; ☎ 03-6224 1117; www.cascadebrewery.com.au; 140 Cascade Rd, South Hobart; 1½hr tours adult/concession/child/family $20/15/10/45; ☾ tours 9.30am, 10am, 1pm & 1.30pm Mon-Fri except public holidays, additional summer tours), in South Hobart is a grand gothic edifice. It's Australia's oldest brewery, established in 1832 next to the clean-running Hobart Rivulet, and still pumps out superb beer and soft drinks today. Tours involve plenty of stair climbing with beer tastings at the end. Visitors must wear flat, enclosed shoes and long trousers (no shorts or skirts), and book in advance. You can take a tour on weekends, but none of the machinery will be operating (brewers have weekends, too).

MOORILLA ESTATE

Moorilla Estate (off Map p638; ☎ 03-6277 9900; www.moorilla.com.au; 655 Main Rd, Berriedale; tastings free; ☾ 10am-5pm) sits on a saucepan-shaped peninsula on the Derwent River 12km north of Hobart's centre. Since its founding in the 1950s, Moorilla has played a prominent role in Hobart society. Stop by for wine and beer

TASMANIA

tastings, have lunch or dinner at the outstanding restaurant **The Source** (mains $25-33; ☯ lunch & dinner) or splash some cash for a night in the deluxe accommodation (doubles $395). Moorilla also plays host to some great summer concerts on its grounds – Grinspoon, Cat Empire and The Pretenders have featured in recent times. Note that the renowned Mona museum here is closed for long-term redevelopment.

Outdoor Stuff

Cloaked in winter snow, **Mt Wellington** (off Map p638; www.wellingtonpark.tas.gov.au) peaks at 1270m, towering above Hobart like a benevolent overlord. The citizens find reassurance in its constant, solid presence, while outdoorsy types find the space to hike and bike on its leafy flanks. And the view from the top is unbelievable! Don't be deterred if the sky is overcast – often the peak rises above cloud level and looks out over a magical ocean of rolling white cloud-tops.

The 22km road to the top was hacked out of the mountainside during the Great Depression – it winds up from the city through thick temperate forest, opening out to lunar rock-scapes at the summit. If you don't have wheels, local buses 48 and 49 stop at Fern Tree halfway up the mountain, from where it's a five- to six-hour return walk to the top. Pick up the *Wellington Park Recreation Map* ($9.95 from the visitor information centre) as a guide.

Some bus-tour companies include Mt Wellington in their itineraries (see p646); another option is the **Mt Wellington Shuttle Bus Service** (☏ 0408 341 804; per person return $25), departing the visitor information centre at 9.30am and 1.30pm daily (city pick-ups by arrangement; bookings essential). See Cycling (right) for information on bike trips down the mountain.

A lower-altitude version of the view is from **Mt Nelson** (off Map p638), where there's an old signal station, a cafe, barbecues and picnic tables. To get here drive up Davey St then take the Southern Outlet towards Kingston and turn left at the top of the hill. Local buses 57, 58, 156 and 158 also come here.

The excellent little **Royal Tasmanian Botanical Gardens** (off Map p638; ☏ 03-6236 3076; tours 6236 3075; www.rtbg.tas.gov.au; Queens Domain; admission free, 1hr tours per person $5; ☯ 8am-6.30pm Oct-Mar, 8am-5.30pm Apr & Sep, 8am-5pm May-Aug, tours 11am Mon, Tue & Thu), established in 1818, showcase more than 6000 exotic and native plant species. Explore the

> ### SALAMANCA MARKET
>
> Colourful hippies and crazy craftspeople have been coming to sell their wares at **Salamanca Market** (Map p640; ☏ 03-6238 2843; www.hobartcity.com.au; ☯ 8.30am-3pm Sat) on Saturday mornings since 1972. They come from all over the state's southern reaches with their fresh produce, secondhand clothes and books, tacky tourist souvenirs, CDs, cheap sunglasses, antiques and bric-a-brac. The buskers and jugglers also come, as do the purveyors of fine food and snake-oil treatments, and everyone enjoys the street-party love-in atmosphere. Rain or shine – don't miss it!

flora in detail at the **Botanical Discovery Centre** (admission free; ☯ 9am-5pm), which also houses a gift shop, kiosk and restaurant.

ACTIVITIES
Cycling

A useful navigational tool is the *Hobart Bike Map* ($4 from the visitor information centre and bike shops), detailing cycle paths and road routes.

Island Cycle Tours (☏ 1300 880 334, 03-6234 4951; www.islandcycletours.com) organises a range of guided and self-guided cycling tours around the state, and runs the brilliant three-hour Mt Wellington Descent (adult/child $75/70, including hotel pick-ups, transport, bikes and safety equipment), departing daily at 9.30am and 1.30pm. You can also combine this with a sea-kayaking experience around the Hobart docks.

Blackaby's Sea-Kayaks & Tours (opposite) also combines a Mt Wellington Descent with kayaking around the Hobart docks.

Bike hire:

Bike Hire Tasmania (Appleby Cycles) (Map p640; ☏ 03-6234 4166, 0400 256 588; www.bikehiretasmania.com.au; 109 Elizabeth St; ☯ 8.30am-6pm Mon-Fri, 9am-4pm Sat) Quality mountain/road bikes from $40/50 per day.

Derwent Bike Hire (Map p640; ☏ 03-6260 4426, 0428 899 169; www.derwentbikehire.com; Regatta Grounds Cycleway; ☯ 10am-4pm Sat & Sun Sep-Nov, Apr & May, daily Dec-Mar) Mountain and touring bikes from $30/140 per day/week.

Sea-Kayaking

Kayaking around the docks in Hobart, particularly at twilight, is a lovely way to get a feel for the city.

There's a couple of operators:

Blackaby's Sea-Kayaks & Tours (☎ 0418 124 072, 0438 671 508; www.blackabyseakayaks.com.au) Morning, afternoon and sunset paddles around the Hobart waterfront, running on demand ($50 per person). Ask about paddling adventures further afield (Port Arthur, Fortescue Bay and Gordon River).

Island Cycle Tours (☎ 1300 880 334, 03-6234 4951; www.islandcycletours.com) The Pedal 'n' Paddle Tour combines its Mt Wellington Descent (see opposite) with a two-hour paddle around the docks, either before or after the cycle. Departures are at 9.30am and 3pm daily; breakfast or lunch included (adult/child $129/119).

WALKING TOUR

Ready for a Hobart history lesson? Begin at **Franklin Square (1)**, where skaters and canoodling school kids mingle beneath the statue of

---

WALK FACTS

Start Franklin Square
Finish Knopwood's Retreat
Distance 3km
Duration three hours

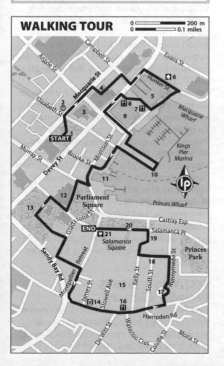

WALKING TOUR

Governor Sir John Franklin. Head northeast on Macquarie St past the **General Post Office (2)** with its 1906 sandstone clock-tower, the 1864 **Town Hall (3**; p643) to the **Tasmanian Museum & Art Gallery (4**; p643) to soak up some culture. Slip out through the cafe into the courtyard and across the car park, and head down Campbell St to the waterfront around **Victoria Dock (5)** where the fishing boats bump and sway.

Head northeast along Davey St and check out the ubertrendy **Henry Jones Art Hotel (6**; p649). This was once the IXL jam factory headed by the excelling Henry Jones and once Tasmania's largest private employer. Cross the swing bridge towards **Mures (7**; p650) or **Flippers Fish Punt (8**; p650) for a fishy takeaway lunch by **Constitution Dock (9)**. This place is party-central for yachties celebrating the finish of the famous Sydney to Hobart Yacht Race (see p634) around New Year's Eve.

Elizabeth St Pier (10) is the next stop, jutting into Sullivans Cove with classy accommodation upstairs, and restaurants and bars downstairs. Walk around **Watermans Dock (11)**, cross Morrison St and then wander through Parliament Sq in front of **Parliament House (12**; p643). Turn right through the undulating lawns and colonial gravestones of **St David's Park (13)**. Hobart Town's original cemetery had become an overgrown eyesore when converted into a park in 1926. Cut through Salamanca Mews, jag right onto Gladstone St, left onto Kirksway Pl then right onto Montpellier Retreat, arcing uphill towards the colonial delights of the 1836 **Narryna Heritage Museum (14**; p642).

Hampden Rd leads you into the heart of **Battery Point (15**; p642), Hobart's oldest 'hood. Enjoy a coffee and croissant at **Jackman & McRoss (16**; p651), then turn left into Runnymede St for **Arthur Circus (17)**, an old-world roundabout encircled with Georgian cottages. After a play on the swings, continue down Runnymede St and turn left into McGregor St, casting an eye up well-preserved **South St (18)**. Turn right onto Kelly St and skip down **Kellys Steps (19)**, an 1839 sandstone link between Battery Point and the warehouses of **Salamanca Place (20**; p642). Not far along is Hobart's best pub, **Knopwood's Retreat (21**; p652). Grab a table out front in the sunshine for a couple of Cascades and regale the locals with tall tales of your adventures.

HOBART FOR CHILDREN

There's always something interesting going on around the waterfront – fishing boats

TASMANIA

chugging in and out of Victoria Dock, yachts tacking and jibing in Sullivans Cove – and you can feed the whole family on a budget at the floating fish punts (p650) at Constitution Dock. There's free Friday-night music in the courtyard at the Salamanca Arts Centre (p653) and the street performers, buskers and sights of Saturday's Salamanca Market (p644) captivate kids of all ages.

Rainy-day attractions include the Tasmanian Museum & Art Gallery (p643), the Maritime Museum of Tasmania (p643), the Cadbury Chocolate Factory (p643) and the Discovery Centre at the Royal Tasmanian Botanical Gardens (p644).

There are crews spruiking boat cruises up or down the river. Or you might assail the heights of Mt Wellington or Mt Nelson or rent a bike and explore the cycling paths. Outside Hobart there's a multitude of kid-friendly options with many animal parks, beaches, caves, nature walks and mazes to explore; see Around Hobart (p654).

TOURS
Bus Tours
Gray Line (☎ 1300 858 687, 03-6234 3336; www.grayline .com.au) City tours in an idiotic bus-dressed-as-a-tram (adult/ child $40/20), plus longer tours to destinations including Mt Wellington ($45/22.50), Mt Field National Park ($134/67) and the Huon Valley ($139/69.50). Free hotel pick-ups.

Red Decker (☎ 03-6236 9116; www.reddecker.com.au) Commentated sightseeing on an old London double-decker bus (sigh). Buy a 20-stop, hop-on-hop-off pass (adult/ concession/child $25/23/15) or do the tour as a 90-minute loop. Pay a bit more and add a Cascade Brewery tour ($44/42/25) or river cruise ($48/46/37) to the deal.

Tasman Island Cruises (☎ 03-6250 2200; www .tasmancruises.com.au; full-day tour adult/child $220/150) Take a bus to Port Arthur for a three-hour ecocruise around Tasman Island, then explore the Port Arthur Historic Site and bus back to town. Includes morning tea, lunch and Port Arthur admission.

TassieLink (☎ 1300 300 520, 03-6230 8900; www .tassielink.com.au) Full-day trips including to Lake St Clair (adult/child $75/38) and Freycinet National Park (adult/ child $85/51), or a half-day trip to Huonville and Franklin ($16/8). Tours depart the terminal at 64 Brisbane St.

Cruises
Captain Fell's Historic Ferries (☎ 03-6223 6893; www.captainfellshistoricferries.com.au) Good-value cruises on cute old ferries (adult/child/family $28/14/70) that can incorporate lunch (from $30/45/100) and dinner ($53/27/140). They also run coach or double-decker bus

sightseeing trips around town and to Mt Wellington and Richmond.

Hobart Harbour Jet Boat (☎ 0404 078 687; www .hobartharbourjet.com.au) Water-taxi rides to Hobart locales (Moorilla, Bellerive and Wrest Point Casino) from $10 per person, plus adrenalin-fuelled jet-boat river tours from adult/child $35/20.

Navigators (☎ 03-6223 1914; www.navigators.net .au) Slick ships sailing north to Moorilla Estate (adult/child $22/11) and south to Port Arthur ($149/110, including site entry and return coach trip) and Storm Bay ($35/18). Also Derwent River cruises ($22/12).

Peppermint Bay Cruise (☎ 1300 137 919; www .peppermintbay.com.au) A five-hour float down the D'Entrecasteaux Channel to the sassy Peppermint Bay development at Woodbridge (p661). Prices start at adult/ child $88/48, including lunch on board.

Wild Thing (☎ 03-6224 2021; www.wildthingadven tures.com.au) A speedy red boat churns up the froth on tours around the Derwent (adult/child $24/15), Bruny Island (from $125/99), Cape Raoul ($125/99) and Iron Pot Lighthouse ($55/35).

Walking Tours
Ghost Tours of Hobart (☎ 0439 335 696; www .ghosttoursofhobart.com.au; adult/child/family $25/15/70) Walking tours with ghoulish commentaries departing the Bakehouse in Salamanca Sq at dusk. Bookings are essential.

Hobart Historic Tours (☎ 03-6278 3338; www.ho barthistorictours.com.au; adult/child $27.50/12) A highly informative 1½-hour Hobart Historic Walk (10am) and a beery Old Hobart Pub Tour (5pm).

Louisa's Walk (☎ 03-6230 8233; www.livehistory.com .au; adult/concession/family $25/20/60) These excellent 1½-hour tours take in Hobart's female convict heritage at the Female Factory (p643), interpreted through 'strolling theatre'. Tours depart Cascade Brewery at 10.30am and 2pm.

Mt Wellington Walks (☎ 0439 551 197; www.mtwel lingtonwalks.com.au; adult/concession $70/60) Four-hour 'easy' or 'adventurous' mountain tours. Minimum age 10; hotel pick-ups 11am daily.

Waterways Tours (☎ 03-6230 8233; www.welcome tohobart.com.au; adult/concession/family $19/13/40) A subterranean tour of the Hobart Rivulet that sluices beneath the CBD. Tours depart the council offices at 16 Elizabeth St, opposite the visitors centre. Bookings are essential.

FESTIVALS & EVENTS
December & January
Falls Festival (www.fallsfestival.com) Tassie's premier outdoor rock-music festival (affiliated with Lorne in Victoria's New Year's Eve event) is a sensation. Three days of live Oz and international acts (John Butler Trio, Franz

Ferdinand, The Hives etc) at Marion Bay, an hour south of Hobart.

Sydney to Hobart Yacht Race (www.rolexsydney hobart.com) Yachts competing in this annual race start arriving in Hobart around 28–29 December, just in time for New Year's Eve! (Yachties sure can party…)

Taste Festival (www.tastefestival.com.au) On either side of New Year's Eve, this week-long, harbourside event is a celebration of Tassie's gastronomic prowess and features theatre, kids' activities, concerts, buskers and New Year's Eve shenanigans. Stalls represent the who's who of Hobart's restaurant scene. BYO plastic wine glass or pay $5 for one.

February

Australian Wooden Boat Festival (www.australian woodenboatfestival.com.au) Biennial event (odd-numbered years) to coincide with the Royal Hobart Regatta. The festival showcases Tasmania's boat-building heritage and maritime traditions.

Royal Hobart Regatta (www.royalhobartregatta.com) Three days of aquatic yacht-watching and mayhem on the Derwent River.

March & April

Ten Days on the Island (www.tendaysontheisland.com) Tasmania's premier cultural festival – a biennial event (odd-numbered years, usually late March to early April) celebrating island culture at state-wide venues. Concerts, exhibitions, dance, film, theatre and workshops.

June

Antarctic Midwinter Festival (www.antarctic-tasma nia.info) Celebrate the winter solstice at this 10-day Hobart festival, designed to highlight and celebrate Tasmania's connection with the Antarctic.

October

Royal Hobart Show (www.hobartshowground.com.au) Enduring rural-meets-urban festival showcasing the state's primary industries. Show bags, hold-onto-your-lunch rides and the fecund aromas of nature.

SLEEPING

Hobart's most interesting neighbourhoods for staying in are the Sullivans Cove waterfront and Salamanca Place (and to a lesser extent Battery Point), but prices here are high and vacancy rates low. There's less atmosphere in the CBD, but it's here you'll find most of the hostels and midrange hotels. North Hobart and New Town are in the city's northern regions, and have plenty of rental apartments and B&Bs within easy walking distance to that area's restaurants and shops. Around at

waterside Sandy Bay there's lots of reasonably priced accommodation, but it's a fair hike from town. Approaching the city from the north, you'll see most of Hobart's motels strung along Brooker Ave, though the ones we've listed below are closer in.

There are no campgrounds within cooee of the city centre. Aside from what's listed here, see Seven Mile Beach (p657).

Top-end Hobart accommodation is often quite reasonable – if your budget stretches to $200 you can afford something quite special: designer hotels, historic guest houses and modern waterside apartments. However, midrange accommodation is sometimes overpriced due to high demand, especially in high season – if you're visiting in January, book as far in advance as humanly possible!

Budget

HOSTELS & HOTELS

Hobart Hostel (Map p638; ☎ 03-6234 6122; www.ho barthostel.com; cnr Goulburn & Barrack Sts; dm $21-26, tw & d with/without bathroom $90/70; 🖳) Hobart Hostel offers clean, cheap 'n' cheerful chock-a-block dorms and good communal facilities in the old converted Doghouse Hotel. There are good-value twins and doubles upstairs, and fine rooftop views from the tiny smoker's deck. Linen included.

Pickled Frog (Map p638; ☎ 03-6234 7977; www .thepickledfrog.com; 281 Liverpool St; dm $23-25, s $60, d & tw $65; 🖳) This is party-central for shaggy backpackers. There's no wowser's wing in this old hotel on the CBD fringe refitted with big-screen TVs, pool tables and kegfuls of Tasmania's cheapest beer. All rooms have shared bathrooms. A happenin' place if you're in the mood.

Central City Backpackers (Map p640; ☎ 1800 811 507, 03-6224 2404; www.centralcityhobart.com; 138 Collins St; dm $23-27, s/d $55/69; 🖳) Spread over floors and hallways smack-bang in the middle of the city, this maze-like hostel has loads of character and communal space, a great kitchen, reasonable rooms, friendly staff and extras such as baggage storage and tour desk. Linen costs extra in the dorms.

Narrara Backpackers (Map p638; ☎ 03-6231 3191; www.narrarabackpackers.com; 88 Goulburn St; dm/s/d $23/60/69; 🖳) Casual Narrara, in a three-level townhouse, gets mixed reports from readers. It's cramped with basic facilities.

Adelphi Court YHA (off Map p638; ☎ 03-6228 4829; www.yha.com.au; 17 Stoke St, New Town; dm $29, d & tw with/without bathroom from $98/82) This was once a 1950s apartment block built around a courtyard behind a Federation manor. It's 2.5km from the city but reasonably close to the North Hobart strip.

Montgomery's Private Hotel & YHA (Map p640; ☎ 03-6231 2660; www.montgomerys.com.au; 9 Argyle St; dm from $30, s & d with/without bathroom $130/112; ☐) Attached to Montgomery's pub, this YHA offers clean, bright, secure and rather characterless accommodation in a great central location. It's spread over three levels with dorms of all sizes, as well as singles, doubles and family rooms. A solid option.

our pick **Astor Private Hotel** (Map p640; ☎ 03-6234 6611; www.astorprivatehotel.com.au; 157 Macquarie St; dm $42, s $63-80, tw/d $76/90, d with bathroom $115-140, all incl breakfast; ☐) The Astor's an authentic old-school 1920s hotel in a great cental location retaining much of its original decor and charm, including wonderful old furniture, stained-glass windows and ornate ceilings. Lovely Tildy is as oddball as her old hotel (free wi-fi in exchange for a chocolate bar). Older-style rooms share facilities. Strict 'No Bogans' policy!

Midrange
GUEST HOUSES & B&BS
Battery Point Manor (Map p638; ☎ 03-6224 0888; www.batterypointmanor.com.au; 13-15 Cromwell St, Battery Point; s/d incl breakfast from $85/95; 🈺) With sweeping views from the outdoor terrace, this pearly-white 1834 Georgian building offers a range of comfortable rooms, all with en suites and some with king-size beds, and a separate two-bedroom cottage. Summertime rates go through the roof, but ask about low-season discounts.

Edinburgh Gallery (Map p638; ☎ 03-6224 9229; www.artacom.com.au; 211 Macquarie St; s $90, d $100-180; ☐) This funky old Federation home, just west of the CBD, has done away with the doilies and instead installed an eclectic collection of tasteful art pieces. Some rooms share bathrooms, but all have a quirky artsy decor and come with complimentary breakfast. Excellent winter reductions and gay-friendly to boot.

Lodge on Elizabeth (Map p638; ☎ 03-6231 3830; www.thelodge.com.au; 249 Elizabeth St, North Hobart; s/d incl breakfast from $130/150, self-contained cottage from $195; ☐) Built in 1829 this old-timer has been a school house, boarding house and halfway house, but is now a value-for-money guest house. The rooms are done out with antiques

and all have en suites. The self-contained cottage overlooks the courtyard out the back (two-night minimum).

HOTELS
Prince of Wales (Map p640; ☎ 03-6223 6355; www.princeofwaleshotel.net.au; 55 Hampden Rd, Battery Point; r $100-120) A kitsch '60s glitch in Battery Point's urban planning, the POW is nonetheless exquisitely located and offers cheery, spotlessly clean and excellent value pub-style rooms, all with en suite. There's a large family room that sleeps six and breakfast is included. The downstairs bistro serves first-class food and there's secure off-street parking.

Leisure Inn Hobart Macquarie (Map p640; ☎ 03-6220 7100; www.leisureinnhotels.com; 167 Macquarie St; d from $105; ☐ 🈺) The original facade was an interesting 1968 edifice, but a recent makeover has 'modernised' the exterior and made over the inside with coffee-and-cream colours, dark timber floors, flat-screen TVs and natty bathrooms. It's comfortable, good value and in a great location close to the city and waterfront (views to either from most rooms). Internet deals sometimes include breakfast.

Hobart Midcity Hotel (Map p640; ☎ 03-6234 6333, 1800 030 966; www.hobartmidcity.com.au; cnr Elizabeth & Bathurst Sts; r $135-215; ☐ 🈺) Don't be put off by the Midcity's graceless '70s stance, because the staff and rooms are great, the location's peerless, there's 24-hour reception and an on-site restaurant and bar. A good all-rounder.

Grand Mercure Hadleys Hotel (Map p640; ☎ 1800 131 689, 03-6223 4355; www.grandmercure.com.au; 34 Murray St; d from $180; ☐ 🈺) This National Trust–listed hotel in the heart of the city was constructed by convicts in 1834 and has been hosting guests ever since. It's acquired many modern accoutrements along the way, including a restaurant and bar, but retained much of its colonial grandeur.

MOTELS
Mayfair Plaza Motel (Map p638; ☎ 03-6220 9900; www.mayfairplaza.com.au; 236 Sandy Bay Rd, Sandy Bay; r $150; 🈺) The rooms are large and comfortable at the Mayfair – its redevelopment in the '90s incorporated a brown-brick courtyard that these days is looking rather lifeless and forlorn. Still, the location is good in the heart of the Sandy Bay shopping and restaurant strip.

Woolmers Inn (Map p638; ☎ 1800 030 780, 03-6223 7355; www.woolmersinn.com; 123-127 Sandy Bay Rd, Sandy Bay; d from $138) With spacious studio and two-bedroom units, all with kitchenette, cable TV and video, this is a good choice despite the brown-brick faux colonial coach-house exterior. Some disabled-access units, too.

APARTMENT HOTELS & SERVICED APARTMENTS

Graham Court Apartments (off Map p638; ☎ 1800 811 915, 03-6278 1333; www.grahamcourt.com.au; 15 Pirie St, New Town; d $120-150, extra person $25) Offering great-value self-contained accommodation, this block of 23 well-maintained family-friendly apartments sits in lovely gardens in the quiet northern suburbs. Units range from one to three bedrooms, with a playground and cots, high chairs and babysitters on call. Wheelchair-accessible units are available.

Grosvenor Court (Map p638; ☎ 03-6223 3422; www.grosvenorcourt.com.au; 42 Grosvenor St, Sandy Bay; d $130-145, q $155-300; 🖳) Grosvenor Court is a curious mix of the good, the bad and the ugly: quiet street, obnoxious tiling; lovely linen, ugly brickwork; exciting leather lounge suites, weary kitchens. The friendly owners lessen any disappointment and make things feel homey. Wireless internet access.

Avon Court Holiday Apartments (Map p640; ☎ 03-6223 4837, 1800 807 257; www.avoncourt.com.au; 4 Colville St; d $150-210, extra adult/child $35/18) Overlook the ugly nouveaux-sandstone exteriors and bland, motel-style interiors and you'll find yourself brilliantly poised in a spacious apartment, right in the heart of Battery Point. Larger apartments sleep up to six. Off-street parking is a bonus.

our pick **The Gables** (off Map p638; ☎ 03-6278 9973; hobartgables@bigpond.com; 2 Stoke St, New Town; d $200, extra persons $33) If you've got wheels and a crew in the back, this place is ideal. It has two large two-bedroom apartments that sleep up to five with full kitchens, spacious lounges and dining areas, plus tasteful furniture and views of Mt Wellington.

Top End

our pick **Corinda's Cottages** (Map p638; ☎ 03-6234 1590; www.corindascottages.com.au; 17 Glebe St, Glebe; d from $220) This renovated Victorian mansion sits high on the Glebe hillside among meticulously maintained parterre gardens, a short (and steep!) walk from town. Three self-contained cottages provide contemporary comforts with none of the twee, old-world guff so much Tasmanian accommodation wallows in. Breakfast is DIY gourmet (eggs,

muffins, fresh coffee etc). Cheaper rates for longer stays. Outstanding.

Somerset on the Pier (Map p640; ☎ 1800 766 377, 03-6220 6600; www.somerset.com; Elizabeth St Pier; apt from $270; 🖳) These luxuriously appointed apartments occupy perhaps Hobart's most prestigious address on the upper level of Elizabeth Pier, and come with glorious harbour views and slick contemporary decor. Balcony rooms come at a premium. Somerset on Salamanca (8 Salamanca Pl; prices as above) is booked through the same management.

Henry Jones Art Hotel (Map p640; ☎ 03-6210 7700; www.thehenryjones.com; 25 Hunter St; d $220-320, ste $490-850; 🖳) Since opening in 2004, super-swish HJs has become famous around Australia as the paradigm of modern style and sophistication. Absolute waterfront in a restored jam factory, it oozes class but is far from intimidating (this is Hobart after all, not Sydney). Modern art enlivens the walls, while facilities and downstairs distractions (bar, restaurant and cafe) are world class.

Camping

Elwick Cabin & Tourist Park (☎ 03-6272 7115; www.islandcabins.com.au; 19 Goodwood Rd, Glenorchy; unpowered/powered sites $20/30, cabins $90-115, 3-bedroom house per d $135) The nearest camping area to town (about 8km north of the centre) has a range of cabins but limited powered sites (book ahead). The three-bedroom houses sleep eight (extra adult/child $25/20).

Barilla Holiday Park (☎ 1800 465 453, 03-6248 5453; www.barilla.com.au; 75 Richmond Rd, Cambridge; unpowered/powered sites $26/28, cabins $77-160; 🖳 🖳) If you have a car, Barilla could be a good option, midway between Hobart (12km) and Richmond (14km). It's close to the airport and some great wineries, and has good facilities including a mini-golf course and an on-site restaurant serving decent wood-fired pizzas.

EATING

Hobart's central area has some good daytime restaurants and cafes providing excellent breakfast and lunch options, but come nightfall dickheads in their muscle cars take over the streets doing endless loops of the city block, leering at women and abusing everyone else – bogans! Make for the harbour or North Hobart for your evening victuals.

The waterfront streets, docks and piers are the main areas of the city's culinary scene and quality seafood is the main theme. Salamanca

---

OYSTER LOVERS

Pacific oysters *(Crassostrea gigaswas)* are farmed at over 100 sites along Tasmania's north and east coasts. They're said to have aphrodisiac properties, but science has found no link between oysters and ever-lovin'. Several oyster farms around Tasmania have farm-gate sales where shucked oysters cost about $13 a dozen or live unshucked babies go for about $8 (buy a shucker from a tackle shop and shuck 'em yourself). **Barilla Bay** (☎ 03-6248 5458; www.barillabay.com.au; 1388 Tasman Hwy, Cambridge) near Hobart, **Get Shucked** (☎ 0428 606 250; www.getshucked.com.au; Great Bay) on Bruny Island, **Aqa Oysters** (www.aqaoysters.com.au; Binalong Bay Rd) in St Helens and **Freycinet Marine Farm** (www.aqaoysters.com.au; 1784 Coles Bay Rd) on Freycinet Peninsula all sell direct to the public.

Freshly shucked with a squeeze of lemon or a slosh of Tabasco sauce or even a little wasabi is the only way to go. Don't make that tragic 'oysters Kilpatrick' mistake – a cooked oyster is a ruined oyster. The best oysters we ever had we picked off the rocks in Great Bay, Bruny Island, off the little rocky point – opened and eaten on the spot, knee-deep in the brine. They say eating oysters is a bit like performing cunnilingus…but we wouldn't know about that.

Place is an almost unbroken string of excellent cafes and restaurants, and Battery Point's Hampden Rd restaurants are always splendid, too. Elizabeth St in North Hobart has evolved into a diverse collation of cosmopolitan cafes, multicultural eateries and pubs.

City Centre

La Cuisine (Map p640; ☎ 03-6231 1274; 85 Bathurst St; meals $5-8; ◐ breakfast & lunch Mon-Fri) With Basque house cakes, stuffed sourdough rolls, juicy quiches and sensational salads, La Cuisine dragged the city out of the white-bread culinary quicksand when it opened in the mid-80s – no one in Hobart had seen a croissant before. Also at 108 Collins St (☎ 03-6224 2587).

South Hobart Food Store (Map p638; ☎ 03-6224 6862; 356 Macquarie St, South Hobart; meals $6-13; ◐ breakfast & lunch) A little way out of the city centre – sure – but a trip to the Food Store is well worth the effort. This old shopfront cafe is full of booths, bookish students, brunching friends and kids under the tables.

Axum Ethiopian Restaurant (☎ 03-6231 5421, Level 1, 112 Liverpool St; meals $8-12; ◐ lunch & dinner) In a space shared with Mouse on Mars internet cafe, Axum is an Ethiopian community centre and Hobart's only African restaurant. The food is dirt cheap and based around dips and stews eaten by hand with *injeera* flat bread.

Sirens (Map p640; ☎ 03-6234 2634; 6 Victoria St; mains $17-19; ◐ dinner Mon-Sat) Sirens is Hobart's best vegetarian restaurant and does creative cuisine that's much more than just tofu and lentils – try the three-cheese beetroot ravioli in champagne, dill and pink peppercorn cream. The service is excellent and the space

is warm, welcoming and full of exotic aromas and happy diners.

The most central self-catering option is **City Supermarket** (Map p640; ☎ 03-6234 4003; 148 Liverpool St; ◐ 8am-7pm Mon-Fri, 9am-5pm Sat, noon-5pm Sun).

Waterfront Area

Flippers Fish Punt (Map p640; ☎ 03-6234 3101; Constitution Dock; meals $7-15; ◐ lunch & dinner) Flippers Fish Punt, with its voluptuous fish-shaped profile and sea-blue exterior, has been floating at Constitution Dock for as long as anyone can remember. Fillets of flathead and curls of calamari – straight from the deep blue sea and into the deep fryer.

Mures (Map p640; ☎ 03-6231 2121; www.mures.com.au; Victoria Dock; ◐ lunch & dinner) Mures is the name in Hobart seafood with its own fishing fleet serving this restaurant as well as local markets. On the ground level is the fishmonger, a sushi bar, ice-cream parlour and the hectic, family-focused bistro Lower Deck (mains $7 to $13), serving fish and chips and salmon burgers to the masses. The Upper Deck (mains $20 to $28) is a sassier affair, with expansive dockside views and à la carte seafood dishes.

Jam Packed (Map p640; ☎ 03-6231 3454; 27 Hunter St; mains $8-18; ◐ breakfast & lunch) This trendy cafe inside the brilliant redeveloped IXL Jam Factory atrium next to the Henry Jones Art Hotel is jam-packed at breakfast time. The BLT is the perfect hangover salve and the prawn spaghetti puttanesca, simmered in olive oil, tomato and caper sauce, makes a filling lunch.

ourpick Fish Frenzy (Map p640; ☎ 03-6231 2134; Elizabeth St Pier; meals $11-32; ◐ lunch & dinner) This casual place at a great location on Elizabeth Pier has a slightly upmarket take on the humble fish and chip, and keeps bringing us back for its waterfront outdoor tables, seafood platters, fishy salads (spicy calamari, smoked salmon and brie), wine by the glass and perky service. The eponymous 'Fish Frenzy' ($16) delivers a bit of everything. It's ridiculously popular, but doesn't take bookings.

Marque IV (Map p640; ☎ 03-6224 4428; Elizabeth St Pier; mains $35-45; ☯ lunch Mon-Fri, dinner Mon-Sat) High-class dining hits waterfront Hobart at Marque IV, a discreet dining room halfway along Elizabeth St Pier. You could start with an 'amuse', but at these prices, it doesn't pay to dally. Perhaps begin with Spring Bay baby abalone ceviche with picked zucchini and zucchini flowers ($28). And then maybe an ocean trout nicoise with pink eye potatoes, beans, olives, fresh white anchovies and salsa verde ($38). Desserts? Superb. Wine list? Select. Service and decor? Sufficient.

See also T-42° (p652).

Salamanca Place

Retro Café (Map p640; ☎ 03-6223 3073; 31 Salamanca Pl; mains $7-20; ☯ breakfast & lunch) Funky Retro is ground zero for Saturday brunch among the market stalls. Masterful breakfasts, bagels, salads and burgers mix it with laughing staff, chilled-out jazz and the whir and bang of the coffee machine in a riot of good vibes.

Vietnamese Kitchen (Map p640; ☎ 03-6223 2188; 61 Salamanca Pl; mains $8-13; ☯ lunch & dinner) This cheap, kitsch Viet canteen, with its glowing drinks fridge and plastic-coated photos of steaming soups and stir-fries, is refreshingly utilitarian among Salamanca's super-cool bars and slick eateries. Eat in or takeaway.

Ciuccio (Map p640; ☎ 03-6224 5690; 9 Salamanca Sq; mains $9-15; ☯ breakfast & lunch) Formerly Sugo, Ciuccio continues the theme of serious coffee and a menu with Italian leanings (pasta, pizza, risotto, panini) – an excellent all-rounder. Licensed Ciuccio is popular for drinks, too.

Machine Laundry Café (Map p640; ☎ 03-6224 9922; 12 Salamanca Sq; mains $9-16; ☯ breakfast & lunch) Is it a cafe or a laundrette? Wash a load ($5) of clothes in this bright retro-style cafe and make a mess of the ones you're wearing slurping your soup and sipping your coffee. The food is first class and the tumble-dryers are strangely soothing and hypnotic.

Sals on the Square (Map p640; ☎ 03-6224 3667; 55 Salamanca Pl; mains $15-28) Part bar, part restaurant and occasional live-music venue, Sals has a takeaway counter on Salamanca Place and a

huge prime possie on Salamanca Sq, where the real serious eating gets done. Pastas, risottos, steaks, burgers and salads rule the roost.

Gourmet self-caterers should head to **Wursthaus** (Map p640; ☎ 03-6224 0644; 1 Montpellier Retreat; ☯ 8am-6pm Mon-Fri, to 5pm Sat, 9.30am-4pm Sun) for superb deli produce, or the **Salamanca Fresh Fruit Market** (Map p640; ☎ 03-6223 2700; 41 Salamanca Pl; ☯ 7am-7pm) for fruit and groceries.

Battery Point

ourpick **Jackman & McRoss** (Map p640; ☎ 03-6223 3186; 57-59 Hampden Rd; meals $7-15; ☯ breakfast & lunch) Apologies to every other Hobart cafe, bakery and pastry chef, but *this* is the best cafe experience in Hobart and perhaps all of Tasmania. Pick from the delicious menu or the display cabinet of delectable pies, tarts, baguettes and pastries. Early-morning cake and coffee may evolve into quiche or soup for lunch. Staff stay cheery despite being run off their feet.

Francisco's on Hampden (Map p640; ☎ 03-6224 7124; 60 Hampden Rd, Battery Point; tapas $9-11, mains $24-27; ☯ lunch Fri, dinner Tue-Sun) This upbeat tapas bar is done out with posters of toreadors and dusky dancing maidens. Try some snacky tapas sloshed down with Rioja, or a larger paella, or seafood or meat platter.

Magic Curries (Map p640; ☎ 03-6223 4500; 41 Hampden Rd, Battery Point; mains $13-22; ☯ dinner) The Indian cricket team eats here when they're in town, so the food gets the stamp of approval. Try a Kingfisher beer and an Indian curry (from aromatic and mild to face-meltingly hot). Excellent vegetarian options and takeaway available.

Da Angelo (Map p640; ☎ 03-6223 7011; 47 Hampden Rd; mains $17-27; ☯ dinner) An enduring (and endearing) Italian *ristorante*, Da Angelo presents an impressively long menu of homemade pastas, veal and chicken dishes, calzone, and pizza with 20 different toppings. Colosseum and Carlton Football Club team photos add authenticity. Takeaway and BYO.

Piccalilly (Map p640; ☎ 03-6224 9900; cnr Hampden Rd & Francis St, Battery Point; 4 courses with/without wine $135/82; ☯ dinner) This historic corner site has seen lots of comings and goings, but it's now home to super-swish Piccalilly. Creative dishes like cannelloni of braised lamb shoulder with mushroom bolognese, and King George whiting with sauce *vierge* and citrus jellyfish are just part of what's on offer.

See also Shipwrights Arms Hotel (p652).

North Hobart

Kaos Café (Map p638; ☎ 03-6231 5699; 237 Elizabeth St; mains $5-19) This laid-back, gay-friendly spot offers up an assortment of tasty burgers, salads and risottos, and keeps serving until around 11.30pm. Soak@Kaos bar (right) is next door.

Onba (Map p638; ☎ 03-6231 5931; 301 Elizabeth St; mains $8-24; ▣) Quirky Onba is a bit of everything – brilliant breakfast cafe, great lunchtime cook-house and happenin' evening tapas and wine bar. Local art adorns the walls and food-art is done in the kitchen. Buy a coffee (or anything) and get 30 minutes complimentary wi-fi.

Raincheck Lounge (Map p638; ☎ 03-6234 5975; 392 Elizabeth St; mains $12-27; ❤ breakfast & lunch Mon-Fri, brunch Sat & Sun, dinner Wed-Sat) This could be Darlinghurst or Fitzroy – Rain Check's cool Moroccan-hewn room and sidewalk tables see punters sipping coffee, reconstituting over big breakfasts and conversing over impressive Mod Oz dinners.

Annapurna (Map p638; ☎ 03-6236 9500; 305 Elizabeth St; mains $13-15; ❤ lunch & dinner) Ever-popular Annapurna consistently rates among Hobartians' fave eateries (bookings advised). Northern and southern Indian options are served with absolute proficiency – Tassie's best Indian food! The *masala dosa* (south Indian crepe filled with curried potato) is a crowd favourite. BYO, and takeaway available. Also at 93 Salamanca Pl (Map p640).

Restaurant 373 (Map p638; ☎ 03-6231 9186; 373 Elizabeth St, North Hobart; mains $28-33; ❤ dinner Tue-Sat) Inhabiting a lovely old shopfront, Restaurant 373 is an artsy, high-end eatery with wide floorboards and splashes of dark red paint and white linen. The young owners give local produce a Mod Oz twist. Excellent service; brilliant wine list and desserts. One of Hobart's best.

Self-caterers should find most of what they need at **Fresco Market** (Map p638; ☎ 03-6234 2710; 346 Elizabeth St; ❤ 8.30am-8pm).

See also Republic Bar & Café (opposite).

DRINKING

Hobart has a long tradition of drinking, but today's pretty young things are 10,000 leagues removed from the rum-addled whalers of the past. Great pubs and bars abound around Salamanca Place and the waterfront, where the outdoors are enjoyed on summer evenings and indoor open fires are cajoled in winter. North Hobart, too, has a good selection of pubs and bars. See p646 for information on a guided pub tour, with lots of historical tales and drinking involved.

Knopwood's Retreat (Map p640; ☎ 03-6223 5808; 39 Salamanca Pl; ❤ 11am-late) Knopwood's is Hobart's holy temple of insobriety, and barmaids – both burly and buxom – have been pulling beers here since 1829. Hobart's best pub is a congenial family-friendly daytime watering hole with an open fire and a few rusted-on locals, but come Friday night the beautiful people swarm and the crowd spills across the street.

Quarry (Map p640; ☎ 03-6223 6552; 27 Salamanca Pl; ❤ 11am-late) This slick Salamanca renovation teems with sassy young Hobart starlets. The dim lighting is kind to the receding hairlines of aging musos and businessmen out too late. There's a great Mod Oz menu too (pan-fried haloumi salad or mussel linguini with tomato, fresh basil and chives).

T-42° (Map p640; ☎ 03-6224 7742; Elizabeth St Pier; ❤ 9am-late) Waterfront T-42° makes a big splash with its new-world fusion food that's heavy on seafood, and attracts late-week barflies with its minimalist interior, spinnaker-shaped bar, muzak and Charlie, the quintessential Hobart barman. If you're out late enough, they do breakfast, too.

Shipwrights Arms Hotel (Map p638; ☎ 03-6223 5551; 29 Trumpeter St, Battery Point) Bend your elbow with the yachties at this beloved 1834 pub, bedecked with nautical paraphernalia and known affectionately as 'Shippies'. A generous seafood counter meal + beer garden = the perfect summer afternoon.

Lizbon (Map p638; ☎ 03-6234 9133; 217 Elizabeth St, North Hobart; ❤ 4pm-late Tue-Sat) Lizbon lures a late-20s set with excellent wines by the glass, antipasto platters, smooth tunes, a pool table and intimate nooks and crannies. Occasional live jazz.

Soak@Kaos (Map p638; ☎ 03-6231 5699; 237 Elizabeth St, North Hobart; ❤ 10am-2pm) Gay- and straight-friendly Soak is a cloistered little lounge bar attached to Kaos Café (left) and makes for an intoxicating place for a tipple. Burgers and cakes are served from the cafe alongside handsome cocktails, and there's DJs on Friday and Saturday nights.

Bar Celona (Map p640; ☎ 03-6224 7557; 23 Salamanca Sq; ❤ 10am-late) The impressive renovation is almost irrelevant here, with the main focus drifting between divorcees eyeing each other across the crowd and the effervescent staff, bubbly as champagne in tight yellow T-shirts. The tapas menu deserves scrutiny, and there's DJs on Saturday nights.

ENTERTAINMENT

The *Mercury* newspaper lists most of Hobart's entertainment options in its Thursday edition. The free monthly *Sauce* entertainment rag provides detailed arts listings. The online gig guide at www.thedwarf.com.au is also worth a look.

Live Music

Republic Bar & Café (Map p638; ☎ 03-6234 6954; www .republicbar.com; 299 Elizabeth St, North Hobart; ☼ 11am-late) The No 1 live-music pub in Hobart, the Republic is a raucous art deco pub hosting live music every night (often free entry). There's an always-interesting line-up of local and international acts of an indie ilk and a loyal clientele.

New Sydney Hotel (Map p640; ☎ 03-6234 4516; www .newsydneyhotel.com; 87 Bathurst St; ☼ noon-10pm Mon, to midnight Tue-Sat, 4-9pm Sun) Low-key folk, jazz, blues and comedy playing Tuesday to Sunday nights (usually free), with the occasional pub-rock outfit and end-of-week crowds adding a few decibels. With 12 beers on tap, it's a sociable place for a drink or three.

Salamanca Arts Centre (Map p640; ☎ 03-6234 8414; www.salarts.org.au; 77 Salamanca Pl; ☼ live music 5.30-7.30pm Fri) There's free live music year-round in the SAC courtyard off Wooby Lane – Afrobeat to rockabilly, folk or gypsy-Latino. Drinks essential (sangria in summer, mulled wine in winter); dancing optional.

Irish Murphy's (Map p640; ☎ 03-6223 1119; www .irishmurphys.com.au; 21 Salamanca Pl; ☼ 11am-late) Pretty much what you'd expect from any out-of-the-box Irish pub – crowded, lively, affable and dripping with Guinness. Free live music of varying repute from Wednesday to Sunday nights; original acts on Thursdays.

Other options include the rowdy pub rock at the **Telegraph Hotel** (Map p640; ☎ 03-6234 6254; telegraph.hotel.hobart@gmail.com; 19 Morrison St) and the nearby **Customs House Hotel** (Map p640; ☎ 03-6234 6645; www.customshousehotel.com; 1 Murray St).

Theatre & Concerts

Theatre Royal (Map p640; ☎ 1800 650 277, 03-6233 2299; www.theatreroyal.com.au; 29 Campbell St; shows $20-60; ☼ box office 10am-5pm) The Theatre Royal is Australia's oldest continually operating theatre, where actors first trod the boards back in

1837. It showcases a range of music, ballet, theatre, opera and university revues. See p643 for backstage tour information.

Federation Concert Hall (Map p640; ☎ 1800 001 190, 03-6235 3633; www.tso.com.au; 1 Davey St; ☼ box office 9am-5pm Mon-Fri) Welded to the Hotel Grand Chancellor, this concert hall resembles a huge aluminium can leaking insulation from gaps in the panelling. Inside, the Tasmanian Symphony Orchestra saw their fiddles and bang their kettle drums (tickets from $55).

Cinema

State Cinema (Map p638; ☎ 03-6234 6318; www .statecinema.com.au; 375 Elizabeth St, North Hobart; tickets adult/concession $15/13; ☼ box office noon-10pm) Saved from the wrecking ball in the '90s, the State shows local and international art-house flicks. There's a great cafe and bar on site (you can take your wine into the cinema).

Village Cinemas (Map p640; ☎ 03-6234 7288; www .villagecinemas.com.au; 181 Collins St; tickets adult/concession/child $15/12/10.50; ☼ box office 10am-10pm) Inner-city multiplex screening mainstream releases. Cheap-arse Tuesday tickets $10.

Nightclubs

Mobius (Map p640; ☎ 03-6224 4411; 7 Despard St; ☼ 9pm-late Thu-Sat) A throbbing dungeon behind the main waterfront area, Mobius pumps relentless break beats, hip hop, and drum 'n' bass while the crowd writhes and wriggles.

Halo (Map p640; ☎ 03-6234 6669; 37a Elizabeth St, access off Purdy's Mart; ☼ 10pm-late Wed-Sun) Halo is Hobart's best-credentialed club and hosts touring and local DJs spinning acid, hard trance, electro and hip hop.

Syrup (Map p640; ☎ 03-6224 8249; www.syrupclub .com; 39 Salamanca Pl; ☼ 9pm-late Thu-Sat) Spreading syrup-like over two floors above Knopwood's Retreat (opposite), this is a great place for late-night drinks and DJs playing to the techno/house crowd.

Isobar (Map p640; ☎ 03-6231 6600; www.isobar .com.au; 11a Franklin Wharf; ☼ 10pm-5am Wed, Fri & Sat) Downstairs here is a shmick bar (open from 5pm Fridays, 7pm Saturdays), while Isobar itself – the club upstairs – plays commercial dance and blows hot and cold with the locals.

SHOPPING

People who've relocated to Hobart from Melbourne or Sydney bemoan the shopping.

Unless you're looking for outdoors gear and fishing equipment or yet another Huon pine-handled cheese knife (see Hugh & Who?, p656) or lathe-turned sassafras bowl, there's not much in the way of shopping opportunities to rival Milan or Paris. There is some outstanding handmade furniture, but that can be hard to get home in your cabin baggage. Head to Salamanca Place for shops stocking Huon pine goods, hand-knitted beanies, superb local wines and cheeses, sauces, jams, fudge and assorted edibles. The hyperactive Salamanca Market (p644), held here every Saturday, overflows with gourmet Tasmanian produce and sassafras cheeseboards.

The CBD shopping area is the place for less specialised needs, extending west from Elizabeth St Mall through the inner-city arcades. On Elizabeth St between Melville and Bathurst Sts is a swath of stores catering to the abovementioned outdoors types.

GETTING THERE & AWAY
Air
There are no direct international flights to/from Tasmania. Airlines with services between Hobart and the mainland are **Qantas** (☎ 13 13 13; www.qantas.com.au), **Jetstar** (☎ 13 15 38; www.jetstar.com.au) and **Virgin Blue** (☎ 13 67 89; www.virginblue.com.au).

Bus
See p636 for information on intrastate bus services.

The main bus companies (and their terminals) operating to/from Hobart are **Redline Coaches** (Map p638; ☎ 1300 360 000; www.tasredline.com.au; Transit Centre, 199 Collins St; ☼ 9am-5.30pm Mon-Fri, to 3pm Sat, to 4pm Sun) and **TassieLink** (Map p640; ☎ 1300 300 520; www.tassielink.com.au; Hobart Bus Terminal, 64 Brisbane St; ☼ 7am-6pm Sun-Fri, to 4pm Sat).

Additionally, **Metro Tasmania** (☎ 13 22 01; www.metrotas.com.au) has regular services to/from Richmond, New Norfolk and Kingston, south along the D'Entrecasteaux Channel and to Cygnet. Timetable and fare information is available online or from Metro Tasmania's Metro Shop (right).

GETTING AROUND
To/From the Airport
The airport is 16km east of the city centre. The **Airporter Shuttle Bus** (Map p638; ☎ 0419 382 240; 199 Collins St; one-way adult/concession/child $15/6/7.50) scoots between the Transit Centre and the airport

(via various city pick-up points), connecting with all flights. Bookings are essential.

A taxi between the airport and the city centre will cost around $33 between 6am and 8pm weekdays, or $38 at other times.

Bicycle
See p644 for details of bicycle-rental options.

Bus
Metro Tasmania (☎ 13 22 01; www.metrotas.com.au) operates the local bus network, which is reliable but infrequent outside business hours. The **Metro Shop** (Map p640; ☼ 8.30am-5.30pm Mon-Fri), inside the GPO on the corner of Elizabeth and Macquarie Sts, handles ticketing and enquiries. Most buses depart from this section of Elizabeth St, or from nearby Franklin Sq.

One-way fares vary with distances ('sections' $2 to $4.50). For $5 you can buy an unlimited-travel Day Rover ticket, valid after 9am Monday to Friday, and all day Saturday, Sunday and public holidays. Buy one-way tickets from the driver (exact change required) or ticket agents (newsagents and most post offices); day passes are only available from ticket agents. Alternatively, buy a book of 10 discounted tickets for use any time of day ($16 to $36).

Car
Timed, metered parking predominates in the CBD and tourist areas like Salamanca and the waterfront. For longer-term parking, large CBD garages (clearly signposted) offer inexpensive rates, often with the first hour free.

The big rental firms (Avis, Budget, Thrifty et al) have airport desks. Cheaper local firms with city offices offer daily rental rates starting at around $35; see p636 for details.

Taxi
You'll have no trouble hailing a cab in the busy, touristed areas. Fares are metered.
City Cabs (☎ 13 10 08)
Maxi-Taxi Services (☎ 03-6234 8061) Wheelchair-accessible vehicles.
Taxi Combined Services (☎ 13 22 27)

AROUND HOBART

Riverside communities, sandy beaches, historic towns, pretty undulating pasturelands and stands of native bush are all just few minutes' drive beyond the Hobart city limits. The ghosts of Tasmania's convict past drag their leg-irons in historic Richmond, while wilderness, wildlife, waterfalls and great short walks at Mt Field National Park make a terrific day trip from the capital.

Without your own wheels, day trips around Hobart are offered by a number of companies (see p646).

RICHMOND

pop 880

Richmond straddles the Coal River 27km northeast of Hobart. It was once a strategic military post and convict station on the road to Port Arthur. With an impressive stock of 19th-century buildings and relics, Richmond parades itself as Tasmania's premier historic town, but like The Rocks in Sydney and Hahndorf in Adelaide, it long ago morphed into a caricature with no organic life of its own – just a leeching tourist industry of trinkets, tea houses and cottage B&Bs.

Nevertheless, Richmond is undeniably attractive, and kids love chasing the ducks that waddle on the grassy riverbanks. It's also quite close to the airport – a happy overnight option if you're on an early flight. See www.richmondvillage.com.au for more information.

Sights & Activities

Richmond Bridge (Wellington St) is the town's proud centrepiece – handsome although rather bovine in its proportions. Built by convicts in 1823, it's purportedly haunted by the 'Flagellator of Richmond', George Grover, who died here in 1832. The northern wing of the remarkably well-preserved **Richmond Gaol** (☎ /fax 6260 2127; 37 Bathurst St; adult/child/family $7/3/18; ☯ 9am-5pm) was built in 1825, five years before the penitentiary at Port Arthur. And like Port Arthur, Richmond Gaol is historically fascinating, but is another macabre reminder of the privations and cruelties the British ruling class imposed upon their proletariat.

Other interesting historic places include the 1836 **St John's Church** (Wellington St), the first Roman Catholic church in Australia; the 1834 **St Luke's Church of England** (Edwards St); the 1825 **courthouse** (Forth St); the 1826 **post office** (Bridge St); the 1888 **Richmond Arms Hotel** (Bridge St); and the 1830 **Prospect House** (Richmond Rd), a historic B&B just south of town.

Loose the kids in wooden-walled **Richmond Maze** (☎ 03-6260 2451; 13 Bridge St; adult/child/family $7/5/20; ☯ 9am-5pm) or visit the curious **Old**

Hobart Town Historic Model Village (☎ 03-6260 2502; www.oldhobarttown.com; 21a Bridge St; adult/family $10/25; ☯ 9am-5pm), a diminutive re-creation of 1820s Hobart.

There are two wildlife parks nearby. **ZooDoo Wildlife Fun Park** (☎ 03-6260 2444; www.zoodoo.com .au; 620 Middle Tea Tree Rd; adult/child $18/10; ☯ 9am-5pm), 6km west of Richmond on the road to Brighton, has miniature horses and Tasmanian devils, wallabies and a nursery farm. **Bonorong Wildlife Centre** (☎ 03-6268 1184; www.bonorong.com.au; 593 Briggs Rd, Brighton; adult/child $16/9; ☯ 9am-5pm), 17km west of Richmond, has devils, koalas, wombats, echidnas and quolls that are fed daily at 11.30am and 2pm, and works to conserve Tasmania's native wildlife.

Richmond is the centre of Tasmania's fastest-growing wine region, the Coal River Valley, with wineries popping up in all directions. Overlooking the Mt Pleasant Observatory 9km southwest of Richmond, **Meadowbank Estate** (☎ 03-6248 4484; www.meadowbankwines.com.au; 699 Richmond Rd, Cambridge; tastings free-$5, mains $16-28; ☯ 10am-5pm) is the area's best-known winery (brilliant Pinot Gris, Sauvignon Blanc and Pinot Noir), with an acclaimed restaurant serving lunch daily, plus an art gallery, kids' play area, tastings and sales. Check out *Flawed History,* an in-floor jigsaw by local artist Tom Samek.

Sleeping & Eating

Richmond Colonial Accommodation (☎ 03-6260 2570; 4 Percy St; d $130-160, extra adult/child $25/15) Manages three well-equipped, family-friendly historic cottages (Willow, Bridge and Poplar) around town. All are self-contained with a roll call of colonial touches.

Richmond Arms Hotel (☎ 03-6260 2109; www .richmondarmshotel.com.au; 42 Bridge St; mains $13-22; ☯ lunch & dinner) This laid-back sandstone pub has four simple units (doubles including breakfast from $100) in a converted stables. The pub is popular with day-tripping, moustachioed bikers, and has a reliable pub-grub menu (plus a kids' menu) with pleasant streetside tables. Coal River Valley wines are available.

Richmond Cabin & Tourist Park (☎ 1800 116 699, 03-6260 2192; www.richmondcabins.com; 48 Middle Tea Tree Rd; unpowered/powered sites $20/26, cabins $60-110; ☒) Over the back fence of Prospect House, this park is 1km south of town but provides affordable accommodation in neat, no-frills cabins. Kids will be happy with the indoor pool and games room.

Richmond Bakery (☎ 03-6260 2628; off Edward St; ☺ breakfast & lunch) Pies, pastries, sandwiches, croissants, muffins and cakes – eat in or takeaway.

Ma Foosies (☎ 03-6260 2412; 46 Bridge St; dishes $5-11; ☺ breakfast & lunch) Cosy tearoom serving breakfast till 11.30am (pancakes, stuffed croissants, bacon and eggs) and an array of light meals, including ploughman's lunch, grilled panini, quiche and lasagne. Gluten-free menu available.

Getting There & Away

Richmond is a 20-minute drive from Hobart. You can get to Richmond on **TassieLink** (☎ 1300 653 633; www.tassielink.com.au) buses that leave the corner of Elizabeth and Macquarie Sts at 7am, 8.30am, noon, 4pm, 5pm and 5.30pm Monday to Friday. TassieLink's east-coast service to Swansea also passes through Richmond, leaving the Hobart Bus Terminal (Map p640) at 4pm Monday to Friday. The one-way fare on either is $7.

The **Richmond Tourist Bus** (☎ 0408 341 804; per person return $25; ☺ 9.15am & 12.20pm) runs a twice-daily service from Hobart, with three hours to explore Richmond before returning. Call for bookings and pick-up locations.

MT FIELD NATIONAL PARK

Declared a national park in 1916, Mt Field is famed for its spectacular mountain scenery, alpine moorlands and lakes, rainforest, waterfalls and abundant wildlife. It's 80km northwest of Hobart and makes a terrific day-trip – on the way you might want to stop at **New Norfolk**, an industrial river town making something of a revival.

The park's **visitor information centre** (☎ 03-6288 1149; www.parks.tas.gov.au; 66 Lake Dobson Rd; ☺ 8.30am-5pm Nov-Apr, 9am-4pm May-Oct) houses a cafe and displays on the park's origins, and provides information on walks. Day-use facilities include barbecues, shelters and a playground.

Skiing at Mt Mawson is sometimes an option, when nature sees fit to deposit snow (infrequently in recent years). Snow reports are available online at www.ski.com.au, or via a **recorded message service** (☎ 03-6288 1166).

Don't miss the magnificently tiered, 45m-high **Russell Falls**, an easy 20-minute return amble from behind the visitor information centre. The path is suitable for prams and wheelchairs. There are also easy walks to

---

HUGH & WHO?

Tasmania's Huon pine (*Lagarostrobos franklinii*) is one of the world's slowest-growing and longest-living trees, and is highly prized for its rich golden hue, rot-resistant oils and fine grain. Trees can take 2000 years to reach 30m in height and live to be 3000 years or more, a fact lost on the 19th-century 'piners' and ship builders who plundered the southwest forests in search of 'Yellow Gold'. Fortunately it's now a protected species – most of the Huon Pine furniture and timberwork you'll see around the state is recycled, or comes from dead trees salvaged from riverbeds and hydro-electric dams.

Lady Barron Falls and Horseshoe Falls, and longer bushwalks.

On the Tyenna River 4km east of Mt Field is **Something Wild** (☎ 03-6288 1013; 2080 Gordon River Rd; www.somethingwild.com.au; adult/concession/child/family $14/12/7/42; ☺ 10am-5pm), a wildlife sanctuary that rehabilitates orphaned and injured wildlife. Visit the animal nursery, see native wildlife (devils, wombats, quolls) and maybe spot a platypus sniffing around the grounds.

Sleeping & Eating

Self-caterers need to buy supplies in New Norfolk before arriving at Mt Field National Park…or go hungry.

Lake Dobson Cabins (☎ 03-6288 1149; www.parks.tas.gov.au; Lake Dobson Rd; cabins up to 6 people $40) These three simple six-bed cabins about 14km inside the park are equipped with mattresses, cold water, wood stove and firewood (there's no power). There's a communal toilet block, and visitors must bring gas lamps, cookers and utensils. Book at the visitors centre.

Russell Falls Holiday Cottages (☎ 03-6288 1198; fax 6288 1341; 40 Lake Dobson Rd; d $110-130) These spotless, self-contained cottages are in a super location next to the park entrance. Ask about low-season and drive-by discounts.

Land of the Giants Campground (☎ 03-6288 1526; unpowered/powered sites $16/25) A privately run, self-registration campground with adequate facilities (toilets, showers, laundry and free barbecues) just inside the park gates. Bookings are not required. Site prices are additional to national park entry fees.

TASMANIA

Celtic Dawn (☎ 03-6288 1058; http://celticdawnx.tripod.com; 2400 Gordon River Rd; meals $8-12) About 600m west of the national park turn-off is this odd octagonal cafe with only a couple of tables serving tacos, soups, filo pastries and good coffee. There are two great-value rooms here: one double room ($70) and one with two singles ($60), and both with bathrooms and a shared outdoor kitchen.

National Park Hotel (☎ 03-6288 1103; Gordon River Rd; d $90; mains $15-27; ☿ dinner) This relaxed rural pub 300m past the park turn-off cooks up mixed grills, chicken dishes and steaks. There are some simple pub rooms with shared facilities.

Getting There & Away
The drive to Mt Field through the Derwent River Valley and Bushy Park is beautiful: river rapids, hop fields, rows of poplars and hawthorn hedgerows. Day tours from Hobart are run by various operators including Bottom Bits Bus (p634) and Gray Line (p646).

TAROONA & KINGSTON
Taroona and Kingston are suburbs of Kingborough, Tasmania's fastest-growing municipality (population 30,900). Taroona, 10km south of Hobart, is a bush-meets-beach hippie 'burb that peaked in the '70s but lost much of its community vibe. It's famously home town of Crown Princess Mary of Denmark (aka Mary Donaldson of Taroona High School).

On Taroona's southern fringe stands the **Shot Tower** (☎ 03-6227 8885; fax 6227 8643; Channel Hwy, Taroona; adult/child $5.50/2.50; ☿ 9am-5pm), a 48m-high, circular sandstone turret built in 1870 to make lead shot for firearms. The river views from atop the 318 steps are wondrous.

Sprawling Kingston, 12km south of Hobart, is headquarters for the **Australian Antarctic Division** (☎ 03-6232 3209; www.aad.gov.au; 203 Channel Hwy; admission free; ☿ 8.30am-5pm Mon-Fri), the department administering Australia's 42% wedge of the frozen continent. There's a small display on Antarctic exploration and ecology.

Kingston Beach is a popular swimming and sailing spot, with steep wooded cliffs at each end of a long arc of sand. Further south by road are **Blackmans Bay**, another swimmable beach, and **Tinderbox Marine Reserve**, where you can snorkel along an underwater trail marked with submerged information plates.

For sleeping and eating options, you'll be far better off back in Hobart. Local buses 56 and 61 run from Hobart through Taroona to Kingston.

SEVEN MILE BEACH
pop 1000
Out near the airport 15km east of Hobart is this safe swimming beach, backed by beach houses, a corner shop and pine-punctured dunes. When the swell is working, the point break here is magic.

A two-minute walk from the beach, **Seven Mile Beach Cabin Park** (☎ 03-6248 6469; www.comfycabins.com.au; 12 Aqua Pl; unpowered/powered sites $20/25, cabins $70-120; ☙) is a spacey patch with blue-painted corrugated iron cabins and free gas barbecues – as low-key as can be.

To get to Seven Mile Beach, drive towards the airport and follow the signs. Local buses 191, 192, 291 and 293 also run here.

THE SOUTHEAST

The southeast offers serene landscapes of rolling hills and valleys, riverside towns, and quiet harbours and inlets – it's a gentle collection of agrarian communities producing cherries, apricots, Atlantic salmon and cool-climate wines, servicing an increasing parade of tourists and recreational yachties and escapees from Hobart. Here, the fruit-filled hillsides of the Huon Valley give way to the sparkling inlets of the D'Entrecasteaux Channel. Bruny Island waits enticingly offshore, and the Hartz Mountains National Park is not far inland.

For further regional low-down see www.huontrail.org.au.

Getting There & Around
The southeast has three distinct areas: the peninsula, including Kettering and Cygnet; Bruny Island; and the Huon Hwy coastal strip linking Huonville with Cockle Creek.

Metro Tasmania (☎ 13 22 01; www.metrotas.com.au) runs several weekday buses from Hobart south to Kettering ($9.30, 50 minutes) and Woodbridge ($9.50, one hour). A bus from Hobart also runs once each weekday to Snug, then inland across to Cygnet ($11.50, one hour).

TassieLink (☎ 1300 300 520; www.tassielink.com.au) buses service the Huon Hwy from Hobart through Huonville ($10.90, one hour) several

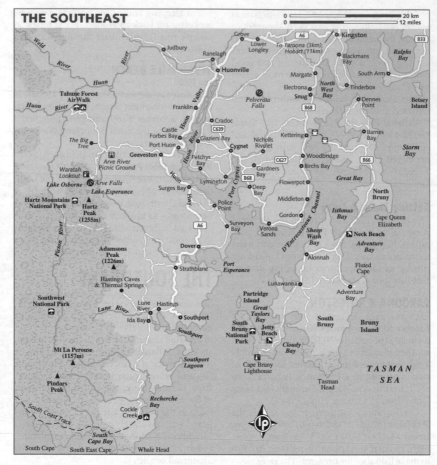

THE SOUTHEAST

times a day (once on Saturday and Sunday), with some continuing to Geeveston ($16.10, 1½ hours) and Dover ($21.40, 1¾ hours, not Sundays). Check the website or call for departure times.

From December to March on Monday, Wednesday and Friday, TassieLink also runs buses from Hobart down to Cockle Creek ($71.30, three hours), returning to Hobart on the same days.

KETTERING
pop 400

Somnolent Kettering is an attractive port town with fishing boats and tethered yachts in its marina. It's a popular launching place for sea-kayakers who come to explore the D'Entrecasteaux Channel, but most people just blow through to board the Bruny Island ferry.

The **Kettering visitor information centre** (☎ 03-6267 4494; www.tasmaniaholiday.com; 81 Ferry Rd; ⏰ 9am-5pm) by the ferry terminal has information on accommodation and services on Bruny Island, including notes on walks and a self-guided driving tour. The Mermaid Café is also here.

Roaring 40s Ocean Kayaking (☎ 03-6267 5000; www.roaring40skayaking.com.au; Oyster Cove Marina, Ferry Rd), at the marina, is Tassie's leading sea-kayaking tour operator. The company offers gear rental to kayakers, and organises a smorgasbord of kayaking trips to suit all levels of experience. A half-day paddle around Oyster Cove costs $95; a full day on D'Entrecasteaux Channel costs $160, including lunch. Overnight trips at venues such as Lake St Clair, Lake Pedder and Maria Island are also available, plus three- to seven-day trips around the southwest wilderness.

A cream-coloured monolith overlooking the boat-cluttered harbour, **Oyster Cove Inn** (☎ 03-6267 4446; www.view.com.au/oyster; 1 Ferry Rd; s/d without bathroom from $45/80) is a large pub with budget singles, twins and doubles upstairs. A mismatch of weird carpet, linen and drape oddments, raggedy bathrooms and occasional antique furniture pieces, Oyster Cove Inn is an eclectically no-frills experience. The restaurant (mains $10 to $25) offers good dinnertime fare, with an extensive menu, local wines, a casual bar and outdoor deck.

Just north of town, **Herons Rise Vineyard** (☎ 03-6267 4339; www.heronsrise.com.au; 1000 Saddle Rd; d $140-160) has two upmarket, self-contained cottages set in lush surroundings among the vines (the third is being built above the Pinot-stacked wine cellar), each featuring a log fire. Breakfast provisions are supplied.

BRUNY ISLAND
pop 600

Bruny Island is almost two islands joined by a narrow, sandy isthmus called The Neck. Famous for its wildlife (fairy penguins, echidnas and mutton birds), it's a windswept, sparsely populated and undeveloped retreat, soaked in ocean rains in the south, and dry and scrubby in the north. It was named after French explorer Bruny D'Entrecasteaux – see www.brunyisland.net.

You really need a few days to appreciate Bruny's isolated coastal communities, swimming and surf beaches, and the forests and walking tracks within the **South Bruny National Park** (www.parks.tas.gov.au) – don't try and cram it into a day trip. Each hour or so another convoy of vehicles alights from the ferry and drives in formation along the main road. Tourism is the mainstay of the island's economy, yet there are no large resorts – just self-contained cottages and guest houses. A car or bicycle is essential for getting around. Supplies are available at the well-stocked Adventure Bay general store and the tiny shops at Alonnah and Lunawanna. Many island roads are unsealed – and not all car rental companies are cool with this concept.

Climb the 273 steps up to the lookout at the **Hummock** at **Bruny Island Neck Game Reserve**.

All around are the rookeries of mutton birds and little penguins that nest in the dunes – the penguins can be seen emerging from the sea at dusk. This is the site of the **Truganini Memorial** and another moment of reflection on Tasmania's grim history; see p660.

The curiosity-arousing **Bligh Museum of Pacific Exploration** (☎ 03-6293 1117; 876 Main Rd, Adventure Bay; adult/child/family $4/2/10; ✆ 10am-4pm) details the local exploits of explorers Bligh, Cook, Furneaux and, of course, Bruny D'Entrecasteaux. Also worth visiting is the 1836 **Cape Bruny Lighthouse** (☎ 03-6298 3114; tours adult/child $5/2) on South Bruny. Take a tour (one day's advance booking required) or wander the surrounding **reserve** (✆ 10am-4pm), with expansive views from the rugged cape headland over mainland Tasmania's southernmost reaches.

From October to April, **Bruny Island Charters** (☎ 03-6293 1465; www.brunycharters.com.au) operates sensational three-hour tours of Bruny's towering southeast coastline, taking in rookeries, seal colonies, bays, caves and high sea cliffs. Trips depart Adventure Bay jetty at 11am daily from October to May, and cost $100/55 per adult/child. Alternatively, take the tour as a full-day trip from Hobart ($165/110), including lunch and transfers.

Travellers without wheels could try Bruny Island Charters' **Bruny Island Bus Service** ($45; ✆ 7.50am). This return bus trip from Hobart to Adventure Bay includes Bligh Museum admission and four hours' exploring time, and returns to Hobart at 5.30pm.

Sleeping

Self-contained cottages are plentiful on Bruny. Bookings are essential, as owners/managers and their keys aren't always easily located – the Kettering visitor information centre (opposite) is a good starting point. The **White Wallaby Café** (☎ 1300 889 557; www.bruny islandaccommodation.com.au) in Adventure Bay (see p661) manages many of Bruny's private rental properties. Most of the accommodation is in Adventure Bay, but there's more at Alonnah, and at Barnes Bay and Dennes Point (pronounced 'Denz') on North Bruny.

Lumeah (☎ 03-6293 1265; www.lumeah-island.com .au; Adventure Bay Rd, Adventure Bay; d $145) Sawmillers built this cottage 115 years ago, and it's since been refitted to comfortably accommodate two couples or two families, with two double rooms, two bathrooms and a bunk room sleeping six (maximum 10 guests). It's fully

TASMANIA

THE SORRY STORY OF TASMANIA'S ABORIGINES

The treatment of Tasmania's Indigenous peoples by early European settlers is a tragic and shameful story. Isolated from the Australian mainland by rising sea levels 10,000 years ago, the island's Aborigines developed a distinct, sustainable, seasonal culture of hunting, fishing and gathering.

When European pastoralists arrived, they fenced off sections of fertile land for farming. Aborigines lost more and more of their traditional hunting grounds, and battles erupted between blacks and whites – the so-called Black Wars. Lieutenant-Governor Arthur declared martial law in 1828 and Aboriginal tribes were systematically murdered, incarcerated or forced at gunpoint from districts settled by whites. Many more succumbed to European diseases.

An attempt to resettle Tasmania's remaining Aborigines to Flinders Island – to 'civilise' and Christianise them – occurred between 1829 and 1834, but most died of despair, poor food or respiratory disease. Of the 135 taken to the island, only 47 survived to be transferred to another settlement at Oyster Cove in Tasmania's south in 1847. Within 32 years, the entire Aboriginal population at Oyster Cove had perished.

European sealers had been working in Bass Strait since 1798 and, although they occasionally raided tribes along the coast, their contact with Aboriginal people was mainly based on trade. Aboriginal women were also traded and many sealers settled on Bass Strait islands with these women and had families.

There's a simple memorial at The Neck (p659) on Bruny Island to Truganini, who was said to be the last full-blood Aborigine. Truganini died in her seventies in Hobart in 1876 (she was, in fact, outlived by two full-blood women). Her sad life and death was reported at the time as 'the end of the native problem' and her skeleton was displayed in the Hobart museum, but she's since become a symbol of the horror of the attempted genocide of Tasmania's Indigenous peoples.

By 1847 an Aboriginal community, with a lifestyle based on both Aboriginal and European ways, had emerged on Flinders and other islands in the Furneaux Group. Although the last full-blooded Tasmanian Aborigines died in the 19th century, the strength of this community helped save the race from oblivion. Today, thousands of descendants of this community live in Tasmania.

For more information contact the **Aboriginal Heritage Office** (☎ 1300 135 513, 03-6216 4471; www.tahl.tas.gov.au) or see the excellent *Deep Time: Continuing Tasmanian Aboriginal Culture* brochure available at the Hobart visitor information centre (p641).

---

self-contained, 50m from the beach, and has a barbecue area and spa.

Explorers' Cottages (☎ 03-6293 1271; www.bruny island.com; 20 Lighthouse Rd, Lunawanna; d $150) Just south of Lunawanna on the way to the lighthouse, these bright, beachy, self-contained cottages sleep four with lounge areas, log fires, board games and outdoor decks.

our pick **The Tree House** (☎ 0405 192 892; www .thetreehouse.com.au; Alonnah; d $185) This wonderful open-plan timber place overlooks romantically named Sheep Wash Bay, with two bedrooms and everything that opens and shuts. The price drops to $165 for stays of two nights or more.

Captain James Cook Memorial Caravan Park (☎ 03-6293 1128; www.capcookolkid.com.au; 786 Main Rd, Adventure Bay; unpowered/powered sites $18/22, on-site caravans from $45, cabins $110-120; ⊠) Bruny's cheapest accommodation offers decent facilities (including wheelchair-accessible cabins) and a great beachside location. There are some

shady tent sites by the creek, but elsewhere it could use a few more trees. The owners are lovely and also run fishing charters.

There's free bush **camping** in South Bruny National Park (national park fees apply) at Jetty Beach, a sheltered cove 3km north of the lighthouse. But the best spot is surf-battered South Cloudy Bay – put your car (not a hire car!) down onto the firm sand at Whalebone Point on Cloudy Bay and drive 3km along the beach to the terrific free-camping area behind the dunes. The drive can be tricky on a high tide and is officially rated 4WD, but plucky types in a standard car should have no problems. There's also free camping outside the national park at Neck Beach, at the southern end of The Neck.

Eating

Hothouse Café (☎ 03-6293 1131; 46 Adventure Bay Rd, South Bruny; snacks & meals $9-23; ⊠ breakfast & lunch, dinner by arrangement) This cafe at Morella Island Retreat occupies a converted hothouse (sit inside on a sunny day and you'll start to sprout). Isthmus views and flappy birdlife complement the interesting menu of omelettes, steaks and flatbread wraps.

Bruny Island Smoke House (☎ 03-6260 6344; 360 Lennon Rd, North Bruny; mains $12-20; ☼ lunch Sat & Sun, dinner Fri) Managed with pizzazz, 'BISH' is a winner – gourmet pizzas, smoked fish and meats, cakes, decent coffee and astounding views from the deck. If only they were open more often!

White Wallaby Café (☎ 03-6293 2096; 710 Main Rd, Adventure Bay; mains $14-28; ☼ lunch & dinner; 🖳) The old Penguin Café next to the Adventure Bay store has new owners who've changed the name, extended the trading hours and menu, ramped up the daytime cafe and evening à la carte offerings, and incorporated a new rental-property-management business.

Bruny Island Hotel (☎ 03-6293 1148; Main Rd, Alonnah; mains $17-24; ☼ lunch & dinner) Australia's southernmost hotel is this unassuming pub in Alonnah, with outdoor water-view seating and a fair menu of mainly local seafood fare. There are also two simple (overpriced) motel-style rooms at single/double $90/100.

Getting There & Around

Access to the island is via **car ferry** (☎ 03-6272 3277) from Kettering across to Roberts Point on the north of the island. There are at least 10 services daily from 7am to 7.30pm, taking 20 minutes one way. Return fares: cars $25 ($30 on public holidays and public holiday weekends), motorcycles $11, bicycles $3 and foot passengers free.

Metro Tasmania (☎ 13 22 01; www.metrotas.com .au) runs weekday-only buses from Hobart to Kettering (see p657), stopping on request at the Kettering ferry terminal. The ferry terminal on Bruny is a long way from anywhere – BYO transport.

WOODBRIDGE
pop 250

Established in 1874 as Peppermint Bay, Woodbridge was eventually renamed by a nostalgic English landowner. It's a quiet village sitting squarely on the tourist trail, thanks to the sexy **Peppermint Bay** (☎ 03-6267 4088; www .peppermintbay.com.au; 3435 Channel Hwy) development that consumed the old Woodbridge pub. On a glorious D'Entrecasteaux Channel inlet,

Peppermint Bay houses a provedore, art gallery, upmarket **Dining Room** (mains $25-30; ☼ lunch daily, dinner Sat), and casual **Terrace Bar** (mains $15-20; ☼ lunch daily, dinner Tue-Sat). Local produce – seafood, fruits, meats, cheeses and other foodstuffs from the region – is used to fantastic effect. You can also take a cruise here from Hobart (p646).

CYGNET
pop 840

Bruny D'Entrecasteaux originally named this little rural neighbourhood Port de Cygne Noir (Port of the Black Swan) because of the swans that proliferate on the bay. Youthfully reincarnated as Cygnet (baby swan), the town has recently evolved into an artsy enclave while still functioning as a major centre for regional fruit production, and these days weathered farmers, dreadlocked hippies and commuting city workers make up a convivial inclusive community. If you're not in a hurry, cruise the scenic Cygnet Coast Rd (C639) between Cradoc and Cygnet. It's 20km longer than the direct A6 route from Hobart that turns off for Cygnet at Huonville, but makes a slow-paced, photo-worthy detour (and then the razorback C627 over the ridge to Woodbridge – another picturesque route).

The ever-popular **Cygnet Folk Festival** (www .cygnetfolkfestival.org) is three days of words, music and dance in January, showcasing bluesy-folksters like Mic Conway, Jeff Lang and Monique Brumby. The warmer months also provide abundant fruit-picking work for backpackers.

The **Cygnet Living History Museum** (☎ 03-6295 1602; 37 Mary St; admission by donation; ☼ 10am-3pm Tue & Wed, 12.30-3pm Fri & Sat), next to the church on the main street, is stuffed with old photos, documents and curios.

Huon Valley (Balfes Hill) Backpackers (☎ 03-6295 1551; www.huonvalleybackpackers.com; 4 Sandhill Rd, Cradoc; unpowered sites $15, dm/d/f $20/50/75; 🖳), off the Channel Hwy 4.5km north of Cygnet, has decent rooms, good facilities, extensive grounds and super views from the large communal area, and is busy (book ahead) from November to May, when backpackers come for fruit-picking work. Courtesy bus to/from Cygnet bus stop; bike hire per half-/full day $15/25.

The pick of Cygnet's three pubs is the **Commercial Hotel** (☎ 03-6295 1296; 2 Mary St; s/d with shared bathroom $50/65) at the bottom of the main street: serviceable pub rooms upstairs, cafe and **bistro** (mains $10-24; ✪ lunch & dinner) downstairs serving mountainous pub classics.

The **Red Velvet Lounge** (☎ 03-6295 0466; 24 Mary St; mains $8-12; ✪ breakfast & lunch), is one of a number of groovy cafes popping up on the main street. This funky wholefood store and coffee-house serves deliciously healthy and hearty meals to a diverse clientele of aforementioned farmers, hippies and city workers.

HUONVILLE & AROUND

Huonville (population 1940), on the banks of the Huon River, is the biggest town south of Hobart and sits in a region of pretty hillside orchards and riverfront villages. The town was traditionally the centre of Tasmania's prodigious apple-growing industry, and while the region's farmers have since diversified into cherries, berries and stone fruit, and the viticulturalists have moved in, Huonville remains largely a functioning farming centre with shops and services, but few attractions. Just down the road, pretty riverside **Franklin** is reinventing itself with a new slew of teahouses, eateries and bric-a-brac stores.

The **Huonville visitor information centre** (☎ 03-6264 1838; www.huonjet.com/trips/viscentre1.html; The Esplanade; ✪ 9am-5pm; ▯) is by the river on the road south to Cygnet. These guys also book the **Huon Jet** (www.huonjet.com; adult/child $62/40), 35-minute, heart-in-your-mouth jet-boat rides, and hire out paddleboats ($15 for 30 minutes).

At Grove, 6km north of Huonville, the **Huon Apple & Heritage Museum** (☎ 03-6266 4345; www.applemuseum.huonvalley.biz; 2064 Main Rd; adult/concession/child/family $6/5/3/15; ✪ 9am-5pm) has displays on 500 apple varieties (count 'em!) and 19th-century orchard life. Skip the tacky gift shop.

The nearby township of Ranelagh (3km northwest of Huonville) is home to the vinewreathed **Home Hill** (☎ 03-6264 1200; www.homehill wines.com.au; 38 Nairn St; ✪ 10am-5pm), producers of award-winning Pinot Noir with free tastings and an outstanding **restaurant** (mains $27-28; ✪ lunch daily, dinner Fri & Sat).

Ranelagh is also home to the 1865 **Matilda's of Ranelagh** (☎ 03-6264 3493; www.matildasofranelagh .com.au; 2 Louisa St; d $165-205), one of Tasmania's finest heritage B&Bs. Huonville's best eatery is hip BYO **Café Motó** (☎ 0400 315 533; 4 Wilmot St; mains $10-14; ✪ breakfast & lunch Mon-Fri), serving excellent coffee, cakes, quiches, pies and pastries – delicious!

GEEVESTON & AROUND

Trying hard to shake its reputation as a redneck logging town, Geeveston (population 760) is pitching itself as a tourist centre for Tassie's deep south, offering some decent accommodation and eateries close to the Hartz Mountains and Tahune Forest AirWalk.

Doubling as a visitor information centre, the **Forest & Heritage Centre** (☎ 03-6297 1836; www .forestandheritagecentre.com.au; 15 Church St; ✪ 9am-5pm; ▯) has forestry displays, a woodturning gallery and accommodation info and bookings. You can buy Tahune Forest AirWalk and Hastings Caves tickets here, and pick up a map detailing short walks en route to the AirWalk.

The hugely popular **Tahune Forest AirWalk** (☎ 03-6297 0068; www.tasforestrytourism.com.au; adult/concession/child/family $22/19.80/10/45; ✪ 9am-5pm), 29km west of town, has 600m of steel wheelchair-accessible walkways suspended 20m above the forest floor. There's a cafe and gift shop here, too. Drive here under your own steam, or take a day trip from Hobart (see Tours, p634). There's a free (unofficial) campsite at the Arve River Picnic Ground about halfway to the AirWalk. Don't miss the **Big Tree**, an enormous swamp gum not far west of the Arve River.

Bears Went Over the Mountain (☎ 03-6297 0110; www.bearsoverthemountain.com; 2 Church St; r $90-150; ▯), in the middle of Geeveston, has four rooms decorated in a whimsical bear theme with lots of lace and four-poster beds – makes us gag on our chawin' tobacco! Offers complimentary port for cold southern nights.

Cambridge House (☎ 03-6297 1561; www.cambridge house.biz; cnr School Rd & Huon Hwy; r $110-160) is an attractive 1930s B&B, with Baltic pine features and staircases, plus upstairs accommodation in three bedrooms with shared facilities (ideal for families), or a downstairs en suite room.

Kyari (☎ 03-6297 1601; 13 Church St; mains $9-14; ✪ breakfast & lunch) is a streamlined eatery in a converted bank, with all-day breakfasts, enticing cafe fare, a kids' menu and an outdoor deck. Hours are subject to wild variations – call in advance before you get your hopes up.

HARTZ MOUNTAINS NATIONAL PARK

The wilderness of this **park** (www.parks.tas.gov.au), part of Tasmania's World Heritage Area, is only 84km from Hobart – easy striking distance for day trippers and weekend walkers. The park is renowned for its jagged peaks, glacial tarns, gorges, alpine moorlands and dense rainforest. Rapid weather changes bluster through – even day-walkers should bring waterproofs and warm clothing.

There are some great hikes and isolated viewpoints in the park. **Waratah Lookout**, 24km from Geeveston, is an easy five-minute shuffle from the road. Other well-surfaced short walks include **Arve Falls** (20 minutes return) and **Lake Osborne** (40 minutes return). The steeper **Lake Esperance** walk (two hours return) takes you through sublime high country that's commonly known as 'God's own'.

There are basic day facilities within the park – toilets, shelters, picnic tables, barbecues – but camping is not allowed. Collect a *Hartz Mountains National Park* brochure from the Geeveston (opposite) or Huonville (opposite) visitor information centres.

DOVER & AROUND

Dover (population 465) is a chilled-out base for exploring the far south. In the 19th century Dover was a timber-milling town, but nowadays fish farms harvest Atlantic salmon for export throughout Asia. This is Tasmania's last vestige of civilisation for travellers heading south, and the place to stock up on fuel and supplies. On the road from Geeveston, take the pretty detour around Police Point, which provides superb views over the lower Huon River and D'Entrecasteaux Channel with its salmon farms and watercraft.

On the Esperance River at Strathblane, 5km south of Dover, **Far South Wilderness Lodge & Backpackers** (☎ 03-6298 1922; www.farsouthwilderness .com.au; Narrows Rd, Strathblane; dm/d $30/80; 💻) provides some of Tasmania's best budget accommodation, with a bushy waterfront setting, cosy lounge, quality accommodation and a strong environmental focus. During the summer months it's often booked solid by school groups so reserve well in advance. There's also a separate self-contained three-bedroom house for $300 per night, plus mountain bikes and kayaks for rent ($15/35 per day).

The huge **Dover Hotel** (☎ 03-6298 1210; www .doverhotel.com.au; Huon Hwy; mains $16-22; 🕑 lunch & dinner) has budget rooms above the bar (singles/ doubles $45/70), motel rooms (doubles $95) out the back and a self-contained unit sleeping up to seven ($190 for four adults). But it's the gourmet pub grub that we call in for – it features local Hastings oysters, Huon Valley produce and fresh fish and seafood from the

local fishing fleet. Kids' menu, tempting desserts and a great wine list, too.

The well-maintained **Dover Beachside Tourist Park** (☎ 03-6298 1301; www.dovercaravanpark.com.au; 27 Kent Beach Rd; unpowered/powered sites $20/27.50, caravans/cabins from $45/85), by a sandy beach, features grassy lawns, good camping facilities, on-site caravans and spotless cabins.

The snug, wood-panelled **Dover Woodfired Pizza** (☎ 03-6298 1905; Main Rd; mains $9-19; 🕑 lunch & dinner Wed-Sun) offers traditional and gourmet wood-fired pizzas, baked spuds and filling pasta dishes. Eat in or takeaway.

HASTINGS CAVES & THERMAL SPRINGS

The **Hastings Caves & Thermal Springs** facility, signposted inland from the Huon Hwy, is 21km south of Dover. The only way to explore the caves is via guided tour; buy tickets at the **Hastings visitor information centre** (☎ 03-6298 3209; www.parks.tas.gov.au; adult/concession/child/family $24/19.20/12/60; 🕑 9am-5pm Mar-Apr & Sep-Dec, 9am-6pm Jan & Feb, 10am-4pm May-Aug). Tours leave on the hour: the first an hour after the visitor centre opens, the last an hour before it closes. Admission includes a 45-minute tour of the amazing dolomite Newdegate Cave, plus entry to the **thermal swimming pool** behind the visitor information centre, filled with 28°C (supposedly) water from thermal springs (pool-only admission adult/concession/child/family $5/4/2.50/12). The pool water is tepid and on a cool day getting down to your togs and into the water seems slightly insane – kids love it while mums and dads watch on from the sidelines.

The wheelchair-friendly 20-minute **Hot Springs Trail** does an interesting loop through the rainforest from the pool area.

COCKLE CREEK

Australia's most southerly drive is a 19km corrugated-gravel stretch from Ida Bay past the gentle waves of **Recherche Bay** (pronounced 'Research Bay') to **Cockle Creek**. A grand grid of streets was once planned for Cockle Creek, but dwindling coal seams and whale numbers poured cold water on that idea. There's free camping along the Recherche Bay foreshore, or pitch tent just within Southwest National Park (national park fees apply). You can walk to windy **Whale Head** and onto the **South East Cape**. Apart from the remote Maatsuyker Islands and Macquarie Island, an Australian

DEFORESTATION IN TASMANIA *Senator Bob Brown*

Tasmania's wild and scenic beauty, along with an Aboriginal heritage dating back 30,000 years, is a priceless heritage available to all of us. The waterfalls, wild rivers, lovely beaches, snow-capped mountains, turquoise seas and wildlife are abundant and accessible for locals and visitors alike.

Because we are all creations of nature – that curl on our ears is fashioned to pick up the faintest sounds from the forest floor – we are all bonded to the wilds. It's no wonder that in this anxiety-ridden world there is such a thirst for remote, pristine, natural places. Yet around the world, wilderness is the fastest disappearing resource and Tasmania is no exception.

Every year more than 100,000 truck-loads of the island's native forests, including giant eucalypt species that are the tallest flowering plants on Earth, will arrive at the woodchip mills en route to Japan. After logging, the forests are firebombed and every fur, feather and flower is destroyed. These great forests are one of the world's best hedges against global warming – they're carbon banks. Yet they are being looted from our fellow creatures and all who come after us. The log trucks on Tasmania's highways are enriching banks of a different kind.

In the 1980s people power saved Tasmania's wild Franklin and Lower Gordon Rivers, which nowadays attract hundreds of thousands of visitors to the west coast. Those visitors, in turn, bring jobs, investment and local prosperity. Saving the environment has been a boon for the economy and employment.

The rescue of Tasmania's forests relies on each of us, and there are plenty of ways we can help. We can help with letters or phone calls to newspapers, radio stations or politicians; with every cent donated to the forest campaigners; and in every well-directed vote. The tourist dollar speaks loudly in Tasmania, so overseas travellers, who cannot vote, make an even greater impression if they write to our newspapers and politicians.

That said, welcome to this lucky, beautiful island: I hope that even if you don't raft a wild river, scale a giant tree or ride one of the world's biggest ocean waves, you find the special magic Tasmania offers every one of us.

Senator Bob Brown was elected to the Tasmanian parliament in 1983 and was first elected to the Senate in 1996. His books include The Valley of the Giants. *Read more about Bob Brown at www.bobbrown.org.au.*

territory halfway to Antarctica, South East Cape is the southernmost point of Australia and is buffeted by the Roaring Forties.

The Cockle Creek area features craggy, clouded mountains, brilliant long beaches and (best of all) hardly any people – perfect for camping and bushwalking. The challenging **South Coast Track** starts (or ends) here, taking you through to Melaleuca in the Southwest National Park. Combined with the **Port Davey Track** you can walk all the way to Port Davey in the southwest; see p714.

TASMAN PENINSULA

Port Arthur Historic Site, Tassie's single biggest tourist attraction, is the Tasman Peninsula's centre of activity. However, the ruins of convict settlement are only part of the peninsula's story. Here, too, are astonishing 300m-high sea cliffs, empty surf beaches, sandy bays and stunning bushwalks through thickly wooded forests and isolated coastlines. Much of the area constitutes the Tasman National Park. The Tasman Peninsula is almost an island – the 1905 Denison Canal was cut across the narrow isthmus at Dunalley to allow boats to pass from Blackman Bay on the peninsula's east to Norfolk Bay in the west. Vehicles access the peninsula by swing bridge.

See www.tasmanregion.com.au and www.portarthur.org.au for more information.

Getting There & Around

TassieLink (☎ 1300 300 520; www.tassielink.com.au) runs a 3.55pm weekday bus from Hobart Bus Terminal (Map p640) to Port Arthur ($26.60, 2¼ hours) during school terms; the Port Arthur–Hobart bus leaves at 6am. The service is reduced to Monday, Wednesday and Friday during school holidays. Buses stop at the main towns en route.

Redline Coaches (☎ 1300 360 000; www.redlinecoaches.com.au) also operates some weekday services between Hobart, Sorell and Dunalley, but go no further.

TOURS

Bottom Bits Bus (☎ 1800 777 103, 03-6229 3540; www.bottombitsbus.com.au; $110) Offers small-group backpacker-focused day trips (daily except Tuesday and Saturday), including Port Arthur entry, and visits to the peninsula's attractions including Tessellated Pavement, Tasman Arch, Devil's Kitchen and Doo Town.

Gray Line (☎ 1300 858 687, 03-6234 3336; www.grayline.com.au; adult/child $98/49) Coach tours including Isle of the Dead harbour cruise, Port Arthur admission and guided tour, and pit stops at Tasman Arch and the Devils' Kitchen.

Navigators (☎ 03-6223 1914; www.navigators.net.au; Brooke St Pier, Hobart; adult/child $229/183) Boat cruises from Hobart returning by bus, departing Wednesday, Friday and Sunday. Includes site entrance, guided tour, morning tea and cruise around Tasman Island.

Port Arthur Bus Service (☎ 03-6250 2200; www.tasmancruises.com.au; adult/child $85/55) Tasman Island Cruises run this return bus service that includes site admission. Departs Hobart visitor centre at 7.45am.

Roaring 40s Ocean Kayaking (☎ 03-6265 5000; www.roaring40stours.com.au; 1-/3-day tour $255/1150)

Based in Kettering (p658), Roaring 40s also conducts epic sea-kayaking tours around the Tasman Peninsula. Prices include equipment, meals, accommodation and transfers from Hobart.

Smash & Grab (☎ 1800 777 103; www.tourstasmania.com.au; $100) Sunday, Monday, Wednesday and Friday day tours ($100) including Port Arthur admission and stops at Eaglehawk Neck, Doo Town, Tasmans Arch and Remarkable Cave.

Tasman Island Cruises (☎ 03-6250 2200; www.tasmancruises.com.au; adult/child $165/110) Take a bus to Port Arthur for a three-hour ecocruise around Tasman Island, then explore the Port Arthur Historic Site and bus back to town. Includes morning tea, lunch and Port Arthur admission. Departs Hobart visitors centre at 8am. You can also take the three-hour ecocruise from Port Arthur (adult/child $100/55).

SORELL
pop 1730

Sorell is the gateway T-junction town for the Tasman Peninsula. It was settled in 1808, making it one of Tasmania's oldest towns, but these days it's a service town with more petrol stations and fast-food joints than anything else. One good reason to stop is the **Sorell Fruit Farm** (☎ 03-6265 3100; www.sorellfruitfarm.com; 174 Pawleena Rd; ☼ 8.30am-5pm late Oct-May). Pick your own fruit (15 different kinds!) from their intensively planted 12½ acres ($6 minimum pick) or enjoy a snack and good coffee in the tearooms. Head east through Sorell towards Port Arthur. After exiting the town you'll see Pawleena signposted on your left.

EAGLEHAWK NECK TO PORT ARTHUR

Most tourists associate the Tasman Peninsula only with Port Arthur, but there are many attractions (natural and otherwise) down this way. Hit the bookshops for *Peninsula Tracks* by Peter and Shirley Storey ($18) for track notes on 35 walks in the area. The *Convict Trail* booklet, available from visitor information centres, covers the peninsula's historic sites.

The general store at Eaglehawk Neck was demolished in a property-development move. As a result the nearest provisions to Eaglehawk Neck are at the shops in Nubeena and Port Arthur.

Approach Eaglehawk Neck from the north, then turn east onto Pirates Bay Dr for the **lookout** – the Pirates Bay views extending to the rugged coastline beyond are truly incredible. Also clearly signposted around Eaglehawk Neck are some bizarre and precipitous coastal

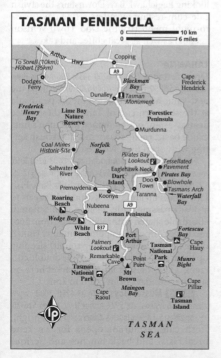

TASMAN PENINSULA

0 — 10 km
0 — 6 miles

To Sorell (10km);
Hobart (35km)

Arthur Hwy

Copping

A9

Dodges Ferry

Blackman Bay

Cape Frederick Hendrick

Dunalley ■ Tasman Monument

Frederick Henry Bay

Lime Bay Nature Reserve

Forestier Peninsula

Murdunna

Coal Mines Historic Site

Norfolk Bay

Pirates Bay Lookout

Tessellated Pavement

Saltwater River

Eaglehawk Neck

Pirates Bay

Dart Island

Doo Town

Blowhole

Premaydena

Koonya

Taranna

Tasmans Arch

Waterfall Bay

Roaring Beach

Nubeena

A9

Tasman Peninsula

Wedge Bay

White Beach

B37

Fortescue Bay

Palmers Lookout

Port Arthur

Tasman National Park

Cape Hauy

Remarkable Cave

Point Puer

Munro Bight

Tasman National Park

Mt Brown

Maingon Bay

Cape Pillar

Cape Raoul

Tasman Island

TASMAN SEA

DOO TOWN

No one is really sure how it all started, but the raggedy collection of fishing shacks at Doo Town, 3km south of Eaglehawk Neck, all contain the word 'Doo' in their names. There's the sexy 'Doo Me', the approving 'We Doo', the unfussy 'Thistle Doo Me', the Beatle-esque 'Love Me Doo' and the melancholic 'Doo Write'. We doo hope the new breed of architectural beach-houses stick with tradition.

---

formations: **Tessellated Pavement**, the **Blowhole**, **Tasmans Arch** and **Waterfall Bay**. South of Port Arthur is the sea-gouged **Remarkable Cave**.

The **Tasman National Park** (www.parks.tas.gov.au) offers some spectacular bushwalking (national park fees apply). From Fortescue Bay, you can walk east to **Cape Hauy** (four to five hours return) – a well-trodden path leading to sea cliffs with sensational rocky sea-stack outlooks. The walk to the exquisitely named **Cape Raoul** (five hours return) is equally rewarding.

You can also visit the remains of **penal outstations** at Eaglehawk Neck, Koonya, Premaydena and Saltwater River, and the restored ruins at the **Coal Mines Historic Site**.

The **Tasmanian Devil Conservation Park** (☎ 03-6250 3230; www.tasmaniandevilpark.com; 5990 Arthur Hwy, Taranna; adult/child/family $26/14/64; ☀ 9am-6pm) functions as a quarantine breeding centre for devils to help protect against devil facila tumour disease (DFTD; see Tigers & Devils, p698). There are plenty of other native animals and birds here, with feedings throughout the day. Scuba diving is popular and certified local operators include **Eaglehawk Dive Centre** (☎ 03-6250 3566; www.eaglehawkdive.com.au; 178 Pirates Bay Dr, Eaglehawk Neck) and **Go Dive Tassie** (☎ 03-6231 9749; www.godivetassie.com; Arthur Hwy, Taranna).

Learn to surf at Eaglehawk Neck with **Island Surf School** (☎ 03-6265 9776, 0400 830 237; www.island surfschool.com.au; 2hr group lessons per person $40); gear is provided. **Sealife Experience** (☎ 0428 300 303; www .sealife.com.au; cruises adult/child/family $99/55/290) runs informative three-hour cruises around the peninsula's east coast departing from Eaglehawk Neck – bring your camera.

Sleeping & Eating

EAGLEHAWK NECK & AROUND

Eaglehawk Neck Budget Accommodation (☎ 03-6250 3248; 94 Old Jetty Rd; unpowered sites/dm $16/20) This

very simple, family-run hostel is in a peaceful location signposted west of the isthmus – just four beds in a dorm, tent spots on the back lawn and a basic camp kitchen in an old garden shed. The owners are lovely and offer $5 bike hire for the duration of your stay.

Lufra Hotel (☎ 03-6250 3262; www.lufrahotel.com; 380 Pirates Bay Dr; d & f $110-180, 2-bedroom ste $240) This chowder-coloured hotel has a million-dollar outlook over Pirates Bay. The newish owners are progressively renovating the rooms in the original building and have built a new wing of roomy self-contained one- and two-bedroom units. The older rooms are modest but comfortable; all have bathrooms and some have fantastic sea views. The downstairs bistro offers interesting dishes from an eclectic menu (mains $20 to $34).

our pick Eaglehawk Café & Guesthouse (☎ 03-6250 3331; www.theneck.com.au; 5131 Arthur Hwy; mains $10-23; ☀ breakfast & lunch year-round, dinner Fri-Sun Dec-Feb) Above this groovy cafe (c 1929) are three lovely B&B rooms (doubles including breakfast $110 to $130) that were once the refuge of sleeping shipwrights. Two of the rooms have French doors opening onto a balcony overlooking Eaglehawk Bay. Downstairs the stylish cafe-cum-restaurant offers a fine day-turns-to-night menu (try the Doo Town venison kebabs) as well as great coffee and cakes.

TARANNA

Teraki Cottages (☎ 03-6250 3435; 996 Arthur Hwy, Taranna; d $80-90, extra adult/child $20/10) Perhaps the best-value accommodation on the peninsula at the southern end of Taranna, these three neat-as-a-pin, self-contained bushman's huts exude basic, rustic charm in a quiet bush setting with open fires. No credit cards.

Fish Lips Café & Accommodation (☎ 03-6250 3066; www.fishlipstasmania.com.au; 5934 Arthur Hwy; mains $12-25; ☀ breakfast & lunch) By Little Norfolk Bay, Fish Lips serves up great snacks and light meals to a steady passing trade. There's a collection of affordable shared-bathroom rooms (from $66) in a huge converted shipping container (much more comfortable than they sound) sleeping up to three, and classier waterside double cottages. There's also a farmers market here on summer Sundays from 10am to 2pm.

our pick Mussel Boys (☎ 03-6250 3088; www .themusselboys.com.au; 5927 Arthur Hwy; mains $16-26; ☀ breakfast Sat & Sun, lunch & dinner daily) This bright, fresh cafe-restaurant opens for weekend breakfasts, laid-back lunches and serious evening à la carte dining that's strong on local produce, seafood and select Tasmanian wines. Try the outstanding signature dish: mussels in dill and coconut curry broth with Asian greens and rice noodles (entrée or main). Or spend an afternoon grazing over the expansive seven-course degustation menu (with/without local wines $124/89). Out back there are five deluxe studios (doubles $240) offering designer-stylin' good looks as well as LCD TVs, king beds and spa baths.

PORT ARTHUR
pop 300

In 1830 Lieutenant-Governor George Arthur chose the Tasman Peninsula to confine prisoners who had committed further crimes in the colony. A 'natural penitentiary', the peninsula is connected to the mainland by a strip of land less than 100m wide – Eaglehawk Neck. To deter escape, ferocious guard dogs were chained across the isthmus.

From 1830 to 1877, 12,500 convicts did hard, brutal prison time at Port Arthur. Port Arthur became the hub of a network of penal stations on the peninsula, its fine buildings sustaining thriving convict-labour industries, including timber milling, shipbuilding, coal mining, shoemaking, and brick and nail production.

Australia's first railway literally 'ran' the 7km between Norfolk Bay and Long Bay: convicts pushed the carriages along the tracks. A semaphore telegraph system allowed instant communication between Port Arthur, other peninsula outstations and Hobart. Convict farms provided fresh vegetables, a boys' prison was built at Point Puer to reform and educate juvenile convicts, and a church was erected.

Although Port Arthur is a hugely popular tourist site – over 300,000 visitors annually – it remains a sombre, confronting and haunting place. Don't come expecting to remain unaffected by what you see – there's a palpable sadness and sense of woe that clouds your senses on the sunniest of days. What makes it all the more poignant is the scale of the penal settlement and its genuine beauty – the stonemasonry work, gothic architecture, lawns and gardens are exquisite – and visitors leave feeling profoundly moved and conflicted by the experience.

The visitor centre at the **Port Arthur Historic Site** (☎ 03-6251 2310, 1800 659 101; www.portarthur.org .au; Arthur Hwy, Port Arthur; adult/child/concession/family $28/14/23/62; ⊙ tours & buildings 9am-5pm, grounds 8.30am-dusk) includes an information counter, cafe, restaurant and gift shop. Downstairs is an excellent interpretation gallery, where you can follow the convicts' journey from England to Tasmania. Buggy transport around the site can be arranged for people with restricted mobility; ask at the information counter.

Worthwhile guided tours (included in admission) leave regularly from the visitor centre. You can visit all the restored buildings, including the Old Asylum (now a museum and cafe) and the Model Prison. Admission tickets, valid for two consecutive days, also entitle you to a short harbour cruise circumnavigating (but not stopping at) the **Isle of the Dead**. For an additional $12/8/34 per adult/child/family, you can visit the island on 40-minute guided tours – count headstones and listen to some stories. You can also tour to **Point Puer** boys' prison for the same additional prices.

Another extremely popular tour is the 90-minute, lantern-lit **Historic Ghost Tour** (☎ 1800 659 101; adult/child/family $20/12/55), which leaves from the visitor centre nightly at dusk (rain or shine) and visits a number of historic buildings, with guides relating spine-chilling occurrences. Bookings are essential.

DON'T ASK – THE PORT ARTHUR MASSACRE

Staff at the Port Arthur Historic Site won't speak of the 1996 massacre. Many lost relatives and colleagues, and Martin Bryant's name will not be spoken. On the morning of Sunday 28 April, 28-year-old Bryant drove from Hobart with a sports bag of semiautomatic weapons. Over the course of the late morning and afternoon he murdered 35 people and injured 37 more in and around the Port Arthur Historic Site. He took a hostage into a local guest house and held off police for a further 18 hours, killing the hostage and setting the guest house on fire before surrendering to police. He remains imprisoned north of Hobart, having received 35 life sentences. The Port Arthur Massacre is the world's worst killing spree in a single event. The incident precipitated Australia's strict gun-control laws.

Sleeping

Port Arthur used to have a YHA, but now there's no budget accommodation other than the caravan park.

Port Arthur Villas (☎ 03-6250 2239, 1800 815 775; www.portarthurvillas.com.au; 52 Safety Cove Rd; d $135-180) This place has reasonable self-contained units sleeping up to four that arc around a garden and outdoor barbecue area. Faux-Victorian lace and brickwork dominate the outside, but inside things are a little more stylish. It's walking distance to the historic site.

Comfort Inn Port Arthur (☎ 03-6250 2101, 1800 030 747; www.portarthur-inn.com.au; 29 Safety Cove Rd; d $145-185; ✖) The superb views over the historic site from the Comfort Inn rooms are more remarkable than the rooms themselves, but the Commandant's Table Restaurant is noteworthy (right). Ask about packages including accommodation, dinner, breakfast and a Port Arthur ghost tour (from $270 for two).

Stewarts Bay Lodge (☎ 03-6250 2888; www .stewartsbaylodge.com; 6955 Arthur Hwy; d $160-200, 2-/3-bedroom cabin from $195/255; ✖ ☐) Deluxe log cabins is not an oxymoron and this place offers one-, two- and three-bedroom self-contained cabins fronting picturesque and swimmable Stewarts Bay.

Port Arthur Caravan & Cabin Park (☎ 03-6250 2340, 1800 620 708; www.portarthurcaravan-cabinpark.com .au; Garden Point Rd; unpowered/powered sites $21/23, dm $19, cabins $105-115) This is a real turn-up: an undulating old-school caravan park with lots of space and shady trees, and fireplaces for each site. The facilities are up to scratch, too, including camp kitchen, laundry and store. It's 2km before Port Arthur, close to a sheltered beach.

Eating

There are a couple of daytime food options at the historic site: a coffee shop in the Old Asylum and a cafe inside the visitor information centre, both serving the usual takeaway suspects.

Lemo's Seafood & Roast (☎ 03-6250 3403; 6555 Arthur Hwy; mains $8-36; ☾ lunch & dinner) On the Long Bay waterfront, Lemo's looks like a displaced fast-food barn with a tiled floor and massive car park. But appearances can deceive – this ambitious enterprise incorporates a trout farm, gift shop and provedore, and the food is excellent featuring authentic Asian dishes, seafood platters and comfort-food roasts. Fully licensed.

Eucalypt (☎ 03-6250 2555; 6962 Arthur Hwy, Port Arthur; mains $11-20; ☾ breakfast & lunch Wed-Mon, dinner Fri) Stylish Eucalypt lives by a creed: 'Coffee, Art, Food'. Hearty organic breakfasts, inventive Mod Oz lunches and casual dinners with a glass of wine. We concur.

Commandant's Table (☎ 03-6250 2101; 29 Safety Cove Rd; mains $17-28, ☾ dinner) The better of the Comfort Inn's two dining options, with broad historic site views. The worldly menu has some tricked-up favourites and Asian-fusion surprises (fish of the day with Nonya sambal, ginger and lemon juice on basmati rice).

Felons (☎ 03-6251 2310; mains $19-27; ☾ dinner) 'Dine with Conviction' at this seafoodie favourite with people heading off on the Ghost Tour. It's at the visitor information centre.

MIDLANDS

Tasmania's Midlands are the very antithesis of the forested wilderness areas the island is famous for. The early settlers comprehensively cleared this area for sheep and cattle grazing, and planted willows, poplars and hawthorn hedgerows around their settlements and along the fertile river valleys. The Midlands' baked, straw-coloured plains and hillsides, and grand Georgian mansions give the area a distinctly English countryside feel. The Midland's agricultural potential fuelled Tasmania's settlement – coach stations, garrison towns, stone villages and pastoral properties sprang up as convict gangs hammered out the road between Hobart and Launceston. By 1821 the Hobart–Launceston road was carrying horses and carriages.

The upgrading of Tasmania's main north–south road – the Midland Hwy (aka Heritage Highway) – bypassed many old towns along the old route. So it's worth pulling off the highway to explore the Georgian main streets, cottage gardens, antique shops and some of Australia's best-preserved colonial architecture.

See www.southernmidlands.tas.gov.au and www.northernmidlands.tas.gov.au for more information.

Getting There & Around

Redline Coaches (☎ 1300 360 000; www.tasredline .com.au) powers along the Midland Hwy several times daily; you can jump off at any of the main towns except on express services. The Hobart to Launceston fare is $38.80

(about 2½ hours). One way from Hobart/ Launceston to Oatlands costs $20.30/23.10; to Ross it's $28.70/13.20 and to Campbell Town $28.70/13.20.

OATLANDS

pop 540

Established as a garrison town in 1832, Oatlands serves a thriving tourist trade, but (thankfully) remains stately, restrained and rather dignified about it. Surveyors proposed 80km of streets for the little town that today contains Australia's largest collection of Georgian architecture and many splendid early dry-stone walls. On the impressive main street alone there are 87 historic buildings, many of which are now galleries and craft stores.

Oatlands visitor information centre (☎ 03-6254 1212; 85 High St; ✆ 9am-5pm) handles accommodation bookings and has a sandstone history room full of photos, relics and knick-knacks. Wander around town by yourself, or take a one-hour **Oatlands Tour** (☎ 03-6254 1135; per person $5), booked through the visitor centre.

Much of Oatlands' sandstone, as featured in the 1881 **Town Hall** (High St), came from the shores of nearby **Lake Dulverton** (now bone dry). **Callington Mill** (☎ 03-6254 0039; fax 6254 5014; Mill Lane; admission free; ✆ 9am-5pm), off High St, was built in 1837 and ground flour until 1891. Restoration work began after a century of neglect. The eerie sounds of chickens and laughing children are piped through restored outbuildings, including the 15m-high mill tower (climb the wobbly stairs to the top).

There are decent rooms in the town's two pubs: **Midlands Hotel** (☎ 03-6254 1103; fax 6254 1450; 91 High St; s/d $50/65), with shared bathroom facilities; and **Kentish Hotel** (☎ 03-6254 1119; www.view .com.au/kentishhotel; 60 High St; s/d $55/75), with en suite rooms and good pub meals.

Elegant sandstone **Oatlands Lodge** (☎ 03-6254 1444; fax 6254 1456; 92 High St; s/d $110/130) was built by convicts in 1837 and is perhaps the pick of the town's accommodation. Rates include a huge breakfast.

There's free camping (one night maximum) at the Lake Dulverton picnic area with toilets and barbecues.

ROSS

pop 270

Another tidy Midlands town is Ross, 120km north of Hobart. Established in 1812 as a garrison town to protect Hobart–Launceston trav-ellers from bushrangers, it quickly became an important coach staging post. Tree-lined streets are wrapped in colonial charm and history.

The crossroads in the middle of town leads you in one of four directions: temptation (represented by the Man O'Ross Hotel), salvation (the Catholic church), recreation (the town hall) and damnation (the old jail). Beyond salvation, the **Ross visitor information centre** (☎ 03-6381 5466; Church St; ✆ 9am-5pm) is inside the **Tasmanian Wool Centre** (www.taswoolcentre.com .au), which sells garments, scarves and beanies made from superfine merino wool. Ross is the centre of Australia's superfine wool industry.

The town is most famous for the superb **Ross Bridge** (1836), the third-oldest bridge in Australia's and one of its most impressive. Designed by colonial architect John Lee Archer and built by skilled convict stonemasons James Colbeck and Daniel Herbert, the bridge is floodlit at night and light reflecting from the water makes eerie shifting shadows on the 186 carvings that decorate the arches. Other notable historic edifices include the 1832 **Scotch Thistle Inn** (Church St), now a private residence; the 1830 **barracks** (Bridge St), restored by the National Trust and also a private residence; the 1885 **Uniting Church** (Church St); the 1868 **St John's Anglican Church** (cnr Church & Badajos Sts); and the still-operating 1896 **post office** (26 Church St).

Off Bond St, the **Ross Female Factory** (☎ 03-6278 7398; www.femalefactory.com.au/FFRG/ross.htm; admission free; ✆ 9am-5pm) was one of only four female convict prisons in the colony. One building is still standing, and archaeological excavations are under way. Descriptive signs and stories provide insights into the prisoners' lives. To get here, walk down the track near the Uniting Church.

Sleeping & Eating

Man O'Ross Hotel (☎ 03-6381 5445; www.manoross .com.au; 35 Church St; s/d/f without bathroom & incl breakfast $75/90/125, self-contained d cottage $125) This gracious 1835 hotel is a fascinating old building – a tunnel (now blocked) runs beneath the street to the old jail so convicts constructing the hotel wouldn't flee. Accommodation prices are a bit steep given the shared bathrooms, but the rooms are better than average. Evening bistro meals (mains $15 to $24) are good, and the pretty beer garden is ideal for lunch or Plenty O'Beer.

TASMANIA

Ross Bakery Inn (☎ 03-6381 5246; www.ross
bakery.com.au; 15 Church St; s/d incl breakfast from $120/150)
This 1830s coaching house adjacent to ex-
cellent Ross Village Bakery has small rooms
but a lovely guest lounge with open fire and
complimentary bakery treats. Breakfast is prepared fresh in a 100-year-old wood-fired oven.
Groups of up to six can bed down in the three-
bedroom, self-contained Kirsty's Cottage
across the street ($175/195/205/215/225 for
two/three/four/five/six people). The bakery is
a top spot for lunch offering wood-fired pizzas,
soups, salads and pies of all denominations.

Ross Motel & Caravan Park (☎ 03-6381 5224; www
.rossmotel.com.au; 2 High St; powered sites/cabins $20/70, d
incl breakfast $135, f $160-185) Pitch your tent on the
banks of the fish-filled Macquarie River, bunk
down in a barracks-style single-bed cabin or
settle into post-colonial comfort in a mod
motel room – the choice is yours.

CAMPBELL TOWN
pop 770

Campbell Town, 12km north of Ross, was
established as yet another garrison settlement. Unlike Oatlands and Ross, however,
the Midlands Hwy still trucks right through
town. The local catch-cry is 'Campbell Town
is reaching out to you!' – perhaps a little evan-
gelic for this small introspective agricultural
town. But it does make a handy pit stop.

The first white settlers here were Irish
timber-workers who spoke Gaelic and had a
particularly debauched reputation. Buildings
dating from the early days are dotted along
High St and Bridge St, including the 1835
St Luke's Church of England (High St); the 1840
Campbell Town Inn (100 High St); the 1834 **Fox
Hunters Return** (132 High St); the **Grange** (87 High
St), an 1847 mansion; and the still-scholarly
1878 **old school** (Hamilton St). Rows of red bricks
set into the High St footpath detail the crimes,
sentences and arrival dates of convicts like
Ephram Brain and English Corney, sent to
Van Diemen's Land for crimes as various as
stealing potatoes, bigamy and murder.

You wouldn't know from the outside, but
parts of the **Campbell Town Hotel** (☎ 03-6381 1158;
www.goodstone.com.au; 118 High St; s/d $65/75) predates
all the other hotels in town. It has 10 simple but
clean motel units out the back and reasonably
priced meals (mains $8 to $18) for lunch and
dinner. The **Fox Hunters Return** (☎ 03-6381 1602;
www.foxhunters.com.au; 132 High St; s/d from $129/149) is a
grand-looking old coaching inn built in 1833.

Modern and jazzy **Zeps** (☎ 03-6381 1344; 92
High St; meals $7-22; 🖥) is the town's best eatery.
Patrons pore over newspapers and cooked
breakfasts, eat stuffed focaccias and pies for
lunch, and tuck into pizzas and Mod Oz mains
at night.

EAST COAST

Tasmania's laid-back east coast is drop-dead
gorgeous. Hardy types will find superb opportunities for swimming in clean, clear
water, while the rest can enjoy walking barefoot along the white-sand beaches, letting the
waves lick at their ankles and shins. Mild,
sunny days lure summer holidaymakers from
Hobart, while mainlanders in campervans
explore the east coast's squeaky beaches and
fishing towns, and enjoy the slow-paced
seaside atmospheria. The voluptuous goblet
of Wineglass Bay and pink granite peaks in
Freycinet National Park are world famous.

Getting There & Around
BICYCLE

The Tasman Hwy along the east coast,
Tasmania's most popular cycle-touring route,
is wonderfully varied, taking in pretty seaside
towns, forests and plenty of places to swim.
Traffic is usually light, and the hills aren't too
steep, particularly the section from Chain of
Lagoons to Falmouth (east of St Marys).

BUS

Redline Coaches (☎ 1300 360 000; www.tasredline.com
.au) runs weekday buses between Launceston
and Swansea, the Coles Bay turn-off and
Bicheno, via the Midland Hwy and the inland B34 road. Services from Hobart connect with these buses at Campbell Town,
where you may have to wait depending on
your particular connection. Redline also
runs daily services (except Saturday) between Launceston and St Helens along the
A4 via St Marys. Hobart buses connect with
this service at Conara on the Midland Hwy.
Redline fares:

Journey	Price ($)	Duration (hr)
Launceston-Bicheno	34	2¾
Launceston-Coles Bay turn-off	34	2½
Launceston-St Helens	32	2¾
Launceston-St Marys	31	2
Launceston-Swansea	31	2

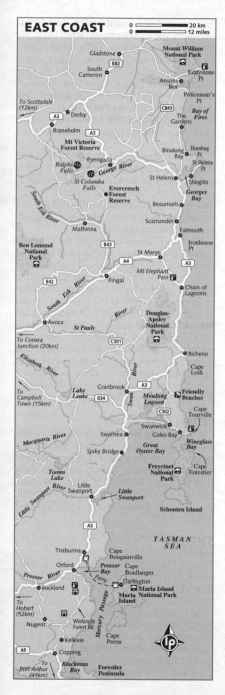

EAST COAST

TassieLink (☎ 1300 300 520; www.tassielink.com.au) also provides east coast services from Hobart, running at least three times per week. Some buses detour through Richmond. Buses also run twice weekly from Launceston to Bicheno via the A4 and St Marys. TassieLink fares:

Journey	Price ($)	Duration (hr)
Hobart-Bicheno	35	3
Hobart-Coles Bay turn-off	34	2¾
Hobart-Orford	19	1¼
Hobart-St Helens	51	4
Hobart-Swansea	29	2¼
Hobart-Triabunna	20	1½
Launceston-Bicheno	34	2½
Launceston-St Marys	26	2

Bicheno Coach Service (☎ 03-6257 0293, 0419 570 293) runs between Bicheno, Coles Bay and Freycinet National Park, connecting with east-coast Redline and TassieLink coaches at the Coles Bay turn-off:

Journey	Price ($)	Duration (min)
Bicheno-Coles Bay	11	35
Bicheno-Freycinet NP	13	45
Coles Bay turn-off-Coles Bay	10	25
Coles Bay turn-off-Freycinet NP	11	35
Coles Bay-Freycinet NP	5	10

ORFORD
pop 550

Orford, built around the wide Prosser river mouth about an hour northeast of Hobart, is a once-busy whaling port that's devolved into a sleepy seaside town. Today Orford is where many Hobartians keep their beachside weekenders and rapid development has seen the recent arrival of some striking architectural homes. The town retains its beachy vibe with excellent fishing, swimming, a couple of B&Bs and greasy cormorants squatting on river jetties. South of town (signposted from the southern end of the bridge over the river) are **Shelly Beach** and **Spring Beach**, both popular swimming and surfing spots. There's a 2km cliff-top walk between the two beaches.

Cream-and-marine **Prosser Holiday Units** (☎ 03-6257 1427; fax 03-6225 4884; cnr Tasman Hwy & Charles St; d $95-105) offers family-friendly, self-contained highwayside accommodation in the middle of town. They're spacious, unfussy (a bit '80s) and sleep up to five.

TASMANIA

Sanda House (☎ 03-6257 1527; www.orfordsanda house.com.au; 33 Walpole St; d $110-140) is a B&B in Orford's oldest residence, a white-painted stone farmhouse dating from 1840. The open fire in the breakfast room smoulders away for most of the year.

Orford offers two great side-by-side eating options by the Prosser River bridge: **Scorchers on the River** (☎ 03-6257 1033; 1 The Esplanade; mains $11-24; ☽ lunch & dinner Sep-Jul) cooks up sizzlin' pizzas, pastas and toasted focaccias, and **Gateway Café** (☎ 03-6257 1539, 1 Charles St; mains $8-24) does all-day breakfasts and great lunches and dinners. There's an array of Tassie gourmet goods for sale and an impressive display of sporting memorabilia.

TRIABUNNA & MARIA ISLAND NATIONAL PARK

About 8km north of Orford is Triabunna (population 800), a flat-grid fishing town with a few historic building but otherwise almost zero appeal. But it's the departure point for ferries to Maria Island National Park (pronounced ma-rye-ah). Book and buy ferry tickets and national park passes at the **Triabunna visitor information centre** (☎ 03-6257 4772; cnr Charles St & The Esplanade; ☽ 9am-4pm), which provides information on Maria Island accommodation, walks, activities and fishing charters.

Triabunna's best place to stay is **Tandara Motor Inn** (☎ 03-6257 3333; www.tandaramotorinn.com.au; Tasman Hwy; d $125; ☒) with modern motels rooms, a restaurant (mains $16 to $26) and a pool.

Triabunna Cabin & Caravan Park (☎ 03-6257 3575; www.mariagateway.com; 4 Vicary St; powered site $23, onsite van from $55, cabin $77-110) is a neat, compact caravan park with decent facilities and a backpacker dorm (linen included).

Clearly visible a few kilometres off shore, car-free **Maria Island** (www.parks.tas.gov.au) was declared a national park in 1972. Its mixed history provides some interesting convict and industrial ruins among some exquisite natural features: forests, fern gullies, fossil-studded sandstone and limestone cliffs, and empty beaches. Maria is popular with bushwalkers, mountain bikers and bird-watchers, and snorkellers and divers are in for a treat (see Scuba Diving, p633). National park fees apply; island info is available at the visitors reception area in the old Commissariat Store near the ferry pier.

From 1825 to 1832 **Darlington** was Tasmania's second penal colony (the first was Sarah Island near Strahan). The remains of the convict village, including the **Commissariat Store** (1825), the **Mill House** (1846) and the **Coffee Palace** (1888), are well preserved and easy to explore. There are no shops on the island so BYO supplies (no, the Coffee Palace doesn't serve coffee). Don't miss walks to the top of **Bishop & Clerk** (four hours return), the **Fossil Cliffs** (two hours return) and **Painted Cliffs** (2½ hours return). Chant monastically in the old **silos** near the pier after dark.

The four-day **Maria Island Walk** (☎ 03-6227 8800; www.mariaislandwalk.com.au; per person $1950) is a guided walk of the island, with the emphasis on nature, history and minimal-impact walking. Trips run from October to April and include transfers from Hobart to the island, meals and accommodation.

Bookings aren't required for Maria's **camping grounds** (unpowered sites per d/f $13/16) at Darlington, French's Farm and Encampment Cove. Only the Darlington site has cooking facilities (gas barbecues); fires are permitted in designated fireplaces but are often banned during summer. The cells in Darlington's old **Penitentiary** (☎ 03-6257 1420; maria.island@parks.tas .gov.au; dm/d/6-bed unit $15/40/80) have been converted into very basic, unpowered bunkhouses (bring gas lamps, utensils and cookers). The bunkhouses tend to overflow with school groups, so book well ahead. Hot showers are available (gold coin donation).

Getting There & Away

The **Maria Island Ferry** (☎ 0419 746 668; www.maria islandferry.com.au) operates from the marina near the Triabunna visitor information centre (left), departing 9.30am and 4pm daily (leaving Maria Island at 10.30am and 5pm). The journey takes 40 minutes; a return ticket per adult/child/concession is $50/25/37, and bikes cost $10.

SWANSEA

pop 560

Founded in 1820, Swansea sits on the western sheltered shores of beautiful Great Oyster Bay with magnificent views over Freycinet Peninsula. There's no surf in Swansea; instead a calm pervades the blue waters towards Freycinet. Once another sleepy seaside village, Swansea's rise and rise has coincided with Tasmania's tourism boom and today offers terrific B&B accommodation, good restaurants and an interesting museum.

EAST COAST SHORTCUT

The **Wielangta Forest Road** leads from the Tasman Highway at Copping to Orford – a beautiful forest drive over 29km of good gravel road with brilliant lookouts and walking trails. The Wielangta Forest is home to many endangered flora and fauna species and has been the focus of a high-profile logging debate. Walks in the forest include a 20-minute rainforest stroll through the **Sandspit Forest Reserve** and the 90-minute-return **Wielangta Walk**, which follows the river valley. A side road 6km south of Orford leads up to **Thumbs Lookout** giving panoramic views over Maria Island. If you've driven from Orford, you'll reach a give-way sign at the southern end of the forest road – turn right and head past nearby Kellevie to reach the turn-off to either Buckland or Copping.

There are many still-functioning historic buildings, including 1860 **Council Chambers** (Noyes St), the 1871 **Anglican Church** (Noyes St) and the red-brick 1838 **Morris' General Store** (13 Franklin St). Around 7km south of town is the 1840s convict-built **Spiky Bridge**. Function or folly, the concept behind the stone spikes has been lost to history.

The **Heritage Centre** (☎ 03-6257 8215; 22 Franklin St; adult/child $3/1; 🕙 9am-5pm Mon-Sat) was a school in the 1860s, but now features local history exhibits and an ancient billiard table. The facility at the **Swansea Bark Mill** (☎ 03-6257 8382; www.swanseabarkmill.com.au; 96 Tasman Hwy) was modernised recently to incorporate a great new bakery-cafe, tavern and backpackers (see below). The excellent **museum** (adult/concession/child/family $10/8/6/23; 🕙 9am-5pm) features working models of black-wattle bark processing equipment used in tanning leather, and displays on Swansea's early history, from French exploration to agriculture and industry.

Sleeping

Swansea Backpackers (☎ 03-6257 8650; www.swansea backpackers.com.au; 96 Tasman Hwy; dm/d/f from $28/75/112; 🖳) This brilliant purpose-built 'flashpacker' place opened in 2006 and is more luxury house than grungy hostel. It has flawless bathrooms, a stainless-steel kitchen, pool table, grassy courtyard and quality mattresses – all surrounded by a burnt-orange, bone and charcoal colour scheme.

Redcliffe House (☎ 03-6257 8557; www.redcliffehouse .com.au; 13569 Tasman Hwy; s $130, d $145-160, all incl breakfast) This restored farmhouse (c 1835) 1.5km north of Swansea sits beside the Meredith River and offers delightful timber-panelled rooms with views over the fields and vineyard. After a swim in the waterhole relax in the guest lounge with its excellent book and DVD collection, or take to the verandah with a little wine and cheese. Very accommodating.

Abbotsford (☎ 03-6257 9092; www.abbotsfordbb .worldstays.com; 50 Gordon St, d incl breakfast $140-170) This wonderful old stone house is one of Swansea's nicest places to stay. With three double bedrooms that share a bathroom and guest lounge, it suits couples or families travelling together.

Tubby & Padman (☎ 03-6257 8901; www.tubbyand padman.com.au; 20 Franklin St; cottage suite $165-195, units $165-175; 🖳) This 1840s former department store has been refitted as a classy, romantic B&B with imaginative decor, fine art and attention to detail. There are also modern, two-bedroom, self-contained units out the back.

Swansea Holiday Park at Jubilee Beach (☎ 03-6257 8177; www.swansea-holiday.com.au; 27 Shaw St; unpowered/powered sites $24/28, cabins from $80; 🖳 🖳) Just north of town, this beachfront caravan park has barbecues, camp kitchen and laundry, and a pool and playground. Prime tent sites are right on the beach.

Eating

Kate's Berry Farm (☎ 03-6257 8428; 12 Addison St; items $4-9; 🕙 9am-5pm) Kate's farm, about 3km south of Swansea, has become an essential stop for east-coast tourers. It sells homemade jams, wines, sauces and divine ice cream, and has a lovely cafe serving berry-heavy afternoon teas.

Trellis (☎ 03-6257 9095; 26 Franklin St; dishes $4-9) Newbie on the Swansea food scene, cafe-bar Trellis offers cooked breakfasts and an interesting all-day tapas-style menu. Gourmet foodie treats are sold, as are local boutique wines from the attached bottle shop.

Banc (☎ 03-6257 8896; cnr Franklin & Maria Sts; lunch mains $8-26, dinner mains $26-40; 🕙 dinner Wed-Mon, brunch & lunch Sun & Mon, closed Tue & Wed Jun-Aug) Ranking among Tasmania's top restaurants, Banc features fresh east-coast produce in dishes like venison steak, slow-roasted

TASMANIA

suckling pig and abalone confit with fresh lime mirin. Lazy late breakfasts are served Sunday and Monday.

Bark Mill Tavern (☎ 03-6257 8382; 96 Tasman Hwy; mains $16-26; ⏱ lunch & dinner) Comfort food and favourites – steaks, pastas, pizza and seafood – are offered at the Bark Mill Tavern, neither too challenging nor poorly prepared. Tasmanian beers and local wines complement a pleasant lunch or evening meal, and there's occasionally live acoustic music to chew to.

our pick **Kabuki by the Sea** (☎ 03-6257 8588; www .kabukibythesea.com.au; Tasman Hwy; mains $24-29; ⏱ lunch daily, dinner Tue-Sat Dec-Apr, Fri & Sat May-Nov) Who'd have thought: build a traditional Japanese restaurant on the clifftops 15km south of a seaside Tasmanian town and they'll come? They did and they do – Kabuki is the real deal preparing some of Tasmania's best Japanese cuisine. Try the marinated *una ju* (eel), the local baby abalone or wallaby *yakiniku*. Kabuki also offers snug clifftop apartments with commanding ocean views and Japanese-style decor (doubles $180).

Ebb (☎ 03-6257 8088; 11 Franklin St; dinner mains $27-33; ⏱ 11.30am-3pm & 6pm-late, Tue-Sun) Ebullient Ebb wins the groovy vote in Swansea – a bright modern waterfront dining room decorated with art and Pacific tapa-cloth serving fresh, light lunches and à la carte dinners big on local seafood.

COLES BAY & FREYCINET NATIONAL PARK

The spectacular 485m-high pinky-orange granite outcrops known as the Hazards dominate the tiny town of Coles Bay (population 473). Brilliant Freycinet Peninsula (pronounced *fray*-sin-ay) is one of Tasmania's principal tourism drawcards, and Coles Bay exists as the gateway and service town for its national park. The peninsula's sublime white-sand beaches, secluded coves, rocky cliffs and outstanding bushwalks make it an essential visit on any east coast itinerary. Be aware, however, that everything in Coles Bay – from petrol to potatoes – is hyperinflated to cash in on captive consumers, and the town is aggressively geared towards tourism. Check out www.freycinetcolesbay.com.

Information

At the park entrance is the professionally run **Freycinet National Park Visitor Centre** (☎ 03-6256 7000; Freycinet Dr; www.parks.tas.gov.au; ⏱ 8am-5pm

Nov-Apr, 9am-4pm May-Oct) – pay your park fees or catch free ranger-led activities in summer.

In Coles Bay itself, jack-of-all-trades **Coles Bay Trading** (☎ 03-6257 0109; 1 Garnet Ave; ⏱ 8am-6pm Mar-Nov, 7am-7pm Dec-Feb) is a general store with a post office, ATM and cafe. Iluka Holiday Centre (opposite) also has a shop with an ATM and fuel. **Freycinet Adventures** (☎ 03-6257 0500; www .freycinetadventures.com; 2 Freycinet Dr) hires out essential camping equipment and also runs a water taxi service that can deliver you to Hazards Beach, Cooks Beach or Schouten Island.

Sights & Activities

Sheathed in coastal heaths, orchids and wildflowers, **Freycinet National Park** (www.parks.tas.gov .au) incorporates Freycinet Peninsula, people-free Schouten Island and the lesser-known Friendly Beaches north of Coles Bay. Black cockatoos, yellow wattlebirds, honeyeaters and Bennett's wallabies flap and bounce between the bushes.

For bushwalkers it's nirvana, with long hikes including the two-day, 31km peninsula circuit. Shorter tracks include the up-and-over saddle climb to the majestic white bowl of **Wineglass Bay**. Ascend the saddle as far as **Wineglass Bay Lookout** (one to 1½ hours return, 600 steps each way) or continue down the other side to the beach (2½ to three hours return). Alternatively, the 500m wheelchair- and pram-friendly lighthouse boardwalk at **Cape Tourville** affords sweeping coastal panoramas and a less-strenuous glimpse of Wineglass Bay. On longer walks, sign in (and out) at the registration booth at the car park; national park fees apply.

Coles Bay Boat Hire (☎ 0419 255 604; fax 03-6257 0344) hires out bikes (half/full day $25/35), canoes (two hours $55), dinghies (two hours including petrol $75) and fishing rods (two rods and tackle $30 per day).

Tours

All4Adventure (☎ 03-6257 0018; www.all4adventure .com.au; Coles Bay Esplanade) Ever-popular two-hour quad-biking tours ($114) departing several times daily, plus half-day tours to Friendly Beaches and Bluestone Bay ($195). A driving licence is essential. Kids can ride as passengers in all-terrain vehicles for $65 (two-hour tours) and $105 (half-day tours).

Freycinet Adventures (☎ 03-6257 0500; www. freycinetadventures.com.au; 2 Freycinet Dr) Get active with this local company – half-day rock climbing and abseiling ($125), half-day sea-kayaking ($90), plus multiday walks and paddle trips.

Freycinet Air (☎ 03-6375 1694; www.freycinetair.com
.au; 109 Friendly Beaches Rd) Scenic flights over the park
from the Friendly Beaches airstrip. Flights start at $95 for
30 minutes.

Freycinet Experience (☎ 1800 506 003, 03-6223
7565; www.freycinet.com.au) From October to April, this
Hobart-based company offers four-day guided walks on
the peninsula (from $2075) with a degree of comfort and
style. Prices include food, wine, accommodation, boat trips
and return transport from Hobart.

Sleeping

Accommodation here is at a premium at
Christmas, January and Easter, so book well
ahead. Everybody and their dog wants to stay
here, so expect higher prices than in other
parts of the state.

BUDGET

The main camping ground is at **Richardsons
Beach** (☎ 03-6256 7000; www.parks.tas.gov.au; unpow-
ered/powered sites $13/16). There are toilets and
water here, but no showers. Due to its popularity, from mid-December to Easter site al-
locations are determined by ballot (drawn
on 1 August). Apply beforehand by post (to
the visitor centre), fax (☎ 03-6256 7090) or
email (freycinet@parks.tas.gov.au). Some
dates may remain unfilled after the ballot,
so it's still worth enquiring about vacancies.
Reservations are still recommended outside
the ballot period.

There's superb walk-in free camping (national park fees apply) at **Wineglass Bay** (1½
hours from the car park), **Hazards Beach** (three
hours), **Cooks Beach** (4½ hours) and **Bryans
Beach** (5½ hours). Further north at **Friendly
Beaches**, Isaacs Point has basic camping with
pit toilets. There's little or no drinking water
at these sites, so carry your own. The park
is a fuel-stove only area – campfires are
banned.

Iluka Holiday Centre (☎ 1800 786 512, 03-6257
0115; http://iluka-holiday-centre.tas.big4.com.au; Coles Bay
Esplanade; unpowered/powered sites $25/30, dm $28-35, cabins & units $100-220; 🖳) This large, bushy park in
the heart of the Iluka village gets crowded, but
it's well maintained and managed, with amenities including camp kitchens and laundry;
a shop, pub and bakery are adjacent. Tents
sites are gravelly; book a decade in advance
for the self-contained cabins. The old Iluka
Backpackers YHA has been subsumed into
the Iluka Holiday Centre, but offers the same
great facilities and YHA discounts.

MIDRANGE & TOP END

Freycinet Rentals (☎ 03-6257 0320; www.freycinetrentals
.com; 5 Garnet Ave, Coles Bay) For Coles Bay holiday
accommodation, this is a good starting point.
The managers have 14 houses/units (sleeping
up to seven) on their books, all with kitchen,
laundry, lounge, TV and barbecue. Summer
prices range from $110 to $295 (most are a flat
rate, but some tariffs are calculated at dual occupancy charging extra adults $15 to $25 and
children $5 to $15). Prices slump from May
to August, and for longer stays. Check the
website for details and property pictures.

Freycinet Getaway (☎ 0417 609 151, www.frey
cinetgetaway.com; d $135-230) Choose from the
two funky Cove Beach Apartments (97 The
Esplanade) and beachfront Azure Beach
House at Swanwick, 7km from Coles Bay. All
are fully self-contained with tasteful decor.

Sheoaks on Freycinet (☎ 03-6257 0049; www
.sheoaks.com; 47 Oyster Bay Crt; s/d incl breakfast $145/180)
With magnificent Nine Mile Beach views,
kid-free Sheoaks is a modern architecturally
designed house with comfortable rooms,
first-class facilities and great breakfasts.
Knowledgeable hosts will send you off for
the day with packed lunches and hampers on
request, and can provide evening meals, too.
Sheoaks manages several other nearby properties with the same aplomb. Take Hazards View
Rd (about 5km before Coles Bay), then turn
left at Oyster Bay Crt.

Freycinet Lodge (☎ 03-6257 0101; www.freycinet
lodge.com.au; d cabins $247-389; 🖳) This is the plush
Freycinet arm of the giant Federal Hotels'
'Pure Tasmania' enterprise and managed
super professionally. It's inside the national
park at the southern end of Richardsons
Beach with 60 deluxe bushland cabins with
balconies, some with self-catering facilities
and/or spas, and several with disabled access.
Activities and walks are organised and there
are two on-site restaurants.

Eating

Freycinet Bakery & Café (☎ 03-6257 0272; Coles Bay
Esplanade; items $3-10, pizzas $9-22; 🕑 breakfast & lunch;
🖳) For years families and outdoorsy types
have fuelled up for daily activities here on
all-day brekkies, pies, pastries, focaccias and
cakes galore. Pizzas are available from 5pm
during extended summer hours (until 8pm).

Oystercatcher (☎ 03-6257 0033; 6 Garnet Ave, Coles
Bay; mains $8-20; 🕑 lunch & dinner Nov-Apr) Local sea-
food is well prepared for diners inside or on

the deck, and for those stopping by for takeaway. Laid-back daytime cafe fare makes this a popular spot for coffee, salads, fish and chips, and classic scallop pies.

Iluka Tavern (☎ 03-6257 0429; Coles Bay Esplanade; lunch mains $10-20, dinner mains $19-27; ☻ lunch & dinner) This popular place packs in locals and visitors alike. The chalkboard menu announces standard pub grub, but has some exotic surprises too – Thai green prawn curry and spicy seafood paella. Kids' menu available.

Madge Malloys (☎ 03-6257 0399; 3 Garnet Ave, Coles Bay; mains $28-35; ☻ dinner Tue-Sat) Madge has her own fishing boat, reeling in your fresh-from-the-sea dinner. The fish o' the day might be poached wrasse or steam-baked bastard trumpeter. Fresh lobster, oysters and east-coast produce round out an innovative and ever-changing menu.

Getting There & Away

Bicheno Coach Service runs between Bicheno, Coles Bay and Freycinet National Park, connecting with east coast Redline and TassieLink coaches at the Coles Bay turn-off. See p670 for details.

BICHENO
pop 640

Unlike Swansea and Coles Bay, Bicheno is still largely a functioning fishing port. It's madly popular with holidaymakers, with brilliant ocean views, lovely beaches and surf and sunshine, but Bicheno never sold its soul and remains rough-edged and unwashed. A busy fishing fleet still comes home to harbour in the Gulch with pots of lobsters and scaly loot. Thankfully, food and accommodation prices in Bicheno are realistic.

The **Bicheno visitor information centre** (☎ 03-6375 1500; 41b Foster St; ☻ 10am-4pm Mon-Fri, 10am-noon Sat, noon-4pm Sun, shorter hours in winter) assists with local information and accommodation bookings.

Sights & Activities

The 3km **Foreshore Footway** extends south from **Redbill Beach**, which has solid sandy breaks, to **Peggys Point**, **the Gulch** and along to the **Blowhole**, returning along footpaths with panoramic town views. **Whalers Hill** is the lookout from where whales were spotted in the old days.

If the tide is low, you can wade over a sandy isthmus to **Diamond Island** at the northern end of Redbill Beach. Keep an eye on the sea

though – the isthmus will ruin your Christmas if you're caught on the island when the tumultuous tide returns. Retro-kitsch **Sea Life Centre** (☎ 03-6375 1121; www.sealifecentre.com.au; 1 Tasman Hwy; adult/child/family $6.50/4/20; ☻ 9am-5pm) has some interesting things on display, a tacky gift shop and a decent on-site seafood restaurant. More to our liking is the dinky little no-name tin-shed **aquarium** (☎ 0418 300 620; www.bichenoaquarium.com.au; Gulch Rd; adult/child $3/2; ☻ 10am-4pm) below Whalers Hill with displays of fish, seahorses, giant crabs and crayfish.

Bicheno Penguin Tours (☎ 03-6375 1333; www.bichenopenguintours.com.au; adult/child $20/10; ☻ dusk nightly) runs informative one-hour tours of the fairy penguin rookery at the northern end of Redbill Beach. This is as close as you'll get to these little creatures as they waddle out of the sea to feed their squeaking chicks. Tours depart the surf shop on the main road in the town centre; bookings are essential.

The **Bicheno Dive Centre** (☎ 03-6375 1138; www.bichenodive.com.au; 2 Scuba Crt; ☻ 9am-5pm) hires diving equipment and organises underwater adventures. Explore the submarine caves and rock formations at **Governor Island Marine Reserve** near the Gulch.

Take the 40-minute coastal tour on the **Bicheno Glass Bottom Boat** (☎ 03-6375 1294; the Gulch; tours adult/child $15/5; ☻ 10am, noon & 2pm), with lots of info provided on the underwater world.

East Coast Natureworld (☎ 03-6375 1311; www.natureworld.com.au; adult/concession/child $15/12.50/7.50; ☻ 9am-5pm), 7km north of Bicheno, is one of Tasmania's best nature parks. Highlights include a walk-through aviary, seething snake pits and plenty of free-roaming native animals. East Coast Natureworld is involved in protecting Tasmanian devils from DFTD (see Tigers & Devils, p698).

Five kilometres north of Bicheno is the turn-off to **Douglas-Apsley National Park** (☎ 03-6256 7000; www.parks.tas.gov.au), protecting undisturbed dry eucalypt forest, waterfalls, gorges and an abundance of birds and animals. Walk to the swimming hole at **Apsley Gorge** (two to three hours return), or to the **Apsley River Waterhole** (15 minutes return). There's basic, walk-in bush camping here, too (free, but national park fees apply).

Sleeping & Eating

Bicheno Backpackers (☎ 03-6375 1651; www.bicheno backpackers.com; 11 Morrison St; dm $23-25, d $62-70, f $70) Bicheno's best budget digs has young, enthusiastic owners, mural-embossed walls and a neat but unfussy atmosphere. The dorms (with linen) are in one lodge and the double rooms are in another, and the front room opens onto a large balcony and sea views. They also hire out bikes/kayaks for $30/35 per day.

Wintersun Gardens Motel (☎ 03-6375 1225; www.wintersunbicheno.com.au; 35 Gordon St; d $94-120, d self-contained unit $120-150; ☒) The rooms in this motel on the edge of town are simple but well equipped and neat as a pin. The grounds have a lovely old-fashioned feel with rose-filled gardens, box hedges and hanging baskets.

Old Tram Road B&B (☎ 03-6375 1298; www.oldtramroad.com.au; 3 Old Tram Rd; d $150-160) This is allegedly the second-oldest house on the coast, dating from 1886. Inside are two large, comfortable rooms only 100m from the beach, accessed via a private track through the back garden. Gourmet cooked breakfasts will get your day started.

Bicheno East Coast Holiday Park (☎ 03-6375 1999; www.bichenoholidaypark.com.au; 4 Champ St; unpowered/powered site $20/30, d apt $85-95, d cabin $108-125) This neat, centrally located park has plenty of trees, green grass and friendly managers. There are sheltered, shady tent spots, barbecues, camp kitchen and laundry, as well as a kids' playground.

Swell Café (☎ 03-6375 1076; 2/70 Burgess St; meals $7-13; ☽ lunch & dinner; ☐) This is where Bicheno's teens hang out sucking on sodas. Variously stuffed wraps and crepes populate the menu, plus there's good coffee, fresh juices and shiny surf posters.

Cod Rock Café (☎ 03-6375 1340; 45 Foster St; meals $7.50-18.50; ☽ 9am-8.30pm) Sells the freshest fish and seafood prepared in various ways – try the crayfish sandwich – with fish and chips cooked to order. Burgers are available for those done with seafood.

our pick **Cyrano** (☎ 03-6375 1137; 77 Burgess St; mains $27-31; ☽ dinner) This fine French restaurant is the classiest eatery in Bicheno. Try the duckling in orange and Cointreau sauce or the scallops à la Cyrano sautéed and flambéed in light cream sauce. Big on rich French flavours –butter, cream and white wine – all dishes are prepared from scratch (so be prepared to wait).

ST MARYS
pop 520

Most of the tourist traffic bypasses St Marys, but the beautiful drive up the mountains from the coast is itself worthwhile. Just 10km from the coast St Mary's is 600m above sea level near the St Nicholas Range. It's a practical, unpretentious little town with weatherboard cottages, a pub and a post office. If you were on the run from the law, this would be the place to disappear, change your name and maybe open a coffee shop.

St Marys Seaview Farm (☎ 03-6372 2341; www.seaviewfarm.com.au; Germantown Rd; dm $30, d $80-95) is on a remote hilltop 8km from St Marys with stunning views of the coastline and mountains. The cosy backpackers cottage has a kitchen and lounge for all guests, and the doubles with bathrooms are great value. Take Franks St opposite St Marys Hotel, which becomes Germantown Rd, and follow the signs. BYO supplies; no kids under 12.

The legendary **Mount Elephant Pancakes** (☎ 03-6372 2263; Elephant Pass; dishes $10-20; ☽ breakfast & lunch) changed hands recently but is still going strong. It's in an unlikely location on a cool mountain pass in the middle of nowhere on the Bicheno road, 8km south of St Marys. Seasonal fruits and local produce dominate the menu, but the house speciality – a smoked salmon, camembert and mushroom pancake – is wonderful. Cash only.

THE NORTHEAST

The northeast gets relatively few travellers, and many that do make it here leave only a day to experience the area on their way through. This gives the northeast a more undeveloped and wild feeling than the rest of the east coast. In 2005 *Condé Nast Traveller* magazine voted the exquisite Bay of Fires the world's second most beautiful beach, and suddenly Tasmania's northeast was on the radar. Pretty seaside St Helens is the main centre and a good base for exploring the region's wildlife-rich national park, waterfalls and miles of empty coastline. Fishing opportunities abound, and needless to say, so does seafood on plates.

A useful local resource is www.northeasttasmania.com.au.

Getting There & Around

The main bus company serving the northeast is **Redline Coaches** (☎ 1300 360 000; www.tasredline.com.au), running daily except Saturday between Launceston and St Helens via St Marys ($31.60, 2¾ hours). Buses also run daily except

Saturday from Launceston to Scottsdale ($18.20, 1¼ hours).

TassieLink (☎ 1300 300 520; www.tassielink.com.au) has Monday to Thursday services between Hobart and St Helens ($50.50, four hours), via the Midlands Hwy connecting with **Calows Coaches** (☎ 03-6372 5166).

ST HELENS

pop 2050

Sprawling around picturesque Georges Bay, St Helens was established as a whaling town in 1830 and soon after 'swanners' came to harvest the downy under-feathers of the bay's black swans. It's long been an important fishing port and today is home to Tasmania's largest fishing fleet. The town's history is recorded through memorabilia and photographs in the **St Helens History & Visitor Information Centre** (☎ 03-6376 1744; 61 Cecilia St; admission by donation; ⏰ 9am-5pm).

Water sports are popular in and around St Helens. **East Lines** (☎ 03-6376 1720; 28 Cecilia St) hires surfboards, wetsuits, snorkelling gear, fishing rods and bicycles. For diving, contact Bay of Fires Dive (opposite) at Binalong Bay. You can hire sea kayaks and aluminium dinghies at the St Helens Youth Hostel (below). Big-game fishing charters in St Helens include **Keen Angler** (☎ 0409 964 847), **Professional Charters** (☎ 03-6376 3083; www.gamefish.net.au) and **Roban Coastal Charters** (☎ 03-6376 3631; www.robancoastalcharters.com.au).

Town beaches are lousy for swimming, but there are superb swimming beaches at **Binalong Bay** (11km north on Binalong Bay Rd), **Jeanneret Beach** and **Sloop Rock** (15km north; take Binalong Bay Rd then The Gardens turnoff for both), **Stieglitz** (7km east on St Helens Point), and at **St Helens Point** and **Humbug Point**. Also on St Helens Point are the wind-weathered **Peron Dunes** (8km east).

About 26km west of St Helens, turn off to tiny **Pyengana** and the feathery 90m-high **St Columba Falls**, the state's highest. Further on is **Derby** (not pronounced 'Darby'), an old tin-mining town with a few B&Bs, galleries and pubs.

Sleeping & Eating

St Helens Youth Hostel (☎ 03-6376 1661; www.yha.com.au; 5 Cameron St; dm/d from $23/60; 🖥️) The bunk and double rooms are simple at this funky '60s-era YHA in quiet Cameron St lined with flowering gums, but there are good facilities as well as bike and kayak hire.

St Helens Backpackers (☎ 03-6376 2017; www.sthelensbackpackers.com.au; 59 Cecilia St; dm/f $24/75, d with/without bathroom $70/60) This family home on the main street has been refitted as great-value budget accommodation. The shared kitchen, lounge and bathroom areas are clean and well equipped, and Paul the manager is friendly and knowledgeable. The hostel also hires out camping kits and provides transport for people looking to experience the wilds of the Bay of Fires.

our pick Kellraine Units (☎ /fax 6376 1169; www.kellraineunits.com.au; 72 Tully St; d $70, extra child/adult $20/40) This unpretentious collection of roomy self-contained units, on the main road 800m northwest of the town centre, is St Helens' best-value digs. More modest than fashionable with discreet decor and charming old-school hosts, Kellraine is popular with returning visitors (book ahead).

Bay of Fires Character Cottages (☎ 03-6376 8262; www.bayoffirescottages.com.au; 64-74 Main Rd, Binalong Bay; d $180-270) Up at Binalong Bay, 11km north of St Helens, these eight colourful, modern one- to three-bedroom cottages are beautifully appointed with kitchens, laundries and barbecues. Best of all are the million-dollar views from the private balconies.

St Helens Caravan Park (☎ 03-6376 1290; www.sthelenscp.com.au; 2 Penelope St; unpowered/powered sites $27/29, cabins $90-140; ♿ 🖥️) With good, clean facilities, oodles of tent and van sites, and old and new cabins, this park is 1km south of the town centre. There's also a playground, camp kitchen, games room and jumping pillow.

our pick Angasi (☎ 03-6376 8222; www.angasi.com.au; 64 Main Rd, Binalong Bay; lunch mains $9-17, dinner mains $22-28) With a breathtaking position overlooking Binalong Bay, Angasi is brilliant – casual cafe by day and smart-casual à la carte dining room by night. Three young locals got a bright idea and have been winning awards and loyal customers ever since. Changing local art is featured in the groovy red-and-black dining room, but most people can't take their eyes off the view. Crafty Mod Oz is accompanied by select Tasmanian wines. Ask about the adjacent Angasi Apartment (from $220 for two).

Captain's Catch (☎ 03-6376 1170; Marine Pde; meals $9-17; ⏰ lunch & dinner) The freshest of the St Helens fishing booty is sold at this fish and chippery/fishmonger. Grab some battered blue eye or a dozen succulent St Helens oysters – superb!

Latris (☎ 03-6376 1170; Marine Pde; mains $28-32; ☻ lunch & dinner) Latris was born when Captain's Catch (above) was made over and extended in 2008 to incorporate this high-end restaurant. Mod Oz mains are not all fishy – wallaby fillets, duck breasts and pork bellies are prepared with skill, and the views over Georges Bay through the giant floor-to-ceiling windows are outstanding.

BAY OF FIRES

Binalong Bay Rd heads northeast from St Helens over a low tidal swamp before it makes its way to lovely Binalong Bay. This is the only permanent community at the Bay of Fires, but it's just a clutch of holiday houses, a phone box and the acclaimed Angasi restaurant. The dive shop, **Bay of Fires Dive** (☎ 03-6376 8173; 0419 372 342; www.bayoffiresdive.com.au), is the only shop of any kind. To get to the Bay of Fires proper, follow the road toward the ramshackle shack-town of **The Gardens**. The Bay of Fires' northern end is reached via the C843, the road to the Ansons Bay settlement and Mt William National Park.

The Bay of Fires is exquisite – powder-white sands and foaming cerulean-blue water is backed by scrubby bush and lagoons. Despite the proliferation of signature bright-orange lichen on the rocky points and headlands, the early explorers named the bay after seeing Aboriginal fires along the shore. Ocean beaches offer reliable surfing but potentially dangerous swimming – beware of rips and currents. The lagoons offer safe swimming.

For those who fancy a deluxe wilderness experiences, the **Bay of Fires Walk** (☎ 03-6391 9339; www.bayoffires.com.au) conducts a fully catered four-day walk ($2000 per person) from Boulder Point south to Ansons Bay. Trips run from October to May, and accommodation includes two nights at the company's magnificent ecofriendly **Bay of Fires Lodge** (☎ 03-6392 2211; www.bayoffireslodge.com.au), where you can otherwise stay for a lazy $450 per person.

Bay of Fires Eco Tours (☎ 03-6376 8262; fax 6376 8261; tours per person $70) runs three- to four-hour return boat trips from Binalong Bay to Eddystone Point, passing seals, dolphins and birdlife along the way. Tours run on Monday, Wednesday and Saturday (weather permitting). Call for bookings and departure times.

There are wonderful free **camping** spots along the bay, mostly without toilets or fresh water. There are good options immediately north of Binalong Bay, accessed by road from St Helens (take the turn-off to The Gardens). The best spots are secret (but if you go to Cosy Corner South leave room for us, eh?). In the northern reaches, there are the sheltered beachfront sites at Policemans Point, reached by a turn-off before Ansons Bay.

MT WILLIAM NATIONAL PARK

The little-known, isolated **Mt William National Park** (www.parks.gov.tas.au) brings together long sandy beaches, low ridges and coastal heathlands – visit during spring or early summer when the wildflowers are at their bloomin' best. The highest point, Mt William (1½-hour return walk), stands only 216m tall, yet projects your gaze over land and sea. The area was declared a national park in 1973, primarily to protect Tasmania's remaining Forester (eastern grey) kangaroos that were nearly wiped out by disease in the 1950s and '60s (they've been breeding themselves silly ever since). Activities on offer in the area include bird-watching and wildlife-spotting, fishing, swimming, surfing and diving.

At Eddystone Point is the impressive **Eddystone Lighthouse**, built from granite blocks in the 1890s. A small picnic spot here overlooks a beach with red granite outcrops. A short drive away beside a tannin-stained creek (and yet another magnificent arc of white sand and aqua water) is the idyllic free campground at **Deep Creek** with pit toilets and fireplaces – bring drinking water and firewood. You can also camp at **Stumpys Bay** and **Musselroe Top Camp**. The park is well off the main roads, accessible from the north or south. The northern end is 17km from Gladstone; the southern end around 60km from St Helens. Try to avoid driving here at night when animals are bounding about.

SCOTTSDALE & AROUND
pop 2500

The northeast's largest town is Scottsdale, servicing some of Tasmania's richest agricultural and forestry country. This unprepossessing town has a few old country pubs, a motel, some teenage mums and other disillusioned youths looking to make a break. The architecturally interesting **Forest EcoCentre** (☎ 03-6352 6466; www.forestrytas.com.au; 88 King St, ☻ 9am-5pm) has an interactive forest interpretation centre and some superbly crafted timber furniture.

The same building houses the **Scottsdale visitor information centre** (☎ 03-6352 6520) with plenty of regional info.

Anabel's of Scottsdale (☎ 03-6352 3277; www.vision .net.au/~anabels; 46 King St, Scottsdale; s/d $110/130) has a high-calibre **restaurant** (mains $18-26; ☽ lunch & dinner Tue-Sat) inside a lovely old Federation home, plus peach-and-pine motel units overlooking a rambling, overgrown garden.

Bridestowe Estate Lavender Farm (☎ 03-6352 8182; www.bridestoweestates.com.au; 296 Gillespies Rd) is near Nabowla, 22km west of Scottsdale. It's the biggest lavender farm in the southern hemisphere. Admission charges (per person/ vehicle $4/12) only apply during flowering season from mid-December to late January (a purple patch?), which covers a guided tour; the rest of the year it's free. Try lavender-flavoured muffins and ice cream at the cafe.

Bridport, 21km northwest of Scottsdale, is a wound-down beach town with plenty of accommodation. The **Pavilion visitor information centre** (☎ 03-6356 1881; Main St, Bridport; ☽ 10am-4pm) has all the local info. The Southern Shipping Company runs a weekly ferry from here to Flinders Island (p717).

Bridport Seaside Lodge (☎ 03-6356 1585; www .bridportseasidelodge.com; 47 Main St, Bridport; dm/s $22/30, d $50-75) is a weatherboard house on the main street. The better doubles have en suites while the dorms are smallish, but tidy.

Bridport Caravan Park (☎ 03-6356 1227; Bentley St; unpowered/powered sites $20/25) stretches fully three kilometres along the foreshore.

An accommodating cafe about 3km south of Bridport, **Flying Teapot** (☎ 03-6356 1918; 1800 Bridport Rd; mains $8-16; ☽ lunch Wed-Sun, closed winter) overlooks a private airstrip. They'll cook whatever they feel like, or whatever you feel like, depending on their mood.

PIPERS RIVER REGION

This region's most famous vineyard is **Pipers Brook** (☎ 03-6382 7527; www.kreglingerwineestates .com; 1216 Pipers Brook Rd; ☽ 10am-5pm) where you can try Pipers Brook, Ninth Island and Krieglinger wines in an architecturally innovative building that also houses the **Winery Café** (mains from $22; ☽ lunch). Also within the Pipers Brook estate, but signposted up a different drive, is the separately run **Jansz Wine Room** (☎ 03-6382 7066; www.jansztas.com; 1216B Pipers Brook Rd, Pipers Brook; ☽ 10am-4.30pm) where you can taste excellent sparklings and enjoy a cheese platter.

Bay of Fires Wines (☎ 03-6382 7622; www.bayof fireswines.com.au; 40 Baxters Rd, Pipers River; ☽ 10am-5pm) is 15km south of Pipers River, and home of recently prestigious Arras Sparkling and a fine Tigress Riesling, as well as a stylish **restaurant** (mains $12-35; ☽ lunch). Other local vineyards include the **Delamere** (☎ 03-6382 7190; www.delamerevineyards.com.au; 4238 Bridport Rd, Pipers Brook; ☽ 10am-5pm), with superb Chardonnay and Pinot varieties, and **Dalrymple** (☎ 03-6382 7222; www.dalrymplevineyards.com.au; 1337 Pipers Brook Rd; ☽ 10am-5pm).

LAUNCESTON

pop 71,400

Locals call this place 'Lonnie' and it sits in a basin at the head of the Tamar Valley where the North and South Esk rivers meet to form the Tamar River. Tasmania's second-largest city is an unhurried and rather diffident place, and while Hobart is more cosmopolitan, Launceston is very likeable with a remarkable stock of Victorian, Federation, Edwardian and art deco architecture that is the rival of any Australian city.

Launceston's beginnings, however, were anything but refined. When the Reverend Horton visited in 1822, he wrote to his superiors: 'The wickedness of the people of Launceston exceeds all description. If you could witness the ignorance, blasphemy, drunkenness, adultery and vice of every description, you would use every effort to send them more missionaries.' Launceston seems to be still emerging from its colonial-outpost roots, and buffing off some rough edges along the way, but transforming itself into a glorious historic town with a glam all its own. The University of Tasmania is here and the many great restaurants, galleries and cultural and sporting institutions testify to modern Lonnie's more worldly outlook.

See www.ltvtasmania.com.au for more on Lonnie and the Tamar Valley.

ORIENTATION

The city grid is around Brisbane St Mall, which runs between Charles and St John Sts. Flanking the old seaport are a string of new eateries and a hotel. West of the city is Cataract Gorge, a rugged ravine that's one of the city's major tourist drawcards. Charles St south of the CBD is the groovy, caffeinated, bohemian strip.

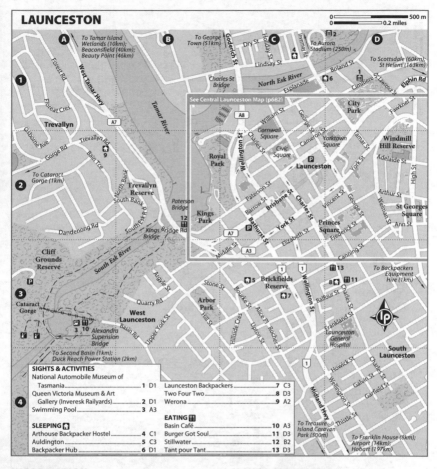

LAUNCESTON

SIGHTS & ACTIVITIES

National Automobile Museum of Tasmania	1 D1
Queen Victoria Museum & Art Gallery (Inveresk Railyards)	2 D1
Swimming Pool	3 A3

SLEEPING

Arthouse Backpacker Hostel	4 C1
Auldington	5 C3
Backpacker Hub	6 D1
Launceston Backpackers	7 C3
Two Four Two	8 D3
Werona	9 A2

EATING

Basin Café	10 A3
Burger Got Soul	11 D3
Stillwater	12 B2
Tant pour Tant	13 D3

INFORMATION

Banks and ATMs are located on St John and Brisbane Sts near the mall. There are post-offices on St John and Cameron Sts.

Birchalls (Map p682; ☎ 03-6331 3011; www.birchalls .com.au; 118-120 Brisbane St; ⏰ 8.30am-6pm Mon-Fri, to 5pm Sat, 10am-4pm Sun) Considered Australia's oldest bookshop (c 1844).

Cyber King (Map p682; ☎ 03-6334 2802; 113 George St; per hr $5; ⏰ 8.30am-7.30pm Mon-Fri, 9.30am-6.30pm Sat & Sun) Internet access.

Launceston visitor information centre (Map p682; ☎ 03-6336 3133; travelcentre@launceston.tas.gov .au; cnr St John & Cimitiere Sts; ⏰ 9am-5pm Mon-Fri, to 3pm Sat, to noon Sun) Pamphlets and state-wide accommodation, tour and transport bookings. Next to the bus terminal.

SIGHTS & ACTIVITIES
Cataract Gorge

A 10-minute walk west of the city is the fabulous **Cataract Gorge** (Map p681; ☎ 03-6331 5915; www.launcestoncataractgorge.com.au; ⏰ 9am-dusk). Surrounded by a wildlife reserve, near-vertical basalt cliffs crowd the banks of the South Esk River as it enters the Tamar. During the day, teens plunge into the river and rock-climbers defy gravity; at night the floodlit cliffs take on a shifty, shadow-strewn countenance.

Walking tracks on either side of the gorge lead from Kings Bridge up to **First Basin**, where there's a **swimming pool** (admission free; ⏰ Nov-Mar), picnic grounds, a quality restaurant with resident peacocks, and trails leading to vista-packed lookouts. Both a suspension bridge and

TASMANIA

CENTRAL LAUNCESTON

TASMANIA

0 ____ 200 m
0 ____ 0.1 miles

Lyttleton St

Clarence St

East Launceston

Hornsey Ave

Adelaide St

St George Square

15

High St

14

St Georges Square

12

St George Square

Parkmere St

Weymouth St

18

Windmill Hill Reserve

Stewart St

Arthur St

My St

Welman St

Agina Place

City Park

8 7

Tamar St

Brisbane St

26 24

33

23

28

York St

Earl St

George St

St Vincent's Hospital

St Johns Anglican Church

Cameron St

Holy Trinity Anglican Church

Yorktown Square

30

13

Vincent St

Princes Square

Charles St

6 32

16

George St

4

20

St Johns St

5

Quadrant Mall

Brisbane St Mall

27

22

Frederick St

Shields St

St Andrews Presbyterian Church

Launceston Library

19

Wm St

1

9

Kingsway

York St

1

William St

Town Hall

Civic Square

Pilgrim Uniting Church

34

29

Brisbane St

Wellington St

Elizabeth St

A3

Cornwall Square

31

Cameron St

Charles St

Paterson St

Barrow St

25

Bathurst St

A7

Lower Charles St

A8

10

Middle St

37

North Esk River
Old Launceston Seaport

21

Seaport Blvd

Royal Park

23

Park St

Paterson St

West Tamar Hwy

West Launceston

Home Point

11

Tamar River

Kings Park

Zig Zig Reserve

INFORMATION					
Birchalls	**1**	C3			
Cyber King	**2**	D2			
Launceston Visitor					
Information Centre	**3**	C2			
Post Office	**4**	C2			
Post Office	**5**	C3			
SIGHTS & ACTIVITIES					
Boag's Centre for Beer					
Lovers	**6**	C1			
Design Centre of					
Tasmania	**7**	D1			
Japanese Macaque					
Enclosure	**8**	D1			
Mountain Bike Tasmania					
(Mountain Designs)	**9**	C3			
Planetarium		(see 10)			
Queen Victoria Museum					
& Art Gallery (Royal					
Park Site)	**10**	B3			

Tamar River Cruises	**11**	A2			
Wood Design					
Collection		(see 7)			
SLEEPING					
Ashton Gate	**12**	E3			
Fiona's B&B	**13**	D3			
Hatherley House	**14**	F3			
Kurrajong House	**15**	F2			
Lloyds Hotel					
Backpackers	**16**	C1			
Old Bakery Inn	**17**	B4			
Sandor's on the Park	**18**	E1			
Star Bar	**19**	C2			
EATING					
Black Cow Bistro	**20**	C2			
Fish 'n' Chips	**21**	A1			
Fresh	**22**	C4			
Hallam's Waterfront	**23**	A3			
Izakaya	**24**	D1			

DRINKING					
Irish Murphy's	**25**	B4			
Royal Oak Hotel	**26**	D1			
ENTERTAINMENT					
Hotel New York	**27**	C3			
Princess Theatre	**28**	D2			
Village Cinemas	**29**	C3			
TRANSPORT					
Bike Hire Tasmania (Appleby					
Cycles)	**30**	D2			
Cornwall Square Transit Centre	**31**	B1			
Economy Car Rentals	**32**	C1			
Lo-Cost Auto Rent	**33**	D1			
Manion's Coaches	**34**	C3			
Mountain Bike Tasmania					
(Mountain Designs)		(see 9)			
Redline Coaches		(see 31)			
Rent-a-Bug		(see 33)			
TassieLink		(see 31)			

a **chairlift** (one way adult/child $10/7, return $12/8; 9am-5pm) sail across First Basin. A walking track (45 minutes one way) leads further up the gorge to **Second Basin** and the old Duck Reach power station. On hot summer days the gorge and swimming pool take on a beach-like scene with sun umbrellas, towels and swimwear, as seemingly all of Launceston comes to cool off. The classy Basin Café (p686) has wonderful views over the pool, river and gorge.

Queen Victoria Museum & Art Gallery

The **Queen Victoria Museum & Art Gallery** (03-6323 3777; www.qvmag.tas.gov.au; admission free; 10am-5pm) has two campuses. The purpose-built 1891 museum at **Royal Park** (Map p682; 2 Wellington St) is currently closed undergoing major refurbishment and will reopen in 2010 as a home for fine arts; the superb remodelled site at the **Inveresk Railyards** (Map p681; 2 Invermay Rd) remains open and showcases an outstanding collection of traditional Aboriginal mareener shell necklaces, an impressive display of early colonial painting, interactive museum spaces with old aeroplanes and railway workshops, and shifting contemporary exhibits. The popular **Planetarium** will be relocated to Inveresk site from the Royal Park campus. Both sites have cafes and access for wheelchairs.

Boag's Brewery

Boag's beer, the northern Tasmanian beer of choice, has been brewed on William St since 1881. One-hour guided 'Discovery Tours' operate from the **Boag's Centre for Beer Lovers** (Map p682; 03-6332 6300; www.boags.com.au; 39 William St; adult/concession/child/family $18/14/14/50; tours from 9am

Mon-Fri), concluding with tastings. For extra gas try the 1½-hour 'Beer Lovers Tour' (adult/concession/child/family $25/22/22/75) with beer *and* cheese tastings. Bookings are essential.

Other Attractions

The **Design Centre of Tasmania** (Map p682; 03-6331 5506; www.designcentre.com.au; cnr Brisbane & Tamar Sts; 9.30am-5.30pm), on the edge of City Park, is a retail outlet displaying high-quality work by Tasmanian craftspeople – if you covet a giant Huon pine clothes peg, the prices here are as good as anywhere in the state. In the same building, the **Wood Design Collection** (adult/concession/child $5/4/free) showcases local designs, with more sassafras, Huon pine and myrtle than your average southwest forest.

The oxymoronic **National Automobile Museum of Tasmania** (Map p681; 03-6334 8888; www.namt .com.au; 86 Cimitiere St; adult/child/family $10.50/6/27; 9am-5pm Sep-May, 10am-4pm Jun-Aug) will excite rev-heads – it has one of Australia's best presentations of classic and historic cars and motorbikes, though it's more Chitty Chitty Bang Bang than bitchin' Camaro.

Franklin House (off Map p681; 03-6344 7824; www.nationaltrusttas.org.au; 413 Hobart Rd, Breadalbane; adult/concession/child/family $8/6/free/16; 9am-5pm Oct-Mar, to 4pm Apr-Sep) is signposted 8km south of Launceston and is one of Tasmania's most attractive Georgian homes. Built in 1838 it's now beautifully restored, furnished and passionately managed by the National Trust.

Parks & Reserves

The 13-hectare, oak-filled **City Park** (Map p682) was established in the 1820. It's a fine example

TASMANIA

of a Victorian garden, with an elegant fountain, mature European trees, a bandstand and an 1832 glass conservatory. A glass-walled enclosure houses Japanese macaques (monkeys) who look sad and listless wondering what the hell they're doing in Tasmania. Pretty **Princes Square** (Map p682) features a bronze fountain purchased at the 1855 Paris Exhibition. **Royal Park** (Map p682), at the North Esk and Tamar River junction, features a Gorge-to-Seaport boardwalk and Launceston's shifting cabal of disaffected skateboarders.

Ten minutes' drive north of the city are the **Tamar Island Wetlands** (off Map p681; ☎ 03-6327 3964; www.parks.tas.gov.au; West Tamar Hwy; adult/concession/child/family $3/2/2/6; ☺ 9am-5pm Apr-Sep, 10am-4pm Oct-Mar), where you'll find an Interpretation Centre and a 2km wheelchair-accessible boardwalk through a significant wetlands reserve, teeming with birds, reptiles and the odd echidna.

TOURS

Launceston City Ghost Tours (☎ 0421 819 373; www.launcestoncityghosttours.com; adult/concession/child/family $25/20/15/55; ☺ dusk) Spooky 90-minute tours around the city's back alleys and lanes with theatrical guides, departing the Royal Oak Hotel (p686); bookings are essential.

Launceston Historic Walks (☎ 03-6336 2213; per person $15; ☺ 4pm Mon, 10am Tue-Sat) One-hour guided architecture and social history walks, departing the 1842 shop, corner St John and Cimitere Sts (diagonally opposite the visitor information centre). Bookings required.

Mountain Bike Tasmania (Mountain Designs) (Map p682; ☎ 03-6334 0977; www.mountainbiketasmania.com.au; 120 Charles St) Guided rides with transport, equipment and lunch/snacks provided: Ben Lomond Descent ($150), Trevallyn Reserve ($90) or North Esk River ($75).

Tamar River Cruises (Map p682; ☎ 03-6334 9900; www.tamarrivercruises.com.au; Home Point Pde) Fifty-minute Cataract Gorge cruises hourly from 9.30am to 3.30pm (adult/concession/child/family $22/19/12/56), plus longer lunch, afternoon and dinner cruises on the Tamar.

FESTIVALS & EVENTS

Festivale (www.festivale.com.au) Three mid-February days devoted to eating, drinking, arts and entertainment, staged in City Park.

Three Peaks Race (www.threepeaks.org.au) Over four days in April, teams sail from Beauty Point (north of Launceston) to Hobart, pausing for runners to scale three mountains along the way.

Royal Launceston Show (☎ 03-6331 6044) Old hands display their herds in October.

Launceston Blues Festival (www.ozblues.net/lbc) In November, blues, roots and funk with local and mainland performers.

SLEEPING
Budget

Launceston Backpackers (Map p681; ☎ 03-6334 2327; www.launcestonbackpackers.com.au; 103 Canning St; dm $20-21, s $48, d with/without bathroom $65/55; ☐) One of several great backpacker options, this large 1904 Federation church-built house is in a good location across the street from shady Brickfields Reserve. Has terrific (huge!) communal areas, great staff and clean spacious rooms. Dorm linen extra.

Lloyds Hotel Backpackers (Map p682; ☎ 1300 858 861; www.backpackers-accommodation.com.au; 23 George St; dm/s/d/f $24/58/75/128; ☐) The backpackers upstairs at Lloyds is a great facility with clean rooms (all with bathroom), full kitchen, capacious communal areas and wi-fi internet. Lloyds Hotel is a jumpin' joint and downstairs goes berserk on Friday and Saturday nights.

Backpacker Hub (Map p681; ☎ 03-6334 9288; www.backpackerhub.com.au; 1 Tamar St; dm/s/d $25/50/58; ☐) This 1888 pub overlooking the river has no-fuss, no-frills backpacker accommodation with clean shared bathrooms. Downstairs the bar, gelati counter and pool tables collide with occasional live music.

ourpick Arthouse Backpacker Hostel (Map p681; ☎ 03-6333 0222; www.arthousehostel.com.au; 20 Lindsay St, 4-/6-/8-bed dm $27/25/23; ☐) Just across the North Esk River is this beautiful old heritage home refitted as a spacious hostel with airy dorms, friendly communal spaces, wide verandah and barbecue courtyard. The friendly young owners also hire bikes and camping equipment. Disabled-traveller-friendly and carbon neutral, too.

Star Bar (Map p682; ☎ 03-6331 6111; www.starbarcafeandhotel.com.au; 113 Charles St; s/d/f $80/100/150) Star Bar is right in the heart of the CBD and has great-value, spic-and-span rooms upstairs, each with its own en suite.

Treasure Island Caravan Park (off Map p681; ☎ 03-6344 2600; www.caravancampingnetwork.com.au; 94 Glen Dhu St; unpowered/powered sites $22/26, on-site caravans $56, cabins $80-90) This park, 2.5km south of town, has reasonable facilities and some shady areas next to the noisy highway.

Midrange

Sandor's on the Park (Map p682; ☎ 1800 030 140, 03-6331 2055; www.sandorsonthepark.com.au; 3 Brisbane St; d

$95-120) This '60s motel is Lonnie's most central. The '80s facelift is starting to sag – gravity always wins. The location is fab with marvellous City Park across the road. The Monkey Bar Café downstairs is a popular business lunch spot.

Fiona's B&B (Map p682; ☎ 03-6334 5965; www.fionas .com.au; 141a George St; s $110-120, d $150-175) In a great central location, some of Fiona's rooms have excellent Launceston views. Deluxe touches include quality linen, claw-foot baths and artsy decor. Most rooms have their own private courtyard or access to the leafy, green garden.

Old Bakery Inn (Map p682; ☎ 1800 641 264, 03-6331 7900; www.oldbakeryinn.com.au; 270 York St; r $115-150; ✖) Curly-iron colonial beds; floral bedspreads, drapes and prints; and ornate ceiling roses and fireplaces – the Old Bakery Inn's 24 rooms are comfortable with minibars and electric blankets, and aren't overly fussy. The old gal's about 130 years old and surprisingly quiet inside given the busy corner location.

Ashton Gate (Map p682; ☎ 03-6331 6180; www.ash tongate.com.au; 32 High St; s $115, d $140-180) This 1880s B&B on the East Launceston hilltop deftly treads the balance between stately period elegance and colonial kitsch, offering a homely sense of calm and tranquillity. The authentic period decor features some impressive antique pieces and the prim gardens bloom with roses and camellias. There's a self-contained apartment too, and a lovely park across the street.

Werona (Map p681; ☎ 03-6334 2272; www.werona .com; 33 Trevallyn Rd; d $130-230; ▢) Werona offers opulent B&B accommodation in a 1908 Federation home with brilliant Launceston views. There are leadlight windows, decorative mouldings and ornate ceilings, and *trompe l'oeil* murals. The Romantic suites are little larger than the Intimate suites, but all have antiques, four-poster beds and en suites. There's a billiard table and a guest lounge on the ground level, and a pretty garden out the back.

Kurrajong House (Map p682; ☎ 03-6331 6655; www .kurrajonghouse.com.au; 18 High St; d $135-180) Roses bloom in the gardens, log fires crackle at night and natural light fills the breakfast dining room. The rooms of this welcoming B&B are large and tastefully decorated, and cooked breakfasts are a sumptuous affair.

Top End

Two Four Two (Map p681; ☎ 03-6331 9242; www.two fourtwo.com.au; 242 Charles St; d incl breakfast $200-220; ✖ ▢) When all that old-world doily-and-lace decor is getting you down, head for Two Four Two. Much-lauded contemporary timber furniture maker Alan Livermore turned his hand to fitting out these three too-cool-for-school self-contained apartments with superb blackwood, myrtle and Tasmanian oak detailing. Flat-screen TVs, stainless-steel kitchens, coffee machines and spa baths complete the experience.

Auldington (Map p681; ☎ 03-6331 2050; www.auld ington.com.au; 110 Frederick St; d $210-300; ▢) Old on the outside and new on the inside – this historic boutique hotel has a light, bright and modern interior filled with tasteful art pieces, contemporary fittings and lots of little luxuries. There's a wheelchair-friendly suite and attentive personal service.

Hatherley House (Map p682; ☎ 03-6334 7727; www .hatherleyhouse.com.au; 43 High St; ste incl breakfast $250-350) Multi-award-winning, über-hip Hatherley is set in an 1830s mansion overlooking expansive lawns and decked out with marble fireplaces and the best furnishings, art and ultra-modern fittings money can buy. You can have the run of the whole house for a lazy $2100 per night. Leave the kiddies at home.

EATING
Restaurants

Izakaya (Map p682; ☎ 03-6331 0613; 25 Yorktown Sq; sushi $4-8, mains $17-22; ⏱ lunch Wed-Sat, dinner Tue-Sun) Chef Caesar Woo makes superior sushi, noodle dishes and mains in this downbeat Japanese canteen-style eatery that has some of Tasmania's best Japanese cuisine.

our pick Stillwater (Map p682; ☎ 03-6331 4153; Ritchies Mill, 2 Bridge Rd; lunch mains $13-27, dinner 2/3/6 courses $70/85/105) Ensconced in the brilliantly renovated 1840s Ritchies riverside flour mill, Stillwater offers one of Tasmania's great culinary experiences. By day it's a stylish but relaxed cafe cooking up superb late breakfasts (perfect eggs, French toast and homemade muesli) and lazy lunches (tapas plates, wraps and salads). Come night-time the dining gets serious with a creative degustation menu featuring the best Tasmanian seafood and produce.

Hallam's Waterfront (Map p682; ☎ 03-6334 0554; 13 Park St; mains $25-30; ⏱ lunch & dinner) With a splendid waterfront location, Hallam's is an upmarket seafood restaurant with a nautical theme and a fresh stash of fish and seafood sizzling in its pans. There's also a takeaway catering for gourmet fish 'n' chip lovers.

Black Cow Bistro (Map p682; ☎ 03-6331 2325; 70 George St; mains $25-35; ◎ dinner Wed-Mon) Black Cow Bistro is the latest of high-end-restaurant incarnation of the wonderful old Luck's butchery art deco corner site. Owned by the folks from Stillwater (p685), Black Cow specialises in premium grass-fed cuts as fat as your forearm, select Tasmanian wines and French-style desserts.

Cafes & Quick Eats

our pick **Tant pour Tant** (Map p681; ☎ 03-6334 9884; 226 Charles St; pastries & baguettes $4-14; ◎ 7.30am-6pm Mon-Fri, 8.30am-4pm Sat & Sun) Your eyes will surely be bigger than your stomach at this wonderful French patisserie. As well as artisan and organic breads, it serves a jaw-dropping range of croissants, cakes and pastries; and does breakfasts and light lunches, too. You'll feel like you're in Paris as you savour your *mille feuille* and coffee at a streetside table.

Fresh (Map p682; ☎ 6331 4299; 178 Charles St; mains $8-16; ◎ breakfast & lunch daily, dinner Fri) A super-friendly hippy hangout, Fresh has a largely organic vegie/vegan (licensed) menu and a committed enviro-crusty clientele. Reclaimed retro furniture and oddball-arty decor set a fun tone, but they're serious about recycling their waste and supporting green community issues.

Fish 'n' Chips (Map p682; ☎ 03-6331 1999; 30 Seaport Blvd; mains $8-17; ◎ lunch & dinner) The late afternoon sunshine on the riverfront deck here makes for a memorable meal. Upmarket fish 'n' chips cooked fresh to order, seafood salads, antipasto platters and wine by the glass. Hard to beat and kid friendly, too.

Burger Got Soul (Map p681; ☎ 03-6334 5204; 243 Charles St; burgers $10-16; ◎ lunch & dinner) Wonderful! Healthy hamburgers, handmade from lean meat served with the freshest breads, crunchy salads and hand-cut chunky chips. Burger Got Soul gets very busy, but the wait is worthwhile. Try the spicy Soul Mama, with chilli sauce and sliced jalapenos, or a Soul Veggie Burger (cooked on a separate grill) for nonmeat-eating people.

Basin Café (☎ 03-6331 5222; Cataract Gorge Reserve, Basin Rd; mains $12-24) With billion-dollar views over Cataract Gorge the classy Basin Café is a great spot for a fortifying coffee and cake,

a gourmet basin burger or more substantial meal from a shifting Mod-Oz menu. Relaxed casual dining.

DRINKING & ENTERTAINMENT

Royal Oak Hotel (Map p682; ☎ 03-6331 5345; 14 Brisbane St; ◎ 11am-late) Hands down Launceston's best pub – grungy, friendly and convivial with stacks of beers on tap, open mic nights (the last Wednesday of the month) and live acoustic rock Wednesday to Sunday. Decent pub meals, too, with a kids' menu and a family-friendly vibe.

Irish Murphy's (Map p682; ☎ 03-6331 4440; www .irishmurphys.com.au; 211 Brisbane St; ◎ 11am-late) A happy watering hole full of Emerald Isle pre-dictabilia, with live music every night (usually free), including Sunday arvo jam sessions. The upstairs accommodation has reasonable bunkrooms and doubles.

Hotel New York (Map p682; ☎ 03-6334 7231; www.ho telnewyork.net.au; 122 York St) The old St James Hotel has been rebadged Hotel New York and hosts a steady stream of local and interstate acoustic and full-blown rock acts (Kate Miller-Heidke et al) plus a wicked line-up of celebrity DJs and special events.

Princess Theatre (Map p682; ☎ 03-6323 3666; www .theatrenorth.com.au; 57 Brisbane St) Built in 1911 and incorporating the smaller Earl Arts Centre, the Princess stages an eclectic mix of local and mainland drama, dance and comedy acts.

Village Cinemas (Map p682; ☎ 03-6331 5066; www.villagecinemas.com.au; 163 Brisbane St; tickets adult/ concession/child $15/12/10.50; ◎ 10am-10pm) Screens mainstream Hollywood fodder. Tuesdays all sessions cost $10.

Aurora Stadium (off Map p681; ☎ 03-6323 3666, 6344 9988; www.aurorastadium.com; admission from adult/con-cession/child/family $21/13/5/40) If you're in town during AFL football season (April to August), see the big men fly. AFL team Hawthorn plays four home games each season at Aurora Stadium. 'BAAAAAALL!!!'

GETTING THERE & AWAY
Air

There are regular direct flights between Launceston and Melbourne, Sydney and Brisbane (see p635).

Bus

Redline Coaches (☎ 1300 360 000; www.tasredline.com.au) and **TassieLink** (☎ 1300 300 520; www.tassielink.com.au) depart Launceston from the **Cornwall Square Transit Centre** (Map p682; cnr St John & Cimitiere Sts), just behind the visitor information centre. **Manion's Coaches** (Map p682; ☎ 03-6383 1221; manions.coaches@tassie.net.au; 168 Brisbane St) have services that run from Launceston up the West Tamar Valley (see Getting There & Around, right).

Redline fares and routes:

Journey	Price ($)	Duration (hr)
Launceston-Bicheno	34	2¾
Launceston-Burnie	37	2¾
Launceston-Deloraine	14	¾
Launceston-Devonport	24	1½
Launceston-George Town	12	¾
Launceston-Hobart	39	2½
Launceston-St Helens	32	2¾
Launceston-Stanley	49	4
Launceston-Swansea	31	2

TassieLink fares and routes:

Journey	Price ($)	Duration (hr)
Launceston-Bicheno	34	2½
Launceston-Cradle Mountain	59	3
Launceston-Devonport (meeting ferries)	24	1¼
Launceston-Hobart	34	2½
Launceston-Queenstown	72	6
Launceston-Sheffield	30	2
Launceston-Strahan	82	8¾

GETTING AROUND
To/From the Airport

Launceston airport is 15km south of town. **The Airporter** (☎ 03-6343 6677; adult/child $12/6) is a door-to-door airport shuttle bus. A taxi to/from the city costs about $40.

Bicycle

Bicycle hirers in Launceston include **Backpackers Equipment Hire** (off Map p681; ☎ 03-6334 9779; www.tasequiphire.com.au; 4 Penquite Rd, Newstead; per day from $20), 2km southeast of the city centre; **Bike Hire Tasmania (Appleby Cycles)** (Map p682; ☎ 03-6331 1311; www.bikehiretasmania.com.au; 83 George St; per day from $25); and **Mountain Bike Tasmania (Mountain Designs)** (Map p682; ☎ 03-6334 0988; www.mountainbiketasmania.com.au; 120 Charles St; per day from $20). Several backpacker hostels also rent bikes, including Arthouse Backpacker Hostel (see p684).

Bus

Local buses are run by **Metro Tasmania** (☎ 13 22 01; www.metrotas.com.au), most departing from St John St between Paterson and York Sts. For $5 you can buy a Day Rover pass for unlimited travel after 9am Monday to Friday, and all day Saturday, Sunday and public holidays. Most services cease after dark; Sunday services are limited.

Car

The big-name rental companies have either Launceston airport or city offices. Smaller operators with cars from around $35 per day:
Economy Car Rentals (Map p682; ☎ 03-6334 3299; fax 6334 1500; 27 William St)
Freedom Rent-A-Car (☎ 0409 933 618; www.freedomrentacar.com.au) Free delivery to airport or city.
Lo-Cost Auto Rent (Map p682; ☎ 1300 883 739, 03-6334 6202; www.rentforless.com.au; 80 Tamar St)
Rent-a-Bug (Map p682; ☎ 03-6334 3437; 80 Tamar St)

AROUND LAUNCESTON

TAMAR VALLEY

The broad Tamar River flows north 64km from Launceston and empties into Bass Strait. Along its flanks are orchards, forests, pastures and vineyards – a charming bucolic region that's home to some of Tasmania's best wineries and where the philosophy is simply 'eat, drink and be merry'. The striking Batman Bridge, the Tamar's only bridge that spans the river near Deviot, is an architecturally interesting construction that recently celebrated its 40th birthday (one of the world's first cable-stayed truss bridges and clearly visible from the air flying from Launceston to the Australian mainland). The **Tamar visitor information centre** (☎ 1800 637 989, 03-6394 4454; www.tamarvalley.com.au; Main Rd, Exeter; ⏱ 8.30am-5pm) is in Exeter in the West Tamar Valley.

GETTING THERE & AROUND

For cyclists, the ride north along the Tamar River is a gem.

Manion's Coaches (Map p682; ☎ 03-6383 1221; manions.coaches@tassie.net.au; 168 Brisbane St) runs buses from Launceston up the West Tamar Valley to Rosevears ($7, 20 minutes), Beaconsfield ($10, 55 minutes) and Beauty Point ($11, one hour).

Redline Coaches (☎ 1300 360 000; www.tasredline.com.au) has three buses on weekdays along the

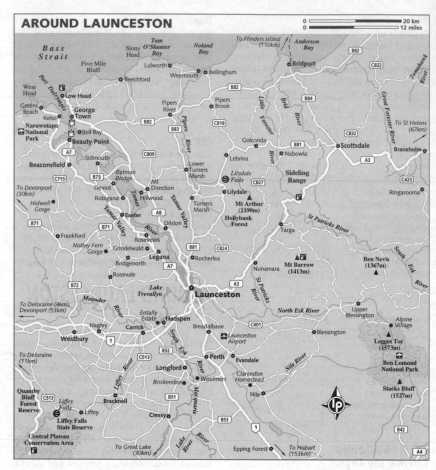

AROUND LAUNCESTON

Tamar's eastern side between Launceston and George Town ($11.80, 45 minutes).

Rosevears
pop 270

This pretty little riverside hamlet is on a side road off the West Tamar Hwy. With some super wineries in the area, this is wine-buff heaven.

Call into **Ninth Island Vineyard Strathlynn** (☎ 03-6330 2388; www.kreglingerwineestates.com; 95 Rosevears Dr; ☺ 10am-5pm), an outlet for Pipers Brook Vineyard (p680) and home to the highly polished restaurant **Daniel Alps at Strathlynn** (mains $23-33; ☺ lunch), one of Tassie's best restaurants with beautiful river views. Daniel is a local boy made good – try the ever-popular

vineyard tasting platter or brave the lambs' tongues on warm potato salad. Daniel runs highly regarded cooking courses (enquire at the restaurant).

Back on the main road, follow the signs to the hilltop HQ of prestigious **Rosevears Estate** (☎ 03-6330 1800; www.rosevears.com.au; 1a Waldhorn Dr; ☺ 10am-5pm). Its stylish restaurant **Estelle** (mains $25-30; ☺ lunch) offers a contemporary menu, and rather than drink and drive you can stay here in plush self-contained **cottages** (1- & 2-bedroom cottages $165-320).

Built in 1831, **Rosevears Waterfront Tavern** (☎ 03-6394 4074; 215 Rosevears Dr; mains $18-24; ☺ lunch & dinner) is a gastronomic pub with superb creative inflections on your chicken parmigiana (with honey and macadamias) and other pub-grub favourites. The river views are superb, the beer terrace lovely and bas-relief murals bizarre.

Beauty Point & Around
pop 1100

At Beauty Point is the coo-inducing **Seahorse World** (☎ 03-6383 4111; www.seahorseworld.com .au; Inspection Head Wharf; adult/concession/child/family $20/18/9/50; ♥ 9.30am-4.30pm), where the cute seahorses are hatched and raised to supply aquariums worldwide. Tours (45 minutes) take you into the world of the *Hippocampus abdominalis* (pot-bellied seahorse). There's a gift shops and cafe with expansive Tamar views.

Located next to Seahorse World is **Platypus House** (☎ 03-6383 4884; www.platypushouse.com.au; Inspection Head Wharf; adult/concession/child/family $18/15/9/46; ♥ 9.30am-3.30pm Apr-Nov, to 4.30pm Dec-Mar), a wildlife centre where you can get an eye-to-eye look at platypuses and pat bumbling echidnas.

South of Beauty Point is **Beaconsfield**, the gold-mining town that made world news after a mine collapse and rescue in April 2006 (see below). At the mine is the **Beaconsfield Mine & Heritage Museum** (☎ 03-6383 1473; www .beaconsfieldheritage.com.au; West St, Beauty Point; adult/ concession/child/family $11/9/4/28; ♥ 9.30am-4.30pm), detailing mining history through interactive exhibits.

You can visit all three of the above attractions with a **Triple Pass** (adult/family $45/114) from the Tamar visitor information centre (p687).

Rowlie's little **Shuttlefish Ferry** (☎ 0412 485 611; www.shuttlefishferry.com.au; 1hr tour $20) runs tours around Beauty Point and out to George Town at 11.30am and 1.30pm when there's a quorum of passengers (three or so). Bookings are essential.

In Beauty Point, readers rave about the food at **Tamar Cove** (☎ 03-6383 4375; www.tamarcove .com; 4421 Main Rd, Beauty Point; d from $95; mains $12-24; 🍴), an inexpensive motel and terrific restaurant that's been recently refurbished. Try the signature seafood chowder. **Beauty Point Tourist Park** (☎ 03-6383 4536; www.beautypointtouristpark.com .au; 36 West Arm Rd, Beauty Point; unpowered/powered sites $20/25, on-site caravans $70, cabins $100-120) offers sheltered camping on the waterfront and a range of vans and cabins. Friendly owners enthusiastically point out the river's best fishing and swimming spots.

George Town
pop 4270

Historic George Town, on the eastern lip of the Tamar river mouth, is Australia's third-oldest settlement (after Sydney and Hobart). George Town was settled in 1804 by Lieutenant Colonel Paterson to guard against the French who were reconnoitring the area. Sadly, little remains of the original township (now defined by an aluminium smelter). The **visitor information centre** (☎ /fax 6382 1700; Main Rd), staffed by volunteers, has the local low-down.

The National Trust–classified 1835 bluestone residence the Grove, at 25 Cimitiere St, recently closed to visitors due to a lack of interest. The **Pier Hotel** (☎ 03-6382 1300; www.pierho tel.com.au; 5 Elizabeth St; motel/villa d $155/180) offers

---

TODD, BRANT & LARRY

On Anzac Day (April 25) 2006, there was a rock fall at the Beaconsfield Mine. Seventeen people were in the mine at the time, 14 of whom escaped immediately following the collapse. But three men remained unaccounted for. As it transpired, one man, Larry Knight, was killed in the initial rock fall. However, five days after the accident the two others, Todd Russell and Brant Webb, were discovered (by a remote-control device) trapped in a metal cage 1km underground. The world's media scrambled and Todd and Brant made global headlines when they were finally rescued two weeks after the collapse.

In perhaps their only moment of mirth and charisma, the two clocked off as they emerged from the mine's lift into a sea of media, family and onlookers. During the two-week media circus journalists drank beer at the Beaconsfield pub, rock band the Foo Fighters got involved and Oprah was mentioned.

Todd and Brant signed lucrative media deals, but turned out to be regular blokes with nothing terribly interesting to say. The mine reopened in April 2007. Tony Wright's *Bad Ground: Inside the Beaconsfield Mine Rescue* is the definitive account of the tragedy. A coroner's report in February 2009 found the mine operator was not directly responsible for Larry Knight's death.

TASMANIA

self-contained villas (sleeping four), spotless motel rooms and a beery **bistro** (mains $15-26; 🕑 lunch & dinner) with outdoor riverfront seating and a decent menu.

Low Head
pop 465

Low Head, sitting on a sandy spit, is north of George Town and virtually contiguous with it. It's much more attractive than George Town – a beachy holiday town centred on the **Low Head Historic Precinct**.

Helping ships navigate into the Tamar, **Low Head Pilot Station** (☎ 03-6382 2826; 399 Low Head Rd; adult/concession/child/family $5/3/3/15; 🕑 9am-6pm) is Australia's oldest (1805) and houses an interesting **maritime museum** cluttered with historical items and displays. There's also colonial cottage accommodation here in the 1860s **Pilot's Row** (d from $120).

On Low Head itself, the view from the 1888 **lighthouse** is a winner. Penguins return to their burrows here every night, and can be viewed with **Low Head Penguin Tours** (☎ 0418 361 860; www .penguintours.lowhead.com; adult/child $16/10; 🕑 dusk). There's good surf at **East Beach** on Bass Strait, and safe swimming in the river.

Low Head Tourist Park (☎ 03-6382 1573; www .lowheadtouristpark.com.au; 136 Low Head Rd; unpowered/ powered sites $23/28.50, cabins $83-98; 🐾) overlooks the Tamar from a bald, treeless position. The better cabins have full kitchens.

WESTBURY
pop 1360

Historic Westbury, 32km west of Launceston, has a crop of old buildings, a village green and some quirky attractions. Across from the green is the 1841, National Trust–listed **White House** (☎ 03-6393 1171; www.nationaltrust .au/pdfs/copytas.pdf; 170 King St; adult/concession/child/family $8/6/free/16; 🕑 10am-4pm Tue-Sun), full of colonial furnishings, vintage cars, antique toys and an intricate dolls' house. The on-site bakery has great fresh bread and pastries.

Lose the kids in the hedges of **Westbury Maze** (☎ 03-6393 1840; dent_wma@vision.net.au; 10 Meander Valley Rd; adult/child/family $6/5/22; 🕑 10am-5pm Sep-Jul) then recover in the tearoom. **Pearn's Steam World** (☎ 03-6397 3313; www.pearnssteamworld.org.au; 65 Meander Valley Rd; adult/child $5/2; 🕑 9am-4pm), across the road, houses puffing steam engines and steam-era relics.

Gingerbread Cottages (☎ 03-6393 1140; www.west burycottages.com.au; 52 William St; d $160-180) is a wee village of renovated colonial cottages dating from the 1850s, all self-contained with breakfast provisions included.

LONGFORD & AROUND

Longford (population 3030), a National Trust–classified town 27km south of Launceston, hosted the 1965 Australian Grand Prix. You wouldn't think it now – the cars are gone – but the area is noted for its historic estates.

Magnificent **Woolmers** (☎ 03-6391 2230; www .woolmers.com.au; Woolmers La, Longford; adult/child/concession/family $14/5/12/30; 🕑 10am-4.30pm) was built in 1819 and features a two-hectare rose garden and buildings full of antiques. Pay a little extra (adult/child/concession/family $20/7/17/45) and enjoy a 40-minute guided tour of the main house and a self-guided tour of the grounds. Nearby is **Brickendon** (☎ 03-6391 1383; www.brick endon.com.au; Woolmers La, Longford; adult/concession/child/ family $12/11/4.50/35; 🕑 9.30am-5pm Tue-Sun), a more modest estate dating from 1824, with heritage gardens and a still-functioning farm village. Both offer self-contained accommodation in restored colonial-era **cottages** (d $115-180).

Around 10km west of Longford, running north towards Launceston, is the gorgeous **Liffey Valley**. It's well worth a short detour to explore the valley, the river and **Liffey Falls State Reserve**.

Grand, government-owned 1819 **Entally Estate** (☎ 03-6393 6201; www.entally.com.au; Old Bass Hwy, Hadspen; adult/concession/family $9/7/20; 🕑 10am-4pm), set in beautiful grounds, is the highlight of Hadspen, 15km north of Longford.

Welcoming (gay-friendly) **Racecourse Inn** (☎ 03-6391 2352; www.racecourseinn.com; 114 Marlborough St, Longford; d $158-198) is a restored Georgian inn with antique-decorated rooms and gourmet à la carte breakfasts. Meals are served most nights in the restaurant, too.

Fine **JJ's Bakery & Old Mill Café** (☎ 03-6391 2364; 52 Wellington St, Longford; mains $10-20; 🕑 breakfast & lunch) is a Longford stalwart in the Old Emerald flour mill, turning out pizzas, salads and splendid baked goods.

EVANDALE
pop 1060

Of all Tasmania's historic towns, immaculately preserved Evandale is our favourite. Less isolated than Oatlands and less corny than Richmond, it's 20km south of Launceston in the South Esk Valley. The large country **Evandale Market** (☎ 03-6391 9191; www.touringtas mania.info/evandale_market.htm; Falls Park; 🕑 8am-2pm

Sun) happens every week. Volunteers staff the **visitor information centre** (☎/fax 6391 8128; 18 High St; 💻) and handle accommodation bookings (B&Bs aplenty).

The highlight of the annual **Evandale Village Fair & National Penny Farthing Championships** (www.evandalevillagefair.com), in February each year, is the penny farthing races. Various age divisions and handicaps race, cheered on by townsfolk in historic dress.

Rising from the plains off Nile Rd, 11km south of Evandale, is the National Trust–listed **Clarendon Homestead** (☎ 03-6398 6220; adult/concession/child $10/7/free; ⏰ 10am-5pm Sep-May, 10am-4pm Jun-Aug), a grand neoclassical mansion (1838) surrounded by impressive parklands. There are three self-contained **cottages** (☎ 03-6398 6190; d from $115) out the back and **Menzies Restaurant** (mains $12-20; ⏰ lunch) out the front.

Clarendon Arms Hotel (☎ 03-6391 8181; 11 Russell St; s/d without bathroom $50/75) is a classic country pub with good-value bistro meals, basic accommodation and a leafy beer garden. Built in 1836, tiny **Wesleyan Chapel** (☎ 03-6331 9337; www.windmillhilllodge.com.au; 28 Russell St; d $115-125) has been used as a Druids hall, an RSL hall and Scouts hall. Now it's stylish accommodation for two.

Ingleside Bakery Café (☎ 03-6391 8682; 4 Russell St; mains $9-20; ⏰ breakfast & lunch) serves all-day breakfasts and light lunches amid local art and antiques.

BEN LOMOND NATIONAL PARK

Tassie's most reliable skiing hot spot (or cold spot), this 165 sq km **park** (www.parks.tas.gov.au), 55km southeast of Launceston, incorporates the entire Ben Lomond Range. Bushwalkers traipse through when the snow melts, swooning over alpine wildflowers during spring and summer. The odd lonesome crow may comment on your arrival on the treeless plateau.

Stay here year-round at Tasmania's highest-altitude pub, the **Creek Inn** (☎ 03-6390 6199; d summer/winter $95/180). There's a fully licensed restaurant and, during ski season (July to September), a kiosk and ski shop. Lift tickets cost adult/child $50/25 per day; ski hire (including lift ticket) is $100/65. See www.ben-lomond.com; national park fees apply.

During the ski season, **McDermotts Coaches** (☎ 03-6394 3535; www.mcdermotts.com.au; return adult/concession/family $27/22/90) depart Launceston at 8am and ascend the mountain, returning at 4pm. Outside the ski season, driving is your only option. The route up to the alpine village includes Jacob's Ladder, a ludicrously steep ascent on an unsealed hairpin-bend road – drive slowly, with snow chains in winter.

THE NORTH

Tasmania's North is a region of populated seaside towns and the vast open reaches and hillside communities of the Great Western Tiers. Much of this area is extensively cultivated – rust-coloured, iron-rich soils and verdant pastures extend north and west of Launceston – but there are also important stands of forest, glacial valleys, dolerite peaks and mighty rivers. Get off the main highway and explore the quiet minor roads and towns.

Getting There & Around

Redline Coaches (☎ 1300 360 000; www.tasredline.com.au) has several northern services daily.

Journey	Price ($)	Duration (hr)
Launceston-Burnie	37	2¾
Launceston-Deloraine	14	¾
Launceston-Devonport	24	1½
Launceston-Penguin	35	2¼
Launceston-Ulverstone	30	2

TassieLink (☎ 1300 300 520; www.tassielink.com.au) runs the daily Main Road Express to meet the Bass Strait ferry – an early-morning express bus runs from Devonport to Launceston and Hobart, returning in the opposite direction in the afternoon to meet evening boat departures. Typical one-way fares:

Journey	Price ($)	Duration (hr)
Devonport-Cradle Mountain	41	1½
Devonport-Hobart	57	4¼
Devonport-Launceston	24	1¼
Devonport-Sheffield	5	½
Devonport-Strahan	82	7¼

DEVONPORT

pop 24,300

Devonport is Tasmania's third-largest city, but it is *much* less interesting than Hobart and Launceston. The *Spirit of Tasmania* Bass Strait ferry arrives from Melbourne every morning (and evening in summer) sounding its huge air-horn thrice as it advances toward its Mersey River dock, whereupon it pirouettes 180 degrees before sailing off again. Locals line the riverbanks to watch, wave and hope that something bright, special and glamorous from the Australian mainland might stay here to cultivate and grow in Devonport – it's like a cargo cult. But keeping people here is a challenge too large, and they only ever come to leave again to other more interesting places.

Devonport remains a sedentary, mildly menacing place: speeding rednecks in muscle cars hurl abuse at unsuspecting pedestrians before lining up at the McDonald's drive-thru.

Information

Backpacker's Barn & Wilderness Centre (☎ 03-6424 3628; www.backpackersbarn.com.au; 12 Edward St; ☽ 8am-5pm Mon-Fri, to 3pm Sat) Greenie bushwalking and tour information, bushwalking gear for sale/hire and accommodation, tour, car-rental and bus bookings.

Devonport visitor information centre (☎ 03-6424 8176; www.dcc.tas.gov.au; 92 Formby Rd; ☽ 7.30am-5pm or 9pm) In the city across the river from the ferry terminal, it opens to meet ferry arrivals.

Online Access Centre (☎ 03-6424 9413; 21 Oldaker St; per hr $2; ☽ 9.30am-5.30pm Mon-Fri, 10.30am-1.30pm Sat; ▣) Internet access at the library.

Sights & Activities

With fine coastal views, attractive lighthouse-topped **Mersey Bluff** is the most striking feature of Devonport, from where you can bid the final farewell to the ferry as it slips away into Bass Strait. The red-and-white-striped lighthouse was built in 1889 to aid

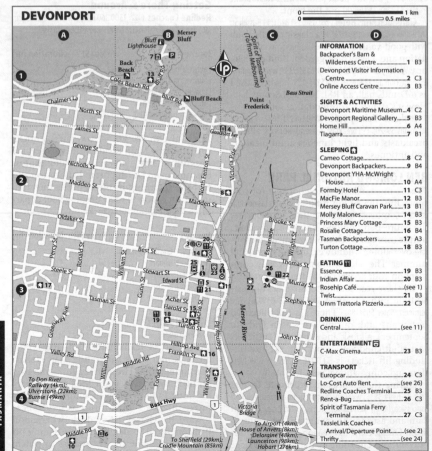

DEVONPORT

0 ————————— 1 km
0 ————————— 0.5 miles

INFORMATION	
Backpacker's Barn & Wilderness Centre	**1** B3
Devonport Visitor Information Centre	**2** C3
Online Access Centre	**3** B3

SIGHTS & ACTIVITIES	
Devonport Maritime Museum	**4** C2
Devonport Regional Gallery	**5** B3
Home Hill	**6** A4
Tiagarra	**7** B1

SLEEPING ☐	
Cameo Cottage	**8** C2
Devonport Backpackers	**9** B4
Devonport YHA-McWright House	**10** A4
Formby Hotel	**11** C3
MacFie Manor	**12** B3
Mersey Bluff Caravan Park	**13** B1
Molly Malones	**14** B3
Princess Mary Cottage	**15** B3
Rosalie Cottage	**16** B4
Tasman Backpackers	**17** A3
Turton Cottage	**18** B3

EATING ☐	
Essence	**19** B3
Indian Affair	**20** B3
Roseship Café	(see 1)
Twist	**21** B3
Umm Trattoria Pizzeria	**22** C3

DRINKING	
Central	(see 11)

ENTERTAINMENT ☐	
C-Max Cinema	**23** B3

TRANSPORT	
Europcar	**24** C3
Lo-Cost Auto Rent	(see 26)
Redline Coaches Terminal	**25** B3
Rent-a-Bug	**26** C3
Spirit of Tasmania Ferry Terminal	**27** C3
TassieLink Coaches Arrival/Departure Point	(see 2)
Thrifty	(see 24)

TASMANIA

navigation into the expanding port, which is still important today, handling much of the produce from northern Tasmania's agricultural areas.

Mersey Bluff is also home to the impressive Aboriginal culture centre and museum, **Tiagarra** (☎ 03-6424 8250; Bluff Rd; adult/child/concession/family $4/2.50/2.50/10; ⊙ 9am-5pm). This museum has a rare collection of more than 250 Indigenous rock engravings, dating back 10,000 years, and a sobering commentary on the near annihilation of Tasmania's Aborigines. Pick up a map for the free geological trail around the Bluff (traditionally a men's ceremonial area), taking in a series of petroglyphs.

The excellent **Devonport Regional Gallery** (☎ 03-6424 8296; www.devonportgallery.com; 45-47 Stewart St; admission free; ⊙ 10am-5pm Mon-Sat, noon-5pm Sun) seems slightly incongruous in this cultural backwater, with permanent and temporary exhibitions and installations of contemporary and Indigenous art.

The passionately run **Devonport Maritime Museum** (☎ 03-6424 7100; 6 Gloucester Ave; adult/child/family $4/1/8; ⊙ 10am-4.30pm Tue-Sun Oct-Mar, 10am-4pm Tue-Sun Apr-Sep) occupies the old harbourmaster's residence and has an excellent collection of maritime and local history paraphernalia, including model ships, knots, flags and chaotic folios of photos.

Four kilometres west of Devonport is the **Don River Railway** (☎ 03-6424 6335; www.donriverrailway.com.au; Forth Main Rd; adult/concession/child/family $10/8/6/25) with a collection of steam locomotives and carriages. Ride a vintage train (steam on Sunday and every day in January, diesel other times; 15 minutes one way) along the banks of the Don River and picnic at Coles Beach. Trains leave hourly from 10am to 4pm.

The National Trust–administered **Home Hill** (☎ 03-6424 3028; 77 Middle Rd; adult/concession/family $8/6/18; ⊙ 1.30-4pm Tue-Thu, Sat & Sun, Sep-Jun), 3km south of town, is the former residence of

Joseph and Dame Enid Lyons. Joe is the only Tasmanian to have been Prime Minister of Australia (1932–39), while Enid raised eyebrows in 1943 as the first female member of the House of Representatives.

About 8km southeast of Devonport, **House of Anvers** (☎ 03-6426 2958; www.anvers-chocolate.com.au; 9025 Bass Hwy, Latrobe; ⊙ 7am-7pm) has become an essential stop on the road to Launceston. It produces Belgian-style chocolates and truffles. See shower-capped workers mixing chocolate vats, and visit the cafe and shop where you can sample and buy chocolates.

Sleeping
BUDGET
Devonport Backpackers (☎ 0400 656 345; 16 Formby Rd; dm $18, d with/without bathroom $50/45) In an amazing Italianate brown-brick building in a central location, it has clean, cheap rooms and reasonable communal lounge and kitchen areas – unremarkable but perfectly adequate.

Tasman Backpackers (☎ 03-6423 2335; www.tasmanbackpackers.com; 114 Tasman St; dm/tw/f $18/20/75, d with/without bathroom $60/45) This huge former nurses' quarters looks like a stark gulag outside, but inside it's colourful and happy. It's a 15-minute trudge from town, or arrange transport when booking. There's a movie room, pool table and a wall of fridges in the kitchen. Managers help guests with seasonal work in nearby fruit and vegetable farms.

Devonport YHA-MacWright House (☎ 03-6424 5696; www.yha.com.au; 115 Middle Rd; dm/s from $20/27) In a large old house 3km from the city centre, this YHA hostel offers simple, clean accommodation and a friendly vibe. It's a 40-minute walk to town or a five-minute ride on bus 40.

Molly Malone's (☎ 03-6424 1898; mollymalones@vantagegroup.com.au; 34 Best St; dm $20, d with/without bathroom $55/45) Another reasonable budget option with basic dorms and doubles above a lively Irish pub. The food downstairs is well regarded; the rooms upstairs a little less so.

Formby Hotel (☎ 03-6424 1601; www.goodstone.com.au; 82 Formby Rd; dm/s/d $45/70/80) The Formby, across the river from the ferry terminal, has good-value en suite rooms with TVs and river views, some with shared facilities. The dorm is men-only.

Mersey Bluff Caravan Park (☎ 03-6424 8655; mbcp1@bigpond.net.au; Bluff Rd; unpowered/powered sites d $16/20, on-site vans/cabins d from $45/65) This is the pick of Devonport's caravan parks in a terrific seaside setting on Mersey Bluff, just steps from the beach and lighthouse. Good facilities include a camp kitchen, laundry and barbecues.

MIDRANGE

MacFie Manor (☎ 03-6424 1719; www.macfiemanor.com .au; 44 MacFie St; s $95, d $100-130) Offering B&B close to the city centre is this beautiful two-storey Federation building, opulently decorated with lacy trim, flowery drapes and antiques (not for the retro-phobic). The views from the balcony are commanding.

our pick **Cameo Cottage** (☎ 03-6427 0991, 0439 658 503; www.devonportbedandbreakfast.com; 27 Victoria Pde; d $140-160) This cottage, tucked in the quiet backstreets, was built in 1914 but is now thoroughly up to date. With two bedrooms, well-equipped kitchen, great lounge with DVD, laundry and a quiet garden with barbecue, it's super comfy.

Devonport Historic Cottages (☎ 03-6424 1560; www.devonportcottages.com; d incl breakfast from $150) This company manages three self-contained cottages: Rosalie Cottage (66 Wenvoe St), Turton Cottage (28 Turton St) and Princess Mary Cottage (42 MacFie St), all comfortably fitted out with period furniture. Breakfast provisions, log fires and overgrown gardens are a bonus.

Eating

Rosehip Café (☎ 03-6424 1917; 12 Edward St; mains $8-12; ☺ breakfast & lunch Mon-Fri) Part of the Backpacker's Barn complex (p692), hip Rosehip does reliable coffee, healthy wraps, crisp salads, and good focaccias and soups with organic products.

Umm Trattoria Pizzeria (☎ 03-6427 7055; 13 Murray St, East Devonport; mains $13-21; ☺ lunch Tue-Fri, dinner Wed-Sat) Authentic Italian fare in East Devonport – wood-fired pizzas as well as pastas, risottos and tasty toasted paninis. A chalkboard announces the daily changing specials. A cool place to cool your heels waiting for the ferry.

Indian Affair (☎ 03-6423 5141; 153 Rooke St; mains $16-20; ☺ dinner) Spicy South Indian curries cooked with chutzpah ensure the round tables in this upbeat eatery are always busy.

Twist (☎ 03-6423 2033; 5 Rooke St; mains $23-20; ☺ lunch & dinner Tue-Fri, dinner Sat, brunch & lunch from 10am Sun) Pan-fried wallaby sirloin served with pepperberry sauce perhaps? Thai-style trevalla with mango and Asian green salad? Twice-cooked duck? Twist is Devonport's grooviest

contemporary restaurant with creative new mains and a new twist on old faves.

Essence (☎ 03-6424 6431; 28 Forbes St; 2/3 courses $55/65; ☺ lunch Wed & Fri, dinner Tue-Sat) You'd hardly expect to find a top-notch restaurant in this suburban-industrial neighbourhood, but Essence offers excellent reasonably priced degustation-style dining to discerning Devonportians.

Drinking & Entertainment

The Hotel Formby's popular bar **Central** (☎ 03-6424 1601; 82 Formby Rd; ☺ 10am-late), across the road from the river, is Devonport's happeningest bar, done out in leather couches with concertina windows opening onto the river on warm summer nights. There are live bands on Friday and Saturday nights, and Sunday arvo is saved for laid-back acoustic music. Popular Molly Malone's (p693) is always lively.

C-Max Cinemas (☎ 03-6420 2111; www.cmax.net .au; 5-7 Best St; tickets adult/child $12/9) screens recent releases. All Tuesday tickets $9.50.

Getting There & Away

AIR

There are regular direct flights between Launceston and Melbourne, Sydney and Brisbane (see p635). **Tasair** (☎ 03-6248 5088; www .tasair.com.au) flies between Devonport and King Island (one way $220).

BOAT

The **Spirit of Tasmania** (☎ 13 20 10; www.spiritoftasma nia.com.au) vehicle/passenger ferry sails between Melbourne and Devonport; see p635 for details. It docks on the eastern side of the river.

BUS

See p691 for details on **Redline Coaches** (☎ 1300 360 000; www.tasredline.com.au) and **TassieLink** (☎ 1300 300 520; www.tassielink.com.au) services between Launceston and Devonport. TassieLink also runs from Devonport to Cradle Mountain, and from Devonport to Burnie continuing to the west coast (Zeehan, Strahan, Queenstown etc).

The Redline Coaches terminal is opposite the Backpacker's Barn on Edward St (also stopping at the ferry terminal); TassieLink coaches stop outside the Devonport visitor information centre and the ferry terminal.

If none of the scheduled services suits your particular bushwalking needs, charter a minibus from **Maxwells** (☎ 6492 1431, 0418 584 004) or through the Backpacker's Barn (p692).

Getting Around

Devonport airport is 5km east of town. A **shuttle bus** (☎ 1300 659 878; per person $10) runs between the airport and ferry terminals, the visitor information centre and city accommodation; bookings are essential. A **taxi** (☎ 03-6424 1431) to/from the airport costs about $18.

A **ferry** (☎ 0418 360 142; one way $2.50; ✆ 9am-5pm Mon-Sat Mar-Nov, 8am-6pm Mon-Sat Dec-Feb) has been running across the Mersey River since 1855 (there was no bridge until 1902). *Torquay* departs on demand from opposite the visitors information centre, docking on the eastern side of the river beside the ferry terminal.

Operating out of the same office are **Rent-a-Bug** (☎ 03-6427 9034; www.rentabug.com.au; 5 Murray St, East Devonport) and **Lo-Cost Auto Rent** (☎ 03-6427 0796; www.locostautorent.com), with older cars from $35 per day. Established internationals at the ferry terminal include **Europcar** (☎ 03-6427 0888; www.europcar.com.au; 11 The Esplanade, East Devonport) and **Thrifty** (☎ 1800 030 730, 03-6427 9119; www.thrifty .com.au; 10 The Esplanade, East Devonport).

DELORAINE

pop 2240

Deloraine, at the foot of the Great Western Tiers, is an artsy rural town of fine Georgian and Victorian buildings set on the tumbling hills around the handsome Meander River. Public sculptures and huge European trees are a feature of the main street, as are Deloraine's groovy eateries, galleries and interesting bric-a-brac stores. The annual four-day **Tasmanian Craft Fair** (www.tascraftfair.com.au) kicks off in late October when thousands of visitors book out accommodation from Launceston to Devonport for the festivities.

The **Great Western Tiers visitor information centre** (☎ 03-6362 3471; www.greatwesterntiers.net.au; 98 Emu Bay Rd; ✆ 9am-5pm) handles accommodation bookings, and gives advice on the many great walks in the area. Also here is the **Deloraine Folk Museum & YARNS: Artwork in Silk** (adult/child/family $7/2/15; ✆ 9.30am-4pm). The centrepiece here is the extraordinary four-panel, quilted and appliquéd tapestry of Meander Valley life through a year of seasonal change. An audiovisual display explains its design and construction (taking 300 locals three years to complete).

Many of the town's Georgian and Victorian buildings have been restored. Those of interest include the whitewashed 1859 **St Mark's Anglican Church** (East Westbury Pl) and the 1853 **Bowerbank Mill** (4455 Meander Valley Hwy), now a gallery, 2km east of town.

At popular **Ashgrove Farm Cheese** (☎ 03-6368 1105; www.ashgrovecheese.com.au; 6173 Bass Hwy, Elizabeth Town; ✆ 9am-5.30pm), 10km north of Deloraine, you can watch the cheeses being made and taste the results. About 6km out of town towards Mole Creek (well signed down Montana Rd) is fascinating **41°South Aquaculture** (☎ 03-6362 4130; www.41south-aquaculture.com; 323 Montana Rd; self-guided tour adult/child/concession/family $10/5/7/25; ✆ 9am-5pm Nov-Mar, 10am-4pm Apr-Oct) where 15,000 salmon are reared in a no-waste, no-chemical fish-farming environment. Ginseng is also grown.

Sleeping & Eating

Highview Lodge YHA (☎ 03-6362 2996; www.yha.com .au; 8 Blake St; dm/d/f from $22/50/66) This ramshackle hillside YHA hostel has warm, timber-floored rooms and friendly staff. It's a steep walk from town, but incredible Great Western Tiers views compensate.

Empire Hotel & Thai Restaurant (☎ 03-6362 2075; 19 Emu Bay Rd; s $90, d $110-125) The beautiful old Empire has quirky upstairs rooms with shared facilities (some done out in pseudo-Japanese decor). The dining rooms downstairs serve cooked breakfasts (summer only) and incorporate authentic Thai dishes alongside traditional gourmet pub evening fare (mains $12 to $26).

Tierview Twin Cottages (☎ 03-6362 2377; 125 Emu Bay Rd; 4-person cottage d $115, 6-person cottage d $135, extra person $20) These identical twin cottages are just off the main street, and offer comfortable self-contained accommodation. One cottage has an open fire and sleeps up to four in two bedrooms, the other sleeps up to six and has a spa bathroom. Get your keys from the Shell service station opposite.

Deloraine Apex Caravan Park (☎ 03-6362 2345; 2 West Goderich St; unpowered/powered sites $21/25) A shady sliver of lush green grass by the Mender River, this park has clean, simple facilities, but no cabins. It's very popular so book ahead. The site floods once in a blue moon and occasional freight trains thunder past on tracks right beside the park…just to keep things interesting.

ourpick **Deloraine Deli** (☎ 03-6362 2127; 36 Emu Bay Rd; mains $7-13; ✆ breakfast & lunch Mon-Sat) What a find! Spread out the weekend papers and enjoy a leisurely cooked breakfast and excellent coffee. Plough into a ploughman's lunch,

TASMANIA

bail up baguettes and bagels, and feed on focaccias. There's spinach lasagne, vegie burgers and dairy- and gluten-free meals, too.

MOLE CREEK
pop 220

Mole Creek, about 25km west of Deloraine, is an unflattering name for this tiny creek-plains town at the feet of the towering cracks of the Great Western Tiers. Tiny though it is, Mole Creek's environs are packed with attractions (it's a favourite area for spelunkers and bushwalkers) and the town makes a great base for exploring the Great Western Tiers and the national parks of the Walls of Jerusalem and Cradle Mountain (the B12 road through Mole Creek is an interesting alternative route to Cradle Mountain). Around Mole Creek (once overrun with thylacines) are limestone caves in the **Mole Creek Karst National Park** (www.parks.tas.gov.au), leatherwood honey apiaries and an excellent wildlife park.

Marakoopa Cave, a wet cave 15km from Mole Creek, features underground streams and glow-worms. **King Solomons Cave**, a dry cave with light-reflecting calcite crystals, has few steps – the better cave for the less energetic. During summer there are at least five tours in each cave daily between 10am and 4.30pm. Each cave costs $16/12/8/40 per adult/concession/child/family; tour times are displayed on access roads, or call the **Mole Creek Caves Ticket Office** (☎ 03-6363 5182; www.parks.tas.gov.au; 330 Mayberry Rd, Mayberry). Wear warm clothes – cave temperatures average 9°C.

There are many magnificent wild caves in the area. **Wild Cave Tours** (☎ 03-6367 8142; www.wildcavetours.com) offers half-/full-day adventures for $95/180, including caving gear.

The leatherwood tree only grows in damp, western Tasmania, and honey from its flowers is uniquely delicious! Tasmanian kids grow up studying the weird bee on the honey labels from **R Stephens Leatherwood Honey Factory** (☎ 03-6363 1170; www.leatherwoodhoney.com.au; 25 Pioneer Dr; admission free; ☼ 9am-4pm Mon-Fri). Visitors can taste and purchase the sticky stuff. At nearby Chudleigh there's a **Honey Farm** (☎ 03-6363 6160; www.thehoneyfarm.com.au; 39 Sorell St; admission free; ☼ Sun-Fri 9am-5pm) with free honey tasting and an interactive beehive.

About 5km east of Mole Creek on the B12 road is the first-rate **Trowunna Wildlife Park** (☎ 03-6363 6162; www.trowunna.com.au; adult/child/family $16/8.50/44; ☼ 9am-5pm), specialising in Tasmanian devils and wombats, where you can pat, feed and hold various critters.

The only road that reaches the top of the Western Tiers plateau is the gravel Lake Mackenzie road that ascends into the alpine reaches (take warm clothes year-round and watch for sudden weather changes). Follow this road to **Devils Gullet**, where there's a 40-minute return walk leading to a platform bolted to the top of a dramatic gorge: looking over the edge is a heart-in-mouth experience.

Sleeping & Eating

Mole Creek Hotel (☎ 03-6363 1102; molecreekhotel2@bigpond.com; Pioneer Dr; s $45, d with/without bathroom $85/65) A classic small-town pub with bright upstairs rooms. The Tiger Bar (mains $15 to $25) is a thylacine shrine wallpapered with old newspaper clippings and serves hearty pub standards.

our pick **Mole Creek Guest House & Laurelberry Restaurant** (☎ 03-6363 1399; www.molecreekgh.com.au; 100 Pioneer Dr; s $110-140, d $120-160, all incl breakfast; ☐) This renovated c 1890 guest house is full of surprises, including Wunderlich pressed-tin panelling, period fretwork and fittings, large comfortable rooms, a huge cinema room and DVD library, and platypuses in the stream out the back! Licensed Laurelberry Restaurant (mains $16 to $28; open for breakfast, lunch and dinner) downstairs is prim and professional (not what you'd expect in backcountry Mole Creek) serving a changing menu based on local produce, and (they reckon) the best fillet steak in Tasmania. Complimentary wi-fi.

Mole Creek Caravan Park (☎ 03-6363 1150; cnr Mole Creek & Union Bridge Rds; unpowered/powered sites $17/20) This grassy, old-fashioned park, about 4km west of town, sits on the bank of the babbling Sassafras Stream.

WALLS OF JERUSALEM NATIONAL PARK

This isolated Central Plateau **national park** (www.parks.tas.gov.au), part of the Tasmanian Wilderness World Heritage Area, features glacial lakes and valleys, alpine flora and the rugged dolerite Mt Jerusalem (1459m). It's a favourite of experienced bushwalkers with a lust for challenging, remote hiking. The most popular walk here is the full-day trek to the 'Walls'; you can also camp in the park. National park fees apply.

If you prefer a guided walk, Tasmanian Expeditions (p635) operates a seven-day Walls trip for $1490. Tarkine Trails (p634) also runs a four-day walking tour here for $1049.

Access to the Walls is from Sheffield or Mole Creek. From Mole Creek take the B12 west, the C138 south then the C171 (Mersey Forest Rd) to Lake Rowallan; remain on this road, following the C171 and/or Walls of Jerusalem signs to the start of the track. Pick up the *Walls of Jerusalem Map* ($10.50) from Mole Creek Caves Ticket Office (opposite).

SHEFFIELD & AROUND
pop 1030

Sheffield was settled in 1859 but by the 1980s it was a failing rural town. Then some bright spark suggested they paint large murals on Sheffield's public walls to attract tourists, and the town's fortunes began to change. These days there are more than 50 murals and Sheffield is a veritable outdoor art gallery with its own annual painting festival **Muralfest** (www.muralfest.com.au). The town is now an interesting conglomerate of rural folks, artsy types and alternative lifestylers. The **Kentish visitor information centre** (☎ 03-6491 1036; www.sheffieldcradleinfo.com.au; 5 Pioneer Cres; ☒ 9am-5pm), just off the main street, has mural maps, mural audio tours and regional information.

The spacious rooms and apartments at **Sheffield Country Motor Inn** (☎ 03-6491 1800; www.sheffieldmotorinn.com.au; 49-53 Main St; motel s/d from $85/90, units d $110-160) are set back from the main street. There are one-, two- and three-bedroom apartments, all clean and well equipped.

Tanglewood (☎ 03-6491 1854; www.tanglewoodtasmania.com; 25 High St; d $110-140) is restored 1906 Federation house with three roomy en suite bedrooms and a large formal lounge with an open fire and old-world decor.

The lacy old **Sheffield Hotel** (☎ 03-6491 1130; 38 Main St; mains $11-23; ☒ lunch & dinner) has good-value counter meals amid the confusing blare of the sound system and multiple TVs. Upstairs **rooms** (s $50, d with/without bathroom $80/70) are better than average, with new beds and decent bathrooms.

There are some excellent eateries in the main street, including French-style **Yvette's** (☎ 03-6491 1893; 43 Main St; mains $9.90-18.90; ☒ lunch Thu-Mon), with groovy red-leather sofas serving classy light meals, and **Bossimi's Bakery** (☎ 03-

6491 1298; 44 Main St; ☒ breakfast & lunch Mon-Fri), with speciality pastries, cakes and bread.

The scenery around Sheffield is lovely – hulking **Mt Roland** (1234m) rises above farmlands, forests and fish-filled rivers. Nearby is deep **Lake Barrington**, an international rowing venue. **Tasmazia** (☎ 03-6491 1934; www.tasmazia.com.au; 500 Staverton Rd; adult/child $16/9; ☒ 9am-5pm), at the wonderfully named Promised Land at the Lake Barrington turn-off, combines leafy mazes, the cheesy-as-hell Lower Crackpot model village, a lavender patch and pancake parlour.

Gowrie Park, 14km southwest of Sheffield below Mt Roland, is an excellent base for mountain walks. Here you'll find **Mt Roland Budget Backpackers** (☎ 03-6491 1385; www.weindorfers.com; 1447 Claude Rd; unpowered & powered sites $10, dm, tw & d per person $15; ☐), a supercasual, vaguely managed operation with basic camping and cheap hostel-style beds.

ULVERSTONE & AROUND

Unhurried Ulverstone (population 9800) has a relaxed, uncommercial atmosphere at the mouth of the Leven River (pronounced *lee*-ven). The town became an important commercial port with the coming of the railway in 1890, but a decade later the rail was extended to Burnie and with it went the shipping activity. Today it's home to a few fishing boats, retirees, some gracious old buildings and a ridiculous clock tower. The **Ulverstone visitor information centre** (☎ 03-6425 2839; www.centralcoast.tas.gov.au; 13 Alexandra Rd; ☒ 9am-5pm; ☐) is a striking piece of architecture and a treasure trove of local knowledge.

The B17 road does a worthwhile loop from the A1 coast highway, and goes to **Gunns Plains**, 25km south of Ulverstone. Take a guided tour of the 'shawl' formations at **Gunns Plains Caves** (☎ 03-6429 1388; adult/concession/child/family $12/10/6/35; ☒ 10am-4pm). Also here is **Wings Wildlife Park** (☎ 03-6429 1151; www.wingswildlife.com.au; 137 Winduss Rd; adult/child $17/8; ☒ 10am-4pm), a family-oriented place where you can interact with farm and native animals, reptiles, birds of prey and a proprietorial rooster. There's riverside **camping** (unpowered/powered sites $10/17) and **backpacker accommodation** (s/d/cabin $15/20/100) here, too.

South of Gunns Plains, the River Leven stutters through a 274m-deep gorge. Follow the 41km road from Ulverstone through Nietta to the jaw-dropping **Leven Canyon Lookout**. A 20-minute return track leads to

---

TIGERS & DEVILS

There are two endings to the story of the Tasmanian tiger (*Thylacinus cynocephalus,* or thylacine). The thylacine – a striped, nocturnal, dog-like predator – was once widespread in Tasmania (and also roamed mainland Australia and New Guinea until about 2000 years ago). Conventional wisdom says that it was hunted to extinction in the 19th and early 20th centuries, and that the last-known specimen died in Hobart Zoo in 1936. Despite hundreds of alleged sighting since, no specimen, living or dead, has been confirmed. The second version of the story is that the shy, illusive tigers still exist in the wilds of Tasmania. Scientists scoff at such suggestions, but Tasmanian folklore seems reluctant to let go of this tantalising possibility. David Owen's *Thylacine* examines this phenomenon and traces the animal's demise.

The obnoxious Tasmanian devil (*Sarcophilus harrisii*) is definitely still alive, but devil facial tumour disease (DFTD, a communicable cancer) infects up to 75% of the wild population (the real beast looks nothing like the Warner Bros cartoon). Quarantined populations have been established around the state, but efforts to find a cure have been depressingly fruitless. In the meantime, you can check them out at wildlife parks around the state.

---

the gorge-top – if you're lucky you'll have the viewing platform to yourself. Are you out there, thylacine?

Sleeping & Eating

Willaway Motel Apartments (☎ 03-6425 2018; www
.willaway.southcom.com.au; 2 Tucker St; d $100-130; 🖳)
This cluster of generic self-contained units looks a little like a retirement village, but they're excellent value and well equipped, with lawns and barbecue facilities, and only a minute to the beach. Wi-fi internet.

Big 4 Ulverstone Holiday Park (☎ 03-6425 2624; www.big4ulverstone.com.au; 57 Water St; unpowered/powered sites $21/25, cabins & units $95-140; 🖳) Fronting East Beach, this friendly park is close to town with good facilities, including camp kitchen, laundry and playgrounds.

Pedro's the Restaurant (☎ 03-6425 6663; Wharf Rd; mains $21-40; 🕑 lunch & dinner) is on stilts above the river and has its own fleet that delivers the daily catch right to the door. This is *the* place to eat in Ulverstone, specialising in upmarket seafood dishes.

Pedro's Takeaway (☎ 03-6425 5181; mains $7-11; 🕑 11am-8pm) Next door to Pedro's the Restaurant, this place does fab fish and chips.

PENGUIN
pop 3050

A quaint little seaside village (complete with huge concrete penguin on the foreshore and penguin-shaped rubbish bins), Penguin lures tourists with its fantastic beaches. The absence of a natural harbour has meant commercial interests have overlooked Penguin – the town remains uncomplicated, unassuming and only half-awake. And we like it that way.

Driving from Ulverstone, take the old Bass Hwy along the coast. As you approach Penguin, the countryside takes on a gentrified, rural feel with cottage gardens, a narrow-gauge railway track and beaches squeezing themselves into the scene. The **Penguin visitor information centre** (☎ 03-6437 1421; fax 6437 1463; 78 Main Rd; 🕑 9am-4pm) does what it's supposed to, but the famous **Penguin Market** (☎ 03-6437 2935; www.penguinmarket.com; cnr Arnold & King Edward Sts; 🕑 9am-3.30pm Sun) has gone off the boil in recent years. Waddle around all you like, but don't expect happy feet. There's still some decent arts and crafts and secondhand wares, but the gourmet foodie stallholders have gone elsewhere.

Treat yourself to a night at the stylish, minimalist **Madsen Guesthouse** (☎ 03-6437 2588; www
.themadsen.com; 64 Main Rd; d $148-195; 🖳). The top rate will score you the spacey front room (a former banking chamber), with sea views and wi-fi internet.

The **Groovy Penguin Café** (☎ 03-6437 2101; 74 Main Rd; mains $8-13; 🕑 breakfast & lunch Tue-Sun; 🖳) is a gay-friendly shrine to all things kitsch and retro, with super-nice staff, cakes, focaccias, soups, salads, great coffee and fold-back windows snaring the sea breeze. We love it!

Wild Café Restaurant (☎ 03-6437 2000; 87 Main Rd; lunch mains $12-19, dinner mains $20-29; 🕑 lunch & dinner Wed-Sun) has made quite a splash on northwest coast, with dishes like Thai-inspired char-grilled calamari, and five-spice brioche with marinated duck, orange and Grand Marnier.

THE NORTHWEST

Tassie's Northwest is lashed by Roaring Forties winds and in excess of 2m of rain each year, and boasts coastal heathlands, wetlands and dense temperate rainforests unchanged from Gondwana times. Communities here are either isolated rural outposts or tricked-up tourist traps, with not much in between. The further west you get, the fewer fellow travellers you'll encounter until you reach the woolly wilds of Tasmania's northwest tip, a region of writhing ocean beaches and tiny communities with no landfall until South America. The Northwest is Tassie magic of a different kind.

Getting There & Around

AIR

Regional Express (REX; ☎ 13 17 13; www.regionalexpress .com.au) flies between Melbourne and Wynyard Airport (aka Burnie/Wynyard Airport or Burnie Airport) from $120 one way.

Tasair (☎ 03-6248 5088; www.tasair.com.au) flights between King Island and Burnie/Wynyard cost $220 one way.

BUS

There are no public transport services to Marrawah or Arthur River, but **Redline Coaches** (☎ 1300 360 000; www.tasredline.com.au) services the Northwest's larger towns:

Journey	Price ($)	Duration (min)
Burnie-Boat Harbour	10	30
Burnie-Smithton	22	90
Burnie-Stanley	20	60
Burnie-Wynyard	80	20
Launceston-Burnie	37	160

On weekdays (except public holidays), **Metro** (☎ 03-6431 3822; www.metrotas.com.au) has regular buses from Burnie to Penguin, Ulverstone and Wynyard (all $4.80 one way), departing from Cattley St. Burnie to Wynyard buses also run on Saturday.

CAR & MOTORCYCLE

The main north-to-west-coast route is the Murchison Hwy (A10) from Somerset west of Burnie, running through to Queenstown. The **Western Explorer** is the inland road from Smithton through the **Tarkine** wilderness area

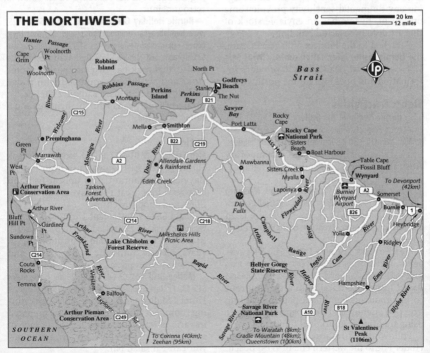

THE NORTHWEST

to the west coast, including a difficult 50km section between Arthur River and Corinna. Promoted as a tourist route, the road is OK for non-4WD vehicles, but it's remote, potholed and mostly unsealed – think twice in bad weather or after dark. Fill up your tank in Marrawah in the north or Zeehan in the south, as there's no petrol in between. The **Arthur River Parks & Wildlife Service** (☎ 03-6457 1225) provides road condition updates.

At Corinna there's a pay-per-crossing vehicle ferry (p705) across the Pieman River, from where you continue to Zeehan and the rest of the west.

BURNIE
pop 19,060

Built over Emu Bay, Burnie is Tasmania's fourth-largest city. It's a deepwater port and shipping is a lynchpin of the local economy. Burnie has also long been home to a huge paper mill, and heavy-machinery manufacturing and agricultural-services industries. The scars of industry and docks piled high with logs and woodchips don't make a great first impression, but a beachy vibe and an emerging environmental sensitivity provide some optimism. Burnie has an enviable stock of fine art deco homes and buildings.

Attached to the Pioneer Village Museum, the **Burnie visitor information centre** (☎ 03-6434 6111; www.burnie.net; Little Alexander St) provides information and bookings for the northwest.

Sights & Activities

The **Burnie Regional Art Gallery** (☎ 03-6431 5918; Civic Centre Precinct, Wilmot St; admission free; ⊗ 10am-4.30pm Mon-Fri, 1.30-4.30pm Sat, Sun & public holidays) has excellent exhibitions of contemporary Australian artworks, including photography, sculpture and painting.

The absorbing **Pioneer Village Museum** (☎ 03-6430 5746; Little Alexander St; adult/child/concession/family $6/2.50/4.50/17; ⊗ 9am-5pm Mon-Fri) is an authentic indoor re-creation of a 1900s village streetscape.

Creative Paper Tasmania (☎ 03-6430 7717; www.creativepapertas.com.au; Bass Hwy; entry by donation, tours adult/child/concession/family $15/8/10/40; ⊗ 9am-5pm Mon-Fri, 10am-4pm Sat & Sun) is an arty, nonprofit co-op producing handmade paper, including 'roo poo', denim and beer paper, and paper using traditional Aboriginal fibres.

Follow the foreshore boardwalk from Hilder Pde to the western end of West Beach,

where there's a **penguin observatory**. Book at the visitor information centre for free dusk tours (October to February).

Sleeping

Regent Hotel Backpackers (☎ 03-6431 1933; fax 6432 2091; 26 North Tce; s/d from $25/40) Perfunctory accommodation in clean dorms and doubles, some with sea views and en suites. The Mallee Grill (below) serves whopping steaks downstairs.

Duck House & Mrs Philpott's (☎ 03-6431 1712; www.ozpal.com/duck; 26-28 Queen St; s/d $100/140) For 30 years the home of Salvation Army stalwarts Bill and Winifred Duck, this charming little two-bedroom cottage, with dinky duck decor, still bears their name. Next door Mrs Philpot's has leadlights, a claw-foot bath and brass beds.

Apartments Down Town (☎ 03-6432 3219; www.apartmentsdowntown.com.au; 52 Alexander St; s/d apt incl breakfast $145/190; 🖥) Happily dwelling in a bygone era, these glorious self-contained art deco apartments are stylish, spacious and well equipped, with two or three bedrooms. Sumptuous 1930s trimmings make an alluring change from the standard Tassie colonial retrogression.

Burnie Holiday Caravan Park (☎ 03-6431 1925; www.burniebeachaccommodation.com.au; 253 Bass Hwy, Cooee; unpowered/powered sites $18/25, dm/on-site van $25/50, cabins $88-110; 🐕) Located 4km west of the centre, this park has two backpacker rooms (four and six bunks) equipped with fridge and stove, some grassy camping sites at the property's rear, vans with kitchenettes and a range of cabins.

Eating

Fish Frenzy (☎ 03-6432 1111; 2 North Terrace; meals $10-24; ⊗ 11am-9pm) Downstairs from fancier Bayviews Restaurant, this upbeat fish and chippery does great fishy favourites, flippin' fillets and choppin' chips.

Rialto Gallery Restaurant (☎ 03-6431 7718; 46 Wilmot St; mains $14-25; ⊗ lunch Mon-Fri, dinner Mon-Sat) Rialto has been a Burnie institution for 28 years, serving authentic Italian pastas and fine wood-oven pizzas.

Mallee Grill (☎ 03-6431 1933; 26 North Tce; mains $15-43; ⊗ lunch Sun-Fri, dinner daily) The Regent Hotel's Mallee Grill is a specialty-steak dining room. Fat rumps and spuds are prepared in various ways, and there's also a range of snags, seafood, pork and chicken, and an all-you-can-eat salad bar.

TASMANIA

WYNYARD

pop 4810

Sheltered by the monolithic Table Cape, the oft-overlooked service town of Wynyard abuts the beach and the Inglis River's tidal estuary. In its heyday it was a timber-milling centre and home Tasmania's first butter factory, but these days most people go to Wynyard to retire. Wynyard services the agricultural lands of the state's northeast, and is an affordable, easy-going base from which to explore the area. Wynyard has some splendid low-cost accommodation options.

The **Wynyard visitor information centre** (☎ 03-6443 8330; www.warwyn.tas.gov.au; 8 Exhibition Link; Ⓨ 9am-5pm) dispenses tourist info on the region. Also here is **Wonders of Wynyard** (admission adult/child/concession/family $6/3/5/15), a polished exhibition of old Fords (Holden fans wait outside). The showpiece is a 1903 Model A Ford, one of only two in the world.

Wynyard's undisputed highlight is **Table Cape**. A hulking igneous plateau 4km north of town, it has unforgettable views, a tulip farm (in bloom and open to the public from late September to mid-October) and an 1888 lighthouse. Sit for a while at the lookout – cloudbanks roll in over the ultramarine sea, fishing boats slice through the shimmer, crows jeer above deep-red soils. You can drive to the lighthouse or walk along the cliff tops from the lookout (30 minutes return).

Fossil Bluff, 3km from town signposted from the Saunders St roundabout, is where the oldest marsupial fossil found in Australia was unearthed (it's an estimated 20 million years old). The soft sandstone here also contains shell fossils deposited when the level of Bass Strait was much higher. Errol Flynn's dad (of all people) spent a lot of time here digging through the dust and bones.

The recently renovated **Wharf Hotel** (☎ 03-6442 2344; www.wharfhotel.net; 10 Goldie St; s/d $49/75) has huge rooms with fridges, quality linen, spotless en suites (some with baths), river views and TVs that actually work (on every channel!). This is the best budget pub accommodation in Tasmania. The downstairs bistro, open for lunch and dinner, does great pub nosh (mains $15 to $25) and there's quality live music in the bar and film screenings for the Lighthouse Film Society in the large theatre space (guests welcome).

In a peaceful beachside spot on neatly manicured grassy grounds, pretty **Beach**

Retreat Tourist Park (☎ 03-6442 1998; 30b Old Bass Hwy; unpowered & powered sites d $24, backpacker s/d $30/45, motel unit/cabin $80/90) deserves more than just an overnight stay. There's great backpacker accommodation in double rooms (no dorms) and a terrific shared kitchen. The self-contained motel rooms are up to scratch, too.

Wynyard has a few cafes and pubs on the main street, but the best choice for a fishy feed is **Buckaneers** (☎ 03-6442 4104; 4 Inglis St; mains $10-27; Ⓨ lunch & dinner).

BOAT HARBOUR

pop 140

It's a bit of a pity the word got out about Boat Harbour – it wasn't *that* long ago that nobody knew about this tiny beach village 14km northwest of Wynyard. Perched on a beautiful bay with gleaming white sand and crystal-clear water, it's still an idyllic spot. But the crusty old fibro fishermen's shacks are slowly being overrun by ugly 'beachside living' townhouses and upmarket B&Bs.

Boat Harbour Beach House (☎ 03-6445 0913; www
.boatharbourbeachhouse.com; d $180-200) is actually two self-contained, multibedroom beach houses: **The View** (12 Moore St) and **The Waterfront** (314 The Esplanade). Both are beautifully renovated, with outdoor decks and barbecues.

Lit with rice-paper lanterns, **Jolly Rogers** (☎ 03-6445 1710; The Esplanade; mains $15-30) is a slick Mod Oz seafood restaurant next to the surf club. They do a noteworthy run of daytime burgers, fish and chips, focaccias and seafood snacks, and offer a more serious à la carte menu at night.

Nearby are the coastal heathlands of the small **Rocky Cape National Park** (www.parks.gov.tas
.au), known for its bushwalking, diving, snorkelling, shipwrecks and sea caves; and **Sisters Beach**, an 8km expanse of bleached sand with safe swimming, good fishing, a boat ramp and a general store.

STANLEY

pop 460

Europeans established Stanley back in 1826 well before any other Northeast settlements and for a long time it was only accessible by sea. The Peerapper people were the original inhabitants of Stanley's little isthmus and peninsula, and back then extraordinary bulbous Circular Head (better known as The Nut) was covered in forest. Oddly treeless little Stanley has a strangely impermanent yesteryear feel to it, as if it's been teleported from Victorian England. Buffeted by cold ocean winds, Stanley lives for two things: fishing (particularly crayfish) and tourism. Every second house is a 'heritage B&B', but there are several good eateries and enough to keep visitors occupied for a few days.

The **Stanley visitor information centre** (☎ 03-6458 1330; www.stanley.com.au; 45 Main Rd) is on your left as you roll into town.

Sights & Activities

Around 13 million years old, **The Nut** is an iconic, 152m-high volcanic table-top formation visible for miles around. It's a steep 20-minute climb to the top, but the view is damn impressive. For the aged, infirm or just lazy, a **chairlift** (☎ /fax 6458 1286; Browns Rd; adult/child/family $10/8/30; ☺ 9.30am-5.30pm Oct-May, 10am-4pm Jun-Sep) also operates, weather permitting.

Popular with kids, **Seaquarium** (☎ 03-6458 2052; Fisherman's Dock; adult/child/family $10/5/25; ☺ 9am-5pm) displays giant crabs, seahorses, fish and crays in tanks in a shed on the waterfront.

The 1844 bluestone building on the seafront was originally the Van Diemen's Land Company Store, and now houses **@VDL Stanley** (☎ 03-6458 2032; 16 Wharf Rd; www.atvdlstanley.com.au; ☺ 10am-5pm), a gallery with ultra-luxe accommodation (see right). The VDL Company's headquarters were at high-brow **Highfield** (☎ 03-6458 1100; www.historic-highfield.com.au; Green Hills Rd; adult/child/family $9/4/22; ☺ 10am-4pm), 2km north of Stanley, a dignified colonial homestead with barns, stables, workers' cottages, a chapel and views.

Back in town near the wharf is the mid-19th-century **Ford's Store**, a two-storey bluestone grain store that's now a restaurant. Other historic buildings include **Joe Lyons Cottage** (☎ 03-6458 1145; 14 Alexander Tce; admission by donation; ☺ 10am-4pm), birthplace of former prime minister Joseph Lyons, and **St James' Presbyterian Church** (Fletcher St), bought in England and transported to Stanley in 1885. **St Paul's Anglican Church** (39 Church St) is around the corner, next to which is the **Stanley Discovery Museum** (☎ 03-6458 1309; rutheslake@yahoo.com.au; 37 Church St; adult/child $3/50c; ☺ 10am-4pm), a one-room folk museum festooned with photos and artefacts.

Tours

Stanley Seal Cruises (☎ 0419 550 134; www.stanley sealcruises.com.au; Fishermans Dock; adult/child/family $49/9/130; ☺ 10am daily, extra 3pm cruise Oct-Apr) See 300 Australian fur seals sunning themselves on Bull Rock on these 75-minute cruises. Cruises run rain or shine, but not if the sea is angry.

Wilderness to West Coast Tours (☎ 03-6458 2038, 0417 593 158; www.wildernesstasmania.com; 8 Church St) Combined platypus and penguin-spotting excursions (adult/child $50/25, September to June) and all-day 4WD wilderness tours ($249 per person) to the Tarkine rainforests and Arthur River beaches with gourmet lunch prepared in the rainforest.

Sleeping

Stanley Hotel (☎ 03-6458 1161; www.stanleytasmania .com.au; 19 Church St; s $45, d with/without bathroom $85/65) A convolution of doorways and halls upstairs connects these brightly painted and comfortable rooms. The shared bathrooms are spotless, the staff are chipper and there's a fantastic verandah overlooking Stanley's goings-on. The pub meals downstairs are excellent and a man comes round with Lions Club raffle tickets for a meat tray.

Abbey's Cottages (☎ 1800 222 397; www.stanleytas mania.com.au; d $95-140, extra person $15-30) Abbey's manages a range of self-contained units and cottages around town of varying sizes, standards and prices – check the website for details.

our pick **@VDL Stanley** (☎ 03-6458 2032; www.atvdl stanley.com.au; 16 Wharf Rd; s $180-220; ☐) If you're gonna splash out this is the place! A stunning contemporary refit of an old 1840s bluestone warehouse, with two ultra-hip suites that are simply exquisite from the fittings, cutlery, towels and linen to the superb choice of artworks. If you've booked just one night you'll be disappointed.

Stanley Cabin & Tourist Park (☎ 03-6458 1266; www.stanleycabinpark.com.au; 1 Wharf Rd; unpowered/powered sites from $22/24, dm/d $24/80, cabins $55-95; ☐) On a grassy flat fronting Tatlows Beach, this park has a brilliant location and good facilities, including camp kitchen, laundry and coin-operated internet kiosk. Sleeping options suit all budgets: doubles are motel-like, cabins are clean and tent sites are almost on the beach.

Eating

Psst…if it's just fresh crays you want the cheapest are sold out of the Seaquarium (left) at around $55 per kg. Expect to pay about $90 per kilogram at Hurseys (opposite).

Moby Dick's Breakfast Bar (☎ 03-6458 1414; 5 Church St; mains $6-15; ☺ breakfast) Moby's mega-breakfast, in this simple pine-panelled room, is the best in Stanley (they don't do anything else!). Waffles, eggs, omelettes and strong coffee.

Hurseys Seafood (☎ 03-6458 1103; 2 Alexander Tce; mains $8-25) Look for the giant orange crayfish adorning the facade of Hurseys on the waterfront, a Stanley institution. There's Kermies Café (meals $5 to $13), serving fish 'n' chip takeaways as well as Julie & Patrick's (mains $19 to $30, open for dinner), a more formal seafood restaurant with cute balcony seats.

Sealer's Cove (☎ 03-6458 1234; 2 Main Rd; mains $11-19; ✆ dinner Tue-Sun) Going green around the gills at the thought of another scallop? Head along to this navy-blue BYO place for some seafood relief: pasta, steaks, gourmet pizza, salads and excellent desserts. It does seafood too, but you don't have to.

SMITHTON & AROUND

Smithton (population 3360), 22km west of Stanley, serves one of Tasmania's largest forestry areas. There's bugger-all to see here, but for a bed and a feed try the **Bridge Hotel/Motel** (☎ 03-6452 1389; www.goodstone.com.au; 2 Montague Rd; hotel s/d $40/60, motel s/d $90/100). Serving dinner, county music boot-scoots through the bistro (mains $10 to $20).

The **Allendale Gardens & Rainforest** (☎ 03-6456 4216; www.allendalegardens.com.au; Allendale La, Edith Creek; adult/child $10/3.50; ✆ 9am-5pm Oct-Apr) is signposted off Blanche Rd (which is off the B22), 12km south of Smithton towards Edith Creek. There are 6.5 acres of bird-filled gardens and 26 hectares of old temperate rainforest to forget yourself in, plus a cafe serving Devonshire tea.

Thirty kilometres southwest of Smithton on the A2 is **Tarkine Forest Adventures** (☎ 03-6456 7199; www.dismalswamp.com.au; Bass Hwy; adult/child/family $20/10/45; ✆ 9am-5pm Nov-Mar, to 4pm Apr-Oct), with a 110m slippery-dip plummeting into a blackwood sinkhole.

MARRAWAH
pop 370

At Marrawah, with its open pastureland punctuated by stands of old conifers, the wild Southern Ocean occasionally coughs up pieces of ships wrecked off the rugged coast. The area's beaches and rocky outcrops are hauntingly beautiful, particularly at dusk, and the seas are often monstrous. In March the **West Coast Classic** (www.ripcurl.com) surf competition carves up the swell.

In the township there is a general store selling petrol and supplies, and the **Marrawah Tavern** (☎ 03-6457 1102; Comeback Rd; mains $10-19; ✆ lunch & dinner), which serves counter meals but doesn't have accommodation. There's a free but very basic (and windy!) camping area with toilets and cold shower by the beach at Green Point, 2km from Marrawah.

Wake up, scratch your head and contemplate a surf at the compact, blue-and-pine **Marrawah Beach House** (☎ 03-6457 1285; 19 Beach Rd; s/d from $90/100), which has amazing views across the beach to oblivion. Fully self-contained, it sleeps four.

About 5km from the beach, **Glendonald Cottage** (☎ /fax 03-6457 1191; 79 Arthur River Rd; d from $95) is a comfortable self-contained cottage sleeping five; the owner also conducts excellent four-hour **wildlife tours** (www.kingsrun.com.au; per person $100) in the area.

ARTHUR RIVER
pop 120

Fifteen kilometres south of Marrawah is the straggly settlement of Arthur River, an isolated bevy of fibro fishing shacks and holiday houses. **Gardiner Point**, signposted off the main road south of the old timber bridge, has been christened the 'Edge of the World' – there's nothing but sea from here to Argentina. The off-shore breeze peels spray from the breakers as they thunder towards the river mouth. From here you can drive 110km south to Corinna on the West Coast via the Western Explorer road (p699).

If you're not into fishing, take a scenic cruise on the Arthur River with either **Arthur River Cruises** (☎ 03-6457 1158; www.arthurrivercruises .com; Arthur River Store, 1414 Arthur River Rd; adult/child $83/35; ✆ 10am-3pm), cruising upriver to the confluence of the Arthur and Frankland Rivers for a barbecue and a rainforest walk; or **AR Reflections River Cruises** (☎ 03-6457 1288; www.arreflections.com; 4 Gardiner St; adult/child $85/44; ✆ 10.15am-4.15pm), where passengers also get a guided rainforest walk and a gourmet lunch.

Arthur River Canoe & Boat Hire (☎ /fax 6457 1312; 1429 Arthur River Rd; ✆ 9am-5pm) hires out motorboats ($25/130 per hour/day), canoes ($16/70) and kayaks ($12/50). You can take the canoes upriver and camp for as long as you like. Waterproof drums are provided; BYO everything else.

There is decent self-catering accommodation in Arthur River, but no eateries (only

TASMANIA

two takeaway stores). Pitch a tent at Manuka, Peppermint or Prickly Wattle **camping grounds** (sites $20) around Arthur River; self-register at the **Arthur River Parks & Wildlife Service** (☎ 03-6457 1225; www.parks.tas.gov.au; ⏰ 24hr registration booth) on the main street.

Just north of town, **Arthur River Caravan Park** (☎ 0429 336 223; www.arthurrivercabinpark.com; 1239 Arthur River Rd; unpowered & powered sites $20, dm $25, cabins $75-85) has old and new cabins, and plenty of wildlife passing through.

Arthur River Holiday Units (☎ 03-6457 1288; www.arholidayunits.com; 2 Gardiner St; powered sites $22; s/d $88/110) has several comfortable (if a little dated) riverside units ranging from one to three bedrooms, as well as a couple of powered sites.

THE WEST

Primeval, tempestuous and elemental – this region of Tasmania is unlike anywhere else in Australia. Towering, jagged mountain ranges, button-grass-covered alpine plateaus, raging tannin-stained rivers, dense impenetrable rainforest and unyielding rain. Humankind never tamed this western wilderness and today much of the region comprises Tasmania's World Heritage Area. Tourist-centric Strahan aside, the few towns and settlements here are rough and primitive, weathered and hardened by wilderness.

Prior to 1932, when the Hobart–Queenstown road was built, the only way

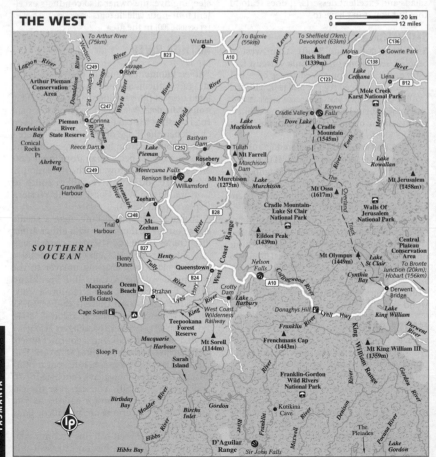

THE WEST

TASMANIA

into the area was by sea, through the dangerous Hells Gates into Strahan's Macquarie Harbour. European settlement brought convicts, soldiers, loggers, prospectors, railway gangs and fishermen to the area. In the 20th century, outdoor adventurers, naturalists and environmental crusaders were lured into the wilderness. The proposed damming of the Franklin and Lower Gordon Rivers in the 1980s sparked the greatest environmental debate in Australian history, and fostered an ecotourism boom around Strahan.

See www.westcoast.tas.gov.au and www.tasmaniaswestcoast.com.au for regional information.

Getting There & Around

TassieLink (☎ 1300 300 520; www.tassielink.com.au) buses run from Hobart to the west coast five times per week. The duration of the Strahan journey varies with Queenstown stopover times.

Journey	Price ($)	Duration (hr)
Hobart-Bronte Junction	37	2¼
Hobart-Derwent Bridge	44	3¼
Hobart-Lake St Clair	51	2¾
Hobart-Queenstown	65	5
Hobart-Strahan	75	6-8¾

From Launceston, TassieLink buses run three times per week:

Journey	Price ($)	Duration (hr)
Launceston-Cradle Mountain	59	3
Launceston-Devonport (meeting ferries)	24	1¼
Launceston-Gowrie Park	40	2¼
Launceston-Queenstown	72	6
Launceston-Sheffield	30	2
Launceston-Strahan	82	8¾
Launceston-Zeehan	62	5½

Drivers heading north along the rugged Western Explorer road (p699) should fill up at Zeehan or Waratah; there's no fuel at Corinna or Arthur River, only at distant Marrawah.

CORINNA
pop 5

Tiny **Corinna** (☎ 03-6446 1170; www.corinna.com.au; Western Explorer Rd; unpowered sites $20, s $50, d cottages $175, d cabins $150-200), on the northern bank of the Pieman River, was once a thriving gold-mining settlement of more than 2500 people, but nowadays the whole town is run as an isolated tourist resort with a strong environmentalist focus. The ambitious owners have renovated the old pub and built 14 new self-contained, solar-powered cabins on the hillside.

Pieman River Cruises (adult/child $79/37; ☼ 10.30am-2.30pm) operates from here – a laid-back, rustic alternative to Strahan's crowded, mass-produced Gordon River cruises. Four-hour cruises on the *Arcadia II* pass an impressive gorge and forests of eucalypts, ferns and Huon pines en route to Pieman Heads, where you can rummage around the log-strewn beaches. Bookings are essential.

The *Fatman* **ferry** (☎ 03-6446 1170; motorcycles & bicycles/standard vehicle/caravan $10/20/25; ☼ 9am-5pm Apr-Sep, to 7pm Oct-Mar) slides across the Pieman on demand (the only way across the river).

ZEEHAN
pop 850

A boom-bust mining town, Zeehan's fortunes have been bound to its deposits of silver, lead, tin and more recently zinc. In the late 1800s the Silver City, as it was dubbed, was home to 10,000 residents, 27 hotels and even its own stock exchange. But by 1908 the mines were failing and Zeehan declined inexorably until the late '60s when the nearby Renison Tin Mine reopened. These days it's the rich Zeehan Zinc open-cut mine that's employing the locals, but Zeehan's never reclaimed the glories of its heyday.

The historic part of Main St is at the northern end of town, not the bit you see when entering from Strahan or Queenstown. Remnant boom-time buildings are the **post office** and **courthouse** (both on Main St) and the concrete **St Luke's Church** on Belstead St.

The excellent **West Coast Pioneers Memorial Museum** (☎ 03-6471 6225; Main St; adult/child/family $10/9/22; ☼ 9am-5pm), in the old School of Mines building, offer insights into mine workings plus old steam trains, a mineral collection and pictorial west coast history. Admission includes access to the magnificently restored, 1000-seat **Gaiety Theatre** (Main St); when it opened in 1898 it was one of the largest, most opulent and modern theatres in the world.

Trial Harbour, Zeehan's original port, is a lonely, end-of-the-world place with bush camping; between Zeehan and Strahan are the desert-like, blindingly white expanses of the **Henty Dunes**.

The redbrick **Hotel Cecil** (☎ 03-6471 6221; www.cecilhotel.com.au; 99 Main St; s $45, d with/without bathroom

$75/65, cottage from $85) has small, well-loved pub rooms and four self-contained miners' cottages on the adjacent block. Hearty pub meals, available for lunch and dinner (mains $12 to $25) from the bistro, are miner-sized.

The **Heemskirk Motor Hotel** (☎ 1800 639 876, 03-6471 6107; heemskirk@tasparkside.com.au; Main St; d $100-115), at the eastern end of town, is no architectural wonder, but it has spacious, clean rooms and decent bistro (mains $18 to $26).

QUEENSTOWN
pop 2120

The extraordinary Lyell Hwy winds down from the mountains into Queenstown through a surreal, apocalyptic moonscape of deep, eroded gullies and bare hillsides bleached and burnt as if by nuclear fallout. This is the legacy of environmentally destructive mining. Mining activities and sulphur emissions are now controlled, and greenery is springing up on the slopes. Ironically, some locals want to keep the green away, believing the bald hills and gravel football field attract the tourists.

Queenstown retains an isolated, impoverished mining-town atmosphere. Kids with hoodies and crooked teeth look cagey and menacing on rusty BMX bikes, and curtains shift in windows as you pass by. Then the weather closes in and you feel like you're in a slasher movie.

Doubling as the Queenstown visitor information centre, the **Eric Thomas Galley Museum** (☎ /fax 6471 1483; 1-7 Driffield St; adult/child/concession/family $4/2.50/3/10; ☻ 9.30am-6pm Mon-Fri, 12.30-6pm Sat & Sun, reduced hours in winter) started life as the Imperial Hotel in 1898. Inside are diverting displays of old photographs with idiosyncratic captions.

The town's biggest (and priciest) attraction is the West Coast Wilderness Railway (see opposite), a restored line traversing the pristine wilderness between Queenstown and Strahan. The station is on Driffield St, opposite the Empire Hotel.

For top-of-the-town views, follow Hunter St uphill, turn left onto Bowes St, then sharp left onto Latrobe St to a small car park. From here a short, steep track ascends **Spion Kop Lookout**.

The abandoned open-cut mine **Iron Blow** can be seen from a lookout off the Lyell Hwy, while mining continues deep beneath the massive West Lyell crater. Take a 2½-hour

tour with **Douggies Mine Tours** (☎ 0407 049 612; tours $70; ☻ 10am & 1pm). Minimum age is 14; bookings are essential.

Sleeping & Eating

Empire Hotel (☎ 03-6471 1699; www.empirehotel.net.au; 2 Orr St; s $25, d with/without bathroom $60/45) 'Almost too friendly' is the motto on Empire's flyer, which is a bit creepy. But the majestic c 1901 Empire Hotel is terrific, with simple, clean, well-priced rooms in the middle of town. Its heritage dining room (mains $14 to $20) serves beefy pub standards to the jingle of gaming machines for lunch and dinner.

Mt Lyell Anchorage (☎ 03-6471 1900; www.mount lyellanchorage.com; 17 Cutten St; s/d $70/100) This place, in an old weatherboard home, has hiked up its prices in recent years and is not the friendly budget bargain place it was. It has clean singles and doubles with a shared bathroom and good kitchen and laundry facilities, just back from the main drag.

Penghana (☎ 03-6471 2560; www.penghana.com.au; 32 The Esplanade; d incl breakfast from $150) Built in 1898 for the Mt Lyell Mining Company's general manager, this National Trust–listed upmarket guest house presides over Queenstown from a treed, grassy hill. The interior is filled with antiques and period fittings, and guest facilities include a lounge with open fire, bar and billiard table, and a grand dining room. Lunch and dinner is by arrangement; access via Preston St.

Queenstown Cabin & Tourist Park (☎ 03-6471 1332; fax 6471 1125; 17 Grafton St; unpowered/powered sites $24/28, on-site caravans $50, cabins $80-100) Set on gravel 500m south of town past some dreary neighbourhoods, this park has decent vans and cabins, a communal kitchen and a riot of mismatched tiles in the amenities block. Barbecue facilities, games room and playground, too.

While there are takeaway shops lining the main street, the Queenstown culinary scene is as dreary as the drizzle outside. **Dotties Coffeeshop** (☎ 03-6471 1700; Driffield St), inside the train station, and **JJ's Coffeeshop** (☎ 03-6471 1793; 13 Orr St) both serve decent earthy food – soups, toasted sandwiches, focaccias and good cooked breakfasts.

STRAHAN
pop 640

They say Federal Hotels 'owns' Strahan, and certainly their Pure Tasmania moniker is

WEST COAST WILDERNESS RAILWAY

The old railway from Queenstown to Strahan was a remarkable engineering feat. Built to transport copper from Queenstown's Mt Lyell mine to the Macquarie Harbour port at Strahan, it passes through dense forest, crosses wild rivers via 40 bridges, and stops at old stations on its route. The rack-and-pinion line opened in 1896, utilising the Abt system (involving a third, toothed, lock-on rail) to allow fully loaded mining carriages to tackle steep 1:16 gradients. After closing in 1963 the railway fell into disrepair.

Today the entire track is magnificently restored, locomotives shuttling passengers along its full length. Trains depart Queenstown and Strahan at the same times (10am daily, plus 3pm December to February), meeting in the rainforest at Dubbil Barril station. You change trains here and continue the full distance (around four hours end to end), then take a later train or bus back to your starting point; or return to your point of origin on the train you rode in on. One way (or return to Dubbil Barril) costs $105/60 per adult/child. The bus costs an additional $18/10.

Purchase tickets at either **Queenstown Station** (☎ 03-6471 1700; Driffield St; ◷ ticket office 9am-5pm, to 7pm Dec-Feb) in the centre of town, the **Strahan Activities Centre** (☎ 03-6471 4300; The Esplanade, Strahan; ◷ 9am-5pm, to 7pm Dec-Feb) or by phone or online at **Pure Tasmania** (☎ 1800 420 155; www.puretasmania.com.au).

stamped on much of the tourist town's accommodation, restaurants, wilderness river cruisers, and tours and activity providers. There are some minor independent players, too, but Federal Hotels is the Goliath of Tasmanian tourism, and Strahan is one of its cash cows and showpieces.

Strahan (pronounced 'Strawn'), 40km southwest of Queenstown on the Macquarie Harbour, is the only vestige of civilisation on Tasmania's wild west coast and the epicentre of west-coast tourism. Visitors come in droves seeking a taste of Tasmania's famous wilderness, whether by seaplane, a Gordon River cruise or the Wilderness Railway.

Macquarie Harbour was discovered in the early 1800s by sailors searching for Huon pine. The area was inaccessible by land and proved difficult to reach by sea – dubious assets that prompted the establishment of a brutal penal colony on Sarah Island in 1821. In the middle of Macquarie Harbour, Sarah Island isolated the colony's worst convicts, their muscle used to harvest Huon pine nearby. Convicts worked 12 hours a day, often in leg irons, felling pines and rafting them back to the island's saw-pits where they were used to build superb ships. In 1834, after the establishment of the Port Arthur penal settlement, Sarah Island was abandoned.

Today, Strahan's harbourside main street is undeniably attractive, but in an artificial, overcommercialised kind of way. Everything is expensive, from fuel to a loaf of bread. It can snow here in summer or blow a blizzard on a whim, so bring winter-weight and waterproof clothing, just in case…

Information

The architecturally innovative **West Coast visitor information centre** (☎ 03-6472 6800; www.westcoast .tas.gov.au; The Esplanade; ◷ 10am-7pm Dec-Mar, to 6pm Apr-Nov; ▯) provides information on accommodation, attractions and activities around town.

The **Parks & Wildlife Service** (☎ 03-6471 7122; www.parks.tas.gov.au; The Esplanade; ◷ 9am-5pm Mon-Fri; ▯) office in the old Customs House on the foreshore also houses the post office and online access centre. There are ATMs in the main street.

Log onto www.destinationstrahan.com.au and www.strahantasmania.com.

Sights & Activities

Beyond the Huon pine reception desk at the visitor information centre is **West Coast Reflections** (☎ 03-6472 6800; The Esplanade), a creative, thought-provoking display on west-coast history, including a refreshingly blunt appraisal of environmental disappointments and achievements.

Nearby is **Strahan Woodworks** (☎ 03-6471 7244; 12 Esplanade; ◷ 8.30am-5pm) with old machine-powered saws and lathes.

The Ship That Never Was (☎ 03-6472 6800; www.roun dearth.com.au; The Esplanade; adult/child/concession $17.50/gold-coin donation/12.50; ◷ 5.30pm, also 8.30pm in Jan) is a pantomime-style show (Australia's longest-running play!) staged daily at the visitor

TASMANIA

information centre's amphitheatre. It tells the story of the last ship built at Sarah Island, and the convicts who stole it and escaped.

Hogarth Falls is at the end of a rainforest walk (40 minutes return) alongside the platypus-inhabited Botanical Creek, starting from People's Park south of town.

Other natural attractions include the storm-battered, 33km-long **Ocean Beach**, 6km from town, where the sunsets have to be seen to be believed. The rips rip and the undertows tow – swimming isn't recommended. From October to April the Ocean Beach dunes become a **mutton bird rookery**, the birds returning from winter migration. Ask at the visitor information centre about ranger-run tours in January and February. **West Strahan Beach**, closer to town, has a gently shelving sandy bottom that's OK for swimming. About 14km along the road from Strahan to Zeehan are the spectacular **Henty Dunes**, impressive 30m-high sand mountains.

Tours

See t p707 for information about the West Coast Wilderness Railway between Strahan and Queenstown. **Strahan Taxis** (☎ 0417 516 071) can run you out to Ocean Beach (about $15 each way) and Henty Dunes ($25 each way).

GORDON RIVER CRUISES

Both cruises include a rainforest walk at Heritage Landing; views of (or passage through) Hells Gates, Macquarie Harbour's narrow entrance; and a land tour of Sarah Island.

Gordon River Cruises (☎ 1800 628 288, 03-6471 4300; www.puretasmania.com.au; The Esplanade) Offers 5½-hour cruises departing 8.30am daily, and also at 2.45pm over summer. Cost depends on where you sit. Standard seats with an excellent buffet lunch cost from $90/35/235 per adult/child/family. You can pay more for window-recliner seats, but the windows fog up and people wander around anyway, and they're not worth the extra. Or you can pay $195 (all tickets) for the Captain's Premier Upper Deck with a swisho lunch, wine and all beverages (no, you're not allowed to drive).

World Heritage Cruises (☎ 1800 611 796, 03-6471 7174; www.worldheritagecruises.com.au; The Esplanade) Take a 5¾-hour morning or afternoon cruise daily costing per adult/child/family $85/45/235 including a fine buffet lunch, or pay $110/60/295 for premium window seats. You can buy Gold Pass tickets that cost $130 (all tickets) and include a few extras like a glass of wine, *Story of Sarah Island* booklet, premium window seats...wouldn't bother.

JET-BOAT RIDES

Wild Rivers Jet (☎ 03-6471 7396; www.wildriversjet .com.au; The Esplanade) Fifty-minute jet-boat rides on the hour from 9am to 4pm up the King River's rainforest-lined gorges. The experience costs $68/40/185 per adult/child/family. Minimum two people; bookings recommended.

SAILING

West Coast Yacht Charters (☎ 03-6471 7422; www .tasadventures.com/wcyc; The Esplanade) Overnight Gordon River sightseeing cruises onboard the 60ft steel ketch *Stormbreaker*. The boat carries just 10 passengers, making it a much more intimate experience. One night, including a visit to Sarah Island and all meals, costs $320/160 per adult/child. Two-day/two-night cruises are $420/210. Also available are three-hour fishing trips ($45/20) and a 2½-hour evening cruise on Macquarie Harbour ($80/50, including crayfish dinner). When docked overnight in Strahan, *Stormbreaker* offers cute B&B accommodation (see below).

SCENIC FLIGHTS

Strahan Seaplanes & Helicopters (☎ 03-6471 7718; www.adventureflights.com.au; The Esplanade) Seaplane and helicopter flights over the region. Seaplane options include 80-minute flights over Frenchmans Cap, the Franklin and Gordon Rivers, and Sarah Island (per adult/child $185/110), and 65-minute flights over the Cradle Mountain region ($195/95). A 60-minute helicopter flight over the Teepookana Forest Reserve costs $185/110, and a quick 15 minutes over Hells Gates and Macquarie Harbour costs $110/95.

Sleeping

The sprawling **Strahan Village** (☎ 1800 628 286, 03-6471 4200; www.puretasmania.com.au) takes up most of the town centre and is a(nother) Federal Hotels enterprise. The booking office is under the clock tower on the Esplanade. Book well ahead.

BUDGET

West Coast Yacht Charters (☎ 03-6471 7422; www .tasadventures.com/wcyc; The Esplanade; r per person incl breakfast $50) The cruising yacht *Stormbreaker* offers its two double cabins and six-bunk dorm as cheery B&B-style accommodation when berthed at the pretty Strahan waterfront. This is a working yacht doing Gordon River cruises (see above), and spends several nights per week on the river, so call ahead. When moored it offers interesting 5pm-to-9am check in/check out accommodation. Linen supplied.

Strahan Wilderness Lodge (☎ 03-6471 7142; www
.bayviewcottages-cabins.com.au; Ocean Beach Rd; lodge d
incl breakfast $60-85, cabins $75-110) This homely old
house was relocated here in 11 sections from
Queenstown in 1982. The '70s decor is cheesy-
authentic and some rooms share bathrooms,
but it's the best value in town and is warm
when the rain sets in. Self-contained timber
cabins are dotted among windswept heathlands – also great value. To get here drive
three minutes along Harvey St west from the
town.

Discovery Holiday Parks Strahan (☎ 03-6471
7239; www.discoveryholidayparks.com.au; cnr Andrew &
Innes Sts; unpowered/powered sites $25/35, cabins $104-
150; 🖵) Neat and friendly on Strahan's West
Beach, this park has good facilities including a kiosk, a camp kitchen, barbecues and
playground.

Strahan Holiday Park (☎ 03-6471 7442; www.island
cabins.com.au; cnr Innes & Jones Sts; powered sites $28, cabins
$95-120, cottages $180) One of a handful of caravan parks, Strahan Holiday Park offers swish
executive cabins and clean standard cabins in
a shady space (platypuses in the creek!) with
good facilities just 130m from the beach.

MIDRANGE & TOP END

Regatta Point Villas (☎ 03-6471 7103; The Esplanade; d
$150) Near the West Coast Wilderness Railway
station at Regatta Point and managed by the
local tavern (right), this place offers eight
roomy, self-contained units with reasonable
views. There are occasionally vacancies in the
cheap worker's dorms here – ask.

Ormiston House (☎ 03-6471 7077; www.ormiston
house.com.au; Esplanade; d $150-250; 🖵) This stun-
ning 1899 mansion was built by Frederick
Ormiston, Strahan's founder, and offers
stately yet relaxed B&B accommodation in
five antique-filled rooms. Climb up to the
widow's walk for some of the best harbour
views in Strahan.

Risby Cove (☎ 03-6471 7572; www.risbycove.com.au;
Esplanade; d $155-250; 🖵) This refurbished wa-
terfront sawmill village is now a handsome
accommodation complex clad in blue corrugated iron with eight rooms and one- and
two-bedroom spa suites. There's also a gallery
and restaurant, Risby Cove (right). Bike and
kayak hire are also available here.

Eating

Fish Café (☎ 03-6471 4386; The Esplanade; mains $14-
22; 🕙 lunch & dinner) This flash harbourside fish

and chippery serves fresh (and overpriced)
fish and chips. Chow down on pink ling,
blue-eye trevalla, prawns or oysters, or try
the 'Fish Café Sampler' ($26.50) with a bit
of everything.

Regatta Point Tavern (☎ 03-6471 7103; The
Esplanade; mains $16-30; 🕙 lunch & dinner) This is the
locals' pub, 2km around the bay from town
near the railway terminus. It's the last bastion
of grit and substance in Strahan. The beery
conversation and working-class atmosphere
are slightly offset by the ring and clatter of
gaming machines, but it's otherwise a nice
antidote to Strahan's pretensions. The bistro
serves substantial mains.

Hamer's Hotel (☎ 03-6471 4335; The Esplanade; mains
$17-35; 🕙 lunch & dinner) Hamer's is an upmarket
waterside family-friendly bistro that serves
first-class dinnertime meals – try the mussels
in Thai coconut, chilli and lime broth or the
wallaby steak on roast-pumpkin mash with
pepperberry relish. At lunch the menu is more
downmarket with burgers, steak sandwiches
and fish and chips.

Risby Cove (☎ 03-6471 7572; The Esplanade; mains
$24-32; 🕙 dinner) Classy and cool it offers con-
sistently excellent food prepared by trained
kitchen staff using the freshest local ingredients. People come from all around to linger
over an excellent menu that includes pan-fried
trout, handmade gnocchi and slow-roasted
duck over an Asian vegetable medley.

FRANKLIN-GORDON WILD RIVERS NATIONAL PARK

Saved from hydroelectric immersion in the
1980s, this World Heritage–listed **national
park** (www.parks.tas.gov.au) embraces the catchment areas of the Franklin and Olga Rivers
and part of the Gordon River – all exceptional
rafting, bushwalking and climbing areas. The
park's snow-capped summit is **Frenchmans Cap**
(1443m; a challenging three- to five-day walk).
The park also boasts a number of unique plant
species and the major Indigenous Australian
archaeological site at **Kutikina Cave**.

Much of the park consists of deep river
gorges and impenetrable rainforest, but the
Lyell Hwy traverses its northern end. There
are a handful of short walks starting from the
highway, including hikes to **Nelson Falls** (20
minutes return), and **Donaghys Hill** (40 minutes
return) from where you can see the Franklin
River and the sky-high white quartzite dome
of Frenchmans Cap.

TASMANIA

Rafting

Rafting the bubbling churns of the Franklin River is thrillingly hazardous; for the inexperienced, tour companies offer complete rafting packages. Whether you go with an independent group or a tour operator, you should contact the park rangers at the **Queenstown Parks & Wildlife Service** (☎ 03-6471 2511; Penghana Rd), or the **Lake St Clair visitor information centre** (☎ 03-6289 1172; Cynthia Bay) for current information on permits, weather, regulations and environmental considerations. Also check the detailed 'Franklin River Rafting Notes' online at www .parks.tas.gov.au/recreation/boating.

Expeditions should register at the booth at the junction of the Lyell Hwy and the Collingwood River, 49km west of Derwent Bridge. Rafting the length of the river, starting at Collingwood River and ending at Sir John Falls, takes between eight and 14 days. It's also possible to do shorter trips. From the exit point, you can be picked up by a **Strahan Seaplanes & Helicopters** (☎ 03-6471 7718; www.adven tureflights.com.au) seaplane or by **West Coast Yacht Charters'** (☎ 03-6471 7422; www.tasadventures.com) *Stormbreaker* for the trip back to Strahan. Or you can paddle 22km further downriver to meet a Gordon River cruise boat at Heritage Landing.

Tours run mainly from December to March. Tour companies with complete rafting packages (departing Hobart) include:

Rafting Tasmania (☎ 03-6239 1080; www.raft ingtasmania.com) Five-/seven-/10-day trips costing $1650/2000/2600.

Tasmanian Expeditions (☎ 1300 666 856, 03-6339 3999; www.tas-ex.com) Nine-/11-day trips for $2450/2650.

Water By Nature (☎ 1800 111 142, 0408 242 941; www.franklinriver.com) Five-/seven-/10-day trips for $1740/2040/2680.

CRADLE MOUNTAIN-LAKE ST CLAIR NATIONAL PARK

Tasmania is world famous for the stunning 168,000-hectare World Heritage area of Cradle Mountain-Lake St Clair. Mountain peaks, dank gorges, pristine lakes, tarns and wild moorlands extend triumphantly from the Great Western Tiers in the north to Derwent Bridge on the Lyell Hwy in the south. It was one of Australia most heavily glaciated areas, and includes Mt Ossa (1617m) – Tasmania's highest peak – and Lake St Clair, Australia's deepest natural freshwater lake (167m).

The preservation of this region as a **national park** (www.parks.tas.gov.au) is due in part to Austrian immigrant Gustav Weindorfer. In 1912 he built a chalet out of King Billy pine, called it Waldheim (German for 'Forest Home') and, from 1916, lived there permanently. Today the site of his chalet at the northern end of the park retains the name Waldheim.

There are fabulous day walks at both Cradle Valley in the north and Cynthia Bay (Lake St Clair) in the south, but it's the outstanding 80.5km Overland Track between the two that has turned this park into a bushwalkers' mecca.

Information

All walking tracks in the park are signposted, well defined and easy to follow, but it's prudent to carry a map – pick one up at park visitor information centres.

CRADLE VALLEY

There are two visitor information centres here. Adjacent to Discovery Holiday Parks Cradle Valley (p712), 3km north of the park's northern boundary, is the privately run **Cradle Information Centre** (☎ 03-6492 1590; Cradle Mountain Rd; ⏰ 8am-5pm) with its vast car park. This is the starting point for the national-park shuttle-bus service (p712). The centre provides bushwalking information and sells park passes, food and fuel. It's more worthwhile to continue onto the mega-helpful Parks & Wildlife Service's own **Cradle Mountain visitor information centre** (☎ 03-6492 1110; www.parks.tas .gov.au; Cradle Mountain Rd; ⏰ 8am-5pm Jun-Aug, 8am-6pm Sep-May), within the park itself, which provides extensive bushwalking information (including national park and Overland Track passes and registration), and informative flora, fauna and park history displays.

Regardless of season, be prepared for cold, wet weather around Cradle Valley. On average it rains here seven days out of 10, is cloudy eight days in 10, the sun shines all day only one day in 10 and it snows on 54 days each year!

LAKE ST CLAIR

Occupying one wing of a large building at Cynthia Bay on the park's southern boundary is the **Lake St Clair visitor information centre** (☎ 03-6289 1172; www.parks.tas.gov.au; Cynthia Bay; ⏰ 8am-5pm), providing rock-solid walking advice, national park passes and displays.

At the adjacent, separately run **Lake St Clair Wilderness Resort** (☎ 03-6289 1137; www.lakestclairresort .com.au; Cynthia Bay; 🕒 8am-5pm Apr-Oct, 7am-8pm Nov-Mar), you can book a range of accommodation (p712), or a seat on a ferry or cruise (p712).

Sights & Activities

Bushwalking is the primary lure of this national park. Aside from the **Overland Track** (see p713), there are dozens of short walks here. For Cradle Valley visitors, behind the Cradle Mountain Visitor Information Centre (opposite) there is an easy but first-rate 20-minute circular boardwalk through the adjacent rainforest, called the **Pencil Pine Falls & Rainforest Walk**, suitable for wheelchairs and prams. Nearby is another trail leading to **Knyvet Falls** (45 minutes return), as well as the **Enchanted Walk** alongside Pencil Pine Creek (20 minutes return), and the **King Billy Walk** (one hour return). The **Cradle Valley Walk** (2½ hours one way) is an 8.5km-long boardwalk linking the Cradle Mountain visitor information centre and Dove Lake. The **Dove Lake Walk** is a 6km lap of the lake, which takes around two hours.

At Cynthia Bay, the **Larmairremener tabelti** is an Aboriginal culture walk that winds through the traditional lands of the Larmairremener, the Indigenous people of the region. The walk (one hour return) starts at the visitor centre. Another way to do some walking here is to catch the ferry service (p712) to either Echo Point Hut or Narcissus Hut and walk back to Cynthia Bay along the lakeshore. From Echo Point it's four to five hours' walk back; from Narcissus five to six hours.

Tours

Most travellers to Tasmania consider Cradle Mountain a must-see, so almost every tour operator in the state offers day trips or longer tours to the area (including guided walks along the Overland Track). Some recommendations:

Craclair (☎ 03-6339 4488; www.craclair.com.au) Craclair has among its many offerings a seven-day/six-night Overland Track tour ($2150 per person including packs, sleeping bags, tents, jackets and over-trousers) and also runs shorter trips.

Cradle Mountain Helicopters (☎ 03-6492 1132; www.adventureflights.com.au; Cradle Mountain Rd; flights Sep-Jun) A thrilling way to see the region's wonders is to take a helicopter flight from beside the Cradle Information Centre. Thirty-minute flights cost $190/140 per adult/child.

Cradle Mountain Huts (☎ 03-6391 9339; www.cra dlehuts.com.au) If camping isn't your bag, from November to May you can take a six-day/five-night, small-group guided walk along the Overland Track with accommodation in plush private huts and others carrying your pack. The fee (from $2500 per person) includes meals, national park fees and transfers to/from Launceston.

Grayline (☎ 03-6234 3336; www.grayline.com.au) Offers a day coach tour from Launceston to Cradle Mountain (adult/child $150/75), including a hike around Dove Lake, on Monday, Wednesday, Friday and Saturday leaving at 8.30am and returning at 5pm.

Tasmanian Expeditions (☎ 1300 666 856, 03-6339 3999; www.tas-ex.com) Does an eight-day/seven-night Overland Track trip for $1850 (November to April), as well as a six-day Cradle Mountain/Walls of Jerusalem walk for $1390.

Sleeping & Eating
CRADLE VALLEY

Waldheim Cabins (☎ 03-6492 1110; cradle@parks.tas .gov.au; Cradle Mountain Rd; d $85) 'This is Waldheim, where there is no time, and nothing matters.' The legacy of pioneering Gustav Weindorfer lives on in these rustic, basic four- to eight-bunk huts near his original hut, 5km into the national park. Each contains a shared bathroom, gas stove, heater and cooking utensils, but no bedding. Book through the Cradle Mountain visitor information centre (opposite).

Cradle Mountain Highlanders Cottages (☎ 03-6492 1116; www.cradlehighlander.com.au; Cradle Mountain Rd; d $120-180) Hospitable Highlanders is a cluster of 10 Germanic, shingle-clad timber cottages straight out of *The Sound of Music*. It's an easy-going, family-run operation. All cottages have a kitchen and lounge; the more luxurious ones have a wood heater and spa. Yodel-lay-hee-hoo…

Cradle Mountain Chateau (☎ 1800 420 155, 03-6492 1404; www.puretasmania.com.au; Cradle Mountain Rd; d $170-370; 🖥) This large edifice is another Federal Hotels enterprise with an attractive foyer and public spaces, including the excellent **Wilderness Gallery** (www.wildernessgallery.com.au), but its rooms are less impressive.

Cradle Mountain Lodge (☎ 1300 134 044, 02-8296 8010; www.cradlemountainlodge.com.au; Cradle Mountain Rd; d $270-750; 🖥) This huge stone-and-timber resort near the national park entrance has nearly 100 cabins surrounding the main chalet lodge. Four types of cabin each have tea- and coffee-making facilities and fridge, but no kitchens. Prices include buffet breakfast.

TASMANIA

There's good eating at the house restaurants – the neat-casual Highland (mains $19 to $28; open for breakfast, lunch and dinner) and the laid-back Tavern (mains $12 to $19; open for lunch and dinner), with pub-style meals and ski-lodge vibes. There's a spa retreat here, too, and heaps of organised activities.

Discovery Holiday Parks Cradle Valley (☎ 03-6492 1395; www.discoveryholidayparks.com.au; Cradle Mountain Rd; unpowered/powered sites $30/45, dm $40, cabins $150-175) This huge bushland area, just 2.5km from the park gates, offers stacks of camping and caravan sites, a good backpacker hostel, clean self-contained cabins and swish spa cottages. It's expensive for a caravan park but offers cheaper off-season rates, and the excellent camp kitchens with huge log fires compensate. Book in advance.

Self-caterers should stock up before heading to Cradle Valley; minimal supplies are sold at the Cradle Mountain Cafe, Discovery Holiday Parks shop and Cradle Mountain Lodge.

CYNTHIA BAY & DERWENT BRIDGE
Derwent Bridge Wilderness Hotel (☎ 03-6289 1144; fax 6289 1173; Lyell Hwy, Derwent Bridge; dm $30, d with/without bathroom $125/105) This is a brilliant spot on a freezing day with roaring log fires, cold beers and man-sized pub meals. The accommodation needs an upgrade, but the bar has a soaring, timber-beamed ceiling, a pool table, jukebox and easy-going vibe. Many a tall story has been told and many a long night has been had in the legendary Derwent Bridge pub.

Derwent Bridge Chalets (☎ 03-6289 1000; www.derwent-bridge.com; Lyell Hwy, Derwent Bridge; d $155-230) These half-dozen roomy, self-contained studios and chalets come with bushy back-porch views. The larger chalets sleep eight (popular with Overland Track groups), and have kitchens and laundries (some with spa). The newer, smaller studio doubles have kitchenettes.

Lake St Clair Wilderness Resort (☎ 03-6289 1137; www.lakestclairresort.com.au; Cynthia Bay; unpowered/powered sites $20/25, dm $28, d cabins $130-190) The bushy lakeside camping area here is lovely, with the calm waters of Lake St Clair in the foreground and the serrated mountain peaks behind. There are decent shower facilities, lots of walking opportunities and plentiful wildlife. There's a simple backpacker lodge and good-quality self-contained cabins on offer too. The licensed shop/restaurant adjoining the Lake St Clair visitor information centre (p710) handles the bookings and serves good light meals and fancier dinnertime fare.

Getting There & Away
TassieLink (☎ 1300 300 520; www.tassielink.com.au) buses service both Cradle Mountain and Lake St Clair; see p705 for details.

Maxwells (☎ /fax 03-6492 1431) runs on-demand services from Devonport to Cradle Mountain (one to four passengers $160; five or more $40 per passenger), Launceston to Cradle Mountain ($240/60), and Devonport or Launceston to Lake St Clair ($280/70).

You might be able to find more convenient or cheaper transport options by talking to staff at bushwalking shops or hostels.

Getting Around
CRADLE VALLEY
Leave your car at the Cradle Information Centre (p710) and jump on a **shuttle bus**, departing at 10-minute intervals (mid-September to late May) and stopping at the visitor information centre inside the park, Snake Hill, Ronny Creek (the Overland Track departure point) and Dove Lake. The service is free, but national park fees apply (p632). Visitors can alight at any bus stop along the way. Contact the Cradle Information Centre for reduced winter service details.

Maxwells (☎ /fax 6492 1431) runs on-demand year-round local shuttles picking up passengers from local accommodation places and taking them into the national park. Bookings are essential.

CYNTHIA BAY & DERWENT BRIDGE
Maxwells (☎ /fax 6492 1431) runs on-demand buses between Cynthia Bay/Lake St Clair and Derwent Bridge ($7 per person one way).

Lake St Clair Wilderness Resort (☎ 03-6289 1137; www.lakestclairresort.com.au; one way/return $25/35) runs the ferry service between Cynthia Bay and Narcissus Hut at the northern end of Lake St Clair. The boat (essentially a water taxi for Overland Track walkers) departs twice daily from April to October (10am and 2pm) and thrice daily from November to March (9am, 12.30pm and 3pm). Bookings are essential and prices rise for fewer than four passengers. If you are taking the ferry to complete your Overland Track opus, you must book in advance and radio the ferry operator to confirm when you reach Narcissus Hut.

THE OVERLAND TRACK

Australia's most famous trek is usually tackled as a six-day, five-night epic, walking 65km between Cradle Valley in the north and Lake St Clair in the south. The scenery is breathtaking and takes in some of Tasmania's highest peaks, through tall eucalypt forests bursting with wildlife, and across exposed alpine moors and buttongrass valleys of unsurpassed beauty.

The Overland Track is at its most picturesque in the summer months when the alpine wildflowers are blooming. This December-to-April period has more daylight hours and warmer temperatures, but there are fewer walkers in the spring and autumn months. Only very experienced walkers should tackle the track in winter. All walkers must register the start and finish of their walk at either end of the track.

In 1953 fewer than 1000 people walked the Overland Track, but by 2004 the trail was being pounded by 9000 hikers annually. To preserve the area's delicate ecology and avoid environmental degradation and overcrowding, some changes to walking conditions have been introduced:

- There's a booking system for the peak walking period (November to April), with walker numbers limited to 34 people departing per day.
- From November to April bushwalkers are required to tackle the track from north to south (Cradle Valley to Lake St Clair).
- In addition to national park fees (p632), a charge of $150/120 for adults/children applies to cover costs of sustainable track management. The additional fees only apply from November to April.

Departing Cradle Valley, walkers sometimes start at Dove Lake, but the recommended route begins at Ronny Creek, around 5km from the Cradle Mountain visitor information centre. There are many secondary paths off the main track, scaling mountains like Mt Ossa and detouring to lakes, waterfalls and valleys, so the length of time you spend on the track is only limited by the amount of supplies you can carry.

Once you reach Narcissus Hut at the northern end of Lake St Clair, you can walk around the lake's edge to Cynthia Bay (a five- to six-hour walk) or take the ferry run by Lake St Clair Wilderness Resort (opposite). To guarantee a seat, you must book the ferry before you start walking, then when you get to Narcissus Hut, use the radio to confirm your booking. The one-way ride costs $25 per person.

You can bunk down in the excellent huts along the track, but in summer they're full of snoring hikers and smelly socks. To preserve your sanity, bring a tent and pitch it on the established timber platforms around each hut. Campfires are banned, so fuel stoves are essential. There's plenty of clean drinking water available along the way, but boil anything you have doubts about.

Book your walk online at www.overlandtrack.com.au, where there's stacks of info and where you can order *The Overland Track – One Walk, Many Journeys* booklet ($12) detailing track sections, flora and fauna. There's also a link to the **Tasmap** (www.tasmap.tas.gov.au) website, where you can buy the 1:100,000 *Lake St Clair Map & Notes* ($14.95). Visitor information centres also sell the booklet and map. Lonely Planet's *Tasmania* and *Walking in Australia* guides have detailed walk descriptions.

THE SOUTHWEST

SOUTHWEST NATIONAL PARK

The **Southwest National Park** (www.parks.tas.gov.au), Tasmania's largest national park, is one of the planet's last great isolated wilderness areas and home to some of the last tracts of virgin temperate rainforest. It's a place of untouched primeval grandeur and extraordinary biodiversity, and part of Tasmania's World Heritage area.

The southwest is the habitat of the endemic Huon pine and the swamp gum, the world's tallest hardwood and tallest flowering plant. Around 300 species of lichen, moss and fern – some of which are rare and endangered – dapple the rainforest with shades of green; glacial tarns seamlessly mirror snowy mountaintops; and in summer, picture-perfect alpine meadows explode with wildflowers. Untamed rivers charge through the landscape, rapids surging

TASMANIA

through gorges and waterfalls plummeting over cliffs.

Activities
BUSHWALKING
The most-trodden walks in the park are the 70km **Port Davey Track** between Scotts Peak Rd and Melaleuca (around five days' duration), and the considerably more popular 85km **South Coast Track** (six to eight days) between Cockle Creek and Melaleuca. You can combine the two (Scotts Peak Rd to Cockle Creek), but it's one hell of a hike!

On both tracks, hikers should be prepared for vicious weather. Light planes airlift bushwalkers into Melaleuca in the southwest (there are no roads), while there's vehicle access and public transport to/from Cockle Creek at the other end of the South Coast Track, and Scotts Peak Rd at the other end of the Port Davey Track. Check out the notes on the **Parks & Wildlife Service** (www.parks.tas.gov.au) website, and the detailed descriptions in Lonely Planet's *Walking in Australia*.

SEA-KAYAKING
Kettering's Roaring 40s Ocean Kayaking (p658) runs three- and seven-day guided kayaking expeditions ($1650/2395 per person) out of Melaleuca, exploring the waterways around Bathurst Harbour and Port Davey. Prices include flights, food and all equipment (except sleeping bags).

Getting There & Around
The most popular way to tackle the South Coast Track is to fly into Melaleuca and walk out to Cockle Creek. **Par Avion** (☎ 1800 144 460, 03-6248 5390; www.paravion.com.au) flies between Hobart and Melaleuca one way for $195. There's also a soft option: scenic flights from Hobart over the southwest, with time spent on the ground. Par Avion's speciality is a four-hour 'Heritage Tour' (adult/child $200/170), passing the big peaks and surf-ravaged south coast, along with a boat trip on Bathurst Harbour and refreshments included. Full-day trips cost $310/260. **Tasair** (☎ 1800 062 900, 03-6248 5088; www.tasair.com.au) offers a two-hour scenic flight with 30 minutes on the ground at Melaleuca (from $298 per person).

From December to March on Monday, Wednesday and Friday, **TassieLink** (☎ 1300 300 520; www.tassielink.com.au) runs buses from Hobart to Cockle Creek ($71.30, 3½ hours), returning to Hobart on the same days. Between November and April, **Evans Coaches** (☎ 03-6297 1335; www.evanscoaches.com.au) also has a Hobart–Cockle Creek service ($75) and runs the only bus service from Hobart to Scotts Peak Rd at the end of the Port Davey Track – this runs as a charter service costing $150 for one and $95 per person for two or more, and takes four hours.

LAKE PEDDER & STRATHGORDON
Lake Pedder sits at the northern edge of the Southwest National Park. It was once a stunning natural lake famed for its beaches, and regarded as the ecological jewel of Tasmania's wilderness region. But in 1972, amid howls of protest from a nascent green movement, it was flooded to become part of the Gordon River power development. Together with nearby Lake Gordon, Pedder now holds 27 times the volume of water in Sydney Harbour and is the largest inland freshwater catchment in Australia.

Built to service employees during construction of the Gordon River Power Scheme, tiny **Strathgordon** (population 30) appears out of nowhere. On a clear day (about one in five!), the drive out here from Mt Field is bedazzling – bleak peaks, empty buttongrass plains, rippling lakes and the Gordon Forests. About 12km west of Strathgordon is the **Gordon Dam Lookout** and **visitor information centre** (☎ 03-6280 1134; www.hydro.com.au; Gordon River Rd; ☒ 10am-5pm Nov-Apr, to 3pm May-Oct), poised above the 140m-high Gordon Dam and providing info on the scheme. The views from atop the dam will make the strongest of knees tremble.

Accommodation-wise, your only options are the free Teds Beach Campground beside Lake Pedder (toilets and electric barbecues; no fires permitted), or the vast **Lake Pedder Chalet** (☎ 03-6280 1166; www.lakepedderchalet.com.au; Gordon River Rd; dm $35, d $90-150; ☒), a low-slung motel hunkering down under the rain clouds. Also at the Chalet is a **restaurant** (mains $12-26; ☒ lunch & dinner) serving dam-busting mains like beef lasagne and steak and Guinness pie.

No bus services run to Strathgordon.

BASS STRAIT ISLANDS

If you find Tassie's laid-back pace too frenetic (spare a thought for those harried mainlanders!) idle away a few days on King and Flinders islands where things are positively sluggish.

The Hunter and Furneaux Groups are the two archipelagos in Bass Strait at the western and eastern entrances of Bass Strait respectively. King Island is the main land mass in the Hunter Group as Flinders is to the Furneaux Group. Once the transient homes of sealers, sailors and prospectors, today these islands harbour an extraordinary array of wildlife, punctuated by small towns caught in a slow-turning 1980s cultural loop – the perfect escape for aspiring novelists, damaged urbanites, mad artists and those in need of some solitude.

Your best bet for visiting King or Flinders Islands is to purchase a package including flights, car rental and accommodation. Enquire with the airlines listed below, or contact Tourism Tasmania (p632).

KING ISLAND
pop 1640

Things are simple on 'KI', as King Island is locally known. It's flat and fertile – just 64km long and 27km wide – with a rocky coastline broken up by beautiful beaches. King Island is world famous for its cheeses and dairy products, and its beef is served in Australia's top restaurants. As well as gourmet food products, King Island exports processed seaweed, about 20% of the world's demand, used to thicken cosmetics and stabilise ice cream.

Discovered in 1798 the island became known as a breeding ground for seals and sea elephants, which were hunted close to extinction by brutal sealers and sailors known as the Straitsmen.

Over the years Bass Strait's heaving seas have wrecked hundreds of ships, around 60 of these off King Island. Australia's worst peace-time catastrophe occurred here in 1845 when the *Cataraqui*, an immigrant ship from Liverpool, went down just 150 yards offshore, drowning 399 people.

The main township is Currie on the west coast, which has a pub, two supermarkets, a petrol station, ATM and post office. Over on the east coast is Naracoopa, a beachy collaboration of holiday shacks with a fabulously derelict jetty that is perfect for fishing. In the southeast is Grassy.

For help planning your trip, contact **King Island Tourism** (☎ 1800 645 014; www.kingisland.org .au). Another useful website is www.kingisland .net.au. For tourist information on KI, visit **The Trend** (☎ 03-6462 1360; trend@kingisland.net.au; 26 Edward St, Currie; ☺ 8.30am-6pm Mon-Fri, 9am-5pm Sat, 9.30am-5pm Sun).

Sights & Activities

King Island Dairy (☎ 1800 004 950, 03-6462 1348; www .kidairy.com.au; North Rd, Loorana; ☺ noon-4.30pm Sun-Fri Oct-Apr, noon-4.30pm Sun-Tue, Thu & Fri May-Sep), 8km north of Currie (just beyond the airport), has free tastings and cheap cheese sales.

The **King Island Historical Museum** (☎ 03-6462 1572; Lighthouse St, Currie; adult/child $4/1; ☺ noon-4.30pm Sun-Fri Oct-Apr, noon-4.30pm Sun-Tue, Thu & Fri May-Sep), inside the former lighthouse-keeper's cottage, features maritime and local history displays, including remnants of maritime disasters (casually displayed on the floor) and absorbing newspaper accounts of the Grassy mine closure.

Kelp Industries Pty Ltd (☎ 03-6462 1340; www .kelpind.com.au; 89 Netherby Rd, Currie; ☺ 8am-4pm Mon-Fri) processes bull kelp seaweed for export to Scotland for alginate extraction. See the kelp drying on racks by the roadside, or duck into the visitor centre for more info.

King Island's four **lighthouses** illuminate the treacherous coastline. The 48m Cape Wickham lighthouse is the southern hemisphere's tallest; the others are at Currie, Stokes Point and south of Naracoopa. **Diving** among the local marine life and shipwrecks is highly recommended, as is **swimming** at deserted beaches and freshwater lagoons, **surfing** and **fishing** from Naracoopa jetty. There are established bush and coastal **walks** here too, including a 20-minute return stroll to the **calcified forest** in the south. King Island **wildlife** is ridiculously healthy; don't miss the **fairy penguin colony** on Grassy breakwater.

Tours

King Island Dive Charter (☎ 03-6461 1133) Single boat dives for $75, plus good-value three- to seven-day packages (including dives on the *Cataraqui* wreck).

Sleeping & Eating

Bass Caravan Park & Cabins (☎ 03-6462 1168; dino john@bigpond.com; 100 Main St, Currie; on-site van/cabin $45/100) KI's only budget option is this doleful little park with a clutch of weary en suite caravans and newer self-contained two-bedroom cabins.

King Island Hotel (☎ 03-6462 1633; www.kingisland hotel.com.au; 7 Main St, Currie; d incl breakfast $125) Also known as Parer's, this double-storey cream-brick hotel was built on the site of the grand old pub that burnt down in 1964. It's clean and central with motel-style suites. There's a sports bar and pokies. The main bar has a large open fireplace and bang-up counter meals (mains $16 to $29).

Devil's Gap Retreat & Craypot Cottage (☎ 03-6462 1180, 0429 621 180; www.kingisland.net.au/~devilsgap; Charles St, Currie; d $100-130) These weathered, one-bedroom cottages on the foreshore 1km northwest of Currie are KI's best place to stay. They're self-contained with ceiling-high stone hearths, open fires and tubs that spy the ocean. The decor is rustic and eclectic (they're owned by a local artist) and the price includes breakfast provisions. Craypot Cottage, in central Currie, is another arty, comfortable option.

Boathouse (☎ 0429 621 180; Lighthouse Rd, Currie; ☽ 24hr) This weather-beaten old boathouse on Currie Harbour has been turned into a free, artsy 'restaurant with no food' – you bring the edibles and wine; the plates, cutlery and glasses are in the cupboard.

Nautilus Coffee Lounge (☎ 03-6462 1868; Edward St, Currie; mains $5-18; ☽ breakfast & lunch Mon-Sat) Nautilus is your best bet for a near-decent coffee and a big island breakfast. Ponder the local art on the crimson walls as you chow into a feta-and-scrambled-egg croissant with orange mustard dressing ($16).

Grassy Club (☎ 03-6461 1341; Main Rd, Grassy; mains $18-25; ☽ lunch Thu-Sun, dinner Wed-Mon) The chef in the restaurant here can be hit-and-miss, but at least he's ambitious. Expect creative mains utilising produce from around the island (often involving cheese) served attentively in discreet surrounds. The bar next door is perfect for a beer.

Getting There & Away

Flying is the only way to access King Island. **Regional Express** (REX; ☎ 13 17 13; www.regionalexpress .com.au) flies from Melbourne, as does **King Island Airlines** (☎ 03-9580 3777; www.kingislandair.com.au) – the latter flies to/from the small Moorabbin airport in Melbourne's southeast. Return flights cost from $290.

Tasair (☎ 1800 062 900, 03-6248 5088; www.tasair .com.au) flies from Devonport and Burnie/ Wynyard to King Island ($440 return from both destinations).

Getting Around

There's no public transport on the island. Car-hire companies will meet you at the airport; bookings are essential. **Cheapa Car Rental**

(☎ 03-6462 1603; kicars@kingisland.net.au; 1 Netherby Rd, Currie) and **King Island Car Rental** (☎ 1800 777 282, 03-6462 1282; kicars@bigpond.com; 2 Meech St, Currie) both have cars from around $65 per day.

FLINDERS ISLAND

pop 860

Flush with natural wonderments, Flinders Island is the largest of the Furneaux Group's 52 islands. First charted in 1798 by British salt Matthew Flinders, the Furneaux Group became a base for the Straitsmen who slaughtered seals in their tens of thousands. Like King Island, Flinders is strewn with shipwrecks, 68 vessels having come to grief here.

The most tragic part of Flinders Island's history, however, was its role in the near-annihilation of Tasmania's Aboriginal people between 1829 and 1834. Of the 135 survivors who were forcibly removed from the Tasmanian mainland to Wybalenna to be 'civilised and educated', only 47 survivors made the journey back to Oyster Cove near Hobart in 1847.

The island runs rampant with wildlife, especially birds, the most famous of which is the Cape Barren Goose.

Whitemark, the main town, is on the west coast. Lady Barron in the south is the main fishing area and deep-water port. Plan your visit with help from the **Flinders Island Area Marketing & Development Office** (☎ 1800 994 477, 03-6359 2380; www.flindersislandonline.com.au). On the island the **Flinders Island visitor information centre** (☎ 03-6359 2160; 6 Patrick St, Whitemark; ☽ 10am-4pm Mon-Fri) provides the local low-down. Another useful website is www.focusonflinders.com .au. There are no ATMs on the island, but there's a Westpac Bank agency and most businesses have Eftpos facilities.

Sights & Activities

Today, all that remains of the sad settlement at **Wybalenna** are the cemetery and chapel, restored by the National Trust. In 1999 the site was returned to the descendants of the Indigenous people who lived there.

Nearby at Emita is the engrossing **Furneaux Museum** (☎ 03-6359 2010; fax 6359 2026; adult/child $4/ free; ☽ 1-5pm daily Dec-Feb, 1-4pm Sat & Sun Mar-Nov), housing a variety of Aboriginal artefacts (including beautiful shell necklaces), sealing and shipwreck relics, and a display on the seasonal mutton-birding industry.

Visitors love to stamp up the 756m-high Mt Strzelecki in **Strzelecki National Park** (www .parks.tas.gov.au). The walk starts 12km south of Whitemark on Trousers Point Rd, from where you point your trousers up the well-signposted track (four to five hours return). The views from the top are gob-smacking. Mt Strzelecki is one of the peaks in the Three Peaks Race (p684).

There are some brilliant, footprint-free **beaches** around the island (particularly the west coast – don't miss Trousers Point), and easily accessible **scuba diving** sites off the northern and western coasts. Rock and beach **fishing** keeps the locals entertained year-round.

Tours
Flinders Island Adventures (☎ 03-6359 4507; www .flindersisland.com.au) Arranges fishing charters, evening mutton bird viewing cruises (December to March, $35), 4WD tours (half- or full-day $100/166 per person) and other customised touring options.

Sleeping & Eating
Flinders Island Cabin Park (☎ 03-6359 2188; www. flindersislandcp.com.au; 1 Bluff Rd; campsites for 2 $14, cabins $35, d $60-95, extra person $15) Close to the airport, this park is about 4km north of Whitemark. Eight family-sized, quality cabins are on offer, some with private bathroom and all with cooker and TV. The friendly owner also has cars ($66 per day) and bikes ($25 per day) for rent.

Interstate Hotel (☎ 03-6359 2114; interstatehotel@ trump.net.au; Patrick St; s $22-65, d $38-95, all incl cooked breakfast) In the centre of Whitemark is this amenable pub, built in 1911 and renovated in Federation green and burgundy, with no-frills budget rooms (shared facilities). Better rooms have private shower and TV. Its dining room serves a range of well-priced lunches and dinners, with the usual array of pub grub on offer and a natural emphasis on local seafood.

Furneaux Tavern (☎ 03-6359 3521; www.focuson flinders.com.au/tavern; Franklin Pde; s/d $80/110, extra person $30) The local drinking hole has 10 spacey, timber-panelled motel cabins with wrap-around decks, set in native gardens behind the bar-restaurant. Each has en suite, TV, fridge, kettle and toaster (continental breakfast provisions cost extra). Note that some road signage still refers to this place as the Flinders Island Lodge. Filling bar meals include the wallaby burgers and steak sandwiches, and the Shearwater restaurant menu has daily specials for the locavore: fish (perhaps ling), scallops or lamb.

Flinders Island Bakery (☎ 03-6359 2105; 4 Lagoon Rd, Whitemark; sandwiches & pies $3-6; ☉ 8.30am-5pm Mon-Fri) The only decent coffee on the island is at the only bakery. Try a wallaby and red-wine pie or pick up some preservative-free bread made with rainwater. Open on weekends in summer.

Walkers Supermarket (☎ 03-6359 2010; Patrick St, Whitemark; ☉ 9am-5.30pm Mon-Fri, 9am-noon Sat, 1-5pm Sun) and the general stores in Lady Barron and Killiecrankie are all open daily.

Getting There & Away
AIR
Airlines of Tasmania (☎ 1800 144 460, 03-6359 2312; www.airtasmania.com.au) flies daily between Launceston and Flinders Island ($320 return), as well as from Moorabbin in Melbourne three times a week ($430 return).

BOAT
Southern Shipping Company (☎ 03-6356 3333; www.southernshipping.com.au; Main St Bridport; ☉ 8am-4.30pm Mon-Fri) operates a weekly ferry (departing Monday) from Bridport in Tasmania's Northeast to Flinders Island; the ferry continues to Port Welshpool in Victoria on demand. A return trip to Flinders Island costs $97 per person (transporting a vehicle costs from $515 to $930 (including driver). The journey takes 8½ hours one way. Bookings essential (at least four weeks in advance).

Getting Around
There's no public transport on the island. Car-hire companies will meet you at the airport; bookings are essential. **Flinders Island Car Rentals** (☎ 03-6359 2168; flindersislandcarrentals@hotmail.com; 21 Memana Rd, Whitemark) has sedans and minivans from $66 to $110 per day.

South Australia

The driest state on the driest continent, South Australia (SA) beats the heat by celebrating life's finer things: fine landscapes, fine festivals, fine food, and (...OK, forget the other three) fine wine. SA isn't an automatic 'must see' on everyone's list – rather, the state has a 'secret' status the locals are only too happy about.

Start your explorations along the sea-salty Limestone Coast. To the north, the Murray River curls Mississippi-like towards the sea; to the northwest, the Fleurieu Peninsula is a decadent weekender for Adelaidians, with Kangaroo Island's wildlife, forests and seafood not far offshore. Adelaide remains near Australia's cultural high-water mark – a chilled-out, gracious city with world-class festivals, restaurants and a hedonistic arts scene: pubs and eat-streets abound. A day trip away, the Barossa and Clare Valleys are self-assured viticulture success stories.

Looking like mini-Italy on the map, Yorke Peninsula makes for a beachy, slow-paced detour. Further west, Gargantuan Eyre Peninsula is fringed with oyster farms and fishing towns, and offers some truly amazing encounters with SA's underwater residents. Wheeling into the Flinders Ranges, wheat fields give way to arid cattle stations beneath russet peaks. Continuing north, the Stuart Hwy tracks across the dead-flat desert, eccentric outback towns like Woomera and Coober Pedy emerging from the heat-haze.

So wind your watch back 30 minutes and slip into SA time. Crowd-free and relaxed, SA makes a perfect escape from the east coast frenzy.

HIGHLIGHTS

- Sniff out the ripest cheese, fullest fruit and strongest coffee at Adelaide's **Central Market** (p729)
- Trundle past pelicans, dunes and lagoons in **Coorong National Park** (p764)
- Watch the little **penguins** (p759) waddle on Kangaroo Island
- Slurp down a dozen briny oysters and watch passing whales at **Coffin Bay** (p790)
- Noodle for opals in the moonscape mullock at **Coober Pedy** (p804)
- Swirl, nose and quaff your way through the wine regions **McLaren Vale** (p750), **Barossa Valley** (p775), **Clare Valley** (p780), **Coonawarra** (p768) and **Adelaide Hills** (p744)
- Kick back with a cold schooner or two in **Adelaide's pubs** (p740)
- Hike up to the lofty, desolate rim of **Wilpena Pound** (p797) in the Flinders Ranges

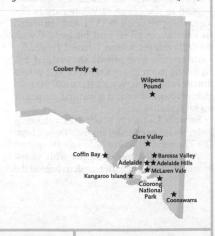

- Coober Pedy ★
- Wilpena Pound ★
- Clare Valley ★
- Coffin Bay ★
- Barossa Valley ★
- Adelaide ★★ Adelaide Hills
- ★ McLaren Vale
- Kangaroo Island ★
- Coorong National Park
- Coonawarra ★

| ▪ TELEPHONE CODE: 08 | ▪ POPULATION: 1.6 MILLION | ▪ AREA: 984,400 SQ KM |

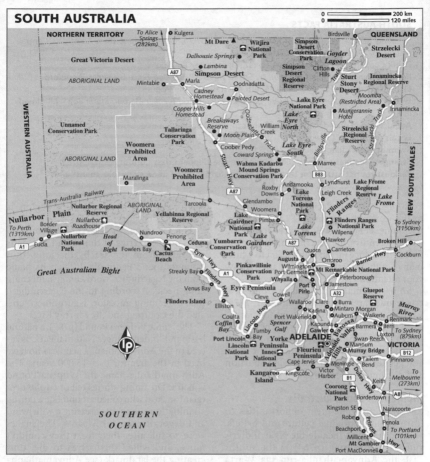

SOUTH AUSTRALIA

HISTORY

South Australia was declared a province on 28 December 1836, when the first British colonists landed at Holdfast Bay. The first governor, Captain John Hindmarsh, named the state capital Adelaide, after the wife of the British monarch, William IV. While the eastern states struggled with the stigma of convict society, SA's colonists were free citizens – a fact to which many South Australians will happily draw your attention.

The founders based the colony on a utopian 19th-century ideal of social engineering. Land was sold at set prices by the British government to help establish mainly young, skilled married couples; the concept was that equal numbers of men and women, free from reli-

gious and political persecution, would create an egalitarian new order.

Between 1838 and 1841, 800 German farmers and artisans (many persecuted Lutherans from Prussia) arrived and settled Hahndorf in the Adelaide Hills – now the best preserved German village in the state. Many more followed over the next decade, bringing vine cuttings with them – SA's famous vineyards began to take root.

The young colony's early progress was slow – only British government funds saved it from bankruptcy – but it became self-supporting by the mid-1840s and self-governing by 1856. Following the successful crossing of the continent by local explorers, SA won the contract to lay the Overland Telegraph from

SOUTH AUSTRALIA

SOUTH AUSTRALIA FACTS

Eat King George Whiting from Kangaroo Island (p760), fresh produce from Adelaide's Central Market (p729), Eyre Peninsula oysters (p790)

Drink Coopers beer, McLaren Vale Shiraz, Clare Valley Riesling

Read *All Things Bright and Beautiful* by Susan Mitchell, *The Dog Fence* by James Woodford

Listen to 'Adelaide' by Paul Kelly, 'South Australia' by the Pogues

Watch *Priscilla, Queen of the Desert; Gallipoli; Pitch Black; Breaker Morant; Storm Boy* – all filmed in SA

Avoid Wearing an Adelaide Crows T-shirt in Port Adelaide

Locals' nickname Croweaters

Swim at Carrickalinga Beach (p753)

Strangest festival Kernewek Lowender (aka the Copper Coast Cornish Festival; p785)

Tackiest tourist attraction Larry the Lobster (p764) – one of SA's few 'big' tourist lures

---

Port Augusta to Darwin, connecting Australia to the world by telegram (1872), and later, telephone. Following a long recession in the late 19th century, the government became the first to introduce income tax – a fact to which many South Australians are hesitant to draw your attention…

SA has maintained its socially progressive creed: trade unions were legalised in 1876; women were permitted to stand for parliament in 1894; and the state was one of the first places in the world to give women the vote and the first state in Australia to outlaw racial and gender discrimination, legalise abortion and decriminalise gay sex.

Indigenous South Australia

SA offers up some great opportunities to learn about Aboriginal culture and beliefs. Some of the best include the Ngarrindjeri-run Camp Coorong (p764) in the southeast; the Adnyamathanha-run Iga Warta (p800) in the Flinders Ranges; and the Yorke Peninsula cultural tours run by Adjahdura Land (p784). In Adelaide there's Tandanya National Aboriginal Cultural Institute (p727); the Australian Aboriginal Cultures Gallery in the South Australian Museum (p727); and the Indigenous-run Bookabee Tours (p734).

SA's best-known Aboriginal language is Pitjantjatjara (also known as Pitjantjara), which is spoken throughout the Anangu-Pitjantjarjara Aboriginal Lands of northern SA, down almost to the Great Australian Bight. The traditional language of the Adelaide area is Kaurna. Many Kaurna-derived place names have survived around the city: Aldinga comes from *Ngultingga*, Onkaparinga from *Ngangkiparringga*, and Noarlunga from

Nurlungga. The Adelaide Hills region is Peramangk country.

The Coorong, in Ngarrindjeri country, is a complex series of dunes and salt pans separated from the sea by the long, thin Younghusband Peninsula. It takes its name from the Ngarrindjeri word *kurangh*, meaning 'long neck'. According to the Ngarrindjeri, their Dreaming ancestor, Ngurundjeri, created the Coorong and the Murray River.

The iconic Wilpena Pound (p797), a natural basin in Flinders Ranges National Park, is sacred to the Adnyamathanha people, who have lived in the area for over 15,000 years. The Adnyamathanha name for Wilpena Pound is Ikara. Dreaming stories tell of two *akurra* (giant snakes) who coiled around Ikara during an initiation ceremony, creating a whirlwind and devouring the participants. The snakes were so full after their feast they couldn't move, and willed themselves to die, thus creating the landmark (see Adnyamathanha Dreaming, p799).

In 1966, SA became the first state to grant Aboriginal people title to their land. In the early '80s most of the land west of the Stuart Hwy and north of the railway to Perth was transferred to Aboriginal ownership. Cultural clashes still occur, exemplified by the politically and culturally divisive Hindmarsh Bridge controversy in the 1990s, which pitted Aboriginal beliefs against development (see Building Bridges (Not…), p755).

GEOGRAPHY & CLIMATE

SA's population is thin on the ground – over 80% of locals live in Adelaide and a handful of mid-sized rural centres. The state's agricultural regions are clustered around the south and in the Murray River irrigation belt. Further north and west the terrain becomes increasingly dry and inhospitable; the outback (more than 75% of the state) is semideserted semidesert. The only hills of any altitude are the Mt Lofty and Flinders ranges – a continuous spine running 800km from southeast of Adelaide into the interior.

The state's biggest river is the mighty Murray, which rises in the Australian Alps and spills into the sea near Lake Alexandrina. The state's low rainfall has necessitated Murray water being piped over huge distances to many communities, including Adelaide: around 90% of South Australians depend either wholly or partly on the Murray for their water supply. The ongoing deterioration of the Murray's water quality and flow is a massive problem.

SA has a Mediterranean climate: hot, dry summers and cool winters, with most rain falling between May and August. It gets hotter than a red-hot chilli pepper in the outback in summer, with daily maximums regularly topping 40°C.

INFORMATION

Department of Environment & Heritage (DEH; Map p728; ☎ 08-8463 3999; www.environment.sa.gov .au; Level 1, 100 Pirie St; ◔ 9am-5pm Mon-Fri) Maps and comprehensive parks information.

Royal Automobile Association of South Australia (RAA; Map p728; ☎ 08-8202 4600; www.raa.net; 55 Hindmarsh Sq; ◔ 8.30am-5pm Mon-Fri, 9am-noon Sat) Auto advice and plenty of maps.

South Australian Visitor & Travel Centre (SATC; Map p728; ☎ 1300 655 276; www.southaustralia.com; 18 King William St; ◔ 8.30am-5pm Mon-Fri, 9am-2pm Sat & Sun) Abundantly stocked with leaflets and publications on Adelaide and SA. Super-patient staff and event ticketing, too.

NATIONAL PARKS

Around 22% of SA's land area is under some form of official conservation management, including national parks, recreation parks, wildlife reserves, waterways and regional reserves. The largest areas are in the outback. Flinders Chase National Park (p762) on Kangaroo Island, Flinders Ranges National Park (p797) and the Great Australian Bight Marine Park (p792) are some of Australia's better-known national parks.

The **Department of Environment & Heritage** (www.environment.sa.gov.au) manages the state's

conservation areas and sells park passes and camping permits. A 'Two Month Holiday Pass' ($30 per vehicle; $50 including camping) covers entry to most SA parks, excluding the desert parks and Flinders Chase on Kangaroo Island.

ACTIVITIES

With hills, beaches, forests, deserts and wide open spaces, there's pretty much nothing you can't do in SA (well, apart from skiing…). The **South Australian Trails** (www.southaustraliantrails .com) website is chockers with activities info, including horse riding, canoeing, bushwalking, cycling and diving, with safety tips, maps and useful links.

Bushwalking

SA's national parks and conservation areas have thousands of kilometres of marked trails traversing eye-popping wilderness. Around Adelaide there are walks to suit all abilities in the Mt Lofty Ranges, including trails in **Belair National Park** (Map p724; www .environment.sa.gov.au/parks/sanpr/belair) and **Morialta Conservation Park** (Map p745; www.environment.sa.gov .au/parks/sanpr/morialta).

In the Flinders Ranges there are outstanding walks in Mt Remarkable National Park (p795) and Flinders Ranges National Park (p798), and further north in Arkaroola Wilderness Sanctuary (p800).

Canoeing & Sailing

Abundant wildlife, good fishing, gorgeous scenery and quiet places to camp make the Murray River (p770) and Coorong (p764) primo canoeing spots. **Canoe South Australia** (☎ 08-8240 3294; www.canoesa.asn.au) lists clubs, equipment and events.

There's breezy sailing all along Adelaide's Gulf St Vincent shoreline; **Yachting South Australia** (☎ 08-8410 2117; www.sa.yachting.org.au) provides contacts for all SA sailing clubs, courses and boat-shaped events.

Diving

This ain't the Great Barrier Reef, but SA's underwater world sustains a great diversity of life. Don your flippers and tanks and check out leafy sea-dragons, seals, nudibranchs, sponge beds, dolphins and endemic species.

Off the Gulf St Vincent coast, top dive sites include Second Valley, Rapid Bay jetty, Cape Jervis and the ex-destroyer **HMAS Hobart**

TAKE THE LONG WAY HOME

South Australia has three fabulous long-distance trails for hiking and cycling:

- **Heysen Trail** (Map p745; www.heysentrail.asn.au) Australia's longest walking trail: 1200km between Cape Jervis on the Fleurieu Peninsula and Parachilna Gorge in the Flinders Ranges. Access points along the way make it ideal for half- and full-day walks. Note that due to fire restrictions, some sections of the trail are closed between December and April.
- **Kidman Trail** (www.kidmantrail.org.au) A 10-section cycling and walking trail between Willunga on the Fleurieu Peninsula and Kapunda north of the Barossa Valley.
- **Mawson Trail** (www.southaustraliantrails.com) A 900km bike trail between Adelaide and Blinman in the Flinders Ranges, via the Adelaide Hills and Clare Valley.

(Map p750; www.diveexhmashobart.com), which was scuttled off Yankalilla Bay in 2002. Pick up a permit from **South Coast Surf** (☎ 08-8558 2822; fax 08-8558 2822; 2/79 Main Rd, Normanville; per dive $12; ✦ seasonal). The **Court House Café** (☎ 08-8558 3532; courthousecafe@optusnet.com.au; 52 Main St, Normanville; s/d $70/80; ☐) has basic diver accommodation in old jail buildings and hires dive gear.

Other good dive sites include the Yorke Peninsula jetties and the reefs off Port Lincoln. Cave diving around Mt Gambier is also fantastic. The **Scuba Divers Federation of SA** (www.sdfsa .net) website has details.

Rock Climbing

Rock spiders keen on 10m to 15m cliffs can clamber over the gorges in Morialta Conservation Park and Onkaparinga River Recreation Park, both on the outskirts of Adelaide. More advanced climbers should head for the Flinders Ranges. SA's premier cliff is at Moonarie on the southeastern side of Wilpena Pound – 120m cliffs! Buckaringa Gorge, close to Quorn and Hawker, is another fave for the more daring. Contact the **Climbing Club of South Australia** (www.climbingclubsouthaustralia .asn.au) for more info.

Swimming & Surfing

Uncrowded, white-sand swimming beaches stretch right along the SA coast; the safest for swimming are along the Gulf St Vincent (p752) and Spencer Gulf coasts. Anywhere exposed to the Southern Ocean and the Backstairs Passage (between Kangaroo Island and the mainland) may have strong rips and undertows. If you're after that all-over-tan look, head for the nudie southern end of Maslin Beach (p752), 40km south of Adelaide.

The SA coast is consistently pummelled by rolling Southern Ocean swells. Pennington

Bay (p758) has the most consistent surf on Kangaroo Island, while Pondalowie Bay (p787) on the Yorke Peninsula has the state's strongest breaks. Other hot-spots are scattered between Port Lincoln on the Eyre Peninsula and the famous Cactus Beach (p792) in the far west. Closer to Adelaide, Port Elliot (p754) and Middleton have some wicked surf, with swells often holding at 3m; other gnarly breaks are Waitpinga Beach and Parsons Beach, 12km southwest of Victor Harbor.

The best surfing season is March to June, when the northerlies doth blow. See www .southaustralia.com/fleurieupeninsulasurfing .aspx for info, and www.surfsouthoz.com for surf reports.

You can learn to surf (around $40 including gear) with the following companies: **South Coast Surf Academy** (☎ 0414 341 545; www .danosurf.com.au) **Surf & Sun Safaris** (☎ 1800 786 386; www.surfnsun .com.au)

Whale Watching

Between July and September, migrating southern right whales cruise within a few hundred metres of SA shores as they head to/from their Great Australian Bight breeding grounds. Once prolific, southern right whales suffered unrestrained slaughter during the 19th century, which reduced the whale population from 100,000 to just a few hundred by 1935. Although an endangered species, they are fighting back and the population worldwide may now be as high as 7000.

Key spots for whale watching include Victor Harbor (p753), Port Lincoln, and Head of Bight (p792) on the far west coast. To find out about current whale action call ☎ 1900 931 223, or contact the South Australian Whale Centre (p753) in Victor Harbor.

TOURS

Whatever your persuasion or destination, there's probably a SA tour to suit you. See p734 for details on tours in and around Adelaide, including day trips to the Adelaide Hills, Fleurieu Peninsula, Murray River and the Barossa and Clare Valleys.

Further afield, outback tours usually include the Flinders Ranges and Coober Pedy, some continuing north to Alice Springs and Uluru in the Northern Territory (NT). Operators include:

Groovy Grape (☎ 1800 661 177, 08-8371 4000; www .groovygrape.com.au) Three days, Melbourne–Adelaide ($345) along the Great Ocean Rd; and seven days, Adelaide–Alice Springs ($865) via the Flinders Ranges, Coober Pedy and Uluru. Includes meals, camping and national park entry fees. Small groups.

Heading Bush (☎ 1800 639 933, 08-8356 5501; www .headingbush.com) Rugged, small-group, 10-day Adelaide–Alice Springs expeditions (with/without VIP or YHA $1470/1595) are all-inclusive. Tours include the Flinders Ranges, Coober Pedy, Simpson Desert, Aboriginal communities, Uluru and West MacDonnell Ranges.

Swagabout Tours (☎ 0408 845 378; www.swagabout tours.com.au) Dependable tours with the option of staying in hotels or camping under the stars. Adelaide–Alice Springs trips (five-/seven-/nine-/10-day tours camping $1350/1850/2400/2690, hotels $1920/2675/3450/3850) take in the Clare Valley, Flinders Ranges, Oodnadatta Track, Dalhousie Springs and Uluru. It also runs one-/two-day Clare Valley trips ($120/440).

Wayward Bus (☎ 1300 653 510, 08-8132 8230; www .waywardbus.com.au) Wide range of backpacker-style bus tours around SA and interstate, including trips from Adelaide to Alice Springs, Uluru, Kangaroo Island and the Great Ocean Rd.

GETTING THERE & AROUND
Air

International, interstate and regional flights service **Adelaide Airport** (Map p724; ☎ 08-8308 9211; www.aal.com.au), 7km west of the city centre. The usual car-rental suspects all have desks here.

Around the state, **Regional Express** (Rex; ☎ 13 17 13; www.regionalexpress.com.au) flies between Adelaide and Kingscote on Kangaroo Island ($90), Coober Pedy ($200), Ceduna ($165), Mt Gambier ($130), Port Lincoln (from $110) and Whyalla ($110). Special fares can be as low as 30% of the price of fully flexible fares.

Bus

Buses are usually the cheapest way of getting from A to B in SA, and the bus companies have more comprehensive networks than the rail system. Adelaide's new **Central Bus Station** (Map p728; 85 Franklin St) has ticket offices and terminals for all major interstate and statewide services. For online bus timetables see the **Bus SA** (www.bussa.com.au) website; see individual destination sections for regional services.

Major operators:

Firefly Express (☎ 1300 730 740; www.fireflyexpress .com.au) Buses from Adelaide to Melbourne ($50, 11 hours, two daily), continuing to Sydney ($110, 24 hours, one daily).

Greyhound Australia (☎ 1300 473 946; www.grey hound.com.au) Services between Adelaide and Melbourne (from $50, 11 hours, two daily), Sydney (from $140, 24 hours, three daily) and Alice Springs ($260, 21 hours, one daily) continuing to Darwin ($560, 42 hours).

Premier Stateliner (☎ 08-8415 5555; www.premier stateliner.com.au) State-wide bus services.

V/Line (☎ 13 61 96, 03-9697 2076; www.vline.com.au) Bus and bus/train services between Adelaide and Melbourne (from $45, 12 hours, three daily).

Car & Motorcycle

Get your camera ready if you're driving between Adelaide and Melbourne. Make sure you go via the **Great Ocean Road** (www.greatoceanrd .org.au) between Torquay and Warrnambool in Victoria – one of the best coastal drives in the world, with awesome views and more twists and turns than a Hitchcock plot.

To hitch a ride (sharing petrol costs) or buy a secondhand car, check out hostel notice-boards (see also p1071).

Train

Interstate trains grind into the recently tarted-up **Adelaide Parklands Terminal** (Map p728; ☎ 13 21 47; www.gsr.com.au; Railway Tce, Keswick), 1km south-west of the city centre. **Skylink** (☎ 08-8413 6196; www.skylinkadelaide.com; adult/child one-way $5/3) runs from the city to Adelaide Parklands Terminal en route to the airport; bookings are essential for all city pick-up locations other than the Central Bus Station.

The following trains depart from Adelaide regularly:

The Ghan To Alice Springs (seat/sleeper $355/720, 19 hours)
The Ghan To Darwin ($710/1440, 47 hours)
The Indian Pacific To Perth ($395/1020, 39 hours)
The Indian Pacific To Sydney ($295/500, 25 hours)
The Overland To Melbourne ($94/152, 11 hours)

The *Ghan* and *Indian Pacific* also offer a scenic way to get from Adelaide to Port Augusta (from $22, 4½ hours). The fastest service between Sydney and Adelaide (around 21 hours) is Speedlink run by **V/Line** (☎ 13 61 96; www.vline .com.au) – you travel from Sydney to Albury ($72) on the XPT train, then from Albury to Adelaide ($43) on a V/Line bus.

ADELAIDE

pop 1.17 million

Sophisticated, cultured, neat casual – this is the self-image Adelaide projects, a nod to the days of free colonisation without the 'penal colony' taint. Adelaidians may remind you of their convict-free status, but the city's stuffy, affluent origins did more to inhibit development than promote it. Bogged down in the old-school doldrums and painfully short on charisma, this was a pious, introspective place. As Paul Kelly sang in 'Adelaide':

> Find me a bar or a girl or guitar
> Where do you go on a Saturday night?
> …And the streets are so wide, everybody's inside
> Sitting in the same chairs they were sitting in last year.

But even Paul would admit that these days – thanks in part to progressive '70s premier Don Dunstan, who wore pink shorts to parliament – things are much improved. Multicultural flavours infuse Adelaide's restaurants; there's a pumping pub, arts and live-music scene; and

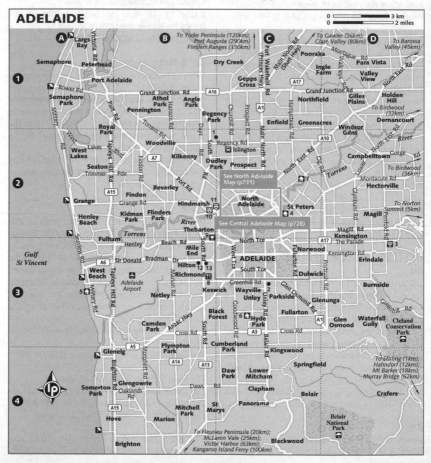

ADELAIDE

the city's festival calendar has vanquished dull Saturday nights. And, of course, there's the local wine. Residents flush with hedonism at the prospect of a punchy McLaren Vale Shiraz or summer-scented Clare Riesling.

That said, a subtle conservatism remains. 'What school did you go to?' is a common salvo from those unsure of your place in the social hierarchy, while countercultural urges bubble up through Adelaide's countless sex shops, kung-fu dojos and canyon-sized bottle shops.

Just down the tram tracks is beachy Glenelg, Adelaide with its guard down and boardshorts up; and Port Adelaide, a historic enclave fast developing into SA's version of Fremantle. Inland, Adelaide's winking plains rise to the Adelaide Hills, just 12 minutes up the freeway. The Hills' gorgeous valley folds, old-fangled towns and cool-climate vineyards are all close at hand.

ORIENTATION
Adelaide's rectangular city grid is bordered by North, East, South and West Tces. King William St dissects the city north–south; most cross streets change names here. Victoria Sq, the city's geographical centre, has bus stops and the Glenelg tram terminus. Franklin St, west of Victoria Sq, has Adelaide's regional bus station.

Heading north, King William St becomes King William Rd and crosses the River Torrens then rises into elevated North Adelaide. In the

East End, Rundle St is Adelaide's social epicentre, dotted with restaurants, bookshops, retro-chic boutiques and independent cinemas. Heading west Rundle St becomes Rundle Mall, the main shopping strip, then Hindley St in the West End, with its grungy ramble of bars, clubs and strip joints.

See p744 for city access details from the airport and interstate train station.

Maps
The free maps from the South Australian Visitor & Travel Centre (p721) are fine for navigating your way around central Adelaide.

For more detailed maps:

Map Shop (Map p728; ☎ 08-8231 2033; www.map shop.net.au; 6-10 Peel St; 🕑 9am-5.30pm Mon-Fri, to 12.30pm Sat) Maps, charts and guides for walking, hiking and touring, plus GPS sales and advice.

Royal Automobile Association of South Australia (p721) RAA, Hema and Westprint maps.

INFORMATION
Bookshops
Dymocks Booksellers (Map p728; ☎ 08-8223 5380; 135 Rundle Mall; 🕑 9am-6pm Mon-Thu, to 9pm Fri, to 5.30pm Sat, 11am-5pm Sun) Mainstream books and mags.

Imprints Booksellers (Map p728; ☎ 08-8231 4454; www.imprints.com.au; 107 Hindley St; 🕑 9am-6pm Mon, Tue & Sat, to 9pm Wed-Fri, 11am-6pm Sun) Jazz, floorboards, Persian rugs and the best books in print.

Mary Martin Bookshop (Map p728; ☎ 08-8359 3525; www.marymartin.com.au; 249 Rundle St; 🕑 10am-late) Adelaide's oldest bookshop (since 1945).

Emergency
Ambulance (☎ emergency 000, non-emergency 13 29 62; www.saambulance.com.au)

Fire (☎ emergency 000, non-emergency 08-8204 3600; www.samfs.sa.gov.au)

Lifeline (☎ 13 11 14; www.lifeline.org.au; 🕑 24hr)

Police (Map p728; ☎ emergency 000, non-emergency 08-8303 0525; www.sapolice.sa.gov.au; 26 Hindley St; 🕑 24hr)

RAA Emergency Roadside Assistance (☎ 13 11 11; www.raa.net)

Internet Access
Arena Internet Café (Map p728; ☎ 08-8223 3481; upstairs, 264 Rundle St; 🕑 11am-midnight Mon-Thu, 10am-late Fri-Sun)

State Library of South Australia (Map p728; ☎ 08-8207 7250; www.slsa.sa.gov.au; 1st fl, cnr North Tce & Kintore Ave; 🕑 10am-8pm Mon-Wed & Fri, to 6pm Thu & Fri, to 5pm Sat & Sun) Free access; book ahead.

SIGHTS & ACTIVITIES	
Coopers Brewery	1 B2
Haigh's Chocolates Visitors Centre	2 C3
Penfolds Magill Estate Winery	3 D3

SLEEPING 🏠	
Adelaide Caravan Park	4 C2
Adelaide Shores Caravan Resort	5 A3
Jasper Motor Inn	6 C3
Levi Park Caravan Park	7 C2

EATING 🍴	
Café de Vili's	8 B3

DRINKING 🍷	
Wheatsheaf	9 B2

ENTERTAINMENT 🎭	
Adelaide Entertainment Centre	10 B2
Governor Hindmarsh Hotel	11 B2

TRANSPORT	
Acacia Car Rentals	12 B3
Cut Price Car & Truck Rentals	13 B3
Koala Car Rentals	(see 13)

ADELAIDE IN...

Two Days

If you're here at Festival, WOMADelaide or Fringe time, lap it up. Otherwise, kick-start your day at the **Central Market** (p729) then wander through the **Botanic Gardens** (p730), finishing up at the **National Wine Centre** (p730). After a few bohemian beers at the **Exeter Hotel** (p740), have a ritzy dinner on **Rundle St** (p738). Next day, visit the **South Australian Museum** (opposite) and the **Bradman Collection Museum** (p730). Check out **Tandanya National Aboriginal Cultural Institute** (opposite) before riding the tram to **Glenelg** (p730) for an evening swim, and fish and chips on the sand.

Four Days

Follow the two-day itinerary – perhaps slotting in the **Art Gallery of South Australia** (opposite) and **Jam Factory Craft & Design Centre** (opposite) – then pack a picnic basket of Central Market produce and day trip out to the nearby **Adelaide Hills** (p744), **McLaren Vale** (p750) or **Barossa** (p775) wine regions. Next day, truck out to the museums and historic centre of **Port Adelaide** (p731), then catch a band at the **Grace Emily Hotel** (p740) back in the city, before dinner on **Gouger St** (p738).

Wireless Café (Map p728; ☎ 08-8212 1266; 53 Hindley St; ☺ 7am-8pm Mon-Fri, from 9am Sat & Sun, open later Dec-Feb)

Media

Adelaide's daily tabloid is the parochial *Advertiser*, though the *Age*, *Australian* and *Financial Review* are also widely available. The free fortnightly **Adelaide Review** (www .adelaidereview.com.au) has highbrow articles, plus culture and arts sections. The *Independent* comes out on Sunday (including articles from the UK paper of the same name). **Rip it Up** (www. ripitup.com.au) and **dB** (ww.dbmagazine.com.au) are the local street mags, loaded with music info. **Blaze** (www.blaze.e-p.net.au) is the local gay-and-lesbian street press.

Medical Services

Corner Chemist (Map p728; ☎ 08-8231 2460; www .cornerchemist.com.au; cnr Pirie & King William Sts; ☺ 7.45am-5.30pm Mon-Fri)

Emergency Dental Service (☎ Mon-Fri 08-8222 822, Sat, Sun & after hours 08-8272 8111)

Royal Adelaide Hospital (Map p728; ☎ 08-8222 4000; www.rah.sa.gov.au; 275 North Tce; ☺ 24hr) Emergencies department (not for blisters!) and STD clinic.

Traveller's Medical & Vaccination Centre (Map p728; ☎ 1300 658 844, 08-8212 7522; www.traveldoctor .com.au; 27 Gilbert Pl; ☺ 9am-5pm Mon-Fri, to 7pm Wed, to 1pm Sat)

Women's & Children's Hospital (Map p731; ☎ 08-8161 7000; www.cywhs.sa.gov.au; 72 King William Rd, North Adelaide; ☺ 24hr) Emergency and sexual assault services.

Money

Banks and ATMs prevail throughout the CBD, particularly around Rundle Mall.

American Express (Map p728; ☎ 1300 139 060; Shop 32, Citi-Centre Arcade, Rundle Mall; ☺ 9am-5pm Mon-Fri, to noon Sat) Foreign currency exchange.

Travelex (Map p728; ☎ 08-8231 6977; www.travelex .com.au; Shop 4, Rundle Mall; ☺ 9am-5.30pm Mon-Fri, to 5pm Sat) Foreign currency exchange.

Post

Australia Post Shop (Map p728; ☎ 13 13 18; www .auspost.com.au; Station Arcade, 136 North Tce; ☺ 9am-5pm Mon-Fri)

Main Post Office (Map p728; ☎ 13 13 18; www .auspost.com.au; 141 King William St; ☺ 8am-5pm Mon-Fri) Poste Restante; have mail addressed to you c/o Poste Restante, Adelaide 5001.

Tourist Information

Adelaide Visitor Information Kiosk (Map p728; ☎ 08-8203 7611; Rundle Mall; ☺ 10am-5pm Mon-Thu, to 8pm Fri, to 3pm Sat & Sun) Adelaide-specific information, and free city-centre walking tours at 9.30am Monday to Friday; at the King William St end of the mall.

Disability Information & Resource Centre (DIRC; Map p728; ☎ 08-8236 0555; www.dircsa.org.au; 195 Gilles St; ☺ 9am-5pm Mon-Fri) Info on accommodation, venues and travel for people with disabilities.

South Australian Visitor & Travel Centre (Map p728; ☎ 1300 655 276; www.southaustralia.com; 18 King William St; ☺ 8.30am-5pm Mon-Fri, 9am-2pm Sat & Sun) Abundantly stocked with leaflets and publications on Adelaide and SA. Super-patient staff and a BASS ticket-selling outlet, too.

Women's Information Service (Map p728; ☎ 1800 188 158, 08-8303 0590; www.wis.sa.gov.au; Station Arcade, 136 North Tce; ☻ 8.30am-5.30pm Mon-Fri; ▣) Information and counselling services.

Volunteering

Conservation Council of SA (Map p728; ☎ 08-8223 5155; www.ccsa.asn.au; 120 Wakefield St; ☻ 9am-5pm Mon-Fri) Volunteer opportunities including restoration of swamps, grasslands and other natural habitats, and recovery programs for threatened bird species.

SIGHTS

Most of Adelaide's big-ticket sights are within walking distance of the city centre, with many strung along North Tce. It's also *de rigeur* to day trip out to beachside Glenelg (p730), historic Port Adelaide (p731), or the nearby Adelaide Hills (p744), Barossa Valley (p775) or McLaren Vale (p750) regions.

The **Adelaide Attractions Pass** (☎ 1300 661 711, 08-9906 2711; www.adelaideattractionspass.com; adult/child $79/59) can be an economical way of seeing the sights; choose six of the 15 wildlife parks, museums and tours available and book online or over the phone.

Art Galleries

Spend a few hushed hours in the vaulted, parquetry-floored **Art Gallery of South Australia** (Map p728; ☎ 08-8207 7000; www.artgallery.sa.gov.au; North Tce; admission free; ☻ 10am-5pm), which represents the big names in Australian art. Permanent exhibitions include Australian, modern Australian, contemporary Aboriginal, Asian, Islamic and European art (with 20 bronze Rodins!). Temporary exhibitions occupy the basement. Free audio tours of the Australian collection are insightful, as are the free guided tours (11am and 2pm daily).

For an insight into Adelaide's **public artworks** – including the infamous **Mall's Balls** (Rundle Mall) – pick up a walking tour map from the visitor centre.

Adelaide's private gallery scene swings between snooty, la-di-dah openings peopled by turtle-necked doyens, and rootsy garage exhibitions in the city's West End. Two West End favourites:

Experimental Art Foundation (Map p728; ☎ 08-8211 7505; www.eaf.asn.au; Lion Arts Centre, cnr Morphett St & North Tce; admission free; ☻ 11am-5pm Tue-Fri, from 2pm Sat) A focus on innovation, with a bookshop specialising in film, architecture, culture and design.

Jam Factory Craft & Design Centre (Map p728; ☎ 08-8410 0727; www.jamfactory.com.au; 19 Morphett St; admission free; ☻ 10am-5pm Mon-Sat, from 1pm Sun) Quality contemporary local arts and crafts, plus a hell-hot glass-blowing studio (watch from the balcony above).

Museums

The **South Australian Museum** (Map p728; ☎ 08-8207 7368; www.samuseum.sa.gov.au; North Tce; admission free; ☻ 10am-5pm) digs into Australia's natural history, with special exhibits on whales and Antarctic explorer Sir Douglas Mawson, and an Aboriginal Cultures Gallery displaying artefacts of the Ngarrindjeri people of the Coorong and lower Murray. Free tours are run at 11am Monday to Friday and 2pm on 3pm Saturday and Sunday (don't miss the giant squid!). There's a cool cafe (mains $10 to $17; open for lunch) here too.

The engaging **Migration Museum** (Map p728; ☎ 08-8207 7580; www.history.sa.gov.au; 82 Kintore Ave; admission by donation; ☻ 10am-5pm Mon-Fri, from 1pm Sat & Sun) tells the social history of the many migrants who have made SA their home. The museum has info on 100-plus nationalities in its database, along with some poignant personal stories.

Only decommissioned as a jail in 1988, the **HM Adelaide Gaol Historic Site** (Map p728; ☎ 08-8231 4062; www.adelaidegaol.org.au; Gaol Rd, Thebarton; admission adult/child/concession $8.50/6.50/7; ☻ 11am-5pm Mon-Fri & Sun, last entry 3.30pm) has a grim vibe, but its displays of homemade bongs, weapons and escape devices are amazing. Commentary tapes are available for self-guided tours; guided tours are offered on Sundays, at 11am, noon and 1pm. Ghost tours by appointment.

See also Bradman Collection Museum (p730).

Tandanya National Aboriginal Cultural Institute

Tandanya (Map p728; ☎ 08-8224 3200; www.tandanya.com.au; 253 Grenfell St; adult/concession/family $5/4/12; ☻ 10am-5pm) offers an insight into the culture of the local Kaurna people, whose territory extends south to Cape Jervis and north to Port Wakefield. Inside the cultural institute there are interactive displays on living with the land, as well as galleries, gifts and a cafe. There are didgeridoo or Torres Strait Islander dance performances at noon from Tuesday to Sunday, plus Indigenous short film and documentary screenings in the theatre.

SOUTH AUSTRALIA

CENTRAL ADELAIDE

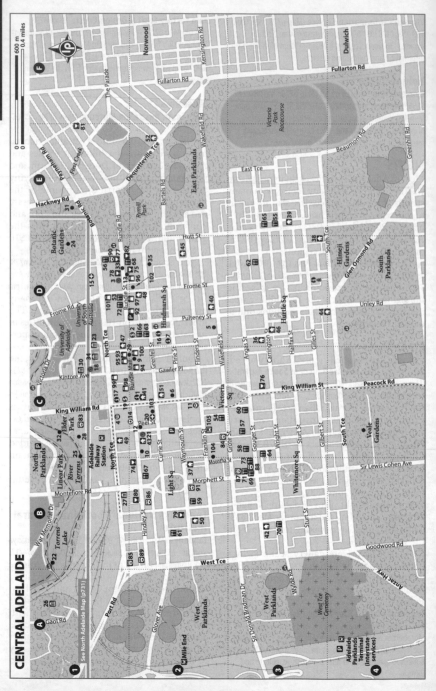

Markets

Satisfy both obvious and obscure culinary cravings at the 250-odd stalls in Adelaide's superb **Central Market** (Map p728; ☎ 08-8203 7203; www.adelaidecentralmarket.com.au; btwn Grote & Gouger Sts; ⏱ 7am-5.30pm Tue, 9am-5.30pm Thu, 7am-9pm Fri, 7am-3pm Sat). A gluten-free snag from the Gourmet Sausage Shop, a sliver of English stilton from the Smelly Cheese Shop, a tub of blueberry yoghurt from the Yoghurt Shop – you name it, it's all here. Good luck making it out without eating anything. For market tour details, see p734.

Over in the East End, don't miss Sunday's **Rundle St Market** (Map p728; ☎ 08-8203 7203; www.cityofadelaide.com.au; Rundle St; ⏱ 11am-4pm Sun), with food stalls, fashion, buskers, jewellery, arts and crafts.

Wine, Beer & Chocolate

Check out the self-guided, interactive 'Wine Discovery Journey' exhibition, paired with tastings of Australian wines, at the very sexy **National Wine Centre of Australia** (Map p728; ☎ 08-8303 3355; www.wineaustralia.com.au; cnr Botanic & Hackney Rds; exhibition free, tastings $8-16; ☑ 10am-5pm). You'll get an insight into the issues winemakers contend with, and even have your own virtual vintage rated. A heady range of wine appreciation courses (from $55) is also available, and there's a cool cafe here too.

The 100-year-old **Penfolds Magill Estate Winery** (Map p724; ☎ 08-8301 5569; www.penfolds.com .au; 78 Penfolds Rd, Magill; tastings free, mains $42-45; ☑ tastings 10am-5pm, lunch Fri, dinner Tue-Sun) is home to Australia's best known wine – the legendary Grange. Taste the product at the cellar door; dine at the slick, glass-fronted restaurant; take the 'Heritage Tour' ($15) or steel your wallet for the 'Great Grange Tour' ($150).

You can't possibly come to Adelaide without entertaining thoughts of touring the **Coopers Brewery** (Map p724; ☎ 08-8440 1800; www .coopers.com.au; 461 South Rd, Regency Park; 1½hr tours per person $20; ☑ tours 1pm Tue-Fri). Tours take you through the brewhouse, bottling hall and history museum, where you can get stuck in to samples of stouts, ales and lagers (some of which are carbon neutral). Bookings required; minimum age 18. The brewery is in the northern suburbs – grab a cab, or walk 1km from Islington train station.

If you've got a chocolate problem, get guilty at the iconic **Haigh's Chocolates Visitors Centre** (Map p724; ☎ 08-8372 7070; www.haighschocolates.com; 154 Greenhill Rd, Parkside; admission free; ☑ 8.30am-5.30pm Mon-Fri, 9am-5pm Sat). Free factory tours (with samples if you're good) take you through the chocolate life-cycle from cacao nut to hand-dipped truffle. Tours run at 11am, 1pm and 2pm Monday to Saturday; bookings essential.

Gardens & Parklands
Meander, jog or chew through your trashy airport novel in the city-fringe **Botanic Gardens** (Map p728; ☎ 08-8222 9311; www.botanicgardens.sa.gov.au; North Tce; admission free; ☑ 7am-sunset Mon-Fri, from 9am Sat & Sun). Highlights include a restored 1877 palm house, the new waterlily pavilion (housing the gigantic *Victoria amazonica*) and the fabulous steel-and-glass arc of the **Bicentennial Conservatory** (adult/child/family $4.50/2.50/10; ☑ 10am-5pm), which recreates a tropical rainforest. Free 1½-hour guided walks depart the garden cafe at 10.30am daily.

The city and ritzy North Adelaide are surrounded by a broad band of **parklands**. Colonel William Light, Adelaide's controversial planner, came up with the concept, which has been both a blessing and a curse for the city. Pros: heaps of green space, clean air and sports grounds for the kids. Cons: bone-dry in summer, perverts loitering and a sense that the city is cut off from its suburbs. Convinced he was right, a **Colonel William Light statue** (Map p731) overlooks the gleaming city office towers from Montefiore Hill.

Adelaide Zoo
Around 1400 exotic and native mammals, birds and reptiles roar, growl and screech at Adelaide's **zoo** (Map p731; ☎ 08-8267 3255; www .adelaidezoo.com.au; Frome Rd; admission adult/child/concession/family $20/12/16/60; ☑ 9.30am-5pm). There are free walking tours half-hourly, feeding sessions and a children's zoo. Until the new pandas arrived (pandemonium!) the major drawcard was the Southeast Asian rainforest exhibit.

You can take a river cruise to the zoo from the Festival Centre on **Pop-eye** (Map p728; ☎ 08-8295 4747; cruises adult/child $10/5; ☑ hourly 11am-3pm Mon-Fri, every 20min 10.30am-5pm Sat & Sun). Weekends only in winter.

Adelaide Oval
Hailed as the world's prettiest cricket ground the **Adelaide Oval** (Map p731; ☎ 08-8300 3800; www .cricketsa.com.au; King William Rd, North Adelaide) hosts interstate and international cricket matches, plus South Australian National Football League (SANFL) games in winter. A bronze statue of 'the Don' (Sir Donald Bradman) cracks a cover drive out the front. When there are no games on you can take a two-hour **tour** (adult/student $10/5; ☑ 10am Mon-Fri), departing the Phil Ridings Gates on War Memorial Dr.

At the **Bradman Collection Museum** (admission free; ☑ 9.30am-4.30pm Mon-Fri, gates open-4.30pm match days) Don devotees can pore over personal items of the cricketing legend. Call or check the website for tour details.

Glenelg
Palindromic Glenelg (Map p724), or 'the Bay' – the site of SA's colonial landing – is Adelaide at its most chilled-out and eccentric. Glenelg beach faces west, and as the sun sinks into the sea, the pubs and bars burgeon with surfies, backpackers and sun-damaged sexagenarians. The tram rumbles in from the city, past the Jetty Rd shopping strip to the alfresco cafes

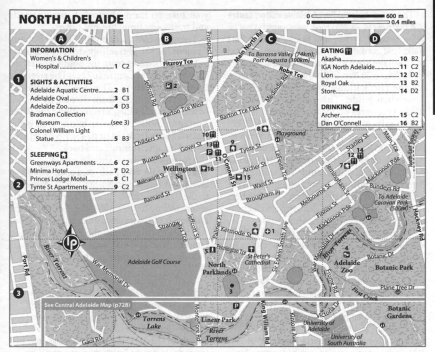

NORTH ADELAIDE

0 ———— 600 m
0 ———— 0.4 miles

INFORMATION	
Women's & Children's Hospital	**1** C2

SIGHTS & ACTIVITIES	
Adelaide Aquatic Centre	**2** B1
Adelaide Oval	**3** C3
Adelaide Zoo	**4** D3
Bradman Collection Museum	(see 3)
Colonel William Light Statue	**5** B3

SLEEPING	
Greenways Apartments	**6** C2
Minima Hotel	**7** D2
Princes Lodge Motel	**8** C1
Tynte St Apartments	**9** C2

EATING	
Akasha	**10** B2
IGA North Adelaide	**11** C2
Lion	**12** D2
Royal Oak	**13** B2
Store	**14** D2

DRINKING	
Archer	**15** C2
Dan O'Connell	**16** B2

To Barossa Valley (74km);
Port Augusta (300km)

See Central Adelaide Map (p728)

around Moseley Sq. **Glenelg visitor centre** (☎ 08-8294 5833; www.glenelgsa.com.au; Moseley Sq; ☺ 9.30am-5pm Mon-Fri, to 3pm Sat, 10am-2pm Sun; ☐) is behind the Town Hall; internet access available.

The **Bay Discovery Centre** (☎ 08-8179 9504; www.baydiscovery.com.au; Town Hall, Moseley Sq; admission free; ☺ 10am-5pm) depicts the social history of Glenelg from colonisation to today, and addresses the plight of the local Kaurna people, who lost both their land and voice. Don't miss the rusty relics dredged up from the original pier, and the spooky old sideshow machines.

Near the visitors centre, **Beach Hire** (☎ 08-8294 1477; Moseley Sq; ☺ sunny days Sep-Apr) hires out wave skis (per hour $14), bodyboards ($5) and bikes ($12), plus deck chairs, umbrellas and cricket sets.

One Hel-a-va Ride (☎ 08-8376 8288; www.helava.com.au; Marina Pier; 20min rides adult/child/concession $70/50/60; ☺ from 10am daily) takes thrill seekers on high-speed jet boat rides (how long since you had breakfast?) and five-hour Port River cruises (adult/child/concession $190/169/180).

Temptation Sailing (☎ 0412 811 838; www.dolphinboat.com.au; Holdfast Shores Marina; 3½hr dolphin watch/swim $58/98; ☺ 8am) runs eco-accredited catamaran cruises to watch or swim with dolphins.

Adventure Blue (☎ 08-8294 7744; www.adventureblue.com.au; Patawalonga Frontage, Glenelg North; ☺ 8.30am-5.30pm Mon-Fri, 8am-5pm Sat & Sun) hires snorkelling gear ($25 per day), and offers one-day Discover Scuba courses ($250) and two-hour kiteboard lessons at West Beach ($199 including transport).

See p744 for details on the Glenelg tram. Alternatively, take bus 135, 167, 168, 190 or 264 from the city down Anzac Hwy to Glenelg.

Port Adelaide

Bogged in boganity for decades, Port Adelaide (Map p724) – 15km northwest of the city – is in the midst of gentrification, morphing its warehouses into art spaces and museums, and its brawl-house pubs into boutique beer emporia. Things are on the up! The Port Adelaide footy team has been kicking goals too, winning the Australian Football League (AFL) premiership in 2004 and making the Grand Final in 2007 (just don't mention the score…).

The mega-helpful **Port Adelaide visitors centre** (☎ 1800 629 888, 08-8405 6560; www.portenf.sa.gov.au; 66 Commercial Rd; ☯ 9am-5pm) books guided **Port Walks** (gold coin donation; ☯ 2pm Thu & Sun) around the heritage area; and **Kaurna Cultural Heritage Walks** (free; ☯ 10.30am 1st Sun of the month), unearthing the Port's Indigenous heritage with an Aboriginal guide. The visitors centre also stocks brochures on local self-guided tours.

The salty **Maritime Museum** (☎ 08-8207 6255; www.history.sa.gov.au; 126 Lipson St; adult/child/concession/family $8.50/3.50/6.50/22; ☯ 10am-5pm daily, lighthouse 10am-20m Sun-Fri) is the oldest of its kind in Australia. Highlights include the iconic Port Adelaide Lighthouse, busty figureheads made everywhere from Londonderry to Quebec, shipwreck and explorer displays, and a computer register of early migrants.

Trainspotters rejoice! The **National Railway Museum** (☎ 08-8341 1690; www.natrailmuseum.org.au; Lipson St Sth; adult/child/concession/family $12/5/9/29; ☯ 10am-5pm) has a hefty collection of railway memorabilia. The **South Australian Aviation Museum** (☎ 08-8240 1230; www.saam.org.au; Lipson St; adult/child/concession/family $8/4/5/16; ☯ 10.30am-4.30pm) has a similarly impressive collection of old birds.

Kids adore the **Seahorse Farm** (☎ 08-8447 7824; www.seahorses.com; adult/child/concession/family $8.50/7.50/8/26; ☯ 11am-4pm), with an educational DVD and walls of aquaria full of the squiggly little critters.

Cruises departing Port Adelaide Wharf to ogle the local bottlenose dolphins are run by **Port Princess Dolphin Cruises** (☎ 08-8447 2366; www.portprincess.com.au) and **Dolphin Explorer Cruises** (☎ 08-8447 2366; www.dolphinexplorer.com.au), both offering 90-minute, two-hour and lunch cruises from $4 per person. Alternatively, **Blue Water Sea Kayaking** (☎ 08-8295 8812; www.adventure-kayak.com.au) runs a range of guided and self-guided kayak tours around the Port River estuary from $50 per adult.

If you're here on a Sunday, the **Fisherman's Wharf Market** (☎ 08-8341 2040; ☯ 9am-5pm Sun) has antiques, bric-a-brac and crappy collectables.

West-bound buses 150 and 153 will get you to Port Adelaide from North Tce, or you can take the train.

ACTIVITIES
Cycling & Walking

Adelaide is pancake flat – perfect for cycling and walking (if it's not too hot!). You can take

your bike on trams during off-peak periods and trains any time, but not buses.

There are free guided walks in the Botanic Gardens (p730), plus self-guided city walks detailed in brochures from the South Australian Visitor & Travel Centre (p721). The riverside **Linear Park** (Map p728) is a 40km walking/cycling path running from Glenelg to the foot of the Adelaide Hills, mainly along the River Torrens. Another popular hiking trail is the **Waterfall Gully Track** (Map p745; 1½ hr return) up to Mt Lofty summit and back.

Mountain bikers should check out the **Eagle Mountain Bike Park** (Map p745; ☎ 08-8416 6677; www.bikesa.asn.au; admission free; ☯ dawn-dusk) in the Adelaide Hills; phone for directions. If you're feeling hyperactive, wheel off along the **Mawson Trail** (www.southaustraliantrails.com), from Adelaide to Blinman in the Flinders Ranges. **Ecotrek** (☎ 08-8346 4155; www.ecotrek.com.au) runs one-day cycling tours of the Adelaide Hills ($207).

Useful organisations:

Bicycle SA (Map p728; ☎ 08-8168 9999; www.bikesa.asn.au; 111 Franklin St; ☯ 9am-5pm) Free city bikes (see p744), cycling maps and info, plus details on the Adelaide–Flinders Ranges Mawson Trail.

Bikeabout (☎ 0413 525 733; www.bikeabout.com.au) Cycling day-trips to the Barossa Valley and coast ($75).

Linear Park Hire (Map p728; ☎ 0400 596 065; Elder Park; bikes per day $20; ☯ 9am-5pm) Bike hire (with helmets and locks).

Trails SA (www.southaustraliantrails.com) SA cycling and hiking trail info. Pick up their *40 Great South Australian Short Walks* brochure.

Water Activities

Adelaide gets *reeeeally* hot in summer. You can swim at the beach at Glenelg (p730), or the closest swimming pool to the city is the **Adelaide Aquatic Centre** (Map p731; ☎ 08-8344 4411; Jeffcott Rd, North Adelaide; casual swim adult/child/concession $6.50/5/5.60; ☯ 5am-10pm Mon-Sat, 7am-8pm Sun), with swimming and diving pools, gym, sauna, spa and other facilities.

Maybe if you squint…no, it still doesn't look like Venice…but cruising the River Torrens on the **Adelaide Gondola** (Map p728; ☎ 08-8358 1800; www.adelaidegondola.com.au; 4 people per 40 min $100) may still float your boat. You can even order a bottle of wine!

For scuba diving, skin diving and kiteboarding opportunities, head to Glenelg (p731). See also Pop-eye (p730) and Captain Jolley's Paddle Boats (p734).

WALKING TOUR

Feel like stretching your legs? Take a stroll around Adelaide's East End and get a feel for the city's architectural cache, its museums, river, parklands and best pub!

Kick things off at the King William St end of **Rundle Mall** (1), Adelaide's main commercial strip. Cruise east past the shops and shoppers and watch your reflection distort the legendary **Malls Balls** (2) sculpture. From the mall head north along Charles St to **North Tce** (3), Adelaide's formal boulevard. Across the street are the hushed, crimson-walled galleries of the **Art Gallery of South Australia** (4; p727). Next door is the **South Australian Museum** (5; p727), with its fantastic Aboriginal Cultures Gallery and natural-history displays. There's a good cafe here too if you need a caffeine hit or some solid fuel.

Continue west along North Tce then jag north along Kintore Ave at the **State Library of South Australia** (6; p725). Further north is the **Migration Museum** (7; p727) – anyone you know on their database?

Follow Kintore Ave down to the **River Torrens** (8), Adelaide's small-but-perfectly-formed waterway (this ain't the Amazon). Follow the river west under the King William Rd Bridge and into **Elder Park** (9), where you can hire a paddleboat or check out the jaunty architectural facets of the **Adelaide Festival Centre** (10; p741).

Across the Torrens is the photogenic **Adelaide Oval** (11; p730). Catch a game or take a tour of the Bradman Collection Museum. From the oval, follow the walking path east along the river's northern bank to Frome Rd and the entrance to the **Adelaide Zoo** (12; p730). Have the pandas arrived yet?

Head south down Frome Rd and turn left onto the walking path following the zoo fence. Fork right onto Plane Tree Dr and truck along to the gates of the expansive **Botanic Gardens** (13; p730). Meander across the lawns to the main gate on North Tce, then trundle east to the **National Wine Centre** (14; p730) and put your viticultural knowledge to the test.

Backtrack to East Tce, then beeline for the cafes, shops and bars on **Rundle St** (15). Order a cold schooner of local ale and pull up a footpath table outside the iconic **Exeter Hotel** (16; p740) – as the day winds down, this is the best place in town to wet your whistle!

ADELAIDE FOR CHILDREN

The free monthly paper **Adelaide's Child** (www .adelaideschild.com.au), available at cafes and libraries, is largely advertorial but contains comprehensive events listings. *Adelaide for Kids: A Guide for Parents,* by James Muecke, has comprehensive details and is available at bookshops.

WALK FACTS

Distance 5km
Duration Allow a full day for browsing, grazing and drinking

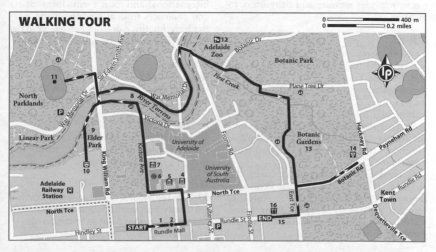

WALKING TOUR

There are few kids who won't love the tram ride from the city to Glenelg (see p744; kids under five ride for free!). You may have trouble getting them off the tram – the lure of a high-speed dash across the bay with One Hel-a-va Ride (p731) jet boats might help. If it's a scorcher, consider a splash in the shallows at Glenelg Beach (p730). You can hire the requisite water toys from Beach Hire (p731), and finish up with some fish and chips on the lawns.

During school holidays, the South Australian Museum (p727), State Library of South Australia (p725), Art Gallery of South Australia (p727), Adelaide Zoo (p730) and Botanic Gardens (p730) run inspired kid- and family-oriented programs with accessible and interactive general displays.

Along North Tce every Sunday, Adelaide City Council runs **Sunday Fundays** (☎ 08-8207 7575; www.adelaidecitycouncil.com; ⊗ 2-4pm Sun), featuring giant games, juggling workshops, clowns and musical entertainment. Not far away, **Captain Jolley's Paddle Boats** (Map p728; ☎ 08-8223 5863; Jolley's La; hire per 30min $12; ⊗ 10am-5pm Sat, Sun & school holidays) make a splash on the River Torrens.

Live out the kids' (or perhaps your own) Charlie and the Chocolate Factory fantasies on a tour at Haigh's Chocolates Visitors Centre (p730). Not the best for young diets, perhaps, but the chocolates sure are Wonka-worthy.

In Port Adelaide, ask the visitors centre about the Kids' Port Walk, and check out the Maritime Museum (p732) and Seahorse Farm (p732).

Dial-An-Angel (☎ 08-8267 3700; www.dialanangel.com.au) provides nannies and babysitters to all areas.

TOURS
You can circle around the main Adelaide sights on the free city buses (p744), or on the **Adelaide Explorer** (☎ 08-8293 2966; www.adelaideexplorer.com.au), a jump-on/jump-off tram-bus. Two-day tickets cover the city and coast (adult/child $30/10), or city only ($25/10); there are three departures daily. For details on boat cruises to Adelaide Zoo see p730; around Port Adelaide see p732; and from Glenelg see p731.

Beyond the city, day-tours cover the Adelaide Hills (p746), Fleurieu Peninsula (above) and Barossa Valley (p777). Note that one-day trips to the Flinders Ranges and Kangaroo Island tend to be rushed and not great value for money.

Adelaide-focused operators:

Adelaide Sightseeing (☎ 1300 769 762, 08-8231 4144; www.adelaidesightseeing.com.au) Runs a city highlights tour ($55) including North Tce, Glenelg, Haigh's Chocolates and the Adelaide Oval (among other sights). Barossa and Clare Valleys and Fleurieu Peninsula tours also available.

Adelaide's Top Food & Wine Tours (☎ 08-8263 0265; www.topfoodandwinetours.com.au) Uncovers SA's gastronomic soul with dawn ($48) and morning ($35) tours of the buzzing Central Market where stallholders introduce their varied produce. Dawn tours include breakfast. McLaren Vale and Clare Valley tours also available.

Bookabee Tours (☎ 08-8235 9954, 0408 209 593; www.bookabee.com.au) Indigenous-run Adelaide tours focusing on bush foods in the Botanic Gardens ($42, two hours), Tandanya & the South Australian Museum ($42, two hours) or Cleland Wildlife Park (half-day from $80), plus half-/full-day city tours ($138/180). A great insight into Kaurna culture. Longer outback tours also available.

Enjoy Adelaide (☎ 08-8332 1401; www.enjoyadelaide.com.au) Runs a half-day city highlights tour ($40) with diversions to Mt Lofty Summit and Hahndorf. Barossa Valley and Fleurieu Peninsula tours also available.

Gray Line (☎ 1300 858 687; www.grayline.com.au) Old-school city coach tours, with extensions to the Adelaide Hills and Glenelg, plus river-cruise and wildlife park options. Barossa Valley tours available too.

Premier Stateliner (☎ 08-8415 5566; www.premierstateliner.com.au) The big bus company runs a 'City Sights & Seaside' tour ($55), plus Barossa Valley and Adelaide Hills day trips.

FESTIVALS & EVENTS
As local licence plates attest, SA is the 'Festival State'. A continuous stream of high-calibre international and local events lures artists and audiences from around the world, particularly for the Adelaide Festival of Arts, WOMADelaide and the Adelaide Fringe.

January
Tour Down Under (www.tourdownunder.com.au) The world's best cyclists sweating in their lycra: six races through SA towns, with the grand finale in Adelaide.

February
Adelaide Fringe (www.adelaidefringe.com.au) This annual independent arts festival in February and March is second only to the Edinburgh Fringe.

March
Adelaide Festival of Arts (www.adelaidefestival.com.au) Culture vultures absorb international and Australian dance, drama, opera and theatre performances in even-numbered years.

Clipsal 500 (www.clipsal500.com.au) Rev-heads flail their mullets as Adelaide's streets become a four-day Holden versus Ford racing track.

WOMADelaide (www.womadelaide.com.au) One of the world's best live-music events, with more than 300 musicians and performers from around the globe.

June

Adelaide Cabaret Festival (www.adelaidecabaret festival.com) The only one of its kind in the country.

July

Adelaide's Festival of Ideas (www.adelaidefestival ofideas.com.au) The glorious, the good and the innovative descend on Adelaide for a biennial talkfest (odd-numbered years).

August

South Australian Living Artists Festival (www .salafestival.com) Progressive exhibitions and displays across town.

September

City to Bay (www.city-bay.org.au) Annual 12km fun run from the city to Glenelg; much sweat and cardiac duress.

Royal Adelaide Show (www.adelaideshowground.com .au) Agricultural and horticultural displays and showbags. Mooo...

SANFL Grand Final (www.sanfl.com.au) Zenith of the local Aussie Rules football season. Can anyone beat Central Districts?

October

Classic Adelaide Rally (www.classicadelaide.com.au) Full of lovingly maintained machines.

November

Christmas Pageant (www.cupageant.com.au) An Adelaide institution for 70-plus years – floats, bands and marching troupes occupy city streets for a day.

Feast Festival (www.feast.org.au) Three-week gay and lesbian festival with a carnival, theatre, dialogue and dance.

December

Adelaide Guitar Festival (www.adelaidefestivalcentre .com.au) Annual axe-fest with a whole lotta rock, classical, country, blues and flamenco.

Bay Sports Festival (www.baysportsfestival.com .au) Sports fest in Glenelg, featuring beach volleyball, an aquathon and surf carnival.

SLEEPING

Most of Adelaide's budget accommodation is in the city centre, but in a town this easy to navigate, staying outside the CBD is viable. For peace and quiet, consider leafy North Adelaide; for beachside accommodation, try Glenelg. 'Motel Alley' is along Glen Osmond Rd, the main southeast city access road. See www.bandbfsa.com.au for B&B listings.

Adelaide's top-end hotels usually offer weekend package deals, when room prices are cheaper than mid-week. Holiday apartments generally offer competitive weekly and monthly rates. Book accommodation ahead during December and January, and expect price spikes during school holidays.

Budget

HOSTELS

Backpack Oz (Map p728; ☎ 08-8223 3551; www.back packoz.com.au; cnr Wakefield & Pulteney Sts; dm/s/d from $25/50/65; ❸ ⬜) It doesn't look like much externally, but this converted pub (the old Orient Hotel) strikes the right balance between party and placid. There are spacious dorms, a guest house over the road (great for couples), and guests can still get a coldie and shoot some pool in the bar. Communal area; free dinner on Wednesday. Linen provided.

our pick **My Place** (Map p728; ☎ 08-8221 5299; www .adelaidehostel.com.au; 257 Waymouth St; dm incl breakfast $24, d incl breakfast & TV $64; ⬜) The antithesis of the big formal operations, My Place has a welcoming, personal vibe and is just a stumble from the Grace Emily, arguably Adelaide's best pub! There's a cosy TV room, barbecue terrace above the street, beach-bus in summer, and regular pizza and pub nights – great for solo travellers. Free bike hire, too.

Hostel 109 (Map p728; ☎ 1800 099 318, 08-8223 1771; www.hostel109.com; 109 Carrington St; dm/s/tw/d $25/50/58/65; ❸ ⬜) A small, well-managed hostel in a quiet corner of town, with a couple of little balconies over the street and a cosy kitchen/communal area. Spotlessly clean and super-friendly, with lockers, travel info, good security and gas cooking. The only negative: rooms open onto light wells rather than the outside world.

Glenelg Beach Hostel & Bar (☎ 1800 359 181, 08-8376 0007; www.glenelgbeachhostel.com.au; 1-7 Moseley St, Glenelg; dm/s/d/f from $27/60/80/120; ⬜) A couple of streets back from the beach, this beaut old terrace (1879) is Adelaide's budget golden child. Fan-cooled rooms maintain period details and are bunk-free. There's cold Coopers in the basement bar, open fireplaces, lofty ceilings, girls-only dorms and a courtyard garden. Book *waaay* in advance in summer.

Adelaide Central YHA (Map p728; ☎ 08-8414 3010; www.yha.com.au; 135 Waymouth St; dm/d/f from $28/80/110; ✖ ⚏) The YHA isn't known for its gregariousness, but you'll get plenty of sleep in the spacious and comfortable rooms here. This is a seriously schmick hostel with great security, roomy kitchen and lounge area and immaculate bathrooms. A real step up from the average backpackers around town.

Other hostels:

Adelaide Backpackers Inn (Map p728; ☎ 1800 247 725, 08-8223 6635; www.adelaidebackpackersinn.net.au; 112 Carrington St; dm/tw incl breakfast $24/48; ✖ ⚏) A relaxed and surprisingly clean place (inside an old pub), with the emphasis on 'free' (pick-ups, breakfast, videos, linen, storage etc).

Blue Galah Backpackers Hostel (Map p728; ☎ 08-8231 9295; www.bluegalah.com.au; Level 1, 62 King William St; dm/tw from $26/70; ✖ ⚏) A friendly, 140-bed hostel with an enormous balcony above King Willie St (perfect for the Oz boutique beers from the bar) and an environmental bent. Rooms have good security and excellent mattresses, but some are sans windows and a little squishy.

Adelaide Travellers Inn (Map p728; ☎ 08-8224 0753; www.adelaidebackpackers.com.au; 220 Hutt St; dm $25, d with/without bathroom $75/60, f $100-125; P ✖) Steps away from the Hutt St eateries, this shabby-but-sociable joint has a maze of dorms and old-time motel units out the back. Rates include linen and light breakfast. Beery balcony above the street.

MOTELS

City Central Motel (Map p728; ☎ 08-8231 4049; www.arta.com.au/ccentral.html; 23 Hindley St; s/d/tw $70/80/80; ✖) Small but clean, secure and comfortable motel-style rooms poised above the Hindley St melee. Have a few beers on the balcony and watch the crowds pass onwards to oblivion. Discounted multistorey parking across the street.

CAMPING & HOLIDAY PARKS

Levi Park Caravan Park (Map p724; ☎ 08-8344 2209; www.levipark.com.au; 69 Lansdowne Tce, Walkerville; unpowered/powered sites $27/31, cabins & ste $86-120; P ✖) This Torrens-side park is 5km from town and loaded with facilities, including tennis courts and a massive oval. Suites are in restored Vale House, purportedly Adelaide's oldest residence!

Adelaide Caravan Park (Map p724; ☎ 08-8363 1566; www.adelaidecaravanpark.com.au; 46 Richmond St, Hackney; powered sites $30-32, cabins/units from $85/113; P ✖)

An orderly park on the River Torrens, just 2km northeast of the city centre. Clean and well run, but not much grass.

Adelaide Shores Caravan Resort (Map p724; ☎ 08-8356 7654; www.adelaideshores.com.au; 1 Military Rd, West Beach; powered sites $34-54, cabins $85-198; P ✖ ⚏ ⚎) Hunkered-down behind the West Beach dunes with a walking/cycling track extending to Glenelg (3.4km) in one direction and Henley Beach (3.5km) in the other, this is a choice spot in summer. There are lush sites, glistening amenities and passing dolphins.

Midrange

HOTELS & MOTELS

Jasper Motor Inn (Map p724; ☎ 08-8271 0377; www.jaspermotorinn.com.au; 17 Jasper St, Hyde Park; s & d $85-120; P ✖ ⚏) Just beyond the city (3.5km), Jasper is off King William Rd in upper-crust Hyde Park. It's a low-slung '70s number without much style, but on a super-quiet street – far preferable to the traffic rumble of Glen Osmond Rd's 'Motel Alley'. Great value.

Princes Lodge Motel (Map p731; ☎ 08-8267 5566; www.princeslodge.com.au; 73 LeFevre Tce, North Adelaide; s/d/f incl breakfast from $65/95/160; P ✖) In a grand 1913 house overlooking the parklands, this friendly (but achingly uncool) lodging has high ceilings and a certain faded grandeur. Close to the chichi North Adelaide restaurants and within walking distance of the city.

Taft Motor Inn (☎ 1800 060 905; 08-8376 1233; www.taftmotorinn.com.au; 18 Moseley St, Glenelg; d from $115, 1-/2-bedroom apt from $145/155; P ✖ ⚎) Revamped motel rooms and apartments with lashings of timber and taupe (did they spend as much on the beds?). Some rooms have kitchenettes, and there's a barbecue and kidney-shaped pool on site.

Minima Hotel (Map p731; ☎ 1800 779 954, 08-8334 7766; www.majestichotels.com.au; 146 Melbourne St, North Adelaide; d from $110, parking per night $8; P ✖ ⚏) A spaceship has landed in ye olde North Adelaide! Minima is so new the paint has barely dried, so you'll be assured of a clean, quality night's stay. Small but super-stylish rooms in a winning Melbourne St location; check-in at 9 Jerningham St.

City Parklands Motel (Map p728; ☎ 08-8223 1444; www.citypark.com.au; 471 Pulteney St; d with/without bathroom from $120/99, tr/f from $130/150; P ✖) Immaculate bathrooms, leather lounges, winsome French prints and an easy walk to the Hutt St restaurants. Free parking, bike hire, DVDs and wireless internet, too.

Mercure Grosvenor Hotel (Map p728; ☎ 08-8407 8888; www.mercuregrosvenorhotel.com.au; 125 North Tce; d $110-270; P ✖ 🖳) This place was built in 1918, but there's not much old-world vibe left inside – slick modern rooms and friendly staff compensate. Kids under 16 stay free.

Royal Coach Motor Inn (Map p728; ☎ 08-8362 5676; www.royalcoach.com.au; 24 Dequetteville Tce, Kent Town; d from $155, extra adult/child $15/10; P ✖ 🐾) Three-storey brick motel monster just beyond the parklands at the eastern end of town, with good facilities and late-'90s decor. There's a restaurant downstairs, but Rundle St is just a 10-minute walk away.

APARTMENTS & COTTAGES

Greenways Apartments (Map p731; ☎ 08-8267 5903; www.greenwaysapartments.com; 41-45 King William Rd, North Adelaide; 1-/2-/3-bedroom apt $95/140/180; P ✖) These 1938 apartments ain't flash (floral tiles and rude '70s laminates), but if you have a pathological hatred of 21st-century open-plan 'lifestyles', then Greenways is for you! And where else can you stay in clean, perfectly operational apartments so close to town at these rates? A must for cricket fans, the Adelaide Oval is a lofted cover drive away – book early for Test Matches.

BreakFree Director's Studios (Map p728; ☎ 08-8213 2500; www.breakfree.com.au; 259 Gouger St; d/studios from $120/145; P ✖) Unfussy but not the slickest, these corporate hotel rooms and studios (with kitchenettes) on the west side of town are a safe business bet. Close the deal, then close your eyes.

Tynte Street Apartments (Map p731; ☎ 1800 779 919, 08-8334 7783; www.majestichotels.com.au; 82 Tynte St, North Adelaide; d from $150, extra adult/child $20/6; P ✖) Comfortable, red-brick, self-contained studio apartments on a tree-lined street near the O'Connell St cafes, sleeping three. Check-in is 1km away at 9 Jerningham St.

Quest on King William (Map p728; ☎ 08-8217 5000; www.questonkingwilliam.com.au; 82 King William St; studio/1-/2-bedroom apt from $150/165/220, parking per night $12; P ✖ 🖳) These immaculate downtown apartments (72 of them over eight levels) are central as can be – perfect for business bods. All have kitchenettes and DVD players. On-site laundry; family units sleep five.

For self-contained beachside apartments in Glenelg, try:

Glenelg Holiday & Corporate Letting (☎ 08-8376 1934; www.glenelgholiday.com.au; 1-bedroom apt from $135; ✖)

Glenelg Letting Agency (☎ 08-8376 0933; www .baybeachfront.com.au; 1-bedroom apt per week from $1204; ✖)

Top End

Hotel Richmond (Map p728; ☎ 08-8223 4044; www.hotel richmond.com.au; 128 Rundle Mall; d from $165; ✖ 🖳) This opulent hotel in a grand 1920s building in the middle of Rundle Mall has mod-minimalist rooms with king-sized beds, marble bathrooms and American oak and Italian furnishings. Oh, and that hotel rarity – opening windows. Rates include breakfast, movies, papers and gym passes. Great value!

our pick Clarion Hotel Soho (Map p728; ☎ 08-8412 5600; www.clarionhotelsoho.com.au; 264 Flinders St; d $170-590; ✖ 🖳 🐾) *Ooh-la-la*! The slick new Clarion attempts to conjure up the vibe of London's Soho district, but it's far more sophisticated than anything on Old Compton St. Thirty very plush suites (some with spas, most with balconies) are complimented by sumptuous linen, 24-hour room service, iPod docks, Italian marble bathrooms, jet pool, a fab restaurant…Rates take a tumble midweek.

Stamford Grand Hotel (☎ 08-8376 1222; www.stam ford.com.au; Moseley Sq, Glenelg; d city/ocean views from $185/220, parking per day $15; P ✖ 🖳) The first Glenelg edifice to scrape the sky with any real authority, this plush, pink-hued hotel overlooks Gulf St Vincent. Dinner, bed and breakfast packages are decent value.

Majestic Roof Garden Hotel (Map p728; ☎ 08-8100 4400; www.majestichotels.com.au; 55 Frome St; d from $199, extra person $30, parking per day $24; ✖ 🖳) Everything looks new in this place – a speck of dirt would feel lonely. Book a room facing Frome St for a balcony and the best views, or take a bottle of wine up to the rooftop garden to watch the sunset.

Adelaide Old Terraces (Map p728; ☎ 08-8364 5437; www.adelaideoldterraces.com.au; 26 Blackburn Street; d $200, extra person $35; ✖) Actually it's just one old terrace house near Hutt St, but it's a good'un: gorgeously furnished, heritage listed, four bedrooms, two bathrooms and plenty of living space – perfect for a group of friends. Continental breakfast provisions included; two-night minimum.

EATING

Eating out in Adelaide is a divine pleasure, with reasonable prices, multicultural offerings and high standards.

Foodies flock to Gouger St (pronounced 'Googer') for **Chinatown**, the food-filled corridors of Central Market, and eclectic international eateries (from Argentine to Vietnamese and everywhere in between). Rundle St in the East End is the place for all-day alfresco cafes and people watching; nearby Hutt St has some quality food rooms. Artsy-alternative Hindley St – Adelaide's dirty little secret – has a smattering of good eateries and some great pubs (in fact, you can get decent pub meals all over Adelaide; see www.beerandburger .info for reviews). Across the river in North Adelaide, Melbourne and O'Connell streets have a healthy spread of bistros, provedores and pubs.

Gouger St, Chinatown & Central Market

Central Market (Map p728; ☎ 08-8203 7203; btwn Grote & Gouger Sts; ☺ 7am-5.30pm Tue, 9am-5.30pm Thu, 7am-9pm Fri, 7am-3pm Sat) This place is an exercise in sensory bombardment: a barrage of smells, colours and yelling stall-holders selling fresh vegetables, breads, cheeses, seafood and gourmet produce. Cafes, hectic food courts and a supermarket too.

Mesa Lunga (Map p728; ☎ 08-8410 7617; cnr Gouger & Morphett Sts; tapas $6-14, mains $19-24; ☺ lunch Wed-Fri & Sun, dinner Tue-Sun, all-day tapas & pizza Fri & Sun) In a fishbowl corner room with an amazing dark-wood wine wall, sassy Mesa Lunga serves tapas and quality pizzas. Order some *queso manchego* (aged sheep cheese with *membrillo*) and anchovies stuffed with Manzanillo olives, washed down with some sparkling sangria. Magic.

Lucia's Pizza & Spaghetti Bar (Map p728; ☎ 08-8251 2303; 2 Western Mall, Central Market; meals $8-10; ☺ breakfast & lunch Tue & Thu-Sat, dinner Fri) This little slice of Italy has been around since Lucia was a lot younger. All her pasta, sauces and pizzas are authentically homemade – perfection any time of day. If you like what you're eating, you can buy fresh pasta next door at Lucia's Pasta.

Ying Chow (Map p728; ☎ 08-8211 7998; 114 Gouger St; mains $10-17; ☺ dinner daily, lunch Fri) This fluoro-lit, utilitarian eatery is a culinary gem; serving cuisine styled from the Guangzhou region, such as crispy salt-and-pepper squid and steamed duck with salty sauce. It gets packed – with queues out the door – but it's well worth the wait.

Ding Hao (Map p728; ☎ 08-8231 6683; 26 Gouger St; mains $10-17; ☺ 11am-3pm & 5pm-late) Ding Hao is *the* place for yum cha. Even if you book a table, you might find yourself waiting outside as reluctant-to-leave diners spin lazy susans full of prawn dumplings, shredded duck, pork buns and (eek…) chicken feet.

Thali Room (Map p728; ☎ 08-8212 2411; 270-276 Morphett St; thalis $21; ☺ dinner Tue-Sun) Tacked onto the more upmarket British India restaurant, the moody Thali Room offers a selection of eight *thalis* (curry platters), all served with dhal, mango chutney, rice and naan. Try the Goan (hot beef) or the Malabar (prawns in mild coconut).

Gaucho's (Map p728; ☎ 08-8331 2299; 91 Gouger St; mains $35-80; ☺ lunch Mon-Fri, dinner daily) Low on iron? Book a seat at this Argentinean meat house and order the 300g full-blood Wagyu steak, grain-fed for 500 days and air-dried for 14. Eighty dollars well spent!

Augé (Map p728; ☎ 08-8410 9332; 22 Grote St; mains from $36, 2/3 courses $59/78; ☺ lunch Tue-Fri, dinner Tue-Sat) 'To continually strive to be at one's peak' is the motto here, and palate-peaking cuisine is what to expect. Try the seared medium-rare pigeon breast with soft parmesan polenta, cured pork-cheek pancetta and confit pigeon legs. WOW! (Augé rhymes with 'R-J', in case you want to name-drop).

East End

Vego and Lovin' It (Map p728; ☎ 08-8223 7411; 1st fl, 240 Rundle St; meals $5-10; ☺ lunch Mon-Fri) Get your weekly vitamin dose disguised in a scrumptious vegie burger, wrap or focaccia at this artsy upstairs kitchen. Dreadlocked urban renegades order 'extra alfalfa but no hummus'.

Biga (Map p728; ☎ 08-8232 8880; cnr Halifax & Hutt Sts; mains $6-18; ☺ breakfast & lunch daily, dinner Wed-Sat) A cool cafe popular with Adelaide's weekend cycling set, who exhaustedly sprawl across the outdoor tables. Head-kicking coffee and creative breakfasts – try the *uova e pancetta* (baked free-range eggs wrapped in pancetta with roasted mushrooms and fat toast).

Amalfi Pizzeria Ristorante (Map p728; ☎ 08-8223 1948; 29 Frome St; mains $13-25; ☺ lunch Mon-Fri, dinner Mon-Sat) What a classic! Authentic pizza and pasta with bentwood chairs, terrazzo floors, red-and-white checked tablecloths, sleep-defeating coffee and imagined Mafioso mutterings in the back room.

Lemongrass Thai Bistro (Map p728; ☎ 08-8223 6627; 289 Rundle St; mains $14-22; ☺ lunch Mon-Fri, dinner daily) Cheap, breezy Thai joint right in the Rundle

St mix. Mango and coconut chicken, red curry beef, clattering chairs and chilli chatter.

ourpick Jasmin Indian Restaurant (Map p728; ☎ 08-8223 7837; basement, 31 Hindmarsh Sq; mains $24-26; ☯ lunch Thu & Fri, dinner Tue-Sat) Magical North Indian curries and consummately professional staff (they might remember your name from when you ate here in 1997). There's nothing too surprising about the menu, but it's done to absolute perfection. Bookings essential.

Farina Kitchen & Bar (Map p728; ☎ 08-8227 1007; basement, 39 Hindmarsh Sq; mains $25-33; ☯ lunch Mon-Fri, dinner Mon-Sat) Wander downstairs into this contemporary Italian restaurant, festooned with white/yellow/black Miro-meets-Rorschach graphics and industrial light globes. Sip a cocktail at the bar while the effortlessly hip staff check if your table's ready.

Enoteca (Map p728; ☎ 08-8359 2255; 262 Carrington St; mains $27-37; ☯ lunch Wed-Fri, dinner Wed-Sat) In a timber-floored glass box dangling off the side of the Italian Chamber of Commerce, Enoteca plates up superb modern Italian. The gnocchi with Spencer Gulf prawns, shredded pork belly, roast tomato, white beans and truffles is heaven-sent. Classy, classy, classy.

Botanic Café (Map p728; ☎ 08-8224 0925; 4 East Tce; mains $27-41; ☯ lunch & dinner) Order from a seasonal menu of quality SA produce in this linen-crisp, modern Italian eatery opposite the Botanic Gardens. Offerings might include goats cheese tartlets with pear chutney, or pappardelle with braised lamb shank and thyme *ragu*. The tasting menu (two courses and a glass of wine for $25) is a steal.

See also Good Life (p740) and Penfolds Magill Estate Winery (p730).

West End

Café de Vili's (Map p724; ☎ 08-8234 2042; 2-14 Manchester St, Mile End Sth; mains $5-15; ☯ 24hr) Vili's pies are a South Australian institution. Next to their factory just west of the West End, this is an all-night cafe serving the equally iconic 'pie floaters' (a meat pie floating in pea soup, topped with mashed potato, gravy and sauce – outstanding!).

Jerusalem Sheshkabab House (Map p728; ☎ 08-8212 6185; 131 Hindley St; mains $10-15; ☯ lunch Tue-Sat, dinner Tue-Sun) A skinny Hindley St room that's been here forever, serving magnificent Middle Eastern and Lebanese delights: falafels, hummus, tabouleh, tahini and (of course) sheshkababs. The plastic furniture and draped tent material are appropriately tacky.

For a bang-up West End pub meal:

Edinburgh Castle (Map p728; ☎ 08-8231 1435; 223 Currie St; mains $10; ☯ lunch & dinner) Super-cheap $10 menu (the students love it) featuring bangers and mash, burgers, vegie lasagne, and beer-battered whiting.

Prince Albert (Map p728; ☎ 08-8212 7912; 254 Wright St; mains $12-25; ☯ lunch & dinner) Cheap pub grub that looms large: steaks, rissoles, hanging-off-the-plate schnitzels and inexplicably popular lambs brains.

Cumberland Arms (Map p728; ☎ 08-8231 3578; 205 Waymouth St; mains $14-21; ☯ lunch & dinner) Ignore the pokies for excellent rump steaks, warm chicken salads and 'Cumby' burgers. Cheap schnitzels Monday and Tuesday; cheap steaks Wednesday.

North Adelaide

Store (Map p731; ☎ 08-8361 6999; 157 Melbourne St; breakfast $8-17, mains $10-28) A much-needed slice of bohemia amid the North Adelaide affluence, Store is a casual corner eatery with a built-in deli, serving great coffee, pastas, risottos and gourmet mains like crispy chicken breast on mascarpone mash with grilled asparagus, prosciutto and sage butter.

Royal Oak (Map p731; ☎ 08-8267 2488; 123 O'Connell St; mains $16-23; ☯ breakfast Sat & Sun, lunch Wed-Sun, dinner daily) Winning pub grub at this enduring pub boozer: steak sangers, vegie lasagne, lamb shank pie, king prawn salad and blueberry pancakes (not all at once). Quirky retro vibe; live jazz/indie-rock Tuesday, Wednesday and Sunday.

Akasha (Map p731; ☎ 08-8267 5000; 8/157 O'Connell St; mains $16-33; ☯ breakfast Fri & Sat, lunch & dinner Tue-Sat) Modern Greek fills a niche on upper O'Connell St at Akasha, a classy glass-fronted restaurant serving meze (tapas-style plates) and hefty platters. Ouzo, ascending bouzouki music and knowledgeable staff. The $36 lunch for two is top value.

Lion (Map p731; ☎ 08-8367 0222; 161 Melbourne St; mains $30-34; ☯ lunch Sun-Fri, dinner Mon-Sat) Off to one side of this popular, upmarket boozer (all big screens, beer terraces and business types) is a sassy restaurant with a cool retro interior and romantic vibes. Hot off the menu are luscious Coorong Angus steaks, market fish and corn-fed chicken breasts, served with a professionalism far exceeding the average pub.

Glenelg

Cafe Zest (☎ 08-8295 3599; 2A Sussex St; meals $5-16; ☯ breakfast & lunch) This cafe-gallery fills a tiny crack between buildings, but its laid-back vibe and brilliant breakfasts more than compensate for any shortcomings in size. Baguettes and bagels are crammed with creative combos, or banish your hangover with some 'Hells Eggs': two potted eggs with tomato, capsicum and rosemary salsa, topped with grilled cheese and Tabasco sauce. Great coffee, arty staff, and vegetarian specials too.

Thuy-Linh (☎ 08-8295 5746; 168C Jetty Rd; mains $11-19; ☺ lunch Tue-Sat, dinner Tue-Sun) Astonishingly unpretentious Vietnamese/Chinese eatery at the city end of Jetty Rd, with attentive service and a swathe of fresh seafood, meat and noodle delights. Bring some mates and spin the lazy susan (banquets $20 per person).

our pick **Good Life** (☎ 08-8376 5900; 1st fl, cnr Jetty Rd & Moseley St; pizzas $13-37; ☺ lunch Tue-Fri & Sun, dinner daily) At this brilliant organic pizzeria above the Jetty Rd tram-scape, thin crusts are stacked with tasty toppings like free-range roast duck, Spencer Gulf 'monster' prawns and spicy Angaston salami. *Ahhh*, life is good… Also at 170 Hutt St in the city (Map p728; ☎ 08-8223 2618).

Gringos (☎ 08-8295 3524; Shop 1, Colley Tce; mains $16-24; ☺ lunch & dinner) Crack a cold Corona and chilli-up in the sun at this casual, good-time Mexican cantina opposite Moseley Sq, or take your bulging burrito down to the beach. Dangling sombreros, and margaritas by the jug.

Zucca Greek Mezze (☎ 08-8376 8222; Shop 5, Marina Pier, Holdfast Shores; meze $17-19, mains $28-43; ☺ lunch & dinner) Spartan linen, marina views, super service and a contemporary menu of tapas-style meze plates – you wouldn't find anything this classy on Santorini. The saganaki is sheer teeth-squeaking joy.

Self-Catering

You can find just about everything at the 250-odd shops in the Central Market (see p738) – fresh organic fruit and vegetables, bread, cheese, seafood, sausages – you name it. Good luck making it out without eating anything!

Supermarkets around town:

Coles (Map p728; ☎ 08-8231 6683; Central Market Arcade, cnr King William & Gouger Sts; ☺ midnight-9pm Mon-Fri, to 5pm Sat, 11am-5pm Sun)

IGA North Adelaide (Map p731; ☎ 08-8223 3114; 113 O'Connell St, North Adelaide; ☺ 8am-10pm)

Woolworths (Map p728; ☎ 08-8232 0787; 86 Rundle Mall; ☺ 7am-9pm Mon-Sat, 11am-5pm Sun)

DRINKING

For a true Adelaide experience, head for the bar and order a schooner of Coopers – the local brew – or a glass of SA's impressive wine. Rundle St has a few iconic pubs, while along Hindley St in the West End, grunge and sleaze collides with student energy and groovy bars. Most bars are closed on Mondays.

our pick **Exeter** (Map p728; ☎ 08-8223 2623; 246 Rundle St; ☺ 11am-1am Mon, to 2am Tue & Wed, to 3am Thu-Sat, to midnight Sun) The best pub in the city, this legendary boozer attracts a kooky mix of post-work, punk and uni drinkers, shaking the day off their backs. Pull up a stool or a table in the grungy beer garden (*sooo* much better without the smokers) and settle in for the evening. Music most nights; curry nights Wednesday and Thursday.

Grace Emily (Map p728; ☎ 08-8231 5500; 232 Waymouth St; ☺ 11am-midnight Mon-Fri, noon-midnight Sat, noon-9pm Sun) Duking it out with the Exeter for 'Adelaide's Best Pub' bragging rights (it pains us to separate the two) the 'Gracie' has live music most nights, featuring up-and-coming Australian acts. Inside it's all kooky '50s-meets-voodoo decor, open fires and great beers. Cult cinema Tuesday nights. Look for the UFO on the roof.

Supermild (Map p728; ☎ 08-8212 8077; 182 Hindley St; ☺ 10pm-late Thu-Sat) A down-sized basement bar that stays and stays while other West End bars come and go. Hip staff, retro-lounge interior, funky tunes – arguably the best bar in town (if you can get in!).

Wheatsheaf (Map p724; ☎ 08-8443 4546; 39 George St, Thebarton; ☺ 11am-midnight Mon-Fri, noon-midnight Sat, noon-9pm Sun) A hidden gem under the flight path in industrial Thebarton, with an artsy crowd of students, jazz musos, lesbians, punks and rockers. Tidy beer garden; live music Friday to Monday.

Distill (Map p728; ☎ 08-8227 0825; 286 Rundle St; ☺ noon-2.30pm & 5pm-late Tue-Sat) Super-sassy Rundle St bar with a tight dress code (to

---

PINT OF COOPERS PALE THANKS!

Things can get confusing at the bar in Adelaide. Aside from 200ml (7oz) 'butchers' – the choice of old men in dim, sticky-carpet pubs – there are three main beer sizes: 285ml (10oz) 'schooners' (pots or middies elsewhere in Australia), 425ml (15oz) 'pints' (schooners elsewhere) and 568ml (20oz) 'imperial pints' (traditional English pints). Now go forth and order with confidence!

the nines) and a kickin' organic cocktail list. Sustainable snacks (sourced within 100 miles) are creatively paired with wines: Limestone Coast cloth cheddar with juicy, 'wet dog Shiraz'; organic basil pesto with 'herbaceous, greasy Riesling'.

Crown & Sceptre (Map p728; ☎ 08-8212 4159; 308 King William St; ⏰ 10am-1am Mon-Wed, 10am-2am Thu, 10am-3am Fri, midday-5am Sat, midday-1am Sun) An urbane boozer drawing all-comers, from legal-eagles on adjournment from trial to ditch diggers in their boots. Ambient tunes, DJs most nights, sidewalk tables, a cool little beer garden and better-than-average pub food (mains $15 to $28).

Universal Wine Bar (Map p728; ☎ 08-8232 5000; 285 Rundle St; ⏰ noon-late) A hip crowd clocks-in to this stalwart bar to select from 200-plus South Australian and international wines, and a menu (mains $22 to $36) packed with SA produce. 'The scene is very Italian', says the barman.

Salt Bar & Restaurant (☎ 08-8376 6887; Holdfast Shores, Glenelg; ⏰ noon-11.30pm Mon-Thu, noon-12.30am Fri, 9am-12.30am Sat, 9am-11.30pm Sun) Sassy Salt pulls the punters to dine (upper-crust oysters, fish and steak) or just for drinks from the island bar. Live DJs and duos Thursday to Saturday; jazz on Sunday afternoon.

Pier One Bar (☎ 08-8350 8188; 18 Holdfast Promenade, Glenelg; ⏰ noon-late) A cavernous sports bar with voyeuristic beach views and fold-back windows for when the sea breeze drops. As many screens as staff (a lot of each), and raucous Sunday sessions.

Other eclectic spots:

Apothecary 1878 (Map p728; ☎ 08-8212 9099; 118 Hindley St; ⏰ 4pm-midnight Tue-Thu, noon-1am Fri & Sat) Classy coffee and wine at this gorgeous chemist-turned-bar. Medicine cabinets, bentwood chairs and Parisian marble-topped tables.

Belgian Beer Café (Map p728; ☎ 08-8359 2233; 27-29 Ebenezer Pl; ⏰ noon-9.30pm Sun-Thu, noon-10.30pm Fri & Sat) Shiny brass, sexy staff, much pre-sluicing of glasses and somewhere upwards of 26 imported Belgian super-brews (we lost count…); off Rundle St.

Tap Inn (Map p728; ☎ 08-8362 2116; 76 Rundle Rd, Kent Town; ⏰ 9am-midnight Sun-Thu, 9am-2am Fri & Sat) A huge pub doubling as a shrine to golf, with an indoor driving range and rooftop putting green.

Worthy drinking dens in North Adelaide:

Dan O'Connell (Map p731; ☎ 08-8267 4034; 165 Tynte St, North Adelaide; ⏰ 11am-midnight Mon-Fri, noon-midnight Sat, noon-10pm Sun) An Irish pub without a whiff of kitsch Celtic cash-in! Just great Guinness, open fires, acoustic music and a house-sized pepper tree in the beer garden (161 years old and counting).

Archer (☎ 08-8361 9300; 47 O'Connell St, North Adelaide; ⏰ 11am-midnight Mon-Thu & Sun, to 2am Fri & Sat) A cool place for SA wines and microbrews, with a jovial big-screen front bar, snooker room, music room (weekend DJs), and fireside lounge with chesterfields. Classy pub food too (mains $15 to $25).

Royal Oak (p739)

Lion (p739)

ENTERTAINMENT

Artsy Adelaide has a phenomenal cultural life that stacks up favourably with much larger cities. The free monthly **Adelaide Review** (www.adelaidereview.com) features theatre and gallery listings, and on Thursday and Saturday the **Advertiser** (www.theadvertiser.news.com.au) newspaper lists events, cinema programs and gallery details. The **Adelaide Theatre Guide** (www.theatreguide.com.au) lists booking details, venues and reviews for comedy, drama, musicals and other performance arts.

Big-ticket events can be booked through **Ticketek** (☎ 13 28 49; www.ticketek.com.au), **Moshtix** (☎ 1300 428 849; www.moshtix.com.au), or **BASS** (☎ 13 12 46; www.bass.sa.com.au), which has outlets at the South Australian Visitor & Travel Centre (p721), and the riverside **Adelaide Festival Centre** (Map p728; ☎ 08-8216 8600; www.adelaidefestivalcentre.com.au). The hub of performing arts in SA, the crystalline white Festival Centre opened in June 1973, four proud months before the Sydney Opera House! The **State Theatre Company** (www.statetheatrecompany.com.au) is based here.

Other entertainment venues:

Adelaide Entertainment Centre (Map p724; ☎ 08-8288 2222; www.theaec.net; Port Rd, Hindmarsh) Everyone from the Wiggles to Stevie Wonder.

Her Majesty's Theatre (Map p728; ☎ 08-8212 8600; 58 Grote St)

Lion Theatre (Map p728; ☎ 08-8231 7760; Lion Arts Centre, cnr North Tce & Morphett St)

Live Music

With serious musical pedigree (from Cold Chisel to the Superjesus and the Audreys), Adelaide knows how to kick out the jams! The free street-press papers **Rip It Up** (www.ripitup.com.au) and **db** (www.dbmagazine.com.au) – available from record shops, pubs and cafes – have band and DJ listings and reviews. Cover charges vary with acts.

Online resources:

Adelaide Symphony Orchestra (www.aso.com.au) Listings for the estimable ASO.

Jazz Adelaide (www.jazz.adelaide.onau.net) Finger-snappin' za-bah-dee-dah.

South Australian Music Online (www.musicsa.com.au) All-genre listings.

our pick **Governor Hindmarsh Hotel** (Map p724; ☎ 08-8340 0744; www.thegov.com.au; 59 Port Rd, Hindmarsh; ⏰ 11am-11pm Mon-Thu, 11am-2am Fri & Sat, 5pm-midnight Sun) Ground Zero for live music in Adelaide, 'The Gov' hosts some legendary local and international acts. The odd Irish band fiddles around in the bar, while the main venue features rock, folk, jazz, blues, salsa, reggae and dance. A huge place with an inexplicably personal vibe.

Jive (Map p728; ☎ 08-8211 6683; www.jivevenue.com; 181 Hindley St; ⏰ 8pm-2am Wed & Sun, to 3am Thu, to 5am Fri & Sat) In a converted theatre, Jive caters to an off-beat crowd of student types who like their tunes funky, left-field and removed from the mainstream. A sunken dance floor = great views from the bar!

HQ Complex (right) Primarily a dance venue, HQ is big and powered-up enough to entice touring rock powerhouses like The Living End and Shihad.

Fowlers Live (Map p728; ☎ 08-8212 0255; www.fowlerslive.com.au; 68 North Tce; ⏰ 6pm-4am Fri & Sat) Inside the former Fowler Flour Factory, this 500-capacity venue is a temple of hard rock, metal and sweaty mayhem.

Pubs around town with regular live gigs (everything from DJs to indie-rock and acoustic duos):

Grace Emily (p740) West End alt-rock, country and acoustic.

Wheatsheaf (p740) Eclectic offerings in the semi-industrial Thebarton wastelands.

Crown & Sceptre (p741) Grooves, beats and funky stuff from resident selectors.

Royal Oak (p739) Lounge and jazz spicing up North Adelaide.

Exeter (p740) The East End's rockin' soul: indie bands, electronica and acoustic.

Cinemas

Check the **Advertiser** (www.theadvertiser.news.com.au) for what's screening around town. Tickets generally cost around adult/child/concession $15/9/11 (cheaper on 'tight-arse' Tuesdays).

Palace Nova Eastend Cinemas (Map p728; ☎ 08-8232 3434; 250 & 251 Rundle St; ⏰ 10am-midnight)

Facing-off across Rundle St, both cinemas feature new-release art-house, foreign-language and independent films as well as some mainstream flicks.

Mercury Cinema (Map p728; ☎ 08-8410 1934; www.mercurycinema.org.au; Lion Arts Centre, 13 Morphett St; ⏰ box office 9.30am-5pm Mon-Fri and 30min before screenings) The Mercury screens art-house releases, and is home to the Adelaide Cinémathèque (classic, cult and experimental flicks).

Moonlight Cinema (Map p728; ☎ 1300 551 908; www.moonlight.com.au; Botanic Gardens; ⏰ mid-Dec–mid-Feb) In summer, pack a picnic and mosquito repellent, and spread out on the lawn to watch old and new classics under the stars.

Glenelg Cinema Centre (☎ 08-8294 3366; www.wallis.com.au; 119 Jetty Rd, Glenelg; ⏰ 11am-midnight) Mainstream films in an old art deco theatre, plus movie-and-meal deals with local restaurants.

Nightclubs

The scene is ever changing, though the West End and Light Sq are safe bets for club activity. Online check out www.pubscene.com.au or **Onion** (www.onion.com.au) for the 'word from the street'. Cover charges can be anything from free to $15, depending on the night; most clubs are closed Monday to Wednesday.

Lotus Lounge (Map p728; ☎ 08-8231 0312; 268 Morphett St; ⏰ 6pm-midnight Tue-Thu, to late Fri & Sat) We like the signage here – a very minimal fluoro martini glass with a flashing olive. Inside it's a glam lounge with cocktails, quality beers and Adelaide dolls cuttin' the rug. Expect queues around the corner on Saturday nights.

Zhivago (Map p728; ☎ 08-8212 0569; 155 Waymouth St, Light Sq; ⏰ 5pm-late Fri-Sun) The pick of the Light Sq clubs (there are quite a few of 'em - some are a bit moron-prone), Zhivago's DJs pump out everything from reggae and dub to quality house. Popular with the 18 to 25 dawn patrol.

Mojo West (Map p728; ☎ 08-8231 9290; 258 Hindley St; ⏰ 3pm-3am Thu & Fri, 9pm-5am Sat) One of the more relaxed clubs around town (dress code and atmosphere), Mojo West has freaky blue light emanating from under the pool table cushions and quasi–Easter Island graffiti art – it certainly looks the part! Thursday university nights attract pretty young things to the lights.

HQ Complex (Map p728; ☎ 08-7221 1245; www.hqcomplex.com.au; 7 West Tce; ⏰ 8pm-3am Wed & Fri, 9pm-6am

Sat) Adelaide's biggest club occupies the bad-old Heaven complex, filling five big rooms with shimmering sound and light. Night time is the right time on Saturdays – the biggest (and trashiest) club night in town.

Mars Bar (Map p728; ☎ 08-8231 9639; www.themars bar.com.au; 120 Gouger St; 10.30pm-5am Wed-Sat) The lynchpin of Adelaide's nocturnal G&L scene, always-busy Mars Bar features glitzy decor, flashy clientele and OTT drag shows.

Sport

As most Australian cities do, Adelaide hangs its hat on the successes of its sporting teams. In the **Australian Football League** (AFL; www.afl.com .au), the Adelaide Crows and Port Adelaide have sporadic success. Suburban Adelaide teams compete in the **South Australian National Football League** (SANFL; www.sanfl.com.au). The foot-ball season runs from March to September.

In the **National Basketball League** (NBL; www.nbl .com.au), the Adelaide 36ers have been a force for decades. In soccer's **A League** (www.a-league.com .au), Adelaide United are always competitive. Under the auspices of **Cricket SA** (www.cricketsa.com .au), the Redbacks play one- and multiday state matches at the Adelaide Oval (p730).

SHOPPING

Shops and department stores (Myer, David Jones, Harris Scarf et al) line Rundle Mall. The beautiful old arcades running between the mall and Grenfell St retain their original splendour, and house eclectic little shops. Rundle St and the surrounding lanes are home to boutique and retro clothing shops.

Tacky souvenir and opal shops cluster around the Rundle Mall and King William St corner. For something a little more classy, try Tandanya National Aboriginal Cultural Institute (p727), or local arts-and-crafts at the Jam Factory Craft & Design Centre (p727) or **T'Arts** (Map p728; ☎ 08-8232 0265; 10G Gays Arcade, Adelaide Arcade, Rundle Mall). The catch-cry at **Urban Cow Studio** (Map p728; ☎ 08-8232 6126; 11 Frome St) is 'Handmade in Adelaide' – a brilliant as-sortment of paintings, jewellery, glassware, ceramics and textiles, plus a gallery upstairs.

An international success story, the gor-geous cosmetics from SA's own **Jurlique** (Map p728; ☎ 08-8410 7180; www.jurlique.com.au; 22-38 Rundle Mall Plaza, Rundle Mall) are pricey but worth every cent. Another SA smash hit is **RM Williams** (Map p728; ☎ 08-8232 3611; 6 Gawler Pl) selling boots handmade from single pieces of leather.

For new and secondhand CDs and vinyl, swing into the excellent **Big Star** (Map p728; ☎ 08-8232 1484; 197 Rundle St). Not far away is **Midwest Trader** (Map p728; ☎ 08-8223 6606; shop 1 & 2 Ebenezer Pl), which stocks a toothy range of punk, rock, skate and rockabilly gear.

Outdoor shops convene around Rundle St:

Annapurna (Map p728; ☎ 08-8223 4633; www.an napurna.com.au; 210 Rundle St)

Mountain Designs (Map p728; ☎ 08-8232 1351; www.mountaindesigns.com; 187 Rundle St)

Paddy Pallin (Map p728; ☎ 08-8232 3155; www .paddypallin.com.au; 228 Rundle St)

GETTING THERE & AWAY

Air

Adelaide is connected by regular air services to all Australian capitals. **Qantas** (☎ 13 13 13; www.qantas.com.au), **Virgin Blue** (☎ 13 67 89; www .virginblue.com.au) and **Tiger Airways** (☎ 03-9335 3033; www.tigerairways.com) operate flights between **Adelaide Airport** (Map p724; ☎ 08-8308 9211; www .aal.com.au) and other capital cities and major centres.

For more details on travelling to and from Adelaide, see p1046.

Bus

Adelaide's new **Central Bus Station** (Map p728; 85 Franklin St) has ticket offices and terminals for all major interstate and statewide services. For online bus timetables see the **Bus SA** (www .bussa.com.au) website.

Car & Motorcycle

If you want to hitch a ride (sharing petrol costs) or buy a secondhand car, check out the hostel noticeboards. See the local *Yellow Pages* for Adelaide car-rental companies, includ-ing the major internationals. Note that some companies don't allow vehicles to be taken to Kangaroo Island. Expect to pay around $45 per day (less for longer rentals) for car hire with the cheaper companies, such as the following:

Acacia Car Rentals (Map p724; ☎ 08-8234 0911; www.acaciacarrentals.com.au; 91 Sir Donald Bradman Dr, Hilton) Cheap rentals for travel within a 100km radius.

Access Rent-a-Car (Map p728; ☎ 1800 812 580, 08-8359 3200; www.accessrentacar.com; 60 Frome St)

Cut Price Car & Truck Rentals (Map p724; ☎ 08-8443 7788; www.cutprice.com.au; cnr Sir Donald Bradman Dr & South Rd, Mile End) 4WD rentals available.

Koala Car Rentals (Map p724; ☎ 08-8352 7299; www .koalarentals.com.au; 41 Sir Donald Bradman Dr, Mile End)

SOUTH AUSTRALIA

Train

The interstate train terminal is **Adelaide Parklands Terminal** (Map p728; ☎ 13 21 47; www.gsr .com.au; Railway Tce, Keswick), 1km southwest of the city centre. See p723 for details of train services to and from Adelaide.

GETTING AROUND
To/from the Airport & Train Station

Skylink (☎ 08-8413 6196; www.skylinkadelaide.com; adult/child one-way $8/3) runs around 20 shuttles between 5.50am and 9.15pm to/from Adelaide Airport via Adelaide Parklands interstate train station (adult/child one-way $5/3). Bookings essential for all city pick-up locations other than the Central Bus Station.

Adelaide Metro's **JetBus** (☎ 1800 182 160, 08-8210 1000; www.adelaidemetro.com.au) runs several routes linking the suburbs, city and airport, starting around 5am and running until 11.30pm. Standard fares apply.

Many hostels will pick you up and drop you off if you're staying with them. Taxis charge around $20 between the airport and city centre.

Bicycle

With a valid photo ID you can borrow a bike for the day (for free!) from **Bicycle SA** (Map p728; ☎ 08-8168 9999; www.bikesa.asn.au; 111 Franklin St; ☺ 9am-5pm). Keep your bike overnight for a $25 charge. Helmet and lock provided.

Down at the beach, hire a bike from **Glenelg Cycles** (☎ 08-8294 4741; www.glenelgcycles.com.au; 754 Anzac Hwy; bikes per day $30; ☺ 9am-5.30pm Mon-Fri, 9am-4pm Sat).

Public Transport

The **Adelaide Metro InfoCentre** (Map p728; ☎ 1800 182 160, 08-8210 1000; www.adelaidemetro.com.au; cnr King William & Currie Sts; ☺ 8am-6pm Mon-Fri, 9am-5pm Sat, 11am-4pm Sun) provides timetables and sells tickets for the integrated city bus, train and Glenelg tram network. Tickets can also be purchased on board, at staffed train stations and in delis and newsagents. There are day-trip ($8), and two-hour peak ($4.20) and off-peak ($2.60) tickets. Train tickets can be purchased from vending machines on board trains, or at staffed train stations. The peak travel time is before 9am and after 3pm. Kids under five ride free!

BUS

Adelaide's clean and reliable suburban buses are the best way to get around town. Most services start around 6am and run until midnight.

The free City Loop bus runs clockwise and anticlockwise around the CBD fringe from Adelaide Train Station on North Tce, passing the Central Market en route. It runs every 15 minutes on weekdays from 8am to 6.15pm (plus every 30 minutes from 6.15pm to 9.15pm on Fridays), and every 30 minutes on Saturday between 8.15am and 5.45pm, and Sunday between 10.15am and 5.45pm.

The free Bee Line bus runs a loop from Victoria Sq, up King William St and past the Adelaide Railway Station on North Tce. It leaves Victoria Sq every five to 10 minutes on weekdays from 7.40am to 6pm (9.20pm Friday), every 15 minutes on Saturday from 8.27am to 5.35pm, and every 15 minutes on Sunday from 10am to 5.30pm.

Saturday night/Sunday morning After Midnight buses run select standard routes (including to Glenelg and the Adelaide Hills), but have an 'N' preceding the route number on their displays. Buses run generally from midnight to 5am; standard ticket prices apply.

TRAIN

Adelaide's hokey old diesel trains depart from **Adelaide Railway Station** (North Tce), plying five suburban routes (Belair, Gawler, Grange, Noarlunga and Outer Harbour). Trains generally run between 6am and midnight (some services start at 4.30am).

TRAM

State-of-the-art trams rumble to/from Moseley Sq in Glenelg, through Victoria Sq in the city and along North Tce, approximately every 15 minutes from 6am to midnight daily. Standard ticket prices apply, but the section between North Tce and South Tce is free.

Taxi

There are licensed taxi ranks all over town.
Adelaide Independent Taxis (☎ 13 22 11, wheelchair users 1300 360 940)
Suburban Taxis (☎ 13 10 08)
Yellow Cabs (☎ 13 22 27)

ADELAIDE HILLS

When the Adelaide plains are desert-hot in the summer months, the Adelaide Hills (technically the Mt Lofty Ranges) are always a few degrees cooler, with crisp air, woodland shade and labyrinthine valleys. Fleeing the sweaty city, early colonists built stately summer houses around Stirling and Aldgate. German settlers escaping religious persecution also arrived, infusing towns like Hahndorf and Lobethal with European values and architecture.

The Hills make a brilliant day trip from Adelaide. Hop from town to town (all with at least one pub), passing carts of fresh produce for sale, stone cottages, olive groves and vineyards along the way. The Hills are especially beautiful in autumn, with fiery red deciduous leaves and rows of hillside vines aglow at sunset. And the Hills are alive

ADELAIDE HILLS

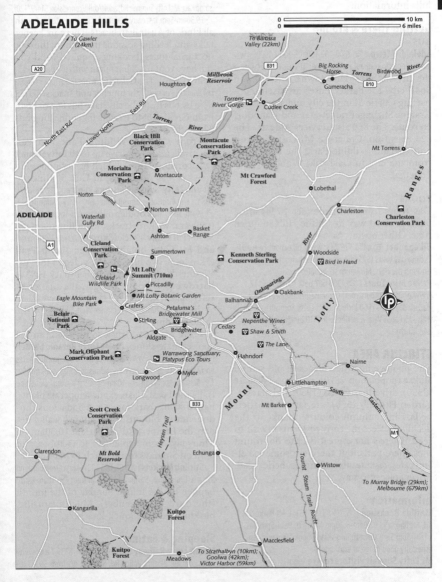

with the sound of clinking wine glasses; pick up the *Adelaide Hills Wine Region Cellar Door Guide* and *Fabulous Adelaide Hills Food Trails* brochures from visitors centres and go exploring. For a more structured, self-drive picnic experience, see www.cheeseand winetrails.com.au/adelaidehills.html. See www.visitadelaidehills.com.au for general hills information.

Getting There & Around

BUS

Adelaide Metro (☎ 1800 182 160, 08-8212 1000; www .adelaidemetro.com.au) runs several buses between the city and most Hills towns. The 864 and 864F city–Mt Barker buses are useful, departing Currie St in the city and stopping at Crafers, Stirling, Bridgewater and Hahndorf en route. The 864 also services Aldgate. The 823 runs from Crafers to Mt Lofty Summit and Cleland Wildlife Park; the 830F runs from the city to Oakbank, Woodside and Lobethal.

TOURS

Day tours from Adelaide (see p734) are a package-sized way to see the Hills in quick time. Other operators:

Bikeabout (☎ 0413 525 733; www.bikeabout.com.au) Cycling day tours ($75 including bikes, helmets and lunch) through the Hills. Minimum six people.

Prime Mini Tours (☎ 1300 667 650, 08-8556 6117; www.primeminitours.com) Combined Hahndorf–Victor Harbor day tours ($60 including Mt Lofty Summit), and a Hills–McLaren Vale wineries tour ($102 including tastings and lunch).

STIRLING AREA

The photogenic little villages of old-school **Stirling** (population 2870), one-horse **Aldgate** (3350), drive-thru **Crafers** (1950) and market-garden **Piccadilly** (530), are famed for their bedazzling autumn colours, thanks to the deciduous trees the early residents saw fit to seed. There's not a great deal to do 'round these here parts, but there are some excellent cafes, restaurants and atmospheric (read: pricey) places to stay.

Information

Matilda Bookshop (☎ 08-8339 3931; 8 Mt Barker Rd, Stirling; ⌚ 9.30am-5.30pm Mon-Fri, 9am-5pm Sat, 11am-5pm Sun) Outstanding village bookshop, with an especially good range of kids' books.

Mt Lofty Summit visitors centre (right)

Sights & Activities

Clambering up the slopes from the foothills to Mt Lofty, **Cleland Conservation Park** (☎ 08-8339 2444; www.environment.sa.gov.au/parks) has some steep bushwalking trails through tall eucalypt forest and cool gullies.

Inside the Conservation Park, the fab **Cleland Wildlife Park** (☎ 08-8339 2444; www.clelandwildlifepark .sa.gov.au; Mt Lofty Summit Rd; adult/child/concession $14/9/120; ⌚ 9.30am-5pm, last entry 4.30pm) lets you interact with all kinds of Australian beasts. There are keeper talks and feeding sessions throughout the day, nocturnal tours (bookings required), and you can have your mugshot taken with a koala ($15, 2pm to 4pm). The **Cleland Café** (meals $3-16; ⌚ breakfast & lunch) serves light lunches and snacks. To get here by bus from the city, take bus 864 or 864F from Grenfell St to Crafers for connecting bus 823 to the park.

From Cleland Wildlife Park you can bushwalk (2km) or drive up to **Mt Lofty Summit** (a surprising 710m), which has eye-popping views across Adelaide and Gulf St Vincent. **Mount Lofty Summit visitors centre** (☎ 08-8370 1054; www.mtloftysummit.com; Mt Lofty Summit Rd; ⌚ 9am-5pm) has oodles of info on local attractions and walking tracks, including the steep Waterfall Gully Track (8km return, 2½ hours) and Mt Lofty Botanic Gardens Loop Trail (7km loop, two hours). The video of the Ash Wednesday bushfires of 16 February 1983 is harrowing. If you're hungry, the snazzy **Mt Lofty Summit Restaurant** (lunch $10-18, dinner $27-33; ⌚ breakfast & lunch daily, dinner Wed-Sun) is in the same building.

From Mt Lofty, truck south 1.5km to the cool-climate slopes of **Mt Lofty Botanic Garden** (☎ 08-8222 9311; www.botanicgardens.sa.gov.au; gates on Mawson Dr & Lampert Rd; admission free, parking $2; ⌚ 8.30am-4pm Mon-Fri, 10am-5pm Sat & Sun). Nature trails wind past a lake, exotic temperate plants, native stringybark forest and bodacious rhododendron blooms. Free guided walks depart the Lampert Rd car park at 10.30am on Thursdays from September to October, and 2pm on Sundays from March to May.

Stirling Markets (☎ 08-8339 3378; brycarm@bigpond .net.au; Druids Ave, Stirling; admission free; ⌚ 10am-4pm) happen on the fourth Sunday of the month (the third in December). Much plant-life, busking and Hills knick-knackery.

Sleeping & Eating

Mount Lofty Railway Station (☎ 08-8339 7400; www .mlrs.com.au; 2 Sturt Valley Rd, Stirling; d/f from $95/110)

With four bedrooms, five bathrooms, two lounges, a kitchen and kitchenette, this disused, heritage-listed train station is affordable and versatile. You can book the whole thing, or divide it into two self-contained apartments. The only catch: the train line is *not* disused (10 trains every 24 hours – bring earplugs). Two night minimum.

Mt Lofty House (☎ 08-8339 6777; www.mtlofty house.com.au; 74 Summit Rd, Crafers; d incl breakfast from $180; ❄ ❋) Proprietarily poised above Mt Lofty Botanic Garden (*awesome* views) this 1850s baronial mansion has lavish heritage rooms and garden suites, plus an upmarket restaurant (also with killer views). The perfect dirty weekender.

Aldgate Creek Cottage B&B (☎ 08-8339 1987; www .aldgatecreekbnb.com; 3 Rugby Rd, Aldgate; d from $210; ❄) A romantic, two-storey cottage-for-two in a grove of vegetation above Aldgate Creek, just across the road from the improving Aldgate Pump Hotel. Bonuses include flat-screen TV in the bedroom, spa and family of resident ducks.

ourpick **Organic Market & Café** (☎ 08-8339 4835; 5 Druids Ave, Stirling; meals $6-12; ❋ breakfast & lunch) Rejecting Stirling's pompous tendencies, hirsute Hill-types flock to this vibrant, hippie cafe. It's the busiest spot in town – and rightly so; the food's delicious and everything's made with love. Gorge on bruschetta, plump savoury muffins, great coffee and wicked Portuguese custard tarts.

Stirling Hotel (☎ 08-8339 2345; 52 Mt Barker Rd, Stirling; bistro $14-26, restaurant $26-36; ❋ lunch & dinner) The owners spent so much money tarting up this gorgeous old dame, it's a wonder they can pay the staff. A runaway success, the free-flowing bistro (classy pub grub) and romantic restaurant (upmarket regional cuisine) are always packed.

Jimmies (☎ 08-8339 1534; 6 Main St, Crafers; mains $17-20; ❋ breakfast Sun, lunch Sat, dinner Tue-Sun) A perennially busy pizza joint (kid friendly) serving fantastic gourmet pizzas. Order a delicious pumpkin, Danish fetta, rocket and *zataar* (Middle Eastern spices) disc and hit the outdoor tables.

See also Petaluma's Bridgewater Mill, in Top Five Adelaide Hills Wineries, p748.

MYLOR
pop 740

The going concern in leafy Mylor is **Warrawong Sanctuary** (☎ 08-8370 9197; www.warrawong.com; Stock Rd, Mylor; admission before 4pm free, adult/child/family $5/3/13 4pm-9pm; ❋ 9am-9pm), 3km from town – a feral-free private wildlife sanctuary with a cafe and accommodation. Take a self-guided walk, check out a wildlife show (adult/child/family $5/3/13, 11am and 2pm daily), or book a 1½-hour guided dusk walk (adult/child/family $25/16/65). Accommodation is in en suite eco tents, each sleeping up to eight. Bed-and-breakfast costs adult/child/family $75/45/195; packages are also available including bed, show, walk, dinner and breakfast (adult/child/family $120/70/350). There's a **cafe** (meals $6-20; ❋ lunch & dinner) here too, but the awful blaring R&B might send you packing.

Never seen a platypus? **Platypus Eco Tours** (☎ 08-8370 8628; www.platypusecotours.com.au; Lot 14, Williams Rd, Mylor; adult/child $40/20; ❋ sunset) runs small-group eco tours – you're guaranteed to see more than just the disappearing splash of a tail! Other critters here include bandicoots, wallabies, kangaroos and koalas. Tours at sunset year-round; call for bookings and times.

HAHNDORF
pop 1700

Like The Rocks in Sydney and Richmond near Hobart, Hahndorf is a 'ye olde worlde' colonial enclave that trades ruthlessly on its history. The town has become a kitsch parody of itself with very little actual 'life', just busloads of tourists picking over the bones of former glories.

That said, Hahndorf is undeniably pretty, with Teutonic sandstone architecture, European trees, and flowers overflowing from half wine-barrels. And it *is* interesting: Australia's oldest surviving German settlement (1839), founded by 50 Lutheran families fleeing religious persecution in Prussia. Hahndorf was placed under martial law during WWI; its Lutheran school was boarded-up and its name changed to 'Ambleside' (renamed Hahndorf in 1935).

Information
Adelaide Hills visitors centre (☎ 1800 353 323; 08-8388 1185; www.visitadelaidehills.com.au; 41 Main St; ❋ 9am-5pm Mon-Fri, 10am-4pm Sat & Sun) Has the usual barrage of brochures, books accommodation and provides internet access.

Sights & Activities
The 1857 **Hahndorf Academy & Heritage Museum** (☎ 08-8388 7250; www.hahndorfacademy.org.au; 68

SOUTH AUSTRALIA

TOP FIVE ADELAIDE HILLS WINERIES

With night mists and reasonable rainfall, the Adelaide Hills' midaltitude slopes sustain one of SA's cooler climates – perfect for producing some complex and truly top-notch white wines, especially Chardonnays and Sauvignon Blancs. There are 20-plus wineries here, but the following are our favourite five:

- **Bird in Hand** (☎ 08-8389 9488; www.birdinhand.com.au; cnr Bird in Hand & Pfeiffer Rds, Woodside; ☷ 11am-5pm Mon-Fri, from 10am Sat & Sun) Brilliant sparkling red, Shiraz, Merlot and blends, plus an olive-oil press. Worth at least two in the bush.

- **The Lane** (☎ 08-8388 1250; www.thelane.com.au; Ravenswood La, Hahndorf; mains $27-35; ☷ 10am-4pm Mon-Thu, to 5pm Fri-Sun) Wow! What a cool building, and what a setting! Camera-conducive views and contemporary varietals (Viognier, Pinot Grigio, Pinot Gris), plus an outstanding restaurant.

- **Nepenthe Wines** (☎ 08-8388 4439; www.nepenthe.com.au; Jones Rd, Balhannah; ☷ 10am-4pm) Homer described nepenthe as a potion to ease grief and banish sorrow from the mind. Accordingly, Nepenthe Wines bring great happiness, especially the Semillon, Chardonnay and (surprisingly) Cabernet Sauvignon.

- **Petaluma's Bridgewater Mill** (☎ 08-8339 9200; www.bridgewatermill.com.au; Mt Barker Rd, Bridgewater; 2/3 courses $68/87; ☷ 10am-5pm Thu-Mon) In a restored 200-year-old flour mill, this is one of SA's premier winery restaurants. Book for a tasting followed by lunch. Exquisite Chardonnay, Riesling and Sauvignon Blanc.

- **Shaw & Smith** (☎ 08-8398 0500; www.shawandsmith.com; Jones Rd, Balhannah; ☷ 11am-4pm Sat & Sun) Picture-perfect Mt Lofty Ranges views almost steal the show at this mod winery, run by two cousins. Outstanding Chardonnays and Sauvignon Blancs, holding hands with grand Shiraz.

Main St; academy free; museum by donation; ☷ 10am-5pm) houses an art gallery with rotating exhibitions and several original sketches by Sir Hans Heysen, the famed landscape artist and Hahndorf homeboy. The museum depicts the lives of early German settlers, with pious church pews, dour dresses, horse-drawn buggies and a collection of bizarrely carved pipes.

You'll see more than 300 of Sir Hans' original doodles on a tour through his studio and house, the **Cedars** (☎ 08-8388 7277; fax 08-8388 1845; Heysen Rd; tours $8; ☷ tours 11am, 1pm & 3pm Sep-May, 11am & 2pm Jun-Aug, Tue-Sun), 2km northwest of town.

Pick your own strawberries between November and May from the famous, family-run **Beerenberg Strawberry Farm** (☎ 08-8388 7272; www.beerenberg.com.au; Mount Barker Rd; strawberries from $9 per kg; ☷ 9am-5pm, last entry 4.15pm), also big-noted for its plethora of jams, chutneys and sauces.

Sleeping & Eating

Stables Inn (☎ 08-8388 7988; www.stablesinncafemotel .websyte.com.au; 74 Main St; d with/without spa $110/85,

f $150, extra person $22; ☒) The most affordable beds within cooee are in this converted 1860s stable, with small but comfy bottle-green motel rooms. The family-sized house out the back sleeps eight.

Manna (☎ 1800 882 682, 08-8388 1000; www.the manna.com.au; 25 & 35a Main St; d with/without spa from $200/140; ☒ ☒) Behind the Hahndorf Inn you'll find a refurbished, exposed-brick motel complex (formerly the Hahndorf Inn Motor Lodge) with an indoor pool, and brand spankin'–new upmarket suites at the Manna.

Chocolate @ No 5 (☎ 08-8388 1835; 5 Main St; items $2-8; ☷ breakfast & lunch Thu-Mon) Everyone knows why you're here, so don't feel embarrassed. Just plough into the homemade choc desserts and delicious milk, dark or white hot chocolates.

Udder Delights (☎ 08-8388 1588; www.udderdelights .com.au; 91a Main St; breakfast $6-10, mains $12-32; ☷ breakfast & lunch) The shining light of Hahndorf's food scene, this udderly delightful cheese cellar-cafe serves salads, tarts, pies, soups, cakes, generous cheese platters and the best coffee this side of Stirling.

For slatherings of sauerkraut, wurst, pretzels, strudel and clinking beer steins, try Hahndorf's pubs:

German Arms Hotel (☎ 08-8388 7013; 69 Main St; mains $12-30; ☿ lunch & dinner) Packed on weekends (with 18-to-25-year-olds, oddly enough), the bratwursts and schnitzels here are legendary.

Hahndorf Inn (☎ 08-8388 1000; 35 Main St; mains $14-30) Heart-clogging cheese kranskys, Vienna sausages, sauerkraut and apple strudels; a friendly buzz and no pokies.

See also The Lane, in Top Five Adelaide Hills Wineries, opposite.

OAKBANK & WOODSIDE

Strung-out **Oakbank** (population 450), lives for the annual **Oakbank Easter Racing Carnival** (www.oakbankracingclub.com.au), said to be the greatest picnic race meeting in the world. It's a two-day festival of equine splendour, risqué dresses and 18-year-olds who can't hold their liquor.

On 200 acres 2km north of Oakbank, the three traditional and two contemporary retreats that make up the **Adelaide Hills Country Cottages** (☎ 08-8388 4193; www.ahcc.com.au; Oakwood Rd, Oakbank; d incl breakfast from $205; ☒) have racked up a wall-full of awards. Open fires, breakfast provisions, spas and wireless internet. Two night minimum.

Agricultural **Woodside** (population 1830) has a few enticements for galloping gourmands:

Melba's Chocolate & Confectionary Factory (☎ 08-8389 7868; www.melbaschocolates.com; 22 Henry St, Woodside; admission & tastings free; ☿ 9am-4.30pm) Watch choc-coated sultanas tumbling in huge cement mixers and stock up on rocky road, scorched almonds and appallingly realistic chocolate cow pats.

Woodside Cheese Wrights (☎ 08-8389 7877; www .woodsidecheesewrights.com.au; 7 Henry St, Woodside; admission & tastings free; ☿ 10am-4pm) A passionate and unpretentious Woodside gem producing classic, artisan and experimental cheeses (soft styles a speciality) from locally grazing sheep and cows.

Woodside Providore (☎ 08-8389 9510; 69 Main Rd, Woodside; mains $10-23; ☿ breakfast & lunch) An understated, organic Hills hit, with super coffee, salads, soups, gourmet pizzas, local wines and international offerings such as osso bucco and Sri Lankan curries.

LOBETHAL

pop 1660

In the 'Valley of Praise', Lobethal was established by Lutheran Pastor Fritzsche and his followers in 1842. The church opened for business in 1843. Like Hahndorf, Lobethal was renamed during WWI – 'Tweedale' was the unfortunate choice. The main street has the usual complement of soporific pubs and hardware stores, but the town really hits its straps during December's **Lights of Lobethal** (www.lightsoflobethal.com.au) festival – a blaze of Christmas lights bringing sightseers from the city.

While you're in town, check out the local arts and crafts at the **Heart of the Hills Market** (☎ 08-8389 5615; www.marketsatheart.com; 1 Adelaide-Lobethal Rd; admission free; ☿ 10am-4pm Fri-Sun) then repair to the streetside terrace of the **Lobethal Bierhaus** (☎ 08-8389 5570; www.bierhaus.com.au; 3a Main St; ☿ noon-10pm Fri & Sat, to 6pm Sun) for some serious microbrewed concoctions. The Red Truck Porter will put hairs on your chest.

The modest **Lobethal Bakery** (☎ 08-8389 6318; 80 Main St; items $2-7; breakfast & lunch Mon-Sat) is a Hills institution, spawning franchises in other towns. Germanic biscuits, cakes, pies and takeaway soup in a cup.

The **Mawson Trail** (see Take the Long Way Home, p722) tracks through here.

GUMERACHA & BIRDWOOD

A scenic drive from Adelaide to Birdwood leads through the **Torrens River Gorge** and **Gumeracha** (population 400), a hardy hillside town with a pub at the bottom (making it hard to roll home). The main lure here is the 18.3m-high **Big Rocking Horse** (admission $2), which doesn't actually rock, but is unusually tasteful as far as Australia's 'big' tourist attractions go. It's part of the **Toy Factory** (☎ 08-8389 1085; www.thetoyfactory.com.au; Main Adelaide Rd, Gumeracha; ☿ 9am-5pm), which turns out quality handmade wooden toys (oh, and Big Rocking Horse stubbie holders).

National Trust–classified buildings line the slumbering main drag of **Birdwood** (population 1130), which began as a wide-awake gold-mining and agricultural centre in the 1850s. Behind the town's impressive old flour mill (1852) is a collection of immaculate vintage and classic cars and motorcycles at the **National Motor Museum** (☎ 08-8568 4000; Shannon St; www.history.sa.gov.au; adult/child/concession/family $9/4/7/24; ☿ 9am-5pm). The museum marks the finishing line for September's **Bay to Birdwood** (www.baytobirdwood .com.au): a convoy of classic cars chugging up from the city.

SOUTH AUSTRALIA

FLEURIEU PENINSULA

Patterned with vineyards, olive groves and almond plantations, the Fleurieu (pronounced *Floo*-ree-oh) is Adelaide's weekend (and often midweek) playground, with straw-coloured hills running down to the sea. The McLaren Vale Wine Region is booming, producing gutsy reds (salubrious Shiraz) to rival those from the Barossa Valley (actually, we think McLaren Vale wins hands down).

Further east, the Fleurieu's Encounter Coast is a curious mix of surf beaches, historic towns and whales cavorting offshore.

Online resources include www.fleurieupeninsula.com.au and www.mclarenvale.info.

MCLAREN VALE
pop 2560

Flanked by the wheat-coloured Willunga Scarp, 'The Vale' rivals the Barossa as SA's most-visited wine region. Just 40 minutes south of Adelaide, it's an easy cruise to SA's version of the Mediterranean. Encircled by vines, McLaren Vale itself is the region's service centre – an energetic, utilitarian town that's not much to look at, but has some great eateries.

Information

McLaren Vale & Fleurieu visitors centre (☎ 08-8323 9944; www.mclarenvale.info; Main Rd, McLaren Vale; ☺ 9am-5pm Mon-Fri, from 10am Sat & Sun) At the northern end of McLaren Vale; can assist with accommodation and Sealink (p758) bus and ferry bookings (to Kangaroo Island).

Sights & Activities

Most people come to McLaren Vale to cruise the wineries (see Top Five McLaren Vale Wineries, opposite). You could spend days doing nothing else!

Another way to get a feel for the area is to take the **walking & cycling track** along the old railway line from McLaren Vale to Willunga, 6km south. Hire a bike from Blessed Cheese (see opposite), or **Oxygen Cycles** (☎ 08-8323 7345; oxygencycles@gmail.com; 143 Main Rd; bike hire per half/full day $15/25; ☺ 10am-6pm Tue-Thu, 9am-6pm Fri, 9am-5pm Sat, 10am-5pm Sun). Helmet, lock and basket (for bottles!) included.

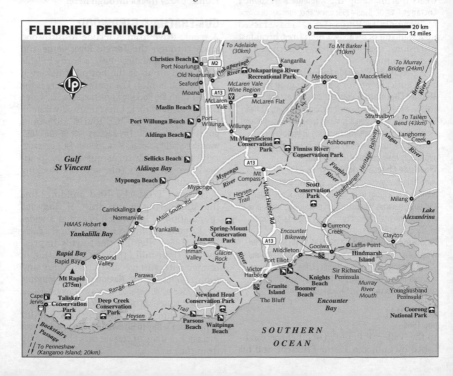

FLEURIEU PENINSULA

TOP FIVE MCLAREN VALE WINERIES

If the Barossa Valley is SA wine's old-school, then McLaren Vale is the upstart teenager smoking cigarettes behind the shed and stealing nips from dad's port bottle. The gorgeous vineyards around here have a Tuscan haze in summer, rippling down to a calm coastline that's similarly Ligurian. This is Shiraz country – solid, punchy and seriously good.

■ **Chapel Hill Winery** (☎ 08-8323 8429; www.chapelhillwine.com.au; cnr Chapel Hill & Chaffey's Rd;   noon-5pm) At the top of the hill is this restored 1865 chapel with vineyard and ocean views. The wines are made for drinking now.

■ **Coriole** (☎ 08-8323 8305; www.coriole.com; Chaffeys Rd, McLaren Vale;   10am-5pm Mon-Fri, from 11am Sat & Sun) Take your regional tasting platter out into the garden of this beautiful cottage cellar door (1860) to share kalamata olives, homemade breads and Adelaide Hills' Woodside cheeses made lovelier by a swill of the Redstone Shiraz or the flagship Chenin Blanc.

■ **d'Arenberg Wines** (☎ 08-8323 8710; www.darenberg.com.au; Osborn Rd;   10am-5pm) A favourite spot in the Vale for lunch, 'd'Arry's' relaxes atop a hillside and enjoys fine views. The wine labels are part of the character of this place: Stump Jump Grenache Shiraz, Dead Arm Shiraz, and the Broken Fishplate Sauvignon Blanc are our faves. Book ahead for lunch.

■ **Wirra Wirra Vineyards** (☎ 08-8323 8414; www.wirrawirra.com; McMurtrie Rd;   10am-5pm Mon-Sat, from 11am Sun) Fancy some *pétanque* with your plonk? This barnlike, 1894 cellar door has a grassy picnic area, and there's a roaring fire inside in winter. Sample reasonably priced stickies (dessert wines) and the popular Reserve Shiraz. Whites include a citrusy Viognier and aromatic Riesling.

■ **Woodstock Winery & Coterie** (☎ 08-8383 0156; www.woodstockwine.com.au; Douglas Gully Rd;   9am-5pm Mon-Fri, from noon Sat & Sun) Their reds are grand but hold out for the stickies and fortified drops. The Coterie does great platters ($30) for lunch, while the surrounding native garden is full of birdlife.

It seems like most of Adelaide gets tizzied-up and buses down to the annual **Sea & Vines Festival** (www.seaandvines.com) over the June long weekend. Local wineries cook up seafood, splash wine around and host live bands.

Sleeping & Eating

McLaren Vale Lakeside Caravan Park (☎ 08-8323 9255; www.mclarenvale.net; Field St; unpowered/powered sites $21/25, vans/cabins with bathroom from $50/80;   ) A short walk from town, this park by an artificial lake (any water this summer?) is as affordable as McLaren Vale accommodation gets. There's a camp kitchen, pool, spa, tennis court and trashy book exchange.

McLaren Vale Motel & Apartments (☎ 1800 631 817; 08-8323 8265; www.mclarenvalemotel.com.au; cnr Main Rd & Caffrey St; s/d/f from $101/116/124;   ) A digestive walk from main-street restaurants, this cheery motel has solid doubles (old fashioned but clean and perfectly adequate), studio apartments and family suites, plus a pool fringed by derelict palms.

Red Poles (☎ 08-8323 8994; www.redpoles.com.au; McMurtrie Rd; d with/without bathroom $125/115) Nooked away in a bushy enclave, Red Poles is a great place to stay (and eat!). Try for the rustic-style en-suite room – it's bigger than its counterparts. Order up some vegetarian moussaka or saltbush lamb salad (mains $23 to $31; open for lunch Wednesday to Sunday, breakfast on Sunday), and check out the local artwork in the gallery while you wait.

Blessed Cheese (☎ 08-8323 7958; 150 Main Rd; mains $7-18;   breakfast & lunch) This blessed cafe cranks out great coffee, croissants, wraps, salads, tarts, burgers, cheese platters and murderous cakes. Join their self-guided Cheese & Wine Trail (www.cheeseandwinetrails.com.au/mclaren.html; $55) and pick up a mini-Esky containing cheeses, crackers, olives and muscatels. Bike hire per day/three hours costs $30/21.

Salopian Inn (☎ 08-8323 8769; cnr Main & McMurtie Rds; mains $32;   lunch Thu-Tue, dinner Fri & Sat) South of town, this vine-covered cottage behind a rosemary hedge has a serious rep. Start with the crumbed lambs brains with roasted cherry tomatoes and lemon, garlic and caper noisette butter, then follow through with the wild

SOUTH AUSTRALIA

rabbit pie with roast vegies. Descend into the cellar for your wine.

See also Top Five McLaren Vale Wineries, p751, for winery restaurant options.

Getting There & Around

Premier Stateliner (☎ 08-8415 5555; www.premierstate liner.com.au) runs up to three buses daily from Adelaide to McLaren Vale ($8, one hour) and Willunga ($9, 70 minutes). Regular **Adelaide Metro** (☎ 1800 182 160, 08-8210 1000; www.adelaidemetro .com.au) suburban trains run between Adelaide and Noarlunga. From here, **Southlink** (☎ 08-8186 2888; www.southlink.com.au) buses 751 and 753 run to McLaren Vale and Willunga. Regular Adelaide Metro ticket prices apply.

For bike hire, see Oxygen Cycles (p750). For McLaren Vale tours ex-Adelaide, see p734.

WILLUNGA
pop 2430

A one-horse town with three pubs (a winning combo!), artsy Willunga took off in 1840 when high-quality slate was discovered nearby and exported across Australia. Today, the pink dollar has helped convert the town's early buildings along sloping High St into gourmet eateries and galleries.

The **Willunga Environment Centre** (☎ /fax 08-8556 4188; 18 High St; ☽ 10am-3pm Mon-Fri, 9.30am-1.30pm Sat) has basic tourist info and details on local flora and fauna. The town blooms into its own during the **Almond Blossom Festival** (www .willungafestivals.com) in July; if you can't wait that long, the **Willunga Farmers Market** (☎ 08-8556 4297; www.willungafarmersmarket.com; High St; ☽ 8am-12.30pm Sat) happens every weekend.

SEASONAL WORK

The Fleurieu Peninsula offers myriad opportunities for harvest work, including picking and pruning work among the almonds, grapes, olives, strawberries and roses. For work leads see www.southaustralia.com, or contact the following agencies:

Cozwine (☎ 08-8555 0103; www.baysidegrp .com.au/cozwine)

Employment Options (☎ 08-8398 2355; www.employmentoptions.com.au)

Trimvine (☎ 08-8537 3221; www.trimvine .com.au)

Workskil (☎ 1300 656 441; www.workskil .com.au)

The **Kidman Trail** (see Take the Long Way Home, p722) kicks off here.

Sleeping & Eating

Willunga Hotel (☎ 08-8556 2135; jhunt@picknowl.com .au; 3-5 High St; s/d $35/60) Straight-up, carpeted pub rooms painted a peachy colour, with clean shared bathrooms and a TV room. Downstairs in the 'Middle Pub' you can get a simple, feed-a-farmer pub meal (mains $16 to $20, lunch and dinner) – schnitzels, steaks and pasta.

Willunga House B&B (☎ 08-8556 2467; www.wil lungahouse.com.au; 1 St Peters Tce; d incl breakfast $190-250; ☒ ☒) If you're looking for a real treat, this graceful 1850 mansion off the main street is for you: Baltic-pine floorboards, Italian cherry-wood beds, open fires, Indigenous art and wireless internet. Breakfast is a feast of organic muesli, fruit salad and poached pears, followed by cooked delights.

ourpick Russell's Pizza (☎ 08-8556 2571; 13 High St; pizzas from $24; ☽ dinner Thu-Sat Dec-Feb, Fri & Sat Mar-Nov) It may look like a ramshackle chicken coop, but Russell's is the place to be on weekends for sensational wood-fired pizza. No one minds the wait for a meal (which could be hours) – it's all about the atmosphere. It's super popular, so book way ahead.

GULF ST VINCENT BEACHES

There are some ace swimming beaches (but no surf) along the Gulf St Vincent coastline, extending from suburban **Christies Beach** onto **Maslin Beach**, the southern end of which is a nudist and a gay hang-out. Maslin is 45 minutes from Adelaide by car – just far enough to escape the sprawling shopping centres and new housing developments trickling south from the city.

Port Willunga is home to the eternally busy, cliff-top seafood shack the **Star of Greece** (☎ 08-8557 7420; 1 The Esplanade, Port Willunga; mains $28-37; ☽ lunch daily, dinner Fri & Sat), with funky decor, great staff and a sunny outdoor patio. We asked the waiter where the whiting was caught: he looked out across the bay and said, 'See that boat out there?'.

On the highway near **Sellicks Beach** is the rowdy, 1858 pub the **Victory** (☎ 08-8556 3083; Main South Rd, Sellicks Beach; mains $10-32; ☽ lunch & dinner). The pub has awesome views of the silvery gulf and a cheery, laid-back vibe. Factor in inspired meals, an impressive cellar and wines by the glass and you're onto a winner. Renovations

---

DETOUR: RAPID BAY

Off the highway 15km south of Normanville is Rapid Bay. In the 1950s this was a boomtown, the local quarry shipping 60,000 tonnes of lime per month from the enormous jetty. When production ceased in 1981, Rapid Bay assumed a gothic, ghost-town atmosphere: empty '50s villas and workers' quarters now line the streets, and the local shop (closed) has signs advertising soft drinks they don't make any more. Without the lime boats, the old jetty has become a popular **fishing** and **diving** site.

---

were afoot when we visited – expect even better views!

About 60km south of Adelaide is **Carrickalinga**, which has a gorgeous arc of white sandy beach. North and south Carrickalinga beaches are separated by the volcanic outcrop Haycock Point. It's a very chilled spot with no shops. For supplies and accommodation, head to **Normanville**, which has a great pub, a supermarket, a couple of caravan parks and the **Jetty Food Store** (☎ 08-8558 2537; 48A Main Rd, Normanville; meals $10-29; ☺ 10am-6pm Mon-Thu, to 7.30pm Fri, 9am-7.30pm Sat, to 6.30pm Sun). The motto here is 'Coastal food hunted and gathered for you'. Grab a dozen Kangaroo Island oysters, some locally caught fish and chips, or a gourmet pizza, from Friday to Sunday.

There's not much at **Cape Jervis**, 107km from Adelaide, other than the Kangaroo Island ferry terminal (see p758), and the start (or end) point for the Heysen Trail (p722). Nearby, **Deep Creek Conservation Park** (☎ 08-8598 0263; www .environment.sa.gov.au/parks/sanpr/deepcreek; admission per car $7.50) has sweeping coastal views, a wicked waterfall, man-size yakkas (*Xanthorrhoea semiplana tateana*), sandy beaches, kangaroos, kookaburras and bush camping areas (per car $15).

Off the road to Deep Creek Conservation Park are the curved roofs of the superb **Ridgetop Retreats** (☎ 08-8598 4169; www.southern oceanretreats.com.au; d $185): three corrugated iron-clad, self-contained luxury units in the bush, with wood heaters, leather lounges and stainless steel benchtops. See the website for more-affordable local options.

See p721 for local diving info.

VICTOR HARBOR
pop 10,400

Oddly detached from its rural setting, Victor Harbor (yes, that's the correct spelling) is the biggest town on the **Encounter Coast** – a raggedy, brawling holiday destination, with three huge pubs and circa-1991 decor. In January the grassy foreshore runs rampant with **schoolies** (www.schoolies.org.au/victor-harbor.htm), teenage school-leavers blowing off hormones.

Information
Victor Harbor visitors centre (☎ 08-8552 5738; www.tourismvictorharbor.com.au; Causeway; ☺ 9am-5pm; ▣) Has internet access, and handles tour and accommodation bookings.

Sights & Activities
Just offshore is the boulder-strewn **Granite Island**, connected to the mainland by an 1875 causeway. Ride out there on the 1894 double-decker **horse-drawn tram** (return adult/child/family $7/5/20; ☺ every 40 min 10am-4pm); tickets from the visitors centre. **Granite Island Nature Park** (☎ 08-8552 7555; www.graniteisland.com.au) runs sunset **penguin tours** (adult/child/concession/family $12.50/7.50/11/36; ☺ nightly) to watch the island's little penguins haul themselves out of the water. Bookings essential.

Victor Harbor is on the migratory path of southern right whales (see www.environment .sa.gov.au/coasts/whales). The **South Australian Whale Centre** (☎ 08-8551 0750; www.sawhalecentre.com; 2 Railway Tce; adult/child/concession/family $8/4/5.50/20; ☺ 9.30am-5pm) has impressive displays on Victor's largest visitors – including a big stinky skull – and can give you the low-down on where to see them.

The much-wheeled **Encounter Bikeway** (www .tourismvictorharbor.com.au/walks_trails.html) extends 30km from Victor Harbor to Laffin Point, past Goolwa. The visitors centre stocks maps. For bike hire, see p754.

Sleeping & Eating
Victor Harbor Holiday & Cabin Park (☎ 08-8552 1949; www.victorharborholiday.com.au; Bay Rd; unpowered/powered sites $24/28, vans/cabins from $52/86; ▣) The friendliest operation in town, with tidy facilities, free barbecues and a rambling grassed area with a few trees to pitch a tent on. Runs rings around Victor's other caravan parks.

Anchorage Seafront Hotel (☎ 08-8552 5970; www
.anchorageseafronthotel.com; 21 Flinders Pde; s/d/tr incl breakfast from $40/70/85) This grand, heritage-listed,
seafront guest house is the pick of the bunch.
Immaculately maintained, great-value rooms
open off jade-painted corridors with fresh
flowers in them. Most rooms face the beach,
and some have a balcony (you'd pay through
the nose for this is Sydney!). The cheapest
rooms share bathrooms. The Ocean Grill cafe-
bar downstairs is a winner too.

Nino's (☎ 08-8552 3501; 17 Albert Pl; mains $14-23;
🕑 lunch & dinner) Nino's cafe has been here since
1974, but it manages to put a contemporary
sheen on downtown VH. Hip young staff and
a mod interior set the scene for gourmet pizzas, pasta, salads, risottos and meaty Italian
mains. Good coffee too.

Ocean Grill @ Anchorage (☎ 08-8552 5970; Anchorage
Seafront Hotel, 21 Flinders Pde; mains $16-26) This salty
sea-cave, with fishing nets trawling from the
ceiling and an old whaling boat for a bar, has
a Med-meets–Mod Oz menu with plenty of
seafood. There's great coffee, tapas, cakes,
Euro beers and a beachside terrace to drink
them on.

Getting There & Around

Premier Stateliner (☎ 08-8415 5555; www.premierstate
liner.com.au) runs buses to Victor Harbor from
Adelaide ($19, 1¾ hours, one to five daily)
continuing on to Goolwa.

On the last Sunday in May and the first
and third Sundays from June to November,
SteamRanger Heritage Railway (☎ 1300 655 991,
08-8263 5621; www.steamranger.org.au) operates the
Southern Encounter (adult/child/conces-
sion/family return $64/35/55/155) tourist
train from Mt Barker in the Adelaide Hills to
Victor Harbor via Strathalbyn, Goolwa and
Port Elliot. The *Cockle Train* (adult/child return $26/15) runs along the Encounter Coast
between Victor Harbor and Goolwa via Port
Elliot every Sunday.

Victor Harbor Cycle & Skate (☎ /fax 08-8552 1417;
73 Victoria St; bike hire per 2hr/day $10/45; 🕑 9am-5.30pm
Mon-Wed & Fri, to 7.30pm Thu, to noon Sat) rents out
mountain bikes.

PORT ELLIOT
pop 3100

About 8km east of Victor Harbor, historic
Port Elliot is set back from **Horseshoe Bay**, an
orange-sand arc with surging surf. Norfolk
Island pines reach for the sky, and there are

whale-spotting updates posted on the pub
wall. **Commodore Point**, at the eastern end of
Horseshoe Bay, and nearby **Boomer Beach** and
Knights Beach have reliable waves for experienced surfers. The beach at otherwise missable
Middleton, the next town towards Goolwa, also
has solid breaks.

For surf-gear hire:
Southern Surf (☎ 08-8554 2375; 36 North Tce, Port
Elliot; 🕑 9am-5pm) Surfboards/bodyboards/wetsuits per
day for $22/11/11.
Big Surf Australia (☎ 08-8554 2399; fax 08-8554
3028; 24 Goolwa Rd, Middleton; 🕑 9am-5pm) Surf-
boards/bodyboards/wetsuits per day for $25/15/10.

Sleeping & Eating

Royal Family Hotel (☎ 08-8554 2219; www.royalfamilyho
tel.com.au; 32 North Tce, Port Elliot; s/d $50/60) It's doubtful
that Prince Chuck has ever stayed here, but if
he did he'd find surprisingly decent pub rooms
with clean shared bathrooms, a TV lounge and
balcony over the main street. Downstairs the
bistro serves counter meals fit for a king (mains
$12 to $24, lunch and dinner).

Port Elliot Holiday Park (☎ 08-8554 2134; www
.portelliotcaravanpark.com.au; Middleton Rd, Port Elliot; un-
powered/powered sites $28/34, cabins/units/cottages from
$110/135/160, extra person $9) In an unbeatable position behind the Horseshoe Bay dunes (it
can be a touch windy), this grassy, 12-acre
park has all the requisite facilities, including
a tennis court and all-weather barbecue area.
Prices plummet in winter.

our pick Flying Fish (☎ 08-8554 3504; 1 The Foreshore,
Port Elliot; lunch $21-28, dinner $29-42; 🕑 lunch & dinner daily,
reduced winter hrs) Sit down for lunch and you'll be
here all day – the views of Horseshoe Bay are
sublime. Otherwise grab some quality takeaway
of Coopers-battered flathead and chips and
head back to the sand. At night things get a
little classier, with à la carte mains or a degustation menu (per person $95, or $130 with wine)
focusing on independent SA producers.

Getting There & Away

Premier Stateliner (☎ 08-8415 5555; www.premier
stateliner.com.au) has up to five daily services
between Adelaide and Port Elliot ($19, two
hours), linking the town with Victor Harbor
and Goolwa.

GOOLWA
pop 6500

Much more low-key and elegant than
kissing-cousin Victor Harbor, Goolwa is an

BUILDING BRIDGES (NOT...)

First proposed in 1988, construction of the Hindmarsh Island Bridge was opposed by Ngarrindjeri women who had concerns about the spiritual and cultural significance of the site. A series of court battles ensued, pitting Aboriginal beliefs against development, and culminating in a Royal Commission (1995) that ruled that the claims of Aboriginal 'secret women's business' were fabricated. Further court appeals were launched, and in August 2001 the Federal Court overturned the Royal Commission, finding the Ngarrindjeri claims to be legitimate. Unfortunately, this vindication came five months after the bridge was officially opened. The decade-long furore was a step backwards for reconciliation, made worse by the media's often-flawed coverage.

unassuming town where the Murray River empties into the sea. Australia's greatest river has been tragically depleted by climate change and upstream irrigation – Goolwa's jetties and marinas have been left high and dry above the shrinking river; a huge banner adorning a local pub says 'We Need Water Now!'. But beyond the dunes is a fantastic beach with ranks of broken surf rolling in from the ocean, same as it ever was...

Information

Goolwa visitors centre (☎ 08-8555 3488; www.visit alexandrina.com; The Wharf; ☷ 9am-5pm) Has plenty of local info (including accommodation), plus the Signal Point River Murray Centre.

Sights & Activities

The **Signal Point River Murray Centre** (adult/child/family $5.50/3/13.50) is in the Goolwa visitors centre. Inside are interpretive and interactive displays on the life and ecology of the Murray.

Down on the wharf, the **Steam Exchange Brewery** (☎ 08-8555 3406; www.steamexchange.com.au; The Wharf; ☷ 10am-5pm) is a locally-run brewery, turning out manly stouts and ales. There's a small fee for tastings; tours by arrangement.

Not far from the brewery, Hindmarsh Island Bridge links the Goolwa with **Hindmarsh Island**; see Building Bridges (Not...), above, for the story behind the bridge.

Spirit of the Coorong (☎ 1800 442 203, 08-8555 2203; www.coorongcruises.com.au; The Wharf) runs eco-cruises on the Murray and into the Coorong National Park, including lunch and guided walks. The 4½-hour Coorong Discovery Cruise (adult/child $74/55) runs on Mondays and Thursdays all year, plus Tuesdays and Saturdays from October to May. The six-hour Coorong Adventure Cruise (adult/child $88/60) runs on Sundays all year, plus Wednesdays from October to May. Bookings essential.

At **Goolwa Beach** a boardwalk traverses the dunes looking out at the barrelling surf. **Barrell Surf & Skate** (☎ 08-8555 5422; www.barrellsurf.com.au; 10C Cadell St; ☷ 9.30am-5.30pm) has gear hire (longboard/bodyboard/wetsuit $25/10/15). See p753 for details on the coastal Encounter Bikeway between Goolwa and Victor Harbor (maps available at the Goolwa visitor centre).

Sleeping

Holiday rentals in and around Goolwa are managed by **LJ Hooker** (☎ 08-8555 1785; www.ljh .com.au/goolwa; 25 Cadell St) and the **Professionals** (☎ 08-8555 2122; www.professionalsgoolwa.com.au; 1 Cadell St), both of whom have houses for as little as $70 per night (mostly around $130) and good weekly rates.

Goolwa Central Motel (☎ 08-8555 1155; www .goolwacentralmotel.com.au; 30 Cadell St; s/d/f from $110/120/160; ☒ ☐ ☒) This two-level motel is next to an Irish pub, and has allowed the emerald roguishness to filter through (rooms are called Tyrone, Fermanagh, etc). Nothing flash, but a solid central option with a tiny pool.

Brooking Cottage B&B (☎ 08-8555 2387; www .brookingcottage.com.au; 28a Brooking St; d incl breakfast $170; ☒) A 2½-year-old B&B with all the trimmings, including an outdoor spa, brekkie provisions, a bottle of decent plonk and a cheese platter. The owner used to drive tractors; now he drives the vacuum cleaner. Sleeps six (but no kids).

Eating

Hector's (☎ 08-8555 5885; The Wharf; mains $8-19; ☷ breakfast & lunch Thu-Tue, dinner daily Jan-Mar) Standing under the ugly (in more ways than one) span of the Hindmarsh Island Bridge, eating at Hector's (festooned with fishing rods) is like hanging out in your mate's boathouse. The seafood chowder and spinach-and-fetta pie sweetly complement the local wines.

Café Lime (☎ 08-8555 5522; 1/11 Goolwa Tce; meals $10-17; ☺ breakfast & lunch) Pick up heat-and-eat gourmet dinners or a takeaway cone of salt-and-pepper squid with lime-salted fries, or nab a table for beer-battered Coorong mullet (not a description of a haircut at the pub), baguettes, curries, soups and pasta. Espresso perfecto.

Southy's Wood Fired Pizzas (☎ 08-8555 5055; 1 Cadell St; pizzas $12-17; ☺ dinner Wed-Sun) All the old faves, plus a few good 'gourmet' selections: satay chicken, tandoori lamb and a yiros pizza (chicken, tomato, Spanish onion, hummus and tzatziki).

Getting There & Around

Premier Stateliner (☎ 08-8415 5555; www.premier stateliner.com.au) runs up to five buses daily between Adelaide and Goolwa ($19, two hours).

For tourist steam-train details between Goolwa, Victor Harbor and the Adelaide Hills, see p754.

KANGAROO ISLAND

From Cape Jervis, car ferries chug across the swells of the Backstairs Passage to Kangaroo Island. Long devoid of tourist trappings, the island these days is a booming destination for fans of wilderness and wildlife – it's a veritable zoo of seals, birds, dolphins, echidnas and roos. Southern Ocean Lodge, a new luxury retreat for the exquisitely rich, has propelled 'KI' onto the international stage – it seems KI is about to boom! But until that happens, it remains low-key, rurally paced and under-developed – the kind of place where kids ride bikes to school and farmers advertise for wives on noticeboards. There's some brilliant accommodation here, and island produce is just as good (if not the restaurants that serve it). Be sure to try the local seafood, marron (freshwater crayfish), honey, cheese and wine.

History

Many KI place names are French, attributable to Gallic explorer Nicholas Baudin who surveyed the coast in 1802 and 1803. Baudin's English rival, Matthew Flinders, named the island in 1802 after his crew feasted on kangaroo meat here. By this stage the island was uninhabited, but archaeologists think Indigenous Australians lived here as recently as 2000 years ago. Why they deserted KI is a matter of conjecture, though the answer is hinted at in the Indigenous name for KI: 'Karta', or 'Land of the Dead.' In the early 1800s an Indigenous presence (albeit a tragically displaced one) was re-established on KI when whalers and sealers abducted Aboriginal women from Tasmania and brought them here.

Kingscote dates from 1836 when it became the first official colony in SA. The settlement struggled bravely for two years, but the lack of fresh water led most colonists to move to Adelaide.

Information

There are bank facilities in Kingscote and Penneshaw, and a hospital in Kingscote. Mobile phone reception on the island is patchy, restricted to Kingscote, Penneshaw, American River, the airport and parts of Emu Bay. There are supermarkets at Penneshaw and Kingscote, and a general store at American River.

Department for Environment & Heritage (DEH; ☎ 08-8553 2381; www.environment.sa.gov.au/parks; 37 Dauncey St, Kingscote) Stocks Island Parks Passes (adult/child/student/family $46.50/28/36.50/126), covering all park and conservation area entry fees, and ranger-guided tours at Seal Bay, Kelly Hill Caves, Cape Borda and Cape Willoughby Lightstations (but not the penguin walks). Passes can also be purchased at most sights.

Kangaroo Island Gateway visitors centre (☎ 08-8553 1185; www.tourkangarooisland.com.au; Howard Dr; ☺ 9am-5pm Mon-Fri, 10am-4pm Sat & Sun) Just outside Penneshaw on the road to Kingscote, this centre is stocked with brochures and maps. It also books accommodation and sells park entry tickets and passes.

Activities

The safest **swimming** is along the north coast, where the water is warmer and there are fewer rips than down south. The easiest beaches to access are Emu Bay, Stokes Bay, Snelling Beach and Western River Cove.

For **surfing**, hit the uncrowded swells along the south coast. Pennington Bay has strong, reliable breaks; Vivonne Bay and Hanson Bay in the southwest also serve up some tasty waves.

There's plenty to see under your own steam on KI. Check out www.tourkangaroo island.com.au/wildlife/walks.aspx for info on **bushwalks** from 1km to 18km.

The waters around KI harbour 230 species of fish, soft and hard corals and around 60 shipwrecks – perfect for **snorkelling** and **diving**. For charters, contact **Kangaroo Island**

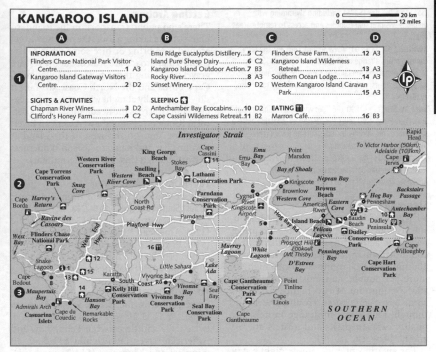

KANGAROO ISLAND

0 — 20 km
0 — 12 miles

INFORMATION	Emu Ridge Eucalyptus Distillery...**5** C2	Flinders Chase Farm..................**12** A3
Flinders Chase National Park Visitor	Island Pure Sheep Dairy..............**6** C2	Kangaroo Island Wilderness
Centre..**1** A3	Kangaroo Island Outdoor Action.**7** B3	Retreat...............................**13** A3
Kangaroo Island Gateway Visitors	Rocky River...............................**8** A3	Southern Ocean Lodge............**14** A3
Centre..**2** D2	Sunset Winery...........................**9** D2	Western Kangaroo Island Caravan
		Park...................................**15** A3
SIGHTS & ACTIVITIES	**SLEEPING**	
Chapman River Wines...............**3** D2	Antechamber Bay Ecocabins......**10** D2	**EATING**
Clifford's Honey Farm...............**4** C2	Cape Cassini Wilderness Retreat.**11** B2	Marron Café...........................**16** B3

Diving Safaris (☎ 0427 102 387; www.kidivingsafaris
.com), which runs boat dives with equipment
($290 per day) and boat-based snorkelling
($137 per day). Scuba gear hire also available
($75). Cooinda Fishing Charters (below) also
run dive trips.

Kangaroo Island Outdoor Action (☎ 08-8559 4296,
0428 822 260; www.kioutdooraction.com.au; Jetty Rd, Vivonne
Bay) rents out sandboards ($29 for four hours)
and toboggans ($39) to skid down the dunes
at Little Sahara, plus single/double kayaks
($39/69). Quad-bike tours are also available.
Vivonne Bay General Store (p762) rents out
sandboards and toboggans at the same rates.

There's plenty of good **fishing** around
the island, including jetties at Kingscote,
Penneshaw, Emu Bay and Vivonne Bay.
Fishing charter tours (half-/full-day from
$90/180) include tackle and refreshments, and
you keep what you catch. Operators include
the following:

Cooinda Fishing Charters (☎ 0439 867 713; www
.kidiving.com) Half-day tours from American River.

Kangaroo Island Fishing Charters (☎ 08-8552
7000; www.kifishchart.com.au) Pick-ups at Penneshaw,
Emu Bay or Kingscote.

Tours

See the Kangaroo Island Gateway visitors
centre or www.tourkangarooisland.com.au
for comprehensive tour listings. Day tours
from Adelaide are hectic – stay at least one
night on the island if you can. Multiday tours
generally include meals and accommodation.
A few operators:

Adventure Tours (☎ 1300 654 604; www.adventure
tours.com.au) Popular two-day tours ($425) ex-Adelaide
with lots of walking and wildlife.

Alkirna Nocturnal Tours (☎ 08-8553 7464; www
.alkirna.com.au) Nightly naturalist-led tours viewing
nocturnal critters around American River (adult/child
$58/37, two hours).

Exceptional Kangaroo Island (☎ 08-8553 9119;
www.exceptionalkangarooisland.com) Small group, deluxe
4WD day tours ($348,) with a wildlife or Flinders Chase
focus. Tours depart KI.

Groovy Grape (☎ 1800 66 11 77, 08-8440 1640; www
.groovygrape.com.au) Two-/three-day small-group wildlife
safaris ($335/435) ex-Adelaide, with sand-boarding,
campfires and all the main sights. The three-day tour runs
October to May only.

Kangaroo Island Marine Tours (☎ 0427 315 286;
www.kimarinetours.com) Water tours from one hour

SOUTH AUSTRALIA

($55) to a full day ($275), including swimming with dolphins, visiting seal colonies and access to remote areas of KI.

Sealink (☎ 13 13 01; www.sealink.com.au) The ferry company runs a range of KI-highlight day tours ($62 to $131) departing Adelaide or Kingscote. Overnight backpacker tours, self-drive tours and multiday tours also available.

Surf 'n' Sun (☺ 1800 786 386; www.surfnsun.com.au) Two-/three-day 4WD tours ($340/399) ex-Adelaide, with a strong focus on wildlife. Includes surfing lesson (three-day tour only) and sand-boarding.

Wayward Bus (☎ 1300 653 510; www.waywardbus .com.au) Two-day backpacker tours (from $397) ex-Adelaide, covering all the big-ticket sights.

Sleeping

KI accommodation is expensive, adding insult to your wallet's injury after the pricey ferry ride across from the mainland. Self-contained cottages, B&Bs and beach houses abound, most charging $150 per night or more per double, and most require guests stay a minimum of two-nights. There are some great campsites around the island though, plus a few midrange motels, but quality caravan parks and hostels are few and far between.

For an atmospheric, remote night's stay, try the historic cottages available for rent through DEH (p756; $48 to $150 for two people).

Accommodation booking resources include the Kangaroo Island Gateway visitors centre (p756), Sealink (below) and **Century 21** (☎ 08-8553 2688; www.century21.com.au/kangarooisland; 66 Dauncey St, Kingscote).

Getting There & Away

For daily flights (one-way from $77 online) between Adelaide and Kingscote, contact **Regional Express Airlines** (Rex; ☎ 13 17 13; www .regionalexpress.com.au) or **Air South** (☎ 1300 247 768, 08-8234 4988; www.airsouth.com.au).

A car ferry operates between Cape Jervis and Penneshaw. **Sealink** (☎ 13 13 01; www.sealink .com.au) runs at least three ferries each way daily (one-way adult/child/concession $43/24/36, bicycles/motorcycles/cars $15/30/84, 45 minutes). One driver is included with the vehicle price (cars only, not bikes). Sealink also operates a morning and afternoon bus service between Cape Jervis and Adelaide's Central Bus Station (adult/child $20/10, 2¼ hours).

Getting Around

There's no public transport on the island, so unless you're taking a tour, the only way to get around is to bring or hire some wheels. The island's main roads are sealed, but the rest are gravel, including those to Cape Willoughby, Cape Borda and the North Coast Rd. Take it slowly, especially at night when roos and wallabies bounce across the headlights. There's petrol at Kingscote, Penneshaw, American River, Parndana, and on the west of the island at Vivonne Bay and Kangaroo Island Wilderness Retreat (though this can be intermittent).

TO/FROM THE AIRPORT

Kingscote Airport is 14km from Kingscote; **Airport Shuttle Services** (☎ 0427 887 575) connects the airport with Emu Bay ($17.50), Kingscote ($20), American River ($25) and Penneshaw ($40). Prices are per person, with a minimum of two people; solo travellers pay double (eg Kingscote $40). Bookings essential.

TO/FROM THE FERRY

Once you're on the island, **Sealink Kangaroo Island** (☎ 13 13 01; www.sealink.com.au) runs a twice-daily shuttle between Penneshaw and American River (adult/child $11/5.50, 30 minutes) and Kingscote ($14/7, one hour). Bookings essential.

CAR HIRE

Not all Adelaide car-rental companies will let you take their cars onto KI; with ferry prices it's often cheaper to hire on the island. **Budget** (☎ 08-8553 3133; www.budgetki.com) and **Hertz** (☎ 13 30 39, 08-8553 2390; www.hertz.com.au) supply cars to Penneshaw, Kingscote and Kingscote Airport. Check if they'll let you drive on unsealed roads.

PENNESHAW & DUDLEY PENINSULA

Looking across Backstairs Passage to the Fleurieu Peninsula, **Penneshaw** (population 300), on the north shore of the **Dudley Peninsula**, is the arrival point for ferries from the mainland. The passing tourist trade lends a certain transience to the businesses here, but the pub, hostel and general store remain authentically grounded. As are the resident fairy penguins: you'll hear their clacking safety call (a cross between a quack and a yap) around town at night.

En route to American River, **Pennington Bay** has consistent surf.

Information

Kangaroo Island Gateway visitors centre (p756)
Penneshaw Business Centre (☎ 08-8553 1020; 99 Middle Tce; ☼ 9am-5pm Mon-Fri, 9am-noon Sat) Acts as a post office, internet cafe and bank agency with cash-withdrawal facilities.

Sights & Activities

On the foreshore near the ferry terminal, **Penneshaw Penguin Centre** (☎ 08-8553 1103; ppen guincentre@bigpond.com.au; adult/child/concession/fam ily $10/9/9/29; ☼ 6-9.30pm Apr-Oct, 8-10.30pm Nov-Mar, tours 7.30pm & 8.30pm Apr-Oct, 8.30pm & 9.30pm Nov-Mar) provides an unobtrusive view of the little wad-dlers that nest along the shore. Book ahead.

The **Penneshaw Maritime & Folk Museum** (☎ 08-8553 1109; www.nationaltrustsa.org.au; 52 Howard Dr; adult/ child/concession/family $3/2/2/7; ☼ 3-5pm Wed-Sun Sep-May) displays artefacts from local shipwrecks and early settlement, plus endearingly geeky models of Flinders' *Investigator* and Baudin's *Geographe*.

About 28km southeast of town, the **Cape Willoughby Lightstation** (☎ 08-8553 1191; www .environment.sa.gov.au/parks/sanpr/capewilloughby; Cape Willoughby Rd; tours adult/child/concession/fam ily $12/9.50/7.50/33) first shone in 1852 and is now used as a weather station. Tours run at 11.30am, 12.30pm and 2pm, also 3pm and 4pm in holiday periods. There's also basic accommodation here; book through DEH (p756; doubles $150).

Chapman River Wines (☎ 08-8553 1371; chapman riverwines@activ8.net.au; Cape Willoughby Rd, Antechamber Bay; ☼ 11am-4.30pm Thu-Mon Sep-Jun) occupies a converted aircraft hangar – an eccentric winery with a mean Merlot. The interior is festooned with art and quirky bits of sal-vage from churches, pubs and homesteads around SA.

Wow, what a view! If you can make it up the steep driveway, **Sunset Winery** (☎ 08-8553 1378; www.sunset-wines.com.au; Penneshaw-Kingscote Rd; platters $7-11; ☼ 11am-5pm) has brilliant Sauvignon Blanc and sparkling Shiraz, and serves savoury platters to go with the panorama.

Sleeping & Eating

See the earlier review of Cape Willoughby Lightstation for details on sleeping there.

Kangaroo Island YHA (☎ 08-8553 1344; www.yha .com.au; 33 Middle Tce; dm/d/f from $26/68/103; ☒ ☐) Occupying an old '60s motel with faux-brick cladding, the island YHA has spacious rooms with en suite bathrooms. There's a small com-munal kitchen, lounge and laundry, and pen-guins at the bottom of the garden.

Antechamber Bay Ecocabins (☎ 08-8553 1557; www.kiecocabins.com; Chapman River East Rd, Antechamber Bay; d from $100, extra adult/child $20/free) Off Cape Willoughby Rd, these two six-bed cabins are run by a couple of IT industry runaways. On 55 acres behind the dunes, the cabins are ru-dimentary but perfectly comfortable, with roofless showers, self-composting toilets and solar power and hot water. Kayaks and fishing gear $20 per stay.

Saar Beach House (☎ 08-8370 7119; www.saar beachhouse.com.au; Island Beach; d from $200, extra person $20; ☒) Saar Beach House is a self-contained architectural stand-out atop the dunes along 'Millionaire's Row' at Island Beach, 15km from Penneshaw. Views from the deck are indeed million-dollar! Sleeps 12; good winter rates.

Fish (☎ 08-8553 1177; 43 North Tce; mains $8-14; ☼ dinner Sep-Jun) Fish and chips like you ain't never had before – grilled, beer-battered or crumbed – plus giant scallops, KI marron and lobster medallions. Free fish-cooking demos at 3.30pm, October to May.

Dudley Cellar Door & Café (☎ 08-8553 1333; www .dudleywines.com.au; cnr North Tce & Thomas Wilson St, Penneshaw; mains $12-25; ☼ 11am-5pm) A brilliant new outlet for one of the KI's pioneering wine growers, serving cheese and seafood platters, curries and buckets o' prawns – perfect with a bottle of Chardonnay on the outdoor deck.

AMERICAN RIVER

pop 230

Between Penneshaw and Kingscote on the way to nowhere in particular, American River squats redundantly by the glassy **Pelican Lagoon**. The town was named after a crew of American sealers who built a trading schooner here in 1804. There's no such industriousness here today, just a daily pelican-feeding frenzy at the pier and wallabies hopping around the streets. The general store is the town's cul-tural zenith.

From the end of Scenic Dr, a fern-fringed **coastal walk** (2km one way) passes through natural scrub, sugar gums and she-oak en route to some old fish cannery ruins.

Sleeping & Eating

American River Campsite (per car $15) A shady, self-registration campsite by the lagoon, with fire pits, showers and toilets.

SOUTH AUSTRALIA

Island Coastal Units (☎ 08-8553 7010; www.kanga
rooislandcoastalunits.com.au; Tangara Dr; d from $115, extra
person $20) A low row of one- and two-bedroom
motel-style units among trees opposite the
foreshore, plus four beautiful self-contained
cabins with solar hot water, gas cooktops and
air-con.

Kangaroo Island Lodge (☎ 08-8553 7053; www
.kilodge.com.au; Scenic Dr; d $155-190; 🗶 🗩) Up-to-
scratch motel suites overlooking either the
pool or lagoon (the rammed-earth wing has
the best rooms). The restaurant plates up
plenty of local seafood (mains $20 to $30;
open for breakfast and dinner).

American River General Store (☎ 08-8553 7051;
Scenic Dr; 🕙 7.30am-6.30pm) Packed to the northern
hemisphere with provisions, bait and tackle,
plus there's an amazing hardware 'cupboard',
petrol and a bottle shop.

KINGSCOTE
pop 1450

Snoozy seaside Kingscote (pronounced,
'Kings-coat') is the main town on KI, and
the hub of island life. It's a photogenic town
with swaying Norfolk Island pines, a couple
of pubs and some decent eateries.

Information
DEH (p756)

Kangaroo Island Hospital (☎ 08-8553 4200; www
.kihealth.sa.gov.au; The Esplanade; 🕙 24hr) Accident and
emergency service.

Kangaroo Island Library (☎ 08-8553 4516; Dauncey
St; 🕙 10am-4.30pm Mon-Fri) Free internet access for
travellers; bookings essential.

Sights & Activities

The **Kangaroo Island Marine Centre** (☎ 08-8553 3112;
www.kimarinecentre.com.au; Kingscote Wharf; adult/child/con-
cession/family $15/6/13/36; 🕙 tours 8.30pm & 9.30pm Nov-
Mar, 7.30pm & 8.30pm Apr-Oct) runs one-hour tours of
their saltwater aquariums and the local penguin
colony. It also runs informative (and comical)
pelican feeding (Kingscote Wharf; admission $2; 🕙 5pm)
sessions at the adjacent wharf.

Hope Cottage Museum (☎ 08-8553 2656; Centenary
Ave; adult/child/concession $5/1/3; 🕙 1-4pm daily, Sat only
Aug) was built in 1857. It's now a fastidiously
maintained National Trust museum decked
out in period style, with a reconstructed lighthouse, an amazing old quilt and KI's first
piano.

Island Beehive (☎ 08-8553 0080; www.island-beehive
.com.au; cnr Playford Hwy & Acacia Dr; tours adult/child/conces-
sion/family $4.50/3/3.50/13; 🕙 9am-5pm) runs factory
tours where you can bone up on Ligurian bees
and beekeeping, then stock up on by-products
(bee-products?), including delicious organic
honey and honeycomb ice cream.

Near Cygnet River, 12km from Kingscote,
Island Pure Sheep Dairy (☎ 08-8553 9110; is_pure@
bigpond.net.au; Gum Creek Rd, Cygnet River; tours adult/
child/concession/family $5.50/4.50/4.50/20; 🕙 1-5pm) is a
family-owned operation where 1500 sheep
line up to be milked (from 3pm). Take a tour
of the factory, which includes yoghurt and
cheese tastings (the haloumi is magic).

Kingscote itself is lousy for swimming; locals usually head 18km northwest to **Emu Bay**,
or the **tidal swimming pool** (admission free; 🕙 daylight
hours) on Chapman Tce.

Sleeping & Eating

Kangaroo Island Central Hostel (☎ 08-8553 2787,
0400 197 231; ki_backpackers@bigpond.com; 19 Murray St;
dm/d from $22/55) Just a couple of blocks from
Kingscote's main strip, this small, innocuous
hostel is clean, cheap and has a cosy lounge.

Aurora Ozone Hotel (☎ 1800 083 133, 08-8553 2011;
www.ozonehotel.com; cnr Commercial St & Kingscote Tce; motel
d/tr/f from $130/180/202, deluxe d from $193; 🗶 🖳 🗩)
Opposite the foreshore with killer views, the
100-year-old Ozone pub has standard motel-
style rooms and stylish deluxe suites in a new
wing across the street. The eternally busy bistro (mains $17 to $30; breakfast, lunch and
dinner) serves farmer-sized grills and seafood,
and you can pickle yourself on KI wines at
the bar.

Seaview Motel (☎ 08-8553 2030; www.seaview.net
.au; 51 Chapman Tce; guest house s/d $72/82, motel $132/142,
extra adult/child $25/15; 🗶) It seems like this place
is always full – a good sign! Choose from
older-style guest house rooms with shared
facilities, or refurbished '80s motel rooms.

Kingscote Nepean Bay Tourist Park (☎ 08-8553
2394; www.kingscotetouristpark.com.au; Third Ave; unpow-
ered/powered sites $27/33; vans & cabins $75-130) You'll
find the standard gamut of caravan park delights behind the dunes in Brownlow, 3km
southwest of Kingscote. You can walk back to
Kingscote via a coastal walking trail.

our pick **Kangaroo Island Fresh Seafood** (☎ 08-
8553 0177; 26 Telegraph Rd; meals $6-16; 🕙 lunch daily,
dinner Tue-Sun) Seriously, this place has the best
seafood you're every likely to taste. A dozen
fat oysters go for around a dollar each, then
there are all manner of cooked and fresh seafood packs and combos. Superb!

ALL CREATURES GREAT & SMALL

You bump into a lot more wildlife here (sometimes literally) than on mainland SA. **Kangaroos**, **wallabies**, **bandicoots** and **possums** come out at night, especially in wilderness areas like Flinders Chase National Park. **Koalas** and the **platypus** were introduced to Flinders Chase in the 1920s when it was feared they would become extinct on the mainland. Ironically, koala numbers have increased to the point where they're at risk of starvation. **Echidnas** mooch around in the undergrowth and are far less obvious.

Of the island's 243 **bird species**, several are rare or endangered. One species – the dwarf emu – has gone the way of the dodo. **Glossy black cockatoos** may soon follow it out the door due to habitat depletion. On the cold-blooded side of the ledger, **goannas** and **tiger snakes** keep KI suitably scaly.

Offshore, **dolphins** and **southern right whales** are often seen cavorting, and there are colonies of **fairy penguins**, **New Zealand fur seals** and **Australian sea lions** here too.

Bella (☎ 08-8553 0400; 54 Dauncey St; pizzas $12-32, mains $30; ☺ lunch & dinner) Sit inside or sidewalk alfresco at Bella, a cheery Italian cafe-restaurant–pizza bar. Pizzas run all day (eat in or takeaway); dinner is à la carte (American River oysters, Spencer Gulf king prawns, local roo and whiting).

NORTH COAST ROAD

Exquisite beaches (much calmer than those on the south coast), bushland and undulating pastures dapple the North Coast Rd, running from Kingscote along the coast to the Playford Hwy 85km west (the bitumen expires at Emu Bay). There's not a whole lot to do here other than swan around on the beach – sounds good!

About 18km from Kingscote, **Emu Bay** is a holiday hamlet with a 5km-long, white-sand beach flanked by dunes – one of KI's best swimming spots. Around 36km further west, **Stokes Bay** has a penguin rookery and broad rock pool you access by scrambling through a 20m tunnel in the cliffs at the bay's eastern end (mind your head!). Beware the rip outside the pool.

You won't be able to prevent the word wow! escaping your lips as you look back over **Snelling Beach** from atop Constitution Hill. Continue 7km west and you'll hit the turn-off to **Western River Cove**, where a small beach is crowded in by sombre basalt cliffs. The ridge-top road in is utterly scenic (and steep!).

Sleeping & Eating

Western River Cove Campsite (unpowered sites per car $5) This self-registration campsite is a short walk from the beach and a footbridge over the river

(so tempting to dangle a line). There's a toilet block and a barbecue hut but no showers.

Emu Bay Holiday Homes (☎ 08-8553 5241; www .emubaysuperviews.com.au; 10 Bayview Rd, Emu Bay; d $80-130, extra person $18) Great-value (if a little frilly) cabins and holiday homes in a large garden set back from the beach (the views are great!). The self-contained cabins (caravan-park cabins with a facelift) sleep four or six; the holiday homes sleep six or ten.

Cape Cassini Wilderness Retreat (☎ 08-8559 2215; www.capecassini.com.au; off North Coast Rd; d incl breakfast $295) The emphasis is on sustainability and wilderness at this remote house, comprising three guest rooms in the owners' rammed-earth and stone home. There are two neat en suite double rooms and a small twin with separate bathroom; the doubles have sensational views. Call for directions or a pick-up.

Rock Pool Café (☎ 08-8559 2277; Stokes Bay; mains $13-23; ☺ lunch Sep-May) Don't worry about sandy feet at this casual, alfresco joint in Stokes Bay. 'What's the house special?', we asked. 'Whatever I feel like doin'!', said the chef (usually seafood, washed down with local wines and decent espresso).

SOUTH COAST ROAD

The south coast is rough and wave swept compared with the north.

A detour off Hog Bay or Birchmore roads takes you past the **Emu Ridge Eucalyptus Distillery** (☎ 08-8553 8228; www.emuridge.com.au; Willsons Rd, MacGillivary; adult/child $4.50/2; ☺ 9am-2pm), a self-sufficient operation extracting eucalyptus oil from Kangaroo Island's narrow-leaf mallee. The attached craft gallery sells lots of eucalyptus oil products.

It's almost worth swimming the Backstairs Passage for the honey ice cream at nearby **Clifford's Honey Farm** (☎ 08-8553 8295; fax 08-8553 8224; Elsegood Rd, Haines; tastings free, self-guided tour adult/child $2/1.50; ☺ 9am-5pm), sourced from a colony of rare Ligurian bees.

A real KI highlight is **Seal Bay Conservation Park** (☎ 08-8559 4207; www.environment.sa.gov.au/parks/sanpr/sealbay; tours adult/child/concession/family beach $14/8.50/11/38, boardwalk $10/6/8/27; ☺ tours 9am-4.15pm year-round, plus 5.15pm Dec-Feb), where ranger-led guided tours stroll along the beach or boardwalk to a colony of (mostly sleeping) Australian sea lions. Tours depart between 9am and 4.15pm daily (plus 5.15pm during summer). 'Observation, not interaction' is the mentality.

Back on South Coast Rd, the next turn-off south (6km from Seal Bay Rd) leads to **Little Sahara**, a rolling dunescape looming above the surrounding scrub. You can hire sand-boards from Vivonne Bay General Store (right) or Kangaroo Island Outdoor Action (p757) for $29 per four hours. Further west, **Vivonne Bay** is a quiet settlement with a beautiful sweeping beach.

Closer to Flinders Chase National Park is **Kelly Hill Conservation Park** (☎ 08-8559 7231; www .environment.sa.gov.au/parks/sanpr/kellyhill; tours adult/child/concession/family $12/7.50/9.50/33; ☺ tours 10.30am then hourly 11.15am-4.15pm), a series of dry limestone caves 'discovered' in the 1880s by a horse named Kelly, who fell into them through a hole. Adventure caving tours (adult/child/concession/family $13/18/24/81.50) leave at 2.15pm daily, following on from the standard tour. Minimum age is eight years; bookings essential. The 9km **Hanson Bay Walk** runs from the caves through mallee scrub and past freshwater wetlands.

Sleeping & Eating

Flinders Chase Farm (☎ 08-8559 7223; www.flinders chasefarm.com.au; West End Hwy; dm/cabins $25/60, d & tw with bathroom $100) A farm with charm! A couple of amiable mutts (and maybe a kangaroo) greet you as you check in here, a short drive from Flinders Chase National Park. Accommodation includes immaculate dorms, a couple of cosy cabins and en suite rooms in a lodge. Outdoors is where it's at: there's a terrific camp kitchen, fire pits and 'tropical' outdoor showers.

Kangaroo Island Wilderness Retreat (☎ 08-8559 7275; www.austdreaming.com.au; South Coast Rd; d $150-420; ☒ ☐) This low-key resort on the Flinders Chase doorstep guarantees guests will see some wildlife: 30 or 40 wallabies graze in the courtyard every evening! Accommodation ranges from basic motel-style rooms to flashy spa suites. There's a restaurant and bar here too, serving breakfast ($12 to $27) and dinner ($28 to $34).

Western Kangaroo Island Caravan Park (☎ 08-8559 7201; www.westernki.com.au; South Coast Rd; unpowered/powered sites $20/25, cabins $110-140; ☒) A few minutes' drive east of Flinders Chase National Park, this ultrafriendly, farm-based park has shady gums and resident roos. Check out the koala and lagoon walks, and the phone booth inside an old bakery truck. The shop sells groceries, homemade heat-and-eats and (for guests only) beer and wine.

Vivonne Bay General Store (☎ 08-8559 4285; South Coast Rd; meals $6-14; ☺ breakfast & lunch) This chipper little fish-and-chipper has an exhaustive menu of all-day breakfasts and takeaways. The whiting burger reigns supreme.

Marron Café (☎ 08-8559 4128; Harriet Rd; mains $20-30; ☺ lunch) Around 15km north of Vivonne Bay you can check out marron in breeding tanks, then eat some! It's a subtle taste, not necessarily enhanced by the heavy sauces issued by the kitchen. Last orders 4pm.

FLINDERS CHASE NATIONAL PARK

Occupying the western end of the island, **Flinders Chase National Park** (www.environment.sa.gov .au/parks/sanpr/flinderschasenp; admission adult/child/concession/family $8/4.50/6.50/21) is one of SA's top national parks. Much of the park is mallee scrub, but there are some beautiful, tall sugar-gum forests, particularly around Rocky River and the Ravine des Casoars, 5km south of Cape Borda. Sadly, around 100,000 acres of bush were burned out by bushfires in 2007. Many walking tracks and campsites are closed for rehabilitation, but there's still plenty to see and do. Contact the park visitors centre or DEH in Kingscote (p756) for updates on closures.

The **Flinders Chase National Park visitor centre** (☎ 08-8559 7235; South Coast Rd, Rocky River; ☺ 9am-5pm) supplies info and park maps, and has a cafe and displays on island ecology.

Sights & Activities

Once a farm, **Rocky River** is a rampant hotbed of wildlife, with kangaroos, wallabies and Cape Barren geese competing for your affections. The roos are particularly brazen – they'll bug

SOUTHERN OCEAN LODGE

Millionaires, start your engines! The shining star in the SA tourism galaxy is **Southern Ocean Lodge** (☎ 08-9918 4355; www.southernoceanlodge.com.au; Hanson Bay; d per night $1800-3600; ✖ ☐ ☎), billing itself as 'Australia's first true luxury lodge'. The lodge is a sexy, low-profile snake tracing the Hanson Bay clifftop, and is an exercise in exclusivity. There's a two-night minimum stay; you get airport transfers, all meals and drinks and guided tours of KI.

If you want a sticky-beak, don't expect to see anything from the road (all you'll find is a steely set of gates and an unreceptive intercom: privacy is what guests are paying for here), but you can catch a sneaky glimpse from Hanson Bay beach.

you for food, but park officers request that you don't feed them. A slew of good walks launch from behind the visitors centre, including one where you might spy a platypus (4.5km return).

From Rocky River, a road runs south to a remote 1906 lighthouse atop wild **Cape du Couedic**. A boardwalk weaves down to **Admirals Arch**, a huge archway ground out by heavy seas, and passes a colony of New Zealand fur seals (sweet smelling they ain't…).

At Kirkpatrick Point, a few kilometres east of Cape du Couedic, the **Remarkable Rocks** are a cluster of hefty, weather-gouged granite boulders atop a rocky dome that arcs 75m down to the sea.

On the northwestern corner of the island, **Cape Borda** is topped by an 1858 lighthouse, standing tall above the rippling iron surface of the Southern Ocean. There are walks here from 1.5km to 9km, and **lighthouse tours** (☎ 08-8559 3257; adult/child/concession/family $12/7.50/9.50/33) departing at 11am, 12.30pm and 2pm daily (plus 3.15pm and 4pm during summer holidays).

At nearby **Harvey's Return** a cemetery speaks poignant volumes about the reality of isolation in the early days. From here you can drive to **Ravine des Casoars** (literally 'Ravine of the Cassowaries', referring to the now-extinct dwarf emus seen here by Baudin's expedition). Check with the visitors centre if the walking trail (6.5km return) down to the coast is open again.

Sleeping & Eating

The 2007 bushfires ravaged many of the park's campsites: the Rocky River, Snake Lagoon and West Bay sites were all closed when we visited, but may have re-opened by the time you read this (check with the park visitors centre). The basic campsite at **Harvey's Return** (per car $10) near Cape Borda is still open; book through DEH in Kingscote (p756).

DEH also runs refurbished cottage accommodation at Rocky River – the budget Postmans Hut (double $48) and family-friendly Mays Homestead (double $115) – and lightkeepers' cottages at Cape du Couedic and Cape Borda (doubles $150).

See opposite for sleeping options just outside the national park.

On the food front, the only option here if you're not self catering is the **cafe** (meals $7-14; ☺ 9am-5pm) at the visitors centre, serving burgers, wraps, soup, coffee, and wines by the glass.

LIMESTONE COAST

The Limestone Coast – strung-out southeastern SA between the flat, olive span of the lower Murray River and the Victorian border – is a curiously engaging place. On the highways you can blow across these flatlands in under a day, no sweat, but around here the delight is in the detail. Detour off-road to check out the area's lagoons, surf beaches and sequestered bays. Also on offer are wine regions, photogenic fishing ports and snoozy agricultural towns. And what's *below* the road is even more amazing: a bizarre subterranean landscape of limestone caves, sinkholes and bottomless crater lakes. For regional information, see www.thelimestonecoast.com.

Festivals & Events

Robe is the main party town in this neck of the woods.

Robe Easter Classic April brings the longest-running surf contest in SA (since 1968); contact Steve's Place (p765) for info.

Robe Village Fair (www.robevillagefair.com.au; weekend tickets adult/child/concession $88/free/44) Weekend food-and-music frenzy with a family bent, in April.

Getting There & Away

The Dukes Hwy is the most direct route between Adelaide and Melbourne (729km), but the coastal Princes Hwy adjacent to the Coorong National Park is definitely more scenic.

Premier Stateliner (☎ 08-8415 5555; www.premier stateliner.com.au) runs two bus routes – coastal and inland – between Adelaide and Mt Gambier ($62, 6¼ hours). From Adelaide along the coast (daily except Saturday) via the Coorong you can stop at Meningie ($31, two hours), Robe ($55, 4½ hours) and Beachport ($58, 5¼ hours). The inland bus runs daily via Bordertown ($47, 3½ hours), Naracoorte ($58, five hours), and Penola ($59, 5½ hours).

V/Line (☎ 1800 817 037, 13 61 96; www.vline.com .au) runs a service between Mt Gambier and Melbourne ($33, seven hours) – you take the bus from Mt Gambier to Ballarat or Warrnambool, where you hop on a train for Melbourne.

If you'd rather wing it, **Regional Express** (Rex; ☎ 13 17 13; www.regionalexpress.com.au) flies daily between Adelaide and Mt Gambier (one-way from $130).

COORONG NATIONAL PARK

The amazing **Coorong** (www.environment.sa.gov.au/ parks/sanpr/coorong) is a fecund lagoon landscape curving along the coast for 145km from Lake Alexandrina towards Kingston SE. A complex series of soaks and salt pans, it's separated from the sea by the chunky dunes of the Younghusband Peninsula. More than 200 species of waterbirds live here. *Storm Boy*, an endearing film about a young boy's friendship with a pelican (based on the novel by Colin Thiele), was filmed on the Coorong.

The name 'Coorong' derives from the Ngarrindjeri Aboriginal word *Karangk*, meaning 'long neck'. In the 1800s the bountiful resources of the Coorong supported a large Ngarrindjeri population. The Ngarrindjeri are still closely connected to the Coorong, and many still live here.

At the edge of the Coorong on Lake Albert (a large arm of Lake Alexandrina), **Meningie** (population 900) was established as a minor port in 1866. It was a blowy sailboarding spot until climate change and shrinking Murray River flows sent the shoreline receding into the distance. The local pelicans seem unfazed.

The Princes Hwy scuttles through the park, but you can't see much from the road.

Instead, take the 13km, unsealed **Coorong Scenic Drive**. Signed as Seven Mile Rd, it starts 10km southwest of Meningie off the Narrung Rd, and takes you right into the landscape, with its stinky lagoons, sea mists, fishing shanties, pelicans and wild emus. The road rejoins the Princes Hwy 10km south of Meningie.

With a 4WD you can access **Ninety Mile Beach**, a well-known surf-fishing spot. The easiest ocean access point is 3km off the Princes Hwy at 42 Mile Crossing, 19km south of Salt Creek.

On the southern fringe of the Coorong is **Kingston SE** (www.kingstonsesa.com) – population 2230. The town is home to the lurid, anatomically correct **Larry the Lobster**, one of Australia's 'big' tourist attractions. Kingston SE is a hotbed of crayfishing and hosts the week-long **Lobsterfest** in the second week of January.

Information

Department for Environment & Heritage (DEH; ☎ 08-8575 1200; www.environment.sa.gov.au; 34 Princes Hwy, Meningie; ☾ 9am-5pm Mon-Fri) Park maps and access, bushwalking, camping, boating and fishing info.

Tours

Adelaide Sightseeing (☎ 1300 769 762, 08-8410 2269; www.adelaidesightseeing.com.au; tours adult/child $167/138; ☾ Mon, Wed, Thu & Sun) Full-day Coorong tours departing Adelaide, with a cruise on the *Spirit of the Coorong* (see following review), a guided walk, picnic lunch and plenty of birdlife.

Ecotrek (☎ 08-8357 3935; www.ecotrek.com.au; tours from $906) Three-day/two-night canoeing trips on the Coorong, including transport, camping accommodation, meals, wine and a guide.

Spirit of the Coorong (☎ 1800 442 203, 08-8555 2203; www.coorongcruises.com.au; The Wharf, Goolwa; ☾ Mon, Wed, Thu & Sun) Popular Coorong cruises departing from Goolwa (p754). Take either a 4½-hour (adult/child $74/55) or six-hour (adult/child $88/60) cruise. Adelaide coach connections available; lunch provided.

Sleeping & Eating

There are 11 bush **campsites** (per car $5) in the park, but you need a permit from DEH in Meningie (above) or Mt Gambier (p767), or the roadhouse at Salt Creek.

Camp Coorong (☎ 08-8575 1557; www.ngarrindjeri.net; Princes Hwy; museum admission per car $5; powered sites/dm/ cabins $20/27/70; ☾ vary) Run by the Ngarrindjeri Lands and Progress Association, 10km south of Meningie, this is the place to learn about the Coorong's Aboriginal history and habitat. Take a guided cultural walk, basket-weaving lesson, museum tour, Coorong tour or session about the Ngarrindjeri's perspective on Australian political history. Call for tour prices, museum hours, and to make bookings. The cabins here are modern, well maintained and good value; BYO linen and food.

Coorong Wilderness Lodge (☎ 08-8575 6001; www .coorongwildernesslodge.com; off the Princes Hwy; unpowered/ powered sites $10/20, dm/d $28/70; 🏊) At Hack Point, 25km south of Meningie, this fish-shaped centre is owned by the Ngarrindjeri community. By the time you read this five amazing new accommodation units should be finished. Until then the ordinary old bunkhouse will have to do, but you can enjoy bush-tucker and bush-medicine walks ($10), walking and kayak tours ($20; kayaks per half-/full day $30/50), and bush-tucker meals (around $20). Book everything in advance.

Lake Albert Caravan Park (☎ 08-8575 1411; lacp@ lm.net.au; 25 Narrung Rd, Meningie; unpowered/powered sites $20/28, cabins with/without bathroom from $80/55; 🏊) An old park with limited facilities, but a beaut aspect overlooking the (ever-shrinking) lake. Cabins 1, 2 and 3 (with bathroom) have the best views.

our pick **Dalton on the Lake** (☎ 0428 737 161; adma son@lm.net.au; 30 Narrung Rd, Meningie; d from $125; 🏊) Generous in spirit and unfailingly clean, this lakeside B&B goes to great lengths to ensure your stay is comfortable. There'll be fresh bread baking when you arrive, jars of homemade biscuits and bountiful bacon and eggs for breakfast. There's a modern self-contained studio off to one side, or a renovated stone cottage – book either, or both.

Cheese Factory (☎ 08-8575 1914; off Narrung Rd, Meningie; mains $8-21; 🕑 lunch & dinner Tue-Sun) In a converted cheese factory (you might have guessed), this outfit gives Meningie pub a run for its money. Lean on the front bar with the locals, or munch into steaks, lasagne, mixed grills, Coorong mullet or a Coorong burger (with mullet!) in the cavernous dining room. There's a very lo-fi history museum here too (admission $2, open 11am to 5pm).

ROBE
pop 1130

Robe is a cherubic little fishing port that's become a holiday hotspot for Adelaidians and Melburnians alike. The sign saying 'Drain Outlet L' as you roll into town doesn't prom-

ise much, but along the main street you'll find quality eateries and boundless accommodation, and there are some magic beaches and lakes around town. Over Christmas and Easter, Robe is packed to the heavens – book *waaay* in advance.

Information

Robe visitors centre (☎ 1300 367 144, 08-8768 2465; www.robe.com.au; Public Library, Mundy Tce; 🕑 9am-5pm Mon-Fri, 10am-4pm Sat & Sun) History displays, brochures and free internet access.

Sights & Activities

Heritage-listed buildings dating from the late 1840s to 1870s litter the streets of Robe, including the 1863 **Customs House** (Royal Circus; 🕑 2-4pm Tue & Sun), which is now a nautical museum. Ask the visitors centre about access.

Little Dip Conservation Park (www.environment .sa.gov.au/parks/sanpr/littledip) runs along the coast for about 13km south of town. It features a variety of habitats including lakes, wetlands and dunes, and some beaut beaches, Aboriginal middens, walks and camping spots ($5 per car). Access is via Nora Creina Rd.

The small town beach has safe swimming, while **Long Beach** (2km from town), is good for surfing, sailboarding and lazy days (safe swimming in some sections – ask at the visitors centre). **Steve's Place** (☎ 08-8762 8094; 26 Victoria St; 🕑 9am-5pm) rents out beginners' boards (per half-/full-day $20/40) and bodyboards ($5/10).

Sleeping

The local real estate office **Raine & Horne** (☎ 08-8768 2028; www.rhsa.com.au/robe; 25 Victoria St; 🕑 9am-5pm Mon-Fri, 9.30am-11am Sat) books holiday rental properties from as little as $60 per night in the off-season.

Lakeside Manor Backpackers Lodge (☎ 1800 155 350, 08-8768 1995; www.lakesidemanorbackpackers.com .au; 22 Main Rd; dm/d $29/77; 💻) In an 1885 sandstone mansion becalmed in faded grandeur, this place has cavernous dorms and doubles. There's an open fireplace, a library, an orchard and a hallway as long as two cricket pitches (we tested it out with a few leg-breaks).

Caledonian Inn (☎ 08-8768 2029; www.caledonian .net.au; 1 Victoria St; hotel/cottage/villa d from $85/185/310) This historic inn has it all under one roof (actually, several roofs). The half-dozen hotel rooms upstairs share bathroom facilities but

SOUTH AUSTRALIA

THE LONG WALK TO BALLARAT

During the 1850s gold rush in Victoria, Robe came into its own when the Victorian government whacked a $10-per-head tax on Chinese gold miners arriving to work the goldfields. Thousands of Chinese miners dodged the tax by landing at Robe in SA, then walking the 400-odd kilometres to Bendigo and Ballarat; 10,000 arrived in 1857 alone. But the flood stalled as quickly as it started when the SA government instituted its own tax on the Chinese. The Chinamen's Wells along their route (including one in the Coorong) can still be seen today.

---

are bright and cosy, while the split-level, self-contained units – all rattan and white-painted wood – are sandwiched between the pub and beach. The plush villa sleeps eight.

Lake View Motel & Apartments (☎ 08-8768 2100; www.robelakeviewmotel.com.au; 2 Lakeside Tce; d/apt from $100/195, extra person $15; ⊠) Overlooking Lake Fellmongery (a waterskiing mecca), the enthusiastically managed Lake View is Robe's best motel. The decor is a little 'peachy', but the rooms are roomy and immaculately clean, and the barbecue area pumps during summer.

For happy campers:

Lakeside Tourist Park (☎ 08-8768 2193; www .lakesiderobe.com.au; 24 Main Rd; unpowered/powered sites from $25/27, cabins & villas $50-150) Right on Lake Fellmongery, this abstractly laid-out park has heritage-listed pine trees, plenty of grass and basic but clean cabins. Bike hire per half/full day is $20/30.

Discovery Holiday Parks Robe (☎ 08-8768 2237; www.discoveryholidayparks.com.au; 70 The Esplanade; unpowered/powered sites from $27/29, cabins & chalets $60-180; ⊠ ☒) This humongous value-for-money park is almost beachside. The self-contained cabins and chalets are big and comfortable, plus there's a heated indoor pool, tennis courts, wireless internet, playground, barbecue and crayfish boiler!

Eating

Union (☎ 08-8768 2627; cnr Victoria & Union Sts; breakfast $5-15, lunch $8-17; ☾ breakfast & lunch) Robe's best coffee is at this curiously angled corner cafe with polished-glass fragments in the floor and Astroturf on the wall. Unionise your hangover with big breakfasts (banana pancakes with bacon and maple syrup), stir-fries, pastas and risottos.

Vic Street Pizzeria (☎ 08-8768 2081; 6 Victoria St; mains $9-22) An exciting addition to Robe's foodie scene, Vic Street is a high-energy, all-day cafe, serving gourmet pizzas, good coffee, and an astoundingly good caesar salad. Mod-Asian interior touches, cool tunes on the stereo and local wines, too.

Caledonian Inn (☎ 08-8768 2029; 1 Victoria St; mains $19-28; ☾ lunch & dinner) First licensed in 1858, the Caledonian has retained its Scottish heritage and has a great atmosphere. There's a beer garden, summer cafe out the back and bar meals aimed towards carnivores and seafood fans.

Gallerie (☎ 08-8768 2256; 2 Victoria St; lunch $16-24, dinner $20-34; ☾ lunch & dinner) Shiny, clattery Gallerie is the most upmarket eatery in Robe, with lots of polished wood and glass. The fish-of-the-day is always good, as is the chicken florentine. Contemporary re-workings of Bob Marley classics add an inauthentic tone.

BEACHPORT
pop 350

'See and be seen: headlights 24 hours!' say billboards on the way into Beachport. A town that's desperate to be noticed? A plaintive cry for attention? We like it the way it is: low-key and beachy, with aquamarine surf, staunch stone buildings and rows of Norfolk Island pines. Take a walk along the jetty, hang out in the old pub, or munch some fish and chips on the grassy foreshore. Forget about being seen – your time here will be perfectly anonymous.

Information

Beachport visitors centre (☎ 08-8735 8029; www .wattlerange.sa.gov.au; Millicent Rd; ☾ 9am-5pm Mon-Fri year-round, 10am-4pm Sat & Sun Dec-Feb, 11am-2pm Sat & Sun Mar-Nov; ⌨) Centrally placed, with internet access.

Sights & Activities

The **Old Wool & Grain Store Museum** (☎ 08-8735 8313; www.nationaltrustsa.org.au; 5 Railway Tce; adult/child/concession/family $5/2/4/10; ☾ 10am-4pm Mon-Wed, Fri & Sat, to 2pm Sun) is in a National Trust building on the main street. Inside are relics from Beachport's whaling days and rooms decked out in 1870s style.

The 800m-long **Beachport Jetty** provides excellent fishing for local pelicans and fishermen: try your luck for some whiting, school shark, squid and the easy-eating Lake George mullet.

There are some great walking tracks in the 710-hectare **Beachport Conservation Park** (www.environment.sa.gov.au/parks/sanpr/beachport), sandwiched between the coast and Lake George 2km north of town. Here you'll find Aboriginal middens, sheltered coves, lagoons and bush camping ($5 per car). There's good surfing, birdwatching and sailboarding at **Lake George**, 5km north of Beachport.

Canunda National Park (www.environment.sa.gov.au/parks/sanpr/canunda), with its giant sand dunes, is 22km south of town.

The hypersaline **Pool of Siloam** in the dunes on the western outskirts of town is great for swimming; the water is seven times saltier than the ocean.

Sleeping & Eating

Our pick Bompas (☎ 08-8735 8333; www.bompas.com.au; 3 Railway Tce; dm/d from $35/85) Brilliant Bompas is an all-in-one small hotel and cosy licensed restaurant-cafe (meals $9 to $29; open for breakfast, lunch and dinner). The dorms have TVs, and all rooms are generously sized and strewn with modern art. If you're after a double try No 3 ($145) – it's more expensive, but well worth it for the million-dollar water views and deep balcony. Menu offerings downstairs include a range of curries, lasagne and lamb shanks, with local and imported beers. The owners live on site, and call you 'Honey' and 'Darl' whether they know you or not.

Southern Ocean Tourist Park (☎ 08-8735 8153; sotp@bigpond.net.au; Somerville St; unpowered/powered sites $17/20, cabins from $60; 🐾) This grassy, well-pruned park sits behind a slope in the town centre. Facilities include a laundry, ice, fuel, bait, covered barbecues, crayfish cookers and a great little playground.

MT GAMBIER
pop 24,500

Strung out along the flatlands below an extinct volcano, Mt Gambier is the Limestone Coast's major town and service hub, and the hometown of musical *bon vivant* Dave Graney. We can see why Dave might have wanted to get to Melbourne in a hurry: 'The Mount' can seem a grim place, short on urban virtues and with a huge derelict hospital glowering over the rooftops. In de-

nial of rising fuel costs, rev-heads cruise the main drag as needless traffic lights blink from green to red.

But it's not what's above the streets that makes Mt Gambier special – it's the deep Blue Lake and the sinkholes and caves that worm their way though the limestone beneath the town. Amazing!

Information

Mt Gambier visitors centre (☎ 1800 087 187, 08-8724 9750; www.mountgambiertourism.com.au; Jubilee Hwy E; ⊗ 9am-5pm) Details on local sights, activities and accommodation, plus a 20-minute video on the town. The Mt Gambier Discovery Centre (see review following) is here too.

Department for Environment & Heritage (☎ 08-8735 1177; www.environment.sa.gov.au; 11 Helen St; ⊗ 8.45am-5pm Mon-Fri)

Sights & Activities

Mt Gambier's big-ticket item is the luminous, 75m-deep **Blue Lake** (John Watson Dr; admission free; ⊗ 24hr) which turns an almost implausible hue of blue during summer. Perplexed scientists think it has to do with calcite crystals suspended in the water, which form at a faster rate during the warmer months. Consequently, if you visit between April and November, the lake will look much like any other – a steely grey. **Acquifer Tours** (☎ 08-8723 1199; www.aquifertours.com; cnr Bay Rd & John Watson Dr; adult/child/family $7/3/19; ⊗ tours 9am-5pm Nov-Jan, to 2pm Feb-May & Sep-Oct, to noon Jun-Aug) runs hourly tours, taking you down near the lake shore in a glass-panelled lift.

If the lake isn't blue, don't feel blue – cheer yourself up with a visit to the outstanding **Riddoch Art Gallery** (☎ 08-8723 9566; www.riddochartgallery.org.au; 8-10 Commercial St E; admission free; ⊗ 10am-5pm Tue-Fri, 11am-3pm Sat & Sun), one of Australia's best regional galleries.

Inside the Mt Gambier visitors centre is the **Mt Gambier Discovery Centre** (adult/child $10/5), which features a replica of the historic brig *Lady Nelson*. An audio-visual display focuses on the devastating impact of European settlement on the local Indigenous people.

The Mt Gambier district is famous for its limestone caves and sinkholes. Have a sticky-beak at these:

Engelbrecht Cave (☎ 0408 133 40; Jubilee Hwy W; tours adult/child/concession $7.50/4/6.50; ⊗ tours 9.30am-5.30pm Dec-Feb, to 3.30pm Apr-Nov) A tour-accessible cave and cave-diving spot. Enter off Chute St.

Umpherston Sinkhole (Jubilee Hwy E; admission free; 24hr) Once 'a pleasant resort in the heat of summer' on James Umpherston's long-since-subdivided estate.

Cave Gardens (cnr Bay Rd & Watson Tce; admission free; 24hr) To say that Mt Gambier is a hole is technically correct: this 50m-deep sinkhole is right in the middle of town.

Sleeping

If nothing here takes your fancy, there are a heap of motels along Jubilee Hwy E. Online, check out www.bnb.limestonecoast.com and www.mountgambieraccommodation.com.au.

Grand Central Motel (08-8725 8844; grandcentralmotel@hotmail.com; 6 Helen St; s/d/f $50/75/125;) A rock-solid, conveniently located cheapie whose managers are Mt Gambier born and bred, and can point you in the right direction on the town map. Rooms are nothing flash and a bit pokey, but clean and well kept.

Park Hotel (08-8725 2430; www.parkhotel.com.au; 163 Commercial St W; d from $130;) In Mt Gambier's western wastelands, this old corner pub has spent a fortune renovating its half-dozen upstairs rooms. Polished timber floors, double glazing, marble bathrooms and coffee-and-cream colour schemes – a really slick product.

Colhurst House (08-8723 1309; www.colhursthouse.com.au; 3 Colhurst Pl; d incl breakfast from $135) Most locals don't know about Colhurst – it's up a laneway off a sidestreet (Wyatt St) and you can't really see it from downtown Mt G. It's an 1878 mansion built by Welsh migrants, and manages to be old-fashioned without being twee. There's a gorgeous wrap-around balcony upstairs with great views over the rooftops. Cooked breakfasts, too.

Blue Lake Holiday Park (1800 676 028, 08-8725 9856; www.bluelakeholidaypark.com.au; Bay Rd; unpowered/powered sites $24/29, cabins/units/bungalows from $82/95/120;) Adjacent to the Blue Lake, a golf course and walking and cycling tracks, this amiable park has some natty grey-and-white cabins and well-weeded lawns. There are also spiffy new contemporary, self-contained 're-treats' (from $149) which sleep four.

Eating & Drinking

Bull Frogs (08-8723 3933; 7 Percy St; lunch $9-19, dinner $16-40; lunch Mon-Sat, dinner daily) Spread over three floors of a fabulous old mill building, this is the place for organic beef and lamb grills, boutique beers, Coonawarra wines, cocktails, trusty coffee and acoustic tunes on weekends. Hard to beat.

Banana Tree Cafe (08-8723 9393; 2/94 Commercial St E; mains $13-20; lunch & dinner) Wow – authentic Thai in Mt Gambier! A colourful, corner eatery with a Thai chef, serving chilli-laden dishes like beef-and-basil stir-fry and a smokin' green chicken curry that will have a memorable effect on your innards.

Sage & Muntries (08-8724 8400; 78 Commercial St W; mains $16-40; lunch & dinner Mon-Sat) An award-winning licensed cafe serving up enticing daily specials like spicy sausages with mash and caramelised onions, plus steaming bowls of homemade pasta and Med-flavoured baguettes, salads and focaccias. Local wines by the bottle or glass.

Flanagan's Irish Pub (08-8725 1671; 6 Ferrers St; mains $10 to $25; lunch & dinner) By far the most palatable place to drink in the Mount, Flanagan's was allegedly the first Irish pub in SA. There's chunky pub food, bands on Saturday night, snooker tables, cold Guinness and warm fires.

PENOLA & THE COONAWARRA WINE REGION

A rural town on the way up (what a rarity!), **Penola** (population 1670) is the kind of place where you walk down the main street and five people say 'Hello!' before you get to the pub. The town has won fame for two things: firstly for its association with the Sisters of St Joseph of the Sacred Heart, the order co-founded by Mother Mary MacKillop in 1867; and secondly for being smack bang in the middle of the Coonawarra Wine Region. Online, check out www.penola.org and www.coonawarra.org.

Information

Penola visitors centre (08-8737 2855; www.wattlerange.sa.gov.au; 27 Arthur St; 9am-5pm Mon-Fri, 10am-4pm Sat & Sun) Services the Coonawarra region. The John Riddoch Interpretative Centre is also here.

Sights & Activities

The **Mary MacKillop Interpretative Centre** (08-8737 2092; www.mackillop-penola.com; cnr Portland St & Petticoat La; adult/child $5/free; 10am-4pm) is a jaunty new building with a gregarious entrance pergola – perhaps not as modest as Mother Mary might have liked! There's oodles of info on Australia's 'Saint-in-Waiting' here, plus the Woods-MacKillop Schoolhouse, the first school in Australia for children from lower socioeconomic backgrounds.

TOP FIVE COONAWARRA WINERIES

When it comes to spicy Cabernet Sauvignon, it's just plain foolish to dispute the virtues of the Coonawarra Wine Region – the *terra rossa* (red earth) region between Penola and Naracoorte. The climate also produces some irresistible Shiraz and Chardonnay. Five of the best:

- **Balnaves of Coonawarra** (☎ 08-8737 2946; www.balnaves.com.au; Riddoch Hwy; ⏰ 9am-5pm Mon-Fri, from noon Sat & Sun) The tasting notes here ooze florid wine speak (dark seaweed, leather or tobacco, anyone?), but even if you're nosing skills aren't that subtle you'll enjoy the Cab Sav and Chardonnay.
- **Majella Wines** (☎ 08-8736 3055; www.majellawines.com.au; Lynn Rd; ⏰ 10am-4.30pm) The family that runs Majella are fourth-generation Coonawarrans, so they know a thing or two about gutsy reds. Their Sparkling Shiraz and Riesling are unexpected bonuses.
- **Rymill Coonawarra** (☎ 08-8736 5001; www.rymill.com.au; Riddoch Hwy; ⏰ 10am-5pm) Down a long avenue of plane trees, Rymill rocks the local boat by turning out some of the best Sauvignon Blanc you'll ever taste. The modern cellar door is fronted by a statue of two duelling steeds – appropriately rebellious.
- **Wynns Coonawarra Estate** (☎ 08-8736 2225; www.wynns.com.au; Memorial Dr; ⏰ 10am-5pm) The oldest Coonawarra winery, Wynns' cellar door dates from 1896 and was built by Penola pioneer John Riddoch. Top-quality Shiraz, fragrant Riesling and golden Chardonnay are the mainstays.
- **Zema Estate** (☎ 08-8736 3219; www.zema.com.au; Riddoch Hwy; ⏰ 9am-5pm) A steadfast, traditional winery started by the Zema family in the early '80s. It's a low-key affair with a handmade vibe infusing the Shiraz and Cab Sav.

In the same building as the visitors centre, the **John Riddoch Interpretative Centre** (admission free) casts a web over local history back to the 1850s, including info on the local Pinejunga people and original Penola pastoralist Riddoch, who 'never gave in to misfortune' and was 'steady and persistent.'

Diminutive **Petticoat Lane** was one of Penola's first streets. Most of the original buildings have been razed, but there are still a few old timber-slab houses and gnarly trees to see.

Sleeping & Eating

Contact **Coonawarra Discovery** (☎ 1800 600 262, 08-8737 2449; www.coonawarradiscovery.com) for local B&B listings.

Heyward's Royal Oak Hotel (☎ 08-8737 2322; www .heywardshotel.com.au; 31 Church St; s $55, d & tw $88) The Royal Oak – a lace-trimmed, main-street megalith – is Penola's community hub. The rooms upstairs are a bit tatty and share bathrooms, but they're a good bang for your buck. Downstairs the huge tartan-carpeted dining room (mains $19 to $28, open for lunch and dinner) serves classy pub food (roo fillets with pepper crust and Cabernet glaze) and schnitzels as big as your head. Summery beer garden, too.

Coonawarra Motor Lodge (☎ 08-8737 2364; www .bushmansinn.com.au; 114 Church St; d/f $120/145; 🖧 🖴) On the way up the winery strip, this refurbished motel (splashes of chocolate and beige) occupies a compact, two-storey building overlooking a pool. There's also a restaurant here (mains $18 to $27), open for dinner from Monday to Saturday, serving fairly predictable pizza, pasta, lamb shanks and fish and chips.

diVine (☎ 08-8737 2122; 39 Church Street; meals $7-15; ⏰ breakfast & lunch) The busiest spot on the main street, diVine is a bright modern cafe serving baguettes, all-day breakfasts (try the pancakes with fresh strawberries, double cream and maple syrup) and great coffee. Nattering Penolans chew muffins and local cheeses, discussing the nuances of various vintages.

Pipers of Penola (☎ 08-8737 3999; 58 Riddoch St; mains $28; ⏰ lunch Fri-Sun, dinner Wed-Sat) This place is a winner: a classy, intimate dining room tastefully constructed inside an old Methodist church, with friendly staff and seasonal fare. The menu is studded with words like 'galette,' 'carpaccio' and 'rotollo' – seriously gourmet indicators! Reasonable prices, voluptuous wine glasses and awesome desserts.

SOUTH AUSTRALIA

NARACOORTE CAVES NATIONAL PARK

About 12km southeast of Naracoorte township, off the Penola road, is the only World Heritage–listed site in SA. The discovery of an ancient fossilised marsupial in these limestone caves raised palaeontologic eyebrows around the world, and featured in the BBC's David Attenborough series *Life on Earth*.

The park visitors centre doubles as the impressive **Wonambi Fossil Centre** (☎ 08-8762 2340; www.naracoortecaves.sa.gov.au; Hynam-Caves Rd; adult/child/concession/family $7.50/4.50/6/20; ⏰ 9am-5pm winter, to sunset summer) – a re-creation of the rainforest that covered this area 200,000 years ago. Follow a ramp down past grunting, life-sized reconstructions of extinct animals, including a marsupial lion, a giant echidna, *Diprotodon australis* (koala meets grizzly bear), and *Megalania prisca* – 500kg of bad-ass goanna.

The 26 limestone **caves** here – including the Victoria Fossil Cave, Alexandra Cave, Blanche Cave, Bat Cave and Wet Cave – have bizarre formations of stalactites and stalagmites. Unless you're Bruce Wayne you can't actually access the Bat Cave, but at dusk during summer you can watch thousands of endangered southern bentwing bats exiting en masse to find dinner. Infrared TV cameras allow you to see them huddled-up inside. You can check out the Wet Cave by self-guided tour, but the others require ranger-guided tours. Single-cave tours cost adult/child/concession/family $12/7.50/9.50/33; and two-cave tours $19.50/12/15.50/53. See the website for further tour and pricing info, including adventure tours of undeveloped caves (booking required). There's also some great-value budget **accommodation** (dm $15) here in an old stone house with a modern kitchen outbuilding.

For more local info and tips on places to stay, contact the **Naracoorte visitors centre** (☎ 1800 244 421, 08-8762 1399; www.naracoortelucindale.com; 36 MacDonnell St, Naracoorte; ⏰ 9am-5pm Mon-Fri, to 4pm Sat & Sun) in Naracoorte.

MURRAY RIVER

On the lowest gradient of any Australian river, the slow-flowing Murray hooks and bows through 650 SA kilometres. Tamed by weirs and locks, the Murray irrigates the fruit trees and vines of the Riverland district to the

north, and winds through the dairy country of the Murraylands district to the south. Raucous flocks of white corellas and pink galahs launch from cliffs and river red gums and dart across lush vineyards and orchards. With well-watered median strips and bubbling fountains, the towns here are also improbably green. But will the waters always flow? See Murray in Meltdown, opposite, for some background on the Murray's flagging fortunes.

Prior to European colonisation, the Murray was home to Meru communities. Then came shallow-draught paddle steamers, carrying wool, wheat and supplies from Murray Bridge as far as central Queensland along the Darling River. With the advent of railways, river transport declined. These days, waterskiers, jet skis and houseboats crowd out the river, especially during summer. If your concept of riverine serenity doesn't include the roar of V8 inboards, then avoid the major towns and caravan parks during holidays and weekends.

Online, sneak a peek at www.murrayriver.com.au, www.murraylands.info, and www.murraycare.com.au for info on how to minimise your impact on the Murray.

Sights & Activities

Houseboat hire is big business on the Murray. 'Simply relax' say the brochures…or relax in a complicated manner if you'd prefer – you just need to be over 18 with a current drivers licence. Despite the hokey marketing, meandering along the Murray River on a houseboat with an unabashedly Australian name like *Scallywag, Gunnadoo* or *Sensational Spirit* is great fun. Book ahead from Adelaide or from most riverside towns, especially if you plan to float off between October and April.

The **Houseboat Hirers Association** (☎ 08-8231 8466; www.houseboatbookings.com) website details departure points, conditions, has pictures of each boat and can make bookings on your behalf. Prices vary, but expect to pay anywhere from $625 per week (off-peak, two people) to $5250 for a luxury boat in peak season (sleeping 10). Most boats sleep at least two couples and there's generally a bond involved (starting at $200). Many provide linen, so all you need to bring is food and fine wine.

Tours

If you don't feel like pottering around in a houseboat, try the following operators (see also Waikerie's Murray River Queen; p772).

BMS Tours (☎ 08-8582 5511, 0408 282 300; www
.houseboatadventure.com.au; 2hr tour $40) Daily Murray
tours from Berri on the custom-built, 48-seat *Missy*.

Riverland Leisure Canoe Tours (☎ 08-8595
5399; www.riverlandcanoes.com.au; 2½-/3½-/8hr tours
$25/50/90) Slow-paced guided canoe tours on the Murray,
departing Paringa across the river from Renmark. Canoe
and kayak hire also available (from $30 per day).

Riverland Wine Experience (☎ 08-8586 6755; www
.renmarkhotel.com.au; tours per person incl lunch from $115)
Wine tasting tours ex-Renmark, run by the Renmark Hotel.

Getting There & Away
BUS
Murray Bridge Passenger Service (☎ 08-8415 5579;
www.murraybridgebus.com.au) runs several daily
services between Adelaide and Murray
Bridge ($19, 1¼ hours) and limited services
to Mannum ($26, 2½ hours) from Monday
to Friday.

Premier Stateliner (☎ 08-8415 5555) has daily
services from Adelaide to Murray Bridge
($15, one hour), on its Mt Gambier service; its
Riverland service stops in Waikerie ($36, 2½
hours), Barmera and Berri ($45, 3½ hours),
and Loxton and Renmark ($45, four hours).

CAR & MOTORCYCLE
Murray Bridge in the Murraylands region is an
hour's drive from Adelaide on the freeway. If
you're heading for the Riverland area further
north, you might want to take the Stuart Hwy
from the Barossa Valley (around three hours'
drive). Once you hit the Murray, you'll find a
lot of river crossings are via ferry rather than
bridge (see Don't Pay the Ferryman, p772).

MURRAY BRIDGE
pop 18,370
SA's largest river town is a rambling regional
hub with lots of old pubs but an underutilised
riverfront, a huge prison and little charm.
The town has however been anointed SA's

'Regional Centre of Culture' for 2010, so
maybe things are looking up. The **Murray Bridge
visitor information centre** (☎ 08-8339 1142; www
.murraybridge.sa.gov.au; 3 South Tce; ☒ 8.30am-5.30pm
Mon-Fri, 9am-4pm Sat, 10am-4pm Sun) stocks the
Murray Bridge Accommodation Guide and
Eating Out in Murray Bridge brochures, and
has info on river cruise operators:

Captain Proud Paddle Boat Cruises (☎ 0433 162
700; www.captainproud.com.au; cruises from $25) Hour-
long weekday cruises, plus three-hour Saturday lunch and
dinner and Sunday breakfast and lunch cruises.

MV Barrangul (☎ 0407 395 385; www.barrangul.com
.au; cruises from $20; ☒ 2pm) Devonshire-tea cruises de-
parting Sturt Reserve. Also offers lunch and dinner cruises.

The epicentre of the town's cultural thrust in
2010 will be the **Murray Bridge Regional Gallery**
(☎ 08-8531 2606; www.murraybridgegallery.com.au; 27 6th
St; admission free; ☒ 10am-4pm Tue-Fri, 9.30am-noon Sat,
1-4pm Sun), a great little space housing touring
and local exhibitions.

About 14km west of town, the excellent
open-range **Monarto Zoo** (☎ 08-8534 4100; www
.monartozoo.com.au; Princes Hwy, Monarto; adult/child/con-
cession/family $26/15/18/68; ☒ 9.30am-5pm) is home
to Australian and African beasts including
cheetahs, rhinos and giraffes. A one-hour
safari bus tour and guided walk are included
in the price; keeper talks happen throughout
the day.

MANNUM TO WAIKERIE
Clinging to a narrow strip of riverbank
84km east of Adelaide, improbably cute
Mannum (population 6750) is the unofficial
houseboat-hiring capital of the world! The *Mary
Ann*, Australia's first riverboat, was knocked
together here in 1853 and made the first paddle-
steamer trip up the Murray. You can make
cruise and houseboat bookings at the **Mannum
visitor information centre** (☎ 1300 626 686; www.ps
marion.com; 6 Randell St, Mannum; ☒ 9am-5pm Mon-Fri,

MURRAY IN MELTDOWN

Old Man Murray keeps on flowin' – but not like he used to, and rarely does he make the distance.
The Murray is heavily tapped for irrigation and SA's domestic water supply, and has been further
depleted by climate-change-induced salinisation and evaporation. Downstream at Goolwa and
the lower lakes, shrinking flows have left jetties high and dry and farmers facing bankruptcy.
Debate rages over solutions: federal control of the Murray-Darling Basin? Stiffer quotas for upstream irrigators? A weir at Wellington? Opening the Goolwa barrages and letting salt water
flood the lower lakes? In these dry lands, the Murray is in dire straits – see www.savethemurray
.com for the latest.

SOUTH AUSTRALIA

DON'T PAY THE FERRYMAN

As the Murray curls abstractly across eastern SA, roads (on far more linear trajectories) invariably bump into it. Dating back to the late 19th century, a culture of free, 24-hour, winch-driven ferries has evolved to shunt vehicles across the water. Your car is guided onto the punts by burly, bearded, fluoro-clad ferrymen, who lock safety gates into position then shunt you across to the other side. There are 11 ferries in operation, the most useful of which are those at Mannum, Swan Reach and Waikerie. Turn off your headlights if you're waiting for the ferry at night so you don't bedazzle the approaching skipper.

10am-4pm Sat & Sun). The centre incorporates the **Mannum Dock Museum of River History** (☎ 08-8569 2733; adult/child/family $5/2.50/13), featuring info on local Ngarrindjeri Aboriginal communities, an 1876 dry dock and the restored 1897 paddle steamer *PS Marion*.

Breeze Holiday Hire (☎ 0439 829 964; www.murrayriver.com.au/breeze-holiday-hire-1052) hires out canoes ($75 per day), dinghies with outboards ($95 per day) and fishing gear ($15 per day), and can get you waterskiing too.

From Mannum to Swan Reach, the eastern riverside road scoots through Bowhill, Purnong and Nildottie. The road often tracks a fair way east of the river, but various lookouts en route help you scan the scene. Around 9km from Swan Reach, the Murray takes a tight meander called **Big Bend**, a sweeping river curve with pock-marked, ochre-coloured cliffs.

Sedentary old **Swan Reach** (population 850), 70km southwest of Waikerie, is a bit of a misnomer: plenty of pelicans, not many swans.

A citrus-growing centre oddly festooned with TV antennas, **Waikerie** (population 4630; www.waikerietourism.com.au) takes its name from the Aboriginal phrase for 'anything that flies'. There's plenty of flap-happy birdlife around here, with 180 species recorded at **Gluepot Reserve** (☎ 08-8892 8600; www.riverland.net.au/gluepot; Gluepot Rd; cars per day/overnight $5/10; ☿ 8am-6pm), a mallee scrub area 64km north of Waikerie (off Lunn Rd) and part of Unesco's Bookmark Biosphere Reserve. Before you head off, check with Waikerie's Shell service station on Peake Tce to see if you'll need a gate key.

Sleeping & Eating

Murray River Queen (☎ 08-8541 4411; www.murrayriverqueen.com.au; Leonard Norman Dve, Waikerie; cabins dm/d from $35/80) When it's not cruising the Murray, this 1974 paddleboat berths at Waikerie and offers basic bunkrooms (a tad shabby and

dim but undeniably novel) and more up-market staterooms with spas. There's a cafe on board if you're in the market for a light lunch (items $5 to $15, open Wednesday to Sunday).

Waikerie Hotel/Motel (☎ 08-8541 2999; www.waikeriehotel.com; 2 McCoy St, Waikerie; s/d hotel $55/65, motel from $75; ☒) Waikerie's humongous pub has clean hotel rooms (all with bathroom) and recently updated motel rooms out the back. The bistro does lots of seafood and pub-grub classics (mains $16 to $24, open for lunch and dinner).

Mannum House B&B (☎ 08-8569 2631; www.mannumhouse.com.au; 33 River La, Mannum; d $135) With glimpses of the river and a five-minute walk from the pub, this spic-and-span (if a little twee) B&B has two cosy rooms with bathrooms and serves generous cooked breakfasts.

Mannum Caravan Park (☎ 08-8569 1402; www.mannumcaravanpark.com.au; Purnong Rd, Mannum; unpowered/powered sites $20/24, cabins/villas from $57/100; ☒) A clean-cut caravan park right on the river next to the Mannum ferry crossing. Ducks and water hens patrol the lawns, and there's a pool table in the games room if it's raining.

Pretoria Hotel (☎ 08-8569 1109; 50 Randell St, Mannum; mains $12-28; ☿ lunch & dinner) The family-friendly Pretoria (built 1900) has a vast bistro and deck fronting the river, and plates up big steaks, saltbush lamb chops and parmas plus Asian salads and Mediterranean antipasti. When the 1956 flood swamped the town they kept pouring beer from the first-floor balcony!

BARMERA & AROUND

On the shallow shores of Lake Bonney (upon which world land-speed record holder Donald Campbell unsuccessfully attempted to break his water-speed record in 1964), snoozy **Barmera** (population 1930) was once a key town on the overland stock route from NSW.

These days Barmera feels a bit depressed – all fishing shops and nowhere to get a decent coffee – but the local passion for both kinds of music (country *and* western) lends a simple optimism to proceedings. **Kingston-On-Murray** (population 260; aka Kingston OM) is a tiny town en route to Waikerie.

Information

Barmera visitors centre (☎ 08-8588 2289; www .berribarmera.sa.gov.au; Barwell Ave, Barmera; ☺ 9am-5.15pm Mon-Fri, 9am-noon Sat, 10am-1pm Sun) The local visitor centre can help with transport and accommodation bookings.

Sights & Activities

The once ephemeral **Lake Bonney** has been transformed into a permanent lake ringed by large, drowned red gums, whose stark branches are often festooned with birds. If you're feeling uninhibited, there's a nudist beach at **Pelican Point Nudist Resort** (☎ 08-8588 7366; www.riverland.net.au/pelicanpoint) on the lake's western shore.

Country music is a big deal in Barmera, with the **South Australian Country Music Festival & Awards** (www.riverlandcountrymusic.com) in June, and **Rocky's Hall of Fame Pioneers Museum** (☎ 08-8588 1463; Barwell Ave, Barmera; adult/child $2/1; ☺ 10am-noon & 1-3pm Wed-Mon) blaring sincere rural twangings down the main street from outdoor speakers. Don't miss the 35m Botanical Garden Guitar out the back, inlayed with the handprints of 160 country musos: Slim Dusty to Kasey Chambers and everyone in between.

There are wildlife reserves with walking trails at **Moorook** (camping per car $5), on the road to Loxton, and **Loch Luna**, across the river from Kingston-On-Murray. Loch Luna backs onto the Overland Corner Hotel (see right). Both reserves have nature trails and are prime spots for birdwatching and canoeing. Self-register camping permits are available at reserve entrances.

Overlooking regenerated wetlands off the Sturt Hwy at Kingston OM, carbon-neutral **Banrock Station Wine & Wetland Centre** (☎ 08-8583 0299; www.banrockstation.com.au; Holmes Rd, Kingston OM; ☺ 9am-5pm) is a stylish, rammed-earth wine-tasting centre and jazzy lunchtime restaurant (mains $18 to $22 – try the Waikerie beef Thai salad). There are three **wetland walks** here: 2.5km and 4km ($3), and 8km ($5).

There are also walking trails at the Overland Corner Hotel (right).

Sleeping & Eating

Barmera Lake Resort Motel (☎ 08-8588 2555; www .barmeralakeresortmotel.com.au; Lakeside Dr, Barmera; s/d from $75/105; ☒ ☒) Right on the lake, this good-value motel has a barbecue, pool, laundry and tennis court. Rooms are nothing flash but immaculate; most have lake views.

Lake Bonney Holiday Park (☎ 08-8588 2234; www .discoveryholidayparks.com.au; Lakeside Dr, Barmera; un-powered/powered sites $25/29, cabins from $68; ☒ ☒) This enthusiastically managed lakeside park has small beaches, an electric barbecue, camp kitchen, laundry and plenty of room for kids to run amuck.

Overland Corner Hotel (☎ 08-8588 7021; Old Coach Rd; meals $8-23; ☺ 11am-6pm Tue, Wed & Sun, to late Thu-Sat) Off the Morgan Rd 19km northwest of Barmera, this moody 1859 boozer is named after a Murray River bend where drovers used to camp. The pub walls ooze character and the pubs meals are drover sized, plus there's a museum, a resident ghost and a beaut beer garden. An 8km self-guided nature trail leads down to the river from the pub past an ochre quarry. Pick up the *Overland Corner Reserve Walking Trails* brochure at the bar or from the info point over the levee bank behind the beer garden.

Banrock Station Wine & Wetland Centre (left) also does a great lunch and fab desserts sourced from local produce.

LOXTON
pop 4100

Sitting above a broad loop of the slow-roaming Murray, Loxton proclaims itself the 'Garden City of the Riverland'. The vibe here is low-key, agricultural and un-touristy, with more tyre distributors, hardware shops and irrigation supply outlets than anything else.

Information

Loxton visitors centre (☎ 08-8584 8071; www .loxtontourism.com.au; Bookpurnong Tce; ☺ 9am-5pm Mon-Fri, 9.30am-12.30pm Sat, 1-4pm Sun; ☐) Accommodation, transport and national park information, plus a small art gallery, friendly staff, internet and bags of sticky nectarines for sale.

Sights & Activities

From Loxton you can canoe across to Katarapko Creek and the **Katarapko Game Reserve** in the **Murray River National Park** (www.environment.sa.gov.au/parks/sanpr/murrayrivernpk); hire canoes from Loxton Riverfront Caravan Park.

The town's other lure is **Loxton Historical Village** (☎ 08-8584 7194; www.loxtonhistoricalvillage .com.au; Scenic Rd; admission adult/child/concession/family $8/4/7/21; 10am-4pm Mon-Fri, to 5pm Sat & Sun), a re-creation time warp of old buildings and costumed staff.

Down by the river near the caravan park, the **Tree of Knowledge** is marked with flood levels from previous years. The bumper flows of 1931, '73, '74 and '75 were totally outclassed by the flood-to-end-all-floods of 1956, marked about 5m up the trunk.

Sleeping & Eating

Harvest Trail Lodge (☎ 08-8584 5646; www.harvesttrail .com; 1 Kokoda Tce; dm per night/week for workers $15/105; dm per night for nonworkers $45;) Inside a converted '60s waterworks office are neat four-bed dorms with TVs and fridges, and a barbecue balcony to boot. Staff will find you fruit-picking work, and shunt you to and from jobs.

Loxton Community Hotel/Motel (☎ 1800 656 686, 08-8584 7266; www.loxtonhotel.com.au; East Tce; hotel s/d $80/90, motel s/d from $95/105;) With all profits syphoned back into the Loxton community, this large, contemporary complex offers immaculate rooms with tasty weekend packages. Bistro meals are tasty too (mains $17 to $28, open for breakfast, lunch and dinner).

Loxton Riverfront Caravan Park (☎ 1800 887 733, 08-8584 7862; www.lrcp.com.au; Riverfront Rd; unpowered/ powered sites from $15/23, cabins with/without bathroom from $60/50, linen $12;) On the gum-studded Habels Bend, 2km from town, this riverside park bills itself as 'The Quiet One'. You can hire a canoe (per hour/day $15/60), and there's a free (sandy) nine-hole golf course.

BERRI

pop 4010

The name Berri derives from the Aboriginal term *berri berri*, meaning 'big bend in the river', and it was once a busy refuelling stop for wood-burning paddle steamers. These days Berri is an affluent regional hub for both state government and agricultural casual-labour agencies, and one of the best places to chase down casual harvest jobs.

Information

Berri visitors centre (☎ 08-8582 5511; www .berribarmera.sa.gov.au; Riverview Dr; 9am-5.30pm Mon-Fri, 10am-4pm Sat & Sun;) Right by the river, with brochures, internet, maps and cluey staff.

Department of Environment & Heritage (DEH; ☎ 08-8595 2111; www.environment.sa.gov.au/parks; 28 Vaughan Tce; 9am-5pm Mon-Fri)

Sights & Activities

A short amble from the visitor centre is **A Special Place for Jimmy James**, a living riverbank memorial to the Aboriginal tracker who could 'read the bush like a newspaper'. Whimsical tracks and traces are scattered around granite boulders.

Berri is an artsy kinda town. Around the base of Berri Bridge, check out the **murals** and **totem poles** created by local artists. The **Berri Arts Centre** (☎ 08-8582 2288; www.countryarts.org.au; 23 Wilson St; admission free; 10am-4pm Mon-Fri) displays local and travelling exhibitions.

Road access to the scenic Katarapko Creek section of the **Murray River National Park** (www .environment.sa.gov.au/parks/sanpr/murrayrivernpk) is off the Stuart Hwy between Berri and Barmera. This is a beaut spot for **bush camping** (per car per night $5), canoeing and birdwatching.

See also BMS Tours (p771).

Sleeping & Eating

our pick **Berri Backpackers** (☎ 08-8582 3144; www .berribackpackers.com.au; Old Sturt Hwy; dm per night/week $25/140;) On the Barmera side of town, this eclectic hostel is destination *numero uno* for work-seeking travellers, who chill out after a hard day's manual toil in quirky new-age surrounds. Facilities include beach volleyball and soccer, tennis, bicycles, canoes, and a post-harvest sauna. Rooms range from messy dorms to doubles, share houses, a tepee, a treehouse and a yurt – all for the same price. The managers can hook you up with harvest work (call in advance).

Berri Resort Hotel (☎ 1800 088 226, 08-8582 1411; www.berriresorthotel.com; Riverview Dr; hotel s/d $70/145, motel d $145-155;) This mustard-and-maroon monolith across the road from the river has hotel rooms with shared bathrooms and a wing of spacious en suite motel rooms. There's a gym, pool, tennis court and the cavernous Riverboat bistro serving upmarket pub grub (mains $12 to $26, open for lunch and dinner daily).

Berri Riverside Caravan Park (☎ 08-8582 3723; www.berricaravanpark.com.au; Riverview Dr; unpowered/ powered sites $20/25, cabins $60-126;) Big on greenery, this well-groomed and patron-ised park is opposite the river, and has an impressive range of cabin configurations (the

---

RIVERLAND FRUIT PICKING

The fruit- and grape-growing centres of Berri, Barmera, Waikerie, Loxton and Renmark are always seeking harvest workers. Work is seasonal but there's usually something that needs picking (stonefruit, oranges, grapes, apples…), except for mid-September to mid-October and mid-April to mid-May when things get a bit quiet. If you have a valid working visa and don't mind sweating it out in the fields, ask the local backpacker hostels about work. Also try Berri's private job agencies **MADEC Jobs Australia Berri Harvest Labour Office** (☎ 08-8582 9307; www.madec.edu.au) and **Mission Australia** (☎ 08-8582 2188). The **National Harvest Telephone Information Service** (☎ 1800 062 332) has general harvest info.

---

top-end ones look like Sydney apartments). Ask about pedal-boat hire (per half/full day $40/60).

Cragg's Creek Café (☎ 08-8582 4466; Riverview Dr; mains $12-25; ☒ breakfast & lunch) Next door to the visitors centre is this cool cafe, functioning as a cellar door for the winery of the same name. A top spot for a light cafe lunch, some tapas, a glass of the aforementioned vino or a caffeine kick-start.

RENMARK
pop 8060

Renmark is the first major river town across from the Victorian border, about 254km from Adelaide. It's not a pumping tourist destination by any means, but has a relaxed vibe and grassy waterfront, where you can pick up a houseboat. This is the hub of the Riverland wine region: lurid signs on the roads into town scream 'Buy 6 Get 1 Free!', '20% Off' and 'Carton of Wine $33!'.

Information

Renmark Paringa visitors centre (☎ 08-8586 6704; www.renmarkparinga.sa.gov.au; 84 Murray Ave; ☒ 9am-5pm Mon-Fri, 9am-4pm Sat, 10am-4pm Sun; ☒) All the usual brochures and info, plus an interpretive centre and the recommissioned 1911 paddle steamer *PS Industry* outside (gold coin donation).

Sights & Activities

Renmark River Cruises (☎ 08-8595 1862; www.renmarkrivercruises.com.au; Main Wharf; adult/concession/family $33/30/75; ☒ 2pm Tue, Thu & Sat, 11am Sun) offers two-hour cruises past the Murray River cliffs on the *MV Big River Rambler*. Guided two-hour tours on the Murray's mildly spooky backwaters in a motorised dinghy also available (adult/family $60/150).

Upstream from town, **Chowilla Game Reserve** (www.environment.sa.gov.au/parks/sanpr/chowillagr; camping per car $5) is great for bush camping, canoeing

and bushwalking. Access is along the north bank from Renmark or along the south bank from Paringa. For more info, contact the DEH in Berri (opposite).

You can hire **canoes** (per hr s/d $10/15) and **pedal boats** (per hr 2-/4-seater $15/25) if you're staying at Renmark Riverfront Caravan Park (see below). Riverland Leisure Canoe Tours (p771) also hires out canoes and kayaks.

See also Riverland Wine Experience (p771).

Sleeping & Eating

Affordable motels and fast-food joints line the highways into own.

Renmark Hotel (☎ 1800 736 627, 08-8586 6755; www.renmarkhotel.com.au; Murray Ave; hotel s/d $70/85, motel s/d from $90/105; ☒ ☒ ☒) Wow, what a beauty! The sexy art deco curves of Renmark's humongous pub are really looking good these days, thanks to a $3.5-million overhaul. Choose from older-style hotel rooms and upmarket motel rooms. On a sultry evening it's hard to beat a cold beer and some grilled barramundi on Nanya bistro's riverfront balcony (mains $16 to $25, open for breakfast, lunch and dinner).

Renmark Riverfront Caravan Park (☎ 1300 664 612, 08-8586 6315; www.big4renmark.com.au; Sturt Hwy; unpowered/powered sites $29/32, cabins $75-150; ☒ ☒) Highlights of this spiffy riverfront park 1km east of town include a camp kitchen, canoe hire and absolute waterfront cabins and powered sites. The new corrugated-iron cabins are top-notch, and look a little 'Riviera' surrounded by scraggly palms. The waterskiing fraternity swarms here during holidays.

BAROSSA VALLEY

With hot, dry summers and cool, moderate winters, the Barossa is one of the world's great wine regions – an absolute must for anyone

SOUTH AUSTRALIA

with even the slightest interest in a good drop. It's a compact valley – just 25km long – yet it manages to produce 21% of Australia's wine, mostly big, luscious reds. The 80-plus wineries here are within easy reach of one another, and make a no-fuss day trip from Adelaide, just 65km to the southwest. This accessibility, combined with the high-volume output,

has fostered a mainstream, commercial scene reminiscent of California's Napa Valley (which is 16 years younger than the Barossa!). The long-established 'Barossa Barons' hold sway – big, ballsy and brassy – while spritely young boutique wineries are harder to sniff out.

The local towns have a distinctly German heritage, dating back to 1842. Fleeing re-

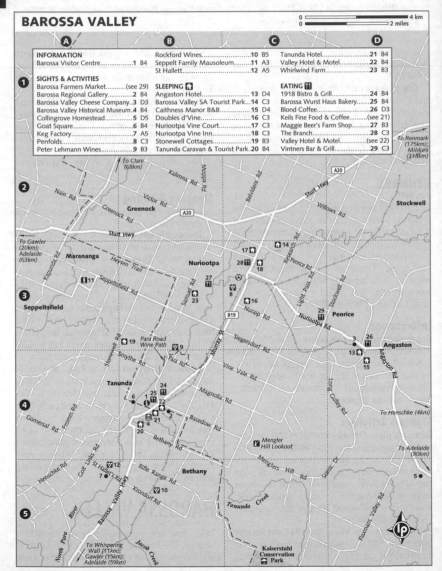

BAROSSA VALLEY

0 — 4 km
0 — 2 miles

INFORMATION
Barossa Visitor Centre..............1 B4

SIGHTS & ACTIVITIES
Barossa Farmers Market..........(see 29)
Barossa Regional Gallery............2 B4
Barossa Valley Cheese Company..3 D3
Barossa Valley Historical Museum..4 B4
Collingrove Homestead................5 D5
Goat Square................................6 B4
Keg Factory.................................7 A5
Penfolds.....................................8 C3
Peter Lehmann Wines..................9 B3

Rockford Wines........................10 B5
Seppelt Family Mausoleum.......11 A3
St Hallett.................................12 A5

SLEEPING
Angaston Hotel.........................13 D4
Barossa Valley SA Tourist Park...14 C3
Caithness Manor B&B...............15 D4
Doubles d'Vine.........................16 C3
Nuriootpa Vine Court................17 C3
Nuriootpa Vine Inn...................18 C3
Stonewell Cottages...................19 B3
Tanunda Caravan & Tourist Park..20 B4

Tanunda Hotel..........................21 B4
Valley Hotel & Motel.................22 B4
Whirlwind Farm........................23 B3

EATING
1918 Bistro & Grill....................24 B4
Barossa Wurst Haus Bakery.......25 B4
Blond Coffee............................26 D3
Keils Fine Food & Coffee..........(see 21)
Maggie Beer's Farm Shop..........27 B3
The Branch................................28 C3
Valley Hotel & Motel................(see 22)
Vintners Bar & Grill...................29 C3

ligious persecution in Prussia and Silesia, settlers (bringing their vine cuttings with them) created a Lutheran heartland where German traditions persist today. The physical remnants of colonisation – gothic church steeples and stone cottages – are everywhere. Cultural legacies of the early days include a dubious passion for oom-pah bands, and an appetite for wurst, pretzels and sauerkraut.

Information

There are ATMs in the main street in Tanunda and Nuriootpa.

Barossa visitor centre (☎ 1300 852 982, 08-8563 0600; www.barossa.com; 66-68 Murray St, Tanunda; 9am-5pm Mon-Fri, 10am-4pm Sat & Sun;) Has the lowdown on the valley, plus internet access, bike hire (see right) and accommodation bookings.

Tours

The Barossa visitor centre has details on organised tours, including the following. For other Barossa tours departing from Adelaide, see p734.

Balloon Adventures (☎ 08-8389 3195; www.balloon adventures.com.au; adult/child $300/195) Fly the sky in a hot-air balloon and sail serenely over the valley. One-hour flights depart Tanunda and include a champagne breakfast.

Barossa Classic Cycle Tours (☎ 0427 000 957; www .bccycletours.com.au; tours per day $225) One- and two-day cycling tours of the valley. Cheaper rates for bigger groups.

Barossa Epicurean Tours (☎ 08-8564 2191, 0402 989 647; www.barossatours.com.au; full-/half-day tours $90/60) Good-value, small-group tours visiting the wineries of your choice and Mengler Hill Lookout.

Barossa Experience Tours (☎ 08-8563 3248, 0418 809 313; www.barossavalleytours.com; full-/half-day tours $105/75) Local small-group operator whisking you around the major sites. The Food & Wine Experience ($210) includes lunch, cheese tastings and a glass of plonk.

Barossa Wine Lovers Tours (☎ 08-8263 1633; tours incl lunch from $65) This tour takes in several wineries, lookouts, shops and heritage buildings – a good blend.

Bikeabout (☎ 0413 525 733; www.bikeabout.com.au) Cycling day trips to the Barossa Valley ($75).

Groovy Grape Getaways (☎ 1800 661 177, 08-8440 1640; www.groovygrape.com.au; full-day tours $75) Backpacker Barossa day tours including the Whispering Wall, Big Rocking Horse, a few wineries and a barbecue lunch.

Prime Mini Tours (☎ 1300 667 650, 08-8556 6117; www.primeminitours.com; tours from $70) Adelaide-based company offering four full-day Barossa tours, all of which include lunch, four or five wineries and pit stops at sights like the Whispering Wall and the Big Rocking Horse. Good value.

Festivals & Events

The Barossa knows how to host a whizz-bang festival or two; here's a handful of the best:

A Day on the Green (www.adayonthegreen.com.au) Mature-age moshpit at Peter Lehmann Wines; acts like Simply Red and Kate Ceberano; held in February.

Barossa Under the Stars (www.barossaunderthestars .com.au) Wine-slurping picnickers watch middle-of-the-road crooners like Chris Isaak, Cliff Richard and Shirley Bassie in March.

Barossa Vintage Festival (www.barossavintagefes tival.com.au) A week-long festival with music, maypole dancing, wineries' tug-of-war contests etc; begins Easter Monday in odd-numbered years.

Barossa Music Festival (www.barossa.org) Picnics, wine, theatre and bands playing classical and jazz in intimate venues; held in October.

Getting There & Around

There are several routes from Adelaide; the most direct is along Main North Rd through Elizabeth and Gawler. If you're coming from the east and want to tour the wineries before hitting Adelaide, the scenic route via Springton and Eden Valley to Angaston is a sure bet.

Barossa Valley Coaches (☎ 08-8564 3022; www.bv coach.com) runs service between Adelaide and Angaston. buses ply the return route twice daily (once on Sunday), stopping at Tanunda ($18, 1¾ hours), Nuriootpa ($20, two hours) and Angaston ($21, 2¼ hours).

The Barossa is pretty good for **cycling**, with routes trundling past a few wineries. The Barossa visitor centre (left) hires out bikes from $44 per eight hours (six hours on weekends), and can point you towards the best routes. You can also rent bikes from Tanunda Caravan & Tourist Park (p778; per half/full day $19/30).

Barossa Valley Taxis (☎ 08-8563 3600) has a 24-hour service.

TANUNDA
pop 4690

At the centre of the valley both geographically and socially, Tanunda is the Barossa's main tourist town. Despite a steady deluge of visitors, Tanunda manages to morph the practicality of Nuriootpa with the charm of Angaston without a sniff of self-importance.

There are a few attractions and artsy shops along Murray St, the main road through town, but the wineries are what you're here for – sip, sip, sip!

The Barossa visitor centre (p777) is located here.

Sights & Activities

Tanunda is flush with historic buildings, including the **cottages** around Goat Sq on John St. This was the *ziegenmarkt*, a meeting and market place, laid-out in 1842 as Tanunda's original town centre.

Access to the **Barossa Valley Historical Museum** (☎ 08-8563 0507; 47 Murray St; adult/child/concession $2/50c/1; ☉ 10am-4pm) is via a secondhand bookshop out the front. Inside are displays of bone-handled cutlery, butter-making gear, photos of top-hatted locals, a recreated colonial bedroom and an amazing map of Germany pinpointing the homelands of Barossa settlers. The Indigenous coverage could use a little help.

The **Barossa Regional Gallery** (☎ 0428 322 871; www.freewebs.com/barossagallery; 3 Basedow Rd; admission free; ☉ 11am-4pm Tue-Sun) has an eclectic collection of paintings, crafts and touring exhibitions, plus an impressive set of organ pipes at the back of the room.

You can watch honest-to-goodness coopers make and repair wine barrels at the **Keg Factory** (☎ 08-8563 3012; www.thekegfactory.com.au; St Halletts Rd; admission free; ☉ 10am-4pm), 4km south of town.

From Tanunda, take the scenic route to Angaston via Bethany and hazy valley views from **Mengler Hill Lookout** (just ignore the naff sculptures in the foreground). The road tracks through beautiful rural country, studded with huge eucalypts. Also en route is the 390-hectare **Kaiserstuhl Conservation Park** (www.environ ment.sa.gov.au/parks/sanpr/kaiserstuhl; Tanunda Creek Rd, Angaston; admission free), with some ace views and walking tracks.

Other worthy detours include the **Para Road Wine Path** between Nuriootpa and Tanunda – a short-and-sweet, walking/cycling trail passing four wineries – and **Seppeltsfield Rd** (www.sep peltsfieldroad.com), an incongruous avenue of huge palm trees meandering through the vineyards. Beyond Marananga the palm rows veer off the roadside and track up a hill to the **Seppelt Family Mausoleum** – a Grecian shrine fronted by chunky Doric columns.

About 7km southwest of Lyndoch, itself 13km south of Tanunda, the Barossa Reservoir

dam is better known as the **Whispering Wall**. The huge concrete curve has amazing acoustics: whispers at one end of the wall can be heard clearly 150m away at the other. The perfect spot to propose?

Sleeping

Tanunda Hotel (☎ 08-8563 2030; www.tanundapub .com; 51 Murray St; d with/without bathroom $80/70; ☒) Opened in 1846, this boisterous ol' pub in the centre of town is a real community centre. Rooms are good value and clean, but nothing out of the ordinary. Downstairs, Duran Duran wails from the jukebox and schnitzels fall off the edges of plates (mains $12 to $26, open for lunch and dinner).

Valley Hotel & Motel (☎ 08-8563 2039; fax 8563 3830; 73 Murray St; s/d $90/110, d with spa $125; ☒) There are only five brick-and-stone rooms here (the smallest motel in Australia?), but they're spotless, modern and great value. Out the front is the Valley Hotel (mains $14 to $30, open for lunch and dinner) if you're keen for a bite or a beer.

Stonewell Cottages (☎ 0417 848 977; www.stonewell cottages.com.au; Stonewell Rd, Tanunda; cottages d incl break-fast from $255; ☒) These romantic, waterfront spa retreats are surrounded by vines and offer unbeatable privacy, comfort and serenity. Pet ducks waddle around rusty old ploughs as waterbirds splash down in the reservoir.

Tanunda Caravan & Tourist Park (☎ 08-8563 2784; www.tanundacaravantouristpark.com.au; Barossa Valley Way; unpowered/powered sites $23/28, vans from $55, cabins with/without bathroom from $85/65; ☒ ▣) This spacious park is dotted with mature trees offering a little shade for your hangover. Facilities include a playground, barbecues, laundry and bike hire (see p777).

Eating

Keils Fine Food & Coffee (☎ 08-8563 1468; Shop 1, 63-67 Murray St; meals $4-10; ☉ breakfast & lunch) Sidestep the coffee mums and their prams; spurn the ugly, humming drinks fridge; and place your order for homemade baguettes, soups, quiches, pies, wraps, quality teas and the punchiest coffee in town.

Barossa Wurst Haus Bakery (☎ 08-8563 3598; 86a Murray St; meals $7-20; ☉ breakfast & lunch) This fast-not-flashy bakery serves *mettwurst* (Bavarian sausage) rolls, cheeses, pies, cakes, strudel and all-day breakfasts. It's hard to go past a trad German roll with kransky sausage, sauer-kraut and mustard, or the *Bayern Schmaus*

(Bavarian feast). An emasculating display of phallic wursts dangles above the counter.

1918 Bistro & Grill (☎ 08-8563 0405; 94 Murray St; mains $24-29; ☺ lunch & dinner) 1918 is an enduring restaurant in a lovely old villa, set back from the main street beneath the boughs of a massive Norfolk Island pine. It's a sassy affair serving adventurous mains like caramelised pork belly with steamed scallop dumplings, star anise broth and coconut caramel. Book a verandah table for a long lunch.

NURIOOTPA
pop 5030

Along an endless main street at the northern end of the valley, Nuriootpa is the Barossa's commercial centre. It's not as immediately endearing as Tanunda or Angaston, but has a certain agrarian appeal. Lutheran spirit runs deep in Nuri: signs say, 'God has invested in you – are you showing any interest?'

Sleeping & Eating

Doubles d'Vine (☎ 08-8562 2260; www.doublesdvine .com.au; Barossa Valley Hwy; cottage/lodge d $80/70; ☒ ☒) Affordable Barossa accommodation at last! About 1.5km south of town is this self-contained, unpretentious cottage and separate 'lodge' (a renovated apricot shed) with two en suite doubles and shared lounge and kitchen. Both have wood heaters, barbecues and access to the pool. Reduced rates for two nights or more; bike hire (guests only) $25 per day.

Nuriootpa Vine Inn & Vine Court (☎ 08-8562 2133; www.vineinn.com.au; 14 & 49 Murray St; s $85-105, d $95-120; ☒ ☒) These two regulation motels share reception at the Vine Inn pub (14 Murray St), out the back of which are the better, pricier rooms and the swimming pool. The pub bistro (mains $10 to $19) serves lunch and dinner amid bright lights, palms and pokies.

Whirlwind Farm (☎ 08-8562 2637; www .whirlwindbb.com; Samuel Rd; s/d incl breakfast from $130/150; ☒) Surrounded by vineyards and native shrubs, this farmhouse B&B has a private guest wing with exposed timber beams, separate guest entry and two country-style rooms. Snooze on the wide verandah and contemplate a day's successful (or imminent) wine touring.

Barossa Valley SA Tourist Park (☎ 08-8562 1404; www.barossatouristpark.com.au; Penrice Rd; unpowered/ powered sites $22/25, cabins with/without bathroom from $56/47; ☒ ☒) There are at least six different kinds of cabins at this shady park, lined with pine trees next to the Nuriootpa football oval

---

TOP FIVE BAROSSA VALLEY WINERIES

From the moment Johann Gramp planted the valley's first grapes on his property at Jacob's Creek in 1847, the Barossa Valley was destined to become a major Australian wine region. The valley is best known for Shiraz, with Riesling the dominant white. There are around 80 vineyards here and 60 cellar doors, ranging from boutique wine rooms to monstrous complexes. Five of the best:

■ **Henschke** (☎ 08-8564 8223; www.henschke.com.au; Henschke Rd, Keyneton; ☺ 9am-4.30pm Mon-Fri, to noon Sat) Henschke, 11km southeast of Angaston in the Eden Valley, is known for its iconic Hill of Grace red, but most of the wines here are classics.

■ **Penfolds** (☎ 08-8568 9408; www.penfolds.com.au; Tanunda Rd, Nuriootpa; ☺ 10am-5pm) You know the name. Book ahead for the 'Make your own Blend' tour ($55) or 'Taste of Grange' tour ($150), which allows you to slide some Grange Hermitage across your lips.

■ **Peter Lehmann Wines** (☎ 08-8563 2100; www.peterlehmannwines.com.au; Para Rd, Tanunda; ☺ 9.30am-5pm Mon-Fri, 10.30am-4.30pm Sat & Sun) The multiaward-winning Shiraz and Riesling vintages here (oh, and the Semillon) are probably the most consistent and affordable wines in the Barossa. Buy a bottle and have a picnic in the grounds.

■ **Rockford Wines** (☎ 08-8563 2720; www.rockfordwines.com.au; Krondorf Rd, Tanunda; ☺ 11am-5pm) This 1850s winery uses traditional winemaking methods and produces a small range of superb wines, including sparkling reds. The Black Shiraz is a smooth and spicy killer; the cellar door in a beautiful old stable is picturesque.

■ **St Hallett** (☎ 08-8563 7000; www.sthallett.com.au; St Halletts Rd, Tanunda; ☺ 10am-5pm) Using only Barossa grapes, St Hallet produces reasonably priced but consistently good whites (try the Poacher's Blend) and the excellent Gamekeeper's Reserve Shiraz-Grenache. Unpretentious and great value for money.

(go Tigers!). All cabins have TVs, fridges, cooking facilities and small balconies.

Maggie Beer's Farm Shop (☎ 08-8562 4477; www.maggiebeer.com.au; Pheasant Farm Rd; items $4-200; ⏰ 10.30am-5pm) Celebrity SA gourmand Maggie (have you seen her on *The Cook & The Chef* on ABC TV?) has been hugely successful with her range of condiments, preserves and pâtés. The vibe here isn't as relaxed as it used to be (there's a hint of 'empire' about proceedings), but stop by for some tastings, an ice cream or a hamper of delicious bites. Off Samuel Rd.

The Branch (☎ 08-8562 4561; 15 Murray St; mains $16-33; ⏰ breakfast & lunch daily, dinner Wed-Sat) A cool conversion of an old redbrick bank on the main street is the backdrop for select Asian and Euro offerings like Kapunda saltbush lamb madras, Thai crispy beef salad, burgers and risottos. The best coffee in town to boot, and a well-considered wine and beer list.

ANGASTON
pop 2215

Photo-worthy Angaston was named after George Fife Angas, a pioneering Barossa pastoralist. An agricultural vibe persists, as there are relatively few wineries on the town doorstep: cows graze in paddocks down the end of every street, and there's a vague whiff of fertiliser in the air. Along the main drag are two pubs, some terrific eateries and a few B&Bs in old stone cottages (check for double glazing and ghosts – we had a sleepless night!).

The **Barossa Farmers Market** (☎ 0402 026 882; www.barossafarmersmarket.com; cnr Stockwell & Nuriootpa Rds; ⏰ 7.30 -11.30am Sat) happens near Vintners Bar & Grill (right) every Saturday.

The **Barossa Valley Cheese Company** (☎ 08-8564 3636; www.barossacheese.com.au; 67b Murray St; ⏰ 10am-5pm Mon-Fri, 10am-4pm Sat, 11am-3pm Sun) is a fabulously stinky room, selling handmade cheeses from local cows and goats. Tastings are free, but it's unlikely you'll leave without buying a wedge of the Washington Washed Rind.

About 6km southeast of town, lavish **Collingrove Homestead** (☎ 08-8564 2061; www.collingrovehomestead.com.au; Eden Valley-Angaston Rd; tours adult/concession $10/5; ⏰ 1-4.30pm Mon-Fri, from noon Sat & Sun) was built by George Angas' son John in 1856. Thirty-minute tours run at 1.30pm, 2.30pm and 3.30pm daily, plus 12.30pm on weekends. Regroup afterwards over Devonshire tea ($10), or consider a night in the B&B wing (doubles from $250).

Sleeping & Eating
Caithness Manor B&B (☎ 08-8564 2761; www.caithness .com.au; 12 Hill St W; d incl breakfast from $175; 🏊) The sign here says 'Ceud Mile Faille', Gaelic for '100,000 Welcomes'. The house is actually a refurbished girls' school, but there's not an ink stain or spitball in sight – just two cottage-style, ground-floor units with hillside views over the town (especially from the pool!).

Angaston Hotel (☎ 08-8564 2428; 60 Murray St; mains $8-20; ⏰ lunch & dinner) The better looking of the town's two pubs, the friendly Angaston serves budget bar meals (sub-$10 burgers and sandwiches) and the cheapest steaks this side of Argentina. The bog-basic pub rooms upstairs were still going cheap when we visited (single/double $50/70), but were about to be overhauled – expect a price hike.

OUR PICK **Blond Coffee** (☎ 08-8564 3444; 60 Murray St; mains $9-16; ⏰ breakfast & lunch) An elegant, breezy room with huge windows facing the main street, Blond serves nutty coffee and all-day cafe fare, including an awesome bacon-and-cheese club sandwich. There's also a cheese-and-smallgoods counter, and a wall full of local produce (vinegar, olive oil, biscuits and confectionery). Fake-blonde botox tourists share the window seats with down-to-earth regulars.

Vintners Bar & Grill (☎ 08-8564 2488; cnr Stockwell & Nuriootpa Rds; mains $21-35; ⏰ lunch daily, dinner Mon-Sat) One of the Barossa's landmark restaurants, Vintners stresses simple elegance in both food and atmosphere. Their dining room has an open fire, vineyard views and bolts of crisp white linen; menus concentrate on local produce.

See also Collingrove Homestead (left).

CLARE VALLEY

Take a couple of days to check out the Clare Valley, about two hours north of Adelaide. At the centre of the fertile Mid-North agricultural district, the skinny valley produces world-class Rieslings and reds. This is gorgeous countryside, with open skies, rounded hills, stands of large gums and wind rippling over wheat fields. The towns around here date from the 1840s, many built to service the Burra copper mines.

Accommodation
Refurbished B&Bs and self-contained cottages prevail around the valley, but unless

you get a good package try to avoid staying here on weekends; Friday and Saturday night rates verge on outright greed. The visitors centre in Clare can assist with accommodation bookings.

Information

Clare Valley visitors centre (☎ 1800 242 131, 08-8842 2131; www.clarevalley.com.au; cnr Spring Gully & Main North Rd; 🕙 9am-5pm Mon-Fri, 10am-4pm Sat & Sun; 🖳) This shiny new centre has local info and internet access, and handles valley-wide accommodation bookings; on the southern edge of Clare itself.

Department for Environment & Heritage (DEH; ☎ 08-8841 3400; www.environment.sa.gov.au/parks; 6/17 Lennon St, Clare; 🕙 9am-5pm Mon-Fri) Information about national parks and reserves in the area.

Tours

For other Clare Valley tours ex-Adelaide, see p734.

Clare Valley Experiences (☎ 08-8842 1880; www .clarevalleyexperiences.com; tours up to 4 people $220) Choose-your-own-adventure Clare tours in a flash Merc to stretch your hedonistic muscles.

Clare Valley Tours (☎ 08-8843 8066, 0418 832 812; www.cvtours.com.au; 4-/6-hr tours $86/100) Mini-bus tours taking in the Clare wineries, Martindale Hall and Burra.

Swagabout Tours (☎ 0408 845 378; www.swagabout tours.com.au) Dependable one-/two-day Clare Valley trips ($120/440).

Festivals& Events

Clare Valley Gourmet Weekend (☎ 08-8843 4222; www.southaustralia.com) A frenzy of wine, food and music in May.

Clare Show (☎ 08-8842 2374) The largest one-day show in SA, held in October.

Getting There & Around

To access the Clare Valley from Adelaide, take Main North Rd to Gawler then take Rte 32, which becomes the Barrier Hwy, into New South Wales.

Yorke Peninsula Coaches (☎ 08-8821 2755; www .ypcoaches.com.au) departs Adelaide daily for Auburn ($21, 2¼ hours) and Clare ($29, 2¾ hours), extending to Burra ($29, 3¼ hours) on Monday and Thursday.

You can hire a bike to pelt around the Clare Valley wineries from either Cogwebs (below) in Auburn or Clare Valley Cycle Hire (p783) in Clare.

Clare Valley Taxis (☎ 0419 847 900) can drop-off or pick-up anywhere along the Riesling Trail.

AUBURN

pop 320

Sleepy, 1849 Auburn – the Clare Valley's southernmost village – is a leave-the-back-door-open-and-the-keys-in-the-ignition kinda town, with a time-warp vibe that makes you feel like you're in an old black-and-white photograph. The streets are defined by beautifully preserved, hand-built stone buildings; cottage gardens overflow with untidy blooms. Pick up a copy of the *Walk with History at Auburn* brochure from the Clare visitors centre (left).

Now on the main route to the valley's wineries, Auburn initially serviced bullockies and South American muleteers whose wagons – up to 100 a day – trundled between Burra's copper mines and Port Wakefield.

Clare Valley's largest winery **Taylors Wines** (see Top Five Clare Valley Wineries, p782) lurks on the edge of town, while the brilliant 25km **Riesling Trail** (below) starts (or ends) at the restored Auburn Train Station.

Cogwebs (☎ 08-8849 2380; www.cogwebs.com.au; 30 Main North Rd; 🕙 8am-6pm Thu-Tue) offers internet access (per 30 minutes/hour $4/6) and bike hire (per half-/full day $25/40).

Sleeping & Eating

Auburn Shiraz Motel (☎ 08-8849 2125; www.auburn shirazmotel.com.au; Main North Rd; d $78-90; 🕃) This small motel on the Adelaide side of town has

---

THE RIESLING TRAIL

Following the course of a disused railway line between Auburn and Clare, the fabulous **Riesling Trail** (www.southaustraliantrails.com.au) is 25km of wines, wheels and wonderment. It's primarily a cycling trail, but the gentle gradient means you can walk or push a pram along it just as easily. It's a two-hour dash end to end on a bike, but why hurry? There are three loop track detours to explore and dozens of cellar doors to tempt you along the way.

For bike hire, see Clare Valley Cycle Hire (p783) in Clare or Cogwebs (above) in Auburn.

SOUTH AUSTRALIA

TOP FIVE CLARE VALLEY WINERIES

Despite a warm climate, the Clare Valley's cool microclimates (around rivers, creeks and gullies) noticeably affect the wines, enabling Clare Valley whites to be laid down for long periods and still be brilliant. The valley produces some of the best Riesling going around, plus grand Semillon and Shiraz. Our favourite cellar doors:

- **Annie's Lane** (☎ 08-8843 2204; www.annieslane.com.au; Quelltaler Rd, Watervale; ☷ 9am-5pm Mon-Fri, 10am-4pm Sat & Sun) Annie's flagship wines are Copper Trail Shiraz and Riesling. The attached winery museum and art gallery contain personal touches like the VE Day closure notice from WWII.

- **Knappstein** (☎ 08-8842 2600; www.knappsteinwines.com.au; 2 Pioneer Ave, Clare; ☷ 9am-5pm Mon-Fri, 11am-5pm Sat, 11am-4pm Sun) Taking a minimal-intervention approach to wine making, Knappstein has built quite a name for itself. Shiraz and Riesling steal the show, but they also make a mighty fine Semillon-Sauvignon Blanc blend (and beer!).

- **Pikes** (☎ 08-8843 4370; www.pikeswines.com.au; Polish Hill River Rd, Sevenhill; ☷ 10am-4pm) The industrious Pike family has been producing wine since 1886, so they know a thing or two about Riesling (and Shiraz, Sangiovese, Pino Grigio, Viognier...). A beautiful cellar door, with Bella the wine dog.

- **our pick** **Skillogalee** (☎ 08-8843 4311; www.skillogalee.com; Trevarrick Rd, Sevenhill; ☷ 10am-5pm) Quite possibly our favourite SA winery (OK, so it is our favourite), Skillogalee is a small family outfit known for its spicy Shiraz, fabulous food and top-notch Riesling (a glass of which is like kissing a pretty girl in summer). Kick back with a long, lazy lunch on the verandah (mains $20 to $30).

- **Taylors Wines** (☎ 08-8849 1111; www.taylorswines.com.au; Taylors Rd, Auburn; ☷ 9am-5pm Mon-Fri, 10am-5pm Sat, 10am-4pm Sun) Sure, it's a massive nation-wide operation with a heinous mock-castle cellar door, but the wine here is fit for royalty (love the Cab Sav).

---

been proudly renovated with Shiraz-coloured render and Cabernet-coloured doors. There are nine bright, spotless units and friendly hosts – great value.

Rising Sun Hotel (☎ 08-8849 2015; rising@capri.net.au; Main North Rd; mains $14-18; ☷ lunch & dinner; ☒) This classic 1850 pub has a huge rep for its atmosphere, food and accommodation. En suite hotel rooms and cottage mews rooms out the back (doubles from $90 and $115 respectively) have solid occupancy – book well in advance (dinner and overnight packages a speciality). The pub food is unpretentious but unremarkable, and (disconcertingly) there was only one Clare Valley wine available by the glass when we visited.

Cygnets at Auburn (☎ 08-8849 2030; www.cygnetsatauburn.com.au; Main North Rd; mains $18-29; ☷ breakfast & lunch daily, dinner Thu-Sun Dec-Mar, Fri & Sat Apr-Nov) This gourmet restaurant-provedore serves and stocks local produce matched with Clare Valley wines. There's a wine and tapas bar for grazers, the best coffee in town, and delicious mains like caramelised pear and blue cheese bruschetta. A good-value B&B wing is out the back (from $160 mid-week).

MINTARO
pop 230

A few kilometres up the road from Auburn, heritage-listed Mintaro (founded 1849) is a stone village that could have been lifted out of the Cotswolds and plonked into the Australian bush. There are very few architectural intrusions from the 1900s – the whole place seems to have been largely left to its own devices. A fact for your next trivia night: Mintaro slate is used internationally in the manufacture of billiard tables.

There's nowhere else in the world quite like **Martindale Hall** (☎ 08-8843 9088; www.martindalehall.com; Manoora Rd; adult/child/concession $10/2.50/7.50; ☷ 11am-4pm Mon-Fri, from noon Sat & Sun), an astonishing 1880 manor 3km from Mintaro. Built for young pastoralist Edmund Bowman Jnr who subsequently partied away the family fortune (OK, so drought and plummeting wool prices played a part...but it was mostly the partying), the manor features original furnishings, a magnificent blackwood staircase, Mintaro-slate billiard table and a museumlike smoking room. The hall starred as Appleyard College in the 1975

Peter Weir film *Picnic at Hanging Rock*. B&B and DB&B packages allow you to spend a spooky night here ($110 and $230 respectively; *Mirandaaa…*).

Hedge your bets at **Mintaro Maze** (☎ 08-8843 9012; www.mintaromaze.com; Jacka Rd; adult/child $7/5; 🕙 10am-4pm Mon-Thu & school holidays) as you try to find your way into the middle and back out again.

Sleeping & Eating

Reilly's Wines & Restaurant (☎ 08-8843 9013; www .reillyswines.com; Burra St; mains $15-25; 🕙 10am-5pm; 🍴) Reilly's started life as a shop for an Irish cobbler in 1856, and has been a winery since the '90s. An organic vegie garden out the back supplies the attached restaurant, which is decorated with local artists and serves creative mod Oz (antipasto, rabbit terrine, vegie lasagne). The owners also rent out a three-bedroom house and three one-bedroom units on Hill St (doubles from $140).

our pick Magpie & Stump Hotel (☎ 08-8843 9014; Burra St; meals $7-25; 🕙 lunch daily, dinner Mon-Sat) The old Magpie & Stump was first licensed in 1851, and was a vital rehydration point for the copper carriers travelling between Burra and Port Wakefield. Schnitzels and steaks, log fires, pool table, Mintaro-slate floors, a beer garden and a lazy black dog – the perfect pub?

See also Martindale Hall (opposite).

CLARE
pop 3070

Named after County Clare in Ireland, this town was founded in 1842 and is the biggest in the valley, but it's a little thin on charm. All the requisite services are here (post, supermarket, fuel, internet etc), but you'll have a more interesting Clare experience sleeping out of town.

Information

Clare Valley visitors centre (p781)
Domain Internet Café (☎ 08-8842 4166; 202 Main North Rd; per 15min $3; 🕙 2.30-5.30pm Mon-Fri) Internet access.

Sights & Activities

Most folks are here for the wine, but Clare does have some worthy heritage-listed buildings. Pick up the *Clare Historic Walk* pamphlet from the visitors centre.

The 1850 cop-shop and courthouse is now the **Old Police Station Museum** (☎ 08-8842 2376; www .nationaltrustsa.org.au; adult/child/concession $2/50c/1.50; 🕙 10am-noon & 2-4pm Sat & Sun), displaying Victorian clothing, old photos, furniture and domestic bits and pieces.

About 3km southwest of Sevenhill, the 400-hectare **Spring Gully Conservation Park** (☎ 08-8892 3025; www.environment.sa.gov.au/parks/sanpr/springully; admission free) features blue-gum forest, red stringybarks and 18m-high winter waterfalls. There are plenty of bird twitters, critters and trails too.

Hit the **Riesling Trail** (p781) with **Clare Valley Cycle Hire** (☎ 08-8842 2782, 0418 802 077; www .clarevalleycyclehire.com.au; 32 Victoria Rd; bike hire per half/ full day $17/25; 🕙 8am-5pm). The operators will also collect and freight any wine you buy en route – bless their cotton socks!

Sleeping

Clare Valley Cabins (☎ 08-8842 1155; www.clarevalley cabins.com.au; Hubbe Rd; d from $99; 🍴) At this 52-acre property 6km north of Clare, secluded cabins come in a variety of packages with breakfast and barbecue provisions. They also have an 1860 stone chapel to sleep/pray/confess in (double from $120 per night).

Clare Valley Motel (☎ 08-8842 2799; clarevalleymo tel@bigpond.com; 74a Main North Rd; d $105-154; 🍴 🐾) Looking like some kind of ranch from

---

DETOUR: BURRA

Bursting at the seams with historic sites, **Burra** (population 1110), 43km northeast of Clare, was a copper mining boomtown between 1847 and 1877 with a burgeoning Cornish community. Towns like Mintaro and Auburn serviced miners travelling between Burra and Port Wakefield, from where the copper was shipped. The miners had it tough here, excavating dugouts for themselves and their families to live in.

Burra visitors centre (☎ 08-8892 2154; www.visitburra.com; 2 Market Sq; 🕙 9am-5pm) sells the self-guided Burra Heritage Pass ($20) providing admission (via a key) to eight historic sights, and the Burra Museum Pass ($15). A two-pass combo costs $30. The visitors centre also handles bike hire (per half-/full day $35/20) and accommodation bookings.

SOUTH AUSTRALIA

Vermont, this huge place has four different wings, offering basic motel rooms up to swish spa suites. The restaurant (mains $25 to $27) serves dinner nightly (except Sunday). Wireless internet available.

Batunga B&B (☎ 08-8843 0120; www.battunga .com.au; Watervale; d incl breakfast $160, extra adult/child $50/40) On a 200-acre farm over the hills 2km west of Watervale (it's a little hard to find – ask for directions), Batunga has four modern apartments in two stone cottages with Mintaro-slate floors, barbecues, kitchenettes and wood fires. This is beautiful country – undulating farmland studded with huge eucalypts.

Clare Caravan Park (☎ 08-8842 2724; www.clare caravanpark.com.au; Main North Rd; unpowered/powered sites $20/27, cabins from $80; ❄ ▣) This huge, dogmatically run park 4km south of town towards Auburn has secluded sites, all en suite cabins, a creek and giant gum trees. There's also an inground pool, plus bike hire (per day $25).

Eating

Citadel (☎ 08-8842 1453; Main North Rd; mains $12-18; ☾ lunch Sat & Sun, dinner Wed-Sun) Before it was an upmarket pizza joint, an old bloke lived here with dirt floors and no electricity! Things have improved: expect tasty pasta and even-better pizzas. Takeaways welcome.

Clare Hotel (☎ 08-8842 2816; 244 Main North Rd; mains $13-25; ☾ lunch & dinner) The Clare (aka the 'Middle Pub') cooks up the best pub food in town, to the blaring soundtrack of horse racing and TVs simultaneously showing all available channels. There are also budget pub rooms upstairs (single/double $30/70) with shared bathrooms.

Salt n Vines Bar & Bistro (☎ 08-8842 1796; Wendouree Rd; mains $22-48; ☾ lunch & dinner) This mod, airy, hillside bar-restaurant has a broad, sunny balcony – the perfect setting for a bottle of local Riesling and an indulgent seafood platter for two (surprisingly good this far inland!). Kids' menu and grown-up desserts, too.

See also Skillogalee, in Top Five Clare Valley Wineries, p782.

YORKE PENINSULA

A couple of hours west of Adelaide, boot-shaped Yorke Peninsula (www.yorkepen insula.com.au) bills itself as 'Agriculturally Rich – Naturally Beautiful'. It does have a certain agrarian beauty – deep azure summer skies and yellow wheat fields on hazy, gently rolling hills – but if you're looking for cosmopolitan riches and tourist trappings, you won't find much here to engage you. Yorkes is as low as low-key can be, with a smattering of farm villages and beach-shack fishing towns, offering little for hedonistic urbanites.

That said, far-flung Innes National Park on the peninsula's southern tip is well worth visiting. The coastline here is gorgeous, with great surf, roaming emus, kangaroos, ospreys and sea eagles, and southern right whales and dolphins cruising by.

For history buffs, the peninsula's north has a trio of towns called the **Copper Triangle**: Moonta (the mine), Wallaroo (the smelter) and Kadina (the service town). Settled by Cornish miners, this area drove the regional economy following a copper boom in the early 1860s.

Adjahdura Land (☎ 0429 367 121; www.adjahdura .com.au) runs highly regarded Aboriginal cultural tours of the peninsula, exploring the incredibly long Indigenous association with this country – walk the land with the traditional owners on one-day tours (adults/children $120/25). Two-, three- and five-day options are also available.

The Yorke Peninsula visitor centre (opposite) is in Kadina.

Getting There & Around

Yorke Peninsula Coaches (☎ 1300 132 932, 08-8821 2755; www.ypcoaches.com.au) services the peninsula daily from Adelaide, stopping at the bigger towns like Kadina ($25, 2¼ hours) and Wallaroo ($25, 2½ hours) and travelling as far south as Warooka and/or Yorketown ($40, four hours). Services from Warooka to Marion Bay near Innes National Park are too sporadic to be useful (first Tuesday of the month, $6, 1½ hours).

SEASA (☎ 08-8823 0777; www.seasa.com.au) runs a vehicle ferry between Wallaroo (on the Yorke Peninsula) and Lucky Bay (on the Eyre Peninsula) – a shortcut shaving around 350km off the drive between the two peninsulas (via Port Augusta). Cars cost $130 one way plus $32.50 for the driver; extra adults/children pay $35/15. Ferries run twice daily Monday to Friday; once daily on weekends. The voyage takes around 1¾ hours one way.

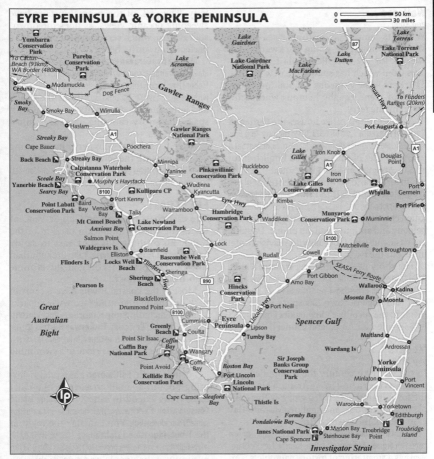

EYRE PENINSULA & YORKE PENINSULA

Based in Moonta, **Copper Coast Eco Bikes** (☎ 0408 859 034; bike hire per hr/half-day $10/50) rents out bicycles.

WEST COAST

Fronting Spencer Gulf, the west coast has a string of shallow swimming beaches, plus the Copper Triangle towns, all a short drive from one other. **Kernewek Lowender** (www.kernewek.org), aka the Copper Coast Cornish Festival, happens around here in May in odd-numbered years.

Kadina
pop 4000

Baking-hot, inland Kadina (pronounced 'Kadeena') calls itself 'Australia's Little Cornwall', and has some impressive copper-era civic buildings and a slew of pubs and petrol stations. The **Yorke Peninsula visitor centre** (☎ 1800 654 991, 08-8821 2333; www.coppercoast.sa.gov .au; Farm Shed, 50 Moonta Rd, Kadina; ☼ 9am-5pm Mon-Fri, 10am-3.30pm Sat & Sun) is here.

Behind the visitor centre, the amazing collection of old farming, mining and domestic bits-and-pieces at the **Farm Shed Museum** (☎ 08-8821 2333; 50 Moonta Rd; adult/child/concession/ family $8/3/6/20; ☼ 9am-5pm Mon-Fri, 10am-3.30pm Sat & Sun) gives an engaging insight into olden days and ways.

Kadina Village Motel (☎ 08-8821 1920; www.kadi navillagemotel.websyte.com.au; 28 Port Rd; d $85;) is a retro, U-shaped joint on the road to Wallaroo; basic, clean motel digs if all you need is a bed.

Wallaroo

pop 3000

With its empty shopfronts, sea-breezy Wallaroo might be going backwards if it weren't for the Eyre Peninsula ferry, business from which has spawned a new marina. There are some gorgeous old buildings here, offset by some equally heinous wheat silos down by the ferry.

A stoic ex–post office houses the **Heritage & Nautical Museum** (☎ 08-8823 3015; cnr Jetty Rd & Emu St; adult/child $5/2; ☼ 10am-4pm Mon-Fri, from 2pm Sat & Sun), with tales of square-rigged English ships and George the pickled giant squid.

Once a grand temperance hotel, **Sonbern Lodge Motel** (☎ 08-8823 2291; www.sonbernlodgemotel .com.au; 18 John Tce; s/d from $75/95; ✖) is an old-fashioned charmer, right down to the old wooden balcony and antique wind-up phone. Upstairs are basic pub-style rooms, with newish motel units out the back.

The shiny new multistorey **Wallaroo Marina Apartments** (☎ 08-8823 4068; www.wallarooa partents.com.au; 11 Heritage Dve; d from $149; ✖) on the northern edge of town has spiffy suites and meals in the 'alehouse' downstairs (mains $15 to $28, open for lunch and dinner).

Moonta

pop 3070

In the late 19th century the Moonta copper mine was the richest in Australia. These days the town maintains a faded glory, with a couple of decent pubs, and shallow Moonta Bay 1km west of the town centre.

Moonta visitor centre (☎ 08-8825 1891; info@moon tatourism.org.au; Old Railway Station, Blanche Tce; ☼ 9am-5pm) has a smattering of history pamphlets, and details on the **Moonta Heritage Site** 1.5km east of town. The site includes the excellent **Moonta Mines Museum** (Verran Tce; adult/child $5/2; ☼ 1-4pm), once a grand school with 1100 pupils; the **Moonta Mines Sweet Shop** (☼ 10am-4pm) across the road; and a fully restored **Miner's Cottage** (Verco St; adult/child $3/1; ☼ 1.30-4pm Wed, Sat & Sun).

Around 3km north of town, the **Wheal Hughes Copper Mine** (☎ 08-8825 1891; Moonta-Wallaroo Rd; adult/child/concession/family $15/8/13/45; ☼ tours 10.30am, 12.30pm & 2.30pm Wed, Sat & Sun) offers a gander at a contemporary mine worked until 1993. Book through the visitor centre.

The flashy **Seagate Bistro Motel** (☎ 08-8825 3270; www.seagatemoontabay.com.au; 171 Bay Rd; d $150-220; ✖) is an octagonal (or is it a squashed dodecahedron?) motel right by Moonta Bay

jetty. The pick of the rooms upstairs have sweeping oceanic views, as does the downstairs bistro, which serves upbeat pub grub – perfect for a sunset beer!

Moonta Bay Caravan Park (☎ 08-8825 2406; www.ad elaidecaravanpark.com.au/moontabay.html; Foreshore, Moonta Bay; unpowered/powered sites $27/29, cabins with/ without spa $139/97; ✖) is handy to the beach and jetty, and has decent luxury cabins with spas. The grassy camping areas are almost on the beach.

After a hard day's copper mining, swing your shovel into the **Cornish Kitchen** (☎ 08-8825 3030; 12 Ellen St; items $2-5; ☼ breakfast & lunch Mon-Sat) for the ultimate Cornish pastie.

EAST COAST

The east-coast road along Gulf St Vincent traces the coast within 1km or 2km of the water. En route, roads dart east to sandy beaches and holiday towns. Like the suburban Adelaide beaches across the gulf, this is prime crab-fishing territory.

Most of the coastal towns have a caravan park or camping ground (see www.ypparks .com.au), including unpretentious **Port Vincent**. Need a bunk? Try cosy **Tuckerway Hostel** (☎ 08-8853 7285; fax 08-8853 7182; 14 Lime Kiln Rd; dm $18), with simple dorms and twins close to a swimming beach.

Further south, **Edithburgh** has a tidal swimming pool in a small cove; from the cliff-tops, views extend to sandy **Troubridge Island Conservation Park** (www.environment.sa.gov.au/parks/ sanpr/troubridgeisland). You can stay the night at the **Troubridge Island Lighthouse** (☎ 08-8852 6290; www.lighthouse.net.au; per person incl transfers $80, q $320): minimum four people and two-night stay; BYO food and linen. Fairy penguins still live here, but the island is steadily eroding – what the sea wants, the sea will have...

Back on the mainland, **Edithburgh House** (☎ 08-8852 6373; www.edithburghhouse.com.au; 7 Edith St; d with/without breakfast $140/110) has sophisticated cottage-style rooms, a homely Scottish vibe and an on-site restaurant.

The district's main business and administrative centre is **Yorketown** (population 750) – you'll usually find a bed here when the seaside towns are packed to the gills in summer.

SOUTH COAST & INNES NATIONAL PARK

The peninsula's south coast is largely sheltered from the Southern Ocean's fury by Kangaroo

Island, so there are some great swimming beaches along here. The surf finds its way through around Troubridge Point and Cape Spencer, where the **Cutloose Rip Curl Yorkes Classic** (☎ 0427 796 845) surf comp happens every October.

Cape Spencer is part of **Innes National Park** (www.environment.sa.gov.au/parks/sanpr/innes; admission per car $7.50), where sheer cliffs plunge into indigo waters and rocky offshore islands hide small coves and sandy beaches. **Stenhouse Bay**, just outside the park, and **Pondalowie Bay**, within the park, are the main local towns. Pondalowie Bay has a bobbing lobster-fishing fleet and a gnarly surf beach (keep one eye on the swell if you're swimming). Fishing charters and reef diving are also an option here.

The rusty ribs of the 711-tonne steel barque *Ethel*, which foundered in 1904, arc forlornly from the sands just south of Pondalowie Bay. Follow the sign just past the Cape Spencer turn-off to the ghost-town ruins of **Inneston**, a gypsum-mining community abandoned in 1930.

The national park also has bushy **campsites** (per car $5-15). Our favourite spot at Pondalowie was closed at the time of research. If it's still closed when you visit, try Cable Bay for beach access, Surfers for surfing or Browns Beach for fishing.

Alternatively, the heritage **lodges** (per night $85-120) at Inneston sleep four to 10 people and have showers and cooking facilities. **Stenhouse Bay Hall** ($260) sleeps 28; **Sheperds Hut** ($35) at Shell Beach sleeps four, but doesn't have power. Book ahead through Stenhouse Bay **DEH** (☎ 08-8854 3200). BYO drinking water in summer.

Rhino's Tavern & Innes Park Trading Post (☎ 08-8854 4078; www.rhinostavern.com.au; 1 Stenhouse Bay Rd, Stenhouse Bay; ☯ 8am-late) is a one-stop shop for fuel, bait, groceries and takeaway food, or kick back with a beer and a pub meal (mains $15 to $30, open for lunch and dinner).

EYRE PENINSULA & THE WEST COAST

The vast, straw-coloured triangle of Eyre Peninsula is Australia's big-sky country, and is considered by galloping gourmands to be the promised land of seafood. Meals out here rarely transpire without the option of trying

the local oysters, tuna and whiting. Sublime national parks punctuate the coast, along with world-class surf breaks and lazy holiday towns, thinning out as you head west towards the Great Australian Bight, the Nullarbor Plain and Western Australia (WA).

Eyre Peninsula's photogenic wild-western flank is an important breeding ground for southern right whales, Australian sea lions and great white sharks (the scariest scenes of *Jaws* were shot here). There are some memorable opportunities to encounter these various submariners along the way.

The quickest route heading west is the Eyre Hwy from Port Augusta to Ceduna (468km), though the coast road via Port Lincoln (763km) is far more interesting.

Online, visit www.southaustralia.com/eyre peninsula.aspx.

Getting There & Away

Regional Express (Rex; ☎ 13 17 13; www.regionalexpress .com.au) operates flights daily from Adelaide to Whyalla (one way from $108), Port Lincoln (from $107) and Ceduna ($160).

See also Adelaide–Eyre Peninsula & the West Coast by Bus, below.

For details of train services in the region, see p723.

ADELAIDE–EYRE PENINSULA & THE WEST COAST BY BUS

Premier Stateliner (☎ 08-8415 5555; www.premierstateliner.com.au) operates daily buses from Adelaide to the following destinations:

Destination	Price ($)	Duration (hr)
Ceduna	131	11¼
Port Augusta	47	4
Port Lincoln	97	9¾
Streaky Bay	102	10
Whyalla	56	5¼

PORT AUGUSTA

pop 13,900

At the head of Spencer Gulf, Port Augusta proudly calls itself the 'Crossroads of Australia'. From here, highways and railways roll west across the Nullarbor into WA, north to Darwin, south to Adelaide, and east to Sydney.

The old town centre has considerable appeal, with some elegant old buildings and a revitalised waterfront: locals cast lines into the blue, and Indigenous kids back-flip off jetties. The town has had problems with alcoholism (the streets are now a dry zone), but the vibe is rarely menacing.

Information

Department for Environment & Heritage (DEH; ☎ 08-8648 5300; Upstairs, 9 Mackay St; ✆ 9am-5pm Mon-Fri) Information, maps and road condition updates for the Flinders Ranges and outback.

Port Augusta visitors centre (☎ 08-8641 9193; www.portaugusta.sa.gov.au; Wadlata Outback Centre, 41 Flinders Tce; ✆ 9am-5.30pm Mon-Fri, 10am-4pm Sat & Sun) The major information outlet for the Flinders Ranges, outback and Eyre Peninsula.

Sights & Activities

The highlights of the **Wadlata Outback Centre** (☎ 08-8641 9193; www.wadlata.sa.gov.au; 41 Flinders Tce; adult/child/concession/family $11/7/10/25; ✆ 9am-5.30pm Mon-Fri, 10am-4pm Sat & Sun) are an old transcontinental train carriage and the 'Outback Tunnel of Time', tracing Aboriginal and European histories using audio-visual displays, interactive exhibits and a distressingly big snake.

Just north of town the excellent **Australian Arid Lands Botanic Garden** (☎ 08-8641 1049; www.australian-aridlands-botanic-garden.org; Stuart Hwy; admission free, tours adult/child/concession $6.50/5/6; ✆ 9am-5pm Mon-Fri, 10am-4pm Sat & Sun, tours 10am Mon-Fri) has 250 hectares of sand hills, clay flats and desert fauna. Explore on your own, or take a guided tour.

Port Augusta Aquatic & Outdoor Adventure Centre (☎ 08-8642 2699, 0427 722 450; paa.oac@bigpond.com; cnr Gibson & El Alamein Sts; ✆ 8am-8pm Oct-Mar, by appointment Apr-Sep) has lessons and gear rental for kayaking, windsurfing, fishing, rock-climbing, abseiling, snorkelling, orienteering, bushwalking, sailing…

Tours

Blue Emu Tours (☎ 0439 346 120; www.blueemutours.com.au) Half-/full-day Flinders Ranges tours ($98/180), plus Port Augusta area tours ($55 per hour).

Flinders Ranges Water Cruises (☎ 08-8642 2488, 0438 857 001; www.augustawestside.com.au; cruises per person from $45) Two-hour morning ecocruises to the top of the Gulf, and two-hour sunset cruises.

Gulf Getaways (☎ 08-8642 6827, 0408 445 133; www.gulfgetaways.com.au; per person cruises incl lunch $45) A 2½-hour ecocruise on the Spencer Gulf, checking out mangroves, dolphins and birdlife.

Wallaby Tracks Adventure Tours (☎ 0428 486 655; www.wallabytracks.com) Small-group 4WD tours through the Southern Flinders Ranges (half-day $110), or north to Wilpena Pound (full day $160).

Sleeping & Eating

Hotel Flinders (☎ 08-8642 2544; www.thehotelflinders.com; 39 Commercial Rd; motel dm/s/d/tr $22/55/70/80; ⌨) This central, 130-year-old pub has a variety of basic rooms upstairs and some clean but weirdly configured motel rooms off to one side. The Italian-prone dining room here is pretty good too (mains $15 to $25, serving lunch and dinner).

Best Western Standpipe (☎ 08-8642 4033; www.standpipe.com.au; cnr Stuart Hwy & Hwy 1; s/d/tr/f/apt $115/125/135/160/240; ⌨ 🖳 🍴) Attracting government delegates and business types with its comfortable 1980s-ish units, this must be the only accommodation in SA that charges less on weekends (singles and doubles $77 and $84 respectively). And the Indian restaurant here (mains $15 to $30; open for lunch and dinner) is unbelievable!

Oasis Apartments (☎ 1800 008 648, 08-8648 9000; www.majestichotels.com.au; foreshore, Marryatt St; apt $135-190; ⌨ 🖳 🍴) A group of 75 luxury units with jaunty designs, right by the water. All rooms have washing machines, dryers, TVs, fridges, microwaves and flashes of interior design.

Shoreline Caravan Park (☎ 08-8642 2965; www.shorelinecaravanpark.com.au; Gardiner Ave; unpowered/powered sites $22/25, dm/cabins $18/55, units $65-85; ⌨ 🍴) It's a grassless, dusty site a fair way from town (and the shore), but the budget cabins here are beaut, plus there are simple four-bed dorm units for backpackers.

Gottabe Fish (☎ 08-8641 3777; 6 Marryatt St; meals $7-14; ✆ lunch & dinner) Here at the top of Spencer Gulf, you expect quality seafood. This sweaty takeaway joint serves fresh king fish, snapper, King George whiting, prawns, butterfish and Smoky Bay oysters, plus burgers, yiros and steak sandwiches.

Getting There & Away

From Port Augusta, **Yorke Peninsula Coaches** (☎ 08-8821 2755; www.ypcoaches.com.au) runs buses to Quorn in the Flinders Ranges ($6, 45 minutes).

The famous *Ghan* train connects Adelaide with Darwin via Port Augusta, and the *Indian Pacific* (between Perth and Sydney) connects with the *Ghan* at Port Augusta. See p723 for details.

For a more scenic trip, **Pichi Richi Railway** (☎ 1800 440 101, 08-8648 6598; www.prr.org.au; one-way adult/child/concession/family $45/17/42/107) runs between Port Augusta and Quorn (2½ hours) on Saturdays.

WHYALLA
pop 21,130

An hour's drive south of Port Augusta is Whyalla – the second-biggest city in SA – its deep-water port sustaining steel mills, oil and gas refineries and an apocalyptic morass of chugging chimneys, hideous portworks and furnaces. There's not a whole lot to see here if you're not into fossil fuels, but the **Whyalla visitor centre** (☎ 08-8645 7900; www.whyalla.com; Lincoln Hwy; ☺ 9am-5pm Mon-Fri, 9am-4pm Sat, 10am-4pm Sun) can help with local info and accommodation listings.

PORT LINCOLN
pop 15,000

Prosperous Port Lincoln, the 'Tuna Capital of the World', overlooks broad Boston Bay on the southern end of Eyre Peninsula. It's still a fairly rough town a long way from anywhere, but the vibe here is energetic (dare we say progressive!). The grassy foreshore is a busy promenade, and there are some good pubs, eateries and aquatic activities here to keep you out of trouble.

If not for a lack of fresh water, Port Lincoln might have become the South Australian capital. These days it's salt water (and the tuna therein) that keeps the town ticking. A guaranteed friend-maker here is to slip Dean Lukin's name into every conversation. Straight off the tuna boats, Big Dean won the Super Heavyweight weightlifting gold medal at the 1984 Olympics in LA – what a champ!

Information

Port Lincoln visitor centre (☎ 1300 788 378, 08-8683 3544; www.visitportlincoln.net; 3 Adelaide Pl; ☺ 9am-5pm; 🖳) This excellent centre books accommodation and has national parks information and passes.

Sights & Activities

The annual **Tunarama Festival** (www.tunarama.net) on the Australia Day weekend in January celebrates every finny facet of the tuna-fishing industry. Highlights include tuna tossing, keg rolling, slippery-pole climbing, boat-building comps, stalls and bands.

Sadly, Port Lincoln hasn't managed to preserve many of its original buildings. In Flinders Park, **Mill Cottage** (☎ 08-8682 4650; 20 Flinders Hwy; adult/child $4/50c; ☺ 10am-2pm Wed, 2-4pm Sun), built in 1866, has somehow survived.

Bite into some extreme underwater adventure with **Calypso Star Charter** (☎ 08-8682 3939; www.sharkcagediving.com.au; 1-day dive $495), which runs cage dives with great white sharks around Neptune Islands. Book in advance.

Short on bravado? Sea lions and tuna might be more your speed. Carbon-neutral **Adventure Bay Charters** (☎ 0409 890 979; www.adventurebaycharters.com.au; half-day tours $160) takes you swimming with sea lions and Port Lincoln's famous tuna, which you hand feed in a fish-farm enclosure.

If you'd rather be near the water but not in it, the local fishing is outstanding. **Spot On Fishing & Camping World** (☎ 08-8683 0021; fishandcamp@ozemail.com.au; 39 Tasman Tce; ☺ 8.30am-5.30pm Mon-Fri, 8am-4pm Sat & Sun) will give you the latest on what's biting where.

For info on local surf and dive opportunities, contact **Port Lincoln Dive & Surf Centre** (☎ 08-8682 4428; ptlincolnsurfdive@bigpond.com; 1 King St; ☺ 9am-5.30pm Mon-Fri, to 12.30pm Sat), where licensed divers can hire scuba equipment (around $100 per day).

Kuju Arts & Crafts (☎ 08-8682; 6677; www.visitaboriginalart.com; 30 Ravendale Rd; ☺ 9am-5pm Mon-Fri) stocks exquisite Indigenous artwork, and you can meet the artists who work on site.

Sleeping & Eating

The visitor centre (left) books self-contained flats overlooking the bay, starting at $95 per night for two people.

Grand Tasman Hotel (☎ 08-8682 2133; www.grandtasmanhotel.com.au; 94 Tasman Tce; s/d $55/80; ☒) The swanky refit downstairs at this foreshore hotel didn't make it upstairs, but the rooms are large, airy and you're smack bang in the middle of town. The bistro's not bad either (mains $16 to $28; open for lunch and dinner).

Limani Motel (☎ 08-8682 2200; www.limanimotel.com.au; 50 Lincoln Hwy; d from $120; ☒) It's a bit architecturally clunky and the decor is a few years behind recent, but the bay-front rooms here are well appointed and spacey. Staff can help plan your Port Lincoln experience.

Port Lincoln Hotel (☎ 1300 766 100, 08-8621 2000; www.portlincolnhotel.com.au; 1 Lincoln Hwy; d $125-300; ☒ 🖳 🖭) Bankrolled by a couple of Adelaide Crows AFL footballers, this ritzy seven-storey hotel lifts Port Lincoln above the fray. It's a classy, contemporary affair, offering a bit of luxury at reasonable prices. Good on-site bars and eateries too – play 'Spot Mark Ricciuto' from behind your menu (restaurant mains $21 to $35, bar meals $11 to $23; open for lunch and dinner).

Port Lincoln Tourist Park (☎ 08-8621 4444; www .saringroup.com.au; cnr New West Rd & Oxford Tce; unpowered/powered sites $23/26, cabins with/without bathroom from $85/65, units $115; ⊠) A breezy waterside park with some beaut new cabins and units and plenty of elbow room.

Cafe Koco (☎ 08-8682 6153; 60 Tasman Tce; mains $6-12; ⊗ breakfast & lunch Mon-Sat) On the waterfront, Koco is a reliable spot for a coffee, a slab of cake, a burger or baguette.

AROUND PORT LINCOLN

For a rugged coastal interlude, **Cape Carnot** (aka Whalers Way) is 32km south of Port Lincoln. It's privately owned but you can visit with a 24-hour permit ($30 per car, plus $10 key deposit) from the Port Lincoln visitor centre (p789). Permits include bush camping at Redbanks or Groper Bay (both of which are a little windy).

The visitor centre also sells permits to **Mikkira Station & Koala Sanctuary** (☎ 08-8685 6020; fax 08-8685 6077; Fishery Bay Rd; day permit/camping $14/20), Eyre Peninsula's first sheep station and home to the endemic Port Lincoln parrot.

The beaches at **Sleaford Bay** – a 3km detour off the Cape Carnot road – are sublime but risky for swimming.

Around 15km south of Port Lincoln is **Lincoln National Park** (www.environment.sa.gov.au/parks/ sanpr/lincoln; admission per car $7.50), with roaming emus, roos and brush-tailed bettongs, safe-swimming coves and pounding surf beaches. Entry is via self-registration on the way in.

If you want to stay the night, the two-bedroom **Donnington Cottage** (per adult/child $39/10) at Spalding Cove, built in 1899, sleeps six and has photo-worthy views. Book through Port Lincoln visitor centre (p789); BYO linen and food. There's also some great **bush camping** (per car $5) to be had here, including the following sites:

Fisherman's Point By a sandy, blue-green bay with a rocky point ideal for throwing a line in.

Memory Cove Tranquil 4WD-accessible site 50km from Port Lincoln. To visit you'll need a Memory Cove Pass from the Port Lincoln visitor centre ($20 key deposit; access and camping $15).

September Beach Excellent facilities (wood barbecues, bench seats) in foreshore scrub just metres from a beaut beach.

Surfleet Cove Basic camping away from the main track; good shade and plenty of solitude.

PORT LINCOLN TO STREAKY BAY

Coffin Bay

pop 650

Oyster lovers rejoice! Deathly-sounding Coffin Bay (named by Matthew Flinders after his buddy Sir Isaac Coffin) is a snoozy fishing village basking languidly in the warm sun…until a 2500-strong holiday horde arrives every January. Slippery, salty oysters from the nearby beds are exported worldwide, but you shouldn't pay more than $1 per oyster around town. Online, see www .coffinbay.net.

Along the ocean side of Coffin Bay there's some wild coastal scenery, most of which is part of **Coffin Bay National Park** (www.environment .sa.gov.au/parks/sanpr/coffinbay; admission per car $7.50), overrun with roos, emus and fat goannas. Access for conventional vehicles is limited: you can get to picturesque **Point Avoid** (coastal lookouts, rocky cliffs, good surf and whales passing between May and October) and **Yangie Bay** (arid-looking rocky landscapes and walking trails), but otherwise you'll need a 4WD. There are some isolated **campsites** (per car $5) within the park, generally with difficult access.

Birdlife, including some unusual migratory species, fills the sky at **Kellidie Bay Conservation Park**, just outside Coffin Bay township.

SLEEPING & EATING

For holiday shacks around town contact **Coffin Bay Holiday Rentals** (☎ 0427 844 568; www.coffinbay holidayrentals.com.au; cottages per night $50-300).

Coffin Bay Hotel/Motel (☎ 08-8685 4111; cbhotel@ bigpond.com; Shepperd Ave; s/d $85/95; ⊠) The local pub has eight roomy units out the back, and plates up regulation counter meals (mains $16 to $24, open for lunch and dinner).

Coffin Bay Caravan Park (☎ 08-8685 4170; www .coffinbay.net/caravanpark; 91 Esplanade; unpowered/powered sites $20/28, on-site vans $59, cabins with/without bathroom $79/69; ⊠) Resident cockatoos and parrots squawk around the shady sheoak sites here, and the cabins are a reasonable bang for your buck (BYO linen).

Oysterbeds Restaurant (☎ 08-8685 4000; 61 Esplanade; mains $20-28; ⊗ lunch & dinner Wed-Sat, lunch Sun) The best food in town; serving the pick of the local seafood. Closed June to mid-August.

Coffin Bay to Point Labatt

There's reliable surf at **Greenly Beach** just past **Coulta**, 40km north of Coffin Bay. There's also good salmon fishing along this wild stretch of coast, notably at **Locks Well**, where a long, steep stairway called the **Staircase to Heaven** (283 steps? Count 'em…), leads from the car park down to the beach. About 15km further north, **Elliston** is a small fishing town on soporific Waterloo Bay, with a beautiful swimming beach and a fishing jetty (hope the tommy ruff and whiting are biting). Waterside **Waterloo Bay Tourist Park** (☎ 08-8687 9076; www.visitelliston .net; Beach Tce, Elliston; unpowered/powered sites $20/24, cabins $50-100; ⊠) is a smallish operation with decent cabins.

Just north of Elliston, take the 7km detour to **Anxious Bay** for some anxiety-relieving ocean scenery (billed as Elliston's 'Great Ocean Drive'). En route you'll pass **Blackfellows**, which boasts some of the west coast's best surf. From here you can eyeball the 9000-acre **Flinders Island** 35km offshore, where there's a sheep station and a self-contained, nine-bed **holiday house** (☎ 0428 261 132; www.flindersgetaway.com; per person from $90). To get here you have to charter a plane from Port Lincoln or a boat from Elliston (additional to accommodation costs); ask for details when you book.

At **Venus Bay** there are sheltered beaches (and the not-so-sheltered Mount Camel Beach), a gaggle of pelicans, a small caravan park and the obligatory fishing jetty.

If you feel like taking a plunge and swimming with sea lions and dolphins, stop by Baird Bay and organise a tour with **Baird Bay Ocean Eco Experience** (☎ 08-8626 5017; www.bairdbay .com; 4hr tours adult/child $120/60). Accommodation is also available.

If you'd rather stay high-and-dry, the road to **Point Labatt**, 38km south of Streaky Bay, takes you to one of the few permanent sea lion colonies on the Australian mainland; ogle them from the clifftops (bring binoculars).

A few kilometres down the Point Labatt road are the globular **Murphy's Haystacks**, an improbable congregation of 'inselbergs' – colourful, weather-sculpted granite outcrops, which are millions of years old.

STREAKY BAY
pop 1150

This endearing little town takes its name from the streaks of seaweed Matt Flinders spied in the bay as he sailed by. Visible at low tide, the seagrass attracts ocean critters and the bigger critters that eat them – first-class fishing. For tourist info, swing by the **Streaky Bay visitor centre** (☎ 08-8626 7033; www. streakybay.com.au; 21 Bay Rd; ⊗ 9am-12.30pm & 1.30-5pm Mon-Fri).

Occupying a 1901 school house, the **Streaky Bay Museum** (☎ 08-8626 1443; www.nationaltrustsa.org .au; 42 Montgomery Tce; adult/child $3.50/50c; ⊗ 2-4pm Tue & Fri) features a fully furnished pug-and-pine hut, an old iron lung and plenty of pioneering history. The museum is also open by appointment.

There's some dramatic cliff scenery around the coast here. **Back Beach**, 4km west of Streaky Bay, is a good spot to hit the surf.

Sleeping & Eating

Streaky Bay Community Hotel/Motel (☎ 08-8626 1008; www.streakybayhotel.com.au; 33 Alfred Tce; budget/ hotel/motel d from $50/90/100) The hotel rooms upstairs here have rip-snorting water views and a large balcony from which to snort them. Breakfast, lunch and dinner happen downstairs daily (mains $16 to $26).

Headland House (☎ 08-8626 1315; headlandhouse@ aapt.net.au; 5 Flinders Dr; d $120; ⊠) A plush, modern place with ace views from the back terrace. The two rooms on offer are smartly decked-out, but the twin is better than the double. Kid-free zone.

Mocean (☎ 08-8626 1775; 34b Alfred Tce; mains $20-26; ⊗ lunch Tue-Sun, dinner Tue-Sat) This stylish cafe is the town's social pacemaker, with water views and an alfresco terrace. Dishes focus on scrumptious seafood (try the abalone).

CEDUNA
pop 3580

Unlike Streaky Bay and Port Lincoln – and despite the locals' best intentions – Ceduna remains a raggedy fishing town that just can't shake its tag as a blow-through pit stop en route to WA.

The **Ceduna visitor centre** (☎ 1800 639 413, 08-8625 2780; www.ceduna.net; 58 Poynton St; ⊗ 9am-5.30pm Mon-Fri, 9.30am-5pm Sat & Sun) can help with local info.

Ceduna Museum (☎ 08-8625 2210; www.nation altrustsa.org.au; 2 Park Tce; adult/child $4/2; ⊗ 10am-noon Mon, Tue & Thu-Sat, 2-4pm Wed & Thu) has pioneer exhibits, Indigenous artefacts and a display on the tragic British nuclear tests at Maralinga.

The sea-inspired works of local Indigenous artists from along the coast steal the show at **Ceduna Aboriginal Arts & Culture Centre** (☎ 08-8625 2487; cnr Eyre Hwy & Kuhlmann St; admission free; ☻ 9am-5pm Mon-Fri).

If you're passing through in early October, check out **Oysterfest** (www.ceduna.net/site/page .cfm?u=167), the undisputed king of Australian bivalve parties.

Sleeping & Eating

East West Motel (☎ 08-8625 2101; www.cedunamoteleast west.com.au; 66-76 McKenzie St; d from $90; ☒ ☒) The ol' East West still makes the grade after some long years in the saddle. Accommodation ranges from simple motel rooms to deluxe apartments (and there's a pool). Evening meals cost $18 to $28.

Ceduna Foreshore Hotel/Motel (☎ 08-8625 2008; www.cedunahotel.com.au; 32 O'Loughlin Tce; d from $100; ☒) The recently renovated Foreshore is the most luxurious option in town, with water views and a bistro zooming in on west coast seafood (mains $19 to $30, open for lunch and dinner).

Ceduna Foreshore Caravan Park (☎ 1300 666 290, 08-8625 2290; www.cedunaforeshorecaravanpark.com .au; 25 Poynton St; unpowered/powered sites $20/23, cabins $65-90; ☒) Right on the foreshore, this small, serviceable park has (mostly) shady sites and cabins that don't skimp on the faux-timber finishes. Linen costs extra.

Ceduna Oyster Bar (☎ 08-8626 9086; Eyre Hwy; 12 oysters $10; ☻ 9.30am-6pm Mon-Sat) Wash down a few snotty molluscs with a glass of wine near the town's (not very) Big Oyster.

CEDUNA TO THE WESTERN AUSTRALIA BORDER

It's 480km from Ceduna to the WA border. Along the stretch you can get a bed and a beer at Penong (72km from Ceduna), Nundroo (151km), the Nullarbor Roadhouse (295km) near Head of Bight, and at Border Village on the border itself.

Wheat and sheep paddocks line the road to Nundroo, after which you're in mallee scrub for another 100km. Around 20km later, the trees thin to low bluebush as you enter the true Nullarbor (Latin for 'no trees'). Road trains, caravans and cyclists of questionable sanity are your only companions as you put your foot down and careen towards the setting sun.

Turn off the highway at **Penong** (population 200), and follow the 20km dirt road to Point Sinclair and **Cactus Beach**, which has three of Australia's most famous surf breaks. Caves is a wicked right-hand break for experienced surfers, but be aware that locals don't take too kindly to tourists dropping in. There's **bush camping** (per person $10) on private property close to the breaks; BYO drinking water.

The viewing platforms at **Head of Bight** (☎ 08-8625 6201; www.yalata.org; adult/child/concession $12/free/10; ☻ 8am-5pm) overlook a major southern right whale breeding ground. Whales migrate here from Antarctica in June, and you can see them cavorting from July to September. The breeding area is protected by the **Great Australian Bight Marine Park** (www .environment.gov.au/coasts/mpa/gab), the world's second-largest marine park after the Great Barrier Reef.

Head of Bight is a part of the Yalata Indigenous Protected Area. After paying your entry fee, stop and get the latest whale information from the **White Well Ranger Station** on the way in to the viewing area. The signposted turn-off is 14km east of the Nullarbor Roadhouse.

While you're in the Head of Bight area, you can also check out **Murrawijinie Cave**, a large overhang behind the Nullarbor Roadhouse, and have a look at the signposted coastal lookouts along the top of the 80m-high **Bunda Cliffs**.

If you're continuing west into WA, dump all fruit, vegetables, cheese and plants at Border Village (as per quarantine regulations), and watch out for animals if you're driving at night. Note that if you're driving east rather than west, SA's quarantine check point isn't until Ceduna.

Sleeping & Eating

Travelling west from towards WA from Ceduna, you'll run into the following places (in this order), where you can grab a meal or put yourself to bed.

Penong Caravan Park (☎ 08-8625 1111; www .nullarbornet.com.au/towns/penong.html; 5 Stiggants Rd; unpowered/powered sites $18/22, on-site vans $38, cabins with/without linen $85/65; ☒) A short hop from Ceduna, this well-kept park is rated by some travellers as the best on the Nullarbor. The cabins are in good shape, and the camping area has pristine facilities.

Fowlers Bay Caravan Park (☎ 08-8625 6143; www .nullarbornet.com.au/towns/fowlersbay; unpowered/powered sites $12/15, on-site vans $35) There's basic accommodation, a shop and takeaway food in this almost-ghost town, plus heritage buildings, good fishing and rambling dunes. Take the Fowlers Bay turn-off 106km from Ceduna.

Nundroo Hotel/Motel (☎ 08-8625 6120; www.nun drooaccommodation.com; Eyre Hwy, Nundroo; unpowered/ powered sites $8/18, on-site vans $30, dm/d $10/77; ⌘) If you're heading west, Nundroo has this decent hotel/motel and the last mechanic until Norseman WA, 1038km away. There's a very basic dorm, and worn but comfy motel rooms with updated bathrooms. There's a bar and restaurant on site (meals $12 to $30; open for breakfast, lunch and dinner).

Nullarbor Roadhouse (☎ 08-8625 6271; www .nullarbornet.com.au/towns/nullarbor.html; Eyre Hwy, Nullarbor; unpowered/powered sites $13/19, backpacker s/d/tr/q $30/42/50/57, motel s/d/tr/q $92/110/128/146; ☺ 7am-11pm) Close to the Head of Bight whale-watching area, this roadhouse is a real oasis for weary road-warriors. The on-site bar and restaurant serves breakfast, lunch and dinner (meals $10 to $25).

Border Village Motel (☎ 08-9039 3474; www.nullar bornet.com.au/towns/bordervillage.html; Eyre Hwy, Border Village; unpowered/powered sites $15/20, backpacker s/d/tr/q $40/60/70/80, motel s/d/tr $95/110/120; ⌘ ▣ ☻) Just 50m from the WA border, this rebuilt motel has a variety of modern rooms and cabins and a licensed restaurant (meals $10 to $25, open for lunch and dinner).

FLINDERS RANGES

Known simply as 'the Flinders', this ancient mountain range is an iconic South Australian environment. Jagged peaks and escarpments rise up north of Port Augusta and track 400km north to Mt Hopeless. The colours here are remarkable: as the day stretches out, the mountains shift from mauve mornings to midday chocolates and ochre-red sunsets.

Before Europeans arrived, the Flinders were prized by the Adnyamathanha peoples for their red ochre deposits, which had medicinal and ritual uses. Sacred caves, rock paintings and carvings exist throughout the region. In the wake of white exploration came villages, farms, country pubs, wheat farms and cattle stations, many of which failed under the unrelenting sun.

The cooler Southern Ranges are studded with stands of river red gums and country hamlets with cherubic appeal. In the arid Northern Ranges, the desert takes a hold: the scenery here is stark, desolate and very beautiful.

Online, it's worth having a look at www .flindersranges.com and www.southern flindersranges.com.au.

Information

There are visitors centres in Quorn (p796) and at Wilpena Pound Resort (p798) inside Flinders Ranges National Park. Also try:

Department of Environment & Heritage (p788) In Port Augusta.

Port Augusta visitors centre (p788) On the Flinders' doorstep, Port Augusta's visitor centre has plenty of Ranges info too.

Tours

Local operators work out of Port Augusta (p788), Quorn (p796), Hawker (p797), Wilpena Pound (p798), Iga Warta (p800) and Arkaroola (p800). The following tours are all ex-Adelaide:

Arabunna Tours (☎ 08-8675 8351; www.southaus tralia.com/S9008383.aspx; 7-day tour $1050) Aboriginal-owned company offering cultural tours from Adelaide to the Flinders Ranges, Marree, Oodnadatta Track and Lake Eyre.

Bookabee Tours (☎ 08-8235 9954, 0408 209 593; www.bookabee.com.au; 4-/5-day tours $1930/2380) Highly rated Indigenous-run tours to the Flinders Ranges and outback ex-Adelaide, including quality accommodation, meals, cultural tours, activities and interpretation.

Ecotrek (☎ 08-8346 4155; www.ecotrek.com; 7-day tour $1548) Excellent all-inclusive tours walking the best sections of the Flinders, with soft beds, hot showers and food and wine at the end of each day. Ex-Adelaide.

Swagabout Tours (☎ 0408 845 378; www.swaga bouttours.com.au) Dependable Flinders Ranges trips (three/four days camping $650/1000, hotels $870/1300) including Quorn and Wilpena (plus Arkaroola and Blinman on the four-day jaunt), and can be extended to Coober Pedy.

Other major operators swinging through the Flinders:

Adventure Tours Australia (☎ 1300 654 604, 08-8132 8130; www.adventuretours.com.au)

Groovy Grape (☎ 1800 661 177, 08-8440 1640; www .groovygrape.com.au)

Wayward Bus (☎ 1300 653 510, 08-8132 8230; www .waywardbus.com.au)

SOUTH AUSTRALIA

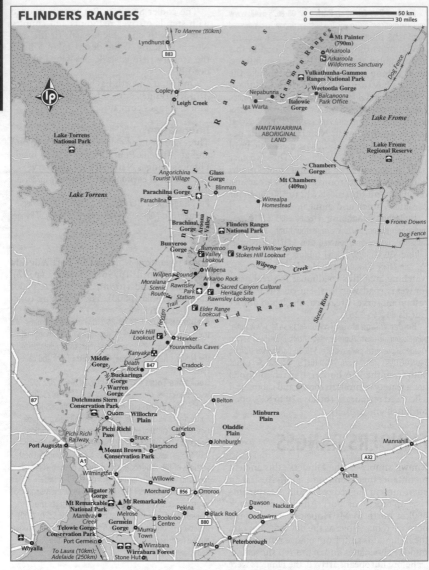

FLINDERS RANGES

0 ____ 50 km
0 ____ 30 miles

Sleeping

Flinders Ranges Accommodation Booking Service
(☎ 1800 777 880, 08-8648 4022; www.frabs.com.au)
The deliciously named FRABS can help
with bookings for various accommodation
options, including rural cottages and shearers' quarters on outback stations around
Hawker.

Getting There & Around

If you're driving, you can access the Flinders
Ranges from Adelaide via sealed roads off
Main North Rd and Hwy 1. The major roads
into Quorn, Hawker, Wilpena Pound, Leigh
Creek and the Southern Ranges towns are all
sealed, but most of the others are gravel (fine
in a regular car if you take 'em slow). This far

north, be prepared for a dearth of drinking water, shops and service stations. Check with DEH offices or call ☎ 1300 361 033 for road-condition updates after rains.

Premier Stateliner (☎ 08-8415 5555; www.premier stateliner.com.au) buses run at least twice daily from Adelaide to Port Augusta ($47, four hours) at the base of the Southern Flinders Ranges. From here, **Yorke Peninsula Coaches** (☎ 08-8821 2755; www.ypcoaches.com.au) runs a Friday bus to Quorn. Yorke Peninsula Coaches also runs a Thursday bus from Port Pirie (south of Port Augusta) to Melrose ($8, 1¼ hours).

Gulf Getaways (☎ 1800 170 170, 08-8642 6827; www .gulfgetaways.com.au) runs a Port Augusta–Wilpena shuttle on Fridays and Sundays, stopping at Quorn ($20, 30 minutes), Hawker ($40, 1¼ hours) and Wilpena Pound ($50, 2¼ hours).

SOUTHERN RANGES TOWNS
Heading north from Adelaide along Main North Rd, you enter the Southern Ranges near **Laura** (population 500), emerging from the wheat fields like Superman's Smallville (all civic pride and 1950s prosperity). There's not a lot to do here, but the long, geranium-adorned main street has a supermarket, chemist, bakery, bank, post office…even a jeweller!

About 10km further north, **Stone Hut** (population 290) doesn't have much on offer other than the amazing **Old Bakery** (☎ 08-8673 2165; www.oldbakerystonehut.com.au; Main North Rd, Stone Hut; items $4-10; ☺ 7am-6pm), which makes legendary chunky beef pies, slices and quandong tart. There's new cabin-style accommodation here too (doubles from $150).

The oldest town in the Flinders (1853) is **Melrose** (population 200), snug in the elbow of the 960m Mt Remarkable. It has the perfect mix of well-preserved architecture, a cracking-good pub, quality accommodation and parks with *actual grass*.

Melrose Caravan Park (☎ 08-8666 2060; mcp@rbe .net.au; Joe's Rd, Melrose; dm $15, unpowered/powered sites $15/20, cabins $45-100; ☒) is a small, tidy park with bush campsites and self-contained cabins (all with TVs and cooking facilities – the cheaper ones are sans bathrooms). The 12km return hike up Mt Remarkable starts on the back doorstep. Next door is a converted agricultural shed with basic dorm facilities (no air-con).

our pick **North Star Hotel** (☎ 08-8666 2110; www .northstarhotel.com.au; Nott St, Melrose; r $90-160, trucks $140-160, ste $195-225; ☒) is as welcome as summer rain: a fabulous, 150-year-old hotel renovated in city-meets-woolshed style. Sit under the hessian sack ceiling and spinning fans for a fresh menu (mains $10 to $29; lunch Wednesday to Sunday, dinner Thursday to Saturday), great coffee and cold Flinders Ranges beer (try the Fargher Lager). Accommodation ranges from rooms in the place next door (TPND) to plush suites above the pub and surprisingly cool metal-clad cabins built on two old trucks out the back.

MT REMARKABLE NATIONAL PARK
Bush boffins rave about this steep, jaggedy park straddling the Southern Flinders. Wildlife and bushwalking are the main lures, with various tracks (including part of the Heysen Trail; see The Long Way Home, p722) meandering through isolated gorges.

From the car park at **Alligator Gorge** take the short, steep walk (2km, two hours) down into the craggy gorge (no sign of any 'gators), the ring route (9km, four hours), or walk to **Hidden Gorge** (18km, seven hours) or **Mambray Creek** (13km, seven hours). From Mambray Creek the track to **Davey's Gully** (2.5km, one hour) is (literally and metaphorically) a walk in the park. Peak baggers sweat up the 960m track to the summit of **Mt Remarkable** (12km, five hours); the trail starts behind Melrose Caravan Park (left).

Pay the park entry fee at the **Park Office** (☎ 08-8634 7068; www.environment.sa.gov.au/parks/ sanpr/mountremarkable; admission per car $7.50; ☺ office 8.30am-4.30pm) at Mambray Creek, off Hwy 1 about 21km north of Port Germein. On the inland route (Main North Rd between Melrose and Wilmington), there's an honour box at Alligator Gorge. Both stations have park info brochures.

If you want to stay the night there's plenty of **bush camping** (per car $15), and two **lodges**: at Mambray Creek (sleeps four; per night $42) and Alligator Gorge (sleeps eight; per night $85). Both are solar powered; Alligator Gorge has better cooking facilities and showers. Book through the Park Office.

QUORN
pop 1010

Is Quorn a film set after the crew has gone home? With more jeering crows than people, it's a cinematographic little outback town. Wheat farming took off here in 1875, and the town prospered with the arrival of the Great

SOUTH AUSTRALIA

GOYDER'S LINE

Just off Main North Rd 3km north of Melrose is a monument heralding the presence of **Goyder's Line**. In 1865, George Woodroffe Goyder drew an imaginary line across the map of SA, delineating drought-prone land to the north and agriculturally viable land (with more than 10 inches of annual rain) to the south. The line arcs up from the Victorian border through Burra then darts down through Melrose, across the top of the Yorke Peninsula and slices off the Eyre Peninsula halfway up. Over time, George W's estimations have proved reliable – farmers ignored his advice at their peril – but all this was before climate change. Where would he draw the line today?

Northern Railway from Port Augusta. Quorn remained an important railroad junction until trains into the Flinders were cut in 1970.

Information

Flinders Ranges visitors centre (☎ 08-8648 6419; www.flindersranges.com; 3 Seventh St; 9am-5pm; 🖳) Maps, brochures, internet access and advice.

Sights & Activities

Quorn's streetscapes, especially **Railway Tce**, are a real history lesson, and have featured in iconic Australian films like *Gallipoli* and *Sunday Too Far Away*. A fragment of the long-defunct railway now conveys the **Pichi Richi Railway** (☎ 1800 440 101, 08-8648 6598; www.prr.org.au) between Port Augusta and Quorn (one-way adult/child/concession/family $45/17/42/107, 2½ hours) on Saturdays.

Kicking off at nearby Woolshed Flat (ask at the visitors centre for directions), the **Waukarie Creek Trail** (9km, five hours) meets up with part of the Heysen Trail (see The Long Way Home, p722) and passes through copses of red gum and wattle. Look out for hollow trees once used as shelters by the Adnyamathanha people. Closer to town are walks at **Dutchman's Stern** and **Devil's Peak**.

Derelict ruins of early settlements litter the Quorn-Hawker road, the most impressive of which is **Kanyaka**, a once-thriving sheep station founded in 1851. From the homestead ruins (41km from Quorn) it's a 20-minute walk to a waterhole, loomed over by the massive **Death Rock**. The story goes that local Aborigines once placed their dying kinsfolk here to see out their last hours.

Tours

Pichi Richi Camel Tours (☎ 08-8648 6640, 0429 998 044; www.pichirichicameltours.com) Saddle up for a one-hour ride ($35) or a longer half-/full-day camel-back tour ($95/175) through the country around Quorn. Overnight safaris and sunset and moonlight rides also available.

Quorn Adventures (www.quornadventures.com) Collaborative website listing tour operators and 4WD tracks around Quorn.

Wallaby Tracks Adventure Tours (☎ 0428 486 655; www.wallabytracks.com) Small-group 4WD tours through the Southern Ranges (half day $110) or extending north to Wilpena Pound (full day $160).

Sleeping & Eating

Austral Inn (☎ 08-8648 6017; www.australinn.com.au; 16 Railway Tce; d motel/pub from $70/100; 🕷) There's always a few locals here giving the jukebox a workout and chatting with the publican. The pub rooms are renovated – simple and clean with new linen – while the motel rooms are more '80s than the menu (standard country-pub fare with a twist: try a camel schnitzel). The pub is purportedly above an old well, so if it's been raining watch out for mozzies.

Quandong Apartments (☎ 08-8648 6155, 0432 113 473; www.quandongapartments.com; 31 First St; d $150; 🕷) Next door to the Quandong Café (and run by the same folks), these two self-contained apartments have full kitchens, big TVs, quality linen and mod-Asian touches. Rates come down for stays of two nights or more.

Quorn Caravan Park (☎ 08-8648 6206; www.quorncaravanpark.com.au; 8 Silo Rd; unpowered/powered sites $18/22, cabins $50-80; 🕷) Fully keyed in to climate change, this passionately run park on Pinkerton Creek is hell bent on reducing emissions and restoring native habitat. Features include spotless cabins, shady sites and a few lazy roos lounging about under the red gums.

Quandong Café (☎ 08-8648 6155; 31 First St; mains $6-12; breakfast & lunch mid-Mar–mid-Dec) A traditional country cafe with creaky floorboards and spinning ceiling fans, serving big breakfasts and light lunches. Try a generously adorned 'Railway Sleeper' (like a pizza sub), or a massive slab of lemon meringue or quandong pie. Good old-fashioned country value!

HAWKER
pop 300

Hawker is the last outpost of civilisation before Wilpena Pound, 55km to the north. Much like Quorn, Hawker has seen better days, most of which were when the old *Ghan* train stopped here. These days Hawker is a pancake-flat, pit-stop town with an ATM and the world's most helpful petrol station. Online, check out www.hawkersa.info.

Information
Teague's Hawker Motors & visitors centre (☎ 08-8648 4014, 08-8648 4022; www.hawkermotors.com.au; cnr Wilpena & Cradock Rds; ☒ 7.30am-6pm; ☐) The town's petrol station (fill up if you're heading north) is also the visitors centre.

Sights & Activities
It's not so much what's in Hawker that's interesting – it's more what's around it – but if you like your great outdoors inside (and a little bit eccentric), **Wilpena Panorama** (☎ 08-8648 4071; www.wilpenapanorama.com; cnr Wilpena & Cradock Rds; adult/child $5.50/3; ☒ 9am-5pm Mon-Sat, noon-4pm Sun) is a large circular room with a painting of Wilpena Pound surrounding you on all sides.

Yourambulla Caves, 12km south of Hawker, have detailed Aboriginal rock paintings (including emu tracks), with three sites open to visitors. **Yourambulla Peak**, a half-hour walk from the car park, is the most accessible spot to check out the paintings.

Around 40km north of Hawker towards Wilpena, **Arkaroo Rock** is a sacred Aboriginal site. The rock art here features reptile and human figures in charcoal, bird-lime and yellow and red ochre. It's a short(ish) return walk from the car park (2km, one hour).

Tours
Derek's 4WD Tours (☎ 0417 475 770; www.dereks 4wdtours.com; tours half-/full day from $105/160) Derek does several good trips with an environmental bent, including to Bunyeroo and Brachina gorges.
Skytrek Willow Springs (☎ 08-8648 0016; www .skytrekwillowsprings.com.au) Six-hour self-drive tours on a working sheep station ($55 per vehicle), or they can hook you up with a tour operator. Self-contained cabin accommodation available ($45 to $160 per double).

Sleeping & Eating
Chapmanton Outback Motel (☎ 08-8648 4100; fax 08-8648 4109; 1 Wilpena Rd; s/d/units $95/105/120; ☒)

A drive-up motel offering the best rooms in town. The two-bedroom units are good value for families.
Hawker Caravan Park (☎ 08-8648 4006; www .hawkerbig4holidaypark.com.au; cnr Wilpena Rd & Chace View Tce; unpowered/powered sites $24/26, en suite sites $30-36, cabins $86-120; ☒ ☒) At the Wilpena end of town, this upbeat acreage with generous sites and a range of cabins is the pick of Hawker's two caravan parks. And there's a pool!
Hawker General Store Café (☎ 08-8648 4005; cnr Wilpena & Cradock Rds; meals $4-12; ☒ breakfast & lunch Mon-Fri, plus Sat & Sun Mar-Nov) A jack-of-all-trades shop serving steak sangers, cooked breakfasts, cakes, coffee and quandong smoothies.
Old Ghan Restaurant (☎ 08-8648 4176; Leigh Creek Rd; mains $20-28; ☒ lunch & dinner Thu-Sat, Mar-Dec) In the old *Ghan* railway station on the outskirts of town, this restaurant is about as upmarket as Hawker gets. Expect mains like barramundi with quince-and-orange glaze, and grilled chicken breast with mango curry sauce.

See also Skytrek Willow Springs (left).

FLINDERS RANGES NATIONAL PARK
One of SA's most treasured parks, **Flinders Ranges National Park** (www.environment.sa.gov .au/parks/sanpr/flindersranges; admission per car $7.50) is laced with craggy gorges, saw-toothed ranges, abandoned homesteads, Aboriginal sites, hyperactive wildlife and, after it rains, carpets of wildflowers. The park's big-ticket drawcard is the 80-sq-km natural basin **Wilpena Pound** – a sunken elliptical valley ringed by gnarled ridges (don't let anyone tell you it's a meteorite crater!).

The Pound is only vehicle accessible on the Wilpena Pound Resort's **shuttle bus** (return adult/child/concession/family $4/2.50/2.50/9), which drops you within 1km of **Wangarra Lookout**. The shuttle runs at 9am, 11am, 1pm, 3pm and 5pm, dropping people off and coming straight back (so if you take the 5pm shuttle and want more than a cursory look around, you'll miss the return bus). Otherwise it's a three-hour, 8km return walk between the resort and lookout.

The 20km **Brachina Gorge Geological Trail** features an amazing layering of exposed sedimentary rock, covering 120 million years of the Earth's history. Grab a brochure from the visitors centre.

The **Bunyeroo-Brachina-Aroona Scenic Drive** is a 110km round trip, passing by Bunyeroo

SOUTH AUSTRALIA

Valley, Brachina Gorge, Aroona Valley and **Stokes Hill Lookout**. There are plenty of short walks along the way; a stop at **Bunyeroo Valley Lookout** is mandatory. The drive starts north of Wilpena off the road to Blinman.

Just beyond the park's southeast corner, a one-hour, 1km return walk leads to the **Sacred Canyon Cultural Heritage Site**, with Aboriginal rock-art galleries featuring animal tracks and designs.

Information

Wilpena Pound visitors centre (☎ 1800 805 802, 08-8648 0004; www.wilpenapound.com.au; Wilpena Pound Resort; ☽ 8am-5.30pm; ☐) Info on the park and district, internet access and bike hire (per half/full day $20/40). Also handles bookings for scenic flights (see right), and 4WD tours and guided walks (see right). If you didn't pay your park entry fees at the self-registration booth, cough up the dosh here ($7.50 per vehicle).

Bushwalking

Before you make happy trails, ensure you've got enough water, sunscreen and a massive hat, and tell someone where you're going and when you'll be back. Pick up the *Bushwalking in Flinders Ranges National Park* brochure/map from the visitors centre, detailing 17 walks in the park. Nine of the walks kick off at Wilpena Pound Resort.

For a really good look at Wilpena, the walk up to **Tanderra Saddle** on the ridge of **St Mary Peak** on the Pound's rim is brilliant, though it's a thigh-pounding scramble at times. The Adnyamathanha people request that you restrict your climbing to the ridge and don't climb St Mary Peak itself, due to its traditional significance to them (see Adnyamathanha Dreaming, opposite). The return walk to the saddle (15km, six hours) opens up some good views of the ABC Ranges and Wilpena. If you have time, take the longer outside track for even more eye-popping vistas. You can keep going on the round trip (22km, nine hours), camping overnight at **Cooinda Camp**.

The quick, tough track up to **Mt Ohlssen Bagge** (6.5km, four hours) rewards the sweaty hiker with a stunning panorama. Good short walks include the stroll to **Hills Homestead** (6.5km, two hours), or the dash up to the **Wilpena Solar Power Station** (500m, 30 minutes).

In the park's north (50km north of Wilpena Pound Resort), the **Aroona Ruins** are the launch pad for a few less-trampled walks. The **Yuluna Hike** (8km, four hours) weaves through a pain-

terly stretch of the ABC Ranges. The challenging **Aroona-Youngoona Track** (one-way 15.5km, seven hours) offers views of the Trezona and Heysen Ranges; cool your boots overnight at Youngoona campsite.

Tours

For **4WD tours**, contact Derek's 4WD Tours or Skytrek Willow Springs (see p797), Wilpena Pound Resort (per adult/child $135/100, morning and afternoon), or Rawnsley Park Station (per half/full day $115/175). Wilpena Pound Resort also runs short 1.5km to 3km **guided walks** into Wilpena Pound ($35 to $50 per person).

Central Air Services (☎ 08-8648 0008, 08-8648 0040; flights 20min/30min/1hr $125/145/215) runs scenic flights over Wilpena Pound departing from the resort and Rawnsley Park Station. Book through Wilpena Pound visitors centre or Rawnsley Park Station.

Sleeping & Eating

our pick **Wilpena Pound Resort** (☎ 1800 805 802, 08-8648 0004; www.wilpenapound.com.au; Wilpena Rd; unpowered/powered sites $20/28, permanent tent with/without linen $90/65, s/d from $170/195; ✗ ☐ ☖) This resort is already pretty plush, but it's slated for an upgrade (which will probably include prices). Accommodation includes motel-style rooms, more upmarket self-contained suites, and a great (although hugely popular) campsite. If you didn't bring your own camping gear, there are permanent tents sleeping four. Purchase your camping permit at the visitors centre, which also sells petrol and basic (and expensive) groceries. Don't miss a swim in the pool, happy hour at the bar (5pm to 6pm) and dinner at the excellent bistro (mains $20 to $30 – the roo is the best we've ever had!).

Rawnsley Park Station (☎ reception 08-8648 0008, caravan park/YHA 08-8648 0030, restaurant 08-8648 0126; www.rawnsleypark.com.au; Wilpena Rd; unpowered/powered sites $20/29, dm $33; cabins/units/villas from $82/112/340; ✗ ☐) This rangy homestead, 35km from Hawker just south of the national park, runs the accommodation gamut from tent sites to luxe ecovillas. The YHA runs some of the caravan park cabins as dorms. Also on offer is a range of outback activities including sheep-shearing demos (per adult/child/family $16/8/40), mountain-bike hire (per hour $15), bushwalking (30 minutes to four hours), 4WD tours and scenic flights (see p793). The Woolshed Restaurant (mains $12 to $28; open

---

ADNYAMATHANHA DREAMING

Land and nature are integral to the culture of the traditional owners of the Flinders Ranges. The people collectively called Adnyamathanha (Hill People) are actually a collection of the Wailpi, Kuyani, Jadliaura, Piladappa and Pangkala tribes, who exchanged and elaborated on stories to explain their spectacular local geography.

The walls of Ikara (Wilpena Pound), for example, are the bodies of two *akurra* (giant snakes), who coiled around Ikara during an initiation ceremony, eating most of the participants. The snakes were so full after their feast they couldn't move and willed themselves to die, creating the landmark. Because of its traditional significance, the Adnyamathanha prefer that visitors don't climb St Mary Peak, reputed to be the head of the female snake.

In another story another *akurra* drank Lake Frome dry, then wove his way across the land creating creeks and gorges. Wherever he stopped, he created a large waterhole, including Arkaroola Springs. The sun warmed the salty water in his stomach causing it to rumble, a noise which can still be heard today in the form of underground springwater flowing.

Colour is essential to the Adnyamathanha as they use the area's red ochre in traditional ceremonies and medicine. Traditional stories say that the vivid orange colour is from the Marrukurli, dangerous dogs who were killed by Adnu, the bearded dragon. When Adnu killed the black Marrukurli the sun went out and he was forced to throw his boomerang in every direction to reawaken the sun. It was only when he threw it to the east that the sun returned. Meanwhile the blood of the Marrukurli had seeped into the earth to create sacred ochre deposits.

---

for lunch and dinner from March to January) does bang-up bush tucker, plus curries, seafood and pizzas.

Permits for **bush camping** (per car $10) within the national park (ie outside the resort) are available from either the visitors centre or self-service booths along the way. Trezona, Aroona and Brachina East have creek-side sites among big gum trees; Youngoona in the park's north is a good base for walks. Remote Wilkawillina is certainly the quietest spot.

BLINMAN & PARACHILNA

North of Wilpena Pound, uber-cute **Blinman** (population 30; www.blinman.org.au) owes its existence to the copper smelter built here in 1903. But the copper boom went bust, and today Blinman's main claim to fame is as SA's highest town (610m above sea level).

Much of the old **Blinman Mine** (☎ 08-8648 4370; admission adult/family $4/10, key deposit $10) has been redeveloped with lookouts and information boards. Pick up a key from the Blinman General Store to access some of the mine shafts (the rest of the site is free).

Chunky slate floors, old-time photographs and luxury rooms collide at the renovated 1869 **Blinman Hotel** (☎ 08-8648 4867; blinman@senet .com.au; Mine Rd, Blinman; unpowered/powered sites $10/20, d hotel/motel/cottage $110/135/135; ❄ ☒). The kitchen (mains $14 to $24; lunch and dinner) serves up bush-hewn delights like saltbush-wrapped

chicken breast and char-grilled eucalyptus lamb. There are raggedy tent and caravan sites out the back.

Run by a jeweller and a painter on the run from suburban Melbourne, the **Wild Lime Café & Gallery** (☎ 08-8648 4679; Mine Rd, Blinman; mains $10-20; Old Schoolhouse, Mine Rd; ☺ breakfast & lunch Tue-Sun, daily school holidays) serves reliable coffee, soups, salads, pies, pasties and great cakes.

The road between Blinman and Parachilna tracks through **Parachilna Gorge**, where you'll find creek-side camping and chill-out spots. The northern end of the Heysen Trail (see Take the Long Way Home, p722) starts/finishes here.

'Real people only, no Yuppies' is the slogan at **Angorichina Tourist Village** (☎ 08-8648 4842; www .angorichinavillage.com.au; Parachilna Gorge; unpowered/powered sites $20/24, on-site vans s/d from $28/38, dm $18, cabins from $75; ☒), 3km east of Parachilna Gorge. It's a rambling joint with a mix of accommodation; the store sells fuel and can fix your flat. The **Blinman Pools Walk** (6km, five hours) starts here, following a creek past abandoned dugouts, river red gums and cypress pines.

On the Hawker–Leigh Creek road, **Parachilna** (population somewhere between four and seven) is an essential Flinders Ranges destination. Aside from a few shacks, a phone booth and some rusty wrecks, the only thing here is the legendary **Prairie Hotel** (☎ 08-8648 4844; www.prairiehotel.com.au; Parachilna; cabins s $45-100,

SOUTH AUSTRALIA

DETOUR: MORALANA SCENIC DRIVE

This sneaky, unsealed 28km back route between the Wilpena and Leigh Creek roads takes in railway ruins, lookouts and the rust-red mountain scenery of the Elder and Wilpena Pound Ranges. If you're heading north from Wilpena to Leigh Creek (or the other way around), it'll save you having to backtrack through Hawker. The turn-off is 24km north of Hawker on the Wilpena road (46km on the Leigh Creek road).

---

cabins d $60-120, hotel d $175-320; ⊠ ⌨). It's looking just a tad weary, but it's still a world-class stay with slick suites out the back and basic cabins across the street. Don't miss a meal and a cold Fargher Lager (or five) in the pub (mains $16 to $28; lunch and dinner). Try the feral mixed grill (camel sausage, kangaroo fillet, emu and bacon). We arrived at 10.42am: 'Too early for a beer!? Whose rules are those?' said the barman.

LEIGH CREEK & COPLEY

In the early 1980s the previously non-existent town of **Leigh Creek** (population 700) was built by the state government: blooming out of the desert, it's an odd, Canberra-like oasis of leafy landscaping and cul-de-sacs (or is that culs-de-sac?). It's a coal-mining town, supplying the Port Augusta power stations. The **Leigh Creek visitors centre** (☎ 08-8675 2723; lcvic@internode.on.net; 13 Black Oak Dr; ⌚ 9am-5pm; ⌨) has the local low-down.

The hub of town life, the **Leigh Creek Tavern** (☎ 08-8675 2025; leighcreektavern@flinderspower.com.au; Leigh Creek Town Shopping Centre; motel s/d $110/135, cabins s/d/f $80/95/120; ⊠) offers jaunty '80s-style motel rooms, cabins and miner-sized bistro meals (mains $10 to $27; lunch and dinner).

About 6km north of Leigh Creek is the sweet meaninglessness of little **Copley** (population 80). **Copley Caravan Park** (☎ 08-8675 2288; www .copleycaravan.com.au; Railway Tce W; unpowered/powered sites $20/25, cabins d $60-130; ⊠) is a going concern: a small, immaculate park that does a bonfire cook-up for guests.

our pick **Iga Warta** (☎ 08-8648 3737; www .igawarta.com; Arkaroola Rd; unpowered sites $22, tents/ bunkhouses/cabins/safari tents d $36/36/104/150, tours $75-138, cultural experiences $25-52; ⊠ ⌨), approximately 60km east of Copley on the way into Vulkathunha-Gammon Ranges National Park, is a superb, Indigenous-run establishment offering Adnyamathanha cultural experiences (including bush-tucker walks and campfire stories) as well as 4WD and bushwalking tours. The various on-site

accommodation is open to all comers (the safari tents are lovely!).

Immediately after Iga Warta is **Nepabunna**, an Adnyamathanha community that manages the land just before the national park.

VULKATHUNHA-GAMMON RANGES NATIONAL PARK

Blanketing 128,200 desert hectares, the remote **Vulkathunha-Gammon Ranges National Park** (www .environment.sa.gov.au/parks/sanpr/vulkathunha_gammon ranges) has deep gorges, rugged ranges yellow-footed rock wallabies and gum-lined creeks. Most of the park is difficult to access (4WDs are near compulsory) and has limited facilities. The rangers hang out at the **Balcanoona Park Office** (☎ 08-8648 0049), 99km from Copley.

The area around **Grindells Hut** has expansive views and stark ridges all around. You can reach it on a 4WD track off the Arkaroola road, or by walking through **Weetootla Gorge**. It's a 13km-return hike – you might want to stay the night at Grindells Hut. Check with the ranger before driving or walking into this area.

The park has six **bush camping** (per car $5) areas, including Italowie Gorge, Grindells Hut, Weetootla Gorge and Arcoona Bluff. Pick up camping permits at Balcanoona Park HQ. There are two huts that can be booked at the ranger's office: **Grindells Hut** (up to 8 people $120) and **Balcanoona Shearer's Quarters** (up to 18 people $220). These prices give you exclusive use of the huts, regardless of how many people are staying.

ARKAROOLA

A privately operated wildlife reserve/resort 129km east of Copley on unsealed roads, **Arkaroola Wilderness Sanctuary** (☎ 1800 676 042, 08-8648 4848; www.arkaroola.com.au) occupies a far-flung and utterly spectacular part of the Flinders Ranges. The **visitors centre** (⌚ 9am-5pm) has displays on local natural history, including a scientific explanation of the tremors that often shake things up hereabouts.

The absolute must-do highlight of Arkaroola is the four-hour 4WD **Ridgetop Tour** ($99) through wild mountain country, complete with white-knuckle climbs and descents towards the freakish Sillers Lookout. Once you've extracted your fingernails from your seat, look for wedge-tailed eagles and yellow-footed rock wallabies. You can also book guided or tag-along **tours** (drives and walks) through the area. Most areas are accessible in a regular car, with some hiking to pump up your pulse.

The **resort** (☎ 1800 676 042, 08-8648 4848; www .arkaroola.com.au; Arkaroola Rd Camp; unpowered/powered sites $15/20, cabins $40, lodges $65-175; ✗ ⬛) includes a motel complex and caravan park. Campsites range from dusty hilltop spots to creekside corners. Comfortable cabins are a good budget bet, while air-con lodges are a self-contained paradise. Other facilities include a woody bar-restaurant (mains $15 to $30; breakfast, lunch and dinner), a supermarket and service station.

OUTBACK

The area north of the Eyre Peninsula and the Flinders Ranges stretches into the vast, empty spaces of SA's outback. If you're prepared, travelling through this sparsely populated and harsh country is utterly rewarding.

Heading into the red heart of Australia on the Stuart Hwy, Woomera is the first pit stop, with its dark legacy of nuclear tests and shiny collection of left-over rockets. Further north, the opal-mining town of Coober Pedy is an absolute one off: a desolate human aberration amid the blistering, arid plains. If you're feeling gung-ho, tackle a section of the iconic Oodnadatta Track, a rugged outback alternative to the Stuart Hwy tarmac. Along the way are warm desert springs, the gargantuan Lake Eyre and some amazing old outback pubs.

National Parks

For outback park information call the **Desert Parks Hotline** (☎ 1800 816 078) or contact the **Department for Environment & Heritage** (DEH; www .environment.sa.gov.au/parks) Adelaide (☎ 08-8821 2270; 91-97 Grenfell St; ⏲ 9am-5pm Mon-Fri) Port Augusta (☎ 08-8648 5300; Upstairs, 9 MacKay St; ⏲ 9am-5pm Mon-Fri).

One way to explore the outback environment is to purchase a **Desert Parks Pass** (per car $105), allowing access to nine outback parks,

with a map and handbook included. Aside from the DEH offices listed previously, passes are available online (www.environment .sa.gov.au/parks/visitor/desertprice.html), or from the following outlets:

Adelaide Royal Automobile Association (p721)
Coober Pedy Underground Books (p804)
Hawker Teague's Hawker Motors & visitors centre (p797)
Innamincka Innamincka Trading Post (p807)
Leigh Creek Leigh Creek visitors centre (opposite)
Mt Dare Mt Dare Hotel (☎ 08-8670 7835; Mt Dare, Witjira National Park)
Oodnadatta Pink Roadhouse (p806)
Port Augusta Port Augusta visitors centre (p788)
Roxby Downs Roxby Downs visitors centre (☎ 08-8671 2001; 1 Richardson Pl)

Tours

Outback tours are a great way to go, particularly if you're not used to driving epic off-road distances. The following options are all ex-Adelaide; see p734 for more.

Arabunna Tours (☎ 08-8675 8351; www.southaus tralia.com/S9008383.aspx; 7-day tour $1050) Aboriginal-owned company offering cultural tours from Adelaide to the Flinders Ranges, Marree, Oodnadatta Track and Lake Eyre.
Big Country Safaris (☎ 08-8538 7105; www.bigcoun trysafaris.com.au; 12-day tour from $1860) Small-group outback-camping 4WD tours ex-Adelaide that take in the Simpson Desert, Coober Pedy and the Birdsville Track.
Great Australian Cattle Drive (☎ 08-8303 2220; www.cattledrive.com.au) From 2010 this epic outback cattle drive will hoof through Coober Pedy, Marree and William Creek. Planning was in the early stages at the time of research; check the website for updates on how to participate.
Just Cruisin 4WD Tours (☎ 08-8383 0962; www. justcruisin4wdtours.com.au; 13-day tour $6650) Aboriginal cultural tours visiting outback Indigenous communities, sites and guides between Adelaide and Uluru.

Getting There & Around
AIR
Regional Express (☎ 13 17 13; www.regionalexpress.com .au) flies daily between Adelaide and Coober Pedy ($199, two hours).

BUS
Greyhound Australia (☎ 1300 473 946; www.greyhound .com.au) operates daily coaches from Adelaide to Alice Springs ($280, 19½ hours), stopping in SA at Pimba ($119, seven hours), Glendambo ($132, 8¼ hours) and Coober Pedy ($168, 10½ hours). Internet fares are much reduced (eg Coober Pedy $94; Alice Springs $157).

CAR & MOTORCYCLE

The Stuart Hwy is sealed all the way from Port Augusta to Darwin. In SA, fuel and accommodation are available at Pimba (171km from Port Augusta), Glendambo (285km), Coober Pedy (535km), Cadney Homestead (689km) and Marla (771km). Pimba, Coober Pedy and Marla have 24-hour fuel sales.

The highway is a long, flat ribbon beating out across the red desert flats. The temptation is to get it over with quickly, but wandering cattle, sheep, emus, kangaroos, camels, wedge-tailed eagles, etc make driving fast a dangerous prospect. Take care and avoid nocturnal driving.

A more adventurous route to/from the NT is the rugged, unsealed Oodnadatta Track (p178) between Marree in the northern Flinders Ranges and Marla on the Stuart Hwy, 180km from the NT border. It's best tackled in a 4WD, but you can do it in a conventional car if you take it slowly. Carry plenty of bottled water and two spare tyres, deflate your tyres to 25psi to avoid punctures, and take a satellite phone or UHF CB radio with you in case you break down. A set of cheap Chinese high-profile tyres (around $80 each) will give your car a little more ground clearance.

Two other interesting outback routes are the legendary Birdsville Track (p807) and Strzelecki Track (p807).

Note that all three tracks are subject to closure after heavy rains – roads can either be washed out or turned into muddy glue. Before you depart, check road conditions with the Royal Automobile Association in Adelaide (p721), or online at www.transport.sa.gov.au.

TRAIN

For information on the *Ghan* train between Adelaide and Alice Springs, see p723.

WOOMERA

pop 300

An 8km detour off the Stuart Hwy from Pimba (485km from Adelaide), Woomera began in 1946 as HQ for experimental British rocket and nuclear tests at notorious sites like Maralinga. Local Indigenous tribes suffered greatly from nuclear fallout. These days Woomera is a drab, oddly artificial government town that's still an active Department of Defence test site.

With displays on Woomera's past and present, the small **Woomera Heritage Centre**

(☎ 1300 761 620, 08-8673 7042; www.woomera.com .au; Dewrang Ave; museum admission adult/child $6/3; ☾ 9am-5pm Mar-Nov, 10am-2pm Dec-Feb) doubles as the visitors centre. Out the front is the **Lions Club Aircraft & Missile Park**, studded with rocket remnants.

The affable **Woomera Travellers' Village** (☎ 08-8673 7800; www.woomera.com; Old Pimba Rd; unpowered/powered sites $20/24, cabins & units $50-75; ☒) has a well-maintained range of budget accommodation. The cheaper cabins and units share bathroom facilities; BYO linen.

Built to house rocket scientists, the **Eldo Hotel** (☎ 08-8673 7867; www.eldohotel.com.au; Kotara Ave; d with/without bathroom $90/80; ☒ ☒) has comfortable budget and motel-style rooms, and serves meaty à la carte meals in the bistro (mains $15 to $30; open for lunch and dinner). Try the kangaroo bratwurst snags!

Continue north through Woomera for 90km (sealed road) and you'll hit **Roxby Downs** (population 4,500; www.roxbydowns.com), a bizarrely affluent desert town servicing the massive Olympic Dam Mine, which digs up untold amounts of copper, silver, gold and uranium.

WOOMERA TO COOBER PEDY

Around 115km northwest of Pimba and 245km shy of Coober Pedy, middle-of-nowhere **Glendambo** (population 30) was established in 1982 as a Stuart Hwy service centre. This is the last fuel stop before Coober Pedy.

You can bunk down at the oasislike **Glendambo Hotel-Motel** (☎ 08-8672 1030; www.glen dambooutback4x4.com.au; Stuart Hwy; unpowered/powered sites $20/24, s/d $85/90; ☒ ☒), which has bars, a restaurant and a bunch of decent motel units. Out the back are campsites without a huge amount of shade.

North of Glendambo the Stuart Hwy enters the government-owned **Woomera Prohibited Area** – the highway itself is unrestricted, but don't go a-wanderin' now, y'hear?

COOBER PEDY

pop 3500

Coming into Coober Pedy the dry, barren desert suddenly becomes riddled with holes and adjunct piles of dirt – reputedly more than a million around the township. The reason for all this rabid digging is opals – the 'fire in the stone' – which have made this small town a mining mecca. This isn't to say it's also a tourist mecca – with swarms of flies, no trees, 50°C summer days, sub-zero winter nights, cave-dwelling locals and rusty car wrecks in every second front yard, you might think you've arrived in a post-apocalyptic hell hole – but it sure is an interesting place!

Coober Pedy is actually very cosmopolitan, with 44 nationalities represented. Greeks, Serbs, Croats and Italians form sizeable groups amongst the mining community, Indians and Sri Lankans run accommodation, and gem buyers come from as far off as Scotland and Hong Kong. The surrounding desert is jaw-droppingly desolate, a fact not overlooked by international filmmakers who've come here to shoot end-of-the-world epics like *Mad Max III*, *Red Planet*, *Ground Zero*, *Pitch Black* and

the slightly more believable *Priscilla, Queen of the Desert*.

Few people make their living solely from mining here, so there's a lot of 'career diversification'. This means the dude who drives the shuttle bus to the airport also loads the baggage onto the plane, mans the hotel reception desk and works his opal claim on weekends (so he can retire from his other jobs!).

Information

24-hour water dispenser (Hutchison St; per 10L 20c) If you're headed into the desert, fill your canteens opposite the Oasis Tourist Park.

Coober Pedy Hospital (☎ 08-8672 5009; goddard .christine@asaugov.sa.gov.au; Hospital Rd; ⏱ 24hr) Accident and emergency.

COOBER PEDY

0 _____ 500 m
0 _____ 0.2 miles

INFORMATION
24-hour Water Dispenser............**1** C1
Coober Pedy Hospital...................**2** D1
Coober Pedy Visitors Centre........**3** C3
Underground Books.......................**4** C3

SIGHTS & ACTIVITIES
Anglican Church............................**5** D1
Big Winch.......................................**6** C2
Coober Pedy Revival
  Fellowship...................................**7** D2
Coober Pedy Swimming Pool.......**8** B3
Faye's Underground Display
  Home..**9** D3
Old Timers Mine.........................**10** D2
Spaceship....................................**11** C2
St Peter & Paul Catholic
  Church.......................................**12** C3

SLEEPING
Desert Cave Hotel......................**13** C3
Mud Hut Motel............................**14** C3
Oasis Caravan Park.....................**15** C1
Opal Inn Hotel/Motel.................**16** C3
Radeka's Downunder
  Underground Backpackers
  & Motel......................................**17** C3
Underground Motel....................**18** D1

EATING
Italo-Australian Miners Club.....**19** C3
John's Pizza Bar..........................**20** C3
Tom & Mary's Greek Taverna....**21** C3
Umberto's................................(see 13)

TRANSPORT
Budget...**22** C3
Coober Pedy Rent-a-Car..........(see 14)

SOUTH AUSTRALIA

Coober Pedy visitors centre (☎ 1800 637 076, 08-8672 5298; www.opalcapitaloftheworld.com.au; Council offices, Hutchison St; ☽ 8.30am-5pm Mon-Fri, 10am-1pm Sat & Sun; ☐) Free 30-minute internet access, history displays and comprehensive tour and accommodation listings and prices.

Underground Books (☎ 08-8672 5558; underground books@bigpond.com; Post Office Hill Rd; ☽ 8.30am-5pm Mon-Fri, 10am-4pm Sat) The town's only bookshop also has loads of regional info.

Sights & Activities
OPAL MINING

There are hundreds of working opal mines around town, the elusive gems at the fore of everyone's consciousness. If you're keen for a fossick, tour operators or locals may invite you out to their claim to 'noodle' through the mullock (waste pile) for stones. Watch out for unmarked shafts, and never wander around the fields at night.

The best place to check out a working excavation is **Tom's Working Opal Mine** (☎ 1800 196 500, 08-8672 3966; www.coobertours.com; Stuart Hwy; tours adult/child/family $25/10/55; ☽ tours 10am, 2pm & 3.30pm), 3km southwest of town. Miners continue their search for the big vein; visitors noodle for small fortunes.

The brilliant **Old Timers Mine** (☎ 08-8672 5555; www.oldtimersmine.com; Crowders Gully Rd; adult/child/ concession/family $10/4.50/9/29; ☽ 9am-5pm) was mined in 1916 but was then hidden by the miners. The mine was rediscovered when a dugout home punched through into the labyrinth of tunnels, which now make a great tour. There's also a museum, a re-created 1920s underground home and free mining equipment demos daily (9.30am, 1.30pm and 3.30pm).

DUGOUT HOMES & CHURCHES

It gets face-meltingly hot out here in summer – it makes sense to live underground! Even when it's a stinker outside, subterranean temperatures never rise above 23°C, and air-conditioning isn't necessary. Many of the early **dugout homes** were simply worked-out mines, but these days they're usually specifically excavated residences. If you want to see one, **Faye's Underground Display Home** (☎ 1800 676 680, 08-8672 5029; Old Water Tank Rd; admission $5; ☽ 8am-5pm Mon-Sat) was hand dug by three women in the 1960s. It's a little chintzy, but the living-room swimming pool is a winner!

You can visit several of Coober Pedy's **underground churches** – these are functioning churches, so be respectful of services and worshippers. The **Serbian Orthodox Church** (☎ 08-8672 3048; off Stuart Hwy; admission free; ☽ 11am-6pm) is the largest and most impressive, with carvings in the rock walls. The **St Peter & Paul Catholic Church** (☎ 08-8672 5011; Oliver St; admission free; ☽ 10am-4pm) was Coober Pedy's first church, and still has a sweet appeal.

OTHER STUFF

You can't miss the **Big Winch**, from which there are sweeping views over Coober Pedy and towards the Breakaways. An optimistic 'if' painted on the side of the big bucket sums up the town's spirit.

Leftover sets and props from the movies that have been filmed here are littered around town. Check out the amazing **spaceship** from *Pitch Black*, which has crash-landed outside the Opal Cave shop on Hutchison St.

When the mercury nudges 50°C, **Coober Pedy Swimming Pool** (☎ 08-8672 5388; Paxton Rd; adult/ child $5/2.50; ☽ 12.45-8.30pm Mon-Fri, 11am-8.30pm Sat & Sun) becomes a splashy human soup.

Tours

There are heaps of tour options that can take you around town or further afield. Most accommodation places also run town tours. Some of the many operators:

Arid Zone Tours (☎ 08-8672 5359, 0417 885 909; www.cooberpedy.info; tours per person from $55) Customised 4WD tours to anywhere you want to go, run by the experienced Merv: around town, Lake Eyre, Painted Desert, the Breakaways, etc.

Desert Cave Tours (☎ 08-8672 5688; www.desert cave.com.au; 4hr tour adult/child $85/42.50) Arguably the most convenient tour, taking in town highlights and a few further out like the Dog Fence, Breakaways and Moon Plain. Also on offer are four-hour 'Down 'N' Dirty' opal-digging tours (per person $98).

Desert Diversity Tours (☎ 1800 069 911, 08-8672 5226; www.desertdiversity.com) Coober Pedy–based full-day Painted Desert tours ($195) and mail-run tours to Oodnadatta and William Creek return ($175).

Oasis Tours (☎ 08-8672 5169; 3hr tour adult/child $35/17.50) A good budget tour taking in the major town sights plus a little fossicking. Two-hour sunset Breakaways tours (adult/child $40/20) also swing by the Dog Fence and the Moon Plain.

Radeka's Downunder Desert Breakaways Tour (☎ 1800 633 891, 08-8672 5223; www.radekadow nunder.com.au; 4hr tour adult/child $50/25) A wandering tour that includes an underground home, fossicking, the Breakaways, an underground church, the Dog Fence and an active opal mine. Stargazing tour also available (adult/child $30/15).

Stuart Range Tours (☎ 08-8672 5179; 3hr tour adult/child $40/20, 4½hr tour adult/child $50/25) A budget-conscious option taking in the main sights and activities, including fossicking, an underground church and a working opal mine.

Sleeping

Radeka's Downunder Underground Backpackers & Motel (☎ 1800 633 891, 08-8672 5223; www.radekadown under.com.au; Hutchison St; dm $25, d & tw $65, motel units $125; ✱ ▨) The owners started excavating this place in 1960 – they haven't found much opal, but have ended up with a beaut backpackers! On multiple levels down 6.5m below the surface are Coober Pedy's best budget beds, plus good individual rooms and motel units. The shared kitchen is handy for self-caterers, and there's a bar, barbecue, snooker room and laundry. Desert and stargazing tours also available (see opposite).

Opal Inn Hotel/Motel (☎ 08-8672 5054; www.opalinn .com.au; Hutchison St; unpowered/powered sites $20/27, hotel s/d $75/80, motel s/d/tr/q $115/125/135/145; ✱ ▨) The rambling Opal Inn is a jack-of-all-trades (we could say master of none…) with basic pub rooms, more sophisticated motel rooms and a dusty caravan park attached. The bistro (mains $15 to $29) does lunch from Monday to Saturday and dinner nightly, and the bar is the best place for a beer in town.

Underground Motel (☎ 08-8672 5324; www.theun dergroundmotel.com.au; Catacomb Rd; s/d/f incl light break-fast from $85/95/105, extra adult/child $30/16) Choose between standard rooms and suites (with separate lounge and kitchen) at this service-able spot with a broad Breakaways panorama. It's a fair walk from town, but friendly and affordable.

Mud Hut Motel (☎ 08-8672 3003; www.mudhutmotel .com.au; St Nicholas St; s/d/units $120/140/200; ✱ ▨) The rustic-looking walls here are actually rammed earth, and despite the grubby name this is one of the cleanest places in town. The two-bedroom units have cooktops, fridges and air-conditioning. The in-house restaurant does dinner most nights (mains $27 to $31).

Down to Erth B&B (☎ 08-8672 5762; www.downto erth.com.au; Monument Rd; s & d incl breakfast $150, extra person $25; ▨) A real dugout gem 4km from town, where you can have your own subterranean two-bedroom bunker. There's a shady plunge pool for cooling off after a day exploring the Earth, and a telescope for exploring the universe.

Desert Cave Hotel (☎ 08-8672 5688; www.desertcave .com.au; Hutchison St; d $218, extra person $35; ✱ ▨ ▣) For a much-needed shot of desert luxury – plus a pool, gym, in-house movies, formidable minibar and great restaurant (see below). Staff are super-courteous and there are plenty of tours on offer (see opposite). Above-ground rooms also available.

Oasis Caravan Park (☎ 08-8672 5169; www.oasiscoo berpedy.com.au; Seventeen Mile Rd; unpowered/powered sites $22/26, r/on-site vans $36/52, cabins $74-109; ✱ ▨ ▣) There are a few places to camp in Coober Pedy, but this place is reasonably central and has the most shade, plus a swimming pool. An affordable tour runs daily (see opposite).

Riba's (☎ 08-8672 5614; www.camp-underground .com.au; William Creek Rd; underground/above-ground sites $24/16, powered sites $22, s/d $45/55; ▨) Around 5km from town, Riba's offers the unique option of underground camping! Extras include an underground TV lounge, budget rooms and nightly opal mine tour (free for campers).

Eating

John's Pizza Bar (☎ 08-8672 5561; Hutchison St; meals $4-30) Serving up table-sized pizzas, hearty pastas and heat-beating gelato, you can't go past John's. Grills, salads, burgers, yiros and fish and chips also available. Sit inside, order some take-aways, or pull up a seat with the bedraggled pot plants by the street.

Tom & Mary's Greek Taverna (☎ 08-8672 5622; Hutchison St; meals $15-25; ☽ lunch & dinner) This busy Greek diner does everything from a superb moussaka to yiros, seafood, Greek salads and pastas with Hellenic zing. Sit back with a cold Coopers or retsina as the red sun sets on another dusty day in Coober Pedy.

Italo-Australian Miners Club (IAMC; ☎ 08-8672 5102; Italian Club Rd; mains $10-15; ☽ dinner Wed-Sat) Vinyl chairs reflect the sunset at this elevated local watering hole, attracting beer bellies most nights. Meals (monster steaks, schnitzels and damn fine pastas) make an appetising appearance from Wednesday to Saturday nights.

Umberto's (☎ 08-8672 5688; Hutchison St; mains $25-46; ☽ dinner) The Desert Cave Hotel's rooftop restaurant maintains the quality with first-class dishes like wallaby shanks with vegetables and char-grilled tomato stew, and their 'Essential Tastes of the Outback' platter: char-grilled kangaroo, camel, emu and beef with bush chutney and hand-cut fries. Swift service, moody desert views and a motivating wine list.

Getting There & Around

Coober Pedy sits just off the Stuart Hwy, 846km northwest of Adelaide and 686km south of Alice Springs (NT). See p801 for transport details.

The Desert Cave Hotel (p805) runs a shuttle van to/from the airport ($10). You can rent cars, 4WDs and campervans here (cars from around $70 per day, with additional fees for distances over 100km):

Budget (☎ 08-8672 5333; www.budget.com.au; 100 Hutchison St)

Coober Pedy Rent-a-Car (☎ 08-8672 3003; Mud Hut Motel, St Nicholas St)

COOBER PEDY TO MARLA

The **Breakaways Reserve** is a stark but colourful area of arid hills and scarps 33km away on a rough road north of Coober Pedy – turn off the highway 22km west of town. You can drive to a lookout in a conventional vehicle and check out the white-and-yellow mesa called the **Castle**, which featured in *Mad Max III* and *Priscilla, Queen of the Desert*. Entry permits ($2.20 per person) are available at the visitors centre in Coober Pedy (see p804).

An interesting 70km loop on mainly unsealed road from Coober Pedy takes in the Breakaways, the **Dog Fence** (built to keep dingos out of southeastern Australia) and the tablelike **Moon Plain** on the Coober Pedy–Oodnadatta Rd. If it's been raining, you'll need a 4WD.

If you're heading for Oodnadatta, turning off the Stuart Hwy at Cadney Homestead (151km north of Coober Pedy) gives you a shorter run on dirt roads than the routes via Marla or Coober Pedy. En route you pass through the aptly named **Painted Desert** (bring your camera).

Cadney Homestead (☎ 08-8670 7994; Stuart Hwy; www.cadneyhomestead.com.au; unpowered/powered sites $14/20, d cabin/motel $55/96.50; ❄ ⬚) itself has caravan and tent sites, serviceable motel rooms and basic (no linen) cabins, plus petrol, puncture repairs, take aways, cold beer, ATM, swimming pool…and they can organise Painted Desert tours.

In mulga scrub about 82km from Cadney Homestead, **Marla** (population 245) replaced Oodnadatta as the official regional centre when the *Ghan* railway line was rerouted in

1980. **Marla Travellers Rest** (☎ 08-8670 7001; Stuart Hwy; unpowered/powered sites $10/18, d $90; ❄ ⬚) has fuel, motel rooms, campsites, a cafe and a supermarket.

Frontier-style **Mintabie** (population 250) is an opal field settlement on Aboriginal land 35km west of Marla – there's a general store, restaurant and basic caravan park here.

From Marla the NT border is another 180km, with a fuel stop 20km beyond that in Kulgera.

OODNADATTA TRACK

The legendary, lonesome Oodnadatta Track is an unsealed, 615km road between Marla (left) on the Stuart Hwy, and Marree in the northern Flinders Ranges. The track traces the route of the old Overland Telegraph Line and the defunct Great Northern Railway. **Lake Eyre** (the world's sixth largest lake) is just off the road. The landscape here is amazingly diverse: floodplains south of Marla, saltbush flats around William Creek, dunes and red gibber plains near Coward Springs.

INFORMATION

Before you hit the Oodnadatta – a rough, rocky and sandy track that's subject to closure after rains – check track conditions with the Pink Roadhouse in Oodnadatta (below), the Coober Pedy visitors centre (p804), the Royal Automobile Association in Adelaide (p721), or online at www.transport.sa.gov .au. If you're finding the dust and dirt heavy going, there are escape routes to Coober Pedy on the Stuart Hwy from William Creek and Oodnadatta. Fuel, accommodation and meals are available at Marla, Oodnadatta, William Creek and Marree.

See the *Oodnadatta Track – String of Springs* booklet from the South Australian Tourism Commission, and the *Travel the Oodnadatta Track* brochure produced by the Pink Roadhouse for detailed track info. See Getting There & Around (p801) for driving tips.

OODNADATTA TO WILLIAM CREEK

Around 209km from Marla, **Oodnadatta** (population 150) is where the main road and the old railway line diverged. The heart of the town today is the **Pink Roadhouse** (☎ 1800 802 074, 08-8670 7822; www.pinkroadhouse.com.au; ❄ 8am-5.30pm), an excellent source of track info, plus they serve meals (try the impressive 'Oodnaburger'). They also run the attached **caravan park** (unpowered/powered sites $15/25, budget cabins s/d/tr $45/60/70, self-contained cabins s/d $80/95; 🞕 🞖), which has basic camping through to self-contained cabins.

In another 70km you'll hit **William Creek** (population 6), best enjoyed in the weather-beaten **William Creek Hotel** (☎ 08-8670 7880; www .williamcreekhotel.net.au; unpowered sites $16/20, cabins s/d $60/70, motel s/d $65/95; 🞕), an iconic 1887 pub with a dusty campground and modest cabins and motel rooms. Also on offer are fuel, cold beer, basic provisions, meals and spare tyres.

COWARD SPRINGS TO MARREE

Some 130km shy of Marree, **Coward Springs Campground** (☎ 08-8675 8336; www.cowardsprings .com.au; unpowered sites $16) is the first stop at the old Coward Springs railway siding. You can soak yourself silly in a natural hot-spring tub made from old rail sleepers, or take a **camel trek** (per person per day from $200) to Lake Eyre from here.

About 60km from Marree there's a sculpture park called **Mutonia** (admission by donation; 🕙 24hr), featuring a gate made from a Kombi van cut in half and several planes welded together with their tails buried in the ground to form 'Planehenge'.

Sleepy **Marree** (population 380) was once a vital hub for Afghan camel teams and the Great Northern Railway. The **Oasis Town Centre Caravan Park & Motel** (☎ 08-8675 8352; Railway Tce; un-powered/powered sites $16/20, s/d $40/60; 🞕) has camp-sites and a camp kitchen, as well as motel-style rooms with TVs and fridges. Alternatively, the 100-year-old **Marree Hotel** (☎ 08-8675 8344; marreepub@bigpond.com; Railway Tce; pub s/d $45/70, motel $75/100; 🞕 🞖) has decent pub rooms and brand new motel units out the back. Both businesses can organise flights out over Lake Eyre and **Marree Man**, the 4.2km-long outline of a Pitjantjatjara Aboriginal warrior etched into the desert near Lake Eyre. It was only dis-covered in 1988, and no-one seems to know who created it.

From Marree it's 80km to Lyndhurst, where the bitumen kicks back in, then 33km down to Copley (p800).

BIRDSVILLE TRACK

This old droving trail runs 520km from Marree in SA to Birdsville, just across the border in Queensland – one of Australia's classic outback routes. See above for details.

STRZELECKI TRACK

Meandering through the sand hills of the **Strzelecki Regional Reserve** (www.environment.sa.gov .au/parks/sanpr/strzeleckirr), the Strzelecki Track spans 460km from Lyndhurst, 80km south of Marree, to the tiny outpost of **Innamincka** (below). Discovery of oil and gas at **Moomba** (a town closed to travellers) saw the upgrading of the road from a camel track to a decent dirt road, though heavy transport travelling along it has created bone-rattling corruga-tions. The newer Moomba–Strzelecki Track is better kept, but longer and less interesting than the old track, which follows Strzelecki Creek. Accommodation, provisions and fuel are available at Lyndhurst and Innamincka, but there's nothing in between.

INNAMINCKA
pop 12

On **Cooper Creek** at the northern end of the Strzelecki Track, Innamincka is near where Burke and Wills' ill-fated 1860 expedition expired. The famous **Dig Tree** marks the ex-pedition's base camp, and although the word 'dig' is no longer visible you can still see the expedition's camp number. The Dig Tree is over the Queensland border, though memo-rials and markers – commemorating where Burke and Wills died, and where sole-survi-vor King was found – are downstream in SA. There's also a memorial where A W Howitt's rescue party made its base on the creek.

Cooper Creek only has water in it after heavy rains across central Queensland, but it has deep, permanent waterholes and the semipermanent **Coongie Lakes**, which are part of the **Innamincka Regional Reserve** (☎ 08-8675 9909; www.environment.sa.gov.au/parks/sanpr/innamincka). Prior to European settlement the area had a large Aboriginal population, so relics such as middens and grinding stones can be seen around the area.

The **Innamincka Trading Post** (☎ 08-8675 9900) sells fuel, Desert Parks passes, camping per-mits and provisions, including fresh bread and rolls.

Westprint's *Innamincka/Coongie Lakes* map is a good source of Innamincka info.

Sleeping & Eating
Cooper Creek Homestay (☎ 08-8675 9591; www .coopercreekhomestay.com; cnr Mitchell & Stuart Sts; s/d $80/95; 🞕) About 400m from Cooper Creek, this homestay has comfy shearing-shed-style

accommodation, and the owners are a wealth of local knowledge. After a dip in the waterhole, eat your cooked dinner (extra cost) under the stars. Breakfast and lunch are also available.

Innamincka Hotel (☎ 08-8675 9901; www.theout back.com.au; 2 South Tce; s/d from $85/130; ☒) This old-fashioned hotel has decent motel-style rooms as well as a cheaper bunkhouse. Choose between take aways and hefty counter meals (mains $18 to $28), or the Sunday-night roast ($25).

There are plenty of shady **bush camping** (per car $30) sites along Cooper Creek – Innamincka Trading Post sells permits. You can also camp on the Town Common (per car $5); there are pit toilets and an honesty box for fees. You can use the hot shower ($2), toilet and laundry tub outside the Trading Post. There's also a laundrette in town.

Northern Territory

From the moment you scoot up the Stuart Hwy, there's an enigmatic, ethereal feel to the Northern Territory (NT) that you'll only find in Australia's remote north. It's the kind of land where clichés are born: endless blue skies collide with flat desert expanse in the Red Centre, while the tropical Top End bursts with birdlife, wild rivers and untamed wilderness. And then there are all of those deadly animals poised to snap, sting and strike.

From desert to the tropics, this is a great place to be in the dry winter months, but the monsoon Wet brings its own excitement in the north, with spectacular thunderstorms, cyclones whipping the coast and dumps of rain that cut road access to many settlements and sights.

Though there's access to the prolific natural areas, the Territory has an undeniable edge. There really are wild crocodiles in the waterways and another car might not come down the desert road for weeks. Then there's Darwin, the most relaxed of Australia's capitals, and Alice Springs, a modern frontier town in the middle of nowhere.

For some travellers, the Northern Territory consists of its spine – the Stuart Hwy – and the must-see side trips to Uluru, Kakadu and Litchfield. But take some time to look around and you can visit remote Aboriginal communities to shop for art, hike through rainforest and rocky gorges, sleep in a swag under a billion stars and dine on bush foods and billy tea.

It's a legendary road trip.

HIGHLIGHTS

- Paddle through ancient gorge country in **Nitmiluk National Park** (p854)

- Imagine the *mimi* spirits while deciphering ancient rock art, then watch the wetlands light up at **Ubirr** (p846), one of Kakadu's rock-art sites

- Hike past beehive domes, ancient ferns and the stunning sheer-sided walls of **Kings Canyon** (p884) on the canyon rim walk

- Learn Uluru's secrets from Anangu guides before watching the Rock glow like a burning ember at sunset at **Uluru-Kata Tjuta National Park** (p885)

- Catch a whiff of the exotic foods on offer while weaving through crowds, buskers, and stalls selling services and handcrafted goodies at one of the markets in **Darwin** (p833)

- Float on your back in the sublime pool at Wangi Falls and bathe in a natural waterfall spa at **Litchfield National Park** (p839)

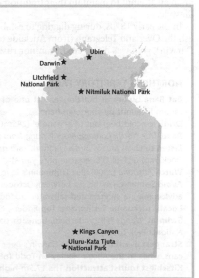

- TELEPHONE CODE: 08
- POPULATION: 221,700
- AREA: 1,349,129 SQ KM

HISTORY

Most experts believe that Australian Aborigines have occupied the Australian landmass for around 60,000 years, although the central regions were not inhabited until about 24,000 years ago. The first significant contact with outsiders was an amicable one, occurring in the 17th century when Macassan traders from modern-day Sulawesi in Indonesia came to collect trepang (sea cucumber).

Early attempts to settle the Top End were mainly due to British fears that the French or Dutch might get a foothold in Australia. The Brits established three forts between 1824 and 1838, but all were short-lived. Then the desire for more grazing land and trade routes spurred speculators from Queensland and South Australia (SA) to explore the vast untamed north. With an eye to development, SA governors annexed the NT in 1863 (it became self-governing only in 1978).

From the mid-1860s to 1895 hundreds of thousands of sheep, cattle and horses were overlanded to immense pastoral settlements. Dislocation and hardship were bedfellows of the industry, with Aborigines forced from their lands and pastoralists confronted by a swath of difficulties. Some Aborigines took employment as stockmen or domestic servants on cattle stations, while others moved on in an attempt to maintain their traditional lifestyle.

In the early 1870s, during digging to establish the Overland Telegraph (from Adelaide to Darwin), gold was discovered. A minor rush ensued, with an influx of Chinese prospectors. Though the gold finds were relatively insignificant, the searches for it unearthed a wealth of natural resources that would lead to mining becoming a major economic presence.

WWII had a significant impact on the Territory. Just weeks after the Japanese bombed Darwin, the entire Territory north of Alice Springs was placed under military control, with 32,000 soldiers stationed in the Top End.

While the process of white settlement in the NT was slower than elsewhere in Australia, it had an equally troubled and violent effect. By the early 20th century, most Aboriginal people were confined to government reserves or Christian missions. During the 1960s Aboriginal people began to demand more rights.

In 1966 a group of Aboriginal stockmen, led by Vincent Lingiari, went on strike on Wave Hill Station, to protest over the low wages and poor conditions that they received compared with white stockmen. The Wave Hill walk-off (still celebrated annually at Kalkaringi) gave rise to the Aboriginal land-rights movement.

In 1976 the Aboriginal Land Rights (Northern Territory) Act was passed in Canberra. It handed over all reserves and mission lands in the NT to Aboriginal people and allowed Aboriginal groups to claim vacant government land if they could prove continuous occupation – provided the land wasn't already leased, in a town or set aside for some other special purpose.

NORTHERN TERRITORY FACTS

Eat Barra burger or buffalo steak at one of NT's many roadhouses; or, better still, baked barramundi caught by your own hand

Drink Ice-cold beer out of a 'handle' (285mL) or 'schooner' (425mL)

Read *True North: Contemporary Writing from the Northern Territory*, edited by Marian Devitt

Listen to Local musos Birdwave (funk, rare groove), Warumpi Band (Indigenous rock), NoKTuRNL (rock, rap) or Phil O'Brien (campfire yarns)

Watch *Australia* (2008), Baz Lurhmann's love story set in Darwin and the Top End

Avoid Swimming in the sea between October and May, and in any waterway without first seeking advice: marine stingers and saltwater crocodiles inhabit these waters

Locals' nickname Territorians, Top Enders, Centralians

Swim at Wangi Falls waterhole, beneath palm trees populated by roosting bats, at Litchfield National Park (p839)

Strangest event Boat races: in Darwin's Beer Can Regatta (p827) they're in boats made from beer cans, while in the Alice's Henley-on-Todd (p870) they're on a river with no water

Kitschiest tourist attraction The 17.5m-high Anmatjere Man (whose left testicle is purported to be a time capsule) at Aileron roadhouse (p862)

NORTHERN TERRITORY

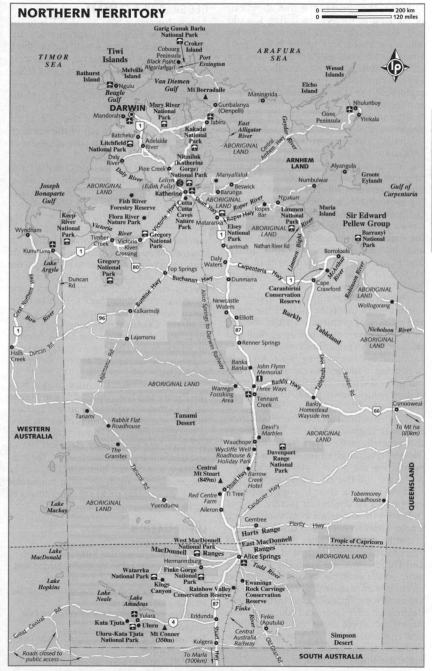

Today, Aboriginal people own about half of the land in the NT, including Kakadu and Uluru-Kata Tjuta National Parks, which are leased back to the federal government. Minerals on Aboriginal land are still government property, though the landowners' permission is usually required for exploration and mining, and landowners are remunerated.

Around 30% of the Territory's 200,000 people are Aborigines. While non-Aboriginal Australia's awareness of the need for reconciliation with the Aboriginal community has increased in recent years, there are still huge gulfs between the cultures. Entrenched disadvantage and substance abuse is causing enormous social problems within some Indigenous communities. A report by the Crown prosecutor in 2006 revealed appalling sexual and violent abuses against women and children in remote NT communities. The Howard federal government in 2007 responded with the Northern Territory National Emergency Response Act, which resulted in an 'intervention' into Aboriginal communities involving police, the army and a flurry of politicians. Part of the Act included a government ban on alcohol and pornography in prescribed areas in the NT – identified by blue warning signs. An audit of policing in Indigenous communities also recommended partially abolishing the permit system (which limits access to Aboriginal lands).

It's often difficult for short-term visitors to make meaningful contact with Aborigines, as they generally prefer to be left to themselves. The impressions given by some Aboriginal people on the streets of Alice Springs, Katherine and Darwin, where social problems and substance abuse among a few people can present an unpleasant picture, are not indicative of Aboriginal communities as a whole. Tours to Aboriginal lands, most operated by the communities themselves, and visits to arts centres (such as at Yuendumu and Gunbalanya) are gradually becoming more widely available, as communities feel more inclined to share their culture. Benefits are numerous: financial gain through self-determined endeavour, and educating non-Aboriginal people about traditional culture and customs, which helps to alleviate the problems caused by the ignorance and misunderstandings of the past.

GEOGRAPHY & CLIMATE

Although roughly 80% of the NT is in the tropics – the Tropic of Capricorn lies just north of Alice Springs – only the northern 25%, known as the Top End, has anything that resembles the popular idea of a tropical climate. It's a distinct region of savannah woodlands and rainforest pockets – in the northeast, the Arnhem Land plateau rises abruptly from the plain and continues to the Gulf of Carpentaria. Much of the southern 75% of the Territory consists of desert or semiarid plain.

The Top End's climate is described in terms of the Dry and the Wet, with year-round maximum temperatures of 30°C to 34°C and minimums between 19°C and 26°C. Roughly, the Dry lasts from April to September and the Wet from October to March, with the heaviest rain falling from January onwards. Indigenous Australians recognise between two and six seasons, which are observed through the movement and cycles of plant and animal species – including us tourists: 'When storm come now they all [go] back to their country' noted one traditional owner.

In the Centre temperatures are much more variable, plummeting below freezing on winter nights (June to August) and soaring above 40°C on summer days (December to March).

The most comfortable time to visit both the Centre and the Top End is late May to early August, though the Centre is pleasant as early as April. The Top End has its good points during the Wet – everything is green, and there are spectacular electrical storms and relatively few tourists. However, the combination of heat and high humidity can be unbearable, dirt roads are often impassable and some national parks are either totally or partly closed.

INFORMATION

Helpful websites:

Exploroz (www.exploroz.com) Handy user-generated site for fuel locations and pricing, weather forecasts, road conditions and more.

Parks & Wildlife Service (www.nt.gov.au/nreta/parks) Details on parks and reserves.

Road Report (www.ntlis.nt.gov.au/roadreport) Road-conditions report.

Tourism Top End (www.tourismtopend.com.au) Darwin-based tourism body.

Travel NT (http://en.travelnt.com) Official tourism site.

Permits

Although changes to the permit system were made by the Howard government in 2007, permits may be required to enter Aboriginal land, unless you are using recognised public roads that cross Aboriginal territory.

The Central Land Council deals with all land south of a line drawn between Kununurra (Western Australia) and Mt Isa (Queensland); the Northern Land Council is responsible for land north of that line, and the Tiwi Land Council deals with Bathurst and Melville Islands. Permits can take four to six weeks to be processed, although for the Injalak arts centre at Gunbalanya (Oenpelli) they are generally issued on the spot in Jabiru.

Central Land Council (Map p864; ☎ 08-8951 6211; www.clc.org.au; 33 Stuart Hwy, Alice Springs)

Northern Land Council (www.nlc.org.au) Darwin (Map pp820-1; ☎ 08-8920 5100; 45 Mitchell St); Jabiru (☎ 08-8979 2410; Flinders St); Katherine (Map p852; ☎ 08-8972 2799; 5 Katherine Tce); Nhulunbuy (☎ 08-8987 2602; Endeavour Sq)

Tiwi Land Council (Map p817; ☎ 08-8981 4898; www.tiwilandcouncil.net.au; Armidale St, Stuart Park, Darwin) Issues permits for the Tiwi Islands.

NATIONAL PARKS

The NT is all about its national parks; it has some of the largest and most famous natural areas in Australia. The **Parks & Wildlife Commission** (www.nt.gov.au/nreta/parks) produces fact sheets, available online or from its various offices.

Gregory (p857) Lying at the nexus between desert and tropics, this little-visited park has a network of walking trails featuring rock art. It's best accessed with a 4WD.

Kakadu (p842) Flush with well-preserved rock-art sites and diverse natural habitats, the World Heritage–listed Kakadu has a well-developed tourist infrastructure. Open year-round, much of the park is accessible to conventional vehicles.

Litchfield (p839) Magnificent rocky swimming holes, waterfalls and termite mounds can be found in this park just outside Darwin.

Nitmiluk (Katherine Gorge) (p854) Great park for walkers, but even better for canoeing trips up through the stunning sandstone gorges.

Uluru-Kata Tjuta (p885) Famous for a certain rock, the park has tours, walking trails, and helicopter and camel rides.

Watarrka (Kings Canyon) (p884) This park is centred on the humbling hugeness of Kings Canyon – one of the best short walks in the Territory.

West MacDonnell (p879) Spectacular gorge country offers excellent camping and bushwalking, including the renowned Larapinta Trail (p880).

ACTIVITIES
Bushwalking

The Territory's national parks offer well-maintained tracks of different lengths and degrees of difficulty that expose walkers to various environments and wildlife habitats. Carry plenty of water, take rubbish out with you and stick to the tracks.

Top bushwalks:

Barrk Sandstone Bushwalk, Kakadu (p848)
Jatbula Trail, Nitmiluk (Katherine Gorge) (p856)
Ormiston Pound, West MacDonnell Ranges (p880)
Trephina Gorge, East MacDonnell Ranges (p877)
Valley of the Winds, Kata Tjuta (p889)

Fishing

No permit is required to fish the Territory's waterways, though there are limits on the minimum size and number of fish per person. Travel NT produces the excellent *Fishing the Territory* booklet (free from information centres), and publishes some info online (http://en.travelnt.com). The **Amateur Fishermen's Association of the Northern Territory** (www.afant.com.au) also has online info.

The feisty barramundi lures most fisher folk to the Top End, particularly to Borroloola, Daly River and Mary River. Increasingly, the recreational-fishing fraternity encourages catch and release to maintain sustainable fish levels. Loads of tours offer transport and gear but start at $250 per person. For more information see http://en.travelnt.com or Tourism Top End (p819).

Swimming

The cool waterfalls, waterholes and rejuvenating thermal pools throughout the NT are perfect spots to soak. Litchfield National Park, in the Top End, and the West MacDonnell Ranges, in the Centre, are particularly rewarding.

Saltwater crocodiles inhabit both salt and fresh waters in the Top End, though there are quite a few safe, natural swimming holes. Before taking the plunge, be sure to read the signs and seek local advice. If in doubt, don't risk it.

Box jellyfish seasonally infest the sea around Darwin; swimming at the city's beaches is safest from May to September.

NORTHERN TERRITORY

ABORIGINAL FESTIVALS & EVENTS

Most of the festivals in the Northern Territory's cities and towns have strong Aboriginal components, plus there's a bunch of annual Aboriginal celebrations to attend. Although these festivals are usually held on restricted Aboriginal land, permit requirements are generally waived for them; this applies to most of the festivals listed below. Bear in mind that alcohol is banned in many communities.

March
Tiwi Grand Final Held at the end of March on Bathurst Island, this sporting spectacle displays the Tiwis' sparkling skills and passion for football. Thousands come from Darwin for the day, which coincides with the **Tiwi Art Sale** (www.tiwiart.com).

June
Barunga Festival (www.barungafestival.com.au) For three days over the Queen's Birthday long weekend (mid-June), Barunga, 80km east of Katherine, displays traditional arts and crafts, dancing, music, and sporting competitions. Bring your own camping equipment; alternatively, visit for the day from Katherine.

Merrepen Arts Festival (www.merrepenarts.com) The Nauiyu community, on the banks of the Daly River, is the venue for this arts festival. On the first weekend in June the Centre showcases its string bags, paintings and prints, while locals show off their sporting prowess in foot races and basketball and softball matches.

August
Stone Country Festival This is an open day and cultural festival in Gunbalanya (Oenpelli) just outside Kakadu National Park. With traditional music, dancing, arts and crafts demonstrations, it's the only day you can visit Gunbalanya without a permit. Camping is allowed but strictly no alcohol.

Walking With Spirits This two-day Indigenous cultural festival is held at Beswick Falls, about 130km from Katherine. In a magical setting, traditional dance and music is combined with theatre, films and a light show. Camping is allowed at the site (only during the festival). A 4WD is recommended for the last 20km to the falls, or a shuttle bus runs from Beswick. See www.djilpinarts.org.au for more information.

Garma Festival (www.garma.telstra.com) This four-day festival is held in August in northeastern Arnhem Land. It's one of the most significant festivals, a large-scale celebration of Yolngu culture that includes ceremonial performances, bushcraft lessons, a *yidaki* (didgeridoo) master class and an academic forum. Serious planning is required to attend, so start early.

Wildlife Watching

The best places for guaranteed wildlife sightings, from bilbies to emus, are at the excellent Territory Wildlife Park (p838) outside Darwin and the Alice Springs Desert Park (p865).

If you prefer to see wildlife in the wild, there are few guarantees; many of the region's critters are nocturnal. One exception is at Kakadu, where you'll certainly see crocodiles at Cahill's Crossing or Yellow Waters and numerous species of birds at its wealth of wetlands. In the arid Centre you'll see wallabies, reptiles and eagles. Good places to keep an eye out include the West MacDonnell Ranges and Watarrka (Kings Canyon) National Park.

SEASONAL WORK

The majority of working-holiday opportunities in the NT for backpackers are in fruit picking, station handing, labouring and hospitality.

Most work is picking mangoes and melons on plantations between Darwin and Katherine. Mango harvesting employs up to 2000 workers each season (late September to November). Station-work wannabes are generally required to have some skills (ie a trade or some experience), as with labouring and hospitality. Employers usually ask workers to commit for at least a month (sometimes three months).

TOURS

Even staunch independent travellers entrust some hard-earned time and money to a carefully selected tour. Tours can provide unmatched insights and access to the Territory, and they support local industry. See specific destination sections of this chapter for details of tours departing from those locations.

Community Project Travel

Conservation Volunteers Australia (CVA; www .conservationvolunteers.com.au) Check the website for current programs, which run year-round throughout the region. Projects are nature based and include weeding, maintenance of walking tracks and wildlife surveys. It's free to join a day trip; bring lunch and water. Multiday projects cost $40 per night and include all meals, accommodation and project-related travel.

World Expeditions (www.worldexpeditions.com) Offers a limited number of projects, such as cleaning up debris along the coast of Arnhem Land.

Indigenous Tours

Anangu Tours (p886) Tours around Uluru, guided by the traditional owners.

Kakadu Animal Tracks (p845) Enviro-focused bushtucker tour in Kakadu; profits support the local Buffalo Farm, which donates food to local communities.

Magela Cultural & Heritage Tours (p846) Aboriginal owned; runs tours into Arnhem Land and around Kakadu.

Tiwi Tours (p826) Trips with local communities to the Tiwi Islands.

Rustic & Remote

Small-group and/or off-road adventures sleeping in a tent or swag.

Venture North (p849) Trips to the remote Cobourg Peninsula.

Willis' Walkabouts (☎ 08-8985 2134; www .bushwalkingholidays.com.au) Multiday guided hikes, carrying your own gear, to Kakadu, Litchfield, Watarrka and the West MacDonnells.

GETTING THERE & AROUND

For an overview of countrywide transport, see p1050. Quarantine restrictions require travellers to surrender all fruit, vegetables, nuts and honey at the NT–Western Australia (WA) border.

Air

International flights arrive at and depart from **Darwin International Airport** (DIA; ☎ 08-8920 1805; www.darwinairport.com.au). Airlines operating flights to their countries of origin and beyond:

Airnorth (www.airnorth.com.au) To/from East Timor and Denpasar.

Qantas (www.qantas.com.au) To/from Asia and Europe.

The following domestic carriers have regular connections to other Australian states.

Airnorth (☎ 1800 627 474; www.airnorth.com.au) From Darwin to Broome and Kununurra.

Jetstar (☎ 13 15 38; www.jetstar.com.au) Services most major Australian cities.

Qantas (☎ 13 13 13; www.qantas.com) Services all major Australian cities.

Virgin Blue (☎ 13 67 89; www.virginblue.com) Direct flights only from Darwin to Brisbane.

For flights between NT centres, see the Darwin (p833), Alice Springs (p875) and Uluru (p892) sections.

Bus

Greyhound Australia (☎ 1300 473 946; www.greyhound .com.au) regularly services the main road routes throughout the Territory, including side trips to Kakadu and Uluru; see Getting There & Away in the relevant destination sections for details.

An alternative is tour-bus companies such as AAT Kings, and backpacker buses that cover vast distances while savouring the sights along the way (see p1069 for more on the latter).

Car

Having your own vehicle in the NT means you can travel at your own pace and branch off the main roads to access less-visited places. To truly explore, you'll need a well-prepared 4WD vehicle and some outback nous. The **Automobile Association of the Northern Territory** (AANT; Map pp820-1; ☎ 08-8981 3837, emergency breakdown service 13 11 11; www.aant.com.au; 79-81 Smith St, Darwin; ◷ 9am-5pm Mon-Fri) can advise on preparation and additional resources; members of automobile associations in other states have reciprocal rights.

Many roads are open to conventional cars and campervans, which can be hired in Darwin and Alice Springs and can work out to be quite economical when split by a group.

Some driving conditions are particular to the NT. While traffic may be light and roads dead straight, distances between places are long. Watch out for the four great NT road hazards: speed (maximum speed on the open highway is now 130km/h), driver fatigue, road trains and animals (driving at night is particularly dangerous).

Roads are regularly closed during the Wet due to flooding.

Train

A trip on the famous **Ghan** (☎ 13 21 47; www.gsr .com.au) is one of the world's great rail adventures. You cross the country from Adelaide to Darwin, stopping at Alice Springs and Katherine. Alice to Darwin seat/sleeper/first class costs $358/656/1019. See the table below for details of services.

The *Ghan* is met in Adelaide by the *Indian Pacific*, which travels to/from Sydney; and the *Overland*, which travels to/from Melbourne.

See p869 for the story of the jinxed *Ghan*.

The Ghan Timetable

depart Alice Springs	6pm Mon	6pm Thu
arrive Katherine	9am Tue	9am Fri
depart Katherine	1pm Tue	2pm Fri
arrive Darwin	5.30pm Tue	6.30pm Fri
depart Darwin	10am Wed	9am Sat
arrive Katherine	1.40pm Wed	12.40pm Sat
depart Katherine	6.20pm Wed	4.45pm Sat
arrive Alice Springs	9.10am Thu	11.15am Sun

DARWIN

pop 73,800

Australia's only tropical capital, Darwin gazes out confidently across the Timor Sea. It's closer to Bali than Bondi, and many from the southern states still see it as some strange frontier outpost or jumping-off point for Kakadu National Park.

But Darwin is a surprisingly affluent, cosmopolitan, youthful and vibrant city, thanks in part to an economic boom fuelled by the mining industry and tourism. It's a city on the move but there's a small-town feel and a laconic, relaxed vibe that fits easily with the tropical climate. Here non-Aboriginal meets Aboriginal (Larrakia), urban meets remote, and industry meets idleness.

Darwin has plenty to offer the traveller. Boats sail around the harbour, chairs and tables spill out of streetside restaurants and bars, museums reveal the city's absorbing past, and galleries showcase the region's rich Indigenous art. Darwin's cosmopolitan mix – more than 50 nationalities are seamlessly represented here – is typified by the wonderful Asian markets held throughout the dry season.

Nature is well and truly part of Darwin's backyard – the famous national parks of Kakadu and Litchfield are only a few hours' drive away and the unique Tiwi Islands a boat-ride away. For locals the perfect weekend is going fishing for barra in a tinny with an esky full of beer.

HISTORY

The Larrakia Aboriginal people lived for thousands of years in Darwin, hunting, fishing and foraging. In 1869 a permanent white settlement was established and the grid for a new town laid out. Originally called Palmerston, and renamed Darwin in 1911, the new town developed rapidly, transforming the physical and social landscape.

The discovery of gold at nearby Pine Creek brought an influx of Chinese, who soon settled into other industries. Asians and Islanders came to work in the pearling industry and on the railway line and wharf. More recently, neighbouring East Timorese and Papuans have sought asylum in Darwin.

During WWII, Darwin was the frontline for the Allied action against the Japanese in the Pacific. It was the only Australian city ever bombed, and official reports of the time downplayed the damage – to buoy Australians' morale. Though the city wasn't destroyed by the 64 attacks, the impact of full-scale military occupation on Darwin was enormous.

More physically damaging was Cyclone Tracy, which hit Darwin at around midnight on Christmas Eve 1974. By Christmas morning, Darwin effectively ceased to exist as a city, with only 400 of its 11,200 homes left standing and 71 people killed. The town was rebuilt to a new, stringent building code and in the past decade has steadily expanded outwards and upwards, with the latest project the multimillion-dollar waterfront development at Darwin Harbour.

ORIENTATION

Darwin sits at the end of a peninsula poking into the turquoise waters of Port Darwin. The main shopping, accommodation and wining and dining area is a remarkably compact grid along the parallel Mitchell, Smith and Cavenagh Sts, including the pedestrianised Smith St Mall, and the intersecting Knuckey St.

Long-distance buses pull in to the Transit Centre off Mitchell St in the city centre. Most places of interest to travellers in central Darwin are within two or three blocks of the Transit

DARWIN

0 ————— 2 km
0 ————— 1 mile

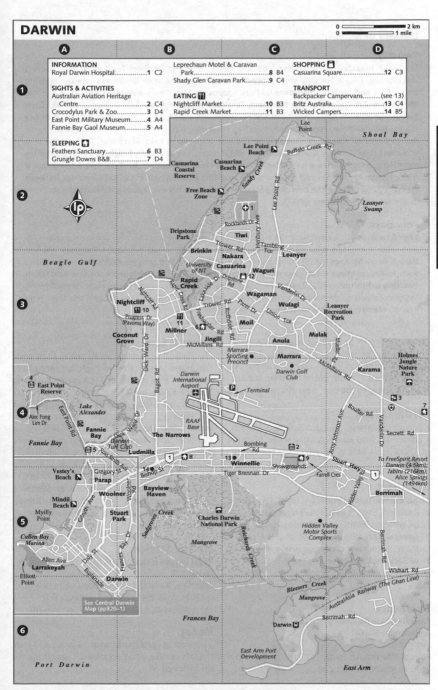

INFORMATION
Royal Darwin Hospital...............1 C2

SIGHTS & ACTIVITIES
Australian Aviation Heritage
   Centre..................................2 C4
Crocodylus Park & Zoo............3 D4
East Point Military Museum.......4 A4
Fannie Bay Gaol Museum..........5 A4

SLEEPING
Feathers Sanctuary..................6 B3
Grungle Downs B&B.................7 D4

Leprechaun Motel & Caravan
   Park...................................8 B4
Shady Glen Caravan Park..........9 C4

EATING
Nightcliff Market....................10 B3
Rapid Creek Market................11 B3

SHOPPING
Casuarina Square.....................12 C3

TRANSPORT
Backpacker Campervans..........(see 13)
Britz Australia.........................13 C4
Wicked Campers......................14 B5

NORTHERN TERRITORY

NORTHERN TERRITORY

DARWIN IN...

Two days
Start with breakfast at **Roma Bar** (p831), lingering over the *Northern Territory News* or surfing the internet. Take a leisurely stroll around some of the downtown landmarks (see our walking tour, p825) and through **Bicentennial Park** (opposite). Don't miss a couple of hours at the free **Museum & Art Gallery of the Northern Territory** (p822), followed by a beer at the **Ski Club** (p831) opposite. At lunchtime, head out to Stokes Hill Wharf for a casual feed, or to Cullen Bay marina for something more upmarket. In the afternoon, hire a bike and ride up through Fannie Bay to **East Point Reserve**, stopping on the way for a dip in Lake Alexander. Try to make it to a **market** (see Darwin's Magical Markets, p833), especially at Mindil Beach or Parap's Saturday morning market, which are packed with flavour-packed food outlets, buskers, take-home tropical fruits, handmade clothes and souvenirs. On your first evening, you could take a sunset **harbour cruise** (p826), then hit the bars along Mitchell St. On another eve, catch a movie under the stars at the **Deckchair Cinema** (p832).

Four days
With four days you can tick off the must-dos at a pace more in sync with Darwin's. Explore (or find some shade and relax in) the **Botanic Gardens** (p823). Head out to the **Territory Wildlife Park & Berry Springs** (p838). Jump on the **Tour Tub** (p826) and take your pick of the attractions, such as **Crocosaurus Cove** (opposite), the **Indo-Pacific Marine Exhibition** and the **Australian Pearling Exhibition** (p822). Feed the fish at **Aquascene** (opposite) and spend some time admiring Indigenous and contemporary art in the city's **art galleries** (p823). Finally, catch the short ferry over to **Mandorah** (p835) for a beer or dinner at the pub.

Centre or Smith St Mall, or a short distance north in the 'suburbs' of Cullen Bay, Fannie Bay, East Point and Parap. Darwin's airport is 12km northeast of the centre; the train station is about 15km to the east, near Berrimah.

INFORMATION
Aboriginal Darwin, by Toni Bauman, is both a guidebook and an alternative social history of Darwin; it makes an excellent travelling companion.

Bookshops
Angus & Robertson (Map pp820-1; ☎ 08-8941 3489; 18 The Galleria, Smith St Mall) Stocks a broad range of fiction, nonfiction, Australiana and travel books.
NT General Store (Map pp820-1; ☎ 08-8981 8242; 42 Cavenagh St) Good range of maps and travel guides.
Read Back Book Exchange (Map pp820-1; ☎ 08-8981 0099; 32 Smith St Mall) Secondhand books, CDs and videos.

Emergency
AANT Roadside Assistance (☎ 13 11 11)
Ambulance (☎ 000)
Fire (☎ 000)
Poisons Information Centre (☎ 13 11 26; ☾ 24hr) Advice on poisons, bites and stings.

Internet Access
Hotels and hostels generally have their own computer terminals and there are numerous internet cafes in the CBD charging between $2 and $5 an hour. A number of cafes and restaurants offer free wi-fi, including Roma Bar (p831).
Global Gossip (Map pp820-1; ☎ 08-8942 3044; 44 Mitchell St; ☾ 9am-midnight Mon-Sat, to 11pm Sun) Darwin's busiest internet cafe, with space for laptops and full phone and scanning services.
Northern Territory Library (Map pp820-1; ☎ 1800 019 155; www.ntl.nt.gov.au; Parliament House, Mitchell St; ☾ 10am-6pm Mon-Fri, 1-5pm Sat & Sun) You'll need to book in advance for a terminal, but access is free and wi-fi available.

Medical Services
Royal Darwin Hospital (Map p817; ☎ 08-8920 6011; Rocklands Dr, Tiwi)
Travellers Medical & Vaccination Centre (Map pp820-1; ☎ 08-8981 7492; 1st fl, 43 Cavenagh St; ☾ appointments 8.30am-noon & 1.30-5pm Mon-Fri)

Money
There are several banks with 24-hour ATMs in the city centre, and private exchange bureaux on Mitchell St.

Post
Main post office (Map pp820-1; ☎ 13 13 18; 48 Cavenagh St; ☼ 9am-5pm Mon-Fri, to 12.30pm Sat) Efficient poste restante.

Tourist Information
Tourism Top End (Map pp820-1; ☎ 08-8980 6000; www.tourismtopend.com.au; 6 Bennett St; ☼ 8.30am-5.30pm Mon-Fri, 9am-3pm Sat, 10am-3pm Sun) Stocks hundreds of brochures and can book tours or accommodation for businesses within its association.

Travel Agencies
To book or confirm flights, bus and train travel, there's no shortage of agents in Darwin.

Backpackers World Travel (Map pp820-1; ☎ 08-8941 5100; www.backpackersworld.com.au; Shop 9, 21 Knuckey St; ☼ 9am-6pm)

Flight Centre (Map pp820-1; ☎ 08-8941 8002; www.flightcentre.com.au; 24 Cavenagh St; ☼ 9am-5pm Mon-Fri, to 1pm Sat)

Qantas Travel (Map pp820-1; ☎ 13 13 13; 16 Bennett St; ☼ 9am-5pm Mon-Fri, to 1pm Sat)

DANGERS & ANNOYANCES
Potentially deadly box jellyfish inhabit shallow coastal waters during the Wet (between October and May). In Darwin, though, the stinger season tends to be longer, making swimming risky year-round. If stung, douse the wound with vinegar and get thee to a doctor.

SIGHTS
The Esplanade
Bicentennial Park (Map pp820–1) runs the length of Darwin's waterfront and Lameroo Beach – a sheltered cove popular in the '20s when it housed the saltwater baths, and traditionally a Larrakia camp area. Shaded by tropical trees, the park is an excellent place to stroll. At the Herbert St end, there's a **cenotaph** commemorating Australians' service to the country's war efforts. Also honoured are **200 Remarkable Territorians**: hand-painted tiles in panels dispersed intermittently along the Esplanade commemorate some of the Territory's 'quiet achievers', including pioneers, publicans and pastoralists.

At Doctors Gully there's a remarkable fish-feeding frenzy daily at **Aquascene** (Map pp820-1; ☎ 08-8981 7837; www.aquascene.com.au; 28 Doctors Gully Rd; adult/child/family $8/5/20; ☼ high tide, check website). Visitors, young and old, wade into the water and hand-feed hordes of mullet, catfish, batfish and big milkfish.

At the end of Mitchell St is the boxlike **Parliament House** (Map pp820-1; ☎ tours 08-8946 1434; ☼ 8am-6pm, tours 9am & 11am Sat), reminiscent of Southeast Asian architecture, that is designed to withstand Darwin's monsoonal climate. Book a free 45-minute tour exploring the cavernous interior. The building also houses the Northern Territory Library (opposite).

Crocosaurus Cove
If the tourists won't go out to see the crocs, then bring the crocs to the tourists. Right in the middle of Mitchell St, **Crocosaurus Cove** (Map pp820-1; ☎ 08-8981 7522; www.crocosauruscove.com; 58 Mitchell St; adult/child $28/16; ☼ 8am-8pm, last admission 6pm) is as up close and personal as you'll ever want to get to these amazing creatures. Six of the largest crocs in captivity can be seen in state-of-the-art aquariums and pools. You can be lowered right into a pool with Snowy, a 600kg 'albino' saltie, in the transparent 'Cage of Death' (one/two people $120/160). If that's too scary, there's another pool where you can swim with a clear tank wall separating you from another big croc. Other aquariums feature barramundi, turtles and stingrays, plus there's an enormous reptile house.

Wharf Precinct
Bold development of the Darwin Harbour is well underway. The first stage of the billion-dollar Darwin City Waterfront development features a new cruise-ship terminal, luxury hotels, boutique restaurants and shopping, and a wave pool. The old **Stokes Hill Wharf** is well worth an afternoon promenade. It's a short stroll down from the Survivors' Lookout at the end of Smith St, past the WWII Oil-Storage Tunnels and the Indo-Pacific Marine Exhibition.

At the end of the jetty an old warehouse houses a food centre that's ideal for an alfresco lunch, cool afternoon beer or a seafood dinner as the sun sets over the harbour. Several harbour cruises and a jet boat also leave from the wharf.

You can escape from the heat of the day and relive your Hitchcockian fantasies by walking through the **WWII oil-storage tunnels** (Map pp820-1; ☎ 08-8985 6333; adult/child $5/3; ☼ 9am-4pm May-Sep, to 1pm Tue-Sun Oct, Nov, Jan, Mar & Apr). Built to store the Navy's oil supplies (but never used), they exhibit wartime photos.

NORTHERN TERRITORY

NORTHERN TERRITORY

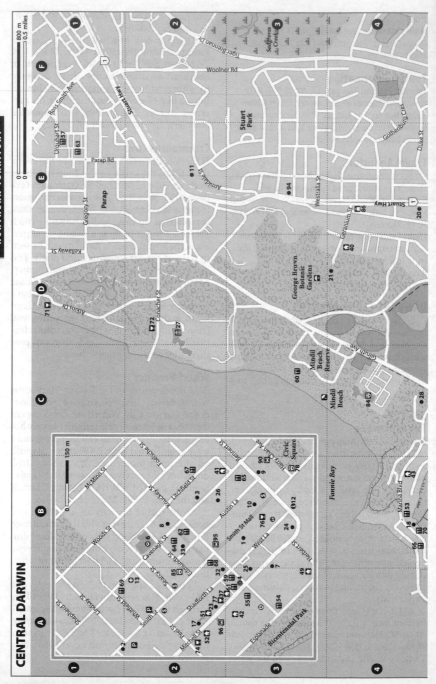

CENTRAL DARWIN

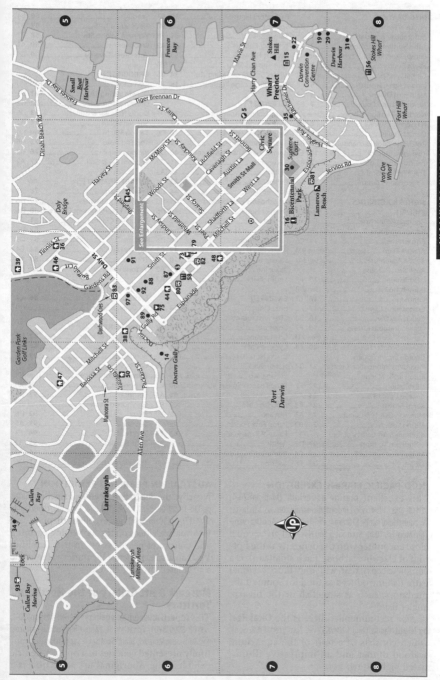

INDO-PACIFIC MARINE EXHIBITION

This excellent **marine aquarium** (Map pp820-1; ☎ 08-8981 1294; www.indopacificmarine.com.au; Kitchener Dr; adult/child/family $18/8/44; ⏲ 10am-5pm Apr-Oct, 9am-1pm Mon-Fri, 10am-5pm Sat & Sun Nov-Mar) gives you a close encounter with the denizens at the bottom of Darwin Harbour. Each small tank is a complete ecosystem, with only the occasional extra fish introduced as food for some of the predators, such as stonefish or the bizarre angler fish.

Also recommended here is the **Coral Reef by Night** (adult/child $104/55; ⏲ 7pm Wed, Fri & Sun), which consists of a tour of the aquarium, seafood dinner and an impressive illuminated night show.

AUSTRALIAN PEARLING EXHIBITION

Nearby, the **Australian Pearling Exhibition** (Map pp820-1; ☎ 08-8981 1294; Kitchener Dr; adult/child/family $7/4/17; ⏲ 10am-5pm) has excellent displays and informative videos on the harvesting, farming and culture of pearl oysters in the Top End. You can also experience life underwater inside a simulated diving helmet.

Museum & Art Gallery of the Northern Territory

This superb **museum and gallery** (MAGNT; Map pp820-1; ☎ 08-8999 8201; Conacher St, Fannie Bay; admission free; ⏲ 9am-5pm Mon-Fri, 10am-5pm Sat & Sun) boasts beautifully presented galleries of Top End–centric exhibits. The Aboriginal art collection is a

NORTHERN TERRITORY

highlight, with carvings from the Tiwi Islands, bark paintings from Arnhem Land and dot paintings from the desert.

An entire room is devoted to Cyclone Tracy, in a display that graphically illustrates life before and after the disaster. You can stand in a darkened room and listen to the whirring sound of Tracy at full throttle – a sound you won't forget in a hurry. The cavernous **Maritime Gallery** houses an assortment of weird and wonderful craft from the nearby islands and Indonesia, as well as a pearling lugger and a Vietnamese refugee boat.

Pride of place among the stuffed animals undoubtedly goes to 'Sweetheart': a 5m-long, 780kg saltwater crocodile. It became a Top End personality after attacking several fishing dinghies on the Finniss River south of Darwin.

The museum has a good bookshop and the Cornucopia Cafe is a great lunch spot.

Galleries

Darwin's commercial and public galleries are a fabulous (and free) way to appreciate the spirit of the Top End, both non-Aboriginal and Aboriginal.

24HR Art (Map pp820-1; ☎ 08-8981 5368; www.24hrart.org.au; Vimy Lane, Parap Shopping Village; 🕑 10am-4pm Wed-Fri, to 2pm Sat) Changing exhibitions by the Northern Territory Centre for Contemporary Art.

Aboriginal Fine Arts (Map pp820-1; ☎ 08-8981 1315; www.aaia.com.au; 1st fl, cnr Mitchell & Knuckey Sts; 🕑 9am-5pm) Displays and sells art from Arnhem Land and the Central Desert region, including the work of high-profile artists such as 'Lofty' Bardayal Nadjamerrek.

Karen Brown Gallery (Map pp820-1; ☎ 08-8981 9985; www.karenbrowngallery.com; 1/22 Mitchell St; 🕑 9am-5pm Mon-Fri, to 3pm Sat) Commercial gallery specialising in changing exhibitions of contemporary Aboriginal art.

Maningrida Arts & Culture (Map pp820-1; ☎ 08-8981 4122; www.maningrida.com; Shop 1, 32 Mitchell St; 🕑 9am-5pm Mon-Sat, to 3pm Sun) Features didgeridoos, weavings and paintings from the Kunibidji community at Maningrida on the banks of the Liverpool River, Arnhem Land.

Mason Gallery (Map pp820-1; ☎ 08-8981 9622; www.masongallery.com.au; Shop 7, 21 Cavenagh St; 🕑 9am-5pm Mon-Fri, 10am-3pm Sat & Sun) Features bold dot paintings from the Western and Central Desert regions.

Territory Colours (Map pp820-1; ☎ 08-8981 1803; www.territorycolours.com; 21 Knuckey St; 🕑 9am-5.30pm) Contemporary paintings and crafts, including glass, porcelain and wood from local artists; features the work of contemporary Indigenous artist Harold Thomas.

Tiwi Art Network (Map pp820-1; ☎ 08-8941 3593; www.tiwiart.com; 3/3 Vickers St, Parap; 🕑 10am-5pm Wed-Fri, to 2pm Sat) The office and showroom for three arts communities on the Tiwi Islands.

George Brown Botanic Gardens

The 42-hectare **Botanic Gardens** (Map pp820-1; ☎ 08-8981 1958; admission free; 🕑 7am-7pm) showcases plants from the Top End and around the world – monsoon vine forest, the mangroves and coastal plants habitat, baobabs and a magnificent collection of native and exotic palms and cycads.

Many of the plants here were traditionally used by the local Aboriginal people, and self-guiding Aboriginal Plant Use trails have been set up – pick up a brochure at the gardens' **Information Centre** (🕑 8am-4pm Mon-Fri, from 8.30am Sat & Sun) near the Geranium St entry.

It's an easy 2km bicycle ride out to the gardens from the centre of town along Gilruth Ave and Gardens Rd, or there's another entrance off Geranium St, which runs off the Stuart Hwy in Stuart Park.

East Point Reserve

North of Fannie Bay, this spit of land is particularly good in the late afternoon when wallabies emerge to feed and you can watch the sun set over the bay. On the northern side there are some wartime gun emplacements and the military museum.

Lake Alexander, a small, recreational saltwater lake, was created so people could enjoy a swim year-round without having to worry about box jellyfish. There's a good children's playground and picnic areas with barbecues. A 1.5km **mangrove boardwalk** (☼ 8am-6pm) leads off from the car park.

On the point's northern side is a series of WWII gun emplacements and the small **East Point Military Museum** (Map p817; ☎ 08-8981 9702; adult/child/family $10/5/28; ☼ 9.30am-5pm). Video footage of Darwin Harbour being bombed is a sobering reminder of Australia's only wartime attack.

Fannie Bay Gaol Museum
This interesting **museum** (Map p817; ☎ 08-8999 8920; cnr East Point Rd & Ross Smith Ave; admission free; ☼ 10am-4.30pm) represents almost 100 years of solitude. Serving as Darwin's main jail from 1883 to 1979, the solid cells contain information panels that provide a window into the region's unique social history. Lepers, refugees and juveniles were among the groups of people confined here, and you can still see the old cells and the gallows constructed for two hangings in 1952.

Myilly Point Historic Precinct
At the far northern end of Smith St is this small but important precinct of four houses built in the 1930s and now on the Register of the National Estate. One of them, **Burnett House** (Map pp820-1; ☎ 08-8981 2848; admission by donation; ☼ 10am-1pm Mon-Sat), operates as a museum. There's a tantalisingly colonial high tea ($7.50) in the gardens on Sunday afternoon from 3.30pm to 6pm.

Crocodylus Park & Zoo
Crocodylus Park & Zoo (Map p817; ☎ 08-8947 2510; www.crocodyluspark.com; McMillans Rd, Berrimah; adult/child/family $28/14/70; ☼ 9am-5pm, tours 10am, noon, 2pm & 3.30pm) showcases hundreds of crocs and a minizoo comprising lions, tigers, a Persian leopard and other big cats, spider monkeys, marmosets, cassowaries and large birds. Allow about two hours to look around the whole park, and you should time your visit with a tour, which includes a feeding demonstration.

The park is about 15km from the city centre. Take bus 5 or 9 from Darwin.

Australian Aviation Heritage Centre
Darwin's **aviation museum** (Map p817; ☎ 08-8947 2145; www.darwinsairwar.com.au; 557 Stuart Hwy, Winnellie; adult/child/family $12/7/30; ☼ 9am-5pm), about 10km from the centre, is one for military aircraft nuts. The centrepiece is a mammoth B52 bomber, one of only a few of its kind displayed outside the USA, which has somehow been squeezed inside. It dwarfs the other aircraft, which include a Japanese Zero fighter shot down in 1942 and the remains of an RAAF Mirage jet that crashed in a nearby swamp. Free guided tours commence at 10am and 2pm.

Buses 5 and 8 run along the Stuart Hwy, and it's on the route of the Tour Tub (p826).

ACTIVITIES
Beaches & Swimming
Darwin is no beach paradise – naturally enough the harbour has no surf – but along the convoluted coastline north of the city centre is a string of sandy beaches. The most popular are **Mindil** and **Vestey's** on Fannie Bay. Further north, a stretch of the 7km **Casuarina Beach** is an official nude beach. Darwin's swimming beaches tend to be far enough away from mangrove creeks to make the threat of meeting a crocodile very remote. A bigger problem is the deadly box jellyfish, which makes swimming decidedly unhealthy between October and May. You can swim year-round without fear of stingers in the western part of **Lake Alexander**, an easy cycle from the centre at East Point.

Cycling
Darwin is great for cycling. Traffic is light and a series of bike tracks covers most of the city, with the main one running from the northern end of Cavenagh St to Fannie Bay, Coconut Grove, Nightcliff and Casuarina. At Fannie Bay, a side track heads out to the East Point Reserve. Consider heading for Charles Darwin National Park, 5km southeast of the city, with a few kilometres of path around the park's wetlands, woodlands and WWII bunkers. Most hostels hire out bicycles for $12 to $20 per day for a mountain bike, or try **Darwin Scooter Hire** (Map pp820-1; ☎ 08-8941 2434; 29 Stuart Hwy), which has mountain bikes for $20 a day ($100 deposit required).

Diving
The Japanese bombs of WWII and Cyclone Tracy have contributed an array of wrecks to

the floor of Darwin Harbour. On the downside Darwin experiences massive tides, which churn the sea floor and restrict diving times, so you will need to plan ahead to catch the best conditions (only during neap tides).

Cullen Bay Dive (Map pp820–1; ☎ 08-8981 3049; www .divedarwin.com; 66 Marina Blvd, Cullen Bay Marina) conducts Professional Association of Diving Instructors (PADI)–affiliated instruction courses and wreck dives throughout the year.

Jet Boating

If a harbour cruise (see p826) is too tame, jump on **Oz Jet** (Map pp820–1; ☎ 1300 13 55 95; www .ozjetboating.com.au; adult/child $60/40) for a thrilling ride around the harbour. Departs from Stokes Hill Wharf.

Sailing

The **Darwin Sailing Club** (Map pp820–1; ☎ 08-8981 1700; www.dwnsail.com.au; Atkins Dr, Fannie Bay) is a good place to meet local yachties, as well as an excellent place to watch the sunset over a beer. Although you can't charter boats here, there is a noticeboard advertising crewing needs and detailing the seasonal race program.

The **Winter School of Sailing** (Map pp820–1; ☎ 08-8981 9368, 0417 818 257; www.darwinsailingschool.com.au; 3hr sailing session $60, overnight cruise from $120, courses from $230) sails the harbour in *Zanzibar*, an 11.6m sloop berthed at Cullen Bay Marina. Regular crewing sessions are held on Wednesday afternoon. Check the website for a timetable of training courses.

Skydiving

Top End Tandems (☎ 0417 190 140; www.topendtandems .com.au; tandem jumps from $310) has tandem skydives starting at Darwin Airport and landing at Lee Point Reserve.

WALKING TOUR

A short walkabout in Darwin's centre will reveal some of the remarkable events and social groups that shape this creative, cosmopolitan city.

Begin at **St Mary's Cathedral (1)**, at the corner of Smith and McLachlan Sts, to see the larger-than-life-sized *Aboriginal Madonna*. Painted by visiting French artist Karel Kupka in the '60s, it depicts Mary and Child as Aboriginal, with a background of totemic abstract designs.

Head southeast along Smith St to the pedestrian **Smith Street Mall (2)**, shaded by banyan

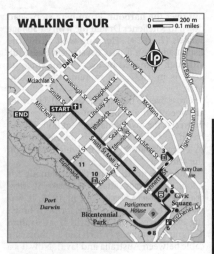

WALKING TOUR

| 0 | 200 m |
| 0 | 0.1 miles |

WALK FACTS

Start St Mary's Cathedral
Finish The Esplanade
Distance 3km to 3.5km
Duration one to 1½ hours

trees and decorated with tiles painted by Tiwi Islanders. Also on the concrete seating is a small tiled mural by Prince of Wales Midpul (1935–2002). Prince's highly regarded paintings interpreted ceremonial body marks. Prince was the son of King George Imabul and grandson of King Miranda – named by the early settlers in recognition of the men's status as Larrakia leaders.

This is a nice segue to the **Chinese Museum & Chung Wah Temple (3**; ☎ 08-8941 0898; Woods St; admission by donation; 🕙 10am-2pm Wed-Mon Apr-Oct), which explores Chinese settlement in the Top End. The sacred tree in the grounds is rumoured to be a direct descendant from the Bodhi tree under which Buddha sat when he attained enlightenment.

Back on Smith St, you'll pass the Civic Square gardens and the former mining exchange **Brown's Mart (4; p832)**, now restored and popular as a theatre venue. Detour through the gardens to the **Tree of Knowledge (5)**, one of the largest banyan figs in Darwin and a significant historical meeting place. Southwest across the Esplanade, perched on the edge of the escarpment, is the **Survivors' Lookout (6)**, with WWII photos and views

NORTHERN TERRITORY

out over the harbour. From here steps lead down to Kitchener Dr and the **WWII Oil-Storage Tunnels (7**; p819). Heading west along the Esplanade, you'll pass **Government House (8)**; although damaged by every event since its genesis in 1877, it's in remarkably good nick.

Cross over to the **Supreme Court (9)**. Hearings are open to the public, but of more general interest is the foyer's magnificent floor mural, based on the *Milky Way Dreaming* painting by Nora Napaltjari Nelson, which hangs on the 4th floor.

Continue north along the Esplanade for a look in at **Lyons Cottage (10**; Knuckey St; admission free; ☉ 10am-4.40pm). Built in 1925, it was Darwin's first stone residence, formerly housing executives from the British Australian Telegraph Company (which laid a submarine cable between Australia and Java). Now it's a museum displaying Darwin in photos from the early days.

Continue along the **Esplanade (11**; p819), with its bevy of sights, or head east along Knuckey St back to the centre of the city.

TOURS

There are dozens of tours in and around Darwin, and lots of combinations covering Kakadu, Arnhem Land, Litchfield and further afield. Tourism Top End (p819) is the best place to start looking and asking questions. Remember that many tours run less frequently (or not at all) in the wet season.

Around Darwin

Darwin Day Tours (☎ 1300 721 365; www.aussieadventure.com.au; afternoon city tour adult/child $59/30) Runs an afternoon city tour at 2pm that takes in all the major attractions, including Stokes Hill Wharf, the Museum & Art Gallery and East Point Reserve, and can be linked with a sunset harbour cruise ($99/48).

Darwin Walking & Bicycle Tours (☎ 08-8942 1022; www.darwinwalkingtours.com.au) Two-/three-hour guided walks of local attractions for $25/35 (children free) and three-hour bike tours ($40) that take you out to Fannie Bay and East Point.

Double Decker Tours (☎ 0416 140 903; www .doubledeckertours.com.au; night tour $50; ☉ 5-10pm Sat) Evening pub crawl on an open double-decker bus with food and a drink at each venue. One for the backpackers.

Tour Tub (Map pp820-1; ☎ 08-8985 6322; www.tourtub.com.au; adult/child $30/20; ☉ 9am-4pm Jan-Nov) This open-sided hop-on, hop-off minibus tours around the various Darwin sights throughout the day.

Harbour Cruises

Between April and October there are plenty of boats based at the Cullen Bay Marina and Stokes Hill Wharf to take you on a cruise of the harbour.

Anniki (☎ 08-8941 4000; www.australianharbourcruises.com.au; adult/child $70/50) Three-hour sunset cruises on this historical pearling lugger depart at 4.45pm from Cullen Bay and include sparkling wine and nibbles. You might recognise the ship from the film *Australia*.

Darwin Harbour Cruises (Map pp820-1; ☎ 08-8942 3131; www.darwinharbourcruises.com.au; Stokes Hill Wharf) Variety of cruises from Stokes Hill Wharf. The 20m schooner *Tumlaren* does a three-hour barbecue lunch cruise at noon (adult/child $75/46), and a sunset cruise departing at 5pm ($66/43). The 30m schooner *Alfred Noble* has a full-dinner cruise departing at 5.45pm ($105/65).

Spirit of Darwin (Map pp820-1; ☎ 08-8981 3711; www.spiritofdarwin.net; Cullen Bay; adult/child $40/18) Fully licensed air-con motor-catamaran does a two-hour sightseeing cruise at 1.40pm and a sunset cruise at 5.30pm daily from Cullen Bay.

Sunset Sail (Map pp820-1; ☎ 0408 795 567; www .sailnt.com.au; Stokes Hill Wharf; adult/child $60/45) This three-hour afternoon cruise aboard the catamaran *Daymirri* departs from Stokes Hill Wharf. Refreshments are included but BYO alcohol.

Territory Trips

Adventure Tours (Map pp820-1; ☎ 08-8132 8230; www.adventuretours.com.au; shop 2, 52 Mitchell St) Range of 4WD tours to suit the adventurous backpacker crowd. Two-/three-day Kakadu tours $325/480; also longer tours.

Aussie Adventure (Map pp820-1; ☎ 1300 721 365; www.aussieadventure.com.au; shop 6, 52 Mitchell St) Trips include half-day Territory Wildlife Park (adult/child $66/33), jumping croc cruise ($92/46), Kakadu ($179/90) and Litchfield ($117/59).

Kakadu Dreams (Map pp820-1; ☎ 1800 813 266; www.kakadudreams.com.au; 50 Mitchell St) Backpacker day tours to Litchfield ($80), and two-/three-/five-day trips to Kakadu ($350/460/680).

Sacred Earth Safaris (☎ 08-8981 8420; www .sacredearthsafaris.com.au) Multiday small group camping tours to Kakadu, Arnhem Land and the Kimberley. Two-day 4WD Kakadu tour starts at $645; the five-day Top End tour is $1850.

Wallaroo Eco Tours (☎ 08-8983 2699; www.litchfielddaytours.com) Small-group tours to Litchfield National Park ($120).

Wilderness 4WD Adventures (☎ 1800 808 288, 08-8941 2161; www.wildernessadventures.com.au; 2/3 days $370/485) Small-group 4WD camping tours into Kakadu and further afield, visiting some out-of-the-way spots; all meals included.

FESTIVALS & EVENTS

May

WordStorm (www.ntwriters.com.au) The annual NT Writers' Festival event, in May, includes song, storytelling, visual-art collaboration, theatre, performance poetry, history, biography, poetry and fiction.

July

Beer Can Regatta (www.beercanregatta.org.au) An utterly insane and typically Territorian festival that features races for boats made out of beer cans. It takes places at Mindil Beach and is a good fun day.

Royal Darwin Show (www.darwinshow.com.au) This agricultural show takes place at the showgrounds in Winnellie on the last weekend of the month. Activities include all the usual rides, as well as demonstrations and competitions.

Darwin Cup Carnival (www.darwinturfclub.org.au) The Darwin Cup racing carnival takes place in July and August at the Darwin Turf Club in Fannie Bay. The highlight of the eight-day program is the running of the Darwin Cup, along with all the fashions and social outings.

August

Darwin Aboriginal Art Fair (www.darwinaborigi nalartfair.com.au) Held at the convention centre, this two-day festival showcases Indigenous art from communities throughout the Territory.

Darwin Festival (www.darwinfestival.org.au) This mainly outdoor arts and culture festival reflects the city's large Aboriginal and Asian populations and runs for about two weeks.

Darwin Fringe Festival (www.darwinfringe.com.au) Showcases eclectic, local performing and visual arts at venues including Brown's Mart Theatre (p832).

SLEEPING

Darwin has a good range of accommodation, most of it handy to the CBD, but finding a bed in the peak May to September period can be difficult at short notice – book ahead, at least for the first night. Accommodation prices vary greatly with the season and de-mand. Prices given here are for high season, but expect big discounts between November and March, especially for midrange and top-end accommodation.

Backpacker hostels fluctuate the least, and prices differ little between places – concen-trated as they are in a small stretch of bar-heavy Mitchell St. They also offer the best value for cheap longer-term accommodation.

Hotels quote inflated rack rates but there are all sorts of specials, including stand-by and internet rates.

Budget

Darwin has about a dozen centrally located backpacker hostels, including a few party places on Mitchell St. If you want a quieter stay, choose one a bit further out – they're still within walking distance of the action. Hostel facilities usually include communal kitchen, pool and laundry facilities and they all have tour-booking desks. Some offer airport, bus or train station pick-ups with advance bookings, and most give YHA/VIP discounts.

Frogshollow Backpackers (Map pp820-1; ☎ 1800 068 686; www.frogs-hollow.com.au; 27 Lindsay St; dm $24-30, d with/without bathroom $100/75; ✴ ☐ ☂) Set in a lush garden opposite parkland, Frogshollow is an easy walk to the city centre but far enough away to have a relaxed atmosphere. The swim-ming pool and spa in the garden and a pool table in the common area give it a sociable feel. The facilities, including kitchen and laun-dry, are good. Dorms can be a bit cramped.

Banyan View Lodge (Map pp820-1; ☎ 08-8981 8644; www .banyanviewlodge.com.au; 119 Mitchell St; dm $25, s/d without bathroom $60/70, d $120; ✴ ☂) The Banyan View suits travellers not into the party scene. It's a big YWCA that welcomes men and has no curfew. Spacious rooms are clean and well kept.

Gecko Lodge (Map pp820-1; ☎ 1800 811 250; www.gecko lodge.com.au; 146 Mitchell St; dm $25-29, tw & d without bathroom $75-92; ✴ ☐ ☂) Want to stay away from the Mitchell St madness? In a pair of well-worn elevated houses halfway to Mindil Beach, this small, personable hostel offers a relaxing stay and a place to park a campervan, and attracts a few long-termers and savvy backpackers. Bike hire and a free pancake breakfast.

Cavenagh (Map pp820-1; ☎ 1300 851 198, 08-8941 6383; www.thecavenagh.com; 12 Cavenagh St; dm $25-30, motel d $160; ✴ ☐ ☂) The Cav is as much motel as hostel – the four- to 12-bed dorms are in converted motel rooms that wrap around a huge central pool. It's a sociable place with a perpetual pool-party atmosphere, a popular bar-restaurant and central location, with the Roma Bar cafe right across the road.

Darwin YHA (Map pp820-1; ☎ 08-8981 5385; www.yha .com.au; 97 Mitchell St; dm $28-32, d $87; ✴ ☐ ☂) One of the newer additions to the hostel scene, the YHA is in a converted motel, so all rooms (in-cluding dorms) have en suite, and they're built around a decent pool. The kitchen and TV room are tiny, but there's the Brit pub–style Globetrotters Bar, with cheap meals and en-tertainment, next door.

Youth Shack (Map pp820-1; ☎ 1300 793 302; www.youth shack.com.au; 69 Mitchell St; dm $29, tw & d without bathroom $77; ✖ ▣ ☎) At one end of the Transit Centre, this popular hostel has a large open kitchen and meals area overlooking a pool big enough to actually swim in. Rooms are a little tired but clean, and the staff are consistently praised for being friendly and helpful; reception is open 24 hours.

Chilli's (Map pp820-1; ☎ 1800 351 313; www.chillis.com .au; 69a Mitchell St; dm $29, tw & d without bathroom $77, d $82; ✖ ▣) Run by the same crew as the Youth Shack – note the colour coordination – Chilli's is a funky place with a small sundeck and spa (use the pool next door), a pool table and a breezy kitchen and meals area overlooking Mitchell St. Rooms are compact but clean.

our pick Melaleuca on Mitchell (Map pp820-1; ☎ 1300 723 437; www.melaleucaonmitchell.com.au; 52 Mitchell St; dm $31, d with/without bathroom $115/95; ✖ ▣ ☎) The highlight at this busy backpackers is the bopping rooftop island bar and pool area overlooking Mitchell St – complete with waterfall spa and big-screen TV. Party heaven! The modern hostel is immaculate but a little sterile with its stark white walls and sparse rooms. Facilities are A1 though and it's very secure – the 3rd floor is female only.

Midrange

Barramundi Lodge (Map pp820-1; ☎ 08-8941 6466; www .barramundilodge.com.au; 4 Gardens Rd, The Gardens; s/d without bathroom $50/100; ✖ ☎) Relatively quiet, secure and comfortable, Barramundi Lodge is a touch above most backpacker places but still caters to a budget crowd. Spotless and spacious, the old-fashioned, louvre-windowed rooms have a TV and kitchenette, though the bathrooms are all communal. It's close to the Botanical Gardens and Mindil Beach.

Ashton Lodge (Map pp820-1; ☎ 08-8941 4866; www .ashtonlodge.com.au; 48 Mitchell St; d without bathroom with/ without air-con $85/65, d $140; ✖ ☎) This warren of compact rooms is squeezed in behind the Wisdom Bar & Cafe. The cheapest rooms are tiny and there's lots of blue in the decor but it's very clean and secure.

Grungle Downs B&B (Map p817; ☎ 08-8947 4440; www.grungledowns.com.au; 945 McMillans Rd, Knuckey Lagoon; d $120-165, cottage $400; ✖ ☎) Set on a five-acre property, this beautiful rural retreat seems a world away from the city but is not that far, and is handy to Crocodylus Park and the airport. Relax in the guest lounge, extensive gardens or by the pool. There are

four lodge rooms (one with en suite) and a gorgeous two-bedroom cottage (which drops to $200 in the low season).

Value Inn (Map pp820-1; ☎ 08-8981 4733; www.valueinn .com.au; 50 Mitchell St; d from $140; ✖ ☎) Also in the thick of the Mitchell St action but quiet and comfortable, Value Inn lives up to its name, especially out of season. En-suite rooms are small but sleep up to three and have fridge and TV.

Cullen Bay Resorts (Map pp820-1; ☎ 1800 625 533; www .cullenbayresortsdarwin.com.au; 26-32 Marina Blvd; hotel d $150, 1-/2-bed apt $240/290; ✖ ☎) Cullen Bay is (or was) Darwin's prime waterfront location and this pair of twin apartment towers boasts million-dollar views over the marina and harbour. You'll pay more than the prices listed here for water views, but the slick hotel rooms and spacious apartments are decent value.

our pick Steeles at Larrakeyah (Map pp820-1; ☎ 08-8941 3636; www.steeles-at-larrakeyah.com.au; 4 Zealandia Cres, Larrakeyah; d $150-190, apt from $250; ✖ ☎) Some B&Bs are business and others feel like staying with friends; Steeles is the latter. With a perfect residential location midway between the city centre, Cullen Bay and Mindil Beach, the three rooms in this pleasant Spanish Mission–style home are equipped with air-con, TV, fridge and private entrance. Enjoy breakfast in the tropical garden.

Palms City Resort (Map pp820-1; ☎ 1800 829 211, 08-8982 9200; www.citypalms.com; 64 The Esplanade; motel d $175-185, villas d $190-285; ✖ ☎) With palm-filled gardens and a fabulous location at the southern end of the Esplanade, Palms City lives up to its name. The superior motel rooms are worth the extra $10 for the extra space. The villas, with solid timber finishes and louvred windows orbit a central pool, while the executive villas with outdoor spa are pure luxury.

Frontier Hotel (Map pp820-1; ☎ 08-8981 5333; www.fron tierdarwin.com.au; 3 Buffalo Crt; d $185, apt $225; ✖ ☎) Towering above other places on the northern edge of town, this block of spacious, stylish rooms boasts excellent views, particularly from the 6th-floor apartments. The rooftop restaurant has stunning harbour views across the golf course.

Alatai Holiday Apartments (Map pp820-1; ☎ 1800 628 833, 08-8981 5188; www.alataiapartments.com.au; cnr McMinn & Finniss Sts; studios/apt $190/295; ⓟ ✖ ☎) This well-kept, leafy complex built around a swimming pool offers a peaceful and private stay at the northern edge of the city centre. The compact studios sleep two, while roomy two-bedroom apartments have their own kitchen and laundry and sleep up to six. There's a garden cafe and a licensed Chinese restaurant.

Top End

Most of the big hotels are gathered along the Esplanade. Weekend and online specials should bring substantial discounts.

Botanic Gardens Apartments (Map pp820-1; ☎ 08-8946 0300; www.botanicgardens.com.au; 17 Geranium St, Stuart Park; motel d $195, apt $245-395; 🟨 🖭 🕿) Location, location. In a unique and peaceful location nudging up against the Botanic Gardens, the motel rooms and roomy one-, two- and three-bedroom apartments here are enveloped in palms and lush tropical gardens, and there are two fabulous pools to cool off in. The best apartment rooms boast prestigious views over the Botanic Gardens to the Timor Sea.

Novotel Atrium (Map pp820-1; ☎ 08-8941 0755; www.novoteldarwin.com.au; 100 The Esplanade; d $200-275, 2-bedroom apt from $295; 🟨 🖭 🕿) This four-star tower of contemporary style has slick hotel rooms and fine views from the upper floors. The well-appointed rooms are arranged around the impressive, verdant namesake atrium, at the bottom of which is the Zest Restaurant and a cocktail bar swathed in palms and vines.

Feathers Sanctuary (Map p817; ☎ 08-8985 2144; www.featherssanctuary.com; 49a Freshwater Rd, Jingili; d $330; 🟨) A sublime retreat for bird enthusiasts and nature lovers, Feathers has beautifully designed timber-and-iron cottages with semi-open-air bathrooms and luxurious interiors. The lush gardens have a private aviary breeding some rare birds, and a waterhole – a setting that belies its proximity to the city.

Camping & Caravan Parks

Some campervanners take their chances staying overnight at parking areas along the beach around Fannie Bay and East Point Reserve, but it's officially a no-no and council officers may move you on or dish out fines. The following caravan parks are within about 10km of the city centre. Prices given below are for two people.

Leprechaun Motel & Caravan Park (Map p817; ☎ 08-8984 3400; 378 Stuart Hwy, Winnellie; unpowered/powered sites $22/27, motel s/d $85/95; 🟨 🕿) The closest caravan park to the city centre is relatively small and simple, but also the cheapest around, and the motel is reasonable value.

Shady Glen Caravan Park (Map p817; ☎ 1800 662 253, 08-8984 3330; www.shadyglen.com.au; cnr Farrell Cres & Stuart Hwy; sites $29, r $59-79, cabins $90-180; 🟨 🕿) Shady by name… Well-treed caravan park with immaculate facilities, camp kitchen, licensed shop and friendly staff.

FreeSpirit Resort Darwin (Map p817; ☎ 1800 350 888; www.freespiritresorts.com.au; 901 Stuart Hwy, Berrimah; unpowered/powered sites $30/38, cabins $125-255; 🟨 🖭 🕿) Impressive park with loads of facilities, including wi-fi from the terrace area, and three pools.

EATING

When it comes to dining, Darwin doesn't pretend to be a Melbourne or Sydney, but it does have by far the best culinary scene between here and Adelaide. Restaurants and cafes make the most of the tropical ambience with alfresco seating, and the quality and diversity of produce tops anywhere else in the Territory.

A few pubs also entice backpackers off the pavement with free barbecues and cheap meals to soak up the beer. Some of the best deals are at the Vic and Shennanigans – see Drinking (p831) for more information.

Apart from the many city-centre restaurants and cafes, Cullen Bay has a hip waterfront dining scene, while the food centre at the end of Stokes Hill Wharf provides cheap-and-cheerful fish and chips and Asian stir-fries, and there are a few gems hidden in the suburbs north of the city.

Restaurants
CITY CENTRE

Vietnam Saigon Star (Map pp820-1; ☎ 08-8981 1420; Shop 4, 21 Smith St; mains $5-20; 🕑 lunch & dinner Mon-Fri, dinner Sat & Sun) Darwin's speedy Vietnamese restaurant serves up inexpensive rice-paper rolls, and beef, pork, chicken and seafood dishes with a multitude of sauces. Vegetarians are well catered for and there are good-value lunch specials.

Moorish Café (Map pp820-1; ☎ 08-8991 0010; 37 Knuckey St; tapas $6.50-11, mains $24-32; 🕑 Mon-Sat) Seductive aromas emanate from this divine cafe fusing North African, Mediterranean and Middle Eastern delights. It's especially popular with the lunchtime crowd for its tantalising tapas and lunch specials, but it's an atmospheric place for dinner, with classical Spanish guitar on Tuesday, salsa dancing Thursday and belly dancers on Saturday night.

NORTHERN TERRITORY

Monsoons (Map pp820-1; ☎ 08-89417188; www.monsoons
.net.au; 46 Mitchell St; mains $13-30) The old Rourke's
Drift pub has been completely remodelled
into a sassy restaurant-bar with an Oriental/
Indian feel – all dark wood, high-back chairs
and bamboo blinds. The bar is enormous, the
terrace relatively small and the fusion menu
features meze plates, lamb kofta and crispy-
skin duckling.

Tim's Surf 'n' Turf (Map pp820-1; ☎ 08-8981 1024; 10
Litchfield St; mains $14-30; ☺ lunch Mon-Fri, dinner daily)
Tim's is a long-standing Darwin diner where
you can enjoy good-value seafood, steak,
schnitzels and pasta in a relaxed, quiet setting – it's squirrelled away in a city backstreet.
Lunch is great value with all meals at $12.50.

Nirvana (Map pp820-1; ☎ 08-8981 2025; 6 Dashwood
Cr; mains $15-30; ☺ dinner Mon-Sat) Excellent Thai,
Malaysian and Indian dishes are only part of
the story at Nirvana – it's also one of Darwin's
best small live-music venues for jazz and
blues. It doesn't look much from the outside,
but inside the fortresslike Smith St door is an
intimate warren of rooms with booth seating
and Oriental decor. Enjoy a Thai green curry,
nasi goreng or fish masala with your music.

Ducks Nuts Bar & Grill (Map pp820-1; ☎ 08-8942
2122; www.ducksnuts.com.au; 76 Mitchell St; mains $15-35)
Slick bistro delivering clever fusion of Top
End produce with that Asian/Mediterranean
blend we like to claim as Modern Australian.
Try the red Thai duck shank and banana
curry, barra wrap or succulent lamb shanks.
The attached Bar Espresso coffee shop delivers
good brekkies and caffeinated brews.

our pick Hanuman (Map pp820-1; ☎ 08-8941 3500;
28 Mitchell St; mains $16-32; ☺ lunch Mon-Fri, dinner daily)
Ask most locals where to find Darwin's top
fine-dining experience and the answer is usually Hanuman. Sophisticated but not stuffy or
pretentious, enticing aromas of innovative
Indian and Thai Nonya dishes waft from the
kitchen to the stylish open dining room and
deck. The signature dish is oysters bathed in
lemon grass, chilli and coriander, or the *meen
mooli* – reef fish in coconut and curry leaves –
but the menu is broad, with exotic vegetarian
choices and banquets available.

Char Restaurant (Map pp820-1; ☎ 08-8981 4544; www
.charrestaurant.com.au; cnr The Esplanade & Knuckey St; mains
$25-40; ☺ lunch & dinner Mon-Fri, dinner Sat & Sun) In the
historic Admiralty House on the Esplanade,
Char is the latest addition to Darwin's culinary
landscape. The speciality here is char-grilled
steaks – aged, grain-fed and cooked to perfec-

tion – but there's also a range of seafood, a
crab-and-croc lasagne and a thoughtful vegetarian menu.

Crustaceans (Map pp820-1; ☎ 08-8981 8658; Stokes
Hill Wharf; mains $25-55; ☺ dinner Mon-Sat) This highly
regarded but rather touristy seafood restaurant perches on the end of Stokes Hill Wharf,
where diners can enjoy the sunset and views
over fresh fish, mud crabs, lobster, crocodile
and oysters.

CULLEN BAY & PARAP

Cullen Bay's eateries centre on the marina,
full of yachts bobbing listlessly below million-
dollar apartments.

Saffron (Map pp820-1; ☎ 08-8981 2383; Shop 14,
34 Parap Rd, Parap; mains $14-20; ☺ dinner Wed-Sun)
Saffron is Darwin's newest Indian restaurant, a
contemporary but intimate dining experience.
The menu spans the subcontinent, from rich
butter chicken to Kerala lamb curry or Goan
beef vindaloo. There are plenty of vegetarian
choices and traditional Indian sweets such as
kulfi (ice cream) and lassi (yoghurt drink).

Buzz Café (Map pp820-1; ☎ 08-8941 1141; 48 Marina
Blvd, Cullen Bay; mains $15-35; ☺ lunch & dinner daily, break-
fast Sat & Sun) This chic bar-restaurant furnished
in Indonesian teak and Mt Bromo lava has a
super multilevel deck overlooking the marina
and makes a lovely, sunny spot for a lazy lunch
and a few drinks. Meals are Mod Oz, with
some excellent salads and dishes to share. The
men's toilets reveal all.

Seadogs (Map pp820-1; ☎ 08-8941 2877; Marina Blvd;
mains $16-24; ☺ lunch & dinner Tue-Sun) It may not
front the marina, but the meals are cheaper
at this popular local restaurant specialising
in pizza, pasta, risotto and a few prawn and
calamari dishes.

Yots Greek Taverna (Map pp820-1; ☎ 08-8981
4433; 54 Marina Blvd, Cullen Bay; mains $24-34; ☺ lunch
& dinner) With a prime deck overlooking the
marina, Yots serves up classic Greek and
Mediterranean fare from saganaki and souvlaki to moussaka and spanakopita, along with
barramundi and prawn dishes – the Greco
barramundi is served on spinach with baked
lemon potatoes and a caper sauce. There's a
cheaper lunch menu.

Cafes & Quick Eats

Darwin has a growing number of cool cafes
serving good coffee and snacks. There are also
several food courts tucked away in the arcade
off Smith St Mall.

Relish (Map pp820-1; ☎ 08-8941 1900; Shop 1, 35 Cavenagh St; meals $4.50-8; ☯ breakfast & lunch Mon-Fri) Hip hole-in-the-wall cafe with a good dose of acoustic music, local artworks and magazines. Gourmet melts, ciabattas, focaccias and salads dominate the blackboard and there's good coffee and spicy chai.

Cyclone Cafe (Map pp820-1; ☎ 08-8941 1992; 8 Urquhart St, Parap; meals $5-9; ☯ 7.30am-3pm Mon-Fri, 8.30am-1pm Sat) Possibly the best coffee in Darwin is brewed at this unassuming local haunt in Parap. The corrugated-iron decor harks back to a simpler time, the coffee is strong and aromatic (try the hypercino), and there's some great breakfast and lunch fare such as croissants, burritos and cheese melts.

our pick Roma Bar (Map pp820-1; ☎ 08-8981 6729; 9-11 Cavenagh St; mains $7-16; ☯ breakfast & lunch; ☐) Roma has long been a local institution and meeting place for Lefties, literati and business types. Well away from the bustle of Mitchell St, the free wi-fi is a bonus, the coffee and juices are great, and you can get anything from muesli and eggs for breakfast to excellent focaccias and wraps for lunch.

Indian Cafe (Map pp820-1; ☎ 08-8941 0752; 1/15 Knuckey St; mains $7.50; ☯ lunch & dinner) Cheap and cheerful, this hole-in-the-wall curry joint has $7.50 two-curries-and-rice meal deals, eat in or take away.

Self-Catering

There are two large supermarkets in the town centre. **Coles** (Map pp820-1; ☎ 08-8941 8055; Mitchell Centre, 55-59 Mitchell St) is open 24 hours, while **Woolworths** (Map pp820-1; ☎ 08-8941 6111; cnr Cavenagh & Whitfield Sts) is open until midnight most nights.

Parap Fine Foods (Map pp820-1; ☎ 08-8981 8597; 40 Parap Rd, Parap) is a gourmet food hall in the Parap shopping centre, stocking organic and health foods, deli items and wine – perfect for a picnic.

DRINKING

Drinking is big business in tropical Darwin and the city has dozens of pubs and terrace bars that make the most of sunny afternoons and balmy evenings. Virtually all bars double as restaurants. Mitchell St has the densest concentration of bars popular with travellers, all within a short walk of each other.

Tap on Mitchell (Map pp820-1; ☎ 08-8981 5521; www .thetap.com.au; 51 Mitchell St; ☯ 8am-10pm) One of the busiest of the terrace bars, the Tap is always

buzzing and there are inexpensive meals of nachos, burgers and calamari to complement a good range of wine and beers.

Wisdom Bar & Grill (Map pp820-1; ☎ 08-8941 4866; www .wisdombar.com.au; 48 Mitchell St; ☯ 9am-1am) Bright blue walls, velour couches and a nice terrace with a tree growing out of it add up to a more intimate version of the Tap. There's an extensive menu of bar food.

Victoria Hotel (The Vic; Map pp820-1; ☎ 08-8981 4011; 27 Smith St; ☯ 11am-late) The Vic is a good place for a drink but these days it's more of an all-round backpacker entertainment venue – see p832.

Top End Hotel (Map pp820-1; ☎ 08-8981 6511; cnr Mitchell & Daly Sts; ☯ 10am-2am) Popular with locals, this busy little entertainment enclave has several clubs and bars, including Lizards Outdoor Bar & Grill, with its lush tropical beer garden; the Rock 'n' Country Bar, with pool tables on the deck and Elvis posters and guitars stuck to the roof (Darwin's version of the Hard Rock Cafe!); and the Beehive Nightclub.

Darwin Ski Club (Map pp820-1; ☎ 08-8981 6630; Conacher St, Fannie Bay; ☯ noon-midnight Sun-Thu, to 1am Fri & Sat) Leave Mitchell St behind and head for a sublime sunset at this laid-back waterski club on Vestey's Beach. The view through the palm trees from the beer garden is sublime and there are often live bands.

Darwin Sailing Club (Map pp820-1; ☎ 08-8981 1700; www .dnwsail.com.au; Atkins Dr, Fannie Bay; mains $10-32; ☯ noon-11pm) More upmarket than the ski club, the sailing club is always filled with yachties and families enjoying sunset over the Timor Sea.

Shenannigans (Map pp820-1; ☎ 08-8981 2100; www .shenannigans.com.au; 69 Mitchell St; ☯ 10am-late) Darwin has a few Irish-theme pubs, but Shenannigans mixes it up with a big Mitchell St terrace, good food and big party nights.

Other popular city watering holes:

Cavenagh (Map pp820-1; ☎ 08-8941 6383; www.thecav enagh.com; 12 Cavenagh St; ☯ 10am-1am) Popular backpackers' and sports bar, the Cav also serves up good food.

Ducks Nuts Bar & Grill (Map pp820-1; ☎ 08-8942 2122; 76 Mitchell St) A big backlit cocktail bar, regular live music and the swanky Tzars vodka bar give the Ducks Nuts plenty of cred.

Mandorah Beach Hotel (☯ lunch & dinner) Reached in just 20 minutes by ferry from Cullen Bay, the Mandorah pub (p835) is well worth a visit for a beer and a meal with views back across the bay to Darwin city.

ENTERTAINMENT

Darwin's balmy nights invite a bit of late-night exploration and while there is only a handful of nightclubs, you'll find something on every night of the week. There's also a thriving arts and entertainment scene of theatre, film and concerts.

Find up-to-date entertainment listings for live music and other attractions in the free what's on guide *Off the Leash.*

Top End Arts (www.topendarts.com .au) lists events happening around town, as does *Darwin Community Arts* (www.darwin communityarts.org.au). Keep an eye out for bills posted on noticeboards and telegraph poles that advertise dance and full-moon parties.

Live Music

Just about every pub/bar in town has some form of live music, mostly on Friday and Saturday nights. Some places also keep their microphones busy with karaoke and DJs on other nights.

Victoria Hotel (The Vic; Map pp820-1; ☎ 08-8981 4011; 27 Smith St; ❤ 11am-late) The Vic has bags of history – the stone building on the Mall dates from 1890 – but it's hard to see it these days. This is Darwin's favourite backpacker pub and goes off every night of the week. Dirt-cheap meals draw the travellers in to the upstairs Banjos Bar, and they stay for the pool tables, DJs and dance floor. Downstairs is a happening bar with a pub quiz on Monday, table dancing, live bands and DJs.

Nirvana (Map pp820-1; ☎ 08-8981 2025; Smith St; ❤ from 6.30pm Mon-Sat) Behind an imposing doorway, this cosy restaurant-bar has live jazz/blues every Thursday, Friday and Saturday night and an open-mic jam session every Tuesday. As well as meals, bar snacks are available at reasonable prices.

Nightclubs

Discovery & Lost Arc (Map pp820-1; ☎ 08-8942 3300; 89 Mitchell St; ❤ 9pm-4am Fri & Sat) Discovery is Darwin's biggest nightclub and dance venue with three levels playing techno, hip hop and R&B tunes. Lost Arc is the neon-lit chill-out bar opening on to Mitchell St, but it starts to rock after 10pm.

Throb (Map pp820-1; ☎ 08-8942 3435; www.throbnight club.com.au; 64 Smith St; admission $10; ❤ 10pm-5am Fri & Sat) Darwin's premier gay- and lesbian-friendly nightclub and cocktail bar, Throb attracts party-goers of all genders and persuasions for its hot DJs and cool atmosphere. Hosts drag shows and touring live acts.

Cinemas

Deckchair Cinema (Map pp820-1; ☎ 08-8981 0700; www .deckchaircinema.com; Jervois Rd, Wharf Precinct; adult/ child/family $13/6/30; ❤ box office from 6.30pm Apr-Nov) During the Dry, the Darwin Film Society runs this fabulous outdoor cinema below the southern end of the Esplanade. Watch a movie under the stars while reclining in a deckchair – bring a cushion for real comfort. There's a licensed bar serving food or you can bring your own picnic (no BYO alcohol). There's usually a double feature on Friday and Saturday (adult/child $20/9). If you're walking, the best way to get here is via the Damoe Ra walkway at the southern end of Bicentennial Park – follow the signs.

Darwin City Cinemas (Map pp820-1; ☎ 08-8981 5999; 76 Mitchell St; adult/child $15/11) This is the city's large cinema complex, screening latest-release films across five theatres. Head down on Tropical Tuesday for $9 entry (all day).

Theatre

Darwin Entertainment Centre (Map pp820-1; ☎ 08-8980 3333; www.darwinentertainment.com.au; 93 Mitchell St; ❤ box office 10am-5.30pm Mon-Fri & 1hr prior to shows) Darwin's main community arts venue houses the Playhouse and Studio Theatres, and hosts events from fashion-award nights to plays, rock operas, comedies and concerts. Check the website for upcoming shows.

Brown's Mart (Map pp820-1; ☎ 08-8981 5522; www .brownsmart.com.au; Harry Chan Ave) This historic venue features live theatre performances, music and short films. An arty crowd congregates here for Bamboo Lounge.

Casino

Skycity Darwin (Map pp820-1; ☎ 08-8943 8888; www.skycity darwin.com.au; Gilruth Ave; ❤ 24hr) On Mindil Beach, this is Darwin's flashy casino complex, with accommodation and three restaurants and all the card tables, roulette wheels and pokie machines you need – all the tools to help you lose your shirt (or win your fortune). To ensure you have a shirt to lose there's a dress code, which means no singlets, thongs or scruffy clothing.

SHOPPING

You don't have to walk far along the Smith St Mall to find a souvenir shop selling Territory-themed knick-knacks: jewellery, pottery, tea towels, T-shirts and cane-toad coin purses (most of it made in China). Also in oversup-

---

DARWIN'S MAGICAL MARKETS

As the sun heads towards the horizon on Thursday and Sunday, half of Darwin descends on **Mindil Beach Sunset Market** (Map pp820-1; ☎ 08-8981 3454; www.mindil.com.au; off Gilruth Ave; ⊗ 5-10pm Thu, 4-9pm Sun May-Oct) with tables, chairs, rugs, grog and kids to settle under the coconut palms for sunset, and decide which of the tantalising food-stall aromas holds the greatest allure. Food is the main attraction and it spans the globe from Thai, Sri Lankan, Indian, Chinese and Malaysian to Brazilian, Greek, Portuguese and more, all at around $5 to $8 a serve. Don't miss a flaming satay stick from Bobby's brazier. Top it off with fresh fruit salad, decadent cakes or luscious crêpes. But that's only half the fun: arts and crafts stalls bulge with handmade jewellery, fabulous rainbow tie-died clothes, Aboriginal artefacts, and wares from Indonesia and Thailand. Patrons peruse and promenade, or stop for a pummelling massage or to listen to rhythmic live music. Mindil Beach is about 2km from the city centre. Buses 4 and 6 go past the market area or you can catch a shuttle ($2).

Similar stalls (you'll recognise many of the stall holders) can be found at various suburban markets from Friday to Sunday.

Nightcliff Market (Map p817; Pavonia Way; ⊗ 8am-2pm Sun) Another popular community market, north of the city in the Nightcliff Shopping Centre.

Parap Village Market (Map pp820-1; ☎ 08-8942 0805; Parap Shopping Village; ⊗ 8am-2pm Sat) This compact but crowded market is a local favourite every Saturday with the full gamut of Southeast Asian cuisine, as well as plenty of ingredients to cook up your own storm.

Rapid Creek Market (Map p817; Trower Rd; ⊗ 5-10pm Fri, 8am-2pm Sun) Darwin's oldest market is another Asian marketplace, with a tremendous range of tropical fruit and vegetables mingled with a heady mixture of spices and swirling satay smoke.

---

ply are outlets selling Aboriginal arts and crafts (see p823). Darwin's fabulous markets (see Darwin's Magical Markets, above) sell unique handcrafted items such as seed-pod hats, shell jewellery, kites, clothing and original photos.

Framed (Map pp820-1; ☎ 08-8981 2994; www.framed .com.au; 55 Stuart Hwy, Stuart Park) A fine range of arts and crafts is presented in this gallery near the entrance to the Botanic Gardens. The eclectic and ever-changing range is typically Territorian and tropical, and includes contemporary Aboriginal art, pottery, jewellery and exquisitely carved furniture.

Casuarina Square (Map p817; ☎ 08-8920 2345; 247 Trower Rd, Casuarina) This shopping complex has 200 mainstream retail outlets, plus cinemas and a foodcourt. Buses 4 and 5 travel the 20 minutes north of Darwin.

NT General Store (Map pp820-1; ☎ 08-8981 8242; 42 Cavenagh St) This store has shelves piled high with camping and bushwalking gear, as well as a range of maps.

GETTING THERE & AWAY
Air

Domestic flights connect Darwin with all other Australian capital cities, as well as Alice Springs, Broome, Cairns, Kununurra and various regions throughout the Top End. A few international flights to Asian destinations also leave Darwin. Fares fluctuate so check websites for current specials.

Apart from the following major carriers, smaller routes are flown by local operators; ask a travel agent.

Airnorth (☎ 1800 627 474; www.airnorth.com .au) Small airline serving the Top End region (including Broome, Gove/Nhulunbuy and Kununurra) and some international destinations, such as Dili (East Timor) and Denpasar (Indonesia).

Jetstar (☎ 13 15 38; www.jetstar.com) Direct flights to Melbourne, Sydney, Brisbane, Cairns and Adelaide, as well as international flights to Singapore, and Ho Chi Minh City (Vietnam).

Qantas (☎ 13 13 13; www.qantas.com.au) Direct daily services to Adelaide, Alice Springs, Brisbane, Cairns, Melbourne, Perth and Sydney.

Skywest (☎ 1300 660 088; www.skywest.com.au) Direct flights to Perth and Broome.

Virgin Blue (☎ 13 67 89; www.virginblue.com.au) Direct flights to Brisbane only.

Bus

There's only one road in and out of Darwin and long-distance bus services are operated by **Greyhound Australia** (Map pp820-1; ☎ 1300 473 946; www.greyhound.com.au; Transit Centre, 69 Mitchell St). At least one service per day travels up and down the Stuart Hwy. Buses depart from the rear of the **Transit Centre** (off Mitchell St) and stop at various points down the Stuart Hwy, including Pine Creek ($65, three hours), Katherine ($84, 4½ hours), Mataranka ($106, seven hours), Tennant Creek ($225, 14½ hours) and Alice Springs ($314, 22 hours).

For Kakadu, there's a daily return service from Darwin to Cooinda ($74, 4½ hours) via Jabiru ($53, 3½ hours).

Backpacker buses such as **Oz Experience** (www.ozexperience.com) and **Adventure Tours** (www.adventuretours.com.au) can also get you to out-of-the-way places.

Car & Campervan

For driving around Darwin, conventional vehicles are cheap enough, but most companies offer only 100km free, which won't get you very far. Rates start at around $35 per day for a small car with 100km per day.

There are also plenty of 4WD vehicles available in Darwin, but you usually have to book ahead and fees and deposits are higher than for 2WD vehicles. Larger companies offer one-way rentals plus better mileage deals for more expensive vehicles. Campervans are a great option for touring around the Territory and you generally get unlimited kilometres even for short rentals. Prices start at around $50 a day for a basic camper or $80 to $100 for a three-berth hi-top camper, to $200-plus for the bigger mobile homes or 4WD bush-campers. Additional insurance cover or excess reduction costs extra.

Most rental companies are open every day and have agents in the city centre. Avis, Budget, Hertz and Thrifty all have offices at the airport.

Advance Car Rentals (Map pp820–1; ☎ 08-8981 2999; www.advancecar.com.au; 86 Mitchell St) Small local operator with some good deals.

Avis (Map pp820–1; ☎ 08-8981 9922; www.avis.com; 89 Smith St)

Backpacker Campervans (Map p817; ☎ 08-8981 2081; www.backpackercampervans.com.au; 17 Bombing Rd, Winnellie) At the same depot as Britz, this is a budget outfit with small campers and hi-tops at reasonable rates.

Britz Australia (Map p817; ☎ 08-8981 2081; www.britz.com.au; 17 Bombing Rd, Winnellie) Britz is a reliable outfit with a big range of campervans and motorhomes, including 4WD bushcampers.

Budget (Map pp820–1; ☎ 08-8981 9800; www.budget.com.au; cnr Daly St & Doctors Gully Rd)

Europcar (Map pp820–1; ☎ 08-8941 0300; www.europcar.com.au; 77 Cavenagh St)

Hertz (Map pp820–1; ☎ 08-8941 0944; www.hertz.com.au; cnr Smith & Daly Sts)

Thrifty (Map pp820–1; ☎ 08-8924 0000; www.rentacar.com.au; 64 Stuart Hwy, Stuart Park)

Travellers Autobarn (Map pp820–1; ☎ 08-8941 7700; www.travellers-autobarn.com.au; 13 Daly St) Campervan specialist.

Wicked Campers (Map p817; ☎ 1800 246 869; www.wickedcampers.com.au; 34 Bishop St, Woolner) Colourfully painted small campers aimed at backpackers.

Train

The famous *Ghan* train operates weekly (twice weekly May to July) between Adelaide and Darwin via Alice Springs. The Darwin terminus is located on Berrimah Rd, about 15km or 20 minutes from the city centre. A taxi fare into the centre is about $30, though there is a shuttle service to/from the Transit Centre for $10. See p1071 for fare details. Bookings (recommended) can be made through **Trainways** (☎ 13 21 47; www.trainways.com.au).

GETTING AROUND
To/From the Airport

Darwin International Airport (Map p817; ☎ 08-8920 1805) is about 12km northeast of the centre of town, and handles both international and domestic flights. **Darwin Airport Shuttle** (☎ 1800 358 945, 08-8981 5066; www.darwinairportshuttle.com.au) will pick up or drop off almost anywhere in the centre for $11. When leaving Darwin book a day before departure. A taxi fare into the centre is about $25.

Public Transport

Darwinbus (Map pp820–1; ☎ 08-8924 7666; Harry Chan Ave) runs a comprehensive bus network that departs from the city bus interchange (Map pp820–1), opposite Brown's Mart.

A $2 adult ticket gives unlimited travel on the bus network for three hours (validate your ticket when you first get on). Daily ($5) and weekly ($15) travel cards are also available from bus interchanges, some newsagencies and the tourist information office. Bus 4 (to Fannie Bay, Nightcliff, Rapid Creek and Casuarina) and bus 6 (Fannie Bay, Parap and Stuart Park) are useful for getting to Aquascene, the Botanic Gardens, Mindil Beach, the Museum & Art Gallery, Fannie Bay Gaol Museum and East Point and the markets.

The **Tour Tub** (☎ 08-8985 6322; www.tourtub.com
.au) hop-on, hop-off minibus tours Darwin's
sights throughout the day.

Scooter

Darwin Scooter Hire (☎ 0418 892 885; www.thescooter
shop.com.au; 29 Stuart Hwy) rents out 50cc scooters
for $30/40 per two/four hours or $50 per day.
Motorbikes are also available for hire, along
with bicycles.

Taxi

Taxis wait along Knuckey St, diagonally opposite the north end of Smith St Mall, and are
usually easy to flag down. Phone **Darwin Radio
Taxis** (☎ 13 10 08).

AROUND DARWIN

MANDORAH

Mandorah is a low-key, relaxed residential
beach suburb looking out across the harbour
to Darwin. It sits on the tip of Cox Peninsula,
128km by road from Darwin but only 6km
across the harbour by regular ferry. The main
reason to visit is for the ferry ride across
the harbour and a few drinks or dinner at
the super-friendly pub. The nearby Wagait
Aboriginal community numbers around 400
residents.

The **Mandorah Beach Hotel** (☎ 08-8978 5044;
d/f $88/110; ❷ ❸) has sublime views over the
beach and turquoise water to Darwin. All
rooms in the refurbished motel have a fridge,
TV and air-con. Even if you don't stay the
night, the pub and restaurant are great. Hearty
meals ($10 to $25) are available for lunch and
dinner and there's live music some weekends
in season.

The **Sea Cat** (Map pp820-1; ☎ 08-8978 5015; www
.seacat.com.au; adult/child/family return $23/12/60) oper-
ates about a dozen daily services, with the
first departure from the Cullen Bay Marina
in Darwin at 6.30am and the last at 10pm
(midnight on Friday and Saturday). The last
ferry from Mandorah is at 10.20pm (12.20am
Saturday and Sunday).

TIWI ISLANDS

The Tiwi Islands – Bathurst and Melville
Islands – lie about 80km north of Darwin,
and are home to the Tiwi Aboriginal people.
The Tiwis ('We People') have a distinct culture
and today are well known for producing vi-

brant art and the odd champion Aussie Rules
football player.

Tourism is restricted on the islands and
for most tourists the only way to visit is on
one of the daily organised tours from Darwin
(see below).

The Tiwis' island homes kept them fairly
isolated from mainland developments until
the 20th century, and their culture has retained several unique features. Perhaps the
best known are the *pukumani* (burial poles),
carved and painted with symbolic and mythological figures, which are erected around
graves. More recently the Tiwis have turned
their hand to art for sale – carving, painting, textile screen-printing, batik and pottery using traditional designs and motifs. The
Bima Wear textile factory was set up in 1969
to employ Tiwi women, and today makes
many bright fabrics in distinctive designs.

The main settlement on the islands is **Nguiu**
in the southeast of Bathurst Island, which was
founded in 1911 as a Catholic mission. On
Melville Island the settlements are **Pularumpi**
and **Milikapiti**.

Most of the 2700 Tiwi Islanders live on
Bathurst Island (there are about 900 people on
Melville Island). Most follow a mainly non-
traditional lifestyle, but they still hunt dugong
and gather turtle eggs, and hunting and gathering usually supplements the mainland diet a
couple of times a week. Tiwis also go back to
their traditional lands on Melville Island for a
few weeks each year to teach and to learn traditional culture. Descendants of the Japanese
pearl divers who regularly visited here early
this century also live on Melville Island.

Aussie Rules football is a passion among
the islanders and one of the biggest events
of the year (and the only time it's possible
to visit without a permit) is the Tiwi football
grand-final day in late March. Given the large
numbers of people coming across from the
mainland for the event, it's still best to organise this through a tour or book well ahead for
the Sea Cat ferry.

Tours

Tiwi Tours (☎ 1300 721 365, 08-8923 6523; www
.aussieadventure.com.au) runs fascinating one- and
two-day Tiwi Island tours, although interaction with the local Tiwi community tends
to be limited to your guides and the local
workshops and showrooms. A one-day tour
(adult/child $414/212) to Bathurst Island

NORTHERN TERRITORY

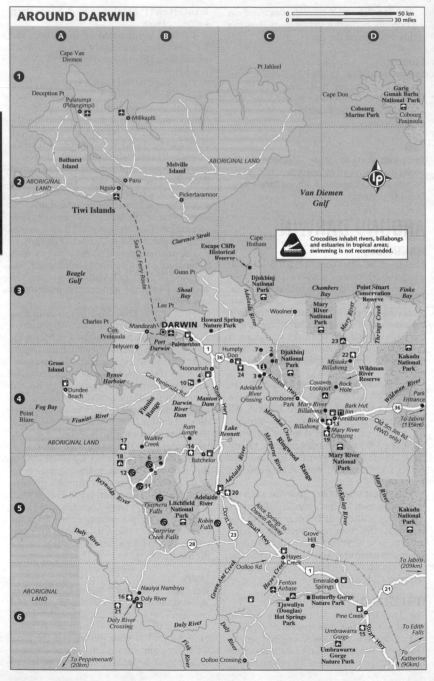

AROUND DARWIN

0 — 50 km
0 — 30 miles

Crocodiles inhabit rivers, billabongs and estuaries in tropical areas; swimming is not recommended.

INFORMATION		
Window on the Wetlands Visitor	Territory Wildlife Park...............**10** B4	Litchfield Tourist & Van Park...(see 14)
Centre......................................**1** C4	Tolmer Falls................................**11** B5	Mary River Park......................... **19** D4
	Wangi Falls.................................**12** B5	Mt Bundy Station.....................**20** C5
SIGHTS & ACTIVITIES		Perry's.......................................**21** B6
Adelaide River Experience............**2** C4	**SLEEPING** 🏠 🛖	Point Stuart Wilderness Lodge..**22** D4
Adelaide River Queen.................**3** C4	Annaburroo Billabong.............. **13** D4	Shady Camp...........................**23** D3
Berry Springs Nature Park...........**4** B4	Banyan Tree Caravan & Tourist	
Buley Rockhole............................**5** B5	Park.......................................**14** B4	**EATING**
Florence Falls..............................**6** B5	Bonrook Country Stay............. **15** D6	Litchfield Cafe.........................(see 18)
Fogg Dam Conservation Reserve..**7** C4	Daly River Mango Farm...........**16** B6	Mary River Park.......................(see 19)
Jumping Crocodile Cruise........... **8** C4	Labelle Downs Station..............**17** B4	
Magnetic Termite Mounds.........**9** B5	Latitude 1308........................(see 18)	**DRINKING** 🍸
	Litchfield Safari Camp.............**18** B5	Humpty Doo Hotel...................**24** C4

includes a charter flight, permit, lunch, tea and damper with Tiwi women, craft workshops, and visits to the early Catholic-mission buildings, the Patakijiyali Museum and a *pukumani* burial site. It departs daily from April to November.

The two-day tour ($704/544) includes overnight camping in a remote location and allows you to get a better experience of the people, culture and the island's environment, with wildlife spotting and searching for turtles' nests. The tour operates on Tuesday from May to October.

Arafura Pearl (Map pp820-1; ☎ 08-8941 1991; seacat .com.au/arafurapearl.htm; adult/child $259/189; ☷ 7.30am Mon, Wed & Fri Mar-Nov) is a cheaper alternative to flying, with daily catamaran tours run in association with Tiwi Tours. Leaving from Cullen Bay ferry terminal at 7.30am and returning at 5pm, the trip takes about two hours, and you spend all of the land time in Nguiu, visiting the church, museum, Tiwi Design and Ngaruwanajirri Art Community. There's an additional permit charge of $17 per person.

ARNHEM HIGHWAY

The Arnhem Hwy branches off towards Kakadu 34km southeast of Darwin. About 10km along the road, in the small agricultural hub of Humpty Doo, the self-proclaimed 'world famous' **Humpty Doo Hotel** (☎ 08-8988 1372; www.humptydoohotel.com.au; Arnhem Hwy; d/cabins $80/95; ☷ lunch & dinner; 🍴 🛖) is a popular local (even with Darwin locals) serving up meals (mains $12 to $20), big Sunday sessions and weekend bands.

About 15km beyond Humpty Doo is the turn-off to the carpet of green that makes up the **Fogg Dam Conservation Reserve**. Bring your binoculars for a closer look at the varieties of waterbirds that call these significant wetlands home. Three nature walks (from 2km

to 3.6km) lead around the rim and along the dam wall. Lotus lilies and bird numbers are richest between December and July.

Window on the Wetlands Visitor Centre (☎ 08-8988 8188; admission free; ☷ 7.30am-7pm), 3km past Fogg Dam, is a modern structure full of displays (static and interactive) that give a great introduction to the wetland ecosystem, as well as the history of the local Aboriginal people. There are great views over the Adelaide River floodplain from the observation deck, and binoculars for studying the waterbirds on Lake Beatrice.

MARY RIVER REGION

Beyond Adelaide River, the Arnhem Hwy passes through the Mary River region with the wetlands and wildlife of the Mary River National Park extending to the north.

Bird Billabong, just off the highway a few kilometres before Mary River Crossing, is a back-flow billabong, filled by creeks flowing off the nearby Mt Bundy Hill during the Wet. It's 4km off the highway and accessible by 2WD year-round. The scenic **loop walk** (4.5km, 1½ hours) passes through tropical woodlands, with a backdrop of Mt Bundy granite rocks.

A little further on is the emerald-green **Mary River Billabong**, with a pleasant barbecue area (no camping); from here a 4WD-only track leads deeper into the national park to Corroboree Billabong and Hardies Lagoon (25km) and Couzens camping area (37km).

Further along and north of the Arnhem Hwy, the partly sealed Point Stuart Rd leads to a number of riverside viewing platforms and to **Shady Camp**. The grassy campsites under banyan trees are beaut, but come prepared to ward off armies of mosquitoes. The causeway barrage here, which stops freshwater flowing into saltwater, creates the ideal feeding environment for barramundi, and the ideal fishing environment.

NORTHERN TERRITORY

THE JUMPING CROC CIRCUS

Few people seem to be able to resist the sight of a 5m-long saltwater crocodile launching itself out of the water towards a hunk of meat. Like a well-trained circus act, these wild crocs know where to get a free feed – and down on the Adelaide River, the croc-jumping show is guaranteed.

Jumping out of the water to grab prey is actually natural behaviour for crocs, usually to take surprised birds or animals from overhanging branches. They use their powerful tails to propel themselves up from a stationary start just below the surface, from where they can see their prey.

Croc-jumping cruises have been going on the Adelaide River for more than 20 years now and there are currently three operators at different locations along the river. The modus operandi is pretty similar – a crew member or lucky tourist gets to hold one end of a long stick that has a couple of metres of string attached to the other end. Tied to the end of the string is a very domesticated-looking pork chop. Not exactly wild bush tucker, but the acrobatic crocs love it. The whole thing is a bit of a circus really, but it is still a thoroughly amazing sight – have your camera at the ready.

Adelaide River Experience (☎ 08-8983 3224; www.adelaiderivercruises.com.au; Anzac Pde; adult/child $30/16; ☼ 9am, 11am, 1pm & 3pm) On a private stretch of river past the Fogg Dam turn-off. Also runs small-group full-day wildlife cruises.

Adelaide River Queen (☎ 08-8988 8144; www.jumpingcrocodilecruises.com.au; all cruises $25; ☼ 9am, 11am, 1pm & 3pm) Well-established operator on the highway just before Adelaide River Crossing. Licensed coffee shop.

Jumping Crocodile Cruise (☎ 08-8988 9077; www.jumpingcrocodile.com.au; adult/child/family $30/15/70; ☼ 9am, 11am, 1pm & 3pm) Along the Window on the Wetlands access road, this outfit runs one-hour tours.

Sleeping & Eating

Annaburroo Billabong (☎ 08-8978 8971; Arnhem Hwy; unpowered sites per adult/family $7.50/20, cabins $70-150; 🅿) With a private billabong, bush camping sites, a wandering menagerie and friendly owners, this place seems a world away from the highway only 2km down the road, and is a great alternative to the roadhouses. The elevated African-style safari cabins with fridge and en suite are cosy, and there are cabins, lodge rooms and immaculate tin-and-bamboo amenity blocks. Free canoes for guests to paddle around the croc-free billabong.

Mary River Park (☎ 1800 788 844, 08-8978 8877; www.maryriverpark.com.au; Arnhem Hwy, Mary River Crossing; unpowered/powered sites $22/30, cabins en-suite/deluxe $99/199; 🅿 🅿), Boasting 3km of Mary River frontage but a location just off the highway, this is a fine bush retreat heading steadily upmarket. New owners have built a slick licensed restaurant (mains $10 to $30) and 10 small but comfortable units around a private pool to complement the cheaper cabins and grassy camping area down by the river. Guided tours include a croc cruise ($45), sunset cruise ($80) and half-day fishing ($160); bookings essential.

Point Stuart Wilderness Lodge (☎ 08-8978 8914; www.pointstuart.com.au; unpowered/powered sites $24/30, d from $85; 🅿 🅿 🅿) This is part of an old cattle station and is a great base from which to explore the Mary River region. Boat hire is available and wetland cruises can be booked here. The lodge is easily accessed by 2WD, 1.5km off the Point Stuart Rd and 5km north of Mistake Billabong. A two-hour wetland cruise (per person $35; 10am and 4pm) on Rockhole Billabong can be arranged here.

There are basic public **camping grounds** (adult/child $3.30/1.65) at Couzens Lookout and Shady Camp.

STUART HIGHWAY TO LITCHFIELD NATIONAL PARK

Territory Wildlife Park & Berry Springs Nature Park

Much like the Alice Springs Desert Park, the **Territory Wildlife Park** (☎ 08-8988 7200; www.territorywildlifepark.com.au; Cox Peninsula Rd; adult/child/concession/family $20/10/14/55; ☼ 8.30am-6pm, last admission 4pm) showcases the best of Aussie wildlife in a state-of-the-art open-air zoo. You can spend years looking around in the wild and still not see half of what's on display here.

Highlights include the Flight Deck, where birds of prey display their intelligence and dexterity (don't miss one of the free-flying birds-of-prey demonstrations at 10am and 3pm daily); the nocturnal house, where you can observe nocturnal fauna such as bilbies and bats; 11 habitat aviaries, each representing a different habitat from mangroves to woodland;

and a huge walk-through aviary, representing a monsoon rainforest. Pride of place must go to the aquarium, where a walk-through clear tunnel puts you among giant barramundi, stingray, sawfish, saratoga and a score of others, while a separate tank holds a 3.8m saltwater crocodile. To see everything you can either walk around the 4km perimeter road, or hop on and off the shuttle trains that run every 15 to 20 minutes and stop at all the exhibits.

Close by is **Berry Springs Nature Park** (admission free; ☺ 8am-6.30pm), a beautiful series of spring-fed swimming holes shaded by paperbarks and pandanus palms and serenaded by abundant birds. Facilities include a kiosk, a picnic area with barbecues, toilets, changing sheds and showers.

The turn-off to Berry Springs is 48km down the Track from Darwin; it's then 10km to the park.

Batchelor
pop 480

The government once gave Batchelor's blocks of land away to encourage settlement in the little town. That was before uranium was discovered and the nearby Rum Jungle mine developed (it closed in '71 after almost 20 years). These days, Batchelor exists as a gateway and service centre for neighbouring Litchfield, and is home to the Batchelor Institute for Indigenous Education. The community-based **Coomalie Cultural Centre** (☎ 08-8939 7404; www.coomalieculturalcentre.com; cnr Awillia Rd & Nurndina St; ☺ 10am-5pm Tue-Sat Apr-Sep, to 4pm Tue-Fri Oct-Mar) displays and sells a range of Indigenous art and crafts from throughout the Territory, and runs an artist-in-residence program, so you'll often see artists at work.

A small **visitor centre** (☺ 8.30am-5pm) stocked with fliers, including national-parks info, is usually open opposite the general store.

SLEEPING & EATING
Although most travellers are naturally headed into Litchfield, this gateway town offers some quality accommodation and a pub. The **Batchelor General Store** (☎ 08-8976 0450; ☺ 7am-6pm) has a well-stocked supermarket, takeaway shop, newsagent and post office.

Batchelor Butterfly & Bird Farm (☎ 08-8976 0199; www.butterflyfarm.net; 8 Meneling Rd; d $85-95, f/bungalows $150/160; ☒ 🖭 🖘) The enthusiastic owner here has been busy building Batchelor's quirkiest accommodation for years now. The self-con-

tained house behind the butterfly enclosure has three colourful rooms with hand-crafted mahogany beds, and there's a pair of cosy en-suite bungalows that sleep up to four. Call into the cafe (mains $12 to $23; open 8am to 8.30pm) for some comfort food, such as nasi goreng, lentil burgers and garlic prawns – it's all very Zen with Buddha statues, sitar music and wicker chairs on the shaded deck.

Historic Retreat B&B (☎ 08-8976 0554; www.historicretreat.com.au; 19 Pinaroo Cres; d $120-180; ☒) The beautifully restored former home of Rum Jungle–mine managers, this elevated tropical-style place has louvred windows, polished floorboards, vintage furniture and your own 'butler'. The five guest rooms share two bathrooms and a modern well-equipped kitchen, with a 'silver service' breakfast included.

Batchelor Resort (☎ 08-8976 0166; www.batchelor-resort.com; 37-49 Rum Jungle Rd; powered sites $30-50, unpowered sites/self-contained cabins/motel d $24/115/168; ☒ 🖭 🖘) On the edge of town, this impressive resort complex has a sprawling caravan park with en-suite sites and cabins, and a separate motel section. It's good for families, with an 18-hole minigolf course, bird feeding and two pools. There are two licensed restaurants, a bar and a shop selling groceries and Batchelor's only takeaway alcohol.

Beyond Batchelor, on the road to Litchfield, are two caravan parks that make good bases for day trips into the park.

Banyan Tree Caravan & Tourist Park (☎ 08-8976 0330; www.banyan-tree.com.au; Litchfield Park Rd; unpowered/powered sites $17/20, budget r $65, cabins $110-135; ☒ 🖘) Located 11km from Batchelor, this place has grassy, shaded sites and clean brightly painted cabins.

Litchfield Tourist & Van Park (☎ 08-8976 0070; www.litchfieldtouristpark.com.au; 2916 Litchfield Park Rd; unpowered/powered sites $18/24, cabins $75-105; ☒ 🖘) Just 2km further on, the stand-out feature here is the two-bedroom ranch-style house that you can rent for $500 (it sleeps 15!) or for $105 per couple. There's also the highly regarded Leslee's on Litchfield Restaurant (mains $12 to $23; open 8am to 8pm).

LITCHFIELD NATIONAL PARK
It may not be as well known as Kakadu, but many Territory locals rate Litchfield even higher. In fact, there's a local saying that goes: 'Litchfield-do, Kaka-don't.' We don't entirely agree – we think Kaka-do-too – but this is certainly one of the best places in the Top End for bushwalking, camping and especially

NORTHERN TERRITORY

swimming, with waterfalls plunging into gorgeous, safe swimming holes.

The 1500-sq-km national park encloses much of the spectacular Tabletop Range, a wide sandstone plateau mostly surrounded by cliffs. The waterfalls that pour off the edge of this plateau are a highlight of the park, feeding crystal-clear cascades and croc-free plunge pools.

The two routes to Litchfield (115km south of Darwin) from the Stuart Hwy join up and loop through the park. The southern access road via Batchelor is all sealed, while the northern access route, off the Cox Peninsula Rd, is partly unsealed, corrugated and often closed in the Wet.

About 17km after entering the park from Batchelor you come to what look like tombstones. Only the very tip of these remarkable **magnetic termite mounds** is used to bury the dead; at the bottom are the king and queen, with workers in between. They're perfectly aligned north to south, designed to regulate the temperature, so the termites' thin skins can cope with the extreme seasonal changes.

Another 6km further along is the turn-off to **Buley Rockhole** (2km), where water cascades through a series of rock pools big enough to lodge your bod in for a pleasant hour or so. This turn-off also takes you to **Florence Falls** (5km), which is accessed by a 15-minute walking trail leading to a deep, beautiful pool surrounded by monsoon forest. There's a walking track (1.6km, 45 minutes) between the two places that follows Florence Creek.

About 18km beyond the turn-off to Florence Falls is the turn-off to the spectacular **Tolmer Falls**, which is for looking only. A 1.5km loop track (45 minutes) offers beautiful views of the valley.

It's a further 7km along the main road to the turn-off for Litchfield's most popular attraction, **Wangi Falls**, 1.5km up a side road. The Wangi (*wong*-guy) Falls flow year-round, filling an enormous swimming hole bordered by rainforest and roosting fruit bats. Bring swimming goggles to spot local fish. It's immensely popular with families during the Dry, but water levels in the Wet can make it unsafe; look for signposted warnings.

The park offers plenty of bushwalking, including the **Tabletop Track** (39km), a circuit of the park that takes three to five days to complete depending on how many side tracks you follow. You can access the track at Florence Falls, Wangi Falls and Walker Creek. Overnight walkers should register (call ☎ 1300 650 730).

Sleeping & Eating

There is excellent public **camping** (adult/child/family $6.60/3.30/16) within the park. Grounds with toilets and fireplaces are located at Florence Falls, Florence Creek (4WD required), Buley Rockhole, Wangi Falls (better for vans than tents) and Tjaynera Falls (Sandy Creek; 4WD required). There are more-basic campsites at Surprise Creek Falls (free) and Walker Creek, with its own swimming hole, where camping involves bushwalking to a series of sublime, isolated riverside sites.

ourpick Labelle Downs Station (☎ 08-8978 2330; www.labelleadventures.com.au; unpowered/powered sites $20/25) For a taste of outback station life, Labelle Downs is well worth a detour. Although well outside the park boundaries, this 100,000-hectare cattle station is only 17km from the turn-off just north of Wangi Falls. Wallabies abound and there's a peaceful atmosphere around the camping area (book ahead for the limited powered sites). The owners run cruises ($50) on their private billabong at 10am, as well as barra fishing trips ($250 per person).

Litchfield Safari Camp (☎ 08-8978 2185; www.litchfieldsafaricamp.com.au; unpowered/powered sites $20/30, safari tents with/without bathroom $130/110) Shady grassed sites make this a good alternative from Litchfield's bush camping sites, especially if you want power (generator). The spacious safari tents are great value as they comfortably sleep up to four people.

Latitude 1308 (☎ 08-8978 2077; www.litchfieldcafe .com.au; s/d incl meals $145/215) Run by the Litchfield Cafe, in a nearby bush clearing, Latitude 1308 is an intimate group of safari tents rented only on a full-board basis.

ourpick Litchfield Cafe (☎ 08-8978 2077; www.litchfieldcafe.com.au; mains $16-26) Filo parcels such as chicken, mango and macadamia are popular for lunch at this excellent licensed cafe, or you could go for a meal of grilled barra or roo fillet, topped with good coffee and a wicked mango cheesecake.

ADELAIDE RIVER TO KATHERINE

Adelaide River

pop 190

Blink and you'll miss this tiny highway town, 111km south of Darwin, once an important point on the Overland Telegraph Line and supply depot during WWII. The town's **War Cemetery** is an important legacy: a sea of white crosses commemorates those killed in the 1942–43 air raids on northern Australia.

If you're into horse riding, fishing or just relaxing with some country-style hospitality, **Mt Bundy Station** (☎ 08-8976 7009; www.mtbundy.com .au; Haynes Rd; unpowered/powered sites $20/24, s/d $35/70, cottage from $165, B&B $260; ✘ ▣) is the perfect detour, just 3km off the highway before Adelaide River. Original station buildings are now a spotless 20-bed bunkhouse with kitchen and a separate cottage sleeping six. Up on the hill in the family residence are two beautiful boutique B&B rooms where you can enjoy sunset drinks and panoramic views from the balcony. There are plenty of animals on the property – guided horse riding costs from $35 for a half-hour to $100 for a half-day, and overnight treks can be arranged.

Adelaide River Inn (☎ 08-8976 7047; unpowered/ powered sites $15/20, cabins $120; ✘ ▣) is an affable little pub (mains $17 to $22) hiding behind the roadhouse, and one worth stopping in for a beer. On the corner of the bar stands Charlie the water buffalo, who lived here in relative obscurity until shooting to fame in *Crocodile Dundee*. When he died the owner had him stuffed for posterity.

Daly River
pop 468

The Daly River is considered some of the best barramundi fishing country in the Territory and the hub is this small community 117km southwest of Hayes Creek, reached by a nar-row sealed road off the Dorat Rd (Old Stuart Hwy).

Most of the population lives in the NauiyauNambiyu Aboriginal community, a few kilometres before Daly River Crossing. There's a shop and fuel here and visitors are welcome without a permit, but note that this is a dry community (no alcohol). The main attraction is **Merrepen Arts** (☎ 08-8978 2533; www .merrepenarts.com; ☺ 10am-5pm), a gallery displaying locally made arts and crafts including etchings, screen printing, acrylic paintings, carvings, weaving and textiles. You can usually see artists at work in the mornings.

The **Merrepen Arts Festival**, held on the first weekend in June, celebrates arts and music from communities around the district, such as Nauiyu, Wadeye and Peppimenarti.

At Daly River itself is the **Daly River Roadside Inn** (☎ 08-8978 2418; unpowered/powered sites $15/25, r $65-95), a boisterous pub with basic rooms, a small camping ground and meals (takeaway or pub food from $6 to $18) and fuel available.

The camping ground at **Daly River Mango Farm** (☎ 1800 000 576, 08-8978 2464; www.mangofarm .com.au; unpowered/powered sites $24/30, d $100-150, cabins $120-180; ✘ ▣), on the Daly River 9km from the crossing, is shaded by a magnificent grove of 90-year-old mango trees. Other accommodation includes self-contained cabins (consider the stone one right on the river).

Perry's (☎ 08-8978 2452; www.dalyriver.com; Mayo Park; unpowered/powered sites $24/30; ▣ ▣) is another peaceful place to get away from it all with 2km of river frontage and gardens where orphaned wallabies bound around. Dick Perry, a well-known fishing expert, operates guided trips.

BONZA BACK ROADS: WATERS OF WAGIMAN COUNTRY

Just south of Adelaide River, Dorat Rd (the old Stuart Hwy) does a scenic, little-trafficked loop south through the traditional territory of the Wagiman before rejoining the main road after 52km. It's beautiful country, endowed with thermal springs, gorges and waterfalls.

Robin Falls, tumbling through a monsoon-forested gorge, are a short, rocky scramble from the car park 15km along Dorat Rd. To reach the searing waters of **Tjuwaliyn (Douglas) Hot Springs Park**, which is watched over by Wagiman women, turn south from Dorat Rd onto Oolloo Rd and continue for 35km. The springs are a further 7km down a dirt track (usually OK for 2WD vehicles). The park includes a section of the Douglas River that burbles up with several hot springs – a bit hot for a dip at 40°C to 60°C; head 200m up or downstream where the waters merge. The **camping ground** (adult/child/family $6.60/3.30/16) has toilets, barbecues and drinking water.

Butterfly Gorge Nature Park is 17km further along a 4WD track accessible only in the Dry. Swim across the main hole and through the narrowest of gorges to the upper pools; clamber across the crinkled pink rock walls to discover one of the Territory's more peaceful and pristine places. As the name suggests, butterflies sometimes gather in the gorge.

Pine Creek

pop 256

A short detour off the Stuart Hwy, Pine Creek was once the scene of a frantic gold rush. The open-cut mine here closed in 1995, but today there's a new influx of mine workers from the recently opened gold and iron-ore mines nearby. A few of the 19th-century timber and corrugated-iron buildings still survive. The Kakadu Hwy branches off the Stuart Hwy here, connecting it to Cooinda and Jabiru.

Dating from 1888, the **railway station** (admission free) has a display on the Darwin to Pine Creek railway (1889–1976). The lovingly restored steam engine, built in Manchester in 1877, sits in its own enclosure next to the museum.

The **Pine Creek Museum** (Railway Tce; adult/child $2.20/free; ⏰ 11am-5pm Mon-Fri, to 1pm Sat & Sun in the Dry) is dedicated to the area's mining history and Chinese population.

Drive or walk up the short but steep hill off Moule St to a **lookout** overlooking the old open-cut mine, now full of water.

The small, well-grassed camping area at **Lazy Lizard Tourist Park & Tavern** (☎ 08-8976 1224; unpowered/ powered sites $15/20; ⚓) is really only secondary to the pulsing pub next door. The open-sided bar supported by carved ironwood pillars is a great local watering hole and the kitchen here serves top-notch pub food (mains $16 to $32), featuring big steaks and barra dishes.

Beautiful **Bonrook Country Stay** (☎ 08-8976 1232; www.bonrook.com; Stuart Hwy; s/d/f $50/60/120, deluxe d $85-120; ⚓ ⚓), 8km south of town, is a tranquil B&B on a wild horse sanctuary where the brumbies are free to roam. The spotless rooms have no TV and no phone – just the sound of the wind in the trees and the birds outside.

About 3km south of Pine Creek on the Stuart Hwy is the turn-off to pretty **Umbrawarra Gorge Nature Park,** with a safe swimming hole, a little beach and a basic **camping ground** (adult/child/family $3.30/1.65/7.70);. It's 22km southwest on a rugged dirt road (OK for 2WDs in the Dry; often impassable in the Wet). Bring plenty of water.

KAKADU & ARNHEM LAND

KAKADU NATIONAL PARK

Kakadu is much more than just a national park. It's an adventure into a natural and cultural landscape that almost defies descrip-tion. Encompassing almost 20,000 sq km, it holds in its boundaries a spectacular ecosystem and a mind-blowing concentration of ancient rock art.

In just a few days you can cruise on billabongs bursting with crocodiles and birdlife, examine 25,000-year-old rock paintings with the help of an Indigenous guide, swim in pools at the foot of tumbling waterfalls and hike through ancient sandstone escarpment country.

Kakadu and neighbouring Arnhem Land epitomise the remarkable landscape and cultural heritage of the Top End. Each is a treasure house of natural history and Aboriginal art, an acknowledgement of the elemental link between the Aboriginal custodians and the country they have nurtured, endured and respected for thousands of generations. The landscape is an ever-changing tapestry – periodically scorched and flooded, apparently desolate or obviously abundant depending on the season.

If Kakadu has a downside – in the dry season at least – it's that it's very popular. Resorts, camping grounds and rock-art sites can get very crowded in peak seasons, but this is a vast park and with a little adventurous spirit you can easily get off the beaten track and be alone with nature.

Geography

The circuitous Arnhem Land escarpment, a dramatic 30m- to 200m-high sandstone cliff line, forms the natural boundary between Kakadu and Arnhem Land and winds 500km through eastern and southeastern Kakadu.

Creeks cut across the rocky plateau and, in the wet season, tumble off it as thundering waterfalls. They then flow across the lowlands to swamp Kakadu's vast northern flood plains. From west to east, the rivers are the Wildman, West Alligator, South Alligator and East Alligator (the latter forming the eastern boundary of the park). The coastal zone has long stretches of mangrove swamp, important for halting erosion and as a breeding ground for bird and marine life. The southern part of the park is dry lowlands with open grassland and eucalypts. Pockets of monsoon rainforest crop up throughout the park.

Over 80% of Kakadu is savannah woodland. It has more than 1000 plant species, many still used by Aboriginal people for food and medicinal purposes.

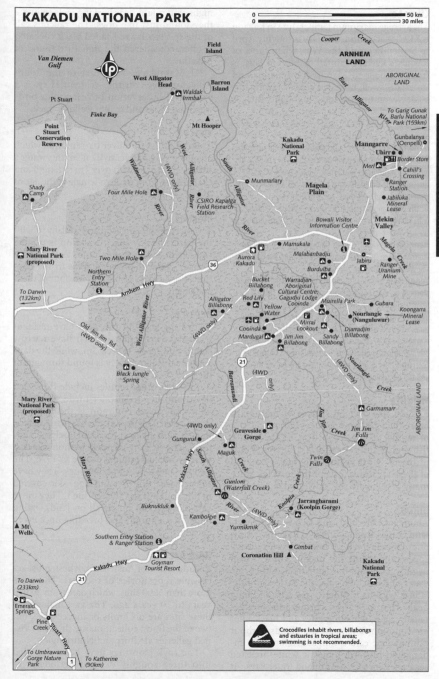

KAKADU NATIONAL PARK

Crocodiles inhabit rivers, billabongs and estuaries in tropical areas; swimming is not recommended.

Climate

The average maximum temperature in Kakadu is 34°C, year-round. The Dry is roughly April to September, and the Wet, when most of Kakadu's average rainfall of 130mm falls, is from October to March. As wetlands and waterfalls swell, unsealed roads become impassable, cutting off some highlights such as Jim Jim Falls.

Local Aboriginal people recognise six seasons in the annual cycle:

Gunumeleng (October to December) The build-up to the Wet. Humidity increases, the temperature rises to 35°C or more and mosquitoes reach near-plague proportions. By November the thunderstorms have started, billabongs are replenished, and waterbirds and fish disperse.

Gudjewg (January to March) The Wet proper continues, with violent thunderstorms, and flora and fauna thriving in the hot, moist conditions.

Banggereng (April) Storms (known as 'knock 'em down' storms) flatten the spear grass, which during the course of the Wet has shot up to 2m high.

Yegge (May to June) The season of mists, when the air starts to dry out. The wetlands and waterfalls still have a lot of water and most of the tracks are open.

Wurrgeng (June to mid-August) The most comfortable time, weather-wise, is the late Dry, beginning in July. This is when wildlife, especially birds, gathers in large numbers around shrinking billabongs, and when most tourists visit.

Gurrung (mid-August to September) The end of the Dry and the beginning of another cycle.

Wildlife

Kakadu has over 60 species of mammals, more than 280 bird species, 120 or so types of reptile, 25 species of frog, 55 freshwater fish species and at least 10,000 different kinds of insect. Most visitors see only a fraction of these creatures (except the insects), since many of them are shy, nocturnal or scarce.

BIRDS

Abundant waterbirds and their beautiful wetland homes are a highlight of Kakadu. This is one of the chief refuges in Australia for several species, including the magpie goose, green pygmy goose and Burdekin duck. Other fine water birds include pelicans, darters and the jabiru, with its distinctive red legs and long beak. Herons, egrets, cormorants, wedgetailed eagles, whistling kites and black kites are common. The open woodlands harbour rainbow bee-eaters, kingfishers and the endangered bustard. Majestic white-breasted sea eagles are seen near inland waterways. At night, you might hear barking owls calling – they sound just like dogs. The raucous call of the spectacular red-tailed black cockatoo is often considered the signature sound of Kakadu.

At Mamukala, 8km east of the South Alligator River on the Arnhem Hwy, is a wonderful observation building, plus birdwatching hides and a 3km walking track.

FISH

You can't miss the silver barramundi, which creates a distinctive swirl near the water's surface. It can grow to over 1m in length and changes sex from male to female at the age of five or six years.

MAMMALS

Several types of kangaroo and wallaby inhabit the park; the shy black wallaroo is unique to Kakadu and Arnhem Land. You may see a sugar glider in wooded areas in the daytime. Kakadu has 26 bat species, four of them endangered.

REPTILES

Twin Falls and Jim Jim Falls have resident freshwater crocodiles, which have narrow snouts and rarely exceed 3m, while the dangerous saltwater variety is found throughout the park.

Kakadu's other reptiles include the frilled lizard and five freshwater turtle species, of which the most common is the northern snake-necked turtle. Kakadu has many snakes, though most are nocturnal and rarely encountered. The striking Oenpelli python was first seen by non-Aboriginal people in 1976. The odd file snake lives in billabongs. They have square heads, tiny eyes and saggy skin covered in tiny rough scales (hence 'file'). They move very slowly (and not at all on land), eating only once a month and breeding once every decade.

Rock Art

Kakadu is one of Australia's richest, most accessible repositories of rock art. There are more than 5000 sites, which date from 20,000 years to 10 years ago. The vast majority of these sites are off limits or inaccessible, but two of the finest collections are the easily visited galleries at Ubirr and Nourlangie.

The rock paintings have been classified into three roughly defined periods: Pre-estuarine, which is from the earliest paintings up to around 6000 years ago; Estuarine, which covers the period from 6000 to around 2000 years ago, when rising sea levels brought the coast to its present level; and Freshwater, from 2000 years ago until the present day.

For local Aboriginal people, these rock-art sites are a major source of traditional knowledge and represent their archives. Aboriginal people rarely paint on rocks any more, as they no longer live in rock shelters and there are fewer people with the requisite knowledge. Some older paintings are believed by many Aboriginal people to have been painted by *mimi* spirits, connecting people with creation legends and the development of Aboriginal law.

As the paintings are all rendered with natural, water-soluble ochres, they are very susceptible to water damage. Drip lines of clear silicon rubber have been laid on the rocks above the paintings to divert rain. As the most accessible sites receive up to 4000 visitors a week, boardwalks have been erected to keep the dust down and to keep people at a suitable distance from the paintings.

Orientation

Kakadu National Park stretches more than 200km south from the coast and 100km from east to west.

Two main roads traverse the park (Arnhem Hwy and Kakadu Hwy); both are sealed and accessible year-round. The 4WD-only Old Jim Jim Rd is an alternative access from the Arnhem Hwy, joining the Kakadu Hwy 7km south of Cooinda.

Information

About 200,000 people visit Kakadu between April and October, so you can expect some tour-bus action at sites such as Ubirr and Yellow Water. Consider spending some time bushwalking and camping in the south of the park – it's less visited but inimitably impressive.

Admission to the park is free: pick up an excellent *Visitor Guide & Maps* booklet from Bowali visitor information centre, or check online at www.environment.gov.au/parks/kakadu or www.kakadunationalpark.com. Fuel is available at Kakadu Resort, Cooinda and Jabiru. Jabiru has a shopping complex with a supermarket, post office, a Westpac bank and newsagency.

Accommodation prices in Kakadu vary tremendously depending on the season – resort rates can drop by as much as 50% during the Wet.

The excellent **Bowali Visitor Information Centre** (☎ 08-8938 1121; Kakadu Hwy, Jabiru; ☽ 8am-5pm) has walk-through displays that sweep you across the land, explaining Kakadu's ecology from Aboriginal and non-Aboriginal perspectives. The helpful staffed info window has 'Park Notes' fliers on all walks, with superb information about plants, animals and salient features you might encounter on each walk, explaining their uses and significance. The 'What's On' flier details where and when to catch a free and informative park ranger talk. The **Marrawuddi Gallery** (www.marrawuddi.com) is good for a souvenir, stocking music, paintings and craft by the countrymen and women of Kakadu and Arnhem Land. The centre is about 2.5km south of the Arnhem Hwy intersection; a 1km walking track connects it with Jabiru.

The **Northern Land Council** (☎ 08-8979 2410; www.nlc.org.au; Flinders St, Jabiru; ☽ 8am-1pm & 2-4.30pm Mon-Fri) issues permits (adult/child $13.20/free) to visit Gunbalanya (Oenpelli), across the East Alligator River.

Tours

Most trips require some notification that you'll be joining them, so book at least a day ahead if possible; operators generally collect you from your accommodation. For tours departing Darwin, see p826.

Arnhemlander (☎ 1800 089 113; www.arnhemlander.com.au; adult/child $195/156) Runs 4WD tours to the Mikinj Valley and Injalak Art Centre at Gunbalanya (Oenpelli).

Kakadu Air (☎ 1800 089 113; www.kakaduair.com.au) Offers 30-minute/one-hour fixed-wing flights for $100/175 per person. Helicopter tours, though more expensive, give a more exciting aerial perspective. They cost from $195 (20 minutes) to $425 (70 minutes) per person.

Kakadu Animal Tracks (☎ 08-8979 0145; www.animaltracks.com.au; adult/child $165/125) Based at Cooinda, this outfit runs highly recommended tours combining a wildlife safari and Aboriginal cultural tour with an Indigenous guide. You'll see thousands of birds on the floodplains in the Dry, and get to hunt and gather, prepare and consume bush tucker and crunch on some green ants.

Kakadu Gorge & Waterfall Tours (☎ 08-8979 0111; www.gagudju-dreaming.com; adult/child $170/145) Operates 4WD tours to Jim Jim Falls.

URANIUM MINING

It's no small irony that some of the world's biggest deposits of uranium lie within one of Australia's most beautiful national parks. In 1953 uranium was discovered in the Kakadu region. Twelve small deposits in the southern reaches of the park were worked in the 1960s, but were abandoned following the declaration of Woolwonga Wildlife Sanctuary.

In 1970 three huge deposits – Ranger, Nabarlek and Koongarra – were found, followed by Jabiluka in 1971. The Nabarlek deposit (in Arnhem Land) was mined in the late '70s, and the Ranger Uranium Mine started producing ore in 1981.

While all mining in the park has been controversial, it was Jabiluka that brought international attention to Kakadu and pitted conservationists and Indigenous owners against the government and mining companies. After uranium was discovered at Jabiluka in 1971, an agreement to mine was negotiated with the local Aboriginal peoples. The Jabiluka mine became the scene of sit-in demonstrations during 1998 that resulted in large-scale arrests. In 2003, stockpiled ore was returned into the mine and the decline tunnel leading into the deposit was backfilled as the mining company moved into dialogue with the traditional landowners, the Mirrar people.

In February 2005 the current owners of the Jabiluka mining lease, Energy Resources of Australia (ERA), signed an agreement that gave the Mirrar the deciding vote on any resumption of this controversial mining project. Under the deal ERA is allowed to continue to explore the lease, subject to Mirrar consent. Meanwhile, the Ranger mine – which is officially not part of the national park but is surrounded by it – is due to close in 2010, but the discovery of further deposits in late 2008 means it is possible the mine could remain operating for another five years, depending on the approval of government and the Northern Land Council.

Lord's Kakadu & Arnhemland Safaris (☎ 08-8948 2200; www.lords-safaris.com; adult/child $195/155) One-day trip into Arnhem Land (Gunbalanya) from Jabiru visits Oenpelli with a guided walk around Injalak Hill. Lord's also has a range of multiday trips covering Kakadu and Arnhem Land departing from Darwin.

Magela Cultural & Heritage Tours (☎ 08-8979 2548; www.kakadutours.com.au; adult/child $235/188) Aboriginal-owned and -operated day tour into northern Kakadu and Arnhem Land, including Injalak Hill and a cruise on Inkiyu billabong. Pick-up from Jabiru.

Murdudjurl Kakadu (☎ 08-8979 0145; www.murdud jurlkakadu.com.au; tours $75) Aboriginal-owned and -run cultural tour that takes you onto private land where you can interact with the traditional owners and learn about bush tucker, basket weaving and painting. The two-hour tours depart from Gagadju Lodge in Cooinda on Monday, Wednesday, Friday and Saturday at 3pm.

WETLAND & RIVER TRIPS

Guluyambi (☎ 1800 089 113; www.guluyambi.com .au; adult/child $45/25; ⏱ 9am, 11am, 1pm & 3pm May-Nov) Launch into an Aboriginal-led river cruise from the upstream boat ramp on the East Alligator River near Cahill's Crossing.

Kakadu Culture Camp (☎ 0428 792 048; www.kak aduculturecamp.com) Aboriginal-owned and -operated cruises on Djarradjin Billabong; two-hour night cruise ($49/30 per adult/child, at 6.20pm daily) and bush tucker and boat cruise ($179/119 per adult/child, from 5pm to

10pm Tuesday). Tours depart from Muirella Park camping ground.

Yellow Water Cruises (☎ 08-8979 0145; www .gagudju-dreaming.com) This is a highlight for many – cruise the South Alligator River and Yellow Water billabong spotting wildlife. Purchase tickets from Gagudju Lodge, Cooinda, where a shuttle bus will deliver you to the departure point. Two-hour cruises ($70/49 per adult/child) depart at 6.45am, 9am and 4.30pm; 1½ hour cruises ($50/35) leave at 11.30am, 1.15pm and 2.45pm.

Ubirr & Around

It'll take a lot more than the busloads of visitors here to disturb Ubirr's inherent majesty and grace. Layers of paintings, in various styles and from various centuries, command a mesmerising stillness. Part of the main gallery reads like a menu, with images of kangaroos, tortoises and fish painted in X-ray, which became the dominant style about 8000 years ago. Predating these are the paintings of *mimi* spirits: cheeky, dynamic figures who, it's believed, were the first of the Creation Ancestors to paint on rock. (Given the lack of cherry pickers in 6000 BC, you have to wonder who else but a spirit could have painted at that height and angle.) Look out for the yam-head figures, where the head is depicted as a yam on the body of a human or animal; these date back around 15,000 years.

The magnificent **Nardab Lookout** is a 250m scramble from the main gallery. Surveying the exotic floodplain and watching the sun set in the west and the moon rise in the east, like they're on an invisible set of scales gradually exchanging weight, is humbling, to say the least.

Ubirr (8.30am-sunset Apr-Nov, from 2pm Dec-Mar) is 39km north of the Arnhem Hwy via a sealed road. On the way you'll pass the turn-off to **Merl** (adult/child $5.40/free) camping ground, which is only open in the Dry and has an amenities block, and the **Border Store** (08-8979 2474; meals $6-18; 8am-5.30pm Apr-Nov), selling a range of groceries, sit-down meals and takeaway food.

WALKS

Bardedjilidji Sandstone Walk (2.5km, 90 minutes, easy) Starting from the upstream picnic-area car park, this walk takes in wetland areas of the East Alligator River and some interesting eroded sandstone outliers of the Arnhem Land escarpment. Informative track notes point out many features on this walk.

Manngarre Monsoon Rainforest Walk (1.5km return, 30 minutes, easy) Mainly sticking to a boardwalk, this walk starts by the boat ramp near the Border Store and winds through heavily shaded vegetation, palms and vines.

Sandstone & River Bushwalk (6.5km, three hours, medium) This extension of the Bardedjilidji Walk features sandstone outcrops, paperbark swamps and riverbanks.

Jabiru
pop 1135

It may seem surprising to find a town of Jabiru's size and structure in the midst of a wilderness national park, but it exists solely because of the nearby Ranger uranium mine. It's Kakadu's major service centre, with a bank, newsagent, medical centre, supermarket, bakery and service station. You can even play a round of golf here.

The **Ranger Uranium Mine Tour** (1800 089 113; adult/child $25/10; 9am, 11am & 1pm Mon-Sat) is an opportunity to see one of the park's controversial mining projects up close and learn some of the issues surrounding uranium mining. Guided tours leave from Jabiru airstrip, about 8km east of town.

SLEEPING & EATING

Kakadu Lodge & Caravan Park (1800 811 154; www.auroraresorts.com.au; Jabiru Dr; unpowered/powered sites $26/32, cabins from $240;) An impeccable resort with shady, grassed sites and a great

lagoon swimming pool. Self-contained cabins sleep up to five people but are booked up well in advance. There's a kiosk, bar and bistro.

our pick Lakeview Park (08-8979 3144; www.lakeviewkakadu.com.au; 27 Lakeside Dr; en-suite powered sites $30, bungalows/d/cabins $95/110/195;) Although there are no lake views as such, this beautifully landscaped Aboriginal-owned park is one of Kakadu's best with a range of comfortable tropical-designed bungalows set in lush gardens. The doubles share a communal kitchen, bathroom and lounge, and also come equipped with their own TV and fridge, while the 'bush bungalows' are stylish elevated safari designs with private external bathroom that sleep up to four.

Gagudju Crocodile Holiday Inn (08-8979 9000; www.gagudju-dreaming.com; Flinders St; d from $300;) Known locally as 'the Croc', this hotel is designed in the shape of a crocodile, which, of course, is only obvious when viewed from the air or Google Earth. The rooms are clean and comfortable if a little pedestrian for the price. Try for one on the ground floor opening out to the central pool. The Escarpment Restaurant here is the best in Jabiru.

Jabiru Sports & Social Club (08-8979 2326; Lakeside Dr; mains $18-32; lunch daily, dinner Mon-Sat) Along with the golf club, this is the place to meet the locals over a beer. The bistro meals are generous and there's a nice outdoor deck overlooking the lake, sports on TV and a TAB.

Superb made-to-order sandwiches on home-baked bread walk out the door at **Kakadu Bakery** (08-8979 2320; Gregory Pl; snacks $2-8; 6.30am-2pm Mon-Fri, 7am-2pm Sat, 9am-1pm Sun), or you can self-cater at the well-stocked **Foodland** (Jabiru Plaza; 9am-5.30pm Mon-Fri, to 3pm Sat, 10am-2pm Sun & public holidays). Note that there's no takeaway alcohol available here or anywhere in Kakadu – if you want a drink back at the campsite, stock up in Darwin.

Nourlangie Area

The sight of this looming outlier of the Arnhem Land escarpment makes it easy to understand its ancient importance to Aboriginal people. Its long red-sandstone bulk, striped in places with orange, white and black, slopes up from surrounding woodland to fall away at one end in stepped cliffs. Below is Kakadu's best-known collection of rock art.

The name Nourlangie is a corruption of *nawulandja*, an Aboriginal word that refers to an area bigger than the rock itself. The 2km looped walking track takes you first to the **Anbangbang rock shelter**, used for 20,000 years as a refuge and canvas. Next is the Anbangbang Gallery, featuring Dreaming characters repainted in the '60s. From here it's a short walk to **Gunwarddehwarde lookout**, with views of the Arnhem Land escarpment.

Nourlangie is at the end of a 12km sealed road that turns east off Kakadu Hwy, 21km south of Arnhem Hwy. Seven kilometres south is the turn-off to **Muirella Park** (adult/child $5.40/free) camping ground, with barbecues and excellent amenities.

WALKS

Anbangbang Billabong Walk (2.5km loop, 45 minutes, easy) This picturesque, lily-filled billabong lies close to Nourlangie, and the picnic tables dotted around its edge make it a popular lunch spot. The track circles the billabong and passes through paperbark swamp.

Barrk Sandstone Bushwalk (12km loop, six to eight hours, difficult) This long day walk will take you away from the crowds on a circuit of the Nourlangie area. Barrk is the male black wallaroo and you might see this elusive marsupial if you set out early. Starting at the Nourlangie car park, this demanding walk passes through the Anbangbang galleries before a steep climb to the top of Nourlangie Rock. Cross the flat top of the rock weaving through sandstone pillars before descending along a wet-season watercourse. The track then follows the rock's base past the Nanguluwur gallery and western cliffs before re-emerging at the car park.

Nanguluwur Gallery (3.5km return, 1½ hours, easy) This outstanding rock-art gallery sees far fewer visitors than Nourlangie simply because it's further to walk and has a gravel access road. Here the paintings cover most of the styles found in the park, including very early dynamic style work, X-ray work and a good example of 'contact art', a painting of a two-masted sailing ship towing a dinghy.

Jim Jim Falls & Twin Falls

Remote and spectacular, these two falls epitomise the rugged Top End. Jim Jim Falls, a sheer 215m drop, is awesome after rain (when it can only be seen from the air), but its waters shrink to a trickle by about June. Twin Falls flows year-round (no swimming), but half the fun is getting there, involving a little boat trip and an over-the-water boardwalk.

These two iconic waterfalls are reached along a 4WD track that turns south off the Kakadu Hwy between the Nourlangie and Cooinda turn-offs. Jim Jim Falls is about 57km from the turn-off (the last 1km on foot),

and it's a further 10 corrugated kilometres to Twin Falls. The track is open in the Dry only and can still be closed into late May; it's off limits to most rental vehicles (check the fine print). A couple of tour companies make trips here in the Dry and there's a camping area near Jim Jim.

Cooinda & Yellow Water

Cooinda is best known for the cruises on the wetland area known as Yellow Water (see Yellow Water Cruises, p846), and has developed into a slick resort. About 1km from the resort, the **Warradjan Aboriginal Cultural Centre** (☎ 08-8975 0051; Yellow Water Area; ⏰ 9am-5pm) depicts creation stories and has an excellent permanent exhibition that includes clap sticks, sugar-bag holders and rock-art samples. You'll be introduced to the moiety system (internal tribal division) and skin names, and there's a minitheatre with a huge selection of films from which to choose. Warradjan is an easy walk (15 minutes) from the Cooinda resort.

Gagudju Lodge Cooinda (☎ 08-8979 0145; www .gagudjulodgecooinda.com.au; unpowered/powered sites $15/35, dm $35, budget/lodge r $85/285; ✗ 🖳 ⏰) is the most popular accommodation resort in the park. It's a modern oasis but, even with 380 campsites, facilities can get very stretched. The budget air-con units are compact and comfortable, and share the camping ground amenities. The lodge rooms are spacious and comfortable, and sleep up to four people. There are two restaurants on site: the casual open-air **Barra Bar & Bistro** (mains $6-25; ⏰ 10am-10pm) and the intimate **Mimi Restaurant** (mains $26-36; ⏰ breakfast & dinner), delivering local produce, such as barramundi and emu prepared with bush fruits and spices.

The turn-off to the Cooinda accommodation complex and Yellow Water wetlands is 47km down the Kakadu Hwy from the Arnhem Hwy intersection. Just off the Kakadu Hwy, 2km south of the Cooinda turn-off, is the National Parks **Mardugal** (adult/child $5.40/free) camping ground – an excellent year-round camping area with shower and toilets.

Cooinda to Pine Creek

This southern section of the park sees far fewer tour buses. Though it's unlikely you'll have dreamy **Maguk** (Barramundi Gorge; 45km south of Cooinda and 10km along a corrugated 4WD track) to yourself, you might time it right to have the glorious natural pool and falls between just a few of you. Conventional-vehicle drivers fear not: 40-odd kilometres further south is the turn-off to **Gunlom** (Waterfall Creek), another superb escarpment waterfall, plunge pool and camping area. It's located 37km along an unsealed, though easily doable, gravel road. Walk the steep Waterfall Walk (1km, one hour) here, which affords incredible views.

YURMIKMIK WALKS
On the road to Gunlom is the start of a series of interconnected walks leading first through woodlands and monsoon forest to **Boulder Creek** (2km, 45 minutes), then on to the **Lookout** (5km, 1½ to two hours), with views over rugged ridges, and **Motor Car Falls** (7.5km, four hours).

Getting There & Around
Without your own wheels it's still possible to explore Kakadu independently. You can combine transport to Jabiru, Ubirr and Cooinda with a couple of tours, such as a trip to Jim Jim Falls, the Yellow Water cruise and an Aboriginal cultural tour.

     Greyhound Australia (☎ 1300 473 946; www .greyhound.com.au) has a daily service between Darwin and Cooinda via Jabiru. Buses reach the Yellow Water wetlands in time for the 1pm cruise, and depart after the cruise, 1½ hours later. The bus leaves Darwin at 8am and Jabiru at 11.30am, arriving at Cooinda at 12.40pm. It departs from Cooinda at 1.15pm and Jabiru at 2.30pm, and arrives in Darwin at 5.30pm. The one-way fare from Darwin to Jabiru is $53, and to Cooinda $74.

ARNHEM LAND
Arnhem Land is a vast, overwhelming and mysterious corner of the Northern Territory. About the size of the state of Victoria and with a population of only around 17,000, mostly Yolngu people, this Aboriginal reserve is one of Australia's last great untouched wilderness areas. Most people live on outstations, combining traditional practices with modern Western ones, so they might go out for a hunt and be back in time to watch the 6pm news. Outside commercial interests and visits are highly regulated through a permit system, designed to protect the environment, the rock art and ceremonial grounds. *Balanda* (white people) are unaware of the locations of burial grounds and ceremonial lands. Basically, you

need a specific purpose for entering, usually to visit an arts centre, in order to be granted a permit. If you're travelling far enough to warrant an overnight stay, you'll need to organise accommodation (which is in short supply). It's easy to visit Gunbalanya (Oenpelli) and its arts centre, just over the border, either on a tour or independently. Elsewhere, it's best to travel with a tour, which will include the necessary permit(s) to enter Aboriginal lands.

TOURS
Arnhemlander (☎ 1800 089 113; www.arnhemlander .com.au; adult/child $195/156) Runs 4WD tours to the Mikinj Valley and Injalak Art Centre at Gunbalanya (Oenpelli).
Davidson's Arnhemland Safaris (☎ 08-8927 5240; www.arnhemland-safaris.com) Experienced operator taking tours to Mt Borradaile, north of Oenpelli. Meals, guided tours, fishing and accommodation in the comfortable safari camp are included in the daily price of around $450; transfers from Darwin can be arranged.
Gove Diving & Fishing Charters (☎ 08-8987 3445; www.govefish.com.au) Variety of fishing, diving and snorkelling, and wilderness trips from Nhulunbuy.
Lord's Kakadu & Arnhemland Safaris (☎ 08-8948 2200; www.lords-safaris.com; adult/child $195/155) Small-group 4WD tours to Gunbalanya (Oenpelli), including an Aboriginal-guided walk to the Injalak Hill rock-art site, lunch and a scout around the Mikinj Valley.
Nomad (☎ 08-8987 8085; www.nomadcharters.com.au; tours $375-1800) Luxury small-group tours from Nhulunbuy including fishing charters and cultural tours.
Venture North Australia (☎ 08-8927 5500; www .northernaustralia.com; 4-/5-day tour $1479/1960) Tours to remote areas; features expert guidance on rock art. It also has a safari camp near Smith Point on the Cobourg Peninsula.

Gunbalanya (Oenpelli)
pop 881
Gunbalanya is a small Aboriginal community 17km into Arnhem Land across the East Alligator River from the Border Store in Kakadu. The drive in itself is worth it with brilliant green wetlands and spectacular escarpments all around. Road access is only possible between May and October: check the tides at Cahill's Crossing on the East Alligator River before setting out so you don't get stuck on the other side.

     A permit is required to visit the town, usually issued for visits to the **Injalak Arts & Crafts Centre** (☎ 08-8979 0190; www.injalak.com; ⏰ 8am-5pm). At this centre, artists and craftspeople produce traditional paintings on bark and paper, plus didgeridoos, pandanus weavings and baskets, and screen-printed fabrics, either at the arts centre or on remote outstations throughout Arnhem Land.

As you walk around the verandah of the arts centre to see the artists at work (morning only), peer out over the wetland at the rear to the escarpment and **Injalak Hill** (Long Tom Dreaming). Knowledgable local guides lead tours to see the fine rock-art galleries here. The two-hour tours (bookings essential) cost $150 per group. Although it may be possible to join a tour as a walk-in, it's generally best to book a tour from Jabiru.

The **Northern Land Council** (☎ 08-8979 2410; Flinders St, Jabiru) issues permits ($12.50) to visit Injalak, usually on the spot. It also provides tide times for the East Alligator, which is impassable at high tide.

Cobourg Peninsula

The entire wilderness of this remote peninsula forms the **Garig Gunak Barlu National Park**, which includes the surrounding sea. In the turquoise water you'll likely see dolphins and turtles, and – what most people come for – a threadfin salmon thrashing on the end of your line.

On the shores of Port Essington are the stone ruins and headstones from Victoria settlement – Britain's 1838 attempt to establish a military outpost.

At Black Point (Algarlarlgarl) there's a **ranger station** (☎ 08-8979 0244) with a visitor information and cultural centre, and the **Garig Store** (☎ 08-8979 0455; 4-6pm Mon-Sat), which sells basic provisions, ice and camping gas. There are two camping grounds in the park with shower, toilet, barbecues and limited bore water; generators are allowed in one area. Camping fees are covered by your vehicle permit but if you fly in the permits cost $16.50 per person per day. Other accommodation is available in pricey fishing resorts.

Two permits are required to visit the Cobourg Peninsula: for a transit pass to drive through Aboriginal land contact the **Northern Land Council** (www.nlc.org.au; passes $12.50); for permission to stay overnight in the National Park contact the **Parks & Wildlife Commission** (☎ 08-8999 4814; www.nt.gov.au). The fee is $232 per vehicle, which covers up to five people for seven days and includes camping.

GETTING THERE & AWAY
The quickest route here is by private charter flight, which can be arranged by accommoda-

tion providers. The track to Cobourg starts at Gunbalanya (Oenpelli) and is accessible by 4WD vehicles only from May to October. The 270km drive to Black Point from the East Alligator River takes about four hours.

Eastern Arnhem Land
The wildly beautiful coast and country of Eastern Arnhem Land (www.ealta.org) is really off the beaten track. About 4000 people live in the region's main settlement, **Nhulunbuy**, built to service the bauxite mine. The 1963 plans to establish a manganese mine were hotly protested by the traditional owners, the Yolngu people; though mining proceeded, the case became an important step in establishing land rights. Some of the country's most respected art comes out of this region too, including bark paintings, carved *mimi* figures, *yidaki* (didgeridoos), woven baskets and mats, and jewellery.

Nambara Arts & Crafts Aboriginal Gallery (☎ 08-8987 2811; Melville Bay Rd, Nhulunbuy) sells art and crafts from northeast Arnhem Land and often has artists in residence. **Buku Larrnggay Mulka Art Centre & Museum** (☎ 08-8987 1701; www.yirrkala .com; Yirrkala; museum admission $2; 8am-4.30pm Mon-Fri, 9am-noon Sat), 20km southeast of Nhulunbuy, is one of Arnhem Land's best. No permit is required to visit from Nhulunbuy or Gove airport.

Overland travel through Arnhem Land from Katherine requires a permit (free) from the **Northern Land Council** (www.nlc.org.au). The **Dhimurru Land Management Aboriginal Corporation** (☎ 08-8987 3992; www.dhimurru.com.au; Arnhem Rd, Nhulunbuy) issues recreation permits ($20/35 for seven days/two months) for visits to particular recreation areas in Eastern Arnhem Land – check the website for details.

GETTING THERE & AWAY
Airnorth (☎ 1800 627 474; www.airnorth.com.au) flies from Darwin to Gove (for Nhulunbuy) daily from $150 one way. Overland, it's a 10-hour 4WD trip and only possible in the Dry. The Central Arnhem Hwy to Gove leaves the Stuart Hwy 52km south of Katherine.

KATHERINE TO ALICE

The Stuart Hwy from Darwin to Alice Springs is still referred to as 'the Track' – it has been since WWII, when it was literally a dirt track connecting the Territory's two main towns, roughly following the Overland Telegraph Line. It's dead straight most of the way and gets progressively drier and flatter as you head south, but there are quite a few notable diversions.

KATHERINE

pop 5850

Katherine is considered a big town in this part of the world and you'll certainly feel like you've arrived somewhere after the long trip up the highway. Its namesake river is the first permanent running water on the road north from Alice Springs. In the Wet the river swells dramatically and has been responsible for some devastating floods – the worst in memory was Australia Day 1998, when rising waters inundated the surrounding countryside and left a mark up to 2m high on Katherine's buildings.

Katherine is probably best known for the Nitmiluk (Katherine Gorge) National Park to the east, and the town makes an obvious base, with plenty of accommodation and some decent restaurants. It also has quite a few attractions of its own, including a thriving Indigenous arts community, thermal springs and a few museums.

The Katherine area is the traditional home of the Jawoyn and Dagoman Aboriginal peoples. Following land claims they have received the title to large parcels of land, including Nitmiluk National Park.

Orientation & Information

The Stuart Hwy is known as Katherine Tce through town – possibly one of the only streets in Australia that pipes music from loudspeakers day and night. It's a disconcerting mix of country and retro pop – whether you like it or not!

Didj Shop Internet Cafe (☎ 0415 461 759; www .didj.com.au; cnr Giles St & Railway Tce; per 15min/hr $2/6; ◷ 10am-7pm Mon-Sat, also 11am-3pm Sun Apr-Oct only) Katherine's best internet cafe – log on, order fine coffee and chat with the gregarious owner. Buy a coffee and get 15 minutes internet free. Access for laptops.

Katherine Hospital (☎ 08-8973 9211; Giles St) About 3km north of town, with an emergency department.

Katherine Visitor Information Centre (☎ 08-8972 2650; www.visitkatherine.com.au; cnr Lindsay St & Katherine Tce; ◷ 8.30am-5pm Mon-Fri, 9am-2pm Sat & Sun, to 5pm Sat & Sun in the Dry) Modern, air-con information centre stocking information on all areas of the NT.

Parks & Wildlife office (☎ 08-8973 8888; 32 Giles St) National park information notes are available here.

Sights & Activities

Katherine Low Level Nature Park is a great spot on the banks of the Katherine River, just off the Victoria Hwy 4km from town. It has a popular dry-season swimming hole linked to crystalline **thermal pools** and town by a tree-lined shared cycle- and footpath.

Katherine Outback Heritage Museum (☎ 08-8972 3945; Gorge Rd; adult/child $5/2; ◷ 9am-4pm) is in the old airport terminal, about 3km from town on the road to the gorge. The original Gypsy Moth biplane flown by Dr Clyde Fenton, the first Flying Doctor, is housed here. There's a good selection of historical photos, including a display on the 1998 flood.

At the **School of the Air** (☎ 08-8972 1833; www .schools.nt.edu.au/ksa; Giles St; adult/child $5/2; ◷ Mar-Nov), 1.5km from the town centre, you can listen in on a class and see how kids in the remote outback are educated in the virtual world. Guided tours are held at 9am, 10am and 11am on weekdays and bookings are preferred.

Alfred Giles established **Springvale Homestead** (☎ 08-8972 1355; Shadforth Rd) in 1879 after he drove 2000 cattle and horses and 12,000 head of sheep from Adelaide to the site in 19 months. It claims to be the oldest cattle station in the Northern Territory. The stone homestead still stands by the river, about 8km southwest of town, and the surrounding riverside property is now a caravan and camping resort. There's a free tour of the homestead at 3pm daily (except Monday) from May to October. Canoes are available for hire from $11 for an hour or $21 for a half-day.

Jurassic Cycad Gardens (☎ 0417 623 014; www .cycadinternational.com.au; 61 Morris Rd; adult/child/family $10/5/25; ◷ 8am-6pm Tue-Sun) is home to over 200 species of prehistoric cycads, collected and seeded from around Australia and overseas. A self-guided tour through the remarkable maze of rare plants also takes you past baobabs, rock figs, ferns and cacti. The attached cafe is a good place for breakfast or lunch.

Tours

Crocodile Night Adventure (☎ 1800 089 103; adult/child $55/29; ◷ 6.30pm May-Oct) At Springvale Homestead, this evening cruise seeks out crocs and other nocturnal wildlife on the Katherine River. Includes barbecue dinner and drinks.

NORTHERN TERRITORY

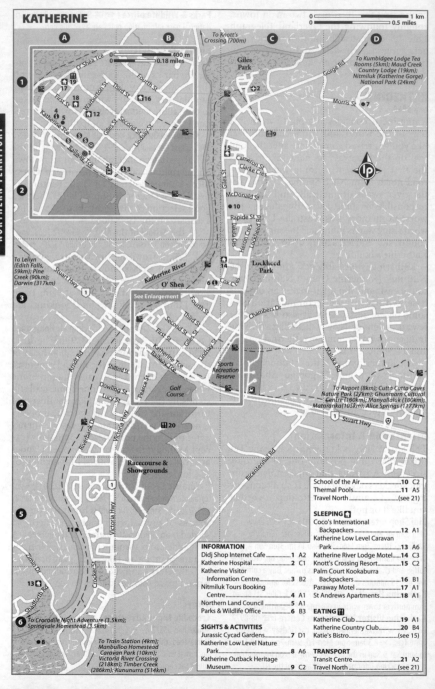

INFORMATION
Didj Shop Internet Cafe **1** A2
Katherine Hospital **2** C1
Katherine Visitor
  Information Centre **3** B2
Nitmiluk Tours Booking
  Centre **4** A1
Northern Land Council **5** A1
Parks & Wildlife Office **6** B3

SIGHTS & ACTIVITIES
Jurassic Cycad Gardens **7** D1
Katherine Low Level Nature
  Park **8** A6
Katherine Outback Heritage
  Museum **9** C2

School of the Air **10** C2
Thermal Pools **11** A5
Travel North ....(see 21)

SLEEPING 🏠
Coco's International
  Backpackers **12** A1
Katherine Low Level Caravan
  Park **13** A6
Katherine River Lodge Motel **14** C3
Knott's Crossing Resort **15** C2
Palm Court Kookaburra
  Backpackers **16** B1
Paraway Motel **17** A1
St Andrews Apartments **18** A1

EATING 🍴
Katherine Club **19** A1
Katherine Country Club **20** B4
Katie's Bistro ....(see 15)

TRANSPORT
Transit Centre **21** A2
Travel North ....(see 21)

Gecko Canoeing (☎ 1800 634 319, 08-8972 2224; www.geckocanoeing.com.au) Exhilarating guided canoe trips on the more remote stretches of the Katherine River. Trips vary from one/three days ($195/720) on the Katherine River to expeditions of up to seven days on the Baines, Wickham and Victoria Rivers. A five-day hike along the Jatbula Trail in Nitmiluk National Park costs $995.

Katherine Town Tour (☎ 08-8971 9999; adult/child $62/32; ☽ Tue, Wed, Fri & Sat) Half-day tours of local and regional attractions.

Manyallaluk Tours (☎ 08-8972 2294) Excellent Aboriginal cultural tours at Manyallaluk, about 100km from Katherine. A one-day cultural experience (adult/child $177/88) departing from Katherine includes a bush-tucker and bush-medicine walk, lunch, and painting and craft activities. The self-drive option is $135/78.

Travel North (☎ 1800 089 103; www.travelnorth .au; Transit Centre, Katherine Tce) Katherine's main tour operator has a range of tours to Kakadu, Arnhem Land, Litchfield, Manyallaluk, Mataranka and the Katherine region. Also booking agent for the *Ghan* and Greyhound.

Festivals & Events

Katherine Country Music Muster (www.kcmm.com .au) Features plenty of live music in the pubs and entertainment at a site on Gorge Rd over the May Day long weekend.

Katherine District Show (www.katherineshow.org .au) An annual agricultural show held at the Katherine Showgrounds in July with rides, stalls and lots of animals.

Sleeping
BUDGET

Coco's International Backpackers (☎ 08-8971 2889; www.21firstst.com; 21 First St; camping per person $13, dm $23) With travellers lounging around amid tents in the backyard, idly strumming on guitars and swapping outback tales, you'll feel like you've walked into an old Asian overland bolthole here. Coco's is a real backpackers, a converted home where the owner chats with the guests and offers sage advice on didgeridoos from his tin shed gallery. Aboriginal artists are often here painting didgeridoos.

Palm Court Kookaburra Backpackers (☎ 1800 626 722; www.travelnorth.com.au; cnr Third & Giles Sts; dm $24, tw & d $54; ☒ ▣ ▣) This well-equipped backpacker hostel is a welcoming place where they pack 'em into the retired motel rooms. Each room has a bathroom, fridge and TV and are four- to eight-share dorms or twin/ double shares.

Springvale Homestead (☎ 08-8972 1355; www .travelnorth.com.au; Shadforth Rd; unpowered/powered sites $10/25, s/tw $51/61; ☒ ▣) This historic home-

stead is a lovely place to camp in a real bushland setting by the Katherine River. There's plenty of space, a palm-shaded pool and a bistro open in the evening. Rooms are motel style and there are free tours of the homestead at 3pm daily in the Dry.

Also recommended:

Katherine Low Level Caravan Park (☎ 08-8972 3962; www.katherinelowlevel.com.au; Shadforth Rd; unpowered/powered sites $27/30, en-suite cabins $130; ☒ ▣) Sprawling manicured park has plenty of shady sites, a great swimming pool adjoining a bar and bistro, and spotless amenities.

Manbulloo Homestead Caravan Park (☎ 08-8972 1559; www.manbulloohomesteadcaravanpark.com.au; unpowered/powered sites $18/22, motel/cabins $80/120) Peaceful cattle station property 12km southwest of Katherine.

MIDRANGE & TOP END

Katherine River Lodge Motel (☎ 08-8971 0266; www.katherineriverlodge.net; 50 Giles St; d $79-89, f $100; ☒ ▣ ▣) One of Katherine's best-value motels, this large complex has spotless rooms in a lush tropical garden. The attached Cheeky Croc Restaurant (mains $17 to $29) serves filling meals from Tuesday to Sunday, including $6.50 kids' meals.

Knott's Crossing Resort (☎ 1800 222 511, 08-8972 2511; www.knottscrossing.com.au; cnr Cameron & Giles Sts; powered sites $30, cabins from $95, motel d from $142; ☒ ▣) Knott's Crossing is more a motel and cabin resort than camping, but it's also a great spot for caravanners and campervans. Set amid lush tropical gardens, everything is packed pretty tightly here but it's very well run with a day spa, bar and the excellent Katie's Bistro.

Paraway Motel (☎ 08-8972 2644; www.parawaymotel .com.au; O'Shea Tce; d $110-150; ☒ ▣) This smart motel is as neat as a pin and its quiet location is handy to the main street shopping. Standard motel rooms are spotless and comfortable and there are spa rooms. There's also the popular Carriage Restaurant.

ourpick **Maud Creek Country Lodge** (☎ 08-8971 1814; www.maudcreeklodge.com.au; Gorge Rd; d/cottage $156/186; ☒ ▣) Set on a former cattle run just 6km from the gorge, this peaceful farmstay puts you in touch with nature. The property reaches down to the river and is ideal for bushwalking, birdwatching and fishing. The three immaculate adjoining lodge rooms share a communal kitchen and TV lounge, but better still is the private self-contained cottage.

It's all set in a lush tropical garden with pool, gazebo and mahogany trees.

St Andrews Apartments (☎ 1800 686 106; www.stan drewsapts.com.au; 27 First St; apt $170-240; ☒ ☒) In the heart of town, these serviced apartments are great for families or if you pine for a few home comforts. Spotless and contemporary, the two-bedroom apartments sleep four (six if you use the sofa bed), and come with fully equipped kitchen and lounge/dining area.

Eating

Katherine has a handful of reasonably good cafes, pubs and motel restaurants. Locals tend to eat out at clubs such as the **Katherine Country Club** (☎ 08-8972 1276; 3034 Pearce St; mains $12-25; ☾ lunch & dinner), overlooking the nine-hole golf course, and the **Katherine Club** (☎ 08-8972 1250; cnr Second St & O'Shea Tce; mains $15-20; ☾ lunch Tue-Fri, dinner Tue-Sat), closer to the town centre. They're nothing fancy but you can rely on inexpensive and satisfying bistro meals such as steak, schnitzel and barra, and kids are welcome.

our pick **Kumbidgee Lodge Tea Rooms** (☎ 08-8971 0699; Gorge Rd; mains $7-18; ☾ 7am-8.30pm) On the road to Nitmiluk, 10km from Katherine, Kumbidgee is a tranquil spot with a big deck overlooking a small pond and a few pet goats to keep the kids happy. It's a great spot to indulge in a hearty 'bush breakfast' ($13) or a Devonshire tea while catching up with the rest of the world in the newspapers. The Sunday buffet breakfast ($12) is a popular local outing.

Katie's Bistro (☎ 08-8972 2511; Knott's Crossing Resort, cnr Giles & Cameron Sts; mains $19-38; ☾ breakfast & dinner) This intimate little bistro at Knott's Crossing Resort is locally regarded as one of Katherine's best. Wagyu beef, lobster and prawn pasta, and grilled outback camel grace the eclectic menu. You can eat inside or alfresco by the pool.

Getting There & Around

Katherine is a major road junction in this part of the Territory: apart from the Stuart Hwy tracking north and south, the Victoria Hwy heads west from here to Kununurra in WA.

Greyhound Australia (☎ 1300 473 946; www.greyhound .com.au) has regular services between Darwin and Alice Springs, Queensland or Western Australia. All buses stop at Katherine's **Transit Centre** (☎ 08-8971 9999; 6 Katherine Tce). Typical one-way fares from Katherine include: Darwin ($84, four hours), Alice Springs ($253, 16 hours), Tennant Creek ($166, 8½ hours) and Kununurra ($130, five hours).

The *Ghan* train travels between Adelaide and Darwin twice a week, stopping at Katherine for four hours – enough for a whistlestop tour to Katherine Gorge; see the Ghan Timetable, p816, for a schedule of services. Katherine train station is off the Victoria Hwy, 9km southwest of town. **Travel North** (☎ 08-8971 9999; Transit Centre) runs shuttles between the station and town.

AROUND KATHERINE
Cutta Cutta Caves Nature Park

Turn your back on the searing sun and dip down 15m below terra firma into this maze-like limestone cave system. The 1499-hectare **Cutta Cutta Caves Nature Park** (☎ 08-8972 1940; adult/ child $14.50/7.25; ☾ 8.30am-4.30pm, guided tours 9am, 10am, 11am, 1pm, 2pm & 3pm) has a unique ecology and you'll be sharing the space with brown tree snakes, plus the endangered ghost bats and orange horseshoe bats that they feed on. Cutta Cutta is a Jawoyn name meaning many stars; it was taboo for Aborigines to enter the cave, which they believed was where the stars were kept during the day.

Nitmiluk (Katherine Gorge) National Park

Spectacular Katherine Gorge forms the backbone of this 2920-sq-km park, about 30km from Katherine. A series of 13 deep sandstone gorges have been carved out by the Katherine River on its journey from Arnhem Land to the Timor Sea. It is a hauntingly beautiful place – though it can get crowded in peak season – and a must-do from Katherine. In the Dry the tranquil river is perfect for a paddle, but in the Wet the deep still waters and dividing rapids are engulfed by an awesome torrent that churns through the gorge. Plan to spend at least a full day canoeing or cruising on the river and bushwalking.

The traditional owners are the Jawoyn Aboriginal people who jointly manage Nitmiluk with Parks & Wildlife.

INFORMATION

The **Nitmiluk Centre** (☎ 1800 089 103, 08-8972 1253; www.nitmiluktours.com.au; ☾ 7am-7pm May-Aug, to 4pm Sep-Apr) has excellent displays and information on the park's geology, wildlife, the traditional owners (the Jawoyn) and European history. There's also a desk for **Parks & Wildlife** (☎ 08-8972 1886), which has information sheets on a wide range of marked walking tracks that

NORTHERN TERRITORY

GHUNMARN & MANYALLALUK CULTURAL CENTRES

If you're interested in seeing genuine Aboriginal art produced by local communities, it's worth detouring off the Stuart Hwy to these two remote cultural centres.

The small community of Beswick is reached via the sealed Central Arnhem Hwy 56km east of the Stuart Hwy on the southern fringes of Arnhem Land. Here you'll find the **Ghunmarn Cultural Centre** (☎ 08-8977 4250; www.djilpinarts.org.au; Beswick; ♥ 10am-4pm Mon-Fri Apr-Nov), opened in 2007, and displaying local artworks, prints, carvings, weaving and didgeridoos from western Arnhem Land. The centre also features the Blanasi Collection, a permanent exhibition of works by elders from the western Arnhem Land region. Visitors are welcome to visit the centre without a permit – call ahead to check that it's open.

A very special festival at Beswick is **Walking With Spirits** (see Aboriginal Festivals & Events, p814), magical performances of traditional corroborees staged in conjunction with the Australian Shakespeare Company. It's held on the first weekend in August. Camping is possible at Beswick Falls over this weekend but advance bookings are essential.

Abutting the eastern edge of Nitmiluk (Katherine Gorge) National Park, the southern edge of Kakadu and the western edge of Arnhem Land, the former 3000-sq-km Eva Valley cattle station is now home to the Jawoyn community of **Manyallaluk**. Unlike Beswick, Manyallaluk can only be visited as part of a guided **cultural tour** (☎ 1800 644 727, 08-8975 4727; self-drive adult/child $135/78, incl transfers to/from Katherine $177/88; ♥ Wed-Sun Apr-Oct). On these highly regarded one-day tours you'll learn about traditional bush tucker and medicine, spear throwing and how to play a didgeridoo from Indigenous Jawoyn guides. Lunch and billy tea is included. **Manyallaluk Art & Craft Centre** has excellent art and crafts at competitive prices, and is included in the tours.

No permits are needed to camp at Manyallaluk, but alcohol is prohibited. The **camping ground** (unpowered/powered sites $12/18) has grassy sites and a community store with basic supplies.

The turn-off to Manyallaluk is 15km along the Central Arnhem Hwy, then 35km along a well-maintained, all-season gravel road. Both Manyalluluk and Beswick are around a 90-minute drive from Katherine.

start here and traverse the picturesque country south of the gorge. Registration for overnight walks and camping permits ($3.30 per night) is from 7am to 1pm; canoeing permits are also issued. Check at the centre for information on ranger talks.

LELIYN (EDITH FALLS)

Reached off the Stuart Hwy 40km north of Katherine and a further 20km along a sealed road, Leliyn is a beautiful, safe place for swimming and hiking. The **Leliyn Trail** (2.6km loop, 1½ hours, easy) climbs into escarpment country through grevillea and spinifex and past scenic lookouts (Bemang is best in the afternoon) to the Upper Pool, where the **Sweetwater Pool Trail** (8.6km return, three to five hours, medium) branches off. The peaceful Sweetwater Pool has a small camping site; overnight permits are available at the kiosk.

The Parks & Wildlife **camping ground** (☎ 08-8975 4869; adult/child/family $9/4.50/20) at the main pool has grassy sites, lots of shade, toilets, showers, a laundry and facilities for the disabled. Fees

are paid at the **kiosk** (♥ 8am-6pm), which sells snacks and basic supplies. Nearby is a picnic area with gas barbecues and tables.

Nitmiluk Tours (Map p852; ☎ 08-8972 1253; www.nitmiluk.com.au) has transfers from Katherine (one way/return $35/45) daily from May to September and by request from October to March.

ACTIVITIES
Bushwalking

The park has around 120km of marked walking tracks, ranging from 2km stretches to 66km multinight hikes. Overnight hikers must register at the Nitmiluk Centre. There's a $50 refundable deposit for any overnight walk and a camping fee of $3.30 per person per night. Visit the centre for the full range of walks and to pick up a map.

Barrawei (Lookout) Loop (3.7km, one hour, medium) A short, steep climb with good views over the Katherine River.
Butterfly Gorge (12km, 4½ hours, difficult) A shady walk through a pocket of monsoon rainforest, often with butterflies, leads to midway along the second gorge and a deep water swimming spot.

Jatbula Trail (58km, four to five days, difficult) This walk to Leliyn (Edith Falls) climbs the Arnhem Land escarpment, taking in features such as the swamp-fed Biddlecombe Cascades, Crystal Falls, the Amphitheatre and the Sweetwater Pool. This walk can only be done one way (ie you can't walk from Leliyn to Katherine Gorge) and a minimum of two people are required to do the walk. A ferry service ($5) takes you across the gorge to begin this walk.

Jawoyn Valley (40km, overnight, difficult) A wilderness loop trail leading off the Eighth Gorge walk into a valley with rock outcrops and rock-art galleries.

Canoeing

Nothing beats exploring the gorges in your own boat, and lots of travellers canoe at least as far as the first or second gorge. Bear in mind the intensity of the sun and heat, and the fact that you may have to carry your canoe over the rock bars and rapids that separate the gorges. Pick up the *Canoeing Guide* at the Nitmiluk Centre.

Nitmiluk Tours (☎ 08-8972 1253) hires out single/double canoes for a half-day ($40/59, departing 8am and 12.30pm) or full day ($51/76, departing 8am), including the use of a splash-proof drum for cameras and other gear (it's not fully waterproof), a map and a life jacket. The half-day hire only allows you to paddle up the first gorge; with the full-day you can get up as far as the fourth gorge depending on your level of fitness – start early. The canoe shed is at the boat ramp by the main car park, about 500m beyond the Nitmiluk Centre.

You also can be a little more adventurous and take the canoes out overnight for $98/220 a single/double, plus $3.30 for a camping permit – there are campsites at the fifth, sixth, eighth and ninth gorges. Bookings are essential as overnight permits are limited and there is a $60 deposit. Don't take this trip lightly though.

Gorge Cruises

A popular way to see far into the gorge is on one of the numerous cruises run by **Nitmiluk Tours** (☎ 1300 146 743, 08-8972 1253; www.nitmiluktours .com.au). Bookings on some cruises can be tight in the peak season, so it's a good idea to make a reservation the day before.

The two-hour cruise (adult/child $53/30) goes to the second gorge and visits a rock-art gallery (including an 800m walk). Departures are at 9am, 11am, 1pm and 3pm daily year-round. There's wheelchair access to the top of the first gorge only. The four-hour cruise

(adult/child $69/32) goes to the third gorge and includes refreshments and a chance to swim. Cruises leave at 9am daily from April to November, plus at 11am and 1pm May to August. Finally, there's the full-day eight-hour trip (adult or child $110), which takes you up to the fifth gorge, involves walking about 5km and includes a barbecue lunch and refreshments. It departs at 8am daily from May to October.

There's also a more leisurely dawn **breakfast cruise** (adult/child $59/47; ⊗ 7am Apr-Nov); a two-hour **lunch cruise** (adult/child $69/40; ⊗ noon Mon-Sat); and a **sunset cruise** (adult/child $116/101; ⊗ 4.30pm Wed & Fri-Mon Apr-Nov), with a candlelit buffet dinner and champagne.

Scenic Flights

Nitmiluk Helicopter Tours (☎ 1300 146 743; www .airbournesolutions.com.au; flights from $75 per person) has a variety of flights ranging from an eight-minute buzz over the first three gorges ($75 per person) to an 18-minute flight over all thirteen gorges ($165). The Adventure Swim Tour ($285) drops you at a secluded swimming hole for an hour or so, and there are broader tours that take in Aboriginal rock-art sites, Kakadu and a cattle station. Book at the Nitmiluk Centre.

SLEEPING

Apart from bush-camping sites established for overnight walkers, there are permanent camping grounds at Leliyn (p855) and at **Nitmiluk Caravan Park** (☎ 08-8972 1253; unpowered/powered sites $19/24, safari tents $80; ⊠), with plenty of grass and shade, hot showers, toilets, barbecues and a laundry. Wallabies and goannas are frequent visitors. There's a 'tent village' here with permanent safari tents sleeping two people. Book at the Nitmiluk Centre.

GETTING THERE & AWAY

It's 30km by sealed road from Katherine to the Nitmiluk Centre, and a few hundred metres further to the car park, where the gorge begins and the cruises start.

Daily transfers between Katherine and the gorge run from the Nitmiluk Town Booking Office for adult/child return $24/12 and pick up at local accommodation places on request. From April to September they leave Katherine at 8am, 12.15pm and 4pm, returning from Nitmiluk at 9am, 1pm and 5pm. From October to March they leave at 8am and 4pm, returning at 9am and 5pm. Seats are usually booked with cruise bookings.

KATHERINE TO WESTERN AUSTRALIA

The sealed Victoria Hwy – part of the Savannah Way – stretches 513km from Katherine to Kununurra in WA. It winds through diverse landscapes, with extensive tracts annexed as cattle stations in the 1880s, these becoming the economy's backbone in the post-war recovery period of the 1950s.

A 4WD will get you into a few out-of-the-way national parks accessed off the Victoria Hwy, or you can meander through semiarid desert and lush sandstone outcrops until bloated baobab trees herald your imminent arrival in WA. All fruits, vegetables, nuts and honey must be left at the quarantine-inspection post on the border. WA time is 1½ hours behind NT time.

Flora River Nature Park

Limestone tufa (spongy rock) outcrops form bars across the mineral-rich Flora River, acting as dams; the effect is a series of pretty cascades running with glowing blue-green water. There's a **camping ground** (adult/child/family $6.60/3.30/16) at Djarrung with an amenities block. The Flora River has crocs, so there's no swimming.

The park turn-off is 90km southwest of Katherine; the park entrance is a further 36km along a passable dirt road.

Victoria River Crossing

The low sandstone cliffs surrounding this spot where the highway crosses the Victoria River (192km southwest of Katherine) create a dramatic setting. Much of this area forms the eastern section of Gregory National Park. The **Victoria River Wayside Inn** (☎ 08-8975 0744; Victoria Hwy; unpowered/powered sites $15/20, d $95), west of the bridge, has a shop, bar and meals ($6 to $25).

Timber Creek

pop 229

Tiny Timber Creek is the only town between Katherine and Kununurra. It has a pretty big history for such a small place, with an early European exploration aboard the *Tom Tough* requiring repairs to be carried out with local timber (hence the town's name). The expedition's leader, AC Gregory, inscribed his arrival date into a baobab; it is still discernable

(and explained in detail through interpretive panels) at **Gregory's Tree**, 15km northwest of town.

The town's **old police station** (adult/child $3.50/ free; ☒ 10am-noon Mon-Fri May-Oct), established to smooth relations with pastoralists and Indigenous people, is now a museum displaying old police and mining equipment.

A highlight of Timber Creek is the **Victoria River Cruise** (adult/child $80/40; ☒ 4pm Mon-Sat), which takes you 40km downriver spotting wildlife and returning in time for a fiery sunset. Book at the **Croc Stock Shop** (☎ 08-8975 0850; Victoria Hwy).

The town is dominated by the roadside **Timber Creek Gunamu Tourist Park** (☎ 08-8975 0722; Victoria Hwy; unpowered/powered sites $15/20, s $45, d $70-90; ☒ ☒). Enormous trees shade the 'Circle F' camping area by a small creek where there's croc feeding every evening. The complex includes the Timber Creek Hotel and Wayside Inn (both have bars and bistros) and a small supermarket.

Gregory National Park

The remote and rugged wilderness of this little-visited national park will swallow you up. Covering 12,860 sq km, it sits at the transitional zone between the tropical and semiarid regions. The park consists of old cattle country and is made up of two separate sections: the eastern (Victoria River) section and the much larger Bullita section in the west. While some parts of the park are accessible by 2WD, it's the rough-as-guts 4WD tracks that provide the most rewarding challenge; for these you need to be self sufficient and to register (call ☎ 1300 650 730) and leave a $50 credit-card deposit – refunded upon deregistration.

The **Parks & Wildlife office** (☎ 08-8975 0888; ☒ 7am-4.30pm) in Timber Creek can provide park notes and a map to the various walks, the historic homestead and ruggedly romantic original stockyards, camping spots and rough tracks – a must before heading in. This is croc country; swimming isn't safe.

There's accessible bush camping at **Big Horse Creek** (adult/child $3.30/1.65), 10km west of Timber Creek.

Keep River National Park

This remote park is noted for its stunning sandstone formations, beautiful desolation and rock art. Pamphlets detailing walks are available at the start of the excellent trails.

Don't miss **Nganalang** (500m, 10 minutes), with an estimated 2500 rock carvings and numerous painted images. **Jinumum** (3km, 1½ hours) is a comfortable walk through the gorge.

The park entrance is just 3km from the WA border. You can reach the park's main points by conventional vehicle during the Dry. A **rangers station** (☎ 08-9167 8827) lies 3km into the park from the main road, and there are basic, sandstone-surrounded **camping grounds** (adult/child/family $3.30/1.65/7.70) at Gurrandalng (15km into the park) and Jarnem (28km). Tank water is available at Jarnem.

MATARANKA
pop 252

With soothing, warm thermal springs set in lush pockets of palms and tropical vegetation, you'd be mad not to pull into Mataranka for at least a few hours to soak away those miles of road travel. The small settlement of Mataranka regularly swells with towel-toting visitors shuffling to the thermal pool or the spring-fed Elsey National Park. If you see Mataranka referred to as the 'capital of the Never Never', it's a reference to Jeannie Gunn's 1908 autobiographical novel *We of the Never Never*, about life as a pioneering woman on nearby Elsey Station – for which the deeds of title have since been returned to the Mangarayi Indigenous owners.

Sights & Activities

Mataranka's crystal-clear **thermal pool**, shrouded in rainforest, is 10km from town beside the Mataranka Homestead Resort. The warm, clear water dappled by filtered light leaking through overhanging palms rejuvenates a lot of bodies on any given day; it's reached via a boardwalk from the resort and can get mighty crowded. About 200m away (keep following the boardwalk) is the **Waterhouse River**, where you can rent canoes for $10 per hour. **Stevie's Hole**, a natural swimming hole in the cooler Waterhouse River, about 1.5km from the homestead, is rarely crowded.

Outside the resort entrance is a replica of the **Elsey Station Homestead**, constructed for the filming of *We of the Never Never* (shown daily at noon in the main homestead).

The **Never Never Museum** (Stuart Hwy; adult/child $2.50/1; ☒ 8.30am-4.30pm Mon-Fri), back in town, has displays on the northern railway, WWII and local history.

Elsey National Park adjoins the thermal-pool reserve and offers peaceful camping, fishing and walking along the Waterhouse and Roper Rivers. **Bitter Springs**, a serene palm-fringed thermal pool within the national park, is accessed via Martin Rd from Mataranka. The almost unnatural blue-green colour of the 34°C water is due to dissolved limestone particles.

Sleeping & Eating

Mataranka Homestead Resort (☎ 08-8975 4544; Homestead Rd; unpowered/powered sites $20/24, dm/d/cabins $19/89/115; ☒) Only metres from the main thermal pool and with a range of accommodation, this is a popular place to stay or to call into for lunch and a quick soak. The large camping ground is a bit dusty but has shady areas, good amenities and barbecues. The fan-cooled hostel rooms are pretty basic but comfortable enough, and linen is provided. The air-con motel rooms have fridge, TV and bathroom, while the cabins have a kitchenette and sleep up to six people. Book ahead.

Down Martins Rd towards Bitter Springs are a couple of good options.

Mataranka Cabins (☎ 08-8975 4838; www.matarankacabins.com.au; Martins Rd, Bitter Springs; unpowered/powered sites $20/24, cabins $110; ☒) On the banks of the Little Roper River, only a few hundred metres from Bitter Springs thermal pool, this quiet bush setting has some amazing termite mounds adorning the front paddock. The secluded, open-plan cabins are equipped with linen, bathrooms and kitchens, and accommodate up to six people.

Jalmurark Camping Ground (adult/child/family $6.60/3.30/16) Located at 12 Mile Yards, this national park camping ground has lots of grass and shade and access to the Roper River and walking trails.

Stockyard Gallery (☎ 08-8975 4530; Stuart Hwy; snacks $3-10; ☒ 9am-4pm) In town, this casual cafe is a little gem. There's a delicious range of homemade snacks such as focaccias and sandwiches, cakes and muffins. Finish with fresh plunger coffee, a divine mango smoothie or the unusual bush-orange ice cream. The art gallery here has Aboriginal art, jewellery and books, and information on the region is also available.

BARKLY TABLELAND & GULF COUNTRY

East of the Stuart Hwy is some of the Territory's most remote cattle country, but parts are accessible by sealed road and the waters of the Gulf coast are regarded as some of the best for isolated fishing in the country.

Roper Highway

Not far south of Mataranka on the Stuart Hwy, the mostly sealed single-lane Roper Hwy strikes 175km eastwards to **Roper Bar**, crossing the paperbark- and pandanus-lined Roper River where freshwater meets saltwater. It's passable only in the Dry and keen fisher folk stop here, with accommodation, fuel and supplies available at the **Roper Bar Store** (☎ 08-8975 4636). Roper Bar is an access point to both Borroloola (head south along the rough-going Nathan River Rd through Limmen National Park – high-clearance with two spares required) and into southeastern Arnhem Land.

Continuing east along the highway for 45km leads to the Aboriginal community of Ngukurr, home to 900 people from nine different language groups and cultures. This cultural diversity informs the unique works on show and available to buy from the **Ngukurr Arts Centre** (☎ 08-8975 4656; www.ngukurrarts.com.au; 🕙 9am-4pm Mon-Fri); no permit is required to visit the centre.

Carpentaria & Tablelands Highways

Just south of Daly Waters, the sealed Carpentaria Hwy (Hwy 1) heads 378km east to Borroloola, near the Gulf of Carpentaria, and one of the NT's top barramundi fishing spots. After 267km the Carpentaria Hwy meets the sealed Tablelands Hwy at Cape Crawford. At this intersection is the legendary **Heartbreak Hotel** (☎ 08-8975 9928; unpowered/powered sites $12/20, dm/s/d $40/65/75; 🗷). Pitch the tent on the shaded grassy lawn, and then park yourself on the wide verandah with a cold beer. Breakfast, lunch and dinner (meals $10 to $22) are available.

Cape Crawford Tourism (☎ 08-8975 9611; www.cape crawfordtourism.com.au; tours $300) runs three-hour tours, including a helicopter ride to see the otherwise inaccessible Lost City sandstone formations.

From here it's a desolate 374km south across the Barkly Tableland to the Barkly Hwy and the 'roadhouse', the **Barkly Homestead Wayside Inn** (☎ 08-8964 4549; unpowered/powered sites $16/24, budget s/d $65/85, motel s/d $95/110; 🗷). Then it's 210km west to Tennant Creek and 252km east to the Queensland border.

Borroloola

pop 773

On the McArthur River close to the bountiful waters of the Gulf, Borroloola is big news for fishing fans, but unless you're keen on baiting a hook (the barramundi season peaks from February to April) or driving the remote (preferably 4WD) Savannah Way to Queensland, it's a long way to go for not much reward.

About three-quarters of the population of Borroloola is Indigenous, and the town's colourful history is displayed at the **Borroloola Museum** (☎ 08-8975 4149; Robinson Rd; admission $2; 🕙 8am-5pm Mon-Fri), within the 1887 police station.

Borroloola Guesthouse (☎ 08-8975 8883; www.bor roloolaaccommodation.com.au; Robinson Rd; r $70-110, cabins $120; 🗷), close to the airport on the main road through town, is clean and comfortable, with cabins and guest-house rooms set in tropical gardens.

There's also a caravan park in town, and meals at the local pub: the rowdy **Borroloola Hotel** (☎ 08-8975 8766; Robinson Rd; meals $10-28; 🕙 lunch & dinner) serves the usual pub fare of burgers, chops and mixed grills within a lounge bar that's heavily reinforced with steel mesh.

MATARANKA TO TENNANT CREEK
Larrimah
pop 13

Once upon a time the railway line from Darwin came as far as Birdum, 8km south of tiny Larrimah. Its **museum** (Mahoney St; admission by donation; 🕙 7am-9pm), in the former telegraph repeater station opposite the Larrimah Hotel, tells of the town's involvement with the railway and WWII.

Larrimah Hotel (☎ 08-8975 9931; unpowered/powered sites $10/15, d $40-45; 🗷 🗷) is a cheerfully rustic and quirky pub offering basic rooms, meals and a small menagerie of animals. **Fran's Devonshire Teahouse** (☎ 08-8975 9945; Stuart Hwy; meals $4-12; 🕙 breakfast & lunch) is in Fran's house, where she cooks up legendary pies and pastries. This is the place to stop for a filling camel or buffalo pie, roast lamb with damper, or just a Devonshire tea or fresh coffee.

Daly Waters
pop 25

About 3km off the highway and 160km south of Mataranka is Daly Waters, an important staging post in the early days of aviation – Amy Johnson landed here on her monster flight from England to Australia in 1930. Just about everyone stops at the famous **Daly Waters Pub** (☎ 08-8975 9927; www.dalywaterspub.com; unpowered/powered sites $10/18, dm/d $15/50, cabins $75-95; ☒ ☒). Decorated with business cards, bras, banknotes and memorabilia from passing travellers, the pub claims to be the oldest in the Territory (its liquor licence has been valid since 1893) and has become a bit of a legend along the Track, although it may be a bit too popular for its own good. Every evening from April to September there's the popular beef 'n' barra barbecue ($25), along with entertainment from the 'Chook Man' or a visiting country muso. Otherwise, hearty meals (mains $10 to $25), including the filling barra burger, are served. Beside the pub is a dustbowl camping ground with a bit of shade – book ahead or arrive early to secure a powered site. Accommodation ranges from basic dongas to spacious self-contained cabins.

Daly Waters to Three Ways

Heading south, you encounter the fascinating ghost town of **Newcastle Waters**, 3km west of the highway. Its atmospheric, historic buildings include the Junction Hotel, cobbled together from abandoned windmills in 1932. South of the cattle town of **Elliott**, the land just gets drier and drier and the vegetation sparser. The mesmerising sameness breaks at **Renner Springs**, generally accepted as the dividing line between the seasonally wet Top End and the dry Centre.

Banka Banka is a historic cattle station 100km north of Tennant Creek, with a grassy camping area (no power), marked walking tracks (one leading to a tranquil waterhole) and a small kiosk selling basic refreshments.

Three Ways, 537km north of Alice, is the junction of the Stuart and Barkly Hwys, from where you can head south to Alice, north to Darwin (988km) or east to Mt Isa in Queensland (643km). **Threeways Roadhouse** (☎ 08-8962 2744; Stuart Hwy; unpowered/powered sites $16/22, donga s/d $43/56, motel d $86-106; ☒ ☐ ☒) is a potential stopover with a bar and restaurant, but Tennant Creek is only 26km further south.

TENNANT CREEK

pop 3427

Servicing a vast region of cattle stations and Aboriginal communities, Tennant Creek is the only town of any size between Katherine,

680km to the north, and Alice Springs, 511km to the south. Many travellers spend a night here to break up the long drive or make a bus connection, and there're a few interesting attractions to visit.

Local legend speaks of Tennant Creek being founded on beer, first settled when the drivers of a broken-down beer-laden wagon settled in to consume the freight. The truth is somewhat more prosaic: Tennant Creek was founded on gold in the early 1930s, with mining leases occasionally spurting into activity when the gold price looks favourable. Tennant Creek wears an air of despair, with many buildings boarded-up with security screens, but there is also a wealth of Aboriginal art and culture to experience. The Warumungu people know Tennant Creek as Jurnkurakurr, the intersection of a number of Dreaming tracks.

Orientation & Information

Tennant Creek's services sprawl along the Stuart Hwy, which is called Paterson St within the town's limits. Long-distance buses stop at the north end of town.

Leading Edge Computers (☎ 08-8962 3907; 145 Paterson St; per 20min $2; ☺ 9am-5pm Mon-Fri, to 12.30pm Sat) Internet access.

Police station (☎ 08-8962 4444; Paterson St)

Tennant Creek hospital (☎ 08-8962 4399; Schmidt St)

Visitor information centre (☎ 08-8962 3388; www .barklytourism.com.au; Peko Rd; ☺ 9am-5pm) Located 2km east of town at Battery Hill.

Sights & Activities

The contemporary focus of the exhibitions at **Nyinkka Nyunyu** (☎ 08-8962 2221; www.nyinkka nyunyu.com.au; Paterson St; adult/child/family $10/5/20; ☺ 8am-5pm Mon-Fri, 9am-4pm Sat May-Sep, 9am-5pm Mon-Fri, 10am-2pm Sat Oct-Apr, 10am-2pm Sun year-round) makes this one of the best gallery-museums in the Territory. Excellent dioramas, prints and paintings produced by local artists show Aboriginal culture as a living culture. Dioramas depict the night patrol bus or the experience of working in local mines. These mingle with other displays of contemporary art and old artefacts – some recently returned by interstate museums. Nyinkka Nyunyu is located beside a sacred sight of the spiky tailed goanna (Nyinkka). There's an indigenous garden, which is sometimes the venue for ceremonies and performances, and the Jajjikari Café, which sells espresso coffee, cakes and snacks.

NORTHERN TERRITORY

The artwork at Nyinkka Nyunyu comes from the **Julalikari Arts Centre** (☎ 08-8962 2163; www.julalikariarts.com; North Stuart Hwy; ✆ 8am-noon Mon-Fri), also known as the Pink Palace, in the Ngalpa Ngalpa community (also known as Mulga Camp) at the northern end of town. Here you can see Aboriginal women painting traditional and contemporary art, chat to the artists and purchase directly from the painter or one of her colleagues.

Gold-bearing ore was originally crushed and treated at what's now **Battery Hill Mining Centre** (☎ 08-8962 1281; Peko Rd; adult/child/family $30/20/60; ✆ 9am-5pm), 1.5km east of town. There are **underground mine tours** (✆ 9.30am & 2.30pm) and surface tours of the 10-head **battery** (✆ 11am & 4pm). In addition there is a superb **Minerals Museum** and you can try your hand at gold panning. The admission price gives access to all of the above, or you can just choose one of the tours (adult/child/family $22/15/55), visit the Minerals and Social History Museums only (adult/family $5/10), or just go panning ($5 per person). While you're here, ask for the key ($20 deposit) to the old **Telegraph Station**, which is just off the highway about 12km north of town. The green-roofed stone buildings look as isolated and forlorn as they must have 135 years ago when they were built. This is one of only four of the original 11 stations remaining in the Territory (the others are at Barrow Creek, Alice Springs and Powell Creek). Just north of the Telegraph Station is the turn-off west to **Kundjarra** (The Pebbles), a formation of granite boulders like a miniaturised version of the better-known Devil's Marbles found 100km south. It's a sacred women's Dreaming site of the Warumungu.

Sleeping & Eating

Tourist's Rest Youth Hostel (☎ 08-8962 2719; www .touristrest.com.au; cnr Leichhardt & Windley Sts; dm/d $18/38; ✆ 🖫 🖳) This small, friendly and slightly ramshackle hostel has bright clean rooms, free breakfast and VIP discounts. The hostel can organise tours of the gold mines and Devil's Marbles and pick-up from the bus stop.

Safari Lodge Motel (☎ 08-8962 2207; safari@switch .com.au; Davidson St; s/d $80/90; 🖫) Part of the Budget chain, this motel is centrally located, family-run and accredited as environmentally friendly. The rooms are fairly standard with phone, fridge and TV. There's also an outdoor spa.

Desert Sands (☎ 08-8962 1346; www.desertsands .com.au; Paterson St; s/d from $85/95, extra person $10; 🖫 🖳) The Desert Sands offers enormous units (sleeping three to eight), each with a fully equipped kitchen, TV (with in-house movies), and a bathroom with a washing machine. This motel is at the southern end of Paterson St and is excellent value for families.

Bluestone Motor Inn (☎ 08-8962 2617; bluestone@ internode.on.net; 1 Paterson St; standard/deluxe d $100/123; 🖫 🖳) At the southern end of town, this 3½-star motel has comfortable standard rooms in leafy surrounds. In addition there are spacious hexagonal deluxe rooms with queen-size beds and a sofa. There are also wheelchair-accessible units and a restaurant.

Outback Caravan Park (☎ 08-8962 2459; www .outbacktennantcreek.com.au; Peko Rd; unpowered/powered sites $21/27, cabins $60-115, serviced apt $95-180; 🖫 🖳) About 1km east of town, this is a pleasant shady park with a kiosk, camp kitchen and fuel. You may even be treated to some bush poetry and bush tucker, courtesy of Jimmy Hooker, at 7.30pm ($5). There are discounts for bookings of more than three nights. The serviced apartments are outside the park, closer to town.

Woks Up (☎ 08-8962 3888; Ambrose St; mains $9-18; ✆ dinner) Inside the fortress that is the Sporties Club you'll find one of the Territory's best Chinese diners with an immense menu and generous portions.

Fernanda's Café & Restaurant (☎ 08-8962 3999; 1 Noble St; mains $9-25; ✆ lunch & dinner) Tucked inside the Tennant Creek squash courts (yes squash courts) is this surprising Mediterranean-themed, licensed restaurant. Among the offerings are Portuguese seafood hotpot and Moroccan kangaroo with roasted vegetables drizzled in honey-yoghurt glaze and herb oil. For lighter lunches there are salads, dips, pastas and burgers.

Margo Miles Restaurant (☎ 08-8962 2227; Tennant Creek Hotel, 146 Paterson St; mains $13-24; ✆ lunch & dinner Wed-Sun) This pleasant pub-restaurant is a welcome change from roadhouse dining rooms. Grab a drink from the Faye Lewis Bar, then settle down in the period dining room for a steak, seafood, pasta, Thai or gourmet pizza. The pizzas here are the best in town.

Tennant Food Barn (☎ 08-8962 2296; 185 Paterson St) Opposite the post office, this supermarket can supply your self-catering needs.

Getting There & Away

All long-distance buses stop at the **BP Service Station** (☎ 08-8962 2626; 218 Paterson St) where you can purchase tickets. **Greyhound Australia** (☎ 1300 473 946; www.greyhound.com.au) has regular buses from Tennant Creek to Alice Springs ($160, six hours), Katherine ($165, 8½ hours), Darwin ($225, 14 hours) and Mount Isa ($135, eight hours).

The weekly *Ghan* rail link between Alice Springs and Darwin can drop off passengers in Tennant Creek, although few people stop here and cars can't be loaded or offloaded. The train station is about 6km south of town and there is no shuttle service. Instead, call a **taxi** (☎ 08-8962 3626, 0432 289 369; ☼ 6am-5.30pm).

Car hire is available from **Thrifty** (☎ 08-8962 2207; Safari Lodge Motel, Davidson St), while for tyres and tyre repairs head to **Bridgestone Tyre Centre** (☎ 08-8962 2361; Paterson St).

TENNANT CREEK TO ALICE SPRINGS

The huge boulders in precarious piles beside the Stuart Hwy, 105km south of Tennant Creek, are called the **Devil's Marbles**; Karlwe Karlwe is their Warumungu name, for whom the site is associated with many stories and traditions. According to scientists, the 'marbles' are the rounded remains of a layer of granite that has eroded over aeons. A 20-minute self-guided walk loops around the main site. This geological phenomenon is particularly beautiful at sunrise and sunset, when these oddballs glow warmly. The **camping ground** (adult/child/family $3.30/1.65/7.70) has remarkably hard ground, pit toilets and fireplaces (BYO firewood).

At Wauchope (*war*-kup), 10km south of the Devil's Marbles, are the well-kept rooms of the **Wauchope Hotel** (☎ 08-8964 1963; Stuart Hwy; unpowered/powered sites $14/18, s $40, cabins s/d $70/80; ❄ ⏦). The budget rooms are dongas and the costlier rooms are more spacious, with bathrooms. Meals from the **restaurant** (dinner mains $15-20) are more than satisfactory.

At **Wycliffe Well Roadhouse & Holiday Park** (☎ 08-8964 1966; www.wycliffe.com.au; unpowered/powered sites $22/26, budget s/d $30/38, donga s/d $55/68, s/d cabins with bathroom $99/112; ☼ 6.30am-9pm; ❄ 🖥 ⏦), 17km south of Wauchope, you can fill up with fuel and food (dinner $16 to $20; open breakfast, lunch and dinner) or stay and spot UFOs that apparently fly over with astonishing regularity. The place is decorated with alien figures, newspaper clippings ('That UFO Was Chasing Us!'), and an international doll collection. On a more down-to-earth note, the park has a pleasant lawn campsite, a kids' playground, a cafe and a range of international beer.

Heading south, you reach the **Barrow Creek Hotel** (☎ 08-8956 9753; Stuart Hwy; powered campsites $10, s/d $45/60; ☼ 7am-midnight), one of the highway's eccentric outback pubs. In the tradition of shearers who'd write their name on a banknote and pin it to the wall to ensure they could afford a drink when next they passed through, travellers have left notes, and photos and bumper stickers. Lunch and dinner are available (meals $10 to $20).

The highway continues through **Ti Tree**, where you'll find the **Red Sand Art Gallery** (☎ 08-8956 9738; www.redsandart.com.au; Stuart Hwy; ☼ 8am-5pm) and its cafe. The art comes mainly from Utopia, a community northeast of Alice Springs set up on traditional land reclaimed from the former Utopia station. The community has produced some renowned Indigenous artists.

Twelve kilometres south of Ti Tree, the **Red Centre Farm** (Shatto Mango; ☎ 08-8956 9828; www.redcentrefarm.com; Stuart Hwy; ☼ 9am-7pm) sells unique Territory-style wine – made from mangoes. If that sounds a bit hard to swallow, try the other mango products, such as toppings, marinades and delicious ice cream.

In the grand Australian tradition of building very big things by the side of the road to pull up drivers, **Aileron**, 135km north of Alice, has **Naked Charlie Quartpot**, the Anmatjere (Anmatyerre) man, who cuts a fine figure at the back of the roadhouse. At the time of research, his larger-than-life family was being constructed beside the art gallery. The **Outback Art Gallery** (☎ 08-8956 9111; Stuart Hwy; ☼ 8am-5pm Mon-Sat, 10am-4pm Sun) sells inexpensive watercolours and dot paintings by the local Anmatyerre community, as well as paintings from the Warlpiri community of Yuendumu. If you're lucky you may see artists at work.

Aileron Hotel Roadhouse (☎ 08-8956 9703; www.aileronroadhouse.com.au; Stuart Hwy; unpowered sites $20, dm $36, s/d $98/100; ☼ 7am-10pm Mon-Sat, to 9pm Sun; ❄ ⏦) has campsites (power available until 10pm), a 10-bed dorm, and decent motel units. There's an ATM, bar, shop and a licensed restaurant. The owner's collection of Namatjira watercolours (at least 10 by Albert) is displayed around the roadhouse's bar and dining area. With all that entertainment, it's only polite to stay for a meal ($10 to $20) and a drink.

About 70km north of Alice, the Plenty Hwy heads off to the east towards the **Harts Range**. The main reason to detour is to fossick in the gem fields about 78km east of the Stuart Hwy, which are well known for garnets and zircons. You're guaranteed to get lucky at the popular **Gemtree Caravan Park** (☎ 08-8956 9855; www.gemtree.com.au; Gemtree; unpowered/powered sites $20/24, cabins $70).

ALICE SPRINGS

pop 26,305

The iconic outback town of Alice Springs is no longer the rough-and-ready frontier settlement of legend, yet the vast surroundings of red desert and barren rocky ranges still underscore its remoteness. No matter where you arrive from, or how you get here, this thriving town makes a welcome halt to a long journey. What began 135 years ago as a lonely telegraph station has developed into a modern country town, firmly on the tourist trail as the service centre to that most popular monolith to the south, Uluru, and the ruggedly beautiful MacDonnell Ranges.

To the Arrernte people, the traditional owners of the Alice Springs area, this place is called Mparntwe. The heart of Mparntwe is the junction of the Charles (Anthelke Ulpeye) and Todd (Lhere Mparntwe) Rivers, just north of Anzac Hill (Untyeyetweleye). All the topographical features of the town were formed by the creative ancestral beings – known as the Yeperenye, Ntyarlke and Utnerrengatye caterpillars – as they crawled across the landscape from Emily Gap (Anthwerrke), in the MacDonnell Ranges southeast of town.

Contemporary Alice is populated by outback characters (where else would you find the biggest boat race on a dry river bed?) and is a hub for the incredibly popular central desert Aboriginal art movement, with numerous galleries and arts-related events.

There are remnants of pioneering times, and fascinating institutions such as the Royal Flying Doctor Service Base and the School of the Air, which serve to highlight just how important this town is to the vast central region of Australia.

ORIENTATION

The centre of Alice Springs is a compact and uniform grid five streets wide, bounded by the (usually dry) Todd River on one side and the Stuart Hwy on the other. Todd St is the main drag, and it's a pedestrian mall from Wills Tce to Gregory Tce.

Greyhound Australia buses arrive at and depart from the terminal office on Todd St. The train station is west of the Stuart Hwy in the town's light industrial area, and the airport is 15km south of town through Heavitree Gap.

INFORMATION

Bookshops

Bookmark It (Map p866; ☎ 08-8953 2465; shop 1, 113 Todd St; ✆ 9am-5pm Mon-Fri, 10am-2pm Sat) Piles of secondhand books to sell and trade, including an extensive foreign-language section.

Dymocks (Map p866; ☎ 08-8952 9111; Alice Plaza, Todd Mall; ✆ 8.30am-5.30pm Mon-Fri, to 5pm Sat, 10am-3pm Sun) Mainstream bookshop with a good selection of central Australian titles.

Red Kangaroo Books (Map p866; ☎ 08-8953 2137; 79 Todd Mall; ✆ 9am-5.30pm Mon-Fri, to 2pm Sat) Excellent bookshop specialising in central Australian titles: history, art, travel, novels, guidebooks and more.

Emergency

Ambulance (☎ 000)

Police (Map p866; ☎ 000, 08-8951 8888; Parsons St)

Internet Access

JPG Computers (Map p866; ☎ 08-8952 2040; Coles Complex, Bath St; per hr $6; ✆ 9am-5.30pm Mon-Fri, 10am-2pm Sat)

Outback Email (Map p866; 2a Gregory Tce; per hr $3; ✆ 9am-6pm) Part of the Outback Travel Shop.

Todd Internet Café (Map p866; ☎ 08-8953 8355; Colocag Plaza, 76 Todd St; per hr $4; ✆ 10am-6pm)

Medical Services

Alice Springs Hospital (Map p864; ☎ 08-8951 7777; Gap Rd)

Alice Springs Pharmacy (Map p866; ☎ 08-8952 1554; Shop 19, Yeperenye Shopping Centre, 36 Hartley St; ✆ 8.30am-7.30pm)

Money

Major banks with ATMs, such as ANZ, Commonwealth, National Australia and Westpac are located in and around Todd Mall in the town centre.

NORTHERN TERRITORY

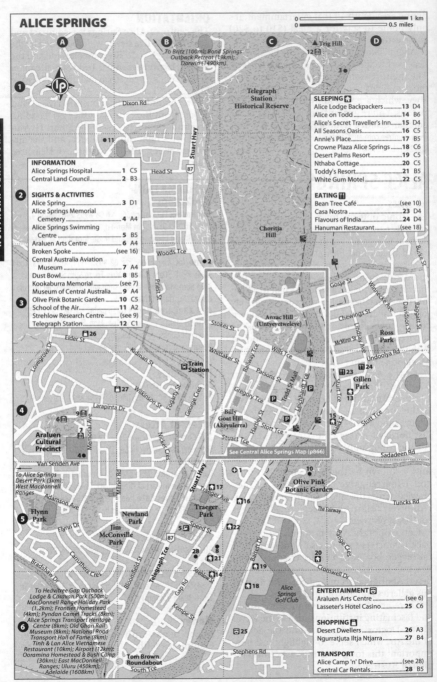

ALICE SPRINGS

0 — 1 km
0 — 0.5 miles

To Britz (100m); Bond Springs
Outback Retreat (19km);
Darwin (1490km)

Telegraph
Station
Historical Reserve

Choritja
Hill

INFORMATION
Alice Springs Hospital 1 C5
Central Land Council 2 B3

SIGHTS & ACTIVITIES
Alice Spring 3 D1
Alice Springs Memorial
  Cemetery 4 A4
Alice Springs Swimming
  Centre 5 B5
Araluen Arts Centre 6 A4
Broken Spoke .... (see 16)
Central Australia Aviation
  Museum 7 A4
Dust Bowl 8 B5
Kookaburra Memorial .... (see 7)
Museum of Central Australia 9 A4
Olive Pink Botanic Garden 10 C5
School of the Air 11 A2
Strehlow Research Centre .... (see 9)
Telegraph Station 12 C1

SLEEPING
Alice Lodge Backpackers 13 D4
Alice on Todd 14 B6
Alice's Secret Traveller's Inn 15 D4
All Seasons Oasis 16 C5
Annie's Place 17 B5
Crowne Plaza Alice Springs 18 C6
Desert Palms Resort 19 C5
Nthaba Cottage 20 C5
Toddy's Resort 21 B5
White Gum Motel 22 C5

EATING
Bean Tree Café .... (see 10)
Casa Nostra 23 D4
Flavours of India 24 D4
Hanuman Restaurant .... (see 18)

Trig Hill

Ross
Park

Gillen
Park

Anzac Hill
(Untyeyetweleye)

Billy
Goat Hill
(Akeyulerra)

See Central Alice Springs Map (p866)

Araluen
Cultural
Precinct

To Alice Springs
Desert Park (3km);
West Macdonnell
Ranges

Flynn
Park

Newland
Park

Jim
McConville
Park

Traeger
Park

Olive Pink
Botanic Garden

Alice
Springs
Golf Club

To Heavitree Gap Outback
Lodge & Caravan Park (500m);
MacDonnell Range Holiday Park
(1.2km); Frontier Homestead
(4km); Pyndan Camel Tracks (8km);
Alice Springs Transport Heritage
Centre (8km); Old Ghan Rail
Museum (8km); National Road
Transport Hall of Fame (8km);
Tinh & Lan Alice Vietnamese
Restaurant (10km); Airport (12km);
Ooramina Homestead & Bush Camp
(30km); East MacDonnell
Ranges; Uluru (450km);
Adelaide (1608km)

Tom Brown
Roundabout

ENTERTAINMENT
Araluen Arts Centre .... (see 6)
Lasseter's Hotel Casino 25 C6

SHOPPING
Desert Dwellers 26 A3
Ngurratjuta Iltja Ntjarra 27 B4

TRANSPORT
Alice Camp 'n' Drive .... (see 28)
Central Car Rentals 28 B5

BONZA BACKROAD: TANAMI ROAD

The Tanami is a rewarding trip for travellers wanting to veer off the beaten track. Heading 1000km through some of the Territory's most remote country, the 'track' connects with Halls Creek in WA, and is essentially a short cut between central Australia and the Kimberley. The Tanami Desert is the traditional homeland of the Warlpiri people and home to the **Bush Mechanics** (www.bushmechanics.com), famous for their ability to resuscitate bush-bombs; they can fix a flat tyre with a shoelace and fashion a new clutch plate from an old boomerang. Permits aren't required for travel on the Tanami Road or to visit the **Yuendumu community** (population 740), about 220km up the track. The community arts centre, **Warlukurlangu** (☎ 08-8956 4133; www .warlu.com; Yuendumu; ☽ 9am-6pm Mon-Fri), is a locally owned venture representing over 150 artists working primarily in acrylics.

Post
Main post office (Map p866; ☎ 13 13 18; 31-33 Hartley St; ☽ 8.15am-5pm Mon-Fri) All the usual services are available here.

Tourist Information
Central Land Council (Map p864; ☎ 08-8951 6211; www.clc.org.au; PO Box 3321, NT 0871, 31-33 Stuart Hwy; ☽ 8.30am-noon & 2-4pm) For Aboriginal land permits and transit permits.
Tourism Central Australia Visitor Information Centre (Map p866; ☎ 1800 645 199, 08-8952 5199; www.centralaustraliantourism.com; 60 Gregory Tce; ☽ 8.30am-5.30pm Mon-Fri, 9am-4pm Sat & Sun) This very helpful centre can load you up with stacks of brochures and the free visitors guide. Weather forecasts and road conditions are posted on the wall, and Mereenie Tour Passes ($2) and fossicking permits (free) are issued. National parks information is also available. Tourism Central Australia desks are also found at the airport and train station.

DANGERS & ANNOYANCES
Avoid walking alone late at night. Catch a taxi back to your accommodation if you're out late.

SIGHTS
Alice Springs Desert Park
Like a kind of Noah's Ark, the **Alice Springs Desert Park** (off Map p864; ☎ 08-8951 8788; www .alicespringsdesertpark.com.au; Larapinta Dr; adult/child/family $20/10/55; ☽ 7.30am-6pm, last entry 4.30pm) has gathered up all the creatures of central Australia and put them on display in one accessible location. So, should the travel itinerary not allow weeks of camping in desert, woodlands and river ecologies to glimpse a spangled grunter or splendid fairy-wren, come here, where the sightings are guaranteed.

The predominantly open-air exhibits faithfully recreate the animals' natural environment with helpful information boards that explain seasonal changes and Aboriginal management. The excellent nocturnal house includes threatened species such as the bilby and ghost bat. Owls, eagles and other birds of prey swoop for food daily at 10am and 3.30pm in the Nature Theatre. Audio guides are available in English, German and Japanese.

It's an easy 2.5km cycle out to the park. Alternatively, **Desert Park Transfers** (☎ 1800 806 641; www.tailormadetours.com.au; adult/child/family $38/26/124) operates five times daily during park hours (between 7.30am and 6pm) and the cost includes park entry and pick-up and drop-off at your accommodation.

Araluen Cultural Precinct
The **precinct** (Map p864; ☎ 08-8951 1120; www.nt.gov .au/nreta/arts/ascp; cnr Larapinta Dr & Memorial Ave; precinct pass adult/child/family $10/7/30; ☽ most attractions 10am-5pm) combines a natural-history collection, a stellar arts centre, a cemetery, a sculpture garden, sacred sites and an aviation museum, all connected by a walking path. You can wander around freely outside, accessing the cemetery and grounds, but a precinct pass provides entry to the exhibitions and displays.

ARALUEN ARTS CENTRE
Alice Springs' **art gallery** (Map p864) shows off an enviable collection of works spanning decades. Permanent exhibitions include the Albert Namatjira Gallery – the Territory's largest collection of the famous watercolourist's works – plus paintings by Albert's mentor Rex Battarbee and other artists from the Hermannsburg School. Other galleries exhibit acrylics from the central desert region, plus European-style oils and outdoor sculptures.

NORTHERN TERRITORY

CENTRAL ALICE SPRINGS

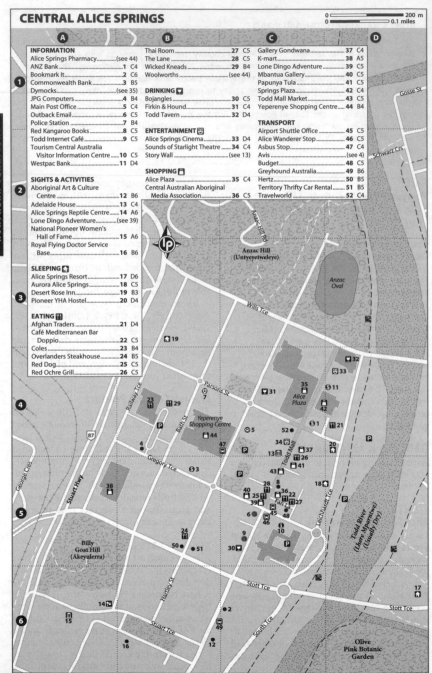

INFORMATION
Alice Springs Pharmacy.............(see 44)
ANZ Bank......................................**1** C4
Bookmark It...................................**2** C6
Commonwealth Bank...................**3** B5
Dymocks.....................................(see 35)
JPG Computers.............................**4** B4
Main Post Office...........................**5** C4
Outback Email..............................**6** C5
Police Station................................**7** B4
Red Kangaroo Books....................**8** C5
Todd Internet Café.......................**9** C5
Tourism Central Australia
   Visitor Information Centre.....**10** C5
Westpac Bank.............................**11** D4

SIGHTS & ACTIVITIES
Aboriginal Art & Culture
   Centre.....................................**12** B6
Adelaide House...........................**13** C4
Alice Springs Reptile Centre......**14** A6
Lone Dingo Adventure.............(see 39)
National Pioneer Women's
   Hall of Fame.........................**15** A6
Royal Flying Doctor Service
   Base.......................................**16** B6

SLEEPING
Alice Springs Resort....................**17** D6
Aurora Alice Springs...................**18** C5
Desert Rose Inn..........................**19** B3
Pioneer YHA Hostel....................**20** D4

EATING
Afghan Traders...........................**21** D4
Café Mediterranean Bar
   Doppio...................................**22** C5
Coles...**23** B4
Overlanders Steakhouse.............**24** B5
Red Dog......................................**25** C5
Red Ochre Grill...........................**26** C5

Thai Room...................................**27** C5
The Lane.....................................**28** C5
Wicked Kneads...........................**29** B4
Woolworths...............................(see 44)

DRINKING
Bojangles....................................**30** C5
Firkin & Hound............................**31** C4
Todd Tavern................................**32** D4

ENTERTAINMENT
Alice Springs Cinema..................**33** D4
Sounds of Starlight Theatre **34** C4
Story Wall.................................(see 13)

SHOPPING
Alice Plaza..................................**35** D4
Central Australian Aboriginal
   Media Association..................**36** C5

Gallery Gondwana......................**37** C4
K-mart...**38** A5
Lone Dingo Adventure................**39** C5
Mbantua Gallery.........................**40** C5
Papunya Tula...............................**41** C5
Springs Plaza...............................**42** C4
Todd Mall Market........................**43** C5
Yeperenye Shopping Centre.......**44** B4

TRANSPORT
Airport Shuttle Office..................**45** C5
Alice Wanderer Stop...................**46** C5
Asbus Stop..................................**47** C4
Avis..(see 4)
Budget..**48** C5
Greyhound Australia...................**49** B6
Hertz...**50** B5
Territory Thrifty Car Rental.........**51** B5
Travelworld.................................**52** C4

MUSEUM OF CENTRAL AUSTRALIA
Deft displays at this **museum** (Map p864) recall the days of megafauna – when hippo-sized wombats and 3m-tall flightless birds roamed the woodlands of 20,000 to 50,000 years ago. Meticulously pinned insects, pieces of meteorite, stuffed reptiles and marsupials, and Indigenous artefacts complete the picture.

Upstairs, the **Strehlow Research Centre** (☎ 08-8951 1111) commemorates the anthropological work of Professor Ted Strehlow among the Arrernte people, particularly at the Hermannsburg Mission where he was born, with a small display of Arrernte artefacts.

CENTRAL AUSTRALIA AVIATION MUSEUM & KOOKABURRA MEMORIAL
The **Aviation Museum** (Map p864; Memorial Ave; admission free; ☾ 9am-5pm Mon-Fri, 10am-5pm Sat & Sun) is in the Connellan Hangar, Alice's original aerodrome. There are exhibits on pioneer aviation in the Territory and, of course, the famous Royal Flying Doctor Service.

A small circular building nearby houses the wreck and story of the **Kookaburra** (Map p864), a tiny plane forced to make an emergency landing in the Tanami Desert in 1929 while searching for Charles Kingsford Smith and Charles Ulm, who had gone down in their plane, the *Southern Cross*. Keith Anderson and Bob Hitchcock perished in the desert, while Kingsford Smith and Ulm were rescued.

ALICE SPRINGS MEMORIAL CEMETERY
The **cemetery** (Map p864) is adjacent to the aviation museum and contains the graves of some prominent locals. The most famous is that of **Albert Namatjira** (1902–59); it's the sandstone one in the middle section to the left as you enter the cemetery. The headstone features a terracotta-tile mural of three of Namatjira's Dreaming sites in the MacDonnell Ranges. Other graves located in the cemetery include that of **Harold Lasseter** (1880–1931), the eccentric prospector whose fervent search for the folkloric reef of gold (Lasseter's Reef) claimed his life. The grave of anthropologist **Olive Pink** (1884–1975), who campaigned for Aboriginal rights, is also here.

Telegraph Station Historical Reserve
Laying the Overland Telegraph Line across Australia's harsh Centre was no easy task, as you'll discover at the small museum at the evocative **Telegraph Station** (Map p864; ☎ 08-8952 3993; adult/child/family $7.80/4.30/21; ☾ 8am-9pm, museum 8.30am-5pm). The old stone station dates to the early 1870s and operated until 1932. It later served as a welfare home for Aboriginal children of mixed descent, until 1963. Guided tours operate between 9am and 4.30pm (April to October); phone for times. There's also an informative station map that guides you through restored homestead buildings, a blacksmith shop and the telegraph station itself. The **spring** called Alice (Thereyurre to the Arrernte Aboriginal people), a semipermanent waterhole in the Todd River after which the town is named, is just behind the station.

It's all set on 450 hectares of shady land embellished with picnic tables, free barbecues and walking trails. The best is the 30-minute loop to **Trig Hill**, returning via the original station cemetery.

It's an easy 4km walk or cycle north to the station from Todd Mall; follow the path on the western side of the riverbed.

Royal Flying Doctor Service Base
These dedicated doctors make house calls in an area covering around 2.3 million sq km. So, it's for more than a headache that they fly out to remote stations and communities. Entry to Alice's **Royal Flying Doctor Service base** (RFDS; Map p866; ☎ 08-8952 1129; www.flyingdoctor.net; Stuart Tce; adult/child $7/3.50; ☾ 9am-4pm Mon-Sat, 1-4pm Sun) is on a half-hour tour; they run continuously all day. Tours include a 10-minute video, a look at an operational control room, and a wander through a museum with historical displays that include ancient medical gear. The adjoining cafe (open 9am to 4.45pm Monday to Saturday) serves light meals, cakes and drinks.

School of the Air
The **School of the Air** (Map p864; ☎ 08-8951 6834; www.assoa.nt.edu.au; 80 Head St; adult/child/family $6.50/4.50/18; ☾ 8.30am-4.30pm Mon-Sat, 1.30-4.30pm Sun), about 1km north of the town centre, is another of those innovations born out of necessity in the remote outback. Started in 1951, this was the first school of its type in Australia, broadcasting lessons to children over an area of 1.3 million sq km. While transmissions were originally all done over high-frequency radio, satellite internet connections and web-cams now mean students and teachers can study in a virtual classroom. You get a guided tour of the centre and during school term you can

view a live broadcast from 8.30am to 2.30pm Monday to Friday.

Alice Springs Reptile Centre

Ever wondered how, in the movies, they happen to be in the right place at the right time to film that lizard scampering across the screen? It's a set-up. And many of the stars are here, in their dressing rooms, glass-fronted for us all to see. The **reptile centre** (Map p866; ☎ 08-8952 8900; www.reptilecentre.com.au; 9 Stuart Tce; adult/child $12/10; ☻ 9.30am-5pm) provides a rare opportunity to see the enormous, magnificently patterned perentie lizard, plus thorny devils, bluetongues, bearded lizards and pythons. A purpose-built fossil cave evidences the reptiles' long history with the land. Handling takes place at 11am, 1pm and 3.30pm.

National Pioneer Women's Hall of Fame

This **tribute** (Map p866; ☎ 08-8952 9006; www.pioneer women.com.au; 2 Stuart Tce; adult/child $6.50/3; ☻ 10am-5pm) to Australia's pioneering women is in the former Alice Springs Gaol, very near the Royal Flying Doctor Service base. Behind the high walls and rolls of barbed wire are stories of the exploits and achievements of women from all over the country, including large pictorial displays on 'Women First in Their Field' and 'Women at the Heart' celebrating outback heroines.

Alice Springs Transport Heritage Centre

At the MacDonnell siding, about 10km south of Alice and 1km west of the Stuart Hwy, are a couple of museums dedicated to big trucks and old trains. If you want to visit both the museums, consider the **half-day tour** (☎ 08-8955 5047; tours $55; ☻ 10am-2pm), which includes entry, a guide and lunch.

The **Old Ghan Rail Museum** (off Map p864; ☎ 08-8955 5047; 1 Norris Bell Ave; adult/child/family $8/5/23; ☻ 9am-5pm) has a collection of restored *Ghan* locos and carriages to please train buffs and anyone interested in this pioneering railway (originally called the *Afghan Express* after the cameleers who forged the route). There's also the Old Ghan Tea Rooms and an ad-hoc collection of railway memorabilia in the lovely Stuart railway station.

If you fancy big trucks, the **National Road Transport Hall of Fame** (off Map p864; ☎ 08-8952 7161; www.roadtransporthall.com; 2 Norris Bell Ave; adult/child/family

$12/6/28; ☻ 9am-5pm) has a fabulous collection, including the chassis of the first Kenworth to come off the production line in 1971, and a few ancient road trains. There are over 100 restored trucks and vintage cars, including many of the outback's pioneering vehicles. Admission is valid for two days so take your time.

Olive Pink Botanic Garden

There's no room for ornament in the hardy native shrubs and trees that thrive in this semi-arid **botanic garden** (Map p864; ☎ 08-8952 2154; www.opbg.com.au; Tuncks Rd; admission by donation; ☻ 10am-6pm). A meandering walkway leads through the garden, which is signposted with plant information and significant details. From Meyers Hill there are fine views over Alice and Ntyarlkarle Tyaneme – one of the first sites created by the caterpillar ancestors (the name indicates that this was the place where caterpillars crossed the river). The small information centre and the excellent Bean Tree Cafe (gourmet fare, coffee and cakes) are both open until 4pm.

Adelaide House

Built in the 1920s as the Australian Inland Mission hospital, **Adelaide House** (Map p866; ☎ 08-8952 1856; Todd Mall; admission by donation; ☻ 10am-4pm Mon-Fri, to noon Sat) was the first hospital in central Australia. Designed by the founding flying doctor Reverend John Flynn, it now displays photographs and implements of pioneering medical practice. At the rear of the building stands a small shed housing the original 'pedal radio' invented by Alfred Traeger.

ACTIVITIES
Ballooning

Outback Ballooning (☎ 1800 809 790; www.outback ballooning.com.au; 30-/60-min flight $240/360, mandatory insurance $25) floats above Alice at sunrise, and includes breakfast and transfer from your accommodation.

Bowling

The **Dust Bowl** (Map p864; ☎ 08-8952 5051; 29 Gap Rd; per game weekday/weekend $7/10; ☻ noon-late) has a kiosk and bar and stays open till the last bowlers leave.

Bushwalking

For an intimate experience of the bush around Alice, there are several easy walks radiating

---

THE GHAN

Cutting across the middle of Australia on the *Ghan* is one of Australia's great railway adventures with a fascinating history featuring many twists and turns.

It started in 1877 with the decision to build a railway line from Adelaide to Darwin. It took more than 50 years for the line to reach Alice Springs, and the final 1500km of track to Darwin was only completed in 2004. The reason the project was so protracted was the placement of the original line. Because all the creek beds north of Marree were bone dry, and because nobody had seen rain, it was presumed that there wouldn't be rain in the future. In fact, the initial stretch of line was laid across a flood plain and, when the rain came, even though it soon dried up, the line was simply washed away. In the century or so that the original *Ghan* line existed, this was a regular occurrence.

Compounding the problem were the original track's flimsy foundations, steep grades and multiple meanderings, all of which explain the old *Ghan*'s top speed of 30km/h. Early rail travellers went from Adelaide to Marree on the broad-gauge line, changed there to narrow gauge as far as Oodnadatta, then made the final journey to Alice Springs by camel train. 'Afghan' (actually most were from Balochistan in present–day Pakistan) cameleers pioneered outback transport and it was from them that the *Ghan* took its name.

In 1929 the line was extended to Alice Springs, but the *Ghan* was still chronically slow and unreliable. Worst of all, heavy rain could strand it at either end or even in the middle. Parachute drops of supplies to stranded train travellers became part of outback legend and on one occasion the *Ghan* rolled in 10 days late.

By 1980 a new standard-gauge line had been laid from Tarcoola (northwest of Port Augusta) to Alice Springs, in a spot where rain wouldn't wash it out. In 1982 the old *Ghan* made its last run and the old line was subsequently torn up.

---

from the Olive Pink Botanic Garden (opposite) and the Telegraph Station (p867), which marks the start of the first stage of the Larapinta Trail (see p880).

Alice Springs Bushwalkers Association (http://home.austarnet.com.au/longwalk) is a group of local bushwalkers that schedules a variety of walks in the area, particularly the West MacDonnell Ranges, from March to November.

If you're keen to tackle part of the Larapinta Trail but don't have your own equipment, **Lone Dingo Adventure** (Map p866; ☎ 08-8953 3866; cnr Todd Mall & Gregory Tce) can put together packs of camping and hiking gear for hire, as well as GPS and EPIRB (Emergency Positioning Indicating Radio Beacon) equipment (see p875).

Camel Riding

Camels played an integral part in pioneering central Australia before roads and railways, and travellers can relive some of that adventure.

Frontier Homestead (off Map p864; ☎ 08-8953 0444; www.ananguwaai.com.au; Ross Hwy; 1hr rides adult/child $55/35; 9am-5pm) stages one-hour rides, with extra options to lollop in the morning with breakfast ($85/53 adult/child) or the evening including dinner ($115/85). Prices include transfers from Alice, and you're also free to

wander around the minimuseum on site. The homestead is on the Ross Hwy about 5km southeast of Heavitree Gap.

Pyndan Camel Tracks (off Map p864; ☎ 0416 170 164; www.cameltracks.com; Jane Rd) offers one-hour rides ($40/20 adult/child), as well as half-day jaunts ($95 per person) and overnight treks ($245 per person all-inclusive) where you can roll out the swag and sleep under the southern sky.

Cycling

Recommended rides include the excellent track beside the Todd River to the Telegraph Station (see p867), west to the Alice Springs Desert Park (p865), or further out on the designated cycle path to Simpsons Gap (p880). Pick up a copy of *Active in Alice* from the visitor information centre for a map of cycling and walking paths and take plenty of water on all rides.

Alice Bike Hire (☎ 0407 324 697; half/full day $15/25) Drop-off/pick-up service, mountain bikes, kids' bikes and baby seats available.

Broken Spoke (Map p864; ☎ 08-8953 8744; 10 Gap Rd; half/full day $25/35; 9am-6pm Mon-Fri, to 2pm Sat) Sells and hires bicycles, stocks accessories and does repairs. Hire bikes include cruisers and tandems.

Swimming

If the pool at your lodgings has become too familiar, consider using the lap lane at the **Alice Springs Swimming Centre** (Map p864; ☎ 08-8953 4633; Speed St; adult/child $3.30/1.70; ⌚ 6am-7pm Mon-Fri, 10am-7pm Sat & Sun).

ALICE SPRINGS FOR CHILDREN

If the idea of handling a 3m-long python at the Alice Springs Reptile Centre (p868) doesn't charm the kids, nothing will. Alice Springs Desert Park (p865) has an impressive collection of creatures on show, or kids can saddle-up on a one-humped friend on a camel ride (p869).

TOURS

Around Alice & MacDonnell Ranges

Aboriginal Art & Culture Centre (Map p866; ☎ 08-8952 3408; www.aboriginalart.com.au; 125 Todd St; half/full day $95/170) Offers the chance to meet with Aboriginal people and learn about their culture. Tours include a bushwalk, dance performance and didgeridoo lesson. Full-day trips can be customised to suit your interest.

Alice Wanderer (☎ 1800 722 111; www.alicewanderer.com.au) Runs day tours into the West MacDonnell Ranges as far as Glen Helen Gorge, including morning tea and lunch (adult/child $105/75), and a half-day trip to Simpsons Gap and Standley Chasm ($62/42). There is also a full-day tour into Palm Valley, including morning tea and lunch ($105/75).

Beanies, Baskets & Bushtucker (☎ 0408 436 928; tours $77) Sit with Pitjantjatjara women around a campfire in the Alice Springs Desert Park (p865) to learn grass weaving and beanie crochet, while listening to stories and tasting bush tucker.

Dreamtime Tours (☎ 08-8955 5095; www.rstours.com.au; adult/child $84/42, self-drive $66/33; ⌚ 8.30-11.30am) Runs the popular three-hour Dreamtime & Bushtucker Tour, where you meet Warlpiri Aboriginal people and learn a little about their traditions. As it caters for large bus groups it can be impersonal, but you can tag along with your own vehicle.

Foot Falcon (☎ 0427 569 531; www.footfalcon.com; 2hr guided walking tour $30) Excellent morning, evening and afternoon walking tours of the Alice covering Aboriginal history, historical buildings and tales of the early days.

Outback Experience (☎ 08-8953 2666; www.outbackexperience.com.au) Day trips to Chambers Pillar and Rainbow Valley ($150), and the East MacDonnells ($130).

Trek Larapinta (☎ 08-8953 2933; www.treklarapinta.com.au; 6 days $1200) Guided multiday walks along sections of the Larapinta Trail.

Uluru, Kings Canyon & Palm Valley

Emu Run Tours (☎ 08-8953 7057; www.emurun.com.au) Operates day tours to Uluru ($199) and two-day tours to Uluru and Kings Canyon ($440). Prices include park entry fees. There are also recommended small-group day tours through the West MacDonnell Ranges or Palm Valley ($100), including morning tea, lunch and entrance fees.

Ossies Outback 4WD Tours (☎ 08-8952 2308; www.ossies.com.au) Ossies promises to get you further off the beaten track than most other tours. There are several excellent 4WD tours, including a three-day trip that goes through Finke Gorge National Park to Kings Canyon and Uluru. It costs from $1650 depending on the accommodation option selected.

Palm Valley Tours (☎ 08-8952 0022; www.palmvalleytours.com.au) Day tours depart daily, taking in Palm Valley National Park and Hermannsburg ($135 including lunch); better two-day tours depart weekly ($325), spending longer in Palm Valley and traversing the Mereenie Loop.

The Rock Tour (☎ 1800 246 345; www.therocktour.com.au) Recommended three-day (two nights) camping safaris ($295) that visit Kings Canyon, Curtin Springs, the 'rock' and Kata Tjuta.

Wayoutback (☎ 1300 551 510, 08-8952 4324; www.wayoutback.com.au) Runs three-day 4WD safaris that traverse 4WD tracks to Uluru and Kings Canyon for $565, and five-day safaris that top it up with the Palm Valley and West MacDonnells for $885.

FESTIVALS & EVENTS

Most of the local community gets involved in Alice's annual antics.

Alice Springs Cup (www.alicespringsturfclub.org.au) In May, don a hat and gallop down to the Pioneer Park Racecourse for the main event.

Finke Desert Race (www.finkedesertrace.com.au) Motorcyclists and buggy drivers vie to take out the title of this crazy June race 240km from Alice along the Old South Rd to Finke; the following day they race back again.

Alice Springs Beanie Festival (www.beaniefest.org) This four-day festival in June/July, held at Araluen Art Centre, celebrates the humble beanie (knitted woollen hat) – handmade by women throughout the central desert.

Camel Cup (www.camelcup.com.au) A carnival atmosphere prevails during the running of the Camel Cup at Blatherskite Park in mid-July.

Alice Springs Rodeo Bareback bull riding, steer wrestling and ladies' barrel races at Blatherskite Park in August.

Alice Desert Festival (www.alicedesertfestival.com.au) A cracker of a festival, including a circus program, music, film, comedy and the highly anticipated Desert Mob art exhibition. It's on in September.

Henley-on-Todd Regatta (www.henleyontodd.com.au) Drawing the biggest crowds of all, this series of boat races in September on the dry bed of the Todd River is a typically Australian light-hearted denial of reality. The boats are bottomless: the crews' legs stick through and they run down the course.

SLEEPING

Alice has lots of sleeping options, from caravan parks and backpacker hostels to luxury hotels. Book ahead during the peak season (June to September), but if you're trying your luck, check the internet for last-minute rates, which often bring top-end places into mid-range reach.

Budget

Alice's Secret Traveller's Inn (Map p864; ☎ 1800 783 633, 08-8952 8686; www.asecret.com.au; 6 Khalick St; dm $20-24, s/tw/d $42/54/62; ✗ ⬛ ⬛) Just across the Todd River from town, this is a recommended 'hideaway' hostel where you can relax around the pool, strum a guitar, or play a game of badminton in the garden. Rooms in the dongas are a bit of a squeeze, and those in the house are simple, comfortable and clean.

Toddy's Resort (Map p864; ☎ 1800 027 027; www.toddys.com.au; 39-41 Gap Rd; dm $20-26, d $58-90; ✗ ⬛ ⬛) Toddy's is a rambling place encompassing two properties and a huge variety of rooms. There are basic four-, six- and eight-bed dorms, family rooms, budget doubles and motel doubles. Toddy's is popular with groups and there's a party atmosphere, spurred on by the all-you-can-eat meals at the outdoor bar every evening. Although there are plenty of beds, the motel-style rooms can be hard to get (book ahead).

Pioneer YHA Hostel (Map p866; ☎ 08-8952 8855; www.yha.com.au; cnr Leichhardt Tce & Parsons St; dm $20-29, tw & d $65-73, q $98; ✗ ⬛ ⬛) There's character in this central city hostel, which retains hints of a previous life as the open-air Pioneer Picture Theatre. Location is the biggest bonus here but it's also spotlessly clean, friendly and well run. The comfortable doubles share bathrooms. There's a good-sized kitchen and a pleasant outdoor area around a small pool.

Alice Lodge Backpackers (Map p864; ☎ 1800 351 925, 08-8953 1975; www.alicelodge.com.au; 4 Mueller St; dm $22-25, d $63; ✗ ⬛ ⬛) Friendly staff are as accommodating as the variety of room options at this small, low-key hostel. The old house has mixed and female, three-, four- and eight-bed dorms as well as comfortable doubles and twins. The Todd River lies between the site and town, a 10-minute walk away.

Annie's Place (Map p864; ☎ 1800 359 089, 08-8952 1255; www.anniesplace.com.au; 4 Traeger Ave; dm $22, d & tw $65; ✗ ⬛ ⬛) Alice's most popular hostel has a cosy feel with converted motel rooms (all with bathroom and some with a fridge) around a

central pool. Rooms vary in quality and cleanliness issues are occasionally raised by readers, so check a few rooms before settling in. Apart from a poky kitchen, the facilities are excellent and the lively Travellers Café & Bar (dinner meals for guests are $5 to $12) is a winner.

Desert Rose Inn (Map p866; ☎ 08-8952 1411; www.desertroseinn.com.au; 15 Railway Tce; budget s/d $45/50, motel r from $85; ✗ ⬛ ⬛) Centrally located, the Desert Rose is a great alternative to the backpacker hostels with spotless budget rooms, a communal kitchen and lounge. Budget rooms are two share, with beds (no bunks) and a shower. No more walking down the corridor in your towel! There are other rooms with double beds, fridges and TVs, and motel rooms with full bathrooms.

Midrange

See p872 for information on comfortable motel units and cabins at camping resorts.

White Gum Motel (Map p864; ☎ 1800 624 110; 08-8952 5144; www.whitegum.com.au; 17 Gap Rd; s/d/tr/q $95/110/125/140; ✗ ⬛ ⬛) This impeccable motel is located 10 to 15 minutes' walk from the mall, and perfect if you want a reasonably priced room with your own full kitchen. The spacious, old-fashioned rooms are self-contained, clean as a whistle, and ideal for families.

All Seasons Oasis (Map p864; ☎ 08-8952 1444; www.allseasons.com.au; 10 Gap Rd; d from $110; ✗ ⬛ ⬛) The well-appointed rooms here are conventional and comfortable and the numerous tour groups coming and going attest to its popularity. Facilities include a sports-themed bar, restaurant and wheelchair-accessible rooms. The large, sail-shaded pool surrounded by palms convincingly recreates the oasis experience. The best rates are available from the website.

Alice on Todd (Map p864; ☎ 08-8953 8033; www.aliceontodd.com; cnr Strehlow St & South Tce; studios $115, 1-/2-bedroom apt $140/175; ✗ ⬛) This attractive and secure apartment complex on the banks of the Todd River offers modern, self-contained rooms with kitchen and lounge. The two-bedroom apartments sleep up to six, and the landscaped grounds enclose a barbecue area, children's playground and a games room. These private, balconied rooms are perfect for families and couples alike, with stand-by and long-term rates available.

Desert Palms Resort (Map p864; ☎ 1800 678 037, 08-8952 5977; www.desertpalms.com.au; 74 Barrett Dr; s/d villas from $120/135; ✗ ⬛ ⬛) True to its name,

NORTHERN TERRITORY

this resort is padded with palms positioned for seclusion. The rows of Indonesian-style villas add to the exotic feel, with cathedral ceilings and tropical-style furnishings. Each has a kitchenette, tiny bathroom, TV, breakfast bar and private balcony. The island swimming pool is a big hit with kids.

Nthaba Cottage B&B (Map p864; ☎ 08-8952 9003; www.nthabacottage.com.au; 83 Cromwell Dr; s/d $145/185; ❄) This floral-furnished family home tucked into Alice's exclusive Golf Course estate, on the east side of town, has a beautiful garden with a separate, self-contained cottage giving ample privacy. A room in the house (private entrance) may also be available if the cottage is booked.

Alice Springs Resort (Map p866; ☎ 08-8951 4545; www.voyages.com.au; 34 Stott Tce; standard/superior/deluxe d $150/180/240; ❄ 🖥 🐾) With a circle of double-storey buildings arranged around a swath of lawns and gum trees, Alice Springs Resort has a relaxed country-club vibe. Handsome rooms become handsomer the higher up from 'standard' you go. Guests tend to gravitate to the cool pool terrace with a poolside bar or the resort's seafood restaurant.

Aurora Alice Springs (Map p866; ☎ 1800 089 644, 08-8950 6666; www.auroraresorts.com.au; 11 Leichhardt Tce; standard/deluxe/executive d $160/180/250; ❄ 🖥 🐾) Right in the town centre (the 'back' door opens out onto Todd Mall), this modern hotel has a relaxed atmosphere and an excellent restaurant, the Red Ochre Grill (see opposite). Standard rooms are nondescript but well-appointed with fridge, phone and free in-house movies.

Crowne Plaza Alice Springs (Map p864; ☎ 1300 666 545, 08-8950 8000; www.crowneplaza.com.au; Barrett Dr; d from $165, ste $250-295; ❄ 🖥 🐾) With spacious resort-style facilities and attentive service, this is one of Alice's best hotels. Choose from the garden-view rooms or the better mountain-range–view rooms – all have a balcony or patio, TV, free movies and bath-tub. A pleasant pool and spa, well-equipped gym and sauna, tennis courts and one of Alice's best restaurants, Hanuman (opposite), complete the picture.

Top End

Bond Springs Outback Retreat (off Map p864; ☎ 08-8952 9888; www.outbackretreat.com.au; 2-/3-bedroom cottages from $230/280; ❄ 🐾) Experience the combination of outback station life and imported luxury at this retreat, about 26km

from town. Two private self-contained cottages are on offer, which are refurbished stockman's quarters. A full breakfast is included but the rest is self-catering. The enormous property provides occasion for walks, including mooching around the original station school, which operated through the School of the Air.

Ooraminna Homestead & Bush Camp (Map p877; ☎ 08-8953 0170; www.ooraminnahomestead.com.au; off Old South Rd; s swag $140, d incl meals $500) This homestead is only 30km south of Alice, and offers a genuine outback station experience. Roll out a swag (provided) or stay in style in the secluded stone or timber cabins converted from buildings originally constructed for a movie set (one is an old gaol!). The cabins have four-poster beds made from desert oak and modern bathrooms. You can relax on the verandah of the family homestead, which has a bar and dining room, take a station tour or go bushwalking.

Camping & Caravanning

Most camping grounds are on the outskirts of Alice.

Heavitree Gap Outback Lodge (off Map p864; ☎ 1800 896 119, 08-8950 4444; www.auroraresorts.com.au; Palm Circuit; unpowered/powered sites $20/22, dm $25, d $125-135; ❄ 🖥 🐾) Several eucalypt-studded acres make a shady place to pitch or park, though the bulk of business here is in the rooms: four-bed dorms, and lodge and kitchenette rooms. The old-fashioned kitchenette rooms that can sleep six are cheaper than the lodge rooms, making them excellent value. There's a knees-up at the neighbouring barn-sized pub most nights.

MacDonnell Range Holiday Park (off Map p864; ☎ 1800 808 373, 08-8952 6111; www.macrange.com.au; Palm Pl; unpowered/powered sites $32/36, cabins d $68-172; ❄ 🖥 🐾) The children can cavort on the adventure playground, BMX track and basketball court, while the adults can kick back around the pool. Those not in the family way will also enjoy the immaculate facilities of this park. Cabins range from simple affairs with no linen or bathroom, to self-contained two-bedroom villas.

EATING

Alice has a reasonable diversity of eateries, with most making an effort to cater for vegetarians. For fine dining the top-end hotel restaurants can't be beaten, and for a range of options for casual breakfasts, brunches and lunches Todd Mall is the place to head.

Restaurants

Thai Room (Map p866; ☎ 08-8952 0191; Fan Lane; mains $10-21; Ⓥ lunch Mon-Fri, dinner Mon-Sat) Perky Thai flavours of tamarind, garlic, basil and coconut milk make the perfect palate freshener in Alice's dry climate. The modest menu mixes its signature spices with a variety of meats or straight veg. There's no need to frock up, and the lunch specials are a bargain.

Red Ochre Grill (Map p866; ☎ 08-8952 9614; Todd Mall; mains $11-31) With innovative fusion cuisine featuring outback meats, as well as traditional favourites, this is one of the better eateries on Todd Mall. As well as familiar dishes of chicken, lamb, barramundi and beef, there's camel, crocodile, emu and kangaroo infused with native berries, fruits and herbs. So there's no chance you'll say, 'It tasted like chicken'.

Flavours of India (Map p864; ☎ 08-8952 3721; 20 Undoolya Rd; mains $14-20; Ⓥ dinner) There's no Bollywood drama in the decor of this humble family restaurant. While covering ubiquitous curries and tandoori favourites, the menu includes a smattering of non-Indian meals. There are several vegetarian dishes, and though fully licensed, BYO is also possible.

Tinh & Lan Alice Vietnamese Restaurant (off Map p864; ☎ 08-8952 8396; 1900 Heffernan Rd; mains $14-20; Ⓥ lunch & dinner Tue-Sun) This atmospheric Vietnamese restaurant is set in a market garden illuminated with lanterns. All the favourites, spring and ricepaper rolls, *pho* (soup) and noodles, are deliciously prepared and the ingredients – growing all around you – couldn't be fresher. Follow the signs off Colonel Rose Dr; it's about 14km south of town.

Casa Nostra (Map p864; ☎ 08-8952 6749; cnr Undoolya Rd & Sturt Tce; mains $14-28; Ⓥ dinner) Choose your pasta and match it with a long list of classic Italian sauces and specials: from bolognese and pesto to a chef's secret-recipe sauce. Thin-crust pizzas and mains dishes also arrive on the red-and-white-checked tablecloths among the plastic grapevines. Note that it's BYO vino.

Hanuman Restaurant (Map p864; ☎ 08-8953 7188; Crowne Plaza Alice Springs, Barrett Dr; mains $14-30; Ⓥ lunch Mon-Fri, dinner daily) Stylish Hanuman tempts with Thai- and Indian-influenced cuisine. The delicate Thai entrées, including the signature dish of oysters, lemon grass and basil, are a real triumph. Although the menu is ostensibly Thai, featuring beef, chicken, seafood, jasmine rice and noodles, there are enough Indian dishes to satisfy a curry craving. There are several vegetarian offerings and a good wine list.

The Lane (Map p866; ☎ 08-8952 5522; 58 Todd Mall; mains $18-35; Ⓥ breakfast Sat & Sun, lunch & dinner Tue-Sun) The licensed Lane has most bases covered, with a stylish restaurant and casual outdoor seating in the hub of the mall, plus a big menu featuring bistro dishes, wood-fired pizzas, tapas and salads.

Overlanders Steakhouse (Map p866; ☎ 08-8952 2159; 72 Hartley St; mains $20-40; Ⓥ dinner) A local institution for big steaks, be they buffalo, kangaroo, crocodile or camel. And why stop at just one? Amid the drover's decor (saddles, branding irons and the like) you can take the challenge of the Drover's Blowout ($65), four courses including a platter of Aussie meats.

Cafes

Bean Tree Cafe (Map p864; ☎ 08-8952 0190; Olive Pink Botanic Garden, Tuncks Rd; mains $9-12; Ⓥ 10am-4pm Tue-Sun) The Bean Tree is a soothing retreat in the Olive Pink Botanic Garden. Choose from a small selection of wholesome dishes, such as kangaroo and rocket salad, Thai chicken pot pie, or a BLT, and order a refreshing iced coffee.

Café Mediterranean Bar Doppio (Map p866; ☎ 08-8952 6525; Fan Lane; mains $10-17; Ⓥ breakfast & lunch) Alice's locals duck down this laneway for huge and wholesome home-style breakfasts (eggs any style, pancakes), pita pizzas, burgers, pies and salads. It's also a favoured meeting place for well-made coffee or fresh-pressed juice, either in the shade of the covered arcade or inside with local-events flyers wallpapering the walls.

Red Dog (Map p866; ☎ 08-8953 1353; 64 Todd Mall; mains $12-15; Ⓥ breakfast & lunch) Join the throng at this Australiana-decorated place pumping out decent coffee and hearty breakfasts (eggs, pancakes or the whole-hog 'bushman's breakfast'), and a range of chicken burgers.

Quick Eats & Self-Catering

Wicked Kneads (Map p866; Coles Complex, Bath St; pastries $3-4.50, focaccias $9; Ⓥ 7am-4pm) This place has an excellent made-to-order sandwich bar, pies (15 varieties), cakes and sourdough bread.

Afghan Traders (Map p866; ☎ 08-8955 5560; Leichtodd Plaza, 7 Leichhardt Tce) Replete with organic and other health foods – follow the laneway behind

NORTHERN TERRITORY

the ANZ bank, or duck through Springs Plaza from Todd Mall.

Large supermarkets include **Woolworths** (Map p866; Yeperenye Shopping Centre; ☽ 7am-midnight Mon-Sat, to 10pm Sun) on Hartley and Bath Sts, and **Coles** (Map p866; Coles Complex, cnr Gregory & Railway Tces; ☽ 24hr).

DRINKING
Bojangles (Map p866; ☎ 08-8952 2873; 80 Todd St; ☽ 11.30am-late) Swing open the saloon doors to boots, barrels and bones – a 'Wild West meets Aussie Outback' theme. Grab a handful of peanuts from the barrel by the door and sidle up to a communal table with a beer in hand. Bojangles is easily the most popular pub in town, beloved of backpacker groups and jumping most nights of the week.

Firkin & Hound (Map p866; ☎ 08-8953 3033; 21 Hartley St; ☽ 11.30am-1am) This low-lit, Brit tavern has snug booths, a large TV fixed on the sports channel and a dozen or so beers on tap. It's a pleasant place to bend the elbow and fill up on hearty meals such as beef and Guinness pie for lunch or dinner (mains $12 to $25).

Todd Tavern (Map p866; ☎ 08-8952 1255; www.todd tavern.com.au; 1 Todd Mall; ☽ 10am-midnight) This enduring, classically Aussie pub is the true 'local' in Alice. There's a lively bar, pokies, pub grub and occasional live music on weekends.

ENTERTAINMENT
The gig guide in the entertainment section of the *Centralian Advocate* (published every Tuesday and Friday) lists what's on in and around town.

Araluen Arts Centre (Map p864; ☎ 08-8951 1122; www.araluenartscentre.nt.gov.au; Larapinta Dr) The cultural heart of Alice, the 500-seat Araluen Theatre hosts a diverse range of performers, from dance troupes to comedians, while the Art House Cinema screens films every Sunday evening (adult/child $12/10). The website has an events calendar.

Alice Springs Cinema (Map p866; ☎ 08-8952 4999; Todd Mall; adult/child $14.50/10, Tue $10/8) Latest-release movies make themselves at home at this multiscreen complex.

Lasseter's Hotel Casino (Map p864; ☎ 08-8950 7777; www.lassetershotelcasino.com.au; 93 Barrett Dr; ☽ 10am-3am Sun-Thu, to 4am Fri & Sat, gaming tables from 2pm) Along with the usual slot and table games, there's the classic Aussie two-up ring (from 9pm Friday and Saturday). The casino is named after a man who died in his quest for riches.

Sounds of Starlight Theatre (Map p866; ☎ 08-8953 0826; www.soundsofstarlight.com; 40 Todd Mall; adult/concession/family $30/25/90; ☽ 8pm Tue, Fri & Sat) This atmospheric 1½-hour musical performance evoking the spirit of the outback with didgeridoo, drums and keyboards and wonderful photography and lighting is an Alice institution.

Story Wall (Map p866; Adelaide House, Todd Mall; ☽ Thu & Fri nights) Park yourself on the grass outside Adelaide House and enjoy free films pertaining to central Australia's heritage screened on an adjacent building's wall.

SHOPPING
Trawl Todd Mall for Aboriginal art, souvenir T-shirts, road signs ('Kangaroos next 14km') and stubby holders. Nearby you'll find the large indoor shopping centres, Alice Plaza (Map p866) and Springs Plaza (Map p866). A block away is Yeperenye Shopping Centre (Map p866). For general items, try **K-mart** (Map p866; ☎ 08-8952 8188; Bath St; ☽ 9am-6pm Mon-Wed & Fri, 8am-8pm Thu, 9am-5pm Sat & Sun).

Aboriginal Arts & Crafts
Alice is the centre for Aboriginal arts from all over central Australia. The places owned and run by community art centres ensure that a better slice of the proceeds goes to the artist and artist's community.

Central Australian Aboriginal Media Association (Caama; Map p866; ☎ 08-8951 9711; www.caama.com .au; 79 Todd Mall; ☽ 9am-5pm Mon-Fri, to 1pm Sat) Here you will find most of the CDs recorded by central Australia's Aboriginal musicians. The Caama studio, which has its own radio network (8KINFM), is just down the road at 101 Todd St. As well as CDs the shop in the mall stocks Aboriginal-design printed material, T-shirts, jewellery and other Indigenous-themed items.

Gallery Gondwana (Map p866; ☎ 08-8953 1577; www .gallerygondwana.com.au; 43 Todd Mall; ☽ 9.30am-6pm Mon-Fri, 10am-5pm Sat) Gondwana is a well-established private gallery, recognised for dealing directly with community art centres and artists. Quality works from leading and emerging Central and Western Desert artists include those from Yuendumu and Utopia.

Mbantua Gallery (Map p866; ☎ 08-8952 5571; www .mbantua.com.au; 71 Gregory Tce; ☽ 9am-6pm Mon-Fri, 9.30am-5pm Sat) This privately owned gallery, which extends through to Todd Mall, includes a cafe and extensive exhibits of works from the renowned Utopia region, as well as watercolour landscapes from the Namatjira school. The upstairs Educational & Permanent Collection (adult/child \$4.60/3.30) is a superb cultural exhibition space with panels explaining Aboriginal mythology and customs.

Ngurratjuta Iltja Ntjarra (Map p864; ☎ 08-8951 1953; www.ngurart.com.au; 29 Wilkinson St; ⊗ 9am-3.30pm Mon-Fri) The 'many hands' art centre is a small gallery and studio for visiting artists from all over Central Australia. Watercolour and dot paintings are reasonably priced and you buy directly from the artists. You can see artists at work from Monday to Thursday, 10am to 3pm.

Papunya Tula Artists (Map p866; ☎ 08-8952 4731; www.papunyatula.com.au; 78 Todd Mall; ⊗ 9am-5pm Mon-Fri, 10am-2pm Sat) The Western Desert art movement began at Papunya Tula in 1971, and today this Aboriginal-owned gallery displays some of this most sought-after art. Papunya Tula works with around 120 artists, most painting at Kintore in the far west.

Outdoor Equipment

Desert Dwellers (Map p864; ☎ 08-8953 2240; 38 Elder St; ⊗ 9am-5pm Mon-Fri, to 2pm Sat) For camping and hiking gear, head to this shop, which has just about everything you need to equip yourself for an outback jaunt – maps, swags, tents, portable fridges, stoves, Larapinta Trail Packs and more.

Lone Dingo Adventure (Map p866; ☎ 08-8953 3866; cnr Todd Mall & Gregory Tce; ⊗ 9am-6pm Mon-Fri, to 4pm Sat, 10am-2pm Sun) Lone Dingo stocks hiking and camping gear, GPS systems and EPIRBs.

Markets

Todd Mall Market (Map p866; ⊗ 9am-1pm 2nd Sun of month, May-Dec) Buskers, craft stalls, sizzling woks, smoky satay stands, clothing racks, Aboriginal art, jewellery and knick-knacks make for interesting mooching.

GETTING THERE & AWAY
Air

Alice Springs is well connected with **Qantas** (☎ 13 13 13, 08-8950 5211; www.qantas.com.au) and **Tiger Airways** (☎ 08-9335 3033; www.tigerairways.com.au) operating daily flights to/from capital cities. Airline representatives are based at Alice Springs airport. One-way fares from Alice include Yulara (\$170), Adelaide (\$250), Melbourne (\$310), Darwin (\$290), Sydney (from \$280), Brisbane (from \$310) and Perth (from \$330). Check websites for latest timetables and fare offers.

Bus

Greyhound Australia (☎ 1300 473 946; www.greyhound.com.au; shop 3, 113 Todd St; ⊗ office 8.30-11.30am & 1.30-4pm Mon-Fri) has regular services from Alice Springs (check the website for timetables). Buses arrive at, and depart from, the Greyhound office in Todd St.

Destination	One-way fare (\$)	Duration (hr)
Adelaide	280	20
Coober Pedy	165	8
Darwin	315	22
Katherine	255	16½
Tennant Creek	160	6½

Austour (☎ 1800 335 009; www.austour.com.au) runs the cheapest daily connections between Alice Springs and Yulara (\$120/60 per adult/child) and Kings Canyon (\$110/60). **AAT Kings** (☎ 08-8952 1700; www.aatkings.com) also runs between Alice Springs and Yulara (adult/child \$135/68), and between Kings Canyon and Alice Springs (\$138/69).

Backpacker buses roam to and from Alice providing a party atmosphere and a chance to see some of the sights on the way. **Desert Venturer** (☎ 1300 858 059; www.desertventurer.com.au) plies the route from Alice to Cairns via the Plenty Hwy. The three-day coach trip costs \$396 plus \$85 for meals. **Groovy Grape Getaways Australia** (☎ 1800 661 177; www.groovygrape.com.au) plies the route from Alice to Adelaide overnighting in Coober Pedy for \$195, plus offers six- and seven-day camping trips from Adelaide to Alice Springs. The **Wayward Bus Touring Company** (☎ 1300 653 510, 08-8410 8833; www.waywardbus.com.au) has a 2½-day 'Just the Centre' trip (\$405) taking in Kings Canyon, Uluru and Rainbow Valley. It also does an eight-day Alice–Adelaide tour (\$1095).

Car & Motorcycle

Alice Springs is a long way from everywhere. It's 1180km to Mt Isa, in Queensland, 1490km to Darwin and 441km (4½ hours) to Yulara (for Uluru). Although the roads to the north and south are sealed and in good condition, these are outback roads, and it's wise to have your vehicle well prepared, particularly as you won't get a mobile phone signal outside Alice or Yulara. Carry plenty of drinking water and emergency food at all times.

All the major car-rental companies have offices in Alice Springs, and Avis, Budget, Europcar, Hertz and Territory Thrifty also have counters at the airport. A conventional (2WD) vehicle will get you to most sights in the MacDonnell Ranges and out to Uluru and Kings Canyon via sealed roads. If you want to go further afield, say to Chambers Pillar, Finke Gorge or even the Mereenie Loop Rd, a 4WD is essential. Rentals don't come cheap, as most firms offer only 100km free a day, which won't get you far. Prices drop by about 20% between November and April.

Alice Camp 'n' Drive (Map p864; ☎ 08-8952 0099; www.alicecampndrive.com; 48 Gap Rd) Provides vehicles fully equipped for camping with swags (or tents), sleeping bags, cooking gear, chairs etc. Rates include unlimited kilometres and vehicles can be dropped off at your accommodation.

Avis (Map p866; ☎ 08-8953 5533; www.avis.com.au; shop 21b, Coles Shopping Complex, Gregory Tce) Also has an airport counter.

Britz (off Map p864; ☎ 08-8952 8814; www.britz.com.au; cnr Stuart Hwy & Power St) Campervans and cars; also at the airport. This is also the base for Maui (www.maui.com.au) and Backpacker (www.backpackercampervans.com) campervans.

Budget (Map p866; ☎ 13 27 27, 08-8952 8899; www.budget.com.au; shop 6, Capricornia Centre, Gregory Tce) Also at the airport.

Central Car Rentals (Map p864; ☎ 08-8952 0098; www.centralcarrentals.com.au; 48 Gap Rd) A local operator (associated with Alice Camp 'n' Drive) with 2WD and 4WD vehicles that can be equipped with camping gear. Unlimited kilometre rates are available.

Europcar (☎ 13 13 90; www.europcar.com.au) At airport only.

Hertz (Map p866; ☎ 08-8952 2644; www.hertz.com; 76 Hartley St)

Territory Thrifty Car Rental (Map p866; ☎ 08-8952 9999; www.rentacar.com.au; cnr Stott Tce & Hartley St)

Train

In Alice, tickets for the classic, Australia-crossing *Ghan* can be booked through **Trainways** (☎ 13 21 47; www.trainways.com.au) or **Travelworld** (Map p866; ☎ 08-8953 0488; 40 Todd Mall). Discounted fares are sometimes offered, especially in the low season (February to June). Bookings are recommended on this popular route. See p816 for a timetable.

The train station (Map p864) is at the end of George Cres off Larapinta Dr.

GETTING AROUND

Alice Springs is compact enough to get to most parts of town on foot, and you can reach quite a few of the closer attractions by bicycle (see p869).

To/From the Airport

Alice Springs airport is 15km south of the town. It's about $30 by taxi. The **airport shuttle** (Map p866; ☎ 08-8953 0310; Gregory Tce; 1/2/3 persons one way $17/29/33) meets flights and drops off passengers at city accommodation. Book a day in advance for pick-up from accommodation.

Bus

The public bus service, **Asbus** (☎ 08-8952 5611), departs from outside the **Yeperenye Shopping Centre** (Hartley St). Buses run about every 1½ hours from 7.45am to 6pm Monday to Friday, and from 9am to 12.45pm on Saturday. The adult/child fare for all routes is $2/50c. There are three routes of interest to travellers: 1 has a detour to the cultural precinct, 3 passes the School of the Air, and 4 passes many southern hotels and caravan parks along Gap Rd and Palm Circuit. The visitor information centre has free timetables.

The **Alice Wanderer** (☎ 1800 722 111, 08-8952 2111; www.alicewanderer.com.au; adult/child $40/30; ⌚ 9am-4pm) sightseeing bus does a loop around the major sights, including the old telegraph station, School of the Air, Old Ghan Museum and the cultural precinct. You can get on and off wherever you like. It runs every 70 minutes from opposite the visitor information centre on Gregory Tce, and you can arrange to be picked up from your accommodation. The ticket is valid for two days.

Taxi

Taxis congregate near the visitor information centre. To book one, call ☎ 13 10 08 or ☎ 08-8952 1877.

MACDONNELL RANGES

The ruggedly beautiful MacDonnell Ranges stretch to the east and west of Alice Springs. Within this ancient, fissured structure there are spectacular gorges with sheer walls of brick-red stone sheltering life-sustaining waterholes. There are many places you can visit within a day from the Alice, but, if you have time, immerse yourself in this primordial landscape by camping under the stars. Walks range from sightseeing strolls to the challenge of the Larapinta Trail. There's no public transport to either the East or West MacDonnell Ranges; see p870 for tours from Alice.

EAST MACDONNELL RANGES

The East MacDonnell Ranges stretch for 100km east of Alice Springs, intersected by a series of scenic gaps and gorges that see far fewer visitors than the West MacDonnell Ranges. The sealed Ross Hwy, accessible through Heavitree Gap south of town, leads to most of the highlights. About 100km from Alice Springs, the unsealed Arltunga Rd becomes Arltunga Tourist Dr (also known as Gardens Rd) northwest of Arltunga. This road, which rejoins the Stuart Hwy 50km north of Alice Springs, is usually OK for 2WDs.

Emily & Jessie Gaps Nature Park

Both of these gaps are associated with the Eastern Arrernte Caterpillar Dreaming trail. **Emily Gap**, 16km out of town, is a pleasant spot with rock art and a fairly deep waterhole in the narrow gorge. Known to the Arrernte as Anthwerrke, this is one of the most important Aboriginal sites in the Alice Springs area; it was from here that the caterpillar ancestral beings of Mparntwe originated before crawling across the landscape to create the topographical features that exist today. The gap is a sacred site with some well-preserved paintings on the eastern wall. **Jessie Gap**, 8km further, is an equally scenic and usually much quieter place. Both sites have toilets.

Corroboree Rock Conservation Reserve

Past Jessie Gap you drive over eroded flats before entering a valley between red ridges. **Corroboree Rock**, 51km from Alice Springs, is one of many strangely shaped dolomite outcrops scattered over the valley floor. Despite the name, it's doubtful the rock was ever used as a corroboree area, but it is associated with the Perentie Dreaming trail. The perentie is one of the world's largest lizards, growing in excess of 2.5m, and takes refuge within the area's rock falls. The rock is looped by a walking track (15 minutes), and there's a toilet.

Trephina Gorge Nature Park

About 70km from Alice Springs you cross the sandy bed of Benstead Creek and shadow a lovely stand of red gums for the 6km from the creek crossing to the Trephina Gorge turn-off; it's then another 8km to the gorge. If you only have time for a couple of stops in the East MacDonnell Ranges, make Trephina Gorge Nature Park one of them. The play between the pale sandy river beds, the red and purple gorge walls, the white tree trunks, the eucalyptus-green foliage and the blue sky is spectacular. You'll also find deep swimming holes and abundant wildlife. Just before the gorge itself is **Trephina Bluff**. The Trephina Gorge Walk (2km, 45 minutes) loops around the gorge's rim. The Ridgetop Walk (10km one way, five hours) traverses the ridges from the gorge to John Hayes Rockhole; the 8km return along the road takes about two hours.

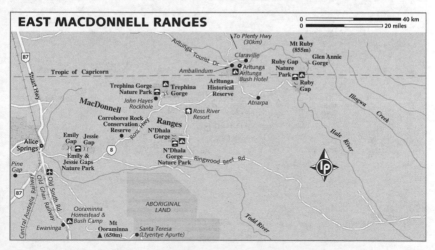

EAST MACDONNELL RANGES

NORTHERN TERRITORY

The delightful **John Hayes Rockhole**, 9km from the Trephina Gorge turn-off (the last 4km is 4WD only) has three very basic **campsites** (adult/child/family $3.30/1.65/7.70). From here, the Chain of Ponds walk (4km loop, 1½ hours) leads through the gorge, past rock pools and up to a lookout above the gorge.

There's a **rangers station** (☎ 08-8956 9765) and **camping grounds** (adult/child/family $3.30/1.65/7.70) with barbecues, water and toilets at Trephina Gorge and the Bluff.

N'Dhala Gorge Nature Park

Nine kilometres along the continuation of the Ross Hwy past the Arltunga turn-off you come to the secluded **Ross River Resort** (☎ 08-8956 9711; www.rossriverresort.com.au; unpowered/powered sites $24/30, bunkhouse $22, d cabins $120; ✂ 🏊). Built around a historic stone homestead, timber cabins encircle a swimming pool. There's a store with fuel, and it's worth the detour to check out the old homestead and maybe grab lunch or a beer in the Stockman's Bar, but it may pay to ring first to check that it is open.

Shortly before the resort, a strictly 4WD-only track leads 11km south to **N'Dhala Gorge**.

Around 5900 ancient Aboriginal rock carvings and some rare endemic plants decorate a deep, narrow gorge, although the art isn't easy to spot. There's a small, exposed **camping ground** (adult/child/family $3.30/1.65/7.70) without reliable water.

Arltunga Historical Reserve

Situated at the eastern end of the MacDonnell Ranges, 110km east of Alice Springs, is the old gold-mining ghost town of **Arltunga**. Its history, from the discovery of alluvial (surface) gold in 1887 until mining activity petered out in 1912, is fascinating. **Old buildings**, a couple of **cemeteries** and the many deserted **mine sites** in this parched landscape give visitors an idea of what life was like for the miners. There are walking tracks (the Government Works area has the best collection of dry-stone buildings) and old mines (with bats!) to explore, so bring a torch.

The unstaffed **visitor information centre** (⏱ 8am-5pm) has many displays and old photographs of the gold-extracting process, plus a slide show on the area's history, and drinking water and toilets. There's no camping in the

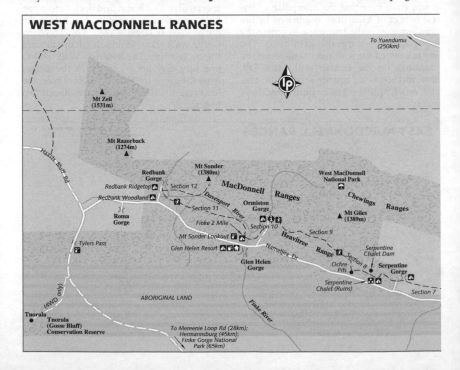

WEST MACDONNELL RANGES

To Yuendumu
(250km)

Mt Zeil
(1531m)

Haasts Bluff Rd

Mt Razorback
(1274m)

Redbank Gorge
Redbank Ridgetop
Redbank Woodland
Section 12
Mt Sonder
(1380m)
Davenport River
MacDonnell   Ranges
West MacDonnell National Park
Chewings   Ranges
Section 11
Ormiston Gorge
Roma Gorge
Finke 2 Mile
Section 10
Mt Giles
(1389m)
Tylers Pass
Mt Sonder Lookout
Section 9
Glen Helen Resort
Heavitree   Range
Section 8
Serpentine Chalet Dam
Namatjira Dr
Glen Helen Gorge
Ochre Pits
Serpentine Gorge
(AWD only)
ABORIGINAL LAND
Serpentine Chalet (Ruins)
Section 7
Tnorala
Tnorala
(Gosse Bluff)
Conservation Reserve
Finke River
To Mereenie Loop Rd (28km);
Hermannsburg (45km);
Finke Gorge National
Park (65km)

reserve itself, but the nearby **Arltunga Bush Hotel** (☎ 08-8956 9797; sites per adult/child $8/4) has a camping ground with showers, toilets, barbecue pits and picnic tables. Fees are collected in the late afternoon. The bar is open for drinks Thursday to Monday, but there were no meals available at the time of writing.

The 40km section of unsealed road between the Ross Hwy and Arltunga can be impassable after heavy rain. From Arltunga it's possible to loop back to the Alice along the Arltunga Tourist Dr.

Ruby Gap Nature Park

This remote, little-visited park rewards visitors with wild and beautiful scenery. The sandy bed of the Hale River sparkles with thousands of tiny garnets. The garnets caused a 'ruby rush' here in the 19th century and some miners did well out of it until it was discovered that the 'rubies' were, in fact, virtually worthless garnets. It's an evocative place and is well worth the considerable effort required to reach it – by high-clearance 4WD. The waterholes at **Glen Annie Gorge** are usually deep enough for a cooling dip.

Camping (adult/child/family $3.30/1.65/7.70) is permitted anywhere along the river; make sure to BYO drinking water and a camp cooker. Allow two hours each way for the 44km trip from Arltunga. It's essential to get a map from Parks & Wildlife Commission (www.nt.gov.au/nreta/parks/find/rubygap.html) and to **register** (☎ 1300 650 730) in Alice Springs before setting out and upon return.

WEST MACDONNELL RANGES

Outstanding in the arid zone for their stunning beauty and rich diversity of plants and animals, the West Macdonnell Ranges are not to be missed. Their easy access by conventional vehicle makes them especially popular with day-trippers. Heading west from Alice, Namatjira Dr turns northwest off Larapinta Dr 6km beyond Standley Chasm and is sealed all the way to Tylers Pass. Roadwork continues to seal it all the way to Larapinta Dr and complete a sealed loop back to Alice, via Hermannsburg.

All the sites mentioned in this section lie within the **West MacDonnell National Park**, except for Standley Chasm, which is privately owned.

NORTHERN TERRITORY

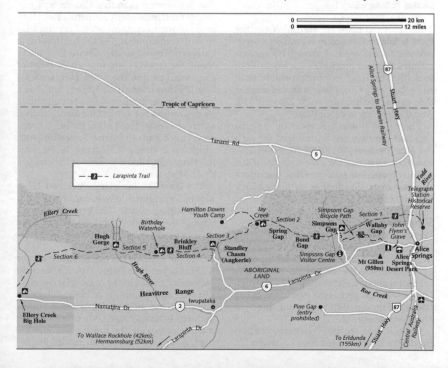

There are ranger stations at Simpsons Gap and Ormiston Gorge.

Larapinta Trail

The Larapinta Trail is a 12-stage, 233.5km track of varying degrees of difficulty along the backbone of the West MacDonnells, stretching from the Telegraph Station in Alice Springs to the craggy 1380m summit of Mt Sonder. The following sections each take one to two days to navigate and pass many of the attractions in the West MacDonnells:

Section 1 Alice Springs Telegraph Station to Simpsons Gap (23.8km)

Section 2 Simpsons Gap to Jay Creek (24.5km)

Section 3 Jay Creek to Standley Chasm (13.6km)

Section 4 Standley Chasm to Birthday Waterhole (17.7km)

Section 5 Birthday Waterhole to Hugh Gorge (16km)

Section 6 Hugh Gorge to Ellery Creek (31.2km)

Section 7 Ellery Creek to Serpentine Gorge (13.8km)

Section 8 Serpentine Gorge to Serpentine Chalet Dam (13.4km)

Section 9 Serpentine Chalet Dam to Ormiston Gorge (28.6km)

Section 10 Ormiston Gorge to Finke River (9.9km)

Section 11 Finke River to Redbank Gorge (25.2km)

Section 12 Redbank Gorge to Mt Sonder (15.8km return)

Trail notes and maps are available from the **Parks & Wildlife Commission** (www.nt.gov.au/nreta/parks/walks/larapinta/index.html), though it is recommended that you purchase a Larapinta Trail Pack ($45) from outdoor equipment shops in Alice Springs (p875). Walkers should register their names and itinerary on ☎ 1300 650 730. And don't forget to deregister.

There's no public transport out to this area, but transfers can be arranged through the **Alice Wanderer** (☎ 1800 722 111, 08-8952 2111; www.alicewanderer.com.au); see the website for the various costs. For guided walks, including transport from Alice Springs, go through Trek Larapinta (p870).

Simpsons Gap

Westbound from Alice Springs on Larapinta Dr you soon come to **John Flynn's Grave**. The flying doctor's final resting place is topped by a boulder donated by the Arrernte people (the original was a since-returned Devil's Marble). Opposite the car park is the start of the **cycling track** to Simpsons Gap, a pleasant three- to four-hour return ride.

By road, **Simpsons Gap** (🕙 5am-8pm) is 22km from Alice Springs and 8km off Larapinta Dr.

It's a popular picnic spot and has some good walks. This towering gap in the range is the result of 60 million years of effort by a creek – a creek that rarely runs. There are often rock wallabies in the jumble of rocks either side of the gap. The visitor information centre is 1km from the park entrance.

Standley Chasm (Angkerle)

Fifty kilometres west of Alice Springs is **Standley Chasm** (☎ 08-8956 7440; adult/senior & child $8/6.50; camping per person $3; 🕙 8am-6pm). This narrow corridor slices neatly through the rocky range and in places the smooth walls rise to 80m. It's usually cool and dark on the chasm floor, except for about an hour either side of midday when the red stone walls are briefly warmed by sunlight. This is when most camera-toting tourists arrive, so early or late in the day is much more peaceful. The rocky path into the gorge (15 minutes) follows a creek bed lined with ghost gums and cycads. You can continue to a second chasm (one hour return). There's a kiosk, picnic facilities and toilets near the car park.

Namatjira Drive

Not far beyond Standley Chasm you can choose the northwesterly Namatjira Dr (which loops down to connect with Larapinta Dr west of Hermannsburg) or the southwesterly Larapinta Dr (opposite). Continuing along Namatjira Dr takes you to a whole series of gorges and gaps in the range. **Ellery Creek Big Hole** is 91km from Alice Springs and has a large permanent waterhole – a popular place for a swim on a hot day, but the usually shaded water is freezing. About 11km further, a rough gravel track leads to narrow **Serpentine Gorge**, which has a waterhole blocking the entrance (no swimming) and a lookout at the end of a short, steep track.

The **Ochre Pits** line a dry creek bed 11km west of Serpentine and were a source of paint for Aboriginal people. The various coloured ochres – mainly yellow, white and red-brown – are weathered limestone, with iron-oxide creating the colours.

The car park for the grand **Ormiston Gorge** is 25km beyond the Ochre Pits. It's the most impressive chasm in the West MacDonnells and well worth a couple of hours. There's a waterhole, and the gorge curls around to the enclosed **Ormiston Pound**. When the pound's waterholes dry up, the fish burrow into the sand, going into a sort of suspended animation only to reappear after rain. There are some excellent **walking tracks**, including the **Ghost Gum Lookout** (20 minutes), which affords brilliant views down the gorge, and the excellent, circuitous **Pound Walk** (7.5km, three hours). There's a **visitor centre** (☎ 08-8956 7799; ☽ 5am-8pm) and a **kiosk** (☽ 10am-4pm).

About 2km further is the turn-off to scenic **Glen Helen Gorge**, where the Finke River cuts through the MacDonnells. Only 1km past Glen Helen is a good **lookout** over Mt Sonder, which was a popular painting subject for Albert Namatjira; sunrise and sunset here are particularly impressive.

If you continue northwest for 25km you'll reach the turn-off (4WD only) to multihued, cathedral-like **Redbank Gorge**, a permanent waterhole. Namatjira Dr then heads south and is sealed as far as **Tylers Pass Lookout**, which provides a dramatic view of **Tnorala (Grosse Bluff)**, the legacy of an earth-shattering comet impact.

SLEEPING & EATING

There are basic **camping grounds** (adult/child/family $3.30/1.65/7.70) at Ellery Creek Big Hole, Redbank Gorge and 6km west of Serpentine Gorge at Serpentine Chalet (a 4WD or high-clearance 2WD vehicle is recommended to reach the chalet ruins). The **camping area** (adult/child/family $6.60/3.30/16) at Ormiston Gorge is the ritziest in the West Macs, with showers, toilets, gas barbecues and picnic tables.

At the edge of the national park is the popular **Glen Helen Resort** (☎ 08-8956 7489; www .glenhelen.com.au; Namatjira Dr; unpowered/powered sites $24/30, dm/r from $30/160; ☒ ☒). There's been a homestead on this superb site, with the sheer walls of the gorge as a spectacular backdrop, since 1905 – the current building dates mainly from the 1980s. This comfortable retreat has a restaurant-bar (breakfast and lunch $5 to $15, dinners $22 to $32) serving delicious and hearty meals. There are also helicopter flights from the homestead ranging from $50 to $375, with the $125 Ormiston Gorge flight representing the best value.

SOUTH OF ALICE SPRINGS

It's worth diverting off the road south from Alice Springs to some of the Centre's more memorable attractions. There are also attrac-

tions to the east of the Stuart Hwy, but to visit most of these requires a 4WD.

LARAPINTA DRIVE

The low-lying **James Ranges** form an east–west band south of the West MacDonnell Ranges. While not as well known as the MacDonnells, the ranges border some of the Centre's top attractions: Hermannsburg, Palm Valley and Kings Canyon.

Taking the alternative road to the south from Standley Chasm (opposite), Larapinta Dr crosses the Hugh River before reaching the turn-off to the Western Arrernte community of **Wallace Rockhole**, 18km off the main road and 109km from Alice Springs.

You'll be virtually guaranteed seclusion at the **Wallace Rockhole Tourist Park** (☎ 08-8956 7993; www.wallacerockholetours.com.au; unpowered/powered sites $20/24, cabins $130; ☒), situated at the end of an 18km dirt road branching off Larapinta Dr. Tours from here include a 1½-hour rock-art tour ($15/13 adult/child) with billy tea and damper.

About 26km from the Wallace Rockhole turn-off, continuing along Larapinta Dr, you will pass the lonely **Namatjira Monument**, which is about 8km from Hermannsburg.

Hermannsburg

pop 460

Hermannsburg (Ntaria) is 125km from Alice Springs. Although the town is restricted Aboriginal land, permits are not required to visit the historic precinct and town shop.

The whitewashed walls of the old **mission** (☎ 08-8956 7402; adult/child/family $10/5/25; ☽ 9am-4pm Mar-Nov, 10am-4pm Dec-Feb) are shaded by tall river gums and date palms. This fascinating monument to the Territory's early Lutheran missionaries includes a school building, a church and various outbuildings. The 'Manse' houses an art gallery and a history of the life and times of Albert Namatjira (a one-time resident) as well as work of 39 Hermannsburg artists.

The **Kata-Anga Tea Room** (meals $7-13; ☽ 9am-4pm), in the old missionary house, serves highly recommended apple strudel and Devonshire tea. Distinctive paintings and pottery by the locals is also on display here and is for sale.

Just west of Hermannsburg is **Namatjira's House**. Albert Namatjira (1902–59), the Aboriginal artist whose European-style watercolours of the region were embedded with depictions of important Dreaming sites, lived in this two-room house (now in disrepair) in the 1920s. Albert did much to change the extremely negative views of Aboriginal people that prevailed during his lifetime.

Finke Gorge National Park

Finke Gorge National Park, south of Hermannsburg, is one of central Australia's premier wilderness reserves, famous for its rare red cabbage palms. The top-billing attraction here is **Palm Valley** with its ribbon of tall palms, ancient cycads, and excellent walks and **camping ground** (adult/child/family $6.60/3.30/16).

Walks include the **Arankaia walk** (2km loop, one hour), which traverses the valley, returning via the sandstone plateau; the **Mpulungkinya track** (5km loop, two hours), heading down the gorge before joining the Arankaia walk; and the **Mpaara track** (5km loop, two hours), taking in the Finke River, Palm Bend and a rugged amphitheatre (a semicircle of sandstone formations sculpted by a now extinct meander of Palm Creek).

Access to the park follows the sandy bed of the Finke River and rocky tracks, and so a high-clearance 4WD is essential. If you don't have one, several tour operators go to Palm Valley from Alice Springs; see p870. The turn-off to Palm Valley starts about 1km west of the Hermannsburg turn-off on Larapinta Dr.

Mereenie Loop Road (Red Centre Way)

From Hermannsburg you can continue west to the turn-off to Areyonga (no visitors) and then take the Mereenie Loop Rd to Kings Canyon. This is an alternative route from Alice to Kings Canyon. Despite government plans to seal this rugged road, work had not started at the time of writing. There are deep sandy patches and countless corrugations (call ☎ 1800 246 199 for the latest road conditions) and it's best travelled in a high-clearance 4WD. Be aware that 2WD hire vehicles will not be covered by insurance on this road.

To travel along this route, which passes through Aboriginal land, you need a Mereenie Tour Pass ($2.20), which is valid for one day and includes a booklet with details about the local Aboriginal culture and a route map. The pass is issued on the spot (usually only on the day of travel) at the visitor information centre in Alice Springs (p865), Glen Helen Resort (p881), Kings Canyon Resort (p885) and Hermannsburg service station.

OLD SOUTH ROAD

The Old South Road, which runs close to the old *Ghan* railway line, is pretty rough and may require a 4WD after rain. It's only 39km from Alice Springs to **Ewaninga**, where prehistoric Aboriginal petroglyphs are carved into sandstone. The rock carvings found here and at N'Dhala Gorge (p878) are thought to have been made by Aboriginal people who lived here before those currently in the region.

The eerie, sandstone **Chambers Pillar**, southwest of Maryvale Station, rises 50m above its surrounding plain and is carved with the names and visit dates of early explorers – and, unfortunately, some far less worthy modern-day graffitists. To the Aboriginal people of the area, Chambers Pillar is the remains of Itirkawara, a powerful gecko ancestor. It's 160km from Alice Springs, and a 4WD is required for the last 44km from the turn-off at Maryvale Station. There's a basic **camping ground** (adult/child/family $3.30/1.65/7.70).

Back on the main track south, you eventually arrive at **Finke (Aputula)**, a small Aboriginal community 230km from Alice Springs. When the old *Ghan* was running, Finke was a thriving town; these days it seems to have drifted into a permanent torpor, except when the Finke Desert Race (p870) is staged. Fuel is sold at the **Aputula Store** (☎ 08-8956 0968; ☼ 9am-noon & 2-4pm Mon-Fri, 9am-noon Sat), which is also an outlet for local artists' work, including carved wooden animals and seed necklaces.

From Finke, you can turn west along the Goyder Stock Rte to join the Stuart Hwy at Kulgera (150km), or east to Old Andado station on the edge of the Simpson Desert (120km). Just 21km west of Finke, and 12km north of the road along a signposted track, is the **Lambert Centre**. The point marks Australia's geographical centre and features a 5m-high version of the flagpole found on top of Parliament House in Canberra.

RAINBOW VALLEY CONSERVATION RESERVE

This series of freestanding sandstone bluffs and cliffs, in shades ranging from cream to red, is one of central Australia's more extraordinary sights. A marked walking trail takes you past clay pans and in between the multi-hued outcrops to the aptly named **Mushroom Rock**. Rainbow Valley is most striking in the early morning or at sunset, but the area's un-

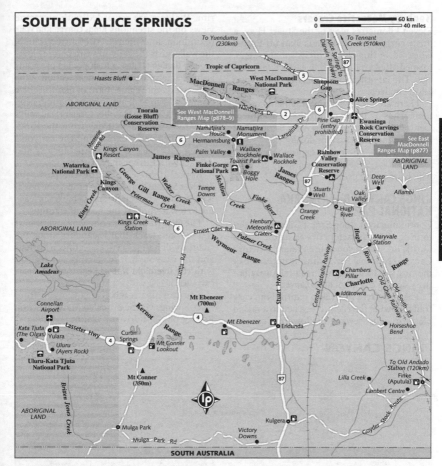

SOUTH OF ALICE SPRINGS

earthly silence will overwhelm you whatever time of day you are here.

The park lies 24km off the Stuart Hwy along a 4WD track that's 77km south of Alice Springs. It has a basic **camping ground** (adult/child/family $3.30/1.65/7.70).

STUARTS WELL

Climb onto a camel at Stuarts Well, 90km south of Alice Springs. At **Camels Australia** (☎ 08-8956 0925; www.camels-australia.com.au) you can take a short ride around the yard for $5, a 30-minute jaunt for $25 or a full-day ride for $165. Extended outback safaris (including meals and swag) of three ($500) to five ($800) days through the gaps and gorges of the James Ranges can also be arranged.

Jim's Place (☎ 08-8956 0808; Stuarts Well; unpowered/powered sites $17/20, budget r with own swag/supplied linen $15/30, cabins s/d $70/85; 🏊 🖥 🍴) is run by well-known outback identity Jim Cotterill, who, along with his father, opened up Kings Canyon to tourism. You might also catch Dinky the singing dingo – rescued and raised from a pup.

ERNEST GILES ROAD

The Ernest Giles Rd heads off to the west of the Stuart Hwy about 140km south of Alice. This shorter but rougher route to Kings Canyon is often impassable after heavy rain and is not recommended for 2WD vehicles. The section along the Luritja Rd to Kings Canyon is sealed.

Henbury Meteorite Craters

Eleven kilometres west of the Stuart Hwy, a dusty corrugated track leads 5km off Ernest Giles Rd to this cluster of 12 small craters, formed after a meteor fell to earth 4700 years ago. The largest of the craters is 180m wide and 15m deep.

There are no longer any fragments of the meteorites at the site, but the Museum of Central Australia (p867) in Alice Springs has a small chunk that weighs 46.5kg.

There are some basic, exposed **campsites** (adult/child/family $3.30/1.65/7.70), on stony ground, which are pretty grim.

KINGS CANYON & WATARRKA NATIONAL PARK

Continuing west along Ernest Giles Rd, or detouring off the Lasseter Hwy along the sealed Luritja Rd, brings you to the Watarrka (Kings Canyon) National Park, which features one of the most spectacular sights in central Australia – the yawning chasm of **Kings Canyon**.

The **Kings Creek Walk** (2km return) is an easy trail following the rocky creek bed to a raised platform with views of the towering canyon

rim. Walkers are rewarded with awesome views on the strenuous **Kings Canyon Rim Walk** (6km loop, four hours). After a steep climb, the walk skirts the canyon's rim before entering the **Garden of Eden**: a lush pocket of cycads around a natural pool. The next section of the walk winds through a maze of giant beehive domes – keep well away from the unfenced edge. From May to October rangers lead walks (on Thursday and Saturday from the Kings Canyon car park) explaining the canyon's geology, its place in Aboriginal history and contact with European explorers.

About 10km east of the car park, the **Kathleen Springs Walk** (2.6km return, one hour) is a pleasant wheelchair-accessible track leading to a waterhole at the head of a gorge.

The **Giles Track** (22km one way, overnight) is a marked track that meanders along the George Gill Range between Kathleen Springs and the canyon; before starting out register with the **Overnight Walker Registration Scheme** (☎ 1300 650 730).

You can also reach Kings Canyon from Alice Springs via the unsealed Mereenie Loop Rd (see p882), a drive of 325km.

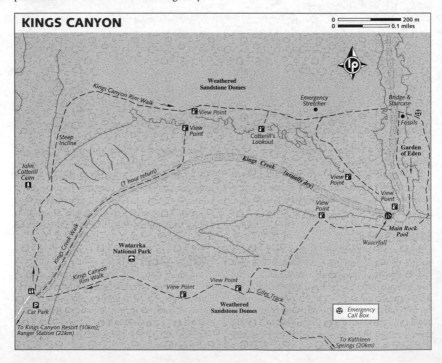

KINGS CANYON

Tours

Several tour companies depart Alice and stop here on the way to/from Uluru (see p870).

Kings Creek Helicopters (☎ 08-8956 7886; flights per person $45-380) Has flights from Kings Creek Station, including 30-minute flights over Kings Canyon for $220.

Professional Helicopter Services (PHS; ☎ 08-8956 7873) Picking up from Kings Canyon Resort; PHS buzzes the canyon for 8/15 minutes ($70/115).

Sleeping & Eating

Kings Canyon Resort (☎ 1300 134 044, 08-8951 4545; www.kingscanyonresort.com.au; Luritja Rd; unpowered/powered sites $27/33, dm $44, budget d $110, r $260-450; ❄ ❑ ❑) This sprawling resort, 10km from the canyon, caters to school groups, honeymooners, folks on a budget and people with no budget. Accommodation options start with a neat rectangle on the lawn for your tent to a deluxe room with an almost-outdoor spa in the most private part of the grounds. Eating and drinking options are as varied, with a cafe, a restaurant for buffet breakfasts and dinner, a bar with pizzas and steaks, and an exclusive candlelit dinner around a campfire ($140 per person). There's a general store with fuel and an ATM at reception.

Kings Creek Station (☎ 08-8956 7474; www.kingscreekstation.com.au; Luritja Rd; per adult/child $16/8, power $5.50, safari cabins s/d incl breakfast $95/145; ❑ ❑) Located outside the national park's eastern boundary, 35km from the canyon, this station has campsites set among desert oaks. Safari-style cabins (small canvas tents on solid floors) share a bathroom block and kitchen-barbecue area. There are camel rides (one-hour ride $50), quad bikes (one-hour ride $78) and helicopter flights (see above). Fuel, ice, beer, wine, snacks, barbecue packs and limited supplies are available at the shop (open 7am to 7pm).

LASSETER HIGHWAY

The Lasseter Hwy connects the Stuart Hwy with Uluru-Kata Tjuta National Park, 244km to the west from the turn-off at Erldunda. There are a couple of roadhouses along the way.

Mount Conner, the large mesa (table-top mountain) that looms 350m out of the desert, is the outback's most photographed red herring. On first sighting many mistake it for Uluru, but other than being a large mass protruding from a flat plain it bears no resemblance. It has great significance to local Aboriginal people, who know it as Atila.

Curtin Springs (☎ 08-8956 2906; www.curtinsprings.com; Lasseter Hwy; unpowered/powered sites free/$25, s/d $65/90, r with bathroom $140-200; ❄) is the last stop before Yulara, and the nearest alternative to Ayers Rock Resort. You can pitch a tent for free or bed down in a well-maintained cabin. There's fuel, a store with limited supplies and takeaway and bistro meals (mains $15 to $25), plus a bar.

ULURU-KATA TJUTA NATIONAL PARK

One of the world's most recognised natural attractions holds pride of place in this fascinating national park. Fascinating, because no picture conveys entirely the multidimensional grandeur of Uluru, or the equally impressive Kata Tjuta (the Olgas). And fascinating because this entire area is of cultural significance to the traditional owners, the Pitjantjatjara and Yankuntjatjara Aboriginal peoples (who refer to themselves as Anangu). The Anangu officially own the national park, which is leased to Parks Australia and jointly administered.

Many of the 500,000 annual visitors spend fewer than two days here, especially those on tours, which generally whiz through in 24 hours. Considering the 445 long, flat kilometres travelled from Alice to arrive here, and the numerous walks and organised activities on offer, it's worth at least that. The only accommodation is the Voyagers Ayers Rock Resort in the Yulara village, 4km from the park boundary.

Information

The **park** (www.environment.gov.au/parks/uluru; adult/child $25/free) is open from half an hour before sunrise to sunset daily (varying between 5am to 9pm November to March and 6.30am to 7.30pm April to October). Entry permits are valid for three days and available at the drive-through entry station on the road from Yulara.

Uluru-Kata Tjuta Cultural Centre (☎ 08-8956 3138; ⏰ 7am-6pm, information desk 8am-noon & 1-5pm) is 1km before Uluru on the road from Yulara and should be your first stop. Displays and exhibits focus on *tjukurpa* (Aboriginal law, religion and custom) and the history and management of the national park. The information desk in the Nintiringkupai building is staffed by

NORTHERN TERRITORY

SORRY ROCKS

If you have the habit of souveniring stones and rocks for the mantelpiece, and feel tempted to take a little piece of this sacred land home, then you should check out the small display in the Nintiringkupai building of the Uluru Cultural Centre. Above a small pile of rocks is a folder of letters from people around the world who – in a fit of guilt or superstition – have returned their ill-gotten souvenirs. The letters contain pleas of forgiveness (hence 'sorry rocks') from people recognising that their geological grab and run speaks of disrespect to the traditional owners and the land itself. Furthermore, a substantial proportion of the letters tell tales of woe and bad luck that have befallen the light-fingered and their immediate family since removing a rock from its rightful place. These make particularly good reading.

Removing rocks is not only disrespectful and potentially ill boding; it is also illegal. Fines for removing rocks, sand or soil from the park range up to $5000. And after all, T-shirts and fridge magnets are more useful and easier to pack.

---

park rangers who can supply the informative *Visitor Guide*, leaflets and walking notes.

The Cultural Centre encompasses the craft outlet **Maruku** (☎ 08-8956 2558; www.maruku.com.au; ☽ 8.30am-5.30pm), owned by about 20 Anangu communities from across central Australia (including the local Mutitjulu community), selling hand-crafted wooden carvings, bowls and boomerangs. **Walkatjara Art Centre** (☎ 08-8956 2537; ☽ 9am-5.30pm) is a working art centre owned by the local Mutitjulu community. It focuses on paintings and ceramics created by women from Mutitjulu. **Ininti Cafe & Souvenirs** (☎ 08-8956 2214; ☽ 7am-5.15pm) sells souvenirs such as T-shirts, ceramics, hats, CDs and a variety of books on Uluru, Aboriginal culture, biographies, bush foods and the flora and fauna of the area. The attached cafe serves ice cream, pies and light meals. The **Liru Walk** (2km, 45 minutes) leads from the Cultural Centre to the start of the Base and Mala Walks.

There's also a visitor information centre in Yulara (see p890).

Tours

Most tour operators have desks at Yulara's Tour & Information Centre (p890) and depart from the resort unless otherwise stated.

BUS TOURS

The small-group operator **Discovery Ecotours** (☎ 08-8956 2563; www.ecotours.com.au) runs a five-hour Uluru circumambulation and breakfast for $115/86 per adult/child; Spirit of Uluru is a four-hour, vehicle-based version for the same price. The Kata Tjuta & Dunes Tour includes a walk into Olga Gorge and sunset at Kata Tjuta for $97/73. There's also a seven-hour tour to **Cave Hill**, across the South Australian

border in Pitjantjatjara land, including lunch for $237.

AAT Kings (☎ 08-8956 2171; www.aatkings.com) operates the biggest range of coach tours. You can choose from a range of half- and full-day tours, or buy one of a selection of three-day tour passes (from $200/98 per adult/child). Check the website or ask at the Tour & Information Centre for details.

CAMEL TOURS

Uluru Camel Tours (☎ 08-8956 2444; www.ananguwaai .com.au; short rides adult/child $10/5; ☽ 10.30am-2.30pm) provides the opportunity to view Uluru and Kata Tjuta from a distance in a novel way: atop a camel ($65, 45 minutes). Most popular, though, are the Camel to Sunrise tours ($99, 2½ hours) and the sunset equivalent with champagne or beer ($99).

CULTURAL TOURS

Anangu Tours (☎ 08-8956 2123; www.ananguwaai.com .au), owned and operated by Anangu from the Mutitjulu community, offers a range of trips led by an Anangu guide and gives an insight into the land through Anangu eyes; tours depart from the Cultural Centre (p885).

The daily, five-hour Aboriginal Uluru Tour ($127/85 per adult/child) starts with sunrise over Uluru and breakfast at the Cultural Centre, followed by a guided stroll down the Liru Walk (including demonstrations of bush skills such as spear-throwing).

The Kuniya Sunset Tour ($106/69, 4½ hours) departs at 2.30pm (3.30pm between November and February) and includes a visit to Mutitjulu Waterhole and the Cultural Centre, finishing with a sunset viewing of Uluru.

Both trips can be combined over 24 hours with an Anangu Culture Pass ($214/140). Self-drive options are also available for $63/32. You can join an Aboriginal guide at 8.30am (7.30am from November to February and 8am in March and October) for the morning walk or at 3.30pm (4.30pm from December to February) for the Kuniya tour.

DINING TOURS

With **Sounds of Silence** (☎ 08-8957 7448; www.ayers rockresort.com.au/sounds-of-silence; adult/child $155/80), snappily dressed waiters serve champagne and canapés on a desert dune with stunning sunset views of Uluru and Kata Tjuta. Then it's a buffet dinner (with emu, croc and roo) beneath the twinkling southern sky, which, after dinner, is dissected and explained with the help of a telescope. If you're more of a morning person, try the similarly styled **Desert Awakenings** (adult/child $146/113). Neither tour is suitable for children under 10 years.

MOTORCYCLE TOURS

Sunrise and sunset tours to Uluru and Kata Tjuta can also be had on the back of a Harley Davidson. **Uluru Motorcycle Tours** (☎ 08-8956 2019; rides $50-295) motors out to Uluru at sunset ($160, 30 minutes).

SCENIC FLIGHTS

While the enjoyment of those on the ground may be diminished by the buzz of light aircraft and helicopters overhead, for those actually up there it's an unforgettable experience. Prices are per person and include airport transfers from Ayers Rock Resort.

Ayers Rock Helicopters (☎ 08-8956 2077) A 15-minute buzz of Uluru costs $110; to include Kata Tjuta costs $220.

Ayers Rock Scenic Flights (☎ 08-8956 2345; www .ayersrockresort.com.au/helicopter-flights) Prices start from $165 for a 40-minute flight over Uluru and Kata Tjuta; it costs $390 for a two-hour flight that also takes in Lake Amadeus and Kings Canyon.

Professional Helicopter Services (PHS; ☎ 08-8956 2003; www.phs.com.au) Charges $115 for its Uluru flight and $220 for its 30-minute Uluru and Kata Tjuta flight.

ULURU (AYERS ROCK)

Nothing in Australia is as readily identifiable as Uluru (Ayers Rock). No matter how many times you've seen it on postcards, nothing prepares you for the hulk on the horizon – so solitary and impressive. Uluru is 3.6km long and rises a towering 348m from the surrounding sandy scrubland (867m above sea level). If that's not impressive enough, it's believed that two-thirds of the rock lies beneath the sand. Closer inspection reveals a

NORTHERN TERRITORY

A QUESTION OF CLIMBING

Many visitors consider climbing Uluru to be a highlight – even a rite of passage – of a trip to the Centre. But for the traditional owners, the Anangu, Uluru is a sacred place. The path up the side of the Rock is part of the route taken by the Mala ancestors on their arrival at Uluru and has great spiritual significance – and is not to be trampled by human feet. When you arrive at Uluru you'll see a sign from the Anangu saying 'We don't climb' and a request that you don't climb either.

The Anangu are the custodians of Uluru and take responsibility for the safety of visitors. Any injuries or deaths that occur (and they do occur – check out the memorial plaques at the base) are a source of distress and sadness to them. For similar reasons of public safety, Parks Australia would (unofficially) prefer that people didn't climb. It's a very steep and taxing ascent, not to be taken lightly, and each year there are several costly air rescues, mostly from people suffering heart attacks. Furthermore, Parks Australia must constantly monitor the climb and close it on days where the temperature is forecast to reach 36°C or strong winds are expected.

So if the Anangu don't want people to climb and Parks Australia would prefer to see it closed, why does it remain open? The answer is tourism. The tourism industry believes visitor numbers would drop significantly – at least initially – if the climb was closed, particularly from overseas visitors thinking there is nothing else to do at Uluru.

The debate has grown louder in recent years and many believe the climb will eventually be closed for good, perhaps as early as 2010. Until such a time, it remains a personal decision and a question of respect. Before deciding, visit the Cultural Centre and perhaps take an Anangu tour. You might just change your mind.

NORTHERN TERRITORY

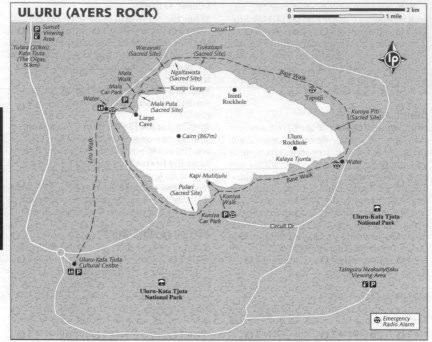

ULURU (AYERS ROCK)

wondrous pitted and contoured surface concealing numerous sacred sites of particular significance to the Anangu people. If your first sight of Uluru is during the afternoon, it appears as an ochre-brown colour, scored and pitted by dark shadows. As the sun sets, it illuminates the rock in burnished orange, then a series of deeper and darker reds before it fades into charcoal. A performance in reverse, with marginally fewer spectators, is given at dawn.

Activities
WALKING

There are walking tracks around Uluru, and ranger-led walks explain the area's plants, wildlife, geology and mythology. All the walks are flat and suitable for wheelchairs. Several areas of spiritual significance to Anangu people are off limits to visitors; these are marked with fences and signs. Photography of sacred sites is also forbidden.

The *Visitor Guide & Maps* brochure, which can be picked up at the Cultural Centre, gives details on the following self-guided walks (except the climb).

Base Walk (10km, three to four hours) A highlight for many, this track circumnavigates the rock, passing caves, paintings, sandstone folds and geological abrasions along the way.

Kuniya Walk (1km return, 45 minutes) A short walk from the car park on the southern side leads to the only permanent waterhole, Mutitjulu, with links to the Kuniya and Liru Tjukurpa.

Liru Walk (4km return, 1½ hours) This walking track links the Cultural Centre with the start of the Mala walk and climb, and passes a number of significant Anangu sites.

Mala Walk (2km return, one hour) From the base of the climbing point, interpretive signs explain the *tjukurpa* of the Mala (hare-wallaby people), which is significant to the Anangu. A ranger-guided walk (free) along this route departs at 10am (8am from October to April) from the car park.

Uluru Climb (1.6km return, two hours) The Anangu ask that visitors respect Aboriginal law and culture by choosing not to climb Uluru (see A Question of Climbing, p887). The steep and demanding path follows the traditional route taken by ancestral Mala men. The climb is often closed (sometimes at short notice) due to strong winds, rain, mist and Anangu business, and on days forecast to reach 36°C or more.

SUNSET & SUNRISE VIEWING

About halfway between Yulara and Uluru, the **sunset viewing area** has plenty of car and coach parking for that familiar postcard view. The **Talnguru Nyakunytjaku viewing area** should be operational by the time you read this. This new area provides a different perspective of Uluru to the postcard profile, and will be of interest for more than just sunrise.

KATA TJUTA (THE OLGAS)

A striking group of domed rocks huddle together about 35km west of Uluru to form Kata Tjuta (the Olgas). There are 36 domed rocks shoulder to shoulder forming deep valleys and steep-sided gorges. Most visitors find them as captivating as their prominent neighbour. The tallest rock, **Mt Olga** (546m, 1066m above sea level) is approximately 200m higher than Uluru. Kata Tjuta means 'many heads' and is of great *tjukurpa* significance, so climbing on the domed rocks is definitely not on.

The main walking track here is the **Valley of the Winds**, a 7.4km loop trail (two to four hours) that traverses varying desert terrain and yields wonderful views of surreal boulders. It's not particularly arduous, but wear sturdy shoes, and take plenty of water and sun protection. Starting this walk at first light may reward you with solitude, enabling you to appreciate the sounds of the wind and bird calls carried up the valley.

The short signposted track beneath towering rock walls into pretty **Walpa Gorge** (2.6km return, 45 minutes) is especially beautiful in the afternoon, when sunlight floods the gorge.

There's a picnic and sunset-viewing area with toilet facilities just off the access road a few kilometres west of the base of Kata Tjuta. Like Uluru, the Olgas are at their glorious, blood-red best at sunset.

HEADING WEST

A lonely sign at the western end of the Kata Tjuta access road signals that there's a hell of a lot of nothing if you travel west – if suitably equipped, you can travel all the way to Kalgoorlie and on to Perth in WA. It's 181km to Kaltukatjara (Docker River), an Aboriginal settlement to the west, and about 1500km to Kalgoorlie. You need a permit from the Central Land Council for this trip – for more information, see p85.

YULARA (AYERS ROCK RESORT)

pop 2080 (including Mutitjulu)

Yulara is the service village for the Uluru-Kata Tjuta National Park and has effectively turned one of the world's least hospitable regions into an easy and comfortable place to visit. Lying just outside the national park, 20km from Uluru and 53km from Kata Tjuta, the complex is the closest base for exploring the area's renowned attractions. The village includes a bank, a petrol station, emergency services, the resort's four hotels, apartments, a lodge, a camping ground and a supermarket. Yulara supplies the only accommodation,

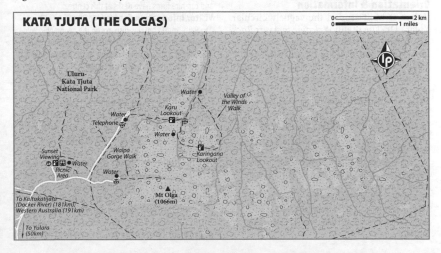

KATA TJUTA (THE OLGAS)

0────2 km
0────1 miles

Uluru-
Kata Tjuta
National Park

Water
Telephone

Water

Karu
Lookout

Valley of
the Winds
Walk

Water

Sunset
Viewing

Water

Walpa
Gorge Walk

Karingana
Lookout

Picnic
Area

Water

To Kaltukatjara
(Docker River) (181km);
Western Australia (191km)

Mt Olga
(1066m)

To Yulara
(50km)

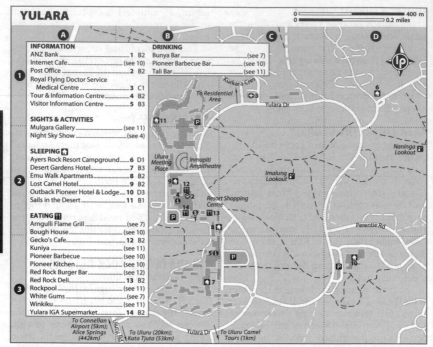

YULARA

0 — 400 m
0 — 0.2 miles

INFORMATION		
ANZ Bank	1	B2
Internet Cafe	(see 10)	
Post Office	2	B2
Royal Flying Doctor Service Medical Centre	3	C1
Tour & Information Centre	4	B2
Visitor Information Centre	5	B3

SIGHTS & ACTIVITIES		
Mulgara Gallery	(see 11)	
Night Sky Show	(see 4)	

SLEEPING		
Ayers Rock Resort Campground	6	D1
Desert Gardens Hotel	7	B3
Emu Walk Apartments	8	B2
Lost Camel Hotel	9	B2
Outback Pioneer Hotel & Lodge	10	D3
Sails in the Desert	11	B1

EATING		
Arngulli Flame Grill	(see 7)	
Bough House	(see 10)	
Gecko's Cafe	12	B2
Kuniya	(see 11)	
Pioneer Barbecue	(see 10)	
Pioneer Kitchen	(see 10)	
Red Rock Burger Bar	(see 12)	
Red Rock Deli	13	B2
Rockpool	(see 11)	
White Gums	(see 7)	
Winkiku	(see 11)	
Yulara IGA Supermarket	14	B2

DRINKING		
Bunya Bar	(see 7)	
Pioneer Barbecue Bar	(see 10)	
Tali Bar	(see 11)	

food outlets and other services available in the region. If it weren't in the middle of the desert within cooee of the rock you'd baulk at the prices here; as it is, you're stuck with them.

Orientation & Information

Yulara is built around the vaguely circular Yulara Dr. The useful *Welcome to Ayers Rock Resort* flyer is available at the visitor information centre and at hotel desks. Most of the village's facilities are in the shopping centre, including a post office and a local job vacancies board.

ANZ bank (☎ 08-8956 2070) Currency exchange and 24-hour ATMs.

Emergency (☎ police 08-8956 2166, ambulance 0420 101 403)

Internet cafe (Outback Pioneer Hotel; per 10min $2; ⏰ 5am-11pm) In the backpacker common room. Internet access is also available at the Tour & Information Centre and all accommodation.

Post office (☎ 08-8956 2288; Resort Shopping Centre; ⏰ 9am-6pm Mon-Fri, 10am-2pm Sat & Sun) An agent for the Commonwealth and NAB banks. Pay phones are outside.

Royal Flying Doctor Service medical centre (☎ 08-8956 2286; ⏰ 9am-noon & 2-5pm Mon-Fri, 10-11am Sat & Sun) The resort's medical centre and ambulance service.

Tour & Information Centre (☎ 08-8957 7324; Resort Shopping Centre; ⏰ 8am-8pm; ⌨) Most tour operators and car-hire firms have desks at this centre.

Visitor Information Centre (☎ 08-8957 7377; ⏰ 9am-5pm) Contains displays on the geography, wildlife and history of the region, and sells books and regional maps. Information is also available at the national park's Uluru-Kata Tjuta Cultural Centre (p885).

Sights & Activities

Check out the **Mulgara Gallery** (found off reception in the Sails in the Desert hotel), where quality handmade Australian arts and crafts are displayed. Each month brings a new artist in residence.

The **Night Sky Show** (☎ 08-8956 2563; www.eco tours.com.au; Discovery Ecotours, Tour & Information Centre; adult/child $33/25) takes an informative one-hour look at the startlingly clear outback night sky with a telescope and an astronomer. Trips in English are at 8.30pm, with a further session at 7.30pm from May to August and 10.15pm from September to April. Prices also include pick-up from your accommodation; bookings are essential.

Sleeping

All of the accommodation in Yulara, including the camping ground and hostel, is owned by the Ayers Rock Resort. And unless the free camping at Curtin Springs station (p885) outweighs the risk of driving in the dark for sunrise/sunset at Uluru, there's no other option. Even though there are almost 5000 beds, it's wise to make a reservation, especially during school holidays. Bookings can be made through **central reservations** (☎ 1300 134 044; www .ayersrockresort.com.au). Substantial discounts are usually offered if you stay for three nights or more, and you can also save a reasonable amount through internet sites offering discount accommodation.

Outback Pioneer Hotel & Lodge (☎ 08-8957 7605; dm $34-42, d $190-430; ✕ 🖳 🕱) With a lively barnlike bar and restaurant, this is the budget (budget for Yulara) choice for noncampers. Accommodation ranges from four-bed mixed-sex dorms and 20-bed unisex dorms to budget rooms with/without bathroom and standard hotel rooms. Rooms are a decent size, and pricier ones are equipped with TV and fridge.

Lost Camel Hotel (☎ 08-8957 7605; d $430; ✕ 🖳 🕱) The funky (though small) rooms available at this boutique hotel come with very comfy beds and stereos – TV addicts, however, will have to head for the plasma screen at reception. A fine courtyard pool and a bar inspire you to do very little.

Emu Walk Apartments (☎ 08-8956 7714; 1-/2-bedroom apt from $490/570; ✕) Comfort and uniformity are the chief characteristics of these modern apartments, each with a lounge room (with TV) and a well-equipped kitchen. The one-bedroom apartment accommodates four people, while the two-bedroom version sleeps six. Check in at the Desert Gardens Hotel reception.

Desert Gardens Hotel (☎ 08-8957 7714; r $490-580; ✕ 🖳 🕱) One of Yulara's originals, this ageing hotel is nothing special, though it has spacious rooms and a great pool. The deluxe rooms feature a balcony with desert or Uluru views.

Sails in the Desert (☎ 08-8956 2200; d $580, with spa $680, ste $930; ✕ 🖳 🕱) This luxurious five-star hotel has several restaurants, a piano bar and

plenty of sunbathing sites around the pool. Standard rooms are spread over three levels, so request an upper berth if you want a balcony to lean over. Deluxe spa rooms feature a balcony spa.

Ayers Rock Resort Campground (☎ 08-8957 7001; camp.ground@ayersrockresort.com.au; unpowered/powered sites $33/38, cabins $150; ✕ 🖳 🕱) A sprawling camping ground with good facilities, including a kiosk, free barbecues, a camp kitchen and a pool. During the peak season it fills up with dusty campervans, tents and tourists, and the inevitable predawn convoy heading for Uluru can provide an unwanted wake-up call. The cabins (shared facilities) sleep six people and are cramped and only really suitable for a family.

Eating

Most eateries in Yulara are part of an accommodation complex and have matching levels of swankiness: from silver service right down to aluminium tongs at the DIY barbecue. For a unique dinner on a dune, try the Sounds of Silence tour (p887).

RESTAURANTS

Geckos Cafe (Resort Shopping Centre; mains $17-30; ☯ lunch & dinner) The bright interior and courtyard tables of this licensed cafe make a popular meeting place. It serves a large range of salads, gourmet wood-fired pizzas, plus more substantial dishes and snacks.

Pioneer Barbecue (Outback Pioneer Hotel & Lodge; mains $18-26, salad only $16; ☯ dinner) Kangaroo skewers, vegie burgers, steaks and emu sausages are among the meats you can grill yourself at this lively tavern, and the deal includes all the salad you can eat. In the same complex are Pioneer Kitchen (meals $10 to $17; open for lunch & dinner), doing brisk business in burgers and kiddie meals, and Bough House (below).

White Gums (☎ 08-8957 7888; Desert Gardens Hotel; dinner mains $20-35; ☯ breakfast & dinner) Hotel guests enjoy a big buffet breakfast and return at night for an à la carte dinner featuring fusion cuisine with Asian, Mediterranean and Australian themes.

Bough House (☎ 08-8956 2170; Outback Pioneer Hotel & Lodge; breakfast/dinner buffets $28/47) This family-friendly, country-style place overlooks the pool at the Outback Pioneer and has buffet spreads for breakfast and dinner. The dinner choices feature Australian fare – kangaroo, emu, crocodile and barramundi. Kids under 12 eat free, making this the place for families.

Rockpool (Sails in the Desert; 3 tapas plates $45, plus dessert $50; ☺ dinner) Located in the resort's port of call for upmarket dining, the Sails in the Desert hotel, Rockpool serves tapas-style dishes on the poolside patio.

Arngulli Flame Grill (☎ 08-8957 7888; Desert Gardens Hotel; 2/3 courses $49/59; ☺ dinner) This seasonal, set-price restaurant features flame-grilled meats and seafood, though note that premium cuts of steak attract a surcharge on the set prices.

Winkiku (☎ 08-8956 2200; Sails in the Desert; breakfast buffets $25-35, dinner buffets $60; ☺ breakfast & dinner) In Yulara's five-star hotel, this casual-yet-stylish restaurant does extravagant buffets with seafood, a meat carvery, and all the trimmings and desserts you can imagine. Kids (under 12) eat free, so it can work out as good value for families.

Kuniya (☎ 08-8956 2200; Sails in the Desert; mains $45-60; ☺ dinner) Yulara's most sophisticated restaurant, Kuniya is the place for romantic candlelit dinners and special occasions. The walls are adorned with contemporary Australian art and the inspired menu features Aussie cuisine infused with native ingredients. Dress smartly and note that reservations are essential.

CAFES & TAKEAWAY

Red Rock Deli (Resort Shopping Centre; snacks $4-10; ☺ 8am-4pm) Chilly mornings see the folks lining up here for steaming-hot espresso and croissants. There're also muffins and sticky cakes for a calorie infusion, and filled panini, wraps and baguettes for a guilt-free lunch.

Red Rock Burger Bar (Resort Shopping Centre; burgers $6.50-10; ☺ lunch) This is the place to head for a no-fuss burger and chips on the run.

SELF-CATERING

Yulara IGA Supermarket (Resort Shopping Centre; ☺ 8am-9pm) This well-stocked supermarket has a delicatessen and sells picnic portions, fresh fruit and vegetables, meat, groceries, ice and camping supplies at reasonable prices.

Drinking

Pioneer Barbecue Bar (Outback Pioneer Hotel & Lodge; ☺ 10am-midnight) Modelled on a big iron shed, this rowdy bar is lined with long benches, with plenty of chances to meet other travellers. It has pool tables, live music nightly (usually a touch of twang) and minimal dress standards.

Tali Bar (Sails in the Desert; ☺ 10am-1am) The cocktails ($15 to $20) at this bar include locally inspired mixtures such as Desert Oasis. The piano gets a workout most nights from 8pm. Dress smart after sunset.

Bunya Bar (Desert Gardens Hotel; ☺ 11am-midnight) This is a rather characterless hotel bar, but it knows the importance of well-chilled beer, and the cocktails are several dollars cheaper than at Tali Bar.

Getting There & Away

AIR

Connellan airport is about 4km north from Yulara. **Qantas** (☎ 13 13 13; www.qantas.com.au) has direct flights from Alice Springs, Melbourne, Perth, Adelaide and Sydney.

BUS

Daily shuttle connections (listed as minitours) between Alice Springs and Yulara are run by **AAT Kings** (☎ 1300 556 100; www.aatkings.com) and cost adult/child $135/68. **Austour** (☎ 1800 335009; www.austour.com.au) runs the cheapest shuttle connections between Alice Springs and Uluru ($120/60). At the time of research, there were no direct services between Adelaide and Yulara.

CAR & MOTORCYCLE

The road from Alice to Yulara is sealed, with regular food and petrol stops along the way. Yulara is 441km from Alice Springs (241km west of Erldunda on the Stuart Hwy), and the direct journey takes four to five hours.

Renting a car in Alice Springs to go to Uluru and back is a reasonably priced option if you make the trip in a group; see p875 for a list of operators.

Getting Around

A free shuttle bus meets all flights and drops off at all accommodation points around the resort; pick-up is 90 minutes before your flight. Another free shuttle bus loops through the resort – stopping at all accommodation points and the shopping centre – every 15 minutes from 10.30am to 6pm and from 6.30pm to 12.30am daily.

Uluru Express (☎ 08-8956 2152; www.uluruexpress .com.au) falls somewhere between a shuttle-bus service and an organised tour. It provides return transport from the resort to Uluru ($40/25 adult/child, $45/25 for the sunrise and sunset shuttles). Morning shuttles to Kata

Tjuta cost $60/35; afternoon shuttles include a stop at Uluru for sunset and cost $65/35. There are also two-day ($145/70) and three-day ($160/70) passes that allow unlimited use of the service. Fares do not include the park entry fee.

Hiring a car will give you the flexibility to visit the Rock and the Olgas as often as and whenever you want. **Hertz** (☎ 08-8956 2244) has a desk at the Tour & Information Centre, which also has direct phones to the **Avis** (☎ 08-8956 2266) and **Thrifty** (☎ 08-8956 2030) desks at Connellan airport.

Bike hire is available at the **Ayers Rock Resort Campground** (☎ 08-8957 7001; per hr $7, per half/full day $15/20, deposit $200 or credit card; ☷ 7am-8pm).

Western Australia

Western Australia (WA) is big. Seriously big. Its size, swaths of gloriously empty outback, small population largely hugging the coast and Perth's distinction as the world's most isolated capital city offer perhaps Australia's best frontier experience. Its residents are defiantly *Western* Australian, with an independence shaped by distance. The state's mining wealth means a booming economy that isn't so dependent on that other Australia on the east coast.

'Up north' you'll encounter unexpected gorges and waterfalls along the coast and in inland national parks on Aboriginal land, and a colourful tourist hub, the historic pearling town of Broome. In the more temperate south, uncrowded beaches, expanses of wildflowers and lush green forests beckon. Around Margaret River, the fruit of the vine keeps winemakers busy, vineyard restaurants offer the freshest food and artisans of all sorts make inspired craft from the salvaged wood of stunning karri, marri and jarrah trees.

Wherever you go, wildlife-watching opportunities are extraordinary, but it's not all beach and bush. Perth and neighbouring Fremantle are both cosmopolitan cities with enough to satisfy the most avid culture vulture, and glimpses of colonial splendour remain in coastal Albany and gold-fevered Kalgoorlie.

Driving distances in WA are mind-boggling, the terrain can be challenging and the elements often unforgiving. The rewards, however, are obvious – hit the road and enjoy the sensation of space around you.

HIGHLIGHTS

- Surf world-class waves before tasting world-class wines around **Margaret River** (p938)
- Wander the **Tree-top Walk** (p944) among tall tingle trees in Walpole's Valley of the Giants
- Snorkel with whale sharks off the colourful coral reefs of **Ningaloo Marine Park** (p988)
- Bask in a blood-red sunset on gorgeous Cable Beach in **Broome** (p998)
- Watch for wildlife in the **Kimberley** (p995): roadside emus and roos, sky-high eagles and waterside crocs
- Explore ghost towns such as **Gwalia** (p961) in the harsh, beautiful northern goldfields
- Bend your elbow to the beer and your ear to the local musicians in the bars and boutique breweries of **Fremantle** (p920)

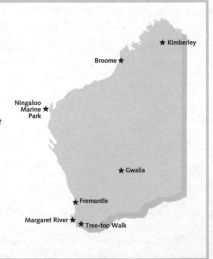

★ Kimberley

Broome ★

Ningaloo Marine ★ Park

★ Gwalia

★ Fremantle

Margaret River ★ ★ Tree-top Walk

■ TELEPHONE CODE: 08   ■ POPULATION: 2.15 MILLION   ■ AREA: 2,529,875 SQ KM

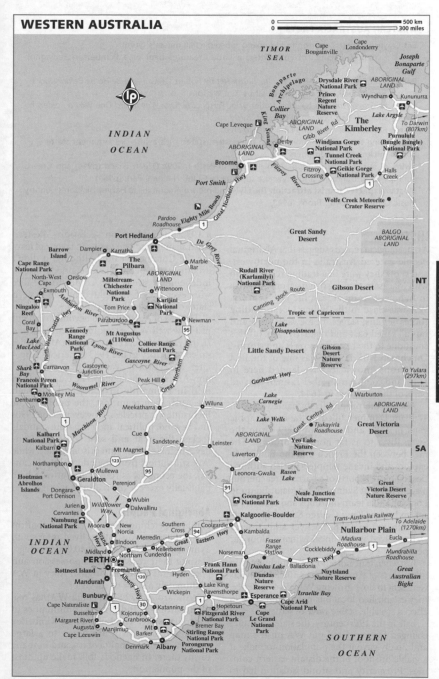

WESTERN AUSTRALIA FACTS

Eat Crayfish (lobster), marron (odd-looking lobster), chilli mussels (yum)

Drink A 'middy' (285mL) of Emu Bitter, a Little Creatures beer or a Pemberton Sauvignon Blanc

Read *A Fortunate Life* by AB Facey, *The Shark Net* by Robert Drewe, *And Be Home Before Dark* by Roland Rocchiccioli, and anything at all by Tim Winton

Listen to *Grand National* by John Butler Trio, *Personality (One Was a Bird One Was a Spider)* by Sleepy Jackson, and *Hollywood* by Little Birdy

Watch *Rabbit-Proof Fence* and *Last Train to Freo*

Avoid Being too complimentary about the eastern states – it's a sure-fire argument starter

Locals' nickname Sandgropers

Swim 'n' surf at Scarborough and Cottesloe in Perth (p909); Ocean Beach (p946) and Greens Pool (p946) in Denmark; and anywhere in Cape Le Grand National Park (p954)

Most unexpected tourist attraction The Elvis-and-more memorabilia at Harvey Dickson's Country Music Centre in Boyup Brook (p942)

HISTORY

Archaeological records suggest that Aboriginal people entered Australia in the northwest, and show they were in a trading relationship with Macassan trepang fishers, from Sulawesi in Indonesia, from at least the 17th century. WA was close to the Indian Ocean trading routes – guns, slaves, homewares, hay and rats all sailed past and regularly sank off this coast due to the hazardous reefs and storms. Dutchman Dirk Hartog was one of the first Europeans known to have landed here in 1616, and countryman Abel Tasman charted parts of the coastline in 1644.

Aboard the prophetically named *Cygnet*, William Dampier filled in the cartographic gaps in 1688 and again in 1699, from the Swan River to as far north as Broome. The race between the French and the English to explore and invade tempted British authorities to ignore reports of a barren, treacherous place. They sent Sydney-based Major Edmund Lockyer and a team of troops and convicts to set up base at King George Sound (present-day Albany) in 1826. Lockyer and co were well received by the local Minang Noongar people.

Just when transportation was finishing up in other parts of Australia, over 10,000 convicts were sent to slow-growing WA. Post-sentence, they established local businesses and were in effect a sizeable, stable wave of settlers.

Late in the 19th century, the state's fortunes changed forever. Gold put WA on the map and finally gave it the population to make it a viable offshoot of the distant eastern colonies. Prosperity and proud isolation led to a 1933 referendum on secession: Western Australians voted two to one in favour of leaving the Commonwealth. Although it didn't eventuate, the people have retained a strong independent streak that comes to the fore whenever they feel slighted by the eastern states or the federal government.

The rest of Australia and beyond found out just how well WA was doing when *Australia II*, the yacht of local entrepreneur Alan Bond, sailed to victory in the 1983 America's Cup – after 132 years it was the first successful non-American challenger. The Cup was then held in Fremantle in 1987, and although the Australian team lost, the publicity for Fremantle was priceless. However, in the 1990s and beyond, political and corporate scandals rocked the boat and sent some modern-day criminals sailing into prison. Today, while WA still suffers from the odd political scandal, the economy is robust and growth here habitually exceeds the national average.

Aboriginal People

Paintings, etchings and stone tools confirm that Indigenous Australians lived as far south as present-day Perth at least 40,000 years ago. Despite their resistance, dispossession and poor treatment, the Aboriginal story in WA is ultimately a story of survival.

With around 72,000 people WA has one of the strongest Indigenous communities in Australia today. The Pilbara and Kimberley regions in the north are home to a large number of Aboriginal peoples, and in many towns there, Indigenous folk make up most of the population.

As elsewhere in Australia, colonisation irrevocably changed Indigenous ways of life in WA. Across the state, the experience was uniform: confrontations led to massacres or jail (see p927). Conflict and assimilation policies plagued Aboriginal people, with tales of 'blackbirding' (kidnapping for the purpose of labour), incarceration, illness, death and the loss of basic rights. Forced off their traditional lands, some communities were practically wiped out by European diseases. The *Aborigines Act 1905* (WA) allowed authorities to remove children, control employment and restrict movement.

After WWII many Aboriginal people banded together in protest against their appalling treatment on cattle stations, in their first public displays of political consciousness. One such resistance legend was Jandamarra. In 1972 there was a full repeal of repressive legislation. Today, with a growing recognition and acceptance of land rights, native-title claims are being made by Aboriginal people across the state.

GEOGRAPHY & CLIMATE

Massive WA covers one-third of Australia's land mass. In the north much of the landscape is barren. The Great Sandy Desert fringes the central-west coast. The Nullarbor, a vast dry plain, sweeps across the south and over the border into South Australia (SA). The southwestern corner of the state is a fertile area of forest and vineyards, and is tiny in comparison to the size of the rest of WA.

Interesting variations in landscape include the Kimberley in the extreme north of the state, a wild and rugged area with a convoluted coastline and stunning inland sandstone gorges. The Pilbara, in the northwest, is magnificent ancient-rock and gorge country, from which the state derives vast mineral wealth. Away from the coast, most of WA is simply a huge empty stretch of outback: along with the Nullarbor Plain and the Great Sandy Desert, the Gibson and Great Victoria Deserts cover much of the state.

It's tropical in the north, where dry and wet seasons replace winter and summer. The Dry lasts from about June to August, and the Wet from about December to February, with monsoonal rain falling from January onwards. The rain can render roads impassable and Port Hedland weathers a serious cyclone at least every two years. In the interior the climate

is semi-arid and arid. The southwest of WA is temperate all year (and often cold and wet in the winter), while the average temperature along the Kimberley coast averages a humid 28°C. Up in the Pilbara summer temperatures can soar to an enthusiasm-depleting 48°C.

INFORMATION

See the comprehensive **Western Australian Tourism Commission** (www.westernaustralia.com) website for general statewide information. Most country towns have their own helpful visitors centres.

The **Royal Automobile Club of Western Australia** (Racwa; Map pp906-7; ☎ 13 17 03; www.rac.com.au; 832 Wellington St, Perth) produces the terrific *Western Australia Experience Guide*, full of accommodation and touring information. Download free basic maps (with distances, en route facilities and road conditions) from its website.

Lonely Planet's *Perth & Western Australia* guidebook gives more comprehensive information about the state.

Permits

To travel through Aboriginal land in WA you need a permit issued by the **Department of Indigenous Affairs** (Map pp906-7; ☎ 08-9235 8000; www .dia.wa.gov.au; 197 St Georges Tce, Perth). Applications can be lodged on the internet.

NATIONAL PARKS

Most of the state's important natural attractions are protected as national parks. The majority are managed by the **Department of Environment & Conservation** (DEC; Map pp906-7; ☎ 08-6467 5000; www.naturebase.net; 168 St Georges Tce, Perth), with offices throughout the state. In recent times up to 30 new national parks have been created to protect old-growth forests in the southwest.

You can camp in designated areas in some parks, and helpful maps, pamphlets and local signage are all produced by DEC. Fees are payable for some parks, from a $10 Day Pass to the good-value $35 Holiday Pass, valid for four weeks.

ACTIVITIES
Birdwatching

Birders delight in the variety of species found in WA. There are **Birds Australia** (www.birdsaustralia.com.au) observatories in Eyre (p963) and Broome (p1005), and there are important freshwater habitats – such as Yalgorup

National Park (p934) – across the state. Twitchers can contact **Birds Australia Western Australia** (BAWA; ☎ 08-9383 7749; www.birdswa.com.au) for site- and species-specific information.

Bushwalking

You can contact the many bushwalking clubs in Perth through the umbrella organisation **Federation of Western Australian Bushwalkers** (www.bushwalkingwa.org.au).

Good bushwalking areas in WA include the Stirling Range and Porongurup National Parks (p947), both northeast of Albany. Walking tracks abound in the coastal parks in the south and southwest, such as Walpole-Nornalup (p944), Fitzgerald River (p951), Cape Le Grand (p954) and Cape Arid (p954). To the north are the Kalbarri (p974), Karijini (p989) and Purnululu National Parks (p1013), which provide a rugged walking environment.

There are also good walks through the hills around Perth. Real enthusiasts undertake the 1000km **Bibbulmun Track** (www.bibbulmuntrack.org.au) from Perth's outskirts to Albany. Catering for walkers of all abilities, it goes through seven rural communities and the loveliest natural areas of the southwest: take a one-day wander or have an eight-week adventure.

Camping

Western Australia is an outstanding place to go camping. Considering that most people go camping to 'get away from it all', WA provides that in spades, especially in the national parks, where sleeping on a swag under the stars is almost obligatory.

Cycling

The **Munda Biddi Mountain Bike Trail** (www.mundabiddi.org.au) will eventually take off-road cyclists some 900km from Mundaring on Perth's outskirts through the beautiful scenic southwest to Albany on the south coast; currently open as far as Nannup, it's scheduled to be completed through to Albany in 2012. Two-wheel enthusiasts always love Rottnest Island (p927) and Perth (p909). **Bicycle Transportation Alliance** (www.btawa.org.au) lists statewide cycle clubs.

Since 1896, when the first bicycle crossing was made, the Nullarbor has continued to entice tenacious cyclists who relish a tremendous physical and mental challenge (1219km in the heat). Preparation and planning are essential (see p963).

Diving

The stunning reefs of the Ningaloo Marine Park (p988), the artificial reefs created by sunken ships at Albany (p949) and Dunsborough (p910), along with colourful corals fed by tropical and temperate currents and older shipwrecks along the coast between Geraldton and Exmouth are all popular.

In Perth, check out the **Australasian Diving Academy** (☎ 08-9389 5018; www.ausdiving.com.au; 4-day open-water dive course with/without Rottnest dive $695/545) with its several dive shops, which hire out equipment and run dive courses.

Fishing

WA is a fishing paradise pretty much anywhere along the west and south coasts. Recreational fishing licences ($24 to $41) are required to catch marron (freshwater crayfish) or rock lobsters, to use a fishing net or to freshwater angle in the southwest. There's an annual licence covering all fishing activities ($81). Buy one from the **Department of Fisheries** (Map pp906-7; ☎ 08-9482 7333; www.fish.wa.gov.au; SGIO Bldg, 168-170 St Georges Tce, Perth) or one of its regional offices. Saltwater angling and crabbing come free.

Rock Climbing & Caving

The southern sea cliffs of Wilyabrup, West Cape Howe and the Gap, and the huge cliffs of the Stirling and Porongurup Ranges attract plenty of climbers. Those with a head for heights will also enjoy scaling the lookout trees in the Valley of the Giants (p944).

The caves of the Margaret River region – for example, near Yallingup (p937) – and the lesser-known 'holes' of Cape Range National Park (p988) offer plenty of opportunities for cavers.

Check out the website of the **Western Australian Speleological Group** (www.wasg.iinet.net.au).

Surfing & Windsurfing

If you're here to surf, WA is simply brilliant. Beginners, intermediates, wannabe pros and adventure surfers will find excellent conditions to suit their skill levels. The southwestern beaches, from Cape Naturaliste to Margaret River (p937), boast some great waves, as do the less-crowded stretches of coast from Geraldton to Kalbarri. Around Perth's beaches, Trigg and Scarborough have decent beach breaks (p910) and Rottnest

Island (p929) is a wave magnet. Check conditions at **Coastalwatch** (www.coastalwatch.com).

Wind- and kitesurfers also have plenty of choice spots to try out in WA, with excellent flat-water and wave sailing. Kitesurfers in particular will appreciate the long, empty beaches and offshore reefs. After trying out Perth's city beaches, head to Lancelin (p931), home to a large population of surfers, especially in summer. Further up the coast, Geraldton (p969) is another hot spot – especially at Coronation Beach. The remote Gnaraloo Station (p980), 150km north of Carnarvon, is a world-renowned wave-sailing spot.

Wildflowers

When spring has sprung in southern WA, wildflowers abound. From about August to about October the bush is ablaze with colour; it's a great time to bushwalk sections of the Bibbulmun track or to drive through inland national parks such as Stirling Range (p947) or Mt Lesueur near Cervantes (p932).

TOURS

Statewide tour operators abound, offering everything from half-day tours to trips lasting several weeks. Check out www.westernaustralia.com for links. Local tours are recommended in relevant sections.

Aboriginal Culture Tours

There are a number of Indigenous tours across the state that look at aspects of Aboriginal life and culture. Here's a sample:

Kodja Place Indigenous Tours (www.kodjaplace .net.au) Noongar elder Jack Cox teaches you traditional practices and tells wonderful Dreaming stories over billy tea at Kojonup (p965).

Wula Guda Nyinda (www.wulaguda.com.au) Let the bush talk to you; learn to love bush tucker and how to identify the size of an animal by its poo! Based at Monkey Mia (p979).

GETTING THERE & AWAY

The east coast of Australia is the most common gateway for international travellers, although there are some airlines that fly direct into **Perth Airport** (code PER; ☎ 08-9478 8888; www .perthairport.com). If you do choose to fly to the east coast first, it's usually possible to book a same-day domestic flight that will wing you across country to Perth.

See Getting There & Away in individual sections for information on domestic transport into WA by air, bus and train.

GETTING AROUND

Air

Qantas (☎ 13 13 13; www.qantas.com.au) has regular flights to Broome and Kalgoorlie; it's also worth checking internet specials to Broome with **Virgin Blue** (☎ 13 67 89; www.virginblue.com.au). **Skywest** (☎ 1300 660 088; www.skywest.com.au) operates flights to many regional centres, including Albany, Esperance, Exmouth, Carnarvon and Kalgoorlie. **Northwest Regional Airlines** (☎ 08-9192 1369; www.northwestregional.com.au) shuttles travellers between Port Hedland, Fitzroy Crossing, Broome, Halls Creek and Karratha, as well as offering scenic flights.

Bus

Greyhound Australia (☎ 13 14 99; www.greyhound.com .au; ⌚ 7am-9pm) buses run from Perth along the coast to Broome (special/standard $241/432, 33 hours) and on to Darwin ($830, 60 hours). Greyhound has a variety of flexible travel passes that are generally much cheaper than buying single trips – check the website for details.

Goldfields Express (☎ 1800 620 440; www.gold rushtours.com.au) runs between Kalgoorlie and Laverton. **Integrity Coach Lines** (☎ 08-9226 1339; www.integritycoachlines.com.au) runs between Perth and Port Hedland. **South West Coachlines** (☎ 08-9324 2333; www.southwestcoachlines.com.au), in the Transperth City Busport, runs services from Perth to southwestern towns such as Augusta, Bunbury, Busselton, Dunsborough, Nannup and Margaret River.

Government-operated **Transwa** (☎ 1300 662 205; www.transwa.wa.gov.au) goes to Albany, Augusta, Esperance, Hyden, Kalgoorlie, Pemberton and York, and north to Geraldton, Kalbarri and Meekatharra.

Car

To really see and explore this enormous state, and for flexibility, many people end up hiring or buying a car (see p74). Bear in mind that WA is not only enormous, but also sparsely populated, so make safety preparations if you plan to travel any significant distance (for more information on outback travel, see p83).

There are many enticing areas of the state that don't have sealed roads, and a 4WD is recommended for many places such as the spectacular Kimberley, even in the Dry.

For up-to-date road information across the state, call **Main Roads WA** (☎ 1800 013 314).

Train

Transwa (☎ 1300 662 205; www.transwa.wa.gov.au) operates WA's domestic rail network. It provides services between Perth and Kalgoorlie (*Prospector*), Northam (*AvonLink*) and Bunbury (*Australind*); for details, see the individual destinations.

PERTH

pop 1.5 million

Laid-back, liveable Perth has wonderful weather, beautiful beaches and an easygoing character. About as close to Southeast Asia as to Australia's eastern state capitals, Perth's combination of big-city attractions with relaxed and informal surrounds offers an appealing lifestyle for locals and a variety of things to do for visitors. It's a sophisticated, cosmopolitan city with myriad bars, restaurants and cultural activities all vying for attention. But the best bit is that when you want to chill out, it's easy to do so. Perth's pristine parkland, nearby bush, and river and ocean beaches – along with a good public transport system – allow its inhabitants to spread out and enjoy what's on offer.

Relaxed doesn't mean static, though. Western Australia's mining boom has seen Perth blossom like WA's wildflowers in spring. Ambitious (and sometimes controversial) citywide development projects are under way. They are intended to increase the residential appeal of the city centre and to further open up the waterfront. Watch this space…

HISTORY

Aboriginal Noongar people lived here for thousands of years, well before the Swan River Settlement developed not quite two hundred years ago. Founded by a hopeful Captain Stirling in 1829, settlers paid for their own passage and that of their families and servants. In return they received 200 acres for every labourer they brought with them. This didn't appease them once they arrived – life was much harder than they had been promised. The settlement was later named Perth, after a dignitary's hometown in Scotland.

The early settlement grew very slowly until 1850, when convicts alleviated the labour shortage and boosted the population. Convict labour was also responsible for constructing the city's substantial buildings such as Government House and the town hall. The discovery of gold inland in the 1890s increased Perth's population fourfold in a decade and initiated a building bonanza, mirrored in the mining and economic boom of the 2000s. Largely excluded from this race to riches were the Noongar people, whose claim to native title of Perth's metropolitan area remains unrecognised.

ORIENTATION

Perth lazes by the wide blue swath of the Swan River to its south. To the east is a gentle backdrop of hills and the vineyards of the Swan Valley. In the city centre, the glass towers of the central business district (CBD) sparkle on the besuited drag of St Georges Tce. North of here, the Hay and Murray St Malls and arcades are abuzz with shoppers who spill over into the streets and eateries of Northbridge, Mount Lawley and Leederville. The high green expanse of Kings Park oversees Perth's western end. Beyond are the Indian Ocean, stylish Subiaco and the beachside suburbs of Cottesloe and Scarborough. Fremantle ('Freo') is only 30 minutes south by train or car.

INFORMATION

Bookshops

It's hard to go far without finding a bookshop, especially around the Hay and Murray St Malls. Independent booksellers include the following:

All Foreign Languages Bookshop (Map pp906-7; ☎ 08-9321 9275; 572 Hay St) Travel books, language guides, books in languages other than English.

Boffins Bookshop (Map pp906-7; ☎ 08-9321 5755; 806 Hay St) Australiana and travel books galore.

Elizabeth's (Map pp906-7; ☎ 08-9481 8848; 820 Hay St) Great selection of second-hand books and a book exchange.

Emergency

Dial ☎ 000 for ambulance, fire or police.

Lifeline (☎ 13 11 14) Crisis counselling.

Police station (Map pp906-7; ☎ 08-9222 1111; Curtin House, 60 Beaufort St)

Racwa Roadside Assistance (☎ 13 11 11)

Sexual Assault Resource Centre (☎ 08-9340 1828; ☉ 24hr)

Internet Access

Plenty of places offer internet access in the city centre, particularly along the roads linking Murray and Wellington Sts.

PERTH IN...

Two Days
Get out and explore Perth with a **walking tour** (p910), winding your way up to vast **Kings Park** (p909) for a picnic. In the evening munch on the multicultural offerings of the restaurants at **Northbridge** (p915), close to the city. Next morning jump on the train to **Fremantle** (p920). After some meandering through Freo's **museums** (p921), make a beeline for an ale at **Little Creatures** (p925). Be sure to find the **Fremantle Markets** (p923), open Friday to Sunday.

Four Days
Do the two-day thing then cruise across to **Rottnest Island** (p927) on the morning ferry for a sunny day of cycling, surfing, snorkelling and quokka spotting. Spend your last day at Cottesloe, where you can warm the soles of your feet on the windowsill of the **Ocean Beach Hotel** (p917) as the sun sets spectacularly over the Indian Ocean.

Maps
Department for Planning & Infrastructure (Map pp906-7; ☎ 08-9216 8000; www.dpi.wa.gov.au; 441 Murray St) Free TravelSmart maps show environmentally-friendly transport options around the city – walking and biking tracks, and public transport routes. Can also be downloaded.

Medical Services
King Edward Memorial Hospital for Women (Map pp904-5; ☎ 08-9340 2222; 347 Bagot Rd, Subiaco)
Lifecare Dental (Map pp906-7; ☎ 08-9221 2777; Forrest Chase; ☉ 8am-8pm)
Royal Perth Hospital (Map pp906-7; ☎ 08-9224 2244; Victoria Sq) In the CBD.
Travel Medicine Centre (Map pp906-7; ☎ 08-9321 7888; 5 Mill St)

Money
ATMs are plentiful; there are currency-exchange facilities at the airport and banks; and the CBD has branches of all the major banks.
American Express (Map pp906-7; ☎ 1300 132 639; Westpac Bldg, 109 St Georges Tce)
Travelex (Map pp906-7; ☎ 08-9321 7811; 267 Murray St; ☉ 9am-5pm Mon-Fri, 10am-3pm Sat, noon-4pm Sun)

Post
Main post office (GPO; Map pp906-7; ☎ 08-9237 5460, info line 13 13 18; 3 Forrest Pl; ☉ 8.30am-5pm Mon-Fri, 9am-12.30pm Sat)

Tourist Information
i-City Information Kiosk (Map pp906-7; Murray St Mall; ☉ 9.30am-4.30pm Mon-Thu & Sat, 9.30am-8pm Fri, 11am-3.30pm Sun) Volunteers answer questions and lead walking tours.

Western Australian Visitors Centre (Map pp906-7; ☎ 1300 361 351; www.westernaustralia.net; cnr Forrest Pl & Wellington St; ☉ 8.30am-5.30pm Mon-Thu, 8.30am-6pm Fri, 9.30am-4.30pm Sat, noon-4.30pm Sun) A good resource for a trip anywhere in WA.

SIGHTS
Most of Perth's attractions are all within easy reach of the CBD and many have their own stops on the free Central Area Transit (CAT) bus service route (see p920). For a pedestrian's perspective of Perth, take in our suggested walking tour (p910).

Perth Cultural Centre
Just north of the Perth train station, between James St Mall and Roe St in Northbridge, you'll find the state museum, art gallery, library and the Perth Institute of Contemporary Arts.

The **Western Australian Museum** (Map pp906-7; ☎ 08-9212 3700; www.museum.wa.gov.au; James St; admission by donation; ☉ 9.30am-5pm, tours 11am & 2pm) includes an excellent 'land and people' display that examines both ancient history and the more recent past; a gallery of dinosaur casts; a good collection of meteorites; and galleries dedicated to mammals, butterflies and birds.

The **Art Gallery of Western Australia** (Map pp906-7; ☎ 08-9492 6600; www.artgallery.wa.gov.au; James St Mall; admission free; ☉ 10am-5pm, tours 11am & 1pm Tue-Thu, 12.30pm & 2pm Fri, 1pm Sat, 11am & 1pm Sun) has a brilliant collection of Aboriginal artworks and a fine permanent exhibition of early Europeans-in-Australia paintings. There are regular exhibitions and a fabulous gift shop.

(Continued on page 909)

GREATER PERTH

WESTERN AUSTRALIA

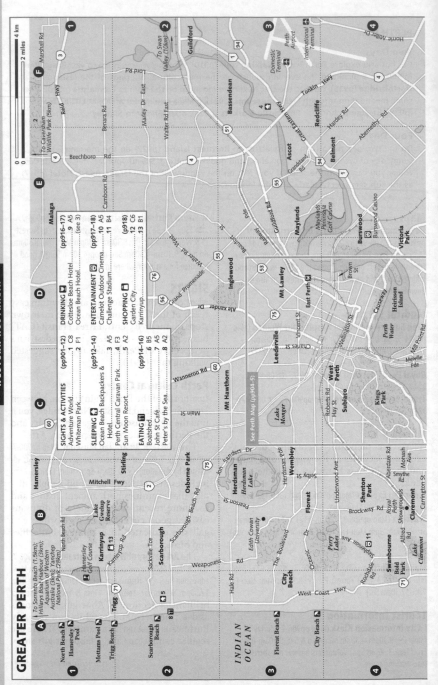

SIGHTS & ACTIVITIES	(pp901–12)
Adventure World	1 C8
Whiteman Park	2 F1

SLEEPING	(pp912–14)
Ocean Beach Backpackers & Hotel	3 A5
Perth Central Caravan Park	4 F3
Sun Moon Resort	5 A2

EATING	(pp914–16)
Boatshed	6 B5
John St Café	7 A5
Peter's by the Sea	8 A2

DRINKING	(pp916–17)
Cottesloe Beach Hotel	9 A5
Ocean Beach Hotel	(see 3)

ENTERTAINMENT	(pp917–18)
Camelot Outdoor Cinema	10 A5
Challenge Stadium	11 B4

SHOPPING	(p918)
Garden City	12 C6
Karrinyup	13 B1

See Perth Map (pp904–5)

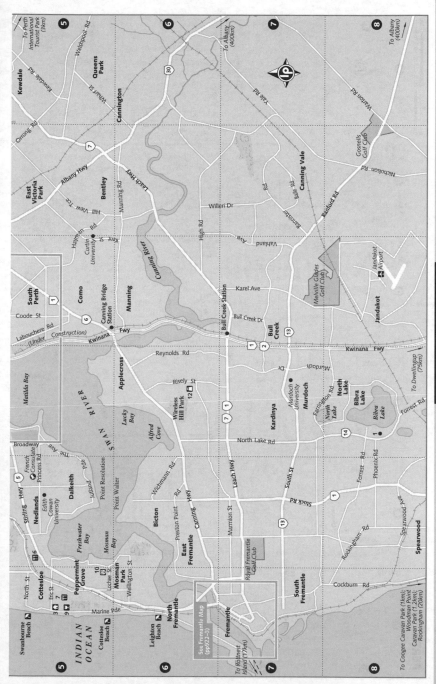

WESTERN AUSTRALIA

WESTERN AUSTRALIA

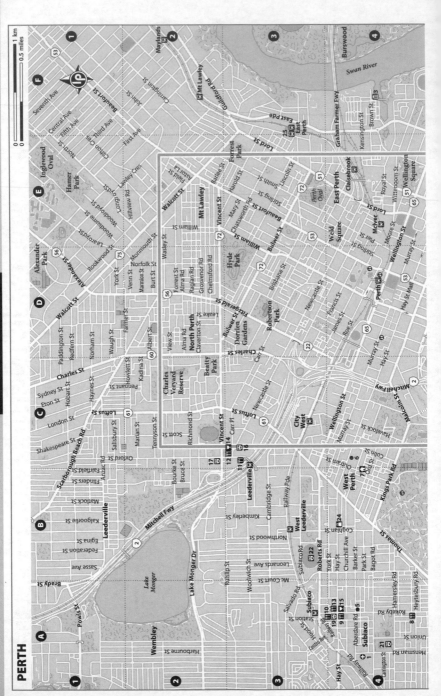

PERTH

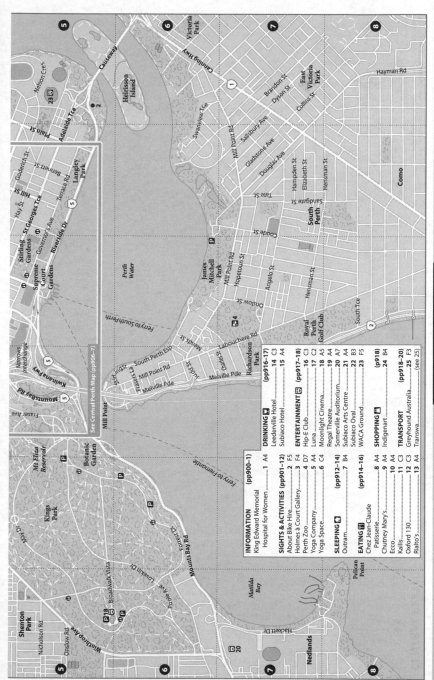

WESTERN AUSTRALIA

INFORMATION (pp900–1)
King Edward Memorial
Hospital for Women.........1 A4

SIGHTS & ACTIVITIES (pp901–12)
About Bike Hire..............2 F5
Holmes a Court Gallery....3 F4
Perth Zoo.....................4 D7
Yoga Company...............5 A4
Yoga Space...................6 C4

SLEEPING (pp912–14)
Outram........................7 B4

EATING (pp914–16)
Chez Jean-Claude
Patisserie....................8 A4
Chutney Mary's..............9 A4
Ecco..........................10 A4
Kailis........................11 C3
Oxford 130...................12 C3
Rialto's......................13 A4

DRINKING (pp916–17)
Leederville Hotel............14 C3
Subiaco Hotel................15 A4

ENTERTAINMENT (pp917–18)
Hip-E Club...................16 C3
Luna..........................17 C2
Moonlight Cinema...........18 A5
Regal Theatre...............19 A4
Somerville Auditorium......20 A7
Subiaco Arts Centre........21 A4
Subiaco Oval................22 B3
WACA Ground................23 F5

SHOPPING (p918)
Indigenart...................24 B4

TRANSPORT (pp918–20)
Greyhound Australia........25 F3
Transwa.....................(see 25)

CENTRAL PERTH

WESTERN AUSTRALIA

CENTRAL PERTH (pp906–7)

(Continued from page 901)

Cutting-edge contemporary art – installations, performance, sculpture, video works – lives at **Perth Institute of Contemporary Arts** (PICA; Map pp906-7; ☎ 08-9227 6144; www.pica.org.au; James St; admission free; ☺ 11am-6pm Tue-Sun). This gallery has long promoted new and experimental art, and exhibits graduate works annually.

The **State Library of Western Australia** (Map pp906-7; www.slwa.wa.gov.au; admission free; ☺ 9am-8pm Mon-Thu, 9am-5.30pm Fri, 10am-5.30pm Sat & Sun) has a great reference section on all things WA.

Kings Park

The green hilltop crown of **Kings Park & Botanic Garden** (Map pp904-5; ☎ 08-9480 3600; www.bgpa.wa.gov .au; Kings Park Rd, West Perth) is set amid 4 sq km of natural bushland. The garden boasts over 2000 Western Australian plant species, which bloom during the September **Perth Wildflower Festival**. The architect-designed **Lotterywest Federation Walkway** (admission free; ☺ 9am-5pm) is a broad 222m-long, glass-and-steel structure that allows you to walk among the treetops – it's a highlight.

Kings Park Visitors Centre (Map pp906-7; ☺ 9.30am-4pm) is opposite the war memorial on Fraser Ave. Free guided walks leave at 10am and 2pm. If you are laden with picnic gear, take the free bus (number 37) from the city to the park entrance.

Holmes à Court Gallery

Idyllically located by the river in East Perth, the **Holmes à Court Gallery** (Map pp904-5; ☎ 08-9218 4540; www.holmesacourtgallery.com.au; 11 Brown St; admission free; ☺ noon-5pm Wed-Sun) was started by the late millionaire industrialist Robert Holmes à Court in the 1970s and today the collection comprises more than 3000 pieces. About one-third is made up of the best collection of canvas and bark paintings by Indigenous artists held in private hands; the remainder includes some of Australia's leading contemporary artworks, and touring exhibitions.

Aquarium of Western Australia

For all things fishy, head to the **Aquarium of Western Australia** (AQWA; off Map pp902-3; ☎ 08-9447 7500; www.aqwa.com.au; Hillarys Boat Harbour, West Coast Dr, Hillarys; adult/child $26/14.50; ☺ 10am-5pm). Here you can wander through a 98m underwater tunnel as gargantuan turtles, stingrays, fish and sharks stealthily glide over the top of you. A series of

mini marine-worlds show off the state's underwater treasures: intriguing sea dragons, moon jellies (which billow, iridescent, through a giant cylinder), venomous fish and sea snakes. Seals play in the underwater-viewing area. The daring can even snorkel or dive with the sharks in the giant aquarium with the in-house divemaster. Book in advance (snorkel/dive including gear $145/165; 1pm and 3pm).

To get here on weekdays, take the Joondalup train to Warwick Interchange and then transfer to bus 423 (roughly hourly). AQWA is by the water, behind Hillarys shopping complex.

Greater Perth

Want to get out of town for a while? Just a 30-minute drive away is the fabulous **Swan Valley**, home to great scenery and many of WA's fine 'food and wineries', most of which are open for cellar door tastings and sales. You really need a car to make the most of the Swan, though many, *many* day tours by road, river, or a combination of both, are offered (see p911). Check out www.swanvalley.com.au.

If bushwalks or cycle trails are more your style, head for the 10,000 acres of **Whiteman Park** (Map pp902-3; ☎ 08-9209 6000; www.whitemanpark .com; admission free; ☺ 8.30am-6pm) with its many outdoor attractions. It also has fantastic child-friendly activities, especially during holidays (see p911).

ACTIVITIES
Cycling

Need some wheels? Try the **Cycle Centre** (Map pp906-7; ☎ 08-9325 1176; 313 Hay St; mountain bikes per day $25; ☺ 9.30am-5.30pm Mon-Fri, 9am-3pm Sat, 1-4pm Sun) or **About Bike Hire** (Map pp904-5; ☎ 08-9221 2665; www.about bikehire.com.au; Causeway Carpark, 1-7 Riverside Dr; bike/inline skates/kayak per day $33/40/55). Bicycle routes follow the Swan River all the way to Fremantle and along the coast. Download city cycling maps from www.dpi.wa.gov.au.

Water Activities

With some of the cleanest water in Australia, many Perthites are devoted to water activity: swimming, surfing, fishing or yachting. You'll see windsurfers flying on the afternoon wind and kitesurfers colouring the beach sky. Weekend snorkellers head north to **Marmion Marine Park** near Scarborough.

Cottesloe Beach (Map pp902–3) and its neighbour **Swanbourne Beach** are surf-and-swim spots popular with families, as is the stretch north towards **Scarborough**, which is like a mini surf city with good waves, surf shops, cafes and bars. The next beach along, **Trigg**, has better surf and a more hard-core group of locals who come out when the surf's up. The comparatively quiet **City** and **Floreat Beaches** are in between. On the way to Yanchep National Park, **Sorrento** (off Map pp902–3) is relaxed and beautiful. Closer to town, surf-free beaches on the Swan River include **Crawley**, **Peppermint Grove** and **Como** (Map pp902–3).

Catch any nonexpress Fremantle-bound train for Cottesloe and Swanbourne – in each case there's a bit of a walk to get to the beach itself. Alternatively, bus 71 or 72 (destination Cottesloe) from the City Busport will get you to Cottesloe and Swanbourne. For Scarborough, take bus 400 from the Wellington St bus station.

Whale Watching

Whales pass by Perth on their annual journey to Antarctic waters from September to December, offering a once-in-a-lifetime encounter. **Mills Charters** (☎ 08-9246 5334; www .millscharters.com.au; adult/child $65/50) runs an informative three-hour whale-watching trip from Hillarys Boat Harbour (off Map pp902–3), as does Oceanic Cruises (p912) from Barrack St jetty in the city.

Yoga

Yoga Company (Map pp904–5; ☎ 08-9388 6683; www .theyogacompany.com.au; 136 Rokeby Rd; class $17) Hatha.

Yoga Space (Map pp904–5; ☎ 08-9243 5114; www .yogaspace.com.au; Shop 6, Seasons Arcade, 1251 Hay St; class $15) Ashtanga.

WALKING TOUR

While Perth is a growing city, it retains remnants of colonial glory. This walk takes you past the best of the (relatively) old and the new, and guides you to great views of the city at Kings Park.

Start in front of the **Art Gallery of WA** (1; p901), where there's good coffee in the cafe. Head over the walkbridge towards the train station; at the newsagency, head down the last set of escalators (don't cross the second walkbridge). Cross Wellington St into Forrest Pl. The Victorian-era **post office (2)** looms to your right. Turn left along Murray St Mall, then right down Barrack St. At the corner of Hay and Barrack Sts you'll find the beautifully restored **town hall (3)**, the only convict-built town hall (1867–70) in the country.

Continue southeast down Hay St, then left into Irwin St. At the corner of Irwin and Murray Sts is the **Fire Safety & Education Museum (4)**, Perth's fire headquarters from 1900 to 1979. Further along you'll pass the red-brick

---

WALK FACTS

Start Art Gallery of WA
Finish Kings Park
Distance 4.5km
Duration two hours minimum

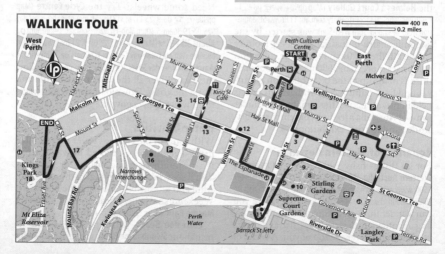

WALKING TOUR

buildings of **Royal Perth Hospital (5)**. Down the end of the street is **St Mary's Cathedral (6)**, sited on its own square and dating from 1863. Wander along Victoria Ave to **Perth Concert Hall (7)**, a fine auditorium and grand structure built in the early 1970s.

Continue along St Georges Tce, with **Government House (8;** ⊙ noon-2pm) to your left, a Gothic-looking fantasy built between 1859 and 1864, followed by the impressive **Council House (9)**, designed by Howlett and Bailey in the early 1960s. Then head southwest through Stirling Gardens to the creamy-yellow **courthouse (10)**, adjacent to the Supreme Court. The courthouse is one of Perth's oldest buildings (1837).

Walk south of the Supreme Court and make for the river. Within moments you'll see the **Swan Bell Tower (11)**, a modern copper-and-glass structure that contains bells dating from the 14th century from London's St Martin-in-the-Fields church. Double back up Barrack St, left along the Esplanade, and right up Howard St. Back on St Georges Tce, bear left: the **Palace Hotel (12)**, now home to Bankwest, is to your right. Continue to King St, noting the **Old Perth Boys School (13)**, a modest structure today dwarfed by gleaming office towers. On the corner of King and Hay, you'll find **His Majesty's Theatre (14)**, where you can look around in the lobby.

If you don't wish to hike up to Kings Park, head up to the King Street Café (p915) and relax with good coffee. Otherwise, return to St Georges Tce, where you'll see **Cloisters (15)** to your right, built in 1858 as a school and notable for its brickwork. Roll down Mill St (not signed), straight for the **Perth Convention Exhibition Centre (16)**, one of Perth's much-vaunted landmarks. Stick to the north side of the road as it winds under the underpass, and keep an eye out for **Jacob's Ladder (17)**, up a path by the Adelphi Hotel. Once you're at the end of Cliff St, head northwest, following Fraser Ave into **Kings Park (18;** p909). Treat yourself to a well-earned cuppa-with-a-view at the Botanical Cafe, next to the Visitors Centre, before enjoying the park's many well-signed attractions.

Walk, or take free-bus number 37 from the Visitors Centre car park, back to the city.

PERTH FOR CHILDREN

There's plenty of free kids' entertainment in Perth: **Cottesloe Beach** (Map pp902–3) has long

been a family favourite and **Leighton Beach** is fairly sheltered and shallow. **Kings Park** (p909) has numerous playgrounds, walking tracks and gardens. And there's always the bike tracks (p909) stretching along the river and the coast, long enough to tire out any young 'un.

The **Royal Perth Show**, held September to October, is an ever-popular family outing, all sideshow rides, show bags and proudly displayed poultry. Many of Perth's big attractions such as **AQWA** (p909), the **Western Australian Museum** (p901) and the **Art Gallery of WA** (p901), cater well for young audiences.

Perth Zoo (Map pp904-5; ☎ 08-9474 3551; www.perthzoo .wa.gov.au; 20 Labouchere Rd, South Perth; adult/child/family $19/9.50/50; ⊙ 9am-5pm) has a number of interesting collections, including a nocturnal house and an 'Australian Bushwalk'. Take the ferry ($3.20 return) across the river from Barrack St jetty to South Perth jetty, where the zoo is within walking distance. Otherwise catch buses to the zoo's entrance: 30/31 from Wellington St bus station or the Esplanade Busport or 730/731 along Adelaide Tce.

Scitech (Map pp906-3; ☎ 08-9481 6295; City West Centre, cnr Sutherland St & Railway Pde, West Perth; adult/ child $14/9; ⊙ 9.30am-4pm Mon-Fri, 10am-5pm Sat & Sun) is another option, especially if it's raining. It has over 160 hands-on, large-scale science and technology exhibits.

Adventure World (Map pp902-3; ☎ 08-9417 9666; 179 Progress Dr, Bibra Lake; adult/child $39/32; ⊙ 10am-5pm Thu-Mon Sep-Apr), packed with kids and teenagers, has white-knuckle rides such as 'Bounty's Revenge', a giant boat that swings around in an arc, plus pools and waterslides. Open daily during school holidays and throughout December, it's 18km south of Perth.

Whiteman Park (Map pp902-3; ☎ 08-9209 6000; www .whitemanpark.com; admission free; ⊙ 8.30am-6pm) is a child's outdoor wonderland (and it's pretty good for adults, too). Within its boundaries are Caversham Wildlife Park with its farm shows and close-up animal encounters, a motor museum, heritage train rides, playgrounds, picnic areas and summer swimming pools, and walk and cycle tracks. Fees apply to some attractions.

TOURS

There are countless tours on offer, so head to the visitors centre (p901) or one of the budget traveller centres for a full list of options. Several companies offer the 'tourist trifecta', including a cruise between Perth and Fremantle, and sightseeing on both Perth's open-top bus and Freo's historic tram (around $85). Others offer day trips to the Pinnacles and Wave Rock, and extended trips elsewhere.

Perth Tram (☎ 08-9322 2006; www.perthtram.com.au; adult/child $30/12) This hop-on hop-off tram is a speedy way to tour some of the city's main attractions (with commentary) between Burswood Casino and Kings Park. It runs at least six times daily.

Planet Perth (☎ 08-9225 6622; www.planettours.com .au) Offers some great day trips for the young fun crowd, including a Pinnacles (with sandboarding) day tour ($145) and up to 10-day tours elsewhere in WA. Offers YHA/VIP discounts.

Rockingham Wild Encounters (☎ 08-9591 1333; www.rockinghamwildencounters.com.au) Offers Perth pick-ups for its various low-impact marine wildlife interaction tours – think seals, penguins and dolphins – at Rockingham (p933), 45 minutes' drive from the city.

Cruises

Several cruise companies run tours from Barrack St Jetty, including **Captain Cook Cruises** (Map pp906-7; ☎ 08-9325 3341; www.captaincookcruises.com .au), **Oceanic Cruises** (Map pp906-7; ☎ 08-9325 1191; www .oceaniccruises.com.au) and the cheaper and less-frills **Golden Sun Cruises** (Map pp906-7; ☎ 08-9325 9916; goldensuncruises@arach.net.au). All offer lunch and dinner cruises on the Swan River, winery visits and trips to Fremantle and Rottnest Island.

Options include cruises around Perth and Fremantle (adult/child $30/30), which will satisfy real-estate-obsessed Australians from the east. There are daily cruises to the Swan Valley vineyards (full day adult/child $130/94). Oceanic Cruises offers a whale-watching tour between September and November (adult/child $59/28).

Rottnest Express (Map pp906-7; ☎ 1300 467 688; www .rottnestexpress.com.au) specialises in transport to and packages on Rottnest Island (p927).

A ferry leaves from Barrack St Jetty for the few minutes' trip to the zoo ($3.20 return, at least every half hour).

FESTIVALS & EVENTS

Perth Cup (www.perthracing.org.au) New Year's Day sees Perth's biggest day at the races, with the party people heading to 'Tentland' for DJs and daiquiris.

Big Day Out (www.bigdayout.com) Held in late-January or early February, this long-standing one-day pop/rock music festival features interesting international and local artists.

Perth International Arts Festival (www.perthfes tival.com.au) Several weeks of multi-arts entertainment from early February to early March, including theatre, dance, music, film and visual arts.

Perth Wildflower Festival (www.bgpa.wa.gov.au) From late September to early October, Kings Park and the Botanic Garden host displays, workshops and guided walks in this annual event celebrating WA's unique and spectacular wildflowers.

Royal Perth Show (www.perthroyalshow.com.au) In October, it's the west's biggest agriculture, food and wine show – with rides and show bags for the kids.

Perth Pride (www.pridewa.asn.au) This gay and lesbian event is in October, as is the annual Pride March.

Blessing of the Fleet Popular historic festival introduced to Fremantle by young Italian fishermen in 1948 and celebrated in mid-October.

SLEEPING

Perth is very spread out so choose your location carefully. Northbridge is backpacker central and is best for those unperturbed by noise. The CBD and Northbridge are close to all forms of public transport, while the beach-side Cottesloe and Scarborough are better for those who just want to loll on the beach.

Note that many hotels adjust their rates daily depending on occupancy, and that internet bookings often offer better value than these published rates.

City Centre

BUDGET

Perth City YHA (Map pp906-7; ☎ 08-9287 3333; www.yha .com.au; 300 Wellington St; dm from $29, r from $85-110; 🖳 🖳) It's a little predictable, with that boarding-school feel (there are 240 beds), but the floorboards of this well-preserved 1940s art deco building gleam, walls are freshly painted and facilities are excellent. Nondorm rooms are decently sized, with TVs and air-con.

Royal Hotel (Map pp906-7; ☎ 08-9481 1000; www .royalhotelperth.com.au; cnr Wellington & William Sts; s with/without bathroom $90/70, d with/without bathroom $120/100; ❸) A creaking, character-filled historic building, the 1890s Royal Hotel is well placed for early-morning trips out of town (the busport and train station are just metres away). Cute though modest single rooms have attic-like roofs.

MIDRANGE

Wentworth Plaza (☎ 08-9338 5000; www.wentworthpla zahotel.com.au; 300 Murray St; s/d without bathroom $90/115) The sister hotel of the Royal Hotel, the 1928

Wentworth helps with overflow bookings, and checks in out-of-hours arrivals.

Riverview on Mount Street (Map pp906-7; ☎ 08-9321 8963; www.riverviewperth.com.au; 42 Mount St; d from $130; P ⊠ ⊑) Riverview stands out as the best personality on this block below Kings Park. The refurbished 1960s bachelor pads are self-contained, spacious, sunny and simple, and there's (limited) free on-site parking. Its attached coffee shop is a popular local meeting place.

Mont Clare Apartments (Map pp906-7; ☎ 08-9225 4300; www.montclareapartments.com; 190 Hay St, East Perth; 1-bedroom apt $145, 2-bedroom apt from $160; P ⊠ ⊑ ☞) Friendly and unfussy, with somewhat casual housekeeping, the self-contained apartments here are spacious and, notably, quiet and private. It's all a bit chalk-white and plain, but in summer the outdoor pool terrace makes this a cool and restful spot.

Melbourne (Map pp906-7; ☎ 08-9320 3333; www.melbournehotel.com.au; cnr Hay & Milligan Sts; d from $160; ⊠) Classic country charm wafts through this gold-rush-era, heritage-listed hotel. Inside you'll find a stylish and serious dining room, and a polished bar and cafe buzzing with office workers. Rooms are gradually undergoing a stylish upgrade, and some have Victorian-era lattice-work balconies.

Goodearth Hotel (Map pp906-7; ☎ 08-9494 7777; www.goodearthhotel.com.au; 195 Adelaide Tce; studio/1-bedroom apt from $175/200; P ⊑) Popular with country folk coming to town, these self-contained units have (tiny) balconies, some with views of the river just a block away, secure parking and a great location near the CAT bus route.

TOP END

Medina Executive Barrack Plaza (Map pp906-7; ☎ 08-9267 0000; www.medina.com.au; 138 Barrack St; d $207-230; ⊠ ☞) The Medina's meticulously decorated apartment-sized hotel rooms are minimalist yet welcoming. All one-bedrooms have balconies, and rooms on Barrack St tend to have more natural light (not always easy to obtain in Perth).

Mantra on Hay (Map pp906-7; ☎ 08-9267 4888; www.mantraresorts.com.au; 201 Hay St; studio/1-bedroom apt from $207/230; ⊠ ☞) With a Tuscan-orange outside, and muted, urban-chic greys and purples inside, the Mantra is low-key and classy. Apartments are roomy, with laundries, dishwashers and good-sized benches and great utensils – plenty of room to prepare some local rock lobster here.

Outram (Map pp904-5; ☎ 08-9322 4888; www.wyndhamvrap.com.au; 32 Outram St, West Perth; s/d from $295/335; ⊠) Discreet and understated, the Outram (now offically 'Wyndham Vacation Resorts Asia Pacific Perth' but – understandably – still known as the Outram) is super-stylish, with compact open-plan rooms, a bathroom with a walk-through shower, king-sized beds draped in white linens, flat-screen TVs and spas.

Northbridge & Around

Most hostels are in Northbridge. You might want to walk around and inspect rooms before putting your money down – some are not up to scratch.

BUDGET

Britannia (Map pp906-7; ☎ 08-9227 6000; www.perthbritannia.com; 253 William St; dm/s/d $22/37/58; ⊑) This no-frills backpackers in the centre of Northbridge has good-value dorms, friendly staff and a busy vibe. The kitchen is a bit of a cramped hot-box, but with some of the area's best cheap eats just up the road, it's no biggie. Unless the carpet cleaner's been, you'll want to wear shoes throughout.

Witch's Hat (Map pp906-7; ☎ 08-9228 4228; www.witchs-hat.com; 148 Palmerston St; dm/d $23/64; ⊠ ⊑) Resembling a gingerbread house, the Witch's Hat is clearly something out of a fairy tale. With its 1897 Edwardian turret beckoning the curious, and founding-family photos overseeing the action, guests are rewarded with light and spacious dorms and plenty of facilities.

Oneworld Backpackers (Map pp906-7; ☎ 08-9228 8206; www.oneworldbackpackers.com.au; 162 Aberdeen St, Northbridge; dm/d $24/71; ⊑) Oneworld is clean, green and beautifully maintained. Polished floorboards beam brightly in all the rooms of this nicely restored old house, the dorms are big and sunny, and the brick garden courtyard is the place to hang out with the hostel's extended family of long-term travellers. It's near enough to the Northbridge action to be convenient, far enough away to be relaxing.

Billabong Backpackers Resort (Map pp906-7; ☎ 08-9328 7720; www.billabongresort.com.au; 381 Beaufort St; dm/d $27/80; ⊑ ☞) This large, relaxed hostel (about 150 beds) is brought to life by Australiana murals along its walls, as well as its poolside activities – it's nice to have some green space to sit in. The well-kept dorms are excellent value, the doubles less so.

Governor Robinsons (Map pp906-7; ☎ 08-9328 3200; www.govrobinsons.com.au; 7 Robinson Ave; dm $28, d from

$75; ☒) In two restored colonial homes, this small, impeccably maintained and beautifully furnished hostel (think Chesterfields, floorboards) is more like a cosy B&B than a backpackers. The kitchen is a foodie's friend, the dorms are fresh and clean, rooms are high and airy, and the clean-as-a-whistle Federation-style bathrooms are a real hit.

MIDRANGE

Emperor's Crown (Map pp906-7; ☎ 08-9227 1400; www .emperorscrown.com.au; 85 Stirling St; dm $30, r with/without bathroom $102/92; ☐) A minimalist and surprisingly stylish taste of urban chic for midrange and budget travellers alike. It has multi-language internet, a chilled-out movie lounge and decent access for disabled guests.

Hotel Northbridge (Map pp906-7; ☎ 08-93285254; www .hotelnorthbridge.com.au; 210 Lake St; d with spa $125-170; ☒ ☐) The Northbridge has long been the star attraction for couples and country folk with its good-value rooms and old-fashioned charm. A recent refurbishment has dropped a spa in every single room, and considering its smack-bang location it's a great midrange choice.

Cottesloe & Scarborough

BUDGET

Ocean Beach Backpackers (Map pp902-3; ☎ 08-9384 5111; www.oceanbeachbackpackers.com; cnr Marine Pde & Eric St, Cottesloe; 8-bed dm $23, s/d $62/67; ☐) Offering (some) ocean views, this big, bright hostel right in the heart of Cottesloe is just a short skip from the sand. Rooms are basic but all have private bathrooms, and you'll probably just be here to sleep given the great location; hire a bike ($20 per day) to get around locally. It's alcohol-free – which is no big deal, given the pub next door.

MIDRANGE & TOP END

Ocean Beach Hotel (Map pp902-3; ☎ 08-9384 2555; www .obh.com.au; cnr Marine Pde & Eric St, Cottesloe; d $145-185; ☒) Overlooking the water, the only boutique-style hotel on Cottesloe Beach features smart, playful colours and contemporary furnishings that bring this art deco building to life. Rooms are big, but get a deluxe or spa room if you want to watch the waves.

Sun Moon Resort (Map pp902-3; ☎ 08-9245 8000; www .arcadiahospitality.com.au; 200 West Coast Hwy, Scarborough; r from $160; ☒ ☒) While this Bali-style resort and Scarborough marriage might appear a mismatch, the two make a lovely couple. The

rooms are enormous, and the terracotta-tiled floor is cool and pleasing under bare feet. Batik furnishings complement the otherwise minimalist rooms, but note there's a busy main road between hotel and beach.

Camping

Perth Central Caravan Park (Map pp902-3; ☎ 08-9277 1704; www.perthcentral.com.au; 34 Central Ave, Ascot; powered sites $33-36, cabins from $120; ☒ ☒) This small caravan park, 8km east of the city, is the closest to Perth, with chalets in functional serried ranks. Weekly rates are good value, and frequent public buses to the city (30 minutes) stop outside.

Perth International Tourist Park (off Map pp902-3; ☎ 1800 626 677; www.discoveryholidayparks.com.au; 186 Hale Rd, Forrestfield; powered sites from $35, cabins from $100; ☒ ☐ ☒) This caravan park, 15km out of the city, is more of a holiday complex than overnight stop. It's big and shady, with plenty of accommodation options, including simple budget rooms ($55) with shared balconies. A huge public pool is up the road and regular public buses travel into the city (40 minutes).

EATING

So much choice, so little time! Perth's city centre offers choices ranging from budget to business lunch. Northbridge is a hub for cheap and cheerful food, with an emphasis on Southeast Asian and Aussie staples; coffee-culture rules in the trendy inner city suburbs of Mount Lawley, Leederville and Subiaco, where restaurants are a step up in ambience and budget range (think gourmet local produce). The beachside 'burbs of Cottesloe (to the south) and Scarborough (to the north) offer outdoor informal.

City Centre

Tiger Tiger (Map pp906-7; ☎ 08-9322 8055; Murray Mews; mains $8-10; ☺ breakfast & lunch Mon-Sat; ☐) While the wi-fi here attracts bespectacled blogger types, the cool feel, with polished concrete floor, communal table and antique-style wooden chairs, might play a part, too. It's signed off Murray St.

Secret Garden (☎ 08-9322 5885; Shop 7, 329 Murray St; mains $10-20; ☺ breakfast & lunch Mon-Fri) This relaxed and relaxing cafe shares a courtyard with Tiger Tiger.

Matsuri (Map pp906-7; ☎ 08-9322 7737; cnr Hay & Milligan Sts; mains $13-21; ☺ lunch Mon-Fri, dinner daily)

You'll feel a bit like a carp in a fish tank here – floor-to-ceiling glass runs the perimeter of this large, long-standing Japanese restaurant. The tempura udon with sushi set ($20) is enough to feed two salarymen.

King Street Café (Map pp906-7; ☎ 08-9321 4476; 44 King St; mains from $24) This Perth stalwart played a crucial role in creating a cafe culture back when only European expats and well-travelled types drank espresso. Great decor, great wine list and an expansive menu that changes monthly.

Annalakshmi (Map pp906-7; ☎ 08-9221 3003; www.annalakshmi.com.au; Jetty 4, Barrack St; prices at customer's discretion; ☺ lunch & dinner Tue-Fri) While the 360-degree views of the Swan River are worth a million dollars, Annalakshmi is actually a vego curry house run by volunteers. Paying by donation, an eclectic mix of hippies, local and visiting Indians, and Perth families line up for spicy curries and fragrant dhal.

Balthazar (Map pp906-7; ☎ 08-9421 1206; cnr Sherwood Ct & The Esplanade; mains from $26, desserts $15; ☺ lunch Mon-Fri, dinner Mon-Sat) Low-lit, discreet and sophisticated, but unpompous. The menu is refreshingly original with a strong European twist, with dishes such as caramelised witlof, Roquefort tempura, and aromatic chai pannacotta accompanying sticky date pudding.

Northbridge

Source (Map pp906-7; ☎ 6468 7100; 289 Beaufort St; mains $6-17; ☺ breakfast & lunch Tue-Sun) Plenty of simple vego options, made from fair-traded organic food that's travelled few food miles.

Good Fortune Roast Duck House (Map pp906-7; ☎ 08-9228 3293; 344 William St; mains from $8; ☺ lunch & dinner Wed-Mon) Locals charge in here for family-sized feeds of barbecue pork, roast duck and noodles. The front window, with its glistening hanging ducks, will make you salivate.

Red Teapot (Map pp906-7; ☎ 08-9228 1981; 413 William St; mains from $8, noodles $9-11; ☺ lunch & dinner Mon-Sat) This intimate restaurant is always busy with diners enjoying stylishly executed Chinese favourites such as fragrant Prosperous Chicken and chilli salt squid.

Viet Hoa (Map pp906-7; ☎ 08-9328 2127; 349 William St; mains $8-16; ☺ lunch & dinner) Don't be fooled by the bare-bones ambience of this always-busy corner Vietnamese restaurant or you'll miss out on the fresh ricepaper rolls and top-notch *pho* (beef-and-rice-noodle soup).

Tarts (Map pp906-7; ☎ 08-9328 6607; 212 Lake St; lunch dishes $10-15; ☺ breakfast & lunch) Tarts is French country style in the city. You'll find exquisite tarts piled with berries, rich scrambled eggs tumbling off toasted sourdough, delicious frittata and salad, and comfy informal indoor/outdoor seating.

Inner-City Suburbs

Soto Espresso (Map pp906-7; ☎ 08-9227 7686; 507 Beaufort St, Mt Lawley; ☺ breakfast $4-10, lunch $9; ☺ 7am-midnight) Modern Soto opens onto the street to welcome its inner-city crowd, from stay-at-home dads to bleary-eyed students. The lime-green banquette is a great spot to watch all the comings and goings, and the large *croque-monsieur* ($10) will cure that super-sized hangover.

Oxford 130 (Map pp904-5; 130 Oxford St, Leederville; sandwiches $8; ☺ 6am-midnight) Boasting one of the best breakfasts in Perth, this is the classic, casual cafe you need in every neighbourhood. Elbow your way into a booth, or pull up a milk crate out front, eavesdrop on the local gossip and let the day slip by.

Chutney Mary's (Map pp904-5; ☎ 08-9381 2099; 67 Rokeby Rd, Subiaco; mains $15-28; ☺ lunch Wed-Sat, dinner daily) The feisty, authentic Indian food here is much loved. The menu is huge, and much of it's devoted to vegetarian favourites such as *malai kofta* and *dal makhani*. The vibe is colourful and casual, with wall-sized scenes of Indian life.

Ecco (Map pp904-5; ☎ 08-9388 6710; 23 Rokeby Rd; pizzas $19; ☺ 11am-late Tue-Sun) With black-and-white prints of Italy slicked along the walls, small and rustic Ecco is all about the perfect Italian pizza. Slip into a wooden table inside, or gaze at passers-by out front, and get busy munching.

Rialto's (Map pp904-5; ☎ 08-9382 3292; 424 Hay St, Subiaco; mains $35; ☺ lunch Mon-Fri, dinner Mon-Sat) Bold red leather, slick black stools, chalk-white walls and chairs: Rialto's is see-and-be-seen Euro chic. The flair extends to the serious menu.

Fraser's Restaurant (Map pp906-7; ☎ 08-9481 7100; Fraser Ave, Kings Park; mains $35-55) Atop Kings Park, overlooking the city and the glittering Swan River, Fraser's location is unrivalled. And the food has enjoyed a good reputation for years, with Mod Oz standards such as chargrilled rock lobster and roast 'roo on beetroot rōsti and polenta. Its more casual sister restaurant next door, Botanical Café, is open for breakfast and lunch.

Must Winebar (Map pp906-7; ☎ 08-9328 8255; 519 Beaufort St, Mt Lawley; mains $38; ☺ noon-late) Arguably Perth's best wine bar, this is a fine restaurant as well. Tuck into local WA speciality produce such as Margaret River Wagyu beef shanks, or simply stop by for a glass of something delicious.

Jackson's (Map pp906-7; ☎ 08-9328 1177; 483 Beaufort St, Highgate; mains $44, 7-course tasting menu $115, with wine $170; ☺ dinner Mon-Sat) Foodies flock to what is one of Perth's top dining experiences: Neal Jackson's tasting menu. À-la-carte highlights include seasonal specials – in winter, think gamey dishes of venison, rabbit and partridge.

Cottesloe & Scarborough

The surf beaches and coastal walk tracks at Cottesloe and Scarborough are fringed by eateries ranging from cheap and cheerful to seriously chic and gourmet.

Peter's by the Sea (Map pp902-3; ☎ 08-9341 1738; 128 The Esplanade, Scarborough; burgers & kebabs from $8; ☺ lunch & dinner) A Perth surfie icon, Peter's bacon-and-egg burgers are the cure for those hangovers or post-surf hunger pangs.

John Street Café (Map pp902-3; ☎ 08-9384 3390; 37 John St, Cottesloe; mains $15-20; ☺ breakfast & lunch) Just two minutes from the beach, cute John St Café is *the* locals' spot for that late-morning brunch-cum-lunch. Dig into divine eggs Benedict or a breakfast bagel of bacon, avocado and cream cheese.

Self-Catering

Supermarkets and corner stores abound. For something different try the following:

Boatshed (Map pp902-3; ☎ 08-9284 5176; 40 Jarrad St, Cottesloe; ☺ 6.30am-8pm) Enormous upmarket shed stacked with fresh produce and fabulous deli and picnic food.

Chez Jean-Claude Patisserie (Map pp904-5; 333 Rokeby Rd, Subiaco; ☺ 6am-6.30pm Mon-Fri) Line up with locals for brioche, baguettes and quichey things.

Kailis (Map pp904-5; ☎ 9443 6300; 101 Oxford St, Leederville; ☺ 9am-6pm) Big fresh-seafood supplier with attached cafe.

Kakulas Bros (Map pp906-7; ☎ 08-9328 5744; 183 William St, Perth; ☺ Mon-Sat) Ramshackle provisions store overflowing with dirt-cheap legumes, nuts and olives.

DRINKING

While the city has a few popular watering holes, the gems of Perth's drinking scene are sprinkled throughout the suburbs. Generally, the mainstream drinking venues are in Northbridge; smaller, more laid-back clubs and bars are in Mt Lawley, Leederville and Subiaco; and big beer gardens are strewn around the suburbs, notably in Cottesloe.

City Centre

Hula Bula Bar (Map pp906-7; ☎ 08-9225 4457; 12 Victoria Ave; ☺ Wed-Sun) This tiny Polynesian-themed bar is decked out in bamboo, palm leaves and totems, and the ostentatious cocktails come in ceramic monkey heads. You won't mind being castaway here, especially on the weekends.

Carnegie's (Map pp906-7; ☎ 08-9481 3222; 356 Murray St; ☺ 11am-1am Mon-Thu, noon-3am Fri & Sat, noon-midnight Sun) Casual and cheerful; the sort of place for when you want to go out, but don't want to dress up. Retro jukebox hits are enjoyed by a mix of locals and travellers.

Tiger Lil's (Map pp906-7; ☎ 08-9481 2008; 437 Murray St; ☺ 11am-late Tue-Sat) Fun, over-the-top decor – think Asian lanterns and tattoo posters – with good dance music and a youngish mix of locals and blow-ins.

Northbridge

Brass Monkey (Map pp906-7; ☎ 08-9227 9596; cnr James & William Sts; ☺ 11am-midnight Mon & Tue, to 1am Wed & Thu, to 2am Fri & Sat, to 10pm Sun) This massive pub, built in 1897, boasts several different areas and vibes. Take your pick: sit up on a stool at the bar, lean back in the relaxed beer garden or hunker down on a sofa by the fire. The food's good, too.

Grapeskin (Map pp906-7; ☎ 08-9227 9596; 215 William St; ☺ noon-midnight Mon & Tue, to 1am Wed & Thu, to 2am Fri & Sat, 11am-10pm Sun) Next door, Grapeskin is the Monkey's somewhat up-market wine-bar cousin. It gets very crowded.

Universal (Map pp906-7; ☎ 08-9227 6771; 221 William St; ☺ to 2am Wed-Sat, to 10pm Sun) The unpretentious Universal is one of Perth's oldest bars and much-loved by jazz and blues enthusiasts.

Deen (Map pp906-7; ☎ 08-9227 9361; 84 Aberdeen St; ☺ 5pm-2am Mon & Thu-Sat) While Monday night's backpacker night is obligatory for travellers, other nights see DJs, pool tables and big lines out the front.

Shed (☎ 08-9228 2200; 84 Aberdeen St; ☺ noon-late) More chilled-out pub than club, the Shed often has live music and a younger crowd of locals and visitors. Big-screen TV shows all international sports.

INNER-CITY SUBURBS

Luxe (Map pp906-7; ☎ 08-9228 9680; 446 Beaufort St, Mt Lawley; ☺ to late Wed-Sun) With retro wood panelling, big sexy lounge chairs and red-velvet curtains, Luxe is knowingly hip. Like any serious bar, it's also armed with turntables and a specialist cocktail bar.

Must Winebar (Map pp906-7; ☎ 08-9328 8255; 519 Beaufort St, Mt Lawley; ⏱ noon-late) With cool house music pulsing through the air and the perfect glass of wine in your hand (40 offerings by the glass, 500 on the list), it's difficult to leave this buzzing bar in the thick of Beaufort St. The food's also excellent.

Brisbane Hotel (Map pp906-7; ☎ 08-9227 2300; 292 Beaufort St, Mt Lawley; ⏱ noon-late) Classic 1898 recently renovated Aussie pub. The busy beer garden is a melting pot of all ages and all interests; the restaurant serves up a storm.

Leederville Hotel (Map pp904-5; ☎ 08-9286 0150; 742 Newcastle St, Leederville; ⏱ noon-midnight Mon-Thu, to 1am Fri & Sat, to 11pm Sun) The something-for-everyone philosophy of the old Leederville is etched out in the sports screens, dance floors and pool tables – and it does them all well.

Subiaco Hotel (Map pp904-5; ☎ 08-9381 3069; cnr Hay St & Rokeby Rd, Subiaco; ⏱ 7am-late) The Subi's a local favourite and the institution of choice for a morning coffee with the papers or a pre-footy beer. It's popular, too, for a Sunday sundowner or an afternoon of quiet beverages and people-watching.

Cottesloe

Ocean Beach Hotel (Map pp902-3; ☎ 08-9384 2555; cnr Marine Pde & Eric St; ⏱ 11am-midnight Mon-Sat, to 10pm Sun) While we love it here during the week when it's comparatively quiet and we can watch the waves roll in, the Sunday 'sesh' at this beachside pub is unmissable.

Cottesloe Beach Hotel (Map pp902-3; ☎ 08-9383 1100; 104 Marine Pde; ⏱ 11am-midnight Mon-Sat, to 10pm Sun) If it's too crowded at the Ocean Beach, check out the competition at the Cott – it's just as good.

ENTERTAINMENT

Most of the big clubs are in Northbridge; Leederville and Mt Lawley are also nightlife spots. Theatre and classical music are found in Subiaco and the city; ring ahead to confirm details and hours. Also check out the free weekly *X Press Magazine* for gig listings for pubs and clubs.

Nightclubs

Geisha (Map pp906-7; ☎ 08-9328 9808; 135a James St, Northbridge; ⏱ 11pm-6am Fri & Sat) Geisha's a small and pumping DJ-driven, gay-friendly club. The vibe's usually music focused and chilled out.

Connections (Map pp906-7; ☎ 08-9328 1870; 81 James St, Northbridge; ⏱ Wed, Fri & Sat) This is Perth's one 'real' gay club, with a mixed crowd mingling on busy Saturday nights – other nights can be hit-or-miss.

Velvet Lounge (Map pp906-7; ☎ 08-9328 6200; 639 Beaufort St, Mt Lawley; ⏱ 11am-midnight Sun-Thu, to 1am Fri & Sat) Out the back of the Flying Scotsman pub is a small, red-velvet-clad lounge with hip hop, drum'n'bass, house and funk. Punters pop in and out of here and the Flying Scotsman all night long.

Other clubs:

Ambar (Map pp906-7; ☎ 08-9325 0000; 100 Murray St, Perth) The place for international DJs.

Hip-E Club (Map pp904-5; ☎ 08-9227 8899; 663 Newcastle St, Leederville; ⏱ Tue-Sun) Thrust about to 'Tainted Love' all night long. Tuesday is backpackers' night.

Moon Cafe (Map pp906-7; ☎ 08-9328 7474; 323 William St, Northbridge; ⏱ 6pm-late Mon & Tue, 11am-late Wed-Sun) Low-key late-night jazz bar.

Rise (Map pp906-7; ☎ 08-9328 7447; 139 James St, Northbridge) Serious clubbers head here for nonstop trance.

Live Music

Amplifier Bar (Map pp906-7; ☎ 08-9321 7606; rear 385 Murray St, Perth; ⏱ 8am-late Fri & Sat) Good old Amplifier is one of the best places for live (mainly indie) bands.

Bakery (Map pp906-7; ☎ 08-9227 0629; 233 James St, Northbridge) Run by Artrage, Perth's contemporary arts festival body, the Bakery draws an arty crowd. Popular indie gigs are held almost every weekend.

Rosemount Hotel (Map pp906-7; ☎ 08-9328 7062; cnr Angove & Fitzgerald Sts, North Perth; ⏱ 11am-late Mon-Sat, to 10pm Sun) Local and international bands play regularly in this spacious pub, which is all wood and floorboards and laid-back beer garden.

Hyde Park Hotel (Map pp906-7; ☎ 08-9328 6166; cnr Bulwer & Fitzgerald Sts, Northbridge) The Hydie does indie and rock bands some evenings, comedy on others. The Perth Jazz Society (www.perthjazzsociety.com) meets here every Monday night to play swing and modern jazz. The Jazz Club of WA, which plays traditional jazz and Dixieland, meets here on Tuesday nights.

Big international acts play at **Metro City** (Map pp906-7; ☎ 08-9228 0500; 146 Roe St, Northbridge).

WESTERN AUSTRALIA

Cinemas

Perth has a couple of art-house cinemas:

Cinema Paradiso (Map pp906-7; ☎ 08-9227 1771; www.lunapalace.com.au; Galleria complex, 164 James St, Northbridge)

Luna (Map pp904-5; ☎ 08-9444 4056; www.lunapalace .com.au; 155 Oxford St, Leederville) Monday twin-features ($10) and a bar.

A number of outdoor cinemas operate in summer:

Camelot Outdoor Cinema (Map pp902-3; ☎ 08-9385 4793; www.camelot.com.au; Memorial Hall, 16 Lochee St, Mosman Park)

Luna (Map pp904-5; ☎ 08-9444 4056; www.lunapalace .com.au; 155 Oxford St, Leederville)

Moonlight Cinema (Map pp904-5; ☎ 1300 551 908; www.moonlight.com.au; Kings Park)

Somerville Auditorium (Map pp902-3; www.perthfes tival.com.au; University of Western Australia, 35 Stirling Hwy, Crawley) A quintessential Perth experience, the art-house Somerville is on beautiful grounds surrounded by pines. Picnicking before the film is a must.

Theatre & Classical Music

Check Saturday's *West Australian* newspaper for theatre programs and other entertainment listings. For theatre, dance and classical music:

His Majesty's Theatre (Map pp906-7; ☎ 08-9265 0900; www.hismajestys.com.au; 825 Hay St, Perth)

Perth Concert Hall (Map pp906-7; ☎ 08-9484 1133; www.perthconcerthall.com.au; 5 St Georges Tce, Perth) Home to the Western Australian Symphony Orchestra (WASO).

Playhouse Theatre (Map pp906-7; ☎ 08-9484 1133; www.playhousetheatre.com.au; 3 Pier St, Perth)

Regal Theatre (Map pp904-5; ☎ 08-9484 1133; www .regaltheatre.com.au; 474 Hay St, Subiaco)

Subiaco Arts Centre (Map pp904-5; ☎ 08-9382 3385; www.subiacoartscentre.com.au; 180 Hamersley Rd, Subiaco)

Sport

During the Australian Football League season it's hard to get footy fans to talk about anything but the two local teams – the Fremantle Dockers and the West Coast Eagles. There's a great atmosphere during the games at **Subiaco Oval** (Map pp904-5; ☎ 08-9381 2187; www.subiacooval.com .au; 250 Roberts Rd, Subiaco).

In summer, cricket fans spend lazy afternoons at the **WACA** (Western Australian Cricket Association ground; Map pp904-5; ☎ 08-9265 7222; www.waca.com.au; Nelson Cres, East Perth) watching the drama unfold

at a test or one-day match – and perhaps having a brew or two.

The Perth Glory soccer team has many obsessive fans. See them in action at **Perth Oval** (Map pp906-7; ☎ 08-9492 6000; Members Equity Stadium, Lord St, East Perth). Perth Wildcats play NBL basketball at **Challenge Stadium** (Map pp902-3; ☎ 08-9441 8222; Stephenson Ave, Mt Claremont).

The *West Australian* has details of all sports games.

SHOPPING

The Hay and Murray St Malls border the city's shopping heartland, while James St Mall has a stylish selection of boutiques. The London Ct arcade has opals and souvenirs, while upmarket Subiaco's Rokeby Rd and Hay St boast high fashion and classy souvenirs. Leederville's Oxford St is the place for groovy boutiques and eclectic music- and bookshops.

78 Records (Map pp906-7; ☎ 08-9322 6384; 914 Hay St, Perth) It's been around since 78s – well, almost. It's as big as a warehouse and has a massive range.

Keith & Lottie (Map pp906-7; ☎ 08-9328 8082; 276 William St, Northbridge) An indie kid's delight, this extremely cute store has journals, badges, necklaces, T-shirts, a few homewares, and coats and tops.

Indigenart (Map pp904-5; ☎ 08-9388 2899; 115 Hay St, Subiaco) Reputable Indigenart carries major Kimberley, Papunya Tula and Arnhem Land artists. Works span weavings, canvases, works on paper and limited-edition prints.

Form (Map pp906-7; ☎ 08-9226 2799; 357 Murray St, Perth) Just around the corner from King St, Form stocks vases and craft pieces by Australian artists as well as design books, broaches, jewellery and bags.

If you need something special to wear, try **Periscope** (Map pp906-7; ☎ 08-9321 6868; 30 King St, Perth) or **Varga Girl** (Map pp906-7; ☎ 08-9321 7838; 349 Murray St, Perth). Both carry Australian designers. Varga Girl has a good range of dresses, some vintage pieces and jeans.

Gargantuan shopping malls are **Garden City** (Map pp902-3; 125 Risely St, Booragoon), south of the city centre, and the more upmarket **Karrinyup** (Map pp902-3; 200 Karrinyup Rd, Karrinyup), to the north.

GETTING THERE & AWAY
Air

Qantas (Map pp906-7; ☎ 13 13 13; www.qantas.com.au; 55 William St) and **Virgin Blue** (☎ 13 67 89; www.virginblue .com.au) fly between Perth and other Australian

HAPPY CAMPERS

If you're heading out of town for, say, more than two weeks, consider hiring a campervan. You won't be hampered by hostel check-in timetables and dorm-snorers, leaving you to stop where you want, when you want. And it can be quite economical once costs are split between two or three people. In general, if you're just planning to tour the southwest of WA, a hire car is better value – accommodation is plentiful, and distances aren't as great.

Mention the word 'budget campervan' to a traveller who's hired one, and wait for the reaction. Some travellers have had a great time of freedom on the road with no hassles; others need to take a deep breath before recounting their tales of woe and disaster. Everyone agrees, reluctantly, that basically you get what you pay for. As we write this, the popular **Wicked Campers** (Map pp906-7; ☎ 1800 246 869; www.wickedcampers.com.au; 49 Shenton St, Northbridge) are the most visible on the road.

Compare deals carefully. You should be able to get unlimited kilometres, roadside assistance, and pick-up and delivery within metropolitan Perth. Oh, and find out who wears the cost if you're unlucky enough to break down 500km from the nearest town and garage.

If you've done the sums and decided to purchase instead, Freo has a number of second-hand car yards, including a cluster in North Freo, near Mojo's on Stirling Hwy. There's also the **Traveller's Autobarn** (Map pp906-7; ☎ 08-9228 9500; www.travellers-autobarn.com.au; 365 Newcastle St, Northbridge).

state capitals. **Jetstar** (www.jetstar.com) runs cheapies to Perth from Avalon, Melbourne.

Skywest (☎ 1300 660 088; www.skywest.com.au) flies between Perth and regional destinations such as Esperance and Broome. Qantas also flies to Broome and Kalgoorlie.

Bus

Greyhound Australia (Map pp904-5; ☎ 13 14 99; www.greyhound.com.au; East Perth terminal, West Pde) has daily services from the East Perth terminal to Darwin via Broome.

Transwa (Map pp904-5; ☎ 1300 662 205; www.transwa.wa.gov.au) operates services from the bus terminal at East Perth train station to many destinations around the state.

South West Coach Lines (☎ 08-9324 2333) focuses on the southwestern corner of WA, doing trips from the Esplanade Busport (Map pp906-7) to most towns in the region, including Bunbury, Busselton and Margaret River.

Integrity Coach Lines (☎ 1800 226 339, 08-9226 1339; www.integritycoachlines.com.au; Wellington St Bus Station) runs services between Perth and Port Hedland via Meekathara and Newman.

Train

The intrastate rail network, run by **Transwa** (Map pp904-5; ☎ 1300 662 205; www.transwa.wa.gov.au), is limited to the Perth–Kalgoorlie–Boulder *Prospector* ($77, one daily), departing from the East Perth terminal.

There is only one interstate rail link: the famous *Indian Pacific* transcontinental train

journey, run by **Great Southern Railway** (☎ 13 21 47; www.trainways.com.au), which leaves from East Perth station (Map pp904–5). One-way fares between Sydney and Perth are about $690 (seat only), $315 (seat only, backpacker rate) or $1350 (sleeper cabin). Between Adelaide and Perth, fares are $395 (seat only), $250 (seat only, backpacker) or $1020 (sleeper cabin). There are connections to the *Ghan* (to Alice Springs and Darwin) and the *Overland* (to Melbourne) trains.

GETTING AROUND
To/From the Airport

The domestic and international terminals of Perth's airport are 10km and 13km east of Perth respectively. Taxi fares to the city are around $25/35 from the domestic/international terminal.

The **Perth Airport City Shuttle** (☎ 08-9277 7958; www.perthshuttle.com.au) provides transport to the city centre, hotels and hostels. It meets incoming domestic and international flights. The shuttle costs $15/20 from the domestic/international terminal. Bookings essential.

Transperth bus 37 travels to the domestic airport from Kings Park (or Esplanade Busport) via St Georges Tce every 20 minutes during weekdays, every 30 to 60 minutes early mornings, evenings and weekends.

Car & Motorcycle

All the major car-rental companies – **Avis** (Map pp906-7; ☎ 13 63 33; 46 Hill St, Perth), **Budget** (Map pp906-7;

☎ 13 27 27; 960 Hay St, Perth), **Hertz** (Map pp906-7; ☎ 13 30 39; 39 Milligan St, Perth) and **Thrifty** (Map pp906-7; ☎ 1300 367 227, within WA 13 61 39; 198 Adelaide Tce) – are in Perth. Some local operators – such as **Bayswater Hire Car** (Map pp906-7; ☎ 08-9325 1000; 160 Adelaide Tce) – can be cheaper, but make sure you read the fine print. Note that some insurance policies, even with the bigger companies, don't cover you outside the metropolitan area after dark – in case you hit a roo.

Public Transport

Transperth (☎ 13 62 13; www.transperth.wa.gov.au) operates buses, trains and ferries. There are Transperth information offices at the Perth train station (Map pp906-7) on Wellington St and at the Esplanade Busport (Map pp906-7) on Mounts Bay Rd, by the convention centre.

There's a free transit zone for all buses and trains within the city. Look for the 'FTZ' sign. On regular Transperth buses and trains, a short ride of one zone costs $2.30, two zones $3.50 and three zones $4.30. Zone 1 includes the city centre and the inner suburbs, and Zone 2 extends to Fremantle, Sorrento and Midland. The DayRider pass ($8.40) is good value, giving you unlimited travel after 9am weekdays and all day on the weekend.

BUS

For travellers, the free Central Area Transit (CAT) services in the city centre are fantastic. There are computer readouts at the stops telling you when the next bus is due. Using the CAT, you can get to most sights in the inner city, and CAT maps are available around town.

The red CAT operates east–west from Outram St, West Perth, to the WACA in East Perth. It runs every five minutes from 6.50am to 6.20pm weekdays, and every 25 minutes from 10am to 6.15pm on weekends.

The blue CAT operates north–south from the river to Northbridge. Services run every seven minutes from 6.50am to 6.20pm weekdays, and on Friday evenings every 15 minutes from 6.20pm to 1am. On weekends, there's a bus every 15 minutes from 8.30am to 1am on Saturday and from 10am to 6.15pm on Sunday.

The yellow CAT runs from East Perth up Wellington St to West Perth every 10 minutes from 6.50am to 6.20pm weekdays, and every 30 minutes from 10am to 6.15pm on weekends.

A wide network of Transperth buses also services the metropolitan area. See the information office at Perth train station for timetables and advice or use the 'journey planner' on its website (www.transperth.wa.gov.au).

FERRY

A popular way of getting to the zoo, Transperth ferries cross the river from the Barrack St jetty (Map pp906-7) in the city to the Mends St jetty in South Perth. Services run every 20 to 30 minutes from 6.50am to 7.24pm weekdays, and from around 8.10am to 9.15pm on weekends.

TAXI

Perth has a decent system of metered taxi cabs, though the distances in Perth make frequent use costly, and on busy nights you may have trouble flagging one down off the street. There are ranks throughout the city and in Fremantle. The two main companies are **Swan Taxis** (☎ 13 13 30, 08-9422 2240) and **Black & White** (☎ 13 10 08, 08-9333 3377); both have wheelchair access.

TRAIN

Transperth also operates suburban train lines to Armadale, Fremantle, Midland, Thornlie and the northern suburb of Clarkson (Joondalup) from around 5.20am to midnight weekdays. The satellite cities of Rockingham and Mandurah are also served by trains. Trains run until about 2am on Saturday and Sunday.

All trains leave from Perth station on Wellington St. Your rail ticket can also be used on Transperth buses and ferries within the ticket's area of validity; the free transit zone extends to Claisebrook and City West stations. You're also free to take your bike on the train in nonpeak times.

FREMANTLE

pop 26,800

'Freo' lies at the mouth of the Swan River, 19km from Perth but a world away in terms of atmosphere. Creative and relaxed, clean and green Freo makes a cosy home for performers, professionals, artists, hippies and more than a few eccentrics. There's a lot to enjoy here – Freo is also home to some fantastic museums, historic buildings, galleries, pubs and a thriving coffee culture. At night on weekends the city's residents vacate the main drag, leaving it to kids from the suburbs, who move in to party hard and loud.

HISTORY

This area was originally settled by Noongar people who used it for ceremony and trade. Aboriginal groups quickly came to occupy various parts of what was known to them as Manjaree. Fremantle's European history began when the ship HMS *Challenger* landed here in 1829. The settlement made little progress until convict labour constructed most of the town's earliest buildings. Today, buildings such as the Round House, Old Fremantle Prison and the Fremantle Arts Centre are among the oldest in WA.

As a port, Fremantle was ineffective until the engineer CY O'Connor created an artificial harbour in the 1890s. Almost one hundred years later the ocean drew crowds when, in 1987, Freo hosted the (unsuccessful) defence of the America's Cup yachting trophy. While Australia lost the Cup, Fremantle was the big winner, having transformed from a sleepy port into today's vibrant city.

INFORMATION

Chart & Map Shop (☎ 08-9335 8665; 14 Collie St; ☘ 9am-5pm Mon-Fri, 9am-4pm Sat, 10am-4pm Sun) Great range of maps and travel guides.

etech (☎ 08-9239 8189; 53 South Tce; per hr $6; ☘ 8am-8.30pm Mon-Thu, 8am-4pm Fri, 8.30am-3pm Sat) Quiet internet access.

Fremantle Hospital (☎ 08-9431 3333; Alma St)

New Edition (☎ 08-9335 2383; 82 High St; ☘ 9am-10.30pm) Excellent independent bookstore.

Post office (☎ 13 13 18; 13 Market St)

Travellers Centre (☎ 08-9335 8776; 16 Market St; ☘ 8am-8pm) Travellers' hang-out with lots of Australian travel information and internet terminals.

Visitors centre (☎ 08-9431 7878; www.fremantlewa .com.au; Kings Sq; ☘ 9am-5pm Mon-Fri, 10am-3pm Sat, 11.30am-2.30pm Sun) Nongovernment visitors centre with excellent online accommodation booking service.

SIGHTS & ACTIVITIES

Western Australian Maritime Museum

Housed in a stunning, architect-designed building on the harbour, just west of the city centre, the **WA Maritime Museum** (☎ 08-9431 8444; www.museum.wa.gov.au; Victoria Quay; museum adult/child $10/3, submarine $8/3, combined ticket $15/5; ☘ 9.30am-5pm) explores WA's relationship with the ocean. It faces out to the sea, which has

shaped so much of the state's, and Fremantle's, destiny.

You can't miss the display of **Australia II**, the famous winged-keel yacht that won the America's Cup yachting race in the 1980s (ending the 132-year American domination). Other boats on show include an **Indonesian fishing boat**, introduced to the Kimberley and used by the Indigenous people, and a **pearl lugger** from Broome. A classic 1970s panel van (complete with fur lining) makes the cut as the surfer's vehicle of choice from that era.

If you're not claustrophobic, take a tour of another ocean-going vessel, the submarine **HMAS Ovens**. The vessel was part of the Australian Navy's fleet from 1969 to 1997. Tours leave every half-hour from 10am to 3.30pm.

Fremantle Arts Centre & History Museum

An impressive neo-Gothic building, the **Fremantle Arts Centre** (☎ 08-9432 9555; www.fac .org.au; cnr Ord & Finnerty Sts; ☘ 10am-5pm) was constructed by convict labourers as a lunatic asylum in the 1860s. Saved from demolition in the late 1960s, the building now also houses the excellent **Fremantle History Museum** (☎ 08-9430 7966). Admission to both is free.

The arts centre hosts interesting temporary exhibitions. During summer it's a hive of cultural activity, with outdoor concerts, courses and workshops.

Old Fremantle Prison

In some ways, the **Old Fremantle Prison** (☎ 08-9336 9200; www.fremantleprison.com.au; 1 The Terrace; adult/child day tours $18/9, night tours $23/13, tunnel tours $59/30; ☘ 10am-6pm), with its foreboding 5m-high walls, dominates present-day Fremantle. Tales of adventures and hardships experienced here have lived on in the city's imagination.

Suitably enough, the prison was built by convict labour, and it operated from 1855 right through to 1991, playing host to people such as bushranger Moondyne Joe, a famed escape artist; Brenden Abbott, a bank robber who escaped in a prison guard's uniform; and Eric Edgar Cooke, the last person to be hanged in WA. Viewing is by tour only, though the gatehouse and exhibition gallery are freely accessible.

Maritime Museum Shipwrecks Galleries

Although the Maritime Museum commands a lot of attention, don't miss the intriguing

FREMANTLE

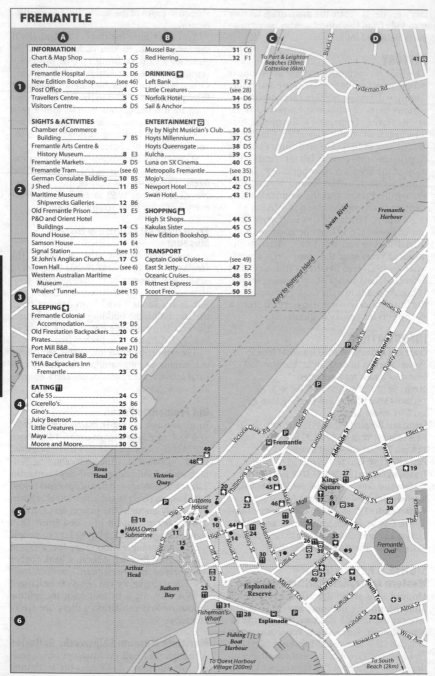

INFORMATION

Chart & Map Shop	**1**	C5
etech	**2**	D5
Fremantle Hospital	**3**	D6
New Edition Bookshop	(see 46)	
Post Office	**4**	C5
Travellers Centre	**5**	C5
Visitors Centre	**6**	D5

SIGHTS & ACTIVITIES

Chamber of Commerce Building	**7**	B5
Fremantle Arts Centre & History Museum	**8**	E3
Fremantle Markets	**9**	D5
Fremantle Tram	(see 6)	
German Consulate Bulding	**10**	B5
J Shed	**11**	B5
Maritime Museum Shipwrecks Galleries	**12**	B6
Old Fremantle Prison	**13**	E5
P&O and Orient Hotel Buildings	**14**	C5
Round House	**15**	B5
Samson House	**16**	E4
Signal Station	(see 15)	
St John's Anglican Church	**17**	C5
Town Hall	(see 6)	
Western Australian Maritime Museum	**18**	B5
Whalers' Tunnel	(see 15)	

SLEEPING

Fremantle Colonial Accommodation	**19**	D5
Old Firestation Backpackers	**20**	C5
Pirates	**21**	C6
Port Mill B&B	(see 21)	
Terrace Central B&B	**22**	D6
YHA Backpackers Inn Fremantle	**23**	C5

EATING

Cafe 55	**24**	C5
Cicerello's	**25**	B6
Gino's	**26**	C5
Juicy Beetroot	**27**	D5
Little Creatures	**28**	C6
Maya	**29**	C5
Moore and Moore	**30**	C5

Mussel Bar	**31**	C6
Red Herring	**32**	F1

DRINKING

Left Bank	**33**	F2
Little Creatures	(see 28)	
Norfolk Hotel	**34**	D6
Sail & Anchor	**35**	D5

ENTERTAINMENT

Fly by Night Musician's Club	**36**	D5
Hoyts Millennium	**37**	D5
Hoyts Queensgate	**38**	D5
Kulcha	**39**	C5
Luna on SX Cinema	**40**	C6
Metropolis Fremantle	(see 35)	
Mojo's	**41**	D1
Newport Hotel	**42**	C5
Swan Hotel	**43**	E1

SHOPPING

High St Shops	**44**	C5
Kakulas Sister	**45**	C5
New Edition Bookshop	**46**	C5

TRANSPORT

Captain Cook Cruises	(see 49)	
East St Jetty	**47**	E2
Oceanic Cruises	**48**	B5
Rottnest Express	**49**	B4
Scoot Freo	**50**	B5

WESTERN AUSTRALIA

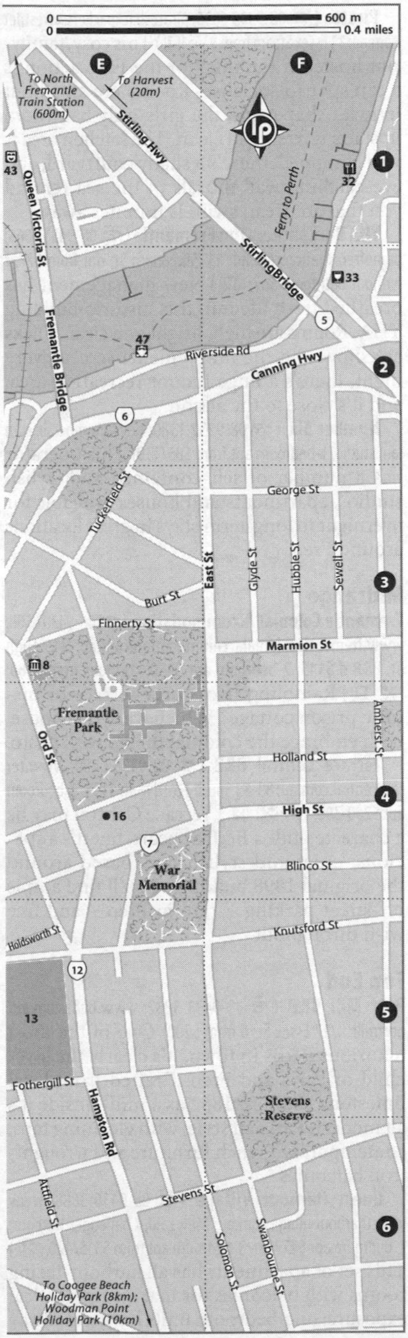

Shipwrecks Galleries (☎ 08-9431 8444; Cliff St; admission by donation; 🕑 9.30am-5pm), where you can learn about gung-ho seafaring adventures and misfortunes. The museum (in a building constructed in 1852 as a commissariat store) has a display on WA's maritime history, with emphasis on the recovery and restoration of the famous wreck *Batavia* (see Shipwrecks & Survivors, p971), in addition to other Dutch merchant ships and some more recent wrecks.

Arthur Head

Out on Arthur Head, the western end of High St near the Maritime Museum, is the **Round House** (☎ 08-9336 6897; admission by donation; 🕑 10.30am-3.30pm). Built in 1831, it's the oldest public building in WA. It was originally a local prison and the site of the colony's first hanging. On the hilltop outside is the **Signal Station**, where at 1pm daily a time ball and cannon blast were used to alert seamen to the correct time – the ceremony is reenacted daily. Later, the building was used for holding Aborigines before they were taken away to Rottnest Island. To the Noongar people, the Round House is a sacred site because of the number of their people killed while incarcerated here.

Beneath it is an impressive 1837 **Whalers' Tunnel** carved through sandstone and used for moving goods from the port into town.

Gold-Rush Buildings

Fremantle boomed during the WA gold rush and many buildings were constructed during, or shortly before, this period. **Samson House** (🕑 1.15-5pm Sun) is a well-preserved 1888 colonial home on Ellen St. **St John's Anglican Church** (1882), on the corner of Adelaide and Queen Sts, contains a large stained-glass window. Fremantle's sturdy **town hall** (1887) is in Kings Sq. A wander around the backstreets near the port will uncover many architectural treasures, including the 1903 former **German consulate building** (5 Mouat St); the (still-in-use) 1873 **Chamber of Commerce building** (16 Phillimore St); the lattice-balconied **P&O Hotel** and **Orient Hotel** on High St; and the 1907 **Fremantle Train Station**.

Other Attractions

Originally opened in 1897, the colourful **Fremantle Markets** (☎ 08-9335 2515; cnr South Tce & Henderson St; 🕑 Fri-Sun) reopened in 1975 and today draws slow-moving crowds combing over souvenirs and depleting the food and fresh produce stalls to the accompaniment of rotating buskers. The huge **Esplanade Reserve**, behind the Fishing Boat Harbour and full of Norfolk Island pines, is a good spot to relax, as is sheltered and swimmable **South Beach** at the turnaround of the free CAT bus service. A surprising drawcard for visitors is the **Bon Scott sculpture** at **J Shed** (www.gregjamessculpture.com; Fleet St; ☺ 10am-4pm Wed-Fri), where music fans can see this memorial to late-lamented local boy and lead singer of rock group AC/DC. A more permanent site is planned at Fishing Boat Harbour.

TOURS

The **Fremantle Tram** (☎ 08-9431 7878; www.fremantle trams.com) is actually a bus resembling an old-fashioned trolley car. It leaves from the town hall on a guided tour of historic Fremantle several times a day and you can hop on and off at other stops around town (adult/child $22/5). There's also a Friday night Ghostly Tour (adult/child $56/42, with fish-and-chip supper).

The **Spectacles Yargan Tours** (☎ 08-9431 7878; www.spectaclestours.com.au; ☺ Oct-Apr) offers a view of life and culture of the Beeliar Aboriginal people around the Kwinana wetlands, 20km south of Freo. The two-hour day/sunset tours ($20/39) include transfers from Freo.

FESTIVALS & EVENTS

Sardine Festival Fun for foodies in January, with a gourmet seafood fiesta.
Busker's Festival March/April.
Blessing of the Fleet October.
Festival of Fremantle This 10-day festival in November is the city's largest annual event, featuring street parades, concerts, exhibitions and free performances.

Check www.fremantlefestivals.com for other annual events.

SLEEPING
Budget

Old Firestation Backpackers (☎ 08-9430 5454; www .old-firestation.net; 18 Phillimore St; dm from $26, d from $70; ☐) The firefighters might have left, but there's still plenty of down-time entertainment in this scarlet converted fire station: free internet, foosball, Playstation and a sunny courtyard. Girls have their own space and the dorms and airy doubles are good value, with natural light and the afternoon sea breeze fluttering in.

Pirates (☎ 08-9335 6635; piratesbackpackers@westnet .com.au; 11 Essex St; dm from $26; ☐) This cosy, family-run hostel is in the thick of the Freo action is a top spot to socialise. Rooms are small but in great shape, and the girls-only bathroom upstairs is fresh and clean. The kitchen area is well equipped, there's a shady courtyard, and eye-catching wall murals of the sea remind you that an ocean swim is minutes away.

YHA Backpackers Inn Fremantle (☎ 08-9431 7065; bpinnfreo@yahoo.com.au; 11 Pakenham St; dm from $27, r without bathroom $67; ☐) New management has breathed fresh life into this historic-building YHA. Rooms are high, bright and clean. Flicks are shown on the mini cinema screen every night, there's a huge indoor recreation area, and it's close to the action.

Number Six (☎ 08-9252 1380; www.numbersix.com .au; studio/1-bedroom apt from $85/130) This operator has a number of self-contained and stylish studios, apartments and houses available for overnight to long-term stays in great locations around Freo.

Midrange

Fremantle Colonial Accommodation (☎ 08-9430 6568; www.fremantlecolonialaccommodation.com.au; 215 High St; B&B d $145, 2-bedroom apt $150, cottages from $180; ☒ ☐) Rambling two-storey terrace or historic prison cottage? Whichever you choose, both embrace the colonial theme with gusto.

Terrace Central B&B (☎ 08-9335 6600; www.ter racecentral.com.au; 83-85 South Tce; d from $155, 3-bedroom apt $200-300; ℗ ☒ ☐) Terrace Central may be a character-filled B&B at heart, but it's a spacious, quiet and stylish one, based around the original 1898 building. You'll find ample off-street parking – rare in Freo – and free wi-fi throughout.

Top End

Port Mill B&B (☎ 08-9433 3832; www.babs.com.au/ portmill; 3/17 Essex St; d from $200) One of the most luxurious B&Bs in town, it's clearly the love-child of Paris and Freo. Crafted from local limestone (built in 1862 as a mill), inside it's all modern Parisian style, with gleaming taps, contemporary French furniture and wrought-iron balconies.

Quest Harbour Village (☎ 08-9430 3888; www .questharbourvillage.com.au; Mews Rd, Challenger Harbour; 1-bedroom apt $277, 2-/3-bedroom apt from $315/420; ☒) This set of apartments has all harbour-facing rooms with balconies for maximum nautical exposure; one-bedroom units have a roadway between them and the ocean, others directly front the marina. Downstairs the rooms are light and simple, if a little dated, and kitchens are fully equipped. Upstairs has a more contemporary, spacious feel.

Camping

Both these caravan parks are pleasantly located along the coast south of Freo – 8km and 10km respectively – and are regularly served by buses along Cockburn Rd. Prices take a 30% or more hike in peak season.

Woodman Point Holiday Park (☎ 08-9434 1433; www.aspenparks.com.au; 132 Cockburn Rd, Munster; unpowered/powered sites from $26/30, chalets from $105; ▨ ▨ ▨) A particularly pleasant spot. It's in a bush setting and is just a short walk through a traffic-free reserve from the beach. Campers can pitch a tent here.

Coogee Beach Holiday Park (☎ 08-9418 1810; www .aspenparks.com.au; Cockburn Rd, Coogee; powered sites $34, cabins from $85) Right on the beach this large, shady, well-established caravan park is a top spot – there are no tent sites, though.

EATING

Eating and drinking your way around town are two of the great pleasures of Freo. The three main areas to browse before you graze are around the town centre, around Fishing Boat Harbour, and around East Freo's George St and riverbank. There's room for only some of our favourites below!

Town Centre

Gino's (☎ 08-9336 1464; 1 South Tce; mains $9-24) Old-school Gino's is Freo's most famous cafe, and while it's become a tourist attraction in its own right, the locals still treat it as their second living room, only with better coffee.

Moore & Moore (☎ 08-9335 8825; 46 Henry St; wraps $10; ▧ breakfast & lunch) An urban-chic cafe that spills into the adjoining art gallery and overflows into a flagstoned courtyard. Great coffee, good pastries, tasty wraps, free wi-fi.

Cafe 55 (☎ 08-9336 2604; 55 High St; soups $10; ▧ breakfast & lunch Mon-Sat) Vietnamese food with a Freo feel. The fragrant soups – *pho, pho ga* and laksa – are fantastic.

Juicy Beetroot (High St; dishes $10; ▧ lunch Mon-Fri) This meat-free zone serves tasty vego and vegan dishes of the wholefood variety, and zingy fresh juices. Read the wall posters for news of Freo's eclectic events. It's tucked up an alley off High St, with outdoor seating.

Maya (☎ 08-9335 2796; 77 Market St; mains from $20; ▧ lunch Fri, dinner Tue-Sun) Maya's white tablecloths and wooden chairs signal classic style. The well-executed Indian favourites make it a very popular local spot; the eggplant pakoras with fennel and tamarind dipping sauce ($12) are truly spectacular.

Fishing Boat Harbour

Cicerello's (☎ 08-9335 1911; mains $12-20; ▧ lunch & dinner) This busy fish 'n' chippery has been around since 1903 and remains a quintessential Freo experience. Choose your fish and chips, then pick a spot out on the boardwalk and soak up the sun – just watch those seagulls.

Little Creatures (☎ 08-9430 5555; www.littlecreatures .com.au; mains $18-25; ▧ lunch & dinner Mon-Fri, brunch & dinner Sat & Sun) Little Creatures is classic Freo: harbour views, fantastic brews (made on the premises) and excellent food. Try the classic chilli tomato mussels ($22) and wood-fired pizzas – the blue cheese, pear and rocket ($18) is sensational – while sampling the boutique beer menu. No bookings.

Mussel Bar (☎ 08-9433 1800; mains from $25; ▧ lunch & dinner Tue-Sun) For a more formal Freo experience, Mussel Bar's large glass windows afford romantic views of the glittering harbour. Mussels, of course, are the go – including traditional *moule marinieres* – or you can shuck fresh oysters ($4 each) with a glass of sunset bubbly.

East Fremantle

Red Herring (☎ 08-9339 1611; 26 Riverside Rd; mains $30; ▧ lunch & dinner daily, breakfast Sun) Set out on a deck with picture windows overlooking the Swan River, this great restaurant offers (mainly) seafood with a view. Fresh and simple is the key, with Asian touches to some dishes. Book well ahead.

DRINKING

Little Creatures (☎ 08-9430 5555; 40 Mews Rd, Fishing Boat Harbour; ▧ 10am-11pm Sun-Wed, to midnight Thu-Sat) In a huge old boatshed by the harbour, this brewery crafts award-winning ales of several different styles. Check out the brewing vats from the 2nd floor, or drink up on the deck and watch the boats out back. Creatures Loft (open Thursday to Sunday), a late-night lounge bar with regular live entertainment – and a great selection of international beers and wine to accompany the view – is attached.

Norfolk Hotel (☎ 08-9335 5405; 47 South Tce; ☯ 11am-midnight Mon-Sat, to 10pm Sun) A great selection of beers on tap – Asahi, Coopers, Becks, James Squire – gives you a good excuse to take your time here. The limestone courtyard, with the sun streaking in through the elms and eucalypts, is downright soporific sometimes.

Sail & Anchor (☎ 08-9335 8433; 64 South Tce; ☯ 11am-midnight Mon-Thu, to 1am Fri & Sat, to 10pm Sun) Built in 1854, this Fremantle landmark has been impressively restored to recall much of its former glory. Downstairs is big and beer-focused; it's more sedate upstairs, where a verandah overlooking the markets provides a perfect people-watching position.

Left Bank (☎ 08-9319 1315; 15 Riverside Rd, East Fremantle; ☯ 7.30am-midnight Mon-Sat, noon-9pm Sun) This Edwardian riverside inn, up from the East St jetty and overlooking the water, is patronised by lively young 'uns in the downstairs cafe and bar; upstairs is a more sedate dining room.

ENTERTAINMENT

Fly by Night Musician's Club (☎ 08-9430 5976; www .flybynight.org; Queen St) Variety is the key at Fly by Night, a not-for-profit club that's been run by musos for musos for years. All kinds perform here, and many – Eskimo Joe, the Waifs, the John Butler Trio – made a start here. It's opposite the car park below the Old Fremantle Prison.

Mojo's (☎ 08-9430 4010; www.mojosbar.com.au; 237 Queen Victoria St, North Fremantle; ☯ 7pm-late) Good old Mojo's is one of Freo's longstanding live-music pubs – a real stalwart. Local and national bands (mainly Australian rock and indie) and DJs play at this small venue, and there's a sociable beer garden out back. Rest one elbow on the bar and turn your attention to an up-and-coming local band. First Friday of the month is reggae night; every Monday is open-mic night.

Kulcha (☎ 08-9336 4544; www.kulcha.com.au; 1st fl, 13 South Tce) World music of all sorts is the focus here. There are also African drumming workshops. Book ahead.

Metropolis Fremantle (☎ 08-9336 1880; www .metropolisfremantle.com.au; 58 South Tce; ☯ 9pm-4am Fri, to 5am Sat) Most international and popular Australian bands and DJs perform here. It's a good space to watch a gig.

Local bands play most Sundays, with DJs other nights, at the **Newport Hotel** (☎ 08-9335 2428; www.thenewport.com; 2 South Tce; ☯ noon-10pm

Sun-Thu, to midnight Fri & Sat). DJs and bands also perform in the basement of the popular **Swan Hotel** (☎ 08-9335 2725; 201 Queen Victoria St, North Fremantle; ☯ 11am-10pm Mon, to midnight Tue-Sat, noon-10pm Sun).

Retro **Luna on SX** (☎ 08-9430 5999; www.lunapal ace.com.au; Essex St) is Freo's great art-house cinema. Blockbusters screen at **Hoyts** (☎ 08-9430 6988; www.hoyts.com.au; Millennium Collie St; Queensgate William St).

SHOPPING

The bottom end of the **High St** is the place for interesting and quirky shopping. Look for **Remedy** (☎ 08-9431 7080; 95 High St) with its eclectic collection of goodies; **New Edition Bookstore** (☎ 08-9335 2383; 82 High St), a bookworm's dream with comfy armchairs for browsing; **Record Finder** (☎ 08-9335 2770; 87 High St) for more vinyl than you thought possible; **Bodkin's Bootery** (☎ 08-9336 1484; 72 High St) for foot fashionistas; **Love in Tokyo** (☎ 08-9433 2110; 61-3 High St) for gorgeously fashioned fabrics; **Japingka** (☎ 08-9335 8265; 47 High St) for quality Aboriginal art; and **Bill Campbell Secondhand Bookseller** (☎ 08-9336 3060; 48 High St) for those out-of-print Penguin classics you always meant to read.

Kakulas Sister (☎ 08-9430 4445; 29-31 Market St) – a provedore packed with nuts, quince paste and Italian rocket seeds – is a cook's dream, and an excellent spot to stock up on energy-filled snacks. If you've been to Kakulas in Northbridge, you'll know the deal.

The Fremantle Markets (p923) are a good spot for clothes, crafts, souvenirs and picnic goodies.

GETTING THERE & AROUND

The **Fremantle Airport Shuttle** (☎ 08-9457 7150; www.fremantleairportshuttle.com.au) leaves to and from the airport several times daily ($35 per person). Services can be a bit erratic – they're often short of drivers – and bookings are essential.

The train between Perth and Fremantle runs every 10 minutes or so throughout the day ($3.50). There are countless buses between Perth city and Fremantle train station; they include buses 103, 106, 111, 158 and 107. Some buses travel via the Canning Hwy; others go via Mounts Bay Rd and Stirling Hwy.

Oceanic Cruises (☎ 08-9325 1191; www.oceaniccruises .com.au) runs several ferries a day from Perth's Barrack St Jetty to Freo (adult/child $21/13, return $31/20).

There is a plethora of one-way streets and parking meters in Freo. It's easy enough to travel by foot or on the free Fremantle CAT bus service, which takes in all the major sights on a continuous route every 10 minutes from 7.30am to 6pm on weekdays and 10am to 6pm on the weekend. A fun way to nip around town is by scooter (single/double $40/45 per two hours, $75/85 per day) or scoot car ($60 per hour) from **Scoot Freo** (☎ 08-9336 5933; www .scootfreo.com.au; 2 Phillimore St).

AROUND PERTH

ROTTNEST ISLAND
pop 475

'Rotto' is the family holiday playground of choice for Perth locals. About 19km from Fremantle, it's ringed by secluded tropical beaches and bays. Outdoor activities rule, and swimming, snorkelling, fishing, surfing and diving are just some of the popular things to do here. Cycling round the 11km-long, 4.5km-wide car-free island is a real pleasure; just ride around and pick your own bit of beach to spend the day on.

Rotto is also the site of annual school leavers' and end-of-uni-exams parties, a time when the island is overrun by kids partying night and day. Depending on your age, it's either going to be the best time you've ever had or the worst – check the calendar before proceeding.

At the time of research, a massive renovation/reconstruction/upgrade program was underway around Thomson Bay – expect further changes to have taken place by the time you read this.

QUOKKAS

The Aborigines knew the cute quokka as the *quak-a*, which was heard by Europeans as 'quokka'. These marsupials of the macropod family (along with kangaroos and wallabies) were once found throughout the southwest but are now confined to forest on the mainland and a population of 8000 to 12,000 on Rottnest Island. You will see plenty during your visit. Don't be surprised if one comes up to you looking for a titbit (don't oblige them, as human food isn't good for them) – many are almost tame.

History

There are signs of Aboriginal occupation on Rottnest dating from 7000 years ago, when a hill on a coastal plain became the island after being cut off by rising seas. It was, however, uninhabited when Europeans arrived. Dutch explorer Willem de Vlamingh claimed discovery of the island in 1696 and named it Rottenest ('rat's nest') because of the numerous king-sized 'rats' (quokkas) he saw there. The Noongar people knew it as Wadjemup.

The island has had a chequered human history. The settlement was originally established in 1838 as a prison for Aborigines from the mainland; Wadjemup Aboriginal Cemetery remembers those who never left. Although there were no new Aboriginal prisoners after 1903 (by which time holiday-makers from the mainland had already dicovered the island), by 1915 during WWI the island was briefly a prisoner-of-war camp. In more peaceful times it became the holiday destination it remains.

Information

At the Thomson Bay settlement, behind the main jetty, there's a shopping area with ATMs, a general store and a bottle shop.
Post office (◷ 9am-1pm & 1.30-4pm Mon-Fri) Inside the gift shop.
Ranger (☎ 08-9372 9788; ◷ 24hr)
Rottnest Island website (www.rottnestisland.com)
Visitors centre (☎ 08-9372 9752; ◷ 7.30am-5pm Sat-Thu, to 7pm Fri) At the main jetty.

Sights & Activities

All year round, the small but informative **Rottnest Museum** (☎ 08-9372 9753; Kitson St; admission by donation; ◷ 11am-3.30pm) has exhibits about the natural and human history of the island.

The photographic exhibition at the 19th-century **Salt Store** (Colebatch Ave; ◷ 8.30am-4pm) deals with a different chapter of local history when, between 1838 and 1950, the island's salt lakes provided all of WA's salt. You can also wander around convict-built buildings such as the octagonal 1864 **Quod** (18th-century British slang for 'prison'), where the prison cells are now hotel rooms. Other **Heritage buildings** and interesting information boards are dotted around town and the island. Not far away is (unsigned) **Vlamingh's Lookout**. Go up past the old cemetery for panoramic views of the island. Also of interest is the **Oliver Hill Battery**, 3.2km from the Thomson Bay settlement. This gun battery was built in the 1930s

AROUND PERTH

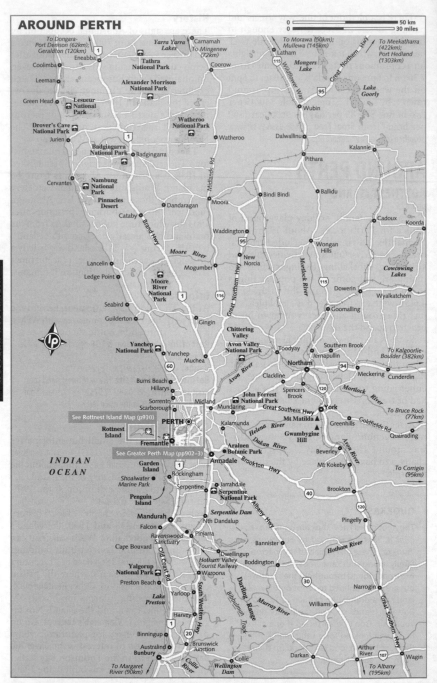

WESTERN AUSTRALIA

and played a major role in the defence of the WA coastline and Fremantle harbour.

Most visitors come for Rottnest's **beaches** and water activities. **Surfing** is big at Strickland, Salmon and Stark Bays at the west end of the island, while **swimmers** prefer the Basin (protected by a ring of reefs) and Longreach and Geordie Bays. Excellent visibility in the temperate waters, coral and shipwrecks appeal to **scuba divers** and **snorkellers**; snorkel trails are at Little Salmon Bay and Parker Point. When we visited, tenders were out for a new island-based dive operator; check the island website for updates.

The **Family Fun Park** (☎ 08-9292 5156; adult/child $9.50/6.50, trampolines per 10min $4; 9am-4pm) is the spot for putt-putt and trampolines. Hire bikes from **Rottnest Bike Hire** (☎ 08-9292 5105; bike.hire@ rottnestisland.com; multigear/single-gear bike per day $24/19, bond $25; 8.30am-4pm).

Tours

From the Salt Store you can join a volunteer guide on one of the **free daily walks** (11am, 1pm & 2pm) that take in a variety of the settlement's historic buildings, the **Wadjemup Aboriginal cemetery**, the sea wall and boat sheds, the **chapel** and the Quod.

A 90-minute **bus tour** (adult/child/family $30/15/67.50; 11am, 1.30pm & 1.45pm) leaves from the main bus stop. There's also an **Oliver Hill Train & Guns tour** (adult/child/family $18/9/44; 1.30pm), which takes you by train to the gun and tunnel on Oliver Hill.

From November to March, **Capricorn Kayak** (☎ 08-6267 8059; www.capricornseakayaking.com.au; half-day tours $99) runs sea-kayaking tours around the Rottnest coastline.

Enjoy the reef and wrecks from above the water in the **Underwater Explorer** (adult/child $23/15). Tours last 45 minutes and leave from the main jetty four times daily September to May; contact the visitors centre for times.

Expect some seasonal variation in all dates and times.

Sleeping & Eating

Rotto is wildly popular in summer and school holidays, when accommodation is booked out months in advance. Prices can rise steeply at these times – low-season rates are given here. Book online at www.rottnestisland.com for the campsites, youth hostel and cottages.

Kingston Barracks Youth Hostel (☎ 08-9432 9111; dm $27;) If you stay in these old army barracks you might find yourself fighting with school groups for a spot in front of the potbelly stove. Check in at the accommodation office at the main jetty before you make the 1.8km walk, bike or bus trip to Kingston.

Rottnest Island Authority Cottages (☎ 08-9432 9111; per night from $51-355) There are more than 250 refurbished houses and cottages around the island to suit all budgets. Some have magnificent beachfront positions and are palatial; others are more like beach shacks. Linen provided. Note that there are off-season discounts.

Rottnest Lodge (☎ 08-9292 5161; www.rottnestlodge .com.au; Kitson St; d/f from $165-225;   ) It's claimed there are ghosts in this cool, comfortable complex, which is based around the former Quod and boys' reformatory school. If that worries you, ask for one of the cheery rooms with a view in the new section fronting the salt lake. Its Marlins restaurant offers a small, creative menu (mains from $25).

Hotel Rottnest (☎ 08-9292 5011; www.hotelrottnest .com.au; 1 Bedford Ave) The 1894 Quokka Arms was once the governor's summer holiday pad. More recently it's been the island's pub, with a few rooms devoted to accommodation. It was closed for major renovations and upgrades when we visited. But by the time you read this, it will have started a new life as Hotel Rottnest, with rooms in the $200 to $300 bracket and a fine-dining restaurant. Try reception@hotelrottnest.com.au for current information.

Camping ground (☎ 08-9432 9111; Thomson Bay; sites per person $9) Camping is restricted to just 18 sites on a small, leafy camping ground that has barbecues. It's known as Tentland by the surfers, students and families who colonise this patch of Rotto. Be vigilant about your belongings.

Most visitors to Rotto self-cater. The general store is like a small supermarket, but if you're staying a while, better bring supplies with you. Day trippers can get by with the coffee shop, bakery and a couple of fast food outlets at the shopping area; there's also a cafe at Geordie Bay that opens in summer.

Getting There & Away

Apart from their points of departure, all ferry services are basically the same. Return trips are around $53/24 per adult/child from Fremantle (25 minutes), $69/34 from Perth (1½ hours) and $72/33 (40 minutes) from Hillarys Boat

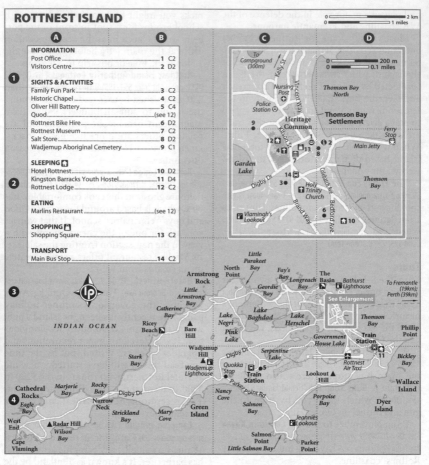

Harbour. Each company offers transfers only, or transfer and accommodation packages.

Rottnest Express (☎ 1300 467 688; www.rottnestexpress.com.au) departs Fremantle (C Shed, Victoria Quay) about five times daily, and Northport terminal, Fremantle, about four times daily. There's a thrice-daily service from Perth. Secure parking is available at Northport.

Oceanic Cruises (☎ 08-9325 1191; www.oceaniccruises.com.au) departs Perth about three times daily. From Fremantle, there's a service from the East St jetty once in the morning and from the B Shed about four times daily.

Rottnest Fast Ferries (☎ 08-9246 1039; www.rottnestfastferries.com.au) runs trips from Hillarys Boat Harbour to Rotto three times daily, from September to June.

Rottnest Air-Taxi (☎ 1800 500 006; www.rottnest.de) has a same-day return fare from Jandakot airport in Perth starting at \$270. Extended return is \$320. This price is for a three-passenger plane.

Getting Around

Bicycles are the time-honoured way of getting around the island. Rotto is just big enough (and with enough hills) to make a day's ride good exercise. Hire a bike from one of the ferry companies or on-island. Helmets (compulsory) and locks (bicycles are often stolen) are provided.

Two bus services leave from the main bus stop. A free shuttle bus runs between the main accommodation areas and the airport, departing about every 30 minutes, with the last bus at 7pm. The **Bayseeker** (day pass adult/child/family $10/5/22.50; ⏱ 8.30am-3.30pm) is a jump-on, jump-off service that does an hourly loop around the island.

NORTH OF PERTH

The coast north of Perth is windswept and barren, and although the sprawling sands look inviting, these beaches are much better for water sports. Expect winter seaweed washed up on the beaches. Popular with day-trippers is **Yanchep National Park** (admission per vehicle $10), 51km north of Perth. It's a pretty bushland park with plentiful wildlife, including a koala compound. Visitors can explore the limestone **Crystal Cave**, row boats ($6.50 per 30 minutes) on **Loch McNess**, or hike some of the nine walking tracks (from 20 minutes up to three days).

Lancelin
pop 700

What do you do when the beach is windy? Harness yourself to a really big kite and strap yourself to a surfboard, of course! Afternoon offshore winds and shallows protected by an outlying reef make for perfect kitesurfing and windsurfing conditions at lazy, low-key Lancelin. The town (130km north of Perth) plays host to action-seekers from around the world because of its consistently windy conditions in summer. In January it's a veritable festival of wind-worshippers during the **Ocean Classic race** (www.lancelinoceanclassic.com.au), which starts at Ledge Point.

SIGHTS & ACTIVITIES

Head to the beach and watch the windsurfers and kitesurfers whoop it up. If you're inspired, **Werner's Hot Spot** (☎ 08-9655 1448) offers windsurfing ($20 per hour) and kitesurfing ($25/70 per hour/day) lessons. Werner also hires out boards and gear from his Kombi parked at the beach from October to March (phone at other times and he'll come to meet you). There are gentle waves at the main beach for 'traditional' surfing; learn to surf locally with **Surfschool** (☎ 1800 198 121; www.surfschool.com), which offers one-off lessons ($55 per 2½ hours) as well as surf and accommodation packages.

Desert Storm Adventures (☎ 08-9655 2550; www.desertstorm.com.au; adult/child $45/30) takes delighted (sometimes shrieking) travellers on a wild ride

daily through the dunes aboard 'the world's largest 4WD tour coach'.

SLEEPING & EATING

Lancelin Lodge YHA (☎ 08-9655 2020; www.lancelinlodge.com.au; 10 Hopkins St; dm $28, d $70; ☐ ☒) This award-winning hostel is well equipped and welcoming, with wide verandahs and lots of communal spaces to spread about. Catering mainly to windsurfers, the excellent facilities include a big kitchen, barbecue, wood-fire pizza oven, decent-sized swimming pool, ping-pong table, volleyball court, and push-bikes and boogie boards!

Windsurfer Beach Chalets (☎ 08-9655 1454; www.lancelinaccommodation.com.au; 1 Hopkins St; d from $140, extra person $30) A good choice for groups of friends and families (each chalet sleeps up to six), these simple, self-contained two-bedroom chalets are the closest accommodation to the windsurfing beach. They're functional and well equipped; book well in advance at holiday time.

Lancelin Caravan Park (☎ 08-9655 1056; Hopkins St; unpowered/powered sites per person $12/14, on-site cabins $70) Sailboarders love camping out at this neat park – not for the facilities and amenities, which are rudimentary, but for the location. This is as close to the beach as you can get.

Eat at Offshore Café, which serves decent coffee and burgers as well as Indonesian and Thai main dishes ($15). Coffee and cake is served among the knick-knacks at Isabella's Cottage. Both the Endeavour Hotel and Lancelin Beach Hotel have beer gardens on the waterfront. There are two small supermarkets, and takeaways along Gingin Rd.

GETTING THERE & AWAY

Catch-a-Bus (☎ 08-9655 2020; fare $30) is the only bus service to Lancelin. It's a private shuttle service run by the Lancelin Lodge YHA for guests, offering drop-offs and pick-ups between Perth and Lancelin on demand (minimum two passengers).

Cervantes & Pinnacles Desert
pop 500

The cruisy crayfishing town **Cervantes**, 245km north of Perth, is a wise overnight stop for enjoying the **Pinnacles Desert** at sunset, full moon or dawn when the light is sublime and the crowds thin. Go during crayfishing season (mid-November to June), when the fresh, sweet crustaceans provide another compelling reason

WESTERN AUSTRALIA

to visit (their almost-as-delicious frozen relatives are available year-round).

Get information on accommodation, and wildflower and Pinnacles tours at Cervantes' combined **post office and visitors centre** (☎ 08-9652 7700; www.visitpinnaclescountry.com.au; Cadiz St; ◷ 7.30am-5pm). The town's general store, liquor shop, internet access and takeaway are also in this small shopping centre.

SIGHTS & ACTIVITIES
Nambung National Park (bus passenger/car $4/10), 17km from Cervantes, is home to the spectacular and otherworldly **Pinnacles Desert**, where thousands of limestone pillars are scattered across a moonlike landscape on a golden desert floor. The lime-rich desert sand originated from seashells, which compacted with rain and subsequently eroded, forming individual pillars, some towering up to 5m. A good gravel loop-road runs through the formations and you can stop to walk among them. Also in the park, and accessible from the main road in, two gravel tracks lead for a kilometre or so to beaches at **Kangaroo Point** and **Hangover Bay**, which is good for a dip. Gas barbecues and tables are in prime locations here.

In town climb the 70 steps to **Hansen Bay Lookout** for fabulous views across the coast, and visit **Lake Thetis** where living **stromatolites** – the world's oldest organisms – can be seen on the edges of the lake when the water level drops in summer. Walkways wend along the town's coastline and to the beaches.

In wildflower season take the gorgeous 18km scenic drive through the remote biodiversity hot spot of **Lesueur National Park**. About 10% of WA's plant species are found here, many bursting into bloom in late winter and spring. It's about 50km northeast of Cervantes via Jurien.

TOURS
Turquoise Coast Enviro Tours (☎ 08-9652 7047; www.pinnacletours.info; 59 Seville St; 3hr Pinnacles tour $40) leads highly regarded 2½-hour walks. Guided by ex-park-ranger Mike Newton, they leave Cervantes at 8am and 2½ hours before sunset.

Along the coast in Jurien, 22km from Cervantes, **Jurien Sea Lion Charters** (☎ 08-9652 1109; www.juriencharters.com; 2hr tours adult/child $85/30) offers an opportunity to visit sea lion colonies on offshore islands.

SLEEPING & EATING
Cervantes Lodge & Pinnacles Beach Backpackers (☎ 1800 245 232, 08-9652 7377; www.cervanteslodge.com .au; 91 Seville St; dm $28, d with/without bathroom $110/75) Travellers love the communal kitchen, the proximity of the beach, and the cosy and comfortable lounge area. The bright, spacious ensuite rooms are in the detached lodge, most with views of heath and ocean.

Pinnacles Caravan Park (☎ 08-9652 7060; www.pin naclespark.com.au; 35 Aragon St; unpowered/powered sites from $18/22, on-site vans/cabins $50/70) This shady park is in prime tent-pitching position next to the beach with simple, good-value accommodation. On-site Seashells Cafe – which has a good collection of shells on display – does a mean coffee and cake on the waterfront patio.

In town eat at the Seabreeze Cafe; the Ronsard Bay Tavern, with its fireplace, bigscreen TV, dartboards and pool table; or the Country Club, where the crayfish platter ($55 for two) is unforgettable.

GETTING THERE & AWAY
Greyhound (☎ 13 20 30; www.greyhound.com.au) has services from Cervantes to Perth ($50, four hours, daily) and Geraldton ($50, 2½ hours, daily) via Jurien (20 minutes) and Leeman (35 minutes).

SOUTH OF PERTH
Holiday homes, tranquil fishing spots and sleepy towns – which turn crazy-busy in school holidays – fringe the soft contours of the coast south of Perth. Here's where many Western Australians spend a lazy week or few at the beach each year.

GETTING THERE & AWAY
Transperth buses buzz back and forth between Fremantle and Rockingham many times a day (number 920 or 825, 45 minutes), with frequent stops en route. From Perth city train station catch one of the frequent Mandurah trains (50 minutes), all of which stop in Rockingham (40 minutes), and which are met by buses to the towns' centres.

The *Australind* train service stops at Pinjarra twice daily, but there's no public transport to Dwellingup.

Rockingham
pop 91,700
The quiet seaside town Rockingham, some 47km south of Perth, was founded in 1872 as

a port, although over time this function was taken over by Fremantle.

Rockingham itself doesn't have much to offer travellers. By contrast, offshore **Shoalwater Marine Park** is one of the great highlights of the region and makes a great day tour from Perth or Freo. Here you can watch dolphins, sea lions and fairy penguins in the wild in a pristine, beautifully preserved environment.

The **visitors centre** (☎ 08-9592 3464; 43 Kent St; ☺ 9am-5pm Mon-Fri, to 4pm Sat & Sun) has plenty of information and accommodation listings if you want to overnight.

SHOALWATER MARINE PARK

Just a few minutes' paddle, swim or boat ride from the mainland is tiny, fabulous and strictly protected **Penguin Island**. Home to – at last count – 600 breeding pairs of seriously cute little penguins, and several thousand pairs of ground-nesting and in-your-face silver gulls, the island also has an informal and informative feeding centre (for long-term injured or orphaned penguins), boardwalks, swimming beaches and picnic tables for day visitors. It's lovely and low-key (but visit out of peak season if you can). Nearby **Seal Island** is home to a haul-out colony of Australian sea lions, visible only on a 45-minute glass-bottom boat tour.

Only one tour operator is licensed to take visitors to the islands. Multi-ecotour-award-winner **Rockingham Wild Encounters** (☎ 08-9591 1333; www.rockinghamwildencounters.com.au) offers an impressive array of low-impact high-experience tours (some of which are seasonal), including dolphin-swim tours (from Perth or Rockingham $195 per adult); dolphin-watch half-day tours (from Perth/Rockingham $75/55 per adult); dolphin, penguin and sea-lion day tours (from Perth/Rockingham $114/94 per adult); and combined penguin and sea-lion cruises (from Rockingham only, adult/child $35/26).

Getting There & Away

From Rockingham train station, buses run roughly every half hour near to Mersey Point Jetty (153 Arcadia Dr).

The *Penguin Express* ferry leaves from the jetty hourly (adult/child return $18/15, includes entry to the feeding centre) between 9am and 3pm (last boat back at 4pm). At low tide it's possible to wade the few hundred metres to the island across the sandbar; if you

get stranded, a one-way ferry ride in either direction is $6.50.

Mandurah
pop 60,600

This formerly sleepy waterside town, 75km south of Perth on the Mandurah Estuary, is booming. Its canals and estuary are popular for fishing, crabbing, prawning (March to April) and dolphin-spotting. It's another good day-trip destination from Perth or Freo.

The **visitors centre** (☎ 08-9550 3999; 75 Mandurah Tce; ☺ 9am-4.30pm Mon-Fri, 9.30am-4pm Sat & Sun), on the estuary boardwalk, is well informed and can set you up with a place to stay if you choose to overnight.

SIGHTS & ACTIVITIES

Take a stroll between the decidedly moneyed marina at **Boat Harbour** and the more relaxed and family-friendly **foreshore**, where a heritage walking trail highlights the town's history. Cafes and boardwalks – both great for people-watching – abound. Start at the centrally located visitors centre, from where you can walk, take short **dolphin-spotting cruises** of the estuary, or check out what's happening at the **Mandurah Performing Arts Centre**.

Dwellingup
pop 835

Dwellingup is a small, forest-covered township with character. Primarily it's a base for hiking, cycling, swimming and canoeing on the Murray – the surrounding area is filled with adventure. It's 97km south of Perth. You'll find good bush camping at Lane Poole Reserve a few kilometres out of town, a gallery or two to browse through, and a couple of stores and cafes.

The **Bibbulmun Track** (www.bibbulmuntrack.org.au) passes through this timber town on its journey southwards, and the **Munda Biddi** (www.mundabiddi.org.au) bike trail passes through here to Collie and will eventually reach Albany. The **Hotham Valley Tourist Railway** (☎ 08-9221 4444; www.hothamvalleyrailway.com.au) runs various steam and other vintage train trips in the valley during weekends and school holidays (adult/child from $18/9). See the **visitors centre** (☎ 08-9538 1108; Marrinup St; ☺ 9am-4.30pm Mon-Fri, 10am-3pm Sat & Sun) for more information.

Don't waste any time getting out to the beautiful Murray. The cheery and efficient

WESTERN AUSTRALIA

Dwellingup Adventures (☎ 08-9538 1127; www.dwell ingupadventures.com.au; ☿ 8.30am-5pm) is the place to hire bikes ($22 per day) and one-person kayaks or two-person canoes ($32 per day). Or join a paddling tour (half-day one-person kayaks $55); white-water rafting tours from June to October start at $110. Camping gear can also be hired, and good river-route and bike-track maps are available.

The **Forest Heritage Centre** (☎ 08-9538 1395; www.forestheritagecentre.com.au; Acacia St; ☿ 10am-5pm) is an interesting architect-designed rammed-earth building in the shape of three gum leaves with a woodwork gallery and workshop – it's home to the Australian School of Fine Wood, which offers occasional weekend courses. Three walking trails (adult/child $5.50/2.20) lead off from the centre.

Yalgorup National Park

Fifty kilometres south of Mandurah is the beautiful coastal Yalgorup National Park, a region of woodlands, tranquil lakes and coastal sand dunes. The park is recognised as a wetland of international significance for seasonally migrating waterbirds, so **birdwatching** here can be rewarding. Amateur scientists can visit the distinctive **thrombalites** of Lake Clifton, descendants of some of the earliest living organisms on earth. These rocklike structures are most easily seen when the water is low, usually in March and April.

THE SOUTHWEST

The farmland, forests, rivers and coast of the lush, green southwestern corner of WA are simply magnificent. Bottlenose dolphins and whales frolic offshore while devoted surfers search for the perfect line on perfect waves. On land, world-class wineries beckon and tall trees provide enticing shade for walking trails and scenic drives. Unusually for WA, distances between the many attractions are short, and drive-time is mercifully limited, making it a fantastic area to explore for a few days – and you will get much more out of your stay here if you have your own wheels. Summer brings hordes of visitors, but in the wintery months from July to September the cosy pot-belly stove rules and visitors are scarce, and while opening hours can be somewhat erratic, the low-season prices shown here are good value.

Getting There & Away

South West Coach Lines (☎ in Perth 08-9324 2333, in Bunbury 08-9791 1955, in Busselton 08-9754 1666; www .southwestcoachlines.com.au) runs daily bus services from Perth to the following places:

Transwa (☎ 1300 662 205; www.transwa.wa.gov.au) buses service Pemberton, and the *Australind* train service travels from Perth to Bunbury ($26, 2½ hours) twice daily.

TRAVELLING THE SOUTHWEST BY BUS		
Destination	Price ($)	Duration (hr)
Augusta	40	6
Balingup	34	5½
Bridgetown	34	4½
Bunbury	25	3
Busselton	30	4
Dunsborough	32	4½
Manjimup	40	5
Margaret River	34	5½

BUNBURY
pop 31,600

Bunbury, 184km south of Perth, is transforming itself from industrial port to seaside holiday destination. This small city centre – with some stately colonial buildings – is bordered by a sweeping coastal walk and bike track, several parks and reserves, and an upgraded and trendy harbour area.

The **visitors centre** (☎ 08-9721 7922; www.vis itbunbury.com.au; Carmody Pl; ☿ 9am-4.30pm Mon-Sat, 10am-2pm Sun) is in the old 1904 train station, with an internet cafe next door.

Activities

Make a morning visit to the **Dolphin Discovery Centre** (☎ 08-9791 3088; www.dolphindiscovery.com.au; Koombana Beach; adult/child $8/4; ☿ 8am-3pm Oct & Nov, 8am-4pm Dec-Apr, 9am-2pm May & Jun), where pods of about 100 bottlenose dolphins regularly feed in the inner harbour, most frequently between November and April. Dolphin interaction tours by boat run from November to April (swim/watch $135/65). Nearby is the **Mangrove Boardwalk**, by the shores of bird-haven Leschenault Inlet.

Sleeping

Dolphin Retreat YHA (☎ 08-9792 4690; www.dol phinretreatbunbury.com.au; 14 Wellington St; dm/s/d $26/45/66; 🖳) Just around the corner from

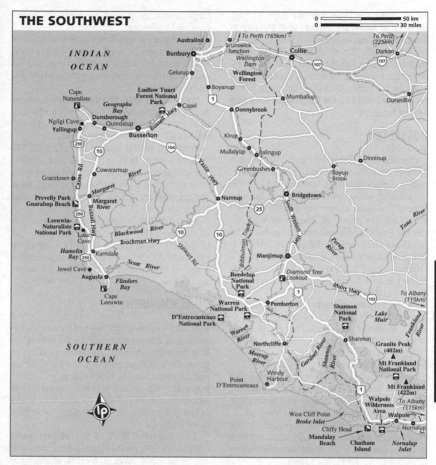

THE SOUTHWEST

WESTERN AUSTRALIA

the beach, this small and popular hostel is well located in a rabbit-warren of an old house, with hammocks and a barbecue on the back verandah.

Wander Inn Backpackers (☎ 08-9721 3242; www .bunburybackpackers.com.au; 16 Clifton St; dm/s/d $27/47/68; 🖳) Down a quiet side street, between the beach and the main strip, this busy hostel has good adventure tours and cruises. Look for the cheerful blue-and-yellow house.

Rose Hotel (☎ 08-9721 4533; www.rosehotel.com .au; cnr Victoria & Wellington Sts; r $75-105) From the chandeliers hanging in the halls to the bloke wearing the armour in the lobby, the 1865 Rose Hotel oozes character. Go for the old-style hotel rooms upstairs – they're charming, even with a shared bathroom. A delightfully

old-fashioned dining room serves tasty and filling meals (mains from $20).

Lighthouse Beach Resort (☎ 08-9721 2700; www .lighthousehotel.com.au; Carey St; r from $110, apt $160; 🖵 🖳) In a fabulous setting above (you guessed it) Lighthouse Beach, the two-room self-contained apartment here is a winner. The small indoor pool means swimming's an option all year.

Eating & Drinking

Mojo's (☎ 08-9792 5900; Victoria St; lunch/dinner from $20/35) Mojo's is stylish and comfortable, whether you go just for coffee or for the full (and very good) fresh-food experience.

At Boat Harbour, check out trendy **VAT Two** (☎ 08-9791 8833; 2 Jetty Rd; mains from $30; 🕑 lunch &

dinner), and be sure to eat fish and chips ($10) on the deck at **Aristos Waterfront** (☎ 08-9791 6477; 15 Bonnefoi Blvd; 🕑 lunch & early dinner). The big beer garden at **Fitzgerald's** (Victoria St; 🕑 6pm-late Thu-Sun) serves traditional pub meals ($13) with a relaxed vibe – go for the ever-popular Sunday session.

For good coffee, breakfast or a light lunch try **Benesse** (Victoria St), **Caf-fez** (20 Prinsep St) or **Café 140** (140 Victoria St).

BUSSELTON
pop 27,500

On the shores of Geographe Bay, 230km south of Perth, Busselton is a popular holiday resort with a slightly faded air. Surrounded by calm waters and white-sand beaches, its famous jetty is the main attraction. Family-friendly Busselton has plenty of diversionary activities for lively kids; think playgrounds on the foreshore, sheltered beaches, waterslides, animal farms and even a classic drive-in cinema. During school holidays, the population increases fourfold, and accommodation is fully booked and pricey.

Busselton's **visitors centre** (☎ 08-9752 1288; www .geographebay.com; cnr Causeway Rd & Peel Tce; 🕑 9am-5pm Mon-Fri, 9am-4pm Sat, 10am-2pm Sun) has a huge range of tourist information.

Sights & Activities

The town boasts the longest **timber jetty** in the southern hemisphere, at 2km. Constructed in 1865, a mammoth closure and renovation program is planned, but at the time of research you could still walk its length. At the shore end is a free and friendly small **museum**; at the ocean end is the **underwater observatory** (adult/child $23/13; 🕑 10.30am-3.30pm).

Diving is popular, especially on Four Mile Reef (a 40km limestone ledge about 6.5km off the coast) and on the scuttled Navy vessel HMAS *Swan* off Dunsborough. The **Dive Shed** (☎ 08-9754 1615; www.diveshed.com.au; 21a Queen St) can take you out.

Sleeping & Eating

Observatory Guesthouse (☎ 1800 180 343; www .observatory-guesthouse.com; 7 Brown St; s/d $90/105) A five-minute walk from the jetty, this friendly B&B guesthouse has bright, cheerful rooms and a communal sea-facing balcony.

Blue Bay Apartments (☎ 08-9751 1796; www.blue bayapartments.com; cnr Brown & Adelaide Sts; apt from $95) Just a stone's throw from the beach, these good-value self-contained apartments are bright and cheery, each with private courtyard and barbecue.

Kookaburra Caravan Park (☎ 08-9752 1516; kook park@compwest.net.au; tents $27, cabins $60-75) In a great location on the waterfront and just a short walk from town, this is a good option for budget travellers.

Equinox Cafe (☎ 08-9752 4641; www.theequinox.com .au; Jetty foreshore; lunches $15) Lower-key and somewhat more relaxed than its goosy neighbour, this is a fine waterfront hang-out.

Vasse (☎ 08-9754 8560; 44 Queen St; mains $20; 🕑 lunch & dinner) Join the locals and sit outside eating good cafe fare and drinking beer, wine or coffee; in the evenings it has a busy bar atmosphere. There are several vego and vegan options.

Goose (☎ 08-9754 7700; www.thegoose.com.au; Jetty foreshore; mains $25; 🕑 Tue-Sat) At the shore end of the jetty, this stylish restaurant offers an eclectic and interesting seasonal menu; coffee is served all day, and there's wireless internet access, too.

DUNSBOROUGH
pop 3200

Relaxed Dunsborough, west of Busselton, has developed into an increasingly chichi destination for affluent Perth weekenders; it's now generally too expensive for the local family holidays that used to be its mainstay. It's also popular with school leavers, thousands of whom descend to party for a couple of weeks in late November/early December – you have been warned.

The cheerful staff at the **visitors centre** (☎ 08-9755 3299; www.geographebay.com; Naturaliste Tce; 🕑 9am-5pm) have a wealth of regional information.

Sights & Activities

Northwest of Dunsborough, Cape Naturaliste Rd leads to the excellent beaches of **Meelup**, **Eagle Bay** and **Bunker Bay** (take a coffee break and absorb the stunning view at Bunkers Beach Café on the way); some fine coastal walks and lookouts; and the **Cape Naturaliste lighthouse** (☎ 08-9755 3955; adult/child $11/9.50; 🕑 9.30am-4pm), built in 1903.

Whale-watching for humpbacks and southern rights is a regular pastime between September and December. **Naturaliste Charters** (☎ 0428 938 056; www.whales-australia.com) offers two-hour whale-watching tours by boat (adult/ child $65/35). The southernmost nesting

---

SURFING THE SOUTHWEST

Known colloquially to surfers as 'Yal's' and 'Margaret's', the beaches between Capes Naturaliste and Leeuwin offer powerful reef breaks, mainly left-handers (the direction you take after catching a wave). The surf at Margaret's has been described by surfing supremo Nat Young as 'epic', and by world surfing champ Mark Richards as 'one of the world's finest'.

The better locations include Rocky Point (short left-hander), the Farm and Bone Yards (right-hander), Three Bears (Papa, Mama and Baby, of course), Yallingup (breaks left and right), Injidup Car Park and Injidup Point (right-hand tube on a heavy swell; left-hander), Guillotine/Gallows (right-hander), South Point (popular break), Left-Handers (the name says it all) and Margaret River (with Southside or 'Suicides').

Pick up a surfing map ($5) from the Dunsborough visitors centre on the way through, and check out **Yallingup Surf School** (www.yallingupsurfschool.com) if you need some help with your technique.

---

colony of the red-tailed tropicbird is at scenic **Sugarloaf Rock**.

There has been excellent diving in Geographe Bay since the decommissioned Navy destroyer HMAS *Swan* was purpose-scuttled in 1997 for use as a dive wreck. It lies at a depth of 30m, 2.5km offshore. **Cape Dive** (☎ 08-9756 8778; www.capedive.com; 222 Naturaliste Tce; 2-tank dive from $195) offers dives and dive courses.

Sleeping & Eating

There are many, many self-contained apartments scattered along the waterfront; the visitors centre can help.

Dunsborough Inn (☎ 08-9756 7277; www.dunsboroughinn.com; 50 Dunn Bay Rd; dm/d $25/50, units $90-139; 🖳) Budget rooms are fine here, but while it's central the surroundings are more concrete than coast; you're only five minutes' walk from the beach, though. Ask for a room away from the road.

Dunsborough Beachouse (☎ 08-9755 3107; www.dunsboroughbeachouse.com.au; 205 Geographe Bay Rd; dm/s/d $27/45/66; 🖳) On the Quindalup beachfront, Dunsborough Beachouse is a friendly hostel with the best beach location in town; plus it's an easy 2km cycle from the town centre.

Dunsborough Rail Carriages & Farm Cottages (☎ 08-9755 3865; www.dunsborough.com; Commonage Rd; rail carriages from $100, cottages from $140) Refurbished rail carriages are dotted about this big bush block near Quindalup, as are self-contained timber cottages, which are spacious for families. Kids will have fun with the friendly sheep and chooks.

Cape Wine Bar (☎ 08-9756 7650; 239 Naturaliste Tce; mains from $20; 🕑 dinner Mon-Thu, tasting plates at the bar Fri & Sat, tapas Sun) Buzzing most nights, this wine bar has a well-deserved reputation for fresh seasonal and regional food.

Artezen (☎ 08-9755 3325; 234 Naturaliste Tce; mains from $20; 🕑 7am-5pm Sun-Thu) This super-cool cafe serves everything from great breakfasts to interesting Asian-influenced dishes such as squid salad with soba.

Other choices include Inji Bar at the Dunsborough Hotel (good counter food and sports TV); Bambooe (cheap and cheerful Asian food); Evviva Café (fresh juices and salads); and Yallingup Coffee Roasting Company (great coffee, no food).

YALLINGUP
pop 1050

Yallingup, surrounded by scenic coastline and fine beaches, is a surfing mecca (see Surfing the Southwest, above); if you prefer dry land, a series of beautiful **walking trails** tracks the coast between here and Smith's Beach.

Between Dunsborough and Yallingup, is mystical **Ngilgi Cave** (☎ 08-9755 1288; adult/child $18/9; 🕑 9.30am-4.30pm, last entry 3.30pm); a series of well-marked bushwalks also starts here. **Wardan Cultural Centre** (☎ 08-9756 6566; www.wardan.com.au; adult/child $15/8; 🕑 10am-4pm, but closed Tue & Sat Apr-Aug, closed July), 6km south, is a place of stories, bush tucker, dancers, didgeridoo and other aspects of the local Wardandi culture.

Sleeping & Eating

Yallingup Beach Caravan Park (☎ 08-9755 2164; www.yallingupbeach.com.au; Valley Rd; sites $28, cabins from $80) You'll sleep to the sound of the surf here, with the beach just across the road from the rolling lawns.

Seashells Caves House Yallingup (☎ 08-9750 1500; www.seashells.com.au; Yallingup Beach Rd; r $175-395) Built in the 1930s, this splendid lodge has undergone a major shift upmarket. Impeccably renovated – think high ceilings, polished wood, comfortable leather sofas – the rooms are gorgeous and the restaurant offers a creative menu.

Drinking

Wicked Ale Brewery (☎ 08-9755 2848; www.wickedalebrewery.com.au; Caves Rd; ☽ 10am-5pm) This is a small-scale and eccentric brewery in a great bush setting.

MARGARET RIVER

pop 4415

The ample attractions of Margaret River – top surf, undulating bushland, some of Australia's best wineries and gourmet local produce – make it one of WA's most popular destinations, and a place where travellers can often find seasonal harvest work. It gets very, *very* busy at Easter and Christmas (when you should book weeks, if not months, ahead), during the annual food and wine bash in November (www.mrwinefest.org.au), during surf competitions in March and November,

and at the time of the renowned Leeuwin Estate open-air concerts in February.

Information

Cybercorner Cafe (2/72 Willmott Ave; ☽ 9am-5pm) Check your email here.
Visitors centre (☎ 08-9757 2911; www.margaretriver .com; Bussell Hwy; ☽ 9am-5pm) This sleek visitors centre has wads of information, as well as an on-site wine centre.

Sights & Activities

You'll find yourself zipping up and down Caves Rd (stretching from Yallingup to Augusta) and the Bussell Hwy, taking in countless attractions in between – there's only room to mention a few here.

Drop by the **Margaret River Regional Wine Centre** (☎ 08-9755 5501; www.mrwines.com; 9 Bussell Hwy, Cowaramup; ☽ 10am-7pm Mon-Sat, to 6pm Sun), where the knowledgeable staff can plan a vineyard itinerary for you and will ship wine to almost anywhere in the world.

Eagles Heritage Raptor Wildlife Centre (☎ 08-9757 2960; www.eaglesheritage.com.au; adult/child $11/5; ☽ 10am-5pm), 5km south of Margaret River on

WESTERN AUSTRALIA

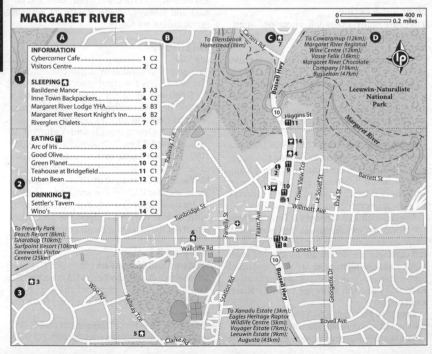

MARGARET RIVER

0 ——— 400 m
0 ——— 0.2 miles

INFORMATION	
Cybercorner Cafe	1 C2
Visitors Centre	2 C2

SLEEPING 🏠	
Basildene Manor	3 A3
Inne Town Backpackers	4 C2
Margaret River Lodge YHA	5 B3
Margaret River Resort Knight's Inn	6 B2
Riverglen Chalets	7 C1

EATING 🍴	
Arc of Iris	8 C3
Good Olive	9 C2
Green Planet	10 C2
Teahouse at Bridgefield	11 C1
Urban Bean	12 C3

DRINKING 🍷	
Settler's Tavern	13 C2
Wino's	14 C2

To Ellensbrook Homestead (8km)

Carters Rd

To Cowaramup (12km);
Margaret River Regional
Wine Centre (12km);
Vasse Felix (16km);
Margaret River Chocolate
Company (19km);
Busselton (47km)

Leeuwin-Naturaliste
National
Park

Margaret River

Higgins St

Barrett St

Railway Tce

Tunbridge St

Farrelly St

Wallcliffe Rd

Fearn Ave

Town View Tce

Le Souëf St

Elva St

Willmott Ave

Forrest St

Georgette Dr

Station Rd

Bussell Hwy

Clarke Rd

Bovell Ave

To Prevelly Park
Beach Resort (8km);
Gnarabup (10km);
Surfpoint Resort (10km);
Caveworks Visitor
Centre (25km)

To Xanadu Estate (3km);
Eagles Heritage Raptor
Wildlife Centre (5km);
Voyager Estate (7km);
Leeuwin Estate (9km);
Augusta (43km)

Wise Rd

Railway Tce

WINING & DINING

A number of great vineyards in Margaret River are equally renowned for their dining. The region produces highly regarded Cabernets and dry whites. Here's some that do both very well:

Leeuwin Estate (☎ 08-9759 0000; www.leeuwinestate.com.au; Stevens Rd, Margaret River) A brilliant estate, with excellent wines (taste the Art Series Chardonnay), a stylish cellar door, a highly regarded restaurant and an annual sell-out concert series.

Vasse Felix (☎ 08-9756 5000; www.vassefelix.com.au; cnr Caves & Harmans Rds, South Cowaramup) A good all-round winery with a fabulous art collection.

Voyager Estate (☎ 08-9757 6354; www.voyagerestate.com.au; Stevens Rd, Margaret River) A true gem, with great wines across the board and an elegant cellar door and restaurant.

Xanadu Estate (☎ 08-9757 2581; www.xanaduwines.com; Terry Rd, Margaret River) A broad range (including its popular Secession label) and a decent cellar door and restaurant.

Boodjidup Rd, rehabilitates birds of prey. There are flight displays at 11am and 1.30pm.

At the **Margaret River Chocolate Company** (☎ 08-9755 6555; www.chocolatefactory.com.au; Harman's South Rd, Willyabrup; 🕑 9am-5pm) sample a bag of chilli choc and macadamia, but try not to loiter by the chocolate massage oil.

A beautiful National Trust property 8km northwest of town, the 1857 **Ellensbrook Homestead** (adult/child $4/2; 🕑 house 10am-4pm Sat, Sun & public holidays, grounds open daily) was the first home of pioneer settlers Alfred and Ellen Bussell, who were led by local Noongar people to this sheltered site, with its supply of fresh water. It's a great picnic spot.

Caveworks visitor centre (☎ 08-9757 7411; www .margaretriver.com; Caves Rd; 🕑 9am-5pm), about 25km from Margaret River, has excellent screen displays about the many caves of the region and cave conservation, a 'cave crawl' experience, and cave tours. Fees apply to some of these.

Tours

Bushtucker Tours (☎ 08-9757 9084; www.bush tuckertours.com; adult/child $80/30) The four-hour trip combines walking and canoeing up the Margaret River, and features aspects of Aboriginal culture along with uses of flora and a bush-tucker lunch.

Margaret River Tours (☎ 0419 917 166; www.marga retrivertours.com) One of the longest-standing local operators; runs combined-wineries-sightseeing tours (half-/ full day $70/110) or can arrange charters.

Wine for Dudes (☎ 0427 774 994; www.winefordudes .com; tours $75) Includes pick-up and drop-off, a tour of a working winery along with tastings and wine blendings, and lunch.

Sleeping

Book well in advance and, except for budget accommodation (where good weekly rates are offered to travellers who stay to work a while), expect to pay at least $30 a night more than in other country towns; low-season rates are given here.

Inne Town Backpackers (☎ 1800 244 115; www.inne town.com; 93 Bussell Hwy; dm/s/d $25/60/65; 🖳) In a converted house between the river and town, this smallish hostel is in a great location; check its noticeboards for work opportunities in town.

Margaret River Lodge YHA (☎ 08-9757 9532; www.mr lodge.com.au; 220 Railway Tce; dm/s/d/f $25/60/65/76; 🖳 🖳) About 1.5km southwest of the town centre, this is clean and modern with a pool and volleyball court in sizeable gardens. Again, you'll find info about available seasonal work here.

Surfpoint Resort (☎ 1800 071 777, 08-9757 1777; www.surfpoint.com.au; Gnarabup Beach; dm/d $25/95; 🖳 🖳) Offers the beach on a budget, rents boogie boards and surfboards, and offers lessons from an expert.

Riverglen Chalets (☎ 08-9757 2101; www.riverg lenchalets.com.au; Carters Rd; chalets $115-220; 🐾) Just north of town, these timber chalets are spacious and fully self-contained, with verandahs looking out onto bushland; there's full disabled access to a couple of them.

Margaret River Resort Knight's Inn (☎ 08-9757 0000; www.mrresort.com.au; 40 Wallcliffe Rd; motel/hotel/villas $130/140/230; 🐾 🖳) Ignore the dinky exterior: the jarrah-dense hotel rooms here are big and gorgeous, and the motel rooms luxurious.

Basildene Manor (☎ 08-9757 3140; www.basildene .com.au; Wallcliffe Rd; d $259-399; 🐾 🖳) Basildene – a historic 1912 home converted into a luxury B&B hotel, set in the middle of landscaped gardens with views of karri forest – is simply magnificent.

Prevelly Park Beach Resort (☎ 08-9757 2374; campsites per person $11-17, vans $50-90, cabins $80-120) It's a good budget option on the hill above the

WESTERN AUSTRALIA

beach, though you'll want your own transport to get to the water.

Eating & Drinking

Sniff out a feast along the Bussell Hwy, which is the town centre.

Urban Bean (☎ 08-9757 3480; 157 Bussell Hwy; lunches $7-10; ☽ 7.30am-4pm) A funky little place serving bleary-eyed locals their first daily brew, selling loose-leaf tea and coffee, and making good fresh things for lunch such as yummy mushroom risotto pie ($8).

Green Planet (Bussell Hwy; dishes $10; ☽ noon-9pm) A cosy vego cafe, doing a relaxed line in tasty tofu burgers, salads and soups. Dreadlocks optional.

Teahouse at Bridgefield (☎ 08-9757 3007; 73 Bussell Hwy; lunch $10-15; ☽ breakfast & lunch) Good country cooking here, with hearty soups to warm the cockles in winter, and great morning and afternoon teas served on the sheltered verandah.

Good Olive (☎ 08-9758 7877; www.tgo.com; 97 Bussell Hwy; mains $15; ☽ breakfast & lunch) An informal cafe-cum-deli serving local produce; try the platter of olives and cheeses.

Arc of Iris (☎ 08-9757 3112; 151 Bussell Hwy; mains $25; ☽ dinner) This lively old favourite has an eclectic, creative menu.

Settler's Tavern (☎ 08-9757 2398; 114 Bussell Hwy; ☽ 11am-late) There's live music regularly at Settler's, so settle in for the evening with good pub grub and a choice of 13 beers and 18 wines by the glass.

Wino's (☎ 08-9758 7155; 85 Bussell Hwy; ☽ 3pm-late) Leather lounges, bentwood chairs and plenty of local wines to sample (choose a taste, a glass or a bottle) make this modern bar a great place in which to wine and dine.

AUGUSTA

pop 1070

Augusta is 5km north of Cape Leeuwin, where the Indian and Southern Oceans meet and the magnificent Blackwood River rolls into the sea. This is the most southwesterly point in Australia and on an exhilarating, wild day you fear being blown off the edge of the earth.

The **visitors centre** (☎ 08-9758 0166; www.marga retriver.com; cnr Blackwood Ave & Ellis St; ☽ 9am-5pm) has a range of information.

Sights & Activities

Whale-watching happens at Cape Leeuwin between June and August. **Naturaliste Charters**

(☎ 08-9758 0111; www.whales-australia.com) offers two-hour whale-watching tours by boat (adult/child $65/35). **Sea Dragon** (☎ 08-9758 4003) and **Miss Flinders** (☎ 0439 424 455; www.missflinders.com) operate Blackwood River 'eco-cruises' (adult/child $25/10), usually leaving mid-morning; both close for a while over winter.

Cape Leeuwin lighthouse (☎ 08-9757 7411; lighthouse tour/grounds only $12/5; ☽ 8.45am-5pm), opened in 1896, has magnificent views of the coastline at the point where the oceans meet. Enjoy a good coffee at the attached cafe.

Augusta Historical Museum (Blackwood Ave; adult/child $3/2; ☽ 10am-noon & 2-4pm Sep-Apr & school holidays, 10am-noon May-Aug) has interesting local exhibits.

Sleeping & Eating

Baywatch Manor Resort (☎ 08-9758 1290; www.bay watchmanor.com.au; 88 Blackwood Ave; dm/s/d $22/55/58, s/d with bathroom $75/78; ☐) Standards are being maintained here with lots of clean, modern rooms and great facilities (including a room equipped for disabled travellers). Ask about the self-contained options around town.

Riverside Cottages (☎ 08-9758 1545; www.riverside cottagesaugusta.com.au; Molloy St; cottages $60-100) A tad tatty but clean and great value, various-sized self-contained cottages sit on the riverbank. Cottage number 8 is perfect for two, with a small balcony overlooking the river.

Augusta Hotel Motel (☎ 08-9758 1944; www.au gusta-resorts.com.au; Blackwood Ave; r from $110) Go for the rooms with river views in this rambling waterside property dating from 1912.

Hamelin Bay Caravan Park (☎ 08-9758 5540; hamelinbay@bordernet.com.au; unpowered/powered sites from $20/25, cabins $60-110) On the beach a few kilometres north of Augusta, this secluded gem of a place gets very busy at holiday times.

Augusta Bakery & Cafe (☎ 08-9758 1664; 121 Blackwood Ave; snacks/meals $5/16; ☽ breakfast & lunch) Bakes good bread daily, with attached cafe where light lunches are served.

Colourpatch Café (☎ 08-9758 1295; 38 Albany Tce; takeaway/dine-in $10/25; ☽ lunch & dinner) Watch the Blackwood River meet the waters of Flinders Bay at the self-styled 'last eating house before the Antarctic', which sells fish from the ocean across the road.

SOUTHERN FORESTS

The tall forests of WA's southwest are world famous, and rightly so. They are simply superb, with a musical combination of karri, jarrah and marri trees sheltering cool undergrowth. Small towns in between the forests bear witness to the region's history of logging and mining; most have redefined themselves as low-key tourist centres from where you can bushwalk, take wine tours or go on canoe trips and trout- and marron-fishing expeditions. Their backdrop is verdant farmland and meandering rivers, such as the Blackwood, making their way through the landscape to the sea.

The area of 'tall trees' lies between the Vasse Hwy and the South Western Hwy, and includes the timber towns of Bridgetown, Manjimup, Nannup, Pemberton and Northcliffe. The back-road drives are truly spectacular.

Nannup

pop 1200

Nannup's historic weatherboard buildings and cottage gardens are in an idyllic bush setting, 290km from Perth on the Blackwood River. It's a good base for bushwalkers and canoeists. The **Nannup Music Festival** (www.nannupmusicfestival.org) is held in early March.

The area is home to the legendary Nannup tiger. It's a striped wolflike animal, 'sighted' so rarely that it's taken on the nature of a rural myth. Check out the tiger press-clippings in the **visitors centre** (☎ 08-9756 1211; www.nannupwa.com; Brockman St; ⏲ 9am-5pm), in the 1922 police station. Garden-lovers should head to **Blythe Gardens** (admission by donation), just across the road, which has a wonderful mix of native and exotic plants. You can walk, cycle, swim and camp in pretty **St John Brook Conservation Park**, 8km west of Nannup.

SLEEPING & EATING

Accommodation in Nannup tends towards B&Bs and self-contained cottages; the visitors centre can find you a bed, or book you a site at the **caravan park** (unpowered/powered sites $19/22, cabins $65) on the riverbank next door.

Maranup Ford (☎ 08-9761 1200; powered sites/cabins $20/65) Out of town, this working farm is part of the Land for Wildlife network, which is committed to sustainable farming practices. It's low-key with a small camping area and one cabin close to the river; canoes are available. It's 30km from Nannup, off the Bridgetown road.

Wilton's Bistro (☎ 08-9756 1287; 1 Warren Rd; mains $25; ⏲ lunch Thu-Mon, dinner Fri & Sat) Serves substantial fare, with local specialities such as lamb on the menu.

There are a couple of decent coffee shops in the main street.

SOUTHWEST HIGHWAY

Winding through a gorgeous setting of karri forests and farmland along the Blackwood River, this main regional road passes through some gems of towns that deserve more than just a pit stop.

Balingup, Bridgetown & Boyup Brook

Balingup (population 443) was first settled in 1859, and is home to a variety of arty, foodie, farming and hippy types. The **visitors centre** (☎ 08-9764 1818; www.ballinguptourism.com.au; ⏲ 10am-3pm) is beside the pub. Cute and tiny **Hiker's Hideaway** (☎ 08-9764 1049; hotbunks@wn.com.au; behind the post office; dm $28) offers budget accommodation – rare around here – and is popular with Bibbulmun Track walkers; book well ahead. Between Balingup and Bridgetown, drop into the historic mining and timber township of **Greenbushes**, where some splendid decaying buildings from the boom days line the road.

Bridgetown (population 2300) is one of the loveliest little towns in the southwest. Despite being busy most weekends, and overrun with visitors on the second weekend of November during its annual **Blues at Bridgetown Festival** (www.bluesatbridgetown.com), it retains a great community feel. The town's **visitors centre** (☎ 08-9761 1740; www.bridgetown.com.au; 54 Hampton St; ⏲ 10am-5pm Mon-Fri, to 1pm Sat & Sun) is on the main road. Bridgetown's historic buildings include **Bridgedale House** (☎ 08-9761 1740; Hampton St; admission $3; ⏲ 10am-2pm Fri-Sun), which was built of mud and clay by the area's first settler in 1862.

In town, stay at **Nelsons of Bridgetown** (☎ 08-9761 1645; www.nelsonsofbridgetown.com.au; 38 Hampton St; r $105-185;). The central location is great, but go for the spacious new rooms built to the side of this 1898 Federation-style hotel. The **caravan park** (☎ 08-9761 1740; www.bridgetowncaravanpark.com.au; powered sites $20, on-site vans $60) is on the riverbank, just over the bridge south of town. Out of town, **Bridgetown Riverside Chalets** (☎ 08-9761 1040; www.bridgetownchalets.com.au; 1338 Brockman Hwy; chalets $105) are on a spectacular farm on the road to Nannup, and come equipped with pot-bellied stoves and washing machines, wide views and friendly cows.

Coffee shops and restaurants abound in Bridgetown. **Bridgetown Pottery & Tearooms** (☎ 08-9761 1038; Hampton St; ⏲ breakfast & lunch), in an 1870s cottage with an outdoor verandah and an indoor open fire, cooks up a storm for locals and visitors alike. **Cidery** (☎ 08-9761 2204; 43 Gifford Rd; ☻ lunch Wed-Mon) serves local alcoholic and nonalcoholic ciders – tasting of delicious Pink Lady apples – and light lunches on outdoor tables by the river. **Bridgetown Hotel** (☎ 08-9761 1034; Hampton St; ☻ lunch & dinner) offers a mix of a restaurant, a bar and regular live bands.

Nearby, the pretty township of **Boyup Brook** (population 530) is the centre of country music in WA. The fantastically over-the-top **Harvey Dickson's Country Music Centre** (☎ 08-9765 1125; www.harveydickson.com.au; adult/child $5/2; ☻ 9am-5pm) comes complete with a life-sized Elvis, an Elvis room and three 13.5m-tall guitar-playing men. It hosts regular rodeos and big-name country music events, as well as the **WA Country Music Festival** in February. Scenic but basic **bush camping** (per site $8) is always available.

Pemberton
pop 750

Deep in the karri forests, and at the centre of yet another promising wine and food industry, is the delightful town of Pemberton; a few days here is time well spent.

INFORMATION
DEC (☎ 08-9776 1207; Kennedy St; ☻ 8am-4.30pm Mon-Fri) Detailed information on the many local parks and walking tracks.
Pemberton Telecentre (Brockman St; ☻ 9am-5pm Mon-Fri, to noon Sat) Check your email here.
Visitors centre (☎ 08-9776 1133; www.pemberton tourist.com.au; Brockman St; ☻ 9am-5pm) Includes a pioneer museum and karri-forest discovery centre; it's also the place for Transwa bookings.

SIGHTS & ACTIVITIES
The forests around Pemberton are simply stunning. Aim to spend at least a day, or preferably two, driving the well-marked **Karri Forest Explorer** tracks, walking the trails and picnicking in the green depths. Popular attractions include the **Gloucester Tree**, laddered with a daunting metal spiral stairway that winds 60m to the top, and the **Dave Evans Bicentennial Tree**, tallest of the 'climbing trees' at 68m, in Warren National Park, 11km south of Pemberton. The Karri Forest Explorer track makes a one-way driving loop via **Maiden Bush** to the **Heartbreak Trail**, passing

through 400-year-old karri stands; nearby **Drafty's Camp** and **Warren Campsite** are delightful for overnighting or bush picnics. Take a short scenic walk at **Beedelup National Park**, 15km west of town, where the bridge that crosses Beedelup Brook near **Beedelup Falls** was built from a single karri log.

Wend through marri and karri forests on the scenic **Pemberton Tramway** (☎ 08-9776 1322; www.pemtram.com.au; Pemberton Railway Station; adult/child $18/9) daily at 10.45am and 2pm.

In lush gardens, the **Fine Woodcraft Gallery** (☎ 08-9776 1399; Dickinson St; ☻ 9am-5pm) has truly beautiful pieces, all mastercrafted from salvaged timber.

Last but by no means least, the wines of Pemberton's burgeoning wine industry attract favourable comparison to those from Burgundy; check at the visitors centre for wineries that are open to visitors. The **Pemberton Wine Centre** (☎ 08-9776 1211; www.marima.com.au; ☻ noon-5pm Mon-Fri, 10am-5pm Sat & Sun), in Warren National Park, offers tastings of most local wines, and can pack a mixed box to your taste.

TOURS
Pemberton Discovery Tours (☎ 08-9776 0484; www.pembertondiscoverytours.com.au) Operates half-day 4WD tours to the stunning Yeagarup sand dunes and the Warren River mouth (adult/child $85/50), and can tailor tours to suit. You're welcome to tag along in your own 4WD. Aiming to be carbon neutral, the company offsets its commercial vehicle use and is privately reforesting property in WA's arid wheatbelt.
Pemberton Hiking & Canoeing (☎ 08-9776 1559; www.pembertonwa.com; half-day tours per adult/child $50/20 per person) Runs long-standing, well-regarded and environmentally sound walks and canoe trips through forest, clear rivers and sand dunes.

SLEEPING & EATING
Pemberton Backpackers YHA (☎ 08-9776 1105; pem bertonbackpackers@wn.com.au; 7 Brockman St; dm/s/d/ cottages $24/38/59/79; ☐) This hostel, right in the centre of town, keeps its finger on the pulse of seasonal work opportunities and has small dorms (weekly rate $165) often full of long-term working travellers. Other guests sleep in the hostel's well-equipped, self-contained two- or three-room cottages, within walking distance around town.

Gloucester Motel (☎ 08-9776 1266; Ellis St; r $77-90) This is the best choice of the motels in town; cheaper rooms are a bit tattier than the others,

BONZA BACKROADS – D'ENTRECASTEAUX NATIONAL PARK

This quiet gem of a national park, named for French admiral Bruny D'Entrecasteaux, who explored here in 1792, stretches for 130km along the coast 60km south of Pemberton. It's a complete contrast to the tall forests, with its wild stretches of heath, sand dunes, cliffs and beaches.

Windy Harbour is a collection of ramshackle holiday shacks with names such as 'Wywurk'. You can camp here as long as you're self-sufficient. A wild and (you guessed it) windy coastal walk stretches about 3km from Windy Harbour to Point D'Entrecasteaux. The roads around this section of the park are sealed.

A series of decent 4WD tracks leads in from the Pemberton–Northcliffe Rd to bush and beach campsites; locals regularly go in to fish. On the way, the tiny timber town of **Northcliffe** has forest walks and a friendly cluster of museum buildings beside the very impressive visitors centre at the junction.

but have a much nicer outlook. The creative restaurant menu offers local goodies including fresh trout ($22).

Marima Cottages (☎ 08-9776 1211; www.marima .com.au; Old Vasse Rd; cottages from $195) Right in the middle of Warren National Park, these four country-style rammed-earth-and-cedar cottages with pot-belly stoves and lots of privacy are luxurious getaways.

Pemberton Caravan Park (☎ 08-9776 1300; www .pembertonpark.com.au; Pump Hill Rd; sites $25, cabins $60-95) Set in a shady clearing beside a creek, this pretty camping area has good-value cabins and is just a walk away from Pemberton's natural swimming pool.

You can also get away from it all at campsites in Warren National Park; contact **DEC** (☎ 08-9776 1207) for details.

Coffee Connection (☎ 08-9776 1159; Dickinson St; mains $8-15; ☼ breakfast & lunch) There are several cafes in town, but this one is our favourite. It is attached to the Fine Woodcraft Gallery, with a garden setting, good coffee, and inexpensive meals with vegetarian and vegan options.

King Trout Restaurant & Marron Farm (☎ 08-9776 1352; cnr Northcliffe & Old Vasse Rds; mains from $15; ☼ 9.30am-5pm Fri-Tue) The menu at this cafe showcases trout and marron prepared in more ways than we previously imagined possible. You can even hire a rod and hook your own; it can be cleaned and cooked on site (for a fee).

Shannon National Park

The 535-sq-km Shannon National Park is on the South Western Hwy, 53km south of Manjimup. Until 1968 Shannon was the site of WA's biggest timber mill, and plants including deciduous trees from the northern hemisphere are some of the few reminders of the old settlement.

The 48km **Great Forest Trees Drive** is a one-way loop, split by the highway. Start at the park day-use area on the north of the highway. From here there's also an easy 3.5km walk to the Shannon Dam (via a quokka observation deck) and a steeper 5.5km loop to Mokare's Rock, with a boardwalk and great views. Further along, the 8km-return **Great Forest Trees Walk** crosses the Shannon River. Off the southern part of the drive, boardwalks look over stands of giant karri at **Snake Gully** and **Big Tree Grove**.

There is one fine and sizeable park camping area in the spot where the original timber-milling town used to be. A self-contained bunkhouse, Shannon Lodge, is available for groups of up to eight people; book this through **DEC** (☎ 08-9776 1207) in Pemberton.

SOUTH COAST

The South Coast, or 'Great Southern', offers all things to all people. Almost everywhere you look is stunning coastline, interspersed with 386,000 hectares of tall forest, including the famous Valley of the Giants; early colonial history and heritage in Albany; and artisanal food, wine and craft. Stretching from Walpole-Nornalup in the west to Cape Arid, east of Esperance, the area is a nature-lover's paradise, with spectacular (and often empty) beaches and some of the best mountainous national parks in Australia, exemplified by the ecological 'islands' of the dramatic Stirling Range and the ancient granite spires of the Porongurups.

Getting There & Away

SkyWest Airlines (☎ 1300 660 088; www.skywest .com.au) flies daily from Perth to Albany and Esperance.

WESTERN AUSTRALIA

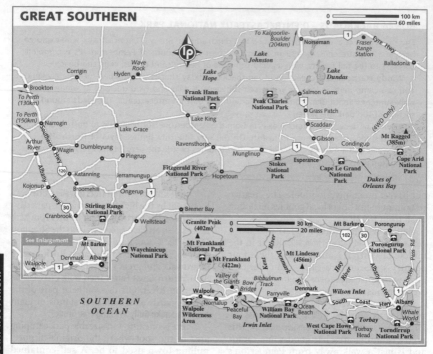

Transwa (☎ 1300 662 205; www.transwa.wa.gov.au) runs bus services between Perth and Denmark ($60, eight hours), Albany ($51, six hours) and Esperance ($77, 10 hours); some services go via Walpole. You can also travel by train from Perth to Bunbury, then by coach from Bunbury to Albany. Transwa runs a service several times a week from Kalgoorlie-Boulder to Esperance ($49, five hours).

To make the most of your time in the region, especially its national parks, your own wheels really are the best option.

WALPOLE-NORNALUP AREA

The peaceful twin inlets of Walpole and Nornalup make good bases from which to explore the heavily forested Walpole Wilderness Area. This surrounds Nornalup Inlet and the town of Walpole with beaches, rugged coastline and inlets, and wanders inland to Mt Frankland and the magnificent Valley of the Giants (when you're under the tall forest canopy, you'll understand the name). The South Western Hwy almost meets the coast at the two inlets, then becomes the South Coast Hwy.

Information

DEC (☎ 08-9840 1027; South Coast Hwy, Walpole; ☷ 9am-4pm Mon-Fri) Has detailed national park and bushwalking information.

Visitors centre (☎ 08-9840 1111; www.walpole.com.au; South Coast Hwy, Walpole; ☷ 9am-5pm Mon-Sat, to 4pm Sun) The helpful Walpole visitors centre is in Pioneer Cottage.

Sights & Activities

The **Tree Top Walk** (☎ 08-9840 8263; adult/child $8/4; ☷ 9am-4.15pm, Christmas school holidays 8am-5.15pm) has become Walpole's main drawcard. A 600m-long ramp gently rises from the floor of the **Valley of the Giants**, allowing visitors access high into the canopy of the giant tingle trees. At its highest point, the ramp is 40m above the ground and the views are simply stunning. The ramp is an engineering feat in itself, though vertigo sufferers might have a few problems; it's designed to sway gently in the breeze, mimicking life in the tree tops. At ground level, the **Ancient Empire** boardwalk meanders around and through the base of veteran red tingles, some of which are 16m in circumference.

The Valley of the Giants is part of the **Walpole Wilderness Area**, which comprises several national parks. Old forests fringe granite peaks, calm rivers and wetlands, sandy beaches and wild coast. Look for *Exploring the Walpole Wilderness and Surrounding Area*, a terrific booklet produced by DEC. There are numerous good walking tracks around, including a section of the **Bibbulmun Track** (see p898), which passes through Walpole to Coalmine Beach (two hours). There are several **scenic drives**, including the Valley of the Giants Rd; the drive through rolling pastoral country to Mt Frankland, 29km north of Walpole, where you can climb to the summit for panoramic views or walk around the trail at its base; and Knoll Dr, 3km east of Walpole, which accesses several beaches. Opposite Knoll Dr, Hilltop Rd leads to a giant tingle tree; this road continues to the **Circular Pool** on the Frankland River, a popular canoeing spot.

A trip to Walpole should include the ever-popular **WOW Wilderness Cruise** (☎ 08-9840 1036; www.wowwilderness.com.au) through the inlets and river systems. This magnificent landscape and its ecology are brought to life with anecdotes about Aboriginal settlement, salmon fishers and shipwrecked pirates. A 2½-hour trip (adult/child $40/15) leaves daily at 10am.

The Frankland River, lined with karri and tingle trees, is peaceful and great for canoeing. Hire canoes from **Nornalup Riverside Chalets** (☎ 08-9840 1107; South Coast Hwy, Nornalup) for $20 per hour or $45/60 per half-/full day.

Midway between Nornalup and Peaceful Bay, check out **Conspicuous Cliffs**. It's a great spot for whale-watching from July to November, with a boardwalk, hilltop lookout and steepish 800m walk to the beach.

Sleeping & Eating

Tingle All Over YHA (☎ 08-9840 1041; tingleallover2000@ yahoo.com.au; Nockolds St, Walpole; dm/s/d $22/44/65) Exercise your brain with the giant chess set in the garden at this clean, comfortable option near the highway.

Walpole Lodge (☎ 08-9840 1244; www.walpolelodge .com.au; cnr Pier St & Park Ave, Walpole; dm/s/d $25/40/55; 🖳) This popular place is basic, open-plan and informal, with great info boards around the walls and casual, cheery owners.

Nornalup Riverside Chalets (☎ 08-9840 1107; www.walpole.org.au/nornalupriversidechalets; Riverside Dr, Nornalup; chalets $80-125) Stay a night in sleepy Nornalup in these comfortable, colourful self-contained chalets, just a rod's throw from the fish in the Frankland River. One is adapted for disabled access.

Riverside Retreat (☎ 08-9840 1255; www.riversideretreat.com.au; chalets from $130) Set up off the road and on the banks of the beautiful Frankland River, these quiet, private and well-equipped chalets are great value, with pot-bellied stoves for cosy winter warmth and tennis and canoeing as outdoor pursuits.

Coalmine Beach (☎ 08-9840 1026; www.coalminebeach .com.au; Knoll Dr, Walpole; sites per 1-2 people unpowered $16-22, powered $19-26, cabins from $68) You couldn't get a better location than this, under shady trees above the sheltered waters of the inlet.

Rest Point Holiday Village (☎ 08-9840 1032; www.rest point.com.au; Rest Point; sites $22, cabins from $65) On wide lawns with direct waterfrontage is a spacious, pet-friendly site, with shade for campers and a range of self-contained accommodation.

See the Walpole office of **DEC** (☎ 08-9840 1027) for wilderness camping options.

In Walpole, stop by for a casual coffee at the Top Deck Café or a filling counter meal at the Walpole Hotel Motel. Better still, head to **Thurlby Herb Farm** (☎ 08-9840 1249; www.thurlbyherb .com.au; Gardiner Rd), 15km north of town, which distils its own essential oils, makes herb-based products including soap, and serves up tasty light lunches and cakes – accompanied by fresh-picked herbal teas ($4) – in a pretty cafe overlooking the garden.

DENMARK
pop 4000
The first wave of sea- and tree-changers looking for an alternative lifestyle found idyllic

---

BONZA BACKROADS – MANDALAY BEACH

About 13km west of Walpole, at Crystal Springs, is a good 8km gravel road to **Mandalay Beach**, where the *Mandalay*, a Norwegian barque, was wrecked on the beach in 1911. As the sand gradually builds and erodes with storms, the wreck eerily appears every 10 years or so, in shallow water that is walkable at low tide (check out the photos at Walpole visitors centre). The beach is glorious, often deserted, and accessed by an impressive boardwalk across sand dunes and cliffs. It's now part of D'Entrecasteaux National Park.

Book your stay at lonelyplanet.com/hotels

Denmark about 20 years ago. Its beaches and coastline, river and sheltered inlet, forested backdrop and rolling hinterland ensure the continuing presence of a varied, creative and environmentally aware community. Farmers, ferals, fishers, families and folk of all sorts mingle during the town's three market weekends each year, when the population and accommodation prices soar.

Denmark was established to supply timber to the early goldfields. Known by Noongar people as Koorabup ('place of the black swan'), there's evidence of early Aboriginal settlement in the 3000-year-old fish traps found in Wilson Inlet.

Information

Denmark Environment Centre (☎ 08-9848 1644; 33 Strickland St; ☽ 10am-4pm Mon-Fri, to noon Sat) Resource for local environmental info, natural history books and green products.

Telecentre (☎ 08-9848 2842; ☽ 10am-4pm Mon-Fri) Internet access; next door to the library.

Visitors Centre (☎ 08-9848 2055; www.denmark.com .au; South Coast Hwy; ☽ 9am-5pm) Good information, accommodation booking service, gift- and bookshop, and temporary local exhibitions.

Sights & Activities

Surfers and anglers usually waste no time in heading to rugged **Ocean Beach**. If you're keen to try surfing, accredited local instructor Mike Neunuebel gives **surf lessons** (☎ 08-9848 2057; 2hr private/group lessons $45/75). More placidly, **Denmark Dinghy Hire** (☎ 0429 421 786; canoe per hr/half-day $20/30, paddle boat per half hr $10; ☽ Sep-May) can set you up with boats for messing about on the river, and can take Bibbulmun Track walkers by boat across the inlet ($40 per transfer).

To get your bearings, walk the **Mokare Heritage Trail** (3km circuit along the Denmark River) or the **Wilson Inlet Trail** (12km return, starting at the river mouth). Put everything into perspective at **Mt Shadforth Lookout**, with its view of fine coastal scenery. The lush **Mt Shadforth Rd**, running from the centre of town and finishing up on the South Coast Hwy west of town makes a great scenic drive, as does the longer pastoral loop of **Scotsdale Rd**. Potter along these, taking your pick of attractions including alpaca farms, wineries, cheese farms, and art and craft galleries.

William Bay National Park, about 20km west of town, offers sheltered swimming in stunning

Greens Pool and **Elephant Rocks**, and has good walking tracks. Swing by **Bartholomews Meadery** (☎ 08-9840 9349; South Coast Hwy; ☽ 9am-4.30pm) for a post-beach treat of house mead – honey wine – or delicious homemade honey-rose-almond ice cream ($4).

Sleeping

Blue Wren Travellers' Rest YHA (☎ 08-9848 3300; www .denmarkbluewren.com.au; 17 Price St; dm/d $26/64; 🖳) Chooks live under this little timber house and everyone spoils the goofy house dog. Great info panels cover the walls, and it's small enough (just 20 beds) to have a homey feel.

Chimes Spa Retreat (☎ 08-9848 2255; www.chimes .com.au; Mt Shadforth Rd; r $230-355; 🔀 🖳) At the top end of the scale, this luxurious, architect-designed and tastefully decorated resort perched above town has a Balinese aesthetic.

Caravan parks in town are in great locations and offer – as well as good tent/van sites (from $20/30 for two people) – the only other budget accommodation in town in the form of on-site vans/cabins (from $50/70). **Ocean Beach Caravan Park** (☎ 08-9848 1105; www .oceanbeachcaravanpark.com.au) is just about on the beach; **Rivermouth Caravan Park** (☎ 08-9848 1262; www.denmarkrivermouthcaravanpark.com.au) is – you guessed it – at the mouth of the river.

Most visitors stay at one of the many many **self-contained cottages** (per night from $100); check with the visitors centre. The perfectly peaceful **Spring Bay Villas** (☎ 08-9848 1211; www.springbayvillas .com; Ocean Beach Rd; villas from $145) is one option, fronting the water and offering good off-season rates.

Eating

Denmark has a decent coffee-shop culture, and several nearby wineries serve great food.

Denmark Bakery (Strickland St; pies around $5; ☽ 7am-5pm) Prize-winning and proud of it; this bakery is an institution, because of its pies – and the bread is also good.

Bibbulmun Cafe (☎ 08-9848 1289; cnr Strickland St & South Coast Hwy; sandwiches from $10; ☽ breakfast & lunch) Stop here to drink the best coffee in town, eavesdrop on the local gossip, and eat great homemade cakes and sandwiches.

Mary Rose Cafe (☎ 08-9848 1260; Mt Shadforth Rd; lunches from $12; ☽ 10am-4.30pm Wed-Mon) A calm gem, with a courtyard for summer and pot-belly stove for winter, perfect for long brunches over the weekend papers.

Southern End Restaurant (☎ 08-9848 2600; Mt Shadforth Rd; mains $20-29; ☻ dinner daily, lunch Sat & Sun) With views to the edge of the world, this eatery is a treat. Light lunches ($13) or at least coffee and cake are a must; check out the occasional Sunday-afternoon live music sessions.

MOUNT BARKER

pop 4000

Bare as a babe's bum, Mt Barker (50km north of Albany) has become the gateway town to the increasingly visited Porongurup and Stirling Range National Parks. There's a panoramic view of the area from the **Mt Barker Lookout**, 5km south of town.

It's also the hub for the rapidly growing local wine industry. **Plantagenet Wines** (☎ 08-9851 3111; www.plantagenetwines.com; Albany Hwy) is in the middle of town; **Goundrey Wines** (☎ 08-9851 1777; www.goundrey.com; Muir Hwy) is 10km west. For a list of vineyards see the **visitors centre** (☎ 08-9851 1163; www.mountbarkertourismwa.com.au; 622 Albany Hwy; ☻ 9am-4pm Mon-Fri, 9am-3pm Sat, 10am-3pm Sun) in the restored train station. Eat at **Old Station Cafe** next door – good fresh lunches for around $10.

The town has been settled since the 1830s and the convict-built 1868 police station and gaol have been preserved as a **museum** (Albany Hwy; adult/child $5/free; ☻ 10am-4pm Sat, Sun & school holidays). All 77 species of weird and wonderful Australian banksia tree have found a home at the **Banksia Farm** (☎ 08-9851 1770; www.banksiafarm.com.au; Pearce Rd; admission $10; ☻ 9.30am-4.30pm, check seasonal closures).

A surprising sight is the authentic Mongolian felt tent – ger – and gallery of eclectic Mongolian and Chinese art in the grounds of **Nomads B&B** (☎ 08-9851 2131; aussie_robyn@yahoo.com.au; 12 Morpeth St; s/d $60/80).

Southwest of Mt Barker, on the rolling grounds of the Egerton-Warburton estate, is the exquisitely photogenic **Saint Werburgh's Chapel**, built between 1872 and 1873.

PORONGURUP & STIRLING RANGE

The region north of Albany is one of spectacular natural beauty with two rugged, mountainous national parks to explore. Albany's **DEC office** (☎ 08-9842 4500; 120 Albany Hwy) has maps and information, and can issue park permits.

Porongurup National Park

The 24 sq km, 12km-long Porongurup National Park has 1100-million-year-old

granite outcrops, panoramic views, beautiful scenery, large karri trees and some excellent bushwalks.

The bushwalks range from the 100m **Tree-in-the-Rock** stroll (just what it sounds like) to the harder **Hayward and Nancy Peaks** (four hours). The **Devil's Slide** (two hours) is a walk of contrasts that takes you through a pass of karri forest and onto the stumpy vegetation of the granite. These walks start from the main day-use area, and the **Castle** and **Balancing Rocks** walks (two hours) are 2km further north. A 6km **scenic drive** along the northern edge of the park starts near the ranger's residence; the effects of a major bushfire in 2007 are still visible.

There is no camping allowed within the national park but you can camp on its doorstep at pretty **Porongurup Range Tourist Park** (☎ 08-9853 1057; www.porongurupprangetouristpark.com.au; powered/unpowered sites $25/24, cabins $75 ☒); no credit cards. The welcoming **Porongurup Shop & Tearooms** (☎ 08-9853 1110; www.porongurupinn.com.au; r/apt/cottages $30/80/100) has grown higgledy-piggledy over the years to include great home-cooked food (lunches $13) with veggies from the organic garden.

One of the oldest country retreats in WA, **Karribank Country Retreat** (☎ 08-9853 1022; www.karribank.com.au; r $90, chalets/cottages from $118/175) offers beautifully decorated rooms in the historic house and its surrounding cottages.

If you're a fan of authentic Thai food, don't miss **Maleeya's Thai Café** (☎ 08-9853 1123; 1376 Porongurup Rd; mains $20; ☻ Thu-Sun). It's just before Porongurup township on the Mt Barker road.

Stirling Range National Park

Ever seen a Queen of Sheba orchid or a Stirling Bell? Here's your chance. Rising abruptly from the surrounding flat and sandy plains, Stirling Range's propensity to change colour through blues, reds and purples will captivate photographers during the spectacular wildflower season from late August to early December. Try to squeeze in at least one half-day walk to **Toll Peak** (plentiful wildflowers), **Toolbrunup Peak** (for views and a good climb) or **Bluff Knoll** (1073m; the highest peak in the range).

Stirling Range Retreat (☎ 08-9827 9229; www.stirlingrange.com.au; Chester Pass Rd; tents per person $12, powered sites $26, budget dm/d $28/65, cabins $65-100) is on the park's northern boundary. There's a

---

FAMILIAR LANDSCAPES

Beloved Australian author Tim Winton makes no secret of his love for WA. Its coast and people wind and spark through the majority of his couple of dozen books. The following, in particular, will give you a strong sense of place:

- *Shallows* (1984) – the fictional town of Angelus is based on the real-life southwestern community of Albany, where Tim spent his late childhood and teenage years. The novel explores the conflict here between whaling and conservation, and the town's convict history.

- *Cloud Street* (1991) – a magnificent, funny, ambitious, beautiful, brawling family saga set in the suburbs of Perth, including Mt Lawley, where Winton was born. Somehow this book is familiar territory for all Australians. It bottles and shelves the essence of this country.

- *Dirt Music* (2001) – fictional White Point is based on a settlement like Lancelin, a coastal cray-potting town ('fish deco') north of Perth, where Winton lived with his family. This is a novel of loneliness, regret, redemption…and music! The CD soundtrack to the book charts the Western Australian landscape and a northbound passage all the way up to Cape Leveque.

- *Breath* (2008) – back in a place much like Albany, this latest novel visits subjects such as adolescence, alienation and surf-and-sex rites of passage.

---

wide range of accommodation, from a backpackers' lodge to self-contained, rammed-earth cabins.

Camp in the national park at **Moingup Springs** on Chester Pass Rd. Another good option is **Mount Trio Bush Camping & Caravan Park** (☎ 08-9827 9270; www.mounttrio.com.au; Salt River Rd; unpowered/powered sites per person $10/12), a big bush block on a farm property close to the walking tracks of the western half of the park. There are decent facilities, including wheelchair access to the showers.

The excellent community-managed and volunteer-run **Yongergnow Malleefowl Centre** (☎ 08-9828 2325; www.yongergnow.com.au; adult/child $6/3) is in Ongerup, about 50km north of the park – check opening hours before visiting.

ALBANY
pop 25,200

Albany is a mixed bag of stately and genteelly decaying colonial quarter, an ongoing sophisticated reclamation and development of the waterfront, and a hectic sprawl of malls and fast food. Established shortly before Perth in 1826, the oldest European settlement in the state is now the bustling commercial centre of the southern region.

This is a place that's seen the violence of weather and whaling on its white beaches and rugged coastline. Whales are still a part of the Albany experience, but these days are seen through a camera lens rather than at the business end of a harpoon.

Information
DEC (☎ 08-9842 4500; 120 Albany Hwy; ☿ 8am-4pm Mon-Fri) For national parks information.
Visitors centre (☎ 1800 644 088, 08-9841 1088; www .amazingalbany.com; Proudlove Pde; ☿ 9am-5pm) The informative visitors centre, and southern terminus of the Bibbulmun Track, is in the old train station.

Sights
HISTORIC BUILDINGS
Near the foreshore you'll see the buildings of the historic precinct. This area is relatively quiet, as if the town's boom years belong to another time. Take a stroll down Stirling Tce – noted for its **Victorian shopfronts**, the **Old Post Office** and the **Courthouse** – and up York St, where you'll see the lovely **Saint John's Anglican Church** and the **town hall**. A guided walking-tour brochure of colonial buildings is available from the visitors centre.

One of the most impressive buildings was turned into the **Albany Residency Museum** (☎ 08-9841 4844; www.museum.wa.gov.au; Residency Rd; admission by donation; ☿ 10am-5pm). Built in the 1850s as the home of the resident magistrate, the museum has displays telling seafaring stories, explaining local natural history, and showing Aboriginal artefacts. Next to the museum is a full-scale replica of the brig **Amity** (adult/child $3/1; ☿ 9am-5pm), which carried Albany's founding party to the area from Sydney in 1826.

Opposite the museum, the 1851 **Old Gaol** (☎ 08-9841 1401; Lower Stirling Tce; adult/child $4/3; ☿ 10am-4.15pm) was constructed as a hiring depot for ticket-of-leave convicts. Most were in private employment by 1855, so it was closed until 1872, when it reopened as a civil gaol. These days it's a folk museum. Nearby is the 1832 wattle-and-daub **Patrick Taylor Cottage** (☎ 08-9841 5403; 39 Duke St; admission by donation; ☉ 11am-3pm), believed to be the oldest colonial dwelling in WA.

The **Old Farm at Strawberry Hill** (☎ 08-9841 3735; 170 Middleton Rd; adult/child $5/3; ☉ 10am-5pm) is one of the earliest in the state. The homestead features antiques and artefacts that belonged to the original owner, and has beautiful gardens and tearooms.

OTHER ATTRACTIONS

The **Desert Mounted Corps Memorial** sits atop Mt Clarence, which you can climb along a track

accessible from the end of Grey St East. Enjoy panoramic views from the **Mount Melville lookout tower**; there's a signposted turn-off from Serpentine Rd.

The **Princess Royal Fortress** (Marine Dr; adult/child $4/2; ☉ 9am-5pm) on Mt Adelaide was built in 1893 as a strategic defence post, and today boasts restored buildings, gun emplacements and fine views. A clifftop **walking track** hugs much of the waterfront between the town centre and Middleton Beach.

Activities

Albany's appeal as a top-class diving destination grew after the 2001 scuttling of the warship HMAS *Perth* to create an artificial reef for divers. Its natural reefs feature temperate and

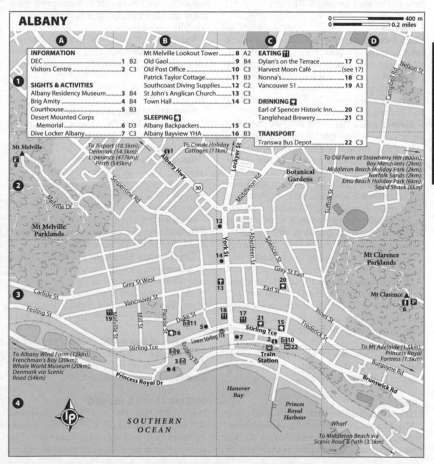

ALBANY

0   400 m
0   0.2 miles

WESTERN AUSTRALIA

INFORMATION		
DEC	1	B2
Visitors Centre	2	C3

SIGHTS & ACTIVITIES		
Albany Residency Museum	3	B4
Brig Amity	4	B4
Courthouse	5	B3
Desert Mounted Corps Memorial	6	D3
Dive Locker Albany	7	C3

Mt Melville Lookout Tower	8	A2
Old Gaol	9	B4
Old Post Office	10	C3
Patrick Taylor Cottage	11	B3
Southcoast Diving Supplies	12	C2
St John's Anglican Church	13	C3
Town Hall	14	C3

SLEEPING		
Albany Backpackers	15	C3
Albany Bayview YHA	16	B3

EATING		
Dylan's on the Terrace	17	C3
Harvest Moon Café	(see 17)	
Nonna's	18	C3
Vancouver 51	19	A3

DRINKING		
Earl of Spencer Historic Inn	20	C3
Tanglehead Brewery	21	C3

TRANSPORT		
Transwa Bus Depot	22	C3

tropical corals, and are home to the bizarre and wonderful leafy and weedy sea dragons. **Dive Locker Albany** (☎ 08-9842 6886; www.albanydive .com.au; cnr York St & Proudlove Pde; ☷ Mon-Sat) and **Southcoast Diving Supplies** (☎ 08-9841 7176; www .divealbany.com.au; 84b Serpentine Rd; ☷ Mon-Fri) will show you the underwater world.

Tours

Kalgan Queen (☎ 08-9844 3166; www.albanyaustralia .com) offers a four-hour sheltered-water cruise ($60) from Emu Point up the Kalgan River in a glass-bottomed boat.

Albany Whale Tours & Sail-A-Way (☎ 0409 107 180; www.albanywhaletours.com.au) and **Silver Star Cruises** (☎ 0428 936 711; www.whales.com.au) both run whale-watching trips in season (roughly June to October, around $70).

Sleeping

Albany Backpackers (☎ 08-9842 5245; www.albanyback packers.com.au; cnr Stirling Tce & Spencer St; dm/s/d $25/60/60; ☐) Bright with murals and with a reputation for partying, this hostel knows how to keep its guests happy with extras such as coffee and cake each afternoon, bike hire ($10 per day) and limited free internet access on arrival.

Albany Bayview YHA (☎ 08-9842 3388; albanyyha@ westnet.com.au; 49 Duke St; dm/s/d $25/60/60; ☐) In a quiet street 400m from the centre, this rambling backpackers has a lazy feel and is less frenzied than the hostel in town.

Norfolk Sands (☎ 08-9841 3585; www.norfolksands .com.au; 18 Adelaide Cres, Middleton Beach; s/d $60/80) Just a few minutes' walk from Middleton Beach, this is simple accommodation with a touch of class. The shared-facility rooms are tastefully decorated with Asian-style furnishings and breakfast is served at the fantastic Bay Merchants cafe next door.

Coraki Holiday Cottages (☎ 08-9844 7068; www .corakicottages.com.au; Lower King Rd; cottages from $125) On the edge of Oyster Bay, between the King and Kalgan Rivers, these light, bright, private cottages with bush surrounds are great value.

Quality B&Bs rule in Albany; check availability with the visitors centre. Expect to pay around $130 for two people.

CAMPING

Middleton Beach Holiday Park (☎ 1800 644 674; www .holidayalbany.com.au; Middleton Beach; unpowered/powered sites $30/32, cabins $90-160, chalets $120-240; ☐ ☒) This beachfront caravan park is sheltered by high sand dunes (a good thing when a gale is raging). Book early.

Emu Beach Holiday Park (☎ 1800 984 411, 08-9844 1147; www.emubeach.com; Emu Point; powered sites $32, cabins from $65, chalets from $100) Families love the relaxed Emu Beach area, and this holiday park, close to the beach, has good facilities, including free barbecues and a kids' playground.

Eating & Drinking

Bay Merchants (☎ 08-9841 7821; 18 Adelaide Cres, Middleton Beach; mains $10-14, ☷ breakfast & lunch) Just a sandy-footed stroll from the beach, this cafe-cum-providore makes good coffee and to-die-for gourmet sandwiches.

Dylan's on the Terrace (☎ 08-9841 8720; 82 Stirling Tce; mains $12-20; ☷ closed Mon) With its 1950s ambience and menu of hamburgers, pancakes and the like, Dylan's is forever family friendly.

Squid Shack (☎ 0417 170 857; Emu Beach; fish & chips $12; ☷ lunch & early dinner) This local institution serves fish straight from the ocean from what is literally a shack at the boat pens; take a bottle of wine and have a sunset picnic on the beach.

Harvest Moon Café (☎ 08-9841 8833; 86 Stirling Tce; mains $13; ☷ lunch Mon-Sat) Does a great line in vegetarian food and fresh juices, in an informal, bookish cafe setting.

Vancouver 51 (☎ 08-9841 2475; 65 Vancouver St; lunches $13; ☷ lunch Tue-Sun, dinner Fri & Sat) This great little cafe is perched above the coast, with balcony views and creative fusion food such as Szechuan duck with spicy plums.

Nonna's (☎ 08-9841 4626; 135 York St; lunch specials $15; ☷ lunch & dinner) This ever-popular eatery serves classic Italian food at reasonable prices.

Earl of Spencer Historic Inn (☎ 08-9841 1322; cnr Earl & Spencer Sts; mains $20; ☷ lunch & dinner) On a cold Albany night, you can't beat the warming qualities of the Earl's famous pie and pint or hearty lamb shanks. It's popular for a quiet drink or, on the weekends, for catching a live band.

Tanglehead Brewery (☎ 08-9841 1733; Stirling Tce; ☷ lunch & dinner) A newish kid on the block, this microbrewery has become a popular local haunt for drinks and dinner.

Getting There & Around

Love's (☎ 08-9841 1211) runs local bus services 301 and 501 around town and to the beaches on weekdays and Saturday morning. The visitors centre has routes and timetables, and information about local car hire. The Transwa Bus Depot is on Proudlove Pde, near the train station.

AROUND ALBANY
Whale World Museum
The **Whale World Museum** (☎ 08-9844 4021; www .whaleworld.org; Frenchman's Bay; adult/child/family $20/9/45; ☺ 9am-5pm), 21km from Albany, is based in Frenchman's Bay at Cheynes Beach Whaling Station, which closed in November 1978. There's the rusting *Cheynes IV* whale chaser and station equipment to inspect outside. The museum screens several 3-D gore-spattered films and other films about whaling operations, and displays harpoons, whaleboat models and scrimshaw (etchings on whalebone). There are free guided tours on the hour.

En route to Whale World, about 12km from Albany, stop off to take a look at the **Albany Wind Farm** (Frenchman's Bay Rd), the biggest in the southwest and an eerily striking sight as you get closer.

National Parks & Reserves
West Cape Howe National Park, 30km west of Albany, is a 35 sq km playground for naturalists, bushwalkers, rock climbers and anglers. Inland, there are areas of coastal heath, lakes, swamp and karri forest. With the exception of the road to Shelley Beach, access is restricted to 4WDs.

Torndirrup National Park, 16km southwest of town, includes the easily accessed – and often windswept and elemental – **Natural Bridge** and the **Gap**. Nearby, the **Blowholes** can put on a show when the surf is up, worth the 80-step stairway up and down. Beautiful **Misery Beach** is often deserted and has an easy drive in/walk down. At **Stony Hill**, a short heritage trail leads around the site of an observatory station from both World Wars. Keen walkers can tackle the hard 10km-return **bushwalk** (over five hours) over Isthmus Hill to Bald Head, at the eastern edge of the park. The views are spectacular pretty much everywhere – look out for whales in season!

Some 20km east of Albany, **Two Peoples Bay** is a 46 sq km nature reserve, sanctuary for the cute and furry Gilbert's potoroo. It has a good swimming beach and a scenic coastline; camping is available further along the coast at **Waychinicup National Park**, home to the rare noisy scrub-bird.

FITZGERALD RIVER NATIONAL PARK
Between Albany and Esperance is this gem of a national park. Its 3300 sq km contains half of the orchid species in WA (more than 80, 70 of which occur nowhere else), 22 mammal species, 200 species of birds and 1700 species of plants. It's also the blossoming ground of the royal hakea (*Hakea victoria*) and qualup bell (*Pimelia physodes*) flowers. Walkers will discover beautiful coastline, sand plains, rugged coastal hills (known as 'the Barrens') and deep, wide river valleys. In season, you'll almost certainly see whales and their calves from the shore at Point Ann, where there's a lookout, and there's a heritage walk that follows a short stretch of the 1164km **No 2 rabbit-proof fence**. For information on wilderness walks check with the rangers on Quiss Rd, **Jerramungup** (☎ 08-9835 5043); Murray Rd, just north of **Bremer Bay** (☎ 08-9837 1022); or at **East Mount Barren** (☎ 08-9838 3060).

The three main 2WD entry points to the park are from the South Coast Hwy (Quiss Rd and Pabelup Dr), Hopetoun (Hamersley Dr) and Bremer Bay (along Swamp and Murray Rds). This last is the prettiest route, winding through acres of flowering shrubs. All roads are gravel, and likely to be impassable after rain, so check locally before you set out.

There are 2WD **campsites** at St Mary Inlet (near Point Ann) and Four Mile Beach, while camping at Hamersley Inlet, Whale Bone Beach, Quoin Head and Fitzgerald Inlet is by 4WD only.

Detours off the South Coast Hwy take you to the quiet fishing community of **Bremer Bay** southwest of the park and, via Ravensthorpe, to the small waterfront town of **Hopetoun**. Both have camping grounds, cabins and long, wild coastlines. The 1833km-long **No 1 rabbit-proof fence** enters the sea in the south at Starvation Bay, east of Hopetoun; it starts at Eighty Mile Beach on the Indian Ocean, north of Port Hedland. The fences were built during the height of the rabbit plague in the early 20th century, but the bunnies beat the fence-builders to the west side so the barriers weren't as effective as hoped.

ESPERANCE
pop 14,650
Esperance sits in solitary splendour on the Bay of Isles, a seascape of aquamarine waters fringed with squeaky white beaches. At first glance, the Norfolk pines are the only stately

WESTERN AUSTRALIA

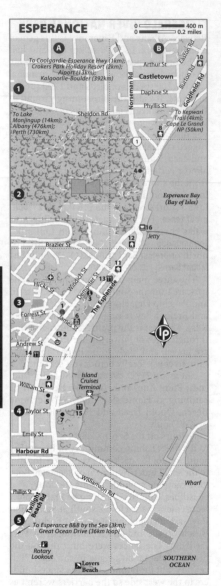

beach retreat for Kalgoorlie locals, and a welcome stop for travellers taking the coast road to the Nullarbor and points north. The pristine coastal environment of the Recherche Archipelago can be wild and windy, or turn on a calmly charming show; it's home to colonies of fur seals, penguins and a variety of sea birds.

Information

Computer Alley (☎ 08-9072 1293; 69c Dempster St; 9am-5pm Mon-Fri, to 4pm Sat) Check your email here.
DEC (☎ 08-9083 2100; 92 Dempster St) For park permits and information about back roads to the Nullarbor.
Visitors centre (☎ 08-9083 1555; www.visitesperance.com; Dempster St; 9am-5pm Mon-Fri, to 2pm Sat, to noon Sun) In the museum village. The helpful staff can book tours and transport.

Sights & Activities

When you hit Esperance, musts are the 36km **Great Ocean Drive**, which includes spectacular vistas from **Observatory Point** and the lookout on **Wireless Hill**; the popular swimming spots at **Blue Haven Beach** and **Twilight Cove**; and a **wind farm**. There's a walking track among the turbines that is quite surreal when it's windy – and it often is, with the farm supplying about 23% of Esperance's electricity.

About 100 small islands are in the **Recherche Archipelago**; you'll see many of them from the

reminder that Esperance has been around just as long as Perth (1863). A port during the gold rush of the 1890s, it continues to rely on the waterfront to export grain and minerals from the region's farms and mines.

The town and surrounds is a low-key and family holiday destination for people who enjoy the sense of community here. It's the

WESTERN AUSTRALIA

waterfront in town. Seals, penguins and many different water birds live on the islands. **Woody Island** is a wildlife sanctuary, which you can visit on cruises and even stay on (see right). A cruise is a must! Walk the 840m **Tanker Jetty** and chat to Sammy, the long-term resident sea lion.

The **Museum Village** (⊙ 10am-4pm Mon-Fri, to 1pm Sat) consists of various restored heritage buildings, including a gallery, smithy's forge, cafe and craft shop. The **Esperance Museum** (☎ 08-9071 1579; cnr James & Dempster Sts; adult/child $5/1; ⊙ 1.30-4.30pm) contains among its local history collection a Skylab display – when the USA's Skylab crashed to earth in 1979, it made its fiery re-entry at Balladonia, east of Esperance. The **Cannery Arts Centre** (☎ 08-9071 3599; Norseman Rd; ⊙ 1-4pm) has artists studios, occasional exhibitions and a shop selling local artwork.

Fun for kids is **Ralph Bower Adventureland Park**, near the Taylor St Jetty, which has a miniature train and playground. Other outdoor activities include Lake Warden wetland's **Kepwari Trail**, off Fisheries Rd in town, with a boardwalk across the lake, interpretive displays and excellent bird-watching. **Lake Monjingup**, 14km out of town on the South Coast Hwy, offers a similar environment.

Tours

Eco-Discovery Tours (☎ 08-9072 1688; www.esper ancetours.com.au) Runs 4WD day tours along the sand to Cape Le Grand National Park (half-/full day $85/150 per person, minimum of two).

Esperance Diving & Fishing (☎ 08-9071 5111; www .esperancedivingandfishing.com.au; 72 The Esplanade) Takes you wreck-diving on the *Sanko Harvest* (two-tank dive including all gear $230) or charter fishing throughout the archipelago.

Kepa Kurl Eco Cultural Discovery Tours (☎ 08-9072 1688; www.kepakurl.com.au; Museum Village) Explore the country from an Aboriginal perspective (half-day adult/child $105/68, minimum of four).

Mackenzie's Island Cruises (☎ 08-9071 5757; www .woodyisland.com.au; 71 The Esplanade) A power catamaran regularly tours Esperance Bay and Woody Island (half-day adult/child $75/26). Morning wildlife tours get close to wild fur seals, sea lions, Cape Barren geese and (with luck) dolphins. Full-day trips ($106/50) also available.

Sleeping

BUDGET

Blue Waters Lodge YHA (☎ 08-9071 1040; yhaesperance@ hotmail.com; 299 Goldfields Rd; dm/s/d $26/40/63; 🖳) On

the beachfront about 1.5km from the centre, this popular rambling place looks out over the water, has a green and welcoming garden, and stokes up wood fires in winter. Hire bikes ($10 per day) to cycle the waterfront.

Goldie's Place (☎ 08-9071 2879; www.goldies placeesperance.com; 51 Goldfields Rd; d from $80) Still a standout in comfort and value, Goldie's is a sizeable, spotless, well-equipped and well-located two-bedroom unit. Helpful young owners live upstairs, with their friendly dog living in the garden.

MIDRANGE

Esperance B&B By the Sea (☎ 08-9071 5640; www .esperancebb.com; Stewart St; s/d $95/140) This beachhouse has a private guest wing, and the views from the deck overlooking Blue Haven Beach are breathtaking, especially at sunset. It's just a stroll from the ocean and a five-minute drive from Dempster St.

Clearwater Motel Apartments (☎ 08-9071 3587; www.clearwatermotel.com.au; 1a William St; s/d from $110/135, 2-bedroom apt $155) The bright and spacious rooms and apartments here have balconies and are fully self-contained, and there's a well-equipped shared barbecue area. It's just a short walk from both waterfront and town.

Jetty Resort (☎ 08-9071 3333; www.thejettyresort.com .au; 1 The Esplanade; r with/without seaview $145/125; 🖳 🍴) You can't miss this white balconied building as you drive along the beachfront Esplanade. There's a variety of rooms from motel-style to very comfortable top-end spa apartments. All have access to the pool. It has a barbecue, comfy outdoor seats, a giant chess set in the garden and a kids playground. A day spa is attached.

TOP END

Island View Esperance (☎ 08-9072 0044; www.esper anceapartments.com.au; 14-16 The Esplanade; apt from $190) It's easy living in these architect-designed and tastefully furnished units, with floor-to-ceiling windows overlooking the beach and a waterfront walking track across the road. The kitchens have all the mod cons, and there's a spacious living area.

CAMPING

Woody Island (☎ 08-9071 5757; www.woodyisland.com .au; tent sites per person $15, on-site tents $30-55, huts $83-126; ⊙ late Sep-Apr) It's not every day you get to stay in an A-class nature reserve. Choose between leafy campsites (very close together) or timber bush cabins; a few have a private deck and their own lighting. Power is mostly solar, and rainwater supplies the island – both are highly valued. A peak season one-way boat transfer costs $18/44 per child/adult, or get dropped off as part of a tour.

Crokers Park Holiday Resort (☎ 08-9071 4100; www .acclaimparks.com.au; 817 Harbour Rd; unpowered/powered sites $29/32, cabins $73-99; 🐾) Of the several very ordinary campsites in town, this stands apart for its clean, shady and decent-sized grounds and pretty pool area. It's a five-minute drive from the waterfront; stay at the back of the site, away from the busy road.

Eating & Drinking

Onshore Cafe (☎ 08-9071 2575; 105 Dempster St; mains $10; 🕑 breakfast & lunch Mon-Sat) A homewares-store-cum-cafe in a breezy modern space next to the cinema, this place serves light lunches, as well as decent coffee and cake.

Taylor Street Jetty Cafe Restaurant (☎ 08-9071 4317; Taylor St Jetty; mains $15-30; 🕑 Wed-Mon) This attractive, sprawling cafe by the jetty serves reliable fare – the whitebait's a winner. Locals hang out at the tables on the grass or read on the covered terrace, wi-fi is free with an order of more than $10, and it's a child-friendly zone.

Ocean Blues (☎ 08-9071 7107; 19 The Esplanade; mains $15-30; 🕑 Tue-Sun) Wander in sandy-footed and order some simple fare for lunch (classic steak sandwiches $12), or shelter from the sea breeze over an afternoon coffee and cake. Early dinner is served until 8.30pm.

Coffee Cat (🕑 7am-2pm Thu-Mon) A red-and-black van parked at the end of Tanker Jetty is the locals' choice before, during or after a daily waterfront promenade. It's the best coffee in town.

CAPE LE GRAND, CAPE ARID & PEAK CHARLES NATIONAL PARKS

An easy day tour from Esperance is Cape Le Grand. It starts 60km east of Esperance and boasts spectacular coastal scenery, turquoise water, dazzling talcum-powder-soft beaches and excellent walking tracks. It offers good fishing, swimming and camping at **Lucky Bay** and **Le Grand Beach**, and day-use facilities at gorgeous **Hellfire Bay**. Make the effort to climb **Frenchman Peak** (a steep 3km return), as the views from the top and through the 'eye', especially during the late afternoon, are superb. **Rossiter Bay** is where explorers Edward John

Eyre and the Aborigine Wylie, during their epic overland crossing in 1841, fortuitously met Captain Rossiter of the French whaler *Mississippi*, on which the pair spent two weeks resting. The roads to all these places are sealed. A 15km **coastal walking track** links the bays; you can do shorter stretches between beaches.

Further east, at the start of the Great Australian Bight, is the coastal **Cape Arid National Park**. The park is rugged and isolated, with good bushwalking, great beaches and campsites. Whales (in season), seals and Cape Barren geese are seen regularly here. Most of the park is 4WD only, although the Thomas River Rd, which leads to the shire campsite, is accessible to all vehicles. For the hardy, there is a tough walk to the top of **Tower Peak** on Mt Ragged (3km return, three hours), where the world's most primitive species of ant was found thriving in 1930.

Peak Charles National Park, 130km to the north, is a granite wilderness area with only basic facilities; you'll need to be completely self-sufficient here. **DEC** (☎ 08-9083 2100) in Esperance has information on each.

Orleans Bay Caravan Park (☎ 08-9075 0033; or leansbay@bigpond.com; unpowered/powered sites $22/25, cabins/chalets $60/90), at Duke of Orleans Bay between Cape Le Grand and Cape Arid, is a shady, child-friendly, fishing-obsessed place to stay, 3km from stunning Wharton Beach with its surfing, swimming, boating and 4WD beach tracks.

For those heading east across the Nullarbor, **Parmango Road**, north of Duke of Orleans Bay, offers an alternative route to the Eyre Hwy; see DEC in Esperance for track information.

SOUTHERN OUTBACK

The stark beauty of the Southern Outback offers an iconic Australian experience. In summer, heat haze shimmers on the desert and the parched voices of crows carry for miles; midyear, a winter chill tones down the landscape's reds and blues to cool purple and grey. Almost-empty roads lead on – and on and on – towards South Australia via the relentless Nullarbor Plain, and up to the Northern Territory. This was (and is) gold-rush country, with the city of Kalgoorlie-Boulder as its centrepiece while smaller, more remote and less sustainable gold towns lie sunstruck and deserted. Aboriginal people have lived for an

SOUTHERN OUTBACK

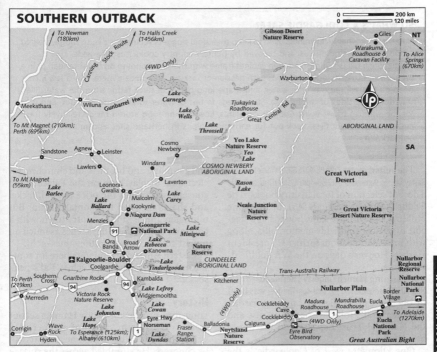

age in this region, which the early colonists found unforgiving – until the rewards of the gold rush made it worth their while to stay.

History

The government in long-suffering Perth was in raptures when gold was discovered at Southern Cross in 1888. In one of the world's last great gold rushes, the next few years drew prospectors from other states – and other nations. Some 50 towns immediately rose up in the Eastern Goldfields, but it was a harsh life on the goldfields. Enthusiasm, or greed, sometimes outweighed common sense. Diseases such as typhoid ran through mining camps. Inadequate water, housing, food and medical supplies led to a dusty death for many.

The area's population dwindled along with the gold itself, and these days Kalgoorlie-Boulder is the only real survivor. You can explore other diminished towns and prodigious mining structures from early last century along the well-sign-posted 965km **Golden Quest Discovery Trail** (www.goldenquesttrail.com).

The 1903 **Golden Pipeline** (www.goldenpipeline.com.au) brought water to the goldfields, stretch-

ing 560km from the Perth foothills, thanks to the vision of engineer CY O'Connor. It was a lifeline for the towns it passed through and filled Kalgoorlie with the sense of a future, with or without gold. The present-day Great Eastern Hwy follows the pipeline's route, with heritage pumping stations and information signs along the way.

COOLGARDIE
pop 4000

Today you wouldn't pick that the quiet, dusty town of Coolgardie was the third-biggest town in WA in 1898. These days it's a pause in the long journey to or from the Nullarbor Plain, or a day trip from Kalgoorlie-Boulder, 39km to the east. Just hours after Arthur Bayley rode into Southern Cross in 1892 and dumped 554 ounces of gold on the mining warden's counter, the greatest movement of people in Australian history began. Bayley had found the gold at Fly Flat, the site that became Coolgardie, and is now the turn-off for Kalgoorlie. Great information panels are dotted around the now-sleepy town, detailing its former glory.

SO WHAT'S A COOLGARDIE SAFE?

Nope, it's not what lucky miners used to keep their gold nuggets secure. It's a bush fridge, created in the Coolgardie goldfields, and beloved by pioneer country cooks Australia-wide.

Imagine a tall-ish thin-ish kitchen cabinet frame with shelves, standing on the verandah or in a breezeway. Cover its sides and door with hessian or sacking, and place a metal tray a few inches deep on top. Fill the tray with water, and drape long pieces of thick fabric from the water-filled tray down the sides of the hessian. Sit the legs in tins of water to keep the ants out, and wait for the wind to blow. Voila! Cool air circulates, keeping the food stored inside relatively fresh and protected from flies. Look out for early prototypes in heritage sites and museums across outback WA.

The **visitors centre** (☎ 08-9026 6090; Warden's Court, Bayley St; ⊙ 9am-noon & 12.30-4pm Mon-Fri) also sells a decent selection of local history books. The **Goldfields Museum** (adult/child $4/2), in the same building and with the same hours, has a sizeable display of goldfields memorabilia, along with information about former US president Herbert Hoover's days on the WA goldfields in Gwalia.

Charming **Warden Finnerty's Residence** (☎ 08-9026 6028; 2 McKenzie St; ⊙ 11am-4pm Thu-Tue) was built in 1895 for Coolgardie's first mining warden and magistrate, John Michael Finnerty, and the National Trust has restored the house beautifully.

One kilometre west of Coolgardie is the **town cemetery**, which includes the graves of explorer Ernest Giles (1835–97) and several Afghan camel drivers. An earlier **pioneer cemetery** (Forrest St) was used from 1892 to 1894.

At the **Camel Farm** (☎ 08-9026 6159; Great Eastern Hwy; adult/child $5/2; ⊙ 10am-4pm school & public holidays, or by appointment), 3km west of town, you can take short camel rides or organise longer treks.

KALGOORLIE-BOULDER
pop 30,100

Kalgoorlie-Boulder ('Kal' to the locals), some 600km from Perth, is an outback success story. The town is prosperous, with streets wide enough to turn a camel-train in – a necessity in turn-of-the-century goldfield towns – and well-preserved historic buildings. The most enduring and productive of WA's gold towns, today it's still the centre for mining in this part of WA.

Kal still feels a bit like the Wild West: a frontier town where bush meets brash. Workers can come straight from the mines in their overalls to spend disposable income at the bars, and are served by 'skimpie' staff wearing only underwear. There are tattoos and gambling and brothels and churches. An electronic display high on the Palace Hotel constantly provides the price of gold, nickel and shares in a red horizontal stream. But ultimately this is still a country town, with a community that these days relies as much on tourist gold as it does on the mines' gold.

Eastern Australians migrate here for some warmth during winter, which is Kal's peak season.

History

Long-time prospector Paddy Hannan set out from Coolgardie in search of another gold strike, and proved that sometimes beggars can be choosers. He stumbled across the surface gold that sparked the 1893 gold rush, and inadvertently chose the site of Kalgoorlie for a township.

When surface sparkles subsided, the miners dug deeper, extracting the precious metal from the rocks by costly and complex processes. Kalgoorlie quickly prospered, and the town's magnificent public buildings, constructed at the end of the 19th century, are evidence of its fabulous wealth.

Despite its slow decline after WWI, Kal is still the largest producer of gold in Australia. What was a Golden Mile of small mining operators' headframes and corrugated-iron shacks is now a mind-boggling Super Pit, which will eventually be 3.8km long, 1.35km wide and 0.5km deep.

Orientation

The town centre in Kalgoorlie is a grid of broad, tree-lined streets. Hannan St is the main street, flanked by imposing public buildings; you'll find most of the town's hotels, restaurants and offices on or close by Hannan. Boulder is about 4km southeast of Hannan St.

KALGOORLIE-BOULDER

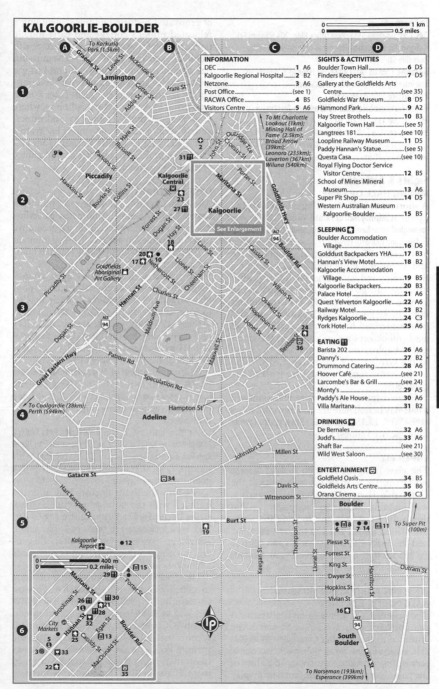

INFORMATION	
DEC	**1** A6
Kalgoorlie Regional Hospital	**2** B2
Netzone	**3** A6
Post Office	(see 1)
RACWA Office	**4** B5
Visitors Centre	**5** A6

SIGHTS & ACTIVITIES	
Boulder Town Hall	**6** D5
Finders Keepers	**7** D5
Gallery at the Goldfields Arts	
Centre	(see 35)
Goldfields War Museum	**8** D5
Hammond Park	**9** A2
Hay Street Brothels	**10** B3
Kalgoorlie Town Hall	(see 5)
Langtrees 181	(see 10)
Loopline Railway Museum	**11** D5
Paddy Hannan's Statue	(see 5)
Questa Casa	(see 10)
Royal Flying Doctor Service	
Visitor Centre	**12** B5
School of Mines Mineral	
Museum	**13** A6
Super Pit Shop	**14** D5
Western Australian Museum	
Kalgoorlie-Boulder	**15** B5

SLEEPING	
Boulder Accommodation	
Village	**16** D6
Golddust Backpackers YHA	**17** B3
Hannan's View Motel	**18** B2
Kalgoorlie Accommodation	
Village	**19** B5
Kalgoorlie Backpackers	**20** B3
Palace Hotel	**21** A6
Quest Yelverton Kalgoorlie	**22** A6
Railway Motel	**23** B2
Rydges Kalgoorlie	**24** C3
York Hotel	**25** A6

EATING	
Barista 202	**26** A6
Danny's	**27** B2
Drummond Catering	**28** A6
Hoover Café	(see 21)
Larcombe's Bar & Grill	(see 24)
Monty's	**29** A5
Paddy's Ale House	**30** A6
Villa Maritana	**31** B2

DRINKING	
De Bernales	**32** A6
Judd's	**33** A6
Shaft Bar	(see 21)
Wild West Saloon	(see 30)

ENTERTAINMENT	
Goldfield Oasis	**34** B5
Goldfields Arts Centre	**35** B6
Orana Cinema	**36** C3

To Karkurla Park (1.5km)

Graeme St
Lewis St
McKenzie St
Keenan St
Lamington
Cotter St
Hare St
Addis St
Hare St
Russell St
John St
Coeus St
Outridge Tce
Porter St
Maritana St

To Mt Charlotte
Lookout (1km);
Mining Hall of
Fame (2.5km);
Broad Arrow
(39km);
Leonora (235km);
Laverton (367km)
Wiluna (540km)

Parsons St
Piccadilly
Hawkins St
Bourke St
Collins St
Kalgoorlie
Central
Goldfields Hwy
Boulder Rd

Kalgoorlie
See Enlargement

Forrest St
Dugan St
Hay St
Lane St
Cassidy St
Wilson St
Lionel St

Goldfields
Aboriginal
Art Gallery
Hannan St
Charles St
Nethercott St
Cheetham St
Maxwell St
Oswald St
Hopetoun St
Lionel St
Davidson St

Piccadilly St
Dugan St
Maldrum Ave
Great Eastern Hwy
Patroni Rd
Speculation Rd
Hampton St
Adeline

To Coolgardie (38km);
Perth (594km)

Johnston St
Millen St
Gatacre St
Davis St
Wittenoom St
Hart Kesplen Dr
Boulder

Burt St
Thompson St
Keegan St
Lionel St

Kalgoorlie
Airport
Piesse St
Forrest St
King St
Dwyer St
Hopkins St
Vivian St
Hamilton St
Outram St
Super Pit
(100m)
South
Boulder

To Norseman (193km);
Esperance (399km)

400 m
0.2 miles
Maritana St
Brookman St
Porter St
Hannan St
City
Markets
Egan St
Cassidy St
Boulder Rd
MacDonald St

WESTERN AUSTRALIA

Information

DEC (☎ 08-9080 5555; Post Office Bldg, 204 Hannan St)
Kalgoorlie Regional Hospital (☎ 08-9080 5888;
Piccadilly St)
Netzone (☎ 08-9091 4178; cnr Hannan & Wilson Sts)
Fast internet access in a central location.
Post office (204 Hannan St)
Royal Automobile Club of Western Australia
(Racwa; ☎ 131 703; cnr Hannan & Porter Sts)
Visitors centre (☎ 08-9021 1966; www.kalgoorlietour
ism.com; Town Hall, cnr Hannan & Wilson Sts; �})8.30am-
5pm Mon-Fri, 10am-2pm Sat & Sun)

Sights & Activities

MINING HALL OF FAME

A shortcut to understanding this town is the
excellent **Mining Hall of Fame** (☎ 08-9026 2700; www
.mininghall.com; Eastern Bypass Rd; adult/child/family incl
underground tour $30/15/70; �} 9am-4.30pm). Located
on the site of Paddy Hannan's original lease
and a working mine until 1952, it explores
the mining industry from the underground
up. You can go 36m below the surface in
a mine shaft (and see why claustrophobics
don't make good miners), pan for gold and
be mesmerised by a gold pour. Kids of all
ages will be kept well occupied in the interactive Exploration Zone, and you can relax
in the Garden of Remembrance, dedicated
to the immigrant Chinese who worked the
goldfields.

If you're into mining history, allow yourself
a half-day here. There are underground tours
at 9.45am, 12.15pm and 2.15pm daily (wear
fully enclosed shoes).

SUPER PIT

The view from the **Super Pit Lookout** (www.su
perpit.com.au; Outram St; �} 7am-9pm), just off the
Goldfields Hwy in Boulder, is staggering,
with building-sized trucks zigzagging up and
down the huge hole and looking like kids'
toys. Good info is given in the on-site signs,
and the **Super Pit Shop** (☎ 08-9093 3488; 2 Burt St;
�} 9am-5pm Mon-Fri) sells souvenirs and offers
more detailed information.

WESTERN AUSTRALIAN MUSEUM
KALGOORLIE-BOULDER

The impressive Ivanhoe mine headframe at
the northern end of Hannan St marks the
entrance to this excellent **museum** (☎ 08-9021
8533; www.museum.wa.gov.au; 17 Hannan St; admission by
donation; �} 10am-4.30pm) of early social history of
the goldfields. Check out the fantastic display

of renovated historic buildings, including a
relocated miner's cottage and early mobile
police station (attached to a train, to deal with
troublemakers in the outback!). The museum
has an underground gold vault and historic
photographs, and an exhibition of Victorian-
era trade-union banners. A lift takes you to
a dizzying lookout on the headframe, where
you can peer out over the city and mines,
and down into delightfully untidy backyards.
Twice-daily guided tours start at 11am and
2.30pm, and the gift shop has a good choice
of local history books.

OTHER ATTRACTIONS

Along Hannan St, you'll find the imposing
town hall and the equally impressive **post office**.
There's an art gallery upstairs in the decorative
town hall, while outside is a drinking fountain
in the form of a **statue** of Paddy Hannan holding a water bag.

Northwest of Hannan St in Hay St is one of
Kalgoorlie-Boulder's most notorious and popular attractions, the **Hay Street brothels**. Brothel
tours of **Langtrees 181** (☎ 08-9026 2181; 181 Hay St;
admission $35; �} 1pm, 3pm & 6pm) and Australia's
oldest operating brothel **Questa Casa** (☎ 08-9021
4897; 133 Hay St; admission $20; �} 2pm) have become
de rigueur for many visitors to Kal.

The small **School of Mines Mineral Museum**
(☎ 08-9088 6001; cnr Egan & Cassidy Sts; �} 8.30am-noon
Mon-Fri, closed school holidays) has a geology display
including replicas of big nuggets discovered
in the area.

At the gallery at the **Goldfields Arts Centre**
(☎ 08-9088 6900; Cheetham St; entry by donation; �} 10am-
3pm Mon-Fri, noon-3pm Sun) you'll find regular exhibitions by local, state and national artists in a
great exhibition space.

See how the flying doctors look after the
outback with the hourly tours at the **Royal
Flying Doctor Service Visitor Centre** (☎ 08-9093
7595; www.flyingdoctor.net; Kalgoorlie-Boulder Airport;
admission by donation; �} 10am-3pm Mon-Fri). Be generous with your donation if you can; it does
a fabulous job.

Head over to Boulder for a couple of hours
to check out the 1908 Goatcher Theatre
Curtain in the 1907 **Boulder Town Hall** (☎ 08-
9021 9600; cnr Burt & Lane Sts, Boulder). Englishman
Philip W Goatcher, one of the great theatrical
scene artists of the Victorian era, painted the
trompe l'œil curtain, which creates an extraordinary illusion of 3-D space. It's dropped
from 10am to 3pm Tuesday to Thursday,

and on the third Sunday of each month from 9.30am to 12.30pm. Nearby, the **Goldfields War Museum** (☎ 08-9093 1083; 106 Burt St; ☒ 10am-4pm Mon-Fri, 9am-1pm Sat & Sun) has a collection of local war memorabilia and military vehicles. The Loopline railway was once the most important urban transport for Kalgoorlie and Boulder, and Boulder's Golden Mile station (1897) once the busiest in WA. Its story is told in the **Loopline railway museum** (☎ 08-9093 3055; www.loopline.com.au; cnr Burt & Hamilton Sts; adult/child $2/1; ☒ 9am-1pm), operating out of the old train station.

Hammond Park (Lyall St; ☒ 9am-5pm), in the west of Kalgoorlie-Boulder, is a good spot for kids, with playgrounds, animals and a miniature Bavarian castle. And if you've had enough of holes in the ground, you can do your bit towards revegetating them in **Karkurla Park**, northwest of town, scattering a packet of native Silky Pear seeds (available at the visitors centre) while enjoying the 4km of walking tracks.

Tours
Finders Keepers (☎ 08-9093 2222; www.finderskeepersgold.com; 20 Burt St, Boulder) You can be inducted into the mysteries of the metal detector on a popular half-day gold-prospecting tour (adult/child $80/40), or journey to the centre of the earth (OK, not quite) on a 2½-hour tour of the Super Pit (adult/child $50/30).

Goldfields Air Services (☎ 08-9093 2116; www.goldfieldsairservices.com) See Kalgoorlie-Boulder and the Golden Mile mining operations from the air. Prices for fixed-wing trips start from $50 per person, with a minimum of two people.

Goldrush Tours (☎ 1800 620 440; www.goldrushtours.com.au) Runs all sorts of tours, including half-day heritage jaunts around Kalgoorlie-Boulder (adult/child $50/25) and day tours to the sculptures on Lake Ballard (adult/child $230/175). Tours are dependent on numbers.

Heliwest (☎ 08-9093 4466; www.heliwest.com.au) Helicopter across the Super Pit for $70 per person (minimum two people), from the chopper pad at the Mining Hall of Fame.

Festivals & Events
The highlight of the social calendar is the annual **Kalgoorlie-Boulder Racing Round** in September, where locals and a huge influx of visitors dress up to the nines to watch horses race on the red dirt. See the racing club's website (www.kbrc.com.au) for coming events. On the third Sunday of the month, **Boulder Market Day** is busy but pleasantly low-key.

Sleeping
BUDGET
Kalgoorlie Backpackers (☎ 0412 110 001; www.kalgoorlie.com/backpackers; 166 Hay St; dm/s/d $28/50/70; ☒ ☐ ☒) Partly located in a former brothel, this rather rundown hostel was under new management when we visited, with plans for improvement. It's in a good location and, like the nearby YHA, is a good place to find out about work opportunities.

Golddust Backpackers YHA (☎ 08-9091 3737; golddust@westnet.com.au; 192 Hay St; dm/s/d $30/40/65; ☒ ☐ ☒) Maintaining standards is this YHA hostel. It's close to town, with clean, basic rooms, good communal areas including a games room, and noticeboards with info about work available in town.

York Hotel (☎ /fax 08-9021 2337; yorkhtl@bigpond.net.au; 259 Hannan St; s/d $55/85) One of Kalgoorlie's most unique heritage buildings, this is a character-filled labyrinth of high rooms, wooden staircases and lacework balconies. It's good value, if a bit worn, with a light breakfast included.

MIDRANGE
Palace Hotel (☎ 08-9021 2788; www.palacehotel.com.au; cnr Hannan & Maritana Sts; s/d $75/85, balcony s/d $110/130, apt $160, ste $160-260; ☒) Climb the magnificent sweeping staircase of this 1897 hotel to reach the accommodation wing, a rabbit warren with various styles of rooms. The suites were formerly early stockbrokers' offices – check out the massive wall safes, which have been converted into wardrobes! There's free wi-fi access in most rooms.

Railway Motel (☎ 08-9088 0000; www.railwaymotel.com.au; 51 Forrest St; r/apt $140/145; ☒ ☒) This complex, opposite the train station and built on the site of the old hotel of the same name, is a cut above the average with bright, spruced-up rooms and comfy reclining chairs. Its well-equipped and self-contained two-bedroom apartments just up the road are spacious and comfortable.

Hannan's View Motel (☎ 08-9091 3333; www.hannansview.com.au; 430 Hannan St; r from $159; ☒) If you're in town for a while, this is a good central location with quiet self-contained units, free in-house movies, and complimentary access to the town's Olympic-sized pool and gym (a five-minute drive away).

TOP END
Quest Yelverton Kalgoorlie (☎ 08-9022 8181; www.kalgoorlieproperty.questwa.com.au; 210 Egan St; s/d from

$165; ⊠ ⊒) Close enough to Hannan St to walk but far enough away to get a quiet night's sleep, the Yelverton's chic, fully self-contained and serviced apartments have all you need – even a lap pool.

Rydges Kalgoorlie (☎ 08-9080 0800; www.rydges.com.au; 21 Davidson St; s/d from $170; ⊠ ⊒ ⊒) This low-key and stylish complex, opposite the cinema in a residential area between Kalgoorlie and Boulder, has big, comfortable rooms with views of the native bush garden and/or the pool area.

CAMPING

Kalgoorlie Accommodation Village (☎ 08-9039 4800; www.discoveryholidayparks.com.au; 286 Burt St; tent/van sites $26/36, chalets/units $99/105; ⊠ ⊒ ⊒) and **Boulder Accommodation Village** (☎ 08-9093 1266; 201 Lane St; same rates) are sister complexes 6km south of Kalgoorlie. Both have sizeable and well-fitted-out A-frame chalets and cabins, grassy tent sites, and a kids' playground and pool, and are fully equipped for disabled travellers. Wi-fi is available.

Eating

Barista 202 (☎ 08-9022 2228; 202 Hannan St; Turkish breads $8; ⊠ breakfast & light lunch Mon-Sat) This buzzing cafe-cum-art-gallery is a welcome addition to the Kal scene; it serves Italian sandwiches and baked goodies to accompany the good coffee.

Drummond Catering (☎ 08-9022 3301; Hannan St; lunch specials $10; ⊠ lunch Mon-Sat) This gourmet deli serves salads ($5) and *very* good sandwiches and daily hot lunch specials. Takeaway, or eat at the tables in the back.

Hoover Café (☎ 08-9021 2788; cnr Hannan & Maritana Sts; mains $15; ⊠ breakfast & lunch) Under the high ceilings and heritage atmosphere of the Palace Hotel, this cafe is a popular local brekkie spot and serves great-value home-cooked lunches, and morning and afternoon teas with fresh-baked scones.

Monty's (☎ 08-9022 8288; cnr Hannan & Porter Sts; mains $15-30; ⊠ 24hr) The servings of standard cafe fare here are tasty, massive and – handily – available round the clock.

Paddy's Ale House (☎ 08-9021 2833; Exchange Hotel, 135 Hannan St; mains $18-30; ⊠ lunch & dinner) With a wide range of tap beers, Paddy's serves up good, classic counter meals such as bangers and mash to the hordes.

Larcombe's Bar & Grill (☎ 08-9080 0800; Rydges Kalgoorlie, 21 Davidson St; mains $18-30) It's worth the

drive from the centre of town to sip a decent coffee or wine on the verandah, and eat at this locally popular restaurant; with the cinema across the road, make it a pre- or post-movie stop.

Villa Maritana (☎ 08-9022 4406; 20 Maritana St; mains from $20; ⊠ dinner Wed-Sun) Just over the railway bridge, locals enthusiastically recommend this Italian addition to Kal's eating scene. Fresh and tasty pastas, and classic Mediterranean meat and fish dishes, are on the menu.

Danny's (☎ 08-9022 7614; 14 Wilson St; mains $30; ⊠ dinner Tue-Sat) Just a walk away from the main drag, Danny's is the place to go for a quality meat fix, with choice cuts of beef featuring heavily on the menu.

The top end of Hannan St also offers long-standing shish-kebab, pizza and Thai options, and all the pubs serve counter meals.

Drinking & Entertainment

Even at the height of a drought there's never been a shortage of watering holes in Kal. The many classic colonial-era pubs of Hannan St are worth a trawl, both to admire from the outside and to venture in to quench your thirst and curiosity. Female bar staff may be clad in underwear, suspenders and high heels – 'skimpies' are the norm here. You'll need to pick your pub carefully if you prefer your bar staff fully clothed.

Wild West Saloon (☎ 08-9021 2833; Exchange Hotel, 135 Hannan St; ⊠ 10am-late) For an anthropological experience, the front bar at the Exchange Hotel provides a window into some locals' lives at all hours of the day, with skimpies, TV sports and mine workers furiously refuelling.

Judd's (☎ 08-9021 3046; Kalgoorlie Hotel, 319 Hannan St) With hot-pink walls and windows that open onto the street, this bar is the place to check out live bands.

De Bernales (☎ 08-9021 4534; 193 Hannan St) For as long as we can remember, De Bernales has been the place for a quiet, comfortable tipple amid the Hannan St hoopla. Sit back and people-watch from the street-side verandah.

Shaft Bar (☎ 08-9021 2788; cnr Hannan & Maritana Sts) At the Palace Hotel, this is where big nights out in Kalgoorlie inevitably end – boogieing in the late-night bar.

You can do a gym workout, swim laps or catch a wave (really!) at **Goldfields Oasis** (☎ 08-9022 2922; 99 Johnston St; adult/child swim $5/3; ⊠ 5.45am-9pm Mon-Fri, 8am-6pm Sat & Sun); catch a flick in air-conditioned comfort at the **Orana Cinema**

(☎ 08-9021 2199; Oswald St); and catch performing arts at the **Goldfields Arts Centre** (☎ 08-9088 6900; Cheetham St).

Getting There & Away

AIR

Skywest (☎ 1300 660 088; www.skywest.com.au) and **Qantas** (☎ 13 13 13; www.qantas.com.au) fly between Kalgoorlie-Boulder and Perth at least twice daily.

BUS & TRAIN

Bus and train services operate from Kalgoorlie Central station on Forrest St.

Transwa (☎ 1300 662 205; www.transwa.wa.gov.au) runs a bus service between Esperance on the south coast and Kalgoorlie ($49) several times a week. It also operates the *Prospector* train from Perth to Kalgoorlie-Boulder ($77, seven hours), which runs daily. It's wise to book, as this service is popular.

The **Indian Pacific** (☎ 13 21 47; www.trainways.com .au) train also goes through Kalgoorlie-Boulder four times a week, twice to Perth and twice from Perth.

Getting Around

Between Kalgoorlie and Boulder there's a regular bus service from 7am to 6pm Monday to Friday and Saturday morning with **TransGoldfields** (☎ 08-9021 2655; adult/child $2/1).

NORTH OF KALGOORLIE-BOULDER

Heading north from Kalgoorlie-Boulder, the Goldfields Hwy is surfaced as far as Wiluna (580km north), which is also the starting point for the 4WD Canning Stock Route and Gunbarrel Hwy. Branching east off the highway, the road from Leonora is sealed as far as Laverton (367km northeast), which is the starting point for the unsealed Great Central Rd (Outback Way).

Off the main road you'll see the occasional mining truck but other traffic is virtually nonexistent – and while many gravel roads are fine for regular cars, rain can quickly close them to all vehicles.

Easy day trips north from Kalgoorlie include the gold ghost towns of **Kanowna** (18km northeast), **Broad Arrow** (38km north) and **Ora Banda** (65km northwest). Little remains of Kanowna apart from the building foundations of its 16 hotels (!) and other public buildings, but its pioneer cemetery – including a couple of early Japanese graves – is

interesting. Broad Arrow was featured in *The Nickel Queen* (1971), the first full-length feature film made in WA. It is a shadow of its former self: at the beginning of the 20th century it had a population of 2400. Now there's just one pub – popular with Kal locals at weekends – and a couple of tumbledown houses. The 1911 **Ora Banda Historic Inn** (☎ 08-9024 2444; r $80) has been rebuilt after a notorious pub-bombing in 2000, and makes a good refreshment or overnight stop.

The once thriving but now tiny township of **Menzies** (www.menzies.wa.gov.au), at 132km, is the turn-off for the stunning **sculptures on Lake Ballard**. They're on an eye-dazzling salt lake 51km northwest of town – don't miss them.

Further north, the largest service centre for mining exploration and the pastoral industry in the area is **Leonora** (237km). Check out the old public buildings and pubs on the main street near the **visitors centre** (☎ 08-9037 6044; www.leonora.wa.gov.au; Tower St; ☼ 9am-4pm Mon-Fri) and hit the telecentre next door for email. Just 4km southwest of town, **Gwalia Historic Site** (☎ 08-9037 7122; www.gwalia.org.au; adult/child/family $5/2/12; ☼ 10am-4pm) was occupied in 1896 and deserted pretty much overnight in 1963, after the pit closed. With houses and household goods disintegrating intact, it's a strange, eerie, fascinating ghost town. There's a **museum** with more weird and wonderful stuff in it than we've ever seen. **Hoover House** – the 1898 mine manager's house, named for Gwalia's first mine manager, Herbert Hoover, who later became the 31st president of the United States – is beautifully restored, and you can B&B here in one of its three exquisite bedrooms (rooms $145). On a gravel road parallel to the main highway, about 60km south of Leonora, is **Kookynie**, where a true outback pub experience can be had at the 1901 **Grand Hotel** (☎ 08-9031 3010; s/d $77/93). Nearby **Niagara Dam** is a top bush camping spot, with walking trails around the water.

Northeast is **Laverton**, crouching on the edge of the Great Victoria Desert. The cheery **visitors centre** (☎ 08-9031 1130; www.visit-laverton .com.au; ☼ 9am-4pm Mon-Fri, 10am-1pm Sat & Sun) is combined with the **Great Beyond – Explorers' Hall of Fame** (admission $10); internet access is at the telecentre. Laverton marks the start of the Great Central Rd (Outback Way) to Yulara (near Uluru, formerly Ayers Rock) via Warburton. Expect to overnight and/or stock up on supplies of fuel and water here, and *definitely* check at the visitors centre for current road conditions.

All the (nonghost) towns have pub accommodation, caravan parks (most with on-site cabins), fuel stops and grocery stores. **Public transport** (☎ 1800 620 440; www.goldrushtours .com.au) is limited to a weekly run between Kalgoorlie and Laverton, which goes out on Thursday and back on Friday. Check out www.northerngoldfields.com.au for more information.

Great Central Road (Outback Way)

The unsealed Great Central Rd – also known as the **Outback Way** (www.outbackway.org.au) – provides rich scenery of red sand, spinifex, mulga and desert oak. It links Laverton with Winton in central Queensland, via the red centre of the Northern Territory. From Laverton it is a mere 1098km to Yulara, 1541km to Alice Springs and 2720km to Winton!

The road is sandy and corrugated in places, but wide and suitable for all vehicles. It can be closed for several days after rain. Diesel is available at roughly 300km intervals on the WA side, and Opal fuel takes the place of unleaded petrol. (Opal is unsniffable, and its provision is one of the measures in place to counteract petrol-sniffing problems in local communities.)

Coming from Laverton, the three **WA roadhouses** (www.ngaanyatjarraku.wa.gov.au) – all of which provide food, fuel and limited mechanical services – are **Tjukayirla** (☎ 08-9037 1108) at 315km, **Warburton** (☎ 08-8956 7656) at 567km and **Warakurna** (☎ 08-8956 7344) at 798km. All have a range of accommodation, from camping (around $12 per person) to budget rooms (around $50) and self-contained units (around $100); you should book ahead, as rooms are limited.

At Warburton take time to visit the **Tjulyuru Cultural & Civic Centre** (☎ 08-8956 7966; www.tjulyuru .com; ☻ 9am-4pm Mon-Fri), near the roadhouse; the art gallery contains an extensive collection of Warburton Aboriginal paintings. At **Giles**, 231km northeast of Warburton and 105km west of the Northern Territory (NT) border, there is a meteorological station that runs an 8am tour daily.

Warakurna, Warburton and Giles run on NT time, 1½ hours ahead of WA time. Permits to travel across Aboriginal land on the Great

Central Rd are needed for both **WA** (Department of Indigenous Affairs; ☎ 08-9235 8000; www.dia.wa.gov. au) and **NT** (Central Land Council; ☎ 08-8951 6320; www .clc.org.au).

SOUTH OF KALGOORLIE-BOULDER
Norseman
pop 1600

From the crossroads township of Norseman you can head south to Esperance or north to Kalgoorlie, westwards to Hyden and Wave Rock via 300km of all-weather gravel road, or begin the long, long trek across the Eyre Hwy (Nullarbor).

The **visitors centre** (☎ 08-9039 1071; www.norse man.info; 68 Roberts St; ☻ 9am-5pm Mon-Fri, 9.30am-4pm Sat & Sun) is a mine of information about the Nullarbor. Stretch your legs at the excellent and well-signed **Beacon Hill Mararoa Lookout**, and stop at the **Historical Museum** (Battery Rd; admission $3; ☻ 10am-1pm Mon-Sat), which showcases all sorts of pioneering items.

SLEEPING & EATING
Lodge 101 (☎ 08-9039 1541; 101 Prinsep St; s/d $45/65) After the relentless road, this colourful guesthouse, with its clean and comfortable rooms, is a cheery place to rest your cramped bones.

Great Western Motel (☎ 08-9039 1633; www .norsemangreatwesternmotel.com.au; Prinsep St; s/d $90/140; ☒ ☒) If you're looking for a cool respite, try these motel rooms constructed of rammed-earth and timber in a leafy setting. There's a restaurant on site.

Gateway Caravan Park (☎ 08-9039 1500; www.ac claimparks.com.au; 23 Prinsep St; unpowered/powered sites $24/26, cabins from $75; ☒) Decent cabins and a bushy atmosphere make this a reliable option. Wi-fi is available, as are a couple of basic twin-bedded on-site vans ($20 per person).

There are a couple of cafes and a supermarket in town, or go for the 24-hour cafe at the BP Service Station.

EYRE HIGHWAY (THE NULLARBOR)

London to Moscow, or Perth to Adelaide? There's not much difference, distance-wise. The 2700km Eyre Hwy crosses the southern edge of the vast **Nullarbor Plain**, parallel with the **Trans-Australia Railway** to the north. One stretch of the railway runs dead straight for 478km – the longest piece of straight railway line in the world.

John Eyre has the highway named after him because he was the first European to cross the stretch in 1841. After the 1877 telegraph line was laid, miners en route to the goldfields trekked its length across the plain and under an unforgiving sun. In 1912 the first car made it across. By 1941 the rough-and-ready transcontinental highway carried a handful of vehicles a day. In 1969 the WA government surfaced the road as far as the South Australian (SA) border. Finally, in 1976, the last stretch was surfaced and now it runs close to the coast on the SA side, with the Nullarbor region ending dramatically at the cliffs of the Great Australian Bight.

From Norseman it's 725km to the South Australian border, near Eucla, and a further 480km to Ceduna (meaning 'a place to sit down and rest' in the local Aboriginal language) in SA. They aren't kidding! From Ceduna, it's still another 793km to Adelaide (a *long* day's drive) via Port Augusta.

Crossing the Nullarbor

Do outback rescue services a big favour and take some simple precautions before hitting the road. This is not the place to run out of petrol: fuel prices are high and there's a distance between fuel stops of about 200km. Getting help for a mechanical breakdown can be expensive and time consuming, so make sure your vehicle is in decent shape and you've got good tyres and basic spare parts. Carry more drinking water than you think you'll need, just in case you breakdown and have to sit it out by the roadside. Book ahead if you're planning to overnight at the roadhouses, and check out www.nullarbornet .com.au for comprehensive information. Oh, and last but not least – take plenty of compilation CDs or audiobooks.

Norseman to Eucla

At the 100km mark from Norseman, **our pick** **Fraser Range Station** (☎ 08-9039 3210; www.fraserrangestation.com.au; unpowered/powered sites $20/25, budget r s/d $55/75, stone cottage r $95) is the first (or last, depending) and best stop on the Nullarbor. This working sheep-station's bush camping ground, heritage buildings and facilities are top-notch (though there's no fuel). Next is **Balladonia** (193km), where the **Balladonia Hotel Motel** (☎ 08-9039 3453; unpowered/ powered sites $13/22, dm $22, s/d from $90/108; ✷ 💻) has a small heritage museum.

Balladonia to Cocklebiddy, some 210km, is a lonely section. The first 160km to **Caiguna**

includes one of the world's longest stretches of straight road – 145km, the so-called Ninety Mile Straight. If you can't face any more road, stay the night at the **John Eyre Motel** (☎ 08-9039 3459; unpowered/powered sites $12/18, budget s/d $58/72, standard s/d $83/99; ✷).

There are shaded picnic tables and a decent playground for kids at **Cocklebiddy**. The **Cocklebiddy Wedgetail Inn** (☎ 08-9039 3462; unpowered/powered sites $16/22, budget s/d $54/72, standard s/d $82/99; ✷) has fuel, a licensed restaurant and a snack bar. Cocklebiddy runs on Central Western time, 45 minutes ahead of Perth time, and 45 minutes behind Adelaide time.

Birds Australia's **Eyre Bird Observatory** (☎ 08-9039 3450; www.eyrebirds.org) is housed in the remote and lovely 1897 former Eyre Telegraph Station, 50km south of Cocklebiddy on the Great Australian Bight. Day visitors are welcome ($10 per vehicle), but the last 10km are soft sand and are 4WD accessible only. If you are in a 2WD and are overnighting, the wardens will pick you up from the observatory car park, 14km off the Eyre Hwy; bookings are essential. Full board is good value at $90 per person per night; Birds Australia members, YHA members and seniors get a discount.

Madura, 91km east of Cocklebiddy, has a population of seven and is close to the Hampton Tablelands (stop at the lookout). If you need a cool night's sleep, the standard rooms at the **Madura Pass Oasis Inn** (☎ 08-9039 3464; unpowered/powered sites $15/25, budget s/d $65/75, standard s/d $95/112; ✷ 💻) are air-conditioned, the campsite is shady and the pool is welcome in summer.

In **Mundrabilla**, 116km further east, is the **Mundrabilla Motel Hotel** (☎ 08-9039 3465; Eyre Hwy; unpowered/powered sites $15/20, r from $85; ✷), where fuel prices are still reputedly the cheapest on the Nullarbor.

Just before the SA border is **Eucla**, surrounded by stunning sand dunes and pristine beaches. Around 5km south of town are the photogenic ruins of the 1877 **telegraph station**, which are gradually being engulfed by the dunes. Campsites and spacious rooms are available at the **Eucla Motor Hotel** (☎ 08-9039 3468; unpowered/powered sites $15/20, budget s/d $35/60, s/d with bathroom $90/105; ✷ 💻).

Eucla to Ceduna

See p792 for details on what you'll find on the section of highway between the border and Ceduna.

WESTERN AUSTRALIA

A FORTUNATE LIFE

The autobiography of AB Facey (1894–1982) relates one of the great coming-of-age stories in 20th-century Australia. Before Facey turned two his father died and his mother abandoned him soon after, leaving his grandmother to raise him until he was eight – at which time he went off to work.

He spent a tough childhood working the outback of WA as a farm labourer, and later fought in a boxing troupe before enlisting at the outbreak of WWI. He landed at Gallipoli where two of his brothers were killed.

Facey was badly injured in WWI, struggled through the Great Depression and lost a son in WWII. However, his optimism rarely wavered. Facey didn't teach himself to write until his return from Gallipoli, but after this he kept copious notes about his experiences. He only stopped writing after the death of Evelyn, his wife of nearly 60 years. In 1979, at the age of 85, Facey had his manuscript accepted for publication by the Fremantle Arts Centre Press.

Facey's autobiography, *A Fortunate Life,* was released in 1981 and he passed away nine months later, just long enough for him to see how deeply affecting the book was to anyone who read it. Apart from its emotional resonance, it's an important historical document, as Facey experienced many of the significant events that helped shape Australia's cultural identity.

THE MIDLANDS & WHEATBELT

This vast rural region expands from the base of the Pilbara down to the Wheatbelt towns some 300km or so south of the Great Eastern Hwy. Visitors come to see vibrant displays of spring wildflowers and dramatic geological formations, particularly the iconic Wave Rock (Map p955).

Getting There & Away

With a vehicle you can move at your own pace through the Central Wheatbelt towns on your way to the Goldfields. Otherwise, the **Transwa Prospector** (☎ 1300 662 205; www.transwa.wa.gov.au) has daily departures connecting Perth and Kalgoorlie. Trains depart from the East Perth terminal and make stops at Cunderdin (two hours), Kellerberrin (2¼ hours), Merredin (3¼ hours) and Southern Cross (4½ hours), before arriving in Kalgoorlie (6¼ hours). Note that not all trains stop at Cunderdin and Kellerberrin.

CUNDERDIN TO SOUTHERN CROSS

Sleepy **Cunderdin** (population 1250), 156km from Perth, is a fine spot to stretch your legs. The visitors centre is handily situated in the **museum** (☎ 08-9635 1291; 100 Forrest St; entry by donation; ☉ 10am-4pm), which features a restored steam water pumping station on the old goldfields pipeline. The building, with its brick chimney stretching skyward, is also the town's icon.

Even if you're not spending the night, don't miss Cunderdin's **Ettamogah Pub** (☎ 08-9635 1777; www.ettamogah.com; 75 Main St; s/d from $70/80; ❂). This wonky waterhole is a replica of an Albury-Wodonga hotel immortalised in Aussie cartoonist Ken Maynard's long-running comic for *Australasian Post* magazine. The Ettamogah does great-value counter meals including satisfying salads, pastas and burgers ($13 to $24).

It's worth stopping at **Kellerberrin** (population 1182), 203km from Perth, to take in the latest exhibition at the cutting-edge **International Artspace Kellerberrin Australia** (Iaska; ☎ 08-9228 2444; www.iaska.com.au; 88-90 Massingham St; admission free; ☉ 1-5pm Thu, Fri & Sun, 10am-5pm Sat). The **visitors centre** (☎ 08-9045 4006; www.kellerberrin .wa.gov.au; 110 Massingham St; ☉ 8.30am-4.30pm Mon-Fri) has info on other attractions.

Merredin (population 3629), 260km east of Perth, is a good place to refuel. The **visitors centre** (☎ 08-9041 1666; www.wheatbelttourism.com; 88 Barrack St; ☉ 10am-4pm Mon-Fri, to 2pm Sat & Sun) has info on wildflower and town tours, and where to see 2500-million-year-old granite rock formations.

You can overnight in Merredin's **Olympic Motel** (☎ 08-9041 1588; www.olympicmotel.com; Great Eastern Hwy; s/d from $80/90), with pleasant, carpeted rooms set with patchwork quilts and splashes of colour. The **Merredin Caravan Park** (☎ 08-9041 1535; 2 Oats St; unpowered/powered sites $20/25; ❂) is another reliable option with a laundry, playground and palm-fringed pool.

Southern Cross (population 708), 370km east of Perth, is the last Wheatbelt town and the first Goldfields town, making a fine living from both. Named after the stars that prospectors Tom Riseley and Mick Toomey used to guide them to discover gold here in 1888, Southern Cross was the state's first gold-rush town. Its spacious streets also bear the names of stars and constellations. The **visitors centre** (☎ 08-9049 1001; www.yilgarn.wa.gov.au; Shire of Yilgarn, Antares St; ☻ 8.30am-4.30pm Mon-Fri) can organise bush tours and make transport bookings.

WAVE ROCK & HYDEN

Perfectly shaped like a wave about to crest, the 15m-high and 110m-long multicoloured granite **Wave Rock** is worth the 350km journey from Perth – we dare you not to strike a surfing pose on this rock-solid wave! Formed some 60 million years ago by weathering and water erosion, Wave Rock's streaks of colour were caused by run-off from local mineral water springs.

The **visitors centre** (☎ 08-9880 5182; www.waverock.com.au; Wave Rock; ☻ 9am-5pm), at the Wildflower Shoppe and Country Kitchen, has plenty of information and souvenirs, and you can stop in the adjoining museum and wildlife park.

Other attractions in the area include several walking tracks, including the excellent, easy 3.5km **Wave Rock Circuit Walk** from the car park through granite country and out over the salt lakes. Some 20km north, visitors can see Aboriginal art – mostly hand stencils – at **Mulka's Cave**.

If you plan to stay, make sure you phone ahead – accommodation can fill with tour groups. Camp amid the gum trees near the rock at **Wave Rock Cabins & Caravan Park** (☎ 08-9880 5022; www.waverock.com.au; unpowered/powered sites $28/33, cabin s/d $100/115; ☒).

In **Hyden** (population 190), 4km east, the **Wave Rock Motel** (☎ 08-9880 5052; hotelmotel@ waverock.com.au; 2 Lynch St; d from $98; ☒ ☒) has well-equipped rooms, a comfy lounge with fireplace, and an indoor bush bistro.

Transwa (☎ 1300 662 205; www.transwa.wa.gov.au) runs a bus from Perth to Hyden ($45, five hours) every Tuesday, with the return service to Perth each Thursday.

OTHER WHEATBELT TOWNS

Narrogin (population 4200), 189km southeast of Perth, is an agricultural centre with a **courthouse museum** (☎ 08-9881 2064; Egerton St; ☻ 9.30am-4.30pm Mon-Fri, to noon Sat). The **visitors centre** (☎ 08-9881 2064; www.dryandratourism.org.au) is next door.

Eucalypt woodlands once covered most of the Wheatbelt. Some 26km north of Narrogin is the magnificent **Dryandra Woodland**, the remnants of an environment in which numbats, many bird species and striking wildflowers survive today. For the full escapist experience, stay at the 1920s forestry settlement of **Lions Dryandra Village** (☎ 08-9884 5231; www.dryandravillage.org.au; midweek adult/child $25/10, weekends & holidays 2-/8-person cabins $75/100), 8km from the animal enclosure, in rustic woodcutters' cabins.

Wickepin, about 45km northeast of Narrogin, is the setting of *A Fortunate Life*, the much-loved, school-of-hard-knocks autobiography of Albert Facey. The **Albert Facey Homestead** (☎ 08-9888 1005; Wogolin Rd; adult/child $3/1; ☻ 10am-4pm daily Mar-Nov, 10am-4pm Fri-Sun Dec-Feb) merits a visit for anyone who's read it.

A favourite slice of Western Australiana is the kitschy 9m-high fibreglass merino, 228km southeast of Perth in **Wagin** (population 1800). It has a rival in Goulburn, New South Wales (see p248). The visitors centre is at **Wagin Historical Village** (☎ 08-9861 1232; www.waginhistoricalvillage.com; Kitchener St; admission free; ☻ 10am-4pm), which contains 26 original and replica buildings showing village life in the early settlement days.

Kojonup (population 2150), 39km southwest of Katanning, was established in 1837 as a military outpost to protect travellers taking the mail run from the Swan Settlement (Perth) to Albany. Kojonup has a cutting-edge museum, the interactive **Kodja Place Interpretive Centre** (☎ 08-9831 0500; www.kojonupvisitors.com; Albany Hwy; adult/child $6/3; ☻ 9am-5pm). You can sit around a Noongar campfire, ride an old school bus and drive a farm ute. Noongar guide Jack Cox also offers excellent Indigenous cultural tours ($5).

WILDFLOWER WAY

One of the best places to see WA's famous carpet of wildflowers, which bloom between August and November, is in the Midlands area north of Perth. There's prime viewing off the three roads running roughly parallel towards Geraldton. Everlasting daisies, kangaroo paws, foxgloves, wattles, featherflowers, banksias and the gorgeous low-lying wreath *Leschenaultia* (see Blooming Wildflowers, p966) blanket the countryside.

WESTERN AUSTRALIA

BLOOMING WILDFLOWERS

WA is famed for its 8000 species of wildflower, which bloom between August and November. Even some of the driest regions put on a colourful display after a little rainfall at any time of the year.

The southwest has over 3000 species, many of which are unique to this region. They're commonly known as everlastings because the petals stay attached after the flowers have died. You can find flowers almost everywhere in the state, but the jarrah forests in the southwest are particularly rich. Coastal national parks such as Fitzgerald River and Kalbarri also have brilliant displays, as do the Stirling Ranges. Near Perth, the Badgingarra, Alexander Morrison, Yanchep and John Forrest national parks are excellent choices. There's also a wildflower display in Kings Park, Perth. As you go further north, they tend to flower earlier in the season. Common flowering plants include mountain bell, Sturt's desert pea and various species of banksia, wattle, kangaroo paw and orchid.

Notable stops along the Brand Hwy (Map p928) between Midland and Dongara include **Moore River National Park**, **Badgingarra National Park**, **Coomallo Nature Reserve** and **Lesueur National Park**, which requires a 4WD. Towns along the way include Cataby, Badgingarra and Eneabba. This road also connects you to the Pinnacles and several coastal towns that have the area's best accommodation; see p968.

From Bindoon on the Great Northern Hwy (Map p928), the Midland Rd heads to Dongara, passing **Alexander Morrison National Park**, **Capamauro Nature Reserve** and **Depot Hill Reserve**, and the towns of Moora, Watheroo, Coorow and Mingenew. The **Yarra Yarra Lakes**, near Carnamah, are noted for their bird life.

The stretch between Wubin, on the Great Northern Hwy, and Mullewa, east of Geraldton, has fewer formal wildflower areas, but there's plenty to see in the fields and along the verges as you drive. The surrounds of the tiny towns of **Mullewa**, **Moora**, **Morawa**, **Wongan Hills** and **Perenjori** are the best places to look.

Pick up a free copy of the *Wildflower Holiday Guide* from the **Western Australian Visitors Centre** (☎ 1300 361 351, 08-9483 1111; www .westernaustralia.com; cnr Forrest Pl & Wellington St, Perth) for more information, or pop into the local visitors centres.

GREAT NORTHERN HIGHWAY

Small mining and agricultural towns dot the Great Northern Hwy on its long stretch from Perth to Port Hedland. This is the quickest way north (and the designated route for long-haul road trains), but little used by travellers as it's less scenic than the coastal route. Undulating pastures and slender eucalypts quickly give way to packed red earth and the scrubby landscape of the Pilbara. The peaceful monastic village (and lovely pub) of New Norcia is an excellent place to overnight.

Getting There & Away

Integrity (☎ 1800 226 339; www.integritycoachlines.com .au) has a service along the Great Northern Hwy that leaves Perth once weekly (currently Wednesdays). It passes through New Norcia ($24, two hours), Mt Magnet ($95, seven hours), Cue ($107, eight hours) and Meekatharra ($124, 10 hours) before reaching Port Headland ($232, 22 hours).

Transwa (☎ 1300 662 205; www.transwa.wa.gov.au) coaches leave Perth on Tuesday, Thursday, Friday and Sunday, arriving in New Norcia two hours later; they return to Perth on Tuesday and Thursday ($20).

NEW NORCIA

pop 70

The idyllic monastery settlement of New Norcia, 132km from Perth, consists of a cluster of ornate Spanish-style buildings set incongruously in the Australian bush. Founded in 1846 by Spanish Benedictine monks as an Aboriginal mission, today the working monastery holds prayers and retreats, alongside a business producing boutique breads and gourmet goodies.

New Norcia Museum & Art Gallery (☎ 08-9654 8056; www.newnorcia.com; Great Northern Hwy; combined museum, town tour & tastings ticket adult/child $23/14; ☯ 9am-4.30pm) traces the history of the monastery and houses impressive art, including works by Charles Blackman and Pro Hart, and one of the country's largest collections of post-Renaissance religious art. The gift shop sells souvenirs, honeys, preserves, and breads baked in the monks' wood-fired oven.

The **abbey church** is also worth a look, particularly for its syncretic artworks. One painting shows Christ's birth among palms, visiting Aboriginal wise men and a kangaroo, emu and kookaburra looking on.

Guided **town tours** (⏲ 11am & 1.30pm) enable you to get a look inside the monks' private chapel within the monastery, the abbey chapel and the frescoed college chapels; purchase tickets from the museum. **Meet a Monk** (admission free; ⏲ 10.30am Mon-Fri, 4.30pm Sat, 10am Sun) gives you the chance to find out what it's like to be a monk. Choral concerts and organ recitals are also held.

our pick **New Norcia Hotel** (☎ 08-9654 8034; www.newnorcia.wa.edu.au/hotel.htm; Great Northern Hwy; s/d without bathroom incl breakfast $75/95) is a grand place, with sweeping staircases, high ceilings and atmospheric public spaces. The understated rooms open onto an enormous verandah. An international menu ($18 to $25) is available at the bar or in the elegant dining room. You can sit outside on the terrace and sample the delicious hand-crafted New Norcia Abbey Ale, a Belgian-style golden ale brewed specially for the abbey.

The abbey also offers lodging in the **Monastery Guesthouse** (☎ 08-9654 8002; guest house@newnorcia.wa.edu.au; full board suggested donation $75) within the walls of the southern cloister, in gender-segregated rooms. Guests can also join in prayers with the monks (and males can dine with them).

NEW NORCIA TO NEWMAN

More than 400km to the north of New Norcia is **Mount Magnet** (population 1180), where mining is the town's lifeblood. Some 11km north of town are the ruins of **Lennonville**. Approximately 80km further north is the old gold-mining town of **Cue** (population350), the route's architectural highlight. It's a pretty, little town of stone buildings, corrugated-tin roofs and a sense of time gone by. The massive red granite monolith of **Walga Rock**, 48km to the west, has a gallery of Aboriginal art, and **Wilgie Mia**, 64km northwest of Cue via Glen Station, is the site of a 30,000-year-old Aboriginal red-ochre quarry.

Meekatharra (population 800), 116km north of Cue, offers fuel; further north, the mining town of **Newman** (population 4245) has all the facilities and is the place to stock up for further travels. Enquire about mine tours through the **visitors centre** (☎ 08-9175 2888; www.newman-wa.org; Fortescue Ave).

Sleeping & Eating

Commercial Hotel (☎ 08-9981 1020; 77 Main St, Meekatharra; hotel s/d from $50/70) Great-value and well-maintained motel rooms, and tasty counter meals ($12 to $25) – the burgers and steaks are memorable.

Outback Gold (☎ 08-9963 4433; 12 Scott Close, Mt Magnet; s/d from $70/80; ⬛ ⬛) Miners and backpackers exchange stories in the communal kitchen and barbecue areas at this good-value place.

Queen of the Murchison Hotel (☎ 08-9963 1625; Austin St, Cue; s/d $85/120; ⬛ ⬛) This classic hotel has cosy and clean rooms.

Mia Mia Hotel (☎ 08-9175 8400; www.miamia.com.au; 32 Kalgan Dr, Newman; d from $120; ⬛) This swish newcomer offers trim contemporary rooms with an earthy colour scheme; photographs of the Pilbara adorn the walls.

Mt Magnet Caravan Park (☎ 08-9963 4198; Hepburn St, Mt Magnet; unpowered/powered sites $15/18) Can provide a patch of dirt to park for the night.

Cue Caravan Park (☎ 08-9963 1107; Austin St, Cue; unpowered/powered sites $18/22) This dusty caravan park has basic facilities.

Dearlove's Caravan Park (☎ 08-9175 2802; Cowra Dr, Newman; unpowered/powered sites $20/26; ⬛) A sprawling, shady, central park with decent facilities, including a campers kitchen and gas barbecues.

Meekatharra Caravan Park (☎ 08-9981 1253; Main St, Meekatharra; powered sites $26) Basic dirt sites behind a service station.

CENTRAL WEST COAST

The sun-kissed Central West Coast is a 550km stretch from the sedate fishing town of Dongara-Port Denison on the Batavia Coast in the south to the agriculturally lush Gascoyne region surrounding Carnarvon in the north. Jagged sea cliffs, historic settlements, craggy national parks and lovely beaches set the stage for some fascinating exploring.

The windswept Batavia Coast and the attractive, up-and-coming town of Geraldton attract windsurfers and anglers. Dramatic coastal scenery lies a bit north in Kalbarri, a sleepy town surrounded by a pristine national park with deep river gorges, jagged sea cliffs and richly hued wildflowers in spring.

For a rewarding aquatic experience, Shark Bay is a major draw, blessed with turquoise waters and prolific land- and marine life. Monkey Mia is the star attraction, made famous by its visiting dolphins and a sizeable dugong population. It's also a fine spot for snorkelling, sailing and lazing about on a calm, pretty beach. The area also has a rich Aboriginal history and geological intrigue, with fossils (stromatolites) related to the earliest life forms on earth.

Getting There & Away

Skywest (☎ 1300 660 088; www.skywest.com.au) has several flights daily from Perth to Geraldton, with links to Kalbarri, Monkey Mia, Carnarvon and Exmouth.

Greyhound Australia (☎ 1300 473 946; www.greyhound.com.au) has northbound buses departing Perth (daily except Tuesday and Sunday) for Dongara ($43, 5¾ hours), Geraldton ($51, 6½ hours), Overlander Roadhouse (for Denham and Monkey Mia; $102, 10½ hours) and Carnarvon ($130, 13½ hours). **Transwa** (☎ 1300 662 205; www.transwa.wa.gov.au) follows three routes to Geraldton: via the Brand Hwy, Midlands Rd and Great Northern Hwy.

JURIEN BAY TO DONGARA-PORT DENISON

Heading straight up the coast from Cervantes, you'll pass the small seaside towns of **Jurien Bay**, **Green Head** and **Leeman** en route to Dongara-Port Denison. Stop off at the Molah Hill Lookout, 11km north of Cervantes, for some spectacular views of the countryside.

Apart from some comely white-sand beaches and great fishing, the main draw is the **Lesueur National Park**, which is home to one of the most diverse and rich wildflower areas of WA (access is via a 4WD track off Cockleshell Gully Rd), and excellent tours to Australian sea-lion populations on offshore islands.

You can snorkel with sea lions and watch humpback whales migrate south (September to December) with **Jurien Charters** (☎ 08-9652 1109; www.juriencharters.com; 3 Dorcas Dr; 3hr sea-lion tours adult/child $90/30).

The popular local watering hole, **Jurien Bay Hotel Motel** (☎ 08-9652 1022; jurienhotel@wn.com.au;

5 White St; s/d $90/105; ☒ ☒), has comfy motel rooms out back, with a decent restaurant (mains $16 to $30) serving prawns with chilli, kangaroo steak and local seafood specialities.

Pitch your tent, camp your van or rent a chalet (which sleep up to six) a short stroll from the beach at the **Jurien Bay Tourist Park** (☎ 08-9652 1595; www.jurienbaytouristpark.com.au; Roberts St; unpowered/powered sites $23/26, chalets $130). There's a laundry, a giant 'jumping pillow' (trampoline of sorts) and two campers kitchens.

DONGARA-PORT DENISON

pop 3500

The tranquil seaside towns of Dongara and Port Denison, 359km from Perth, have attractive beaches and a laid-back atmosphere. Dongara's charming main street, Moreton Tce, is shaded by century-old fig trees that set this old town apart from its younger sibling. There are superlative beaches for swimming, surfing, fishing and strolling, such as South Beach, Seaspray Beach and Surf Beach.

The **visitors centre** (☎ 08-9927 1404; www.irwin.wa.gov.au/tourism; 9 Waldeck St; ☒ 9am-5pm Mon-Fri, to noon Sat) is in Dongara's old post office. Moreton Tce has several banks with ATMs and a **telecentre** (☎ 08-9927 2111; 11 Moreton Tce; per hr $8; ☒ 9am-4pm Mon-Fri).

Pick up the free *Walk Dongara-Denison* brochure from the visitors centre and choose from 12 historic- or nature-based rambles. Wildlife lovers should stroll the **Irwin River Nature Trail** for black swans, pelicans and cormorants.

Historic buildings include **Russ Cottage** (Pt Leander Dr; adult/child $2.50/50c; ☒ 10am-noon Sun & by appointment), built in the late 1860s, with a kitchen floor made from compacted anthills, and the sandstone **Royal Steam Flour Mill** (Brand Hwy; no public access). Its steam engines ground wheat from surrounding farms between 1894 and 1935. In the old police station, the cells of the **Irwin District Museum** (☎ 08-9927 1404; admission $2.50; ☒ 10am-noon Mon-Sat) hold interesting historical displays.

Denison Beach Marina brims with boats that haul crayfish, the towns' livelihood. Enjoy the views from the **Fisherman's Lookout Obelisk** at Port Denison.

Sleeping & Eating

Dongara Tourist Park (☎ 08-9927 1210; www.dongaratouristpark.com.au; 8 George St, Port Denison; unpowered/

powered sites $30/40, on-site vans/cabins $70/145; ▨) The best option for camping or caravanning, this place offers shaded, spacious sites protected by dunes (with South Beach on the other side). The cabins are comfy and colourful, some with beach views.

Dongara Old Mill Motel (☎ 08-9927 1200; www .dongaraoldmillmotel.com.au; 58 Waldeck St, Dongara; d $88; ▨ ▣) Just off the Brand Hwy, the Old Mill Motel offers modern, nicely renovated rooms with small kitchen units. There's a communal barbecue and an enticing pool.

Priory Hotel (☎ 08-9927 1090; www.prioryhotel.com .au; 11 St Dominics Rd, Dongara; d/f/apt from $100/120/140; ▨ ▣) A former nunnery and ladies college, the Priory Lodge boasts charming period furniture, polished floorboards, black-and-white photos, and wide verandahs. There's a big swimming pool, leafy grounds, and an atmospheric restaurant and bar.

Dongara Hotel (☎ 08-9927 1023; dhm@westnet.com .au; 12 Moreton Tce, Dongara; d $105) In the centre of town, Dongara Hotel is a clean if predictable option, with simple, carpeted rooms with minifridges and a popular restaurant with a wide verandah (but no view).

Port Denison Holiday Units (☎ 08-9927 1104; 14 Carnarvon St, Port Denison; d $110-120; ▨) Run by a friendly Scottish soul, these eight spotless, spacious units are just a block from the beach; ask for a room with marina views.

Southerleys (☎ 08-9927 2207; Point Leander Dr, Port Denison; mains $17-30; �YY lunch & dinner) Soak up the rays on the sunny terrace while you enjoy fresh seafood at this casual bistro. Licensed and BYO.

Little Starfish (☎ 0448 344 215; White Tops Rd, Port Denison; mains $6-28; �YY breakfast & lunch) Hanging buoys are strung like Christmas lights along the roof at this casual snack shack above South Beach. The menu features big breakfasts, prawn-and-cheese sandwiches, burgers and lobsters in season (December to June).

The Season Tree (☎ 08-9927 1400; 8 Moreton Tce, Dongara; mains $16-25) The Season Tree serves coffee, cakes, smoothies and assorted Thai and Chinese dishes. You can order takeout pad thai, curry and *tom yum* or enjoy a meal at an outdoor table beneath an enormous fig tree. BYO.

GREENOUGH
pop 100

Historic, windswept Greenough was an active administrative centre in its 1860s hey-

day. Nearly a dozen of its traditional stone buildings have been preserved at the charming **Central Greenough Historic Settlement** (☎ 08-9926 1084; Brand Hwy; adult/child $6/3; �YY 9am-4pm). You can freely wander the buildings, getting a glimpse of early pioneer days in the village through informative displays. The visitors centre has a stylish cafe (mains $15 to $20) serving Devonshire tea and scones, tasty vegetable curry (and other meals) plus homemade desserts; it also sells local products such as beeswax candles and handmade soaps.

The **Pioneer Museum** (☎ 08-9926 1058; www .greenough-pioneer-museum.com; Phillips Rd; adult/child $5/free; �YY 10am-4pm) recreates life in an 1880s homestead with displays of period pieces and local artefacts. John and Elizabeth Maley – and their 14 children – were the cottage's original owners and early pioneers in the area.

The small **Greenough Wildlife & Bird Park** (☎ 08-9926 1171; www.wildlifeandbirdpark.com.au; Company Rd; adult/child/teen $8/4.50/6; �YY 9am-5pm) provides close encounters with kangaroos, wallabies, emus, cockatoos and other animal life. Most animals are tame enough to feed by hand (feed bags cost 50c) – the dingoes and crocodile excepted, of course.

Rock of Ages Bed & Breakfast (☎ 08-9926 1154; rock ofages@westnet.com.au; Phillips Rd; s/d $70/80), next door to the Pioneer Museum, offers three handsome rooms with wood floors and shared bathrooms in an 1857 sandstone cottage. Guests can use the dining room and outdoor spa, and watch the moon rise from the back patio.

Hampton Arms Inn (☎ 08-9926 1057; www.hampton arms.com.au; Company Rd; s/d $70/90) is a classic Aussie inn (1863) with delightfully old-fashioned rooms (some with a fireplace), a cluttered bookshop crammed with rare titles, a quaint restaurant (mains $10 to $25) and an atmospheric bar.

Transwa (☎ 1300 662 205; www.transwa.wa.gov.au) services along the Kalbarri–Geraldton route stop at Greenough on the Brand Hwy daily.

GERALDTON
pop 19,200

Capital of the midwest, Geraldton is an intriguing seaside town well worth exploring. It's home to classic 19th-century pubs, a European-influenced cathedral and picturesque neighbourhoods. Geraldton's waterfront houses a sizeable fishing industry, while its wind-whipped beaches are major destinations for wind- and kitesurfers.

A good place to begin an exploration of Geraldton is along Marine Tce, one street back from the sleek new waterfront promenade. Here you'll find pubs, restaurants, shops and cafes providing a window into this old-fashioned town on the edge of reinvention.

Information

Batavia Coast Air Charter (166 Marine Tce; per hr $5; 9am-5pm Mon-Fri, 9.30am-noon Sat) Convenient internet cafe, with an adjoining shop full of eye-catching knick-knacks and enticing confections. Here you can also book a flight to the Abrolhos (p973).

Book Tree (176 Marine Tce; 9.30am-4pm Mon-Fri, to noon Sat) Scour the floor-to-ceiling shelves of preloved books for some road reading.

Geraldton Regional Hospital (08-9956 2222; Shenton St) Has 24-hour emergency facilities.

Sun City Books (08-9964 7258; 49 Marine Tce; 9am-5pm Mon-Fri, to 1pm Sat) Decent selection of books plus internet.

Visitors centre (08-9921 3999; www.gerald tontourist.com.au; Bill Sewell Complex, Chapman Rd; 9am-5pm Mon-Fri, 10am-4pm Sat & Sun) Provides lots of great info and staff will book accommodation, tours and transport.

Sights & Activities

One not-to-be-missed attraction is the **Western Australian Museum Geraldton** (08-9921 5080; www .museum.wa.gov.au; 1 Museum Pl; admission by donation; 9.30am-4.30pm). Here you'll find engaging multimedia displays on the area's natural and

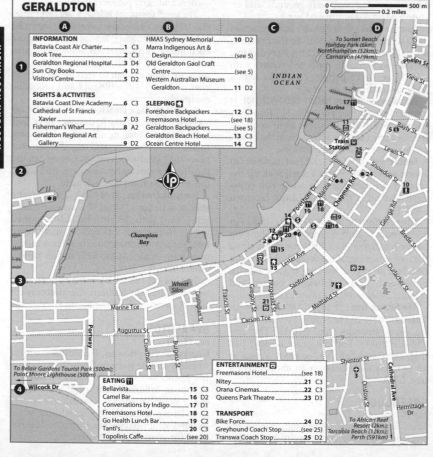

GERALDTON

0 — 500 m
0 — 0.2 miles

INFORMATION	
Batavia Coast Air Charter	1 C3
Book Tree	2 C3
Geraldton Regional Hospital	3 D4
Sun City Books	4 D2
Visitors Centre	5 D2

SIGHTS & ACTIVITIES	
Batavia Coast Dive Academy	6 C3
Cathedral of St Francis Xavier	7 C3
Fisherman's Wharf	8 A2
Geraldton Regional Art Gallery	9 D2

HMAS Sydney Memorial	10 D2
Marra Indigenous Art & Design	(see 5)
Old Geraldton Gaol Craft Centre	(see 5)
Western Australian Museum Geraldton	11 D2

SLEEPING	
Foreshore Backpackers	12 C3
Freemasons Hotel	(see 18)
Geraldton Backpackers	13 C3
Geraldton Beach Hotel	13 C3
Ocean Centre Hotel	14 C2

EATING	
Bellavista	15 C3
Camel Bar	16 D2
Conversations by Indigo	17 D1
Freemasons Hotel	18 C2
Go Health Lunch Bar	19 C2
Tanti's	20 C3
Topolinis Caffe	(see 20)

ENTERTAINMENT	
Freemasons Hotel	(see 18)
Nitey	21 C3
Orana Cinemas	22 C3
Queens Park Theatre	23 D3

TRANSPORT	
Bike Force	24 D2
Greyhound Coach Stop	(see 25)
Transwa Coach Stop	25 D2

INDIAN OCEAN

To Sunset Beach Holiday Park (6km); Northhampton (52km); Carnarvon (479km);

Marina

Train Station

Champion Bay

Wheat Silos

Marine Tce

Augustus St

Portway

To Belair Gardens Tourist Park (500m); Point Moore Lighthouse (500m)

Wilcock Dr

Shenton St

To African Reef Resort (2km); Tarcoola Beach (12km); Perth (591km)

WESTERN AUSTRALIA

SHIPWRECKS & SURVIVORS

Early in the morning on 4 June 1629, the Dutch East India Company's ship *Batavia* ran aground on a reef of the Abrolhos Islands, off the coast of Terra Australis Incognita, as Australia was then known. The ship was taking the fastest route to Batavia (Jakarta) in Java – heading due east once around the Cape of Good Hope and then along the WA coast to Indonesia. Quite often these ships were caught in storms or they misjudged the depth of the reefs close to the Australian coast, which earned this stretch of coastline the name Shipwreck Coast.

The captain of the *Batavia*, Francis Pelsaert, sailed a boat to the Dutch East India Company's base at Batavia to get help and supplies. While his back was turned a gruesome mutiny took place, and on the captain's return he executed all those involved, apart from two young men who were left ashore, becoming perhaps the first white men on Australian soil.

Another notable wreck was the *Zuytdorp*, which ran aground beneath the towering cliffs about 65km north of Kalbarri in 1712. Wine bottles, other relics and the remains of fires have been found on the cliff top, and the discovery of the extremely rare Ellis van Creveld syndrome (rife in Holland at the time the ship ran aground) in Aboriginal children suggests that *Zuytdorp* survivors lasted long enough to introduce the gene into Australia.

The remains of the *Batavia* and other wrecks can be seen at the Western Australian Museum in Geraldton (opposite) and in Fremantle's Maritime Museum Shipwrecks Galleries (p921).

Batavia Coast Dive Academy (below) offers diving tours to a more recent shipwreck, the *South Tomi*, which sank off the Geraldton coast in 2004.

cultural history with exhibits on Aborigines, pioneers and early explorers. The atmospheric Shipwreck Gallery documents the tragic story of the *Batavia* (see Shipwrecks & Survivors, above). There's also video footage of the sunken HMAS *Sydney*, which was only located in 2008.

The elaborate **Cathedral of St Francis Xavier** (☎ 08-9921 3221; Cathedral Ave; tours $2) is the finest example of the architectural achievements of the multitalented Monsignor Hawes. Construction began in 1916, but the plans were so grandiose for what was essentially a country-town church that it wasn't completed until 1938. Its most striking features include imposing twin towers with arched openings, a central dome, Romanesque columns and boldly striped walls. Guided tours are available at 10am Monday, Wednesday and Friday.

Geraldton Regional Art Gallery (☎ 08-9964 7170; 24 Chapman Rd; admission free; ☒ 10am-4pm Tue-Sat, 1-4pm Sun) has an excellent permanent collection, including paintings by Norman Lindsay and Elizabeth Durack, along with engaging temporary exhibitions.

If you want to take a bit of Yamatji culture home with you, check out **Marra Indigenous Art & Design** (☎ 08-9965 3440; www.marra.com.au; Bill Sewell Complex, Chapman Rd; ☒ 10am-2pm Mon-Fri), which sells vibrant paintings, woven bowls, wooden artefacts, didgeridoos, beaded necklaces and CDs.

Old Geraldton Gaol Craft Centre (☎ 08-9921 1614; Bill Sewell Complex, Chapman Rd; admission free; ☒ 10am-4pm) has local crafts for sale, but more compelling are the gloomy cells that housed prisoners from 1858 to 1986, and the historic documents detailing their grim circumstances.

At **Fisherman's Wharf** (☎ 08-9921 3999; Geraldton Harbour; tours adult/child $5/3; ☒ 9.30am Mon-Fri Nov-Jun) you can follow the lobsters' journey from fishing boat to dinner plate and buy fresh seafood from the market.

Discover the region's aquatic splendour with **Batavia Coast Dive Academy** (☎ 08-9921 4229; www.bcda.com.au; 153 Marine Tce; local dive with/without equipment $115/75), which offers open-water courses and a range of diving trips, including three-day chartered trips to the Abrolhos ($900 per person).

The monument on the hill overlooking town is the **HMAS Sydney Memorial** (signposted from George St), commemorating the 1941 loss of the ship and its 645 men after a skirmish with a German ship. There are free daily tours of the complex at 10.30am (donations accepted).

Sleeping

BUDGET

Foreshore Backpackers (☎ 08-9921 3275; 172 Marine Tce; dm/s/d $24/35/55; ☐) In an elegant old building, Foreshore has high ceilings and wooden floors, plus a central location and great sea views. Reception hours are from 8am to noon and 4pm to 8pm.

WESTERN AUSTRALIA

Geraldton Backpackers (☎ 08-9964 3001; Bill Sewell Complex, Chapman Rd; dm/s/d $25/30/60; 💻) Geraldton Backpackers has small dorm rooms and basic doubles, set in an attractive 1897 colonial building. Some travellers complain that it's less guesthouse and more halfway house. Reception hours are 8.30am to 12.30pm and 3pm to 8pm.

Freemasons Hotel (☎ 08-9964 3457; www.free masonshotel.com.au; cnr Marine Tce & Durlacher St; dm/s/d $30/70/80) The 1895 heritage hotel is better known for its bar, though rooms are fair value, with a spare design and tall ceilings. Some rooms open onto the shared verandah.

Geraldton Beach Hotel (☎ 08-9921 4444; 15 Fitzgerald St; s/d with shared bathroom $45/60; 💻) Set in a rather uninspiring building, this affordable place has clean, airy rooms with carpeting and shared bathrooms.

MIDRANGE & TOP END

African Reef Resort (☎ 08-9964 5566; www.african reef.com.au; 5 Broadhead Ave; s/d from $110/130; ✖ 🖳) Overlooking Tarcoola Beach, the recently renovated African Reef Resort is a relaxing spot for enjoying the beauty of the coastline. The self-contained rooms are the best bet – ask for ocean views.

Ocean Centre Hotel (☎ 08-9921 7777; www.oce ancentrehotel.com.au; cnr Foreshore Dr & Cathedral Ave; d standard/deluxe/deluxe with view $130/140/160; ✖ 💻) This waterfront hotel boasts a convenient central location and spacious, if minimalist rooms. Other bonuses include sunset views from the balcony and wireless internet access (although it costs).

CAMPING

Belair Gardens Tourist Park (☎ 08-9921 1997; www .belairbig4geraldton.com.au; 463 Marine Tce; unpowered/powered sites $23/26, cabins $81-125; 🖳) Near the lighthouse and across from Point Moore beach, this shady park has cramped sites, but extensive facilities, including a campers kitchen, barbecue area and tennis court.

Sunset Beach Holiday Park (☎ 08-9938 1655; sun setbeach@bigpond.com; Bosley St; powered sites $30, cabins $80-145) About 6km north of the town centre, Sunset Beach has roomier, shaded sites just a few steps from the beach.

Eating & Drinking

Geraldton has myriad takeaways, coffee lounges, bakeries, supermarkets and, of course, a great fish market.

Go Health Lunch Bar (☎ 08-9965 5200; 122 Marine Tce; light meals around $9; 💻) Fresh juices and smoothies, excellent espresso, healthy burritos, lentil burgers, focaccia sandwiches and other light meals are served over the cool corrugated-iron counter of this splashy cafe.

our pick Bellavista (☎ 08-9964 2681; cnr Marine Tce & Fitzgerald St; mains $10-30; ☀ breakfast & lunch Mon-Sat, dinner Fri & Sat) Serving Geraldton's best coffee, this small stylish cafe with its sidewalk seating is a great place for a pick-me-up. Former Melburnian John Todaro also prepares some of the city's best Italian and seafood dishes here.

Topolinis Caffe (☎ 08-9964 5866; 158 Marine Tce; mains $11-30; ☀ 8.30am-late) A favourite local haunt for afternoon coffee or an evening meal, this relaxed licensed eatery serves tasty specials such as mahi mahi served with mussel and prawn polenta and mustard-seared kangaroo. There's a $29 dinner-and-movie deal Monday through Thursday.

Tanti's (☎ 08-9964 2311; 174 Marine Tce; mains $12-18; ☀ lunch Wed-Fri, dinner Mon-Sat) This casual BYO restaurant is packed every night with Thai-loving regulars. Tanti's also offers good-value three-course lunch specials ($12) and takeaway.

Camel Bar (☎ 08-9965 5500; 20 Chapman Rd; mains $15-32; ☀ lunch & dinner Sun-Thu, to midnight Fri & Sat) In a Federalist-style building on Chapman, the sun-drenched Camel Bar serves up fresh salads, garlic prawns, curry and other bistro fare, but is best known for its inventive wood-fired pizzas.

Freemasons Hotel (☎ 08-9964 3457; cnr Marine Tce & Durlacher St; mains $18-30; ☀ 11am-midnight Mon-Sat, to 10pm Sun) This classic old Aussie pub with sidewalk seating has a modern brasserie where seafood, steak and lamb shanks are cooked up on a sizzling stone grill tableside. There are great WA beers such as the honeyed Beez Neez on tap and a decent wine list.

our pick Conversations by Indigo (☎ 08-9965 0800; Bayly St, Batavia Coast Marina; mains $29-41; ☀ 10.30am-late Mon-Sat, 8.30am-late Sun) In a stunning contemporary building overlooking the new marina, Geraldton's best restaurant has an inventive global menu highlighting fresh seafood and a great selection of WA wines.

Entertainment

Freemasons Hotel (above) is a favourite drinking spot with regular live music and occasional DJ and dance nights. Also popular is

Nitey (☎ 08-9921 1400; 60 Fitzgerald St; ◷ 10pm-lateThu-Sat), which sees locals lining up until late to boogie away in this red-walled club.

If you fancy a film, **Orana Cinemas** (☎ 08-9965 0568; www.oranacinemas.com.au; cnr Marine Tce & Fitzgerald St) screens the latest flicks, while **Queens Park Theatre** (☎ 08-9956 6662; www.queensparktheatre.com .au; cnr Cathedral Ave & Maitland St) stages theatre, comedy, concerts and films.

Getting There & Around

Skywest (☎ 1300 660 088; www.skywest.com.au) has flights to and from Perth daily, as well as regular flights to Carnarvon, Denham (for Monkey Mia), Exmouth and Karratha.

Greyhound (☎ 1300 473 946; www.greyhound.com .au) buses run from the old train station on Chapman Rd to Perth daily ($66, 6½ hours), as well as Broome ($264, 26 hours) and all points in between. **Transwa** (☎ 1300 662 205) goes from the same location daily to Perth ($50, six hours) and three times weekly to Kalbarri ($22, 2½ hours).

Geraldton Bus Service (☎ 08-9923 1100) operates eight routes to local suburbs (all-day ticket $4). **Bike Force** (☎ 08-9921 3279; 58 Chapman Rd) hires bikes for $20/80 per day/week.

HOUTMAN ABROLHOS ISLANDS

Better known as 'the Abrolhos', this archipelago of 122 coral islands is about 60km off the coast of Geraldton. While they're home to sealion colonies, a host of sea birds, golden-orb spiders, carpet pythons and the Tammar wallabies, much of the beauty of the Abrolhos lies beneath the water. Here *Acropora* genus corals abound and, thanks to the warm Leeuwin Current, a rare and spectacular mix of tropical and temperate fish species thrives.

The beautiful but treacherous reefs surrounding the islands have claimed many ships over the years, including the ill-fated *Batavia* (see Shipwrecks & Survivors, p971).

As the islands are protected and there are no tourist facilities, you can't stay overnight. Only licensed crayfishing families are permitted to shack-up on the islands in season (March to June). But you can go on bushwalks and picnics, and you can fly over, dive, snorkel, surf or fish the Abrolhos. A number of boats and light planes leave from Geraldton.

Flights for a half-/full-day tour cost around $200/250 per person. Try **Geraldton Air Charter** (☎ 08-9923 3434; www.geraldtonaircharter.com.au) or **Batavia Coast Air Charter** (☎ 08-9921 5168; www.abrolhosbat.com.au; 166 Marine Tce).

Abrolhos Odyssey Charters (☎ 0428 382 505; www .abrolhoscharters.com.au) runs popular fishing, diving and snorkelling trips.

Pick up the excellent *Houtman Abrolhos Islands Visitors Guide* from Geraldton's visitors centre.

NORTHAMPTON TO KALBARRI

Charming **Northampton**, a National Trust–classified town, was established to exploit lead and copper deposits discovered in 1848, and its historic stone architecture is splendid. It's worth calling in if you're around during the annual **Airing of the Quilts** in October, when Northampton's heritage buildings are draped with beautiful patchwork bed covers.

All of the town's attractions are sprinkled along Hampton Rd (the highway). Pick up a

---

PRINCE LEONARD'S LAND

One of Australia's more eccentric challenges to statehood lies along a dusty dirt road, 75km northwest of Northampton. Here the **Principality of Hutt River** (☎ 08-9936 6035; www.principality-hutt -river.com; ◷ 10am-4pm), Australia's 'second-largest country', formed when farmer Leonard Casley, appalled by new government quotas on wheat production, seceded from the Commonwealth of Australia on 21 April 1970.

Although the Australian government does not legally recognise the principality, they've largely left Prince Leonard and his Princess Shirley alone to preside over their small but growing kingdom. With four sons, three daughters, 24 grandchildren and 22 great-grandchildren, the family tree would suggest that the principality's borders will not be compromised any time soon.

Despite his busy schedule, HRH Prince Leonard takes time out for the little people – both loyal subjects and visitors are welcome to call on the residence. Increasingly, the kingdom has turned its focus to tourism rather than farming. Stamps, currency, even royal passports are all for sale. Phone ahead to ensure that one of the royals is at home – royalty with a delicious sense of the absurdity of it all!

free *Heritage Walk* pamphlet from the **visitors centre** (☎ 08-9934 1488; www.northamptonwa.com.au; Hampton Rd; ☽ 9am-3pm Mon-Fri, to noon Sat), in the old police station. Also check out **Chiverton House** (☎ 08-9934 1215; Hampton Rd; admission $3; ☽ 10am-noon & 2-4pm Fri-Mon), an early mining cottage dating to 1896, which has been converted into a fascinating pioneer museum. Don't miss the vintage tractors and Model-T Ford out back.

The stately **Old Convent** (☎ 08-9934 1692; 61 Hampton Rd; dm $15) was designed by Monsignor Hawes and later converted to a backpacker accommodation. Next door, the striking **St Mary's Church** (☽ 9am-5pm), Hawes again, was built from hammer-dressed red sandstone in 1936.

The town's three pubs – all on Hampton Rd – serve hearty counter meals. The **Railway Tavern** (☎ 08-9934 1120; www.railwaytavern.com.au; 71 Hampton Rd; d $95-110) is a reliable favourite with spacious rooms and a satisfying menu of homemade pies, quiches and other pub fare (mains $10 to $17). If you're camping or caravanning, try **Northampton Caravan Park** (☎ 0439 979 489; Hampton Rd; unpowered/powered sites $15/20).

Greyhound (☎ 1300 473 946; www.greyhound.com.au) stops at the Miners Arms Hotel daily (Perth to Northampton; $94, eight hours).

The coastal road is the more scenic option to get to Kalbarri – with good detours through the tiny coastal towns of **Horrocks** and **Port Gregory** on the way, and superb coastal gorges in the southern reaches of Kalbarri National Park.

Pitch a tent or camp your van at the small, laid-back **Port Gregory Caravan Park** (☎ 08-9935 1052; powered sites $25, cabins $70-150).

The Hutt River Province (see Prince Leonard's Land, p973) is accessible from Ogilvie Rd; look for the blue signs.

KALBARRI
pop 2000

Kalbarri is located on an idyllic stretch of waterfront, where the Murchison River meets Gantheaume Bay. Outside of the busy school holidays, the town remains a pleasant and sleepy destination, and an excellent base to explore the empty windswept beaches, dramatically carved sea cliffs, wildflower-filled meadows and river gorges just outside of town. National park surrounds Kalbarri, and the natural world seems ever present here, including pelicans and flocks of pink-and-grey galahs that linger along the riverfront. Surfing,

fishing, bushwalking, horse riding and canoeing down the Murchison are a few ways to experience Kalbarri's natural beauty.

Information

There are ATMs at the shopping centres on Grey and Porter Sts.

Kalbarri Café (☎ 08-9937 1045; Porter St; ☽ 8.30am-8pm Thu-Tue) Has internet terminals.

Traveller's Book Exchange (☎ 08-9937 2676; Kalbarri Lane; ☽ 9am-5pm Mon-Fri, to noon Sat) Internet plus paperback books.

Visitors centre (☎ 1800 639 468, 08-9937 1104; www .kalbarriwa.info; Grey St; ☽ 9am-5pm) Kalbarri's busy visitors centre has lots of info on the national park and activities around town, and can book accommodation and tours.

Sights & Activities
KALBARRI NATIONAL PARK

With its magnificent river red gums and Tumblagooda sandstone, the ruggedly beautiful **national park** (admission per car $10) contains over 1000 sq km of bushland, stunning river gorges and jagged coastal cliffs. There's abundant wildlife, including 200 species of birds, and spectacular wildflowers such as banksias, grevilleas and kangaroo paws between July and November.

To get to the river gorges from Kalbarri, head 11km east along Ajana Kalbarri Rd to the turn-off, and follow the 20km stretch of dirt to the gorges. A number of lookouts provide superb gorge vistas: at the **Loop** (400m from the car park) there's a natural rock arch, 'nature's window', framing the view upstream (and an 8km walk for the more adventurous); from **Z-Bend** (500m from the car park) the gorge plunges 150m to the river below; at **Hawk's Head** there are great views from the picnic grounds; and from **Ross Graham** you can access the river.

The park extends south of Kalbarri to a string of rugged coastal cliff faces, including **Red Bluff**, **Rainbow Valley**, **Pot Alley**, **Eagle Gorge** and **Natural Bridge**. A walking/cycling path from town goes as far as Red Bluff (5.5km), passing **Jakes Point**, an excellent surf break. From the cliff tops you may spot humpback whales (August to November) and dolphins (year-round).

OTHER SIGHTS & ACTIVITIES

Kalbarri's most popular attraction is the **pelican feeding** (☎ 08-9937 1104; Grey St waterfront; admission free; ☽ 8.45am).

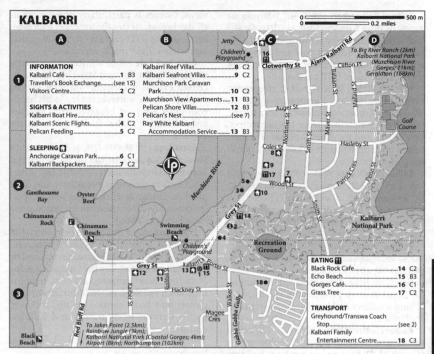

KALBARRI

INFORMATION	
Kalbarri Café	1 B3
Traveller's Book Exchange	(see 15)
Visitors Centre	2 C2

SIGHTS & ACTIVITIES	
Kalbarri Boat Hire	3 C2
Kalbarri Scenic Flights	4 C2
Pelican Feeding	5 C2

SLEEPING	
Anchorage Caravan Park	6 C1
Kalbarri Backpackers	7 C2

Kalbarri Reef Villas	8 C2
Kalbarri Seafront Villas	9 C2
Murchison Park Caravan Park	10 C2
Murchison View Apartments	11 B3
Pelican Shore Villas	12 B3
Pelican's Nest	(see 7)
Ray White Kalbarri Accommodation Service	13 B3

EATING	
Black Rock Cafe	14 C2
Echo Beach	15 B3
Gorges Café	16 C1
Grass Tree	17 C2

TRANSPORT	
Greyhound/Transwa Coach Stop	(see 2)
Kalbarri Family Entertainment Centre	18 C3

To Big River Ranch (2km); Kalbarri National Park (Murchison River Gorges; 11km); Geraldton (168km)

To Jakes Point (2.5km); Rainbow Jungle (3km); Kalbarri National Park (Coastal Gorges; 4km); Airport (8km); Northampton (102km)

WESTERN AUSTRALIA

Rainbow Jungle (☎ 08-9937 1248; www.rainbowjun glekalbarri.com; Red Bluff Rd; adult/child $14/5; 9am-5pm Mon-Sat, 10am-5pm Sun) is a bird habitat and breeding centre set in luxuriant tropical gardens 4km south of Kalbarri. At night, Rainbow Jungle hosts outdoor film screenings.

Kalbarri Boat Hire (☎ 08-9937 1245; www.ka lbarriboathire.com; Grey St waterfront; kayak/canoe/surf cat/powerboat per hr $15/15/35/50) on the foreshore hires out kayaks, canoes, surf cats, paddle bikes/boats and powerboats to explore the Murchison River. You can also join one of its four-hour canoe trips ($65 per person) down the Murchison River.

Other activities include fishing, surfing, sandboarding, deep-sea fishing, charters, horse riding and camel rides; see the visitors centre for more details.

Tours

There's a host of daily tours covering scenic, adventure and wildlife activities (including whale-watching tours).

Big River Ranch (☎ 08-9937 1214; off Ajana Kalbarri Rd; 1-/2-hr rides $50/80) Offers horse-riding trips through pretty countryside.

Kalbarri Abseil (☎ 08-9937 1618; www.abseilaus tralia.com.au; half-/full-day tours $80/125) Stages abseiling tours amid the gorges of Kalbarri National Park.

Kalbarri Adventure Tours (☎ 08-9937 1677; www .kalbarritours.com.au) Popular all-day bushwalking (adult/ child $65/50) and canoeing trips (adult/child $65/50) through the national park.

Kalbarri Scenic Flights (☎ 08-9937 1130; www .kalbarriaircharter.com.au; 62 Grey St; flights per person $59-225) Six different scenic flights, including 20-minute coastal cliff tours, 45-minute Murchison River gorges flyovers and trips to the Abrolhos Islands.

Kalbarri Wilderness Cruises (☎ 08-9937 2259; cruises adult/child $40/26) Runs popular cruises down the Murchison River to the Loop and Z-Bend.

Sleeping

Kalbarri accommodation is often full during school holidays. The visitors centre (opposite) has a list of places it can book for you.

Big River Ranch (☎ 08-9937 1214; www.bigriverranch .net; off Ajana Kalbarri Rd; campsites per person $8, r per person $25;) This horse ranch 2km out of town offers riding trips as well as basic dormitory-style accommodation and camping. There's a campers kitchen, pool and barbecue.

Kalbarri Backpackers (☎ 08-9937 1430; www.yha .com.au; cnr Woods & Mortimer Sts; dm/d $27/73; 🖳 🛄 �екс) While the atmosphere is uninspiring, the facilities are good (decent pool and barbecue) and the location is excellent. Guests can book tours or hire bikes ($10 per day).

Pelican's Nest (☎ 08-9937 1430; pelicansnest@ westnet.com.au; cnr Woods & Mortimer Sts; d $100-160; 🔲 🛄 🛄) Adjoining Kalbarri Backpackers, this nicely maintained place has contemporary rooms and excellent facilities. The best rooms open onto private balconies overlooking gum trees.

Kalbarri Reef Villas (☎ 08-9937 1165; www.reefvillas .com.au; cnr Coles & Mortimer Sts; 2-bedroom apt from $150; 🔲 🛄) One block inland, Kalbarri Reef Villas has attractive two-bedroom apartments with kitchens and small patios (or balconies) facing a palm-filled garden.

Pelican Shore Villas (☎ 08-9937 1708; pelican shores@westnet.com.au; cnr Grey & Kaiber Sts; 2-bedroom villas $150-180; 🔲) These stylish, contemporary-design units have all the mod cons (including DVD, microwave, private laundry), floor-to-ceiling windows and big balconies overlooking the sea.

Kalbarri Seafront Villas (☎ 08-9937 1025; www.ka lbarriseafrontvillas.com.au; 108 Grey St; 1-/2-bedroom apt from $175/195; 🔲 🛄 🛄) In a low-rise brick building facing the waterfront, these spacious, clean and comfortable units come with TV, DVD players and small kitchens.

Ray White Kalbarri Accommodation Service (☎ 08-9937 1700; www.kalbarriaccommodation.com.au; Kalbarri Arcade, 44 Grey St; holiday houses per week $350-1200) Has a wide range of self-contained apartments and houses.

Murchison Park Caravan Park (☎ 08-9937 1005; www.murcp.com; cnr Woods & Grey Sts; unpowered/powered sites $24/28, cabins with/without bathroom $105/85; 🔲) This central, family-owned park opposite Kalbarri's waterfront has good facilities, but it gets packed and there's not much space between sites.

Anchorage Caravan Park (☎ 08-9937 1181; anchor@ wn.com.au; cnr Anchorage Lane & Grey St; unpowered/powered sites $25/28, cabins with/without bathroom $100/70; 🛄) The best option for caravan and campsites, Anchorage has roomy, nicely shaded sites overlooking the waterfront.

Eating

Gorges Café (☎ 08-9937 1200; Marina Complex, Grey St; mains $7-22; 🕙 breakfast & lunch Wed-Mon) A friendly, laid-back spot with outdoor seating and river views, Gorges is particularly popular for its all-day breakfasts (try the pancakes with blueberries). The BYO cafe also serves wraps and sandwiches, light meals and cakes.

Black Rock Cafe (☎ 08-9937 1062; 80 Grey St; mains $10-28; 🕙 Tue-Sat, 7am-noon Sun) This casual, licensed eatery, with sunny outdoor seating overlooking the water, keeps the locals happy with great gourmet breakfasts and lunches, and a creative global fusion menu in the evening.

Grass Tree (☎ 08-9937 2288; 94-96 Grey St; mains $10-30; 🕙 10am-late Fri-Tue, 6pm-late Thu) While this licensed cafe-restaurant opposite the waterfront serves delicious breakfasts and light lunches, dinner is what it does best – expect innovative Asian-inspired global fusion using fresh local produce.

Echo Beach (☎ 08-9937 1033; Porter St; mains $26-38; 🕙 10am-late) This stylish upstairs restaurant serves delicious Mod Oz cuisine matched by an eclectic wine list. Try the Outback Tasting Plate (barbecue kangaroo skewers, tempura crocodile, smoked rabbit, Murchison goat cutlets and bush tomato relish!) followed by Carnarvon tiger prawns and Kalbarri dhufish.

There are supermarkets and takeaways at the shopping centres.

Getting There & Around

Buses stop and depart from the visitors centre. **Greyhound** (☎ 1300 473 946; www.greyhound .com.au) buses head to Perth ($143, 9¼ hours), Exmouth ($210, 11 hours) and Broome ($373, 26 hours), while **Transwa** (☎ 1300 662 205) services Perth several days a week ($68, 9½ hours).

Kalbarri Auto Centre (☎ 08-9937 1290) rents 4WDs and sedans from $40 a day and picks up and delivers to your door, while **Kalbarri Family Entertainment Centre** (☎ 08-9937 1105; 15 Magee Cres) rents bikes from $20 per day.

SHARK BAY

The spectacular World Heritage–listed site of Shark Bay contains more than 1500km of coastline stretching along two jagged peninsulas and numerous islands. Its natural beauty – white-sand beaches, fiery red cliffs and turquoise lagoons – is only one part of its allure. This is also one of WA's most biologically rich habitats with an array of plant and animal life found nowhere else on earth. Lush beds of seagrass and sheltered bays nourish dugongs, sea turtles, humpback whales, dolphins, rays, sharks and other aquatic life. On land, Shark Bay's biodiversity has benefited from Project Eden, an ambitious ecosystem regeneration program that has sought to eradicate feral animals and reintroduce endemic species. Shark Bay has some other surprising attractions, including stromatolites (see below).

Shark Bay was originally inhabited by the Malgana, Nhanda and Inggarda peoples, who depended on both the sea and bush for their subsistence; visitors can take Indigenous cultural tours to learn about the land from their perspective. The local people were probably the first Indigenous Australians to encounter Europeans – Shark Bay was the site of the first recorded landing by a European on Australian soil when, in 1616, Dutch explorer Dirk Hartog anchored at the island that now bears his name, just off Denham, Shark Bay's main town.

Overlander Roadhouse to Denham

Leaving the highway just after the Overlander Roadhouse, the first turn-off (about 27km along) takes you to **Hamelin Pool**, a marine reserve containing the world's best-known colony of **stromatolites**. These brown rocklike formations are made up of modest microbes almost identical to organisms that existed 3500 million years ago. Although they aren't the most dazzling of sites, the stromatolite role in evolutionary history is profound. For 2900 million years, these microbes were the only life on earth. By consuming carbon dioxide and releasing oxygen, they were largely responsible for creating earth's atmosphere, and set the stage for other life forms to emerge. They're extremely fragile, so there's a boardwalk (with information panels) that allows no-impact viewing; visit at low tide.

The nearby 1884 **Postmasters Residence & Telegraph Office** (☎ 08-9942 5905; admission $5; ◷ 9am-4pm) served as a telephone exchange until 1977. This unassuming little outpost was also unwittingly responsible for transmitting messages from NASA's Gemini space-mission craft in 1964 after communications between the tracking station and Carnarvon's dish went down. It now serves Devonshire tea (tea, scones and jam) and has displays on the stromatolites. Campers and caravan travellers can stay at the **Hamelin Pool Caravan Park** (☎ 08-9942 5905; unpowered/powered sites $18/20).

The miniature cockleshells that cover the extraordinary **Shell Beach**, 50km from Hamelin,

are 10m deep in places. These shells are peculiar to Shark Bay and cement together after rain, making sturdy white bricks – look out for them in Denham.

At the next turn-off, the sleepy **Nanga Bay Resort** (☎ 08-9948 3992; www.nangabayresort.com.au; unpowered/powered sites $25/30, d backpackers/cabins/motel $40/90/165; ⊠ ⊠) is a former sheep station with a range of accommodation, from motel units to fishing huts. Facilities include a shop, barbecue, pool and rustic bar and restaurant. You'll need your own wheels.

At **Eagle Bluff**, there are spectacular cliff-top views, wonderful bird life and sharks swimming in the clear waters below.

Denham

pop 1140

Australia's most westerly town, laid-back Denham, with its crystal-clear water and charming beachfront, makes a decent base for visiting the marine park, nearby Francois Peron National Park and Monkey Mia, 26km away. Originally established as a pearling town, Denham was paved with pearl shell, according to old-timers. These days, all you'll see is bitumen, but some shell-brick buildings still stand.

INFORMATION

Almost all visitor facilities are on the main thoroughfare, Knight Tce. There's an ATM at Heritage Resort.

Post office (Knight Tce; ◷ 8am-5pm Mon-Fri, 9am-1pm Sat & Sun) Also has a pharmacy and internet access.

Shark Bay visitors centre (☎ 08-9948 1590; 53 Knight Tce; ◷ 8am-5pm Mon-Fri) Has plenty of information on the World Heritage area and national park.

SIGHTS & ACTIVITIES

In a striking contemporary building, the cutting-edge **Shark Bay World Heritage Discovery Centre** (☎ 08-9948 1590; www.sharkbayinterpretivecentre.com.au; 53 Knight Tce; adult/child $10/6; ◷ 9am-6pm) is one of WA's best museums, with compelling exhibitions on Shark Bay's natural environment, its Indigenous people, the many explorers who've ventured here and how understanding these entanglements can help us experience a sense of place.

On the way into town, **Ocean Park** (☎ 08-9948 1765; www.oceanpark.com.au; Shark Bay Rd; adult/child $15/10; ◷ 10am-3.30pm) is a locally run aquaculture farm featuring an artificial lagoon where you can observe sharks, turtles, stingrays and fish on guided 45-minute tours. The cafe has panoramic views.

TOURS

Majestic Tours (☎ 08-9948 1627; www.sharkbay holiday.com.au; tours $75-170) Has various full-day 4WD tours, including François Péron National Park and Shell Beach.

Shark Bay Coaches & Tours (☎ 08-9948 1081; www .sbcoaches.com; tours $70) Runs half-day tours to all key sights.

Shark Bay Scenic Flights (☎ 08-9948 1773; www .sharkbayair.com.au) Offers seven different scenic flights including 15-minute Monkey Mia flyovers ($55), 40-minute trips over Zuytdorp Cliffs ($150) and half-day flying/4WD excursions visiting Dirk Hartog Island ($255).

Shark Bay Sea Kayaking (☎ 08-9948 1952; shark bayseakayaking@hotmail.com; 113 Knight Tce) This outfit runs five-hour kayak tours, taking in the rugged coastal scenery of Eagle Bluff, Wilson Island and Ticklebelly Flats. Based out of Bay Lodge.

SLEEPING & EATING

Bay Lodge (☎ 08-9948 1278; www.baylodge.info; 113 Knight Tce; dm/d from $22/55; 🖳 🐾) Every room at this YHA hostel has its own bathroom, kitchen, and living and dining facilities with TV and DVD. The owners will also spoil you, taking you on complimentary 4WD fishing, swimming and wildlife-spotting tours, and holding bush barbecue nights. They also provide a shuttle bus to Monkey Mia.

Oceanside Village (☎ 08-9948 3003; www.oceanside .com.au; 117 Knight Tce; houses $135-175; 🕸 🐾) The friendly, Dutch-owned Oceanside Village consists of trim freestanding blue-and-white cottages, most with waterfront views. All have kitchen units, free wi-fi access and small balconies.

Denham Villas (☎ 08-9948 1264; www.denhamvillas .com; 4 Durlacher St; villas $140-155; 🕸) The spacious, fully self-contained villas (with proper kitchen and laundry) are excellent value and ideal for families.

Seaside Tourist Village (☎ 1300 133 733, 08-9948 1242; www.sharkbayfun.com; Knight Tce; unpowered/ powered sites $25/30, cabins d $70, 1-/2-bedroom chalets $110/125; 🕸) This big beachside park has good facilities, including barbecues and self-contained chalets with verandahs overlooking the sea.

Shark Bay Hotel (☎ 08-9948 1203; 43 Knight Tce; mains $12-26; 🕸) While this typical Aussie pub bistro is nothing flash, it's a decent spot to eat a hearty counter meal and play a few rounds

of pool. Rooms (doubles $85) are small, clean and basic.

Old Pearler Restaurant (☎ 08-9948 1373; Knight Tce; mains $29-45) Built from seashell bricks, this splendid building houses one of WA's most atmospheric old restaurants. Its cosy interior, with fireplace, rustic wooden furniture and candlesticks on the walls, is the perfect place to feast on delicious fresh seafood.

There is a supermarket, bakery, cafe and takeaways on Knight Tce.

GETTING THERE & AROUND

Skywest (☎ 1300 660 088; www.skywest.com.au) has flights from Geraldton and Carnarvon, linking to Perth, Exmouth and Karratha.

Daily shuttle buses head to the Overlander Roadhouse on the main highway – from Denham ($67, 1½ hours) and Monkey Mia ($68, two hours) – to connect with the north- and south-bound **Greyhound** (☎ 1300 473 946; www. greyhound.com.au) services, including Denham to Carnarvon ($115, four hours).

Bay Lodge (☎ 08-9948 1278) runs a shuttle bus to Monkey Mia (Monday, Wednesday, Friday and Saturday; return for nonguests $20) that leaves from the Shell service station on Knight Tce; bookings essential.

Francois Peron National Park

Renowned for its dramatic golden cliffs, pristine white-sand beaches, salt lakes and rare marsupial species, this **national park** (per bus passenger/car $4/10), 4km from Denham on Monkey Mia Rd, will reward those with 4WD vehicles and an adventurous spirit. There's a visitors centre at the old Péron Homestead, 6km from the main road, where a former artesian bore has been converted to a 35°C **hot tub**, a novel spot for a sunset soak. There are **campsites** ($7) with limited facilities at Big Lagoon, Gregories, Bottle Bay and Herald Bight. If you don't have your own wheels, take a tour to the park (see left).

Monkey Mia

World-famous for the wild dolphins that turn up in the shallow water for feeding each day, the beach resort of **Monkey Mia** (adult/child/family $6/2/12), 26km northeast of Denham, now tops many travellers' list of things to do. The morning feeding session (around 7.45am) can get packed, but often the dolphins return for a second feeding later in the morning. Aside from dolphins, the resort offers plenty of other diversions, including Aboriginal heritage walks, sailing, camel trips, diving and stargazing.

The **Monkey Mia Visitors Centre** (☎ 08-9948 1366; ◷ 7.30am-4pm) has lots of info; it also shows videos and hosts presentations. There are great books for sale in the shop and you can also buy tour tickets here.

You can **volunteer** to work full-time with the dolphins for a period of up to two weeks – it's understandably popular, so apply several months in advance. Contact volunteer coordinator **Alison True** (☎ 08-9948 1366; alison.true@ dec.wa.gov.au).

TOURS
Aristocat II (☎ 08-9948 1446; 1½-3½hr tours $54-89) On these wonderful wildlife-spotting cruises on the *Shotover* catamaran you'll get to see dugongs, dolphins, loggerhead turtles, sea snakes and perhaps even tiger sharks.

Astronomy on the Beach (☎ 1800 241 481; per person $29) Gives visitors a deeper understanding of the star-filled heavens. Held most nights from 8.30pm to 10pm.

Blue Lagoon Pearl Farm (☎ 08-9948 1325; www .bluelagoon.com.au; 1hr tours adult/child $30/10; ◷ 11am) Take an eight-minute boat ride from Monkey Mia jetty across to the floating pearl farm to learn how the beautiful black pearls are cultured.

Power Dive (☎ 08-9948 3031; www.divefun.com .au; tours $70-120) Offers snorkelling and diving safaris in Francois Peron National Park. Transport from Denham can also be arranged.

Wildsights (☎ 1800 241 481, 08-9948 1481; www .monkeymiawildsights.com.au) Offers similar trips to Aristocat II, at similar prices.

Wula Guda Nyinda Aboriginal Cultural Tours
(☎ 0429 708 847, 08-9948 1320; www.monkeymia.com .au; daytime tours adult/child $30/15, dusk tours $35/17,

night tours $30/15) Local Aboriginal guide Darren 'Capes' Capewell (see Meeting the Malgana Mob, below) leads excellent bushwalks where he teaches you 'how to let the bush talk to you'. You'll learn some local Malgana language, and identify bush tucker and native medicine. The evening 'Didgeridoo Dreaming' walks are magical.

SLEEPING & EATING
Monkey Mia is a resort and not a town, so eating and sleeping options are limited. Self-catering is a good option.

Monkey Mia Dolphin Resort (☎ 1800 653 611, 08-9948 1320; www.monkeymia.com.au; tent sites $14, van sites $31-37, dm/d $25/80, garden units $233, beachfront villas $285; ☒ ▣ ▣) This leafy resort offers a range of accommodation, from popular tent and van sites to top-end villas with verandahs overlooking the beach. Backpackers can overnight in dorms or in simple doubles with shared bathrooms. You can rent kayaks and snorkelling gear, play tennis, watch free films playing daily or just soak up rays on the pretty beach.

Monkey Bar (☎ 08-9948 1320; mains $7-18) This casual bar serves good counter meals and snacks, and is a popular spot for a round of pool and a few drinks. Open late.

Bough Shed Restaurant (☎ 08-9948 1171; mains $15-34) Boasting splendid waterfront views, the Bough Shed offers a tasty selection of seafood and grill items, including Shark Bay snapper, sesame-toasted prawns, Moroccan lamb and vegetarian quesadillas.

GETTING THERE & AWAY
Greyhound (☎ 1300 473 946; www.greyhound .com.au) travels between Monkey Mia and Denham ($30 return, 30 minutes, Mondays, Wednesdays and Fridays), as does the Bay Lodge shuttle (see opposite).

WESTERN AUSTRALIA

MEETING THE MALGANA MOB

Darren 'Capes' Capewell is like a one-man Aboriginal Embassy in Monkey Mia – except that this is his country, Malgana country. The fit, 30-something ex–Aussie Rules player has run his own cultural walks, Wula Guda Nyinda ('you come this way'), here since late 2004.

Capes takes visitors on fascinating and information-overload-inducing walks covering Malgana language, 'respect for country', bush medicine, bush survival, tracking, local history and the obligatory bush tucker. At night, he brings out the didgeridoo and tells Dreaming stories around a campfire.

Capes had strong support from Waitoc (the Western Australian Indigenous Tour Operators Committee; www.waitoc.com) through training, networking and mentoring when setting up his business. And at last count, he had ambitious plans for the future – expanding his tours and perhaps even adding a multiday kayak excursion.

CARNARVON

pop 6900

At the mouth of the Gascoyne River, fertile Carnarvon, with its fruit and vegetable plantations and thriving fishing industry, makes a good stopover between Denham and Exmouth. This lush centre of the dry Gascoyne has a variety of decent accommodation and well-stocked supermarkets.

Information

There are a couple of ATMs on Robinson St.

Post office (Camel Lane)

Visitors centre (☎ 08-9941 1146; www.carnarvon.org .au; Civic Centre, 11 Robinson St; ☒ 9am-5pm Mon-Fri, 9am-noon Sat, 10am-1pm Sun) Has lots of information on the town and region, and can provide maps of walking trails and driving tours. It also sells unique local products, such as the tasty dried 'Mango Leather'. Internet available.

Sights & Activities

On the outskirts of town the **OTC Dish** (Mahoney Ave) was established by NASA in 1966 as a tracking station for the Gemini and Apollo space missions, and tracked Halley's Comet in 1986. It was closed in 1987 although you can still wander around the site.

Carnarvon's luxuriant plantations provide nearly 70% of the state's tropical fruits and vegetables. A handful of growers offer plantation tours, including **Bumbak's** (449 North River Rd; ☒ shop 9am-4pm Mon-Fri Apr-Jan, plantation tours 10am Mon-Fri Apr-Oct), which sells a variety of fresh and dried fruit as well as chutneys, jams, ice cream and honey from the shop. You can get a taste of everyone's delicious produce at the **Gascoyne Growers Market** (Civic Centre car park; ☒ 8-11.30am Sat May-Oct).

The **Heritage Precinct** is an intriguing place to learn about the region's history. The area, once the city's port, houses the **Lighthouse Keepers Cottage Museum** (☒ 10am-1pm), **Railway Station Museum** (☒ 9am-4.30pm) and the **One Mile Jetty** (admission tram/walking $3/2; ☒ 9am-4.30pm), where locals fish for mulloway; you can either walk or take a vintage tram to the end of the jetty. Although the train from the footbridge to the Heritage Precinct is no longer running, a walking trail runs the 2.5km length of the old tracks.

The multicultural **Carnarvon Pioneer Cemetery** (Crowther St) is worth a wander; it's the final resting place of pioneers from as far away as Afghanistan and China.

Tours

Carnarvon Charter Fishing (☎ 08-9941 1375, 0407 995 432; day trips $170) Offers fishing trips and whale watching; includes bait, ice and fishing gear.

Outback Coast Safaris (☎ 08-9941 3448; www. outbackcoastsafaris.com.au; Aboriginal Heritage tour

---

BACKROAD RAMBLING – BLOWHOLES AND SHEEP STATIONS

About 20km north of Carnarvon along the main highway is the Blowhole Rd turn-off. This sealed road leads 49km to the frenzied **blowholes** and swaths of desolate, windswept coastline. Keep a sharp eye on the ocean: as the sign says, 'king waves kill'. Just 1km further south is **Point Quobba**, where locals have beach shacks and come for the fishing and swimming. You can often spot turtles, whales (June to September) and sea eagles. There are rocky **campsites** ($6), but no facilities. With all of the following places, you'll need to bring your own food and drinking water.

Around 10km further north (mostly unsealed) you'll find **Quobba Station** (☎ 08-9948 5098; www.quobba.com.au; unpowered/powered sites $8/10, cabins per person $30-50), an ocean-front property with plenty of rustic accommodation, a small store and legendary fishing.

Also part of Quobba Station, but 60km north of the Quobba homestead, is **Red Bluff** (☎ 08-9948 5001; www.quobba.com.au; unpowered sites per person $10, shacks per person $20, d bungalows/safari retreats $160/345), another spectacularly sited place with great surfing, fishing and snorkelling. Accommodation runs a wide spectrum: there are 'luxury safari retreats' (tented dwellings with wood floors, private bathrooms, verandahs and kitchen units), bungalows (smaller but with the same set-up), palm-frond shacks and campsites.

A further 70km up the coast (150km from Carnarvon), **Gnaraloo** (☎ 08-9942 5927; www.gnaraloo .com; unpowered sites per person $20, cabins d $70-180) is a working sheep station (with 3000 head of sheep) on 91,000 hectares of land. The coastline here is spectacular and campsites at Gnaraloo's 3-mile camp enjoy pristine views. There's also a range of other accommodation from small basic cabins to spacious houses. Gnaraloo often needs help for station work, an option for those looking to stay a while.

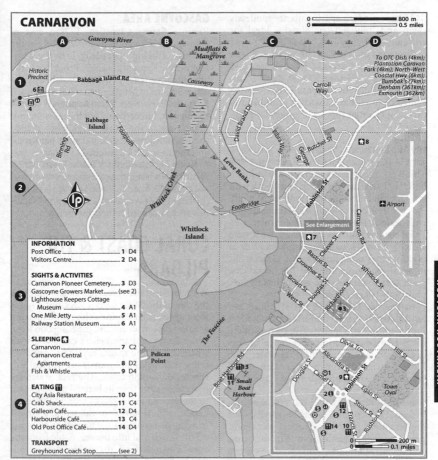

CARNARVON

0 — 800 m
0 — 0.5 miles

To OTC Dish (4km);
Plantation Caravan
Park (4km); North-West
Coastal Hwy (6km);
Bumbak's (7km);
Denham (361km);
Exmouth (362km)

INFORMATION
Post Office **1** D4
Visitors Centre **2** D4

SIGHTS & ACTIVITIES
Carnarvon Pioneer Cemetery **3** D3
Gascoyne Growers Market ... (see 2)
Lighthouse Keepers Cottage
    Museum **4** A1
One Mile Jetty **5** A1
Railway Station Museum **6** A1

SLEEPING
Carnarvon **7** C2
Carnarvon Central
    Apartments **8** D2
Fish & Whistle **9** D4

EATING
City Asia Restaurant **10** D4
Crab Shack **11** C4
Galleon Café **12** D4
Harbourside Café **13** C4
Old Post Office Café **14** D4

TRANSPORT
Greyhound Coach Stop .... (see 2)

adult/child $140/110, Sunset Dreaming tours $35/18, Kennedy Range tours $130/110, 2-day Mt Augustus tours $280/220) A small outfit running walking and 4WD tours, the best of which have a focus on Aboriginal heritage (and feature Aboriginal guides). Outback also heads to the Kennedy Range, and offers a two-day Mt Augustus trip with overnight camping.

Stockman Safaris (☎ 08-9941 2421; stockmansafaris@ wn.com.au; town tours adult/child $50/25, Blowholes, Quobba & Salt Mine tours $90/50, Kennedy Range $130/65) Runs a variety of tours that take in the town and local and regional sites.

Sleeping

There are numerous caravan parks and a growing range of other accommodation options.

Fish & Whistle (☎ 08-9941 1704; 35 Robinson St; dm/s/d without bathroom $25/40/50, d with bathroom $80-100;) This big, breezy backpackers is a hit with travellers for its enormous communal spaces, excellent kitchen, barbecue area and big verandahs, not to mention private rooms and bunk-free shares. The owners can help guests find seasonal jobs, and provide transport to work every day ($15 per week).

Carnarvon (☎ 08-9941 1181; 121 Olivia Tce; dm/s/d $30/72/96;) Home to the town's favourite pub (and the TAB), the Carnarvon also has clean, basic rooms and backpacker dorms at fair prices. The restaurant and bar enjoy a fine view of the waterfront.

Carnarvon Central Apartments (☎ 08-9941 1317; www.carnarvonholidays.com; 120 Robinson St; apt from $115;

😵) These modern apartments are spotlessly clean and fully self-contained – ideal for self-caterers.

Plantation Caravan Park (☎ 08-9941 8100; www .plantation-caravanpark.com.au; 589 Robinson St; unpowered/ powered sites d $25/28, cabins $150-180; 😵 💻) This lush, pleasantly shaded park 5km from the centre of town has expansive grounds and excellent facilities (pool, playground, wi-fi).

Eating

City Asia Restaurant (☎ 08-9941 4078; 18 Francis St; mains $7-17; 🕑 lunch Mon & Wed-Fri, dinner Wed-Mon) This BYO eatery serves a small but tasty lunch buffet of barbecue ribs, duck, roast pork with crackling and other meaty standouts. At night, the chef showcases mostly Vietnamese dishes, with seafood playing a prominent role.

Galleon Café (☎ 08-9941 2531; 26 Robinson St; mains $7-18; 🕑 breakfast & lunch) Among a handful of inviting cafes along Robinson St, Galleon has its local following, lured by big breakfasts, good coffee, sandwiches and light lunches, plus fresh-baked goodies.

Harbourside Café (☎ 08-9941 4111; Small Boat Harbour; mains $11-32; 🕑 11am-3pm & 5-8pm Tue-Sun) Fresh seafood and imaginative recipes make for a rewarding dining experience at this casual, sunny restaurant near the water. The Eastern-accented menu includes Asian-spiced calamari, Thai shrimp salad and Carnarvon snapper.

Old Post Office Café (☎ 08-9941 1800; 10 Robinson St; mains $14-28; 🕑 dinner Tue-Sat) This stylish but unpretentious place has excellent pizzas and pastas as well as lamb, fresh fish, kangaroo and decadent desserts. You can dine on the verandah. Licensed and BYO.

Crab Shack (☎ 08-9941 4078; Small Boat Harbour; 🕑 9am-5pm) Self-catering seafood lovers shouldn't miss this takeaway stand, with freshly steamed fresh blue crabs and prawns.

Getting There & Around

Skywest (☎ 1300 660 088; www.skywest.com.au) flies from Carnarvon to Perth ($354) daily, and has less-frequent flights to Geraldton and Exmouth. Daily **Greyhound Australia** (☎ 1300 473 946; www.greyhound.com.au) buses to Perth ($130, 13 hours), and Broome ($201, 20 hours) via Port Hedland ($100, 12 hours), stop at the visitors centre. Bicycle hire is available at the visitors centre (p980) for around $20 per half day.

GASCOYNE AREA

Remote **Gascoyne Junction**, 177km east of Carnarvon on a good unsealed road (in the process of being upgraded), is in the gemstone-rich Kennedy Range. From here, the adventurous can continue northeast another 300km to Mt Augustus (Burringurrah) National Park to see **Mount Augustus** (1106m), the biggest, but certainly not the most memorable, rock in the world. Highlights include the outstanding Aboriginal rock paintings, and the rock can be climbed in a day.

Mount Augustus Outback Tourist Resort (☎ 08-9943 0527; www.mtaugustusresort.com.au; unpowered/powered sites $18/22, dongas $70, units $175; 😵) is right at the base of Mt Augustus and has good facilities and a licensed restaurant on site.

CORAL COAST & THE PILBARA

Western Australia's great reef system may lack the size of the Great Barrier Reef, but it holds some spectacular marine riches. Brilliant coral gardens bloom all around the Ningaloo Reef, while divers and snorkellers can swim with whale sharks and manta rays, and seek dugongs, sea turtles and numerous tropical fish species on sailing tours. The reef is also far more accessible than its better-known cousin to the east. In many places around the Coral Coast, exploring one of the world's largest fringing reefs entails little more than stepping off the beach and into the sea. Aside from the aquatic wonderland, the region offers excellent surfing, tranquil swimming coves, lovely beaches and, not surprisingly, excellent fresh seafood.

The sparkling coastline provides a marked contrast to the sun-scorched interior of the Pilbara, a vast region of desiccated red earth, big skies and iron-ore ranges that keep the wheels of heavy industry turning.

The real reason to venture inland, however, is to visit the carved gorges, waterfalls and lush swimming holes of Karijini National Park, a long but highly rewarding inland detour from the coast.

Getting There & Away

Skywest (☎ 1300 660 088; www.skywest.com.au) has daily flights between Perth and Port Hedland, sometimes via Karratha. There are also daily

CORAL COAST & THE PILBARA

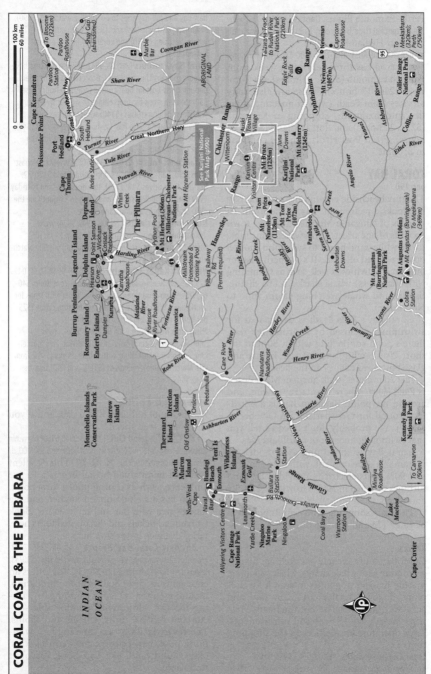

Perth–Exmouth flights. **Qantas** (☎ 13 13 13; www .qantas.com.au) flies between Perth and Karratha and Port Hedland.

Greyhound Australia (☎ 1300 473 946; www.greyhound.com.au) has three services a week from Perth to Exmouth ($258, 19 hours), via Coral Bay ($230, 17 hours). There are also daily services from Perth (with connecting shuttles into Exmouth) stopping at Karratha ($258, 22 hours) and Port Hedland ($296, 26 hours). From Port Hedland buses continue to Broome.

CORAL BAY
pop 190

The tiny beachside community of Coral Bay overlooks a picturesque bay in the southern reaches of Ningaloo Marine Park. The town consists of one street, down which you amble to the white-sand beach to swim and snorkel on the reef just offshore. It's a superb base for outer-reef activities as well, such as swimming with (harmless) whale sharks, scuba diving, fishing and whale watching (from June to November).

Coral Bay's **Main Beach** is designated for swimming; enclosed by a protective reef, there's good snorkelling within 50m of the shore. You can hire snorkel gear, kayaks and glass-bottomed canoes on the beach.

Just 20 minutes' walk north of Main Beach is **Point Maud**, where manta rays swim, and around the point, Bateman Bay is a breeding ground for reef sharks from October to March. We probably don't need to tell you that swimming here is not a brilliant idea.

Coral Bay is something of a model for sustainable development, with between 50% and 90% of its electricity provided by wind turbines installed in 2007. Growth is carefully contained.

The main shopping centre on Robinson St has an ATM and newsagent.

Tours

Coral Bay tours include snorkelling, diving, swimming with whale sharks, whale watching, marine-life-spotting tours to search for dolphins, dugongs, turtles and manta rays, and coral viewing from glass-bottom boats. Most trips include equipment and refreshments. Tour operators have offices in the shopping centre.

Coral Bay Adventures (☎ 08-9942 5955; www .coralbayadventures.com.au) This excellent company offers half-day and full-day trips to go wildlife watching ($190), swimming with whale sharks ($345) or manta rays ($150), whale watching ($110) and coral viewing on a glass-bottom boat ($32).

Coral Bay Ecotours (☎ 08-9942 5870; www.coralbayecotours.com.au) This respected, ecocertified outfit offers popular glass-bottom boat cruises (one/two hour cruise $30/45) with stops for snorkelling, as well as five-hour wildlife-watching cruises ($140) where you can swim with manta rays. It also has 1½-hour sunset cruises ($40), whale-watching cruises in season ($125), and you can book scenic flights here.

Coral Coast Tours (☎ 08-9948 5052; www.coralcoasttours.com; half-day wildlife safaris adult/child $120/72, full-day Cape drives $185/124) Also does full- and half-day 4WD outback wildlife safaris and tours to Exmouth via the 4WD coastal tracks around Cape Range.

Ningaloo Experience (☎ 08-9942 5824; www .ningalooexperience.com; adult/child from $145/105) Offers officially ecocertified tours, including wildlife watching/snorkelling tours.

Ningaloo Kayak Adventures (☎ 08-9948 5034; 0429 425 889; www.ningalookayakadventures.com; tours $40-60) Offers two- and three-hour kayak tours with stops for snorkelling. You can also hire a glass-bottom canoe ($25 per hour), wetsuit and snorkelling gear.

Ningaloo Reef Dive (☎ 08-9942 5824; www .ningalooreefdive.com) Specialises in diving and snorkelling, and offers snorkelling with whale sharks ($365; from late March to June), reef dives ($160) and PADI courses from $445.

Sleeping & Eating

Avoid school holidays if you can, and if you can't, book well ahead.

OUR PICK **Ningaloo Club** (☎ 08-9948 5100; www.ningalooclub.com; dm $24-26, d/tr without bathroom $80/100, d/tr with bathroom $100/120; 🐾 🖳 🖴) This excellent and well-maintained hostel boasts a festive ambience, with its central pool a focal point. It also has a well-equipped kitchen and big lounge area with bar and table tennis. Book Greyhound tickets and discounted tours here. Long-distance buses stop here.

Bayview Coral Bay Resort (☎ 08-9385 7411; www.coralbaywa.com; unpowered/powered sites $30/33, cabins d from $95, chalets $125-270; 🐾 🖳) Offers an enormous range of quality accommodation, including grassy sites for camping or parking the van, along with comfortable self-contained villas, units, chalets and cabins. The resort facilities are far-ranging: swimming pool, barbecues, tennis courts, kids' playground, and you can book discount tours here.

Ningaloo Reef Resort (☎ 08-9942 5934; www.nin galooreefresort.com.au; d/apt from $191/243; 🔀 🔊 🏊) On a fine grassy site above the beach, this laid-back resort, pub and bottle shop has a range of accommodation, from motel-style rooms to spacious apartments. The pub, Coral Bay's only drinking spot, is particularly popular on Thursdays when there's live music.

Bullara Station (☎ 08-9942 5938; www.bullara-sta tion.com.au; cnr Truscott Cres & Murat Rd; unpowered sites per person $11, d without bathroom $110) Located sixty kilometres north of Coral Bay, Bullara is a working cattle station that offers a rustic overnight experience amid pretty country-side. You can camp, park the van or stay in the old shearers' quarters (pleasant cabins with verandahs and shared bathrooms). There's a kitchen, dining room and outdoor barbecue for guests (bring your own food and drink).

People's Park Caravan Village (☎ 08-9942 5933; www.peoplesparkcoralbay.com; powered sites $32-36, cabins 1-/2-bedroom $200/220) This excellent caravan park has grassy, shaded sites with waterfront views. You can also rent a trim cabin, each with a kitchen and verandah. There's a campers kitchen and barbecue.

Fins Cafe (☎ 08-9942 5900; mains lunch $9-18, dinner $28-36) Coral Bay's best restaurant, Fins has standard pub fare by day and more eclectic dishes by night (New Orleans–style seafood gumbo, grilled local snapper, Thai red beef curry). Book ahead at this BYO spot.

Reef Cafe (☎ 08-9942 5882; mains $12-24) This casual family-friendly spot serves seafood and the usual suspects, though it's best known for filling pizzas.

There's a good **bakery** (🕑 6.30am-5.30pm) and supermarket at the shopping centre but prices are high. If you're self-catering, stock up in Carnarvon or Exmouth.

Getting There & Away

Coral Bay is 1200km north of Perth, and is accessible from north and south by a sealed road off the Manilya-Exmouth Rd.

Skywest Airlines (☎ 1300 660 088; www.skywest.com .au) flies into Exmouth's Learmonth Airport, about a 75-minute drive from Coral Bay; most Coral Bay resorts can arrange a private taxi service on request. **Greyhound** (☎ 1300 473 946; www.greyhound.com.au) has regular bus services via Exmouth and, along with Easyrider and Western Exposure buses, stops at the Ningaloo Club.

EXMOUTH

pop 2500

Gateway to the magnificent Ningaloo Marine Park and Cape Range National Park, Exmouth is a lively little place where the natural world frequently interacts with small-town life. Emus still wander through the main streets and parks of Exmouth, while pink-breasted galahs rule the skies and kangaroos and goannas keep watch over the highway leading into town. Exmouth sees a growing number of tourists, who come to book excursions in the park, surf waves off the cape and sample the prawns (produce of a thriving local industry).

Exmouth's shopping centre on Maidstone Cres has banks with ATMs (as does the visitors centre) as well as stores selling surfing, camping and diving gear.

Information

Department of Environment & Conservation office (DEC; ☎ 08-9949 8000; www.dec.wa.gov.au; 20 Nimitz St; 🕑 8.30am-5pm Mon-Fri) Supplies maps and brochures. Pick up the excellent brochures covering area marine life and purchase national park passes here. Those interested in Ningaloo's turtle monitoring program should contact Jamie Campbell (jamie.campbell@dec.wa.gov.au).

Exmouth District Hospital (☎ 08-9949 3666; Lyon St)

Post office (Maidstone Cres)

Tours 'N' Travel (☎ 08-9949 4748; www.ningaloo -tours-travel.com.au; 102 Murat Rd; 🕑 8.30am-7pm) A requisite stop in Ningaloo, with an internet cafe, tour-booking agency and secondhand bookshop, plus scooter, car, boat and camping gear hire.

Visitors centre (☎ 1800 287 328, 08-9949 1176; www .exmouthwa.com.au; Murat Rd; 🕑 9am-5pm Mon-Fri, to noon Sat & Sun) Has lots of info on the national parks and good fishing spots, and can book tours, flights, bus tickets and accommodation.

Tours

Memorable tours from Exmouth include swimming with whale sharks, whale watching, wildlife spotting, scuba diving, sea kayaking, fishing and coral viewing from glass-bottom boats. There are many more tours than those listed here – see the visitors centre.

Capricorn Sea Kayaking (☎ 08-6267 8059; www .capricornseakayaking.com.au; one-/two-/five-day tours $149/595/1495) Offers coastal and camping tours by sea kayak from April to October, including one-, two- and five-day tours, with stops for snorkelling and lunch. Also offers multiday kayaking trips in Shark Bay.

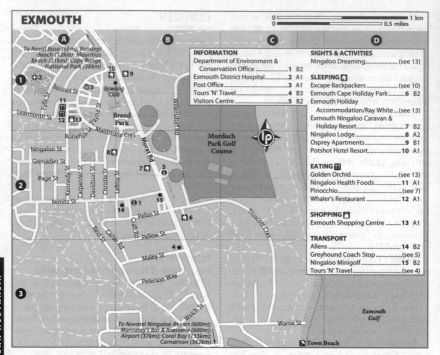

EXMOUTH

Exmouth Sailing (☎ 08-9721 7664; www.swyachtch
arters.com.au) Small-group sailing adventures with a focus
on learning to sail. There are two-hour twilight cruises
($150 per person), all-day cruises ($400) and live-aboard
sailing trips lasting two days ($790) or five days ($1390).

Ningaloo Dreaming (☎ 08-9949 4777; www
.ningaloodreaming.com; Exmouth Shopping Centre,
Maidstone Cres; from $135) This ecocertified company of-
fers whale-shark cruises, wildlife spotting, trips to Muiron
Islands, scuba-diving courses and dives off biologically rich
Exmouth Navy Pier.

Ningaloo Ecology Cruises (☎ 08-9949 2255; www
.ecology.com.au; tours from $60) Operates one- to 2½-
hour glass-bottom boat trips to view coral in the Ningaloo
Reef, leaving from Tatabiddi on the west coast of the cape
(free bus transfers).

Sleeping

Accommodation is limited; don't even think
about arriving in Exmouth without a booking
during the high season (April to October).

Potshot Hotel Resort (☎ 08-9949 1200; www.pot
shotresort.com; Murat Rd; dm/d $28/65, motel d $68, studios
$164, apt from $175; 🗙 🗔 🗩) This bustling resort, with several bars, two eateries, a swimming pool and a bottle shop, offers a range

of clean and comfortable sleeps, from simple
motel rooms to the trim and stylish Osprey
Apartments across the road. Potshot's laid-
back Excape Backpackers is a particularly
popular option.

Ningaloo Lodge (☎ 08-9949 4949; www.ninga
loolodge.com.au; Lefroy St; d $110; 🗙 🗩) These basic
rooms with fridge and TV – and commu-
nal kitchen, barbecue and pool – are the best
budget motel deal in town.

Novotel Ningaloo Resort (☎ 08-9949 0000; www
.novotelningaloo.com.au; Madaffari Dr; d/apt from $275/355;
🗙 🗩) Opened in 2006, the Novotel Ningaloo
Resort has brought a new level of sophistication (and expense) to Exmouth. Handsomely
designed rooms feature tasteful fabrics and
ample natural light, and even the standards
are spacious and well equipped. All have
balconies, while the best rooms sport ocean
views. There's a private beach, a large pool
and an excellent restaurant.

Wilderness Island (☎ 0409 430 688; www.wilderness
-island.com.au; all-inclusive per person per day $350) Some
26km off the mainland in the Exmouth Gulf,
this island retreat offers a completely different
experience. Guests stay overnight in one of

four low-impact safari tents and spend their days fishing, kayaking, snorkelling, taking wildlife-watching boat tours and exploring the remote and pristine environment. The price includes boat transport to and from the island, all meals, plus one tour per day. Special rates for backpackers.

Exmouth Holiday Accommodation/Ray White (☎ 08-9949 1144; www.raywhiteexmouth.com.au; holiday houses per week $500-1750; 😖) If you're planning a longer getaway, Ray White Real Estate has a wide range of weekly rentals, from fibro shacks to enormous two-storey homes with verandahs all around. The average price is $1000 per week.

Exmouth Cape Holiday Park (☎ 08-9949 1101; www.aspenparks.com.au; cnr Truscott Cres & Murat Rd; unpowered/powered sites $25/33, dm $27, cabins d $70; 😖 🖥 😫) This popular park has shady campsites, backpacker dorms, cabins and good facilities (barbecues, campers kitchen and swimming pool), plus it's just a short stroll to the beach.

Exmouth Ningaloo Caravan & Holiday Resort (☎ 08-9949 2377; www.exmouthresort.com; Murat Rd; unpowered/powered sites $30/35, dm/d $28/77, chalets $145-170; 😖 😫) Across from the visitors centre, this 23-acre site has grassy camping and caravan sites, self-contained chalets, dorms and extensive facilities (pool, barbecue, playground, wi-fi), along with a good Italian restaurant.

Eating & Drinking

There are several popular cafes, a bakery and two supermarkets at the Exmouth Shopping Centre on Maidstone Cres.

Ningaloo Health Foods (☎ 08-9949 1400; 3a Kennedy St; mains $8-14; 😊 9am-5pm Mon-Fri, to 1pm Sat & Sun) This charming little cafe serves delicious breakfasts (pancakes with berries and maple syrup), light lunches (Thai salads, chicken or tofu wraps), plus mango lassis, fresh juices, smoothies and excellent coffees.

Golden Orchid (☎ 08-9949 1740; Exmouth Shopping Centre, Maidstone Cres; mains $10-24; 😊 lunch Mon-Fri, dinner daily) If you're craving Chinese food, head here for tasty king-prawn chow mein, tofu and vegetables and Szechuan seafood. The $9 lunch specials are excellent value. BYO.

Pinocchio (☎ 08-9949 2577; Murat Rd; mains $15-35; 😊 dinner) Across from the visitors centre, Pinocchio is a warmly lit BYO spot that whips up tasty pastas and pizzas. Outdoor dining on the deck.

our pick **Whaler's Restaurant** (☎ 08-9949 2416; 5 Kennedy St; mains lunch $15-22, dinner $24-32; 😊 lunch & dinner Tue-Sun) Exmouth's long-time culinary favourite, Whaler's serves delicious eclectic fare such as New Orleans seafood gumbo, gnocchi with tiger prawns, smoked kangaroo loin and Mexican fajitas. Lunch is more-mainstream bistro fare. Dine on the breezy terrace. Licensed and BYO.

Mantaray's Bar & Brasserie (☎ 08-9949 0003; Madaffari Dr; mains lunch $14-24, dinner $34-45; 😊 lunch & dinner) Inside the Novotel Ningaloo Resort, Mantaray's offers delectable cuisine amid an elegantly set dining room. Seafood risotto, marinated lamb rump, and pumpkin ravioli are among the varied selections.

The Potshot Hotel is the town's main watering hole, with a pool table, darts, a juke box and live music.

Getting There & Away

From the North-West Coastal Hwy take the turn-off to Exmouth (200km) at the Minilya Roadhouse.

Exmouth's Learmonth Airport is 37km south of town and there are daily **Skywest** (☎ 1300 660 088; www.skywest.com.au) flights to and from Perth.

Buses stop at the visitors centre. **Greyhound** (☎ 1300 473 946; www.greyhound.com.au) has three services a week from Perth ($252, 20 hours). From Exmouth there are three services per week to Coral Bay ($68, two hours). Northbound buses go three times weekly from Exmouth to Port Hedland ($228, 11 hours) and Broome ($311, 21 hours).

Red Earth Safaris (☎ 08-9279 9011; www.redearth safaris.com.au) runs six- or eight-day tours ($655 to $795) from Perth to Exmouth, along with a weekly 1½-day Perth Express service departing on Sunday at 7am ($180). **Easyrider Backpacker Tours** (☎ 08-9227 0824; www.easyridertours .com.au) stop at Exmouth at least once a week on the three-day Coastal cruiser route to Perth ($379). Easyrider's Perth Express ($139) stops here once or twice a week (but there's no service July through October). Easyrider also has three-day Broome-bound trips taking in Karijini ($409).

Getting Around

The **Airport Shuttle Bus** (☎ 08-9949 1101; one way $25) meets all flights and shuttles the 37km into town; reservations are required for a ride back to the airport.

WESTERN AUSTRALIA

Tours 'N' Travel (☎ 08-9949 4748; www.ningaloo -tours-travel.com.au; 102 Murat Rd) rents mopeds (from $39/53 for five/24 hours) and cars (from $50 per day). **Allens** (☎ 08-9949 2403; 24 Nimitz St) also rents cars, starting at $45 per day. Rent a mountain bike ($20 per day) or a kayak ($50 per day) from **Ningaloo Minigolf** (☎ 08-9949 4644; Murat Rd; ☺ 9am-8pm).

NINGALOO MARINE PARK

The spectacular Ningaloo Marine Park protects more than 250km of waters and foreshore areas from Bundegi Reef in the northeast of the North-West Cape peninsula to Amherst Point in the southwest.

The Ningaloo reef is amazingly accessible, lying only 100m offshore from some parts of the peninsula, and is home to a staggering array of marine life. There are sharks, manta rays, humpback whales, turtles, dugongs and more than 500 species of fish.

There's wonderful marine activity to enjoy year-round:

November to February Turtles – four species are known to nestle and hatch in the sands.
March & April Coral spawning – a dazzling, but difficult to predict, event 10 to 12 days after the full moon.
May to July Whale sharks – these behemoths follow the coral spawning.
May to November Manta rays – dramatic migrations in big schools.
July to November Humpback whales – migrating south, they have fun splashing about on the way.

What also makes Ningaloo special is its **coral**. Over 220 species of hard coral have been recorded in the waters, ranging from the slow-growing bommies to delicate branching varieties. The hard corals found here are less colourful than soft corals, but have amazing formations. For eight or nine nights after the full moon in March and April there is a synchronised mass spawning, when branches of hermaphroditic coral simultaneously eject eggs and sperm into the water.

It's this coral that attracts the park's biggest drawcard, the speckled **whale shark** (*Rhiniodon typus*). Ningaloo is the only place in the world where these solitary gentle giants arrive like clockwork each year to feed on plankton and small fish, making it a mecca for marine biologists and visitors alike. The largest fish in the world, whale sharks can reach up to 18m in length and weigh up to 21 tonnes, although most weigh between 13 and 15 tonnes.

Activities

Most people visit Ningaloo Marine Park to snorkel. Stop at the **Milyering visitors centre** (☎ 08-9949 2808; ☺ 9am-3.45pm) to get maps, information and an eyeful of dangerous critters in glass bottles. Informative staff can tell you which beaches are best for snorkelling; be sure to ask about dangerous currents off the reefs. The shop at the visitors centre sells and rents snorkelling equipment.

The best snorkelling spots:

Lakeside Snorkel out with the current before returning to the original point.
Oyster Stacks Just metres offshore, the Oyster Stacks shelter many species of fish.
Turquoise Bay Everyone's favourite: walk 300m south along the beach, swim out for about 40m and float face down – the current will carry you over coral bommies and abundant sea life. Get out at the sand bar then run back along the beach and start all over!

There are plenty of other water- and land-based tours from Coral Bay (p984) and Exmouth (p985).

CAPE RANGE NATIONAL PARK

Stunning **Cape Range National Park** (admission per vehicle $10) covers 510 sq km, about a third of the North-West Cape peninsula, and is rich in wildlife – kangaroos, emus, echidnas and lizards are easily spotted on a walk or drive through the park. Spectacular deep canyons and rugged red limestone gorges dramatically cut into the range and flow with deep blue water that mirrors the cliffs when calm. The gorges gradually give way to white sand, which leads to the crystal waters of Ningaloo Reef.

The park is accessible from the east coast from the unsealed Charles Knife Rd and Shothole Canyon Rd, which in turn are accessed from Minilya-Exmouth Rd, although these roads won't take you through to the west coast. From the west coast the park is accessible from Yardie Creek Rd.

The excellent **Milyering visitors centre** (☎ 08-9949 2808; ☺ 9am-3.45pm) has a comprehensive display of the area's natural and cultural history, and great maps and publications.

Sights & Activities

On the east coast, the scenic drive to **Charles Knife Canyon** along Charles Knife Rd, 23km south of Exmouth, dramatically follows the ridges of the range with breathtaking views below. **Shothole Canyon** is reached from Shothole

---

WARNING

While swimming and snorkelling are the highlights of Cape Range, please be aware that strong currents do occur at beaches everywhere in the park, including the popular Turquoise Bay. Be attentive.

Canyon Rd, 16km south of Exmouth, along a dry creek-bed of a road that gets you up close to the colourful canyon walls.

On the west coast, you can drive to the start of the walk into **Mandu Mandu gorge** (3km return) via an access road 20km south of the Milyering visitors centre, for fantastic panoramic vistas of the gorge.

Drive to **Yardie Creek**, where the sealed Yardie Creek Rd ends, to do the easy 1.5km return walk to the creek. You can take a very pleasant one-hour **Yardie Creek Cruise** (☎ 08-9949 2808; adult/child $25/12; ☾ 11am) up the short, sheer gorge to see rare black-footed rock wallabies and lots of bird life. The cruise runs daily April to September.

Passing through Yardie Creek to southern points is rarely possible even with a good 4WD. Check road conditions with the Milyering visitors centre.

Sleeping

There are many compact **camping grounds** (per adult/child $7/2) nicely situated along the coast. Facilities and shade are minimal, but most have toilets. Sites are limited and allocated upon arrival (no advance bookings). Milyering visitors centre has a list of sites with photos of the beaches. Get info in advance from **DEC** (☎ 08-9949 8000; 20 Nimitz St, Exmouth).

Getting There & Away

If you're not on a tour, you'll need your own transport to explore Ningaloo Marine Park and Cape Range National Park.

KARIJINI NATIONAL PARK

One of WA's most impressive attractions, **Karijini National Park** (per car $10) provides an idyllic setting for hiking, swimming and soaking up the incredible scenery. Deep gorges, spectacular waterfalls, pristine swimming holes, along with stunning wildflowers and abundant wildlife have made the place a deservedly popular, if still remote, destination.

Most of Karijini's attractions are located in the park's north, off the 67km-long Banyjima Dr. The quality of this unsealed road varies, depending on how deep into the tourist season it is; it's not easy-going for conventional vehicles and it's advisable to do it in a 4WD.

The state-of-the-art **Karijini visitors centre** (☎ 08-9189 8121; Banyjima Dr; ☾ 9am-4pm May-Oct, 10am-2pm Nov-Apr), in the northeastern corner of the park, is managed by the traditional owners of Karijini, the Banyjima, and it's a stunner! The slick interpretive displays give a thought-provoking overview of the natural and cultural history of the park.

Pick up trail maps and walking information here. Do be sensible about what walks you select, and take care: the trails through the park are more dangerous than they appear – particularly after rain when they get slippery, and flash flooding can occur. Rescues of injured tourists happen all too often.

Entering Banyjima Dr from the east, you soon reach the turn-off to beautiful **Dales Gorge**, where you can camp. A short, sharp descent takes you to **Fortescue Falls**, behind which lies the beautiful swimming hole of **Fern Pool**. There's also a path from Fortescue Falls that follows the stream to picturesque **Circular Pool**; you can return via a sunny trail along the cliff top.

From Kalimina Rd a 30-minute walk takes you into the depths of **Kalimina Gorge**, where there's a small tranquil pool. Another 11km along is Joffre Falls Rd, which leads to **Knox Gorge**, passing the lookout over the spectacular **Joffre Falls**.

The final turn-off is Weano Rd, which takes you to the park's signature attraction, the breathtaking **Oxers Lookout**, where there are extraordinary views of the junction of the Red, Weano, Joffre and Hancock Gorges.

While it's technically possible to climb down into **Hancock Gorge** from here, locals advise against it, and guides will no longer take you. You'll notice a touching memorial to Jim Regan, a volunteer SES rescuer who died on 3 April 2004 rescuing a couple of backpackers here.

Other attractions include **Hamersley Gorge** off Nanutarra-Wittenoom Rd in the park's northwest.

Tours

For an adrenalin rush, go abseiling with **West Oz Active Adventure Tours** (☎ 0438 913 713;

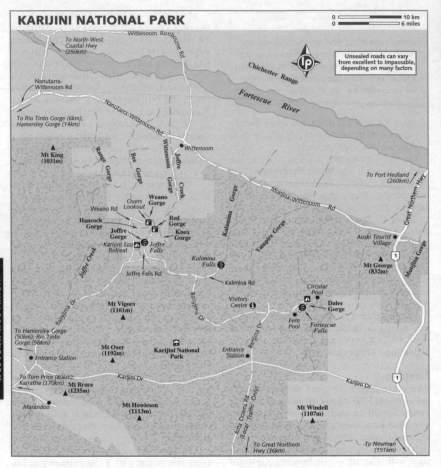

KARIJINI NATIONAL PARK

www.westozactive.com.au; half-/full day excursion $140/215).
These gorge tours combine hiking, swimming,
climbing, sliding off waterfalls and abseiling.
You can also contact the company at Eco-
Retreat Karijini (see right).

Lestok Tours (☎ 08-9188 1112; www.lestoktours.com
.au; full-day Karijini tours $130, 1½hr Pilbara Iron mine tours
$21) runs full-day outings to Karijini from Tom
Price, as well as mine tours.

Also in Tom Price, you can arrange a two-
hour walking tour with **Wilanah Walkabouts**,
learning about dreaming sites as well as
plants, animals and bush medicines from
Vivienne Cook, a traditional owner of the
land. Contact her through **Tom Price visitor
centre** (☎ 08-9188 1112; www.tompricewa.com.au;
Central Rd).

Sleeping & Eating

At Dales Gorge inside Karijini, there's a basic
camping ground (☎ 08-9189 8157; sites per adult/child
$8/2), where dingoes and other wildlife hap-
pily roam.

Eco Retreat Karijini (☎ 08-9425 5591; www.ka
rijiniecoretreat.com.au; campsites $25; d high/low season
$270/149) Also in Karijini, this handsomely set
bush retreat offers lodging in 'eco tents'. These
boast a Zenlike design, excellent beds and
fine views of the spinifex-laced countryside.
There's also a traditional camping ground, a
bush kitchen and a good restaurant (mains
$25 to $29), where guests grill up their own
barramundi, lamb and rump steak.

Auski Tourist Village (☎ 08-9176 6988; Great Northern
Hwy; s/d $55/65, motel d $150; ✕ ⌨ ▨) On the high-

way, 35km north of the Karijini Dr turn-off, this place provides simple lodging and serves typical roadhouse fare (mains $9 to $30).

Getting There & Away

Access to the Karijini National Park is via Karijini Dr, which leaves the Great Northern Hwy 226km south of Port Hedland and 162km northwest of Newman. Greyhound buses stop at the Auski Tourist Village, 35km north of the turn-off, on Saturday.

The unsealed Pilbara Railway Rd takes you between Tom Price and Karratha, but it's a private road and you must get a (free) permit from the visitors centres at **Tom Price** (☎ 08-9188 1112; www.tompricewa.com.au; Central Rd; ⏰ 9.30am-3.30pm Mon-Fri and 9am-noon Sat; 🖳) or **Karratha** (☎ 08-9144 4600; Karratha Rd).

KARRATHA

pop 11,700

Avoided by most travellers, Karratha ('good country') is a rugged industrial town that supports a plethora of companies and industries, including iron, salt, gas and fertiliser.

Karratha visitors centre (☎ 08-9144 4600; info@tourist.karratha.com; Karratha Rd; ⏰ 8.30am-5pm Mon-Fri, 9am-3pm Sat & Sun, shorter hours Dec-Mar) has internet access and lots of local info and can organise fishing charters and dives in the Dampier Archipelago or Montebello Islands (from $150). It can also supply permits (free) to use the private company road to Tom Price.

The visitors centre can book cruises run by **Discovery Sailing Adventure** (☎ 0408 801 040; beaumont2@westnet.com.au). The 12m sailing ketch heads out on sunset cruises ($50), five-hour daytime cruises ($70) and overnight trips ($250). There are also industrial tours, including iron-ore tours, Dampier Salt and Dampier Port. One of Karratha's best attractions is free: the 3.5km-long **Jaburara Heritage Trail** takes visitors through significant traditional sites and details Karratha's history, from the displacement and eventual extinction of the Jaburara people to the development of billion-dollar industries. The trail starts near the visitors centre.

The shopping centre has ATMs and a newsagent.

Sleeping & Eating

Hotels in Karratha cater mostly to corporate and government guests, and are often fully booked. Call ahead if you are planning to stay the night.

Karratha Backpackers (☎ 08-9144 4904; 110 Wellard Way; dm/d $25/65; 🏠 🖳) The only budget place in town is a mellow, fairly basic affair with rooms set around a courtyard. There's a communal kitchen and a lively lounge.

All Seasons Karratha (☎ 08-9159 1000; www.allseasons.com.au; Searipple Rd; d $245-265; 🏠 🖳 🏊) Just behind the shopping centre, this central hotel has spacious, comfortable rooms with fridge, TV and phone. The hotel's Hearson's Bistro (mains $18 to $32) is one of Karratha's best eateries and has a pleasant poolside setting.

Pilbara Holiday Park (☎ 08-9185 1855; www.aspenparks.com.au; Rosemary Rd; unpowered/powered sites $34/42, motel/studio d from $190/215; 🏠 🖳 🏊) This neat, leafy park has a range of good self-contained accommodation, shady sites, a kids' playground, campers kitchen, TV room and kiosk.

For a little more natural beauty, head to the rugged coastline at **Gnoorea Point** (also known as 40-Mile Beach), where you can camp for $7 per night. There's no water or facilities of any kind. It's located 70km south of Karratha.

In the main shopping centre are a supermarket, takeaways and cafes.

Getting There & Around

Qantas (☎ 13 13 13; www.qantas.com.au) flies daily from Perth and twice weekly from Brisbane, while **Northwest Regional Airlines** (☎ 08-9192 1369) has flights to Port Hedland and Broome three times a week. **Virgin Blue** (☎ 13 67 89) has daily flights to Perth.

Greyhound (☎ 1300 473 946; www.greyhound.com.au) has daily services to Perth ($296, 22 hours) and Broome ($153, 11 hours) departing from Welcome Rd, opposite the Catholic church.

DAMPIER

Dampier, some 25km from Karratha, is the region's main port. Spread around King Bay, it overlooks the 42 pristine islands of the **Dampier Archipelago** and supports a wealth of marine life in its coral waters, but heavy industry has blighted Dampier's shores. The archipelago is popular with anglers, and a number of charter boat operators head there; contact the Karratha visitors centre (left) for details.

The **Dampier Transit Caravan Park** (☎ 08-9183 1109; The Esplanade; unpowered/powered sites $18/22) has a handful of grassy caravan sites overlooking the water and the Pilbara Iron works.

WONDERS OF THE MURUJUGA

Northeast of Dampier lies the Burrup Peninsula, or Murujuga by its Aboriginal name. It is the focal point for a great deal of Karratha's industry and also houses one of the great and least-known wonders of Western Australia. On a drive through the area, you'll pass Pilbara Iron facilities, quarries, an enormous ammonia plant – one of the world's largest – and finally the vast sprawl of the space-age Liquefied Natural Gas Plant. Here visitors can learn all about the science of the plant, hydrocarbons in general and how it all fits together in a sleek multimedia visitors centre. The Burrup also houses some other intriguing sites, including Hearson's Cove, an attractive (though rocky) swimming beach on the east side of the peninsula. As in Broome, you can see the 'Staircase to the Moon' here from May through October (see p1004).

The real reason to come up the peninsula, however, is to visit the incredible collection of petroglyphs, lying in a gorge not far from Hearson's Cove. These are just one small part of an enormous rock-art collection – hundreds of thousands of pieces stretching over 88 sq km. According to the National Trust of Australia, the Burrup probably contains the largest collection of petroglyphs on the planet. Some of the rock art here dates back 20,000 years or more, including perhaps the first representation of a human face in history. Other pieces show kangaroos, whales, emus, abstract symbols, Aboriginal ceremonies, and even thylacines (Tasmanian tigers), animals that left no record of ever having lived in this part of Australia. Visitors can freely wander through the gorge, taking in thousands of rock engravings.

Unfortunately, the future of the site remains at risk, as six new gas processing plants are planned for construction in the coming years. Thousands of pieces have already been destroyed – estimates range from 5% to 25% of the original collection. Learn more about the petroglyphs at www.burrup.org.au.

Dampier Mermaid (☎ 08-9183 1222; www.damp iermermaid.com.au; The Esplanade; d $185-240; ✖ ▯ ▨) has basic but comfortable rooms, with the best having great ocean views. It's mostly occupied by contract workers, so book ahead. There's also a bar and bistro. **Road Runner** (☎ 08-9183 0445; The Esplanade; mains $7-15; ☯ breakfast & lunch daily, dinner Fri-Sun), overlooking Dampier Harbour, has typical pub fare and outdoor seating.

ROEBOURNE AREA

While atmospheric Roebourne and Cossack are the sites of the first European settlements in the Pilbara, seaside Point Samson is a fine spot for doing nothing but marking the time with the tides. The area gets busy during school holidays, and swelteringly hot in summer.

Roebourne (population 970), 40km east of Karratha, is the oldest Pilbara town still in existence (1866) and home to a large Aboriginal community. Once a grazing and copper-mining centre, it has some grand buildings, several of which house small art galleries. The region's **visitors centre** (☎ 08-9182 1060; Queen St; ☯ 9am-3pm, shorter hours Nov-Apr) is housed in the Old Gaol, which is also a **museum** (admission by donation). Other historic buildings include the **Holy Trinity Church** (1894) and **Victoria Hotel**, the last of five original pubs.

Cossack is a ghost town with a lovely riverside location and historic bluestone buildings (1870–98). At the mouth of the Harding River, it was the district's main port from the mid- to late 19th century, but was supplanted by Point Samson and then abandoned. Attractions include the **Social History Museum** (adult/child $2/1; ☯ 9am-4pm), which celebrates the town's halcyon days. The pioneer cemetery has a tiny Japanese section dating from the days when Cossack was WA's first major pearl-fishing town. **Cossack Budget Accommodation** (☎ 08-9182 1190; d with/without air-con $80/60; ✖) has clean rooms in the atmospheric old police barracks, but you'll need to bring your own food as there are no restaurants in Cossack. A **kiosk** (☯ 10am-3pm May-Oct) selling snack food keeps minimal hours in season.

Point Samson (population 230) is a tiny seaside town that supports a substantial commercial fishing industry. There's good **snorkelling** off Point Samson and Honeymoon Cove, a picture-perfect beach featured on myriad tourist brochures (bring your own gear). Swish **Point Samson Resort** (☎ 08-9187 1052; www.pointsamson.com; 56 Samson Rd; d $273; ✖ ▨) has comfortable, nicely equipped rooms amid tropical gardens. **Samson Beach Caravan Park** (☎ 08-9187 1414; Samson Rd; powered sites $30) is a tiny park in leafy surrounds, conveniently close to the water and the tavern. Bookings are essential during school holidays. Point Samson Resort has one of the region's best restaurants, **Ta Ta's** (mains around $40), with a creative, mainly seafood menu and stylish surroundings. Adjacent to the caravan park, **Moby's Kitchen** (☎ 08-9187 1435; mains $18-24; ☺ 11am-2.30pm & 5-8.30pm Mon-Fri, 11am-8pm Sat & Sun) fries up good old-fashioned takeaway fish and chips, and has a popular outdoor verandah overlooking the sea.

MILLSTREAM-CHICHESTER NATIONAL PARK

The tranquil waterholes of the Fortescue River are cool, lush oases in the midst of arid spinifex-covered plateaus and basalt ranges. Around 120km south of Roebourne, this 2000-sq-km **park** (per vehicle $10) is well worth a detour – you'll be rewarded by panoramic vistas reminiscent of the USA's Monument Valley.

The unstaffed Millstream **visitors centre** (☺ 8am-4pm) was once the homestead of a pastoral station and now has excellent displays on the park's history, ecosystems and traditional owners, the Yindjibarndi people.

In the park's north, the enchanting **Python Pool** (just a two-minute walk from the car park) is worth a look, and a swim if it's warm enough. It's linked to Mt Herbert by the **Chichester Range Camel Trail** (8km, three hours one way), from where it's a further 45-minute clamber (one way) to the peak. Further south, **Chinderwarriner Pool** and **Crossing Pool** are lovely waterholes with lilies and shady palms. The **Murlunmunyjurna Trail** (7km, two hours return) features river crossings over palm-trunk bridges and interpretive plaques next to vegetation explaining the plants' uses by the Yindjibarndi people. Pick up a park map from the visitors centre.

Shady bush **campsites** (☎ 08-9184 5144; per person $7) are located at Snake Creek, Crossing Pool and Deep Reach Pool; all have pit toilets and the latter two sites have gas barbecues.

MARBLE BAR
pop 200

This sleepy, dusty town was born around the time gold was discovered in the surrounding hills. Marble Bar boomed in the 1890s (population 5000) when fortune seekers from across Australia flooded the area. Today, the place is famous not for its minerals but its relentless heat. Following a long summer in 1924, when for 161 consecutive days the temperature never dipped below 100°F (37.8°C), Marble Bar became known as the hottest place in Australia.

It's appropriate then that the main attraction here is a natural pool, 5km west of town. **Chinaman Pool** is just beyond the 'marble bar' in a rock face for which the town is named, which is actually a 'bar' of jasper that pioneers mistook for marble. At the one-room museum of the **Comet Gold Mine** (☎ 08-9176 1015; Hillside Rd; admission $2; ☺ 9am-4pm), visitors can look at old relics from the gold mines, photos of aviator Kingsford Smith and the Corunna Downs secret airbase, plus displays of local rocks and minerals. You can also camp or park your caravan here for $10 per person. It's 8km west of town. The **Ironclad Hotel** (☎ 08-9176 1066; www.geocities.com/ironcladhotel; 15 Francis St; d $66-110; ☒) is a classic old pub that's the heart and soul of Marble Bar, with well-used pool tables, a likeable beer garden and home-cooked counter meals (mains $7 to $19). The homemade pizzas are particularly well liked.

PORT HEDLAND
pop 15,000

The industrious town of Port Hedland, with its low-rise corrugated-iron buildings and fibro houses, is caked in dark red dirt. Its massive dock handles the iron ore mined at Newman and exports more tonnage than any other Australian port. The stockpiles of ore dominating the skyline are the source of the layer of dust that coats the town.

Information

There are ATMs along Wedge St and in the Boulevard shopping centre (cnr Wilson and McGregor Sts).

Hospital (☎ 08-9158 1666; Sutherland St)

Visitors centre (☎ 08-9173 1711; 13 Wedge St; ☺ 8.30am-4.30pm Mon-Fri, 10am-2pm Sat & Sun, shorter hours Nov-May) The helpful visitors centre has internet access and can advise of iron-ore plant tours, turtle monitoring (November to February) and reef walks.

Sights & Activities

Charming **Dalgety House Museum** (☎ 08-9173 4300; cnr Wedge & Anderson Sts; admission $2; ☺ 10am-2pm Mon-Fri), dating to 1903, is one of the few remaining examples of early-20th-century architecture.

WESTERN AUSTRALIA

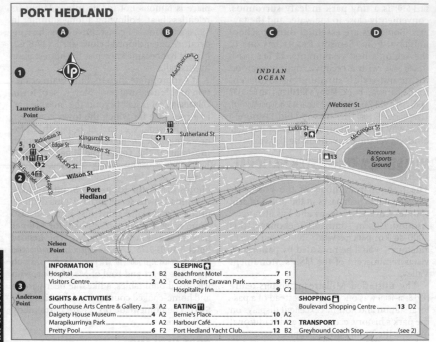

PORT HEDLAND

INFORMATION		SLEEPING	
Hospital	1 B2	Beachfront Motel	7 F1
Visitors Centre	2 A2	Cooke Point Caravan Park	8 F2
		Hospitality Inn	9 C2
SIGHTS & ACTIVITIES			
Courthouse Arts Centre & Gallery	3 A2	EATING	
Dalgety House Museum	4 A2	Bernie's Place	10 A2
Marapikurrinya Park	5 A2	Harbour Café	11 A2
Pretty Pool	6 F2	Port Hedland Yacht Club	12 B2
		SHOPPING	
		Boulevard Shopping Centre	13 D2
		TRANSPORT	
		Greyhound Coach Stop	(see 2)

Displays tell the story of Port Hedland's early development days.

The visitors centre is the departure point for massive **BHP Billiton iron-ore plant tours** (adult/child $26/20; ☺ 9.30am Mon-Fri).

Courthouse Arts Centre & Gallery (☎ 08-9173 1064; Edgar St; ☺ 9am-4.30pm Mon-Fri) has a rotation of contemporary art exhibitions, as well as a gallery shop that sells Aboriginal and local art and crafts.

Between November and February **flatback turtles** nest on nearby beaches. The best spot to see them is Cemetery Beach, but make sure you follow the code of conduct; the visitors centre has detailed information.

Pretty Pool, 7km east of the town centre, is a popular fishing and picnicking spot (beware of stonefish). Just to the north, Goode St is the best place to view Port Hedland's **Staircase to the Moon** (see p1004).

From **Marapikurrinya Park** at the end of Wedge St, you can watch impossibly large tankers glide in and out of port during the day, and see BHP's Hot Briquetted Iron plant on Finucane Island glow like a warlock's castle at night.

Sleeping & Eating

Budget accommodation is extremely limited in Port Hedland.

Beachfront Motel (☎ 08-9173 2000; www.beach frontvillage.com.au; Webster St; s/d $185/205, s/d without bathroom $140/165; ⊠) This former correctional facility received a slight makeover to offer small, spotless rooms with flat-screen TVs for mostly contract workers in the area. It's backed by sand dunes and still bears the aura (and high-security fencing) of its not-so-distant past.

Hospitality Inn (☎ 08-9173 1044; www.hospitalityinns .com.au; Webster St; d $225; ⊠ ⊡ ⊠) This exceptional motel has spacious, spotless rooms with loads of equipment. Some rooms boast ocean views. There's also a good in-house restaurant serving duck confit, prawn risotto and other international fare (mains $19 to $32).

Cooke Point Caravan Park (☎ 08-9173 1271; www .aspenparks.com.au; cnr Athol & Taylor Sts; powered sites $39, d without bathroom $80, motel/unit d $190-220; ⊠ ⊠) Park your van or pitch your tent on the red dirt at this tidy, but pricey caravan park overlooking Pretty Pool and the ocean. Expect good amenities including a campers kitchen

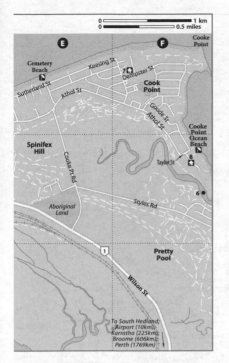

and pool, and a range of decent motel-style accommodation.

Bernie's Place (☎ 08-9173 4342; Edgar St; mains $6-9; ✆ breakfast & lunch Mon-Fri) The sweet Philippine owner whips up tasty, nicely spiced Asian dishes at this homey restaurant. The menu changes regularly, but usually includes spring rolls, curry puffs, chilli mussels and vegetarian options.

Harbour Café (☎ 08-9173 2630; Wedge St; mains around $15; ✆ 5am-4pm Mon-Fri, 7am-2pm Sat & Sun) Near the visitors centre, the Harbour Café cooks satisfying breakfasts (eggs Benedict, Mexican wraps) as well as hearty lunch fare (meat pies, sausage rolls, tandoori chicken) and decent coffee.

Port Hedland Yacht Club (☎ 08-9173 3398; Sutherland St; mains $12-20) This is a popular spot with local families for traditional fish and chips wrapped in butcher paper. It's licensed and has outdoor seating on a terrace overlooking the port.

There is a supermarket and cafe at the **Boulevard shopping centre** (cnr Wilson & McGregor Sts).

Getting There & Away

Qantas (☎ 13 13 13; www.qantas.com.au) flies between Port Hedland and Perth daily, while **Northwest**

Regional Airlines (☎ 1300 136 629) goes to Broome and Karratha from Perth three times a week.

Greyhound (☎ 1300 473 946; www.greyhound.com.au) has buses to Perth ($328, 26 hours) and Broome ($109, 7½ hours); both go daily except Monday and Wednesday and depart from the visitors centre and the South Hedland shopping centre. **Integrity** (☎ 1800 226 339; www.integritycoachlines.com.au) has a slightly quicker inland service to Perth ($232, 22 hours) via Newman and Mt Magnet on Friday, departing from the visitors centre.

Getting Around

The airport is 13km from town; **Hedland Taxis** (☎ 08-9172 1010) charges around $30. **Hedland Bus Lines** (☎ 08-9172 1394) runs limited weekday services between Port Hedland and Cooke Point, and on to South Hedland ($3); services stop at the visitors centre.

PORT HEDLAND TO BROOME

The highway runs inland from Port Hedland to Broome for 611km. Dust devils whip through flat, featureless terrain while the coast to the west is lovely and unspoilt.

If you want to break the journey, there are some fine spots near picturesque beaches. The exit to **Cape Keraudren Reserve** is 154km from Port Hedland, near Pardoo Roadhouse; there are **campsites** (per vehicle $7.50) with toilet facilities here. Shady **Eighty Mile Beach Caravan Park** (☎ 08-9176 5941; www.eightymilebeach.com.au; unpowered/powered sites $29/33, cabins d $90-190; ✪ ▣) backs onto the beautiful white-sand beach, 245km from Port Hedland; there's a shop for essentials. **Barn Hill Station** (☎ 08-9192 4975; unpowered/powered sites $20/24, cabins d $75), 490km from Port Hedland, is a working cattle station 10km off the highway (it's barely marked so stay alert). Campsites are once again set near untouched beachfront. All get packed from June to September.

THE KIMBERLEY

The vast and rugged Kimberley holds some of Australia's most spectacular – and remote – scenery. With just two opposing seasons, the Wet and the Dry, the Kimberley is a land of extremes: semiarid plains dotted with spinifex, outback roads that flow like rivers, panoramic ranges cut by steep stony gorges and dramatic waterfalls surrounded by tropical rainforest.

WESTERN AUSTRALIA

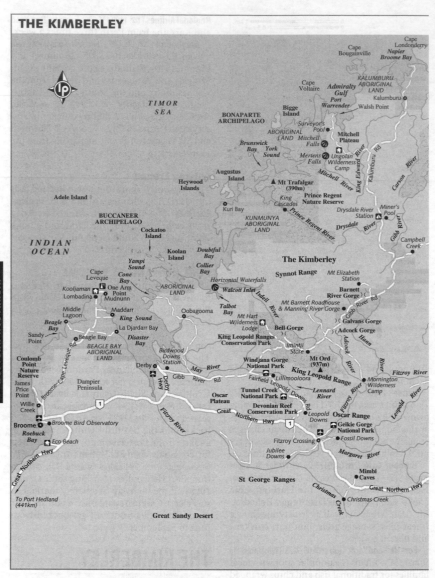

THE KIMBERLEY

Exploring this region means big adventure: taking on the Gibb River Rd in a well-equipped 4WD, camping out under magnificently starlit skies and gazing upon ancient natural wonders in this 420,000 sq km wilderness (that's three times the size of England). These attractions come in many forms – from the pristine and largely Indigenous Dampier Peninsula to the magnificent gorges of Geike and Windjana. There's the surreal 'beehive' domes of Purnululu, mysterious rock art dating back millennia and thundering Mitchell Falls. Gateway to the region is laid-back Broome, with a rich Indigenous history and exotic 19th-century pearling past. Today, the town is well loved for the white sands and

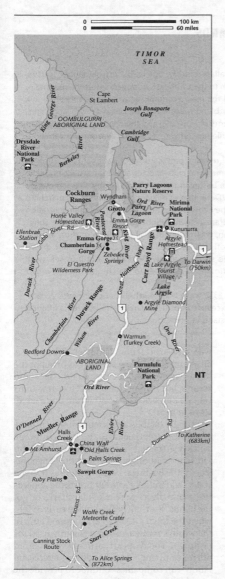

clear waters of Cable Beach, while its excellent restaurants and lively resorts make it a fine place to linger before or after a big journey into the outback.

Tours

Numerous multiday tours explore the Kimberley. Itineraries, prices and dates vary; shop around and ask questions before committing. Prices usually include meals, accommodation (which means camping for budget tours) and park fees.

Kimberley Wild (☎ 08-9193 7778; www.kimberley wild.com) An award-winner for ecotourism, Kimberley Wild offers a wide assortment of tours from Broome including day trips to Windjana/Tunnel Creek ($229), Geike Gorge ($259) and Cape Leveque ($239), and three-day West Kimberley trips with a focus on Indigenous heritage ($795).

Kimberley Wilderness Adventures (☎ 1800 804 005, 08-9192 5741; www.kimberleywilderness.com.au) Award-winning outfit offers multiday tours, including the popular 13-day Kimberley Complete (s/d per person $7030/5895).

Wilderness 4WD Adventures (☎ 1800 808 288, 08-8941 2161; www.wildernessadventures.com.au) This ecocertified company offers one-way Broome-to-Darwin trips through the Kimberley, with trips of six days ($825) to nine days ($1525), taking in Purnululu National Park, various gorges and El Questro Station. There's also a two-day Darwin-to-Broome trip ($225).

Other companies offering 4WD Broome-to-Darwin trips:

Kimberley Adventure Tours (☎ 1800 083 368, 08-9191 2655; www.kimberleyadventures.com.au; 9 days $1395)

Western Xposure (☎ 1800 621 200, 08-9371 3695; www.westernxposure.com.au; 6 days $825)

For a different perspective on the Kimberley:

Alligator Airways (☎ 1800 632 533; www.alligatorai rways.com.au) Offers a variety of air trips from Kununurra, including a full-day Lake Argyle and Bungle Bungles tour ($440) and 30-minute float plane flights ($120).

King Leopold Air (☎ 08-9193 7155; www.kingle opoldair.com.au) Air tours of western Kimberley including the half-day Buccaneer Explorer ($430), over Horizontal Falls, and the full-day Prince Regent Explorer via Mitchell Falls ($780).

Willis's Walkabouts (☎ 08-8985 2134; www .bushwalkingholidays.com.au) Multiday bushwalking tours all over the Kimberley, ranging from rugged six-week trips along the coast ($7650) to one-week trips through the Cockburn Range ($1125).

Getting There & Away

Qantas (☎ 13 13 13; www.qantas.com.au) has daily flights from Perth to Broome as well as several flights per week to Kununurra. Partner airline **Airnorth** (☎ 08-8920 4001; www.airnorth.com.au) flies from Broome to Darwin and Kununurra, as well as Kununurra to Darwin.

WESTERN AUSTRALIA

CHRISTMAS & COCOS (KEELING) ISLANDS
CHRISTMAS ISLAND
pop 1600

Remote Christmas Island (CI) may be an Australian territory, but its closest neighbour is Java, Indonesia, 360km to the north; Perth lies 2600km to the southeast. A rugged limestone mountain, CI was settled in 1888 to mine phosphate – still the main economic activity. Its people are a mix of Chinese, Malays and European-Australians, a blend reflected in the island's food, languages, customs and religions. All are permanent residents of Australia, and the majority hold Australian citizenship. Several Singapore-style colonial buildings remain, as do traces from the Japanese occupation in WWII.

In spite of mining activity, 63% of the island remains protected by CI National Park. There is tall rainforest on the plateau, and a series of limestone cliffs and terraces that attract endemic nesting sea birds, including the gorgeous golden bosun and rare Abbott's booby. CI is famous for the spectacular annual movement in November/December of millions of red land crabs marching from the forest down to the coast to breed. They cover everything in sight on their migration routes, including the roads. Marine life is also dramatic, with bright corals and fish on the fringing reefs attracting snorkellers in the dry season, when international yachties also drop anchor. Divers come throughout the year for the drop-off wall and cave dives, and are especially drawn to the possibility of diving with seasonal whale sharks (roughly October to April). A sea swell can bring decent surf during the wet season (roughly December to March) and there's a surf shop on the island.

Christmas Island **visitors centre** (☎ 08-9164 8382; www.christmas.net.au) can coordinate accommodation, diving, fishing and car hire. Visit its excellent website for links to travel agents offering packages, other local businesses and detailed island information.

Greyhound Australia (☎ 1300 473 946; www.greyhound.com.au) stops at the Broome visitors centre on its daily Perth–Darwin service. From Darwin, destinations include Kununurra ($215, 11 hours), Derby ($362, 22 hours) and Broome ($397, 26 hours). From Broome, destinations include Perth ($432, 33 hours), Port Hedland ($108, 7½ hours), Derby ($69, 2½ hours) and Kununurra ($237, 14 hours).

BROOME
pop 14,800

Broome's peninsula setting is undoubtedly dramatic, from the powdery white sands of its famous Cable Beach to the deep aquamarine hues of Roebuck Bay. Surrounding the town is the arid clay-baked landscape of the Kimberley, which turns lush when the thundering storms of the Wet arrive. The natural world is very much a part of Broome's allure, from fiery red sunsets over the beach to enchanting full-moon rises over the mud flats. Perhaps one of Broome's most captivating features is something intangible – a unique energy and atmosphere found nowhere else in WA. Despite its obvious allure, Broome has a complicated soul, and many visitors arrive with false expectations about what the town is all about. A boom in tourism has brought the openings of some fine restaurants, bars and resorts, but Broome hasn't lost touch with its remote outback roots, and it remains a small town at heart.

Initially established as a pearling centre by Japanese entrepreneurs in the 1880s, Broome quickly attracted Chinese and Malays who joined local Aboriginal divers in the dangerous side of the business. Pearl diving was in open water, and initially without breathing apparatus; many divers were taken by sharks or got the bends. Pearling peaked in the early 1900s, when the town's 400 luggers supplied 80% of the world's mother-of-pearl (mainly used for buttons). Today, pearl farms have replaced open-sea diving and a handful of successful family-run companies continue to provide the world with exquisite Broome pearls.

During the Dry, Broome buzzes; this is the liveliest time to visit. During the Wet, prices drop, opening hours are shorter, and locals breathe a collective sigh of relief and get on with their lives. While some like visiting during this time, keep in mind many attractions shut and roads can close.

WESTERN AUSTRALIA

Visitor accommodation is in self-contained units, motel-style rooms or resort-style suites ranging from $90 to $180 per night. Expect to pay about $6 to $12 for lunch and $18 to $30 for dinner in the several Chinese and European-Australian restaurants.

COCOS (KEELING) ISLANDS
pop 600
Some 900km further west are the Cocos (Keeling) Islands (CKI), a necklace of low-lying islands around a blue lagoon that inspired Charles Darwin's theory of coral atoll formation. CKI was settled by John Clunies-Ross in 1826 (and briefly by a huge contingent of British forces during WWII), and his family remained in control of the islands and their Malay workers until 1978, when CKI became part of Australia's Indian Ocean territories. Today about 500 Malays and 100 European-Australians live on the two settled islands. It's a very low-key place in which to walk, snorkel, dive, fish, surf and relax. Check out the two island-information websites: www.cocos-tourism.cc and www.cocos-solutions.com.

Getting There & Away
National Jet Systems, booked through **Qantas** (☎ 13 13 13; www.qantas.com.au), flies a circle from Perth via the CKI to CI two or three times a week (five to seven hours depending on the route). Return tickets to CI or CKI start at $1880. There is also a return charter flight at least once a week from Kuala Lumpur (return $840, 2½ hours) operated by **Australia Indian Ocean Territories Airline** (AIOTA; ☎ 08-9164 7096; enquiries@travelxch.com.cx). Visa requirements are as for Australia, and Australians should bring their passports.

Orientation
Broome is situated on the west coast of the Dampier Peninsula. Within Broome, Chinatown, the commercial heart, and Old Broome, the administrative and residential centre, are in the town's east, overlooking Roebuck Bay. Hamersley St runs from Chinatown, south through Old Broome to Town Beach, while Frederick St leaves Chinatown heading west to meet Cable Beach Rd, which leads to Cable Beach, and runs into Port Dr, which leads to Broome's deep-water port in the south.

Information
BOOKSHOPS
Kimberley Bookshop (☎ 08-9192 1944; 4 Napier Tce; ⏲ 9am-5pm Mon-Fri, to 2pm Sat) Stocks an extensive range of books on Broome, the Kimberley and Aboriginal art, as well as fiction, nonfiction and travel guides.

EMERGENCY
Broome District Hospital (☎ 08-9192 9222; 28 Robinson St) Open 24 hours.

INTERNET ACCESS
Internet access costs anything from $5 to $10 per hour.

Galactica DMZ Internet Café (☎ 08-9192 5897; 4/2 Hamersley St; per hr $5; ⏲ 8am-8pm) Broome's best, with 40 terminals with internet access, Skype and webcams; BYO laptop for wi-fi access. Next to McDonald's.

INTERNET RESOURCES
Kimberley Tourism Association (www.kimberleytourism.com)

MONEY
There are ATMs in Carnarvon St, Napier Tce and Short St.

POST
The post office is in Chinatown's Paspaley shopping centre.

TOURIST INFORMATION
Visitors centre (☎ 08-9192 2222; www.broomevisitor centre.com.au; 1 Hamersley St; ⏲ 8.30am-4.30pm Mon-Fri, 9.30am-2.30pm Sat & Sun Apr-Nov, 9am-4pm Mon-Fri, 10am-2pm Sat & Sun Dec-Mar) Just off the first roundabout on the way into town, the visitors centre has masses of info on the Kimberley and Broome, and books transport, accommodation and tours.

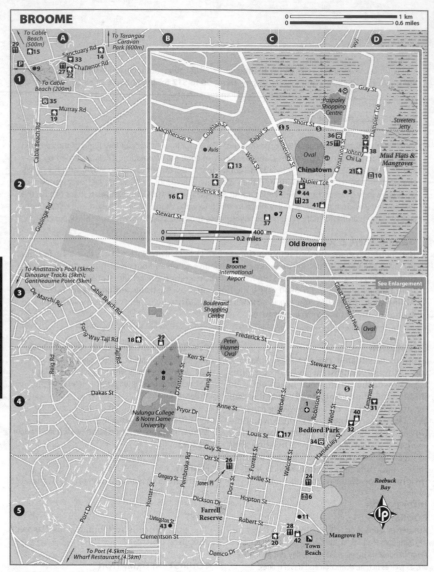

Sights & Activities

CABLE BEACH

About 4km west of town, Cable Beach is one of Australia's finest beaches, with azure waters and a wide, unblemished stretch of white sand as far as the eye can see. Red dunes rise behind the beach, with marked walking paths leading to **Gantheaume Point**, 7km south of Broome.

Here, the striking cliffs have eroded into curious shapes, revealing beautiful layers of reds, oranges and yellows that emit a lovely hue at sunset. At extremely low tides 120-million-year-old **dinosaur tracks** are exposed (at high tide check out the concrete casts on the cliff-top). **Anastasia's Pool** is a rock pool built by the lighthouse keeper to soothe his wife's arthritis.

INFORMATION		Kimberley Klub	**16** B2	Sunset Bar & Grill	(see 15)
Broome District Hospital	**1** C4	McAlpine House	**17** C4	Tides Bar	(see 31)
Galactica DMZ Internet		Ocean Lodge	**18** B3	ZeeBar	**33** A1
Café	**2** C2	Palm Grove Holiday Resort	**19** A1		
Kimberley Bookshop	**3** D2	Roebuck Bay Caravan Park	**20** C5	ENTERTAINMENT ☺	
Post Office	**4** D1	Roebuck Bay Hotel	**21** D2	Capt'n Murphy's Irish Bar	**34** C4
Visitors Centre	**5** C1	Seashells Resort	**22** A1	Diver's Tavern	**35** A1
				Sun Pictures	**36** D2
SIGHTS & ACTIVITIES		EATING 🍴			
Broome Museum	**6** C5	Aarli Bar	**23** C2	SHOPPING 🛒	
Courthouse	**7** C2	Black Pearl	**24** C5	Courthouse Market	**37** C2
Japanese, Chinese &		Blooms	**25** D2	Galway Pearls	**38** D2
Muslim Cemeteries	**8** B4	Café Carlotta	**26** C5	Kimberley Camping &	
Malcolm Douglas		Noodlefish	(see 23)	Outback Supplies	**39** B3
Crocodile Park	**9** A1	Old Zoo Café	**27** A1	Monsoon Gallery	**40** D4
Pearl Luggers	**10** D2	Town Beach Cafe	**28** C5	Old Broome Lockup	
Pioneer Cemetery	**11** C5	Zanders	**29** A1	Gallery	**41** C2
Sun Pictures	(see 36)			Town Beach Market	**42** C5
		DRINKING 🍷			
SLEEPING 🛏		Bungalow Bar	**30** D2	TRANSPORT	
Broome Motel	**12** B2	Mangrove Hotel	**31** D4	Britz	**43** B5
Broome's Last Resort	**13** C2	Matso's Broome Brewery	**32** D4	Broome Broome	(see 44)
Cable Beach Backpackers	**14** A1	Palms	(see 31)	Broome Cycles	**44** C2
Cable Beach Club Resort	**15** A1	Roebuck Bay Hotel	(see 21)	Greyhound Coach Stop	(see 5)

Just back from Cable Beach is the **Malcolm Douglas Crocodile Park** (☎ 08-9192 1489; www.malcol mdouglas.com.au;.cnr Cable Beach Rd & Sanctuary Dr; adult/ child/family $25/20/65; ☉ 10am-5pm Mon-Fri, 2-5pm Sat & Sun Apr-Nov, 4.15-5.45pm daily Dec-Mar). Australia's original crocodile hunter was making classic Aussie adventure films *Across the Top* and *Follow the Sun* back in the 1960s. To get the most out of your visit, time it with a feeding tour (3pm daily in the dry season; alligator-feeding tours 11am Monday to Friday). Douglas' latest project is a new wildlife park 16km north of Broome (see p1005).

CHINATOWN & TOWN BEACH

Enchanting **Chinatown** is Broome's historical and commercial heart; there's scant evidence of the Chinese now, its atmosphere coming from the vernacular architecture. Corrugated-iron buildings with lattice, louvres and veran-dahs line Carnarvon St, Short St, Dampier Tce and Napier Tce. Open-air **Sun Pictures** (p1004) is the highlight. This was once home to boarding houses, tailors and grocers (and in nearby Sheba Lane, brothels, opium dens and gambling joints). Today, the buildings house boutiques, cafes and art galleries.

Pearl Luggers (☎ 08-9192 2059; www.pearlluggers .com.au; 31 Dampier Tce; admission free, 75min tours adult/ child $19/free; ☉ tours 9am, 11am, 1pm & 3pm) offers compelling tours covering Broome's pearl-ing past, including a glimpse of restored sail-ing vessels, rare archival footage of divers at work, and a taster of flavourful pearl meat. Tour times vary at weekends and in the Wet;

book ahead. If you enjoy this don't miss **Willie Creek Pearl Farm** (see p1006). Equally fascinat-ing is **Broome Museum** (☎ 08-9192 2075; 67 Robinson St; adult/child/concession $5/1/3; ☉ 10am-4pm Mon-Fri, to 1pm Sat & Sun Jun-Oct, to 1pm Nov-May), with a collec-tion of early photos documenting the town's multicultural history and exhibits on pearling and luggers.

A number of cemeteries attest to Broome's multicultural roots. There's a small **pioneer cem-etery** overlooking Roebuck Bay by Town Beach, while on Frederick St there's a **Japanese Cemetery** with 919 graves (mostly pearl divers), a **Chinese Cemetery** with more than 90 graves and several monuments, and a **Muslim Cemetery**.

The elegant old teak **courthouse** on Hamersley St was built in 1889 to house staff from the Eastern Extension Australasian and China Telegraph Company, which linked Broome to Java by an underwater cable – it came ashore at Cable Beach, ran across the current airport site and finished here! Markets are held in the court-house gardens every Saturday (see p1004).

Tiny **Town Beach** is fine for a dip, while the **port** has a pleasant sandy beach from where you can swim across to the rocks, and good fishing from the jetty.

Tours

Astro Tours (☎ 0417 949 958; www.astrotours.net; adult/child $75/45; ☉ Apr-Nov) A fascinating two-hour 'tour' of the night sky, with a look (through telescopes) at planets, constellations and other astronomic highlights. Price includes transport to a dark site 10km from Broome (self-drive adult/child $65/35).

WESTERN AUSTRALIA

Broome Sightseeing Tours (☎ 08-9192 5041; www
.broomesightseeingtours.com; adult/child $90/70) Award-
winning, comprehensive four-hour guided multimedia
tour.

Hovercraft Tours (☎ 08-9193 5025; www.broome
hovercraft.com.au; 1hr tour adult/child $90/60, sunset BYO
tour $132/80) 'Fly' over tidal flats to visit historical sights
and see magnificent sunsets. You can also book a tour
followed by a barbecue on its beachside verandah facing
Roebuck Bay.

Red Sun Camels (☎ 08-9193 7423; www.redsun
camels.com.au; 40min morning ride adult/child $45/30,
1hr sunset ride $60/40) Seeing Cable Beach from atop a
slow-moving dromedary is an essential Broome experience,
particularly for the youngest of travellers.

Taste of Broome (☎ 08-9193 7778; www.kimberley
wild.com.au; adult/child $129/49) Half-day culinary tour
visiting mango orchards, the wharf for oysters, Matso's
brewery and Minyirr Park for Indigenous bush tucker,
finishing with a minibarbecue overlooking Cable Beach.

Turtle Bay Kayak (☎ 1300 665 888; www.broomead
venture.com.au; adult/child $70/55) Offers three-hour
kayaking trips through the turquoise waters of Broome's
coastline.

Willie Creek Pearl Farm (☎ 08-9192 0000; www
.williecreekpearls.com.au) A fascinating insight into
modern pearl farming, with compelling presentations on
oyster insemination, plus a boat ride on the azure-coloured
estuary to see an active pearl farm. Take a half-day bus
tour from Broome (adult/child $80/40), or self-drive (4WD
recommended) then join the two-hour tour at the farm
($40/20). You can also sign up for a helicopter tour over
the coastline.

Willie Pearl Lugger Cruises (☎ 0428 919 781;
www.williecruises.com.au; adult/child $95/50) Sail on a
traditional 25m topsail schooner, with the chance to see
humpback whales (July to September) and other marine
life, plus great sunsets. Price includes transport and
barbecue finger food. Cocktails available.

Other activities include fishing charters, kayaking, birdwatching, trike flights, Harley tours
and skydiving. See the visitors centre (p999)
for details.

Festivals & Events

Staircase to the Moon Three magical nights each
month from March to October (p1004).

Big Race Round Broome's unique and highly social
horse-racing season kicks off in late May or early June and
culminates with the Broome Cup in early August.

Naidoc Week Big cultural fest celebrating Aboriginal and
Torres Strait Islander heritage in July.

Opera Under the Stars (www.operaunderthestars.com
.au) On Cable Beach in August.

Shinju Matsuri Festival of the Pearl (www.shinju
matsuri.com) Broome's big 10-day event in September
with a parade, food festival, concerts, fireworks and dragon
boat races.

Worn Art A colourful spectacle of fashion, performance,
music and dance in September.

Mango Festival A celebration of the fruit in all its forms
takes place in November.

Sleeping

Prices skyrocket during the Dry. If you're here
in the Wet, compare deals as many places
slash their rates (some by 50%). Prices listed
in this section are for the high season (June
to October).

BUDGET

Broome's Last Resort (☎ 08-9193 5000; www
.broomeslastresort.com.au; 2 Bagot St; dm $22-28, d $70;
❄ ▯ ▣) The 'Lasty' has plenty of enduring
charm thanks to its wide verandahs, palm-
shaded swimming pool, hammocks, bar, pool
tables and jukebox. There's also free breakfast,
town tours, barbecues, beach trips and a daily
happy hour.

Cable Beach Backpackers (☎ 08-9193 5511; www
.cablebeachbackpackers.com; 12 Sanctuary Rd; dm $25-28,
s/d $50/65; ❄ ▯ ▣) Within walking distance
of Cable Beach, this relaxed place has a lush
tropical courtyard, swimming pool, big communal kitchen and bar. The friendly management can provide anything from shuttle buses
to free sausage sizzles and surfboards.

Kimberley Klub (☎ 08-9192 3233; www.kimberleyklub
.com; 62 Frederick St; dm $28-30, d/apt $120/160; ❄ ▯ ▣)
This big, breezy backpackers exudes a laid-
back tropical vibe and is a good place to meet
other travellers. There are myriad common
areas, a poolside bar, hammock spaces, a massive kitchen, table tennis, beach volleyball, free
beach shuttle and barbecues most nights.

MIDRANGE

Roebuck Bay Hotel (☎ 08-9192 1221; www.roebuckbay
hotel.com.au; Carnarvon St; dm $25, budget/standard/supe-
rior motel d $150/160/180; ❄ ▣) Broome's oldest
hotel, built in 1890, has comfortable rooms
surrounding a tropical swimming pool (take
an upstairs room), while the budget sleeps
back onto the pub's noisy band area. The
backpackers lodge is in a separate building
next to the live gig/dance space and attracts
a party crowd.

Broome Motel (☎ 08-9192 7775; www.broomemo
tel.com.au; 51-57 Frederick St; d $175, self-contained r $225;

⊠ ⊠) This pleasant two-storey motel has clean, comfortable rooms with TV, fridge and tea and coffee facilities; it's just a short stroll into Chinatown.

Ocean Lodge (☎ 08-9193 1700; www.oceanlodge .com.au; 1 Cable Beach Rd; d/f $185/230; ⊠ ⊠) Halfway between Cable Beach and Chinatown, the Ocean Lodge offers a mix of ageing and renovated rooms, the latter with wood floors, new beds and a warm contemporary look. The swimming pool, expansive tropical garden, in-room wi-fi and sizeable barbecues are a nice bonus.

TOP END

Eco Beach (☎ 08-9193 8015; www.ecobeach.com.au; 323 Thangoo Station, Great Northern Hwy; safari tent/villa d from $270/450; ⊠ ⊠) New in 2009, this luxury resort and ecologically sustainable retreat is set on a secluded stretch of coastline 130km southwest of Broome. Guests stay in safari tents or more lavish villas with outdoor showers and verandahs. There's a top-notch restaurant and a host of tours and activities. From Broome, reach the resort by catamaran ($50), shuttle bus ($50) or your own vehicle.

Seashells Resort (☎ 08-9192 6111; www.seashells .com.au; 4 Challenor Dr; 1-/2-/3-bedroom apt $295/345/425; ⊠ ⊠) A short walk to Cable Beach, Seashells has spacious, attractive apartments and bungalows, each with a verandah and a fully equipped kitchen. Landscaped garden surrounds the place, and there's a partially shaded pool and several barbecues.

Cable Beach Club Resort (☎ 08-9192 0400; www .cablebeachclub.com; Cable Beach Rd; d/bungalows/villas from $376/529/846; ⊠ ⊡ ⊠) Broome architecture plus touches of Eastern exoticism create an idyllic retreat at this beautifully set resort near the edge of Cable Beach. Lush gardens, serene swimming pools, fine restaurants, a spa and numerous other facilities add to the appeal.

McAlpine House (☎ 08-9192 3886; www.mcalpine house.com; 84 Herbert St; d from $500; ⊠ ⊡ ⊠) Set in a grand 1910 residence once owned by a pearling captain, McAlpine House is a boutique guest house with wide timber verandahs, lush tropical surroundings and handsomely furnished rooms.

CAMPING

Tarangau Caravan Park (☎ 08-9193 5084; tarangau@tpg. com.au; 16 Millington Rd; unpowered/powered sites $26/29) A quiet alternative to often noisy Cable Beach caravan parks, Tarangau is a laid-back spot

with pleasant grassy sites. It's about 1km from the beach.

Roebuck Bay Caravan Park (☎ 08-9192 1366; 91 Walcott St; unpowered/powered sites $29/33, on-site vans d $80; ⊠) On the milky waters of Roebuck Bay's Town Beach, and short bus rides to Chinatown and Cable Beach, this shady park has good facilities, including a communal kitchen and barbecue area.

Palm Grove Holiday Resort (☎ 08-9192 3336; www .palmgrove.com.au; cnr Cable Beach & Murray Rds; unpowered/ powered sites $34/38, studio d $175, 2-bedroom units $190; ⊠ ⊡) Across the road from Cable Beach, this verdant caravan park has free barbecues, a campers kitchen and a gorgeous swimming pool.

Eating

Broome has the only serious dining scene between Perth and Darwin. During the Wet some eateries close, keep shorter hours or only offer takeaway. Chinatown has the densest concentration of restaurants, particularly on Napier Tce and neighbouring Carnarvon St.

Aarli Bar (☎ 08-9192 5529; cnr Frederick & Hamersley Sts; tapas & mains $9-16, pizzas $16) Like a cosy trattoria with outdoor seating under frangipanis, Aarli Bar isn't actually a bar – it's BYO only. What it does have though is large portions of modern Med-influenced tapas as well as authentic wood-fired pizzas and, of course, its speciality, whole fresh fish ('*aarli*' means 'fish' in the Aboriginal Bardi language).

Wharf Restaurant (☎ 08-9192 5800; Port of Pearls House, Port Dr; mains $9-20; ☺ 10am-10pm) Experience 'Broome time' with a glass of white wine and a dozen fresh oysters overlooking Roebuck Bay. The owners here have been keeping locals and tourists sated since 2000 with fabulous quality seafood and a great list of WA wines by the glass.

Town Beach Café (☎ 08-9193 5585; Robinson St; mains $10-20; ☺ breakfast & lunch Mon-Sat) This busy BYO seafood cafe overlooking the beach does excellent tempura king prawns or beer-battered fish and chips.

Black Pearl (☎ 08-9192 1779; 4/63 Robinson St; mains $12-29) Overlooking Roebuck Bay, Black Pearl has inviting terrace seating and decent – though unsurprising – bistro fare. Late risers take note: breakfast served till 5.30pm.

Blooms (☎ 08-9193 6366; 12 Carnarvon St; mains $13-28) Blooms is a popular spot for its big breakfasts, outdoor seating and casual country-classic ambience. It does decent sandwiches, light dishes (salt-and-pepper squid, fish cakes etc) and pastas, with decent wines and fresh juices.

Café Carlotta (☎ 08-9192 7606; Jones Pl; mains $14-23; ☻ dinner Mon-Sat) Owners Mick and Charlotte make regular research trips to Italy and it shows with their daily handmade pastas and authentic wood-fired pizzas. Dine on the terrace surrounded by lush gardens.

Old Zoo Café (☎ 08-9193 6200; 2 Challenor Dr; mains $15-32) This small, charming bistro has outdoor tables and delectable fusion fare, with tasty tapas selections (including crab croquettes, scallops and crocodile) as well as nicely presented grills and seafood. Fully licensed (try the fresh mango cocktail).

Noodle Fish (☎ 08-9192 1697; cnr Frederick & Hamersley Sts; mains $18-29; ☻ dinner Mon-Sat) A local favourite for its eclectic menu with Eastern accents, Noodle Fish is a friendly BYO spot with outdoor dining under palms. Satisfying dishes include green paw paw salad, grilled threadfin salmon and the Malay fish curry.

our pick Zanders (☎ 08-9193 5090; Cable Beach Reserve, Cable Beach Rd; mains $18-32) Boasting a fantastic sunset spot overlooking the ocean, Zanders serves tasty seafood, excellent salads and a few international selections such as Moroccan lamb rump and prawns in red curry with coconut milk. There's outdoor seating and a traditional fish-and-chips takeaway next door.

Self-caterers should visit well-stocked supermarkets and bakeries at the Paspaley and Boulevard shopping centres.

Drinking

Matso's Broome Brewery (☎ 08-9193 5811; 60 Hamersley St; ☻ 7am-late) There's no better spot in Broome to kick back with a beer than Matso's wide verandahs overlooking Roebuck Bay. The wonderful award-winning beers are brewed on site – the Monsoonal Blonde is sensational – and there's live music on Sundays in the courtyard from 4pm to 7pm, and occasional DJs and bands on weekend nights.

Sunset Bar & Grill (☎ 08-9192 0400; Cable Beach Club Resort, Cable Beach Rd; ☻ 4-10pm) Arrive early to snag a prime seat on the terrace and catch one of Broome's famous sunsets. The vibe is casual and the drinks are fine, but the food doesn't quite match the views.

Roebuck Bay Hotel (☎ 08-9192 1221; 45 Dampier Tce; ☻ noon-late) The 'Roey' is your typical Aussie pub with a blokes' sports bar, a band venue (Pearlers Lounge) and an open-air club/concert

> **STAIRCASE TO THE MOON**
>
> The reflections of the rising full moon hitting the rippled Roebuck Bay mud flats, exposed at low tide, create the optical illusion of a golden stairway leading to the moon, called (naturally) the Staircase to the Moon. It has quite an impact on Broome's locals and visitors alike. If you're in town for the few days around the full moon, between March and October (the visitors centre publishes the exact dates and times), the town will be abuzz with everyone eager to see the spectacle. At Town Beach there's a lively evening market with food stalls and people bring their fold-up chairs and a bottle of something.

venue (Oasis), with live music and dance parties with DJs.

Bungalow Bar (☎ 08-9192 1941; 18 Dampier Tce; ☻ 10pm-late) Next door to the Roebuck Bay Hotel, Bungalow is a popular late-night destination that draws a better-dressed crowd, which comes for cocktails and electronica.

ZeeBar (☎ 08-9193 6511; 4 Sanctuary Rd; ☻ 10pm-late) This stylish bar and bistro near Cable Beach mixes up tasty cocktails (matched by good tapas) and hosts live music and DJs on Friday and Saturday nights plus trivia nights on Tuesdays.

Tides Bar (☎ 08-9192 1303; 47 Carnarvon St; ☻ noon-10pm) On Friday nights locals like to sink a few beers here on the outdoor terrace overlooking Roebuck Bay; in the Mangrove Hotel.

Entertainment

Aside from watching a Cable Beach sunset, Broome's other requisite experience is catching a film at historic **Sun Pictures** (☎ 08-9192 3738; www.sunpictures.com.au; 27 Carnarvon St; adult/child/concession/family $15/10/12/42), the world's oldest operating picture gardens.

The Tuesday jam nights at **Capt'n Murphy's Irish Bar** (☎ 08-9195 5900; Mercure Hotel, Weld St) are a local favourite, as are the Vegemite Jam Nights on Wednesday nights at traditional pub **Diver's Tavern** (☎ 08-9193 6066; Cable Beach Rd), where you can bring your own instruments and join in.

Shopping

Broome specialises in pearls and Aboriginal art, with pieces for every budget ($100 pearl earrings and $90 limited-edition art prints included). There's also a burgeoning craft industry, which you can catch at the **Courthouse Market** on Saturdays (year-round) and Sundays (May to September). Another good place to browse for locally made soaps, incense, vintage clothes and knick-knacks is the **Town Beach Market**, held during the Staircase to the Moon (opposite).

Monsoon Gallery (☎ 08-9193 5379; www.monsoongal lery.com.au; Hammersley St; ☽ 10am-5pm) Has an eclectic range of art by Aboriginal and other local artists, along with quality prints, photography, sculpture, textiles, glass and ceramics.

Old Broome Lockup Gallery (☎ 08-9193 5633; www.lockup.groovylips.com; Carnarvon St; ☽ 10am-5pm) In the building that was a jail for Aborigines up until the 1950s, this gallery sells art by local Indigenous painters, along with photography, carvings, didgeridoos and music created by resident artists.

Galway Pearls (☎ 08-9192 2414; Dampier Tce; ☽ 9.30am-4.30pm Mon-Fri, to 1pm Sat) One of Broome's most popular and approachable pearl shops, with a small but well-curated selection and good prices.

Kimberley Camping & Outback Supplies (☎ 08-9193 5909; www.kimberleycamping.com.au; cnr Frederick St & Cable Beach Rd) This well-stocked store sells everything you need for a successful journey into the Kimberley.

Kimberley Camping Hire (☎ 08-9192 5282; www .kimberleycampinghire.com.au) This long-time outfit hires out sleeping bags, tents, stoves, satellite phones, generators and more. Free delivery and pick-up.

Getting There & Away

Broome is a regional hub with flights or links to all Australian capitals, including Perth and several towns in the Kimberley. **Greyhound Australia** (☎ 1300 473 946; www.greyhound.com.au) stops at the visitors centre. See p998 for details of fares.

Getting Around

The **Town Bus Service** (☎ 08-9193 6585; www.broome bus.com.au; adult/child $3.50/1.50, hop-on hop-off day pass $10) links Chinatown with Cable Beach every hour (7.10am to 6.12pm year-round), with a half-hourly service (8.30am to 4pm) from May to mid-October. Children (age 16 and under) ride free when accompanied by an adult. Get timetables from the visitors centre.

Broome Broome (☎ 08-9192 2210; www.broome broome.com.au; 3/15 Napier Tce) hires air-conditioned cars from $58 a day and 4WDs from $99 including insurance; scooters run $35 per day. **Britz** (☎ 08-9192 2647; www.britz.com; 10 Livingston St) hires campervans and rugged 4WD Toyota Land Cruisers (starting at $129 per day) – essential for Gibb River Rd.

Broome Cycles (Chinatown ☎ 9192 1871, Cable Beach ☎ 0409 192 289) rents bicycles for $24/84 per day/week ($50 deposit). For taxis phone **Broome Taxis** (☎ 08-9192 1133) or **Chinatown Taxis** (☎ 1800 811 772).

AROUND BROOME
Malcolm Douglas Wildlife Park

Entering through the jaws of a giant crocodile, visitors arrive at this 30-hectare animal refuge and **wildlife park** (☎ 08-9193 6580; www.mal colmdouglas.com.au; Great Northern Hwy; adult/child/family $30/20/80; ☽ 2-5pm Apr-Nov) opened by Malcolm Douglas in 2005. This naturally designed park, 16km north of Broome, is home to dozens of crocs at two billabongs (feedings at 3pm), as well as kangaroos, cassowaries, emus, dingoes, jabirus and numerous bird species.

Broome Bird Observatory

This wonderful **bird observatory** (☎ 08-9193 5600; Crab Creek Rd; admission by donation; ☽ 8am-5pm) on the Roebuck Bay shores, 25km from Broome, is a vital staging post for hundreds of migratory species, including 49 waders (nearly a quarter of the world's total species). An incredible 800,000 birds arrive each year, some travelling 12,000km to get here. Join an excellent two-hour tour ($75); a full-day tour of the freshwater lakes ($150; BYO lunch); or do a five-day all-inclusive course ($1000 including transfers, accommodation and meals). Binoculars available to visitors.

You can rent a room (singles $40, doubles with air-con $75) or fully self-contained chalet ($140), or camp (per person $14) on site. Transfers from Broome cost $45. If you're driving, access is via a decent dirt road, which can be closed in the Wet.

Dampier Peninsula

The Dampier Peninsula is synonymous with aquamarine waters, white-sand beaches and red rock formations; it's also home to thriving Indigenous settlements of the Ngumbarl, Jabirrjabirr, Nyul Nyul, Nimanburu and Bardi peoples.

Access to the isolated Aboriginal communities is by 4WD only, along the rough,

---

WET OR DRY?

The climatic extremes of the Kimberley make for very different travel experiences, depending on the time of year you visit. The best, but busiest, time to visit is April to September (the Dry). There's little rain, the temperatures are low and all the roads are likely to be open. By October it's already getting hot as the build-up starts, and throughout the Wet (roughly November to March) temperatures of more than 40°C are common.

Probably the Wet's major drawback is the closure of the Gibb River Rd, which blocks exploration of the magnificent northern Kimberley. In addition, opening hours for visitors centres and attractions are reduced and tours run less frequently or not at all. Otherwise, the Wet is definitely not to be sneezed at. It's as hot as blazes, and humid to boot, but the locals are more relaxed, there's plenty of elbow room and the lack of crowds makes accommodation prices plummet. And when the rains do arrive, you'll be glad you were here to see the spectacle – low, black clouds come at a pace, dumping massive volumes of water during huge thunderstorms with awesome lightning displays. Rivers and creeks can rise rapidly and become impassable torrents within 15 minutes.

---

corrugated, red pindan 200km-long Cape Leveque Rd (turn-off 9km east of Broome). Many communities require visitors to obtain permission and pay a visitor fee upon arrival (road signs will alert you of this as you arrive), which helps support the community and the natural environment. Some communities may close to visitors owing to funerals or other events. Check road conditions and get other information from the Broome visitors centre, which can make accommodation arrangements for you. A good booklet to the area (not always available) is the *Ardi – Dampier Peninsula Travellers Guide* (www.ardi.com. au), which costs $3. You need to be largely self-sufficient and take fuel, food and water to last the period you'll be away.

The first turn-off, Manari Rd, takes you to the Willie Creek Pearl Farm (see p1002), while another 40km north is **Coulomb Point Nature Reserve**, which protects unique pindan vegetation and the rare bilby. Isolated campsites sprinkle the coast between the two.

Back on Cape Leveque Rd, it's around 110km to **Beagle Bay** (☎ 08-9192 4913), notable for the extraordinarily beautiful mother-of-pearl altar at Beagle Bay church, built by Pallotine monks in 1918. There are no public facilities or accommodation, just a shop and fuel (weekdays only). Contact the office on arrival.

Tranquil, unspoilt **Middle Lagoon** (☎ 08-9192 4002; www.users.bigpond.com/pindan; entry per car $8; unpowered/powered sites per person $15/20, beach shelter d $50, cabin d $150-250), 170km from Broome, is ideal for swimming, snorkelling and fishing, and is popular with Broome families. There's no fuel here.

Between Middle Lagoon and Cape Leveque, **Lombadina** (☎ 08-9192 4936; www.lombadina.com.au; entry per car $10, dm/s/d $44/77/99, unit d $165), 200km from Broome, has fishing, whale watching, mudcrabbing and Indigenous 'footprint' **tours** (1hr/2hr guided walks $35/55, boat tours per person from $154). It's a beautiful little village, where residents take obvious pride in the place. There's fuel here Monday to Friday. Nearby, tiny **Chile Creek** (☎ 08-9192 4141; www.chilecreek.com; sites per person $17, bush shelters per person $25), 7km from Lombadina, offers basic bush shelters and a rustic camp kitchen, all just a short stroll to a lovely beach. You can arrange a two-hour mud-crabbing tour here (adult/child $55/25).

our pick **Kooljaman** (☎ 08-9192 4970; www.kool jaman.com.au; unpowered/powered sites d $32/37, beach shelters d $60, cabins with/without bathroom d $160/140, safari tents d $250) is the most sophisticated of the communities on spectacular Cape Leveque, which has pristine beaches and stunning red cliffs. This ecotourism-award-winning place has accommodation ranging from hilltop resort-style safari tents with panoramic views to thatched beach huts. It gets busy June to October, but is almost deserted off-season. **Dinkas** (mains $25-30; ☼ Apr-Oct) is a BYO restaurant overlooking the sea; you can dine on the enclosed porch or order bush butler service.

Tour operators to Cape Leveque from Broome include Indigenous-owned **Chomley's Tours** (☎ 08-9192 6195; www.chomleystours.com.au; 1-/2-/3-/4-day tour $230/400/560/580), offering one- to four-day tours of the peninsula, as well as one-way transfers ($180). Chomley's also offers a one-day 4WD tour up to the Cape, followed by a scenic flight back to Broome ($430).

Other companies offering Cape Leveque tours include **Kimberley Wild Expeditions** (☎ 08-9193 7778; www.kimberleywild.com.au; 1-/2-day Cape Leveque tour $239/465) and **Australian Pinnacle Tours** (☎ 08-9192 8080; www.pinnacletours.com.au; 1-/3-/4-day Cape Leveque tour $245/740/895).

Mamabulanjin (☎ 08-9192 1662) provides transport from Broome to Beagle Bay ($55), Cape Leveque ($100) and other Dampier towns departing Sundays, Tuesdays and Thursdays; it returns on the same days.

DERBY
pop 5000

Drowsy Derby, the administrative centre for west Kimberley, sits astride a peninsula jutting into King Sound, surrounded by tidal mud flats. Its mangroves attract over 200 bird species, including migratory waders. This is crocodile country so squeeze the last bit of beach out of Broome (219km south) before heading here. Derby is short on sights but makes a decent base for trips to the national parks of the ancient Devonian Reef (see p1010) and the islands of the Buccaneer Archipelago; it's also the western entrance to the Gibb River Rd.

Orientation & Information

The post office, supermarkets and ATMs are on Loch and Clarendon Sts. The **visitors centre** (☎ 1800 621 426, 08-9191 1426; www.derbytourism.com.au; 2 Clarendon St; ☺ 8.30am-4.30pm Mon-Fri & 9am-noon Sat year-round, 9am-1pm Sun Apr-Sep) sells bus tickets, advises on road conditions, and books local fishing and mud-crabbing tours, and scenic flights.

Sights & Activities

Derby's first wooden jetty was built in 1894 to serve the growing pastoral population and gold rush, while the current **wharf** opened in 1964 to export cattle; nowadays it's mainly for lead and zinc. Locals like to fish here for northwest salmon, shark and mud crabs, and it's the best place to see the colossal 11m tides. There are crocodiles, so if you want to swim head for the swimming pool on Clarendon St.

The **Old Derby Gaol** (Loch St), next to the police station, is the town's oldest building, dating to 1906, and is a grim reminder of the hostility and violence between the Indigenous people and European settlers that racked the town from the late 1800s.

The **Boab Prison Tree**, 7km south of town, is Derby's most famous attraction. With a girth of 14m and a hollow trunk, it's said to be over 1000 years old. Prisoners were locked up here en route to Old Derby Gaol.

Begun in 1960, the **Boab Festival** (July) entertains locals with concerts, sports (including mud footy) and street parades.

Tours

Derby's biggest drawcard is its proximity to the natural splendours of remote King Sound and the Buccaneer Archipelago, uninhabited islands that are best viewed from the air or sea.

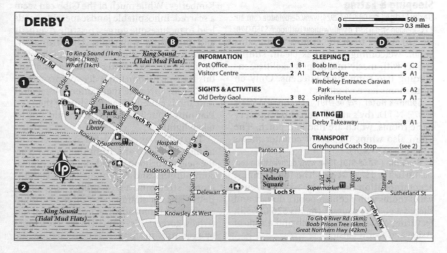

DERBY

0 ——— 500 m
0 ——— 0.3 miles

INFORMATION	
Post Office	1 B1
Visitors Centre	2 A1

SIGHTS & ACTIVITIES	
Old Derby Gaol	3 B2

SLEEPING	
Boab Inn	4 C2
Derby Lodge	5 A1
Kimberley Entrance Caravan Park	6 A2
Spinifex Hotel	7 A1

EATING	
Derby Takeaway	8 A1

TRANSPORT	
Greyhound Coach Stop	(see 2)

To King Sound (1km);
Point (1km);
Wharf (1km)

King Sound
(Tidal Mud Flats)

Jetty Rd

Elder St

Johnston St

Villiers St

Hardman St

Lions Park

Pool

Derby Library

Rowan St

Supermarket

Loch St

Nevill St

Hospital

Hensman St

Clarendon St

Anderson St

Panton St

Stanley St

Nelson Square

Loch St

Supermarket

Sutures St

Ashley St

Fairbairn St

Delewarr St

Marmion St

Knowsley St West

Reid St

Wayott St

Stanwell St

Sutherland St

Derby Hwy

To Gibb River Rd (5km);
Boab Prison Tree (6km);
Great Northern Hwy (42km)

King Sound
(Tidal Mud Flats)

LP

HORIZONTAL WATERFALLS

One of the most intriguing features of the Kimberley coastline is the phenomenon known as 'horizontal waterfalls'. Despite the name, the falls are simply tides gushing through narrow coastal gorges in the Buccaneer Archipelago, north of Derby. What makes it such a spectacle are the huge tides, often reaching up to 11m: the rate of flow reaches an astonishing 30 knots as the water is forced in and out of the constricted sandstone gorges. The two narrow gaps, the first being 20m wide and the second 10m wide, often see the 'waterfall' reach a height of 4m. The falls are best seen by air and form part of many tour operators' itineraries; see p1007 or inquire at the visitors centres in Derby (p1007) or Broome (p999).

Buccaneer Sea Safaris (☎ 0419 917 797, 08-9191 1991; www.buccaneerseasafaris.com; 5 days from Derby/Broome $2800/3000) Offers tours combining sea and sky vistas.

Bush Flight (☎ 08-9193 2680; www.caneflight.com; 30min flights from Derby $100)

Kimberley Seaplanes (☎ 08-9192 2885; www .horizontalfalls.com.au; 5hr/overnight fly-cruise-fly tour $495/595)

One Tide Charters (☎ 08-9193 1358; www.onetide .com; 5/8/12 days $3200/5120/7700) Offers all-inclusive multiday 'sea safaris' with camping overnight at idyllic spots.

Sleeping & Eating

Derby Lodge (☎ 08-9193 2924; www.derbylodge.com.au; 15 Clarendon St; dm $30, d with/without bathroom $150/120; ✗ ▯) Across from the visitors centre, this small, welcoming place has clean, simple rooms with nicely maintained facilities, including two communal kitchens. Only en suite rooms have windows.

Spinifex Hotel (☎ 08-9191 1233; Clarendon St; s/d $60/75; ✗) Derby's affable pub also rents very basic rooms, which are fine in a pinch. The Spini also whips up decent counter meals (mains $12 to $24).

Boab Inn (☎ 08-9191 1044; www.derbyboabinn.com .au; 100 Loch St; d $200; ✗ ▣) The town's finest accommodation has comfy, recently renovated rooms with a contemporary design, and there's a good restaurant (mains $26 to $35), featuring oysters, rack of lamb and a mix of Asian and world cuisine.

Kimberley Entrance Caravan Park (☎ 08-9193 1055; www.kimberleyentrancecaravanpark.com; 2 Rowan St; unpowered/powered sites $21/27) Friendly managers Ian and Julie provide great facilities in a quiet stretch of Derby. The surrounding trees are leafy for all but four weeks of the year.

Derby Takeaway (☎ 08-9191 1131; 4 Clarendon St; mains $6-18) This no-nonsense counter whips up grilled burgers, fish and chips, sausage rolls and decent coffee. Eat-in or takeaway.

Point (☎ 08-9191 1195; mains $12-28; ☯ lunch & dinner Tue-Sun) In a prime sunset-watching spot overlooking the jetty, this BYO place is Derby's best, with delicious seafood. The barramundi and croc steaks are popular. It also does takeaway.

Getting There & Away

Daily **Greyhound** (☎ 1300 473 946; www.greyhound .com.au) buses to Darwin and Perth stop at the visitors centre – where you can also book a once-weekly flight on the mail plane headed north or south. **Ozjet Airlines** (☎ 1300 737 000; www .ozjet.com.au) flies three times weekly between Derby and Perth. **Golden Eagle Airlines** (☎ 08-9172 1777; www.goldeneagleairlines.com.au) flies twice weekly between Derby and Broome.

GIBB RIVER ROAD

Stretching some 660km between Derby and Kununurra, the unpaved Gibb River Rd ('the Gibb') is one of the great outback highways of Australia. Expect an endless sea of red dirt, big open skies and dramatic terrain on this rugged journey into the heart of the Kimberley. While much of the Gibb can seem a scarred, inhospitable landscape, side roads lead to picturesque gorges, pristine riverbeds and pounding waterfalls. Unfortunately, these roads are often the most challenging to negotiate. No matter your destination, this is a rough, sometimes deeply corrugated, 4WD-only dirt road that's often closed after rain and is closed altogether during the Wet. Planning your journey here should not be taken lightly.

The Gibb was constructed as a 'beef road' to move cattle to and from the area. Today the neighbourhood is made up of Aboriginal communities and enormous cattle stations (some stretching for a million hectares). Better known stations also offer overnight accommodation and attractions (hiking, waterfalls, gorges). It's essential to reserve a room or a campsite in advance, as many stations are booked solid during the peak months (June to August). Most places open in mid- to late April and close in mid-October.

If you want just a taste of back-country adventure, do the 'tourist loop' that takes you 125km along the Gibb River Rd from Derby to the Fairfield Leopold Downs Rd turn-off, then 124km past Windjana Gorge and Tunnel Creek (see the Devonian Reef National Parks, p1010) to the Great Northern Hwy, 43km west of Fitzroy Crossing.

If you plan to visit Aboriginal communities, you'll need permission first from the **Department of Indigenous Affairs** (☎ 1300 651 077; www.dia.wa.gov.au); a permit may take around three days to be processed.

By far, the most comprehensive guide to the area is *The Kimberley Atlas & Guide* ($30) published by Hema maps. Here you'll find detailed maps and sight descriptions, info on all lodging and camping grounds in the area, plus coverage of wildlife, fuel stops and everything else Kimberley-related. The *Gibb River & Kalumburu Roads Travellers Guide* ($5 from visitors centres) is also helpful. Make sure you're driving a high-clearance 4WD, have spare tyres and tools, and stock up on several days' food and water in case you get stranded. Before leaving, check road conditions with **Mainroads Western Australia** (☎ 24hr 13 81 38; www.mainroads.wa.gov.au). You can hire a solid 4WD from Broome – most travellers opt for a Toyota Land Cruiser (smaller 4WDs are rarely insured for the Gibb River Rd). In Broome, a reputable hire outfit is Britz (p1005). Broome is also the best place to gather supplies for a trip (p1005).

There are also many organised tours that travel the road (see p997).

For online information about travel along the Gibb, visit www.gibbriverroad.net and www.kimberleyaustralia.com.

Derby to Wyndham-Kununurra Road

Mowanjum Wandjina Art (☎ 08-9191 1008; www .mowanjumarts.com; ☾ 8am-3pm Mon-Fri), about 4km along Gibb River Rd, is an Aboriginal community renowned for its artists painting in the Wandjina style.

The 5000-acre **Birdwood Downs Station** (☎ 08-9191 1275; www.birdwooddowns.com; Gibb River Rd; camping per person $12, savannah huts per person incl breakfast & dinner $125), about 20km from Derby, offers outback accommodation and a range of tours. It's also the Kimberley School of Horsemanship, with

lessons, riding camps and trail rides (two-hour sunset ride $90).

After crossing the Lennard River bridge (120km from Derby) you'll come to the Yamarra Gap in the King Leopold Range (145km). Narrow 5km-long **Lennard River Gorge**, 8km off Gibb River Rd, has a refreshing pool and waterfall, but it's a rocky, unshaded 1.5km walk from the car park to the gorge and a steep descent from there.

At 184km you'll see the turn-off (and 50km rough drive) to enchanting **Mount Hart Wilderness Lodge** (☎ 08-9191 4645; www.mthart.com.au; campsites per person $20; d per person incl dinner & breakfast $205), where guests can hike along gorges, cool off in refreshing streams and fish for black bream.

At 26km past the Mt Hart turn-off is stunning **Bell Gorge**, 29km down a rough track, with a picturesque waterfall and camping at **Silent Grove** (adult/child $10/2).

Refuel and meet some locals at characterful **Imintji Store** (☎ 08-9191 7471; ☾ 7am-5pm), your last chance to get supplies. Next door is a **repair shop** (☎ 08-9191 7887).

our pick **Mornington Wilderness Camp** (☎ 08-9191 7406; www.awc.org.au; campsites per adult/child $15/7, safari tents incl full board s/d $285/480), part of the Australian Wildlife Conservancy, lies on the Fitzroy River, a rough 95km drive south of the Gibb's 247km mark. Guests can camp or stay in spacious tents with verandahs. There's excellent birdwatching, canoeing and bush walks, with gorges and waterfalls among the scenery.

Horseshoe-shaped **Galvans Gorge** has a swimming hole less than 1km off the road at the 286km mark. It's an easy 15-minute walk from the car park.

Mount Barnett Roadhouse (☎ 08-9191 7007), at the 306km point, is owned by the Kupingarri Aboriginal community and has fuel and a store. Pay at the roadhouse for a campsite at **Manning River Gorge** (per person $13), another swimming and hiking spot. Another 30km up the road is **Mount Barnett River Gorge**, a deep river gorge surrounded by sandstone cliffs. It's 5km off the main road, reachable along a dodgy sandy track.

A little further up the Gibb (at the 345km point) is the turn-off (and 30km drive) to **Mount Elizabeth Station** (☎ 08-9191 4644; mtelizabeth@ bigpond.com; campsites per person $14, s/d incl breakfast & dinner $275/350), a good base for exploring the gorges, waterfalls and Indigenous rock art on the 200,000-hectare property.

WESTERN AUSTRALIA

At 406km you reach the Kalumburu turn-off (see below). The Gibb River Rd continues through spectacular country; at 579km there are views of the Cockburn Ranges, the Cambridge Gulf and the Pentecost and Durack Rivers. Just 2km further is wonderful **Home Valley Homestead** (☎ 08-9161 4322; www.homevalley.com.au; campsites adult/child $15/5, homestead $230) with swimming, fishing, horse riding, station tours, bushwalks and gorge canoeing.

At 590km is the infamous **Pentecost River** crossing. Take care: water levels are hard to predict and saltwater crocs love it here. Beyond El Questro, at 630km you cross King River and at 647km you finally hit bitumen: Wyndham is 48km to the northwest (see p1013), Kununurra 52km east (see p1014).

El Questro

The million-acre **El Questro Wilderness Park** (☎ 08-9169 1777; www.elquestro.com.au; 7-day park permit $15; ☼ Apr-Nov) is a tourist attraction all of its own and many travellers make the trip from Kununurra just to visit this vast former cattle station. Highlights include boat tours up the wonderful **Chamberlain Gorge** (adult/child $49/25) to see Indigenous art and the odd croc, the 40-minute bushwalk along **Emma Gorge** to a shaded plunge pool and waterfall, and the thermal waters and lush palms at **Zebedee Springs**. Organised tours include fishing, horse riding and chopper flights.

The place to start any visit is **El Questro Station Township** (campsites per person $15, safari tents d $140, bungalows d $312; ☒), where there's a bar, restaurant, tour desk and camping. There's more accommodation in safari-style tent-cabins at the **Emma Gorge Resort** (d $270; ☒ ☲). The luxurious hilltop **El Questro Homestead** (2 nights all-inclusive $3800-5000; ☒) is only for the rich and famous!

KALUMBURU ROAD

Kalumburu Rd is often in abysmal condition, and generally opens later than the Gibb River Rd owing to washed-out sections and impassable river crossings. Distances are given from the junction of the Gibb River and Kalumburu Rds, which is 419km from the Derby Hwy and 248km from the Wyndham–Kununurra Rd.

You need two permits to visit the Kalumburu community; the first one is available for free from the **Department of Indigenous Affairs** (☎ 1300 651 077; www.dia.wa.gov.au); the second permit (valid for seven days) is available from the Kununurra visitors centre (p1014) or from the **Kalumburu community** (☎ 08-9161 4300; kalumburumission@bigpond .com; per car $35) upon arrival.

Gibb River Road to Mitchell Plateau

After crossing the Gibb River at 3km, and Plain Creek at 16km, you reach the first fuel stop at 59km, **Drysdale River Station** (☎ 08-9161 4326; www.drysdaleriver.com.au; campsites per person $9-20, d $130), where you can get basic supplies, meals and, in the Dry, set up scenic flights to Mitchell Falls ($325).

The Mitchell Plateau turn-off is at 172km, from where it's 70km to the turn-off to the spectacular **Mitchell Falls**, 16km downhill; you have to walk the final 3km. In the Dry, the water spills down the terraces; in the Wet, it thunders over the escarpments and a scenic flight from Kununurra is the only way to see the spectacle. There is a spacious but popular camping ground here ($7 per person), which can be noisy owing to the nearby helicopter pad. While the pools are undoubtedly enticing, don't swim here. It's a sacred Aboriginal site and inhabited by saltwater crocodiles. **Slingair** (☎ 08-9161 5412; www.slingair.com.au; 6/18/48min flight per person from $100/170/350) operates scenic flights over the falls. At the turn-off to the falls is the **Ungolan Wilderness Camp** (☎ 1800 335 003; www.kimberleywilderness.com.au; safari tents incl breakfast & dinner s/d $385/450); there's also camping ($7 per person) back at King Edward River. Keep in mind that this river can be a tough crossing early in the season, when it's rocky and deep. Near the crossing there is also some exceptional ancient Aboriginal art, which is well worth a stop to look at.

Mitchell Plateau Turn-Off to Kalumburu

From the Mitchell Plateau turn-off the road heads northeast, crossing **Carson River** at 247km. In another 20km you'll arrive at **Kalumburu Aboriginal Community** (☎ 08-9161 4333), a picturesque mission nestled among giant mango trees and coconut palms, with a shop, food and **fuel** (☼ 8am-4pm Mon-Fri). You can pitch a tent at **Honeymoon Bay** (☎ 08-9161 4378; sites $10).

DEVONIAN REEF NATIONAL PARKS

West Kimberley's three national parks feature stunning gorges that were once part of a western 'great barrier reef' in the Devonian

THE MYSTERIOUS AND WONDROUS PAINTINGS OF THE KIMBERLEY

In 1891 Joseph Bradshaw, an early settler in the Kimberley region, lost his way while exploring the Prince Regent River area. While walking through a gorge, he stumbled upon a wall of colourful paintings, and was utterly struck by what he saw. In numerous caves and recesses in the rocks were drawings of elaborately adorned human figures, some life-sized, with aquiline features and elegant poses that reminded Bradshaw, as he later described, of paintings in Egyptian temples.

His serendipitous discovery was just the first piece of an enormous gallery of rock art stretching across the Kimberley. Today they are known as the 'Bradshaw paintings', called Gwion Gwion by the Aborigines, and have been found in tens of thousands of sites covering an area roughly the size of Spain. The works are nothing like Aboriginal art found in other parts of the country and show no relationship to the ethereal forms of Wandjina art of the Kimberley, a fact that has led to a great deal of controversy surrounding their origins.

The paintings show a remarkable level of artistry – and have even been compared to pieces by Matisse. They depict a people with a high level of culture; the figures appear to be clothed, wearing tassels, armbands and sashes. Some wear elaborate headdresses. They are shown in ceremony, some dancing, some paying homage. One painting depicts figures in a large boat, possibly an ocean-going vessel, while another depicts people cultivating root crops. Most surprising of all is their age. A fossilised wasps' nest partially covering one painting was dated to over 17,000 years old. At over four times the age of classic Egypt, this collection comprises the oldest known rock art of such advanced artistry found anywhere in the world.

Yet, the million-dollar question that has stirred up so much controversy remains: who were the creators of these unique and extraordinary paintings? The foremost expert on the Bradshaw art is the amateur archaeologist and self-taught art historian Grahame Walsh, who first began exploring the Kimberley in 1977. Walsh suggests that the drawings were created not by Aborigines, but rather by an advanced people from somewhere else – Southeast Asia, perhaps – who came, flourished and mysteriously disappeared. Ian Wilson, in *The Lost World of the Kimberley* (2006), goes further, advancing theories of links to pygmylike tribes from the Andaman Islands, Saharan peoples and South American tribes. He even suggests the Kimberley might be where human civilisation first began. Regardless of the provenance of these stunning artworks, they deserve to be studied and discussed in much greater detail. They are one of Australia's great and little known artistic treasures.

Learn more about the Bradshaw paintings and other fascinating Palaeolithic art of the world on the Bradshaw Foundation website (www.bradshawfoundation.com).

WESTERN AUSTRALIA

era, 350 million years ago. Windjana Gorge and Tunnel Creek national parks are accessed via Fairfield Leopold Downs Rd (linking the Great Northern Hwy with Gibb River Rd), while Geikie Gorge National Park is just north of Fitzroy Crossing.

The walls of beautiful **Windjana Gorge** soar 100m above the Lennard River, which surges in the Wet but is a series of pools in the Dry. Scores of freshwater crocodiles sunbake on its banks and lurk in the water. Bring plenty of water for the 7km return walk from the **camping ground** (adult/child $10/2) to the end of the gorge. The ruins of **Lillimooloora** homestead (1893), once a police outpost, are 3km from Lennard River.

Tunnel Creek is a 750m-long passage, 3m to 15m wide, created by the creek cutting through a spur of the Napier Range. In the Dry, you can walk all the way to the end; be prepared to meet bats along the way and wade through cold, knee-deep water in places. Take a strong torch and change of shoes. There are Aboriginal paintings at either end. No camping.

The magnificent **Geikie Gorge** is 18km north of Fitzroy Crossing on a sealed road. The best way to enjoy this incredible gorge and its abundance of wildlife (including bull sharks and crocs – no swimming!) is on an entertaining one-hour **DEC boat tour** (☎ 08-9191 5121; adult/child $25/5; ⏰ 8am & 3pm daily May-Oct, additional trips & times Jun-Sep); get tickets from the DEC kiosk at Geikie Gorge. You can also take cultural bushwalks and boat tours with an Indigenous guide through **Darngku Heritage Tours** (☎ 08-9191 5355; 2hr walk adult/child $55/45, 3hr boat cruise $70/55).

FITZROY CROSSING
pop 1100

This rugged outback town is located where the Great Northern Hwy crosses the Fitzroy River, with a large Aboriginal population hailing from the Gooniyandi, Bunuba, Walmatjarri and Wangkajungka communities. Fitzroy Crossing is a good access point for Geikie and Windjana Gorges and Tunnel Creek. The **visitors centre** (☎ 08-9191 5355; fxinfo@sdwk.wa.gov.au; ○ 8.30am-4.30pm Mon-Fri year-round, 9am-1pm Sat Apr-Sep) is on the highway.

One of the Kimberley's best-kept secrets is the vast subterranean labyrinth of the **Mimbi caves**, located 90km southeast of Fitzroy Crossing. Located within Mt Pierre Station, on Gooniyandi land, the caves house a significant collection of Aboriginal rock art and some of the most impressive fish fossils in the southern hemisphere. Sign up for a tour with Aboriginal-owned **Girloorloo Tours** (mimbi@bigpond.com; adult/child $65/35), which includes an introduction to local Dreamtime stories, bush tucker and traditional medicines. Billy tea and damper are also served. You can book through the Fitzroy Crossing visitors centre.

The oldest pub in the Kimberley, lively **Crossing Inn** (☎ 08-9191 5080; crossinginn@bigpond.com.au; Skuthorpe Rd; unpowered/powered sites $20/25, s/d $125/135; ⓧ) provides a chance to meet locals inside its tin shed and across the road at the billabong. Basic accommodation is at the back of the pub.

Fitzroy River Lodge Motel Hotel & Caravan Park (☎ 08-9191 5141; Great Northern Hwy; unpowered/powered sites d $22/27, safari tents d $135, motel d $185; ⓧ ⓡ) has comfortable motel rooms, safari tents and camping spots, plus a friendly bar with decent counter meals (mains $12 to $26). Sometimes the park has infestations of Singapore ants; if this is the case, campers should not stay here.

Golden Eagle Airlines (☎ 08-9172 1777) has flights from Fitzroy Crossing to Broome ($265) and Halls Creek ($145), departing four times weekly. **Northwest Regional Airlines** (☎ 08-9192 1369) also flies regularly to Broome and Halls Creek at similar prices. **Greyhound** (☎ 1300 473 946; www.greyhound.com.au) has daily buses to Broome ($148, 5½ hours) and Darwin ($307, 20 hours), with four weekly Perth-bound buses ($581, 39 hours); buses stop at the visitors centre and upon request at the Fitzroy River Lodge.

HALLS CREEK
pop 1590

On the edge of the Great Sandy Desert, Halls Creek is a small town with communities of Kija, Jaru and Gooniyandi people. The town has a user-friendly layout, with most services on the highway or Roberta Ave. Pick up local information at the **visitors centre** (☎ 08-9168 6007; Great Northern Hwy; ○ 8am-4pm Mon-Fri Apr-Nov). Check email next door at the **TelCentre** (Great Northern Hwy; per 20min $2; ○ 8.15am-3.45pm Mon-Fri) in the Shire Office.

From Halls Creek there are tours and scenic flights over Purnululu National Park (Bungle Bungle Range) and the Wolfe Creek Meteorite Crater, while **China Wall**, 5km east and about 1.5km off the road, is a small but picturesque subvertical quartz vein protruding 6m off the ground.

Best Western Halls Creek Motel (☎ 08-9168 6001; www.bestwestern.com.au/hallscreek; 194 Great Northern Hwy; budget s/d $100/110, d $165-250; ⓧ ⓡ) has clean, well-equipped rooms, including decent budget rooms, and serves hearty meals at **Russian Jack's** (mains $12-28).

Kimberley Hotel (☎ 08-9168 6101; www.kimberleyhotel.com.au; Roberta Ave; budget/motel d $99/175; ⓧ ⓡ) has comfortable rooms with all the mod cons, and a sports bar and restaurant (mains $16 to $31) with tables on a shaded terrace overlooking the pool.

Halls Creek Caravan Park (☎ 08-9168 6169; lanus@bigpond.com.au; 4 Roberta Ave; unpowered/powered sites $24/26) is an OK place to camp, though there isn't much shade.

Northwest Regional Airlines (☎ 08-9192 1369) and **Golden Eagle Airlines** (☎ 08-9172 1777) have regular flights to Fitzroy Crossing and Broome. **Greyhound Australia** (☎ 1300 473 946; www.greyhound.com.au) buses run to Perth ($633, 42 hours) and Darwin ($244, 16 hours); they stop at the Poinciana Roadhouse.

WOLFE CREEK METEORITE CRATER

The world's second largest meteorite crater (measuring 850m wide and 50m deep) was probably formed when a meteorite plunged into earth more than a million years ago. According to the local Jaru people's Dreaming, the crater, Kandimalal, marks the spot where a huge rainbow snake emerged from the ground.

The crater is best appreciated from the air. **Northwest Regional Airlines** (☎ 08-9168 5211; www.northwestregional.com.au; 70min flight $270) offers scenic flights from Halls Creek. Otherwise,

WESTERN AUSTRALIA

it's a challenging drive along a rough 4WD road. The turn-off is 16km west of Halls Creek, from where it's 137km south along the Tanami Rd. You'll need plenty of food, water and fuel.

PURNULULU NATIONAL PARK – BUNGLE BUNGLE RANGE

The **Purnululu National Park** (per car $10), 3000 sq km of ancient country, is home to the wonderful ochre and black striped 'beehive' domes of the Bungle Bungle Range.

The distinctive rounded rock towers are made of sandstone and rough conglomerates (rocks comprised of pebbles and boulders), moulded by rainfall over millions of years. Their stripes are caused by differences in clay content and porosity of the layers; the rock within the dark stripes is more permeable, allowing algae to flourish, while the lighter layers consist of oxidised iron compounds.

While the local Kija people have always known about them – *purnululu* means 'sandstone' in the Kija language and Bungle Bungle is thought to be a misspelling of 'bundle bundle', a common grass – the formations were only 'discovered' during the mid-1980s; the park was created in 1987, and added to the World Heritage list in 2003.

The park has wonderful **Aboriginal art galleries**, gorgeous **swimming holes** within the gorges and a wide array of wildlife, including over 130 bird species.

The stunning **Echidna Chasm** in the north and **Cathedral Gorge** in the south are about an hour's walk from the car parks, while the soaring **Piccaninny Gorge** is an 18km circuit that takes a full day to walk. The restricted gorges in the northern part of the park can only be seen from the air.

The park is open April to December; rangers are based here during these months. If you're driving you'll need a high-clearance 4WD, as there are five deep creek crossings. The turn-off from the highway is 53km south of Warmun, then it's 52km along a very rough 4WD-only track to the Three Ways junction. Allow at least 2½ hours to get to the visitors centre. **Kurrajong Camp** and **Walardi Camp** have fresh water and toilets (campsites per adult/child $10/2).

Tours

East Kimberley Tours (☎ 08-9168 2213; www.eastkimberleytours.com.au; 2-day tour $715) has many tours

from Kununurra, and several operators include Purnululu in multiday Kimberley tours (see p997). You can also do scenic flights from Kununurra in helicopters with **Slingair** (☎ 08-9169 1300; www.slingair.com.au; 18/30min $205/295) and light planes with **Alligator Airways** (☎ 1800 632 533, 08-9168 1333; www.alligatorairways.com.au; 2¼hr $265). Sadly, three tourists died in a Slingair crash in 2008, temporarily suspending all Purnululu flights.

WYNDHAM

pop 670

A languid little town at the confluence of five rivers, Wyndham is WA's northernmost and oldest town (1885). Although the port, 5km from the main town, is still in use, Wyndham's heyday is long gone. The town has a rugged frontier feel, but there's plenty to see in the surrounding area.

Kimberley Motors (☎ 08-9161 1281; Great Northern Hwy; ☎ 6am-6pm) has tourist information, maps and tide charts, and can book fishing and 4WD tours.

Don't miss the excellent **Wyndham Crocodile Farm** (☎ 08-9161 1124; Barytes Rd, Wyndham Port; adult/child $17/10; ☀ 10am-2pm Mar-Nov, to noon Dec-Feb) with some astonishing salties. The guides get up close during an entertaining tour at feeding time (11am daily).

Five Rivers Lookout on Mt Bastion is a visual highlight here. Drive to the top for superb views of the King, Pentecost, Durack, Forrest and Ord Rivers converging on the Cambridge Gulf; the views are best at sunrise and sunset.

About 15km from Wyndham is **Parry Lagoons Nature Reserve**, a beautiful wetland area teeming with birds in the Wet, particularly at lovely Marlgu Billabong (4WD access). Nearby, the **Grotto** is a popular swimming hole where 140 steps lead down to a peaceful pool surrounded by lush vegetation in a small gorge.

Wyndham Town Hotel (☎ 08-9161 1202; O'Donnell St; d $130; ☒), near Wyndham Port, has basic, overpriced motel-style rooms, but the pub is the best place to meet locals over a beer and the bistro cooks up generous home-style steaks, fish and chips and salads (mains $15 to $35).

Parry Creek Farm (☎ 08-9161 1139; www.parrycreekfarm.com.au; unpowered/powered sites $28/33, r $85, cabins $195; ☒), at Parry Lagoons Nature Reserve, is a lovely place to stay, with its own billabong

WESTERN AUSTRALIA

and loads of bird and animal life. A raised boardwalk leads to comfy cabins and there's a cafe.

KUNUNURRA

pop 6000

Kununurra is a relaxed town in the midst of an oasis of lush farmland and tropical fruit plantations, thanks to the Ord River irrigation scheme. There is literally water everywhere – with the Lily Creek Lagoon and Lake Kununurra feeding off the Ord River and Lake Argyle just down the road. The town has a few worthwhile sights of its own – don't miss the red sandstone domes of Mirima National Park – and if you've just dusted yourself off after the Gibb River Rd trip from Broome, it's a good place to unwind and recharge. For backpackers there's plenty of seasonal fruit-picking work in the area.

Information

There are ATMs at the shopping centres.

District Hospital (☎ 08-9166 4222; 96 Coolibah Dr) Has a 24-hour emergency department.

Kununurra telecentre (☎ 08-9169 1868; Coolibah Dr; per hr $7; 🕒 8.30am-5pm Mon-Fri, 9am-noon Sat) Access the internet here, including laptop access ($6 per hour).

Visitors centre (☎ 08-9168 1177, 1800 586 868; www.kununurratourism.com; Coolibah Dr; 🕒 8am-5pm Mon-Fri year-round, 8am-4pm Sat Dry, 9am-1pm Sat Wet) Has tonnes of information, and can advise on road conditions and book tours.

Sights & Activities

Across the highway from the township, **Lily Creek Lagoon** is a miniwetlands with lots of wonderful bird life, boating and freshwater crocs. Lake Kununurra, also called **Diversion Dam**, has pleasant picnic spots and great fishing.

For a bird's-eye view of the town and surrounding lakes and farmland, **Kelly's Knob** is a favourite sunset viewpoint on the town's northern fringe. During the Wet, distant thunderstorms are spectacular from here. You can drive to the top or it's an easy 20-minute walk from town.

Waringarri Aboriginal Arts Centre (☎ 08-9168 2212; 16 Speargrass Rd; 🕒 8.30am-4pm Mon-Fri) is an Aboriginal-owned art gallery and studio where some 50 local artists work in their unique

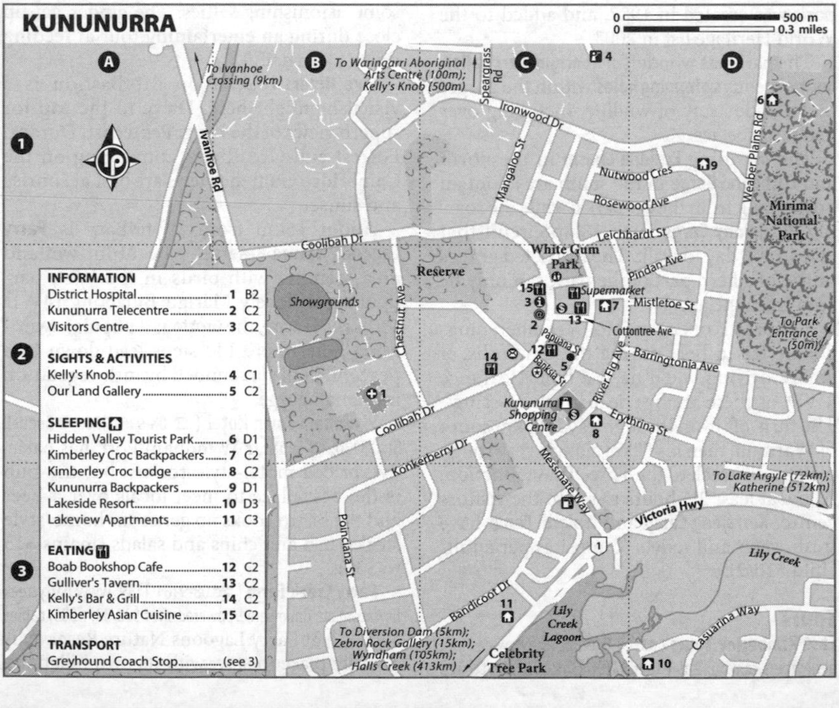
KUNUNURRA
0 500 m
0 0.3 miles
To Ivanhoe Crossing (9km)
To Waringarri Aboriginal Arts Centre (100m); Kelly's Knob (500m)
Speargrass Rd
Ironwood Dr
Ivanhoe Rd
Mangaloo St
Nutwood Cres
Rosewood Ave
Weaber Plains Rd
Mirima National Park
Leichhardt St
Coolibah Dr
White Gum Park
Reserve
Pindan Ave
Supermarket
Mistletoe St
Showgrounds
Chestnut Ave
Cottontree Ave
Papuana St
Barringtonia Ave
To Park Entrance (50m)
Banksia St
River Fig Ave
Kununurra Shopping Centre
Erythrina St
Konkerberry Dr
Messmate Way
To Lake Argyle (72km); Katherine (512km)
Victoria Hwy
Poinciana St
Lily Creek
Bandicoot Dr
Lily Creek Lagoon
Casuarina Way
To Diversion Dam (5km); Zebra Rock Gallery (15km); Wyndham (105km); Halls Creek (413km)
Celebrity Tree Park
INFORMATION
District Hospital 1 B2
Kununurra Telecentre 2 C2
Visitors Centre 3 C2
SIGHTS & ACTIVITIES
Kelly's Knob 4 C1
Our Land Gallery 5 C2
SLEEPING
Hidden Valley Tourist Park 6 D1
Kimberley Croc Backpackers 7 C2
Kimberley Croc Lodge 8 C2
Kununurra Backpackers 9 D1
Lakeside Resort 10 D3
Lakeview Apartments 11 C3
EATING
Boab Bookshop Cafe 12 C2
Gulliver's Tavern 13 C2
Kelly's Bar & Grill 14 C2
Kimberley Asian Cuisine 15 C2
TRANSPORT
Greyhound Coach Stop (see 3)

abstract style using ochre pigments. **Our Land Gallery** (☎ 08-9168 1881; 10 Papuana St; ☺ 9am-5pm Mon-Fri, to 2pm Sat & Sun) has a great range of ochre paintings from the Kimberley as well as did-geridoos and acrylics from the Territory. **Zebra Rock Gallery** (☎ 08-9168 1114; Packsaddle Rd; adult/child $1/50c; ☺ 8am-6pm), on the Ord River about 15km from Kununurra, produces jewellery and sculptures from the unique zebra rock found around Argyle Downs Station.

MIRIMA NATIONAL PARK

A short stroll east of town (1.5km), this **national park** (per car $10) is a stunning area of rugged sedimentary formations that look like mini Bungle Bungles. The 350-million-year-old sandstone rock has taken shape by uplift over the past 20 million years.

The splendid gorges of Hidden Valley are home to spinifex-covered hills, boab trees and wonderful wildlife. The two well-marked walking-track loops take around 30 minutes each – head here a couple of hours before sunset so you can see the magic the sun's light works on the rocks.

Tours

Alligator Airways (☎ 1800 632 533; www.alligator airways.com.au) Scenic flights to the Bungle Bungles (adult/child $265/185) and the Kimberley ($595).

Go Wild (☎ 1300 663 369; www.gowild.com.au) Canoe trips (1/2/3 days from $150/180/200) and abseiling tours (from $95).

Kununurra Cruises (☎ 08-9168 1718; www.thebbq boat.com.au; adult/child $85/40) Popular sunset 'BBQ Boat' cruises on Lily Creek Lagoon and the Ord River.

Sleeping

Kununurra has a pair of excellent backpacker hostels and a half-dozen motels.

Kununurra Backpackers (☎ 1800 641 998, 08-9169 1998; www.kununurrabackpackers.com.au; 22 Nutwood Cres; dm $22-25, d $56; ☒ ☐ ☒) The more laid-back of the two hostels, this place has a cool garden, minicinema and organises three-day self-guided canoe safaris ($175).

Kimberley Croc Backpackers (☎ 1300 136 702, 08-9168 2702; www.kimberleycroc.com.au; 120 Konkerberry Dr; dm $28-30, d $90-110; ☒ ☒) More central, this slick, modern YHA has a large pool and bar-becue area and excellent kitchen facilities. Same owners run Kimberley Croc Lodge, a motel at 2 River Fig Ave.

Lakeview Apartments (☎ 08-9168 0000; www .lakeviewapartments.net; 224 Victoria Hwy; 1-/2-/3-bedroom apt $200/240/300; ☒ ☒) Spacious self-contained apartments looking across the highway over Lily Creek Lagoon. The larger ones sleep up to six.

Kununurra has a good range of caravan parks.

Hidden Valley Tourist Park (☎ 08-9168 1790; www .hiddenvalleytouristpark.com; Weaber Plains Rd; un-powered/powered sites $22/26, cabins d $120; ☒ ☒) Excellent park bordering Mirima National Park.

Lakeside Resort (☎ 08-9169 1092; www.lakeside .com.au; Casuarina Way; unpowered/powered sites $24/28, studio/motel d $165/185; ☒ ☒) Serene location by Lily Creek Lagoon.

Eating

Kununurra has two well-stocked supermar-kets, bakeries and a couple of takeaways.

Gulliver's Tavern (☎ 08-9168 1666; 196 Cottontree Ave; mains $10-30) The alfresco back bar is the best place in town for a beer, and the kitchen serves up hearty counter meals – from bar snacks and barra burgers to steaks and Asian dishes.

Boab Bookshop Cafe (☎ 08-9169 2574; 4a Papuana St; mains $12-25; ☺ 6am-9pm) Kununurra's best cafe is part bookshop and internet cafe (with wi-fi; per hr $5) and delivers great coffee, smoothies, breakfast fare, pastas and focaccias.

Kimberley Asian Cuisine (☎ 08-9169 3698; 75 Coolibah Dr; mains $12-25; ☺ lunch & dinner Mon-Fri, din-ner only Sat & Sun) Next to the visitors centre, this pan-Asian place is informal and serves good Aussie versions of Chinese and Thai.

Kelly's Bar & Grill (☎ 08-9168 1024; 47 Coolibah Dr; mains $18-36; ☺ lunch & dinner) At the Country Club Hotel, Kelly's serves up some of the best mod-ern Australian cuisine in town: try the saltwa-ter croc skewers, lamb rack or Muscovy duck breast and sit inside or out on the pool deck.

Getting There & Around

Qantas (☎ 13 13 13; www.qantas.com.au) flies to Broome ($280, five weekly) and Darwin ($250, six weekly).

Greyhound Australia (☎ 1300 473 946; www.grey hound.com.au) has daily buses between Darwin ($208, 12 hours) and Perth that stop at the visitors centre. Destinations include Katherine ($130, eight hours), Derby ($241, 10 hours) and Broome ($246, 13 hours).

LAKE ARGYLE

Enormous Lake Argyle is a spectacular sight. Australia's second-largest reservoir, it was created by the Ord River Dam in 1972 and can hold around 18 times the water of Sydney Harbour. The results have been amazing: 58,000 hectares of dry clay plains have been irrigated, the riverside ecology has improved and wildlife numbers have increased, with some being struck off endangered species lists (for example, the buff-sided robin). It's possible to drive across the dam wall and walk to various lookout points: the scenery is awesome, with high, steep red ridges plunging into the lake's deep blue waters.

Atmospheric **Argyle Homestead** (☎ 08-9167 8088; adult/child $3/1; ☻ 9am-3pm Apr-Oct), home of the remarkable Durack pastoral family, was moved here when its original site was flooded and now opens as a museum in the Dry. Fascinating old black-and-white photos, artworks and memorabilia are displayed and there's a small family cemetery where some of the pioneering Duracks are buried.

Lake Argyle Cruises (☎ 08-9168 7687; www.lakear gylecruises.com) offers several cruises – morning (adult/child $65/40), sunset ($85/50) and full day ($145/87) – but book ahead as trips are cancelled if there aren't enough numbers. Transfers from Kununurra are available for the day and afternoon cruises. **Triple J Tours** (☎ 08-9168 2682; www.triplejtours.net.au; adult/child $145/105) offers a retrun trip from Kununurra to Lake Argyle including a 55km cruise on the Ord River.

Lake Argyle Tourist Village (☎ 08-9168 7777; www .lakeargyle.com; Parker Rd; unpowered/powered sites $20/30, dm $25, safari tents $99, cabins $155; ☒ ▢ ▣) enjoys a fabulous location high on the edge of the lake. As well as a camping ground, there are lake-view cabins, a backpacker bunkhouse and a new hotel section is under construction. It's a friendly place with a restaurant (mains $14 to $25) serving the local lake fish, silver cobbler. All tours can be booked here.

Directory

CONTENTS

ACCOMMODATION

It's easy to get a good night's sleep in Australia, as it offers everything from the tent-pegged confines of camping grounds and the communal space of hostels to gourmet breakfasts in guesthouses, chaperoned farm stays and everything-at-your-fingertips resorts, plus the gamut of hotel and motel lodgings.

The accommodation listings in this book are organised into budget, midrange and top-end sections. These listings are in order of budget, and are selected based on a mixture of atmosphere, cleanliness, facilities, location and authorial mood of the day. Places that primarily offer tent and campervan sites (eg camping grounds and holiday parks) appear at the tail of the accommodation section.

We generally treat any place that charges up to $90 per double as budget accommodation. Midrange facilities are usually in the range of $90 to $180 per double, although B&Bs (considered midrange) often go for as much as $200 for a double. The top-end tag is mostly applied to places charging more than $180 per double. In more expensive areas, however, such as Far North Queensland, Kangaroo Island, metropolitan Sydney and Melbourne, and the tourist towns surrounding these cities, budget can mean paying up to $110 per double, and midrange places can charge up to $200 for a double.

In most areas you'll find seasonal price variations. During the high season over summer (December to February) and at other peak times, particularly school and public holidays, prices are usually at their highest, whereas outside these times you will find useful discounts and lower walk-in rates. An exception is the Top End, where the wet season (roughly October to March) is the low season, and prices can drop substantially. Another exception is the ski resorts whose high season is winter.

Low- or normal-season prices (as opposed to high-season prices) are quoted in this guidebook unless otherwise indicated. High season generally encompasses Christmas to New Year and school holidays (see p1032). The weekend escape is a notion that figures prominently in the Australian psyche, meaning accommodation from Friday night through to Sunday can be in greater demand (and pricier) in major holiday areas.

BOOK YOUR STAY ONLINE

For more accommodation reviews and recommendations by Lonely Planet authors, check out the online booking service at www.lonelyplanet.com/hotels. You'll find the true, insider low-down on the best places to stay. Reviews are thorough and independent. Best of all, you can book online.

DIRECTORY

B&Bs

The local 'bed and breakfast' (guest house) industry is thriving. Options include everything from restored miners' cottages, converted barns, rambling old houses, upmarket country manors and beachside bungalows to a simple bedroom in a family home. In areas that tend to attract weekenders – quaint historic towns, wine regions, accessible forest regions such as the Blue Mountains in New South Wales (NSW) and the Dandenongs in Victoria – B&Bs are often upmarket and will charge a small fortune for stays between Friday and Sunday in high season. Tariffs are typically in the $100 to $200 (per double) bracket, but can be higher.

Local tourist offices can usually provide a list of places.

Online resources:

australianbandb.com.au (www.australianbandb .com.au)

babs.com.au (www.babs.com.au)

OZBedandBreakfast.com (www.ozbedandbreakfast.com)

Camping & Caravanning

The cheapest accommodation lies outdoors, where the nightly cost of camping for two people is usually between $15 and $30, slightly more for a powered site. Whether you're packing a tent, driving a campervan or towing a caravan ('trailer' in North American–speak), camping in the bush is a highlight of travelling in Australia. In the outback and northern Australia, you often won't even need a tent, and nights spent around a camp fire under the stars are unforgettable. Staying at designated sites in national parks normally costs between $6 and $11 per person. Note that most city camping grounds lie at least several kilometres from the town centre, so they're a more convenient option if you have wheels.

Almost all caravan or holiday parks are equipped with hot showers, flushing toilets and laundry facilities, and frequently a pool. Some still have old on-site caravans for rent, and most have on-site cabins. Cabin sizes and facilities vary, but expect to pay $70 to $80 for a small cabin with a kitchenette and up to $150 for a two-bedroom cabin with a fully-equipped kitchen, lounge room, TV and stereo, verandah, and beds for up to six people. Regardless of the vintage or style of cabin, they're generally excellent value if you're on the road for a while, are travelling in a group, or have a family in tow. They allow you to be completely self-sufficient and often provide more space than a motel or hotel room.

Caravan parks, which encompass tent sites, caravan sites and cabins, are popular along coastal areas. In summer months and school holidays they're often booked out well in advance. Well-touristed areas (other than cities) have the greatest number of parks.

If you intend on doing a lot of caravanning/camping, consider joining one of the major chains, such as **Big 4** (www.big4.com.au), which offer discounts at member parks.

It's also useful to get your hands on **Camps Australia Wide** (www.campsaustraliawide.com) a handy publication containing maps and information about campsites and rest stops that are either free, or have a capped rate for the 12 months following publication.

Western Australia (WA) has roadside overnight stops (designated by a '24' symbol) for

---

PRACTICALITIES

- Leaf through the daily *Sydney Morning Herald,* Melbourne's *Age* or the national *Australian* broadsheets.

- Tune in to ABC on the radio – pick a program and frequency from www.abc.net.au/radio.

- On the box watch the ad-free ABC, the government-sponsored and multicultural SBS, or one of three commercial TV stations; Seven, Nine and Ten.

- DVDs sold in Australia can be watched on players accepting region 4 DVDs (the same as Mexico, South America, Central America, New Zealand, the Pacific and the Caribbean). The USA and Canada are region 1 countries, and Europe and Japan are region 2.

- Use a three-pin adaptor (different to British three-pin adaptors) to plug into the electricity supply (240V AC, 50Hz).

- For weights and measures, use the metric system.

> **CAMPSITES**
>
> Unless otherwise stated, prices for camp-sites listed throughout this book are for two people.

travellers on the road that are free and usually well positioned to break up a long drive. A handy brochure put out by WA Main Roads covers these and includes what facilities are available at each stop. It is available at most WA visitors centres.

Bear in mind that camping is best done during winter (the dry season) across the north of Australia, and during summer in the south of the country.

Holiday Apartments

Self-contained holiday apartments or flats are another mainstay on the Australian landscape. They range from simple, studio-like rooms with a small kitchenette, to two-bedroom apartments with full laundries and state of the art entertainment systems. They are great value for multinight stays. Sometimes they come in small, single-storey blocks but in tourist hotspots such as the Gold Coast expect a sea of high-rises. For a two-bedroom flat, you're looking at anywhere from $100 to $160 per night (but much higher in high season). The other alternative in major cities is to take out a serviced apartment.

Hostels

Backpacker hostels are exceedingly popular in Australian cities, and along coastal tourist trails. In the outback and rural areas you'll be hard pressed to find one. Highly social affairs, they're generally overflowing with 18- to 30-year olds, but some have reinvented themselves to attract other travellers who simply want to sleep for cheap.

Hostels provide varying levels of accommodation, from the austere simplicity of wilderness hostels to city-centre buildings with a cafe-bar and some en suite rooms. Most of the accommodation is in dormitories (bunk rooms), which can range in size from four bunk beds to 60. Many hostels also provide twin rooms and doubles. Typically a dorm bed costs $20 to $30 per night and a double (usually without bathroom) $70 to $90. Hostels generally have cooking facilities, a communal area with a TV, laundry facilities

and sometimes travel offices and job centres. There's often a maximum-stay period (usually five to seven days). Bed linen is often provided; sleeping bags are not welcome due to hygiene concerns and the risk of introducing bed bugs.

Some places will only admit overseas backpackers; this mainly applies to city hostels that have had problems with locals sleeping over and bothering the backpackers. Hostels that discourage or ban Aussies say it's only a rowdy minority that makes trouble, and will often just ask for identification in order to deter potential troublemakers, but it can be annoying and discriminatory for genuine people trying to travel in their own country. Also watch out for hostels catering expressly to working backpackers, where facilities can be minimal but rent can be high.

HOSTEL ORGANISATIONS & CHAINS

Australia has over 130 hostels that are part of the **Youth Hostels Association** (YHA; ☎ 02-9261 1111; www.yha.com.au). The YHA is part of **Hostelling International** (HI; www.hihostels.com), also known as the International Youth Hostel Federation (IYHF), so if you're already a member of that organisation in your own country, your membership entitles you to YHA rates in the relevant Australian hostels. Nightly charges are between $15 and $30 for members; most hostels also take non-YHA members for an extra $5. Preferably, visitors to Australia should purchase an HI card in their country of residence, but you can also buy one at major local YHA hostels at a cost of $37 for 12 months; see the HI or YHA websites for further details. Australian residents can become full YHA members for $42/80 for one/two years; join online, at a state office or at any youth hostel.

A new trend in hostels is represented by **base BACKPACKERS** (www.basebackpackers.com), an upmarket hostel chain that emphasises comfort and offers extensive facilities – one of its innovations is a women-only floor.

More information on useful international hostel organisations:

Nomads Backpackers (☎ 1800 091 905, 02-9280 4110; www.nomadsworld.com) Membership ($35 for 12 months) entitles you to numerous discounts.

VIP Backpacker Resorts (☎ 07-3395 6111; www .vipbackpackers.com) Membership is $43/57 for one/two years and entitles you to many discounts.

Hotels & Motels

Except for pubs, the hotels that exist in cities or well-touristed places are generally of the business or luxury variety (insert the name of your favourite chain here), where you get a comfortable, anonymous and mod con–filled room in a multistorey block. These places tend to have a pool, restaurant-cafe, room service and various other facilities. For these hotels we quote 'rack rates' (official advertised rates), though significant discounts can be offered when business is quiet.

Motels (or motor inns) offer comfortable budget to midrange accommodation and are found all over Australia. Prices vary and there's rarely a cheaper rate for singles, so motels are better for couples or groups of three. Most motels are modern, low rise, and have similar facilities (tea- and coffee-making, fridge, TV, air-con, bathroom) but the price will indicate the standard. You'll mostly pay between $70 and $130 for a room.

Useful booking agencies that can save you some dosh:

Lastminute.com (www.lastminute.com.au)
Quickbeds.com (www.quickbeds.com.au)
Wotif.com (www.wotif.com.au)

Pubs

For the budget traveller, hotels in Australia are the ones that serve beer, and are commonly known as pubs (from the term 'public house'). In country towns, pubs are invariably found in the town centre. Many were built during boom times, so they're often among the largest, most extravagant buildings in town. In tourist areas some of these pubs have been restored as heritage buildings, but generally, the rooms remain small, old-fashioned and weathered, with a long amble down the hall to the bathroom. They're usually cheap and central, but if you're a light sleeper, avoid booking a room right above the bar and check whether a band is playing downstairs that night.

Standard pubs have singles/doubles with shared facilities starting at around $45/80, more if you want a private bathroom.

Rental & Long-Term Accommodation

If you're in Australia for a while (visas permitting), then a rental property or room in a shared flat or house will be an economical option. Delve into the classified advertisement sections of the daily newspapers; Wednesday and Saturday are usually the best days. Notice boards in universities, hostels, bookshops and cafes are also good to check out. Properties that are listed through a real estate agent necessitate at least a six-month lease, plus a bond and first month's rent up front.

Useful websites:

CityHobo (www.cityhobo.com) Excellent website using your shoes to match your personality to the perfect suburb for you to live in Melbourne or Sydney.
Couch Surfing (www.couchsurfing.com) Hooks you up with spare couches and new friends around the world.
Domain.com.au (www.domain.com.au) Lists holiday and long-term rentals.
Flatmate Finders (www.flatmatefinders.com.au) Good site for long-term share accommodation in Sydney and Melbourne.
Gumtree (http://sydney.gumtree.com.au) Great site for flat shares, jobs and other classifieds in capital cities.
Sleeping with the Enemy (www.sleepingwiththeenemy.com) Another good site for long-term accommodation in Sydney and Cairns.

Other Accommodation

There are lots of less-conventional and, in some cases, uniquely Australian accommodation possibilities scattered across the country.

A decent number of the country's farms offer a bed for a night. A couple of remote outback stations also allow you to stay in homestead rooms or shearers' quarters and try activities such as horseback riding. Check out **Australian Farmstays** (www.australiafarmstay.com.au) for your options. State tourist offices can also tell you what's available.

Back within city limits, it's sometimes possible to stay in the hostels and halls of residence normally occupied by university students, though you'll need to time your stay to coincide with the longer university holiday periods.

ACTIVITIES

Although Australia provides plenty of excuses to sit back and do little more than roll your eyes across some fine landscape, that same landscape lends itself very well to any number of energetic pursuits, whether it's on the rocks, wilderness trails and mountains of dry land, or on the offshore swells and reefs. The following is a general rundown of what's possible; for more detail read the individual Activities sections at the start of each state and territory chapter.

Adrenalin-Charged Activities

Fantastic sites for rock climbing and abseiling include the Blue Mountains (p156) in NSW, Victoria's Mt Arapiles (p571), Grampians National Park (p566) and Mt Buffalo in the High Country (p608). In Tasmania head to the spectacular Hazards at Coles Bay (p674) in Freycinet National Park, and in WA, West Cape Howe National Park (p951). In Queensland there's excellent abseiling on offer at Kangaroo Point (p310). For online info on rock climbing in Australia, visit www.climbing .com.au.

Tandem paragliding and flights are available anywhere there are good take-off and landing points, and thermal winds. A good place to learn is Bright (p609) in the Victorian High Country; the national paragliding championships are held annually in Manilla (p207) in NSW.

Skydiving and parachuting are also widely practised; try Coffs Harbour in NSW (p187) and Mission Beach (p428) and Caloundra (p346) in Queensland. Most clubs are listed in the *Yellow Pages* telephone directory.

Elastic entertainment is all the rage in Queensland with bungee jumping in Cairns (p442); on the Gold Coast (p338) there's also an assortment of stomach-churning rides.

Bushwalking

Bushwalking is supremely popular in Australia and vast tracts of untouched scrub and forest provide ample opportunity. The best time to go varies significantly from state to state, but a general rule is that the further north you go the more tropical and humid the climate gets; June to August are the best walking months up top and in the south, summer – December to March – is better. See Responsible Bushwalking, p62.

You can follow fantastic trails through many national parks. Notable walks include the Overland Track (p713), and the South Coast Track (p714) in Tasmania, the Australian Alps Walking Track (p620) and Great South West Walk (p564) in Victoria, the Bibbulmun Track (p898) in WA, and the Thorsborne Trail (p427) across Hinchinbrook Island or the Gold Coast Hinterland's Great Walk (p343) in Queensland.

In NSW you can trek between Sydney and Newcastle on the Great North Walk (p163), tackle the Royal National Park's coastal walking trail (p147), the 42km Six Foot Track (p161) or trek Mt Kosciuszko (p242). In South Australia (SA) there's the epic 1200km Heysen Trail (p722) and in the Northern Territory (NT) there's the majestic, 233.5km Larapinta Trail (p880), the 39km Tabletop Track (p840), and beautifully remote tracks in Nitmiluk (Katherine Gorge) National Park (p854).

Walking in Australia by Lonely Planet provides good detailed information about bushwalking around the country.

Cycling

Avid cyclists have access to lots of great cycling routes and can tour the country for days, weekends or even make multiweek trips.

Standout routes for longer rides include the Murray to the Mountains Rail Trail (p601)

SAFETY GUIDELINES FOR WALKING

Before embarking on a walking trip, consider the following points to ensure a safe and enjoyable experience (these are particularly important if you're considering an unguided trek):

■ Pay any fees and possess any permits required by local authorities.

■ Be sure you are healthy and feel comfortable walking for a sustained period.

■ Obtain reliable information about physical and environmental conditions along your intended route (eg from park authorities).

■ Be aware of local laws, regulations and etiquette about wildlife and the environment.

■ Walk only in regions, and on tracks, within your realm of expertise.

■ Be aware that weather conditions and terrain vary significantly from one region, or even from one track, to another. Seasonal changes can significantly alter any track. These differences influence the way walkers dress and the equipment they carry.

■ Ask before you set out about the environmental characteristics that can affect your walk and how local, experienced walkers deal with these considerations.

and the East Gippsland Rail Trail (p622) in Victoria.

In WA, the Munda Biddi Mountain Bike Trail (p898) offers 900km of pedal power and you can tackle the same distance on the Mawson Trail (p722) in SA.

Individual chapters list bike-hire companies where relevant. Rates charged by most outfits for renting road or mountain bikes (not including the discounted fees offered by budget accommodation to their guests) are anywhere from $8 to $14 per hour, and $18 to $40 per day. Security deposits can range from $50 to $200, depending on the rental period.

Most states have helpful bicycle organisations that provide maps and advice; see p1051 and each destination chapter for more information. More information and news on local pedal power is available online at www.bicycles.net.au.

Diving & Snorkelling

The Great Barrier Reef has more dazzling dive sites than you can poke a fin at; see The Great Barrier Reef, p410 and Diving in Queensland – Five of the Best, p295.

In WA the Ningaloo Reef (p988) is every bit as interesting as the east-coast reefs, without the tourist numbers, and there are spectacular artificial reefs created by sunken ships at Albany (p949) and Dunsborough (p936).

The Rapid Bay jetty off the Gulf St Vincent coast (p721) in SA is renowned for its abundant marine life and in Tasmania, the Bay of Fires (p679) and Eaglehawk Neck (p666) are popular spots. In NSW, Jervis Bay (p233) and Fish Rock Cave off South West Rocks (p184) are fantastic spots.

Professional Association of Diving Instructors (PADI) dive courses are offered throughout the country and on the east coast you don't have to travel far before stumbling across one. They are particularly prevalent in diving meccas such as Cairns and Port Douglas. Also, don't forget it's cheap to hire a mask, snorkel and fins and you can enjoy the marine life by snorkelling.

Fishing

Barramundi fishing is hugely popular across the Top End, particularly around Borroloola (p859) in the NT, and Karumba (p434) and Lake Tinaroo (p458) in Queensland.

Ocean fishing is possible right around the country, from a pier or a beach, or on an organised deep-sea charter. There are magnificent glacial lakes and clear streams for fishing in Tasmania (p633).

Before casting a line, be warned that strict limits to catches and sizes apply in Australia, and many species are threatened and therefore protected. Check local guidelines via fishing equipment stores or through individual state's government fishing bodies for information. The uninitiated may think the website **Fishnet** (www.fishnet.com.au) is devoted to stockings, but those keen on all aspects of Australian fishing know better.

Skiing & Snowboarding

Australia has a small but enthusiastic skiing industry, with snowfields straddling the NSW–Victoria border. The season is relatively short, however, running from about mid-June to early September, and snowfalls can be unpredictable. The top places to ski are within Kosciuszko National Park in the Snowy Mountains (p239) in NSW (see p242), and Mt Buller, Falls Creek and Mt Hotham in Victoria's High Country (see Ski Resorts, p605).

The website www.ski.com.au has links to major resorts and snow reports.

Surfing

World-class waves can be ridden all around Australia, from Queensland's Gold Coast (p336), along the entire NSW coast (p96) and at fine beaches in Victoria (p491). In Tasmania head to Bruny Island (p659) or Marrawah (p703) and in SA try Cactus Beach (p792). Southern WA is a surfing mecca, and Margaret River (p938) is the heartland.

See the Where to Surf in Australia (p490) for more detail on surfing sites.

The *Surfer's Travel Guide,* published by **Liquid Addictions** (www.liquidaddictions.com.au), provides a detailed description of just about every break along the Australian coast, and is a must-have tome for avid surfers.

(More) Water Sports

The places with the most activities on offer are those with the most visitors, such as Airlie Beach (p404), and Cairns (p442).

Sailing is a popular activity around the islands of the Great Barrier Reef (see Sailing the Whitsundays, p412) and all along the east coast, where you can take lessons or sometimes just pitch in and help crew a yacht. The best places for info are the local sailing clubs.

Canoeing and kayaking can be enjoyed on rivers at Katherine Gorge (p856) in the NT, the Murray River (p770) in SA, and Barrington Tops National Park (p176) in NSW. Sea kayaking is big at Byron Bay (p197) in NSW, around Tasmania's D'Entrecasteaux Channel (p658) and Freycinet Peninsula (p674) and at Mission Beach (p428) in Queensland.

For rafting head to the upper Murray River (p241) and Coffs Harbour (p186) in NSW, the Tully River (p427) in north Queensland and the Franklin River (p710) in Tasmania.

Whale, Dolphin & Marine-Life Watching

Southern right and humpback whales pass close to Australia's southern coast on their migratory route between the Antarctic and warmer waters. The best spots for whale-watching cruises are Hervey Bay (p363) in Queensland, Eden (p238) in southern NSW, the midnorth coast of NSW (p175), Warrnambool (p560) in Victoria, Albany (p948) on WA's southwest cape, and numerous places in SA (p722). Whale-watching season is roughly May to October on the west coast and in southwestern Victoria, September to November on the east coast, and July to September off the SA coast.

· Dolphins can be seen year-round along the east coast at Jervis Bay (p233), Port Stephens (p174) and Byron Bay (p195) in NSW; and off the coast of WA at Bunbury (p934) and Rockingham (p932). Fur seals and sea lions can be seen at Esperance (p953) and all manner of beautiful sea creatures can be seen at Monkey Mia (p978).

Wildlife Watching

Wildlife is one of Australia's top selling points and justifiably so. The vast majority of national parks are home to native fauna, although much of it is nocturnal so you may need to hone your torch (flashlight) skills to spot it.

Australia is a twitcher's haven, with a wide variety of habitats and bird life, particularly water birds. **Birds Australia** (☎ 1300 730 075; www .birdsaustralia.com.au) publishes the informative quarterly magazine *Wingspan*.

In the NT the best parks to spot wildlife are in the tropical north, particularly Kakadu (p842), where the birdlife in particular is brilliant and abundant. You've also got a good chance of spotting crocs up here. See p814

for more wildlife-watching opportunities in the territory.

In NSW there are platypuses and gliders to be found in New England National Park (p210), and 120 bird species in Dorrigo National Park (p211). The Border Ranges National Park (p204) is home to a quarter of all of Australia's bird species. Willandra National Park (p254) is World Heritage–listed and encompasses dense temperate wetlands and wildlife. WA (p897) also has ample bird watching hotspots.

In Victoria, Wilsons Promontory National Park (p617) teems with wildlife – in fact, wombats seem to have right of way.

In SA make a beeline for Flinders Chase National Park (p762). In Queensland, head to Malanda (p460) for birdlife, turtles and pademelons, Cape Tribulation (p467) for even better birdlife, or hike around Magnetic Island (p418) for superb koala spotting. In Tasmania, Maria Island (p672) is another twitcher's paradise, while Mt William (p679) and Mt Field National Parks (p656) and Bruny Island (p659) teem with native fauna.

BUSINESS HOURS

Hours vary a little from state to state but most shops and businesses open about 9am and close at 5pm Monday to Friday, with Saturday hours usually from 9am to either noon or 5pm. Sunday trading is becoming increasingly common but is currently limited to major cities, urban areas and tourist towns. In most towns there are usually one or two late shopping nights a week, normally Thursday and/ or Friday, when doors stay open until about 9pm. Most supermarkets are open till at least 8pm and are sometimes open 24 hours. Milk bars (general stores) and convenience stores are often open until late.

Banks are normally open from 9.30am to 4pm Monday to Thursday and until 5pm on Friday. Some large city branches are open from 8am to 6pm weekdays, and a few are also open until 9pm on Friday. Post offices are open from 9am to 5pm Monday to Friday, but you can also buy stamps on Saturday morning at post-office agencies (operated from news-agencies) and from Australia Post shops in all the major cities.

Restaurants typically open from 8am to 10.30am for breakfast, at noon for lunch and between 6pm and 7pm for dinner; most dinner bookings are made for 6.30pm to 8pm.

See p69 for more information about restaurants, cafes, pubs and general dining hours.

Nearly all attractions across Australia are closed on Christmas Day, and many also close on New Years Day and Good Friday.

CHILDREN
Practicalities

All cities and most major towns have centrally located public rooms where mothers (and sometimes fathers) can go to nurse their baby or change its nappy; check with the local tourist office or city council for details. While many Australians have a relaxed attitude about breastfeeding or nappy changing in public, some do frown on it.

Most motels and the better-equipped caravan parks have playgrounds and swimming pools, and can supply cots and baby baths – motels may also have in-house children's videos and child-minding services. Top-end hotels and many (but not all) midrange hotels are well versed in the needs of guests with children. B&Bs, on the other hand, often market themselves as sanctuaries from all things child related. Many cafes and restaurants lack a specialised children's menu, but many others do have kids' meals, or will provide small serves from the main menu. Some also supply high chairs.

If you want to leave Junior behind for a few hours, some of Australia's numerous licensed childcare agencies offer casual care. Check under 'Baby Sitters' and 'Child Care Centres' in the *Yellow Pages* telephone directory, or phone the local council for a list. Licensed centres are subject to government regulations and usually adhere to high standards; to be on the safe side, avoid unlicensed ones.

Child concessions (and family rates) often apply to accommodation, tours, admission fees, and transport, with some discounts as high as 50% of the adult rate. However, the definition of 'child' varies from under 12 to under 18 years. Accommodation concessions generally apply to children under 12 years sharing the same room as adults. On the major airlines, infants travel free provided they don't occupy a seat – child fares usually apply between the ages of two and 11 years.

Australia has high-standard medical services and facilities, and items such as baby formula and disposable nappies are widely available in urban and regional centres. Major

hire-car companies will supply and fit booster seats, charging around $18 for up to three days' use, with an additional daily fee for longer periods.

Lonely Planet's *Travel with Children* contains plenty of useful information.

Sights & Activities

There's no shortage of active, interesting or amusing things for children to focus on in Australia. Plenty of museums, zoos, aquariums, interactive technology centres and pioneer villages have historical, natural or science-based exhibits to get kids thinking. And of course outdoor destinations are always a winner. This guide has hot tips for keeping kids occupied in Sydney (p122), Canberra (p277), Melbourne (p513), Adelaide (p733), Perth (p911), Brisbane (p313), Alice Springs (p870) and Hobart (p645).

Elsewhere, in Victoria, Wilsons Promontory National Park (p617) is a favourite family haunt and keeps knee-biters occupied with bush walks, swimming, surfing and wildlife spotting. The Penguin Parade of Philip Island (p548) is also a must for families.

In NSW, some surf schools in Byron Bay (p198) run camps specifically for kids during school holidays, and the Art Gallery of NSW (p114) runs the excellent GalleryKids program on Sundays.

In the NT you can take them wildlife spotting in Territory Wildlife Park (p838). Not quite as wild, but a family must nevertheless, is the world-famous Australia Zoo (p345) in Queensland, the Alice Springs Desert Park (p865) in the NT and East Coast Natureworld (p676) in Tasmania.

For synthetic but scintillating fun spend a day at the Gold Coast theme parks (p335) in Queensland.

CLIMATE

Australia's size means there's a lot of climatic variation, but without severe extremes. The southern third of the country has cold (though generally not freezing) winters (June to August). Tasmania and the alpine country in Victoria and NSW get particularly chilly. Summers (December to February) range from pleasantly warm to sweltering. Spring (September to November) and autumn (March to May) are transition months, much the same as in Europe and North America.

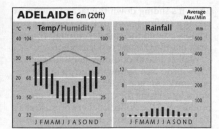

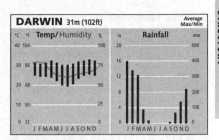

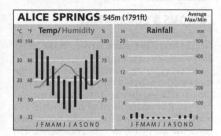

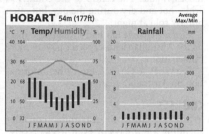

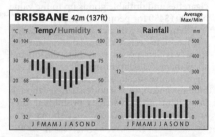

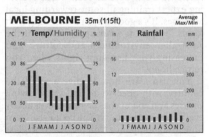

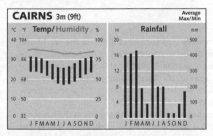

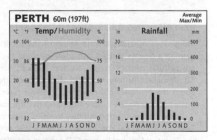

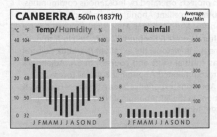

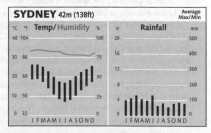

DIRECTORY

As you head north, the climate changes dramatically. Seasonal variations become fewer until, in the far north, around Darwin and Cairns, you're in the monsoon belt with just two seasons: hot and wet, and hot and dry. The Dry lasts roughly from April to September, and the Wet from October to March; the build-up to the Wet (from early October) is when the humidity is at its highest and when the locals confess to being at their most irritable. The centre of the country is arid – hot and dry during the day, but often bitterly cold at night.

Climate change has had a tangible impact on the Australian landscape; see p59 for more information.

See When to Go, p22, for further information on Australia's seasons.

COURSES

While travelling in Australia, consider spending a few days or even weeks receiving expert training in some rewarding local activities. It's a good way of connecting with locals, deepening your appreciation of the Australian environment and culture, and increasing your bragging rights when you return home.

You can learn how to dive around the country, with open-water and shore diving courses available at coastal locations in nearly every state and territory. You could also learn how to stand up on a thin piece of fibreglass while it's sliding down the face of a wave by taking a surfing lesson or two. There are surf schools around the country, though the east coast has the greatest concentration.

Well-fed cosmopolitan habitats such as Melbourne and Sydney offer plenty of opportunities for you to learn how to cook up a storm by utilising the wonderful array of local produce and the skilled cookery of Australia's many imported ethnic cuisines. For more on cooking courses, see p72.

CUSTOMS & QUARANTINE

For information on customs regulations, contact the **Australian Customs Service** (☎ 1300 363 263, 02-6275 6666; www.customs.gov.au).

When entering Australia you can bring most articles in free of duty provided that customs is satisfied they are for personal use and that you'll be taking them with you when you leave. There's a duty-free quota per person (over the age of 18) of 2.25L of alcohol, 250 cigarettes and dutiable goods up to the value of $900 ($450 for people under 18).

When arriving or departing the country, you'll need to declare all animal and plant material (wooden spoons, straw hats, the lot) and show them to a quarantine officer. And if you lug in a souvenir, such as a drum with animal hide for a skin, or a wooden article (though these items are not strictly prohibited, they are subject to inspection) that shows signs of insect damage, it won't get through. Some

---

EXPERIENCING ABORIGINAL AUSTRALIA

Indigenous Australians have some of the most complex and ancient cultures in the world and gaining a deeper insight into some of them is one of the highlights of a visit to Australia. There are cultural centres, museums and festivals across the country that enable you to experience Aboriginal art, history, tradition, diversity and life. You can also take an Indigenous tour and learn about the centuries-old relationship tribes have with the land, how to play a didgeridoo, throw a spear or recognise edible flora and natural medicines out in the bush.

There are ample opportunities to enjoy these experiences in the Top End, such as at the Northern Territory Aboriginal community of Manyallaluk (p855). In Queensland, Guurrbi Tours (p474) and the Tjapukai Cultural Park (p437) are two excellent projects operated by Indigenous communities. The Laura Aboriginal Dance Festival (p479) is another excellent Aboriginal experience.

There are also opportunities in NSW, including the Muru Mittigar Aboriginal Cultural Centre (p156) near the Blue Mountains, the Aboriginal Cultural Centre & Keeping Place (p209) in Armidale, and the Umbarra Cultural Centre (p237) near Bermagui. In Victoria, the excellent Brambuk Cultural Centre (p569) in the Grampians National Park has cultural tours and courses. In SA, Adjahdura Land on the Yorke Peninsula (p784) runs highly recommended Aboriginal cultural tours.

Individual chapters provide greater detail about Aboriginal experiences; see Aboriginal Festivals & Events (p814) and Indigenous Tours (p815) for options in the NT, Aboriginal NSW (p95), Aboriginal Victoria (p489), and Aboriginal Culture Tours (p899) in WA.

items may require treatment to make them safe before they are allowed in. The authorities are naturally keen to protect Australia's unique environment and important agricultural industries by preventing weeds, pests or diseases from getting into the country. Food is also prohibited, particularly meat, cheese, fruit, vegetables and flowers; plus, there are restrictions on taking fruit and vegetables between states.

You also need to declare currency in excess of $10,000 (including foreign currency) and all medicines.

There are strong restrictions on the possession and use of weapons in Australia. If you plan to travel with weapons of any sort contact the customs service or consult their website well before departure, as permits may be required.

Unless you want to make a first-hand investigation of conditions in Australian jails, don't bring illegal drugs in with you. Customs authorities are adept at searching for them and those cute sniffer dogs are a permanent fixture in arrival and baggage halls.

Australia takes quarantine very seriously. All luggage is screened or X-rayed – if you fail to declare quarantine items on arrival and are caught, you risk a hefty on-the-spot fine or prosecution, which may result in much more significant fines and up to 10 years imprisonment. For more information on quarantine regulations contact the **Australian Quarantine and Inspection Service** (AQIS; ☎ 1800 020 504, 02-6272 3933; www.aqis.gov.au).

DANGERS & ANNOYANCES

See p82 for important information on road hazards in Australia.

Animal Hazards

Australia's profusion of dangerous creatures is legendary. Apart from the presence of poisonous snakes and spiders, the country has its share of shark and crocodile attacks and, to top it off, it's home to the world's deadliest creature, the box jellyfish (p386). Travellers don't need to be constantly alarmed, however – you're unlikely to see many of these creatures in the wild, much less be attacked by one. For some reassuring statistics, see A Bit of Perspective, p1028.

Hospitals have antivenin on hand for all common snake and spider bites, but it helps to know what it was that bit you.

BOX JELLYFISH

There have been numerous fatal encounters between swimmers and these large jellyfish on the northern coast. Also known as the sea wasp or 'stinger', their venomous tentacles can grow up to 3m long. You can be stung during any month, but the worst time is from November to the end of April, when you should stay out of the water unless you're wearing protective clothing such as a 'stinger suit', available from swimwear and sporting shops in the stinger zone. The box jellyfish also has a tiny, lethal relative called an irukandji, though to date only two north-coast deaths have been directly attributed to it.

CROCODILES

In northern Australia, saltwater crocodiles ('salties') are a real danger. As well as living around the coast they can be found in estuaries, creeks and rivers, sometimes a long way inland. Observe safety signs or ask locals whether an inviting water hole or river is croc-free before plunging in – these precautions have been fatally ignored in the past.

INSECTS

For four to six months of the year you'll have to cope with the two banes of the Australian outdoors: the fly and the mosquito ('mozzie'). Flies aren't too bad in the cities but they start getting out of hand in the outback. In central Australia the flies emerge with the warmer spring weather (late August), particularly if there has been good winter rain, and last until the next frost kills them off. Flies also tend to be bad in various coastal areas. The humble fly net fits on a hat and is very effective (albeit utterly unfashionable). Widely available repellents, such as Aerogard and Rid, may also help to deter the little bastards, but don't count on it.

Mozzies are a problem in summer, especially near wetlands in tropical areas, and some species are carriers of viral infections; see p1075. Try to keep your arms and legs covered as soon as the sun goes down and make liberal use of insect repellent. For details of what ticks can get up to, see p1076.

SNAKES

There are many venomous snakes in the Australian bush, the most common being brown and tiger snakes, but few are aggressive – unless you're interfering with one,

A BIT OF PERSPECTIVE

There's approximately one shark-attack fatality per year in Australia, and a similar number of croc-attack deaths. Every now and then the number increases slightly, but usually because people have become complacent about impinging on these creatures' territories. Blue-ringed octopus deaths are even rarer – only two in the last century – and there's only ever been one confirmed death from a cone shell. Jellyfish do better, disposing of about two people each year. However, you're still over 100 times more likely to drown than be killed by one of these creatures.

On land, snakes kill one or two people per year (about the same as bee stings, or less than one-thousandth of those killed on the roads). There hasn't been a recorded death from a tick bite for over 50 years, nor from spider bites in the last 20.

or have the misfortune to stand on one, it's extremely unlikely that you'll be bitten. The golden rule if you see a snake is to do a Beatles and *let it be*.

For information on treating snake bites, see p1077.

SPIDERS

The deadly funnel-web spider is found in NSW (including Sydney) and its bite is treated in the same way as a snake bite. Another eight-legged critter to stay away from is black with a distinctive red stripe on its body. Called the redback spider for obvious reasons; if bitten apply ice and seek medical attention. The white tail is a long, thin black spider with, you guessed it, a white tail, and has a fierce bite that can lead to local inflammation and ulceration. The disturbingly large huntsman spider, which often enters homes, is harmless, though seeing one for the first time can affect your blood pressure and/or your underpants.

Bushfires & Blizzards

Bushfires are a regular occurrence in Australia, and every state aside from the NT has experienced severe fires in recent years. In the summer of 2009 Victoria was particularly ravaged, with numerous fires raging out of control. The devastation claimed 173 lives and quite literally wiped towns from the map; see Black Saturday, p545. It's important to remember that the Australian bush is designed to thrive from fire but common sense will put you well out of harms way. In hot, dry and windy weather, be extremely careful with any naked flame – cigarette butts thrown out of car windows have started many a fire. On a total fire ban day it's forbidden to use a camping stove, campfires or solid fuel barbecue and the penalties for doing so are severe. Given that people have

lost their homes and worse to bushfires in rural Australia, locals will not be amused if they catch you breaking this law, and they'll happily turn you in.

When a total fire ban is in place, bushwalkers should delay their trip until the weather improves. If you're out in the bush and you see smoke, even a long way away, take it seriously – bushfires move quickly and change direction with the wind. Go to the nearest open space, downhill if possible. A forested ridge, on the other hand, is the most dangerous place to be.

If you're road-tripping in a bushfire-prone area heed the local warnings. Most importantly, take the authorities' advice seriously and leave threatened towns early.

More bushwalkers actually die of cold than in bushfires. Even in summer temperatures can drop below freezing at night in the mountains and the weather can change very quickly. Blizzards in the mountains of Tasmania, Victoria and NSW can occur at almost any time of the year. Exposure in even moderately cool temperatures can sometimes result in hypothermia – for more information on hypothermia and how to minimise its risk, see p1077.

Crime

Australia is a relatively safe place to visit but you should still take reasonable precautions. Don't leave hotel rooms or cars unlocked, and don't leave your valuables unattended or visible through a car window. Sydney, the Gold Coast, Cairns and Byron Bay all get a dishonourable mention when it comes to theft, so keep a careful eye on your belongings in these areas.

Some pubs in Sydney and other major cities carry posted warnings about drugged drinks, after several reported cases in the past few years of women accepting a drink from a stranger only to later fall unconscious and be sexually assaulted. Regardless of whether you're male or female, it's advisable to refuse drinks offered by strangers in bars and to drink bottled alcohol rather than from a glass.

Swimming

Popular beaches are patrolled by surf life savers and patrolled areas are marked off by flags. Even so, surf beaches can be dangerous places to swim if you aren't used to the conditions. Undertows (or 'rips') are the main problem. If you find yourself being carried out by a rip, the important thing to do is just keep afloat; don't panic or try to swim against the rip, which will exhaust you. In most cases the current stops within a couple of hundred metres of the shore and you can then swim parallel to the shore for a short way to get out of the rip and make your way back to land.

A number of people are also paralysed every year by diving into waves in shallow water and hitting a sand bar; check the depth of the water before you leap.

DISCOUNT CARDS
Senior Cards

Senior travellers with some form of identification are often eligible for concession prices. Overseas pensioners are entitled to discounts of at least 10% on most express bus fares with Greyhound. Travellers over 60 years of age (both Australian residents and visitors) will simply need to present current age-proving identification to be eligible for discounts on full economy air fares.

Student & Youth Cards

The **International Student Travel Confederation** (ISTC; www.istc.org) is an international collective of specialist student travel organisations. It's also the body behind the internationally recognised International Student Identity Card (ISIC), which is only issued to full-time students aged 12 years and over, and gives the bearer discounts on accommodation, transport and admission to various attractions. The ISTC also produces the International Youth Travel Card (IYTC), which is issued to people under 26 years of age and not fulltime students, and has benefits equivalent to the ISIC. A similar ISTC brainchild is the International Teacher Identity Card (ITIC), available to teaching professionals. All three cards are chiefly available from student travel companies.

EMBASSIES & CONSULATES

The main diplomatic representations are in Canberra. There are also representatives in other major cities, particularly from countries with a strong link to Australia, such as the USA, the UK or New Zealand, or in cities with important connections, such as Darwin, which has an Indonesian consulate.

Addresses of major offices include the following. Look in the *Yellow Pages* phone directories of the capital cities for a more complete listing.

Canada Canberra (Map p270; ☎ 02-6270 4000; www .australia.gc.ca; Commonwealth Ave, Yarralumla, ACT 2600); Sydney (Map pp102-3; ☎ 02-9364 3000; Level 5, 111 Harrington St, Sydney, NSW 2000)

China (Map p270; ☎ 02-6273 4780; http://au.china -embassy.org/eng/; 15 Coronation Dr, Yarralumla, Canberra, ACT 2600)

France Canberra (Map p270; ☎ 02-6216 0100; www .ambafrance-au.org; 6 Perth Ave, Yarralumla, ACT 2600); Sydney (Map pp102-3; ☎ 02-92668 2400; Level 26, St Martins Tower, 31 Market St, Sydney, NSW 2000)

Germany Canberra (Map p270; ☎ 02-6270 1911; www .canberra.diplo.de; 119 Empire Circuit, Yarralumla, ACT 2600); Sydney (Map pp100-1; ☎ 02-9328 7733; 13 Trelawney St, Woollahra, NSW 2025); Melbourne (Map pp494-5; ☎ 03-9864 6888; 480 Punt Rd, South Yarra, Vic 3141)

Ireland (Map p270; ☎ 02-6273 3022; www.embas syofireland.au.com; 20 Arkana St, Yarralumla, Canberra, ACT 2600)

Japan Canberra (Map p270; ☎ 02-6273 3244; www .au.emb-japan.go.jp; 112 Empire Circuit, Yarralumla, ACT 2600); Sydney (Map pp102-3; ☎ 02-9231 3455; Level 34, Colonial Centre, 52 Martin Pl, Sydney, NSW 2000)

Malaysia (Map p268; ☎ 02-6273 1543; www.malaysia .org.au; 7 Perth Ave, Yarralumla, Canberra, ACT 2600)

Netherlands Canberra (Map p270; ☎ 02-6220 9400; www.netherlands.org.au; 120 Empire Circuit, Yarralumla, ACT 2600); Sydney (Map pp100-1; ☎ 02-9387 6644; Level 23, Tower 2, 101 Grafton St, Bondi Junction, NSW 2022)

New Zealand Canberra (Map p270; ☎ 02-6270 4211; www.nzembassy.com/australia; Commonwealth Ave, Canberra, ACT 2600); Sydney (Map pp102-3; ☎ 02-8256 2000; Level 10, 55 Hunter St, Sydney, NSW 2001)

Singapore (Map p270; ☎ 02-6271 2000; www.mfa .gov.sg/canberra; 17 Forster Cres, Yarralumla, Canberra, ACT 2600)

South Africa (Map p270; ☎ 02-6272 7300; www.sahc .org.au; cnr Rhodes Pl & State Circle, Yarralumla, Canberra, ACT 2600)

Thailand Canberra (Map p270; ☎ 02-6273 1149; http://
canberra.thaiembassy.org; 111 Empire Circuit,
Yarralumla, ACT 2600); Sydney (Map pp102-3; ☎ 02-9241
2542; http://thaisydney.idx.com.au; Level 8, 131
Macquarie St, Sydney, NSW 2000)

UK Canberra (Map p270; ☎ 02-6270 6666; www.britaus
.net; Commonwealth Ave, Yarralumla, ACT 2600); Sydney
(Map pp102-3; ☎ 02-9247 7521; 16th fl, 1 Macquarie
Pl, Sydney, NSW 2000); Melbourne (Map pp496-7; ☎ 03-
9652 1600; 17th fl, 90 Collins St, Melbourne, Vic 3000)

USA Canberra (Map p270; ☎ 02-6214 5600; http://can
berra.usembassy.gov; 1 Moonah Pl, Yarralumla, ACT 2600);
Sydney (Map pp102-3; ☎ 02-9373 9184; Level 59, 19-29
Martin Pl, Sydney, NSW 2000); Melbourne (Map pp494-5;
☎ 03-9526 5900; Level 6, 553 St Kilda Rd, Melbourne,
Vic 3004)

It's important to realise what your own embassy – the embassy of the country of which
you are a citizen – can and can't do to help you
if you get into trouble. Generally speaking,
it won't be much help in emergencies if the
trouble you're in is even remotely your own
fault. Remember that while in Australia you
are bound by Australian laws. Your embassy
will not be sympathetic if you end up in jail
after committing a crime locally, even if such
actions are legal in your own country.

In genuine emergencies you might get
some assistance, but only if other channels
have been exhausted. For example, if you need
to get home urgently, a free ticket is exceedingly unlikely – the embassy would expect you
to have insurance. If you have all your money
and documents stolen, it might assist with
getting a new passport, but a loan for onward
travel is out of the question.

FESTIVALS & EVENTS

Some of the most enjoyable Australian festivals are also the most typically Australian –
such as the surf life-saving competitions on
beaches all around the country during summer, or outback race meetings, which draw
together isolated communities. There are
also big city-based street festivals, sporting
events and arts festivals that showcase comedy, music and dance, and some important
commemorative get-togethers.

Details of festivals and events that are
grounded in a single place – be it a city, town,
valley or reserve – are provided throughout the
destination chapters of this book. The following events are pursued throughout a particular
region or state, or even around the country.

January & February

Big Day Out (www.bigdayout.com) This huge open-air
music concert tours Sydney, Melbourne, Adelaide, Perth
and the Gold Coast, and attracts big-name international
acts and dozens of local bands and DJs.

Australia Day This national holiday, commemorating
the arrival of the First Fleet in 1788, is observed on 26
January.

Tropfest (www.tropfest.com.au) The world's largest
short-film festival is held in Sydney, but is broadcast
throughout the country.

St Jerome's Laneway Festival (www.lanewayfestival
.com.au) An iconic indie festival crammed into laneways in
Melbourne, Sydney, Brisbane, Perth and Adelaide, featuring a local and international music line-up.

March & April

Ten Days on the Island (www.tendaysontheisland
.org) Major biennial Tasmanian cultural festival. Held in
odd-numbered years in venues around the state.

WOMADelaide (www.womadelaide.com.au) Annual
festival of world music, arts and dance, held over three
days in Adelaide and attracting crowds from around the
country.

Anzac Day National holiday held on April 25, commemorating the Australian and New Zealand Army Corps (Anzacs)
who have served and are serving for their countries. Dawn
services and marches take place around the country.

May

Sorry Day (www.nsdc.org.au) On 26 May each year (the
anniversary of the tabling in 1997 of the *Bringing Them
Home* report), concerned Australians acknowledge the
continuing pain and suffering of Indigenous Australians affected by Australia's one-time child-removal practices and
policies. Events are held in most cities countrywide.

June

Antarctic Midwinter Festival (www.antarctic-tasma
nia.info) A 10-day festival in Hobart celebrating the winter
solstice and Tasmania's connection with the Antarctic.

July

Naidoc Week (www.naidoc.org.au) Communities across
Australia celebrate the National Aboriginal and Islander
Day of Celebration (inaugurated in 1957), from local street
festivals to the annual Naidoc Ball (held in a different
location each year).

November

Melbourne Cup (www.melbournecup.com) On the first
Tuesday in November, Australia's premier horse race is run
in Melbourne. Many country towns schedule racing events
to coincide with the day and the nation does actually stop
for the big race.

December

Sydney to Hobart Yacht Race (http://rolexsydneyho bart.com) Sydney Harbour is a fantastic sight as hundreds of boats farewell competitors in the gruelling Sydney to Hobart Yacht Race.

FOOD

Australian cuisine may not have a high profile internationally, but visitors to Australian cities will find a huge range and wealth of food available in restaurants, markets, delicatessens (delis) and cafes. Competition for the custom of savvy tastebuds is increasingly high and so too are the resulting standards. This is evident most in Sydney and Melbourne, but the case will be the same in all cities, large urban areas and well-tourist destinations. In regional areas the variety diminishes with the population.

Vegetarian eateries and vegetarian selections in non-veg places (including menu choices for vegans and coeliac sufferers) are becoming more common in large cities and are forging a stronger presence in the smaller towns visited by tourists, though rural Australia – as exemplified by pub grub – continues its stolid dedication to meat. Those who enjoy a pre- or post-digestive puff will need to go outside, as smoking has been made illegal in most enclosed public places in all Australian states and territories, including indoor cafes, restaurants, clubs and pubs.

When it comes to cities, the eating recommendations provided in this book are often broken down into the main food-infatuated areas or suburbs and listed in order of price. The innovative food offered in top-quality Australian eateries doesn't necessarily cost a fortune. Best value are the modern cafes where you can get a good meal in casual surroundings for around $20.

For this book, eating venues are open for breakfast, lunch and dinner unless otherwise stated. See Food & Drink (p65) for more comprehensive information on Australian cuisine and where best to enjoy it.

GAY & LESBIAN TRAVELLERS

Australia is a popular destination for gay and lesbian travellers, with the so-called 'pink tourism' appeal of Sydney especially big, thanks largely to the city's annual, high-profile and spectacular Sydney Gay & Lesbian Mardi Gras. Throughout the country, but particularly on the east coast, there are tour operators, travel agents and accommodation places that make a point of welcoming gay men and lesbians.

Certain regions are the focus of gay and lesbian communities, among them Cairns (p436) in Queensland; Oxford St and King's Cross in Sydney (see Gay & Lesbian Sydney, p136), the Blue Mountains (p153), and the Hunter Valley (p168) in NSW; the Melbourne suburbs of Prahran, St Kilda and Collingwood (see Gay & Lesbian Melbourne, p521) and Daylesford and Hepburn Springs (p588) in Victoria.

Major gay and lesbian events include the aforementioned **Sydney Gay & Lesbian Mardi Gras** (www.mardigras.org.au) held annually in February and March, Melbourne's **Midsumma Festival** (www.midsumma.org.au) from mid-January to mid-February, Adelaide's **Feast** (www.feast.org.au) held in November, and Perth's Pride March and **Perth Pride** (www.pridewa.asn.au) festival – both held in October.

In general Australians are open minded about homosexuality, but the further into the country you get, the more likely you are to run into overt homophobia. Having said that, you will find active gay communities in places such as Alice Springs and Darwin. Even Tasmania, once a bastion of sexual conservatism, now actively encourages gay and lesbian tourism. Homosexual acts are legal in all states but the age of consent for sodomy varies: in the Australian Capital Territory (ACT), Victoria, NSW, NT and WA it's 16 years; in SA and Tasmania it's 17; and in Queensland it's 18.

Publications & Contacts

All major cities have gay newspapers, available from gay and lesbian venues and from newsagents in popular gay and lesbian residential areas. Gay lifestyle magazines include *DNA, Lesbians on the Loose,* the monthly *Queensland Pride* and the bimonthly *Blue.* Perth has the free *OutinPerth* and Adelaide has *Blaze.*

The website of **Gay and Lesbian Tourism Australia** (Galta; www.galta.com.au) has general information, and **Pinkboard** (www.pinkboard.com.au) is also helpful. **Gay and Lesbian Counselling and Community Services of Australia** (GLCCS; www.glccs.org .au) telephone counselling services are often a useful source of general information. It has a switchboard in every capital city and toll-free numbers for rural areas.

HOLIDAYS
Public Holidays
The following is a list of the main national and state public holidays (* indicates holidays that are only observed locally). As the timing can vary from state to state, check locally for precise dates.

National
New Year's Day 1 January
Australia Day 26 January
Easter (Good Friday to Easter Monday inclusive) March/April
Anzac Day 25 April
Queen's Birthday (except WA) Second Monday in June
Queen's Birthday (WA) Last Monday in September
Christmas Day 25 December
Boxing Day 26 December

Australian Capital Territory
Canberra Day March
Bank Holiday First Monday in August
Labour Day First Monday in October

New South Wales
Bank Holiday First Monday in August
Labour Day First Monday in October

Northern Territory
May Day First Monday in May
Show Day* (Alice Springs) First Friday in July; (Tennant Creek) Second Friday in July; (Katherine) Third Friday in July; (Darwin) Fourth Friday in July
Picnic Day First Monday in August

Queensland
Labour Day First Monday in May
RNA Show Day* (Brisbane only) August

South Australia
Adelaide Cup Day Third Monday in May
Labour Day First Monday in October
Proclamation Day Last Tuesday in December

Tasmania
Regatta Day 14 February
Launceston Cup Day Last Wednesday in February
Eight Hours Day First Monday in March
Bank Holiday Tuesday following Easter Monday
King Island Show First Tuesday in March
Launceston Show Day Thursday preceding second Saturday in October
Hobart Show Day Thursday preceding fourth Saturday in October
Recreation Day* (northern Tasmania only) First Monday in November

Victoria
Labour Day Second Monday in March
Melbourne Cup Day* (Melbourne only) First Tuesday in November

Western Australia
Labour Day First Monday in March
Foundation Day First Monday in June

School Holidays
The Christmas holiday season, from mid-December to late January, is part of the summer school holidays – it's also the time you are most likely to find transport and accommodation booked out, and long, restless queues at tourist attractions. There are three shorter school holiday periods during the year, but they vary by a week or two from state to state. They fall roughly from early to mid-April, late June to mid-July, and late September to early October. Even though they don't coincide nationwide, accommodation in tourist hotspots like the north and south coasts of NSW and Queensland's Gold and Sunshine Coasts will still be booked out.

INSURANCE
Don't underestimate the importance of a good travel insurance policy that covers theft, loss and medical problems – nothing is guaranteed to ruin your holiday plans quicker than an accident or having that brand new digital camera stolen. Most policies offer lower and higher medical-expense options; the higher ones are chiefly for countries that have extremely high medical costs, such as the USA. There is a wide variety of policies available, so compare the small print.

Some policies specifically exclude designated 'dangerous activities' such as scuba diving, bungee jumping, motorcycling, skiing and even bushwalking. If you plan on doing any of these things, make sure the policy you choose fully covers you for your activity of choice.

You may prefer a policy that pays doctors or hospitals directly rather than requiring you to pay on the spot and claim later. If you have to claim later make sure you keep all documentation. Check that the policy covers ambulances and emergency medical evacuations by air.

See also Before You Go (p1073) for details on health insurance. For information on insurance matters relating to cars that are bought or rented, see p80.

INTERNET ACCESS

Internet addicts will find it fairly easy to get connected throughout Australia.

Internet Cafes

Most internet cafes in Australia now have broadband access, but prices vary significantly depending on where you are. Most public libraries also have internet access, but this is provided primarily for research needs, not for travellers to check their email, so head for an internet cafe first. You'll find these in cities, sizable towns and pretty much anywhere else that travellers congregate. The cost ranges from $3 per hour in cut-throat places in Sydney's King's Cross to $10 per hour in more remote locations. The average is about $6 per hour, usually with a minimum of 10 minutes' access. Most youth hostels and backpacker places can hook you up, as can many hotels and caravan parks. Telecentres (community centres providing web access and other hi-tech facilities to locals and visitors) provide internet access in remote areas of WA, SA and NSW, while Tasmania has set up access centres in numerous local libraries and schools.

Hooking Up

If you've brought your palmtop or notebook computer and want to get connected to a local internet service provider (ISP), there are plenty of options – some ISPs do limit their dial-up areas to major cities or particular regions. Whatever enticements a particular ISP offers, make sure it has local dial-up numbers for the places where you intend to use it – the last thing you want is to be making timed long-distance calls every time you connect to the internet. Another useful tip when dialling up from a hotel room is to put 0 in front of your dial-up number to enable your modem to dial an outside line.

Some major ISPs:

Australia On Line (☎ 1300 650 661; www.ozonline.com.au)

Dodo (☎ 13 24 73; www.dodo.com.au)

iinet (☎ 13 19 17; www.iinet.net.au)

iPrimus (☎ 13 17 89; www.iprimus.com.au)

Optus (☎ 13 33 45; www.optus.com.au)

Telstra BigPond (☎ 13 76 63; www.bigpond.com)

An increasing number of hotels, cafes and bars in cities offer wi-fi (wireless) access. Some charge a fee so make sure you ask the price before connecting. These locations are most prevalent in Sydney and Melbourne but they're on the rise elsewhere. The following websites are helpful for sourcing locations:

Azure Wireless (www.azure.com.au)

Free WiFi (www.freewifi.com.au)

Wi-Fi HotSpotList (www.wi-fihotspotlist.com/browse/au)

Australia uses RJ-45 telephone plugs and Telstra EXI-160 four-pin plugs, but neither is universal – electronics shops such as Tandy and Dick Smith should be able to help. You'll also need a plug adaptor, and a universal AC adaptor will enable you to plug in without frying the innards of your machine.

Keep in mind that your PC-card modem may not work in Australia. The safest option is to buy a reputable 'global' modem before you leave home or buy a local PC-card modem once you get to Australia.

For a list of useful Australia-savvy websites, see p25.

LEGAL MATTERS

Most travellers will have no contact with the Australian police or any other part of the legal system. Those that do are likely to experience it while driving. There is a significant police presence on the country's roads, with the power to stop your car and ask to see your licence (you're required to carry it at all times), check your vehicle for roadworthiness, and insist that you take a breath test for alcohol – needless to say, drink-driving offences are taken very seriously here.

First offenders caught with small amounts of illegal drugs are likely to receive a fine rather than go to jail; nonetheless the recording of a conviction against you may affect your visa status.

If you remain in Australia beyond the life of your visa, you will officially be an 'overstayer' and could face detention and expulsion, and then be prevented from returning to Australia for up to three years.

If you are arrested, it's your right to telephone a friend, relative or lawyer before any formal questioning begins. Legal Aid is available only in serious cases and only to the truly needy (for links to Legal Aid offices see www.nla.aust.net.au). However, many solicitors do not charge for an initial consultation.

MAPS

Good-quality road and topographical maps are plentiful and readily available. The various state motoring organisations are a dependable source of road maps, while local tourist offices usually supply free maps, though the quality varies.

Authors on this book got off the beaten track and scrutinised the maps in this book. City street guides, such as those produced by Ausway (publishers of *Melway* and *Sydway*), Gregorys and UBD are useful for in-depth urban navigation, but they're expensive, bulky and only worth getting if you intend to do a lot of city driving. Useful websites for locating urban points of interest and specific addresses include www.whereis.com.au and http://maps.google.com.au.

Bushwalkers and others undertaking outdoor activities for which large-scale maps are essential should browse the topographic sheets published by **Geoscience Australia** (☎ 1800 800 173, 02-6249 9111; www.ga.gov.au). The more popular topographic sheets are usually available over the counter at shops selling specialist bushwalking gear and outdoor equipment.

MONEY
ATMs, Eftpos & Bank Accounts

Branches of the ANZ, Commonwealth, National Australia, Westpac and affiliated banks are found all over Australia, and many provide 24-hour automated teller machines (ATMs). But don't expect to find ATMs *everywhere*, certainly not off the beaten track or in very small towns. Most ATMs accept cards issued by other banks and are linked to international networks.

Eftpos (Electronic Funds Transfer at Point of Sale) is a convenient service that most Australian businesses have embraced. It means you can use your bank card (credit or debit) to pay for services or purchases directly, and often withdraw cash as well. Eftpos is available practically everywhere these days, even in outback roadhouses where it's a long way between banks. Just like using an ATM, you need to know your personal identification number (PIN) to use Eftpos.

Bear in mind that withdrawing cash via ATMs or Eftpos may attract significant fees – check the associated costs with your bank first.

OPENING A BANK ACCOUNT

If you're planning on staying in Australia a while (on a Working Holiday Maker visa for instance) it makes sense to open up a local bank account. This is easy enough for overseas visitors provided it's done within six weeks of arrival. Simply present your passport and provide the bank with a postal address and they'll open the account and send you an ATM card.

After six weeks it's much more complicated. A points system operates and you need to score a minimum of 100 points before you can have the privilege of letting the bank take your money. Passports or birth certificates are worth 70 points; an international driving licence with photo earns you 40 points; and minor IDs, such as credit cards, get you 25 points. You must have at least one ID with a photograph. Once the account is open, you should be able to have money transferred across from your home account (for a fee, of course).

It's possible to set up an Australian bank account before you embark on your international trip and applications can be made online; check the following bank websites for details:

ANZ (www.anz.com)
Commonwealth Bank (www.commbank.com.au)
National Australia Bank (www.nab.com.au)
Westpac (www.westpac.com.au)

If you don't have an Australian Tax File Number (TFN) you may end up paying up to twice as much tax, depending on the income bracket you fall into. See p1044 for tax-related information.

Credit & Debit Cards

Arguably the best way to carry most of your money around is in the form of a plastic card. Australia is well and truly a card-carrying society; it is becoming unusual to line up at a supermarket checkout, petrol station or department store and see someone actually paying with cash these days. Credit cards such as Visa and MasterCard are widely accepted for everything from a hostel bed or a restaurant meal to an adventure tour, and are pretty much essential (in lieu of a large deposit) for hiring a car. They can also be used to get cash advances over the counter at banks and from many ATMs, depending on the card, though these transactions incur immediate interest. Charge cards such as Diners Club and American Express (Amex) are not as widely accepted.

The obvious danger with credit cards is maxing out your limit and going home to a steaming pile of debt and interest charges. A safer option is a debit card with which you can withdraw money directly from your home bank account using ATMs, banks or Eftpos devices. Any card connected to the international banking networks (Cirrus, Maestro, Plus and Eurocard) should work, provided you know your PIN. Fees for using your card at a foreign bank or ATM vary depending on your home bank; ask before your leave.

The most flexible option is to carry both a credit and a debit card.

Currency

Australia's currency is the Australian dollar, made up of 100 cents. There are 5c, 10c, 20c, 50c, $1 and $2 coins, and $5, $10, $20, $50 and $100 notes. Although the smallest coin in circulation is 5c, prices are often still marked in single cents and then rounded to the nearest 5c when you come to pay.

Cash amounts equal to or in excess of the equivalent of A$10,000 (in any currency) must be declared on arrival or departure.

In this book, unless otherwise stated, all prices given in dollars refer to Australian dollars. For an idea of local costs, see p23.

Exchanging Money

Changing foreign currency or travellers cheques is usually no problem at banks throughout Australia or at licensed money-changers such as Travelex or Amex in cities and major towns.

Taxes & Refunds

The Goods and Services Tax (GST) is a flat 10% tax on all goods and services – accommodation, eating out, transport, electrical and other goods, books, furniture, clothing etc. There are exceptions, however, such as basic foods (milk, bread, fruits and vegetables etc). By law the tax is included in the quoted or shelf prices, so all prices in this book are GST-inclusive. International air and sea travel to/from Australia is GST-free, as is domestic air travel when purchased outside Australia by nonresidents.

If you purchase new or secondhand goods with a total minimum value of $300 from any

one supplier no more than 30 days before you leave Australia, you are entitled under the Tourist Refund Scheme (TRS) to a refund of any GST or WET (wine equalisation tax) paid. The scheme doesn't apply to all goods, and those that do qualify you must be able to wear or take as hand luggage onto the plane or ship. Also note that the refund is valid for goods bought from more than one supplier, but only if at least $300 is spent in each. For more details, contact the **Australian Customs Service** (☎ 1300 363 263, 02-6275 6666; www.customs .gov.au).

See p1044 for details on income tax refunds.

Travellers Cheques

The ubiquity and convenience of internationally linked credit and debit card facilities in Australia means that travellers cheques are virtually redundant. However Amex and Travelex will exchange their associated travellers cheques, and major banks will change travellers cheques also. In all instances you'll need to present your passport for identification when cashing them.

There are no notable restrictions on importing or exporting travellers cheques.

PHOTOGRAPHY & VIDEO

Digital cameras, memory sticks and batteries are sold prolifically in cities and urban centres. Electronics stores such as Dick Smith will stock everything you need, as will the larger departments stores. The availability of batteries and memory sticks in more rural or remote areas is far diminished so if you're planning to get trigger happy it's best to stock up in the cities. Many internet cafes, camera stores and large stationers such as **Officeworks** (www .officeworks.com.au) have facilities that enable you to produce prints directly from your memory stick or to burn CDs.

Film and slide film are still available and developing standards are high. You can get your shots processed at any camera store and just about any chemist. Video cassettes are widely available at camera and electronics stores.

As in any country, politeness goes a long way when taking photographs; ask before taking pictures of people. Particularly bear in mind that Indigenous Australians are not objects of curiosity; they are people like you and photography can be highly intrusive.

Regardless of whether the purpose is personal or commercial, always ask permission before photographing or videoing a person, group or residence and offer to return copies of photographs or footage (and get an address). Taking photographs of cultural places, practices and images, sites of significance and ceremonies may also be a sensitive matter. Always ask and always respect the right to say no.

Useful Lonely Planet titles for the budding photographer include *Travel Photography, Urban Travel Photography, Wildlife Travel Photography* and *People Photography*.

POST

Australia Post (www.auspost.com.au) has divided international destinations into four parcel zones. You can send parcels by sea mail to anywhere in the world except countries in the Asia-Pacific region (including New Zealand); it's cheap but they can take forever.

Sending & Receiving Mail

All post offices hold mail for visitors. You need to provide some form of identification (such as a passport) to collect mail. You can also have mail sent to you at city Amex offices if you have an Amex card or travellers cheques.

See p1023 for post office opening times.

SHOPPING

Australians are fond of spending money, a fact evidenced by the huge variety of local- and international-brand shops, and the feverish crowds that gather at every clearance sale. Big cities can satisfy most consumer appetites with everything from high-fashion boutiques to secondhand emporia, while many smaller places tend towards speciality retail, be it home-grown produce, antiques or arts and crafts. Markets are a great place to shop and most cities have at least one permanent bazaar.

You may be able to get a refund on the tax you pay on goods; see p1035.

Aboriginal Art & Artefacts

An Aboriginal artwork or artefact makes an evocative reminder of your trip. By buying authentic items you are supporting Aboriginal culture and helping to ensure that traditional and contemporary expertise and designs continue to be of economic and cultural benefit for Aboriginal individuals and their commu-

nities. Unfortunately, much of the so-called Aboriginal art sold as souvenirs is ripped off, consisting of appropriated designs illegally taken from Aboriginal people; or it's just plain fake, and usually made overseas by underpaid workers.

The best place to buy artefacts is either directly from the communities that have art-and-craft centres or from galleries and outlets that are owned, operated or supported by Aboriginal communities. There are also many reputable galleries that have long supported the Aboriginal arts industry, usually members of the **Australian Commercial Galleries Association** (ACGA; www.acga.com.au), that will offer certificates of authenticity with their goods. See Buying Aboriginal Art (p823) for more information.

Didgeridoos are in high demand, but you should decide whether you want a decorative piece or a functional musical instrument. The didgeridoos on the market are not always made by Aboriginal people, which means that at a nonsupportive souvenir shop in Darwin or Cairns you could pay anything from $250 to $400 or more for something that looks pretty but is little more than a painted bit of wood. Buying from a community outlet such as Manyallaluk (p855) or Julalikari (p861) in the NT is your best opportunity to purchase a functional, authentic didgeridoo painted with natural pigments such as ochre.

Australiana

The cheapest souvenirs, usually mass produced and with little to distinguish them, are known collectively by the euphemism 'Australiana'. They are supposedly representative of Australia and its culture, but in reality are just lowest-common-denominator trinkets, often made in Asia rather than Australia (check the label).

Genuine Australian offerings include the seeds of native plants – try growing kangaroo paws back home (if your own country will allow them in). You could also consider a bottle of fine Australian wine, honey (leatherwood honey is one of many powerful local varieties), macadamia nuts (native to Queensland), Bundaberg Rum with its unusual sweet flavour, or genuine Ugg boots (sheepskin boots that conquer any winter).

Opals & Gemstones

The opal, Australia's national gemstone, is a popular souvenir, as is the jewellery made with it. It's a beautiful stone but buy wisely and shop around, as quality and prices vary widely from place to place. Coober Pedy (p804) in SA and Lightning Ridge (p223) and White Cliffs (p259) in NSW are opal-mining towns where you can buy the stones or fossick for your own.

On the Torres Strait Islands (p482) look out for South Sea pearls, while in Broome (p1004) in WA, cultured pearls are sold in many local shops.

Australia is a mineral-rich country and semiprecious gemstones such as topaz, garnets, sapphires, rubies, zircon and others can sometimes be found lying around in piles of dirt at various locations. There are sites around rural and outback Australia where you can pay a few dollars and fossick for your own stones. The gem fields around Emerald, Anakie and Rubyvale in Queensland's Capricorn Hinterland (p389) are a good place to shop for jewellery and gemstones.

TELEPHONE

The two main telecommunication companies are **Telstra** (www.telstra.com.au) and **Optus** (www.optus .com.au). Both are also major players in the mobile (cell) market, along with **Vodafone** (www .vodafone.com.au) – other mobile operators include **Virgin** (www.virginmobile.com.au) and **3** (www .three.com.au).

Information & Toll-Free Calls

Numbers starting with ☎ 190 are usually recorded information services, charged at anything from 35c to $5 or more per minute (more from mobiles and payphones). To make a reverse-charge (collect) call from any public or private phone, dial ☎ 1800 REVERSE (☎ 1800 738 3773), or ☎ 12 550.

Toll-free numbers (prefix ☎ 1800) can be called free of charge from almost anywhere in Australia – they may not be accessible from certain areas or from mobile phones. Calls to numbers beginning with ☎ 13 or ☎ 1300 are charged at the rate of a local call – the numbers can usually be dialled Australia-wide, but may be applicable only to a specific state or STD district. Telephone numbers beginning with either ☎ 1800, ☎ 13 or ☎ 1300 cannot be dialled from outside Australia.

International Calls

Most payphones allow international subscriber dialling (ISD) calls, the cost and international dialling code of which will vary depending on which international phone card provider you are using. International phone cards are readily available from internet cafes and small independent stores. Check the fine print on your phone card to ensure you aren't paying a hefty trunk charge every time you make a call. International calls from landlines in Australia are also relatively cheap and subject to special deals, so if you're paying for residential phone rental it's worth shopping around – look in the *Yellow Pages* for a list of telephone service providers and compare their international rates.

The **Country Direct service** (☎ 1800 801 800) connects callers in Australia with operators in nearly 60 countries to make reverse-charge (collect) or credit-card calls.

When calling overseas you will need to dial the international access code from Australia (☎ 0011 or ☎ 0018), the country code and then the area code (without the initial 0). So for a London telephone number you'll need to dial ☎ 0011-44-20, then the number. In addition, certain operators will have you dial a special code to access their service.

Some country codes:

Country	International Country Code
France	☎ 33
Germany	☎ 49
Ireland	☎ 353
Japan	☎ 81
Netherlands	☎ 31
New Zealand	☎ 64
UK	☎ 44
USA & Canada	☎ 1

If dialling Australia from overseas, the country code is ☎ 61 and you need to drop the 0 in state/territory area codes.

Local Calls

Calls from private phones cost 15c to 30c, while local calls from public phones cost 50c; both involve unlimited talk time. Calls to mobile phones attract higher rates and are timed.

Long-Distance Calls & Area Codes

Long-distance calls (over around 50km) are timed. Australia uses four subscriber trunk dialling (STD) area codes. These STD calls can be made from any public phone and are cheaper during off-peak hours – generally between 7pm and 7am and on weekends. Broadly, the main area codes are as follows.

State/Territory	Area code
ACT	☎ 02
NSW	☎ 02
NT	☎ 08
QLD	☎ 07
SA	☎ 08
TAS	☎ 03
VIC	☎ 03
WA	☎ 08

Area code boundaries don't necessarily coincide with state borders; for example some remote parts of NSW and Victoria use neighbouring state's area codes.

Mobile (Cell) Phones

Local numbers with the prefixes ☎ 04xx or ☎ 04xxx belong to mobile phones. Australia's GSM and 3G mobile networks service more than 90% of the population but leave vast tracts of the country uncovered. The east coast, southeast and southwest get good reception, but elsewhere (apart from major towns) it can be haphazard or nonexistent. It is improving however.

Australia's digital network is compatible with GSM 900 and 1800 (used in Europe), but generally not with the systems used in the USA or Japan. It's easy and cheap enough to get connected short-term, as prepaid mobile systems are offered by providers such as **Telstra** (www.telstra.com.au), **Optus** (www.optus.com .au), **Vodafone** (www.vodafone.com.au), **Virgin** (www .virginmobile.com.au) and **3** (www.three.com.au).

Phonecards

A variety of phonecards can be bought at newsagents, hostels and post offices for a fixed dollar value (usually $10, $20 etc) and can be used with any public or private phone by dialling a toll-free access number and then the PIN number on the card. Some public phones also accept credit cards.

TIME

Australia is divided into three time zones: the Western Standard Time zone (GMT/UTC plus eight hours) covers WA; Central Standard Time (plus 9½ hours) covers the NT and SA; and Eastern Standard Time (plus 10 hours) covers Tasmania, Victoria, NSW, the ACT and Queensland. There are minor exceptions

– Broken Hill (NSW) for instance is on Central Standard Time. For international times, see www.timeanddate.com/worldclock.

'Daylight saving', for which clocks are put forward an hour, operates in some states during the warmer months (October to early April). However, things can get pretty confusing, with WA, the NT and Queensland staying on standard time, while in Tasmania daylight saving starts a month earlier than in SA, Victoria, the ACT and NSW.

TIPPING

It's common but by no means obligatory to tip in restaurants and upmarket cafes if the service warrants it – a gratuity of between 5% and 10% of the bill is the norm. Taxi drivers will also appreciate you rounding up the fare.

TOILETS

One of the pleasures of travelling in a 'first world' country is the abundance of hygienic and free public toilets. These can be found in shopping centres, parks and just about any other public space in the country.

TOURIST INFORMATION

Australia's highly self-conscious tourism infrastructure means that when you head out looking for information, you can easily end up being buried neck deep in brochures, booklets, maps and leaflets, or that you can get utterly swamped with detail during an online surf.

The **Australian Tourist Commission** (www.australia .com) is the national government tourist body, and has a good website for pretrip research.

Local Tourist Offices

Within Australia, tourist information is disseminated by various regional and local offices. In this book, the main state and territory tourism authorities are listed in the introductory information section of each destination chapter. Almost every major town in Australia seems to maintain a tourist office of some type and in many cases they are very good, with friendly staff (often volunteers) providing local info not readily available from the state offices. If booking accommodation or tours from local offices, bear in mind that they often only promote businesses that are paying members of the local tourist association. Details of local tourism offices are given in the relevant city and town sections throughout this book.

AUSTRALIA FOR THE TRAVELLER WITH A DISABILITY

Information

Reliable information is the key ingredient for travellers with a disability and the best source is the **National Information Communication & Awareness Network** (Nican; ☎ 02-6241 1220, TTY 1800 806 769; www.nican.com.au). It's an Australia-wide directory providing information on access issues, accessible accommodation, sporting and recreational activities, transport and specialist tour operators.

Another source of quality information is the **Disability Information & Resource Centre** (DIRC; Map p728; ☎ 08-8236 0555, TTY 08-8223 7579; www.dircsa.org.au; 195 Gilles St, Adelaide, SA 5000). The website of **e-bility** (www.e-bility.com/travel/) provides lots of info on accessible holidays in Australia, including listings of tour operators and accommodation.

The publication **Easy Access Australia** (www.easyaccessaustralia.com.au), by Bruce Cameron, is available from various bookshops and provides details on easily accessible transport, accommodation and attraction options.

The comprehensive website www.toiletmap.gov.au lists over 14,000 public and private toilets, including those with wheelchair access.

Air

Qantas (☎ 13 13 13, TTY 133 677; www.qantas.com.au) entitles a disabled person and the carer travelling with them to a discount on full economy fares; contact Nican (see above) for eligibility and an application form. Guide dogs travel for free on **Qantas** (☎ 13 13 13; www.qantas.com.au), **Jetstar** (☎ 13 15 38; www.jetstar.com.au) and **Virgin Blue** (☎ 13 67 89; www.virginblue.com.au), and their affiliated carriers. All of Australia's major airports have dedicated parking spaces, wheelchair access to terminals, accessible toilets, and skychairs to convey passengers onto planes via airbridges.

Train

In NSW, CountryLink's XPT trains have at least one carriage (usually the buffet car) with a seat removed for a wheelchair, and an accessible toilet. Queensland Rail's *Tilt Train* from Brisbane to Cairns has a wheelchair-accessible carriage.

Melbourne's suburban rail network is accessible and guide dogs and hearing dogs are permitted on all public transport in Victoria. **Metlink** (☎ 13 16 38, TTY 03-9619 2727; www.metlinkmelbourne.com .au) also offers a free travel pass to visually impaired people for transport in Melbourne.

Tourist Offices Abroad

The federal government body charged with improving relationships with foreign tourists is **Tourism Australia** (☎ 02-9360 1111; www.australia.com). A good place to start some pretrip research is on its website, which provides information about many aspects of visiting Australia in 10 languages (including French, German, Japanese and Spanish).

Some countries with Tourism Australia offices:

Germany (☎ 069-274 00622; Neue Mainzer Strasse 22, Frankfurt D 60311)

Japan (☎ 13-5214 0720; Australian Business Centre, New Otani Garden Court Bldg 28F, 4-1 Kioi-cho Chiyoda-ku, Tokyo 102-0094)

New Zealand (☎ 09-915 2826; Level 3, 125 The Strand, Parnell, Auckland)

Singapore (☎ 6255 4555; 101 Thomson Rd, United Sq 08-03, Singapore 307591)

Thailand (☎ 02 670 0640; 16th fl, Unit 1614, Empire Tower, 195 South Sathorn Rd, Yannawa, Sathorn, Bangkok 10120)

UK (☎ 020-7438 4601; 6th fl, Australia House, Melbourne Place/Strand, London WC2B 4LG)

USA (☎ 310-695 3200; Suite 1150, 6100 Center Dr, Los Angeles CA 90045)

TRAVELLERS WITH DISABILITIES

Disability awareness in Australia is pretty high and getting higher. Legislation requires that new accommodation meets accessibility standards for mobility-impaired travellers, and discrimination by tourism operators is illegal. Many of Australia's key attractions, including many national parks, provide access for those with limited mobility and a number of sites also address the needs of visitors with visual or aural impairments; contact attractions in advance to confirm the facilities. Tour operators with vehicles catering to mobility-impaired travellers operate from most capital cities. Facilities for wheelchairs are improving in accommodation, but there are still far too many older (particularly 'historic') establishments where the necessary upgrades haven't been done.

VISAS

All visitors to Australia need a visa – only New Zealand nationals are exempt, and even they receive a 'special category' visa on arrival. Application forms for the several types of visa are available from Australian diplomatic missions overseas, travel agents or the website of the **Department of Immigration & Citizenship** (☎ 13 18 81; www.immi.gov.au).

eVisitor

Many European passport holders are eligible for an eVisitor, which is free and allows visitors to stay in Australia for up to three months. eVisitors must be applied for online and they are electronically stored and linked to individual passport numbers, so no stamp in your passport is required. It's advisable to apply at least 14 days prior to the proposed date of travel to Australia. Applications are made on the Department of Immigration & Citizenship website.

Electronic Travel Authority (ETA)

Some visitors who aren't eligible for an eVisitor can get an ETA through any International Air Transport Association (IATA)–registered travel agent, overseas airline or Australian visa office outside Australia. They make the application direct when you buy a ticket and issue the ETA, which replaces the usual visa stamped in your passport – it's common practice for travel agents to charge a fee, in the vicinity of US$25, for issuing an ETA. This system is available to passport holders of eight countries: Brunei, Canada, Hong Kong, Japan, Malaysia, Singapore, South Korea and the USA.

You can also apply for the ETA online (www.eta.immi.gov.au), which attracts a nonrefundable service charge of $20.

Tourist Visas

Short-term tourist visas have largely been replaced by the eVisitor and ETA. However, if you are from a country not covered by either, or you want to stay longer than three months,

you'll need to apply for a visa. Standard Tourist Visas (which cost $100) allow one (in some cases multiple) entry, for a stay of up to 12 months, and are valid for use within 12 months of issue.

Visa Extensions

A Further Stay visa can be applied for within Australia through the Department of Immigration & Citizenship. It's best to apply at least two or three weeks before your visa expires. The application fee is $240 and is nonrefundable, even if your application is rejected.

Working Holiday Maker (WHM) Visas (417)

Young (aged 18 to 30) visitors from Belgium, Canada, Cyprus, Denmark, Estonia, Finland, France, Germany, Hong Kong, Ireland, Italy, Japan, Korea, Malta, the Netherlands, Norway, Sweden, Taiwan and the UK are eligible for a WHM visa, which allows you to visit for up to one year and gain casual employment.

The emphasis of this visa is on casual and not full-time employment, so you're only supposed to work for any one employer for a maximum of six months. A first WHM visa must be obtained prior to entry to Australia and can be applied for at Australian diplomatic missions abroad or online (www.immi .gov.au/visitors/working-holiday). You can't change from a tourist visa to a WHM visa once you're in Australia.

You can apply for this visa up to a year in advance, which is worthwhile as there's a limit on the number issued each year. Conditions include having a return air ticket or sufficient funds for a return or onward fare, and an application fee of $195 is charged. For details of what sort of employment is available and where, see Seasonal Work, p1042.

Visitors who have worked as a seasonal worker in regional Australia for a minimum of three months while on their first WHM are eligible to apply for a second WHM while still in Australia. 'Regional Australia' encompasses the vast majority of the country, excepting major cities; the definition of 'seasonal work' is a little more specific. The Department of Immigration has good information and straightforward facts that are easy to understand. Tourism Australia also has a dedicated website with helpful information – www.work.australia.com.

See p1044 for information regarding income tax refunds, which holders of a WHM are eligible for.

Work & Holiday Visas (462)

Nationals from Chile, Malaysia, Thailand, Turkey and the USA between the ages of 18 and 30 can apply for a Work and Holiday visa prior to entry to Australia. Once granted this visa allows the holder to enter Australia within three months of issue, stay for up to 12 months, leave and re-enter Australia any number of times within that 12 months, undertake temporary employment to supplement a trip, and study for up to four months.

General Skilled Migration Visas

Some visitors may be eligible for a Skilled Migrant visa. Applicants must be between 18 and 45 years of age and possess skills and qualifications in fields such as engineering, nursing, child care, sales and marketing, education, human resources and a surprisingly long and diverse list of others. Skilled migrant visas can be applied for on or offshore (other conditions apply of course) and the Department of Immigration & Citizenship's website has more information.

WOMEN TRAVELLERS

Australia is generally a safe place for women travellers, although the usual sensible precautions apply. It's best to avoid walking alone late at night in any of the major cities and towns. And if you're out on the town, always keep enough money aside for a taxi back to your accommodation. The same applies to outback and rural towns where there are often a lot of unlit, semideserted streets between you and your temporary home. When the pubs and bars close and there are inebriated people roaming around, it's not a great time to be out and about. Lone women should also be wary of staying in basic pub accommodation unless it looks safe and well managed.

Sexual harassment is an ongoing problem, be it via an aggressive metropolitan male or a rural bloke living a less-than-enlightened pro forma bush existence. Stereotypically, the further you get from 'civilisation' (ie the big cities), the less enlightened your average Aussie male is probably going to be about women's issues. Having said that, many women travellers say that they have met the friendliest, most down-to-earth blokes in outback pubs and remote roadhouse stops. And cities still have to put up with their unfortunate share of 'ocker' males who regard a bit of sexual harassment as a right, and chauvinism as a desirable trait.

Lone female hitchers are tempting fate – hitching with a male companion is safer. See Crime (p1028) for a warning on drugged drinks.

WORK

If you come to Australia on a tourist visa then you're not allowed to work for pay – working for approved volunteer organisations (for details see p1044) in exchange for board is OK. If you're caught breaching your visa conditions, you can be expelled from the country and placed on a banned list for up to three years.

Equipped with a WHM visa (see opposite), you can begin to sniff out the possibilities for temporary employment. Casual work can often be found during peak season at the major tourist centres. Places such as Alice Springs, Cairns and various resort towns along the Queensland coast, and the ski fields of Victoria and NSW are all good prospects when the country is in holiday mode.

Many travellers have found work cleaning or attending the reception desk at backpacker hostels, which usually means free accommodation. Most hostels, however, are now employing their own locally based staff.

Other prospects for casual employment include factory work, labouring, bar work, waiting tables, domestic chores at outback roadhouses, nanny work, working as a station hand (jackaroo/jillaroo) and collecting for charities. People with computer, secretarial, nursing and teaching skills can find work temping in the major cities by registering with a relevant agency.

Information

Backpacker accommodation, magazines and newspapers are good resources for local work opportunities.

Useful websites:

Career One (www.careerone.com.au) General employment site, good for metropolitan areas.

Face2Face Fundraising (www.face2facefundraising .com.au) Fundraising jobs for charities and not-for-profits.

Gumtree (http://sydney.gumtree.com.au) Great classified site with jobs, accommodation and items for sale.

DIRECTORY

SEASONAL WORK

Seasonal fruit picking (harvesting) relies on casual labour and there is always something that needs to be picked, pruned or farmed somewhere in Australia all year round. It's definitely hard work that involves early-morning starts, and you're usually paid by how much you pick (per bin, bucket or whatever). Expect to earn about $50 to $60 a day to start with, more when you get quicker and better at it. Some work, such as pruning or sorting, is paid by the hour at around $12 or $13.

Throughout this book you'll find separate seasonal work information for towns where there is an abundance of this type of employment. You can also call the **National Harvest Labour Information Service** (☎ 1800 062 332) for more information about when and where you're likely to pick up this sort of work. Useful websites:

Harvest Trail (www.jobsearch.gov.au/harvesttrail) Harvest jobs around Australia.

Workabout Australia (www.workaboutaustralia.com.au) State-by-state breakdown of seasonal work opportunities.

Grunt Labour (www.gruntlabour.com) Specialises in labour, manufacturing and agricultural-based recruitment.

The following table indicates some of the more prominent areas and details general work seasons.

New South Wales

The NSW ski fields have seasonal work (June to September), particularly around Thredbo (p242). There's also harvest work around Narrabri and Moree (p222), and grape picking in the Hunter Valley (p170). Fruit picking is all the go near Tenterfield (p213), Orange (p215) and Young (p218).

Industry	Time	Region(s)
tomatoes	Jan-Mar	Forbes
grapes	Feb-Mar	Griffith, Hunter Valley
apples	Feb-Apr	Orange, Batlow, Gundagai
asparagus	Oct-Dec	Jugiong (northeast of Gundagai)
cotton	Oct-Jan	Narrabri
bananas	Nov-Jan	North Coast
cherries	Nov-Jan	Orange, Batlow, Young
apples	Dec-Jan	Forbes
citrus	Dec-Mar	Griffith

Northern Territory

For information on seasonal work in the Northern Territory, see p814.

Industry	Time	Region(s)
tourism	May-Sep	Darwin, Alice Springs, Katherine
mangoes	Sep-Nov	Darwin, Katherine

Queensland

Farm work and fruit picking is available in north Queensland around Cardwell (p426) and Tully (p427), near the Atherton Tablelands at Mareeba (p456) and Atherton (p457), and in Cooktown (p472). Further south there's seasonal work on the Fraser Coast (p371) and in the Darling Downs (p357).

Those looking for sturdier (and much better paying) work should keep an eye on mining opportunities in growth mining towns such as Weipa (p480), Boodjamulla (p435) and Cloncurry (p392).

Industry	Time	Region(s)
grapes	Jan-Apr	Stanthorpe
apples	Feb-Mar	Warwick
tourism	Apr-Oct	Cairns
fishing trawlers	May-Aug	Cairns
vegies	May-Nov	Bowen
asparagus	Aug-Dec	Warwick
tomatoes	Oct-Dec	Bundaberg
mangoes	Dec-Jan	Atherton, Mareeba
bananas	year-round	Tully, Innisfail

South Australia

Good seasonal work opportunities can be found on the Fleurieu Peninsula (p752), and some can still be found on the Limestone Coast and along the Murray River.

Industry	Time	Region(s)
tomatoes	Jan-Feb	Riverland
grapes	Feb-Apr	Riverland, Barossa, Clare
peaches	Feb-Jun	Riverland
apples/pears	Feb-Jul	Adelaide Hills
citrus	May-Dec	Berri, Riverland
pruning	Aug-Dec	Adelaide Hills
apricots	Dec	Riverland

Tasmania

The apple orchards in the south, especially around Cygnet (p661), and Huonville (p662) are your best bet for work in Tassie.

Industry	Time	Region(s)
strawberries/raspberries	Jan-Apr	Huonville
apples/pears	Mar-Apr	Huon/Tamar Valleys
grapes	Mar-Apr	Tamar Valley
cherries	Dec-Jan	Huonville

Victoria

There's plenty of harvest work in Mildura (p577) and Shepparton (p600).

Industry	Time	Region(s)
tomatoes	Jan-Mar	Shepparton, Echuca
grapes/oranges	Jan-Mar	Mildura
peaches/pears	Feb-Apr	Shepparton
apples	Mar-May	Bendigo
ski fields	Jun-Oct	Wangaratta/Alps
strawberries	Oct-Dec	Echuca, Dandenongs
cherries	Nov-Dec	Dandenongs

Western Australia

WA is in a labour shortage and a wealth of opportunities exist for travellers (both Australian and foreign) for paid work year-round.

In Perth, plenty of temporary work is available in tourism and hospitality, administration, IT, nursing, childcare, factories and labouring. Outside of Perth, travellers can easily get jobs in tourism and hospitality, plus a variety of seasonal work. For grape-picking work in Margaret River, see Inne Town Backpackers, p939.

Industry	Time	Region(s)
grapes	Feb-Mar	Albany, Margaret River, Mt Barker, Manjimup
apples/pears	Feb-Apr	Donnybrook, Manjimup
prawn trawlers	Mar-June	Carnarvon
bananas	Apr-Dec	Kununurra
bananas	year-round	Carnarvon
vegies	May-Nov	Kununurra, Carnarvon
tourism	May-Dec	Kununurra
flowers	Sep-Nov	Midlands
lobsters	Nov-May	Esperance

MyCareer (www.mycareer.com.au) General employment site, good for metropolitan areas.

Recruit Oz (www.recruitoz.com) Helpful online job agency for skilled migrants and working holiday visa holders looking for employment in Australia.

Seek (www.seek.com.au) General employment site, good for metropolitan areas.

Travellers at Work (www.taw.com.au) Excellent site for working travellers in Australia.

Tax

PAYING TAX & TAX REFUNDS

Even with a tax file number (TFN), nonresidents (including WHM visa holders) pay a considerably higher rate of tax than Australian residents, especially those on a low income. For a start, there's no tax-free threshold – you pay tax on every dollar you earn.

Because you have been paid wages in Australia, you must lodge a tax return with the **Australian Taxation Office** (ATO; ☎ 13 28 61; www .ato.gov.au). To lodge a tax return, you will need your TFN and also a Group Certificate (an official summary of your earnings and tax payments) provided by your employer – give them written advice at least 14 days in advance that you want the certificate on your last day at work, otherwise you may have to wait until the end of the financial year.

You should lodge your tax return by 31 October, unless you have been granted an extension to lodge at a later date. If you leave Australia permanently before the end of the tax year the Australian Tax Office may accept an early lodgement (ie before June 30). It can take up to six weeks to process your tax return, so make sure you write an address on your tax return where it can send your notice of assessment.

It's important to bear in mind that you are not entitled to a refund for the tax you paid – you will only receive a refund if too much tax was withheld from your pay. If you didn't pay enough while you were working then you will have to pay more. You are, however, entitled to any superannuation that has been deducted from your pay. You may hear rumours of a 'harvest tax' – ignore them – this doesn't exist and you aren't eligible for a great refund by doing harvest work.

For more information contact the ATO, which can provide advice over the phone and has an informative website. Another good website is www.taxsites.com/international /australia.html.

TAX FILE NUMBER

If you have a WHM visa, you should apply for a TFN. Without it, tax will be deducted from any wages you receive at the maximum rate. Apply for a TFN online via the ATO; it takes about four weeks to be issued.

Volunteering

Mainly involved in recruiting Australians to work overseas, **Australian Volunteers International** (AVI; ☎ 1800 331 282, 03-9279 1788; www .australianvolunteers.com) does also place skilled volunteers into Aboriginal communities in northern and central Australia. Most of the placements are paid contracts for a minimum of a year and you will need an appropriate work visa. There are, however, occasional short-term placements, especially in the medical or accounting fields, and short-term unskilled jobs, usually helping out at community-run roadhouses.

In Tasmania you can volunteer for the state's Parks and Wildlife Service – see p633. A similar vehicle for environmental volunteering is **Conservation Volunteers Australia** (CVA; ☎ 1800 032 501, 03-5330 2600; www.conservationvolun teers.com.au), a nonprofit organisation focussing on practical conservation projects such as tree planting, walking-track construction, and flora and fauna surveys. It's an excellent way to get involved with conservation-minded people and visit some interesting areas of the country. Most projects are either for a weekend or a week and all food, transport and accommodation is supplied in return for a small contribution to help cover costs ($40 per day, $210 per week).

Willing Workers on Organic Farms (WWOOF; ☎ 03-5155 0218; www.wwoof.com.au) is well established in Australia. The idea is that you do a few hours work each day on a farm in return for bed and board, often in a family home. Almost all places have a minimum stay of two nights. As the name states, the farms are supposed to be organic (including permaculture and biodynamic growing), but that isn't always so. Some places aren't even farms – you might help out at a pottery or do the books at a seed wholesaler. Whether participants in the scheme have a farm or just a vegie patch, most are concerned to some extent with alternative lifestyles. You can join online or through various WWOOF agents (see the website for details) for a fee of $60/70 per single/couple. You'll get a membership number and a booklet that lists participating enterprises. If you need these posted overseas, add another $5.

The **Earthwatch Institute** (www.earthwatch.org) offers volunteer 'expeditions' that focus on conservation and wildlife.

STA (www.statravel.com.au) is another great resource for international travellers seeking volunteer holiday opportunities in Australia – click on 'Experiences' on their website and go to the volunteer link. Lonely Planet's *Volunteer: A Traveller's Guide to Making a Difference Around the World* also provides useful information about volunteering.

Other useful organisations:

Go Volunteer (www.govolunteer.com.au) National website listing volunteer opportunities.

i-to-i (www.i-to-i.com) Conservation-based volunteer holidays in Australia.

Nature Conservation Society of South Australia (www.ncssa.asn.au) Survey fieldwork volunteer opportunities in SA.

Reef Watch (www.reefwatch.asn.au) Surveys sightings of introduced marine pests and endangered native species.

Responsible Travel (www.responsibletravel.com) Volunteer travel opportunities.

Scientific Expedition Group (www.communitywebs .org/scientificexpeditiongroup) Loads of different scientific and cultural data collection volunteer opportunities in SA.

Threatened Species Network SA (www.wwf.org .au/tsn) Volunteer opportunities in SA focusing on the monitoring and conservation of threatened species.

Volunteering Australia (www.volunteeringaustralia .org) Support, advice and volunteer training.

Transport

CONTENTS

> **THINGS CHANGE...**
>
> The information in this chapter is particularly vulnerable to change. Check directly with the airline or a travel agent to make sure you understand how a fare (and ticket you may buy) works and be aware of the security requirements for international travel. Shop carefully. The details given in this chapter should be regarded as pointers and are not a substitute for your own careful, up-to-date research.

GETTING THERE & AWAY

They don't call Australia the land 'down under' for nothing. It's a long way from just about everywhere, and getting here is usually going to mean a long-haul flight. That 'over the horizon' feeling doesn't stop once you're here, either – the distances between key cities (much less opposing coastlines) can be vast, requiring a minimum of an hour or two of air time but up to several days of highway cruising or dirt-road jostling to traverse.

ENTERING THE COUNTRY

Disembarkation in Australia is a straightforward affair, with only the usual customs declarations (p1026) and the fight to be first to the luggage carousel to endure. However, global instability in the last few years has resulted in conspicuously increased security in Australian airports, and you may find that customs procedures are now more time-consuming.

Passport

There are no restrictions when it comes to citizens of foreign countries entering Australia. If you have a visa (p1040), you should be fine.

AIR

There are lots of competing airlines and a wide variety of air fares to choose from if you're flying in from Asia, Europe or North America, but you'll still pay a lot for a flight.

Because of Australia's size and diverse climate, any time of year can prove busy for inbound tourists – if you plan to fly at a particularly popular time of year (Christmas is notoriously difficult for Sydney and Melbourne) or on a particularly popular route (such as Hong Kong, Bangkok or Singapore to Sydney or Melbourne), make your arrangements well in advance of your trip.

The high season for flights into Australia is roughly over the country's summer (December to February), with slightly less of a premium on fares over the shoulder months (October/ November and March/April). The low season generally tallies with the winter months (June to August), though this is actually the peak tourist season in central Australia and the Top End.

Airports & Airlines

Australia has several international gateways, with Sydney and Melbourne being the busiest. The full list of international airports follows.

Adelaide (code ADL; ☎ 08-8308 9211; www.aal.com.au)
Brisbane (code BNE; ☎ 07-3406 3000; www.brisbaneairport.com.au)
Cairns (code CNS; ☎ 07-4080 6703; www.cairnsport.com.au/airport)
Darwin (code DRW; ☎ 08-8920 1811; www.ntapl.com.au)
Melbourne (Tullamarine; code MEL; ☎ 03-9297 1600; www.melbourneairport.com.au)
Perth (code PER; ☎ 08-9478 8888; www.perthairport.net.au)
Sydney (Kingsford Smith; code SYD; ☎ 02-9667 9111; www.sydneyairport.com.au)

CLIMATE CHANGE & TRAVEL

Climate change is a serious threat to the ecosystems that humans rely upon, and air travel is the fastest-growing contributor to the problem. Lonely Planet regards travel, overall, as a global benefit, but believes we all have a responsibility to limit our personal impact on global warming.

Flying & Climate Change

Pretty much every form of motor travel generates CO_2 (the main cause of human-induced climate change) but planes are far and away the worst offenders, not just because of the sheer distances they allow us to travel, but because they release greenhouse gases high into the atmosphere. The statistics are frightening: two people taking a return flight between Europe and the US will contribute as much to climate change as an average household's gas and electricity consumption over a whole year.

Carbon Offset Schemes

Climatecare.org and other websites use 'carbon calculators' that allow jetsetters to offset the greenhouse gases they are responsible for with contributions to energy-saving projects and other climate-friendly initiatives in the developing world – including projects in India, Honduras, Kazakhstan and Uganda.

Lonely Planet, together with Rough Guides and other concerned partners in the travel industry, supports the carbon offset scheme run by climatecare.org. Lonely Planet offsets all of its staff and author travel.

For more information check out our website: lonelyplanet.com.

Australia's international carrier Qantas flies chiefly to runways across Europe, North America, Asia and the Pacific.

Airlines that fly in and out of Australia include the following (all phone numbers listed here are for dialling from within Australia).

Air Canada (airline code AC; ☎ 1300 655 767; www .aircanada.ca)

Air New Zealand (airline code NZ; ☎ 13 24 76; www .airnz.com.au)

Air Pacific (airline code FJI; ☎ 1800 230 150; www .airpacific.com)

American Airlines (airline code AAL: ☎ 1800 673 486; www.aa.com)

British Airways (airline code BA; ☎ 1300 767 177; www.britishairways.com)

Cathay Pacific (airline code CX; ☎ 13 17 47; www .cathaypacific.com)

Emirates (airline code EK; ☎ 1300 303 777; www .emirates.com)

Garuda Indonesia (airline code GA; ☎ 1300 365 330; www.garuda-indonesia.com)

Hawaiian Airlines (airline code HA; ☎ 1300 669 106; www.hawaiianairlines.com.au)

Japan Airlines (airline code JL; ☎ 1300 525 287; www .jal.com)

Jetstar (airline code JST; ☎ 131 538; www.jetstar.com)

KLM (airline code KL; ☎ 1300 392 192; www.klm.com)

Korean Air (airline code KAL; ☎ 02-9262 6000; www .koreanair.com)

Lufthansa (airline code LH; ☎ 1300 655 727; www .lufthansa.com)

Malaysia Airlines (airline code MH; ☎ 13 26 27; www .malaysiaairlines.com)

Pacific Blue (airline code DJ; ☎ 13 16 45; www .flypacificblue.com)

Qantas (airline code QF; ☎ 13 13 13; www.qantas .com.au)

Royal Brunei Airlines (airline code BI; ☎ 1300 721 271; www.bruneiair.com)

Singapore Airlines (airline code SQ; ☎ 13 10 11; www.singaporeair.com.au)

South African Airways (airline code SA; ☎ 1300 435 972; www.flysaa.com)

Thai Airways International (airline code TG; ☎ 1300 651 960; www.thaiairways.com.au)

Tiger Airways (airline code TR; ☎ 03-9335 3033; www .tigerairways.com)

United Airlines (airline code UA; ☎ 13 17 77; www .unitedairlines.com.au)

Tickets

Automated online ticket sales work well if you're doing a simple one-way or return trip on specified dates, but are no substitute for a travel agent with the low-down on special deals, strategies for avoiding stopovers and other useful advice.

Paying by credit card offers some protection if you unwittingly end up dealing with a rogue fly-by-night agency, as most card is-suers provide refunds if you can prove you didn't get what you paid for. Alternatively, buy a ticket from a bonded agent, such as one covered by the **Air Travel Organiser's Licence** (ATOL; www.atol.org.uk) scheme in the UK. If you have doubts about the service provider, at the very least call the airline and confirm that your booking has been made.

CIRCLE PACIFIC TICKETS
A Circle Pacific ticket is similar to a round-the-world (RTW) ticket but covers a more limited region, using a combination of airlines to connect Australia, New Zealand, North America and Asia, with stopover options in the Pacific islands. As with RTW tickets, there are restrictions on how many stopovers you can take.

ROUND THE WORLD (RTW) TICKETS
If you are flying to Australia from the other side of the world, RTW tickets can be real bargains. They're generally put together by the three biggest airline alliances – **Star Alliance** (www.staralliance.com), **Oneworld** (www.oneworldalliance .com) and **Skyteam** (www.skyteam.com) – and give you a limited period (usually a year) in which to circumnavigate the globe. You can go anywhere the participating airlines go, as long as you stay within the prescribed kilometre extents or number of stops and don't backtrack when flying between continents. Backtracking is generally permitted within a single continent, though with certain restrictions; see the relevant websites for details.

An alternative type of RTW ticket is one put together by a travel agent. These used to be more expensive but individual airlines are increasingly teaming up to make this a competitive option to the large alliances.

ONLINE TICKET SITES
For online ticket bookings, including RTW fares, start with the following websites:
Air Brokers (www.airbrokers.com) This US company specialises in cheap RTW tickets such as Los Angeles–Fiji–Aukland–Sydney–Bangkok–Athens–Copenhagen–Amsterdam–New York.
Cheap Flights (www.cheapflights.com) Informative site with specials, airline information and flight searches from the USA and other regions.
Cheapest Flights (www.cheapestflights.co.uk) Cheap worldwide flights from the UK; get in early for the bargains.
ebookers (www.ebookers.com) UK-based.

Expedia (www.expedia.com) Mainly USA-related but has international sites.
Flight Centre International (www.flightcentre.com) Respected operator handling direct flights, with sites for Australia, New Zealand, the UK, the USA, Canada and South Africa.
Flights.com (www.flights.com) International site for flights; offers cheap fares and an easy-to-search database.
Roundtheworldflights.com (www.roundtheworld flights.com) This excellent site allows you to build your own trips from the UK with up to six stops.
STA Travel (www.statravel.com) Prominent in international student travel but you don't have to be a student; site linked to worldwide STA sites.
Travel.com.au (www.travel.com.au) Good Australian site; look up fares and flights to/from the country.
Webjet (www.webjet.com) Great resource for booking flights out of Australia, New Zealand and the Pacific.
Zuji (www.zuji.com) Excellent online travel site with links to Asian, Indian and other sites.

Africa
Rennies Travel (www.renniestravel.com) and **STA Travel** (www.statravel.co.za) have offices throughout Southern Africa. Check their websites for branch locations.

Asia
Most Asian countries offer competitive airfare deals, but Bangkok, Singapore and Hong Kong are the best places to shop around for discount tickets.

Flights between Hong Kong and Australia are notoriously heavily booked. Flights to/from Bangkok and Singapore are often part of the longer Europe-to-Australia route so they are also in demand. Plan your preferred itinerary well in advance.

You can get cheap short-hop flights between Darwin and Indonesia, a route serviced by Garuda Indonesia and Qantas. Airnorth runs flights between Darwin and Dili, East Timor (see p1051).

Royal Brunei Airlines flies between Darwin and Bandar Seri Begawan Airport, while Malaysia Airlines flies from Kuala Lumpur.

Tiger Airways, a budget carrier, flies from Singapore to Australian cities via Darwin and Perth.

Useful agencies:
STA Travel Bangkok (☎ 02-236 0262; www.statravel .co.th); Singapore (☎ 6737 7188; www.statravel.com.sg); Hong Kong (☎ 2736 1618; www.statravel.com.hk); Tokyo (☎ 03-5391-2922; www.statravel.co.jp) A good option with numerous offices throughout Asia.

No 1 Travel (☎ 03-3205-6073; www.no1-travel.com)
In Japan.
Four Seas Tours (☎ 2200 7760; www.fourseastravel
.com/english) In Hong Kong.

Canada

The air routes from Canada are similar to
those from mainland USA, with most Toronto
and Vancouver flights stopping in one US
city such as Los Angeles or Honolulu before
heading on to Australia.

The air fares sold by Canadian discount
air-ticket sellers (consolidators) tend to be
about 10% higher than those sold in the USA.
Travel Cuts (☎ 866-246-9762; www.travelcuts.com) is
Canada's national student travel agency and
has offices in all major cities.

Continental Europe

From major European destinations, most
flights travel to Australia via one of the
Asian capitals. Some flights are also routed
through London before arriving in Australia
via Singapore, Bangkok, Hong Kong or Kuala
Lumpur.

Recommended agencies in Germany:
Adventure Travel (www.adventure-holidays.com)
Expedia (www.expedia.de)
Lastminute (☎ 01805-284 366; www.lastminute.de)
STA Travel (☎ 069-743 032 92; www.statravel.de) For
travellers under the age of 26 years.

In France:
Anyway (☎ 08 92 30 23 01; http://voyages.anyway
.com)
Lastminute (☎ 04 66 92 30 29; www.lastminute.fr)
Odysia (www.odysia.fr)
Nouvelles Frontiéres (☎ 01 49 20 65 87; www
.nouvelles-frontieres.fr)
Enjoy France (www.enjoyfrance.com) Also a useful site
for finding individual travel agencies in France.
Voyageurs du Monde (www.vdm.com/vdm)

In the Netherlands:
Airfair (☎ 09007717717; www.airfair.nl)
BarronTravel (www.barron.nl)
Holland International (www.hollandinternational.nl)
Wereldcontact (☎ 0885305305; www.wereld
contact.nl)

A recommended agent in Italy is **CTS Viaggi**
(☎ 06 44 11 11; www.cts.it), specialising in student
and youth travel.

In Spain try **Barcelo Viajes** (☎ 902 20 04 00; www
.barceloviajes.com).

India

STIC Travels (www.stictravel.com) Delhi (☎ 11-462 06
600); Mumbai (☎ 22-221 82 628) Has offices in dozens of
Indian cities.

Middle East

Recommended agencies:
Al-Rais Travels (☎ 800 25 7247; www.alrais.com) In
Dubai.
Egypt Panorama Tours (☎ 2-2359 0200; www
.eptours.com) In Cairo.
Israel Student Travel Association (ISTA; ☎ 03-777
7111; www.issta.co.il) In Jerusalem.
Orion-Tour (www.oriontour.com) In Istanbul.

New Zealand

Air New Zealand and Qantas operate a network of flights linking key New Zealand cities
with most major Australian gateway cities.
Quite a few other international airlines also
include New Zealand and Australia on their
Asia–Pacific routes.

Another trans-Tasman option is the no-
frills budget airline Freedom Air, an Air New
Zealand subsidiary that offers direct flights
between destinations on Australia's east coast
and main New Zealand cities.

Pacific Blue, a subsidiary of budget air-
line Virgin Blue, flies between Christchurch,
Auckland and Wellington and several
Australian cities, including Sydney and
Brisbane.

There's usually not a significant difference
in price between seasons, as this is a popular
route year-round.

For reasonably priced fares, try one of the
numerous branches of **Flight Centre** (☎ 0800 243
544; www.flightcentre.co.nz) and **STA Travel** (☎ 0800
474 400; www.statravel.co.nz) or **House of Travel** (www
.houseoftravel.co.nz).

South America

Recommended agencies include the
following:
ASATEJ (☎ 011 4114-7528; www.asatej.com) In
Argentina.
IVI Tours (www.ivivenezuela.com) In Venezuela.
Student Travel Bureau (☎ 0xx11-3038 1555; www
.stb.com.br) In Brazil.

UK & Ireland

There are two routes for flights from the
UK: the western route via the USA and the
Pacific; and the eastern route via the Middle
East and Asia. Flights are usually cheaper

TRANSPORT

INTERSTATE QUARANTINE

When travelling in Australia, whether by land or air, you'll come across signs (mainly in airports, in interstate train stations and at state borders) warning of the possible dangers of carrying fruit, vegetables and plants (which may be infected with a disease or pest) from one area to another. Certain pests and diseases – such as fruit fly, cucurbit thrips, grape phylloxera and potato cyst nematodes, to name a few – are prevalent in some areas but not in others, and so for obvious reasons authorities would like to limit them spreading.

There are quarantine inspection posts on some state borders and occasionally elsewhere. While quarantine control often relies on honesty, many posts are staffed and officers are entitled to search your car for undeclared items. Generally they will confiscate all fresh fruit and vegetables, so it's best to leave shopping for these items until the first town past the inspection point.

---

and more frequent on the latter route. Some of the best deals around are with Emirates, Gulf Air, Malaysia Airlines, Japan Airlines and Thai Airways International. British Airways, Singapore Airlines and Qantas generally have higher fares but may offer a more direct route.

Discount air travel is big business in London. Advertisements for travel agencies appear in the travel pages of the weekend broadsheet newspapers, in *Time Out*, in the *Evening Standard* and in the free online magazine **TNT** (www.tntmagazine.com).

At peak times such as mid-December, fares go up by as much as 30%. Recommended travel agencies (all phone numbers UK-based) include the following:

ebookers (☎ 0871 223 5000; www.ebookers.com)

Flight Centre (☎ 0870 499 0040; flightcentre.co.uk)

North-South Travel (☎ 01245-608291; www.north southtravel.co.uk) North-South Travel donate part of their profit to projects in the developing world.

Quest Travel (☎ 08745 263 6963; www.questtravel .com)

STA Travel (☎ 0871 2300 040; www.statravel.co.uk) For travellers under the age of 26.

Trailfinders (www.trailfinders.co.uk)

Travel Bag (☎ 0871 703 4700; www.travelbag.co.uk)

USA

Discount travel agents in the USA are known as consolidators (although you won't see a sign on the door saying 'Consolidator'). San Francisco is the ticket consolidator capital of America, although some good deals can be found in Los Angeles, New York and other big cities.

The following agencies are recommended for online bookings:

cheaptickets.com (www.cheaptickets.com)

expedia.com (www.expedia.com)

lowestfare.com (www.lowestfare.com)

orbitz.com (www.orbitz.com)

sta.com (www.sta.com); For travellers under 26 years of age.

travelocity.com (www.travelocity.com)

SEA

It's possible (though by no means easy or safe) to make your way between Australia and countries such as Papua New Guinea and Indonesia, and between New Zealand and Australia and some smaller Pacific islands, by hitching rides or crewing on yachts – usually you have to at least contribute towards food. Ask around at harbours, marinas and sailing clubs.

Good places on the Australian east coast include Coffs Harbour, Great Keppel Island, Airlie Beach and the Whitsundays, and Cairns – basically anywhere boats call. Darwin could yield Indonesia-bound possibilities. A lot of boats move north to escape the winter, so April is a good time to look for a berth in the Sydney area.

P&O Cruises (www.pocruises.com.au) operates holiday cruises between Brisbane or Sydney and destinations in New Zealand and the Pacific. There are no other passenger liners operating regularly to/from Australia and finding a berth on a cargo ship is difficult – that's if you actually wanted to spend months at sea aboard an enormous metal can.

GETTING AROUND

AIR

Time pressures combined with the vastness of the Australian continent may lead you to consider taking to the skies at some point in your trip. Nicotine fiends should note that all domestic flights are nonsmoking.

Both **STA Travel** (☎ 134 782; www.statravel.com.au) and **Flight Centre** (☎ 133 133; www.flightcentre.com.au) have offices throughout Australia. For online bookings, try www.travel.com.au.

Airlines in Australia

Qantas is the country's chief domestic airline, represented at the budget end by its subsidiary Jetstar. Another highly competitive carrier that flies all over Australia is Virgin Blue. Keep in mind if flying with Jetstar or Virgin Blue that these no-frills airlines close check-in 30 minutes prior to a flight.

Australia also has many smaller operators flying regional routes. In many places, such as remote outback destinations or islands, these are the only viable transport option. Many of these airlines operate as subsidiaries or commercial partners of Qantas.

Some regional airlines:

Aeropelican (☎ 02-4928 9600; www.aeropelican .com.au) Flies between Newcastle (Williamtown Airport), Inverell and Sydney.

Airnorth (☎ 1800 627 464; www.airnorth.com.au) Flies across northern Australia between Darwin, Kununurra, Broome and Gove; also flies to Perth and across the Timor Sea to Dili (East Timor) and to Denpasar (Indonesia).

Alliance Airlines (☎ 07-3212 1212; www.allianceair lines.com.au) Charter flights between Brisbane, Townsville and Cairns.

Brindabella Airlines (☎ 1300 668 824; www.brinda bellaairlines.com.au) Flies to Canberra, Albury, Newcastle, Port Macquarie, Coffs Harbour and Brisbane.

Golden Eagle Airlines (☎ 08-9172 1777; www .goldeneagleairlines.com) Offers services in the northwest of WA to destinations including Broome, Derby, Fitzroy Crossing and Halls Creek.

Jetstar (☎ 13 15 38; www.jetstar.com.au) Budget-oriented Qantas subsidiary flying to all the capital cities and around 15 east-coast destinations from Cairns to Hobart.

Macair (☎ 1300 622 247; www.macair.com.au) Commercially partnered with Qantas, this Townsville-based airline flies throughout western and northern Queensland.

Norfolk Air (☎ 1300 663 913; www.norfolkair.com) Flies from Norfolk Island to Brisbane, Melbourne, Newcastle and Sydney.

Qantas (☎ 13 13 13; www.qantas.com.au) Australia's chief domestic airline.

QantasLink (☎ 13 13 13; www.qantas.com.au) Flying across Australia under this Qantas subsidiary brand is a collective of regional airlines that includes Eastern Australia Airlines, Airlink and Sunstate Airlines.

Regional Express (Rex; ☎ 13 17 13; www.regionalex press.com.au) Flies from Sydney, Melbourne, Burnie and Adelaide to around 25 other destinations in New South Wales (NSW), Victoria, South Australia (SA) and Tasmania.

Regional Pacific Airlines (☎ 1300 797 667, 07-4040 1400; www.regionalpacific.com.au) Flies between Cairns and Bamaga and throughout the Torres Strait.

Skippers (☎ 1300 729 924; www.skippers.com.au) Flies between a half-dozen Western Australian (WA) destinations, including Perth, Laverton, Meekatharra and Wiluna.

Skytrans (☎ 1300 759 872; www.skytrans.com.au) Charter service flying from Cairns to Coen, Aurukun, Cooktown and Lockhart River.

Skywest (☎ 1300 660 088; www.skywest.com.au) Flies from Perth to western towns including Albany, Esperance, Exmouth, Carnarvon, Kalgoorlie and Broome, plus Darwin up north.

Tasair (☎ 02-6248 5088; www.tasair.com.au) Flies within Tasmania.

Tiger Airways (www.tigerairways.com) A subsidiary of Singapore Airlines, this budget carrier flies between a handful of major capital cities in Australia.

Virgin Blue (☎ 13 67 89; www.virginblue.com.au) Highly competitive, Virgin Blue flies all over Australia – Virgin fares are cheaper if booked online (discount per ticket $10).

Air Passes

With discounting being the norm these days, air passes are not great value. Qantas' **Boomerang Pass** (☎ 13 13 13) can only be purchased overseas and involves buying coupons for either short-haul flights (up to 1200km, eg Hobart to Melbourne) or multizone sectors (including New Zealand and the Pacific). You must purchase a minimum of two coupons before you arrive in Australia, and once here you can buy more.

Regional Express (Rex) has the **Rex Backpacker** (☎ 13 17 13) scheme, where international travellers clutching a VIP, YHA, ISIC, Nomad or IYTC card (Australian residents are not eligible) buy one or two months' worth of unlimited travel on the airline; it applies to standby fares only.

BICYCLE

Australia has much to offer cyclists, from leisurely bike paths winding through most major cities to thousands of kilometres of good country roads where you can wear out your chain wheels. There's lots of flat countryside and gently rolling hills to explore and although Australia is not as mountainous as say Switzerland or France, mountain bikers can find plenty of forestry trails and high country.

TRANSPORT

Bike helmets are compulsory in all states and territories, as are white front lights and red rear lights for riding at night.

If you are bringing in your own bike, check with your airline for costs and the degree of dismantling and packing required. Within Australia, bus companies require you to dismantle your bike and some don't guarantee that it will travel on the same bus as you. On trains supervise the loading (if possible tie your bike upright) and check for possible restrictions: most intercity trains carry only two to three boxed bikes per service.

Eastern Australia was settled on the principle of not having more than a day's horse ride between pubs, so it's possible to plan even ultralong routes and still get a shower at the end of each day. Most riders carry camping equipment but, on the east coast at least, it's feasible to travel from town to town staying in hostels, hotels or caravan parks.

You can get by with standard road maps but, if you want to avoid both highways and low-grade unsealed roads, the government series is best. The 1:250,000 scale is the most suitable, though you'll need a lot of maps if you're going far. The next scale up, 1:1,000,000, is adequate and is widely available in speciality map shops.

Carry plenty of water to avoid dehydration. Cycling in the summer heat can be made more endurable by wearing a helmet with a peak (or a cap under your helmet), using plenty of sunscreen, not cycling in the middle of the day, and drinking lots of water (not soft drinks). It can get very cold in the mountains, so pack appropriate clothing. In the south, beware the blistering hot northerlies that can make a north-bound cyclist's life hell in summer. The southeast trade winds begin to blow in April, when you can have (theoretically at least) tailwinds all the way to Darwin.

Outback travel needs to be properly planned, with the availability of drinking water the main concern (remember that most of the country is in a drought) – those isolated water sources (bores, tanks, creeks and the like) shown on your map may be dry or undrinkable, so you can't depend entirely on them. Also make sure you've got the necessary spare parts and bike-repair knowledge. Check with locals if you're heading into remote areas, and let someone know where you're headed before setting off.

Bicycle hire in cities is easy to access (look under Activities headings in destination chapters), but if you're planning to ride for more than a few hours or even a day it's far more economical to invest in your own set of wheels. Additionally, if you're planning to ride beyond urban areas make sure you buy a bicycle that will match the conditions.

Information

The national cycling body is the **Bicycle Federation of Australia** (☎ 02-6249 6761; www.bfa .asn.au). Each state and territory has a touring organisation that can also help with cycling information and put you in touch with touring clubs.

Bicycle New South Wales (☎ 02-9218 5400; www .bicyclensw.org.au)

Bicycle Queensland (☎ 07-3844 1144; www.bq.org.au)

Bicycle SA (☎ 08-8168 9999; www.bikesa.asn.au)

Bicycle Tasmania (www.biketas.org.au)

Bicycle Transportation Alliance (☎ 08-9420 7210; www.btawa.org.au) In WA.

Bicycle Victoria (☎ 03-8636 8888; www.bv.com.au)

Northern Territory Cycling Association (www .nt.cycling.org.au)

Pedal Power ACT (☎ 02-6248 7995; www.pedalpower .org.au)

Purchase

If you arrive in the country without a set of wheels and want to buy a reliable new road cycle or mountain bike, your absolute bottom-level starting point is $500 to $650. To set yourself up with a new bike, plus all the requisite on-the-road equipment such as panniers, helmet etc, your starting point becomes $1500 to $2000. Secondhand bikes are worth checking out in the cities, as are the post-Christmas sales and midyear stocktakes, when newish cycles can be heavily discounted.

Your best bet for reselling your bike is via the **Trading Post** (www.tradingpost.com.au), which is distributed in newspaper form in many urban centres and also has a busy online trading site.

BOAT

There's a hell of a lot of water around Australia but unless you're fortunate enough to hook up with a yacht, it's not a feasible way of getting around. The only regular passenger services of note are run by **TT-Line** (☎ 1800 634 906; www .spiritoftasmania.com.au), which dispatches two high-speed, vehicle-carrying ferries – *Spirit of Tasmania I* and *II* – between Devonport and Melbourne. See p635 for more details.

(Continued on page 1069)

Road Maps

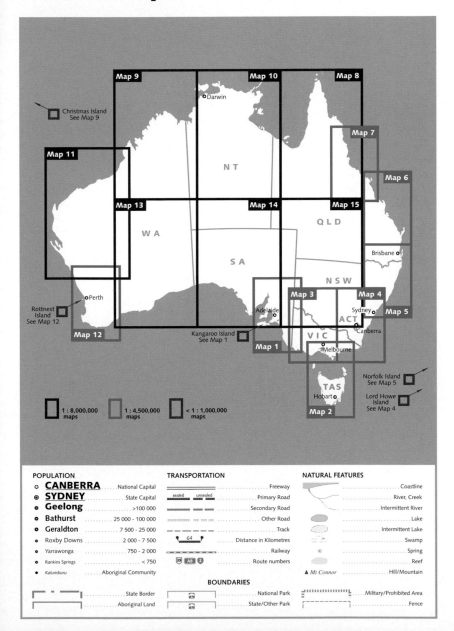

Map 9

Christmas Island
See Map 9

Darwin

Map 10

Map 8

Map 7

Map 11

N T

Map 6

Map 13

Map 14

Map 15

Q L D

W A

S A

Brisbane

N S W

Map 3

Map 4

Perth

Adelaide

Sydney

Map 5

Rottnest
Island
See Map 12

ACT

Canberra

Map 12

Kangaroo Island
See Map 1

V I C

Map 1

Melbourne

Norfolk Island
See Map 5

TAS

Hobart

Lord Howe
Island
See Map 4

Map 2

1 : 8,000,000
maps

1 : 4,500,000
maps

< 1 : 1,000,000
maps

POPULATION

⊙	**CANBERRA**	National Capital
◉	**SYDNEY**	State Capital
●	**Geelong**	>100 000
●	**Bathurst**	25 000 - 100 000
●	**Geraldton**	7 500 - 25 000
●	Roxby Downs	2 000 - 7 500
●	Yarrawonga	750 - 2 000
●	Rankins Springs	< 750
●	*Kalumburu*	Aboriginal Community

State Border

Aboriginal Land

TRANSPORTATION

Freeway

sealed   unsealed   Primary Road

Secondary Road

Other Road

Track

64   Distance in Kilometres

Railway

39 A8 2   Route numbers

BOUNDARIES

National Park

State/Other Park

NATURAL FEATURES

Coastline

River, Creek

Intermittent River

Lake

Intermittent Lake

Swamp

Spring

Reef

▲ *Mt Connor*   Hill/Mountain

Military/Prohibited Area

Fence

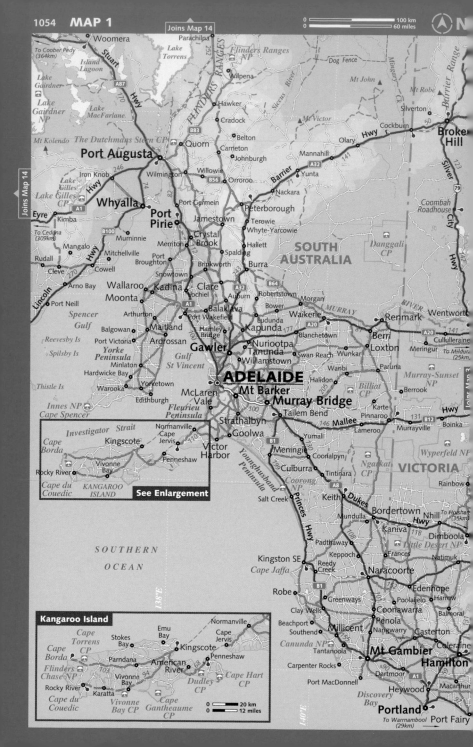

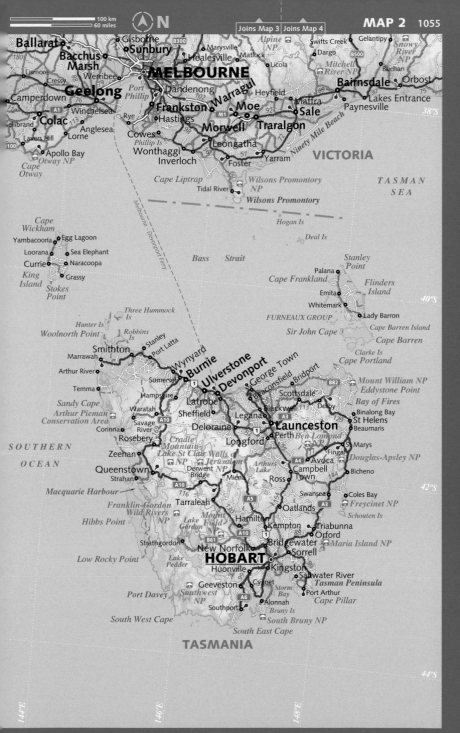

MAP 2 1055

100 km
60 miles

N

Ballarat
Bacchus
Marsh
Werribee
Lismore
Cressy
Camperdown
Winchelsea
Colac
Anglesea
Lorne
Lavers Hill
Apollo Bay
Cape
Otway
Otway NP
Ellibrand
Geelong

Gisborne
Sunbury
Marysville
Healesville
Matlock
MELBOURNE
Dandenong
Frankston
Hastings
Rye
Cowes
Phillip Is
Wonthaggi
Inverloch
Port
Phillip

Alpine
NP
Swifts Creek
Gelantipy
Dargo
Licola
Heyfield
Warragul
Moe
Morwell
Traralgon
Leongatha
Foster
Yarram
Maffra
Sale
Traralgon

Snowy
River
NP
Buchan
Bairnsdale
Orbost
Lakes Entrance
Paynesville
Mitchell
River NP

Ninety Mile Beach

VICTORIA

Cape Liptrap
Tidal River
Wilsons Promontory
NP
Wilsons Promontory

TASMAN
SEA

Hogan Is
Deal Is

Cape
Wickham
Yambacoona
Egg Lagoon
Loorana
Sea Elephant
Currie
Naracoopa
King
Island
Grassy
Stokes
Point

Bass   Strait

Stanley
Point
Palana
Cape Frankland
Emita
Whitemark
Flinders
Island
Lady Barron
FURNEAUX GROUP
Sir John Cape
Cape Barren Island
Cape Barren

Three Hummock
Is
Hunter Is
Woolnooth Point
Robbins
Is
Stanley
Port Latta
Smithton
Marrawah
Arthur River
Temma
Sandy Cape
Arthur Pieman
Conservation Area
Corinna

SOUTHERN

OCEAN

Zeehan
Queenstown
Strahan
Macquarie Harbour
Franklin-Gordon
Wild Rivers
NP
Hibbs Point
Tarraleah
Strathgordon
Low Rocky Point

Wynyard
Burnie
Ulverstone
Devonport
Somerset
George Town
Beaconsfield
Bridport
Scottsdale
Derby
Latrobe
Blackwall 113
Sheffield
Legana
Launceston
Deloraine
Perth
Longford
Cradle
Mountain-
Lake St Clair
NP
Jerusalem
NP
Derwent
Bridge
Miena
Arthurs
Lake
Ross
Campbell
Town
Avoca
Fingal
St Marys
Bicheno
Lake
Gordon
Mount
Field
Hamilton
Kempton
Oatlands
Swansea
Coles Bay
Freycinet NP
Schouten Is
Lake
Pedder
New Norfolk
Bridgewater
Sorrell
Triabunna
Orford
Maria Island NP
HOBART
Huonville
Kingston
Salt water River
Tasman Peninsula
Port Arthur
Cape Pillar
Geeveston
Cygnet
Storm
Bay
Alonnah
Southport
Bruny Is
South Bruny NP
Southwest
NP
Port Davey
South West Cape
South East Cape

Clarke Is
Cape Portland
Mount William NP
Eddystone Point
Bay of Fires
Binalong Bay
St Helens
Beaumaris
Ben Lomond
NP
Douglas-Apsley NP

TASMANIA

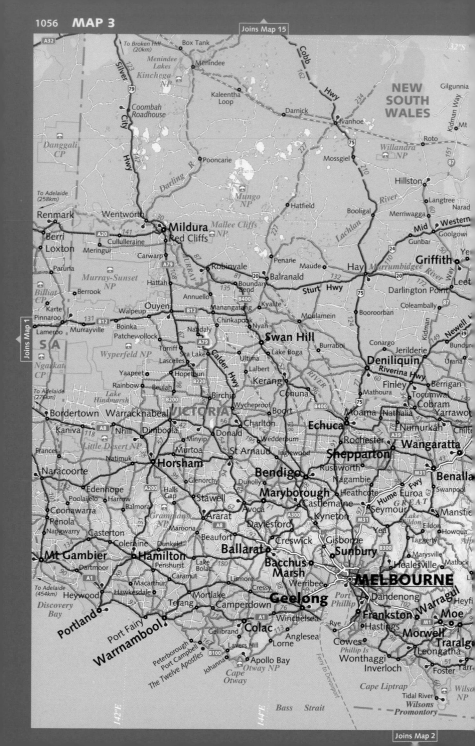

Joins Map 15

Joins Map 1

Joins Map 2

MAP 4 1057

100 km
60 miles

N

Joins Map 15 | Joins Map 5

Joins Map 5

To Tamworth
(15km)

Warren
Buddabaddah
Nevertire
Gilgandra
Breelong
Binnaway
Quirindi
Weetaliba
Coolah Tops
NP
Ben Halls Gap NP
Woko NP
ymagee
Tabratong
Trangie
Mitchell Hwy
Eumungerie
Mendooran
Coolah
Dunedoo
Cassilis
Merriwa
Gungal
Murrurundi
Barrington
Wingen Tops
NP
Scone
Gloucester
badah
Tottenham
Narromine
Dubbo
Birriwa
Turill
Baerami
Denman
Muswellbrook
Kerein Hills
Tullamore
Toongi
Wellington
Gulgong
Mudgee
Breakfast Creek
Rylstone
Olinda
Dungog
Stroud
Fifield
Peak Hill
Tomingley
Yeoval
Stuart
Town
Sallys
Flat
Ilford
Glen Alice
Wollemi
NP
Singleton
Maitland
Raymond
Terrace
Condobolin
Trundle
Goonumbla
Parkes
Molong
Sofala
Capertee
Cessnock
Newcastle
Euabalong
ke Cargelligo
Forbes
Orange
Bathurst
Wallerawang
Lithgow
Yenga NP
Wyong
Gosford
Swansea
bigeal
Bena
Canowindra
Cargo
Blayney
Rockley
Katoomba
Lawson
Blue Mountains
NP
Windsor
Penrith
Toukley
Ungarie
Yalgogrin
West
Wyalong
Marsden
Caragabal
Grenfell
Trunkey
Creek
Tuena
Camden
Picton
Bargo
Helensburgh
Stanwell Park
SYDNEY
rellan
Barmedman
Quandialla
Bribbaree
Young
Godfreys
Creek
Crookwell
Bowral
Moss
Vale
Wollongong
34°S
narah
Grogan
Wombat
Boorowa
Marulan
Kiama
Temora
Coolamon
Cootamundra
Goulburn
Yass
Murrumbateman
Tarago
Nowra
Shoalhaven Heads
Junee
Olympic
Gundagai
CANBERRA
Queanbeyan
Huskisson
Sussex Inlet
To Lord Howe
Island (800km)
NB: distance taken
from Sydney.
See map below
Wagga Wagga
Forest
Hill
Tarcutta
Tumut
Talbingo
Braidwood
Michelago
Araluen
Ulladulla
Bawley Point
TASMAN
Henty
Kyeamba
Batlow
Namadgi
NP
Bredbo
Batemans Bay
Malua Bay
Mossy Point
SEA
Holbrook
Tumbarumba
Towong
Kiandra
Moruya
Albury
Wodonga
Tallangatta
Corryong
Adaminaby
Mt Kosciuszko
(2228m)
Cooma
Jindabyne
Bodalla
Tuross Head
Narooma
36°S
echworth
Myrtleford
Benambra
Thredbo
Nimmitabel
Wadbilliga
NP
Bermagui
Cobargo
Mt Bogong
(1986m)
Hotham
Heights
Omeo
Suggan Buggan
Candelo
Bega
Tathra
Swifts Creek
Dargo
Gelantipy
Delegate
River
South East
Forests
NP
Bombala
Merimbula
Pambula
Eden
Mitchell
River NP
Buchan
Cann
River
Genoa
Narrabarba
152°E
Bairnsdale
Orbost
Cape Howe
Croajingolong NP
38°S
Maffra
Sale
Paynesville
Lakes Entrance
Point
Hicks
Ninety Mile Beach
romontory

Lord Howe Island

Admiralty
Islands
0 2 km
0 1 mile
31°30'S
North
Head
Clear Place
Point
Blackburn
Island
Transit Hill
(120m)
The Lagoon
Mutton
Bird Is
Mt Lidgbird
(777m)
East
Point
Mt Gower
(875m)
31°35'S
King Point
159°05'E

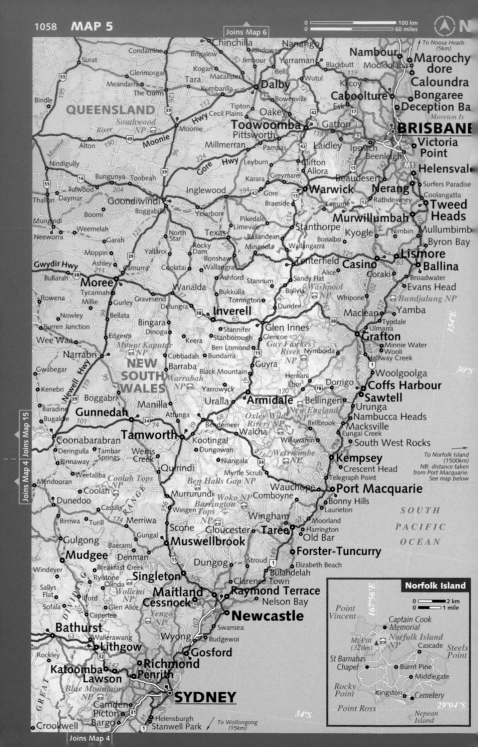

Joins Map 6

100 km
60 miles

N

MAP 6 1059

100 km
60 miles

N

To Townsville
(140km)
Cape Upstart NP

Bowen
Delta

Mt Aberdeen NP

Airlie
Beach

Hayman Is

THE
WHITSUNDAY
ISLANDS

Whitsunday Island

Proserpine
Collinsville

Conway NP

Hamilton Is
Lindeman Is

Midge Point

Bloomsbury

Yalboroo
Calen

Brampton Is

Mt Sugarloaf
Eungella NP

Newlands
Coal Mine
Eungella

Seaforth

Walkerston
Bucasia

Mackay

Glenden
Elphinstone

Sarina Beach

Sarina
Koumala

Nebo

Ilbilbie

NORTHUMBERLAND
ISLANDS

Peak Downs

Dipperu NP

Moranbah

Clairview
Kalarka

Stanage

Shoalwater Bay

Cape Townshend

Coxens
Peak

St Lawrence

Dysart

SHOALWATER BAY
MILITARY
TRAINING AREA

Cape Clinton

Ogmore

Middlemount

Bruce

Marlborough

Byfield

Byfield NP

Tieri

Hwy

CORAL
SEA

SOUTH
PACIFIC
OCEAN

20°S

Great Barrier Reef Marine Park

GREAT

BARRIER

REEF

Swain Reefs

22°S

Emerald

Blackwater

Capricorn

Comet

Foleyvale

The Caves

Yeppoon

Emu Park

Great Keppel Island

Hwy

Dingo

Gracemere

Rockhampton

Westwood
Bouldercombe

Mt Morgan
Marmor

Duaringa

Blackdown
Tableland
NP

Wowan

Dululu

Raglan

Mt Larcom

Cape Capricorn

Curtis
Island

Gladstone

Tannum Sands

Tropic of Capricorn

Bunker Group

24°S

Lady Elliot Is

Woorabinda

Rannes

Calliope

Rolleston

Baralaba
Goovigen

Callide

Turkey Beach

Dawson

Banana

Biloela

Bororen

Town of 1770
Agnes Water

Mt Carnarvon

Moura
Thangool

Nagoorin

Mt Nicholson

Kianga

Burnett

Cania

Miriam
Vale

Lowmead

Rosedale

Carnarvon
NP

Expedition
NP

Theodore

Hwy

Isla Gorge
NP

Kalpawar
Monto

Lake
Monduran

Gin Gin

Wolca

Burnett Heads

Bundaberg

Cooloola
(Great
Sandy)
NP

Mt Bassett

Roma
Wallumbilla

Lake
Wuruma

Cracow

Eidsvold

Coldalba

Booyal

Hervey Bay

Childers

Dallarnil

Hervey
Bay

Fraser
Island

Taroom

Mundubbera

Torbanlea

Maryborough

Injune
Gunnewin

Lake
Boondooma

Windera

Gayndah

Tiaro
Gundiah

Tin Can Bay

Mt Eumamurran

Tansey

Gunalda

Rainbow
Beach

Wandoan

Guluguba

QUEENSLAND

Barakula

Dulacca

Murgon
Wondai

Goomeri
Cherbourg

Gympie

Warrego
Yuleba

Fairyland

Durong

Noosa
Heads

To
Brisbane
(105km)

To St George
(120km)

Miles

Columboola

Chinchilla

Kingaroy

Jandowae

Cooroy

Tewantin

Condamine

Brigalow

Nanango

Nambour

Joins Map 5

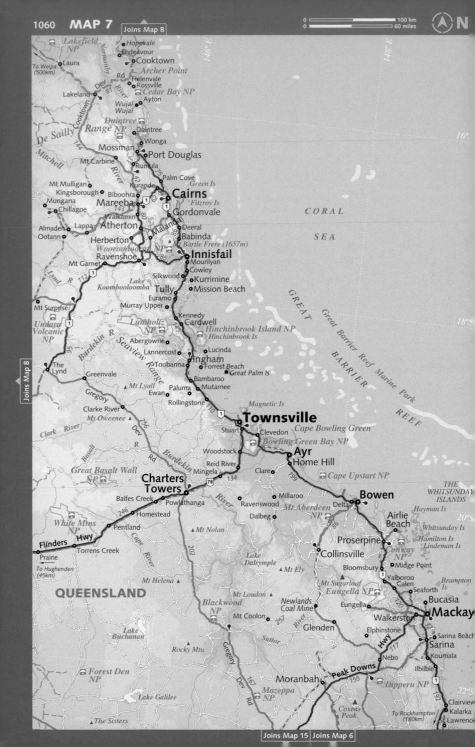

Joins Map 8

100 km
60 miles

N

Lakefield NP

To Weipa (500km)

Hopevale
Endeavour
Laura
Cooktown
Archer Point
Lakeland
Helenvale
Rossville
Cedar Bay NP
Ayton
Wujal Wujal
Daintree Range NP
Daintree
Wonga
Mossman
Port Douglas
Mt Carbine
Rumula
Palm Cove
Mt Mulligan
Kuranda
Green Is
Kingsborough
Biboohra
Cairns
Mungana
Mareeba
Gordonvale
Chillagoe
Fitzroy Is
Walkamin
Atherton
Deeral
Almaden
Herberton
Babinda
Mt Bartle Frere (1657m)
Ootann
Wooroonooran NP
Innisfail
Lappa
Ravenshoe
Mourilyan
Mt Garnet
Cowley
Silkwood
Kurrimine
Lake Koombooloomba
Tully
Mission Beach
Euramo
Mt Surprise
Murray Upper
Kennedy
Undara Volcanic NP
Lumholtz NP
Cardwell
Abergowrie
Hinchinbrook Island NP
Hinchinbrook Is
Lannercost
Lucinda
Seaview Range
Toobanna
Ingham
The Lynd
Greenvale
Forrest Beach
Bambaroo
Great Palm Is
Mt Lyall
Paluma
Mutarnee
Ewan
Rollingstone
Gregory
Clarke River
Magnetic Is
Mt Oweenee
Townsville
Stuart
Cape Bowling Green
Clevedon
Bowling Green Bay NP
Woodstock
Ayr
Reid River
Home Hill
Mingela
Clare
Cape Upstart NP
Charters Towers
134
Millaroo
Bowen
Balfes Creek
Powlathanga
Ravenswood
Mt Aberdeen NP
Delta
THE WHITSUNDAY ISLANDS
Dalbeg
Hayman Is
White Mtns NP
Homestead
Mt Nolan
Airlie Beach
Pentland
Whitsunday Is
Flinders Hwy
Proserpine
Hamilton Is
Lindeman Is
Prairie
Torrens Creek
Collinsville
Conway NP
To Hughenden (45km)
Lake Dalrymple
Mt Ely
Bloomsbury
Brampton Is
Yalboroo
Calen
Mt Helena
QUEENSLAND
Eungella NP
Seaforth
Mt Sugarloaf
Blackwood NP
Mt Loudon
Newlands Coal Mine
Eungella
Bucasia
Mt Coolon
Walkerston
Mackay
Lake Buchanan
Glenden
Elphinstone
Sarina Beach
Rocky Mtn
Sarina
Nebo
Koumala
Forest Den NP
Lake Galilee
Peak Downs
Ilbilbie
Moranbah
Mazeppa NP
Dipperu NP
The Sisters
Coxens Peak
To Rockhampton (180km)
Clairview
Kalarka
St Lawrence

CORAL SEA

Great Barrier Reef Marine Park

GREAT BARRIER REEF

Joins Map 15 | Joins Map 6

Joins Map 8

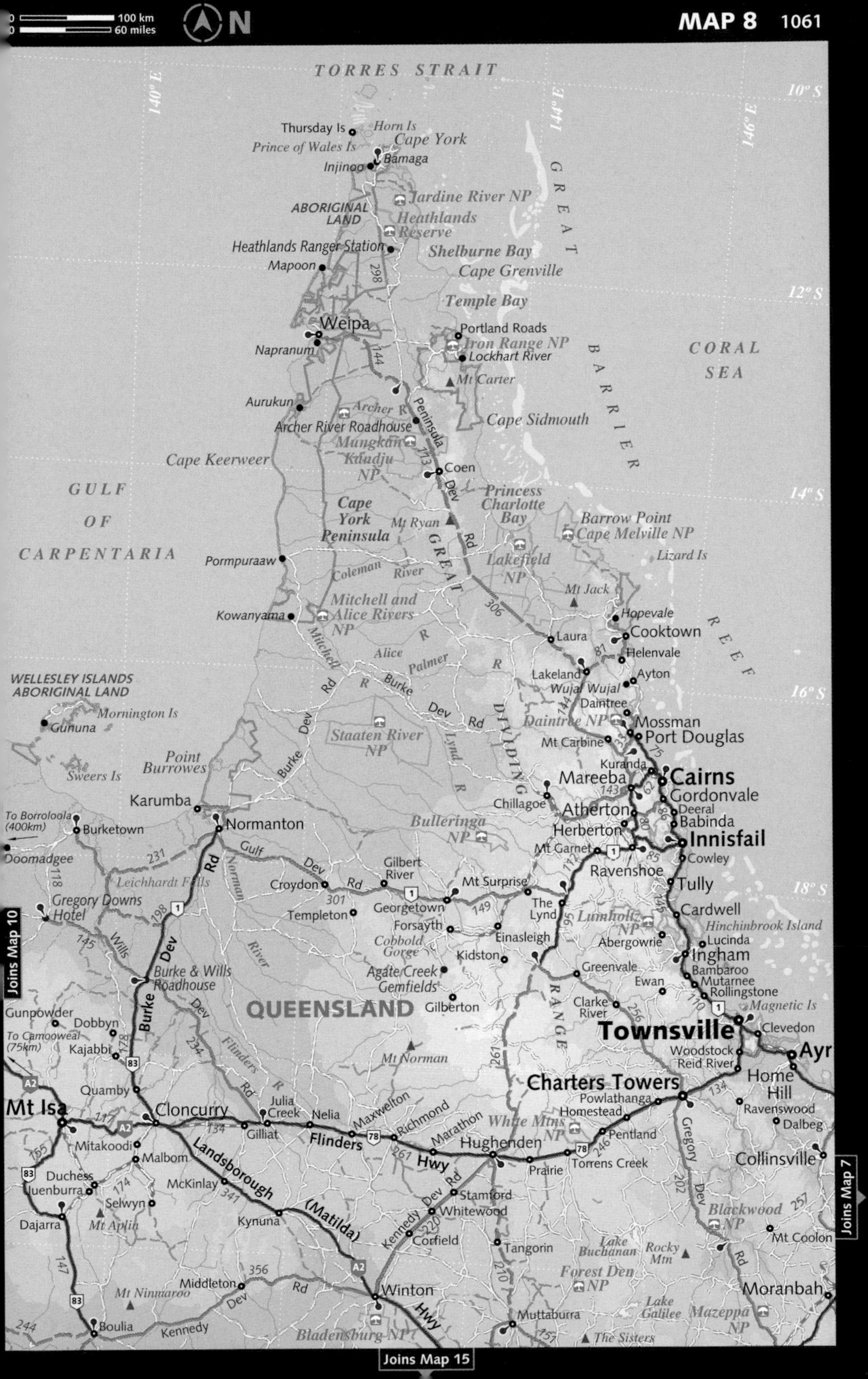

MAP 8 1061

100 km
60 miles

N

TORRES STRAIT

10° S

Thursday Is Horn Is Cape York
Prince of Wales Is
Injinoo Bamaga

Jardine River NP
ABORIGINAL Heathlands
LAND Reserve

Heathlands Ranger Station Shelburne Bay
Mapoon Cape Grenville

12° S

Temple Bay

Weipa Portland Roads
Iron Range NP
Napranum Lockhart River

Mt Carter

CORAL
SEA

Aurukun Archer R
Archer River Roadhouse Mangkan
Kaladju
NP Coen

Cape Keerweer Cape Sidmouth

Princess
Charlotte
Bay Barrow Point
Cape Melville NP

14° S

GULF Cape
OF York
CARPENTARIA Peninsula Mt Ryan
Pormpuraaw Lizard Is
Lakefield
NP
Coleman River

Mitchell and Mt Jack
Kowanyama Alice Rivers
NP Alice

WELLESLEY ISLANDS
ABORIGINAL LAND Palmer Hopevale
Cooktown
Mornington Is Laura Helenvale
Gununa Burke Lakeland Ayton
Wuja Wujal
Sweers Is Point Daintree
Burrowes Mt Carbine Daintree NP
Karumba Staaten River Mossman
NP Port Douglas
To Borroloola Kuranda
(400km) Normanton Mareeba Cairns
Burketown Chillagoe Gordonvale
Doomadgee Bulleringa Atherton Deeral
NP Herberton Babinda
Gregory Downs Gilbert Mt Garnet Innisfail
Hotel River Mt Surprise Cowley
Croydon Ravenshoe Tully
Georgetown The
Gunpowder Templeton Forsayth Lynd Lumholtz Cardwell
To Camooweal Cobbold NP Hinchinbrook Island
(75km) Dobbyn Gorge Einasleigh Abergowrie Lucinda
Kajabbi Burke & Wills Agate Creek Kidston Ingham
Roadhouse Gemfields Greenvale Bambaroo
Gilberton Mutarnee
Quamby QUEENSLAND Ewan Rollingstone
Mt Norman Clarke Magnetic Is
Mt Isa River Townsville Clevedon
Mitakoodi Woodstock Ayr
Malbom Reid River Home
Duchess Cloncurry Charters Towers Hill
Juenburra McKinlay Powlathanga Ravenswood
Selwyn Julia Nelia Homestead Dalbeg
Dajarra Mt Aplin Creek Maxwelton Pentland
Gilliat Richmond Collinsville
Flinders Marathon White Mtns
Landsborough Hughenden NP Torrens Creek
Kynuna Prairie
(Matilda) Stamford Blackwood
Whitewood NP Mt Coolon
Middleton Corfield
Boulia Tangorin Lake Rocky Moranbah
Buchanan Mtn
Winton Forest Den Lake
NP Galilee Mazeppa
Mt Ninmaroo Muttaburra NP
Bladensburg NP The Sisters

Joins Map 10
Joins Map 7
Joins Map 15

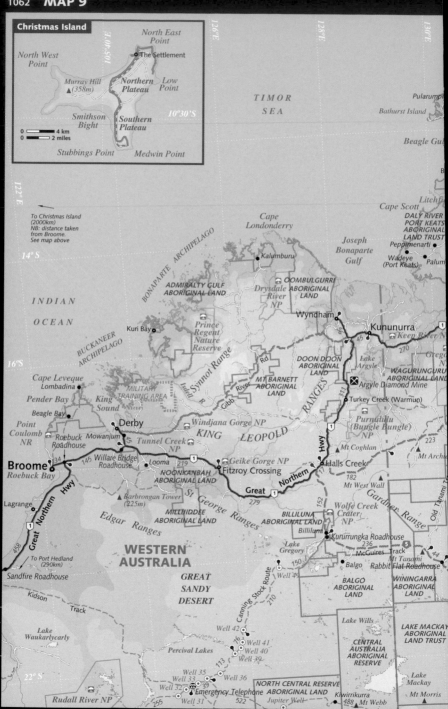

Christmas Island

North West Point

North East Point

o The Settlement

105°40'E

Murray Hill
▲(358m)

Northern Plateau

Low Point

Smithson Bight

Southern Plateau

10°30'S

0 ———— 4 km
0 ———— 2 miles

Stubbings Point   Medwin Point

TIMOR
SEA

Pularumpi

Bathurst Island

Beagle Gul

B

122°E

Cape Scott

Litchfi

DALY RIVER
PORT KEATS
ABORIGINAL
LAND TRUST

Peppimenarti ●

14°S

To Christmas Island
(2000km)
NB: distance taken
from Broome.
See map above

Kalumburu ●

Cape
Londonderry

Joseph
Bonaparte
Gulf

Wadeye
(Port Keats)

Palum

INDIAN

ADMIRALTY GULF
ABORIGINAL LAND

Drysdale
River
NP

OOMBULGURRI
ABORIGINAL
LAND

OCEAN

Kuri Bay ●

Prince
Regent
Nature
Reserve

Wyndham ●

56

Kununurra

Keep River N

1

BONAPARTE ARCHIPELAGO

DOON DOON
ABORIGINAL
LAND

45

270

Grego

16°S

BUCKANEER
ARCHIPELAGO

MT BARNETT
ABORIGINAL
LAND

Lake
Argyle

WAGURUNGURU
ABORIGINAL LAND

Cape Leveque

Isdell

Synnot Range

River

✕ Argyle Diamond Mine

Lombadina ●

MILITARY
TRAINING
AREA

Gibb

311

Turkey Creek (Warmun) ●

Pender Bay

King
Sound

Windjana Gorge NP

LEOPOLD

Purnululu
(Bungle Bungle)
NP

223

Beagle Bay ●

Derby ●

KING

RANGES

▲ Mt Coghlan

▲ Mt Archi

Point
Coulomb
NR

Roebuck
Roadhouse

Mowanjum

Tunnel Creek
NP

Hwy

34

145

Willare Bridge
Roadhouse

Looma

219

Geike Gorge NP

Halls Creek

182

▲ Mt West Wall

Broome ●

Roebuck Bay

Fitzroy Crossing

Northern

17

Gardner

Range

NOONKANBAH
ABORIGINAL LAND

Great

152

Wolfe Creek
Crater
NP

Old Tanami T

Lagrange ●

Great

Northern

Hwy

▲ Barbrongan Tower
(225m)

St George Ranges

279

1

BILLILUNA
ABORIGINAL LAND

Mt Tanami

44

1

458

Edgar
Ranges

MILLIJIDDEE
ABORIGINAL LAND

Billiluna ●

236

Kururrungka Roadhouse

5

To Port Hedland
(290km)

WESTERN
AUSTRALIA

Lake
Gregory

McGuires Track

Balgo ●

Mt Tanami
Rabbit Flat Roadhouse

Sandfire Roadhouse ●

GREAT
SANDY
DESERT

150

Well 49

BALGO
ABORIGINAL
LAND

WININGARRA
ABORIGINAL
LAND

Kidson

Track

Canning Stock Route

210

Lake Wills

LAKE MACKAY
ABORIGINAL
LAND TRUST

Lake
Waukarlycarly

76

Well 42

Well 41

CENTRAL
AUSTRALIA
ABORIGINAL
RESERVE

22°S

Percival Lakes

Well 40

Well 39

Lake
Mackay

Well 35

113

Well 36

Well 33

39

NORTH CENTRAL RESERVE

Kiwirrkurra ●

▲ Mt Morris

Rudall River NP

Well 32

255

Well 31

Emergency Telephone

ABORIGINAL LAND

Jupiter Well ●

488 ▲ Mt Webb

522

MAP 10 1063

100 km
60 miles

N

ARAFURA SEA

Cobourg
Peninsula Croker
Island
Marchinbar Is

le Island
kapiti
Garig Gunak
Barlu NP WESSEL
ISLANDS Guluwuru Is

ertaramoor
Braithwaite
Point

Van Diemen Gulf Maningrida Galiwinku Nhulunbuy

DARWIN Oenpelli Ramingining Dhupuma

Palmerston Gapuwiyak *Gove*
Peninsula Garrthalala
Noonamah Jabiru Arnhem
Land
gs 262 36
Nourlangie ARNHEM LAND *Cape Grey*
ABORIGINAL
Bark Hut Inn LAND TRUST
Adelaide River Kakadu Mt Gilruth
NP
aly 28 1 Bulman Mt Marumba Alyangula
River 21 Mary River Roadhouse
Daly Pine Creek Nitmiluk Angurugu GULF
River Butterfly (Katherine Gorge) Mt Furner
Gorge NP 24 Numbulwar GROOTE OF
Katherine Roper EYLANDT
Bar Ngukurr
Beswick Port Roper CARPENTARIA
Gregory Stuart Mataranka Maria Is
NP Hwy MARRA ABORIGINAL LAND TRUST
125 Elsey 127 SIR EDWARD
er NP HODGSON DOWNS PELLEW GROUP
k 131 Larrimah ABORIGINAL LAND
164 1 ALAWA Vanderlin Is
160 ABORIGINAL
Victoria LAND TRUST Borroloola
Daly Waters Mt Brown
Top Springs Dunmarra 269 1 Cape Crawford GARAWA Mornington Is
181 ABORIGINAL Gununa
169 109 BARKLY TABLELAND LAND TRUST
uragu 96 87 Tablelands Hell's Gate
Kalkarinji Newcastle Waters Elliott NORTHERN Roadhouse
Mt Searle TERRITORY 1
Mt Reid Lake Hwy WAANYI / Doomadgee
Lajamanu Woods GARAWA Gregory
ABORIGINAL Mt Steiglitz Downs
181 Renner Springs LAND Hotel
Mirrinyungu Mt Hawker Tarrabool 376 Lawn Hill
KARLANTUPA NORTH Lake Mt Morgan NP
ABORIGINAL LAND TRUST
Winnecke 45 183 Lake
CENTRAL DESERT Sylvester 11 Mt Oxide
ABORIGINAL Threeways Barkly Mt Lamb Gunpowder
LAND TRUST Tennant Creek MUNGKARTA Barkly Homestead Roadhouse Camooweal
TANAMI DESERT ABORIGINAL 66 Wunura Store A2
LAND TRUST 87 Hwy Camooweal
Mt Solitaire KARLANTUPA SOUTH Devils Marbles WAKAYA ABORIGINAL Caves Mt Isa
ABORIGINAL Conservation Reserve LAND TRUST NP
Mt Rawlins Wycliffe Well Wauchope Alpurrurulam QLD
ami Track WIRLYAJARRAYI Davenport Range 139 83
313 Mt Theo ABORIGINAL All-Curung NP 155
LAND Barrow Creek Mt Alone Urandangi
Mt Leichhardt 5 203 231 Dajarra
Stuart Mt Dixon Honeymoon 14 Sandover Hwy Mt Hogarth To Boulia
Yuendumu Ti Tree Bore (147 km)
Tanami Hwy Arlparra Store
Rd Urapuntja 226 Leslie Peak
lmouth Well Roadhouse Aileron Mt Sainthill
To Alice 274 Mt Guide 244
Springs 125 180 12 Plenty Hwy
(68 km)

Joins Map 5

Joins Map 14

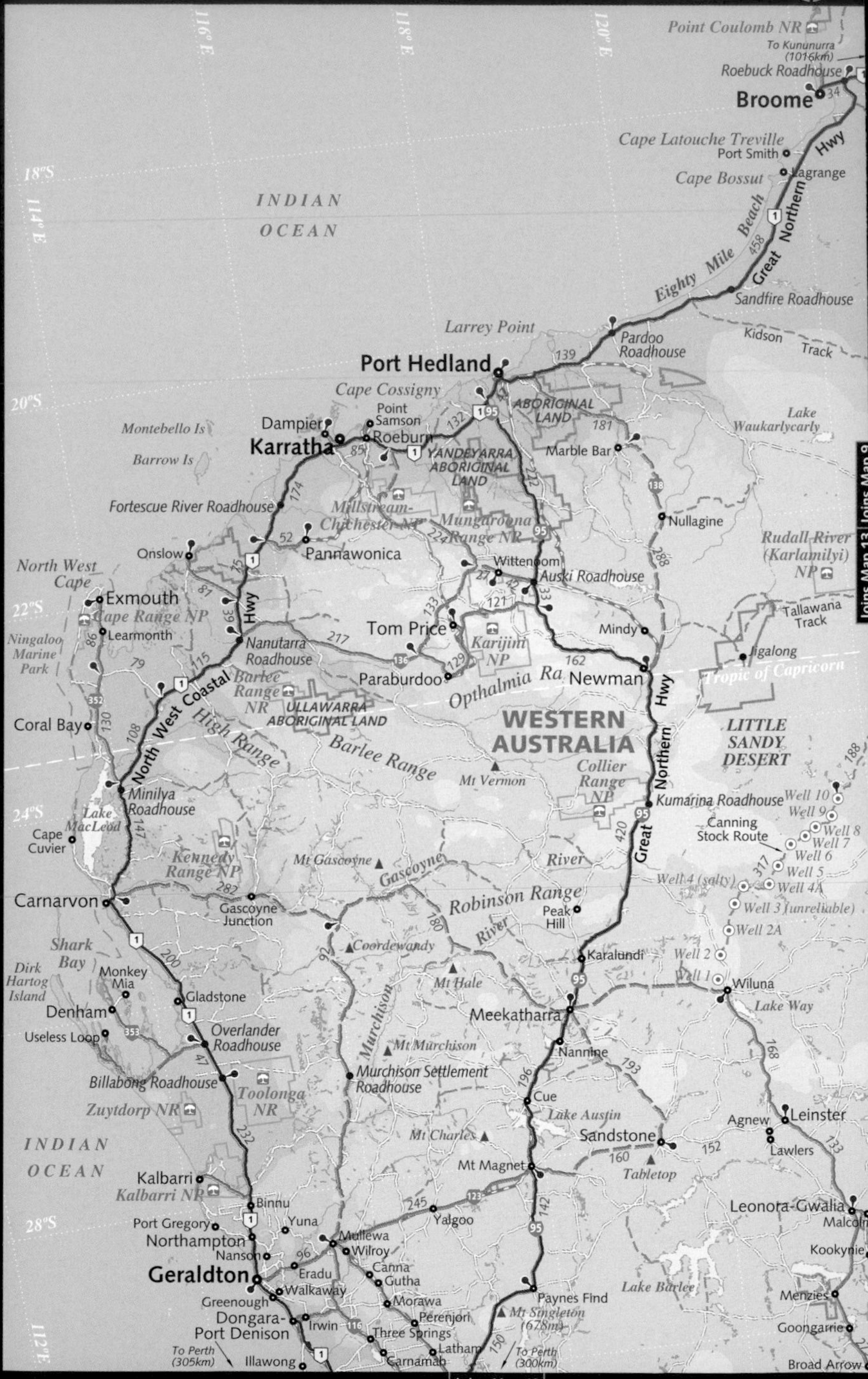

0 | 100 km
0 | 60 miles

N

INDIAN OCEAN

18°S

116°E
118°E
120°E

114°E

20°S

112°E

22°S

24°S

26°S

28°S

Point Coulomb NR
To Kununurra (1016km)
Roebuck Roadhouse
Broome
34

Cape Latouche Treville
Port Smith
Cape Bossut
Lagrange
Eighty Mile Beach
458
Great Northern Hwy
Sandfire Roadhouse
Kidson Track

Larrey Point
Pardoo Roadhouse
139
Port Hedland
Lake Waukarlycarly

Cape Cossigny
Point Samson
132
165
ABORIGINAL LAND
181
Dampier
Roeburn
Marble Bar
Karratha
85
YANDEYARRA ABORIGINAL LAND
Montebello Is
Barrow Is
222
188
Nullagine
Rudall River (Karlamilyi) NP

Fortescue River Roadhouse
174
Millstream-Chichester NP
Mungaroona Range NR
224
95
Tallawana Track
52
Wittenoom
Onslow
75
Pannawonica
222
Auski Roadhouse
233
Jigalong
North West Cape
87
39
121
Tom Price
Mindy
Exmouth
Cape Range NP
Learmonth
86
217
Karijini NP
129
162
Tropic of Capricorn
Ningaloo Marine Park
79
Nanutarra Roadhouse
136
Paraburdoo
Opthalmia Ra
Newman
LITTLE SANDY DESERT

Barlee Range NR
High Range
Ra
188

Coral Bay
130
352
108
North West Coastal Hwy
ULLAWARRA ABORIGINAL LAND
WESTERN AUSTRALIA
Collier Range NP
Great Northern Hwy

Barlee Range
Mt Vernon
Kumarina Roadhouse
Well 10

24°S
Minilya Roadhouse
147
Kennedy Range NP
Mt Gascoyne
Gascoyne
River
420
95
Canning Stock Route
Well 9
Well 8
Well 7
Well 6
Well 5
317
Well 4A
Well 4 (salty)

Cape Cuvier
Lake MacLeod
282
Robinson Range
Well 3 (unreliable)
Well 2A

Carnarvon
Gascoyne Junction
Peak Hill
Well 2

Shark Bay
200
Coordewandy
Murchison
River
260
Karalundi
Well 1
Wiluna
Lake Way

Dirk Hartog Island
Monkey Mia
Mt Hale
95
Meekatharra
168

Denham
Gladstone
353
Overlander Roadhouse
Mt Murchison
Nannine
193
Agnew
Leinster

Useless Loop
47
Murchison Settlement Roadhouse
Cue
Lake Austin
Lawlers
133

Billabong Roadhouse
Toolonga NR
Mt Charles
Sandstone
160
152

Zuytdorp NR
272
Mt Hale
Mt Magnet
Tabletop
Leonora-Gwalia

INDIAN OCEAN
Kalbarri
Kalbarri NP
Binnu
245
121
Yalgoo
Malcolm
Kookynie

Port Gregory
Yuna
142
95
Northampton
Nanson
96
Mullewa
Wilroy
Menzies
Nanson
Canna
Gutha
Morawa
Paynes Find
Goongarrie

Geraldton
Eradu
Walkaway
Perenjori
Mt Singleton (678m)
Lake Barlee

Greenough
Irwin
116
Latham
150
To Perth (300km)
Broad Arrow

Dongara-Port Denison
Three Springs
Carnamah

To Perth (305km)
Illawong

Joins Map 12
Joins Map 13
Joins Map 9

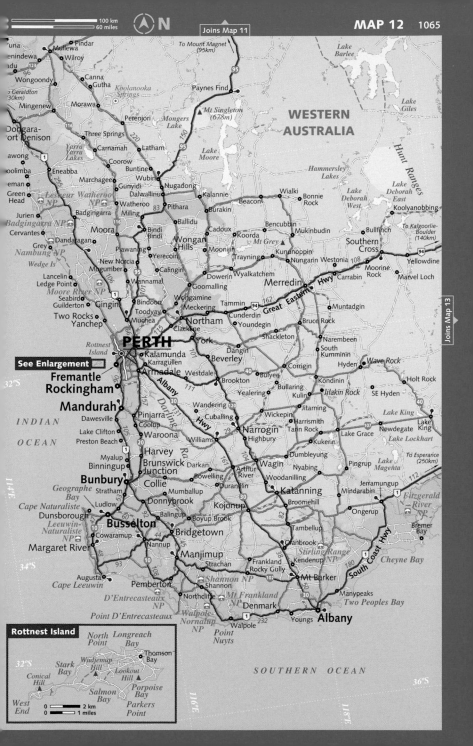

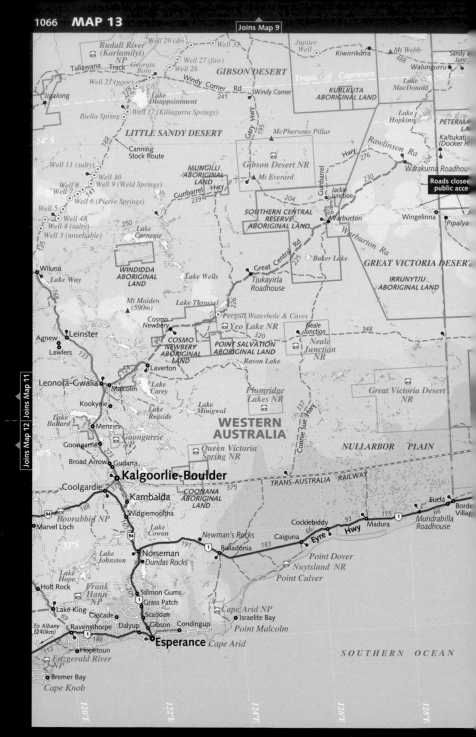

Rudall River
(Karlamilyi)
NP
Tallawana Track
Georgia Bore
Well 29 (dry)
Well 31
Jupiter Well
Kiwirrikurra
Mt Webb 489
Sandy Junc
Walungurru

GIBSON DESERT
Well 27 (fair)
Well 26
Windy Corner Rd
241
Windy Corner
KURLKUTA ABORIGINAL LAND
Tropic of Capricorn
Lake MacDonald

Jigalong
Well 21 (poor)
178
Lake Disappointment
Gary Hwy 195
McPhersons Pillar
Lake Hopkins
PETERMA
LA

Biella Spring
Well 17 (Killagurra Springs)
188
Hwy 276
Rawlinson Ra 704
Kaltukatja (Docker R

LITTLE SANDY DESERT
Canning Stock Route
MUNGILLI ABORIGINAL LAND
Gibson Desert NR
Mt Everard
Gunbarrel
230
Warakurna Roadhou

Roads close
public acce

Well 11 (salty)
Well 10
Well 9 (Weld Springs)
141
Well 8
Well 7
Well 6 (Pierre Springs)
Gunbarrel Hwy 239
204
Jackie Junction
66
Warburton
Wingelinna
Pipalya

SOUTHERN CENTRAL RESERVE ABORIGINAL LAND
Warburton Ra

Well 5
Well 4A
Well 4 (salty)
Well 3 (unreliable)
135
350
Lake Carnegie
225
Baker Lake
GREAT VICTORIA DESER

Wiluna
Lake Way
188
WINDIDDA ABORIGINAL LAND
Lake Wells
Great Tjukayirla Roadhouse
IRRUNYTJU ABORIGINAL LAND

Mt Maiden 590m
Lake Throssel
226
Peegull Waterhole & Caves
Neale Junction
348

Agnew
Leinster
Cosmo Newbery
389
Yeo Lake NR 320
Neale Junction NR

Lawlers
133
COSMO NEWBERY ABORIGINAL LAND
POINT SALVATION ABORIGINAL LAND
Rason Lake

Leonora-Gwalia
Malcolm
Laverton
Lake Carey
Plumridge Lakes NR
Great Victoria Desert NR

Kookynie
Lake Reaside
Lake Minigwal
337
Connie Sue Hwy

Lake Ballard
Menzies
Goongarrie NP
WESTERN AUSTRALIA

Goongarrie
Broad Arrow
Gudarra
Queen Victoria Spring NR
NULLARBOR PLAIN

Kalgoorlie-Boulder
TRANS-AUSTRALIA RAILWAY

Coolgardie
Kambalda
COONANA ABORIGINAL LAND
375
Eucla
Borde
Villag

Boorabbin NP
188
94
Widgiemooltha
Cocklebiddy
66
93
Eyre Hwy
115
1
Madura
Mundrabilla Roadhouse
66

Marvel Loch
Lake Cowan
262
Caiguna
Newman's Rocks
791
Balladonia
183

Lake Johnston
1
Norseman
Dundas Rocks
Point Dover
Nuytsland NR
Point Culver

Lake Hope
Holt Rock
Frank Hann NP
Salmon Gums
Grass Patch

Lake King
Cascade
Scaddan
Cape Arid NP
Israelite Bay
Point Malcolm

To Albany (240km)
Ravensthorpe
Dalyup
Gibson
Condingup
186
1
Hopetoun
112
Esperance
Cape Arid

Fitzgerald River NP
Bremer Bay
Cape Knob
SOUTHERN OCEAN

Joins Map 12 | Joins Map 11
Joins Map 11

100 km
60 miles

N

Tilmouth Well Roadhouse
Papunya
To Tennant Creek (405km)
Tanami Rd
Plenty
Hwy
274
244
Mt Wooldridge
Mt Gerald
MacDonnell West MacDonnell NP
Ranges
Alice Springs
Mt Isabel
ATNETYE ABORIGINAL LAND
QLD
it required for access along eenie Loop Rd
Areyonga
Santa Teresa
Watarrka NP
Finke Gorge NP
Stuart Hwy
NORTHERN TERRITORY
Bedourie
RIGINAL T
Kings Canyon
Illpurla
Stuarts Well
Mt Rodinga
Alice Well
222
246
Lake Amadeus
Tjuta Olgas)
Yulara
Erldunda
Mt Hakea
SIMPSON DESERT
Simpson Desert NP
Eyre Dev Rd
Uluru- Kata Tjuta NP
Mt Connor (Artula)
Mt Kingston
Finke
Mt Peebles
Uluru rs Rock)
Mt Reynolds
75
Kulgera
150
Mt Etingimbra
Poeppel Corner
160
Birdsville
Amata
Ernabella (Pukatja)
Bagot Range
Mt Alberga
Witjira NP
272
(4WD only)
757
198
Mt Kintore
Fregon
Indulkana
Oodnadatta
216
Dalhousie Springs
Simpson Desert Regional Reserve
Track
199
PITJANTJATJARA ABORIGINAL LAND
Mimili
Mintabie
Marla
Stuart Hwy
Mt Waddikee
Oodnadatta
88
Mirra Mitta Bore
eservation Park
Cadney Homestead Roadhouse
235
Mt Euee
Giles Memorial
190
Lake Eyre North
Mungeranie Roadhouse
Birdsville Tk
199
A87
Lake Eyre NP
Strzelecki Regional Reserve
MARALINGA TJARUTJA BORIGINAL LAND
Tallaringa CP
Coober Pedy
William Creek
Lake Eyre South
217
Maralinga (Restricted Area)
WOOMERA PROHIBITED AREA (Stuart Hwy unrestricted)
SOUTH AUSTRALIA
Dog Fence
251
Marree
FLINDERS RANGES
Arkaroola
Lake Frome
llarbor RR
Yellabinna RR
Mt Finke
Tarcoola
Olympic Dam
Roxby Downs
Andamooka
Leigh Creek
Gammon Ranges NP
Blinman
Kingoonya
Glendambo
Woomera
Pimba
B83
Parachilna
Wilpena
Flinders Ranges NP
ullarbor NP
Nullarbor Roadhouse & Hotel
A1
Yalata Roadhouse
93
Head of Bight
Fowlers Bay
Nundroo Roadhouse & Hotel
Penong
88
74
Pureba CP
Mt Hiltaba
Lake Everard
Lake Gairdner NP
Lake Gairdner
Lake Torrens NP
773
Lake Torrens
A87
Hawker
Cradock
Great Australian Bight
Ceduna
Smoky Bay
Haslam
Streaky Bay
Wirrula
Poochera
Minnipa
221
Kyancutta
Eyre
A1
Hwy
Port Augusta
Iron Knob
246
Whyalla
Quorn
Carrieton
Wilmington
Orroroo
Melrose
Yunta
A32
Venus Bay
Talia
B100
Lock
Rudall
B100
Port Pirie
Peterborough
Eyre Peninsula
Elliston
Sheringa
296
Toologie
Snowtown
Crystal Brook
Spalding
Burra
Yeelanna
Arno Bay
Port Neill
Kadina
Clare
Morgan
Coffin Bay NP
Tumby Bay
Spencer Gulf
Maitland
Port Wakefield
Kapunda
Port Lincoln
Louth Bay
Yorke Peninsula
A1
Gawler
Lincoln NP
ADELAIDE
Murray Bridge
Innes NP
Investigator Strait
Tailem Bend
B1
A8
KANGAROO ISLAND
Kingscote
Victor Harbor
Kiki
Culburra
Rocky River

130°E
132°E
134°E

(Continued from page 1052)

BUS

Australia's extensive bus network is a relatively cheap and reliable way to get around, though it can be a tedious means of travel and requires planning if you intend to do more than straightforward city-to-city trips. Most buses are equipped with air-con, toilets and videos, and all are smoke-free zones. The smallest towns eschew formal bus terminals for a single drop-off/pick-up point, usually outside a post office, newsagent or shop.

A national bus network is provided by **Greyhound Australia** (☎ 1300 473 946; www.greyhound.com.au). Fares purchased online are roughly 5% cheaper than over-the-counter tickets; fares purchased by phone incur a $4 booking fee.

Due to convoluted licensing arrangements involving some regional bus operators, there are some states and smaller areas in Australia – namely SA, Victoria and parts of NSW and northern Queensland – where you cannot buy a Greyhound ticket to travel between two destinations within that state/area. Rather, your ticket needs to take you out of the region or across a state/territory border. This situation does not apply to bus passes (p1070), which can be used freely.

Small regional operators running key routes or covering a lot of ground include the following:

Crisps' Coaches (☎ 07-4661 8333; www.crisps.com.au) Throughout Queensland.

Emerald Coaches (☎ 1800 28737, 07-4982 4444; www.emeraldcoaches.com.au) Outback Queensland.

Firefly Express (☎ 1300 730 740; www.fireflyexpress.com.au) Runs between Sydney, Melbourne and Adelaide.

Integrity Coach Lines (☎ 1800 226 339, 08-9226 1339; www.integritycoachlines.com.au) Heads north from Perth up to Port Hedland.

Northern Rivers Buslines (☎ 02-6626 1499; www.nrbuslines.com.au) Northern NSW.

Premier Motor Service (☎ 13 34 10; www.premierms.com.au) Runs along the east coast between Cairns and Melbourne.

Premier Stateliner (☎ 08-8415 5555; www.premierstateliner.com.au) Services towns around SA.

Redline Coaches (☎ 1300 360 000; www.tasredline.com.au) Services Hobart and Tasmania's northern and eastern coasts.

TassieLink (☎ 1300 300 520; www.tassielink.com.au) Criss-crosses Tasmania, with extra summer links to bushwalking locales.

Transnorth (☎ 07-4776 5124, www.transnorthbus.com) Northern Queensland.

Transwa (☎ 1300 662 205; www.transwa.wa.gov.au) Hauls itself around the southern half of WA.

V/Line (☎ 13 61 96; www.vline.com.au) Runs to most major towns and cities in Victoria.

Backpacker Buses

While the companies offering transport options for budget travellers in various parts of Australia are pretty much organised-tour operators, they do also get you from A to B (sometimes with hop-on, hop-off services) and so can be a cost-effective alternative to the big bus companies. The buses are usually smaller, you'll meet lots of other travellers, and the drivers sometimes double as tour guides; conversely, some travellers find the tour-group mentality and inherent limitations don't suit them. Discounts for card-carrying students and members of hostel organisations are usually available.

Adventure Tours Australia (☎ 1300 654 604; www.adventuretours.com.au) This company does budget tours in all states. A two-day Red Centre tour starting/finishing in Alice Springs and taking in Uluru, Kata Tjuta and Kings Canyon costs $445 (plus national park entry fees), while a 10-day trip from Perth to Broome costs $1495.

Autopia Tours (☎ 03-9419 8878; www.autopiatours.com.au) Autopia runs three-day trips along the Great Ocean Rd from Melbourne to Adelaide via the Grampians, and from Melbourne to Sydney via Wilsons Promontory, the Snowy Mountains and Canberra, for $395.

Easyrider Backpacker Tours (☎ 1300 308 477; www.easyridertours.com.au) A true hop-on, hop-off bus, but you can also do trips as tours. It covers the west coast from Esperance to Broome, with trips out of Perth. The Southern Curl goes Perth–Margaret River–Albany–Perth ($300) in three days. A trip from Perth to Exmouth costs $400 and Exmouth to Broome costs $390.

Groovy Grape Getaways Australia (☎ 1800 661 177, 08-8371 4000; www.groovygrape.com.au) This SA-based operator offers three-day Melbourne–Adelaide tours ($345) along the Great Ocean Rd and seven-day Adelaide–Alice Springs tours ($865), stopping in the Flinders Ranges, Coober Pedy and Uluru. Small groups.

Nullarbor Traveller (☎ 1800 816 858; www.the-traveller.com.au) This small, ecocertified company runs relaxed minibus trips across the Nullarbor. Nine-day laid-back camping and hostelling trips between Adelaide and Perth ($1295) include bushwalking, surfing, whale watching, accommodation, national park entry fees and almost all meals. Swimming with sea lions and dolphins is also possible.

TRANSPORT

PRINCIPAL BUS ROUTES & RAILWAYS

Oz Experience (☎ 1300 300 028; www.ozexperience.com)
This is one of those hop-on, hop-off services you will either
love or hate. In the past many travellers have complained
about seat availability and a boozy culture, while others rave
about it as a highly social experience. The Oz Experience network covers central, northern and eastern Australia. Travel is
one-directional and passes are valid for up to six months with
unlimited stops. A Sydney–Cairns pass is $600, and the 'Fish
Hook' pass from Sydney or Melbourne to Darwin is $1650.

Wayward Bus Touring Company (☎ 1300 653 510;
www.waywardbus.com.au) Most trips with this reputable
company allow you to get on or off where you like. The Classic
Coast runs between Melbourne and Adelaide via the Coorong
and Great Ocean Rd ($365, 3½ days). Their longest tour is
the Face the Outback route, running between Adelaide and
Alice Springs ($945, eight days) via the Clare Valley, Flinders
Ranges, Oodnadatta Track, Coober Pedy and Uluru.

Greyhound Bus Passes

The following Greyhound passes are subject
to a 10% discount for members of YHA, VIP,
Nomads and other approved organisations, as
well as card-carrying seniors and pensioners.

EXPLORER PASSES

These hop-on, hop-off passes are matched to
the most popular itineraries. You don't have
the backtracking flexibility of the Kilometre
Pass (see opposite), but if you can find a route
that suits you it generally works out cheaper.
Validity is based on the distance travelled.

The Aussie Highlights pass allows you
to loop around the eastern half of Australia
from Sydney, taking in Melbourne, Adelaide,
Coober Pedy, Alice Springs, Darwin, Cairns,

Townsville, the Whitsundays, Brisbane and Surfers Paradise for $1600, including tours of Uluru-Kata Tjuta and Kakadu National Parks. Or there are one-way passes, such as the Best of the Outback, which goes from Sydney to Darwin via Melbourne, Adelaide and Alice Springs for $950.

KILOMETRE PASS

This is the simplest pass and gives you a specified amount of travel, starting at 500km ($99), going up in increments of 1000km to a maximum of 20,000km ($2210). It's valid for 12 months and you can travel where and in what direction you please, and stop as many times as you like. For example, a 2000km pass ($360) will get you from Cairns to Brisbane, a 4000km pass ($660) will get you from Airlie Beach to Adelaide, and a 12,000km pass ($1560) will cover a loop from Sydney through Melbourne, Adelaide, central Australia, Darwin, Cairns and back to Sydney.

Phone at least a day ahead to reserve a seat if you're using this pass, and bear in mind that side trips or tours off the main route (say to Kakadu, Uluru or Shark Bay) will be calculated at double the actual kilometre distance to the site so as to account for the journey there and back.

Classes

There are no separate classes on buses, and the vehicles of the different companies all look pretty similar and are equipped with air-con, toilets and videos. Smoking isn't permitted on Australian buses.

Costs

Following are the average, nondiscounted, one-way bus fares on some well-travelled Australian routes.

Route	Adult/Child/Concession
Adelaide-Darwin	$605/530/550
Adelaide-Melbourne	$70/60/65
Brisbane-Cairns	$280/250/255
Cairns-Sydney	$420/370/395
Canberra-Melbourne	$80/70/75
Canberra-Sydney	$36/30/30
Sydney-Brisbane	$140/110/115
Sydney-Melbourne	$65/60/60

Reservations

Over summer, school holidays and public holidays, book well ahead on the more popular routes, including intercity and east-coast services. Make a reservation at least a day in advance if you're using a Greyhound pass.

CAR & MOTORCYCLE

See p74 for comprehensive information about getting around Australia by car and motorcycle, and road distance charts.

HITCHING

Hitching is never entirely safe in any country in the world, and we don't recommend it. Travellers who decide to hitch should understand that they are taking a small but potentially serious risk. People who do choose to hitch will be safer if they travel in pairs and let someone know where they are planning to go.

In Australia, the hitching signal can be a thumbs up or a downward-pointed finger.

TRAIN

Long-distance rail travel in Australia is something you do because you really want to – not because it's cheaper or more convenient, and certainly not because it's fast. That said, trains are more comfortable than buses, and on some of Australia's long-distance train journeys the romance of the rails is alive and kicking. The *Indian Pacific* across the Nullarbor Plain and the *Ghan* from Adelaide to Darwin are two of Australia's great rail journeys.

Rail services within each state are run by that state's rail body, either government or private – see the introductory transport section of the relevant state or territory chapter for details.

The three major interstate services in Australia are operated by **Great Southern Railways** (☎ 13 21 47; www.gsr.com.au), namely the *Indian Pacific* between Sydney and Perth, the *Overland* between Melbourne and Adelaide, and the *Ghan* between Adelaide and Darwin via Alice Springs.

Costs

Following are some standard one-way train fares. Note that 'rail saver' tickets are nonrefundable, no changes are permitted, they are only available on travel seats and payment has to be made at the time of the booking.

Adelaide–Darwin Adult/child/concession in an economy seat $700/350/440, from $1415/860/860 in a cabin.

Adelaide–Melbourne Adult/child/rail saver in a travel seat $90/45/60, from $140/100 in a cabin.

TRANSPORT

Adelaide–Perth Adult/child/rail saver in a travel seat $395/190/245, from $1350/660 in a cabin.

Brisbane–Cairns $212 to $311 per adult (economy seat).

Canberra–Melbourne $102 per adult (economy seat); involves a bus ride from Canberra to Cootamundra, then a train to Melbourne.

Canberra–Sydney $40 per adult (economy seat).

Sydney–Brisbane $100 (economy seat).

Sydney–Melbourne $91 per adult (economy seat).

Sydney–Perth Adult/child/rail saver in a travel seat $680/275/300, from $1330/860 in a cabin.

Reservations

As the railway-booking system is computerised, any station (other than those on metropolitan lines) can make a booking for any journey throughout the country. For reservations call ☎ 13 22 32; this will connect you to the nearest main-line station.

Discounted tickets work on a first-come, first-served quota basis; it helps to book in advance.

Train Passes

The **Great Southern Rail Rail Explorer Pass** (☎ 13 21 47; www.gsr.com.au), which is available only to non-Australian residents equipped with a passport, allows unlimited travel on the rail network for a period of six months. The pass costs $690/590 per adult/concession (relatively inexpensive considering the amount of ground you could cover over the life of the pass), but note that you'll be travelling in a Daynighter reclining seat and not a cabin. You need to prebook all seats at least 24 hours in advance.

CountryLink (☎ 13 22 32; www.countrylink.info) is a rail and coach operation that visits destinations in NSW, the ACT, Queensland and Victoria, and offers two passes to foreign nationals with valid passports. The East Coast Discovery Pass allows one-way economy travel between Melbourne and Cairns (in either direction) with unlimited stopovers, and is valid for six months – the full trip costs $500, while Sydney to Cairns is $410 and Brisbane to Cairns is $280. The Backtracker Rail Pass allows for travel on the entire CountryLink network and has four versions: a 14-day/one-/three-/six-month pass costing $235/275/300/420.

Health Dr David Millar

CONTENTS

Healthwise, Australia is a remarkably safe country in which to travel, considering that such a large portion of it lies in the tropics. Tropical diseases such as malaria and yellow fever are unknown; diseases of insanitation such as cholera and typhoid are unheard of. Thanks to Australia's isolation and quarantine standards, even some animal diseases such as rabies and foot-and-mouth disease have yet to be recorded.

Few travellers to Australia will experience anything worse than an upset stomach or a bad hangover, and, if you do fall ill, the standard of hospitals and health care is high.

BEFORE YOU GO

Since most vaccines don't produce immunity until at least two weeks after they're given, visit a physician four to eight weeks before departure. Ask your doctor for an International Certificate of Vaccination (otherwise known as 'the yellow booklet'), which will list all the vaccinations you've received. This is mandatory for countries that require proof of yellow fever vaccination upon entry (sometimes required in Australia, see Required & Recommended Vaccinations, right), but it's a good idea to carry a record of all your vaccinations wherever you travel.

Bring medications in their original, clearly labelled containers. A signed and dated letter from your physician describing your medical conditions and medications, including generic names, is also a good idea. If carrying syringes or needles, be sure to have a physician's letter documenting their medical necessity.

INSURANCE

If your health insurance doesn't cover you for medical expenses abroad, consider getting extra insurance – check www.lonelyplanet.com for more information. Find out in advance if your insurance plan will make payments directly to providers or if it will reimburse you later for overseas health expenditures. In Australia, as in many countries, doctors expect payment at the time of consultation. Make sure you get an itemised receipt detailing the service and keep the contact details of the health provider. See p1074 for details of health care in Australia.

REQUIRED & RECOMMENDED VACCINATIONS

If you're entering Australia within six days of having stayed overnight or longer in a yellow fever–infected country, you'll need proof of yellow fever vaccination. For a full list of these countries visit the **World Health Organization** (WHO; www.who.int/wer) or **Centers for Disease Control & Prevention** (www.cdc.gov/travel) websites.

If you're really worried about health when travelling, there are a few vaccinations you could consider for Australia. The WHO recommends that all travellers should be covered for diphtheria, tetanus, measles, mumps, rubella, chickenpox and polio, as well as hepatitis B, regardless of their destination. While you're making plans to travel is a great time to ensure that all routine vaccination cover is complete. The consequences of these diseases can be severe, and while Australia has high levels of childhood vaccination coverage, outbreaks of these diseases do occur.

HEALTH

MEDICAL CHECKLIST

- acetaminophen (paracetamol) or aspirin
- adhesive or paper tape
- antibacterial ointment in case of cuts or abrasions
- antibiotics
- antidiarrhoeal drugs (eg loperamide)
- antihistamines (for hayfever and allergic reactions)
- anti-inflammatory drugs (eg ibuprofen)
- bandages, gauze, gauze rolls
- DEET-containing insect repellent for the skin
- iodine tablets or water filter (for water purification)
- oral rehydration salts
- permethrin-containing insect spray for clothing, tents and bed nets
- pocket knife
- scissors, safety pins, tweezers
- steroid cream or cortisone (for allergic rashes)
- sun block
- sunglasses
- thermometer

INTERNET RESOURCES

There is a wealth of travel health advice to be found on the internet. For further information, **Lonely Planet** (www.lonelyplanet .com) is a good place to start. The **WHO** (www .who.int/ith) publishes a superb book called *International Travel and Health*, which is revised annually and is available online at no cost. Another website of general interest is **MD Travel Health** (www.mdtravelhealth.com), which provides complete travel health recommendations for every country and is updated daily.

It's usually a good idea to consult your government's travel health website before departure, if one is available:

Australia (www.dfat.gov.au/travel)
Canada (www.travelhealth.gc.ca)
UK (www.nhs.uk/livewell/travelhealth)
USA (www.cdc.gov/travel)

FURTHER READING

Travel with Children, published by Lonely Planet, includes handy advice on travel health for younger children. Other recommended references include *Traveller's Health* by Dr Richard Dawood and *International Travel Health Guide* by Stuart R Rose, MD.

IN TRANSIT

DEEP VEIN THROMBOSIS (DVT)

Blood clots (thromboses) may form in the legs during plane flights, chiefly because of prolonged immobility. The longer the flight, the greater the risk. Though most blood clots are reabsorbed uneventfully, some may break off and travel through the blood vessels to the lungs, where they could cause life-threatening complications.

The chief symptom of DVT is swelling or pain of the foot, ankle or calf, usually – but not always – on just one side. When a blood clot travels to the lungs, it may cause chest pain and breathing difficulties. Travellers with any of these symptoms should immediately seek medical attention.

To prevent the development of DVT on long flights, you should walk about the cabin, perform isometric compressions of the leg muscles (ie flex the leg muscles while sitting), drink plenty of fluids and avoid alcohol and tobacco.

JET LAG & MOTION SICKNESS

Jet lag is a common problem when crossing more than five time zones, and it results in insomnia, fatigue, malaise or nausea. To avoid jet lag, try drinking plenty of (nonalcoholic) fluids and eating light meals. On arrival, expose yourself to sunlight and readjust your schedule (for meals, sleep etc) as soon as possible.

Antihistamines such as dimenhydrinate and meclizine are usually the first choice for treating motion sickness. Their main side effect is drowsiness. A herbal alternative is ginger, which works like a charm for some people.

IN AUSTRALIA

AVAILABILITY & COST OF HEALTH CARE

Health insurance is essential for all travellers. While health care in Australia is of a high standard and not overly expensive by international standards, considerable costs can build up and repatriation is extremely expensive. Make sure your existing health insurance will cover you – if not, organise extra insurance.

Australia has an excellent health-care system. It's a mixture of privately run medical clinics and hospitals alongside a system of public hospitals funded by the Australian government. There are excellent specialised, public health facilities for women and children in Australia's major centres.

The Medicare system covers Australian residents for some of their health-care costs. Visitors from countries with which Australia has a reciprocal health-care agreement are eligible for benefits specified under the Medicare program. There are agreements currently in place with Finland, Ireland, Italy, Malta, the Netherlands, New Zealand, Norway, Sweden and the UK – check the details before departing from these countries. In general, the agreements provide for any episode of ill-health that requires prompt medical attention. For further information, visit www.medicareaustralia.gov.au/public/migrants/visitors.

Over-the-counter medications are widely available at privately owned chemists throughout Australia. These include painkillers, antihistamines for allergies, and skin-care products.

You may find that medications readily available over the counter in some countries are only available in Australia by prescription. These include the oral contraceptive pill, most medications for asthma and all antibiotics. If you take medication on a regular basis, bring an adequate supply and ensure you have details of the generic name as brand names may differ between countries.

Health Care in Remote Areas

In Australia's remote locations, it is possible there'll be a significant delay in emergency services reaching you in the event of serious accident or illness. Do not underestimate the vastness between most major outback towns; an increased level of self-reliance and preparation is essential.

Consider taking a wilderness first-aid course, such as those offered at the **Equip Wilderness First Aid Institute** (www.wmi.net.au). Take a comprehensive first-aid kit that is appropriate for the activities planned, and ensure that you have adequate means of communication. Australia has extensive mobile phone coverage but additional radio communication is important for remote areas. The **Royal Flying Doctor Service** (www.flyingdoctor.net) provides an important back-up for remote communities.

INFECTIOUS DISEASES
Bat Lyssavirus

This disease is related to rabies and some deaths have occurred after bites. The risk is greatest for animal handlers and vets. The rabies vaccine is effective, but the risk of travellers contracting bat lyssavirus is very low.

Dengue Fever

Dengue fever occurs in northern Queensland, particularly from October to March, during the wet season. Also known as 'breakbone fever', because of the severe muscular pains that accompany it, this viral disease is spread by a species of mosquito that feeds primarily during the day. Most people recover in a few days but more severe forms of the disease can occur, particularly in residents who are exposed to another strain of the virus (there are four types) in a subsequent season.

Giardiasis

Giardia is widespread in waterways around Australia. Drinking untreated water from streams and lakes is not recommended. Use water filters and boil or treat water with iodine to help prevent giardisis. Symptoms consist of intermittent bad-smelling diarrhoea, abdominal bloating and wind. Effective treatment is available (tinidazole or metronidazole).

Hepatitis C

This is still a growing problem among intravenous drug users. Blood transfusion services fully screen all blood before use.

Human Immunodeficiency Virus (HIV)

In Australia HIV rates have stabilised and levels are similar to other Western countries. Clean needles and syringes are widely available at all chemists.

Malaria

Although isolated cases have occurred in northern Queensland, malaria is not an ongoing problem in Australia. The risk to travellers is low.

Meningococcal Disease

This disease occurs worldwide and is a risk if you have prolonged stays in dormitory-style accommodation. A vaccine exists for some types of this disease, namely meningococcal A, C, Y and W. There is no vaccine presently available for the viral type of meningitis.

HEALTH

Ross River Fever

The Ross River virus is widespread throughout Australia and is spread by mosquitoes living in marshy areas. In addition to fever, it causes headache, joint and muscular pains, and a rash that resolves after five to seven days.

Sexually Transmitted Diseases (STDs)

Rates of STD infection are similar to most other Western countries. The most common symptoms are pain while passing urine, and a discharge. Infection can be present without symptoms, so seek medical screening after any unprotected sex with a new partner. Throughout the country you'll find sexual health clinics in all of the major hospitals. Always use a condom with any new sexual partner. Condoms are readily available in chemists and through vending machines in many public places, including toilets.

Tick Typhus

Cases of tick typhus have been reported throughout Australia, but are predominantly found in Queensland and New South Wales. A week or so after being bitten, a dark area forms around the bite, followed by a rash and possible fever, headache and inflamed lymph nodes. The disease is treatable with antibiotics (doxycycline), so see a doctor if you suspect you have been bitten.

Viral Encephalitis

Also known as Murray Valley encephalitis virus, this is spread by mosquitoes and is most common in northern Australia, especially during the wet season (October to March). This potentially serious disease is normally accompanied by headache, muscle pains and sensitivity to light. Residual neurological damage can occur and no specific treatment is available. However, the risk to most travellers is low.

TRAVELLERS' DIARRHOEA

Tap water is universally safe in Australia. All water other than tap water should be boiled, filtered or chemically disinfected (with iodine tablets) to prevent travellers' diarrhoea and giardisis.

If you develop diarrhoea, be sure to drink plenty of fluids – preferably an oral rehydration solution containing lots of salt and sugar. A few loose stools don't require treatment but if you start having more than four or five stools a day, you should begin taking an antibiotic (usually a quinolone drug) and an antidiarrhoeal agent (such as loperamide). If diarrhoea is bloody, persists for more than 72 hours or is accompanied by fever, shaking chills or severe abdominal pain, you should seek medical attention.

ENVIRONMENTAL HAZARDS
Bites & Stings
MARINE ANIMALS

Marine spikes, such as those found on sea urchins, stonefish, scorpion fish, catfish and stingrays, can cause severe local pain. If this occurs, immediately immerse the affected area in hot water (as high a temperature as can be tolerated). Keep topping up with hot water until the pain subsides and medical care can be reached. The stonefish is found only in tropical Australia, from northwestern Australia around the coast to northern Queensland. An antivenin is available.

Marine stings from jellyfish such as box jellyfish and irukandji also occur in Australia's tropical waters, particularly during the wet season (October to March). Box jellyfish and irukandji have an incredibly potent sting and have been known to cause fatalities. Warning signs exist at affected beaches, and stinger nets are in place at the more popular beaches. Never dive into water unless you have checked – with local beach life-savers – that it's safe. 'Stinger suits' (full-body Lycra swimsuits) prevent stinging, as do wetsuits. If you are stung, first aid consists of washing the skin with vinegar, which may prevent further discharge of the remaining stinging cells, followed by rapid transfer to a hospital; treatment is widely available.

SHARKS & CROCODILES

Despite extensive media coverage, the risk of shark attack in Australian waters is no greater than in other countries with extensive coastlines. There's also low risk of an attack by tropical sharks on scuba divers in northern Australian waters. Great white sharks are now few in number in the temperate southern waters. Check with surf life-saving groups about local risks. See A Bit of Perspective, p1028.

The risk of crocodile attack in tropical northern Australia is real but predictable and largely preventable. Discuss the local risk with police or tourist agencies in the area before swimming in rivers, water holes and the sea.

SNAKES

Australian snakes have a fearful reputation that is justified in terms of the potency of their venom, but unjustified in terms of the actual risk to travellers and locals. Snakes are usually quite timid in nature and, in most instances, will move away if disturbed. They have only small fangs, making it easy to prevent bites to the lower limbs (where 80% of bites occur) by wearing protective clothing (such as gaiters) around the ankles when bushwalking. The bite marks are very small and may even go unnoticed.

In all cases of confirmed or suspected bites, preventing the spread of toxic venom can be achieved by applying pressure to the wound and immobilising the area with a splint or sling before seeking medical attention. Firmly wrap an elastic bandage (you can improvise with a T-shirt) around the entire limb, but not so tight as to cut off the circulation. Along with immobilisation, this is a life-saving first-aid measure.

SPIDERS

Australia has a number of poisonous spiders. The Sydney funnel-web spider causes severe local pain, as well as generalised symptoms (vomiting, abdominal pain, sweating). An antivenin exists, so apply pressure to the wound and immobilise the area before transferring to a hospital.

Redback spiders are found throughout the country. Bites cause increasing pain at the site, followed by profuse sweating and generalised symptoms (including muscular weakness, sweating at the site of the bite, nausea). First aid includes application of ice or cold packs to the bite, then transfer to hospital.

White-tailed spider bites may cause an ulcer that is very slow and difficult to heal. Clean the wound thoroughly and seek medical assistance.

Heat Exhaustion & Heatstroke

Very hot weather is experienced all year round in northern Australia and during the summer months for most of the country. Conditions vary from tropical in the Northern Territory and Queensland to hot desert in northwestern Australia and central Australia. When arriving from a temperate or cold climate, remember that it takes two weeks for acclimatisation to occur. Before the body is acclimatised, an excessive amount of salt is lost in perspiration, so increasing the salt in your diet is essential.

Heat exhaustion occurs when fluid intake does not keep up with fluid loss. Symptoms include dizziness, fainting, fatigue, nausea or vomiting. The skin is usually pale, cool and clammy. Treatment consists of rest in a cool, shady place and fluid replacement with water or diluted sports drinks.

Heatstroke is a severe form of heat illness that occurs after fluid depletion or extreme heat challenge from heavy exercise. This is a true medical emergency, with heating of the brain leading to disorientation, hallucinations and seizures. Prevent heatstroke by maintaining an adequate fluid intake to ensure the continued passage of clear and copious urine, especially during physical exertion.

A number of unprepared travellers die from dehydration each year in outback Australia. This can be prevented by following some simple rules:

- Carry sufficient water for any trip, including extra in case your vehicle breaks down.
- Always let someone, such as the local police, know where you are going and when you expect to arrive.
- Carry communications equipment of some form.
- Stay with your vehicle rather than walking for help.

Hypothermia

Hypothermia is a significant risk, especially during the winter months in southern parts of Australia. Despite the absence of high mountain ranges, strong winds produce a high chill factor that can result in hypothermia even in moderately cool temperatures. Early signs include the inability to perform fine movements (such as doing up buttons), shivering and a bad case of the 'umbles' (fumbles, mumbles, grumbles, stumbles). The key elements of treatment include moving out of the cold, changing out of any wet clothing into dry clothes with windproof and waterproof layers, adding insulation and providing fuel (water and carbohydrate) to allow shivering, which builds the internal temperature. In severe hypothermia, shivering actually stops – this is a medical emergency requiring rapid medical attention in addition to the above measures.

HEALTH

Insect-Borne Illnesses

Various insects can be a source of irritation and, in Australia, may transfer specific diseases (dengue fever, Ross River fever, tick typhus, viral encephalitis). Protection from mosquitoes, sandflies, ticks and leeches can be achieved by a combination of the following strategies:

- Wear loose-fitting, long-sleeved clothing.
- Apply 30% DEET to all exposed skin and reapply every three to four hours.
- Impregnate clothing with permethrin (an insecticide that is believed to be safe for humans).

Surf Beaches & Drowning

Australia has exceptional surf, particularly on the eastern, southern and western coasts. Beaches vary enormously in their underwater conditions: the slope offshore can result in changeable and often powerful surf. It's a good idea to check with local surf lifesaving organisations and be aware of your own expertise and limitations before entering the water.

Ultraviolet Light Exposure

Australia has one of the highest rates of skin cancer in the world. Monitor your exposure to direct sunlight closely. Ultraviolet (UV) exposure is greatest between 10am and 4pm, so avoid skin exposure during these times. Always use 30+ sunscreen; apply it 30 minutes before going into the sun and repeat applications regularly to minimise damage.

HEALTH

Glossary

AUSTRALIAN ENGLISH

Any visitor from abroad who thinks that Australian (that's 'Strine') is simply a weird-sounding variant of English is in for a surprise. The colloquial language may mean you'll be lost in a strange maze of Australian words. The meaning of some words in Australia is completely different from that in other English-speaking countries – some commonly used words have been shortened almost beyond recognition, while others are derived from Aboriginal languages, or from the slang used by early convict settlers.

If you want to pass for an Aussie, just try speaking slightly nasally, shortening any word of more than two syllables and then adding a vowel to the end of it. Then pepper your speech with expletives.

Lonely Planet's *Australian Language & Culture Travel Guide* is an introduction to both Australian English and some Aboriginal languages. The list that follows may also help.

ACT – Australian Capital Territory
Akubra hat – Traditional Australian bushman's hat now seen more frequently atop retired German tourists
arvo – afternoon
Aussie rules – Australian Rules football

B&B – 'bed and breakfast' accommodation
back o' Bourke – back of beyond, middle of nowhere, *outback*
Banana Bender – resident of Queensland
barbie – barbecue; also BBQ
bastard – general form of address which can mean many things, from high praise or respect ('He's the bravest bastard I know!') to dire insult ('You bastard!'); avoid use if unsure
bathers – swimming costume (in Victoria)
battler – struggler, someone who tries hard
beaut, beauty, bewdie – great, fantastic
bevan – see *bogan* (in Queensland)
billabong – waterhole in a riverbed formed by waters receding in the *Dry*
billy – tin container used to boil water in the *bush*
block, do your – lose your temper
bloke – man
blowies, blow flies – large flies

bludger – lazy person, one who refuses to work
blue – argument or fight
bodyboard – half-sized surfboard
bogan – unsophisticated person
bonzer – great, *ripper*
boogie board – see *bodyboard*
boomer – very big; a particularly large male kangaroo
boomerang – a curved, flat, wooden instrument used by Aborigines for hunting
booner – *bogan* (in ACT)
booze bus – police van used for random breath testing for alcohol
brekky – breakfast
Buckley's – no chance at all
bulldust – fine, sometimes deep, dust on *outback* roads; also bullshit
bullroarer – instrument often used in Aboriginal men's initiation ceremonies; a long piece of wood on a string swung around the head to create an eerie roar
bunyip – mythical bush spirit
burl – have a try ('give it a burl')
bush, the – country, anywhere away from the city
bushranger – Australia's equivalent of the outlaws of the American Wild West
BYO – 'bring your own'; a restaurant licence permitting customers to drink *grog* they've purchased elsewhere

camp oven – large, cast-iron pot with lid used for cooking on an open fire
cask wine – wine packaged in a plastic bladder surrounded by a cardboard box (a great Australian invention)
chiga – see *bogan* (in Tasmania)
chockers – completely full (from 'chock-a-block')
chook – chicken
chuck a U-ey – make a U-turn, turn a car around within a road
clap stick – percussion instrument used in Aboriginal societies, either sticks (one or two) or a pair of boomerangs
clobber – to hit; clothes
Cockroach – resident of NSW
c'mon – come on, encouragement in an endeavour usually heard at the sidelines at a sporting event
cobber – see *mate* (archaic)
cooee – a long, loud high-pitched call
corroboree – Aboriginal festival or gathering for ceremonial or spiritual reasons
counter meal – pub meal
cozzie – swimming costume (in NSW)
crack the shits – lose one's temper
crook – ill or substandard

Croweater – resident of SA

crikey – an exclamation of surprise, as in 'crikey these shorts are tight!'

dag – dirty lump of wool at a sheep's rear; also an affectionate or mildly abusive term for a socially inept person

daks – trousers, *strides*

damper – bush loaf made from flour and water, often cooked in a *camp oven*

dead horse – tomato sauce

dead set – true, *dinkum*

deli – see *milk bar* (in SA and WA); also delicatessen

didgeridoo – wind instrument made from a hollow piece of wood, traditionally played by Aboriginal men

digger – soldier; *mate*

dillybag – Aboriginal carry bag

dinkum – honest, genuine

dinky-di – the real thing

donga – small, transportable building widely used in the *outback*

Dreaming – complex concept that forms the basis of Aboriginal spirituality, incorporating the creation of the world and the spiritual energies operating around us; often preferred to 'Dreamtime' as it avoids the association with time

drongo – worthless or stupid person

drop bear – imaginary Australian bush creature

Dry, the – dry season in northern Australia (April to October)

dunny – outdoor lavatory

earbash – to talk nonstop

Esky – large insulated ice chest for keeping food and drinks cold

fair dinkum – see *dinkum*

fair go! – give us a break!

flat out – very busy or fast

flog – sell; steal

football, footy – for *Mexicans, Croweaters, Taswegians* and *Sand Gropers*: Aussie Rules. For *Banana Benders* and *Cockroaches*: rugby league. Almost never soccer.

fossick – hunt for gems or semiprecious stones

freshie – freshwater crocodile (usually harmless, unless provoked); new *tinny* of beer

galah – noisy parrot, thus noisy idiot

gander – to look ('have a gander')

g'day – good day, traditional Australian greeting

grazier – large-scale sheep or cattle farmer

grog – general term for alcoholic drinks

hicksville – derogatory term usually employed by urbanites to describe a country town

hotel more often a pub than a place to sleep

hoon – idiot, hooligan

icy pole – frozen lollipop, ice lolly

iffy – dodgy, questionable

indie – independent music and film

jackaroo – male trainee on an *outback station*

jillaroo – female trainee on an *outback station*

journo – journalist

jumped-up – self-important, arrogant

kali – jumbo-sized boomerang

karri – eucalyptus tree of southern WA

Kiwi – New Zealander

knacker – testicle

knackered – broken, tired

knock – to criticise, deride

knocker – one who *knocks*; woman's breast

kombi – a classic (hippies') type of van made by Volkswagen

Koories – Aboriginal people of southeastern Australia

Kooris – Aboriginal people of NSW

lamington – square of sponge cake covered in chocolate icing and desiccated coconut

larrikin – hooligan, mischievous youth

lemon – faulty product, a dud

little ripper – extremely good thing

loo – toilet

mate – general term of familiarity, correctly pronounced 'maaaaate'

Mexicans – Victorians

milk bar – small shop selling milk and other basic provisions; see also *deli*

mobile phone – cell phone

mozzies – mosquitoes

Murri – collective term used to identify Aborigines from Queensland

musos – musicians

never-never – remote country in the *outback*

no-hoper – hopeless case

no worries! – No problems! That's OK!

Noongar – collective term used to identify Aborigines from WA

NSW – New South Wales

NT – Northern Territory

Nunga – collective term used to identify Aborigines from SA

ocker – uncultivated or boorish Australian; a *knocker* or derider

oi oi oi – the second stanza of the traditional Australian ballad that starts 'Aussie Aussie Aussie'

outback – remote part of the *bush*, *back o'Bourke*

pavlova – traditional Australian meringue, fruit and cream dessert, named after Russian ballerina Anna Pavlova; also 'pav'

pay out – to make fun of, deride

perve – to gaze with lust

piker – someone who doesn't pull their weight, or chickens out

piss – beer

piss up – boozy party

piss weak – no good, gutless

pissed – drunk

pissed off – annoyed

plonk – cheap wine

pokies – poker machines

Pom – English person

pot – medium beer glass (in Victoria and Tasmania); beer gut; to sink a billiard ball

Queenslander – high-set weatherboard house, noted for its wide verandah

rarrk – cross-hatching designs used in Arnhem Land paintings and body art

ratbag – friendly term of abuse

ratshit – lousy

rego – vehicle registration

ridgy-didge – original, genuine

ring-in – substitute or outsider

rip – a strong ocean current or undertow

ripper – good; see also *little ripper*

road train – semitrailer truck towing several trailers

roos – kangaroos

root – to have sexual intercourse

rooted – tired, broken

ropable – very bad-tempered or angry

RSL – Returned Servicemen's League or community venue operated by same

SA – South Australia

saltie – saltwater crocodile (the dangerous one)

Sand Groper – resident of WA

schooner – large beer glass in NSW, medium beer glass in SA

session – lengthy period of heavy drinking

shark biscuit – inexperienced surfer

sheila – woman

she'll be right – no problems, *no worries*

shellacking – comprehensive defeat

shonky – unreliable

shoot through – to leave in a hurry

shout – to buy a round of drinks ('Your shout!')

skimpy – scantily clad female bar person in WA

slab – two dozen *stubbies* or *tinnies*

smoko – tea break

snag – sausage

sparrow's fart – dawn

station – large farm

stickybeak – nosy person; to snoop or pry

stolen generations – Aboriginal and Torres Strait Islander children forcibly removed from their families during the government's policy of assimilation

strides – trousers, *daks*

stroppy – bad-tempered

stubby – 375mL bottle of beer

sundowner – alcoholic drink consumed at sunset

surf 'n' turf – a slab of steak topped with seafood, usually served in pubs

swag – canvas-covered bed roll used in the *outback*; a large amount

ta thank you

TAB local betting parlour

tackers – young children

take the piss – friendly derision

tall poppies – achievers (*knockers* like to cut them down)

Taswegian – resident of Tasmania

tea – evening meal

thingo – thing, whatchamacallit, doovelacki, thingumajig

thongs – flip-flops, an *ocker*'s idea of formal footwear

tinny – 375mL can of beer; small aluminium fishing dinghy

tjukurpa – Aboriginal law, religion and custom

toastie – toasted sandwich

togs – swimming costume (in Queensland and Victoria)

Top End – northern part of the NT

true blue – see *dinkum*

tucker – food

two-pot screamer – person unable to hold their drink

two-up – traditional heads-or-tails coin gambling game

ute – utility; pick-up truck

WA – Western Australia

wag – to skip school or work

walkabout – lengthy solitary walk

weatherboard – timber cladding on a house

Wet, the – rainy season in the north (November to March)

whoop-whoop – *outback*, miles from anywhere

wobbly – disturbing, unpredictable behaviour

woomera – stick used by Aborigines to propel spears

wowser – someone who doesn't believe in having fun, spoilsport, teetotaller

yabbie – small freshwater crayfish

yobbo – uncouth, aggressive person

yonks – a long time

youse – plural form of 'you' (pronounced 'yooze'), used by the grammatically challenged

The Authors

JUSTINE VAISUTIS
Coordinating Author, Victoria (Melbourne)

Despite the world's best efforts, Justine is tragically in love with her own country. Having chartered vast sections of it numerous times in many directions, her wonder at Australia's beauty is ceaseless. This love affair began on a New South Wales beach when she was a tiny tacker – she still returns to her favourite secret there whenever possible. For the most part Melbourne is now home and she revelled in the opportunity to rediscover her own city again for this guide, not to mention fuel her passion for beer, coffee, live music and art. This is Justine's 13th Lonely Planet title. She now devotes most of her time to improving her manners (tough ask) and working at the Australian Conservation Foundation with truly inspiring folk. Justine also wrote Destination Australia, Getting Started, Itineraries, the Culture, Food & Drink, Driving in Australia, Directory and Transport chapters.

LINDSAY BROWN
Northern Territory (Tennant Creek to Uluru-Kata Tjuta National Park)

A former conservation biologist and Publishing Manager of Outdoor Activity Guides at Lonely Planet, Lindsay enjoys nothing more than heading into the outback to explore and photograph Australia's heartland. As a Lonely Planet author and photographer Lindsay has contributed to several titles covering South Asia and Australia including Central Australia – Adelaide to Darwin, Queensland & the Great Barrier Reef, East Coast Australia, and Sydney & New South Wales.

JAYNE D'ARCY
Queensland (North Coast to Far North Queensland)

Still carrying the juggling skills she picked up from hippies at the Kuranda market as a 12-year-old, Jayne finally got the chance to return to the land of crocs, stingers and laid-back locals as a grown-up, and see who'd changed the most. When she's not discovering her own backyard and teaching her four-year-old how to read maps, Jayne writes on travel, design, the environment and homes for newspapers, magazines and her blog.

LONELY PLANET AUTHORS

Why is our travel information the best in the world? It's simple: our authors are passionate, dedicated travellers. They don't take freebies in exchange for positive coverage so you can be sure the advice you're given is impartial. They travel widely to all the popular spots, and off the beaten track. They don't research using just the internet or phone. They discover new places not included in any other guidebook. They personally visit thousands of hotels, restaurants, palaces, trails, galleries, temples and more. They speak with dozens of locals every day to make sure you get the kind of insider knowledge only a local could tell you. They take pride in getting all the details right, and in telling it how it is. Think you can do it? Find out how at **lonelyplanet.com**.

THE AUTHORS

KATJA GASKELL   New South Wales (Sydney to Upper Hunter Valley)

Having spent the last three years living in Sydney, Katja jumped at the chance to spend even more time at the beach – all in the name of research, of course. In addition to comparing the surf and sand of the north shore versus the eastern suburbs, Katja had the tough task of sampling the many bars, restaurants and cafes that make Sydney such a fabulous city. Add to that magical weekends on the Hawkesbury and wine-soaked trips to the Hunter Valley and she's suddenly beginning to wonder quite why she's leaving Australia… By the time this is published, Katja, along with her boys Nick and Alfie, will have embarked on a new adventure living in Delhi, India.

SARAH GILBERT   Australian Capital Territory

Sarah moved to Canberra at the age of 18, and has barely stopped moving since. After studying at the Australian National University, she returned to her native Sydney but her restlessness sent her on to Amsterdam, and later New York, where she earned her masters in journalism at New York's Columbia University and cut her teeth on the Big Apple's tabloids, then on to Buenos Aires, and many other places in between. Sarah is now living in Sydney, where she works as a freelance journalist.

PAUL HARDING   Victoria (Around Melbourne to Gippsland), Northern Territory (Darwin to Katherine to Alice)

Melbourne-born and raised in central Victoria, Paul spent childhood summer holidays in the Gippsland Lakes and indulged in many years of camping and fishing trips along the Murray River. He has since travelled to many parts of Australia and the world, but still finds Australia one of the world's greatest countries to explore and was intrigued to find so many gems in his own backyard of Victoria. Paul also packed the campervan and travelled to the Northern Territory's Top End and Western Australia's east Kimberley for this edition. Paul has worked on numerous Lonely Planet titles. When not travelling, he lives by the beach in Melbourne. Paul also contributed to the Kimberleys section of the Western Australia chapter.

VIRGINIA JEALOUS   Western Australia (Perth to Southern Outback)

Virginia was thrilled to hit the road locally from her base in Denmark – that's Denmark on Western Australia's stunning south coast. After years of overseas contracts – with LP, aid agencies and development NGOs – it was great to simply pack up the car and go bush. A birder from way back, she's happiest with a pair of binoculars to hand, and over the 6000km travelled enjoyed spotting new birds (emu wrens at last!) and spending time with old ones like the kooky Cape Barren geese, last seen when she contributed to Lonely Planet's *Perth & Western Australia*.

THE AUTHORS

ROWAN MCKINNON   Tasmania

A Melburnian through and through, Rowan got the Tasmania bug on his first trip across Bass Strait decades ago and keeps going back with his partner and children (he'd move to Tassie's northeast coast if he didn't love Melbourne so much). A freelance writer and lapsed rock musician, Rowan has contributed to many Lonely Planet titles on his native Australia as well as the island states of the South Pacific and the Caribbean.

OLIVIA POZZAN   Queensland (Cape York Peninsula)

Olivia's unusual knack for attracting adventure has seen her caving in Oman, expedition racing in Morocco and trekking mountain ranges from the Himalayas to the Alps. Her veterinary career has seen her darting lions in South Africa, riding camels in central Australia and working for an Arabian prince in the Middle East. Having travelled most of Australia and written for both the *Queensland & the Great Barrier Reef* and *East Coast Australia* guidebooks, this Queensland-based author couldn't resist the chance to experience one of Australia's last great frontiers. For this edition, Olivia shared memorable moments with outback heroes and wacky characters on an unforgettable overland pilgrimage to Cape York.

CHARLES RAWLINGS-WAY   South Australia (coauthor)

As a likely lad, Charles suffered in shorts through Tasmanian winters and in summer counted the days until he visited is grandparents in Adelaide. With desert-hot days, cool swimming pools, pasties with sauce squirted into the middle and four TV stations, this flat city held paradisaical status. In teenage years he realised that girls from Adelaide – with their Teutonic cheekbones and fluoridated teeth – were better looking than anywhere else in Australia. These days he lives with a girl from Adelaide in the Adelaide Hills and has developed an unnatural appreciation for Coopers Pale Ale. An underrated rock guitarist and proud new dad, this is Charles's 14th book for Lonely Planet. Charles also covered Norfolk and Lord Howe Islands in the New South Wales chapter, and wrote Great Aussie Trips.

ROWAN ROEBIG   Queensland (Brisbane to Gold Coast Hinterland)

A Melbourne-based writer and editor, Rowan jumped at the chance to return to his native southeast Queensland for this book. Raised in Brisbane, his writing career began with a journalism degree at the University of Queensland, followed by stints at various local newspapers. Passion for travel led him around the world and on one occasion to Ireland for a week – but he stayed for two years, working as a scribe for a magazine in Dublin. He eventually moved back to Australia and, with travel obsession intact, worked as a digital content producer for Lonely Planet, then joined the guidebook-author ranks.

THE AUTHORS

TOM SPURLING   Queensland (Sunshine Coast to Whitsunday Coast)

It took an anarchic German vegan with a penchant for Bundy Rum to remind Tom that thumbs out, balls 'n' all, Australia is bloody unreal for travel. Tom came to writing guidebooks after reading them cover to cover in 30 countries, including Guatemala, Mozambique and Portugal. He's worked on Lonely Planet guides to India and Turkey and spent a year in rural South Africa on a project supported by the LP Foundation. For *Australia*, he went without socks for six weeks. Back in Melbourne, Tom lives with his wife, Lucy, and their son, Oliver, and teaches high school boys that it pays to have a second job.

REGIS ST LOUIS   Western Australia (The Midlands & Wheatbelt to
Purnululu National Park)

Regis has always been captivated by rugged wilderness and big journeys, which made his 9000km road trip around Western Australia one of his all-time favourites. Memorable moments from his travels include stargazing beside remote billabongs in the Kimberley, watching dramatic sunsets along the Coral Coast and introducing his daughter to emus, galahs and other Australian wildlife. When not out travelling the world for Lonely Planet, he splits his time between New York City and Sydney, but seems increasingly drawn to the big skies out west.

PENNY WATSON   New South Wales (Port Stephens to
Around Broken Hill)

Penny Watson grew up on the New South Wales–Victoria border in Albury. Her frequent family holidays instilled an early love of New South Wales' many and varied landscapes, from coastal, outback and river country to the hinterlands, highlands and Snowies. Penny covered the South Coast, Riverina and snowfields for Lonely Planet's *Sydney & New South Wales*. For *Australia*, she has chartered more territory, clocking up almost 10,000km twisting and turning around alpine bends, pot-holing through isolated national parks and slip-sliding over the red-earthy roads of the outback. She is a trained journalist and travel writer and her work (www.pennywatson.com.au) appears in magazines, newspapers and guidebooks in Australia, Asia, Europe and the US.

MEG WORBY   South Australia (coauthor)

After six years at Lonely Planet in the languages, editorial and publishing teams, Meg swapped the desktop for a laptop in order to write about her home state, South Australia. After 10 years away, she was stoked to find that King George Whiting is still every bit as fresh on Kangaroo Island, there are the same endless roads to cruise down in the Flinders Ranges, and the Adelaide Hills now has more wineries. In fact, obvious wine analogies aside, she found that most places in South Australia just keep getting better. This is Meg's fourth Australian guidebook for Lonely Planet.

THE AUTHORS

CONTRIBUTING AUTHORS

Bob Brown wrote the Deforestation in Tasmania boxed text (p664). Bob was elected to the Tasmanian parliament on the first day after his release from Risdon Prison, during the Franklin Dam blockade in 1983. He was first elected to the Senate in 1996. His books include *Memo for a Saner World* (Penguin, 2004) and a guide to the Styx River forests with Vica Bayley, entitled *The Valley of the Giants* (The Wilderness Society, 2005).

Dr Michael Cathcart wrote the History chapter. Michael teaches history at the Australian Centre, the University of Melbourne. He is well known as a broadcaster on ABC Radio National and has presented history programs on ABC TV. His most recent book is *The Water Dreamers* (2009), a history of how water shaped the history of Australia.

Dr Tim Flannery wrote the Environment chapter. Tim is a naturalist, explorer and writer. He is the author of a number of award-winning books, including *The Future Eaters* and *Throwim Way Leg* (an account of his adventures as a biologist working in New Guinea) and the landmark ecological history of North America, *The Eternal Frontier*. Tim lives in Adelaide where he is director of the South Australian Museum and a professor at the University of Adelaide.

Alan Fletcher wrote the Just for *Neighbours* Fans boxed text (p518). Alan has worked in every branch of the performing arts for 30 years. He has played Dr Karl Kennedy on *Neighbours* since 1994.

Dr David Millar wrote the Health chapter. David is a travel-medicine specialist, diving doctor and lecturer in wilderness medicine who graduated in Hobart, Tasmania. He has worked as an expedition doctor with the Maritime Museum of Western Australia, accompanying a variety of expeditions around Australia. David is currently a medical director with the Travel Doctor in Auckland.

Janelle White wrote the Bush Tucker: Australian Native Foods boxed text (p67). Janelle is an applied anthropologist, currently completing a PhD on Aboriginal peoples' involvement in a variety of desert-based bush produce industries, including bush foods, bush medicines and bush jewellery. She lives and works between Adelaide and territory 200km northwest of Alice Springs.

Thanks also to Katie Horner (boxed texts, Australiana on the Page, p52, and Best of the West, p514), Jeanie Menzies (boxed texts, Australiana on the Big Screen, p50, and Australiana on the Speakers, p54) and Andrew Tudor (boxed text, Where to Surf in Australia, p490).

Behind the Scenes

THIS BOOK

Lonely Planet's guide to its home country, Australia, was first published in 1977, when the company's cofounder Tony Wheeler covered the entire country on his own. In the 32 years since then we've sent literally hundreds of authors around Australia to check every dusty nook and cranny of the world's largest island for Lonely Planet guidebooks.

This 15th edition of the Australia guide combined the efforts of 15 fabulous Lonely Planet writers, who spent a total of 65 weeks on the road. To see who did what, see the Authors (p1082). We'd also like to thank the following people for their contributions to this guide: Bob Brown, Dr Michael Cathcart, Dr Tim Flannery, Alan Fletcher, Dr David Millar and Janelle White. And lastly, we'd also like to thank all those who contributed to the Highlights section, so thanks to Jimmy Barnes, Layne Beachley, Kenny Bedford, Bob Brown, Jill Dupleix, Moira Finucane, Catherine Freeman, Steve Kinnane, Will Minson, Tristan Mungatopi and Rockie Stone for sharing with us all their favourite parts of Australia; to check them out see p7.

This guidebook was commissioned in Lonely Planet's Melbourne office (of course!), and produced by the following:

Commissioning Editors Rebecca Chau, Errol Hunt
Coordinating Editor David Carroll
Coordinating Cartographer Amanda Sierp
Coordinating Layout Designer Nicholas Colicchia
Managing Editor Brigitte Ellemor
Managing Cartographers David Connolly, Adrian Persoglia
Managing Layout Designer Sally Darmody
Assisting Editors Michelle Bennett, Monique Choy, Peter Cruttenden, Kirsten Rawlings, Angela Tinson, Simon Williamson
Assisting Cartographers Hunor Csutoros, Xavier Di Toro, Alex Leung, Marc Milinkovic, Jacqueline Nguyen, Andrew Smith, Brendan Streager
Assisting Layout Designer Carlos Solarte
Cover Image research provided by lonelyplanetimages.com
Project Manager Rachel Imeson

Thanks to Lucy Birchley, Jessica Boland, Emma Gilmour, Penny, Trent Paton, Chris Rennie, Jeanette Wall, Tashi Wheeler

THANKS
JUSTINE VAISUTIS

My greatest respect goes to Charles, Meg, Katja, Lindsay, Penny, Paul (Union Saturday?), Rowan M, Rowan R, Sarah, Tom, Virginia (my turn to cook?), Regis, Olivia and Jayne for your professionalism,

---

THE LONELY PLANET STORY

Fresh from an epic journey across Europe, Asia and Australia in 1972, Tony and Maureen Wheeler sat at their kitchen table stapling together notes. The first Lonely Planet guidebook, *Across Asia on the Cheap*, was born.

Travellers snapped up the guides. Inspired by their success, the Wheelers began publishing books to Southeast Asia, India and beyond. Demand was prodigious, and the Wheelers expanded the business rapidly to keep up. Over the years, Lonely Planet extended its coverage to every country and into the virtual world via lonelyplanet.com and the Thorn Tree message board.

As Lonely Planet became a globally loved brand, Tony and Maureen received several offers for the company. But it wasn't until 2007 that they found a partner whom they trusted to remain true to the company's principles of travelling widely, treading lightly and giving sustainably. In October of that year, BBC Worldwide acquired a 75% share in the company, pledging to uphold Lonely Planet's commitment to independent travel, trustworthy advice and editorial independence.

Today, Lonely Planet has offices in Melbourne, London and Oakland, with over 500 staff members and 300 authors. Tony and Maureen are still actively involved with Lonely Planet. They're travelling more often than ever, and they're devoting their spare time to charitable projects. And the company is still driven by the philosophy of *Across Asia on the Cheap*: 'All you've got to do is decide to go and the hardest part is over. So go!'

support and brilliance. At Lonely Planet big cheers to Bec Chau, Emma Gilmour, Ezza Hunt (Prudence Friday?) and Dave Connolly. Massive thanks to my beloved and inspiring ACF colleagues, particularly David McLean, Anna Molan, Jen, Josh, Julie and Loveliest Aria. Thanks to Katie and Jeanie for their prose and eternal mischief and, most importantly, love and hugs always to Mum, Bill, Dad, Aidy, Alan, Simon & the crew, Margie and Ange.

LINDSAY BROWN
Thanks to the helpful folks at the Northern Territory Tourist Commission and the various visitor information centres around the Red Centre. A special thanks to David Duffy of Parks Australia and Lizzie Gilliam and family (Phoebe, Harry and Sam) in Alice Springs. Thanks to Errol and Davids Carroll and Connolly at Lonely Planet and fellow 'lonely' traveller Paul Harding. Last but not least, thanks to Jenny, Patrick and Sinead at home.

JAYNE D'ARCY
Thanks to young Miles D'Arcy for keeping a constant lookout for cassowaries, and to Sharik Billington and Jocelyn Hardie for keeping a constant lookout for Miles and sharing the trip. Thanks also to Tovit Nizer, Peter at Villa Marine, Chris at Ahoy Plane Sailing Seaplanes, Commissioning Editor Rebecca Chau and my fellow authors.

KATJA GASKELL
A huge thank you to the Lonely Planet team that worked on this guide including Rebecca Chau, Errol Hunt, David Connolly and the mapping team. Thanks also to Justine Vaisutis and my fellow New South Wales author Penny Watson. I owe a massive thank you – and a round of drinks – to all the Sydneysiders who so willingly shared their favourite beaches, bars and restaurants, in particular George and Fiona. Thanks to Alastair, my very own restaurant critic, Belinda for art and entertainment insight, and grandparents Gaskell and Panes for stellar babysitting duties. Finally, the biggest thank you goes to my wonderful boys Nick and Alfie; you two rock.

SARAH GILBERT
Thanks to Misha, Jamie and Elijah for putting me up. Thanks to my Lonely Planet colleagues. Thanks to Kyles, Mel, Pen, Bill, BJ, Jane and the rest for generating all those Canberra memories, happy wafts of which arose to meet me while I was researching the chapter. I'll always be grateful to my loving and beloved parents, Danny and Kathleen, and my brother and sister James and Mary. Thanks most of all to Nico for his company on the road, and in life.

PAUL HARDING
In Victoria, thanks to Mary and Brian Harding in Castlemaine; James, Kylie, Amy, Parker and Will in Bendigo; Philip, Dan and Ashleigh in Sunbury and for help with the campervan; Matt, Simone and Xavier in Yackandandah during tough bushfire times; Brian, Kerry, Martyn, Braidyn and Sarah in Swan Hill; Kate Sloggett for coming along with an open mind; and David, Kay and the Blackie family for time spent in Lorne. In the Northern Territory thanks to Graham Steele and his family in Darwin. Big thanks to my wife Hannah who joined me for a few memorable trips in Victoria.

VIRGINIA JEALOUS
To Libby thanks, as always, for my home away from home in Dunsborough and to Judy Q for the same in Freo. Brian and Margaret Winchcombe's winter trip across the Great Central Rd and the Gerrard-Green family's summer one across the Nullarbor filled in some gaps and saved me another long long drive the length of both – believe me when I say I'm grateful! And to Matt and Kylie, cheers for the insider look at Perth's entertainment scene.

ROWAN MCKINNON
Huge thanks to my partner Jane Hart and our kids Lauren and Wesley who travelled with me for the first fortnight. We saw in the new year in Hobart, watched the yachts arriving and enjoyed the Taste Festival before shootin' through in a campervan. Massive thanks and kudos to Charles Rawlings-Way, whose work on Tasmania for this guidebook's last edition was a hard act to follow. Thanks to Jenny Jones and Glenn van der Knijff for insights, to Rebecca Chau for commissioning me, Davids Connolly and Carroll, and Lewis and Eadie McKinnon. Thanks to my daughter Lauren for the lame penguin joke.

OLIVIA POZZAN
The friendly smiles and cheery hellos I encountered in the isolated frontier of Cape York Peninsula deserve a special mention. Many thanks to the Wilderness Challenge team for an adventurous and memorable trip to the Tip. Special thanks to Tom-Tom, a true-blue Aussie larrikin and Cape York hero; to Carmel for her spontaneity in sharing this adventure with me (and for being so much fun!); and to the wonderful strangers who shared our journey and left as friends. Finally, thanks to Justine and the Lonely Planet team.

CHARLES RAWLINGS-WAY
Maximal thanks to Emma and Kerryn for the gig, Bec for the brief and Tashi and Errol for the follow

through. Thanks also to Andrew McEvoy and Sigrid Frede at the SATC, Professor Lester-Irabinna Rigney for the Indigenous overview, Gus and Lyn for the King George Whiting, John Teague for expert radiator wranglings and the all-star in-house Lonely Planet production staff. Most of all, thanks to my sweetheart Meg and the ultimate travelling companion – our one-year-old daughter Ione – who provided countless laughs, unscheduled pit stops and ground-level perspectives along the way.

ROWAN ROEBIG
I tip my hat to: the friendly folks of southeast Queensland; Justine Vaisutis for great support during write-up; and the Lonely Planet digital content team for three fun years working in-house. Huge thanks to: Suzanne Swords for shuttling me around Brisbane; Trevor & Donna Roebig for Gold Coast advice and navigation; and Peter Golikov for the inside word on the Valley. A wisened nod to any friends and family I haven't mentioned, and an enormous thank you to Rama Nicholas for patience and amazing support from first kilometre travelled to last word written.

TOM SPURLING
Thanks to Rebecca Chau for taking a chance on a kid from Geelong. To Justine Vaisutis for her good-natured guidance. In the Whitsundays, thanks to Rachel. In Mt Isa, thanks to the O'Neill family. Near Carnarvon Gorge, thanks to the cop for slowing me down. To Nob Creek Pottery in Byfield, keep fighting for Shoalwater Bay! In 1770, thanks to Reiki Greg. In Noosa, thanks to the Smiths and to Tropicsurf. In Woodford, much love to Haydo and Sandra. Lastly, to my wife Lucy for indulging an errant husband and for moving house (with child!). Baba Nam Kevalam!

REGIS ST LOUIS
A huge thank you to Cassandra and Magdalena who joined me on the epic road trip around Western Australia. I also thank Katrina Hetherington and Jeena Cramer for helpful Kimberley tips, Capes for a fascinating Dreaming tour and the many travellers and visitors centres in Western Australia who plied me with information. In Sydney, warm thanks go to Leonie, Col, Nadina and Luca for a delightful stay after the journey. I'd also like to thank Tim, Leone and Ladd for memorable conversations over a cuppa. Thanks to Virginia Jealous for Wave Rock insight and the rest of the team at Lonely Planet.

PENNY WATSON
Am always grateful to my road-trip companions: thanks especially to Jo McKenzie-McHarg, who chose 'flight' over 'fight' when confronted with a snake in the outback; and to Steph Smiedt who was trampled – rugby-style – in the process. As always, mountains of 'I am not worthy' gratitude to Pipster King, who counted down the miles with me on that gruelling coastal ride from Port Macquarie to Byron Bay. Tough love.

MEG WORBY
Backslaps to Lizzie for tips on drinking and clubbing, Davis Love Jnr for live-music knowledge, Dad and Lynny for the low-down on Burra and KI company, and Georgy and Luke for Clare Valley insights. Thanks also to Mum for Fridays and to Lauren for being there. Grateful thanks to Emma and Kerryn for the gig and to the in-house team at Lonely Planet Footscray for their hard work. Thank you to our sunny travelling companion, Ione, and to my beautiful Grandma, Mary Kupa (1918-2008) for the genetic urge to travel. Heartfelt thanks, as ever, to Charles.

OUR READERS

Many thanks to the travellers who used the last edition and wrote to us with helpful hints, useful advice and interesting anecdotes:

A Nelleke Aben, Dawn Agg, David Alexander, Boberg Alina, Kelly Allen, Sue Allison, Nicole Allmann, Claire Ashard, Nikhil Asthana **B** Gary B, Andreas Badelt, Lee Bailey, Allison Bandy, Nicky Barber, Horst Bardof, Peter Bartels, Anne Batalibasi, Jayne Bates, Julia Baumhoegger, Rosemary Baxter, Janine Beck, Don Beer, Mary Bennie, Ian Bennie, Kurt Bieder, Niall Bishop, David Bissett, Nick Bloxham, Vera Blum, Linda Boekensteijn, Dorothee Boesing, Brigitte Born, Peter Boulton, David Bowman, Tom Bradbury, Paolo Bragantini, Judith Brandmeier, Mark Brandmeier, Dara Bridgewater, Jeremy Brock, Lizanne Bromley, Shane Burke, Robert Burrows, Dick Butters **C** Andy Caldwell, Claire Cambournac, Auburn Carr, Tannith Cattermole, Duncan Chanbers, Nigel Cockburn, Samantha Collins, Laurel Colton, Carmel Conlon, Annie Cook, Rose Crawford, Gary Cullinan **D** Michael Davenport, Mark Davey, Anouk De Leeuw, Lydie De Negri, Martin Decker, William Dempsey, Marjolaine Dey, Sarah Dickinson, Anke Dijkstra, Judith Dolling, Martin Donegan, Kim Dorin, Vivienne Dubourdieu **E** Sally Edsall, Chris Edwards, Caitlyn Eide, David Elliot, Caroline Elliott, Christine Ellis, Nora Evans **F** David Fay, Frans Flippo, Wilbur Floss, Richard Folley, Neil Forbes, Annett Forman, Nathan Francis, Svea Fraser, Michael Fredericks, Kayleigh Freeland **G** Laurie George, Elizabeth Gleeson, David Gohla, Lucy Gower, Michael Grandbois, Kim Grayson, Peter Gremse, Jean-Francois Guibourt **H** Angus Hamilton, Nicole Hansen, Isabelle Harder, Edward Hardy, Lynn Hawkes, Ursula Head, Sean Heanen,

Linda Hein, Gitta Heitmann, Mike Henderson, Sally Henery, Michael Herrmann, Sarah Hewitt, Elizabeth Hodgson, Lucy Holpin, Suzanne Houthuyse, Denis Howe, Paul Huber, Mara Hudson, Gail Hunt, Paula Hurley, Nicole Hurni, Rachelle Hynds **I** Amy Iacopi, Hilary Ilott **J** Jan-Ulrich, Ian James, Rowena Jameson, Line Kyndi Jensen, Bradley Jordan **K** Daniela Kallenbach, Louise Kavanagh, James Keddie, Jos Keijsper, Karolina Kiraga, Christoph Knop, Angkana Koelnsperger, Torhild Kraft, Jean-Marc Krupa **L** Lucas Labute, Matthew Lafontaine, Robert-Jan Lambrichs, Gavin Langcake, Charlotte Langmead, Cath Lanigan, Valda Lavoipierre, Mark Lawrence, Jarrod Lea, Vicki Leblanc, Thomas Lee, Kevin Leonard, Lianne Lewis, Patrick Linehan, Antonio Lovric, Janet Lyke, Aoife Lynch **M** Nick M, Mally Maccarthy, Vince Macdonald, Claire Mackie, Claire Mallinson, Matteo Malvezzi, Gottfried Mammone, Lena Mannerstrale, Kelly Manning, Brina Marks, David Marquard, Brian Mason, Chris May, Jack Mc Ilroy, Maree Mccaskill, Georgina Mckay, Hayley Mckee, Philip W Mclarty, Paul Mclaughlin, Derek Mcmahon, Eddie Mcnally, Rob Menown, Bettina Mestenhauser, Scott Meyer, Pippa Micklem, Robert Miller, Adriana Miosga, Stephen Morey, Annette Morgan, John Morrow, Rebecca Mowat, Susie Munday, Oliver Munn, Mikkel Mynster, **N** Alexandra Nisbeck, Sabrina Nitzsche **O** Carol O'Byrne, John O'Connor, Danny O'Donnell, Tommy Odenhamn, Maria Olsen, Paul Ossieur, Madeline Oziewicz **P** Esther Papas, Seth Patla, Trent Paton, John Pennefather, Deborah Perry, Soren Petersen, Stefano Petroli, Mitchell Phillips, James, John Phillips, Marnie Phillips, Margaret Phipps, Ricky Picky, Rochelle Pincini, Jenny Platt, Stephen Platt, Michael Poesen, Kirstie Power, Julie Prive **Q** Nicky Quinn **R** Joshua Radke, Annemarie Rehders, Hayley Robbins, Cristina Rodriguez, Monika Ruhnke, Michelle Rush, Adrian Rys **S** Anjana Sahu, Terry Sanbrook, Fiona Sandhurst, Rich Sayette, Danielle Schembri, Andre Schmidt, Ulla Schmitt, Tobias Schmitz, Pamela And Gerhard Schoene, Lee Scott, Tara Shanes-Hernandez, Elinor Sheargold, Kate Simpson, Monte Simpson, Frank Sinclair, Edgar Skipsey, Eric Slipp, Marie Sloan, Olivia Slonim, Annie Smeaton, Sara Smith, Peggy Spruit, Chris Stephen, Rogowski Stephen, Gemma Stephenson, Richard Steves, Miriam Steyer, Bianca Stimpson, Pamela Stokes, Christine Stokes, Harriet Stone, Simone Stuewe, Deepak Subramanian, Deepak Subramanian, Candise Sullivan, Ann Sutherland, **T** Remie (Lemiaye) Taylor, Daniela Thies, Rupert Thomas, Kristy Thomas, Tony, Rebecca Tornqvist, Laura Town, Caroline Trenfield, Neil Turner, S Turner **V** Ivan Valencic, Sandra Vallaure, Karine Van Oeteren, Gert-Jan Van Rootselaar, Jessica Veloza, Annette Vickers, Annalise Vogel **W** Montgomery Walker, Matthew Waller, Sylvia Walters, Luke Wang, Mukund Wankhede, Steve Waters, Sharon Watson, Paul Wellington, Sue Whigham, Ann Whittaker, David Williams, Simon Williamson, Myrtle Wilson, Graham Wilson, Jo Winston, Linda Wotherspoon, Heather Wright **Y** David Yalin **Z** Frances Zeeman, Michael Zimmerman, Michael Zimmerman & Theo Zuiderduin.

ACKNOWLEDGMENTS

Many thanks to the following for the use of their content:

Globe on title page ©Mountain High Maps 1993 Digital Wisdom, Inc.

Internal photographs by Lonely Planet Images, and by Juliet Coombe p376; Jason Edwards p378 (#4); Manfred Gottschal p378 (#1); Christopher Groen p374 (#2), p379 (#3); Robert Halstead p375 (#9); John Hay p375 (#6); Richard I'Anson p379 (#6); Holger Leue p380; Chris Mellor p374 (#1); Will Saller p377 (#3); Oliver Strewe p373, p377 (#2); David Wall p377 (#1).

Additional photographs: Kenny Bedford taken by Nicolette Körmendy p11; Moira Finucane taken by Yvette Coppersmith p9; Steve Kinnane taken by Tom Vigilante p11.

All images are the copyright of the photographers unless otherwise indicated. Many of the images in this guide are available for licensing from Lonely Planet Images: www.lonelyplanetimages.com.

Index

INDEX

INDEX

INDEX

INDEX

INDEX

INDEX

GreenDex

Choosing ecofriendly tours and accommodation is one of the best ways you can limit your impact on the environment. But what is ecotourism? Basically any tourism venture that is ecologically sustainable, focuses on experiencing natural areas, and fosters environmental and cultural understanding and conservation. In Australia, look for operators sporting the eco-tick assurance, determined by Ecotourism Australia (www.ecotourism.org.au). This accreditation is rigorous and graded.

The following choices have all been selected by Lonely Planet authors because they demonstrate an active sustainable-tourism policy. It's not an exhaustive list and we want to continue developing our sustainable-tourism content. If you have a suggestion or amendment, email us at www .lonelyplanet.com/feedback.

For more information:

Lonely Planet (www.lonelyplanet.com/responsibletravel) Advice on how to travel responsibly.
Sustainable Travel International (www.sustainabletravelinternational.org) Has developed an ecocertification program.
Green Building Council of Australia (www.gbcaus.org) Has a green star rating for buildings (examining design and construction).

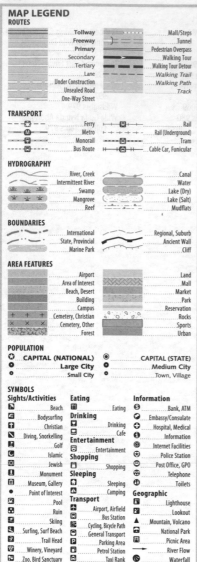

MAP LEGEND

ROUTES

Tollway · Mall/Steps · Freeway · Tunnel · Primary · Pedestrian Overpass · Secondary · Walking Tour · Tertiary · Walking Tour Detour · Lane · Walking Trail · Under Construction · Walking Path · Unsealed Road · Track · One-Way Street

TRANSPORT

Ferry · Rail · Metro · Rail (Underground) · Monorail · Tram · Bus Route · Cable Car, Funicular

HYDROGRAPHY

River, Creek · Canal · Intermittent River · Water · Swamp · Lake (Dry) · Mangrove · Lake (Salt) · Reef · Mudflats

BOUNDARIES

International · Regional, Suburb · State, Provincial · Ancient Wall · Marine Park · Cliff

AREA FEATURES

Airport · Land · Area of Interest · Mall · Beach, Desert · Market · Building · Park · Campus · Reservation · Cemetery, Christian · Rocks · Cemetery, Other · Sports · Forest · Urban

POPULATION

CAPITAL (NATIONAL) · CAPITAL (STATE) · Large City · Medium City · Small City · Town, Village

SYMBOLS

Sights/Activities
Beach · Bodysurfing · Christian · Diving, Snorkelling · Golf · Islamic · Jewish · Monument · Museum, Gallery · Point of Interest · Pool · Ruin · Skiing · Surfing, Surf Beach · Trail Head · Winery, Vineyard · Zoo, Bird Sanctuary

Eating
Eating

Drinking
Drinking · Cafe

Entertainment
Entertainment

Shopping
Shopping

Sleeping
Sleeping · Camping

Transport
Airport, Airfield · Bus Station · Cycling, Bicycle Path · General Transport · Parking Area · Petrol Station · Taxi Rank

Information
Bank, ATM · Embassy/Consulate · Hospital, Medical · Information · Internet Facilities · Police Station · Post Office, GPO · Telephone · Toilets

Geographic
Lighthouse · Lookout · Mountain, Volcano · National Park · Picnic Area · River Flow · Waterfall

---

LONELY PLANET OFFICES

Australia
Head Office
Locked Bag 1, Footscray, Victoria 3011
☎ 03 8379 8000, fax 03 8379 8111
talk2us@lonelyplanet.com.au

USA
150 Linden St, Oakland, CA 94607
☎ 510 250 6400, toll free 800 275 8555
fax 510 893 8572
info@lonelyplanet.com

UK
2nd fl, 186 City Rd,
London EC1V 2NT
☎ 020 7106 2100, fax 020 7106 2101
go@lonelyplanet.co.uk

Published by Lonely Planet Publications Pty Ltd
ABN 36 005 607 983

© Lonely Planet 2009

© photographers as indicated 2009

Cover photograph: Hanging Rock, Grose Valley, Blue Mountains, New South Wales, Phillip Hayson/Photolibrary. Many of the images in this guide are available for licensing from Lonely Planet Images: www .lonelyplanetimages.com.

Printed by Toppan Security Printing Pte. Ltd., Singapore.

Mixed Sources
Product group from well-managed forests and other controlled sources
www.fsc.org   Cert no. SGS-COC-005002
© 1996 Forest Stewardship Council
FSC
